UTAH CRIMINAL AND TRAFFIC CODE

2005 EDITION

Complete Through the 2005 1st Special Session
of the Utah State Legislature

Prepared and distributed by Utah Safety Council
1574 West 1700 South, Salt Lake City, Utah 84104
(801) 262-5400
Email: safety@utahsafetycouncil.org
Web: www.utahsafetycouncil.org

QUESTIONS ABOUT THIS PUBLICATION?

For CUSTOMER SERVICE ASSISTANCE concerning replacement pages,
shipments, billing, reprint permission, or other matters,

please call Customer Service Department at 800-833-9844
email *customer.support@lexisnexis.com*
or visit our interactive customer service website at *www.lexisnexis.com/printcdsc*

For EDITORIAL **content questions** concerning this publication,

please call 800-446-3410 ext. 7447
or email: *LLP.CLP@lexisnexis.com*

For **information on other LEXISNEXIS MATTHEW BENDER publications**,

please call us at 800-223-1940
or visit our online bookstore at *www.lexisnexis.com/bookstore*

ISBN: 0-8205-7883-5

Matthew Bender & Company, Inc.
Editorial Offices
P.O. Box 7587
Charlottesville, VA 22906-7587
800-446-3410
www.lexisnexis.com

Product Number 3380521

(Pub. 33805)

Table of Contents

Page

Sections Affected by 2005 Legislation

Utah Code	Action	Ch. No.	Chapter Sec. No.	Bill No.
13-20-2	Amended	2	2	SB 5
13-32a-102	Amended	256	2	SB 62
13-32a-102.5	Enacted	256	3	SB 62
13-32a-106	Amended	256	4	SB 62
13-32a-106.5	Enacted	256	5	SB 62
13-32a-107	Amended	256	6	SB 62
13-32a-110	Amended	256	7	SB 62
13-32a-111	Amended	256	8	SB 62
13-32a-112	Amended	256	9	SB 62
13-32a-113	Amended	256	10	SB 62
13-32a-114	Amended	256	11	SB 62
17-43-201	Amended	2	4	SB 5
17-43-201	Amended	71	6	HB 176
23-13-17	Amended	2	7	SB 5
26-1-30	Amended	2	8	SB 5
26-6a-1	Repealed	243	12	SB 19
26-6a-1.5	Repealed	243	12	SB 19
26-6a-2	Repealed	243	12	SB 19
26-6a-3	Repealed	243	12	SB 19
26-6a-4	Repealed	243	12	SB 19
26-6a-5	Repealed	243	12	SB 19
26-6a-6	Repealed	243	12	SB 19
26-6a-7	Repealed	243	12	SB 19
26-6a-8	Repealed	243	12	SB 19
26-6a-9	Repealed	243	12	SB 19
26-6a-10	Renumbered	243	2	SB 19
26-6a-11	Renumbered	243	3	SB 19
26-6a-12	Renumbered	243	4	SB 19
26-6a-13	Renumbered	243	5	SB 19
26-6a-14	Renumbered	243	6	SB 19
30-6-4.2	Amended	156	1	SB 104
31A-21-303	Amended	123	7	HB 195
31A-21-303	Amended	247	1	SB 48
31A-22-302	Amended	124	4	HB 200
31A-22-303	Amended	295	1	SB 207
31A-22-305.5	Amended	37	1	SB 4
31A-22-321	Enacted	177	1	HB 235
32A-1-105	Amended	152	1	SB 65
32A-1-115	Amended	2	9	SB 5
32A-12-212	Amended	152	7	SB 65
32A-12-301	Amended	152	8	SB 65
32A-12-505	Amended	71	19	HB 176
34A-2-901	Enacted	243	2	SB 19
34A-2-901	Amended	243	2	SB 19
34A-2-902	Amended	243	3	SB 19
34A-2-903	Amended	243	4	SB 19
34A-2-904	Amended	243	5	SB 19
34A-2-905	Amended	243	6	SB 19
41-1a-202	Amended	2	11	SB 5
41-1a-203	Amended	2	12	SB 5
41-1a-205	Amended	2	13	SB 5
41-1a-209	Amended	47	1	SB 98
41-1a-217	Amended	2	14	SB 5
41-1a-222	Amended	217	2	HB 53
41-1a-222	Amended	244	2	SB 23
41-1a-405	Amended	148	22	HB 318
41-1a-407	Amended	2	15	SB 5
41-1a-418	Amended	63	1	HB 91
41-1a-420	Amended	207	1	HB 5
41-1a-421	Amended	63	2	HB 91
41-1a-506	Amended	47	2	SB 98
41-1a-802	Amended	32	1	HB 149
41-1a-1101	Amended	2	16	SB 5

Utah Code	Action	Ch. No.	Chapter Sec. No.	Bill No.
41-1a-1101	Amended	56	1	HB 67
41-1a-1103	Amended	56	2	HB 67
41-1a-1104	Amended	56	3	HB 67
41-1a-1201	Amended	1	1	HB 1008
41-1a-1206	Amended	2	17	SB 5
41-1a-1222	Enacted	284	1	SB 8
41-1a-1314	Amended	71	24	HB 176
41-3-105	Amended	57	1	HB 68
41-3-205	Amended	90	1	SB 37
41-3-209	Amended	144	1	HB 299
41-3-303	Amended	2	18	SB 5
41-3-603	Amended	57	2	HB 68
41-6-1	Renumbered	2	20	SB 5
41-6-1.5	Renumbered	2	47	SB 5
41-6-11	Renumbered	2	21	SB 5
41-6-12	Renumbered	2	22	SB 5
41-6-13	Renumbered	2	29	SB 5
41-6-13.5	Renumbered	2	30	SB 5
41-6-13.7	Renumbered	2	31	SB 5
41-6-14	Renumbered	2	32	SB 5
41-6-15	Renumbered	2	33	SB 5
41-6-16	Renumbered	2	27	SB 5
41-6-17	Renumbered	2	28	SB 5
41-6-17.5	Renumbered	2	34	SB 5
41-6-18	Renumbered	2	35	SB 5
41-6-19	Renumbered	2	36	SB 5
41-6-19.5	Renumbered	2	37	SB 5
41-6-20	Renumbered	2	38	SB 5
41-6-20.1	Renumbered	2	40	SB 5
41-6-21	Renumbered	2	39	SB 5
41-6-22	Repealed	2	315	SB 5
41-6-23	Renumbered	2	41	SB 5
41-6-24	Renumbered	2	42	SB 5
41-6-25	Renumbered	2	43	SB 5
41-6-26	Renumbered	2	44	SB 5
41-6-26.5	Renumbered	2	45	SB 5
41-6-27	Renumbered	2	46	SB 5
41-6-28	Renumbered	2	48	SB 5
41-6-29	Repealed	2	315	SB 5
41-6-30	Repealed	2	315	SB 5
41-6-31	Renumbered	2	49	SB 5
41-6-32	Repealed	2	315	SB 5
41-6-35	Renumbered	2	50	SB 5
41-6-35.5	Renumbered	2	51	SB 5
41-6-37	Repealed	2	315	SB 5
41-6-38	Renumbered	2	55	SB 5
41-6-38.5	Renumbered	2	56	SB 5
41-6-39	Renumbered	2	53	SB 5
41-6-40	Renumbered	2	52	SB 5
41-6-41	Renumbered	2	54	SB 5
41-6-42	Repealed	2	315	SB 5
41-6-43	Renumbered	2	66	SB 5
41-6-43.5	Repealed	2	315	SB 5
41-6-43.7	Renumbered	2	67	SB 5
41-6-43.8	Renumbered	2	69	SB 5
41-6-44	Renumbered	2	58	SB 5
41-6-44.1	Renumbered	2	70	SB 5
41-6-44.3	Renumbered	2	71	SB 5
41-6-44.5	Renumbered	2	72	SB 5
41-6-44.6	Renumbered	2	73	SB 5
41-6-44.7	Renumbered	2	74	SB 5
41-6-44.8	Renumbered	2	75	SB 5
41-6-44.10	Renumbered	2	76	SB 5
41-6-44.12	Renumbered	2	81	SB 5
41-6-44.20	Renumbered	2	82	SB 5
41-6-44.30	Renumbered	2	83	SB 5
41-6-45	Renumbered	2	84	SB 5
41-6-46	Renumbered	2	85	SB 5
41-6-47	Renumbered	2	86	SB 5

Utah Code	Action	Ch. No.	Chapter Sec. No.	Bill No.
41-6-48	Renumbered	2	87	SB 5
41-6-48.5	Renumbered	2	88	SB 5
41-6-49	Renumbered	2	89	SB 5
41-6-50	Repealed	2	315	SB 5
41-6-51	Renumbered	2	90	SB 5
41-6-52	Renumbered	2	91	SB 5
41-6-52.5	Renumbered	2	92	SB 5
41-6-52.7	Renumbered	2	93	SB 5
41-6-53	Renumbered	2	94	SB 5
41-6-53.5	Renumbered	2	95	SB 5
41-6-54	Renumbered	2	96	SB 5
41-6-55	Renumbered	2	97	SB 5
41-6-56	Renumbered	2	98	SB 5
41-6-57	Renumbered	2	99	SB 5
41-6-58	Renumbered	2	100	SB 5
41-6-59	Renumbered	2	101	SB 5
41-6-60	Renumbered	2	102	SB 5
41-6-61	Renumbered	2	103	SB 5
41-6-62	Renumbered	2	104	SB 5
41-6-63.10	Renumbered	2	105	SB 5
41-6-63.30	Renumbered	2	106	SB 5
41-6-64	Renumbered	2	107	SB 5
41-6-65	Renumbered	2	108	SB 5
41-6-66	Renumbered	2	109	SB 5
41-6-67	Renumbered	2	110	SB 5
41-6-68	Renumbered	2	111	SB 5
41-6-69	Renumbered	2	112	SB 5
41-6-70	Repealed	2	315	SB 5
41-6-71	Repealed	2	315	SB 5
41-6-72	Renumbered	2	113	SB 5
41-6-72.10	Renumbered	2	114	SB 5
41-6-73	Renumbered	2	115	SB 5
41-6-75	Repealed	2	315	SB 5
41-6-75.5	Repealed	2	315	SB 5
41-6-76	Renumbered	2	116	SB 5
41-6-76.10	Renumbered	2	117	SB 5
41-6-77	Renumbered	2	119	SB 5
41-6-78	Renumbered	2	120	SB 5
41-6-79	Renumbered	2	121	SB 5
41-6-79.10	Renumbered	2	122	SB 5
41-6-79.20	Renumbered	2	123	SB 5
41-6-80	Renumbered	2	124	SB 5
41-6-80.1	Renumbered	2	125	SB 5
41-6-80.5	Renumbered	2	126	SB 5
41-6-82	Renumbered	2	127	SB 5
41-6-82.10	Renumbered	2	128	SB 5
41-6-82.50	Renumbered	2	129	SB 5
41-6-83	Renumbered	2	130	SB 5
41-6-84	Renumbered	2	131	SB 5
41-6-85	Renumbered	2	132	SB 5
41-6-86	Renumbered	2	133	SB 5
41-6-87	Renumbered	2	134	SB 5
41-6-87.3	Renumbered	2	135	SB 5
41-6-87.4	Renumbered	2	136	SB 5
41-6-87.5	Renumbered	2	137	SB 5
41-6-87.7	Renumbered	2	138	SB 5
41-6-87.8	Renumbered	2	139	SB 5
41-6-87.9	Renumbered	2	140	SB 5
41-6-88	Renumbered	2	141	SB 5
41-6-89	Renumbered	2	142	SB 5
41-6-90	Renumbered	2	143	SB 5
41-6-90.5	Renumbered	2	144	SB 5
41-6-93	Renumbered	2	146	SB 5
41-6-94	Renumbered	2	147	SB 5
41-6-95	Renumbered	2	148	SB 5
41-6-95.5	Renumbered	2	149	SB 5
41-6-97	Renumbered	2	150	SB 5
41-6-98	Renumbered	2	151	SB 5
41-6-99	Renumbered	2	118	SB 5

Utah Code	Action	Ch. No.	Chapter Sec. No.	Bill No.
41-6-100	Renumbered	26	2	HB 24
41-6-100.10	Renumbered	2	153	SB 5
41-6-100.15	Renumbered	2	154	SB 5
41-6-101	Renumbered	2	162	SB 5
41-6-102	Renumbered	2	163	SB 5
41-6-102.5	Renumbered	2	164	SB 5
41-6-102.7	Renumbered	2	165	SB 5
41-6-103	Renumbered	2	159	SB 5
41-6-103.5	Renumbered	2	158	SB 5
41-6-104	Renumbered	2	160	SB 5
41-6-105	Renumbered	2	161	SB 5
41-6-106	Renumbered	2	219	SB 5
41-6-106.10	Renumbered	2	220	SB 5
41-6-107	Renumbered	2	167	SB 5
41-6-107.2	Renumbered	2	168	SB 5
41-6-107.4	Renumbered	2	169	SB 5
41-6-107.6	Renumbered	2	170	SB 5
41-6-107.8	Renumbered	2	171	SB 5
41-6-108	Renumbered	2	221	SB 5
41-6-108.10	Renumbered	2	222	SB 5
41-6-109	Renumbered	2	223	SB 5
41-6-109.5	Renumbered	2	224	SB 5
41-6-109.10	Renumbered	2	225	SB 5
41-6-110	Renumbered	2	226	SB 5
41-6-111	Renumbered	2	227	SB 5
41-6-112	Renumbered	2	228	SB 5
41-6-113	Renumbered	2	229	SB 5
41-6-114	Renumbered	2	230	SB 5
41-6-114.1	Renumbered	2	231	SB 5
41-6-114.2	Renumbered	2	232	SB 5
41-6-115	Renumbered	2	155	SB 5
41-6-116	Renumbered	2	156	SB 5
41-6-116.1	Renumbered	2	157	SB 5
41-6-116.10	Renumbered	2	166	SB 5
41-6-117	Renumbered	2	175	SB 5
41-6-117.5	Renumbered	2	176	SB 5
41-6-117.6	Renumbered	2	174	SB 5
41-6-118	Renumbered	2	177	SB 5
41-6-119	Renumbered	2	178	SB 5
41-6-120	Repealed	2	315	SB 5
41-6-121.10	Repealed	2	315	SB 5
41-6-122	Repealed	2	315	SB 5
41-6-127	Renumbered	2	179	SB 5
41-6-128	Renumbered	2	180	SB 5
41-6-129	Renumbered	2	181	SB 5
41-6-130	Renumbered	2	182	SB 5
41-6-130.5	Renumbered	2	183	SB 5
41-6-131	Renumbered	2	184	SB 5
41-6-132	Repealed	2	315	SB 5
41-6-133	Renumbered	2	185	SB 5
41-6-133.5	Renumbered	2	186	SB 5
41-6-135	Renumbered	2	187	SB 5
41-6-135.5	Renumbered	2	188	SB 5
41-6-139	Repealed	2	315	SB 5
41-6-140	Renumbered	2	190	SB 5
41-6-140.10	Renumbered	2	152	SB 5
41-6-140.20	Renumbered	2	191	SB 5
41-6-141	Renumbered	2	192	SB 5
41-6-141.5	Renumbered	2	193	SB 5
41-6-142	Repealed	2	315	SB 5
41-6-142	Amended	24	1	HB 16
41-6-143	Renumbered	2	194	SB 5
41-6-143.5	Renumbered	2	195	SB 5
41-6-144	Renumbered	2	196	SB 5
41-6-145	Renumbered	2	197	SB 5
41-6-145.5	Renumbered	2	198	SB 5
41-6-146	Renumbered	2	199	SB 5
41-6-147	Renumbered	2	200	SB 5
41-6-148	Renumbered	2	201	SB 5

Utah Code	Action	Ch. No.	Chapter Sec. No.	Bill No.
41-6-148.10	Renumbered	2	202	SB 5
41-6-148.29	Renumbered	2	203	SB 5
41-6-148.31	Renumbered	2	204	SB 5
41-6-148.32	Renumbered	2	205	SB 5
41-6-148.33	Renumbered	2	206	SB 5
41-6-148.40	Renumbered	2	208	SB 5
41-6-149	Renumbered	2	209	SB 5
41-6-150	Renumbered	2	210	SB 5
41-6-150.10	Renumbered	2	207	SB 5
41-6-152	Renumbered	2	211	SB 5
41-6-153	Renumbered	2	212	SB 5
41-6-154	Renumbered	2	213	SB 5
41-6-154.10	Renumbered	2	214	SB 5
41-6-154.20	Renumbered	2	215	SB 5
41-6-154.50	Renumbered	2	172	SB 5
41-6-155	Repealed	2	315	SB 5
41-6-155.5	Renumbered	2	173	SB 5
41-6-163.6	Renumbered	2	216	SB 5
41-6-163.7	Renumbered	2	217	SB 5
41-6-163.8	Renumbered	2	218	SB 5
41-6-164.5	Renumbered	2	23	SB 5
41-6-165	Renumbered	2	24	SB 5
41-6-165.5	Renumbered	2	25	SB 5
41-6-166	Repealed	2	315	SB 5
41-6-167	Renumbered	2	308	SB 5
41-6-168	Repealed	2	315	SB 5
41-6-169	Repealed	2	315	SB 5
41-6-170	Repealed	2	315	SB 5
41-6-171	Repealed	2	315	SB 5
41-6-172	Renumbered	2	310	SB 5
41-6-173	Renumbered	2	309	SB 5
41-6-175	Renumbered	2	19	SB 5
41-6-175.5	Renumbered	2	26	SB 5
41-6-181	Renumbered	2	233	SB 5
41-6-181.5	Renumbered	2	234	SB 5
41-6-182	Renumbered	2	235	SB 5
41-6-183	Renumbered	2	236	SB 5
41-6-185	Renumbered	2	237	SB 5
41-6-186	Renumbered	2	238	SB 5
41-6a-101	Enacted	2	19	SB 5
41-6a-101	Amended	2	19	SB 5
41-6a-102	Amended	2	20	SB 5
41-6a-102	Amended	111	1	HB 159
41-6a-201	Enacted	2	21	SB 5
41-6a-201	Amended	2	21	SB 5
41-6a-202	Amended	2	22	SB 5
41-6a-203	Amended	2	23	SB 5
41-6a-204	Amended	2	24	SB 5
41-6a-205	Amended	2	25	SB 5
41-6a-206	Amended	2	26	SB 5
41-6a-207	Amended	2	27	SB 5
41-6a-208	Amended	2	28	SB 5
41-6a-209	Amended	2	29	SB 5
41-6a-210	Amended	2	30	SB 5
41-6a-211	Amended	2	31	SB 5
41-6a-212	Amended	2	32	SB 5
41-6a-213	Amended	2	33	SB 5
41-6a-214	Amended	2	34	SB 5
41-6a-215	Amended	2	35	SB 5
41-6a-216	Amended	2	36	SB 5
41-6a-217	Amended	2	37	SB 5
41-6a-301	Enacted	2	38	SB 5
41-6a-301	Amended	2	38	SB 5
41-6a-302	Amended	2	39	SB 5
41-6a-303	Amended	2	40	SB 5
41-6a-304	Amended	2	41	SB 5
41-6a-305	Amended	2	42	SB 5
41-6a-306	Amended	2	43	SB 5
41-6a-307	Amended	2	44	SB 5

Utah Code	Action	Ch. No.	Chapter Sec. No.	Bill No.
41-6a-308	Amended	2	45	SB 5
41-6a-309	Amended	2	46	SB 5
41-6a-310	Amended	2	47	SB 5
41-6a-311	Amended	2	48	SB 5
41-6a-401	Enacted	2	49	SB 5
41-6a-401	Amended	2	49	SB 5
41-6a-401	Amended	26	1	HB 24
41-6a-402	Amended	2	50	SB 5
41-6a-403	Amended	2	51	SB 5
41-6a-404	Amended	2	52	SB 5
41-6a-405	Amended	2	53	SB 5
41-6a-406	Amended	2	54	SB 5
41-6a-407	Amended	2	55	SB 5
41-6a-408	Amended	2	56	SB 5
41-6a-501	Enacted	2	57	SB 5
41-6a-501	Enacted	2	57	SB 5
41-6a-502	Amended	2	58	SB 5
41-6a-502	Amended	91	1	SB 42
41-6a-503	Enacted	2	59	SB 5
41-6a-503	Amended	91	2	SB 42
41-6a-504	Enacted	2	60	SB 5
41-6a-505	Enacted	2	61	SB 5
41-6a-506	Enacted	2	62	SB 5
41-6a-507	Enacted	2	63	SB 5
41-6a-508	Enacted	2	64	SB 5
41-6a-509	Enacted	2	65	SB 5
41-6a-510	Amended	2	66	SB 5
41-6a-511	Amended	2	67	SB 5
41-6a-512	Enacted	2	68	SB 5
41-6a-513	Amended	2	69	SB 5
41-6a-514	Amended	2	70	SB 5
41-6a-515	Amended	2	71	SB 5
41-6a-516	Amended	2	72	SB 5
41-6a-517	Amended	2	73	SB 5
41-6a-517	Amended	283	1	HB 311
41-6a-518	Amended	2	74	SB 5
41-6a-519	Amended	2	75	SB 5
41-6a-520	Amended	2	76	SB 5
41-6a-520	Amended	91	3	SB 42
41-6a-521	Enacted	2	77	SB 5
41-6a-521	Amended	91	4	SB 42
41-6a-522	Enacted	2	78	SB 5
41-6a-523	Enacted	2	79	SB 5
41-6a-524	Enacted	2	80	SB 5
41-6a-524	Amended	91	5	SB 42
41-6a-525	Amended	2	81	SB 5
41-6a-526	Amended	2	82	SB 5
41-6a-527	Amended	2	83	SB 5
41-6a-527	Amended	91	6	SB 42
41-6a-528	Amended	2	84	SB 5
41-6a-529	Enacted	91	7	SB 42
41-6a-530	Enacted	91	8	SB 42
41-6a-601	Enacted	2	85	SB 5
41-6a-601	Amended	2	85	SB 5
41-6a-602	Amended	2	86	SB 5
41-6a-603	Amended	2	87	SB 5
41-6a-604	Amended	2	88	SB 5
41-6a-605	Amended	2	89	SB 5
41-6a-606	Amended	2	90	SB 5
41-6a-607	Amended	2	91	SB 5
41-6a-608	Amended	2	92	SB 5
41-6a-609	Amended	2	93	SB 5
41-6a-701	Enacted	2	94	SB 5
41-6a-701	Amended	2	94	SB 5
41-6a-702	Amended	2	95	SB 5
41-6a-702	Amended	108	1	HB 96
41-6a-703	Amended	2	96	SB 5
41-6a-704	Amended	2	97	SB 5
41-6a-705	Amended	2	98	SB 5

Utah Code	Action	Ch. No.	Chapter Sec. No.	Bill No.
41-6a-706	Amended	2	99	SB 5
41-6a-706.5	Enacted	216	1	HB 49
41-6a-707	Amended	2	100	SB 5
41-6a-708	Amended	2	101	SB 5
41-6a-709	Amended	2	102	SB 5
41-6a-710	Amended	2	103	SB 5
41-6a-711	Amended	2	104	SB 5
41-6a-712	Amended	2	105	SB 5
41-6a-713	Amended	2	106	SB 5
41-6a-714	Amended	2	107	SB 5
41-6a-715	Amended	2	108	SB 5
41-6a-716	Enacted	245	9	SB 25
41-6a-801	Enacted	2	109	SB 5
41-6a-801	Amended	2	109	SB 5
41-6a-802	Amended	2	110	SB 5
41-6a-803	Amended	2	111	SB 5
41-6a-804	Amended	2	112	SB 5
41-6a-901	Enacted	2	113	SB 5
41-6a-901	Amended	2	113	SB 5
41-6a-902	Amended	2	114	SB 5
41-6a-903	Amended	2	115	SB 5
41-6a-904	Amended	2	116	SB 5
41-6a-905	Amended	2	117	SB 5
41-6a-906	Amended	2	118	SB 5
41-6a-907	Amended	26	2	HB 24
41-6a-1001	Enacted	2	119	SB 5
41-6a-1001	Amended	2	119	SB 5
41-6a-1002	Amended	2	120	SB 5
41-6a-1003	Amended	2	121	SB 5
41-6a-1004	Amended	2	122	SB 5
41-6a-1005	Amended	2	123	SB 5
41-6a-1006	Amended	2	124	SB 5
41-6a-1007	Amended	2	125	SB 5
41-6a-1008	Amended	2	126	SB 5
41-6a-1009	Amended	2	127	SB 5
41-6a-1010	Amended	2	128	SB 5
41-6a-1011	Amended	2	129	SB 5
41-6a-1101	Enacted	2	130	SB 5
41-6a-1101	Amended	2	130	SB 5
41-6a-1102	Amended	2	131	SB 5
41-6a-1103	Amended	2	132	SB 5
41-6a-1104	Amended	2	133	SB 5
41-6a-1105	Amended	2	134	SB 5
41-6a-1106	Amended	2	135	SB 5
41-6a-1107	Amended	2	136	SB 5
41-6a-1108	Amended	2	137	SB 5
41-6a-1109	Amended	2	138	SB 5
41-6a-1110	Amended	2	139	SB 5
41-6a-1111	Amended	2	140	SB 5
41-6a-1112	Amended	2	141	SB 5
41-6a-1113	Amended	2	142	SB 5
41-6a-1114	Amended	2	143	SB 5
41-6a-1115	Amended	2	144	SB 5
41-6a-1115	Amended	111	2	HB 159
41-6a-1116	Enacted	2	145	SB 5
41-6a-1116	Amended	111	3	HB 159
41-6a-1117	Enacted	111	4	HB 159
41-6a-1201	Enacted	2	146	SB 5
41-6a-1201	Amended	2	146	SB 5
41-6a-1202	Amended	2	147	SB 5
41-6a-1203	Amended	2	148	SB 5
41-6a-1204	Amended	2	149	SB 5
41-6a-1205	Amended	2	150	SB 5
41-6a-1206	Amended	2	151	SB 5
41-6a-1301	Enacted	2	152	SB 5
41-6a-1301	Amended	2	152	SB 5
41-6a-1302	Amended	2	153	SB 5
41-6a-1303	Amended	2	154	SB 5
41-6a-1304	Amended	2	155	SB 5

Utah Code	Action	Ch. No.	Chapter Sec. No.	Bill No.
41-6a-1305	Amended	2	156	SB 5
41-6a-1306	Amended	2	157	SB 5
41-6a-1307	Amended	2	158	SB 5
41-6a-1401	Enacted	2	159	SB 5
41-6a-1401	Amended	2	159	SB 5
41-6a-1402	Amended	2	160	SB 5
41-6a-1403	Amended	2	161	SB 5
41-6a-1404	Amended	2	162	SB 5
41-6a-1405	Amended	2	163	SB 5
41-6a-1406	Amended	2	164	SB 5
41-6a-1406	Amended	56	4	HB 67
41-6a-1407	Amended	2	165	SB 5
41-6a-1408	Amended	2	166	SB 5
41-6a-1501	Enacted	2	167	SB 5
41-6a-1501	Amended	2	167	SB 5
41-6a-1502	Amended	2	168	SB 5
41-6a-1503	Amended	2	169	SB 5
41-6a-1504	Amended	2	170	SB 5
41-6a-1505	Amended	2	171	SB 5
41-6a-1506	Amended	2	172	SB 5
41-6a-1507	Amended	2	173	SB 5
41-6a-1508	Amended	2	174	SB 5
41-6a-1601	Enacted	2	175	SB 5
41-6a-1601	Amended	2	175	SB 5
41-6a-1602	Amended	2	176	SB 5
41-6a-1603	Amended	2	177	SB 5
41-6a-1604	Amended	2	178	SB 5
41-6a-1605	Amended	2	179	SB 5
41-6a-1606	Amended	2	180	SB 5
41-6a-1607	Amended	2	181	SB 5
41-6a-1608	Amended	2	182	SB 5
41-6a-1609	Amended	2	183	SB 5
41-6a-1610	Amended	2	184	SB 5
41-6a-1611	Amended	2	185	SB 5
41-6a-1612	Amended	2	186	SB 5
41-6a-1613	Amended	2	187	SB 5
41-6a-1614	Amended	2	188	SB 5
41-6a-1615	Amended	2	189	SB 5
41-6a-1615	Repealed	26	6	HB 24
41-6a-1616	Amended	2	190	SB 5
41-6a-1617	Amended	2	191	SB 5
41-6a-1618	Amended	2	192	SB 5
41-6a-1619	Amended	2	193	SB 5
41-6a-1620	Amended	2	194	SB 5
41-6a-1621	Amended	2	195	SB 5
41-6a-1622	Amended	2	196	SB 5
41-6a-1623	Amended	2	197	SB 5
41-6a-1624	Amended	2	198	SB 5
41-6a-1625	Amended	2	199	SB 5
41-6a-1626	Amended	2	200	SB 5
41-6a-1627	Amended	2	201	SB 5
41-6a-1628	Amended	2	202	SB 5
41-6a-1629	Amended	2	203	SB 5
41-6a-1629	Amended	26	3	HB 24
41-6a-1630	Amended	2	204	SB 5
41-6a-1631	Amended	2	205	SB 5
41-6a-1632	Amended	2	206	SB 5
41-6a-1632	Amended	26	4	HB 24
41-6a-1633	Amended	2	207	SB 5
41-6a-1634	Amended	2	208	SB 5
41-6a-1635	Amended	2	209	SB 5
41-6a-1635	Amended	26	5	HB 24
41-6a-1636	Amended	2	210	SB 5
41-6a-1637	Amended	2	211	SB 5
41-6a-1638	Amended	2	212	SB 5
41-6a-1639	Amended	2	213	SB 5
41-6a-1640	Amended	2	214	SB 5
41-6a-1641	Amended	2	215	SB 5
41-6a-1642	Amended	2	216	SB 5

Utah Code	Action	Ch. No.	Chapter Sec. No.	Bill No.
41-6a-1642	Amended	229	1	HB 93
41-6a-1643	Amended	2	217	SB 5
41-6a-1644	Amended	2	218	SB 5
41-6a-1701	Enacted	2	219	SB 5
41-6a-1701	Amended	2	219	SB 5
41-6a-1702	Amended	2	220	SB 5
41-6a-1703	Amended	2	221	SB 5
41-6a-1704	Amended	2	222	SB 5
41-6a-1705	Amended	2	223	SB 5
41-6a-1706	Amended	2	224	SB 5
41-6a-1707	Amended	2	225	SB 5
41-6a-1708	Amended	2	226	SB 5
41-6a-1709	Amended	2	227	SB 5
41-6a-1710	Amended	2	228	SB 5
41-6a-1711	Amended	2	229	SB 5
41-6a-1712	Amended	2	230	SB 5
41-6a-1713	Amended	2	231	SB 5
41-6a-1714	Amended	2	232	SB 5
41-6a-1801	Enacted	2	233	SB 5
41-6a-1801	Amended	2	233	SB 5
41-6a-1802	Amended	2	234	SB 5
41-6a-1803	Amended	2	235	SB 5
41-6a-1804	Amended	2	236	SB 5
41-6a-1805	Amended	2	237	SB 5
41-6a-1806	Amended	2	238	SB 5
41-6a-1901	Enacted	127	1	HB 212
41-6a-1901	Enacted	127	1	HB 212
41-12a-202	Amended	2	239	SB 5
41-12a-301	Amended	2	240	SB 5
41-12a-407	Amended	102	13	SB 123
41-12a-501	Amended	2	241	SB 5
41-12a-502	Amended	2	242	SB 5
41-15-1	Repealed	24	2	HB 16
41-15-2	Repealed	24	2	HB 16
41-15-3	Repealed	24	2	HB 16
41-15-4	Repealed	24	2	HB 16
41-15-5	Repealed	24	2	HB 16
41-15-6	Repealed	24	2	HB 16
41-15-7	Repealed	24	2	HB 16
41-15-8	Repealed	24	2	HB 16
41-15-9	Repealed	24	2	HB 16
41-15-10	Repealed	24	2	HB 16
41-15-11	Repealed	24	2	HB 16
41-15-12	Repealed	24	2	HB 16
41-22-2	Amended	2	243	SB 5
41-22-10.2	Amended	2	244	SB 5
41-22-10.6	Amended	2	245	SB 5
41-22-16	Amended	2	246	SB 5
41-22-31	Amended	102	14	SB 123
41-22-32	Amended	2	247	SB 5
53-1-106	Amended	2	248	SB 5
53-1-106	Amended	169	15	HB 109
53-1-108	Amended	2	249	SB 5
53-1-109	Amended	2	250	SB 5
53-2-102	Amended	214	1	HB 34
53-2-102.5	Enacted	1	1	HB 240
53-2-104	Amended	214	2	HB 34
53-2-107	Amended	71	33	HB 176
53-2-108	Amended	62	1	HB 90
53-2-110	Enacted	214	3	HB 34
53-3-104	Amended	2	251	SB 5
53-3-104	Amended	20	1	SB 227
53-3-104	Amended	34	1	HB 223
53-3-105	Amended	2	252	SB 5
53-3-106	Amended	2	253	SB 5
53-3-202	Amended	2	254	SB 5
53-3-204	Amended	20	2	SB 227
53-3-205	Amended	20	3	SB 227
53-3-205	Amended	34	2	HB 223

Utah Code	Action	Ch. No.	Chapter Sec. No.	Bill No.
53-3-207	Amended	20	4	SB 227
53-3-214	Amended	2	255	SB 5
53-3-214	Amended	34	3	HB 223
53-3-218	Amended	2	256	SB 5
53-3-220	Amended	2	257	SB 5
53-3-220	Amended	91	9	SB 42
53-3-220	Amended	220	1	HB 65
53-3-221	Amended	197	1	SB 167
53-3-222	Amended	2	258	SB 5
53-3-223	Amended	2	259	SB 5
53-3-223.5	Amended	2	260	SB 5
53-3-226	Amended	2	261	SB 5
53-3-227	Amended	2	262	SB 5
53-3-227	Amended	91	10	SB 42
53-3-227	Amended	220	2	HB 65
53-3-229	Amended	197	2	SB 167
53-3-231	Amended	2	263	SB 5
53-3-232	Amended	2	264	SB 5
53-3-232	Amended	91	11	SB 42
53-3-232	Amended	220	3	HB 65
53-3-233	Repealed	91	13	SB 42
53-3-233	Amended	220	4	HB 65
53-3-402	Amended	220	5	HB 65
53-3-404	Amended	220	6	HB 65
53-3-408	Amended	220	7	HB 65
53-3-410	Amended	220	8	HB 65
53-3-412	Amended	220	9	HB 65
53-3-413	Amended	220	10	HB 65
53-3-414	Amended	2	265	SB 5
53-3-414	Amended	220	11	HB 65
53-3-418	Amended	2	266	SB 5
53-3-804	Amended	20	5	SB 227
53-3-804	Amended	34	4	HB 223
53-3-807	Amended	20	6	SB 227
53-3-807	Amended	34	5	HB 223
53-3-810	Amended	197	3	SB 167
53-5-702	Amended	282	1	HB 276
53-5-704	Amended	282	2	HB 276
53-5-705	Amended	282	3	HB 276
53-6-104	Amended	181	4	HB 319
53-8-105	Amended	2	267	SB 5
53-8-202	Amended	2	268	SB 5
53-8-213	Amended	2	269	SB 5
53-10-601	Amended	169	16	HB 109
53-10-605	Amended	169	17	HB 109
53A-1-402	Amended	227	1	HB 86
53A-3-402	Amended	2	7	HB 1001
53A-3-402	Amended	2	270	SB 5
53A-11-102	Amended	253	1	SB 59
53B-3-106	Amended	2	271	SB 5
58-37-2	Amended	283	2	HB 311
58-37-6	Amended	248	2	SB 50
58-37-7.5	Amended	248	3	SB 50
58-37-8	Amended	30	1	HB 55
58-63-302	Amended	81	12	SB 12
58-63-304	Amended	307	2	SB 71
59-13-302	Amended	198	8	SB 170
59-13-303	Amended	198	9	SB 170
59-13-304	Amended	1	4	HB 1008
59-13-304	Amended	108	4	HB 96
59-13-305	Amended	198	10	SB 170
59-13-308	Amended	198	11	SB 170
62A-4a-201	Amended	304	1	HB 338
62A-4a-202.3	Amended	286	3	SB 72
62A-4a-410	Amended	102	17	SB 123
62A-7-106	Renumbered	13	14	HB 28
62A-15-105	Amended	2	276	SB 5
63-2-304	Amended	2	278	SB 5
63-2-304	Amended	131	1	HB 226

Utah Code	Action	Ch. No.	Chapter Sec. No.	Bill No.
63-2-304	Amended	201	6	SB 179
63-2-304	Amended	214	4	HB 34
63-2-304	Amended	256	12	SB 62
63-2-304	Amended	297	2	SB 212
63-30d-301	Amended	2	279	SB 5
63-30d-301	Amended	99	1	SB 106
63-46b-1	Amended	33	1	HB 157
63-46b-1	Amended	102	20	SB 123
63-63a-1	Amended	2	281	SB 5
72-1-209	Amended	148	163	HB 318
72-1-211	Enacted	245	10	SB 25
72-4-102.5	Amended	245	14	SB 25
72-4-114	Amended	21	1	HB 6
72-4-119	Amended	21	2	HB 6
72-4-122	Amended	21	3	HB 6
72-4-128	Amended	21	4	HB 6
72-4-129	Amended	21	5	HB 6
72-4-132	Amended	21	6	HB 6
72-4-302	Amended	148	164	HB 318
72-5-304	Amended	169	68	HB 109
72-5-306	Amended	102	24	SB 123
72-5-401	Amended	254	156	SB 60
72-6-107	Amended	25	116	HB 19
72-6-109	Amended	2	282	SB 5
72-6-114	Amended	2	283	SB 5
72-6-118	Amended	245	15	SB 25
72-7-107	Amended	2	284	SB 5
72-7-401	Amended	2	285	SB 5
72-7-403	Amended	2	286	SB 5
72-7-407	Amended	2	287	SB 5
72-7-502	Amended	254	157	SB 60
72-7-504	Amended	148	165	HB 318
72-9-501	Amended	2	288	SB 5
72-9-502	Amended	161	1	SB 144
72-9-601	Amended	2	289	SB 5
72-9-602	Amended	2	290	SB 5
72-9-603	Amended	2	291	SB 5
72-10-501	Amended	2	292	SB 5
72-10-502	Amended	2	293	SB 5
72-12-110	Amended	2	294	SB 5
73-18-13	Amended	2	295	SB 5
73-18-15.5	Amended	2	296	SB 5
73-18-20	Amended	2	297	SB 5
73-18-20.1	Amended	2	298	SB 5
73-18a-15	Amended	2	299	SB 5
73-18c-306	Amended	102	25	SB 123
76-1-302	Amended	59	1	HB 76
76-1-302	Amended	270	1	SB 177
76-2-101	Amended	2	300	SB 5
76-3-203.1	Amended	93	9	SB 47
76-3-203.5	Amended	59	2	HB 76
76-5-102.6	Amended	230	1	HB 98
76-5-109	Amended	95	4	SB 83
76-5-110	Amended	95	5	SB 83
76-5-202	Amended	143	1	HB 297
76-5-207	Amended	2	301	SB 5
76-6-503	Repealed	93	12	SB 47
76-6-503.5	Enacted	93	10	SB 47
76-6-504	Amended	93	11	SB 47
76-6-702	Amended	72	1	HB 185
76-6-703	Amended	72	2	HB 185
76-6-1102	Amended	101	1	SB 118
76-7-203	Amended	137	2	HB 259
76-7-204	Repealed	150	100	SB 14
76-8-305.5	Enacted	288	1	SB 146
76-8-306	Amended	13	27	HB 28
76-8-418	Amended	13	28	HB 28
76-8-506	Amended	92	1	SB 43
76-8-510.5	Amended	41	1	SB 73

Utah Code	Action	Ch. No.	Chapter Sec. No.	Bill No.
76-9-201	Amended	128	1	HB 221
76-9-704	Amended	143	2	HB 297
76-10-201	Amended	215	11	HB 38
76-10-202	Amended	215	12	HB 38
76-10-203	Amended	215	13	HB 38
76-10-504	Amended	2	302	SB 5
76-10-508	Amended	220	12	HB 65
76-10-528	Amended	2	303	SB 5
76-10-1204	Amended	281	3	HB 260
76-10-1205	Amended	281	4	HB 260
76-10-1206	Amended	281	5	HB 260
76-10-1230	Enacted	281	6	HB 260
76-10-1231	Enacted	281	7	HB 260
76-10-1232	Enacted	281	8	HB 260
76-10-1233	Enacted	281	9	HB 260
76-10-1311	Amended	102	27	SB 123
76-10-1506	Amended	2	304	SB 5
77-2-4.2	Amended	2	305	SB 5
77-2a-3.1	Amended	2	306	SB 5
77-7-18	Amended	2	307	SB 5
77-18-12	Amended	2	311	SB 5
77-23-204	Repealed and Reenacted	87	1	SB 30
77-23-209	Amended	87	2	SB 30
77-36-1.1	Amended	55	1	HB 59
77-37-3	Amended	13	29	HB 28
77-38a-102	Amended	96	3	SB 94
77-38a-203	Amended	96	4	SB 94
77-38a-302	Amended	96	5	SB
78-1-2.3	Amended	77	1	HB 218
78-3a-102	Amended	304	2	HB 338
78-3a-103	Amended	95	6	SB 83
78-3a-104	Amended	2	312	SB 5
78-3a-109	Amended	156	3	SB 104
78-3a-113	Amended	13	30	HB 28
78-3a-504	Amended	156	4	SB 104
78-3a-604	Enacted	106	2	HB 54
78-18-1	Amended	2	313	SB 5
78-29-101	Amended	243	7	SB 19
78-29-102	Amended	243	8	SB 19
78-29-103	Amended	243	9	SB 19
78-29-104	Enacted	243	10	SB 19
78-29-105	Enacted	243	11	SB 19
78-57-102	Amended	2	314	SB 5

UTAH CRIMINAL AND TRAFFIC CODE

TITLE 10

UTAH MUNICIPAL CODE

CHAPTER 3

MUNICIPAL GOVERNMENT

Part 7

Municipal Ordinances, Resolutions, and Procedure

Part 9

Appointed Officials and Their Duties

PART 7

MUNICIPAL ORDINANCES, RESOLUTIONS, AND PROCEDURE

10-3-701. Legislative power exercised by ordinance.

Except as otherwise specifically provided, the governing body of each municipality shall exercise its legislative powers through ordinances.   1977

10-3-702. Extent of power exercised by ordinance.

The governing body may pass any ordinance to regulate, require, prohibit, govern, control or supervise any activity, business, conduct or condition authorized by this act or any other provision of law. An officer of the municipality shall not be convicted of a criminal offense where he relied on or enforced an ordinance he reasonably believed to be a valid ordinance. It shall be a defense to any action for punitive damages that the official acted in good faith in enforcing an ordinance or that he enforced an ordinance on advice of legal counsel.   1977

10-3-703. Criminal penalties for violation of ordinance — Civil penalties prohibited — Exceptions.

(1) The governing body of each municipality may impose a minimum criminal penalty for the violation of any municipal ordinance by a fine not to exceed the maximum class B misdemeanor fine under Section 76-3-301 or by a term of imprisonment up to six months, or by both the fine and term of imprisonment.

(2) (a) Except as provided in Subsection (2)(b), the governing body may prescribe a minimum civil penalty for the violation of any municipal ordinance by a fine not to exceed the maximum class B misdemeanor fine under Section 76-3-301.

(b) A municipality may not impose a civil penalty and adjudication for the violation of a municipal moving traffic ordinance.   2003

10-3-703.5. Repealed.   2002

10-3-703.7. Administrative proceedings — Procedures — Appeals.

(1) As used in this section, "administrative proceeding" means an adjudicative hearing for a violation of a civil municipal ordinance.

(2) An administrative proceeding:

(a) shall be a public meeting with business transacted during regularly scheduled hours;

(b) shall be conducted by an administrative law judge;

(c) shall provide due process for the parties;

(d) shall be recorded or otherwise documented so that a true and correct transcript may be made of its proceedings; and

(e) may not be held for a civil violation that occurs in conjunction with another criminal violation as part of a single criminal episode that will be prosecuted in a criminal proceeding.

(3) An administrative law judge:

(a) shall be appointed by the municipality to conduct administrative proceedings;

(b) may be an employee of the municipality; and

(c) shall make a final administrative determination for each administrative proceeding.

(4) (a) A final administrative determination under this section may be an order for the municipality to abate the violation.

(b) If a final administrative determination under this section is for a violation, the final administrative determination may be appealed by a party in accordance with Subsection (5).

(5) (a) (i) Any person adversely affected by an administrative proceeding may petition a district court for review of the administrative determination.

(ii) In the petition, the petitioner may only allege that the administrative proceeding's decision was arbitrary, capricious, or illegal.

(iii) The petition is barred unless it is filed within 30 days after the administrative determination is final.

(b) (i) The administrative proceeding shall transmit to the reviewing district court the record of its proceedings, including its findings, orders, and a true and correct transcript of its proceedings.

(ii) The district court may not accept or consider any evidence that is not included in the administrative proceeding's record unless the evidence was offered to the administrative proceeding and the district court determines that the evidence was improperly excluded by the administrative proceeding.

2003

PART 9

APPOINTED OFFICIALS AND THEIR DUTIES

10-3-913. Authority of chief of police.

(1) The chief of police has the same authority as the sheriff within the boundaries of the municipality of appointment. The chief has authority to:

(a) suppress riots, disturbances, and breaches of the peace;

(b) apprehend all persons violating state laws or city ordinances;

(c) diligently discharge his duties and enforce all ordinances of the city to preserve the peace, good order, and protection of the rights and property of all persons; and

(d) attend the municipal justice court located within the city when required, provide security for the court, and obey its orders and directions.

(2) This section is not a limitation of a police chief's statewide authority as otherwise provided by law.

(3) The chief of police shall, on or before January 1, 2003, adopt a written policy that prohibits the stopping, detention, or search of any person when the action is solely motivated by considerations of race, color, ethnicity, age, or gender.

2002

10-3-918. Chief of police or marshal in a city of the third, fourth, or fifth class or town.

The chief of police or marshal in each city of the third, fourth, or fifth class or town:

(1) shall:

(a) exercise and perform the duties that are prescribed by the legislative body;

(b) be under the direction, control, and supervision of the person or body that appointed the chief or marshal; and

(c) on or before January 1, 2003, adopt a written policy that prohibits the stopping, detention, or search of any person when the action is solely motivated by considerations of race, color, ethnicity, age, or gender; and

(2) may, with the consent of the person or body that appointed the chief or marshal, appoint assistants to the chief of police or marshal. 2003

TITLE 13

COMMERCE AND TRADE

CHAPTER 20

NEW MOTOR VEHICLE WARRANTIES

13-20-2. Definitions.

As used in this chapter:

(1) "Consumer" means an individual who has entered into an agreement or contract for the transfer, lease, or purchase of a new motor vehicle other than for purposes of resale, or sublease,

during the duration of the period defined under Section 13-20-5.

(2) "Manufacturer" means manufacturer, importer, distributor, or anyone who is named as the warrantor on an express written warranty on a motor vehicle.

(3) "Motor home" means a self-propelled vehicular unit, primarily designed as a temporary dwelling for travel, recreational, and vacation use.

(4) (a) "Motor vehicle" includes:

(i) a motor home, as defined in this section, but only the self-propelled vehicle and chassis sold in this state;

(ii) a motor vehicle, as defined in Section 41-1a-102, sold in this state; and

(iii) a motorcycle, as defined in Section 41-1a-102, sold in this state if the motorcycle is designed primarily for use and operation on paved highways.

(b) "Motor vehicle" does not include:

(i) those portions of a motor home designated, used, or maintained primarily as a mobile dwelling, office, or commercial space;

(ii) farm tractor, road tractor, or truck tractor as defined in Section 41-1a-102;

(iii) mobile home as defined in Section 41-1a-102;

(iv) any motor vehicle with a gross laden weight of over 12,000 pounds, except a motor home as defined under Subsection (3);

(v) a motorcycle, as defined in Section 41-1a-102, if the motorcycle is designed primarily for use or operation over unimproved terrain;

(vi) an electric assisted bicycle as defined in Section 41-6a-102;

(vii) a moped as defined in Section 41-6a-102;

(viii) a motor assisted scooter as defined in Section 41-6a-102; or

(ix) a motor-driven cycle as defined in Section 41-6a-102. 2005

CHAPTER 32a

PAWNSHOP TRANSACTION INFORMATION ACT

13-32a-101.   Title.

This chapter is known as the "Pawnshop Transaction Information Act."   2004

13-32a-102.   Definitions.

As used in this chapter:

(1) "Account" means the Pawnbroker Operations Restricted Account created in Section 13-32a-113.

(2) "Board" means the Pawnshop Advisory Board created by this chapter.

(3) "Central database" or "database" means the electronic database created and operated under Section 13-32a-105.

(4) "Division" means the Division of Consumer Protection in Title 13, Chapter 1, Department of Commerce.

(5) "Identification" means a form of positive identification issued by a governmental entity that:

    (a) contains a numerical identifier and a photograph of the person identified; and

    (b) may include a state identification card, a state drivers license, a United States military identification card, or a United States passport.

(6) "Local law enforcement agency" means a law enforcement agency that has jurisdiction over the location where the pawnshop is located.

(7) "Misappropriated" means stolen, embezzled, converted, obtained by theft, or otherwise appropriated without authority of the lawful owner.

(8) "Original victim" means a victim who is not a party to the pawn transaction.

(9) "Pawnbroker" means a person whose business engages in the following activities:

    (a) loans money on one or more deposits of personal property;

    (b) deals in the purchase, exchange, or possession of personal property on condition of selling the same property back again to the pledgor or depositor;

    (c) loans or advances money on personal property by taking chattel mortgage security on the property and takes or receives the personal property into his possession, and who sells the unredeemed pledges; or

    (d) engages in a licensed business enterprise as a pawnshop.

(10) "Pawn ticket" means a document upon which information regarding a pawn transaction is entered when the pawn transaction is made.

(11) "Pawn transaction" means an extension of credit in which an individual delivers property to a pawnbroker for an advance of money or sells property to a pawnbroker and retains the right to redeem or repurchase the property for the redemption price within a fixed period of time.

(12) "Pawnshop" means the physical location or premises where a pawnbroker conducts business.

(13) "Property" means any tangible personal property.

(14) "Register" means the record of information required under this chapter to be maintained by the pawnbroker. The register is an electronic record that is in a format that is compatible with the central database.   2005

13-32a-102.5.   Administration and enforcement.

(1) The division shall administer and enforce this chapter in accordance with the authority under Title 13, Chapter 2, Division of Consumer Protection.

(2) The attorney general, upon request, shall give legal advice to, and act as counsel for, the division in the exercise of its responsibilities under this chapter.

(3) Reasonable attorney's fees, costs, and interest shall be awarded to the division in any action brought to enforce the provisions of this chapter.   2005

13-32a-103.   Compliance with criminal code.

Every pawnbroker shall, regarding each article of property a person pawns or sells, comply with the requirements of Subsections 76-6-408(2)(c)(i) through (iii) regarding the person's:

(1) legal right to the property;

(2) fingerprint; and

(3) picture identification.   2004

13-32a-104.   Register required to be maintained — Contents — Identification of items.

(1) Every pawnbroker shall keep a register of pawn transactions, in which the pawnbroker or his employee shall enter the following information regarding every article pawned to him:

    (a) the date and time of the transaction;

    (b) the pawn transaction ticket number;

    (c) the date by which the article must be redeemed;

    (d) the following information regarding the person who pawns the article:

       (i) the person's name, residence address, and date of birth;

       (ii) the number of the driver license or other form of positive identification presented by the person, and notations of discrepancies if the person's physical description, including gender, height, weight, race, age, hair color, and eye color, does not correspond with identification provided by the person;

       (iii) the person's signature; and

       (iv) a legible fingerprint of the person's right thumb, or if the right thumb cannot be fingerprinted, a legible fingerprint of the person with a written notation identifying the fingerprint and the reason why the thumb print was unavailable;

    (e) the amount loaned on or paid for the article, or the article for which it was traded;

    (f) the identification of the pawnbroker or his employee, whoever is making the register entry; and

    (g) an accurate description of the article of property, including available identifying marks such as:

       (i) names, brand names, numbers, serial numbers, model numbers, color, manufacturers' names, and size;

       (ii) metallic composition, and any jewels, stones, or glass;

       (iii) any other marks of identification or indicia of ownership on the article;

(iv) the weight of the article, if the payment is based on weight;

(v) any other unique identifying feature;

(vi) gold content, if indicated; and

(vii) if multiple articles of a similar nature are delivered together in one transaction and the articles do not bear serial or model numbers and do not include precious metals or gemstones, such as musical or video recordings, books, or hand tools, the description of the articles is adequate if it includes the quantity of the articles and a description of the type of articles delivered.

(2) A pawnshop may not accept any personal property if, upon inspection, it is apparent that serial numbers, model names, or identifying characteristics have been intentionally defaced on that article of property.   2004

13-32a-105.   Central database.

(1) There is created under this section a central database as a statewide repository for all information pawnbrokers are required to submit in accordance with this chapter and for the use of all participating law enforcement agencies whose jurisdictions include one or more pawnshops.

(2) The Division of Purchasing and General Services created in Title 63A, Chapter 2, shall:

(a) meet with the board to determine the required elements of the database; and

(b) conduct a statewide request for proposal for the creation of and maintenance of the central database.

(3) Funding for the creation and operation of the central database shall be from the account.

(4) (a) Any entity submitting a bid to create, maintain, and operate the database pursuant to the request for proposal conducted by the Division of Purchasing and General Services may not hold any financial or operating interest in any pawnshop in any state.

(b) The Division of Purchasing and General Services, in conjunction with the Pawnshop Advisory Board, shall verify before a bid is awarded that the selected entity meets the requirements of Subsection (4)(a).

(c) If any entity is awarded a bid under this Subsection (4) and is later found to hold any interest in violation of Subsection (4)(a), the award is subject to being opened again for request for proposal.

(5) Information entered in the database shall be retained for five years and shall then be deleted.
                                          2004

13-32a-106.   Transaction information provided to the central database — Protected information.

(1) The information required to be recorded under Sections 13-32a-103 and 13-32a-104 that is capable of being transmitted electronically shall be transmitted electronically to the central database on the next business day following the transaction.

(2) The pawnbroker shall maintain all pawn tickets generated by the pawnshop and shall maintain the tickets in a manner so that the tickets are available to local law enforcement agencies as required by this chapter and as requested by any law enforcement agency as part of an investigation or reasonable random inspection conducted pursuant to this chapter.

(3) (a) If a pawnshop experiences a computer or electronic malfunction that affects its ability to report transactions as required in Subsection (1), the pawnshop shall immediately notify the local law enforcement agency of the malfunction.

(b) The pawnshop shall solve the malfunction within three business days or notify law enforcement under Subsection (4).

(4) If the computer or electronic malfunction under Subsection (3) cannot be solved within three business days, the pawnshop shall notify the local law enforcement agency of the reasons for the delay and provide documentation from a reputable computer maintenance company of the reasons why the computer or electronic malfunction cannot be solved within three business days.

(5) A computer or electronic malfunction does not suspend the pawnshop's obligation to comply with all other provisions of this chapter.

(6) During the malfunction under Subsections (3) and (4), the pawnshop shall:

(a) maintain the pawn tickets and other information required under this chapter in a written form; and

(b) arrange with the local law enforcement agency a mutually acceptable alternative method by which the pawnshop provides the required information to the local law enforcement official.

(7) A pawnshop that violates the electronic transaction reporting requirement of this section is subject to an administrative fine of $50 per day if:

(a) the pawnshop is unable to submit the information electronically due to a computer or electronic malfunction;

(b) the three business day period under Subsection (3) has expired; and

(c) the pawnshop has not provided documentation regarding its inability to solve the malfunction as required under Subsection (4).

(8) A pawnshop is not responsible for a delay in transmission of information that results from a malfunction in the central database.   2005

13-32a-106.5.   Confidentiality of pawn and purchase transactions.

(1) All pawn and purchase transaction records delivered to a local law enforcement official or transmitted to the central database pursuant to Section 13-32a-106 are protected records under Section 63-2-304. These records may be used only by law enforcement officials and the division and only for the law enforcement and administrative enforcement purposes of:

(a) investigating possible criminal conduct involving the property delivered to the pawnbroker in a pawn or purchase transaction;

(b) investigating a pawnbroker's possible violation of the record keeping or reporting requirements of this chapter when the local law enforcement official, based on a review of the records and information received, has reason to believe that a violation has occurred;

(c) responding to an inquiry from a person claiming ownership of described property by searching the database to determine if property matching the description has been delivered to a pawnbroker by another person in a pawn or purchase transaction and if so, obtaining from the database:

(i) a description of the property;

(ii) the name and address of the pawnbroker who received the property; and

(iii) the name, address, and date of birth of the conveying person; and

(d) take enforcement action under Section 13-2-5 against a pawnbroker.

(2) (a) A person may not knowingly and intentionally use, release, publish, or otherwise make available to any person or entity any information obtained from the database for any purpose other than those specified in Subsection (1).

(b) Each separate violation of this Subsection (2) is subject to a civil penalty not to exceed $250.

2005

13-32a-107. Deadline for registers to be electronic — Notice for updating.

(1) On and after January 1, 2005, each pawnbroker in the state that generates ten or more pawn transactions per month shall maintain the register in an electronic format that is compatible with the central database computer system.

(2) (a) On and after January 15, 2005, pawnbrokers under Subsection (1) are subject to an administrative fine of $50 a day for each daily report required under Section 13-32a-106 that is submitted as a written report rather than electronically.

(b) Fines imposed under this section shall be paid to the division, which shall deposit the fines in the account.

(3) The operators of the central database shall establish written procedures in conjunction with the Pawnshop Advisory Board to ensure that when the central database is upgraded, the affected pawnbrokers will receive adequate notice, information, and time to upgrade their computer systems so the systems are compatible with the upgraded central database.

2005

13-32a-108. Retention of records — Reasonable inspection.

(1) The pawnbroker or law enforcement agency, whichever has custody of pawn tickets, shall retain them for no less than three years from the date of the transaction.

(2) (a) A law enforcement agency may conduct random reasonable inspections of pawnshops for the purpose of monitoring compliance with the reporting requirements of this chapter. The inspections may be conducted to:

(i) confirm that pawned items match the description reported to the database by the pawnshop; and

(ii) make spot checks of property at the pawnshop to determine if the property is appropriately reported.

(b) Inspections under Subsection (2)(a) shall be performed during the regular business hours of the pawnshop.

2004

13-32a-109. Holding period for pawned articles.

(1) (a) The pawnbroker shall hold all articles pawned or sold to him for not fewer than 30 days after the date of receipt of the article, except that the pawnbroker may within this time period return an article to the person who pawned it.

(b) This Subsection (1) does not preclude a law enforcement agency from requiring a pawnbroker to hold an article longer than 30 days if necessary in the course of an investigation.

(2) If a law enforcement agency seizes an article or requires the pawnbroker to hold an article as part of an investigation, the agency shall provide to the pawnbroker a hold ticket issued by the agency, which:

(a) states the active case number;

(b) confirms the date of the hold request and the article to be held; and

(c) facilitates the pawnbroker's ability to track the article when the prosecution takes over the case.

(3) If an article is not seized by a law enforcement agency that has placed a hold on the property, the property may remain in the custody of the pawnbroker until further disposition by the law enforcement agency, and as consistent with this chapter.

(4) The initial hold by a law enforcement agency is for a period of 45 days. If the article is not seized by the law enforcement agency, the article shall remain in the custody of the pawnshop and is subject to the hold unless exigent circumstances require the pawned article to be seized by the law enforcement agency.

(5) (a) A law enforcement agency may extend any hold for up to an additional 45 days when exigent circumstances require the extension.

(b) When there is an extension of a hold under Subsection (5)(a), the requesting law enforcement agency shall notify the pawnshop subject to the hold prior to the expiration of the initial 45 days.

(c) A law enforcement agency may not hold an item for more than the 90 days allowed under Subsections (5)(a) and (b) without obtaining a court order authorizing the hold.

(6) A hold on an article under Subsection (2) takes precedence over any request to claim or purchase the article subject to the hold.

(7) When the purpose for the hold on or seizure of an article is terminated, the law enforcement agency requiring the hold or seizure shall within 15 days after the termination:

(a) notify the pawnshop in writing that the hold or seizure has been terminated;

(b) return the article subject to the seizure to the pawnbroker; or

(c) if the article is not returned to the pawnbroker, advise the pawnbroker either in writing or electronically of the specific alternative disposition of the article.

(8) If the article is subject to an investigation and a criminal prosecution results, the prosecuting agency shall, upon disposition of the case, request restitution to the pawnbroker for the crimes perpetrated against the pawnshop as a victim of theft by deception in addition to the request for restitution to the original victim.

(9) If the original victim of the theft of the property files a police report and the property is subsequently located at a pawnshop, the victim must fully cooperate with the prosecution of the crimes perpetrated against the pawnshop as a victim of theft by deception, in order to qualify for restitution regarding the property.

(10) If the victim does not wish to pursue criminal charges or does not cooperate in the prosecution of the property theft against the defendant and the theft by deception committed against the pawnshop, then the original victim must pay to the pawnshop the amount of money financed by the pawnshop to the defendant in order to obtain the property.

(11) (a) The victim's cooperation in the prosecution of the property crimes and in the prosecution of the theft by deception offense committed against the pawnshop suspends the requirements of Subsections (9) and (10).

(b) If the victim cooperates in the prosecution under Subsection (11)(a) and the defendants are convicted, the prosecuting agency shall direct the pawnshop to turn over the property to the victim.

(c) Upon receipt of notice from the prosecuting agency that the property must be turned over to the victim, the pawnshop shall return the property to the victim as soon as reasonably possible.

(12) A pawnshop must fully cooperate in the prosecution of the property crimes committed against the original victim and the property crime of theft by deception committed against the pawnshop in order to participate in any court-ordered restitution.

(13) At all times during the course of a criminal investigation and subsequent prosecution, the article subject to a law enforcement hold shall be kept secure by the pawnshop subject to the hold unless the pawned article has been seized by the law enforcement agency.   2004

13-32a-110. Penalties.

(1) A violation of any of the following sections is subject to a civil penalty of not more than $500:

(a) Section 13-32a-104, register required to be maintained;

(b) Section 13-32a-106, transaction information provided to law enforcement;

(c) Section 13-32a-108, retention of records; or

(d) Section 13-32a-109, holding period for pawned articles.

(2) This section does not prohibit civil action by a governmental entity regarding the pawnbroker's business operation or licenses.   2005

13-32a-111. Fees to fund training and central database.

(1) On and after January 1, 2005, each pawnshop in operation shall annually pay $250 to the division, to be deposited in the account.

(2) On and after January 1, 2005, each law enforcement agency that participates in the use of the database shall annually pay to the division a fee of $2 per sworn law enforcement officer who is employed by the agency as of January 1 of that year. The fee shall be deposited in the account.

(3) The fees under Subsections (1) and (2) shall be paid to the account annually on or before January 30.   2005

13-32a-112. Pawnshop Advisory Board — Membership — Duties — Provide training — Records of compliance.

(1) There is created within the division the Pawnshop Advisory Board. The board consists of ten voting members and one nonvoting member:

(a) one representative of the Utah Chiefs of Police Association;

(b) one representative of the Utah Sheriffs Association;

(c) one representative of the Statewide Association of Prosecutors;

(d) five representatives from the pawnshop industry who are appointed by the director of the Utah Commission on Criminal and Juvenile Justice (CCJJ) and who represent five separate pawnshops, each owned by a separate person or entity;

(e) one law enforcement officer who is appointed by the board members under Subsections (1)(a) through (d);

(f) one law enforcement officer whose work regularly involves pawnshops and who is appointed by the board members under Subsections (1)(a) through (d); and

(g) one representative from the central database, who is nonvoting.

(2) (a) The board shall elect one voting member as the chair of the board by a majority of the members present at the board's first meeting each year.

(b) The chair shall preside over the board for a period of one year.

(c) The advisory board shall meet quarterly upon the call of the chair.

(3) (a) The board shall conduct quarterly training sessions regarding compliance with this chapter and other applicable state laws for any person defined as a pawnbroker in this chapter.

(b) Each training session shall provide not fewer than two hours of training.

(4) (a) Each pawnbroker in operation as of January 1 shall ensure one or more persons employed by the pawnshop each participate in no fewer than four hours of compliance training within that year.

(b) This requirement does not limit the number of employees, directors, or officers of a pawnshop who attend the compliance training.

(5) The board shall monitor and keep a record of the hours of compliance training accrued by each pawnshop.

(6) The board shall provide each pawnshop with a certificate of compliance upon completion by an employee of the four hours of compliance training.

(7) (a) Each law enforcement agency that has a pawnshop located within its jurisdiction shall ensure that at least one of its officers completes four hours of compliance training yearly.

(b) This requirement does not limit the number of law enforcement officers who attend the compliance training.   2005

13-32a-113. Pawnbroker Operations Restricted Account.

(1) There is created within the General Fund a restricted account known as the Pawnbroker Operations Restricted Account.

(2) (a) The account shall be funded from the fees and administrative fines imposed and collected under Sections 13-32a-106, 13-32a-107, 13-32a-110, and 13-32a-111. These fees and administrative fines shall be paid to the division, which shall deposit them in the account.

(b) The Legislature may appropriate the funds in this account:

(i) to the board for the costs of providing training required under this chapter, costs of the central database created in Section 13-32a-105, and for costs of operation of the board; and

(ii) to the division for management of fees and penalties paid under this chapter.

(c) The board shall account to the division for expenditures.

(d) The board shall account separately for expenditures for:

(i) training required under this chapter;

(ii) operation of the database;

(iii) operation of the board; and

(iv) costs of operation of the board.   2005

13-32a-114. Preemption of local ordinances — Exceptions.

(1) This chapter preempts all city, county, and other local ordinances governing pawnshops, pawnbrokers, and pawnbroking transactions, if the ordinances are more restrictive than the provisions of this chapter or are not consistent with this chapter.

(2) Subsection (1) does not preclude a city, county, or other local governmental unit from:

(a) enacting or enforcing local ordinances concerning public health, safety, or welfare, if the ordinances are uniform and equal in application to pawnshops and pawnbrokers and other retail businesses or activities;

(b) requiring a pawnshop or pawnbroker to obtain and maintain a business license; and

(c) enacting zoning ordinances that restrict areas where pawnshops and other retail businesses or activities can be located.   2005

TITLE 17

COUNTIES

CHAPTER 22

SHERIFF

17-22-2. Sheriff — General duties.

(1) The sheriff shall:

(a) preserve the peace;

(b) make all lawful arrests;

(c) attend in person or by deputy the Supreme Court and the Court of Appeals when required or when the court is held within his county, all courts of record, and court commissioner and referee sessions held within his county, obey their lawful orders and directions, and comply with the court security rule, Rule 3-414, of the Utah Code of Judicial Administration;

(d) upon request of the juvenile court, aid the court in maintaining order during hearings and transport a minor to and from youth corrections facilities, other institutions, or other designated places;

(e) attend county justice courts if the judge finds that the matter before the court requires the sheriff's attendance for security, transportation, and escort of jail prisoners in his custody, or for the custody of jurors;

(f) command the aid of as many inhabitants of his county as he considers necessary in the execution of these duties;

(g) take charge of and keep the county jail and the jail prisoners;

(h) receive and safely keep all persons committed to his custody, file and preserve the commitments of those persons, and record the name, age, place of birth, and description of each person committed;

(i) release on the record all attachments of real property when the attachment he receives has been released or discharged;

(j) endorse on all process and notices the year, month, day, hour, and minute of reception, and, upon payment of fees, issue a certificate to the person delivering process or notice showing the names of the parties, title of paper, and the time of receipt;

(k) serve all process and notices as prescribed by law;

(l) if he makes service of process or notice, certify on the process or notices the manner, time, and place of service, or, if he fails to make service, certify the reason upon the process or notice, and return them without delay;

(m) extinguish fires occurring in the undergrowth, trees, or wooded areas on the public land within his county;

(n) perform as required by any contracts between the county and private contractors for management, maintenance, operation, and construction of county jails entered into under the authority of Section 17-53-311;

(o) manage search and rescue services in his county;

(p) obtain saliva DNA specimens as required under Section 53-10-404;

(q) on or before January 1, 2003, adopt a written policy that prohibits the stopping, detention, or search of any person when the action is solely motivated by considerations of race, color, ethnicity, age, or gender; and

(r) perform any other duties that are required by law.

(2) Violation of Subsection (1)(j) is a class C misdemeanor. Violation of any other subsection under Subsection (1) is a class A misdemeanor.   2002

CHAPTER 43

LOCAL HUMAN SERVICES ACT

Part 2

Local Substance Abuse Authorities

PART 2

LOCAL SUBSTANCE ABUSE AUTHORITIES

17-43-201. Local substance abuse authorities — Responsibilities.

(1) (a) (i) In each county operating under a county executive-council form of government under Section 17-52-504, the county legislative body is the local substance abuse authority, provided however that any contract for plan services shall be administered by the county executive.

(ii) In each county operating under a council-manager form of government under Section 17-52-505, the county manager is the local substance abuse authority.

(iii) In each county other than a county described in Subsection (1)(a)(i) or (ii), the county legislative body is the local substance abuse authority.

(b) Within legislative appropriations and county matching funds required by this section, and under the policy direction of the board and the administrative direction of the division, each local substance abuse authority shall:

(i) develop substance abuse prevention and treatment services plans; and

(ii) provide substance abuse services to residents of the county.

(2) (a) By executing an interlocal agreement under Title 11, Chapter 13, Interlocal Cooperation Act,

two or more counties may join to provide substance abuse prevention and treatment services.

(b) The legislative bodies of counties joining to provide services may establish acceptable ways of apportioning the cost of substance abuse services.

(c) Each agreement for joint substance abuse services shall:

(i) (A) designate the treasurer of one of the participating counties or another person as the treasurer for the combined substance abuse authorities and as the custodian of moneys available for the joint services; and

(B) provide that the designated treasurer, or other disbursing officer authorized by the treasurer, may make payments from the moneys for the joint services upon audit of the appropriate auditing officer or officers representing the participating counties;

(ii) provide for the appointment of an independent auditor or a county auditor of one of the participating counties as the designated auditing officer for the combined substance abuse authorities;

(iii) (A) provide for the appointment of the county or district attorney of one of the participating counties as the designated legal officer for the combined substance abuse authorities; and

(B) authorize the designated legal officer to request and receive the assistance of the county or district attorneys of the other participating counties in defending or prosecuting actions within their counties relating to the combined substance abuse authorities; and

(iv) provide for the adoption of management, clinical, financial, procurement, personnel, and administrative policies as already established by one of the participating counties or as approved by the legislative body of each participating county or interlocal board.

(d) An agreement for joint substance abuse services may provide for joint operation of services and facilities or for operation of services and facilities under contract by one participating local substance abuse authority for other participating local substance abuse authorities.

(3) (a) Each local substance abuse authority is accountable to the department, the Department of Health, and the state with regard to the use of state and federal funds received from those departments for substance abuse services, regardless of whether the services are provided by a private contract provider.

(b) Each local substance abuse authority shall comply, and require compliance by its contract provider, with all directives issued by the department and the Department of Health regarding the use and expenditure of state and federal funds received from those departments for the purpose of providing substance abuse programs and services. The department and Department of Health shall ensure that those directives are not duplicative or conflicting, and shall consult and coordinate with local substance abuse authorities with regard to programs and services.

(4) Each local substance abuse authority shall:

(a) review and evaluate substance abuse prevention and treatment needs and services, including substance abuse needs and services for individuals incarcerated in a county jail or other county correctional facility;

(b) annually prepare and submit to the division a plan approved by the county legislative body for funding and service delivery that includes:

(i) provisions for services, either directly by the substance abuse authority or by contract, for adults, youth, and children, including those incarcerated in a county jail or other county correctional facility; and

(ii) primary prevention, targeted prevention, early intervention, and treatment services;

(c) establish and maintain, either directly or by contract, programs licensed under Title 62A, Chapter 2, Licensure of Programs and Facilities;

(d) appoint directly or by contract a full or part time director for substance abuse programs, and prescribe the director's duties;

(e) provide input and comment on new and revised policies established by the board;

(f) establish and require contract providers to establish administrative, clinical, procurement, personnel, financial, and management policies regarding substance abuse services and facilities, in accordance with the policies of the board, and state and federal law;

(g) establish mechanisms allowing for direct citizen input;

(h) annually contract with the division to provide substance abuse programs and services in accordance with the provisions of Title 62A, Chapter 15, Substance Abuse and Mental Health Act;

(i) comply with all applicable state and federal statutes, policies, audit requirements, contract requirements, and any directives resulting from those audits and contract requirements;

(j) promote or establish programs for the prevention of substance abuse within the community setting through community-based prevention programs;

(k) provide funding equal to at least 20% of the state funds that it receives to fund services described in the plan;

(l) comply with the requirements and procedures of Title 11, Chapter 13, Interlocal Cooperation Act, Title 17A, Chapter 1, Part 4, Uniform Fiscal Procedures for Special Districts Act, and Title 51, Chapter 2a, Accounting Reports from Political Subdivisions, Interlocal Organizations, and Other Local Entities Act;

(m) for persons convicted of driving under the influence in violation of Section 41-6a-502 or 41-6a-517, conduct the following as defined in Section 41-6a-501:

(i) a screening;

(ii) an assessment;

(iii) an educational series; and

(iv) substance abuse treatment; and

(n) utilize proceeds of the accounts described in Subsection 62A-15-503(1) to supplement the cost of providing the services described in Subsection (4)(m).

(5) Before disbursing any public funds, each local substance abuse authority shall require that each entity that receives any public funds from the local substance abuse authority agrees in writing that:

(a) the entity's financial records and other records relevant to the entity's performance of the services provided to the local substance abuse authority shall be subject to examination by:

(i) the division;

(ii) the local substance abuse authority director;

(iii) (A) the county treasurer and county or district attorney; or

(B) if two or more counties jointly provide substance abuse services under an agreement under Subsection (2), the designated treasurer and the designated legal officer;

(iv) the county legislative body; and

(v) in a county with a county executive that is separate from the county legislative body, the county executive;

(b) the county auditor may examine and audit the entity's financial and other records relevant to the entity's performance of the services provided to the local substance abuse authority; and

(c) the entity will comply with the provisions of Subsection (3)(b).

(6) A local substance abuse authority may receive property, grants, gifts, supplies, materials, contributions, and any benefit derived therefrom, for substance abuse services. If those gifts are conditioned upon their use for a specified service or program, they shall be so used.

(7) (a) As used in this section, "public funds" means the same as that term is defined in Section 17-43-203.

(b) Public funds received for the provision of services pursuant to the local substance abuse plan may not be used for any other purpose except those authorized in the contract between the local substance abuse authority and the provider for the provision of plan services.   2005

TITLE 23

WILDLIFE RESOURCES CODE

CHAPTER 13

GENERAL PROVISIONS

23-13-1. Short title — "Wildlife Resources Code of Utah."

This act shall be known and may be cited as the "Wildlife Resources Code of Utah."   1971

23-13-2. Definitions.

As used in this title:

(1) "Activity regulated under this title" means any act, attempted act, or activity prohibited or regulated under any provision of Title 23 or the rules, and proclamations promulgated thereunder pertaining to protected wildlife including:

(a) fishing;

(b) hunting;

(c) trapping;

(d) taking;

(e) permitting any dog, falcon, or other domesticated animal to take;

(f) transporting;

(g) possessing;

(h) selling;

(i) wasting;

(j) importing;

(k) exporting;

(l) rearing;

(m) keeping;

(n) utilizing as a commercial venture; and

(o) releasing to the wild.

(2) "Aquatic animal" has the meaning provided in Section 4-37-103.

(3) "Aquatic wildlife" means species of fish, mollusks, crustaceans, aquatic insects, or amphibians.

(4) "Aquaculture facility" has the meaning provided in Section 4-37-103.

(5) "Bag limit" means the maximum limit, in number or amount, of protected wildlife that one person may legally take during one day.

(6) "Big game" means species of hoofed protected wildlife.

(7) "Carcass" means the dead body of an animal or its parts.

(8) "Certificate of registration" means a document issued under this title, or any rule or proclamation of the Wildlife Board granting authority to engage in activities not covered by a license, permit, or tag.

(9) "Closed season" means the period of time during which the taking of protected wildlife is prohibited.

(10) "Conservation officer" means a full-time, permanent employee of the Division of Wildlife Resources who is POST certified as a peace or a special function officer.

(11) "Dedicated hunter program" means a program that provides:

(a) expanded hunting opportunities;

(b) opportunities to participate in projects that are beneficial to wildlife; and

(c) education in hunter ethics and wildlife management principles.

(12) "Division" means the Division of Wildlife Resources.

(13) (a) "Domicile" means the place:

(i) where an individual has a fixed permanent home and principal establishment;

(ii) to which the individual if absent, intends to return; and

(iii) in which the individual, and the individual's family voluntarily reside, not for a special or temporary purpose, but with the intention of making a permanent home.

(b) To create a new domicile an individual must:

(i) abandon the old domicile; and

(ii) be able to prove that a new domicile has been established.

(14) "Endangered" means wildlife designated as such pursuant to Section 3 of the federal Endangered Species Act of 1973.

(15) "Fee fishing facility" has the meaning provided in Section 4-37-103.

(16) "Feral" means an animal which is normally domesticated but has reverted to the wild.

(17) "Fishing" means to take fish or crayfish by any means.

(18) "Furbearer" means species of the Bassariscidae, Canidae, Felidae, Mustelidae, and Castoridae families, except coyote and cougar.

(19) "Game" means wildlife normally pursued, caught, or taken by sporting means for human use.

(20) (a) "Guide" means a person who receives compensation or advertises services for assisting another person to take protected wildlife.

(b) Assistance under Subsection (20)(a) includes the provision of food, shelter, or transportation, or any combination of these.

(21) "Guide's agent" means a person who is employed by a guide to assist another person to take protected wildlife.

(22) "Hunting" means to take or pursue a reptile, amphibian, bird, or mammal by any means.

(23) "Intimidate or harass" means to physically interfere with or impede, hinder, or diminish the efforts of an officer in the performance of the officer's duty.

(24) "Nonresident" means a person who does not qualify as a resident.

(25) "Open season" means the period of time during which protected wildlife may be legally taken.

(26) "Pecuniary gain" means the acquisition of money or something of monetary value.

(27) "Permit" means a document, including a stamp, which grants authority to engage in specified activities under this title or a rule or proclamation of the Wildlife Board.

(28) "Person" means an individual, association, partnership, government agency, corporation, or an agent of the foregoing.

(29) "Possession" means actual or constructive possession.

(30) "Possession limit" means the number of bag limits one individual may legally possess.

(31) (a) "Private fish installation" means a body of water where privately owned, protected aquatic wildlife are propagated or kept.

(b) "Private fish installation" does not include any aquaculture facility or fee fishing facility.

(32) "Private wildlife farm" means an enclosed place where privately owned birds or furbearers are propagated or kept and which restricts the birds or furbearers from:

(a) commingling with wild birds or furbearers; and

(b) escaping into the wild.

(33) "Proclamation" means the publication used to convey a statute, rule, policy, or pertinent information as it relates to wildlife.

(34) (a) "Protected aquatic wildlife" means aquatic wildlife as defined in Subsection (3), except as provided in Subsection (34)(b).

(b) "Protected aquatic wildlife" does not include aquatic insects.

(35) (a) "Protected wildlife" means wildlife as defined in Subsection (49), except as provided in Subsection (35)(b).

(b) "Protected wildlife" does not include coyote, field mouse, gopher, ground squirrel, jack rabbit, muskrat, and raccoon.

(36) "Released to the wild" means to be turned loose from confinement.

(37) (a) "Resident" means a person who:

(i) has been domiciled in the state of Utah for six consecutive months immediately preceding the purchase of a license; and

(ii) does not claim residency for hunting, fishing, or trapping in any other state or country.

(b) A Utah resident retains Utah residency if that person leaves this state:

(i) to serve in the armed forces of the United States or for religious or educational purposes; and

(ii) complies with Subsection (37)(a)(ii).

(c) (i) A member of the armed forces of the United States and dependents are residents for the purposes of this chapter as of the date the member reports for duty under assigned orders in the state if the member:

(A) is not on temporary duty in this state; and

(B) complies with Subsection (37)(a)(ii).

(ii) A copy of the assignment orders must be presented to a wildlife division office to verify the member's qualification as a resident.

(d) A nonresident attending an institution of higher learning in this state as a full-time student may qualify as a resident for purposes of this chapter if the student:

(i) has been present in this state for 60 consecutive days immediately preceding the purchase of the license; and

(ii) complies with Subsection (37)(a)(ii).

(e) A Utah resident license is invalid if a resident license for hunting, fishing, or trapping is purchased in any other state or country.

(f) An absentee landowner paying property tax on land in Utah does not qualify as a resident.

(38) "Sell" means to offer or possess for sale, barter, exchange, or trade, or the act of selling, bartering, exchanging, or trading.

(39) "Small game" means species of protected wildlife:

    (a) commonly pursued for sporting purposes; and

    (b) not classified as big game, aquatic wildlife, or furbearers and excluding turkey, cougar, and bear.

(40) "Spoiled" means impairment of the flesh of wildlife which renders it unfit for human consumption.

(41) "Spotlighting" means throwing or casting the rays of any spotlight, headlight, or other artificial light on any highway or in any field, woodland, or forest while having in possession a weapon by which protected wildlife may be killed.

(42) "Tag" means a card, label, or other identification device issued for attachment to the carcass of protected wildlife.

(43) "Take" means to:

    (a) hunt, pursue, harass, catch, capture, possess, angle, seine, trap, or kill any protected wildlife; or

    (b) attempt any action referred to in Subsection (43)(a).

(44) "Threatened" means wildlife designated as such pursuant to Section 3 of the federal Endangered Species Act of 1973.

(45) "Trapping" means taking protected wildlife with a trapping device.

(46) "Trophy animal" means an animal described as follows:

    (a) deer — any buck with an outside antler measurement of 24 inches or greater;

    (b) elk — any bull with six points on at least one side;

    (c) bighorn, desert, or rocky mountain sheep — any ram with a curl exceeding half curl;

    (d) moose — any bull;

    (e) mountain goat — any male or female;

    (f) pronghorn antelope — any buck with horns exceeding 14 inches; or

    (g) bison — any bull.

(47) "Waste" means to abandon protected wildlife or to allow protected wildlife to spoil or to be used in a manner not normally associated with its beneficial use.

(48) "Water pollution" means the introduction of matter or thermal energy to waters within this state which:

    (a) exceeds state water quality standards; or

    (b) could be harmful to protected wildlife.

(49) "Wildlife" means:

    (a) crustaceans, including brine shrimp and crayfish;

    (b) mollusks; and

    (c) vertebrate animals living in nature, except feral animals. 2004

23-13-3. Wildlife declared property of the state.

All wildlife existing within this state, not held by private ownership and legally acquired, is the property of the state. 1992

23-13-4. Captivity of protected wildlife unlawful.

It is unlawful for any person to hold in captivity at any time any protected wildlife except as provided by this code or rules and regulations of the Wildlife Board. 1971

23-13-5. Importation or exportation and release of wildlife unlawful.

It is unlawful for any person to import into or export from the state of Utah any species of live native or exotic wildlife or to possess or release from captivity any such imported live wildlife except as provided in this code or the rules and regulations of the Wildlife Board without first securing written permission from the Division of Wildlife Resources. 1973

23-13-6. Taking of wildlife by division.

The Division of Wildlife Resources may take wildlife of any kind from any place and in any manner for purposes deemed by the director to be in the interest of wildlife conservation. 1995

23-13-7. Use of fireworks and explosives by division employees and certain federal game agents.

Notwithstanding any other provision of law, employees of the Division of Wildlife Resources and federal game agents charged with the duty of managing wildlife resources may, without obtaining a permit, use fireworks and explosives to rally, drive, or otherwise disperse concentrations of wildlife as may be necessary to protect property or wildlife resources. 1986

23-13-8. Private wildlife farms.

(1) Any person may establish and maintain private wildlife farms for propagating, rearing, and keeping furbearers or birds classified as protected wildlife and may sell or dispose of wildlife reared upon such farms except that disposal may not include release to the wild without first securing written permission from the Wildlife Board. Before establishing such farm, a person shall obtain written authorization from the Division of Wildlife Resources in accordance with rules established by the Wildlife Board. Any wildlife which escapes from private wildlife farms becomes the property of the state.

(2) This section does not apply to private fur farms established and maintained for rearing domesticated, privately owned mink or chinchilla which were not acquired as wild animals from any state or country, nor does it provide for the propagating, rearing, and keeping of any protected wildlife other than those specified in this section. 1986

23-13-9, 23-13-10. Repealed. 1986

23-13-11. Violations.

(1) Unless otherwise provided, a violation of any provision of this title is a class B misdemeanor.

(2) A violation of any rule or proclamation of the Wildlife Board is a class C misdemeanor. 1995

23-13-12. Repealed. 2000

23-13-12.5. Agreement with a tribe.

(1) As used in this section, "tribe" means a federally recognized:

    (a) Indian tribe; or

    (b) Indian band.

(2) (a) Subject to the requirements of this section, the governor may enter into an agreement with a tribe to settle a dispute between the state and the tribe concerning a hunting, fishing, or trapping right claim that is:

      (i) based on:

        (A) a treaty;

        (B) an aboriginal right; or

        (C) other recognized federal right; and

      (ii) on lands located within the state.

(b) Except as provided in Subsection (2)(c), an agreement permitted under Subsection (2)(a) may not exempt any person from the requirements of this title.

(c) An agreement permitted under Subsection (2)(a) may exempt or partially exempt a tribe that is a party to the agreement or a member of that tribe from:

(i) Section 23-16-5, placing a limit of one of any species of big game during a license year;

(ii) Section 23-16-6, commencement date of the general deer season;

(iii) a hunter or furharvester education requirement under Chapter 19, Licenses, Permits, and Tags;

(iv) an age restriction under Chapter 19, Licenses, Permits, and Tags;

(v) paying a fee required under this title to obtain a hunting, fishing, or trapping license or permit;

(vi) obtaining a license or permit required under this title to hunt, trap, or fish; or

(vii) complying with a rule or proclamation of the Wildlife Board if the exemption is not inconsistent with this title.

(d) An agreement permitted under Subsection (2)(a) shall:

(i) be in writing;

(ii) be signed by:

(A) the governor; and

(B) the governing body of the tribe that:

(I) is designated by the tribe; and

(II) may bind the tribe to the terms of the agreement;

(iii) be conditioned on obtaining any approval required by federal law;

(iv) state the effective date of the agreement;

(v) provide that the governor shall renegotiate the agreement if the agreement is or becomes inconsistent with a state statute for which an exemption is not authorized under this section; and

(vi) include any accommodation made by the tribe that:

(A) is agreed to by the tribe;

(B) is reasonably related to the agreement; and

(C) concerns the management and use of wildlife resources or habitat.

(e) Prior to executing an agreement under this Subsection (2), the governor shall consult with:

(i) the division; and

(ii) the chair of the Wildlife Board created in Section 23-14-2.

(f) At least 30 days before the agreement under this Subsection (2) is executed, the governor or the governor's designee shall provide a copy of the agreement in the form that the agreement will be executed to:

(i) the chairs of the Native American Legislative Liaison Committee; and

(ii) the Office of Legislative Research and General Counsel.   2002

23-13-13. Commercialization of wildlife unlawful.

It shall be unlawful for any person to utilize wildlife as a commercial venture for financial gain except as provided in this code or under rules and regulations of the Wildlife Board.   1975

23-13-14. Release of wildlife unlawful — Penalty.

It is unlawful for any person to release any terrestrial or aquatic wildlife into the wild except as provided in this title. Any person who violates the provisions of this section is guilty of a class A misdemeanor.   1986

23-13-15. Hunting and Fishing Day.

In recognition of the substantial and continued contribution by hunters and fishermen toward the sound management of wildlife in Utah, the fourth Saturday of September of each year is hereby established as Utah State Hunting and Fishing Day.   1973

23-13-16. Judicial notice of proclamations.

The courts shall take judicial notice of any proclamation published under the authority of this title.   1992

23-13-17. Spotlighting of coyote, red fox, striped skunk, and raccoon — County ordinances — Permits.

(1) Spotlighting may be used to hunt coyote, red fox, striped skunk, or raccoon where allowed by a county ordinance enacted pursuant to this section.

(2) The ordinance shall provide that:

(a) any artificial light used to spotlight coyote, red fox, striped skunk, or raccoon must be carried by the hunter;

(b) a motor vehicle headlight or light attached to or powered by a motor vehicle may not be used to spotlight the animal; and

(c) while hunting with the use of an artificial light, the hunter may not occupy or operate any motor vehicle.

(3) For purposes of the county ordinance, "motor vehicle" shall have the meaning as defined in Section 41-6a-102.

(4) The ordinance may specify:

(a) the time of day and seasons when spotlighting is permitted;

(b) areas closed or open to spotlighting within the unincorporated area of the county;

(c) safety zones within which spotlighting is prohibited;

(d) the weapons permitted; and

(e) penalties for violation of the ordinance.

(5) (a) A county may restrict the number of hunters engaging in spotlighting by requiring a permit to spotlight and issuing a limited number of permits.

(b) (i) A fee may be charged for a spotlighting permit.

(ii) Any permit fee shall be established by the county ordinance.

(iii) Revenues generated by the permit fee shall be remitted to the Division of Wildlife Resources for deposit into the Wildlife Resources Account, except the Wildlife Board may allow any county that enacts an ordinance pursuant to this section to retain a reasonable amount to pay for the costs of administering and enforcing the ordinance, provided this use of the permit revenues does not affect federal funds received by the state under 16 U.S.C. Sec. 669 et seq., Wildlife Restoration Act and 16 U.S.C. Sec. 777 et seq., Sport Fish Restoration Act.

(6) A county may require hunters to notify the county sheriff of the time and place they will be engaged in spotlighting.

(7) The requirement that a county ordinance must be enacted before a person may use spotlighting to hunt coyote, red fox, striped skunk, or raccoon does not apply to:

(a) a person or his agent who is lawfully acting to protect his crops or domestic animals from predation by those animals; or

(b) an animal damage control agent acting in his official capacity under a memorandum of agreement with the division.   2005

CHAPTER 15

AQUATIC WILDLIFE

Section

23-15-2.   Jurisdiction of division over public or private land and waters.

All wildlife within this state, including but not limited to wildlife on public or private land or in public or private waters within this state, shall fall within the jurisdiction of the Division of Wildlife Resources.   1971

23-15-6.   Pollution of waters unlawful.

It is unlawful for any person to pollute any waters deemed necessary by the Wildlife Board for wildlife purposes or any waters containing protected aquatic wildlife and stoneflies (Plecoptera), mayflies (Ephemoptera), dragonflies and damsel flies (Odonata), water bugs (Hemiptera), caddis flies (Trichoptera), spongilla flies (Neuroptera), and crustaceans. Provided further that each day of pollution shall constitute a separate offense.   1971

23-15-7.   Taking protected aquatic wildlife or eggs unlawful except as authorized.

It is unlawful for any person to take any protected aquatic wildlife or eggs of same in any of the waters of this state, except as provided by this code or the rules and regulations of the Wildlife Board.   1971

23-15-8.   Seining or selling aquatic wildlife unlawful except as authorized.

It is unlawful for any person to seine for any kind of protected aquatic wildlife in any of the waters of this state or to sell protected aquatic wildlife except as prescribed by this title or rules of the Wildlife Board.   1994

23-15-9.   Possession or transportation of live aquatic wildlife unlawful except as authorized — Exceptions.

It is unlawful for any person to possess or transport live protected aquatic wildlife except as provided by this code or the rules and regulations of the Wildlife Board. This section shall not apply to tropical and goldfish species intended for exhibition or commercial purposes. Operators of properly registered private fish installations may transport live aquatic wildlife specified by the Wildlife Board in the operator's certificate of registration.   1971

CHAPTER 16

BIG GAME

Section

23-16-5.   Limit of one of any species of big game during license year.

A person may take only one of any species of big game during a license year, regardless of how many licenses or permits he purchases, except as otherwise provided by this code or proclamations of the Wildlife Board.   1995

CHAPTER 19

LICENSES, PERMITS AND TAGS

Section

23-19-1.   Possession of licenses, certificates of registration, permits, and tags required — Nonassignability — Exceptions — Free fishing day.

(1) A person may not engage in hunting, trapping, fishing, or seining protected wildlife or in the sale, trade, or barter of protected wildlife or their parts without first having procured the necessary licenses, certificates of registration, permits, and tags as provided under this chapter and having at the same time the licenses, certificates of registration, permits, and tags on his or her person, except as provided under Subsection (3).

(2) (a) Except as provided in Subsection (2)(b) a person may not:

(i) lend, transfer, sell, give, or assign licenses, certificates of registration, permits, or tags belonging to the person or the rights granted by licenses, certificates of registration, permits, or tags; or

(ii) use or attempt to use a license, certificate of registration, permit, or tag of another person.

(b) The Wildlife Board may make exceptions to the prohibitions specified in Subsection (2)(a) for purposes of:

(i) transporting wildlife;

(ii) taking protected wildlife for a person who has a permanent physical impairment due to injury or disease, congenital or acquired, which renders the person so severely disabled as to be physically unable to use a legal hunting weapon or fishing device; or

(iii) transferring a certificate of registration to harvest brine shrimp and brine shrimp eggs to another person, if the certificate is transferred in connection with the sale or transfer of the brine shrimp harvest operation or the harvesting equipment, subject to the restrictions referred to under Subsection (2)(c).

(c) (i) A certificate of registration to harvest brine shrimp and brine shrimp eggs may not be transferred without the approval of the division.

(ii) Application to allow the transfer of a certificate of registration to harvest brine shrimp and brine shrimp eggs shall be made to the division on a form prescribed and furnished by it.

(iii) The division may grant a transfer of a certificate of registration to harvest brine shrimp and brine shrimp eggs if the proposed transferee meets all the requirements necessary to obtain an original certificate of registration.

(3) No license, certificate of registration, permit, or tag is required to:

(a) fish on a free fishing day which the Wildlife Board may establish each year under rules prescribed by the board;

(b) fish at a private fish installation operated in accordance with Section 23-15-10; or

(c) hunt birds on a commercial hunting area that the owner or operator is authorized to propagate, keep, and release for shooting pursuant to a certificate of registration issued under Section 23-17-6. 2003

23-19-5. Fraud, deceit, or misrepresentation in obtaining a license, permit, tag, or certificate of registration unlawful — Violation — Penalty.

It is unlawful for any person to obtain or attempt to obtain a license, permit, tag, or certificate of registration by fraud, deceit, or misrepresentation. It is unlawful for a nonresident to purchase a resident license. It is unlawful for a resident to purchase a nonresident license. Any person violating provisions of this section is guilty of a class B misdemeanor. 1986

23-19-6. Imitating or counterfeiting license unlawful — Violation — Penalty.

It is unlawful to imitate or counterfeit any license, permit, tag, or certificate of registration for the purpose of defrauding the state of Utah or for evading the purposes and provisions of this code. Any person who violates any provision of this section is guilty of a class A misdemeanor. 1979

23-19-8. Signature on documents — Considered under oath — Prohibition on use of unsigned documents.

(1) A person's signature on a license, permit, tag, or certificate of registration is certification of that person's eligibility to use the license, permit, tag, or certificate of registration for the purpose intended by this title.

(2) The signature need not be notarized but shall be considered to be made under oath.

(3) A person may not use an unsigned license, permit, tag, or certificate of registration. 2000

23-19-14. Persons residing in certain institutions authorized to fish without license.

(1) The Division of Wildlife Resources shall permit a person to fish without a license if:

(a) (i) the person resides in:

(A) the Utah State Developmental Center in American Fork;

(B) the state hospital;

(C) a veteran's hospital;

(D) a veteran's nursing home;

(E) a mental health center;

(F) an intermediate care facility for the mentally retarded;

(G) a group home licensed by the Department of Human Services and operated under contract with the Division of Services for People with Disabilities;

(H) a group home or other community-based placement licensed by the Department of Human Services and operated under contract with the Division of Juvenile Justice Services;

(I) a private residential facility for at-risk youth licensed by the Department of Human Services; or

(J) another similar institution approved by the division; or

(ii) the person is a youth who participates in a work camp operated by the Division of Juvenile Justice Services;

(b) the person is properly supervised by a representative of the institution; and

(c) the institution obtains from the division a certificate of registration that specifies:

(i) the date and place where the person will fish; and

(ii) the name of the institution's representative who will supervise the person fishing.

(2) The institution must apply for the certificate of registration at least ten days before the fishing outing.

(3) (a) An institution that receives a certificate of registration authorizing at-risk youth to fish shall provide instruction to the youth on fishing laws and regulations.

(b) The division shall provide educational materials to the institution to assist it in complying with Subsection (3)(a). 2003

23-19-18. Fishing license — Season [Repealed effective December 1, 2005].

(1) A person 14 years of age or older shall purchase a fishing license before engaging in any regulated fishing activity.

(2) A person 14 years of age or older, upon payment of the fee prescribed by the Wildlife Board, may receive a season fishing license.

(3) A person under 14 years of age may fish without a license pursuant to rules, proclamations, and orders set forth by the Wildlife Board.

(4) A resident 65 years of age or older, upon payment of the fee prescribed by the Wildlife Board, may receive a season fishing license. 2002

23-19-36. Disabled, mentally impaired, terminally ill persons, and children in the custody of the state — License to fish for free.

(1) A resident who is blind, paraplegic, or otherwise permanently disabled so as to be permanently con-

fined to a wheelchair or the use of crutches, or who has lost either or both lower extremities, may receive a free license to fish upon furnishing satisfactory proof of this fact to the Division of Wildlife Resources.

(2) A resident who is a mentally retarded person and is not eligible under Section 23-19-14 to fish without a license may receive a free license to fish upon furnishing verification of mental retardation, as defined in Section 62A-5-101, from a physician.

(3) A resident who is terminally ill, and has less than five years to live, may receive a free license to fish:

(a) upon furnishing verification from a physician; and

(b) if he qualifies for assistance under any low income public assistance program administered by a state agency.

(4) A child placed in the custody of the state by a court order may receive a free fishing license upon furnishing verification of custody to the Division of Wildlife Resources.   1999

CHAPTER 20

ENFORCEMENT — VIOLATIONS AND PENALTIES

23-20-1. Enforcement authority of conservation officers — Seizure and disposition of property.

(1) Conservation officers of the division shall enforce the provisions of this title with the same authority and following the same procedures as other law enforcement officers.

(2) (a) Conservation officers shall seize any protected wildlife illegally taken or held.

(b) (i) Upon determination of a defendant's guilt by the court, the protected wildlife shall be confiscated by the court and sold or otherwise disposed of by the division.

(ii) Proceeds of the sales shall be deposited in the Wildlife Resources Account.

(iii) Migratory wildfowl may not be sold, but must be given to a charitable institution or used for other charitable purposes.

(3) Materials and devices used for the unlawful taking or possessing of protected wildlife shall be seized, and upon a finding by the court that they were used in the unlawful taking or possessing of protected wildlife, the materials and devices shall be subject to criminal or civil forfeiture under the procedures and substantive protections established in Title 24, Chapter 1, Utah Uniform Forfeiture Procedures Act.

(4) (a) Conservation officers may seize and impound a vehicle used for the unlawful taking or possessing of protected wildlife for any of the following purposes:

(i) to provide for the safekeeping of the vehicle, if the owner or operator is arrested;

(ii) to search the vehicle as provided in Subsection (2)(a) or as provided by a search warrant; or

(iii) to inspect the vehicle for evidence that protected wildlife was unlawfully taken or possessed.

(b) The division shall store any seized vehicle in a public or private garage, state impound lot, or other secured storage facility.

(5) A seized vehicle shall be released to the owner no later than 30 days after the date the vehicle is seized, unless the vehicle was used for the unlawful taking or possessing of wildlife by a person who is charged with committing a felony under this title.

(6) (a) Upon a finding by a court that the person who used the vehicle for the unlawful taking or possessing of wildlife is guilty of a felony under this title, the vehicle may be subject to criminal or civil forfeiture under the procedures and substantive protections established in Title 24, Chapter 1, Utah Uniform Forfeiture Procedures Act.

(b) The owner of a seized vehicle is liable for the payment of any impound fee if he used the vehicle for the unlawful taking or possessing of wildlife and is found by a court to be guilty of a violation of this title.

(c) The owner of a seized vehicle is not liable for the payment of any impound fee or, if the fees have been paid, is entitled to reimbursement of the fees paid, if:

(i) no charges are filed or all charges are dropped which involve the use of the vehicle for the unlawful taking or possessing of wildlife;

(ii) the person charged with using the vehicle for the unlawful taking or possessing of wildlife is found by a court to be not guilty; or

(iii) the owner did not consent to a use of the vehicle which violates this chapter.   2002

23-20-1.5. Powers of law enforcement section — Employees.

(1) The chief and assistant chief of the law enforcement section, enforcement agents, and conservation officers of the law enforcement section within the Division of Wildlife Resources are vested with the powers of law enforcement officers throughout all of the counties of the state with exception of the power to serve civil process and:

(a) may serve criminal process, arrest, and prosecute violators of any law of this state; and

(b) shall have the same right as other law enforcement officers to require aid in executing their duties.

(2) The powers and duties conferred by this section upon employees of the law enforcement section of the Division of Wildlife Resources shall be supplementary to and in no way a limitation on the powers and duties of other law enforcement officers in the state.   1998

23-20-2. Special deputies — Appointment — Duties.

The director of the Division of Wildlife Resources is authorized to appoint persons, on a temporary basis, as special deputies. These special deputies shall have the authority to enforce provisions of this code and all rules and regulations promulgated under this code.
1971

23-20-3. Taking, transporting, selling, or purchasing protected wildlife illegal except as authorized — Penalty.

(1) Except as provided in this title or a rule, proclamation, or order of the Wildlife Board, a person may not:

(a) take or permit his dog to take:

(i) protected wildlife or their parts;

(ii) an occupied nest of protected wildlife; or

(iii) an egg of protected wildlife;

(b) transport, ship, or cause to be shipped protected wildlife or their parts;

(c) sell or purchase protected wildlife or their parts; or

(d) possess protected wildlife or their parts unaccompanied by a valid license, permit, tag, certificate of registration, bill of sale, or invoice.

(2) Possession of protected wildlife without a valid license, permit, tag, certificate of registration, bill of sale, or invoice is prima facie evidence that the protected wildlife was illegally taken and is illegally held in possession.

(3) A person is guilty of a class B misdemeanor if he:

(a) violates any provision of Subsection (1); and

(b) does so with criminal negligence as defined in Subsection 76-2-103(4).   1995

23-20-3.5. Taking protected wildlife while trespassing — Penalty.

(1) A person may not take or permit his dog to take, while in violation of Subsection 23-20-14(2):

(a) protected wildlife or their parts;

(b) an occupied nest of protected wildlife; or

(c) an egg of protected wildlife.

(2) A person is guilty of a class B misdemeanor if he or she violates any provision of Subsection (1).   2000

23-20-4. Wanton destruction of protected wildlife — Penalties.

(1) A person is guilty of wanton destruction of protected wildlife if that person:

(a) commits an act in violation of Section 23-13-4, 23-13-5, 23-13-13, 23-15-6 through 23-15-9, 23-16-5, or Subsection 23-20-3(1);

(b) captures, injures, or destroys protected wildlife; and

(c) (i) does so with intentional, knowing, or reckless conduct as defined in Section 76-2-103;

(ii) intentionally abandons protected wildlife or a carcass;

(iii) commits the offense at night with the use of a weapon;

(iv) is under a court or division revocation of a license, tag, permit, or certificate of registration; or

(v) acts for pecuniary gain.

(2) Subsection (1) does not apply to actions taken which are in accordance with the following:

(a) Title 4, Chapter 14, Utah Pesticide Control Act;

(b) Title 4, Chapter 23, Agriculture and Wildlife Damage Prevention Act; or

(c) Section 23-16-3.1.

(3) Wanton destruction of wildlife is punishable:

(a) as a third degree felony if:

(i) the aggregate value of the protected wildlife determined by the values in Subsection (4) is more than $500; or

(ii) a trophy animal was captured, injured, or destroyed;

(b) as a class A misdemeanor if the aggregate value of the protected wildlife, other than any trophy animal, determined by the values established in Subsection (4) is more than $250, but does not exceed $500; and

(c) as a class B misdemeanor if the aggregate value of the protected wildlife determined by the values established in Subsection (4) is $250 or less.

(4) Regardless of the restitution amounts imposed under Subsection 23-20-4.5(2), the following values are assigned to protected wildlife for the purpose of determining the offense for wanton destruction of wildlife:

(a) $1,000 per animal for:
    (i) bison;
    (ii) bighorn sheep;
    (iii) rocky mountain goat;
    (iv) moose;
    (v) bear;
    (vi) peregrine falcon; or
    (vii) endangered species;
(b) $750 per animal for:
    (i) elk; or
    (ii) threatened species;
(c) $500 per animal for:
    (i) cougar;
    (ii) golden eagle;
    (iii) river otter; or
    (iv) gila monster;
(d) $400 per animal for:
    (i) pronghorn antelope; or
    (ii) deer;
(e) $350 per animal for bobcat;
(f) $100 per animal for:
    (i) swan;
    (ii) sandhill crane;
    (iii) turkey;
    (iv) pelican;
    (v) loon;
    (vi) egrets;
    (vii) herons;
    (viii) raptors, except those that are threatened or endangered;
    (ix) Utah milk snake; or
    (x) Utah mountain king snake;
(g) $35 per animal for furbearers, except:
    (i) bobcat;
    (ii) river otter; and
    (iii) threatened or endangered species;
(h) $25 per animal for trout, char, salmon, grayling, tiger muskellunge, walleye, largemouth bass, smallmouth bass, and wiper;
(i) $15 per animal for game birds, except:
    (i) turkey;
    (ii) swan; and
    (iii) sandhill crane;
(j) $10 per animal for game fish not listed in Subsection (4)(h);
(k) $8 per pound dry weight of processed brine shrimp including eggs; and
(l) $5 per animal for protected wildlife not listed.
(5) For purposes of sentencing for a wildlife violation, a person who has been convicted of a third degree felony under Subsection (3)(a) is not subject to the mandatory sentencing requirements prescribed in Subsection 76-3-203.8(4).
(6) As part of any sentence imposed, the court shall impose a sentence of incarceration of not less than 20 consecutive days for any person convicted of a third degree felony under Subsection (3)(a)(ii) who captured, injured, or destroyed a trophy animal for pecuniary gain.
(7) If a person has already been convicted of a third degree felony under Subsection (3)(a)(ii) once, each separate further offense under Subsection (3)(a)(ii) is punishable by, as part of any sentence imposed, a sentence of incarceration of not less than 20 consecutive days.
(8) The court may not sentence a person subject to Subsection (6) or (7) to less than 20 consecutive days of incarceration or suspend the imposition of the sentence unless the court finds mitigating circumstances justifying lesser punishment and makes that finding a part of the court record.   2004

23-20-4.5. Illegal taking, possession, or wanton destruction of protected wildlife — Restitution — Reimbursable damages — Assessment by magistrates — Disposition of monies.

(1) When a person is adjudged guilty of illegal taking, illegal possession, or wanton destruction of protected wildlife, other than any trophy animal, the court may order the defendant to pay restitution as set forth in Subsection (2), or a greater or lesser amount, for the value of each animal taken, possessed, or destroyed, unless the court finds that restitution is inappropriate.
(2) Suggested minimum restitution values for protected wildlife are as follows:
(a) $1,000 per animal for:
    (i) bison;
    (ii) bighorn sheep;
    (iii) rocky mountain goat;
    (iv) moose;
    (v) bear;
    (vi) peregrine falcon; or
    (vii) endangered species;
(b) $750 per animal for:
    (i) elk; or
    (ii) threatened species;
(c) $500 per animal for:
    (i) golden eagle;
    (ii) river otter; or
    (iii) gila monster;
(d) $400 per animal for:
    (i) pronghorn antelope; or
    (ii) deer;
(e) $350 per animal for:
    (i) cougar; or
    (ii) bobcat;
(f) $100 per animal for:
    (i) swan;
    (ii) sandhill crane;
    (iii) turkey;
    (iv) pelican;
    (v) loon;
    (vi) egrets;
    (vii) herons;
    (viii) raptors, except those that are threatened or endangered;
    (ix) Utah milk snake; or
    (x) Utah mountain king snake;
(g) $35 per animal for furbearers, except:
    (i) bobcat;
    (ii) river otter; and
    (iii) threatened or endangered species;
(h) $25 per animal for trout, char, salmon, grayling, tiger muskellunge, walleye, largemouth bass, smallmouth bass, and wiper;
(i) $15 per animal for game birds, except:
    (i) turkey;
    (ii) swan; and
    (iii) sandhill crane;
(j) $10 per animal for game fish not listed in Subsection (2)(h);
(k) $8 per pound dry weight of processed brine shrimp including eggs; and
(l) $5 per animal for protected wildlife not listed.
(3) If the court finds that restitution is inappropriate or if the value imposed is less than the suggested minimum value as provided in Subsection (2), the court shall make the reasons for the decision part of the record.
(4) The court shall order any person convicted of a third degree felony under Subsection 23-20-4(3)(a)(ii)

to pay restitution. Minimum restitution values for trophy animals are as follows:

(a) $30,000 per animal for bighorn, desert, or rocky mountain sheep;

(b) $8,000 per animal for deer;

(c) $8,000 per animal for elk;

(d) $6,000 per animal for moose or mountain goat;

(e) $6,000 per animal for bison; and

(f) $2,000 per animal for pronghorn antelope.

(5) Any restitution shall be remitted to the division and deposited in the Wildlife Resources Account.

(6) Restitution monies shall be used by the division for activities and programs to help stop poaching, including:

(a) educational programs on wildlife crime prevention;

(b) acquisition and development of wildlife crime detection equipment;

(c) operation and maintenance of anti-poaching projects; and

(d) wildlife law enforcement training.

(7) If restitution is required it shall be in addition to:

(a) any other fine or penalty imposed for a violation of any provision of this title; and

(b) any remedial action taken to revoke or suspend a person's license, permit, tag, or certificate of registration.

(8) A judgment imposed under this section constitutes a lien when recorded in the judgment docket and shall have the same effect and is subject to the same rules as a judgment for money in a civil action. 2004

23-20-5 to 23-20-7. Repealed. 1992

23-20-8. Waste of wildlife unlawful.

It is unlawful to waste or permit to be wasted or spoiled any protected wildlife or any part of them. 1971

23-20-9. Donating protected wildlife.

(1) A person may donate protected wildlife or their parts to another person only at the following places:

(a) the residence of the donor;

(b) the residence of the person receiving protected wildlife or their parts;

(c) a meat locker;

(d) a storage plant; or

(e) a meat processing facility.

(2) A written statement of donation must be kept with the protected wildlife or parts showing:

(a) the number and species of protected wildlife or parts donated;

(b) the date of donation;

(c) the license or permit number of the donor; and

(d) the signature of the donor.

(3) Notwithstanding Subsections (1) and (2), a person may donate the hide of a big game animal to another person or organization at any place without a donation slip. 1993

23-20-10. Butcher, locker or storage plant to require proper tag or donation slip.

It is unlawful for any butcher or owner or employee of a locker plant or storage plant to receive for processing or storage the carcass of any protected wildlife which by law or regulation is required to be tagged, unless the carcass has attached to it the required tag or proper donation slip. 1971

23-20-11. Repealed. 1995

23-20-12. Airplanes or terrestrial or aquatic vehicles — Use in taking wildlife unlawful — Exceptions.

It is unlawful for any person to take any wildlife from an airplane or any other airborne vehicle or device or any motorized terrestrial or aquatic vehicle, including snowmobiles and other recreational vehicles, except as provided by this code or in the rules and regulations of the Wildlife Board. Provided, however, that an individual validly licensed to hunt who is a paraplegic, or otherwise permanently disabled so as to be permanently confined to a wheelchair or the use of crutches, may be authorized to hunt from a vehicle under terms and conditions specified by the Wildlife Board. 1975

23-20-13. Signs or equipment — Damage or destruction unlawful.

A person may not:

(1) shoot at, shoot, deface, damage, remove, or destroy any division signs or placards located in any part of this state; or

(2) damage, destroy, remove, or cause to be damaged, destroyed, or removed any equipment or devices owned, controlled, or operated by the Division of Wildlife Resources. 1995

23-20-14. Definitions — Posted property — Hunting by permission — Entry on private land while hunting or fishing — Violations — Penalty — Prohibitions inapplicable to officers — Promotion of respect for private property.

(1) As used in this section:

(a) "Division" means the Division of Wildlife Resources.

(b) "Cultivated land" means land which is readily identifiable as:

(i) land whose soil is loosened or broken up for the raising of crops;

(ii) land used for the raising of crops; or

(iii) pasturage which is artificially irrigated.

(c) "Permission" means written authorization from the owner or person in charge to enter upon private land that is either cultivated or properly posted, and must include:

(i) the signature of the owner or person in charge;

(ii) the name of the person being given permission;

(iii) the appropriate dates; and

(iv) a general description of the property.

(d) "Properly posted" means that "No Trespassing" signs or a minimum of 100 square inches of bright yellow, bright orange, or fluorescent paint are displayed at all corners, fishing streams crossing property lines, roads, gates, and rights-of-way entering the land. If metal fence posts are used, the entire exterior side must be painted.

(2) (a) While taking wildlife or engaging in wildlife related activities, a person may not:

(i) without the permission of the owner or person in charge, enter upon privately owned land that is cultivated or properly posted;

(ii) refuse to immediately leave the private land if requested to do so by the owner or person in charge; or

(iii) obstruct any entrance or exit to private property.

(b) "Hunting by permission cards" will be provided to landowners by the division upon request.

(c) A person may not post:

(i) private property he does not own or legally control; or

(ii) land that is open to the public as provided by Section 23-21-4.

(3) (a) A person convicted of violating any provision of Subsection (2) may have his license, tag, certificate of registration, or permit, relating to the activity engaged in at the time of the violation, revoked by a hearing officer.

(b) A hearing officer may construe any subsequent conviction which occurs within a five-year period as a flagrant violation and may prohibit the person from obtaining a new license, tag, certificate of registration, or permit for a period of up to five years.

(4) Subsection (2)(a) does not apply to peace or conservation officers in the performance of their duties.

(5) (a) The division shall provide information regarding owners' rights and sportsmen's duties:

(i) to anyone holding licenses, certificates of registration, tags, or permits to take wildlife; and

(ii) by using the public media and other sources.

(b) The restrictions in this section relating to trespassing shall be stated in all hunting and fishing proclamations issued by the Wildlife Board.

(6) Any person who violates any provision of Subsection (2) is guilty of a class B misdemeanor.   2000

23-20-15. Destruction of signs or inclosure on private land unlawful.

It is unlawful for any person, without the consent of the owner or person in charge of any privately owned land, to tear down, mutilate, or destroy any sign, signboard or other notice which regulates trespassing for purposes of hunting, trapping, or fishing on this land; or to, without such consent, tear down, deface, or destroy any fence or other inclosure on this privately owned land, or any gate or bars belonging to any such fence or inclosure.   1971

23-20-16. Enforcement — Procedure.

In enforcing the misdemeanor or felony provisions of this code, the peace officer shall follow the procedures and requirements of Title 53, Chapter 13, Peace Officer Classifications.   1998

23-20-17. Repealed.   1992

23-20-18. Interference with, intimidation or harassment of officer unlawful.

It is unlawful for any person to interfere with, intimidate or harass a conservation officer or special deputy in the lawful performance of his duty.   1975

23-20-19. Failure to stop at road blocks or checking stations unlawful.

It is unlawful for any person to fail to stop at Division of Wildlife Resources road blocks or checking stations where a stop sign or red or blue light is displayed.   1975

23-20-20. Children accompanied by adults while hunting with weapon.

(1) As used in this section, "accompanied" means at a distance within which visual and verbal communication is maintained for the purposes of advising and assisting.

(2) A person under the age of 14 years must be accompanied by his parent or legal guardian, or other responsible person of the age of 21 years or older and approved by his parent or guardian, while hunting with any weapon.

(3) A person of at least 14 years of age and under 16 years of age must be accompanied by his parent or legal guardian, or other responsible person of the age of 21 years or older and approved by his parent or guardian, while hunting big game with any weapon.

(4) A person of at least 14 years of age and under 16 years of age must be accompanied by a person of the age of 21 years or older while hunting wildlife, other than big game, with any weapon.

(5) A person under the age of 12 years is not permitted to hunt for protected wildlife except as provided by rules of the Wildlife Board.   1988

23-20-21, 23-20-22. Repealed.   1990

23-20-23. Aiding or assisting violation unlawful.

It is unlawful for any person to aid or assist any other person to violate any provisions of this code or any rules or regulations promulgated under it. The penalty for violating this section is the same as for the provision or regulation for which aid or assistance is given.   1971

23-20-24. Failure to stop vehicle when ordered — Operation of vehicle in dangerous manner — Attempt to flee officer — Penalty.

It is unlawful for any driver, who having received a visual or audible signal from a conservation officer to bring his vehicle to a stop, to operate his vehicle in willful or wanton disregard of the signal so as to endanger or harm a conservation officer or other person, to interfere with the operation of the conservation officer's vehicle, or any other vehicle or to increase his speed and attempt to flee or elude the conservation officer. A person who violates this section is guilty of a class A misdemeanor; a fine imposed under this section shall be not less than $250, and a penalty of imprisonment shall be for not less than 60 days.   1986

23-20-25. Exhibition of license, permit, tag or device required — Misdemeanor.

(1) Any person while engaged in any activity regulated under this title, shall be required upon demand of any conservation officer or any other peace officer to exhibit:

(a) the required license, permit, or tag;

(b) any device or apparatus in that person's possession used for any activity regulated under this title; or

(c) any wildlife in that person's possession.

(2) Any conservation officer who has a reasonable belief that a person is engaged in any activity regulated under this title may stop and temporarily detain that person in order to demand and inspect:

(a) the required license, permit, or tag;

(b) any device or apparatus in that person's possession used for any activity regulated under this title; or

(c) any wildlife in that person's possession.

(3) Any person who fails to produce for examination to an officer any of the required licenses, permits, tags, devices or apparatuses used for any activity regulated under this title or any wildlife in that person's possession is guilty of a class B misdemeanor.   1994

23-20-26. Repealed.   1998

23-20-27. Alteration of license, permit, tag or certificate a misdemeanor.

Any person who at any time alters or changes in any manner, with intent to defraud, any license, permit, tag or certificate of registration issued under provisions of this code or action of the Wildlife Board is guilty of a misdemeanor.   1973

23-20-28. Search warrants.

(1) A search warrant may be issued by a magistrate to search for any property which may constitute evidence of any violation of the provisions of this code, rules, regulations, or proclamations of the Wildlife Board upon an affidavit of any person.

(2) The search warrant shall be directed to a conservation officer or a peace officer, directing him to search for evidence and to bring it before the magistrate.

(3) A search warrant shall not be issued except upon probable cause supported by oath or affirmation, particularly describing the place, person, or thing to be searched for and the person or thing to be seized.

(4) The warrant shall be served in the daytime, unless there is reason to believe that the service of the search warrant is required immediately because a person may:

(a) flee the jurisdiction to avoid prosecution or discovery of a violation noted above;

(b) destroy or conceal evidence of the commission of any violation; or

(c) injure another person or damage property.

(5) The search warrant may be served at night if:

(a) there is reason to believe that a violation may occur at night; or

(b) the evidence of the violation may not be available to the officers serving the warrant during the day.   1995

23-20-29. Interference with hunting prohibited — Action to recover damages — Exceptions.

(1) A person is guilty of a class B misdemeanor who intentionally interferes with the right of a person licensed and legally hunting under Title 23, Chapter 19, to take wildlife by driving, harassing, or intentionally disturbing any species of wildlife for the purpose of disrupting a legal hunt, trapping, or predator control.

(2) Any directly affected person or the state may bring an action to recover civil damages resulting from a violation of Subsection (1) or a restraining order to prevent a potential violation of Subsection (1).

(3) This section does not apply to incidental interference with a hunt caused by lawful activities including, but not limited to, ranching, mining, and recreation.   1986

23-20-29.5. Interference with hunters or hunting activity — Prosecution under criminal code.

A person who intentionally interferes with a person who is licensed and taking wildlife legally under the provision of Title 23, Chapter 19, or disrupts an activity involving a legal hunt, trapping, falconry, or predator control may be charged with a violation under Section 76-9-102 if that interference or disruption constitutes a violation under Section 76-9-102.   1994

23-20-30. Tagging requirements.

(1) The Wildlife Board may make rules that require the carcass of certain species of protected wildlife to be tagged.

(2) The carcass of any species of protected wildlife required to be tagged must be tagged before the carcass is moved from or the hunter leaves the site of kill.

(3) To tag a carcass, a person shall:

(a) completely detach the tag from the license or permit;

(b) completely remove the appropriate notches to correspond with:

(i) the date the animal was taken; and

(ii) the sex of the animal; and

(c) attach the tag to the carcass so that the tag remains securely fastened and visible.

(4) A person may not:

(a) remove more than one notch indicating date or sex; or

(b) tag more than one carcass using the same tag.   1995

23-20-31. Requirement to wear hunter orange.

(1) As used in this section:

(a) (i) "Centerfire rifle hunt" means a hunt for which a hunter may use a centerfire rifle, except as provided in Subsection (1)(a)(ii).

(ii) "Centerfire rifle hunt" does not include:

(A) a bighorn sheep hunt;

(B) a mountain goat hunt;

(C) a hunt requiring the hunter to possess a statewide conservation permit; or

(D) a hunt requiring the hunter to possess a statewide sportsman permit.

(b) "Statewide conservation permit" means a permit:

(i) issued by the division;

(ii) distributed through a nonprofit organization founded for the purpose of promoting wildlife conservation; and

(iii) valid:

(A) on open hunting units statewide; and

(B) for the species of big game and time period designated by the Wildlife Board.

(c) "Statewide sportsman permit" means a permit:

(i) issued by the division through a public draw; and

(ii) valid:

(A) on open hunting units statewide; and

(B) for the species of big game and time period designated by the Wildlife Board.

(2) (a) A person shall wear a minimum of 400 square inches of hunter orange material while hunting any species of big game, except as provided in Subsection (3).

(b) Hunter orange material must be worn on the head, chest, and back.

(c) A camouflage pattern in hunter orange does not meet the requirements of Subsection (2)(a).

(3) A person is not required to wear hunter orange material during an archery, muzzle-loader, mountain goat, or bighorn sheep hunt, unless a centerfire rifle hunt is in progress in the same area.   2001

TITLE 24

FORFEITURE PROCEDURES

24-1-1. Title.

This chapter is known as the "Utah Uniform Forfeiture Procedures Act."   2002

24-1-2. Purpose.

It is the intent of this chapter to:

(1) provide a uniform set of procedures and substantive standards for the criminal and civil forfeiture of property within the state of Utah;

(2) permit law enforcement personnel to deter crime by lawfully seizing and forfeiting contraband and the instrumentalities and proceeds of criminal conduct;

(3) protect innocent owners and innocent interest holders from the forfeiture of their property;

(4) ensure that seizures and forfeitures of property from private citizens are in proportion to the violation or crime committed;

(5) ensure direct control and accountability over the use and sale of forfeited property and the revenue resulting from the disposal of forfeited property;

(6) ensure the revenue resulting from property forfeiture allows continued:

(a) law enforcement, crime prevention, and drug courts; and

(b) other appropriate activities related to the functions under Subsection (6)(a);

(7) maximize the benefits of, and accountability for, federal asset forfeiture sharing for the citizens of the state; and

(8) direct that any and all revenues resulting from the sale of forfeited property be allocated to the Utah Commission on Criminal and Juvenile Justice for grants to state and local law enforcement agencies according to specified guidelines.

2004

24-1-3. Definitions.

As used in this section:

(1) "Account" means the Criminal Forfeiture Restricted Account created in Section 24-1-18.

(2) "Agency" means any agency of municipal, county, or state government, including law enforcement agencies, law enforcement personnel, and multi-jurisdictional task forces.

(3) "Claimant" means:

(a) any owner of property as defined in this section;

(b) any interest holder as defined in this section; and

(c) any other person or entity who asserts a claim to any property seized for forfeiture under this section.

(4) "Complaint" means a civil complaint seeking the forfeiture of any real or personal property pursuant to this chapter.

(5) "Constructive seizure" means a seizure of property where the property is left in the control of the owner and the seizing agency posts the property with notice of seizure by that agency for forfeiture.

(6) "Contraband" means any property, item, or substance which is unlawful to produce or to possess under state or federal law.

(7) (a) "Innocent owner" means an owner or interest holder who held an ownership interest in property at the time the conduct subjecting the property to seizure occurred, and:

(i) did not have actual knowledge of the conduct subjecting the property to seizure; or

(ii) upon learning of the conduct subjecting the property to seizure, took reasonable steps to prohibit the illegal use of the property.

(b) "Innocent owner" means an owner or interest holder who acquired an ownership interest in the property and who had no knowledge that the illegal conduct subjecting the property to seizure had occurred or that the property had been seized for forfeiture, and:

(i) acquired the property in a bona fide transaction for value;

(ii) was a person, including a minor child, who acquired an interest in the property through probate or inheritance; or

(iii) was a spouse who acquired an interest in property through dissolution of marriage or by operation of law.

(8) (a) "Interest holder" means a secured party as defined in Subsection 70A-9a-102(72), a mortgagee, lien creditor, or the beneficiary of a security interest or encumbrance pertaining to an interest in property, whose interest would be perfected against a good faith purchaser for value.

(b) "Interest holder" does not mean a person who holds property for the benefit of or as an agent or nominee for another person, or who is not in substantial compliance with any statute requiring an interest in property to be recorded or reflected in public records in order to perfect the interest against a good faith purchaser for value.

(9) "Legal costs" means the costs and expenses incurred by the prosecuting agency, not to exceed 20% of the net value of the forfeited property.

(10) "Legislative body" means:
(a) (i) the state Legislature, county commission, county council, city commission, city council, or town council that has fiscal oversight and budgetary approval authority over a seizing agency; or
(ii) the seizing agency's governing political subdivision; or
(b) the lead governmental entity of a multijurisdictional task force, as designated in a memorandum of understanding executed by the agencies participating in the task force.
(11) "Multijurisdictional task force" means a law enforcement task force or other agency comprised of persons who are employed by or acting under the authority of different governmental authorities, including federal, state, county or municipal governments, or any combination of these agencies.
(12) "Owner" means any person or entity, other than an interest holder as defined in this section, that possesses a bona fide legal or equitable interest in real or personal property.
(13) "Program" means the Crime Reduction Assistance Program created in Section 24-1-19.
(14) "Property" means all property, whether real or personal, tangible or intangible.
(15) "Prosecuting attorney" means:
(a) the state attorney general and any assistant attorney general;
(b) any district attorney or deputy district attorney; and
(c) any county attorney or assistant county attorney;
(d) any other attorney authorized to commence an action on behalf of the state under this chapter or other provisions of state law.
(16) "Seize for forfeiture" means seizure of property:
(a) by a law enforcement officer or law enforcement agency, including a constructive seizure; and
(b) accompanied by an assertion by the officer or agency or by a prosecuting attorney that the property is seized for forfeiture in accordance with this chapter. 2004

24-1-3.5. Jurisdiction and venue.
(1) A state district court has jurisdiction over any action filed in accordance with this chapter regarding:
(a) all interests in property if the property for which forfeiture is sought is within this state at the time the action is filed; and
(b) the interests of owners or interest holders in the property, if the owner or interest holder is subject to the personal jurisdiction of the district court.
(2) (a) In addition to the venue provided for under Title 78, Chapter 13, Place of Trial — Venue, or any other provisions of law, a proceeding for forfeiture under this chapter may be maintained in the judicial district in which:
(i) any part of the property is found; or
(ii) a civil or criminal action could be maintained against an owner or interest holder for the conduct alleged to give cause for the forfeiture.
(b) A claimant may obtain a change of venue under Section 78-13-9. 2004

24-1-4. Civil Procedures.
(1) An agency which seizes property under any provision of state law subjecting the property to forfeiture shall, as soon as practicable, but in no case more than 30 days after seizure:
(a) prepare a detailed inventory of all property seized and transfer the seized property to a designated official within the agency, who shall be responsible for holding and maintaining seized property pending a court order of release or final determination of forfeiture and disposition of property under this chapter;
(b) notify the prosecuting attorney for the appropriate jurisdiction who is responsible for initiating forfeiture proceedings under this chapter of the items of property seized, the place of the seizure and any persons arrested at the time of seizure; and
(c) give written notice to all owners and interest holders known, or reasonably discoverable after due diligence, of:
(i) the date of the seizure and the property seized;
(ii) the owner's or interest holder's rights and obligations under this chapter, including the availability of hardship relief in appropriate circumstances; and
(iii) a brief description of the statutory basis for the forfeiture and the judicial proceedings by which property is forfeited under this chapter.
(2) (a) If the seizing agency fails to provide notice as required in Subsection (1), an owner or interest holder entitled to notice who does not receive notice may void the forfeiture with respect to the owner's or interest holder's interest in the property by bringing a motion before the appropriate district court and serving it upon the seizing agency. The motion may be brought at any time prior to the final disposition of the property under this chapter.
(b) If an owner or interest holder brings a motion to void the forfeiture for lack of the notice required under Subsection (1), the court shall void the forfeiture unless the seizing agency demonstrates:
(i) good cause for the failure to give notice to that owner; or
(ii) that the owner otherwise had actual notice of the seizure.
(3) (a) Within 60 days of any seizure, the prosecuting attorney shall file a complaint for forfeiture in the appropriate district court and serve a summons and notice of intent to seek forfeiture with a copy of the complaint upon all owners and interest holders known to the prosecuting attorney to have an interest in the property. Service shall be by one of the following methods:
(i) if the owner's or interest holder's name and current address are known, either by personal service by any person qualified to serve process, by a law enforcement officer, or by certified mail, return receipt requested, to that address;
(ii) if the owner's or interest holder's name and address are required by law to be on record with any state agency in order to perfect an interest in property and the owner's or interest holder's current address is not known, by mailing a copy of the notice by certified mail, return receipt requested, to the most recent address listed by any of those agencies; or
(iii) if the owner's or interest holder's address is not known and is not on record as

provided in Subsection (3)(a)(i) or (ii), by publication for two successive weeks in a newspaper of general circulation in the county in which the seizure occurred.

(b) Notice is effective upon the earlier of personal service, publication, or the mailing of a written notice.

(c) The summons and notice of intent to seek forfeiture shall:

(i) be addressed to the known owners and interest holders of the seized property, and to the person from whom the property was seized;

(ii) contain the name, business address, and business telephone number of the prosecuting attorney seeking the forfeiture; and

(iii) contain:

(A) a description of the property which is the subject matter of the forfeiture proceeding;

(B) notice that a complaint for forfeiture has been or will be filed;

(C) the time and procedural requirements for filing an answer or claim;

(D) notice of the availability of hardship or bond release of the property; and

(E) notice that failure to file an answer or other claim regarding the seized property will result in a default judgment against the seized property.

(d) The complaint shall describe with reasonable particularity:

(i) the property which is the subject matter of the forfeiture proceeding;

(ii) the date and place of seizure; and

(iii) the allegations which constitute a basis for forfeiture.

(4) (a) If the prosecuting attorney does not timely file a complaint for forfeiture of the property in accordance with Subsection (3), the agency shall promptly return the property to its owner and the prosecuting attorney may take no further action to effect the forfeiture of the property.

(b) If the agency knows of more than one owner, it shall return the property to the owner who was in possession at the time of the seizure.

(5) (a) In any case where the prosecuting attorney files a complaint for forfeiture of property, an owner or interest holder may file a claim and an answer to the complaint.

(b) The claim and answer shall be filed within 30 days after the complaint is served in person or by mail, or where applicable, within 30 days after publication under Subsection (3).

(6) (a) Except as otherwise provided in this chapter, forfeiture proceedings are governed by the Utah Rules of Civil Procedure.

(b) The court shall take all reasonable steps to expedite forfeiture proceedings and shall give these proceedings the same priority as is given to criminal cases.

(c) In all suits or actions brought for the civil forfeiture of any property under this chapter, the burden of proof is on the prosecuting attorney to establish, by clear and convincing evidence, to what extent, if any, property is subject to forfeiture.

(d) The right to trial by jury applies to forfeiture proceedings under this chapter.   2004

24-1-5. No bond required in civil cases.

Any person may assert an interest in seized property or file an answer to a complaint for civil forfeiture

without posting bond with respect to the property which is the subject of the seizure or forfeiture action.   2000

24-1-6. Innocent owners.

(1) An innocent owner's or interest holder's interest in property may not be forfeited under any provision of state law.

(2) The prosecuting attorney has the burden of establishing by clear and convincing evidence that an owner or interest holder:

(a) is criminally responsible for the conduct giving rise to the forfeiture, subject to Subsection (4);

(b) knew of the conduct giving rise to the forfeiture, and allowed the property to be used in furtherance of the conduct;

(c) acquired the property with notice of its actual or constructive seizure for forfeiture under this chapter;

(d) acquired the property knowing the property was subject to forfeiture under this chapter; or

(e) acquired the property in an effort to conceal, prevent, hinder, or delay its lawful seizure or forfeiture under any provision of state law.

(3) For purposes of this chapter, an owner or interest holder may not be required to take steps that he reasonably believes would be likely to result in physical harm or danger to any person. An owner or interest holder may demonstrate that he took reasonable action to prohibit the illegal use of the property by, for example:

(a) timely notifying a law enforcement agency of information that led the owner to know that conduct subjecting the property to seizure would occur, was occurring, or has occurred;

(b) timely revoking or attempting to revoke permission for those engaging in the illegal conduct to use the property; or

(c) taking reasonable actions to discourage or prevent the illegal use of the property.

(4) If the state relies on Subsection (2)(a) to establish that a person is not an innocent owner or interest holder, and if the owner or the interest holder is criminally charged with the conduct giving rise to the forfeiture and is acquitted of that charge on the merits:

(a) the property subject to the forfeiture or the value of the property, if the property has been disposed of under Subsection 24-1-7(15), shall be returned to the owner or interest holder; and

(b) any payments required under this chapter regarding holding the property shall be paid to the owner or interest holder.

(5) No owner may assert, under this section, an ownership interest in contraband.

(6) Property is presumed to be subject to forfeiture under this chapter if the prosecuting attorney establishes, by clear and convincing evidence, that:

(a) the owner or interest holder has engaged in conduct giving cause for forfeiture;

(b) the property was acquired by the owner or interest holder during that period of the conduct giving cause for forfeiture or within a reasonable time after that period; and

(c) there was no likely source for the purchase or acquisition of the property other than the conduct giving cause for forfeiture.

(7) A finding that property is the proceeds of conduct giving cause for forfeiture does not require proof that the property was the proceeds of any particular exchange or transaction.   2004

24-1-7. Hardship release of seized property.

(1) After property is seized for forfeiture, a person or entity may not alienate, convey, sequester, or attach that property until the court issues a final order of dismissal or an order of forfeiture regarding the property.

(2) The seizing agency or the prosecuting attorney may authorize the release of property seized for forfeiture to its owner if retention of actual custody is unnecessary.

(3) With the consent of a court of competent jurisdiction, the prosecuting attorney may discontinue forfeiture proceedings and transfer the action to another state or federal agency which has initiated forfeiture proceedings involving the same property.

(4) Property seized for forfeiture is considered to be in the custody of the district court and subject only to:

(a) the orders and decrees of the court having jurisdiction over the property or the forfeiture proceedings; and

(b) the acts of the seizing agency or the prosecuting attorney pursuant to this chapter.

(5) (a) An owner of property seized pursuant to this chapter may obtain release of the property by posting with the district court a surety bond or cash in an amount equal to the current fair market value of the property as determined by the court or by the parties' stipulation.

(b) The district court may refuse to order the release of the property if:

(i) the bond tendered is inadequate;

(ii) the property is contraband or is retained as evidence; or

(iii) the property is particularly altered or designed for use in conduct giving cause for forfeiture.

(c) If a surety bond or cash is posted and the property seized and then released on a bond or cash is forfeited, the court shall order the forfeiture of the surety bond or cash in lieu of the property.

(6) (a) As soon as practicable after seizure for forfeiture, and in no case later than 30 days after seizure for forfeiture, the seizing agency shall conduct a written inventory of the property seized.

(b) The seizing agency shall deposit property that is in the form of cash or other readily negotiable instruments into a restricted account maintained by the agency solely for the purpose of managing and protecting the property from commingling, loss, or devaluation during the pendency of the forfeiture proceedings.

(c) The seizing agency shall have in place written policy for the identification, tracking, management, and safekeeping of seized property, which shall include a prohibition against the transfer, sale, or auction of forfeited property to any employee of the seizing agency.

(d) An agency may not be awarded any funds from forfeiture through the Crime Reduction Assistance Program under Section 24-1-19 if the agency has not established or maintained the inventory policy, restricted account, and written policies required by this Subsection (6).

(7) An owner is entitled to the immediate release of seized property from the seizing agency pending the final determination of forfeiture if:

(a) the owner had a possessory interest in the property at the time of seizure;

(b) continued possession by the agency or the state pending the final disposition of the forfeiture proceedings will cause substantial hardship to the owner, such as:

(i) preventing the functioning of a legitimate business;

(ii) preventing any individual from working;

(iii) preventing any minor child or student from attending school;

(iv) preventing or hindering any person from receiving necessary medical care;

(v) hindering the care of an elderly or disabled dependent child or adult;

(vi) preventing an owner from retaining counsel to provide a defense in the forfeiture proceeding; or

(vii) leaving any individual homeless, or any other condition that the court determines causes a substantial hardship;

(c) the hardship from the continued possession by the agency of the seized property outweighs the risk that the property will be destroyed, damaged, lost, concealed, or transferred if it is returned to the owner during the pendency of the proceeding; and

(d) determination of substantial hardship under this Subsection (7) is based upon the property's use prior to the seizure.

(8) The right to appointed counsel under Section 24-1-9 applies throughout civil forfeiture proceedings, including an owner's motion for hardship release.

(9) An owner may file a motion for hardship release:

(a) in the court in which forfeiture proceedings have commenced; or

(b) in any district court having jurisdiction over the property, if forfeiture proceedings have not yet commenced.

(10) The motion for hardship release shall also be served upon the prosecuting attorney or the seizing agency within ten days after filing the motion.

(11) The court shall render a decision on a motion for hardship filed under this section not later than 20 days after the date of filing, or ten days after service upon the prosecuting attorney or seizing agency, whichever is earlier, unless this period is extended by the parties or by the court for good cause shown.

(12) (a) If the owner demonstrates substantial hardship pursuant to this section, the court shall order the property immediately released to the owner pending completion of proceedings by the government to obtain forfeiture of the property.

(b) The court may place conditions on release of the property as it finds necessary and appropriate to preserve the availability of the property or its equivalent for forfeiture.

(13) The hardship release does not apply if the seized property is:

(a) contraband;

(b) currency or other monetary instrument or electronic funds, unless the property is used to pay for the reasonable costs of defending against the forfeiture proceeding or constitutes the assets of a legitimate business; or

(c) likely to be used to commit additional illegal acts if returned to the owner.

(14) (a) The court may order property which has been seized for forfeiture to be sold as allowed by Subsection (15), leased, rented, or operated to satisfy a specified interest of any owner or interest holder, or to preserve the interests of any party on motion of that party.

(b) The court may enter orders under Subsection (14)(a) after notice to persons known to have an interest in the property, and after an opportunity for a hearing.

(15) (a) A sale may be ordered under Subsection (14) when the property is liable to perish, waste, or be significantly reduced in value, or when the expenses of maintaining the property are disproportionate to its value.

(b) A third party designated by the court shall dispose of the property by commercially reasonable public sale and distribute the proceeds in the following order of priority:

(i) first, for the payment of reasonable expenses incurred in connection with the sale;

(ii) second, for the satisfaction of any interests, including those of interest holders, in the order of their priority as determined by Title 70A, Uniform Commercial Code; and

(iii) third, any balance of the proceeds shall be preserved in the actual or constructive custody of the court, in an interest-bearing account, subject to further proceedings under this chapter.   2004

24-1-8. Criminal procedures.

(1) In cases where an owner is criminally prosecuted for conduct giving rise to forfeiture, the prosecuting attorney may elect to forfeit the owner's interest in the property civilly or criminally, provided that no civil forfeiture judgment may be entered with respect to the property of a defendant who is acquitted of the offense on which the forfeiture claim is based.

(2) If the prosecuting attorney elects to criminally forfeit the owner's interest in the property, the information or indictment must state that the owner's interest in the specifically described property is subject to criminal forfeiture and the basis for the forfeiture.

(3) (a) Upon application of the prosecuting attorney, the court may enter restraining orders or injunctions, or take other reasonable action to preserve for forfeiture under this section any forfeitable property if, after notice to persons known, or discoverable after due diligence, to have an interest in the property and after affording them an opportunity for a hearing, the court determines that:

(i) there is a substantial probability that the state will prevail on the issue of forfeiture and that failure to enter the order will result in the property being sold, transferred, destroyed or removed from the jurisdiction of the court or otherwise made unavailable for forfeiture; and

(ii) the need to preserve the availability of the property or prevent its sale, transfer, destruction or removal through the entry of the requested order outweighs the hardship against any party against whom the order is to be entered.

(b) A temporary restraining order may be entered ex parte upon application of the prosecuting attorney before or after an information or indictment has been filed with respect to the property, if the prosecuting attorney demonstrates that:

(i) there is probable cause to believe that the property with respect to which the order is sought would, in the event of a conviction, be subject to forfeiture under this section; and

(ii) provision of notice would jeopardize the availability of the property for forfeiture or would jeopardize an ongoing criminal investigation.

(c) The temporary order expires not more than ten days after entry unless extended for good cause shown or unless the party against whom it is entered consents to an extension. An adversarial hearing concerning an order entered under this paragraph shall be held as soon as practicable and prior to the expiration of the temporary order.

(d) The court is not bound by the Utah Rules of Evidence regarding evidence it may receive and consider at any hearing under this paragraph.

(4) (a) Upon conviction by a jury of an owner for conduct giving rise to criminal forfeiture, the jury shall be instructed and asked to return a special verdict as to the extent of the property identified in the information or indictment, if any, that is forfeitable.

(b) Whether property is forfeitable shall be proven beyond a reasonable doubt.

(5) Upon conviction of a person for violating any provision of state law subjecting an owner's property to forfeiture and upon the jury's special verdict that the property is forfeitable, the court shall enter a judgment and order the property forfeited to the state treasurer upon the terms stated by the court in its order. Following the entry of an order declaring property forfeited, the court may, upon application of the prosecuting attorney, enter appropriate restraining orders or injunctions, require the execution of satisfactory performance bonds, appoint receivers, conservators, appraisers, accountants, or trustees, or take any other action to protect the interest of the state in property ordered forfeited.

(6) (a) After property is ordered forfeited under this section, the state treasurer shall direct the disposition of the property under Section 24-1-16. Any property right or interest not exercisable by or transferable for value to the state expires and does not revert to the defendant. The defendant or any person acting in concert with or on behalf of the defendant is not eligible to purchase forfeited property at any sale held by the state treasurer unless approved by the judge.

(b) The court may stay the sale or disposition of the property pending the conclusion of any appeal of the criminal case giving rise to the forfeiture if the defendant demonstrates that proceeding with the sale or disposition of the property may result in irreparable injury, harm or loss to him.

(7) Except under Subparagraphs (3) or (10), a party claiming an interest in property subject to criminal forfeiture under this section:

(a) may not intervene in a trial or appeal of a criminal case involving the forfeiture of property under this section; and

(b) may not commence an action at law or equity against the state or the county concerning the validity of his alleged interests in the property subsequent to the filing of an indictment or an information alleging that the property is subject to forfeiture under this section.

(8) The district court of the state which has jurisdiction of a case under this part may enter orders under this section without regard to the location of any property which may be subject to forfeiture under this section, or which has been ordered forfeited under this section.

(9) To facilitate the identification or location of property declared forfeited and to facilitate the disposition of petitions for remission or mitigation of forfeiture, after the entry of an order declaring property forfeited to the state treasurer, the court, may upon application of the prosecuting attorney, order that the testimony of any witness relating to the property forfeited be taken by deposition, and that any book, paper, document, record, recording, or other material not privileged shall be produced as provided for depositions and discovery under the Utah Rules of Civil Procedure.

(10) (a) Following the entry of an order of forfeiture under this section, the prosecuting attorney shall publish notice of the order's intent to dispose of the property as the court may direct. The prosecuting attorney shall also provide direct written notice to any person known to have an alleged interest in the property subject to the order of forfeiture.

(b) Any person, other than the defendant, asserting a legal interest in property which has been ordered forfeited to the state treasurer under this section may, within 30 days of the final publication of notice or his receipt of written notice under Subparagraph (a), whichever is earlier, petition the court for a hearing to adjudicate the validity of his alleged interest in the property. Any genuine issue of material fact, including issues of standing, is triable to a jury upon demand of any party.

(c) The petition shall be in writing and signed by the petitioner under penalty of perjury. It shall set forth the nature and extent of the petitioner's right, title, or interest in the property, the time and circumstances of the petitioner's acquisition of the right, title, or interest in the property, and any additional facts supporting the petitioner's claim and the relief sought.

(d) The trial or hearing on the petition shall be expedited to the extent practicable. The court may consolidate a trial or hearing on the petition and any petition filed by any other person under this section other than the defendant. The court shall permit the parties to conduct pretrial discovery pursuant to the Utah Rules of Civil Procedure.

(e) At the trial or hearing, the petitioner may testify and present evidence and witnesses on his own behalf and cross-examine witnesses who appear at the hearing. The prosecuting attorney may present evidence and witnesses in rebuttal and in defense of the claim to the property and cross-examine witnesses who appear. In addition to testimony and evidence presented at the trial or hearing, the court may consider the relevant portion of the record of the criminal case which resulted in the order of forfeiture. Any trial or hearing shall be conducted pursuant to the Utah Rules of Evidence.

(f) The court shall amend the order of forfeiture in accordance with its determination, if after the trial or hearing, the court or jury determines that the petitioner has established by a preponderance of the evidence that:

(i) the petitioner has a legal right, title, or interest in the property, and the right, title, or interest renders the order of forfeiture invalid in whole or in part because the right, title, or interest was vested in the petitioner rather than the defendant or was superior to any right, title, or interest of the defendant at the time of the commission of the acts or conduct which gave rise to the forfeiture of the property under this section; or

(ii) the petitioner acquired the right, title or interest in the property in a bona fide transaction for value and, at the time of such acquisition, the petitioner did not know that the property was subject to forfeiture.

(g) Following the court's disposition of all petitions filed under this paragraph, or if no petitions are filed following the expiration of the period provided in Subparagraph (b) for the filing of petitions, the state treasurer has clear title to property subject to the order of forfeiture and may warrant good title to any subsequent purchaser or transferee.   2002

24-1-9. Appointment of counsel for indigent claimants in civil and criminal forfeiture proceedings.

(1) The court may appoint counsel to represent indigent persons in civil and criminal forfeiture proceedings, including owners in criminal forfeiture proceedings who are not charged as criminal defendants. In determining whether to appoint counsel, the court shall take into account such factors as:

(a) the person's asserted interest in the property;

(b) the person's standing to contest the forfeiture; and

(c) whether the person's allegations appear to be in good faith or to be frivolous.

(2) The court shall set compensation for counsel in forfeiture proceedings at a level equivalent to compensation provided for counsel appointed in criminal cases.   2000

24-1-10. Prejudgment and postjudgment interest.

In any proceeding to forfeit currency or other negotiable instruments under this chapter, the court shall award a prevailing party prejudgment and postjudgment interest on the currency or negotiable instruments at the legal rate of interest established by Section 15-1-1.   2004

24-1-11. Attorneys' fees and costs.

In any proceeding to forfeit seized property under this chapter, the court shall award a prevailing party reasonable attorneys' fees and other costs of litigation reasonably incurred by the owner. An owner who prevails only in part is entitled to recover reasonable attorneys' fees and reasonable costs of suit related to those issues on which he prevailed.   2004

24-1-12. Compensation for damaged property.

(1) If property seized for forfeiture is returned by operation of this chapter, an owner has a civil right of action against a seizing agency for any claim based upon the negligent destruction, loss, damage, or other injury to seized property while in the possession or custody of the agency.

(2) As used in this section, "damage or other injury" does not include normal depreciation, deterioration, or ordinary wear and tear.   2004

24-1-13. Limitation on fees for holding seized property.

In any civil or criminal proceeding under this chapter in which a judgment is entered in favor of an owner, or where a forfeiture proceeding against an owner is voluntarily dismissed by the prosecuting attorney, the seizing agency shall be prohibited from charging that owner any fee for holding seized property.   2000

24-1-14. Proportionality.

(1) (a) An owner's interest in property, excluding contraband, is not subject to forfeiture under any provision of state law if the forfeiture is substantially disproportional to the use of the property in committing or facilitating a violation of state law and the value of the property.

(b) Forfeiture of property used solely in a manner that is merely incidental and not instrumental to the commission or facilitation of a violation of law is not proportional.

(2) (a) In determining proportionality, the court shall consider:

(i) the conduct giving cause for the forfeiture;

(ii) what portion of the forfeiture, if any, is remedial in nature;

(iii) the gravity of the conduct for which the claimant is responsible in light of the offense; and

(iv) the value of the property.

(b) If the court finds that the forfeiture is substantially disproportional to the conduct for which the claimant is responsible, it shall reduce or eliminate the forfeiture, as it finds appropriate.

(3) The prosecuting attorney has the burden to demonstrate that any forfeiture is proportional to an alleged violation of state law. It is the province of the court, not the jury, to decide questions of proportionality.   2004

24-1-15. Transfer and sharing procedures.

(1) For purposes of this section, property is considered to be "seized" whenever any agency takes possession of the property or exercises any degree of control over the property.

(2) (a) Seizing agencies or prosecuting attorneys authorized to bring civil or criminal forfeiture proceedings under this chapter may not directly or indirectly transfer seized property to any federal agency or any governmental entity not created under and subject to state law unless the court enters an order, upon petition of the prosecuting attorney, authorizing the property to be transferred. The court may not enter an order authorizing a transfer unless:

(i) the activity giving rise to the investigation or seizure is interstate in nature and sufficiently complex to justify the transfer;

(ii) the seized property may only be forfeited under federal law; or

(iii) pursuing forfeiture under state law would unreasonably burden prosecuting attorneys or state law enforcement agencies.

(b) Notwithstanding Subsection (2)(a), the court may refuse to enter an order authorizing a transfer to the federal government if the transfer would circumvent the protections of the Utah Constitution or of this chapter that would otherwise be available to the property owner.

(c) Prior to granting any order to transfer pursuant to Subsection (2)(a), the court must give any owner the right to be heard with regard to the transfer.

(3) (a) Subject to Subsection (3)(b), all property, money, or other things of value received by an agency pursuant to federal law which authorizes the sharing or transfer of all or a portion of forfeited property or the proceeds of the sale of forfeited property to an agency:

(i) shall be used in compliance with federal rules and regulations relating to equitable sharing;

(ii) shall be used only for those law enforcement purposes specified in Subsection 24-1-19(8); and

(iii) may not be used for those law enforcement purposes prohibited in Subsection 24-1-19(9).

(b) If an agency receives forfeiture proceeds under Subsection (3)(a) that equal an amount that is more than 25% greater than the annual budget of the receiving agency, the amount of the proceeds that is in excess of 125% of the agency's annual budget shall be passed through by the agency to the Commission on Criminal and Juvenile Justice to be used for the purposes under Section 24-1-19.

(c) Subject to Subsection (3)(a), state agencies are encouraged to seek an equitable share of property forfeited by the federal government and to cooperate with federal law enforcement agencies in all cases in which cooperation is in the interest of this state.

(d) A law enforcement agency awarded any equitable share of property forfeited by the federal government may only use the award monies after approval or appropriation by the agency's legislative body.

(e) Law enforcement agencies are entitled to their equitable share of property forfeited by the federal government since March 29, 2001.

(f) (i) Each agency awarded any equitable share of property forfeited by the federal government shall file copies of all federal equitable sharing certifications, applications, and reports with the state auditor and the Commission on Criminal and Juvenile Justice at least annually.

(ii) This information shall provide details of all awards received from the federal government during the preceding reporting period, including for each award:

(A) the agency's case number or other identification;

(B) the amount of the award;

(C) the date of the award;

(D) the identity of the federal agency involved in the forfeiture;

(E) how the awarded property has been used; and

(F) a statement signed by both the agency's executive officer or designee and by the agency's legal counsel, that the agency has only used the awarded property for crime reduction or law enforcement purposes authorized under Section 24-1-19, and only upon approval or appropriation by the agency's legislative body.

(4) (a) Any agency that violates Subsection (2) or (3) is civilly liable to the state for three times the amount of the forfeiture diverted and for costs of suit and reasonable attorneys' fees.

(b) Any damages awarded to the state shall be paid to the Criminal Forfeiture Restricted Account created in Section 24-1-18.

(c) Any agent, including a state law enforcement officer, detached to, deputized or commissioned by, or working in conjunction with a federal agency, who knowingly transfers or otherwise trades seized property in violation of Subsection (2)(a) or who receives property, money, or other things of value under Subsection (3)(a) and knowingly fails to transfer the property in accordance with this section is guilty of a class B misdemeanor.   2004

24-1-16. Repealed.   2004

24-1-17. Disposition and allocation of forfeiture property.

(1) Upon finding that property is subject to forfeiture under this chapter, the court shall order the property forfeited to the state, and the seizing agency shall then:

(a) make the payments as required under this chapter; and

(b) transfer possession, custody, and control of the net forfeiture property or proceeds immediately to the Criminal Forfeiture Restricted Account created under Section 24-1-18.

(2) If the forfeiture arises from any violation of Section 23-20-1 relating to wildlife resources, the court shall:

(a) direct that the legal costs of the forfeiture proceeding be paid to the prosecuting agency; and

(b) direct that the net forfeited property after the legal costs shall be deposited in the Wildlife Resources Account created in Section 23-14-13.

(3) (a) Prior to transferring forfeited property, the seizing agency shall authorize a public or otherwise commercially reasonable sale of that property which is not required by law to be destroyed and that is not harmful to the public.

(b) The proceeds of the forfeited property shall remain segregated from other property, equipment, or assets of the seizing agency until transferred to the state in accordance with this chapter.

(4) From the forfeited property, both currency and the proceeds or revenue from the property, the seizing agency shall:

(a) deduct the seizing agency's direct costs and expenses, as approved by the court, of obtaining and maintaining the property pending forfeiture; and

(b) pay the legal costs to the prosecuting agency for the prosecution of the forfeiture proceeding.

(5) The remaining forfeited property shall then be deposited in the Criminal Forfeiture Restricted Account created in Section 24-1-18.

(6) All property and proceeds awarded to the state through forfeiture proceedings under this chapter shall be deposited in the Criminal Forfeiture Restricted Account created in Section 24-1-18.   2004

24-1-18. Criminal Forfeiture Restricted Account.

(1) There is created within the General Fund a restricted account known as the Criminal Forfeiture Restricted Account.

(2) Proceeds from forfeited property and forfeited monies through state forfeitures shall be deposited in this account.

(3) Money in the account shall be appropriated to the Commission on Criminal and Juvenile Justice for implementing the Crime Reduction Assistance Program under Section 24-1-19.   2004

24-1-19. Crime Reduction Assistance Program.

(1) There is created the Crime Reduction Assistance Program.

(2) The program shall fund crime prevention and law enforcement activities that have the purpose of:

(a) deterring crime by depriving criminals of the profits and proceeds of their illegal activities;

(b) weakening criminal enterprises by removing the instrumentalities of crime;

(c) reducing crimes involving substance abuse by supporting the creation, administration, or operation of drug court programs throughout the state;

(d) encouraging cooperation between local, state, and multijurisdictional law enforcement agencies;

(e) allowing the costs and expenses of law enforcement to be defrayed by the forfeited proceeds of crime; and

(f) increasing the equitability and accountability of the use of forfeited property used to assist law enforcement in reducing and preventing crime.

(3) (a) When property is forfeited under this chapter and transferred to the fund, the Commission on Criminal and Juvenile Justice shall make awards of monies from the fund to state, local, or multijurisdictional law enforcement agencies or political subdivisions of the state in compliance with this section and to further the program purposes under Subsection (2).

(b) In granting the awards, the Commission on Criminal and Juvenile Justice shall ensure that the amount of each award takes into consideration:

(i) the demonstrated needs of the agency;

(ii) the demonstrated ability of the agency to appropriately use the award;

(iii) the degree to which the agency's need is offset through the agency's participation in federal equitable sharing or through other federal and state grant programs; and

(iv) the agency's cooperation with other state and local agencies and task forces.

(4) Agencies or political subdivisions shall apply for program awards by completing and submitting forms specified by the Commission on Criminal and Juvenile Justice.

(5) Applying agencies or political subdivisions shall demonstrate compliance with all reporting and policy requirements applicable under this chapter and under Title 63, Chapter 25a, Criminal Justice and Substance Abuse, in order to qualify as a potential award recipient.

(6) Recipient law enforcement agencies may only use program award monies after approval or appropriation by the agency's legislative body, and the award monies are nonlapsing.

(7) A recipient law enforcement agency or political subdivision shall use program awards only for law enforcement or controlled substance law enforcement purposes as described in Subsection (8), and only as these purposes are specified by the agency or political subdivision in its application for the award.

(8) Permissible law enforcement purposes for which award monies may be used include:

(a) controlled substance interdiction and enforcement activities;

(b) drug court programs;

(c) activities calculated to enhance future investigations;

(d) law enforcement training that includes:

(i) implementation of the Fourth Amendment of the federal constitution and Utah Constitution Article I, Section 7, and addresses the protection of the individual's rights of due process;

(ii) protection of the rights of innocent property holders; and

(iii) the Tenth Amendment of the federal constitution regarding states' sovereignty and the states' reserved rights;

(e) law enforcement or detention facilities;

(f) law enforcement operations or equipment which are not routine costs or operational expenses;

(g) drug, gang, or crime prevention education programs which are sponsored in whole or in part by the law enforcement agency or its legislative body; and

(h) matching funds for other state or federal law enforcement grants.

(9) Law enforcement purposes for which award monies may not be granted or used include:

(a) payment of salaries, retirement benefits, or bonuses to any person;

(b) payment of enforcement expenses not related to law enforcement;

(c) uses not specified in the agency's award application;

(d) uses not approved or appropriated by the agency's legislative body;

(e) payments, transfers, or pass-through funding to entities other than law enforcement agencies; or

(f) uses, payments, or expenses that are not within the scope of the agency's functions.

(10) For each fiscal year, any state, local, or multi-jurisdictional agency or political subdivision that received a program award shall prepare, and file with the Utah Commission on Criminal and Juvenile Justice and the state auditor, a report in a form specified by the Utah Commission on Criminal and Juvenile Justice. The report shall include the following regarding each award:

(a) the agency's name;

(b) the amount of the award;

(c) the date of the award;

(d) how the award has been used; and

(e) a statement signed by both the agency's or political subdivision's executive officer or designee and by the agency's legal counsel, that:

(i) the agency or political subdivision has complied with all inventory, policy, and reporting requirements of this chapter;

(ii) all program awards were used for crime reduction or law enforcement purposes as specified in the application; and

(iii) and only upon approval or appropriation by the agency's or political subdivision's legislative body.

(11) The Utah Commission on Criminal and Juvenile Justice shall report in writing to the legislative Law Enforcement and Criminal Justice Interim Committee annually regarding the forfeited property transferred to the fund, awards made by the program, uses of program awards, and any equitable share of property forfeited by the federal government as reported by agencies pursuant to Subsection 24-1-15(3).

2004

24-1-20. State Law Enforcement Forfeiture Account created — Revenue sources — Use of account designated.

(1) (a) There is created in the General Fund a restricted account called the State Law Enforcement Forfeiture Account.

(b) All monies awarded to the Department of Public Safety or the Department of Corrections, or any division or agency within either department, through the Crime Reduction Assistance Program created in Section 24-1-19 shall be deposited into the State Law Enforcement Forfeiture Account.

(c) All monies previously deposited, or currently held in the Drug Forfeiture Account created in Section 58-37-20, and that were in that account when it was repealed by Initiative B, which passed in 2000, and which became effective March 29, 2001, shall be transferred to and deposited in the State Law Enforcement Forfeiture Account created in this Subsection (1).

(2) The Department of Public Safety and the Department of Corrections may expend amounts as appropriated by the Legislature from the State Law Enforcement Forfeiture Account for law enforcement purposes or controlled substance law enforcement purposes as specified in Section 24-1-19.

(3) That portion of funds forfeited or that are required to be disbursed to other governmental entities under existing contractual agreements or Utah statutory requirements are exempt from this section.

(4) Funds forfeited as a result of the Salt Lake Airport Drug Program operated by the Department of Public Safety, not to exceed the Department of Public Safety's expenditure to that program, are exempt from this section.

(5) The Department of Public Safety and the Department of Corrections, as part of the annual legislative budget hearings, shall provide to the legislative Executive Offices and Criminal Justice Appropriations Subcommittee a complete accounting of expenditures and revenues from the funds received under this section.

(6) The Legislature may annually provide, in an appropriations act, legislative direction for anticipated expenditures of the monies received under this section.

2004

TITLE 26

UTAH HEALTH CODE

CHAPTER 1

DEPARTMENT OF HEALTH ORGANIZATION

26-1-1. Title cited as "Utah Health Code."

This title shall be known and may be cited as the "Utah Health Code."

1981

26-1-2. Definitions.

Subject to additional definitions contained in the chapters of this title which are applicable to specific chapters, as used in this title:

(1) "Department" means the Department of Health created in Section 26-1-4.

(2) "Executive director" means the executive director of the department appointed pursuant to Section 26-1-8.

(3) "Council" means the Utah Health Advisory Council. 1991

26-1-30. Powers and duties of department.

(1) The department shall:

(a) enter into cooperative agreements with the Department of Environmental Quality to delineate specific responsibilities to assure that assessment and management of risk to human health from the environment are properly administered; and

(b) consult with the Department of Environmental Quality and enter into cooperative agreements, as needed, to ensure efficient use of resources and effective response to potential health and safety threats from the environment, and to prevent gaps in protection from potential risks from the environment to specific individuals or population groups.

(2) In addition to all other powers and duties of the department, it shall have and exercise the following powers and duties:

(a) promote and protect the health and wellness of the people within the state;

(b) establish, maintain, and enforce rules necessary or desirable to carry out the provisions and purposes of this title to promote and protect the public health or to prevent disease and illness;

(c) investigate and control the causes of epidemic, infectious, communicable, and other diseases affecting the public health;

(d) provide for the detection, reporting, prevention, and control of communicable, infectious, acute, chronic, or any other disease or health hazard that the department considers to be dangerous, important, or likely to affect the public health;

(e) collect and report information on causes of injury, sickness, death, and disability and the risk factors that contribute to the causes of injury, sickness, death, and disability within the state;

(f) collect, prepare, publish, and disseminate information to inform the public concerning the health and wellness of the population, specific hazards, and risks that may affect the health and wellness of the population and specific activities which may promote and protect the health and wellness of the population;

(g) establish and operate programs necessary or desirable for the promotion or protection of the public health and the control of disease or which may be necessary to ameliorate the major causes of injury, sickness, death, and disability in the state, except that the programs shall not be established if adequate programs exist in the private sector;

(h) establish, maintain, and enforce isolation and quarantine, and for this purpose only, exercise physical control over property and individuals as the department finds necessary for the protection of the public health;

(i) close theaters, schools, and other public places and forbid gatherings of people when necessary to protect the public health;

(j) abate nuisances when necessary to eliminate sources of filth and infectious and communicable diseases affecting the public health;

(k) make necessary sanitary and health investigations and inspections in cooperation with local health departments as to any matters affecting the public health;

(l) establish laboratory services necessary to support public health programs and medical services in the state;

(m) establish and enforce standards for laboratory services which are provided by any laboratory in the state when the purpose of the services is to protect the public health;

(n) cooperate with the Labor Commission to conduct studies of occupational health hazards and occupational diseases arising in and out of employment in industry, and make recommendations for elimination or reduction of the hazards;

(o) cooperate with the local health departments, the Department of Corrections, the Administrative Office of the Courts, the Division of Juvenile Justice Services, and the Crime Victims Reparations Board to conduct testing for HIV infection of convicted sexual offenders and any victims of a sexual offense;

(p) investigate the cause of maternal and infant mortality;

(q) establish, maintain, and enforce a procedure requiring the blood of adult pedestrians and drivers of motor vehicles killed in highway accidents be examined for the presence and concentration of alcohol;

(r) provide the commissioner of public safety with monthly statistics reflecting the results of the examinations provided for in Subsection (2)(q) and provide safeguards so that information derived from the examinations is not used for a purpose other than the compilation of statistics authorized in this Subsection (2)(r);

(s) establish qualifications for individuals permitted to draw blood pursuant to Section 41-6a-523, and to issue permits to individuals it finds qualified, which permits may be terminated or revoked by the department;

(t) establish a uniform public health program throughout the state which includes continuous service, employment of qualified employees, and a basic program of disease control, vital and health statistics, sanitation, public health nursing, and other preventive health programs necessary or desirable for the protection of public health;

(u) adopt rules and enforce minimum sanitary standards for the operation and maintenance of:

(i) orphanages;

(ii) boarding homes;

(iii) summer camps for children;

(iv) lodging houses;

(v) hotels;

(vi) restaurants and all other places where food is handled for commercial purposes, sold, or served to the public;

(vii) tourist and trailer camps;

(viii) service stations;

(ix) public conveyances and stations;

(x) public and private schools;

(xi) factories;

(xii) private sanatoria;

(xiii) barber shops;

(xiv) beauty shops;

(xv) physicians' offices;

(xvi) dentists' offices;

(xvii) workshops;

(xviii) industrial, labor, or construction camps;

(xix) recreational resorts and camps;

(xx) swimming pools, public baths, and bathing beaches;

(xxi) state, county, or municipal institutions, including hospitals and other buildings, centers, and places used for public gatherings; and

(xxii) of any other facilities in public buildings and on public grounds;

(v) conduct health planning for the state;

(w) monitor the costs of health care in the state and foster price competition in the health care delivery system;

(x) adopt rules for the licensure of health facilities within the state pursuant to Title 26, Chapter 21, Health Care Facility Licensing and Inspection Act;

(y) license the provision of child care;

(z) accept contributions to and administer the funds contained in the Organ Donation Contribution Fund created in Section 26-18b-101; and

(aa) serve as the collecting agent, on behalf of the state, for the nursing care facility assessment fee imposed under Title 26, Chapter 35a, Nursing Care Facility Assessment Act, and adopt rules for the enforcement and administration of the nursing facility assessment consistent with the provisions of Title 26, Chapter 35a.   2005

26-1-34. Restricted account created to fund drug testing for law enforcement agencies.

(1) There is created within the General Fund a restricted account known as the State Laboratory Drug Testing Account.

(2) The account consists of a specified portion of fees generated under Subsection 53-3-106(5) from the reinstatement of certain licenses, which shall be deposited in this account.

(3) The Department of Health shall use funds in this account solely for the costs of performing drug and alcohol analysis tests for state and local law enforcement agencies, and may not assess any charge or fee to the law enforcement agencies for whom the analysis tests are performed.   1998

CHAPTER 6

COMMUNICABLE DISEASE CONTROL ACT

Section
26-6-11.   Rabies or other animal disease — Investigation and order of quarantine.
26-6-12.   Rabies or other animal disease — Investigation following order of quarantine.
26-6-13.   Rabies or other animal disease — Authority of peace officer to kill or capture animals.
26-6-14.   Rabies or other animal disease — Quarantine defined.
26-6-15.   Rabies or other animal disease — Possession of animal in violation of chapter a misdemeanor.

26-6-11. Rabies or other animal disease — Investigation and order of quarantine.

Whenever rabies or any other animal disease dangerous to the health of human beings is reported, the department shall investigate to determine whether such disease exists, and the probable area of the state in which man or beast is thereby endangered. If the department finds that such disease exists, a quarantine may be declared against all animals designated in the quarantine order and within the area specified in the order. If the quarantine is for the purpose of preventing the spread of rabies or hydrophobia, the order shall contain a warning to the owners of dogs within the quarantined area to confine or muzzle all dogs to prevent biting. Any dog not muzzled found running at large in a quarantined area or any dog known to have been removed from or escaped from such area, may be killed by any person without liability therefor.   1981

26-6-12. Rabies or other animal disease — Investigation following order of quarantine.

Following the order of quarantine the department shall make a thorough investigation as to the extent of the disease, the probable number of persons and beasts exposed, and the area involved.   1981

26-6-13. Rabies or other animal disease — Authority of peace officer to kill or capture animals.

During the period any quarantine order is in force all peace officers may kill or capture and hold for further action by the department all animals in a quarantined area not held in restraint on private premises.   1981

26-6-14. Rabies or other animal disease — Quarantine defined.

Quarantine for the purposes of Sections 26-6-11 through 26-6-13 means strict confinement upon the private premises of the owners, under restraint by leash, closed cage or paddock of all animals specified by the order.   1981

26-6-15. Rabies or other animal disease — Possession of animal in violation of chapter a misdemeanor.

Any person in possession of any animal being held in violation of this chapter is guilty of a class C misdemeanor.   1981

CHAPTER 6a

DISEASE TESTING AND WORKERS' COMPENSATION PRESUMPTION FOR BENEFIT OF EMERGENCY MEDICAL SERVICES PROVIDERS [RENUMBERED]

26-6a-1 to 26-6a-14. Renumbered as §§ 34A-2-901 to 34A-2-905.   2005

CHAPTER 18b

ORGAN DONATION CONTRIBUTION FUND

Section
26-18b-101.   Organ Donation Contribution Fund created.

26-18b-101. Organ Donation Contribution Fund created.

(1) (a) There is created a restricted special revenue fund known as the Organ Donation Contribution Fund.

(b) The Organ Donation Contribution Fund shall consist of:

(i) private contributions;

(ii) donations or grants from public or private entities;

(iii) voluntary donations collected under Sections 41-1a-230.5 and 53-3-214.7; and

(iv) interest and earnings on fund monies.

(c) The cost of administering the Organ Donation Contribution Fund shall be paid from monies in the fund.

(2) The Department of Health shall:

(a) administer the funds deposited in the Organ Donation Contribution Fund;

(b) select qualified organizations and distribute the funds in the Organ Donation Contribution Fund in accordance with Subsection (3); and

(c) make an annual report on the fund to the Health and Human Services Appropriations Subcommittee.

(3) (a) The funds in the Organ Donation Contribution Fund may be distributed to a selected organization that:

(i) promotes and supports organ donation;

(ii) assists in maintaining and operating a statewide organ donation registry; and

(iii) provides donor awareness education.

(b) An organization that meets the criteria of Subsections (3)(a)(i) through (iii) may apply to the Department of Health, in a manner prescribed by the department, to receive a portion of the monies contained in the Organ Donation Contribution Fund.   2002

CHAPTER 20

FALSE CLAIMS ACT

26-20-13. Medicaid fraud enforcement.

(1) This chapter shall be enforced in accordance with this section.

(2) The department shall be responsible for:

(a) investigating and prosecuting all civil violations of this chapter; and

(b) promptly referring suspected criminal violations of this chapter to the attorney general for criminal investigation and prosecution.

(3) The attorney general shall be responsible for:

(a) investigating criminal violations of this chapter that are reported to the attorney general by the department or others;

(b) promptly referring probable civil violations of this chapter that are not related to a criminal investigation or prosecution to the department for civil investigation and prosecution; and

(c) prosecuting criminal violations of this chapter.

(4) The department and the attorney general may enter into an interagency agreement regarding the investigation and prosecution of violations of this chapter in accordance with this section, the requirements of Title XIX of the federal Social Security Act, and applicable federal regulations.   2000

CHAPTER 23b

DETECTION OF PUBLIC HEALTH EMERGENCIES ACT

26-23b-101. Title.

This chapter is known as the "Detection of Public Health Emergencies Act."   2002

26-23b-102. Definitions.

As used in this chapter:

(1) "Bioterrorism" means:

(a) the intentional use of any microorganism, virus, infectious substance, or biological product to cause death, disease, or other biological malfunction in a human, an animal, a plant, or another living organism in order to influence, intimidate, or coerce the conduct of government or a civilian population; and

(b) includes anthrax, botulism, small pox, plague, tularemia, and viral hemorrhagic fevers.

(2) "Department" means the Department of Health created in Section 26-1-4 and a local health department as defined in Section 26A-1-102.

(3) "Diagnostic information" means a clinical facility's record of individuals who present for treatment, including the reason for the visit, chief complaint, presenting diagnosis, final diagnosis, and any pertinent lab results.

(4) "Epidemic or pandemic disease":

(a) means the occurrence in a community or region of cases of an illness clearly in excess of normal expectancy; and

(b) includes diseases designated by the Department of Health which have the potential to cause serious illness or death.

(5) "Health care provider" shall have the meaning provided for in Section 78-14-3.

(6) "Public health emergency" means an occurrence or imminent credible threat of an illness or health condition, caused by bioterrorism, epidemic or pandemic disease, or novel and highly fatal infectious agent or biological toxin, that poses a substantial risk of a significant number of human fatalities or incidents of permanent or long-term disability. Such illness or health condition includes an illness or health condition resulting from a natural disaster.

(7) "Reportable emergency illness and health condition" includes the diseases, conditions, or syndromes designated by the Utah Department of Health.   2002

26-23b-103. Mandatory reporting requirements — Contents of reports — Penalties.

(1) (a) A health care provider shall report to the department any case of any person who the provider knows has a confirmed case of, or who the provider believes in his professional judgment

is sufficiently likely to harbor any illness or health condition that may be caused by:

    (i) bioterrorism;

    (ii) epidemic or pandemic disease; or

    (iii) novel and highly fatal infectious agents or biological toxins which might pose a substantial risk of a significant number of human fatalities or incidences of permanent or long-term disability.

    (b) A health care provider shall immediately submit the report required by Subsection (1)(a) within 24 hours of concluding that a report is required under Subsection (1)(a).

(2) (a) A report required by this section shall be submitted electronically, verbally, or in writing to the department or appropriate local health department.

    (b) A report submitted pursuant to Subsection (1) shall include, if known:

        (i) diagnostic information on the specific illness or health condition that is the subject of the report, and, if transmitted electronically, diagnostic codes assigned to the visit;

        (ii) the patient's name, date of birth, sex, race, occupation, and current home and work address and phone number;

        (iii) the name, address, and phone number of the health care provider; and

        (iv) the name, address, and phone number of the reporting individual.

(3) The department may impose a sanction against a health care provider for failure to make a report required by this section only if the department can show by clear and convincing evidence that a health care provider willfully failed to file a report.   2002

26-23b-104. Authorization to report.

(1) A health care provider is authorized to report to the department any case of a reportable emergency illness or health condition in any person when:

    (a) the health care provider knows of a confirmed case; or

    (b) the health care provider believes, based on his professional judgment that a person likely harbors a reportable emergency illness or health condition.

(2) A report pursuant to this section shall include, if known:

    (a) the name of the facility submitting the report;

    (b) a patient identifier that allows linkage with the patient's record for follow-up investigation if needed;

    (c) the date and time of visit;

    (d) the patient's age and sex;

    (e) the zip code of the patient's residence;

    (f) the reportable illness or condition detected or suspected;

    (g) diagnostic information and, if available, diagnostic codes assigned to the visit; and

    (h) whether the patient was admitted to the hospital.

(3) (a) If the department determines that a public health emergency exists, the department may, with the concurrence of the governor and the executive director or in the absence of the executive director, his designee, issue a public health emergency order and mandate reporting under this section for a limited reasonable period of time, as necessary to respond to the public health emergency.

    (b) The department may not mandate reporting under this subsection for more than 90 days. If more than 90 days is needed to abate the public health emergency declared under Subsection (3)(a), the department must obtain the concurrence of the governor to extend the period of time beyond 90 days.

(4) (a) Unless the provisions of Subsection (3) apply, a health care provider is not subject to penalties for failing to submit a report under this section.

    (b) If the provisions of Subsection (3) apply, a health care provider is subject to the penalties of Subsection 26-23b-103(3) for failure to make a report under this section.   2002

26-23b-105. Pharmacy reporting requirements.

(1) Notwithstanding the provisions of Subsection 26-23b-103(1)(a), a pharmacist shall report unusual drug-related events as described in Subsection (2).

(2) Unusual drug-related events that require a report include:

    (a) an unusual increase in the number of prescriptions filled for antimicrobials;

    (b) any prescription that treats a disease that has bioterrorism potential if that prescription is unusual or in excess of the expected frequency; and

    (c) an unusual increase in the number of requests for information about or sales of over-the-counter pharmaceuticals to treat conditions which may suggest the presence of one of the illnesses or conditions described in Section 26-23b-103 or 26-23b-104 and which are designated by department rule.

(3) (a) A pharmacist shall submit the report required by this section within 24 hours after the pharmacist suspects, in his professional judgement, that an unusual drug-related event has occurred.

    (b) If a pharmacy is part of a health care facility subject to the reporting requirements of this chapter, the pharmacist in charge shall make the report under this section on behalf of the health care facility.

(4) (a) The report required by this section shall be submitted in accordance with Subsection 26-23b-103(2)(a).

    (b) A report shall include the name and location of the reporting pharmacist, the name and type of pharmaceuticals that are the subject of the unusual increase in use, and if known, the suspected illness or health condition that is the subject of the report.

(5) A pharmacist is subject to the penalties under Subsection 26-23b-103(3) for failing to make a report required by this section.   2002

26-23b-106. Medical laboratory reporting requirements.

(1) Notwithstanding the provisions of Subsection 26-23b-103(1), the director of a medical laboratory located in this state is responsible for reporting results of a laboratory test that confirm a condition or illness described in Subsection 26-23b-103(1) within 24 hours after obtaining the results of the test. This reporting requirement also applies to results obtained on specimens sent to an out-of-state laboratory for analysis.

(2) The director of a medical laboratory located outside this state that receives a specimen obtained inside this state is responsible for reporting the results of any test that confirm a condition or illness

described in Subsection 26-23b-103(1), within 24 hours of obtaining the results, provided that the laboratory that performs the test has agreed to the reporting requirements of this state.

(3) If a medical laboratory is part of a health care facility subject to the reporting requirements of this chapter, the director of the medical laboratory shall make the report required by this section on behalf of the health care facility.

(4) The report required by this section shall be submitted in accordance with Subsection 26-23b-103(2).

(5) The director of a medical laboratory is subject to the penalties of Subsection 26-23b-103(3) for failing to make a report required by this section.   2002

26-23b-107. Exemptions from liability.

(1) A health care provider may not be discharged, suspended, disciplined, or harassed for making a report pursuant to this chapter.

(2) A health care provider may not incur any civil or criminal liability as a result of making any report under this chapter so long as the report is made in good faith.   2002

26-23b-108. Investigation   of   suspected   bioterrorism and diseases.

(1) The department shall:

(a) ascertain the existence of cases of an illness or condition caused by the factors described in Subsections 26-23b-103(1) and 26-23b-104(1);

(b) investigate all such cases for sources of infection or exposure;

(c) ensure that any cases, suspected cases, and exposed persons are subject to proper control measures; and

(d) define the distribution of the suspected illness or health condition.

(2) (a) Acting on information received from the reports required by this chapter, or other reliable information, the department shall identify all individuals thought to have been exposed to an illness or condition described in Subsection 26-23b-103(1).

(b) The department may request information from a health care provider concerning an individual's identifying information as described in Subsection 26-23b-103(2)(b) when:

(i) the department is investigating a potential illness or condition described in Subsection 26-23b-103(1) and the health care provider has not submitted a report to the department with the information requested; or

(ii) the department has received a report from a pharmacist under Section 26-23b-105, a medical laboratory under Section 26-23b-106, or another health care provider under Subsection 26-23b-104(1) and the department believes that further investigation is necessary to protect the public health.

(c) A health care provider shall submit the information requested under this section to the department within 24 hours after receiving a request from the department.

(3) The department shall counsel and interview identified individuals as appropriate to:

(a) assist in the positive identification of other cases and exposed individuals;

(b) develop information relating to the source and spread of the illness or condition; and

(c) obtain the names, addresses, phone numbers, or other identifying information of any other person from whom the illness or health condition may have been contracted and to whom the illness or condition may have spread.

(4) The department shall, for examination purposes, close, evacuate, or decontaminate any facility when the department reasonably believes that such facility or material may endanger the public health due to a condition or illness described in Subsection 26-23b-103(1).

(5) The department will destroy personally identifying health information about an individual collected by the department as a result of a report under this chapter upon the earlier of:

(a) the department's determination that the information is no longer necessary to carry out an investigation under this chapter; or

(b) 180 days after the information is collected.   2002

26-23b-109. Enforcement.

The department may enforce the provisions of this chapter in accordance with existing enforcement laws and regulations.   2002

26-23b-110. Information sharing with public safety authorities.

(1) For purposes of this section, "public safety authority" means a local, state, or federal law enforcement authority including the division of emergency services homeland security, emergency medical services personnel, and firefighters.

(2) Notwithstanding the provisions of Title 63, Chapter 2, Government Records Access and Management Act:

(a) whenever a public safety authority suspects a case of a reportable illness or condition under the provisions of this chapter, it shall immediately notify the department;

(b) whenever the department learns of a case of a reportable illness or condition under this chapter that it reasonably believes has the potential to be caused by one of the factors listed in Subsection 26-23b-103(1), it shall immediately notify the appropriate public safety authority; and

(c) sharing of information reportable under the provisions of this chapter between persons authorized by this chapter shall be limited to information necessary for the treatment, control, investigation, and prevention of a public health emergency.

(3) Except to the extent inconsistent with this chapter, Sections 26-6-27 and 26-6-28 apply to this chapter.   2002

CHAPTER 28

UNIFORM ANATOMICAL GIFT ACT

Section
26-28-6.   Routine inquiry and required request — Search and notification.

26-28-6. Routine inquiry and required request — Search and notification.

(1) At or near the time of a patient's death, the administrator of the hospital where the patient is being treated or a representative designated by the administrator shall:

(a) notify the appropriate organ procurement organization of the imminent or actual death of the patient;

(b) ensure, in collaboration with the organ procurement organization, tissue bank, and eye bank that readily available persons listed as having priority in Section 26-28-4 are informed of the option to make or refuse to make an anatomical gift in accordance with Section 26-28-4, with reasonable discretion and sensitivity appropriate to the circumstances of the family;

(c) enter the required information on a Utah Anatomical Consent Form or hospital death form as adopted by the department, which may include the patient's name and demographic information, medical suitability of the patient, the response of the person to whom the request was made and the person's relationship to the patient, and if the patient does not meet the medical criteria, the reasons he did not meet the criteria;

(d) obtain the signature or verbal confirmation of the one having the highest priority of the readily available persons listed as having priority in Section 26-28-4, signifying whether he consented or declined to consent to the making of an anatomical gift on behalf of the patient; and

(e) obtain verbal or written confirmation from the organ procurement organization, tissue bank, or eye bank, including name and organization, indicating whether the patient is eligible or not to make an anatomical gift.

(2) For purposes of Subsection (1)(b), the individual designated by the hospital to initiate the request to the family must be an organ procurement entity representative or an individual who has completed a course offered or approved by the organ procurement organization and designed in conjunction with the tissue and eye bank community in the methodology for approaching potential donor families.

(3) (a) A law enforcement officer, fireman, emergency medical services provider, or other emergency rescuer who finds an individual who is deceased or near death, and a hospital, upon the admission of an individual at or near death, shall:

(i) make a reasonable search for a document of gift or other information identifying whether the individual has made or refused to make an anatomical gift; and

(ii) if he finds a document of gift, evidence of a document of gift, or evidence of refusal, notify the hospital to which the individual is taken and deliver the evidence to the hospital.

(b) When a law enforcement officer, fireman, emergency medical services provider, or other emergency rescuer finds an individual who is deceased at the scene of a motor vehicle accident, and when the deceased individual is transported from the scene of the accident to a funeral establishment licensed under Title 58, Chapter 9, Funeral Services Licensing Act:

(i) the law enforcement officer, firemen, emergency medical services provider, or other emergency rescuer shall as soon as reasonably possible, notify the appropriate organ procurement organization, tissue bank, or eye bank of:

(A) the identity of the deceased individual, if known; and

(B) information, if known, pertaining to the deceased individual's legal next-of-kin in accordance with Subsection 26-28-4(1);

(C) the name and location of the funeral establishment which received custody of and transported the deceased individual; and

(ii) the funeral establishment receiving custody of the deceased individual under this Subsection (3) may not embalm the body of the deceased individual until:

(A) the funeral establishment receives notice from the organ procurement organization, tissue bank, or eye bank that the readily available persons listed as having priority in Section 26-28-4 have been informed by the individual described in Subsection (2) of the option to make or refuse to make an anatomical gift in accordance with Section 26-28-4, with reasonable discretion and sensitivity appropriate to the circumstances of the family;

(B) in accordance with federal law, prior approval for embalming has been obtained from a family member or other authorized person; and

(C) the period of time in which embalming is prohibited under Subsection (3)(b)(ii) may not exceed 24 hours after death.

(4) A hospital shall notify the appropriate organ procurement organization that a part is available if a person known to be a donor, and at or near death, is in transit to the hospital.

(5) The hospital and funeral establishment shall cooperate in the release and removal of the anatomical gift.

(6) A person who fails to discharge the duties imposed by this section is not subject to civil or criminal liability but is subject to appropriate administrative sanctions against the professional certification or license and against the facility's license.   2004

TITLE 30

HUSBAND AND WIFE

Chapter
6. Cohabitant Abuse Act.

CHAPTER 6

COHABITANT ABUSE ACT

30-6-1. Definitions.

As used in this chapter:

(1) "Abuse" means intentionally or knowingly causing or attempting to cause a cohabitant physical harm or intentionally or knowingly placing a cohabitant in reasonable fear of imminent physical harm.

(2) "Cohabitant" means an emancipated person pursuant to Section 15-2-1 or a person who is 16 years of age or older who:

(a) is or was a spouse of the other party;

(b) is or was living as if a spouse of the other party;

(c) is related by blood or marriage to the other party;

(d) has one or more children in common with the other party;

(e) is the biological parent of the other party's unborn child; or

(f) resides or has resided in the same residence as the other party.

(3) Notwithstanding Subsection (2), "cohabitant" does not include:

(a) the relationship of natural parent, adoptive parent, or step-parent to a minor; or

(b) the relationship between natural, adoptive, step, or foster siblings who are under 18 years of age.

(4) "Court clerk" means a district court clerk.

(5) "Domestic violence" means the same as that term is defined in Section 77-36-1.

(6) "Ex parte protective order" means an order issued without notice to the defendant in accordance with this chapter.

(7) "Foreign protective order" means a protective order issued by another state, territory, or possession of the United States, tribal lands of the United States, the Commonwealth of Puerto Rico, or the District of Columbia which shall be given full faith and credit in Utah, if the protective order is similar to a protective order issued in compliance with Title 30, Chapter 6, Cohabitant Abuse Act, or Title 77, Chapter 36, Cohabitant Abuse Procedures Act, and includes the following requirements:

(a) the requirements of due process were met by the issuing court, including subject matter and personal jurisdiction;

(b) the respondent received reasonable notice; and

(c) the respondent had an opportunity for a hearing regarding the protective order.

(8) "Law enforcement unit" or "law enforcement agency" means any public agency having general police power and charged with making arrests in connection with enforcement of the criminal statutes and ordinances of this state or any political subdivision.

(9) "Peace officer" means those persons specified in Title 53, Chapter 13, Peace Officer Classifications.

(10) "Protective order" means an order issued pursuant to this chapter subsequent to a hearing on the petition, of which the petitioner and respondent have been given notice in accordance with this chapter. **2003**

30-6-2. Abuse or danger of abuse — Protective orders.

(1) Any cohabitant who has been subjected to abuse or domestic violence, or to whom there is a substantial likelihood of abuse or domestic violence, may seek an ex parte protective order or a protective order in accordance with this chapter, whether or not that person has left the residence or the premises in an effort to avoid further abuse.

(2) A petition for a protective order may be filed under this chapter regardless of whether an action for divorce between the parties is pending.

(3) A petition seeking a protective order may not be withdrawn without approval of the court. **2003**

30-6-3. Venue of action.

(1) The district court has jurisdiction of any action brought under this chapter.

(2) An action brought pursuant to this chapter shall be filed in the county where either party resides or in which the action complained of took place. **2003**

30-6-4. Forms for petitions and protective orders — Assistance.

(1) (a) The offices of the court clerk shall provide forms and nonlegal assistance to persons seeking to proceed under this chapter.

(b) The Administrative Office of the Courts shall develop and adopt uniform forms for petitions and orders for protection in accordance with the provisions of this chapter on or before September 1, 1995. That office shall provide the forms to the clerk of each court authorized to issue protective orders. The forms shall include:

(i) a statement notifying the petitioner for an ex parte protective order that knowing falsification of any statement or information provided for the purpose of obtaining a protective order may subject the petitioner to felony prosecution;

(ii) a separate portion of the form for those provisions, the violation of which is a criminal offense, and a separate portion for those provisions, the violation of which is a civil violation, as provided in Subsection 30-6-4.2(5);

(iii) language in the criminal provision portion stating violation of any criminal provision is a class A misdemeanor, and language in the civil portion stating violation of or failure to comply with a civil provision is subject to contempt proceedings;

(iv) a space for information the petitioner is able to provide to facilitate identification of the respondent, such as social security number, driver license number, date of birth, address, telephone number, and physical description;

(v) a space for the petitioner to request a specific period of time for the civil provisions to be in effect, not to exceed 150 days, unless the petitioner provides in writing the reason for the requested extension of the length of time beyond 150 days;

(vi) a statement advising the petitioner that when a minor child is included in an ex parte protective order or a protective order, as part of either the criminal or the civil portion of the order, the petitioner may provide a copy of the order to the principal of the school where the child attends; and

(vii) a statement advising the petitioner that if the respondent fails to return custody of a minor child to the petitioner as ordered in a protective order, the petitioner may obtain from the court a writ of assistance.

(2) If the person seeking to proceed under this chapter is not represented by an attorney, it is the responsibility of the court clerk's office to provide:

(a) the forms adopted pursuant to Subsection (1);

(b) all other forms required to petition for an order for protection including, but not limited to, forms for service;

(c) clerical assistance in filling out the forms and filing the petition, in accordance with Subsection (1)(a). A court clerk's office may designate any other entity, agency, or person to provide that service, but the court clerk's office is responsible to see that the service is provided;

(d) information regarding the means available for the service of process;

(e) a list of legal service organizations that may represent the petitioner in an action brought under this chapter, together with the telephone numbers of those organizations; and

(f) written information regarding the procedure for transporting a jailed or imprisoned respondent to the protective order hearing, including an explanation of the use of transportation order forms when necessary.

(3) No charges may be imposed by a court clerk, constable, or law enforcement agency for:

(a) filing a petition under this chapter;

(b) obtaining an ex parte protective order;

(c) obtaining copies, either certified or not certified, necessary for service or delivery to law enforcement officials; or

(d) fees for service of a petition, ex parte protective order, or protective order.

(4) A petition for an order of protection shall be in writing and verified.

(5) (a) All orders for protection shall be issued in the form adopted by the Administrative Office of the Courts pursuant to Subsection (1).

(b) Each protective order issued, except orders issued ex parte, shall include the following language:

"Respondent was afforded both notice and opportunity to be heard in the hearing that gave rise to this order. Pursuant to the Violence Against Women Act of 1994, P.L. 103-322, 108 Stat. 1796, 18 U.S.C.A. 2265, this order is valid in all the United States, the District of Columbia, tribal lands, and United States territories." **1997**

30-6-4.1. Continuing duty to inform court of other proceedings — Effect of other proceedings.

(1) At any hearing in a proceeding to obtain an order for protection, each party has a continuing duty to inform the court of each proceeding for an order for protection, any civil litigation, each proceeding in juvenile court, and each criminal case involving either party, including the case name, the file number, and the county and state of the proceeding, if that information is known by the party.

(2) (a) An order for protection issued pursuant to this chapter is in addition to and not in lieu of any other available civil or criminal proceeding.

(b) A petitioner is not barred from seeking a protective order because of other pending proceedings.

(c) A court may not delay granting relief under this chapter because of the existence of a pending civil action between the parties.

(3) A petitioner may omit his or her address from all documents filed with the court under this chapter, but shall separately provide the court with a mailing address that is not to be made part of the public record, but that may be provided to a peace officer or entity for service of process.   **1998**

30-6-4.2. Protective orders — Ex parte protective orders — Modification of orders — Service of process — Duties of the court.

(1) If it appears from a petition for an order for protection or a petition to modify an order for protection that domestic violence or abuse has occurred or a modification of an order for protection is required, a court may:

(a) without notice, immediately issue an order for protection ex parte or modify an order for protection ex parte as it considers necessary to protect the petitioner and all parties named to be protected in the petition; or

(b) upon notice, issue an order for protection or modify an order after a hearing, whether or not the respondent appears.

(2) A court may grant the following relief without notice in an order for protection or a modification issued ex parte:

(a) enjoin the respondent from threatening to commit or committing domestic violence or abuse against the petitioner and any designated family or household member;

(b) prohibit the respondent from harassing, telephoning, contacting, or otherwise communicating with the petitioner, directly or indirectly;

(c) order that the respondent is excluded from the petitioner's residence and its premises, and order the respondent to stay away from the residence, school, or place of employment of the petitioner, and the premises of any of these, or any specified place frequented by the petitioner and any designated family or household member;

(d) upon finding that the respondent's use or possession of a weapon may pose a serious threat of harm to the petitioner, prohibit the respondent from purchasing, using, or possessing a firearm or other weapon specified by the court;

(e) order possession and use of an automobile and other essential personal effects, and direct the appropriate law enforcement officer to accompany the petitioner to the residence of the parties to ensure that the petitioner is safely restored to possession of the residence, automobile, and other essential personal effects, or to supervise the petitioner's or respondent's removal of personal belongings;

(f) grant to the petitioner temporary custody of any minor children of the parties;

(g) order any further relief that the court considers necessary to provide for the safety and welfare of the petitioner and any designated family or household member; and

(h) if the petition requests child support or spousal support, at the hearing on the petition order both parties to provide verification of current income, including year-to-date pay stubs or employer statements of year-to-date or other period of earnings, as specified by the court, and complete copies of tax returns from at least the most recent year.

(3) A court may grant the following relief in an order for protection or a modification of an order after notice and hearing, whether or not the respondent appears:

(a) grant the relief described in Subsection (2); and

(b) specify arrangements for parent-time of any minor child by the respondent and require supervision of that parent-time by a third party or deny parent-time if necessary to protect the safety of the petitioner or child.

(4) Following the protective order hearing, the court shall:

(a) as soon as possible, deliver the order to the county sheriff for service of process;

(b) make reasonable efforts to ensure that the order for protection is understood by the petitioner, and the respondent, if present;

(c) transmit, by the end of the next business day after the order is issued, a copy of the order for protection to the local law enforcement agency or agencies designated by the petitioner; and

(d) transmit a copy of the order to the statewide domestic violence network described in Section 30-6-8.

(5) (a) Each protective order shall include two separate portions, one for provisions, the violation of which are criminal offenses, and one for provisions, the violation of which are civil violations, as follows:

(i) criminal offenses are those under Subsections (2)(a) through (e), and under Subsection (3)(a) as it refers to Subsections (2)(a) through (e); and

(ii) civil offenses are those under Subsections (2)(f) through (h), and Subsection (3)(a) as it refers to Subsections (2)(f) through (h).

(b) The criminal provision portion shall include a statement that violation of any criminal provision is a class A misdemeanor.

(c) The civil provision portion shall include a notice that violation of or failure to comply with a civil provision is subject to contempt proceedings.

(6) The protective order shall include:

(a) a designation of a specific date, determined by the court, when the civil portion of the protective order either expires or is scheduled for review by the court, which date may not exceed 150 days after the date the order is issued, unless the court indicates on the record the reason for setting a date beyond 150 days;

(b) information the petitioner is able to provide to facilitate identification of the respondent, such as Social Security number, driver license number, date of birth, address, telephone number, and physical description; and

(c) a statement advising the petitioner that:

(i) after two years from the date of issuance of the protective order, a hearing may be held to dismiss the criminal portion of the protective order;

(ii) the petitioner should, within the 30 days prior to the end of the two-year period, advise the court of the petitioner's current address for notice of any hearing; and

(iii) the address provided by the petitioner will not be made available to the respondent.

(7) Child support and spouse support orders issued as part of a protective order are subject to mandatory income withholding under Title 62A, Chapter 11, Part 4, Income Withholding in IV-D Cases, and Title 62A, Chapter 11, Part 5, Income Withholding in Non IV-D Cases, except when the protective order is issued ex parte.

(8) (a) The county sheriff that receives the order from the court, pursuant to Subsection (5)(a), shall provide expedited service for orders for protection issued in accordance with this chapter, and shall transmit verification of service of process, when the order has been served, to the statewide domestic violence network described in Section 30-6-8.

(b) This section does not prohibit any law enforcement agency from providing service of process if that law enforcement agency:

(i) has contact with the respondent and service by that law enforcement agency is possible; or

(ii) determines that under the circumstances, providing service of process on the respondent is in the best interests of the petitioner.

(9) (a) When an order is served on a respondent in a jail or other holding facility, the law enforcement agency managing the facility shall make a reasonable effort to provide notice to the petitioner at the time the respondent is released from incarceration.

(b) Notification of the petitioner shall consist of a good faith reasonable effort to provide notification, including mailing a copy of the notification to the last-known address of the victim.

(10) A court may modify or vacate an order of protection or any provisions in the order after notice and hearing, except that the criminal provisions of a protective order may not be vacated within two years of issuance unless the petitioner:

(a) is personally served with notice of the hearing as provided in Rules 4 and 5, Utah Rules of Civil Procedure, and the petitioner personally appears before the court and gives specific consent to the vacation of the criminal provisions of the protective order; or

(b) submits a verified affidavit, stating agreement to the vacation of the criminal provisions of the protective order.

(11) A protective order may be modified without a showing of substantial and material change in circumstances.

(12) Insofar as the provisions of this chapter are more specific than the Utah Rules of Civil Procedure, regarding protective orders, the provisions of this chapter govern.   2005

30-6-4.3. Hearings on ex parte orders.

(1) (a) When a court issues an ex parte protective order the court shall set a date for a hearing on the petition within 20 days after the ex parte order is issued.

(b) If at that hearing the court does not issue a protective order, the ex parte protective order shall expire, unless it is otherwise extended by the court.

(c) If at that hearing the court issues a protective order, the ex parte protective order remains in effect until service of process of the protective order is completed.

(d) A protective order issued after notice and a hearing is effective until further order of the court.

(e) If the hearing on the petition is heard by a commissioner, either the petitioner or respondent may file an objection within ten days of the entry of the recommended order and the assigned judge shall hold a hearing within 20 days of the filing of the objection.

(2) Upon a hearing under this section, the court may grant any of the relief described in Section 30-6-4.2.

(3) When a court denies a petition for an ex parte protective order or a petition to modify an order for protection ex parte, the court shall set the matter for hearing upon notice to the respondent.

(4) A respondent who has been served with an ex parte protective order may seek to vacate the ex parte protective order prior to the hearing scheduled pursuant to Subsection (1)(a) by filing a verified motion to vacate. The respondent's verified motion to vacate and a notice of hearing on that motion shall be personally served on the petitioner at least two days prior to the hearing on the motion to vacate.   2001

30-6-4.4. No denial of relief solely because of lapse of time.

The court may not deny a petitioner relief requested pursuant to this chapter solely because of a lapse of time between an act of domestic violence or abuse and the filing of the petition for an order of protection.   1995

30-6-4.5. Mutual protective orders prohibited.

(1) A court may not grant a mutual order or mutual orders for protection to opposing parties, unless each party:

(a) has filed an independent petition against the other for a protective order, and both petitions have been served;

(b) makes a showing at a due process protective order hearing of abuse or domestic violence committed by the other party; and

(c) demonstrates the abuse or domestic violence did not occur in self-defense.

(2) If the court issues mutual protective orders, the circumstances justifying those orders shall be documented in the case file.   1996

30-6-4.6. Prohibition of court-ordered or court-referred mediation.

In any case brought under the provisions of this chapter, the court may not order the parties into mediation for resolution of the issues in a petition for an order for protection.   1995

30-6-4.8 to 30-6-7. Repealed.   1993, 1995, 2003

30-6-8. Statewide domestic violence network — Peace officers' duties — Prevention of abuse in absence of order — Limitation of liability.

(1) (a) On or before January 1, 1996, law enforcement units, the Department of Public Safety, and the Administrative Office of the Courts shall utilize statewide procedures to ensure that peace officers at the scene of an alleged violation of a protective order have immediate access to information necessary to verify the existence and terms of that order, and other orders of the court required to be made available on the network by the provisions of this chapter or Title 77, Chapter 36, Cohabitant Abuse Procedures Act. Those officers shall use every reasonable means to enforce the court's order, in accordance with the requirements and procedures of this chapter and Title 77, Chapter 36.

(b) The Administrative Office of the Courts, in cooperation with the Department of Public Safety and the Criminal Investigations and Technical Services Division, established in Section 53-10-103, shall provide for a single, statewide network containing:

(i) all orders for protection issued by a court of this state; and

(ii) all other court orders or reports of court action that are required to be available on the network under this chapter and Title 77, Chapter 36.

(c) The entities described in Subsection (b) may utilize the same mechanism as the statewide warrant system, described in Section 53-10-208.

(d) All orders and reports required to be available on the network shall be available within 24 hours after court action. If the court that issued the order is not part of the state court computer system, the orders and reports shall be available on the network within 72 hours.

(e) The information contained in the network shall be available to a court, law enforcement officer, or agency upon request.

(2) When any peace officer has reason to believe a cohabitant or child of a cohabitant is being abused, or that there is a substantial likelihood of immediate danger of abuse, although no protective order has been issued, that officer shall use all reasonable means to prevent the abuse, including:

(a) remaining on the scene as long as it reasonably appears there would otherwise be danger of abuse;

(b) making arrangements for the victim to obtain emergency medical treatment;

(c) making arrangements for the victim to obtain emergency housing or shelter care;

(d) explaining to the victim his or her rights in these matters;

(e) asking the victim to sign a written statement describing the incident of abuse; or

(f) arresting and taking into physical custody the abuser in accordance with the provisions of Title 77, Chapter 36.

(3) No person or institution may be held criminally or civilly liable for the performance of, or failure to perform, any duty established by this chapter, so long as that person acted in good faith and without malice.   1998

30-6-9, 30-6-10. Repealed.   1995

30-6-11. Division of Child and Family Services — Development and assistance of volunteer network.

(1) The Division of Child and Family Services within the Department of Human Services shall, either directly or by contract:

(a) develop a statewide network of volunteers and community resources to support, assist, and advocate on behalf of victims of domestic violence;

(b) train volunteers to provide clerical assistance to persons seeking orders for protection under this chapter;

(c) coordinate the provision of volunteer services with Utah Legal Services and the Legal Aid Society; and

(d) assist local government officials in establishing community based support systems for victims of domestic violence.

(2) Volunteers shall provide additional nonlegal assistance to victims of domestic violence, including providing information on the location and availability of shelters and other community resources.   1996

30-6-12. Full faith and credit for foreign protective orders.

(1) A foreign protective order is enforceable in this state as long as it is in effect in the issuing state or political entity.

(2) (a) A person entitled to protection under a foreign protective order may file the order in any district court by filing with the court a certified copy of the order. A filing fee may not be required.

(b) The person filing the foreign protective order shall swear under oath in an affidavit, that to the best of the person's knowledge the order is presently in effect as written and the respondent was personally served with a copy of the order.

(c) The affidavit shall be in the form adopted by the Administrative Office of the Courts, consistent with its responsibilities to develop and adopt forms under Section 30-6-4.

(d) The court where the order is filed shall transmit a copy of the order to the statewide domestic violence network described in Section 30-6-8.

(e) Upon inquiry by a law enforcement agency, the clerk of the district court shall make a copy of the foreign protective order available.

(3) Law enforcement personnel may rely:

(a) upon a certified copy of any foreign protective order which has been provided to the peace officer by any source; and

(b) on the statement of the person protected by the order that the order is in effect and the respondent was personally served with a copy of the order.

(4) A violation in Utah of a foreign protective order is subject to the same penalties as the violation of a protective order issued in Utah.   1996

30-6-14. Authority to prosecute class A misdemeanor violations.

Alleged class A misdemeanor violations of this chapter may be prosecuted by city attorneys.   1996

30-6-15. Dismissal of protective order when divorce is final.

When a protective order exists and a divorce proceeding is pending between the same parties named in the protective order, the protective order shall be dismissed when the court issues a decree of divorce for the parties if the petitioner in the protective order action is present or has been given notice in both the divorce and protective order action of the hearing, and the court specifically finds that the order need not continue. If the court dismisses the protective order, the court shall immediately issue an order of dismissal to be filed in the protective order action and transmit a copy of the order of dismissal to the statewide domestic violence network as described in Section 30-6-8.   2003

TITLE 31A

INSURANCE CODE

Chapter

CHAPTER 19a

UTAH RATE REGULATION ACT

Part 2

General Rate Regulation

PART 2

GENERAL RATE REGULATION

31A-19a-211. Premium rate reduction for seniors — Motor vehicle accident prevention course — Curriculum — Certificate — Exception.

(1) (a) Each rate, rating schedule, and rating manual for the liability, personal injury protection, and collision coverages of private passenger motor vehicle insurance policies submitted to or filed with the commissioner shall provide for an appropriate reduction in premium charges for those coverages if the principal operator of the covered vehicle:

(i) is a named insured who is 55 years of age or older; and

(ii) has successfully completed a motor vehicle accident prevention course as outlined in Subsection (2).

(b) Any premium reduction provided by an insurer under this section is presumed to be appropriate unless credible data demonstrates otherwise.

(2) (a) The curriculum for a motor vehicle accident prevention course under this section shall include:

(i) how impairment of visual and audio perception affects driving performance and how to compensate for that impairment;

(ii) the effects of fatigue, medications, and alcohol on driving performance, when experienced alone or in combination, and precautionary measures to prevent or offset ill effects;

(iii) updates on rules of the road and equipment, including safety belts and safe, efficient driving techniques under present day road and traffic conditions;

(iv) how to plan travel time and select routes for safety and efficiency; and

(v) how to make crucial decisions in dangerous, hazardous, and unforeseen situations.

(b) (i) In accordance with Title 63, Chapter 46a, Utah Administrative Rulemaking Act, the Department of Public Safety may make rules to establish and clarify standards pertaining to the curriculum and teaching methods of a course under this section.

(ii) These rules may include provisions allowing the department to conduct on-site visits to ensure compliance with agency rules and this chapter.

(iii) These rules shall be specific as to time and manner of visits and provide for methods to prohibit or remedy forcible visits.

(3) (a) The premium reduction required by this section shall be effective for a named insured for

a three-year period after successful completion of the course outlined in Subsection (2).

(b) The insurer may require, as a condition of maintaining the premium reduction, that the named insured not be convicted or plead guilty or nolo contendere to a moving traffic violation for which points may be assessed against the named insured's driver license except for a violation under Subsection 53-3-221(11).

(4) Each person who successfully completes the course outlined in Subsection (2) shall be issued a certificate by the organization offering the course. The certificate qualifies the person for the premium reduction required by this section.

(5) This section does not apply if the approved course outlined in Subsection (2) is attended as a penalty imposed by a court or other governmental entity for a moving traffic violation.   1999

CHAPTER 22

CONTRACTS IN SPECIFIC LINES

Part 3

Motor Vehicle Insurance

PART 3

MOTOR VEHICLE INSURANCE

31A-22-301.   Definitions.

As used in this part:

(1) "Motor vehicle" has the same meaning as under Subsection 41-12a-103(4).

(2) "Motor vehicle business" means a motor vehicle sales agency, repair shop, service station, storage garage, or public parking place.

(3) "Motor vehicle liability policy" means a policy which satisfies the requirements of Sections 31A-22-303 and 31A-22-304.

(4) "Occupying" means being in or on a motor vehicle as a passenger or operator, or being engaged in the immediate acts of entering, boarding, or alighting from a motor vehicle.

(5) "Operator" has the same meaning as under Subsection 41-12a-103(7).

(6) "Owner" has the same meaning as under Subsection 41-12a-103(8).

(7) "Pedestrian" means any natural person not occupying a motor vehicle.   1987

31A-22-302.   Required components of motor vehicle insurance policies — Exceptions.

(1) Every policy of insurance or combination of policies purchased to satisfy the owner's or operator's security requirement of Section 41-12a-301 shall include:

(a) motor vehicle liability coverage under Sections 31A-22-303 and 31A-22-304;

(b) uninsured motorist coverage under Section 31A-22-305, unless affirmatively waived under Subsection 31A-22-305(4);

(c) underinsured motorist coverage under Section 31A-22-305, unless affirmatively waived under Subsection 31A-22-305(9); and

(d) except as provided in Subsection (2) and subject to Subsection (3), personal injury protection under Sections 31A-22-306 through 31A-22-309.

(2) A policy of insurance or combination of policies, purchased to satisfy the owner's or operator's security requirement of Section 41-12a-301 for a motorcycle, trailer, or semitrailer is not required to have personal injury protection under Sections 31A-22-306 through 31A-22-309.

(3) (a) First party medical coverages may be offered or included in policies issued to motorcycle, trailer, and semitrailer owners or operators.

(b) Owners and operators of motorcycles, trailers, and semitrailers are not covered by personal injury protection coverages in connection with injuries incurred while operating any of these vehicles.

(4) First party medical coverage expenses shall be governed by the relative value study provisions under Subsections 31A-22-307(2) and (3).   2005

31A-22-303.   Motor vehicle liability coverage.

(1) (a) In addition to complying with the requirements of Chapter 21, Insurance Contracts in General, and Chapter 22, Part 2, Liability Insurance in General, a policy of motor vehicle liability coverage under Subsection 31A-22-302(1)(a) shall:

(i) name the motor vehicle owner or operator in whose name the policy was purchased, state that named insured's address, the coverage afforded, the premium charged, the policy period, and the limits of liability;

(ii) (A) if it is an owner's policy, designate by appropriate reference all the motor vehicles on which coverage is granted, insure the person named in the policy, insure any other person using any named motor vehicle with the express or implied permission of the named insured, and, except as provided in Subsection (7), insure any person included in Subsection (1)(a)(iii) against loss from the liability imposed by law for damages arising out of the ownership, maintenance, or use of these motor vehicles within the United States and Canada, subject to limits exclusive of interest and costs, for each motor vehicle, in amounts not less than the minimum limits specified under Section 31A-22-304; or

(B) if it is an operator's policy, insure the person named as insured against loss from the liability imposed upon him by law for damages arising out of the insured's use of any motor vehicle not owned by him, within the same territorial limits and with the same limits of liability as in an owner's policy under Subsection (1)(a)(ii)(A);

(iii) except as provided in Subsection (7), insure persons related to the named insured by blood, marriage, adoption, or guardianship who are residents of the named insured's household, including those who usually make their home in the same household but temporarily live elsewhere, to the same extent as the named insured;

(iv) where a claim is brought by the named insured or a person described in Subsection (1)(a)(iii), the available coverage of the policy may not be reduced or stepped-down because:

(A) a permissive user driving a covered motor vehicle is at fault in causing an accident; or

(B) the named insured or any of the persons described in this Subsection (1)(a)(iii) driving a covered motor vehicle is at fault in causing an accident; and

(v) cover damages or injury resulting from a covered driver of a motor vehicle who is stricken by an unforeseeable paralysis, seizure, or other unconscious condition and who is not reasonably aware that paralysis, seizure, or other unconscious condition is about to occur to the extent that a person of ordinary prudence would not attempt to continue driving.

(b) The driver's liability under Subsection (1)(a)(v) is limited to the insurance coverage.

(2) (a) A policy containing motor vehicle liability coverage under Subsection 31A-22-302(1)(a) may:

(i) provide for the prorating of the insurance under that policy with other valid and collectible insurance;

(ii) grant any lawful coverage in addition to the required motor vehicle liability coverage;

(iii) if the policy is issued to a person other than a motor vehicle business, limit the coverage afforded to a motor vehicle business or its officers, agents, or employees to the minimum limits under Section 31A-22-304, and to those instances when there is no other valid and collectible insurance with at least those limits, whether the other insurance is primary, excess, or contingent; and

(iv) if issued to a motor vehicle business, restrict coverage afforded to anyone other than the motor vehicle business or its officers, agents, or employees to the minimum limits under Section 31A-22-304, and to those instances when there is no other valid

and collectible insurance with at least those limits, whether the other insurance is primary, excess, or contingent.

(b) (i) The liability insurance coverage of a permissive user of a motor vehicle owned by a motor vehicle business shall be primary coverage.

(ii) The liability insurance coverage of a motor vehicle business shall be secondary to the liability insurance coverage of a permissive user as specified under Subsection (2)(b)(i).

(3) Motor vehicle liability coverage need not insure any liability:

(a) under any workers' compensation law under Title 34A, Utah Labor Code;

(b) resulting from bodily injury to or death of an employee of the named insured, other than a domestic employee, while engaged in the employment of the insured, or while engaged in the operation, maintenance, or repair of a designated vehicle; or

(c) resulting from damage to property owned by, rented to, bailed to, or transported by the insured.

(4) An insurance carrier providing motor vehicle liability coverage has the right to settle any claim covered by the policy, and if the settlement is made in good faith, the amount of the settlement is deductible from the limits of liability specified under Section 31A-22-304.

(5) A policy containing motor vehicle liability coverage imposes on the insurer the duty to defend, in good faith, any person insured under the policy against any claim or suit seeking damages which would be payable under the policy.

(6) (a) If a policy containing motor vehicle liability coverage provides an insurer with the defense of lack of cooperation on the part of the insured, that defense is not effective against a third person making a claim against the insurer, unless there was collusion between the third person and the insured.

(b) If the defense of lack of cooperation is not effective against the claimant, after payment, the insurer is subrogated to the injured person's claim against the insured to the extent of the payment and is entitled to reimbursement by the insured after the injured third person has been made whole with respect to the claim against the insured.

(7) A policy of motor vehicle liability coverage under Subsection 31A-22-302(1) may specifically exclude from coverage a person who is a resident of the named insured's household, including a person who usually makes his home in the same household but temporarily lives elsewhere, if:

(a) at the time of the proposed exclusion, each person excluded from coverage satisfies the owner's or operator's security requirement of Section 41-12a-301, independently of the named insured's proof of owner's or operator's security;

(b) the named insured and the person excluded from coverage each provide written consent to the exclusion; and

(c) the insurer includes the name of each person excluded from coverage in the evidence of insurance provided to an additional insured or loss payee.

(8) A policy of motor vehicle liability coverage may limit coverage to the policy minimum limits under Section 31A-22-304 if the insured motor vehicle is

operated by a person who has consumed any alcohol or any illegal drug or illegal substance if the policy or a specifically reduced premium was extended to the insured upon express written declaration executed by the insured that the insured motor vehicle would not be so operated.

(9) (a) When a claim is brought exclusively by a named insured or a person described in Subsection (1)(a)(iii) and asserted exclusively against a named insured or an individual described in Subsection (1)(a)(iii), the claimant may elect to resolve the claim:

(i) by submitting the claim to binding arbitration; or

(ii) through litigation.

(b) Once the claimant has elected to commence litigation under Subsection (9)(a)(ii), the claimant may not elect to resolve the claim through binding arbitration under this section without the written consent of both parties and the defendant's liability insurer.

(c) (i) Unless otherwise agreed on in writing by the parties, a claim that is submitted to binding arbitration under Subsection (9)(a)(i) shall be resolved by a panel of three arbitrators.

(ii) Unless otherwise agreed on in writing by the parties, each party shall select an arbitrator. The arbitrators selected by the parties shall select a third arbitrator.

(d) Unless otherwise agreed on in writing by the parties, each party will pay the fees and costs of the arbitrator that party selects. Both parties shall share equally the fees and costs of the third arbitrator.

(e) Except as otherwise provided in this section, an arbitration procedure conducted under this section shall be governed by Title 78, Chapter 31a, Utah Uniform Arbitration Act, unless otherwise agreed on in writing by the parties.

(f) (i) Discovery shall be conducted in accordance with Rules 26b through 36, Utah Rules of Civil Procedure.

(ii) All issues of discovery shall be resolved by the arbitration panel.

(g) A written decision of two of the three arbitrators shall constitute a final decision of the arbitration panel.

(h) Prior to the rendering of the arbitration award:

(i) the existence of a liability insurance policy may be disclosed to the arbitration panel; and

(ii) the amount of all applicable liability insurance policy limits may not be disclosed to the arbitration panel.

(i) The amount of the arbitration award may not exceed the liability limits of all the defendant's applicable liability insurance policies, including applicable liability umbrella policies. If the initial arbitration award exceeds the liability limits of all applicable liability insurance policies, the arbitration award shall be reduced to an amount equal to the liability limits of all applicable liability insurance policies.

(j) The arbitration award is the final resolution of all claims between the parties unless the award was procured by corruption, fraud, or other undue means.

(k) If the arbitration panel finds that the action was not brought, pursued, or defended in good faith, the arbitration panel may award reasonable fees and costs against the party that failed to bring, pursue, or defend the claim in good faith.

(l) Nothing in this section is intended to limit any claim under any other portion of an applicable insurance policy.

(10) An at-fault driver or an insurer issuing a policy of insurance under this part that is covering an at-fault driver may not reduce compensation to an injured party based on the injured party not being covered by a policy of insurance that provides personal injury protection coverage under Sections 31A-22-306 through 31A-22-309. 2005

31A-22-304. Motor vehicle liability policy minimum limits.

Policies containing motor vehicle liability coverage may not limit the insurer's liability under that coverage below the following:

(1) (a) $25,000 because of liability for bodily injury to or death of one person, arising out of the use of a motor vehicle in any one accident;

(b) subject to the limit for one person in Subsection (a), in the amount of $50,000 because of liability for bodily injury to or death of two or more persons arising out of the use of a motor vehicle in any one accident; and

(c) in the amount of $15,000 because of liability for injury to, or destruction of, property of others arising out of the use of a motor vehicle in any one accident; or

(2) $65,000 in any one accident whether arising from bodily injury to or the death of others, or from destruction of, or damage to, the property of others. 1993

31A-22-305. Uninsured and underinsured motorist coverage.

(1) As used in this section, "covered persons" includes:

(a) the named insured;

(b) persons related to the named insured by blood, marriage, adoption, or guardianship, who are residents of the named insured's household, including those who usually make their home in the same household but temporarily live elsewhere;

(c) any person occupying or using a motor vehicle:

(i) referred to in the policy; or

(ii) owned by a self-insured; and

(d) any person who is entitled to recover damages against the owner or operator of the uninsured or underinsured motor vehicle because of bodily injury to or death of persons under Subsection (1)(a), (b), or (c).

(2) As used in this section, "uninsured motor vehicle" includes:

(a) (i) a motor vehicle, the operation, maintenance, or use of which is not covered under a liability policy at the time of an injury-causing occurrence; or

(ii) (A) a motor vehicle covered with lower liability limits than required by Section 31A-22-304; and

(B) the motor vehicle described in Subsection (2)(a)(ii)(A) is uninsured to the extent of the deficiency;

(b) an unidentified motor vehicle that left the scene of an accident proximately caused by the motor vehicle operator;

(c) a motor vehicle covered by a liability policy, but coverage for an accident is disputed by the liability insurer for more than 60 days or continues to be disputed for more than 60 days; or

(d) (i) an insured motor vehicle if, before or after the accident, the liability insurer of the motor vehicle is declared insolvent by a court of competent jurisdiction; and

(ii) the motor vehicle described in Subsection (2)(d)(i) is uninsured only to the extent that the claim against the insolvent insurer is not paid by a guaranty association or fund.

(3) (a) Uninsured motorist coverage under Subsection 31A-22-302(1)(b) provides coverage for covered persons who are legally entitled to recover damages from owners or operators of uninsured motor vehicles because of bodily injury, sickness, disease, or death.

(b) For new policies written on or after January 1, 2001, the limits of uninsured motorist coverage shall be equal to the lesser of the limits of the insured's motor vehicle liability coverage or the maximum uninsured motorist coverage limits available by the insurer under the insured's motor vehicle policy, unless the insured purchases coverage in a lesser amount by signing an acknowledgment form provided by the insurer that:

(i) waives the higher coverage;

(ii) reasonably explains the purpose of uninsured motorist coverage; and

(iii) discloses the additional premiums required to purchase uninsured motorist coverage with limits equal to the lesser of the limits of the insured's motor vehicle liability coverage or the maximum uninsured motorist coverage limits available by the insurer under the insured's motor vehicle policy.

(c) A self-insured, including a governmental entity, may elect to provide uninsured motorist coverage in an amount that is less than its maximum self-insured retention under Subsections (3)(b) and (4)(a) by issuing a declaratory memorandum or policy statement from the chief financial officer or chief risk officer that declares the:

(i) self-insured entity's coverage level; and

(ii) process for filing an uninsured motorist claim.

(d) Uninsured motorist coverage may not be sold with limits that are less than the minimum bodily injury limits for motor vehicle liability policies under Section 31A-22-304.

(e) The acknowledgment under Subsection (3)(b) continues for that issuer of the uninsured motorist coverage until the insured, in writing, requests different uninsured motorist coverage from the insurer.

(f) (i) In conjunction with the first two renewal notices sent after January 1, 2001, for policies existing on that date, the insurer shall disclose in the same medium as the premium renewal notice, an explanation of:

(A) the purpose of uninsured motorist coverage; and

(B) the costs associated with increasing the coverage in amounts up to and including the maximum amount available by the insurer under the insured's motor vehicle policy.

(ii) The disclosure required under this Subsection (3)(f) shall be sent to all insureds that carry uninsured motorist coverage limits in an amount less than the insured's motor vehicle liability policy limits or the maximum uninsured motorist coverage limits available by the insurer under the insured's motor vehicle policy.

(4) (a) (i) Except as provided in Subsection (4)(b), the named insured may reject uninsured motorist coverage by an express writing to the insurer that provides liability coverage under Subsection 31A-22-302(1)(a).

(ii) This rejection shall be on a form provided by the insurer that includes a reasonable explanation of the purpose of uninsured motorist coverage.

(iii) This rejection continues for that issuer of the liability coverage until the insured in writing requests uninsured motorist coverage from that liability insurer.

(b) (i) All persons, including governmental entities, that are engaged in the business of, or that accept payment for, transporting natural persons by motor vehicle, and all school districts that provide transportation services for their students, shall provide coverage for all motor vehicles used for that purpose, by purchase of a policy of insurance or by self-insurance, uninsured motorist coverage of at least $25,000 per person and $500,000 per accident.

(ii) This coverage is secondary to any other insurance covering an injured covered person.

(c) Uninsured motorist coverage:

(i) is secondary to the benefits provided by Title 34A, Chapter 2, Workers' Compensation Act;

(ii) may not be subrogated by the workers' compensation insurance carrier;

(iii) may not be reduced by any benefits provided by workers' compensation insurance;

(iv) may be reduced by health insurance subrogation only after the covered person has been made whole;

(v) may not be collected for bodily injury or death sustained by a person:

(A) while committing a violation of Section 41-1a-1314;

(B) who, as a passenger in a vehicle, has knowledge that the vehicle is being operated in violation of Section 41-1a-1314; or

(C) while committing a felony; and

(vi) notwithstanding Subsection (4)(c)(v), may be recovered:

(A) for a person under 18 years of age who is injured within the scope of Subsection (4)(c)(v) but limited to medical and funeral expenses; or

(B) by a law enforcement officer as defined in Section 53-13-103, who is injured within the course and scope of the law enforcement officer's duties.

(d) As used in this Subsection (4), "motor vehicle" has the same meaning as under Section 41-1a-102.

(5) When a covered person alleges that an uninsured motor vehicle under Subsection (2)(b) proximately caused an accident without touching the covered person or the motor vehicle occupied by the covered person, the covered person must show the existence of the uninsured motor vehicle by clear and convincing evidence consisting of more than the covered person's testimony.

(6) (a) The limit of liability for uninsured motorist coverage for two or more motor vehicles may not be added together, combined, or stacked to determine the limit of insurance coverage available to an injured person for any one accident.

    (b) (i) Subsection (6)(a) applies to all persons except a covered person as defined under Subsection (7)(b)(ii).

    (ii) A covered person as defined under Subsection (7)(b)(ii) is entitled to the highest limits of uninsured motorist coverage afforded for any one motor vehicle that the covered person is the named insured or an insured family member.

    (iii) This coverage shall be in addition to the coverage on the motor vehicle the covered person is occupying.

    (iv) Neither the primary nor the secondary coverage may be set off against the other.

    (c) Coverage on a motor vehicle occupied at the time of an accident shall be primary coverage, and the coverage elected by a person described under Subsections (1)(a) and (b) shall be secondary coverage.

(7) (a) Uninsured motorist coverage under this section applies to bodily injury, sickness, disease, or death of covered persons while occupying or using a motor vehicle only if the motor vehicle is described in the policy under which a claim is made, or if the motor vehicle is a newly acquired or replacement motor vehicle covered under the terms of the policy. Except as provided in Subsection (6) or this Subsection (7), a covered person injured in a motor vehicle described in a policy that includes uninsured motorist benefits may not elect to collect uninsured motorist coverage benefits from any other motor vehicle insurance policy under which the person is a covered person.

    (b) Each of the following persons may also recover uninsured motorist benefits under any one other policy in which they are described as a "covered person" as defined in Subsection (1):

    (i) a covered person injured as a pedestrian by an uninsured motor vehicle; and

    (ii) except as provided in Subsection (7)(c), a covered person injured while occupying or using a motor vehicle that is not owned, leased, or furnished:

        (A) to the covered person;

        (B) to the covered person's spouse; or

        (C) to the covered person's resident parent or resident sibling.

    (c) (i) A covered person may recover benefits from no more than two additional policies, one additional policy from each parent's household if the covered person is:

        (A) a dependent minor of parents who reside in separate households; and

        (B) injured while occupying or using a motor vehicle that is not owned, leased, or furnished:

            (I) to the covered person;

            (II) to the covered person's resident parent; or

            (III) to the covered person's resident sibling.

    (ii) Each parent's policy under this Subsection (7)(c) is liable only for the percentage of the damages that the limit of liability of each parent's policy of uninsured motorist coverage bears to the total of both parents' uninsured coverage applicable to the accident.

    (d) A covered person's recovery under any available policies may not exceed the full amount of damages.

    (e) A covered person in Subsection (7)(b) is not barred against making subsequent elections if recovery is unavailable under previous elections.

    (f) (i) As used in this section, "interpolicy stacking" means recovering benefits for a single incident of loss under more than one insurance policy.

    (ii) Except to the extent permitted by Subsection (6) and this Subsection (7), interpolicy stacking is prohibited for uninsured motorist coverage.

(8) (a) As used in this section, "underinsured motor vehicle" includes a motor vehicle, the operation, maintenance, or use of which is covered under a liability policy at the time of an injury-causing occurrence, but which has insufficient liability coverage to compensate fully the injured party for all special and general damages.

    (b) The term "underinsured motor vehicle" does not include:

    (i) a motor vehicle that is covered under the liability coverage of the same policy that also contains the underinsured motorist coverage;

    (ii) an uninsured motor vehicle as defined in Subsection (2); or

    (iii) a motor vehicle owned or leased by:

        (A) the named insured;

        (B) the named insured's spouse; or

        (C) any dependent of the named insured.

(9) (a) (i) Underinsured motorist coverage under Subsection 31A-22-302(1)(c) provides coverage for covered persons who are legally entitled to recover damages from owners or operators of underinsured motor vehicles because of bodily injury, sickness, disease, or death.

    (ii) A covered person occupying or using a motor vehicle owned, leased, or furnished to the covered person, the covered person's spouse, or covered person's resident relative may recover underinsured benefits only if the motor vehicle is:

        (A) described in the policy under which a claim is made; or

        (B) a newly acquired or replacement motor vehicle covered under the terms of the policy.

    (b) For new policies written on or after January 1, 2001, the limits of underinsured motorist coverage shall be equal to the lesser of the limits of the insured's motor vehicle liability coverage or the maximum underinsured motorist coverage limits available by the insurer under the insured's motor vehicle policy, unless the insured purchases coverage in a lesser amount by signing an acknowledgment form provided by the insurer that:

    (i) waives the higher coverage;

    (ii) reasonably explains the purpose of underinsured motorist coverage; and

    (iii) discloses the additional premiums required to purchase underinsured motorist coverage with limits equal to the lesser of the limits of the insured's motor vehicle liability coverage or the maximum underinsured motorist coverage limits available by the insurer under the insured's motor vehicle policy.

(c) A self-insured, including a governmental entity, may elect to provide underinsured motorist coverage in an amount that is less than its maximum self-insured retention under Subsections (9)(b) and (9)(g) by issuing a declaratory memorandum or policy statement from the chief financial officer or chief risk officer that declares the:

    (i) self-insured entity's coverage level; and

    (ii) process for filing an underinsured motorist claim.

(d) Underinsured motorist coverage may not be sold with limits that are less than:

    (i) $10,000 for one person in any one accident; and

    (ii) at least $20,000 for two or more persons in any one accident.

(e) The acknowledgment under Subsection (9)(b) continues for that issuer of the underinsured motorist coverage until the insured, in writing, requests different underinsured motorist coverage from the insurer.

(f) (i) The named insured's underinsured motorist coverage, as described in Subsection (9)(a), is secondary to the liability coverage of an owner or operator of an underinsured motor vehicle, as described in Subsection (8).

    (ii) Underinsured motorist coverage may not be set off against the liability coverage of the owner or operator of an underinsured motor vehicle, but shall be added to, combined with, or stacked upon the liability coverage of the owner or operator of the underinsured motor vehicle to determine the limit of coverage available to the injured person.

(g) (i) A named insured may reject underinsured motorist coverage by an express writing to the insurer that provides liability coverage under Subsection 31A-22-302(1)(a).

    (ii) This written rejection shall be on a form provided by the insurer that includes a reasonable explanation of the purpose of underinsured motorist coverage and when it would be applicable.

    (iii) This rejection continues for that issuer of the liability coverage until the insured in writing requests underinsured motorist coverage from that liability insurer.

(h) (i) In conjunction with the first two renewal notices sent after January 1, 2001, for policies existing on that date, the insurer shall disclose in the same medium as the premium renewal notice, an explanation of:

    (A) the purpose of underinsured motorist coverage; and

    (B) the costs associated with increasing the coverage in amounts up to and including the maximum amount available by the insurer under the insured's motor vehicle policy.

    (ii) The disclosure required by this Subsection (9)(h) shall be sent to all insureds that carry underinsured motorist coverage limits in an amount less than the insured's motor vehicle liability policy limits or the maximum underinsured motorist coverage limits available by the insurer under the insured's motor vehicle policy.

(10) (a) (i) Except as provided in this Subsection (10), a covered person injured in a motor vehicle described in a policy that includes underinsured motorist benefits may not elect to collect underinsured motorist coverage benefits from any other motor vehicle insurance policy.

    (ii) The limit of liability for underinsured motorist coverage for two or more motor vehicles may not be added together, combined, or stacked to determine the limit of insurance coverage available to an injured person for any one accident.

    (iii) Subsection (10)(a)(ii) applies to all persons except a covered person described under Subsections (10)(b)(i) and (ii).

(b) (i) Except as provided in Subsection (10)(b)(ii), a covered person injured while occupying, using, or maintaining a motor vehicle that is not owned, leased, or furnished to the covered person, the covered person's spouse, or the covered person's resident parent or resident sibling, may also recover benefits under any one other policy under which they are a covered person.

    (ii) (A) A covered person may recover benefits from no more than two additional policies, one additional policy from each parent's household if the covered person is:

        (I) a dependent minor of parents who reside in separate households; and

        (II) injured while occupying or using a motor vehicle that is not owned, leased, or furnished to the covered person, the covered person's resident parent, or the covered person's resident sibling.

    (B) Each parent's policy under this Subsection (10)(b)(ii) is liable only for the percentage of the damages that the limit of liability of each parent's policy of underinsured motorist coverage bears to the total of both parents' underinsured coverage applicable to the accident.

    (iii) A covered person's recovery under any available policies may not exceed the full amount of damages.

    (iv) Underinsured coverage on a motor vehicle occupied at the time of an accident shall be primary coverage, and the coverage elected by a person described under Subsections (1)(a) and (b) shall be secondary coverage.

    (v) The primary and the secondary coverage may not be set off against the other.

    (vi) A covered person as described under Subsection (10)(b)(i) is entitled to the highest limits of underinsured motorist coverage under only one additional policy per household applicable to that covered person as a named insured, spouse, or relative.

    (vii) A covered injured person is not barred against making subsequent elections if recovery is unavailable under previous elections.

    (viii) (A) As used in this section, "interpolicy stacking" means recovering benefits for a single incident of loss under more than one insurance policy.

    (B) Except to the extent permitted by this Subsection (10), interpolicy stacking is prohibited for underinsured motorist coverage.

(c) Underinsured motorist coverage:

(i) is secondary to the benefits provided by Title 34A, Chapter 2, Workers' Compensation Act;

(ii) may not be subrogated by the workers' compensation insurance carrier;

(iii) may not be reduced by any benefits provided by workers' compensation insurance;

(iv) may be reduced by health insurance subrogation only after the covered person has been made whole;

(v) may not be collected for bodily injury or death sustained by a person:

(A) while committing a violation of Section 41-1a-1314;

(B) who, as a passenger in a vehicle, has knowledge that the vehicle is being operated in violation of Section 41-1a-1314; or

(C) while committing a felony; and

(vi) notwithstanding Subsection (10)(c)(v), may be recovered:

(A) for a person under 18 years of age who is injured within the scope of Subsection (10)(c)(v) but limited to medical and funeral expenses; or

(B) by a law enforcement officer as defined in Section 53-13-103, who is injured within the course and scope of the law enforcement officer's duties.

(11) The inception of the loss under Subsection 31A-21-313(1) for underinsured motorist claims occurs upon the date of the last liability policy payment.

(12) (a) Within five business days after notification in a manner specified by the department that all liability insurers have tendered their liability policy limits, the underinsured carrier shall either:

(i) waive any subrogation claim the underinsured carrier may have against the person liable for the injuries caused in the accident; or

(ii) pay the insured an amount equal to the policy limits tendered by the liability carrier.

(b) If neither option is exercised under Subsection (12)(a), the subrogation claim is considered to be waived by the underinsured carrier.

(13) Except as otherwise provided in this section, a covered person may seek, subject to the terms and conditions of the policy, additional coverage under any policy:

(a) that provides coverage for damages resulting from motor vehicle accidents; and

(b) that is not required to conform to Section 31A-22-302. 2004

31A-22-305.5. Uninsured motorist property damage coverage — Coverage limitations.

(1) (a) At the request of the named insured, every motor vehicle liability policy of insurance under Sections 31A-22-303 and 31A-22-304 or combination of policies purchased to satisfy the owner's or operator's security requirement of Section 41-12a-301 which policy does not provide insurance for collision damage shall provide uninsured motorist property damage coverage for property damage to the motor vehicle described in the policy.

(b) The uninsured motorist property damage coverage provided under Subsection (1)(a) shall be for the benefit of covered persons, as defined under Section 31A-22-305, who are legally entitled to recover damages:

(i) from the owner or operator of an uninsured motor vehicle, as defined under Subsections 31A-22-305(2)(a), (c), and (d); and

(ii) arising out of the operation, maintenance, or use of an uninsured motor vehicle.

(2) (a) Except as provided under Subsection (5), the coverage provided under this section shall include payment for loss or damage to the motor vehicle described in the policy, not to exceed the motor vehicle's actual cash value or $3,500, whichever is less.

(b) Property damage does not include compensation for loss of use of the motor vehicle.

(3) The coverage provided under this section shall be payable only if:

(a) the occurrence causing the property damage involves actual physical contact between the covered motor vehicle and an uninsured motor vehicle;

(b) the owner, operator, or license plate number of the uninsured motor vehicle is identified; and

(c) the insured or someone on his behalf reports the occurrence within ten days to the insurer or his agent.

(4) Except as provided under Subsection (5), the coverage provided under this section shall be subject to a $250 deductible and shall be excess to any other insurance covering property damage to the motor vehicle described in the policy.

(5) The insurer providing coverage under this section may, at appropriate premium rates, make available additional:

(a) coverage above the limits provided under Subsection (2); and

(b) deductibles for the coverage under Subsection (5)(a) above the limits provided under Subsection (4).

(6) A rating surcharge may not be applied to any policy of motor vehicle insurance issued in this state as a result of payment of a claim made under this section. 2005

31A-22-306. Personal injury protection.

Personal injury protection under Subsection 31A-22-302(2) provides the coverages and benefits described under Section 31A-22-307 to persons described under Section 31A-22-308, but is subject to the limitations, exclusions, and conditions set forth in Section 31A-22-309. 1986

31A-22-307. Personal injury protection coverages and benefits.

(1) Personal injury protection coverages and benefits include:

(a) the reasonable value of all expenses for necessary medical, surgical, X-ray, dental, rehabilitation, including prosthetic devices, ambulance, hospital, and nursing services, not to exceed the total minimum required coverage of $3,000 per person;

(b) (i) the lesser of $250 per week or 85% of any loss of gross income and loss of earning capacity per person from inability to work, for a maximum of 52 consecutive weeks after the loss, except that this benefit need not be paid for the first three days of disability, unless the disability continues for longer than two consecutive weeks after the date of injury; and

(ii) a special damage allowance not exceeding $20 per day for a maximum of 365 days, for services actually rendered or expenses reasonably incurred for services that, but for the injury, the injured person would have performed for the injured person's household, except that this benefit need not be paid for the first three days after the date of injury unless the person's inability to perform these services continues for more than two consecutive weeks;

(c) funeral, burial, or cremation benefits not to exceed a total of $1,500 per person; and

(d) compensation on account of death of a person, payable to the person's heirs, in the total of $3,000.

(2) (a) (i) To determine the reasonable value of the medical expenses provided for in Subsection (1) and under Subsection 31A-22-309(1)(a)(v), the commissioner shall conduct a relative value study of services and accommodations for the diagnosis, care, recovery, or rehabilitation of an injured person in the most populous county in the state to assign a unit value and determine the 75th percentile charge for each type of service and accommodation.

(ii) The relative value study shall be updated every other year.

(iii) In conducting the relative value study, the department may consult or contract with appropriate public and private medical and health agencies or other technical experts.

(iv) The costs and expenses incurred in conducting, maintaining, and administering the relative value study shall be funded by the tax created under Section 59-9-105.

(v) Upon completion of the relative value study, the department shall prepare and publish a relative value study which sets forth the unit value and the 75th percentile charge assigned to each type of service and accommodation.

(b) (i) The reasonable value of any service or accommodation is determined by applying the unit value and the 75th percentile charge assigned to the service or accommodation under the relative value study.

(ii) If a service or accommodation is not assigned a unit value or the 75th percentile charge under the relative value study, the value of the service or accommodation shall equal the reasonable cost of the same or similar service or accommodation in the most populous county of this state.

(c) This Subsection (2) does not preclude the department from adopting a schedule already established or a schedule prepared by persons outside the department, if it meets the requirements of this Subsection (2).

(d) Every insurer shall report to the commissioner any pattern of overcharging, excessive treatment, or other improper actions by a health provider within 30 days after the insurer has knowledge of the pattern.

(e) (i) In disputed cases, a court on its own motion or on the motion of either party may designate an impartial medical panel of not more than three licensed physicians to examine the claimant and testify on the issue of the reasonable value of the claimant's medical services or expenses.

(ii) An impartial medical panel designated under Subsection (2)(e)(i) shall consist of a majority of health care professionals within the same license classification and specialty as the provider of the claimant's medical services or expenses.

(3) Medical expenses as provided for in Subsection (1)(a) and in Subsection 31A-22-309(1)(a)(v) include expenses for any nonmedical remedial care and treatment rendered in accordance with a recognized religious method of healing.

(4) The insured may waive for the named insured and the named insured's spouse only the loss of gross income benefits of Subsection (1)(b)(i) if the insured states in writing that:

(a) within 31 days of applying for coverage, neither the insured nor the insured's spouse received any earned income from regular employment; and

(b) for at least 180 days from the date of the writing and during the period of insurance, neither the insured nor the insured's spouse will receive earned income from regular employment.

(5) This section does not:

(a) prohibit the issuance of policies of insurance providing coverages greater than the minimum coverage required under this chapter; or

(b) require the segregation of those minimum coverages from other coverages in the same policy.

(6) Deductibles are not permitted with respect to the insurance coverages required under this section.

2004

31A-22-308. Persons covered by personal injury protection.

The following may receive benefits under personal injury protection coverage:

(1) the named insured, when injured in an accident involving any motor vehicle, regardless of whether the accident occurs in this state, the United States, its territories or possessions, or Canada, except where the injury is the result of the use or operation of the named insured's own motor vehicle not actually insured under the policy;

(2) persons related to the insured by blood, marriage, adoption, or guardianship who are residents of the insured's household, including those who usually make their home in the same household but temporarily live elsewhere under the circumstances described in Section (1), except where the person is injured as a result of the use or operation of his own motor vehicle not insured under the policy; and

(3) any other natural person whose injuries arise out of an automobile accident occurring while the person occupies a motor vehicle described in the policy with the express or implied consent of the named insured or while a pedestrian if he is injured in an accident occurring in Utah involving the described motor vehicle. 1990

31A-22-309. Limitations, exclusions, and conditions to personal injury protection.

(1) (a) A person who has or is required to have direct benefit coverage under a policy which includes personal injury protection may not maintain a cause of action for general damages arising out of personal injuries alleged to have been caused by an automobile accident, except where the person has sustained one or more of the following:

(i) death;

(ii) dismemberment;

(iii) permanent disability or permanent impairment based upon objective findings;

(iv) permanent disfigurement; or

(v) medical expenses to a person in excess of $3,000.

(b) Subsection (1)(a) does not apply to a person making an uninsured motorist claim.

(2) (a) Any insurer issuing personal injury protection coverage under this part may only exclude from this coverage benefits:

(i) for any injury sustained by the insured while occupying another motor vehicle owned by or furnished for the regular use of the insured or a resident family member of the insured and not insured under the policy;

(ii) for any injury sustained by any person while operating the insured motor vehicle without the express or implied consent of the insured or while not in lawful possession of the insured motor vehicle;

(iii) to any injured person, if the person's conduct contributed to his injury:

(A) by intentionally causing injury to himself; or

(B) while committing a felony;

(iv) for any injury sustained by any person arising out of the use of any motor vehicle while located for use as a residence or premises;

(v) for any injury due to war, whether or not declared, civil war, insurrection, rebellion or revolution, or to any act or condition incident to any of the foregoing; or

(vi) for any injury resulting from the radioactive, toxic, explosive, or other hazardous properties of nuclear materials.

(b) The provisions of this subsection do not limit the exclusions which may be contained in other types of coverage.

(3) The benefits payable to any injured person under Section 31A-22-307 are reduced by:

(a) any benefits which that person receives or is entitled to receive as a result of an accident covered in this code under any workers' compensation or similar statutory plan; and

(b) any amounts which that person receives or is entitled to receive from the United States or any of its agencies because that person is on active duty in the military service.

(4) When a person injured is also an insured party under any other policy, including those policies complying with this part, primary coverage is given by the policy insuring the motor vehicle in use during the accident.

(5) (a) Payment of the benefits provided for in Section 31A-22-307 shall be made on a monthly basis as expenses are incurred.

(b) Benefits for any period are overdue if they are not paid within 30 days after the insurer receives reasonable proof of the fact and amount of expenses incurred during the period. If reasonable proof is not supplied as to the entire claim, the amount supported by reasonable proof is overdue if not paid within 30 days after that proof is received by the insurer. Any part or all of the remainder of the claim that is later supported by reasonable proof is also overdue if not paid within 30 days after the proof is received by the insurer.

(c) If the insurer fails to pay the expenses when due, these expenses shall bear interest at the rate of 1 ½% per month after the due date.

(d) The person entitled to the benefits may bring an action in contract to recover the expenses plus the applicable interest. If the insurer is required by the action to pay any overdue benefits and interest, the insurer is also required to pay a reasonable attorney's fee to the claimant.

(6) Every policy providing personal injury protection coverage is subject to the following:

(a) that where the insured under the policy is or would be held legally liable for the personal injuries sustained by any person to whom benefits required under personal injury protection have been paid by another insurer, including the Workers' Compensation Fund created under Chapter 33, the insurer of the person who would be held legally liable shall reimburse the other insurer for the payment, but not in excess of the amount of damages recoverable; and

(b) that the issue of liability for that reimbursement and its amount shall be decided by mandatory, binding arbitration between the insurers. 2001

31A-22-310. Assigned risk plan.

(1) After consultation with insurers authorized to issue policies containing the provisions specified under Section 31A-22-302, the insurance commissioner shall approve a reasonable plan for the equitable apportionment among the insurers of applicants for those policies who are in good faith entitled to, but are unable to procure, these policies through ordinary methods.

(2) Upon the commissioner's approval of a plan under this section, all insurers issuing policies described under Section 31A-22-302 shall subscribe to and participate in the commissioner's approved plan.

(3) Any applicant for a policy under the commissioner's plan, any person insured under the plan, and any insurer affected by the commissioner's plan may appeal to the insurance commissioner from any ruling or decision of the manager or committee designated to operate the plan.

(4) Section 31A-2-306 applies to the commissioner's decision on this appeal. 1987

31A-22-311. Definitions.

As used in Sections 31A-22-312 and 31A-22-314:

(1) "Authorized driver" means the person to whom the vehicle is rented and includes:

(a) his spouse if a licensed driver satisfying the rental company's minimum age requirement;

(b) his employer or coworker if engaged in business activity with the renter and if they are licensed drivers satisfying the rental company's minimum age requirement;

(c) any person who operates the vehicle during an emergency situation;

(d) any person who operates the vehicle while parking the vehicle at a commercial establishment; or

(e) any person expressly listed by the rental company on the rental agreement as an authorized driver.

(2) "Damage" means any damage or loss to the rented vehicle resulting from a collision, including loss of use and any costs and expenses incident to the damage or loss.

(3) "Rental agreement" means any written agreement stating the terms and conditions governing the use of a private passenger motor vehicle provided by a rental company.

(4) "Rental company" means any person or organization in the business of providing private passenger motor vehicles to the public.

(5) "Renter" means any person or organization obtaining the use of a private passenger motor vehicle from a rental company under the terms of a rental agreement.   1994

31A-22-312.   Liability for collision damage — No security required — No waiver — Section inapplicable to rental companies disclosing charges.

(1) No rental company may, in rental agreements of 30 continuous days or less, hold any authorized driver liable for any damage except when:

(a) the damage is caused intentionally by an authorized driver or as a result of his willful and wanton misconduct;

(b) the damage arises out of the authorized driver's operation of the vehicle while illegally intoxicated or under the influence of any illegal drug as defined or determined under the law of the state where the damage occurred;

(c) the damage is caused while the authorized driver is engaged in any speed contest;

(d) the rental transaction is based on information supplied by the renter with the intent to defraud the rental company;

(e) the damage arises out of the use of the vehicle while committing or otherwise engaged in a criminal act in which the use of the motor vehicle is substantially related to the nature of the criminal activity;

(f) the damage arises out of the use of the motor vehicle to carry persons or property for hire; or

(g) the damage arises out of the use of the motor vehicle outside of the United States or Canada unless the use is specifically authorized by the rental agreement.

(2) No security or deposit for damage in any form may be required or requested by the rental company during the rental period, or pending the resolution of any dispute.

(3) No waiver may be offered to provide coverage for any of the exceptions listed in this section.

(4) This section does not apply to any rental company:

(a) whose advertising in this state clearly discloses all charges and costs incidental to the basic daily rental rate; and

(b) that provides written notice to renters clearly printed on the rental agreement and prominently displayed at its place of business, that the renter's own motor vehicle insurance or his credit card agreement may cover any damage or loss to the rental vehicle.   1989

31A-22-313.   Repealed.   1994

31A-22-314.   Mandatory coverage.

(1) A rental company shall provide its renters with primary coverage meeting the requirements of Title 41, Chapter 12a, Financial Responsibility of Motor Vehicle Owners and Operators Act, unless there is other valid or collectible insurance coverage.

(2) All coverage shall include primary defense costs and may not be waived.   1998

31A-22-315.   Motor vehicle insurance reporting — Penalty.

(1) (a) Each insurer that issues a policy that includes motor vehicle liability coverage, uninsured motorist coverage, underinsured motorist coverage, or personal injury coverage under this part shall before the seventh day of each calendar month provide to the Department of Public Safety's designated agent selected in accordance with Title 41, Chapter 12a, Part 8, Uninsured Motorist Identification Database Program, a record of each motor vehicle insurance policy in effect for vehicles registered or garaged in Utah as of the previous month that was issued by the insurer.

(b) This Subsection (1) does not preclude more frequent reporting.

(2) The record shall include:

(a) the name, date of birth, and driver license number of each insured owner or operator, and the address of the named insured;

(b) the make, year, and vehicle identification number of each insured vehicle; and

(c) the policy number, effective date, and expiration date of each policy.

(3) Each insurer shall provide this information on magnetic tape or in another form the Department of Public Safety's designated agent agrees to accept.

(4) (a) The commissioner may, following procedures set forth in Title 63, Chapter 46b, Administrative Procedures Act, assess a fine against an insurer of up to $250 for each day the insurer fails to comply with this section.

(b) If an insurer shows that the failure to comply with this section was inadvertent, accidental, or the result of excusable neglect, the commissioner shall excuse the fine.   2004

31A-22-316.   Title.

Sections 31A-22-316 through 31A-22-319 are known as the "Aftermarket Crash Parts Act."   1995

31A-22-317.   Definitions.

As used in Sections 31A-22-316 through 31A-22-319:

(1) "Aftermarket crash part" means a replacement for any of the nonmechanical sheet metal or plastic parts that generally constitute the exterior of a motor vehicle, including inner and outer panels.

(2) "Installer" means an individual who replaces or repairs the parts of a motor vehicle.

(3) "Insurer" means an insurance company and any person authorized to represent the insurer with respect to a claim.

(4) "Nonoriginal equipment manufacturer" or "non-OEM" means a manufacturer of replacement parts for a different manufacturer's equipment.

(5) "Non-OEM aftermarket crash part" means an aftermarket crash part not made for or by the manufacturer of the motor vehicle.

(6) "Repair facility" means any motor vehicle dealer, garage, body shop, or other commercial entity that repairs or replaces those parts that generally constitute the exterior of a motor vehicle.   1995

31A-22-318.   Identification.

(1) Any aftermarket crash part supplied by a nonoriginal equipment manufacturer for use in a motor vehicle in this state shall have the logo or name of the nonoriginal equipment manufacturer affixed or inscribed on the aftermarket crash part.

(2) The nonoriginal equipment manufacturer's logo or name shall be visible after installation whenever practicable.   1995

31A-22-319. Prohibition on insurer requiring certain parts — Disclosure.

(1) Unless the insured is given notice in writing an insurer may not specify the use of non-OEM aftermarket crash parts in the repair of an insured's motor vehicle. The notice required by Subsection (1) shall identify non-OEM parts as not made for or by the vehicle manufacturer.

(2) Unless the consumer is given notice in writing prior to installation, a repair facility or installer may not use non-OEM aftermarket parts to repair a vehicle.

(3) In all instances where non-OEM aftermarket crash parts are intended for use by an insurer:

(a) the written estimate shall clearly identify each non-OEM aftermarket crash part; and

(b) a disclosure document containing the following statements in ten point or larger type shall appear on or be attached to the insured's copy of the estimate: "This estimate has been prepared based on the use of crash parts supplied by a source other than the manufacturer of your motor vehicle. Warranties applicable to these replacement parts are provided by the manufacturer or distributor of these parts rather than the manufacturer of your vehicle."   1995

31A-22-320. Use of credit information.

(1) For purposes of this section:

(a) "Credit information" means:

(i) a consumer report;

(ii) a credit score;

(iii) any information obtained by the insurer from a consumer report;

(iv) any part of a consumer report; or

(v) any part of a credit score.

(b) (i) Except as provided in Subsection (1)(b)(ii), "consumer report" is as defined in 15 U.S.C. 1681a.

(ii) "Consumer report" does not include:

(A) a motor vehicle record obtained from a state or an agency of a state; or

(B) any information regarding an applicant's or insured's insurance claim history.

(c) (i) "Credit score" means a numerical value or a categorization that is:

(A) derived from information in a consumer report;

(B) derived from a statistical tool or modeling system; and

(C) developed to predict the likelihood of:

(I) future insurance claims behavior; or

(II) credit behavior.

(ii) "Credit score" includes:

(A) a risk predictor; or

(B) a risk score.

(iii) A numerical value or a categorization described in Subsection (1)(c)(i) is a credit score if it is developed to predict the behavior described in Subsection (1)(c)(i)(C) regardless of whether it is developed to predict other factors in addition to predicting the behavior described in Subsection (1)(c)(i)(C).

(d) "Motor vehicle related insurance policy" means:

(i) a motor vehicle liability policy;

(ii) a policy that contains uninsured motorist coverage;

(iii) a policy that contains underinsured motorist coverage;

(iv) a policy that contains property damage coverage under this part; or

(v) a policy that contains personal injury coverage under this part.

(2) An insurer that issues a motor vehicle related insurance policy:

(a) except as provided in Subsection (2)(b), may not use credit information for the purpose of determining for the motor vehicle related insurance policy:

(i) renewal;

(ii) nonrenewal;

(iii) termination;

(iv) eligibility;

(v) underwriting; or

(vi) rating; and

(b) notwithstanding Subsection (2)(a), may use credit information for the purpose of:

(i) if risk related factors other than credit information are considered, determining initial underwriting; or

(ii) providing to an insured:

(A) a reduction in rates paid by the insured for the motor vehicle related insurance policy; or

(B) any other discount similar to the reduction in rates described in Subsection (2)(b)(ii)(A).

(3) In accordance with Title 63, Chapter 46a, Utah Administrative Rulemaking Act, the commissioner may make rules necessary to enforce this section.   2002

31A-22-321. Use of arbitration in third party motor vehicle accident cases.

(1) A person injured as a result of a motor vehicle accident may elect to submit all third party claims to arbitration by filing a notice of the submission of the claim to binding arbitration in a district court if:

(a) the claimant or the claimant's representative has:

(i) previously and timely filed a complaint in a district court that includes a third party claim; and

(ii) filed a notice to submit the claim to arbitration before the plaintiff's initial disclosures have been filed under Rule 26, Utah Rules of Civil Procedure; and

(b) the notice required under Subsection (1)(a)(ii) is filed while the action under Subsection (1)(a)(i) is still pending.

(2) If a party submits a claim to arbitration under Subsection (1), the party submitting the claim or the party's representative is limited to an arbitration award that does not exceed $25,000.

(3) A claim for punitive damages may not be made in an arbitration proceeding under Subsection (1), even if the claim is later resolved through a trial de novo under Subsection (9).

(4) (a) Unless otherwise agreed to in writing by the parties, a claim that is submitted to arbitration under this section shall be resolved by a single arbitrator.

(b) All parties shall agree on the single arbitrator selected under Subsection (4)(a).

(c) If the parties are unable to agree on a single arbitrator as required under Subsection (4)(b), the parties shall select a panel of three arbitrators.

(d) If the parties select a panel of three arbitrators under Subsection (4)(c):

(i) each side shall select one arbitrator; and

(ii) the arbitrators appointed under Subsection (4)(d)(i) shall select one additional arbitrator to be included in the panel.

(5) Unless otherwise agreed to in writing:

(a) each party shall pay an equal share of the fees and costs of the arbitrator selected under Subsection (4)(a); and

(b) if an arbitration panel is selected under Subsection (4)(d):

(i) each party shall pay the fees and costs of the arbitrator selected by that party's side; and

(ii) each party shall pay an equal share of the fees and costs of the arbitrator selected under Subsection (4)(d)(ii).

(6) Except as otherwise provided in this section and unless otherwise agreed to in writing by the parties, an arbitration proceeding conducted under this section shall be governed by Title 78, Chapter 31a, Utah Uniform Arbitration Act.

(7) (a) Subject to the provisions of this section, the Utah Rules of Civil Procedure and Utah Rules of Evidence apply to the arbitration proceeding.

(b) The Utah Rules of Civil Procedure and Utah Rules of Evidence shall be applied liberally with the intent of concluding the claim in a timely and cost-efficient manner.

(c) Discovery shall be conducted in accordance with Rules 26 through 37 of the Utah Rules of Civil Procedure and shall be subject to the jurisdiction of the district court in which the matter is filed.

(d) Dispositive motions shall be filed, heard, and decided by the district court prior to the arbitration proceeding in accordance with the court's scheduling order.

(8) A written decision by a single arbitrator or by a majority of the arbitration panel shall constitute a final decision.

(9) An arbitration award issued under this section shall be the final resolution of all claims between the parties unless either party, within 20 days after service of the arbitration award:

(a) files a notice requesting a trial de novo in the district court; and

(b) serves the nonmoving party with a copy of the notice requesting a trial de novo under Subsection (9)(a).

(10) (a) Upon filing a notice requesting a trial de novo under Subsection (9), the claim shall proceed through litigation pursuant to the Utah Rules of Civil Procedure and Utah Rules of Evidence in the district court.

(b) In accordance with Rule 38, Utah Rules of Civil Procedure, either party may request a jury trial with a request for trial de novo filed under Subsection (9)(a).

(11) (a) If the plaintiff, as the moving party in a trial de novo requested under Subsection (9), does not obtain a verdict that is at least $5,000 and is at least 20% greater than the arbitration award, the plaintiff is responsible for all of the nonmoving party's costs.

(b) Except as provided in Subsection (11)(c), the costs under Subsection (11)(a) shall include:

(i) any costs set forth in Rule 54(d), Utah Rules of Civil Procedure; and

(ii) the costs of expert witnesses and depositions.

(c) An award of costs under this Subsection (11) may not exceed $2,500.

(12) (a) If a defendant, as the moving party in a trial de novo requested under Subsection (9), does not obtain a verdict that is at least 20% less than the arbitration award, the defendant is responsible for all of the nonmoving party's costs.

(b) Except as provided in Subsection (12)(c), the costs under Subsection (12)(a) shall include:

(i) any costs set forth in Rule 54(d), Utah Rules of Civil Procedure; and

(ii) the costs of expert witnesses and depositions.

(c) An award of costs under this Subsection (12) may not exceed $2,500.

(13) For purposes of determining whether a party's verdict is greater or less than the arbitration award under Subsections (11) and (12), a court may not consider any recovery or other relief granted on a claim for damages if the claim for damages:

(a) was not fully disclosed in writing prior to the arbitration proceeding; or

(b) was not disclosed in response to discovery contrary to the Utah Rules of Civil Procedure.

(14) If a district court determines, upon a motion of the nonmoving party, that the moving party's use of the trial de novo process was filed in bad faith as defined in Section 78-27-56, the district court may award reasonable attorney fees to the nonmoving party.

(15) Nothing in this section is intended to affect or prevent any first party claim from later being brought under any first party insurance policy under which the injured person is a covered person.

(16) (a) If a defendant requests a trial de novo under Subsection (9), the verdict at trial may not exceed $40,000.

(b) If a plaintiff requests a trial de novo under Subsection (9), the verdict at trial may not exceed $25,000.

(17) All arbitration awards issued under this section shall bear postjudgment interest pursuant to Section 15-1-4.   **2005**

CHAPTER 35

BAIL BOND ACT

Part 7

Prohibitions and Penalties

Section
31A-35-701.   Prohibited acts.

PART 7

PROHIBITIONS AND PENALTIES

31A-35-701. Prohibited acts.

(1) A bail bond producer or bail bond surety may not:

(a) solicit business in or about:

(i) any place where persons in the custody of the state or any local law enforcement or correctional agency are confined; or

(ii) any court;

(b) pay a fee or rebate or give or promise anything of value to any person in order to secure a settlement, compromise, remission, or reduction of the amount of any undertaking or bail bond;

(c) pay a fee or rebate or give anything of value to an attorney in regard to any bail bond matter, except payment for legal services actually rendered for the bail bond producer or bail bond surety;

(d) pay a fee or rebate or give or promise anything of value to the principal or anyone in the principal's behalf; or

(e) engage in any other act prohibited by the commissioner by rule.

(2) The following persons may not act as bail bond producers and may not, directly or indirectly, receive any benefits from the execution of any bail bond:

(a) a person employed at any jail, correctional facility, or other facility used for the incarceration of persons;

(b) a peace officer;

(c) a judge; and

(d) a trusty or prisoner incarcerated in any jail, correctional facility, or other facility used for the incarceration of persons.

(3) A bail bond producer may not:

(a) sign or countersign in blank any bail bond; or

(b) give the power of attorney to, or otherwise authorize anyone to, countersign in the bail bond producer's name to a bail bond.

(4) A bail bond producer may not advertise or hold himself out to be a bail bond surety.

(5) The following persons or members of their immediate families may not solicit business on behalf of a bail bond surety or bail bond producer:

(a) a person employed at any jail, correctional facility, or other facility used for the incarceration of persons;

(b) a peace officer;

(c) a judge; and

(d) a trusty or prisoner incarcerated in any jail, correctional facility, or other facility used for the incarceration of persons.   2004

TITLE 32A

ALCOHOLIC BEVERAGE CONTROL ACT

CHAPTER 1

GENERAL PROVISIONS

Part 1

Administration

Part 3

Proof of Age

PART 1

ADMINISTRATION

32A-1-105. Definitions.

As used in this title:

(1) "Airport lounge" means a place of business licensed to sell alcoholic beverages, at retail, for consumption on its premises located at an international airport with a United States Customs office on the premises of the international airport.

(2) "Alcoholic beverages" means "beer" and "liquor" as the terms are defined in this section.

(3) (a) "Alcoholic products" means all products that:

(i) contain:

(A) at least $\frac{63}{100}$ of 1% of alcohol by volume; or

(B) at least $\frac{1}{2}$ of 1% by weight; and

(ii) are obtained by fermentation, infusion, decoction, brewing, distillation, or any other process that uses any liquid or combinations of liquids, whether drinkable or not, to create alcohol in an amount greater than the amount prescribed in Subsection (3)(a)(i).

(b) "Alcoholic products" does not include any of the following common items that otherwise come within the definition of alcoholic products:

(i) extracts;

(ii) vinegars;

(iii) ciders;

(iv) essences;

(v) tinctures;

(vi) food preparations; or

(vii) over-the-counter drugs and medicines.

(4) "Bar" means a counter or similar structure:

(a) at which alcoholic beverages are:

(i) stored; or

(ii) dispensed; or

(b) from which alcoholic beverages are served.

(5) (a) "Beer" means any product that contains:

(i) $\frac{63}{100}$ of 1% of alcohol by volume or $\frac{1}{2}$ of 1% of alcohol by weight, but not more than 4% of alcohol by volume or 3.2% by weight; and

(ii) is obtained by fermentation, infusion, or decoction of any malted grain.

(b) Beer may or may not contain hops or other vegetable products.

(c) Beer includes a product that:

(i) contains alcohol in the percentages described in Subsection (5)(a); and

(ii) is referred to as:

(A) malt liquor;

(B) malted beverages; or

(C) malt coolers.

(6) (a) "Beer retailer" means any business establishment that is:

(i) engaged, primarily or incidentally, in the retail sale of beer to public patrons, whether for consumption on or off the establishment's premises; and

    (ii) licensed to sell beer by:

        (A) the commission;

        (B) a local authority; or

        (C) both the commission and a local authority.

  (b) (i) "On-premise beer retailer" means any beer retailer engaged, primarily or incidentally, in the sale of beer to public patrons for consumption on the beer retailer's premises.

    (ii) "On-premise beer retailer" includes a tavern.

(7) "Billboard" means any public display used to advertise including:

  (a) a light device;

  (b) a painting;

  (c) a drawing;

  (d) a poster;

  (e) a sign;

  (f) a signboard; or

  (g) a scoreboard.

(8) "Brewer" means any person engaged in manufacturing beer.

(9) "Cash bar" means the service of alcoholic beverages:

  (a) at:

    (i) a banquet; or

    (ii) a temporary event for which a permit is issued under this title; and

  (b) if an attendee at the banquet or temporary event is charged for the alcoholic beverage.

(10) "Chartered bus" means a passenger bus, coach, or other motor vehicle provided by a bus company to a group of persons pursuant to a common purpose:

  (a) under a single contract;

  (b) at a fixed charge in accordance with the bus company's tariff; and

  (c) for the purpose of giving the group of persons the exclusive use of the bus and a driver to travel together to a specified destination or destinations.

(11) "Church" means a building:

  (a) set apart for the purpose of worship;

  (b) in which religious services are held;

  (c) with which clergy is associated; and

  (d) which is tax exempt under the laws of this state.

(12) "Club" and "private club" means any of the following organized primarily for the benefit of its members:

  (a) a social club;

  (b) a recreational association;

  (c) a fraternal association;

  (d) an athletic association; or

  (e) a kindred association.

(13) "Commission" means the Alcoholic Beverage Control Commission.

(14) "Department" means the Department of Alcoholic Beverage Control.

(15) "Distressed merchandise" means any alcoholic beverage in the possession of the department that is saleable, but for some reason is unappealing to the public.

(16) "General food store" means any business establishment primarily engaged in selling food and grocery supplies to public patrons for off-premise consumption.

(17) "Guest" means a person accompanied by an active member or visitor of a club who enjoys only those privileges derived from the host for the duration of the visit to the club.

(18) (a) "Heavy beer" means any product that:

    (i) contains more than 4% alcohol by volume; and

    (ii) is obtained by fermentation, infusion, or decoction of any malted grain.

  (b) "Heavy beer" is considered "liquor" for the purposes of this title.

(19) "Hosted bar" means the service of alcoholic beverages:

  (a) without charge; and

  (b) at a:

    (i) banquet; or

    (ii) privately hosted event.

(20) "Identification card" means the identification card issued under Title 53, Chapter 3, Part 8, Identification Card Act.

(21) "Interdicted person" means a person to whom the sale, gift, or provision of an alcoholic beverage is prohibited by:

  (a) law; or

  (b) court order.

(22) "Intoxicated" means that to a degree that is unlawful under Section 76-9-701 a person is under the influence of:

  (a) an alcoholic beverage;

  (b) a controlled substance;

  (c) a substance having the property of releasing toxic vapors; or

  (d) a combination of Subsections (22)(a) through (c).

(23) "Licensee" means any person issued a license by the commission to sell, manufacture, store, or allow consumption of alcoholic beverages on premises owned or controlled by the person.

(24) "Limousine" means any motor vehicle licensed by the state or a local authority, other than a bus or taxicab:

  (a) in which the driver and passengers are separated by a partition, glass, or other barrier; and

  (b) that is provided by a company to an individual or individuals at a fixed charge in accordance with the company's tariff for the purpose of giving the individual or individuals the exclusive use of the limousine and a driver to travel to a specified destination or destinations.

(25) (a) "Liquor" means alcohol, or any alcoholic, spirituous, vinous, fermented, malt, or other liquid, or combination of liquids, a part of which is spirituous, vinous, or fermented, and all other drinks, or drinkable liquids that contain more than ½ of 1% of alcohol by volume and is suitable to use for beverage purposes.

  (b) "Liquor" does not include any beverage defined as a beer, malt liquor, or malted beverage that has an alcohol content of less than 4% alcohol by volume.

(26) "Local authority" means:

  (a) the governing body of the county if the premises are located in an unincorporated area of a county; or

  (b) the governing body of the city or town if the premises are located in an incorporated city or a town.

(27) "Manufacture" means to distill, brew, rectify, mix, compound, process, ferment, or otherwise make an alcoholic product for personal use or for sale or distribution to others.

(28) "Member" means a person who, after paying regular dues, has full privileges of a club under this title.

(29) (a) "Military installation" means a base, air field, camp, post, station, yard, center, or homeport facility for any ship:

(i) (A) under the control of the United States Department of Defense; or

(B) of the National Guard;

(ii) that is located within the state; and

(iii) including any leased facility.

(b) "Military installation" does not include any facility used primarily for:

(i) civil works;

(ii) rivers and harbors projects; or

(iii) flood control projects.

(30) "Minor" means any person under the age of 21 years.

(31) "Outlet" means a location other than a state store or package agency where alcoholic beverages are sold pursuant to a license issued by the commission.

(32) "Package" means any of the following containing liquor:

(a) a container;

(b) a bottle;

(c) a vessel; or

(d) other receptacle.

(33) "Package agency" means a retail liquor location operated under a contractual agreement with the department, by a person other than the state, who is authorized by the commission to sell package liquor for consumption off the premises of the agency.

(34) "Package agent" means any person permitted by the commission to operate a package agency pursuant to a contractual agreement with the department to sell liquor from premises that the package agent shall provide and maintain.

(35) "Permittee" means any person issued a permit by the commission to perform acts or exercise privileges as specifically granted in the permit.

(36) "Person" means any individual, partnership, firm, corporation, limited liability company, association, business trust, or other form of business enterprise, including a receiver or trustee, and the plural as well as the singular number, unless the intent to give a more limited meaning is disclosed by the context.

(37) "Premises" means any building, enclosure, room, or equipment used in connection with the sale, storage, service, manufacture, distribution, or consumption of alcoholic products, unless otherwise defined in this title or in the rules adopted by the commission.

(38) "Prescription" means a writing in legal form, signed by a physician or dentist and given to a patient for obtaining an alcoholic beverage for medicinal purposes only.

(39) (a) "Privately hosted event" or "private social function" means a specific social, business, or recreational event for which an entire room, area, or hall has been leased or rented, in advance by an identified group, and the event or function is limited in atten-

dance to people who have been specifically designated and their guests.

(b) "Privately hosted event" and "private social function" does not include events or functions to which the general public is invited, whether for an admission fee or not.

(40) "Proof of age" means:

(a) an identification card;

(b) an identification that:

(i) is substantially similar to an identification card;

(ii) is issued in accordance with the laws of a state other than Utah in which the identification is issued;

(iii) includes date of birth; and

(iv) has a picture affixed;

(c) a valid driver license certificate that:

(i) includes date of birth;

(ii) has a picture affixed; and

(iii) is issued:

(A) under Title 53, Chapter 3, Uniform Driver License Act; or

(B) in accordance with the laws of the state in which it is issued;

(d) a military identification card that:

(i) includes date of birth; and

(ii) has a picture affixed; or

(e) a valid passport.

(41) (a) "Public building" means any building or permanent structure owned or leased by the state, a county, or local government entity that is used for:

(i) public education;

(ii) transacting public business; or

(iii) regularly conducting government activities.

(b) "Public building" does not mean or refer to any building owned by the state or a county or local government entity when the building is used by anyone, in whole or in part, for proprietary functions.

(42) "Representative" means an individual who is compensated by salary, commission, or any other means for representing and selling the alcoholic beverage products of a manufacturer, supplier, or importer of liquor, wine, or heavy beer.

(43) "Residence" means the person's principal place of abode within Utah.

(44) "Restaurant" means any business establishment:

(a) where a variety of foods is prepared and complete meals are served to the general public;

(b) located on a premises having adequate culinary fixtures for food preparation and dining accommodations; and

(c) that is engaged primarily in serving meals to the general public.

(45) "Retailer" means any person engaged in the sale or distribution of alcoholic beverages to the consumer.

(46) (a) "Sample" includes:

(i) a department sample; and

(ii) an industry representative sample.

(b) "Department sample" means liquor, wine, and heavy beer that has been placed in the possession of the department for testing, analysis, and sampling.

(c) "Industry representative sample" means liquor, wine, and heavy beer that has been placed in the possession of the department for testing, analysis, and sampling by local industry representatives on the premises of the department to educate the local industry representatives of the quality and characteristics of the product.

(47) (a) "School" means any building used primarily for the general education of minors.

   (b) "School" does not include:

     (i) a nursery school;

     (ii) an infant day care center; or

     (iii) a trade or technical school.

(48) "Sell," "sale," and "to sell" means any transaction, exchange, or barter whereby, for any consideration, an alcoholic beverage is either directly or indirectly transferred, solicited, ordered, delivered for value, or by any means or under any pretext is promised or obtained, whether done by a person as a principal, proprietor, or as an agent, servant, or employee, unless otherwise defined in this title or the rules made by the commission.

(49) "Small brewer" means a brewer who manufactures less than 60,000 barrels of beer and heavy beer per year.

(50) (a) "Spirituous liquor" means liquor that is distilled.

   (b) "Spirituous liquor" includes an alcohol product defined as a "distilled spirit" by 27 U.S.C. 211 and 27 C.F.R. Sections 5.11 through 5.23.

(51) (a) "State label" means the official label designated by the commission affixed to all liquor containers sold in the state.

   (b) "State label" includes the department identification mark and inventory control number.

(52) (a) "State store" means a facility for the sale of package liquor:

     (i) located on premises owned or leased by the state; and

     (ii) operated by state employees.

   (b) "State store" does not apply to any:

     (i) licensee;

     (ii) permittee; or

     (iii) package agency.

(53) "Supplier" means any person selling alcoholic beverages to the department.

(54) (a) "Tavern" means any business establishment that is:

     (i) engaged primarily in the retail sale of beer to public patrons for consumption on the establishment's premises; and

     (ii) licensed to sell beer under Chapter 10, Part 2, On-Premise Beer Retailer Licenses.

   (b) "Tavern" includes the following if the revenue from the sale of beer exceeds the revenue of the sale of food, although food need not be sold in the establishment:

     (i) a beer bar;

     (ii) a parlor;

     (iii) a lounge;

     (iv) a cabaret; or

     (v) a nightclub.

(55) "Temporary domicile" means the principal place of abode within Utah of a person who does not have a present intention to continue residency within Utah permanently or indefinitely.

(56) "Unsaleable liquor merchandise" means merchandise that:

   (a) is unsaleable because the merchandise is:

     (i) unlabeled;

     (ii) leaky;

     (iii) damaged;

     (iv) difficult to open; or

     (v) partly filled;

   (b) is in a container:

     (i) having faded labels or defective caps or corks;

     (ii) in which the contents are:

       (A) cloudy;

       (B) spoiled; or

       (C) chemically determined to be impure; or

     (iii) that contains:

       (A) sediment; or

       (B) any foreign substance; or

   (c) is otherwise considered by the department as unfit for sale.

(57) "Visitor" means an individual that in accordance with Section 32A-5-107 holds limited privileges in a private club by virtue of a visitor card.

(58) "Warehouser" means any person, other than a licensed manufacturer, engaged in the importation for sale, storage, or distribution of liquor regardless of amount.

(59) "Wholesaler" means any person engaged in the importation for sale, or in the sale of beer in wholesale or jobbing quantities to retailers, other than a small brewer selling beer manufactured by that brewer.

(60) (a) "Wine" means any alcoholic beverage obtained by the fermentation of the natural sugar content of fruits, plants, honey, or milk, or any other like substance, whether or not other ingredients are added.

   (b) "Wine" is considered "liquor" for purposes of this title, except as otherwise provided in this title.   2005

32A-1-115. Alcoholic Beverage Enforcement and Treatment Restricted Account — Distribution to municipalities and counties.

(1) As used in this section:

   (a) "Account" means the Alcoholic Beverage Enforcement and Treatment Restricted Account created in this section.

   (b) "Alcohol-related offense" means:

     (i) a violation of:

       (A) Section 41-6a-502; or

       (B) an ordinance that complies with the requirements of:

         (I) Subsection 41-6a-510(1); or

         (II) Section 76-5-207; or

     (ii) an offense involving the:

       (A) illegal sale of alcohol;

       (B) illegal distribution of alcohol;

       (C) illegal transportation of alcohol;

       (D) illegal possession of alcohol; or

       (E) illegal consumption of alcohol.

   (c) "Annual conviction time period" means the time period that:

     (i) begins on July 1 and ends on June 30; and

     (ii) immediately precedes the fiscal year for which an appropriation under this section is made.

   (d) "Coordinating council" means the Utah Substance Abuse and Anti-Violence Coordinating Council created in Section 63-25a-201.

   (e) "Municipality" means:

(i) a city; or

(ii) a town.

(2) (a) There is created in the General Fund a restricted account called the "Alcoholic Beverage Enforcement and Treatment Restricted Account."

(b) The account shall be funded from:

(i) amounts deposited by the state treasurer in accordance with Section 59-15-109;

(ii) any appropriations made to the account by the Legislature; and

(iii) interest described in Subsection (2)(c).

(c) Interest earned on the account shall be deposited into the account.

(d) (i) The revenues in the account shall be used exclusively for programs or projects related to prevention, treatment, detection, prosecution, and control of violations of this title and other offenses in which alcohol is a contributing factor except as provided in Subsection (2)(d)(ii).

(ii) The portion distributed under this section to counties may also be used for the confinement or treatment of persons arrested for or convicted of offenses in which alcohol is a contributing factor.

(iii) Any municipality or county entitled to receive funds shall use the funds exclusively as required by this Subsection (2)(d).

(iv) The appropriations provided for under Subsection (3) are:

(A) intended to supplement the budget of the appropriate agencies of each municipality and county within the state to enable the municipalities and counties to more effectively fund the programs and projects described in this Subsection (2)(d); and

(B) not intended to replace funds that would otherwise be allocated for the programs and projects in this Subsection (2)(d).

(3) (a) The revenues deposited into the account shall be distributed to municipalities and counties:

(i) to the extent appropriated by the Legislature except that the Legislature shall appropriate each fiscal year an amount equal to at least the amount deposited in the account in accordance with Section 59-15-109; and

(ii) as provided in this Subsection (3).

(b) The amount appropriated from the account shall be distributed as follows:

(i) 25% to municipalities and counties based upon the percentage of the state population residing in each municipality and county;

(ii) 30% to municipalities and counties based upon each municipality's and county's percentage of the statewide convictions for all alcohol-related offenses;

(iii) 20% to municipalities and counties based upon the percentage of all state stores, package agencies, liquor licensees, and beer licensees in the state that are located in each municipality and county; and

(iv) 25% to the counties for confinement and treatment purposes authorized by this section based upon the percentage of the state population located in each county.

(c) (i) Except as provided in Subsection (3)(c)(iii), a municipality that does not have a

law enforcement agency may not receive monies under this section.

(ii) The State Tax Commission:

(A) may not distribute the monies the municipality would receive but for the municipality not having a law enforcement agency to that municipality; and

(B) shall distribute the monies that the municipality would have received but for it not having a law enforcement agency to the county in which the municipality is located for use by the county in accordance with this section.

(iii) Notwithstanding Subsections (3)(c)(i) and (ii), if the coordinating council finds that a municipality described in Subsection (3)(c)(i) demonstrates that the municipality can use the monies that the municipality is otherwise eligible to receive in accordance with this section, the coordinating council may direct the State Tax Commission to distribute the money to the municipality.

(4) To determine the distributions required by Subsection (3)(b)(ii), the State Tax Commission shall annually:

(a) for an annual conviction time period:

(i) multiply by two the total number of convictions in the state obtained during the annual conviction time period for violation of:

(A) Section 41-6a-502; or

(B) an ordinance that complies with the requirements of Subsection 41-6a-510(1) or Section 76-5-207; and

(ii) add to the number calculated under Subsection (4)(a)(i) the number of convictions obtained during the annual conviction time period for all alcohol-related offenses other than the alcohol-related offenses described in Subsection (4)(a)(i);

(b) divide an amount equal to 30% of the appropriation for that fiscal year by the sum obtained in Subsection (4)(a); and

(c) multiply the amount calculated under Subsection (4)(b), by the number of convictions obtained in each municipality and county during the annual conviction time period for alcohol-related offenses.

(5) For purposes of this section:

(a) the number of state stores, package agencies, and licensees located within the limits of each municipality and county:

(i) is the number determined by the department to be so located;

(ii) includes all:

(A) private clubs;

(B) restaurants;

(C) airport lounges;

(D) package agencies; and

(E) state stores; and

(iii) does not include on-premise beer retailer licensees;

(b) the number of state stores, package agencies, and licensees in a county consists only of that number located within unincorporated areas of the county;

(c) population figures shall be determined according to the most current population estimates prepared by the Utah Population Estimates Committee;

(d) a county's population figure for the 25% distribution to municipalities and counties under Subsection (3)(b)(i) shall be determined only with reference to the population in the unincorporated areas of the county;

(e) a county's population figure under Subsection (3)(b)(iv) for the 25% distribution to counties only shall be determined with reference to the total population in the county, including that of municipalities;

(f) a conviction occurs in the municipality or county that actually prosecutes the offense to judgment; and

(g) in the case of a conviction based upon a guilty plea, the conviction is considered to occur in the municipality or county that, except for the guilty plea, would have prosecuted the offense.

(6) By not later than September 1 each year:

(a) the state court administrator shall certify to the State Tax Commission the number of convictions obtained for alcohol-related offenses in each municipality or county in the state during the annual conviction time period; and

(b) the coordinating council shall notify the State Tax Commission of any municipality that does not have a law enforcement agency.

(7) By not later than December 1 of each year, the coordinating council shall notify the State Tax Commission for the fiscal year of appropriation of:

(a) any municipality that may receive a distribution under Subsection (3)(c)(iii);

(b) any county that may receive a distribution allocated to a municipality described in Subsection (3)(c)(ii);

(c) any municipality or county that may not receive a distribution because the coordinating council has suspended the payment under Subsection (10)(a)(i); and

(d) any municipality or county that receives a distribution because the suspension of payment has been cancelled under Subsection (10)(a)(ii).

(8) (a) By not later than January 1 of the fiscal year of appropriation, the State Tax Commission shall annually distribute to each municipality and county the portion of the appropriation that the municipality or county is eligible to receive under this section, except for any municipality or county that the coordinating council notifies the State Tax Commission in accordance with Subsection (7) may not receive a distribution in that fiscal year.

(b) (i) The State Tax Commission shall prepare forms for use by municipalities and counties in applying for distributions under this section.

(ii) The forms described in this Subsection (8) may require the submission of information the State Tax Commission considers necessary to enable the State Tax Commission to comply with this section.

(9) A municipality or county that receives any monies under this section during a fiscal year shall by no later than October 1 following the fiscal year:

(a) report to the coordinating council:

(i) the programs or projects of the municipality or county that receive monies under this section;

(ii) if the monies for programs or projects were exclusively used as required by Subsection (2)(d);

(iii) indicators of whether the programs or projects that receive monies under this section are effective; and

(iv) if any monies received under this section were not expended by the municipality or county; and

(b) provide the coordinating council a statement signed by the chief executive officer of the county or municipality attesting that the monies received under this section were used in addition to any monies appropriated or otherwise available for the county's or municipality's law enforcement and were not used to supplant those monies.

(10) (a) The coordinating council may, by a majority vote:

(i) suspend future payments under Subsection (8) to a municipality or county that:

(A) does not file a report that meets the requirements of Subsection (9); or

(B) the coordinating council finds does not use the monies as required by Subsection (2)(d) on the basis of the report filed by the municipality or county under Subsection (9); and

(ii) cancel a suspension under Subsection (10)(a)(i).

(b) The State Tax Commission shall:

(i) retain monies that a municipality or county does not receive under Subsection (10)(a); and

(ii) notify the coordinating council of the balance of retained monies under this Subsection (10)(b) after the annual distribution under Subsection (8).

(11) (a) Subject to the requirements of this Subsection (11), the coordinating council shall award the balance of retained monies under Subsection (10)(b):

(i) as prioritized by majority vote of the coordinating council; and

(ii) as grants to:

(A) a county;

(B) a municipality; or

(C) the Department of Public Safety.

(b) By not later than May 30 of the fiscal year of the appropriation, the coordinating council shall notify the State Tax Commission of any grants awarded under this Subsection (11).

(c) The State Tax Commission shall make payments of grants:

(i) upon receiving notice as provided under Subsection (11)(b); and

(ii) by not later than June 30 of the fiscal year of the appropriation.

(d) An entity that receives a grant under this Subsection (11) shall use the grant monies exclusively for programs or projects described in Subsection (2)(d).   2005

PART 3

PROOF OF AGE

32A-1-301. Unlawful transfer or use of proof of age — False information.

(1) (a) It is unlawful for a person to transfer that person's proof of age to any other person to aid that person:

(i) in procuring alcoholic beverages or products;

(ii) to gain admittance to a place where alcoholic beverages or products are sold or consumed; or

(iii) to obtain any employment that under this title may not be obtained by a minor.

(b) Any person who permits that person's proof of age to be used by another for any purpose stated in Subsection (1)(a) is guilty of a class B misdemeanor.

(2) (a) It is unlawful for a person to use a proof of age containing false information with the intent to:

(i) procure alcoholic beverages or products;

(ii) gain admittance to a place where alcoholic beverages or products are sold or consumed; or

(iii) obtain any employment that under this title may not be obtained by a minor.

(b) A person who violates this Subsection (2) is guilty of a class A misdemeanor.   2004

32A-1-302. Presentation of proof of age upon request.

(1) To obtain one or more of the following, a person shall present proof of age at the request of a person listed in Subsection (2):

(a) an alcoholic beverage or product; or

(b) employment that under this title may not be obtained by a minor.

(2) To determine whether the person described in Subsection (1) is 21 years of age, the following may request a person described in Subsection (1) to present proof of age:

(a) a person authorized by law to sell or otherwise handle alcoholic beverages or products;

(b) a peace officer;

(c) a representative of the State Bureau of Investigation of the Department of Public Safety, established in Section 53-10-301; or

(d) an authorized employee of the department.   2002

32A-1-303. Additional requirements when age is in question.

(1) In addition to requesting the presentation of proof of age under Section 32A-1-302, any person authorized to sell or otherwise handle alcoholic beverages or products shall require any person whose age is in question to sign a statement of age on the form provided under Subsection (2) that includes:

(a) the date the statement of age is signed; and

(b) the number assigned to the person's proof of age by the issuing authority.

(2) (a) At the request of a licensee, the commissioner of public safety shall provide to a licensee under this title the form for the statement of age described in Subsection (1).

(b) The person authorized to sell or otherwise handle alcoholic beverages or products shall:

(i) file in alphabetical order any statement of age obtained under Subsection (1) by no later than the close of business on the day on which the statement is executed; and

(ii) maintain on file for three years any statement of age obtained under Subsection (1).

(c) The statement of age obtained under Subsection (1) is subject to examination by:

(i) a peace officer;

(ii) a representative of the State Bureau of Investigation of the Department of Public Safety, established in Section 53-10-301; or

(iii) an authorized employee of the department.   2002

32A-1-304. Acceptance of identification — Evidence.

(1) A person authorized by law to sell or otherwise handle alcoholic beverages or products may accept as evidence of the legal age of the person presenting the following:

(a) proof of age; or

(b) if a statement of age is required under Subsection 32A-1-303(1):

(i) proof of age; and

(ii) a statement of age obtained under Section 32A-1-303.

(2) A statement of age described in Section 32A-1-303, if properly completed, signed, and filed in accordance with Section 32A-1-303, may be offered as a defense in any case where there is at issue the legality of:

(a) selling or otherwise furnishing an alcoholic beverage or product to the person who signed the statement of age; or

(b) allowing the person who signed the statement of age to be employed in any employment that under this title may not be obtained by a minor.

(3) A person may not be subject to a penalty for a violation of this part if it is proved to the commission or the court hearing the matter that the person charged with the violation acted in good faith.   2002

32A-1-305. Penalty.

Unless otherwise provided in this title, any person who violates this part is guilty of a class B misdemeanor.   1990

CHAPTER 12

CRIMINAL OFFENSES

Part 1

General Provisions

PART 1

GENERAL PROVISIONS

32A-12-101. Utah Criminal Code applicable.

Title 76, Chapters 1, 2, 3, and 4, the Utah Criminal Code, relating to principles of construction, jurisdiction, venue, limitations of actions, multiple prosecutions, double jeopardy, burdens of proof, definitions, principles of criminal responsibility, punishments, and inchoate offenses apply to any criminal offense defined in this title, except as otherwise provided.

1990

32A-12-102. Special burdens of proof — Inferences and presumptions.

(1) In any prosecution of an offense defined in this title or in any proceeding brought to enforce this title:

(a) it is not necessary that the state or commission establish the precise description or quantity of the alcoholic beverages or products or the precise consideration, if any, given or received for the alcoholic beverages or products;

(b) there is an inference, absent proof to the contrary, that the alcoholic beverage or product in question is an alcoholic beverage or product if the witness describes it:

(i) as an alcoholic beverage or product;

(ii) by a name that is commonly applied to an alcoholic beverage or product; or

(iii) as intoxicating;

(c) if it is alleged that an association or corporation has violated this title, the fact of the incorporation of the association or corporation is presumed absent proof to the contrary;

(d) a certificate or report signed or purporting to be signed by any state chemist, assistant state chemist, or state crime laboratory chemist, as to the analysis or ingredients of any alcoholic beverage or product is:

(i) prima facie evidence:

(A) of the facts stated in that certificate or report; and

(B) of the authority of the person giving or making the report; and

(ii) admissible in evidence without any proof of appointment or signature absent proof to the contrary; and

(e) a copy of entries made in the records of the United States internal revenue collector, certified by the collector or a qualified notary public, showing the payment of the United States internal revenue special tax for the manufacture or sale of alcoholic beverages or products is prima facie evidence of the manufacture or sale by the party named in the entry within the period set forth in the record.

(2) (a) In proving the unlawful sale, disposal, gift, or purchase, gratuitous or otherwise, or consumption of alcoholic beverages or products, it is not necessary that the state or commission establish that any money or other consideration actually passed or that an alcoholic beverage or product was actually consumed if the court or trier of fact is satisfied that:

(i) a transaction in the nature of a sale, disposal, gift, or purchase actually occurred; or

(ii) any consumption of alcoholic beverages or products was about to occur.

(b) Proof of consumption or intended consumption of an alcoholic beverage or product on premises on which consumption is prohibited, by some person not authorized to consume alcoholic beverages or products on those premises, is evidence that an alcoholic beverage or product was sold or given to or purchased by the person consuming, about to consume, or carrying away the alcoholic beverage or product as against the occupant of the premises.

2004

32A-12-103. Criminal responsibility for conduct of another.

In addition to Title 76, Chapter 2, Part 2, Criminal Responsibility for the Conduct of Another, the following principles apply to violations of this title:

(1) If a violation of this title is committed by any person in the employ of the occupant of any premises in which the offense is committed, or by any person who is required by the occupant to be

or remain in or upon the premises, or to act in any way for the occupant, the occupant is prima facie considered a party to the offense committed, and is liable as a principal offender, notwithstanding the fact that the offense was committed by a person who is not proved to have committed it under or by the direction of the occupant. Nothing in this section relieves the person actually committing the offense from liability.

(2) If a violation of this title is committed by a corporation, association, partnership, or limited liability company, the officer or agent of the corporation or association, partner, manager, or member of the limited liability company in charge of the premises in which the offense is committed is prima facie considered a party to the offense committed, and is personally liable to the penalties prescribed for the offense as a principal offender. Nothing in this section relieves the corporation, association, partnership, or limited liability company, or the person who actually committed the offense from liability.   2003

32A-12-104.   Violation of title a misdemeanor.
Any person who violates this title or the commission rules adopted under this title is guilty of a class B misdemeanor, unless otherwise provided in this title.
1990

32A-12-105.   Additional criminal penalties.
In addition to the penalties provided in Title 76, Chapter 3, Penalties:

(1) Upon any defendant's conviction of any offense defined in this title, the court may also order the defendant to make restitution or pay costs in accordance with Title 77, Chapter 32A, Defense Costs.

(2) (a) Upon a corporation's, association's, partnership's, or limited liability company's conviction of any offense defined in this title, and a failure of the corporation, partnership, association, or limited liability company to pay a fine imposed upon it, the powers, rights, and privileges of the corporation, association, partnership, or limited liability company, if it is a domestic corporation, association, partnership, or limited liability company may be suspended or revoked, and if a foreign corporation, association, partnership, or limited liability company, it forfeits its right to do intrastate business in this state.

(b) The department shall transmit the name of each corporation, association, partnership, or limited liability company to the Division of Corporations and Commercial Code, which shall immediately record the action in a manner that makes the information available to the public. The suspension, revocation, or forfeiture is effective from the time the record is made, and the certificate of the Division of Corporations and Commercial Code is prima facie evidence of the suspension, revocation, or forfeiture. Nothing contained in this section may be construed as affecting, limiting, or restricting any proceedings that otherwise may be taken for the imposition of any other punishment or the modes of enforcement or recovery of fines or penalties.

(3) Upon the conviction of any business entity required to have a business license to operate its business activities, or upon the conviction of any

of its agents, employees, or officers of any offense defined in this title, with the knowledge, consent, or acquiescence of the business entity, the department shall forward a copy of the judgment of conviction to the appropriate governmental entity responsible for issuing and revoking the business licenses. That governmental entity may institute appropriate proceedings to revoke the business' license, and upon revocation, a license may not be granted to the business entity for at least one year from the date of revocation. Upon the conviction for a second or other offense, a license may not be granted for at least two years from the date of revocation.

(4) Upon conviction of any physician, pharmacist, druggist, dentist, or veterinarian of any offense defined in this title, the department shall forward a certified copy of the judgment of conviction to the Division of Occupational and Professional Licensing. That department may institute appropriate proceedings to revoke the defendant's license, and upon revocation, a license may not be granted to the defendant by the department for at least one year from the date of revocation. Upon the defendant's conviction for a second or other offense, a license may not be granted for at least two years from the date of revocation.   2003

PART 2

SALE, PURCHASE, POSSESSION, AND CONSUMPTION

32A-12-201.   Unlawful sale or furnishing.
(1) It is unlawful for any person in the business of selling liquor, or any manufacturer, supplier, or importer of liquor, or their officers, managers, employees, or agents to sell, ship, transport, or cause to be sold, shipped, or transported any liquor from an out-of-state location directly or indirectly into this state except to the extent authorized by this title to:

(a) the department;

(b) a military installation;

(c) a holder of a special use permit to the extent authorized by the commission in the permit; or

(d) a bonded liquor warehouse licensed by the commission to distribute and transport liquor to:

(i) the department; or

(ii) an out-of-state wholesaler or retailer.

(2) (a) It is unlawful for any person in the business of selling beer, or any manufacturer, supplier, or importer of beer, or their officers, managers, employees, or agents to sell, ship, transport, or cause to be sold, shipped, or transported any beer from an out-of-state location directly or indirectly into this state except to the extent authorized by this title to:

(i) a licensed beer wholesaler;

(ii) a military installation; or

(iii) a holder of a special use permit to the extent authorized by the commission in the permit.

(b) Subsection (2)(a) does not preclude a small brewer that holds a certificate of approval under Subsection 32A-8-101(4) from selling, shipping, or transporting beer directly to a licensed beer retailer to the extent authorized by Subsection 32A-8-401(5).

(3) (a) It is unlawful for any manufacturer, supplier, or importer of liquor in this state, or their officers, managers, employees, or agents to sell, ship, transport, or cause to be sold, shipped, or

transported any liquor directly or indirectly to any person in this state except to the extent authorized by this title to:

    (i) the department;

    (ii) a military installation;

    (iii) a holder of a special use permit to the extent authorized by the commission in the permit; or

    (iv) a bonded liquor warehouse licensed by the commission to distribute and transport liquor to:

        (A) the department; or

        (B) an out-of-state wholesaler or retailer.

  (b) Subsection (3)(a) does not preclude a winery licensed under this title and located in this state from selling wine to persons on its winery premises:

    (i) to the extent authorized by Subsection 32A-8-201(4)(c); or

    (ii) under a package agency established by the commission on the winery premises.

(4) (a) It is unlawful for any manufacturer, supplier, or importer of beer in this state, or their officers, managers, employees, or agents to sell, ship, transport, or cause to be sold, shipped, or transported any beer directly or indirectly to any person in this state except to the extent authorized by this title to:

    (i) a licensed beer wholesaler;

    (ii) a military installation; or

    (iii) a holder of a special use permit to the extent authorized by the commission in the permit.

  (b) Subsection (4)(a) does not preclude:

    (i) a small brewer licensed under this title and located in this state from selling, shipping, and transporting beer directly to a licensed beer retailer in this state to the extent authorized by Subsection 32A-8-401(5); or

    (ii) a brewer licensed under this title from selling beer to persons on its manufacturing premises under Subsection 32A-8-401(4)(c).

(5) It is unlawful for any person other than a person described in Subsection (1) or (2) to sell, ship, transport, or cause to be sold, shipped, or transported any alcoholic beverage or product from an out-of-state location directly or indirectly into this state, except as otherwise provided by this title.

(6) It is unlawful for any person in this state other than a person described in Subsection (3) or (4) to sell, ship, transport, or cause to be sold, shipped, or transported any alcoholic beverage or product directly or indirectly to any other person in this state, except as otherwise provided by this title.

(7) It is unlawful for any retail licensee or permittee in this state, or their officers, managers, employees, or agents, to keep for sale, or to directly or indirectly, sell, offer to sell, or otherwise furnish to another, any alcoholic beverage or product, except as otherwise provided by this title.

(8) (a) A violation of Subsection (1), (2), (3), or (4) is a third degree felony.

  (b) A violation of Subsection (5) or (6) is a class B misdemeanor.

  (c) A violation of Subsection (7) is a class B misdemeanor, except where otherwise provided by this title.   2004

32A-12-202. Unauthorized sale or supply.

A person authorized by this title to sell any alcoholic beverage or product, and an officer, manager, employee, or agent of that person may not sell, offer to sell, or otherwise furnish or supply, any alcoholic beverage or product in any place, or at any day or time other than as authorized by this title or the rules of the commission.   1990

32A-12-203. Unlawful sale or furnishing to minors.

(1) A person may not sell, offer to sell, or otherwise furnish any alcoholic beverage or product to any minor.

(2) (a) Except as otherwise provided in Subsection (4), a person is guilty of a class B misdemeanor if that person:

    (i) sells, offers to sell, or otherwise furnishes any alcoholic beverage or product to any minor; and

    (ii) negligently or recklessly fails to determine whether the recipient of the alcoholic beverage or product is a minor.

  (b) As used in this Subsection (2), "negligently" means with simple negligence.

(3) Except as otherwise provided in Subsection (4), a person who sells, offers to sell, or otherwise furnishes any alcoholic beverage or product to any minor knowing that the recipient of the alcoholic beverage or product is a minor is guilty of a class A misdemeanor.

(4) This section does not apply to the furnishing of an alcoholic beverage or product to a minor in accordance with this title:

  (a) for medicinal purposes by:

    (i) the parent or guardian of the minor; or

    (ii) the minor's physician or dentist; or

  (b) as part of a church's or religious organization's religious services.   2003

32A-12-204. Unlawful sale or furnishing to intoxicated persons.

(1) A person may not sell, offer to sell, or otherwise furnish any alcoholic beverage or product to:

  (a) any person who is actually or apparently intoxicated; or

  (b) a person whom the person furnishing the alcoholic beverage knew or should have known from the circumstances was actually or apparently intoxicated.

(2) (a) A person who negligently or recklessly violates Subsection (1) is guilty of a class B misdemeanor.

  (b) A person who knowingly violates Subsection (1) is guilty of a class A misdemeanor.

(3) As used in Subsection (2)(a), "negligently" means with simple negligence.   2003

32A-12-205. Unlawful sale or supply to interdicted persons.

(1) A person may not sell, offer to sell, or otherwise furnish or supply any alcoholic beverage or product to any known interdicted person.

(2) This section does not apply to the furnishing or supplying of an alcoholic beverage or product to an interdicted person upon the prescription of a physician, or administered by a physician, dentist, or hospital under this title.   1990

32A-12-206. Unlawful sale or supply of beer.

(1) A person may not sell, offer to sell, or otherwise furnish or supply beer to the general public in containers larger than two liters. This does not preclude licensed beer wholesalers from selling, offering to sell, or otherwise furnishing or supplying beer in containers larger than two liters to beer retailers authorized

by this title to dispense beer on draft for consumption on the beer retailer's licensed premises.

(2) A person may not purchase or possess beer in containers larger than two liters unless the person is a beer retailer authorized by this title to dispense beer on draft for consumption on the beer retailer's licensed premises. 1991

32A-12-207. Unlawful sale or furnishing during emergency.

During a period of emergency proclaimed by the governor to exist in an area of the state, it is unlawful for a person to sell, offer to sell, or otherwise furnish any alcoholic product in that area if the director of the department has publicly announced and directed that alcoholic products may not be sold, offered for sale, or otherwise furnished in that area during the period of emergency. 2003

32A-12-208. Unlawful purchase or acceptance.

It is unlawful for any person, or the person's officer, manager, employee, or agent, directly or indirectly or upon any pretense or device, to purchase, take, or accept any alcoholic beverage or product from any other person, except as provided by this title or the rules of the commission adopted under this title. 1990

32A-12-209. Unlawful purchase, possession, consumption by minors — Measurable amounts in body.

(1) Unless specifically authorized by this title, it is unlawful for any minor to:

(a) purchase any alcoholic beverage or product;

(b) attempt to purchase any alcoholic beverage or product;

(c) solicit another person to purchase any alcoholic beverage or product;

(d) possess any alcoholic beverage or product;

(e) consume any alcoholic beverage or product; or

(f) have measurable blood, breath, or urine alcohol concentration in the minor's body.

(2) It is unlawful for the purpose of purchasing or otherwise obtaining an alcoholic beverage or product for a minor for:

(a) any minor to misrepresent the minor's age; or

(b) any other person to misrepresent the age of a minor.

(3) It is unlawful for a minor to possess or consume any alcoholic beverage while riding in a limousine or chartered bus.

(4) When a person who is at least 13 years old, but younger than 18 years old, is found by the court to have violated this section, the provisions regarding suspension of the driver's license under Section 78-3a-506 apply to the violation.

(5) When the court has issued an order suspending a person's driving privileges for a violation of this section, the Driver License Division shall suspend the person's license under the provisions of Section 53-3-219.

(6) When the Department of Public Safety receives the arrest or conviction record of a person for a driving offense committed while the person's license is suspended pursuant to this section, the department shall extend the suspension for an additional like period of time.

(7) This section does not apply to a minor's consumption of an alcoholic beverage or product in accordance with this title:

(a) for medicinal purposes if the alcoholic beverage or product is furnished by:

(i) the parent or guardian of the minor; or

(ii) the minor's physician or dentist; or

(b) as part of a church's or religious organization's religious services. 2004

32A-12-210. Unlawful purchase by intoxicated persons.

A person may not purchase any alcoholic beverage or product when the person is intoxicated. 2003

32A-12-211. Unlawful purchase by interdicted persons.

A person may not purchase or possess any alcoholic beverage or product if he is an interdicted person, except as prescribed or administered by a physician, dentist, or hospital under this title. 1990

32A-12-212. Unlawful possession — Exceptions.

(1) A person may not have or possess within this state any liquor unless authorized by this title or the rules of the commission, except that:

(a) a person who clears United States Customs when entering this country may have or possess for personal consumption and not for sale or resale, a maximum of two liters of liquor purchased from without the United States;

(b) a person who moves the person's residence to this state from outside of this state may have or possess for personal consumption and not for sale or resale, any liquor previously purchased outside the state and brought into this state during the move, if:

(i) the person first obtains department approval prior to moving the liquor into the state;

(ii) the department affixes the official state label to the liquor; and

(iii) the person pays the department a reasonable administrative handling fee as determined by the commission;

(c) a person who as a beneficiary inherits as part of an estate liquor that is located outside the state, may have or possess the liquor and transport or cause the liquor to be transported into the state if:

(i) the person first obtains department approval prior to moving the liquor into the state;

(ii) the person provides sufficient documentation to the department to establish the person's legal right to the liquor as a beneficiary;

(iii) the department affixes the official state label to the liquor; and

(iv) the person pays the department a reasonable administrative handling fee as determined by the commission; or

(d) a person may transport, have, or possess liquor if:

(i) the person transports, has, or possesses the liquor:

(A) for personal household use and consumption; and

(B) not for:

(I) sale;

(II) resale;

(III) gifting to another; or

(IV) consumption on a premise licensed by the commission;

(ii) the liquor is purchased from a store or outlet on a military installation; and

(iii) the maximum amount the person transports, has, or possesses under this Subsection (1)(d) is:

    (A) two liters of:

        (I) spirituous liquor;

        (II) wine; or

        (III) a combination of spirituous liquor and wine; and

    (B) one case of heavy beer that does not exceed 288 ounces.

(2) (a) Approval under Subsection (1)(b) may be obtained by a person who:

    (i) is transferring the person's permanent residence to this state; or

    (ii) maintains separate residences both in and out of this state.

(b) A person may not obtain approval to transfer liquor under Subsection (1)(b) more than once.

2005

32A-12-213. Unlawful bringing onto premises for consumption.

(1) Except as provided in Subsection (3), a person may not bring for on-premise consumption any alcoholic beverage onto the premises of any:

    (a) licensed or unlicensed restaurant;

    (b) licensed or unlicensed private club;

    (c) airport lounge licensee;

    (d) on-premise banquet licensee;

    (e) on-premise beer retailer licensee;

    (f) event where alcoholic beverages are sold or served under a single event permit or temporary special event beer permit issued under this title; or

    (g) any establishment open to the general public.

(2) Except as provided in Subsection (3), a licensed or unlicensed restaurant or private club, airport lounge licensee, on-premise banquet licensee, on-premise beer retailer licensee, or holder of a single event permit or temporary special event beer permit issued under this title, or its officers, managers, employees, or agents may not allow a person to bring onto its premises any alcoholic beverage for on-premise consumption or allow consumption of any such alcoholic beverage in violation of this section.

(3) (a) A person may bring bottled wine onto the premises of any restaurant liquor licensee, limited restaurant licensee, or private club licensee and consume the wine pursuant to the applicable restrictions contained in Subsection 32A-4-106(14), 32A-4-307(14), or 32A-5-107(32);

(b) a passenger of a limousine may bring onto, have, and consume any alcoholic beverage on the limousine if:

    (i) the travel of the limousine begins and ends at:

        (A) the residence of the passenger;

        (B) the hotel of the passenger, if the passenger is a registered guest of the hotel; or

        (C) the temporary domicile of the passenger; and

    (ii) the driver of the limousine is separated from the passengers by partition or other means approved by the department;

(c) a passenger of a chartered bus may bring onto, have, and consume any alcoholic beverage on the chartered bus:

    (i) (A) but may consume only during travel to a specified destination of the chartered bus and not during travel back to the place where the travel begins; or

        (B) if the travel of the chartered bus begins and ends at:

            (I) the residence of the passenger;

            (II) the hotel of the passenger, if the passenger is a registered guest of the hotel; or

            (III) the temporary domicile of the passenger; and

    (ii) the chartered bus has a nondrinking designee other than the driver traveling on the chartered bus to monitor consumption; and

(d) a person may bring onto any premises, have, and consume any alcoholic beverage at a privately hosted event that is not open to the general public.

(4) Except as provided in Subsection (3)(c)(i)(A), the consumption of alcoholic beverages in limousines and chartered buses is not allowed if the limousine or chartered bus drops off passengers at locations from which they depart in private vehicles.

2004

32A-12-214. Unlawful possession by licensees or permittees.

A licensee or permittee of the commission may not have, possess, store, or allow consumption on its premises any liquor not purchased from the department, a state store, or a package agency, except as authorized by Section 32A-12-213, other provisions of this title, or the rules of the commission.

1995

32A-12-215. Unlawful storage.

It is unlawful for any person to store liquor in any establishment that is authorized to sell beer for on-premise consumption but is not licensed by the commission to sell liquor.

2003

32A-12-216. Unlawful permitting of intoxication.

(1) A person may not permit any other person to become intoxicated or any intoxicated person to consume any alcoholic beverage in:

    (a) any premises of which the person is the owner, tenant, or occupant; or

    (b) in any chartered bus or limousine of which the person is the owner or operator.

(2) A violation of Subsection (1) is a class C misdemeanor.

2003

32A-12-217. Unlawful permitting of consumption by minors.

(1) A person may not permit any minor to consume any alcoholic beverage in any chartered bus or limousine of which the person is the owner or operator.

(2) A violation of Subsection (1) is an infraction.

1990

32A-12-218. Unlawful labeling or lack of label.

(1) Unless otherwise provided by this title or the rules of the commission, it is unlawful for any person to possess any liquor unless:

    (a) the liquor is contained in its original package; and

    (b) the package has affixed to it the official commission label and markings as required by this title and the rules of the commission.

(2) Unless authorized by the department, it is unlawful for any person to be in possession of or use an official commission label, marking, or equipment that is used by the department, a state store, or a package agency to label or mark original liquor bottles or packages.

(3) A violation of Subsection (2) is a third degree felony.   2003

32A-12-219. Unlawful adulteration.

A person may not, for any purpose, mix or allow to be mixed any drug, methylic alcohol, any crude, unrectified, or impure form of ethylic alcohol, or any other deleterious substance or liquid with an alcoholic beverage sold or supplied by the person as a beverage.   1990

32A-12-220. Unlawful consumption in public places.

(1) A person may not consume liquor in a public building, park, or stadium, except as provided by this title.

(2) A violation of this section is a class C misdemeanor.   1990

32A-12-221. Lawful detention.

(1) (a) For the purpose of informing a peace officer of a suspected violation and subject to the requirements of Subsection (1)(c), a person described in Subsection (1)(b) may:

    (i) detain a person; and

    (ii) hold any form of identification presented by the person.

(b) The following may take an action described in Subsection (1)(a):

    (i) a state store employee;

    (ii) a package agent;

    (iii) a licensee or permittee under this title;

    (iv) a beer retailer; or

    (v) an employee of a person described in Subsections (1)(b)(i) through (iv).

(c) A person described in Subsection (1)(b) may take an action described in Subsection (1)(a) only:

    (i) if that person has reason to believe that the person against whom the action is taken is:

        (A) in a facility where liquor or beer is sold; and

        (B) in violation of Section 32A-12-209, 32A-12-210, or 32A-12-211; and

    (ii) (A) in a reasonable manner; and

        (B) for a reasonable length of time.

(2) Unless the detention is unreasonable under all circumstances, the detention or failure to detain does not create criminal or civil liability for:

    (a) false arrest;

    (b) false imprisonment;

    (c) slander; or

    (d) unlawful detention.   2002

32A-12-222. Unlawful dispensing.

(1) For purposes of this section:

    (a) "primary spirituous liquor" means the main distilled spirit in a beverage; and

    (b) "primary spirituous liquor" does not include any secondary alcoholic product used as flavorings in conjunction with the primary distilled spirit in the beverage.

(2) A licensee licensed under this title to sell, serve, or otherwise furnish spirituous liquor for consumption on the licensed premises, or any officer, manager, employee, or agent of the licensee may not:

    (a) sell, serve, dispense, or otherwise furnish any primary spirituous liquor to any person on the licensed premises except in a quantity that does not exceed one ounce per beverage dispensed through a calibrated metered dispensing system approved by the department;

    (b) sell, serve, dispense, or otherwise furnish more than a total of 2.75 ounces of spirituous liquor per beverage;

    (c) allow any person on the licensed premises to have more than two alcoholic beverages containing spirituous liquor at a time; or

    (d) allow any person on the licensed premises to have more than a total of 2.75 ounces of spirituous liquor at a time.

(3) Any of the following or an officer, manager, employee, or agent of the following may not allow any person on the premises of the following to have more than one spirituous liquor beverage at a time:

    (a) a restaurant liquor licensee;

    (b) limited restaurant licensee;

    (c) an on-premise banquet licensee; or

    (d) a single event permittee.

(4) A violation of this section is a class C misdemeanor.   2004

PART 3

OPERATIONS

32A-12-301. Operating without a license or permit.

Except as provided by this title or the rules of the commission, a person may not operate the following if that establishment allows patrons, customers, members, guests, visitors, or other persons to purchase or consume alcoholic beverages on the premises:

    (1) a restaurant;

    (2) an airport lounge;

    (3) a private club;

    (4) an on-premise beer retailer outlet;

    (5) on-premise banquet premises; or

    (6) an establishment similar to one listed in Subsections (1) through (5).   2005

32A-12-302. Storing or possessing pursuant to federal stamp.

(1) It is unlawful for any person, not acting for or licensed by the commission, who holds a stamp issued by the Bureau of Internal Revenue of the United States as a retail dealer in fermented malt liquor, or the person's operators or employees, to have, hold, store, or possess liquor in or on premises described in the stamp while the stamp remains in effect, except as otherwise provided by statute.

(2) Nothing in this section may be construed to prevent persons other than the owner or operator, or employees of either, from possessing and consuming, but not storing, liquor on premises described by the fermented malt liquor stamp.   1990

32A-12-303. Tampering with records.

(1) Any official or employee of the commission or the department who has custody of any writing or record required to be filed or deposited with the commission or the department under this title, and who steals, falsifies, alters, willfully destroys, mutilates, defaces, removes, or conceals in whole or in part that writing or record, or who knowingly permits any other person to do so, is guilty of a third degree felony.

(2) Any person not an official or employee of the commission or the department who commits any of the acts specified in Subsection (1) is guilty of a class B misdemeanor.   2000

32A-12-304. Making false statements.

(1) (a) Any person who makes any false material statement under oath or affirmation in any official proceeding before the commission or the department is guilty of a second degree felony.

(b) As used in Subsection (1)(a), "material" statement is as defined in Section 76-8-501.

(2) A person is guilty of a class B misdemeanor if that person knowingly:

(a) makes a false statement under oath or affirmation in any official proceeding before the commission or the department;

(b) makes a false statement with a purpose to mislead a public servant in performing that servant's official functions under this title;

(c) makes a false statement and the statement is required by this title to be sworn or affirmed before a notary or other person authorized to administer oaths;

(d) makes a false written statement on or pursuant to any application, form, affidavit, or document required by this title;

(e) creates a false impression in a written application, form, affidavit, or document required by this title by omitting information necessary to prevent statements in them from being misleading;

(f) makes a false written statement with intent to deceive a public servant in the performance of that servant's official functions under this title; or

(g) submits or invites reliance on any writing or document required under this title which he knows to be lacking in authenticity.

(3) A person is not guilty under Subsection (2) if that person retracts the falsification before it becomes apparent that the falsification was or would be exposed.   2000

32A-12-305. Obstructing an officer making a search or an official proceeding or investigation.

(1) A person in or having charge of any premises may not refuse or fail to admit to the premises or obstruct the entry of any member of the commission, authorized representative of the commission or department, or any law enforcement officer who demands entry when acting under this title.

(2) A person in or having charge of any premises may not interfere with any of the following who is conducting an investigation under this title at the premises:

(a) a member of the commission;

(b) an authorized representative of the commission or department; or

(c) any law enforcement officer.

(3) A person is guilty of a second degree felony if, believing that an official proceeding or investigation is pending or about to be instituted under this title, that person:

(a) alters, destroys, conceals, or removes any writing or record with a purpose to impair its verity or availability in the proceeding or investigation; or

(b) makes, presents, or uses anything that the person knows to be false with a purpose to deceive any commissioner, department official or employee, law enforcement official, or other person who may be engaged in a proceeding or investigation under this title.   2003

32A-12-306. Conflicting interests.

(1) A member of the commission, the department director, or any employee of the department may not be directly or indirectly interested or engaged in any other business or undertaking dealing in alcoholic products, whether as owner, part owner, partner, member of syndicate, shareholder, agent, or employee and whether for the member's own benefit or in a fiduciary capacity for some other person or entity.

(2) A member of the commission, the department director, or any employee of the department may not enter into or participate in any business transaction as a partner, co-owner, joint venturer, or shareholder with any agent, representative, employee, or officer of any supplier of alcoholic products to the department.

(3) The following are governed by Title 67, Chapter 16, Utah Public Officers' and Employees' Ethics Act:

(a) a member of the commission;

(b) the department director; or

(c) any employee of the department.

(4) This section does not prevent the purchase of alcoholic products by any commission member, the department director, or any employee of the department as authorized by this title.   2003

32A-12-307. Interfering with suppliers.

A member of the commission, the department director, or an employee of the department may not directly or indirectly participate in any manner, by recommendation or otherwise, in the appointment, employment, or termination of appointment or employment of any agent, representative, employee, or officer of any manufacturer, supplier, or importer of liquor, wine, or heavy beer to the department except to determine qualifications for licensing under Chapter 8, Part 5, Local Industry Representative Licenses, and to enforce compliance with this title.   2003

32A-12-308. Offering or soliciting bribes or gifts.

(1) A person having sold, selling, or offering any alcoholic product for sale to the commission or department may not offer, make, tender, or in any way deliver or transfer any bribe, gift as defined in Section 67-16-5, or share of profits to:

(a) any commissioner;

(b) the department director;

(c) any department employee; or

(d) any law enforcement officer responsible for the enforcement of this title.

(2) A commissioner, the department director, any department employee, or any law enforcement officer responsible for the enforcement of this title may not knowingly solicit, receive, accept, take, or seek, directly or indirectly, any commission, compensation as defined in Section 67-16-3, gift as defined in Section 67-16-5, or loan whatsoever from any person, association, or corporation having sold, selling, or offering any alcoholic product for sale.

(3) A violation of this section is punishable under the provisions of Section 67-16-12.   2003

32A-12-309. Repealed.   2003

32A-12-310. Forgery.

(1) (a) Any person, with a purpose to defraud the commission or the department or with knowledge that he is facilitating a fraud to be perpetrated by anyone, who forges any writing required under this title, is guilty of forgery as provided under Section 76-6-501.

(b) A violation of Subsection (1)(a) is a second degree felony.

(2) Any person, with intent to defraud the commission or the department, who knowingly possesses any writing that is a forgery as defined in Section 76-6-501, is guilty of a third degree felony.   2000

PART 4

ADVERTISING AND SOLICITING

32A-12-401. Advertising prohibited — Exceptions.

(1) The advertising of liquor by the department is prohibited, except:

    (a) the department may provide for an appropriate sign in the window or on the front of a state store or package agency denoting that it is a state authorized liquor outlet;

    (b) the department may provide printed price lists to the public; and

    (c) the department may authorize the use of price posting and floor stacking of liquor within state stores.

(2) (a) The department may not advertise alcoholic beverages on billboards.

    (b) A package agency may not advertise alcoholic beverages on billboards except to the extent allowed by the commission by rule.

(3) (a) The department may not display liquor or price lists in windows or showcases visible to passersby.

    (b) A package agency may not display liquor or price lists in windows or showcases visible to passersby except to the extent allowed by the commission by rule.

(4) Except to the extent prohibited by this title, the advertising of alcoholic beverages is allowed under guidelines established by the commission by rule.

(5) The advertising or use of any means or media to offer alcoholic beverages to the general public without charge is prohibited.   2003

32A-12-402, 32A-12-403. Repealed.   1993

PART 5

TRANSPORTATION AND DISTRIBUTION

32A-12-501. Disposition of liquor items shipped to the department.

(1) Any liquor item received by the department from a supplier as a sample or as an item not specifically listed on a department purchase order shall be handled in accordance with and subject to Subsection 32A-12-603(4)(c)(ix).

(2) Funds of the department may not be used to pay freight or charges on a sample or any liquor item:

    (a) shipped to the department by suppliers; and

    (b) not listed on a department purchase order.   2004

32A-12-502. Unlawful removal from conveyance or diversion of shipments.

(1) It is unlawful for any motor carrier or other person transporting any alcoholic product in interstate or other commerce intended for, or consigned to, or claimed to be intended for or consigned to any person without this state, to remove or to permit any person to remove the alcoholic product or any part of the alcoholic product from the conveyance in which it is carried while within this state.

(2) Removal from the conveyance may be allowed if a motor carrier or other person notifies the department in writing at least 24 hours before the intended removal and complies with the instructions given by the department. The department shall, upon receiving this notice or a notice under Subsection (4), take precautions as necessary to ensure compliance with the laws of this state relating to alcoholic products.

(3) It is unlawful for any person to receive for storage or other purpose, or to possess any alcoholic product that has been removed from a car or other conveyance in violation of this section.

(4) It is unlawful for any motor carrier, or any other person, to divert to any place within this state, or to deliver to any person in this state, any alcoholic product that has been consigned for shipment to any place without this state, unless the carrier or other person first notifies the department in writing at least 24 hours before the intended diversion or delivery, and complies with the instructions given by the department.   1996

32A-12-503. Repealed.   2003

32A-12-504. Unlawful transportation.

It is unlawful for any person, including a motor carrier, or any officer, agent, or employee of a motor carrier, to order or purchase any alcoholic product or to cause any alcoholic product to be shipped, carried, or transported into this state, or from one place to another within this state except as otherwise authorized by this title.   2003

32A-12-505. Lawful transportation.

Nothing contained in Section 32A-12-504 prohibits any carrier from:

    (1) transporting alcoholic products in the course of export from the state; or

    (2) transporting alcoholic products across any part of this state while in transit pursuant to a bona fide consignment of the alcoholic products to a person outside of this state.   2005

32A-12-506. Carriers' records.

(1) All motor carriers and other persons transporting alcoholic products into or within this state shall keep books in which is entered, immediately on the receipt of any products, the name of every person to whom the products are consigned, the amount and kind received, and the date when delivered. The consignee shall sign the consignee's name, or in the case of a partnership or corporation, an agent authorized in writing, shall sign their name in the books.

(2) The books shall be open to inspection by any authorized official of the state or local authority at any time during business hours of the motor carrier. The books constitute prima facie evidence of the facts stated in the books and are admissible as evidence in any court proceeding to enforce this title.   1996

PART 6

TRADE PRACTICES

32A-12-601. Definitions.

As used in this part:

    (1) (a) For purposes of Section 32A-12-602, "exclusion" is as defined in 27 C.F.R. Sections 8.51 through 8.54.

    (b) For purposes of Section 32A-12-603, "exclusion" is as defined in 27 C.F.R. Sections 6.151 through 6.153.

    (2) (a) "Industry member" means:

        (i) an alcoholic beverage manufacturer;

        (ii) a producer;

        (iii) a supplier;

        (iv) an importer;

        (v) a wholesaler;

        (vi) a bottler;

        (vii) a warehouser and bottler; or

(viii) for a person described in Subsections (2)(a)(i) through (vii), any of its:

    (A) affiliates;

    (B) subsidiaries;

    (C) officers;

    (D) directors;

    (E) partners;

    (F) agents;

    (G) employees; or

    (H) representatives.

(b) "Industry member" does not include:

    (i) the commission;

    (ii) the department; or

    (iii) any of the commission's or department's officers or employees.

(3) "Retailer" means:

(a) the holder of an alcoholic beverage license or permit issued by the commission or by local authority to allow the holder to engage in the sale of alcoholic beverages to consumers whether for consumption on or off the premises; or

(b) any of the holder's, agents, officers, directors, shareholders, partners, or employees.

                             2004

32A-12-602.   Exclusive outlets.

(1) It is unlawful for any industry member, directly or indirectly or through an affiliate, to require, by agreement or otherwise, that the department or a retailer purchase any alcoholic beverage products from the industry member or the department to the exclusion in whole or in part of any of those products sold or offered for sale by other persons.

(2) (a) Subsection (1) applies only to a transaction between:

    (i) one or more industry members; and

    (ii) (A) the department; or

        (B) one or more retailers.

(b) Subsection (1) does not apply to a transaction between two or more industry members including between a manufacturer and a wholesaler.

(3) Subsection (1) includes purchases coerced by industry members through acts or threats of physical or economic harm, as well as voluntary industry member-retailer purchase agreements.

(4) (a) Subsection (1) includes any contract or agreement, written or unwritten, that has the effect of requiring the department or retailer to purchase alcoholic beverages from the industry member beyond a single sales transaction.

(b) Examples of a contract described in Subsection (4)(a) include:

    (i) an advertising contract between an industry member and a retailer with the express or implied requirement of the purchase of the advertiser's products; or

    (ii) a sales contract awarded on a competitive bid basis that has the effect of prohibiting the department or retailer from purchasing from other industry members by:

        (A) requiring that the retailer purchase a product or line of products exclusively from the industry member for the period of the agreement; or

        (B) requiring that the retailer purchase a specific or minimum quantity during the period of the agreement.

(5) (a) Subsection (1) includes any contract, agreement, or other arrangement between an industry member and a third party nonretailer that re-

quires the department or a retailer to purchase the industry member's products to the exclusion in whole or in part of any alcoholic beverage products sold or offered for sale by other persons.

(b) This Subsection (5) applies whether the contract, agreement, or other arrangement originates with the industry member or the third party.

(c) Examples of a contract, agreement, or other arrangement described in this Subsection (5) include:

    (i) a contract, agreement, or arrangement:

        (A) with a third party such as a ball club or municipal or private corporation that is not a retailer;

        (B) under which the third party leases the concession rights and is able to control the purchasing decisions of a retailer; and

        (C) that requires the retailer to purchase the industry member's products to the exclusion in whole or in part of any alcoholic beverage products sold or offered for sale by other persons; or

    (ii) a contract, agreement, or arrangement with a third party nonretailer that in return requires a retailer to purchase the industry member's products to the exclusion in whole or in part of any alcoholic beverage products sold or offered for sale by other persons in return for which the third party provides a service or other thing of value such as:

        (A) sponsoring radio or television broadcasting;

        (B) paying for advertising; or

        (C) providing other services or things of value.   2003

32A-12-603.   Tied house — Prohibitions.

(1) (a) It is unlawful for any industry member, directly or indirectly or through an affiliate, to induce any retailer to purchase any alcoholic beverages from the industry member or from the department to the exclusion in whole or in part of any of those products sold or offered for sale by other persons by acquiring or holding any interest in any license with respect to the premises of a retailer, except where the license is held by a retailer that is completely owned by the industry member.

(b) Interest in any retail license includes any interest acquired by a corporate official, partner, employee, or other representative of the industry member.

(c) Any interest in a retail license acquired by a separate corporation in which the industry member or the industry member's officials hold ownership or are otherwise affiliated is an interest in a retail license.

(d) Less than complete ownership of a retail business by an industry member constitutes an interest in a retail license within the meaning of Subsection (1)(a).

(2) (a) It is unlawful for any industry member, directly or indirectly or through an affiliate, to induce any retailer to purchase any alcoholic beverages from the industry member or from the department to the exclusion in whole or in part of any of those products sold or offered for sale by other persons by acquiring any interest in real or personal property owned, occupied, or used by the retailer in the conduct of the retailer's business.

(b) For purposes of Subsection (2)(a):

(i) "interest" does not include complete ownership of a retail business by an industry member;

(ii) interest in retail property includes any interest acquired by a corporate official, partner, employee, or other representative of the industry member;

(iii) any interest in a retail license acquired by a separate corporation in which the industry member or its officials hold ownership or are otherwise affiliated is an interest in the retailer's property;

(iv) less than complete ownership of a retail business by an industry member constitutes an interest in retail property;

(v) the acquisition of a mortgage on a retailer's real or personal property by an industry member constitutes an interest in the retailer's property; and

(vi) the renting of display space by an industry member at a retail establishment constitutes an interest in the retailer's property.

(3) (a) It is unlawful for any industry member, directly or indirectly or through an affiliate, to induce any retailer to purchase any alcoholic beverages from the industry member or from the department to the exclusion in whole or in part of any of those products sold or offered for sale by other persons by furnishing, giving, renting, lending, or selling to the retailer any equipment, fixtures, signs, supplies, money, services, or other thing of value, subject to the exceptions enumerated in Subsection (4).

(b) (i) For purposes of this Subsection (3), indirect inducement includes:

(A) furnishing things of value to a third party where the benefits resulting from the things of value flow to individual retailers; and

(B) making payments for advertising to a retailer association or a display company where the resulting benefits flow to individual retailers.

(ii) Notwithstanding Subsection (3)(b)(i), an indirect inducement does not arise if:

(A) the thing of value was furnished to a retailer by the third party without the knowledge or intent of the industry member; or

(B) the industry member did not reasonably foresee that the thing of value would have been furnished to a retailer.

(iii) Anything that may lawfully be furnished, given, rented, lent, or sold by industry members to retailers under Subsection (4) may be furnished directly by a third party to a retailer.

(c) (i) A transaction in which equipment is sold to a retailer by an industry member, except as provided in Subsection (4), is the selling of equipment within the meaning of Subsection (3)(a) regardless of how the equipment is sold.

(ii) The negotiation by an industry member of a special price to a retailer for equipment from an equipment company is the furnishing of a thing of value within the meaning of Subsection (3)(a).

(d) The furnishing of free warehousing by delaying delivery of alcoholic beverages beyond the time that payment for the product is received, or if a retailer is purchasing on credit, delaying final delivery of products beyond the close of the period of time for which credit is lawfully extended, is the furnishing of a service or thing of value within the meaning of Subsection (3)(a).

(e) Any financial, legal, administrative, or influential assistance given a retailer by an industry member in the retailer's acquisition of the retailer's license is the furnishing of a service or thing of value within the meaning of Subsection (3)(a).

(4) (a) Notwithstanding Subsection (3), things of value may be furnished by industry members to retailers under the conditions and within the limitations prescribed in:

(i) this Subsection (4); and

(ii) the applicable federal laws cited in this Subsection (4).

(b) (i) The following may be furnished by an industry member:

(A) a product display as provided in 27 C.F.R. Sec. 6.83;

(B) point of sale advertising materials and consumer advertising specialties as provided in 27 C.F.R. Sec. 6.84;

(C) things of value to a temporary retailer to the extent allowed in 27 C.F.R. Sec. 6.85;

(D) equipment and supplies as provided in 27 C.F.R. Sec. 6.88;

(E) combination packaging as provided in 27 C.F.R. Sec. 6.93;

(F) educational seminars as provided in 27 C.F.R. Sec. 6.94;

(G) consumer promotions as provided in 27 C.F.R. Sec. 6.96;

(H) advertising service as provided in 27 C.F.R. Sec. 6.98;

(I) stocking, rotation, and pricing service as provided in 27 C.F.R. Sec. 6.99;

(J) merchandise as provided in 27 C.F.R. Sec. 6.101; and

(K) outside signs as provided in 27 C.F.R. Sec. 6.102.

(ii) The following exceptions provided in federal law are not adopted:

(A) the exception for samples provided in 27 C.F.R. Sec. 6.91;

(B) the exception for consumer tasting or sampling at retail establishments provided in 27 C.F.R. Sec. 6.95; and

(C) the exception for participation in retailer association activities provided in 27 C.F.R. Sec. 6.100.

(iii) To the extent required by 27 C.F.R. Sec. 6.81(b) an industry member shall keep and maintain a record:

(A) of all items furnished to a retailer;

(B) on premises of the industry member; and

(C) for a three-year period.

(c) Samples of liquor, wine, and heavy beer may be provided to the department under the conditions listed in this Subsection (4)(c).

(i) With the department's permission, an industry member may submit department samples to the department for product testing, analysis, and sampling.

(ii) No more than two department samples of a particular type, vintage, and production lot of a particular branded product may be submitted to the department for department testing, analysis, and sampling within a consecutive 120-day period.

    (iii) (A) Each sample of liquor may not exceed 1 liter.

        (B) Each sample of wine and heavy beer may not exceed 1.5 liters unless that exact product is only commercially packaged in a larger size, not to exceed 5 liters.

    (iv) (A) Department samples submitted to the department:

        (I) shall be shipped prepaid by the industry member by common carrier; and

        (II) may not be shipped by United States mail directly to the department's central administrative warehouse office.

        (B) Department samples may not be shipped to any other location within the state.

    (v) Department samples submitted to the department shall be accompanied by a letter from the industry member:

        (A) clearly identifying the product as a "department sample"; and

        (B) clearly stating the FOB case price of the product.

    (vi) (A) The department may transfer listed items from current stock for use as comparison control samples or to verify product spoilage as deemed appropriate.

        (B) Each sample transferred under Subsection (4)(c)(vi)(A) shall be charged back to the respective industry member.

    (vii) The department shall:

        (A) account for, label, and record all department samples received or transferred;

        (B) account for the department sample's disposition; and

        (C) maintain a record:

        (I) of the samples and their disposition; and

        (II) for a two-year period.

    (viii) The department shall affix to each bottle or container a label clearly identifying the product as a "department sample".

    (ix) Each department sample delivered to the department or transferred from the department's current stock shall be disposed of at the discretion of the department in one of the following ways:

        (A) tested and analyzed with the remaining contents destroyed under controlled and audited conditions established by the department;

        (B) entire contents destroyed under controlled and audited conditions established by the department; or

        (C) added to the inventory of the department for sale to the public.

    (x) Persons other than authorized department officials may not be in possession of department samples except as otherwise provided.

(d) Samples of beer may be provided by a beer industry member to a retailer under the conditions listed in this Subsection (4)(d).

    (i) Samples of beer may be provided by an industry member only to a retailer who has not purchased the brand of beer from that industry member within the last 12 months.

    (ii) For each retailer, the industry member may give not more than three gallons of any brand of beer, except that if a particular product is not available in a size within the quantity limitation an industry member may furnish the next largest size.

(e) Educational seminars may involve an industry member under the conditions listed in this Subsection (4)(e).

    (i) An industry member may provide or participate in educational seminars:

        (A) involving:

        (I) the department;

        (II) retailers;

        (III) holders of educational or scientific special use permits;

        (IV) other industry members; or

        (V) employees of the persons listed in Subsections (4)(e)(i)(A)(I) through (IV); and

        (B) regarding such topics as:

        (I) merchandising and product knowledge;

        (II) use of equipment; and

        (III) tours of alcoholic beverage manufacturing facilities.

    (ii) An industry member may not pay a department employee's, retailer's, or permittee's expenses or compensate them for attending a seminar or tour described in Subsection (4)(e)(i).

    (iii) (A) A liquor, wine, and heavy beer industry member may conduct tastings of the industry member's products:

        (I) for the department, at the department's request; and

        (II) for licensed industry representatives, but only at the department's central administrative warehouse office.

        (B) The industry member may only use department or industry representative samples when conducting any tasting of the industry member's products.

    (iv) A beer industry member may conduct tastings of beer products for a licensed beer retailer either at:

        (A) the industry member's premises; or

        (B) a retail establishment.

    (v) Except to the extent authorized by commission rule, an alcoholic beverage industry member may not conduct tasting or sampling activities with:

        (A) a retailer; or

        (B) a member of the general public.

(f) A beer industry member may participate in beer retailer association activities to the extent authorized by 27 C.F.R. Sec. 6.100.

(g) (i) An industry member may contribute to charitable, civic, religious, fraternal, educational, or community activities.

    (ii) A contribution described in Subsection (4)(g)(i) may not be given to influence a retailer in the selection of the alcoholic beverage products that may be sold at these activities and events.

    (iii) An industry member or retailer violates this section if:

(A) the industry member's contribution described in Subsection (4)(g)(i) influences, directly or indirectly, the retailer in the selection of alcoholic beverage products; and

(B) a competitor's alcoholic beverage products are excluded in whole or in part from sale at the activity or event.

(h) (i) An industry member may lease or furnish equipment listed in Subsection (4)(h)(ii) to a retailer if:

(A) the equipment is leased or furnished for a special event;

(B) a reasonable rental or service fee is charged for the equipment; and

(C) the period for which the equipment is leased or furnished does not exceed 30 days.

(ii) This Subsection (4)(h) applies to the following equipment:

(A) a picnic pump;

(B) a cold plate;

(C) a tub;

(D) a keg box;

(E) a refrigerated trailer;

(F) a refrigerated van; or

(G) a refrigerated draft system.

(i) (i) A liquor, wine, and heavy beer industry member may assist the department in:

(A) ordering, shipping, and delivering merchandise;

(B) new product notification;

(C) listing and delisting information;

(D) price quotations;

(E) product sales analysis;

(F) shelf management; and

(G) educational seminars.

(ii) (A) Subject to Subsection (4)(i)(ii)(B), a liquor, wine, and heavy beer industry member may, for the purpose of acquiring new listings:

(I) solicit orders from the department; and

(II) submit to the department samples of their products under Subsection (4)(c) and price lists.

(B) An industry member may not solicit either in person, by mail, or otherwise, any state store personnel for the purpose or with the intent of furthering the sale of a particular brand or brands of alcoholic beverage product as against another brand or brands.

(iii) (A) Any visitations to a state store or package agency by an industry member shall be confined to the customer areas of the store unless otherwise approved.

(B) Calls on the state warehouse by industry members are to be confined to the office area only unless otherwise approved.

(iv) A beer industry member may assist licensed retailers in:

(A) ordering, shipping, and delivering beer merchandise;

(B) new product notification;

(C) listing and delisting information;

(D) price quotations;

(E) product sales analysis;

(F) shelf management; and

(G) educational seminars.

(v) A beer industry member may, for the purpose of acquiring new listings:

(A) solicit orders from licensed retailers; and

(B) submit to licensed retailers samples of their beer products under Subsection (4)(c) and price lists.

(5) It is unlawful for any industry member, directly or indirectly or through an affiliate, to induce any retailer to purchase any alcoholic beverages from the industry member or from the department to the exclusion in whole or in part of any of those products sold or offered for sale by other persons by paying or crediting the retailer for any advertising, display, or distribution service:

(a) as defined in and to the extent restricted by 27 C.F.R. Sections 6.51 through 6.56; and

(b) subject to the exceptions:

(i) for newspaper cuts listed in 27 C.F.R. Sec. 6.92; and

(ii) for advertising services listed in 27 C.F.R. Sec. 6.98.

(6) It is unlawful for any industry member, directly or indirectly or through an affiliate, to induce any retailer to purchase any alcoholic beverages from the industry member or from the department to the exclusion in whole or in part of any of those products sold or offered for sale by other persons by guaranteeing any loan or the repayment of any financial obligation of the retailer.

(7) (a) It is unlawful for any industry member, directly or indirectly or through an affiliate, to induce any retailer to purchase any beer from the industry member to the exclusion in whole or in part of any beer products sold or offered for sale by other persons by extending to any retailer credit for a period in excess of 15 days from the date of delivery to the date of full legal discharge of the retailer through the payment of cash or its equivalent, from all indebtedness arising from the transaction, so long as that beer purchased or delivered during the first 15 days of any month is paid for in cash or its equivalent on or before the 25th day of the same month, and beer purchased or delivered after the 15th day of any month is paid for in cash or its equivalent on or before the 10th day of the next succeeding month.

(b) First party in-state checks are considered cash payment if the checks:

(i) are honored on presentment; and

(ii) received under the terms prescribed in Subsection (7)(a).

(c) An extension of credit for product purchased by an industry member to a retailer whose account is in arrears does not constitute a violation of Subsection (7)(a) if the retailer pays in advance or on delivery an amount equal to or greater than the value of each order, regardless of the manner in which the industry member applies the payment in its records.

(8) (a) It is unlawful for any industry member, directly or indirectly or through an affiliate, to induce any retailer to purchase any alcoholic beverages from the industry member or from the department to the exclusion in whole or in part of any of those products sold or offered for sale by other persons by requiring:

(i) the department to take and dispose of a certain quota of any alcoholic products; or

(ii) a beer retailer to take and dispose of a certain quota of any beer products.

(b) (i) It is an unlawful means to induce to require:

(A) the department to purchase one product in order to purchase another; or

(B) a beer retailer to purchase one beer product in order to purchase another.

(ii) This Subsection (8)(b) includes:

(A) the requirement to take a minimum quantity of a product in standard packaging in order to obtain the same product in some type of premium package such as:

(I) a distinctive decanter; or

(II) a wooden or tin box; or

(B) combination sales if one or more products may be purchased only in combination with other products and not individually.

(c) This Subsection (8) does not preclude the selling, at a special combination price, two or more kinds or brands of products so long as the department or beer retailer:

(i) has the option of purchasing either product at the usual price; and

(ii) is not required to purchase any product the department or beer retailer does not want.

(d) An industry member may package and distribute alcoholic beverages in combination with other nonalcoholic items or products.

(e) The combination package shall be designed to be delivered intact to the consumer and the additional cost incurred by the industry member shall be included in the cost to the department or beer retailer. 2004

32A-12-604. Commercial bribery.

This section adopts and makes applicable to all industry members, including beer industry members, doing business in this state 27 U.S.C. Section 205(c) and 27 C.F.R. Sections 10.1 through 10.54 which make it unlawful for any industry member, directly or indirectly or through an affiliate, to induce a wholesaler or retailer engaged in the sale of alcoholic beverages to purchase the industry member's products, to the complete or partial exclusion of alcoholic beverages sold or offered for sale by other persons, by commercial bribery, or by offering or giving a bonus, premium, compensation, or other thing of value, to any officer, employee, or representative of the wholesaler or retailer. 2003

32A-12-605. Consignment sales.

(1) This section adopts and makes applicable to all industry members, including beer industry members, doing business in this state 27 U.S.C. Section 205(d) and 27 C.F.R. Sections 11.1 through 11.46, which make it unlawful for an industry member, directly or indirectly or through an affiliate to sell, offer for sale, or contract to sell to any wholesaler or retailer engaged in the sale of alcoholic beverages, or for any wholesaler or retailer to purchase, offer to purchase, or contract to purchase any of those products on consignment or under conditional sale or with the privilege of return or on any basis otherwise than a bona fide sale, or where any part of the transaction involves, directly or indirectly, the acquisition by that person from the wholesaler or retailer or that person's agreement to acquire from the wholesaler or retailer other alcoholic beverages, if the sale, purchase, offer, or contract is made in the course of interstate or foreign commerce, or if the person or wholesaler or

retailer engages in such practice to an extent so as substantially to restrain or prevent transactions in interstate or foreign commerce in any of those products or if the direct effect of the sale, purchase, offer, or contract is to prevent, deter, hinder, or restrict other persons from selling or offering for sale any of those products to the wholesaler or retailer in interstate or foreign commerce.

(2) This section does not apply to transactions involving solely the bona fide return of merchandise for ordinary and usual commercial reasons arising after the merchandise has been sold. 2003

32A-12-606. Unlawful acts involving consumers.

(1) (a) It is unlawful for any industry member, directly or indirectly or through an affiliate, to give away any of its alcoholic products to any person except for testing, analysis, and sampling purposes by the department and local industry representative licensees to the extent authorized by this title.

(b) This Subsection (1) does not preclude an industry member from serving its alcoholic products to others at private social functions hosted by the industry member in the member's home or elsewhere so long as the product is not served:

(i) as part of a promotion of the industry member's products; or

(ii) as a subterfuge to provide samples to others for product testing, analysis, or sampling purposes.

(2) It shall be unlawful for any industry member or retailer, directly or indirectly or through an affiliate, to engage in any advertisement or promotional scheme that requires the purchase or sale of an alcoholic beverage, or consumption of an alcoholic beverage in order to participate in any promotion, program, or other activity.

(3) It shall be unlawful for any industry member or retailer, directly or indirectly or through an affiliate, to pay, give, or deliver to any person any money or any other thing of value, including rebates, refunds, or prizes, based upon the purchase, display, use, sale, or consumption of alcoholic beverages.

(4) It shall be unlawful for any industry member or retailer to sponsor or underwrite any athletic, theatrical, scholastic, artistic, or scientific event that:

(a) overtly promotes the consumption of alcoholic products;

(b) offers alcoholic products to the general public without charge; or

(c) takes place on the premises of a school, college, university, or other educational institution. 2003

CHAPTER 13

CRIMINAL PROCEDURE

32A-13-101. Utah Code of Criminal Procedure applicable.

Except as otherwise provided in this title, the procedure in all criminal cases arising under this title shall be as prescribed in Title 77, Utah Code of Criminal Procedure, and any other rules adopted by the Utah Supreme Court. 1992

32A-13-102. Arrests.

Except as otherwise provided in this chapter, all arrests of persons for any violation of this title shall be made in accordance with Title 77, Chapter 7, Utah Code of Criminal Procedure, and Rules 6 and 7, Utah Rules of Criminal Procedure. All summons in lieu of warrants of arrest shall be in accordance with Rule 6, Utah Rules of Criminal Procedure. 1990

32A-13-103. Searches, seizures, and forfeitures.

(1) The following are subject to forfeiture pursuant to the procedures and substantive protections established in Title 24, Chapter 1, Utah Uniform Forfeiture Procedures Act:

(a) all alcoholic products possessed, used, offered for sale, sold, given, furnished, supplied, received, purchased, stored, warehoused, manufactured, adulterated, shipped, carried, transported, or distributed in violation of this title or commission rules;

(b) all packages or property used or intended for use as a container for an alcoholic product in violation of this title or commission rules;

(c) all raw materials, products, and equipment used, or intended for use, in manufacturing, processing, adulterating, delivering, importing, or exporting any alcoholic product in violation of this title or commission rules;

(d) all implements, furniture, fixtures, or other personal property used or kept for any violation of this title or commission rules;

(e) all conveyances including aircraft, vehicles, or vessels used or intended for use, to transport or in any manner facilitate the transportation, sale, receipt, possession, or concealment of property described in Subsection (1)(a), (b), (c), or (d); and

(f) all books, records, receipts, ledgers, or other documents used or intended for use in violation of this title or commission rules.

(2) Any of the property subject to forfeiture under this title may be seized by any peace officer of this state or any other person authorized by law upon process issued by any court having jurisdiction over the property in accordance with the procedures provided in Title 77, Chapter 23, Part 2, Search Warrants. However, seizure without process may be made when:

(a) the seizure is incident to an arrest or search under a search warrant or an inspection under an administrative inspection warrant;

(b) the property subject to seizure has been the subject of a prior judgment in favor of the state in a criminal injunction or forfeiture proceeding under this title;

(c) the peace officer or other person authorized by law has probable cause to believe that the property is directly or indirectly dangerous to health or safety; or

(d) the peace officer or other person authorized by law has probable cause to believe that the property is being or has been used, intended to be used, held, or kept in violation of this title or commission rules.

(3) If the property is seized pursuant to a search or administrative warrant, the peace officer or other person authorized by law shall make a proper receipt, return, and inventory and ensure the safekeeping of the property as required by Sections 77-23-206 through 77-23-208. If the magistrate who issued the warrant is a justice court judge, upon the filing of the return the jurisdiction of the justice court shall cease and the magistrate shall certify the record and all files without delay to the district court of the county in which the property was located. From the time of this filing, the district court has jurisdiction of the case.

(4) In the event of seizure of property without process, the peace officer or other person authorized by law shall make a return of his acts without delay directly to the district court of the county in which the property was located, and the district court shall have jurisdiction of the case. The return shall describe all property seized, the place where it was seized, and any persons in apparent possession of the property. The officer or other person shall also promptly deliver a written inventory of anything seized to any person in apparent authority at the premises where the seizure was made, or post it in a conspicuous place at the premises. The inventory shall state the place where the property is being held.

(5) Property taken or detained under this section is not repleviable but is considered in custody of the law enforcement agency making the seizure subject only to the orders of the court or the official having jurisdiction. When property is seized under this title, the appropriate person or agency may:

(a) place the property under seal;

(b) remove the property to a place designated by it or the warrant under which it was seized; or

(c) take custody of the property and remove it to an appropriate location for disposition in accordance with law.

(6) When any property is subject to forfeiture under this section, proceedings shall be instituted in accordance with the procedures and substantive protections of Title 24, Chapter 1, Utah Uniform Forfeiture Procedures Act.

(7) When any property is ordered forfeited under Title 24, Chapter 1, Utah Uniform Forfeiture Procedures Act, by a finding of the court that no person is entitled to recover the property, the property, if an alcoholic product or a package used as a container for an alcoholic product, shall be disposed of as follows:

(a) If the alcoholic product is unadulterated, pure, and free from crude, unrectified, or impure form of ethylic alcohol, or any other deleterious substance or liquid, and is otherwise in saleable condition, sold in accordance with Section 24-1-16.

(b) If the alcoholic product is impure, adulterated, or otherwise unfit for sale, it and its package or container shall be destroyed by the department under competent supervision. 2002

32A-13-104. Prosecutions.

(1) All prosecutions for violations of this title or commission rules shall be in the name of the state of Utah. A criminal action for violation of any county or municipal ordinance enacted in furtherance of this title shall be in the name of the governmental entity involved.

(2) (a) Prosecution for violation of any provision of this title or commission rule shall be brought by the county attorney of the county or district attorney of the prosecution district where the violation occurs. If any county attorney or district attorney fails to initiate or diligently pursue any prosecution authorized and warranted under this

title, the attorney general shall exercise supervisory authority over the county attorney or district attorney to ensure prosecution is initiated and diligently pursued.

(b) If a violation occurs within a city or town, prosecution may be brought by either the county, district, or city attorney, notwithstanding any provision of law limiting the powers of city attorneys.

(c) Local city and town prosecutors also have the responsibility of initiating and diligently pursuing prosecutions for violations of any local ordinances enacted in furtherance of this title or commission rules.

(3) Prosecutions for violations of this title or commission rules shall be commenced by the return of an indictment or the filing of an information with the district court of the county in which the offense occurred or where the premises are located upon which any alcoholic product was seized, if the offense involves an alcoholic product. All other offenses prescribed by this title shall be filed before any court having jurisdiction of the offense committed.

(4) Unless otherwise provided by law, no information may be filed charging the commission of any felony or class A misdemeanor under this title unless authorized by a prosecuting attorney. This restriction does not apply in cases where the magistrate has reasonable cause to believe that the person to be charged may avoid apprehension or escape before approval can be obtained.

(5) In describing an offense respecting the sale, keeping for sale, or other disposal of alcoholic products, or the having, keeping, giving, purchasing, or the consumption of alcoholic products in any information, indictment, summons, judgment, warrant, or proceeding under this title, it is sufficient to state the sale, keeping for sale, or disposal, having, keeping, giving, purchasing, or consumption of the alcoholic product without stating the name or kind of the alcoholic product or the price of the alcoholic product, or any person to whom it was sold or disposed of, or by whom it was taken or consumed, or from whom it was purchased or received. It is not necessary to state the quantity of alcoholic beverage so sold, kept for sale, disposed of, had, kept, given, purchased, or consumed, except in the case of offenses where the quantity is essential, and then it is sufficient to allege the sale or disposal of more or less than the quantity.

(6) If an offense is committed under a local ordinance enacted to carry out this title, it is sufficient if the charging document refers to the chapter and section of the ordinance under which the offense is committed. 1993

32A-13-105. Fines and forfeitures.

Except where otherwise provided, all fines and forfeitures levied under this title shall be paid to the county treasurer of the county in which the prosecution occurred. 1990

32A-13-106. Nuisances.

(1) Any room, house, building, structure, place, aircraft, vehicle, vessel, or other conveyance, where alcoholic products are possessed, kept, used, offered for sale, sold, given, furnished, supplied, received, purchased, stored, warehoused, manufactured, adulterated, shipped, carried, transported, or distributed in violation of this title or commission rules, and all alcoholic products, packages, equipment, or other property kept or used in maintaining the same, are common nuisances. Any person who maintains or assists in maintaining any common nuisance is guilty of a class B misdemeanor.

(2) If any person has knowledge, or has reason to believe that the person's room, house, building, structure, place, aircraft, vehicle, vessel, or other conveyance is occupied or used in violation of this title or commission rules as described in this section, or allows it to be so occupied or used, it is subject to a lien for and may be sold to pay all fines and costs assessed against the person guilty of the nuisance. This lien may be enforced by action in any court having jurisdiction.

(3) Any action to abate any nuisance defined in this title shall be brought in the name of the department in any court having jurisdiction. It shall be tried as an action in equity. No bond is required to initiate proceedings.

(4) The court may issue a temporary writ of injunction, if it appears that the nuisance exists, restraining the defendant from conducting or permitting the continuance of the nuisance until the conclusion of the trial. The court may also issue an order restraining the defendant and all other persons from removing or interfering with the alcoholic products, packages, equipment, or other property kept or used in violation of this title or commission rules.

(5) (a) In any action to abate or enjoin any nuisance, the court need not find that the property involved was being unlawfully used at the time of the hearing.

(b) On finding that the material allegations of the petition or complaint are true, the court shall order that no alcoholic product may be possessed, kept, used, offered for sale, sold, given, furnished, supplied, received, purchased, stored, warehoused, manufactured, adulterated, shipped, carried, transported, or distributed in the room, house, building, structure, place, aircraft, vehicle, vessel, or other conveyance or in any part of these.

(c) Upon judgment of the court ordering abatement of the nuisance, the court may order that the premises or conveyance in question may not be occupied or used for any purpose for one year.

(d) The court may permit the premises or conveyance to be occupied or used if its owner, lessee, tenant, or occupant gives bond in an appropriate amount with sufficient surety, approved by the court, payable to the state of Utah, and on the conditions that alcoholic products will not be present therein or thereon, and that payment of all fines, costs, and damages that may be assessed for any violation of this title or commission rules upon the property will be made.

(6) If a tenant of any premises uses the premises or any part of them in maintaining a common nuisance as defined in this section, or knowingly permits use by another, the lease is rendered void and the right to possession reverts to the owner or lessor who is entitled to the remedy provided by law for forcible detention of the premises.

(7) Any person who knowingly permits any building or premises owned or leased by the person, or under the person's control, or any part of any building or premises, to be used in maintaining a common nuisance as defined in this section, or who, after being notified in writing by a prosecuting officer or any citizen of the unlawful use, and who fails to take all proper measures, either to abate the nuisance or to remove the person or persons from the premises, is guilty of assisting in the maintaining of the nuisance as provided in Section 76-10-804. 1991

32A-13-107. Right of appeal.

In all cases arising under this title, the commission or the state has the right of appeal as to questions of law.   1990

32A-13-108. Duties to enforce this title.

(1) It is the duty of the governor, the commissioners, the director and all officials, inspectors, and employees of the department, all prosecuting officials of the state and its political subdivisions and of counties, cities, and towns, all peace officers, sheriffs, deputy sheriffs, constables, marshals, law enforcement officials, state health officials, and all clerks of the courts to diligently enforce this title in their respective capacities.

(2) Immediately upon conviction of any person for violation of this title or commission rules, or for violation of any local ordinance relating to alcoholic products, it is the duty of the clerk of the court to notify the department of the conviction in writing on forms supplied by the department.   1990

32A-13-109. Authority to inspect.

(1) For purposes of enforcing this title and commission rules, all members of the commission, authorized representatives of the commission or department, or any law enforcement or peace officer shall be accorded access, ingress, and egress to and from all premises or conveyances used in the manufacture, storage, transportation, service, or sale of any alcoholic product. They also may open any package containing, or supposed to contain, any article manufactured, sold, or exposed for sale, or held in possession with intent to sell in violation of this title or commission rules, and may inspect its contents and take samples of the contents for analysis.

(2) All dealers, clerks, bookkeepers, express agents, railroad and airline officials, common and other carriers, and their employees shall assist, when so requested by any authorized person specified in Subsection (1), in tracing, finding, or discovering the presence of any article prohibited by this title or commission rules to the extent assistance would not infringe upon the person's federal and state constitutional rights.   2000

CHAPTER 14a

ALCOHOLIC BEVERAGE LIABILITY

32A-14a-101. Definitions.

As used in this chapter:

(1) "Death of a third person" includes recovery for all damages, special and general, resulting from such death, except punitive damages.

(2) (a) "Injury" includes injury in person, property, or means of support.

(b) "Injury" also includes recovery for intangibles such as mental and emotional injuries, loss of affection, and companionship.
                                                    2000

32A-14a-102. Liability for injuries and damage resulting from distribution of alcoholic beverages — Causes of action — Statute of limitations — Employee protections.

(1) (a) Except as provided in Section 32A-14a-103, a person described in Subsection (1)(b) is liable for:

(i) any and all injury and damage, except punitive damages to:

(A) any third person; or

(B) the heir, as defined in Section 78-11-6.5, of that third person; or

(ii) for the death of a third person.

(b) A person is liable under Subsection (1)(a) if:

(i) the person directly gives, sells, or otherwise provides an alcoholic beverage:

(A) to a person described in Subsection (1)(b)(ii); and

(B) as part of the commercial sale, storage, service, manufacture, distribution, or consumption of alcoholic products;

(ii) those actions cause the intoxication of:

(A) any individual under the age of 21 years;

(B) any individual who is apparently under the influence of intoxicating alcoholic products or drugs;

(C) any individual whom the person furnishing the alcoholic beverage knew or should have known from the circumstances was under the influence of intoxicating alcoholic beverages or products or drugs; or

(D) any individual who is a known interdicted person; and

(iii) the injury or death described in Subsection (1)(a) results from the intoxication of the individual who is provided the alcoholic beverage.

(2) (a) A person 21 years of age or older who is described in Subsection (2)(b) is liable for:

(i) any and all injury and damage, except punitive damages to:

(A) any third person; or

(B) the heir, as defined in Section 78-11-6.5, of that third person; or

(ii) for the death of the third person.

(b) A person is liable under Subsection (2)(a) if:

(i) that person directly gives or otherwise provides an alcoholic beverage to an individual who the person knows or should have known is under the age of 21 years;

(ii) those actions caused the intoxication of the individual provided the alcoholic beverage;

(iii) the injury or death described in Subsection (2)(a) results from the intoxication of the individual who is provided the alcoholic beverage; and

(iv) the person is not liable under Subsection (1), because the person did not directly give or provide the alcoholic beverage as part of the commercial sale, storage, service, manufacture, distribution, or consumption of alcoholic products.

(3) Except for a violation of Subsection (2), an employer is liable for the actions of its employees in violation of this chapter.

(4) A person who suffers an injury under Subsection (1) or (2) has a cause of action against the person who provided the alcoholic beverage in violation of Subsection (1) or (2).

(5) If a person having rights or liabilities under this chapter dies, the rights or liabilities provided by this chapter survive to or against that person's estate.

(6) The total amount that may be awarded to any person pursuant to a cause of action for injury and damage under this chapter that arises after January 1, 1998, is limited to $500,000 and the aggregate amount which may be awarded to all persons injured as a result of one occurrence is limited to $1,000,000.

(7) An action based upon a cause of action under this chapter shall be commenced within two years after the date of the injury and damage.

(8) (a) Nothing in this chapter precludes any cause of action or additional recovery against the person causing the injury.

(b) Any cause of action or additional recovery against the person causing the injury and damage, which action is not brought under this chapter, is exempt from the damage cap in Subsection (6).

(c) Any cause of action brought under this chapter is exempt from Sections 78-27-37 through 78-27-43.

(9) This section does not apply to a general food store or other establishment licensed under Chapter 10, Part 1, to sell beer at retail for off-premise consumption. 2000

32A-14a-103. Employee protected in exercising judgment.

(1) An employer may not sanction or terminate the employment of an employee of a restaurant, airport lounge, private club, on-premise beer retailer, or any other establishment serving alcoholic beverages as a result of the employee having exercised the employee's independent judgment to refuse to sell alcoholic beverages to any person the employee considers to meet one or more of the conditions described in Subsection 32A-14a-102(1).

(2) Any employer who terminates an employee or imposes sanctions on the employee contrary to this section is considered to have discriminated against that employee and is subject to the conditions and penalties set forth in Title 34A, Chapter 5, Utah Antidiscrimination Act. 2000

32A-14a-104. Governmental immunity.

No provision of this title creates any civil liability on the part of the state or its agencies and employees, the commission, the department, or any political subdivision arising out of their activities in regulating, controlling, authorizing, or otherwise being involved in the sale or other distribution of alcoholic beverages. 2000

32A-14a-105. Action for contribution by provider of alcoholic beverages.

(1) (a) Except as provided in Subsections (2) and (3), a person, as defined under Subsection 32A-14a-102(1), (2), or (3), against whom an award has been made under this chapter, may bring a separate cause of action for contribution against any person causing the injury and damage.

(b) The maximum amount for which any person causing the injury and damage may be liable to any person seeking contribution is that per-

centage or proportion of the damages equivalent to the percentage or proportion of fault attributed to that person causing the injury and damage.

(2) This action for contribution under this section may not be brought against:

(a) any person entitled to recovery as described in Subsection 32A-14a-102(1)(a)(i) or (ii); or

(b) any person entitled to recover as described in Subsection 32A-14a-102(2)(a)(i) or (ii).

(3) An action for contribution under this section may not diminish the amount of recovery for injury or damages awarded and received to any person entitled to recover as described in Subsection 32A-14a-102(1)(a)(i) or (ii) or 32A-14a-102(2)(a)(i) or (ii):

(a) in a cause of action brought under this chapter; or

(b) in a separate cause of action for injury and damage that is not brought under this chapter. 2000

TITLE 34A

UTAH LABOR CODE

Chapter
2. Workers' Compensation Act.

CHAPTER 2

WORKERS' COMPENSATION ACT

Part 9

Presumptions for Emergency Medical Services Providers

Section
34A-2-901. Workers' compensation presumption for emergency medical services providers.
34A-2-902. Workers' compensation claims by emergency medical services providers — Time limits.
34A-2-903. Failure to be tested — Time limit for death benefits.
34A-2-904. Volunteer emergency medical services providers — Workers' compensation premiums.
34A-2-905. Rulemaking authority — Rebuttable presumption.

PART 9

PRESUMPTIONS FOR EMERGENCY MEDICAL SERVICES PROVIDERS

34A-2-901. Workers' compensation presumption for emergency medical services providers.

(1) An emergency medical services provider who claims to have contracted a disease, as defined by Section 78-29-101, as a result of a significant exposure in the performance of his duties as an emergency medical services provider, is presumed to have contracted the disease by accident during the course of his duties as an emergency medical services provider if:

(a) his employment or service as an emergency medical services provider in this state commenced prior to July 1, 1988, and he tests positive for a disease during the tenure of his employment or service, or within three months after termination of his employment or service; or

(b) the individual's employment or service as an emergency medical services provider in this state commenced on or after July 1, 1988, and he tests negative for any disease at the time his employment or service commenced, and again three months later, and he subsequently tests positive during the tenure of his employment or service, or within three months after termination of his employment or service.

(2) Each emergency medical services agency shall inform the emergency medical services providers that it employs or utilizes of the provisions and benefits of this section at commencement of and termination of employment or service.   2005

34A-2-902. Workers' compensation claims by emergency medical services providers — Time limits.

(1) For all purposes of establishing a workers' compensation claim, the "date of accident" is presumed to be the date on which an emergency medical services provider first tests positive for a disease, as defined in Section 78-29-101. However, for purposes of establishing the rate of workers' compensation benefits under Subsection 34A-2-702(5), if a positive test for a disease occurs within three months after termination of employment, the last date of employment is presumed to be the "date of accident."

(2) The time limits prescribed by Section 34A-2-417 do not apply to an employee whose disability is due to a disease, so long as the employee who claims to have suffered a significant exposure in the service of his employer gives notice, as required by Section 34A-3-108, of the "date of accident."

(3) Any claim for workers' compensation benefits or medical expenses shall be filed with the Division of Adjudication of the Labor Commission within one year after the date on which the employee first becomes disabled or requires medical treatment for a disease, or within one year after the termination of employment as an emergency medical services provider, whichever occurs later.   2005

34A-2-903. Failure to be tested — Time limit for death benefits.

(1) An emergency medical services provider who refuses or fails to be tested in accordance with Section 34A-2-901 is not entitled to any of the presumptions provided by this part.

(2) Death benefits payable under Section 34A-2-702 are payable only if it can be established by competent evidence that death was a consequence of or result of the disease and, notwithstanding Subsection 34A-2-702(5), that death occurred within six years from the date the employee first became disabled or required medical treatment for the disease that caused his death.   2005

34A-2-904. Volunteer emergency medical services providers — Workers' compensation premiums.

(1) For purposes of receiving workers' compensation benefits, any person performing the services of an emergency medical services provider is considered an employee of the entity for whom it provides those services.

(2) (a) With regard to emergency medical services providers who perform those services for minimal or no compensation on a volunteer basis, and who are primarily employed other than as emergency medical services providers, the amount of workers' compensation benefits shall be based on that primary employment. Any excess premiums necessary for workers' compensation shall be paid by the entity that utilized that individual as an emergency medical services provider.

(b) With regard to emergency medical services providers who perform those services for minimal or no compensation or on a volunteer basis, and who have no other employment, the amount of workers' compensation benefits shall be the minimum benefit. Any premium necessary for workers' compensation shall be paid by the entity that utilizes that individual as an emergency medical services provider.

(3) Workers' compensation benefits are the exclusive remedy for all injuries and occupational diseases, as provided by Title 34A, Chapters 2 and 3. However, emergency medical services providers described in Subsection (2) are not precluded from utilizing insurance benefits provided by a primary employer, or any other insurance benefits, in addition to workers' compensation benefits.   2005

34A-2-905. Rulemaking authority — Rebuttable presumption.

(1) The Labor Commission has authority to establish rules necessary for the purposes of this part.

(2) The presumption provided by this part is a rebuttable presumption.   2005

TITLE 41

MOTOR VEHICLES

CHAPTER 1

MOTOR VEHICLE ACT [RENUMBERED]

41-1-1 to 41-1-231.   Renumbered as §§ 41-1a-101 to 41-1a-1402.   1992

PART 1

ADMINISTRATION

41-1a-101. Short title.

This chapter is known as the "Motor Vehicle Act."

1992

41-1a-102. Definitions.

As used in this chapter:

(1) "Actual miles" means the actual distance a vehicle has traveled while in operation.

(2) "Actual weight" means the actual unladen weight of a vehicle or combination of vehicles as operated and certified to by a weighmaster.

(3) "Affidavit of Mobile Home Affixture" means the affidavit of affixture described in Title 59, Chapter 2, Part 6, Mobile Homes.

(4) "All-terrain type I vehicle" has the same meaning provided in Section 41-22-2.

(5) "All-terrain type II vehicle" has the same meaning provided in Section 41-22-2.

(6) "Amateur radio operator" means any person licensed by the Federal Communications Commission to engage in private and experimental two-way radio operation on the amateur band radio frequencies.

(7) "Branded title" means a title certificate that is labeled:

(a) rebuilt and restored to operation;

(b) flooded and restored to operation; or

(c) not restored to operation.

(8) "Camper" means any structure designed, used, and maintained primarily to be mounted on or affixed to a motor vehicle that contains a floor and is designed to provide a mobile dwelling, sleeping place, commercial space, or facilities for human habitation or for camping.

(9) "Certificate of title" means a document issued by a jurisdiction to establish a record of ownership between an identified owner and the described vehicle, vessel, or outboard motor.

(10) "Certified scale weigh ticket" means a weigh ticket that has been issued by a weighmaster.

(11) "Commercial vehicle" means a motor vehicle, trailer, or semitrailer used or maintained for the transportation of persons or property that operates:

(a) as a carrier for hire, compensation, or profit; or

(b) as a carrier to transport the vehicle owner's goods or property in furtherance of the owner's commercial enterprise.

(12) "Commission" means the State Tax Commission.

(13) "Dealer" means a person engaged or licensed to engage in the business of buying, selling, or exchanging new or used vehicles, vessels, or outboard motors either outright or on conditional sale, bailment, lease, chattel mortgage, or otherwise or who has an established place of business for the sale, lease, trade, or display of vehicles, vessels, or outboard motors.

(14) "Division" means the Motor Vehicle Division of the commission, created in Section 41-1a-106.

(15) "Essential parts" means all integral and body parts of a vehicle of a type required to be registered in this state, the removal, alteration, or substitution of which would tend to conceal the identity of the vehicle or substantially alter its appearance, model, type, or mode of operation.

(16) "Farm tractor" means every motor vehicle designed and used primarily as a farm implement for drawing plows, mowing machines, and other implements of husbandry.

(17) (a) "Farm truck" means a truck used by the owner or operator of a farm solely for his own use in the transportation of:

(i) farm products, including livestock and its products, poultry and its products, floricultural and horticultural products;

(ii) farm supplies, including tile, fence, and every other thing or commodity used in agricultural, floricultural, horticultural, livestock, and poultry production; and

(iii) livestock, poultry, and other animals and things used for breeding, feeding, or other purposes connected with the operation of a farm.

(b) "Farm truck" does not include the operation of trucks by commercial processors of agricultural products.

(18) "Fleet" means one or more commercial vehicles.

(19) "Foreign vehicle" means a vehicle of a type required to be registered, brought into this state from another state, territory, or country other than in the ordinary course of business by or through a manufacturer or dealer, and not registered in this state.

(20) "Gross laden weight" means the actual weight of a vehicle or combination of vehicles, equipped for operation, to which shall be added the maximum load to be carried.

(21) "Highway" or "street" means the entire width between property lines of every way or place of whatever nature when any part of it is open to the public, as a matter of right, for purposes of vehicular traffic.

(22) (a) "Identification number" means the identifying number assigned by the manufacturer or by the division for the purpose of identifying the vehicle, vessel, or outboard motor.

(b) "Identification number" includes a vehicle identification number, state assigned identification number, hull identification number, and motor serial number.

(23) "Implement of husbandry" means every vehicle designed or adapted and used exclusively for an agricultural operation and only incidentally operated or moved upon the highways.

(24) (a) "In-state miles" means the total number of miles operated in this state during the preceding year by fleet power units.

(b) If fleets are composed entirely of trailers or semitrailers, "in-state miles" means the total number of miles that those vehicles were towed on Utah highways during the preceding year.

(25) "Interstate vehicle" means any commercial vehicle operated in more than one state, province, territory, or possession of the United States or foreign country.

(26) "Jurisdiction" means a state, district, province, political subdivision, territory, or possession of the United States or any foreign country.

(27) "Lienholder" means a person with a security interest in particular property.

(28) "Manufactured home" means a transportable factory built housing unit constructed on or after June 15, 1976, according to the Federal Home Construction and Safety Standards Act of 1974 (HUD Code), in one or more sections, which, in the traveling mode, is eight body feet or more in width or 40 body feet or more in length, or when erected on site, is 400 or more square feet, and which is built on a permanent chassis and designed to be used as a dwelling with or without a permanent foundation when connected to the required utilities, and includes the plumbing, heating, air-conditioning, and electrical systems.

(29) "Manufacturer" means a person engaged in the business of constructing, manufacturing, assembling, producing, or importing new or unused vehicles, vessels, or outboard motors for the purpose of sale or trade.

(30) "Mobile home" means a transportable factory built housing unit built prior to June 15, 1976, in accordance with a state mobile home code which existed prior to the Federal Manufactured Housing and Safety Standards Act (HUD Code).

(31) "Motorboat" has the same meaning as provided in Section 73-18-2.

(32) "Motorcycle" means a motor vehicle having a saddle for the use of the rider and designed to travel on not more than three wheels in contact with the ground.

(33) (a) "Motor vehicle" means a self-propelled vehicle intended primarily for use and operation on the highways.

(b) "Motor vehicle" does not include an off-highway vehicle.

(34) (a) "Nonresident" means a person who is not a resident of this state as defined by Section 41-1a-202, and who does not engage in intrastate business within this state and does not operate in that business any motor vehicle, trailer, or semitrailer within this state.

(b) A person who engages in intrastate business within this state and operates in that business any motor vehicle, trailer, or semitrailer in this state or who, even though engaging in interstate commerce, maintains any vehicle in this state as the home station of that vehicle is considered a resident of this state, insofar as that vehicle is concerned in administering this chapter.

(35) "Odometer" means a device for measuring and recording the actual distance a vehicle travels while in operation, but does not include any auxiliary odometer designed to be periodically reset.

(36) "Off-highway implement of husbandry" has the same meaning as provided in Section 41-22-2.

(37) "Off-highway vehicle" has the same meaning as provided in Section 41-22-2.

(38) "Operate" means to drive or be in actual physical control of a vehicle or to navigate a vessel.

(39) "Outboard motor" means a detachable self-contained propulsion unit, excluding fuel supply, used to propel a vessel.

(40) (a) "Owner" means a person, other than a lienholder, holding title to a vehicle, vessel, or outboard motor whether or not the vehicle, vessel, or outboard motor is subject to a security interest.

(b) If a vehicle is the subject of an agreement for the conditional sale or installment sale or mortgage of the vehicle with the right of purchase upon performance of the conditions stated in the agreement and with an immediate right of possession vested in the conditional vendee or mortgagor, or if the vehicle is the subject of a security agreement, then the conditional vendee, mortgagor, or debtor is considered the owner for the purposes of this chapter.

(c) If a vehicle is the subject of an agreement to lease, the lessor is considered the owner until the lessee exercises his option to purchase the vehicle.

(41) "Personalized license plate" means a license plate that has displayed on it a combination of letters, numbers, or both as requested by the owner of the vehicle and assigned to the vehicle by the division.

(42) (a) "Pickup truck" means a two-axle motor vehicle with motive power manufactured, remanufactured, or materially altered to provide an open cargo area.

(b) "Pickup truck" includes motor vehicles with the open cargo area covered with a camper, camper shell, tarp, removable top, or similar structure.

(43) "Pneumatic tire" means every tire in which compressed air is designed to support the load.

(44) "Preceding year" means a period of 12 consecutive months fixed by the division that is within 16 months immediately preceding the commencement of the registration or license year in which proportional registration is sought. The division in fixing the period shall conform it to the terms, conditions, and requirements of any applicable agreement or arrangement for the proportional registration of vehicles.

(45) "Public garage" means every building or other place where vehicles or vessels are kept and stored and where a charge is made for the storage and keeping of vehicles and vessels.

(46) "Reconstructed vehicle" means every vehicle of a type required to be registered in this state that is materially altered from its original construction by the removal, addition, or substitution of essential parts, new or used.

(47) "Recreational vehicle" has the same meaning as provided in Section 13-14-102.

(48) "Registration" means a document issued by a jurisdiction that allows operation of a vehicle or vessel on the highways or waters of this state for the time period for which the registration is

valid and that is evidence of compliance with the registration requirements of the jurisdiction.

(49) (a) "Registration year" means a 12 consecutive month period commencing with the completion of all applicable registration criteria.

(b) For administration of a multistate agreement for proportional registration the division may prescribe a different 12-month period.

(50) "Repair or replacement" means the restoration of vehicles, vessels, or outboard motors to a sound working condition by substituting any inoperative part of the vehicle, vessel, or outboard motor, or by correcting the inoperative part.

(51) "Road tractor" means every motor vehicle designed and used for drawing other vehicles and constructed so it does not carry any load either independently or any part of the weight of a vehicle or load that is drawn.

(52) "Sailboat" has the same meaning as provided in Section 73-18-2.

(53) "Security interest" means an interest that is reserved or created by a security agreement to secure the payment or performance of an obligation and that is valid against third parties.

(54) "Semitrailer" means every vehicle without motive power designed for carrying persons or property and for being drawn by a motor vehicle and constructed so that some part of its weight and its load rests or is carried by another vehicle.

(55) "Special group license plate" means a type of license plate designed for a particular group of people or a license plate authorized and issued by the division in accordance with Section 41-1a-418.

(56) (a) "Special interest vehicle" means a vehicle used for general transportation purposes and that is:

    (i) 20 years or older from the current year; or

    (ii) a make or model of motor vehicle recognized by the division director as having unique interest or historic value.

(b) In making his determination under Subsection (56)(a), the division director shall give special consideration to:

    (i) a make of motor vehicle that is no longer manufactured;

    (ii) a make or model of motor vehicle produced in limited or token quantities;

    (iii) a make or model of motor vehicle produced as an experimental vehicle or one designed exclusively for educational purposes or museum display; or

    (iv) a motor vehicle of any age or make that has not been substantially altered or modified from original specifications of the manufacturer and because of its significance is being collected, preserved, restored, maintained, or operated by a collector or hobbyist as a leisure pursuit.

(57) (a) "Special mobile equipment" means every vehicle:

    (i) not designed or used primarily for the transportation of persons or property;

    (ii) not designed to operate in traffic; and

    (iii) only incidentally operated or moved over the highways.

(b) "Special mobile equipment" includes:

    (i) farm tractors;

    (ii) off-road motorized construction or maintenance equipment including backhoes, bulldozers, compactors, graders, loaders, road rollers, tractors, and trenchers; and

    (iii) ditch-digging apparatus.

(c) "Special mobile equipment" does not include a commercial vehicle as defined under Section 72-9-102.

(58) "Specially constructed vehicle" means every vehicle of a type required to be registered in this state, not originally constructed under a distinctive name, make, model, or type by a generally recognized manufacturer of vehicles, and not materially altered from its original construction.

(59) "Title" means the right to or ownership of a vehicle, vessel, or outboard motor.

(60) (a) "Total fleet miles" means the total number of miles operated in all jurisdictions during the preceding year by power units.

(b) If fleets are composed entirely of trailers or semitrailers, "total fleet miles" means the number of miles that those vehicles were towed on the highways of all jurisdictions during the preceding year.

(61) "Trailer" means a vehicle without motive power designed for carrying persons or property and for being drawn by a motor vehicle and constructed so that no part of its weight rests upon the towing vehicle.

(62) "Transferee" means a person to whom the ownership of property is conveyed by sale, gift, or any other means except by the creation of a security interest.

(63) "Transferor" means a person who transfers his ownership in property by sale, gift, or any other means except by creation of a security interest.

(64) "Travel trailer," "camping trailer," or "fifth wheel trailer" means a portable vehicle without motive power, designed as a temporary dwelling for travel, recreational, or vacation use that does not require a special highway movement permit when drawn by a self-propelled motor vehicle.

(65) "Truck tractor" means a motor vehicle designed and used primarily for drawing other vehicles and not constructed to carry a load other than a part of the weight of the vehicle and load that is drawn.

(66) "Vehicle" includes a motor vehicle, trailer, semitrailer, off-highway vehicle, manufactured home, and mobile home.

(67) "Vessel" has the same meaning as provided in Section 73-18-2.

(68) "Vintage vehicle" has the same meaning as provided in Section 41-21-1.

(69) "Waters of this state" has the same meaning as provided in Section 73-18-2.

(70) "Weighmaster" means a person, association of persons, or corporation permitted to weigh vehicles under this chapter.   2003

41-1a-103. Commission to administer chapter.

The commission shall administer and enforce this chapter.   1992

41-1a-104. Commission powers.

The commission may:

(1) enter into agreements with other jurisdictions:

(a) relating to proportional registration to facilitate administration;

(b) for the exchange of information for audit and enforcement activities; and

(c) for cooperation with other jurisdictions;

(2) confer and advise with the proper officers, officials, and legislative bodies of other jurisdictions to promote agreements under which the registration of vehicles owned in this state is recognized by the other jurisdictions;

(3) make and enforce rules necessary to effectuate this chapter; and

(4) adopt an official seal for the use of the division.   1992

41-1a-105. Commission to create forms.

The commission shall prescribe and provide suitable forms of applications, certificates of title, registration cards, and all other forms necessary to carry out the provisions of this chapter.   1992

41-1a-106. Division created.

There is created within the commission the Motor Vehicle Division with the duties and powers provided in Sections 41-1a-107 through 41-1a-119.   1992

41-1a-107. Commission, division, and officers to enforce chapter — Duties.

The commission and the officers and inspectors of the division designated by the commission, peace officers, and others authorized by the division or by law shall:

(1) enforce the provisions of this chapter and of all other laws regulating the registration of motor vehicles, trailers, or semitrailers; and

(2) inspect any motor vehicle, trailer, or semitrailer of a type required to be registered in any public garage or repair shop or in any place where the motor vehicle, trailer, or semitrailer is held for sale or wrecking, for the purpose of locating and investigating the title and registration of stolen motor vehicles, trailers, and semitrailers.   1992

41-1a-108. Division inspection of applications for registration, certificate of title, or license plate.

(1) The division shall examine and determine the genuineness, regularity, and legality of each application for:

(a) registration of a vehicle;

(b) a certificate of title for a vehicle, vessel, or outboard motor;

(c) license plates; and

(d) any other request lawfully made to the division.

(2) The division may investigate or require additional information on any application or request necessary to implement this chapter.

(3) When the division is satisfied as to the genuineness, regularity, and legality of an application and that the applicant is entitled to register the vehicle and to the issuance of a certificate of title, the division shall register the vehicle, issue a certificate of title and issue license plates.   1992

41-1a-109. Grounds for division refusing registration or certificate of title.

(1) The division shall refuse registration or issuance of a certificate of title or any transfer of registration upon any of the following grounds:

(a) the application contains any false or fraudulent statement;

(b) the applicant has failed to furnish required information or reasonable additional information requested by the division;

(c) the applicant is not entitled to the issuance of a certificate of title or registration of the vehicle under this chapter;

(d) the division has reasonable grounds to believe that the vehicle is a stolen vehicle or that the granting of registration or the issuance of a certificate of title would constitute a fraud against the rightful owner or other person having a valid lien upon the vehicle;

(e) the registration of the vehicle is suspended or revoked for any reason provided in the motor vehicle laws of this state; or

(f) the required fees have not been paid.

(2) The division shall also refuse registration or any transfer of registration if the vehicle is mechanically unfit or unsafe to be operated or moved upon the highways.

(3) The division shall refuse registration or any transfer of registration of a vehicle upon notification by the Department of Transportation that the vehicle or owner is not in compliance with Title 72, Chapter 9, Motor Carrier Safety Act.

(4) The division may not register a vehicle if the registration of the vehicle is revoked under Subsection 41-1a-110(2) until the applicant provides proof:

(a) of owner's or operator's security in a form allowed under Subsection 41-12a-303.2(4);

(b) of exemption from the owner's or operator's security requirements; or

(c) that the applicant was not an owner of the vehicle at the time of the alleged violation or on the day following the time limit provided after the second notice under Subsection 41-12a-804(2).   2000

41-1a-110. Authority of division to suspend or revoke registration, certificate of title, license plate, or permit.

(1) Except as provided in Subsections (3) and (4), the division may suspend or revoke a registration, certificate of title, license plate, or permit if:

(a) the division is satisfied that a registration, certificate of title, license plate, or permit was fraudulently procured or erroneously issued;

(b) the division determines that a registered vehicle is mechanically unfit or unsafe to be operated or moved upon the highways;

(c) a registered vehicle has been dismantled;

(d) the division determines that the required fee has not been paid and the fee is not paid upon reasonable notice and demand;

(e) a registration decal, license plate, or permit is knowingly displayed upon a vehicle other than the one for which issued;

(f) the division determines that the owner has committed any offense under this chapter involving the registration, certificate of title, registration card, license plate, registration decal, or permit; or

(g) the division receives notification by the Department of Transportation that the owner has committed any offence under Title 72, Chapter 9, Motor Carrier Safety Act.

(2) The division shall revoke the registration of a vehicle if the division receives notification by the:

(a) Department of Public Safety that a person:

(i) has been convicted of operating a registered motor vehicle in violation of Section 41-12a-301 or 41-12a-303.2; or

(ii) is under an administrative action taken by the Department of Public Safety for operating a registered motor vehicle in violation of Section 41-12a-301; or

(b) designated agent that the owner of a motor vehicle:

(i) has failed to provide satisfactory proof of owner's or operator's security to the designated agent after the second notice provided under Section 41-12a-804; or

(ii) provided a false or fraudulent statement to the designated agent.

(3) The division may not suspend or revoke the registration of a vessel or outboard motor unless authorized under Section 73-18-7.3.

(4) The division may not suspend or revoke the registration of an off-highway vehicle unless authorized under Section 41-22-17.

(5) The division shall charge a registration reinstatement fee under Section 41-1a-1220, if the registration is revoked under Subsection (1)(f).   2000

41-1a-111. Cancellation, suspension, or revocation of registration — Return of registration items.

If the division cancels, suspends, or revokes a registration, certificate of title, license plate, or permit under this chapter, the owner or person in possession of it shall immediately return the canceled, suspended, or revoked item to the division.   1992

41-1a-112. Authority to administer oaths.

Officers and employees of the division designated by the commission for the purpose of administering the motor vehicle laws may administer oaths and acknowledge signatures and shall do so without fee.
          1992

41-1a-113. Power to summon witnesses and take testimony — Service of summons — Witness fees — Failure to appear.

(1) The commission and officers of the division designated by the commission may summon witnesses to give testimony under oath or to give written deposition upon any matter under the jurisdiction of the division.

(2) The summons may require the production of relevant books, papers, or records.

(3) Every summons shall be served at least five days before the return date, either by personal service made by any person over 18 years of age or by registered mail, but return acknowledgment is required to prove the latter service.

(4) The fees for the attendance and travel of witnesses are the same as for witnesses before the district court.

(5) Failure to obey a summons served is a class C misdemeanor.   1992

41-1a-114. Method of giving notice.

(1) If the division is required to give any notice under this chapter or other law regulating the operation of vehicles, vessels, and outboard motors, unless a different method of giving the notice is expressly prescribed, the notice shall be given either by:

(a) personal delivery to the person to be notified; or

(b) deposit in the United States mail of the notice in an envelope with postage prepaid, addressed to the person at the address shown by the records of the division.

(2) Notice by mail is complete upon the expiration of four days after deposit of the notice.

(3) Proof of the giving of notice in either manner specified in Subsection (1) may be made by the certificate of any officer or employee of the division or affidavit of any person over 18 years of age, naming the person to whom the notice was given and specifying the time, place, and manner of giving the notice.
          1992

41-1a-115. Division records — Copies.

(1) The division shall file each application received.

(2) The division shall keep a record of each registration on a calendar year basis as follows:

(a) under a distinctive registration number assigned to the vehicle, vessel, or outboard motor;

(b) alphabetically, under the name of the owner of the vehicle, vessel, or outboard motor;

(c) under the identification number of the vehicle, vessel, or outboard motor; and

(d) in any manner the division finds desirable for compiling statistical information or of comparative value for use in determining registration fees in future years.

(3) (a) The division shall maintain a current record of each certificate of title it issues.

(b) (i) The division shall file and retain every surrendered certificate of title and every application for title to permit the tracing of title of the vehicles designated in them.

(ii) The retention period for division records shall be set by the Division of Archives and Records Service in accordance with Title 63, Chapter 2, Government Records Access and Management Act.

(4) (a) The commission and officers of the division the commission designates may prepare under the seal of the division and deliver upon request a certified copy of any record of the division, including microfilmed records, charging a fee, determined by the commission pursuant to Section 63-38-3.2, for each document authenticated.

(b) The application shall include the requested information to identify the applicant.

(c) Each certified copy is admissible in any proceeding in any court in the same manner as the original.

(5) The division shall comply with Title 63, Chapter 2, Government Records Access and Management Act.
          1994

41-1a-116. Records — Access to records — Fees.

(1) (a) All motor vehicle title and registration records of the division are protected unless the division determines based upon a written request by the subject of the record that the record is public.

(b) In addition to the provisions of this section, access to all division records is permitted for all purposes described in the federal Driver's Privacy Protection Act of 1994, 18 U.S.C. Chapter 123.

(2) (a) Access to public records is determined by Section 63-2-201.

(b) A record designated as public under Subsection (1)(a) may be used for advertising or solicitation purposes.

(3) Access to protected records, except as provided in Subsection (4), is determined by Section 63-2-202.

(4) In addition to those persons granted access to protected records under Section 63-2-202, the division may disclose a protected record to a licensed private investigator, holding a valid agency or registrant license, with a legitimate business need, a person with a bona fide security interest, or the owner of a mobile home park subject to Subsection (5), only upon receipt

of a signed acknowledgment that the person receiving that protected record may not:

(a) resell or disclose information from that record to any other person except as permitted in the federal Driver's Privacy Protection Act of 1994; or

(b) use information from that record for advertising or solicitation purposes.

(5) The division may disclose the name or address, or both, of the lienholder or mobile home owner of record, or both of them, to the owner of a mobile home park, if all of the following conditions are met:

(a) a mobile home located within the mobile home park owner's park has been abandoned under Section 57-16-13 or the resident is in default under the resident's lease;

(b) the mobile home park owner has conducted a reasonable search, but is unable to determine the name or address, or both, of the lienholder or mobile home owner of record; and

(c) the mobile home park owner has submitted a written statement to the division explaining the mobile home park owner's efforts to determine the name or address, or both, of the lienholder or mobile home owner of record before the mobile home park owner contacted the division.

(6) The division may provide protected information to a statistic gathering entity under Subsection (4) only in summary form.

(7) A person allowed access to protected records under Subsection (4) may request motor vehicle title or registration information from the division regarding any person, entity, or motor vehicle by submitting a written application on a form provided by the division.

(8) If a person regularly requests information for business purposes, the division may by rule allow the information requests to be made by telephone and fees as required under Subsection (9) charged to a division billing account to facilitate division service. The rules shall require that the:

(a) division determine if the nature of the business and the volume of requests merit the dissemination of the information by telephone;

(b) division determine if the credit rating of the requesting party justifies providing a billing account; and

(c) requestor submit to the division an application that includes names and signatures of persons authorized to request information by telephone and charge the fees to the billing account.

(9) (a) The division shall charge a reasonable search fee determined under Section 63-38-3.2 for the research of each record requested.

(b) Fees may not be charged for furnishing information to persons necessary for their compliance with this chapter.

(c) Law enforcement agencies have access to division records free of charge.   2004

41-1a-117.   Adjudicative proceedings.

The commission and the division shall comply with the procedures and requirements of Title 63, Chapter 46b, Administrative Procedures Act, in all adjudicative proceedings conducted under this chapter.   1992

41-1a-118.   Seizure of documents and plates — Grounds — Receipt.

(1) The division and peace officers may take possession of any certificate of title, registration card, registration decal, permit, license plate, or any other article issued by the division:

(a) upon expiration, suspension, revocation, alteration, or cancellation of it;

(b) that is fictitious;

(c) that has been unlawfully or erroneously issued; or

(d) that is unlawfully or erroneously displayed.

(2) A receipt shall be issued for any confiscated item.   1992

41-1a-119.   Emergency procedures for collection of fees.

(1) If the commission finds that the owner or operator of a vehicle who is liable for the payment of any registration fee required by this chapter plans to depart quickly from the state, to remove his property from the state, to conceal himself or his property, or do any other act tending to prejudice or render wholly or partially ineffectual proceedings to collect the registration fees, the commission shall follow the emergency procedures set forth in Title 63, Chapter 46b, Administrative Procedures Act, and declare that the registration fees are immediately due and payable.

(2) When the commission issues its emergency order, the registration fees are immediately due and payable after notice is given to the owner or operator of the vehicle.   1992

41-1a-120.   Participation in Uninsured Motorist Identification Database Program.

(1) The division shall provide the Department of Public Safety's designated agent, as defined in Section 41-12a-802, with a record of all current motor vehicle registrations.

(2) The division shall perform the duties specified in:

(a) Title 41, Chapter 12a, Part 8, Uninsured Motorist Identification Database Program; and

(b) Sections 41-1a-109 and 41-1a-110.

(3) The division shall cooperate with the Department of Public Safety in making rules and developing procedures to use the Uninsured Motorist Identification Database.   2004

PART 2

REGISTRATION

41-1a-201.   Function of registration — Registration required.

Unless exempted, a person may not operate and an owner may not give another person permission to operate a motor vehicle, combination of vehicles, trailer, semitrailer, vintage vehicle, off-highway vehicle, or vessel in this state unless it has been registered in accordance with this chapter, Title 41, Chapter 22, Off-Highway Vehicles, or Title 73, Chapter 18, State Boating Act.   1992

41-1a-202.   Definitions — Vehicles exempt from registration — Registration of vehicles after establishing residency.

(1) In this section:

(a) "Domicile" means the place:

(i) where an individual has a fixed permanent home and principal establishment;

(ii) to which the individual if absent, intends to return; and

(iii) in which the individual and his family voluntarily reside, not for a special or temporary purpose, but with the intention of making a permanent home.

(b) (i) "Resident" means any of the following:

(A) an individual who:

(I) has established a domicile in this state;

(II) regardless of domicile, remains in this state for an aggregate period of six months or more during any calendar year;

(III) engages in a trade, profession, or occupation in this state or who accepts employment in other than seasonal work in this state and who does not commute into the state;

(IV) declares himself to be a resident of this state for the purpose of obtaining a driver license or motor vehicle registration; or

(V) declares himself a resident of Utah to obtain privileges not ordinarily extended to nonresidents, including going to school, or placing children in school without paying nonresident tuition or fees;

(B) any individual, partnership, limited liability company, firm, corporation, association, or other entity that:

(I) maintains a main office, branch office, or warehouse facility in this state and that bases and operates a motor vehicle in this state; or

(II) operates a motor vehicle in intrastate transportation for other than seasonal work.

(ii) "Resident" does not include any of the following:

(A) a member of the military temporarily stationed in Utah;

(B) an out-of-state student, as classified by the institution of higher education, enrolled with the equivalent of seven or more quarter hours, regardless of whether the student engages in a trade, profession, or occupation in this state or accepts employment in this state; and

(C) an individual domiciled in another state or a foreign country that:

(I) is engaged in public, charitable, educational, or religious services for a government agency or an organization that qualifies for tax-exempt status under Internal Revenue Code Section 501(c)(3);

(II) is not compensated for services rendered other than expense reimbursements; and

(III) is temporarily in Utah for a period not to exceed 24 months.

(2) Registration under this chapter is not required for any:

(a) vehicle registered in another state and owned by a nonresident of the state or operating under a temporary registration permit issued by the division or a dealer authorized by this chapter, driven or moved upon a highway in conformance with the provisions of this chapter relating to manufacturers, transporters, dealers, lien holders, or interstate vehicles;

(b) vehicle driven or moved upon a highway only for the purpose of crossing the highway from one property to another;

(c) implement of husbandry, whether of a type otherwise subject to registration or not, that is only incidentally operated or moved upon a highway;

(d) special mobile equipment;

(e) vehicle owned or leased by the federal government;

(f) motor vehicle not designed, used, or maintained for the transportation of passengers for hire or for the transportation of property if the motor vehicle is registered in another state and is owned and operated by a nonresident of this state;

(g) vehicle or combination of vehicles designed, used, or maintained for the transportation of persons for hire or for the transportation of property if the vehicle or combination of vehicles is registered in another state and is owned and operated by a nonresident of this state and if the vehicle or combination of vehicles has a gross laden weight of 26,000 pounds or less;

(h) trailer of 750 pounds or less unladen weight and not designed, used, and maintained for hire for the transportation of property or person;

(i) manufactured home or mobile home;

(j) off-highway vehicle currently registered under Section 41-22-3 if the off-highway vehicle is:

(i) being towed;

(ii) operated on a street or highway designated as open to off-highway vehicle use; or

(iii) operated in the manner prescribed in Section 41-22-10.3;

(k) off-highway implement of husbandry operated in the manner prescribed in Subsections 41-22-5.5(3) through (5);

(l) modular and prebuilt homes conforming to the uniform building code and presently regulated by the United States Department of Housing and Urban Development that are not constructed on a permanent chassis;

(m) electric assisted bicycle defined under Section 41-6a-102;

(n) motor assisted scooter defined under Section 41-6a-102; or

(o) personal motorized mobility device defined under Section 41-6a-102.

(3) Unless otherwise exempted under Subsection (2), registration under this chapter is required for any motor vehicle, combination of vehicles, trailer, semitrailer, or vintage vehicle within 60 days of the owner establishing residency in this state.

(4) A motor vehicle that is registered under Section 41-3-306 is exempt from the registration requirements of this part for the time period that the registration under Section 41-3-306 is valid.   2005

41-1a-203.   Prerequisites for registration.

(1) Except as otherwise provided, prior to registration a vehicle must have:

(a) an identification number inspection under Section 41-1a-204;

(b) passed the safety inspection, if required in the current year, as provided under Sections 41-1a-205 and 53-8-205;

(c) passed the emissions inspection, if required in the current year, as provided under Section 41-6a-1642;

(d) paid property taxes, the in lieu fee, or received a property tax clearance under Section 41-1a-206 or 41-1a-207;

(e) paid the automobile driver education tax required by Section 41-1a-208;

(f) paid the applicable registration fee under Part 12, Fee and Tax Requirements;

(g) paid the uninsured motorist identification fee under Section 41-1a-1218, if applicable; and

(h) paid the motor carrier fee under Section 41-1a-1219, if applicable.

(2) In addition to the requirements in Subsection (1), an owner whose vehicle has not been previously registered or that is currently registered under a previous owner's name must also apply for a valid certificate of title in the owner's name prior to registration.

(3) A new registration, transfer of ownership, or registration renewal under Section 73-18-7 may not be issued for a vessel or outboard motor that is subject to the title provisions of this chapter unless a certificate of title has been or is in the process of being issued in the same owner's name.

(4) A new registration, transfer of ownership, or registration renewal under Section 41-22-3 may not be issued for an off-highway vehicle that is subject to the titling provisions of this chapter unless a certificate of title has been or is in the process of being issued in the same owner's name.   2005

41-1a-204. Identification number inspection.

An application for first registration in this state of any vehicle may not be accepted by the division unless the identification number of that vehicle, other than new vehicles sold by dealers licensed in this state, has been inspected by a qualified identification number inspector under Part 8, Identification Numbers.   1992

41-1a-205. Safety inspection certificate required for renewal or registration of motor vehicle — Exemptions.

(1) If required in the current year, a safety inspection certificate, as required by Section 53-8-205, or proof of exemption from safety inspection shall be presented at the time of, and as a condition of, registration or renewal of a motor vehicle.

(2) (a) Except as provided in Subsections (2)(b), (c), and (d), the safety inspection required under this section may be made no more than two months prior to the renewal of registration.

   (b) (i) If the title of a used motor vehicle is being transferred, a safety inspection certificate issued for the motor vehicle during the previous two months may be used to satisfy the requirement under Subsection (1).

    (ii) If the transferor is a licensed and bonded used motor vehicle dealer, a safety inspection certificate issued for the motor vehicle in a licensed and bonded motor vehicle dealer's name during the previous six months may be used to satisfy the requirement under Subsection (1).

   (c) If the title of a leased vehicle is being transferred to the lessee of the vehicle, a safety inspection certificate issued during the previous six months may be used to satisfy the requirement under Subsection (1).

   (d) If the motor vehicle is part of a fleet of 101 or more vehicles, the safety inspection required under this section may be made no more than 11 months prior to the renewal of registration.

(3) The following motor vehicles are exempt from this section:

   (a) a new motor vehicle when registered the first time, if:

    (i) a new car predelivery inspection has been made by a dealer;

    (ii) the dealer provides a written disclosure statement listing any known deficiency, existing with the new motor vehicle at the time of delivery, that would cause the motor vehicle to fail a safety inspection given in accordance with Section 53-8-205; and

    (iii) the buyer signs the disclosure statement to acknowledge that the buyer has read and understands the listed deficiencies; and

   (b) a motor vehicle required to be registered under this chapter that bears a dealer plate or other special plate under Title 41, Chapter 3, Part 5, Special Dealer License Plates, except that if the motor vehicle is propelled by its own power and is not being moved for repair or dismantling, the motor vehicle shall comply with Section 41-6a-1601 regarding safe mechanical condition.

(4) (a) A safety inspection certificate shall be displayed on:

    (i) all registered commercial motor vehicles with a gross vehicle weight rating of 26,000 pounds or more;

    (ii) a motor vehicle with three or more axles, pulling a trailer, or pulling a trailer with multiple axles;

    (iii) a combination unit; and

    (iv) a bus or van for hire.

   (b) A commercial vehicle under Subsection (4)(a) is exempt from the requirements of Subsection (1).

(5) A motor vehicle may be sold and the title assigned to the new owner without a valid safety inspection, but the motor vehicle may not be registered in the new owner's name until the motor vehicle complies with this section.   2005

41-1a-206. Payment of property taxes or in lieu fees before registration.

(1) Except as provided in Subsection (2), the division before issuing any registration shall require from every applicant for the registration a certificate from the county assessor in which the vehicle has situs for taxation that:

   (a) the property tax or in lieu fee on the vehicle for the current year has been paid;

   (b) in the assessor's opinion the tax or in lieu fee is a lien on real property sufficient to secure the payment of the tax; or

   (c) the vehicle is exempt by law from payment of property tax or the in lieu fee for the current year.

(2) The requirements of Subsection (1) do not apply to the registration of ambulances, peace officer patrol vehicles, fire engines, passenger cars and trucks owned and used by the United States government or by the state of Utah or by any of its political subdivisions, and motor vehicles assessed by the commission under Section 59-2-201.   1992

41-1a-207. Vehicles assessed by commission.

If the vehicle is assessed by the commission under Section 59-2-201, the commission before issuing a registration shall be satisfied that the:

(1) property tax or in lieu fee on the vehicle has been paid;

(2) vehicle is exempt from the payment of the tax or in lieu fee; or

(3) tax or in lieu fee is secured by a lien on real estate or by a bond.   1992

41-1a-208. Payment of automobile driver education tax prerequisite to registration of motor vehicle.

(1) The collection and payment of the automobile driver education tax is a prerequisite to the registration of any motor vehicle.

(2) Except as provided under Subsection (3), the automobile driver education tax accrues and is collectible upon each motor vehicle, subject to the same exemptions, and payable in the same manner and time as motor vehicle registration fees under Section 41-1a-1206.

(3) The automobile driver education tax:

(a) shall be paid in full at the time the motor vehicle is first registered in a calendar year; and

(b) is not collectible or payable upon the transfers of registration, issuance, reissuance of certificates of registration, titles, or plates contemplated by Sections 41-1a-301, 41-1a-1207, 41-1a-1210, and 41-1a-1211.   1996

41-1a-209. Application for registration — Contents.

(1) An owner of a vehicle subject to registration under this part shall apply to the division for registration on forms furnished by the division.

(2) The application for registration shall include:

(a) the signature of an owner of the vehicle to be registered;

(b) the name, bona fide residence and mailing address of the owner, or business address of the owner if the owner is a firm, association, or corporation;

(c) a description of the vehicle including the make, model, type of body, the model year as specified by the manufacturer, the number of cylinders, and the identification number of the vehicle; and

(d) other information required by the division to enable it to determine whether the owner is lawfully entitled to register the vehicle.   2005

41-1a-210. Examination of registration records and indices of stolen and recovered vehicles.

The division upon receiving application for original registration of a vehicle shall first check the identification number shown in the application against the indices of registered vehicles and against indices of stolen and recovered vehicles.   1992

41-1a-210.5. Driver license required on new registrations.

The division, before issuing any new registration on the sale of a vehicle not sold by a vehicle dealer, shall require the applicant or person making the application to show proof that the applicant or person making the application has a valid driver license.   2001

41-1a-211. Temporary permits — Other laws applied.

(1) (a) The division may grant a temporary permit to operate a vehicle for which:

(i) application for registration has been made, or, in the case of a newly purchased vehicle, will be made;

(ii) evidence of ownership is provided; and

(iii) the proper fees have been paid.

(b) The temporary permit allows the vehicle to be operated pending complete registration by displaying:

(i) the temporary permit; or

(ii) other evidence of the application under rules made by the commission.

(2) If a vehicle is operated on a temporary permit issued under this section or Section 41-3-302, that vehicle is subject to all other statutes, rules, and regulations intended to control the use and operation of vehicles on the highways.   1998

41-1a-212. Division to issue registration card.

The division upon registering a vehicle shall issue a registration card.   1992

41-1a-213. Contents of registration cards.

(1) The registration card shall be delivered to the owner and shall contain:

(a) the date issued;

(b) the name and address of the owner;

(c) a description of the vehicle registered including the year, the make, the identification number, and the license plate assigned to the vehicle;

(d) the expiration date; and

(e) other information as determined by the commission.

(2) If a vehicle is leased for a period in excess of 30 days, the registration shall contain:

(a) the owner's name;

(b) the name of the lessee; and

(c) the bona fide residence address of the lessee.

(3) On all vehicles registered under Subsections 41-1a-1206(1)(d) and (1)(e), the registration card shall also contain the gross laden weight as given in the application for registration.   1994

41-1a-214. Registration card to be signed, carried, and exhibited.

(1) A registration card shall be signed by the owner in ink in the space provided.

(2) A registration card shall be carried at all times in the vehicle to which it was issued.

(3) The person driving or in control of a vehicle shall display the registration card upon demand of a peace officer or any officer or employee of the division.   1992

41-1a-215. Staggered registration dates — Exceptions.

(1) (a) Except under Subsections (2) and (3), every vehicle registration, every registration card, and every registration plate issued under this chapter for the first registration of the vehicle in this state, continues in effect for a period of 12 months beginning with the first day of the calendar month of registration and does not expire until the last day of the same month in the following year.

(b) If the last day of the registration period falls on a day in which the appropriate state or county offices are not open for business, the registration of the vehicle is extended to midnight of the next business day.

(2) The provisions of Subsection (1) do not apply to the following:

(a) registration issued to government vehicles under Section 41-1a-221;

(b) registration issued to apportioned vehicles under Section 41-1a-301;

(c) multiyear registration issued under Section 41-1a-222;

(d) lifetime trailer registration issued under Section 41-1a-1206;

(e) partial year registration issued under Section 41-1a-1207;

(f) vintage vehicle registration issued under Section 41-1a-226; or

(g) plates issued to a dealer, dismantler, manufacturer, remanufacturer, and transporter under Title 41, Chapter 3, Part 5, Special Dealer License Plates.

(3) Upon application of the owner or lessee of a fleet of commercial vehicles not apportioned under Section 41-1a-301 and required to be registered in this state, the State Tax Commission may permit the vehicles to be registered for a registration period commencing on the first day of March, June, September, or December of any year and expiring on the last day of March, June, September, or December in the following year.

(4) When the expiration of a registration plate is extended by affixing a registration decal to it, the expiration of the decal governs the expiration date of the plate. 1999

41-1a-216. Renewal of registration.

(1) The division may receive applications for registration renewal and issue new registration cards at any time prior to the expiration of the registration, subject to the availability of renewal materials.

(2) (a) The new registration shall retain the same expiration month as recorded on the original registration even if the registration has expired, except as provided in Subsection (3).

(b) The year of registration expiration shall be changed to reflect the renewed registration period.

(3) Subsection (2) does not apply if the owner can verify to the satisfaction of the division that the vehicle registration was not renewed prior to its expiration due to the fact that the vehicle was in storage, inoperable, or otherwise out of service.

(4) If the registration renewal application is an application generated by the division through its automated system, the owner need not surrender the last registration card or duplicate. 1996

41-1a-217. Application for renewal of registration.

(1) Renewal of a vehicle registration shall be made by the owner upon application and by payment of the fees or taxes required under Subsection 41-1a-203(1).

(2) The application for registration renewal and applicable fees or taxes shall be accompanied by a:

(a) safety inspection certificate as required under Section 41-1a-205; and

(b) certificate of emissions inspection as required under Section 41-6a-1642.

(3) The new registration card issued shall show:

(a) the identical information with respect to the owner and the vehicle description required by Section 41-1a-213; and

(b) the new expiration date. 2005

41-1a-218. Notice of change of address.

If a person after making application for or obtaining a vehicle registration moves from the address named in the application or shown upon a registration card the person shall within ten days of moving notify the division of his old and new addresses. 1992

41-1a-219. Change of name — New registration.

(1) If the name of any person who has applied for or obtained the registration of a vehicle is changed the person shall surrender the last registration card and file an application for a new registration card.

(2) The division upon receipt of the required fees shall issue a new registration card. 1992

41-1a-220. Lost or damaged registration card.

If a registration card is lost, mutilated, or becomes illegible the owner of the vehicle for which the registration card was issued, as shown by the records of the division, shall immediately:

(1) apply for a duplicate;

(2) furnish the information satisfactory to the division; and

(3) pay the proper fees. 1992

41-1a-221. Registration of vehicles of political subdivisions or state — Renewal of registration — Expiration of registration — Certification of information — Failure to comply.

(1) (a) An entity referred to in Subsection 41-1a-407(1) shall register by June 30 of each year each vehicle that it owns, operates, or leases.

(b) This section does not apply to unmarked vehicles referred to in Section 41-1a-407, which shall be registered by the expiration date on the registration card.

(2) (a) The entity shall apply to the division to renew registration pursuant to Section 41-1a-217.

(b) The division shall renew registration pursuant to Section 41-1a-216.

(3) A registration card and license plate issued to an entity under this section are in full force and effect until:

(a) the registration expires;

(b) the vehicle is no longer owned or operated by that entity; or

(c) the division takes action as provided in Subsection (6).

(4) (a) If the owner of a vehicle subject to the provisions of this section transfers or assigns title or interest in the vehicle, the registration of that vehicle expires.

(b) The transferor shall remove the license plates and within 20 days from the date of transfer forward them to the division to be destroyed.

(5) Each entity shall:

(a) account to the division annually for all "EX" license plates issued to it; and

(b) certify to the division that the information is correct.

(6) If an entity fails to comply with this section, the division may:

(a) refuse to renew the registration of its vehicles;

(b) refuse to issue it additional license plates;

(c) suspend all its vehicle registrations; and

(d) recall license plates issued to an entity refusing to comply with this section. 1999

41-1a-222. Application for multiyear registration — Payment of taxes — Penalties [Effective until January 1, 2006].

(1) The owner of any intrastate fleet of commercial vehicles which is based in the state may apply to the commission for registration in accordance with this section.

(a) The application shall be made on a form prescribed by the commission.

(b) Upon payment of required fees and meeting other requirements prescribed by the commission, the division shall issue, to each vehicle for which application has been made, a multiyear license plate and registration card.

(i) The license plate decal and the registration card shall bear an expiration date fixed by the division and are valid until ownership of the vehicle to which they are issued is transferred by the applicant or until the expiration date, whichever comes first.

(ii) An annual renewal application must be made by the owner if registration identification has been issued on an annual installment fee basis and the required fees must be paid on an annual basis.

(iii) License plates and registration cards issued pursuant to this section are valid for an eight-year period, commencing with the year of initial application in this state.

(c) When application for registration or renewal is made on an installment payment basis, the applicant shall submit acceptable evidence of a surety bond in a form, and with a surety, approved by the commission and in an amount equal to the total annual fees required for all vehicles registered to the applicant in accordance with this section.

(2) Each vehicle registered as part of a fleet of commercial vehicles must be titled in the name of the fleet.

(3) Each owner who registers fleets pursuant to this section shall pay the taxes or in lieu fees otherwise due pursuant to:

(a) Section 41-1a-206;

(b) Section 41-1a-207;

(c) Section 59-2-405.1; or

(d) Subsection 41-1a-301(11).

(4) An owner who fails to comply with the provisions of this section is subject to the penalties in Section 41-1a-1301 and, if the commission so determines, will result in the loss of the privileges granted in this section.   1998

Application for multiyear registration — Payment of taxes — Penalties [Effective January 1, 2006].

(1) The owner of any intrastate fleet of commercial vehicles which is based in the state may apply to the commission for registration in accordance with this section.

(a) The application shall be made on a form prescribed by the commission.

(b) Upon payment of required fees and meeting other requirements prescribed by the commission, the division shall issue, to each vehicle for which application has been made, a multiyear license plate and registration card.

(i) The license plate decal and the registration card shall bear an expiration date fixed by the division and are valid until ownership of the vehicle to which they are issued is transferred by the applicant or until the expiration date, whichever comes first.

(ii) An annual renewal application must be made by the owner if registration identification has been issued on an annual installment fee basis and the required fees must be paid on an annual basis.

(iii) License plates and registration cards issued pursuant to this section are valid for an eight-year period, commencing with the year of initial application in this state.

(c) When application for registration or renewal is made on an installment payment basis, the applicant shall submit acceptable evidence of a surety bond in a form, and with a surety, approved by the commission and in an amount equal to the total annual fees required for all vehicles registered to the applicant in accordance with this section.

(2) Each vehicle registered as part of a fleet of commercial vehicles must be titled in the name of the fleet.

(3) Each owner who registers fleets pursuant to this section shall pay the taxes or in lieu fees otherwise due pursuant to:

(a) Section 41-1a-206;

(b) Section 41-1a-207;

(c) Subsection 41-1a-301(11);

(d) Section 59-2-405.1;

(e) Section 59-2-405.2; or

(f) Section 59-2-405.3.

(4) An owner who fails to comply with the provisions of this section is subject to the penalties in Section 41-1a-1301 and, if the commission so determines, will result in the loss of the privileges granted in this section.   2005

41-1a-223. Registration without Utah title.

(1) (a) If the owner of a vehicle operating interstate and registered in another state desires to retain registration of the vehicle in the other state, the applicant need not surrender but shall submit for inspection evidences of out-of-state registration.

(b) The division upon a proper showing shall register the vehicle in this state.

(2) (a) If a person is relocating from another jurisdiction and establishing residence in this state, whether temporary or permanent, and that person has a vehicle registered and titled in another jurisdiction and is not able to surrender title to the vehicle being registered in Utah because title is physically held by a lienholder, the division may register the vehicle without issuing a Utah title.

(b) Notwithstanding Section 70A-9a-316, the registration of a vehicle under this section does not alter or affect the rights or security interest of any lienholder in another jurisdiction.   2000

41-1a-224. Registration of specially constructed, reconstructed, or foreign vehicles — Surrender of foreign registration.

(1) If the vehicle to be registered is a specially constructed, reconstructed, or foreign vehicle, that fact shall be stated in the application.

(2) The owner of a foreign vehicle that has been registered outside of this state shall surrender to the division all registration cards, certificates of title, or other evidence of foreign registration in his possession or under his control, except as provided in Section 41-1a-223.   1992

41-1a-225. Foreign vehicle compliance with federal law — English translation — Temporary permit.

(1) Before a vehicle with a gross vehicle weight of less than 6,000 pounds that was not originally manufactured for sale in the United States may be registered in this state, the applicant shall provide at the time of registration, a signed statement certifying that the vehicle complies with all federal laws and regulations applicable to the vehicle.

(2) If the certificate of title, manufacturer's certificate of origin, or other document purported to evidence ownership is not printed in the English language, the applicant shall obtain a certified

translation of that document in the English language and provide it to the division at the time of registration.

(3) The division may issue the applicant a temporary permit, not to exceed 120 days, as provided in Section 41-1a-211, pending compliance with federal emission and safety standards. 1999

41-1a-226. Vintage vehicle — Signed statement — Registration certificate.

(1) The owner of a vintage vehicle applying for registration under this part shall provide a signed statement certifying that the vintage vehicle is owned and operated for the purposes enumerated in Section 41-21-1 and that the vintage vehicle has been inspected and found safe to operate on the highways of this state.

(2) The registration certificate issued under this part need not specify the weight of the vintage vehicle. 1999

41-1a-227. Campers — Registration and display of decal — Nonresident exceptions.

A person may not operate a vehicle with a camper mounted on it in this state unless:

(1) the camper is currently registered and the appropriate decal, obtained under Section 59-2-330, is attached in plain sight to the rear of the camper; or

(2) the vehicle is currently registered and licensed in another state with an out-of-state camper mounted on it. 1992

41-1a-228. Special lifetime trailer registration — Property tax or in lieu fees.

(1) The owner of a trailer or semitrailer used as a commercial vehicle may obtain an alternative special registration and license plate valid for the life of the trailer while the trailer is possessed by the registrant.

(2) The owner must file, on or before January 31 of each year after the year of issuance of the special registration and license plate, a certificate from the assessing authority to the effect that any property tax or in lieu fee due for the current year has been paid.

(3) If property tax or the in lieu fee is not paid, registration is suspended or revoked. 1997

41-1a-229. Display of gross laden weight.

(1) Each vehicle registered by gross laden weight and exceeding 12,000 pounds of gross laden weight shall have the gross laden weight for which it is registered painted, stenciled, or shown by decal upon both the left and right sides of the vehicle, in a conspicuous place, in letters of a reasonable size as determined by the commission.

(2) If vehicles are registered in combination, the gross laden weight for which the combination of vehicles is registered shall be displayed upon the power unit.

(3) An owner or operator of a vehicle or combination of vehicles may not display a gross laden weight other than that shown on the certificate of registration of the vehicle. 1992

41-1a-230. Registration checkoff for vision screening.

(1) A person who applies for a motor vehicle registration or registration renewal may designate a voluntary contribution for vision screening of $2.

(2) This contribution shall be:

(a) collected by the division;

(b) treated as a voluntary contribution to Friends For Sight to provide blindness prevention education, screening, and treatment and not as a motor vehicle registration fee; and

(c) transferred to Friends For Sight at least monthly, less actual administrative costs associated with collecting and transferring the contributions. 2003

41-1a-230.5. Registration checkoff for promoting and supporting organ donation.

(1) A person who applies for a motor vehicle registration or registration renewal may designate a voluntary contribution of $2 for the purpose of promoting and supporting organ donation.

(2) This contribution shall be:

(a) collected by the division;

(b) treated as a voluntary contribution to the Organ Donation Contribution Fund created in Section 26-18b-101 and not as a motor vehicle registration fee; and

(c) transferred to the Organ Donation Contribution Fund created in Section 26-18b-101 at least monthly, less actual administrative costs associated with collecting and transferring the contributions. 2002

41-1a-231. Special mobile equipment status.

(1) "Special mobile equipment" status as defined under Section 41-1a-102 shall be approved by the Department of Transportation in consultation with the Motor Carrier Advisory Board created under Section 72-9-201.

(2) In accordance with Title 63, Chapter 46a, Utah Administrative Rulemaking Act, the Department of Transportation in consultation with the State Tax Commission shall make rules establishing procedures for application, identification, approval, denial, and appeal of special mobile equipment status. 2000

PART 3

PROPORTIONAL REGISTRATION

41-1a-301. Apportioned registration and licensing of interstate vehicles.

(1) (a) An owner or operator of a fleet of commercial vehicles based in this state and operating in two or more jurisdictions may register commercial vehicles for operation under the International Registration Plan or the Uniform Vehicle Registration Proration and Reciprocity Agreement by filing an application with the division.

(b) The application shall include information that identifies the vehicle owner, the vehicle, the miles traveled in each jurisdiction, and other information pertinent to the registration of apportioned vehicles.

(c) Vehicles operated exclusively in this state may not be apportioned.

(2) (a) If no operations were conducted during the preceding year, the application shall contain a statement of the proposed operations and an estimate of annual mileage for each jurisdiction.

(b) The division may adjust the estimate if the division is not satisfied with its correctness.

(c) At renewal, the registrant shall use the actual mileage from the preceding year in computing fees due each jurisdiction.

(3) The registration fee for apportioned vehicles shall be determined as follows:

(a) divide the in-jurisdiction miles by the total miles generated during the preceding year;

(b) total the fees for each vehicle based on the fees prescribed in Section 41-1a-1206; and

(c) multiply the sum obtained under Subsection (3)(b) by the quotient obtained under Subsection (3)(a).

(4) Trailers or semitrailers of apportioned fleets may be listed separately as "trailer fleets" with the fees paid according to the total distance those trailers were towed in all jurisdictions during the preceding year mileage reporting period.

(5) (a) (i) When the proper fees have been paid and the property tax or in lieu fee has been cleared under Section 41-1a-206 or 41-1a-207, a registration card, annual decal, and where necessary, license plate, will be issued for each unit listed on the application.

(ii) An original registration must be carried in each vehicle at all times.

(b) Original registration cards for trailers or semitrailers may be carried in the power unit.

(c) (i) In lieu of a permanent registration card or license plate, the division may issue one temporary permit authorizing operation of new or unlicensed vehicles until the permanent registration is completed.

(ii) Once a temporary permit is issued, the registration process may not be cancelled. Registration must be completed and the fees and any property tax or in lieu fee due must be paid for the vehicle for which the permit was issued.

(iii) Temporary permits may not be issued for renewals.

(d) (i) The division shall issue one distinctive license plate that displays the letters APP for apportioned vehicles.

(ii) The plate shall be displayed on the front of an apportioned truck tractor or power unit or on the rear of any apportioned vehicle.

(iii) Distinctive decals displaying the word "apportioned" and the month and year of expiration shall be issued for each apportioned vehicle.

(e) A nonrefundable administrative fee, determined by the commission pursuant to Section 63-38-3.2, shall be charged for each temporary permit, registration, or both.

(6) Vehicles that are apportionally registered are fully registered for intrastate and interstate movements, providing the proper interstate and intrastate authority has been secured.

(7) (a) Vehicles added to an apportioned fleet after the beginning of the registration year shall be registered by applying the quotient under Subsection (3)(a) for the original application to the fees due for the remainder of the registration year.

(b) (i) The owner shall maintain and submit complete annual mileage for each vehicle in each jurisdiction, showing all miles operated by the lessor and lessee.

(ii) The fiscal mileage reporting period begins July 1, and continues through June 30 of the year immediately preceding the calendar year in which the registration year begins.

(c) (i) An owner-operator, who is a lessor, may be the registrant and the vehicle may be registered in the name of the owner-operator.

(ii) The identification plates and registration card shall be the property of the lessor and may reflect both the owner-operator's name and that of the carrier as lessee.

(iii) The allocation of fees shall be according to the operational records of the owner-operator.

(d) (i) The lessee may be the registrant of a leased vehicle at the option of the lessor.

(ii) If a lessee is the registrant of a leased vehicle, both the lessor's and lessee's name shall appear on the registration.

(iii) The allocation of fees shall be according to the records of the carrier.

(8) (a) Any registrant whose application for apportioned registration has been accepted shall preserve the records on which the application is based for a period of three years after the close of the registration year.

(b) The records shall be made available to the division upon request for audit as to accuracy of computations, payments, and assessments for deficiencies, or allowances for credits.

(c) An assessment for deficiency or claim for credit may not be made for any period for which records are no longer required.

(d) Interest in the amount prescribed by Section 59-1-402 shall be assessed or paid from the date due until paid on deficiencies found due after audit.

(e) Registrants with deficiencies are subject to the penalties under Section 59-1-401.

(f) The division may enter into agreements with other International Registration Plan jurisdictions for joint audits.

(9) (a) Except as provided in Subsection (9)(b), all state fees collected under this section shall be deposited in the Transportation Fund.

(b) The following fees may be used by the commission as a dedicated credit to cover the costs of electronic credentialing as provided in Section 41-1a-303:

(i) $5 of each temporary registration permit fee paid under Subsection (12)(a)(i) for a single unit; and

(ii) $10 of each temporary registration permit fee paid under Subsection (12)(a)(ii) for multiple units.

(10) If registration is for less than a full year, fees for apportioned registration shall be assessed according to Section 41-1a-1207.

(a) (i) If the registrant is replacing a vehicle for one withdrawn from the fleet and the new vehicle is of the same weight category as the replaced vehicle, the registrant must file a supplemental application.

(ii) A registration card that transfers the license plate to the new vehicle shall be issued.

(iii) When a replacement vehicle is of greater weight than the replaced vehicle, additional registration fees are due.

(b) If a vehicle is withdrawn from an apportioned fleet during the period for which it is registered, the registrant shall notify the division and surrender the registration card and license plate of the withdrawn vehicle.

(11) (a) An out-of-state carrier with an apportionally registered vehicle who has not presented a certificate of property tax or in lieu fee as required by Section 41-1a-206 or 41-1a-207, shall pay, at the time of registration, a proportional part of an equalized highway use tax computed as follows:

(i) Multiply the number of vehicles or combination vehicles registered in each weight class by the equivalent tax figure from the following tables:

Vehicle or Combination Registered Weight	Age of Vehicle	Equivalent Tax
12,000 pounds or less	12 or more years	$10
12,000 pounds or less	9 or more years but less than 12 years	$50
12,000 pounds or less	6 or more years but less than 9 years	$80
12,000 pounds or less	3 or more years but less than 6 years	$110
12,000 pounds or less	Less than 3 years	$150

Vehicle or Combination Registered Weight	Equivalent Tax
12,001 — 18,000 pounds	$150
18,001 — 34,000 pounds	200
34,001 — 48,000 pounds	300
48,001 — 64,000 pounds	450
64,001 pounds and over	600

(ii) Multiply the equivalent tax value for the total fleet determined under Subsection (11)(a)(i) by the fraction computed under Subsection (3) for the apportioned fleet for the registration year.

(b) Fees shall be assessed as provided in Section 41-1a-1207.

(12) (a) Commercial vehicles meeting the registration requirements of another jurisdiction may, as an alternative to full or apportioned registration, secure a temporary registration permit for a period not to exceed 96 hours or until they leave the state, whichever is less, for a fee of:

(i) $25 for a single unit; and

(ii) $50 for multiple units.

(b) A state temporary permit or registration fee is not required from nonresident owners or operators of vehicles or combination of vehicles having a gross laden weight of 26,000 pounds or less for each single unit or combination. 2003

41-1a-302. Repealed. 1996

41-1a-303. Cooperation for electronic credentialing.

The commission shall cooperate with the Department of Transportation and federal agencies to assist in providing electronic credentialing of motor carriers to facilitate implementation, compliance, and enforcement of vehicle registration, special fuel tax payment, and other registration or taxation provisions including the provisions of the International Registration Plan and the International Fuel Tax Agreement. 2003

PART 4

LICENSE PLATES AND REGISTRATION INDICIA

41-1a-401. License plates — Number of plates — Reflectorization — Indicia of registration in lieu of or used with plates.

(1) (a) The division upon registering a vehicle shall issue to the owner one license plate for a motorcycle, trailer, or semitrailer and two identical license plates for every other vehicle.

(b) The license plate shall be issued for the particular vehicle registered and may not be removed during the term for which the license plate is issued or used upon any other vehicle than the registered vehicle.

(2) The division may receive applications for registration renewal, renew registration, and issue new license plates or decals at any time prior to the expiration of registration.

(3) (a) All license plates to be manufactured and issued by the division shall be treated with a fully reflective material on the plate face that provides effective and dependable reflective brightness during the service period of the license plate.

(b) The division shall prescribe all license plate material specifications and establish and implement procedures for conforming to the specifications.

(c) The specifications for the materials used such as the aluminum plate substrate, the reflective sheeting, and glue shall be drawn in a manner so that at least two manufacturers may qualify as suppliers.

(d) The granting of contracts for the materials shall be by public bid.

(4) (a) The commission may issue, adopt, and require the use of indicia of registration it considers advisable in lieu of or in conjunction with license plates as provided in this part.

(b) All provisions of this part relative to license plates apply to these indicia of registration, so far as the provisions are applicable. 1992

41-1a-402. Required colors, numerals, and letters — Expiration.

(1) (a) Except as provided in Subsection (3) and in Section 41-1a-407, each license plate shall be in colors selected by the commission and shall have displayed on it:

(i) the registration number assigned to the vehicle for which it is issued;

(ii) the name of the state;

(iii) a registration decal showing the date of expiration; and

(iv) a slogan determined as provided in Section 41-1a-405.

(b) A special group license plate issued under Section 41-1a-418 is exempt from the slogan requirement under Subsection (1)(a)(iv).

(2) If registration is extended by affixing a registration decal to the license plate, the expiration date of the decal governs the expiration date of the license plate.

(3) Each original license plate that is not one of the special group license plates issued under Section 41-1a-418 shall be a:

(a) statehood centennial license plate with the same color, design, and slogan as the plates issued in conjunction with the statehood centennial; or

(b) Ski Utah license plate. 2003

41-1a-403. Plates to be legible from 100 feet.

License plates and the required letters and numerals on them, except the decals and the slogan, shall be of sufficient size to be plainly readable from a distance of 100 feet during daylight. 1992

41-1a-404. Location and position of plates.

(1) License plates issued for a vehicle other than a motorcycle, trailer, or semitrailer shall be attached to the vehicle, one in the front and the other in the rear.

(2) The license plate issued for a motorcycle, trailer, or semitrailer shall be attached to the rear of the motorcycle, trailer, or semitrailer.

(3) Every license plate shall at all times be:

(a) securely fastened:

(i) in a horizontal position to the vehicle for which it is issued to prevent the plate from swinging;

(ii) at a height of not less than 12 inches from the ground, measuring from the bottom of the plate; and

(iii) in a place and position to be clearly visible; and

(b) maintained:

(i) free from foreign materials; and

(ii) in a condition to be clearly legible.

1992

41-1a-405. License plate slogan — Purpose — Selection.

(1) The slogan required by Section 41-1a-402 shall be a brief slogan designed to promote the recreational, scenic, historic, or tourist attractions of the state.

(2) (a) The slogan shall be selected by the commission pursuant to its procedures.

(b) The commission in selecting the slogan shall consult with all interested state agencies including:

(i) the Utah Highway Patrol;

(ii) the Governor's Office of Economic Development; and

(iii) the Division of Parks and Recreation.

2005

41-1a-406. Repealed.　　　　2002

41-1a-407. Plates issued to political subdivisions or state — Use of "EX" letters — Confidential information.

(1) Except as provided in Subsection (2), each municipality, board of education, school district, state institution of learning, county, other governmental division, subdivision, or district, and the state shall:

(a) place a license plate displaying the letters, "EX" on every vehicle owned and operated by it or leased for its exclusive use; and

(b) display an identification mark designating the vehicle as the property of the entity in a conspicuous place on both sides of the vehicle.

(2) The entity need not display the "EX" license plate or the identification mark required by Subsection (1) if:

(a) the vehicle is in the direct service of the governor, lieutenant governor, attorney general, state auditor, or state treasurer of Utah;

(b) the vehicle is used in official investigative work where secrecy is essential;

(c) the vehicle is used in an organized Utah Highway Patrol operation that is:

(i) conducted within a county of the first or second class as defined under Section 17-50-501, unless no more than one unmarked vehicle is used for the operation;

(ii) approved by the Commissioner of Public Safety;

(iii) of a duration of 14 consecutive days or less; and

(iv) targeted toward aggressive driving and accidents involving:

(A) violations of Title 41, Chapter 6a, Part 5, Driving Under the Influence and Reckless Driving;

(B) speeding violations for exceeding the posted speed limit by 21 or more miles per hour;

(C) speeding violations in a reduced speed school zone under Section 41-6a-604;

(D) violations of Section 41-6a-1002 related to pedestrian crosswalks; or

(E) violations of Section 41-6a-702 related to lane restrictions;

(d) the vehicle is provided to an official of the entity as part of a compensation package allowing unlimited personal use of that vehicle; or

(e) the personal security of the occupants of the vehicle would be jeopardized if the "EX" license plate were in place.

(3) Plates issued to Utah Highway Patrol vehicles may bear the capital letters "UHP," a beehive logo, and the call number of the trooper to whom the vehicle is issued.

(4) (a) The commission shall issue "EX" and "UHP" plates.

(b) In accordance with Title 63, Chapter 46a, Utah Administrative Rulemaking Act, the commission shall make rules establishing the procedure for application for and distribution of the plates.

(5) For a vehicle that qualifies for "EX" or "UHP" license plates, the entity is not required to display an annual registration decal.

(6) (a) Information shall be confidential for vehicles that are not required to display the "EX" license plate or the identification mark under Subsections (2)(a), (b), (d), and (e).

(b) (i) If a law enforcement officer's identity must be kept secret, his agency head may request in writing that the division remove the license plate information of the officer's personal vehicles from all public access files and place it in a confidential file until the assignment is completed.

(ii) The agency head shall notify the division when the assignment is completed.

(7) A peace officer engaged in an organized operation under Subsection (2)(c) shall be in a uniform clearly identifying the law enforcement agency the peace officer is representing during the operation.

2005

41-1a-408, 41-1a-409. Repealed.　　2003

41-1a-410. Eligibility for personalized plates.

(1) A person who is the registered owner of a vehicle not subject to registration under Section 41-1a-301, registered with the division, or who applies for an original registration of a vehicle not subject to registration under Section 41-1a-301, may upon payment of the fee prescribed in Section 41-1a-1211 apply to the division for personalized license plates.

(2) Application shall be made in accordance with Section 41-1a-411.

(3) The personalized plates shall be affixed to the vehicle for which registration is sought in lieu of the regular license plates.

(4) Personalized license plates shall be issued only to the registered owner of the vehicle on which they are to be displayed.　　　　1993

41-1a-411. Application for personalized plates — Refusal authorized.

(1) An applicant for personalized license plates or renewal of the plates shall file an application for the plates in the form and by the date the division requires, indicating the combination of letters, numbers, or both requested as a registration number.

(2) The division may refuse to issue any combination of letters, numbers, or both that may carry connotations offensive to good taste and decency or that would be misleading.　　　1992

41-1a-412. Design of personalized plates.

The personalized license plates shall be the same color and design as regular license plates designed for the type of vehicle being licensed and shall consist of numbers, letters, or any combination as fixed by the division, provided that there are no conflicts with existing or anticipated license plate series.   1992

41-1a-413. Personalized plates — Sale of vehicle — Transfer of plates — Release of priority.

If a person who has been issued personalized license plates sells, trades, or otherwise releases ownership of the vehicle for which the personalized license plates have been issued, that person shall immediately:

(1) apply to display the license plates on a different vehicle owned by the person; or

(2) surrender the license plates to the division and release his priority to the letters and numbers displayed on the personalized license plates.
                1993

41-1a-414. Parking privileges for persons with disabilities.

(1) As used in this section, "accessible parking space" means a parking space that is clearly identified as reserved for use by a person with a disability and includes:

(a) vertical signage, including the international symbol of accessibility, that is visible from a passing vehicle; and

(b) a clearly marked access aisle, if provided, that is adjacent to and considered part of the parking space.

(2) Except in parking areas designated for emergency use, a person with a disability, qualifying under rules made in accordance with Section 41-1a-420, may park an appropriately marked vehicle for reasonable periods without charge in metered parking zones and restricted parking areas, in a manner that allows proper access to the vehicle by the person with a disability.

(3) Only those vehicles carrying a person with a disability special group license plate, temporary removable windshield placard, or removable windshield placard and transporting a qualifying person with a disability may park in an accessible parking space.

(4) This section applies to and may be enforced on public property and on private property that is used or intended for use by the public.

(5) The parking privileges granted by this section also apply to vehicles displaying a person with a disability special group license plate, temporary removable windshield placard, or removable windshield placard issued by another jurisdiction if displayed on a vehicle being used by a person with a disability.
                2003

41-1a-415. Lost or damaged license plate.

If a license plate is lost or becomes illegible, the owner of the vehicle for which the license plate was issued shall immediately apply for and obtain a replacement license plate upon the applicant furnishing information satisfactory to the division and paying the applicable fee.   1992

41-1a-416. Original issue license plates — Alternative stickers — Rulemaking.

(1) The owner of a motor vehicle that is a model year 1973 or older may apply to the division for permission to display an original issue license plate of a format and type issued by the state in the same year as the model year of the vehicle.

(2) The owner of a motor vehicle who desires to display original issue license plates instead of license plates issued under Section 41-1a-401 shall:

(a) complete an application on a form provided by the division;

(b) supply and submit the original license plates that the owner desires to display to the division for approval; and

(c) pay the fees prescribed in Sections 41-1a-1206 and 41-1a-1211.

(3) The division, prior to approval of an application under this section, shall determine that the original issue license plates:

(a) are of a format and type issued by the state for use on a motor vehicle in this state;

(b) have numbers and characters that are unique and do not conflict with existing license plate series in this state;

(c) are legible, durable, and otherwise in a condition that serves the purposes of this chapter, except that original issue license plates are exempt from the provision of Section 41-1a-401 regarding reflectorization and Section 41-1a-403 regarding legibility from 100 feet; and

(d) are from the same year of issue as the model year of the motor vehicle on which they are to be displayed.

(4) An owner of a motor vehicle displaying original issue license plates approved under this section is not exempt from any other requirement of this chapter except as specified under this section.

(5) (a) An owner of a motor vehicle currently registered in this state whose original issue license plates are not approved by the division because of the requirement in Subsection (3)(b) may apply to the division for a sticker to allow the temporary display of the original issue license plates if:

(i) the plates otherwise comply with this section;

(ii) the plates are only displayed when the motor vehicle is used for participating in motor vehicle club activities, exhibitions, tours, parades, and similar activities and are not used for general daily transportation;

(iii) the license plates and registration issued under this chapter for normal use of the motor vehicle on the highways of this state are kept in the motor vehicle and shown to a peace officer on request; and

(iv) the sticker issued by the division under this subsection is properly affixed to the face of the original issue license plate.

(b) The sticker issued under this section shall be the size and form customarily furnished by the division.

(6) In accordance with Title 63, Chapter 46a, Utah Administrative Rulemaking Act, the division may make rules for the implementation of this section.
                2001

41-1a-417. Repealed.   2003

41-1a-418. Authorized special group license plates [Effective until October 1, 2005].

(1) The division shall only issue special group license plates in accordance with Sections 41-1a-418 through 41-1a-422 to a person who is specified under this section within the categories listed as follows:

(a) disability special group license plates issued in accordance with Section 41-1a-420;

(b) honor special group license plates, as in a war hero, which plates are issued for a:

(i) survivor of the Japanese attack on Pearl Harbor;

(ii) former prisoner of war; or

(iii) recipient of a Purple Heart;

(c) unique vehicle type special group license plates, as for historical, collectors value, or other unique vehicle type, which plates are issued for a:

(i) special interest vehicle;

(ii) vintage vehicle;

(iii) farm truck; or

(iv) vehicle powered by clean fuel and for which a current clean special fuel certificate is maintained as provided in Section 59-13-304;

(d) recognition special group license plates, as in a public official or an emergency service giver, which plates are issued for a:

(i) current member of the Legislature;

(ii) current member of the United States Congress;

(iii) current member of the National Guard;

(iv) licensed amateur radio operator;

(v) currently employed, volunteer, or retired firefighter;

(vi) emergency medical technician;

(vii) current member of a search and rescue team; or

(viii) current honorary consulate designated by the United States Department of State; and

(e) support special group license plates, as for a contributor to an institution or cause, which plates are issued for a contributor to:

(i) an institution's scholastic scholarship fund;

(ii) the Division of Wildlife Resources;

(iii) the Office of Veterans' Affairs;

(iv) the Division of Parks and Recreation;

(v) the Department of Agriculture and Food;

(vi) the Guardian Ad Litem Services Account and the Children's Museum of Utah;

(vii) the Boy Scouts of America;

(viii) spay and neuter programs through No More Homeless Pets in Utah;

(ix) the Boys and Girls Clubs of America; or

(x) Utah public education.

(2) Beginning January 1, 2003, the division may not issue a new type of special group license plate unless the division receives:

(a) a start-up fee established under Section 63-38-3.2 for production and administrative costs for providing the new special group license plates; or

(b) a legislative appropriation for the start-up fee provided under Subsection (2)(a).

(3) (a) A sponsoring organization that qualifies for tax-exempt status under Internal Revenue Code Section 501(c)(3) may request the commission to authorize a new type of special group license plate for the sponsoring organization. The sponsoring organization shall:

(i) collect a minimum of 200 applications; and

(ii) pay a start-up fee established under Section 63-38-3.2 for production and administrative costs for providing the new type of special group license plates.

(b) If the provisions of Subsection (3)(a) are met, the commission shall approve the request and the division shall:

(i) design a license plate in accordance with Section 41-1a-419; and

(ii) issue the new type of special group license plates.   2003

Authorized special group license plates [Effective October 1, 2005].

(1) The division shall only issue special group license plates in accordance with Sections 41-1a-418 through 41-1a-422 to a person who is specified under this section within the categories listed as follows:

(a) disability special group license plates issued in accordance with Section 41-1a-420;

(b) honor special group license plates, as in a war hero, which plates are issued for a:

(i) survivor of the Japanese attack on Pearl Harbor;

(ii) former prisoner of war;

(iii) recipient of a Purple Heart; or

(iv) disabled veteran;

(c) unique vehicle type special group license plates, as for historical, collectors value, or other unique vehicle type, which plates are issued for a:

(i) special interest vehicle;

(ii) vintage vehicle;

(iii) farm truck; or

(iv) vehicle powered by clean fuel and for which a current clean special fuel certificate is maintained as provided in Section 59-13-304;

(d) recognition special group license plates, as in a public official or an emergency service giver, which plates are issued for a:

(i) current member of the Legislature;

(ii) current member of the United States Congress;

(iii) current member of the National Guard;

(iv) licensed amateur radio operator;

(v) currently employed, volunteer, or retired firefighter;

(vi) emergency medical technician;

(vii) current member of a search and rescue team; or

(viii) current honorary consulate designated by the United States Department of State; and

(e) support special group license plates, as for a contributor to an institution or cause, which plates are issued for a contributor to:

(i) an institution's scholastic scholarship fund;

(ii) the Division of Wildlife Resources;

(iii) the Office of Veterans' Affairs;

(iv) the Division of Parks and Recreation;

(v) the Department of Agriculture and Food;

(vi) the Guardian Ad Litem Services Account and the Children's Museum of Utah;

(vii) the Boy Scouts of America;

(viii) spay and neuter programs through No More Homeless Pets in Utah;

(ix) the Boys and Girls Clubs of America; or

(x) Utah public education.

(2) Beginning January 1, 2003, the division may not issue a new type of special group license plate unless the division receives:

(a) a start-up fee established under Section 63-38-3.2 for production and administrative costs for providing the new special group license plates; or

(b) a legislative appropriation for the start-up fee provided under Subsection (2)(a).

(3) (a) A sponsoring organization that qualifies for tax-exempt status under Internal Revenue Code Section 501(c)(3) may request the commission to authorize a new type of special group license plate for the sponsoring organization. The sponsoring organization shall:

(i) collect a minimum of 200 applications; and

(ii) pay a start-up fee established under Section 63-38-3.2 for production and administrative costs for providing the new type of special group license plates.

(b) If the provisions of Subsection (3)(a) are met, the commission shall approve the request and the division shall:

(i) design a license plate in accordance with Section 41-1a-419; and

(ii) issue the new type of special group license plates.   2005

41-1a-419. Plate design — Vintage vehicle certification and registration — Personalized special group license plates — Rulemaking.

(1) (a) The design and maximum number of numerals or characters on special group license plates shall be determined by the division in accordance with the requirements under Subsection (1)(b).

(b) Each special group license plate shall display:

(i) the word Utah;

(ii) the name or identifying slogan of the special group;

(iii) a symbol decal not exceeding two positions in size representing the special group; and

(iv) the combination of letters, numbers, or both uniquely identifying the registered vehicle.

(2) (a) The division shall, after consultation with a representative designated by the special group, specify the word or words comprising the special group name and the symbol decal to be displayed upon the special group license plates.

(b) A special group license plate symbol decal may not be redesigned:

(i) unless the division receives a redesign fee established by the division under Section 63-38-3.2; and

(ii) more frequently than every five years.

(c) A special group license plate symbol decal may not be reordered unless the division receives a symbol decal reorder fee established by the division under Section 63-38-3.2.

(3) The license plates issued for horseless carriages prior to July 1, 1992, are valid without renewal as long as the vehicle is owned by the registered owner and the license plates may not be recalled by the division.

(4) A person who meets the criteria established under Sections 41-1a-418 through 41-1a-422 for issuance of special group license plates may make application in the same manner provided in Sections 41-1a-410 and 41-1a-411 for personalized special group license plates.

(5) The commission shall make rules in accordance with Title 63, Chapter 46a, Utah Administrative Rulemaking Act, to:

(a) establish qualifying criteria for persons to receive, renew, or surrender special group license plates; and

(b) establish the maximum number of numerals or characters for special group license plates.   2004

41-1a-420. Disability special group license plates — Application and qualifications — Rulemaking.

(1) The division shall issue a disability special group license plate, a temporary removable windshield placard, or a removable windshield placard to:

(a) a qualifying person with a disability; or

(b) the registered owner of a vehicle that an organization uses primarily for the transportation of persons with disabilities that limit or impair the ability to walk.

(2) (a) The initial application of a person with a disability shall be accompanied by the certification of a licensed physician:

(i) that the applicant meets the definition of a person with a disability that limits or impairs the ability to walk as defined in the federal Uniform System for Parking for Persons with Disabilities, 23 C.F.R. Ch. 11, Subch. B, Pt. 1235.2 (1991); and

(ii) containing the period of time that the physician determines the applicant will have the disability, not to exceed six months in the case of a temporary disability.

(b) The division shall issue a person with a disability special group license plate or a removable windshield placard to a person with a permanent disability.

(c) The issuance of a person with a disability special group license plate does not preclude the issuance to the same applicant of a removable windshield placard.

(d) On request of an applicant with a disability special group license plate, temporary removable windshield placard, or a removable windshield placard the division shall issue one additional placard.

(e) A disability special group license plate, temporary removable windshield placard, or removable windshield placard may be used to allow one motorcycle to share a parking space reserved for persons with a disability if:

(i) the person with a disability:

(A) is using a motorcycle; and

(B) displays on the motorcycle a disability special group license plate, temporary removable windshield placard, or a removable windshield placard;

(ii) the person who shares the parking space assists the person with a disability with the parking accommodation; and

(iii) the parking space is sufficient size to accommodate both motorcycles without interfering with other parking spaces or traffic movement.

(3) (a) The temporary removable windshield placard or removable windshield placard shall be hung from the front windshield rearview mirror when the vehicle is parked in a parking space reserved for persons with disabilities so that it is visible from the front and rear of the vehicle.

(b) If a motorcycle is being used, the temporary removable windshield placard or removable windshield placard shall be displayed in plain sight on or near the handle bars of the motorcycle.

(4) The commission shall make rules in accordance with Title 63, Chapter 46a, Utah Administrative Rule-making Act, to:

(a) establish qualifying criteria for persons to receive, renew, or surrender special group license plates, a temporary removable windshield placard, or a removable windshield placard in accordance with this section;

(b) establish the maximum number of numerals or characters for disability special group license plates; and

(c) require all temporary removable windshield placards and removable windshield placards to include:

(i) an identification number;

(ii) an expiration date not to exceed:

(A) six months for a temporary removable windshield placard; and

(B) two years for a removable windshield placard; and

(iii) the seal or other identifying mark of the division.   2005

41-1a-421. Honor special group license plates — Personal identity requirements [Effective until October 1, 2005].

(1) (a) The requirements of this Subsection (1) apply to a vehicle displaying a:

(i) survivor of the Japanese attack on Pearl Harbor license plate;

(ii) former prisoner of war license plate; or

(iii) Purple Heart license plate.

(b) The vehicle shall be titled in the name of the veteran or the veteran and spouse.

(c) Upon the death of the veteran, the surviving spouse may, upon application to the division, retain the special group license plate decal so long as the surviving spouse remains unmarried.

(d) The division shall require the surviving spouse to make a sworn statement that the surviving spouse is unmarried before renewing the registration under this section.

(2) Proper evidence of a Purple Heart is either:

(a) a membership card in the Military Order of the Purple Heart; or

(b) an original or certificate in lieu of the applicant's military discharge form, DD-214, issued by the National Personnel Records Center.

(3) The Purple Heart license plates shall bear:

(a) the words "Purple Heart" at the bottom of the plate;

(b) a logo substantially depicting a Purple Heart award; and

(c) the letter and number combinations assigned by the division.   2003

Honor special group license plates — Personal identity requirements [Effective October 1, 2005].

(1) (a) The requirements of this Subsection (1) apply to a vehicle displaying a:

(i) survivor of the Japanese attack on Pearl Harbor license plate;

(ii) former prisoner of war license plate;

(iii) Purple Heart license plate; or

(iv) disabled veteran license plate.

(b) The vehicle shall be titled in the name of the veteran or the veteran and spouse.

(c) Upon the death of the veteran, the surviving spouse may, upon application to the division, retain the special group license plate decal so long as the surviving spouse remains unmarried.

(d) The division shall require the surviving spouse to make a sworn statement that the surviving spouse is unmarried before renewing the registration under this section.

(2) Proper evidence of a Purple Heart is either:

(a) a membership card in the Military Order of the Purple Heart; or

(b) an original or certificate in lieu of the applicant's military discharge form, DD-214, issued by the National Personnel Records Center.

(3) The Purple Heart license plates shall bear:

(a) the words "Purple Heart" at the bottom of the plate;

(b) a logo substantially depicting a Purple Heart award; and

(c) the letter and number combinations assigned by the division.

(4) Proper evidence that a person is a disabled veteran is a written document issued by a military entity certifying that the person is disabled as a result of service in a branch of the United States Military.

(5) A disabled veteran seeking a disabled veteran license plate shall request the Division of Veterans' Affairs to provide the verification required under Subsection (4).   2005

41-1a-422. Support special group license plates — Contributor — Voluntary contribution collection procedures.

(1) As used in this section:

(a) (i) Except as provided in Subsection (1)(a)(ii), "contributor" means a person who has donated or in whose name at least $25 has been donated to:

(A) a scholastic scholarship fund of a single named institution;

(B) the Division of Veterans' Affairs in the Utah National Guard for veterans' programs;

(C) the Division of Wildlife Resources for the Wildlife Resources Account created in Section 23-14-13, for conservation of wildlife and the enhancement, preservation, protection, access, and management of wildlife habitat;

(D) the Department of Agriculture and Food for the benefit of soil conservation districts;

(E) the Division of Parks and Recreation for the benefit of snowmobile programs;

(F) the Guardian Ad Litem Services Account and the Children's Museum of Utah, with the donation evenly divided between the two;

(G) the Boy Scouts of America for the benefit of a Utah Boy Scouts of America council as specified by the contributor;

(H) No More Homeless Pets in Utah for distribution to organizations or individuals that provide spay and neuter programs that subsidize the sterilization of domestic animals;

(I) the Utah Alliance of Boys and Girls Clubs, Inc. to provide and enhance youth development programs; or

(J) the Utah Association of Public School Foundations to support public education.

(ii) For a veterans' special group license plate, "contributor" means a person who has donated or in whose name at least a $25 donation at the time of application and $10 annual donation thereafter has been made.

(b) "Institution" means a state institution of higher education as defined under Section 53B-3-102 or a private institution of higher education in the state accredited by a regional or national accrediting agency recognized by the United States Department of Education.

(2) (a) An applicant for original or renewal collegiate special group license plates under Subsection (1)(a)(i) must be a contributor to the institution named in the application and present the original contribution verification form under Subsection (2)(b) or make a contribution to the division at the time of application under Subsection (3).

(b) An institution with a support special group license plate shall issue to a contributor a verification form designed by the commission containing:

(i) the name of the contributor;

(ii) the institution to which a donation was made;

(iii) the date of the donation; and

(iv) an attestation that the donation was for a scholastic scholarship.

(c) The state auditor may audit each institution to verify that the moneys collected by the institutions from contributors are used for scholastic scholarships.

(d) After an applicant has been issued collegiate license plates or renewal decals, the commission shall charge the institution whose plate was issued, a fee determined in accordance with Section 63-38-3.2 for management and administrative expenses incurred in issuing and renewing the collegiate license plates.

(e) If the contribution is made at the time of application, the contribution shall be collected, treated, and deposited as provided under Subsection (3).

(3) (a) An applicant for original or renewal support special group license plates under this section must be a contributor to the sponsoring organization associated with the license plate.

(b) This contribution shall be:

(i) unless collected by the named institution under Subsection (2), collected by the division;

(ii) considered a voluntary contribution for the funding of the activities specified under this section and not a motor vehicle registration fee; and

(iii) deposited into the appropriate account less actual administrative costs associated with issuing the license plates.

(c) The donation described in Subsection (1)(a) must be made in the 12 months prior to registration or renewal of registration.

(d) The donation described in Subsection (1)(a) shall be a one-time donation made to the division when issuing original:

(i) snowmobile license plates; or

(ii) soil conservation license plates.

(4) Veterans' license plates shall display one of the symbols representing the Army, Navy, Air Force, Marines, Coast Guard, or American Legion.   2004

PART 5

TITLING REQUIREMENT

41-1a-501.   Certificate of title required.

Unless exempted, each owner of a motor vehicle, vessel, outboard motor, trailer, semitrailer, manufactured home, mobile home, or off-highway vehicle shall apply to the division for a certificate of title on forms furnished by the division as evidence of ownership.   1992

41-1a-502.   Repealed.   1992

41-1a-503.   Certificate of title or Affidavit of Mobile Home Affixture required — Application by owner.

(1) The owner of a manufactured home or mobile home shall apply to the division for a certificate of title or an Affidavit of Mobile Home Affixture.

(2) (a) An owner of a manufactured home or mobile home previously issued a certificate of title who attaches that home to real property shall apply for an Affidavit of Mobile Home Affixture within 30 days of attaching to the property.

(b) Upon application, the division shall issue an Affidavit of Mobile Home Affixture in lieu of a certificate of title.

(c) However, manufactured homes and mobile homes are not exempt from the other requirements of this part.

(3) (a) The owner of a manufactured home or mobile home previously issued an Affidavit of Mobile Home Affixture who separates that home from the real property shall apply for a certificate of title within 30 days of the separation, prior to any transfer of ownership of that home.

(b) Upon application, the division shall issue a certificate of title in lieu of an Affidavit of Mobile Home Affixture.   1992

41-1a-504.   Exceptions to title requirements for vehicles.

Each vehicle operated in this state is subject to the titling provisions of this part except:

(1) special mobile equipment;

(2) a vehicle owned or leased by the federal government;

(3) a trailer of 750 pounds or less unladen weight and not designed, used, and maintained for hire for the transportation of property or persons; and

(4) modular and prebuilt homes conforming to the Uniform Building Code and presently regulated by the United States Department of Housing and Urban Development that are not constructed on a permanent chassis.   1992

41-1a-505.   Exceptions to title requirements for vessels and outboard motors.

(1) Each vessel or outboard motor, identified by the manufacturer as a 1985 year model or newer, operated on the waters of this state is subject to the title provisions of this part except:

(a) vessels that have valid marine documents issued by the United States Coast Guard;

(b) canoes;

(c) inflatable vessels powered by an outboard motor with a manufacturer's listed horsepower of 25 or less;

(d) outboard motors with a manufacturer's listed horsepower of 25 or less;

(e) vessels and outboard motors owned and operated by nonresidents of the state;

(f) vessels or outboard motors owned and operated by the federal government; or

(g) vessels exempt from registration under Section 73-18-9.

(2) The division may not provide a title on vessels and outboard motors identified by the manufacturer as a 1984 year model or older.   1992

41-1a-506. Exceptions to title requirements for manufactured homes or mobile homes.

(1) Each manufactured home or mobile home in this state is subject to the titling provisions of this part except:

(a) manufactured homes and mobile homes owned and operated by the federal government; and

(b) manufactured homes and mobile homes that have been converted to real property under Section 70D-1-20 if:

(i) an Affidavit Of Mobile Home Affixture has been issued by the division for that home; and

(ii) the home is permanently affixed to real property.

(2) A manufactured home or mobile home previously converted to real property but that has been separated from the real property is subject to the titling provisions of this part upon separation.   2005

41-1a-507. Exceptions to title requirements for off-highway vehicles.

(1) Each off-highway vehicle operated in this state and identified by the manufacturer as a 1988 year model or newer is subject to the titling provisions of this part except:

(a) off-highway vehicles owned and operated by nonresidents of the state;

(b) off-highway vehicles owned and operated by the federal government; and

(c) off-highway vehicles that are registered for highway use.

(2) The division may not provide title to an off-highway vehicle identified by the manufacturer as a 1987 year model or older.   1992

41-1a-508. Prerequisites for titling.

(1) Except as otherwise provided, prior to titling a vehicle, vessel, or outboard motor an owner must provide evidence of:

(a) title or ownership under Section 41-1a-509;

(b) payment of sales taxes in accordance with Section 41-1a-510;

(c) payment of all applicable fees under Part 12, Fee and Tax Requirements;

(d) the identification number inspection required under Section 41-1a-511;

(e) the odometer statement required under Section 41-1a-902; and

(f) evidence of property tax clearance for manufactured homes and mobile homes.

(2) An application for registration or current registration is not a prerequisite for obtaining a title.   1992

41-1a-509. Manufacturer's certificate of origin or title.

(1) If a vehicle other than an off-highway vehicle older than a 1988 model year, or a vessel or outboard motor older than a 1985 model year has not been previously titled, the application for certificate of title shall include the manufacturer's certificate of origin properly endorsed for transfer.

(2) The manufacturer's certificate of origin shall show:

(a) the date of sale to the dealer or person first receiving it from the manufacturer;

(b) the name of the dealer or person;

(c) a description sufficient to identify the vehicle, vessel, or outboard motor; and

(d) a certification by the dealer that the vehicle, vessel, or outboard motor was new when sold to the applicant.

(3) (a) If the vehicle, vessel, or outboard motor is from a state or foreign country that does not issue or require certificates of title, the owner shall submit a bill of sale, sworn statement of ownership, or any other evidence of ownership required by the division.

(b) The division may refuse to issue a certificate of title or an affidavit of Mobile Home Affixture if the applicant fails to submit the evidence of ownership required.   1992

41-1a-510. Sales tax payment required.

(1) (a) Except as provided in Subsection (b), the division before issuing a certificate of title to a vehicle, vessel, or outboard motor shall require from every applicant:

(i) a receipt from the division showing that the sales tax has been paid to the state on the sale of the vehicle, vessel, or outboard motor upon which application for certificate of title has been made; or

(ii) a certificate from the division showing that no sales tax is due.

(b) If a licensed dealer has made a report of sale, no receipt or certificate is required.

(2) The division may also issue an Affidavit of Mobile Home Affixture for a manufactured home or mobile home if the applicant complies with Subsection (1).   1992

41-1a-511. Identification number inspection.

An application for a certificate of title for a vehicle, vessel, or outboard motor not previously titled in this state shall be accompanied by a certificate of identification number inspection obtained in accordance with Section 41-1a-802, unless the vehicle, vessel, or outboard motor is new and was acquired from an in-state dealer or in-state manufacturer.   1992

41-1a-512. Application for title.

(1) The application for a certificate of title shall include:

(a) the signature of a person to be recorded on the certificate as owner;

(b) the name, bona fide residence and mailing address of the owner, or business address of the owner if the owner is a firm, association, or corporation;

(c) a description of the vehicle, vessel, or outboard motor, including the make, model, type of body, the model year as specified by the manufacturer, the number of cylinders, the identification number of the vehicle, vessel, or outboard motor, as applicable, and other information the division may require;

(d) other information required by the division to enable it to determine whether the owner is entitled to a certificate of title;

(e) a statement of one lien or encumbrance, if any, upon the vehicle, vessel, or outboard motor; and

(f) the names and addresses of all persons having any ownership interest in the vehicle, vessel, or outboard motor and the nature of the ownership interest.

(2) An application for a certificate of title for a new vehicle, vessel, or outboard motor purchased from a dealer shall be accompanied by a statement by the dealer or a bill of sale showing any lien retained by the dealer.   2002

41-1a-513. Examination of registration records and indices of stolen and recovered vehicles, vessels, and outboard motors.

The division upon receiving application for any certificate of title shall first check the identification number shown in the application against the indices of registered vehicles, vessels, and outboard motors and against indices of stolen and recovered vehicles, vessels, and outboard motors. 1992

41-1a-514. Certificate of title — Contents.

(1) The division upon approving an application for a certificate of title shall issue a certificate of title. The face of the certificate of title shall include:

(a) the date issued;

(b) the name and address of the owner;

(c) a description of the vehicle, vessel, or outboard motor titled, including the year, make, and identification number;

(d) a statement of the owner's title and of one lien or encumbrance, if any, upon the vehicle, vessel, or outboard motor;

(e) any brand on the title; and

(f) an odometer statement, if applicable.

(2) The certificate of title shall bear the seal of the division.

(3) The certificate of title shall contain adequate space for:

(a) the assignment and warranty of title or interest by the owner;

(b) the release of interest by a recorded lien holder; and

(c) the notation of one lien or encumbrance, if any, existing at the time of transfer. 1992

41-1a-515. Delivery of certificate by division.

(1) The division shall deliver the certificate of title to the owner if no lien or encumbrance is recorded on it. The division shall deliver the certificate to the person holding the first lien or encumbrance as recorded on the certificate.

(2) The certificate of title shall be delivered:

(a) in person;

(b) through the United States mail; or

(c) electronically.

(3) If delivered through the United States mail, receipt of the certificate of title is presumed four days after the mail has been posted. 2004

41-1a-516. Annual renewal of titles unnecessary — Superseded certificates invalid.

(1) Certificates of title need not be renewed annually but shall remain valid until canceled by the division for cause or upon a transfer of any interest shown on the certificate.

(2) A certificate of title is invalid when superseded by a duplicate certificate issued under Section 41-1a-518 or when the certificate has been superseded by a certificate issued by another state or country. 1992

41-1a-517. Change of name — New title.

(1) If the name of any person who has made application for or obtained a certificate of title is legally changed, the person shall surrender the certificate and file an application for a new certificate of title.

(2) The division upon receipt of the required fees shall issue a new certificate of title. 1992

41-1a-518. Duplicate titles.

(1) (a) If a certificate of title is lost, stolen, mutilated, or becomes illegible, the owner, legal representative, or successor in interest of the owner of the vehicle, vessel, or outboard motor for which the certificate was issued, as shown by the records of the division, shall immediately apply for and may obtain a duplicate upon furnishing information satisfactory to the division.

(b) A certificate of title issued under this section shall have printed or stamped in ink upon its face "duplicate".

(c) The duplicate certificate, when properly issued, supersedes and invalidates all other certificates previously issued.

(2) (a) When the application for a duplicate certificate of title is accompanied by a proper release of interest from the owner or owners of record and a proper release of interest from the lienholder of record and the release is accompanied by a proper application to title the vehicle, vessel, or outboard motor in the name of the new owner or owners, a duplicate certificate need not be made.

(b) The division may issue a certificate of title in the name of the new owner or owners.

(c) The duplicate title fees provided under Part 12, Fee and Tax Requirements, apply. 1992

41-1a-519. Dealer requirements for certificate of title or Affidavit of Mobile Home Affixture.

(1) If a dealer delivers a new off-highway vehicle, vessel, or outboard motor to the purchaser, the dealer shall apply for issuance of a certificate of title or Affidavit of Mobile Home Affixture, as appropriate, in the purchaser's name within 30 days of the date of sale.

(2) A dealer who purchases or takes in trade a used off-highway vehicle, vessel, or outboard motor on which a certificate of title has previously been issued is not required to apply for a certificate of title. 1993

41-1a-520. Registration without issuing Utah title.

(1) If a person is relocating from another jurisdiction and establishing residence in this state, whether temporary or permanent, and that person has a vehicle registered and titled in another jurisdiction and is not able to surrender title to the vehicle being registered in the state because title is physically held by a lienholder, the division may register the vehicle without issuing a title.

(2) Upon satisfaction of the lien outstanding against the vehicle in the other jurisdiction, the registered owner shall within ten days of receipt surrender the title from the other jurisdiction to the division and make application for a title. 1992

41-1a-521. Release of prior certificate of title.

Every application for a certificate of title for a vehicle, vessel, or outboard motor for which a certificate of title has previously been issued in this state or another jurisdiction shall be accompanied by the certificate of title. 1992

41-1a-522. Record of nonconforming vehicle — Access — Brand — Unbranding.

(1) The definitions in Section 41-3-407 apply to this section.

(2) Upon receipt of a copy of an original certificate of title, Manufacturer's Statement of Origin, or other evidence of ownership of a nonconforming vehicle in accordance with Section 41-3-409, the division shall:

(a) establish a record of the reported nonconforming vehicle;

(b) consider the record a public record with public access under Sections 41-1a-116 and 63-2-201;

(c) allow access to the record upon written application to the division; and

(d) upon request for a new certificate of title for a nonconforming vehicle, brand the certificate of title with the words "MANUFACTURER BUYBACK NONCONFORMING VEHICLE" clearly and conspicuously on the face of the new certificate of title.

(3) Upon receipt of the branded certificate of title, the division shall:

(a) follow the procedures established in Subsection (2); or

(b) if the record of the nonconforming vehicle contains an application for an unbranded certificate of title that meets the requirements of Section 41-3-409.5:

(i) update the record to show that all nonconformities have been cured;

(ii) consider the record a public record with public access under Sections 41-1a-116 and 63-2-201;

(iii) allow access to the complete record upon written application to the division; and

(iv) upon request for a new certificate of title, issue an unbranded certificate of title.

1994

PART 6

LIENS AND SECURITY INTERESTS

41-1a-601. Lien validity — Security interest.

(1) Except as provided under Subsection (2), a lien upon a vehicle, vessel, or outboard motor, except a lien dependent upon possession, is not valid against the creditors of an owner acquiring a lien by levy or attachment, or subsequent purchasers, or encumbrancers without notice until Sections 41-1a-602 through 41-1a-606 have been complied with.

(2) Security interests in inventory consisting in part of vehicles subject to registration under this chapter, that are held for sale by a person in the business of selling goods of that kind, shall be perfected under Section 70A-9a-310, except that buyers in the ordinary course of business, as defined in Section 70A-1-201, take free of the security interests as provided in Section 70A-9a-320.   2000

41-1a-602. Application for original registration.

(1) (a) If a vehicle is of a type subject to registration but has not been registered and no certificate of title has been issued, or if the vehicle has been registered or titled in another state or country, the owner shall file an application in the form for an original registration and issuance of an original certificate of title.

(b) If the vehicle ownership has changed, the owner shall file an application in the form for an original certificate of title.

(2) Each application shall be accompanied by all applicable taxes and fees under Part 12, Fee and Tax Requirements.   1992

41-1a-603. Issuance of new certificate of title — Lienholder.

(1) Upon receipt of a title application the division shall file the application, and when satisfied as to the authenticity of the application, shall issue a new certificate of title in usual form, giving the name of the owner and a statement of one lien or encumbrance, if any, certified to the division as existing against the vehicle, vessel, or outboard motor.

(2) If a certificate of title has been issued, and the same lienholder as shown by the records of the division only grants additional funds to the same owner as shown by the records of the division, no further recording is required and no subsequent certificate of title need be applied for or issued, if the original certificate or valid duplicate has remained in possession of the lienholder and the lien has not been released and the certificate has not been delivered to the owner.   1992

41-1a-604. Filing effective to give notice of liens.

The filing and the issuance of a new certificate of title under Sections 41-1a-602 and 41-1a-603 constitute constructive notice of all liens and encumbrances against the vehicle, vessel, and outboard motor to creditors of the owner and to subsequent purchasers and encumbrancers.   1992

41-1a-605. Date of constructive notice.

If the documents referred to in Section 41-1a-602 are received and filed with the division within 30 days after the date the documents were executed, the constructive notice dates from the time of the execution of the documents; otherwise, constructive notice dates from the time of receipt and filing of the documents by the division as shown by its endorsement.   1992

41-1a-606. Method of giving notice — Exceptions.

The method provided in Sections 41-1a-602 through 41-1a-605, for giving constructive notice of a lien or encumbrance upon a registered vehicle is exclusive except for liens dependent upon possession and any lien or encumbrance filed as provided under this chapter, which are exempt from the provisions of Section 70A-9a-311, and other provisions of law that otherwise require or relate to the recording or filing of instruments creating or evidencing title retention or other liens or encumbrances upon vehicles of a type subject to registration under this chapter.   2000

41-1a-607. Assignment by lienholder.

(1) (a) Any person holding a lien or encumbrance upon a vehicle, vessel, or outboard motor, other than a lien dependent solely upon possession, may assign his title or interest in or to the vehicle, vessel, or outboard motor to a person other than the owner without the consent of and without affecting the interest of the owner or the registration of the vehicle, vessel, or outboard motor.

(b) If assignment of the lien or encumbrance in any way modifies or affects the owner's repayment agreement, the lien or encumbrance holder shall give to the owner a written notice of the assignment.

(2) Upon request to the division and upon receipt of a certificate of title assigned by the holder of a lien or encumbrance shown on it and giving the name and address of the assignee, accompanied by the fee provided by law, the division shall issue a new certificate of title.   1992

41-1a-608. Release by lienholder to owner.

(1) A person holding a lien or encumbrance as shown upon a certificate of title upon a vehicle or vessel may release the lien or encumbrance or assign his interest to the owner without affecting the registration of the vehicle or vessel.

(2) The division shall issue a new certificate of title without a lien previously recorded upon receiving:

(a) a certificate of title:

(i) upon which a lienholder has released or assigned his interest to the owner; or

(ii) not so endorsed but accompanied by a legal release from a lienholder of his interest in or to a vehicle, vessel, or outboard motor;

(b) an application properly completed; and

(c) the proper fee.   1992

41-1a-609. Terminal rental adjustment clauses.

(1) As used in this section, "terminal rental adjustment clause" means a provision of an agreement that permits or requires the rental price to be adjusted upward or downward by reference to the amount realized by the lessor under the agreement upon sale or other disposition of the property.

(2) Notwithstanding any other provision of law, a motor vehicle or trailer lease agreement that is subject to a terminal rental adjustment clause does not create a sale or security interest.

(3) The provisions of this section do not affect:

(a) the rights and obligations of a valid security interest under this chapter; or

(b) the calculation of sales and use tax payable under Title 59, Chapter 12, Sales and Use Tax Act.   2003

PART 7

TRANSFER OF OWNERSHIP

41-1a-701. Transfer by owner — Removal of plates.

(1) If the owner of a registered vehicle transfers his title or interest to the vehicle the registration of the vehicle expires. The owner shall remove the license plates from the transferred vehicle.

(2) Within 20 days from the date of transfer the owner shall forward the plates to the division to be destroyed or may have the plates and the registration number assigned to another vehicle, subject to the rules of the division.   1993

41-1a-702. Endorsement of assignment and warranty of title — Co-owners.

(1) (a) To transfer a vehicle, vessel, or outboard motor the owner shall endorse the certificate of title issued for the vehicle, vessel, or outboard motor in the space for assignment and warranty of title.

(b) The endorsement and assignment shall include a statement of all liens or encumbrances on the vehicle, vessel, or outboard motor.

(2) (a) If a title certificate reflects the names of two or more people as co-owners in the alternative by use of the word "or" or "and/or," each co-owner is considered to have granted the other co-owners the absolute right to endorse and deliver title and to dispose of the vehicle, vessel, or outboard motor.

(b) If the title certificate reflects the names of two or more people as co-owners in the conjunctive by use of the word "and," or the title does not reflect any alternative or conjunctive word, the endorsement of each co-owner is required to transfer title to the vehicle, vessel, or outboard motor.

(3) The owner shall deliver the certificate of title containing the odometer disclosure statement required under Section 41-1a-902 and the certificate of registration to the purchaser or transferee at the time of, or within 48 hours after delivering the vehicle, vessel, or outboard motor, as applicable, except as provided for under Sections 41-3-301, 41-1a-519, and 41-1a-709.   1993

41-1a-703. New owner to secure new registration and new certificate of title.

The transferee before operating or permitting the operation of a transferred vehicle on a highway shall present to the division the certificate of registration and the certificate of title, properly endorsed, and shall apply for a new certificate of title and obtain a new registration for the transferred vehicle, as upon an original registration, except as permitted under Sections 41-1a-223, 41-1a-520, and 41-1a-704.   1992

41-1a-704. Transfer by operation of law.

(1) Except as provided under Subsection (2), if the title or interest of an owner in or to a registered vehicle passes to another person other than by voluntary transfer:

(a) the registration of the vehicle expires; and

(b) the vehicle may not be operated upon a highway until the person entitled to possession of the vehicle applies for and obtains a valid registration or temporary permit.

(2) (a) A vehicle under Subsection (1) may be operated on the highways by the person entitled to its possession or his legal representative, for a distance not exceeding 75 miles, upon displaying on the vehicle the license plates issued to the former owner.

(b) If title is vested in a person holding a lien or encumbrance on the vehicle, the new title holder may apply to the Motor Vehicle Enforcement Division for special plates issued under Section 41-3-505 to transporters and may operate the repossessed vehicle under the special plate for the purposes of:

(i) transporting the vehicle to a garage or warehouse; or

(ii) demonstrating the vehicle for sale.   1992

41-1a-705. New owner may register and title or upon transfer execute an assignment.

(1) The new owner of a transferred vehicle, vessel, or outboard motor may either obtain a new registration and certificate of title for the vehicle, vessel, or outboard motor transferred to him or transfer his title or interest in that vehicle, vessel, or outboard motor to a third party.

(2) A transferee may title a vehicle, vessel, or outboard motor by completing an application and presenting to the division a properly endorsed certificate of title, duplicate certificate of title, or other document of authority along with any additional documents the division may require to transfer the title.   1992

41-1a-706. When division to transfer and issue new certificate.

The division shall reregister a vehicle in the name of the new owner and issue a new certificate of registration and a new certificate of title:

(1) upon receipt of the:

(a) properly endorsed certificate of title;

(b) certificate of registration;

(c) proper application for registration; and

(d) required fee; and

(2) when satisfied as to the genuineness and regularity of the transfer and the right of the transferee to a certificate of title.   1992

41-1a-707. Repealed.   1995

41-1a-708. Owner not liable for negligent operation after transfer.

The owner of a vehicle or vessel who has made a bona fide sale or transfer of his title or interest and who has delivered to the purchaser or transferee possession of the vehicle or vessel, the certificate of registration, and the properly endorsed certificate of title to the vehicle or vessel is not liable for any damages thereafter resulting from negligent operation of the vehicle or vessel by another.   1992

41-1a-709. Dealer transfer of used off-highway vehicle, vessel, or outboard motor.

Upon the resale or subsequent transfer by a dealer of a used off-highway vehicle, vessel, or outboard motor, the dealer shall endorse the certificate of title and forward it, accompanied by the transferee's application for a certificate of title, or if desired by the purchaser, and as applicable, an affidavit of Mobile Home Affixture, to the division.   1993

41-1a-710. Certificate of origin required for acquisition or resale of vehicle, vessel, or outboard motor.

(1) A dealer may not acquire a new vehicle, vessel, or outboard motor without obtaining a manufacturer's or importer's certificate of origin.

(2) A manufacturer, importer, dealer, or other person may not sell or otherwise dispose of a vehicle, vessel, or outboard motor for purposes of resale without delivering a manufacturer's or importer's certificate of origin to the purchaser or the new owner.

(3) The division may prescribe uniform standards for the size and content of certificates of origin.   1992

41-1a-711. Compliance of foreign motor vehicle required prior to sale — Penalty.

(1) A person may not knowingly sell or offer for sale in this state any vehicle referred to in Section 41-1a-225 without providing to the purchaser at the time of purchase evidence of:

    (a) legal entry of the vehicle into the United States from the United States Customs Service; and

    (b) compliance with the United States Environmental Protection Agency and the United States Department of Transportation requirements applicable to the vehicle.

(2) It is a class A misdemeanor to violate this section.   1993

41-1a-712. Foreign vehicle disclosure requirements — Penalties — Civil damages.

(1) A person may not knowingly sell or offer for sale in this state any vehicle that was initially delivered for disposition or sale in a country other than the United States of America unless, prior to the sale, the person provides written notice to the purchaser on a separate form furnished by the Motor Vehicle Enforcement Division that indicates:

    (a) that the vehicle was initially delivered for disposition or sale in a country outside of the United States as indicated on the Manufacturer's Statement of Origin or similar ownership document;

    (b) the country where the vehicle was initially delivered for the disposition or sale; and

    (c) any other information required by the commission under rules made by the commission in accordance with Title 63, Chapter 46a, Utah Administrative Rulemaking Act.

(2) A person who violates this section is guilty of a class B misdemeanor.

(3) (a) In addition to any other penalties, a purchaser may bring a civil action to recover damages resulting from a seller's failure to provide notice as required under this section.

    (b) The amount of damages that may be recovered in a civil action are the actual damages or $1,500, whichever is greater.   2003

PART 8

IDENTIFICATION NUMBERS

41-1a-801. Altered or changed identification number — State assigned identification number.

(1) The owner of a vehicle required to be registered under this chapter, the identification number of which has been altered, removed, defaced, or has not been placed on it shall make application in the form prescribed by the division for a state assigned identification number.

(2) The owner shall furnish information that will satisfy the division that he is the owner of the vehicle and furnish information to identify the vehicle with the registration of the vehicle for the current year, at which time the division shall assign a state identification number for the vehicle.

(3) A record of state assigned numbers shall be maintained by the division.

(4) The state assigned identification number is the identification number of the vehicle when:

    (a) the owner has stamped the state assigned identification number upon the vehicle as directed by the division;

    (b) a qualified identification number inspector has inspected and found the state assigned identification number stamped upon the vehicle as directed;

    (c) the owner has provided the division with a certificate of inspection; and

    (d) the owner has submitted an application for a certificate of title.   1992

41-1a-802. Identification number inspectors — Duties.

(1) The following are qualified identification number inspectors:

    (a) the commission;

    (b) designated officers and employees of the division;

    (c) a person operating a safety inspection station under Title 53, Chapter 8, Part 2, Motor Vehicle Safety Inspection Act;

    (d) an official inspection station certified inspector;

    (e) a dealer licensed under Subsection 41-3-202(1), (2), (3), or (4); and

    (f) all peace officers of the state.

(2) The qualified identification number inspectors shall, upon the application for the first registration in this state of any vehicle:

    (a) inspect the identification number of the vehicle;

    (b) make a record of the identification number inspection upon an application form provided by the division; and

    (c) verify the facts in the application.   2005

41-1a-803. Identification numbers — Assigning numbers — Requirement for sale.

(1) (a) If a vehicle, vessel, or outboard motor has a permanent manufacturer's identification number, the number shall be used as the vehicle's, vessel's, or outboard motor's identification number.

    (b) If it has no permanent manufacturer's identification number, the division shall assign an identification number to it.

(c) An identification number assigned by the division shall be permanently affixed or imprinted on the vehicle, vessel, or outboard motor as directed by the division.

(2) A person may not sell or offer for sale in this state a new vehicle, vessel, or outboard motor without an identification number.

(3) (a) Each permanent manufacturer's identification number for a vehicle shall be clearly marked in an accessible place on a vehicle.

(b) (i) Each permanent manufacturer's identification number for a vessel shall be clearly marked in an accessible place on the starboard outboard side of the transom or to the starboard outboard side of the hull.

(ii) If the permanent manufacturer's identification number is displayed in a location other than on or near the starboard outboard side of the transom, the manufacturer shall notify the division of its location.

(4) A person may not destroy, remove, alter, or cover an identification number.   1992

41-1a-804. Garagemen, repair shops, and service stations — Duty to report number violations.

A person owning, conducting, managing, or operating a service station, marina, marine dealership, public garage, paint shop, or repair shop for vehicles, vessels, or outboard motors shall immediately notify the local peace officers of any vehicle, vessel, or outboard motor that has any identification number that has apparently been altered, obliterated, or removed.   1992

PART 9

ODOMETERS

41-1a-901. Odometer required.

Each motor vehicle required to be registered under this chapter shall be equipped with a properly functioning odometer.   1992

41-1a-902. Odometer disclosure statement — Contents — Receipt — Exceptions.

(1) Each motor vehicle certificate of title, at the time it is issued to the transferee, shall contain:

(a) the mileage disclosed by the transferor when ownership of the motor vehicle was transferred; and

(b) a space for the information required to be disclosed under this section at the time of future transfer of ownership.

(2) At the time of any sale or transfer of a motor vehicle, the transferor shall furnish to the transferee a written odometer disclosure statement in a form prescribed by the division. This statement shall be signed and certified as to its truthfulness by the transferor, stating:

(a) the date of transfer;

(b) the transferor's name and address;

(c) the transferee's name and address;

(d) the identity of the motor vehicle, including its make, model, year, body type, and identification number;

(e) the odometer reading at the time of transfer, not including tenths of miles or tenths of kilometers;

(f) (i) that to the best of the transferor's knowledge, the odometer reading reflects the amount of miles or kilometers the motor vehicle has actually been driven;

(ii) that the odometer reading reflects the amount of miles or kilometers in excess of the designed mechanical odometer limit; or

(iii) that the odometer reading is not the actual amount of miles or kilometers; and

(g) a warning to alert the transferee if a discrepancy exists between the odometer reading and the actual mileage.

(3) (a) Each transferee of a motor vehicle shall acknowledge receipt of the odometer disclosure statement required by Subsection (2) by signing it, and the transferor shall deliver to the transferee the original odometer disclosure statement. Both the transferor and the transferee shall retain a legible copy of the odometer disclosure statement for not less than four years.

(b) A dealer who is required under Section 41-3-301 to title and register a motor vehicle sold to a customer shall surrender the original odometer disclosure statement to the division and deliver a copy to the transferee.

(4) Notwithstanding the requirements of this section, the odometer mileage need not be disclosed by a transferor of:

(a) a single motor vehicle having a manufacturer specified gross laden weight rating of more than 16,000 pounds, or a motor vehicle registered in this state for a gross laden weight of 18,000 pounds or more;

(b) a motor vehicle that is ten years old or older;

(c) a motor vehicle sold directly by the manufacturer to any agency of the United States in conformity with contractual specifications; or

(d) a new motor vehicle prior to its first transfer for purposes other than resale.

(5) If the motor vehicle has not been titled or if the certificate of title does not contain a space for the information required, the written disclosure shall be executed as a separate document.

(6) A person may not sign an odometer disclosure statement as both the transferor and the transferee in the same transaction.   1992

41-1a-903. Leased motor vehicles — Disclosure of odometer information.

(1) (a) Before executing any transfer of ownership document, each lessor of a leased motor vehicle shall notify the lessee in writing that the lessee is required to provide a written disclosure to the lessor regarding the mileage.

(b) This notice shall state that failure to complete or providing false information may result in fines, imprisonment, or both.

(2) (a) In connection with the transfer of ownership of the leased motor vehicle, the lessee shall furnish to the lessor a written statement regarding the mileage of the motor vehicle.

(b) This statement must be signed by the lessee and shall contain all of the information required by Section 41-1a-902 and in addition the name and address of the lessee and the lessor.

(c) The statement shall be signed and certified as to its truthfulness by the lessee.   1992

41-1a-904. Retention of statements by dealers — Inspection.

(1) Each dealer required to execute and furnish an odometer mileage disclosure statement under Section 41-1a-902 shall retain at its primary place of business for four years after each transfer of a motor vehicle each statement that he receives and a legible copy of

each statement that he issues in connection with those transfers.

(2) These statements shall be available for inspection by, and copies shall be furnished to, any peace officer during reasonable business hours.   1992

41-1a-905. Division to print mileage on certificate of title — Exceptions — Owner to record mileage on application.

(1) The division, before accepting an application for transfer of ownership of a motor vehicle under Part 7, Transfer of Ownership, shall require the transferee to furnish the completed odometer disclosure statement required by Section 41-1a-902 and shall, upon the transfer of ownership, print the mileage on the new certificate of title.

(2) This section does not apply to motor vehicles exempted from mileage disclosure statements under Section 41-1a-902.

(3) The division, before accepting any application for renewal of registration of a motor vehicle, shall require the owner to record the actual miles on the application.   1992

41-1a-906. Repair or replacement of odometer — Notice affixed to motor vehicle.

(1) Sections 41-1a-902 through 41-1a-905 do not prevent the repair or replacement of an odometer, provided the mileage indicated on the odometer remains the same as before the repair or replacement.

(2) Where the odometer is incapable of registering the same mileage as before the repair or replacement, the odometer shall be adjusted to zero and a notice in writing shall be affixed by the owner to the left door frame of the motor vehicle specifying the mileage prior to repair or replacement of the odometer and the date it was repaired or replaced.   1992

PART 10

SALVAGE VEHICLES — JUNK AND DISMANTLED VEHICLES

41-1a-1001. Definitions.

As used in Sections 41-1a-1001 through 41-1a-1008:

(1) "Certified vehicle inspector" means a person employed by the Motor Vehicle Enforcement Division as qualified through experience, training, or both to identify and analyze damage to vehicles with either unibody or conventional frames.

(2) "Major component part" means:

(a) the front body component of a motor vehicle consisting of the structure forward of the firewall;

(b) the passenger body component of a motor vehicle including the firewall, roof, and extending to and including the rear-most seating;

(c) the rear body component of a motor vehicle consisting of the main cross member directly behind the rear-most seating excluding any auxiliary seating and structural body assembly rear of the cross members; and

(d) the frame of a motor vehicle consisting of the structural member that supports the auto body.

(3) (a) "Major damage" means damage to a major component part of the motor vehicle requiring ten or more hours to repair or replace, as determined by a collision estimating guide recognized by the Motor Vehicle Enforcement Division.

(b) For purposes of Subsection (a) repair or replacement hours do not include time spent on cosmetic repairs.

(4) "Owner" means the person who has the legal right to possession of the vehicle.

(5) (a) "Salvage certificate" means a certificate of ownership issued for a salvage vehicle before a new certificate of title is issued for the vehicle.

(b) A salvage certificate is not valid for registration purposes.

(6) "Salvage vehicle" means any vehicle:

(a) damaged by collision, flood, or other occurrence to the extent that the cost of repairing the vehicle for safe operation exceeds its fair market value; or

(b) that has been declared a salvage vehicle by an insurer or other state or jurisdiction, but is not precluded from further registration and titling.

(7) "Unbranded title" means a certificate of title for a previously damaged motor vehicle without any designation that the motor vehicle has been damaged.

(8) "Vehicle damage disclosure statement" means the form designed and furnished by the Motor Vehicle Enforcement Division for a damaged motor vehicle inspection under Section 41-1a-1002.   1994

41-1a-1002. Unbranded title — Prerepair inspections — Interim repair inspections — Repair.

(1) To obtain an unbranded title to a salvage vehicle:

(a) the vehicle must:

(i) be a motor vehicle;

(ii) (A) have an unbranded Utah title or a Utah salvage certificate issued to replace an unbranded Utah title at the time the motor vehicle is inspected under Subsection (iii); or

(B) have an unbranded title from another jurisdiction and the motor vehicle shall have been damaged in Utah as evidenced by an accident report;

(iii) be inspected by a certified vehicle inspector prior to any repairs on the motor vehicle following any major damage; and

(iv) have major damage in no more than one major component part;

(b) the major damage identified by a certified vehicle inspector under Subsection (a) must be repaired in accordance with standards established by the Motor Vehicle Enforcement Division;

(c) any interim inspection required by a certified vehicle inspector must be completed in accordance with the directions of the initial certified vehicle inspector and to the satisfaction of the interim certified vehicle inspector; and

(d) the owner must apply to the Motor Vehicle Enforcement Division for authorization to obtain an unbranded title under Section 41-1a-1003.

(2) A flood damaged motor vehicle does not qualify for an unbranded title.

(3) A salvage vehicle that is seven years old or older at the time of application for unbranding does not qualify for an unbranded title.

(4) The prerepair motor vehicle inspection required under Subsection (1) shall include examination of the

motor vehicle and its major component parts to determine:

    (a) the extent and location of the major damage to the motor vehicle;

    (b) that the identification numbers of the vehicle or its parts have not been removed, falsified, altered, defaced, or destroyed; and

    (c) there are no indications that the vehicle or any of its parts are stolen.

(5) If the certified vehicle inspector determines in an inspection under Subsection (1) that the motor vehicle has major damage:

    (a) in more than one major component part, the certified vehicle inspector shall notify the Motor Vehicle Enforcement Division and the owner that the motor vehicle does not qualify for an unbranded title; or

    (b) requiring repair or replacement in one or no major component part he shall:

        (i) record on the vehicle damage disclosure statement the:

            (A) date of the inspection;

            (B) description of the motor vehicle including its vehicle identification number, make, model, and year of manufacture;

            (C) owner of the motor vehicle and name of the lienholder, if any, shown on the salvage certificate; and

            (D) major damage to the motor vehicle requiring repair or replacement;

        (ii) indicate that the motor vehicle may qualify for an unbranded title if the major damage is repaired or the damaged part is replaced;

        (iii) sign the vehicle damage disclosure statement and attest to the information's accuracy;

        (iv) indicate whether an interim inspection of the motor vehicle damage repairs is required and which repairs require inspection prior to completion of repair work;

        (v) give to the owner a copy of the vehicle damage disclosure statement and deliver or mail a copy of the statement to the lienholder, if any, shown on the salvage certificate; and

        (vi) file the original vehicle damage disclosure statement with the Motor Vehicle Enforcement Division.

(6) (a) Upon receipt by the Motor Vehicle Enforcement Division of notification from a certified vehicle inspector that a motor vehicle has had a prepair inspection, the Motor Vehicle Enforcement Division shall make a record of the inspection.

    (b) Any subsequent prepair inspections shall be disregarded by the Motor Vehicle Enforcement Division in evaluating the major damage to the motor vehicle and the repairs required.

(7) A person who repairs or replaces major damage identified by a certified vehicle inspector on a motor vehicle in accordance with Subsection (1) shall:

    (a) record on the vehicle damage disclosure statement:

        (i) a description of the repairs made to the motor vehicle including how they were made; and

        (ii) his signature following the repair description with an attestation that the description is accurate;

    (b) obtain the signature of the certified vehicle inspector who performs an interim inspection,

attesting that the repairs identified for interim inspection were satisfactorily completed;

    (c) file the original vehicle damage disclosure statement containing the repair information with the Motor Vehicle Enforcement Division; and

    (d) give a copy of the vehicle damage disclosure statement to the owner.   1994

41-1a-1003. Unbranded certificate of title — Application.

(1) If the certified vehicle inspector determines under Section 41-1a-1002 that a motor vehicle may qualify for an unbranded title, following repair or replacement of the damaged major component part of the vehicle identified by the certified vehicle inspector, the owner may submit an application to the Motor Vehicle Enforcement Division for issuance of an unbranded title.

(2) The applicant for an unbranded title shall submit to the Motor Vehicle Enforcement Division an application together with the vehicle damage disclosure statement and other supporting documents required by the Motor Vehicle Enforcement Division.

(3) The Motor Vehicle Enforcement Division shall make an independent determination based on the vehicle damage disclosure statement and other relevant documents whether the motor vehicle is qualified to receive an unbranded title.   1993

41-1a-1004. Certificate of title — Salvage vehicles.

(1) If the division is able to ascertain the fact, at the time application is made for initial registration or transfer of ownership of a salvage vehicle, the title shall be branded:

    (a) rebuilt and restored to operation;

    (b) in a flood and restored to operation; or

    (c) not restored to operation.

(2) Before the sale of a vehicle for which a salvage certificate or branded title has been issued, the seller shall provide the prospective purchaser with written notification that a salvage certificate or a branded title has been issued for the vehicle.   1992

41-1a-1005. Salvage vehicle — Declaration by insurance company — Surrender of title — Salvage certificate of title.

(1) (a) (i) If an insurance company declares a vehicle a salvage vehicle and takes possession of the vehicle for disposal, or an insurance company pays off the owner of a vehicle that is stolen and not recovered, the insurance company shall within ten days from the settlement of the loss surrender to the division the outstanding certificate of title, properly endorsed, or other evidence of ownership acceptable to the division.

        (ii) The division shall then issue a salvage certificate in the insurance company's name.

    (b) (i) If the owner of a salvage vehicle retains possession of the vehicle, the insurance company shall within ten days from the settlement of the loss notify the division of the retention on a form prescribed by the division.

        (ii) The insurance company shall notify the owner of the vehicle of his responsibility to comply with this section.

        (iii) The owner shall within ten days from the settlement of the loss surrender to the division the properly endorsed certificate of title or other evidence of ownership acceptable to the division.

(iv) The division shall then issue a salvage certificate in the owner's name.

(c) (i) When a salvage vehicle is not the subject of an insurance settlement, a self-insurer or an owner who is uninsured shall within ten days of the theft or major damage surrender to the division the properly endorsed certificate of title or other evidence of ownership acceptable to the division.

(ii) The division shall then issue a salvage certificate in the owner's name.

(d) (i) If a dealer licensed under Title 41, Chapter 3, Part 2, Licensing, takes possession of any salvage vehicle for which there is not already issued a branded title or salvage certificate from the division or another jurisdiction, the dealer shall within ten days surrender to the division the certificate of title or other evidence of ownership acceptable to the division.

(ii) The division shall then issue a salvage certificate in the applicant's name.

(2) Any person, insurance company, or dealer licensed under Title 41, Chapter 3, Part 2, Licensing, who fails to obtain a salvage certificate as required in this section or who sells a salvage vehicle without first obtaining a salvage certificate is guilty of a class B misdemeanor.

(3) This section does not apply to a vehicle:

(a) that has an undamaged, wholesale value of $2,000 or less; or

(b) if a salvage certificate has been issued by another state or jurisdiction for the salvage vehicle.

(4) Upon sale or disposal of a salvage vehicle, the seller shall deliver to the purchaser the properly endorsed salvage certificate within 48 hours as required in Section 41-1a-1310, or if the seller is a dealer licensed under Title 41, Chapter 3, Part 2, Licensing, the dealer shall comply with Section 41-3-301.

(5) Except as provided in Subsection (1), this chapter does not apply to a motor vehicle that has been stolen or taken without the consent of the owner until the motor vehicle has been recovered, and then it applies only if the motor vehicle is a salvage vehicle.
1992

41-1a-1006. Vehicle damaged out-of-state — Division to make a record.

(1) If a vehicle that is titled in this state is damaged in another state or jurisdiction but would require a salvage certificate in this state and the vehicle is not returned to the state, the owner of the vehicle must notify the purchaser and the division that if the vehicle is subsequently titled in Utah the certificate of title will be branded as a salvage vehicle.

(2) The division shall make a record of the damage.
1992

41-1a-1007. Fees.

(1) A certified vehicle inspector may charge a fee in accordance with Section 63-38-3.2 for each inspection under Subsection 41-1a-1002(1).

(2) To cover the costs of inspection and to defray the cost of certification, the fee charged under this section by a certified vehicle inspector shall be retained by the Motor Vehicle Enforcement Division as a dedicated credit.
1995

41-1a-1008. Criminal penalty for violation.

It is a class A misdemeanor to knowingly violate Sections 41-1a-1001 through 41-1a-1007, unless another penalty is specifically provided.
1992

41-1a-1009. Abandoned and inoperable vehicles, vessels, and outboard motors — Determination by commission — Disposal of vehicles.

(1) A vehicle, vessel, or outboard motor is abandoned and inoperable when:

(a) the vehicle, vessel, or outboard motor has been inspected by an authorized investigator or agent appointed by the commission; and

(b) the authorized investigator or agent has made a written determination that the vehicle, vessel, or outboard motor cannot be rebuilt or reconstructed in a manner that allows its use as designed by the manufacturer.

(2) (a) Before issuing a written determination under Subsection (1), a signed statement is required from the purchaser of the vehicle, vessel, or outboard motor for salvage, identifying the vehicle, vessel, or outboard motor by identification number and certifying that the inoperable vehicle, vessel, or outboard motor will not be rebuilt, reconstructed, or in any manner allowed to operate as designed by the manufacturer.

(b) The operator of the junk or salvage yard disposing of an inoperable vehicle, vessel, or outboard motor is required to keep copies of the signed statements and other written records required by the commission.

(3) Upon a determination that a vehicle, vessel, or outboard motor is inoperable and cannot be rebuilt or reconstructed, the vehicle, vessel, or outboard motor may be converted to scrap or otherwise disposed of without necessity of compliance with the requirements of Sections 41-1a-1010 and 41-1a-1011. 1999

41-1a-1010. Permit required to dismantle vehicle — Duties upon receiving the permit — Exceptions.

(1) (a) A person may not scrap, dismantle, destroy, or otherwise change any vehicle so that it loses its character, until the person submits to the division:

(i) the certificate of title for the vehicle for cancellation; and

(ii) an application for a permit to dismantle the vehicle.

(b) Upon approval of the application, the division shall issue a permit to dismantle the vehicle.

(2) Except as provided in Subsection (3), if a permit to dismantle is issued under this section, the vehicle shall be destroyed and may not be rebuilt or reconstructed and may not be retitled or registered.

(3) A vehicle for which a permit to dismantle has been issued by the division may be retitled and the permit to dismantle rescinded if:

(a) prior to receiving a dismantling permit the vehicle had a Utah certificate of title;

(b) the vehicle has not been dismantled;

(c) an investigator for the Motor Vehicle Enforcement Division of the commission determines after a physical inspection of the vehicle that it is the same vehicle for which the permit to dismantle was issued; and

(d) the applicant pays the fee under Subsection (4).

(4) The commission may collect a fee established in accordance with Section 63-38-3.2 to cover the expenses of an inspection under Subsection (3). 1995

41-1a-1011. Use of dismantling permit.

The permit to dismantle issued under Section 41-1a-1010:

(1) requires the owner to dismantle the vehicle described in the permit unless the vehicle is retitled as provided in Subsection 41-1a-1010(3); and

(2) entitles the owner of the vehicle to transport the vehicle to the place of business of a dismantler, crusher, or salvage dealer licensed under the provisions of Title 41, Chapter 3, Part 2, Licensing.   1993

41-1a-1012. Destruction or change of vessel or outboard motor — Cancellation of certificate of title.

Within 15 days after a vessel or outboard motor is scrapped, dismantled, destroyed, or changed so that it loses its character as a vessel or outboard motor, the title holder to the vessel or outboard motor shall mail or deliver the certificate of title to the division for cancellation.   1992

PART 11

IMPOUNDED VEHICLES, VESSELS, OR OUTBOARD MOTORS

41-1a-1101. Seizure — Circumstances where permitted — Impound lot standards.

(1) The division or any peace officer, without a warrant, may seize and take possession of any vehicle, vessel, or outboard motor:

(a) that the division or the peace officer has reason to believe has been stolen;

(b) on which any identification number has been defaced, altered, or obliterated;

(c) that has been abandoned in accordance with Section 41-6a-1408;

(d) for which the applicant has written a check for registration or title fees that has not been honored by the applicant's bank and that is not paid within 30 days;

(e) that is placed on the water with improper registration; or

(f) that is being operated on a highway:

(i) with registration that has been expired for more than three months;

(ii) having never been properly registered by the current owner; or

(iii) with registration that is suspended or revoked.

(2) If necessary for the transportation of a seized vessel, the vessel's trailer may be seized to transport and store the vessel.

(3) Any peace officer seizing or taking possession of a vehicle, vessel, or outboard motor under this section shall comply with the provisions of Section 41-6a-1406.

(4) (a) In accordance with Title 63, Chapter 46a, Utah Administrative Rulemaking Act, the commission shall make rules setting standards for public garages, impound lots, and impound yards that may be used by peace officers and the division.

(b) The standards shall be equitable, reasonable, and unrestrictive as to the number of public garages, impound lots, or impound yards per geographical area.

(5) (a) Except as provided under Subsection (5)(b), a person may not operate or allow to be operated a vehicle stored in a public garage, impound lot, or impound yard regulated under this part without prior written permission of the owner of the vehicle.

(b) Incidental and necessary operation of a vehicle to move the vehicle from one parking space to another within the facility and that is necessary for the normal management of the facility is not prohibited under this Subsection (5)(a).

(6) A person who violates the provisions of Subsection (5) is guilty of a class C misdemeanor.

(7) The division or the peace officer who seizes a vehicle shall record the mileage shown on the vehicle's odometer at the time of seizure, if:

(a) the vehicle is equipped with an odometer; and

(b) the odometer reading is accessible to the division or the peace officer.   2005

41-1a-1102. Storage — Establishing ownership.

(1) The division may store a seized vehicle, vessel, or outboard motor in a public or private garage, state impound lot, or other approved storage facility until the vehicle's, vessel's, or outboard motor's registration has been properly completed and the appropriate fees have been paid or until the ownership of the vehicle, vessel, or outboard motor is established to the satisfaction of the division.

(2) If the identification number has been defaced, altered, or obliterated, the vehicle, vessel, or outboard motor may not be released until the identification number has been replaced or until a new number assigned by the division has been provided and has been affixed to the vehicle, vessel, or outboard motor.   1992

41-1a-1103. Sale.

(1) If the owner or lienholder of a seized vehicle, vessel, or outboard motor does not recover the vehicle, vessel, or outboard motor within 30 days from the date of seizure, or if the division is unable to determine the owner or lienholder through reasonable efforts, the division shall sell the vehicle, vessel, or outboard motor.

(2) The sale shall:

(a) be held in the form of a public auction at the place of storage; and

(b) at the discretion of the division, be conducted by:

(i) an authorized representative of the division; or

(ii) a public garage, impound lot, or impound yard that:

(A) is authorized by the division;

(B) meets the standards under Subsection 41-1a-1101(4); and

(C) complies with the requirements of Section 72-9-603.

(3) At least five days prior to the date set for sale, the division shall publish a notice of sale in a newspaper of general statewide circulation setting forth the date, time, and place of sale and a description of the vehicle, vessel, or outboard motor to be sold.

(4) At the time of sale the division or other person authorized to conduct the sale shall tender to the highest bidder a certificate of sale conveying all rights, title, and interest in the vehicle, vessel, or outboard motor.

(5) The proceeds from the sale of a vehicle, vessel, or outboard motor under this section shall be distributed as provided under Section 41-1a-1104.

(6) If the owner or lienholder of a vehicle, vessel, or outboard motor seized under Section 41-1a-1101 and subsequently released by the division fails to take possession of the vehicle, vessel, or outboard motor and satisfy the amount due to the place of storage

within 30 days from the date of release, the division shall renotify the owner or lienholder and sell the vehicle, vessel, or outboard motor, in accordance with this section, 30 days from the date of the notice.   2005

41-1a-1104. Disposition of proceeds from sale.

(1) If, for purposes of this part and Section 41-1a-1301, the ownership of a vehicle, vessel, or outboard motor seized cannot be determined, the excess of the proceeds of any sale over the fees for registration or transfer and penalties and costs shall be deposited with the state treasurer in a suspense account.

(2) (a) If the owner or the owner's heirs or assigns file a claim for the excess of the proceeds within one year of date of sale of the vehicle, vessel, or outboard motor, the excess of the proceeds shall be refunded to the claimant.

(b) If a claim is not filed in accordance with Subsection (2)(a), then the moneys shall be deposited in the General Fund.   2005

41-1a-1105. Records to be kept by public garage, impound lot, or impound yard.

(1) (a) Each person engaged in the business of operating a public garage, impound lot, or impound yard shall keep a record of every vehicle, vessel, or outboard motor stored in it for compensation for a period longer than 12 hours.

(b) The record shall include:

(i) the name and address of the person storing the vehicle, vessel, or outboard motor;

(ii) a brief description of the vehicle, vessel, or outboard motor, including the name or make, identification number, and license number shown by the license plates; and

(iii) the mileage shown on the vehicle's odometer both upon arrival at and upon its release from the public garage, impound lot, or impound yard, if the vehicle is equipped with an odometer.

(2) Every record kept under Subsection (1) shall be open to inspection by any peace officer.   1998

41-1a-1106. Storage of vehicles, vessels, and outboard motors — Reports required.

If any vehicle, vessel, or outboard motor has been stored in a public garage, state impound lot, or other storage facility for ten days and the owner is unknown to the proprietor, on the 11th day of storage the proprietor shall report the presence of the vehicle, vessel, or outboard motor to the law enforcement agency in the city or county where the garage, lot, or facility is located.   1992

PART 12

FEE AND TAX REQUIREMENTS

41-1a-1201. Disposition of fees.

(1) All fees received and collected under this part shall be transmitted daily to the state treasurer.

(2) Except as provided in Subsections (3), (4), and (6), and Sections 41-1a-422, 41-1a-1220, and 41-1a-1221, all fees collected under this part shall be deposited in the Transportation Fund.

(3) (a) Funds generated under Subsections 41-1a-1211(1)(a), (6)(a), and (7) and Section 41-1a-1212 may be used by the commission as a dedicated credit to cover the costs incurred in issuing license plates under Part 4, License Plates and Registration Indicia.

(b) Fees for statehood centennial license plates shall be collected and deposited in the Transpor-

tation Fund, less production and administrative costs incurred by the commission.

(4) All funds available to the commission for purchase and distribution of license plates and decals are nonlapsing.

(5) Except as provided in Subsection (3) and Section 41-1a-1205, the expenses of the commission in enforcing and administering this part shall be provided for by legislative appropriation from the revenues of the Transportation Fund.

(6) (a) Except as provided in Subsection (6)(b), the following portions of the registration fees imposed under Section 41-1a-1206 for each vehicle shall be deposited in the Centennial Highway Fund Restricted Account created under Section 72-2-118:

(i) $10 of the registration fees imposed under Subsections 41-1a-1206(1)(a), (1)(b), (2), and (5);

(ii) $1 of the registration fees imposed under Subsections 41-1a-1206(1)(c)(i), (1)(c)(ii), and (1)(d)(ii);

(iii) $2 of the registration fee imposed under Subsection 41-1a-1206(1)(e)(ii);

(iv) $3 of the registration fee imposed under Subsection 41-1a-1206(1)(d)(i); and

(v) $4.50 of the registration fee imposed under Subsection 41-1a-1206(1)(e)(i).

(b) When the highway general obligation bonds have been paid off and the highway projects completed that are intended to be paid from revenues deposited in the Centennial Highway Fund Restricted Account as determined by the Executive Appropriations Committee under Subsection 72-2-118(6)(d), the portions of the registration fees deposited under Subsection (6)(a) for each vehicle shall be deposited in the Transportation Investment Fund of 2005 created by Section 72-2-124.   2005 (1st S.S.)

41-1a-1202. Refused or rejected application — Refunds.

If an application to the division is accompanied by any fees required by law and the application is refused or rejected, the fees shall be returned immediately to the applicant.   1992

41-1a-1203. Application for refund.

If the division through error collects any fee not required to be paid, the fee shall be refunded to the person paying the fee upon written application for a refund made within six months after date of the payment.   1992

41-1a-1204. Automobile driver education fee — Amount — When paid — Exception.

(1) Each year there is levied and shall be paid to the commission the automobile driver education fee.

(2) (a) Except as provided in Subsection (b), the fee is $2.50 upon each motor vehicle to be registered.

(b) Motorcycle registration is exempt from the fee in Subsection (a).   1993

41-1a-1205. Disposition of driver education tax — Expense appropriation.

(1) The automobile driver education tax collected under Section 41-1a-1204 shall be placed to the credit of the Automobile Driver Education Tax Account within the Uniform School Fund.

(2) The necessary expenses of the commission incurred in the administration and collection of the tax shall be paid from its legislative appropriation in the General Fund, which fund shall be reimbursed by a transfer for the expenses from the legislative appropriation of the Uniform School Fund.   1992

41-1a-1206. Registration fees — Fees by gross laden weight.

(1) Except as provided in Subsection (2), at the time application is made for registration or renewal of registration of a vehicle or combination of vehicles under this chapter, a registration fee shall be paid to the division as follows:

(a) $22.50 for each motorcycle;

(b) $21 for each motor vehicle of 12,000 pounds or less gross laden weight, excluding motorcycles;

(c) unless the semitrailer or trailer is exempt from registration under Section 41-1a-202 or is registered under Section 41-1a-301:

(i) $11 for each trailer or semitrailer over 750 pounds gross unladen weight; or

(ii) $8.50 for each commercial trailer or commercial semitrailer of 750 pounds or less gross unladen weight;

(d) (i) $33 for each farm truck over 12,000 pounds, but not exceeding 14,000 pounds gross laden weight; plus

(ii) $9 for each 2,000 pounds over 14,000 pounds gross laden weight; and

(e) (i) $49.50 for each motor vehicle or combination of motor vehicles, excluding farm trucks, over 12,000 pounds, but not exceeding 14,000 pounds gross laden weight; plus

(ii) $18.50 for each 2,000 pounds over 14,000 pounds gross laden weight.

(2) The initial registration fee for a vintage vehicle is $20.

(3) If a motor vehicle is operated in combination with a semitrailer or trailer, each motor vehicle shall register for the total gross laden weight of all units of the combination if the total gross laden weight of the combination exceeds 12,000 pounds.

(4) (a) Registration fee categories under this section are based on the gross laden weight declared in the licensee's application for registration.

(b) Gross laden weight shall be computed in units of 2,000 pounds. A fractional part of 2,000 pounds is a full unit.

(5) The owner of a commercial trailer or commercial semitrailer may, as an alternative to registering under Subsection (1)(c), apply for and obtain a special registration and license plate for a fee of $110.

(6) Except as provided in Section 41-6a-1642, a truck may not be registered as a farm truck unless:

(a) the truck meets the definition of a farm truck under Section 41-1a-102; and

(b) (i) the truck has a gross vehicle weight rating of more than 12,000 pounds; or

(ii) the truck has a gross vehicle weight rating of 12,000 pounds or less and the owner submits to the division a certificate of emissions inspection or a waiver in compliance with Section 41-6a-1642.

(7) A violation of Subsection (6) is a class B misdemeanor that shall be punished by a fine of not less than $200.

(8) Trucks used exclusively to pump cement, bore wells, or perform crane services with a crane lift capacity of five or more tons, are exempt from 50% of the amount of the fees required for those vehicles under this section.　　　　　2005

41-1a-1207. Reduced fees for portion of year.

If a motor vehicle exceeding 12,000 pounds gross laden weight is registered for less than a 12-month registration period, the registration fees are:

(1) for not more than three months, 30% of the regular registration fee;

(2) for in excess of three months but not more than six months, 60% of the regular registration fee;

(3) for in excess of six months and not more than nine months, 90% of the regular registration fee; and

(4) for anything in excess of nine months but not more than 12 months, the entire registration fee.　　　　　1992

41-1a-1208. Fees for duplicate certificates of registration.

A duplicate certificate of registration may be issued upon application and payment of $4 to the division.　　　　　1993

41-1a-1209. Exemptions from registration fees — Vintage vehicle information renewal.

(1) A fee may not be charged for the registration of ambulances, law enforcement vehicles, fire engines, and passenger cars and trucks owned and used by the United States government or by the state of Utah or any of its political subdivisions.

(2) A fee may not be charged municipal corporations for the issuance of any certificate of title or registration or a duplicate certificate of title or registration.

(3) An annual renewal of registration is not required for a vintage vehicle but registration information for vintage vehicle special group license plates must be updated every five years.　　　　　1993

41-1a-1210. Fees for original and duplicate certificates of title.

A fee of $6 shall be paid to the division for the issuance of each original and duplicate certificate of title for a vehicle, vessel, or outboard motor.　　　　　1993

41-1a-1211. License plate fees — Application fees for issuance and renewal of personalized and special group license plates — Replacement fee for license plates — Postage fees.

(1) A license plate fee of $5 per set shall be paid to the division for the issuance of any new license plate under Part 4, License Plates and Registration Indicia, except for license plates issued under Section 41-1a-407. The license plate fee shall be deposited as follows:

(a) $4 as provided in Section 41-1a-1201; and

(b) $1 in the Transportation Fund.

(2) An applicant for original issuance of personalized license plates issued under Section 41-1a-410 shall pay a $50 per set license plate application fee in addition to the fee required in Subsection (1).

(3) Beginning July 1, 2003, a person who applies for a special group license plate shall pay a $5 fee for the original set of license plates in addition to the fee required under Subsection (1).

(4) An applicant for original issuance of personalized special group license plates shall pay the license plate application fees required in Subsection (2) in addition to the license plate fees and license plate application fees established under Subsections (1) and (3).

(5) An applicant for renewal of personalized license plates issued under Section 41-1a-410 shall pay a $10 per set application fee.

(6) A fee of $5 shall be paid to the division for the replacement of any license plate issued under Part 4, License Plates and Registration Indicia. The license plate fee shall be deposited as follows:

(a) $4 as provided in Section 41-1a-1201; and

(b) $1 in the Transportation Fund.

(7) The division may charge a fee established under Section 63-38-3.2 to recover its costs for the replacement of decals issued under Section 41-1a-418.

(8) The division may charge a fee established under Section 63-38-3.2 to recover the cost of issuing stickers under Section 41-1a-416.

(9) In addition to any other fees required by this section, the division shall assess a fee established under Section 63-38-3.2 to cover postage expenses if new or replacement license plates are mailed to the applicant.

(10) The fees required under this section are separate from and in addition to registration fees required under Section 41-1a-1206.   2003

41-1a-1212. Fee for replacement of license plate decals.

A fee established in accordance with Section 63-38-3.2 shall be paid to the division for the replacement of a license plate decal required by Section 41-1a-402.
1995

41-1a-1213. No fee for identification number inspection.

A fee may not be charged an applicant for vehicle registration under this chapter for an identification number inspection.   1993

41-1a-1214 to 41-1a-1217. Repealed.   1993, 1996

41-1a-1218. Uninsured motorist identification fee for tracking motor vehicle insurance — Exemption — Deposit.

(1) (a) At the time application is made for registration or renewal of registration of a motor vehicle under this chapter, the applicant shall pay an uninsured motorist identification fee of $1 on each motor vehicle.

(b) A commercial vehicle registered as part of a fleet under Section 41-1a-222 or Section 41-1a-301 is exempt from the uninsured motorist identification fee required by this section.

(c) A motor vehicle that is exempt from the registration fee under Section 41-1a-1209 or Subsection 41-1a-419(3) is also exempt from the uninsured motorist identification fee required by this section.

(2) The revenue generated under this section shall be deposited in the Uninsured Motorist Identification Restricted Account created in Section 41-12a-806.
2003

41-1a-1219. Motor carrier fee.

(1) At the time application is made for registration or renewal of registration of a motor vehicle or combination of motor vehicles over 12,000 pounds gross laden weight, the applicant shall pay a motor carrier fee of $6 for each motor vehicle or combination of motor vehicles.

(2) This fee is in addition to the registration fees under Subsections 41-1a-1206(1)(d) and (e).   1996

41-1a-1220. Registration reinstatement fee.

(1) At the time application is made for reinstatement or renewal of registration of a motor vehicle after a revocation of the registration under Subsection 41-1a-110(2), the applicant shall pay a registration reinstatement fee of $100.

(2) The fee imposed under Subsection (1):

(a) is in addition to any other fee imposed under this chapter; and

(b) shall be deposited in the Uninsured Motorist Identification Restricted Account created in Section 41-12a-806.

(3) The division shall waive the registration reinstatement fee imposed under this section if:

(a) the registration was revoked under Subsection 41-1a-110(2)(b); and

(b) a person had owner's or operator's security in effect for the vehicle at the time of the alleged violation or on the day following the time limit provided after the second notice under Subsection 41-12a-804(2).   2000

41-1a-1221. Fees to cover the cost of electronic payments.

(1) In accordance with Section 63-38a-105, the Division of Motor Vehicles may collect an electronic payment fee on all registrations and renewals of registration under Subsections 41-1a-1206(1)(a), 41-1a-1206(1)(b), and 41-1a-1206(2).

(2) The division shall establish the fee according to the procedures and requirements of Section 63-38-3.2.
2003

41-1a-1222. Local option transportation corridor preservation fee — Exemptions — Deposit — County ordinance — Notice [Effective January 1, 2006].

(1) (a) (i) A county legislative body may impose a local option transportation corridor preservation fee of up to $10 on each motor vehicle registration within the county.

(ii) A fee imposed under Subsection (1)(a)(i) shall be set in whole dollar increments.

(b) If imposed under Subsection (1)(a), at the time application is made for registration or renewal of registration of a motor vehicle under this chapter, the applicant shall pay the local option transportation corridor preservation fee established by the county legislative body.

(c) A motor vehicle that is exempt from the registration fee under Section 41-1a-1209 or Subsection 41-1a-419(3) is also exempt from the local option transportation corridor preservation fee required by this section.

(d) A commercial motor vehicle with an apportioned registration under Section 41-1a-301 is exempt from the local option transportation corridor preservation fee required by this section.

(2) The revenue generated under this section shall be:

(a) deposited in the Local Transportation Corridor Preservation Fund created in Section 72-2-117.5;

(b) credited to the county from which it is generated; and

(c) used and distributed in accordance with Section 72-2-117.5.

(3) To impose or change the amount of a fee under this section, the county legislative body shall pass an ordinance:

(a) approving the fee;

(b) setting the amount of the fee; and

(c) providing an effective date for the fee as provided in Subsection (4).

(4) (a) If a county legislative body enacts, changes, or repeals a fee under this section, the enactment, change, or repeal shall take effect on July 1 if the commission receives notice meeting the requirements of Subsection (4)(b) from the county prior to April 1.

(b) The notice described in Subsection (4)(a) shall:

(i) state that the county will enact, change, or repeal a fee under this part;

(ii) include a copy of the ordinance imposing the fee; and

(iii) if the county enacts or changes the fee under this section, state the amount of the fee.   2005

PART 13

OFFENSES AND PENALTIES

41-1a-1301.   Unpaid fees and penalty — Lien — Seizure and sale.

(1) (a) Every registration fee and penalty not paid by the due date is a lien upon all:

(i) the unexempt personal property of the owner or operator of the vehicle, vessel, or outboard motor; and

(ii) interest or equity of the owner or operator in all personal property, including vehicles, vessels, or outboard motors used by the owner or operator in the conduct or operation of his business.

(b) The properties and vehicles, vessels, or outboard motors may be held under warrant, issued by the commission, and sold in accordance with the law applicable to personal property taxes.

(2) Delinquency is a ground for the issuance of a writ of attachment against the owner or operator.   1992

41-1a-1302.   Violation — Class C misdemeanor.

A violation of any provision of this chapter is a class C misdemeanor, unless otherwise provided.   1992

41-1a-1303.   Driving without registration or certificate of title — Class B or C misdemeanor.

(1) (a) Except as provided in Subsection (2) or Section 41-1a-211, a person may not drive or move, or an owner may not knowingly permit to be driven or moved upon any highway any vehicle of a type required to be registered in this state:

(i) that is not properly registered or for which a certificate of title has not been issued or applied for; or

(ii) for which the required fee has not been paid.

(b) A violation of this Subsection (1) is a class C misdemeanor.

(2) (a) A violation of Subsection 41-1a-202(3), related to registration of vehicles after establishing residency, is a class B misdemeanor and except as provided in Subsection (2)(b), has a minimum fine of $1000.

(b) A court may not dismiss an action brought for a violation of Subsection 41-1a-202(3) merely because the defendant has obtained the appropriate registration subsequent to violating the section. The court may, however, reduce the fine to $200 if the violator presents evidence at the time of his hearing that:

(i) the vehicle is currently registered properly; and

(ii) the violation has not existed for more than one year.

(3) A court may require proof of proper motor vehicle registration as part of any sentence imposed under this section.   2002

41-1a-1304.   Operating motor vehicle, trailer, or semitrailer in excess of registered gross laden weight — Class C misdemeanor.

It is a class C misdemeanor for a person to operate, or cause to be operated, a motor vehicle, trailer, or semitrailer, or combination of them the gross laden weight of which is in excess of the gross laden weight for which the motor vehicle, trailer, or semitrailer, or combination of vehicles is registered.   1992

41-1a-1305.   License plate and registration card violations — Class C misdemeanor.

It is a class C misdemeanor:

(1) to break, injure, interfere with, or remove from any vehicle any seal, lock, or device on it for holding or displaying any license plate or registration card attached for denoting registration and identity of the vehicle;

(2) to remove from any registered vehicle the license plate or registration card issued or attached to it for its registration;

(3) to place or display any license plate or registration card upon any other vehicle than the one for which it was issued by the division;

(4) to use or permit the use or display of any license plate, registration card, or permit upon or in the operation of any vehicle other than that for which it was issued;

(5) to operate upon any highway of this state any vehicle required by law to be registered without having the license plate or plates securely attached, and the registration card issued by the division carried in the vehicle, except that the registration card issued by the division to all trailers and semitrailers shall be carried in the towing vehicle;

(6) for any weighmaster to knowingly make any false entry in his record of weights of vehicles subject to registration or to knowingly report to the commission or division any false information regarding the weights;

(7) for any inspector, officer, agent, employee, or other person performing any of the functions required for the registration or operation of vehicles subject to registration, to do, permit, cause, connive at, or permit to be done any act with the intent, or knowledge that the probable effect of the act would be to injure any person, deprive him of his property, or to injure or defraud the state with respect to its revenues relating to title or registration of vehicles;

(8) for any person to combine or conspire with another to do, attempt to do, or cause or allow any of the acts in this chapter classified as a misdemeanor;

(9) to operate any motor vehicle with a camper mounted on it upon any highway without displaying a current decal in clear sight upon the rear of the camper, issued by the county assessor of the county in which the camper has situs for taxation;

(10) to manufacture, use, display, or sell any facsimile or reproduction of any license plate issued by the division or any article that would appear to be a substitute for a license plate; or

(11) to fail to return to the division any registration card, license plate or plates, decal, permit, or title that has been canceled, suspended, voided, or revoked.   1992

41-1a-1306.   Abuse of persons with disabilities parking privileges — Revocation of special plate or transferable ID card — Fine.

(1) A person with a disability who abuses the rights and privileges conferred under Section 41-1a-414 or allows an individual who is not a person with a disability to use those parking privileges may have his person with a disability special group license plate,

temporary removable windshield placard, or removable windshield placard revoked by the division.

(2) A person who violates Section 41-1a-414 shall pay a minimum fine of $125.   2003

41-1a-1307. Operation of motor vehicles, trailers, or semitrailers without payment of fees — Class C misdemeanor.

(1) It is a class C misdemeanor for a person to operate a motor vehicle, trailer, or semitrailer upon the highways without having paid the title and registration or transfer fees and taxes required by law.

(2) In addition to any other penalty, the owner of a motor vehicle, trailer, or semitrailer operated in violation of this section shall pay a penalty equal to title and registration fees in addition to any other fee required under this chapter.

(3) A court may require proof of proper vehicle registration as part of any sentence imposed under this section.   2002

41-1a-1308. Repealed.   1998

41-1a-1309. Boarding with intent to commit injury to motor vehicle, trailer, or semitrailer — Class C misdemeanor.

It is a class C misdemeanor for a person with intent to commit any malicious mischief, injury, or other crime to:

(1) climb into or upon a motor vehicle, trailer, or semitrailer, whether it is in motion or at rest;

(2) attempt to manipulate any of the levers, starting mechanism, brakes, or other mechanism or device of a motor vehicle, trailer, or semitrailer while the same is at rest and unattended; or

(3) set in motion any motor vehicle, trailer, or semitrailer while the same is at rest and unattended.   1992

41-1a-1310. Class B misdemeanors.

It is a class B misdemeanor for any person to:

(1) fail to properly endorse and deliver a valid certificate of title to a vehicle, vessel, or outboard motor to a transferee or owner lawfully entitled to it in accordance with Section 41-1a-702, except as provided for under Sections 41-3-301, 41-1a-519, and 41-1a-709;

(2) fail to give an odometer disclosure statement to the transferee as required by Section 41-1a-902;

(3) operate, or cause to be operated, a motor vehicle knowing that the odometer is disconnected or nonfunctional, except while moving the motor vehicle to a place of repair;

(4) offer for sale, sell, use, or install on any part of a motor vehicle or on an odometer in a motor vehicle any device that causes the odometer to register miles or kilometers other than the true miles or kilometers driven as registered by the odometer within the manufacturer's designed tolerance;

(5) fail to adjust an odometer or affix a notice as required by Section 41-1a-906 regarding the adjustment;

(6) remove, alter, or cause to be removed or altered any notice of adjustment affixed to a motor vehicle as required by Section 41-1a-906;

(7) fail to record the odometer reading on the certificate of title at the time of transfer; or

(8) accept or give an incomplete odometer statement when an odometer statement is required under Section 41-1a-902.   1992

41-1a-1311, 41-1a-1312. Repealed.   1993, 1998

41-1a-1313. Third degree felony to possess motor vehicle, trailer, semitrailer, or parts without identification number — Presumption of knowledge.

(1) It is a third degree felony for a person to have in his possession any motor vehicle, trailer, or semitrailer, or any part or parts of a motor vehicle, trailer, or semitrailer, from which any identification number has been removed, defaced, destroyed, obliterated, or so covered as to be concealed, or where the identification number has been altered or changed in any manner.

(2) A person having possession of any motor vehicle, trailer, or semitrailer or part of them under this section is presumed prima facie to have knowledge of this condition.   1992

41-1a-1314. Unauthorized control for extended time.

(1) Except as provided in Subsection (3), it is a class A misdemeanor for a person to exercise unauthorized control over a motor vehicle that is not his own, without the consent of the owner or lawful custodian, and with the intent to temporarily deprive the owner or lawful custodian of possession of the motor vehicle.

(2) The consent of the owner or legal custodian of a motor vehicle to its control by the actor is not in any case presumed or implied because of the owner's or legal custodian's consent on a previous occasion to the control of the motor vehicle by the same or a different person.

(3) Violation of this section is a third degree felony if:

(a) the person does not return the motor vehicle to the owner or lawful custodian within 24 hours after the exercise of unlawful control; or

(b) regardless of the mental state or conduct of the person committing the offense:

(i) the motor vehicle is damaged in an amount of $500 or more;

(ii) the motor vehicle is used to commit a felony; or

(iii) the motor vehicle is damaged in any amount to facilitate entry into it or its operation.

(4) It is not a defense to Subsection (3)(a) that someone other than the person, or an agent of the person, returned the motor vehicle within 24 hours.

(5) A violation of this section is a lesser included offense of theft under Section 76-6-404, when the theft is of an operable motor vehicle under Subsection 76-6-412(1)(a)(ii).   2005

41-1a-1315. Second degree felony — False evidences of title and registration.

It is a second degree felony for a person with respect to a motor vehicle, trailer, or semitrailer to:

(1) fraudulently use a false or fictitious name in an application for registration, a certificate of title, or for a duplicate certificate of title;

(2) knowingly make a false statement or knowingly conceal a material fact in an application under this chapter;

(3) otherwise commit a fraud in an application under this chapter;

(4) alter with fraudulent intent a certificate of title, registration card, license plate, or permit issued by the division;

(5) forge or counterfeit a document or license plate purporting to have been issued by the division;

(6) alter, falsify, or forge an assignment upon a certificate of title;

(7) hold or use a document or license plate under this chapter knowing it has been altered, forged, or falsified; and

(8) file an application for a certificate of title providing false lien information, when the person named on the application as lienholder does not hold a valid security interest. 1992

41-1a-1316. Receiving or transferring stolen motor vehicle, trailer, or semitrailer — Penalty.

It is a second degree felony for a person:

(1) with intent to procure or pass title to a motor vehicle, trailer, or semitrailer that he knows or has reason to believe has been stolen or unlawfully taken to receive or transfer possession of the motor vehicle, trailer, or semitrailer from or to another; or

(2) to have in his possession any motor vehicle, trailer, or semitrailer that he knows or has reason to believe has been stolen or unlawfully taken if he is not a peace officer engaged at the time in the performance of his duty. 1992

41-1a-1317. Selling or buying without identification numbers — Penalty.

It is a second degree felony for a person to knowingly buy, receive, dispose of, sell, offer for sale, or have in his possession any motor vehicle, trailer, semitrailer, or engine removed from a motor vehicle, from which the identification number has been removed, defaced, covered, altered, or destroyed for the purpose of concealing or misrepresenting the identity of the motor vehicle or engine. 1992

41-1a-1318. Second degree felony — Fraudulent alteration of identification number.

(1) It is a second degree felony for a person with fraudulent intent to:

(a) deface, destroy, or alter the identification number or state assigned identification number of a motor vehicle, trailer, or semitrailer;

(b) place or stamp, without authority by the division, something other than the original identification or state assigned identification number upon a motor vehicle, trailer, or semitrailer; or

(c) sell or offer for sale a motor vehicle, trailer, or semitrailer bearing an altered or defaced identification or state assigned identification number other than the original or the state assigned identification number.

(2) This section does not prevent any manufacturer, importer, or any agent, other than a dealer, from placing or stamping in the ordinary course of business numbers on motor vehicles, trailers, or semitrailers registered under this chapter.

(3) This section does not prohibit the restoration by an owner of an original identification number when the restoration is made under permit issued by the division. 1992

41-1a-1319. Third degree felony — Odometer violation.

It is a third degree felony for a person, with intent to defraud, to:

(1) disconnect, turn back, replace, or reset or cause to be disconnected, turned back, replaced, or reset, the odometer of any motor vehicle with the intent to reduce the true number of miles or kilometers indicated on it;

(2) knowingly sell, transfer, or exchange, or cause to be sold, transferred, or exchanged without the disclosure required by Section 41-1a-902, any motor vehicle on which the odometer has been disconnected, turned back, replaced, or reset; or

(3) give or cause to be given a false odometer mileage disclosure statement when an odometer statement is required by Section 41-1a-902. 1992

41-1a-1320. Tax clearance required to move manufactured home or mobile home.

(1) A manufactured home or mobile home may not be transported by any person, including its owner, unless a tax clearance has been obtained from the assessor of the county in which the real property upon which the manufactured home or mobile home was last located showing that all property taxes, including any interest and penalties, have been paid.

(2) The tax clearance described in Subsection (1):

(a) is proof of having paid all property taxes, interest, and penalties; and

(b) shall be displayed in a conspicuous place on the rear of the manufactured home or mobile home so as to be plainly visible while in transit.

(3) (a) Any person, including the owner, who transports a manufactured home or mobile home without a valid tax clearance is:

(i) in violation of Section 59-2-309; and

(ii) subject to the penalty provisions of Section 59-2-309.

(b) In addition to the penalty provided in Subsection (3)(a), any commercial mover who transports any manufactured home or mobile home without a valid tax clearance is guilty of a class B misdemeanor. 2003

PART 14

LAW ENFORCEMENT

41-1a-1401. Report of stolen and recovered vehicles, vessels, and outboard motors by officials.

(1) (a) A peace officer, upon receiving reliable information that a vehicle, vessel, or outboard motor has been stolen, shall immediately report the theft to the Criminal Investigations and Technical Services Division of the Department of Public Safety, established in Section 53-10-103.

(b) An officer, upon receiving information that a vehicle, vessel, or outboard motor, which he has previously reported as stolen, has been recovered, shall immediately report the recovery to the local law enforcement agency and to the Criminal Investigations and Technical Services Division.

(2) A report of a stolen vehicle, vessel, or outboard motor taken by a law enforcement agency shall include a written advisement to the reporting party of the provisions of Section 76-8-506, and a statement affirming the theft of the vehicle, vessel, or outboard motor signed by the person reporting the theft and witnessed by the person taking the report.

(3) The following information regarding the vehicle, vessel, or outboard motor shall be included in the report and shall be sent to the Criminal Investigations and Technical Services Division:

(a) the registered owner;

(b) the person reporting the theft;

(c) the year, make, model, and color;

(d) the identification number;

(e) the estimated present value;

(f) the license number and state of registration;

(g) the date, time, and place of the theft; and

(h) the name, address, telephone number, policy number, and agent's name of the insurance company insuring the vehicle, vessel, or outboard motor.

(4) If a member of any law enforcement agency confirms that a stolen vehicle, vessel, or outboard motor has been recovered, he shall send the following information regarding the recovered vehicle, vessel, or outboard motor to the Criminal Investigations and Technical Services Division:

(a) the date, time, and place of recovery;

(b) the condition of the vehicle, vessel, or outboard motor; and

(c) the names of peace officers and any other persons involved in the recovery.

(5) (a) Upon receipt of a report of a stolen vehicle, vessel, or outboard motor, the Criminal Investigations and Technical Services Division shall place a notice of theft in the master file computer.

(b) Upon receipt of a report that a stolen vehicle, vessel, or outboard motor has been recovered, the Criminal Investigations and Technical Services Division shall remove the notice of theft of the vehicle, vessel, or outboard motor from the master file computer.

(6) (a) Except as provided in Section 41-1a-1005, the division shall refuse to register or transfer title to a stolen vehicle until the vehicle is recovered.

(b) (i) If the recovered vehicle is a salvage vehicle as defined in Section 41-1a-1001, then Title 41, Chapter 1a, Part 10, Salvage Vehicles — Junk and Dismantled Vehicles, applies.

(ii) The division may issue an unbranded certificate of title for a recovered vehicle if the vehicle has not suffered major damage in more than one major component part.   1998

41-1a-1402.   Report by owners or lienholders of thefts and recoveries.

(1) (a) The owner, or person having a lien or encumbrance upon a vehicle, vessel, or outboard motor that has been stolen, may notify the law enforcement agency having jurisdiction where the theft occurred.

(b) In the event of an embezzlement the owner or person may make a report only after having procured the issuance of a warrant for the arrest of the person charged with embezzlement.

(2) (a) If a vehicle, vessel, or outboard motor is recovered, an owner or other person who has given any notice under Subsection (1) shall notify the law enforcement agency where the theft or embezzlement was reported.

(b) The law enforcement agency shall notify the Criminal Investigations and Technical Services Division, established in Section 53-10-103, of recovery.   1998

CHAPTER 2

OPERATORS' LICENSE ACT [RENUMBERED]

41-2-101 to 41-2-720.   Renumbered as § 53-3-101 et seq.   1993

CHAPTER 3

MOTOR VEHICLE BUSINESS REGULATION

Section
41-3-1 to 41-3-39. Renumbered.

Part 1

Administration

Part 2

Licensing

Part 3

Temporary Permits

41-3-1 to 41-3-39. Renumbered as §§ 41-3-101 to 41-3-702. 1992

PART 1

ADMINISTRATION

41-3-101. Short title.
This chapter is known as the Motor Vehicle Business Regulation Act. 1992

41-3-102. Definitions.
As used in this chapter:
(1) "Administrator" means the motor vehicle enforcement administrator.
(2) "Agent" means a person other than a holder of any dealer's or salesperson's license issued under this chapter, who for salary, commission, or compensation of any kind, negotiates in any way for the sale, purchase, order, or exchange of three or more motor vehicles for any other person in any 12-month period.
(3) "Auction" means a dealer engaged in the business of auctioning motor vehicles, either owned or consigned, to the general public.
(4) "Board" means the advisory board created in Section 41-3-106.
(5) "Body shop" means a business engaged in rebuilding, restoring, repairing, or painting primarily the body of motor vehicles damaged by collision or natural disaster.
(6) "Commission" means the State Tax Commission.
(7) "Crusher" means a person who crushes or shreds motor vehicles subject to registration under Title 41, Chapter 1a, Motor Vehicle Act, to reduce the useable materials and metals to a more compact size for recycling.
(8) (a) "Dealer" means a person:
(i) whose business in whole or in part involves selling new, used, or new and used motor vehicles or off-highway vehicles; and
(ii) who sells, displays for sale, or offers for sale or exchange three or more new or used motor vehicles or off-highway vehicles in any 12-month period.
(b) "Dealer" includes a representative or consignee of any dealer.
(9) (a) "Dismantler" means a person engaged in the business of dismantling motor vehicles

subject to registration under Title 41, Chapter 1a, Motor Vehicle Act, for the resale of parts or for salvage.

(b) "Dismantler" includes a person who dismantles three or more motor vehicles in any 12-month period.

(10) "Distributor" means a person who has a franchise from a manufacturer of motor vehicles to distribute motor vehicles within this state and who in whole or in part sells or distributes new motor vehicles to dealers or who maintains distributor representatives.

(11) "Distributor branch" means a branch office similarly maintained by a distributor for the same purposes a factory branch is maintained.

(12) "Distributor representative" means a person and each officer and employee of the person engaged as a representative of a distributor or distributor branch of motor vehicles to make or promote the sale of the distributor or the distributor branch's motor vehicles, or for supervising or contacting dealers or prospective dealers of the distributor or the distributor branch.

(13) "Division" means the Motor Vehicle Enforcement Division created in Section 41-3-104.

(14) "Factory branch" means a branch office maintained by a person who manufactures or assembles motor vehicles for sale to distributors, motor vehicle dealers, or who directs or supervises the factory branch's representatives.

(15) "Factory representative" means a person and each officer and employee of the person engaged as a representative of a manufacturer of motor vehicles or by a factory branch to make or promote the sale of the manufacturer's or factory branch's motor vehicles, or for supervising or contacting the dealers or prospective dealers of the manufacturer or the factory branch.

(16) "Franchise" means a contract or agreement between a dealer and a manufacturer of new motor vehicles or its distributor or factory branch by which the dealer is authorized to sell any specified make or makes of new motor vehicles.

(17) "Manufacturer" means a person engaged in the business of constructing or assembling new motor vehicles, ownership of which is customarily transferred by a manufacturer's statement or certificate of origin, or a person who constructs three or more new motor vehicles in any 12-month period.

(18) "Motorcycle" has the same meaning as defined in Section 41-1a-102.

(19) (a) "Motor vehicle" means a vehicle intended primarily for use and operation on the highway that is:

(i) self-propelled; or

(ii) a trailer, travel trailer, or semitrailer.

(b) "Motor vehicle" does not include:

(i) mobile homes as defined in Section 41-1a-102;

(ii) trailers of 750 pounds or less unladen weight; and

(iii) farm tractors and other machines and tools used in the production, harvesting, and care of farm products.

(20) "New motor vehicle" means a motor vehicle that has never been titled or registered and has been driven less than 7,500 miles, unless the motor vehicle is a trailer, travel trailer, or semitrailer, in which case the mileage limit does not apply.

(21) "Off-highway vehicle" has the same meaning as provided in Section 41-22-2.

(22) "Pawnbroker" means a person whose business is to lend money on security of personal property deposited with him.

(23) "Principal place of business" means a site or location in this state:

(a) devoted exclusively to the business for which the dealer, manufacturer, remanufacturer, transporter, dismantler, crusher, or body shop is licensed, and businesses incidental to them;

(b) sufficiently bounded by fence, chain, posts, or otherwise marked to definitely indicate the boundary and to admit a definite description with space adequate to permit the display of three or more new, or new and used, or used motor vehicles; and

(c) that includes a permanent enclosed building or structure large enough to accommodate the office of the establishment and to provide a safe place to keep the books and other records of the business, at which the principal portion of the business is conducted and the books and records kept and maintained.

(24) "Remanufacturer" means a person who reconstructs used motor vehicles subject to registration under Title 41, Chapter 1a, Motor Vehicle Act, to change the body style and appearance of the motor vehicle or who constructs or assembles motor vehicles from used or new and used motor vehicle parts, or who reconstructs, constructs, or assembles three or more motor vehicles in any 12-month period.

(25) "Salesperson" means an individual who for a salary, commission, or compensation of any kind, is employed either directly, indirectly, regularly, or occasionally by any new motor vehicle dealer or used motor vehicle dealer to sell, purchase, or exchange or to negotiate for the sale, purchase, or exchange of motor vehicles.

(26) "Semitrailer" has the same meaning as defined in Section 41-1a-102.

(27) "Small trailer" means a trailer that has an unladen weight of more than 750 pounds, but less than 2,000 pounds.

(28) "Special equipment" includes a truck mounted crane, cherry picker, material lift, post hole digger, and a utility or service body.

(29) "Special equipment dealer" means a new or new and used motor vehicle dealer engaged in the business of buying new incomplete motor vehicles with a gross vehicle weight of 12,000 or more pounds and installing special equipment on the incomplete motor vehicle.

(30) "Trailer" has the same meaning as defined in Section 41-1a-102.

(31) "Transporter" means a person engaged in the business of transporting motor vehicles as described in Section 41-3-202.

(32) "Travel trailer" has the same meaning as provided in Section 41-1a-102.

(33) "Used motor vehicle" means a vehicle that has been titled and registered to a purchaser other than a dealer or has been driven 7,500 or more miles, unless the vehicle is a trailer, or semitrailer, in which case the mileage limit does not apply.

(34) "Wholesale motor vehicle auction" means a dealer primarily engaged in the business of auctioning consigned motor vehicles to dealers or dismantlers who are licensed by this or any other jurisdiction. 2003

41-3-103. Exceptions to "dealer" definition — Dealer licensed in other state.

Under this chapter:

(1) (a) An insurance company, bank, finance company, public utility company, commission impound yard, federal or state governmental agency, or any political subdivision of any of them or any other person coming into possession of a motor vehicle as an incident to its regular business, that sells the motor vehicle under contractual rights that it may have in the motor vehicle is not considered a dealer.

(b) A person who sells or exchanges only those motor vehicles that he has owned for over 12 months is not considered a dealer.

(2) (a) A person engaged in leasing motor vehicles is not considered as coming into possession of the motor vehicles incident to his regular business; and

(b) a pawnbroker engaged in selling, exchanging, or pawning motor vehicles is not considered as coming into possession of the motor vehicles incident to his regular business.

(3) A person currently licensed as a dealer or salesperson by another state or country and not currently under license suspension or revocation by the administrator may only sell motor vehicles in this state to licensed dealers, dismantlers, or manufacturers, and only at their places of business. 1992

41-3-104. Division creation — Administrator appointed.

(1) There is created within the commission the Motor Vehicle Enforcement Division with the powers and duties provided in this chapter.

(2) The division shall be administered by the motor vehicle enforcement administrator.

(3) The administrator shall be appointed by the commission and is subject to the commission's supervision and direction. 1992

41-3-105. Administrator's powers and duties — Administrator and investigators to be law enforcement officers.

(1) The administrator may make rules to carry out the purposes of this chapter and Sections 41-1a-1001 through 41-1a-1007 according to the procedures and requirements of Title 63, Chapter 46a, Utah Administrative Rulemaking Act.

(2) (a) The administrator may employ clerks, deputies, and assistants necessary to discharge the duties under this chapter and may designate the duties of those clerks, deputies, and assistants.

(b) The administrator, assistant administrator, and all investigators shall be law enforcement officers certified by peace officer standards and training as required by Section 53-13-103.

(3) (a) The administrator may investigate any suspected or alleged violation of:

(i) this chapter;

(ii) Title 41, Chapter 1a, Motor Vehicle Act;

(iii) any law concerning motor vehicle fraud; or

(iv) any rule made by the administrator.

(b) The administrator may bring an action in the name of the state against any person to enjoin a violation found under Subsection (3)(a).

(4) (a) The administrator may prescribe forms to be used for applications for licenses.

(b) The administrator may require information from the applicant concerning the applicant's fitness to be licensed.

(c) Each application for a license shall contain:

(i) if the applicant is an individual, the name and residence address of the applicant and the trade name, if any, under which he intends to conduct business;

(ii) if the applicant is a partnership, the name and residence address of each partner, whether limited or general, and the name under which the partnership business will be conducted;

(iii) if the applicant is a corporation, the name of the corporation, and the name and residence address of each of its principal officers and directors;

(iv) a complete description of the principal place of business, including:

(A) the municipality, with the street and number, if any;

(B) if located outside of any municipality, a general description so that the location can be determined; and

(C) any other places of business operated and maintained by the applicant in conjunction with the principal place of business; and

(v) if the application is for a new motor vehicle dealer's license, the name of each motor vehicle the applicant has been enfranchised to sell or exchange, the name and address of the manufacturer or distributor who has enfranchised the applicant, and the names and addresses of the individuals who will act as salespersons under authority of the license.

(5) The administrator may adopt a seal with the words "Motor Vehicle Enforcement Administrator, State of Utah," to authenticate the acts of his office.

(6) (a) The administrator may require that the licensee erect or post signs or devices on his principal place of business and any other sites, equipment, or locations operated and maintained by the licensee in conjunction with his business.

(b) The signs or devices shall state the licensee's name, principal place of business, type and number of licenses, and any other information that the administrator considers necessary to identify the licensee.

(c) The administrator may make rules in accordance with Title 63, Chapter 46a, Utah Administrative Rulemaking Act, determining allowable size and shape of signs or devices, their lettering and other details, and their location.

(7) (a) The administrator shall provide for quarterly meetings of the advisory board and may call special meetings.

(b) Notices of all meetings shall be sent to each member not fewer than five days prior to the meeting.

(8) The administrator, the officers and inspectors of the division designated by the commission, and peace officers shall:

(a) make arrests upon view and without warrant for any violation committed in their presence of any of the provisions of this chapter, or Title 41, Chapter 1a, Motor Vehicle Act;

(b) when on duty, upon reasonable belief that a motor vehicle, trailer, or semitrailer is being operated in violation of any provision of Title 41, Chapter 1a, Motor Vehicle Act, require the driver of the vehicle to stop, exhibit his driver's license and the registration card issued for the vehicle and submit to an inspection of the vehicle, the license plates, and registration card;

(c) serve all warrants relating to the enforcement of the laws regulating the operation of motor vehicles, trailers, and semitrailers;

(d) investigate traffic accidents and secure testimony of witnesses or persons involved; and

(e) investigate reported thefts of motor vehicles, trailers, and semitrailers.

(9) The administrator may contract with a public prosecutor to provide additional prosecution of this chapter.   2005

41-3-106. Board — Creation and composition — Appointment, terms, compensation, and expenses of members — Meetings — Quorum — Powers and duties — Officers' election and duties — Voting.

(1) (a) There is created an advisory board of five members that shall assist and advise the administrator in the administration and enforcement of this chapter.

(b) The members shall be appointed by the governor from among the licensed motor vehicle manufacturers, distributors, factory branch and distributor branch representatives, dealers, dismantlers, transporters, remanufacturers, and body shops.

(c) (i) Except as required by Subsection (ii), each member shall be appointed for a term of four years or until his successor is appointed and qualified.

(ii) Notwithstanding the requirements of Subsection (i), the governor shall, at the time of appointment or reappointment, adjust the length of terms to ensure that the terms of board members are staggered so that approximately half of the board is appointed every two years.

(d) Three members of the board shall be selected as follows:

(i) one from new motor vehicle dealers;

(ii) one from used motor vehicle dealers; and

(iii) one from manufacturers, transporters, dismantlers, crushers, remanufacturers, and body shops.

(e) (i) Members shall receive no compensation or benefits for their services, but may receive per diem and expenses incurred in the performance of the member's official duties at the rates established by the Division of Finance under Sections 63A-3-106 and 63A-3-107.

(ii) Members may decline to receive per diem and expenses for their service.

(f) A majority of the members of the board constitutes a quorum and may act upon and resolve in the name of the board any matter, thing, or question referred to it by the administrator, or that the board has power to determine.

(g) When a vacancy occurs in the membership for any reason, the replacement shall be appointed for the unexpired term.

(2) (a) The board shall on the first day of each July, or as soon thereafter as practicable, elect a chair, vice chair, secretary, and assistant secretary from among its members, who shall each hold office until his successor is elected.

(b) As soon as the board elects its officers, the elected secretary shall certify the results of the election to the administrator.

(c) The chair shall preside at all meetings of the board and the secretary shall make a record of the proceedings, which shall be preserved in the office of the administrator.

(d) If the chair is absent from any meeting of the board, his duties shall be discharged by the vice chair, and if the secretary is absent, his duties shall be discharged by the assistant secretary.

(e) All members of the board may vote on any question, matter, or thing that properly comes before it.   1996

41-3-107. Attorney general — Duty to render opinions and to represent or appear for administrator or board.

The attorney general shall:

(1) represent the administrator, the division, and the board;

(2) give opinions on all questions of law relating to the interpretation of this chapter or arising out of the administration of this chapter; and

(3) appear on behalf of the administrator, the division, or the board in all actions brought by or against the administrator, the division, or board, whether under the provisions of this chapter or otherwise.   1992

41-3-108. Copies of records and papers — Admissibility in evidence.

Certified copies of all records and papers prepared in the office of the administrator under seal of the administrator are admissible in evidence in any case in the same manner as the original.   1993

41-3-109. Adjudicative proceedings — Hearings.

(1) The commission, the division, the board, and the administrator shall comply with the procedures and requirements of Title 63, Chapter 46b, Administrative Procedures Act, in all adjudicative proceedings conducted under the authority of this chapter and Sections 41-1a-1001 through 41-1a-1008.

(2) The administrator may request the attendance of the board at any hearing, or he may direct that any hearing be held before the board.   1992

PART 2

LICENSING

41-3-201. Licenses required — Restitution — Education.

(1) As used in this section, "new applicant" means a person who is applying for a license that the person has not been issued during the previous licensing year.

(2) A person may not act as any of the following without having procured a license issued by the administrator: a dealer, salvage vehicle buyer, salesperson, manufacturer, transporter, dismantler, distributor, factory branch and representative, distributor branch and representative, crusher, remanufacturer, and body shop.

(3) (a) A person may not bid on or purchase a vehicle with a salvage certificate as defined in

Section 41-1a-1001 at or through any motor vehicle auction unless the person is a licensed salvage vehicle buyer.

(b) A person may not offer for sale, sell, or exchange a vehicle with a salvage certificate as defined in Section 41-1a-1001 at or through any motor vehicle auction except to a licensed salvage vehicle buyer.

(4) A supplemental license shall be secured by a dealer, manufacturer, remanufacturer, transporter, dismantler, crusher, or body shop for each additional place of business maintained by him.

(5) A person who has been convicted of any law relating to motor vehicle commerce or motor vehicle fraud may not be issued a license unless full restitution regarding those convictions has been made.

(6) (a) The division may not issue a license to a new applicant for a new or used motor vehicle dealer license unless the new applicant completes an eight-hour orientation class approved by the division that includes education on motor vehicle laws and rules.

(b) The approved costs of the orientation class shall be paid by the new applicant.

(c) The class shall be completed by the new applicant and the applicant's partners, corporate officers, bond indemnitors, and managers.

(d) The division shall approve:

(i) providers of the orientation class; and

(ii) costs of the orientation class.   2000

41-3-201.5. Brokering of a new motor vehicle without a license prohibited.

(1) A person, may not, for a fee, commission, or other form of compensation, arrange, offer to arrange, or broker a transaction involving the sale or lease of more than two new motor vehicles in any 12 consecutive month period, unless the person is licensed under Subsection 41-3-202(1).

(2) A person who violates this section is guilty of a class B misdemeanor.   1997

41-3-202. Licenses — Classes and scope.

(1) A new motor vehicle dealer's license permits the licensee to:

(a) offer for sale, sell, or exchange new motor vehicles if the licensee possesses a franchise from the manufacturer of the motor vehicle offered for sale, sold, or exchanged by the licensee;

(b) offer for sale, sell, or exchange used motor vehicles;

(c) operate as a body shop; and

(d) dismantle motor vehicles.

(2) A used motor vehicle dealer's license permits the licensee to:

(a) offer for sale, sell, or exchange used motor vehicles;

(b) operate as a body shop; and

(c) dismantle motor vehicles.

(3) A new motorcycle, off-highway vehicle, and small trailer dealer's license permits the licensee to:

(a) offer for sale, sell, or exchange new motorcycles, off-highway vehicles, or small trailers if the licensee possesses a franchise from the manufacturer of the motorcycle, off-highway vehicle, or small trailer offered for sale, sold, or exchanged by the licensee;

(b) offer for sale, sell, or exchange used motorcycles, off-highway vehicles, or small trailers; and

(c) dismantle motorcycles, off-highway vehicles, or small trailers.

(4) A used motorcycle, off-highway vehicle, and small trailer dealer's license permits the licensee to:

(a) offer for sale, sell, or exchange used motorcycles, off-highway vehicles, and small trailers; and

(b) dismantle motorcycles, off-highway vehicles, or small trailers.

(5) A salesperson's license permits the licensee to act as a motor vehicle salesperson and is valid for employment with only one dealer at a time.

(6) (a) A manufacturer's license permits the licensee to construct or assemble motor vehicles subject to registration under Title 41, Chapter 1a, Motor Vehicle Act, at an established place of business and to remanufacture motor vehicles.

(b) Under rules made by the administrator, the licensee may issue and install vehicle identification numbers on manufactured motor vehicles.

(c) The licensee may franchise and appoint dealers to sell manufactured motor vehicles by notifying the division of the franchise or appointment.

(7) A transporter's license permits the licensee to transport or deliver motor vehicles subject to registration under Title 41, Chapter 1a, Motor Vehicle Act, from a manufacturing, assembling, or distributing point or from a dealer, to dealers, distributors, or sales agents of a manufacturer or remanufacturer, to or from detail or repair shops, and to financial institutions or places of storage from points of repossession.

(8) A dismantler's license permits the licensee to dismantle motor vehicles subject to registration under Title 41, Chapter 1a, Motor Vehicle Act, for the purpose of reselling parts or for salvage, or selling dismantled or salvage vehicles to a crusher or other dismantler.

(9) A distributor or factory branch and distributor branch's license permits the licensee to sell and distribute new motor vehicles, parts, and accessories to their franchised dealers.

(10) A representative's license, for factory representatives or distributor representatives permits the licensee to contact his authorized dealers for the purpose of making or promoting the sale of motor vehicles, parts, and accessories.

(11) (a) (i) A remanufacturer's license permits the licensee to construct, reconstruct, assemble, or reassemble motor vehicles subject to registration under Title 41, Chapter 1a, Motor Vehicle Act, from used or new motor vehicles or parts.

(ii) Evidence of ownership of parts and motor vehicles used in remanufacture shall be available to the division upon demand.

(b) Under rules made by the administrator, the licensee may issue and install vehicle identification numbers on remanufactured motor vehicles.

(12) A crusher's license permits the licensee to engage in the business of crushing or shredding motor vehicles subject to registration under Title 41, Chapter 1a, Motor Vehicle Act, for the purpose of reducing the useable materials and metals to a more compact size for recycling.

(13) A body shop's license permits the licensee to rebuild, restore, repair, or paint primarily the body of motor vehicles damaged by collision or natural disaster, and to dismantle motor vehicles.

(14) A special equipment dealer's license permits the licensee to:

(a) buy incomplete new motor vehicles with a gross vehicle weight of 12,000 or more pounds from a new motor vehicle dealer and sell the new vehicle with the special equipment installed without a franchise from the manufacturer;

(b) offer for sale, sell, or exchange used motor vehicles;

(c) operate as a body shop; and

(d) dismantle motor vehicles.

(15) (a) A salvage vehicle buyer license permits the licensee to bid on or purchase a vehicle with a salvage certificate as defined in Section 41-1a-1001 at any motor vehicle auction.

(b) A salvage vehicle buyer license may only be issued to a motor vehicle dealer, dismantler, or body shop who qualifies under rules made by the division and is licensed in any state as a motor vehicle dealer, dismantler, or body shop.

(c) The division may not issue more than two salvage vehicle buyer licenses to any one dealer, dismantler, or body shop.

(d) In accordance with Title 63, Chapter 46a, Utah Administrative Rulemaking Act, the administrator shall make rules establishing qualifications of an applicant for a salvage vehicle buyer license. The criteria shall include:

(i) business history;

(ii) salvage vehicle qualifications;

(iii) ability to properly handle and dispose of environmental hazardous materials associated with salvage vehicles; and

(iv) record in demonstrating compliance with the provisions of this chapter.   2003

41-3-203. Licenses — Form — Seal — Custody of salesperson's license — Display of salesperson and dealer licenses — Licensee's pocket card.

(1) (a) The administrator shall prescribe the form of each license and the seal of his office shall be imprinted on each license.

(b) The license of each salesperson shall be delivered or mailed to the dealer employing the salesperson and it shall be kept in the custody and control of the dealer and conspicuously displayed in the dealer's place of business.

(c) Each licensee shall display conspicuously his own license in his place of business.

(2) (a) The administrator shall prepare and deliver a pocket card, certifying that the person whose name is on the card is licensed under this chapter.

(b) Each salesperson's card shall also contain the name and address of the dealer employing him.

(c) Each salesperson shall on request display his pocket card.   1992

41-3-204. Licenses — Principal place of business as prerequisite — Change of location — Relinquishment on loss of principal place of business.

(1) (a) The following licensees must maintain a principal place of business: dealers, special equipment dealers, manufacturers, transporters, remanufacturers, dismantlers, crushers, and body shops.

(b) The administrator may not issue a license under Subsection (1)(a) to an applicant who does not have a principal place of business.

(c) If a licensee changes the location of his principal place of business, he shall immediately notify the administrator and a new license shall be granted for the unexpired portion of the term of the original license at no additional fee.

(2) (a) If a licensee loses possession of a principal place of business, the license is automatically suspended and he shall immediately notify the administrator and upon demand by the adminis-

trator deliver the license, pocket cards, special plates, and temporary permits to the administrator.

(b) The administrator shall hold the licenses, cards, plates, and permits until the licensee obtains a principal place of business.   1998

41-3-205. Licenses — Bonds required — Maximum liability — Action against surety — Loss of bond.

(1) (a) Before a dealer's, special equipment dealer's, crusher's, or body shop's license is issued, the applicant shall file with the administrator a corporate surety bond in the amount of:

(i) $50,000 until June 30, 2006, and $75,000 on or after July 1, 2006, for a motor vehicle dealer's license;

(ii) $20,000 until June 30, 2006, and $75,000 on or after July 1, 2006, for a special equipment dealer's license;

(iii) $10,000 for a motorcycle, off-highway vehicle, or small trailer dealer's or crusher's license; or

(iv) $20,000 for a body shop's license.

(b) The corporate surety shall be licensed to do business within the state and have a rating of at least B+ by the A.M. Best Company.

(c) The form of the bond:

(i) shall be approved by the attorney general;

(ii) shall be conditioned upon the applicant's conducting business as a dealer without:

(A) fraud;

(B) fraudulent representation; or

(C) violating Subsection 41-3-301(1) which requires a dealer to submit or deliver a certificate of title or manufacturer's certificate of origin; and

(iii) may be continuous in form.

(d) The total aggregate liability on the bond to all persons making claims, regardless of the number of claimants or the number of years a bond remains in force, may not exceed the amount of the bond.

(2) (a) A cause of action under Subsection (1) may not be maintained against a surety unless:

(i) a claim is filed in writing with the administrator within one year after the cause of action arose; and

(ii) the action is commenced within two years after the claim was filed with the administrator.

(b) The surety or principal shall notify the administrator if a claim on the bond is successfully prosecuted or settled against the surety or principal.

(3) A person making a claim on the bond shall be awarded attorneys' fees in cases successfully prosecuted or settled against the surety or principal if the bond has not been depleted.

(4) (a) (i) If a dealer, body shop, or crusher loses possession of the bond required by this chapter, the dealer, body shop, or crusher license is automatically suspended.

(ii) All licenses, pocket cards, temporary permits, and special plates issued to the licensee shall be immediately returned to the administrator.

(b) A dealer, body shop, or crusher may not continue to use or permit to be used licenses, pocket cards, temporary permits, or special plates until the required bond is on file with the administrator and the license has been reinstated.

(5) A representative or consignee of a dealer is not required to file a bond if the dealer for whom the representative or consignee acts fully complies with the provisions of this chapter.   2005

41-3-206. Duration of licenses — Expiration date — Renewal.

(1) Except as provided in Subsection (2), each license issued under this chapter expires on June 30 of each year and may be renewed upon application and payment of a fee required under Section 41-3-601, if the license has not been suspended or revoked.

(2) A motor vehicle salesperson's license expires as provided under Subsection (1) or when the salesperson terminates employment with the dealer with whom he is licensed, whichever comes first.

(3) (a) Beginning July 1, 1999, the division may not renew a license for a new or used motor vehicle dealer's license unless the renewal applicant completes a three-hour class approved by the division that includes education on new motor vehicle laws and rules.

(b) The approved costs of the class shall be paid by the renewal applicant.

(c) The class shall be completed by the renewal applicant or any designated representative of the renewal applicant dealer.

(d) The division shall approve:

(i) the class providers; and

(ii) costs of the class.   1999

41-3-207. New motor vehicle dealer's license — Change, addition, or loss of franchise — Notification — Relinquishment of license and relicensing as used motor vehicle dealer — Continuance in business to dispose of stock.

(1) If a dealer changes to, adds, cancels, or loses a franchise for the sale of new motor vehicles he shall immediately notify the administrator.

(2) (a) If the dealer has cancelled or lost a franchise, the administrator shall determine whether the dealer should be licensed as a used motor vehicle dealer.

(b) If the administrator determines that the dealer should be licensed as a used motor vehicle dealer, he shall issue to the dealer a used motor vehicle dealer's license.

(c) A dealer relicensed as a used motor vehicle dealer may continue to sell new motor vehicles for up to six months from the date of the relicensing, to enable the dealer to dispose of his existing stock of new motor vehicles.   1992

41-3-208. Salesperson's license — Relinquishment upon loss or change of employment — Notice to salesperson — New license required.

(1) If a salesperson is discharged from or leaves his employer, the dealer who last employed the salesperson shall return the salesperson's license to the administrator.

(2) The salesperson shall be notified at his last known place of residence that his license has been returned to the administrator.

(3) A person may not act as a motor vehicle salesperson until a new license is procured.   1992

41-3-209. Administrator's findings — Suspension and revocation of license.

(1) If the administrator finds that an applicant is not qualified to receive a license, a license may not be granted.

(2) (a) If the administrator finds that there is reasonable cause to deny, suspend, or revoke a license issued under this chapter, the administrator shall deny, suspend, or revoke the license.

(b) Reasonable cause for denial, suspension, or revocation of a license includes, in relation to the applicant or license holder or any of its partners, officers, or directors:

(i) lack of a principal place of business;

(ii) lack of a sales tax license required under Title 59, Chapter 12, Sales and Use Tax Act;

(iii) lack of a bond in effect as required by this chapter;

(iv) current revocation or suspension of a dealer, dismantler, auction, or salesperson license issued in another state;

(v) nonpayment of required fees;

(vi) making a false statement on any application for a license under this chapter or for special license plates;

(vii) a violation of any state or federal law involving motor vehicles;

(viii) a violation of any state or federal law involving controlled substances;

(ix) charges filed with any county attorney, district attorney, or U.S. attorney in any court of competent jurisdiction for a violation of any state or federal law involving motor vehicles;

(x) a violation of any state or federal law involving fraud; or

(xi) a violation of any state or federal law involving a registerable sex offense under Section 77-27-21.5.

(c) Any action taken by the administrator under Subsection (2)(b)(ix) shall remain in effect until a final resolution is reached by the court involved or the charges are dropped.

(3) If the administrator finds that the license holder has been convicted by a court of competent jurisdiction of violating any of the provisions of this chapter or any rules made by the administrator, or finds other reasonable cause, the administrator may, by complying with the emergency procedures of Title 63, Chapter 46b, Administrative Procedures Act:

(a) suspend the license on terms and for a period of time he finds reasonable; or

(b) revoke the license.

(4) (a) After suspending or revoking a license, the administrator may take reasonable action to:

(i) notify the public that the licensee is no longer in business; and

(ii) prevent the former licensee from violating the law by conducting business without a license.

(b) Action under Subsection (4)(a) may include signs, banners, barriers, locks, bulletins, and notices.

(c) Any business being conducted incidental to the business for which the former licensee was licensed may continue to operate subject to the preventive action taken under this subsection.   2005

41-3-210. License holders — Prohibitions.

(1) The holder of any license issued under this chapter may not:

(a) intentionally publish, display, or circulate any advertising that is misleading or inaccurate in any material fact or that misrepresents any of the products sold, manufactured, reman-ufactured, handled, or furnished by a licensee;

(b) intentionally publish, display, or circulate any advertising without identifying the seller as the licensee by including in the advertisement the full name under which the licensee is licensed or the licensee's number assigned by the division;

(c) violate this chapter or the rules made by the administrator;

(d) violate any law of the state respecting commerce in motor vehicles or any rule respecting commerce in motor vehicles made by any licensing or regulating authority of the state;

(e) engage in business as a new motor vehicle dealer, special equipment dealer, used motor vehicle dealer, motor vehicle crusher, or body shop without having in effect a bond as required in this chapter;

(f) act as a dealer, dismantler, crusher, manufacturer, transporter, remanufacturer, or body shop without maintaining a principal place of business;

(g) engage in a business respecting the selling or exchanging of new or new and used motor vehicles for which he is not licensed, including selling or exchanging a new motor vehicle for which the licensee does not have a franchise, but this Subsection (1)(g) does not apply to a special equipment dealer who sells a new special equipment motor vehicle with a gross vehicle weight of 12,000 or more pounds after installing special equipment on the motor vehicle;

(h) dismantle or transport to a crusher for crushing or other disposition any motor vehicle without first obtaining a dismantling or junk permit under Section 41-1a-1009, 41-1a-1010, or 41-1a-1011;

(i) as a new motor vehicle dealer, special equipment dealer, or used motor vehicle dealer fail to give notice of sales or transfers as required in Section 41-3-301;

(j) advertise or otherwise represent, or knowingly allow to be advertised or represented on his behalf or at his place of business, that no down payment is required in connection with the sale of a motor vehicle when a down payment is required and the buyer is advised or induced to finance a down payment by a loan in addition to any other loan financing the remainder of the purchase price of the motor vehicle;

(k) as a crusher, crush or shred a motor vehicle brought to the crusher without obtaining proper evidence of ownership of the motor vehicle; proper evidence of ownership is a certificate of title endorsed according to law or a dismantling or junk permit issued under Section 41-1a-1009, 41-1a-1010, or 41-1a-1011;

(l) as a manufacturer or remanufacturer assemble a motor vehicle that does not comply with construction, safety, or vehicle identification number standards fixed by law or rule of any licensing or regulating authority;

(m) as anyone other than a salesperson licensed under this chapter, be present on a dealer display space and contact prospective customers to promote the sale of the dealer's vehicles;

(n) sell, display for sale, or offer for sale motor vehicles at any location other than the principal place of business or additional places of business licensed under this chapter; this provision is construed to prevent dealers, salespersons, or any other representative of a dealership from selling, displaying, or offering motor vehicles for sale from their homes or other unlicensed locations;

(o) (i) as a dealer, dismantler, body shop, or manufacturer, maintain a principal place of business or additional place of business that shares any common area with a business or activity not directly related to motor vehicle commerce; or

(ii) maintain any places of business that share any common area with another dealer, dismantler, body shop, or manufacturer;

(p) withhold delivery of license plates obtained by the licensee on behalf of a customer for any reason, including nonpayment of any portion of the vehicle purchase price or down payment;

(q) issue a temporary permit for any vehicle that has not been sold by the licensee;

(r) alter a temporary permit in any manner;

(s) operate any principal place of business or additional place of business in a location that does not comply with local ordinances, including zoning ordinances; or

(t) sell, display for sale, offer for sale, or exchange any new motor vehicle if the licensee does not:

(i) have a new motor vehicle dealer's license under Section 41-3-202; and

(ii) possess a franchise from the manufacturer of the new motor vehicle sold, displayed for sale, offered for sale, or exchanged by the licensee.

(2) (a) If a new motor vehicle is constructed in more than one stage, such as a motor home, ambulance, or van conversion, the licensee shall advertise, represent, sell, and exchange the vehicle as the make designated by the final stage manufacturer, except in those specific situations where the licensee possesses a franchise from the initial or first stage manufacturer, presumably the manufacturer of the motor vehicle's chassis.

(b) Sales of multiple stage manufactured motor vehicles shall include the transfer to the purchaser of a valid manufacturer's statement or certificate of origin from each manufacturer under Section 41-3-301.

(3) Each licensee, except salespersons, shall maintain and make available for inspection by peace officers and employees of the division:

(a) a record of every motor vehicle bought, or exchanged by the licensee or received or accepted by the licensee for sale or exchange;

(b) a record of every used part or used accessory bought or otherwise acquired;

(c) a record of every motor vehicle bought or otherwise acquired and wrecked or dismantled by the licensee;

(d) all buyers' orders, contracts, odometer statements, temporary permit records, financing records, and all other documents related to the purchase, sale, or consignment of motor vehicles; and

(e) a record of the name and address of the person to whom any motor vehicle or motor vehicle body, chassis, or motor vehicle engine is sold or otherwise disposed of and a description of the motor vehicle by year, make, and vehicle identification number.

(4) Each licensee required by this chapter to keep records shall:

(a) be kept by the licensee at least for five years; and

(b) furnish copies of those records upon request to any peace officer or employee of the division during reasonable business hours.

(5) A manufacturer, distributor, distributor representative, or factory representative may not induce or attempt to induce by means of coercion, intimidation, or discrimination any dealer to:

(a) accept delivery of any motor vehicle, parts, or accessories or any other commodity or commodities, including advertising material not ordered by the dealer;

(b) order or accept delivery of any motor vehicle with special features, appliances, accessories, or equipment not included in the list price of the motor vehicle as publicly advertised by the manufacturer;

(c) order from any person any parts, accessories, equipment, machinery, tools, appliances, or any other commodity;

(d) enter into an agreement with the manufacturer, distributor, distributor representative, or factory representative of any of them, or to do any other act unfair to the dealer by threatening to cancel any franchise or contractual agreement between the manufacturer, distributor, distributor branch, or factory branch and the dealer;

(e) refuse to deliver to any dealer having a franchise or contractual arrangement for the retail sale of new and unused motor vehicles sold or distributed by the manufacturer, distributor, distributor branch or factory branch, any motor vehicle, publicly advertised for immediate delivery within 60 days after the dealer's order is received; or

(f) unfairly, without regard to the equities of the dealer, cancel the franchise of any motor vehicle dealer; the nonrenewal of a franchise or selling agreement without cause is a violation of this subsection and is an unfair cancellation.

(6) A dealer may not assist an unlicensed dealer or salesperson in unlawful activity through active or passive participation in sales, or by allowing use of his facilities or dealer license number, or by any other means.

(7) (a) The holder of any new motor vehicle dealer license issued under this chapter may not sell any new motor vehicle to:

(i) another dealer licensed under this chapter who does not hold a valid franchise for the make of new motor vehicles sold, unless the selling dealer licenses and titles the new motor vehicle to the purchasing dealer; or

(ii) any motor vehicle leasing or rental company located within this state, or who has any branch office within this state, unless the dealer licenses and titles the new motor vehicle to the purchasing, leasing, or rental company.

(b) Subsection (7)(a)(i) does not apply to the sale of a new incomplete motor vehicle with a gross vehicle weight of 12,000 or more pounds to a special equipment dealer licensed under this chapter.

(8) A dealer licensed under this chapter may not take on consignment any new motor vehicle from anyone other than a new motor vehicle dealer, factory, or distributor who is licensed and franchised to distribute or sell that make of motor vehicle in this or any other state.

(9) A body shop licensed under this chapter may not assist an unlicensed body shop in unlawful activity through active or passive means or by allowing use of its facilities, name, body shop number, or by any other means.

(10) A used motor vehicle dealer licensed under this chapter may not advertise, offer for sale, or sell a new motor vehicle that has been driven less than 7,500 miles by obtaining a title only to the vehicle and representing it as a used motor vehicle.

(11) (a) Except as provided in Subsection (11)(c), or in cases of undue hardship or emergency as provided by rule by the division, a dealer or salesperson licensed under this chapter may not, on consecutive days of Saturday and Sunday, sell, offer for sale, lease, or offer for lease a motor vehicle.

(b) Each day a motor vehicle is sold, offered for sale, leased, or offered for lease in violation of Subsection (11)(a) and each motor vehicle sold, offered for sale, leased, or offered for lease in violation of Subsection (11)(a) shall constitute a separate offense.

(c) The provisions of Subsection (11)(a) shall not apply to a dealer participating in a trade show or exhibition if:

(i) there are five or more dealers participating in the trade show or exhibition; and

(ii) the trade show or exhibition takes place at a location other than the principal place of business of one of the dealers participating in the trade show or exhibition. **2000**

PART 3

TEMPORARY PERMITS

41-3-301. Sale by dealer, sale by auction — Temporary permit — Delivery of certificate of title or origin — Notice to division.

(1) (a) Each dealer licensed under Part 2, Licensing, upon the sale and delivery of any motor vehicle for which a temporary permit is issued under Section 41-3-302 shall within 30 days submit a certificate of title or manufacturer's certificate of origin for that motor vehicle, endorsed according to law, to the Motor Vehicle Division, accompanied by all documents required to obtain a new certificate of title and registration in the new owner's name.

(b) If a temporary permit is not issued, the certificate of title or manufacturer's certificate of origin shall be delivered to the vendee, endorsed according to law, within 48 hours, unless the vendee is a dealer or dismantler in which case the title or manufacturer's certificate of origin shall be delivered within 21 days.

(c) A motor vehicle consigned to an auction and sold is considered sold by the consignor to the auction and then sold by the auction to the consignee. Both the consignor and auction are subject to this section.

(d) (i) (A) A motor vehicle consigned to a wholesale motor vehicle auction and sold to a licensed dealer or dismantler is considered sold by the consignor to the licensed dealer or dismantler.

(B) Both the consignor and the wholesale motor vehicle auction are subject to the title delivery requirements of Subsection (1)(b).

(C) The consignor, or the wholesale motor vehicle auction as the consignor's agent, shall endorse the certificate of title according to law. By endorsing the certificate of title as agent of the consignor, the wholesale motor vehicle auction does not become the owner, seller, or assignor of title.

(ii) (A) A wholesale motor vehicle auction may purchase or sell motor vehicles in its own name.

(B) If a wholesale motor vehicle auction purchases or sells a motor vehicle in its own name, the wholesale motor vehicle auction is subject to Subsections (1)(a) and (1)(b).

(2) (a) (i) Each dealer licensed under Part 2, Licensing, upon the sale and delivery of a motor vehicle for which a temporary permit is issued under Section 41-3-302, shall within 30 days give written notice of the sale to the Motor Vehicle Division upon a form provided by the Motor Vehicle Division.

(ii) The notice shall contain:

(A) the date of the sale;

(B) the names and addresses of the dealer and the purchaser;

(C) a description of the motor vehicle;

(D) the motor vehicle's odometer reading at the time of the sale; and

(E) other information required by the division.

(b) If no temporary permit is issued, the notice shall be filed with the division within 30 days after the sale, and a duplicate copy shall be given to the purchaser at the time of sale, unless the purchaser is a dealer or dismantler.

(c) The administrator may make rules in accordance with Title 63, Chapter 46a, Utah Administrative Rulemaking Act, providing that the notice required under Subsections (2)(a) and (2)(b) may be filed in electronic form or on magnetic media.

1995

41-3-302. Temporary permits — Purchasers of motor vehicles — Penalty for use after expiration — Sale and rescission.

(1) (a) Under rules made by the administrator, dealers and the division may issue temporary permits, the forms for which are furnished by the division to dealers.

(b) Dealers may issue temporary permits to bona fide purchasers of motor vehicles for use for a period not to exceed 30 days on a motor vehicle sold to the purchaser by the dealer.

(c) The dealer is responsible and liable for the registration fee of each motor vehicle for which the permit is issued.

(d) All issued temporary permits that are outstanding after 30 days from the date they are issued are delinquent and a penalty equal to the registration fee shall be collected from the issuing dealer.

(2) If a temporary permit is issued by a dealer under this section and the sale of the motor vehicle is subsequently rescinded, the temporary permit may be voided and the issuing dealer is not liable for the registration fee or penalty.

1992

41-3-303. Temporary permits — Inspections required before issuance.

(1) A dealer licensed in accordance with this chapter may not issue a temporary permit under Section 41-3-302 unless:

(a) (i) the motor vehicle for which the temporary permit is issued has received and passed the safety inspection required by Section 53-8-205 within the previous six months;

(ii) the safety inspection certificate was issued in the name of a licensed and bonded dealer; and

(iii) a copy of the safety inspection certificate is given to the customer; and

(b) the motor vehicle passed the emission inspection test required by Section 41-6a-1642.

(2) Notwithstanding Subsection (1)(a), a dealer may issue a temporary permit without a safety inspection certificate if the motor vehicle complies with the safety inspection as provided in Section 41-1a-205.

(3) Notwithstanding Subsection (1)(b), a dealer may issue a temporary permit without proof of an emission inspection if:

(a) the motor vehicle is exempt from emission inspection as provided in Section 41-6a-1642;

(b) the purchaser is a resident of a county that does not require emission inspections; or

(c) the motor vehicle is otherwise exempt from emission inspections.

(4) Notwithstanding Subsection (1), a dealer may sell a motor vehicle as is without having it safety or emission inspected provided that no temporary permit is issued.

2005

41-3-304. Temporary permits — Temporary sports event registration certificate — Suspension or revocation of dealer's authority to issue — Return of temporary permits to division — Refunds — Appeal.

(1) The division may suspend or revoke a dealer's authority to issue a temporary permit or a temporary sports event registration certificate under this part if the division determines the dealer has failed to comply with this chapter or with any rules made by the commission under this part.

(2) (a) Suspension or revocation of authority to issue a temporary permit or a temporary sports event registration certificate takes effect immediately upon written notification to the dealer by the division.

(b) Upon notification, the dealer shall immediately return all temporary permits to the division.

(c) Subject to Subsection (2)(d), if the authority to issue a temporary permit under Section 41-3-302 is revoked or suspended for more than 30 days, the dealer may apply for a refund of the money paid to the division only for temporary permits described in Section 41-3-302 that are returned prior to issuance.

(d) Temporary permits being returned may not have ever been issued, written on, or separated from their stubs, and shall be in useable condition.

(3) If the division suspends or revokes a dealer's authority to issue a temporary permit or a temporary sports event registration certificate as provided in this section, each of the following is a violation of this chapter and grounds for automatic suspension of the dealer's license:

(a) failure to return a temporary permit to the division as provided in this section; or

(b) issuing a:

(i) temporary permit; or

(ii) temporary sports event registration certificate.

(4) (a) A dealer may appeal the division's suspension or revocation by filing a written appeal with

the administrator within ten days of the suspension or revocation.

(b) Upon receiving the dealer's written appeal, the administrator shall set a hearing for not more than 20 days from the date the written appeal is received.

(c) A hearing or appeal under this section shall be conducted in accordance with Title 63, Chapter 46b, Administrative Procedures Act. 2001 (1st S.S.)

41-3-305. In-transit permits — Limits — Tax provision.

(1) Under rules made by the administrator, in-transit permits may be issued by the division or its authorized representatives.

(2) In-transit permits allow use of the highways for a time period not to exceed 96 hours.

(3) Before issuing any in-transit permit, the division or its authorized representative shall be satisfied that the person applying for the permit is the owner of the motor vehicle or the owner's representative, and if the owner or driver is a Utah resident, that the motor vehicle complies with the security requirements of Sections 31A-22-302 and 31A-22-303.

(4) The division or its authorized representative may issue in-transit permits without requiring a property tax clearance for the motor vehicle on which the permit is to be used. 1992

41-3-306. Temporary sports event registration — Definitions — Issuance — Fees — Expiration — Rulemaking authority.

(1) As used in this section:

(a) "Distributor-provided vehicle" means a motor vehicle:

(i) that has never been titled or registered in any state; and

(ii) the use of which is donated by a distributor licensed under Part 2, Licensing, through a dealer licensed under Part 2, Licensing.

(b) (i) "Event period" means a time period:

(A) during which a sports event takes place;

(B) not to exceed 180 consecutive calendar days; and

(C) specified by the division on a temporary sports event registration certificate.

(ii) "Event period" may include one or more of the following time periods if the division determines that good cause exists for including the time period within the event period:

(A) a reasonable time period before a sports event as determined by the division; or

(B) a reasonable time period after a sports event as determined by the division.

(c) (i) Notwithstanding Section 41-3-102 and except as provided in Subsection (1)(c)(ii), "motor vehicle" means a motor vehicle that is subject to the uniform fee imposed by Section 59-2-405.1.

(ii) "Motor vehicle" does not include a state-assessed commercial vehicle as defined in Section 59-2-102.

(d) (i) "Sports event" means an amateur or professional:

(A) sports:

(I) game;

(II) race; or

(III) contest; or

(B) athletic:

(I) game;

(II) race; or

(III) contest.

(ii) "Sports event" includes a game, race, or contest described in Subsection (1)(d)(i) that is:

(A) an independent game, race, or contest; or

(B) a part of another event or activity regardless of whether the other event or activity is an event or activity relating to sports or athletics.

(e) "Temporary sports event registration certificate" means a motor vehicle certificate of registration issued by the division to a dealer in accordance with this section.

(2) Beginning on September 1, 2001, the division may register a motor vehicle for an event period by issuing to a dealer licensed under Part 2, Licensing, a temporary sports event registration certificate if the division determines that:

(a) the motor vehicle is a distributor-provided vehicle;

(b) the motor vehicle will be used for a sports event within the state during the event period; and

(c) the dealer provides the division an application stating:

(i) the person to whom the distributor is donating use of the motor vehicle;

(ii) the motor vehicle identification number;

(iii) the motor vehicle:

(A) make;

(B) model; and

(C) year;

(iv) the name of the sports event;

(v) the beginning date and ending date of the sports event; and

(vi) any other information the division requires.

(3) If the division issues a temporary sports event registration certificate to a dealer licensed under Part 2, Licensing:

(a) the division:

(i) shall specify the event period on the temporary sports event registration certificate; and

(ii) may specify any other information on the temporary sports event registration certificate as determined by the division; and

(b) the dealer shall for each motor vehicle for which the division issues a temporary sports event registration certificate:

(i) pay the:

(A) registration fees required by Chapter 1a, Part 12, Fee and Tax Requirements; and

(B) uniform fee required by Section 59-2-405.1; and

(ii) place the temporary sports event registration certificate in the rear license plate holder of the motor vehicle.

(4) A temporary sports event registration certificate issued by the division under this section is valid for the event period specified on the temporary sports event registration certificate.

(5) In accordance with Title 63, Chapter 46a, Utah Administrative Rulemaking Act, the commission may make rules:

(a) specifying the information to be provided to the division by a dealer or a person using a distributor-provided vehicle in connection with the issuance of a temporary sports event registration certificate;

(b) specifying the form for a temporary sports event registration certificate; or

(c) defining the terms:

(i) "reasonable time period before a sports event"; and

(ii) "reasonable time period after a sports event."   2001 (1st S.S.)

PART 4

DISCLOSURE REQUIREMENTS — PURCHASER'S RIGHTS

41-3-401. Disclosure of financing arrangements relating to the sale of motor vehicles.

(1) (a) A dealer may not issue a temporary permit or release possession of a motor vehicle that the dealer has sold to someone other than another dealer unless the document of sale contains one of the disclosures listed in Subsection (2).

(b) The disclosures shall be set forth clearly and conspicuously on the first or front page of the sale document at the time of sale, executed by the purchaser, and for Subsection (2)(b), executed by the seller also.

(2) (a) The form to be used when financing is the purchaser's responsibility shall read as follows:

"THE PURCHASER OF THE MOTOR VEHICLE DESCRIBED IN THIS CONTRACT ACKNOWLEDGES THAT THE SELLER OF THE MOTOR VEHICLE HAS MADE NO PROMISES, WARRANTIES, OR REPRESENTATIONS REGARDING SELLER'S ABILITY TO OBTAIN FINANCING FOR THE PURCHASE OF THE MOTOR VEHICLE. FURTHERMORE, PURCHASER UNDERSTANDS THAT IF FINANCING IS NECESSARY IN ORDER FOR THE PURCHASER TO COMPLETE THE PAYMENT TERMS OF THIS CONTRACT ALL THE FINANCING ARRANGEMENTS ARE THE SOLE RESPONSIBILITY OF THE PURCHASER.

_____
(Signature of the purchaser)"

(b) The form to be used when the seller agrees to seek arrangements for financing shall read as follows:

"(1) THE PURCHASER OF THE MOTOR VEHICLE DESCRIBED IN THIS CONTRACT HAS EXECUTED THE CONTRACT IN RELIANCE UPON THE SELLER'S REPRESENTATION THAT THE SELLER CAN PROVIDE FINANCING ARRANGEMENTS FOR THE PURCHASE OF THE MOTOR VEHICLE. THE PRIMARY TERMS OF THE FINANCING ARE AS FOLLOWS:

INTEREST RATE BETWEEN ___ % AND ___ % PER ANNUM, TERM BETWEEN _____ MONTHS AND _____ MONTHS. MONTHLY PAYMENTS BETWEEN $ _____ PER MONTH AND $ _____ PER MONTH BASED ON A DOWN PAYMENT OF $ _____.

(2)(a) IF SELLER IS NOT ABLE TO ARRANGE FINANCING WITHIN THE TERMS DISCLOSED, THEN SELLER MUST WITHIN SEVEN CALENDAR DAYS OF THE DATE OF SALE MAIL NOTICE TO THE PURCHASER THAT HE HAS NOT BEEN ABLE TO ARRANGE FINANCING.

(b) PURCHASER THEN HAS 14 DAYS FROM THE DATE OF SALE TO ELECT, IF PURCHASER CHOOSES, TO RESCIND THE CONTRACT OF SALE PURSUANT TO SECTION 41-3-401.

(c) IN ORDER TO RESCIND THE CONTRACT OF SALE, THE PURCHASER SHALL:

(i) RETURN TO SELLER THE MOTOR VEHICLE HE PURCHASED;

(ii) PAY THE SELLER AN AMOUNT EQUAL TO THE CURRENT STANDARD MILEAGE RATE FOR THE COST OF OPERATING A MOTOR VEHICLE ESTABLISHED BY THE FEDERAL INTERNAL REVENUE SERVICE FOR EACH MILE THE MOTOR VEHICLE HAS BEEN DRIVEN; AND

(iii) COMPENSATE SELLER FOR ANY PHYSICAL DAMAGE TO THE MOTOR VEHICLE.

(3) IN RETURN, SELLER SHALL GIVE BACK TO THE PURCHASER ALL PAYMENTS OR OTHER CONSIDERATION PAID BY THE PURCHASER, INCLUDING ANY DOWN PAYMENT AND ANY MOTOR VEHICLE TRADED IN.

(4) IF THE TRADE-IN HAS BEEN SOLD OR OTHERWISE DISPOSED OF BEFORE THE PURCHASER RESCINDS THE TRANSACTION, THEN THE SELLER SHALL RETURN TO THE PURCHASER A SUM EQUIVALENT TO THE ALLOWANCE TOWARD THE PURCHASE PRICE GIVEN BY THE SELLER FOR THE TRADE-IN, AS NOTED IN THE DOCUMENT OF SALE.

(5) IF PURCHASER DOES NOT ELECT TO RESCIND THE CONTRACT OF SALE AS PROVIDED IN SUBSECTION (2)(b) OF THIS FORM:

(a) THE PURCHASER IS RESPONSIBLE FOR ADHERENCE TO THE TERMS AND CONDITIONS OF THE CONTRACT OR RISKS BEING FOUND IN DEFAULT OF THE TERMS AND CONDITIONS;

(b) THE TERMS AND CONDITIONS OF THE DISCLOSURES SET FORTH IN SECTION (1) OF THIS FORM ARE NOT BINDING ON THE SELLER; AND

(c) IF FINANCING IS NECESSARY FOR THE PURCHASER TO COMPLETE THE PAYMENT TERMS OF THE CONTRACT OF SALE, THE PURCHASER IS SOLELY RESPONSIBLE FOR MAKING ALL THE FINANCING ARRANGEMENTS.

(6) SIGNING THIS DISCLOSURE DOES NOT PROHIBIT THE PURCHASER FROM SEEKING HIS OWN FINANCING.

_____
(Signature of the purchaser)

_____
(Signature of the seller)"

(3) (a) (i) In addition to the penalties in this chapter, if the disclosures in Subsection (2) are not properly executed or if the seller is unable to provide the financing arrangements for the purchaser as provided in Subsection (2)(b) within seven calendar days immediately following the sale date disclosed on the document of sale, then in either case the purchaser may return the purchased motor vehicle to the dealer and receive a complete refund of all money and other consideration

given to the dealer for the purchase, including any motor vehicle or property used as a trade-in.

(ii) If the motor vehicle or property used as a trade-in has been sold or otherwise disposed of, the seller shall return to the purchaser the amount of money equivalent to the allowance towards the purchase price given by the dealer for the motor vehicle or property traded in, as noted in the document of sale.

(b) If the purchaser qualifies for the remedies set forth in Subsection (3)(a) and if the purchaser elects to rescind by returning the purchased motor vehicle to the dealer within the prescribed time frame, then the purchaser is liable to the dealer:

(i) for all physical damage to the motor vehicle while in the possession of the purchaser; and

(ii) in an amount equal to the current standard mileage rate for the cost of operating a motor vehicle established by the federal Internal Revenue Service for each mile the motor vehicle was driven between the date the purchaser first acquired possession and the date when the purchaser returned the motor vehicle to the dealer.

(c) The purchaser is not entitled to the remedy set forth in Subsections (3)(a) and (b) if the purchaser materially misrepresents in writing any information requested by the dealer in an application for financing, financial statement, or similar document customarily used to elicit personal and financial data upon which a credit decision is normally predicated.

(4) (a) A dealer who has complied with Subsection (2)(b), but who has not been able to secure financing as set forth in the disclosure, shall within seven days of the date of sale mail written notice to the purchaser:

(i) disclosing that the dealer has not been able to secure financing as set forth in the disclosure; and

(ii) instructing the purchaser of his right to rescind the contract of sale within 14 calendar days of the date of sale, as provided for in Subsection (2).

(b) (i) The dealer shall mail notification to the purchaser within seven calendar days following the date of sale as set forth in the contract of sale.

(ii) This notice complies with Subsection (4)(b)(i) if it is postmarked before the end of the seventh day following the date of sale and addressed to the purchaser at the address contained in the document of sale.

(iii) If the purchaser's address is not contained on the document of sale, then proof of compliance with the notification provision of this Subsection (4)(b) shall be borne by the dealer.

(iv) If a dealer gives notice in the manner prescribed, the purchaser has 14 calendar days from the date of sale to elect to rescind the contract of sale, in accordance with Subsection (2).

(c) (i) If a dealer executes the disclosure required by Subsection (2)(b), but is not able to secure financing as set forth in the disclosure, and the dealer fails to give written notice to the purchaser within seven days, as

provided for in Subsections (4)(a) and (b), then the purchaser may rescind within seven days of the date he first learns that the dealer has not been able to secure financing as set forth in the disclosure.

(ii) Except as provided in this Subsection (4)(c), the purchaser's option to rescind shall be exercised in the manner prescribed in Subsection (3).

(d) If the purchaser does not exercise the option to rescind within the specified time limits in Subsections (3) and (4)(c):

(i) the purchaser is responsible for adherence to the terms and conditions of the contract of sale;

(ii) the dealer is not subject to the financing terms set forth in the disclosure; and

(iii) if financing is necessary for the purchaser to complete the payment terms of the contract of sale, the purchaser is solely responsible for making all the financing arrangements.

(5) A dealer's failure to execute the disclosure required by Subsection (2), or its failure to provide written notice to the purchaser within the time frame specified in this section, subject the dealer to the sanctions in Section 41-3-701.

(6) Either the purchaser or a dealer may bring an action to enforce his rights under this section. The prevailing party in the action is entitled to reasonable attorneys' fees as part of the costs of suit.

(7) A motor vehicle returned by the purchaser to the dealer in accordance with the rescission provisions of this section is not considered sold for purposes of notice of sale under Section 41-3-301 and for purposes of sales tax under Title 59, Chapter 12, Sales and Use Tax Act.   2003

41-3-402. Payoff of liens on motor vehicles traded in.

(1) If a dealer takes a trade-in from a retail customer as part of the sale of a motor vehicle and there is an outstanding loan balance owing on the trade-in, then:

(a) the dealer, within seven calendar days of the date of sale, must give written notice to the lienholder, as designated by the purchaser, that the vehicle has been traded in;

(b) the dealer, within 21 calendar days of the date of sale, or within 15 calendar days of receiving payment in full for the motor vehicle it sold, whichever date is earlier, shall remit payment to the lienholder sufficient to pay off the lien on the traded-in motor vehicle, unless the underlying contract of sale has been rescinded before expiration of the 21 days;

(c) if the underlying contract of sale has for any reason been rescinded before the expiration of 21 days, the dealer within five calendar days after the rescission shall give written notice to the lienholder that the contract of sale has been rescinded and that the motor vehicle originally traded in has been returned to the purchaser.

(2) A lienholder who has been paid in full by a dealer in accordance with the terms of this section shall deliver to the dealer a properly executed title that releases the lien within:

(a) one business day after the business day on which the funds are received when the funds are in cash, cashier's check, certified check, teller's check, or other certified source of funds;

(b) three business days after the business day on which the funds are received when the funds are in the form of a check drawn on a local originating depository institution; or

(c) six business days after the business day on which the funds are received when the funds are in the form of a check drawn on a nonlocal originating depository institution.

(3) If the final day for performing an act under this section falls on a Saturday, Sunday, or a legal holiday, then the time for performance is extended to the immediately following business day.

(4) A dealer's failure to comply with the provisions of this section subjects the dealer to the sanctions set forth in Section 41-3-701.

(5) A person who trades in a motor vehicle to a dealer and who thereafter sustains loss or damage as a result of a dealer's failure to pay off a properly recorded lien on the traded-in motor vehicle within the time specified by Subsection (1)(b), may bring an action against the offending dealer to recover damages proximately caused by the dealer's failure to comply with the provisions of this section, together with costs and reasonable attorneys' fees.   1992

41-3-403. Dealer noncompliance — Rights of purchaser — Penalties.

(1) (a) Subject to the provisions of Subsection (4), if a dealer fails to comply with Subsection 41-3-301(1), the purchaser may return the purchased motor vehicle to the dealer and receive a complete refund of all money and other consideration given for the purchase, including any motor vehicles or property traded in.

(b) If the motor vehicle or property traded in has been sold by the dealer, he shall return to the purchaser the amount of money equivalent to the value of the motor vehicle or property as allowed toward the purchase.

(c) Demand for the return may be made directly by the customer, his attorney, or the administrator.

(d) Any loan payments or interest due between the sale date and the return date on either the motor vehicle purchased or a motor vehicle traded in, are the responsibility of the dealer.

(2) Failure of a dealer to comply with this section:

(a) is a violation of Subsection 41-3-301(1);

(b) is a ground for immediate dealer license suspension; and

(c) allows the customer a cause of action against the dealer to recover all consideration owed under Subsection (1).

(3) A motor vehicle returned under the provisions of this section is not considered to be sold for purposes of:

(a) notice of sale under Subsection 41-3-301(2); and

(b) sales tax under Title 59, Chapter 12, Sales and Use Tax Act.

(4) If a dealer fails to comply with Subsection 41-3-301(1), the dealer shall accept the return of a purchased motor vehicle under this section if the purchaser:

(a) returns the motor vehicle to the dealer and requests in writing that the purchase be rescinded, prior to the time the dealer submits a certificate of title or manufacturer's certificate of origin for that motor vehicle, endorsed according to law, to the Motor Vehicle Division, accompanied by all documents required to obtain a new

certificate of title and registration in the new owner's name;

(b) furnishes to the dealer a written odometer disclosure statement in accordance with Section 41-1a-902; and

(c) pays the dealer an amount equal to the current standard mileage rate for the cost of operating a motor vehicle established by the federal Internal Revenue Service for each mile the motor vehicle was driven between the date the purchaser first acquired possession and the date when the purchaser returned the motor vehicle to the dealer.   2004

41-3-404. Right of action against dealer, salesperson, crusher, body shop, or surety on bond.

(1) A person may maintain an action against a dealer, crusher, or body shop on the corporate surety bond if:

(a) the person suffers a loss or damage because of:

(i) fraud;

(ii) fraudulent representation; or

(iii) a violation of Section 41-3-210; and

(b) the loss or damage results from the action of:

(i) a licensed dealer;

(ii) a licensed dealer's salesperson acting on behalf of the dealer or within the scope of the salesperson's employment;

(iii) a licensed crusher; or

(iv) a body shop.

(2) Successive recovery against a surety on a bond is permitted, but the total aggregate liability on the bond to all persons making claims, regardless of the number of claimants or the number of years a bond remains in force, may not exceed the amount of the bond.

(3) A cause of action may not be maintained against any surety under any bond required under this chapter except as provided in Section 41-3-205.   1999

41-3-405. Sale of third party warranty or service contract — Remission of fee.

(1) If a dealer licensed under this chapter sells a third party warranty or service contract to a customer, the dealer shall within 15 days remit the fee paid by the customer to the warranty or service contract company.

(2) Failure of a dealer to remit the fee within 15 days is a ground for dealer license suspension and allows the customer a cause of action against the dealer for damages that otherwise would have been covered by the warranty or service contract.   1992

41-3-406. Short title.

Sections 41-3-406 through 41-3-414 are known as the "Motor Vehicle Buyback Disclosure Act."   1993

41-3-407. Definitions.

As used in Sections 41-3-406 through 41-3-414:

(1) "Buyback vehicle" means a motor vehicle with an alleged nonconformity that has been replaced or repurchased by a manufacturer as the result of a court judgment, arbitration, or any voluntary agreement entered into between the manufacturer or its agent and a consumer.

(2) "Consumer" means an individual who has entered into an agreement or contract for the transfer, lease, or purchase of a new motor vehicle other than for the purposes of resale, or sublease,

during the duration of the period defined under Section 13-20-5.

(3) "Manufacturer" means any manufacturer, importer, distributor, or anyone who is named as the warrantor on an express written warranty on a motor vehicle.

(4) (a) "Motor vehicle" includes:

(i) a motor home, as defined in Section 13-20-2, but only the self-propelled vehicle and chassis; and

(ii) a motor vehicle, as defined in Section 41-1a-102.

(b) "Motor vehicle" does not include:

(i) those portions of a motor home designated, used, or maintained primarily as a mobile dwelling, office, or commercial space;

(ii) farm tractor, motorcycle, road tractor, or truck tractor as defined in Section 41-1a-102;

(iii) mobile home as defined in Section 41-1a-102; or

(iv) any motor vehicle with a gross laden weight of over 12,000 pounds, except a motor home as defined under Subsection (4)(a)(i).

(5) "Nonconforming vehicle" means a buyback vehicle that has been investigated and evaluated pursuant to Title 13, Chapter 20, New Motor Vehicles Warranties Act, or a similar law of another state or federal government.

(6) (a) "Nonconformity" means a defect, malfunction, or condition that fails to conform to the express warranty, or substantially impairs the use, safety, or value of a motor vehicle.

(b) "Nonconformity" does not include a defect, malfunction, or condition that results from an accident, abuse, neglect, modification, or alteration of a motor vehicle by a person other than the manufacturer, its authorized agent, or a dealer.

(7) "Seller" means any person selling, auctioning, leasing, or exchanging a motor vehicle.

(8) "Violation" means each failure to comply with the obligations imposed by Sections 41-3-406 through 41-3-413. In the case of multiple failures to comply resulting from a single transaction, each failure to comply is a separate violation.

1998

41-3-408. Resale of buyback or nonconforming vehicles — Disclosure Statements.

(1) (a) A motor vehicle may not be offered, auctioned, sold, leased, transferred, or exchanged by a manufacturer or dealer with the knowledge that it is a buyback vehicle or a nonconforming vehicle without prior written disclosure in a clear and conspicuous manner, in accordance with this section.

(b) This section also applies to buyback vehicles or nonconforming vehicles originally returned to a manufacturer or its agent in another state and subsequently resold, leased, or offered or displayed for resale or lease in this state.

(c) An owner of a motor vehicle who is not a manufacturer or dealer, but who has been given information as required by Subsection (a) or (b) shall give the information, in writing, to any prospective purchaser of the vehicle.

(2) (a) The following disclosure language shall be contained in each contract for the sale or lease of a buyback vehicle or a nonconforming vehicle to a consumer or shall be contained in a form affixed to a contract, lease, bill of sale, or any other document that transfers title:

"DISCLOSURE STATEMENT

Vehicle Identification Number (VIN):
Year: Make: Model:
Prior Title Number: State of Title:
Odometer Reading:

This is a used motor vehicle. It was previously returned to the manufacturer or its agent in exchange for a replacement motor vehicle or a refund because it was alleged or found to have the following nonconformities:

1.
2.
3.
4.
5.

THIS DISCLOSURE MUST BE GIVEN BY THE
SELLER TO THE BUYER
EVERY TIME THIS VEHICLE IS RESOLD

_____   _____
(Buyer's Signature)   Date"

(b) The text of the disclosure shall be printed in 12 point boldface type except the heading, which shall be in 16 point extra boldface type.

(c) The entire notice shall be boxed.

(d) Each nonconformity shall be listed separately on a numbered line.

(e) A seller must obtain the consumer's acknowledgment of this written disclosure prior to completing a sale, lease, or other transfer of title as evidenced by the consumer's signature within the box containing the disclosure.

(f) Within 30 days after the sale, lease, or other transfer of title of a nonconforming vehicle, the seller shall deliver to the Motor Vehicle Division a copy of the signed written disclosure required for the sale, lease, or other transfer of title of the nonconforming vehicle. The Motor Vehicle Division shall include the disclosure in the nonconforming vehicle's records.

(3) (a) There shall be affixed to the lower corner of the windshield furthest removed from the driver's side of a nonconforming vehicle, a disclosure statement form which shall be readily visible from the exterior of the vehicle. The form shall be in the following configuration and shall state:

"DISCLOSURE STATEMENT

Vehicle Identification Number (VIN): _____
Year: _____ Make: _____
Model: _____
Prior Title Number: _____ State of Title: ____
Odometer Reading: _____
Warning: This motor vehicle was previously sold as new. It was subsequently alleged or found to have the following defect(s), malfunction(s), or conditions:

1.
2.
3.
4.
5.   "

THIS DISCLOSURE MUST BE GIVEN BY THE
SELLER TO THE BUYER
EVERY TIME THIS VEHICLE IS RESOLD

(b) The disclosure statement shall be at least 4 ½ inches wide and 5 inches long.

(c) The heading shall be boldface type in capital letters not smaller than 18 point in size and the body copy shall be regular or medium face type not smaller than 12 point in size.

(d) Each nonconformity shall be listed separately on a numbered line.

(e) The motor vehicle and title identification information must be inserted in the spaces provided.   1994

41-3-409.   Certificate of title — Brand — Reporting requirements.

A manufacturer, its agent, or a dealer who accepts the return of a nonconforming vehicle, shall:

(1) immediately upon receipt, cause the words "MANUFACTURER BUYBACK NONCONFORMING VEHICLE" to be clearly and conspicuously stamped on the face of the original certificate of title, the Manufacturer's Statement of Origin, or other evidence of ownership; and

(2) within ten days of receipt of the certificate of title, Manufacturer's Statement of Origin, or other evidence of ownership, submit a copy of the face of that stamped document to the Motor Vehicle Division of the Tax Commission.   1993

41-3-409.5.   Unbranded certificate of title — Application requirements — Recording requirements — Recurrence of nonconformities.

(1) To obtain an unbranded certificate of title to a nonconforming vehicle:

(a) the vehicle must have been originally titled in Utah;

(b) the vehicle must have been originally branded in Utah under Section 41-1a-522; and

(c) the manufacturer must submit to the Motor Vehicle Enforcement Division an original application, completed by the manufacturer, for an unbranded certificate of title that meets the requirements of Subsection (2) and a copy of the application to the owner of the motor vehicle and to the lienholder, if any, shown on the certificate of title.

(2) The form of the application shall be approved by the Motor Vehicle Enforcement Division and shall include:

(a) the manufacturer's certification that:

(i) all nonconformities listed in the disclosure under Section 41-3-408 are completely cured;

(ii) the manufacturer warrants to all subsequent purchasers that the nonconformities are cured for the greater of:

(A) the remaining balance of the manufacturer's original express warranty period; or

(B) one year from the date of the first subsequent retail sale or lease; and

(iii) the vehicle identification number has not been removed, falsified, altered, defaced, or destroyed;

(b) a description of the motor vehicle, including its vehicle identification number, make, model, and year of manufacture;

(c) the owner of the motor vehicle and name of the lienholder, if any, shown on the branded certificate of title; and

(d) a description of the repairs made to cure the nonconformities of the motor vehicle, including how they were made.

(3) If an application for an unbranded certificate of title meets all the requirements of this section, the Motor Vehicle Enforcement Division shall submit the completed application to the Motor Vehicle Division for issuance of an unbranded title in accordance with Section 41-1a-522.

(4) If a motor vehicle certificate of title is unbranded pursuant to this section and a subsequent purchaser or lessee of the vehicle prevails against a manufacturer in any action involving a nonconformity that was certified as cured pursuant to this section, that purchaser or lessee is entitled to court costs and reasonable attorney's fees.   1994

41-3-410.   State civil enforcement.

(1) If a person violates Sections 41-3-406 through 41-3-409, the attorney general may bring an action to:

(a) temporarily or permanently restrain or enjoin the violation;

(b) recover any amounts for the benefit of injured consumers for which the violator is liable under Section 41-3-411;

(c) recover a civil penalty of up to $10,000 for each violation that is committed; and

(d) obtain any other equitable relief the court determines to be proper, in addition to damages and civil penalties.

(2) An action under Subsection (1) must be brought within two years from the date on which the violation is discovered and disclosed to the attorney general.   1993

41-3-411.   Private remedy.

(1) Any seller who violates Sections 41-3-406 through 41-3-409 is liable to the purchaser for:

(a) actual damages if the purchaser elects to retain the buyback vehicle, or the value of the consideration paid for the buyback vehicle if the purchaser elects rescission;

(b) the costs of the action and reasonable attorney fees;

(c) up to three times the value of the actual damages or the consideration as exemplary damages; and

(d) other equitable relief, including rescission and restitution, the court determines to be proper in addition to damages and costs.

(2) Actual damages include the difference between the actual market value of the buyback vehicle or nonconforming vehicle at the time of purchase and the contract price, towing, repair, and storage expenses, rental of substitute transportation, food and lodging expenses, lost wages, finance charges, sales or use tax, other governmental fees, lease charges, and other incidental and consequential damages.

(3) Lack of privity is not a bar to any action under this section.

(4) (a) A permanent injunction, final judgment, or final order of the court obtained by the attorney general under Section 41-3-410 is prima facie evidence, in an action brought under this section, that the defendant has violated Sections 41-3-406 through 41-3-409.

(b) This section does not apply to consent orders or stipulated judgments in which there is no admission of liability by the defendant.

(5) Any action to enforce liability under this section must be brought within two years from the date of discovery by the consumer of the facts underlying the cause of action.   1993

41-3-412.   Unfair trade practices.

A violation of Sections 41-3-406 through 41-3-409 is an unfair or deceptive practice under Title 13, Chapter 11, Utah Consumer Sales Practices Act.   1993

41-3-413. Criminal penalties — Nonexclusive.

(1) Knowing or intentional concealment, removal, destruction, or alteration of a disclosure statement or of a certificate of title branded under Section 41-1a-522 is a second degree felony.

(2) Criminal penalties under this chapter are not exclusive, but are in addition to those under Section 76-10-1801.

(3) The remedies provided in Sections 41-3-410 through this section are not exclusive but are in addition to any other remedies provided by law. 1993

41-3-414. Application.

Sections 41-3-406 through 41-3-414 apply to automobiles repurchased on or after July 1, 1993. 1993

PART 5

SPECIAL DEALER LICENSE PLATES

41-3-501. Special plates — Dealers — Dismantlers — Manufacturers — Remanufacturers — Transporters — Restrictions on use.

(1) Except as provided under this chapter, a dealer may operate or move a motor vehicle displaying a dealer plate issued by the division upon the highways without registering it under Title 41, Chapter 1a, Motor Vehicle Act, if the dealer owns or possesses the motor vehicle by consignment for resale.

(2) A dismantler may operate or move a motor vehicle displaying a dismantler plate issued by the division without registering it as required under Title 41, Chapter 1a, Motor Vehicle Act, upon the highways solely to transport the motor vehicle:

(a) from the place of purchase or legal acquisition to the place of business for dismantling; or

(b) to the place of business of a licensed crusher for disposal.

(3) A manufacturer or remanufacturer may operate or move a manufactured or remanufactured motor vehicle displaying a manufacturer plate issued by the division upon the highways without registering it as required under Title 41, Chapter 1a, Motor Vehicle Act, solely to:

(a) deliver the motor vehicle to a dealer; or

(b) demonstrate a motor vehicle to a dealer or prospective dealer.

(4) (a) A transporter may operate or move a motor vehicle displaying a transporter plate issued by the division upon the highways without registering it as required under Title 41, Chapter 1a, Motor Vehicle Act, solely:

(i) from the point of repossession to a financial institution or to the place of storage, so that a financial institution may provide for operation of a repossessed motor vehicle by a prospective purchaser;

(ii) to and from a detail or repair shop for the purpose of detailing or repairing the motor vehicle; or

(iii) to a delivery point in, out, or through the state.

(b) This subsection does not include loaded motor vehicles subject to the gross laden weight provision of Title 41, Chapter 1a, Motor Vehicle Act.

(5) Dealer plates may not be used:

(a) (i) on a motor vehicle leased or rented for compensation; or

(ii) in lieu of registration, on a motor vehicle sold by the dealer; or

(b) on a loaded motor vehicle over 12,000 pounds gross laden weight unless a special loaded demonstration permit is obtained from the division. 1994

41-3-502. Special plates — Permit to use dealer plate to demonstrate loaded motor vehicle.

(1) Under rules established by the administrator, the division may issue a permit to a dealer to use a dealer plate to demonstrate a loaded motor vehicle to a bona fide prospective purchaser.

(2) To obtain a permit, the dealer or his authorized representative shall apply on a form prescribed by the division.

(3) If approved and issued, the permit shall be carried in the motor vehicle for which it is issued during the demonstration trip and shall be returned to the division properly completed and signed within ten days after its expiration date. 1992

41-3-503. Special plates — Issuance.

(1) Subject to the provisions of Subsections (3), (4), and (5), the division may issue special plates under Section 41-3-501 as necessary to conduct the business of the dealer, dismantler, manufacturer, remanufacturer, or transporter applying for the plates.

(2) Each plate issued shall contain a number or symbol distinguishing it from every other plate.

(3) Except as provided under Subsection (4), the division may issue two special dealer plates to each dealer licensed under this chapter plus one additional special dealer plate for every 25 motor vehicles sold by the dealer each year.

(4) A dealer licensed under this chapter who does not sell at least three new or used motor vehicles in any 12-month period may not be issued or have renewed any special dealer plates.

(5) The division shall determine, at least annually, the number of special dealer plates to be issued or renewed to each dealer prior to issuing or renewing any special dealer plates. In determining the number of special plates to be issued to a dealer, the division shall use the past motor vehicle sales history of the dealer. If no sales history is available, the division may use generally accepted motor vehicle sales projections based on:

(a) written forecasts submitted by the dealer to motor vehicle manufacturers, financial institutions, or bonding and insurance companies;

(b) the dealer's inventory of motor vehicles available for sale; or

(c) written verification of credit extended to the dealer by financial institutions for financing the dealer's inventory of motor vehicles available for sale.

(6) (a) The division may recall, redesign, and reissue special plates under this part, as needed to administer the provisions of this title.

(b) All special plates shall be designed in conformity with Sections 41-1a-401, 41-1a-402, and 41-1a-403. 1996

41-3-504. Special plates — Display.

Special plates issued to dealers, dismantlers, manufacturers, remanufacturers, and transporters for the purpose of operating or moving motor vehicles on the highway under the provisions of this chapter shall be:

(1) prominently displayed on the rear of the motor vehicle where clearly visible;

(2) free from foreign materials; and

(3) clearly legible; and

(4) securely fastened in a horizontal position.

1992

41-3-505. Special plates — Application — Security requirements.

(1) A dealer, dismantler, manufacturer, remanufacturer, or transporter may apply to the division upon the appropriate form for one or more special plates.

(2) The applicant shall also submit proof of his status as a licensed dealer, dismantler, manufacturer, remanufacturer, or transporter as required by the division.

(3) The applicant shall also establish to the satisfaction of the division that he complies with the security requirements of Sections 31A-22-302 and 31A-22-303.

1992

41-3-506. Special plates — Expiration.

(1) A special plate issued expires:

    (a) on June 30 each year; or

    (b) upon the cancellation, suspension, or revocation of the licensee's license.

(2) Under Subsection (1)(b), the plates shall be returned to the licensee upon reinstatement of his license.

(3) A new plate or plates, or renewal decal, for the ensuing year may be obtained by the licensee submitting a new application to the division and paying the dealer, dismantler, manufacturer, or transporter plate fee provided by law.

1992

41-3-507. Special plates — Record to be kept by users — Reporting lost or stolen plates.

(1) Each dealer, dismantler, manufacturer, remanufacturer, and transporter shall keep a written record of each special plate issued to it.

(2) The record shall contain the name and address of any person to whom the plate has been assigned to be used.

(3) The record shall account at all times for every special plate issued to the licensee, and shall be open to inspection by any peace officer or any officer or employee of the division.

(4) Lost or stolen special plates shall be reported immediately to the division.

1992

41-3-508. Special plates — Suspension or revocation — Grounds — Procedure — Appeal — Confiscation.

(1) The division may suspend or revoke the special plate or plates issued to a dealer, dismantler, manufacturer, remanufacturer, or transporter if it determines that the person:

    (a) is not lawfully entitled to them;

    (b) has made or knowingly permitted illegal use of the plates;

    (c) has committed fraud in the registration of motor vehicles; or

    (d) failed to give notices of sales or transfers required under this chapter.

(2) (a) Suspension or revocation of special plates takes effect immediately upon written notification to the licensee by the division.

    (b) Upon notification, the licensee shall immediately return all special plates to the division.

    (c) Failure to return the plates or permitting their continued use is a violation of this chapter.

(3) (a) If a licensee desires to appeal the division's suspension or revocation, he shall file a written notice of appeal with the administrator within ten days of the suspension or revocation.

    (b) Upon receipt of the notice, the administrator shall schedule a hearing for not more than 20 days from the date the written appeal is received.

    (c) The licensee may not continue to use or possess any special plates that have been suspended or revoked.

    (d) The hearing and subsequent appeal process are in accordance with the procedures in this chapter.

(4) (a) A peace officer may confiscate any special plate that he has reason to believe is being used illegally.

    (b) A special plate confiscated under this chapter or Title 41, Chapter 1a, Motor Vehicle Act, may not be returned to the licensee if the administrator determines that the plate was being used illegally.

1992

PART 6

FEES

41-3-601. Fees.

(1) To pay for administering and enforcing this chapter, the administrator shall collect fees determined by the commission under Section 63-38-3.2 for each of the following:

    (a) new motor vehicle dealer's license;

    (b) used motor vehicle dealer's license;

    (c) new motorcycle, off-highway vehicle, and small trailer dealer;

    (d) used motorcycle, off-highway vehicle, and small trailer dealer;

    (e) motor vehicle salesperson's license;

    (f) motor vehicle salesperson's transfer or reissue fee;

    (g) motor vehicle manufacturer's license;

    (h) motor vehicle transporter's license;

    (i) motor vehicle dismantler's license;

    (j) motor vehicle crusher's license;

    (k) motor vehicle remanufacturer's license;

    (l) body shop's license;

    (m) distributor or factory branch and distributor branch's license;

    (n) representative's license;

    (o) dealer plates;

    (p) dismantler plates;

    (q) manufacturer plates;

    (r) transporter plates;

    (s) damaged plate replacement;

    (t) in-transit permits;

    (u) loaded demonstration permits;

    (v) additional place of business; and

    (w) special equipment dealer's license.

(2) To pay for training certified vehicle inspectors and enforcement under Sections 41-1a-1001 through 41-1a-1008, the State Tax Commission shall establish and the administrator shall collect inspection fees determined by the commission under Section 63-38-3.2.

(3) (a) At the time of application, the administrator shall collect a fee of $200 for each salvage vehicle buyer license.

    (b) The administrator may retain a portion of the fee under Subsection (3)(a) to offset the administrator's actual costs of administering and enforcing salvage vehicle buyer licenses.

2003

41-3-602. Disposition of fees and penalties.

All fees and penalties collected under this chapter

shall be paid to the state treasurer who shall deposit them in the General Fund. 1992

41-3-603. Fees for temporary permits and temporary sports event registration certificates — Dedicated credits — Use of fees.

(1) A fee of $6.75 shall be paid to the division for each of the following:

(a) a temporary permit under Section 41-3-302; or

(b) a temporary sports event registration certificate under Section 41-3-306.

(2) The division may use fees collected under Subsection (1) as dedicated credits to be used toward the costs of the division.

(3) The division shall use 75 cents of the fees collected under Subsection (1) as dedicated credits for increased enforcement of this chapter. 2005

41-3-604. Fee to cover the cost of electronic payments.

(1) In accordance with Section 63-38a-105, the division may collect a fee to cover the cost of electronic payments on the following transactions:

(a) each purchase of a book of temporary permits under Section 41-3-302;

(b) each penalty issued for a delinquent temporary permit under Section 41-3-302; and

(c) each purchase of a salvage vehicle buyer license under Section 41-3-202.

(2) The division shall establish the fee according to the procedures and requirements of Section 63-38-3.2. 2004

PART 7

PENALTIES

41-3-701. Violations as misdemeanors.

(1) Except as otherwise provided in this chapter, any person who violates this chapter or any rule made by the administrator is guilty of a class B misdemeanor.

(2) A person who violates Section 41-3-201 is guilty of a class A misdemeanor.

(3) A person who violates Section 41-3-301 is guilty of a class A misdemeanor unless the selling dealer complies with the requirements of Section 41-3-403. 1993

41-3-702. Civil penalty for violation.

(1) The following are civil violations under this chapter and are in addition to criminal violations under this chapter:

(a) Level I:

(i) failure to display business license;

(ii) failure to surrender license of salesperson because of termination, suspension, or revocation;

(iii) failure to maintain a separation from nonrelated motor vehicle businesses at licensed locations;

(iv) issuing a temporary permit improperly;

(v) failure to maintain records;

(vi) selling a new motor vehicle to a nonfranchised dealer or leasing company without licensing the motor vehicle;

(vii) special plate violation; and

(viii) failure to maintain a sign at principal place of business.

(b) Level II:

(i) failure to report sale;

(ii) dismantling without a permit;

(iii) manufacturing without meeting construction or vehicle identification number standards;

(iv) withholding customer license plates; or

(v) selling a motor vehicle on consecutive days of Saturday and Sunday.

(c) Level III:

(i) operating without a principal place of business;

(ii) selling a new motor vehicle without holding the franchise;

(iii) crushing a motor vehicle without proper evidence of ownership;

(iv) selling from an unlicensed location;

(v) altering a temporary permit;

(vi) refusal to furnish copies of records;

(vii) assisting an unlicensed dealer or salesperson in sales of motor vehicles; and

(viii) advertising violation.

(2) (a) The schedule of civil penalties for violations of Subsection (1) is:

(i) Level I: $25 for the first offense, $100 for the second offense, and $250 for the third and subsequent offenses;

(ii) Level II: $100 for the first offense, $250 for the second offense, and $1,000 for the third and subsequent offenses; and

(iii) Level III: $250 for the first offense, $1,000 for the second offense, and $5,000 for the third and subsequent offenses.

(b) When determining under this section if an offense is a second or subsequent offense, only prior offenses committed within the 12 months prior to the commission of the current offense may be considered.

(3) The following are civil violations in addition to criminal violations under Section 41-1a-1008:

(a) knowingly selling a salvage vehicle, as defined in Section 41-1a-1001, without disclosing that the salvage vehicle has been repaired or rebuilt;

(b) knowingly making a false statement on a vehicle damage disclosure statement, as defined in Section 41-1a-1001; or

(c) fraudulently certifying that a damaged motor vehicle is entitled to an unbranded title, as defined in Section 41-1a-1001, when it is not.

(4) The civil penalty for a violation under Subsection (3) is:

(a) not less than $1,000, or treble the actual damages caused by the person, whichever is greater; and

(b) reasonable attorneys' fees and costs of the action.

(5) A civil action may be maintained by a purchaser or by the administrator. 2003

41-3-703. Violations as felonies.

(1) A person may not forge, falsify, or counterfeit any license, special plate, temporary permit, in-transit permit, decal, or other document issued by the division or any other state or jurisdiction.

(2) A person may not hold or use any license, special plate, temporary permit, in-transit permit, decal, or other document issued by the division or any other state or jurisdiction knowing it to have been forged, falsified, or counterfeited.

(3) A violation of Subsection (1) or (2) is a third degree felony. 1998

PART 8

CONSIGNMENT SALES ACT

41-3-801. Short title.

This part shall be known as the "Consignment Sales Act." 1993

41-3-802. Definitions.

As used in this part:

(1) (a) "Consignee" means a dealer who accepts vehicles for sale under an agreement that the dealer will pay the consignor for any sold vehicle and will return any unsold vehicles.

(b) "Consignee" does not include a wholesale motor vehicle auction.

(2) "Consignor" means a person who places a vehicle with a consignee for consignment sale. 1995

41-3-803. Consignment sales.

(1) A consignor may take possession of his consigned vehicle at any time the consigned vehicle is in the possession of a consignee, provided that the consignor:

(a) has notified the consignee in writing that he will take possession of the consigned vehicle; and

(b) has paid all outstanding charges owing to the consignee that have been agreed to by the consignor in accordance with Subsection (2).

(2) The agreed upon charges under Subsection (1)(b) shall be:

(a) stated on a form designed by the department; and

(b) included with the written consignment agreement.

(3) A consignee who sells a consigned vehicle shall report to the consignor in writing the exact selling price of the consigned vehicle under either of the following circumstances:

(a) the consignor and consignee agree in writing that the consignor shall receive a percentage of the selling price upon the sale of the vehicle; or

(b) the consignor and consignee renegotiate in writing the selling price of the vehicle.

(4) When a consignee sells a consigned vehicle:

(a) the consignee, within seven calendar days of the date of sale, must give written notice to the consignor that the consigned vehicle has been sold; and

(b) the consignee, within 21 calendar days of the date of sale, or within 15 calendar days of receiving payment in full for the consigned vehicle, whichever date is earlier, shall remit the payment received to the consignor, unless the agreement to purchase the consigned vehicle has been rescinded before expiration of the 21 days.

(5) If the agreement to purchase the consigned vehicle has for any reason been rescinded before the expiration of 21 calendar days of the date of sale, the consignee shall within five calendar days thereafter give written notice to the consignor that the agreement to purchase has been rescinded.

(6) Vehicles on consignment shall be driven with the consignee's dealer plates. All other license plates or registration indicia must be removed from the vehicle.

(7) Prior to driving a consigned vehicle on the consignee's dealer plates, the consignee and the consignor shall execute a written consignment agreement that states:

(a) the party responsible for damage or misuse to a consigned vehicle; and

(b) the permitted uses a consignee may make of a consigned vehicle.

(8) The consignee shall keep the written consignment agreement on file at his principal place of business. 2000

CHAPTER 4

FINANCING DEALERS AND PURCHASERS

41-4-1. Agreements to finance through designated source which lessen competition or create monopoly declared void.

It shall be unlawful for any person who is engaged, either directly or indirectly, in the manufacture or distribution of motor vehicles, to sell or enter into a contract to sell motor vehicles, whether patented or unpatented, to any person who is engaged or intends to engage in the business of selling such motor vehicles at retail in this state, on the condition or with an agreement or understanding, either express or implied, that such person so engaged in selling motor vehicles at retail shall in any manner finance the purchase or sale of any one or number of motor vehicles only with or through a designated person or class of persons or shall sell and assign the conditional sales contracts, chattel mortgages or leases arising from the sale of motor vehicles or any one or number thereof only to a designated person or class of persons, when the effect of the condition, agreement or understanding so entered into may be to lessen or eliminate competition, or create or tend to create a monopoly in the person or class of persons who are designated, by virtue of such condition, agreement or understanding to finance the purchase or sale of motor vehicles or to purchase such conditional sales contracts, chattel mortgages or leases, and any such condition, agreement or understanding is hereby declared to be void and against the public policy of this state. 1953

41-4-2. Threat to discontinue sales to retail seller prima facie evidence of violation.

Any threat, expressed or implied, made directly or indirectly, to any person engaged in the business of selling motor vehicles at retail in this state by any person engaged, either directly or indirectly, in the manufacture or distribution of motor vehicles, that such person will discontinue or cease to sell, or refuse to enter into a contract to sell, or will terminate a contract to sell motor vehicles, whether patented or unpatented, to such person who is so engaged in the business of selling motor vehicles at retail, unless such person finances the purchase or sale of any one or number of motor vehicles only with or through a designated person or class of persons or sells and assigns the conditional sales contracts, chattel mortgages or leases arising from his retail sales of motor vehicles or any one or number thereof only to a designated person or class of persons shall be prima facie evidence of the fact that such person so engaged in the manufacture or distribution of motor vehicles has sold or intends to sell the same on the condition or with the agreement or understanding prohibited in Section 41-4-1. 1953

41-4-3. Threat to discontinue sales to person engaged in business of financing who is affiliated with manufacturer or distributor.

Any threat, expressed or implied, made directly or indirectly, to any person engaged in the business of selling motor vehicles at retail in this state by any person, or any agent of any such person, who is engaged in the business of financing the purchase or sale of motor vehicles or of buying conditional sales contracts, chattel mortgages or leases on motor vehicles in this state and is affiliated with or controlled by any person engaged, directly or indirectly, in the manufacture or distribution of motor vehicles, that such person so engaged in such manufacture or distribution shall terminate his contract with or cease to sell motor vehicles to such person engaged in the sale of motor vehicles at retail in this state unless such person finances the purchase or sale of any one or number of motor vehicles only or through a designated person or class of persons or sells and assigns the conditional sales contracts, chattel mortgages, or leases arising from his retail sale of motor vehicles or any one or any number thereof only to such person so engaged in financing the purchase or sale of motor vehicles or in buying conditional sales contracts, chattel mortgages or leases on motor vehicles, shall be presumed to be made at the direction of and with the authority of such person so engaged in such manufacture or distribution of motor vehicles, and shall be prima facie evidence of the fact that such person so engaged in the manufacture or distribution of motor vehicles has sold or intends to sell the same on the condition or with the agreement or understanding prohibited in Section 41-4-1. 1953

41-4-4. Giving of gratuity by manufacturer or wholesaler to one financing sales which lessens competition, unlawful.

It shall be unlawful for any person who is engaged, directly or indirectly, in the manufacture or wholesale distribution only of motor vehicles, whether patented or unpatented, to pay or give, or contract to pay or give any thing or service of value to any person who is engaged in the business of financing the purchase or sale of motor vehicles or of buying conditional sales contracts, chattel mortgages or leases on motor vehicles sold at retail within this state if the effect of any such payment or the giving of any such thing or service of value may be to lessen or eliminate competition, or tend to create or create a monopoly in the person or class of persons who receive or accept such thing or service of value. 1953

41-4-5. Unlawful for person financing sales to accept gratuity.

It shall be unlawful for any person who is engaged in the business of financing the purchase or sale of motor vehicles or of buying conditional sales contracts, chattel mortgages or leases on motor vehicles sold at retail within this state to accept or receive, or contract or agree to accept or receive, either directly or indirectly, any payment, thing, or service of value from any person who is engaged, either directly or indirectly, in the manufacture or wholesale distribution only of motor vehicles, whether patented or unpatented, if the effect of the acceptance or receipt of any such payment, thing, or service of value may be to lessen or eliminate competition, or to create or tend to create a monopoly in the person who accepts or receives such payment, thing, or service of value, or contracts or agrees to accept or receive the same. 1953

41-4-6. Accepting gratuity, unlawful thereafter to finance sales.

It shall be unlawful for any person who hereafter so accepts or receives, either directly or indirectly, any payment, thing, or service of value, as set forth in Section 41-4-5, or hereafter so contracts, either directly or indirectly, to receive any such payment or thing or service of value to thereafter finance or attempt to finance the purchase or sale of any motor vehicle or buy or attempt to buy any conditional sales contracts, chattel mortgages or leases on motor vehicles sold at retail in this state. 1953

41-4-7. Violation by corporation — Penalty.

For a violation of any of the provisions of this act by any corporation or association mentioned herein, it shall be the duty of the attorney general or the district attorney of the proper county, to institute proper suits or quo warranto proceedings in any court of competent jurisdiction for the forfeiture of its charter rights, franchises or privileges and powers exercised by such corporation or association, and for the dissolution of the same under the general statutes of the state. 1953

41-4-8. Violation by foreign corporation — Penalty.

Every foreign corporation, as well as every foreign association, exercising any of the powers, franchises, or functions of a corporation in this state, violating any of the provisions of this act, is hereby denied the right and prohibited from doing any business in this state, and it shall be the duty of the attorney general to enforce this provision by bringing proper proceedings by injunction or otherwise. The Division of Corporations and Commercial Code shall be authorized to revoke the license of any such corporation or association heretofore authorized by it to do business in this state. 1984

41-4-9. Persons violating provisions — Penalty.

Any person who violates any of the provisions of this act, any person who is a party to any agreement or understanding, or to any contract prescribing any condition prohibited by this act, and any employee, agent or officer of any such person who shall participate, in any manner, in making, executing, enforcing, performing or in urging, aiding or abetting in the performance of any such contract, condition, agreement or understanding and any person who pays or gives or contracts to pay or give any thing or service of value prohibited by this act, and any person who receives or accepts or contracts to receive or accept any thing or service of value prohibited by this act, shall be deemed guilty of a felony and upon conviction thereof shall be punished by a fine of not less than $50 nor more than $5,000, or be imprisoned not less than six months nor more than one year, or by both such fine and imprisonment. Each day's violation of this provision shall constitute a separate offense.   1953

41-4-10. Agreements in violation of provisions are void.

Any contract or agreement in violation of the provisions of this act, shall be absolutely void and shall not be enforceable either in law or equity.   1953

41-4-11. Provisions cumulative.

The provisions hereof shall be held cumulative of each other and of all other laws in any way affecting them now in force in this state.   1953

41-4-12. Actions for damages.

In addition to the criminal and civil penalties herein provided, any person who is injured in his business or property by any other person or corporation or association or partnership, by reason of anything forbidden or declared to be unlawful by this act, may sue therefor in any court having jurisdiction thereof in the county where the defendant resides or is found, or any agent resides or is found, or where service may be obtained, without respect to the amount in controversy, and to recover twofold the damages by him sustained, and the costs of suit. Whenever it shall appear to the court before which any proceeding under this act is pending, that the ends of justice require that other parties shall be brought before the court, the court may cause them to be made parties defendant and summoned, whether they reside in the county where such action is pending, or not.   1953

41-4-13. Definitions.

(a) The term "person," as used in this act, means any individual, firm, corporation, partnership, association, trustee, receiver or assignee for the benefit of creditors.

(b) The terms "sell," "sold," "buy," and "purchase," as used in this act, include exchange, barter, gift, and offer or contract to sell or buy.   1953

41-4-14. Separability clause.

If any section, subsection, sentence, clause or phrase of this act is for any reason held to be unconstitutional, such decision shall not affect the validity of the remaining portions of this act. The Legislature hereby declares that it would have passed this act, and each section, subsection, sentence, clause and phrase thereof irrespective of the fact that any one or more other sections, subsections, sentences, clauses or phrases be declared unconstitutional.   1953

CHAPTER 5

MOTOR VEHICLE INSURANCE [REPEALED]

41-5-1 to 41-5-4. Repealed.   1985

CHAPTER 6

TRAFFIC RULES AND REGULATIONS [RENUMBERED]

41-6-1 to 41-6-193. Renumbered as §§ 53-3-231, 53-8-203 et seq., 72-9-601 to 72-9-605, and Title 41, Chapter 6a.

1975, 1977, 1978, 1979,
1985 (1st S.S.), 1986, 1987, 1989,
1991, 1993, 1996, 1998, 2000, 2005

CHAPTER 6a

TRAFFIC CODE

Part 1

General Provisions

Part 2

Applicability and Obedience to Traffic Laws

PART 1

GENERAL PROVISIONS

41-6a-101. Title.

This chapter is known as the "Traffic Code."   2005

41-6a-102. Definitions.

As used in this chapter:

(1) "Alley" means a street or highway intended to provide access to the rear or side of lots or buildings in urban districts and not intended for through vehicular traffic.

(2) "All-terrain type I vehicle" has the same meaning as defined in Section 41-22-2.

(3) "Authorized emergency vehicle" includes:

(a) fire department vehicles;

(b) police vehicles;

(c) ambulances; and

(d) other publicly or privately owned vehicles as designated by the commissioner of the Department of Public Safety.

(4) (a) "Bicycle" means every device:

(i) propelled by human power;

(ii) upon which a person may ride; and

(iii) having two tandem wheels.

(b) "Bicycle" does not include scooters and similar devices.

(5) (a) "Bus" means a motor vehicle:

(i) designed for carrying more than 15 passengers and used for the transportation of persons; or

(ii) designed and used for the transportation of persons for compensation.

(b) "Bus" does not include a taxicab.

(6) (a) "Circular intersection" means an intersection that has an island, generally circular in design, located in the center of the intersection where traffic passes to the right of the island.

(b) "Circular intersection" includes:

(i) roundabouts;

(ii) rotaries; and

(iii) traffic circles.

(7) "Commissioner" means the commissioner of the Department of Public Safety.

(8) "Controlled-access highway" means a highway, street, or roadway:

(a) designed primarily for through traffic; and

(b) to or from which owners or occupants of abutting lands and other persons have no legal right of access, except at points as determined by the highway authority having jurisdiction over the highway, street, or roadway.

(9) "Crosswalk" means:

(a) that part of a roadway at an intersection included within the connections of the lateral lines of the sidewalks on opposite sides of the highway measured from:

(i) (A) the curbs; or

(B) in the absence of curbs, from the edges of the traversable roadway; and

(ii) in the absence of a sidewalk on one side of the roadway, that part of a roadway included within the extension of the lateral lines of the existing sidewalk at right angles to the centerline; or

(b) any portion of a roadway at an intersection or elsewhere distinctly indicated for pedestrian crossing by lines or other markings on the surface.

(10) "Department" means the Department of Public Safety.

(11) "Direct supervision" means oversight at a distance within which:

(a) visual contact is maintained; and

(b) advice and assistance can be given and received.

(12) "Divided highway" means a highway divided into two or more roadways by:

(a) an unpaved intervening space;

(b) a physical barrier; or

(c) a clearly indicated dividing section constructed to impede vehicular traffic.

(13) "Electric assisted bicycle" means a moped:

(a) with an electric motor with a power output of not more than 1,000 watts; and

(b) which is not capable of:

(i) propelling the device at a speed of more than 20 miles per hour on level ground; and

(ii) increasing the speed of the device when human power is used to propel the device at more than 20 miles per hour.

(14) "Explosives" means any chemical compound or mechanical mixture commonly used or intended for the purpose of producing an explosion and which contains any oxidizing and combustive units or other ingredients in proportions, quantities, or packing so that an ignition by fire, friction, concussion, percussion, or detonator of any part of the compound or mixture may cause a sudden generation of highly heated gases, and the resultant gaseous pressures are capable of producing destructive effects on contiguous objects or of causing death or serious bodily injury.

(15) "Farm tractor" means a motor vehicle designed and used primarily as a farm implement, for drawing plows, mowing machines, and other implements of husbandry.

(16) "Flammable liquid" means a liquid which has a flashpoint of 100 degrees F. or less, as determined by a tagliabue or equivalent closed-cup test device.

(17) "Freeway" means a controlled-access highway that is part of the interstate system as defined in Section 72-1-102.

(18) "Gore area" means the area delineated by two solid white lines that is between a continuing lane of a through roadway and a lane used to enter or exit the continuing lane including similar areas between merging or splitting highways.

(19) "Gross weight" means the weight of a vehicle without a load plus the weight of any load on the vehicle.

(20) "Highway" means the entire width between property lines of every way or place of any nature when any part of it is open to the use of the public as a matter of right for vehicular travel.

(21) "Highway authority" has the same meaning as defined in Section 72-1-102.

(22) (a) "Intersection" means the area embraced within the prolongation or connection of the lateral curblines, or, if none, then the lateral boundary lines of the roadways of two or more highways which join one another.

(b) Where a highway includes two roadways 30 feet or more apart:

(i) every crossing of each roadway of the divided highway by an intersecting highway is a separate intersection; and

(ii) if the intersecting highway also includes two roadways 30 feet or more apart, then every crossing of two roadways of the highways is a separate intersection.

(c) "Intersection" does not include the junction of an alley with a street or highway.

(23) "Island" means an area between traffic lanes or at an intersection for control of vehicle movements or for pedestrian refuge designated by:

(a) pavement markings, which may include an area designated by two solid yellow lines surrounding the perimeter of the area;

(b) channelizing devices;

(c) curbs;

(d) pavement edges; or

(e) other devices.

(24) "Law enforcement agency" has the same meaning as defined in Section 53-1-102.

(25) "Limited access highway" means a highway:

(a) that is designated specifically for through traffic; and

(b) over, from, or to which neither owners nor occupants of abutting lands nor other persons have any right or easement, or have only a limited right or easement of access, light, air, or view.

(26) "Local highway authority" means the legislative, executive, or governing body of a county, municipal, or other local board or body having authority to enact laws relating to traffic under the constitution and laws of the state.

(27) (a) "Low-speed vehicle" means a four wheeled electric motor vehicle that:

(i) is designed to be operated at speeds of not more than 25 miles per hour; and

(ii) has a capacity of not more than four passengers, including the driver.

(b) "Low-speed vehicle" does not include a golfcart or an off-highway vehicle.

(28) "Metal tire" means a tire, the surface of which in contact with the highway is wholly or partly of metal or other hard nonresilient material.

(29) (a) "Mini-motorcycle" means a motorcycle or motor-driven cycle that has a seat or saddle that is less than 24 inches from the ground as measured on a level surface with properly inflated tires.

(b) "Mini-motorcycle" does not include a moped or a motor assisted scooter.

(c) "Mini-motorcycle" does not include a motorcycle that is:

(i) designed for off-highway use; and

(ii) registered as an off-highway vehicle under Section 41-22-3.

(30) "Mobile home" means:

(a) a trailer or semitrailer which is:

(i) designed, constructed, and equipped as a dwelling place, living abode, or sleeping place either permanently or temporarily; and

(ii) equipped for use as a conveyance on streets and highways; or

(b) a trailer or a semitrailer whose chassis and exterior shell is designed and constructed for use as a mobile home, as defined in Subsection (30)(a), but which is instead used permanently or temporarily for:

(i) the advertising, sale, display, or promotion of merchandise or services; or

(ii) any other commercial purpose except the transportation of property for hire or the transportation of property for distribution by a private carrier.

(31) (a) "Moped" means a motor-driven cycle having:

(i) pedals to permit propulsion by human power; and

(ii) a motor which:

(A) produces not more than two brake horsepower; and

(B) is not capable of propelling the cycle at a speed in excess of 30 miles per hour on level ground.

(b) If an internal combustion engine is used, the displacement may not exceed 50 cubic centimeters and the moped shall have a power drive system that functions directly or automatically without clutching or shifting by the operator after the drive system is engaged.

(c) "Moped" includes an electric assisted bicycle and a motor assisted scooter.

(32) "Motor assisted scooter" means a self-propelled device with:

    (a) at least two wheels in contact with the ground;

    (b) a braking system capable of stopping the unit under typical operating conditions;

    (c) a gas or electric motor not exceeding 40 cubic centimeters;

    (d) either:

        (i) a deck design for a person to stand while operating the device; or

        (ii) a deck and seat designed for a person to sit, straddle, or stand while operating the device; and

    (e) a design for the ability to be propelled by human power alone.

(33) (a) "Motor vehicle" means a vehicle which is self-propelled and every vehicle which is propelled by electric power obtained from overhead trolley wires, but not operated upon rails.

    (b) "Motor vehicle" does not include vehicles moved solely by human power and motorized wheel chairs.

(34) "Motorcycle" means a motor vehicle, other than a tractor, having a seat or saddle for the use of the rider and designed to travel with not more than three wheels in contact with the ground.

(35) "Motor-driven cycle" means every motorcycle, motor scooter, personal motorized mobility device, moped, electric assisted bicycle, motor assisted scooter, and every motorized bicycle having:

    (a) an engine with less than 150 cubic centimeters displacement; or

    (b) a motor which produces not more than five horsepower.

(36) "Off-highway implement of husbandry" has the same meaning as defined under Section 41-22-2.

(37) "Off-highway vehicle" has the same meaning as defined under Section 41-22-2.

(38) "Operator" means a person who is in actual physical control of a vehicle.

(39) (a) "Park" or "parking" means the standing of a vehicle, whether occupied or not.

    (b) "Park" or "parking" does not include the standing of a vehicle temporarily for the purpose of and while actually engaged in loading or unloading property or passengers.

(40) "Peace officer" means a peace officer authorized under Title 53, Chapter 13, Peace Officer Classifications, to direct or regulate traffic or to make arrests for violations of traffic laws.

(41) "Pedestrian" means a person traveling:

    (a) on foot; or

    (b) in a wheelchair.

(42) "Pedestrian traffic-control signal" means a traffic-control signal used to regulate pedestrians.

(43) "Person" means every natural person, firm, copartnership, association, or corporation.

(44) (a) "Personal motorized mobility device" means a self-propelled device with:

        (i) two nontandem wheels in contact with the ground;

        (ii) a system capable of steering and stopping the unit under typical operating conditions;

        (iii) a motor not exceeding one horse power or 750 watts; and

        (iv) a deck design for a person to stand while operating the device.

    (b) "Personal motorized mobility device" does not include a wheelchair.

(45) "Pole trailer" means every vehicle without motive power:

    (a) designed to be drawn by another vehicle and attached to the towing vehicle by means of a reach, or pole, or by being boomed or otherwise secured to the towing vehicle; and

    (b) that is ordinarily used for transporting long or irregular shaped loads including poles, pipes, or structural members generally capable of sustaining themselves as beams between the supporting connections.

(46) "Private road or driveway" means every way or place in private ownership and used for vehicular travel by the owner and those having express or implied permission from the owner, but not by other persons.

(47) "Railroad" means a carrier of persons or property upon cars operated on stationary rails.

(48) "Railroad sign or signal" means a sign, signal, or device erected by authority of a public body or official or by a railroad and intended to give notice of the presence of railroad tracks or the approach of a railroad train.

(49) "Railroad train" means a locomotive propelled by any form of energy, coupled with or operated without cars, and operated upon rails.

(50) "Right-of-way" means the right of one vehicle or pedestrian to proceed in a lawful manner in preference to another vehicle or pedestrian approaching under circumstances of direction, speed, and proximity which give rise to danger of collision unless one grants precedence to the other.

(51) (a) "Roadway" means that portion of highway improved, designed, or ordinarily used for vehicular travel.

    (b) "Roadway" does not include the sidewalk, berm, or shoulder, even though any of them are used by persons riding bicycles or other human-powered vehicles.

    (c) "Roadway" refers to any roadway separately but not to all roadways collectively, if a highway includes two or more separate roadways.

(52) "Safety zone" means the area or space officially set apart within a roadway for the exclusive use of pedestrians and which is protected, marked, or indicated by adequate signs as to be plainly visible at all times while set apart as a safety zone.

(53) (a) "School bus" means a motor vehicle that:

        (i) complies with the color and identification requirements of the most recent edition of "Minimum Standards for School Buses"; and

        (ii) is used to transport school children to or from school or school activities.

    (b) "School bus" does not include a vehicle operated by a common carrier in transportation of school children to or from school or school activities.

(54) (a) "Semitrailer" means a vehicle with or without motive power:

        (i) designed for carrying persons or property and for being drawn by a motor vehicle; and

(ii) constructed so that some part of its weight and that of its load rests on or is carried by another vehicle.

(b) "Semitrailer" does not include a pole trailer.

(55) "Shoulder area" means:

(a) that area of the hard-surfaced highway separated from the roadway by a pavement edge line as established in the current approved "Manual on Uniform Traffic Control Devices"; or

(b) that portion of the road contiguous to the roadway for accommodation of stopped vehicles, for emergency use, and lateral support.

(56) "Sidewalk" means that portion of a street between the curb lines, or the lateral lines of a roadway, and the adjacent property lines intended for the use of pedestrians.

(57) "Solid rubber tire" means a tire of rubber or other resilient material which does not depend on compressed air for the support of the load.

(58) "Stand" or "standing" means the temporary halting of a vehicle, whether occupied or not, for the purpose of and while actually engaged in receiving or discharging passengers.

(59) "Stop" when required means complete cessation from movement.

(60) "Stop" or "stopping" when prohibited means any halting even momentarily of a vehicle, whether occupied or not, except when:

(a) necessary to avoid conflict with other traffic; or

(b) in compliance with the directions of a peace officer or traffic-control device.

(61) "Traffic" means pedestrians, ridden or herded animals, vehicles, and other conveyances either singly or together while using any highway for the purpose of travel.

(62) "Traffic-control device" means a sign, signal, marking, or device not inconsistent with this chapter placed or erected by a highway authority for the purpose of regulating, warning, or guiding traffic.

(63) "Traffic-control signal" means a device, whether manually, electrically, or mechanically operated, by which traffic is alternately directed to stop and permitted to proceed.

(64) "Traffic signal preemption device" means an instrument or mechanism designed, intended, or used to interfere with the operation or cycle of a traffic-control signal.

(65) (a) "Trailer" means a vehicle with or without motive power designed for carrying persons or property and for being drawn by a motor vehicle and constructed so that no part of its weight rests upon the towing vehicle.

(b) "Trailer" does not include a pole trailer.

(66) "Truck" means a motor vehicle designed, used, or maintained primarily for the transportation of property.

(67) "Truck tractor" means a motor vehicle:

(a) designed and used primarily for drawing other vehicles; and

(b) constructed to carry a part of the weight of the vehicle and load drawn by the truck tractor.

(68) "Two-way left turn lane" means a lane:

(a) provided for vehicle operators making left turns in either direction;

(b) that is not used for passing, overtaking, or through travel; and

(c) that has been indicated by a lane traffic-control device which may include lane markings.

(69) "Urban district" means the territory contiguous to and including any street, in which structures devoted to business, industry, or dwelling houses are situated at intervals of less than 100 feet, for a distance of a quarter of a mile or more.

(70) "Vehicle" means a device in, on, or by which a person or property is or may be transported or drawn on a highway, except devices used exclusively on stationary rails or tracks.

2005

PART 2

APPLICABILITY AND OBEDIENCE TO TRAFFIC LAWS

41-6a-201. Chapter relates to vehicles on highways — Exceptions.

The provisions of this chapter relating to the operation of vehicles refer exclusively to the operation of vehicles upon highways, except:

(1) when a different place is specifically identified; or

(2) under the provisions of Section 41-6a-210, Part 4, Accident Responsibilities, and Part 5, Driving Under the Influence and Reckless Driving, which apply upon highways and elsewhere throughout the state.   2005

41-6a-202. Violations of chapter — Penalties.

(1) A violation of any provision of this chapter is a class C misdemeanor, unless otherwise provided.

(2) A violation of any provision of Parts 2, 11, 17, and 18 of this chapter is an infraction, unless otherwise provided.   2005

41-6a-203. Violation of chapter.

(1) A person who commits, attempts to commit, conspires to commit, or aids or abets in the commission of, an act that is a crime under this chapter, whether individually or in connection with one or more other persons or as a principal, agent, or accessory, is guilty of the offense.

(2) A person who falsely, fraudulently, forcibly, or willfully induces, causes, coerces, requires, permits, or directs another to violate a provision of this chapter is guilty of the offense.   2005

41-6a-204. Requiring or knowingly permitting driver to unlawfully operate vehicle.

A person employing or otherwise directing the operator of a vehicle may not require or knowingly permit the operation of the vehicle on a highway in a manner contrary to law.   2005

41-6a-205. Government-owned vehicles subject to chapter.

Except as specifically exempted, the provisions of this chapter applicable to an operator of a vehicle on the highway apply to an operator of a vehicle owned or operated by the United States, this state or any county, city, town, district or any other political subdivision of the state.   2005

41-6a-206. Conflict with Federal Motor Carrier Safety Regulations.

Federal Motor Carrier Safety Regulations supercede any conflicting provisions of this chapter pertaining to commercial motor carriers.   2005

41-6a-207. Uniform application of chapter — Effect of local ordinances.

(1) The provisions of this chapter are applicable throughout this state and in all of its political subdivisions and municipalities.

(2) A local highway authority may not enact or enforce any rule or ordinance in conflict with the provisions of this chapter.

(3) A local highway authority may adopt:

(a) ordinances consistent with this chapter; and

(b) additional traffic ordinances not in conflict with this chapter.   2005

41-6a-208. Regulatory powers of local highway authorities — Traffic-control device affecting state highway — Necessity of erecting traffic-control devices.

(1) The provisions of this chapter do not prevent a local highway authority for a highway under its jurisdiction and within the reasonable exercise of police power, from:

(a) regulating or prohibiting stopping, standing, or parking;

(b) regulating traffic by means of a peace officer or a traffic-control device;

(c) regulating or prohibiting processions or assemblages on a highway;

(d) designating particular highways or roadways for use by traffic moving in one direction under Section 41-6a-709;

(e) establishing speed limits for vehicles in public parks, which supersede Section 41-6a-603 regarding speed limits;

(f) designating any highway as a through highway or designating any intersection or junction of roadways as a stop or yield intersection or junction;

(g) restricting the use of a highway under Section 72-7-408;

(h) regulating the operation of a bicycle and requiring the registration and inspection of bicycles, including requiring a registration fee;

(i) regulating or prohibiting:

(i) certain turn movements of a vehicle; or

(ii) specified types of vehicles;

(j) altering or establishing speed limits under Section 41-6a-603;

(k) requiring written accident reports under Section 41-6a-403;

(l) designating no-passing zones under Section 41-6a-708;

(m) prohibiting or regulating the use of controlled-access roadways by any class or kind of traffic under Section 41-6a-715;

(n) prohibiting or regulating the use of heavily traveled streets by any class or kind of traffic found to be incompatible with the normal and safe movement of traffic;

(o) establishing minimum speed limits under Subsection 41-6a-605(3);

(p) prohibiting pedestrians from crossing a highway in a business district or any designated highway except in a crosswalk under Section 41-6a-1001;

(q) restricting pedestrian crossings at unmarked crosswalks under Section 41-6a-1010;

(r) regulating persons using skates, coasters, sleds, skateboards, and other toy vehicles;

(s) adopting and enforcing temporary or experimental ordinances as necessary to cover emergencies or special conditions;

(t) prohibiting drivers of ambulances from exceeding maximum speed limits; or

(u) adopting other traffic ordinances as specifically authorized by this chapter.

(2) In accordance with Title 72, Chapter 3, Part 1, Highways in General, a local highway authority may not erect or maintain any official traffic-control device at any location which regulates the traffic on a highway not under the local highway authority's jurisdiction, unless written approval is obtained from the highway authority having jurisdiction over the highway.

(3) An ordinance enacted under Subsection (1)(d), (e), (f), (g), (i), (j), (l), (m), (n), or (q) is not effective until official traffic-control devices giving notice of the local traffic ordinances are erected upon or at the entrances to the highway or part of it affected as is appropriate.   2005

41-6a-209. Obedience to peace officer or other traffic controllers — Speeding in construction zones.

(1) A person may not willfully fail or willfully refuse to comply with any lawful order or direction of a:

(a) peace officer;

(b) firefighter;

(c) flagger at a highway construction or maintenance site using devices and procedures conforming to the standards adopted under Section 41-6a-301; or

(d) uniformed adult school crossing guard invested by law with authority to direct, control, or regulate traffic.

(2) (a) If a person commits a speeding violation in a highway construction or maintenance site where workers are present, the court shall impose a fine for the offense that is at least double the fine in the uniform recommended fine schedule established under Section 76-3-301.5.

(b) The highway construction or maintenance site under Subsection (2)(a) shall be clearly marked and have signs posted that warn of the doubled fine.   2005

41-6a-210. Failure to respond to officer's signal to stop — Fleeing — Causing property damage or bodily injury — Suspension of driver's license — Forfeiture of vehicle — Penalties.

(1) (a) An operator who receives a visual or audible signal from a peace officer to bring the vehicle to a stop may not:

(i) operate the vehicle in willful or wanton disregard of the signal so as to interfere with or endanger the operation of any vehicle or person; or

(ii) attempt to flee or elude a peace officer by vehicle or other means.

(b) (i) A person who violates Subsection (1)(a) is guilty of a felony of the third degree.

(ii) The court shall, as part of any sentence under this Subsection (1), impose a fine of not less than $1,000.

(2) (a) An operator who violates Subsection (1) and while so doing causes death or serious bodily injury to another person, under circumstances not amounting to murder or aggravated murder, is guilty of a felony of the second degree.

(b) The court shall, as part of any sentence under this Subsection (2), impose a fine of not less than $5,000.

(3) (a) In addition to the penalty provided under this section or any other section, a person who

violates Subsection (1)(a) or (2)(a) shall have the person's driver license revoked under Subsection 53-3-220(1)(a)(ix) for a period of one year.

(b) (i) The court shall forward the report of the conviction to the division.

(ii) If the person is the holder of a driver license from another jurisdiction, the division shall notify the appropriate officials in the licensing state.   2005

41-6a-211. Vehicle subject to forfeiture — Seizure — Procedure.

(1) Any conveyance, including a vehicle, aircraft, water craft, or other vessel used in violation of Section 41-6a-210, is subject to forfeiture under the procedures and substantive protections established in Title 24, Chapter 1, Utah Uniform Forfeiture Procedures Act.

(2) Property subject to forfeiture under this section may be seized by a peace officer:

(a) upon notice and service of process issued by a court having jurisdiction over the property; or

(b) without notice and service of process if:

(i) the seizure is incident to an arrest under a search warrant or an inspection under an administrative inspection warrant;

(ii) the property subject to seizure has been the subject of a prior judgment in favor of the state in a criminal injunction or forfeiture proceeding under this section; or

(iii) the peace officer has probable cause to believe that the property has been used in violation of the provisions of Section 41-6a-210.

(3) (a) Property taken or detained under this section is not repleviable but is in custody of the law enforcement agency making the seizure, subject only to the orders and decrees of the court or the official having jurisdiction.

(b) When property is seized under this section, the appropriate person or agency may:

(i) place the property under seal;

(ii) remove the property to a place designated by the warrant under which it was seized; or

(iii) take custody of the property and remove it to an appropriate location for disposition in accordance with law.   2005

41-6a-212. Emergency vehicles — Policy regarding vehicle pursuits — Applicability of traffic law to highway work vehicles — Exemptions.

(1) Subject to Subsections (2) through (5), the operator of an authorized emergency vehicle may exercise the privileges granted under this section when:

(a) responding to an emergency call;

(b) in the pursuit of an actual or suspected violator of the law; or

(c) responding to but not upon returning from a fire alarm.

(2) The operator of an authorized emergency vehicle may:

(a) park or stand, irrespective of the provisions of this chapter;

(b) proceed past a red or stop signal or stop sign, but only after slowing down as may be necessary for safe operation;

(c) exceed the maximum speed limits, unless prohibited by a local highway authority under Section 41-6a-208; or

(d) disregard regulations governing direction of movement or turning in specified directions.

(3) Privileges granted under this section to the operator of an authorized emergency vehicle, who is not involved in a vehicle pursuit, apply only when:

(a) the operator of the vehicle sounds an audible signal under Section 41-6a-1625; or

(b) uses a visual signal with emergency lights in accordance with rules made under Section 41-6a-1601, which is visible from in front of the vehicle.

(4) Privileges granted under this section to the operator of an authorized emergency vehicle involved in any vehicle pursuit apply only when:

(a) the operator of the vehicle:

(i) sounds an audible signal under Section 41-6a-1625; and

(ii) uses a visual signal with emergency lights in accordance with rules made under Section 41-6a-1601, which is visible from in front of the vehicle;

(b) the public agency employing the operator of the vehicle has, in effect, a written policy which describes the manner and circumstances in which any vehicle pursuit should be conducted and terminated;

(c) the operator of the vehicle has been trained in accordance with the written policy described in Subsection (4)(b); and

(d) the pursuit policy of the public agency is in conformance with standards established under Subsection (5).

(5) In accordance with Title 63, Chapter 46a, Utah Administrative Rulemaking Act, the Department of Public Safety shall make rules providing minimum standards for all emergency pursuit policies that are adopted by public agencies authorized to operate emergency pursuit vehicles.

(6) The privileges granted under this section do not relieve the operator of an authorized emergency vehicle of the duty to act as a reasonably prudent emergency vehicle operator in like circumstances.

(7) Except for Sections 41-6a-210, 41-6a-502, and 41-6a-528, this chapter does not apply to persons, motor vehicles, and other equipment while actually engaged in work on the surface of a highway.   2005

41-6a-213. Persons riding or driving animals subject to chapter — Exceptions.

(1) Except as provided under Subsection (2), a person who is riding an animal or who is driving an animal-drawn vehicle on a roadway is subject to this chapter.

(2) Driver license sanctions for alcohol or drug related traffic offenses do not apply to a person specified under Subsection (1).   2005

41-6a-214. Quasi-public roads and parking areas — Local ordinances.

(1) As used in this section, "quasi-public road or parking area" means a privately owned and maintained road or parking area that is generally held open for use of the public for purposes of vehicular travel or parking.

(2) (a) Any municipality or county may by ordinance provide that a quasi-public road or parking area within the municipality or county is subject to this chapter.

(b) An ordinance may not be enacted under this section without:

(i) a public hearing; and

(ii) the agreement of a majority of the owners of the quasi-public road or parking area involved.

(3) This section:

(a) supercedes conflicting provisions under Section 41-6a-215;

(b) does not require a peace officer to patrol or enforce any provisions of this chapter on any quasi-public road or parking area; or

(c) does not affect the duty of a peace officer to enforce those provisions of this chapter applicable to private property other than under this section.

2005

41-6a-215. Right of real property owner to regulate traffic.

Except as provided under Section 41-6a-214, this chapter does not prevent the owner of real property used by the public for purposes of vehicular travel by permission of the owner and not as matter of right from:

(1) prohibiting the use;

(2) requiring other conditions not specified in this chapter; or

(3) otherwise regulating the use as preferred by the owner.

2005

41-6a-216. Removal of plants or other obstructions impairing view — Notice to owner — Penalty.

(1) The owner of real property shall remove from his property any tree, plant, shrub, or other obstruction, or part of it that constitutes a traffic hazard by obstructing the view of an operator of a vehicle on a highway.

(2) When a highway authority determines on the basis of an engineering and traffic investigation that a traffic hazard exists, it shall notify the owner and order that the hazard be removed within ten days.

(3) The failure of the owner to remove the traffic hazard within ten days is a class C misdemeanor.

2005

41-6a-217. Volunteers may be authorized to enforce certain parking provisions.

(1) Any law enforcement agency authorized to enforce parking laws in this state may appoint volunteers to issue citations for violations of:

(a) the provisions of Subsections 41-1a-414(3) and (4) related to parking for a person with a disability;

(b) any municipal or county accessible parking privileges ordinance for a person with a disability; or

(c) the provisions of Subsection 41-6a-1307(4) related to parking in a school bus parking zone.

(2) A volunteer appointed under this section must be at least 21 years of age.

(3) The law enforcement agency appointing a volunteer may establish any other qualification for the volunteer that the agency finds desirable.

(4) A volunteer may not issue citations until the volunteer has received training from the appointing law enforcement agency.

(5) A citation issued by a volunteer under this section has the same force and effect as a citation issued by a peace officer for the same offense.

2005

PART 3

TRAFFIC-CONTROL DEVICES

41-6a-301. Standards and specifications for uniform system of traffic-control devices and school crossing guards.

(1) In accordance with Title 63, Chapter 46a, Utah Administrative Rulemaking Act, the Department of Transportation shall make rules consistent with this chapter adopting standards and establishing specifications for a uniform system of traffic-control devices used on a highway.

(2) The standards and specifications adopted under Subsection (1) shall:

(a) include provisions for school crossing zones and use of school crossing guards; and

(b) correlate with, and where possible conform to, the system set forth in the most recent edition of the "Manual on Uniform Traffic Control Devices for Streets and Highways" and other standards issued or endorsed by the federal highway administrator.

2005

41-6a-302. Placing and maintenance on state highways — Restrictions on local authorities.

In accordance with Section 72-3-109, a highway authority shall place and maintain traffic-control devices:

(1) in conformance with the standards and specifications adopted under Section 41-6a-301 on all highways under the highway authority's jurisdiction; and

(2) as the highway authority finds necessary to:

(a) carry out the provisions of:

(i) this chapter; or

(ii) a local traffic ordinance if the highway authority is a local highway authority; or

(b) regulate, warn, or guide traffic.

2005

41-6a-303. Definition of reduced speed school zone — Operation of warning lights — School crossing guard requirements — Responsibility provisions — Rulemaking authority.

(1) As used in this section "reduced speed school zone" means a designated length of a highway extending from a school zone speed limit sign with warning lights operating to an end school zone sign.

(2) The Department of Transportation for state highways and local highway authorities for highways under their jurisdiction:

(a) shall establish reduced speed school zones at elementary schools after written assurance by a local highway authority that the local highway authority complies with Subsections (3) and (4); and

(b) may establish reduced speed school zones for secondary schools at the request of the local highway authority.

(3) For all reduced speed school zones on highways, including state highways within the jurisdictional boundaries of a local highway authority, the local highway authority shall:

(a) (i) provide shuttle service across highways for school children; or

(ii) provide, train, and supervise school crossing guards in accordance with this section;

(b) provide for the:

(i) operation of reduced speed school zones, including providing power to warning lights and turning on and off the warning lights as required under Subsections (4) and (5); and

(ii) maintenance of reduced speed school zones except on state highways as provided in Section 41-6a-302; and

(c) notify the Department of Transportation of reduced speed school zones on state highways that are in need of maintenance.

(4) While children are going to or leaving school during opening and closing hours all reduced speed school zones shall have:

(a) the warning lights operating on each school zone speed limit sign; and

(b) a school crossing guard present if the reduced speed school zone is for an elementary school.

(5) The warning lights on a school zone speed limit sign may not be operating except as provided under Subsection (4).

(6) In accordance with Title 63, Chapter 46a, Utah Administrative Rulemaking Act, the Department of Transportation shall make rules establishing criteria and specifications for the:

(a) establishment, location, and operation of school crosswalks, school zones, and reduced speed school zones;

(b) training, use, and supervision of school crossing guards at elementary schools and secondary schools; and

(c) content and implementation of child access routing plans under Section 53A-3-402.

(7) Each local highway authority shall pay for providing, training, and supervising school crossing guards in accordance with this section.   2005

41-6a-304. Obeying devices — Effect of improper position, illegibility, or absence — Presumption of lawful placement and compliance with chapter.

(1) Except as otherwise directed by a peace officer or other authorized personnel under Section 41-6a-209 and except as provided under Section 41-6a-212 for authorized emergency vehicles, the operator of a vehicle shall obey the instructions of any traffic-control device placed or held in accordance with this chapter.

(2) (a) Any provision of this chapter, for which a traffic-control device is required, may not be enforced if at the time and place of the alleged violation the traffic-control device is not in proper position and sufficiently legible to be seen by an ordinarily observant person.

(b) The provisions of this chapter are effective independently of the placement of a traffic-control device unless the provision requires the placement of a traffic-control device prior to its enforcement.

(3) A traffic-control device placed or held in a position approximately conforming to the requirements of this chapter is presumed to have been placed or held by the official act or direction of a highway authority or other lawful authority, unless the contrary is established by competent evidence.

(4) A traffic-control device placed or held under this chapter and purporting to conform to the lawful requirements of the device is presumed to comply with the requirements of this chapter, unless the contrary is established by competent evidence.   2005

41-6a-305. Traffic-control signal — At intersections — At place other than intersection — Color of light signal — Inoperative traffic-control signals.

(1) (a) Green, red, and yellow are the only colors that may be used in a traffic-control signal, except for a:

(i) pedestrian traffic-control signal that may use white and orange; and

(ii) rail vehicle that may use white.

(b) Traffic-control signals apply to the operator of a vehicle and to a pedestrian as provided in this section.

(2) (a) (i) Except as provided in Subsection (2)(a)(ii), the operator of a vehicle facing a circular green signal may:

(A) proceed straight through the intersection;

(B) turn right; or

(C) turn left.

(ii) The operator of a vehicle facing a circular green signal, including an operator turning right or left:

(A) shall yield the right-of-way to other vehicles and to pedestrians lawfully within the intersection or an adjacent crosswalk at the time the signal is exhibited; and

(B) may not turn right or left if a sign at the intersection prohibits the turn.

(b) The operator of a vehicle facing a green arrow signal shown alone or in combination with another indication:

(i) may cautiously enter the intersection only to make the movement indicated by the arrow or other indication shown at the same time; and

(ii) shall yield the right-of-way to pedestrians lawfully within an adjacent crosswalk and to other traffic lawfully using the intersection.

(c) Unless otherwise directed by a pedestrian traffic-control signal under Section 41-6a-306, a pedestrian facing any green signal other than a green turn arrow may proceed across the roadway within any marked or unmarked crosswalk.

(3) (a) The operator of a vehicle facing a steady circular yellow or yellow arrow signal is warned that the allowable movement related to a green signal is being terminated.

(b) Unless otherwise directed by a pedestrian traffic-control signal under Section 41-6a-306, a pedestrian facing a steady circular yellow or yellow arrow signal is advised that there is insufficient time to cross the roadway before a red indication is shown, and a pedestrian may not start to cross the roadway.

(4) (a) Except as provided in Subsection (4)(c), the operator of a vehicle facing a steady circular red or red arrow signal:

(i) may not enter the intersection unless entering the intersection to make a movement is permitted by another indication; and

(ii) shall stop at a clearly marked stop line, but if none, before entering the marked or unmarked crosswalk on the near side of the intersection and shall remain stopped until an indication to proceed is shown.

(b) Unless otherwise directed by a pedestrian traffic-control signal under Section 41-6a-306, a pedestrian facing a steady red signal alone may not enter the roadway.

(c) (i) Except when facing a red arrow signal or when a sign is in place prohibiting a turn, the operator of a vehicle facing any steady circular red signal may cautiously enter the intersection to turn right, or may turn left from a one-way street into a one-way street, after stopping as required by Subsection (4)(a).

(ii) The operator of a vehicle shall yield the right-of-way to:

(A) another vehicle moving through the intersection in accordance with an official traffic-control signal; and

(B) a pedestrian lawfully within an adjacent crosswalk.

(5) (a) This section applies to a highway or rail line where a traffic-control signal is erected and maintained.

(b) Any stop required shall be made at a sign or marking on the highway pavement indicating where the stop shall be made, but, in the absence of any sign or marking, the stop shall be made at the signal.

(6) The operator of a vehicle approaching an intersection that has an inoperative traffic-control signal shall:

(a) stop before entering the intersection; and

(b) yield the right-of-way to any vehicle as required under Section 41-6a-901.   2005

41-6a-306. Pedestrian traffic-control signals — Rights and duties.

(1) A pedestrian facing a steady "Walk" or symbol of "Walking Person" of a pedestrian traffic-control signal has the right-of-way and may proceed across the roadway in the direction of the signal.

(2) A pedestrian facing a flashing "Don't Walk" or "Upraised Hand" of a pedestrian traffic-control signal may not start to cross the roadway in the direction of the signal, but a pedestrian who has partially completed crossing on the walk signal shall proceed to a sidewalk or safety island.

(3) A pedestrian facing a steady "Don't Walk" or "Upraised Hand" of a pedestrian traffic-control signal may not enter the roadway in the direction of the signal.   2005

41-6a-307. Flashing red or yellow signals — Rights and duties of operators — Railroad grade crossings excluded.

Except as provided under Section 41-6a-1203 regarding railroad grade crossing, the:

(1) operator of a vehicle facing an illuminated flashing red stop signal used in a traffic-control signal or with a traffic sign shall stop at a clearly marked stop line, but if none, before entering the crosswalk on the nearest side of the intersection, or if none, then at a point nearest the intersecting roadway where the operator has a view of approaching traffic on the intersecting roadway before entering;

(2) right to proceed is subject to the rules applicable after making a stop at a stop sign; and

(3) operator of a vehicle facing an illuminated flashing yellow caution signal may cautiously proceed through the intersection or cautiously proceed past the signal.   2005

41-6a-308. Lane use control signals — Colors.

The operator of a vehicle facing a traffic-control signal placed to control individual lane use shall obey the signal as follows:

(1) Green signal — vehicular traffic may travel in any lane over which a green signal is shown.

(2) Steady yellow signal — vehicular traffic is warned that a lane control change is being made.

(3) Steady red signal — vehicular traffic may not enter or travel in any lane over which a red signal is shown.

(4) Flashing yellow signal — vehicular traffic may use the lane only for the purpose of approaching and making a left turn.   2005

41-6a-309. Prohibition of unauthorized signs, signals, lights, or markings — Commercial advertising — Public nuisance — Removal.

(1) Except as provided in Section 41-6a-310, a person may not place, maintain, or display upon or in view of any highway any unauthorized sign, signal, light, marking, or device which:

(a) purports to be or which resembles a traffic-control device or railroad sign or signal, or authorized emergency vehicle flashing light;

(b) attempts to direct the movement of traffic;

(c) hides from view or interferes with the effectiveness of a traffic-control device or any railroad sign or signal; or

(d) blinds or dazzles an operator on any adjacent highway.

(2) Except as provided under Section 72-7-504 regarding logo advertising, a person may not place or maintain any commercial advertising on any traffic-control device.

(3) The provisions of Subsections (1) and (2) do not prohibit a sign on private property adjacent to a highway providing directional information in a manner that may not be mistaken for a traffic-control device.

(4) Every prohibited sign, signal, or light, or marking is a public nuisance and the highway authority having jurisdiction over the highway may remove it or cause it to be removed without notice.   2005

41-6a-310. Private vehicle as emergency vehicle — Rules.

(1) The commissioner of the Department of Public Safety may make rules, consistent with this chapter, governing the use, in emergencies, of signal lights on privately owned vehicles.

(2) The rules under Subsection (1) may authorize a privately owned vehicle to be designated for part-time emergency use.   2005

41-6a-311. Interference with traffic-control devices prohibited — Traffic signal preemption device prohibited — Exceptions — Defense.

(1) Except as provided in Subsection (3), a person may not alter, deface, damage, knock down, or remove any:

(a) traffic-control device;

(b) traffic-monitoring device; or

(c) railroad traffic-control device.

(2) Except as provided in Subsection (3), a person may not:

(a) knowingly use a traffic signal preemption device to interfere with the authorized operation or the authorized cycle of a traffic-control signal; or

(b) operate a motor vehicle on a highway while in possession of a traffic signal preemption device.

(3) The provisions of Subsections (1) and (2) do not apply to a person authorized by the highway authority or railroad authority with jurisdiction over the device.

(4) It is an affirmative defense to a charge under Subsection (2)(b) that the traffic signal preemption device was inoperative and could not be readily used at the time of the citation or arrest.   2005

PART 4

ACCIDENT RESPONSIBILITIES

41-6a-401. Accident involving injury, death, or property damage — Duties of operator, occupant, and owner — Exchange of information — Notification of law enforcement — Penalties.

(1) The operator of a vehicle involved in an accident resulting in injury to or death of a person or damage to another vehicle or other property shall:

(a) immediately stop the vehicle at the scene of the accident or as close as possible without obstructing traffic more than is necessary; and

(b) remain at the scene of the accident until the operator has fulfilled the requirements of this section.

(2) Except as provided under Subsection (6), if the vehicle or other property is operated, occupied, or attended by any person or if the owner of the vehicle or property is present, the operator of the vehicle involved in the accident shall:

(a) give to the persons involved:

(i) the operator's name, address, and the registration number of the vehicle being operated; and

(ii) the name of the insurance provider covering the vehicle being operated including the phone number of the agent or provider;

(b) upon request and if available, exhibit the operator's license to:

(i) any investigating peace officer present;

(ii) the person struck;

(iii) the operator, occupant of, or person attending the vehicle or other property damaged in the accident; and

(iv) the owner of property damaged in the accident, if present; and

(c) render to any person injured in the accident reasonable assistance, including transporting or making arrangements for transporting, of the injured person to a physician or hospital for medical treatment if:

(i) it is apparent that treatment is necessary; or

(ii) transportation is requested by the injured person.

(3) The operator of a vehicle involved in an accident shall immediately and by the quickest means of communication available give notice or cause to give notice of the accident to the nearest office of a law enforcement agency if the accident resulted in:

(a) injury or death of any person; or

(b) property damage to an apparent extent of $1,000 or more.

(4) The occupant of a vehicle involved in an accident who is not the operator of the vehicle shall give or cause to give the immediate notice required under Subsection (3) if:

(a) the operator of a vehicle involved in an accident is physically incapable of giving the notice; and

(b) the occupant is capable of giving an immediate notice.

(5) Except as provided under Subsection (6), if the vehicle or other property is unattended, the operator of the vehicle involved in the accident shall:

(a) locate and notify the operator or owner of the vehicle or the owner of other property damaged in the accident of the operator's name, address, and the registration number of the vehicle causing the damage; or

(b) attach securely in a conspicuous place on the vehicle or other property a written notice giving the operator's name, address, and the registration number of the vehicle causing the damage.

(6) The operator of a vehicle that provides the information required under this section to an investigating peace officer at the scene of the accident is exempt from providing the information to other persons required under this section.

(7) (a) A person who violates the provisions of Subsection (1) is guilty of a class A misdemeanor and shall be fined not less than $750 if the accident results in injury or death of a person.

(b) A person who violates the provisions of Subsection (1) is guilty of a class B misdemeanor if the accident results only in damage to a vehicle or other property.

(c) A person who violates the provision of Subsection (5) is guilty of a class B misdemeanor.

2005

41-6a-402. Accident reports — Duty of operator and investigative officer to forward or render.

(1) The department may require any operator of a vehicle involved in an accident resulting in injury to or death of any person or total property damage to the apparent extent of $1,000 or more to file within ten days after the request:

(a) a report of the accident to the department in a manner specified by the department; and

(b) a supplemental report when the original report is insufficient in the opinion of the department.

(2) The department may require witnesses of accidents to file reports to the department.

(3) (a) An accident report is not required under this section from any person who is physically incapable of making a report, during the period of incapacity.

(b) If the operator is physically incapable of making an accident report under this section and the operator is not the owner of the vehicle, the owner of the vehicle involved in the accident shall within 15 days after becoming aware of the accident make the report required of the operator under this section.

(4) (a) The department shall, upon request, supply to law enforcement agencies, justice court judges, sheriffs, garages, and other appropriate agencies or individuals forms for accident reports required under this part.

(b) A request for an accident report form under Subsection (4)(a) shall be made in a manner specified by the division.

(c) The accident reports shall:

(i) provide sufficient detail to disclose the cause, conditions then existing, and the persons and vehicles involved in the accident; and

(ii) contain all of the information required that is available.

(5) (a) A person shall file an accident report if required under this section.

(b) The department shall suspend the license or permit to operate a motor vehicle and any nonresident operating privileges of any person failing to file an accident report in accordance with this section.

(c) The suspension under Subsection (5)(b) shall be in effect until the report has been filed except that the department may extend the suspension not to exceed 30 days.

(6) (a) A peace officer who, in the regular course of duty, investigates a motor vehicle accident described under Subsection (1) shall file the original or an electronic copy of the report of the accident with the department within ten days after completing the investigation.

(b) The accident report shall be made either at the time of and at the scene of the accident or later by interviewing participants or witnesses.

(7) The accident reports required to be filed with the department under this section and the information in them are protected and confidential and may be disclosed only as provided in Section 41-6a-404.

(8) (a) In addition to the reports required under this part, a local highway authority may, by ordinance, require that for each accident that occurs within its jurisdiction, the operator of a vehicle involved in an accident, or the owner of the vehicle involved in an accident, shall file with the local law enforcement agency a report of the accident or a copy of any report required to be filed with the department under this part.

(b) All reports are for the confidential use of the municipal department and are subject to the provisions of Section 41-6a-404.   2005

41-6a-403. Vehicle accidents — Investigation and report of operator security — Agency action if no security — Surrender of plates — Penalties.

(1) (a) Upon request of a peace officer investigating an accident involving a motor vehicle, the operator of the motor vehicle shall provide evidence of the owner's or operator's security required under Section 41-12a-301.

(b) The evidence of owner's or operator's security includes information specified under Section 41-12a-303.2.

(2) The peace officer shall record on a form approved by the department:

(a) the information provided by the operator;

(b) whether the operator provided insufficient or no information;

(c) whether the officer finds reasonable cause to believe that any information given is not correct; and

(d) whether other information available to the peace officer indicates that owner's or operator's security is in effect.

(3) The peace officer shall deposit all completed forms with the peace officer's law enforcement agency, which shall forward the forms to the department no later than ten days after receipt.

(4) (a) The department shall within ten days of receipt of the forms from the law enforcement agency take action as follows:

(i) if the operator provided no information under Subsection (1) and other information available to the peace officer does not indicate that owner's or operator's security is in effect, the department shall take direct action under Subsection 53-3-221(12); or

(ii) if the peace officer noted or the department determines that there is reasonable cause to believe that the information given under Subsection (1) is not correct, the department shall contact directly the insurance company or other provider of security as described in Section 41-12a-303.2 and request verification of the accuracy of the infor-

mation submitted as of the date of the accident.

(b) The department may require the verification under Subsection (4)(a)(ii) to be in a form specified by the department.

(c) The insurance company or other provider of security shall return the verification to the department within 30 days of receipt of the request.

(d) If the department does not receive verification within 35 days after sending the request, or within the 35 days receives notice that the information was not correct, the department shall take action under Subsection 53-3-221(12).

(5) (a) The owner of a vehicle with unexpired license plates for which security is not provided as required under this chapter shall return the plates for the vehicle to the Motor Vehicle Division unless specifically permitted by statute to retain them.

(b) If the owner fails to return the plates as required, the plates shall be confiscated under Section 53-3-226.

(6) In accordance with Title 63, Chapter 46a, Utah Administrative Rulemaking Act, the department may make rules for the enforcement of this section.

(7) A person is guilty of a class B misdemeanor, and shall be fined not less than $100, who:

(a) when requested to provide security information under Subsection (1), or Section 41-12a-303.2, provides false information;

(b) falsely represents to the department that security required under this chapter is in effect; or

(c) sells a vehicle to avoid the penalties of this section as applicable either to himself or a third party.   2005

41-6a-404. Accident reports — When confidential — Insurance policy information — Use as evidence — Penalty for false information.

(1) As used in this section:

(a) "Agent" means a person's:

(i) attorney;

(ii) insurer; or

(iii) any other individual or entity with signed permission from the person to receive the person's accident report.

(b) "Accompanying data" means all materials gathered by the investigating peace officer in an accident investigation including:

(i) the identity of witnesses and, if known, contact information;

(ii) witness statements;

(iii) photographs and videotapes;

(iv) diagrams; and

(v) field notes.

(2) Except as provided in Subsection (3), all accident reports required in this part to be filed with the department:

(a) are without prejudice to the reporting individual;

(b) are protected and for the confidential use of the department or other state, local, or federal agencies having use for the records for official governmental statistical, investigative, and accident prevention purposes; and

(c) may be disclosed only in a statistical form that protects the privacy of any person involved in the accident.

(3) (a) Subject to the provisions of this section, the department or the responsible law enforcement

agency employing the peace officer that investigated the accident shall disclose an accident report to:

    (i) a person involved in the accident, excluding a witness to the accident;

    (ii) a person suffering loss or injury in the accident;

    (iii) an agent, parent, or legal guardian of a person described in Subsections (3)(a)(i) and (ii);

    (iv) subject to Subsection (3)(d), a member of the press or broadcast news media;

    (v) a state, local, or federal agency that uses the records for official governmental, investigative, or accident prevention purposes;

    (vi) law enforcement personnel when acting in their official governmental capacity; and

    (vii) a licensed private investigator.

(b) The responsible law enforcement agency employing the peace officer that investigated the accident:

    (i) shall in compliance with Subsection (3)(a):

        (A) disclose an accident report; or

        (B) upon written request disclose an accident report and its accompanying data within ten business days from receipt of a written request for disclosure; or

    (ii) may withhold an accident report, and any of its accompanying data if disclosure would jeopardize an ongoing criminal investigation or criminal prosecution.

(c) In accordance with Subsection (3)(a), the department or the responsible law enforcement agency employing the investigating peace officer shall disclose whether any person or vehicle involved in an accident reported under this section was covered by a vehicle insurance policy, and the name of the insurer.

(d) Information provided to a member of the press or broadcast news media under Subsection (3)(a)(iv) may only include:

    (i) the name, age, sex, and city of residence of each person involved in the accident;

    (ii) the make and model year of each vehicle involved in the accident;

    (iii) whether or not each person involved in the accident was covered by a vehicle insurance policy;

    (iv) the location of the accident; and

    (v) a description of the accident that excludes personal identifying information not listed in Subsection (3)(d)(i).

(e) The department shall disclose to any requesting person the following vehicle accident history information, excluding personal identifying information, in bulk electronic form:

    (i) any vehicle identifying information that is electronically available, including the make, model year, and vehicle identification number of each vehicle involved in an accident;

    (ii) the date of the accident; and

    (iii) any electronically available data which describes the accident, including a description of any physical damage to the vehicle.

(f) The department may establish a fee under Section 63-38-3.2 based on the fair market value

of the information for providing bulk vehicle accident history information under Subsection (3)(e).

(4) (a) Except as provided in Subsection (4)(b), accident reports filed under this section may not be used as evidence in any civil or criminal trial arising out of an accident.

    (b) (i) Upon demand of any party to the trial or upon demand of any court, the department shall furnish a certificate showing that a specified accident report has or has not been made to the department in compliance with law.

    (ii) If the report has been made, the certificate furnished by the department shall show:

        (A) the date, time, and location of the accident;

        (B) the names and addresses of the drivers;

        (C) the owners of the vehicles involved; and

        (D) the investigating peace officers.

    (iii) The reports may be used as evidence when necessary to prosecute charges filed in connection with a violation of Subsection (5).

(5) A person who gives information in reports as required in this part knowing or having reason to believe that the information is false is guilty of a class A misdemeanor.

(6) The department and the responsible law enforcement agency employing the investigating peace officer may charge a reasonable fee determined by the department under Section 63-38-3.2 for the cost incurred in disclosing an accident report or an accident report and any of its accompanying data under Subsections (3)(a) and (b).   2005

41-6a-405. Garage keeper to report damaged vehicle without damage sticker.

(1) (a) The person in charge of any garage or repair shop shall make a report to the nearest law enforcement agency within 24 hours of receiving a vehicle which shows evidence of having been:

    (i) involved in an accident for which an accident report may be requested under Section 41-6a-402; or

    (ii) struck by any bullet.

    (b) The report required under Subsection (1)(a) shall include the:

    (i) vehicle identification number;

    (ii) registration number; and

    (iii) name and address of the owner or operator of the vehicle.

(2) If a damaged vehicle sticker describing the damage is affixed to the vehicle by a peace officer, a report under Subsection (1) is not required.   2005

41-6a-406. Statistical information regarding accidents — Annual publication.

(1) The department may analyze all accident reports.

(2) (a) The department shall tabulate and publish statistical information as to the number and circumstances of traffic accidents.

    (b) The publication under Subsection (2)(a) shall be at least annually.   2005

41-6a-407. Livestock on highway — Restrictions — Collision, action for damages.

(1) (a) A person who owns or is in possession or control of any livestock may not willfully or negligently permit any of the livestock to stray or

remain unaccompanied on a highway, if both sides of the highway are separated from adjoining property by a fence, wall, hedge, sidewalk, curb, lawn, or building.

(b) Subsection (1)(a) does not apply to range stock drifting onto any highway moving to or from their accustomed ranges.

(2) (a) A person may not drive any livestock upon, over, or across any highway during the period from half an hour after sunset to half an hour before sunrise.

(b) Subsection (2)(a) does not apply if the person has a sufficient number of herders with warning lights on continual duty to open the road to permit the passage of vehicles.

(3) In any civil action brought for damages caused by collision with any domestic animal or livestock on a highway, there is no presumption that the collision was due to negligence on behalf of the owner or the person in possession of the domestic animal or livestock.   2005

41-6a-408. Peace officer investigating accident to notify owner if livestock or broken fence involved — Exempt from liability.

(1) A peace officer investigating an accident resulting in injury or death of any livestock shall make reasonable efforts as soon as possible to locate the owner of the livestock and inform the owner of the injured or dead animal.

(2) A peace officer investigating an accident resulting in a broken fence, if it appears the fence contains or controls the movement of livestock, shall make reasonable efforts as soon as possible to locate the owner of the property and inform the owner of the broken fence.

(3) (a) Civil or criminal liability for claims does not arise against any peace officer for failure to locate the owner of the livestock or property.

(b) Subsection (3)(a) does not preclude disciplinary action by the law enforcement agency against a peace officer for failure to perform duties required by this section.   2005

PART 5

DRIVING UNDER THE INFLUENCE AND RECKLESS DRIVING

41-6a-501. Definitions.

(1) As used in this part:

(a) "Assessment" means an in-depth clinical interview with a licensed mental health therapist:

(i) used to determine if a person is in need of:

(A) substance abuse treatment that is obtained at a substance abuse program;

(B) an educational series; or

(C) a combination of Subsections (1)(a)(i)(A) and (B); and

(ii) that is approved by the Board of Substance Abuse and Mental Health in accordance with Section 62A-15-105.

(b) "Educational series" means an educational series obtained at a substance abuse program that is approved by the Board of Substance Abuse and Mental Health in accordance with Section 62A-15-105.

(c) "Negligence" means simple negligence, the failure to exercise that degree of care that an ordinarily reasonable and prudent person exercises under like or similar circumstances.

(d) "Screening" means a preliminary appraisal of a person:

(i) used to determine if the person is in need of:

(A) an assessment; or

(B) an educational series; and

(ii) that is approved by the Board of Substance Abuse and Mental Health in accordance with Section 62A-15-105.

(e) "Serious bodily injury" means bodily injury that creates or causes:

(i) serious permanent disfigurement;

(ii) protracted loss or impairment of the function of any bodily member or organ; or

(iii) a substantial risk of death.

(f) "Substance abuse treatment" means treatment obtained at a substance abuse program that is approved by the Board of Substance Abuse and Mental Health in accordance with Section 62A-15-105.

(g) "Substance abuse treatment program" means a state licensed substance abuse program.

(h) (i) "Vehicle" or "motor vehicle" means a vehicle or motor vehicle as defined in Section 41-6a-102; and

(ii) "Vehicle" or "motor vehicle" includes:

(A) an off-highway vehicle as defined under Section 41-22-2; and

(B) a motorboat as defined in Section 73-18-2.

(2) As used in Section 41-6a-503:

(a) "Conviction" means any conviction for a violation of:

(i) driving under the influence under Section 41-6a-502;

(ii) alcohol, any drug, or a combination of both-related reckless driving under Sections 41-6a-512 and 41-6a-528;

(iii) driving with any measurable controlled substance that is taken illegally in the body under Section 41-6a-517;

(iv) local ordinances similar to Section 41-6a-502 or alcohol, any drug, or a combination of both-related reckless driving adopted in compliance with Section 41-6a-510;

(v) automobile homicide under Section 76-5-207;

(vi) Subsection 58-37-8(2)(g);

(vii) a violation described in Subsections (2)(a)(i) through (vi), which judgment of conviction is reduced under Section 76-3-402; or

(viii) statutes or ordinances previously in effect in this state or in effect in any other state, the United States, or any district, possession, or territory of the United States which would constitute a violation of Section 41-6a-502 or alcohol, any drug, or a combination of both-related reckless driving if committed in this state, including punishments administered under 10 U.S.C. Sec. 815.

(b) A plea of guilty or no contest to a violation described in Subsections (2)(a)(i) through (viii) which plea is held in abeyance under Title 77, Chapter 2a, Pleas in Abeyance, is the equivalent of a conviction, even if the charge has been subsequently reduced or dismissed in accordance with the plea in abeyance agreement, for purposes of:

(i) enhancement of penalties under:

(A) this Chapter 6a, Part 5, Driving Under the Influence and Reckless Driving; and

(B) automobile homicide under Section 76-5-207; and

(ii) expungement under Section 77-18-12.

2005

41-6a-502. Driving under the influence of alcohol, drugs, or a combination of both or with specified or unsafe blood alcohol concentration.

(1) A person may not operate or be in actual physical control of a vehicle within this state if the person:

(a) has sufficient alcohol in the person's body that a subsequent chemical test shows that the person has a blood or breath alcohol concentration of .08 grams or greater at the time of the test;

(b) is under the influence of alcohol, any drug, or the combined influence of alcohol and any drug to a degree that renders the person incapable of safely operating a vehicle;

(c) has a blood or breath alcohol concentration of .08 grams or greater at the time of operation or actual physical control; or

(d) (i) is 21 years of age or older;

(ii) has a passenger under 16 years of age in the vehicle at the time of operation or actual physical control;

(iii) has committed a violation of this Subsection (1)(d) within ten years of a prior conviction as defined in Subsection 41-6a-501(2); and

(iv) (A) has sufficient alcohol in the person's body that a subsequent chemical test shows that the person has a blood or breath alcohol concentration of .05 grams or greater at the time of the test; or

(B) has a blood or breath alcohol concentration of .05 grams or greater at the time of operation or actual physical control.

(2) Alcohol concentration in the blood shall be based upon grams of alcohol per 100 milliliters of blood, and alcohol concentration in the breath shall be based upon grams of alcohol per 210 liters of breath.

(3) A violation of this section includes a violation under a local ordinance similar to this section adopted in compliance with Section 41-6a-510.

2005

41-6a-503. Penalties for driving under the influence violations.

(1) A person convicted the first or second time of a violation of Section 41-6a-502 is guilty of a:

(a) class B misdemeanor; or

(b) class A misdemeanor if the person:

(i) has also inflicted bodily injury upon another as a proximate result of having operated the vehicle in a negligent manner;

(ii) had a passenger under 16 years of age in the vehicle at the time of the offense; or

(iii) was 21 years of age or older and had a passenger under 18 years of age in the vehicle at the time of the offense.

(2) A person convicted of a violation of Section 41-6a-502 is guilty of a third degree felony if:

(a) the person has also inflicted serious bodily injury upon another as a proximate result of having operated the vehicle in a negligent manner;

(b) the conviction under Section 41-6a-502 is within ten years of two or more prior convictions as defined in Subsection 41-6a-501(2); or

(c) the conviction under Section 41-6a-502 is at any time after a conviction of:

(i) automobile homicide under Section 76-5-207 that is committed after July 1, 2001;

(ii) a felony violation of Section 41-6a-502 or a statute previously in effect in this state that would constitute a violation of Section 41-6a-502 that is committed after July 1, 2001; or

(iii) any conviction described in Subsection (2)(c)(i) or (ii) which judgment of conviction is reduced under Section 76-3-402.

(3) A person convicted of a violation of Subsection 41-6a-502(1)(d) is guilty of:

(a) a class B misdemeanor; or

(b) a class A misdemeanor if the person has also inflicted bodily injury upon another as a proximate result of having operated the vehicle in a negligent manner.

2005

41-6a-504. Defense not available for driving under the influence violation.

The fact that a person charged with violating Section 41-6a-502 is or has been legally entitled to use alcohol or a drug is not a defense against any charge of violating Section 41-6a-502.

2005

41-6a-505. Sentencing requirements for driving under the influence of alcohol, drugs, or a combination of both violations.

(1) As part of any sentence for a first conviction of Section 41-6a-502:

(a) the court shall:

(i) (A) impose a jail sentence of not less than 48 consecutive hours;

(B) require the person to work in a compensatory-service work program for not less than 48 hours; or

(C) require the person to participate in home confinement through the use of electronic monitoring in accordance with Section 41-6a-506;

(ii) order the person to participate in a screening;

(iii) order the person to participate in an assessment, if it is found appropriate by a screening under Subsection (1)(a)(ii);

(iv) order the person to participate in an educational series if the court does not order substance abuse treatment as described under Subsection (1)(b);

(v) impose a fine of not less than $700; and

(vi) order probation for the person in accordance with Section 41-6a-507, if there is admissible evidence that the person had a blood alcohol level of .16 or higher; and

(b) the court may:

(i) order the person to obtain substance abuse treatment if the substance abuse treatment program determines that substance abuse treatment is appropriate; or

(ii) order probation for the person in accordance with Section 41-6a-507.

(2) If a person is convicted under Section 41-6a-502 within ten years of a prior conviction as defined in Subsection 41-6a-501(2):

(a) the court shall:

(i) (A) impose a jail sentence of not less than 240 consecutive hours;

(B) require the person to work in a compensatory-service work program for not less than 240 hours; or

(C) require the person to participate in home confinement through the use of electronic monitoring in accordance with Section 41-6a-506;

(ii) order the person to participate in a screening;

(iii) order the person to participate in an assessment, if it is found appropriate by a screening under Subsection (2)(a)(ii);

(iv) order the person to participate in an educational series if the court does not order substance abuse treatment as described under Subsection (2)(b);

(v) impose a fine of not less than $800; and

(vi) order probation for the person in accordance with Section 41-6a-507; and

(b) the court may order the person to obtain substance abuse treatment if the substance abuse treatment program determines that substance abuse treatment is appropriate.

(3) Under Subsection 41-6a-503(2), if the court suspends the execution of a prison sentence and places the defendant on probation:

(a) the court shall impose:

(i) a fine of not less than $1,500;

(ii) a jail sentence of not less than 1,500 hours;

(iii) supervised probation; and

(iv) an order requiring the person to obtain a screening and assessment and substance abuse treatment at a substance abuse treatment program providing intensive care or inpatient treatment and long-term closely supervised follow-through after treatment for not less than 240 hours; and

(b) the court may require the person to participate in home confinement through the use of electronic monitoring in accordance with Section 41-6a-506.

(4) (a) The requirements of Subsections (1)(a), (2)(a), and (3)(a) may not be suspended.

(b) Probation or parole resulting from a conviction for a violation under this section may not be terminated.

(5) If a person is convicted of a violation of Section 41-6a-502 and there is admissible evidence that the person had a blood alcohol level of .16 or higher, the court shall order the following, or describe on record why the order or orders are not appropriate:

(a) treatment as described under Subsection (1)(b), (2)(b), or (3)(a)(iv); and

(b) one or both of the following:

(i) the installation of an ignition interlock system as a condition of probation for the person in accordance with Section 41-6a-518; or

(ii) the imposition of home confinement through the use of electronic monitoring in accordance with Section 41-6a-506. 2005

41-6a-506. Electronic monitoring requirements for certain driving under the influence violations.

(1) If the court orders a person to participate in home confinement through the use of electronic monitoring, the electronic monitoring shall alert the appropriate corrections, probation monitoring agency, law enforcement units, or contract provider of the defendant's whereabouts.

(2) The electronic monitoring device shall be used under conditions which require:

(a) the person to wear an electronic monitoring device at all times;

(b) that a device be placed in the home or other specified location of the person, so that the person's compliance with the court's order may be monitored; and

(c) the person to pay the costs of the electronic monitoring.

(3) The court shall order the appropriate entity described in Subsection (5) to place an electronic monitoring device on the person and install electronic monitoring equipment in the residence of the person or other specified location.

(4) The court may:

(a) require the person's electronic home monitoring device to include a substance abuse testing instrument;

(b) restrict the amount of alcohol the person may consume during the time the person is subject to home confinement;

(c) set specific time and location conditions that allow the person to attend school educational classes, or employment and to travel directly between those activities and the person's home; and

(d) waive all or part of the costs associated with home confinement if the person is determined to be indigent by the court.

(5) The electronic monitoring described in this section may either be administered directly by the appropriate corrections agency, probation monitoring agency, or by contract with a private provider.

(6) The electronic monitoring provider shall cover the costs of waivers by the court under Subsection (4)(d). 2005

41-6a-507. Supervised probation for certain driving under the influence violations.

(1) If supervised probation is ordered under Section 41-6a-505 or 41-6a-517:

(a) the court shall specify the period of the probation;

(b) the person shall pay all of the costs of the probation; and

(c) the court may order any other conditions of the probation.

(2) The court shall provide the probation described in this section by contract with a probation monitoring agency or a private probation provider.

(3) The probation provider described in Subsection (2) shall monitor the person's compliance with all conditions of the person's sentence, conditions of probation, and court orders received under this part and shall notify the court of any failure to comply with or complete that sentence or those conditions or orders.

(4) (a) The court may waive all or part of the costs associated with probation if the person is determined to be indigent by the court.

(b) The probation provider described in Subsection (2) shall cover the costs of waivers by the court under Subsection (4)(a). 2005

41-6a-508. Arrest without a warrant for a driving under the influence violation.

A peace officer may, without a warrant, arrest a person for a violation of Section 41-6a-502 when the peace officer has probable cause to believe the violation has occurred, although not in the peace officer's presence, and if the peace officer has probable cause to believe that the violation was committed by the person.   2005

41-6a-509. Driver license suspension or revocation for a driving under the influence violation.

(1) (a) The Driver License Division shall:

(i) suspend for 90 days the operator's license of a person convicted for the first time under Section 41-6a-502;

(ii) revoke for one year the license of a person convicted of any subsequent offense under Section 41-6a-502 or if the person has a prior conviction as defined under Subsection 41-6a-501(2) if the violation is committed within a period of ten years from the date of the prior violation; and

(iii) suspend or revoke the license of a person as ordered by the court under Subsection (2).

(b) The Driver License Division shall subtract from any suspension or revocation period the number of days for which a license was previously suspended under Section 53-3-223 or 53-3-231, if the previous suspension was based on the same occurrence upon which the record of conviction is based.

(2) (a) (i) In addition to any other penalties provided in this section, a court may order the operator's license of a person who is convicted of a violation of Section 41-6a-502 to be suspended or revoked for an additional period of 90 days, 180 days, one year, or two years to remove from the highways those persons who have shown they are safety hazards.

(ii) The additional suspension or revocation period provided in this Subsection (2) shall begin the date on which the individual would be eligible to reinstate the individual's driving privilege for a violation of Section 41-6a-502.

(b) If the court suspends or revokes the person's license under this Subsection (2), the court shall prepare and send to the Driver License Division an order to suspend or revoke that person's driving privileges for a specified period of time.

(3) (a) The court shall notify the Driver License Division if a person fails to:

(i) complete all court ordered:

(A) screening;

(B) assessment;

(C) educational series;

(D) substance abuse treatment; and

(E) hours of work in a compensatory-service work program; or

(ii) pay all fines and fees, including fees for restitution and treatment costs.

(b) Upon receiving the notification described in Subsection (3)(a), the division shall suspend the person's driving privilege in accordance with Subsections 53-3-221(2) and (3).   2005

41-6a-510. Local DUI and related ordinances and reckless driving ordinances — Consistent with code.

(1) An ordinance adopted by a local authority that governs the following matters shall be consistent with the provisions in this code which govern the following matters:

(a) a person's operating or being in actual physical control of a motor vehicle while having alcohol in the blood or while under the influence of alcohol or any drug or the combined influence of alcohol and any drug; or

(b) in relation to any of the matters described in Subsection (1)(a), the use of:

(i) a chemical test or chemical tests;

(ii) evidentiary presumptions;

(iii) penalties; or

(iv) any combination of the matters described in Subsection (1).

(2) An ordinance adopted by a local authority that governs reckless driving, or operating a vehicle in willful or wanton disregard for the safety of persons or property shall be consistent with the provisions of this code which govern those matters.   2005

41-6a-511. Courts to collect and maintain data.

(1) The state courts shall collect and maintain data necessary to allow sentencing and enhancement decisions to be made in accordance with this part.

(2) (a) Each justice court shall transmit dispositions electronically to the Department of Public Safety in accordance with the requirement for recertification established by the Judicial Council.

(b) Immediately upon filling the requirements under Subsection (2)(a), a justice court shall collect and report the same DUI related data elements collected and maintained by the state courts under Subsection (1).

(3) The department shall maintain an electronic data base for DUI related records and data including the data elements received or collected from the courts under this section.

(4) (a) The Commission on Criminal and Juvenile Justice shall prepare an annual report of DUI related data including the following:

(i) the data collected by the courts under Subsections (1) and (2); and

(ii) any measures for which data are available to evaluate the profile and impacts of DUI recidivism and to evaluate the DUI related processes of:

(A) law enforcement;

(B) adjudication;

(C) sanctions;

(D) drivers' license control; and

(E) alcohol education, assessment, and treatment.

(b) The report shall be provided to the Judiciary and Transportation Interim Committees no later than the last day of October following the end of the fiscal year for which the report is prepared.   2005

41-6a-512. Factual basis for alcohol or drug-related reckless driving plea.

(1) (a) The prosecution shall state for the record a factual basis for a plea, including whether or not there had been consumption of alcohol, drugs, or a combination of both, by the defendant in connection with the violation when the prosecution agrees to a plea of guilty or no contest to a charge of a violation of the following in satisfaction of, or as a substitute for, an original charge of a violation of Section 41-6a-502:

(i) reckless driving under Section 41-6a-528; or

(ii) an ordinance enacted under Section 41-6a-510.

(b) The statement under Subsection (1)(a) is an offer of proof of the facts that shows whether there was consumption of alcohol, drugs, or a combination of both, by the defendant, in connection with the violation.

(2) The court shall advise the defendant before accepting the plea offered under this section of the consequences of a violation of Section 41-6a-528.

(3) The court shall notify the Driver License Division of each conviction of Section 41-6a-528 entered under this section.

(4) (a) The provisions in Subsections 41-6a-505(1), (2), and (3) that require a sentencing court to order a convicted person to participate in a screening, an assessment, or an educational series or obtain substance abuse treatment or do a combination of those things, apply to a conviction for a violation of Section 41-6a-528 under Subsection (1).

(b) The court shall render the same order regarding screening, assessment, an educational series, or substance abuse treatment in connection with a first, second, or subsequent conviction under Section 41-6a-528 under Subsection (1), as the court would render in connection with applying respectively, the first, second, or subsequent conviction requirements of Subsections 41-6a-505(1), (2), and (3).   2005

41-6a-513. Acceptance of plea of guilty to DUI — Restrictions — Verification of prior violations — Prosecutor to examine defendant's record.

(1) A court may not accept a plea of guilty or no contest to a charge under Section 41-6a-502 unless:

(a) the prosecutor agrees to the plea:

(i) in open court;

(ii) in writing; or

(iii) by another means of communication which the court finds adequate to record the prosecutor's agreement;

(b) the charge is filed by information as defined under Section 77-1-3; or

(c) the court receives verification from a law enforcement agency that the defendant's driver license record contains no record of a conviction, arrest, or charge for:

(i) more than one prior violation within the previous ten years of any offense which, if the defendant were convicted, would qualify as a "conviction" as defined under Subsection 41-6a-501(2);

(ii) a felony violation of Section 41-6a-502; or

(iii) automobile homicide under Section 76-5-207.

(2) A verification under Subsection (1)(c) may be made by:

(a) a written indication on the citation;

(b) a separate written document; or

(c) any other means which the court finds adequate to record the law enforcement agency's verification.

(3) (a) Prior to agreeing to a plea of guilty or no contest or to filing an information under Subsection (1), the prosecutor shall examine the criminal history or driver license record of the defendant.

(b) If the defendant's record contains a conviction or unresolved arrest or charge for an offense listed in Subsections (1)(c)(i) through (iii), a plea may only be accepted if:

(i) approved by:

(A) a district attorney;

(B) a deputy district attorney;

(C) a county attorney;

(D) a deputy county attorney;

(E) the attorney general; or

(F) an assistant attorney general; and

(ii) the attorney giving approval under Subsection (3)(b)(i) has felony jurisdiction over the case.

(4) A plea of guilty or no contest is not made invalid by the failure of the court, prosecutor, or law enforcement agency to comply with this section.   2005

41-6a-514. Procedures — Adjudicative proceedings.

The department shall comply with the procedures and requirements of Title 63, Chapter 46b, Administrative Procedures Act, in its adjudicative proceedings.   2005

41-6a-515. Standards for chemical breath or oral fluids analysis — Evidence.

(1) The commissioner of the department shall establish standards for the administration and interpretation of chemical analysis of a person's breath or oral fluids, including standards of training.

(2) In any action or proceeding in which it is material to prove that a person was operating or in actual physical control of a vehicle while under the influence of alcohol or any drug or operating with a blood or breath alcohol content statutorily prohibited, documents offered as memoranda or records of acts, conditions, or events to prove that the analysis was made and the instrument used was accurate, according to standards established in Subsection (1), are admissible if:

(a) the judge finds that they were made in the regular course of the investigation at or about the time of the act, condition, or event; and

(b) the source of information from which made and the method and circumstances of their preparation indicate their trustworthiness.

(3) If the judge finds that the standards established under Subsection (1) and the conditions of Subsection (2) have been met, there is a presumption that the test results are valid and further foundation for introduction of the evidence is unnecessary.   2005

41-6a-516. Admissibility of chemical test results in actions for driving under the influence — Weight of evidence.

(1) (a) In any civil or criminal action or proceeding in which it is material to prove that a person was operating or in actual physical control of a vehicle while under the influence of alcohol or drugs or with a blood or breath alcohol content statutorily prohibited, the results of a chemical test or tests as authorized in Section 41-6a-520 are admissible as evidence.

(b) (i) In a criminal proceeding, noncompliance with Section 41-6a-520 does not render the results of a chemical test inadmissible.

(ii) Evidence of a defendant's blood or breath alcohol content or drug content is admissible except when prohibited by Rules of Evidence or the constitution.

(2) This section does not prevent a court from receiving otherwise admissible evidence as to a defendant's blood or breath alcohol level or drug level at the time relevant to the alleged offense.   2005

41-6a-517. Definitions — Driving with any measurable controlled substance in the body — Penalties — Arrest without warrant.

(1) As used in this section:

(a) "Controlled substance" means any substance scheduled under Section 58-37-4.

(b) "Practitioner" has the same meaning as provided in Section 58-37-2.

(c) "Prescribe" has the same meaning as provided in Section 58-37-2.

(d) "Prescription" has the same meaning as provided in Section 58-37-2.

(2) In cases not amounting to a violation of Section 41-6a-502, a person may not operate or be in actual physical control of a motor vehicle within this state if the person has any measurable controlled substance or metabolite of a controlled substance in the person's body.

(3) It is an affirmative defense to prosecution under this section that the controlled substance was involuntarily ingested by the accused or prescribed by a practitioner for use by the accused.

(4) (a) A person convicted of a violation of Subsection (2) is guilty of a class B misdemeanor.

(b) A person who violates this section is subject to conviction and sentencing under both this section and any applicable offense under Section 58-37-8.

(5) A peace officer may, without a warrant, arrest a person for a violation of this section when the officer has probable cause to believe the violation has occurred, although not in the officer's presence, and if the officer has probable cause to believe that the violation was committed by the person.

(6) The Driver License Division shall:

(a) suspend, for 90 days, the driver license of a person convicted under Subsection (2);

(b) revoke, for one year, the driver license of a person convicted of a second or subsequent offense under Subsection (2) or if the person has a prior conviction as defined under Subsection 41-6a-501(2), if the violation is committed within a period of ten years after the date of the prior violation; and

(c) subtract from any suspension or revocation period the number of days for which a license was previously suspended under Section 53-3-223 or 53-3-231, if the previous suspension was based on the same occurrence upon which the record of conviction is based.

(7) (a) The court shall notify the Driver License Division if a person fails to:

(i) complete all court ordered screening and assessment, educational series, and substance abuse treatment; or

(ii) pay all fines and fees, including fees for restitution and treatment costs.

(b) Upon receiving the notification, the division shall suspend the person's driving privilege in accordance with Subsections 53-3-221(2) and (3).

(8) The court shall order supervised probation in accordance with Section 41-6a-507 for a person convicted under Subsection (2).   2005

41-6a-518. Ignition interlock devices — Use — Probationer to pay cost — Impecuniosity — Fee.

(1) As used in this section:

(a) "Commissioner" means the commissioner of the Department of Public Safety.

(b) "Ignition interlock system" or "system" means a constant monitoring device or any similar device certified by the commissioner that prevents a motor vehicle from being started without first determining the driver's breath alcohol concentration.

(c) "Probation provider" means the supervisor and monitor of the ignition interlock system required as a condition of probation who contracts with the court in accordance with Subsections 41-6a-507(2) and (3).

(2) (a) In addition to any other penalties imposed under Sections 41-6a-503 and 41-6a-505, and in addition to any requirements imposed as a condition of probation, the court may require that any person who is convicted of violating Section 41-6a-502 and who is granted probation may not operate a motor vehicle during the period of probation unless that motor vehicle is equipped with a functioning, certified ignition interlock system installed and calibrated so that the motor vehicle will not start if the operator's blood alcohol concentration exceeds a level ordered by the court.

(b) If a person convicted of violating Section 41-6a-502 was under the age of 21 when the violation occurred, the court shall order the installation of the ignition interlock system as a condition of probation.

(c) (i) If a person is convicted of a violation of Section 41-6a-502 within ten years of a prior conviction as defined in Subsection 41-6a-501(2), the court shall order the installation of the ignition interlock system, at the person's expense, for all motor vehicles registered to that person and all motor vehicles operated by that person for the period of probation.

(ii) The division shall post the ignition interlock restriction on the electronic record available to law enforcement.

(d) This section does not apply to a person convicted of a violation of Section 41-6a-502 whose violation involves drugs other than alcohol.

(3) Except as provided in Subsection (2)(c), if the court imposes the use of an ignition interlock system as a condition of probation, the court shall:

(a) stipulate on the record the requirement for and the period of the use of an ignition interlock system;

(b) order that an ignition interlock system be installed on each motor vehicle owned or operated by the probationer, at the probationer's expense;

(c) order the probationer to submit his driver license to the Driver License Division in accordance with Subsection (5);

(d) immediately notify the Driver License Division and the person's probation provider of the order; and

(e) require the probationer to provide proof of compliance with the court's order to the probation provider within 30 days of the order.

(4) (a) The probationer shall provide timely proof of installation within 30 days of an order imposing the use of a system or show cause why the order was not complied with to the court or to the probationer's probation provider.

(b) The probation provider shall notify the court of failure to comply under Subsection (4)(a).

(c) For failure to comply under Subsection (4)(a) or upon receiving the notification under Subsection (4)(b), the court shall order the Driver

License Division to suspend the probationer's driving privileges for the remaining period during which the compliance was imposed.

(d) Cause for failure to comply means any reason the court finds sufficiently justifiable to excuse the probationer's failure to comply with the court's order.

(5) (a) If use of an ignition interlock system is required under this section, the division may not issue, reinstate, or renew the driver license of that person unless that requirement is coded on the person's driver license.

(b) (i) If the division receives a notice that a person with a valid driver license that does not require a driver license withdrawal is required to use an ignition interlock system, the division shall notify the person that he has ten calendar days to apply to the division for an ignition interlock system requirement coded on the license.

(ii) The division shall suspend the driver license of the person after the ten-day period until the person applies to the division for an ignition interlock system requirement coded on the license.

(6) (a) Any probationer required to install an ignition interlock system shall have the system monitored by the manufacturer or dealer of the system for proper use and accuracy at least semiannually and more frequently as the court may order.

(b) (i) A report of the monitoring shall be issued by the manufacturer or dealer to the court or the person's probation provider.

(ii) The report shall be issued within 14 days following each monitoring.

(7) (a) If an ignition interlock system is ordered installed, the probationer shall pay the reasonable costs of leasing or buying and installing and maintaining the system.

(b) A probationer may not be excluded from this section for inability to pay the costs, unless:

(i) the probationer files an affidavit of impecuniosity; and

(ii) the court enters a finding that the probationer is impecunious.

(c) In lieu of waiver of the entire amount of the cost, the court may direct the probationer to make partial or installment payments of costs when appropriate.

(d) The ignition interlock provider shall cover the costs of waivers by the court under this Subsection (7).

(8) (a) If a probationer is required in the course and scope of employment to operate a motor vehicle owned by the probationer's employer, the probationer may operate that motor vehicle without installation of an ignition interlock system only if:

(i) the motor vehicle is used in the course and scope of employment;

(ii) the employer has been notified that the employee is restricted; and

(iii) the employee has proof of the notification in his possession while operating the employer's motor vehicle.

(b) (i) To the extent that an employer-owned motor vehicle is made available to a probationer subject to this section for personal use, no exemption under this section shall apply.

(ii) A probationer intending to operate an employer-owned motor vehicle for personal use and who is restricted to the operation of a motor vehicle equipped with an ignition interlock system shall notify the employer and obtain consent in writing from the employer to install a system in the employer-owned motor vehicle.

(c) A motor vehicle owned by a business entity that is all or partly owned or controlled by a probationer subject to this section is not a motor vehicle owned by the employer and does not qualify for an exemption under this Subsection (8).

(9) Upon conviction for violation of this section, the court shall notify the Driver License Division to immediately suspend the probationer's license to operate a motor vehicle for the remainder of the period of probation.

(10) (a) It is a class B misdemeanor for a person to:

(i) circumvent or tamper with the operation of an ignition interlock system;

(ii) knowingly furnish a motor vehicle without an ignition interlock system to someone who is not authorized to drive a motor vehicle unless the motor vehicle is equipped with an ignition interlock system that is in working order;

(iii) rent, lease, or borrow a motor vehicle without an ignition interlock system if a driving restriction is imposed under this section;

(iv) request another person to blow into an ignition interlock system, if the person is required to have a system and the person requests or solicits another to blow into the system to start the motor vehicle in order to circumvent the system;

(v) blow into an ignition interlock system or start a motor vehicle equipped with an ignition interlock system for the purpose of providing an operable motor vehicle to another person required to have a system;

(vi) advertise for sale, offer for sale, sell, or lease an ignition interlock system unless the system has been certified by the commissioner and the manufacturer of the system has affixed a warning label, as approved by the commissioner on the system, stating that the tampering, circumventing, or other misuse of the system is a class B misdemeanor; or

(vii) operate a motor vehicle in violation of any ignition interlock restriction.

(b) This Subsection (10) does not apply if the starting of a motor vehicle, or the request to start a motor vehicle, equipped with an ignition interlock system is done for the purpose of safety or mechanical repair of the system or the motor vehicle and the person subject to the court order does not drive the motor vehicle.

(11) (a) In accordance with Title 63, Chapter 46a, Utah Administrative Rulemaking Act, the commissioner shall make rules setting standards for the certification of ignition interlock systems.

(b) The standards shall require that the system:

(i) not impede the safe operation of the motor vehicle;

(ii) have features that make circumventing difficult and that do not interfere with the normal use of the motor vehicle;

(iii) require a deep lung breath sample as a measure of breath alcohol concentration;

(iv) prevent the motor vehicle from being started if the driver's breath alcohol concentration exceeds an ordered level;

(v) work accurately and reliably in an unsupervised environment;

(vi) resist tampering and give evidence if tampering is attempted;

(vii) operate reliably over the range of motor vehicle environments; and

(viii) be manufactured by a party who will provide liability insurance.

(c) The commissioner may adopt in whole or in part, the guidelines, rules, studies, or independent laboratory tests relied upon in certification of ignition interlock systems by other states.

(d) A list of certified systems shall be published by the commissioner and the cost of certification shall be borne by the manufacturers or dealers of ignition interlock systems seeking to sell, offer for sale, or lease the systems.

(e) (i) In accordance with Section 63-38-3.2, the commissioner may establish an annual dollar assessment against the manufacturers of ignition interlock systems distributed in the state for the costs incurred in certifying.

(ii) The assessment under Subsection (11)(e)(i) shall be apportioned among the manufacturers on a fair and reasonable basis.

(12) There shall be no liability on the part of, and no cause of action of any nature shall arise against, the state or its employees in connection with the installation, use, operation, maintenance, or supervision of an interlock ignition system as required under this section.   2005

41-6a-519. Municipal attorneys for specified offenses may prosecute for certain DUI offenses and driving while license is suspended or revoked.

The following class A misdemeanors may be prosecuted by attorneys of cities and towns and other prosecutors authorized elsewhere in this code to prosecute these alleged violations:

(1) alleged class A misdemeanor violations of Section 41-6a-502; and

(2) alleged violations of Section 53-3-227, which consist of the person operating a vehicle while the person's driving privilege is suspended or revoked for:

(a) a violation of Section 41-6a-502;

(b) a local ordinance which complies with the requirements of Section 41-6a-510, 41-6a-520, or 76-5-207; or

(c) a criminal prohibition that the person was charged with violating as a result of a plea bargain after having been originally charged with violating one or more of the sections or ordinances identified in Subsection (2)(a) or (b).   2005

41-6a-520. Implied consent to chemical tests for alcohol or drug — Number of tests — Refusal — Warning, report.

(1) (a) A person operating a motor vehicle in this state is considered to have given the person's consent to a chemical test or tests of the person's breath, blood, urine, or oral fluids for the purpose of determining whether the person was operating or in actual physical control of a motor vehicle while:

(i) having a blood or breath alcohol content statutorily prohibited under Section 41-6a-502, 41-6a-530, 53-3-231, or 53-3-232;

(ii) under the influence of alcohol, any drug, or combination of alcohol and any drug under Section 41-6a-502; or

(iii) having any measurable controlled substance or metabolite of a controlled substance in the person's body in violation of Section 41-6a-517.

(b) A test or tests authorized under this Subsection (1) must be administered at the direction of a peace officer having grounds to believe that person to have been operating or in actual physical control of a motor vehicle while in violation of any provision under Subsections (1)(a)(i) through (iii).

(c) (i) The peace officer determines which of the tests are administered and how many of them are administered.

(ii) If a peace officer requests more than one test, refusal by a person to take one or more requested tests, even though the person does submit to any other requested test or tests, is a refusal under this section.

(d) (i) A person who has been requested under this section to submit to a chemical test or tests of the person's breath, blood, or urine, or oral fluids may not select the test or tests to be administered.

(ii) The failure or inability of a peace officer to arrange for any specific chemical test is not a defense to taking a test requested by a peace officer, and it is not a defense in any criminal, civil, or administrative proceeding resulting from a person's refusal to submit to the requested test or tests.

(2) (a) A peace officer requesting a test or tests shall warn a person that refusal to submit to the test or tests may result in revocation of the person's license to operate a motor vehicle and a five or ten-year prohibition of the person driving with any measurable or detectable amount of alcohol in the person's body depending on the person's prior driving history if the person:

(i) has been placed under arrest;

(ii) has then been requested by a peace officer to submit to any one or more of the chemical tests under Subsection (1); and

(iii) refuses to submit to any chemical test requested.

(b) (i) Following the warning under Subsection (2)(a), if the person does not immediately request that the chemical test or tests as offered by a peace officer be administered, a peace officer shall, on behalf of the Driver License Division and within 24 hours of the arrest, give notice of the Driver License Division's intention to revoke the person's privilege or license to operate a motor vehicle.

(ii) When a peace officer gives the notice on behalf of the Driver License Division, the peace officer shall:

(A) take the Utah license certificate or permit, if any, of the operator;

(B) issue a temporary license certificate effective for only 29 days from the date of arrest; and

(C) supply to the operator, in a manner specified by the Driver License Division, basic information regarding how to obtain a hearing before the Driver License Division.

(c) A citation issued by a peace officer may, if provided in a manner specified by the Driver License Division, also serve as the temporary license certificate.

(d) As a matter of procedure, the peace officer shall submit a signed report, within ten calendar days after the day on which notice is provided under Subsection (2)(b), that:

(i) the peace officer had grounds to believe the arrested person was in violation of any provision under Subsections (1)(a)(i) through (iii); and

(ii) the person had refused to submit to a chemical test or tests under Subsection (1).

(3) Upon the request of the person who was tested, the results of the test or tests shall be made available to the person.

(4) (a) The person to be tested may, at the person's own expense, have a physician of the person's own choice administer a chemical test in addition to the test or tests administered at the direction of a peace officer.

(b) The failure or inability to obtain the additional test does not affect admissibility of the results of the test or tests taken at the direction of a peace officer, or preclude or delay the test or tests to be taken at the direction of a peace officer.

(c) The additional test shall be subsequent to the test or tests administered at the direction of a peace officer.

(5) For the purpose of determining whether to submit to a chemical test or tests, the person to be tested does not have the right to consult an attorney or have an attorney, physician, or other person present as a condition for the taking of any test. 2005

41-6a-521. Revocation hearing for refusal — Appeal.

(1) (a) A person who has been notified of the Driver License Division's intention to revoke the person's license under Section 41-6a-520 is entitled to a hearing.

(b) A request for the hearing shall be made in writing within ten calendar days after the day on which notice is provided.

(c) Upon request in a manner specified by the Driver License Division, the Driver License Division shall grant to the person an opportunity to be heard within 29 days after the date of arrest.

(d) If the person does not make a request for a hearing before the Driver License Division under this Subsection (1), the person's privilege to operate a motor vehicle in the state is revoked beginning on the 30th day after the date of arrest for a period of:

(i) 18 months unless Subsection (1)(d)(ii) applies; or

(ii) 24 months if the person has had a previous:

(A) license sanction for an offense that occurred within the previous ten years from the date of arrest under Section 41-6a-517, 41-6a-520, 41-6a-530, 53-3-223, 53-3-231, or 53-3-232; or

(B) conviction for an offense that occurred within the previous ten years from the date of arrest under Section 41-6a-502 or a statute previously in effect in this state that would constitute a violation of Section 41-6a-502.

(2) (a) Except as provided in Subsection (2)(b), if a hearing is requested by the person, the hearing shall be conducted by the Driver License Division in the county in which the offense occurred.

(b) The Driver License Division may hold a hearing in some other county if the Driver License Division and the person both agree.

(3) The hearing shall be documented and shall cover the issues of:

(a) whether a peace officer had reasonable grounds to believe that a person was operating a motor vehicle in violation of Section 41-6a-502, 41-6a-517, 41-6a-530, 53-3-231, or 53-3-232; and

(b) whether the person refused to submit to the test or tests under Section 41-6a-520.

(4) (a) In connection with the hearing, the division or its authorized agent:

(i) may administer oaths and may issue subpoenas for the attendance of witnesses and the production of relevant books and papers; and

(ii) shall issue subpoenas for the attendance of necessary peace officers.

(b) The Driver License Division shall pay witness fees and mileage from the Transportation Fund in accordance with the rates established in Section 78-46-28.

(5) (a) If after a hearing, the Driver License Division determines that the person was requested to submit to a chemical test or tests and refused to submit to the test or tests, or if the person fails to appear before the Driver License Division as required in the notice, the Driver License Division shall revoke the person's license or permit to operate a motor vehicle in Utah beginning on the date the hearing is held for a period of:

(i) 18 months unless Subsection (5)(a)(ii) applies; or

(ii) 24 months if the person has had a previous:

(A) license sanction for an offense that occurred within the previous ten years from the date of arrest under Section 41-6a-517, 41-6a-520, 41-6a-530, 53-3-223, 53-3-231, or 53-3-232; or

(B) conviction for an offense that occurred within the previous ten years from the date of arrest under Section 41-6a-502 or a statute previously in effect in this state that would constitute a violation of Section 41-6a-502.

(b) The Driver License Division shall also assess against the person, in addition to any fee imposed under Subsection 53-3-205(13), a fee under Section 53-3-105, which shall be paid before the person's driving privilege is reinstated, to cover administrative costs.

(c) The fee shall be cancelled if the person obtains an unappealed court decision following a proceeding allowed under Subsection (2) that the revocation was improper.

(6) (a) Any person whose license has been revoked by the Driver License Division under this section may seek judicial review.

(b) Judicial review of an informal adjudicative proceeding is a trial.

(c) Venue is in the district court in the county in which the offense occurred. 2005

41-6a-522. Person incapable of refusal.

Any person who is dead, unconscious, or in any other condition rendering the person incapable of refusal to submit to any chemical test or tests is considered to not have withdrawn the consent provided for in Subsection 41-6a-520(1), and the test or tests may be administered whether the person has been arrested or not.   2005

41-6a-523. Persons authorized to withdraw blood — Immunity from liability.

(1) (a) Only a physician, registered nurse, practical nurse, or person authorized under Section 26-1-30, acting at the request of a peace officer, may withdraw blood to determine the alcoholic or drug content.

(b) The limitation in Subsection (1)(a) does not apply to taking a urine, breath, or oral fluid specimen.

(2) Any physician, registered nurse, practical nurse, or person authorized under Section 26-1-30 who, at the direction of a peace officer, draws a sample of blood from any person whom a peace officer has reason to believe is driving in violation of this chapter, or hospital or medical facility at which the sample is drawn, is immune from any civil or criminal liability arising from drawing the sample, if the test is administered according to standard medical practice.   2005

41-6a-524. Refusal as evidence.

If a person under arrest refuses to submit to a chemical test or tests or any additional test under Section 41-6a-520, evidence of any refusal is admissible in any civil or criminal action or proceeding arising out of acts alleged to have been committed while the person was operating or in actual physical control of a motor vehicle while:

(1) under the influence of:

(a) alcohol;

(b) any drug; or

(c) a combination of alcohol and any drug;

(2) having any measurable controlled substance or metabolite of a controlled substance in the person's body;

(3) having any measurable or detectable amount of alcohol in the person's body if the person is an alcohol restricted driver as defined under Section 41-6a-529; or

(4) having any measurable or detectable amount of alcohol in the person's body if the person has been issued a conditional license under Section 53-3-232.   2005

41-6a-525. Reporting test results — Immunity from liability.

(1) As used in this section, "health care provider" means a person licensed under:

(a) Title 58, Chapter 31b, Nurse Practice Act;

(b) Title 58, Chapter 67, Utah Medical Practice Act; or

(c) Title 58, Chapter 68, Utah Osteopathic Medical Practice Act.

(2) A health care provider who is providing medical care to any person involved in a motor vehicle crash may notify, as soon as reasonably possible, the nearest peace officer or law enforcement agency if the health care provider has reason to believe, as a result of any test performed in the course of medical treatment, that the:

(a) person's blood alcohol concentration meets or exceeds the limits under Subsection 41-6a-502(1)(a);

(b) person is younger than 21 years of age and has any measurable blood, breath, or urine alcohol concentration in the person's body; or

(c) person has any measurable controlled substance or metabolite of a controlled substance in the person's body which could be a violation of Subsection 41-6a-502(1)(b) or Section 41-6a-517.

(3) The report under Subsection (2) shall consist of the:

(a) name of the person being treated;

(b) date and time of the administration of the test; and

(c) results disclosed by the test.

(4) A health care provider participating in good faith in making a report or assisting an investigator from a law enforcement agency pursuant to this section is immune from any liability, civil or criminal, that otherwise might result by reason of those actions.

(5) A report under Subsection (2) may not be used to support a finding of probable cause that a person who is not a driver of a vehicle has committed an offense.   2005

41-6a-526. Drinking alcoholic beverage and open containers in motor vehicle prohibited — Definitions — Exceptions.

(1) As used in this section:

(a) "Alcoholic beverage" has the same meaning as defined in Section 32A-1-105.

(b) "Chartered bus" has the same meaning as defined in Section 32A-1-105.

(c) "Limousine" has the same meaning as defined in Section 32A-1-105.

(d) (i) "Passenger compartment" means the area of the vehicle normally occupied by the operator and passengers.

(ii) "Passenger compartment" includes areas accessible to the operator and passengers while traveling, including a utility or glove compartment.

(iii) "Passenger compartment" does not include a separate front or rear trunk compartment or other area of the vehicle not accessible to the operator or passengers while inside the vehicle.

(2) A person may not drink any alcoholic beverage while operating a motor vehicle or while a passenger in a motor vehicle, whether the vehicle is moving, stopped, or parked on any highway.

(3) A person may not keep, carry, possess, transport, or allow another to keep, carry, possess, or transport in the passenger compartment of a motor vehicle, when the vehicle is on any highway, any container which contains any alcoholic beverage if the container has been opened, its seal broken, or the contents of the container partially consumed.

(4) Subsections (2) and (3) do not apply to a passenger:

(a) in the living quarters of a motor home or camper;

(b) who has carried an alcoholic beverage onto a limousine or chartered bus that is in compliance with Subsections 32A-12-213(3)(b) and (c); or

(c) in a motorboat or on the waters of this state as these terms are defined in Section 73-18-2.

(5) Subsection (3) does not apply to passengers traveling in any licensed taxicab or bus.   2005

41-6a-527. Seizure and impoundment of vehicles by peace officers — Impound requirements — Removal of vehicle by owner.

(1) If a peace officer arrests or cites the operator of a vehicle for violating Section 41-6a-502, 41-6a-517, 41-6a-520, 41-6a-530, 53-3-231, 53-3-232, Subsection 41-6a-518(10), or a local ordinance similar to Section

41-6a-502 which complies with Subsection 41-6a-510(1), the peace officer shall seize and impound the vehicle in accordance with Section 41-6a-1406, except as provided under Subsection (2).

(2) If a registered owner of the vehicle, other than the operator, is present at the time of arrest, the peace officer may release the vehicle to that registered owner, but only if:

    (a) the registered owner:

        (i) requests to remove the vehicle from the scene; and

        (ii) presents to the peace officer sufficient identification to prove ownership of the vehicle or motorboat;

    (b) the registered owner identifies a driver with a valid operator's license who:

        (i) complies with all restrictions of his operator's license; and

        (ii) would not, in the judgment of the officer, be in violation of Section 41-6a-502, 41-6a-517, 41-6a-520, 41-6a-530, 53-3-231, 53-3-232, Subsection 41-6a-518(10), or a local ordinance similar to Section 41-6a-502 which complies with Subsection 41-6a-510(1) if permitted to operate the vehicle; and

    (c) the vehicle itself is legally operable.

(3) If necessary for transportation of a motorboat for impoundment under this section, the motorboat's trailer may be used to transport the motorboat.   2005

41-6a-528. Reckless driving — Penalty.

(1) A person is guilty of reckless driving who operates a vehicle:

    (a) in willful or wanton disregard for the safety of persons or property; or

    (b) while committing three or more moving traffic violations under Title 41, Chapter 6a, Traffic Code, in a series of acts within a single continuous period of driving.

(2) A person who violates Subsection (1) is guilty of a class B misdemeanor.   2005

41-6a-529. Definitions — Alcohol restricted drivers.

(1) As used in this section and section 41-6a-530, "alcohol restricted driver" means a person who:

    (a) within the last two years:

        (i) has been convicted of:

            (A) a misdemeanor violation of Section 41-6a-502;

            (B) alcohol, any drug, or a combination of both-related reckless driving under Section 41-6a-512;

            (C) local ordinances similar to Section 41-6a-502 or alcohol, any drug, or a combination of both-related reckless driving adopted in compliance with Section 41-6a-510;

            (D) a violation described in Subsections (1)(a)(i)(A) through (C), which judgment of conviction is reduced under Section 76-3-402; or

            (E) statutes or ordinances previously in effect in this state or in effect in any other state, the United States, or any district, possession, or territory of the United States which would constitute a violation of Section 41-6a-502 or alcohol, any drug, or a combination of both-related reckless driving if committed in this state, including punishments administered under 10 U.S.C. Sec. 815; or

        (ii) has had the person's driving privilege suspended under Section 53-3-223 based on an arrest which occurred on or after July 1, 2005;

    (b) within the last five years:

        (i) has had the person's driving privilege revoked for refusal to submit to a chemical test under Section 41-6a-520, which refusal occurred on or after July 1, 2005; or

        (ii) (A) has been convicted of an offense described in Subsection (1)(a)(i); and

            (B) at the time of operation or actual physical control of a vehicle the person:

                (I) is 21 years of age or older;

                (II) has a passenger under 16 years of age in the vehicle;

    (c) within the last ten years:

        (i) has been convicted of an offense described in Subsection (1)(a)(i) which conviction was within ten years of a prior conviction for an offense described in Subsection (1)(a)(i); or

        (ii) has had the person's driving privilege revoked for refusal to submit to a chemical test and the refusal is within ten years after:

            (A) a prior refusal to submit to a chemical test under Section 41-6a-520; or

            (B) a prior conviction for an offense described in Subsection (1)(a)(i) which is not based on the same arrest as the refusal; or

    (d) at any time has been convicted of:

        (i) automobile homicide under Section 76-5-207 for an offense that occurred on or after July 1, 2005; or

        (ii) a felony violation of Section 41-6a-502 for an offense that occurred on or after July 1, 2005.

(2) For purposes of this section and Section 41-6a-530, a plea of guilty or no contest to a violation described in Subsection (1)(a)(i) which plea is held in abeyance under Title 77, Chapter 2a, Pleas in Abeyance, is the equivalent of a conviction, even if the charge has been subsequently reduced or dismissed in accordance with the plea in abeyance agreement.

   2005

41-6a-530. Alcohol restricted drivers — Prohibited from operating a vehicle while having any measurable or detectable amount of alcohol in the person's body — Penalties.

(1) An alcohol restricted driver who operates or is in actual physical control of a vehicle in this state with any measurable or detectable amount of alcohol in the person's body is guilty of a class B misdemeanor.

(2) A "measurable or detectable amount" of alcohol in the person's body may be established by:

    (a) a chemical test;

    (b) evidence other than a chemical test; or

    (c) a combination of Subsections (2)(a) and (b).

   2005

PART 6

SPEED RESTRICTIONS

41-6a-601. Speed regulations — Safe and appropriate speeds at certain locations — Prima facie speed limits — Emergency power of the governor.

(1) A person may not operate a vehicle at a speed greater than is reasonable and prudent under the

existing conditions, giving regard to the actual and potential hazards then existing, including when:

(a) approaching and crossing an intersection or railroad grade crossing;

(b) approaching and going around a curve;

(c) approaching a hill crest;

(d) traveling upon any narrow or winding roadway; and

(e) approaching other hazards that exist due to pedestrians, other traffic, weather, or highway conditions.

(2) Subject to Subsections (1) and (4) and Sections 41-6a-602 and 41-6a-603, the following speeds are lawful:

(a) 20 miles per hour in a reduced speed school zone as defined in Section 41-6a-303;

(b) 25 miles per hour in any urban district; and

(c) 55 miles per hour in other locations.

(3) Except as provided in Section 41-6a-604, any speed in excess of the limits provided in this section or established under Sections 41-6a-602 and 41-6a-603 is prima facie evidence that the speed is not reasonable or prudent and that it is unlawful.

(4) The governor by proclamation in time of war or emergency may change the speed limits on the highways of the state.   2005

41-6a-602. Speed limits established on state highways.

(1) (a) The Department of Transportation may determine the reasonable and safe speed limit for each highway or section of highway under its jurisdiction.

(b) Each speed limit shall be based on traffic engineering and safety studies for each highway or section of the highway.

(c) The traffic engineering and safety studies shall include:

(i) the design speed;

(ii) prevailing vehicle speeds;

(iii) accident history;

(iv) highway, traffic, and roadside conditions; and

(v) other highway safety factors.

(2) In addition to the provisions of Subsection (1), the Department of Transportation may establish different speed limits on a highway or section of highway based on:

(a) time of day;

(b) highway construction;

(c) type of vehicle;

(d) weather conditions; and

(e) other highway safety factors.

(3) (a) Except as provided in Subsection (3)(b), a posted speed limit may not exceed 65 miles per hour.

(b) A posted speed limit on a freeway or other limited access highways may not exceed 75 miles per hour.

(c) This Subsection (3) is an exception to the provisions of Subsections (1) and (2).

(4) When establishing or changing a speed limit, the Department of Transportation shall consult with the following entities prior to erecting or changing a speed limit sign:

(a) the county for state highways in an unincorporated area of the county;

(b) the municipality for state highways within the municipality's incorporated area;

(c) the Department of Public Safety; and

(d) the Transportation Commission.

(5) The speed limit is effective when appropriate signs giving notice are erected along the highway or section of the highway.   2005

41-6a-603. Speed limits established by counties and municipalities.

(1) A county or municipality may determine the reasonable and safe speed limit for each highway or section of highway under its jurisdiction as specified under Title 72, Chapter 3, Highway Jurisdiction and Classification Act.

(2) Each speed limit shall be established in accordance with the provisions of Subsections 41-6a-602(1), (2), (3), and (5).   2005

41-6a-604. Maximum speed in a school zone — Penalty — Minimum fines — Compensatory service — Waiver — Recordkeeping.

(1) A person may not operate a vehicle at a speed greater than 20 miles per hour in a reduced speed school zone as defined in Section 41-6a-303.

(2) (a) A violation of Subsection (1) is a class C misdemeanor and the minimum fine:

(i) for a first offense shall be calculated according to the following schedule:

Vehicle Speed	Minimum Fine
21 — 29 MPH	$ 50
30 — 39 MPH	$ 125
40 MPH and greater	$ 275

(ii) for a second and subsequent offense within three years of a previous conviction or bail forfeiture shall be calculated according to the following schedule:

Vehicle Speed	Minimum Fine
21 — 29 MPH	$ 50
30 — 39 MPH	$ 225
40 MPH and greater	$ 525

(b)(i) Except as provided under Subsection (2)(a)(ii), the court may order the person to perform compensatory service in lieu of the fine or any portion of the fine.

(ii) The court shall order the person to perform compensatory service observing a crossing guard if the conviction is for a:

(A) first offense with a vehicle speed of 30 miles per hour or more; or

(B) second and subsequent offense within three years of a previous conviction or bail forfeiture.

(iii) The court may waive the compensatory service required under Subsection (2)(b)(ii) if the court makes the reasons for the waiver part of the record.

(3) The Driver License Division shall develop and implement a record system to distinguish:

(a) a conviction or bail forfeiture under this section from other convictions; and

(b) between a first and subsequent conviction or bail forfeiture under this section.

(4) The provisions of this section take precedence over the provisions of Sections 41-6a-601, 41-6a-602, 41-6a-603, and 76-3-301.   2005

41-6a-605. Minimum speed regulations.

(1) A person may not operate a motor vehicle at a speed so slow as to impede or block the normal and reasonable movement of traffic except when:

(a) a reduced speed is necessary for safe operation;

(b) upon a grade; or

(c) in compliance with a traffic-control device.

(2) Operating a motor vehicle on a limited access highway at less than the speed limit side by side with and at the same speed as a vehicle operated in the adjacent right lane is evidence of a violation of Subsection (1).

(3) (a) If, based on an engineering and traffic investigation, a highway authority determines that slow speeds on any part of a highway under its jurisdiction consistently impede the normal and reasonable movement of traffic, the highway authority may post a minimum speed limit.

(b) If a minimum speed limit is posted under this Subsection (3), a person may not operate a vehicle at a speed below the posted minimum speed limit except:

(i) when necessary for safe operation; or

(ii) in accordance with Section 41-6a-205.

(c) The minimum speed limit is effective when appropriate signs giving notice are erected along the highway or section of the highway.   2005

41-6a-606. Speed contest or exhibition on highway — Barricade or obstruction.

(1) A person may not:

(a) engage in any motor vehicle speed contest or exhibition of speed on a highway; or

(b) aid or abet in any motor vehicle speed contest or exhibition on any highway.

(2) A person may not, in any manner, obstruct or place any barricade or obstruction or assist or participate in placing any barricade or obstruction upon any highway for any purpose prohibited under Subsection (1).   2005

41-6a-607. Speed violation — Complaint — Civil negligence.

(1) For a charge of violation of a speed provision under this part, the citation or information shall specify the:

(a) speed at which the defendant is alleged to have operated a vehicle; and

(b) speed limit applicable to the section of the highway where the violation is alleged to have occurred.

(2) The provisions of this part declaring prima facie speed limitations do not relieve the plaintiff in any civil action from the burden of proving negligence on the part of the defendant as the proximate cause of an accident.   2005

41-6a-608. Photo radar — Restrictions on use.

(1) "Photo radar" means a device used primarily for highway speed limit enforcement substantially consisting of a low power doppler radar unit and camera mounted in or on a vehicle, which automatically produces a photograph of a vehicle traveling in excess of the legal speed limit, with the vehicle's speed, the date, time of day, and location of the violation printed on the photograph.

(2) Photo radar may not be used except:

(a) (i) in school zones; or

(ii) in other areas that have a posted speed limit of 30 miles per hour or less;

(b) when a peace officer is present with the photo radar unit;

(c) when signs are posted on the highway providing notice to a motorist that photo radar may be used;

(d) when use of photo radar by a local highway authority is approved by the local highway authority's governing body; and

(e) when the citation is accompanied by the photograph produced by photo radar.

(3) The restrictions under Subsection (2) on the use of photo radar do not apply when the information gathered is used for highway safety research or to issue warning citations not involving a fine, court appearance, or a person's driving record.

(4) A contract or agreement regarding the purchase, lease, rental, or use of photo radar by the department or by a local highway authority may not specify any condition for issuing a citation.

(5) The department and any local highway authority using photo radar, upon request, shall make the following information available for public inspection during regular office hours:

(a) the terms of any contract regarding the purchase, lease, rental, or use of photo radar;

(b) the total fine revenue generated by using photo radar;

(c) the number of citations issued by the use of photo radar; and

(d) the amount paid to the person providing the photo radar unit.

(6) A moving traffic violation obtained through the use of photo radar is not a reportable violation as defined under Section 53-3-102, and points may not be assessed against a person for the violation.   2005

41-6a-609. Radar jamming devices and jamming radar prohibited — Defense — Exceptions — Penalties.

(1) As used in this section, "radar jamming device" means any instrument or mechanism designed or intended to interfere with the radar or any laser that is used by law enforcement personnel to measure the speed of a motor vehicle on a highway.

(2) (a) A person may not operate a motor vehicle on a highway with a radar jamming device in the motor vehicle.

(b) A person may not knowingly use a radar jamming device to interfere with the radar signals or lasers used by law enforcement personnel to measure the speed of a motor vehicle on a highway.

(3) It is an affirmative defense to a charge under Subsection (2)(a) that the radar jamming device was in an inoperative condition or could not be readily used at the time of the arrest or citation.

(4) This section does not apply to law enforcement personnel acting in their official capacity.

(5) A person who violates this section is guilty of a class C misdemeanor.   2005

PART 7

DRIVING ON RIGHT SIDE OF HIGHWAY AND PASSING

41-6a-701. Duty to operate vehicle on right side of roadway — Exceptions.

(1) On all roadways of sufficient width, a person operating a vehicle shall operate the vehicle on the right half of the roadway, except:

(a) when overtaking and passing another vehicle proceeding in the same direction under the rules governing that movement;

(b) when an obstruction requires operating the vehicle to the left of the center of the roadway subject to the provisions of Subsection (2);

(c) on a roadway divided into three marked lanes for traffic under the applicable rules; or

(d) on a roadway designed and signposted for one-way traffic.

(2) A person operating a vehicle shall yield the right-of-way to a vehicle:

    (a) traveling in the proper direction on a roadway; and

    (b) that is within a distance constituting an immediate hazard.

(3) A person operating a vehicle on a roadway at less than the normal speed of traffic shall operate the vehicle in the right-hand lane then available for traffic, or as close as practicable to the right-hand curb or edge of the roadway, except when:

    (a) overtaking and passing another vehicle proceeding in the same direction;

    (b) preparing to turn left; or

    (c) taking a different highway or an exit on the left.   2005

41-6a-702. Left lane restrictions — Exceptions — Other lane restrictions — Penalties.

(1) As used in this section and Section 41-6a-704, "general purpose lane" means a highway lane open to vehicular traffic but does not include a designated:

    (a) high occupancy vehicle (HOV) lane; or

    (b) auxiliary lane that begins as a freeway on-ramp and ends as part of the next freeway off-ramp.

(2) On a freeway or section of a freeway which has three or more general purpose lanes in the same direction, a person may not operate a vehicle in the left most general purpose lane if the person's:

    (a) vehicle is drawing a trailer or semitrailer regardless of size; or

    (b) vehicle or combination of vehicles has a gross vehicle weight of 12,001 or more pounds.

(3) Subsection (2) does not apply to a person operating a vehicle who is:

    (a) preparing to turn left or taking a different highway split or an exit on the left;

    (b) responding to emergency conditions;

    (c) avoiding actual or potential traffic moving onto the highway from an acceleration or merging lane; or

    (d) following direction signs that direct use of a designated lane.

(4) (a) A highway authority may designate a specific lane or lanes of travel for any type of vehicle on a highway or portion of a highway under its jurisdiction for the:

        (i) safety of the public;

        (ii) efficient maintenance of a highway; or

        (iii) use of high occupancy vehicles.

    (b) The lane designation under Subsection (4)(a) is effective when appropriate signs giving notice are erected on the highway or portion of the highway.

(5) (a) Subject to Subsection (5)(b), the lane designation under Subsection (4)(a) shall allow a vehicle with clean fuel special group license plates issued in accordance with Section 41-1a-418 to travel in lanes designated for the use of high occupancy vehicles regardless of the number of occupants to the extent authorized or permitted by federal law or federal regulation.

    (b) In accordance with Title 63, Chapter 46a, Utah Administrative Rulemaking Act, the Department of Transportation may make rules to allow a vehicle with clean fuel special group license plates issued in accordance with Section 41-1a-418 to travel in lanes designated for the use of high occupancy vehicles regardless of the number of occupants to the extent authorized or permitted by federal law or federal regulation.

(6) A person who operates a vehicle in violation of Subsection (2) or in violation of the restrictions made under Subsection (4) is guilty of a class C misdemeanor.   2005

41-6a-703. Passing vehicles proceeding in opposite directions.

(1) In accordance with Section 41-6a-701, a person operating a vehicle proceeding in an opposite direction from another vehicle shall pass the other vehicle to the right.

(2) On a roadway having width for not more than one line of traffic in each direction, the operator of a vehicle shall, as nearly as possible, give to the other at least ½ of the main traveled portion of the roadway.   2005

41-6a-704. Overtaking and passing vehicles proceeding in same direction.

(1) On any highway:

    (a) the operator of a vehicle overtaking another vehicle proceeding in the same direction:

        (i) shall, except as provided under Section 41-6a-705, pass the overtaken vehicle on the left at a safe distance; and

        (ii) may not drive to the right side of the roadway until safely clear of the overtaken vehicle;

    (b) the operator of an overtaken vehicle:

        (i) shall give way to the right in favor of the overtaking vehicle; and

        (ii) may not increase the speed of the vehicle until completely passed by the overtaking vehicle.

(2) On a highway having more than one lane in the same direction, the operator of a vehicle traveling in the left general purpose lane:

    (a) shall, upon being overtaken by another vehicle in the same lane, yield to the overtaking vehicle by moving safely to a lane to the right; and

    (b) may not impede the movement or free flow of traffic in the left general purpose lane.

(3) The provisions of Subsection (2) do not apply to an operator of a vehicle traveling in the left general purpose lane when:

    (a) overtaking and passing another vehicle proceeding in the same direction in accordance with Subsection (1)(a);

    (b) preparing to turn left or taking a different highway or an exit on the left;

    (c) responding to emergency conditions;

    (d) avoiding actual or potential traffic moving onto the highway from an acceleration or merging lane; or

    (e) following the direction of a traffic-control device that directs the use of a designated lane.   2005

41-6a-705. Passing upon right — When permissible.

(1) The operator of a vehicle may overtake and pass on the right of another vehicle only:

    (a) when the vehicle overtaken is making or preparing to make a left turn; or

    (b) on a roadway with unobstructed pavement of sufficient width for two or more lines of vehicles moving lawfully in the direction being traveled by the overtaking vehicle.

(2) The operator of a vehicle may overtake and pass another vehicle on the right only under conditions permitting the movement with safety.

(3) The operator of a vehicle may not overtake and pass another vehicle if the movement is made by driving off the roadway.   2005

41-6a-706. Limitation on passing — Prohibitions.

(1) Subject to the provisions of Section 41-6a-707, on a two-way highway, a person may not operate a vehicle to the left side of the center of the roadway to pass another vehicle proceeding in the same direction unless the left side is:

(a) clearly visible; and

(b) free of oncoming traffic for a sufficient distance to permit the passing movement to be completed without interfering with the operation of any vehicle approaching from the opposite direction in accordance with Subsection (2).

(2) The person operating the overtaking vehicle shall return the vehicle to an authorized lane of travel:

(a) as soon as practical; and

(b) if the passing movement involves the use of a lane authorized for vehicles approaching in the opposite direction, before coming within 200 feet of any vehicle approaching from the opposite direction. 2005

41-6a-706.5. Operation of motor vehicle near bicycle prohibited.

An operator of a motor vehicle may not knowingly, intentionally, or recklessly operate a motor vehicle within three feet of a moving bicycle, unless the operator of the motor vehicle operates the motor vehicle within a reasonable and safe distance of the bicycle. 2005

41-6a-707. Limitations on driving on left side of road — Exceptions.

(1) A person may not operate a vehicle on the left side of the roadway:

(a) when approaching or on a crest of a grade or a curve on the highway where the person's view is obstructed within a distance which creates a hazard if another vehicle approached from the opposite direction;

(b) when approaching within 100 feet of or traversing any intersection or railroad grade crossing unless otherwise indicated by a traffic-control device or a peace officer; or

(c) when the view is obstructed while approaching within 100 feet of any bridge, viaduct, or tunnel.

(2) Subsection (1) does not apply:

(a) on a one-way roadway;

(b) under the conditions described in Subsection 41-6a-701(1)(b); or

(c) to a person operating a vehicle turning left onto or from an alley, private road, or driveway. 2005

41-6a-708. Signs and markings on roadway — No-passing zones — Exceptions.

(1) (a) A highway authority may designate no-passing zones on any portion of a highway under its jurisdiction if the highway authority determines passing is especially hazardous.

(b) A highway authority shall designate a no-passing zone under Subsection (1)(a) by placing appropriate traffic-control devices on the highway.

(2) A person operating a vehicle may not drive on the left side of:

(a) the roadway within the no-passing zone; or

(b) any pavement striping designed to mark the no-passing zone.

(3) Subsection (2) does not apply:

(a) under the conditions described under Subsection 41-6a-701(1)(b); or

(b) to a person operating a vehicle turning left onto or from an alley, private road, or driveway. 2005

41-6a-709. One-way traffic.

(1) A highway authority may designate any highway, roadway, part of a roadway, or specific lanes under the highway authority's jurisdiction for one direction of vehicle travel at all times as indicated by traffic-control devices.

(2) On a roadway designated for one-way traffic, a person operating a vehicle shall operate the vehicle in the direction indicated by traffic-control devices.

(3) A person operating a vehicle in a roundabout shall operate the vehicle only to the right of the roundabout island. 2005

41-6a-710. Roadway divided into marked lanes — Provisions — Traffic-control devices.

On a roadway divided into two or more clearly marked lanes for traffic the following provisions apply:

(1) A person operating a vehicle:

(a) shall keep the vehicle as nearly as practical entirely within a single lane; and

(b) may not move the vehicle from the lane until the operator has determined the movement can be made safely.

(2) On a roadway divided into three or more lanes and providing for two-way movement of traffic, a person operating a vehicle may not drive in the center lane except:

(a) when overtaking and passing another vehicle traveling in the same direction, and when the center lane is:

(i) clear of traffic within a safe distance; and

(ii) not a two-way left turn lane;

(b) in preparation of making or completing a left turn in compliance with Section 41-6a-801; or

(c) where the center lane is allocated exclusively to traffic moving in the same direction that the vehicle is proceeding as indicated by traffic-control devices.

(3) (a) A highway authority may erect traffic-control devices directing specified traffic to use a designated lane or designating those lanes to be used by traffic moving in a particular direction regardless of the center of the roadway.

(b) An operator of a vehicle shall obey the directions of a traffic-control device erected under Subsection (3)(a). 2005

41-6a-711. Following another vehicle — Safe distance — Exceptions.

(1) The operator of a vehicle:

(a) may not follow another vehicle more closely than is reasonable and prudent, having regard for the:

(i) speed of the vehicles;

(ii) traffic upon the highway; and

(iii) condition of the highway; and

(b) shall allow sufficient space in front of the vehicle to enable any other vehicle to enter and occupy the space.

(2) Subsection (1)(b) does not apply to funeral processions or to congested traffic conditions resulting in prevailing vehicle speeds of less than 35 miles per hour. 2005

41-6a-712. Divided highway — Use of right-hand side — Crossing only where permitted.

(1) A person operating a vehicle on a divided highway shall use the right-hand roadway unless directed or permitted to use another roadway by a traffic-control device or a peace officer.

(2) A person operating a vehicle may not operate the vehicle over, across, or within any dividing space, median, or barrier of a divided highway, except where authorized by a traffic-control device or a peace officer.

2005

41-6a-713. Driving over gore area or island prohibited — Exceptions — Penalties.

(1) (a) A person may not operate a vehicle over, across, or within any part of a gore area or an island.

(b) Subsection (1)(a) does not apply to:

(i) a person operating a vehicle that is disabled; or

(ii) an operator of an authorized emergency vehicle under conditions described under Section 41-6a-208.

(2) A person who violates Subsection (1) is guilty of class C misdemeanor.   2005

41-6a-714. Freeway and controlled-access highways — Driving onto and from highways where permitted.

A person may not operate a vehicle onto or from any freeway or other controlled-access highway except at entrances and exits established by the highway authority having jurisdiction over the highway.   2005

41-6a-715. Controlled-access highways — Prohibiting use by class or kind of traffic — Traffic-control devices.

(1) A highway authority may regulate or prohibit the use of any controlled-access highway within its respective jurisdiction by any class or kind of traffic which is found to be incompatible with the normal and safe movement of traffic.

(2) The highway authority shall erect and maintain traffic-control devices on the controlled-access highway on which the regulations or prohibitions are applicable.   2005

41-6a-716. Driving on tollway without paying toll prohibited.

(1) As used in this section, "tollway" has the same meaning as defined in Section 72-6-118.

(2) The operator of a vehicle traveling on a tollway shall pay the toll imposed by the department or other entity for that tollway under Section 72-6-118.

(3) A person who violates Subsection (2) is guilty of a class C misdemeanor.   2005

PART 8

TURNING AND SIGNALING FOR TURNS

41-6a-801. Turning — Manner — Traffic-control devices.

The operator of a vehicle shall make turns as follows:

(1) Right turns: both a right turn and an approach for a right turn shall be made as close as practical to the right-hand curb or edge of the roadway.

(2) Left turns:

(a) the operator of a vehicle intending to turn left shall approach the turn from the

extreme left-hand lane for traffic moving in the same direction;

(b) whenever practicable, shall be made by turning onto the roadway being entered in the extreme left-hand lane for traffic moving in the new direction, unless otherwise directed by a traffic-control device; and

(c) may be made on a highway across solid double yellow line pavement markings indicating a two-direction, no-passing zone.

(3) Two-way left turn lanes:

(a) where a two-way left turn lane is provided, a left turn may not be made from any other lane;

(b) a vehicle may not be driven in the two-way left turn lane except when preparing for or making:

(i) a left turn from or into the roadway; or

(ii) a U-turn except when prohibited by a traffic-control device;

(c) (i) except as provided under Subsection (3)(c)(ii), the operator of a vehicle intending to turn left may not enter a two-way left turn lane more than 500 feet prior to making the turn;

(ii) if traffic in the two-way left turn lane extends beyond 500 feet, the operator of a vehicle intending to turn left may enter the two-way left turn lane immediately upon reaching the last vehicle in the two-way left turn lane;

(d) the operator of a vehicle that has turned left into the two-way left turn lane may not travel in the lane more than 500 feet unless the operator intends to turn left and Subsection (3)(c)(ii) applies; and

(e) the operator of a vehicle may not travel straight through an intersection in a two-way left turn lane.

(4) (a) A highway authority in its jurisdiction may provide exceptions to the provisions of this section by erecting traffic-control devices directing a different course to be traveled by turning vehicles.

(b) The operator of a vehicle may not turn a vehicle in violation of a traffic-control device erected under Subsection (4)(a).   2005

41-6a-802. Turning around — Where prohibited — Visibility.

The operator of a vehicle may not make a U-turn or turn the vehicle to proceed in the opposite direction:

(1) unless the movement can be made safely and without interfering with other traffic; or

(2) on any curve, or upon the approach to, or near the crest of a grade, if the vehicle is not visible at a distance of 500 feet by the operator of any other vehicle approaching from either direction.   2005

41-6a-803. Moving a vehicle — Safety.

A person may not move a vehicle which is stopped, standing, or parked until the movement may be made with reasonable safety.   2005

41-6a-804. Turning or changing lanes — Safety — Signals — Stopping or sudden decrease in speed — Signal flashing — Where prohibited.

(1) (a) A person may not turn a vehicle or move right or left on a roadway or change lanes until:

(i) the movement can be made with reasonable safety; and

(ii) an appropriate signal has been given as provided under this section.

(b) A signal of intention to turn right or left or to change lanes shall be given continuously for at least the last three seconds preceding the beginning of the movement.

(2) A person may not stop or suddenly decrease the speed of a vehicle without first giving an appropriate signal to the operator of any vehicle immediately to the rear when there is opportunity to give a signal.

(3) (a) A stop or turn signal when required shall be given either by the hand and arm or by signal lamps.

(b) If hand and arm signals are used, a person operating a vehicle shall give the required hand and arm signals from the left side of the vehicle as follows:

(i) Left turn: hand and arm extended horizontally;

(ii) Right turn: hand and arm extended upward; and

(iii) Stop or decrease speed: hand and arm extended downward.

(c) (i) A person operating a bicycle or device propelled by human power may give the required hand and arm signals for a right turn by extending the right hand and arm horizontally to the right.

(ii) This Subsection (3)(c) is an exception to the provision of Subsection (3)(b)(ii).

(4) A person required to make a signal under this section may not flash a signal:

(a) on one side only on a disabled vehicle;

(b) as a courtesy or "do pass" to operators of other vehicles approaching from the rear; or

(c) on one side only of a parked vehicle.   2005

PART 9

RIGHT-OF-WAY

41-6a-901. Right-of-way between vehicles — Unregulated intersection.

(1) The operator of a vehicle approaching an intersection not regulated by a traffic-control device shall yield the right-of-way to any vehicle that has entered the intersection from a different highway.

(2) Except as specified in Subsection (3) and unless otherwise directed by a peace officer, the operator of the vehicle on the left shall yield the right-of-way to the vehicle on the right when:

(a) more than one vehicle enters or approaches an intersection from different highways at approximately the same time; and

(b) the intersection:

(i) is not regulated by a traffic-control device;

(ii) is not regulated because the traffic-control signal is inoperative; or

(iii) is regulated from all directions by stop signs.

(3) The operator of a vehicle approaching an intersection not regulated by a traffic-control device:

(a) from a highway that does not continue beyond the intersection, shall yield the right-of-way to the operator of any vehicle on the intersecting highway; and

(b) from a highway that is not paved, shall yield the right-of-way to the operator of any vehicle on a paved intersecting highway.   2005

41-6a-902. Right-of-way — Stop or yield signals — Yield — Collisions at intersections or junctions of roadways — Evidence.

(1) Preferential right-of-way may be indicated by stop signs or yield signs under Section 41-6a-906.

(2) (a) Except when directed to proceed by a peace officer, every operator of a vehicle approaching a stop sign shall stop:

(i) at a clearly marked stop line;

(ii) before entering the crosswalk on the near side of the intersection if there is not a clearly marked stop line; or

(iii) at a point nearest the intersecting roadway where the operator has a view of approaching traffic on the intersecting roadway before entering it if there is not a clearly marked stop line or a crosswalk.

(b) After having stopped at a stop sign, the operator of a vehicle shall yield the right-of-way to any vehicle in the intersection or approaching on another roadway so closely as to constitute an immediate hazard.

(c) The operator of a vehicle approaching a stop sign shall yield the right-of-way to pedestrians within an adjacent crosswalk.

(3) (a) The operator of a vehicle approaching a yield sign shall:

(i) slow down to a speed reasonable for the existing conditions; and

(ii) if required for safety, stop as provided under Subsection (2).

(b) (i) After slowing or stopping at a yield sign, the operator of a vehicle shall yield the right-of-way to any vehicle in the intersection or approaching on another roadway so closely as to constitute an immediate hazard during the time the operator is moving across or within the intersection or junction of roadways.

(ii) The operator of a vehicle approaching a yield sign shall yield to pedestrians within an adjacent crosswalk.

(4) (a) A collision is prima facie evidence of an operator's failure to yield the right-of-way after passing a yield sign without stopping if the operator is involved in a collision:

(i) with a vehicle in the intersection or junction of roadways; or

(ii) with a pedestrian at an adjacent crosswalk.

(b) A collision under Subsection (4)(a) is not considered negligence per se in determining liability for the accident.   2005

41-6a-903. Yield right-of-way — Vehicle turning left — Entering or crossing highway other than from another roadway — Merging lanes.

The operator of a vehicle:

(1) intending to turn to the left shall yield the right-of-way to any vehicle approaching from the opposite direction which is so close to the turning vehicle as to constitute an immediate hazard;

(2) about to enter or cross a highway from any place other than another highway shall yield the right-of-way to all vehicles approaching on the highway to be entered or crossed; and

(3) traveling in a lane that is about to merge into a continuing lane, shall yield the right-of-way to all vehicles traveling in the continuing lane and which are so close as to be an immediate hazard.   2005

41-6a-904. **Approaching emergency vehicle — Necessary signals — Stationary emergency vehicle — Duties of respective operators.**

(1) Except when otherwise directed by a peace officer, the operator of a vehicle, upon the immediate approach of an authorized emergency vehicle using audible or visual signals under Section 41-6a-212 or 41-6a-1625, shall:

    (a) yield the right-of-way and immediately move to a position parallel to, and as close as possible to, the right-hand edge or curb of the highway, clear of any intersection; and

    (b) then stop and remain stopped until the authorized emergency vehicle has passed.

(2) The operator of a vehicle, upon approaching a stationary authorized emergency vehicle that is displaying alternately flashing red, red and white, or red and blue lights, shall:

    (a) reduce the speed of the vehicle;

    (b) provide as much space as practical to the stationary authorized emergency vehicle; and

    (c) if traveling in a lane adjacent to the stationary authorized emergency vehicle and if practical, with due regard to safety and traffic conditions, make a lane change into a lane not adjacent to the authorized emergency vehicle.

(3) The operator of a vehicle, upon approaching a stationary tow truck or highway maintenance vehicle that is displaying flashing amber lights, shall:

    (a) reduce the speed of the vehicle; and

    (b) provide as much space as practical to the stationary tow truck or highway maintenance vehicle.

(4) This section does not relieve the operator of an authorized emergency vehicle, tow truck, or highway maintenance vehicle from the duty to drive with regard for the safety of all persons using the highway.   **2005**

41-6a-905. **Vehicle or pedestrian working upon highway — Right-of-way.**

The operator of a vehicle shall yield the right-of-way to an:

    (1) authorized vehicle or pedestrian actually engaged in work on a highway within a highway construction or maintenance area indicated by a traffic-control device; or

    (2) authorized vehicle obviously and actually engaged in work on a highway when the vehicle displays lights in accordance with Section 41-6a-1617.   **2005**

41-6a-906. **Designation of through highways — Stop signs, yield signs, and traffic-control devices — Designation of intersections as locations for preferential right-of-way treatment.**

A highway authority, with reference to highways under its jurisdiction, may erect and maintain stop signs, yield signs, or other traffic-control devices to designate:

    (1) through highways; or

    (2) intersections or other roadway junctions at which vehicular traffic on one or more of the roadways should yield or stop and yield before entering the intersection or junction.   **2005**

41-6a-907. **Vehicles emerging from alleys, buildings, private roads, or driveways must stop prior to sidewalk area or street.**

The operator of a vehicle emerging from an alley, building, private road or driveway within a business or residence district shall stop:

    (1) the vehicle immediately prior to driving onto a sidewalk or onto the sidewalk area extending across the alley, building, private road, or driveway; or

    (2) if there is no sidewalk area, at the point nearest the street to be entered where the operator has a view of approaching traffic.   **2005**

PART 10

PEDESTRIANS' RIGHTS AND DUTIES

41-6a-1001. **Pedestrians subject to traffic-control devices — Other controls.**

(1) A pedestrian shall obey the instructions of a traffic-control device specifically applicable to the pedestrian unless otherwise directed by a peace officer.

(2) A pedestrian is subject to traffic and pedestrian-control signals under Sections 41-6a-305 and 41-6a-306.   **2005**

41-6a-1002. **Pedestrians' right-of-way — Duty of pedestrian.**

(1) (a) Except as provided under Subsection (2), when traffic-control signals are not in place or not in operation, the operator of a vehicle shall yield the right-of-way by slowing down or stopping if necessary:

        (i) to a pedestrian crossing the roadway within a crosswalk when the pedestrian is on the half of the roadway upon which the vehicle is traveling; or

        (ii) when the pedestrian is approaching so closely from the opposite half of the roadway as to be in danger.

    (b) Subsection (1)(a) does not apply under conditions of Subsection 41-6a-1003(2).

    (c) A pedestrian may not suddenly leave a curb or other place of safety and walk or run into the path of a vehicle which is so close as to constitute an immediate hazard.

(2) The operator of a vehicle approaching a school crosswalk shall come to a complete stop at the school crosswalk if:

    (a) a school speed limit sign has the warning lights operating; and

    (b) the crosswalk is occupied by a person.

(3) If a vehicle is stopped at a marked crosswalk or at any unmarked crosswalk at an intersection to permit a pedestrian to cross the roadway, the operator of any other vehicle approaching from the rear may not overtake and pass the stopped vehicle.   **2005**

41-6a-1003. **Pedestrians yielding right-of-way — Limits on pedestrians.**

(1) A pedestrian crossing a roadway at any point other than within a marked crosswalk or within an unmarked crosswalk at an intersection shall yield the right-of-way to all vehicles on the roadway.

(2) A pedestrian crossing a roadway at a point where there is a pedestrian tunnel or overhead pedestrian crossing shall yield the right-of-way to all vehicles on the roadway.

(3) Between adjacent intersections at which traffic-control signals are in operation, a pedestrian may not cross at any place except in a marked crosswalk.

(4) (a) A pedestrian may not cross a roadway intersection diagonally unless authorized by a traffic-control device.

    (b) If a pedestrian is authorized to cross diagonally under Subsection (4)(a), the pedestrian shall cross only as directed by the appropriate traffic-control device.   **2005**

41-6a-1004. Emergency vehicle — Necessary signals — Duties of operator — Pedestrian to yield.

(1) A pedestrian shall yield the right-of-way to an authorized emergency vehicle upon the immediate approach of an authorized emergency vehicle using audible or visual signals in accordance with Section 41-6a-212 or 41-6a-1625.

(2) This section does not relieve the operator of an authorized emergency vehicle from:

(a) the duty to drive with regard for the safety of all persons using the highway; nor

(b) from the duty to exercise care to avoid colliding with a pedestrian. 2005

41-6a-1005. Passing closed railroad or bridge gate or barrier prohibited.

A pedestrian may not pass through, around, over, under, or remain on a crossing gate or barrier at a railroad crossing or bridge while the gate or barrier is closed or is being opened or closed. 2005

41-6a-1006. Vehicles to exercise due care to avoid pedestrians — Audible signals and caution.

(1) The operator of a vehicle shall:

(a) exercise care to avoid colliding with a pedestrian;

(b) give an audible signal when necessary; and

(c) exercise appropriate precaution if the operator of the vehicle observes a child or an obviously confused, incapacitated, or intoxicated person.

(2) This section supersedes any conflicting provision of:

(a) this chapter; or

(b) a local ordinance in accordance with Section 41-6a-208. 2005

41-6a-1007. Operators to yield right-of-way to blind pedestrian — Duties of blind pedestrian — Use of cane — Failure to yield — Liability.

(1) (a) The operator of a vehicle shall yield the right-of-way to a blind or visually impaired pedestrian:

(i) carrying a clearly visible white cane; or

(ii) accompanied by a guide dog specially trained for that purpose and equipped with a harness.

(b) (i) Except as provided in Subsection (1)(b)(ii), a person who fails to yield the right-of-way is liable for any loss or damage which results as a proximate cause of the failure to yield the right-of-way to blind or visually impaired persons.

(ii) Blind or visually impaired persons shall:

(A) exercise due care in approaching and crossing roadways; and

(B) yield the right-of-way to authorized emergency vehicles giving an audible warning signal.

(2) A pedestrian other than a blind or visually impaired person may not carry a cane as described in Subsection (1). 2005

41-6a-1008. Vehicle crossing sidewalk — Operator to yield.

The operator of a vehicle crossing a sidewalk shall yield the right-of-way to any pedestrian and all other traffic on the sidewalk. 2005

41-6a-1009. Use of roadway by pedestrians — Prohibited activities.

(1) Where there is a sidewalk provided and its use is practicable, a pedestrian may not walk along or on an adjacent roadway.

(2) Where a sidewalk is not provided, a pedestrian walking along or on a highway shall walk only on the shoulder, as far as practicable from the edge of the roadway.

(3) Where a sidewalk or a shoulder is not available, a pedestrian walking along or on a highway shall:

(a) walk as near as practicable to the outside edge of the roadway; and

(b) if on a two-way roadway, walk only on the left side of the roadway facing traffic.

(4) A person may not sit, stand, or loiter on or near a roadway for the purpose of soliciting from the occupant of a vehicle:

(a) a ride;

(b) contributions;

(c) employment;

(d) the parking, watching, or guarding of a vehicle; or

(e) other business.

(5) A pedestrian who is under the influence of alcohol or any drug to a degree which renders the pedestrian a hazard may not walk or be on a highway except on a sidewalk or sidewalk area.

(6) Except as otherwise provided in this chapter, a pedestrian on a roadway shall yield the right-of-way to all vehicles on the roadway. 2005

41-6a-1010. Unmarked crosswalk locations — Restrictions on pedestrian.

(1) A highway authority in its respective jurisdiction may, after an engineering and traffic investigation, designate unmarked crosswalk locations where:

(a) pedestrian crossing is prohibited; or

(b) pedestrians shall yield the right-of-way to vehicles.

(2) The restrictions in Subsection (1) are effective only when traffic-control devices indicating the restrictions are in place. 2005

41-6a-1011. Pedestrian vehicles.

(1) As used in this section:

(a) (i) "Pedestrian vehicle" means a self-propelled conveyance designed, manufactured, and intended for the exclusive use of a person with a physical disability.

(ii) A "pedestrian vehicle" may not:

(A) exceed 48 inches in width;

(B) have an engine or motor with more than 300 cubic centimeters displacement or with more than 12 brake horsepower; and

(C) be capable of developing a speed in excess of 30 miles per hour.

(b) "Physical disability" means any bodily impairment which precludes a person from walking or otherwise moving about as a pedestrian.

(2) (a) A pedestrian vehicle operated by a physically disabled person is exempt from vehicle registration, inspection, and operator license requirements.

(b) Authority to operate a pedestrian vehicle on public highways or sidewalks shall be granted according to rules promulgated by the commissioner of public safety.

(3) (a) A physically disabled person may operate a pedestrian vehicle with a motor of not more than .5 brake horsepower capable of developing a speed of not more than eight miles per hour:

(i) on the sidewalk; and

(ii) in all places where pedestrians are allowed.

(b) A permit, license, registration, authority, application, or restriction may not be required or imposed on a physically disabled person operating a pedestrian vehicle under this Subsection (3).

(c) The provisions of this Subsection (3) supercede the provision of Subsection (2)(b).   2005

PART 11

BICYCLES, REGULATION OF OPERATION

41-6a-1101.   Parents and guardians may not authorize child's violation of chapter.

The parent or guardian of a child may not authorize or knowingly permit the child to violate any of the provisions of this chapter.   2005

41-6a-1102.   Bicycle and device propelled by human power and moped riders subject to chapter — Exception.

(1) Except as provided under Subsection (2) or as otherwise specified under this part, a person operating a bicycle, a vehicle or device propelled by human power, or a moped has all the rights and is subject to the provisions of this chapter applicable to the operator of any other vehicle.

(2) A person operating a nonmotorized bicycle or a vehicle or device propelled by human power is not subject to the penalties related to operator licenses under alcohol and drug-related traffic offenses.   2005

41-6a-1103.   Carrying more persons than design permits prohibited — Exception.

(1) Except as provided in Subsection (2), a bicycle or moped may not be used to carry more persons at one time than the number for which it is designed or equipped.

(2) An adult rider may carry a child securely attached to the adult rider's person in a back pack or sling.   2005

41-6a-1104.   Persons on bicycles, mopeds, skates, and sleds not to attach to moving vehicles — Exception.

(1) A person riding a bicycle, moped, coaster, skate board, roller skates, sled, or toy vehicle may not attach it or a person to any moving vehicle on a highway.

(2) This section does not prohibit attaching a trailer or semitrailer to a bicycle or moped if that trailer or semitrailer has been designed for attachment.   2005

41-6a-1105.   Operation of bicycle or moped on and use of roadway — Duties, prohibitions.

(1) A person operating a bicycle or a moped on a roadway at less than the normal speed of traffic at the time and place and under the conditions then existing shall ride as near as practicable to the right-hand edge of the roadway except when:

(a) overtaking and passing another bicycle or vehicle proceeding in the same direction;

(b) preparing to make a left turn at an intersection or into a private road or driveway;

(c) traveling straight through an intersection that has a right-turn only lane that is in conflict with the straight through movement; or

(d) reasonably necessary to avoid conditions that make it unsafe to continue along the right-hand edge of the roadway including:

(i) fixed or moving objects;

(ii) parked or moving vehicles;

(iii) bicycles;

(iv) pedestrians;

(v) animals;

(vi) surface hazards; or

(vii) a lane that is too narrow for a bicycle and a vehicle to travel safely side by side within the lane.

(2) A person operating a bicycle or moped on a highway shall operate in the designated direction of traffic.

(3) (a) A person riding a bicycle or moped on a roadway may not ride more than two abreast with another person except on paths or parts of roadways set aside for the exclusive use of bicycles.

(b) If allowed under Subsection (3)(a), a person riding two abreast with another person may not impede the normal and reasonable movement of traffic and shall ride within a single lane.

(4) If a usable path for bicycles has been provided adjacent to a roadway, a bicycle rider may be directed by a traffic-control device to use the path and not the roadway.   2005

41-6a-1106.   Bicycles and human powered vehicle or device to yield right-of-way to pedestrians on sidewalks, paths, or trails — Uses prohibited — Negligent collision prohibited — Speed restrictions — Rights and duties same as pedestrians.

(1) A person operating a bicycle or a vehicle or device propelled by human power shall:

(a) yield the right-of-way to any pedestrian; and

(b) give an audible signal before overtaking and passing a pedestrian.

(2) A person may not operate a bicycle or a vehicle or device propelled by human power on a sidewalk, path, or trail, or across a roadway in a crosswalk, where prohibited by a traffic-control device or ordinance.

(3) A person may not operate a bicycle or a vehicle or device propelled by human power in a negligent manner so as to collide with a:

(a) pedestrian; or

(b) person operating a:

(i) bicycle; or

(ii) vehicle or device propelled by human power.

(4) A person operating a bicycle or a vehicle or device propelled by human power on a sidewalk, path, or trail, or across a driveway, or across a roadway on a crosswalk may not operate at a speed greater than is reasonable and prudent under the existing conditions, giving regard to the actual and potential hazards then existing.

(5) Except as provided under Subsections (1) and (4), a person operating a bicycle or a vehicle or device propelled by human power on a sidewalk, path, or trail, or across a roadway on a crosswalk, has all the rights and duties applicable to a pedestrian under the same circumstances.   2005

41-6a-1107.   Bicycles — Parking on sidewalk, roadway — Prohibitions.

(1) A person may park a bicycle on a sidewalk unless prohibited or restricted by a traffic-control device.

(2) A bicycle parked on a sidewalk may not impede the normal and reasonable movement of pedestrian or other traffic.

(3) A bicycle may be parked on the roadway at any location where parking is allowed:

    (a) at any angle to the curb or edge of the roadway; and

    (b) abreast of another bicycle or bicycles near the side of the roadway.

(4) A bicycle may not be parked on a roadway in a manner as to obstruct the movement of a legally parked motor vehicle.

(5) In all other respects, bicycles parked anywhere on a highway shall conform with the provisions of Part 14, Stopping, Standing, and Parking, regarding the parking of vehicles. 2005

41-6a-1108. Bicycles and mopeds — Turns — Designated lanes.

(1) A person riding a bicycle or moped and intending to turn left shall comply with Section 41-6a-801 or Subsection (2).

(2) (a) A person riding a bicycle or moped intending to turn left shall approach the turn as close as practicable to the right curb or edge of the roadway.

    (b) After proceeding across the intersecting roadway, to the far corner of the curb or intersection of the roadway edges, the bicyclist or moped operator shall stop, as far out of the way of traffic as practical.

    (c) After stopping, the bicyclist or moped operator shall yield to any traffic proceeding in either direction along the roadway he had been using.

    (d) After yielding and complying with any traffic-control device or peace officer regulating traffic, the bicyclist or moped operator may proceed in the new direction.

(3) (a) Notwithstanding Subsections (1) and (2), a highway authority in its respective jurisdiction may place traffic-control devices that require and direct turning bicyclists and moped operators to travel a specific course.

    (b) When the devices are placed under Subsection (3)(a), a person may not turn a bicycle other than as directed by the devices. 2005

41-6a-1109. Bicycles and mopeds — Turn signals — Exceptions.

(1) Except as provided in this section, a person riding a bicycle or moped shall comply with Section 41-6a-804 regarding turn signals and turning.

(2) A person is not required to signal by hand and arm continuously if the hand is needed in the control or operation of the bicycle or moped.

(3) A person operating a bicycle or moped who is stopped in a lane designated for turning traffic only is not required to signal prior to making the turning movement. 2005

41-6a-1110. Bicycle and moped inspections — At request of officer.

A peace officer may at any time require a person riding a bicycle or moped to stop and submit the bicycle or moped to an inspection and a test as appropriate if the officer has reasonable cause to believe that:

    (1) the bicycle or moped is unsafe or not equipped as required by law; or

    (2) the bicycle or moped's equipment is not in proper adjustment or repair. 2005

41-6a-1111. Bicycle racing — When approved — Prohibitions — Exceptions — Authorized exemptions from traffic laws.

(1) Bicycle racing on highways is prohibited under Section 41-6a-606, except as authorized in this section.

(2) (a) Bicycle racing on a highway is permitted when a racing event is approved by a highway authority on a highway under its jurisdiction.

    (b) Approval of bicycle highway racing events may be granted only under conditions:

        (i) which assure reasonable safety for all race participants, spectators, and other highway users; and

        (ii) which prevent unreasonable interference with traffic flow which would seriously inconvenience other highway users.

(3) Participants in an approved bicycle highway racing event may be exempted from compliance with any traffic laws otherwise applicable:

    (a) by agreement with the approving highway authority; and

    (b) if traffic control is adequate to assure the safety of all highway users. 2005

41-6a-1112. Bicycles and mopeds — Carrying bundle — One hand on handlebars.

(1) A person operating a bicycle or moped may not carry any package, bundle, or article which prevents the use of both hands in the control and operation of the bicycle or moped.

(2) A person operating a bicycle or moped shall keep at least one hand on the handlebars at all times. 2005

41-6a-1113. Bicycle — Prohibited equipment — Brakes required.

(1) A bicycle may not be equipped with, and a person may not use on a bicycle, a siren or whistle.

(2) Every bicycle shall be equipped with a brake or brakes which enable its driver to stop the bicycle within 25 feet from a speed of ten miles per hour on dry, level, clean pavement. 2005

41-6a-1114. Bicycles — Lamps and reflective material required.

(1) Every bicycle in use at the times described in Section 41-6a-1603 shall be equipped with a:

    (a) lamp of a type approved by the department which is on the front emitting a white light visible from a distance of at least 500 feet to the front; and

    (b) (i) red reflector of a type approved by the department which is visible for 500 feet to the rear when directly in front of lawful lower beams of head lamps on a motor vehicle; or

        (ii) red taillight designed for use on a bicycle and emitting flashing or nonflashing light visible from a distance of 500 feet to the rear.

(2) Every bicycle when in use at the times described in Section 41-6a-1603 shall be equipped with:

    (a) reflective material of sufficient size and reflectivity to be visible from both sides for 500 feet when directly in front of lawful lower beams of head lamps on a motor vehicle; or

    (b) in lieu of reflective material, a lighted lamp visible from both sides from a distance of at least 500 feet.

(3) A bicycle or its rider may be equipped with lights or reflectors in addition to those required by Subsections (1) and (2). 2005

41-6a-1115. Motor assisted scooters — Conflicting provisions — Restrictions — Penalties.

(1) (a) Except as otherwise provided in this section, a motor assisted scooter is subject to the provisions under this chapter for a bicycle, moped, or a motor-driven cycle.

(b) For a person operating a motor assisted scooter, the following provisions do not apply:

(i) seating positions under Section 41-6a-1501;

(ii) required lights, horns, and mirrors under Section 41-6a-1506;

(iii) entitlement to full use of a lane under Subsection 41-6a-1502(1); and

(iv) driver licensing requirements under Section 53-3-202.

(2) A person under 15 years of age may not operate a motor assisted scooter using the motor unless the person is under the direct supervision of the person's parent or guardian.

(3) A person under eight years of age may not operate a motor assisted scooter with the motor running on any public property, highway, path, or sidewalk.

(4) A person may not operate a motor assisted scooter:

(a) in a public parking structure;

(b) on public property posted as an area prohibiting skateboards;

(c) on a highway consisting of a total of four or more lanes designated for regular vehicular traffic;

(d) on a highway with a posted speed limit greater than 25 miles per hour;

(e) while carrying more persons at one time than the number for which it is designed; or

(f) that has been structurally or mechanically altered from the original manufacturer's design.

(5) Except where posted or prohibited by rule or local ordinance, a motor assisted scooter is considered a nonmotorized vehicle if it is being used with the motor turned off.

(6) An owner may not authorize or knowingly permit a person to operate a motor assisted scooter in violation of this section.

(7) A person who violates this section is guilty of a class C misdemeanor.   2005

41-6a-1116. Personal motorized mobility devices — Conflicting provisions — Restrictions — Penalties.

(1) (a) Except as otherwise provided in this section, a personal motorized mobility device is subject to the provisions under this chapter for a bicycle, moped, or a motor-driven cycle.

(b) For a person operating a personal motorized mobility device, the following provisions do not apply:

(i) seating positions under Section 41-6a-1501;

(ii) required lights, horns, and mirrors under Section 41-6a-1506;

(iii) entitlement to full use of a lane under Subsection 41-6a-1502(1); and

(iv) driver licensing requirements under Section 53-3-202.

(2) A person under 15 years of age may not operate a personal motorized mobility device using the motor unless the person is under the direct supervision of the person's parent or guardian.

(3) A person may not operate a personal motorized mobility device:

(a) on a highway consisting of a total of four or more lanes designated for regular vehicular traffic;

(b) on a highway with a posted speed limit greater than 35 miles per hour; or

(c) that has been structurally or mechanically altered from the original manufacturer's design.

(4) An owner may not authorize or knowingly permit a person to operate a personal motorized mobility device in violation of this section.

(5) A person who violates this section is guilty of a class C misdemeanor.   2005

41-6a-1117. Mini-motorcycle restrictions — Exceptions.

(1) A person may not operate a mini-motorcycle on any public property, highway, path, or sidewalk unless:

(a) the mini-motorcycle is registered for highway use in accordance with Title 41, Chapter 1a, Motor Vehicle Act; and

(b) the operator is licensed to operate a motorcycle in accordance with Title 53, Chapter 3, Uniform Driver License Act.

(2) An owner may not authorize or knowingly permit a person to operate a mini-motorcycle in violation of this section.

(3) A person who violates this section is guilty of a class C misdemeanor.   2005

PART 12

RAILROAD TRAINS, RAILROAD GRADE CROSSINGS, AND SAFETY ZONES

41-6a-1201. Driving on tracks.

(1) The operator of a vehicle proceeding on any track in front of a railroad train on a highway shall remove the vehicle from the track as soon as practicable after signal from the operator of the train.

(2) When a railroad train has started to cross an intersection, an operator of a vehicle may not drive:

(a) on or across the tracks; or

(b) in the path of the train within the intersection in front of the train.   2005

41-6a-1202. Driving through safety zone.

The operator of a vehicle may not drive through or within a safety zone.   2005

41-6a-1203. Railroad grade crossing — Duty to stop — Malfunctions and school buses — Driving through, around, or under gate or barrier prohibited.

(1) Whenever a person operating a vehicle approaches a railroad grade crossing, the operator of the vehicle shall stop within 50 feet but not less than 15 feet from the nearest rail of the railroad track and may not proceed if:

(a) a clearly visible electric or mechanical signal device gives warning of the immediate approach of a train;

(b) a crossing gate is lowered, or when a human flagman gives or continues to give a signal of the approach or passage of a train;

(c) a railroad train approaching within approximately 1,500 feet of the highway crossing emits a signal audible and the train by reason of its speed or nearness to the crossing is an immediate hazard;

(d) an approaching train is plainly visible and is in hazardous proximity to the crossing; or

(e) there is any other condition that makes it unsafe to proceed through the crossing.

(2) (a) An operator of a vehicle who suspects a false activation or malfunction of a railroad grade crossing signal device may drive a vehicle, including a school bus, through the railroad grade crossing after stopping if:

(i) the operator of a vehicle has a clear line of sight of at least one mile of the railroad tracks in all directions;

(ii) there is no evidence of an approaching train;

(iii) the vehicle can cross over the tracks safely; and

(iv) the operator of a vehicle does not violate Subsection (3).

(b) As soon as is reasonably possible, the operator of a school bus shall notify the driver's dispatcher and the dispatcher shall notify the owner of the railroad track where the grade crossing signal device is located of the false activation or malfunction.

(3) A person may not drive a vehicle through, around, or under a crossing gate or barrier at a railroad crossing while the gate or barrier is closed or is being opened or closed.   2005

41-6a-1204. Trains — Interference with vehicles limited.

A person or government agency may not operate a train in a manner to prevent vehicular use of a roadway for a period of time in excess of five consecutive minutes except:

(1) when necessary to comply with signals affecting the safety of the movement of trains;

(2) when necessary to avoid striking any object or person on the track;

(3) when the train is disabled;

(4) when the train is in motion or while engaged in switching operations;

(5) when there is no vehicular traffic waiting to use the crossing;

(6) when necessary to comply with a governmental safety regulation; or

(7) as determined by a highway authority.   2005

41-6a-1205. Railroad grade crossings — Certain vehicles must stop — Exceptions — Rules.

(1) An operator of a commercial motor vehicle, as defined under Section 53-3-102, shall upon approaching a railroad grade crossing:

(a) unless Subsection (2) applies, slow down and check that the tracks are clear of an approaching train;

(b) stop within 50 feet, but not closer than 15 feet, from the nearest rail of the railroad track before reaching the crossing if the tracks are not clear;

(c) obey all traffic control devices or the directions of a peace officer, or other crossing official at the crossing; and

(d) before proceeding over a railroad grade crossing:

(i) ensure that the vehicle has sufficient space to drive completely through a railroad grade crossing without stopping; and

(ii) ensure that the vehicle has sufficient undercarriage clearance to safely and completely pass through the crossing.

(2) (a) Except as provided in Subsection (3), the operator of a vehicle described in 49 CFR 392.10 shall stop within 50 feet, but not closer than 15 feet, from the nearest rail of the railroad track before crossing, at grade, any track of a railroad.

(b) While stopped, the operator shall look in both directions along the track for any sign of an approaching train and look and listen for signals indicating the approach of any train.

(c) The operator may proceed across the railroad track only when the movement may be made with reasonable safety.

(d) After stopping as required and upon safely proceeding, the operator shall only cross the railroad track in a gear that ensures no necessity for manually changing gears while traversing the crossing.

(e) The operator may not manually shift gears while crossing the railroad track.

(3) This section does not apply at a:

(a) railroad grade crossing where traffic is controlled by a peace officer or other crossing official;

(b) railroad grade crossing where traffic is regulated by a traffic-control signal;

(c) railroad grade crossing where a traffic-control device gives notice that the stopping requirements of this section are not applicable; or

(d) other railroad grade crossings excluded under 49 CFR 392.10.   2005

41-6a-1206. Railroad crossing duties respecting crawler type tractor, power shovel, derrick, or other equipment or structure.

(1) A person may not operate or move the following on or across any tracks at a railroad grade crossing without first complying with this section:

(a) a crawler type tractor;

(b) a power shovel;

(c) a derrick;

(d) a roller; or

(e) any equipment or structure having:

(i) normal operating speed of ten or less miles per hour; or

(ii) a vertical body or load clearance of less than:

(A) $\frac{1}{2}$ inch per foot of the distance between any two adjacent axles; or

(B) in any event, nine inches measured above the level surface of a roadway.

(2) Notice of an intended crossing under this section shall be given to the railroad and a reasonable time shall be given to the railroad to provide proper protection at the crossing.

(3) (a) Before making a crossing under this section the person operating or moving the vehicle or equipment shall first stop within 50 feet but not closer than 15 feet from the nearest rail of the railway.

(b) While stopped, the operator of the vehicle shall listen and look in both directions along the track for any approaching train and for signals indicating the approach of a railroad train.

(c) The operator may proceed across the track only when the crossing can be made safely.

(4) The operator of a vehicle shall obey all traffic control devices or the directions of a peace officer or other crossing official at the crossing.   2005

PART 13

SCHOOL BUSES AND SCHOOL BUS PARKING ZONES

41-6a-1301. Standards and specifications for lighting and special warning devices on school buses.

(1) (a) A school bus shall be equipped with red signal lamps mounted as high and as widely spaced laterally as practicable.

(b) The red signal lamps shall display two alternately flashing red lights, located at the same level, to the front and rear of the school bus.

(c) The red signal lamps shall be visible at 500 feet in normal sunlight.

(2) (a) A school bus shall be equipped with yellow signal lamps mounted near each of the four red signal lamps and at the same level but closer to the vertical centerline of the bus.

(b) The yellow signal lamps shall display two alternately flashing yellow lights to the front and rear of the school bus.

(c) The yellow signal lamps shall be visible at 500 feet in normal sunlight.

(3) A school bus driver shall activate the yellow signal lamps at least 100 feet, but not more than 500 feet, before every stop at which the alternately flashing red lights are activated. 2005

41-6a-1302. School bus — Signs and light signals — Flashing amber lights — Flashing red lights — Passing school bus — Duty to stop — Travel in opposite direction — Penalties.

(1) A school bus, when operated for the transportation of school children, shall:

(a) bear on the front and rear of the bus a plainly visible sign containing the words "school bus" in letters not less than eight inches in height, which shall be removed or covered when the vehicle is not in use for the transportation of school children; and

(b) be equipped with alternating flashing amber and red light signals visible from the front and rear, of a type approved and mounted as required under Section 41-6a-1301 and prescribed by the department under Section 41-6a-1601.

(2) The operator of a vehicle on a highway, upon meeting or overtaking a school bus equipped with signals required under this section which is displaying alternating flashing:

(a) amber warning light signals, shall slow the vehicle, but may proceed past the school bus using due care and caution at a speed not greater than specified in Subsection 41-6a-601(2) for school zones for the safety of the school children that may be in the vicinity; or

(b) red light signals visible from the front or rear, shall stop immediately before reaching the bus and may not proceed until the flashing red light signals cease operation.

(3) The operator of a vehicle need not stop upon meeting or passing a school bus displaying alternating flashing red light signals if the school bus is traveling in the opposite direction when:

(a) traveling on a divided highway;

(b) the bus is stopped at an intersection or other place controlled by a traffic-control signal or by a peace officer; or

(c) on a highway of five or more lanes, which may include a left-turn lane or two-way left turn lane.

(4) (a) The operator of a school bus shall operate alternating flashing red light signals at all times when:

(i) children are unloading from a school bus to cross a highway;

(ii) a school bus is stopped for the purpose of loading children who must cross a highway to board the bus; or

(iii) it would be hazardous for vehicles to proceed past the stopped school bus.

(b) The alternating flashing red light signals may not be operated except:

(i) when the school bus is stopped for loading or unloading school children; or

(ii) for an emergency purpose.

(5) The operator of a school bus being operated on a highway shall have the headlights of the school bus lighted.

(6) (a) A violation of Subsection (2) or (3) is a class C misdemeanor and the minimum fine is:

(i) $100 for a first offense;

(ii) $200 for a second offense within three years of a previous conviction or bail forfeiture; and

(iii) $500 for a third or subsequent offense within three years of a previous conviction or bail forfeiture.

(b) A violation of Subsection (5) is a class C misdemeanor and the fine is $50.

(c) The court may order the person to perform compensatory service in lieu of the fine or any portion of the fine if the court makes the reasons for the waiver part of the record.

(7) The Driver License Division shall develop and implement a record system to distinguish:

(a) a conviction or bail forfeiture under this section from other convictions; and

(b) between a first and subsequent conviction or bail forfeiture under this section. 2005

41-6a-1303. Passing a school bus complaint procedure.

(1) (a) An operator of a school bus who observes a violation of Subsection 41-6a-1302(2) or (3) may prepare a report, in a manner specified by the school district, to the school district transportation coordinator no more than two working days after the alleged violation occurred.

(b) The report under Subsection (1)(a) shall contain:

(i) the date, time, and location of the violation;

(ii) the license plate number and state and description of the offending vehicle;

(iii) as much as practical, a description of the operator of the offending vehicle;

(iv) a description of the incident involving the violation;

(v) information on how to contact the school bus operator who witnessed the offense; and

(vi) the signature of the operator of the school bus who witnessed the offense attesting to the accuracy of the report.

(2) (a) Upon receipt of a report in accordance with Subsection (1), the school district transportation coordinator shall promptly send a notification letter to the last-known registered owner of the vehicle.

(b) The notification letter shall include:

(i) the applicable information on the school bus operator's report stating that the vehicle was observed passing a school bus displaying alternating flashing red lights in violation of state law;

(ii) a complete explanation of the applicable provisions of Section 41-6a-1302; and

(iii) an explanation that the notification letter is not a peace officer citation but is an effort to call attention to the seriousness of the incident.

(c) The school district transportation coordinator may file the report with the local law enforcement agency that has jurisdiction for the alleged violation.

(3) A law enforcement agency that receives a report in accordance with Subsection (2) may have a peace officer initiate an investigation of the reported violation. 2005

41-6a-1304. School buses — Rules regarding design and operation.

(1) (a) In accordance with Title 63, Chapter 46a, Utah Administrative Rulemaking Act, the Department of Transportation by and with the advice of the State Board of Education and the Department of Public Safety shall adopt and enforce rules, not inconsistent with this chapter, to govern the design and operation of all school buses in this state when:

(i) owned and operated by any school district;

(ii) privately owned and operated under contract with a school district; or

(iii) privately owned for use by a private school.

(b) The rules under this Subsection (1) shall by reference be made a part of any contract with a school district or private school to operate a school bus.

(2) Every school district or private school, its officers and employees, and every person employed under contract by a school district or private school shall be subject to the rules under Subsection (1). 2005

41-6a-1305. Violation of rules — Penalty.

(1) An officer or employee of a school district who violates any of the rules provided under Section 41-6a-1304 or fails to include the obligation to comply with the rules in a contract executed by that person on behalf of a school district is guilty of misconduct and subject to removal from office or employment.

(2) A person operating a school bus under contract with a school district who fails to comply with any rules provided under Section 41-6a-1304 is guilty of breach of contract, and the contract shall be canceled after notice and hearing by the responsible officers of the school district. 2005

41-6a-1306. School buses removed from service — Removal of markings — Repainting — School district not to bear expense — Infraction.

(1) (a) As used in this section, "old school bus" means a school bus that has been removed from service and is operated on the highways, streets, or roads of this state for a nonschool permanent commercial use.

(b) A person who acquires an old school bus shall cause:

(i) identifying markings be removed; and

(ii) the bus be painted a color other than school-bus yellow.

(c) The school districts may not be charged any expense related to removing markings from the school bus removed from service.

(2) A person who violates this section is guilty of an infraction. 2005

41-6a-1307. School bus parking zones — Establishment — Uniform markings — Penalty.

(1) As used in this section, "school bus parking zone" means a parking space that is clearly identified as reserved for use by a school bus.

(2) A highway authority for highways under its jurisdiction and school boards for roadways located on school property may establish and locate school bus parking zones in accordance with specifications established under Subsection (3).

(3) In accordance with Title 63, Chapter 46a, Utah Administrative Rulemaking Act, the Department of Transportation, after consultation with local highway authorities and school boards which may include input from school traffic safety committees established under Section 53A-3-402, shall make rules establishing specifications for uniform signage or markings to clearly identify school bus parking zones.

(4) A person may not stop, stand, or park a vehicle other than a school bus, whether occupied or not, in a clearly identified school bus parking zone.

(5) A person who violates Subsection (4) shall pay a minimum fine of $75. 2005

PART 14

STOPPING, STANDING, AND PARKING

41-6a-1401. Standing or parking vehicles — Restrictions and exceptions.

(1) Except when necessary to avoid conflict with other traffic, or in compliance with law, the directions of a peace officer, or a traffic-control device, a person may not:

(a) stop, stand, or park a vehicle:

(i) on the roadway side of any vehicle stopped or parked at the edge or curb of a street;

(ii) on a sidewalk;

(iii) within an intersection;

(iv) on a crosswalk;

(v) between a safety zone and the adjacent curb or within 30 feet of points on the curb immediately opposite the ends of a safety zone, unless a different length is indicated by signs or markings;

(vi) alongside or opposite any street excavation or obstruction when stopping, standing, or parking would obstruct traffic;

(vii) on any bridge or other elevated structure, on a highway, or within a highway tunnel;

(viii) on any railroad tracks;

(ix) on any controlled-access highway;

(x) in the area between roadways of a divided highway, including crossovers; or

(xi) any place where a traffic-control device prohibits stopping, standing, or parking; or

(b) stand or park a vehicle, whether occupied or not, except momentarily to pick up or discharge a passenger or passengers:

(i) in front of a public or private driveway;

(ii) within 15 feet of a fire hydrant;

(iii) within 20 feet of a crosswalk;

(iv) within 30 feet upon the approach to any flashing signal, stop sign, yield sign, or traffic-control signal located at the side of a roadway;

(v) within 20 feet of the driveway entrance to any fire station and on the side of a street opposite the entrance to any fire station within 75 feet of the entrance when properly signposted; or

(vi) at any place where a traffic-control device prohibits standing; or

(c) park a vehicle, whether occupied or not, except temporarily for the purpose of and while actually engaged in loading or unloading property or passengers:

>   (i) within 50 feet of the nearest rail of a railroad crossing; or

>   (ii) at any place where traffic-control devices prohibit parking.

(2) A person may not move a vehicle that is not lawfully under the person's control into any prohibited area or into an unlawful distance from the curb.

2005

41-6a-1402. Stopping or parking on roadways — Angle parking — Traffic-control devices prohibiting or restricting.

(1) Except as otherwise provided in this section, a vehicle stopped or parked on a two-way roadway shall be stopped or parked with the right-hand wheels:

>   (a) parallel to and within twelve inches of the right-hand curb; or

>   (b) as close as practicable to the right edge of the right-hand shoulder.

(2) Except when otherwise provided by local ordinance, a vehicle stopped or parked on a one-way roadway shall be stopped or parked parallel to the curb or edge of the roadway in the direction of authorized traffic movement with its:

>   (a) right-hand wheels:

>>   (i) within twelve inches of the right-hand curb; or

>>   (ii) as close as practicable to the right edge of the right-hand shoulder; or

>   (b) left-hand wheels:

>>   (i) within twelve inches of the left-hand curb; or

>>   (ii) as close as practicable to the left edge of the left-hand shoulder.

(3) (a) Except as provided in Subsection (3)(b), local highway authorities may by ordinance permit angle parking on any roadway.

>   (b) Angle parking is not permitted on any federal-aid or state highway unless the Department of Transportation has determined that the roadway is of sufficient width to permit angle parking without interfering with the free movement of traffic.

(4) (a) The Department of Transportation, with respect to highways under its jurisdiction, may place traffic-control devices prohibiting or restricting the stopping, standing, or parking of vehicles on a highway where:

>>   (i) the stopping, standing, or parking is dangerous to those using the highway; or

>>   (ii) the stopping, standing, or parking of vehicles would unduly interfere with the free movement of traffic.

>   (b) A person may not stop, stand, or park a vehicle in violation of the restriction indicated by the devices under Subsection (4)(a).   2005

41-6a-1403. Motor vehicle left unattended — Requirements.

(1) A person operating or in charge of a motor vehicle may not permit the vehicle to stand unattended without:

>   (a) stopping the engine;

>   (b) locking the ignition and removing the key;

>   (c) placing the transmission in "park" or the gears in "low" or "reverse" if the vehicle has a manual shift; or

>   (d) effectively setting the brakes thereon.

(2) A person shall turn the front wheels to the curb or side of the highway when standing a vehicle on any perceptible grade.   2005

41-6a-1404. Stopping or parking on roadway outside business or residential district.

(1) Outside a business or residence district, a person may not stop, park, or leave standing a vehicle, whether attended or unattended, on the roadway when it is practical to stop, park, or leave the vehicle off the roadway.

(2) A person who stops, parks, or leaves a vehicle standing on a roadway shall:

>   (a) leave an unobstructed width of the highway opposite the vehicle for the free passage of other vehicles; and

>   (b) leave the vehicle so that other vehicle operators have a clear view of the stopped vehicle from a distance of 200 feet in each direction on the roadway.

(3) This section and Sections 41-6a-1401 and 41-6a-1402 do not apply to the operator of a vehicle if the vehicle becomes disabled while on the paved or main traveled portion of a roadway in a manner and to the extent that it is impossible to avoid stopping and temporarily leaving the disabled vehicle on the paved or main traveled portion of the roadway.   2005

41-6a-1405. Peace officer authorized to move vehicle.

(1) If a peace officer finds a vehicle in violation of Section 41-6a-1404, the officer may move the vehicle, cause the vehicle to be moved, or require the operator or other person responsible for the vehicle to move the vehicle to a safe position off the highway.

(2) A peace officer may remove or cause to be removed to a place of safety an unattended vehicle left standing on a highway in:

>   (a) violation of this part; or

>   (b) a position or under circumstances that the vehicle obstructs the normal movement of traffic.

(3) In accordance with Section 41-6a-1406, a peace officer may remove or cause to be removed to the nearest garage or other place of safety a vehicle found on a highway when:

>   (a) the vehicle has been reported stolen or taken without the consent of its owner;

>   (b) the person responsible for the vehicle is unable to provide for its custody or removal; or

>   (c) the person operating the vehicle is arrested for an alleged offense for which the peace officer is required by law to take the person arrested before a proper magistrate without unnecessary delay.

2005

41-6a-1406. Removal and impoundment of vehicles — Reporting and notification requirements — Administrative impound fee — Refunds — Possessory lien — Rulemaking.

(1) If a vehicle, vessel, or outboard motor is removed or impounded as provided under Section 41-1a-1101, 41-6a-527, 41-6a-1405, 41-6a-1408, or 73-18-20.1 by an order of a peace officer or by an order of a person acting on behalf of a law enforcement agency or highway authority, the removal or impoundment of the vehicle, vessel, or outboard motor shall be at the expense of the owner.

(2) The vehicle, vessel, or outboard motor under Subsection (1) shall be removed or impounded to:

>   (a) a state impound yard; or

>   (b) if none, a garage, docking area, or other place of safety.

(3) The peace officer may move a vehicle, vessel, or outboard motor or cause it to be removed by a tow truck motor carrier that meets standards established:

(a) under Title 72, Chapter 9, Motor Carrier Safety Act; and

(b) by the department under Subsection (10).

(4) (a) Immediately after the removal of the vehicle, vessel, or outboard motor, a report of the removal shall be sent to the Motor Vehicle Division by:

(i) the peace officer or agency by whom the peace officer is employed; and

(ii) the tow truck operator or the tow truck motor carrier by whom the tow truck operator is employed.

(b) The report shall be in a form specified by the Motor Vehicle Division and shall include:

(i) the operator's name, if known;

(ii) a description of the vehicle, vessel, or outboard motor;

(iii) the vehicle identification number or vessel or outboard motor identification number;

(iv) the license number or other identification number issued by a state agency;

(v) the date, time, and place of impoundment;

(vi) the reason for removal or impoundment;

(vii) the name of the tow truck motor carrier who removed the vehicle, vessel, or outboard motor; and

(viii) the place where the vehicle, vessel, or outboard motor is stored.

(c) Until the tow truck operator or tow truck motor carrier reports the removal as required under this Subsection (4), a tow truck motor carrier or impound yard may not:

(i) collect any fee associated with the removal; and

(ii) begin charging storage fees.

(5) (a) Upon receipt of the report, the Motor Vehicle Division shall give notice to the registered owner of the vehicle, vessel, or outboard motor and any lien holder in the manner prescribed by Section 41-1a-114.

(b) The notice shall:

(i) state the date, time, and place of removal, the name, if applicable, of the person operating the vehicle, vessel, or outboard motor at the time of removal, the reason for removal, and the place where the vehicle, vessel, or outboard motor is stored;

(ii) state that the registered owner is responsible for payment of towing, impound, and storage fees charged against the vehicle, vessel, or outboard motor;

(iii) inform the registered owner of the vehicle, vessel, or outboard motor of the conditions that must be satisfied before the vehicle, vessel, or outboard motor is released; and

(iv) inform the registered owner and lienholder of the division's intent to sell the vehicle, vessel, or outboard motor, if within 30 days from the date of the removal or impoundment under this section, the owner, lien holder, or the owner's agent fails to make a claim for release of the vehicle, vessel, or outboard motor.

(c) If the vehicle, vessel, or outboard motor is not registered in this state, the Motor Vehicle Division shall make a reasonable effort to notify the registered owner and any lien holder of the removal and the place where the vehicle, vessel, or outboard motor is stored.

(d) The Motor Vehicle Division shall forward a copy of the notice to the place where the vehicle, vessel, or outboard motor is stored.

(6) (a) The vehicle, vessel, or outboard motor shall be released after the registered owner, lien holder, or the owner's agent:

(i) makes a claim for release of the vehicle, vessel, or outboard motor at any office of the State Tax Commission;

(ii) presents identification sufficient to prove ownership of the impounded vehicle, vessel, or outboard motor;

(iii) completes the registration, if needed, and pays the appropriate fees;

(iv) if the impoundment was made under Section 41-6a-527, pays an administrative impound fee of $230; and

(v) pays all towing and storage fees to the place where the vehicle, vessel, or outboard motor is stored.

(b) (i) Twenty-nine dollars of the administrative impound fee assessed under Subsection (6)(a)(iv) shall be dedicated credits to the Motor Vehicle Division;

(ii) $97 of the administrative impound fee assessed under Subsection (6)(a)(iv) shall be deposited in the Department of Public Safety Restricted Account created in Section 53-3-106; and

(iii) the remainder of the administrative impound fee assessed under Subsection (6)(a)(iv) shall be deposited in the General Fund.

(c) The administrative impound fee assessed under Subsection (6)(a)(iv) shall be waived or refunded by the State Tax Commission if the registered owner, lien holder, or owner's agent presents written evidence to the State Tax Commission that:

(i) the Driver License Division determined that the arrested person's driver license should not be suspended or revoked under Section 53-3-223 or 41-6a-521 as shown by a letter or other report from the Driver License Division presented within 30 days of the final notification from the Driver License Division; or

(ii) the vehicle was stolen at the time of the impoundment as shown by a copy of the stolen vehicle report presented within 30 days of the impoundment.

(7) (a) An impounded vehicle, vessel, or outboard motor not claimed by the registered owner or the owner's agent within the time prescribed by Section 41-1a-1103 shall be sold in accordance with that section and the proceeds, if any, shall be disposed of as provided under Section 41-1a-1104.

(b) The date of impoundment is considered the date of seizure for computing the time period provided under Section 41-1a-1103.

(8) The registered owner who pays all fees and charges incurred in the impoundment of the owner's vehicle, vessel, or outboard motor, has a cause of action for all the fees and charges, together with damages, court costs, and attorney fees, against the operator of the vehicle, vessel, or outboard motor whose actions caused the removal or impoundment.

(9) Towing, impound fees, and storage fees are a possessory lien on the vehicle, vessel, or outboard motor.

(10) In accordance with Title 63, Chapter 46a, Utah Administrative Rulemaking Act, the department shall make rules setting the performance standards for towing companies to be used by the department.

(11) (a) The Motor Vehicle Division may specify that a report required under Subsection (4) be submitted in electronic form utilizing a database for submission, storage, and retrieval of the information.

(b) (i) Unless otherwise provided by statute, the Motor Vehicle Division or the administrator of the database may adopt a schedule of fees assessed for utilizing the database.

(ii) The fees under this Subsection (11)(b) shall:

(A) be reasonable and fair; and

(B) reflect the cost of administering the database.   2005

41-6a-1407. Removal of unattended vehicles prohibited without authorization — Penalties.

(1) In cases not amounting to burglary or theft of a vehicle, a person may not remove an unattended vehicle without prior authorization of:

(a) a peace officer;

(b) a law enforcement agency;

(c) a highway authority having jurisdiction over the highway on which there is an unattended vehicle; or

(d) the owner or person in lawful possession or control of the real property.

(2) (a) An authorization from a person specified under Subsection (1)(a), (b), or (c) shall be in a form specified by the Motor Vehicle Division.

(b) The removal of the unattended vehicle shall comply with requirements of Section 41-6a-1406.

(3) The removal of the unattended vehicle authorized under Subsection (1)(d) shall comply with requirements of Section 72-9-603.

(4) A person who violates Subsections (1) or (3) is guilty of a class C misdemeanor.   2005

41-6a-1408. Abandoned vehicles — Removal by peace officer — Report — Vehicle identification.

(1) As used in this section, "abandoned vehicle" means a vehicle that is left unattended:

(a) on a highway for a period in excess of 48 hours; or

(b) on public or private property for a period in excess of seven days without express or implied consent of the owner or person in lawful possession or control of the property.

(2) A person may not abandon a vehicle on a highway.

(3) A person may not abandon a vehicle on public or private property without the express or implied consent of the owner or person in lawful possession or control of the property.

(4) A peace officer who has reasonable grounds to believe that a vehicle has been abandoned may remove the vehicle or cause it to be removed in accordance with Section 41-6a-1406.

(5) If the motor number, manufacturer's number or identification mark of the abandoned vehicle has been defaced, altered or obliterated, the vehicle may not be released or sold until:

(a) the original motor number, manufacturer's number or identification mark has been replaced; or

(b) a new number assigned by the Motor Vehicle Division has been stamped on the vehicle.   2005

PART 15

SPECIAL VEHICLES

41-6a-1501. Motorcycle or motor-driven cycle — Place for operator to ride — Passengers.

(1) A person operating a motorcycle or motor-driven cycle shall ride only on the permanent and regular seat attached to the motorcycle or motor-driven cycle.

(2) (a) Except as provided in Subsection (2)(b):

(i) a person operating a motorcycle or motor-driven cycle may not carry any other person on the motorcycle or motor-driven cycle; and

(ii) a passenger may not ride on a motorcycle or a motor-driven cycle.

(b) If a motorcycle or motor-driven cycle is designed to carry more than one person, a passenger may ride on:

(i) the permanent and regular seat, if designed for two persons; or

(ii) another seat firmly attached to the motorcycle or motor-driven cycle at the rear or side of the operator.

(3) A person shall ride on a motorcycle or motor-driven cycle only while sitting astride the seat, facing forward, with one leg on either side of the motorcycle or motor-driven cycle.

(4) A person may not operate a motorcycle or motor-driven cycle while carrying a package, bundle, or other article which prevents the person from keeping both hands on the handlebars.

(5) An operator of a motorcycle or motor-driven cycle may not carry a person and a person may not ride in a position that interferes with:

(a) the operation or control of the motorcycle or motor-driven cycle; or

(b) the view of the operator.   2005

41-6a-1502. Motorcycles, motor-driven cycles, or all-terrain type I vehicles — Operation on public highways.

(1) (a) A motorcycle or a motor-driven cycle is entitled to full use of a lane.

(b) A person may not operate a motor vehicle in a manner that deprives a motorcycle or motor-driven cycle of the full use of a lane.

(c) This Subsection (1) does not apply to motorcycles or motor-driven cycles operated two abreast in a single lane.

(2) The operator of a motorcycle or motor-driven cycle may not overtake and pass in the same lane occupied by the vehicle being overtaken.

(3) A person may not operate a motorcycle or motor-driven cycle between:

(a) lanes of traffic; or

(b) adjacent lines or rows of vehicles.

(4) Motorcycles or motor-driven cycles may not be operated more than two abreast in a single lane.

(5) Subsections (2) and (3) do not apply to peace officers acting in the peace officers' official capacities.

(6) The provisions of this section also apply to all-terrain type I vehicles.   2005

41-6a-1503. Motorcycle or motor-driven cycle — Attaching to another vehicle prohibited.

A person riding on a motorcycle or motor-driven cycle may not attach himself to any other vehicle on a roadway.   2005

41-6a-1504. Motorcycle or motor-driven cycle — Footrests for passenger — Height of handlebars limited.

(1) A motorcycle or motor-driven vehicle carrying a passenger on a public highway, other than in a sidecar or enclosed cab, shall be equipped with footrests for the passenger.

(2) A person may not operate a motorcycle or motor-driven cycle with handlebars above shoulder height.

2005

41-6a-1505. Motorcycle or motor-driven cycle — Protective headgear — Closed cab excepted — Electric assisted bicycles, motor assisted scooters, personal motorized mobility devices.

(1) A person under the age of 18 may not operate or ride on a motorcycle or motor-driven cycle on a highway unless the person is wearing protective headgear which complies with specifications adopted under Subsection (3).

(2) This section does not apply to persons riding within an enclosed cab.

(3) The following standards and specifications for protective headgear are adopted:

(a) 49 C.F.R. 571.218 related to protective headgear for motorcycles; and

(b) 49 C.F.R. 1203 related to protective headgear for bicycles, motor assisted scooters, and personal motorized mobility devices. 2005

41-6a-1506. Motorcycles — Required equipment — Brakes.

(1) A motorcycle and a motor-driven cycle shall be equipped with the following items:

(a) one head lamp which, when factory equipped with an automatic lighting ignition system, may not be disconnected;

(b) one tail lamp;

(c) either a tail lamp or a separate lamp which illuminates the rear license plate with a white light;

(d) one red reflector on the rear, either separate or as part of the tail lamp;

(e) one stop lamp;

(f) a braking system, other than parking brake, in accordance with Section 41-6a-1623;

(g) a horn or warning device in accordance with Section 41-6a-1625;

(h) a muffler and emission control system in accordance with Section 41-6a-1626;

(i) a mirror in accordance with Section 41-6a-1627; and

(j) tires in accordance with Section 41-6a-1636.

(2) The department may require an inspection of the braking system on a motor-driven cycle and disapprove a braking system that is not designed or constructed as to insure reasonable and reliable performance in actual use in accordance with Section 41-6a-1623.

(3) A person may not operate a motor-driven cycle on a highway if the department has disapproved the braking system on the motor-driven cycle.

(4) (a) Upon notice to the party to whom the motor-driven cycle is registered, the department may suspend the registration of a motor-driven cycle if the department has disapproved the braking system under this section.

(b) The Motor Vehicle Division shall, under Subsection 41-1a-109(1)(e) or (2), refuse to register a motor-driven cycle if it has reason to believe the motor-driven cycle has a braking system disapproved under this section. 2005

41-6a-1507. Replica vehicles — Defined — Compliance with all laws and standards — Exceptions — Revocation — Signed statement required.

(1) (a) As used in this section, "replica vehicle" means a motor vehicle:

(i) with a body that is or resembles the body of a motor vehicle with a model year prior to 1975; and

(ii) that may have a significant drive train or equipment upgrade.

(b) A replica vehicle is for occasional pleasure rides and is not used for general daily transportation.

(c) A replica vehicle does not include a vintage vehicle as defined in Section 41-21-1, nor a special interest vehicle as defined in Section 41-1a-102.

(2) Except as specified under this section, a replica vehicle shall meet all safety, emissions, registration, insurance, fees, and taxes required under this title.

(3) (a) Except as provided in Subsection (3)(b), all safety equipment of a replica vehicle shall at least meet the safety standards applicable to the model year of the vehicle being replicated. Any replacement equipment shall comply with the design standards of the replacement equipment's manufacture.

(b) A replica vehicle shall comply with current vehicle brake and stopping standards.

(c) A replica vehicle shall comply with emissions standards applicable to the model year of the engine of the replica vehicle.

(4) The tax commission may revoke the registration of a replica vehicle for failure to comply with this section.

(5) The owner of a replica vehicle shall provide a signed statement certifying that the replica vehicle is owned and operated for the purposes enumerated in this section to the safety inspection and emissions inspection station in order to qualify for the exceptions provided under this section. 2005

41-6a-1508. Low-speed vehicle.

(1) Except as otherwise provided in this section, a low-speed vehicle is considered a motor vehicle for purposes of the Utah Code including requirements for:

(a) traffic rules under Title 41, Chapter 6a, Traffic Code;

(b) driver licensing under Title 53, Chapter 3, Uniform Driver License Act;

(c) motor vehicle insurance under Title 41, Chapter 12a, Financial Responsibility of Motor Vehicle Owners and Operators Act;

(d) vehicle registration, titling, odometer statements, vehicle identification numbers, license plates, and registration fees under Title 41, Chapter 1a, Motor Vehicle Act;

(e) vehicle taxation under Title 59, Chapter 13, Motor and Special Fuel Tax Act, and fee in lieu of property taxes or in lieu fees under Section 59-2-405;

(f) motor vehicle dealer licensing under Title 41, Chapter 3, Motor Vehicle Business Regulation Act;

(g) motor vehicle safety inspection requirements under Section 53-8-205; and

(h) safety belt requirements under Title 41, Chapter 6a, Part 18, Motor Vehicle Safety Belt Usage Act.

(2) (a) A low-speed vehicle shall comply with federal safety standards established in 49 C.F.R. 571.500 and shall be equipped with:

(i) headlamps;

(ii) front and rear turn signals, tail lamps, and stop lamps;

(iii) turn signal lamps;

(iv) reflex reflectors one on the rear of the vehicle and one on the left and right side and as far to the rear of the vehicle as practical;

(v) a parking brake;

(vi) a windshield that meets the standards under Section 41-6a-1635, including a device for cleaning rain, snow, or other moisture from the windshield;

(vii) an exterior rearview mirror on the driver's side and either an interior rearview mirror or an exterior rearview mirror on the passenger side;

(viii) a speedometer and odometer; and

(ix) braking for each wheel.

(b) A low-speed vehicle that complies with this Subsection (2) and Subsection (3) and that is not altered from the manufacturer is considered to comply with equipment requirements under Part 16, Vehicle Equipment.

(3) A person may not operate a low-speed vehicle that has been structurally altered from the original manufacturer's design.

(4) A user of a low-speed vehicle shall obtain an annual clean special fuel tax certificate for each low-speed vehicle as required under Section 59-13-304.

(5) A low-speed vehicle is exempt from a motor vehicle emissions inspection and maintenance program requirements under Section 41-6a-1642.

(6) (a) Except to cross a highway at an intersection, a low-speed vehicle may not be operated on a highway with a posted speed limit of more than 35 miles per hour.

(b) In addition to the restrictions under Subsection (6)(a), a highway authority, may prohibit or restrict the operation of a low-speed vehicle on any highway under its jurisdiction, if the highway authority determines the prohibition or restriction is necessary for public safety.

(7) A person may not operate a low-speed vehicle on a highway without displaying on the rear of the low-speed vehicle, a slow-moving vehicle identification emblem that complies with the Society of Automotive Engineers standard SAE J943.

(8) A person who violates Subsection (2), (3), (6), or (7) is guilty of a class C misdemeanor.   2005

PART 16

VEHICLE EQUIPMENT

41-6a-1601. Operation of unsafe or improperly equipped vehicles on public highways — Exceptions.

(1) (a) A person may not operate or move and an owner may not cause or knowingly permit to be operated or moved on a highway a vehicle or combination of vehicles which:

(i) is in an unsafe condition that may endanger any person;

(ii) does not contain those parts or is not at all times equipped with lamps and other equipment in proper condition and adjustment as required in this chapter;

(iii) is equipped in any manner in violation of this chapter; or

(iv) emits pollutants in excess of the limits allowed under the rules of the Air Quality Board created under Title 19, Chapter 2, Air Conservation Act, or under rules made by local health departments.

(b) A person may not do any act forbidden or fail to perform any act required under this chapter.

(2) (a) In accordance with Title 63, Chapter 46a, Utah Administrative Rulemaking Act, and in coordination with the rules made under Section 53-8-204, the department shall make rules setting minimum standards covering the design, construction, condition, and operation of vehicle equipment for safely operating a motor vehicle on the highway as required under this part.

(b) The rules under Subsection (2)(a):

(i) shall conform as nearly as practical to Federal Motor Vehicle Safety Standards and Regulations;

(ii) may incorporate by reference, in whole or in part, the federal standards under Subsection (2)(b)(i) and nationally recognized and readily available standards and codes on motor vehicle safety;

(iii) shall include provisions for the issuance of a permit under Section 41-6a-1602;

(iv) shall include standards for the emergency lights of authorized emergency vehicles;

(v) may provide standards and specifications applicable to lighting equipment on school buses consistent with:

(A) this part;

(B) federal motor vehicle safety standards; and

(C) current specifications of the Society of Automotive Engineers;

(vi) shall provide procedures for the submission, review, approval, disapproval, issuance of an approval certificate, and expiration or renewal of approval of any part as required under Section 41-6a-1620;

(vii) shall establish specifications for the display or etching of a vehicle identification number on a vehicle;

(viii) shall establish specifications in compliance with this part for a flare, fusee, electric lantern, warning flag, or portable reflector used in compliance with this part;

(ix) shall establish approved safety and law enforcement purposes when video display is visible to the motor vehicle operator; and

(x) shall include standards and specifications for both original equipment and parts included when a vehicle is manufactured and aftermarket equipment and parts included after the original manufacture of a vehicle.

(c) The following standards and specifications for vehicle equipment are adopted:

(i) 49 C.F.R. 571.209 related to safety belts;

(ii) 49 C.F.R. 571.213 related to child restraint devices;

(iii) 49 C.F.R. 393, 396, and 396 Appendix G related to commercial motor vehicles and trailers operated in interstate commerce;

(iv) 49 C.F.R. 571 Standard 108 related to lights and illuminating devices; and

(v) 40 C.F.R. 82.30 through 82.42 and Part 82, Subpart B, Appendix A and B related to air conditioning equipment.

(3) Nothing in this chapter or the rules made by the department prohibit:

(a) equipment required by the United States Department of Transportation; or

(b) the use of additional parts and accessories on a vehicle not inconsistent with the provisions of this chapter or the rules made by the department.

(4) Except as specifically made applicable, the provisions of this chapter and rules of the department with respect to equipment required on vehicles do not apply to:

(a) implements of husbandry;

(b) road machinery;

(c) road rollers;

(d) farm tractors;

(e) motorcycles;

(f) motor-driven cycles;

(g) vehicles moved solely by human power;

(h) off-highway vehicles registered under Section 41-22-3 either:

(i) on a highway designated as open for off-highway vehicle use; or

(ii) in the manner prescribed by Section 41-22-10.3; or

(i) off-highway implements of husbandry when operated in the manner prescribed by Subsections 41-22-5.5 (3) through (5).

(5) The vehicles referred to in Subsections (4)(h) and (i) are subject to the equipment requirements of Title 41, Chapter 22, Off-highway Vehicles, and the rules made under that chapter.

(6) (a) A federal motor vehicle safety standard supersedes any conflicting provision of this chapter.

(b) The department:

(i) shall report any conflict found under Subsection (6)(a) to the appropriate committees or officials of the Legislature; and

(ii) may adopt a rule to replace the superseded provision.   2005

41-6a-1602. Permit to operate vehicle in violation of equipment regulations.

(1) The department may issue a permit which will allow temporary operation of a vehicle in violation of the provisions of this chapter or in violation of rules made by the department.

(2) The permit shall be carried in the vehicle and shall be displayed upon demand of a magistrate or peace officer.

(3) (a) The department may limit the time, manner, or duration of operation and may otherwise prescribe conditions of operation that are necessary to protect the safety of highway users or efficient movement of traffic.

(b) Any conditions shall be stated on the permit and a person may not violate them.   2005

41-6a-1603. Lights and illuminating devices — Duty to display — Time.

(1) (a) The operator of a vehicle shall turn on the lamps or lights of the vehicle on a highway at any time from a half hour after sunset to a half hour before sunrise and at any other time when, due to insufficient light or unfavorable atmospheric conditions, persons and vehicles on the highway are not clearly discernible at a distance of 1,000 feet ahead.

(b) The lights, lighted lamps, and other lamps and illuminating devices under Subsection (1)(a) shall be lighted as respectively required for different classes of vehicles, subject to the exceptions for parked vehicles under Section 41-6a-1607.

(2) Whenever a requirement is made as to distance from which certain lamps and devices shall render objects visible or within which the lamps or devices shall be visible, the provisions apply during the times specified under Subsection (1)(a) for a vehicle without load on a straight, level, unlighted highway under normal atmospheric conditions, unless a different time or condition is expressly stated.

(3) Whenever a requirement is made as to the mounted height of lamps or devices it shall mean from the center of the lamp or device to the level ground upon which the vehicle stands when the vehicle is without a load.   2005

41-6a-1604. Motor vehicle head lamp, tail lamps, stop lamps, and other lamps — Requirements.

(1) A motor vehicle shall be equipped with at least two head lamps with at least one on each side of the front of the motor vehicle.

(2) (a) A motor vehicle, trailer, semitrailer, pole trailer, and any other vehicle which is being drawn at the end of a combination of vehicles, shall be equipped with at least two tail lamps and two or more red reflectors mounted on the rear.

(b) (i) Except as provided under Subsections (2)(b)(ii), (2)(c), and Section 41-6a-1612, all stop lamps or other lamps and reflectors mounted on the rear of a vehicle shall display or reflect a red color.

(ii) A turn signal or hazard warning light may be red or yellow.

(c) Either a tail lamp or a separate lamp shall be so constructed and placed as to illuminate with a white light the rear registration plate.

(3) (a) A motor vehicle, trailer, semitrailer, and pole trailer shall be equipped with two or more stop lamps and flashing turn signals.

(b) A supplemental stop lamp may be mounted on the rear of a vehicle, if the supplemental stop lamp:

(i) emits a red light;

(ii) is mounted:

(A) and constructed so that no light emitted from the device, either direct or reflected, is visible to the driver;

(B) not lower than 15 inches above the roadway; and

(C) on the vertical center line of the vehicle; and

(iii) is the size, design, and candle power that conforms to federal standards regulating stop lamps.

(4) (a) Each head lamp, tail lamp, supplemental stop lamp, flashing turn lamp, other lamp, or reflector required under this part shall comply with the requirements and limitations established under Section 41-6a-1601.

(b) The department, by rules made under Section 41-6a-1601, may require trucks, buses, motor homes, motor vehicles with truck-campers, trailers, semitrailers, and pole trailers to have additional lamps and reflectors.

(5) The department, by rules made under Section 41-6a-1601, may allow:

(a) one tail lamp on any vehicle equipped with only one when it was made;

(b) one stop lamp on any vehicle equipped with only one when it was made; and

(c) passenger cars and trucks with a width less than 80 inches and manufactured or assembled prior to January 1, 1953, need not be equipped with electric turn signal lamps.   2005

41-6a-1605. Vehicles operated in combination.

If a motor vehicle and other vehicles are operated in combination during the time that lights are required under Section 41-6a-1603, a lamp that is obscured by another vehicle of the combination is not required to be lighted.   2005

41-6a-1606. Load extending beyond rear of vehicle — Duty to display lamps and reflectors or flag.

(1) If a load on a vehicle extends to the rear four feet or more beyond the bed or body of the vehicle, the operator shall display lamps, reflectors, or flags at the extreme rear end of the load in accordance with this section.

(2) During hours of darkness as specified in Section 41-6a-1603, the following shall be displayed:

(a) two red reflectors located so as to indicate maximum width; and

(b) two red lamps, one on each side with one red lamp located so as to indicate maximum overhang.

(3) (a) At a time other than the time indicated under Subsection (2), on a vehicle having a load which extends beyond its sides or more than four feet beyond its rear, red flags shall be displayed marking the extremities of the load, at each point where a lamp or reflector is required under Subsection (2).

(b) The red flags shall be at least 12 inches square.   2005

41-6a-1607. Parking lamps required — Use when vehicle parked at night — Head lamps dimmed.

(1) (a) A vehicle shall be equipped with one or more parking lamps.

(b) The parking lamps shall comply with requirements established under Section 41-6a-1601.

(2) A vehicle parked or stopped on a roadway or shoulder, whether attended or unattended, shall display lighted parking lamps if conditions exist as specified under Subsection 41-6a-1603(1)(a).

(3) Any lighted head lamps on a parked vehicle shall be dimmed.   2005

41-6a-1608. Farm tractors and equipment — Lamps and reflectors — Slow-moving vehicle emblem.

(1) (a) A farm tractor and a self-propelled implement of husbandry manufactured or assembled after January 1, 1970, shall be equipped with hazard warning lights of a type described in Section 41-6a-1611.

(b) The hazard warning lights shall be:

(i) visible from a distance of not less than 1,000 feet to the front and rear in normal sunlight; and

(ii) displayed whenever a farm tractor or self-propelled implement of husbandry is operated on a highway.

(2) (a) A farm tractor and a self-propelled implement of husbandry manufactured or assembled after January 1, 1970, shall be equipped with lamps and reflectors as required under this section.

(b) A farm tractor and a self-propelled implement of husbandry manufactured or assembled prior to January 1, 1970 shall be equipped with lamps and reflectors as required in this section if operated on a highway under the conditions specified under Subsection 41-6a-1603(1)(a).

(3) Subject to the provisions of Subsection (2), a farm tractor and an implement of husbandry shall be equipped with:

(a) at least two head lamps;

(b) at least one red lamp visible when lighted from a distance of not less than 1,000 feet to the rear mounted as far to the left of the center of the vehicle as practicable; and

(c) at least two red reflectors visible from all distances within 600 feet to 100 feet to the rear when directly in front of lawful lower beams of head lamps.

(4) Towed farm equipment or a towed implement of husbandry shall be equipped with lamps and reflectors as provided under this Subsection (4), if operated on a highway under the conditions specified under Subsection 41-6a-1603(1)(a).

(a) If the towed unit or its load extends more than four feet to the rear of the tractor or obscures any light on a tractor, the towed unit shall be equipped on the rear with at least two red reflectors visible from all distances within 600 feet to 100 feet to the rear when directly in front of lawful lower beams of head lamps.

(b) (i) If the towed unit extends more than four feet to the left of the center line of the tractor, the towed unit shall be equipped on the front with an amber reflector visible from all distances within 600 feet to 100 feet to the front when directly in front of lawful lower beams of head lamps.

(ii) The reflector under Subsection (4)(b)(i) shall be positioned to indicate, as nearly as practicable, the extreme left projection of the towed unit.

(c) If the towed unit or its load obscures either of the vehicle hazard warning lights on the tractor, the towed unit shall be equipped with vehicle hazard warning lights described in Subsection (1).

(5) (a) The two red reflectors required under Subsections (3) and (4) shall be positioned to show, as nearly as practicable, the extreme width of the vehicle or combination of vehicles as viewed from the rear of the vehicle or combination of vehicles.

(b) Reflective tape or paint may be used in lieu of the reflectors required under this section.

(6) (a) A slow-moving vehicle emblem mounted on the rear is required on:

(i) a farm tractor and a self-propelled implement of husbandry designed for operation at speeds not in excess of 25 miles per hour; or

(ii) towed farm equipment or a towed implement of husbandry if the towed unit or any load on it obscures the slow-moving vehicle emblem on the farm tractor or self-propelled implement of husbandry.

(b) The slow-moving vehicle emblem's design, size, mounting, and position on the vehicle required under this Subsection (6), shall:

(i) comply with current standards and specifications of the American Society of Agricultural Engineers; and

(ii) be approved by the department.

(c) A slow-moving vehicle identification emblem may not be:

(i) used except as required under this section and Sections 41-6a-1508 and 41-6a-1609; or

(ii) displayed on a vehicle traveling at a speed in excess of 25 miles per hour.   2005

41-6a-1609. Lamps and reflectors on vehicles not otherwise specified — Slow-moving vehicle identification emblems on animal-drawn vehicles.

(1) An animal-drawn vehicle, a vehicle under Section 41-6a-1604, and a vehicle not specifically required by the provisions of other sections in this chapter to be equipped with lamps or other lighting devices, shall be equipped with lamps or other lighting devices if operated on a highway under the conditions specified under Subsection 41-6a-1603(1)(a) as follows:

(a) at least one lamp displaying a white light visible from a distance of not less than 1,000 feet to the front of the vehicle; and

(b) (i) two lamps displaying red light visible from a distance of not less than 1,000 feet to the rear of the vehicle; or

(ii) one lamp displaying a red light visible from a distance of not less than 1,000 feet to the rear and two red reflectors visible from all distances of 600 to 100 feet to the rear when illuminated by the lawful lower beams of head lamps.

(2) An animal-drawn vehicle shall at all times be equipped with a slow-moving vehicle identification emblem as provided under Section 41-6a-1608. 2005

41-6a-1610. Spot lamps.

(1) A motor vehicle may not be equipped with more than two spot lamps.

(2) A lighted spot lamp may not be aimed or used so that any part of the high intensity portion of the beam strikes the windshield, or any windows, mirror, or occupant of another vehicle in use.

(3) This section does not apply to spot lamps on an authorized emergency vehicle. 2005

41-6a-1611. Hazard warning lamps.

(1) A vehicle manufactured with hazard warning lights, shall be equipped with hazard warning lights for the purpose of warning the operators of other vehicles of the presence of a vehicular traffic hazard requiring the exercise of unusual care in approaching, overtaking, or passing.

(2) In addition to the requirements of Subsection (1), a bus, truck, truck-tractor, trailer, semitrailer, or pole trailer shall be equipped with hazard warning lights if the bus, truck, truck-tractor, trailer, semitrailer, or pole trailer is 80 inches or more in overall width or 30 feet or more in overall length.

(3) The hazard warning lights required under this section shall comply with rules made by the department under Section 41-6a-1601. 2005

41-6a-1612. Back-up lamps — Side marker lamps.

(1) (a) A motor vehicle may be equipped with one or more back-up lamps either separately or in combination with other lamps.

(b) A back-up lamp or lamps may not be lighted when the motor vehicle is in forward motion.

(c) A lighted back-up lamp shall emit a white light.

(2) A vehicle may be equipped with one or more side marker lamps that may be flashed in conjunction with turn or vehicular hazard warning signals.

(3) A back-up lamp and side marker lamp under this section shall comply with rules made by the department under Section 41-6a-1601. 2005

41-6a-1613. Lamp required for operation of vehicle on highway or adjacent shoulder — Dimming of lights.

(1) (a) If a vehicle is operated on a highway or shoulder adjacent to the highway under the conditions specified under Subsection 41-6a-1603(1)(a), the operator of a vehicle shall use a high or low beam distribution of light or composite beam except as provided under Subsection (1)(c).

(b) Except as provided under Subsection (1)(c), the distribution of light or composite beam shall be directed high enough and of sufficient intensity to reveal persons and vehicles at a safe distance in advance of the vehicle.

(c) The operator of a vehicle shall use a low beam distribution of light or composite beam if the vehicle approaches:

(i) an oncoming vehicle within 500 feet; or

(ii) another vehicle from the rear within 300 feet.

(2) (a) The low beam distribution of light or composite beam shall be aimed to avoid projecting glaring rays into the:

(i) eyes of an oncoming operator; or

(ii) rearview mirror of a vehicle approached from the rear.

(b) A vehicle is not in violation of Subsection (2)(a) if:

(i) the vehicle has not been significantly altered from the original vehicle manufacturer's specifications; or

(ii) the glaring rays result from road contour or a temporary load on the vehicle. 2005

41-6a-1614. Head lamps on farm tractors — Motor vehicles sold prior to certain date.

(1) Head lamp systems which provide only a single distribution of light shall be permitted on:

(a) a farm tractor; and

(b) other motor vehicles manufactured and sold prior to July 1, 1980.

(2) Head lamp systems authorized under this section shall comply with rules made by the department under Section 41-6a-1601. 2005

41-6a-1615. Repealed. 1979

41-6a-1616. High intensity beams — Red or blue lights — Flashing lights — Color of rear lights and reflectors.

(1) (a) Except as provided under Subsection (1)(b), under the conditions specified under Subsection 41-6a-1603(1)(a), a lighted lamp or illuminating device on a vehicle, which projects a beam of light of an intensity greater than 300 candlepower shall be directed so that no part of the high intensity portion of the beam will strike the level of the roadway on which the vehicle stands at a distance of more than 75 feet from the vehicle.

(b) The provisions of Subsection (1)(a) do not apply to head lamps, spot lamps, auxiliary lamps, flashing turn signals, hazard warning lamps, and school bus warning lamps.

(c) A motor vehicle on a highway may not have more than a total of four lamps lighted on the front of the vehicle including head lamps, auxiliary lamps, spot lamps, or any other lamp if the lamp projects a beam of an intensity greater than 300 candlepower.

(2) Except for an authorized emergency vehicle and a school bus, a person may not operate or move any vehicle or equipment on a highway with a lamp or device capable of displaying a red or blue light that is visible from directly in front of the center of the vehicle.

(3) A person may not use flashing lights on a vehicle except for:

(a) taillights of bicycles under Section 41-6a-1114;

(b) authorized emergency vehicles under rules made by the department under Section 41-6a-1601;

(c) turn signals under Section 41-6a-1604;

(d) hazard warning lights under Sections 41-6a-1608 and 41-6a-1611;

(e) school bus flashing lights under Section 41-6a-1302; and

(f) vehicles engaged in highway construction or maintenance under Section 41-6a-1617.

(4) A person may not use a rotating light on any vehicle other than an authorized emergency vehicle.

2005

41-6a-1617. Highway construction and maintenance vehicles — Transportation department to adopt rules for lighting.

(1) In accordance with Title 63, Chapter 46a, Utah Administrative Rulemaking Act, the Department of Transportation shall make rules providing specifications governing the design and use of special flashing lights on vehicles engaged in highway construction or maintenance operations.

(2) The standards and specifications adopted under Subsection (1) shall correlate with, and where possible conform to, the standards set forth in the most recent edition of the "Manual on Uniform Traffic Control Devices for Streets and Highways" and other standards issued or endorsed by the federal highway administrator.

(3) The operator of a vehicle engaged in highway construction or maintenance operations shall comply with rules adopted under this section.   2005

41-6a-1618. Sale or use of unapproved lighting equipment or devices prohibited.

(1) Except as provided under Subsection (2), a person may not use, have for sale, sell, or offer for sale for use on or as a part of the equipment of a motor vehicle, trailer, semitrailer, or pole trailer any head lamp, auxiliary fog lamp, rear lamp, signal lamp, required reflector, or any parts of that equipment which tend to change the original design or performance, unless the part or equipment complies with the specifications adopted under Section 41-6a-1601.

(2) The provisions of Subsection (1) do not apply to equipment in actual use prior to July 1, 1979 or to replacement parts of this equipment.

(3) A person may not use on a motor vehicle, trailer, semitrailer, or pole trailer any lamps under this section unless the lamps are mounted, adjusted, and aimed in accordance with this part.   2005

41-6a-1619. Sale of unapproved equipment prohibited — Trademark or brand name.

(1) A person shall not sell or offer for sale any equipment or parts that do not comply with the standards adopted under Section 41-6a-1601 including any lamp, reflector, hydraulic brake fluid, seat belt, safety glass, emergency disablement warning device, studded tire, motorcycle helmet, eye protection device for motorists, or red rear bicycle reflector.

(2) Any equipment described under Subsection (1) or Section 41-6a-1618 or any package containing the equipment shall bear the manufacturer's trademark or brand name unless it complies with identification requirements of the United States Department of Transportation or other federal agencies.   2005

41-6a-1620. Departmental approval of lighting devices or safety equipment.

(1) (a) The department shall approve or disapprove any lighting device or other safety equip-

ment, component or assembly of a type for which approval is specifically required under this part.

(b) The department shall consider the part for approval within a reasonable time after approval has been requested.

(2) (a) The department shall establish a procedure for the submission, review, approval, disapproval, issuance of an approval certificate, and the expiration or renewal of approval for any part under Subsection (1).

(b) (i) The procedure may provide for submission of the part to the American Association of Motor Vehicle Administrators as the agent of the department.

(ii) Approval issued by the association under Subsection (1)(b)(i) shall have the same force and effect as if it has been issued by the department.

(c) The department shall maintain and publish lists of all parts, devices, components, or assemblies which have been approved by the department.

(d) A part approved under this section is valid unless revoked under Section 41-6a-1621 or unless the department requires it to be renewed under rules made under Section 41-6a-1601.

2005

41-6a-1621. Departmental hearings — Compliance of approved devices — Revocation of approval — Reapproval.

(1) If the department has reason to believe that a part approved under Section 41-6a-1620 should no longer be approved, the department shall, upon 30 days' notice to the applicant to whom approval was issued, conduct a hearing on the question of whether the part should remain approved.

(2) (a) After the hearing, the department shall determine whether the device meets the requirements of the applicable standard.

(b) If the device does not meet those requirements, the department shall give notice to the applicant to whom the approval was issued of the department's intention to revoke the approval.

(c) If the applicant to whom the approval was issued fails to satisfy the department that the device being sold or offered for sale meets the applicable standard within 90 days of the notice of the department's intention to revoke the approval, the department shall revoke the approval.

(3) When an approval has been revoked under this section:

(a) the department:

(i) shall require the withdrawal of all the parts from the market; and

(ii) may require that all devices sold since the notification of the department's intention to revoke the approval be replaced by parts that are approved.

(b) A part that has been revoked under this section may not be approved again unless a new application and approval is received.

(c) The department may require that as a condition for a new approval of the same or similar part all previously revoked parts are effectively recalled and removed from the market.   2005

41-6a-1622. Purchase and testing of equipment by department — Prohibition against sale of substandard devices — Injunction — Review — Appeal.

(1) The department may purchase and test equipment described in Section 41-6a-1619 to determine

whether it complies with the standards under this part.

(2) Upon identification of unapproved or substandard devices being sold or offered for sale, the department shall give notice to the person selling them that the person is in violation of Section 41-6a-1619 and that selling or offering them for sale is prohibited.

(3) (a) In order to enforce the prohibition against the sale or offer for sale of unapproved or substandard devices, the department may file a petition in the district court of the county in which the person maintains a place of business to enjoin any further sale or offer of sale of the unapproved or substandard product.

(b) An injunction under Subsection (3)(a) shall be issued upon a prima facie showing that:

(i) the part is of a type required to be approved by the department under this part;

(ii) the part has not been approved; and

(iii) the part is being sold or offered for sale.

(4) (a) Any person enjoined under Subsection (3) may file a petition for a review of the court's order in the county in which the injunction was issued.

(b) A copy of the petition shall be served on the department and the department shall have 30 days after the service to file an answer, but the petition shall not act as a stay of the injunction.

(c) At the hearing on the petition, the judge shall sit without intervention of a jury and shall only receive evidence as to whether the parts in question:

(i) are of a type for which approval by the department is required;

(ii) have not been approved; and

(iii) are being sold or offered for sale in violation of Section 41-6a-1619.

(d) Following a hearing under Subsection (4)(c), the injunction shall be continued if the court finds that each condition under Subsection (4)(c) has been met.

(5) Either party may appeal the decision of the court in the same manner as in other civil appeals from the district court.   2005

41-6a-1623. Braking systems required — Adoption of performance requirements by department.

(1) A motor vehicle and a combination of vehicles shall have a service braking system which will stop the motor vehicle or combination of vehicles within:

(a) 40 feet from an initial speed of 20 miles per hour on a level, dry, smooth, hard surface; or

(b) a shorter distance as may be specified by the department in accordance with federal standards.

(2) A motor vehicle and a combination of vehicles shall have a parking brake system:

(a) adequate to hold the motor vehicle or combination of vehicles on any grade on which it is operated under all conditions of loading on a surface free from snow, ice or loose material; or

(b) which complies with performance standards issued by the department in accordance with federal standards.

(3) In addition to the requirements of Subsections (1) and (2), if necessary for safe operation, the department may by rule require additional braking systems in accordance with federal standards.   2005

41-6a-1624. Failure to repair a damaged or deployed airbag — Penalty.

(1) As used in this section, "person" includes the owner or lessee of a motor vehicle, a body shop, dealer, remanufacturer, salvage rebuilder, vehicle service maintenance facility, or any entity or individual engaged in the repair or replacement of motor vehicles or airbag passive restraint systems.

(2) Except as provided under Subsection (3), if a repair to a vehicle to be used on a highway is initiated, a person who has actual knowledge that a motor vehicle's airbag passive restraint system is damaged or has been deployed may not fail or cause another person to fail to fully restore, arm, and return to original operating condition, the motor vehicle's airbag passive restraint system.

(3) In the course of repairing a motor vehicle, a person who has actual knowledge that the motor vehicle's airbag passive restraint system is damaged or has been deployed shall notify the owner or lessee of the vehicle, in a form approved by the Department of Public Safety, that the failure to repair and fully restore the motor vehicle's airbag passive restraint system is a class B misdemeanor.

(4) Unless acting under a dismantling permit under Section 41-1a-1010, a person may not remove or modify a motor vehicle's airbag passive restraint system with the intent of rendering the motor vehicle's airbag passive restraint system inoperable.

(5) A person who violates this section is guilty of a class B misdemeanor.   2005

41-6a-1625. Horns and warning devices — Emergency vehicles.

(1) (a) A motor vehicle operated on a highway shall be equipped with a horn or other warning device in good working order.

(b) The horn or other warning device:

(i) shall be capable of emitting sound audible under normal conditions from a distance of not less than 200 feet; and

(ii) may not emit an unreasonably loud or harsh sound or a whistle.

(c) The operator of a motor vehicle:

(i) when reasonably necessary to insure safe operation, shall give audible warning with the horn; and

(ii) except as provided under Subsection (1)(c)(i), may not use the horn on a highway.

(2) Except as provided under this section, a vehicle may not be equipped with and a person may not use on a vehicle a siren, whistle, or bell.

(3) (a) A vehicle may be equipped with a theft alarm signal device if it is arranged so that it cannot be used by the operator as an ordinary warning signal.

(b) A theft alarm signal device may:

(i) use a whistle, bell, horn or other audible signal; and

(ii) not use a siren.

(4) (a) An authorized emergency vehicle shall be equipped with a siren, whistle, or bell capable of emitting sound audible under normal conditions from a distance of not less than 500 feet.

(b) The type of sound shall be approved by the department based on standards adopted by rules under Section 41-6a-1601.

(c) The siren on an authorized emergency vehicle may not be used except:

(i) when the vehicle is operated in response to an emergency call; or

(ii) in the immediate pursuit of an actual or suspected violator of the law.

(d) The operator of an authorized emergency vehicle shall sound the siren in accordance with this section when reasonably necessary to warn pedestrians and other vehicle operators of the approach of the authorized emergency vehicle.

2005

41-6a-1626. Mufflers — Prevention of noise, smoke, and fumes — Air pollution control devices.

(1) (a) A vehicle shall be equipped, maintained, and operated to prevent excessive or unusual noise.

(b) A motor vehicle shall be equipped with a muffler or other effective noise suppressing system in good working order and in constant operation.

(c) A person may not use a muffler cut-out, bypass, or similar device on a vehicle.

(2) (a) Except while the engine is being warmed to the recommended operating temperature, the engine and power mechanism of a:

(i) gasoline-powered motor vehicle may not emit visible contaminants during operation;

(ii) diesel engine manufactured on or after January 1, 1973, may not emit visible contaminants of a shade or density darker than 20% opacity; and

(iii) diesel engine manufactured before January 1, 1973, may not emit visible contaminants of a shade or density darker than 40% opacity.

(b) A person who violates the provisions of Subsection (2)(a) is guilty of a class C misdemeanor.

(3) (a) A motor vehicle equipped by a manufacturer with air pollution control devices shall maintain the devices in good working order and in constant operation.

(b) For purposes of the first sale of a vehicle at retail, an air pollution control device may be substituted for the manufacturer's original device if the substituted device is at least as effective in the reduction of emissions from the vehicle motor as the air pollution control device furnished by the manufacturer of the vehicle as standard equipment for the same vehicle class.

(c) A person who renders inoperable an air pollution control device on a motor vehicle is guilty of a class B misdemeanor.

(4) Subsection (3) does not apply to a motor vehicle altered and modified to use clean fuel, as defined under Section 59-13-102, when the emissions from the modified or altered motor vehicle are at levels that comply with existing state or federal standards for the emission of pollutants from a motor vehicle of the same class.

2005

41-6a-1627. Mirrors.

(1) (a) A motor vehicle shall be equipped with a mirror mounted on the left side of the vehicle.

(b) A mirror under Subsection (1)(a) shall be located to reflect to the driver a view of the highway to the rear of the vehicle.

(2) (a) Except for a motorcycle, in addition to the mirror required under Subsection (1), a motor vehicle shall be equipped with a mirror mounted either inside the vehicle approximately in the center or outside the vehicle on the right side.

(b) The mirror under Subsection (2)(a) shall be located to reflect to the driver a view of the highway to the rear of the vehicle.

2005

41-6a-1628. Seat belts — Design and installation — Specifications or requirements.

(1) A safety belt installed in a vehicle to accommodate an adult person shall be designed and installed to prevent or materially reduce the movement of the person using the safety belt in the event of collision or upset of the vehicle.

(2) A person may not sell, offer, or keep for sale a safety belt or attachments for use in a vehicle that does not comply with the specifications under Section 41-6a-1601.

2005

41-6a-1629. Vehicles subject to Sections 41-6a-1629 through 41-6a-1633 — Definitions.

(1) As used in Sections 41-6a-1629 through 41-6a-1633:

(a) "Frame" means the main longitudinal structural members of the chassis of the vehicle or, for vehicles with unitized body construction, the lowest longitudinal structural member of the body of the vehicle.

(b) "Frame height" means the vertical distance between the ground and the lowest point on the frame. The distance is measured when the vehicle is unladen and on a level surface.

(c) "Gross vehicle weight rating (GVWR)" means the original manufacturer's gross vehicle weight rating, whether or not the vehicle is modified by use of parts not originally installed by the original manufacturer.

(d) "Manufacturer" means any person engaged in manufacturing or assembling new motor vehicles utilizing new parts or components, or a person defined as a manufacturer in current applicable Federal Motor Vehicle Safety Standards and Regulations.

(e) "Mechanical alteration" or "mechanical lift" means modification or alteration of the axles, chassis, suspension, or body by any means, including tires and wheels, and excluding any load, which affects the frame height of the motor vehicle.

(f) "O.E.M." means original equipment manufacturer.

(g) "Original equipment" means an item of motor vehicle equipment, including tires, which were installed in or on a motor vehicle or available as an option for the particular vehicle from the original manufacturer at the time of its delivery to the first purchaser.

(h) "Wheel track" means the shortest distance between the center of the tire treads on the same axle. On vehicles having dissimilar axle widths, the axle with the widest distance is used for all calculations.

(2) (a) Except as provided in Subsection (2)(b), the provisions of Sections 41-6a-1629 through 41-6a-1633 apply to all motor vehicles operated or parked on a highway.

(b) The provisions of Sections 41-6a-1629 through 41-6a-1633 do not apply to the following vehicles:

(i) implements of husbandry;

(ii) farm tractors;

(iii) road machinery;

(iv) road rollers; and

(v) historical vehicles or horseless carriages that have been restored as near to original condition as is reasonably possible.

2005

41-6a-1630. Standards applicable to vehicles.

(1) The following standards apply to vehicles under Sections 41-6a-1629 through 41-6a-1633:

(a) A replacement part and equipment used in a mechanical alteration shall be:

(i) designed and capable of performing the function for which they are intended; and

(ii) equal to or greater in strength and durability than the original parts provided by the original manufacturer.

(b) Except for original equipment, a person may not use spacers to increase wheel track width of a vehicle.

(c) A person may not use axle blocks to alter the suspension on the front axle of a vehicle.

(d) A person may not stack two or more axle blocks of a vehicle.

(2) (a) In doubtful or unusual cases, or to meet specific industrial requirements, personnel of the Utah Highway Patrol shall inspect the vehicle to determine:

(i) the road worthiness and safe condition of the vehicle; and

(ii) whether it complies with Sections 41-6a-1629 through 41-6a-1633.

(b) If the vehicle complies, the Utah Highway Patrol shall issue a permit of approval that shall be carried in the vehicle.

(3) (a) Upon notice to the party to whom the motor vehicle is registered, the department shall suspend the registration of any motor vehicle equipped, altered, or modified in violation of Sections 41-6a-1629 through 41-6a-1633.

(b) The Motor Vehicle Division shall, under Subsection 41-1a-109(1)(e) or (2), refuse to register any motor vehicle it has reason to believe is equipped, altered, or modified in violation of Sections 41-6a-1629 through 41-6a-1633.   2005

41-6a-1631. Prohibitions.

(1) A person may not operate on a highway a motor vehicle that is mechanically altered or changed:

(a) in any way that may under normal operation:

(i) cause the motor vehicle body or chassis to come in contact with the roadway;

(ii) expose the fuel tank to damage from collision; or

(iii) cause the wheels to come in contact with the body;

(b) in any manner that may impair the safe operation of the vehicle;

(c) so that any part of the vehicle other than tires, rims, and mudguards are less than three inches above the ground;

(d) to a frame height of more than 24 inches for a motor vehicle with a gross vehicle weight rating of less than 4,500 pounds;

(e) to a frame height of more than 26 inches for a motor vehicle with a gross vehicle weight rating of at least 4,500 pounds and less than 7,500 pounds;

(f) to a frame height of more than 28 inches for a motor vehicle with a gross vehicle weight rating of at least 7,500 pounds;

(g) by stacking or attaching vehicle frames (one from on top of or beneath another frame); or

(h) so that the lowest portion of the body floor is raised more than three inches above the top of the frame.

(2) If the wheel track is increased beyond the O.E.M. specification, the top 50% of the tires shall be covered by the original fenders, by rubber, or other flexible fender extenders under any loading condition.   2005

41-6a-1632. Bumpers.

(1) A motor vehicle shall be equipped with a bumper on both front and rear of the motor vehicle, except a motor vehicle that was not originally designed or manufactured with a bumper or bumpers.

(2) (a) On a motor vehicle required to have bumpers under Subsection (1), a bumper shall be:

(i) at least 4.5 inches in vertical height;

(ii) centered on the vehicle's center line; and

(iii) extend no less than the width of the respective wheel track distance.

(b) A bumper shall be securely mounted, horizontal load bearing, and attached to the motor vehicle's frame to effectively transfer impact when engaged.

(3) If a motor vehicle is originally or later equipped with a bumper, the bumper shall:

(a) be maintained in operational condition; and

(b) comply with this section.   2005

41-6a-1633. Mudguards or flaps at rear wheels of trucks, trailers, truck tractors, or altered motor vehicles — Exemptions.

(1) (a) Except as provided in Subsection (2), when operated on a highway, the following vehicles shall be equipped with wheel covers, mudguards, flaps, or splash aprons behind the rearmost wheels to prevent, as far as practicable, the wheels from throwing dirt, water, or other materials on other vehicles:

(i) a vehicle that has been altered:

(A) from the original manufacturer's frame height; or

(B) in any other manner so that the motor vehicle's wheels may throw dirt, water, or other materials on other vehicles;

(ii) any truck with a gross vehicle weight rating of 10,500 pounds or more;

(iii) any truck tractor; and

(iv) any trailer or semitrailer with an unladen weight of 750 pounds or more.

(b) The wheel covers, mudguards, flaps, or splash aprons shall:

(i) be at least as wide as the tires they are protecting;

(ii) be directly in line with the tires; and

(iii) have a ground clearance of not more than 50% of the diameter of a rear-axle wheel, under any conditions of loading of the motor vehicle.

(2) Wheel covers, mudguards, flaps, or splash aprons are not required:

(a) if the motor vehicle, trailer, or semitrailer is designed and constructed so that the requirements of Subsection (1) are accomplished by means of fenders, body construction, or other means of enclosure; or

(b) on a vehicle operated or driven during fair weather on well-maintained, hard-surfaced roads if the motor vehicle:

(i) was made in America prior to 1935;

(ii) is registered as a vintage vehicle; or

(iii) is a replica vehicle as defined under Section 41-6a-1507.

(3) Except as provided in Subsection (2)(b), rear wheels not covered at the top by fenders, bodies, or other parts of the vehicle shall be covered at the top by protective means extending rearward at least to the center line of the rearmost axle.   2005

41-6a-1634. Safety chains on towed vehicles required — Exceptions.

(1) A towed vehicle shall be coupled by means of a safety chain, cable or equivalent device, in addition to the regular trailer hitch or coupling.

(2) Except as provided under Subsection (3), a safety chain, cable or equivalent device shall be:

(a) securely connected with the chassis of the towing vehicle, the towed vehicle, and the drawbar;

(b) of sufficient material and strength to prevent the two vehicles from becoming separated; and

(c) attached to:

(i) have no more slack than is necessary for proper turning;

(ii) the trailer drawbar to prevent it from dropping to the ground; and

(iii) assure the towed vehicle follows substantially in the course of the towing vehicle in case the vehicles become separated.

(3) The provisions of Subsection (2) do not apply to a:

(a) semitrailer having a connecting device composed of a fifth wheel and king pin assembly; or

(b) pole trailer.   2005

41-6a-1635. Windshields and windows — Tinting — Obstructions reducing visibility — Wipers — Prohibitions.

(1) Except as provided in Subsections (2) and (3), a person may not operate a motor vehicle with:

(a) a windshield that allows less than 70% light transmittance;

(b) a front side window that allows less than 43% light transmittance;

(c) any windshield or window that is composed of, covered by, or treated with any material or component that presents a metallic or mirrored appearance; or

(d) any sign, poster, or other nontransparent material on the windshield or side windows of the motor vehicle except:

(i) a certificate or other paper required to be so displayed by law; or

(ii) the vehicle's identification number displayed or etched in accordance with rules made by the department under Section 41-6a-1601.

(2) Nontransparent materials may be used:

(a) along the top edge of the windshield if the materials do not extend downward more than four inches from the top edge of the windshield or beyond the AS-1 line whichever is lowest;

(b) in the lower left-hand corner of the windshield provided they do not extend more than three inches to the right of the left edge or more than four inches above the bottom edge of the windshield; or

(c) on the rear windows including rear side windows located behind the vehicle operator.

(3) A windshield or other window is considered to comply with the requirements of Subsection (1) if the windshield or other window meets the federal statutes and regulations for motor vehicle window composition, covering, light transmittance, and treatment.

(4) Except for material used on the windshield in compliance with Subsections (2)(a) and (b), a motor vehicle with tinting or nontransparent material on any window shall be equipped with rear-view mirrors mounted on the left side and on the right side of the motor vehicle to reflect to the driver a view of the highway to the rear of the motor vehicle.

(5) (a) (i) The windshield on a motor vehicle shall be equipped with a device for cleaning rain, snow, or other moisture from the windshield.

(ii) The device shall be constructed to be operated by the operator of the motor vehicle.

(b) A windshield wiper on a motor vehicle shall be maintained in good working order.

(6) A person may not have for sale, sell, offer for sale, install, cover, or treat a windshield or window in violation of this section.

(7) Notwithstanding this section, any person subject to the federal Motor Vehicle Safety Standards, including motor vehicle manufacturers, distributors, dealers, importers, and repair businesses, shall comply with the federal standards on motor vehicle window tinting.   2005

41-6a-1636. Tires which are prohibited — Regulatory powers of state transportation department — Winter use of studs — Special permits — Tread depth.

(1) A solid rubber tire on a vehicle shall have rubber on its entire traction surface at least one inch thick above the edge of the flange of the entire periphery.

(2) A person may not operate or move on a highway a motor vehicle, trailer, or semitrailer having a metal tire in contact with the roadway.

(3) Except as otherwise provided in this section, a person may not have a tire on a vehicle that is moved on a highway that has on the tire's periphery a block, stud, flange, cleat, or spike or any other protuberances of any material other than rubber which projects beyond the tread of the traction surface of the tire.

(4) In accordance with Title 63, Chapter 46a, Utah Administrative Rulemaking Act, the Department of Transportation may make rules to permit the use of tires on a vehicle having protuberances other than rubber, if the department concludes that protuberances do not:

(a) damage the highway significantly; or

(b) constitute a hazard to life, health, or property.

(5) Notwithstanding any other provision of this section, a person may use:

(a) a tire with protuberances consisting of tungsten carbide studs on a vehicle if the studs:

(i) are only used during the winter periods of October fifteenth through December thirty-first and January first through March thirty-first of each year;

(ii) do not project beyond the tread of the traction surface of the tire more than .050 inches; and

(iii) are not used on a vehicle with a maximum gross weight in excess of 9,000 pounds unless the vehicle is an emergency vehicle or school bus;

(b) farm machinery with tires having protuberances which will not injure the highway; and

(c) tire chains of reasonable proportions on a vehicle when required for safety because of snow, ice, or other conditions tending to cause a vehicle to skid.

(6) Notwithstanding any other provision of this chapter, a highway authority, for a highway under its jurisdiction, may issue special permits authorizing the operation on a highway of:

(a) farm tractors;

(b) other farm machinery; or

(c) traction engines or tractors having movable tracks with transverse corrugations on the periphery of the movable tracks.

(7) (a) A person may not operate a vehicle if one or more of the tires in use on the vehicle:

(i) is in an unsafe operating condition; or

(ii) has a tread depth less than ²⁄₃₂ inch measured in any two adjacent tread grooves at three equally spaced intervals around the circumference of the tire.

(b) The measurement under Subsection (7)(a) may not be made at the location of any tread wear indicator, tie bar, hump, or fillet.

(8) A person in the business of selling tires may not sell or offer for sale for highway use any tire prohibited for use under Subsection (7).   2005

41-6a-1637. Flares, fusees, or electric lanterns and flags — Alternative reflector units — Duty to carry in trucks and buses — Requirements.

(1) Except as provided under Subsection (2) and unless the vehicle is carrying the equipment required under this section, a person may not operate a truck, bus or truck-tractor, or a motor vehicle towing a house trailer:

(a) on a highway outside an urban district; or

(b) on a divided highway during hours of darkness specified under Section 41-6a-1603.

(2) (a) The vehicle shall carry at least:

(i) three flares;

(ii) three red electric lanterns;

(iii) three portable red emergency reflectors; or

(iv) three red-burning fusees.

(b) The equipment required under Subsections (2)(a)(i) and (ii) shall be capable of being seen and distinguished at a distance of not less than 600 feet under normal atmospheric conditions during the hours of darkness.

(c) The equipment required under Subsection (2)(a)(iii) shall be capable of reflecting red light clearly visible from a distance of not less than 600 feet under normal atmospheric conditions during the hours of darkness when directly in front of lawful lower beams of head lamps.

(3) A flare, fusee, electric lantern, warning flag, or portable reflector used under this section or Section 41-6a-1638 shall comply with specifications adopted under Section 41-6a-1601.

(4) (a) A person may not operate a motor vehicle used for the transportation of explosives or any cargo tank truck used for the transportation of flammable liquids or compressed gases under the conditions specified under Subsections (1)(a) and (b) unless there is carried in the vehicle:

(i) three red electric lanterns; or

(ii) three portable red emergency reflectors.

(b) A person operating a vehicle specified under Subsection (4)(a) or a vehicle using compressed gas as a motor fuel may not carry in the vehicle a flare, fusee, or signal produced by flame.

(5) A person may not operate a vehicle described under this section on a highway outside of an urban district or on a divided highway during daylight hours unless at least two red flags, not less than 12 inches square, with standards to support the flags are carried in the vehicle.   2005

41-6a-1638. Warning signal around disabled vehicle — Time and place.

(1) (a) When a truck, bus, truck-tractor, trailer, semitrailer, or pole trailer 80 inches or more in over-all width or 30 feet or more in over-all length is stopped on a roadway or adjacent shoulder, the operator shall immediately actuate vehicular hazard warning signal lamps meeting the requirements of Section 41-6a-1611.

(b) The signal lights need not be displayed by a vehicle:

(i) parked lawfully in an urban district;

(ii) stopped lawfully to receive or discharge passengers;

(iii) stopped to avoid conflict with other traffic or to comply with the directions of a peace officer or an official traffic-control device; or

(iv) while the devices specified in Subsections (2) through (6) are in place.

(2) (a) Except as provided in Subsection (3), if a vehicle of a type specified under Subsection (1) is disabled or stopped for more than ten minutes on a roadway outside of an urban district under the conditions specified under Subsection 41-6a-1603(1), the operator of the vehicle shall display the following warning devices:

(i) a lighted fusee, a lighted red electric lantern, or a portable red emergency reflector shall immediately be placed at the traffic side of the vehicle in the direction of the nearest approaching traffic; and

(ii) as soon as possible after placing the warning devices under Subsection (2)(a)(i) but within the burning period of the fusee (15 minutes), the driver shall place three liquid-burning flares (pot torches), or three lighted red electric lanterns, or three portable red emergency reflectors on the roadway in the following order:

(A) one approximately 100 feet from the disabled vehicle in the center of the lane occupied by the vehicle and toward traffic approaching in that lane;

(B) one approximately 100 feet in the opposite direction from the disabled vehicle and in the center of the traffic lane occupied by the vehicle; and

(C) one at the traffic side of the disabled vehicle not less than ten feet rearward or forward of the disabled vehicle in the direction of the nearest approaching traffic.

(b) If a lighted red electric lantern or a red portable emergency reflector has been placed at the traffic side of the vehicle in accordance with Subsection (2)(a)(ii)(A), a rearward lantern or reflector under Subsection (2)(a)(ii)(C) is not required.

(3) If a vehicle specified under this section is disabled, or stopped for more than ten minutes:

(a) within 500 feet of a curve, hillcrest, or other obstruction to view, the warning device in that direction shall be placed to afford ample warning to other users of the highway, but in no case less than 100 feet or more than 500 feet from the disabled vehicle;

(b) on a roadway of a divided highway under the conditions specified under Subsection 41-6a-1603(1), the appropriate warning devices required under Subsections (2) and (4) shall be placed as follows:

(i) one at a distance of approximately 200 feet from the vehicle in the center of the lane occupied by the stopped vehicle and in the direction of traffic approaching in that lane;

(ii) one at a distance of approximately 100 feet from the vehicle, in the center of the lane occupied by the vehicle and in the direction of traffic approaching in that lane; and

(iii) one at the traffic side of the vehicle and approximately ten feet from the vehicle in the direction of the nearest approaching traffic; or

(c) on a roadway outside of an urban district or on the roadway of a divided highway not under the conditions specified under Subsection 41-6a-1603(1), the driver of the vehicle shall display two red flags as follows:

(i) if traffic on the roadway moves in two directions, one flag shall be placed approximately 100 feet to the rear and one flag approximately 100 feet in advance of the vehicle in the center of the lane occupied by the vehicle; or

(ii) on a one-way roadway, one flag shall be placed approximately 100 feet and one flag approximately 200 feet to the rear of the vehicle in the center of the lane occupied by the vehicle.

(4) When a motor vehicle used in the transportation of explosives or any cargo tank truck used for the transportation of any flammable liquid or compressed gas is disabled, or stopped for more than ten minutes, at any time and place specified under Subsection (2) or (3), the operator of the vehicle shall immediately display red electric lanterns or portable red emergency reflectors in the same number and manner as specified in Subsection (2) or (3).

(5) The warning devices specified under Subsections (2) through (4) are not required to be displayed where there is sufficient light to reveal persons and vehicles within a distance of 1,000 feet.

(6) If a vehicle described under this section is stopped entirely off the roadway and on an adjacent shoulder, the warning devices shall be placed, as nearly as practicable, on the shoulder near the edge of the roadway.   2005

41-6a-1639. Hazardous materials — Transportation regulations — Fire extinguishers.

(1) (a) In accordance with Title 63, Chapter 46a, Utah Administrative Rulemaking Act, the Department of Transportation shall make rules for the safe transportation of hazardous materials.

(b) The rules shall adopt by reference or be consistent with current Hazardous Materials Regulations of the United States Department of Transportation.

(c) An adoption by reference under Subsection (1)(b) shall be construed to incorporate amendments thereto as may be made from time to time.

(2) A person operating a vehicle transporting any hazardous material as a cargo or part of a cargo on a highway shall at all times comply with rules made by the Department of Transportation under this section including being:

(a) marked or placarded; and

(b) equipped with fire extinguishers:

(i) of a type, size, and number approved by rule; and

(ii) that are filled, ready for immediate use, and placed at a convenient point on the vehicle.   2005

41-6a-1640. Air conditioning equipment — Requirements.

(1) As used in this section, "air conditioning equipment" means mechanical vapor compression refriger-

ation equipment used to cool the operator or passenger compartment of a motor vehicle.

(2) Air conditioning equipment shall:

(a) be manufactured, installed, and maintained with due regard for the safety of the occupants of the vehicle and the public; and

(b) not contain any refrigerant which is toxic to persons or which is flammable.

(3) A person may not have for sale, offer for sale, sell, or equip any motor vehicle with air conditioning equipment unless it complies with the specifications adopted under Section 41-6a-1601 and this section.

(4) A person may not operate a motor vehicle on a highway if the motor vehicle is equipped with air conditioning equipment unless the air conditioning equipment complies with the specifications adopted under Section 41-6a-1601 and this section.   2005

41-6a-1641. Video display in motor vehicles prohibited if visible to driver — Exceptions.

(1) A motor vehicle may not be operated on a highway if the motor vehicle is equipped with a video display located so that the display is visible to the operator of the vehicle.

(2) This section does not prohibit the use of a video display used exclusively for:

(a) safety or law enforcement purposes if the use is approved by rule of the department under Section 41-6a-1601;

(b) motor vehicle navigation; or

(c) monitoring of equipment and operating systems of the motor vehicle.   2005

41-6a-1642. Emissions inspection — County program.

(1) The legislative body of each county required under federal law to utilize a motor vehicle emissions inspection and maintenance program or in which an emissions inspection and maintenance program is necessary to attain or maintain any national ambient air quality standard shall require:

(a) a certificate of emissions inspection, a waiver, or other evidence the motor vehicle is exempt from emissions inspection and maintenance program requirements be presented:

(i) as a condition of registration or renewal of registration; and

(ii) at other times as the county legislative body may require to enforce inspection requirements for individual motor vehicles, except that the county legislative body may not routinely require a certificate of emission inspection, or waiver of the certificate, more often than required under Subsection (6); and

(b) compliance with this section for a motor vehicle registered or principally operated in the county and owned by or being used by a department, division, instrumentality, agency, or employee of:

(i) the federal government;

(ii) the state and any of its agencies; or

(iii) a political subdivision of the state, including school districts.

(2) (a) The legislative body of a county identified in Subsection (1), in consultation with the Air Quality Board created under Section 19-1-106, shall make regulations or ordinances regarding:

(i) emissions standards;

(ii) test procedures;

(iii) inspections stations;

(iv) repair requirements and dollar limits for correction of deficiencies; and

(v) certificates of emissions inspections.

(b) The regulations or ordinances shall:

(i) be made to attain or maintain ambient air quality standards in the county, consistent with the state implementation plan and federal requirements; and

(ii) may allow for a phase-in of the program by geographical area.

(c) The county legislative body and the Air Quality Board shall give preference to an inspection and maintenance program that is:

(i) decentralized, to the extent the decentralized program will attain and maintain ambient air quality standards and meet federal requirements;

(ii) the most cost effective means to achieve and maintain the maximum benefit with regard to ambient air quality standards and to meet federal air quality requirements as related to vehicle emissions; and

(iii) providing a reasonable phase-out period for replacement of air pollution emission testing equipment made obsolete by the program.

(d) The provisions of Subsection (2)(c)(iii) apply only to the extent the phase-out:

(i) may be accomplished in accordance with applicable federal requirements; and

(ii) does not otherwise interfere with the attainment and maintenance of ambient air quality standards.

(3) The following vehicles are exempt from the provisions of this section:

(a) an implement of husbandry; and

(b) a motor vehicle that:

(i) meets the definition of a farm truck under Section 41-1a-102; and

(ii) has a gross vehicle weight rating of 12,001 pounds or more.

(4) (a) The legislative body of a county identified in Subsection (1) shall exempt a pickup truck, as defined in Section 41-1a-102, with a gross vehicle weight of 12,000 pounds or less from the emission inspection requirements of this section, if the registered owner of the pickup truck provides a signed statement to the legislative body stating the truck is used:

(i) by the owner or operator of a farm located on property that qualifies as land in agricultural use under Sections 59-2-502 and 59-2-503; and

(ii) exclusively for the following purposes in operating the farm:

(A) for the transportation of farm products, including livestock and its products, poultry and its products, floricultural and horticultural products; and

(B) in the transportation of farm supplies, including tile, fence, and every other thing or commodity used in agricultural, floricultural, horticultural, livestock, and poultry production and maintenance.

(b) The county shall provide to the registered owner who signs and submits a signed statement under this section a certificate of exemption from emission inspection requirements for purposes of registering the exempt vehicle.

(5) (a) Subject to Subsection (5)(c), the legislative body of each county required under federal law to utilize a motor vehicle emissions inspection and maintenance program or in which an emissions inspection and maintenance program is necessary to attain or maintain any national ambient air quality standard may require each college or university located in a county subject to this section to require its students and employees who park a motor vehicle not registered in a county subject to this section to provide proof of compliance with an emissions inspection accepted by the county legislative body if the motor vehicle is parked on the college or university campus or property.

(b) College or university parking areas that are metered or for which payment is required per use are not subject to the requirements of this Subsection (5).

(c) The legislative body of a county shall make the reasons for implementing the provisions of this Subsection (5) part of the record at the time that the county legislative body takes its official action to implement the provisions of this Subsection (5).

(6) (a) An emissions inspection station shall issue a certificate of emissions inspection for each motor vehicle that meets the inspection and maintenance program requirements established in rules made under Subsection (2).

(b) The frequency of the emissions inspection shall be determined based on the age of the vehicle as determined by model year and shall be required annually subject to the provisions of Subsection (6)(c).

(c) (i) To the extent allowed under the current federally approved state implementation plan, in accordance with the federal Clean Air Act, 42 U.S.C. Sec. 7401 et seq., the legislative body of a county identified in Subsection (1) shall only require the emissions inspection every two years for each vehicle.

(ii) The provisions of Subsection (6)(c)(i) apply only to a vehicle that is less than six years old on January 1.

(d) If an emissions inspection is only required every two years for a vehicle under Subsection (6)(c), the inspection shall be required for the vehicle in:

(i) odd-numbered years for vehicles with odd-numbered model years; or

(ii) in even-numbered years for vehicles with even-numbered model years.

(7) The emissions inspection shall be required within the same time limit applicable to a safety inspection under Section 41-1a-205.

(8) (a) A county identified in Subsection (1) shall collect information about and monitor the program.

(b) A county identified in Subsection (1) shall supply this information to an appropriate legislative committee, as designated by the Legislative Management Committee, at times determined by the designated committee to identify program needs, including funding needs.

(9) If approved by the county legislative body, a county that had an established emissions inspection fee as of January 1, 2002, may increase the established fee that an emissions inspection station may charge by $2.50 for each year that is exempted from emissions inspections under Subsection (6)(c) up to a $7.50 increase.

41-6a-1643. Development of standardized emissions inspection and maintenance program.

(1) The county legislative body of each county in which an emissions inspection and maintenance program for motor vehicles is implemented to meet National Ambient Air Quality Standards may enter into an agreement under Title 11, Chapter 13, Interlocal Cooperation Act, to develop an emissions inspection and maintenance program that:

(a) requires standardized, computerized testing equipment;

(b) provides for reciprocity, so that a person required to submit an emissions certificate for vehicle registration may obtain an emissions certificate from any county in which a vehicle emissions inspection and maintenance program is in operation; and

(c) requires standardized emissions standards for all counties entering into an agreement under this section.

(2) Emissions standards set under Subsection (1) shall allow all counties identified in Subsection (1) to meet the National Ambient Air Quality Standards.

(3) Each county legislative body entering into an agreement under Subsection (1) shall make regulations or ordinances to implement the emissions inspection and maintenance program developed under Subsection (1).   2005

41-6a-1644. Diesel emissions program — Implementation — Monitoring.

The legislative body of each county required by the comprehensive plan for air pollution control developed by the Air Quality Board under Subsection 19-2-104(3)(e) to use an emissions opacity inspection and maintenance program for diesel-powered motor vehicles shall:

(1) make regulations or ordinances to implement and enforce the requirement established by the Air Quality Board;

(2) collect information about and monitor the program; and

(3) by August 1 of each year supply written information to the Department of Environmental Quality to identify program status.   2005

PART 17

MISCELLANEOUS RULES

41-6a-1701. Backing — When permissible.

(1) The operator of a vehicle may not back the vehicle unless the movement can be made with safety and without interfering with other traffic.

(2) The operator of a vehicle may not back the vehicle on a shoulder or roadway of a limited-access roadway.   2005

41-6a-1702. Sidewalk — Driving prohibited — Exception.

(1) Except for a bicycle or device propelled by human power, a person may not operate a vehicle on a sidewalk or sidewalk area.

(2) The provisions of Subsection (1) do not apply on a driveway.   2005

41-6a-1703. Prohibition as to passenger riding on improper portion of motor vehicle — Exceptions.

(1) A person may not ride and a person operating a motor vehicle may not knowingly permit a person to ride on any portion of a vehicle not designed or intended for the use of passengers.

(2) This provision does not apply to:

(a) a vehicle that is not being operated on a highway;

(b) an employee engaged in the necessary discharge of the employee's duty; or

(c) a person riding within or on a motor vehicle in a space intended for a load on the vehicle.   2005

41-6a-1704. Vehicle door — Prohibited opening.

(1) A person may not open the door of a motor vehicle on a side available to moving traffic unless it can be done safely and without interfering with the movement of other traffic.

(2) A person may not leave a door open on a side of a vehicle available to moving traffic for a period of time longer than necessary to load or unload passengers.   2005

41-6a-1705. Obstruction to driver's view or driving mechanism.

(1) A person may not operate a vehicle when it is loaded or when there are in the front seat more than three persons that:

(a) obstruct the view of the operator to the front or sides of the vehicle;

(b) interfere with the operator's control over the driving mechanism of the vehicle.

(2) A passenger in a vehicle may not ride in a position that interferes with the operator's:

(a) view ahead or to the sides; or

(b) control over the driving mechanism of the vehicle.   2005

41-6a-1706. Occupancy of a trailer or semitrailer while being moved on highway prohibited.

(1) A person may not occupy a trailer or semitrailer while it is being drawn by a motor vehicle on a public highway.

(2) This section does not apply to a:

(a) livestock trailer or livestock semitrailer;

(b) trailer or semitrailer being used for participation in a parade; or

(c) trailer or semitrailer being used in an agricultural operation.   2005

41-6a-1707. Entering intersection, crosswalk, or railroad grade — Sufficient space required.

The operator of a vehicle may not enter an intersection or a marked crosswalk or drive onto any railroad grade crossing unless there is sufficient space on the other side of the intersection, crosswalk, or railroad grade crossing to accommodate the vehicle without obstructing the passage of other vehicles, pedestrians, or railroad trains notwithstanding any traffic-control signal indication to proceed.   2005

41-6a-1708. Driving in canyons and on mountain highways.

The operator of a motor vehicle traveling through defiles or canyons or on mountain highways shall:

(1) hold the motor vehicle under control and as near the right-hand edge of the roadway as reasonably possible; and

(2) except when driving entirely on the right of the center of the roadway, give an audible warning with the horn of the motor vehicle upon approaching any curve where the view is obstructed within a distance of 200 feet along the highway.   2005

41-6a-1709. Coasting prohibited.

(1) The operator of a motor vehicle, when traveling on a downgrade, may not coast with the gears or transmission of the vehicle in neutral.

(2) The operator of a truck or bus, when traveling on a downgrade, may not coast with the clutch disengaged. 2005

41-6a-1710. Following or parking near fire apparatus prohibited.

Except for an authorized emergency vehicle, the operator of a vehicle may not:

(1) follow closer than 500 feet any fire apparatus traveling in response to a fire alarm; or

(2) stop the vehicle within 500 feet of a fire apparatus which has stopped in answer to a fire alarm. 2005

41-6a-1711. Driving over firehose.

The operator of a vehicle may not drive over an unprotected hose of a fire department when laid down on a street, private road, or driveway to be used at a fire or alarm of fire, without the consent of the fire department official in command. 2005

41-6a-1712. Destructive or injurious materials on highways, parks, recreation areas, waterways, or other public or private lands — Throwing lighted material from moving vehicle — Enforcement officers — Litter receptacles required.

(1) A person may not throw, deposit, or discard, or to permit to be dropped, thrown, deposited, or discarded on any public road, highway, park, recreation area, or other public or private land, or waterway, any glass bottle, glass, nails, tacks, wire, cans, barbed wire, boards, trash or garbage, paper or paper products, or any other substance which would or could mar or impair the scenic aspect or beauty of the land in the state whether under private, state, county, municipal, or federal ownership without the permission of the owner or person having control or custody of the land.

(2) A person who drops, throws, deposits, or discards, or permits to be dropped, thrown, deposited, or discarded, on any public road, highway, park, recreation area, or other public or private land or waterway any destructive, injurious, or unsightly material shall:

(a) immediately remove the material or cause it to be removed; and

(b) deposit the material in a receptacle designed to receive the material.

(3) A person distributing commercial handbills, leaflets, or other advertising shall take whatever measures are reasonably necessary to keep the material from littering public or private property or public roadways.

(4) A person removing a wrecked or damaged vehicle from a public road, highway, park, recreation area, or other public or private land shall remove any glass or other injurious substance dropped from the vehicle on the road or highway or in the park, recreation area, or other public or private land.

(5) A person may not throw any lighted material from a moving vehicle.

(6) Except as provided in Section 72-7-409, any person transporting loose cargo by truck, trailer, or other motor vehicle shall secure the cargo in a reasonable manner to prevent the cargo from littering or spilling on both public and private property or public roadways.

(7) A person in charge of a construction or demolition site shall take reasonable steps to prevent the accumulation of litter at the construction or demolition site.

(8) (a) A law enforcement officer as defined in Section 53-13-103, within the law enforcement officer's jurisdiction, shall enforce the provisions of this section.

(b) Each officer in Subsection (8)(a) is empowered to issue citations to a person who violates any of the provisions of this section and may serve and execute all warrants, citations, and other process issued by any court in enforcing this section.

(9) An operator of a park, campground, trailer park, drive-in restaurant, gasoline service station, shopping center, grocery store parking lot, tavern parking lot, parking lots of industrial firms, marina, boat launching area, boat moorage and fueling station, public and private pier, beach, and bathing area shall maintain sufficient litter receptacles on the premises to accommodate the litter that accumulates.

(10) A municipality within its corporate limits and a county outside of incorporated municipalities may enact local ordinances to carry out the provisions of this section. 2005

41-6a-1713. Penalty for littering.

(1) A person who violates any of the provisions of Section 41-6a-1712 is guilty of a class C misdemeanor and shall be fined not less than $100 for each violation.

(2) The sentencing judge may require that the offender devote at least four hours in cleaning up:

(a) litter caused by him; and

(b) existing litter from a safe area designated by the sentencing judge. 2005

41-6a-1714. Warning signs.

The Department of Transportation shall place adequate warning signs wherever it considers proper within the state notifying all persons using the public roads, highways, parks, or recreation areas of the provisions of Sections 41-6a-1712 and 41-6a-1713. 2005

PART 18

MOTOR VEHICLE SAFETY BELT USAGE ACT

41-6a-1801. Short title.

This part is known as the "Motor Vehicle Safety Belt Usage Act." 2005

41-6a-1802. Definitions.

As used in this part:

(1) "Child restraint device" means a child restraint device that meets standards adopted under Section 41-6a-1601.

(2) "Motor vehicle" means a vehicle defined in Section 41-1a-102, except vehicles that are not equipped with safety belts by the manufacturer.

(3) "Safety belt" means a safety belt or seat belt system that meets standards adopted under Section 41-6a-1601.

(4) "Seating position" means any area within the passenger compartment of a motor vehicle in which the manufacturer has installed a safety belt. 2005

41-6a-1803. Driver and passengers — Seat belt or child restraint device required.

(1) The operator of a motor vehicle operated on a highway shall:

(a) wear a properly adjusted and fastened safety belt;

(b) provide for the protection of each person younger than five years of age by using a child restraint device to restrain each person in the manner prescribed by the manufacturer of the device; and

(c) provide for the protection of each person five years of age up to 16 years of age by:

(i) using an appropriate child restraint device to restrain each person in the manner prescribed by the manufacturer of the device; or

(ii) securing, or causing to be secured, a properly adjusted and fastened safety belt on each person.

(2) A passenger who is 16 years of age or older of a motor vehicle operated on a highway shall wear a properly adjusted and fastened safety belt.

(3) If more than one person is not using a child restraint device or wearing a safety belt in violation of Subsection (1), it is only one offense and the driver may receive only one citation.

(4) For a person 19 years of age or older who violates Subsection (1)(a) or (2), enforcement by a state or local law enforcement officer shall be only as a secondary action when the person has been detained for a suspected violation of Title 41, Motor Vehicles, other than Subsection (1)(a) or (2), or for another offense.   2005

41-6a-1804. Exceptions.

(1) This part does not apply to an operator or passenger of:

(a) a motor vehicle manufactured before July 1, 1966;

(b) a motor vehicle in which the operator or passengers possess a written verification from a licensed physician that the person is unable to wear a safety belt for physical or medical reasons; or

(c) a motor vehicle or seating position which is not required to be equipped with a safety belt system under federal law.

(2) This part does not apply to a passenger if all seating positions are occupied by other passengers.
                                              2005

41-6a-1805. Penalty for violation.

(1) (a) A person who violates Section 41-6a-1803 is guilty of an infraction and shall be fined a maximum of $45.

(b) The court shall waive all but $15 of the fine for a violation of Section 41-6a-1803 if a person:

(i) shows evidence of completion of a two-hour course approved by the commissioner of the Department of Public Safety that includes education on the benefits of using a safety belt and child restraint device; and

(ii) if the violation is for an offense under Subsection 41-6a-1803(1)(b), submits proof of acquisition, rental, or purchase of a child restraint device.

(2) Points for a motor vehicle reportable violation, as defined under Section 53-3-102, may not be assessed against a person for a violation of Section 41-6a-1803.   2005

41-6a-1806. Compliance — Civil litigation.

The failure to use a child restraint device or to wear a safety belt:

(1) does not constitute contributory or comparative negligence on the part of a person seeking recovery for injuries; and

(2) may not be introduced as evidence in any civil litigation on the issue of negligence, injuries, or the mitigation of damages.   2005

PART 19

TRAFFIC VIOLATIONS BY DIPLOMATS

41-6a-1901. Applicability — Law enforcement officer duties — Documents and records — Notice to Department of State.

(1) As used in this section, "diplomat" means an individual who:

(a) has a driver license issued by the United States Department of State; or

(b) claims immunities or privileges under 22 U.S.C. Sections 254a through 258a with respect to:

(i) a moving traffic violation under this title or a moving traffic violation of an ordinance of a local authority; or

(ii) operating a motor vehicle while committing any of the following offenses:

(A) automobile homicide under Section 76-5-207;

(B) manslaughter under Section 76-5-205;

(C) negligent homicide under Section 76-5-206;

(D) aggravated assault under Section 76-5-103; or

(E) reckless endangerment under Section 76-5-112.

(2) A law enforcement officer who stops a motor vehicle and has probable cause to believe that the driver is a diplomat that has committed a violation described under Subsection (1)(b)(i) or (ii) shall:

(a) as soon as practicable, contact the United States Department of State in order to verify the driver's status and immunity, if any;

(b) record all relevant information from any driver license or identification card, including a driver license or identification card issued by the United States Department of State; and

(c) within five working days after the date the officer stops the driver, forward all of the following to the Department of Public Safety:

(i) if the driver is involved in a vehicle accident, the vehicle accident report;

(ii) if a citation or other charging document was issued to the driver, a copy of the citation or other charging document; and

(iii) if a citation or other charging document was not issued to the driver, a written report of the incident.

(3) The Department of Public Safety shall:

(a) file each vehicle accident report, citation or other charging document, and incident report that the Department of Public Safety receives under this section;

(b) keep convenient records or make suitable notations showing each:

(i) conviction;

(ii) finding of responsibility; and

(iii) vehicle accident; and

(c) within five working days after receipt, send a copy of each document and record described in Subsection (3) to the Bureau of Diplomatic Security, Office of Foreign Missions, of the United States Department of State.

(4) This section does not prohibit or limit the application of any law to a criminal or motor vehicle violation committed by a diplomat.   2005

CHAPTER 7

PUBLICLY OWNED MOTOR VEHICLES [REPEALED AND RENUMBERED]

Section
41-7-1 to 41-7-2. Repealed.
41-7-3. Renumbered.
41-7-4 to 41-7-8. Repealed.

41-7-1 to 41-7-2. Repealed. 1987, 1996

41-7-3. Renumbered as § 53-8-211. 1993

41-7-4 to 41-7-8. Repealed. 1996

CHAPTER 8

DRIVING BY MINORS

Section
41-8-1. Operation of vehicle by persons under 16 prohibited — Exceptions for off-highway vehicles, and off-highway implements of husbandry.
41-8-2. Operation of vehicle by persons under 17 during night hours prohibited — Exceptions.
41-8-3. Operation of vehicle by persons under 16 and six months — Passenger limitations — Exceptions — Penalties.

41-8-1. Operation of vehicle by persons under 16 prohibited — Exceptions for off-highway vehicles, and off-highway implements of husbandry.

(1) A person under 16 years of age, whether resident or nonresident of this state, may not operate a motor vehicle upon any highway of this state.

(2) This section does not apply to a person operating:

(a) a motor vehicle under a permit issued under Section 53-3-210 or 53A-13-208;

(b) an off-highway vehicle registered under Section 41-22-3 either:

(i) on a highway designated as open for off-highway vehicle use; or

(ii) in the manner prescribed by Section 41-22-10.3; or

(c) an off-highway implement of husbandry in the manner prescribed by Subsections 41-22-5.5(3) through (5). 2003

41-8-2. Operation of vehicle by persons under 17 during night hours prohibited — Exceptions.

(1) In addition to the provisions of Title 53, Chapter 3, Uniform Driver License Act, a person younger than 17 years of age, whether resident or nonresident of this state, may not operate a motor vehicle upon any highway of this state between the hours of 12:00 a.m. and 5:00 a.m.

(2) It is an affirmative defense to a charge under Subsection (1) that the person is operating a motor vehicle:

(a) accompanied by a licensed driver at least 21 years of age who is occupying a seat next to the driver;

(b) for the driver's employment, including the trip to and from the driver's residence and the driver's employment;

(c) to and from the driver's religion-sponsored activity or own school-sponsored activity and the driver's residence;

(d) on assignment of a farmer or rancher and the driver is engaged in an agricultural operation; or

(e) in an emergency.

(3) In addition to any penalties imposed under Title 53, Chapter 3, Uniform Driver License Act, a violation of this section is a class C misdemeanor. 1999

41-8-3. Operation of vehicle by persons under 16 and six months — Passenger limitations — Exceptions — Penalties.

(1) In addition to the provisions of Title 53, Chapter 3, Uniform Driver License Act, a person, whether resident or nonresident of this state, may not operate a motor vehicle upon any highway of this state with any passenger who is not an immediate family member of the driver until the earlier of:

(a) six months from the date the person's driver license was issued; or

(b) the person reaches 18 years of age.

(2) It is an affirmative defense to a charge under Subsection (1) that the person is operating a motor vehicle:

(a) accompanied by a licensed driver at least 21 years of age who is occupying a seat next to the driver;

(b) on assignment of a farmer or rancher and the driver is engaged in an agricultural operation;

(c) with the written consent of the driver's parent or guardian to and from the driver's school, own school-sponsored activity, or religion-sponsored activity and the driver's residence; or

(d) in an emergency.

(3) In addition to any penalties imposed under Title 53, Chapter 3, Uniform Driver License Act, a violation of this section is a class C misdemeanor.

(4) Enforcement of this section by state or local law enforcement officers shall be only as a secondary action when an operator of a motor vehicle has been detained for a suspected violation of Title 41, other than this section, or for another offense. 2001

CHAPTER 9

GUEST STATUTE [REPEALED]

41-9-1, 41-9-2. Repealed. 1988

CHAPTER 10

STATE VEHICLE DEPARTMENT

Section
41-10-1. State Tax Commission designated vehicle department.

41-10-1. State Tax Commission designated vehicle department.

The State Tax Commission is hereby designated as the vehicle department of this state referred to in Chapters 43, 44 and 45, Laws of Utah, 1933. 1953

CHAPTER 11

MOTOR FUELS [REPEALED]

41-11-1 to 41-11-93. Repealed.
1953, 1971, 1979, 1981, 1986, 1987

Section
41-12a-806. Restricted Account — Creation — Funding — Interest — Purposes.

PART 1

GENERAL PROVISIONS

41-12a-101. Short title.

This chapter may be cited as the "Financial Responsibility of Motor Vehicle Owners and Operators Act."

1985

41-12a-102. References to former provisions.

References to the former "Safety Responsibility Act" under former Title 41, Chapter 12, are considered to refer to the corresponding provisions under this chapter.

1985

41-12a-103. Definitions.

As used in this chapter:

(1) "Department" means the Department of Public Safety.

(2) "Judgment" means any judgment that is final by:

(a) expiration without appeal of the time within which an appeal might have been perfected; or

(b) final affirmation on appeal, rendered by a court of competent jurisdiction of any state or of the United States, upon a cause of action for damages:

(i) arising out of the ownership, maintenance, or use of any motor vehicle, including damages for care and loss of services because of bodily injury to or death of any person, or because of injury to or destruction of property including the loss of use of the property; or

(ii) on a settlement agreement.

(3) "License" or "license certificate" have the same meanings as under Section 53-3-102.

(4) (a) "Motor vehicle" means every self-propelled vehicle that is designed for use upon a highway, including trailers and semitrailers designed for use with other motorized vehicles.

(b) "Motor vehicle" does not include traction engines, road rollers, farm tractors, tractor cranes, power shovels, and well drillers, and every vehicle that is propelled by electric power obtained from overhead wires but not operated upon rails.

(5) "Nonresident" means every person who is not a resident of Utah.

(6) "Nonresident's operating privilege" means the privilege conferred upon a person who is not a resident of Utah by the laws of Utah pertaining to the operation by him of a motor vehicle, or the use of a motor vehicle owned by him, in Utah.

(7) "Operator" means every person who is in actual physical control of a motor vehicle.

(8) "Owner" means:

(a) a person who holds legal title to a motor vehicle;

(b) a lessee in possession;

(c) a conditional vendee or lessee if a motor vehicle is the subject of a conditional sale or lease with the right of purchase upon performance of the conditions stated in the agreement and with an immediate right of possession in the conditional vendee or lessee; or

(d) a mortgagor if a motor vehicle is the subject of a mortgage with the mortgagor entitled to possession.

(9) "Owner's or operator's security," "owner's security," or "operator's security" means any of the following:

(a) an insurance policy or combination of policies conforming to Section 31A-22-302, which is issued by an insurer authorized to do business in Utah;

(b) a surety bond issued by an insurer authorized to do a surety business in Utah in which the surety is subject to the minimum coverage limits and other requirements of policies conforming to Section 31A-22-302, which names the department as a creditor under the bond for the use of persons entitled to the proceeds of the bond;

(c) a deposit with the state treasurer of cash or securities complying with Section 41-12a-406;

(d) maintaining a certificate of self-funded coverage under Section 41-12a-407;

(e) a policy conforming to Section 31A-22-302 issued by the Risk Management Fund created in Section 63A-4-201.

(10) "Registration" means the issuance of the certificates and registration plates issued under the laws of Utah pertaining to the registration of motor vehicles.

(11) "Self-insurance" has the same meaning as provided in Section 31A-1-301.

1993

41-12a-104. Rules of construction.

(1) If a person maintains owner's security under this chapter, it does not limit his liability to the face amount of the owner's security.

(2) Nothing in this chapter prevents the plaintiff in any action at law from relying for relief upon the other processes provided by law.

(3) This chapter is cumulative with the requirements of the laws of this state requiring policies of motor vehicle insurance against liability. This subsection does not preclude compliance through a single policy which, by its terms or by an appropriate endorsement, satisfies the requirements of both applicable laws.

1986

PART 2

ADMINISTRATION

41-12a-201. Administration of laws under Title 41, Chapter 12a — Compliance with Administrative Procedures Act.

(1) The department shall administer and enforce the provisions of this chapter and may adopt rules as necessary for its administration.

(2) The department shall comply with the procedures and requirements of Title 63, Chapter 46b, in its adjudicative proceedings.

1987

41-12a-202. Access to accident reports.

(1) Accident reports and supplemental information as required under this chapter are protected and are for the confidential use of the department and other state, local, or federal government agencies and may be disclosed only as provided in Section 41-6a-404.

(2) (a) Any person entitled to the disclosure of an accident report, as provided in Section 41-6a-404, may obtain a photocopy by paying the department a fee established under Section 63-38-3.2.

(b) These fees shall be deposited in the General Fund.

2005

PART 3

OWNER'S OR OPERATOR'S SECURITY REQUIREMENT

41-12a-301. Definition — Requirement of owner's or operator's security — Exceptions.

(1) As used in this section:

(a) "highway" has the same meaning as provided in Section 41-1a-102; and

(b) "quasi-public road or parking area" has the same meaning as provided in Section 41-6a-214.

(2) Except as provided in Subsection (5):

(a) every resident owner of a motor vehicle shall maintain owner's or operator's security in effect at any time that the motor vehicle is operated on a highway or on a quasi-public road or parking area within the state; and

(b) every nonresident owner of a motor vehicle that has been physically present in this state for:

(i) 90 or fewer days during the preceding 365 days shall maintain the type and amount of owner's or operator's security required in his place of residence, in effect continuously throughout the period the motor vehicle remains within Utah; or

(ii) more than 90 days during the preceding 365 days shall thereafter maintain owner's or operator's security in effect continuously throughout the period the motor vehicle remains within Utah.

(3) (a) Except as provided in Subsection (5), the state and all of its political subdivisions and their respective departments, institutions, or agencies shall maintain owner's or operator's security in effect continuously for their motor vehicles.

(b) Any other state is considered a nonresident owner of its motor vehicles and is subject to Subsection (2)(b).

(4) The United States, any political subdivision of it, or any of its agencies may maintain owner's or operator's security in effect for their motor vehicles.

(5) Owner's or operator's security is not required for any of the following:

(a) off-highway vehicles registered under Section 41-22-3 when operated either:

(i) on a highway designated as open for off-highway vehicle use; or

(ii) in the manner prescribed by Section 41-22-10.3;

(b) off-highway implements of husbandry operated in the manner prescribed by Subsections 41-22-5.5(3) through (5);

(c) electric assisted bicycles as defined under Section 41-6a-102;

(d) motor assisted scooters as defined under Section 41-6a-102; or

(e) personal motorized mobility device as defined under Section 41-6a-102.   2005

41-12a-302. Operating motor vehicle without owner's or operator's security — Penalty.

(1) Any owner of a motor vehicle on which owner's or operator's security is required under Section 41-12a-301, who operates his vehicle or permits it to be operated on a highway in this state without owner's security being in effect is guilty of a class B misdemeanor, and the fine shall be not less than:

(a) $400 for a first offense; and

(b) $1,000 for a second and subsequent offense within three years of a previous conviction or bail forfeiture.

(2) (a) Except as provided under Subsection (2)(b), any other person who operates a motor vehicle upon a highway in Utah with the knowledge that the owner does not have owner's security in effect for the motor vehicle is also guilty of a class B misdemeanor, and the fine shall be not less than:

(i) $400 for a first offense; and

(ii) $1,000 for a second and subsequent offense within three years of a previous conviction or bail forfeiture.

(b) A person that has in effect owner's security on a Utah-registered motor vehicle or its equivalent that covers the operation, by the person, of the motor vehicle in question is exempt from this Subsection (2).   1998

41-12a-303. Condition to obtaining registration, license plates, or safety inspection.

The owner of a motor vehicle required to maintain owner's security under Section 41-12a-301 may be required to swear or affirm, in a manner specified by the State Tax Commission, or present other reasonable evidence that he has owner's security in effect at the time of registering, obtaining license plates for, or a safety inspection of the motor vehicle.   2001

41-12a-303.2. Evidence of owner's or operator's security to be carried when operating motor vehicle — Defense — Penalties.

(1) As used in this section:

(a) "Division" means the Motor Vehicle Division of the State Tax Commission.

(b) "Registration materials" means the evidences of motor vehicle registration, including all registration cards, license plates, temporary permits, and nonresident temporary permits.

(2) (a) (i) A person operating a motor vehicle shall:

(A) have in the person's immediate possession evidence of owner's or operator's security for the motor vehicle the person is operating; and

(B) display it upon demand of a peace officer.

(ii) A person is exempt from the requirements of Subsection (2)(a)(i) if the person is operating:

(A) a government-owned or leased motor vehicle; or

(B) an employer-owned or leased motor vehicle and is driving it with the employer's permission.

(b) Evidence of owner's or operator's security includes any one of the following:

(i) a copy of the operator's valid:

(A) insurance policy;

(B) insurance policy declaration page;

(C) binder notice;

(D) renewal notice; or

(E) card issued by an insurance company as evidence of insurance;

(ii) a certificate of insurance issued under Section 41-12a-402;

(iii) a certified copy of a surety bond issued under Section 41-12a-405;

(iv) a certificate of the state treasurer issued under Section 41-12a-406;

(v) a certificate of self-funded coverage issued under Section 41-12a-407; or

(vi) information that the vehicle or driver is insured from the Uninsured Motorist Identification Database Program created under Title 41, Chapter 12a, Part 8.

(c) Evidence of owner's or operator's security from the Uninsured Motorist Identification Database Program described under Subsection (2)(b)(vi) supercedes any evidence of owner's or operator's security described under Subsection (2)(b)(i)(D) or (E).

(3) It is an affirmative defense to a charge under this section that the person had owner's or operator's security in effect for the vehicle the person was operating at the time of the person's citation or arrest.

(4) (a) Evidence of owner's or operator's security as defined under Subsection (2)(b) except Subsections (2)(b)(i)(D) and (E) or a written statement from an insurance producer or company verifying that the person had the required motor vehicle insurance coverage on the date specified is considered proof of owner's or operator's security for purposes of Subsection (3) and Section 41-12a-804.

(b) The court considering a citation issued under this section shall allow the evidence or a written statement under Subsection (4)(a) and a copy of the citation to be faxed or mailed to the clerk of the court to satisfy Subsection (3).

(c) The notice under Section 41-12a-804 shall specify that the written statement under Subsection (4)(a) and a copy of the notice shall be faxed or mailed to the designated agent to satisfy the proof of owner's or operator's security required under Section 41-12a-804.

(5) A violation of this section is a class B misdemeanor, and the fine shall be not less than:

(a) $400 for a first offense; and

(b) $1,000 for a second and subsequent offense within three years of a previous conviction or bail forfeiture.

(6) Upon receiving notification from a court of a conviction for a violation of this section, the department:

(a) shall suspend the person's driver license; and

(b) may not renew the person's driver license or issue a driver license to the person until the person gives the department proof of owner's or operator's security.

(i) This proof of owner's or operator's security shall be given by any of the ways required under Section 41-12a-401.

(ii) This proof of owner's or operator's security shall be maintained with the department for a three-year period.

(iii) An insurer that provides a certificate of insurance as provided under Section 41-12a-402 or 41-12a-403 may not terminate the insurance policy unless notice of termination is filed with the department no later than ten days after termination as required under Section 41-12a-404.

(iv) If a person who has canceled the certificate of insurance applies for a license within three years from the date proof of owner's or operator's security was originally required, the department shall refuse the application unless the person reestablishes proof of owner's or operator's security and maintains the proof for the remainder of the three-year period. 2003

41-12a-303.3. Providing false evidence of owner's or operator's security — Penalty.

A person who provides evidence of owner's or operator's security to a peace officer under Section 41-12a-303.2 knowing or having reason to believe that the evidence of owner's or operator's security is false or that it is evidence of owner's or operator's security that is not in effect is guilty of a class B misdemeanor. 1994

41-12a-304. No-fault tort immunity ineffective.

The owner of a motor vehicle on which owner's or operator's security is required under Section 41-12a-301 who fails to have the security in effect at the time of an accident does not have immunity from tort liability under Subsection 31A-22-309(1). This owner is personally liable for the payment of the benefits provided for under Section 31A-22-307 to persons entitled to receive them under Section 31A-22-308. 1985

41-12a-305. Assigned risk plan.

Section 31A-22-310 applies to an assigned risk plan. This continues the assigned risk plan established under former Section 41-12-35, with any modifications from Title 31A. 1985

41-12a-306. Claims adjustment by persons with owner's or operator's security other than insurance.

(1) An owner or operator of a motor vehicle with respect to whom owner's or operator's security is maintained by a means other than an insurance policy under Subsection 41-12a-103(9)(a), shall refer all bodily injury claims against the owner's or operator's security to an independent adjuster licensed under Title 31A, Chapter 26, Insurance Adjusters, or to an attorney.

(2) Unless otherwise provided by contract, any motor vehicle claim adjustment expense incurred by a person maintaining owner's or operator's security by a means other than an insurance policy under Subsection 41-12a-103(9)(a), shall be paid by the person who maintains this type of owner's or operator's security.

(3) Owners and operators of motor vehicles maintaining owner or operator's security by a means other than an insurance policy under Subsection 41-12a-103(9)(a) are subject to the claim adjustment provisions of Title 31A, Chapter 26, Part 3, Claim Practices, in connection with claims against such persons which arise out of the ownership, maintenance, or use of a motor vehicle.

(4) In addition to other penalties and remedies available for failure to abide by this section, the department may require any person violating this section to maintain owner's or operator's security only in the manner specified under Subsection 41-12a-103(9)(a). 2004

PART 4

PROOF OF OWNER'S OR OPERATOR'S SECURITY

41-12a-401. Means of providing proof of owner's or operator's security.

(1) Whenever proof of owner's or operator's security is required under this chapter, it may be provided by filing with the department any of the following:

(a) a certificate of insurance under Section 41-12a-402 or 41-12a-403;

(b) a copy of a surety bond under Section 41-12a-405;

(c) a certificate of deposit of money or securities issued by the state treasurer under Section 41-12a-406; or

(d) a certificate of self-funded coverage under Section 41-12a-407.

(2) Whenever the term "proof of financial responsibility" is used in this title, it shall be read as "proof of owner's or operator's security." 1991

41-12a-402. Insurance certificate as proof of owner's or operator's security — Resident.

Proof of owner's or operator's security may be furnished by filing with the department the written certificate of any insurer licensed in Utah certifying that there is in effect an insurance policy or combination of policies conforming to Section 31A-22-302 for the benefit of the person required to furnish proof of owner's or operator's security. This certificate shall be furnished to the department in the form of an SR-22 issued by any insurer licensed in Utah. The certificate shall give each policy number and the effective date of each policy. The effective date of the policy may not be later than the effective date of the certificate. The certificate shall designate by explicit description or by appropriate reference all motor vehicles covered, unless the policy is issued to a person who is not the owner of a motor vehicle. Certificates filed under this section continue in force until cancelled under Section 41-12a-404, or until the requirement for a certificate is waived under Section 41-12a-411. 1985

41-12a-403. Insurance certificate as proof of owner's or operator's security — Nonresident.

(1) The nonresident owner of a motor vehicle not registered in Utah may give proof of owner's or operator's security by filing with the department the written certificate of an insurer licensed in the state in which the motor vehicle described in the certificate is registered, or if the nonresident does not own a motor vehicle, then in the state in which the insured resides, provided the certificate otherwise conforms to the provisions of this chapter. The department shall accept the certificate if the insurer:

(a) executes a power of attorney authorizing the department to accept service on its behalf of notice or process in any action arising out of a motor vehicle accident in Utah; and

(b) agrees in writing that the policies certified are considered to conform with the provisions required under Sections 31A-22-303 and 31A-22-304.

(2) If an insurer which is not licensed in Utah but which has qualified to furnish proof of owner's or operator's security under Subsection (1), defaults in any such undertaking or agreement, the department may not thereafter accept as proof of security any certificate of the insurer, so long as the default continues. 1985

41-12a-404. Limitation on cancellation of coverage specified in certificate.

When an insurer has certified an insurance policy under Sections 41-12a-402 or 41-12a-403, the policy may not be terminated unless notice of termination is filed with the department no later than ten days after termination. However, this type of policy which is subsequently procured and certified shall, on the effective date of its certificate, terminate the insurance previously certified. 1985

41-12a-405. Surety bond as proof of owner's or operator's security.

(1) Proof of owner's or operator's security may be furnished by filing with the department a copy of a surety bond, certified by the surety, which conforms to Subsection 41-12a-103(9)(b). The bond may not be canceled except after ten days' written notice to the department.

(2) If a judgment rendered against the principal within the coverage of the bond is not satisfied within 60 days after judgment becomes final, the judgment creditor may, for his own use and benefit and at his sole expense, bring an action in the name of the department against the surety executing the bond. 1991

41-12a-406. State treasurer's certificate as proof of owner's or operator's security.

(1) Proof of owner's or operator's security may be furnished by delivering to the department the certificate of the state treasurer certifying that the person named in it has deposited in trust with the state treasurer cash in an amount equal to twice the single limit under Subsection 31A-22-304(2) or securities with a fair market value of a similar amount, which securities are legal investments for insurers under Section 31A-18-105. The state treasurer may not accept a deposit and issue a certificate for it, unless the deposit is accompanied by evidence that there are no unsatisfied liens of any character on the assets deposited.

(2) The deposit shall be held by the state treasurer in trust to satisfy any execution on a judgment that would be paid under an insurance policy conforming to Section 31A-22-302 had the treasurer issued such a policy.

(3) Except as provided under Subsection (2), assets deposited with the treasurer under this chapter are exempt from attachment or execution. 1985

41-12a-407. Certificate of self-funded coverage as proof of owner's or operator's security.

(1) The department may, upon the application of any person, issue a certificate of self-funded coverage when it is satisfied that the person has:

(a) more than 24 motor vehicles; and

(b) deposits, in a form approved by the department, securities in an amount of $200,000 plus $100 for each motor vehicle up to and including 1,000 motor vehicles and $50 for every motor vehicle over 1,000 motor vehicles.

(2) Persons holding a certificate of self-funded coverage under this chapter shall pay benefits to persons injured from the self-funded person's operation, maintenance, and use of motor vehicles as would an insurer issuing a policy to the self-funded person containing the coverages under Section 31A-22-302.

(3) In accordance with Title 63, Chapter 46b, Administrative Procedures Act, the department may, upon reasonable grounds, cancel the certificate. Failure to pay any judgment up to the limit under Subsection 31A-22-304(2) within 30 days after the judgment is final is a reasonable ground to cancel the certificate.

(4) Any government entity with self-funded coverage for government-owned motor vehicles under Title 63, Chapter 30d, Governmental Immunity Act of Utah, meets the requirements of this section. 2005

41-12a-408. Substitution of forms of proof of owner's or operator's security.

The department shall consent to the cancellation of any bond or certificate of insurance or the department shall direct and the state treasurer shall return any money or securities to the person entitled to them upon the substitution and acceptance of other adequate proof of owner's or operator's security in a manner allowed under Section 41-12a-401. 1985

41-12a-409. Power to require proof of owner's or operator's security in other form.

If, after a hearing, the department determines that a particular proof of owner's or operator's security filed under this chapter no longer fulfills the purposes for which it is required, the department shall require proof of security in another permitted form. Pending the filing of the other proof, the department shall suspend the license and registration or the nonresident's operating privilege.   1985

41-12a-410. Employee and family relationships.

Whenever any person required to give proof of owner's or operator's security is an operator in the employ of any owner, or is a member of the immediate family or household of the owner, the department shall accept proof of security by the owner in lieu of proof by the employee, family, or household member. The department shall indicate by restriction on the operator's license the vehicles the operator may operate on the basis of that proof of security.   1985

41-12a-411. Duration of proof of owner's or operator's security.

(1) Except as otherwise provided under this section, any person required to give proof of owner's or operator's security shall maintain that proof with the department for a period of three years from the date the filing of proof was last requested. Subject to Subsection (2), the department shall:

(a) upon request, consent to the immediate cancellation of any bond or certificate of insurance;

(b) direct the state treasurer to return to the person entitled to it any money or securities deposited pursuant to this chapter as proof of owner's or operator's security; or

(c) waive the requirement of filing proof, if the person on whose behalf the proof was filed dies or becomes permanently incapacitated to operate a motor vehicle or if the person who has given proof surrenders his registration to the department, except that if he applies for a registration within three years from the date proof was originally required, the application shall be refused unless the applicant reestablishes proof of owner's or operator's security and maintains the proof for the remainder of the three-year period.

(2) (a) The department may not consent to the cancellation of any bond or the return of any money or securities if any action for damages upon a liability covered by that proof is then pending, if:

(i) any judgment of liability is unsatisfied; or

(ii) the person who filed the bond or deposited the money or securities has, within one year immediately preceding the request, been involved as an operator or owner in any motor vehicle accident resulting in injury or damage to the person or property of others.

(b) An affidavit of the applicant is sufficient evidence in the absence of contrary evidence in the records of the department if the affidavit declares:

(i) the nonexistence of liability or accidents;

(ii) that the person has been released from all liability; or

(iii) that the person has been finally adjudicated not to be liable for the injury or damage.   1999

41-12a-412. Repealed.   1997

PART 5

POST-ACCIDENT SECURITY REQUIREMENTS AND SATISFACTION OF JUDGMENTS

41-12a-501. Post-accident security.

(1) (a) Unless excepted under Subsection (2), the operator of a motor vehicle involved in an accident in the state and any owner who has not previously satisfied the requirement of security under Section 41-12a-301 shall file post-accident security with the department for the benefit of persons obtaining judgments against the operator on account of bodily injury, death, or property damage caused by the accident.

(b) The security shall be in an amount determined by the department to be sufficient to satisfy judgments arising from bodily injury, death, or property damage resulting from the accident that may be recovered against the operator, but may not exceed the minimum single limit under Subsection 31A-22-304(2).

(c) The department shall determine the amount of post-accident security on the basis of reports and other evidence submitted to the department by interested parties, including officials investigating the accident.

(d) In setting the amount of post-accident security, the department may not take into account alleged damages resulting from pain and suffering.

(e) Persons who fail to file required post-accident security are subject to the penalties under Subsection (3).

(2) The operator is exempted from the post-accident requirement under Subsection (1) if any of the following conditions are satisfied:

(a) No bodily injury, death, or damage to the property of one person in excess of the damage limit specified under Section 41-6a-401 resulted from the accident.

(b) No injury, death, or property damage was suffered by any person other than the owner or operator.

(c) The owner of the motor vehicle was in compliance with the owner's security requirement under Section 41-12a-301 at the time of the accident and the operator had permission from the owner to operate the motor vehicle.

(d) The operator was in compliance with the operator's security requirement under Section 41-12a-301 at the time of the accident.

(e) The operator has filed satisfactory evidence with the department that the operator has been released from liability, has been finally adjudicated not to be liable, or has executed a duly acknowledged written agreement providing for the payment of an agreed amount in installments with respect to all claims for injuries or damages resulting from the accident and is not in default on that agreement.

(f) The motor vehicle involved in the accident was operated by a nonresident who had an insurance policy or bond covering the accident, but not fully complying with the policy provision requirements under Section 31A-22-302, if the policy or bond is sufficient to provide full recovery for claimants and the policy or bond is issued by an insurer licensed in the state.

(g) The operator at the time of the accident was operating a motor vehicle owned or leased by the operator's employer and driven with the employer's permission.

(h) Evidence as to the extent of injuries or property damage caused by the accident has not been submitted by or on behalf of any person affected by the accident within six months following the date of the accident.

(i) The motor vehicle was legally parked at the time of the accident.

(j) The motor vehicle was an emergency vehicle acting in the line of duty at the time of the accident.

(k) The motor vehicle involved in the accident is owned by the United States, this state, or any political subdivision of this state, if the operator was using the vehicle with the permission of the owner.

(l) The motor vehicle was legally stopped at a stop sign, traffic signal, or at the direction of a peace officer at the time of the accident.

(3) (a) If an operator who is required to file post-accident security under Subsection (1) does not do so within ten days after receiving notice of the requirement of security, the department shall suspend the driver's license of the operator and all registrations of the owner, if he is a resident of the state.

(b) If the operator is not a resident of Utah, the department shall suspend the privilege of operating a motor vehicle within the state and of using, in the state, any owned motor vehicle.

(c) Notice of these suspensions shall be sent to the owner or operator no less than 15 days prior to the effective date of the suspension.   2005

41-12a-502. Accident reports.

(1) (a) Accident reports required under Section 41-6a-402 shall contain information to enable the department to determine whether the owner and operator of the automobile involved in the accident were in compliance with the security requirement of Section 41-12a-301.

(b) The information may consist of identifying the policy, bond, or certificate's issuer and number.

(c) The department may rely upon the accuracy of the information unless it has reason to believe that it is erroneous.

(2) (a) The operator of a motor vehicle involved in an accident shall, unless physically incapable, make an accident report.

(b) If the operator is physically incapable, the owner shall, if physically capable, make a report within ten days of learning of the accident.

(c) The operator and owner shall furnish any additional relevant information the department reasonably requests.

(3) Failure to report an accident as required under Section 41-6a-402 shall be punished as set forth under Subsection 41-6a-402(5).   2005

41-12a-503. Conditions to license, registration, and privilege renewal.

The license, registration, and nonresident's operating privilege suspended under Subsection 41-12a-501(3) remain suspended and may not be renewed nor may that license or registration be issued until one of the following is satisfied:

(1) The person deposits or has deposited on his behalf the post-accident security required under Subsection 41-12a-501(1).

(2) One year has elapsed following the effective date of the suspension and evidence satisfactory to the department has been filed that during that period no action for damages arising out of the accident has been commenced.

(3) Evidence satisfactory to the department has been filed with it of a release from liability, of a final adjudication of nonliability, or of a duly acknowledged written agreement providing for the payment of an agreed amount in installments with respect to all claims for injuries or damages resulting from the accident. In the event of default in the payment of any installment under such an agreement, upon receiving notice of the default, the department shall suspend the license and registration or nonresident's operating privilege of the person defaulting. This license, registration, or nonresident's operating privilege may not be restored until either:

(a) The person deposits and thereafter maintains security as required under Subsection 41-12a-501(1).

(b) One year has elapsed following the date when the security was required and during that period no action upon the agreement has been instituted in a Utah court.   1985

41-12a-504. Payments by insurers as evidence to the department.

(1) The department may accept evidence of a payment to an operator or owner of a motor vehicle involved in an accident by the insurer of any other person involved in the accident on account of damage to property as effective to relieve the operator from the post-accident security and suspension provisions of this chapter in respect to any claim for property damage by the person on whose behalf the payment has been made. A payment to the insurer of an operator or owner under its right of subrogation is the equivalent of a payment to the operator or owner.

(2) The department may accept evidence of a payment on account of bodily injury to a person involved in an accident by the insurer of any other person involved in the accident as effective to relieve the person to whom the payment is made from the post-accident security and suspension provisions of this chapter in respect to any claim for bodily injury by the person on whose behalf the payment is made.   1985

41-12a-505. Effect upon nonresident of use of state highways.

(1) The use and operation by a nonresident or his agent, or of a resident who has departed Utah, of a motor vehicle on Utah highways is an appointment of the Division of Corporations and Commercial Code as the true and lawful attorney for service of legal process in any action or proceeding against him arising from the use or operation of a motor vehicle over Utah highways which use or operation results in damages or loss to person or property. That use or operation is an agreement that process shall, in any action against him in which there is such service, be of the same legal force and validity as if served upon him personally in Utah.

(2) Service of process under Subsection (1) is made by serving a copy upon the Division of Corporations and Commercial Code or by filing a copy in that office with payment of a $5 fee. The plaintiff shall, within ten days after service of process, send notice of the process together with plaintiff's affidavit of compliance with this section to the defendant by registered mail at his last-known address.

(3) The court in which the action is pending may order any continuance necessary to afford the defendant reasonable opportunity to defend the action, but

not exceeding 90 days from the date of filing the action in court. The $5 fee paid by the plaintiff to the Division of Corporations and Commercial Code shall be taxed as costs if the plaintiff prevails. The division shall keep a record of all process served showing the day and hour of service.   1989

41-12a-506. Application to persons without license or registration.

If the operator or the owner of a motor vehicle involved in an accident in Utah has no license or registration in Utah, or is a nonresident, he may not obtain a license or registration in Utah until he has complied with the requirements of this chapter to the extent that would be necessary if, at the time of the accident, he held a Utah license and registration.
                                              1985

41-12a-507. Cooperation with other states.

(1) When a nonresident's operating privilege is suspended under this chapter, the department shall send a certified copy of the record of the action to the official in charge of the issuance of licenses and registration certificates in the state in which the nonresident resides, if the law of the other state provides for action similar to that provided for in Subsection (2).

(2) Upon receipt of certification from the official of another state that the operating privilege of a Utah resident has been suspended in the other state for failure to deposit post-accident security for the payment of judgments arising out of a motor vehicle accident, under circumstances which would require the deposit in Utah, the department shall suspend the license of the resident if he was the operator, and all of his registrations if he was the owner of a motor vehicle involved in the accident. These suspensions continue until the Utah resident furnishes evidence of his compliance with the law of the other state relating to the deposit of post-accident security.   1985

41-12a-508. Form and amount of post-accident security.

(1) The post-accident security required under Subsection 41-12a-501(1) shall be in the form of cash, cashier's check, a national or Utah bank's clean and irrevocable letter of credit, or the assignment of a bank's certificate of deposit. The department may not require a deposit in excess of the minimum single limit under Subsection 31A-22-304(2). The person depositing security shall specify in a manner specified by the department the persons on whose behalf the deposit is made and may, at any time while the deposit is in the custody of the department or state treasurer, in a manner specified by the department amend the specification of the persons on whose behalf the deposit is made. However, a single deposit of security is applicable only on behalf of persons required to furnish security because of the same accident.

(2) Subject to Subsection (1), the department may alter the amount of post-accident security required if, in its judgment, the amount previously ordered is excessive or inadequate. If the security originally ordered is determined to be excessive, the excess deposited over the reduced amount ordered shall be returned to the depositor or his personal representative as soon as possible, notwithstanding the provisions of Section 41-12a-509. If the security originally ordered is determined to be inadequate, the depositor may be required to increase the deposit within 20 days or be subject to the penalties under Subsection 41-12a-501(3).   2001

41-12a-509. Custody and terms of post-accident security deposits.

Post-accident security deposited in compliance with Subsection 41-12a-501(1) shall be placed by the department in the custody of the state treasurer and may be applied only to the payment of judgments rendered against the persons on whose behalf the deposit was made, for damages arising out of the accident in question in an action at law, begun not later than one year after the date of the accident, or within one year after the date of deposit of any security under Subsection 41-12a-503(3)(a), or to the payment in settlement, agreed to by the depositor, of claims arising out of the accident. The deposit or any balance of it shall be returned to the depositor or his personal representative when evidence satisfactory to the department has been provided that the conditions of either Subsection 41-12a-503(2) or (3) have been satisfied.   1985

41-12a-510. Report, findings, action, and security as evidence.

Neither the report required under Section 41-12a-502, nor the department's findings, action, or requirement of post-accident security under this chapter may be referred to in any way, nor be any evidence of negligence or due care of either party, at the trial of any action at law to recover damages.   1985

41-12a-511. Failure to satisfy judgment.

(1) Whenever any person fails within 60 days to satisfy any judgment, it is the duty of the clerk of the court or of the judge of a court which has no clerk in which any such judgment is rendered in Utah, upon the written request of the judgment creditor or his attorney, to forward to the department immediately after the expiration of the 60 days, a certified copy of the judgment.

(2) The department, upon the receipt of a certified copy of a judgment, shall suspend the license and registration and any nonresident's operating privilege of any person against whom the judgment was rendered, except as provided in Subsection (5) and Section 41-12a-513.

(3) Except as provided under Subsection (5) and Section 41-12a-513, a license, registration, and nonresident's operating privilege suspended under Subsection (2) remains suspended and may not be renewed nor may that license or registration be thereafter issued in the name of the same person, including a person not previously licensed, unless every such judgment is stayed or satisfied in full within the meaning of Section 41-12a-512, and until the person files proof of owner's or operator's security.

(4) If the judgment debtor named in any certified copy of a judgment reported to the department is a nonresident, the department shall transmit a certified copy of the judgment to the official in charge of the issuance of licenses and registration certificates of the state of which the judgment debtor is a resident.

(5) If the judgment creditor consents in writing, in a form the department prescribes, that the judgment debtor be allowed license and registration or nonresident's operating privilege, they may be allowed by the department for six months from the date of the consent and thereafter until that consent is revoked in writing, notwithstanding the default in the payment of the judgment or of any installments thereof prescribed in Section 41-12a-513, if the judgment debtor furnishes proof of owner's security.   1985

41-12a-512. When judgments deemed satisfied.

Judgments arising from a single accident which in the aggregate are in excess of the minimum single limit under Subsection 31A-22-304(2) shall be considered satisfied in full, for the purpose of this chapter only, when payments equal to that limit have been credited to the judgment. Payments made by the judgment debtor prior to the judgment, but on the claim which arose out of the bodily injury, death, or property damage caused by a motor vehicle accident shall be credited in reduction of the amount necessary for the judgment to be considered satisfied in full for purposes of this chapter. If multiple judgments against a depositor of post-accident security arise out of the same accident, and in the aggregate the several claims exceed the amount deposited, then the deposit shall be distributed pro rata, based upon each judgment creditor's portion of the total judgments arising from the accident. Any punitive or exemplary damages awarded a judgment creditor may not be considered in determining the claimant's pro rata share.

1985

41-12a-513. Payment of judgment in installments.

(1) A judgment debtor upon due notice to the judgment creditor may apply to the court in which the judgment was rendered for the privilege of paying the judgment in installments. The court, in its discretion and without prejudice to any other legal remedies the judgment creditor may have, may so order and fix the amounts and times of payment of the installments.

(2) Subject to Subsection (3), the department may not suspend a license, registration, or a nonresident's operating privilege, and it shall restore them if previously suspended for nonpayment of a judgment, if the judgment debtor:

    (a) obtains orders under Subsection (1) as to all unsatisfied judgments; and

    (b) provides and maintains proof of owner's or operator's security.

(3) If the judgment debtor fails to pay any installment as specified by an order under Subsection (1), then upon notice of that default, the department shall suspend the license, registration, or nonresident's operating privilege of the judgment debtor until the judgment is satisfied.

1985

PART 6

MISCELLANEOUS ENFORCEMENT PROVISIONS

41-12a-601. Collusive transfers prohibited.

If an owner's registration has been suspended under this chapter, the registration may not be transferred nor the motor vehicle registered in any other name until the department is satisfied that the transfer or registration is proposed in good faith and not with the intent or the effect of defeating the purposes of this chapter. This section does not affect the rights of a conditional vendor, chattel mortgagee, or lessor of a motor vehicle registered in the name of another as owner who becomes subject to the provisions of this chapter.

1985

41-12a-602. Filing of false report.

Any person who gives information required in a report provided for under Section 41-12a-502, knowing or having reason to believe that the information is false, or who shall forge or, without authority, sign any evidence of proof of owner's or operator's security, or who files or offers for filing any such evidence of proof, knowing or having reason to believe that it is forged or signed without authority, or who falsely swears or affirms when obtaining license plates, a safety inspection, or a registration under Section 41-12a-303, is guilty of a class A misdemeanor.

1985

41-12a-603. Operating motor vehicle without license or registration.

Any person whose license or registration or nonresident's operating privilege has been suspended or revoked under this chapter and who, during the suspension or revocation drives any motor vehicle upon any highway or knowingly permits any motor vehicle owned by the person to be operated by another upon any highway, except as permitted under this chapter, is guilty of a class C misdemeanor.

1991

41-12a-604. Suspension of license.

(1) A person convicted of a class A or a class B misdemeanor under this chapter, in addition to any other penalties which are imposed by law, shall have his operator's license suspended by the department.

(2) Whenever any person is convicted of an offense for which this chapter mandates the suspension of his license or the registration of his motor vehicle, and that person does not produce proof of owner's or operator's security at the time of his appearance, the court in which the conviction takes place shall require the surrender to it of all pertinent evidences of registration, including all registration cards, license plates, nonresident temporary permits, and other similar materials then held by the person so convicted. This court shall then forward the registration materials to the Motor Vehicle Division of the State Tax Commission and send the Driver License Division a record of the conviction. If the person so convicted secures a judgment of acquittal or reversal of this conviction in any appellate court, the department shall reinstate his driver license or privilege and the Motor Vehicle Division shall reinstate the registration of his motor vehicle immediately upon receipt of a certified copy of the judgment of acquittal or reversal.

(3) If the owner has surrendered the owner's registration materials to the Motor Vehicle Division, the owner may, unless otherwise prohibited by law, apply for a new registration, by providing proof of owner's security.

1999

41-12a-605. Other violations.

Any person who violates any provision of this chapter for which no penalty is otherwise provided is guilty of a class C misdemeanor.

1985

41-12a-606. Authority of political subdivisions to adopt ordinances.

The provisions of this chapter shall be applied uniformly throughout the state and in all municipalities and other political subdivisions. Local authorities may, however, adopt regulations or ordinances consistent with this chapter and additional traffic regulations which are not in conflict with this chapter.

1985

PART 7

DETECTION OF UNINSURED MOTORISTS [REPEALED]

41-12a-701 to 41-12a-706. Repealed.   1988

PART 8

UNINSURED MOTORIST IDENTIFICATION DATABASE PROGRAM

41-12a-801. Title.

This part is known as the "Uninsured Motorist Identification Database Program."

1994

41-12a-802. Definitions.

As used in this part:

(1) "Account" means the Uninsured Motorist Identification Restricted Account created in Section 41-12a-806.

(2) "Database" means the Uninsured Motorist Identification Database created in Section 41-12a-803.

(3) "Designated agent" means the third party the department contracts with under Section 41-12a-803.

(4) "Division" means the Driver License Division created in Section 53-3-103.

(5) "Motor vehicle" has the same meaning as set forth in Section 41-1a-102.

(6) "Motor Vehicle Division" means the Motor Vehicle Division of the State Tax Commission created in Section 41-1a-106.

(7) "Program" means the Uninsured Motorist Identification Database Program created in Section 41-12a-803. 1998

41-12a-803. Program creation — Administration — Selection of designated agent — Duties — Rulemaking — Audits.

(1) There is created the Uninsured Motorist Identification Database Program to:

(a) establish an Uninsured Motorist Identification Database to verify compliance with motor vehicle owner's or operator's security requirements under Section 41-12a-301 and other provisions under this part;

(b) assist in reducing the number of uninsured motor vehicles on the highways of the state;

(c) assist in increasing compliance with motor vehicle registration and sales and use tax laws; and

(d) assist in protecting a financial institution's bona fide security interest in a motor vehicle.

(2) The program shall be administered by the department with the assistance of the designated agent and the Motor Vehicle Division.

(3) (a) The department shall contract in accordance with Title 63, Chapter 56, Utah Procurement Code, with a third party to establish and maintain an Uninsured Motorist Identification Database for the purposes established under this part.

(b) The contract may not obligate the department to pay the third party more monies than are available in the account.

(4) (a) The third party under contract under this section is the department's designated agent, and shall develop and maintain a computer database from the information provided by:

(i) insurers under Section 31A-22-315;

(ii) the division under Subsection (6); and

(iii) the Motor Vehicle Division under Section 41-1a-120.

(b) (i) The database shall be developed and maintained in accordance with guidelines established by the department so that state and local law enforcement agencies and financial institutions as defined in Section 7-1-103 can efficiently access the records of the database, including reports useful for the implementation of the provisions of this part.

(ii) (A) The reports shall be in a form and contain information approved by the department.

(B) The reports may be made available through the Internet or through other electronic medium, if the department determines that sufficient security is provided to ensure compliance with Section 41-12a-805 regarding limitations on disclosure of information in the database.

(5) With information provided by the department and the Motor Vehicle Division, the designated agent shall, at least monthly:

(a) update the database with the motor vehicle insurance information provided by the insurers in accordance with Section 31A-22-315; and

(b) compare all current motor vehicle registrations against the database.

(6) The division shall provide the designated agent with the name, date of birth, address, and driver license number of all persons on the driver license database.

(7) In accordance with Title 63, Chapter 46a, Utah Administrative Rulemaking Act, the department shall make rules and develop procedures in cooperation with the Motor Vehicle Division to use the database for the purpose of administering and enforcing this part.

(8) (a) The designated agent shall archive computer data files at least semi-annually for auditing purposes.

(b) The internal audit unit of the tax commission provided under Section 59-1-206 shall audit the program at least annually. The audit shall include verification of:

(i) billings made by the designated agent; and

(ii) the accuracy of the designated agent's matching of vehicle registration with insurance data. 2003

41-12a-804. Notice — Proof — Revocation of registration — False statements — Penalties — Exemptions — Sales tax enforcement.

(1) If the comparison under Section 41-12a-803 shows that a motor vehicle is not insured for three consecutive months, the Motor Vehicle Division shall direct that the designated agent provide notice to the owner of the motor vehicle that the owner has 15 days to provide:

(a) proof of owner's or operator's security in a form allowed under Subsection 41-12a-303.2(4); or

(b) proof of exemption from the owner's or operator's security requirements.

(2) If an owner of a motor vehicle fails to provide satisfactory proof of owner's or operator's security to the designated agent, the designated agent shall:

(a) provide a second notice to the owner of the motor vehicle that the owner now has 15 days to provide:

(i) proof of owner's or operator's security in a form allowed under Subsection 41-12a-303.2(4); or

(ii) proof of exemption from the owner's or operator's security requirements;

(b) for each notice provided, indicate information relating to the owner's failure to provide proof of owner's or operator's security in the database; and

(c) provide this information to state and local law enforcement agencies as requested in accordance with the provisions under Section 41-12a-805.

(3) The Motor Vehicle Division:

(a) shall revoke the registration upon receiving notification under Subsection 41-1a-110(2); and

(b) shall provide appropriate notices of the revocation, the legal consequences of operating a vehicle with revoked registration and without owner's or operator's security and instructions on how to get the registration reinstated;

(c) may direct the designated agent to provide the notices under this Subsection (3).

(4) Any action by the Motor Vehicle Division to revoke the registration of a motor vehicle under this section may be in addition to an action by a law enforcement agency to impose the penalties under Section 41-12a-302 or 41-12a-303.2.

(5) (a) A person may not provide a false or fraudulent statement to the Motor Vehicle Division or designated agent.

(b) In addition to any other penalties, a person who violates Subsection (5)(a) is guilty of a class B misdemeanor.

(6) The department and the Motor Vehicle Division shall direct the designated agent to exempt from this section a farm truck that:

(a) meets the definition of a farm truck under Section 41-1a-102; and

(b) is registered as a farm truck under Title 41, Chapter 1a, Motor Vehicle Act.

(7) This part does not affect other actions or penalties that may be taken or imposed for violation of the owner's and operator's security requirements of this chapter.

(8) If a comparison under Section 41-12a-803 shows that a motor vehicle may not be in compliance with motor vehicle registration or sales and use tax laws, the Motor Vehicle Division may direct that the designated agent provide notice to the owner of a motor vehicle that information exists which indicates the possible violation.   2000

41-12a-805. Disclosure of insurance information — Penalty.

(1) Information in the database established under Section 41-12a-803 provided by a person to the designated agent is considered to be the property of the person providing the information. The information may not be disclosed from the database under Title 63, Chapter 2, Government Records Access and Management Act, or otherwise, except as follows:

(a) for the purpose of investigating, litigating, or enforcing the owner's or operator's security requirement under Section 41-12a-301, the designated agent shall verify insurance information through the state computer network for a state or local government agency or court;

(b) for the purpose of investigating, litigating, or enforcing the owner's or operator's security requirement under Section 41-12a-301, the designated agent shall, upon request, issue to any state or local government agency or court a certificate documenting the insurance information, according to the database, of a specific individual or motor vehicle for the time period designated by the government agency;

(c) upon request, the department or its designated agent shall disclose whether or not a person is an insured individual and the insurance company name to:

(i) that individual or, if that individual is deceased, any interested person of that individual, as defined in Section 75-1-201;

(ii) the parent or legal guardian of that individual if the individual is an unemancipated minor;

(iii) the legal guardian of that individual if the individual is legally incapacitated;

(iv) a person who has power of attorney from the insured individual;

(v) a person who submits a notarized release from the insured individual dated no more than 90 days before the date the request is made; or

(vi) a person suffering loss or injury in a motor vehicle accident in which the insured individual is involved, but only as part of an accident report as authorized in Section 41-12a-202;

(d) for the purpose of investigating, enforcing, or prosecuting laws or issuing citations by state or local law enforcement agencies related to the:

(i) registration and renewal of registration of a motor vehicle under Title 41, Chapter 1a, Motor Vehicle Act;

(ii) purchase of a motor vehicle under Title 59, Chapter 12, Sales and Use Tax Act; and

(iii) owner's or operator's security requirements under Section 41-12a-301;

(e) upon request of a peace officer acting in an official capacity under the provisions of Subsection (1)(d), the department or the designated agent shall, upon request, disclose relevant information for investigation, enforcement, or prosecution;

(f) for the purpose of the state auditor, the legislative auditor general, or other auditor of the state conducting audits of the program; and

(g) upon request of a financial institution as defined under Section 7-1-103 for the purpose of protecting the financial institution's bona fide security interest in a motor vehicle.

(2) (a) The department may allow the designated agent to prepare and deliver upon request, a report on the insurance information of a person or motor vehicle in accordance with this section.

(b) The report may be in the form of:

(i) a certified copy that is considered admissible in any court proceeding in the same manner as the original; or

(ii) information accessible through the Internet or through other electronic medium if the department determines that sufficient security is provided to ensure compliance with this section.

(c) The department may allow the designated agent to charge a fee established by the department under Section 63-38-3.2 for each:

(i) document authenticated, including each certified copy;

(ii) record accessed by the Internet or by other electronic medium; and

(iii) record provided to a financial institution under Subsection (1)(g).

(3) Any person who knowingly releases or discloses information from the database for a purpose other than those authorized in this section or to a person who is not entitled to it is guilty of a third degree felony.

(4) An insurer is not liable to any person for complying with Section 31A-22-315 by providing information to the designated agent.

(5) Neither the state nor the department's designated agent are liable to any person for gathering, managing, or using the information in the database as provided in Section 31A-22-315 and this part.   2003

41-12a-806. Restricted Account — Creation — Funding — Interest — Purposes.

(1) There is created within the Transportation Fund a restricted account known as the "Uninsured Motorist Identification Restricted Account."

(2) The account consists of monies generated from the following revenue sources:

(a) monies received by the state under Section 41-1a-1218, the uninsured motorist identification fee;

(b) monies received by the state under Section 41-1a-1220; and

(c) appropriations made to the account by the Legislature.

(3) (a) The account shall earn interest.

(b) All interest earned on account monies shall be deposited into the account.

(4) Monies shall be appropriated from the account by the Legislature to:

(a) the department to fund the contract with the designated agent;

(b) the department to offset the costs to state and local law enforcement agencies of using the information for the purposes authorized under this part; and

(c) the Tax Commission to offset the costs to the Motor Vehicle Division for revoking and reinstating vehicle registrations under Subsection 41-1a-110(2)(b).   2000

CHAPTER 13

DEPARTMENT OF PUBLIC SAFETY [RENUMBERED]

41-13-1 to 41-13-15. Renumbered as § 53-1-103 et seq.   1990, 1993

CHAPTER 13a

SECURITY PERSONNEL LICENSING AND REGULATION [RENUMBERED]

41-13a-1 to 41-13a-20. Renumbered as §§ 53-5-401 to 53-5-420.   1993

CHAPTER 14

TRAFFIC SAFETY COORDINATING COMMITTEE [REPEALED]

41-14-1 to 41-14-3. Repealed.   1987

CHAPTER 15

VEHICLE EQUIPMENT SAFETY COMPACT [REPEALED]

41-15-1 to 41-15-12. Repealed.   2005

CHAPTER 16

MOTOR CLUBS [REPEALED]

41-16-1 to 41-16-35. Repealed.   1986

CHAPTER 17

DRIVERS' LICENSE COMPACT [REPEALED]

41-17-1 to 41-17-7. Repealed.   1987

CHAPTER 18

COMMERCIAL DRIVER TRAINING SCHOOLS [REPEALED]

41-18-1 to 41-18-9. Repealed.   1987

CHAPTER 19

FEDERAL HIGHWAY SAFETY ACT

41-19-1. Powers and duties of governor.

The governor, in addition to other duties and responsibilities conferred upon him by the Constitution and laws of the state of Utah is hereby empowered to contract and to do all other things necessary in behalf of the state to secure the full benefits available to this state under the federal Highway Safety Act of 1966, and any amendments thereto, and in so doing, to cooperate with the federal and state agencies, agencies private and public, interested organizations, and with individuals, to effectuate the purposes of that enactment, and any and all subsequent amendments thereto. The governor shall be the official having the ultimate responsibility for dealing with the United States Government with respect to programs and activities pursuant to the federal Highway Safety Act of 1966, and any amendments thereto. To that end he shall be responsible for activities of any and all departments and agencies of this state and its subdivisions, relating thereto. He may designate an appropriate person, commission or board to assist him in coordinating the activities and programs contemplated under this section.   1967

41-19-2. Participation by political subdivisions.

The Legislature of the state of Utah hereby authorizes the political subdivisions of this state to participate in the state highway safety program as contemplated by the federal Highway Safety Act of 1966, and any amendments thereto, and to do all things necessary to secure benefits available under that act.   1967

CHAPTER 20

RECREATIONAL VEHICLES [REPEALED]

41-20-1 to 41-20-7. Repealed.   1990, 1998

CHAPTER 21

VINTAGE VEHICLES

41-21-1. Vintage vehicle defined.

"Vintage vehicle" means a motor vehicle that is 40 years old or older, from the current year, primarily a collector's item, and used for participation in club activities, exhibitions, tours, parades, occasional transportation, and similar uses, but that is not used for general daily transportation.   1992

41-21-2. Renumbered as § 41-1a-226.   1992

41-21-3. Minimum speed inapplicable.

The provisions of this title relating to minimum speed provisions upon highways do not apply to vehicles properly registered under Title 41, Chapter 1a, Motor Vehicle Act while the vehicles are being driven to or from an assembly, convention, or other meeting where the vehicles and their ownership are of primary interest, or while they are being driven to or from, or while on local, state, or national tours held primarily for the exhibition and enjoyment of the vehicles by their owners, and so long as the vehicle or group of vehicles are not operated in a manner which would constitute a public nuisance or create a hazard to other automobiles or persons.   1992

41-21-4. Minimum safety equipment inapplicable.

The provisions of this title relating to minimum safety equipment are not applicable to vehicles properly registered under Title 41, Chapter 1a, Part 2, Registration, so long as the original equipment, on the vehicle at the time of its manufacture, is in good operating condition or has been replaced by equal or more efficient equipment in good working order and the vehicle is not operated in a manner or at a time that would constitute a public nuisance or create a hazard to other automobiles or persons.   1992

41-21-5. Operation on public highways.

Any motor vehicle properly registered under this chapter may be operated or moved on the streets and highways for going to or from an assembly, convention, parade, or other meeting where the vehicles and their ownership are of primary interest, or while they are being driven to or from, or while on local, state, or national tours held primarily for the exhibition and enjoyment of the vehicles by their owners, and so long as the vehicle or group of vehicles are not operated in a manner which would constitute a public nuisance or create a hazard to other automobiles or persons.   1971

41-21-6. Revocation of registration — Powers of tax commission.

The tax commission may revoke the registration of a vintage vehicle for failure to comply with this chapter.   1993

CHAPTER 22

OFF-HIGHWAY VEHICLES

41-22-1. Policy declaration.

It is the policy of this state to promote safety and protection for persons, property, and the environment connected with the use, operation, and equipment of off-highway vehicles, to promote uniformity of laws, to adopt and pursue a safety education program, and to develop trails and other facilities for the use of these vehicles.   1987

41-22-2. Definitions.

As used in this chapter:

(1) "Advisory council" means the Off-highway Vehicle Advisory Council appointed by the Board of Parks and Recreation.

(2) "All-terrain type I vehicle" means any motor vehicle 52 inches or less in width, having an unladen dry weight of 800 pounds or less, traveling on three or more low pressure tires, having a seat designed to be straddled by the operator, and designed for or capable of travel over unimproved terrain.

(3) "All-terrain type II vehicle" means any other motor vehicle, not defined in Subsection (2), (9), or (20), designed for or capable of travel over unimproved terrain. This term does not include golf carts, any vehicle designed to carry a disabled person, any vehicle not specifically designed for recreational use, or farm tractors as defined under Section 41-1a-102.

(4) "Board" means the Board of Parks and Recreation.

(5) "Dealer" means a person engaged in the business of selling off-highway vehicles at wholesale or retail.

(6) "Division" means the Division of Parks and Recreation.

(7) "Low pressure tire" means any pneumatic tire six inches or more in width designed for use on wheels with rim diameter of 12 inches or less and utilizing an operating pressure of ten pounds per square inch or less as recommended by the vehicle manufacturer.

(8) "Manufacturer" means a person engaged in the business of manufacturing off-highway vehicles.

(9) "Motorcycle" means every motor vehicle having a saddle for the use of the operator and designed to travel on not more than two tires.

(10) "Motor vehicle" means every vehicle which is self-propelled.

(11) "Off-highway vehicle" means any snowmobile, all-terrain type I vehicle, all-terrain type II vehicle, or motorcycle.

(12) "Off-highway implement of husbandry" means every all-terrain type I vehicle, motorcycle, or snowmobile which is used by the owner or his agent for agricultural operations.

(13) "Operate" means to control the movement of or otherwise use an off-highway vehicle.

(14) "Operator" means the person who is in actual physical control of an off-highway vehicle.

(15) "Organized user group" means an off-highway vehicle organization incorporated as a nonprofit corporation in the state under Title 16, Chapter 6a, Utah Revised Nonprofit Corporation Act, for the purpose of promoting the interests of off-highway vehicle recreation.

(16) "Owner" means a person, other than a person with a security interest, having a property interest or title to an off-highway vehicle and entitled to the use and possession of that vehicle.

(17) "Public land" means land owned or administered by any federal or state agency or any political subdivision of the state.

(18) "Register" means the act of assigning a registration number to an off-highway vehicle.

(19) "Roadway" is used as defined in Section 41-6a-102.

(20) "Snowmobile" means any motor vehicle designed for travel on snow or ice and steered and supported in whole or in part by skis, belts, cleats, runners, or low pressure tires.

(21) "Street or highway" means the entire width between boundary lines of every way or place of whatever nature, when any part of it is open to the use of the public for vehicular travel.   2005

41-22-3. Registration of vehicles — Application — Issuance of sticker and card — Proof of property tax payment — Records.

(1) (a) Unless exempted under Section 41-22-9, a person may not operate or transport and an owner may not give another person permission to operate or transport any off-highway vehicle on any public land, trail, street, or highway in this state unless the off-highway vehicle is registered under this chapter for the current year.

(b) Unless exempted under Section 41-22-9, a dealer may not sell an off-highway vehicle which can be used or transported on any public land, trail, street, or highway in this state, unless the off-highway vehicle is registered or is in the process of being registered under this chapter for the current year.

(2) The owner of an off-highway vehicle subject to registration under this chapter shall apply to the Motor Vehicle Division for registration on forms approved by the Motor Vehicle Division.

(3) Each application for registration of an off-highway vehicle shall be accompanied by:

(a) evidence of ownership, a title, or a manufacturer's certificate of origin, and a bill of sale showing ownership, make, model, horsepower or displacement, and serial number;

(b) the past registration card; or

(c) the fee for a duplicate.

(4) (a) Upon each annual registration, the Motor Vehicle Division shall issue a registration sticker and a registration card for each off-highway vehicle registered.

(b) The registration sticker shall:

(i) contain a unique number using numbers, letters, or combination of numbers and letters to identify the off-highway vehicle for which it is issued;

(ii) be affixed to the off-highway vehicle for which it is issued in a plainly visible position as prescribed by rule of the board under Section 41-22-5.1; and

(iii) be maintained free of foreign materials and in a condition to be clearly legible.

(c) At all times, a registration card shall be kept with the off-highway vehicle and shall be available for inspection by a law enforcement officer.

(5) (a) An applicant for a registration card and registration sticker shall provide the Motor Vehicle Division a certificate, described under Subsection (5)(b), from the county assessor of the county in which the off-highway vehicle has situs for taxation.

(b) The certificate required under Subsection (5)(a) shall state one of the following:

(i) the property tax on the off-highway vehicle for the current year has been paid;

(ii) in the county assessor's opinion, the tax is a lien on real property sufficient to secure the payment of the tax; or

(iii) the off-highway vehicle is exempt by law from payment of property tax for the current year.

(6) (a) All records of the division made or kept under this section shall be classified by the Motor Vehicle Division in the same manner as motor vehicle records are classified under Section 41-1a-116.

(b) Division records are available for inspection in the same manner as motor vehicle records under Section 41-1a-116.   2004

41-22-3.1. Off-highway vehicle registration number — Assignment — Display.

(1) Beginning on January 1, 2005, the Motor Vehicle Division shall assign an off-highway vehicle registration number to each off-highway vehicle registered under Section 41-22-3.

(2) The off-highway vehicle registration number shall be:

(a) a unique number using numbers, letters, or combination of numbers and letters to identify the off-highway vehicle;

(b) assigned to the off-highway vehicle for the useful life of the off-highway vehicle or until the ownership of the off-highway vehicle changes, whichever occurs first;

(c) assigned by the Motor Vehicle Division in consultation with the division; and

(d) printed on the registration card.

(3) The owner of an off-highway vehicle shall:

(a) affix and display the off-highway vehicle registration number assigned under Subsection (1) on the off-highway vehicle in a manner that is plainly visible from a distance of at least 50 feet during daylight by position, size, and color as prescribed by rule of the board under Section 41-22-5.1; and

(b) maintain the off-highway vehicle registration number in a condition that is free of foreign materials and clearly legible.   2004

41-22-3.5. Staggered registration dates — Registration renewal.

(1) Unless exempted under Section 41-22-9, every off-highway vehicle registration, every registration card, and every registration sticker issued under this chapter for the first registration of the off-highway vehicle in this state, continues in effect for a period of 12 months beginning with the first day of the calendar month of registration and does not expire until the last day of the same month in the following year.

(2) If the last day of the registration period falls on a day in which the appropriate state or county offices are not open for business, the registration of the off-highway vehicle is extended to 12 midnight of the next business day.

(3) (a) The division may receive applications for registration renewal and issue new registration cards at any time prior to the expiration of the registration, subject to the availability of renewal materials.

(b) Applications for registration renewal shall be made in accordance with Section 41-22-3.

(4) (a) The new registration shall retain the same expiration month as recorded on the original registration even if the registration has expired.

(b) The year of registration expiration shall be changed to reflect the renewed registration period.

(5) If the registration renewal application is an application generated by the division through its automated system, the owner need not surrender the last registration card or duplicate.   2003

41-22-4. Falsification of documents unlawful — Alteration or removal of serial number unlawful — Display of sticker.

A person may not:

(1) knowingly falsify an application for registration, affidavit of ownership, or bill of sale for any off-highway vehicle;

(2) alter, deface, or remove any manufacturer's serial number on any off-highway vehicle;

(3) use or permit the use or display of any registration sticker, registration card, permit, or off-highway vehicle registration number upon an off-highway vehicle or in the operation of any off-highway vehicle other than the vehicle for which it was issued or assigned; or

(4) alter or deface a registration sticker, registration card, permit, or off-highway vehicle registration number issued or assigned to an off-highway vehicle.   2004

41-22-5. Repealed.   2004

41-22-5.1. Rules of board relating to display of registration stickers.

In accordance with Title 63, Chapter 46a, Utah Administrative Rulemaking Act, the board shall make rules for the display of:

(1) a registration sticker on an off-highway vehicle in accordance with Section 41-22-3; and

(2) an off-highway vehicle registration number in accordance with Section 41-22-3.1.   2004

41-22-5.5. Off-highway husbandry vehicles.

(1) (a) The owner of an all-terrain type I vehicle, motorcycle, or snowmobile used for agricultural purposes may apply to the Motor Vehicle Division for an off-highway implement of husbandry sticker. Each application shall be accompanied by evidence of ownership, a title, or a manufacturer's certificate of origin, and a signed statement certifying that the off-highway vehicle is used for agricultural purposes. The owner shall receive an off-highway implement of husbandry sticker upon production of the documents required above and payment of an off-highway implement of husbandry sticker fee established by the board not to exceed $10.

(b) If the vehicle is also used for recreational purposes on public lands, trails, streets, or highways, it shall also be registered under Section 41-22-3.

(c) The off-highway implement of husbandry sticker shall be displayed in a manner prescribed by the board and shall identify the all-terrain type I vehicle, motorcycle, or snowmobile as an off-highway implement of husbandry.

(2) The off-highway implement of husbandry sticker is valid only for the life of the ownership of the

all-terrain type I vehicle, motorcycle, or snowmobile and is not transferable.

(3) The off-highway implement of husbandry sticker is valid for an all-terrain type I vehicle, motorcycle, or snowmobile which is being operated adjacent to a roadway:

(a) when the all-terrain type I vehicle, motorcycle, or snowmobile is only being used to travel from one parcel of land owned or operated by the owner of the vehicle to another parcel of land owned or operated by the owner; and

(b) when this operation is necessary for the furtherance of agricultural purposes.

(4) If the operation of an off-highway implement of husbandry adjacent to a roadway is impractical, it may be operated on the roadway if the operator exercises due care towards conventional motor vehicle traffic.

(5) It is unlawful to operate an off-highway implement of husbandry along, across, or within the boundaries of an interstate freeway. 1999

41-22-6. Repealed. 1986 (2nd S.S.)

41-22-7. Duplicate registration cards and registration stickers.

(1) If a registration card is lost or destroyed, or if an owner changes the owner's address from the address shown on the owner's registration card, the owner shall, within 15 days, apply for a duplicate registration card.

(2) If a registration sticker is lost, stolen, or becomes illegible, the owner of the off-highway vehicle shall immediately apply for and obtain a replacement registration sticker. 2004

41-22-8. Registration fees.

(1) The board shall establish the fees which shall be paid in accordance with this chapter, subject to the following:

(a) The fee for each registration may not exceed $17.

(b) The fee for each duplicate registration card may not exceed $3.

(c) The fee for each duplicate registration sticker may not exceed $5.

(2) A fee may not be charged for an off-highway vehicle that is owned and operated by the United States Government, this state, or its political subdivisions. 2004

41-22-9. Vehicles exempt from registration.

The following off-highway vehicles are exempt from the registration requirements of this chapter:

(1) vehicles that are currently registered for highway use, have a valid motor vehicle safety inspection sticker or certificate, and on which the required safety equipment has not been subsequently modified;

(2) off-highway vehicles that are owned by a nonresident and that are displaying a current annual off-highway vehicle user decal in accordance with Section 41-22-35;

(3) off-highway vehicles sold by a dealer to a person who is not a resident of this state;

(4) off-highway implements of husbandry operated in the manner prescribed by Subsections 41-22-5.5(3) through (5); and

(5) new off-highway vehicles being transported to an off-highway vehicle dealership by the dealer, employee of the dealership, or agent for the dealership. 2004

41-22-10. Powers of board relating to off-highway vehicles.

The board may:

(1) appoint and seek recommendations from the Off-highway Vehicle Advisory Council representing the various off-highway vehicle, conservation, and other appropriate interests; and

(2) adopt a uniform marker and sign system for use by agents of appropriate federal, state, county, and city agencies in areas of off-highway vehicle use. 1987

41-22-10.1. Vehicles operated on posted public land.

(1) Currently registered off-highway vehicles may be operated on public land, trails, streets, or highways that are posted by sign or designated by map or description as open to off-highway vehicle use by the controlling federal, state, county, or municipal agency.

(2) The controlling federal, state, county, or municipal agency may:

(a) provide a map or description showing or describing land, trails, streets, or highways open to off-highway vehicle use; or

(b) post signs designating lands, trails, streets, or highways open to off-highway vehicle use.

(3) Liability may not be imposed on any federal, state, county, or municipality relating to the designation or maintenance of any land, trail, street, or highway open for off-highway vehicle use. 1999

41-22-10.2. Off-highway vehicles — Prohibited on interstate freeway.

It is unlawful for an off-highway vehicle to operate along, across, or within the boundaries of an interstate freeway or controlled access highway, as defined in Section 41-6a-102. 2005

41-22-10.3. Operation of vehicles on highways — Limits.

No person may operate an off-highway vehicle upon any street or highway, not designated as open to off-highway vehicle use, except:

(1) when crossing a street or highway and the operator comes to a complete stop before crossing, proceeds only after yielding the right of way to oncoming traffic, and crosses at a right angle;

(2) when loading or unloading an off-highway vehicle from a vehicle or trailer, which shall be done with due regard for safety, and at the nearest practical point of operation; or

(3) when an emergency exists, during any period of time and at those locations when the operation of conventional motor vehicles is impractical or when the operation is directed by a peace officer or other public authority.

1986 (2nd S.S.)

41-22-10.4. Snowmobiles.

Snowmobiles may be operated on streets or highways which have been officially closed for the season to conventional motor vehicle traffic because snow removal is no longer provided for the season by the public authority having jurisdiction. 1986 (2nd S.S.)

41-22-10.5. Local ordinances — Designating routes — Supervision.

(1) A municipality or county may adopt ordinances designating certain streets and highways under its respective jurisdiction as off-highway vehicle routes to allow off-highway vehicle operators to gain direct access to or from a private or public area open for off-highway vehicle use.

(2) A municipality or a county may adopt an ordinance requiring an operator who is under 16 years of age to be under the direct visual supervision of an adult who is at least 18 years of age while using a route designated under Subsection (1).

(3) A route designated under Subsection (1) may not be along, across, or within the boundaries of an interstate freeway or limited access highway.

(4) Except as provided under Section 41-22-10.3, a person may not operate an off-highway vehicle on any street or highway that is not designated or posted as open for off-highway vehicle use in accordance with Subsection (1) or Section 41-22-10.1.

(5) Subsection (4) does not apply to off-highway implements of husbandry used in accordance with Section 41-22-5.5.   2004

41-22-10.6. Requiring compliance with traffic laws.

Any person operating an off-highway vehicle is subject to the provisions of Title 41, Chapter 6a, Traffic Code, unless specifically excluded.   2005

41-22-10.7. Vehicle equipment requirements — Rulemaking — Exceptions.

(1) Except as provided under Subsection (3), an off-highway vehicle shall be equipped with:

(a) brakes adequate to control the movement of and to stop and hold the vehicle under normal operating conditions;

(b) headlights and taillights when operated between sunset and sunrise;

(c) a noise control device and except for a snowmobile, a spark arrestor device; and

(d) a safety flag, red or orange in color and a minimum of six by 12 inches, attached to the off-highway vehicle at least eight feet above the surface of level ground, when operated on sand dunes designated by the board.

(2) In accordance with Title 63, Chapter 46a, Utah Administrative Rulemaking Act, the board may make rules which set standards for the equipment and which designate sand dunes where safety flags are required under Subsection (1).

(3) An off-highway implement of husbandry used only in agricultural operations and not operated on a highway, is exempt from the provisions of this section.   2002

41-22-10.8. Protective headgear requirements — Owner duty — Penalty for violation.

(1) A person under the age of 18 may not operate or ride on all-terrain type I vehicles, snowmobiles, or motorcycles on public land unless the person is wearing a properly fitted and fastened, United States Department of Transportation safety-rated protective headgear designed for motorized vehicle use.

(2) The owner of an off-highway vehicle or any other person may not give permission to a person who is under 18 years of age to operate or ride on an off-highway vehicle in violation of this section.

(3) An operator and passengers of off-highway implements of husbandry operated in the manner prescribed by Subsections 41-22-5.5(3) and (4) are exempt from the requirements of this section.

(4) Any person convicted of violations of this section is guilty of an infraction and shall be fined not more than $50 per offense.   2002

41-22-10.9. Repealed.   1997

41-22-11. Agencies authorized to erect regulatory signs on public land.

No person, except an agent of an appropriate federal, state, county, or city agency, operating within that agency's authority, may place a regulatory sign governing off-highway vehicle use on any public land.
                                               1986 (2nd S.S.)

41-22-12. Restrictions on use of public lands.

(1) Except as provided in Section 63-11-17, federal agencies are encouraged and agencies of the state and its subdivisions shall refrain from closing any public land to responsible off-highway vehicle use.

(2) A person may not operate and an owner of an off-highway vehicle may not give another person permission to operate an off-highway vehicle on any public land which is closed to off-highway vehicles.
                                                          1999

41-22-12.1. Restrictions on use of snowmobile trails.

A person may not operate a wheeled vehicle with a gross vehicle weight of 800 pounds or more on any snowmobile trail that the division has marked, posted, designated, or maintained as a snowmobile trail.   2002

41-22-12.5. Restrictions on use of privately-owned lands without permission — Unlawful for person to tamper with signs or fencing on privately-owned land.

(1) (a) No person shall operate or accompany a person operating an off-highway vehicle upon privately-owned land of any other person, firm, or corporation without permission from the owner or person in charge.

(b) It is unlawful for any person operating or accompanying a person operating an off-highway vehicle to refuse to immediately leave private land upon request of the owner or person in charge of such land.

(c) Subsections (a) and (b) shall not apply to prescriptive easements on privately owned land.

(d) No person operating or accompanying a person operating an off-highway vehicle shall obstruct any entrance or exit to private property without the owner's permission.

(2) It is unlawful for any person to tear down, mutilate, or destroy any sign, signboards, or other notice which regulates trespassing for purposes of operating an off-highway vehicle on land; or to tear down, deface, or destroy any fence or other enclosure or any gate or bars belonging to any such fence or enclosure.   1989

41-22-13. Prohibited uses.

No person may operate an off-highway vehicle in connection with acts of vandalism, harassment of wildlife or domestic animals, burglaries or other crimes, or damage to the environment which includes excessive pollution of air, water, or land, abuse of the watershed, impairment of plant or animal life, or excessive mechanical noise.   1986 (2nd S.S.)

41-22-14. Repealed.   1996

41-22-15. Permission required for race or organized event.

No person may organize, promote, or hold an off-highway vehicle race or other organized event on any land or highway within this state, except as permitted by the appropriate agency or landowner having jurisdiction over the land or highway.   1989

41-22-16. Authorized peace officers — Arrest provisions.

(1) Any peace officer authorized under Title 53, Chapter 13, Peace Officer Classifications, may enforce

the provisions of this chapter and the rules promulgated under this chapter.

(2) Whenever any person is arrested for any violation of the provisions of this chapter or of the rules promulgated under this chapter, the procedure for the arrest is the same as outlined in Sections 77-7-22, 77-7-23, and 77-7-24. 2005

41-22-17. Penalties for violations.

(1) Except as otherwise provided, a person who violates the provisions of this chapter is guilty of a class C misdemeanor.

(2) The division may revoke or suspend the registration of any off-highway vehicle whose application for registration has been falsified. The owner shall surrender to the division, within 15 days of suspension or revocation, the suspended or revoked registration card and registration sticker. 2004

41-22-18. Ordinances or local laws relating to operation and equipment of vehicles.

The provisions of this chapter and other applicable laws of this state govern the operation, equipment, registration, and all other matters relating to the use of off-highway vehicles on public land. Nothing in this chapter may be construed to prevent the adoption of any ordinance or local law relating to the operation and equipment of off-highway vehicles in which the provisions are identical to the provisions of this chapter or the rules promulgated under this chapter, but these ordinances or local laws shall be operative only as long as and to the extent that they continue to be identical to the provisions of this chapter or the rules promulgated under this chapter. 1986

41-22-19. Deposit of fees and related moneys in Off-highway Vehicle Account — Use for facilities, costs and expenses of division, and education — Request for matching funds.

(1) Except as provided under Subsection (3) and Sections 41-22-34 and 41-22-36, all registration fees and related moneys collected by the Motor Vehicle Division or any agencies designated to act for the Motor Vehicle Division under this chapter shall be deposited as restricted revenue in the Off-highway Vehicle Account in the General Fund less the costs of collecting off-highway vehicle registration fees by the Motor Vehicle Division. The balance of the monies may be used by the division as follows:

(a) for the construction, improvement, operation, or maintenance of publicly owned or administered off-highway vehicle facilities;

(b) for the mitigation of impacts associated with off-highway vehicle use;

(c) as grants or as matching funds with any federal agency, state agency, political subdivision of the state, or organized user group for the construction, improvement, operation, acquisition, or maintenance of publicly owned or administered off-highway vehicle facilities including public access facilities;

(d) for the administration and enforcement of the provisions of this chapter; and

(e) for the education of off-highway vehicle users.

(2) All agencies or political subdivisions requesting matching funds shall submit plans for proposed off-highway vehicle facilities to the division for review and approval.

(3) (a) One dollar and 50 cents of each annual registration fee collected under Subsection 41-22-8(1) and each off-highway vehicle user fee col-

lected under Subsection 41-22-35(2) shall be deposited in the Land Grant Management Fund created under Section 53C-3-101.

(b) The Utah School and Institutional Trust Lands Administration shall use the monies deposited under Subsection (3)(a) for costs associated with off-highway vehicle use of legally accessible lands within its jurisdiction as follows:

(i) to improve recreational opportunities on trust lands by constructing, improving, maintaining, or perfecting access for off-highway vehicle trails; and

(ii) to mitigate impacts associated with off-highway vehicle use.

(c) Any unused balance of the monies deposited under Subsection (3)(a) exceeding $350,000 at the end of each fiscal year shall be deposited in the Off-highway Vehicle Account under Subsection (1). 2004

41-22-20. Public land administrating agencies to develop facilities and programs.

All public land administering agencies are encouraged:

(1) to develop and maintain trails, parking areas, rest rooms, and other related facilities appropriate to off-highway vehicle use; and

(2) to promote the safety, enjoyment, and responsible use of all forms of this recreational activity. 1997

41-22-21. Publication of rules and amendments.

The rules promulgated under this chapter and any amendments to those rules shall be published as required by the Utah Administrative Rulemaking Act. 1986 (2nd S.S.)

41-22-22 to 41-22-28. Repealed. 1986 (2nd S.S.), 1987

41-22-29. Operation by persons under eight years of age prohibited — Definitions — Exception — Penalty.

(1) As used in this section:

(a) "Organized practice" means a scheduled motorcycle practice held in an off-road vehicle facility designated by the division and conducted by an organization carrying liability insurance in at least the amounts specified by the division under Subsection (5) covering all activities associated with the practice.

(b) "Sanctioned race" means a motorcycle race conducted on a closed course and sponsored and sanctioned by an organization carrying liability insurance in at least the amounts specified by the division under Subsection (5) covering all activities associated with the race.

(2) Except as provided under Subsection (3), a person under eight years of age may not operate and an owner may not give another person who is under eight years of age permission to operate an off-highway vehicle on any public land, trail, street, or highway of this state.

(3) A child under eight years of age may participate in a sanctioned race or organized practice if:

(a) the child is under the immediate supervision of an adult;

(b) advanced life support personnel, as defined in Section 26-8-2, are on the premises and immediately available to provide assistance at all times during the sanctioned race or organized practice; and

(c) ambulance service, as defined in Section 26-8-2, is on the premises and immediately available to provide assistance for a sanctioned race.

(4) Any person convicted of a violation of this section is guilty of an infraction and shall be fined not more than $50 per offense.

(5) In accordance with Title 63, Chapter 46a, Utah Administrative Rulemaking Act, the division shall make rules specifying the minimum amounts of liability coverage for an organized practice or sanctioned race.   1999

41-22-30. Supervision, safety certificate, or driver license required — Penalty.

(1) A person may not operate and an owner may not give that person permission to operate an off-highway vehicle on any public land, trail, street, or highway of this state unless the person:

(a) is under the direct supervision of a certified off-highway vehicle safety instructor during a scheduled safety training course;

(b) has in his possession the appropriate safety certificate issued or approved by the division; or

(c) has in his immediate possession a valid motor vehicle operator's license, as provided in Title 53, Chapter 3, Uniform Driver License Act.

(2) (a) Any person convicted of a violation of this section is guilty of an infraction and shall be fined not more than $50 per offense.

(b) It is a defense to a charge under this section, if the person charged produces in court a license or an appropriate safety certificate that was:

(i) valid at the time of the citation or arrest; and

(ii) issued to the person operating the off-highway vehicle.

(3) The requirements of this section do not apply to an operator of an all-terrain type I vehicle with a properly displayed and current off-highway implement of husbandry sticker.   2004

41-22-31. Board to set standards for safety program — Safety certificates issued — Cooperation with public and private entities — State immunity from suit.

(1) The board shall establish curriculum standards for a comprehensive off-highway vehicle safety education and training program and shall implement this program.

(a) The program shall be designed to develop and instill the knowledge, attitudes, habits, and skills necessary for the safe operation of an off-highway vehicle.

(b) Components of the program shall include the preparation and dissemination of off-highway vehicle information and safety advice to the public and the training of off-highway vehicle operators.

(c) Off-highway vehicle safety certificates shall be issued to those who successfully complete training or pass the knowledge and skills test established under the program.

(2) The division shall cooperate with appropriate private organizations and associations, private and public corporations, and local government units to implement the program established under this section.

(3) In addition to the governmental immunity granted in Title 63, Chapter 30d, Governmental Immunity Act of Utah, the state is immune from suit for any act, or failure to act, in any capacity relating to the off-highway vehicle safety education and training program. The state is also not responsible for any insufficiency or inadequacy in the quality of training provided by this program.   2005

41-22-32. Certification of safety instructors.

(1) The division may certify certain qualified persons as off-highway vehicle safety instructors. An instructor certified by the division may act in behalf of the division as an agent in:

(a) conducting off-highway vehicle safety classes and examinations; and

(b) issuing safety certificates.

(2) A certified off-highway vehicle safety instructor shall:

(a) successfully complete an off-highway vehicle safety instructor program for the type of vehicle instruction to be given through a program:

(i) of the division; or

(ii) recognized by the division which is conducted by an off-highway vehicle safety organization;

(b) be at least 18 years of age and hold a valid motor vehicle operator's license;

(c) have no convictions as defined in Subsection 41-6a-501(2) for driving under the influence of alcohol or drugs during the previous five years; and

(d) have no convictions for a sexual offense against a minor or a violent crime against a minor.   2005

41-22-33. Fees for safety and education program — Penalty — Unlawful acts.

(1) A $2 fee shall be added to the registration fee required to register an off-highway vehicle under Section 41-22-8 to help fund the off-highway vehicle safety and education program. The division may also collect a fee not to exceed $10 from each person who receives the training and takes the knowledge and skills test, or a fee not to exceed $5 from each person who takes the knowledge and skills test for off-highway vehicle use.

(2) (a) To help defray instructors' costs, the division may reimburse volunteer certified off-highway vehicle safety instructors up to $6 for each student who receives the training and takes the knowledge and skills test.

(b) On or before the 10th day of each calendar month, volunteer off-highway vehicle safety instructors shall report to the division all fees collected and students trained and shall accompany the report with all money received for off-highway vehicle training.

(c) If a volunteer off-highway vehicle safety instructor intentionally or negligently fails to pay the amount due, the division may assess a penalty of 20% of the amount due. All delinquent payments shall bear interest at the rate of 1% per month. If the amount due is not paid because of bad faith or fraud, the division shall assess a penalty of 100% of the total due together with interest.

(d) All fees collected from students shall be kept separate and apart from private funds of the instructor and shall at all times belong to the state. In case of an assignment for the benefit of creditors, receivership, or bankruptcy, the state shall have a preferred claim against the instructor, receiver, or trustee for all money owing the state for training and shall not be stopped from asserting the claim by reason of commingling of funds or otherwise.

(e) A person may not:

(i) willfully misdate an off-highway vehicle education safety certificate;

(ii) issue an incomplete certificate; or

(iii) issue a receipt in lieu of a certificate.

2002

41-22-34. Search and rescue fee — Amount — Deposition.

(1) In addition to the fees imposed under Sections 41-22-8 and 41-22-33, there is imposed a search and rescue fee of 50 cents on each off-highway vehicle required to be registered or renewed under Section 41-22-3.

(2) The fees imposed under this section shall be collected in the same manner and by the same agency designated to collect the fees imposed under this chapter.

(3) The fees collected under this section shall be deposited in the General Fund as dedicated credits for the Search and Rescue Financial Assistance Program created under Section 53-2-107.

1997

41-22-35. Off-highway vehicle user fee — Decal — Agents — Penalty for fraudulent issuance of decal — Deposit and use of fee revenue.

(1) (a) Except as provided in Subsection (1)(b), any nonresident owning an off-highway vehicle who operates or gives another person permission to operate the off-highway vehicle on any public land, trail, street, or highway in this state shall:

(i) apply for an off-highway vehicle decal issued exclusively for an off-highway vehicle owned by a nonresident of the state;

(ii) pay an annual off-highway vehicle user fee; and

(iii) provide evidence that:

(A) the person is a nonresident; and

(B) the person is the owner of the off-highway vehicle.

(b) The provisions of Subsection (1)(a) do not apply to an off-highway vehicle if the off-highway vehicle is:

(i) registered in another state that offers reciprocal operating privileges to Utah residents under rules made by the board; or

(ii) used exclusively for the purposes of a scheduled competitive event sponsored by a public or private entity or another event sponsored by a governmental entity under rules made by the board.

(2) The off-highway vehicle user fee is $30.

(3) Upon compliance with the provisions of Subsection (1)(a), the nonresident shall:

(a) receive a nonresident off-highway vehicle user decal indicating compliance with the provisions of Subsection (1)(a); and

(b) display the decal on the off-highway vehicle in accordance with rules made by the board.

(4) In accordance with Title 63, Chapter 46a, Utah Administrative Rulemaking Act, the board shall make rules establishing:

(a) procedures for:

(i) the payment of off-highway vehicle user fees; and

(ii) the display of a decal on an off-highway vehicle as required under Subsection (3)(b);

(b) acceptable evidence indicating compliance with Subsection (1);

(c) eligibility requirements for reciprocal operating privileges for nonresident users; and

(d) eligibility for scheduled competitive events or other events under Subsection (1)(b)(ii).

(5) (a) An off-highway vehicle user decal may be issued and the off-highway vehicle user fee may be collected by the division or agents of the division.

(b) An agent shall retain 10% of all off-highway vehicle user fees collected.

(c) The division may require agents to obtain a bond in a reasonable amount.

(d) On or before the tenth day of each month, each agent shall:

(i) report all sales to the division; and

(ii) submit all off-highway vehicle user fees collected less the remuneration provided in Subsection (5)(b).

(e) (i) If an agent fails to pay the amount due, the division may assess a penalty of 20% of the amount due.

(ii) Delinquent payments shall bear interest at the rate of 1% per month.

(iii) If the amount due is not paid because of bad faith or fraud, the division shall assess a penalty of 100% of the total amount due together with interest.

(f) All fees collected by an agent, except the remuneration provided in Subsection (5)(b), shall:

(i) be kept separate and apart from the private funds of the agent; and

(ii) belong to the state.

(g) An agent may not issue an off-highway vehicle user decal to any person unless the person furnishes evidence of compliance with the provisions of Subsection (1)(a).

(h) A violation of any provision of this Subsection (5) is a class B misdemeanor and may be cause for revocation of the agent authorization.

(6) Revenue generated by off-highway vehicle user fees shall be deposited in the Off-highway Vehicle Account created in Section 41-22-19.

2004

41-22-36. Fees to cover the costs of electronic payments.

(1) In accordance with Section 63-38a-105, the Division of Motor Vehicles may collect an electronic payment fee on all registrations and renewals of registration under Section 41-22-8.

(2) The division shall establish the fee according to the procedures and requirements of Section 63-38-3.2.

2003

CHAPTER 23

MULTISTATE HIGHWAY TRANSPORTATION AGREEMENT

41-23-1. Enactment.

The Multistate Highway Transportation Agreement is hereby enacted into law and entered into with all other jurisdictions legally joining therein.

1981

41-23-2. Text.

The text of this agreement is as follows:

MULTISTATE HIGHWAY TRANSPORTATION AGREEMENT

Pursuant to and in conformity with the laws of their respective jurisdictions, the participating jurisdictions, acting by and through their officials lawfully authorized to execute this agreement, do mutually agree as follows:

ARTICLE I

Findings and Purposes

Section 1. Findings. The participating jurisdictions find that:

(a) The expanding regional economy depends on expanding transportation capacity;

(b) Highway transportation is the major mode for movement of people and goods in the western states;

(c) Uniform application in the West of more adequate vehicle size and weight standards will result in a reduction of pollution, congestion, fuel consumption, and related transportation costs, which are necessary to permit increased productivity;

(d) A number of western states, already having adopted substantially the 1964 Bureau of Public Roads recommended vehicle size and weight standards, still find current federal limits more restrictive; and

(e) The participating jurisdictions are most capable of developing vehicle size and weight standards most appropriate for their economy and transportation requirements, consistent with and in recognition of principles of highway safety.

Section 2. Purposes. The purposes of this agreement are to:

(a) Adhere to the principle that each participating jurisdiction should have the freedom to develop vehicle size and weight standards that it determines to be most appropriate to its economy and highway system.

(b) Establish a system recommending the operation of vehicles traveling between two or more participating jurisdictions at more adequate size and weight standards.

(c) Promote uniformity among participating jurisdictions in vehicle size and weight standards on the basis of the objectives set forth in this agreement.

(d) Secure uniformity insofar as possible, of administrative procedures in the enforcement of recommended vehicle size and weight standards.

(e) Provide means for the encouragement and utilization of research which will facilitate the achievement of the foregoing purposes, with due regard for the findings set forth in section 1 of this article.

(f) Study and recommend appropriate highway user fees.

(g) Facilitate communication between legislators, state transportation administrators, and commercial industry representatives in addressing the emerging highway transportation issues in participating jurisdictions.

ARTICLE II

Definitions

Section 1. As used in this agreement:

(a) "Cooperating Committee" means a body composed of the designated representatives from the participating jurisdictions.

(b) "Designated representative" means a legislator or other person authorized under Article XII to represent the jurisdiction.

(c) "Jurisdiction" means a state of the United States or the District of Columbia.

(d) "Vehicle" means any vehicle as defined by statute to be subject to size and weight standards which operates in two or more participating jurisdictions.

ARTICLE III

General Provisions

Section 1. Qualifications for Membership. Participation in this agreement is open to jurisdictions which subscribe to the findings, purposes, and objectives of this agreement and will seek legislation necessary to accomplish these objectives.

Section 2. Cooperation. The participating jurisdictions, working through their designated representatives, shall cooperate and assist each other in achieving the desired goals of this agreement pursuant to appropriate statutory authority.

Section 3. Effect of Headings. Article and section headings contained herein shall not be deemed to govern, limit, modify, or in any manner affect the scope, meaning, or intent of the provisions of any article or section hereof.

Section 4. Vehicle Laws and Regulations. This agreement shall not authorize the operation of a vehicle in any participating jurisdiction contrary to the laws or regulations thereof.

Section 5. Interpretation. The final decision regarding interpretation of questions at issue relating to this agreement shall be reached by unanimous joint action of the participating jurisdictions, acting through the designated representatives. Results of all such actions shall be placed in writing.

Section 6. Amendment. This agreement may be amended by unanimous joint action of the participating jurisdictions, acting through the officials thereof authorized to enter into this agreement, subject to the requirements of section 4, article III. Any amendment shall be placed in writing and become a part hereof.

Section 7. Restrictions, Conditions or Limitations. Any jurisdiction entering this agreement shall provide each other participating jurisdiction with a list of any restriction, condition or limitation on the general terms of this agreement, if any.

Section 8. Additional Jurisdictions. Additional jurisdictions may become members of this agreement by signing and accepting the terms of the agreement.

ARTICLE IV

Cooperating Committee

Section 1. Each participating jurisdiction shall have two designated representatives. Pursuant to section 2, article III, the designated representatives of the participating jurisdictions shall constitute the Cooperating Committee which shall have the power to:

(a) Collect, correlate, analyze, and evaluate information resulting or derivable from research and testing activities in relation to vehicle size and weight related matters.

(b) Recommend and encourage the undertaking of research and testing in any aspect of vehicle size and weight or related matter when, in their collective judgment, appropriate or sufficient research or testing has not been undertaken.

(c) Recommend changes in law or policy with emphasis on compatibility of laws and uniformity of administrative rules or regulations which would promote effective governmental action or coordination in the field of vehicle size and weight related matters.

(d) Recommend improvements in highway operations, in vehicular safety, and in state administration of highway transportation laws.

(e) Perform functions necessary to facilitate the purposes of this agreement.

Section 2. Each designated representative of a participating jurisdiction shall be entitled to one vote only. No action of the committee shall be approved unless a majority of the total number of votes cast by the designated representatives of the participating jurisdictions are in favor of the action.

Section 3. The committee shall meet at least once annually and shall elect, from among its members, a chairman, a vice-chairman, and a secretary.

Section 4. The committee shall submit annually to the legislature of each participating jurisdiction a report setting forth the work of the committee during the preceding year and including recommendations developed by the committee. The committee may submit such additional reports as it deems appropriate or desirable.

ARTICLE V

Objectives of the Participating Jurisdictions

Section 1. Objectives. The participating jurisdictions hereby declare that:

(a) It is the objective of the participating jurisdictions to obtain more efficient and more economical transportation by motor vehicles between and among the participating jurisdictions by encouraging the adoption of standards that will, as minimums, allow the operation on all state highways, except those determined through engineering evaluation to be inadequate, with a single-axle weight of 20,000 pounds, a tandem-axle weight of 34,000 pounds, and a gross vehicle or combination weight not in excess of that resulting from application of the formula:

$$W = 500 \{LN/(N - 1) + 12N + 36\}$$

where W = maximum weight in pounds carried on any group of two or more consecutive axles computed to nearest 500 pounds.

L = distance in feet between the extremes of any group of two or more consecutive axles.

N = number of axles in group under consideration.

(b) It is the further objective of the participating jurisdictions that the operation of a vehicle or combination of vehicles in interstate commerce according to the provisions of subsection (a) of this section be authorized under special permit authority by each participating jurisdiction for vehicle combinations in excess of statutory weights of 80,000 pounds or statutory lengths.

(c) It is the further objective of the participating jurisdictions to facilitate and expedite the operation of any vehicle or combination of vehicles between and among the participating jurisdictions under the provisions of subsection (a) or (b) of this section, and to that end the participating jurisdictions hereby agree, through their designated representatives, to meet and cooperate in the consideration of vehicle size and weight related matters including, but not limited to, the development of: uniform enforcement procedures; additional vehicle size and weight standards; operational standards; agreements or compacts to facilitate regional application and administration of vehicle size and weight standards; uniform permit procedures; uniform application forms; rules and regulations for the operation of vehicles, including equipment requirements, driver qualifications, and operating practices; and such other matters as may be pertinent.

(d) The Cooperating Committee may recommend that the participating jurisdictions jointly secure congressional approval of this agreement and, specifically of the vehicle size and weight standards set forth in subsection (a) of this section.

(e) It is the further objective of the participating jurisdictions to:

(1) Establish transportation laws and regulations to meet regional and economic needs and to promote an efficient, safe, and compatible transportation network;

(2) Develop standards that facilitate the most efficient and environmentally sound operation of vehicles on highways, consistent with and in recognition of principles of highway safety; and

(3) Establish programs to increase productivity and reduce congestion, fuel consumption, and related transportation costs and enhance air quality through the uniform application of state vehicle regulations and laws.

ARTICLE VI

Entry Into Force and Withdrawal

Section 1. This agreement shall enter into force when enacted into law by any two or more jurisdictions. Thereafter, this agreement shall become effective as to any other jurisdiction upon its enactment thereof, except as otherwise provided in section 8, article III.

Section 2. Any participating jurisdiction may withdraw from this agreement by cancelling the same but no such withdrawal shall take effect until 30 days after the designated representative of the withdrawing jurisdiction has given notice in writing of the withdrawal to all other participating jurisdictions.

ARTICLE VII

Construction and Severability

Section 1. This agreement shall be liberally construed so as to effectuate the purposes thereof.

Section 2. The provisions of this agreement shall be severable and if any phrase, clause, sentence or provision of this agreement is declared to be contrary to the constitution of any participating jurisdiction or the applicability thereto to any government, agency, person or circumstance is held invalid, the validity of the remainder of this agreement shall not be affected thereby. If this agreement shall be held contrary to the constitution of any jurisdiction participating herein, the agreement shall remain in full force and effect as to the jurisdictions affected as to all severable matters.

ARTICLE VIII

Filing of Documents

Section 1. A copy of this agreement, its amendments, and rules or regulations adopted thereunder and interpretations thereof shall be filed in the highway department in each participating jurisdiction and shall be made available for review by interested parties.

ARTICLE IX

Existing Statutes Not Repealed

Section 1. All existing statutes prescribing weight and size standards and all existing statutes relating to special permits shall continue to be of force and effect until amended or repealed by law.

ARTICLE X

State Government Departments Authorized to Cooperate with Cooperating Committee

Section 1. Within appropriations available therefor, the departments, agencies and officers of the government of this state shall cooperate with and assist the Cooperating Committee within the scope contemplated by article IV, section 1 (a) and (b) of the agreement. The departments, agencies and officers of the government of this state are authorized generally to cooperate with said Cooperating Committee.

ARTICLE XI

Funding Section

Section 1. Funds for the administration of this agreement, including participation in the Cooperating Committee and the actual expenses of the designated representatives, shall be budgeted or expensed as determined appropriate.

ARTICLE XII

Selection of Designated Representatives

Section 1. The process for selecting the designated representatives to the Cooperating Committee shall be established by law under this section.

Section 2. The persons authorized to represent the state of Utah as the designated representatives to the committee shall be the chairperson of the Senate Transportation Committee and the chairperson of the House Transportation Committee or a legislator or a state agency official that the chairperson assigns.

Section 3. The transportation chairpersons in each house shall also designate one alternative designated representative who shall also be a legislator or state agency official to serve in their absence.   2001

CHAPTER 24

NONRESIDENT VIOLATOR COMPACT [REPEALED]

41-24-1 to 41-24-9. Repealed.   1987

CHAPTER 25

VICTIM RESTITUTION [REPEALED]

41-25-1 to 41-25-8. Repealed.   1987, 1992

TITLE 53

PUBLIC SAFETY CODE

CHAPTER 1

ADMINISTRATION

Part 1

Department Administration

Part 2

Administrative Services

Part 3

Management Information Services

PART 1

DEPARTMENT ADMINISTRATION

53-1-101. Title.
This title is known as the "Public Safety Code."
1993

53-1-102. Definitions.
(1) As used in this title:

(a) "Commissioner" means the commissioner of public safety appointed under Section 53-1-107.

(b) "Department" means the Department of Public Safety created in Section 53-1-103.

(c) "Law enforcement agency" means an entity of the federal government, a state, or a political subdivision of a state, including a state institution of higher education, that exists primarily to prevent and detect crime and enforce criminal laws, statutes, and ordinances.

(d) "Law enforcement officer" has the same meaning as provided in Section 53-13-103.

(e) "Motor vehicle" means every self-propelled vehicle and every vehicle propelled by electric power obtained from overhead trolley wires, but not operated upon rails, except motorized wheel chairs and vehicles moved solely by human power.

(f) "Peace officer" means any officer certified in accordance with Title 53, Chapter 13, Peace Officer Classifications.

(g) "State institution of higher education" has the same meaning as provided in Section 53B-3-102.

(h) "Vehicle" means every device in, upon, or by which any person or property is or may be transported or drawn upon a highway, excepting devices used exclusively upon stationary rails or tracks.

(2) The definitions provided in Subsection (1) are to be applied throughout this title in addition to definitions that are applicable to specific chapters or parts.
1998

53-1-103. Creation of department.

(1) There is created within state government the Department of Public Safety.

(2) The department has all of the policymaking functions, regulatory and enforcement powers, rights, duties, and responsibilities specified in this title.
1993

53-1-104. Boards, bureaus, councils, divisions, and offices.

(1) The following are the policymaking boards within the department:

(a) the Driver License Medical Advisory Board, created in Section 53-3-303;

(b) the Concealed Weapon Review Board, created in Section 53-5-703;

(c) the Utah Fire Prevention Board, created in Section 53-7-203;

(d) the Liquified Petroleum Gas Board, created in Section 53-7-304; and

(e) the Private Investigator Hearing and Licensure Board, created in Section 53-9-104.

(2) The following are the councils within the department:

(a) the Peace Officer Standards and Training Council, created in Section 53-6-106; and

(b) the Motor Vehicle Safety Inspection Advisory Council, created in Section 53-8-203.

(3) The following are the divisions within the department:

(a) the Administrative Services Division, created in Section 53-1-203;

(b) the Management Information Services Division, created in Section 53-1-303;

(c) the Division of Emergency Services and Homeland Security, created in Section 53-2-103;

(d) the Driver License Division, created in Section 53-3-103;

(e) the Criminal Investigations and Technical Services Division, created in Section 53-10-103;

(f) the Peace Officers Standards and Training Division, created in Section 53-6-103;

(g) the State Fire Marshal Division, created in Section 53-7-103; and

(h) the Utah Highway Patrol Division, created in Section 53-8-103.

(4) The Office of Executive Protection is created in Section 53-1-112.

(5) The following are bureaus within the department:

(a) Bureau of Criminal Identification, created in Section 53-10-201;

(b) State Bureau of Investigation, created in Section 53-10-301;

(c) Bureau of Forensic Services, created in Section 53-10-401; and

(d) Bureau of Communications, created in Section 53-10-501.
2004

53-1-105. Rulemaking — Adjudicative proceedings — Meetings.

The commissioner and the department and its boards, councils, divisions, and offices shall comply with the procedures and requirements of:

(1) Title 63, Chapter 46a, Utah Administrative Rulemaking Act, in their rulemaking;

(2) Title 63, Chapter 46b, Administrative Procedures Act, in their adjudicative proceedings; and

(3) Title 52, Chapter 4, Open and Public Meetings, in their meetings.
1993

53-1-106. Department duties — Powers.

(1) In addition to the responsibilities contained in this title, the department shall:

(a) make rules and perform the functions specified in Title 41, Chapter 6a, Traffic Code, including:

(i) setting performance standards for towing companies to be used by the department, as required by Section 41-6a-1406; and

(ii) advising the Department of Transportation regarding the safe design and operation of school buses, as required by Section 41-6a-1304;

(b) make rules to establish and clarify standards pertaining to the curriculum and teaching methods of a motor vehicle accident prevention course under Section 31A-19a-211;

(c) aid in enforcement efforts to combat drug trafficking;

(d) meet with the Department of Technology Services to formulate contracts, establish priorities, and develop funding mechanisms for dispatch and telecommunications operations;

(e) provide assistance to the Crime Victims' Reparations Board and Reparations Office in conducting research or monitoring victims' programs, as required by Section 63-25a-405;

(f) develop sexual assault exam protocol standards in conjunction with the Utah Hospital Association;

(g) engage in emergency planning activities, including preparation of policy and procedure and rulemaking necessary for implementation of the federal Emergency Planning and Community Right to Know Act of 1986, as required by Section 63-5-5;

(h) implement the provisions of Section 53-2-202, the Emergency Management Assistance Compact; and

(i) (i) maintain a database of the information listed below regarding each driver license or state identification card status check made by a law enforcement officer:

    (A) the agency employing the law enforcement officer;

    (B) the name of the law enforcement officer or the identifying number the agency has assigned to the law enforcement officer;

    (C) the race and gender of the law enforcement officer;

    (D) the purpose of the law enforcement officer's status check, including but not limited to a traffic stop or a pedestrian stop; and

    (E) the race of the individual regarding whom the status check is made, based on the information provided through the application process under Section 53-3-205 or 53-3-804;

(ii) provide access to the database created in Subsection (1)(i)(i) to the Commission on Criminal and Juvenile Justice for the purpose of:

    (A) evaluating the data;

    (B) evaluating the effectiveness of the data collection process; and

    (C) reporting and making recommendations to the Legislature; and

(iii) classify any personal identifying information of any individual, including law enforcement officers, in the database as protected records under Subsection 63-2-304(9).

(2) (a) The department may establish a schedule of fees as required or allowed in this title for services provided by the department.

(b) The fees shall be established in accordance with Section 63-38-3.2.   2005

53-1-107. Commissioner of public safety — Appointment — Qualifications — Salary.

(1) The chief executive officer of the department is the commissioner.

(2) (a) Every fourth year after the year 1989, the governor shall appoint a commissioner with the consent of the Senate.

(b) The commissioner shall serve for a period of four years from July 1 of the year of his appointment.

(3) The commissioner shall:

(a) be an individual of recognized executive and administrative capacity;

(b) be selected solely with regard to his qualifications and fitness to discharge the duties of the commissioner's office;

(c) be of high moral character;

(d) be of good standing in the community in which he lives; and

(e) have been a resident of this state for a period of at least five years immediately prior to his appointment.

(4) The commissioner shall devote full time to the duties of the office.

(5) The governor shall establish the commissioner's salary within the salary range fixed by the Legislature in Title 67, Chapter 22, State Officer Compensation.   2002

53-1-108. Commissioner's powers and duties.

(1) In addition to the responsibilities contained in this title, the commissioner shall:

(a) administer and enforce this title and Title 41, Chapter 12a, Financial Responsibility of Motor Vehicle Owners and Operators Act;

(b) appoint deputies, inspectors, examiners, clerical workers, and other employees as required to properly discharge the duties of the department;

(c) make rules:

    (i) governing emergency use of signal lights on private vehicles; and

    (ii) allowing privately owned vehicles to be designated for part-time emergency use, as provided in Section 41-6a-310;

(d) set standards for safety belt systems, as required by Section 41-6a-1803;

(e) serve as the chairman of the Disaster Emergency Advisory Council, as required by Section 63-5-4;

(f) designate vehicles as "authorized emergency vehicles," as required by Section 41-6a-102; and

(g) on or before January 1, 2003, adopt a written policy that prohibits the stopping, detention, or search of any person when the action is solely motivated by considerations of race, color, ethnicity, age, or gender.

(2) The commissioner may:

(a) subject to the approval of the governor, establish division headquarters at various places in the state;

(b) issue to a special agent a certificate of authority to act as a peace officer and revoke that authority for cause, as authorized in Section 56-1-21.5;

(c) create specialized units within the commissioner's office for conducting internal affairs and aircraft operations as necessary to protect the public safety;

(d) cooperate with any recognized agency in the education of the public in safety and crime prevention and participate in public or private partnerships, subject to Subsection (3);

(e) cooperate in applying for and distributing highway safety program funds; and

(f) receive and distribute federal funding to further the objectives of highway safety in compliance with the Federal Assistance Management Program Act.

(3) (a) Money may not be expended under Subsection (2)(d) for public safety education unless it is specifically appropriated by the Legislature for that purpose.

(b) Any recognized agency receiving state money for public safety shall file with the auditor of the state an itemized statement of all its receipts and expenditures.   2005

53-1-109. Security for capitol complex — Traffic and parking rules enforcement for division — Security personnel as law enforcement officers.

(1) As used in this section, "capitol hill facilities" and "capitol hill grounds" have the same meaning as provided in Section 63C-9-102.

(2) (a) The commissioner, under the direction of the State Capitol Preservation Board, shall:

    (i) provide for the security of capitol hill facilities and capitol hill grounds; and

    (ii) enforce traffic provisions under Title 41, Chapter 6a, Traffic Code, and parking rules, as adopted by the State Capitol Preservation Board, for capitol hill facilities and capitol hill grounds.

(b) The commissioner, in cooperation with the director of the Division of Facilities Construction and Management shall provide for the security of all grounds and buildings under the jurisdiction of the Division of Facilities Construction and Management.

(3) Security personnel required in Subsection (2) shall be law enforcement officers as defined in Section 53-13-103.

(4) Security personnel who were actively employed and had five or more years of active service with Protective Services within the Utah Highway Patrol Division as special function officers, as defined in Section 53-13-105, on June 29, 1996, shall become law enforcement officers:

(a) without a requirement of any additional training or examinations, if they have completed the entire law enforcement officer training of the Peace Officers Standards and Training Division; or

(b) upon completing only the academic portion of the law enforcement officer training of the Peace Officers Standards and Training Division.

(5) An officer in a supervisory position with Protective Services within the Utah Highway Patrol Division shall be allowed to transfer the job title that the officer held on April 28, 1996, into a comparable supervisory position of employment as a peace officer for as long as the officer remains with Protective Services within the Utah Highway Patrol Division.

2005

53-1-110. Compilation of highway, traffic, and driver licensing laws — Printing and distribution — Fees.

(1) (a) The commissioner shall compile an edition of the general highway, traffic, and driver licensing laws of the state as soon as practicable after each regular session of the Legislature.

(b) The edition shall include laws enacted or amended by the most recent session of the Legislature.

(2) (a) The Division of Finance shall print a sufficient quantity of the compiled highway, traffic, and driver licensing laws to distribute copies to all state, county, and local enforcement agencies, courts, legislators, and other agencies as necessary.

(b) A fee may be assessed for each copy of the compilation issued by the Division of Finance. The fee shall be established by the Division of Finance in accordance with Section 63-38-3.2.

1995

53-1-111. Crime prevention month — Department of Public Safety to coordinate.

(1) The month of October is designated as "Crime Prevention Month."

(2) The department shall coordinate all activities, special programs, and promotional information to heighten public awareness and involvement in the prevention of crime in each community.

1993

53-1-112. Office of Executive Protection — Creation.

There is created within the department the Office of Executive Protection.

1993

53-1-113. Office of Executive Protection — Personnel.

(1) The commissioner shall select personnel for the Office of Executive Protection primarily from the ranks of the Highway Patrol without competitive examination.

(2) Selection of personnel from other than these ranks may be made at the commissioner's discretion, provided the persons selected are peace officers.

1993

53-1-114. Office of Executive Protection — Security and protection for governor and family — Protection for other officials.

(1) The Office of Executive Protection shall provide all necessary security and protection for the governor and the governor's immediate family.

(2) (a) Subject to the direction of the commissioner, the Office of Executive Protection may provide protection to other public officials.

(b) That protection may not extend for more than 15 days without review and approval by majority vote of the president of the Senate, the speaker of the House, and the commissioner.

(c) Review and approval by the same majority vote shall be required at the end of each 15-day period.

2000

53-1-115. Office of Executive Protection — Closure of property to protect governor — Violation of order of closure.

(1) As used in this section:

(a) "Office" includes the governor's official office and any other location not generally open to the public in which the governor is conducting the business of the state.

(b) "Parking space" includes any space occupied or to be occupied by the governor's vehicle when parked, regardless of whether it is the regular parking space of the governor's vehicle.

(c) "Premises" includes:

(i) the governor's official residence, private residence, and any temporary residence owned by the governor or the governor's family; and

(ii) any temporary lodging or residence where the governor is staying or intends to stay, regardless of whether the stay is for official or other purposes.

(d) "Vehicle" includes an automobile, airplane, or other mode of conveyance in which the governor is traveling or intends to travel.

(2) A member of the Office of Executive Protection may order the closure of or restriction of access to the governor's premises or office when in the member's discretion that action is necessary to insure the safety of the governor, the governor's immediate family, or other persons within the premises or office.

(3) A member of the Office of Executive Protection may order restriction of access to the governor's vehicle by ordering closure of or restriction of access to areas surrounding the vehicle, the vehicle's parking space, or the vehicle's routes of ingress or egress, when in the member's discretion that action is necessary to ensure the safety of the governor, the governor's immediate family, other persons within the vehicle, or the safe passage of persons in or out of or to or from the vehicle.

(4) A member of the Office of Executive Protection may order closure or restriction of access to any public property when in the member's discretion that action is necessary in the discharge of the duty to protect the governor, the governor's immediate family, or other persons for whom protection may be provided under Section 53-1-114.

(5) (a) A member of the Office of Executive Protection may order closure of or restriction of access to

privately owned property to the same extent and for the same purposes as for publicly owned property with the consent of the owner, tenant, or occupant of the private property.

(b) The owner, tenant, or occupant may:

(i) expressly ratify consent that was previously implicit; and

(ii) withdraw consent by informing a member of the Office of Executive Protection.

(6) An order of closure or restriction remains in effect for up to three consecutive days and may be extended beyond three days:

(a) with the commissioner's approval; or

(b) without the commissioner's approval if immediate circumstances warrant the extension.

(7) (a) An order closing or restricting access to property shall be posted by placing a copy of it at the primary entrance to the property.

(b) An order restricting access to a vehicle shall be posted by placing a copy of it in the area to be closed or restricted, including the area surrounding the vehicle, the vehicle's parking space, or the vehicle's routes of ingress or egress.

(c) An order is not invalidated for failure to comply with the procedures of Subsection (7)(a) or (7)(b) if notice to the public of the order is otherwise sufficient and reasonable under the circumstances.

(8) An order shall specify the extent of the closure or restriction.

(9) A person who intentionally or knowingly enters or remains within public property in violation of an order of closure or restricted access is guilty of a class B misdemeanor.

(10) This section does not restrict or limit a member of the Office of Executive Protection in exercising any other power available to the member as an officer of the law to provide for the security of the governor or the safety of the public.   2000

53-1-116. Violations.

A violation of this title, except for a violation under Chapter 3, Part 2, Driver Licensing Act, is a class C misdemeanor, unless otherwise provided.   1997

53-1-117. Alcohol or drug enforcement funding — Rulemaking — Legislative findings.

(1) From monies appropriated by the Legislature and any other funds made available for the purposes described under this section, the department shall assist the law enforcement agencies of the state and its political subdivisions in the enforcement of alcohol or drug-related offenses.

(2) In accordance with Title 63, Chapter 46a, Utah Administrative Rulemaking Act, the commissioner shall make rules establishing criteria and procedures for granting monies under this section to law enforcement agencies for:

(a) providing equipment, including drug and alcohol testing equipment;

(b) funding the training and overtime of peace officers; and

(c) managing driving under the influence related abandoned vehicles.

(3) The Legislature finds that these monies are for a general and statewide public purpose.   2000

PART 2

ADMINISTRATIVE SERVICES

53-1-201. Short title.

This part is known as "Administrative Services."   1993

53-1-202. Definitions.

As used in this part:

(1) "Director" means the division director appointed under Section 53-1-203.

(2) "Division" means the Administrative Services Division created in Section 53-1-203.   1993

53-1-203. Creation of Administrative Services Division — Appointment of director — Qualifications — Term — Compensation.

(1) There is created within the department the Administrative Services Division.

(2) The division shall be administered by a director appointed by the commissioner with the approval of the governor.

(3) The director is the executive and administrative head of the division and shall be experienced in administration and possess additional qualifications as determined by the commissioner and as provided by law.

(4) The director acts under the supervision and control of the commissioner and may be removed from his position at the will of the commissioner.

(5) The director shall receive compensation as provided by Title 67, Chapter 19, Utah State Personnel Management Act.   1993

53-1-204. Division duties.

The division shall:

(1) provide administrative and staff support to the commissioner;

(2) ensure that all departmental administrative processes are in compliance with state law, rules, and procedures;

(3) administer all human resource related matters throughout the department;

(4) make deposits, pay all claims and obligations of the department, and conduct all treasury transactions;

(5) prepare the department budget, review department expenditures, prepare financial reports, and offer general assistance with financial matters to the department;

(6) coordinate and review department purchases and monitor department purchasing practices to ensure compliance with state procurement rules;

(7) coordinate the purchase, operation, maintenance, records, and final disposal of the department's vehicle fleet;

(8) make capital facility plans for the department, maintain a capital equipment inventory system, coordinate risk management records, and organize waste paper recycling; and

(9) make rules for the department authorized by this title.   1993

PART 3

MANAGEMENT INFORMATION SERVICES

53-1-301. Short title.

This part is known as "Management Information Services."   1993

53-1-302. Definitions.

As used in this part:

(1) "Director" means the division director appointed under Section 53-1-303.

(2) "Division" means the Management Information Services Division created in Section 53-1-303.   1993

53-1-303. Creation of Management Information Services Division — Appointment of director — Qualifications — Term — Compensation.

(1) There is created within the department the Management Information Services Division.

(2) The division shall be administered by a director appointed by the commissioner with the approval of the governor.

(3) The director is the executive and administrative head of the division and shall be experienced in administration and possess additional qualifications as determined by the commissioner and as provided by law.

(4) The director acts under the supervision and control of the commissioner and may be removed from his position at the will of the commissioner.

(5) The director shall receive compensation as provided by Title 67, Chapter 19, Utah State Personnel Management Act. 1993

53-1-304. Division duties.

The division shall:

(1) provide technical support for the department's various computer systems, including computer software, hardware, and networking support;

(2) provide access to the National Crime Information Center, National Law Enforcement Telecommunication System, which provides electronic mail messaging capabilities to law enforcement agencies throughout the nation, and to National Commercial Driver License Information;

(3) create information systems for public safety information;

(4) provide programming support as required by the department;

(5) design systems and programs to maximize the efficiency of the department;

(6) provide law enforcement officers and criminal justice agencies access to public safety information that will assist in protecting the public; and

(7) other duties as assigned by the commissioner. 1993

CHAPTER 2

EMERGENCY MANAGEMENT

Part 1

Emergency Services and Homeland Security

Part 2

Emergency Management Assistance Compact

Part 3

Authority of the Governor to Enter Into Compact

PART 1

EMERGENCY SERVICES AND HOMELAND SECURITY

53-2-101. Title.

This part is known as the "Emergency Services and Homeland Security Act." 2002

53-2-102. Definitions.

As used in this part:

(1) "Attack" means a nuclear, conventional, biological, or chemical warfare action against the United States of America or this state.

(2) "Director" means the division director appointed under Section 53-2-103.

(3) "Disaster" means a situation causing, or threatening to cause, widespread damage, social disruption, or injury or loss of life or property resulting from attack, internal disturbance, natural phenomena, or technological hazard.

(4) "Division" means the Division of Emergency Services and Homeland Security created in Section 53-2-103.

(5) "Energy" includes the energy resources defined in Section 63-53a-1.

(6) "Expenses" means actual labor costs of government and volunteer personnel, including workers compensation benefits, fringe benefits, administrative overhead, cost of equipment, cost of equipment operation, cost of materials, and the cost of any contract labor and materials.

(7) "Hazardous materials emergency" means a sudden and unexpected release of any substance that because of its quantity, concentration, or physical, chemical, or infectious characteristics presents a direct and immediate threat to public safety or the environment and requires immediate action to mitigate the threat.

(8) "Internal disturbance" means a riot, prison break, disruptive terrorism, or strike.

(9) "Natural phenomena" means any earthquake, tornado, storm, flood, landslide, avalanche, forest or range fire, drought, or epidemic.

(10) "State of emergency" means a condition in any part of this state that requires state government emergency assistance to supplement the local efforts of the affected political subdivision to save lives and to protect property, public health, welfare, or safety in the event of a disaster, or to avoid or reduce the threat of a disaster.

(11) "Technological hazard" means any hazardous materials accident, mine accident, train derailment, air crash, radiation incident, pollution, structural fire, or explosion. 2005

53-2-102.5. Loan program for disasters.

(1) The director may make loans to local governments as provided in this section when:

(a) the governor has issued a proclamation declaring a state of emergency because of a natural disaster;

(b) the Legislature has appropriated monies to the division explicitly for that purpose; and

(c) threats to the public health and safety, or damages to flood control systems or the transportation infrastructure exist.

(2) (a) In order to qualify for loans under this section, the county and each political subdivision within the county shall:

(i) pass a resolution that:

(A) requests a loan;

(B) identifies the loan amount that is requested; and

(C) describes, in as much detail as possible, how the entity will spend the loan proceeds; and

(ii) complete the application for funds provided by the director.

(b) Each political subdivision other than the county shall submit a copy of its resolution and application to the county legislative body.

(c) The county legislative body shall file with the director:

(i) a letter identifying the total loan amount sought by the county and its political subdivisions; and

(ii) a copy of the county's resolution and application and a copy of the resolution and application of each political subdivision seeking loan funds.

(3) (a) To the extent appropriated funds are available, the director shall prepare a promissory note lending the county the total amount requested by the county for itself and its political subdivisions.

(b) The director shall ensure that the promissory note contains:

(i) an annual percentage rate of 2%;

(ii) a requirement that the principal and interest on the note are due on the May 1 in the calendar year after the year in which the note is signed;

(iii) terms allowing the county to prepay some or all of the note's principal, interest, or both before the date that the note is due;

(iv) terms that require repayment of the principal and interest on the note be made to the General Fund Budget Reserve Account established in Section 63-38-2.5; and

(v) terms that limit the use of note proceeds to the repair and reconstruction of infrastructures owned by local governments located within the county.

(c) After an authorized representative of the county signs the promissory note, the director shall disburse the loan funds to the county.

(4) The county and any participating political subdivision may not use loan proceeds for costs:

(a) that could have been paid from other available funding sources if the county or participating political subdivision had applied for those funds; or

(b) to compensate private businesses or private persons for damages incurred in the disaster by those private businesses or persons.

(5) After receiving the loan proceeds from the state, the county shall, before disbursing loan proceeds to the other county political subdivisions, obtain signed promissory notes from each participating political subdivision that include terms substantially similar to the terms contained in the promissory note signed by the county.

(6) The county shall, on behalf of itself and any participating political subdivision, file a report with the director every three months, that:

(a) specifies each project on which loan funds were expended, classified by the name of the local entity that expended the funds; and

(b) identifies the amount expended for that project.

(7) If the county or one of its participating political subdivisions has not expended or committed the funds by the date that the promissory note is due, the county or participating political subdivision shall return the unused or uncommitted funds to the director for redeposit into the fund.   2005

53-2-103. Division of Emergency Services and Homeland Security — Creation — Director — Appointment — Term — Compensation.

(1) There is created within the department the Division of Emergency Services and Homeland Security.

(2) The division shall be administered by a director appointed by the commissioner with the approval of the governor.

(3) The director is the executive and administrative head of the division and shall be experienced in administration and possess additional qualifications as determined by the commissioner and as provided by law.

(4) The director acts under the supervision and control of the commissioner and may be removed from his position at the will of the commissioner.

(5) The director shall receive compensation as provided by Title 67, Chapter 19, Utah State Personnel Management Act.   2002

53-2-104. Division duties — Powers.

(1) The division shall:

(a) respond to the policies of the governor and the Legislature;

(b) perform functions relating to emergency services and homeland security matters as directed by the commissioner;

(c) prepare, implement, and maintain programs and plans to provide for:

(i) prevention and minimization of injury and damage caused by disasters;

(ii) prompt and effective response to and recovery from disasters;

(iii) identification of areas particularly vulnerable to disasters;

(iv) coordination of hazard mitigation and other preventive and preparedness measures designed to eliminate or reduce disasters;

(v) assistance to local officials, state agencies, and the business and public sectors, in developing emergency action plans;

(vi) coordination of federal, state, and local emergency activities;

(vii) coordination of emergency operations plans with emergency plans of the federal government;

(viii) coordination of search and rescue activities;

(ix) coordination of rapid and efficient communications in times of emergency; and

(x) other measures necessary, incidental, or appropriate to this part; and

(d) coordinate with local officials, state agencies, and the business and public sectors in developing, implementing, and maintaining a state energy emergency plan in accordance with Section 53-2-110.

(2) The division may consult with the Legislative Management Committee, the Judicial Council, and legislative and judicial staff offices to assist them in preparing emergency succession plans and procedures under Title 63, Chapter 5b, Emergency Interim Succession Act.   2005

53-2-105. Hazardous materials emergency — Recovery of expenses.

(1) (a) The director may recover from those persons whose negligent actions caused the hazardous materials emergency, expenses incurred by state agencies directly associated with a response to a hazardous materials emergency taken under authority of this part, Title 63, Chapter 5, Emergency Management, or Title 63, Chapter 5a, Disaster Response and Recovery.

(b) The payment of expenses under this subsection does not constitute an admission of liability or negligence in any legal action for damages.

(c) The director may obtain assistance from the attorney general or a county attorney of the affected jurisdiction to assist the director in recovering expenses and legal fees.

(d) Any recovered costs shall be deposited in the General Fund as dedicated credits to be used by the division to reimburse state and local government agencies for the costs they have incurred.

(2) (a) If the cost directly associated with emergency response exceeds all available funds of the division within a given fiscal year, the division, with approval from the governor, may incur a deficit in its line item budget.

(b) The Legislature shall provide a supplemental appropriation in the following year to cover the deficit.

(c) The division shall deposit all costs associated with any emergency response that are collected in subsequent fiscal years into the General Fund.

(3) Any political subdivision may enact local ordinances pursuant to existing statutory or constitutional authority to provide for the recovery of expenses incurred by the political subdivision.   1993

53-2-106. Expenditures authorized by "state of emergency" declaration.

(1) (a) The director may use funds authorized under Title 63, Chapter 5a, Disaster Response and Recovery, to provide:

(i) transportation to and from the disaster scene;

(ii) accommodations at the disaster scene for prolonged incidents; and

(iii) emergency purchase of response equipment and supplies in direct support of a disaster.

(b) The commissioner may authorize the use of funds accrued under Title 63, Chapter 5a, only if the governor declares a state of emergency as provided in Title 63, Chapter 5a, Disaster Response and Recovery.

(2) These funds may not be allocated to a political subdivision unless the political subdivision has demonstrated that it is beyond its capability to respond to the disaster and that no other resources are available in sufficient amount to meet the disaster.   1993

53-2-107. Search and Rescue Financial Assistance Program — Uses — Rulemaking — Distribution.

(1) "Reimbursable expenses," as used in this section, means those reasonable costs incidental to search and rescue activities, not including any salary or overtime paid to any person on a regular or permanent payroll, including permanent part-time employees, of any agency or political subdivision of the state, including:

(a) rental for fixed wing aircraft, helicopters, snowmobiles, boats, and generators;

(b) replacement and upgrade of search and rescue equipment;

(c) training of search and rescue volunteers; and

(d) any other equipment or expenses necessary or appropriate for conducting search and rescue activities.

(2) There is created the Search and Rescue Financial Assistance Program within the division.

(3) (a) The program shall be funded from the following revenue sources:

(i) any voluntary contributions to the state received for search and rescue operations;

(ii) monies received by the state under Section 23-19-42 and Section 41-22-34; and

(iii) appropriations made to the program by the Legislature.

(b) All funding for the program shall be nonlapsing.

(4) The director shall use the monies to reimburse counties for all or a portion of each county's reimbursable expenses for search and rescue operations subject to:

(a) the approval of the Search and Rescue Advisory Board as provided in Section 53-2-109;

(b) monies available in the program; and

(c) rules made under Subsection (7).

(5) Program monies may not be used to reimburse for any paid personnel costs or paid man hours spent in emergency response and search and rescue related activities.

(6) The Legislature finds that these funds are for a general and statewide public purpose.

(7) The division, with the approval of the Search and Rescue Advisory Board, shall make rules in accordance with Title 63, Chapter 46a, Utah Administrative Rulemaking Act, consistent with this act, establishing:

(a) the costs that qualify as reimbursable expenses;

(b) the procedures of agencies to submit expenses and be reimbursed; and

(c) a formula to govern the distribution of available monies between counties based on:

(i) the total qualifying expenses submitted;

(ii) the number of search and rescue incidents per county population;

(iii) the number of victims that reside outside the county; and

(iv) the number of volunteer hours spent in each county in emergency response and search and rescue related activities per county population.   2005

53-2-108. Search and Rescue Advisory Board — Members — Compensation.

(1) There is created the Search and Rescue Advisory Board consisting of seven members appointed as follows:

(a) two representatives designated by the Utah Search and Rescue Association, one of whom is from a county having a population of 75,000 or more; and one from a county having a population of less than 75,000;

(b) three representatives designated by the Utah Sheriff's Association, at least one of whom shall be a member of a voluntary search and rescue unit operating in the state, at least one of whom shall be from a county having a population of 75,000 or more, and at least one of whom shall be from a county having a population of less than 75,000;

(c) one representative of the Division of Emergency Services and Homeland Security designated by the director; and

(d) one private citizen appointed by the governor with the consent of the Senate.

(2) (a) The term of each member of the board is four years.

(b) A member may be reappointed to successive terms.

(c) When a vacancy occurs in the membership for any reason, the replacement shall be appointed for the unexpired term.

(d) In order to stagger the terms of membership, the members appointed or reappointed to represent the Utah Sheriff's Association on or after May 2, 2005, shall serve a term of two years, and all subsequent terms shall be four years.

(3) Members who are not government employees do not receive compensation or benefits for their services, but may receive per diem and travel expenses incurred in the performance of the member's official duties at the rates established by the Division of Finance under Sections 63A-3-106 and 63A-3-107.
2005

53-2-109. General duties of the Search and Rescue Advisory Board.

The duties of the Search and Rescue Advisory Board shall include:

(1) conducting a board meeting at least once per quarter;

(2) receiving applications for reimbursement of eligible expenses from county search and rescue operations by the end of the first quarter of each calendar year;

(3) determining the reimbursement to be provided from the Search and Rescue Financial Assistance Program to each applicant;

(4) standardizing the format and maintaining key search and rescue statistical data from each county within the state; and

(5) disbursing funds accrued in the Search and Rescue Financial Assistance Program, created under Section 53-2-107, to eligible applicants until the program monies are depleted in that fiscal year.   1997

53-2-110. Energy emergency plan.

(1) The division shall develop an energy emergency plan consistent with Title 63, Chapter 53a, Energy Emergency Powers of Governor.

(2) In developing the energy emergency plan, the division shall coordinate with:

(a) the Division of Public Utilities;

(b) the Division of Oil, Gas, and Mining;

(c) the Division of Air Quality; and

(d) the Department of Agriculture and Food with regard to weights and measures.

(3) The energy emergency plan shall:

(a) designate the division as the entity that will coordinate the implementation of the energy emergency plan;

(b) provide for annual review of the energy emergency plan;

(c) provide for cooperation with public utilities and other relevant private sector persons;

(d) provide a procedure for maintaining a current list of contact persons required under the energy emergency plan; and

(e) provide that the energy emergency plan may only be implemented if the governor declares:

(i) a state of emergency as provided in Title 63, Chapter 5a, Disaster Response and Recovery; or

(ii) a state of emergency related to energy as provided in Title 63, Chapter 53a, Energy Emergency Powers of Governor.

(4) If an event requires the implementation of the energy emergency plan, the division shall report on that event and the implementation of the energy emergency plan to:

(a) the governor; and

(b) the Public Utilities and Technology Interim Committee.

(5) If the energy emergency plan includes a procedure for obtaining information, the energy emergency plan shall incorporate reporting procedures that conform to existing requirements of federal, state, and local regulatory authorities wherever possible.   2005

PART 2

EMERGENCY MANAGEMENT ASSISTANCE COMPACT

53-2-201. Title.

This part is known as the "Emergency Management Assistance Compact."   2001

53-2-202. Compact.

(1) Article I. Purposes and Authorities.

(1) (a) This compact is made and entered into by and between the participating member states which enact this compact, hereinafter called party states. For the purposes of this agreement, the term "states" is taken to mean the several states, the Commonwealth of Puerto Rico, the District of Columbia, and all U.S. territorial possessions.

(b) The purpose of this compact is to provide for mutual assistance between the states entering into this compact in managing any emergency or disaster that is duly declared by the governor of the affected state, whether arising from natural disaster, technological hazard, man-made disaster, civil emergency aspects of resources shortages, community disorders, insurgency, or enemy attack.

(c) This compact shall also provide for mutual cooperation in emergency-related exercises, testing, or other training activities using equipment and personnel simulating performance of any aspect of the giving and receiving of aid by party states or subdivisions of party states during emergencies, such actions occurring outside actual declared emergency periods. Mutual assistance in this compact may include the use of the states' national guard forces, either in accordance with the National Guard Mutual Assistance Compact or by mutual agreement between states.

(2) Article II. General Implementation.

(2) (a) Each party state entering into this compact recognizes many emergencies transcend political jurisdictional boundaries and that intergovernmental coordination is essential in managing these and other emergencies under this compact. Each state further recognizes that there will be emergencies which require immediate access and present procedures to apply outside resources to make a prompt and effective response to such an emergency. This is because few, if any, individual states have all the resources they may need in all types of emergencies or the capability of delivering resources to areas where emergencies exist.

(b) The prompt, full, and effective utilization of resources of the participating states, including any resources on hand or available from the federal government or any other source, that are essential to the safety, care, and welfare of the people in the event of any emergency or disaster declared by a party state, shall be the underlying principle on which all articles of this compact shall be understood.

(c) On behalf of the governor of each state participating in the compact, the legally designated state official who is assigned responsibility for emergency management will be responsible for formulation of the appropriate interstate mutual aid plans and procedures necessary to implement this compact.

(3) Article III. Party State Responsibilities.

(3) (a) It shall be the responsibility of each party state to formulate procedural plans and programs for interstate cooperation in the performance of the responsibilities listed in this article. In formulating such plans, and in carrying them out, the party states, insofar as practical, shall:

(i) review individual state hazards analyses and, to the extent reasonably possible, determine all those potential emergencies the party states might jointly suffer, whether due to natural disaster, technological hazard, man-made disaster, emergency aspects of resource shortages, civil disorders, insurgency, or enemy attack;

(ii) review party states' individual emergency plans and develop a plan which will determine the mechanism for the interstate management and provision of assistance concerning any potential emergency;

(iii) develop interstate procedures to fill any identified gaps and to resolve any identified inconsistencies or overlaps in existing or developed plans;

(iv) assist in warning communities adjacent to or crossing the state boundaries;

(v) protect and assure uninterrupted delivery of services, medicines, water, food, energy and fuel, search and rescue, and critical lifeline equipment, services, and resources, both human and material;

(vi) inventory and set procedures for the interstate loan and delivery of human and material resources, together with procedures for reimbursement or forgiveness; and

(vii) provide, to the extent authorized by law, for temporary suspension of any statutes.

(b) The authorized representative of a party state may request assistance of another party state by contacting the authorized representative of that state. The provisions of this agreement shall only apply to requests for assistance made by and to authorized representatives. Requests may be verbal or in writing. If verbal, the request shall be confirmed in writing within 30 days of the verbal request. Requests shall provide the following information:

(i) a description of the emergency service function for which assistance is needed, such as, but not limited to, fire services, law enforcement, emergency medical, transportation, communications, public works and engineering, building inspection, planning and information assistance, mass care, resource support, health and medical services, and search and rescue;

(ii) the amount and type of personnel, equipment, materials and supplies needed, and a reasonable estimate of the length of time they will be needed; and

(iii) the specific place and time for staging of the assisting party's response and a point of contact at that location.

(c) There shall be frequent consultation between state officials who have assigned emergency management responsibilities and other appropriate representatives of the party states with affected jurisdictions and the United States government, with free exchange of information, plans, and resource records relating to emergency capabilities.

(4) Article IV. Limitations.

(4) (a) Any party state requested to render mutual aid or conduct exercises and training for mutual aid shall take such action as is necessary to provide and make available the resources covered by this compact in accordance with the terms hereof; provided that it is understood that the state rendering aid may withhold resources to the extent necessary to provide reasonable protection for such state.

(b) Each party state shall afford to the emergency forces of any party state, while operating within its state limits under the terms and conditions of this compact, the same powers, except that of arrest unless specifically authorized by the receiving state, duties, rights, and privileges as are afforded forces of the state in which they are performing emergency services. Emergency forces will continue under the command and control of their regular leaders, but the organizational units will come under the operational control of the emergency services authorities of the state receiving assistance. These conditions may be activated, as needed, only subsequent to a declaration of a state of emergency or disaster by the governor of the party state that is to receive assistance or commencement of exercises or training for mutual aid and shall continue so long as the exercises or training for mutual aid are in progress, the state of emergency or disaster remains in effect, or loaned resources remain in the receiving state, whichever is longer.

(5) Article V. Licenses and Permits.

Whenever any person holds a license, certificate, or other permit issued by any state party to the compact evidencing the meeting of qualifications for professional, mechanical, or other skills, and when such assistance is requested by the receiving party state, such person shall be deemed licensed, certified, or permitted by the state requesting assistance to render aid involving such skill to meet a declared emergency or disaster, subject to such limitations and conditions as the governor of the requesting state may prescribe by executive order or otherwise.

(6) Article VI. Liability.

Officers or employees of a party state rendering aid in another state pursuant to this compact shall be considered agents of the requesting state for tort liability and immunity purposes; and no party state or its officers or employees rendering aid in another state pursuant to this compact shall be liable on account of any act or omission in good faith on the part of such forces while so engaged or on account of the maintenance or use of any equipment or supplies in connection therewith. Good faith in this article shall not include willful misconduct, gross negligence, or recklessness.

(7) Article VII. Supplementary Agreements.

Inasmuch as it is probable that the pattern and detail of the machinery for mutual aid among two or more states may differ from that among the states that are party hereto, this instrument contains elements of a broad base common to all states, and nothing herein contained shall preclude any state from entering into supplementary agreements with another state or affect any other agreements already in force between states. Supplementary agreements may comprehend, but shall not be limited to, provisions for evacuation and reception of injured and other persons and the exchange of medical, fire, police, public utility, reconnaissance, welfare, transportation and communications personnel, and equipment and supplies.

(8) Article VIII. Compensation.

Each party state shall provide for the payment of compensation and death benefits to injured members of the emergency forces of that state and representatives of deceased members of such forces in case such members sustain injuries or are killed while rendering aid pursuant to this compact, in the same manner and on the same terms as if the injury or death were sustained within their own state.

(9) Article IX. Reimbursement.

Any party state rendering aid in another state pursuant to this compact shall be reimbursed by the party state receiving such aid for any loss or damage to or expense incurred in the operation of any equipment and the provision of any service in answering a request for aid and for the costs incurred in connection with such requests; provided, that any aiding party state may assume in whole or in part such loss, damage, expense, or other cost, or may loan such equipment or donate such services to the receiving party state without charge or cost; and provided further, that any two or more party states may enter into supplementary agreements establishing a different allocation of costs among those states. Article VIII expenses shall not be reimbursable under this provision.

(10) Article X. Evacuation.

(10) (a) Plans for the orderly evacuation and interstate reception of portions of the civilian population as the result of any emergency or disaster of sufficient proportions to so warrant shall be worked out and maintained between the party states and the emergency management or services directors of the various jurisdictions where any type of incident requiring evacuations might occur.

(b) Such plans shall be put into effect by request of the state from which evacuees come and shall include the manner of transporting such evacuees, the number of evacuees to be received in different areas, the manner in which food, clothing, housing, and medical care will be provided, the registration of the evacuees, the providing of facilities for the notification of relatives or friends, and the forwarding of such evacuees to other areas or the bringing in of additional materials, supplies, and all other relevant factors.

(c) Such plans shall provide that the party state receiving evacuees and the party state from which the evacuees come shall mutually agree as to reimbursement of out-of-pocket expenses incurred in receiving and caring for such evacuees, for expenditures for transportation, food, clothing, medicines and medical care, and like items. Such expenditures shall be reimbursed as agreed by the party state from which the evacuees come. After the termination of the emergency or disaster, the party state from which the evacuees come shall assume the responsibility for the ultimate support of repatriation of such evacuees.

(11) Article XI. Implementation.

(11) (a) This compact shall become operative immediately upon its enactment into law by any two states; thereafter, this compact shall become effective as to any other state upon its enactment by such state.

(b) Any party state may withdraw from this compact by enacting a statute repealing the same, but no such withdrawal shall take effect until 30 days after the governor of the withdrawing state has given notice in writing of such withdrawal to the governors of all other party states. Such action shall not relieve the withdrawing state from obligations assumed hereunder prior to the effective date of withdrawal.

(c) Duly authenticated copies of this compact and of such supplementary agreements as may be entered into shall, at the time of their approval, be deposited with each of the party states and with the federal emergency management agency and other appropriate agencies of the United States government.

(12) Article XII. Validity.

This act shall be construed to effectuate the purposes stated in Article I hereof. If any provision of this compact is declared unconstitutional, or the applicability thereof to any person or circumstances is held invalid, the constitutionality of the remainder of this act and the applicability thereof to other persons and circumstances shall not be affected thereby.

(13) Article XIII. Additional Provisions.

Nothing in this compact shall authorize or permit the use of military force by the National Guard of a state at any place outside that state in any emergency for which the President is authorized by law to call into federal service the militia, or for any purpose for which the use of the Army or the Air Force would in the absence of express statutory authorization be prohibited under Section 1385 of Title 18, United States Code.   2001

PART 3

AUTHORITY OF THE GOVERNOR TO ENTER INTO COMPACT

53-2-301. Authority of governor to join compact.

The governor of Utah is authorized and directed to execute a compact on behalf of this state with any other state or states joining the Emergency Management Assistance Compact as provided in Section 53-2-202.   2001

53-3-101.   Short title.

This chapter is known as the "Uniform Driver License Act." 1993

53-3-102.   Definitions.

As used in this chapter:

(1) "Cancellation" means the termination by the division of a license issued through error or fraud or for which consent under Section 53-3-211 has been withdrawn.

(2) "Class D license" means the class of license issued to drive motor vehicles not defined as commercial motor vehicles or motorcycles under this chapter.

(3) "Class M license" means the class of license issued to drive a motorcycle as defined under this chapter.

(4) "Commercial driver license" or "CDL" means a license issued substantially in accordance with the requirements of Title XII, Pub. L. 99-570, the Commercial Motor Vehicle Safety Act of 1986, and in accordance with Part 4, Uniform Commercial Driver License Act, which authorizes the holder to drive a class of commercial motor vehicle.

(5) (a) "Commercial motor vehicle" means a motor vehicle or combination of motor vehicles designed or used to transport passengers or property if the motor vehicle:

(i) has a gross vehicle weight rating of 26,001 or more pounds or a lesser rating as determined by federal regulation;

(ii) is designed to transport 16 or more passengers, including the driver; or

(iii) is transporting hazardous materials and is required to be placarded in accordance with 49 C.F.R. Part 172, Subpart F.

(b) The following vehicles are not considered a commercial motor vehicle for purposes of Part 4, Uniform Commercial Driver License Act:

(i) equipment owned and operated by the United States Department of Defense when driven by any active duty military personnel and members of the reserves and national guard on active duty including personnel on full-time national guard duty, personnel on part-time training, and national guard military technicians and civilians who are required to wear military uniforms and are subject to the code of military justice;

(ii) vehicles controlled and driven by a farmer to transport agricultural products, farm machinery, or farm supplies to or from a farm within 150 miles of his farm but not in operation as a motor carrier for hire;

(iii) firefighting and emergency vehicles; and

(iv) recreational vehicles that are not used in commerce and are driven solely as family or personal conveyances for recreational purposes.

(6) "Conviction" means any of the following:

(a) an unvacated adjudication of guilt or a determination that a person has violated or failed to comply with the law in a court of original jurisdiction or an administrative proceeding;

(b) an unvacated forfeiture of bail or collateral deposited to secure a person's appearance in court;

(c) a plea of guilty or nolo contendere accepted by the court;

(d) the payment of a fine or court costs; or

(e) violation of a condition of release without bail, regardless of whether the penalty is rebated, suspended, or probated.

(7) "Denial" or "denied" means the withdrawal of a driving privilege by the division to which the provisions of Title 41, Chapter 12a, Part 4, Proof of Owner's or Operator's Security, do not apply.

(8) "Director" means the division director appointed under Section 53-3-103.

(9) "Disqualification" means either:

(a) the suspension, revocation, cancellation, denial, or any other withdrawal by a state of a person's privileges to drive a commercial motor vehicle;

(b) a determination by the Federal Highway Administration, under 49 C.F.R. Part 386, that a person is no longer qualified to drive a commercial motor vehicle under 49 C.F.R. Part 391; or

(c) the loss of qualification that automatically follows conviction of an offense listed in 49 C.F.R. Part 383.51.

(10) "Division" means the Driver License Division of the department created in Section 53-3-103.

(11) "Drive" means:

(a) to operate or be in physical control of a motor vehicle upon a highway; and

(b) in Subsections 53-3-414(1) through (3), Subsection 53-3-414(5), and Sections 53-3-417 and 53-3-418, the operation or physical control of a motor vehicle at any place within the state.

(12) (a) "Driver" means any person who drives, or is in actual physical control of a motor vehicle in any location open to the general public for purposes of vehicular traffic.

(b) In Part 4, Uniform Commercial Driver License Act, "driver" includes any person who is required to hold a CDL under Part 4 or federal law.

(13) "Extension" means a renewal completed in a manner specified by the division.

(14) "Farm tractor" means every motor vehicle designed and used primarily as a farm implement for drawing plows, mowing machines, and other implements of husbandry.

(15) "Highway" means the entire width between property lines of every way or place of any nature when any part of it is open to the use of the public, as a matter of right, for traffic.

(16) "License" means the privilege to drive a motor vehicle.

(17) "License certificate" means the evidence of the privilege issued under this chapter to drive a motor vehicle.

(18) "Motorboat" has the same meaning as provided under Section 73-18-2.

(19) "Motorcycle" means every motor vehicle, other than a tractor, having a seat or saddle for the use of the rider and designed to travel with not more than three wheels in contact with the ground.

(20) (a) "Owner" means a person other than a lienholder having an interest in the property or title to a vehicle.

(b) "Owner" includes a person entitled to the use and possession of a vehicle subject to a security interest in another person but excludes a lessee under a lease not intended as security.

(21) "Renewal" means to validate a license certificate so that it expires at a later date.

(22) "Reportable violation" means an offense required to be reported to the division as determined by the division and includes those offenses against which points are assessed under Section 53-3-221.

(23) (a) "Resident" means an individual who:

(i) has established a domicile in this state, as defined in Section 41-1a-202, or regardless of domicile, remains in this state for an aggregate period of six months or more during any calendar year;

(ii) engages in a trade, profession, or occupation in this state, or who accepts employment in other than seasonal work in this state, and who does not commute into the state;

(iii) declares himself to be a resident of this state by obtaining a valid Utah driver license certificate or motor vehicle registration; or

(iv) declares himself a resident of this state to obtain privileges not ordinarily extended to nonresidents, including going to school, or placing children in school without paying nonresident tuition or fees.

(b) "Resident" does not include any of the following:

(i) a member of the military, temporarily stationed in this state;

(ii) an out-of-state student, as classified by an institution of higher education, regardless of whether the student engages in any type of employment in this state;

(iii) a person domiciled in another state or country, who is temporarily assigned in this state, assigned by or representing an employer, religious or private organization, or a governmental entity; or

(iv) an immediate family member who resides with or a household member of a person listed in Subsections (23)(b)(i) through (iii).

(24) "Revocation" means the termination by action of the division of a licensee's privilege to drive a motor vehicle.

(25) (a) "School bus" means a commercial motor vehicle used to transport pre-primary, primary, or secondary school students to and from home and school, or to and from school sponsored events.

(b) "School bus" does not include a bus used as a common carrier as defined in Section 59-12-102.

(26) "Suspension" means the temporary withdrawal by action of the division of a licensee's privilege to drive a motor vehicle.

(27) "Taxicab" means any class D motor vehicle transporting any number of passengers for hire and that is subject to state or federal regulation as a taxi.   2004

53-3-103. Driver License Division — Creation — Director — Appointment — Term — Compensation.

(1) There is created within the department the Driver License Division.

(2) The division shall be administered by a director appointed by the commissioner with the approval of the governor.

(3) The director is the executive and administrative head of the division and shall be experienced in administration and possess additional qualifications as determined by the commissioner and as provided by law.

(4) The director acts under the supervision and control of the commissioner and may be removed from his position at the will of the commissioner.

(5) The director shall receive compensation as provided by Title 67, Chapter 19, Utah State Personnel Management Act.   1993

53-3-104. Division duties.

The division shall:

(1) in accordance with Title 63, Chapter 46a, Utah Administrative Rulemaking Act, make rules:

(a) for examining applicants for a license, as necessary for the safety and welfare of the traveling public;

(b) for acceptable documentation of an applicant's identity, Utah resident status, Utah residence address, proof of legal presence, proof of citizenship of a country other than the United States, and other proof or documentation required under this chapter;

(c) regarding the restrictions to be imposed on a person driving a motor vehicle with a temporary learner permit; and

(d) for exemptions from licensing requirements as authorized in this chapter;

(2) examine each applicant according to the class of license applied for;

(3) license motor vehicle drivers;

(4) file every application for a license received by it and shall maintain indices containing:

(a) all applications denied and the reason each was denied;

(b) all applications granted; and

(c) the name of every licensee whose license has been suspended, disqualified, or revoked by the division and the reasons for the action;

(5) suspend, revoke, disqualify, cancel, or deny any license issued in accordance with this chapter;

(6) file all accident reports and abstracts of court records of convictions received by it under state law;

(7) maintain a record of each licensee showing his convictions and the traffic accidents in which he has been involved where a conviction has resulted;

(8) consider the record of a licensee upon an application for renewal of a license and at other appropriate times;

(9) search the license files, compile, and furnish a report on the driving record of any person licensed in the state in accordance with Section 53-3-109;

(10) develop and implement a record system as required by Section 41-6a-604;

(11) in accordance with Section 53A-13-208, establish:

(a) procedures and standards to certify teachers of driver education classes to administer knowledge and skills tests;

(b) minimal standards for the tests; and

(c) procedures to enable school districts to administer or process any tests for students to receive a class D operator's license;

(12) in accordance with Section 53-3-510, establish:

(a) procedures and standards to certify licensed instructors of commercial driver training school courses to administer the skills test;

(b) minimal standards for the test; and

(c) procedures to enable licensed commercial driver training schools to administer or process skills tests for students to receive a class D operator's license; and

(13) provide administrative support to the Driver License Medical Advisory Board created in Section 53-3-303. 2005

53-3-105. Fees for licenses, renewals, extensions, reinstatements, rescheduling, and identification cards.

The following fees apply under this chapter:

(1) An original class D license application under Section 53-3-205 is $20.

(2) An original class M license application under Section 53-3-205 is $22.50.

(3) An original provisional license application for a class D license under Section 53-3-205 is $25.

(4) An original provisional license application for a class M license under Section 53-3-205 is $27.50.

(5) An original application for a motorcycle endorsement under Section 53-3-205 is $7.50.

(6) An original application for a taxicab endorsement under Section 53-3-205 is $5.

(7) A renewal of a class D license under Section 53-3-214 is $20 unless Subsection (13) applies.

(8) A renewal of a class M license under Section 53-3-214 is $22.50.

(9) A renewal of a provisional license application for a class D license under Section 53-3-214 is $20.

(10) A renewal of a provisional license application for a class M license under Section 53-3-214 is $22.50.

(11) A renewal of a motorcycle endorsement under Section 53-3-214 is $7.50.

(12) A renewal of a taxicab endorsement under Section 53-3-214 is $5.

(13) A renewal of a class D license for a person 65 and older under Section 53-3-214 is $8.

(14) An extension of a class D license under Section 53-3-214 is $15 unless Subsection (20) applies.

(15) An extension of a class M license under Section 53-3-214 is $17.50.

(16) An extension of a provisional license application for a class D license under Section 53-3-214 is $15.

(17) An extension of a provisional license application for a class M license under Section 53-3-214 is $17.50.

(18) An extension of a motorcycle endorsement under Section 53-3-214 is $7.50.

(19) An extension of a taxicab endorsement under Section 53-3-214 is $5.

(20) An extension of a class D license for a person 65 and older under Section 53-3-214 is $6.

(21) An original or renewal application for a commercial class A, B, or C license or an original or renewal of a provisional commercial class A or B license under Part 4, Uniform Commercial Driver License Act, is:

(a) $35 for the knowledge test; and

(b) $55 for the skills test.

(22) Each original CDL endorsement for passengers, hazardous material, double or triple trailers, or tankers is $5.

(23) An original CDL endorsement for a school bus under Part 4, Uniform Commercial Driver License Act, is $5.

(24) A renewal of a CDL endorsement under Part 4, Uniform Commercial Driver License Act, is $5.

(25) A retake of a CDL knowledge or a CDL skills test provided for in Section 53-3-205 is $15.

(26) A retake of a CDL endorsement test provided for in Section 53-3-205 is $5.

(27) A duplicate class A, B, C, D, or M license certificate under Section 53-3-215 is $13.

(28) (a) A license reinstatement application under Section 53-3-205 is $25.

(b) A license reinstatement application under Section 53-3-205 for an alcohol, drug, or combination of alcohol and any drug-related offense is $25 in addition to the fee under Subsection (28)(a).

(29) (a) An administrative fee for license reinstatement after an alcohol, drug, or combination of alcohol and any drug-related offense under Section 41-6a-520, 53-3-223, or 53-3-231 or an alcohol, drug, or combination of alcohol and any drug-related offense under Part 4, Uniform Commercial Driver License Act, is $150.

(b) This administrative fee is in addition to the fees under Subsection (28).

(30) (a) An administrative fee for providing the driving record of a driver under Section 53-3-104 or 53-3-420 is $4.

(b) The division may not charge for a report furnished under Section 53-3-104 to a municipal, county, state, or federal agency.

(31) A rescheduling fee under Section 53-3-205 or 53-3-407 is $25.

(32) An identification card application under Section 53-3-808 is $8.   2005

53-3-106. Disposition of revenues under this chapter — Restricted account created — Uses as provided by appropriation — Nonlapsing.

(1) There is created within the Transportation Fund a restricted account known as the "Department of Public Safety Restricted Account."

(2) The account consists of monies generated from the following revenue sources:

(a) all monies received under this chapter;

(b) administrative fees received according to the fee schedule authorized under this chapter and Section 63-38-3.2; and

(c) any appropriations made to the account by the Legislature.

(3) (a) The account shall earn interest.

(b) All interest earned on account monies shall be deposited in the account.

(4) The expenses of the department in carrying out this chapter shall be provided for by legislative appropriation from this account.

(5) The amount in excess of $35 of the fees collected under Subsection 53-3-105(29) shall be appropriated by the Legislature from this account to the department to implement the provisions of Section 53-1-117, except that of the amount in excess of $35, $30 shall be deposited in the State Laboratory Drug Testing restricted account created in Section 26-1-34.

(6) All monies received under Subsection 41-6a-1406(6)(b)(ii) shall be appropriated by the Legislature from this account to the department to implement the provisions of Section 53-1-117.

(7) Appropriations to the department from the account are nonlapsing.   2005

53-3-107. Repealed.   1999

53-3-108. Authority to administer oaths.

Officers and employees of the division designated by the director for the purpose of administering this chapter may administer oaths and acknowledge signatures and shall do so without fee.   1999

53-3-109. Records — Access — Fees — Rulemaking.

(1) (a) Except as provided in this section, all records of the division shall be classified and disclosed in accordance with Title 63, Chapter 2, Government Records Access and Management Act.

(b) The division may only disclose personal identifying information:

(i) when the division determines it is in the interest of the public safety to disclose the information; and

(ii) in accordance with the federal Driver's Privacy Protection Act of 1994, 18 U.S.C. Chapter 123.

(c) The division may disclose personal identifying information to a licensed private investigator holding a valid agency or registrant license, with a legitimate business need.

(2) A person who receives personal identifying information shall be advised by the division that the person may not:

(a) disclose the personal identifying information from that record to any other person; or

(b) use the personal identifying information from that record for advertising or solicitation purposes.

(3) The division may:

(a) collect fees in accordance with Section 53-3-105 for searching and compiling its files or furnishing a report on the driving record of a person; and

(b) prepare under the seal of the division and deliver upon request, a certified copy of any record of the division, and charge a fee under Section 63-38-3.2 for each document authenticated.

(4) Each certified copy of a driving record furnished in accordance with this section is admissible in any court proceeding in the same manner as the original.

(5) (a) A driving record furnished under this section may only report on the driving record of a person for a period of ten years.

(b) Subsection (5)(a) does not apply to court or law enforcement reports and to reports of commercial driver license violations.

(6) In accordance with Title 63, Chapter 46a, Utah Administrative Rulemaking Act, the division may make rules to designate:

(a) what information shall be included in a report on the driving record of a person;

(b) the form of a report or copy of the report which may include electronic format;

(c) the form of a certified copy, as required under Section 53-3-216, which may include electronic format;

(d) the form of a signature required under this chapter which may include electronic format; and

(e) the form of written request to the division required under this chapter which may include electronic format.   2004

PART 2

DRIVER LICENSING ACT

53-3-201. Short title.

This part is known as the "Driver Licensing Act."   1993

53-3-202. Drivers must be licensed — Taxicab endorsement — Violation.

(1) A person may not drive a motor vehicle on a highway in this state unless the person is:

(a) granted the privilege to operate a motor vehicle by being licensed as a driver by the division under this chapter;

(b) driving an official United States Government class D motor vehicle with a valid United States Government driver permit or license for that type of vehicle;

(c) driving a road roller, road machinery, or any farm tractor or implement of husbandry temporarily drawn, moved, or propelled on the highways;

(d) a nonresident who is at least 16 years of age and younger than 18 years of age who has in his immediate possession a valid license certificate issued to him in his home state or country and is driving as a class D or M driver;

(e) a nonresident who is at least 18 years of age and who has in his immediate possession a valid license certificate issued to him in his home state or country if driving in the class or classes identified on the home state license certificate, except those persons referred to in Part 6 of this chapter;

(f) driving under a temporary learner permit, instruction permit, or practice permit in accordance with Section 53-3-210 or 53A-13-208;

(g) driving with a temporary license certificate issued in accordance with Section 53-3-207; or

(h) exempt under Title 41, Chapter 22, Off-highway Vehicles.

(2) A person may not drive or, while within the passenger compartment of a motor vehicle, exercise any degree or form of physical control of a motor vehicle being towed by a motor vehicle upon a highway unless the person:

(a) holds a valid license issued under this chapter for the type or class of motor vehicle being towed; or

(b) is exempted under either Subsection (1)(b) or (1)(c).

(3) A person may not drive a motor vehicle as a taxicab on a highway of this state unless the person has a taxicab endorsement issued by the division on his license certificate.

(4) (a) A person may not operate an electric assisted bicycle as defined under Section 41-6a-102 unless the person has a valid class M or class D license issued under this chapter.

(b) Subsection (4)(a) is an exception to the provisions of Section 53-3-104.

(5) A person who violates this section is guilty of a class C misdemeanor.   2005

53-3-203. Authorizing or permitting driving in violation of chapter — Renting of motor vehicles — License requirements — Employees must be licensed — Violations.

(1) A person may not authorize or knowingly permit a motor vehicle owned by him or under his control to be driven by a person in violation of this chapter.

(2) (a) A person may not rent a motor vehicle to another person unless the person who will be the driver is licensed in this state, or in the case of a nonresident, licensed under the laws of the state or country of his residence.

(b) A person may not rent a motor vehicle to another person until he has inspected the license certificate of the person who will be the driver and verified the signature on the license certificate by comparison with the signature of the person who will be the driver written in his presence.

(c) A person renting a motor vehicle to another shall keep a record of the:

(i) registration number of the rented motor vehicle;

(ii) name and address of the person to whom the motor vehicle is rented;

(iii) number of the license certificate of the renter; and

(iv) date and place the license certificate was issued.

(d) The record is open to inspection by any peace officer or officer or employee of the division.

(3) A person may not employ a person to drive a motor vehicle who is not licensed as required under this chapter.

(4) A person who violates Subsection (1), (2)(a), or (3) is guilty of a class C misdemeanor.   1997

53-3-204. Persons who may not be licensed.

(1) (a) The division may not license a person who:

(i) is younger than 16 years of age;

(ii) has not completed a course in driver training approved by the commissioner; or

(iii) if the person is a minor, has not completed the driving requirement under Section 53-3-211; or

(iv) is not a resident of the state of Utah.

(b) Subsections (1)(a)(i), (ii), and (iii) do not apply to a person:

(i) who has been licensed before July 1, 1967;

(ii) who is 16 years of age or older making application for a license who has been licensed in another state or country; or

(iii) who is applying for a permit under Section 53-3-210 or 53A-13-208.

(2) The division may not issue a license certificate to a person:

(a) whose license has been suspended, denied, cancelled, or disqualified during the period of suspension, denial, cancellation, or disqualification;

(b) whose privilege has been revoked, except as provided in Section 53-3-225;

(c) who has previously been adjudged mentally incompetent and who has not at the time of application been restored to competency as provided by law;

(d) who is required by this chapter to take an examination unless the person successfully passes the examination; or

(e) whose driving privileges have been denied or suspended under:

(i) Section 78-3a-506 by an order of the juvenile court; or

(ii) Section 53-3-231.

(3) The division may grant a class D or M license to a person whose commercial license is disqualified under Part 4 of this chapter if the person is not otherwise sanctioned under this chapter.   2005

53-3-205. Application for license or endorsement — Fee required — Tests — Expiration dates of licenses and endorsements — Information required — Previous licenses surrendered — Driving record transferred from other states — Reinstatement — Fee required — License agreement.

(1) An application for any original license, provisional license, or endorsement shall be:

(a) made upon a form furnished by the division; and

(b) accompanied by a nonrefundable fee set under Section 53-3-105.

(2) An application and fee for an original provisional class D license or an original class D license entitle the applicant to:

(a) not more than three attempts to pass both the knowledge and skills tests for a class D license within six months of the date of the application;

(b) a learner permit if needed after the knowledge test is passed; and

(c) an original class D license and license certificate after all tests are passed.

(3) An application and fee for an original class M license entitle the applicant to:

(a) not more than three attempts to pass both the knowledge and skills tests for a class M license within six months of the date of the application;

(b) a learner permit if needed after the knowledge test is passed; and

(c) an original class M license and license certificate after all tests are passed.

(4) An application and fee for a motorcycle or taxicab endorsement entitle the applicant to:

(a) not more than three attempts to pass both the knowledge and skills tests within six months of the date of the application;

(b) a motorcycle learner permit if needed after the motorcycle knowledge test is passed; and

(c) a motorcycle or taxicab endorsement when all tests are passed.

(5) An application and fees for a commercial class A, B, or C license entitle the applicant to:

(a) not more than two attempts to pass a knowledge test and not more than two attempts to pass a skills test within six months of the date of the application;

(b) a commercial driver instruction permit if needed after the knowledge test is passed; and

(c) an original commercial class A, B, or C license and license certificate when all applicable tests are passed.

(6) An application and fee for a CDL endorsement entitle the applicant to:

(a) not more than two attempts to pass a knowledge test and not more than two attempts to pass a skills test within six months of the date of the application; and

(b) a CDL endorsement when all tests are passed.

(7) If a CDL applicant does not pass a knowledge test, skills test, or an endorsement test within the number of attempts provided in Subsection (5) or (6), each test may be taken two additional times within the six months for the fee provided in Section 53-3-105.

(8) (a) Except as provided under Subsections (8)(f) and (g), an original license expires on the birth date of the applicant in the fifth year following the year the license certificate was issued.

(b) Except as provided under Subsections (8)(f) and (g), a renewal or an extension to a license expires on the birth date of the licensee in the fifth year following the expiration date of the license certificate renewed or extended.

(c) Except as provided under Subsections (8)(f) and (g), a duplicate license expires on the same date as the last license certificate issued.

(d) An endorsement to a license expires on the same date as the license certificate regardless of the date the endorsement was granted.

(e) A license and any endorsement to the license held by a person ordered to active duty and stationed outside Utah in any of the armed forces of the United States, which expires during the time period the person is stationed outside of the state, is valid until 90 days after the person has been discharged or has left the service, unless the license is suspended, disqualified, denied, or has been cancelled or revoked by the division, or the licensee updates the information or photograph on the license certificate.

(f) An original license or a renewal to an original license obtained using proof under Subsection (9)(a)(i)(E)(III) expires on the date of the expiration of the applicant's foreign visa, permit, or other document granting legal presence in the United States or on the date provided under this Subsection (8), whichever is sooner.

(g) (i) An original license or a renewal or a duplicate to an original license expires on the next birth date of the applicant or licensee beginning on July 1, 2005 if:

(A) the license was obtained without using a Social Security number as required under Subsection (9); and

(B) the license certificate or driving privilege card is not clearly distinguished as required under Subsection 53-3-207(6).

(ii) A driving privilege card issued or renewed under Section 53-3-207 expires on the birth date of the applicant in the first year following the year that the driving privilege card was issued or renewed.

(iii) The expiration dates provided under Subsections (8)(g)(i) and (ii) do not apply to an original license or driving privilege card or to the renewal of an original license or driving privilege card with an expiration date provided under Subsection (8)(f).

(9) (a) In addition to the information required by Title 63, Chapter 46b, Administrative Procedures Act, for requests for agency action, each applicant shall have a Utah residence address and each applicant shall:

(i) provide the applicant's:

(A) full legal name;

(B) birth date;

(C) gender;

(D) between July 1, 2002 and July 1, 2007, race in accordance with the categories established by the United States Census Bureau;

(E) (I) Social Security number;

(II) temporary identification number (ITIN) issued by the Internal Revenue Service for a person who does not qualify for a Social Security number; or

(III) (Aa) proof that the applicant is a citizen of a country other than the United States;

(Bb) proof that the applicant does not qualify for a Social Security number; and

(Cc) proof of legal presence in the United States, as authorized under federal law; and

(F) Utah residence address as documented by a form acceptable under rules made by the division under Section 53-3-104;

(ii) provide a description of the applicant;

(iii) state whether the applicant has previously been licensed to drive a motor vehicle and, if so, when and by what state or country;

(iv) state whether the applicant has ever had any license suspended, cancelled, revoked, disqualified, or denied in the last six years, or whether the applicant has ever had any license application refused, and if so, the date of and reason for the suspension, cancellation, revocation, disqualification, denial, or refusal;

(v) state whether the applicant intends to make an anatomical gift under Title 26, Chapter 28, Uniform Anatomical Gift Act, in compliance with Subsection (16);

(vi) provide all other information the division requires; and

(vii) sign the application which signature may include an electronic signature as defined in Section 46-4-102.

(b) The division shall maintain on its computerized records an applicant's:

(i) Social Security number;

(ii) temporary identification number (ITIN); or

(iii) other number assigned by the division if Subsection (9)(a)(i)(E)(III) applies.

(c) An applicant may not be denied a license for refusing to provide race information required under Subsection (9)(a)(i)(D).

(10) The division shall require proof of every applicant's name, birthdate, and birthplace by at least one of the following means:

(a) current license certificate;

(b) birth certificate;

(c) Selective Service registration; or

(d) other proof, including church records, family Bible notations, school records, or other evidence considered acceptable by the division.

(11) When an applicant receives a license in another class, all previous license certificates shall be surrendered and canceled. However, a disqualified commercial license may not be canceled unless it expires before the new license certificate is issued.

(12) (a) When an application is received from a person previously licensed in another state to drive a motor vehicle, the division shall request a copy of the driver's record from the other state.

(b) When received, the driver's record becomes part of the driver's record in this state with the same effect as though entered originally on the driver's record in this state.

(13) An application for reinstatement of a license after the suspension, cancellation, disqualification, denial, or revocation of a previous license shall be accompanied by the additional fee or fees specified in Section 53-3-105.

(14) A person who has an appointment with the division for testing and fails to keep the appointment or to cancel at least 48 hours in advance of the appointment shall pay the fee under Section 53-3-105.

(15) A person who applies for an original license or renewal of a license agrees that the person's license is subject to any suspension or revocation authorized under this title or Title 41, Motor Vehicles.

(16) (a) The indication of intent under Subsection (9)(a)(v) shall be authenticated by the licensee in accordance with division rule.

(b) (i) Notwithstanding Title 63, Chapter 2, Government Records Access and Management Act, the division may, upon request, release to an organ procurement organization, as defined in Section 26-28-2, the names and addresses of all persons who under Subsection (9)(a)(v) indicate that they intend to make an anatomical gift.

(ii) An organ procurement organization may use released information only to:

(A) obtain additional information for an anatomical gift registry; and

(B) inform licensees of anatomical gift options, procedures, and benefits.

(17) The division and its employees are not liable, as a result of false or inaccurate information provided under Subsection (9)(a)(v), for direct or indirect:

(a) loss;

(b) detriment; or

(c) injury.   2005

53-3-206. Examination of applicant's physical and mental fitness to drive a motor vehicle.

(1) The division shall examine every applicant for a license, including a test of the applicant's:

(a) eyesight either:

(i) by the division; or

(ii) by allowing the applicant to furnish to the division a statement from a physician licensed under Title 58, Chapter 67, Utah Medical Practice Act, or an optometrist licensed under Title 58, Chapter 16a, Utah Optometry Practice Act;

(b) ability to read and understand highway signs regulating, warning, and directing traffic;

(c) ability to read and understand simple English used in highway traffic and directional signs;

(d) knowledge of the state traffic laws;

(e) other physical and mental abilities the division finds necessary to determine the applicant's fitness to drive a motor vehicle safely on the highways; and

(f) ability to exercise ordinary and responsible control driving a motor vehicle, as determined by actual demonstration or other indicator.

(2) The division shall determine whether any facts exist that would bar granting a license under Section 53-3-204.

(3) The division shall examine each applicant according to the class of license applied for.

(4) An applicant for a CDL shall meet all additional requirements of Part 4 of this chapter.   1993

53-3-207. License certificates or driving privilege cards issued to drivers by class of motor vehicle — Contents — Release of anatomical gift information — Temporary licenses or driving privilege cards — Minors' licenses, cards, and permits — Violation.

(1) As used in this section:

(a) "driving privilege" means the privilege granted under this chapter to drive a motor vehicle;

(b) "driving privilege card" means the evidence of the privilege granted and issued under this chapter to drive a motor vehicle;

(c) "governmental entity" means the state and its political subdivisions as defined in this Subsection (1);

(d) "political subdivision" means any county, city, town, school district, public transit district, redevelopment agency, special improvement or taxing district, special district, an entity created by an interlocal agreement adopted under Title 11, Chapter 13, Interlocal Cooperation Act, or other governmental subdivision or public corporation; and

(e) "state" means this state, and includes any office, department, agency, authority, commission, board, institution, hospital, college, university, children's justice center, or other instrumentality of the state.

(2) (a) The division shall issue to every person privileged to drive a motor vehicle, a license certificate or a driving privilege card indicating the type or class of motor vehicle the person may drive.

(b) A person may not drive a class of motor vehicle unless granted the privilege in that class.

(3) (a) Every license certificate or driving privilege card shall bear:

(i) the distinguishing number assigned to the person by the division;

(ii) the name, birth date, and Utah residence address of the person;

(iii) a brief description of the person for the purpose of identification;

(iv) any restrictions imposed on the license under Section 53-3-208;

(v) a photograph of the person;

(vi) a photograph or other facsimile of the person's signature; and

(vii) an indication whether the person intends to make an anatomical gift under Title 26, Chapter 28, Uniform Anatomical Gift Act, unless the driving privilege is extended under Subsection 53-3-214(3).

(b) A new license certificate issued by the division may not bear the person's Social Security number.

(c) (i) The license certificate or driving privilege card shall be of an impervious material, resistant to wear, damage, and alteration.

(ii) Except as provided under Subsection (4)(b), the size, form, and color of the license certificate or driving privilege card shall be as prescribed by the commissioner.

(iii) The commissioner may also prescribe the issuance of a special type of limited license certificate or driving privilege card under Subsection 53-3-220(4) and may authorize the issuance of a renewed or duplicate license certificate or driving privilege card without a picture if the applicant is not then living in the state.

(4) (a) (i) The division upon determining after an examination that an applicant is mentally and physically qualified to be granted a driving privilege may issue to an applicant a receipt for the fee.

(ii) The receipt serves as a temporary license certificate or temporary driving privilege card allowing the person to drive a motor vehicle while the division is completing its investigation to determine whether the person is entitled to be granted a driving privilege.

(b) The receipt shall be in the person's immediate possession while driving a motor vehicle, and it is invalid when the person's license certificate or driving privilege card has been issued or when, for good cause, the privilege has been refused.

(c) The division shall indicate on the receipt a date after which it is not valid as a license certificate or driving privilege card.

(5) (a) The division shall distinguish learner permits, temporary permits, license certificates, and driving privilege cards issued to any person younger than 21 years of age by use of plainly printed information or the use of a color or other means not used for other license certificates or driving privilege cards.

(b) The division shall distinguish a license certificate or driving privilege card issued to any person:

(i) younger than 21 years of age by use of a portrait-style format not used for other license certificates or driving privilege cards and by plainly printing the date the license certificate or driving privilege card holder is 21 years of age, which is the legal age for purchasing an alcoholic beverage or product under Section 32A-12-203; and

(ii) younger than 19 years of age, by plainly printing the date the license certificate or driving privilege card holder is 19 years of age, which is the legal age for purchasing tobacco products under Section 76-10-104.

(6) (a) The division shall only issue a driving privilege card to a person whose privilege was obtained without using a Social Security number as required under Subsection 53-3-205(9).

(b) The division shall distinguish a driving privilege card from a license certificate by:

(i) use of a format, color, font, or other means; and

(ii) clearly displaying on the front of the driving privilege card a phrase substantially similar to "FOR DRIVING PRIVILEGES ONLY — NOT VALID FOR IDENTIFICATION".

(7) The provisions of Subsection (5)(b) do not apply to a learner permit, temporary permit, or any other temporary permit or receipt issued by the division.

(8) The division shall issue temporary license certificates or temporary driving privilege cards of the same nature, except as to duration, as the license certificates or driving privilege cards that they temporarily replace, as are necessary to implement applicable provisions of this section and Section 53-3-223.

(9) A governmental entity may not accept a driving privilege card as proof of personal identification.

(10) A person who violates Subsection (2)(b) is guilty of a class C misdemeanor.

(11) Except as provided under this section, the provisions, requirements, classes, endorsements, fees, restrictions, and sanctions under this code apply to a:

(a) driving privilege in the same way as a license issued under this chapter; and

(b) driving privilege card in the same way as a license certificate issued under this chapter.   2005

53-3-208.   Restrictions.

(1) (a) When granting a license, the division may for good cause impose restrictions, suitable to the licensee's driving ability, for the type of motor vehicle or special mechanical control devices required on a motor vehicle that the licensee may drive.

(b) The division may impose other restrictions on the licensee as it determines appropriate to assure safe driving of a motor vehicle by the licensee.

(2) The division may either grant a special restricted license or may set forth restrictions upon the regular license certificate.

(3) (a) The division may suspend or revoke any license upon receiving satisfactory evidence of any violation of the restrictions imposed on the license.

(b) Each licensee is entitled to a hearing for a suspension or revocation under this chapter.

(4) It is a class C misdemeanor for a person to drive a motor vehicle in violation of the restrictions imposed on his license under this section.   1993

53-3-209.   Provisional licenses only for persons under 21 — Separate point system — Denial and suspension procedures.

(1) The division may only grant a provisional license to a person younger than 21 years of age.

(2) (a) The division shall make rules for the establishment and administration of a separate point system for persons granted provisional licenses to facilitate counseling, penalization, or both earlier than for persons 21 years of age or older.

(b) The rules shall establish point thresholds at which each of the following actions are taken:

(i) a warning letter;

(ii) a request to appear for a hearing;

(iii) a denial of the driving privilege for first or second actions where the point total established under Section 53-3-221 does not exceed the point threshold under which a person 21 years or older may be suspended; and

(iv) a suspension of the driving privilege.

(c) The rules shall require:

(i) an extension of the denial or suspension period for further violations within the three-year period; and

(ii) denial or suspension of the driving privilege for failure to appear for a hearing required under this section. 1993

53-3-210. Temporary learner permit — Instruction permit — Commercial driver instruction permit — Practice permit.

(1) (a) The division upon receiving an application for a class D or M license from a person 16 years of age or older may issue a temporary learner permit after the person has successfully passed all parts of the examination not involving actually driving a motor vehicle.

(b) The temporary learner permit allows the applicant, while having the permit in the applicant's immediate possession, to drive a motor vehicle upon the highways for six months from the date of the application in conformance with the restrictions indicated on the permit.

(2) (a) The division, upon receiving an application, may issue an instruction permit effective for one year to an applicant who is at least 15 years and six months of age and who is enrolled in a driver education program that includes practice driving, if the program is approved by the State Board of Education or the division, even though the applicant has not reached the legal age to be eligible for a license.

(b) The instruction permit entitles the applicant, while having the permit in his immediate possession, to drive a motor vehicle, only if an approved instructor is occupying a seat beside the applicant.

(3) The division may issue a commercial driver instruction permit under Title 53, Chapter 3, Part 4, Uniform Commercial Driver License Act.

(4) (a) The division shall issue a practice permit to an applicant who:

(i) is at least 15 years and six months of age;

(ii) has been issued an instruction permit under this section;

(iii) is enrolled in a driver education program or has successfully completed a driver education course in a:

(A) commercial driver training school licensed under Title 53, Chapter 3, Part 5, Commercial Driver Training Schools Act; or

(B) driver education program approved by the division;

(iv) has passed the knowledge test required by the division;

(v) has passed the physical and mental fitness tests; and

(vi) has submitted the nonrefundable fee for a class D license.

(b) The division shall supply the practice permit form. The form shall include the following information:

(i) the applicant's full name, date of birth, sex, home address, height, weight, and eye color;

(ii) the name of the school providing the driver education course;

(iii) the dates of issuance and expiration of the permit;

(iv) the statutory citation authorizing the permit; and

(v) the conditions and restrictions contained in this section for operating a class D motor vehicle.

(c) The practice permit is valid for up to six months from the date of issuance. The practice permit allows the person, while having the permit in the applicant's immediate possession, to operate a class D motor vehicle when the person's parent, legal guardian, or adult spouse, who must be a licensed driver, is occupying a seat next to the person.

(d) If an applicant has been issued a practice permit by the division, the applicant may obtain an original or provisional class D license from the division upon passing the skills test administered by the division and reaching 16 years of age.

2004

53-3-211. Application of minors — Liability of person signing application — Cancellation of cosigning adult's liability — Behind-the-wheel driving certification.

(1) As used in this section, "minor" means any person younger than 18 years of age who is not married or has not been emancipated by adjudication.

(2) (a) The application of a minor for a temporary learner permit, practice permit, or provisional license shall be signed by the parent or guardian of the applicant.

(b) If the minor applicant does not have a parent or guardian, then a responsible adult who is willing to assume the obligation imposed under this chapter may sign the application.

(3) (a) Except as provided in Subsection (4), the liability of a minor for civil compensatory damages caused when operating a motor vehicle upon a highway is imputed to the person who has signed the application of the minor under Subsection (2).

(b) The person who has signed the application under Subsection (2) is jointly and severally liable with the minor as provided in Subsections (3)(a) and (c).

(c) The liability imposed under Subsections (3)(a) and (b) is limited to the policy minimum limits established in Section 31A-22-304.

(d) The liability provisions in this Subsection (3) are in addition to the liability provisions in Section 53-3-212.

(4) If owner's or operator's security covering the minor's operation of the motor vehicle is in effect in amounts as required under Section 31A-22-304, the person who signed the minor's application under Subsection (2) is not subject to the liability imposed under Subsection (3).

(5) (a) A person who has signed the application of a minor under Subsection (2) may file with the division a verified written request that the permit or license of the minor be canceled.

(b) The division shall then cancel the permit or license of the minor, and the person who signed the application of the minor under Subsection (2) is relieved from the liability imposed under Subsection (3) or the minor operating a motor vehicle subsequent to the cancellation.

(6) (a) The division upon receipt of satisfactory evidence of the death of the person who signed the application of a minor under Subsection (2) shall cancel the permit or license and may not issue a new permit or license until a new application, signed and verified, is made under this chapter.

(b) This Subsection (6) does not apply to an application of a person who is no longer a minor.

(7) (a) In addition to the liability assumed under this section, the person who signs the application of a minor for a provisional license must certify that the minor applicant, under the authority of a permit issued under this chapter, has completed at least 40 hours of driving a motor vehicle, of which at least ten hours shall be during night hours after sunset.

(b) The hours of driving a motor vehicle required under Subsection (7)(a) may include:

(i) hours completed in a driver education course as required under Subsection 53-3-505.5(1); and

(ii) up to five hours completed by driving simulation practice on a fully interactive driving simulation device at the substitution rate provided under Subsection 53-3-505.5(2)(b).   2004

53-3-212. Owner giving permission and minor liable for damages caused by minor driving a motor vehicle.

(1) The owner of a motor vehicle causing or knowingly permitting a person younger than 18 years of age to drive the motor vehicle on a highway, or a person who gives or furnishes a motor vehicle to the minor, are each jointly and severally liable with the minor for any damages caused by the negligence of the minor in driving the motor vehicle.

(2) This liability provision is in addition to the liability provisions in Section 53-3-211.   1993

53-3-213. Age and experience requirements to drive school bus or certain other carriers — Misdemeanor to drive unauthorized class of motor vehicle — Waiver of driving examination by third party certification.

(1) (a) A person must be at least 21 years of age:

(i) to drive any school bus;

(ii) to drive any commercial motor vehicle outside this state; or

(iii) while transporting passengers for hire or hazardous materials.

(b) Subject to the requirements of Subsection (a), the division may grant a commercial driver license to any applicant who is at least 18 years of age and has had at least one year of previous driving experience.

(c) It is a class C misdemeanor for any person to drive a class of motor vehicle for which he is not licensed.

(2) (a) At the discretion of the commissioner and under standards established by the division, persons employed as commercial drivers may submit a third party certification as provided in Part 4 of this chapter in lieu of the driving segment of the examination.

(b) The division shall maintain necessary records and set standards to certify companies desiring to qualify under Subsection (a).   1993

53-3-214. Renewal — Fees required — Extension without examination.

(1) (a) The holder of a valid license may renew his license and any endorsement to the license by applying:

(i) at any time within six months before the license expires; or

(ii) more than six months prior to the expiration date if the applicant furnishes proof that he will be absent from the state during the six-month period prior to the expiration of the license.

(b) The application for a renewal of, extension of, or any endorsement to a license shall be accompanied by a fee under Section 53-3-105.

(2) (a) Except as provided under Subsections (2)(b) and (3), upon application for renewal of a license, provisional license, and any endorsement to a license, the division shall reexamine each applicant as if for an original license and endorsement to the license, if applicable.

(b) The division may waive any or all portions of the test designed to demonstrate the applicant's ability to exercise ordinary and reasonable control driving a motor vehicle.

(3) (a) Except as provided under Subsection (3)(b), the division shall extend a license, any endorsement to the license, a provisional license, and any endorsement to a provisional license for five years without examination for licensees whose driving records for the five years immediately preceding the determination of eligibility for extension show:

(i) no suspensions;

(ii) no revocations;

(iii) no conviction for reckless driving under Section 41-6a-528; and

(iv) no more than four reportable violations in the preceding five years.

(b) (i) After the expiration of a license, a new license certificate and any endorsement to a license certificate may not be issued until the person has again passed the tests under Section 53-3-206 and paid the required fee.

(ii) A person 65 years of age or older shall take and pass the eye examination specified in Section 53-3-206.

(iii) An extension may not be granted to any person:

(A) who is identified by the division as having a medical impairment that may represent a hazard to public safety;

(B) holding a CDL issued under Part 4 of this chapter; or

(C) whose original license was obtained using proof under Subsection 53-3-205(9)(a)(i)(E)(III).

(c) The division shall allow extensions:

(i) by mail at the appropriate extension fee rate under Section 53-3-105;

(ii) only if the applicant qualifies under this section; and

(iii) for only one extension.   2005

53-3-214.5. License or identification card checkoff for vision screening.

(1) A person who applies for a license or identification card or a renewal of a license or identification card may designate a voluntary contribution for vision screening of $2.

(2) This contribution shall be:

(a) collected by the division;

(b) treated as a voluntary contribution to Friends For Sight to provide blindness prevention education, screening, and treatment and not as a license fee; and

(c) transferred to Friends For Sight at least monthly, less actual administrative costs associated with collecting and transferring the contributions. 2003

53-3-214.7. License or identification card checkoff for promoting and supporting organ donation.

(1) A person who applies for a license or identification card or a renewal of a license or identification card may designate a voluntary contribution of $2 for the purpose of promoting and supporting organ donation.

(2) This contribution shall be:

(a) collected by the division;

(b) treated as a voluntary contribution to the Organ Donation Contribution Fund created in Section 26-18b-101 and not as a license fee; and

(c) transferred to the Organ Donation Contribution Fund created in Section 26-18b-101 at least monthly, less actual administrative costs associated with collecting and transferring the contributions. 2003

53-3-214.8. License or identification card checkoff for public transportation for seniors or people with disabilities.

(1) A person who applies for a license or identification card or a renewal of a license or identification card may designate a voluntary contribution of $1 for public transportation assistance for seniors or people with disabilities.

(2) This contribution shall be:

(a) collected by the division;

(b) treated as a voluntary contribution to the "Out and About" Homebound Transportation Assistance Fund created in Section 62A-3-110 to provide public transportation assistance for seniors or people with disabilities and not as a license fee; and

(c) transferred to the "Out and About" Homebound Transportation Assistance Fund created in Section 62A-3-110 at least monthly, less actual administrative costs associated with collecting and transferring the contributions. 2003

53-3-215. Duplicate license certificate — Fee.

(1) If a license certificate issued under this chapter is lost, stolen, or destroyed, the person to whom the license certificate was issued may obtain a duplicate upon furnishing proof satisfactory to the division that the license certificate has been lost, stolen, or destroyed and upon payment of a duplicate fee under Section 53-3-105.

(2) When the division is advised that a license certificate has been lost, stolen, or destroyed, the license certificate is then void. 1993

53-3-216. Change of address — Duty of licensee to notify division within ten days — Change of name — Proof necessary — Method of giving notice by division.

(1) If a person, after applying for or receiving a license, moves from the address named in the application or in the license certificate issued to him, the person shall within ten days of moving, notify the division in a manner specified by the division of his new address and the number of any license certificate held by him.

(2) If a person requests to change the surname on the applicant's license, the division shall issue a substitute license with the new name upon receiving an application and fee for a duplicate license and any of the following proofs of the applicant's full legal name:

(a) an original or certified copy of the applicant's marriage certificate;

(b) a certified copy of a court order under Title 42, Chapter 1, Change of Name, showing the name change;

(c) an original or certified copy of a birth certificate issued by a government agency;

(d) a certified copy of a divorce decree or annulment granted the applicant that specifies the name change requested; or

(e) a certified copy of a divorce decree that does not specify the name change requested together with:

(i) an original or certified copy of the applicant's birth certificate;

(ii) the applicant's marriage license;

(iii) a driver license record showing use of a maiden name; or

(iv) other documentation the division finds acceptable.

(3) (a) If the division is authorized or required to give any notice under this chapter or other law regulating the operation of vehicles, the notice shall, unless otherwise prescribed, be given by:

(i) personal delivery to the person to be notified; or

(ii) deposit in the United States mail with postage prepaid, addressed to the person at his address as shown by the records of the division.

(b) The giving of notice by mail is complete upon the expiration of four days after the deposit of the notice.

(c) Proof of the giving of notice in either manner may be made by the certificate of any officer or employee of the division or affidavit of any person older than 18 years of age, naming the person to whom the notice was given and specifying the time, place, and manner of giving the notice.

(4) The division may use state mailing or United States Postal Service information to:

(a) verify an address on an application or on records of the division; and

(b) correct mailing addresses in the division's records.

(5) A violation of the provisions of Subsection (1) is an infraction. 2001

53-3-217. License to be carried when driving motor vehicle — Production in court — Violation.

(1) (a) The licensee shall have his license certificate in his immediate possession at all times when driving a motor vehicle.

(b) A licensee shall display his license certificate upon demand of a justice of peace, a peace officer, or a field deputy or inspector of the division.

(2) It is a defense to a charge under this section that the person charged produces in court a license certificate issued to him and valid at the time of his citation or arrest.

(3) A person who violates Subsection (1)(a) is guilty of a class C misdemeanor. 1997

53-3-218. Court to report convictions and may recommend suspension of license — Severity of speeding violation defined.

(1) As used in this section, "conviction" means conviction by the court of first impression or final administrative determination in an administrative traffic proceeding.

(2) (a) A court having jurisdiction over offenses committed under this chapter or any other law of this state, or under any municipal ordinance regulating driving motor vehicles on highways or driving motorboats on the water, shall forward to the division within ten days, an abstract of the court record of the conviction or plea held in abeyance of any person in the court for a reportable traffic or motorboating violation of any laws or ordinances, and may recommend the suspension of the license of the person convicted.

(b) When the division receives a court record of a conviction or plea in abeyance for a motorboat violation, the division may only take action against a person's driver license if the motorboat violation is for a violation of Title 41, Chapter 6a, Part 5, Driving Under the Influence and Reckless Driving.

(3) The abstract shall be made in the form prescribed by the division and shall include:

(a) the name and address of the party charged;

(b) the number of his license certificate, if any;

(c) the registration number of the motor vehicle or motorboat involved;

(d) whether the motor vehicle was a commercial motor vehicle;

(e) whether the motor vehicle carried hazardous materials;

(f) the nature of the offense;

(g) the date of the hearing;

(h) the plea;

(i) the judgment or whether bail was forfeited; and

(j) the severity of the violation, which shall be graded by the court as "minimum," "intermediate," or "maximum" as established in accordance with Subsection 53-3-221(4).

(4) When a convicted person secures a judgment of acquittal or reversal in any appellate court after conviction in the court of first impression, the division shall reinstate his license immediately upon receipt of a certified copy of the judgment of acquittal or reversal.   2005

53-3-219. Suspension of minor's driving privileges.

(1) The division shall immediately suspend all driving privileges of any person upon receipt of an order suspending driving privileges under Section 32A-12-209, Subsection 76-9-701(1), or Section 78-3a-506.

(a) Upon receipt of the first order suspending a person's driving privileges, the division shall impose a suspension for 90 days or, if the person is under the age of eligibility for a driver license, the suspension shall begin on the date of conviction and continue for the first 90 days following the date of eligibility.

(b) Upon receipt of a second order suspending a person's driving privileges, the division shall impose a suspension for six months or, if the person is under the age of eligibility for a driver license, the suspension shall begin on the date of conviction and continue for the first six months following the date of eligibility.

(c) Upon receipt of a third or subsequent order suspending a person's driving privileges, the division shall impose a suspension for one year or, if the person is under the age of eligibility for a driver license, the suspension shall begin on the date of conviction and continue for one year beginning on the date of eligibility.

(2) After reinstatement of the license under Subsection (1)(a), a report authorized under Section 53-3-104 may not contain evidence of the suspension of a minor's license under this section if the minor has not been convicted of any other offense for which the suspension under Subsection (1)(a) may be extended.   2004

53-3-220. Offenses requiring mandatory revocation, denial, suspension, or disqualification of license — Offense requiring an extension of period — Hearing — Limited driving privileges.

(1) (a) The division shall immediately revoke or, when this chapter or Title 41, Chapter 6a, Traffic Code, specifically provides for denial, suspension, or disqualification, the division shall deny, suspend, or disqualify the license of a person upon receiving a record of the person's conviction for any of the following offenses:

(i) manslaughter or negligent homicide resulting from driving a motor vehicle, or automobile homicide under Section 76-5-207;

(ii) driving or being in actual physical control of a motor vehicle while under the influence of alcohol, any drug, or combination of them to a degree that renders the person incapable of safely driving a motor vehicle as prohibited in Section 41-6a-502 or as prohibited in an ordinance that complies with the requirements of Subsection 41-6a-510(1);

(iii) driving or being in actual physical control of a motor vehicle while having a blood or breath alcohol content prohibited in Section 41-6a-502 or as prohibited in an ordinance that complies with the requirements of Subsection 41-6a-510(1);

(iv) perjury or the making of a false affidavit to the division under this chapter, Title 41, Motor Vehicles, or any other law of this state requiring the registration of motor vehicles or regulating driving on highways;

(v) any felony under the motor vehicle laws of this state;

(vi) any other felony in which a motor vehicle is used to facilitate the offense;

(vii) failure to stop and render aid as required under the laws of this state if a motor vehicle accident results in the death or personal injury of another;

(viii) two charges of reckless driving committed within a period of 12 months; but if upon a first conviction of reckless driving the judge or justice recommends suspension of the convicted person's license, the division may after a hearing suspend the license for a period of three months;

(ix) failure to bring a motor vehicle to a stop at the command of a peace officer as required in Section 41-6a-210;

(x) any offense specified in Part 4, Uniform Commercial Driver License Act, that requires disqualification;

(xi) discharging or allowing the discharge of a firearm from a vehicle in violation of Subsection 76-10-508(2);

(xii) using, allowing the use of, or causing to be used any explosive, chemical, or incendiary device from a vehicle in violation of Subsection 76-10-306(4)(b);

(xiii) operating or being in actual physical control of a motor vehicle while having any measurable controlled substance or metabolite of a controlled substance in the person's body in violation of Section 41-6a-517;

(xiv) until July 30, 2015, operating or being in actual physical control of a motor vehicle while having any alcohol in the person's body in violation of Section 53-3-232; and

(xv) operating or being in actual physical control of a motor vehicle while having any measurable or detectable amount of alcohol in the person's body in violation of Section 41-6a-530.

(b) The division shall immediately revoke the license of a person upon receiving a record of an adjudication under Title 78, Chapter 3a, Juvenile Court Act of 1996, for any of the following offenses:

(i) discharging or allowing the discharge of a firearm from a vehicle in violation of Subsection 76-10-508(2); and

(ii) using, allowing the use of, or causing to be used any explosive, chemical, or incendiary device from a vehicle in violation of Subsection 76-10-306(4)(b).

(c) Except when action is taken under Section 53-3-219 for the same offense, the division shall immediately suspend for six months the license of a person upon receiving a record of conviction for any of the following offenses:

(i) any violation of:

(A) Title 58, Chapter 37, Utah Controlled Substances Act;

(B) Title 58, Chapter 37a, Utah Drug Paraphernalia Act;

(C) Title 58, Chapter 37b, Imitation Controlled Substances Act;

(D) Title 58, Chapter 37c, Utah Controlled Substance Precursor Act; or

(E) Title 58, Chapter 37d, Clandestine Drug Lab Act; or

(ii) any criminal offense that prohibits:

(A) possession, distribution, manufacture, cultivation, sale, or transfer of any substance that is prohibited under the acts described in Subsection (1)(c)(i); or

(B) the attempt or conspiracy to possess, distribute, manufacture, cultivate, sell, or transfer any substance that is prohibited under the acts described in Subsection (1)(c)(i).

(2) The division shall extend the period of the first denial, suspension, revocation, or disqualification for an additional like period, to a maximum of one year for each subsequent occurrence, upon receiving:

(a) a record of the conviction of any person on a charge of driving a motor vehicle while the person's license is denied, suspended, revoked, or disqualified;

(b) a record of a conviction of the person for any violation of the motor vehicle law in which the person was involved as a driver;

(c) a report of an arrest of the person for any violation of the motor vehicle law in which the person was involved as a driver; or

(d) a report of an accident in which the person was involved as a driver.

(3) When the division receives a report under Subsection (2)(c) or (d) that a person is driving while the person's license is denied, suspended, disqualified, or revoked, the person is entitled to a hearing regarding the extension of the time of denial, suspension, disqualification, or revocation originally imposed under Section 53-3-221.

(4) (a) The division may extend to a person the limited privilege of driving a motor vehicle to and from the person's place of employment or within other specified limits on recommendation of the trial judge in any case where a person is convicted of any of the offenses referred to in Subsections (1) and (2) except:

(i) automobile homicide under Subsection (1)(a)(i);

(ii) those offenses referred to in Subsections (1)(a)(ii), (a)(iii), (a)(xi), (a)(xii), (a)(xiii), (1)(b), and (1)(c); and

(iii) those offenses referred to in Subsection (2) when the original denial, suspension, revocation, or disqualification was imposed because of a violation of Section 41-6a-502, 41-6a-517, a local ordinance which complies with the requirements of Subsection 41-6a-510(1), Section 41-6a-520, or Section 76-5-207, or a criminal prohibition that the person was charged with violating as a result of a plea bargain after having been originally charged with violating one or more of these sections or ordinances.

(b) This discretionary privilege is limited to when undue hardship would result from a failure to grant the privilege and may be granted only once to any individual during any single period of denial, suspension, revocation, or disqualification, or extension of that denial, suspension, revocation, or disqualification.

(c) A limited CDL may not be granted to an individual disqualified under Part 4, Uniform Commercial Driver License Act, or whose license has been revoked, suspended, cancelled, or denied under this chapter.   2005

53-3-221. Offenses which may result in denial, suspension, disqualification, or revocation of license without hearing — Additional grounds for suspension — Point system for traffic violations — Notice and hearing — Reporting of traffic violation procedures.

(1) By following the emergency procedures in Title 63, Chapter 46b, Administrative Procedures Act, the division may immediately deny, suspend, disqualify, or revoke the license of any person without hearing and without receiving a record of the person's conviction of crime when the division has been notified or has reason to believe the person:

(a) has committed any offenses for which mandatory suspension or revocation of a license is required upon conviction under Section 53-3-220;

(b) has, by reckless or unlawful driving of a motor vehicle, caused or contributed to an accident resulting in death or injury to any other person, or serious property damage;

(c) is incompetent to drive a motor vehicle or is afflicted with mental or physical infirmities or disabilities rendering it unsafe for the person to drive a motor vehicle upon the highways;

(d) has committed a serious violation of the motor vehicle laws of this state;

(e) has knowingly acquired, used, displayed, or transferred an item that purports to be an authentic driver license certificate issued by a governmental entity if the item is not an authentic driver license certificate or has permitted an unlawful use of the license as prohibited under Section 53-3-229; or

(f) has been convicted of serious offenses against traffic laws governing the movement of motor vehicles with a frequency that indicates a disrespect for traffic laws and a disregard for the safety of other persons on the highways.

(2) (a) The division may suspend the license of a person under Subsection (1) when the person has failed to comply with the terms stated on a traffic citation issued in this state, except this Subsection (2) does not apply to highway weight limit violations or violations of law governing the transportation of hazardous materials.

(b) This Subsection (2) applies to parking and standing violations only if a court has issued a warrant for the arrest of a person for failure to post bail, appear, or otherwise satisfy the terms of the citation.

(c) (i) This Subsection (2) may not be exercised unless notice of the pending suspension of the driving privilege has been sent at least ten days previously to the person at the address provided to the division.

(ii) After clearance by the division, a report authorized by Section 53-3-104 may not contain any evidence of a suspension that occurred as a result of failure to comply with the terms stated on a traffic citation.

(3) (a) The division may suspend the license of a person under Subsection (1) when the division has been notified by a court that the person has an outstanding unpaid fine, an outstanding incomplete restitution requirement, or an outstanding warrant levied by order of a court.

(b) The suspension remains in effect until the division is notified by the court that the order has been satisfied.

(c) After clearance by the division, a report authorized by Section 53-3-104 may not contain any evidence of the suspension.

(4) The division shall make rules establishing a point system as provided for in this Subsection (4).

(a) (i) The division shall assign a number of points to each type of moving traffic violation as a measure of its seriousness.

(ii) The points shall be based upon actual relationships between types of traffic violations and motor vehicle traffic accidents.

(b) Every person convicted of a traffic violation shall have assessed against his driving record the number of points that the division has assigned to the type of violation of which the person has been convicted, except that the number of points assessed shall be decreased by 10% if on the abstract of the court record of the conviction the court has graded the severity of violation as minimum, and shall be increased by 10% if on the abstract the court has graded the severity of violation as maximum.

(c) (i) A separate procedure for assessing points for speeding offenses shall be established by the division based upon the severity of the offense.

(ii) The severity of a speeding violation shall be graded as:

(A) "minimum" for exceeding the posted speed limit by up to ten miles per hour;

(B) "intermediate" for exceeding the posted speed limit by from 11 to 20 miles per hour; and

(C) "maximum" for exceeding the posted speed limit by 21 or more miles per hour.

(iii) Consideration shall be made for assessment of no points on minimum speeding violations, except for speeding violations in school zones.

(d) (i) Points assessed against a person's driving record shall be deleted for violations occurring before a time limit set by the division.

(ii) The time limit may not exceed three years.

(iii) The division may also delete points to reward violation-free driving for periods of time set by the division.

(e) (i) By publication in two newspapers having general circulation throughout the state, the division shall give notice of the number of points it has assigned to each type of traffic violation, the time limit set by the division for the deletion of points, and the point level at which the division will generally take action to deny or suspend under this section.

(ii) The division may not change any of the information provided above regarding points without first giving new notice in the same manner.

(5) (a) (i) Upon denying or suspending the license of a person under this section, the division shall immediately notify the licensee in a manner specified by the division and afford him an opportunity for a hearing in the county where the licensee resides.

(ii) The hearing shall be documented, and the division or its authorized agent may administer oaths, may issue subpoenas for the attendance of witnesses and the production of relevant books and papers, and may require a reexamination of the licensee.

(iii) One or more members of the division may conduct the hearing, and any decision made after a hearing before any number of the members of the division is as valid as if made after a hearing before the full membership of the division.

(iv) After the hearing the division shall either rescind its order of denial or suspension, extend the denial or suspension of the license, or revoke the license.

(b) The denial or suspension of the license remains in effect pending qualifications determined by the division regarding a person:

(i) whose license has been denied or suspended following reexamination;

(ii) who is incompetent to drive a motor vehicle;

(iii) who is afflicted with mental or physical infirmities that might make him dangerous on the highways; or

(iv) who may not have the necessary knowledge or skill to drive a motor vehicle safely.

(6) (a) The division may suspend or revoke the license of any resident of this state upon receiving notice of the conviction of that person in another state of an offense committed there that, if committed in this state, would be grounds for the suspension or revocation of a license.

(b) The division may, upon receiving a record of the conviction in this state of a nonresident driver of a motor vehicle or motorboat of any offense under the motor vehicle laws of this state, forward a certified copy of the record to the motor vehicle administrator in the state where the person convicted is a resident.

(7) (a) The division may suspend or revoke the license of any nonresident to drive a motor vehicle in this state for any cause for which the license of a resident driver may be suspended or revoked.

(b) Any nonresident who drives a motor vehicle upon a highway when his license has been suspended or revoked by the division is guilty of a class C misdemeanor.

(8) (a) The division may not deny or suspend the license of any person for a period of more than one year except:

(i) for failure to comply with the terms of a traffic citation under Subsection (2);

(ii) upon receipt of a second or subsequent order suspending juvenile driving privileges under Section 53-3-219;

(iii) when extending a denial or suspension upon receiving certain records or reports under Subsection 53-3-220(2); and

(iv) for failure to give and maintain owner's or operator's security under Section 41-12a-411.

(b) The division may suspend the license of a person under Subsection (2) until he shows satisfactory evidence of compliance with the terms of the traffic citation.

(9) (a) By following the emergency procedures in Title 63, Chapter 46b, Administrative Procedures Act, the division may immediately suspend the license of any person without hearing and without receiving a record of his conviction for a crime when the division has reason to believe that the person's license was granted by the division through error or fraud or that the necessary consent for the license has been withdrawn or is terminated.

(b) The procedure upon suspension is the same as under Subsection (5), except that after the hearing the division shall either rescind its order of suspension or cancel the license.

(10) (a) The division, having good cause to believe that a licensed driver is incompetent or otherwise not qualified to be licensed, may upon notice in a manner specified by the division of at least five days to the licensee require him to submit to an examination.

(b) Upon the conclusion of the examination the division may suspend or revoke the person's license, permit him to retain the license, or grant a license subject to a restriction imposed in accordance with Section 53-3-208.

(c) Refusal or neglect of the licensee to submit to an examination is grounds for suspension or revocation of his license.

(11) A report authorized by Section 53-3-104 may not contain any evidence of a conviction for speeding on an interstate system in this state if the conviction was for a speed of ten miles per hour or less, above the posted speed limit and did not result in an accident, unless authorized in a manner specified by the division by the individual whose report is being requested.

(12) (a) By following the emergency procedures in Title 63, Chapter 46b, Administrative Procedures Act, the division may immediately suspend the license of a person if it has reason to believe that the person is the owner of a motor vehicle for which security is required under Title 41, Chapter 12a, Vehicle Financial Responsibility of Motor Vehicle Owners and Operators Act, and has driven the motor vehicle or permitted it to be driven within this state without the security being in effect.

(b) Section 41-12a-411 regarding the requirement of proof of owner's or operator's security applies to persons whose driving privileges are suspended under this Subsection (12).

(c) If the division exercises the right of immediate suspension granted under this Subsection (12), the notice and hearing provisions of Subsection (5) apply.

(d) A person whose license suspension has been sustained or whose license has been revoked by the division under this subsection may file a request for agency action requesting a hearing.

(13) Any suspension or revocation of a person's license under this section also disqualifies any license issued to that person under Part 4 of this chapter.

2005

53-3-222. Purpose of revocation or suspension for driving under the influence.

The Legislature finds that the purpose of this title relating to suspension or revocation of a person's license or privilege to drive a motor vehicle for driving with a blood alcohol content above a certain level or while under the influence of alcohol, any drug, or a combination of alcohol and any drug, or for refusing to take a chemical test as provided in Section 41-6a-520, is protecting persons on highways by quickly removing from the highways those persons who have shown they are safety hazards.

2005

53-3-223. Chemical test for driving under the influence — Temporary license — Hearing and decision — Suspension and fee — Judicial review.

(1) (a) If a peace officer has reasonable grounds to believe that a person may be violating or has violated Section 41-6a-502, prohibiting the operation of a vehicle with a certain blood or breath alcohol concentration and driving under the influence of any drug, alcohol, or combination of a drug and alcohol or while having any measurable controlled substance or metabolite of a controlled substance in the person's body in violation of Section 41-6a-517, the peace officer may, in connection with arresting the person, request that the person submit to a chemical test or tests to be administered in compliance with the standards under Section 41-6a-520.

(b) In this section, a reference to Section 41-6a-502 includes any similar local ordinance adopted in compliance with Subsection 41-6a-510(1).

(2) The peace officer shall advise a person prior to the person's submission to a chemical test that a test result indicating a violation of Section 41-6a-502 or 41-6a-517 shall, and the existence of a blood alcohol content sufficient to render the person incapable of safely driving a motor vehicle may, result in suspension or revocation of the person's license to drive a motor vehicle.

(3) If the person submits to a chemical test and the test results indicate a blood or breath alcohol content in violation of Section 41-6a-502 or 41-6a-517, or if a peace officer makes a determination, based on reasonable grounds, that the person is otherwise in violation of Section 41-6a-502, a peace officer shall, on behalf of the division and within 24 hours of arrest, give notice of the division's intention to suspend the person's license to drive a motor vehicle.

(4) (a) When a peace officer gives notice on behalf of the division, the peace officer shall:

    (i) take the Utah license certificate or permit, if any, of the driver;

    (ii) issue a temporary license certificate effective for only 29 days from the date of arrest; and

    (iii) supply to the driver, in a manner specified by the division, basic information regarding how to obtain a prompt hearing before the division.

(b) A citation issued by a peace officer may, if provided in a manner specified by the division, also serve as the temporary license certificate.

(5) As a matter of procedure, a peace officer shall send to the division within ten calendar days after the day on which notice is provided:

(a) the person's license certificate;

(b) a copy of the citation issued for the offense;

(c) a signed report in a manner specified by the division indicating the chemical test results, if any; and

(d) any other basis for the peace officer's determination that the person has violated Section 41-6a-502 or 41-6a-517.

(6) (a) Upon request in a manner specified by the division, the division shall grant to the person an opportunity to be heard within 29 days after the date of arrest. The request to be heard shall be made within ten calendar days of the day on which notice is provided under Subsection (5).

(b) (i) Except as provided in Subsection (6)(b)(ii), a hearing, if held, shall be before the division in the county in which the arrest occurred.

    (ii) The division may hold a hearing in some other county if the division and the person both agree.

(c) The hearing shall be documented and shall cover the issues of:

    (i) whether a peace officer had reasonable grounds to believe the person was driving a motor vehicle in violation of Section 41-6a-502 or 41-6a-517;

    (ii) whether the person refused to submit to the test; and

    (iii) the test results, if any.

(d) (i) In connection with a hearing the division or its authorized agent:

    (A) may administer oaths and may issue subpoenas for the attendance of witnesses and the production of relevant books and papers; or

    (B) may issue subpoenas for the attendance of necessary peace officers.

    (ii) The division shall pay witness fees and mileage from the Transportation Fund in accordance with the rates established in Section 78-46-28.

(e) The division may designate one or more employees to conduct the hearing.

(f) Any decision made after a hearing before any designated employee is as valid as if made by the division.

(g) After the hearing, the division shall order whether the person's license to drive a motor vehicle is suspended or not.

(h) If the person for whom the hearing is held fails to appear before the division as required in the notice, the division shall order whether the person's license to drive a motor vehicle is suspended or not.

(7) (a) A first suspension, whether ordered or not challenged under this Subsection (7), is for a period of 90 days, beginning on the 30th day after the date of the arrest.

(b) A second or subsequent suspension for an offense that occurred within the previous ten years under this Subsection (7) is for a period of one year, beginning on the 30th day after the date of arrest.

(8) (a) The division shall assess against a person, in addition to any fee imposed under Subsection 53-3-205(13) for driving under the influence, a fee under Section 53-3-105 to cover administrative costs, which shall be paid before the person's driving privilege is reinstated. This fee shall be cancelled if the person obtains an unappealed division hearing or court decision that the suspension was not proper.

(b) A person whose license has been suspended by the division under this section may file a petition within 30 days after the suspension for a hearing on the matter which, if held, is governed by Section 53-3-224.   2005

53-3-223.5. Telephonic or live audiovisual testimony at hearings.

In any division hearing authorized under this chapter or Title 41, Chapter 6a, Part 5, Driving Under the Influence and Reckless Driving, the division may permit a party or witness to attend or to testify by telephone or live audiovisual means.   2005

53-3-224. Filing a petition for hearing — Judicial review of license cancellation, revocation, or suspension — Scope of review.

(1) A person denied a license or whose license has been cancelled, suspended, or revoked by the division may seek judicial review of the division's order.

(2) (a) Venue for judicial review of informal adjudicative proceedings is in the district court in the county where the offense occurred, which resulted in the cancellation, suspension, or revocation.

(b) Persons not residing in the state shall file in Salt Lake County or the county where the offense occurred, which resulted in the cancellation, suspension, or revocation.   1999

53-3-225. Eligibility for new license after revocation.

(1) (a) Except as provided in Subsections (b) and (c), a person whose license has been revoked under this chapter may not apply for or receive any new license until the expiration of one year from the date the former license was revoked.

(b) A person's license may be revoked for a longer period as provided in:

    (i) Section 53-3-220, for driving a motor vehicle while the person's license is revoked, or involvement as a driver in an accident or violation of the motor vehicle laws; and

    (ii) Section 53-3-221, for failing to comply with the terms of a traffic citation.

(c) (i) The length of the revocation required by Subsection 53-3-220(1)(a)(xi), (a)(xii), (b)(i), or (b)(ii) shall be specified in an order of the court adjudicating or convicting the person of the offense.

(ii) If the person adjudicated of the offense is younger than 16 years of age, the license or driving privilege shall be revoked for a minimum of one year, from age 16, but not to exceed the date the person turns 21 years of age.

(iii) If the person adjudicated or convicted of the offense is 16 years of age or older, the license or driving privilege shall be revoked for a minimum of one year, but not to exceed five years.

(d) A revoked license may not be renewed.

(e) Application for a new license shall be filed in accordance with Section 53-3-205.

(f) The new license is subject to all provisions of an original license.

(g) The division may not grant the license until an investigation of the character, driving abilities, and habits of the driver has been made to indicate whether it is safe to grant him a license.

(2) Any resident or nonresident whose license to drive a motor vehicle in this state has been suspended or revoked under this chapter may not drive a motor vehicle in this state under a license, permit, or registration certificate issued by any other jurisdiction or other source during suspension or after revocation until a new license is obtained under this chapter.

1993 (2nd S.S.)

53-3-226. Grounds for confiscation of licenses, plates, and other articles issued by state.

(1) The division or a peace officer acting in his official capacity may take possession of any certificate of title, registration card, decal, permit, license certificate, permit, registration plate, or any other article issued by the state:

(a) that is fictitious or altered;

(b) that has been unlawfully or erroneously issued;

(c) that is unlawfully or erroneously displayed; or

(d) as required under Section 41-6a-520, 53-3-223, 53-3-231, or 53-3-418.

(2) A receipt shall be issued that describes each confiscated item. 2005

53-3-227. Driving a motor vehicle prohibited while driving privilege denied, suspended, disqualified, or revoked — Penalties.

(1) A person whose driving privilege has been denied, suspended, disqualified, or revoked under this chapter or under the laws of the state in which the person's driving privilege was granted and who drives any motor vehicle upon the highways of this state while that driving privilege is denied, suspended, disqualified, or revoked shall be punished as provided in this section.

(2) A person convicted of a violation of Subsection (1), other than a violation specified in Subsection (3), is guilty of a class C misdemeanor.

(3) (a) A person is guilty of a class B misdemeanor if the person's conviction under Subsection (1) is based on the person driving a motor vehicle while the person's driving privilege is suspended, disqualified, or revoked for:

(i) a refusal to submit to a chemical test under Section 41-6a-520;

(ii) a violation of Section 41-6a-502;

(iii) a violation of a local ordinance that complies with the requirements of Section 41-6a-510;

(iv) a violation of Section 41-6a-517;

(v) a violation of Section 76-5-207;

(vi) a criminal action that the person plead guilty to as a result of a plea bargain after having been originally charged with violating one or more of the sections or ordinances under this Subsection (3);

(vii) a revocation or suspension which has been extended under Subsection 53-3-220(2); or

(viii) where disqualification is the result of driving a commercial motor vehicle while the person's CDL is disqualified, suspended, canceled, or revoked under Subsection 53-3-414(1).

(b) A person is guilty of a class B misdemeanor if the person's conviction under Subsection (1) is based on the person driving a motor vehicle while the person's driving privilege is suspended, disqualified, or revoked by any state, the United States, or any district, possession, or territory of the United States for violations corresponding to the violations listed in Subsections (3)(a)(i) through (viii).

(c) A fine imposed under this Subsection (3) shall be at least the maximum fine for a class C misdemeanor under Section 76-3-301. 2005

53-3-228. Repealed. 1997

53-3-229. Prohibited uses of license certificate — Penalty.

(1) It is a class C misdemeanor for a person to:

(a) lend or knowingly permit the use of a license certificate issued to the person, by a person not entitled to it;

(b) display or to represent as the person's own a license certificate not issued to the person;

(c) refuse to surrender to the division or a peace officer upon demand any license certificate issued by the division;

(d) use a false name or give a false address in any application for a license or any renewal or duplicate of the license certificate, or to knowingly make a false statement, or to knowingly conceal a material fact or otherwise commit a fraud in the application;

(e) display a canceled, denied, revoked, suspended, or disqualified driver license certificate as a valid driver license certificate;

(f) knowingly acquire, use, display, or transfer an item that purports to be an authentic driver license certificate issued by a governmental entity if the item is not an authentic driver license certificate issued by that governmental entity; or

(g) alter any information on an authentic driver license certificate so that it no longer represents the information originally displayed.

(2) The provisions of Subsection (1)(e) do not prohibit the use of a person's driver license certificate as a means of personal identification.

(3) It is a class A misdemeanor to:

(a) knowingly issue a driver license certificate with false or fraudulent information;

(b) knowingly issue a driver license certificate to a person younger than 21 years of age if the driver license certificate is not distinguished as required for a person younger than 21 years of age under Section 53-3-207; or

(c) knowingly acquire, use, display, or transfer a false or altered driver license certificate to procure cigarettes, tobacco, or tobacco products.

(4) A person may not use, display, or transfer a false or altered driver license certificate to procure alcoholic beverages, gain admittance to a place where alcoholic beverages are sold or consumed, or obtain employment that may not be obtained by a minor in violation of Section 32A-1-301.

(5) It is a third degree felony if a person's acquisition, use, display, or transfer of a false or altered driver license certificate:

(a) aids or furthers the person's efforts to fraudulently obtain goods or services; or

(b) aids or furthers the person's efforts to commit a violent felony.   2005

53-3-230. Repealed.   1997

53-3-231. Person under 21 may not operate a vehicle or motorboat with detectable alcohol in body — Chemical test procedures — Temporary license — Hearing and decision — Suspension of license or operating privilege — Fees — Judicial review — Referral to local substance abuse authority or program.

(1) (a) As used in this section:

(i) "Local substance abuse authority" has the same meaning as provided in Section 62A-15-102.

(ii) "Substance abuse program" means any substance abuse program licensed by the Department of Human Services or the Department of Health and approved by the local substance abuse authority.

(b) Calculations of blood, breath, or urine alcohol concentration under this section shall be made in accordance with the procedures in Subsection 41-6a-502(1).

(2) (a) A person younger than 21 years of age may not operate or be in actual physical control of a vehicle or motorboat with any measurable blood, breath, or urine alcohol concentration in the person's body as shown by a chemical test.

(b) (i) A person with a valid operator license who violates Subsection (2)(a), in addition to any other applicable penalties arising out of the incident, shall have the person's operator license denied or suspended as provided in Subsection (2)(b)(ii).

(ii) (A) For a first offense under Subsection (2)(a), the division shall deny the person's operator license if ordered or not challenged under this section for a period of 90 days beginning on the 30th day after the date of the arrest under Section 32A-12-209.

(B) For a second or subsequent offense under Subsection (2)(a), within three years of a prior denial or suspension, the division shall suspend the person's operator license for a period of one year beginning on the 30th day after the date of arrest.

(c) (i) A person who has not been issued an operator license who violates Subsection (2)(a), in addition to any other penalties arising out of the incident, shall be punished as provided in Subsection (2)(c)(ii).

(ii) For one year or until the person is 17, whichever is longer, a person may not operate a vehicle and the division may not issue the person an operator license or learner's permit.

(3) (a) When a peace officer has reasonable grounds to believe that a person may be violating or has violated Subsection (2), the peace officer may, in connection with arresting the person for a violation of Section 32A-12-209, request that the person submit to a chemical test or tests to be administered in compliance with the standards under Section 41-6a-520.

(b) The peace officer shall advise a person prior to the person's submission to a chemical test that a test result indicating a violation of Subsection (2)(a) will result in denial or suspension of the person's license to operate a motor vehicle or a refusal to issue a license.

(c) If the person submits to a chemical test and the test results indicate a blood, breath, or urine alcohol content in violation of Subsection (2)(a), or if a peace officer makes a determination, based on reasonable grounds, that the person is otherwise in violation of Subsection (2)(a), a peace officer shall, on behalf of the division and within 24 hours of the arrest, give notice of the division's intention to deny or suspend the person's license to operate a vehicle or refusal to issue a license under Subsection (2).

(4) When a peace officer gives notice on behalf of the division, the peace officer shall:

(a) take the Utah license certificate or permit, if any, of the operator;

(b) issue a temporary license certificate effective for only 29 days from the date of arrest if the driver had a valid operator's license; and

(c) supply to the operator, in a manner specified by the division, basic information regarding how to obtain a prompt hearing before the division.

(5) A citation issued by a peace officer may, if provided in a manner specified by the division, also serve as the temporary license certificate under Subsection (4)(b).

(6) As a matter of procedure, a peace officer shall send to the division within ten calendar days after the day on which notice is provided:

(a) the person's driver license certificate, if any;

(b) a copy of the citation issued for the offense;

(c) a signed report in a manner specified by the Driver License Division indicating the chemical test results, if any; and

(d) any other basis for a peace officer's determination that the person has violated Subsection (2).

(7) (a) (i) Upon request in a manner specified by the division, the Driver License Division shall grant to the person an opportunity to be heard within 29 days after the date of arrest under Section 32A-12-209.

(ii) The request shall be made within ten calendar days of the day on which notice is provided.

(b) (i) Except as provided in Subsection (7)(b)(ii), a hearing, if held, shall be before the division in the county in which the arrest occurred.

(ii) The division may hold a hearing in some other county if the division and the person both agree.

(c) The hearing shall be documented and shall cover the issues of:

(i) whether a peace officer had reasonable grounds to believe the person was operating a motor vehicle or motorboat in violation of Subsection (2)(a);

(ii) whether the person refused to submit to the test; and

(iii) the test results, if any.

(d) In connection with a hearing, the division or its authorized agent may administer oaths and may issue subpoenas for the attendance of witnesses and the production of relevant books and papers and records as defined in Section 46-4-102.

(e) One or more members of the division may conduct the hearing.

(f) Any decision made after a hearing before any number of the members of the division is as valid as if made after a hearing before the full membership of the division.

(g) After the hearing, the division shall order whether the person:

(i) with a valid license to operate a motor vehicle will have the person's license denied or not or suspended or not; or

(ii) without a valid operator license will be refused a license under Subsection (2)(c).

(h) If the person for whom the hearing is held fails to appear before the division as required in the notice, the division shall order whether the person shall have the person's license denied, suspended, or not denied or suspended, or whether an operator license will be refused or not refused.

(8) (a) (i) Following denial or suspension the division shall assess against a person, in addition to any fee imposed under Subsection 53-3-205(13), a fee under Section 53-3-105, which shall be paid before the person's driving privilege is reinstated, to cover administrative costs.

(ii) This fee shall be canceled if the person obtains an unappealed division hearing or court decision that the suspension was not proper.

(b) A person whose operator license has been denied, suspended, or postponed by the division under this section may file a petition within 30 days after the suspension for a hearing on the matter which, if held, is governed by Section 53-3-224.

(9) After reinstatement of an operator license for a first offense under this section, a report authorized under Section 53-3-104 may not contain evidence of the denial or suspension of the person's operator license under this section if the person has not been convicted of any other offense for which the denial or suspension may be extended.

(10) (a) In addition to the penalties in Subsection (2), a person who violates Subsection (2)(a) shall:

(i) obtain an assessment and recommendation for appropriate action from a substance abuse program, but any associated costs shall be the person's responsibility; or

(ii) be referred by the division to the local substance abuse authority for an assessment and recommendation for appropriate action.

(b) Reinstatement of the person's operator license or the right to obtain an operator license is contingent upon successful completion of the action recommended by the local substance abuse authority or the substance abuse program.

(ii) The local substance abuse authority's or the substance abuse program's recommended action shall be determined by an assessment of the person's alcohol abuse and may include:

(A) a targeted education and prevention program;

(B) an early intervention program; or

(C) a substance abuse treatment program.

(iii) Successful completion of the recommended action shall be determined by standards established by the Division of Substance Abuse and Mental Health.

(c) At the conclusion of the penalty period imposed under Subsection (2), the local substance abuse authority or the substance abuse program shall notify the division of the person's status regarding completion of the recommended action.

(d) The local substance abuse authorities and the substance abuse programs shall cooperate with the division in:

(i) conducting the assessments;

(ii) making appropriate recommendations for action; and

(iii) notifying the division about the person's status regarding completion of the recommended action.

(e) (i) The local substance abuse authority is responsible for the cost of the assessment of the person's alcohol abuse, if the assessment is conducted by the local substance abuse authority.

(ii) The local substance abuse authority or a substance abuse program selected by a person is responsible for:

(A) conducting an assessment of the person's alcohol abuse; and

(B) for making a referral to an appropriate program on the basis of the findings of the assessment.

(iii) (A) The person who violated Subsection (2)(a) is responsible for all costs and fees associated with the recommended program to which the person selected or is referred.

(B) The costs and fees under Subsection (10)(e)(iii)(A) shall be based on a sliding scale consistent with the local substance abuse authority's policies and practices regarding fees for services or determined by the substance abuse program.   **2005**

53-3-232.   Conditional license — May not operate a vehicle or motorboat with alcohol in body — Penalty.

(1) As used in this section, "qualifying conviction" means:

(a) a conviction of a violation of Section 41-6a-502, Section 41-6a-517, a local ordinance which complies with the requirements of Subsection 41-6a-510(1), Section 76-5-207, or of alcohol-related reckless driving as described under Subsection 41-6a-512(1);

(b) a revocation under Section 41-6a-521 if the revocation is not based on the same arrest as a conviction under Subsection (1)(a); or

(c) a violation of Subsection (3).

(2) (a) Until June 30, 2005, the division may only issue, reinstate, or renew a driver license in the form of a no alcohol conditional license to a person who has a qualifying conviction for a period of:

(i) two years after issuance of a Utah driver license or permit following a first qualifying conviction for an offense, the arrest for which occurred within the previous ten years; and

(ii) ten years after issuance of a Utah driver license or permit following a second or subsequent qualifying conviction for an offense, the arrest for which occurred within the previous ten years.

(b) Beginning on July 1, 2005, the division may not issue, reinstate, or renew a driver license in the form of a no alcohol conditional license.

(3) A no alcohol conditional license shall be issued on the condition that the person may not operate or be in actual physical control of a vehicle or motorboat in this state with any alcohol in the person's body.

(4) It is a class B misdemeanor for a person who has been issued a no alcohol conditional license to operate or be in actual physical control of a vehicle or motorboat in this state in violation of Subsection (3).   2005

53-3-233. Repealed.   2005

53-3-234. Driver license application — Selective Service Registration — Statement.

(1) The following information for each male United States citizen or immigrant under the age of 26 shall be electronically transmitted by the division to the Selective Service System:

(a) name;

(b) address;

(c) Social Security number; and

(d) date of birth.

(2) Each application for any type of license to operate a motor vehicle in this state shall contain the following statement which must be acknowledged by the applicant:

"By submitting this application, I am consenting to registration with the Selective Service System, if required by federal law."

(3) Refusal to consent to the release of information to the Selective Service System shall result in the denial of the license.   2001

PART 3

IMPAIRED PERSONS LICENSING

53-3-301. Short title.

This part is known as the "Impaired Persons Licensing Act."   1993

53-3-302. Definitions.

As used in this part:

(1) "Board" means the Driver License Medical Advisory Board created in Section 53-3-303.

(2) "Health care professional" means a physician or surgeon licensed to practice medicine in the state, or when recommended by the Medical Advisory Board, may include other health care professionals licensed to conduct physical examinations in this state.

(3) (a) "Impaired person" means a person who has a mental, emotional, or nonstable physical disability or disease that may impair the person's ability to exercise reasonable and ordinary control at all times over a motor vehicle while driving on the highways.

(b) "Impaired person" does not include a person having a nonprogressive or stable physical impairment that is objectively observable and that may be evaluated by a functional driving examination.   1993

53-3-303. Driver License Medical Advisory Board — Membership — Guidelines for licensing impaired persons — Recommendations to division.

(1) There is created within the division the Driver License Medical Advisory Board.

(2) (a) The board is comprised of three regular members appointed by the Commissioner of Public Safety to four-year terms.

(b) The board shall be assisted by expert panel members nominated by the board as necessary and as approved by the Commissioner of Public Safety.

(c) Notwithstanding the requirements of Subsection (2)(a), the executive director shall, at the time of appointment or reappointment, adjust the length of terms to ensure that the terms of board members are staggered so that approximately half of the board is appointed every two years.

(d) When a vacancy occurs in the membership for any reason, the replacement shall be appointed for the unexpired term.

(e) The expert panel members shall recommend medical standards in the areas of the panel members' special competence for determining the physical, mental, and emotional capabilities of applicants for licenses and licensees.

(3) In reviewing individual cases, a panel acting with the authority of the board consists of at least two members, of which at least one is a regular board member.

(4) The director of the division or his designee serves as secretary to the board and its panels.

(5) Members of the board and expert panel members nominated by them shall be health care professionals.

(6) (a) (i) Members who are not government employees shall receive no compensation or benefits for their services, but may receive per diem and expenses incurred in the performance of the member's official duties at the rates established by the Division of Finance under Sections 63A-3-106 and 63A-3-107.

(ii) Members may decline to receive per diem and expenses for their service.

(b) (i) State government officer and employee members who do not receive salary, per diem, or expenses from their agency for their service may receive per diem and expenses incurred in the performance of their official duties from the board at the rates established by the Division of Finance under Sections 63A-3-106 and 63A-3-107.

(ii) State government officer and employee members may decline to receive per diem and expenses for their service.

(7) The board shall meet from time to time when called by the director of the division.

(8) (a) The board shall recommend guidelines and standards for determining the physical, mental, and emotional capabilities of applicants for licenses and for licensees.

(b) The guidelines and standards are applicable to all Utah licensees and for all individuals who hold learner permits and are participating in driving activities in all forms of driver education.

(c) The guidelines and standards shall be published by the division.

(9) If the division has reason to believe that an applicant or licensee is an impaired person, it may:

(a) act upon the matter based upon the published guidelines and standards; or

(b) convene a panel to consider the matter and submit findings and a recommendation; the division shall consider the recommendation along with other evidence in determining whether a license should be suspended, revoked, denied, disqualified, canceled, or restricted.

(10) (a) If the division has acted under Subsection (9) to suspend, revoke, deny, disqualify, cancel, or restrict the driving privilege without the convening of a panel, the affected applicant or licensee may within ten days of receiving notice of the action request in a manner prescribed by the division a review of the division's action by a panel.

(b) The panel shall review the matters and make written findings and conclusions.

(c) The division shall affirm or modify its previous action.

(11) (a) Actions of the division are subject to judicial review as provided in this part.

(b) The guidelines, standards, findings, conclusions, and recommendations of the board or of a panel are admissible as evidence in any judicial review.

(12) Members of the board and its panels incur no liability for recommendations, findings, conclusions, or for other acts performed in good faith and incidental to membership on the board or a panel.

(13) The division shall provide forms for the use of health care professionals in depicting the medical history of any physical, mental, or emotional impairment affecting the applicant's or licensee's ability to drive a motor vehicle.

(14) (a) (i) Individuals who apply for or hold a license and have, or develop, or suspect that they have developed a physical, mental, or emotional impairment that may affect driving safety are responsible for reporting this to the division or its agent.

(ii) If there is uncertainty, the individual is expected to seek competent medical evaluation and advice as to the significance of the impairment as it relates to driving safety, and to refrain from driving until a clarification is made.

(b) Health care professionals who care for patients with physical, mental, or emotional impairments that may affect their driving safety, whether defined by published guidelines and standards or not, are responsible for making available to their patients without reservation their recommendations and appropriate information related to driving safety and responsibilities.

(c) A health care professional or other person who becomes aware of a physical, mental, or emotional impairment that appears to present an imminent threat to driving safety and reports this information to the division in good faith has immunity from any damages claimed as a result of making the report.   2001

53-3-303.5. Driver License Medical Advisory Board — Medical waivers.

(1) The Driver License Medical Advisory Board shall:

(a) advise the director of the division; and

(b) establish and recommend in a manner specified by the board functional ability profile guidelines and standards for determining the physical, mental, and emotional capabilities of applicants for specific types of licenses, appropriate to various driving abilities.

(2) (a) The Driver License Medical Advisory Board shall establish fitness standards, including provisions for a waiver of specified federal driver's physical qualifications under 49 CFR 391.41, for intrastate commercial driving privileges.

(b) The standards under this Subsection (2) may only be implemented if the United States Department of Transportation (USDOT) will not impose any sanctions, including funding sanctions, against the state.

(3) In case of uncertainty of interpretation of these guidelines and standards, or in special circumstances, applicants may request a review of any division decision by a panel of board members. All of the actions of the director and board are subject to judicial review.

(4) (a) If a person applies for a waiver established under Subsection (2), the applicant shall bear any costs directly associated with the cost of administration of the waiver program, with respect to the applicant's application, in addition to any fees required under Section 53-3-105.

(b) The division shall establish any additional fee necessary to administer the license under this Subsection (4) in accordance with Section 63-38-3.2.   2001

53-3-304. Licensing of impaired persons — Medical review — Restricted license — Procedures.

(1) (a) If the division has reason to believe that an applicant for a license is an impaired person, the division may require one or both of the following:

(i) a physical examination of the applicant by a health care professional and the submittal by the health care professional of a signed medical report indicating the results of the physical examination;

(ii) a follow-up medical review of the applicant by a health care professional and completion of a medical report at intervals established by the division under standards recommended by the board.

(b) The format of the medical report required under Subsection (a) shall be devised by the division with the advice of the board and shall elicit the necessary medical information to determine whether it would be a public safety hazard to permit the applicant to drive a motor vehicle on the highways.

(2) (a) The division may grant a restricted license to an impaired person who is otherwise qualified to obtain a license.

(b) The license continues in effect until its expiration date so long as the licensee complies with the requirements set forth by the division.

(c) The license renewal is subject to the conditions of this section.

(d) Any physical, mental, or emotional impairment of the applicant that in the opinion of the division does not affect the applicant's ability to exercise reasonable and ordinary control at all times in driving a motor vehicle upon the highway, does not prevent granting a license to the applicant.

(3) (a) If an examination is required under this section, the division is not bound by the recom-

mendation of the examining health care professional but shall give fair consideration to the recommendation in acting upon the application. The criterion is whether upon all the evidence it is safe to permit the applicant to drive a motor vehicle.

(b) In deciding whether to grant or deny a license, the division may be guided by the opinion of experts in the fields of diagnosing and treating mental, physical, or emotional disabilities and may take into consideration any other factors that bear on the issue of public safety.

(4) Information provided under this section relating to physical, mental, or emotional impairment is classified under Title 63, Chapter 2, Government Records Access and Management Act.　　　1993

PART 4

UNIFORM COMMERCIAL DRIVER LICENSE ACT

53-3-401.　Short title.

This part is known as the "Uniform Commercial Driver License Act."　　　1993

53-3-402.　Definitions.

As used in this part:

(1) "Alcohol" means any substance containing any form of alcohol, including ethanol, methanol, propanol, and isopropanol.

(2) "Alcohol concentration" means the number of grams of alcohol per:

(a) 100 milliliters of blood;

(b) 210 liters of breath; or

(c) 67 milliliters of urine.

(3) "Commercial driver instruction permit" or "CDIP" means a permit issued under Section 53-3-408.

(4) "Commercial driver license information system" or "CDLIS" means the information system established under Title XII, Pub. L. 99-570, the Commercial Motor Vehicle Safety Act of 1986, as a clearinghouse for information related to the licensing and identification of commercial motor vehicle drivers.

(5) "Controlled substance" means any substance so classified under Section 102(6) of the Controlled Substance Act, 21 U.S.C. 802(6), and includes all substances listed on the current Schedules I through V of 21 C.F.R., Part 1308 as they may be revised from time to time.

(6) "Employee" means any driver of a commercial motor vehicle, including:

(a) full-time, regularly employed drivers;

(b) casual, intermittent, or occasional drivers;

(c) leased drivers; and

(d) independent, owner-operator contractors while in the course of driving a commercial motor vehicle who are either directly employed by or under lease to an employer.

(7) "Employer" means any individual or person including the United States, a state, or a political subdivision of a state, who owns or leases a commercial motor vehicle, or assigns an individual to drive a commercial motor vehicle.

(8) "Felony" means any offense under state or federal law that is punishable by death or imprisonment for a term of more than one year.

(9) "Foreign jurisdiction" means any jurisdiction other than the United States or a state of the United States.

(10) "Gross vehicle weight rating" or "GVWR" means the value specified by the manufacturer as the maximum loaded weight of a single vehicle or GVWR of a combination or articulated vehicle, and includes the GVWR of the power unit plus the total weight of all towed units and the loads on those units.

(11) "Hazardous material" has the same meaning as defined under 49 U.S.C. Sec. 5101 et seq., Hazardous Materials Transportation Act.

(12) "Imminent hazard" means the existence of a condition, practice, or violation that presents a substantial likelihood that death, serious illness, severe personal injury, or a substantial endangerment to health, property, or the environment is expected to occur immediately, or before the condition, practice, or violation can be abated.

(13) "NDR" means the National Driver Register.

(14) "Nonresident CDL" means a commercial driver license issued by a state to an individual who resides in a foreign jurisdiction.

(15) "Out-of-service order" means a temporary prohibition against driving a commercial motor vehicle.

(16) "Port-of-entry agent" has the same meaning as provided in Section 72-1-102.

(17) "Serious traffic violation" means a conviction of any of the following:

(a) speeding 15 or more miles per hour above the posted speed limit;

(b) reckless driving as defined by state or local law;

(c) improper or erratic traffic lane changes;

(d) following the vehicle ahead too closely;

(e) any other motor vehicle traffic law which arises in connection with a fatal traffic accident;

(f) operating a commercial motor vehicle without a CDL or a CDIP;

(g) operating a commercial motor vehicle without the proper class of CDL or CDL endorsement for the type of vehicle group being operated or for the passengers or cargo being transported;

(h) operating a commercial motor vehicle without a CDL or CDIP license certificate in the driver's possession in violation of Section 53-3-404; or

(i) all other violations under Section 53-3-220 for which mandatory suspension or revocation are required.

(18) "State" means a state of the United States, the District of Columbia, any province or territory of Canada, or Mexico.

(19) "United States" means the 50 states and the District of Columbia.　　　2005

53-3-403.　Superseding clause.

This part supersedes the general licensing provisions of state law contained in Parts 1 and 2 of this chapter.　　　1993

53-3-404.　Requirements to drive commercial motor vehicle.

(1) A person may not drive a commercial motor vehicle, unless the person has been issued and is in immediate possession of:

(a) a CDL license certificate valid for the commercial motor vehicle the person is driving; or

(b) a valid CDIP license certificate in accordance with Section 53-3-408.

(2) (a) A licensee shall display a CDL or CDIP license certificate upon demand of a justice court judge, a peace officer, a special function officer, a port-of-entry officer, or a designee of the division.

(b) It is a defense to a charge under this section that the person charged produces in court a CDL or CDIP license certificate that is issued to the person and valid at the time of the citation or arrest.

(3) A person may not drive a commercial motor vehicle if the person's privilege to drive a commercial motor vehicle is:

(a) suspended, revoked, or canceled;

(b) subject to a disqualification; or

(c) subject to an out-of-service order.　2005

53-3-405. Authority to drive commercial motor vehicle in Utah.

(1) A person who holds or is required to hold a CDL may drive a commercial motor vehicle in this state if:

(a) the person has a CDL issued by any state in accordance with the minimum federal standards for the issuance of commercial motor vehicle driver licenses;

(b) the person's license is not suspended, revoked, canceled, or disqualified; and

(c) he is not disqualified from driving a commercial motor vehicle.

(2) This section supersedes any provision to the contrary.　1993

53-3-406. Commercial motor vehicle driver — Only one license.

Any person who drives a commercial motor vehicle may only have one license.　1993

53-3-407. Qualifications for commercial driver license — Fee — Third parties may administer skills test.

(1) A CDL may be issued only to a person who:

(a) is a resident of this state or qualifies as a nonresident under Section 53-3-409;

(b) has passed a test of knowledge and skills for driving a commercial motor vehicle, that complies with minimum standards established by federal regulation in 49 C.F.R., Part 383, Subparts G and H; and

(c) has complied with all requirements of 49 C.F.R., Part 383 and other applicable state laws and federal regulations.

(2) Tests required under this section shall be prescribed and administered by the division.

(3) The division shall authorize a person, an agency of this or another state, an employer, a private driver training facility or other private institution, or a department, agency, or entity of local government to administer the skills test required under this section if:

(a) the test is the same test as prescribed by the division, and is administered in the same manner; and

(b) the party authorized under this section to administer the test has entered into an agreement with the state that complies with the requirements of 49 C.F.R., Part 383.75.

(4) A person who has an appointment with the division for testing and fails to keep the appointment or to cancel at least 48 hours in advance of the appointment shall pay the fee under Section 53-3-105.

(5) A person authorized under this section to administer the skills test is not criminally or civilly liable for the administration of the test unless he administers the test in a grossly negligent manner.

(6) The division shall waive the skills test required under this section if it determines that the applicant meets the requirements of 49 C.F.R., Part 383.77.　1993

53-3-408. Qualifications for commercial driver instruction permit.

(1) A CDIP may be issued to a person who:

(a) holds a valid license;

(b) has at least one year of driving experience; and

(c) has passed the vision and knowledge test for the class of license for which he is applying.

(2) A CDIP may be:

(a) issued only for a period not to exceed six months; and

(b) renewed or issued again only once within a two-year period.

(3) The holder of a CDIP may drive a commercial motor vehicle on a highway only when accompanied by a person who:

(a) (i) holds a CDL valid for the type of commercial motor vehicle driven; or

(ii) is certified by the division to administer driver licensing examinations to CDL applicants; and

(b) occupies a seat beside the individual for the purpose of:

(i) giving the driver instruction regarding the driving of the commercial motor vehicle; or

(ii) administering a driver licensing examination to a CDL applicant.

(4) A CDL or CDIP may not be issued to a person:

(a) subject to disqualification from driving a commercial motor vehicle; or

(b) whose license is suspended, revoked, or canceled in any state.

(5) A CDL or CDIP may not be issued to a person until the person has surrendered all license certificates the person holds to the division for cancellation.　2005

53-3-409. Nonresident CDL — Qualifications.

(1) The division may issue a nonresident CDL to a resident of a foreign jurisdiction if the United States Secretary of Transportation has determined that the commercial motor vehicle testing and licensing standards in the foreign jurisdiction do not meet the testing standards in 49 C.F.R., Part 383.

(2) An applicant for a nonresident CDL shall surrender any nonresident CDL he holds to the issuing state for cancellation.

(3) The word "nonresident" shall be printed clearly on the face of a nonresident CDL issued by the division.

(4) The holder of a nonresident CDL is subject to the same rules, regulations, and laws as a resident CDL holder.　1993

53-3-410. Applicant information required for CDIP and CDL — State resident to have state CDL.

(1) The application for a CDL or CDIP shall include the following information regarding the applicant:

(a) full legal name and current mailing and Utah residential address;

(b) physical description, including sex, height, weight, and eye color;

(c) date of birth;

(d) Social Security number, unless the application is for a nonresident license;

(e) a complete list of all states in which the applicant was issued a driver license in the previous ten years; and

(f) the applicant's signature.

(2) An application under this section shall also include all certifications required by 49 C.F.R., Part 383.71.

(3) When the holder of a license under this part changes the holder's name, mailing address, or residence, the holder shall make application for a duplicate license within 30 days of the change.

(4) A person who has been a resident of this state for 30 consecutive days may not drive a commercial motor vehicle under the authority of a commercial driver license issued by another jurisdiction.   2005

53-3-411.   Description of CDL — Information to be included.

(1) The CDL certificate shall be printed with the identifying words "Commercial Driver License" or "CDL".

(2) To the maximum extent practicable, the CDL certificate shall be resistant to alteration.

(3) The CDL certificate shall include:

(a) the legal name and principal place of residence of the holder;

(b) the holder's photograph in color;

(c) a physical description of the holder, including sex and height;

(d) the holder's birth date;

(e) the holder's Utah license certificate number;

(f) the holder's signature;

(g) the class or type of commercial motor vehicle or vehicles the holder is authorized to drive;

(h) any endorsements or restrictions to which the holder is subject;

(i) the name of the issuing state; and

(j) the dates between which the CDL is valid.

(4) The CDL may not include the holder's Social Security number.   2004

53-3-412.   CDL classifications, endorsements, and restrictions.

A CDL may be granted with the following classifications, endorsements, and restrictions:

(1) Classifications:

(a) Class A: any combination of vehicles with a GVWR of 26,001 pounds or more, if the GVWR of the one or more vehicles being towed is in excess of 10,000 pounds;

(b) Class B: any single motor vehicle with a GVWR of 26,001 pounds or more, including that motor vehicle when towing a vehicle with a GVWR of 10,000 pounds or less; and

(c) Class C: any single motor vehicle with a GVWR of less than 26,001 pounds or that motor vehicle when towing a vehicle with a GVWR of 10,000 pounds or less when the vehicle is designed or used:

(i) to transport more than 15 passengers, including the driver;

(ii) as a school bus, and weighing less than 26,001 pounds GVWR; or

(iii) to transport hazardous materials that requires the vehicle to be placarded under 49 C.F.R., Part 172, Subpart F.

(2) Endorsements:

(a) "H" authorizes the driver to drive a commercial motor vehicle transporting hazardous materials.

(b) "N" authorizes the driver to drive a tank vehicle.

(c) "P" authorizes the driver to drive a motor vehicle carrying more than 15 passengers including the driver.

(d) "S" authorizes the driver to drive a school bus or a motor vehicle carrying more than 15 passengers including the driver.

(e) "T" authorizes the driver to drive a commercial motor vehicle with a double or triple trailer.

(f) "X" authorizes the driver to drive a tank vehicle and transport hazardous materials.

(3) Restrictions:

(a) "K" restricts the driver to driving intrastate only any commercial motor vehicle as defined by Title 49, C.F.R., Parts 383 and 390.

(b) "L" restricts the driver to driving a commercial motor vehicle not equipped with air brakes.

(c) "J" provides for other CDL restrictions.   2005

53-3-413.   Issuance of CDL by division — Driving record — Expiration date — Renewal — Hazardous materials provision.

(1) Before the division may grant a CDL, the division shall obtain the driving record information regarding the applicant through the CDLIS, the NDR, and from each state where the applicant has been licensed.

(2) Within ten days after issuing a CDL, the division shall notify the CDLIS and provide all information required to ensure identification of the CDL holder.

(3) The expiration date for a CDL is the birth date of the holder in the fifth year following the year of issuance of the CDL.

(4) The applicant for a renewal of a CDL shall complete the application form required by Section 53-3-410 and provide updated information and required certification.

(5) (a) The division may not issue a hazardous materials endorsement on a CDL unless the applicant meets the security threat assessment standards of the federal Transportation Security Administration.

(b) The division shall revoke the hazardous materials endorsement on a CDL upon receiving notice from the federal Transportation Security Administration that the person holding a hazardous materials endorsement does not meet Transportation Security Administration security threat assessment standards.

(c) To retain a hazardous materials endorsement upon CDL renewal, the applicant must take and pass the knowledge test for hazardous materials endorsement in addition to any other testing required by the division.   2005

53-3-414.   CDL disqualification or suspension — Grounds and duration — Procedure.

(1) A person who holds or is required to hold a CDL is disqualified from driving a commercial motor vehicle for a period of not less than one year if convicted of a first offense of:

(a) driving a motor vehicle while under the influence of alcohol, drugs, a controlled substance, or more than one of these;

(b) driving a commercial motor vehicle while the concentration of alcohol in the person's blood, breath, or urine is .04 grams or more;

(c) leaving the scene of an accident involving a motor vehicle the person was driving;

(d) using a motor vehicle in the commission of a felony;

(e) refusal to submit to a test to determine the concentration of alcohol in the person's blood, breath, or urine;

(f) driving a commercial motor vehicle while the person's commercial driver license is disqualified, suspended, canceled, or revoked; or

(g) operating a commercial motor vehicle in a negligent manner causing the death of another including the offenses of automobile homicide under Section 76-5-207, manslaughter under Section 76-5-205, or negligent homicide under Section 76-5-206.

(2) If any of the violations under Subsection (1) occur while the driver is transporting a hazardous material required to be placarded, the driver is disqualified for not less than three years.

(3) (a) Except as provided under Subsection (4), a driver of a motor vehicle who holds or is required to hold a CDL is disqualified for life from driving a commercial motor vehicle if convicted of two or more of any of the offenses under Subsection (1) arising from two or more separate incidents.

(b) Subsection (3)(a) applies only to those offenses committed after July 1, 1989.

(4) (a) Any driver disqualified for life from driving a commercial motor vehicle under this section may apply to the division for reinstatement of the driver's CDL if the driver:

(i) has both voluntarily enrolled in and successfully completed an appropriate rehabilitation program that:

(A) meets the standards of the division; and

(B) complies with 49 C.F.R. Part 383.51;

(ii) has served a minimum disqualification period of ten years; and

(iii) has fully met the standards for reinstatement of commercial motor vehicle driving privileges established by rule of the division.

(b) If a reinstated driver is subsequently convicted of another disqualifying offense under this section, the driver is permanently disqualified for life and is ineligible to again apply for a reduction of the lifetime disqualification.

(5) A driver of a motor vehicle who holds or is required to hold a CDL is disqualified for life from driving a commercial motor vehicle if the driver uses a motor vehicle in the commission of any felony involving the manufacturing, distributing, or dispensing of a controlled substance, or possession with intent to manufacture, distribute, or dispense a controlled substance.

(6) (a) Subject to Subsection (6)(b), a driver of a commercial motor vehicle who holds or is required to hold a CDL is disqualified for not less than:

(i) 60 days from driving a commercial motor vehicle if the driver is convicted of two serious traffic violations; and

(ii) 120 days if the driver is convicted of three or more serious traffic violations.

(b) The disqualifications under Subsection (6)(a) are effective only if the serious traffic violations:

(i) occur within three years of each other;

(ii) arise from separate incidents; and

(iii) involve the use or operation of a commercial motor vehicle.

(7) A driver of a commercial motor vehicle who is convicted of violating an out-of-service order while driving a commercial motor vehicle is disqualified from driving a commercial motor vehicle for a period not less than:

(a) 90 days but not more than one year if the driver is convicted of a first violation;

(b) one year but not more than five years if, during any ten-year period, the driver is convicted of two violations of out-of-service orders in separate incidents;

(c) three years but not more than five years if, during any ten-year period, the driver is convicted of three or more violations of out-of-service orders in separate incidents;

(d) 180 days but not more than two years if the driver is convicted of a first violation of an out-of-service order while transporting hazardous materials required to be placarded or while operating a motor vehicle designed to transport 16 or more passengers, including the driver; or

(e) three years but not more than five years if, during any ten-year period, the driver is convicted of two or more violations, in separate incidents, of an out-of-service order while transporting hazardous materials required to be placarded or while operating a motor vehicle designed to transport 16 or more passengers, including the driver.

(8) A driver of a commercial motor vehicle who holds or is required to hold a CDL is disqualified for not less than 60 days if the division determines, in its check of the driver's driver license status, application, and record prior to issuing a CDL or at any time after the CDL is issued, that the driver has falsified information required to apply for a CDL in this state.

(9) A driver of a commercial motor vehicle who is convicted of violating a railroad-highway grade crossing provision under Section 41-6a-1205, while driving a commercial motor vehicle is disqualified from driving a commercial motor vehicle for a period not less than:

(a) 60 days if the driver is convicted of a first violation;

(b) 120 days if, during any three-year period, the driver is convicted of a second violation in separate incidents; or

(c) one year if, during any three-year period, the driver is convicted of three or more violations in separate incidents.

(10) (a) The division shall update its records and notify the CDLIS within ten days of suspending, revoking, disqualifying, denying, or cancelling a CDL to reflect the action taken.

(b) When the division suspends, revokes, cancels, or disqualifies a nonresident CDL, the division shall notify the licensing authority of the issuing state or other jurisdiction and the CDLIS within ten days after the action is taken.

(c) When the division suspends, revokes, cancels, or disqualifies a CDL issued by this state, the division shall notify the CDLIS within ten days after the action is taken.

(11) (a) The division may immediately suspend or disqualify the CDL of a driver without a hearing or receiving a record of the driver's conviction when the division has reason to believe that the:

(i) CDL was issued by the division through error or fraud;

(ii) applicant provided incorrect or incomplete information to the division;

(iii) applicant cheated on any part of a CDL examination;

(iv) driver no longer meets the fitness standards required to obtain a CDL; or

(v) driver poses an imminent hazard.

(b) Suspension of a CDL under this Subsection (11) shall be in accordance with Section 53-3-221.

(c) If a hearing is held under Section 53-3-221, the division shall then rescind the suspension order or cancel the CDL.

(12) (a) Subject to Subsection (12)(b), a driver of a motor vehicle who holds or is required to hold a CDL is disqualified for not less than:

(i) 60 days from driving a commercial motor vehicle if the driver is convicted of two serious traffic violations; and

(ii) 120 days if the driver is convicted of three or more serious traffic violations.

(b) The disqualifications under Subsection (12)(a) are effective only if the serious traffic violations:

(i) occur within three years of each other;

(ii) arise from separate incidents; and

(iii) result in a denial, suspension, cancellation, or revocation of the non-CDL driving privilege from at least one of the violations.

2005

53-3-415. Limitations on employment of commercial motor vehicle drivers.

(1) An employer shall require each applicant for employment as a commercial motor vehicle driver to provide the information required in Section 53-3-416 regarding the applicant's employment history.

(2) An employer may not knowingly allow, permit, or authorize a driver to drive a commercial motor vehicle during any period when the driver has:

(a) a CDL that is suspended, revoked, or canceled by any state;

(b) lost the privilege to drive a commercial motor vehicle in a state;

(c) been disqualified from driving a commercial motor vehicle; or

(d) more than one license.

(3) An employer who violates Subsection (2)(a), (b), or (c) during the period the driver has been disqualified under Subsection 53-3-414(9), is subject to a civil penalty of not more than $10,000.

2001

53-3-416. Driving record and other information to be provided to employer.

(1) Each person who drives a commercial motor vehicle who has a CDL issued by this state and who is convicted of violating, in any type of motor vehicle, a state or local law relating to motor vehicle traffic, other than a parking violation, in this or any other state or jurisdiction, shall notify both the division and his current employer of the conviction within 30 days of the date of conviction.

(2) A driver shall notify his current employer before the end of the business day following the day he receives notice that:

(a) his CDL is suspended, revoked, or canceled by any state;

(b) he loses the privilege to drive a commercial motor vehicle in any state or other jurisdiction for any period; or

(c) he is disqualified from driving a commercial motor vehicle for any period.

(3) A person who applies to be a commercial motor vehicle driver shall at the time of application provide

to the employer the following information for the ten years prior to the date of application:

(a) a list of the names and addresses of the applicant's previous employers for which the applicant was a driver of a commercial motor vehicle as any part of his employment;

(b) the dates between which the applicant drove for each employer listed under Subsection (a); and

(c) the reason the applicant's employment with each employer listed was terminated.

(4) (a) An applicant shall certify that all information provided under this section is true and complete to the best of his knowledge.

(b) An employer receiving information under this section may require that an applicant provide additional information.

1993

53-3-417. Measurable alcohol amount consumed — Penalty — Refusal to take test for alcohol.

(1) A person who holds or is required to hold a CDL may not drive a commercial motor vehicle while there is any measurable or detectable alcohol in his body.

(2) The division, a port-of-entry agent, or a peace officer shall place a person out-of-service for 24 consecutive hours who:

(a) violates Subsection (1); or

(b) refuses a request to submit to a test to determine the alcohol concentration of his blood, breath, or urine.

1998

53-3-418. Prohibited alcohol level for drivers — Procedures, including hearing.

(1) A person who holds or is required to hold a CDL may not drive a commercial motor vehicle in this state if the person:

(a) has sufficient alcohol in the person's body that a subsequent chemical test shows that the person has a blood or breath alcohol concentration of .04 grams or greater at the time of the test after the alleged driving of the commercial motor vehicle;

(b) is under the influence of alcohol, any drug, or the combined influence of alcohol and any drug to degree that renders the person incapable of safely driving a commercial motor vehicle; or

(c) has a blood or breath alcohol concentration of .04 grams or greater at the time of driving the commercial motor vehicle.

(2) A person who holds or is required to hold a CDL and who drives a commercial motor vehicle in this state is considered to have given the person's consent to a test or tests of the person's blood, breath, or urine to determine the concentration of alcohol or the presence of other drugs in the person's physical system.

(3) If a peace officer or port-of-entry agent has reasonable cause to believe that a person may be violating this section, the peace officer or port-of-entry agent may request the person to submit to a chemical test to be administered in compliance with Section 41-6a-515.

(4) When a peace officer or port-of-entry agent requests a person to submit to a test under this section, the peace officer or port-of-entry agent shall advise the person that test results indicating .04 grams or greater alcohol concentration or refusal to submit to any test requested will result in the person's disqualification under Section 53-3-414 from driving a commercial motor vehicle.

(5) If test results under this section indicate .04 grams or greater of alcohol concentration or the person refuses to submit to any test requested under this

section, a peace officer or port-of-entry agent shall, on behalf of the division and within 24 hours of the arrest, give the person notice of the division's intention to disqualify the person's privilege to drive a commercial motor vehicle.

(6) When a peace officer or port-of-entry agent gives notice under Subsection (5), the peace officer or port-of-entry agent shall:

(a) take any Utah license certificate or permit held by the driver;

(b) issue to the driver a temporary license certificate effective for 29 days from the date of arrest;

(c) provide the driver, in a manner specified by the division, basic information regarding how to obtain a prompt hearing before the division; and

(d) issue a 24-hour out-of-service order.

(7) A notice of disqualification issued under Subsection (6) may serve also as the temporary license certificate under that subsection, if provided in a manner specified by the division.

(8) As a matter of procedure, a peace officer or port-of-entry agent shall, within ten calendar days after the day on which notice is provided, send to the division the person's license certificate, a copy of the notice, and a report signed by the peace officer or port-of-entry agent that indicates the results of any chemical test administered or that the person refused a test.

(9) (a) A person disqualified under this section has the right to a hearing regarding the disqualification.

(b) The request for the hearing shall be submitted to the division in a manner specified by the division and shall be made within ten calendar days of the date the notice was issued. If requested, the hearing shall be conducted within 29 days after the date of arrest.

(10) (a) (i) Except as provided in Subsection (10)(a)(ii), a hearing held under this section shall be held before the division and in the county where the notice was issued.

(ii) The division may hold a hearing in some other county if the division and the person both agree.

(b) The hearing shall be documented and shall determine:

(i) whether the peace officer or port-of-entry agent had reasonable grounds to believe the person had been driving a motor vehicle in violation of this section;

(ii) whether the person refused to submit to any requested test; and

(iii) any test results obtained.

(c) In connection with a hearing the division or its authorized agent may administer oaths and may issue subpoenas for the attendance of witnesses and the production of relevant books and documents.

(d) One or more members of the division may conduct the hearing.

(e) A decision made after a hearing before any number of members of the division is as valid as if the hearing were held before the full membership of the division.

(f) After a hearing under this section the division shall indicate by order if the person's CDL is disqualified.

(g) If the person for whom the hearing is held fails to appear before the division as required in the notice, the division shall indicate by order if the person's CDL is disqualified.

(11) (a) If the division disqualifies a person under this section, the person may petition for a hearing under Section 53-3-224.

(b) The petition shall be filed within 30 days after the division issues the disqualification.

(12) (a) A person who violates this section shall be punished in accordance with Section 53-3-414.

(b) (i) In accordance with Section 53-3-414, the first disqualification under this section shall be for one year, and a second disqualification shall be for life.

(ii) A disqualification under Section 53-3-414 begins on the 30th day after the date of arrest.

(13) (a) In addition to the fees imposed under Section 53-3-205 for reinstatement of a CDL, a fee under Section 53-3-105 to cover administrative costs shall be paid before the driving privilege is reinstated.

(b) The fees under Sections 53-3-105 and 53-3-205 shall be canceled if an unappealed hearing at the division or court level determines the disqualification was not proper. 2005

53-3-419. Nonresident driver violations reported to resident state.

(1) When the division receives a report of the conviction of a nonresident holder of a CDL for a violation of a state law or local ordinance relating to traffic control, the division shall notify the driver licensing authority in the licensing state within ten days of receipt of the report.

(2) This section does not apply to parking violations. 1993

53-3-420. Driver's driving record available for certain purposes.

The division shall provide full information regarding the driving record of any holder of a CDL to:

(1) the driver license administrator of any other state requesting that information;

(2) any employer or prospective employer of a person to drive a commercial motor vehicle upon request and payment of a fee under Section 53-3-105; and

(3) insurers of commercial motor vehicle drivers upon request and payment of a fee under Section 53-3-105. 1993

PART 5

COMMERCIAL DRIVER TRAINING SCHOOLS

53-3-501. Short title.

This part is known as the "Commercial Driver Training Schools Act." 1993

53-3-502. Definitions.

As used in this part:

(1) "Commercial driver training school" or "school" means a business enterprise conducted by an individual, association, partnership, or corporation for the education and training of persons, either practically or theoretically, or both, to drive motor vehicles, including motorcycles, and to prepare an applicant for an examination given by the state for a license or learner permit, and charging a consideration or tuition for those services.

(2) "Instructor" means any person, whether acting for himself as operator of a commercial driver training school or for any school for compensation, who teaches, conducts classes of, gives demonstrations to, or supervises practice of per-

sons learning to drive motor vehicles, including motorcycles, or preparing to take an examination for a license or learner permit, and any person who supervises the work of any other instructor.

1993

53-3-503. Exemption for college, university, and high school programs.

This part does not apply to any person giving driver training lessons to schools or classes conducted by colleges, universities, and high schools for regularly enrolled full-time students as a part of the normal program for the institutions.

1993

53-3-504. Licenses required — Inspections.

(1) A commercial driver training school may be established only if the school applies for and obtains a license from the division.

(2) A person may act as an instructor only if the person applies for and obtains a license from the division.

(3) The division shall inspect the school facilities and equipment of applicants and licensees and examine applicants for instructor's licenses.

(4) The division shall administer and enforce this part.

1993

53-3-505. School license — Contents of rules.

(1) In accordance with Title 63, Chapter 46a, Utah Administrative Rulemaking Act, the commissioner shall make rules regarding the requirements for:

  (a) a school license, including requirements concerning:

    (i) locations;

    (ii) equipment;

    (iii) courses of instruction;

    (iv) instructors;

    (v) previous records of the school and instructors;

    (vi) financial statements;

    (vii) schedule of fees and charges;

    (viii) character and reputation of the operators and instructors;

    (ix) insurance as the commissioner determines necessary to protect the interests of the public; and

    (x) other provisions the commissioner may prescribe for the protection of the public; and

  (b) an instructor's license, including requirements concerning:

    (i) moral character;

    (ii) physical condition;

    (iii) knowledge of the courses of instruction;

    (iv) motor vehicle laws and safety principles and practices;

    (v) previous personnel and employment records; and

    (vi) other provisions the commissioner may prescribe for the protection of the public;

  (c) applications for licenses; and

  (d) minimum standards for:

    (i) driving simulation devices that are fully interactive under Subsection 53-3-505.5(2)(b); and

    (ii) driving simulation devices that are not fully interactive under Subsection 53-3-505.5(2)(c).

(2) Rules made by the commissioner shall require that a commercial driver training school offering motorcycle rider education meet or exceed the standards established by the Motorcycle Safety Foundation.

(3) Rules made by the commissioner shall require that an instructor of motorcycle rider education meet or exceed the standards for certification established by the Motorcycle Safety Foundation.

(4) The commissioner may call upon the state superintendent of public instruction for assistance in formulating appropriate rules.

2003

53-3-505.5. Behind-the-wheel training requirements.

(1) Except as provided under Subsection (2), a driver education course under this part or Title 53A, Chapter 13, Part 2, Driver Education Classes that is used to satisfy the driver training requirement under Section 53-3-204 shall require each student to complete at least six hours of behind-the-wheel driving a dual-control motor vehicle with a certified instructor seated in the front seat next to the student driver.

(2) Up to three hours of the behind-the-wheel driving may be substituted as follows:

  (a) two hours of range driving on an approved driving range under Section 53A-13-201 equals one hour of the behind-the-wheel driving required under Subsection (1);

  (b) two hours of driving simulation practice on a driving simulation device that is fully interactive as set forth in rules made under Section 53-3-505, equals one hour of the behind-the-wheel driving required under Subsection (1); and

  (c) four hours of driving simulation practice on a driving simulation device that is not fully interactive as set forth in rules made under Section 53-3-505, equals one hour of the behind-the-wheel driving required under Subsection (1), with a maximum of one hour of the behind-the-wheel driving required under Subsection (1) that may be substituted under this Subsection (2)(c).

(3) The behind-the-wheel driving required under Subsection (1) shall include, if feasible, driving on interstate and other multilane highways.

2003

53-3-506. License expiration and renewal — Fee required — Disposition of revenue.

(1) (a) All commercial driver training school licenses and instructor licenses expire on the last day of the calendar year and may be renewed upon application to the commissioner as prescribed by rule.

  (b) Each application for an original or renewal school license or original or renewal instructor license shall be accompanied by a fee determined by the department under Section 63-38-3.2.

  (c) A license fee may not be refunded if the license is rejected, suspended, or revoked.

(2) The license fees collected under this part shall be placed in a fund designated as the "Commercial Driver Training Law Fund" and shall be used under the supervision and direction of the director of the Division of Finance for the administration of this part.

1995

53-3-507. Licenses — Cancellation, revocation, or refusal to issue or renew — Ineligibility for license.

(1) The department may cancel, revoke, or refuse to issue or renew a school or instructor license if it finds that the licensee or applicant has not complied with, or has violated this part or any rule made by the division.

(2) Any canceled or revoked license shall be returned to the division by the licensee, who is not

eligible to apply for a license under this part until six months have elapsed since the date of the cancellation or revocation. 1993

53-3-508. Local boards of education may conduct class for adults.

Local boards of education, with the consent of the division, may conduct classes in driver education for adult members of the district in those areas of the state where no commercial driver training course is available, and may charge a fee not to exceed the cost of the training. 1993

53-3-509. Violations — Penalties.

A violation of this part is a class C misdemeanor. 1993

53-3-510. Instructors certified to administer skills tests.

(1) (a) The division shall establish procedures and standards to certify licensed instructors of driver training courses under this part to administer skills tests.

(b) An instructor may not administer a skills test under this section to a student that took the course from the same school or the same instructor.

(2) The division is the certifying authority.

(3) (a) Subject to Subsection (1), an instructor certified under this section may give skills tests designed for driver training courses authorized under this part.

(b) The division shall establish minimal standards for the test that is at least as difficult as those required to receive a class D operator's license under Title 53, Chapter 3, Uniform Driver License Act.

(c) A student who fails the skills test given by an instructor certified under this section may apply for a class D operator's license under Title 53, Chapter 3, Part 2, Driver Licensing Act, and complete the skills test at a division office.

(4) A student who successfully passes the test given by a certified driver training instructor under this section satisfies the driving parts of the test required for a class D operator's license.

(5) The division shall establish procedures to enable licensed commercial driver training schools to administer or process the skills test authorized under this section for a class D operator's license.

(6) The division shall establish the standards and procedures required under this section by rules made in accordance with Title 63, Chapter 46a, Utah Administrative Rulemaking Act. 2000

PART 6

DRIVERS' LICENSE COMPACT

53-3-601. Short title.

This part is known as the "Drivers' License Compact." 1993

53-3-602. Definitions.

As used in this part:

(1) "Executive head" means the governor.

(2) "Licensing authority" means the department, the division, or both as the text may require. 1993

53-3-603. Ratification.

The Drivers' License Compact is ratified for the state and is entered into with all other jurisdictions legally joining in the compact. 1993

53-3-604. Text of compact — Party states to report traffic violations and exchange driving record information in home state of driver.

DRIVERS' LICENSE COMPACT

ARTICLE I

Findings and Declaration of Policy

(1) The party states find that:

(a) The safety of their streets and highways is materially affected by the degree of compliance with state and local ordinances relating to the operation of motor vehicles.

(b) Violation of a law or ordinance relating to the operation of motor vehicles is evidence that the violator engages in conduct that is likely to endanger the safety of persons and property.

(c) A license to drive is predicated upon compliance with laws and ordinances relating to the operation of motor vehicles, in whichever jurisdiction the vehicle is operated.

(2) It is the policy of each of the party states to:

(a) promote compliance with the laws, ordinances, and administrative rules and regulations relating to the operation of motor vehicles by their operators in each of the jurisdictions where the operators drive motor vehicles; and

(b) make the reciprocal recognition of licenses to drive and eligibility for licenses more just and equitable by considering the over-all compliance with motor vehicle laws, ordinances, and administrative rules and regulations as a condition precedent to renewing a license authorizing or permitting operation of a motor vehicle in any of the party states.

ARTICLE II

Definitions

As used in this compact:

(1) "State" means a state, territory, or possession of the United States, the District of Columbia, or the Commonwealth of Puerto Rico.

(2) "Home state" means the state that has issued and has the power to suspend or revoke the use of the license or permit to operate a motor vehicle.

(3) "Conviction" means a conviction of any offense related to the use or operation of a motor vehicle that is prohibited by state law, municipal ordinance, or administrative rule or regulation, or a forfeiture of bail, bond, or other security deposited to secure appearance by a person charged with having committed any offense, and which conviction or forfeiture is required to be reported to the licensing authority.

ARTICLE III

Reports of Conviction

(1) The licensing authority of a party state shall report each conviction of a person from another party state occurring within its jurisdiction to the licensing authority of the home state of the licensee.

(2) The report shall clearly:

(a) identify the person convicted;

(b) describe the violation specifying the section of the statute, code, or ordinance violated;

(c) identify the court in which action was taken;

(d) indicate whether a plea of guilty or not guilty was entered, or the conviction was a result of the forfeiture of bail, bond, or other security; and

(e) include any special findings made in connection with the conviction.

ARTICLE IV

Effect of Conviction

(1) The licensing authority in the home state, for the purposes of suspension, revocation, or limitation of the license to operate a motor vehicle, shall give the same effect to the conduct reported, pursuant to Article III of this compact, as it would if the conduct had occurred in the home state, in the case of convictions for:

(a) manslaughter or negligent homicide resulting from the operation of a motor vehicle;

(b) driving a motor vehicle while under the influence of intoxicating liquor or a narcotic drug, or under the influence of any other drug to a degree that renders the driver incapable of safely driving a motor vehicle;

(c) any felony in the commission of which a motor vehicle is used; and

(d) failure to stop and render aid in the event of a motor vehicle accident resulting in the death or personal injury of another.

(2) As to other convictions, reported pursuant to Article III, the licensing authority in the home state shall give the same effect to the conduct as provided by laws of the home state.

(3) If the laws of a party state do not provide for offenses or violations denominated or described in precisely the words employed in Subsection (1) of this article, the party state shall construe the denominations and descriptions appearing in Subsection (1) as applying to and identifying those offenses or violations of a substantially similar nature and the laws of the party state shall contain provisions as necessary to ensure that full force and effect is given in this article.

ARTICLE V

Applications for New Licenses

(1) Upon application for a license to drive, the licensing authority in a party state shall ascertain whether the applicant has ever held, or is the holder of a license to drive issued by any other party state.

(2) The licensing authority in the state where application is made shall not issue a license to drive to the applicant if the applicant:

(a) has held a license, but the license has been suspended by reason, in whole or in part, of a violation and if the suspension period has not terminated;

(b) has held a license, but the license has been revoked by reason, in whole or in part, of a violation and if the revocation has not terminated, except that after the expiration of one year from the date the license was revoked, the person may make application for a new license if permitted by law, which the authority may refuse to issue if, after investigation, the licensing authority determines that it will not be safe to grant to

the person the privilege of driving a motor vehicle on the public highways; or

(c) is the holder of a license to drive issued by another party state and currently in force unless the applicant surrenders the license.

ARTICLE VI

Applicability of Other Laws

Except as expressly required by this compact, nothing in this part affects the right of any party state to apply any of its other laws relating to licenses to drive to any person or circumstance, or invalidates or prevents any driver license agreement or other cooperative arrangement between a party state and a non-party state.

ARTICLE VII

Compact Administrator and Interchange of Information

(1) (a) The head of the licensing authority of each party state is the administrator of this compact for his state.

(b) The administrators, acting jointly have the power to formulate all necessary and proper procedures for the exchange of information under this compact.

(2) The administrator of each party state shall furnish to the administrator of each other party state any information or documents reasonably necessary to facilitate the administration of this compact.

ARTICLE VIII

Entry into Force and Withdrawal

(1) This compact shall enter into force and become effective as to any state when it has enacted the compact into law.

(2) Any party state may withdraw from this compact by enacting a statute repealing the compact, but no withdrawal takes effect until six months after the executive head of the withdrawing state has given notice of the withdrawal to the executive heads of all other party states.

(3) A withdrawal may not affect the validity or applicability by the licensing authorities of states remaining party to the compact of any report of conviction occurring prior to the withdrawal.

ARTICLE IX

Construction and Severability

(1) This compact shall be liberally construed to effectuate the purposes of the compact.

(2) The provisions of this compact are severable and if any phrase, clause, sentence, or provision of this compact is declared to be contrary to the constitution of any party state or of the United States or the applicability of the compact to any government, agency, person, or circumstance is held invalid, the validity of the remainder of this compact and the applicability thereof to any government, agency, person, or circumstance is not affected by the holding.

(3) If this compact is held contrary to the constitution of any party state, the compact remains in full force and effect as to the remaining states and in full force and effect as to the state affected as to all severable matters.   1993

53-3-605. Furnishing information and documents.

The department shall furnish to the appropriate authorities of other party states any information or documents reasonably necessary to facilitate the administration of Articles III, IV, and V of the compact.

1993

53-3-606. Expenses of compact administrator.

The compact administrator provided for in Article VII of the compact is not entitled to any additional compensation on account of his service as administrator, but is entitled to expenses incurred in connection with his duties and responsibilities as administrator, in the same manner as for expenses incurred in connection with any other duties or responsibilities of his office or employment.

1993

53-3-607. Court and agency reporting of actions to department.

Any court or other agency of this state, or a subdivision of the state that has jurisdiction to take any action suspending, revoking, or otherwise limiting a license to drive, shall report any action suspending, revoking, or limiting a license to drive and the adjudication upon which it is based, to the department within ten days, in a manner specified by the department.

2001

PART 7

NONRESIDENT VIOLATOR COMPACT

53-3-701. Short title.

This part is known as the "Nonresident Violator Compact."

1993

53-3-702. Definitions.

As used in this part:

(1) "Citation" means a summons, ticket, or other official document issued by a peace officer for a traffic violation, containing an order that requires the motorist to respond.

(2) "Collateral" means cash or other security deposited to secure an appearance for trial, following the issuance by a peace officer of a citation for a traffic violation.

(3) "Court" means a court of law or traffic tribunal.

(4) "Driver license" means a license or privilege to operate a motor vehicle issued under the laws of the home jurisdiction.

(5) "Home jurisdiction" means the jurisdiction that issued the driver's license of the traffic violator.

(6) "Issuing jurisdiction" means the jurisdiction in which the traffic citation was issued to the motorist.

(7) "Jurisdiction" means a state, territory, or possession of the United States, the District of Columbia, or the Commonwealth of Puerto Rico.

(8) "Motorist" means a driver of a motor vehicle operating in a party jurisdiction other than the home jurisdiction.

(9) "Personal recognizance" means an agreement by a motorist made at the time of issuance of the traffic citation that he will comply with the terms of that traffic citation.

(10) "Terms of the citation" means those options expressly stated upon the citation.

1998

53-3-703. Violations exempted from compact.

This compact does not apply to:

(1) parking or standing violations;

(2) highway weight limit violations; and

(3) violations of law governing the transportation of hazardous materials.

1993

53-3-704. Authority to enter compact.

The director of the division shall execute all documents and perform all other acts necessary to enter into and carry out this part.

1993

53-3-705. Procedures for issuing traffic citation.

The following is the procedure of the issuing jurisdiction:

(1) When issuing a citation for a traffic violation, a peace officer shall issue the citation to a motorist who possesses a driver license issued by a party jurisdiction and shall not, subject to the exceptions noted in Subsection (2), require the motorist to post collateral to secure appearance if the officer receives the motorist's personal recognizance that he or she will comply with the terms of the citation.

(2) Personal recognizance is acceptable only if not prohibited by law. If mandatory appearance is required, it must take place immediately following issuance of the citation.

(3) (a) Upon failure of a motorist to comply with the terms of a traffic citation, the appropriate official shall report the failure to comply to the licensing authority of the jurisdiction in which the traffic citation was issued.

(b) The report shall be made in accordance with procedures specified by the issuing jurisdiction and shall contain information as specified in the compact manual as minimum requirements for effective processing by the home jurisdiction.

(4) Upon receipt of the report, the licensing authority of the issuing jurisdiction shall transmit to the licensing authority in the home jurisdiction of the motorist the information in a form and content contained in the compact manual.

(5) The licensing authority of the issuing jurisdiction may not suspend the privilege of a motorist for whom a report has been transmitted.

(6) The licensing authority of the issuing jurisdiction may not transmit a report on any violation if the date of transmission is more than six months after the date on which the traffic citation was issued.

(7) The licensing authority of the issuing jurisdiction shall not transmit a report on any violation where the date of issuance of the citation predates the most recent of the effective dates of entry for the two jurisdictions affected.

1993

53-3-706. Procedure for home jurisdictions upon report of a licensee's failure to comply with out-of-state authority.

The following is the procedure for the home jurisdiction:

(1) (a) Upon receipt of a report of a failure to comply from the licensing authority of the issuing jurisdiction, the licensing authority of the home jurisdiction may notify the motorist and initiate a suspension action, in accordance with the home jurisdiction's procedures, and suspend the motorist's driver license until satisfactory evidence of compliance with the terms of the traffic citation has been furnished to the home jurisdiction licensing authority.

(b) Due process safeguards will be accorded.

(2) The licensing authority of the home jurisdiction shall maintain a record of actions taken and make reports to issuing jurisdictions as provided in the compact manual.

1993

53-3-707. Rights of party jurisdictions not affected by compact.

Except as expressly required by the compact, nothing contained in this part affects the right of any party jurisdiction to apply any of its other laws relating to licenses to drive to any person or circumstance, or to invalidate or prevent any driver license agreement or other cooperative arrangement between a party jurisdiction and a nonparty jurisdiction.   1993

53-3-708. Compact administrator.

The director of the division is the compact administrator for the state.   1993

53-3-709. Amendment of compact.

(1) (a) This compact may be amended from time to time.

(b) Amendments shall be presented in resolution form to the chairman of the board of compact administrators and may be initiated by one or more party jurisdictions.

(2) Adoption of an amendment requires endorsement of all party jurisdictions and becomes effective 30 days after the date of the last endorsement.

(3) (a) Failure of a party jurisdiction to respond to the compact chairman within 120 days after receipt of the proposed amendment constitutes endorsement.

(b) A report authorized by Section 53-3-104 may not contain any evidence of a suspension that occurred as a result of failure to comply with the requirements of this part.   1993

PART 8

IDENTIFICATION CARDS

53-3-801. Short title.

This part is known as the "Identification Card Act."   1993

53-3-802. Definitions.

As used in this part:

(1) "Adult" means a person 21 years of age or older.

(2) "Identification card" means a card for identification issued under this part.

(3) "Minor" means a person younger than 21 years of age.   1993

53-3-803. Application for identification card — Age requirements — Application on behalf of others.

(1) A person at least 16 years of age or older may apply to the division for an identification card.

(2) A person younger than 16 years of age may apply to the division for an identification card with the consent of the applicant's parent or guardian.

(3) (a) If a person is unable to apply for the card due to his youth or incapacitation, the application may be made on behalf of that person by his parent or guardian.

(b) A parent or guardian applying for an identification card on behalf of a child or incapacitated person shall provide:

(i) identification, as required by the commissioner; and

(ii) the consent of the incapacitated person, as required by the commissioner.   1993

53-3-804. Application for identification card — Required information — Release of anatomical gift information.

(1) To apply for an identification card, the applicant shall:

(a) be a Utah resident;

(b) have a Utah residence address; and

(c) appear in person at any license examining station.

(2) The applicant shall provide the following information to the division:

(a) true and full legal name and Utah residence address;

(b) date of birth as set forth in a certified copy of the applicant's birth certificate, or other satisfactory evidence of birth, which shall be attached to the application;

(c) Social Security number;

(d) place of birth;

(e) height and weight;

(f) color of eyes and hair;

(g) between July 1, 2002 and July 1, 2007, race in accordance with the categories established by the United States Census Bureau;

(h) signature;

(i) photograph; and

(j) an indication whether the applicant intends to make an anatomical gift under Title 26, Chapter 28, Uniform Anatomical Gift Act.

(3) The requirements of Section 53-3-234 apply to this section for each person, age 16 and older, applying for an identification card. Refusal to consent to the release of information shall result in the denial of the identification card.

(4) An applicant may not be denied an identification card for refusing to provide race information required under Subsection (2)(g).   2005

53-3-805. Identification card — Contents — Specifications.

(1) The division shall issue an identification card that:

(a) provides all the information contained in the application, except the identification card may not bear the applicant's:

(i) Social Security number; and

(ii) place of birth;

(b) contains a photograph of the applicant; and

(c) contains a facsimile of the applicant's signature.

(2) (a) The card shall be of an impervious material, resistant to wear, damage, and alteration.

(b) Except as provided under Section 53-3-806, the size, form, and color of the card is prescribed by the commissioner.

(3) At the applicant's request, the card may include a statement that the applicant has a special medical problem or allergies to certain drugs, for the purpose of medical treatment.

(4) (a) The indication of intent under Subsection 53-3-804(2)(j) shall be authenticated by the applicant in accordance with division rule.

(b) (i) Notwithstanding Title 63, Chapter 2, Government Records Access and Management Act, the division may, upon request, release to an organ procurement organization, as defined in Section 26-28-2, the names and addresses of all persons who under Subsection 53-3-804(2)(j) indicate that they intend to make an anatomical gift.

(ii) An organ procurement organization may use released information only to:

(A) obtain additional information for an anatomical gift registry; and

(B) inform applicants of anatomical gift options, procedures, and benefits.

(5) The division and its employees are not liable, as a result of false or inaccurate information provided under Subsection 53-3-804(2)(j), for direct or indirect:

    (a) loss;

    (b) detriment; or

    (c) injury.   2004

53-3-806. Portrait-style format — Minor's card distinguishable.

(1) The division shall use a portrait-style format for all identification cards, similar to the format used for license certificates issued to a person younger than 21 years of age under Section 53-3-207.

(2) The identification card issued to a person younger than 21 years of age shall be distinguished by use of plainly printed information or by the use of a color or other means not used for the identification card issued to a person 21 years of age or older.

(3) The division shall distinguish an identification card issued to any person:

    (a) younger than 21 years of age by plainly printing the date the identification card holder is 21 years of age, which is the legal age for purchasing an alcoholic beverage or product under Section 32A-12-203; and

    (b) younger than 19 years of age by plainly printing the date the identification card holder is 19 years of age, which is the legal age for purchasing tobacco products under Section 76-10-104.   2003

53-3-807. Expiration — Address and name change — Extension for disabled.

(1) The identification card expires on the birth date of the applicant in the tenth year following the issuance of the identification card, except as provided under Subsection (6).

(2) If a person has applied for and received an identification card and subsequently moves from the address shown on the application or on the card, the person shall within ten days notify the division in a manner specified by the division of his new address.

(3) If a person has applied for and received an identification card and subsequently changes his name under Title 42, Chapter 1, Change of Name, he:

    (a) shall surrender the card to the division; and

    (b) may apply for a new card in his new name by:

        (i) furnishing proper documentation to the division as provided in Section 53-3-804; and

        (ii) paying the fee required under Section 53-3-105.

(4) A person older than 21 years of age with a disability, as defined under the Americans with Disabilities Act of 1990, Pub. L. 101-336, may extend the expiration date on an identification card for ten years if the person with a disability or an agent of the person with a disability:

    (a) requests that the division send the application form to obtain the extension or requests an application form in person at the division's offices;

    (b) completes the application;

    (c) certifies that the extension is for a person 21 years of age or older with a disability; and

    (d) returns the application to the division together with the identification card fee required under Section 53-3-105.

(5) (a) An identification card may only be extended once.

    (b) After an extension an application for an identification card must be applied for in person at the division's offices.

(6) An identification card issued to a person 65 years of age or older does not expire, but continues in effect until the death of that person.

(7) Notwithstanding the provisions of this section, an identification card that was obtained without using a Social Security number as required under Subsection 53-3-804(2) expires on July 1, 2005.   2005

53-3-808. Fee required.

The commissioner shall charge and collect a fee under Section 53-3-105 when an application for an identification card is submitted.   1993

53-3-809. Revocation of card for providing false information or altering card.

The commissioner shall revoke and repossess the identification card of any person who has:

    (1) furnished false or forged information or evidence in support of any application for any identification card; or

    (2) altered any information or photograph on an identification card.   1993

53-3-810. Prohibited uses of identification card — Penalties.

(1) It is a class C misdemeanor to:

    (a) lend or knowingly permit the use of an identification card issued to the person, by a person not entitled to it;

    (b) display or to represent as the person's own an identification card not issued to the person;

    (c) refuse to surrender to the division or a peace officer upon demand any identification card issued by the division;

    (d) use a false name or give a false address in any application for an identification card or any renewal or duplicate of the identification card, or to knowingly make a false statement, or to knowingly conceal a material fact in the application;

    (e) display a revoked identification card as a valid identification card;

    (f) knowingly acquire, use, display, or transfer an item that purports to be an authentic identification card issued by a governmental entity if the item is not an authentic identification card issued by that governmental entity; or

    (g) alter any information contained on an authentic identification card so that it no longer represents the information originally displayed.

(2) It is a class A misdemeanor to:

    (a) knowingly issue an identification card with false or fraudulent information;

    (b) knowingly issue an identification card to any person younger than 21 years of age if the identification card is not distinguished as required for a person younger than 21 years of age under Section 53-3-806; or

    (c) knowingly acquire, use, display, or transfer a false or altered identification card to procure cigarettes, tobacco, or tobacco products.

(3) A person may not knowingly use, display, or transfer a false or altered identification card to procure alcoholic beverages, gain admittance to a place where alcoholic beverages are sold or consumed, or obtain employment that may not be obtained by a minor in violation of Section 32A-1-301.

(4) It is a third degree felony if a person's acquisition, use, display, or transfer of a false or altered identification card:

    (a) aids or furthers the person's efforts to fraudulently obtain goods or services; or

    (b) aids or furthers the person's efforts to commit a violent felony.   2005

PART 9

MOTORCYCLE RIDER EDUCATION ACT

53-3-901. Title.

This part is known as the "Motorcycle Rider Education Act."   1999

53-3-902. Definitions.

As used in this part:

(1) "Motorcycle" has the same meaning as provided in Section 41-1a-102.

(2) "Program" means the motorcycle rider education program for training and information disbursement created under Section 53-3-903.

(3) "Rider training course" means a motorcycle rider education curriculum and delivery system approved by the division as meeting national standards designed to develop and instill the knowledge, attitudes, habits, and skills necessary for the safe operation of a motorcycle.   1999

53-3-903. Motorcycle Rider Education Program.

(1) (a) The division shall develop standards for and administer the Motorcycle Rider Education Program.

(b) The division shall make rules in accordance with Title 63, Chapter 46a, Utah Administrative Rulemaking Act, to implement this chapter.

(2) The program shall include:

(a) a novice rider training course;

(b) a rider training course for experienced riders; and

(c) an instructor training course.

(3) The division may expand the program to include:

(a) enhancing public awareness of motorcycle riders;

(b) increasing the awareness of motorcycle riders of the effects of alcohol and drugs;

(c) motorcycle rider skills improvement;

(d) program and other motorcycle safety promotion; and

(e) improvement of motorcycle licensing efforts.

(4) (a) Rider training courses shall be open to all residents of the state who either hold a valid driver's license for any classification or are eligible for a temporary motorcycle learner's permit.

(b) An adequate number of novice rider training courses shall be provided to meet the reasonably anticipated needs of all persons in the state who are eligible and who desire to participate in the program.

(c) Program delivery may be phased in over a reasonable period of time.

(5) (a) The division may enter into contracts with either public or private institutions to provide a rider training course approved by the division.

(b) The institution shall issue certificates of completion in the manner and form prescribed by the director to persons who satisfactorily complete the requirements of the course.

(c) An institution conducting a rider training course may charge a reasonable tuition fee to cover the cost of offering the course.

(d) (i) The division may use program funds to defray its own expenses in administering the program.

(ii) The division may reimburse entities that offer approved courses for actual expenses incurred in offering the courses, up to a limit established by the division based upon available program funds.

(iii) Any reimbursement paid to an entity must be entirely reflected by the entity in reduced course enrollment fees for students.

(6) (a) Standards for the motorcycle rider training courses, including standards for course curriculum, materials, and student evaluation, and standards for the training and approval of instructors shall meet or exceed established national standards for motorcycle rider training courses prescribed by the Motorcycle Safety Foundation.

(b) Motorcycle rider training courses shall be taught only by instructors approved under Section 53-3-904.

(c) Motorcycle rider training courses for novices shall include at least eight hours of practice riding.

(7) The commissioner shall appoint a full-time program coordinator to oversee and direct the program.   1994

53-3-904. Instructor training and approval.

(1) The program coordinator shall approve instructors for the motorcycle rider training courses.

(2) A person may not be approved as an instructor unless the person holds a current instructor certification issued by the Motorcycle Safety Foundation or another nationally recognized motorcycle safety instructor certifying body.

(3) (a) The program shall include instructor training courses as necessary.

(b) Prior to completion of an instructor training course, the participant shall demonstrate:

(i) knowledge of the course material;

(ii) knowledge of proper motorcycle operation;

(iii) proficiency in riding motorcycles; and

(iv) the necessary aptitude for instructing students.

(4) An applicant for an instructor training course shall:

(a) have a high school diploma or its equivalent;

(b) be at least 18 years of age;

(c) have a valid endorsement to his driver's license for motorcycles; and

(d) have at least two years of recent motorcycle riding experience.

(5) The division shall refuse to certify or revoke certification of an instructor if the applicant:

(a) has had his driver's license suspended or revoked during the preceding two years or within the preceding five years if the suspension or revocation was for an alcohol or drug-related offense;

(b) fails to successfully complete an instructor course or required course updates; or

(c) no longer meets the requirements of this section.   1993

53-3-905. Dedication of fees.

(1) Five dollars of the annual registration fee imposed under Section 41-1a-1206 for each registered motorcycle and $2.50 of the fee imposed under Section 53-3-105 for an original, renewal, or extension of a class M license or provisional class M license application shall be deposited as dedicated credits in the

Transportation Fund to be used by the division for the program.

(2) Appropriations to the program are nonlapsing.

(3) Appropriations may not be used for assistance to, advocacy of, or lobbying for any legislation unless the legislation would enhance or affect the financial status of the program or the program's continuation.

1994

53-3-906. Repealed. 1997

53-3-907. Licensing skills test exemption.

(1) The division may exempt an applicant for a motorcycle operator license or endorsement from the licensing skills test if he presents proof of successful completion of a rider training course approved by the division that includes a similar test of skills.

(2) The exemption provided in Subsection (1) applies only if the applicant applies for a motorcycle operator license or endorsement within six months of completion of an approved rider training course. 1993

53-3-908. Advisory committee.

(1) The governor shall appoint a five-member program advisory committee to assist in the development and implementation of the program.

(2) The committee members shall be appointed by the governor as follows:

(a) one representative of motorcycle retail dealers;

(b) one representative of peace officers;

(c) one citizen not affiliated with a motorcycle dealer, manufacturer, or association;

(d) one motorcycle safety foundation instructor or chief instructor; and

(e) one member of an incorporated motorcycle rider organization.

(3) All members of the advisory committee shall be licensed motorcyclists.

(4) (a) Except as required by Subsection (b), as terms of current committee members expire, the governor shall appoint each new member or re-appointed member to a four-year term.

(b) Notwithstanding the requirements of Subsection (a), the governor shall, at the time of appointment or reappointment, adjust the length of terms to ensure that the terms of committee members are staggered so that approximately half of the committee is appointed every two years.

(c) The committee shall meet at the call of the director.

(5) When a vacancy occurs in the membership for any reason, the replacement shall be appointed for the unexpired term.

(6) (a) Members shall receive no compensation or benefits for their services, but may receive per diem and expenses incurred in the performance of the member's official duties at the rates established by the Division of Finance under Sections 63A-3-106 and 63A-3-107.

(b) Members may decline to receive per diem and expenses for their service. 1996

53-3-909. Program exemption.

An entity offering a motorcycle rider training course approved by the division and an instructor providing instruction as part of an approved motorcycle rider training course are exempt from the requirements of Title 53, Chapter 3, Part 5, Commercial Driver Training Schools Act. 1994

CHAPTER 4

INVESTIGATIONS [RENUMBERED]

Part 1

Investigations Division Administration [Renumbered]

Part 2

Narcotics and Alcoholic Beverage Enforcement [Renumbered]

PART 1

INVESTIGATIONS DIVISION ADMINISTRATION [RENUMBERED]

53-4-101, 54-4-102. Repealed. 1998, 1999

53-4-103 to 53-4-105. Renumbered as §§ 53-10-301 to 53-10-303. 1998

PART 2

NARCOTICS AND ALCOHOLIC BEVERAGE ENFORCEMENT [RENUMBERED]

53-4-201. Repealed. 1998

53-4-202 to 53-4-205. Renumbered as §§ 53-10-304, 53-10-305, 53-10-112, 53-10-113. 1998

CHAPTER 5

LAW ENFORCEMENT AND TECHNICAL SERVICES

Part 7

Concealed Weapons

PART 7

CONCEALED WEAPONS

53-5-701. Short title.

This part is known as the "Concealed Weapon Act."

1993

53-5-702. Definitions.

(1) As used in this part:

(a) "Board" means the Concealed Weapon Review Board created in Section 53-5-703.

(b) "Commissioner" means the commissioner of the Department of Public Safety.

(c) "Conviction" means criminal conduct where the filing of a criminal charge has resulted in:

(i) a finding of guilt based on evidence presented to a judge or jury;

(ii) a guilty plea;

(iii) a plea of nolo contendere;

(iv) a plea of guilty or nolo contendere which is held in abeyance pending the successful completion of probation;

(v) a pending diversion agreement; or

(vi) a conviction which has been reduced pursuant to Section 76-3-402.

(d) "Division" means the Criminal Investigations and Technical Services Division created in Section 53-10-103.

(2) The definitions in Section 76-10-501 apply to this part.

2005

53-5-703. Board — Membership — Compensation — Terms — Duties.

(1) There is created within the division the Concealed Weapon Review Board.

(2) (a) The board is comprised of not more than five members appointed by the commissioner on a bipartisan basis.

(b) The board shall include a member representing law enforcement and at least two citizens, one of whom represents sporting interests.

(3) (a) Except as required by Subsection (b), as terms of current board members expire, the commissioner shall appoint each new member or reappointed member to a four-year term.

(b) Notwithstanding the requirements of Subsection (a), the commissioner shall, at the time of appointment or reappointment, adjust the length of terms to ensure that the terms of board members are staggered so that approximately half of the board is appointed every two years.

(4) When a vacancy occurs in the membership for any reason, the replacement shall be appointed for the unexpired term.

(5) (a) (i) Members who are not government employees shall receive no compensation or benefits for their services, but may receive per diem and expenses incurred in the performance of the member's official duties at the rates established by the Division of Finance under Sections 63A-3-106 and 63A-3-107.

(ii) Members may decline to receive per diem and expenses for their service.

(b) (i) State government officer and employee members who do not receive salary, per diem, or expenses from their agency for their service may receive per diem and expenses incurred in the performance of their official duties from the board at the rates established by the Division of Finance under Sections 63A-3-106 and 63A-3-107.

(ii) State government officer and employee members may decline to receive per diem and expenses for their service.

(6) The board shall meet at least quarterly, unless the board has no business to conduct during that quarter.

(7) The board, upon receiving a timely filed petition for review, shall review within a reasonable time the denial, suspension, or revocation of a permit or a temporary permit to carry a concealed firearm.   1997

53-5-704. Division duties — Permit to carry concealed firearm — Certification for concealed firearms instructor — Requirements for issuance — Violation — Denial, suspension, or revocation — Appeal procedure.

(1) (a) The division or its designated agent shall issue a permit to carry a concealed firearm for lawful self defense to an applicant who is 21 years of age or older within 60 days after receiving an application, unless during the 60-day period the division finds proof that the applicant is not of good character.

(b) The permit is valid throughout the state, without restriction except as provided by Section 53-5-710 for five years.

(2) An applicant satisfactorily demonstrates good character if the applicant:

(a) has not been convicted of a felony;

(b) has not been convicted of a crime of violence;

(c) has not been convicted of an offense involving the use of alcohol;

(d) has not been convicted of an offense involving the unlawful use of narcotics or other controlled substances;

(e) has not been convicted of an offense involving moral turpitude;

(f) has not been convicted of an offense involving domestic violence;

(g) has not been adjudicated by a court of a state or of the United States as mentally incompetent, unless the adjudication has been withdrawn or reversed; and

(h) is qualified to purchase and possess a dangerous weapon and a handgun pursuant to Section 76-10-503 and federal law.

(3) (a) The division may deny, suspend, or revoke a concealed firearm permit if the licensing authority has reasonable cause to believe that the applicant has been or is a danger to self or others as demonstrated by evidence including, but not limited to:

(i) past pattern of behavior involving unlawful violence or threats of unlawful violence;

(ii) past participation in incidents involving unlawful violence or threats of unlawful violence; or

(iii) conviction of an offense in violation of Title 76, Chapter 10, Part 5, Weapons.

(b) The division may not deny, suspend, or revoke a concealed firearm permit solely for a single conviction for an infraction violation of Title 76, Chapter 10, Part 5, Weapons.

(c) In determining whether the applicant has been or is a danger to self or others, the division may inspect:

(i) expunged records of arrests and convictions of adults as provided in Section 77-18-15; and

(ii) juvenile court records as provided in Section 78-3a-206.

(d) (i) If a person granted a permit under this part has been charged with a crime of violence in any state, the division shall suspend the permit.

(ii) Upon notice of the acquittal of the person charged, or notice of the charges having been dropped, the division shall immediately reinstate the suspended permit.

(4) A former peace officer who departs full-time employment as a peace officer, in an honorable manner, shall be issued a concealed firearm permit within five years of that departure if the officer meets the requirements of this section.

(5) In assessing good character under Subsection (2), the licensing authority shall consider mitigating circumstances.

(6) Except as provided in Subsection (7), the licensing authority shall also require the applicant to provide:

(a) address of applicant's permanent residence;

(b) one recent dated photograph;

(c) one set of fingerprints; and

(d) evidence of general familiarity with the types of firearms to be concealed as defined in Subsection (8).

(7) An applicant who is a law enforcement officer under Section 53-13-103 may provide a letter of good standing from the officer's commanding officer in place of the items required by Subsection (6)(d).

(8) (a) General familiarity with the types of firearms to be concealed includes training in:

(i) the safe loading, unloading, storage, and carrying of the types of firearms to be concealed; and

(ii) current laws defining lawful use of a firearm by a private citizen, including lawful self-defense, use of force by a private citizen including use of deadly force, transportation, and concealment.

(b) Evidence of general familiarity with the types of firearms to be concealed may be satisfied by one of the following:

(i) completion of a course of instruction conducted by any national, state, or local firearms training organization approved by the division;

(ii) certification of general familiarity by a person who has been certified by the division, which may include a law enforcement officer, military or civilian firearms instructor, or hunter safety instructor; or

(iii) equivalent experience with a firearm through participation in an organized shooting competition, law enforcement, or military service.

(c) Any instruction taken by a student under Subsection (8)(b) shall be in person and not through electronic means.

(9) An applicant for certification as a Utah concealed firearms instructor shall:

(a) be at least 21 years of age; and

(b) be currently eligible to possess a firearm under Section 76-10-503 and federal law.

(10) Each certified concealed firearms instructor shall provide each of the instructor's students with the required course of instruction outline approved by the division.

(11) All concealed firearms instructors are required to provide a signed certificate to persons completing the course of instruction, which certificate shall be provided by the applicant to the division.

(12) The division may deny, suspend, or revoke the certification of a concealed firearms instructor if the licensing authority has reason to believe the applicant has:

(a) become ineligible to possess a firearm under Section 76-10-503 or federal law; or

(b) knowingly and willfully provided false information to the division.

(13) A concealed firearms instructor has the same appeal rights as set forth in Subsection (16).

(14) In issuing a permit under this part, the licensing authority is not vicariously liable for damages caused by the permit holder.

(15) If any person knowingly and willfully provides false information on an application filed under this part, he is guilty of a class B misdemeanor, and his application may be denied, or his permit may be suspended or revoked.

(16) (a) In the event of a denial, suspension, or revocation by the agency, the applicant may file a petition for review with the board within 60 days from the date the denial, suspension, or revocation is received by the applicant by certified mail, return receipt requested.

(b) The denial of a permit shall be in writing and shall include the general reasons for the action.

(c) If an applicant appeals his denial to the review board, the applicant may have access to the evidence upon which the denial is based in accordance with Title 63, Chapter 2, Government Records Access and Management Act.

(d) On appeal to the board, the agency shall have the burden of proof by a preponderance of the evidence.

(e) (i) Upon a ruling by the board on the appeal of a denial, the division shall issue a final order within 30 days stating the board's decision.

(ii) The final order shall be in the form prescribed by Subsection 63-46b-5(1)(i).

(iii) The final order is final agency action for purposes of judicial review under Section 63-46b-15.

(17) The commissioner may make rules in accordance with Title 63, Chapter 46a, Utah Administrative Rulemaking Act, necessary to administer this chapter. 2005

53-5-705. Temporary permit to carry concealed firearm — Denial, suspension, or revocation — Appeal.

(1) The division or its designated agent may issue a temporary permit to carry a concealed firearm to a person who:

(a) has applied for a permit under Section 53-5-704;

(b) has applied for a temporary permit under this section; and

(c) meets the criteria required in Subsections (2) and (3).

(2) To receive a temporary permit under this section, the applicant shall demonstrate in writing to the satisfaction of the licensing authority extenuating circumstances that would justify issuing a temporary permit.

(3) A temporary permit may not be issued under this section until preliminary record checks regarding the applicant have been made with the National

Crime Information Center and the division to determine any criminal history.

(4) A temporary permit is valid only for a maximum of 90 days or any lesser period specified by the division, or until a permit under Section 53-5-704 is issued to the holder of the temporary permit, whichever period is shorter.

(5) The licensing authority may deny, suspend, or revoke a temporary permit prior to expiration if the commissioner determines:

(a) the circumstances justifying the temporary permit no longer exist; or

(b) the holder of the temporary permit does not meet the requirements for a permit under Section 53-5-704.

(6) (a) The denial, suspension, or revocation of a temporary permit shall be in writing and shall include the reasons for the action.

(b) The licensing authority's decision to deny, suspend, or revoke a temporary permit may not be appealed to the board.

(c) Denial, suspension, or revocation under this subsection is final action for purposes of judicial review under Section 63-46b-15.   2005

53-5-706. Permit — Fingerprints transmitted to division — Report from division.

(1) (a) Except as provided in Subsection (2), the fingerprints of each applicant shall be taken on a form prescribed by the division and shall be forwarded to the division.

(b) Upon receipt of the fingerprints and the fee prescribed in Section 53-5-707, the division shall conduct a search of its files for criminal history information pertaining to the applicant, and shall request the Federal Bureau of Investigation to conduct a similar search through its files.

(c) The division shall promptly furnish the forwarding licensing authority a report of all data and information pertaining to any applicant of which there is a record in its office, or of which a record is found in the files of the Federal Bureau of Investigation.

(d) A permit may not be issued by any licensing authority until receipt of the report from the division.

(2) If the permit applicant has previously applied to the same licensing authority for a permit to carry concealed firearms and the applicant's fingerprints and fee have been previously forwarded within one year to the division, the licensing authority shall note the previous identification numbers and other data which would provide positive identification in the files of the division on the copy of any subsequent permit submitted to the division in accordance with this section, and no additional application form, fingerprints, or fee are required.   2004

53-5-707. Permit — Fees — Disposition.

(1) Each applicant for a permit shall pay a fee of $35 at the time of filing an application. The initial fee shall be waived for an applicant who is a law enforcement officer under Section 53-13-103.

(2) The renewal fee for the permit is $10.

(3) The replacement fee for the permit is $10.

(4) The late fee for the renewal permit is $7.50.

(5) All fees shall promptly be deposited in the state treasury and credited to the General Fund.

(6) The division may collect any fees charged by an outside agency for additional services required by statute as a prerequisite for issuance of a permit. The division shall promptly forward any fees collected to the appropriate agency.   1999

53-5-708. Permit — Names private.

(1) When any permit is issued, a record shall be maintained in the office of the licensing authority. Notwithstanding the requirements of Subsection 63-2-301(1)(b), the names, addresses, telephone numbers, dates of birth, and Social Security numbers of persons receiving permits are protected records under Subsection 63-2-304(10).

(2) Copies of each permit issued shall be filed immediately by the licensing authority with the division.   2002

53-5-709. Repealed.   1997

53-5-710. Cross-references to concealed firearm permit restrictions.

A person with a permit to carry a concealed firearm may not carry a concealed firearm in the following locations:

(1) any secure area prescribed in Section 76-10-523.5 in which firearms are prohibited and notice of the prohibition posted;

(2) in any airport secure area as provided in Section 76-10-529; or

(3) in any house of worship or in any private residence where dangerous weapons are prohibited as provided in Section 76-10-530.   1999

53-5-711. Law enforcement officials and judges — Training requirements — Qualification — Revocation.

(1) For purposes of this section and Section 76-10-523:

(a) "Judge" means a judge or justice of a court of record or court not of record, but does not include a judge pro tem or senior judge.

(b) "Law enforcement official of this state" means:

(i) a member of the Board of Pardons and Paroles;

(ii) a district attorney, deputy district attorney, county attorney or deputy county attorney of a county not in a prosecution district;

(iii) the attorney general;

(iv) an assistant attorney general designated as a criminal prosecutor; or

(v) a city attorney or a deputy city attorney designated as a criminal prosecutor.

(2) To qualify for the exemptions enumerated in Section 76-10-523, a law enforcement official or judge shall complete the following training requirements:

(a) meet the requirements of Sections 53-5-704, 53-5-706, and 53-5-707; and

(b) successfully complete an additional course of training as established by the commissioner of public safety designed to assist them while carrying out their official law enforcement and judicial duties as agents for the state or its political subdivisions.

(3) Annual requalification requirements for law enforcement officials and judges shall be established by the:

(a) Board of Pardons and Paroles by rule for its members;

(b) Judicial Council by rule for judges; and

(c) the district attorney, county attorney in a county not in a prosecution district, the attorney general, or city attorney by policy for prosecutors under their jurisdiction.

(4) The division may:

(a) issue a certificate of qualification to a judge or law enforcement official who has completed the requirements of Subsection (1), which certificate of qualification is valid until revoked;

(b) revoke the certificate of qualification of a judge or law enforcement official who fails to meet the annual requalification criteria established pursuant to Subsection (3); and

(c) certify instructors for the training requirements of this section. 1998

CHAPTER 6

PEACE OFFICER STANDARDS AND TRAINING

Part 1

Peace Officer Standards and Training Division Administration

Part 2

Peace Officer Training and Certification

Part 3

Dispatcher Training and Certification

PART 1

PEACE OFFICER STANDARDS AND TRAINING DIVISION ADMINISTRATION

53-6-101. Short title.

This chapter is known as the "Peace Officer Standards and Training Act." 1993

53-6-102. Definitions.

As used in this chapter:

(1) "Certified academy" means a peace officer training institution certified in accordance with the standards developed under Section 53-6-105.

(2) "Council" means the Peace Officer Standards and Training Council created in Section 53-6-106.

(3) "Director" means the director of the Peace Officer Standards and Training Division appointed under Section 53-6-104.

(4) "Dispatcher" means an employee of a public safety agency of the state or any of its political subdivisions and whose primary duties are to:

(a) (i) receive calls for one or a combination of, emergency police, fire, and medical services, and to dispatch the appropriate personnel and equipment in response to the calls; and

(ii) make urgent decisions affecting the life, health, and welfare of the public and public safety employees; or

(b) supervise dispatchers or direct a dispatch communication center.

(5) "Division" means the Peace Officer Standards and Training Division created in Section 53-6-103.

(6) "POST" means the division. 1995

53-6-103. Peace Officer Standards and Training Division — Creation — Administration — Duties.

(1) There is created within the department the Peace Officer Standards and Training Division.

(2) The division shall be administered by a director acting under the supervision and control of the commissioner.

(3) The division shall promote and ensure the safety and welfare of the citizens of this state in their respective communities and provide for efficient and professional law enforcement by establishing minimum standards and training for peace officers and dispatchers throughout the state.   1995

53-6-104. Appointment of director of division — Qualifications — Appointment of employees — Term of office — Compensation [Effective until July 1, 2006].

(1) The commissioner, upon recommendation of the council and with the approval of the governor, shall appoint a director of the division.

(2) The director is the executive and administrative head of the division and shall be experienced in administration and possess additional qualifications as determined by the commissioner and as provided by law.

(3) The director shall be a full-time officer of the state.

(4) The director may appoint deputies, consultants, clerks, and other employees from eligibility lists authorized by the Department of Human Resource Management.

(5) The director may be removed from his position at the will of the commissioner.

(6) The director shall receive compensation as provided by Title 67, Chapter 19, Utah State Personnel Management Act.   1993

Appointment of director of division — Qualifications — Appointment of employees — Term of office — Compensation [Effective July 1, 2006].

(1) The commissioner, upon recommendation of the council and with the approval of the governor, shall appoint a director of the division.

(2) The director is the executive and administrative head of the division and shall be experienced in administration and possess additional qualifications as determined by the commissioner and as provided by law.

(3) The director shall be a full-time officer of the state.

(4) The director may appoint deputies, consultants, clerks, and other employees from eligibility lists authorized by the Division of Human Resource Management.

(5) The director may be removed from his position at the will of the commissioner.

(6) The director shall receive compensation as provided by Title 67, Chapter 19, Utah State Personnel Management Act.   2005

53-6-105. Duties of director — Powers — Rulemaking.

(1) The director, with the advice of the council, shall:

(a) prescribe standards for the certification of a peace officer training academy, certify an academy that meets the prescribed standards, and prescribe standards for revocation of certification for cause;

(b) prescribe minimum qualifications for certification of peace officers appointed or elected to enforce the laws of this state and its subdivisions and prescribe standards for revocation of certification for cause;

(c) establish minimum requirements for the certification of training instructors and establish standards for revocation of certification;

(d) provide for the issuance of appropriate certificates to those peace officers completing the basic training programs offered by a certified academy or those persons who pass a certification examination as provided for in this chapter;

(e) consult and cooperate with certified academy administrators and instructors for the continued development and improvement of the basic training programs provided by the certified academy and for the further development and implementation of advanced in-service training programs;

(f) consult and cooperate with state institutions of higher education to develop specialized courses of study for peace officers in the areas of criminal justice, police administration, criminology, social sciences, and other related disciplines;

(g) consult and cooperate with other departments, agencies, and local governments concerned with peace officer training;

(h) perform any other acts necessary to develop peace officer training programs within the state;

(i) report to the council at regular meetings of the council and when the council requires;

(j) recommend peace officer standards and training requirements to the commissioner, governor, and the Legislature; and

(k) make rules as provided in this chapter.

(2) With the permission of the commissioner, the director may execute contracts on behalf of the division with criminal justice agencies to provide training for employees of those agencies if:

(a) the employees or the employing agency pay a registration fee equivalent to the cost of the training; and

(b) the contract does not reduce the effectiveness of the division in its primary responsibility of providing training for peace officers of the state.

(3) The director may:

(a) revoke certification of a certified academy for cause; and

(b) make training aids and materials available to local law enforcement agencies.

(4) In accordance with Title 63, Chapter 46a, Utah Administrative Rulemaking Act, and consistent with Title 53, Chapter 6, Part 3, Dispatcher Training and Certification Act, the director shall, with the advice of the council, make rules:

(a) establishing minimum requirements for the certification of dispatcher training instructors in a certified academy or interagency program and standards for revocation of this certification;

(b) establishing approved curriculum and a basic schedule for the basic dispatcher training course and the content of the dispatcher certification examination;

(c) providing for the issuance of appropriate certificates to a person who completes the basic dispatcher course or who passes a dispatcher certification examination as provided for in this chapter;

(d) establishing approved courses for certified dispatchers' annual training; and

(e) establishing a reinstatement procedure for a certified dispatcher who has not obtained the required annual training hours.   1995

53-6-106. Creation of Peace Officer Standards and Training Council — Purpose — Membership — Quorum — Meetings — Compensation.

(1) There is created the Peace Officer Standards and Training Council.

(2) The council shall serve as an advisory board to the director of the division on matters relating to peace officer and dispatcher standards and training.

(3) The council includes:

(a) the attorney general or his designated representative;

(b) the superintendent of the highway patrol;

(c) the executive director of the Department of Corrections or his designated representative; and

(d) 14 additional members appointed by the governor having qualifications, experience, or education in the field of law enforcement as follows:

(i) one incumbent mayor;

(ii) one incumbent county commissioner;

(iii) three incumbent sheriffs, one of whom is a representative of the Utah Sheriffs Association, one of whom is from a county having a population of 100,000 or more, and one of whom is from a county having a population of less than 100,000;

(iv) three incumbent police chiefs, one of whom is a representative of the Utah Chiefs of Police Association, one of whom is from a city of the first or second class, and one of whom is from a city of the third, fourth, or fifth class or town;

(v) one officer from the Federal Bureau of Investigation appointed by the governor upon the recommendation of the agency;

(vi) a representative of the Utah Peace Officers Association;

(vii) an educator in the field of public administration, criminal justice, or related area; and

(viii) three persons selected at large by the governor.

(4) (a) Except as required by Subsection (4)(b), the 14 members of the council shall be appointed by the governor for four-year terms.

(b) Notwithstanding the requirements of Subsection (4)(a), the governor shall, at the time of appointment or reappointment, adjust the length of terms to ensure that the terms of council members are staggered so that approximately half of the council is appointed every two years.

(c) A member may be reappointed for additional terms.

(d) When a vacancy occurs in the membership for any reason, the replacement shall be appointed for the unexpired term by the governor from the same category in which the vacancy occurs.

(5) A member of the council ceases to be a member:

(a) immediately upon the termination of his holding the office or employment that was the basis for his eligibility to membership on the council; or

(b) upon two unexcused absences in one year from regularly scheduled council meetings.

(6) The council shall select a chair and vice chair from among its members.

(7) Ten members of the advisory council constitute a quorum.

(8) (a) Meetings may be called by the chair, the commissioner, or the director and shall be called by the chair upon the written request of nine members.

(b) Meetings shall be held at the times and places determined by the director.

(9) The council shall meet at least two times per year.

(10) (a) (i) Members who are not government employees shall receive no compensation or benefits for their services, but may receive per diem and expenses incurred in the performance of the member's official duties at the rates established by the Division of Finance under Sections 63A-3-106 and 63A-3-107.

(ii) Members may decline to receive per diem and expenses for their service.

(b) (i) State government officer and employee members who do not receive salary, per diem, or expenses from their agency for their service may receive per diem and expenses incurred in the performance of their official duties from the council at the rates established by the Division of Finance under Sections 63A-3-106 and 63A-3-107.

(ii) State government officer and employee members may decline to receive per diem and expenses for their service.

(c) (i) Local government members who do not receive salary, per diem, or expenses from the entity that they represent for their service may receive per diem and expenses incurred in the performance of their official duties at the rates established by the Division of Finance under Sections 63A-3-106 and 63A-3-107.

(ii) Local government members may decline to receive per diem and expenses for their service.

(11) Membership on the council does not disqualify any member from holding any other public office or employment. 2003

53-6-107. General duties of council.

(1) The council shall:

(a) advise the director regarding:

(i) the approval, certification, or revocation of certification of any certified academy established in the state;

(ii) the refusal, suspension, or revocation of certification of a peace officer;

(iii) minimum courses of study, attendance requirements, and the equipment and facilities to be required at a certified academy;

(iv) minimum qualifications for instructors at a certified academy;

(v) the minimum basic training requirements that peace officers shall complete before receiving certification;

(vi) the minimum basic training requirements that dispatchers shall complete before receiving certification; and

(vii) categories or classifications of advanced in-service training programs and minimum courses of study and attendance requirements for the categories or classifications;

(b) recommend that studies, surveys, or reports, or all of them be made by the director concerning the implementation of the objectives and purposes of this chapter;

(c) make recommendations and reports to the commissioner and governor from time to time; and

(d) perform other acts as necessary to carry out the duties of the council in this chapter.

(2) The council may approve special function officers for membership in the Public Safety Retirement System in accordance with Sections 49-14-201 and 49-15-201.   2002

53-6-108. Donations, contributions, grants, gifts, bequests, devises, or endowments — Authority to accept — Disposition.

(1) The division may accept any donations, contributions, grants, gifts, bequests, devises, or endowments of money or property, which shall be the property of the state.

(2) (a) If the donor directs that the money or property be used in a specified manner, then the division shall use it in accordance with these directions and state law.

(b) All money and the proceeds from donated property not disposed of under Subsection (a) shall be deposited in the General Fund as restricted revenue for the division.   1993

PART 2

PEACE OFFICER TRAINING AND CERTIFICATION

53-6-201. Short title.

This part is known as the "Peace Officer Training and Certification Act."   1993

53-6-202. Basic training course — Completion required — Annual training — Prohibition from exercising powers — Reinstatement.

(1) (a) The director shall:
(i) (A) suggest and prepare subject material; and
(B) schedule instructors for basic training courses; or
(ii) review the material and instructor choices submitted by a certified academy.

(b) The subject material, instructors, and schedules shall be approved or disapproved by a majority vote of the council.

(2) The materials shall be reviewed and approved by the council on or before July 1st of each year and may from time to time be changed or amended by majority vote of the council.

(3) The basic training in a certified academy shall be appropriate for the basic training of peace officers in the techniques of law enforcement in the discretion of the director.

(4) (a) All peace officers must satisfactorily complete the basic training course or the waiver process provided for in this chapter as well as annual certified training of not less than 40 hours as the director, with the advice and consent of the council, directs.

(b) A peace officer who fails to satisfactorily complete the annual training shall automatically be prohibited from exercising peace officer powers until any deficiency is made up.

(5) The director, with the advice of the council, may make rules relating to the reinstatement of powers of peace officers who have been prohibited from exercising those powers under this part.   1993

53-6-203. Applicants for admission to training programs or for certification examination — Requirements.

(1) Before being accepted for admission to the training programs conducted by a certified academy, and before being allowed to take a certification examination, each applicant for admission or certification examination shall meet the following requirements:

(a) be a United States citizen;

(b) be at least 21 years old at the time of appointment as a peace officer;

(c) be a high school graduate or furnish evidence of successful completion of an examination indicating an equivalent achievement;

(d) have not been convicted of a crime for which the applicant could have been punished by imprisonment in a federal penitentiary or by imprisonment in the penitentiary of this or another state;

(e) have demonstrated good moral character, as determined by a background investigation; and

(f) be free of any physical, emotional, or mental condition that might adversely affect the performance of his duty as a peace officer.

(2) (a) An application for admission to a training program shall be accompanied by a criminal history background check of local, state, and national criminal history files and a background investigation.

(b) The costs of the background check and investigation shall be borne by the applicant or the applicant's employing agency.

(i) Conviction of any offense not serious enough to be covered under Subsection (1)(d), involving dishonesty, unlawful sexual conduct, physical violence, or the unlawful use, sale, or possession for sale of a controlled substance is an indication that an applicant may not be of good moral character and may be grounds for denial of admission to a training program or refusal to take a certification examination.

(ii) An applicant may be admitted to a training program provisionally, pending completion of any background check or investigation required by this subsection.

(3) (a) Notwithstanding any expungement statute or rule of any other jurisdiction, any conviction obtained in this state or other jurisdiction, including a conviction that has been expunged, dismissed, or treated in a similar manner to either of these procedures, may be considered for purposes of this section.

(b) This provision applies to convictions entered both before and after the effective date of this section.

(4) Any background check or background investigation performed pursuant to the requirements of this section shall be to determine eligibility for admission to training programs or qualification for certification examinations and may not be used as a replacement for any background investigations that may be required of an employing agency.   1998

53-6-204. Time of application for admission to training program.

At the time a person is employed or appointed as a peace officer, the chief executive officer of the agency employing or appointing shall submit to a certified academy an application together with the required background information required under Section 53-6-203.   1993

53-6-205. Completion of training course or passing of certificate examination required — Persons affected.

(1) (a) Except as provided in Subsection (2), a peace officer in this state must successfully com-

plete the basic course at a certified academy, or successfully pass a state certification examination according to the requirements of Section 53-6-206, before that person can be certified.

(b) A person may not exercise peace officer powers until certified.

(2) Subsection (1) applies only to persons not previously certified and who receive their first employment appointment or election as a peace officer in this state on or after January 1, 1985.   1993

53-6-206. Waiver of training course requirement — Certification exam.

(1) The director may waive the required basic peace officer training and certify each applicant who passes a written examination, an oral examination, or both a written and oral examination that affirms the applicant's ability in law enforcement.

(2) A waiver applicant shall:

(a) furnish evidence of satisfactory completion of a peace officer training program that, in the director's judgment, is equivalent to the program required for certification in this state; and

(b) furnish evidence that the requirements of Section 53-6-203, relating to qualifications for admission to the Utah training programs have been met.

(3) A waiver applicant may not exercise peace officer powers until all waiver process requirements have been met.

(4) An applicant who fails the certification examination must complete the basic training course required by this part and be certified in order to become a peace officer authorized to exercise peace officer powers.   1993

53-6-207. Municipalities may set higher minimum standards.

The minimum standards in this part concerning peace officer qualifications and training do not preclude counties, cities, or towns from establishing standards higher than the minimum standards contained in this part.   1993

53-6-208. Inactive certificates — Lapse of certificate — Reinstatement.

(1) (a) The certificate of a peace officer who has not been actively engaged in performing the duties of a peace officer for one year shall be designated "inactive."

(b) If a peace officer having an inactive certificate becomes reemployed or subsequently reengaged as a peace officer, his certificate may be reissued or reinstated by the director upon successful completion by that peace officer of the waiver process established by the director.

(c) The director may require a peace officer with an inactive certificate to successfully complete the basic training course before reissuing or reinstating certification.

(2) (a) The certificate of a peace officer lapses if he has not been actively engaged in performing the duties of a peace officer for four continuous years.

(b) Subject to Section 53-6-206, the peace officer shall successfully complete the basic training course before the certificate may be reissued or reinstated.   1993

53-6-209. Termination of employment — Change of status form.

(1) When a peace officer's employment terminates, the employing agency shall submit a change of status form noting the termination of the peace officer to the division.

(2) The change of status form shall:

(a) be completed and submitted within seven days of the peace officer's termination date;

(b) identify the circumstances of the peace officer's status change by indicating that the peace officer has resigned, retired, terminated, transferred, deceased, or that the peace officer's name has changed;

(c) indicate the effective date of action; and

(d) indicate the name of the new employer, if the status change is due to a transfer.

(3) Any person or agency who intentionally falsifies, misrepresents, or fails to give notice of the change of status of a peace officer is liable to the division for any damages that may be sustained by the failure to make the notification.   1993

53-6-210. Investigations and certification hearings — Powers of division — Violation.

(1) For investigations by the division and for certification hearings or other testimony before the council, the division may administer oaths and affirmations, subpoena witnesses, take evidence, and require by subpoena duces tecum the production of relevant papers, records, or other documents or information, whether filed or kept in original form, or electronically stored or recorded.

(2) A person who willfully disobeys a properly served subpoena issued by the division is guilty of a class B misdemeanor.   1993

53-6-211. Revocation, suspension, or refusal of certification — Hearings — Grounds — Notice to employer — Reporting.

(1) (a) The director may, upon the concurrence of the majority of the council, revoke, refuse, or suspend certification of a peace officer for cause.

(b) Except as provided under Subsection (6), the council shall give the person or peace officer involved prior notice and an opportunity for a full hearing before the council.

(c) The director, with the concurrence of the council, may by rule designate a presiding officer to represent the council in adjudicative proceedings or hearings before the council.

(d) Any of the following constitute cause for action under Subsection (1)(a):

(i) willful falsification of any information to obtain certified status;

(ii) physical or mental disability affecting the employee's ability to perform his duties;

(iii) addiction to or the unlawful sale, possession, or use of narcotics, drugs, or drug paraphernalia;

(iv) conviction of a felony or any crime involving dishonesty, unlawful sexual conduct, physical violence, or driving under the influence of alcohol or drugs; or

(v) any conduct or pattern of conduct that would tend to disrupt, diminish, or otherwise jeopardize public trust and fidelity in law enforcement.

(2) (a) Notwithstanding any expungement statute or rule of any other jurisdiction, any conviction obtained in this state or other jurisdiction may be considered for purposes of this section.

(b) In this section, "conviction" includes a conviction that has been expunged, dismissed, or treated in a similar manner to either of these procedures.

(c) This provision applies to convictions entered both before and after April 25, 1988.

(3) The director shall send notice to the governing body of the political subdivision employing the peace officer and shall receive information or comments concerning the peace officer from the governing body or the agency employing the officer before suspending or revoking that peace officer's certification.

(4) Denial, suspension, or revocation procedures may not be initiated by the council when an officer is terminated for infraction of his agency's policies, general orders, or similar guidelines of operation that do not amount to any of the causes for denial, suspension, or revocation enumerated in Subsection (1).

(5) (a) Termination of a peace officer, whether voluntary or involuntary, does not preclude revocation or subsequent denial of peace officer certification status by the council if the peace officer was terminated for any of the reasons under Subsection (1).

(b) Employment by another agency, or reinstatement of a peace officer by his parent agency after termination, whether the termination was voluntary or involuntary, does not preclude revocation or subsequent denial of peace officer certification status by the council if the peace officer was terminated for any of the reasons under Subsection (1).

(6) (a) When the cause for action is conviction of a felony, the proceedings prior to a recommendation shall be limited to an informal review of written documentation by the presiding officer.

(b) If the presiding officer determines that the peace officer has been convicted of a felony, then the presiding officer shall recommend revocation.

(c) The peace officer may request an informal hearing before the presiding officer solely to present evidence that there was no felony conviction.

(d) At the conclusion of an informal hearing, the presiding officer shall make a recommendation to the director and the council.

(7) The chief, sheriff, or administrative officer of a law enforcement agency is required to report to Peace Officer Standards and Training all conduct of employees who are peace officers, as provided in Subsection (1)(d) above.   1998

53-6-212. Responsibility for training — Certification.

(1) The division is not responsible for providing basic or in-service training for peace officers defined and designated in Sections 53-13-104 through 53-13-106 except for approval of the instructors and content of training where required by this chapter, Title 53, Chapter 13, Peace Officer Classifications, or division rules.

(2) Where this chapter or Title 53, Chapter 13, Peace Officer Classifications, requires an agency head to certify that a member has completed required training, the division shall rely on the certification, as provided, to be accurate.   1999

53-6-213. Appropriations from reparation fund.

(1) The Legislature shall appropriate from the fund established in Title 63, Chapter 25a, Part 4, the Crime Victims' Reparations Act, to the division, funds for training of law enforcement officers in the state.

(2) The department shall make an annual report to the Legislature, which includes the amount received during the previous fiscal year.   2002

PART 3

DISPATCHER TRAINING AND CERTIFICATION

53-6-301. Title.

This part is known as the "Dispatcher Training and Certification Act."   1995

53-6-302. Applicants for certification examination — Requirements.

(1) Before being allowed to take a dispatcher certification examination, each applicant shall meet the following requirements:

(a) be a United States citizen;

(b) be 18 years of age or older at the time of employment as a dispatcher;

(c) be a high school graduate or have a G.E.D. equivalent;

(d) have not been convicted of a crime for which the applicant could have been punished by imprisonment in a federal penitentiary or by imprisonment in the penitentiary of this or another state;

(e) have demonstrated good moral character, as determined by a background investigation; and

(f) be free of any physical, emotional, or mental condition that might adversely affect the performance of the applicant's duty as a dispatcher.

(2) (a) An application for certification shall be accompanied by a criminal history background check of local, state, and national criminal history files and a background investigation.

(b) The costs of the background check and investigation shall be borne by the applicant or the applicant's employing agency.

(i) Conviction of any offense not serious enough to be covered under Subsection (1)(d), involving dishonesty, unlawful sexual conduct, physical violence, or the unlawful use, sale, or possession for sale of a controlled substance is an indication that an applicant may not be of good moral character and may be grounds for denial of certification or refusal to give a certification examination.

(ii) An applicant may be allowed to take a certification examination provisionally, pending completion of any background check or investigation required by this subsection.

(3) (a) Notwithstanding Sections 77-18-9 through 77-18-17 regarding expungements, or a similar statute or rule of any other jurisdiction, any conviction obtained in this state or other jurisdiction, including a conviction that has been expunged, dismissed, or treated in a similar manner to either of these procedures, may be considered for purposes of this section.

(b) Subsection (a) applies to convictions entered both before and after May 1, 1995.

(4) Any background check or background investigation performed pursuant to the requirements of this section shall be to determine eligibility for admission to training programs or qualification for certification examinations and may not be used as a replacement for any background investigations that may be required of an employing agency.   1995

53-6-303. Completion of certification examination required — Persons affected.

(1) Except as provided in Subsection (2), a person must successfully complete the basic dispatcher training course and pass the certification examination

according to the requirements of this part before that person can be a certified dispatcher.

(2) Subsection (1) applies only to persons not previously certified and who receive their first employment as a dispatcher in this state on or after July 1, 1996. 1995

53-6-304. Waiver of training course requirement.

(1) The director may waive the required basic dispatcher training course and certify an applicant who:

(a) provides evidence that the applicant meets the requirements under Section 53-6-302, relating to qualifications for admission to the training course;

(b) provides evidence that the applicant has completed a basic dispatcher training program that, in the director's judgment, is equivalent to the course required for certification under this part; and

(c) passes a written examination, an oral examination, or both, that affirms the applicant's ability in public safety communications.

(2) An applicant who fails the examination under Subsection (1)(c) shall complete the basic dispatcher training course and pass the dispatcher certification examination to become certified. 1995

53-6-305. Local governments — Option — Higher minimum standards.

(1) Participation in dispatcher training and certification under this part is at the option of the legislative body of each county or municipality that employs dispatchers.

(2) The minimum standards in this part concerning dispatcher qualifications and training do not preclude counties or municipalities from establishing standards higher than the minimum standards contained in this part. 1995

53-6-306. Inactive and lapsed certificates — Reinstatement — Continuing education requirements.

(1) (a) The certificate of a dispatcher who has not been actively engaged in performing the duties of a dispatcher for one year shall be designated "inactive."

(b) If a dispatcher having an inactive certificate becomes reemployed or subsequently reengaged as a dispatcher, the dispatcher's certificate may be reissued or reinstated by the director upon successful completion by that dispatcher of the certification examination.

(c) The director may require a dispatcher with an inactive certificate to successfully complete the basic dispatcher training course before reissuing or reinstating certification.

(2) (a) The certificate of a dispatcher who has not been actively engaged in performing the duties of a dispatcher for four continuous years shall be designated "lapsed."

(b) Subject to Section 53-6-305, a dispatcher having a lapsed certificate shall successfully complete the basic training course and pass the certification examination before the certificate may be reissued or reinstated.

(3) (a) A certified dispatcher shall complete annual training approved by the director of 20 hours or more.

(b) (i) If a certified dispatcher does not complete the annual training requirement, then that dispatcher's certificate shall be designated "inactive," and after one year, shall be designated "lapsed."

(ii) The reinstatement of an inactive or a lapsed certificate under Subsection (3) shall be governed by rules made by the director. 1995

53-6-307. Termination of employment — Change of status form.

(1) When a certified dispatcher's employment terminates or a certified dispatcher's status changes, the employing agency shall submit a change of status form noting the termination of the certified dispatcher to the division.

(2) The change of status form shall:

(a) be completed and submitted within 30 days of the certified dispatcher's termination date;

(b) identify the circumstances of the certified dispatcher's status change by indicating that the certified dispatcher has resigned, retired, terminated, transferred, deceased, or that the certified dispatcher's name has changed;

(c) indicate the effective date of action; and

(d) indicate the name of the new employer, if the status change is due to a transfer.

(3) Any person or agency who intentionally falsifies, misrepresents, or fails to give notice of the change of status of a certified dispatcher is liable to the division for any damages that may be sustained by the failure to make the notification. 1995

53-6-308. Investigations and certification hearings — Powers of division — Violation.

(1) For investigations by the division and for certification hearings or other testimony before the council, the division may administer oaths and affirmations, subpoena witnesses, take evidence, and require by subpoena duces tecum the production of relevant papers, records, or other documents or information, whether filed or kept in original form, or electronically stored or recorded.

(2) A person who willfully disobeys a properly served subpoena issued by the division is guilty of a class B misdemeanor. 1995

53-6-309. Revocation, suspension, or refusal of certification — Hearings — Grounds — Notice to employer.

(1) (a) The director may, upon the concurrence of the majority of the council, revoke, refuse, or suspend certification of a dispatcher for cause.

(b) The council shall give the person or dispatcher involved prior notice and an opportunity for a full hearing before the council.

(c) The director, with the concurrence of the council, may by rule designate a presiding officer to represent the council in adjudicative proceedings or hearings before the council.

(d) Any of the following constitute cause for action under Subsection (1)(a):

(i) willful falsification of any information to obtain certified status;

(ii) physical or mental disability affecting the employee's ability to perform his duties;

(iii) addiction to or the unlawful sale, possession, or use of narcotics, drugs, or drug paraphernalia;

(iv) conviction of a felony or any crime involving dishonesty, unlawful sexual conduct, physical violence, or driving under the influence of alcohol or drugs; or

(v) any conduct or pattern of conduct that would tend to disrupt, diminish, or otherwise jeopardize public trust and fidelity in law enforcement.

(2) (a) Notwithstanding Title 77, Chapter 18 regarding expungements, or a similar statute or rule of any other jurisdiction, any conviction obtained in this state or other jurisdiction may be considered for purposes of this section.

(b) In this section, "conviction" includes a conviction that has been expunged, dismissed, or treated in a similar manner to either of these procedures.

(c) This provision applies to convictions entered both before and after May 1, 1995.

(3) The director shall send notice to the governing body of the political subdivision employing the certified dispatcher and shall receive information or comments concerning the certified dispatcher from the governing body or the agency employing the dispatcher before suspending or revoking that dispatcher's certification.

(4) Denial, suspension, or revocation procedures may not be initiated by the council when a dispatcher is terminated for infraction of his agency's policies, general orders, or similar guidelines of operation that do not amount to any of the causes for denial, suspension, or revocation enumerated in Subsection (1).

(5) (a) Termination of a certified dispatcher, whether voluntary or involuntary, does not preclude revocation or subsequent denial of dispatcher certification status by the council if the dispatcher was terminated for any of the reasons under Subsection (1).

(b) Employment by another agency, or reinstatement of a certified dispatcher by the certified dispatcher's parent agency after termination, whether the termination was voluntary or involuntary, does not preclude revocation or subsequent denial of dispatcher certification status by the council if the certified dispatcher was terminated for any of the reasons under Subsection (1).

1995

53-6-310. Responsibility for training — Certification.

(1) The division is not responsible for providing basic or in-service training for certified dispatchers except for approval of the instructors and content of training where required by this chapter or division rules.

(2) Where this chapter requires an agency head to certify that a member has completed required training, the division shall rely on the certification, as provided, to be accurate.

1995

CHAPTER 7

UTAH FIRE PREVENTION AND SAFETY

Part 1

State Fire Marshal Division Administration

Part 2

Fire Prevention and Fireworks

Part 3

Liquefied Petroleum Gas

PART 1

STATE FIRE MARSHAL DIVISION ADMINISTRATION

53-7-101. Short title.

This chapter is known as the "Utah Fire Prevention and Safety Act."   1993

53-7-102. Definitions.

As used in this chapter:

(1) "Director" means the state fire marshal appointed in accordance with Section 53-7-103.

(2) "Division" means the State Fire Marshal Division created in Section 53-7-103.

(3) "Fire officer" means:

(a) the state fire marshal;

(b) the state fire marshal's deputies or salaried assistants;

(c) the fire chief or fire marshal of any county, city, or town fire department;

(d) the fire officer of any fire district;

(e) the fire officer of any special service district organized for fire protection pur-poses; and

(f) authorized personnel of any of the per-sons specified in Subsections (a) through (e).

(4) "State fire marshal" means the fire marshal appointed director by the commissioner under Section 53-7-103.   1993

53-7-103. State Fire Marshal Division — Cre-ation — State fire marshal — Appoint-ment, qualifications, duties, and com-pensation.

(1) There is created within the department the State Fire Marshal Division.

(2) (a) The director of the division is the state fire marshal, who shall be appointed by the commis-sioner upon the recommendation of the Utah Fire Prevention Board created in Section 53-7-203 and with the approval of the governor.

(b) The state fire marshal is the executive and administrative head of the division, and shall be qualified by experience and education to enforce rules made under this chapter and perform the duties prescribed by the commissioner.

(3) The state fire marshal acts under the supervi-sion and control of the commissioner and may be removed from his position at the will of the commis-sioner.

(4) The state fire marshal shall:

(a) enforce rules made under this chapter as provided in accordance with Section 53-7-104;

(b) complete the duties assigned by the com-missioner;

(c) examine plans and specifications for school buildings, as required by Section 53A-20-104;

(d) approve criteria established by the state superintendent for building inspectors;

(e) promote and support injury prevention public education programs; and

(f) perform all other duties provided in this chapter.

(5) The state fire marshal shall receive compensa-tion as provided by Title 67, Chapter 19, Utah State Personnel Management Act.   2002

53-7-104. Enforcement of rules — Division of authority and responsibility.

(1) The authority and responsibility for enforcing rules made under this chapter is divided as provided in this section.

(2) The fire officers of any city or county shall enforce the rules of the state fire marshal in their respective areas.

(3) The state fire marshal may enforce the rules in:

(a) areas outside of corporate cities, fire protec-tion districts, and special districts organized for fire protection purposes; and

(b) state-owned property, school district owned property, and privately owned property used for schools located within corporate cities and county fire protection districts, asylums, mental hospi-tals, hospitals, sanitariums, homes for the aged, residential health-care facilities, children's homes or institutions, or similar institutional type occu-pancy of any capacity.

(4) The state fire marshal may enforce the rules in corporate cities, counties, and fire protection districts, and special service districts organized for fire protec-tion purposes upon receiving a request from the chief fire official or the local governing body.   2001

53-7-105. State fire marshal, deputies, and in-vestigators — Status of law enforce-ment officers — Inclusion in Public Safety Retirement — Training.

(1) The state fire marshal, his deputies, and inves-tigators, for the purpose of enforcing and investigat-ing violations of fire related statutes and ordinances, have the status of law enforcement officers.

(2) Inclusion under Title 49, Chapter 14, Public Safety Contributory Retirement Act, or Title 49, Chapter 15, Public Safety Noncontributory Retire-ment Act, is not authorized by Subsection (1) except as provided in those chapters.

(3) The commissioner, with the concurrence of the Peace Officer Standards and Training Advisory Board may require peace officer standards and training for the state fire marshal, his deputies, and investigators.   2002

53-7-106. Adoption of fire code.

(1) A fire code promulgated by a nationally recog-nized code authority and adopted by the Utah Fire Prevention Board pursuant to Section 53-7-204 is the state fire code, to which cities, counties, fire protection districts, and the state shall adhere in safeguarding life and property from the hazards of fire and explo-sion.

(2) (a) The legislative body of a political subdivision may make ordinances that are more restrictive in its fire code requirements than the state fire code, in order to meet the public safety needs of the political subdivision.

(b) The legislative body of a political subdivision shall provide to the Utah Fire Prevention Board one copy of each ordinance enacted under Subsection (2)(a).

(c) The state fire marshal shall keep an indexed copy of the ordinances.

(d) Copies of the ordinances are available from the state fire marshal on request.   2001

53-7-107. Electronic writing.

(1) Any writing required or permitted by this chapter may be filed or prepared in an electronic medium and by electronic transmission subject to the ability of the recipient to accept and process the electronic writing.

(2) Any writing required by this chapter to be signed that is in an electronic medium shall be signed by digital signature in accordance with Title 46, Chapter 3, Utah Digital Signature Act.   2000

53-7-108. Repealed.   2002

PART 2

FIRE PREVENTION AND FIREWORKS

53-7-201. Short title.

This part is known as the "Fire Prevention and Fireworks Act."   1993

53-7-202. Definitions.

As used in this part:

(1) "Agricultural and wildlife fireworks" means a class C dangerous explosive that:

(a) uses sound or light when deployed; and

(b) is designated to prevent crop damage or unwanted animals from entering a specified area.

(2) "Board" means the Utah Fire Prevention Board created in Section 53-7-203.

(3) "Class A explosive" means a class A explosive as defined by the U.S. Department of Transportation in Part 173, Title 49, Code of Federal Regulations.

(4) "Class B explosive" means a class B explosive as defined by the U.S. Department of Transportation in Part 173, Title 49, Code of Federal Regulations.

(5) "Class C explosive" means a class C explosive as defined by the U.S. Department of Transportation in Part 173, Title 49, Code of Federal Regulations.

(6) (a) "Class C common state approved explosive" means a class C explosive that is:

(i) a cardboard or heavy paper cylindrical tube or cone that:

(A) produces a shower of color and sparks that reach a maximum height of 15 feet;

(B) may whistle or pop; and

(C) is not designed to explode or leave the ground;

(ii) a pyrotechnic wheel device that:

(A) may be attached to a post or tree; and

(B) contains up to six "driver" units or tubes;

(iii) any device that:

(A) spins, jumps, or emits popping sounds when placed on the ground;

(B) does not exceed a height of 15 feet when discharged; and

(C) does not travel laterally more than ten feet on a smooth surface when discharged;

(iv) a morning glory, suzuki, or flitter sparkler; and

(v) a single tube day type parachute that does not carry any flare or flame upon descent.

(b) "Class C common state approved explosive" does not mean:

(i) class C dangerous explosives; or

(ii) exempt explosives.

(7) (a) "Class C dangerous explosive" means a class C explosive that is:

(i) a firecracker, cannon cracker, salute, cherry bomb, or other similar explosive;

(ii) a skyrocket or any device other than a model rocket that uses combustible or explosive material and rises more than 15 feet when discharged;

(iii) a roman candle or other device that discharges balls of fire over 15 feet in height;

(iv) a tube or cone aerial firework that propels comets, shells, salutes, flash shells, or similar devices more than 15 feet into the air; and

(v) a chaser, whistler, or other device that darts or travels more than ten feet laterally on a smooth surface or exceeds 15 feet in height when discharged.

(b) A "Class C dangerous explosive" does not mean:

(i) class C common state approved explosives; or

(ii) exempt explosives.

(8) "Display fireworks" means an aerial shell, salute, flash shell, comet, sky battle, mine, and any similar class C explosive or class B explosive.

(9) (a) "Display operator" means the person who purchases and is responsible for setting up and discharging display fireworks.

(b) "Display operator" does not mean a fire department.

(10) "Exempt explosive" means a model rocket, toy pistol cap, emergency signal flare, snake or glow worm, party popper, trick noisemaker, match, and wire sparkler under 12 inches in length.

(11) (a) "Fireworks" means:

(i) class C explosives;

(ii) class C dangerous explosives; and

(iii) class C common state approved explosives.

(b) "Fireworks" does not mean:

(i) exempt explosives;

(ii) class A explosives; and

(iii) class B explosives.

(12) "Importer" means a person who brings class B or class C explosives into Utah for the general purpose of resale within the state or exportation to other states.

(13) (a) "Pyrotechnic" means any composition or device manufactured or used to produce a visible or audible effect by combustion, deflagration, or detonation.

(b) "Pyrotechnic" does not mean exempt explosives.

(14) "Retail seller" means a person who sells class C common state approved explosives to the public during the period authorized under Section 53-7-225.

(15) "State fire code" means a nationally recognized fire code adopted by the Utah Fire Prevention Board pursuant to Section 53-7-204.

(16) "Trick noisemaker" includes a:

(a) tube or sphere containing pyrotechnic composition that produces a white or colored smoke as its primary effect when ignited; and

(b) device that produces a small report intended to surprise the user, including a:

(i) "booby trap," which is a small tube with a string protruding from both ends that ignites the friction sensitive composition in the tube when the string is pulled;

(ii) "snapper," which is a small paper-wrapped device containing a minute quantity of explosive composition coated on bits of sand that explodes producing a small report;

(iii) "trick match," which is a kitchen or book match coated with a small quantity of explosive or pyrotechnic composition that produces a small shower of sparks when ignited;

(iv) "cigarette load," which is a small wooden peg coated with a small quantity of explosive composition that produces a small report when the cigarette is ignited; and

(v) "auto burglar alarm," which is a tube that:

(A) contains pyrotechnic composition that produces a loud whistle and smoke when ignited;

(B) may contain a small quantity of explosive to produce a small explosive noise; and

(C) is ignited by a squib.

(17) "Unclassified fireworks" means any of the following:

(a) a pyrotechnic device that is used, given away, or offered for sale, that has not been tested, approved, and classified by the U.S. Department of Transportation;

(b) an approved device that has been altered or redesigned since obtaining approval by the U.S. Department of Transportation;

(c) a pyrotechnic device that is being tested by a manufacturer, importer, or wholesaler before receiving approval by the U.S. Department of Transportation.

(18) "Wholesaler" means any of the following:

(a) a person who sells class C common state approved explosives to a retailer;

(b) a person who sells class B explosives or class C dangerous explosives for display use.

2001

53-7-203. Utah Fire Prevention Board — Creation — Members — Terms — Selection of chair and officers — Quorum — Meetings — Compensation — Division's duty to implement board rules.

(1) There is created within the division the Utah Fire Prevention Board.

(2) The board shall be nonpartisan and be composed of ten members appointed by the governor as follows:

(a) a city or county official;

(b) a licensed architect;

(c) a licensed engineer;

(d) a member of the Utah State Firemen's Association;

(e) the state forester;

(f) the commissioner of the Labor Commission or the commissioner's designee;

(g) a member of the Utah State Fire Chiefs Association;

(h) a member of the Utah Fire Marshal's Association;

(i) a building inspector; and

(j) a citizen appointed at large.

(3) (a) Except as required by Subsection (3)(b), as terms of current board members expire, the governor shall appoint each new member or reappointed member to a four-year term.

(b) Notwithstanding the requirements of Subsection (3)(a), the governor shall, at the time of appointment or reappointment, adjust the length of terms to ensure that the terms of board members are staggered so that approximately half of the board is appointed every two years.

(4) When a vacancy occurs in the membership for any reason, the replacement shall be appointed for the unexpired term.

(5) A member whose term has expired may continue to serve until a replacement is appointed pursuant to Subsection (3).

(6) The board shall select from its members a chair and other officers as the board finds necessary.

(7) A majority of the members of the board is a quorum.

(8) The board shall hold regular semiannual meetings for the transaction of its business at a time and place to be fixed by the board and shall hold other meetings as necessary for proper transaction of business.

(9) (a) (i) Members who are not government employees shall receive no compensation or benefits for their services, but may receive per diem and expenses incurred in the performance of the member's official duties at the rates established by the Division of Finance under Sections 63A-3-106 and 63A-3-107.

(ii) Members may decline to receive per diem and expenses for their service.

(b) (i) State government officer and employee members who do not receive salary, per diem, or expenses from their agency for their service may receive per diem and expenses incurred in the performance of their official duties from the board at the rates established by the Division of Finance under Sections 63A-3-106 and 63A-3-107.

(ii) State government officer and employee members may decline to receive per diem and expenses for their service.

(c) (i) Local government members who do not receive salary, per diem, or expenses from the entity that they represent for their service may receive per diem and expenses incurred in the performance of their official duties at the rates established by the Division of Finance under Sections 63A-3-106 and 63A-3-107.

(ii) Local government members may decline to receive per diem and expenses for their service.

(10) The division shall implement the rules of the board and perform all other duties delegated by the board. 2001

53-7-204. Duties of Utah Fire Prevention Board — Local administrative duties.

(1) The board shall:

(a) make rules in accordance with Title 63, Chapter 46a, Utah Administrative Rulemaking Act:

(i) adopting a nationally recognized fire code and the specific edition of that fire code as the state fire code to be used as the standard;

(ii) establishing minimum standards for the prevention of fire and for the protection of life and property against fire and panic in any:

(A) publicly owned building, including all public and private schools, colleges, and university buildings;

(B) building or structure used or intended for use as an asylum, a mental hospital, a hospital, a sanitarium, a home for the aged, an assisted living facility, a children's home or day care center, or any similar institutional type occupancy of any capacity; and

(C) place of assemblage where 50 or more persons may gather together in a building, structure, tent, or room for the purpose of amusement, entertainment, instruction, or education;

(iii) establishing safety and other requirements for placement and discharge of display fireworks based upon:

(A) the specific edition of the nationally recognized fire code selected by the board under Subsection (1)(a)(i); and

(B) relevant publications of the National Fire Protection Association;

(iv) establishing minimum safety standards for retail storage, handling, and sale of class C common state approved explosives;

(v) defining methods to establish proof of competence to place and discharge display fireworks;

(vi) for deputizing qualified persons to act as deputy fire marshals, and to secure special services in emergencies;

(vii) implementing Sections 53-7-106 and 53-7-205;

(viii) setting guidelines for use of funding; and

(ix) establishing criteria for training and safety equipment grants for fire departments enrolled in firefighter certification;

(b) recommend to the commissioner a state fire marshal;

(c) develop policies under which the state fire marshal and his authorized representatives will perform;

(d) provide for the employment of field assistants and other salaried personnel as required;

(e) prescribe the duties of the state fire marshal and his authorized representatives;

(f) establish a statewide fire prevention, fire education, and fire service training program in cooperation with the Board of Regents;

(g) establish a statewide fire statistics program for the purpose of gathering fire data from all political subdivisions of the state;

(h) establish a fire academy in accordance with Section 53-7-204.2;

(i) coordinate the efforts of all people engaged in fire suppression in the state;

(j) work aggressively with the local political subdivisions to reduce fire losses;

(k) regulate the sale and servicing of portable fire extinguishers and automatic fire suppression systems in the interest of safeguarding lives and property; and

(l) establish a certification program for persons who inspect and test automatic fire sprinkler systems.

(2) The board may incorporate in its rules by reference, in whole or in part, nationally recognized and readily available standards and codes pertaining to the protection of life and property from fire, explosion, or panic.

(3) (a) The board may only make amendments to the state fire code adopted under Subsection (1)(a)(i) in accordance with Section 53-7-205.

(b) The amendments may be applicable to the entire state or within a city, county, or fire protection district.

(4) The following functions shall be administered locally by a city, county, or fire protection district:

(a) issuing permits, including open burning permits pursuant to Sections 11-7-1 and 19-2-114;

(b) creating a local board of appeals in accordance with the state fire code; and

(c) establishing, modifying, or deleting fire flow and water supply requirements. 2003

53-7-204.2. Fire Academy — Establishment — Fire Academy Support Account — Funding.

(1) In this section:

(a) "Account" means the Fire Academy Support Account created in Subsection (4).

(b) "Property insurance premium" means premium paid as consideration for property insurance as defined in Section 31A-1-301.

(2) The board shall:

(a) establish a fire academy that:

(i) provides instruction and training for paid, volunteer, institutional, and industrial firefighters;

(ii) develops new methods of firefighting and fire prevention;

(iii) provides training for fire and arson detection and investigation;

(iv) provides public education programs to promote fire safety;

(v) provides for certification of firefighters, pump operators, instructors, and officers; and

(vi) provides facilities for teaching firefighting skills;

(b) establish a cost recovery fee in accordance with Section 63-38-3.2 for training commercially employed firefighters; and

(c) request funding for the academy.

(3) The board may:

(a) accept gifts, donations, and grants of property and services on behalf of the fire academy; and

(b) enter into contractual agreements necessary to facilitate establishment of the school.

(4) (a) To provide a funding source for the academy and for the general operation of the State Fire Marshal Division, there is created in the General

Fund a restricted account known as the Fire Academy Support Account.

(b) The following revenue shall be deposited in the account to implement this section:

(i) the percentage specified in Subsection (5) of the annual tax for each year that is levied, assessed, and collected under Title 59, Chapter 9, Taxation of Admitted Insurers, upon property insurance premiums and as applied to fire and allied lines insurance collected by insurance companies within the state;

(ii) the percentage specified in Subsection (6) of all money assessed and collected upon life insurance premiums within the state;

(iii) the cost recovery fees established by the board;

(iv) gifts, donations, and grants of property on behalf of the fire academy; and

(v) appropriations made by the Legislature.

(5) The percentage of the tax specified in Subsection (4)(b)(i) to be deposited in the account each fiscal year is 25%.

(6) The percentage of the money specified in Subsection (4)(b)(ii) to be deposited in the account each fiscal year is 5%.   2003

53-7-205. State fire code amendments — Board duties and responsibilities.

(1) The board shall receive from a city, county, or fire protection district requests for amendments to the state fire code.

(2) The division or the board on its own initiative may make recommendations to the division for amendments to the state fire code.

(3) (a) Within 45 days after receipt of a request or recommendation concerning an amendment, the board shall direct the division to convene an informal hearing concerning the amendment.

(b) The hearing shall be conducted in accordance with the rules of the board.

(c) The board shall decide to accept, modify, or reject the amendment.

(4) Within 15 days following the completion of the hearing, the board shall direct the division to send written notification, in a form prescribed by the board, to the city, county, or fire protection district of its decision.

(5) The board shall make rules incorporating the amendments accepted or modified under Subsection (3).   2001

53-7-206. Equipment for new fire protection systems — Standard equipment.

All equipment for fire protective purposes, purchased in connection with the installation of completely new fire protection systems by any authorities having charge of public property, shall be equipped with the standard hydrant stem and cap nuts and standard threads for fire hose and fire hydrant couplings and fittings designated as the national standard, as adopted by the board, which standard is designated as the standard for the equipment in the state.   1993

53-7-207. Selling or offering for sale nonstandard equipment unlawful — Exception.

(1) A person may not sell or offer for sale any fire hose, fire hydrant, fire engine, or other equipment with threaded parts unless the equipment is fitted and equipped with the threads designated as national standard and adopted by the board and designated by law as the standard of the equipment in the state.

(2) Subsection (1) does not apply to:

(a) equipment sold or offered for sale to a local governing body for the purposes of maintaining, repairing, replacing, or extending existing fire protection equipment as provided in Section 11-4-2; and

(b) adapters and caps for fire protective purposes.   1993

53-7-208. Penalty and punishment.

(1) Any person who violates Sections 53-7-206 and 53-7-207, requiring standard equipment, is guilty of a class B misdemeanor.

(2) A violator shall be punished by:

(a) a fine of not less than $25 nor more than $250;

(b) imprisonment in the county jail for not less than ten days, nor more than sixty days; or

(c) both a fine and imprisonment.   1996

53-7-209. Inspection of buildings by officials.

(1) A fire chief or officer may enter any building or premises not used as a private dwelling at any reasonable hour to inspect the building or premises and enforce the rules made under this part, including the state fire code adopted under Section 53-7-204.

(2) The owner, lessee, manager, or operator of any building or premises not used as a private dwelling shall permit inspections under this section.   2001

53-7-210. Fire investigations by local officers — Notification to division.

(1) The chief fire officer of any city, town, or county fire department, or of any fire district or special service district organized for fire protection purposes, or his authorized representative shall investigate the cause, origin, and circumstances of each fire occurring in his jurisdiction when property has been destroyed or damaged.

(2) The fire officer shall:

(a) begin the investigation immediately after the occurrence of the fire; and

(b) attempt to determine, among other things, whether the fire was the result of carelessness or of design.

(3) If the fire officer making this investigation determines that the fire appears to be suspicious, or of unknown origin, the officer may notify the division to request assistance.   2001

53-7-211. Fire investigations by fire marshal.

(1) If the division is of the opinion that further investigation of a fire is necessary, the state fire marshal, his deputy, or representative may:

(a) join the investigation in cooperation with the fire officers who have been conducting it;

(b) upon the request of the chief fire official of the political subdivision, assume control of the investigation and direct it; or

(c) conduct an independent investigation if necessary.

(2) A fire officer who has conducted or is conducting the investigation shall cooperate in every possible way with the state fire marshal, his deputy, and representative to further the purpose of the investigation.

(3) The county attorney or district attorney of the county in which the fire occurred shall, upon the request of the state fire marshal, his deputy, or representative, assist in the investigation.   1993

53-7-212. Powers of fire marshal in respect to investigation.

In investigating any fire the state fire marshal and his deputy may:

(1) subpoena witnesses;

(2) compel their attendance and testimony; and

(3) require the production of books, papers, documents, records, and other tangible items that constitute or may contain evidence relevant to the investigation in the judgment of the state fire marshal or his deputy.   1993

53-7-213. Criminal charges resulting from investigation — Procedure.

If the state fire marshal, his deputy, or representative, or any other officer participating in the investigation of any fire believes that there is evidence sufficient to charge a person with arson, burning with intent to defraud or prejudice the insurer, or a similar crime, he shall furnish the county attorney or district attorney of the county in which the crime occurred with his evidence and request the county attorney or district attorney to commence the proper procedures to charge the person with the appropriate crime.
1993

53-7-214. Insurance company reports of fires.

(1) The state fire marshal, his deputy, and investigator may, in writing, require any insurance company transacting business in this state to release to the state fire marshal all relevant information or evidence found important by the state fire marshal, his deputy, and investigator that the company may have in its possession, relating to any fire loss in this state in which the company has an insuring interest. Relevant information includes:

(a) insurance policy information related to a fire loss under investigation and any application for the policy;

(b) available policy premium payment records;

(c) history of previous claims made by the insured; and

(d) material relating to the investigation of the loss, including statements of any person, proof of loss, and any other evidence related to the investigation.

(2) (a) Every insurance company transacting business in the state must file with the division a report of any fire of suspicious origin.

(b) The report shall show:

(i) the name of the insured;

(ii) the location of the property burned;

(iii) the probable cause of the fire;

(iv) the occupancy of the property burned;

(v) the construction of the building or structure burned;

(vi) the market value of the property involved;

(vii) the actual loss;

(viii) the insurance carried;

(ix) the insurance paid;

(x) the apportionment of loss where more than one company was on the risk; and

(xi) if a motor vehicle or building is involved in any fire loss, a description of the motor vehicle or building.

(c) In case of a fire of suspicious or incendiary origin, a preliminary report shall be made immediately through some officer or representative of the insurance company, showing:

(i) the name of the insured;

(ii) the date of the fire;

(iii) the location;

(iv) occupancy; and

(v) other facts and circumstances tending to establish the cause or origin of the fire.

(3) All persons making an adjustment occasioned by a loss due to a fire of suspicious or incendiary origin in this state shall, upon written request, send to the division a copy of the final adjustment immediately after the adjustment is made, signed by the person making the adjustment.

(4) Any insurance company or person acting in its behalf or any person making adjustments occasioned by a loss due to fire who releases information, whether oral or written, pursuant to Subsection (1), (2), or (3) is immune from any liability for the release of this information arising out of a civil action or penalty resulting from a criminal prosecution.   1993

53-7-215. Portable fire extinguishers — Persons not subject to part.

(1) The filling or charging of portable fire extinguishers prior to initial sale by the manufacturer is not subject to this part.

(2) Any firm that maintains its own fully equipped and specially staffed fire prevention, fire protection, and fire extinguisher servicing facilities is not subject to the licensing provisions of this part if it services only its own portable fire extinguishers.

(3) Individuals shall maintain a current certificate of registration.   1993

53-7-216. Portable fire extinguishers — Certification required to service.

(1) Each firm engaged in the business of servicing portable fire extinguishers or automatic fire suppression systems that automatically detect fire and discharge an approved fire extinguishing agent onto or in the area of the fire shall be certified by the state fire marshal.

(2) An application for certification shall be in writing, on forms prescribed by the board, and require evidence of competency.

(3) The board may establish a fee under Section 63-38-3.2 to be paid upon application for certification.

(4) This section does not apply to standpipe systems, deluge systems, or automatic fire sprinkler systems.   1995

53-7-217. Portable fire extinguishers — Permit required to perform hydrostatic testing.

Each firm performing hydrostatic testing of portable fire extinguishers shall:

(1) perform the tests in accordance with the specifications of the United States Department of Transportation for compressed gas cylinders; and

(2) obtain a permit from the division by applying in writing on forms provided by the division.
1993

53-7-218. Portable fire extinguishers — Sale or lease without approval prohibited.

A portable fire extinguisher may not be sold or leased in the state unless it is approved, labeled, or listed by a nationally recognized testing laboratory approved by the division as qualified to test portable fire extinguishers.   1993

53-7-219. Portable fire extinguishers — Hearings authorized.

The state fire marshal may conduct hearings or proceedings concerning the renewal, revocation, or refusal to issue permits.   1993

53-7-220. Short title.

Sections 53-7-220 through 53-7-225 are known as the "Utah Fireworks Act."   1993

53-7-221. Exceptions from Utah Fireworks Act.

(1) Sections 53-7-220 through 53-7-225 do not apply to class A, class B, and class C explosives that are not for use in Utah, but are manufactured, stored, warehoused, or in transit for destinations outside of Utah.

(2) Sections 53-7-220 through 53-7-225 do not supersede Section 23-13-7, regarding use of fireworks and explosives by the Division of Wildlife Resources and federal game agents. 1993

53-7-222. Restrictions on the sale or use of fireworks.

(1) (a) The division shall test and approve a representative sample of each class C common state approved explosive before the explosive may be sold to the public.

(b) The division shall publish a list of all class C explosives that are approved for sale to the public each year.

(2) (a) Except as provided in Subsection (b), class C dangerous explosives may not be possessed, discharged, sold, or offered for retail sale.

(b) (i) The following persons may purchase, possess, or discharge class C dangerous explosives:

(A) display operators who receive a license from the division in accordance with Section 53-7-223 and approval from their local licensing authority in accordance with Section 11-3-3.5; and

(B) operators approved by the Division of Wildlife Resources or Department of Agriculture and Food to discharge agricultural and wildlife fireworks.

(ii) Importers and wholesalers licensed under Section 53-7-224 may possess, sell, and offer to sell class C dangerous explosives.

(3) Unclassified fireworks may not be sold, or offered for sale. 1997

53-7-223. State license for display or special effects operators — Permit — Fee — Division duties — Revocation.

(1) A person may not purchase, possess, or discharge display or special effects fireworks unless the person has obtained a display or special effects operator license from the division.

(2) The division shall:

(a) issue an annual license to any display or special effects operator who:

(i) applies for the permit;

(ii) pays a $10 fee;

(iii) demonstrates proof of competence; and

(iv) certifies that he will comply with the rules governing placement and discharge of fireworks established by the board;

(b) provide the licensee with a copy of the rules governing placement and discharge of fireworks made under Section 53-7-204; and

(c) together with county and municipal officers enforce Sections 53-7-220 through 53-7-225.

(3) The division may:

(a) revoke a license issued under this section for cause;

(b) seize display and special effects fireworks, fireworks, and unclassified fireworks that are offered for sale, sold, or in the possession of an individual in violation of Sections 53-7-220 through 53-7-225; and

(c) create application and certification forms. 1995

53-7-224. Licensing importers and wholesalers — Fee.

The division shall:

(1) annually license each importer and wholesaler of pyrotechnic devices; and

(2) charge an annual license fee of $250. 1993

53-7-225. Times for sale and discharge of fireworks.

Class C common state approved explosives may be:

(1) sold:

(a) after June 19 and before July 26;

(b) after December 19 and before January 3; and

(c) 15 days before and on the Chinese New Year;

(2) discharged three days before, on the day of, and three days following:

(a) July 4;

(b) July 24;

(c) January 1; and

(d) the Chinese New Year. 1993

53-7-225.5. Inspection and testing of automatic fire sprinkler systems — Certification required.

(1) Each person engaged in the inspection and testing of automatic fire sprinkler systems shall be certified by the state fire marshal.

(2) The board shall by rule prescribe an application form and standards for certification qualification and for renewal and revocation.

(3) Applicants for certification as an automatic fire sprinkler system inspector and tester shall:

(a) submit a written application on the form prescribed by the board;

(b) provide evidence of competency as required by the board; and

(c) submit the fee established under Subsection (4).

(4) The board may establish an application fee under Section 63-38-3.2. 2003

53-7-226. Violations — Misdemeanor.

A person is guilty of a class B misdemeanor if he:

(1) violates this part;

(2) violates any order made under this part;

(3) produces, reproduces, or uses the official seal of registration of the division in any manner or for any purpose inconsistent with the rules of the board;

(4) removes, uses, or damages service tags or other labels or markings required by the board in a manner inconsistent with the rules of the board;

(5) engages in the sale, storage, or handling of class C fireworks without a permit where a local government requires a permit;

(6) sells at retail, transports, or discharges fireworks that are not approved under rules made by the board;

(7) performs or intends to perform services or induces the public to enter into any obligation relating to the performance of those services that are untrue, misleading, or reasonably known to be untrue or misleading; or

(8) builds in violation of the division's plan review or written instructions conducted on

building specifications, building plans, or amendments of those specifications or plans as required under this part.   1993

PART 3

LIQUEFIED PETROLEUM GAS

53-7-301. Short title.

This part is known as the "Liquefied Petroleum Gas Act."   1993

53-7-302. Definitions.

As used in this part:

(1) "Board" means the Liquefied Petroleum Gas Board created in Section 53-7-304.

(2) "Container" means any vessel, including cylinders, tanks, portable tanks, and cargo tanks used for transporting or storing liquefied petroleum gases, except containers subject to regulation and inspection by the Department of Transportation and under federal laws or regulations.

(3) "Distributor" means any person engaged in the distribution of liquefied petroleum gas, either wholesale or retail, including a commercial carrier, as identified by the Department of Transportation or the Interstate Commerce Commission, who transports or hauls liquefied petroleum gas that is to be distributed or sold within this state.

(4) "Enforcing authority" means the division, the municipal or county fire department, another fire-prevention agency acting within its jurisdiction, or the building official of any city or county and his authorized representatives.

(5) "Gas appliance" means any device that uses liquefied petroleum gas to produce light, heat, power, steam, hot water, refrigeration, or air conditioning.

(6) "Installer" means any person who has satisfactorily passed an examination under the supervision of the board, testing his knowledge and ability to install or properly repair domestic systems, industrial systems, liquefied petroleum gas carburetion systems, bulk plant systems, standby plant systems, or other similar systems, and who holds an installer's certificate under this part.

(7) "Licensee" means a person licensed by the board to engage in the liquefied petroleum gas business.

(8) "Liquefied petroleum gas" means any material having a vapor pressure not exceeding that allowed for commercial propane and composed predominantly of the following hydrocarbons, either by themselves or as mixtures: propane, propylene, butane, normal butane, or isobutane, and butylene, including isomers.

(9) "Liquefied petroleum gas carburetion system" means any carburetion system using liquefied petroleum gas as a fuel in a motor vehicle.

(10) "Liquefied petroleum gas fueling system" means an assembly consisting of compressors, containers, piping, and other delivery devices for the purpose of dispensing liquefied petroleum gas for use as a fuel in a motor vehicle.

(11) "LPG" means liquefied petroleum gas.

(12) "Person" means any individual, firm, partnership, joint venture, association, corporation, estate, trust, or any other group or combination acting as a unit, and includes:

(a) a husband, wife, or both where joint benefits are derived from the operation of a business or activity subject to this part; and

(b) any state, county, municipality, or other agency engaged in a business or activity subject to this part.

(13) "Red tag" means a card or device, red in color, containing printed notice of the condemnation of a liquefied petroleum gas system as a result of a violation of this part, or any rules or orders made by the board; the tag, when attached to the system, is official notice of condemnation and of the prohibition of further use, so long as the red tag remains lawfully affixed.

(14) "System" means an assembly consisting of one or more containers with a means for conveying LPG from the container or containers to dispensing or consuming devices, either continuously or intermittently, and that incorporates components intended to achieve control of quantity, flow, and pressure or state, either liquid or vapor.   1994

53-7-303. Exclusions from part.

This part does not apply to any of the following:

(1) the production, refining, or manufacture of LPG;

(2) the storage, sale, or transportation of LPG by pipeline or railroad tank car by a pipeline company, producer, refiner, or manufacturer;

(3) equipment used by a pipeline company, producer, refiner, or manufacturer in a producing, refining, or manufacturing process or in the storage, sale, or transportation by pipeline or railroad tank car;

(4) any deliveries of LPG to another person at the place of production, refining, or manufacturing;

(5) underground storage facilities other than LPG containers designed for underground use;

(6) refineries, pipeline terminals, or natural gas processing plants.   1993

53-7-304. Liquefied Petroleum Gas Board — Creation — Composition — Appointment — Terms of officers — Meetings — Compensation.

(1) (a) There is created within the division the Liquefied Petroleum Gas Board.

(b) The board is composed of seven members:

(i) two Utah fire chiefs or marshals;

(ii) two members of the general public; and

(iii) three members who are representatives of the LPG industry.

(2) The fire chiefs or marshals and the members of the general public shall be appointed by the governor, on a nonpartisan basis.

(3) Members of the board who are representatives of the LPG industry shall have been legal residents of the state for at least one year immediately preceding the date of appointment and have been actively engaged in the LPG industry for a period of at least five years.

(4) The LPG industry representatives shall be appointed by the governor from a list of at least five but no more than the 12 nominees receiving the largest number of votes according to written ballots executed by representatives of the licensees under Subsection (7).

(5) (a) Except as required by Subsection (5)(b), as terms of current board members expire, the governor shall appoint each new member or reappointed member to a four-year term.

(b) Notwithstanding the requirements of Subsection (5)(a), the governor shall, at the time of appointment or reappointment, adjust the length of terms to ensure that the terms of board members are staggered so that approximately half of the board is appointed every two years.

(c) Members serve from the date of appointment until a replacement is appointed.

(6) When a vacancy occurs in the membership for any reason, the replacement shall be appointed for the unexpired term.

(7) (a) The balloting of licensees shall be conducted by the division.

(b) For the appointments, the division shall forward to each licensee by registered or certified United States mail an official ballot for each staffed plant or facility held under Section 53-7-309, with instructions for executing the ballot and returning it to the division.

(8) (a) The board shall elect its own chair and vice chair at its first regular meeting each calendar year.

(b) All meetings of the board shall be held on a prescribed date, at least quarterly, and at any time a majority of the board members sends a request to the board chair.

(c) A majority of the members of the board is a quorum for the transaction of business.

(9) (a) (i) Members who are not government employees shall receive no compensation or benefits for their services, but may receive per diem and expenses incurred in the performance of the member's official duties at the rates established by the Division of Finance under Sections 63A-3-106 and 63A-3-107.

(ii) Members may decline to receive per diem and expenses for their service.

(b) (i) State government officer and employee members who do not receive salary, per diem, or expenses from their agency for their service may receive per diem and expenses incurred in the performance of their official duties from the board at the rates established by the Division of Finance under Sections 63A-3-106 and 63A-3-107.

(ii) State government officer and employee members may decline to receive per diem and expenses for their service. 2001

53-7-305. Board rulemaking — Notice.

(1) (a) The board shall make rules as reasonably necessary for the protection of the health, welfare, and safety of the public and persons using LPG.

(b) The rules shall be in substantial conformity with the generally accepted standards of safety concerning LPG, and shall include the following conditions:

(i) the rules relating to safety in the storage, distribution, dispensing, transporting, and use of LPG in this state and in the manufacture, fabrication, assembly, sale, installation, and use of LPG systems, containers, apparatus, or appliances shall be reasonable; and

(ii) the rules shall conform as nearly as possible to the standards of the National Fire Protection Association, relating to the design, construction, installation, and use of systems, containers, apparatus, appliances, and pertinent equipment for the storage, transportation, dispensation, and use of LPG.

(2) The board may make rules:

(a) setting minimum general standards covering the design, construction, location, installation, and operation of equipment for storing, handling, transporting by tank truck or tank trailer, or using LPG;

(b) specifying the odorization of the gases and the degree of odorization;

(c) governing LPG distributors and installers and the installation of LPG systems, carburetion systems, and fueling systems; and

(d) prescribing maximum container removal rates.

(3) (a) When a proposed rule is filed, the board shall give at least ten days' notice to all license applicants and licensees under this chapter by sending a notice of the proposed new, revised, or amended rule together with a notice of hearing to the licensee's current address on file with the board.

(b) Any person affected by rulemaking under this part may submit comment, in a format prescribed by the board, on the rule.

(c) A certificate citing the adoption and the effective date of a rule shall be signed by the members comprising a majority of the board.

(d) Within ten days after the adoption of the rule, the board shall send to each license applicant or licensee, at his current address on file, a notice of the adoption of the rule, including its effective date.

(e) A facsimile of any member's signature may be used under this section if authorized by the member. 2001

53-7-306. Duties and powers of the board — Fee setting.

(1) The board shall monitor rates charged in the industry for container removal.

(2) The board may:

(a) set civil penalties for violation of any rule or order made under this part;

(b) in conducting hearings on the issuance or revocation of any license:

(i) compel the attendance of witnesses by subpoena;

(ii) require the production of any records or documents determined by it to be pertinent to the subject matter of the hearing; and

(iii) apply to the district court of the county where the hearing is held for an order citing any applicant or witness for contempt, and for failure to attend, testify, or produce required documents;

(c) suspend or revoke licenses and refuse renewals of licenses if the applicant or licensee has been guilty of conduct harmful to either the safety or protection of the public;

(d) adopt bylaws for its procedures and methods of operation; and

(e) at the request of the enforcing authority, grant exceptions from its rules to accommodate local needs as it determines to be in the best interest of public safety or the persons using LPG materials or services.

(3) The board shall, in accordance with Section 53-7-314, establish fees to cover the cost of administering this section. 1993

53-7-307. Duties of the division.

The division shall:

(1) prescribe the method and form to apply for a LPG license, with the approval of the board;

(2) investigate the experience, reputation, and background of applicants;

(3) recommend to the board issuing, suspending, revoking, and denying licenses;

(4) assist the board in conducting hearings in connection with the applications for, or revocation of, licenses;

(5) submit to the governor a biennial report before September 1 of each even-numbered year, covering the board's transactions during the biennium ending June 30 of that year, including a complete statement of the receipts and expenditures of the board during that period;

(6) keep accurate records and minutes of all meetings, which shall be open to public inspection at all reasonable times, and keep a public record of all applications for licenses and licenses issued by the board;

(7) conduct examinations of every license applicant to determine the responsibility, ability, knowledge, experience, or other qualifications of the applicant for a license;

(8) require competency testing for all employees and subcontractors of licensees engaged in transporting or dispensing LPG or installing, servicing, or repairing an LPG fueling or carburetion system under this part;

(9) prepare applications, collect fees, and issue licenses for any facility that handles LPG;

(10) provide for or direct the inspection of the site of any facility that stores, dispenses, services, or handles LPG;

(11) provide inspections to any facility where a qualified authority does not exist; and

(12) prepare and administer examinations, collect fees, and issue LPG certificates to personnel who handle or work with LPG.   1993

53-7-308. Licenses and certificates.

A person may not engage in any of the following activities related to LPG unless he has obtained an authorizing license or certification from the board:

(1) container activities: the manufacture, assembly, repair, sale, installation, or subframing of containers for use in this state, except that a license is not required for the sale of new containers of 96 pounds water capacity or less;

(2) systems activities: the installation, service, or repair of LPG systems for use in this state, including the laying or connecting of pipes and fittings connecting with or to systems or servicing a system and appliances to be used with LPG as a fuel;

(3) appliance activities: the service, installation, or repair of appliances used or to be used in this state in connection with systems using LPG as a fuel; or

(4) product activities: the sale, transportation, dispensation, or storage of LPG in this state, except that a license is not required to sell LPG where the vendor never obtains possessory rights to the product sold or where the product is transported or stored by the ultimate consumer for personal consumption only.   1993

53-7-309. Classification of applicants and licensees.

(1) To administer this part, the board shall classify all applicants and licensees as follows:

(a) Class 1: a licensed dealer who:

(i) is engaged in the business of installing gas appliances or systems for the use of LPG;

(ii) sells, fills, refills, delivers, or is permitted to deliver any LPG; or

(iii) is involved under both Subsection (i) and (ii).

(b) Class 2: a business engaged in the sale, transportation, and exchange of cylinders, or engaged in more than one of these, but not transporting or transferring gas in liquid.

(c) Class 3: a business not engaged in the sale of LPG, but engaged in the sale and installation of gas appliances or LPG systems.

(d) Class 4: those businesses not specifically within classification 1, 2, or 3 may at the discretion of the board be issued special licenses.

(2) (a) Any license granted under this section entitles the licensee to operate a staffed plant or facility consistent with the license at one location, which is stated in the license, under Section 53-7-310.

(b) For each additional staffed plant or facility owned or operated by the licensee, the licensee shall register the additional location with the board and pay an additional annual fee, to be set in accordance with Section 53-7-314.   1993

53-7-310. License specifications and limits.

(1) (a) A license issued under this part shall state the name of the person or persons to whom it is issued.

(b) The license shall specify the location, by street and number, of the premises for which it is issued and the particular classification of the license authorizing the type of staffed plant or facility to be conducted.

(c) The registration of additional staffed plants or facilities, under Subsection 53-7-309(2), shall specify the location, by street and number, of the premises for which it is issued and the particular classification of the license authorizing the type of business to be conducted.

(2) (a) Any license issued under this part is not transferable by the licensee or licensees to any other person, firm, association, partnership, or corporation, and is valid only for the particular premises and particular persons described on the license.

(b) If there is any transfer or change in the ownership, the change shall be reported to the board within 30 days.

(c) A license or registration fee paid under this part may not be refunded when any license issued is no longer valid because of:

(i) a voluntary transfer of any nature;

(ii) revocation under this part;

(iii) death of the holder;

(iv) insolvency;

(v) assignment for the benefit of creditors; or

(vi) for any other reason determined by rule of the board.   1993

53-7-311. Certification of licensees for certain activities.

(1) A person that transports or dispenses LPG or that installs, repairs, or services appliances, containers, equipment, systems, or piping for the use of LPG shall be certified by the division by passing an appropriate examination based on the safety requirements of the board.

(2) (a) A trainee employee is exempt from this examination for 45 working days, and until examined by a representative of the board. A trainee employee, during the 45-day period, shall be supervised by a qualified instructor.

(b) Any LPG licensee hiring a trainee shall, within 20 days of the commencement of employment, notify the board, so that an examination may be scheduled. If the trainee fails to pass the examination, the trainee may retake it after additional instruction. Prior to retaking the exam, the trainee shall again be supervised by a qualified instructor.

(3) (a) The board shall establish a reasonable fee in accordance with Section 53-7-314 to cover the costs of administering the examination.

(b) All examinations shall be administered by the division.   1993

53-7-312. Division approval of certain storage system plans — Procedure.

(1) (a) The complete plans and specifications for all systems involving the storage of more than 5,000 water gallons of LPG shall be submitted to the division by a person licensed under this part, and receive approval by the division before installation is started. The plans shall be drawn to scale and contain sufficient detail and clarity as necessary to indicate the nature and character of the proposed system and its compliance with this part.

(b) Two copies of the plans shall be submitted to the division and one copy shall be returned to the applicant with approval or disapproval indicated on it.

(2) (a) For dispensing systems for 5,000 water gallons or less of LPG, a detailed sketch or plan shall be submitted to the division by a person licensed under this part, and receive approval by the division before installation is started.

(b) Two copies of the plans shall be submitted to the division and one copy shall be returned to the applicant with approval or disapproval indicated on it.   1995

53-7-313. Removal of LPG containers — Reasonableness of rates.

(1) Rates charged for removal of leased LPG containers shall be reasonable.

(2) The lessor of an LPG container shall credit the lessee's account the current retail price for the amount of LPG remaining in the leased container at the time the container is removed.   1993

53-7-314. Fees — Setting — Deposit — Use.

(1) The board shall establish fees authorized in this part in accordance with the procedures specified in Section 63-38-3.2, but the fees shall be deposited as provided in Subsection (2).

(2) Fees collected by the division under this part, shall be deposited with the state treasurer as a nonlapsing dedicated credit, to be used for the implementation of this part.   1995

53-7-315. Enforcement of part and rules.

(1) Except as provided in Subsection (6), this part, the rules made under it, and orders issued by the board are enforced by:

(a) the enforcing authority, unless otherwise provided by the board; and

(b) the board.

(2) (a) A person who knowingly violates or fails to comply with this part is guilty of a class B misdemeanor and is punishable by a fine of not less than $50 nor more than $500.

(b) A person previously convicted under Subsection (a) who knowingly violates or fails to comply with this part is guilty of a class B

misdemeanor and is punishable by a fine of not less than $200 nor more than $2,000.

(c) Each day the violation or failure to comply continues constitutes a separate offense.

(3) The enforcing authority may enter the premises of a licensee under this part, or any building or other premises open to the public, at any reasonable time, for the purpose of determining and verifying compliance with this part and the rules and orders of the board.

(4) An enforcing authority may declare any container, appliance, equipment, transport, or system that does not conform to the safety requirements of this part or the rules or orders of the board, or that is otherwise defective, as unsafe or dangerous for LPG service, and shall attach a red tag in a conspicuous location.

(5) (a) A person who knowingly sells, furnishes, delivers, or supplies LPG for storage in, or use or consumption by, or through, a container, appliance, transport, or system to which a red tag is attached is guilty of a class B misdemeanor punishable by a fine of not less than $100 and not more than $2,000.

(b) Liquefied petroleum gas shall be removed from a container to which a red tag is attached only as provided by rules made by the board.

(c) An unauthorized person who knowingly removes, destroys, or in any way obliterates a red tag attached to a container, appliance, transport, or system is guilty of a class B misdemeanor punishable by a fine of not less than $50 and not more than $2,000.

(d) The enforcing authority may establish and collect a fee for any services or inspections required by this part, the rules made under it, and orders issued by the board. The fee shall be reasonable and may not exceed the amount of the cost of service or inspection provided. Fees collected under this subsection may be retained by the enforcing authority, and shall be applied to the expenses of providing these services.

(6) (a) Except as provided in Subsection (c), a person who fills a leased container in violation of the terms of a written lease is liable in an action by the container lessor for the greater of:

(i) the actual damages to the container lessor, including incidental and consequential damages and attorneys' fees; or

(ii) $500 for each violation.

(b) (i) The burden of ascertaining the terms of a written lease for purposes of Subsection (a) is on the person filling the container.

(ii) A person has ascertained the terms of a written lease if he has:

(A) read the lease;

(B) received the assurance of the container owner that the lease does not prohibit the person from filling the container;

(C) obtained a signed, written statement from the lessee that the written lease does not prohibit the person from filling the container; or

(D) the leased container is clearly labelled as a container subject to lease terms prohibiting the filling of the container without the lessor's permission.

(c) If a lessee or lessor misrepresents his ownership or the terms of his written lease under Subsection (b), the lessee or lessor who made the misrepresentation, and not the person filling the tank, is liable for the damages under Subsection (a).

(7) If a written container lease entered into after May 1, 1992, restricts the right to fill a leased container, the restriction shall be plainly stated in the lease in any manner designed to draw the attention of the lessee to the lease provision, including:

(a) typing the restriction in at least two point larger type than the majority of the document type;

(b) underlining the restriction; or

(c) typing the restriction in boldface type.

(8) A lessor whose container lease does not comply with Subsection (7) is disqualified from protection under Subsection (6).   1993

53-7-316. Effect of part on state and local provision.

(1) This part supersedes all other conflicting state laws or rules concerning LPG as regulated under this part.

(2) A municipality or other political subdivision may not adopt or enforce any ordinance or rule in conflict with this part, or with the rules made under this part.   1993

CHAPTER 8

UTAH HIGHWAY PATROL

Part 1

Utah Highway Patrol Division Administration

Part 2

Motor Vehicle Safety Inspection

PART 1

UTAH HIGHWAY PATROL DIVISION ADMINISTRATION

53-8-101. Short title.

This chapter is known as the "Utah Highway Patrol Act."   1993

53-8-102. Definitions.

As used in this chapter:

(1) "Division" means the Utah Highway Patrol Division created in Section 53-8-103.

(2) "Highway Patrol" means the Highway Patrol troopers employed under Section 53-8-104.

(3) "Superintendent" means the director of the division, appointed under Section 53-8-103.   1993

53-8-103. Utah Highway Patrol Division — Creation — Appointment of superintendent — Powers — Qualifications — Term — Compensation.

(1) There is created the Utah Highway Patrol Division.

(2) The director of the division shall be the superintendent appointed by the commissioner with the approval of the governor.

(3) The superintendent is the executive and administrative head of the division and shall be experienced in administration and possess additional qualifications as determined by the commissioner.

(4) The superintendent acts under the supervision and control of the commissioner and may be removed from his position at the will of the commissioner.

(5) The superintendent shall receive compensation as provided by Title 67, Chapter 19, Utah State Personnel Management Act.   1993

53-8-104. Superintendent's duties.

The superintendent shall:

(1) divide the state highways into sections for the purpose of patrolling and policing;

(2) employ peace officers known as highway patrol troopers to patrol or police the highways within this state and to enforce the state statutes as required;

(3) establish ranks, grades, and positions in the Highway Patrol and designate the authority and responsibility in each rank, grade, and position;

(4) establish for the Highway Patrol standards and qualifications and fix prerequisites of training, education, and experience for each rank, grade, and position;

(5) appoint personnel to each rank, grade, and position necessary for the efficient operation and administration of the Highway Patrol;

(6) devise and administer examinations designed to test applicants for positions with the Highway Patrol;

(7) make rules governing the Highway Patrol as appear to the superintendent advisable;

(8) discharge, demote, or temporarily suspend any employee in the Highway Patrol for cause;

(9) prescribe the uniforms to be worn and the equipment to be used by employees of the Highway Patrol;

(10) charge against each employee of the Highway Patrol the value of any property of the state lost or destroyed through the carelessness of the employee;

(11) establish, with the approval of the Division of Finance, the terms and conditions under which expense allowance should be paid to any employee of the Highway Patrol while away from his station;

(12) station the Highway Patrol in localities as he finds advisable for the enforcement of the laws of this state;

(13) conduct in conjunction with the State Board of Education in and through all state schools an educational campaign in highway safety and work in conjunction with civic organizations, churches, local units of government, and other organizations that may function in accomplishing the purposes of reducing highway accidents;

(14) provide the initial mandatory uniform items for each new trooper hired after July 1, 1998;

(15) determine by rule a basic uniform allowance system which includes the manner in which troopers may receive maintenance services and vouchers for basic uniforms and administer any funds appropriated by the Legislature to the division for that purpose; and

(16) on or before January 1, 2003, adopt a written policy that prohibits the stopping, detention, or search of any person when the action is solely motivated by considerations of race, color, ethnicity, age, or gender.   2002

53-8-105. Duties of Highway Patrol.

In addition to the duties in this chapter, the Highway Patrol shall:

(1) enforce the state laws and rules governing use of the state highways;

(2) regulate traffic on all highways and roads of the state;

(3) assist the governor in an emergency or at other times at his discretion;

(4) in cooperation with federal, state, and local agencies, enforce and assist in the enforcement of all state and federal laws related to the operation of a motor carrier on a highway, including all state and federal rules and regulations;

(5) inspect certain vehicles to determine road worthiness and safe condition as provided in Section 41-6a-1630;

(6) upon request, assist with any condition of unrest existing or developing on a campus or related facility of an institution of higher education;

(7) assist the Alcoholic Beverage Control Commission in an emergency to enforce the state liquor laws;

(8) provide security and protection for both houses of the Legislature while in session as the speaker of the House of Representatives and the president of the Senate finds necessary; and

(9) carry out the following for the Supreme Court and the Court of Appeals:

(a) provide security and protection to those courts when in session in the capital city of the state;

(b) execute orders issued by the courts; and

(c) carry out duties as directed by the courts.   2005

53-8-106. Vested with powers of peace officers.

(1) The commissioner, superintendent, and each member of the Highway Patrol have the powers of peace officers in each county of the state with the exception of the power to serve civil process.

(2) They may serve criminal process, arrest and prosecute violators of any law of this state, and have the same right as other peace officers to require aid in executing their duties.

(3) The powers and duties conferred upon the superintendent and members of the Highway Patrol are supplementary to and not a limitation on the powers and duties of other peace officers in the state.   1993

53-8-107. Cooperation with other officers.

To secure information in order to achieve greater success in prevention and detection of crime and apprehension of criminals, the Highway Patrol shall cooperate and exchange information with:

(1) any other departments of the state;

(2) other law enforcement agencies, both within and outside this state; and

(3) federal law enforcement agencies.   1993

PART 2

MOTOR VEHICLE SAFETY INSPECTION

53-8-201. Short title.

This part is known as the "Motor Vehicle Safety Inspection Act."   1993

53-8-202. Definitions.

(1) The definitions in Section 41-6a-102 apply to this part.

(2) As used in this part, "council" means the Motor Vehicle Safety Inspection Advisory Council created in Section 53-8-203.   2005

53-8-203. Council created — Members — Term — Meetings — Duties.

(1) There is created within the division the Motor Vehicle Safety Inspection Advisory Council.

(2) (a) The council shall be composed of seven members.

(b) The governor shall appoint:

(i) one representative from the Department of Commerce with experience in consumer protection administration;

(ii) two representatives from motor vehicle mechanics and motor vehicle repair business owners;

(iii) one member of the motoring public with no former or current affiliation with the motor vehicle sales, repair, or fuel industry or its regulation;

(iv) one peace officer with experience in motor vehicle law enforcement;

(v) one representative of the commercial trucking industry; and

(vi) one representative of the staff of the attorney general who shall serve without voting privileges.

(3) Each member of the council shall:

(a) be selected on a nonpartisan basis;

(b) be appointed by the governor; and

(c) have been a legal resident of the state for at least one year immediately preceding the date of appointment.

(4) (a) Except as required by Subsection (b), as terms of current council members expire, the governor shall appoint each new member or reappointed member to a four-year term.

(b) Notwithstanding the requirements of Subsection (a), the governor shall, at the time of appointment or reappointment, adjust the length of terms to ensure that the terms of council members are staggered so that approximately half of the council is appointed every two years.

(c) Members serve from the date of appointment until a replacement is appointed.

(5) When a vacancy occurs in the membership for any reason, the replacement shall be appointed for the unexpired term.

(6) The council shall elect its own chair and vice-chair at its first regular meeting each calendar year.

(7) All meetings of the council shall be called by the superintendent of the highway patrol as needed.

(8) Any three voting members constitute a quorum for the transaction of business that comes before the council.

(9) (a) (i) Members who are not government employees shall receive no compensation or benefits for their services, but may receive per diem and expenses incurred in the performance of the member's official duties at the rates established by the Division of Finance under Sections 63A-3-106 and 63A-3-107.

(ii) Members may decline to receive per diem and expenses for their service.

(b) (i) State government officer and employee members who do not receive salary, per diem, or expenses from their agency for their service may receive per diem and expenses incurred in the performance of their official duties from the council at the rates established by the Division of Finance under Sections 63A-3-106 and 63A-3-107.

(ii) State government officer and employee members may decline to receive per diem and expenses for their service.

(10) The council shall:

(a) hear appeals of administrative actions regarding the suspension or revocation of safety inspection station permits and safety inspector certificates;

(b) advise the division on interpretation, adoption, and implementation of motor vehicle safety inspection standards; and

(c) advise the division on other motor vehicle safety inspection issues as requested by the superintendent.

(11) In conducting appeal hearings on the suspension or revocation of any safety inspection station permit or safety inspector certificate the council may:

(a) compel the attendance of witnesses by subpoena;

(b) require the production of any records or documents determined by it to be pertinent to the subject matter of the hearing; and

(c) apply to the district court of the county where the hearing is held for an order citing any applicant or witness for contempt and for failure to attend, testify, or produce required documents.

1996

53-8-204. Division duties — Official inspection stations — Permits — Fees — Suspension or revocation — Utah-based interstate commercial motor carriers.

(1) The division shall:

(a) conduct examinations of every safety inspection station permit applicant and safety inspector certificate applicant to determine whether the applicant is properly equipped and qualified to make safety inspections;

(b) issue safety inspection station permits and safety inspector certificates to qualified applicants;

(c) establish application, renewal, and reapplication fees in accordance with Section 63-38-3.2 for safety inspection station permits and safety inspector certificates;

(d) provide instructions and all necessary forms, including safety inspection certificates, to safety inspection stations for the inspection of motor vehicles and the issuance of the safety inspection certificates;

(e) charge a $2 fee for each safety inspection certificate;

(f) investigate complaints regarding safety inspection stations and safety inspectors;

(g) compile and publish all applicable safety inspection laws, rules, instructions, and standards and distribute them to all safety inspection stations and provide updates to the compiled laws, rules, instructions, and standards as needed;

(h) establish a fee in accordance with Section 63-38-3.2 to cover the cost of compiling and publishing the safety inspection laws, rules, instructions, and standards and any updates; and

(i) assist the council in conducting its meetings and hearings.

(2) (a) (i) Receipts from the fees established in accordance with Subsection (1)(h) are fixed collections to be used by the division for the expenses of the Utah Highway Patrol incurred under Subsection (1)(h).

(ii) Funds received in excess of the expenses under Subsection (1)(h) shall be deposited in the Transportation Fund.

(b) (i) The first $.75 of the fee under Subsection (1)(e) is a dedicated credit to be used solely by the Utah Highway Patrol for the expenses of administering this section.

(ii) The remaining funds collected under Subsection (1)(e) shall be deposited in the Transportation Fund.

(iii) The dedicated credits described under Subsection (2)(b)(i) are in addition to any other appropriations provided to administer the safety inspection program duties under this section.

(3) The division may:

(a) before issuing a safety inspection permit, require an applicant, other than a fleet station or government station, to file a bond that will provide a guarantee that the applicant safety inspection station will make compensation for any damage to a motor vehicle during an inspection or adjustment due to negligence on the part of an applicant or his employees;

(b) establish procedures governing the issuance of safety inspection certificates to Utah-based interstate commercial motor carriers; and

(c) suspend, revoke, or refuse renewal of any safety inspection station permit issued when the division finds that the safety inspection station is not:

(i) properly equipped; or

(ii) complying with rules made by the division; and

(d) suspend, revoke, or refuse renewal of any safety inspection station permit or safety inspector certificate issued when the station or inspector has violated any safety inspection law or rule.

(4) The division shall maintain a record of safety inspection station permits and safety inspector certificates issued, suspended, revoked, or refused renewal under Subsection (3)(c).

(5) In accordance with Title 63, Chapter 46a, Utah Administrative Rulemaking Act, the division shall make rules:

(a) setting minimum standards covering the design, construction, condition, and operation of motor vehicle equipment for safely operating a motor vehicle on the highway;

(b) establishing motor vehicle safety inspection procedures to ensure a motor vehicle can be operated safely;

(c) establishing safety inspection station building, equipment, and personnel requirements necessary to qualify to perform safety inspections;

(d) establishing age, training, examination, and renewal requirements to qualify for a safety inspector certificate;

(e) establishing program guidelines for a school district that elects to implement a safety inspection apprenticeship program for high school students;

(f) establishing requirements:

(i) designed to protect consumers from unwanted or unneeded repairs or adjustments;

(ii) for maintaining safety inspection records;

(iii) for providing reports to the division; and

(iv) for maintaining and protecting safety inspection certificates;

(g) establishing procedures for a motor vehicle that fails a safety inspection;

(h) setting bonding amounts for safety inspection stations if bonds are required under Subsection (3)(a); and

(i) establishing procedures for a safety inspection station to follow if the station is going out of business.

(6) The rules of the division:

(a) shall conform as nearly as practical to federal motor vehicle safety standards including 49 CFR 393, 396, 396 Appendix G, and Federal Motor Vehicle Safety Standards 205; and

(b) may incorporate by reference, in whole or in part, the federal standards under Subsection (6)(a) and nationally recognized and readily available standards and codes on motor vehicle safety.

2002

53-8-205.   **Safety inspection required — Frequency of safety inspection — Safety inspection certificate required — Out-of-state permits.**

(1) (a) Except as provided in Subsection (1)(b), a person may not operate on a highway a motor vehicle required to be registered in this state unless the motor vehicle has passed a safety inspection.

(b) Subsection (1)(a) does not apply to:

(i) vehicles exempt from registration under Section 41-1a-205; and

(ii) off-highway vehicles.

(2) Except as provided in Subsection (3), the frequency of the safety inspection shall be determined based on the age of the vehicle determined by model year and shall:

(a) be required each year for a vehicle that is eight or more years old on January 1; or

(b) every two years for each vehicle that is less than eight years old on January 1 as follows:

(i) in odd-numbered years for a vehicle with an odd-numbered model year; and

(ii) in even-numbered years for a vehicle with an even-numbered model year;

(c) be made by a safety inspector certified by the division at a safety inspection station authorized by the division;

(d) cover an inspection of the motor vehicle mechanism, brakes, and equipment to ensure proper adjustment and condition as required by department rules; and

(e) include an inspection for the display of license plates in accordance with Section 41-1a-404.

(3) (a) A salvage vehicle as defined in Section 41-1a-1001 is required to pass a safety inspection when an application is made for initial registration as a salvage vehicle.

(b) After initial registration as a salvage vehicle, the frequency of the safety inspection shall correspond with the model year, as provided in Subsection (2).

(4) A safety inspection station shall issue a safety inspection certificate to the owner of each motor vehicle that passes a safety inspection under this section.

(5) The division may:

(a) authorize the acceptance in this state of a safety inspection certificate issued in another state having a safety inspection law similar to this state; and

(b) extend the time within which a safety inspection certificate must be obtained by the resident owner of a vehicle that was not in this state during the time a safety inspection was required.

2003

53-8-206.   **Safety inspection — Station requirements — Permits not transferable — Certificate of inspection — Fees — Unused certificates — Suspension or revocation of permits.**

(1) The safety inspection required under Section 53-8-205 may only be performed:

(a) by a person certified by the division as a safety inspector; and

(b) at a safety inspection station with a valid safety inspection station permit issued by the division.

(2) A safety inspection station permit may not be assigned or transferred or used at any location other than a designated location, and every safety inspection station permit shall be posted in a conspicuous place at the location designated.

(3) If required by the division, a record and report shall be made of every safety inspection and every safety inspection certificate issued.

(4) A safety inspection station holding a safety inspection station permit issued by the division may charge:

(a) a fee as reimbursement for the safety inspection certificate fee as specified in Subsection 53-8-204(1)(e); and

(b) a reasonable fee for labor in performing safety inspections, not to exceed:

(i) $7 or less for motorcycles;

(ii) unless Subsection (4)(b)(i) or (iii) applies, $15 or less for motor vehicles; or

(iii) $20 or less for 4-wheel drive, split axle, and any motor vehicles that necessitate disassembly of front hub or removal of rear axle for inspection.

(5) A safety inspection station may return unused safety inspection certificates in a quantity of ten or more and shall be reimbursed by the division for the cost of the safety inspection certificates.

(6) (a) Upon receiving notice of the suspension or revocation of a safety inspection station permit, the safety inspection station permit holder shall immediately terminate all safety inspection activities and return all safety inspection certificates and the safety inspection station permit to the division.

(b) The division shall issue a receipt for all unused safety inspection certificates.   2002

53-8-207. Falsely representing to be official station or safety inspector.

(1) A person may not in any manner represent any place as a safety inspection station unless the station is operating under a valid permit issued by the division.

(2) A person may not issue a safety inspection certificate unless the person:

(a) is a safety inspector certified by the division;

(b) is operating under a valid safety inspection station permit issued by the division; and

(c) performs the safety inspection on the motor vehicle in compliance with Section 53-8-205.

(3) An unauthorized person may not knowingly possess safety inspection certificates.   1993

53-8-208. Counterfeit certificates of inspection.

(1) A person may not make, issue, or knowingly use any imitation or counterfeit of a safety inspection certificate.

(2) A person may not present or cause or permit to be presented any safety inspection certificate knowing the certificate to be fictitious, issued for another motor vehicle, or issued without a safety inspection having been made and passed.   1993

53-8-209. Inspection by officers — Certificate of inspection.

(1) A peace officer may stop, inspect, and test a vehicle at any time upon reasonable cause to believe that:

(a) a vehicle is unsafe or not equipped as required by law; or

(b) that its equipment is not in proper adjustment or repair.

(2) (a) (i) If a vehicle is found to be in unsafe condition or any required part or equipment is not present or is not in proper repair and adjustment, the officer shall give a written notice to the driver and shall send a copy to the division.

(ii) The notice shall:

(A) require that the vehicle be placed in safe condition and its equipment in proper repair and adjustment;

(B) specify the repairs and adjustments needed; and

(C) require that a safety inspection certificate be obtained within five days.

(b) If a vehicle is, in the reasonable judgment of the peace officer, hazardous to operate, the peace officer may require that the vehicle:

(i) not be operated under its own power; or

(ii) be driven to the nearest garage or other place of safety.

(c) If the owner or driver does not comply with the notice requirements and secure a safety inspection certificate within five days, the vehicle may not be operated on the highways of this state.   1993

53-8-210. Enforcement of inspection requirements.

(1) A person operating a vehicle shall submit the vehicle to a safety inspection when required to do so by a peace officer.

(2) (a) An owner or driver, upon receiving a notice as provided in Section 53-8-209, shall within five days secure a safety inspection certificate, which shall be issued in duplicate, one copy to be retained by the owner or driver and the other copy to be forwarded to the division.

(b) In lieu of compliance with this subsection, the vehicle may not be operated, except as provided in Subsection (3).

(3) (a) A person may not operate any vehicle after receiving a notice from a peace officer that the vehicle is in need of repair or adjustment, except that a peace officer may allow the vehicle to be driven to the residence or place of business of the owner or driver or to the nearest garage where repairs are available if driving the vehicle is not excessively dangerous.

(b) The vehicle may not be operated again on the highways until its equipment has been placed in proper repair and adjustment and otherwise conforms to the requirements of this part and Title 41, Chapter 6, Traffic Rules and Regulations, and a safety inspection certificate is obtained as promptly as possible.

(4) If repair or adjustment of any vehicle or its equipment is necessary, the owner of the vehicle may obtain repair or adjustment at any place he may choose.   1993

53-8-211. Safety inspection of school buses and other vehicles.

(1) (a) The Highway Patrol shall:

(i) perform safety inspections at least twice each school year on all school buses operated by each school district and each private school in the state for the transportation of students, except as otherwise provided in Subsection (1)(b); and

(ii) cause to be removed from the public highways any vehicle found to have mechanical or other defects under Subsection (1)(a) endangering the safety of passengers and the public until the defects have been corrected.

(b) (i) A school district or private school may perform the safety inspections of a school bus that it operates in accordance with rules made by the division under Title 63, Chapter 46a, Utah Administrative Rule Making Act, and after consultation with the State Board of Education.

(ii) The rules under Subsection (b)(i) shall include provisions for:

(A) maintaining school bus drivers' hours of service records;

(B) requiring school bus drivers to maintain vehicle condition reports;

(C) maintaining school bus maintenance and repair records; and

(D) validating that defects discovered during the inspection process have been corrected prior to returning a school bus to service.

(iii) (A) The division shall audit school bus safety operations of each school district and private school performing inspections under Subsection (b)(i) to ensure compliance with the rules made under that subsection.

(B) The audit may include both a formal examination of the district's or school's inspection records and a random physical inspection of buses that have been safety inspected by the district or the school.

(iv) A school district or school must have a comprehensive school bus maintenance plan approved by the division in order to participate in the safety inspection program.

(v) A school district or private school may not operate any vehicle found to have mechanical or other defects that would endanger the safety of passengers and the public until the defects have been corrected.

(2) Motor vehicles operated by private schools or school districts, and not used for the transportation of students, are subject to Section 53-8-205. **1999**

53-8-211.5. School bus safety standards — Exceptions.

(1) Beginning July 1, 2003, a school district or private school may not use a vehicle with a seating capacity of 11 or more, including the driver, for the transportation of its students unless the vehicle meets federal school bus safety standards under 49 U.S.C. Sec. 30101, et seq.

(2) Subsection (1) does not apply to a vehicle operated by a common carrier, as defined in Section 59-12-102, if the common carrier is not exclusively engaged in the transportation of students. **2001**

53-8-212. Suspension of registration.

The State Tax Commission shall suspend the registration of any vehicle the division determines is in an unsafe condition or which after notice and demand is not equipped as required in this part and Title 41, Motor Vehicles. **1993**

53-8-213. Special function officer status for certain employees — Retirement provisions.

(1) The commissioner may designate an employee of the Utah Highway Patrol Division as a special function officer, as defined in Section 53-13-105, for the purpose of enforcing all laws relating to vehicle parts and equipment, including the provisions of this part and Title 41, Chapter 6a, Part 16, Vehicle Equipment.

(2) Notwithstanding Section 49-15-201, a special function officer designated under this section may not become or be designated as a member of the Public Safety Retirement Systems. **2005**

CHAPTER 9

PRIVATE INVESTIGATOR REGULATION ACT

53-9-101. Title.

This chapter is known as the "Private Investigator Regulation Act." **1995**

53-9-102. Definitions.

In this chapter, unless otherwise stated:

(1) "Adequate records" means records containing, at a minimum, sufficient information to identify the client, the dates of service, the fee for service, the payments for service, the type of service given, and copies of any reports that may have been made.

(2) "Advertising" means the submission of bids, contracting or making known by any public notice, publication, or solicitation of business, directly or indirectly, that services regulated under this chapter are available for consideration.

(3) "Agency" means a person who holds an agency license pursuant to this chapter, and includes one who employs an individual for wages and salary, and withholds all legally required deductions and contributions, or contracts with a registrant or an apprentice on a part-time or case-by-case basis to conduct an investigation on behalf of the agency.

(4) "Applicant" means any person who has submitted a completed application and all required fees.

(5) "Apprentice" means a person who holds an apprentice license pursuant to this chapter, has not met the requirements for registration, and works under the direct supervision and guidance of an agency.

(6) "Board" means the Private Investigator Hearing and Licensure Board created in Section 53-9-104.

(7) "Bureau" means the Bureau of Criminal Identification created in Section 53-10-201.

(8) "Commissioner" means the commissioner of the Department of Public Safety.

(9) "Conviction" means an adjudication of guilt by a federal, state, or local court resulting from trial or plea, including a plea of no contest, regardless of whether the imposition of sentence was suspended.

(10) "Department" means the Department of Public Safety.

(11) "Direct supervision" means that the agency or employer:

(a) is responsible for, and authorizes, the type and extent of work assigned;

(b) reviews and approves all work produced by the apprentice before it goes to the client;

(c) closely supervises and provides direction and guidance to the apprentice in the performance of his assigned work; and

(d) is immediately available to the apprentice for verbal contact, including by electronic means.

(12) "Emergency action" means a summary suspension of a license pending revocation, suspension, or probation in order to protect the public health, safety, or welfare.

(13) "Employee" means an individual who works for an agency or other employer, is listed on the agency's or employer's payroll records, and is under the agency's or employer's direction and control. An employee is not an independent contractor.

(14) "Identification card" means a card issued by the commissioner to a qualified applicant for an agency, registrant, or apprentice license.

(15) "Letter of concern" means an advisory letter to notify a licensee that while there is insufficient evidence to support probation, suspension, or revocation of a license, the department informs the licensee of the need to modify or eliminate certain practices and that continuation of the activities that led to the information being submitted to the department may result in further disciplinary action against the licensee.

(16) "Licensee" means a person to whom an agency, registrant, or apprentice license is issued by the department.

(17) (a) "Private investigator or private detective" means any person, except collection agencies and credit reporting agencies, who, for consideration, engages in business or accepts employment to conduct any investigation for the purpose of obtaining information with reference to:

(i) crime, wrongful acts, or threats against the United States or any state or territory of the United States;

(ii) the identity, reputation, character, habits, conduct, business occupation, honesty, integrity, credibility, knowledge, trustworthiness, efficiency, loyalty, activity, movements, whereabouts, affiliations, associations, or transactions of any person or group of persons;

(iii) the credibility of witnesses or other persons;

(iv) the whereabouts of missing persons or owners of abandoned property;

(v) the causes and origin of, or responsibility for a fire, libel, slander, a loss, an accident, damage, or an injury to real or personal property;

(vi) the business of securing evidence to be used before investigating committees or boards of award or arbitration or in the trial of civil or criminal cases and the trial preparation;

(vii) the prevention, detection, and removal of installed devices for eavesdropping or observation;

(viii) the business of "skip tracing" persons who have become delinquent in their lawful debts, either when hired by an individual, collection agency, or through the direct purchase of the debt from a financial institution or entity owning the debt or judgment; or

(ix) serving civil process.

(b) "Private investigator or private detective" does not include:

(i) any person or employee conducting an investigation on the person's or employee's own behalf or on behalf of the employer if the employer is not a private investigator under this chapter; or

(ii) an employee of an attorney licensed to practice law in this state.

(18) "Qualifying party" means the individual meeting the qualifications under this chapter for a private investigator license.

(19) "Registrant" means any person who holds a registrant license pursuant to this chapter. The registrant performs private investigative work either as an employee on an employer's payroll or, on a contract with an agency, part-time, or case-by-case basis, with a minimum amount of direction.

(20) "Restructuring" means any change in the legal status of a business.

(21) "Unprofessional conduct" means any of the following:

(a) engaging or offering to engage by fraud or misrepresentation in any activities regulated by this chapter;

(b) aiding or abetting a person who is not licensed pursuant to this chapter in representing that person as a private investigator or registrant in this state;

(c) gross negligence in the practice of a private investigator or registrant;

(d) failing or refusing to maintain adequate records and investigative findings on a subject of investigation or a client;

(e) committing a felony or a misdemeanor involving any crime that is grounds for denial, suspension, or revocation of an agency, registrant, or apprentice license. In all cases, conviction by a court of competent jurisdiction or a plea of no contest is conclusive evidence of the commission of the crime; or

(f) making a fraudulent or untrue statement to the bureau, board, department, or its investigators, staff, or consultants.   2003

53-9-103. Commissioner of Public Safety to administer — Bureau to issue licenses — Records — Bonds — Rulemaking.

(1) The commissioner of the Department of Public Safety shall administer this chapter.

(2) (a) The bureau, acting at the direction of the commissioner, shall issue a private investigator license to any applicant who meets qualifications for licensure under Section 53-9-108.

(b) The bureau shall issue the license to a qualified applicant within five business days of receipt of the application.

(3) (a) The bureau shall keep records of:

(i) all applications for licenses under this chapter; and

(ii) all bonds and proof of workers' compensation required to be filed.

(b) The records shall include statements as to whether a license or renewal license has been issued for each application and bond.

(4) If a license is revoked, suspended, canceled, or denied or if a licensee is placed on probation, the date of filing the order for revocation, suspension, cancellation, denial, or probation shall be included in the records.

(5) The bureau shall maintain a list of all licensees that have had a license revoked, suspended, placed on probation, or canceled and a written record of complaints filed against licensees.

(6) The commissioner may make rules in accordance with Title 63, Chapter 46a, Utah Administrative Rulemaking Act, necessary to administer this chapter.   2003

53-9-104. Board — Creation — Qualifications — Appointments — Terms — Immunity.

(1) There is established a Private Investigator Hearing and Licensure Board consisting of five members appointed by the commissioner.

(2) Each member of the board shall be a citizen of the United States and a resident of this state at the time of appointment.

(a) Two members shall be qualifying parties who are licensed as provided in this chapter.

(b) One member shall be a supervisory investigator from the commissioner's office.

(c) One member shall be a chief of police or sheriff.

(d) One member shall be a public member who shall not have a financial interest in a private investigative agency and shall not have an immediate family member or a household member or friend who is licensed or registered under this chapter.

(3) (a) Each member of the board shall serve four-year staggered terms beginning and ending on January 1.

(b) Notwithstanding the term requirements of Subsection (3)(a), the commissioner may adjust the length of terms to ensure the terms of board members are staggered so that approximately one member of the board is appointed every year.

(4) When a vacancy occurs in the membership for any reason, the replacement shall be appointed for the unexpired term.

(5) At its first meeting every year, the board shall elect a chair, vice chair, and secretary from its membership.

(6) (a) (i) Members who are not government employees shall receive no compensation or benefits for their services, but may receive per diem and expenses incurred in the performance of the member's official duties at the rates established by the Division of Finance under Sections 63A-3-106 and 63A-3-107.

(ii) Members may decline to receive per diem and expenses for their service.

(b) (i) State government officer and employee members who do not receive salary, per diem, or expenses from their agency for their service may receive per diem and expenses in-

curred in the performance of their official duties from the board at the rates established by the Division of Finance under Sections 63A-3-106 and 63A-3-107.

(ii) State government officer and employee members may decline to receive per diem and expenses for their service.

(7) A member shall not serve more than one term, except that a member appointed to fill a vacancy or appointed for an initial term of less than four years may be reappointed for one full term.

(8) The commissioner, after a board hearing and recommendation, may remove any member of the board for misconduct, incompetency, or neglect of duty.

(9) Members of the board are immune from suit with respect to all acts done and actions taken in good faith in furtherance of the purposes of this chapter.   1998

53-9-105. Powers and duties of the board.

(1) The board shall:

(a) review all applications for licenses and renewals of licenses for private investigators and make recommendations to the commissioner for approval or disapproval;

(b) upon receiving a timely filed petition, review within a reasonable time the denial, suspension, or revocation of a private investigator license; and

(c) review all complaints and make recommendations to the commissioner regarding disciplinary action.

(2) The board may take and hear evidence, administer oaths and affirmations, and compel by subpoena the attendance of witnesses and the production of books, papers, records, documents, and other information relating to a formal complaint against or department investigation of a private investigator.   2003

53-9-106. Meetings — Hearings.

(1) The board shall meet quarterly, unless the board has no business to conduct during that quarter, and shall also meet at the call of the chair.

(2) A quorum consists of three members.

(3) If a member has three unexcused absences within a 12-month period, the board may hold a hearing to determine if that board member should be released from board duties.   2003

53-9-107. Classification of licenses — License required to act.

(1) Every person applying for a license under this chapter shall indicate on the application which of the following licenses the applicant is applying for:

(a) an agency license shall be issued to an applicant who meets the requirements of Subsection 53-9-108(1) and Section 53-9-109;

(b) a registrant license shall be issued to an applicant who meets the requirements of Subsection 53-9-108(2) and Section 53-9-110; or

(c) an apprentice license shall be issued to an applicant who meets the requirements of Subsection 53-9-108(3) and Section 53-9-110.

(2) Unless licensed under this chapter, a person may not:

(a) act or assume to act as, or represent himself to be:

(i) a licensee; or

(ii) a private investigator or private detective as defined in Subsection 53-9-102(16) or conduct any investigation as provided in Subsection 53-9-102(16); or

(b) falsely represent to be employed by or for an independent contractor for an agency.　**1998**

53-9-108.　Qualifications for licensure.

(1) (a) An applicant for an agency license under this chapter shall be at least 21 years of age, a citizen or legal resident of the United States, and of good moral character.

(b) An applicant may not have been:

(i) convicted of a felony;

(ii) convicted of an act involving illegally using, carrying, or possessing a dangerous weapon;

(iii) convicted of an act of personal violence or force on any person or convicted of threatening to commit an act of personal violence or force against another person;

(iv) convicted of an act constituting dishonesty or fraud;

(v) convicted of an act involving moral turpitude;

(vi) placed on probation or parole;

(vii) named in an outstanding arrest warrant; or

(viii) convicted of illegally obtaining or disclosing private, controlled, or protected records as provided in Section 63-2-801.

(c) In assessing good moral character under Subsection (1)(b), the board shall consider mitigating circumstances presented by an applicant regarding information under Subsections (1)(b)(vi) and (viii).

(d) If previously or currently licensed in another state or jurisdiction, the applicant shall be in good standing within that state or jurisdiction.

(e) An applicant shall have completed a minimum of two years, or 2,000 hours, of investigative experience that consists of actual work performed as a private investigator for a private agency, the federal government, or a state, county, or municipal government.

(f) (i) An applicant for an agency license shall substantiate investigative work experience claimed as years of qualifying experience and provide the exact details as to the character and nature of the experience on a form prescribed by the department and certified by the applicant's employers.

(ii) If the applicant is unable to supply written certification from an employer in whole or in part, the applicant may offer written certification from persons other than an employer covering the same subject matter for consideration by the board.

(iii) The applicant shall prove completion of the required experience to the satisfaction of the board and the board may independently verify the certification offered on behalf of the applicant.

(2) (a) (i) An applicant for a registrant license shall meet all qualification standards of this section, except Subsection (1)(d).

(ii) An applicant shall have a minimum of one year, or 1,000 hours, of investigative experience that consists of actual work performed as a private investigator for a private agency, the federal government, a state, county, or municipal government.

(b) A licensed registrant shall only work as an employee of, or an independent contractor with, licensed agencies as provided in Subsection 53-9-102(19), and may not:

(i) advertise his services or conduct investigations for the general public; or

(ii) employ other private investigators or hire them as independent contractors.

(3) (a) An applicant for an apprentice license, lacking the experience required for a registrant license, shall meet all of the qualification standards in Subsection (1), except Subsection (1)(d) and complete an apprentice application.

(b) (i) An apprentice shall work under the direct supervision and guidance of a licensed agency, full-time for one year, or 1,000 hours, prior to eligibility for a registrant license.

(ii) A licensed apprentice shall only work under the direction of a licensed agency as provided in Subsection 53-9-102(5), and may not:

(A) advertise his services or conduct investigations for the general public;

(B) employ other private investigators; or

(C) obtain information from the Utah State Tax Commission Motor Vehicle Division or Driver License Division within the Department of Public Safety, except the apprentice may utilize such information for a legitimate business need under the direct supervision of a licensed agency.

(4) (a) An applicant for an agency, registrant, or apprentice license may be eligible for a license without meeting all or part of the investigative work experience required by this section if the applicant:

(i) has a criminal justice degree from an accredited college or university;

(ii) is certified by Peace Officer Standards and Training; or

(iii) can substantiate other similar law enforcement or investigative training in the areas set forth in Subsection 53-9-102(17).

(b) The board shall determine whether or not training may replace the work experience requirement and to what extent.　**2004**

53-9-109.　Application for agency license — Bond — Workers' compensation.

(1) Every application for an agency license to engage in the private investigative business shall set forth information to assist the commissioner in determining the applicant's ability to meet the requirements prescribed in this chapter and contain the following:

(a) the full name and business address of the applicant;

(b) two passport-size color photographs of the applicant;

(c) the name under which the applicant intends to do business;

(d) a statement that the applicant intends to engage in the private investigative business;

(e) a verified statement of the applicant's experience and qualifications as provided in Section 53-9-108; and

(f) the fee prescribed in Section 53-9-111.

(2) Before the issuance of an original or renewal agency license, the applicant shall provide to the department:

(a) a surety bond in the amount of $10,000; and

(b) a certificate of workers' compensation insurance, if applicable.

(3) The bond required by this section shall be:

(a) executed and acknowledged by the applicant as principal and by a corporation licensed to transact fidelity and surety business in this state as surety;

(b) continuous in form and run concurrently with the license period;

(c) in favor of the state for the benefit of any person injured by any acts of a private investigator, his agency, or his employees; and

(d) subject to claims by any person who is injured by those acts.

(4) (a) The commissioner shall cancel the agency license of any licensed agency on the cancellation of the surety bond.

(b) The license may be reinstated when the qualifying party:

(i) files a surety bond that is concurrent with the remainder of the license period; and

(ii) pays the reinstatement fee prescribed in Section 53-9-111. **1998**

53-9-110. Application for registrant or apprentice license.

(1) Every application for a registrant or apprentice license shall provide information to assist the commissioner in determining the applicant's ability to meet the requirements prescribed in this chapter and contain the following:

(a) the full name and address of the applicant;

(b) two passport-size color photographs of the applicant;

(c) the name of the licensed agency for which the applicant will be an employee, apprentice, or contract registrant, if applicable;

(d) authorization of the licensed agency or its designee to employ the apprentice or contract with the registrant, if applicable;

(e) a verified statement of the applicant's experience and qualifications as provided in Section 53-9-108; and

(f) the fee prescribed in Section 53-9-111.

(2) An application for a registrant or apprentice license or renewal shall be accompanied by a surety bond in the amount of $10,000. **1998**

53-9-111. License and registration fees — Deposit in General Fund.

(1) Fees for licensure and renewal shall be as follows:

(a) for an original agency license application and license, $200, plus an additional fee for the costs of fingerprint processing and background investigation;

(b) for the renewal of an agency license, $100;

(c) for an original registrant or apprentice license application and license, $100, plus an additional fee for the costs of fingerprint processing and background investigation;

(d) for the renewal of a registrant or apprentice license, $50;

(e) for filing an agency renewal application more than 30 days after the expiration date of the license, a delinquency fee of $50;

(f) for filing a registrant or apprentice renewal application more than 30 days after the expiration date of the registration, a delinquency fee of $30;

(g) for the reinstatement of any license, $50;

(h) for a duplicate identification card, $10; and

(i) for the fingerprint processing fee, an amount that does not exceed the cost to the department charged by the Federal Bureau of Investigation for fingerprint processing for the

purpose of obtaining federal criminal history record information.

(2) (a) The commissioner may renew a license granted under this chapter upon receipt of a renewal application on forms as prescribed by the commissioner and upon receipt of the fees prescribed in Subsection (1).

(b) The renewal of a license requires the filing of a surety bond as described in Subsections 53-9-109(2) and (3). Renewal of a license shall not be granted more than 90 days after expiration.

(c) A licensee may not engage in any activity subject to this chapter during any period between the date of expiration of the license and the renewal of the license.

(3) (a) The commissioner shall renew a suspended license if:

(i) the period of suspension has been completed;

(ii) the commissioner has received a renewal application from the applicant on forms prescribed by the commissioner; and

(iii) the applicant has:

(A) filed a surety bond as described by Subsections 53-9-109(2) and (3); and

(B) paid the fees required by this section for renewal, including a delinquency fee if the application is not received by the commissioner within 30 days of the termination of the suspension.

(b) Renewal of the license does not entitle the licensee, while the license remains suspended and until it is reinstated, to engage in any activity regulated by this chapter, or in any other activity or conduct in violation of the order or judgment by which the license was suspended.

(4) The commissioner shall not reinstate a revoked license or accept an application for a license from a person whose license has been revoked for at least one year from the date of revocation.

(5) All fees, except the fingerprint processing fee, collected by the department under this section shall be deposited in the General Fund. **1998**

53-9-112. Issuance of license and identification card to applicant — License period — Expiration of application — Transfer of license prohibited.

(1) The commissioner shall issue a license to an applicant who complies with the provisions of this chapter. Each license issued under this chapter shall:

(a) contain the name and address of the licensee and the number of the license, its agency, registrant, or apprentice license designation; and

(b) be issued for a period of two years.

(2) On the issuance of a license, an identification card shall:

(a) be issued without charge to the licensee; and

(b) state on its face whether the bearer holds an agency, registrant, or apprentice license.

(3) (a) A registrant identification card shall state that the licensee is under the direction of a licensed agency and may not do investigative work independently for the public.

(b) An apprentice identification card shall state that the licensee is under the direct supervision of a licensed agency and may not do investigative work independently for the public.

(4) Upon request by any person, the licensee shall immediately identify the name, business address, and

phone number of the licensed agency for which the licensee is an employee or independent contractor.

(5) (a) On notification by the commissioner to an applicant that the license is not complete, or is not ready for issuance pending additional information, the applicant shall complete the application process and provide the additional information within 90 days.

(b) Failure to complete the process shall result in the application being cancelled and all fees forfeited.

(c) Subsequent application by the same applicant requires the payment of all application and license fees prescribed in Section 53-9-111.

(6) A licensee shall notify the commissioner of any change in the name or address of his business within 60 days of the change and failure to so notify will result in the automatic suspension of the license. To relieve the suspension, the licensee must apply for reinstatement and pay the fee prescribed in Section 53-9-111.

(7) A license issued under this chapter is not transferable or assignable.   1998

53-9-113. Grounds for denial of a license — Appeal.

(1) The board may deny a license or the renewal of a license if the applicant has:

(a) committed an act that, if committed by a licensee, would be grounds for probation, suspension, or revocation of a license under this chapter;

(b) employed or contracted with a person who has been refused a license under this chapter or who has had a license revoked;

(c) while not licensed under this chapter, committed, or aided and abetted the commission of, any act for which a license is required by this chapter; or

(d) knowingly made a material misstatement in connection with an application for a license or renewal of a license.

(2) (a) The board's denial of a license under this chapter shall:

(i) be in writing;

(ii) describe the basis for the denial; and

(iii) inform the applicant that if the applicant desires a hearing to contest the denial, the applicant shall submit a request in writing to the board within 30 days after the denial has been sent by the department by certified mail to the applicant.

(b) The board shall schedule a hearing on the denial for the next board meeting after the applicant's request for a hearing has been received by the board.

(3) The decision of the board may be appealed to the commissioner, who may:

(a) return the case to the board for reconsideration;

(b) modify the board's decision; or

(c) reverse the board's decision.

(4) The department shall promptly issue a final order of the commissioner and send the order to the applicant.

(5) Decisions of the commissioner are subject to judicial review pursuant to Section 63-46b-15.   1998

53-9-114. Repealed.   1998

53-9-115. Business name and address — Posting of license — Advertising.

(1) (a) Subject to the provisions of this chapter, a licensee may conduct an investigative business under a name other than the licensee's by:

(i) complying with the requirements of Title 42, Chapter 2, Conducting Business Under Assumed Name; and

(ii) providing a copy of the filed certificate to the commissioner.

(b) Failure to comply with Subsection (1)(a) shall result in the suspension of the license.

(2) Each licensee shall have at least one physical location from which the normal business of the agency is conducted. The address of this location shall be on file with the commissioner at all times and is not a public record pursuant to Subsection 63-2-301(1)(b)(ii).

(3) The license certificate issued by the commissioner shall be posted in a conspicuous place in the principal office of the licensee.

(4) Subject to the provisions of this chapter, a licensee may solicit business through any accepted form of advertising.

(a) Any advertisement shall contain the licensee's name and license number as it appears on the license certificate.

(b) A licensee may not use false, deceptive, or misleading advertising.   1998

53-9-116. Divulging investigative information — False reports prohibited.

(1) Except as otherwise provided by this chapter, a licensee may not divulge or release to anyone other than his client or employer the contents of an investigative file acquired in the course of licensed investigative activity. However, the board shall have access to investigative files if the client for whom the information was acquired, or his lawful representative, alleges a violation of this chapter by the licensee or if the prior written consent of the client to divulge or release the information has been obtained.

(2) A licensee may not willfully make a false statement or report to a client, employer, the board, or any authorized representative of the department, concerning information acquired in the course of activities regulated by this chapter.

(3) The licensee shall submit investigative reports to a client at times and in the manner agreed upon between the licensee and the client.

(4) Upon demand by the client, the licensee shall divulge to the client the results of an investigation if payment in full has been tendered for the charges levied.

(5) The licensee has full right to withdraw from any case and refund any portion of a retainer for which investigative work has not been completed.   1998

53-9-117. Authority to investigate complaint — Filing of complaints — Response — Retention of records — Appeal — Fines collected.

(1) The commissioner or board may initiate an investigation of any person advertising services or engaged in performing services that require a license under this chapter and shall investigate if a licensee is engaged in activities that do not comply with or are prohibited by this chapter.

(2) The commissioner shall enforce the provisions of this chapter without regard to the place or location in which a violation may have occurred, and on the complaint of any person, may investigate any alleged violation of this chapter or the business and business methods of any licensee or applicant for licensure under this chapter.

(3) Complaints against any licensee shall be filed

with the commissioner in writing on forms prescribed by the commissioner.

(a) Upon receipt of a complaint, or at the request of the board, the commissioner shall assign the complaint to an investigator within the department.

(b) The department will provide a copy of the complaint to the licensee who shall answer the complaint in writing within 15 working days of the date the complaint is sent by the department by certified mail.

(4) In any investigation undertaken by the department, each licensee on request shall provide records and truthfully respond to questions concerning activities regulated under this chapter.

(a) These records shall be maintained for five years at the principal place of business of the licensee or at another location approved by the board for a person whose license has been terminated, canceled, or revoked.

(b) On request by the department the licensee shall:

(i) during normal business hours or other time acceptable to the parties, make its records available immediately to the department unless the department determines that an extension may be granted; and

(ii) provide copies of any business records requested by the department.

(5) Upon completion of the investigation, the department shall report its findings of fact to the board, and shall make a recommendation as to whether disciplinary action is warranted under Subsection 53-9-118(1), including whether emergency action should be taken under Subsection 53-9-118(2).

(6) (a) If the department recommends disciplinary action, a notice of the recommendations in Subsection (5) shall be sent by the department to the licensee by certified mail.

(b) The notice shall include the right to request a hearing before the board, and require that any such request shall be in writing and received by the board within 30 working days of the date the notice of recommendations was sent by the department to the licensee by certified mail.   1998

53-9-118. Grounds for disciplinary action — Types of action.

(1) The board may suspend or revoke a license or registration or deny an application for a license if a person engages in any of the following:

(a) fraud or willful misrepresentation in applying for an original license or renewal of an existing license;

(b) using any letterhead, advertising, or other printed matter in any manner representing that the licensee is an instrumentality of the federal government, a state, or any political subdivision of a state;

(c) using a name different from that under which the licensee is currently licensed for any advertising, solicitation, or contract to secure business unless the name is an authorized fictitious name;

(d) impersonating, permitting, or aiding and abetting an employee or independent contractor to impersonate a peace officer or employee of the United States, any state, or a political subdivision of a state;

(e) knowingly violating, advising, encouraging, or assisting the violation of any statute, court order, or injunction in the course of a business regulated under this chapter;

(f) falsifying fingerprints or photographs while operating under this chapter;

(g) conviction of a felony;

(h) conviction of any act involving illegally using, carrying, or possessing a dangerous weapon;

(i) conviction of any act involving moral turpitude;

(j) conviction of any act of personal violence or force against any person or conviction of threatening to commit any act of personal violence or force against any person;

(k) soliciting business for an attorney in return for compensation;

(l) conviction of any act constituting dishonesty or fraud;

(m) being placed on probation, parole, or named in an outstanding arrest warrant;

(n) committing or permitting any employee or independent contractor to commit any act during the period when the license is expired or suspended;

(o) willfully neglecting to render to a client services or a report as agreed between the parties and for which compensation has been paid or tendered in accordance with the agreement of the parties unless the licensee chooses to withdraw from the case and returns the funds for work not yet completed;

(p) the unauthorized release of information acquired on behalf of a client by a licensee, or its employee or contract agent as a result of activities regulated under this chapter;

(q) failing to cooperate with, misrepresenting to, or refusing access to business or investigative records requested by the board or an authorized representative of the department engaged in an official investigation pursuant to this chapter;

(r) employing or contracting with any unlicensed or improperly licensed person or agency to conduct activities regulated under this chapter if the licensure status was known or could have been ascertained by reasonable inquiry;

(s) permitting, authorizing, aiding, or in any way assisting an employee to conduct services as described in this chapter on an independent contractor basis and not under the authority of the licensed agency;

(t) failure to maintain in full force and effect workers' compensation insurance, if applicable;

(u) conducting private investigation services regulated by this chapter on a revoked or suspended license;

(v) accepting employment, contracting, or in any way engaging in employment that has an adverse impact on investigations being conducted on behalf of clients;

(w) advertising in a false, deceptive, or misleading manner;

(x) refusing to display the identification card issued by the department to any person having reasonable cause to verify the validity of the license;

(y) committing any act of unprofessional conduct;

(z) conviction of any act of illegally obtaining or disseminating private, controlled, or protected records under Section 63-2-801; or

(aa) engaging in any other conduct prohibited by this chapter.

(2) (a) If the board finds, based on the investigation, that the public health, safety, or welfare requires emergency action, the board may order a summary suspension of a license pending proceedings for revocation or other action.

(b) If the board issues a summary suspension order, the commissioner shall issue to the licensee a written notice of the order and indicate the licensee's right to request a formal hearing before the board.

(c) The licensee's request for a formal hearing shall be in writing and received by the department within 30 working days of the date the summary suspension was sent by the department to the licensee by certified mail.

(3) If the board finds, based on the investigation or hearing, that a violation under Subsection (1) has occurred, notice will be sent to the licensee of the board's decision by mailing a true copy to the licensee's last-known address in the department's files by certified mail, return receipt requested.

(4) Based on information the board receives from the investigation or during a hearing, it may do any of the following:

(a) dismiss the complaint if the board believes it is without merit;

(b) take emergency action;

(c) issue a letter of concern, if applicable;

(d) impose a civil fine not to exceed $500;

(e) place the license on suspension for a period of not more than 12 months;

(f) revoke the license or registration; and

(g) place all records, evidence findings, and conclusion, and any other information pertinent to the investigation, in a confidential and protected records section of the file maintained at the department.

(5) A letter of concern issued pursuant to Section 53-9-118 is a document that is retained by the department and may be used in future disciplinary actions against a licensee.

(6) Appeal of the board's decision shall be made in writing to the commissioner within 15 days of the date of issuance of the board's decision. The commissioner shall review the finding by the board and may affirm, return to the board for reconsideration, reverse, adopt, modify, supplement, amend, or reject the recommendation of the board.

(7) The department shall issue a final written order within 30 days outlining the commissioner's decision on the appeal. The final order is final agency action for purposes of judicial review under Section 63-46b-15.

(8) All fines collected under this section shall be deposited in the General Fund.   1998

53-9-119.   Violation — Penalty.

Any person who violates any provision of this chapter is guilty of a class A misdemeanor.   1998

CHAPTER 10

CRIMINAL INVESTIGATIONS AND TECHNICAL SERVICES DIVISION

Part 1

General Provisions

Part 2

Bureau of Criminal Identification

Part 3

State Bureau of Investigation

Part 4

Bureau of Forensic Services

Part 5

Bureau of Communications

Part 6

Coordination of Statewide 911 Emergency Communications

PART 1

GENERAL PROVISIONS

53-10-101. Short title.

This chapter is known as the "Criminal Investigations and Technical Services Act." 1998

53-10-102. Definitions.

As used in this chapter:

(1) "Administration of criminal justice" means performance of any of the following: detection, apprehension, detention, pretrial release, post-trial release, prosecution, adjudication, correctional supervision, or rehabilitation of accused persons or criminal offenders.

(2) "Alcoholic beverages" has the same meaning as provided in Section 32A-1-105.

(3) "Alcoholic products" has the same meaning as provided in Section 32A-1-105.

(4) "Commission" means the Alcoholic Beverage Control Commission.

(5) "Communications services" means the technology of reception, relay, and transmission of information required by public safety agencies in the performance of their duty.

(6) "Conviction record" means criminal history information indicating a record of a criminal charge which has led to a declaration of guilt of an offense.

(7) "Criminal history record information" means information on individuals consisting of identifiable descriptions and notations of:

(a) arrests, detentions, indictments, informations, or other formal criminal charges, and any disposition arising from any of them; and

(b) sentencing, correctional supervision, and release.

(8) "Criminalist" means the scientific discipline directed to the recognition, identification, individualization, and evaluation of physical evidence by application of the natural sciences in law-science matters.

(9) "Criminal justice agency" means courts or a government agency or subdivision of a government agency that administers criminal justice under a statute, executive order, or local ordinance and that allocates greater than 50% of its annual budget to the administration of criminal justice.

(10) "Department" means the Department of Public Safety.

(11) "Director" means the division director appointed under Section 53-10-103.

(12) "Division" means the Criminal Investigations and Technical Services Division created in Section 53-10-103.

(13) "Executive order" means an order of the president of the United States or the chief executive of a state that has the force of law and that is published in a manner permitting regular public access to it.

(14) "Forensic" means dealing with the application of scientific knowledge relating to criminal evidence.

(15) "Missing child" means any person under the age of 18 years who is missing from his or her home environment or a temporary placement facility for any reason and whose location cannot be determined by the person responsible for the child's care.

(16) "Missing person" has the same meaning as provided in Section 26-2-27.

(17) "Pathogens" means disease-causing agents.

(18) "Physical evidence" means something submitted to the bureau to determine the truth of a matter using scientific methods of analysis.

(19) "Qualifying entity" means a business, organization, or a governmental entity which employs persons who deal with:

(a) national security interests;

(b) care, custody, or control of children;

(c) fiduciary trust over money; or

(d) health care to children or vulnerable adults.   2000

53-10-103. Division — Creation — Director appointment and qualifications.

(1) There is created within the department the Criminal Investigations and Technical Services Division.

(2) The division shall be administered by a director appointed by the commissioner with the approval of the governor.

(3) The director is the executive and administrative head of the division and shall be experienced in administration and possess additional qualifications as determined by the commissioner and as provided by law.

(4) The director acts under the supervision and control of the commissioner and may be removed from his position at the will of the commissioner.

(5) The director shall receive compensation as provided by Title 67, Chapter 19, Utah State Personnel Management Act.   1998

53-10-104. Division duties.

The division shall:

(1) provide and coordinate the delivery of support services to law enforcement agencies;

(2) maintain and provide access to criminal records for use by law enforcement agencies;

(3) publish law enforcement and statistical data;

(4) maintain dispatch and communications services for public safety communications centers and provide emergency medical, fire suppression, highway maintenance, public works, and law enforcement communications for municipal, county, state, and federal agencies;

(5) analyze evidence from crime scenes and crime-related incidents for criminal prosecution;

(6) provide criminalistic laboratory services to federal, state, and local law enforcement agencies, prosecuting attorneys' and agencies, and public defenders, with the exception of those services provided by the state medical examiner in accordance with Title 26, Chapter 4, Utah Medical Examiner Act;

(7) establish satellite laboratories as necessary to provide criminalistic services;

(8) safeguard the public through licensing and regulation of activities that impact public safety, including concealed weapons, emergency vehicles, and private investigators;

(9) provide investigative assistance to law enforcement and other government agencies;

(10) collect and provide intelligence information to criminal justice agencies;

(11) investigate crimes that jeopardize the safety of the citizens, as well as the interests, of the state;

(12) regulate and investigate laws pertaining to the sale and distribution of liquor;

(13) make rules to implement this chapter;

(14) perform the functions specified in this chapter; and

(15) comply with the requirements of Section 11-40-103.   2003

53-10-105. Assistance to law enforcement agencies — Investigation of crimes — Laboratory facilities.

(1) The commissioner may assist any law enforcement agency in:

(a) establishing identification and investigation records systems;

(b) establishing uniform crime reporting systems;

(c) investigating any crime;

(d) coordinating the exchange of criminal identification, intelligence, and investigation information among law enforcement agencies; and

(e) providing the agencies with equipment, technical assistance, and instruction.

(2) (a) At the governor's direction, the commissioner shall assign division employees to investigate any crime within this state for the purpose of identifying, apprehending, and convicting the perpetrator or perpetrators of that crime even if the commissioner has not received a request from a law enforcement agency.

(b) The governor may establish a time period for the commissioner to pursue the investigation.

(c) To accomplish the purposes of this section, the commissioner may provide, through the division, crime detection laboratory facilities.   1998

53-10-106. Cooperation with agencies of any state or nation.

The division shall cooperate with appropriate agencies of any state or nation in developing uniform systems of criminal identification, crime reporting, and information exchange.   1998

53-10-107. Admissibility in evidence of certified copies of division files.

A copy of any fingerprint, record, document, or other evidence in the files of the division, certified by the commissioner to be a true copy of the original, is admissible in evidence in the same manner as the original.   1998

53-10-108. Restrictions on access, use, and contents of division records — Limited use of records for employment purposes — Challenging accuracy of records — Usage fees — Missing children records.

(1) Dissemination of information from a criminal history record or warrant of arrest information from division files is limited to:

(a) criminal justice agencies for purposes of administration of criminal justice and for employment screening by criminal justice agencies;

(b) noncriminal justice agencies or individuals for any purpose authorized by statute, executive order, court rule, court order, or local ordinance;

(c) agencies or individuals for the purpose of obtaining required clearances connected with foreign travel or obtaining citizenship;

(d) (i) agencies or individuals pursuant to a specific agreement with a criminal justice agency to provide services required for the administration of criminal justice; and

(ii) the agreement shall specifically authorize access to data, limit the use of the data to purposes for which given, and ensure the security and confidentiality of the data;

(e) agencies or individuals for the purpose of a preplacement adoptive study, in accordance with the requirements of Section 78-30-3.5;

(f) (i) agencies and individuals as the commissioner authorizes for the express purpose of research, evaluative, or statistical activities pursuant to an agreement with a criminal justice agency; and

(ii) private security agencies through guidelines established by the commissioner for employment background checks for their own employees and prospective employees;

(g) a qualifying entity for employment background checks for their own employees and persons who have applied for employment with the qualifying entity; and

(h) other agencies and individuals as the commissioner authorizes and finds necessary for protection of life and property and for offender identification, apprehension, and prosecution pursuant to an agreement.

(2) An agreement under Subsection (1)(f) or (1)(h) shall specifically authorize access to data, limit the use of data to research, evaluative, or statistical purposes, preserve the anonymity of individuals to whom the information relates, and ensure the confidentiality and security of the data.

(3) (a) Before requesting information under Subsection (1)(g), a qualifying entity must obtain a signed waiver from the person whose information is requested.

(b) The waiver must notify the signee:

(i) that a criminal history background check will be conducted;

(ii) who will see the information; and

(iii) how the information will be used.

(c) Information received by a qualifying entity under Subsection (1)(g) may only be:

(i) available to persons involved in the hiring or background investigation of the employee; and

(ii) used for the purpose of assisting in making an employment or promotion decision.

(d) A person who disseminates or uses information obtained from the division under Subsection (1)(g) for purposes other than those specified under Subsection (3)(c), in addition to any penalties provided under this section, is subject to civil liability.

(e) A qualifying entity that obtains information under Subsection (1)(g) shall provide the employee or employment applicant an opportunity to:

(i) review the information received as provided under Subsection (8); and

(ii) respond to any information received.

(f) In accordance with Title 63, Chapter 46a, Utah Administrative Rulemaking Act, the division may make rules to implement this Subsection (3).

(g) (i) The applicant fingerprint card fee under Subsection (1)(g) is $15.

(ii) The name check fee under Subsection (1)(g) is $10.

(iii) These fees remain in effect until changed by the division through the process under Section 63-38-3.2.

(iv) Funds generated under Subsections (3)(g)(i), (3)(g)(ii), and (8)(b) shall be deposited in the General Fund as a dedicated credit by the department to cover the costs incurred in providing the information.

(h) The division or its employees are not liable for defamation, invasion of privacy, negligence, or any other claim in connection with the contents of information disseminated under Subsection (1)(g).

(4) Any criminal history record information obtained from division files may be used only for the purposes for which it was provided and may not be further disseminated, except that a criminal history provided to an agency pursuant to Subsection (1)(e) may be provided by the agency to the person who is the subject of the history, another licensed child-placing agency, or the attorney for the adoptive parents for the purpose of facilitating an adoption.

(5) If an individual has no prior criminal convictions, criminal history record information contained in the division's computerized criminal history files may not include arrest or disposition data concerning an individual who has been acquitted, his charges dismissed, or when no complaint against him has been filed.

(6) (a) This section does not preclude the use of the division's central computing facilities for the storage and retrieval of criminal history record information.

(b) This information shall be stored so it cannot be modified, destroyed, or accessed by unauthorized agencies or individuals.

(7) Direct access through remote computer terminals to criminal history record information in the division's files is limited to those agencies authorized by the commissioner under procedures designed to prevent unauthorized access to this information.

(8) (a) The commissioner shall establish procedures to allow an individual right of access to review and receive a copy of his criminal history report.

(b) A processing fee for the right of access service, including obtaining a copy of the individual's criminal history report under Subsection (8)(a) is $10. This fee remains in effect until changed by the commissioner through the process under Section 63-38-3.2.

(c) (i) The commissioner shall establish procedures for an individual to challenge the completeness and accuracy of criminal history record information contained in the division's computerized criminal history files regarding that individual.

(ii) These procedures shall include provisions for amending any information found to be inaccurate or incomplete.

(9) The private security agencies as provided in Subsection (1)(f)(ii):

(a) shall be charged for access; and

(b) shall be registered with the division according to rules made by the division under Title 63, Chapter 46a, Utah Administrative Rulemaking Act.

(10) Before providing information requested under this section, the division shall give priority to criminal justice agencies needs.

(11) (a) Misuse of access to criminal history record information is a class B misdemeanor.

(b) The commissioner shall be informed of the misuse.   2004

53-10-109. Telecommunications systems.

For the purpose of expediting local, state, national, and international efforts in the detection and apprehension of criminals, the division may operate and coordinate telecommunications systems as may be required in the conduct of its duties under this part.
                                              1998

53-10-110. Authority of officers and officials to take fingerprints, photographs, and other data.

The officers and officials described in Sections 53-10-207 through 53-10-209 shall take, or cause to be taken, fingerprints, photographs, and other related data of persons under this part.   1998

53-10-111. Refusal to provide information — False information — Misdemeanor.

It is a class B misdemeanor for a person to:

(1) neglect or refuse to provide, or willfully withhold any information under this part;

(2) willfully provide false information;

(3) willfully fail to do or perform any act required under this part;

(4) hinder or prevent another from doing an act required under this part; or

(5) willfully remove, destroy, alter, mutilate, or disclose the contents of any file or record of the division unless authorized by and in compliance with procedures established by the commissioner.

1998

53-10-112. Director and officers to have peace officer powers.

The director and enforcement officers:

(1) are vested with the powers of peace officers throughout the several counties of the state, with the exception of the power to serve civil process;

(2) have the powers and duties of inspectors under Title 32A, Alcoholic Beverage Control Act;

(3) may serve criminal process and arrest and prosecute violators of any law of this state; and

(4) have the same rights as other peace officers to require aid in executing their duties.   1998

53-10-113. Other agencies to cooperate with division.

(1) All agencies of the state and local governments shall cooperate with the division in discharging its responsibilities under this chapter, Title 32A, Alcoholic Beverage Control Act, Title 58, Chapter 37, Utah Controlled Substance Act, Title 58, Chapter 37a, Utah Drug Paraphernalia Act, Title 58, Chapter 37b, Imitation Controlled Substances Act, and Title 58, Chapter 37c, Utah Controlled Substance Precursor Act.

(2) This part does not relieve local law enforcement agencies or officers of the responsibility of enforcing laws relating to alcoholic beverages and products or any other laws.

(3) The powers and duties conferred upon the director and the officers of the division are not a limitation upon the powers and duties of other peace officers in the state.   1998

53-10-114. Authority regarding drug precursors.

(1) As used in this section, "acts" means:

(a) Title 58, Chapter 37c, Utah Controlled Substance Precursor Act; and

(b) Title 58, Chapter 37d, Clandestine Drug Lab Act.

(2) The division has authority to enforce the drug lab and precursor acts. To carry out this purpose, the division may:

(a) inspect, copy, and audit any records, inventories of controlled substance precursors, and reports required under the acts and rules adopted under the acts;

(b) enter the premises of regulated distributors and regulated purchasers during normal business hours to conduct administrative inspections;

(c) assist the law enforcement agencies of the state in enforcing the acts;

(d) conduct investigations to enforce the acts;

(e) present evidence obtained from investigations conducted in conjunction with appropriate county and district attorneys and the Office of the Attorney General for civil or criminal prosecution

or for administrative action against a licensee; and

(f) work in cooperation with the Division of Occupational and Professional Licensing, created under Section 58-1-103, to accomplish the purposes of this section.   1998

PART 2

BUREAU OF CRIMINAL IDENTIFICATION

53-10-201. Bureau of Criminal Identification — Creation — Bureau Chief appointment, qualifications, and compensation.

(1) There is created within the division the Bureau of Criminal Identification.

(2) The bureau shall be administered by a bureau chief appointed by the division director with the approval of the commissioner.

(3) The bureau chief shall be experienced in administration and possess additional qualifications as determined by the commissioner or division director and as provided by law.

(4) The bureau chief acts under the supervision and control of the division director and may be removed from his position at the will of the commissioner.

(5) The bureau chief shall receive compensation as provided by Title 67, Chapter 19, Utah State Personnel Management Act.   1998

53-10-202. Criminal identification — Duties of bureau.

The bureau shall:

(1) procure and file information relating to identification and activities of persons who:

(a) are fugitives from justice;

(b) are wanted or missing;

(c) have been arrested for or convicted of a crime under the laws of any state or nation; and

(d) are believed to be involved in racketeering, organized crime, or a dangerous offense;

(2) establish a statewide uniform crime reporting system that shall include:

(a) statistics concerning general categories of criminal activities;

(b) statistics concerning crimes that exhibit evidence of prejudice based on race, religion, ancestry, national origin, ethnicity, or other categories that the division finds appropriate; and

(c) other statistics as required by the Federal Bureau of Investigation;

(3) make a complete and systematic record and index of the information obtained under this part;

(4) subject to the restrictions in this part, establish policy concerning the use and dissemination of data obtained under this part;

(5) publish an annual report concerning the extent, fluctuation, distribution, and nature of crime in Utah;

(6) establish a statewide central register for the identification and location of missing persons, which may include:

(a) identifying data including fingerprints of each missing person;

(b) identifying data of any missing person who is reported as missing to a law enforcement agency having jurisdiction;

(c) dates and circumstances of any persons requesting or receiving information from the register; and

(d) any other information, including blood types and photographs found necessary in furthering the purposes of this part;

(7) publish a quarterly directory of missing persons for distribution to persons or entities likely to be instrumental in the identification and location of missing persons;

(8) list the name of every missing person with the appropriate nationally maintained missing persons lists;

(9) establish and operate a 24-hour communication network for reports of missing persons and reports of sightings of missing persons;

(10) coordinate with the National Center for Missing and Exploited Children and other agencies to facilitate the identification and location of missing persons and the identification of unidentified persons and bodies;

(11) receive information regarding missing persons, as provided in Sections 26-2-27 and 53A-11-502, and stolen vehicles, vessels, and outboard motors, as provided in Section 41-1a-1401;

(12) adopt systems of identification, including the fingerprint system, to be used by the division to facilitate law enforcement; and

(13) assign a distinguishing number or mark of identification to any pistol or revolver, as provided in Section 76-10-520.   1998

53-10-202.5. Bureau services — Fees.

The bureau shall collect fees for the following services:

(1) applicant fingerprint card as determined by Section 53-10-108;

(2) bail enforcement licensing as determined by Section 53-11-115;

(3) concealed firearm permit as determined by Section 53-5-707;

(4) expungement certificate of eligibility as determined by Section 77-18-11;

(5) firearm purchase background check as determined by Section 76-10-526;

(6) name check as determined by Section 53-10-108;

(7) private investigator licensing as determined by Section 53-9-111; and

(8) right of access as determined by Section 53-10-108.   1999

53-10-203. Missing persons — Reports — Notification.

(1) Each law enforcement agency that is investigating the report of a missing person shall provide information regarding that report to the division. The report shall include descriptive information and the date and location of the last-known contact with the missing person.

(2) The division shall notify the state registrar of Vital Statistics and the FBI National Crime Information Center of all missing persons reported in accordance with Subsection (1) and shall provide the state registrar with information concerning the identity of those missing persons.

(3) If the division has reason to believe that a missing person reported in accordance with Subsection (1) has been enrolled in a specific school in this state, the division shall also notify the last-known school of that report.

(4) Upon learning of the recovery of a missing person, the division shall notify the state registrar and any school that it has previously informed of the person's disappearance.

(5) The division shall, by rule, determine the manner and form of reports, notices, and information required by this section.

(6) Upon notification by the state registrar or school personnel that a request for a birth certificate, school record, or other information concerning a missing person has been made, or that an investigation is needed in accordance with Section 53A-11-503, the division shall immediately notify the local law enforcement authority.   1998

53-10-204. Missing person records — Confidentiality — Availability.

Inquiries made regarding missing persons are confidential and are available only to:

(1) a law enforcement agency investigating a report of a missing person;

(2) an agency having the responsibility or authority to care for, treat, or supervise a person who is the subject of a placement in temporary or substitute care or an adoption proceeding;

(3) a court, upon a finding that access to the records may be necessary for the determination of an issue before it;

(4) the office of the public prosecutor or its deputies;

(5) any person engaged in bona fide research when approved by the director of the division, excluding names and addresses; and

(6) entities or persons authorized to receive the information in accordance with Section 53-10-203.   1998

53-10-205. Uniform crime reporting system — Use of data.

The data acquired under the statewide uniform crime reporting system shall be used only for research or statistical purposes and may not contain any information that may reveal the identity of an individual victim of a crime.   1998

53-10-206. Collection of information.

The commissioner and persons designated by him may require all peace officers, the warden of the state prison, the keeper of any jail or correctional institution, or superintendent of the state hospital to obtain information that will aid in establishing the records required to be kept.   1998

53-10-207. Peace officers, prosecutors, and magistrates to supply information to state and F.B.I. — Notification of arrest based on warrant.

(1) Every peace officer shall:

(a) cause fingerprints of persons he has arrested to be taken on forms provided by the division and the Federal Bureau of Investigation;

(b) supply information requested on the forms; and

(c) forward without delay both copies to the division, which shall forward the F.B.I. copy to the Identification Division of the Federal Bureau of Investigation.

(2) If, after fingerprints have been taken in accordance with Subsection (1), the prosecutor declines to prosecute, or investigative action as described in Section 77-2-3 is terminated, the prosecutor or law enforcement agency shall notify the division of this action within 14 working days.

(3) At the preliminary hearing or arraignment of a felony case, the prosecutor shall ensure that each felony defendant has been fingerprinted and an arrest and fingerprint form is transmitted to the division. In

felony cases where fingerprints have not been taken, the judge shall order the chief law enforcement officer of the jurisdiction or the sheriff of the county to:

(a) cause fingerprints of each felony defendant to be taken on forms provided by the division;

(b) supply information requested on the forms; and

(c) forward without delay both copies to the division.

(4) If an arrest is based upon information about the existence of a criminal warrant of arrest or commitment under Rule 6, Utah Rules of Criminal Procedure, every peace officer shall without delay notify the division of the service of each warrant of arrest or commitment, in a manner specified by the division.

1998

53-10-208. Definition — Offenses included on statewide warrant system — Transportation fee to be included — Statewide warrant system responsibility — Quality control — Training — Technical support — Transaction costs.

(1) "Statewide warrant system" means the portion of the state court computer system that is accessible by modem from the state mainframe computer and contains:

(a) records of criminal warrant information; and

(b) after notice and hearing, records of protective orders issued pursuant to:

(i) Title 30, Chapter 6, Cohabitant Abuse Act; or

(ii) Title 77, Chapter 36, Cohabitant Abuse Procedures Act.

(2) (a) (i) The division shall include on the statewide warrant system all warrants issued for felony offenses and class A, B, and C misdemeanor offenses in the state.

(ii) For each offense the division shall indicate whether the magistrate ordered under Section 77-7-5 and Rule 6, Utah Rules of Criminal Procedure, that the accused appear in court.

(b) Infractions shall not be included on the statewide warrant system, including any subsequent failure to appear warrants issued on an infraction.

(3) The division is the agency responsible for the statewide warrant system and shall:

(a) ensure quality control of all warrants of arrest or commitment and protective orders contained in the statewide warrant system by conducting regular validation checks with every clerk of a court responsible for entering the information on the system;

(b) upon the expiration of the protective orders and in the manner prescribed by the division, purge information regarding protective orders described in Subsection 53-10-208.1(4) within 30 days of the time after expiration;

(c) establish system procedures and provide training to all criminal justice agencies having access to information contained on the state warrant system;

(d) provide technical support, program development, and systems maintenance for the operation of the system; and

(e) pay data processing and transaction costs for state, county, and city law enforcement agencies and criminal justice agencies having access to

information contained on the state warrant system.

(4) (a) Any data processing or transaction costs not funded by legislative appropriation shall be paid on a pro rata basis by all agencies using the system during the fiscal year.

(b) This Subsection (4) supersedes any conflicting provision in Subsection (3)(e).   2000

53-10-208.1. Magistrates and court clerks to supply information.

Every magistrate or clerk of a court responsible for court records in this state shall, within 30 days of the disposition and on forms and in the manner provided by the division, furnish the division with information pertaining to:

(1) all dispositions of criminal matters, including:

(a) guilty pleas;

(b) convictions;

(c) dismissals;

(d) acquittals;

(e) pleas held in abeyance;

(f) judgments of not guilty by reason of insanity for a violation of:

(i) a felony offense;

(ii) Title 76, Chapter 5, Offenses Against the Person; or

(iii) Title 76, Chapter 10, Part 5, Weapons;

(g) judgments of guilty and mentally ill;

(h) finding of mental incompetence to stand trial for a violation of:

(i) a felony offense;

(ii) Title 76, Chapter 5, Offenses Against the Person; or

(iii) Title 76, Chapter 10, Part 5, Weapons; or

(i) probations granted; and

(2) orders of civil commitment under the terms of Section 62A-15-631;

(3) the issuance, recall, cancellation, or modification of all warrants of arrest or commitment as described in Rule 6, Utah Rules of Criminal Procedure and Section 78-32-4, within one day of the action and in a manner provided by the division; and

(4) protective orders issued after notice and hearing, pursuant to:

(a) Title 30, Chapter 6, Cohabitant Abuse Act; or

(b) Title 77, Chapter 36, Cohabitant Abuse Procedures Act.   2002 (5th S.S.)

53-10-209. Penal institutions and state hospital to supply information.

(1) The warden of the state prison, keeper of any jail or correctional institution, and superintendent of the state hospital shall forward to the division:

(a) the fingerprints and recent photographs of all persons confined in each institution under criminal commitment;

(b) information relating to the parole, termination or expiration of sentence, or any other release of each person from confinement during the preceding month; and

(c) a photograph taken near the time of release.

(2) The adult probation and parole section of the Department of Corrections shall furnish to the division:

(a) information relating to the revocation or termination of probation or parole; and

(b) upon request, the names, fingerprints, photographs, and other data.

(3) The chair of the Board of Pardons and Parole shall provide to the division information regarding the issuance, recall, cancellation, or modification of any warrant issued by members of the Board of Pardons and Parole, under Section 77-27-11, within one day of issuance.

(4) Information provided to the division under this section shall be on forms designated by the division.

1998

53-10-210. Response for requests — Fees.

(1) In responding to requests for criminal background checks, the division shall make an earnest effort to provide the requested information within three weeks of receipt of a request.

(2) Fees and other payments received by the division in payment for criminal background check services shall be deposited in the General Fund and the Legislature shall make an annual appropriation for payment of personnel and other costs incurred in providing those services. 1998

53-10-211. Notice required of arrest of school employee for controlled substance or sex offense.

(1) The chief administrative officer of the law enforcement agency making the arrest or receiving notice under Subsection (2) shall immediately notify the following individuals:

(a) the administrator of teacher certification in the State Office of Education; and

(b) the superintendent of schools of the employing public school district or, if the offender is an employee of a private school, the administrator of that school.

(2) Subsection (1) applies upon:

(a) the arrest of any school employee for any offense:

(i) in Section 58-37-8;

(ii) in Title 76, Chapter 5, Part 4, Sexual Offenses; or

(iii) involving sexual conduct; or

(b) upon receiving notice from any other jurisdiction that a school employee has committed an act which would, if committed in Utah, be an offense under Subsection (a). 1998

53-10-212. Supplies and equipment for compliance by reporting agencies.

All governing boards or commissions of each city, town, county, or correctional institution of the state shall furnish the appropriate officials with supplies and equipment necessary to perform the duties prescribed in this part. 1998

PART 3

STATE BUREAU OF INVESTIGATION

53-10-301. State Bureau of Investigation — Creation — Bureau chief appointment, qualifications, and compensation.

(1) There is created within the division the State Bureau of Investigation.

(2) The bureau shall be administered by a bureau chief appointed by the division director with the approval of the commissioner.

(3) The bureau chief shall be experienced in administration and possess additional qualifications as determined by the division director and as provided by law.

(4) The bureau chief acts under the supervision and control of the division director and may be removed from his position at the will of the commissioner.

(5) The bureau chief shall receive compensation as provided by Title 67, Chapter 19, Utah State Personnel Management Act. 2002

53-10-302. Bureau duties.

The bureau shall:

(1) upon request, provide assistance and specialized law enforcement services to local law enforcement agencies;

(2) conduct financial investigations regarding suspicious cash transactions, fraud, and money laundering;

(3) investigate organized crime, extremist groups, and others promoting violence;

(4) investigate criminal activity of terrorist groups;

(5) enforce the Utah Criminal Code;

(6) cooperate and exchange information with other state agencies and with other law enforcement agencies of government, both within and outside of this state, to obtain information that may achieve more effective results in the prevention, detection, and control of crime and apprehension of criminals;

(7) create and maintain a statewide criminal intelligence system;

(8) provide specialized case support and investigate illegal drug production, cultivation, and sales;

(9) investigate, follow-up, and assist in highway drug interdiction cases;

(10) make rules to implement this chapter; and

(11) perform the functions specified in Part 2, Narcotics and Alcoholic Beverage Law Enforcement Act. 2000

53-10-303. Repealed. 2000

53-10-304. Narcotics and alcoholic beverage enforcement — Responsibility and jurisdiction.

The bureau shall:

(1) have specific responsibility for the enforcement of all laws of the state pertaining to alcoholic beverages and products;

(2) have general law enforcement jurisdiction throughout the state;

(3) have concurrent law enforcement jurisdiction with all local law enforcement agencies and their officers;

(4) cooperate and exchange information with any other state agency and with other law enforcement agencies of government, both within and outside this state, to obtain information that may achieve more effective results in the prevention, detection, and control of crime and apprehension of criminals;

(5) sponsor or supervise programs or projects related to prevention, detection, and control of violations of:

(a) Title 32A, Alcoholic Beverage Control Act;

(b) Title 58, Chapter 37, Utah Controlled Substance Act;

(c) Title 58, Chapter 37a, Utah Drug Paraphernalia Act;

(d) Title 58, Chapter 37b, Imitation Controlled Substances Act;

(e) Title 58, Chapter 37c, Utah Controlled Substance Precursor Act; and

(f) Title 58, Chapter 37d, Clandestine Drug Lab Act; and

(6) assist the governor in an emergency or as the governor may require.   2000

53-10-305. Duties of bureau chief.

The bureau chief, with the consent of the commissioner, shall do the following:

(1) conduct in conjunction with the state boards of education and higher education in state schools, colleges, and universities, an educational program concerning alcoholic products, and work in conjunction with civic organizations, churches, local units of government, and other organizations in the prevention of alcoholic product and drug violations;

(2) coordinate law enforcement programs throughout the state and accumulate and disseminate information related to the prevention, detection, and control of violations of this chapter and Title 32A, Alcoholic Beverage Control Act, as it relates to storage or consumption of alcoholic beverages on premises maintained by social clubs, recreational, athletic, and kindred associations;

(3) make inspections and investigations as required by the commission and the Department of Alcoholic Beverage Control;

(4) perform other acts as may be necessary or appropriate concerning control of the use of alcoholic beverages and products and drugs; and

(5) make reports and recommendations to the Legislature, the governor, the commissioner, the commission, and the Department of Alcoholic Beverage Control as may be required or requested.   2000

PART 4

BUREAU OF FORENSIC SERVICES

53-10-401. Bureau of Forensic Services — Creation — Bureau Chief appointment, qualifications, and compensation.

(1) There is created within the division the Bureau of Forensic Services.

(2) The bureau shall be administered by a bureau chief appointed by the division director with the approval of the commissioner.

(3) The bureau chief shall be experienced in administration of criminal justice and possess additional qualifications as determined by the commissioner or division director and as provided by law.

(4) The bureau chief acts under the supervision and control of the division director and may be removed from his position at the will of the commissioner.

(5) The bureau chief shall receive compensation as provided by Title 67, Chapter 19, Utah State Personnel Management Act.   1998

53-10-402. Bureau duties.

The bureau shall:

(1) provide quality, timely, and comprehensive analysis of physical evidence from crime scenes and crime-related incidents submitted by federal, state, county, and municipal criminal justice agencies;

(2) provide expert testimony in courts of law regarding the scientific analysis and conclusion of forensic evidence using the most current and advanced analytical techniques and technology;

(3) ensure the safety of all laboratory employees against exposure to blood-borne pathogens, infectious materials, and any other biochemical or toxic hazard which may pose a threat to the safety and well-being of bureau employees;

(4) protect the chain of incoming evidence by ensuring all items are properly packaged, sealed, marked, stored, and delivered back to the submitting agency using established legal guidelines;

(5) adopt systems of identification, including blood and firearms analysis, to be used by the division to facilitate law enforcement;

(6) participate in establishing satellite laboratories in designated locations throughout the state;

(7) provide assistance to the medical community in establishing guidelines for the proper handling of individuals who are the victims of sexual assault; and

(8) upon request, provide law enforcement agencies technical and analytical support in the processing of crime scenes.   1998

53-10-403. DNA specimen analysis — Application to offenders, including minors.

(1) Sections 53-10-404, 53-10-405, and 53-10-406 apply to any person who:

(a) has pled guilty to or has been convicted of any of the offenses under Subsection (2) and who is on probation, parole, or incarcerated for any offense under Subsection (2) on or after July 1, 2002;

(b) has pled guilty to or has been convicted by any other state or by the United States government of an offense which if committed in this state would be punishable as one or more of the offenses listed in Subsection (2), and who is on probation, parole, or incarcerated in this state for the offense on or after July 1, 2003; or

(c) is a minor under Subsection (3).

(2) Offenses referred to in Subsection (1) are:

(a) any felony under the Utah Code, and any violation of Section 76-5-401.1, sexual abuse of a minor;

(b) an attempt to commit a burglary, or any class A burglary offense; or

(c) any offense under Subsection (2)(a) or (b):

(i) for which the court enters a judgment for conviction to a lower degree of offense under Section 76-3-402; or

(ii) regarding which the court allows the defendant to enter a plea in abeyance as defined in Section 77-2a-1.

(3) A minor under Subsection (1) is a minor 14 years of age or older whom a Utah court has adjudicated to be within the jurisdiction of the juvenile court due to the commission of any offense described in Subsection (2), and who is:

(a) within the jurisdiction of the juvenile court on or after July 1, 2002 for an offense under Subsection (2); or

(b) in the legal custody of the Division of Juvenile Justice Services on or after July 1, 2002 for an offense under Subsection (2).   2003

53-10-403.5. Definitions.

As used in Sections 53-10-404, 53-10-405, and 53-10-406:

(1) "DNA" means deoxyribonucleic acid.

(2) "DNA specimen" or "specimen" means a sample of a person's saliva or blood.   2002

53-10-404. DNA specimen analysis — Requirement to obtain the specimen.

(1) As used in this section, "person" refers to any person described under Section 53-10-403.

(2) (a) A person under Section 53-10-403 or any person added to the sex offender register as defined in Section 77-27-21.5 shall provide a DNA specimen and shall reimburse the responsible agency $75 for the cost of obtaining the DNA specimen unless the agency determines the person lacks the ability to pay.

(b) (i) The responsible agencies shall establish guidelines and procedures for determining if the person is able to pay the fee. An agency's implementation of Subsection (2)(b)(ii) meets an agency's obligation to determine an inmate's ability to pay.

(ii) An agency's guidelines and procedures may provide for the assessment of $75 on the inmate's county trust fund account and may allow a negative balance in the account until the $75 is paid in full.

(3) (a) All fees collected under Subsection (2) shall be deposited in the DNA Specimen Restricted Account created in Section 53-10-407, except that sheriffs collecting the fee shall deposit $60 of the fee in the DNA Specimen Restricted Account and retain the balance of $15 for the costs of obtaining the saliva DNA specimen.

(b) The responsible agency shall determine the method of collecting the DNA specimen. Unless the responsible agency determines there are substantial reasons for using a different method of collection or the person refuses to cooperate with the collection, the preferred method of collection shall be obtaining a saliva specimen.

(c) The responsible agencies may use reasonable force, as established by their individual guidelines and procedures, to collect the DNA sample if the person refuses to cooperate with the collection.

(d) If the judgment places the person on probation, the person shall submit to the obtaining of a DNA specimen as a condition of the probation.

(e) Under this section a person is required to provide one DNA specimen. The person shall provide an additional DNA specimen only if the DNA specimen previously provided is not adequate for analysis.

(4) (a) The responsible agency shall cause a DNA specimen to be obtained as soon as possible after conviction, plea, or finding of jurisdiction by the juvenile court, and transmitted to the Department of Public Safety.

(b) If notified by the Department of Public Safety that a DNA specimen is not adequate for analysis, the agency shall obtain and transmit an additional DNA specimen.

(5) (a) The Department of Corrections is the responsible agency whenever the person is committed to the custody of or is under the supervision of the Department of Corrections.

(b) The juvenile court is the responsible agency regarding a minor under Subsection 53-10-403(3), but if the minor has been committed to the legal custody of the Division of Juvenile Justice Services, that division is the responsible agency if a DNA specimen of the minor has not previously been obtained by the juvenile court under Section 78-3a-118.

(c) The sheriff operating a county jail is the responsible agency regarding the collection of DNA specimens from persons who:

(i) have pled guilty to or have been convicted of an offense listed under Subsection 53-10-403(2) but who have not been commit-

ted to the custody of or are not under the supervision of the Department of Corrections; and

(ii) are incarcerated in the county jail:

(A) as a condition of probation for a felony offense; or

(B) for a misdemeanor offense for which collection of a DNA specimen is required.

(d) The sheriff under Subsection (5)(c) shall:

(i) designate employees to obtain the saliva DNA specimens required under Section 53-10-403; and

(ii) ensure that employees designated to collect the DNA specimens receive appropriate training and that the specimens are obtained in accordance with accepted protocol.

(6) (a) As used in this Subsection (6), "department" means the Department of Corrections.

(b) Priority of obtaining DNA specimens by the department is:

(i) first, to obtain DNA specimens of persons who as of July 1, 2002, are in the custody of or under the supervision of the department before these persons are released from incarceration, parole, or probation, if their release date is prior to that of persons under Subsections (6)(b)(ii), but in no case later than July 1, 2004; and

(ii) second, the department shall obtain DNA specimens from persons who are committed to the custody of the department or who are placed under the supervision of the department after July 1, 2002, within 120 days after the commitment, if possible, but not later than prior to release from incarceration if the person is imprisoned, or prior to the termination of probation if the person is placed on probation.

(c) The priority for obtaining DNA specimens from persons under Subsection (6)(b)(ii) is:

(i) persons on probation;

(ii) persons on parole; and

(iii) incarcerated persons.

(d) Implementation of the schedule of priority under Subsection (6)(c) is subject to the priority of Subsection (6)(b)(i), to ensure that the Department of Corrections obtains DNA specimens from persons in the custody of or under the supervision of the Department of Corrections as of July 1, 2002, prior to their release.

(7) (a) As used in this Subsection (7), "court" means the juvenile court and "division" means the Division of Juvenile Justice Services.

(b) Priority of obtaining DNA specimens by the court from minors under Section 53-10-403 who are under the jurisdiction of the court but who are not in the legal custody of the division shall be:

(i) first, to obtain specimens from minors who as of July 1, 2002, are within the court's jurisdiction, prior to termination of the court's jurisdiction over these minors; and

(ii) second, to obtain specimens from minors who are found to be within the court's jurisdiction after July 1, 2002, within 120 days of the minor's being found to be within the court's jurisdiction, if possible, but not later than prior to termination of the court's jurisdiction over the minor.

(c) Priority of obtaining DNA specimens by the division from minors under Section 53-10-403 who are committed to the legal custody of the division shall be:

(i) first, to obtain specimens from minors who as of July 1, 2002, are within the division's legal custody and who have not previously provided a DNA specimen under this section, prior to termination of the division's legal custody of these minors; and

(ii) second, to obtain specimens from minors who are placed in the legal custody of the division after July 1, 2002, within 120 days of the minor's being placed in the custody of the division, jurisdiction, if possible, but not later than prior to termination of the court's jurisdiction over the minor.

(8) (a) The Department of Corrections, the juvenile court, and the Division of Juvenile Justice Services shall by policy establish procedures for obtaining saliva DNA specimens, and shall provide training for employees designated to collect saliva DNA specimens.

(b) The department may designate correctional officers, including those employed by the adult probation and parole section of the Department of Corrections, to obtain the saliva DNA specimens required under this section. The department shall ensure that the designated employees receive appropriate training and that the specimens are obtained in accordance with accepted protocol.

(c) Blood DNA specimens shall be obtained in accordance with Section 53-10-405.   2004

53-10-405. DNA specimen analysis — Saliva sample to be obtained by agency — Blood sample to be drawn by professional.

(1) (a) A blood sample shall be drawn in a medically acceptable manner by a licensed professional nurse, a licensed practical nurse, a paramedic, a qualified medical technician, a licensed physician, or other person licensed by the state for this purpose.

(b) A person authorized by this section to draw a blood sample may not be held civilly liable for drawing a sample in a medically acceptable manner.

(2) (a) A saliva sample shall be obtained by the responsible agency, as provided under Subsection 53-10-404(5).

(b) The sample shall be obtained in a professionally acceptable manner, using appropriate procedures to ensure the sample is adequate for DNA analysis.

(3) A test result or opinion based upon a test result regarding a DNA specimen may not be rendered inadmissible as evidence solely because of deviations from procedures adopted by the department that do not affect the reliability of the opinion or test result.

(4) A DNA specimen is not required to be obtained if:

(a) the department notifies the court or the responsible agency that it has previously received an adequate DNA specimen obtained from the convicted person in accordance with this section; or

(b) the court determines that obtaining a DNA specimen would create a substantial and unreasonable risk to the health of the convicted person.   2002

53-10-406. DNA specimen analysis — Bureau responsibilities.

(1) The bureau shall:

(a) store all DNA specimens received and other physical evidence obtained from analysis of those specimens;

(b) analyze the specimens to establish the genetic profile of the donor or to otherwise determine the identity of persons or contract with other qualified public or private laboratories to conduct the analysis;

(c) maintain a criminal identification data base containing information derived from DNA analysis;

(d) utilize the specimens to create statistical population frequency data bases, provided that genetic profiles or other information in a population frequency data base may not be identified with specific individuals;

(e) ensure that the DNA identification system does not provide information allowing prediction of genetic disease or predisposition to illness; and

(f) make rules in accordance with Title 63, Chapter 46a, Utah Administrative Rulemaking Act, establishing procedures for obtaining, transmitting, and analyzing DNA specimens and for storing and destroying DNA specimens and other physical evidence and criminal identification information obtained from the analysis.

(2) Procedures for DNA analysis may include all techniques which the Department of Public Safety determines are accurate and reliable in establishing identity, including but not limited to, analysis of DNA, antigen antibodies, polymorphic enzymes, or polymorphic proteins.

(3) (a) In accordance with Section 63-2-304, all DNA specimens received shall be classified as protected.

(b) The Department of Public Safety may not transfer or disclose any DNA specimen, physical evidence, or criminal identification information obtained, stored, or maintained under this section, except under its provisions.

(4) Notwithstanding the provisions of Subsection 63-2-202(1), the department may deny inspection if it determines that there is a reasonable likelihood that the inspection would prejudice a pending criminal investigation.

(5) The department shall adopt procedures governing the inspection of records, DNA specimens, and challenges to the accuracy of records. The procedures shall accommodate the need to preserve the materials from contamination and destruction.

(6) (a) Whenever a court reverses the conviction, judgment, or order that created an obligation to provide a DNA specimen, the person who provided the specimen may request destruction of the specimen and any criminal identification record created in connection with that specimen.

(b) Upon receipt of a written request for destruction pursuant to this section and a certified copy of the court order reversing the conviction, judgment, or order, the Department of Public Safety shall destroy any specimen received from the person, any physical evidence obtained from that specimen, and any criminal identification records pertaining to the person, unless the department determines that the person has otherwise become obligated to submit a DNA specimen as a result of a separate conviction or juvenile adjudication for an offense listed in Section 53-10-403.

(7) The department is not required to destroy any item of physical evidence obtained from a DNA specimen if evidence relating to another person subject to

the provisions of Sections 53-10-404 and 53-10-405 would as a result be destroyed.

(8) A DNA specimen, physical evidence, or criminal identification record may not be affected by an order to set aside a conviction, except under the provisions of this section.

(9) If funding is not available for analysis of any of the DNA specimens collected under this part, the bureau shall store the collected specimens until funding is made available for analysis through state or federal funds.   2003

53-10-407. DNA Specimen Restricted Account.

(1) There is created the DNA Specimen Restricted Account, which is referred to in this section as "the account."

(2) The sources of monies for the account are:

(a) DNA collection fees paid under Section 53-10-404;

(b) any appropriations made to the account by the Legislature; and

(c) all federal monies provided to the state for the purpose of funding the collection or analysis of DNA specimens collected under Section 53-10-403.

(3) The account shall earn interest, and this interest shall be deposited in the account.

(4) The Legislature may appropriate monies from the account solely for the following purposes:

(a) to the Department of Corrections for the costs of collecting DNA specimens as required under Section 53-10-403;

(b) to the juvenile court for the costs of collecting DNA specimens as required under Sections 53-10-403 and 78-3a-118;

(c) to the Division of Juvenile Justice Services for the costs of collecting DNA specimens as required under Sections 53-10-403 and 62A-7-104; and

(d) to the Department of Public Safety for the costs of storing and analyzing DNA specimens in accordance with the requirements of this part.

(5) Appropriations from the account to the Department of Corrections, the juvenile court, the Division of Juvenile Justice Services, and to the Department of Public Safety are nonlapsing.   2003

PART 5

BUREAU OF COMMUNICATIONS

53-10-501. Bureau of Communications — Creation — Bureau Chief appointment, qualifications, and compensation.

(1) There is created within the division the Bureau of Communications.

(2) The bureau shall be managed by a bureau chief selected by the division director, with the approval of the commissioner.

(3) The bureau chief should be experienced in communications and administration, and possess additional qualifications as determined by the commissioner or division director and as provided by law.

(4) The bureau chief acts under the supervision and control of the division director.   1998

53-10-502. Bureau duties.

The bureau:

(1) maintains dispatch and communications services for regional public safety consolidated communications centers;

(2) provides facilities and acts as a public safety answering point to answer and respond to 911 calls from a region;

(3) provides professional emergency dispatch and communications support for law enforcement, emergency medical, fire suppression, highway maintenance, public works, and public safety agencies representing municipal, county, state, and federal governments; and

(4) coordinates incident response.   1999

53-10-503. Repealed.   2004

PART 6

COORDINATION OF STATEWIDE 911 EMERGENCY COMMUNICATIONS

53-10-601. Utah 911 Committee.

(1) There is created within the division, the Utah 911 Committee consisting of the following 15 members:

(a) a representative from each of the following primary emergency public safety answering points:

(i) Salt Lake County;

(ii) Davis County;

(iii) Utah County; and

(iv) Weber County;

(b) four members representing the following primary emergency public safety answering points:

(i) Bear River Association;

(ii) Uintah Basin Association;

(iii) South East Association;

(iv) Six County Association;

(v) Five County Association; and

(vi) Mountainlands Association, not including Utah County;

(c) the following people with knowledge of technology and equipment that might be needed for an emergency public safety answering system:

(i) a representative from a local exchange carrier;

(ii) a representative from a rural incumbent local exchange carrier; and

(iii) two representatives from radio communications services as defined in Section 69-2-2;

(d) two representatives from the Department of Public Safety, one of whom represents urban Utah and the other rural Utah; and

(e) a representative from the Department of Technology Services, created in Title 63F, Chapter 1.

(2) (a) Each committee member shall be appointed as follows:

(i) a member described in Subsection (1)(a) shall be appointed by the governor from a nominee or nominees submitted to the governor by the council of government for that member's county;

(ii) the four members described in Subsection (1)(b) shall be appointed by the governor from a nominee or nominees submitted to the governor by the associations described in Subsection (1)(b) as follows:

(A) the six associations shall select by lot, the first four associations to begin the rotation of membership as required by Subsection (2)(b)(i); and

(B) as each association is represented on the commission in accordance with Subsection (2)(b)(i), that association shall select the person to represent it on the commission;

(iii) the members described in Subsection (1)(c) shall be appointed by the governor with the consent of the Senate; and

(iv) the members described in Subsections (1)(d) and (e) shall be appointed by the governor.

(b) The term of office of each member is four years, except as provided in Subsections (2)(b)(ii) through (iv).

(i) The representatives from Subsection (1)(b) must rotate to provide each geographic location at least one representative every four years, except as provided for the initial appointment under Subsection (2)(b)(ii).

(ii) The associations listed in Subsection (1)(b) shall select by lot, two of its members to an initial two-year term.

(iii) The governor shall appoint two representatives from Subsection (1)(c) to initial two-year terms.

(iv) The public service answering points listed in Subsection (1)(a) shall, by lot, select two members to serve an initial two-year term.

(c) No member of the committee may serve more that two consecutive four-year terms.

(d) Each mid-term vacancy shall be filled for the unexpired term in the same manner as an appointment under Subsection (2)(a).

(3) (a) Committee members shall elect a chair from their number and establish rules for the organization and operation of the committee, with the chair rotating among representatives from Subsections (1)(a), (b), and (d) every year.

(b) Staff services to the committee:

(i) shall be provided by the division; and

(ii) may be provided by local entities through the Utah Association of Counties and the Utah League of Cities and Towns.

(c) Funding for staff services shall be provided with funds approved by the committee from those identified under Section 53-10-605.

(4) (a) No member may receive compensation or benefits for the member's service on the committee.

(b) A member is not required to give bond for the performance of official duties.   2005

53-10-602. Committee's duties and powers.

(1) The committee shall:

(a) review and make recommendations to the division, the Bureau of Communications, public safety answering points, and the Legislature on:

(i) technical and operational issues for the implementation of a unified statewide wireless and land-based E-911 emergency system;

(ii) specific technology and standards for the implementation of a unified statewide wireless and land-based E-911 emergency system;

(iii) expenditures by local public service answering points to assure implementation of a unified statewide wireless and land-based E-911 emergency system and standards of operation; and

(iv) mapping systems and technology necessary to implement the unified statewide wireless and land-based E-911 emergency system;

(b) administer the fund as provided in this part;

(c) assist as many local entities as possible, at their request, to implement the recommendations of the committee; and

(d) fulfill all other duties imposed on the committee by the Legislature by this part.

(2) The committee may sell, lease, or otherwise dispose of equipment or personal property belonging to the committee, the proceeds from which shall return to the fund.

(3) The committee shall issue the reimbursement allowed under Subsection 53-10-605(1)(b) provided that:

(a) the reimbursement is based on aggregated cost studies submitted to the committee by the wireless carriers seeking reimbursement; and

(b) the reimbursement to any one carrier does not exceed 125% of the wireless carrier's contribution to the fund.

(4) The committee shall adopt rules in accordance with Title 63, Chapter 46a, Utah Administrative Rulemaking Act, to administer the fund created in Section 53-10-603 including rules that establish the criteria, standards, technology, and equipment that a local entity or state agency must adopt in order to qualify for grants from the fund.   2004

53-10-603. Creation of Statewide Unified E-911 Emergency Service Fund.

(1) There is created a restricted account in the General Fund entitled the "Statewide Unified E-911 Emergency Service Fund," or "fund" consisting of:

(a) proceeds from the fee imposed in Section 69-2-5.6;

(b) money appropriated or otherwise made available by the Legislature;

(c) proceeds from the levy imposed in Section 69-2-5, as required by Subsection 69-2-5(3)(c)(iii); and

(d) contributions of money, property, or equipment from federal agencies, political subdivisions of the state, persons, or corporations.

(2) The moneys in this fund shall be used exclusively for the following statewide public purposes:

(a) enhancing public safety as provided in this chapter;

(b) providing a statewide, unified, wireless E-911 service available to public service answering points; and

(c) providing reimbursement to providers for certain costs associated with Phase 1 wireless E-911 service.   2004

53-10-604. Committee expenses — Tax Commission expenses — Division of Finance responsibilities.

(1) Committee expenses and the costs of administering grants from the fund, as provided in Subsection (3), shall be paid from the fund.

(2) (a) The expenses and costs of the State Tax Commission to administer and enforce the collection of the telephone levy imposed by Section 69-2-5.6 shall be paid from the fund.

(b) (i) The State Tax Commission may charge the fund the administrative costs incurred in discharging the responsibilities imposed by Section 69-2-5.6.

(ii) The charges in Subsection (2)(b)(i) may not exceed an amount equal to 1.5% of the charges imposed under Section 69-2-5.6.

(3) (a) The Division of Finance shall be responsible for the care, custody, safekeeping, collection, and accounting for grants issued by the committee under the provisions of Section 53-10-605.

(b) The Division of Finance may charge the fund the administrative costs incurred in discharging the responsibilities imposed by Subsection (3)(a). 2004

53-10-605. Use of money in fund — Criteria — Administration.

(1) Subject to an annual legislative appropriation from the fund to:

(a) the committee, the committee shall:

(i) authorize the use of the money in the fund, by grant to a local entity or state agency in accordance with this Subsection (1) and Subsection (2);

(ii) grant to state agencies and local entities an amount not to exceed the per month fee levied on telephone services under Section 69-2-5.6 for installation, implementation, and maintenance of unified, statewide 911 emergency services and technology; and

(iii) in addition to any money under Subsection (1)(a)(ii), grant to counties of the third through sixth class the amount dedicated for rural assistance, which is at least 3 cents per month levied on telephone services under Section 69-2-5.6 to:

(A) enhance the 911 emergency services with a focus on areas or counties that do not have E-911 services; and

(B) where needed, assist the counties, in cooperation with private industry, with the creation or integration of wireless systems and location technology in rural areas of the state; and

(b) the committee, the committee shall:

(i) include reimbursement to a provider of radio communications service, as defined in Section 69-2-2, for costs as provided in Subsections (1)(b)(ii) and (iii);

(ii) an agreement to reimburse costs to a provider of radio communications services must be a written agreement among the committee, the local public safety answering point and the carrier; and

(iii) shall include reimbursement to the provider for the cost of design, development, and implementation of equipment or software necessary to provide Phase I, wireless E-911 service to public service answering points, provided:

(A) the reimbursement under this Subsection (1)(b) does not exceed the amount allowed by Subsection 53-10-602(3);

(B) the provider submits an invoice for the reimbursement to the committee; and

(C) the provider has not been reimbursed by the consumer for the costs submitted to the committee; and

(c) the state's Automated Geographic Reference Center in the Division of Integrated Technology of the Department of Technology Services, an amount equal to 1 cent per month levied on telephone services under Section 69-2-5.6 shall be used to enhance and upgrade statewide digital mapping standards.

(2) (a) Beginning July 1, 2007, the committee may not grant the money in the fund to a local entity unless the local entity is in compliance with Phase I, wireless E-911 service.

(b) Beginning July 1, 2009, the committee may not grant money in the fund to a local entity unless the local entity is in compliance with Phase II, wireless E-911 service.

(3) A local entity must deposit any money it receives from the committee into a special emergency telephone service fund in accordance with Subsection 69-2-5(4).

(4) For purposes of this part, "local entity" means a county, city, town, special district, local district, or interlocal entity created under Title 11, Chapter 13, Interlocal Cooperation Act. 2005

53-10-606. Committee to report annually.

(1) The committee shall submit an annual report to the Executive Appropriations Committee of the Legislature which shall include:

(a) the total aggregate surcharge collected by local entities and the state in the last fiscal year under Sections 69-2-5 and 69-2-5.6;

(b) the amount of each disbursement from the fund;

(c) the recipient of each disbursement and describing the project for which money was disbursed;

(d) the conditions, if any, placed by the committee on disbursements from the fund;

(e) the planned expenditures from the fund for the next fiscal year;

(f) the amount of any unexpended funds carried forward;

(g) a cost study to guide the Legislature towards necessary adjustments of both the Statewide Unified E-911 Emergency Service Fund and the monthly emergency services telephone charge imposed under Section 69-2-5; and

(h) a progress report of local government implementation of wireless and land-based E-911 services including:

(i) a fund balance or balance sheet from each agency maintaining its own emergency telephone service fund;

(ii) a report from each public safety answering point of annual call activity separating wireless and land-based 911 call volumes; and

(iii) other relevant justification for ongoing support from the Statewide Unified E-911 Emergency Service Fund.

(2) (a) The committee may request information from a local entity as necessary to prepare the report required by this section.

(b) A local entity imposing a levy under Section 69-2-5 or receiving a grant under Section 53-10-605 shall provide the information requested pursuant to Subsection (2)(a). 2004

CHAPTER 11

BAIL BOND RECOVERY

53-11-101.   Title.

This chapter is known as the "Bail Bond Recovery Act."   1998

53-11-102.   Definitions.

As used in this chapter:

(1) "Applicant" means a person who has submitted to the department a completed application and all required application and processing fees.

(2) "Bail bond agency" means a bail enforcement agent licensed under this chapter who operates a business to carry out the functions of a bail enforcement agent, and to conduct this business:

(a) employs one or more persons licensed under this chapter for wages or salary, and withholds all legally required deductions and contributions; or

(b) contracts with a bail recovery agent or bail recovery apprentice on a part-time or case-by-case basis.

(3) "Bail enforcement agent" means an individual licensed under this chapter as a bail enforcement agent to enforce the terms and conditions of a defendant's release on bail in a civil or criminal proceeding, to apprehend a defendant or surrender a defendant to custody, or both, as is appropriate, and who:

(a) is appointed by a bail bond surety; and

(b) receives or is promised monies or other things of value for this service.

(4) "Bail recovery agent" means an individual employed by a bail enforcement agent to assist the bail enforcement agent regarding civil or criminal defendants released on bail by:

(a) presenting a defendant for required court appearances;

(b) apprehending or surrendering a defendant to a court; or

(c) keeping the defendant under necessary surveillance.

(5) "Bail recovery apprentice" means any individual licensed under this chapter as a bail recovery apprentice, and who:

(a) has not met the requirements for licensure as a bail recovery agent or bail enforcement agent; and

(b) is employed by a bail enforcement agent, and works under the direct supervision of a bail enforcement agent or bail recovery agent employed also by the bail enforcement agent, unless the bail recovery apprentice is conducting activities at the direction of the employing bail enforcement agent that under this chapter do not require direct supervision.

(6) "Board" means the Bail Bond Recovery Licensure Board created under Section 53-11-104.

(7) "Commissioner" means the commissioner of public safety as defined under Section 53-1-107, or his designee.

(8) "Contract employee" or "independent contractor" means a person who works for an agency as an independent contractor.

(9) "Conviction" means an adjudication of guilt by a federal, state, or local court resulting from a trial or plea, including a plea of no contest or nolo contendere, regardless of whether the imposition of sentence was suspended.

(10) "Department" means the Department of Public Safety.

(11) "Direct supervision" means a bail enforcement agent employing or contracting with a bail recovery apprentice, or a bail recovery agent employed by or contracting with that bail enforcement agent who:

(a) takes responsibility for and assigns the work a bail recovery apprentice may conduct; and

(b) closely supervises, within close physical proximity, and provides direction and guidance to the bail recovery apprentice regarding the assigned work.

(12) "Emergency action" means a summary suspension of a license issued under this chapter pending revocation, suspension, or probation, in order to protect the public health, safety, or welfare.

(13) "Identification card" means a card issued by the commissioner to an applicant qualified for licensure under this chapter.

(14) "Letter of concern" means an advisory letter to notify a licensee that while there is insufficient evidence to support probation, suspension, or revocation of a license, the department believes:

(a) the licensee should modify or eliminate certain practices; and

(b) continuation of the activities that led to the information being submitted to the department may result in further disciplinary action against the license.

(15) "Occupied structure" means any edifice, including residential and public buildings, ve-

hicles, or any other structure that could reasonably be expected to house or shelter persons.

(16) "Supervision" means the employing bail enforcement agent is responsible for and authorizes the type and extent of work assigned to a bail recovery agent who is his employee or contract employee.

(17) "Unprofessional conduct" means:

(a) engaging or offering to engage by fraud or misrepresentation in any activities regulated by this chapter;

(b) aiding or abetting a person who is not licensed pursuant to this chapter in representing that person as a bail recovery agent in this state;

(c) gross negligence in the practice of a bail recovery agent;

(d) committing a felony or a misdemeanor involving any crime that is grounds for denial, suspension, or revocation of a bail recovery license, and conviction by a court of competent jurisdiction or a plea of no contest is conclusive evidence of the commission; or

(e) making a fraudulent or untrue statement to the board, department, its investigators, or staff.   1998

53-11-103. Commissioner of Public Safety administers — Licensure — Rulemaking.

(1) The commissioner administers this chapter, including keeping records of:

(a) all applications for licenses under this chapter; and

(b) proof of workers' compensation required to be filed.

(2) Records shall include statements as to whether a license or renewal license has been issued for each application and bond.

(3) If a license is revoked, suspended, or canceled, or a license is denied or placed on probation, the commissioner shall ensure the date of filing the order for revocation, suspension, cancellation, denial, or probation is included in the records.

(4) The commissioner shall maintain a list of all individuals, firms, partnerships, associations, or corporations that have had a license revoked, suspended, placed on probation, or canceled and a written record of complaints filed against licensees.

(5) (a) The commissioner may make rules in accordance with Title 63, Chapter 46a, Utah Administrative Rulemaking Act, as necessary to administer this chapter.

(b) These rules shall include a requirement that all providers offering instruction or continuing instruction required for licensure under this chapter shall offer the courses to all applicants at the same course fees, in order to be qualified by the board.

(6) All records referred to under this section are open to the public under Title 63, Chapter 2, Government Records Access and Management Act, except licensees' residential addresses and telephone numbers.   1998

53-11-104. Board.

(1) (a) There is established under the Department of Public Safety a Bail Bond Recovery Licensure Board consisting of five members appointed by the commissioner.

(b) The commissioner may appoint, in accordance with this section, persons who are also serving in the same capacity on the Private Investigator Hearing and Licensure Board under Section 53-9-104.

(2) Each member of the board shall be a citizen of the United States and a resident of this state at the time of appointment:

(a) one member shall be a person who is qualified for and is licensed under this chapter;

(b) one member shall be a an attorney licensed to practice in the state;

(c) one member shall be a chief of police or sheriff;

(d) one member shall be an owner of a bail bond surety company who is not a bail enforcement agent or a bail recovery agent; and

(e) one member shall be a public member who does not have:

(i) a financial interest in a bail bond surety or bail bond recovery business; and

(ii) an immediate family member or a household member, or a personal or professional acquaintance who is licensed or registered under this chapter.

(3) (a) As terms of current board members expire, the commissioner shall appoint each new member or reappointed member to a four-year term, except as required by Subsection (3)(b).

(b) The commissioner shall, at the time of appointment or reappointment, adjust the length of terms to ensure that the terms of board members are staggered so that approximately half of the board is appointed every two years.

(4) When a vacancy occurs in the membership for any reason, the replacement shall be appointed for the unexpired term.

(5) At its first meeting every year, the board shall elect a chair and vice chair from its membership.

(6) (a) (i) Members who are not government employees receive no compensation or benefits for their services, but may receive per diem and expenses incurred in the performance of the member's official duties at the rates established by the Division of Finance under Sections 63A-3-106 and 63A-3-107.

(ii) Members may decline to receive per diem and expenses for their service.

(b) (i) State government officer and employee members who do not receive salary, per diem, or expenses from their agency for their service may receive per diem and expenses incurred in the performance of their official duties from the board at the rates established by the Division of Finance under Sections 63A-3-106 and 63A-3-107.

(ii) State government officer and employee members may decline to receive per diem and expenses for their service.

(7) A member may not serve more than one term, except that a member appointed to fill a vacancy or appointed for an initial term of less than four years under Subsection (3) may be reappointed for one additional full term.

(8) The commissioner, after a board hearing and recommendation, may remove any member of the board for misconduct, incompetency, or neglect of duty.

(9) Members of the board are immune from suit with respect to all acts done and actions taken in good faith in carrying out the purposes of this chapter.   1998

53-11-105. Powers and duties of board.

(1) The board shall:

(a) review all applications for licensing and renewals of licenses under this chapter and approve or disapprove all applications;

(b) review all complaints and take disciplinary action; and

(c) establish standards for and approve providers of courses required for licensure under this section.

(2) The board may take and hear evidence, administer oaths and affirmations, and compel by subpoena the attendance of witnesses and the production of books, papers, records, documents, and other information relating to:

(a) investigation of an applicant for licensure under this chapter; or

(b) a formal complaint against or department investigation of a bail enforcement agent, bail recovery agent, or bail recovery apprentice.   1998

53-11-106. Board meetings and hearings — Quorum.

(1) The board shall meet at the call of the chair, but not less often than once each quarter.

(2) A quorum consists of three members, but the quorum shall include one peace officer, one person licensed under this chapter and one public member.

(3) If a member has three or more unexcused absences within a 12-month period, the commissioner shall determine if that board member should be released from board duties.   1998

53-11-107. Licenses — Classifications — Prohibited acts.

(1) Licenses under this chapter are issued in the classifications of:

(a) bail enforcement agent;

(b) bail recovery agent; or

(c) bail recovery apprentice.

(2) A person may not:

(a) act or assume to act as, or represent himself to be, a licensee unless he is licensed under this chapter; or

(b) falsely represent that he is employed by a licensee.

(3) The commissioner shall issue licenses to applicants who qualify for them under this chapter.

(4) A license issued under this chapter is not transferable or assignable.   1998

53-11-108. Licensure — Basic qualifications.

An applicant for licensure under this chapter shall meet the following qualifications:

(1) An applicant shall be:

(a) at least 21 years of age;

(b) a citizen or legal resident of the United States; and

(c) of good moral character.

(2) An applicant may not:

(a) have been convicted of:

(i) a felony;

(ii) any act involving illegally using, carrying, or possessing a dangerous weapon;

(iii) any act of personal violence or force on any person or convicted of threatening to commit any act of personal violence or force against another person;

(iv) any act constituting dishonesty or fraud;

(v) impersonating a peace officer; or

(vi) any act involving moral turpitude;

(b) be on probation, parole, community supervision, or named in an outstanding arrest warrant; or

(c) be employed as a peace officer.

(3) If previously or currently licensed in another state or jurisdiction, the applicant shall be in good standing within that state or jurisdiction.

(4) (a) The applicant shall also have completed a training program of not less than 16 hours that is approved by the board and includes:

(i) instruction on the duties and responsibilities of a licensee under this chapter, including:

(A) search, seizure, and arrest procedure;

(B) pursuit, arrest, detainment, and transportation of a bail bond suspect; and

(C) specific duties and responsibilities regarding entering an occupied structure to carry out functions under this chapter;

(ii) the laws and rules relating to the bail bond business;

(iii) the rights of the accused; and

(iv) ethics.

(b) The program may be completed after the licensure application is submitted, but shall be completed before a license may be issued under this chapter.

(5) If the applicant desires to carry a firearm as a licensee, the applicant shall:

(a) successfully complete a course regarding the specified types of weapons he plans to carry. The course shall:

(i) be not less than 16 hours;

(ii) be conducted by any national, state, or local firearms training organization approved by the Criminal Investigations and Technical Services Division created in Section 53-10-103; and

(iii) provide training regarding general familiarity with the types of firearms to be carried, including:

(A) the safe loading, unloading, storage, and carrying of the types of firearms to be concealed; and

(B) current laws defining lawful use of a firearm by a private citizen, including lawful self-defense, use of deadly force, transportation, and concealment; and

(b) shall hold a valid license to carry a concealed weapon, issued under Section 53-5-704.   1999

53-11-109. Licensure — Bail enforcement agent.

(1) (a) In addition to the requirements in Sections 53-11-108 and 53-11-110, an applicant for licensure as a bail enforcement agent shall have a minimum of 2,000 hours of experience consisting of either actual bail recovery work, or work as a law enforcement officer for a federal, state, or local governmental agency.

(b) The applicant shall substantiate the experience claimed under Subsection (1) as qualifying experience and shall provide:

(i) the exact details as to the character and nature of the experience on a form prescribed by the department; and

(ii) certification by the applicant's employers, which is subject to independent verification by the board.

(c) If an applicant is unable to supply written certification of experience from an employer in whole or in part, an applicant may offer written certification from persons other than an employer covering the same subject matter for consideration by the board.

(d) The burden of proving completion of the required experience is on the applicant.

(2) An applicant for license renewal shall have completed not less than eight hours of continuing classroom instruction. 1998

53-11-110. Bail enforcement agent as agency — Bond — Workers' compensation.

(1) An applicant for licensure as a bail enforcement agent who will operate a bail bond recovery agency shall provide the following information as part of the application:

(a) the full name and business address of the applicant;

(b) two passport-size color photographs of the applicant;

(c) the name under which the applicant intends to conduct the business;

(d) a statement that the applicant intends to engage in the bail bond recovery business;

(e) a notarized statement of the applicant's qualifications as required by Sections 53-11-108 and 53-11-109;

(f) the fee required by Section 53-11-115;

(g) a certificate of workers' compensation insurance, if applicable; and

(h) proof of completion of a training program approved by the board.

(2) The license for a bail enforcement agent shall indicate on its face if the holder is licensed to act as a bail bond recovery agency. 1998

53-11-111. Licensure — Bail recovery agent — Requirements and limitations.

(1) (a) In addition to the requirements in Sections 53-11-108 and 53-11-113, an applicant for licensure as a bail recovery agent shall meet all of the requirements under Section 53-11-109, but instead of the experience requirement under Subsection 53-11-109(1)(a), a bail recovery agent applicant shall have a minimum of 1,000 hours of experience consisting of either actual bail recovery work, or work as a law enforcement officer for a federal, state, or local governmental agency.

(b) The applicant shall substantiate the experience claimed under Subsection (1) as qualifying experience and shall provide:

(i) the exact details as to the character and nature of the experience on a form prescribed by the department; and

(ii) certification by the applicant's employers, which is subject to independent verification by the board.

(c) If an applicant is unable to supply written certification of experience from an employer in whole or in part, an applicant may offer written certification from persons other than an employer covering the same subject matter for consideration by the board.

(d) The burden of proving completion of the required experience is on the applicant.

(2) An applicant for license renewal shall have completed not less than eight hours of continuing classroom instruction.

(3) A bail recovery agent may work as a licensee under this chapter only as an employee of or as an independent contractor with a bail bond agency. A bail recovery agent may not:

(a) advertise his services;

(b) provide services as a licensee under this chapter directly for members of the public; or

(c) employ or hire as independent contractors bail enforcement agents, bail recovery agents, or bail recovery apprentices. 1998

53-11-112. Licensure — Bail recovery apprentices — Requirements and limitations.

(1) In addition to the requirements in Sections 53-11-108 and 53-11-113, an applicant for licensure as a bail recovery apprentice shall meet all of the requirements under Section 53-11-109, except the applicant is not subject to the experience requirement under Subsection 53-11-109(1)(a).

(2) A bail recovery apprentice may work as a licensee only:

(a) as an employee or contract employee of a bail bond agency; and

(b) under the direct supervision of a bail enforcement agent or bail recovery agent employed also by the bail enforcement agent, unless the bail recovery apprentice is conducting activities at the direction of the employing bail enforcement agent that under this chapter do not require direct supervision.

(3) A bail recovery apprentice may not:

(a) advertise his services;

(b) provide services as a licensee under this chapter directly for members of the public; or

(c) employ or hire as independent contractors bail enforcement agents, bail recovery agents, or bail recovery apprentices. 1998

53-11-113. Bail recovery agent and bail recovery apprentice licensure — Liability insurance — Fee — Workers' compensation.

(1) An applicant for licensure as a bail recovery agent or as a bail recovery apprentice shall provide as part of the application:

(a) the full name and address of the applicant;

(b) two passport-size color photographs of the applicant;

(c) the name of the bail bond recovery agency for which the applicant will be an employee or with which the applicant will be an independent contractor;

(d) written indication by a bail bond recovery agency or its designee that it intends to employ or contract with the applicant; and

(e) a notarized statement of the applicant's experience and qualifications required under Section 53-11-111 or 53-11-112, as appropriate.

(2) The licensure application or renewal shall be accompanied by the fee required under Section 53-11-115.

(3) (a) A license or a license renewal for a bail recovery agent or a bail recovery apprentice may not be granted to an applicant unless the employing bail bond recovery agency has on file with the department evidence of current workers' compensation coverage.

(b) A bail recovery agent or bail recovery apprentice license may not be reinstated without providing verification of the reinstatement of the workers' compensation coverage and payment of the reinstatement fee required in Section 53-11-115.

(c) The provisions of this Subsection (3) do not apply to a bail recovery agent or bail recovery apprentice who is working for a bail bond recovery agency as an independent contractor.   1998

53-11-114. Licensure — Qualification credit for specified training.

(1) An applicant under this chapter may be exempt from meeting all or a portion of the experience or training requirements for licensure if the applicant:

(a) holds a criminal justice bachelor's degree from an accredited college or university;

(b) is certified to have successfully completed the state Peace Officers Standards and Training basic training course provided under Section 53-6-202; or

(c) provides adequate proof of having successfully completed a training course which the board finds is essentially similar to the training course under Subsection (1)(b).

(2) The board determines to what extent training listed under this section may meet the experience or training requirements for licensure under this chapter.   1998

53-11-115. License fees — Deposit in General Fund.

(1) Fees for licensure, registration, and renewal are:

(a) for an original bail enforcement agent license application and license, $250, which shall include the costs of fingerprint processing and background investigation;

(b) for the renewal of a bail enforcement agent or bail bond recovery agency license, $150;

(c) for an original bail recovery agent license application and license, $150, which shall include the costs of fingerprint processing and background investigation;

(d) for the renewal of each bail recovery agent license, $100;

(e) for an original bail recovery apprentice license application and license, $150, which shall include the costs of fingerprint processing and background investigation;

(f) for the renewal of each bail recovery apprentice license, $100;

(g) for filing a renewal application under Subsection (1)(b) more than 30 days after the expiration date of the license, a delinquency fee of $50;

(h) for filing a renewal application under Subsection (1)(d) more than 30 days after the expiration date of the registration, a delinquency fee of $30;

(i) for filing a renewal application under Subsection (1)(f) more than 30 days after the expiration date of the apprentice license, a delinquency fee of $30;

(j) for the reinstatement of a bail enforcement agent or bail bond recovery agency license, $50;

(k) for a duplicate identification card, $10; and

(l) for reinstatement of an identification card, $10.

(2) (a) The board may renew a license granted under this chapter upon receipt of an application on forms as prescribed by the board and upon receipt of the fees prescribed in Subsection (1).

(b) The renewal of a bail enforcement agent, bail recovery agent, or bail recovery apprentice license requires the filing of a liability insurance policy as described in Subsections 53-9-109(2) and (3).

(c) A license may not be renewed more than 90 days after its expiration.

(d) A licensee may not engage in any activity subject to this chapter during any period between the date of expiration of the license and the renewal of the license.

(3) (a) The board may reinstate a suspended license upon completion of the term of suspension.

(b) Renewal of the license does not entitle the licensee, while the license remains suspended and until it is reinstated, to engage in any activity regulated by this chapter, or in any other activity or conduct in violation of the order or judgment by which the license was suspended.

(4) The board may not reinstate a revoked license or accept an application for a license from a person whose license has been revoked for at least one year after the date of revocation.

(5) All fees collected by the department under this section shall be deposited in the General Fund.   1998

53-11-116. Issuance of license and card to applicant — License period — Expiration of application — Transfer of license prohibited.

(1) (a) The board shall issue a license to an applicant who complies with the provisions of this chapter.

(b) Each license shall:

(i) contain the name and address of the licensee, the classification of license, and the number of the license; and

(ii) be issued for a period of two years.

(2) (a) When the board issues the license, it shall also issue an identification card the design of which shall be approved by the commissioner in accordance with Section 53-11-116.5.

(b) The identification card shall be issued without charge to the licensee if an individual, or if the licensee is an agency, to each of its licensed employees and contract employees, and is evidence the licensee and his employees and contract employees are licensed under this chapter.

(3) (a) If an identification card issued to a person states on it any bail bond agencies for which the cardholder works, that person shall return the card to the employer upon termination of his work relationship with the bail bond agency licensee.

(b) Within five days the licensee shall mail or deliver the card to the commissioner for cancellation.

(4) (a) When the commissioner notifies an applicant that licensure as a bail bond recovery agency is ready for issuance, the applicant shall complete the application process within 90 days.

(b) Failure to complete the process results in cancellation of the application and forfeiture of all fees paid to that point.

(c) Subsequent application by the same applicant requires the payment of all application and license fees prescribed in Section 53-11-115.

(5) A bail bond agency licensee shall notify the commissioner of any change in the name or address of his business and of any change of employees or contract employees within 30 days after the change.

(6) (a) All new employees and contract employees of an agency who are licensed under this chapter shall submit applications on forms prescribed by the board.

(b) Upon board approval, identification cards shall be issued without charge.   1999

53-11-116.5. Identification cards.

(1) A person licensed under this chapter as a bail enforcement agent or a bail recovery agent shall carry an identification card issued under this section.

(2) (a) Bail bond agencies may submit designs for an identification card that shall be used for identification purposes by bail enforcement agents and bail recovery agents licensed under this chapter.

(b) The commissioner shall establish a procedure for the submitting of identification card designs and shall select one design to be used for all identification cards issued under this section.

(c) The identification card design:

(i) may not resemble any identification card currently in use by a law enforcement agency within the state; and

(ii) shall include:

(A) the licensee's classification of licensure;

(B) the license number; and

(C) a current photo of the licensee.

(d) The department of public safety shall issue identification cards, upon notification by the board that a license has been issued. **1999**

53-11-117. Workers' compensation requirements for employees' licensure.

(1) An applicant for licensure under this section who is employed by a bail bond recovery agency may not obtain or renew a license unless the employer has on file with the department evidence of current workers' compensation coverage.

(2) The applicant's license may only be reinstated upon verification by the department of the reinstatement of the workers' compensation coverage and payment of the reinstatement fee required under Section 53-11-115.

(3) This section does not apply to contract employees. **1998**

53-11-118. Grounds for denial of license — Appeal.

(1) The board may deny a license application or a license renewal if the applicant has:

(a) committed an act that, if committed by a licensee, would be grounds for probation, suspension, or revocation of a license under this chapter;

(b) employed as a bail recovery agent or bail recovery apprentice employee or contract employee a person who has been refused a license under this chapter or who has had a license revoked in any state;

(c) committed, or aided and abetted the commission of, any act for which a license is required by this chapter, while not licensed under this chapter; or

(d) knowingly made a material misstatement in connection with an application for a license or renewal of a license under this chapter.

(2) The issuance of an identification card shall be denied to an applicant if the applicant fails to meet the required licensure qualifications.

(3) (a) The denial of the issuance of a license under this chapter shall be in writing and describe the basis for the denial.

(b) The board's denial shall inform the applicant in writing that if the applicant desires a hearing to contest the denial, he shall submit a request in writing to the commissioner within 30 days after the issuance of the denial.

(c) The hearing shall be scheduled not later than 60 days after receipt of the request.

(4) The commissioner shall hear the appeal, and may:

(a) return the case to the board for reconsideration;

(b) modify the board's decision; or

(c) reverse the board's decision.

(5) Decisions of the commissioner are subject to judicial review pursuant to Section 63-46b-15. **1998**

53-11-119. Grounds for disciplinary action.

(1) The board may take disciplinary action under Subsection (2), (4), or (5) regarding a license granted under this chapter if the board finds the licensee commits any of the following while engaged in activities regulated under this chapter:

(a) fraud or willful misrepresentation in applying for an original license or renewal of an existing license;

(b) using any letterhead, advertising, or other printed matter in any manner representing that he is an instrumentality of the federal government, a state, or any political subdivision of a state;

(c) using a name different from that under which he is currently licensed for any advertising, solicitation, or contract to secure business unless the name is an authorized fictitious name;

(d) impersonating, permitting, or aiding and abetting an employee to impersonate a law enforcement officer or employee of the United States, any state, or a political subdivision of a state;

(e) knowingly violating, advising, encouraging, or assisting in the violation of any statute, court order, or injunction in the course of conducting an agency regulated under this chapter;

(f) falsifying fingerprints or photographs while operating under this chapter;

(g) has a conviction for:

(i) a felony;

(ii) any act involving illegally using, carrying, or possessing a dangerous weapon;

(iii) any act involving moral turpitude;

(iv) any act of personal violence or force against any person or conviction of threatening to commit any act of personal violence or force against any person;

(v) any act constituting dishonesty or fraud;

(vi) impersonating a peace officer; or

(vii) any act of illegally obtaining or disseminating private, controlled, or protected records under Section 63-2-801;

(h) soliciting business for an attorney in return for compensation;

(i) being placed on probation, parole, compensatory service, or named in an outstanding arrest warrant;

(j) committing, or permitting any employee or contract employee to commit any act during the period between the expiration of a license for failure to renew within the time fixed by this chapter, and the reinstatement of the license, that would be cause for the suspension or revocation of the license or grounds for denial of the application for the license;

(k) willfully neglecting to render to a client services or a report as agreed between the parties and for which compensation has been paid or tendered in accordance with the agreement of the parties, but if the investigator chooses to withdraw from the case and returns the funds for work not yet done, no violation of this section exists;

(l) failing or refusing to cooperate with, failing to provide truthful information to, or refusing access to an authorized representative of the department engaged in an official investigation;

(m) employing or contracting with any unlicensed or improperly licensed person or agency to conduct activities regulated under this chapter if the licensure status was known or could have been ascertained by reasonable inquiry;

(n) permitting, authorizing, aiding, or in any way assisting a licensed employee to conduct services as described in this chapter on an independent contractor basis and not under the authority of the licensed agency;

(o) failure to maintain in full force and effect workers' compensation insurance, if applicable;

(p) advertising in a false, deceptive, or misleading manner;

(q) refusing to display the identification card issued by the department to any person having reasonable cause to verify the validity of the license;

(r) committing any act of unprofessional conduct; or

(s) engaging in any other conduct prohibited by this chapter.

(2) On completion of an investigation, the board may:

(a) dismiss the case;

(b) take emergency action;

(c) issue a letter of concern, if applicable;

(d) impose a civil penalty not to exceed $500;

(e) place all records, evidence, findings, and conclusions and any other information pertinent to the investigation in the confidential and protected records section of the file maintained at the department; or

(f) if the board finds, based on the investigation, that a violation of Subsection (1) has occurred, notice shall be sent to the licensee of the results of the hearing by mailing a true copy to the licensee's last-known address in the department's files by certified mail, return receipt requested.

(3) A letter of concern shall be retained by the commissioner and may be used in future disciplinary actions against a licensee.

(4) (a) If the board finds, based on its investigation under Subsection (1), that the public health, safety, or welfare requires emergency action, the board may order a summary suspension of a license pending proceedings for revocation or other action.

(b) If the board issues an order of summary suspension, the board shall issue to the licensee a written notice of complaint and formal hearing, setting forth the charges made against the licensee and his right to a formal hearing before the board within 60 days.

(5) Based on information the board receives during a hearing it may:

(a) (i) dismiss the complaint if the board believes it is without merit;

(ii) fix a period and terms of probation best adapted to educate the licensee;

(iii) place the license on suspension for a period of not more than 12 months; or

(iv) revoke the license; and

(b) impose a civil penalty not to exceed $500.

(6) (a) On a finding by the board that a bail recovery agency licensee committed a violation of Subsection (1), the probation, suspension, or revocation terminates the employment of all licensees employed or employed by contract by the bail bond agency.

(b) If a licensee who is an employee or contract employee of a bail bond agency committed a violation of Subsection (1), the probation, suspension, or revocation applies only to the license held by that individual under this chapter.

(7) (a) Appeal of the board's decision shall be made in writing to the commissioner within 30 days after the date of issuance of the board's decision.

(b) The hearing shall be scheduled not later than 60 days after receipt of the request.

(c) The commissioner shall review the finding by the board and may affirm, return to the board for reconsideration, reverse, adopt, modify, supplement, amend, or reject the recommendation of the board.

(8) A person may appeal the commissioner's decision to the district court pursuant to Section 63-46b-15.

(9) All penalties collected under this section shall be deposited in the General Fund.   1999

53-11-120. Requirement to identify employing agency.

Upon request, a licensee shall immediately identify the name, business address, and telephone number of the bail bond agency for which the licensee is an employee or an independent contractor.   1998

53-11-121. False representation as a licensee.

A licensee under this chapter may not wear a uniform, use a title, insignia, badge, or identification card other than the one issued under this chapter, or make any statement that would lead a reasonable person to believe the licensee is connected in any way with the federal government or any state or local governmental entity, unless the licensee has received authorization in writing by one of those governmental authorities to do so.   1998

53-11-122. Requirements during search and seizure — Notification of law enforcement agency.

A bail enforcement agent, bail recovery agent, or bail recovery apprentice shall observe the following requirements before taking action authorized under this chapter:

(1) identify himself as a "bail enforcement agent," "bail recovery agent," or "bail recovery apprentice"; and

(2) comply with the notification requirements of Section 53-11-123.   1998

53-11-123. Notification of local law enforcement.

(1) (a) A bail enforcement agent or bail recovery agent who is searching for or planning to apprehend a person shall notify the local law enforcement agency if the search or apprehension will be conducted in an occupied structure within that law enforcement agency's jurisdiction.

(b) When possible, notification shall be provided before taking action, but always within 24 hours of taking action.

(c) When a bail enforcement agent or bail recovery agent is preparing to enter an occupied structure to carry out an arrest, he shall verbally advise the local law enforcement agency of his location and intended action prior to acting.

(2) A bail enforcement agent, bail recovery agent, and bail recovery apprentice shall each carry with him a written document providing proof and cause for the actions he is taking as a licensee, and shall make the document available to local law enforcement agencies upon request. 1999

53-11-124. Penalties.

Any violation of this chapter is a class A misdemeanor, unless the circumstances of the violation amount to an offense subject to a greater criminal penalty under Title 76, Utah Criminal Code. 1998

CHAPTER 12

STATE OLYMPIC PUBLIC SAFETY COMMAND ACT [REPEALED]

53-12-101 to 53-12-303. Repealed. 2002, 2003

CHAPTER 13

PEACE OFFICER CLASSIFICATIONS

53-13-101. Definitions.

As used in this chapter:

(1) "Auxiliary officer" means a sworn, certified, and supervised special function officer, as described by Section 53-13-112.

(2) "Certified" means recognized and accepted by the division as having successfully met and maintained the standards and training requirements set and approved by the director of the division with the advice and consent of the council.

(3) "Collateral duty" means a duty to corroborate and support a peace officer function that is secondary and supplemental to the primary duty of the position.

(4) "Council" means the Peace Officer Standards and Training Council created in Section 53-6-106.

(5) "Director" means the director of the Peace Officer Standards and Training Division appointed under Section 53-6-104.

(6) "Division" means the Peace Officer Standards and Training Division created in Section 53-6-103.

(7) "Local law enforcement agency" means a law enforcement agency of any political subdivision of the state.

(8) "Primary duties" means those duties which come first in degree of effort and importance.

(9) "Principal duties" means those duties which are the highest and foremost in responsibility.

(10) "Reserve officer" means a sworn and certified peace officer, whether paid or voluntary, who:

(a) is serving in a reserve capacity for a law enforcement agency that is part of or administered by the state or any of its political subdivisions; and

(b) meets the basic and in-service training requirements of the peace officer classification in which the officer will function.

(11) "Spectrum" means that which encompasses the scope of authority. "Full spectrum" encompasses total 24-hour authority; while anything less than full authority is contained or restricted within certain limits as set forth by statute, ordinance, policy, or rule.

(12) "Sworn" means having taken the oath of office set forth in Utah Constitution Article IV, Section 10, administered by the law enforcement agency for whom a peace officer works.

(13) "Volunteer" means an officer who donates service without pay or other compensation except expenses actually and reasonably incurred as approved by the supervising agency.

(14) (a) "While on duty" means while an officer is actually performing the job duties and work activities assigned by the employing agency and for which the officer is trained and certified, and may include time spent outside those duties and activities if that additional time involves an activity that is an integral and necessary part of the job, and is spent for the benefit, and under the direction of, the employing agency.

(b) "While on duty" does not include the time an officer spends commuting between the officer's home and place of employment unless that time involves an activity in Subsection (14)(a). 1999

53-13-102. Peace officer classifications.

The following officers may exercise peace officer authority only as specifically authorized by law:

(1) law enforcement officers;

(2) correctional officers;

(3) special function officers; and

(4) federal officers. 1998

53-13-103. Law enforcement officer.

(1) (a) "Law enforcement officer" means a sworn and certified peace officer who is an employee of a law enforcement agency that is part of or administered by the state or any of its political subdivisions, and whose primary and principal duties consist of the prevention and detection of crime and the enforcement of criminal statutes or ordinances of this state or any of its political subdivisions.

(b) "Law enforcement officer" specifically includes the following:

(i) any sheriff or deputy sheriff, chief of police, police officer, or marshal of any county, city, or town;

(ii) the commissioner of public safety and any member of the Department of Public Safety certified as a peace officer;

(iii) all persons specified in Sections 23-20-1.5 and 63-11-17.2;

(iv) any police officer employed by any college or university;

(v) investigators for the Motor Vehicle Enforcement Division;

(vi) special agents or investigators employed by the attorney general, district attorneys, and county attorneys;

(vii) employees of the Department of Natural Resources designated as peace officers by law;

(viii) school district police officers as designated by the board of education for the school district;

(ix) the executive director of the Department of Corrections and any correctional enforcement or investigative officer designated by the executive director and approved by the commissioner of public safety and certified by the division;

(x) correctional enforcement, investigative, or adult probation and parole officers employed by the Department of Corrections serving on or before July 1, 1993;

(xi) members of a law enforcement agency established by a private college or university provided that the college or university has been certified by the commissioner of public safety according to rules of the Department of Public Safety; and

(xii) airport police officers of any airport owned or operated by the state or any of its political subdivisions.

(2) Law enforcement officers may serve criminal process and arrest violators of any law of this state and have the right to require aid in executing their lawful duties.

(3) (a) A law enforcement officer has statewide full-spectrum peace officer authority, but the authority extends to other counties, cities, or towns only when the officer is acting under Title 77, Chapter 9, Uniform Act on Fresh Pursuit, unless the law enforcement officer is employed by the state.

(b) (i) A local law enforcement agency may limit the jurisdiction in which its law enforcement officers may exercise their peace officer authority to a certain geographic area.

(ii) Notwithstanding Subsection (3)(b)(i), a law enforcement officer may exercise his authority outside of the limited geographic area, pursuant to Title 77, Chapter 9, Uniform Act on Fresh Pursuit, if the officer is pursuing an offender for an offense that occurred within the limited geographic area.

(c) The authority of law enforcement officers employed by the Department of Corrections is regulated by Title 64, Chapter 13, Department of Corrections — State Prison.

(4) A law enforcement officer shall, prior to exercising peace officer authority, satisfactorily complete:

(a) the basic course at a certified law enforcement officer training academy or pass a certification examination as provided in Section 53-6-206, and be certified; and

(b) annual certified training of at least 40 hours per year as directed by the director of the division, with the advice and consent of the council.

                                  2001

53-13-104. Correctional officer.

(1) (a) "Correctional officer" means a sworn and certified officer employed by the Department of Corrections, any political subdivision of the state, or any private entity which contracts with the state or its political subdivisions to incarcerate inmates who is charged with the primary duty of providing community protection.

(b) "Correctional officer" includes an individual assigned to carry out any of the following types of functions:

(i) controlling, transporting, supervising, and taking into custody of persons arrested or convicted of crimes;

(ii) supervising and preventing the escape of persons in state and local incarceration facilities;

(iii) guarding and managing inmates and providing security and enforcement services at a correctional facility; and

(iv) employees of the Board of Pardons and Parole serving on or before September 1, 1993, whose primary responsibility is to prevent and detect crime, enforce criminal statutes, and provide security to the Board of Pardons and Parole, and who are designated by the Board of Pardons and Parole, approved by the commissioner of public safety, and certified by the Peace Officer Standards and Training Division.

(2) (a) Correctional officers have peace officer authority only while on duty. The authority of correctional officers employed by the Department of Corrections is regulated by Title 64, Chapter 13, Department of Corrections — State Prison.

(b) Correctional officers may carry firearms only if authorized by and under conditions specified by the director of the Department of Corrections or the chief law enforcement officer of the employing agency.

(3) (a) An individual may not exercise the authority of an adult correctional officer until the individual has satisfactorily completed a basic training program for correctional officers and the director of the Department of Corrections has certified the completion of training to the director of the division.

(b) An individual may not exercise the authority of a county correctional officer until:

(i) the individual has satisfactorily completed a basic training program for correctional officers and any other specialized training required by the local law enforcement agency; and

(ii) the chief administrator of the local law enforcement agency has certified the completion of training to the director of the division.

(4) (a) The Department of Corrections of the state shall establish and maintain a correctional officer basic course and in-service training programs as approved by the director of the division with the advice and consent of the council.

(b) The in-service training shall:

(i) consist of no fewer than 40 hours per year; and

(ii) be conducted by the agency's own staff or other agencies.

(5) The local law enforcement agencies may establish correctional officer basic, advanced, or in-service training programs as approved by the director of the division with the advice and consent of the council.

                                  1999

53-13-105. Special function officer.

(1) (a) "Special function officer" means a sworn and certified peace officer performing specialized in-

vestigations, service of legal process, security functions, or specialized ordinance, rule, or regulatory functions.

(b) "Special function officer" includes:

(i) state military police;

(ii) constables;

(iii) port-of-entry agents as defined in Section 72-1-102;

(iv) authorized employees or agents of the Department of Transportation assigned to administer and enforce the provisions of Title 72, Chapter 9, Motor Carrier Safety Act;

(v) school district security officers;

(vi) Utah State Hospital security officers designated pursuant to Section 62A-15-603;

(vii) Utah State Developmental Center security officers designated pursuant to Subsection 62A-5-206(9);

(viii) fire arson investigators for any political subdivision of the state;

(ix) ordinance enforcement officers employed by municipalities or counties may be special function officers;

(x) employees of the Department of Natural Resources who have been designated to conduct supplemental enforcement functions as a collateral duty;

(xi) railroad special agents deputized by a county sheriff under Section 17-30-2, or appointed pursuant to Section 56-1-21.5;

(xii) auxiliary officers, as described by Section 53-13-112;

(xiii) special agents, process servers, and investigators employed by city attorneys;

(xiv) criminal tax investigators designated under Section 59-1-206; and

(xv) all other persons designated by statute as having special function officer authority or limited peace officer authority.

(2) (a) A special function officer may exercise that spectrum of peace officer authority that has been designated by statute to the employing agency, and only while on duty, and not for the purpose of general law enforcement.

(b) If the special function officer is charged with security functions respecting facilities or property, the powers may be exercised only in connection with acts occurring on the property where the officer is employed or when required for the protection of the employer's interest, property, or employees.

(c) A special function officer may carry firearms only while on duty, and only if authorized and under conditions specified by the officer's employer or chief administrator.

(3) (a) A special function officer may not exercise the authority of a peace officer until:

(i) the officer has satisfactorily completed an approved basic training program for special function officers as provided under Subsection (4); and

(ii) the chief law enforcement officer or administrator has certified this fact to the director of the division.

(b) City and county constables and their deputies shall certify their completion of training to the legislative governing body of the city or county they serve.

(4) (a) The agency that the special function officer serves may establish and maintain a basic special function course and in-service training programs

as approved by the director of the division with the advice and consent of the council.

(b) The in-service training shall consist of no fewer than 40 hours per year and may be conducted by the agency's own staff or by other agencies.   2002 (5th S.S.)

53-13-106. Federal officers — State law enforcement authority.

(1) (a) "Federal officer" includes:

(i) a special agent of the Federal Bureau of Investigation;

(ii) a special agent of the United States Secret Service;

(iii) a special agent of the United States Department of Homeland Security, excluding a customs inspector or detention removal officer;

(iv) a special agent of the Bureau of Alcohol, Tobacco and Firearms;

(v) a special agent of the Federal Drug Enforcement Agency;

(vi) a United States marshal, deputy marshal, and special deputy United States marshal; and

(vii) a U.S. Postal Inspector of the United States Postal Inspection Service.

(b) Notwithstanding Subsection (2), federal officers listed in Subsection (1)(a) have statewide law enforcement authority relating to felony offenses under the laws of this state.

(c) The council may designate other federal peace officers, as necessary, if the officers:

(i) are persons employed full-time by the United States government as federally recognized law enforcement officers primarily responsible for the investigation and enforcement of the federal laws;

(ii) have successfully completed formal law enforcement training offered by an agency of the federal government consisting of not less than 400 hours; and

(iii) maintain in-service training in accordance with the standards set forth in Section 53-13-103.

(2) Except as otherwise provided under Title 63, Chapter 8, Federal Jurisdiction, and Title 77, Chapter 9, Uniform Act on Fresh Pursuit, a federal officer may exercise state law enforcement authority only if:

(a) the state law enforcement agencies and county sheriffs with jurisdiction enter into an agreement with the federal agency to be given authority; and

(b) except as provided in Subsection (3), each federal officer employed by the federal agency meets the waiver requirements set forth in Section 53-6-206.

(3) A federal officer working as such in the state on or before July 1, 1995, may exercise state law enforcement authority without meeting the waiver requirement.

(4) At any time, consistent with any contract with a federal agency, a state or local law enforcement authority may withdraw state law enforcement authority from any individual federal officer by sending written notice to the federal agency and to the division.

(5) The authority of a federal officer under this section is limited to the jurisdiction of the authorizing state or local agency, and may be further limited by the state or local agency to enforcing specific statutes, codes, or ordinances.   **2004**

53-13-107. Basic training requirements for position — Peace officers temporarily in the state.

(1) (a) Any person who has satisfactorily completed, before the effective date of this chapter, an approved basic training program required of the person's position may act in a certified capacity without completion of an additional basic training program.

(b) Any person hired, appointed, or elected to any position designated in this chapter, except federal officer, shall satisfactorily complete the required basic training required of that position before the person is authorized to exercise peace officer powers under this chapter.

(2) Any peace officer employed by a law enforcement agency of another state and functioning in that capacity within Utah on a temporary basis is considered certified under Utah law:

(a) while functioning as a peace officer within the state at the request of a Utah law enforcement agency; or

(b) when conducting business as a representative of a law enforcement agency from another state. 2004

53-13-108. Retirement.

Eligibility for coverage under the Public Safety Contributory Retirement System or Public Safety Noncontributory Retirement System for persons and political subdivisions included in this chapter is governed by Title 49, Chapter 14, Public Safety Contributory Retirement Act, and Chapter 15, Public Safety Noncontributory Retirement Act. 2002

53-13-109. References in other provisions.

When the term peace officer is used in any other provision of law, the term includes anyone authorized to exercise authority as provided in this chapter, except federal officers. 1998

53-13-110. Duties to investigate specified instances of abuse or neglect.

In accordance with the requirements of Section 62A-4a-202.5, law enforcement officers shall investigate alleged instances of abuse or neglect of a child that occur while the child is in the custody of the Division of Child and Family Services, within the Department of Human Services. 1998

53-13-111. Peace officers serving in a reserve or auxiliary capacity.

(1) (a) Nothing in this chapter shall preclude any law enforcement agency of the state or any of its political subdivisions from utilizing a sworn and certified peace officer in a reserve or auxiliary capacity.

(b) A reserve or auxiliary officer has peace officer authority only while engaged in the reserve or auxiliary activities authorized by the chief or administrator of the agency the officer serves and shall only exercise that spectrum of peace officer authority:

(i) that the supervising agency is empowered to delegate; and

(ii) for which the officer has been trained and certified.

(2) While serving as a nonpaid volunteer in a reserve or auxiliary capacity, or working part-time for fewer hours than that which would qualify the officer as an "employee" under state or federal law, a peace officer is entitled to benefits in accordance with Title 67, Chapter 20, Volunteer Government Workers Act.

(3) The agency the reserve or auxiliary officer serves shall ensure that the officer meets the basic and in-service training requirements of the peace officer classification in which the officer will function. 1999

53-13-112. Auxiliary officer.

(1) An auxiliary officer is a specific category of special function officer and is required to have the level of training of a special function officer as provided in Section 53-13-105, including no fewer than 40 hours per year of in-service training.

(2) An auxiliary officer:

(a) shall work under the direction and immediate supervision of a certified law enforcement officer as defined in Section 53-13-103;

(b) is limited to the role of back-up officer to a law enforcement officer;

(c) may not initiate any action authorized for a law enforcement officer in Section 53-13-103; and

(d) may be separated from a law enforcement officer only under exigent circumstances or when engaged in functions not exclusive to law enforcement, which functions are defined by the division by rule. 1999

53-13-113. Authority of peace officers to administer oaths.

A peace officer, as defined in Section 53-1-102, who is acting within the scope of his or her official duties may administer oaths. 2000

CHAPTER 14

PEACE OFFICER CANDIDATE BACKGROUND INVESTIGATION

Section

53-14-101. Law enforcement and training academy applicants — Employer background information.

53-14-101. Law enforcement and training academy applicants — Employer background information.

(1) As used in this section:

(a) "Director" means the director of a certified law enforcement officer training academy.

(b) "Employer" includes a public employer and a private employer.

(c) "Law enforcement agency" has the same definition as in Section 53-1-102.

(d) "Law enforcement officer" has the same definition as in Section 53-13-103, and includes those officers in administrative positions.

(e) "Training academy" means a peace officer training institution certified in accordance with the standards developed under Section 53-6-105.

(2) A current or former employer and the director of any training academy an applicant has attended or graduated from shall provide available information in accordance with this section regarding an applicant if the request complies with Subsection (3) and is submitted by:

(a) a law enforcement agency regarding an applicant for an employment position; or

(b) the director of a law enforcement training academy for which the applicant requests admission under Section 53-6-203.

(3) The request for information pursuant to Subsection (2) shall be:

(a) in writing;

(b) accompanied by an authorization signed by the applicant and notarized by a notary public, in which the applicant consents to the release of the requested information and releases the employer or training academy providing the information from liability; and

(c) addressed to the employer or director and signed by a sworn officer or other authorized representative of the requesting law enforcement agency or the academy.

(4) The information that a law enforcement agency or the director of an academy may request pursuant to Subsection (2) includes:

(a) the date on which the applicant began his employment and, if applicable, the date on which the employment of the applicant was terminated;

(b) a list of the compensation that the employer provided to the applicant during the course of the employment;

(c) a copy of the application for a position of employment that the applicant submitted to the employer;

(d) a written evaluation of the performance of the applicant;

(e) a record of the attendance of the applicant;

(f) a record of disciplinary action taken against the applicant;

(g) a statement regarding whether the employer would rehire the applicant and, if the employer would not rehire the applicant, the reasons why;

(h) if applicable, a record setting forth the reason that the employment of the applicant was terminated and whether the termination was voluntary or involuntary;

(i) the record of any final action regarding an applicant's peace officer certification that is based on an investigation concerning the applicant's qualification for certification; and

(j) notice of any pending or ongoing investigation regarding the applicant's certification as a peace officer.

(5) (a) In the absence of fraud or malice, an employer or training academy is not subject to any civil liability for any relevant cause of action by releasing employment information requested under this section.

(b) This section does not in any way or manner abrogate or lessen the existing common law or statutory privileges and immunities of an employer.

(c) An employer or training academy may not provide information pursuant to Subsection (2) if the disclosure of the information is prohibited pursuant to federal or state law.

(6) An employer's refusal to disclose information to a law enforcement agency in accordance with this section constitutes grounds for a civil action by the requesting agency for injunctive relief requiring disclosure on the part of an employer.

(7) (a) (i) A law enforcement agency may use the information received pursuant to this section only to determine the suitability of an applicant for employment.

(ii) A director may use the information received pursuant to this section only to determine the suitability of an applicant for acceptance at the training academy.

(b) Except as otherwise provided in Subsection (7)(c), a law enforcement agency and a director shall maintain the confidentiality of information received pursuant to this section.

(c) (i) A law enforcement agency may share information regarding an applicant that it receives pursuant to this section with another law enforcement agency if:

(A) the applicant is also an applicant for any employment position with the other law enforcement agency; and

(B) the confidentiality of the information is otherwise maintained.

(ii) A director may share information regarding an applicant that is received pursuant to this section with another training academy if:

(A) the applicant is an applicant for acceptance at the other training academy; and

(B) the confidentiality of the information is otherwise maintained.

(iii) A director may share information regarding an applicant, attendee, or graduate of a training academy that is received pursuant to this section with a law enforcement agency if:

(A) the applicant is applying for a position as a peace officer with the law enforcement agency; and

(B) the confidentiality of the information is otherwise maintained.

(8) This section applies to requests submitted to employers on and after July 1, 2003 for employment information under this section.   **2004**

TITLE 53A

STATE SYSTEM OF PUBLIC EDUCATION

CHAPTER 1

ADMINISTRATION OF PUBLIC EDUCATION AT THE STATE LEVEL

Part 4

Powers and Duties

PART 4

POWERS AND DUTIES

53A-1-402. Board to establish minimum standards for public schools.

(1) The State Board of Education shall establish rules and minimum standards for the public schools that are consistent with this title, including rules and minimum standards governing the following:

(a) (i) the qualification and certification of educators and ancillary personnel who provide direct student services;

(ii) required school administrative and supervisory services; and

(iii) the evaluation of instructional personnel;

(b) (i) access to programs;

(ii) attendance;

(iii) competency levels;

(iv) graduation requirements; and

(v) discipline and control;

(c) (i) school accreditation;

(ii) the academic year;

(iii) alternative and pilot programs;

(iv) curriculum and instruction requirements;

(v) school libraries; and

(vi) services to:

(A) persons with a disability as defined by and covered under:

(I) the Americans with Disabilities Act of 1990, 42 U.S.C. 12102;

(II) the Rehabilitation Act of 1973, 29 U.S.C. 705(20)(A); and

(III) the Individuals with Disabilities Education Act, 20 U.S.C. 1401(3); and

(B) other special groups;

(d) (i) state reimbursed bus routes;

(ii) bus safety and operational requirements; and

(iii) other transportation needs; and

(e) (i) school productivity and cost effectiveness measures;

(ii) federal programs;

(iii) school budget formats; and

(iv) financial, statistical, and student accounting requirements.

(2) The board shall determine if:

(a) the minimum standards have been met; and

(b) required reports are properly submitted.

(3) The board may apply for, receive, administer, and distribute to eligible applicants funds made available through programs of the federal government.

(4) (a) The Utah College of Applied Technology shall provide competency-based career and technical education courses that fulfill high school graduation requirements, as requested and authorized by the State Board of Education.

(b) A school district may grant a high school diploma to a student participating in courses described under Subsection (4)(a) that are provided by the Utah College of Applied Technology.

2005

CHAPTER 3

LOCAL SCHOOL BOARDS

Part 4

Powers and Responsibilities of Local Boards

PART 4

POWERS AND RESPONSIBILITIES OF LOCAL BOARDS

53A-3-402. Powers and duties generally.

(1) Each local school board shall:

(a) implement the core curriculum utilizing instructional materials that best correlate to the core curriculum and graduation requirements;

(b) administer tests, required by the State Board of Education, which measure the progress of each student, and coordinate with the state superintendent and State Board of Education to assess results and create plans to improve the student's progress which shall be submitted to the State Office of Education for approval;

(c) use progress-based assessments as part of a plan to identify schools, teachers, and students that need remediation and determine the type and amount of federal, state, and local resources to implement remediation;

(d) develop early warning systems for students or classes failing to make progress;

(e) work with the State Office of Education to establish a library of documented best practices, consistent with state and federal regulations, for use by the local districts; and

(f) implement training programs for school administrators, including basic management training, best practices in instructional methods, budget training, staff management, managing for learning results and continuous improvement, and how to help every child achieve optimal learning in core academics.

(2) Local school boards shall spend minimum school program funds for programs and activities for which the State Board of Education has established minimum standards or rules under Section 53A-1-402.

(3) (a) A board may purchase, sell, and make improvements on school sites, buildings, and equipment and construct, erect, and furnish school buildings.

(b) School sites or buildings may only be conveyed or sold on board resolution affirmed by at least two-thirds of the members.

(4) (a) A board may participate in the joint construction or operation of a school attended by children residing within the district and children residing in other districts either within or outside the state.

(b) Any agreement for the joint operation or construction of a school shall:

(i) be signed by the president of the board of each participating district;

(ii) include a mutually agreed upon pro rata cost; and

(iii) be filed with the State Board of Education.

(5) A board may establish, locate, and maintain elementary, secondary, and applied technology schools.

(6) A board may enroll children in school who are at least five years of age before September 2 of the year in which admission is sought.

(7) A board may establish and support school libraries.

(8) A board may collect damages for the loss, injury, or destruction of school property.

(9) A board may authorize guidance and counseling services for children and their parents or guardians prior to, during, or following enrollment of the children in schools.

(10) (a) A board shall administer and implement federal educational programs in accordance with Title 53A, Chapter 1, Part 9, Implementing Federal Programs Act.

(b) Federal funds are not considered funds within the school district budget under Title 53A, Chapter 19, School District Budgets.

(11) (a) A board may organize school safety patrols and adopt rules under which the patrols promote student safety.

(b) A student appointed to a safety patrol shall be at least ten years old and have written parental consent for the appointment.

(c) Safety patrol members may not direct vehicular traffic or be stationed in a portion of a highway intended for vehicular traffic use.

(d) Liability may not attach to a school district, its employees, officers, or agents or to a safety patrol member, a parent of a safety patrol member, or an authorized volunteer assisting the program by virtue of the organization, maintenance, or operation of a school safety patrol.

(12) (a) A board may on its own behalf, or on behalf of an educational institution for which the board is the direct governing body, accept private grants, loans, gifts, endowments, devises, or bequests that are made for educational purposes.

(b) These contributions are not subject to appropriation by the Legislature.

(13) (a) A board may appoint and fix the compensation of a compliance officer to issue citations for violations of Subsection 76-10-105(2).

(b) A person may not be appointed to serve as a compliance officer without the person's consent.

(c) A teacher or student may not be appointed as a compliance officer.

(14) A board shall adopt bylaws and rules for its own procedures.

(15) (a) A board shall make and enforce rules necessary for the control and management of the district schools.

(b) All board rules and policies shall be in writing, filed, and referenced for public access.

(16) A board may hold school on legal holidays other than Sundays.

(17) (a) Each board shall establish for each school year a school traffic safety committee to implement this Subsection (17).

(b) The committee shall be composed of one representative of:
(i) the schools within the district;
(ii) the Parent Teachers' Association of the schools within the district;
(iii) the municipality or county;
(iv) state or local law enforcement; and
(v) state or local traffic safety engineering.

(c) The committee shall:
(i) receive suggestions from parents, teachers, and others and recommend school traffic safety improvements, boundary changes to enhance safety, and school traffic safety program measures;
(ii) review and submit annually to the Department of Transportation and affected municipalities and counties a child access routing plan for each elementary, middle, and junior high school within the district;
(iii) consult the Utah Safety Council and the Division of Family Health Services and provide training to all school children in kindergarten through grade six, within the district, on school crossing safety and use; and
(iv) help ensure the district's compliance with rules made by the Department of Transportation under Section 41-6a-303.

(d) The committee may establish subcommittees as needed to assist in accomplishing its duties under Subsection (17)(c).

(e) The board shall require the school community council of each elementary, middle, and junior high school within the district to develop and submit annually to the committee a child access routing plan.

(18) (a) Each school board shall adopt and implement a comprehensive emergency response plan to prevent and combat violence in its public schools, on school grounds, on its school vehicles, and in connection with school-related activities or events.

(b) The board shall implement its plan by July 1, 2000.

(c) The plan shall:
(i) include prevention, intervention, and response components;
(ii) be consistent with the student conduct and discipline polices required for school districts under Title 53A, Chapter 11, Part 9, School Discipline and Conduct Plans;
(iii) require inservice training for all district and school building staff on what their roles are in the emergency response plan; and
(iv) provide for coordination with local law enforcement and other public safety representatives in preventing, intervening, and responding to violence in the areas and activities referred to in Subsection (18)(a).

(d) The State Board of Education, through the state superintendent of public instruction, shall develop comprehensive emergency response plan models that local school boards may use, where appropriate, to comply with Subsection (18)(a).

(e) Each local school board shall, by July 1 of each year, certify to the State Board of Education that its plan has been practiced at the school level and presented to and reviewed by its teachers, administrators, students, and their parents and local law enforcement and public safety representatives.

(19) (a) Each local school board may adopt an emergency response plan for the treatment of sports-related injuries that occur during school sports practices and events.

(b) The plan may be implemented by each secondary school in the district that has a sports program for students.

(c) The plan may:
(i) include emergency personnel, emergency communication, and emergency equipment components;
(ii) require inservice training on the emergency response plan for school personnel who are involved in sports programs in the district's secondary schools; and

(iii) provide for coordination with individuals and agency representatives who:

(A) are not employees of the school district; and

(B) would be involved in providing emergency services to students injured while participating in sports events.

(d) The board, in collaboration with the schools referred to in Subsection (19)(b), may review the plan each year and make revisions when required to improve or enhance the plan.

(e) The State Board of Education, through the state superintendent of public instruction, shall provide local school boards with an emergency plan response model that local boards may use to comply with the requirements of this Subsection (19).

(20) A board shall do all other things necessary for the maintenance, prosperity, and success of the schools and the promotion of education.   2005 (1st S.S.)

PART 5

OFFENSES

53A-3-501. Possession or consumption of alcoholic beverages at school or school-sponsored activities — Penalty.

(1) Except as approved by a local school board as part of the curriculum, a person may not possess or drink an alcoholic beverage:

(a) inside or on the grounds of any building owned or operated by a part of the public education system; or

(b) in those portions of any building, park, or stadium which are being used for an activity sponsored by or through any part of the public education system.

(2) (a) Subsection (1)(a) does not apply to property owned by a school district in contemplation of future use for school purposes while the property is under lease to another party.

(b) (i) For purposes of Subsection (2)(a), a lease must be full time for a period of not less than two years.

(ii) The property may not be used for school purposes at any time during the lease period.

(3) Violation of this section is a class B misdemeanor.   1998

53A-3-502. Repealed.   2003

53A-3-503. Criminal trespass upon school property — Penalty.

(1) A person is guilty of criminal trespass upon school property if the person does the following:

(a) enters or remains unlawfully upon school property, and:

(i) intends to cause annoyance or injury to a person or damage to property on the school property;

(ii) intends to commit a crime; or

(iii) is reckless as to whether the person's presence will cause fear for the safety of another; or

(b) enters or remains without authorization upon school property if notice against entry or remaining has been given by:

(i) personal communication to the person by a school official or an individual with apparent authority to act for a school official;

(ii) the posting of signs reasonably likely to come to the attention of trespassers;

(iii) fencing or other enclosure obviously designed to exclude trespassers; or

(iv) a current order of suspension or expulsion.

(2) As used in this section:

(a) "Enter" means intrusion of the entire body.

(b) "School official" means a public or private school administrator or person in charge of a school program or activity.

(c) "School property" means real property owned or occupied by a public or private school, including real property temporarily occupied for a school activity or program.

(3) Violation of this section is a class B misdemeanor.   1990

53A-3-504. Traffic ordinances on school property — Enforcement.

(1) A local political subdivision in which real property is located that belongs to, or is controlled by, the State Board of Education, a local board of education, an area vocational center, or the Schools for the Deaf and the Blind may, at the request of the responsible board of education or institutional council, adopt ordinances for the control of vehicular traffic on that property.

(2) A law enforcement officer whose jurisdiction includes the property in question may enforce an ordinance adopted under Subsection (1).   1988

CHAPTER 6

EDUCATOR LICENSING AND PROFESSIONAL PRACTICES ACT

Part 4

Licensing and Background Checks

PART 4

LICENSING AND BACKGROUND CHECKS

53A-6-401. Background checks.

(1) (a) A license applicant shall submit to a background check as a condition for licensing.

(b) As used in this section, licensing includes reinstatement of a lapsed, suspended, or revoked license.

(2) (a) The office shall establish a procedure for obtaining and evaluating relevant information concerning license applicants, including fingerprinting the applicant and submitting the prints to the Criminal Investigations and Technical Services Division of the Department of Public Safety for checking against applicable state, regional, and national criminal records files.

(b) The Criminal Investigations and Technical Services Division shall release to the office all information received in response to the office's request.

(c) The Criminal Investigations and Technical Services Division shall maintain a separate file of fingerprints submitted under Subsection (2)(a) and notify the office when a new entry is made against a person whose fingerprints are held in the file regarding any matters involving an alleged:

    (i) sexual offense;

    (ii) felony or class A misdemeanor drug offense; or

    (iii) offense against the person under Title 76, Chapter 5, Offenses Against the Person.

    (d) The cost of maintaining the separate file shall be paid by the office from fees charged to those submitting fingerprints.

(3) An applicant shall have opportunity to respond to any information received by the office as a result of the background check.

(4) In preparing recommendations concerning licensing for submission to the board, the office shall consider only the following matters obtained through fingerprint checks to the extent that they are relevant to the license sought by the applicant:

    (a) convictions;

    (b) any matters involving an alleged sexual offense;

    (c) any matters involving an alleged felony or class A misdemeanor drug offense;

    (d) any matters involving an alleged offense against the person under Title 76, Chapter 5;

    (e) any matters involving a felony;

    (f) any matters involving a class A misdemeanor property offense alleged to have occurred within the previous three years; and

    (g) any matters involving any other type of criminal offense, if more than one occurrence of the same type of offense is alleged to have taken place within the previous eight years.

(5) If a recommendation is made for denial of licensure because of information obtained through a background check, the person shall receive written notice of the reasons for the recommendation and have an opportunity to respond in accordance with procedures set forth under board rules.

(6) Information obtained under this section is confidential and may only be disclosed as provided in this part.

(7) The applicant shall pay the costs of conducting the background check.

(8) This section applies to matters occurring both before and after the effective date of this section.

2000

53A-6-402. Evaluation information on current or prospective school employees — Notice to employee — Exemption from liability.

(1) (a) The office's administrator of teacher licensing may provide the appropriate administrator of a public or private school or of an agency outside the state which is responsible for licensing or certification of educators with any recommendation or other information possessed by the office which has significance in evaluating the employment or license of a current or prospective school employee, license holder, or applicant for licensing.

    (b) Information supplied under Subsection (1)(a) may include the complete record of a hearing or the investigative report for matters which:

        (i) the educator has had an opportunity to contest; and

        (ii) did not proceed to a hearing.

(2) At the request of the office's administrator of teacher licensing, an administrator of a public school or school district shall, and an administrator of a private school may, provide any recommendation or other information possessed by the school or school district which has significance in evaluating the employment or licensure of a current or prospective school employee, license holder, or applicant for licensing.

(3) If a decision is made to deny licensure, to not hire a prospective employee, or to take action against a current employee or educator based upon information provided under this section, the affected individual shall receive notice of the information and be given an opportunity to respond to the information.

(4) A person who, in good faith, provides a recommendation or discloses or receives information under this section is exempt from civil and criminal liability relating to that recommendation, receipt, or disclosure.

(5) For purposes of this section, "employee" includes a volunteer.   1999

53A-6-403. Office tie-in with the Criminal Investigations and Technical Services Division.

(1) The office shall:

    (a) be an online terminal agency with the Department of Public Safety's Criminal Investigations and Technical Services Division under Section 53-10-108; and

    (b) provide relevant information concerning current or prospective employees or volunteers upon request to other school officials as provided in Section 53A-6-402.

(2) The cost of the online service shall be borne by the entity making the inquiry, using funds available to the entity, which may include funds authorized under Section 53A-6-401.   1999

CHAPTER 11

STUDENTS IN PUBLIC SCHOOLS

Part 1

Compulsory Education Requirements

Part 5

Identification of Missing Children

Part 11

Weapons on School Property

PART 1

COMPULSORY EDUCATION REQUIREMENTS

53A-11-101. Responsibility for minor required to attend school — Penalty for violation.

(1) For purposes of this part:

(a) "Habitual truant" is a school-age minor who has received more than two truancy citations within one school year from the school in which the minor is or should be enrolled and eight absences without a legitimate or valid excuse or who, in defiance of efforts on the part of school authorities to resolve a student's attendance problem as required under Section 53A-11-103, refuses to regularly attend school or any scheduled period of the school day.

(b) "Minor" means a person under the age of 18 years.

(c) "Parent" includes:

(i) a custodial parent of the minor;

(ii) a legally appointed guardian of a minor; or

(iii) any other person purporting to exercise any authority over the minor which could be exercised by persons listed under Subsections (1)(c)(i) and (ii) above.

(d) "School-age minor" means a minor who has reached the age of six years but has not reached the age of eighteen years, but does not include a minor emancipated by marriage.

(e) "Truancy citation" is an administrative notice to a truant minor requiring an appearance before the school truancy control officer or body from which the minor is truant.

(f) "Truant minor" is any school-age minor who is subject to the state's compulsory education law and who is absent from school without a legitimate or valid excuse.

(2) A parent shall enroll and send a school-age minor to a public or regularly established private school during the school year of the district in which the minor resides.

(3) It is a class B misdemeanor for a parent to knowingly:

(a) fail to enroll a school-age minor in school; or

(b) refuse to respond to a written request which is delivered to the parent pursuant to the provisions of Subsection 53A-11-103(1)(b) by a local school board or school district.

(4) The provisions of this section do not apply to a parent of a school-age minor who has been declared by the local school board to be exempt from school attendance in conformity with Section 53A-11-102.

(5) A local board of education or school district shall report violations of Subsection (3) to the appropriate city, county, or district attorney. **1999**

53A-11-102. Minors exempt from school attendance.

(1) (a) A school-age minor may be excused from attendance by the local board of education and a parent exempted from application of Subsections 53A-11-101(2) and (3) for any of the following reasons:

(i) a minor over age 16 may receive a partial release from school to enter employment if the minor has completed the eighth grade; or

(ii) on an annual basis, a minor may receive a full release from attending a public, regularly established private, or part-time school or class if:

(A) the minor has already completed the work required for graduation from high school, or has demonstrated mastery of required skills and competencies in accordance with Subsection 53A-15-102(1);

(B) the minor is in a physical or mental condition, certified by a competent physician if required by the district board, which renders attendance inexpedient and impracticable;

(C) proper influences and adequate opportunities for education are provided in connection with the minor's employment; or

(D) the district superintendent has determined that a minor over the age of 16 is unable to profit from attendance at school because of inability or a continuing negative attitude toward school regulations and discipline.

(b) Minors receiving a partial release from school under Subsection (1)(a)(i) are required to attend:

(i) school part-time as prescribed by the local school board; or

(ii) a home school part-time.

(c) In each case, evidence of reasons for granting an exemption under Subsection (1) must be sufficient to satisfy the local board.

(2) (a) On an annual basis, a school-age minor shall be excused from attendance by a local board of education and a parent exempted from application of Subsections 53A-11-101(2) and (3), if the minor's parent files a signed affidavit with the minor's school district of residence, as defined in Section 53A-2-201, that the minor will attend a home school and receive instruction as required by Subsection (2)(b).

(b) Each minor who attends a home school shall receive instruction:

(i) in the subjects the State Board of Education requires to be taught in public schools in accordance with the law; and

(ii) for the same length of time as minors are required by law to receive instruction in public schools, as provided by rules of the State Board of Education.

(c) Subject to the requirements of Subsection (2)(b), a parent of a minor who attends a home school is solely responsible for:

(i) the selection of instructional materials and textbooks;

(ii) the time, place, and method of instruction, and

(iii) the evaluation of the home school instruction.

(d) A local school board may not:

(i) require a parent of a minor who attends a home school to maintain records of instruction or attendance;

(ii) require credentials for individuals providing home school instruction;

(iii) inspect home school facilities; or

(iv) require standardized or other testing of home school students.

(3) Boards excusing minors from attendance as provided by Subsections (1) and (2) shall issue a certificate stating that the minor is excused from attendance during the time specified on the certificate.

(4) Nothing in this section may be construed to prohibit or discourage voluntary cooperation, resource sharing, or testing opportunities between a school or school district and a parent or guardian of a minor attending a home school. 2005

53A-11-102.5. Dual enrollment.

(1) A person having control of a minor under this part who is enrolled in a regularly established private school or a home school may also enroll the minor in a public school for dual enrollment purposes.

(2) The minor may participate in any academic activity in the public school available to students in the minor's grade or age group, subject to compliance with the same rules and requirements that apply to a full-time student's participation in the activity.

(3) Except as otherwise provided in Sections 53A-11-101 and 53A-11-102, a student enrolled in a public school may also be enrolled in a private school or a home school for dual enrollment purposes.

(4) A student enrolled in a dual enrollment program is considered a student of the district in which the public school of attendance is located for purposes of state funding to the extent of the student's participation in the public school programs.

(5) In accordance with Title 63, Chapter 46a, Utah Administrative Rulemaking Act, the State Board of Education shall make rules for purposes of dual enrollment to govern and regulate the transferability of credits toward graduation that are earned in a private or home school.

(6) The State Board of Education shall determine the policies and procedures necessary to permit students enrolled under Subsection (1) to participate in public school extracurricular activities. 2003

53A-11-103. Duties of boards of education in resolving child's attendance problems — Parental involvement — Issuance of truancy citations — Procedure for contesting citations — Liability not imposed.

(1) For each school-age minor who is or should be enrolled within that school district, the local school board or school district shall make efforts to resolve a minor's school attendance problems. Those efforts shall include, as reasonably feasible:

(a) counseling of the minor by school authorities;

(b) a written request for parental support in securing regular attendance by the minor delivered by certified mail, containing notice of the requirements of this section and stating that refusal to respond to the notice is a class B misdemeanor;

(c) at least one meeting with the minor and the parents;

(d) any necessary adjustment to the curriculum and schedule to meet special needs of the minor; and

(e) monitoring school attendance of the minor for a period not to exceed 30 days.

(2) In addition to the efforts listed in Subsection (1), the local school board or school district may enlist the assistance of community and law enforcement agencies as appropriate and reasonably feasible.

(3) In the event that the minor's school attendance problem cannot be resolved by the efforts of the local school board or school district, the local school board or school district shall refer the school-age minor to the appropriate district or county attorney or juvenile court as a habitual truant.

(4) Any parent of a school-age minor shall, upon written request from a local school board or school district, cooperate with school authorities in resolving the minor's school attendance problem.

(5) A local school board may authorize the issuance of truancy citations by school administrators and appointed truancy specialists. Recipients of truancy citations may be subjected to administrative penalties.

(6) A local school board that authorizes the issuance of truancy citations shall establish a procedure for students to contest citations. Any minor having received three prior truancy citations within a single school year and for whom reasonable efforts to resolve the attendance problem have failed, shall be issued a habitual truancy citation and referred by the local school board or school district to the appropriate county or district attorney or juvenile court as a habitual truant. Proceedings for habitual truancy shall be expedited by the court.

(7) This section shall not impose any civil liability on boards of education or their employees. Proceedings initiated under this part do not obligate or preclude action by the Division of Child and Family Services under Section 78-3a-316. 2003

53A-11-104. Truant officers.

A local school board may appoint and fix the compensation of a truant officer to assist in enforcing laws related to school attendance and to perform other duties prescribed by law or the board. 1988

53A-11-105. Taking custody of person believed to be truant child — Disposition — Receiving centers — Reports — Immunity from liability.

(1) A peace officer, truant officer, or public school administrator may take a minor into temporary custody or issue a truancy citation, or both, if there is reason to believe the minor is a truant minor. A truancy citation issued by a truant officer shall be approved by the school administrator.

(2) An individual taking a school-age minor into custody under Subsection (1) shall, without unnecessary delay, release the minor to:

(a) the principal of the minor's school;

(b) a person who has been designated by the local school board to receive and return the minor to school; or

(c) a receiving center established under Subsection (5).

(3) If the minor refuses to return to school or go to the receiving center, the officer or administrator shall, without unnecessary delay, notify the minor's parents and release the minor to their custody.

(4) If the parents cannot be reached or are unable or unwilling to accept custody, the minor shall be referred to the Division of Child and Family Services.

(5) (a) A local school board, singly or jointly with another school board, may establish or designate receiving centers within existing school buildings and staff the centers with existing teachers or staff to provide educational guidance and coun-

seling for truant minors. Upon receipt of a truant minor, the center shall, without unnecessary delay, notify and direct the minor's parents to come to the center, pick up the minor, and return the minor to the school in which he is enrolled.

(b) If the parents cannot be reached or are unable or unwilling to comply with the request within a reasonable time, the center shall take such steps as are reasonably necessary to insure the safety and well being of the minor, including, when appropriate, returning the minor to school or referring the minor to the Division of Child and Family Services. A minor taken into custody under this section may not be placed in a detention center or other secure confinement facility.

(6) Action taken under this section shall be reported to the appropriate school district. The district shall promptly notify the minor's parents of the action taken.

(7) The Utah Governmental Immunity Act applies to all actions taken under this section.

(8) Nothing in this section may be construed to grant authority to a public school administrator or truant officer to place a minor in the custody of the Division of Child and Family Services, without complying with the provisions of Title 62A, Chapter 4a, Parts 2 and 2A, and of Title 78, Chapter 3a, Parts 3 and 3A.   1999

53A-11-106. Truancy support centers.

(1) A school district may establish one or more truancy support centers for:

(a) truant students taken into custody under Section 53A-11-105; or

(b) students suspended or expelled from school.

(2) A truancy support center shall provide a wide spectrum of services to the truant student and the student's family, including:

(a) assessments of the student's needs and abilities;

(b) support for the parents and student through counseling and community programs; and

(c) tutoring for the student during the time spent at the center.

(3) For the suspended or expelled student, the truancy support center shall provide an educational setting, staffed with certified teachers and aides, to provide the student with ongoing educational programming appropriate to their grade level.

(4) In a district with a truancy support center, all students suspended or expelled from school shall be referred to the center. A parent or guardian shall appear with the student at the center within 48 hours of the suspension or expulsion, not including weekends or holidays. The student shall register and attend classes at the truancy support center for the duration of the suspension or expulsion unless the parent or guardian demonstrates that alternative arrangements have been made for the education or supervision of the student during the time of suspension or expulsion.

(5) The truancy support center may provide counseling and other support programming for students suspended or expelled from school and their parents or guardian.   1997

PART 5

IDENTIFICATION OF MISSING CHILDREN

53A-11-501. Definitions.

As used in this chapter:

(1) "Division" means the Criminal Investigations and Technical Services Division of the Department of Public Safety, established in Section 53-10-103.

(2) "Missing child" has the same meaning as provided in Section 26-2-27.

(3) "State registrar" means the State Registrar of Vital Statistics within the Department of Health.   1998

53A-11-502. Identifying records — Reporting requirements.

(1) Upon notification by the division of a missing child in accordance with Section 53-10-203, a school in which that child is currently or was previously enrolled shall flag the record of that child in a manner that whenever a copy of or information regarding the record is requested, the school is alerted to the fact that the record is that of a missing child.

(2) The school shall immediately report any request concerning flagged records or knowledge as to the whereabouts of any missing child to the division.

(3) Upon notification by the division that a missing child has been recovered, the school shall remove the flag from that child's record.   1998

53A-11-503. Requirement of birth certificate for enrollment of students — Procedures.

(1) Upon enrollment of a student for the first time in a particular school, that school shall notify in writing the person enrolling the student that within 30 days he must provide either a certified copy of the student's birth certificate, or other reliable proof of the student's identity and age, together with an affidavit explaining the inability to produce a copy of the birth certificate.

(2) (a) Upon the failure of a person enrolling a student to comply with Subsection (1), the school shall notify that person in writing that unless he complies within 10 days the case shall be referred to the local law enforcement authority for investigation.

(b) If compliance is not obtained within that ten day period, the school shall refer the case to the division.

(3) The school shall immediately report to the division any affidavit received pursuant to this subsection which appears inaccurate or suspicious.   1993

53A-11-504. Requirement of school record for transfer of student — Procedures.

(1) Within 14 days after enrolling a transfer student, a school shall request, directly from the student's previous school, a certified copy of his record.

(2) The requesting school shall exercise due diligence in obtaining that record.

(3) Any school requested to forward a copy of a transferring student's record to the new school shall comply unless the record has been flagged pursuant to Section 53A-11-502, in which case the copy shall not be forwarded and the requested school shall notify the division of the request.   1993

PART 11

WEAPONS ON SCHOOL PROPERTY

53A-11-1101. Notification of teachers of weapons on school property — Immunity from civil and criminal liability.

(1) Whenever a student is found on school property during school hours or at a school-sponsored activity in possession of a dangerous weapon and that infor-

mation is reported to or known by the principal, the principal shall notify law enforcement personnel and school or district personnel who, in the opinion of the principal, should be informed.

(2) A person who in good faith reports information under Subsection (1) and any person who receives the information is immune from any liability, civil or criminal, that might otherwise result from the reporting or receipt of the information.   1994

CHAPTER 13

CURRICULUM IN THE PUBLIC SCHOOLS

Part 2

Driver Education Classes

PART 2

DRIVER EDUCATION CLASSES

53A-13-201. Driver education established by school districts.

(1) As used in this part:

(a) "driver education" includes classroom instruction and driving and observation in a dual-controlled motor vehicle; and

(b) "driving" or "behind-the-wheel driving" means operating a dual-controlled motor vehicle under the supervision of a certified instructor.

(2) (a) Local school districts may establish and maintain driver education for pupils.

(b) A school or local school district that provides driver education shall provide an opportunity for each pupil enrolled in that school or local school district to take the written test and be issued a practice permit when the pupil is 15 years and nine months of age.

(c) Notwithstanding the provisions of Subsection (2)(b), a school or local school district that provides driver education may provide an opportunity for each pupil enrolled in that school or school district to be issued a practice permit when the pupil is 15 years and six months of age.

(3) The purpose of driver education is to help develop the knowledge, attitudes, habits, and skills necessary for the safe operation of motor vehicles.

(4) In accordance with Title 63, Chapter 46a, Utah Administrative Rulemaking Act, the State Board of Education shall make rules for driver education offered in the public schools.

(5) The rules under Subsection (4) shall:

(a) require at least one hour of classroom training on the subject of railroad crossing safety for each driver education pupil; and

(b) establish minimum standards for approved driving ranges under Section 53-3-505.5.

(6) The requirements of Section 53-3-505.5 apply to any behind-the-wheel driving training provided as part of driver education offered under this part and used to satisfy the driver training requirement under Section 53-3-204.   2004

53A-13-202. Driver education funding — Reimbursement of school districts for driver education class expenses — Limitations — Excess funds — Student fees.

(1) (a) Except as provided in Subsection (1)(b), a school district that provides driver education shall fund the program solely through:

(i) funds provided from the Automobile Driver Education Tax Account in the Uniform School Fund as created under Section 41-1a-1205; and

(ii) student fees collected by each school.

(b) In determining the cost of driver education, a school district may exclude:

(i) the full-time equivalent cost of a teacher for a driver education class taught during regular school hours; and

(ii) classroom space and classroom maintenance.

(c) A school district may not use any additional school funds beyond those allowed under Subsection (1)(b) to subsidize driver education.

(2) (a) The state superintendent of public instruction shall, prior to September 2nd following the school year during which it was expended, or may at earlier intervals during that school year, reimburse each school district that applied for reimbursement in accordance with this section.

(b) A school district that maintains driver education classes that conform to this part and the rules prescribed by the board may apply for reimbursement for the actual cost of providing the behind-the-wheel and observation training incidental to those classes.

(3) Under the state board's supervision for driver education, a school district may:

(a) employ personnel who are not licensed by the board under Section 53A-6-104; or

(b) contract with private parties or agencies licensed under Section 53-3-504 for the behind-the-wheel phase of the driver education program.

(4) The reimbursement amount shall be paid out of the Automobile Driver Education Tax Account in the Uniform School Fund and may not exceed:

(a) $100 per student who has completed driver education during the school year;

(b) $30 per student who has only completed the classroom portion in the school or through the electronic high school during the school year; or

(c) $70 per student who has only completed the behind-the-wheel and observation portion in the school during the school year.

(5) If the amount of money in the account at the end of a school year is less than the total of the reimbursable costs, the state superintendent of public instruction shall allocate the money to each school district in the same proportion that its reimbursable costs bear to the total reimbursable costs of all school districts.

(6) If the amount of money in the account at the end of any school year is more than the total of the reimbursement costs provided under Subsection (4), the superintendent may allocate the excess funds to school districts:

(a) to reimburse each school district that applies for reimbursement of the cost of a fee waived under Section 53A-12-103 for driver education; and

(b) to aid in the procurement of equipment and facilities which reduce the cost of behind-the-wheel instruction.

(7) A local school board shall establish the student fee for driver education for the school district. Student fees shall be reasonably associated with the costs of driver education that are not otherwise covered by reimbursements and allocations made under this section.   2003

53A-13-203. Enrollment of private school pupils.

(1) A school district maintaining driver education classes shall allow pupils enrolled in grades nine to 12 of regularly established private schools located within the school district to enroll in the most accessible public school in the school district to receive driver education.

(2) Enrollment is on the same terms and conditions as applies to students in public schools within the district, as such terms and conditions relate to the driver education classes only.   1988

53A-13-204. Reports as to costs of driver training programs.

A local school board seeking reimbursement shall, at the end of each school year and at other times as designated by the State Board of Education, report the following to the state superintendent of public instruction:

(1) the costs of providing driver education including a separate accounting for:

(a) course work; and

(b) behind-the-wheel and observation training to students;

(2) the costs of fees waived under Section 53A-12-103 for driver education including a separate accounting for:

(a) course work; and

(b) behind-the-wheel and observation training to students;

(3) the number of students who completed driver education including a separate accounting for:

(a) course work; and

(b) behind-the-wheel and observation training to students;

(4) whether or not a passing grade was received; and

(5) any other information the State Board of Education may require for the purpose of administering this program.   2003

53A-13-205. Promoting the establishment and maintenance of classes — Payment of costs.

(1) The superintendent of public instruction shall promote the establishment and maintenance of driver education classes in school districts under rules adopted by the State Board of Education.

(2) The state board may employ personnel and sponsor experimental programs considered necessary to give full effect to this program.

(3) The costs of implementing this section shall be paid from the legislative appropriation to the board made from the Automobile Driver Education Tax Account in the Uniform School Fund.   1988

53A-13-206. Appropriations from Automobile Driver Education Tax Account.

There is appropriated to the State Board of Education from the Automobile Driver Education Tax Account, annually, all money in the account, in excess of the expense of administering the collection of the tax, for use and distribution in the administration and maintenance of driver education classes and programs with respect to classes offered in the school district and the establishment of experimental programs, including the purchasing of equipment, by the board.   1988

53A-13-207. Repealed.   1997

53A-13-208. Driver education teachers certified as license examiners.

(1) The Driver License Division of the Department of Public Safety and the State Board of Education through the State Office of Education shall establish procedures and standards to certify teachers of driver education classes under this part to administer written and driving tests and to issue practice permits.

(2) The division is the certifying authority.

(3) (a) A teacher certified under this section shall give written and driving tests designed for driver education classes authorized under this part.

(b) The Driver License Division shall, in conjunction with the State Office of Education, establish minimal standards for the driver education class tests that are at least as difficult as those required to receive a class D operator's license under Title 53, Chapter 3, Uniform Drivers License Act.

(c) A student who passes the written test but fails the driving test given by a teacher certified under this section may apply for a class D operator's license under Title 53, Chapter 3, Part 2, Driver Licensing Act, and complete the driving test at a Driver License Division office.

(4) (a) A certified driver education teacher shall issue a practice permit to a student who:

(i) is at least 15 years and nine months of age;

(ii) passes the written test given by the teacher under this section;

(iii) has been issued an instruction permit under Subsection 53-3-210(2); and

(iv) has passed the physical and mental fitness tests as required by the division.

(b) Notwithstanding the provisions of Subsection (4)(a)(i), a certified driver education teacher may issue a practice permit to a student who is at least 15 years and six months of age and who meets the requirements of Subsections (4)(a)(ii) and (iii).

(c) The State Office of Education shall supply the practice permit form. The form shall include the following information:

(i) the student's full name, date of birth, sex, home address, height, weight, and eye color;

(ii) the name of the school or local school district providing the driver education program;

(iii) the name and signature of a driver education teacher;

(iv) the dates of issuance and expiration of the permit;

(v) the statutory citation authorizing the permit; and

(vi) the conditions and restrictions contained in this section for operating a class D motor vehicle.

(d) The practice permit is valid for up to six months from the date of issuance. The practice permit allows the student to operate a class D motor vehicle when the student's parent, legal guardian, or adult spouse, who must be a licensed driver, is occupying a seat next to the student.

(e) A student shall have the practice permit in his immediate possession at all times when operating a motor vehicle under this section.

(5) A student who successfully passes the tests given by a certified driver education teacher under this section satisfies the written and driving parts of the test required for a class D operator's license.

(6) The Driver License Division and the State Board of Education shall establish procedures to enable school districts to administer or process any tests for students to receive a class D operator's license.

(7) The division and board shall establish the standards and procedures required under this section by rules made in accordance with Title 63, Chapter 46a, Utah Administrative Rulemaking Act.   2004

53A-13-209. Programs authorized — Minimum standards.

(1) Local school districts may:

(a) allow students to complete the classroom training portion of driver education through the following programs:

(i) home study; or

(ii) the electronic high school;

(b) provide each parent with driver education instructional materials to assist in parent involvement with driver education including behind-the-wheel driving materials;

(c) offer driver education outside of school hours in order to reduce the cost of providing driver education;

(d) offer driver education through community education programs;

(e) offer the classroom portion of driver education in the public schools and allow the student to complete the behind-the-wheel portion with a private provider:

(i) licensed under Section 53-3-504; and

(ii) not associated with the school or under contract with the school under Subsection 53A-13-202(3); or

(f) any combination of Subsections (1)(a) through (e).

(2) In accordance with Title 63, Chapter 46a, Utah Administrative Rulemaking Act, the State Board of Education shall establish minimum standards for the school-related programs under Subsection (1).   2003

TITLE 53B

STATE SYSTEM OF HIGHER EDUCATION

Chapter
3. Enforcement of Regulations at Institutions.

CHAPTER 3

ENFORCEMENT OF REGULATIONS AT INSTITUTIONS

Section
53B-3-101. Purpose of chapter.
53B-3-102. "State institution of higher education" defined.
53B-3-103. Power of board to adopt rules and enact regulations.
53B-3-104. Establishment of police or security departments.
53B-3-105. Appointment of police or security personnel — Powers.
53B-3-106. Criminal and traffic laws in full force and effect.
53B-3-107. Traffic violations — Notice of rule or regulation.
53B-3-108. Violation of chapter a misdemeanor.
53B-3-109. Jurisdiction of district and justice courts.
53B-3-110. Fines and forfeitures — Disposition.

53B-3-101. Purpose of chapter.

(1) It is the purpose of this chapter to confirm and clarify the power vested in the board to pass rules and regulations governing parking and traffic on campuses and related facilities and to enforce the rules and regulations by all appropriate methods.

(2) The board may delegate this authority and other authority granted under this chapter to the president of each institution so long as the rules and regulations are approved by the institution's board of trustees.   1991

53B-3-102. "State institution of higher education" defined.

(1) As used in this chapter, "state institution of higher education" means the University of Utah, Utah State University, Southern Utah University, Weber State University, Snow College, Dixie State College of Utah, the College of Eastern Utah, Utah Valley State College, Salt Lake Community College, and any other university or college which may be established and maintained by the state.

(2) It includes any branch or affiliated institution and any campus or facilities owned, operated, or controlled by the governing board of the university or college.   2000

53B-3-103. Power of board to adopt rules and enact regulations.

(1) The board may enact regulations governing the conduct of university and college students, faculty, and employees.

(2) (a) The board may:

(i) enact and authorize higher education institutions to enact traffic, parking, and related regulations governing all individuals on campuses and other facilities owned or controlled by the institutions or the board; and

(ii) authorize higher education institutions to establish no more than one secure area at each institution as a hearing room as prescribed in Section 76-8-311.1, but not otherwise restrict the lawful possession or carrying of firearms.

(b) In addition to the requirements and penalty prescribed in Subsections 76-8-311.1(3), (4), (5), and (6), the board shall make rules to ensure that:

    (i) reasonable means such as mechanical, electronic, x-ray, or similar devices are used to detect firearms, ammunition, or dangerous weapons contained in the personal property of or on the person of any individual attempting to enter a secure area hearing room;

    (ii) an individual required or requested to attend a hearing in a secure area hearing room is notified in writing of the requirements related to entering a secured area hearing room under this Subsection (2)(b) and Section 76-8-311.1;

    (iii) the restriction of firearms, ammunition, or dangerous weapons in the secure area hearing room is in effect only during the time the secure area hearing room is in use for hearings and for a reasonable time before and after its use; and

    (iv) reasonable space limitations are applied to the secure area hearing room as warranted by the number of individuals involved in a typical hearing.

(3) The board and institutions may enforce these rules and regulations in any reasonable manner, including the assessment of fees, fines, and forfeitures, the collection of which may be by withholding from moneys owed the violator, the imposition of probation, suspension, or expulsion from the institution, the revocation of privileges, the refusal to issue certificates, degrees, and diplomas, through judicial process or any reasonable combination of these alternatives.
          2002

53B-3-104. Establishment of police or security departments.

The board may establish and maintain police or security departments for the purpose of enforcing the regulations of each institution of higher education and the laws of the state.   1987

53B-3-105. Appointment of police or security personnel — Powers.

(1) Members of the police or security department of any college or university are appointed by the board.

(2) Upon appointment, they are peace officers and have all the powers possessed by policemen in cities and by sheriffs, including the power to make arrests on view or on warrant of violation of state statutes and city or county ordinances.

(3) Members of the police or security department of any college or university also have the power to enforce all rules and regulations promulgated by the board as related to the institution.   1987

53B-3-106. Criminal and traffic laws in full force and effect.

(1) All of the criminal laws of this state, including the traffic laws, are in full force and effect on the campuses of state institutions of higher education and upon all other property or facilities owned by the institutions or operated or controlled by the governing board of the institution.

(2) (a) State institutions of higher education are "political subdivisions" and the board of the institutions is a "local authority."

(b) All streets, roadways, alleys, and parking lots on property owned or controlled by state institutions of higher education are "streets or highways" as these terms are used in Title 41, Chapter 6a, Traffic Code.   2005

53B-3-107. Traffic violations — Notice of rule or regulation.

(1) It is a violation of this section for any person to operate or park a vehicle upon any property owned or controlled by a state institution of higher education contrary to posted signs authorized by the published rules and regulations of the institution or to block or impede traffic through or on any of these properties.

(2) Notice of a rule or regulation to all persons is sufficient if the rule or regulation is published in one issue of a newspaper of general circulation in the county or counties in which the institution and the campus or facility is located.   1997

53B-3-108. Violation of chapter a misdemeanor.

A violation of this chapter is a misdemeanor.   1987

53B-3-109. Jurisdiction of district and justice courts.

Any district court or any justice court of any city or county in which property owned or controlled by a state institution of higher education is located has jurisdiction to hear and determine cases involving an alleged violation of this chapter.   1996

53B-3-110. Fines and forfeitures — Disposition.

All fines and forfeitures collected by any justice court judge and one-half of all the fines and forfeitures collected by the clerk of any district court for a violation of any of this chapter are remitted to the state treasurer to be credited to the general operating fund of the state institution of higher education complaining of the violation.   1996

TITLE 54

PUBLIC UTILITIES

Chapter
4. Authority of Commission Over Public Utilities.

CHAPTER 4

AUTHORITY OF COMMISSION OVER PUBLIC UTILITIES

54-4-1. General jurisdiction.

The commission is hereby vested with power and jurisdiction to supervise and regulate every public utility in this state, and to supervise all of the business of every such public utility in this state, and to do all things, whether herein specifically designated or in addition thereto, which are necessary or convenient in the exercise of such power and jurisdiction; provided, however, that the Department of Transportation shall have jurisdiction over those safety functions transferred to it by the Department of Transportation Act.

1975

54-4-1.1. Wholesale electrical cooperative exempt from rate regulation — Requirements for rate increase.

The commission does not have the authority under the provisions of this title to regulate, fix, or otherwise approve or establish the rates, fares, tolls, or charges of a wholesale electrical cooperative. A wholesale electrical cooperative shall not vary its charges within any type or classification of service to any member or the public, one from the other, or from schedules of rates, fares, tolls, or charges which schedules shall be filed at least annually with the Division of Public Utilities for informational purposes only. The prohibition of this section applies only to the rates, fares, tolls, or charges and does not exempt wholesale electrical cooperatives from other areas of regulation under this title including, but not limited to, regulation having an indirect effect on rates, fares, tolls, or charges but which does not constitute an approval or establishment of them.

A wholesale electrical cooperative must, prior to the implementation of any rate increase after January 1, 1984, hold a public meeting for all its customers and members. Notice must be mailed at least ten days prior to the meeting. In addition, any schedule of new rates or other change that results in new rates must be approved by the board of directors of the wholesale electrical cooperative.

1984

54-4-1.5. Investigations, providing information, audits and recommendations by director.

In addition to its other powers and duties provided by law, the Public Service Commission may, with respect to any matter within its jurisdiction, order the director of the Division of Public Utilities to:

(1) conduct research, studies, and investigations;

(2) provide information, documents or records in compliance with the provisions regarding ex parte communications set forth in Section 54-7-1.5;

(3) conduct audits and inspections or take other enforcement actions to assure compliance with commission decisions and state and federal laws; and

(4) make recommendations regarding public utility regulations.

1983

54-4-14. Safety regulation.

The commission shall have power, by general or special orders, rules or regulations, or otherwise, to require every public utility to construct, maintain and operate its line, plant, system, equipment, apparatus, tracks and premises in such manner as to promote and safeguard the health and safety of its employees, passengers, customers and the public, and to this end to prescribe, among other things, the installation, use, maintenance and operation of appropriate safety or other devices or appliances including interlocking and other protective devices at grade crossings or junctions, and block or other system of signaling, and to establish uniform or other standards of construction

and equipment, and to require the performance of any other acts which the health or safety of its employees, passengers, customers or the public may demand, provided, however, that the department of transportation shall have jurisdiction over those safety functions transferred to it by the Department of Transportation Act.

1975

54-4-15. Establishment and regulation of grade crossings.

(1) No track of any railroad shall be constructed across a public road, highway or street at grade, nor shall the track of any railroad corporation be constructed across the track of any other railroad or street railroad corporation at grade, nor shall the track of a street railroad corporation be constructed across the track of a railroad corporation at grade, without the permission of the Department of Transportation having first been secured; provided, that this subsection shall not apply to the replacement of lawfully existing tracks. The department shall have the right to refuse its permission or to grant it upon such terms and conditions as it may prescribe.

(2) The department shall have the power to determine and prescribe the manner, including the particular point of crossing, and the terms of installation, operation, maintenance, use and protection of each crossing of one railroad by another railroad or street railroad, and of a street railroad by a railroad and of each crossing of a public road or highway by a railroad or street railroad, and of a street by a railroad or vice versa, and to alter or abolish any such crossing, to restrict the use of such crossings to certain types of traffic in the interest of public safety and is vested with power and it shall be its duty to designate the railroad crossings to be traversed by school buses and motor vehicles carrying passengers for hire, and to require, where in its judgment it would be practicable, a separation of grades at any such crossing heretofore or hereafter established, and to prescribe the terms upon which such separation shall be made and the proportions in which the expense of the alteration or abolition of such crossings or the separation of such grades shall be divided between the railroad or street railroad corporations affected, or between such corporations and the state, county, municipality or other public authority in interest.

(3) Whenever the department shall find that public convenience and necessity demand the establishment, creation or construction of a crossing of a street or highway over, under or upon the tracks or lines of any public utility, the department may by order, decision, rule or decree require the establishment, construction or creation of such crossing, and such crossing shall thereupon become a public highway and crossing.

(4) (a) The commission retains exclusive jurisdiction for the resolution of any dispute upon petition by any person aggrieved by any action of the department pursuant to this section, except as provided under Subsection (4)(b).

(b) If a petition is filed by a person or entity engaged in a subject activity, as defined in Section 19-3-318, the commission's decision under Subsection (4)(a) regarding resolution of a dispute requires the concurrence of the governor and the Legislature in order to take effect.

1999

54-4-15.1. Signals or devices at grade crossings — Duty to provide.

The Department of Transportation so as to promote the public safety shall as prescribed in this act provide for the installing, maintaining, reconstructing, and improving of automatic and other safety appliances, signals or devices at grade crossings on public highways or roads over the tracks of any railroad or street railroad corporation in the state. 1975

54-4-15.2. Signals or devices at grade crossings — Funds for payment of costs.

The funds provided by the state for purposes of this act shall be used in conjunction with other available moneys, including those received from federal sources, to pay all or part of the cost of the installation, maintenance, reconstruction or improvement of any signals or devices described in Section 54-4-15.1 at any grade crossing of a public highway or any road over the tracks of any railroad or street railroad corporation in this state. 1973

54-4-15.3. Signals or devices at grade crossings — Apportionment of costs.

The Department of Transportation, in accordance with the provisions of Section 54-4-15, shall apportion the cost of the installation, maintenance, reconstruction or improvement of any signals or devices described in Section 54-4-15.1 between the railroad or street railroad and the public agency involved. Unless otherwise ordered by the department, the liability of cities, towns and counties to pay the share of maintenance cost assigned to the local agencies by the department shall be limited to the funds provided under this act. Payment of any moneys from the funds provided shall be made on the basis of verified claims filed with the Department of Transportation by the railroad or street railroad corporation responsible for the physical installation, maintenance, reconstruction or improvement of the signal or device. 1975

54-4-15.4. Signals or devices at grade crossings — Provision of costs.

The Department of Transportation shall provide in its annual budget for the costs to be incurred under this act. 1975

54-4-16. Investigation and report of accidents.

The commission shall investigate the cause of all accidents occurring within this state upon the property of any public utility, or directly or indirectly arising from or connected with its maintenance or operation, resulting in loss of life or injury to persons or property and requiring in the judgment of the commission investigation by it, and shall have the power to make such order or recommendation with respect thereto as in its judgment may seem just and reasonable; provided, that neither the order nor recommendation of the commission nor any accident report filed with the commission shall be admitted as evidence in any action for damage based on or arising out of the loss of life or injury to person or property in this section referred to. Every public utility is hereby required to file with the commission, under such rules and regulations as the commission may prescribe, a report of each accident so occurring of such kinds or classes as the commission may from time to time designate. The Department of Transportation where private and public carriers are involved shall have and assume all powers heretofore held by the commission pursuant to this section; provided that the commission shall retain exclusive jurisdiction for the resolution of any dispute upon petition by any person aggrieved by any order of the department issued pursuant thereto. 1975

TITLE 56

RAILROADS

Chapter
1. General Provisions.
2. Movement of Defective Rolling Stock and Fencing Right-of-Way.
3. Offensive Substances on Right-of-Way.

CHAPTER 1

GENERAL PROVISIONS

56-1-1. Railroad corporations — Powers and duties.

Railroad corporations heretofore organized and now existing or hereafter organized under the laws of this state shall be subject to all the duties imposed and shall have and possess all the powers and privileges conferred by this title, as well as the powers and privileges conferred by the laws under which said corporations were organized or which are contained in their articles of incorporation and are not inconsistent with the laws and Constitution of this state.   1953

56-1-2. Articles of incorporation — Contents.

The articles of incorporation of a railroad corporation proposing to purchase or construct a railroad shall include, in addition to the matters required to be stated in the articles of incorporation of corporations organized for pecuniary profit, the names of the places between which and of the counties through or in which such railroad lies or will be constructed, and a statement of its length as near as may be.   1953

56-1-3. Stock subscriptions — Minimum requirements.

The Division of Corporations and Commercial Code shall not issue a certificate of incorporation to any railroad corporation which proposes to construct a railroad until it shall appear by the affidavit of at least three of the incorporators that $1,000 for each mile in length of the railroad proposed to be constructed shall have been subscribed, and that 10% of the stock subscribed by each stockholder has been paid in.   1984

56-1-4. Construction required within limited time.

If a railroad corporation which proposes to construct a railroad shall not within three years after its incorporation begin the construction of its railroad and expend thereon an amount equal to at least $300 for each mile of the proposed line referred to in its articles of incorporation, or if it shall fail to finish the road and put the same into full operation within ten years after its incorporation, its franchise as to all parts of its line not then constructed shall be deemed forfeited.   1953

56-1-5. General powers enumerated.

Every railroad corporation organized under the laws of this state shall, except as otherwise provided in this title and subject to the limitations and requirements hereof, have all the rights, privileges and powers, and be subject to all the duties and obligations of corporations organized under Title 16, Chapter 10a, Utah Revised Business Corporation Act, and in addition thereto such railroad corporation shall have the following powers:

(1) To lay out, locate, relocate, construct, reconstruct, purchase, lease or otherwise acquire, and to own, maintain and operate railroads situated wholly or partly within or without this state and any branch or branches of such railroads, together with all such turnouts, yards and other facilities as shall be deemed necessary or convenient for use in connection therewith, and all property appurtenant to, or necessary or useful in connection with the construction, maintenance or operation of, such railroads; and in the case of purchase, to exercise and enjoy all the rights, powers, privileges and franchises, which at the time of the sale belonged to or were vested in the corporation or corporations last owning the properties sold, not inconsistent with the Constitution or laws of this state.

(2) To construct, purchase or lease spurs or branch lines of railroad connecting with its main line or any branch thereof, and to relocate any section or sections of its line, with the same power as in the case of original or first location, though such spurs or branch lines or relocated sections are not named or described in the articles of incorporation.

(3) To enter by its servants upon the real property of any person for the purpose of selecting an advantageous route for its main line or any extension or branch thereof or for the purpose of relocating the same, subject to responsibility for all damages resulting therefrom; and to condemn in the manner provided by law a right of way, not to exceed nine rods in width, with such additional lands as shall be necessary for depot grounds, roundhouses, shops and other necessary uses, or for the purpose of constructing necessary embankments, excavations, ditches, drains and culverts, or for the procuring of timber, stone, gravel or other essential materials, including water and water rights for its locomotives, cars, shops, depots or yards, together with all lands and rights of way necessary for the construction and maintenance of reservoirs or pipe or conduit lines for the storage and conveyance of such waters to the places where the same are required.

(4) To acquire by purchase, donation or otherwise all such real and personal property as shall be necessary for, or shall be given to aid or encourage the construction and maintenance of, its railroad, buildings and yards.

(5) To cross natural or artificial streams or bodies of water, streets, highways or railroads, which its road shall intersect, in such manner as to afford security for life and property; subject to the duty of immediately restoring such stream or body of water, street, highway or railroad to its former condition as nearly as may be.

(6) To join or unite its railroad with any other railroad, either before or after construction, at any points upon its route and upon the grounds of such other railroad corporation, with the necessary turnouts, sidings, switches and other conveniences in furtherance of the objects of its connection; and every corporation whose railroad is or shall be hereafter intersected by any new railroad shall join with the owners of such new railroad in forming such intersections and connections, and grant facilities therefor.

(7) To take and transport persons and property by steam, electric, animal or other power, or by any combination thereof, and to receive such compensation therefor as shall be reasonable and conformable to law, and to make such regulations regarding the movement of its trains or cars and the manner of transporting passengers and

freight, the management of its property and the conduct of its business, as shall be reasonable and conformable to law.

(8) To merge or to consolidate with any other railroad corporation or corporations organized or existing under the laws of this or any other state or territory, or of the United States; provided, that the lines of such corporations shall not be competing but shall be substantially continuous or connective either by means of actual union of track or through the medium of any bridge, ferry, or line of railroad leased, operated or otherwise controlled by any or either of said corporations, or which any such corporations shall have the right by contract or otherwise to use or operate. If one or more of the corporations merging or consolidating is a foreign corporation, such merger or consolidation shall be authorized and ratified by such foreign corporation in the manner required by the laws of the jurisdiction under which it is incorporated.

(9) To lease, sell, convey and transfer its property and franchises or any part thereof to any railroad corporation not owning any competitive line in this state, whether organized under the laws of this state or of any other state, or of the United States, and to sell, convey and transfer to a corporation organized under the laws of any foreign country the lines of railroad owned by it and situated wholly in such foreign country.

(10) To acquire, own, maintain, operate and navigate steamships, sailing vessels and boats of every description, and generally to carry on the business of a common carrier by water.

(11) To issue bonds for such sums and payable at such times and places and drawing interest at such rates as the board of directors shall deem expedient, and for the purpose of securing the payment of such bonds and interest to execute trust deeds or mortgages or both upon the whole or any part of its lines, real property, rolling stock, vessels, machinery, franchises, income, profits and other personal property then owned or thereafter acquired. Such bonds and trust deeds or mortgages shall be valid according to their terms, notwithstanding the fact that the bonds may be sold below par value. A trust deed or mortgage made as aforesaid, to operate as notice to third persons, shall be recorded in the office of the recorder of each county in which any of the property affected by such trust deed or mortgage shall be situated, and need not be left or filed in said office. Any such mortgage or trust deed when made shall be a valid lien upon the real and personal property and chattels included therein, notwithstanding the fact that the possession of such personal property may remain with the mortgagor; and when recorded as aforesaid such record shall be notice to all persons of the existence of such mortgage or deed of trust according to its terms; provided, that corporations organized under the laws of this state, owning and operating street, suburban, or interurban railroads, including those that own and operate, with such railroads, power and lighting plants shall be deemed railroad companies, and their properties, railroad properties, within the meaning of this subdivision.

(12) To create, issue and dispose of preferred stock, special stock and income certificates, to such amounts and in such form and for such purposes, and as between the stockholders themselves, to make the same payable in respect of principal and dividends out of such class or character of assets and income, as shall be determined upon by its board of directors with the assent thereto of the holders of at least a majority in amount of the common stock; provided, that no increase of any preferred or special stock, or of any income certificates issued pursuant to this title, shall at any time be made without the assent thereto of the holders of at least a majority in amount of the preferred stock or special stock, or of the income certificates to be affected by such issue, as the case may be.

(13) To purchase or otherwise lawfully acquire, and to own, hold, pledge or otherwise dispose of, the stock or any part of the stock, bonds or other obligations of any corporation organized under the laws of this state or of the United States or of any other state or territory of the United States, which owns or operates by lease or otherwise any line or lines of steam, electric, street or interurban railroad or which directly or indirectly conducts any transportation business by land, water, or air and by whatever motive power or which owns or operates any union depot or station, any railroad terminal, wharves, docks or other shipping facilities, any steamships, steamboats or other watercraft or any aircraft, landing field or other aviation facilities, or which may carry on an express or refrigeration business, or furnish cars or other facilities for refrigeration or storage of freight, or which may manufacture, sell, lease, or otherwise provide railroad equipment; and upon the pledge or sale of such bonds or other obligations to guarantee the same in the discretion of its board of directors.

(14) To receive subscriptions for increases of stock on such terms as the board of directors or the stockholders shall authorize, payable in shares of the stock or in bonds or other obligations of any other corporation organized under the laws of this state or of the United States, or of any other state or territory of the United States, whose stock, bonds, or other obligations are authorized to be purchased or acquired by railroad corporations of this state; provided, that the stocks, bonds or other obligations of such other corporations to be received in payment and exchange for the stock so subscribed shall be of a par value at least equal to the par value of the stock subscribed, or of an actual or market value equal in the opinion of the board of directors to that of the stock so subscribed and issued, and such stock so issued shall for all purposes be deemed full-paid.   1992 (3rd S.S.)

56-1-6. Repealed.   1961

56-1-7. Purpose unaltered by amendment of articles.

Amending the articles of incorporation by adding new lines of route, altering the original route, or changing the termini shall not be deemed an alteration of the original purpose of the corporation.   1953

56-1-8. Use of local streets.

No railroad shall use any road, street, alley or highway within any county, city or town except with the consent of the authorities of such county, city or town as provided by law; provided, that this section shall not be construed to prevent railroads from crossing at right angles, or as nearly as may be, any street, alley or highway across which its located line may pass. 1953

56-1-9. Right of way in canyons.

No railroad company whose right of way or whose track or roadbed upon such right of way passes through any canyon, pass or defile shall exclude any other railroad company from the use and occupancy of such canyon, pass or defile, for the purposes of its road, in common with the road first located, or from crossing its road at grade. And the location of such right of way through any canyon, pass or defile shall not cause the disuse of any wagon road or other public highway now located therein, nor prevent the location through the same of any such wagon road or highway where such road or highway may be necessary for the public accommodation; and where any change in the location of any such wagon road or highway is necessary to permit the passage of any railroad through any canyon, pass or defile, said railroad company shall before entering upon the ground occupied by such wagon road or highway cause the same to be reconstructed at its own expense in the most favorable location, and in as perfect a manner as the original road; provided, that such expenses shall be equitably divided between any number of railroad companies occupying and using the same canyon, pass or defile. 1953

56-1-10. Maps of final location to be filed.

Every company constructing or operating a railroad in this state shall within a reasonable time after the final location of the road file with the Division of Corporations and Commercial Code a map thereof showing the route decided upon and the land obtained for the use thereof; and like maps of the several parts thereof located in the several counties through or into which the road may be extended shall be filed in the offices of the recorders of such counties respectively. Maps and profiles certified by the chief engineer, the president, and the secretary of the company shall be filed in the office of the company subject to examination by any person interested. 1984

56-1-11. Maintenance of crossings.

Every railroad company shall be liable for damages caused by its neglect to make and maintain good and sufficient crossings at points where any line of travel crosses its road. 1953

56-1-12. Injury to livestock — Notice.

Every person operating a railroad within this state that injures or kills any livestock of any description by the running of any engine or engines, car or cars, over or against any such livestock shall within three days thereafter post at the first railroad station in each direction from the place of such injury or killing in some conspicuous place on the outside of such station a notice in writing of the number and kind of animals so injured or killed, with a full description of each, and the time and place as near as may be of such injury or killing. Such notice shall be dated and signed by some officer or agent of such railroad, and a duplicate thereof shall be filed with the county clerk of the county in which stock is so injured or killed. Every person willfully failing, neglecting or refusing to comply with the provisions of this section is guilty of a misdemeanor and shall be fined in any sum not exceeding $50. 1953

56-1-13. Fencing right of way — Gates.

Every railroad company shall erect and maintain a fence on each side of its rights of way where the same passes through lands owned and improved by private owners, and at all public road crossings shall connect the same with cattle guards. Such fence shall not be less than four and one-half feet in height and may be constructed of barbed or other fencing wire with not less than five wires, and good, substantial posts not more than one rod apart with a stay midway between the posts attached to the wires to keep said wires in place; and whenever such railroad company shall provide gates for private crossings for the convenience of the owners of the land through which such railroad passes, such gates shall be so constructed that they may be easily operated; and every railroad company shall be liable for all damages sustained by the owner of any domestic animal killed or injured by such railroad in consequence of the failure to build or maintain such fence. The owner of such lands shall keep such gate closed at all times when not in actual use, and if such owner fails to keep such gates closed, and in consequence thereof, any animal owned by him strays upon such railroad, and is killed or injured, such owner shall not be entitled to recover damages therefor. 1953

56-1-14. Procedures at grade crossings.

Every locomotive shall be provided with a bell which shall be rung continuously from a point not less than eighty rods from any city or town street or public highway grade crossing until such city or town street or public highway grade crossing shall be crossed, but, except in towns and at terminal points, the sounding of the locomotive whistle or siren at least one-fourth of a mile before reaching any such grade crossing shall be deemed equivalent to ringing the bell as aforesaid; during the prevalence of fogs, snow and dust storms, the locomotive whistle shall be sounded before each street crossing while passing through cities and towns. All locomotives with or without trains before crossing the main track at grade of any other railroad must come to a full stop at a distance not exceeding 400 feet from the crossing, and must not proceed until the way is known to be clear; two blasts of the whistle or two sounds of the siren shall be sounded at the moment of starting; provided, that whenever interlocking signal apparatus and derailing switches or any other crossing protective device approved by the Department of Transportation is adopted such stop shall not be required.

Provided, that local authorities in their respective jurisdiction may by ordinance approved by the Department of Transportation provide more restricted sounding of bells or whistles or sirens than is provided herein and may prescribe points different from those herein set forth at which such signals shall be given and may further restrict such ringing of bells or sounding of whistles or sirens so as to provide for either the ringing of a bell or the sounding of a whistle or of a siren or the elimination of the sounding of such bells or whistles or sirens or either of them, except in case of emergency.

The term locomotive as used herein shall mean every self-propelled steam engine, electrically propelled interurban car and so-called diesel operated locomotive.

Every person in charge of a locomotive violating the provisions of this section is guilty of a misdemeanor, and the railroad company shall be liable for all damages which any person may sustain by reason of such violation. 1975 (1st S.S.)

56-1-15. Fire caused by sparks emitted.

In any action for damages on account of fire caused by sparks emitted from locomotive engines on a steam railroad proof that the fire occurred and was caused by sparks emitted from a locomotive engine operated by such railroad shall constitute prima facie evidence of negligence on the part of such railroad.   1953

56-1-16. Time schedules to be maintained — Notice of delays.

Every railroad company shall start and run its trains for the transportation of persons and property at such regular times as it shall fix by public notice, and the station agents thereof shall announce on a bulletin board, placed in a conspicuous and public place at each station not less than fifteen minutes before the regular time of departure of each passenger train, the time of such departure, or if the train is delayed, the probable duration of such delay, and on failure to do so is guilty of a misdemeanor. The railroad company shall be liable for all damages that may be sustained by any person by reason of the failure of any of its station agents to observe the requirements of this section.   1953

56-1-17. Adequate accommodations and regular stops required.

Every railroad company shall furnish sufficient accommodations for the transportation of all passengers and property as shall, within a reasonable time previous to the departure of any train, offer or be offered for transportation at any station, siding or stopping place established for receiving and discharging passengers and freight, and at any railroad junction; and shall take, transport and discharge such passengers and property at, from and to such places, on the due payment of tolls, freight or fare therefor; and if the company or its agents shall refuse to take and transport any passenger or property or to deliver the same at the regular appointed places, it shall be liable to the party aggrieved for all accruing damages.   1953

56-1-18. Injury to passenger riding outside regular cars.

In case a passenger on a train of a railroad company shall suffer personal injury while riding on the platform of any car or on any baggage, wood, gravel or freight car in violation of the company's printed regulations posted at that time in a conspicuous place inside its passenger cars then in such train, or in violation of verbal instructions given by any officer of such train or company, the railroad company shall not be liable for such injury provided at the time it had furnished and had available room inside of its passenger cars then in such train sufficient for the accommodation of the passengers.   1953

56-1-18.5. Railroad property — Duty of care.

(1) A person may not ride or climb or attempt to ride or climb on, off, under, over, or across a railroad locomotive, car, or train.

(2) A person may not walk, ride, or travel across, along, or upon railroad yards, tracks, bridges, or active rights-of-way at any location other than public crossings.

(3) A person may not intentionally obstruct or interfere with train operations or use railroad property for recreational purposes.

(4) (a) Except as provided under Subsection (b), an owner or operator of a railroad, including its officers, agents, and employees, owes no duty of care to keep railroad yards, tracks, bridges, or active rights-of-way safe for entry for any person violating this section.

(b) The owner or operator of a railroad may not intentionally, willfully, or maliciously injure a person if the owner or operator has actual knowledge of the person's presence on the property.

(5) This section does not apply to a railroad employee, business invitee, or other person with express written or oral authorization to enter upon railroad property by the owner or operator of the railroad.

(6) This section does not modify any rights or duties of federal, state, county, or municipal officials in the performance of their duties.   1996

56-1-19. Right to eject passenger.

If any passenger refuses to pay his fare or exhibit or surrender his ticket when requested so to do, or if he behaves in a disorderly manner, the conductor and employees of a railroad company may, on stopping the train, put him and his baggage out of the cars, using no unnecessary force, at any usual stopping place or in sight of a dwelling.   1953

56-1-20. Operating employees to wear insignia.

Every conductor, baggage master, engineer, brakeman or other employee of a railroad company, employed in a passenger train or at the stations for passengers, shall wear upon his hat or cap or in some conspicuous place on the breast of his coat a badge indicating his office or station, and, by its initial letters, the name of the company by which he is employed; and no collector or conductor without such badge shall demand or be entitled to receive from any passenger any fare or ticket or exercise any of the powers of his office or station or interfere with any passenger or his property.   1953

56-1-21. Checking baggage.

A check shall be affixed by the agents or employees of a railroad company to every package or parcel of baggage when taken for transportation and a duplicate thereof given to the passenger or person delivering the same.   1953

56-1-21.5. Railroad special agents.

(1) (a) A railroad company may appoint one or more persons to be designated by the railroad company as a railroad special agent for the protection of railroad property and the protection of the persons and property of railroad passengers and employees.

(b) While engaged in the conduct of employment, each appointed railroad special agent may possess and exercise the powers of a special function officer.

(c) The special function officer authority may be exercised only:

   (i) in the protection of passengers and employees on or about railroad premises and in the protection of property belonging to passengers, or belonging to or under the control of the railroad employing the special agents; and

   (ii) in preventing and making arrest for a violation of law upon the premises or in connection with the property.

(2) (a) A person appointed by a railroad company to act as a railroad special agent shall, prior to appointment, meet the qualifications established for special function officers, pursuant to Section 53-13-105, or as otherwise provided by law.

(b) (i) Before the appointee performs any duties as a special agent, the railroad company shall file the name of the appointee with the commissioner of the Department of Public Safety.

(ii) If the appointee meets qualifications for a special function officer, the commissioner of the Department of Public Safety shall issue to the special agent a certificate of authority to act as a peace officer, to continue in effect during his employment by the railroad unless revoked by the commissioner for cause.

(3) (a) A railroad company appointing a special agent is responsible for any liability arising from the acts or omissions of the special agent within the scope of railroad employment, but is entitled to any defense to liability that may be available to other peace officers.

(b) Neither the state nor any of its political subdivisions is liable for any act or omission of a railroad special agent.   1998

56-1-22. Applicability of public utility provisions.

Nothing contained in this title shall be so construed as to dispense with the necessity for railroad companies to comply with the provisions of the title relating to public utilities applicable to such companies and the conduct of their business. Provided, however, that railroad companies subject to regulation by the Interstate Commerce Commission, shall not be required to comply with the provisions of Sections 54-4-28 through 54-4-30 of said title.   1961

56-1-22.5. Procedures — Adjudicative proceedings.

The Public Service Commission shall comply with the procedures and requirements of Title 63, Chapter 46b, in its adjudicative proceedings.   1987

56-1-23, 56-1-24. Repealed.   1965

56-1-25. Track motor cars — Installation of head and rear lights, canopies, side curtains, windshield and wiper, and heaters.

(1) Every person operating or controlling any railroad running through or within the state shall equip each of its track motor cars used during the period from 30 minutes before sunset to 30 minutes after sunrise, with:

(a) an electric headlight of such construction and with sufficient candle power to render plainly visible at a distance of not less than 300 feet in advance of such track motor car, any track obstruction, landmark, warning sign, or grade crossing;

(b) a canopy or top of such construction as to adequately protect the occupants of such cars from rain, snow, and inclement weather;

(c) side curtains;

(d) a windshield equipped with a windshield wiper device, which must be kept in good working order, with which the operator can clear rain, snow, and other moisture from the windshield; and

(e) a red rear electric light of such construction and with sufficient candle power to be plainly visible at a distance of 300 feet.

(2) It is unlawful for any person operating or controlling any railroad running through or within this state to operate or use any track motor car from 30 minutes before sunset to 30 minutes after sunrise, unless the track motor car is equipped with lights of

the candle power, construction, and utility described in Subsection (1), a windshield, and a windshield wiper.

(3) Track motor cars need to be equipped with canopies and side curtains required by Subsection (1) only when requested in writing by a majority of the employees regularly using the cars. The railroad company shall have not less than 90 days after such request to make the installation required by this section.

(4) Any person operating or controlling a railroad running through or within the state shall equip its track motor cars with heaters while in use during the time period of November 1 through March 31.   1990

56-1-26. Violations — Penalty.

Any person, firm or corporation operating or controlling any railroad running through or within this state using or permitting to be used on its line in this state a track motor car in violation of the provisions of this act shall be liable to a penalty of one hundred dollars for each violation to be recovered in a suit or suits to be brought by the prosecuting attorney in the district court of the county having jurisdiction in the locality where such violation occurred.   1953

56-1-27. First-aid kits — Installation in cabooses.

For the purpose of protecting the health and safety of employees of railroads, the Public Service Commission, hereinafter called the commission, shall prescribe standards of health, sanitation and safety requiring the installation and the maintenance of first-aid kits within cabooses of a type and with contents, as shall be determined by the commission, for use in administering first-aid to employees.   1961

56-1-28. Report made when first-aid kit opened for use.

The employee of the railroad in charge of the train shall report to the office designated by the company whenever any such kit has been opened for use.   1961

56-1-29. Removal or use of first-aid kit except for proper purpose — Misdemeanor.

Any person or any employee of the railroad company who shall remove, carry away from its proper place or use any emergency first-aid kit provided for in this act, except for the purpose of administering first-aid in the event of injury to any passenger, employee, or other person in any accident whereby said kit may be made available at once, shall be deemed guilty of a misdemeanor.   1961

56-1-30. First-aid kits — Duty of railroads to comply — Inspection by commission.

It shall be the duty of all persons engaged in the operation of railroads to comply with any regulation or order of the commission issued under the provisions of this act, and to furnish any information required by the commission for purposes of this act. The commission or its authorized agent may, during reasonable hours, enter the place of operation of any person engaged in the operation of railroads for the purpose of ascertaining whether the standards prescribed by authority of this act are being complied with.   1961

56-1-31. Agency actions.

An employee may file a request for agency action with the commission charging violation of a commission rule, or the commission may initiate an action by filing a notice of agency action.   1987

56-1-32. Judicial review.

(1) Any party aggrieved by any order of the commission may obtain judicial review.

(2) Venue for judicial review of informal adjudicative proceedings is in the district court of the county in which the place of employment is located.   1987

56-1-33. First-aid kits — Failure to comply with order or regulation — Penalty.

Any person failing to comply with an order or regulation of the commission authorized by this act shall be liable to a penalty of twenty-five dollars for each day of noncompliance. The attorney general shall file suit on behalf of the state for any unpaid penalty within one year after the penalty accrues.   1961

56-1-34. First-aid kits — Extension of time for equipping cabooses.

Any common carrier railroad which is unable on or before the effective date of this act to equip its cabooses as prescribed herein may apply to the Public Service Commission for extension of time. The commission may grant additional time, not to exceed six months from the effective date of this act, and during such period the common carrier railroad shall not be subject to the penalty prescribed by Section 56-1-33.   1961

56-1-35. Cabooses and locomotives — Safety, health, and comfort rules — Issuance by commission.

The Public Service Commission shall issue general or special orders, rules, regulations, or otherwise; establishing minimum safety, health and comfort for railroad cabooses and locomotives.   1965

56-1-36. Cabooses and locomotives — Safety, health, and comfort rules — Committee to compile and codify.

The commission shall appoint a committee of equal numbers from railroad management and labor to assist in compiling and coding these rules and regulations.   1965

56-1-37. Cabooses and locomotives — Safety, health, and comfort rules — Provisions to be included.

These rules and regulations should include the following provisions:

(a) Drinking water facilities shall be installed and maintained so as to provide fresh and pure drinking water. When ice is used for water cooling purposes, the containers shall be so arranged that the drinking water will not come in contact with the ice. Containers used for storing or dispensing potable water shall be kept clean at all times and shall be subjected to effective bacterial treatment as often as may be necessary to prevent the contamination of the water so stored and dispensed.

(b) A heating facility shall be maintained and shall be capable of producing a temperature of at least 65 degrees Fahrenheit in a standard caboose and 53 degrees in the locomotive cab.

(c) Weather stripping or weatherproof sash shall be installed and maintained at all windows and doors and other openings, to protect against weather and seepage of dirt and dust.

(d) Toilets will be installed in each caboose of the flush, chemical, incinerating, or other effective type and where toilets are installed on cabooses or locomotives, they shall be maintained in a clean and sanitary condition.   1965

56-1-38. Cabooses and locomotives — Safety, health, and comfort rules — Application of chapter — Exceptions.

The provisions of Section 56-1-37 shall not apply to industrial or interplant operations and to cabooses or yard engines used in yard movements within switching limits having a one-way route mileage of 25 miles or less. The provisions of this act shall not apply to cabooses or locomotives presently operated by railroads having less than 100 miles of main and branch line trackage; provided, however, that any additional cabooses acquired by said railroads shall comply with all of the provisions of this act.   1965

CHAPTER 2

MOVEMENT OF DEFECTIVE ROLLING STOCK AND FENCING RIGHT-OF-WAY

56-2-1. Definitions.

As used in this chapter:

(1) "Broken or defective" means any defects in the wheels, trucks, draft gears, couplers, brakes, draft and center sills, of any car, coach, locomotive, or other rolling stock of a railroad company and every other defect in any car, coach, locomotive or other rolling stock which would be dangerous to the public or to any employee of a railroad company while said car is being moved, hauled or transported.

(2) "Local yard service" means the movement of any car, coach, locomotive or other rolling stock in the railroad yards of any railroad company and between the railroad yards of one or more railroad companies where the distance does not exceed eight miles.   1987

56-2-2. Movement of defective rolling stock prohibited — Exceptions.

It shall be unlawful for any railroad corporation operating or in control of the operation of any railroad within the state of Utah to haul or transport or cause to be hauled or transported any broken or defective car, coach, locomotive or other rolling stock owned, leased or controlled by said railroad company or any broken or defective car, coach, locomotive or other rolling stock in the control or subject to the orders of said railroad company within the state of Utah, except that this act shall not apply to prevent the movement of such defective cars or equipment in case of fire, strikes or by an act of God where the movement of such defective equipment is required by any statute of the Congress of the United States, or where such cars or equipment are loaded for movement and will not move on their own wheels in such transportation. This act shall not be applicable to the movement of defective cars or equipment in local yard service or where the defects in the rolling stock shall occur while in transit, but such defective cars and equipment shall not be moved or transported a greater distance than the nearest repair point within this state where said company maintains shops equipped to repair such defect. 1953

56-2-3. Penalties.

Every railroad corporation guilty of transporting defective cars or equipment within the state is guilty of a class B misdemeanor. Every offense is punishable by a fine not less than $250, and the person or employee of the corporation responsible for permitting the broken or defective car to go into transit and to be transported within the state of Utah is guilty of a class A misdemeanor. 1991

56-2-4. Enforcement of provisions.

The Department of Transportation shall investigate and the Public Service Commission of Utah is hereby required to enforce the provisions of this act, within their respective jurisdictions, and for such purposes are hereby authorized to employ such necessary officials, investigators and inspectors as shall be necessary to provide for the enforcement thereof. And said commission and department are hereby empowered to prescribe the salaries and duties of such officers, investigators and inspectors. 1975 (1st S.S.)

56-2-5. Construction of chapter.

It is hereby declared that this act is passed for the purpose of preserving the safety of the public and of employees engaged in the service of railroad companies and to render less dangerous the performance of duties of such employees. 1953

56-2-6. Fencing rights of way to protect livestock — Power of Public Service Commission to require.

The Public Service Commission shall have the jurisdiction and authority to require every railroad company or corporation operating any steam or electric railroad in this state to erect and maintain fences on each side or either side of such railroad, where such railroad is not now required by law to erect and maintain fences, at such places as the commission shall determine such fences to be necessary to protect sheep, cattle, horses or mules or any other domestic animal being driven, ranged or grazed upon lands adjacent to such railroad from being wounded, maimed or killed by the operation or management of engines, cars or other rolling stock upon or over such railroad, with necessary openings and gates in such fences, and crossings and cattle guards. 1953

56-2-7. Exercise of fencing power by commission — Necessity of application by livestock owners.

The Public Service Commission may exercise the jurisdiction and authority granted in Section 56-2-6 only when at least three persons with the right to drive, range, or graze sheep, cattle, horses, or mules upon land adjacent to the portion of the railroad sought to be fenced file a request for agency action with the Public Service Commission. 1987

56-2-8. Contents of livestock owners' application for fencing.

In addition to the information required by Title 63, Chapter 46b, the request for agency action shall:

(1) identify the lands;

(2) identify the name and address of the owner of the lands;

(3) if any of the lands are owned by the United States or the state of Utah, designate the agency or department of government that administers the lands;

(4) identify the nature of the right of each petitioner to drive, range, or graze sheep, cattle, horses, or mules on the lands; and

(5) specify the ownership of the railroad sought to be fenced. 1987

56-2-9, 56-2-10. Repealed. 1987

56-2-11. Modification or revocation of commission's orders requiring fencing.

Such commission shall also have the jurisdiction and authority to modify or revoke any such order when upon its determination the necessity for any such fence shall cease to exist. 1953

56-2-12. Liability for railroad's noncompliance with commission's fencing orders.

The failure of any railroad company or corporation to comply with any order of the commission authorized by this act shall not subject such noncomplying railroad company or corporation, or any of its officers, agents or employees, to any of the penalties prescribed in Sections 54-7-25 and 54-7-26, Utah Code Annotated 1953, but shall subject such company or corporation to the liability prescribed by Section 56-1-13, Utah Code Annotated 1953. 1953

CHAPTER 3

OFFENSIVE SUBSTANCES ON RIGHT-OF-WAY

Section
56-3-1. Definitions.
56-3-2. Disposal of human waste from passenger train prohibited.
56-3-3. Penalty.
56-3-4. Enforcement.

56-3-1. Definitions.

As used in this chapter:

(1) "Human waste" means excrement, feces, gray water, or other waste material discharged from the human body.

(2) "Person" means an individual, trust, firm, joint stock company, corporation, partnership, association, state, state or federal agency or entity, municipality, commission, or political subdivision of a state.

(3) "Passenger train" means any train operated by a railroad company or corporation pursuant to Title 56, Chapter 1 for the primary purpose of transporting passengers for hire. 1989

56-3-2. Disposal of human waste from passenger train prohibited.

No person operating or controlling any passenger train through or within this state may knowingly place, throw, release, discharge, or deposit human waste from a passenger train upon the right-of-way over which it operates. 1989

56-3-3. Penalty.

Any person who violates any provision of this chapter is guilty of a class B misdemeanor. 1991

56-3-4. Enforcement.

The state and local health departments shall enforce this chapter. 1989

TITLE 58

OCCUPATIONS AND PROFESSIONS

CHAPTER 37

CONTROLLED SUBSTANCES

58-37-1. Short title.

This act shall be known and may be cited as the "Utah Controlled Substances Act." 1971

58-37-2. Definitions.

(1) As used in this chapter:

(a) "Administer" means the direct application of a controlled substance, whether by injection, inhalation, ingestion, or any other means, to the body of a patient or research subject by:

(i) a practitioner or, in his presence, by his authorized agent; or

(ii) the patient or research subject at the direction and in the presence of the practitioner.

(b) "Agent" means an authorized person who acts on behalf of or at the direction of a manufacturer, distributor, or practitioner but does not include a motor carrier, public warehouseman, or employee of any of them.

(c) "Consumption" means ingesting or having any measurable amount of a controlled substance in a person's body, but this Subsection (1)(c) does not include the metabolite of a controlled substance.

(d) "Continuing criminal enterprise" means any individual, sole proprietorship, partnership, corporation, business trust, association, or other legal entity, and any union or groups of individuals associated in fact although not a legal entity, and includes illicit as well as licit entities created or maintained for the purpose of engaging in conduct which constitutes the commission of episodes of activity made unlawful by Title 58, Chapters 37, 37a, 37b, 37c, or 37d, which episodes are not isolated, but have the same or similar purposes, results, participants, victims, methods of commission, or otherwise are interrelated by distinguishing characteristics. Taken together, the episodes shall demonstrate continuing unlawful conduct and be related either to each other or to the enterprise.

(e) "Control" means to add, remove, or change the placement of a drug, substance, or immediate precursor under Section 58-37-3.

(f) (i) "Controlled substance" means a drug or substance included in Schedules I, II, III, IV, or V of Section 58-37-4, and also includes a drug or substance included in Schedules I, II, III, IV, or V of the federal Controlled Substances Act, Title II, P.L. 91-513, or any controlled substance analog.

(ii) "Controlled substance" does not include:

(A) distilled spirits, wine, or malt beverages, as those terms are defined or used in Title 32A, regarding tobacco or food;

(B) any drug intended for lawful use in the diagnosis, cure, mitigation, treatment, or prevention of disease in man or other animals, which contains ephedrine, pseudoephedrine, norpseudoephedrine, or phenylpropanolamine if the drug is lawfully purchased, sold, transferred, or furnished as an over-the-counter medication without prescription; or

(C) dietary supplements, vitamins, minerals, herbs, or other similar substances including concentrates or extracts, which are not otherwise regulated by law, which may contain naturally occurring amounts of chemical or substances listed in this chapter, or in rules adopted pursuant to Title 63, Chapter 46a, Utah Administrative Rulemaking Act.

(g) (i) "Controlled substance analog" means a substance the chemical structure of which is substantially similar to the chemical structure of a controlled substance listed in Schedules I and II of Section 58-37-4, or in Schedules I and II of the federal Controlled Substances Act, Title II, P.L. 91-513:

(A) which has a stimulant, depressant, or hallucinogenic effect on the central nervous system substantially similar to the stimulant, depressant, or hallucinogenic effect on the central nervous system of controlled substances in the schedules set forth in Subsection (1)(f); or

(B) which, with respect to a particular individual, is represented or intended to have a stimulant, depressant, or hallucinogenic effect on the central nervous system substantially similar to the stimulant, depressant, or hallucinogenic effect on the central nervous system of controlled substances in the schedules set forth in this Subsection (1).

(ii) "Controlled substance analog" does not include:

(A) a controlled substance currently scheduled in Schedules I through V of Section 58-37-4;

(B) a substance for which there is an approved new drug application;

(C) a substance with respect to which an exemption is in effect for investigational use by a particular person under Section 505 of the Food, Drug, and Cosmetic Act, 21 U.S.C. 366, to the extent the conduct with respect to the substance is permitted by the exemption;

(D) any substance to the extent not intended for human consumption before an exemption takes effect with respect to the substance;

(E) any drug intended for lawful use in the diagnosis, cure, mitigation, treatment, or prevention of disease in man or other animals, which contains ephedrine, pseudoephedrine, norpseudoephedrine, or phenylpropanolamine if the drug is lawfully purchased, sold, transferred, or furnished as an over-the-counter medication without prescription; or

(F) dietary supplements, vitamins, minerals, herbs, or other similar substances including concentrates or extracts, which are not otherwise regulated by law, which may contain naturally occurring amounts of chemical or substances listed in this chapter, or in rules adopted pursuant to Title 63, Chapter 46a, Utah Administrative Rulemaking Act.

(h) "Conviction" means a determination of guilt by verdict, whether jury or bench, or plea, whether guilty or no contest, for any offense proscribed by Title 58, Chapters 37, 37a, 37b, 37c, or 37d, or for any offense under the laws of the United States and any other state which, if committed in this state, would be an offense under Title 58, Chapters 37, 37a, 37b, 37c, or 37d.

(i) "Counterfeit substance" means:

(i) any substance or container or labeling of any substance that without authorization bears the trademark, trade name, or other identifying mark, imprint, number, device, or any likeness of them, of a manufacturer, distributor, or dispenser other than the person or persons who in fact manufactured, distributed, or dispensed the substance which falsely purports to be a controlled substance distributed by, any other manufacturer, distributor, or dispenser; or

(ii) any substance that is represented to be a controlled substance.

(j) "Deliver" or "delivery" means the actual, constructive, or attempted transfer of a controlled substance or a listed chemical, whether or not an agency relationship exists.

(k) "Department" means the Department of Commerce.

(l) "Depressant or stimulant substance" means:

(i) a drug which contains any quantity of barbituric acid or any of the salts of barbituric acid;

(ii) a drug which contains any quantity of:

(A) amphetamine or any of its optical isomers;

(B) any salt of amphetamine or any salt of an optical isomer of amphetamine; or

(C) any substance which the Secretary of Health and Human Services or the Attorney General of the United States after investigation has found and by regulation designated habit-forming because of its stimulant effect on the central nervous system;

(iii) lysergic acid diethylamide; or

(iv) any drug which contains any quantity of a substance which the Secretary of Health and Human Services or the Attorney General of the United States after investigation has found to have, and by regulation designated as having, a potential for abuse because of its depressant or stimulant effect on the central nervous system or its hallucinogenic effect.

(m) "Dispense" means the delivery of a controlled substance by a pharmacist to an ultimate user pursuant to the lawful order or prescription of a practitioner, and includes distributing to, leaving with, giving away, or disposing of that substance as well as the packaging, labeling, or compounding necessary to prepare the substance for delivery.

(n) "Dispenser" means a pharmacist who dispenses a controlled substance.

(o) "Distribute" means to deliver other than by administering or dispensing a controlled substance or a listed chemical.

(p) "Distributor" means a person who distributes controlled substances.

(q) "Division" means the Division of Occupational and Professional Licensing created in Section 58-1-103.

(r) "Drug" means:

(i) articles recognized in the official United States Pharmacopoeia, Official Homeopathic Pharmacopoeia of the United States, or Official National Formulary, or any supplement to any of them;

(ii) articles intended for use in the diagnosis, cure, mitigation, treatment, or prevention of disease in man or other animals;

(iii) articles, other than food, intended to affect the structure or function of man or other animals; and

(iv) articles intended for use as a component of any articles specified in Subsection (1)(r)(i), (ii), or (iii); but does not include devices or their components, parts, or accessories.

(s) "Drug dependent person" means any individual who unlawfully and habitually uses any controlled substance to endanger the public morals, health, safety, or welfare, or who is so dependent upon the use of controlled substances as to have lost the power of self-control with reference to his dependency.

(t) "Food" means:

(i) any nutrient or substance of plant, mineral, or animal origin other than a drug as specified in this chapter, and normally ingested by human beings; and

(ii) foods for special dietary uses as exist by reason of a physical, physiological, pathological, or other condition including but not limited to the conditions of disease, convalescence, pregnancy, lactation, allergy, hypersensitivity to food, underweight, and overweight; uses for supplying a particular dietary need which exist by reason of age including but not limited to the ages of infancy and childbirth, and also uses for supplementing and for fortifying the ordinary or unusual diet with any vitamin, mineral, or other dietary property for use of a food. Any particular use of a food is a special dietary use regardless of the nutritional purposes.

(u) "Immediate precursor" means a substance which the Attorney General of the United States has found to be, and by regulation designated as being, the principal compound used or produced primarily for use in the manufacture of a controlled substance, or which is an immediate chemical intermediary used or likely to be used in the manufacture of a controlled substance, the control of which is necessary to prevent, curtail, or limit the manufacture of the controlled substance.

(v) "Manufacture" means the production, preparation, propagation, compounding, or processing of a controlled substance, either directly or indirectly by extraction from substances of natural origin, or independently by means of chemical synthesis or by a combination of extraction and chemical synthesis.

(w) "Manufacturer" includes any person who packages, repackages, or labels any container of any controlled substance, except pharmacists who dispense or compound prescription orders for delivery to the ultimate consumer.

(x) "Marijuana" means all species of the genus cannabis and all parts of the genus, whether growing or not; the seeds of it; the resin extracted from any part of the plant; and every compound, manufacture, salt, derivative, mixture, or preparation of the plant, its seeds, or resin. The term does not include the mature stalks of the plant, fiber produced from the stalks, oil or cake made from the seeds of the plant, any other compound, manufacture, salt, derivative, mixture, or preparation of the mature stalks, except the resin extracted from them, fiber, oil or cake, or the sterilized seed of the plant which is incapable of germination. Any synthetic equivalents of the substances contained in the plant cannabis sativa or any other species of the genus cannabis which are chemically indistinguishable and pharmacologically active are also included.

(y) "Money" means officially issued coin and currency of the United States or any foreign country.

(z) "Narcotic drug" means any of the following, whether produced directly or indirectly by extraction from substances of vegetable origin, or independently by means of chemical synthesis, or by a combination of extraction and chemical synthesis:

(i) opium, coca leaves, and opiates;

(ii) a compound, manufacture, salt, derivative, or preparation of opium, coca leaves, or opiates;

(iii) opium poppy and poppy straw; or

(iv) a substance, and any compound, manufacture, salt, derivative, or preparation of the substance, which is chemically identical with any of the substances referred to in Subsection (1)(z)(i), (ii), or (iii), except narcotic drug does not include decocainized coca leaves or extracts of coca leaves which do not contain cocaine or ecgonine.

(aa) "Negotiable instrument" means documents, containing an unconditional promise to pay a sum of money, which are legally transferable to another party by endorsement or delivery.

(bb) "Opiate" means any drug or other substance having an addiction-forming or addiction-sustaining liability similar to morphine or being capable of conversion into a drug having addiction-forming or addiction-sustaining liability.

(cc) "Opium poppy" means the plant of the species papaver somniferum L., except the seeds of the plant.

(dd) "Person" means any corporation, association, partnership, trust, other institution or entity or one or more individuals.

(ee) "Poppy straw" means all parts, except the seeds, of the opium poppy, after mowing.

(ff) "Possession" or "use" means the joint or individual ownership, control, occupancy, holding, retaining, belonging, maintaining, or the application, inhalation, swallowing, injection, or consumption, as distinguished from distribution, of controlled substances and includes individual, joint, or group possession or use of controlled substances. For a person to be a possessor or user of a controlled substance, it is not required that he be shown to have individually possessed, used, or controlled the substance, but it is sufficient if it is shown that the person jointly participated with one or more persons in the use, possession, or control of any substances with knowledge that the activity was occurring, or the controlled substance is found in a place or under circumstances indicating that the person had the ability and the intent to exercise dominion and control over it.

(gg) "Practitioner" means a physician, dentist, veterinarian, pharmacist, scientific investigator, pharmacy, hospital, or other person licensed, registered, or otherwise permitted to distribute, dispense, conduct research with respect to, administer, or use in teaching or chemical analysis a controlled substance in the course of professional practice or research in this state.

(hh) "Prescribe" means to issue a prescription orally or in writing.

(ii) "Prescription" means an order issued by a licensed practitioner, in the course of that practitioner's professional practice, for a controlled substance, other drug, or device which it dispenses or administers for use by a patient or an animal. The order may be issued by word of mouth, written document, telephone, facsimile transmission, computer, or other electronic means of communication as defined by rule.

(jj) "Production" means the manufacture, planting, cultivation, growing, or harvesting of a controlled substance.

(kk) "Securities" means any stocks, bonds, notes, or other evidences of debt or of property.

(ll) "State" means the state of Utah.

(mm) "Ultimate user" means any person who lawfully possesses a controlled substance for his own use, for the use of a member of his household, or for administration to an animal owned by him or a member of his household.

(2) If a term used in this chapter is not defined, the definition and terms of Title 76, Utah Criminal Code, shall apply.   2005

58-37-2.5.   Restricted applicability.

This chapter does not restrict the sale and use of herbs, herbal products, or food supplements that are not scheduled in this chapter as controlled substances.   1990

58-37-3.   Substances considered controlled.

(1) All substances listed in Section 58-37-4 are considered controlled.

(2) All substances listed in the federal Controlled Substances Act, Title II, P.L. 91-513, are considered controlled.   1997

58-37-4.   Schedules of controlled substances — Schedules I through V — Findings required — Specific substances included in schedules.

(1) There are established five schedules of controlled substances known as Schedules I, II, III, IV, and V which shall consist of substances listed in this section.

(2) Schedules I, II, III, IV, and V consist of the following drugs or other substances by the official name, common or usual name, chemical name, or brand name designated:

(a) Schedule I:

(i) Unless specifically excepted or unless listed in another schedule, any of the following opiates, including their isomers, esters, ethers, salts, and salts of isomers, esters, and ethers, when the existence of the isomers, esters, ethers, and salts is possible within the specific chemical designation:

(A) Acetyl-alpha-methylfentanyl (N-[1-(1-methyl-2-phenethyl)-4-piperidinyl]-N-phenylacetamide);

(B) Acetylmethadol;

(C) Allylprodine;

(D) Alphacetylmethadol, except levo-alphacetylmethadol also known as levo-alpha-acetylmethadol, levomethadyl acetate, or LAAM;

(E) Alphameprodine;

(F) Alphamethadol;

(G) Alpha-methylfentanyl (N-[1-(alpha-methyl-beta-phenyl) ethyl-4-piperidyl] propionanilide; 1-(1-methyl-2-phenylethyl)-4-(N-propanilido) piperidine);

(H) Alpha-methylthiofentanyl (N-[1-methyl-2-(2-thienyl)ethyl-4-piperidinyl]-N-phenylpropanamide);

(I) Benzethidine;

(J) Betacetylmethadol;

(K) Beta-hydroxyfentanyl (N-[1-(2-hydroxy-2-phenethyl)-4- piperidinyl]-N-phenylpropanamide);

(L) Beta-hydroxy-3-methylfentanyl, other name: N-[1-(2-hydroxy-2-phenethyl)-3-methyl-4-piperidinyl]-N-phenyl-propanamide;

(M) Betameprodine;

(N) Betamethadol;

(O) Betaprodine;

(P) Clonitazene;

(Q) Dextromoramide;

(R) Diampromide;

(S) Diethylthiambutene;

(T) Difenoxin;

(U) Dimenoxadol;

(V) Dimepheptanol;

(W) Dimethylthiambutene;

(X) Dioxaphetyl butyrate;

(Y) Dipipanone;

(Z) Ethylmethylthiambutene;

(AA) Etonitazene;

(BB) Etoxeridine;

(CC) Furethidine;

(DD) Hydroxypethidine;

(EE) Ketobemidone;

(FF) Levomoramide;

(GG) Levophenacylmorphan;

(HH) Morpheridine;

(II) MPPP (1-methyl-4-phenyl-4-propionoxypiperidine);

(JJ) Noracymethadol;

(KK) Norlevorphanol;

(LL) Normethadone;

(MM) Norpipanone;

(NN) Para-fluorofentanyl (N-(4-fluorophenyl)-N-[1-(2-phenethyl)-4-piperidinyl] propanamide;

(OO) PEPAP (1-(-2-phenethyl)-4-phenyl-4-acetoxypiperidine);

(PP) Phenadoxone;

(QQ) Phenampromide;

(RR) Phenomorphan;

(SS) Phenoperidine;

(TT) Piritramide;

(UU) Proheptazine;

(VV) Properidine;

(WW) Propiram;

(XX) Racemoramide;

(YY) Thiofentanyl (N-phenyl-N-[1-(2-thienyl)ethyl-4-piperidinyl]-propanamide;

(ZZ) Tilidine;

(AAA) Trimeperidine;

(BBB) 3-methylfentanyl, including the optical and geometric isomers (N-[3-methyl-1-(2-phenylethyl)-4-piperidyl]-N-phenylpropanamide); and

(CCC) 3-methylthiofentanyl (N-[(3-methyl-1-(2-thienyl)ethyl-4-piperidinyl]-N-phenylpropana mide).

(ii) Unless specifically excepted or unless listed in another schedule, any of the following opium derivatives, their salts, isomers, and salts of isomers when the existence of the salts, isomers, and salts of isomers is possible within the specific chemical designation:

(A) Acetorphine;

(B) Acetyldihydrocodeine;

(C) Benzylmorphine;

(D) Codeine methylbromide;

(E) Codeine-N-Oxide;

(F) Cyprenorphine;

(G) Desomorphine;

(H) Dihydromorphine;

(I) Drotebanol;

(J) Etorphine (except hydrochloride salt);

(K) Heroin;

(L) Hydromorphinol;

(M) Methyldesorphine;

(N) Methylhydromorphine;

(O) Morphine methylbromide;

(P) Morphine methylsulfonate;

(Q) Morphine-N-Oxide;

(R) Myrophine;

(S) Nicocodeine;

(T) Nicomorphine;

(U) Normorphine;

(V) Pholcodine; and

(W) Thebacon.

(iii) Unless specifically excepted or unless listed in another schedule, any material, compound, mixture, or preparation which contains any quantity of the following hallucinogenic substances, or which contains any of their salts, isomers, and salts of isomers when the existence of the salts, isomers, and salts of isomers is possible within the specific chemical designation; as used in this Subsection (2)(iii) only, "isomer" includes the optical, position, and geometric isomers:

(A) Alpha-ethyltryptamine, some trade or other names: etryptamine; Monase; α-ethyl-1H-indole-3-ethan-amine; 3-(2-aminobutyl) indole; α-ET; and AET;

(B) 4-bromo-2,5-dimethoxy-amphet-amine, some trade or other names: 4-bromo-2,5-dimethoxy-α-methylphenethyla-mine; 4-bromo-2,5-DMA;

(C) 4-bromo-2,5-dimethoxypenethylamine, some trade or other names: 2-(4-bromo-2,5-dimeth-oxyphenyl)-1-aminoethane; alpha-des-methyl DOB; 2C-B, Nexus;

(D) 2,5-dimethoxyamphetamine, some trade or other names: 2,5-dime-thoxy-α-methylphenethylamine; 2,5-DMA;

(E) 2,5-dimethoxy-4-ethylamphet-amine, some trade or other names: DOET;

(F) 4-methoxyamphetamine, some trade or other names: 4-methoxy-α-methylphenethylamine; paramethoxy-amphetamine, PMA;

(G) 5-methoxy-3,4-methylenedioxyamphetamine;

(H) 4-methyl-2,5-dimethoxy-amphet-amine, some trade and other names: 4-methyl-2,5-dimethoxy-α-methylphene-thylamine; "DOM"; and "STP";

(I) 3,4-methylenedioxy amphetamine;

(J) 3,4-methylenedioxymethamphet-amine (MDMA);

(K) 3,4-methylenedioxy-N-ethylamphetamine, also known as N-ethyl-alpha-methyl-3,4(methylene-dioxy)phenethylamine, N-ethyl MDA, MDE, MDEA;

(L) N-hydroxy-3,4-methylene-dioxyamphetamine, also known as N-hydroxy-alpha-methyl-3,4(methylenedi-oxy)phenethylamine, and N-hydroxy MDA;

(M) 3,4,5-trimethoxy amphetamine;

(N) Bufotenine, some trade and other names: 3-(β-Dimethylaminoethyl)-5-hy-droxyindole; 3-(2-dimethylaminoethyl)-5-indolol; N, N-dimethylserotonin; 5-hy-droxy-N,N-dimethyltryptamine; mappine;

(O) Diethyltryptamine, some trade and other names: N,N-Diethyltrypta-mine; DET;

(P) Dimethyltryptamine, some trade or other names: DMT;

(Q) Ibogaine, some trade and other names: 7-Ethyl-6,6β,7,8,9,10,12,13-octa-hydro-2-methoxy-6,9-methano-5 H-pyrido [1′, 2′:1,2] azepino [5,4-b] indole; Tabernanthe iboga;

(R) Lysergic acid diethylamide;

(S) Marijuana;

(T) Mescaline;

(U) Parahexyl, some trade or other names: 3-Hexyl-1-hydroxy-7,8,9,10-tet-rahydro-6,6,9-trimethyl-6H-dibenzo[b,d]pyran; Synhexyl;

(V) Peyote, meaning all parts of the plant presently classified botanically as Lophophora williamsii Lemaire, whether growing or not, the seeds thereof, any extract from any part of such plant, and every compound, manufacture, salts, de-rivative, mixture, or preparation of such plant, its seeds or extracts (Interprets 21 USC 812(c), Schedule I(c)(12));

(W) N-ethyl-3-piperidyl benzilate;

(X) N-methyl-3-piperidyl benzilate;

(Y) Psilocybin;

(Z) Psilocyn;

(AA) Tetrahydrocannabinols, syn-thetic equivalents of the substances con-tained in the plant, or in the resinous extractives of Cannabis, sp. and/or syn-thetic substances, derivatives, and their isomers with similar chemical structure and pharmacological activity such as the following: Δ1 cis or trans tetrahydrocan-nabinol, and their optical isomers Δ6 cis or trans tetrahydrocannabinol, and their optical isomers Δ3,4 cis or trans tetrahy-drocannabinol, and its optical isomers, and since nomenclature of these substances is not internationally standardized, compounds of these structures, regardless of numerical designation of atomic positions covered;

(BB) Ethylamine analog of phencyclidine, some trade or other names: N-ethyl-1-phenylcyclohexylamine, (1-phenylcyclohexyl)ethylamine, N-(1-phenylcyclohexyl)ethylamine, cyclohexamine, PCE;

(CC) Pyrrolidine analog of phencyclidine, some trade or other names: 1-(1-phenylcyclohexyl)-pyrrolidine, PCPy, PHP;

(DD) Thiophene analog of phencyclidine, some trade or other names: 1-[1-(2-thienyl)-cyclohexyl]-piperidine, 2-thienylanalog of phencyclidine, TPCP, TCP; and

(EE) 1-[1-(2-thienyl)cyclohexyl]pyrrolidine, some other names: TCPy.

(iv) Unless specifically excepted or unless listed in another schedule, any material compound, mixture, or preparation which contains any quantity of the following substances having a depressant effect on the central nervous system, including its salts, isomers, and salts of isomers when the existence of the salts, isomers, and salts of isomers is possible within the specific chemical designation:

(A) Mecloqualone; and

(B) Methaqualone.

(v) Any material, compound, mixture, or preparation containing any quantity of the following substances having a stimulant effect on the central nervous system, including their salts, isomers, and salts of isomers:

(A) Aminorex, some other names: aminoxaphen; 2-amino-5-phenyl-2-oxazoline; or 4,5-dihydro-5-phenyl-2-oxazolamine;

(B) Cathinone, some trade or other names: 2-amino-1-phenyl-1-propanone, alpha-aminopropiophenone, 2-aminopropiophenone, and norephedrone;

(C) Fenethylline;

(D) Methcathinone, some other names: 2-(methylamino)-propiophenone; alpha-(methylamino)propiophenone; 2-(methylamino)-1-phenylpropan-1-one; alpha-N-methylaminopropiophenone; monomethylpropion; ephedrone; N-methylcathinone; methylcathinone; AL-464; AL-422; AL-463 and UR1432, its salts, optical isomers, and salts of optical isomers;

(E) (±)cis-4-methylaminorex ((±)cis-4,5-dihydro-4-methyl-5-phenyl-2-oxazolamine);

(F) N-ethylamphetamine; and

(G) N,N-dimethylamphetamine, also known as N,N-alpha-trimethyl-benzene-ethanamine; N,N-alpha-trimethyl-phenethylamine.

(vi) Any material, compound, mixture, or preparation which contains any quantity of the following substances, including their optical isomers, salts, and salts of isomers, subject to temporary emergency scheduling:

(A) N-[1-benzyl-4-piperidyl]-N-phenylpropanamide (benzylfentanyl); and

(B) N-[1-(2-thienyl)methyl-4-piperidyl]-N-phenylpropanamide (thenylfentanyl).

(vii) Unless specifically excepted or unless listed in another schedule, any material, compound, mixture, or preparation which contains any quantity of gamma hydroxy butyrate (gamma hydrobutyric acid), including its salts, isomers, and salts of isomers.

(b) Schedule II:

(i) Unless specifically excepted or unless listed in another schedule, any of the following substances whether produced directly or indirectly by extraction from substances of vegetable origin, or independently by means of chemical synthesis, or by a combination of extraction and chemical synthesis:

(A) Opium and opiate, and any salt, compound, derivative, or preparation of opium or opiate, excluding apomorphine, dextrorphan, nalbuphine, nalmefene, naloxone, and naltrexone, and their respective salts, but including:

(I) Raw opium;

(II) Opium extracts;

(III) Opium fluid;

(IV) Powdered opium;

(V) Granulated opium;

(VI) Tincture of opium;

(VII) Codeine;

(VIII) Ethylmorphine;

(IX) Etorphine hydrochloride;

(X) Hydrocodone;

(XI) Hydromorphone;

(XII) Metopon;

(XIII) Morphine;

(XIV) Oxycodone;

(XV) Oxymorphone; and

(XVI) Thebaine;

(B) Any salt, compound, derivative, or preparation which is chemically equivalent or identical with any of the substances referred to in Subsection (2)(b)(i)(A), except that these substances may not include the isoquinoline alkaloids of opium;

(C) Opium poppy and poppy straw;

(D) Coca leaves and any salt, compound, derivative, or preparation of coca leaves, and any salt, compound, derivative, or preparation which is chemically equivalent or identical with any of these substances, and includes cocaine and ecgonine, their salts, isomers, derivatives, and salts of isomers and derivatives, whether derived from the coca plant or synthetically produced, except the substances may not include decocainized coca leaves or extraction of coca leaves, which extractions do not contain cocaine or ecgonine; and

(E) Concentrate of poppy straw, which means the crude extract of poppy straw in either liquid, solid, or powder form which contains the phenanthrene alkaloids of the opium poppy.

(ii) Unless specifically excepted or unless listed in another schedule, any of the following opiates, including their isomers, esters, ethers, salts, and salts of isomers, esters, and ethers, when the existence of the isomers, esters, ethers, and salts is possible within the specific chemical designation, except dextrorphan and levopropoxyphene:

(A) Alfentanil;

(B) Alphaprodine;

(C) Anileridine;

(D) Bezitramide;

(E) Bulk dextropropoxyphene (non-dosage forms);

(F) Carfentanil;

(G) Dihydrocodeine;

(H) Diphenoxylate;

(I) Fentanyl;

(J) Isomethadone;

(K) Levo-alphacetylmethadol, some other names: levo-alpha-acetylmethadol, levomethadyl acetate, or LAAM;

(L) Levomethorphan;

(M) Levorphanol;

(N) Metazocine;

(O) Methadone;

(P) Methadone-Intermediate, 4-cyano-2-dimethylamino-4, 4-diphenyl butane;

(Q) Moramide-Intermediate, 2-methyl-3-morpholino-1, 1-diphenylpropane-carboxylic acid;

(R) Pethidine (meperidine);

(S) Pethidine-Intermediate-A, 4-cyano-1-methyl-4-phenylpiperidine;

(T) Pethidine-Intermediate-B, ethyl-4-phenylpiperidine-4-carboxylate;

(U) Pethidine-Intermediate-C, 1-methyl-4-phenylpiperidine-4-carboxylic acid;

(V) Phenazocine;

(W) Piminodine;

(X) Racemethorphan;

(Y) Racemorphan;

(Z) Remifentanil; and

(AA) Sufentanil.

(iii) Unless specifically excepted or unless listed in another schedule, any material, compound, mixture, or preparation which contains any quantity of the following substances having a stimulant effect on the central nervous system:

(A) Amphetamine, its salts, optical isomers, and salts of its optical isomers;

(B) Methamphetamine, its salts, isomers, and salts of its isomers;

(C) Phenmetrazine and its salts; and

(D) Methylphenidate.

(iv) Unless specifically excepted or unless listed in another schedule, any material, compound, mixture, or preparation which contains any quantity of the following substances having a depressant effect on the central nervous system, including its salts, isomers, and salts of isomers when the existence of the salts, isomers, and salts of isomers is possible within the specific chemical designation:

(A) Amobarbital;

(B) Glutethimide;

(C) Pentobarbital;

(D) Phencyclidine;

(E) Phencyclidine immediate precursors: 1-phenylcyclohexylamine and 1-piperidinocyclohexanecarbonitrile (PCC); and

(F) Secobarbital.

(v) Unless specifically excepted or unless listed in another schedule, any material, compound, mixture, or preparation which contains any quantity of Phenylacetone.

Some of these substances may be known by trade or other names: phenyl-2-propanone, P2P; benzyl methyl ketone, methyl benzyl ketone.

(vi) Nabilone, another name for nabilone: ($\pm$)-trans-3-(1,1-dimethylheptyl)-6,6a,7,8,10,10a-hexahydro-1-hydroxy-6,6-dimethyl-9H-dibenzo[b,d]pyran-9-one.

(c) Schedule III:

(i) Unless specifically excepted or unless listed in another schedule, any material, compound, mixture, or preparation which contains any quantity of the following substances having a stimulant effect on the central nervous system, including its salts, isomers whether optical, position, or geometric, and salts of the isomers when the existence of the salts, isomers, and salts of isomers is possible within the specific chemical designation:

(A) Those compounds, mixtures, or preparations in dosage unit form containing any stimulant substances listed in Schedule II, which compounds, mixtures, or preparations were listed on August 25, 1971, as excepted compounds under Section 1308.32 of Title 21 of the Code of Federal Regulations, and any other drug of the quantitive composition shown in that list for those drugs or which is the same except that it contains a lesser quantity of controlled substances;

(B) Benzphetamine;

(C) Chlorphentermine;

(D) Clortermine; and

(E) Phendimetrazine.

(ii) Unless specifically excepted or unless listed in another schedule, any material, compound, mixture, or preparation which contains any quantity of the following substances having a depressant effect on the central nervous system:

(A) Any compound, mixture, or preparation containing amobarbital, secobarbital, pentobarbital, or any salt of any of them, and one or more other active medicinal ingredients which are not listed in any schedule;

(B) Any suppository dosage form containing amobarbital, secobarbital, or pentobarbital, or any salt of any of these drugs which is approved by the Food and Drug Administration for marketing only as a suppository;

(C) Any substance which contains any quantity of a derivative of barbituric acid or any salt of any of them;

(D) Chlorhexadol;

(E) Buprenorphine;

(F) Any drug product containing gamma hydroxybutyric acid, including its salts, isomers, and salts of isomers, for which an application is approved under the federal Food, Drug, and Cosmetic Act, Section 505;

(G) Ketamine, its salts, isomers, and salts of isomers, some other names for ketamine: ± -2-(2-chlorophenyl)-2-(methylamino)-cyclohexanone.

(H) Lysergic acid;

(I) Lysergic acid amide;

(J) Methyprylon;

(K) Sulfondiethylmethane;

(L) Sulfonethylmethane;

(M) Sulfonmethane; and

(N) Tiletamine and zolazepam or any of their salts, some trade or other names for a tiletamine-zolazepam combination product: Telazol, some trade or other names for tiletamine: 2-(ethylamino)-2-(2-thienyl)-cyclohexanone, some trade or other names for zolazepam: 4-(2-fluorophenyl)-6,8-dihydro-1,3,8-trimethylpyrazolo-[3,4-e] [1,4]-diazepin-7(1H)-one, flupyrazapon.

(iii) Dronabinol (synthetic) in sesame oil and encapsulated in a soft gelatin capsule in a U.S. Food and Drug Administration approved drug product, some other names for dronabinol: (6aR-trans)-6a,7,8,10a-tetrahydro-6,6,9-trimethyl-3-pentyl-6H-dibenzo[b, d]pyran-1-ol, or (-)-delta-9-(trans)-tetrahydrocannabinol.

(iv) Nalorphine.

(v) Unless specifically excepted or unless listed in another schedule, any material, compound, mixture, or preparation containing limited quantities of any of the following narcotic drugs, or their salts calculated as the free anhydrous base or alkaloid:

(A) Not more than 1.8 grams of codeine per 100 milliliters or not more than 90 milligrams per dosage unit, with an equal or greater quantity of an isoquinoline alkaloid of opium;

(B) Not more than 1.8 grams of codeine per 100 milliliters or not more than 90 milligrams per dosage unit, with one or more active non-narcotic ingredients in recognized therapeutic amounts;

(C) Not more than 300 milligrams of dihydrocodeinone per 100 milliliters or not more than 15 milligrams per dosage unit, with a fourfold or greater quantity of an isoquinoline alkaloid of opium;

(D) Not more than 300 milligrams of dihydrocodeinone per 100 milliliters or not more than 15 milligrams per dosage unit, with one or more active, non-narcotic ingredients in recognized therapeutic amounts;

(E) Not more than 1.8 grams of dihydrocodeine per 100 milliliters or not more than 90 milligrams per dosage unit, with one or more active non-narcotic ingredients in recognized therapeutic amounts;

(F) Not more than 300 milligrams of ethylmorphine per 100 milliliters or not more than 15 milligrams per dosage unit, with one or more active, non-narcotic ingredients in recognized therapeutic amounts;

(G) Not more than 500 milligrams of opium per 100 milliliters or per 100 grams, or not more than 25 milligrams per dosage unit, with one or more active, non-narcotic ingredients in recognized therapeutic amounts; and

(H) Not more than 50 milligrams of morphine per 100 milliliters or per 100 grams with one or more active, non-narcotic ingredients in recognized therapeutic amounts.

(vi) Unless specifically excepted or unless listed in another schedule, anabolic steroids including any of the following or any isomer, ester, salt, or derivative of the following that promotes muscle growth:

(A) Boldenone;

(B) Chlorotestosterone (4-chlortestosterone);

(C) Clostebol;

(D) Dehydrochlormethyltestosterone;

(E) Dihidrotestosterone (4-dihydrotestosterone);

(F) Drostanolone;

(G) Ethylestrenol;

(H) Fluoxymesterone;

(I) Formebulone (formebolone);

(J) Mesterolone;

(K) Methandienone;

(L) Methandranone;

(M) Methandriol;

(N) Methandrostenolone;

(O) Methenolone;

(P) Methyltestosterone;

(Q) Mibolerone;

(R) Nandrolone;

(S) Norethandrolone;

(T) Oxandrolone;

(U) Oxymesterone;

(V) Oxymetholone;

(W) Stanolone;

(X) Stanozolol;

(Y) Testolactone;

(Z) Testosterone; and

(AA) Trenbolone.

Anabolic steroids expressly intended for administration through implants to cattle or other nonhuman species, and approved by the Secretary of Health and Human Services for use, may not be classified as a controlled substance.

(d) Schedule IV:

(i) Unless specifically excepted or unless listed in another schedule, any material, compound, mixture, or preparation containing not more than 1 milligram of difenoxin and not less than 25 micrograms of atropine sulfate per dosage unit, or any salts of any of them.

(ii) Unless specifically excepted or unless listed in another schedule, any material, compound, mixture, or preparation which contains any quantity of the following substances, including its salts, isomers, and salts of isomers when the existence of the salts, isomers, and salts of isomers is possible within the specific chemical designation:

(A) Alprazolam;

(B) Barbital;

(C) Bromazepam;

(D) Butorphanol;

(E) Camazepam;

(F) Chloral betaine;

(G) Chloral hydrate;

(H) Chlordiazepoxide;

(I) Clobazam;

(J) Clonazepam;

(K) Clorazepate;

(L) Clotiazepam;

(M) Cloxazolam;

(N) Delorazepam;

(O) Diazepam;

(P) Dichloralphenazone;

(Q) Estazolam;

(R) Ethchlorvynol;

(S) Ethinamate;

(T) Ethyl loflazepate;

(U) Fludiazepam;

(V) Flunitrazepam;

(W) Flurazepam;

(X) Halazepam;

(Y) Haloxazolam;

(Z) Ketazolam;

(AA) Loprazolam;

(BB) Lorazepam;

(CC) Lormetazepam;

(DD) Mebutamate;

(EE) Medazepam;

(FF) Meprobamate;

(GG) Methohexital;

(HH) Methylphenobarbital (mephobarbital);

(II) Midazolam;

(JJ) Nimetazepam;

(KK) Nitrazepam;

(LL) Nordiazepam;

(MM) Oxazepam;

(NN) Oxazolam;

(OO) Paraldehyde;

(PP) Pentazocine;

(QQ) Petrichloral;

(RR) Phenobarbital;

(SS) Pinazepam;

(TT) Prazepam;

(UU) Quazepam;

(VV) Temazepam;

(WW) Tetrazepam;

(XX) Triazolam;

(YY) Zaleplon; and

(ZZ) Zolpidem.

(iii) Any material, compound, mixture, or preparation of fenfluramine which contains any quantity of the following substances, including its salts, isomers whether optical, position, or geometric, and salts of the isomers when the existence of the salts, isomers, and salts of isomers is possible.

(iv) Unless specifically excepted or unless listed in another schedule, any material, compound, mixture, or preparation which contains any quantity of the following substances having a stimulant effect on the central nervous system, including its salts, isomers whether optical, position, or geometric isomers, and salts of the isomers when the existence of the salts, isomers, and salts of isomers is possible within the specific chemical designation:

(A) Cathine ((+)-norpseudoephedrine);

(B) Diethylpropion;

(C) Fencamfamine;

(D) Fenproprex;

(E) Mazindol;

(F) Mefenorex;

(G) Modafinil;

(H) Pemoline, including organometallic complexes and chelates thereof;

(I) Phentermine;

(J) Pipradrol;

(K) Sibutramine; and

(L) SPA ((-)-1-dimethylamino-1,2-diphenylethane).

(v) Unless specifically excepted or unless listed in another schedule, any material, compound, mixture, or preparation which contains any quantity of dextropropoxyphene (alpha-(+)-4-dimethylamino-1, 2-diphenyl-3-methyl-2-propionoxybutane), including its salts.

(e) Schedule V: Any compound, mixture, or preparation containing any of the following limited quantities of narcotic drugs, or their salts calculated as the free anhydrous base or alkaloid, which includes one or more non-narcotic active medicinal ingredients in sufficient proportion to confer upon the compound, mixture, or preparation valuable medicinal qualities other than those possessed by the narcotic drug alone:

(i) not more than 200 milligrams of codeine per 100 milliliters or per 100 grams;

(ii) not more than 100 milligrams of dihydrocodeine per 100 milliliters or per 100 grams;

(iii) not more than 100 milligrams of ethylmorphine per 100 milliliters or per 100 grams;

(iv) not more than 2.5 milligrams of diphenoxylate and not less than 25 micrograms of atropine sulfate per dosage unit;

(v) not more than 100 milligrams of opium per 100 milliliters or per 100 grams;

(vi) not more than 0.5 milligram of difenoxin and not less than 25 micrograms of atropine sulfate per dosage unit; and

(vii) unless specifically exempted or excluded or unless listed in another schedule, any material, compound, mixture, or preparation which contains Pyrovalerone having a stimulant effect on the central nervous system, including its salts, isomers, and salts of isomers.   2003

58-37-5. Repealed.   1979

58-37-5.5. Recognized controlled substance analogs.

(1) A substance listed under Subsection (2) is an analog, as defined in Subsection 58-37-2(1)(f), if the substance, in any quantity, and in any material, compound, mixture, or preparation, is present in:

(a) any product manufactured, distributed, or possessed for the purpose of human consumption; or

(b) any product, the use or administration of which results in human consumption.

(2) Substances referred to in Subsection (1) include, but are not limited to:

(a) gamma butyrolactone (GBL);

(b) butyrolactone;

(c) 1,2 butanolide;

(d) 2-oxanolone;

(e) tetrahydro-2-furanone;

(f) dihydro-2 (3H)-furanone;

(g) tetramethylene glycol;

(h) 1,4 butanediol; and

(i) gamma valerolactone.   2003

58-37-6. License to manufacture, produce, distribute, dispense, administer, or conduct research — Issuance by division — Denial, suspension, or revocation — Records required — Prescriptions.

(1) (a) The division may adopt rules relating to the licensing and control of the manufacture, distribution, production, prescription, administration, dispensing, conducting of research with, and performing of laboratory analysis upon controlled substances within this state.

(b) The division may assess reasonable fees to defray the cost of issuing original and renewal licenses under this chapter pursuant to Section 63-38-3.2.

(2) (a) (i) Every person who manufactures, produces, distributes, prescribes, dispenses, administers, conducts research with, or performs laboratory analysis upon any controlled substance in Schedules II through V within this state, or who proposes to engage in manufacturing, producing, distributing, prescribing, dispensing, administering, conducting research with, or performing laboratory analysis upon controlled substances included in Schedules II through V within this state shall obtain a license issued by the division.

(ii) The division shall issue each license under this chapter in accordance with a two-year renewal cycle established by rule. The division may by rule extend or shorten a renewal period by as much as one year to stagger the renewal cycles it administers.

(b) Persons licensed to manufacture, produce, distribute, prescribe, dispense, administer, conduct research with, or perform laboratory analysis upon controlled substances in Schedules II through V within this state may possess, manufacture, produce, distribute, prescribe, dispense, administer, conduct research with, or perform laboratory analysis upon those substances to the extent authorized by their license and in conformity with this chapter.

(c) The following persons are not required to obtain a license and may lawfully possess controlled substances under this section:

(i) an agent or employee, except a sales representative, of any registered manufacturer, distributor, or dispenser of any controlled substance, if the agent or employee is acting in the usual course of his business or employment; however, nothing in this subsection shall be interpreted to permit an agent, employee, sales representative, or detail man to maintain an inventory of controlled substances separate from the location of his employer's registered and licensed place of business;

(ii) a motor carrier or warehouseman, or an employee of a motor carrier or warehouseman, who possesses any controlled substance in the usual course of his business or employment; and

(iii) an ultimate user, or any person who possesses any controlled substance pursuant to a lawful order of a practitioner.

(d) The division may enact rules waiving the license requirement for certain manufacturers, producers, distributors, prescribers, dispensers, administrators, research practitioners, or laboratories performing analysis if consistent with the public health and safety.

(e) A separate license is required at each principal place of business or professional practice where the applicant manufactures, produces, distributes, dispenses, conducts research with, or performs laboratory analysis upon controlled substances.

(f) The division may enact rules providing for the inspection of a licensee or applicant's establishment, and may inspect the establishment according to those rules.

(3) (a) Upon proper application, the division shall license a qualified applicant to manufacture, produce, distribute, conduct research with, or perform laboratory analysis upon controlled substances included in Schedules I through V, unless it determines that issuance of a license is inconsistent with the public interest. The division shall not issue a license to any person to prescribe, dispense, or administer a Schedule I controlled substance. In determining public interest, the division shall consider whether or not the applicant has:

(i) maintained effective controls against diversion of controlled substances and any Schedule I or II substance compounded from any controlled substance into other than legitimate medical, scientific, or industrial channels;

(ii) complied with applicable state and local law;

(iii) been convicted under federal or state laws relating to the manufacture, distribution, or dispensing of substances;

(iv) past experience in the manufacture of controlled dangerous substances;

(v) established effective controls against diversion; and

(vi) complied with any other factors that the division establishes that promote the public health and safety.

(b) Licenses granted under Subsection (3)(a) do not entitle a licensee to manufacture, produce, distribute, conduct research with, or perform laboratory analysis upon controlled substances in Schedule I other than those specified in the license.

(c) (i) Practitioners shall be licensed to administer, dispense, or conduct research with substances in Schedules II through V if they are authorized to administer, dispense, or conduct research under the laws of this state.

(ii) The division need not require a separate license for practitioners engaging in research with nonnarcotic controlled substances in Schedules II through V where the licensee is already licensed under this act in another capacity.

(iii) With respect to research involving narcotic substances in Schedules II through V, or where the division by rule requires a separate license for research of nonnarcotic substances in Schedules II through V, a practitioner shall apply to the division prior to conducting research.

(iv) Licensing for purposes of bona fide research with controlled substances by a practitioner considered qualified may be denied only on a ground specified in Subsection (4), or upon evidence that the applicant will abuse or unlawfully transfer or fail to safeguard adequately his supply of substances against diversion from medical or scientific use.

(v) Practitioners registered under federal law to conduct research in Schedule I substances may conduct research in Schedule I substances within this state upon furnishing the division evidence of federal registration.

(d) Compliance by manufacturers, producers, and distributors with the provisions of federal law respecting registration, excluding fees, entitles them to be licensed under this chapter.

(e) The division shall initially license those persons who own or operate an establishment engaged in the manufacture, production, distribution, dispensation, or administration of controlled substances prior to April 3, 1980, and who are licensed by the state.

(4) (a) Any license pursuant to Subsection (2) or (3) may be denied, suspended, placed on probation, or revoked by the division upon finding that the applicant or licensee has:

(i) materially falsified any application filed or required pursuant to this chapter;

(ii) been convicted of an offense under this chapter or any law of the United States, or any state, relating to any substance defined as a controlled substance;

(iii) been convicted of a felony under any other law of the United States or any state within five years of the date of the issuance of the license;

(iv) had a federal license denied, suspended, or revoked by competent federal authority and is no longer authorized to engage in the manufacturing, distribution, or dispensing of controlled substances;

(v) had his license suspended or revoked by competent authority of another state for violation of laws or regulations comparable to those of this state relating to the manufacture, distribution, or dispensing of controlled substances;

(vi) violated any division rule that reflects adversely on the licensee's reliability and integrity with respect to controlled substances;

(vii) refused inspection of records required to be maintained under this chapter by a person authorized to inspect them; or

(viii) prescribed, dispensed, administered, or injected an anabolic steroid for the purpose of manipulating human hormonal structure so as to:

(A) increase muscle mass, strength, or weight without medical necessity and without a written prescription by any practitioner in the course of his professional practice; or

(B) improve performance in any form of human exercise, sport, or game.

(b) The division may limit revocation or suspension of a license to a particular controlled substance with respect to which grounds for revocation or suspension exist.

(c) (i) Proceedings to deny, revoke, or suspend a license shall be conducted pursuant to this section and in accordance with the procedures set forth in Title 58, Chapter 1, Division of Occupational and Professional Licensing Act, and conducted in conjunction with the appropriate representative committee designated by the director of the department.

(ii) Nothing in this Subsection (4)(c) gives the Division of Occupational and Professional Licensing exclusive authority in proceedings to deny, revoke, or suspend licenses, except where the division is designated by law to perform those functions, or, when not designated by law, is designated by the executive director of the Department of Commerce to conduct the proceedings.

(d) (i) The division may suspend any license simultaneously with the institution of proceedings under this section if it finds there is an imminent danger to the public health or safety.

(ii) Suspension shall continue in effect until the conclusion of proceedings, including judicial review, unless withdrawn by the division or dissolved by a court of competent jurisdiction.

(e) (i) If a license is suspended or revoked under this Subsection (4), all controlled substances owned or possessed by the licensee may be placed under seal in the discretion of the division.

(ii) Disposition may not be made of substances under seal until the time for taking an appeal has lapsed, or until all appeals have been concluded, unless a court, upon application, orders the sale of perishable substances and the proceeds deposited with the court.

(iii) If a revocation order becomes final, all controlled substances shall be forfeited.

(f) The division shall notify promptly the Drug Enforcement Administration of all orders suspending or revoking a license and all forfeitures of controlled substances.

(5) (a) Persons licensed under Subsection (2) or (3) shall maintain records and inventories in conformance with the record keeping and inventory requirements of federal and state law and any additional rules issued by the division.

(b) (i) Every physician, dentist, veterinarian, practitioner, or other person who is authorized to administer or professionally use a controlled substance shall keep a record of the drugs received by him and a record of all drugs administered, dispensed, or professionally used by him otherwise than by a prescription.

(ii) A person using small quantities or solutions or other preparations of those drugs for local application has complied with this Subsection (5)(b) if he keeps a record of the quantity, character, and potency of those solutions or preparations purchased or prepared by him, and of the dates when purchased or prepared.

(6) Controlled substances in Schedules I through V may be distributed only by a licensee and pursuant to an order form prepared in compliance with division rules or a lawful order under the rules and regulations of the United States.

(7) (a) A person may not write or authorize a prescription for a controlled substance unless he is:

(i) a practitioner authorized to prescribe drugs and medicine under the laws of this state or under the laws of another state having similar standards; and

(ii) licensed under this chapter or under the laws of another state having similar standards.

(b) A person other than a pharmacist licensed under the laws of this state, or his licensed intern, as required by Sections 58-17b-303 and 58-17b-304, may not dispense a controlled substance.

(c) (i) A controlled substance may not be dispensed without the written prescription of a practitioner, if the written prescription is required by the federal Controlled Substances Act.

(ii) That written prescription shall be made in accordance with Subsection (7)(a) and in conformity with Subsection (7)(d).

(iii) In emergency situations, as defined by division rule, controlled substances may be dispensed upon oral prescription of a practitioner, if reduced promptly to writing on forms designated by the division and filed by the pharmacy.

(iv) Prescriptions reduced to writing by a pharmacist shall be in conformity with Subsection (7)(d).

(d) Except for emergency situations designated by the division, a person may not issue, fill, compound, or dispense a prescription for a controlled substance unless the prescription is signed by the prescriber in ink or indelible pencil or is signed with an electronic or digital signature of the prescriber as authorized by division rule, and contains the following information:

(i) the name, address, and registry number of the prescriber;

(ii) the name, address, and age of the person to whom or for whom the prescription is issued;

(iii) the date of issuance of the prescription; and

(iv) the name, quantity, and specific directions for use by the ultimate user of the controlled substance.

(e) A prescription may not be written, issued, filled, or dispensed for a Schedule I controlled substance.

(f) Except when administered directly to an ultimate user by a licensed practitioner, controlled substances are subject to the following restrictions:

(i) (A) A prescription for a Schedule II substance may not be refilled.

(B) A Schedule II controlled substance may not be filled in a quantity to exceed a one-month's supply, as directed on the daily dosage rate of the prescriptions.

(ii) A Schedule III or IV controlled substance may be filled only within six months of issuance, and may not be refilled more than six months after the date of its original issuance or be refilled more than five times after the date of the prescription unless renewed by the practitioner.

(iii) All other controlled substances in Schedule V may be refilled as the prescriber's prescription directs, but they may not be refilled one year after the date the prescription was issued unless renewed by the practitioner.

(iv) Any prescription for a Schedule II substance may not be dispensed if it is not presented to a pharmacist for dispensing by a pharmacist or a pharmacy intern within 30 days after the date the prescription was issued, or 30 days after the dispensing date, if that date is specified separately from the date of issue.

(v) A practitioner may issue more than one prescription at the same time for the same Schedule II controlled substance, but only under the following conditions:

(A) no more than three prescriptions for the same Schedule II controlled substance may be issued at the same time;

(B) no one prescription may exceed a 30-day supply;

(C) a second or third prescription shall include the date of issuance and the date for dispensing; and

(D) unless the practitioner determines there is a valid medical reason to the contrary, the date for dispensing a second or third prescription may not be fewer than 30 days from the dispensing date of the previous prescription.

(vi) Each prescription for a controlled substance may contain only one controlled substance per prescription form and may not contain any other legend drug or prescription item.

(g) An order for a controlled substance in Schedules II through V for use by an inpatient or an outpatient of a licensed hospital is exempt from all requirements of this Subsection (7) if the order is:

(i) issued or made by a prescribing practitioner who holds an unrestricted registration with the federal Drug Enforcement Administration, and an active Utah controlled substance license in good standing issued by the division under this section, or a medical resident who is exempted from licensure under Subsection 58-1-307(1)(c);

(ii) authorized by the prescribing practitioner treating the patient and the prescribing practitioner designates the quantity ordered;

(iii) entered upon the record of the patient, the record is signed by the prescriber affirming his authorization of the order within 48 hours after filling or administering the order, and the patient's record reflects the quantity actually administered; and

(iv) filled and dispensed by a pharmacist practicing his profession within the physical structure of the hospital, or the order is taken from a supply lawfully maintained by the hospital and the amount taken from the supply is administered directly to the patient authorized to receive it.

(h) A practitioner licensed under this chapter may not prescribe, administer, or dispense a controlled substance to a minor, without first obtaining the consent required in Section 78-14-5 of a parent, guardian, or person standing in loco parentis of the minor except in cases of an emergency. For purposes of this Subsection (7)(h), "minor" has the same meaning as defined in Section 78-3a-103, and "emergency" means any physical condition requiring the administration of a controlled substance for immediate relief of pain or suffering.

(i) A practitioner licensed under this chapter may not prescribe or administer dosages of a controlled substance in excess of medically recognized quantities necessary to treat the ailment, malady, or condition of the ultimate user.

(j) A practitioner licensed under this chapter may not prescribe, administer, or dispense any controlled substance to another person knowing that the other person is using a false name, address, or other personal information for the purpose of securing the controlled substance.

(k) A person who is licensed under this chapter to manufacture, distribute, or dispense a controlled substance may not manufacture, distribute, or dispense a controlled substance to another licensee or any other authorized person not authorized by this license.

(l) A person licensed under this chapter may not omit, remove, alter, or obliterate a symbol required by this chapter or by a rule issued under this chapter.

(m) A person licensed under this chapter may not refuse or fail to make, keep, or furnish any record notification, order form, statement, invoice, or information required under this chapter.

(n) A person licensed under this chapter may not refuse entry into any premises for inspection as authorized by this chapter.

(o) A person licensed under this chapter may not furnish false or fraudulent material information in any application, report, or other document required to be kept by this chapter or willfully make any false statement in any prescription, order, report, or record required by this chapter.

(8) (a) (i) Any person licensed under this chapter who is found by the division to have violated any of the provisions of Subsections (7)(k) through (7)(o) is subject to a penalty not to exceed $5,000. The division shall determine the procedure for adjudication of any violations in accordance with Sections 58-1-106 and 58-1-108.

(ii) The division shall deposit all penalties collected under Subsection (8)(a)(i) in the General Fund as a dedicated credit to be used by the division under Subsection 58-37-7.7(1).

(b) Any person who knowingly and intentionally violates Subsections (7)(h) through (7)(j) is:

(i) upon first conviction, guilty of a class B misdemeanor;

(ii) upon second conviction, guilty of a class A misdemeanor; and

(iii) on third or subsequent conviction, guilty of a third degree felony.

(c) Any person who knowingly and intentionally violates Subsections (7)(k) through (7)(o) shall upon conviction be guilty of a third degree felony.

(9) Any information communicated to any licensed practitioner in an attempt to unlawfully procure, or to procure the administration of, a controlled substance is not considered to be a privileged communication.

2005

58-37-7. Labeling and packaging controlled substance.

(1) A person licensed pursuant to this act may not distribute a controlled substance unless it is packaged and labeled in compliance with the requirements of Section 305 of the Federal Comprehensive Drug Abuse Prevention and Control Act of 1970.

(2) No person except a pharmacist for the purpose of filling a prescription shall alter, deface, or remove any label affixed by the manufacturer.

(3) Whenever a pharmacist sells or dispenses any controlled substance on a prescription issued by a practitioner, he shall affix to the container in which the substance is sold or dispensed:

(a) a label showing the:

(i) pharmacy name and address;

(ii) serial number; and

(iii) date of initial filling;

(b) the prescription number, the name of the patient, or if the patient is an animal, the name of the owner of the animal and the species of the animal;

(c) the name of the practitioner by whom the prescription was written;

(d) any directions stated on the prescription; and

(e) any directions required by rules and regulations promulgated by the department.

(4) A person may not alter the face or remove any label so long as any of the original contents remain.

(5) (a) An individual to whom or for whose use any controlled substance has been prescribed, sold, or dispensed by a practitioner and the owner of any animal for which any controlled substance has been prescribed, sold, or dispensed by a veterinarian may lawfully possess it only in the container in which it was delivered to him by the person selling or dispensing it.

(b) It is a defense to a prosecution under this subsection that the person being prosecuted produces in court a valid prescription for the controlled substance or the original container with the label attached.

2004

58-37-7.5. Controlled substance database — Advisory committee — Pharmacy reporting requirements — Access — Penalties.

(1) As used in this section:

(a) "Committee" means the Controlled Substance Database Advisory Committee created in this section.

(b) "Database" means the controlled substance database created in this section.

(c) "Database manager" means the person responsible for operating the database, or his designee.

(d) "Division" means the Division of Occupational and Professional Licensing created in Section 58-1-103.

(e) "Health care facility" has the same definition as in Section 26-21-2.

(f) "Pharmacy or pharmaceutical facility" has the same definition as in Section 58-17b-102.

(2) (a) There is created within the division a controlled substance database.

(b) The division shall administer and direct the functioning of the database in accordance with this section. The division may under state procurement laws contract with another state agency or private entity to establish, operate, or maintain the database. The division in collaboration with the board shall determine whether to operate the database within the division or contract with another entity to operate the database, based on an analysis of costs and benefits.

(c) The purpose of the database is to contain data as described in this section regarding every prescription for a controlled substance dispensed in the state to any person other than an inpatient in a licensed health care facility.

(d) Data required by this section shall be submitted in compliance with this section to the manager of the database by the pharmacist in charge of the drug outlet where the controlled substance is dispensed.

(3) The Utah State Board of Pharmacy created in Section 58-17b-201 shall advise the division regarding:

(a) establishing, maintaining, and operating the database;

(b) access to the database and how access is obtained; and

(c) control of information contained in the database.

(4) The pharmacist in charge shall, regarding each controlled substance dispensed by a pharmacist under his supervision other than those dispensed for an inpatient at a health care facility, submit to the manager of the database the following information, by a procedure and in a format established by the division:

(a) name of the prescribing practitioner;

(b) date of the prescription;

(c) date the prescription was filled;

(d) name of the person for whom the prescription was written;

(e) positive identification of the person receiving the prescription, including the type of identification and any identifying numbers on the identification;

(f) name of the controlled substance;

(g) quantity of controlled substance prescribed;

(h) strength of controlled substance;

(i) quantity of controlled substance dispensed;

(j) dosage quantity and frequency as prescribed;

(k) name of drug outlet dispensing the controlled substance;

(l) name of pharmacist dispensing the controlled substance; and

(m) other relevant information as required by division rule.

(5) The division shall maintain the database in an electronic file or by other means established by the division to facilitate use of the database for identification of:

(a) prescribing practices and patterns of prescribing and dispensing controlled substances;

(b) practitioners prescribing controlled substances in an unprofessional or unlawful manner;

(c) individuals receiving prescriptions for controlled substances from licensed practitioners, and who subsequently obtain dispensed controlled substances from a drug outlet in quantities or with a frequency inconsistent with generally recognized standards of dosage for that controlled substance; and

(d) individuals presenting forged or otherwise false or altered prescriptions for controlled substances to a pharmacy.

(6) (a) The division shall by rule establish the electronic format in which the information required under this section shall be submitted to the administrator of the database.

(b) The division shall ensure the database system records and maintains for reference:

(i) identification of each person who requests or receives information from the database;

(ii) the information provided to each person; and

(iii) the date and time the information is requested or provided.

(7) The division shall make rules in collaboration with the committee to:

(a) effectively enforce the limitations on access to the database as described in Subsection (8); and

(b) establish standards and procedures to ensure accurate identification of individuals requesting information or receiving information without request from the database.

(8) The manager of the database shall make information in the database available only to the following persons, and in accordance with the limitations stated and division rules:

(a) personnel of the division specifically assigned to conduct investigations related to controlled substances laws under the jurisdiction of the division;

(b) authorized division personnel engaged in analysis of controlled substance prescription information as a part of the assigned duties and responsibilities of their employment;

(c) employees of the Department of Health whom the director of the Department of Health assigns to conduct scientific studies regarding the use or abuse of controlled substances, provided that the identity of the individuals and pharmacies in the database are confidential and are not disclosed in any manner to any individual who is not directly involved in the scientific studies;

(d) a licensed practitioner having authority to prescribe controlled substances, to the extent the information relates specifically to a current patient of the practitioner, to whom the practitioner is prescribing or considering prescribing any controlled substance;

(e) a licensed pharmacist having authority to dispense controlled substances to the extent the information relates specifically to a current patient to whom that pharmacist is dispensing or considering dispensing any controlled substance;

(f) federal, state, and local law enforcement authorities engaged as a specified duty of their employment in enforcing laws regulating controlled substances; and

(g) an individual who is the recipient of a controlled substance prescription entered into the database, upon providing evidence satisfactory to the database manager that the individual requesting the information is in fact the person about whom the data entry was made.

(9) Any person who knowingly and intentionally releases any information in the database in violation of the limitations under Subsection (8) is guilty of a third degree felony.

(10) Any person who obtains or attempts to obtain information from the database by misrepresentation or fraud is guilty of a third degree felony.

(11) (a) A person may not knowingly and intentionally use, release, publish, or otherwise make available to any other person or entity any information obtained from the database for any purpose other than those specified in Subsection (8). Each separate violation of this Subsection (11) is a third degree felony and is also subject to a civil penalty not to exceed $5,000.

(b) The procedure for determining a civil violation of this Subsection (11) shall be in accordance with Section 58-1-108, regarding adjudicative proceedings within the division.

(c) Civil penalties assessed under this Subsection (11) shall be deposited in the General Fund as a dedicated credit to be used by the division under Subsection 58-37-7.7(1).

(12) (a) The failure of a pharmacist in charge to submit information to the database as required under this section after the division has submitted a specific written request for the information or when the division determines the individual has a demonstrable pattern of failing to submit the information as required is grounds for the division to take the following actions in accordance with Section 58-1-401:

(i) refuse to issue a license to the individual;

(ii) refuse to renew the individual's license;

(iii) revoke, suspend, restrict, or place on probation the license;

(iv) issue a public or private reprimand to the individual;

(v) issue a cease and desist order; and

(vi) impose a civil penalty of not more than $1,000 for each dispensed prescription regarding which the required information is not submitted.

(b) Civil penalties assessed under Subsection (12)(a)(vi) shall be deposited in the General Fund as a dedicated credit to be used by the division under Subsection 58-37-7.7(1).

(c) The procedure for determining a civil violation of this Subsection (12) shall be in accordance with Section 58-1-108, regarding adjudicative proceedings within the division.

(13) An individual who has submitted information to the database in accordance with this section may not be held civilly liable for having submitted the information.

(14) All department and the division costs necessary to establish and operate the database shall be funded by appropriations from:

(a) the Commerce Service Fund; and

(b) the General Fund.

(15) All costs associated with recording and submitting data as required in this section shall be assumed by the submitting pharmacy.   2005

58-37-7.7. Use of dedicated credits — Controlled Substance Database — Collection of penalties.

(1) The director may, with concurrence of the Controlled Substance Database Advisory Committee created in Section 58-37-7.5, use the monies deposited in the General Fund as a dedicated credit under Subsections 58-37-6(8)(a), 58-37-7.5(11)(c), and 58-37-7.5(12)(b) for the following purposes:

(a) maintenance and replacement of the database equipment, including hardware and software;

(b) training of staff; and

(c) pursuit of external grants and matching funds.

(2) The director of the division may collect any penalty imposed under Subsections 58-37-6(8)(a), 58-37-7.5(11)(c), and 58-37-7.5(12)(b) and which is not paid by:

(a) referring the matter to the Office of State Debt Collection or a collection agency; or

(b) bringing an action in the district court of the county in which the person owing the debt resides or in the county where the office of the director is located.

(3) The director may seek legal assistance from the attorney general or the county or district attorney of the district in which the action is brought to collect the fine.

(4) The court shall award reasonable attorney's fees and costs to the division for successful collection actions under Subsection (2)(b).

(5) All funding of the controlled substance database as defined under Section 58-37-7.5 is nonlapsing.   2003

58-37-8. Prohibited acts — Penalties.

(1) Prohibited acts A — Penalties:

(a) Except as authorized by this chapter, it is unlawful for any person to knowingly and intentionally:

(i) produce, manufacture, or dispense, or to possess with intent to produce, manufacture, or dispense, a controlled or counterfeit substance;

(ii) distribute a controlled or counterfeit substance, or to agree, consent, offer, or arrange to distribute a controlled or counterfeit substance;

(iii) possess a controlled or counterfeit substance with intent to distribute; or

(iv) engage in a continuing criminal enterprise where:

(A) the person participates, directs, or engages in conduct which results in any violation of any provision of Title 58, Chapters 37, 37a, 37b, 37c, or 37d that is a felony; and

(B) the violation is a part of a continuing series of two or more violations of Title 58, Chapters 37, 37a, 37b, 37c, or 37d on separate occasions that are undertaken in concert with five or more persons with respect to whom the person occupies a position of organizer, supervisor, or any other position of management.

(b) Any person convicted of violating Subsection (1)(a) with respect to:

(i) a substance classified in Schedule I or II, a controlled substance analog, or gammahydroxybutyric acid as listed in Schedule III is guilty of a second degree felony and upon a second or subsequent conviction is guilty of a first degree felony;

(ii) a substance classified in Schedule III or IV, or marijuana, is guilty of a third degree felony, and upon a second or subsequent conviction is guilty of a second degree felony; or

(iii) a substance classified in Schedule V is guilty of a class A misdemeanor and upon a second or subsequent conviction is guilty of a third degree felony.

(c) Any person who has been convicted of a violation of Subsection (1)(a)(ii) or (iii) may be sentenced to imprisonment for an indeterminate term as provided by law, but if the trier of fact finds a firearm as defined in Section 76-10-501 was used, carried, or possessed on his person or in his immediate possession during the commission or in furtherance of the offense, the court shall additionally sentence the person convicted for a term of one year to run consecutively and not concurrently; and the court may additionally sentence the person convicted for an indeterminate term not to exceed five years to run consecutively and not concurrently.

(d) Any person convicted of violating Subsection (1)(a)(iv) is guilty of a first degree felony punishable by imprisonment for an indeterminate term of not less than seven years and which may be for life. Imposition or execution of the sentence may not be suspended, and the person is not eligible for probation.

(2) Prohibited acts B — Penalties:

(a) It is unlawful:

(i) for any person knowingly and intentionally to possess or use a controlled substance analog or a controlled substance, unless it was obtained under a valid prescription or order, directly from a practitioner while acting in the course of his professional practice, or as otherwise authorized by this chapter;

(ii) for any owner, tenant, licensee, or person in control of any building, room, tenement, vehicle, boat, aircraft, or other place knowingly and intentionally to permit them to be occupied by persons unlawfully possessing, using, or distributing controlled substances in any of those locations; or

(iii) for any person knowingly and intentionally to possess an altered or forged prescription or written order for a controlled substance.

(b) Any person convicted of violating Subsection (2)(a)(i) with respect to:

(i) marijuana, if the amount is 100 pounds or more, is guilty of a second degree felony;

(ii) a substance classified in Schedule I or II, marijuana, if the amount is more than 16 ounces, but less than 100 pounds, or a controlled substance analog, is guilty of a third degree felony; or

(iii) marijuana, if the marijuana is not in the form of an extracted resin from any part of the plant, and the amount is more than one ounce but less than 16 ounces, is guilty of a class A misdemeanor.

(c) Upon a person's conviction of a violation of this Subsection (2) subsequent to a conviction under Subsection (1)(a), that person shall be sentenced to a one degree greater penalty than provided in this Subsection (2).

(d) Any person who violates Subsection (2)(a)(i) with respect to all other controlled substances not included in Subsection (2)(b)(i), (ii), or (iii), including less than one ounce of marijuana, is guilty of a class B misdemeanor. Upon a second conviction the person is guilty of a class A misdemeanor, and upon a third or subsequent conviction the person is guilty of a third degree felony.

(e) Any person convicted of violating Subsection (2)(a)(i) while inside the exterior boundaries of property occupied by any correctional facility as defined in Section 64-13-1 or any public jail or other place of confinement shall be sentenced to a penalty one degree greater than provided in Subsection (2)(b), and if the conviction is with respect to controlled substances as listed in:

(i) Subsection (2)(b), the person may be sentenced to imprisonment for an indeterminate term as provided by law, and:

(A) the court shall additionally sentence the person convicted to a term of one year to run consecutively and not concurrently; and

(B) the court may additionally sentence the person convicted for an indeterminate term not to exceed five years to run consecutively and not concurrently; and

(ii) Subsection (2)(d), the person may be sentenced to imprisonment for an indeterminate term as provided by law, and the court shall additionally sentence the person convicted to a term of six months to run consecutively and not concurrently.

(f) Any person convicted of violating Subsection (2)(a)(ii) or (2)(a)(iii) is:

(i) on a first conviction, guilty of a class B misdemeanor;

(ii) on a second conviction, guilty of a class A misdemeanor; and

(iii) on a third or subsequent conviction, guilty of a third degree felony.

(g) A person is subject to the penalties under Subsection (4)(c) who, in an offense not amounting to a violation of Section 76-5-207:

(i) violates Subsection (2)(a)(i) by knowingly and intentionally having in his body any measurable amount of a controlled substance; and

(ii) operates a motor vehicle as defined in Section 76-5-207 in a negligent manner, causing serious bodily injury as defined in Section 76-1-601 or the death of another.

(3) Prohibited acts C — Penalties:

(a) It is unlawful for any person knowingly and intentionally:

(i) to use in the course of the manufacture or distribution of a controlled substance a license number which is fictitious, revoked, suspended, or issued to another person or, for the purpose of obtaining a controlled substance, to assume the title of, or represent himself to be, a manufacturer, wholesaler, apothecary, physician, dentist, veterinarian, or other authorized person;

(ii) to acquire or obtain possession of, to procure or attempt to procure the administration of, to obtain a prescription for, to prescribe or dispense to any person known to be attempting to acquire or obtain possession of, or to procure the administration of any controlled substance by misrepresentation or failure by the person to disclose his receiving any controlled substance from another source, fraud, forgery, deception, subterfuge, alteration of a prescription or written order for a controlled substance, or the use of a false name or address;

(iii) to make any false or forged prescription or written order for a controlled substance, or to utter the same, or to alter any prescription or written order issued or written under the terms of this chapter; or

(iv) to make, distribute, or possess any punch, die, plate, stone, or other thing designed to print, imprint, or reproduce the trademark, trade name, or other identifying mark, imprint, or device of another or any likeness of any of the foregoing upon any drug or container or labeling so as to render any drug a counterfeit controlled substance.

(b) Any person convicted of violating Subsection (3)(a) is guilty of a third degree felony.

(4) Prohibited acts D — Penalties:

(a) Notwithstanding other provisions of this section, a person not authorized under this chapter who commits any act declared to be unlawful under this section, Title 58, Chapter 37a, Utah Drug Paraphernalia Act, or under Title 58, Chapter 37b, Imitation Controlled Substances Act, is upon conviction subject to the penalties and classifications under this Subsection (4) if the trier of fact finds the act is committed:

    (i) in a public or private elementary or secondary school or on the grounds of any of those schools;

    (ii) in a public or private vocational school or postsecondary institution or on the grounds of any of those schools or institutions;

    (iii) in those portions of any building, park, stadium, or other structure or grounds which are, at the time of the act, being used for an activity sponsored by or through a school or institution under Subsections (4)(a)(i) and (ii);

    (iv) in or on the grounds of a preschool or child-care facility;

    (v) in a public park, amusement park, arcade, or recreation center;

    (vi) in or on the grounds of a house of worship as defined in Section 76-10-501;

    (vii) in a shopping mall, sports facility, stadium, arena, theater, movie house, playhouse, or parking lot or structure adjacent thereto;

    (viii) in a public parking lot or structure;

    (ix) within 1,000 feet of any structure, facility, or grounds included in Subsections (4)(a)(i) through (viii);

    (x) in the immediate presence of a person younger than 18 years of age, regardless of where the act occurs; or

    (xi) for the purpose of facilitating, arranging, or causing the transport, delivery, or distribution of a substance in violation of this section to an inmate or on the grounds of any correctional facility as defined in Section 76-8-311.3.

(b) A person convicted under this Subsection (4) is guilty of a first degree felony and shall be imprisoned for a term of not less than five years if the penalty that would otherwise have been established but for this subsection would have been a first degree felony. Imposition or execution of the sentence may not be suspended, and the person is not eligible for probation.

(c) If the classification that would otherwise have been established would have been less than a first degree felony but for this Subsection (4), a person convicted under Subsection (2)(g) or this Subsection (4) is guilty of one degree more than the maximum penalty prescribed for that offense.

    (d) (i) If the violation is of Subsection (4)(a)(xi):

        (A) the person may be sentenced to imprisonment for an indeterminate term as provided by law, and the court shall additionally sentence the person convicted for a term of one year to run consecutively and not concurrently; and

        (B) the court may additionally sentence the person convicted for an indeterminate term not to exceed five years to run consecutively and not concurrently; and

    (ii) the penalties under this Subsection (4)(d) apply also to any person who, acting with the mental state required for the commission of an offense, directly or indirectly solicits, requests, commands, coerces, encourages, or intentionally aids another person to commit a violation of Subsection (4)(a)(xi).

(e) It is not a defense to a prosecution under this Subsection (4) that the actor mistakenly believed the individual to be 18 years of age or older at the time of the offense or was unaware of the individual's true age; nor that the actor mistakenly believed that the location where the act occurred was not as described in Subsection (4)(a) or was unaware that the location where the act occurred was as described in Subsection (4)(a).

(5) Any violation of this chapter for which no penalty is specified is a class B misdemeanor.

(6) (a) Any penalty imposed for violation of this section is in addition to, and not in lieu of, any civil or administrative penalty or sanction authorized by law.

(b) Where violation of this chapter violates a federal law or the law of another state, conviction or acquittal under federal law or the law of another state for the same act is a bar to prosecution in this state.

(7) In any prosecution for a violation of this chapter, evidence or proof which shows a person or persons produced, manufactured, possessed, distributed, or dispensed a controlled substance or substances, is prima facie evidence that the person or persons did so with knowledge of the character of the substance or substances.

(8) This section does not prohibit a veterinarian, in good faith and in the course of his professional practice only and not for humans, from prescribing, dispensing, or administering controlled substances or from causing the substances to be administered by an assistant or orderly under his direction and supervision.

(9) Civil or criminal liability may not be imposed under this section on:

    (a) any person registered under the Controlled Substances Act who manufactures, distributes, or possesses an imitation controlled substance for use as a placebo or investigational new drug by a registered practitioner in the ordinary course of professional practice or research; or

    (b) any law enforcement officer acting in the course and legitimate scope of his employment.

(10) If any provision of this chapter, or the application of any provision to any person or circumstances, is held invalid, the remainder of this chapter shall be given effect without the invalid provision or application.   2005

58-37-8.5. Applicability of Title 76 prosecutions under this chapter.

Unless specifically excluded in or inconsistent with the provisions of this chapter, the provisions of Title 76, Chapters 1, 2, 3, and 4, are fully applicable to prosecutions under this chapter.   1997

58-37-9. Investigators — Status of peace officers.

Investigators for the Department of Commerce shall, for the purpose of enforcing the provisions of this chapter, have the status of peace officers.   1995

58-37-10. Search warrants — Administrative inspection warrants — Inspections and seizures of property without warrant.

(1) Search warrants relating to offenses involving controlled substances may be authorized in the same manner as provided in Title 77, Chapter 23.

(2) Issuance and execution of administrative inspection warrants shall be as follows:

(a) Any judge or magistrate of this state within his jurisdiction upon proper oath or affirmation showing probable cause, may issue warrants for the purpose of conducting administrative inspections authorized by this act or regulations thereunder and seizures of property appropriate to such inspections. Probable cause for purposes of this act exists upon showing a valid public interest in the effective enforcement of the act or rules promulgated thereunder sufficient to justify administrative inspection of the area, premises, building, or conveyance in the circumstances specified in the application for the warrant.

(b) A warrant shall issue only upon an affidavit of an officer or employee duly designated and having knowledge of the facts alleged sworn to before a judge or magistrate which establish the grounds for issuing the warrant. If the judge or magistrate is satisfied that grounds for the application exist or that there is probable cause to believe they exist, he shall issue a warrant identifying the area, premises, building, or conveyance to be inspected, the purpose of the inspection, and if appropriate, the type of property to be inspected, if any. The warrant shall:

(i) state the grounds for its issuance and the name of each person whose affidavit has been taken to support it;

(ii) be directed to a person authorized by Section 58-37-9 of this act to execute it;

(iii) command the person to whom it is directed to inspect the area, premises, building, or conveyance identified for the purpose specified and if appropriate, direct the seizure of the property specified;

(iv) identify the item or types of property to be seized, if any;

(v) direct that it be served during normal business hours and designate the judge or magistrate to whom it shall be returned.

(c) A warrant issued pursuant to this section must be executed and returned within ten days after its date unless, upon a showing of a need for additional time, the court instructs otherwise in the warrant. If property is seized pursuant to a warrant, the person executing the warrant shall give to the person from whom or from whose premises the property was taken a copy of the warrant and a receipt for the property taken or leave the copy and receipt at the place where the property was taken. Return of the warrant shall be made promptly and be accompanied by a written inventory of any property taken. The inventory shall be made in the presence of the person executing the warrant and of the person from whose possession or premises the property was taken, if they are present, or in the presence of at least one credible person other than the person executing the warrant. A copy of the inventory shall be delivered to the person from whom or from whose premises the property was taken and to the applicant for the warrant.

(d) The judge or magistrate who issued the warrant under this section shall attach a copy of the return and all other papers to the warrant and file them with the court.

(3) The department is authorized to make administrative inspections of controlled premises in accordance with the following provisions:

(a) For purposes of this section only, "controlled premises" means:

(i) Places where persons licensed or exempted from licensing requirements under this act are required to keep records.

(ii) Places including factories, warehouses, establishments, and conveyances where persons licensed or exempted from licensing requirements are permitted to possess, manufacture, compound, process, sell, deliver, or otherwise dispose of any controlled substance.

(b) When authorized by an administrative inspection warrant a law enforcement officer or employee designated in Section 58-37-9, upon presenting the warrant and appropriate credentials to the owner, operator, or agent in charge, has the right to enter controlled premises for the purpose of conducting an administrative inspection.

(c) When authorized by an administrative inspection warrant, a law enforcement officer or employee designated in Section 58-37-9 has the right:

(i) To inspect and copy records required by this act.

(ii) To inspect within reasonable limits and a reasonable manner, the controlled premises and all pertinent equipment, finished and unfinished material, containers, and labeling found, and except as provided in Subsection (3)(e), all other things including records, files, papers, processes, controls, and facilities subject to regulation and control by this act or by rules promulgated by the department.

(iii) To inventory and stock of any controlled substance and obtain samples of any substance.

(d) This section shall not be construed to prevent the inspection of books and records without a warrant pursuant to an administrative subpoena issued by a court or the department nor shall it be construed to prevent entries and administrative inspections including seizures of property without a warrant:

(i) With the consent of the owner, operator, or agent in charge of the controlled premises;

(ii) In situations presenting imminent danger to health or safety;

(iii) In situations involving inspection of conveyances where there is reasonable cause to believe that the mobility of the conveyance makes it impracticable to obtain a warrant;

(iv) In any other exceptional or emergency circumstance where time or opportunity to apply for a warrant is lacking; and

(v) In all other situations where a warrant is not constitutionally required.

(e) No inspection authorized by this section shall extend to financial data, sales data, other than shipment data, or pricing data unless the owner, operator, or agent in charge of the controlled premises consents in writing. 1987

58-37-11. District court jurisdiction to enjoin violations — Jury trial.

(1) The district courts of this state shall have jurisdiction in proceedings in accordance with the rules of those courts to enjoin violations of this act.

(2) If an alleged violation of an injunction or restraining order issued under this section occurs, the accused may demand a jury trial in accordance with the rules of the district courts.   1971

58-37-12. Enforcement — Coordination and cooperation of federal and state agencies — Powers.

The department and all law enforcement agencies charged with enforcing this act shall cooperate with federal and other state agencies in discharging their responsibilities concerning traffic in controlled substances and in suppressing the abuse of controlled substances. To this end, they are authorized to:

(1) Arrange for the exchange of information between governmental officials concerning the use and abuse of dangerous substances.

(2) Coordinate and cooperate in training programs in controlled substance law enforcement at the local and state levels.

(3) Cooperate with the United States Department of Justice and the Utah Department of Public Safety by establishing a centralized unit which will receive, catalog, file, and collect statistics, including records of drug-dependent persons and other controlled substance law offenders within the state, and make the information available for federal, state, and local law enforcement purposes.

(4) Conduct programs of eradication aimed at destroying the wild or illicit growth of plant species from which controlled substances may be extracted.   1997

58-37-13. Property subject to forfeiture — Seizure — Procedure.

(1) As used in this section:

(a) "Claimant" means:

(i) any owner as defined in this section; or

(ii) any interest holder as defined in this section and any other person or entity who asserts a claim to any property seized for forfeiture under this section;

(b) "Drug distributing paraphernalia" means any property used or designed to be used in the illegal transportation, storage, shipping, or circulation of a controlled substance. Property is considered "designed to be used" for one or more of the above-listed purposes if the property has been altered or modified to include a feature or device which would actually promote or conceal a violation of this chapter.

(c) "Drug manufacturing equipment or supplies" includes any illegally possessed controlled substance precursor, or any chemical, laboratory equipment, or laboratory supplies possessed with intent to engage in clandestine laboratory operations as defined in Section 58-37d-3.

(d) "Interest holder" means a secured party as defined in Section 70A-9a-102, a mortgagee, lien creditor, or the beneficiary of a security interest or encumbrance pertaining to an interest in property, whose interest would be perfected against a good faith purchaser for value. A person who holds property for the benefit of or as an agent or nominee for another, or who is not in substantial compliance with any statute requiring an interest in property to be recorded or reflected in public records in order to perfect the interest against a good faith purchaser for value, is not an interest holder.

(e) "Owner" means an individual or entity who possesses a legal or equitable ownership in real or personal property.

(f) "Proceeds" means property acquired directly or indirectly from, produced through, realized through, or caused by an act or omission and includes any property of any kind without reduction for expenses incurred in the acquisition, maintenance, or production of that property, or any other purpose.

(g) "Real Property" means:

(i) land; and

(ii) any building, fixture, improvement, appurtenance, structure, or other development that is affixed permanently to land.

(h) "Resolution of criminal charges" occurs at the time a claimant who is also charged with violations under Chapter 37, 37a, 37b, 37c, or 37d enters a plea, upon return of a jury verdict or court ruling in a criminal trial, or upon dismissal of the criminal charge.

(i) "Violation of this chapter" means any conduct prohibited by Chapter 37, 37a, 37b, 37c, or 37d or any conduct occurring outside the state which would be a violation of the laws of the place where the conduct occurred and which would be a violation of Chapter 37, 37a, 37b, 37c, or 37d if the conduct had occurred in this state.

(2) The following are subject to criminal or civil forfeiture pursuant to Title 24, Chapter 1, Utah Uniform Forfeiture Procedures Act:

(a) all controlled substances which have been manufactured, distributed, dispensed, or acquired in violation of this chapter;

(b) all raw materials, products, and equipment of any kind used, or intended for use, in manufacturing, compounding, processing, delivering, importing, or exporting any controlled substance in violation of this chapter;

(c) all property used or intended for use as a container for property described in Subsections (2)(a) and (2)(b);

(d) all hypodermic needles, syringes, and other paraphernalia, not including capsules used with health food supplements and herbs, used or intended for use to administer controlled substances in violation of this chapter;

(e) all conveyances including aircraft, vehicles, or vessels used or intended to be used to facilitate the distribution or possession with intent to distribute the property described in Subsections (2)(a) and (2)(b);

(f) all books, records, and research, including formulas, microfilm, tapes, and data used or intended for use in violation of this chapter;

(g) everything of value furnished or intended to be furnished in exchange for a controlled substance in violation of this chapter, and all moneys, negotiable instruments, and securities used or intended to be used to facilitate any violation of this chapter. An interest in property may not be civilly forfeited under this Subsection (2) unless it is proven by clear and convincing evidence that the owner or any interest holder knew of the conduct which made the property subject to forfeiture. The burden of presenting this evidence is on the state;

(h) all imitation controlled substances as defined in Section 58-37b-2, Imitation Controlled Substances Act;

(i) (i) all warehousing, housing, and storage facilities, or interest in real property of any kind used, or intended for use, in producing, cultivating, warehousing, storing, distributing or manufacturing any controlled substances in violation of this chapter but only if:

(A) the cumulative sales of controlled substances on the property within a two-month period total or exceed $1,000; or

(B) the street value of any controlled substances found on the premises at any given time totals or exceeds $1,000, but only after the judge makes a specific finding of proportionality under Section 24-1-14, and subject to the condition that even if proportionality is found, the judge shall have discretion not to forfeit real property which is a primary residence.

(ii) A narcotics officer experienced in controlled substances law enforcement may testify to establish the street value of the controlled substances for purposes of this Subsection (2);

(j) any firearm, weapon, or ammunition carried or used in connection with a violation of this chapter or any firearm, weapon, or ammunition kept or located within the proximity of controlled substances;

(k) all proceeds traceable to any violation of this chapter.

(3) Property subject to forfeiture under this chapter may be seized by any peace officer of this state upon process issued by any court having jurisdiction over the property. However, seizure without process may be made when:

(a) the seizure is incident to an arrest or search under a search warrant or an inspection under an administrative inspection warrant;

(b) the property subject to seizure has been the subject of a prior judgment in favor of the state in a criminal injunction or forfeiture proceeding under this chapter;

(c) the peace officer has probable cause to believe that the property is directly or indirectly dangerous to health or safety; or

(d) the peace officer has probable cause to believe that the property has been used or intended to be used in violation of this chapter and has probable cause to believe the property will be damaged, intentionally diminished in value, destroyed, concealed, or removed from the state.

(4) Property taken or detained under this section is not repleviable but is in custody of the law enforcement agency making the seizure, subject only to the orders and decrees of the court or the official having jurisdiction. When property is seized under this chapter, the appropriate person or agency may:

(a) place the property under seal;

(b) remove the property to a place designated by it or the warrant under which it was seized; or

(c) take custody of the property and remove it to an appropriate location for disposition in accordance with law.

(5) All substances listed in Schedule I that are possessed, transferred, distributed, or offered for distribution in violation of this chapter are contraband and no property right shall exist in them. All substances listed in Schedule I which are seized or come into the possession of the state may be retained for any evidentiary or investigative purpose, including sampling or other preservation prior to disposal or destruction by the state.

(6) All marijuana or any species of plants from which controlled substances in Schedules I and II are derived which have been planted or cultivated in violation of this chapter, or of which the owners or cultivators are unknown, or are wild growths, may be seized and retained for any evidentiary or investigative purpose, including sampling or other preservation prior to disposal or destruction by the state. Failure, upon demand by the department or its authorized agent, of any person in occupancy or in control of land or premises upon which species of plants are growing or being stored, to produce an appropriate license or proof that he is the holder of a license, is authority for the seizure and forfeiture of the plants.

(7) Forfeiture proceedings shall conform with the procedures and substantive protections of Title 24, Chapter 1, Utah Uniform Forfeiture Procedures Act.
                                                            2002

58-37-14. Resort for illegal use or possession of controlled substances deemed common nuisance — District court power to suppress and enjoin.

(1) Any store, shop, warehouse, dwelling house, building, vehicle, boat, aircraft, or other place to which users or possessors of any controlled substances, listed in schedules I through V, resort or where use or possession of any substances violates this act, or which is used for illegal keeping, storing, or selling any substances listed as controlled substances in schedules I through V shall be deemed a common nuisance. No person shall open, keep, or maintain any such place.

(2) The district court has the power to make any order necessary or reasonable to suppress any nuisance and to enjoin any person or persons from doing any act calculated to cause, or permit the continuation of a nuisance.   1971

58-37-15. Burden of proof in proceedings on violations — Enforcement officers exempt from liability.

(1) It is not necessary for the state to negate any exemption or exception set forth in this act in any complaint, information, indictment or other pleading or trial, hearing, or other proceeding under this act, and the burden of proof of any exemption or exception is upon the person claiming its benefit.

(2) In absence of proof that a person is the duly authorized holder of an appropriate license, registration, order form, or prescription issued under this act, he shall be presumed not to be the holder of a license, registration, order form, or prescription, and the burden of proof is upon him to rebut the presumption.

(3) No liability shall be imposed upon any duly authorized state or federal officer engaged in the enforcement of this act who is engaged in the enforcement of any law, municipal ordinance, or regulation relating to controlled substances.   1971

58-37-16. Repealed.   1997

58-37-17. Judicial review.

(1) Any person aggrieved by a department's final order may obtain judicial review.

(2) Venue for judicial review of informal adjudicative proceedings is in the district court of Salt Lake County.   1987

58-37-18. Prior prosecutions and proceedings continued — Uniform construction.

(1) (a) Prosecution for violation of any law or offense occurring prior to the effective date of this

act shall not be affected by this act; provided, that sentences imposed after the effective date of this act may not exceed the maximum terms specified and the judge has discretion to impose any minimum sentence.

(b) Civil seizures, forfeitures, and injunctive proceedings commenced prior to the effective date of this act shall not be affected by this act.

(c) All administrative proceedings pending before any agency or court on the effective date of this act shall be continued and brought to final determination in accordance with laws and regulations in effect prior to the effective date of this act. Drugs placed under control prior to enactment of this act which are not listed within schedules I through V shall be automatically controlled and listed in the appropriate schedule without further proceedings.

(2) This act does not affect rights and duties that mature, penalties that are incurred, and proceedings that are begun before its effective date.

(3) This act shall be construed to effectuate its general purpose to make uniform the law of those states which enact it where laws are similar to this act.   1971

58-37-19, 58-37-20.   Repealed.   1992, 2000

58-37-21.   Admissibility of Utah State Crime Laboratory documents — Drug analysis in criminal pretrial proceedings.

The commissioner of the Department of Public Safety shall establish standards for administration and interpretation of chemical and forensic analysis in accordance with Title 63, Chapter 46a, Utah Administrative Rulemaking Act, of:

(1) controlled substances as provided in Title 58, Chapter 37;

(2) drug paraphernalia as provided in Title 58, Chapter 37a;

(3) imitation controlled substances as provided in Title 58, Chapter 37b; and

(4) controlled substance precursors as provided in Title 58, Chapter 37d.   1995

CHAPTER 37a

DRUG PARAPHERNALIA

58-37a-1.   Short title.

This chapter shall be known and may be cited as the "Utah Drug Paraphernalia Act."   1981

58-37a-2.   Purpose.

It is the intent of this chapter to discourage the use of narcotics by eliminating paraphernalia designed for processing, ingesting, or otherwise using a controlled substance.   1981

58-37a-3.   "Drug paraphernalia" defined.

As used in this chapter:

"Drug paraphernalia" means any equipment, product, or material used, or intended for use, to plant, propagate, cultivate, grow, harvest, manufacture, compound, convert, produce, process, prepare, test, analyze, package, repackage, store, contain, conceal, inject, ingest, inhale, or to otherwise introduce a controlled substance into the human body in violation of Title 58, Chapter 37, and includes, but is not limited to:

(1) Kits used, or intended for use, in planting, propagating, cultivating, growing, or harvesting any species of plant which is a controlled substance or from which a controlled substance can be derived;

(2) Kits used, or intended for use, in manufacturing, compounding, converting, producing, processing, or preparing a controlled substance;

(3) Isomerization devices used, or intended for use, to increase the potency of any species of plant which is a controlled substance;

(4) Testing equipment used, or intended for use, to identify or to analyze the strength, effectiveness, or purity of a controlled substance;

(5) Scales and balances used, or intended for use, in weighing or measuring a controlled substance;

(6) Diluents and adulterants, such as quinine hydrochloride, mannitol, mannited, dextrose and lactose, used, or intended for use to cut a controlled substance;

(7) Separation gins and sifters used, or intended for use to remove twigs, seeds, or other impurities from marihuana;

(8) Blenders, bowls, containers, spoons and mixing devices used, or intended for use to compound a controlled substance;

(9) Capsules, balloons, envelopes, and other containers used, or intended for use to package small quantities of a controlled substance;

(10) Containers and other objects used, or intended for use to store or conceal a controlled substance;

(11) Hypodermic syringes, needles, and other objects used, or intended for use to parenterally inject a controlled substance into the human body; and

(12) Objects used, or intended for use to ingest, inhale, or otherwise introduce marihuana, cocaine, hashish, or hashish oil into the human body, including but not limited to:

(a) Metal, wooden, acrylic, glass, stone, plastic, or ceramic pipes with or without screens, permanent screens, hashish heads, or punctured metal bowls;

(b) Water pipes;

(c) Carburetion tubes and devices;

(d) Smoking and carburetion masks;

(e) Roach clips: meaning objects used to hold burning material, such as a marihuana cigarette, that has become too small or too short to be held in the hand;

(f) Miniature cocaine spoons and cocaine vials;

(g) Chamber pipes;

(h) Carburetor pipes;

(i) Electric pipes;

(j) Air-driven pipes;

(k) Chillums;

(l) Bongs; and

(m) Ice pipes or chillers.   1981

58-37a-4. Considerations in determining whether object is drug paraphernalia.

In determining whether an object is drug paraphernalia, the trier of fact, in addition to all other logically relevant factors, should consider:

(1) statements by an owner or by anyone in control of the object concerning its use;

(2) prior convictions, if any, of an owner, or of anyone in control of the object, under any state or federal law relating to a controlled substance;

(3) the proximity of the object, in time and space, to a direct violation of this chapter;

(4) the proximity of the object to a controlled substance;

(5) the existence of any residue of a controlled substance on the object;

(6) instructions whether oral or written, provided with the object concerning its use;

(7) descriptive materials accompanying the object which explain or depict its use;

(8) national and local advertising concerning its use;

(9) the manner in which the object is displayed for sale;

(10) whether the owner or anyone in control of the object is a legitimate supplier of like or related items to the community, such as a licensed distributor or dealer of tobacco products;

(11) direct or circumstantial evidence of the ratio of sales of the object to the total sales of the business enterprise;

(12) the existence and scope of legitimate uses of the object in the community; and

(13) expert testimony concerning its use. 1981

58-37a-5. Unlawful acts.

(1) It is unlawful for any person to use, or to possess with intent to use, drug paraphernalia to plant, propagate, cultivate, grow, harvest, manufacture, compound, convert, produce, process, prepare, test, analyze, pack, repack, store, contain, conceal, inject, ingest, inhale or otherwise introduce a controlled substance into the human body in violation of this chapter. Any person who violates this subsection is guilty of a class B misdemeanor.

(2) It is unlawful for any person to deliver, possess with intent to deliver, or manufacture with intent to deliver, any drug paraphernalia, knowing that the drug paraphernalia will be used to plant, propagate, cultivate, grow, harvest, manufacture, compound, convert, produce, process, prepare, test, analyze, pack, repack, store, contain, conceal, inject, ingest, inhale, or otherwise introduce a controlled substance into the human body in violation of this act. Any person who violates this subsection is guilty of a class A misdemeanor.

(3) Any person 18 years of age or over who delivers drug paraphernalia to a person under 18 years of age who is three years or more younger than the person making the delivery is guilty of a third degree felony.

(4) It is unlawful for any person to place in this state in any newspaper, magazine, handbill, or other publication any advertisement, knowing that the purpose of the advertisement is to promote the sale of drug paraphernalia. Any person who violates this subsection is guilty of a class B misdemeanor. 1981

58-37a-6. Seizure — Forfeiture — Property rights.

Drug paraphernalia is subject to seizure and forfeiture in accordance with the procedures and substantive protections of Title 24, Chapter 1, Utah Uniform Forfeiture Procedures Act. 2002

CHAPTER 37b

IMITATION CONTROLLED SUBSTANCES

58-37b-1. Short title.

This act shall be known and may be cited as the "Imitation Controlled Substances Act." 1982

58-37b-2. Definitions.

As used in this chapter:

(1) "Controlled substance" has the same meaning as provided in Section 58-37-2.

(2) "Distribute" means the actual, constructive, or attempted sale, transfer, delivery, or dispensing to another of an imitation controlled substance.

(3) "Imitation controlled substance" means a substance that is not a controlled substance or counterfeit controlled substance, and which by overall dosage unit substantially resembles a specific controlled substance in appearance, including its color, shape, or size.

(4) "Manufacture" means the production, preparation, compounding, processing, encapsulating, tableting, packaging or repackaging, labeling or relabeling, of an imitation controlled substance. 1997

58-37b-3. Considerations in determining whether substance is imitation controlled substance.

If the appearance of the dosage unit is not reasonably sufficient to establish that the substance is an imitation controlled substance, as in liquids or powders, the following factors should be considered:

(1) statements made by an owner or by anyone else in control of the substance, concerning the nature of the substance, its use or effect, or its similarity to a controlled substance;

(2) statements made to the recipient that the substance may be resold at a price substantially higher than the usual and customary price for the ingredients contained in the substance;

(3) whether the substance is packaged or labeled in a manner similar to that generally used for controlled substances;

(4) evasive tactics or actions utilized by the owner or person in control of the substance to avoid detection by law enforcement authorities;

(5) prior convictions of an owner or anyone in control of the object, under state or federal law related to controlled substances or fraud; and

(6) the proximity of the substances to controlled substances. 1987

**58-37b-4. Manufacture, distribution or posses-
sion of substance unlawful — Penalty.**

It is unlawful for any person to manufacture, distribute, or possess with intent to distribute, an imitation controlled substance. Any person who violates
this section is guilty of a class A misdemeanor.   1991

58-37b-5. Repealed.   1987

58-37b-6. Use of substance unlawful — Penalty.

It is unlawful for any person to use, or to possess
with intent to use, an imitation controlled substance.
Any person who violates this section is guilty of a class
C misdemeanor.   1986

**58-37b-7. Advertisement of substance unlawful
— Penalty.**

It is unlawful for any person to place any newspaper, magazine, handbill, or other publication, or to
post or distribute in any public place, any advertisement or solicitation with reasonable knowledge that
the purpose of the advertisement or solicitation is to
promote the distribution of imitation controlled substances. Any person who violates this section is guilty
of a class A misdemeanor.   1991

**58-37b-8. Exemption of persons registered un-
der Controlled Substances Act.**

No civil or criminal liability shall be imposed by
virtue of this act on any person registered under the
Controlled Substances Act who manufactures, distributes, or possesses an imitation controlled substance
for use as a placebo or investigational new drug by a
registered practitioner in the ordinary course of professional practice or research or on any law enforcement officer acting in the course and legitimate scope
of that employment.   1982

CHAPTER 37c

CONTROLLED SUBSTANCE PRECURSOR
ACT

58-37c-1. Short title.

This act shall be known as the "Utah Controlled
Substance Precursor Act."   1992

58-37c-2. Purpose.

The purpose of this act is to provide for the licensure
of regulated distributors and regulated purchasers
engaged in regulated transactions of listed controlled
substance precursor chemicals as they are identified
in the act or rules adopted pursuant to the act, to
provide for maintaining of records and submission of
reports with respect to regulated transactions, to
provide for reasonable and necessary regulation of
defined types of transactions, to provide that violation
of the provisions of this act shall be unlawful and
unprofessional conduct, and to provide for criminal
and administrative actions for that conduct.   1992

58-37c-3. Definitions.

In addition to the definitions in Section 58-1-102, as
used in this chapter:

(1) "Board" means the Controlled Substance
Precursor Advisory Board created in Section 58-
37c-4.

(2) "Controlled substance precursor" includes a
chemical reagent and means any of the following:

(a) Phenyl-2-propanone;

(b) Methylamine;

(c) Ethylamine;

(d) D-lysergic acid;

(e) Ergotamine and its salts;

(f) Diethyl malonate;

(g) Malonic acid;

(h) Ethyl malonate;

(i) Barbituric acid;

(j) Piperidine and its salts;

(k) N-acetylanthranilic acid and its salts;

(l) Pyrrolidine;

(m) Phenylacetic acid and its salts;

(n) Anthranilic acid and its salts;

(o) Morpholine;

(p) Ephedrine;

(q) Pseudoephedrine;

(r) Norpseudoephedrine;

(s) Phenylpropanolamine;

(t) Benzyl cyanide;

(u) Ergonovine and its salts;

(v) 3,4-Methylenedioxyphenyl-2-propa-
none;

(w) propionic anhydride;

(x) Insosafrole;

(y) Safrole;

(z) Piperonal;

(aa) N-Methylephedrine;

(bb) N-ethylephedrine;

(cc) N-methylpseudoephedrine;

(dd) N-ethylpseudoephedrine;

(ee) Hydriotic acid;

(ff) gamma butyrolactone (GBL), including butyrolactone, 1,2 butanolide, 2-oxanolone, tetrahydro-2-furanone, dihydro-2(3H)-furanone, and tetramethylene glycol, but not including gamma aminobutric acid (GABA);

(gg) 1,4 butanediol;

(hh) any salt, isomer, or salt of an isomer of the chemicals listed in Subsections (2)(a) through (gg);

(ii) Crystal iodine;

(jj) Iodine at concentrations greater than 1.5% by weight in a solution or matrix;

(kk) Red phosphorous, except as provided in Section 58-37c-19.7;

(ll) anhydrous ammonia, except as provided in Section 58-37c-19.9;

(mm) any controlled substance precursor listed under the provisions of the Federal Controlled Substances Act which is designated by the director under the emergency listing provisions set forth in Section 58-37c-14; and

(nn) any chemical which is designated by the director under the emergency listing provisions set forth in Section 58-37c-14.

(3) "Deliver," "delivery," "transfer," or "furnish" means the actual, constructive, or attempted transfer of a controlled substance precursor.

(4) "Matrix" means something, as a substance, in which something else originates, develops, or is contained.

(5) "Person" means any individual, group of individuals, proprietorship, partnership, joint venture, corporation, or organization of any type or kind.

(6) "Practitioner" means a physician, dentist, podiatric physician, veterinarian, pharmacist, scientific investigator, pharmacy, hospital, pharmaceutical manufacturer, or other person licensed, registered, or otherwise permitted to distribute, dispense, conduct research with respect to, administer, or use in teaching, or chemical analysis a controlled substance in the course of professional practice or research in this state.

(7) (a) "Regulated distributor" means a person within the state who provides, sells, furnishes, transfers, or otherwise supplies a listed controlled substance precursor chemical in a regulated transaction.

(b) "Regulated distributor" does not include any person excluded from regulation under this chapter.

(8) (a) "Regulated purchaser" means any person within the state who receives a listed controlled substance precursor chemical in a regulated transaction.

(b) "Regulated purchaser" does not include any person excluded from regulation under this chapter.

(9) "Regulated transaction" means any actual, constructive or attempted:

(a) transfer, distribution, delivery, or furnishing by a person within the state to another person within or outside of the state of a threshold amount of a listed precursor chemical; or

(b) purchase or acquisition by any means by a person within the state from another person within or outside the state of a threshold amount of a listed precursor chemical.

(10) "Retail distributor" means a grocery store, general merchandise store, drug store, or other entity or person whose activities as a distributor are limited almost exclusively to sales for personal use:

(a) in both number of sales and volume of sales; and

(b) either directly to walk-in customers or in face-to-face transactions by direct sales.

(11) "Threshold amount of a listed precursor chemical" means any amount of a controlled substance precursor or a specified amount of a controlled substance precursor in a matrix; however, the division may exempt from the provisions of this chapter a specific controlled substance precursor in a specific amount and in certain types of transactions which provisions for exemption shall be defined by the division by rule adopted pursuant to Title 63, Chapter 46a, Utah Administrative Rulemaking Act.

(12) "Unlawful conduct" as defined in Section 58-1-501 includes knowingly and intentionally:

(a) engaging in a regulated transaction without first being appropriately licensed or exempted from licensure under this chapter;

(b) acting as a regulated distributor and selling, transferring, or in any other way conveying a controlled substance precursor to a person within the state who is not appropriately licensed or exempted from licensure as a regulated purchaser, or selling, transferring, or otherwise conveying a controlled substance precursor to a person outside of the state and failing to report the transaction as required;

(c) acting as a regulated purchaser and purchasing or in any other way obtaining a controlled substance precursor from a person within the state who is not a licensed regulated distributor, or purchasing or otherwise obtaining a controlled substance precursor from a person outside of the state and failing to report the transaction as required;

(d) engaging in a regulated transaction and failing to submit reports and keep required records of inventories required under the provisions of this chapter or rules adopted pursuant to this chapter;

(e) making any false statement in any application for license, in any record to be kept, or on any report submitted as required under this chapter;

(f) with the intent of causing the evasion of the recordkeeping or reporting requirements of this chapter and rules related to this chapter, receiving or distributing any listed controlled substance precursor chemical in any manner designed so that the making of records or filing of reports required under this chapter is not required;

(g) failing to take immediate steps to comply with licensure, reporting, or recordkeeping requirements of this chapter because of lack of knowledge of those requirements, upon becoming informed of the requirements;

(h) presenting false or fraudulent identification where or when receiving or purchasing a listed controlled substance precursor chemical;

(i) creating a chemical mixture for the purpose of evading any licensure, reporting or recordkeeping requirement of this chapter or rules related to this chapter, or receiving a chemical mixture created for that purpose;

(j) if the person is at least 18 years of age, employing, hiring, using, persuading, inducing, enticing, or coercing another person under 18 years of age to violate any provision of this chapter, or assisting in avoiding detection or apprehension for any violation of this chapter by any federal, state, or local law enforcement official; and

(k) obtaining or attempting to obtain or to possess any controlled substance precursor or any combination of controlled substance precursors knowing or having a reasonable cause to believe that the controlled substance precursor is intended to be used in the unlawful manufacture of any controlled substance.

(13) "Unprofessional conduct" as defined in Section 58-1-102 and as may be further defined by rule includes the following:

(a) violation of any provision of this chapter, the Controlled Substance Act of this state or any other state, or the Federal Controlled Substance Act; and

(b) refusing to allow agents or representatives of the division or authorized law enforcement personnel to inspect inventories or controlled substance precursors or records or reports relating to purchases and sales or distribution of controlled substance precursors as such records and reports are required under this chapter.   2000

58-37c-4. Board.

(1) There is hereby established a Controlled Substance Precursor Advisory Board which shall consist of four individuals representing distributors and purchasers of controlled substance precursors and one member from the general public.

(2) The board shall be appointed and serve in accordance with Section 58-1-201.

(3) The duties and responsibilities of the board shall be in accordance with Sections 58-1-202 and 58-1-203.   1993

58-37c-5. Responsibility of Department of Commerce — Delegation to the Division of Occupational and Professional Licensing — Rulemaking authority of the division.

(1) Responsibility for the enforcement of the licensing and reporting provisions of this chapter shall be with the Department of Commerce.

(2) The executive director shall delegate specific responsibility within the department to the Division of Occupational and Professional Licensing.

(3) The division shall make, adopt, amend, and repeal rules necessary for the proper administration and enforcement of this chapter.   1992

58-37c-6. Division duties.

The division shall be responsible for the licensing and reporting provisions of this chapter and those duties shall include:

(1) providing for a system of licensure of regulated distributors and regulated purchasers;

(2) refusing to renew a license or revoking, suspending, restricting, placing on probation, issuing a private or public letter of censure or reprimand, or imposing other appropriate action against a license;

(3) with respect to the licensure and reporting provisions of this chapter, investigating or causing to be investigated any violation of this chapter by any person and to cause, when necessary, appropriate administrative action with respect to the license of that person;

(4) presenting evidence obtained from investigations conducted by appropriate county attorneys and the Office of the Attorney General for civil or criminal prosecution or for administrative action against a licensee;

(5) conducting hearings for the purpose of revoking, suspending, placing on probation, or imposing other appropriate administrative action against the license of regulated distributors or regulated purchasers in accordance with the provisions of Title 58, Chapter 1, Division of Occupational and Professional Licensing Act, and Title 63, Chapter 46b, Administrative Procedures Act;

(6) assisting all other law enforcement agencies of the state in enforcing all laws regarding controlled substance precursors;

(7) specifying reports, frequency of reports, and conditions under which reports are to be submitted and to whom reports are to be submitted by regulated distributors and regulated purchasers with respect to transactions involving threshold amounts of controlled substance precursors; and

(8) performing all other functions necessary to fulfill division duties and responsibilities as outlined under this chapter or rules adopted pursuant to this chapter.   1992

58-37c-7. License classifications.

(1) The division shall issue to persons qualified under the provisions of this chapter and rules adopted a license in the classifications:

(a) controlled substance precursor distributor; or

(b) controlled substance precursor purchaser.

(2) It is unlawful for a person to engage in the distribution, sale, transfer, or in the purchase or obtaining of a controlled substance precursor in a regulated transaction without being licensed or excepted from licensure under this chapter.   1992

58-37c-8. License — Exceptions from licensure or regulation.

(1) Any person engaged in a regulated transaction must be appropriately licensed under this chapter as a regulated distributor and regulated purchaser unless excepted from licensure under this chapter.

(2) The division shall:

(a) establish the form of application for a license, the requirements for licensure, and fees for initial licensure and renewal; and

(b) identify required information to be contained in the application as a condition of licensure.

(3) A practitioner who holds a Utah Controlled Substance License and a Controlled Substance Registration issued by the Drug Enforcement Administration of the U.S. Government is excepted from licensure under this chapter.

(4) Any purchase, sale, transfer, furnishing, or receipt of any drug intended for lawful use in the diagnosis, cure, mitigation, treatment, or prevention of disease in man or other animals, which contains ephedrine, pseudoephedrine, norpseudoephedrine, or phenylpropanolamine if such drug is lawfully purchased, sold, transferred, or furnished as an over-the-counter medication without prescription pursuant to

the federal Food, Drug and Cosmetic Act, 21 USC, Sec. 301 et seq., or regulations adopted thereunder are excepted from licensure, reporting, and recordkeeping under this chapter.

(5) Any purchase, sale, transfer, receipt, or manufacture of any dietary supplement, vitamins, minerals, herbs, or other similar substances including concentrates or extracts, which are not otherwise prohibited by law, which may contain naturally occurring amounts of chemicals or substances listed in this chapter, or in rules adopted pursuant to Title 63, Chapter 46a, Utah Administrative Rulemaking Act, are exempt from licensure under this chapter.

(6) A purchaser of two ounces or less of crystal iodine in a single transaction is not required to be licensed as a regulated purchaser if the transaction complies with Section 58-37c-18.

(7) Any purchase, sale, transfer, receipt, or manufacture of any product that contains any precursor chemical listed in Subsection 58-37c-3(2)(ff) or (gg) and that is not intended for human consumption is exempt from licensure, regulation, or criminal penalties under this chapter. **2000**

58-37c-9. Term of license — Expiration — Renewal.

(1) Each license issued under this chapter shall be issued in accordance with a two-year renewal cycle established by rule. A renewal period may be extended or shortened by as much as one year to maintain established renewal cycles or to change an established renewal cycle.

(2) Each license automatically expires on the expiration date shown on the license unless renewed by the licensee in accordance with Section 58-1-308. **1993**

58-37c-10. Reporting and recordkeeping.

(1) Any person who engages in a regulated transaction, unless excepted under the provisions of Subsections 58-37c-8(3) and (4), shall submit a report with respect to such transaction and shall maintain records of inventories in accordance with rules adopted by the division.

(2) The division shall provide reporting forms upon which regulated transactions shall be reported.

(3) The division shall furnish copies of reports of transactions under this section to appropriate law enforcement agencies.

(4) The division shall adopt rules regulating:

(a) records which shall be maintained and reports which shall be submitted by regulated distributors and regulated purchasers with respect to listed controlled substance precursors obtained, distributed, and held in inventory;

(b) records which shall be maintained and reports which shall be submitted by regulated distributors and regulated purchasers with respect to extraordinary or unusual regulated transactions and a requirement that in such cases the report must be received at least three working days prior to transfer of the listed controlled substance precursor;

(c) identification which must be presented by a purchaser of any listed controlled substance precursor before the sale or transfer can be completed and recordkeeping requirements related to such identification presented;

(d) filing by each licensee the identification of all locations where any listed controlled substance precursor is held in inventory or stored and amending such filing when any change in location is made;

(e) reports and actions which must be taken by a regulated distributor or regulated purchaser in the event of any theft, loss, or shortage of a listed controlled substance precursor;

(f) reports and actions which must be taken by a regulated distributor relating to a regulated transaction with an out-of-state purchaser;

(g) reports and actions which must be taken by a regulated purchaser relating to a regulated transaction with an out-of-state distributor; and

(h) regulated transactions to the extent such regulation is reasonable and necessary to protect the public health, safety, or welfare. **1992**

58-37c-11. Penalty for unlawful conduct.

(1) Any person who violates the unlawful conduct provision defined in Subsections 58-37c-3(12)(a) through (j) is guilty of a class A misdemeanor.

(2) Any person who violates the unlawful conduct provisions defined in Subsection 58-37c-3(12)(k) is guilty of a second degree felony. **1999**

58-37c-12. Grounds for denial of license — Disciplinary proceedings.

Grounds for refusal to issue a license to an applicant, for refusal to renew the license of a licensee, to revoke, suspend, restrict, or place on probation the license of a licensee, to issue a public or private reprimand to a licensee, and to issue cease and desist orders shall be in accordance with Section 58-1-401. **1993**

58-37c-13. License does not authorize possession of controlled substances.

Nothing in the provisions of this chapter shall authorize persons not licensed under provisions of Title 58, Chapter 37, Utah Controlled Substance Act, to distribute, possess, dispense, administer, or otherwise deal in controlled substances as defined in the Utah Controlled Substance Act. **1992**

58-37c-14. Emergency listing provision.

(1) Upon a written finding of cause by the director that the listing of a chemical as a controlled substance precursor is necessary to protect the public health, safety, or welfare, the director may make an emergency listing of that chemical as a controlled substance precursor by adopting a rule pursuant to the provisions of Title 63, Chapter 46a, Utah Administrative Rulemaking Act.

(2) Such listing shall have effect until the close of the next immediately succeeding regular session of the Legislature. In the event the Legislature adopts the chemical as a controlled precursor by amendment to this chapter, the chemical shall remain listed under emergency provisions until the effective date of the amendment.

(3) Any violation of this chapter dealing with a controlled substance precursor listed under the emergency listing provisions of this section shall constitute a violation subject only to civil or administrative penalties. **1992**

58-37c-15. Civil forfeiture.

The following shall be subject to forfeiture in accordance with the procedures and substantive protections of Title 24, Chapter 1, Utah Uniform Forfeiture Procedures Act:

(1) all listed controlled substance precursor chemicals regulated under the provisions of this chapter which have been distributed, possessed, or are intended to be distributed or otherwise transferred in violation of any felony provision of this chapter; and

(2) all property used by any person to facilitate, aid, or otherwise cause the unlawful distribution, transfer, possession, or intent to distribute, transfer, or possess a listed controlled substance precursor chemical in violation of any felony provision of this chapter. 2002

58-37c-16. Civil penalties.

Any person who is a regulated distributor or a regulated purchaser who acts in violation of the provisions of Section 58-37c-10 in addition to any criminal penalties, shall be subject to a civil penalty of not more than $25,000 for each offense. 1992

58-37c-17. Inspection authority.

For the purpose of inspecting, copying, and auditing records and reports required under this chapter and rules adopted pursuant thereto, and for the purpose of inspecting an auditing inventories of listed controlled substance precursors, the director, or his authorized agent, and law enforcement personnel of any federal, state, or local law enforcement agency is authorized to enter the premises of regulated distributors and regulated purchasers during normal business hours to conduct administrative inspections. 1992

58-37c-18. Recordkeeping requirements for sale of crystal iodine.

(1) Any person licensed to engage in a regulated transaction and who sells crystal iodine to another person shall:

(a) comply with the recordkeeping requirements of Section 58-37c-10;

(b) require photo identification of the purchaser;

(c) obtain from the purchaser a signature on a certificate of identification provided by the seller; and

(d) obtain from the purchaser a legible fingerprint, preferably of the right thumb, which shall be placed on the certificate next to the purchaser's signature.

(2) Any failure to comply with Subsection (1) is a class B misdemeanor. 1999

58-37c-19. Possession or sale of crystal iodine.

(1) Any person licensed to engage in a regulated transaction is guilty of a class B misdemeanor who, under circumstances not amounting to a violation of Subsection 58-37d-4(1)(c), offers to sell, sells, or distributes more than two ounces of crystal iodine to another person who is:

(a) not licensed as a regulated purchaser of crystal iodine;

(b) not excepted from licensure; or

(c) not excepted under Subsection (3).

(2) Any person who is not licensed to engage in regulated transactions and not excepted from licensure is guilty of a class A misdemeanor who, under circumstances not amounting to a violation of Subsection 58-37c-3(12)(k) or Subsection 58-37d-4(1)(a):

(a) possesses more than two ounces of crystal iodine; or

(b) offers to sell, sells, or distributes crystal iodine to another.

(3) Subsection (2)(a) does not apply to:

(a) a chemistry laboratory maintained by:

(i) a public or private regularly established secondary school; or

(ii) a public or private institution of higher education that is accredited by a regional or national accrediting agency recognized by the United States Department of Education;

(b) a veterinarian licensed to practice under Title 58, Chapter 28, Veterinary Practice Act; or

(c) a general acute hospital. 2000

58-37c-19.5. Iodine solution greater than 1.5% — Prescription or permit required — Penalties.

(1) As used in this section, "iodine matrix" means iodine at concentrations greater than 1.5% by weight in a matrix or solution.

(2) A person may offer to sell, sell, or distribute an iodine matrix only:

(a) as a prescription drug, pursuant to a prescription issued by a veterinarian or physician licensed within the state; or

(b) to a person who is actively engaged in the legal practice of animal husbandry of livestock, as defined in Section 4-1-8.

(3) Prescriptions issued under this section:

(a) shall provide for a specified number of refills;

(b) may be issued by electronic means, in accordance with Title 58, Chapter 17b, Pharmacy Practice Act; and

(c) may be filled by a person other than the veterinarian or physician issuing the prescription.

(4) A retailer offering iodine matrix for sale:

(a) shall store the iodine matrix so that the public does not have access to the iodine matrix without the direct assistance or intervention of a retail employee;

(b) shall keep a record, which may consist of sales receipts, of each person purchasing iodine matrix; and

(c) may, if necessary to ascertain the identity of the purchaser, ask for proof of identification from the purchaser.

(5) A person engaging in a regulated transaction under Subsection (2) is guilty of a class B misdemeanor if the person, under circumstances not amounting to a violation of Subsection 58-37d-4(1)(c), offers to sell, sells, or distributes an iodine matrix to a person who:

(a) does not present a prescription or is not engaged in animal husbandry, as required under Subsection (2); or

(b) is not excepted under Subsection (7).

(6) A person is guilty of a class A misdemeanor who, under circumstances not amounting to a violation of Subsection 58-37c-3(12)(k) or 58-37d-4(1)(a):

(a) possesses an iodine matrix without proof of obtaining the solution in compliance with Subsection (2); or

(b) offers to sell, sells, or distributes an iodine matrix in violation of Subsection (2).

(7) Subsection (6)(a) does not apply to:

(a) a chemistry or chemistry-related laboratory maintained by:

(i) a public or private regularly established secondary school; or

(ii) a public or private institution of higher education that is accredited by a regional or national accrediting agency recognized by the United States Department of Education;

(b) a veterinarian licensed to practice under Title 58, Chapter 28, Veterinary Practice Act;

(c) a general acute hospital; or

(d) a veterinarian, physician, pharmacist, retail distributor, wholesaler, manufacturer, warehouseman, or common carrier, or an agent of any

of these persons who possesses an iodine matrix in the regular course of lawful business activities.
2004

58-37c-19.7. Red phosphorus is a precursor — Affirmative defense.

(1) A person is guilty of a class A misdemeanor who is not licensed to engage in a regulated transaction and is not excepted from licensure who, under circumstances not amounting to a violation of Subsection 58-37c-3(12)(k) or 58-37d-4(1)(a), possesses any amount of red phosphorus.

(2) It is an affirmative defense to a charge under Subsection (1) that the person in possession of red phosphorus:

(a) is conducting a licensed business which involves red phosphorus in the manufacture of any of the following:

(i) the striking surface used for lighting matches, which is sometimes referred to as the striker plate;

(ii) flame retardant in polymers; or

(iii) fireworks, for which the person or entity possesses a federal license to manufacture explosives as required under 27 CFR Chapter 1, Part 55, Commerce in Explosives; or

(b) (i) is a wholesaler, manufacturer, warehouseman, or common carrier handling red phosphorus, or is an agent of any of these persons; and

(ii) possesses the substances in the regular course of lawful business activities.

(3) (a) The defendant shall provide written notice of intent to claim an affirmative defense under this section as soon as practicable, but not later than ten days prior to trial. The court may waive the notice requirement in the interest of justice for good cause shown, if the prosecutor is not unfairly prejudiced by the lack of timely notice.

(b) The notice shall include the specifics of the affirmative defense.

(c) The defendant shall establish the affirmative defense by a preponderance of the evidence. If the defense is established, it is a complete defense to the charges.

(4) Subsection (1) does not apply to:

(a) a chemistry or chemistry-related laboratory maintained by:

(i) a public or private regularly established secondary school; or

(ii) a public or private institution of higher education that is accredited by a regional or national accrediting agency recognized by the United States Department of Education; or

(b) a retail distributor, wholesaler, manufacturer, warehouseman, or common carrier, or an agent of any of these persons who possesses red phosphorus in the regular course of lawful business activities.
2000

58-37c-19.9. Anhydrous ammonia is a precursor — Requirements regarding purposes and containers.

(1) A person is guilty of a class A misdemeanor who is not licensed to engage in a regulated transaction and is not excepted from licensure or exempted under Subsection (2), and who possesses any amount of anhydrous ammonia under circumstances not amounting to a violation of Subsection 58-37c-3(12)(k) or 58-37d-4(1)(a).

(2) A person who possesses anhydrous ammonia has an affirmative defense to a charge under Subsection (1) if the person is:

(a) directly involved in or actively operating land in agricultural use as defined in Section 59-2-502;

(b) a retail distributor, wholesaler, manufacturer, warehouseman, or common carrier, or an agent of any of these persons, who possesses anhydrous ammonia in the regular course of lawful business activities;

(c) directly involved in or actively operating a business or other lawful activity providing or using anhydrous ammonia for refrigeration applications; or

(d) directly involved in or actively operating a lawful business enterprise, including an industrial enterprise, that uses anhydrous ammonia in the regular course of its business activities.
2000

58-37c-20. Possession of ephedrine or pseudoephedrine — Penalties.

(1) Any person who is not licensed to engage in regulated transactions and not excepted from licensure who, under circumstances not amounting to a violation of Subsection 58-37c-3(12)(k) or Subsection 58-37d-4(1)(a), possesses more than 12 grams of ephedrine or pseudoephedrine, their salts, isomers, or salts of isomers, or a combination of any of these substances, is guilty of a class A misdemeanor.

(2) (a) It is an affirmative defense to a charge under Subsection (1) that the person in possession of ephedrine or pseudoephedrine, or a combination of these two substances:

(i) is a physician, pharmacist, retail distributor, wholesaler, manufacturer, warehouseman, or common carrier, or an agent of any of these persons; and

(ii) possesses the substances in the regular course of lawful business activities.

(b) (i) The defendant shall provide written notice of intent to claim an affirmative defense under this section as soon as practicable, but not later than ten days prior to trial. The court may waive the notice requirement in the interest of justice for good cause shown, if the prosecutor is not unfairly prejudiced by the lack of timely notice.

(ii) The notice shall include the specifics of the asserted defense.

(iii) The defendant shall establish the affirmative defense by a preponderance of the evidence. If the defense is established, it is a complete defense to the charges.

(3) This section does not apply to dietary supplements, herbs, or other natural products, including concentrates or extracts, which:

(a) are not otherwise prohibited by law; and

(b) may contain naturally occurring ephedrine, ephedrine alkaloids, or pseudoephedrine, or their salts, isomers, or salts of isomers, or a combination of these substances, that:

(i) are contained in a matrix of organic material; and

(ii) do not exceed 15% of the total weight of the natural product.
2000

58-37c-21. Department of Public Safety enforcement authority.

(1) As used in this section, "division" means the Criminal Investigations and Technical Services Division of the Department of Public Safety, created in Section 53-10-103.

(2) The division has authority to enforce this chapter. To carry out this purpose, the division may:

(a) inspect, copy, and audit records, inventories of controlled substance precursors, and reports required under this chapter and rules adopted under this chapter;

(b) enter the premises of regulated distributors and regulated purchasers during normal business hours to conduct administrative inspections;

(c) assist the law enforcement agencies of the state in enforcing this chapter;

(d) conduct investigations to enforce this chapter;

(e) present evidence obtained from investigations conducted in conjunction with appropriate county and district attorneys and the Office of the Attorney General for civil or criminal prosecution or for administrative action against a licensee; and

(f) work in cooperation with the Division of Occupational and Professional Licensing, created under Section 58-1-103, to accomplish the purposes of this section.   1999

CHAPTER 37d

CLANDESTINE DRUG LAB ACT

58-37d-1.   Short title.

This act shall be known as the "Clandestine Drug Lab Act."   1992

58-37d-2.   Purpose.

The clandestine production of methamphetamine, other amphetamines, phencyclidine, narcotic analgesic analogs so called "designer drugs", various hallucinogens, cocaine and methamphetamine base "crack" cocaine and methamphetamine "ice" respectively, has increased dramatically throughout the western states and Utah. These highly technical illegal operations create substantial dangers to the general public and environment from fire, explosions, and the release of toxic chemicals. By their very nature these activities often involve a number of persons in a conspiratorial enterprise to bring together all necessary components for clandestine production, to thwart regulation and detection, and to distribute the final product. Therefore, the Legislature enacts the following Utah Clandestine Laboratory Act for prosecution of specific illegal laboratory operations. With regard to the controlled substances specified herein, this act shall control, notwithstanding the prohibitions and penalties in Title 58, Chapter 37, Utah Controlled Substances Act.   1992

58-37d-3.   Definitions.

(1) As used in this chapter:

(a) "Booby trap" means any concealed or camouflaged device designed to cause bodily injury when triggered by any action of a person making contact with the device. This term includes guns, ammunition, or explosive devices attached to trip wires or other triggering mechanisms, sharpened stakes, nails, spikes, electrical devices, lines or wires with hooks attached, and devices for the production of toxic fumes or gases.

(b) "Clandestine laboratory operation" means the:

(i) purchase or procurement of chemicals, supplies, equipment, or laboratory location for the illegal manufacture of specified controlled substances;

(ii) transportation or arranging for the transportation of chemicals, supplies, or equipment for the illegal manufacture of specified controlled substances;

(iii) setting up of equipment or supplies in preparation for the illegal manufacture of specified controlled substances;

(iv) activity of compounding, synthesis, concentration, purification, separation, extraction, or other physical or chemical processing of any substance, including a controlled substance precursor, or the packaging, repackaging, labeling, or relabeling of a container holding a substance that is a product of any of these activities, when the substance is to be used for the illegal manufacture of specified controlled substances;

(v) illegal manufacture of specified controlled substances; or

(vi) distribution or disposal of chemicals, equipment, supplies, or products used in or produced by the illegal manufacture of specified controlled substances.

(c) "Controlled substance precursor" means those chemicals designated in Title 58, Chapter 37c, Controlled Substance Precursor Act, except those substances designated in Subsections 58-37c-3(2)(kk) and (ll).

(d) "Disposal" means the abandonment, discharge, deposit, injection, dumping, spilling, leaking, or placing of any hazardous or dangerous material into or on any property, land or water so that the material may enter the environment, be emitted into the air, or discharged into any waters, including groundwater.

(e) "Hazardous or dangerous material" means any substance which because of its quantity, concentration, physical characteristics, or chemical characteristics may cause or significantly contribute to an increase in mortality, an increase in serious illness, or may pose a substantial present or potential future hazard to human health or the environment when improperly treated, stored, transported, disposed of, or otherwise improperly managed.

(f) "Illegal manufacture of specified controlled substances" means in violation of Title 58, Chapter 37, Utah Controlled Substances Act, the:

(i) compounding, synthesis, concentration, purification, separation, extraction, or other physical or chemical processing for the purpose of producing methamphetamine, other amphetamine compounds as listed in Schedule I of the Utah Controlled Substances Act, phencyclidine, narcotic analgesic analogs as listed in Schedule I of the Utah Controlled Substances Act, lysergic acid diethylamide, or mescaline;

    (ii) conversion of cocaine or methamphetamine to their base forms; or

    (iii) extraction, concentration, or synthesis of marijuana as that drug is defined in Section 58-37-2.

(2) Unless otherwise specified, the definitions in Section 58-37-2 also apply to this chapter.   2003

58-37d-4. Prohibited acts — Second degree felony.

(1) It is unlawful for any person to knowingly or intentionally:

    (a) possess a controlled substance precursor with the intent to engage in a clandestine laboratory operation;

    (b) possess laboratory equipment or supplies with the intent to engage in a clandestine laboratory operation;

    (c) sell, distribute, or otherwise supply a precursor chemical, laboratory equipment, or laboratory supplies knowing or having reasonable cause to believe it will be used for a clandestine laboratory operation;

    (d) evade recordkeeping provisions of Title 58, Chapter 37c, Utah Controlled Substance Precursor Act, or the regulations issued under that act, knowing or having reasonable cause to believe that the material distributed or received will be used for a clandestine laboratory operation;

    (e) conspire with or aid another to engage in a clandestine laboratory operation;

    (f) produce or manufacture, or possess with intent to produce or manufacture a controlled or counterfeit substance except as authorized under Title 58, Chapter 37, Utah Controlled Substances Act;

    (g) transport or convey a controlled or counterfeit substance with the intent to distribute or to be distributed by the person transporting or conveying the controlled or counterfeit substance or by any other person regardless of whether the final destination for the distribution is within this state or any other location; or

    (h) engage in compounding, synthesis, concentration, purification, separation, extraction, or other physical or chemical processing of any substance, including a controlled substance precursor, or the packaging, repackaging, labeling, or relabeling of a container holding a substance that is a product of any of these activities, knowing or having reasonable cause to believe that the substance is a product of any of these activities and will be used in the illegal manufacture of specified controlled substances.

(2) A person who violates any provision of Subsection (1) is guilty of a second degree felony.   2004

58-37d-5. Prohibited acts — First degree felony.

(1) A person who violates Subsection 58-37d-4(1)(a), (b), (e), (f), or (h) is guilty of a first degree felony if the trier of fact also finds any one of the following conditions occurred in conjunction with that violation:

    (a) possession of a firearm;

    (b) use of a booby trap;

    (c) illegal possession, transportation, or disposal of hazardous or dangerous material or while transporting or causing to be transported materials in furtherance of a clandestine laboratory operation, there was created a substantial risk to

human health or safety or a danger to the environment;

    (d) intended laboratory operation was to take place or did take place within 500 feet of a residence, place of business, church, or school;

    (e) clandestine laboratory operation actually produced any amount of a specified controlled substance; or

    (f) intended clandestine laboratory operation was for the production of cocaine base or methamphetamine base.

(2) If the trier of fact finds that two or more of the conditions listed in Subsections (1)(a) through (f) of this section occurred in conjunction with the violation, at sentencing for the first degree felony:

    (a) probation shall not be granted;

    (b) the execution or imposition of sentence shall not be suspended; and

    (c) the court shall not enter a judgment for a lower category of offense.   2003

58-37d-6. Legal inference of intent — Illegal possession of a controlled substance precursor or clandestine laboratory equipment.

The trier of fact may infer that the defendant intended to engage in a clandestine laboratory operation if the defendant:

    (1) is in illegal possession of a controlled substance precursor; or

    (2) illegally possesses or attempts to illegally possess a controlled substance precursor and is in possession of any one of the following pieces of equipment:

    (a) glass reaction vessel;

    (b) separatory funnel;

    (c) glass condenser;

    (d) analytical balance; or

    (e) heating mantle.   1992

58-37d-7. Seizure and forfeiture.

Chemicals, equipment, supplies, vehicles, aircraft, vessels, and personal and real property used in furtherance of a clandestine laboratory operation are subject to seizure and forfeiture under the procedures and substantive protections of Title 24, Chapter 1, Utah Uniform Forfeiture Procedures Act.   2002

58-37d-8. Applicability of Title 76 prosecutions under this chapter.

Unless specifically excluded in or inconsistent with the provisions of this chapter, the provisions of Title 76, Chapters 1, 2, 3, and 4, are fully applicable to prosecutions under this chapter.   1997

58-37d-9. Department of Public Safety enforcement authority.

(1) As used in this section, "division" means the Criminal Investigations and Technical Services Division of the Department of Public Safety, created in Section 53-10-103.

(2) The division has authority to enforce this chapter. To carry out this purpose, the division may:

    (a) assist the law enforcement agencies of the state in enforcing this chapter;

    (b) conduct investigations to enforce this chapter;

    (c) present evidence obtained from investigations conducted in conjunction with appropriate county and district attorneys and the Office of the Attorney General for civil or criminal prosecution or for administrative action against a licensee; and

(d) work in cooperation with the Division of Occupational and Professional Licensing, created under Section 58-1-103, to accomplish the purposes of this section.   1999

CHAPTER 37e

DRUG DEALER'S LIABILITY ACT

58-37e-1.   Title.

This chapter is known as the "Drug Dealer's Liability Act."   1997

58-37e-2.   Definitions.

As used in this chapter:

(1) "Illegal drug" means a drug or controlled substance whose distribution is a violation of state law.

(2) "Illegal drug market" means the support system of illegal drug-related operations, from production to retail sales, through which an illegal drug reaches the user.

(3) "Illegal drug market target community" is the area described in Section 58-37e-7.

(4) "Individual drug user" means the individual whose illegal drug use is the basis of an action brought under this chapter.

(5) "Level 1 offense" means possession of 16 ounces or more or distribution of four ounces or more of a mixture containing a specified illegal drug or possession of 16 pounds or more or 100 plants or more or distribution of ten pounds or more of marijuana.

(6) "Level 2 offense" means possession of eight ounces or more, but less than 16 ounces, or distribution of two ounces or more, but less than four ounces, of a mixture containing a specified illegal drug or possession of eight pounds or more or 75 plants or more, but less than 16 pounds or 100 plants, or distribution of more than five pounds, but less than ten pounds of marijuana.

(7) "Level 3 offense" means possession of four ounces or more, but less than eight ounces, or distribution of one ounce or more, but less than two ounces, of a mixture containing a specified illegal drug or possession of four pounds or more or 50 plants or more, but less than eight pounds or 75 plants, or distribution of more than one pound, but less than five pounds of marijuana.

(8) "Level 4 offense" means possession of ¼ ounce or more, but less than four ounces, or distribution of less than one ounce of a mixture containing a specified illegal drug or possession of one pound or more or 25 plants or more, but less than four pounds or 50 plants, or distribution of less than one pound of marijuana.

(9) "Participate in the illegal drug market" means to distribute, possess with an intent to distribute, commit an act intended to facilitate the marketing or distribution of, or agree to distribute, possess with an intent to distribute, or commit an act intended to facilitate the marketing and distribution of an illegal drug. "Participate in the illegal drug market" does not include the purchase or receipt of an illegal drug for personal use only.

(10) "Period of illegal drug use" means, in relation to the individual drug user, the time of the individual's first use of an illegal drug to the accrual of the cause of the action. The period of illegal drug use is presumed to commence two years before the cause of action accrues unless the defendant proves otherwise by clear and convincing evidence.

(11) "Person" means an individual, governmental entity, corporation, firm, trust, partnership, or incorporated or unincorporated association, existing under or authorized by the laws of this state, another state, or foreign country.

(12) "Place of illegal drug activity" means, in relation to the individual drug user, each county in which the individual possesses or uses an illegal drug or in which the individual resides, attends school, or is employed during the period of the individual's illegal drug use, unless the defendant proves otherwise by clear and convincing evidence.

(13) "Place of participation" means, in relation to a defendant in an action brought under this chapter, each county in which the person participates in the illegal drug market or in which the person resides, attends school, or is employed during the period of the person's participation in the illegal drug market.

(14) "Specified illegal drug" means cocaine, heroin, or methamphetamine and any other controlled substance the distribution of which is a violation of state law.   1997

58-37e-3.   Liability for participation in the illegal drug market.

(1) A person who knowingly participates in the illegal drug market within this state is liable for civil damages as provided in this chapter. A person may recover damages under this chapter for injury resulting from an individual's use of an illegal drug.

(2) A law enforcement officer or agency, the state, or a person acting at the direction of a law enforcement officer or agency or the state is not liable for participating in the illegal drug market, if the participation is in furtherance of an official investigation.   1997

58-37e-4.   Recovery of damages.

(1) One or more of the following persons may bring an action for damages caused by an individual's use of an illegal drug:

(a) a parent, legal guardian, child, spouse, or sibling of the individual drug user;

(b) an individual who was exposed to an illegal drug in utero;

(c) an employer of the individual drug user;

(d) a medical facility, insurer, governmental entity, employer, or other entity that funds a drug treatment program or employee assistance program for the individual drug user or that otherwise expended money on behalf of the individual drug user; or

(e) a person injured as a result of the willful, reckless, or negligent actions of an individual drug user.

(2) A person entitled to bring an action under this section may seek damages from one or more of the following:

(a) a person who knowingly distributed, or knowingly participated in the chain of distribution of, an illegal drug that was actually used by the individual drug user;

(b) a person who knowingly participated in the illegal drug market if:

(i) the place of illegal drug activity by the individual drug user is within the illegal drug market target community of the defendant;

(ii) the defendant's participation in the illegal drug market was connected with the same type of illegal drug used by the individual drug user; and

(iii) the defendant participated in the illegal drug market at any time during the individual drug user's period of illegal drug use.

(3) A person entitled to bring an action under this section may recover all of the following damages:

(a) economic damages, including the cost of treatment and rehabilitation, medical expenses, loss of economic or educational potential, loss of productivity, absenteeism, support expenses, accidents or injury, and any other pecuniary loss proximately caused by the illegal drug use;

(b) noneconomic damages, including physical and emotional pain, suffering, physical impairment, emotional distress, mental anguish, disfigurement, loss of enjoyment, loss of companionship, services and consortium, and other nonpecuniary losses proximately caused by an individual's use of an illegal drug;

(c) exemplary damages;

(d) reasonable attorney's fees; and

(e) costs of suit, including reasonable expenses for expert testimony.   1997

58-37e-5. Limited recovery of damages.

(1) An individual drug user may not bring an action for damages caused by the use of an illegal drug, except as otherwise provided in this section. An individual drug user may bring an action for damages caused by the use of an illegal drug only if all of the following conditions are met:

(a) the individual personally discloses to narcotics enforcement authorities, more than six months before filing the action, all of the information known to the individual regarding all that individual's sources of illegal drugs;

(b) the individual has not used an illegal drug within the six months before filing the action; and

(c) the individual continues to remain free of the use of an illegal drug throughout the pendency of the action.

(2) A person entitled to bring an action under this section may seek damages only from a person who distributed, or is in the chain of distribution of, an illegal drug that was actually used by the individual drug user.

(3) A person entitled to bring an action under this section may recover only the following damages:

(a) economic damages, including the cost of treatment, rehabilitation, and medical expenses, loss of economic or educational potential, loss of productivity, absenteeism, accidents or injury, and any other pecuniary loss proximately caused by the person's illegal drug use;

(b) reasonable attorney's fees; and

(c) costs of suit, including reasonable expenses for expert testimony.   1997

58-37e-6. Third party cases.

A third party may not pay damages awarded under this chapter, or provide a defense or money for a defense, on behalf of an insured under a contract of insurance or indemnification.   1997

58-37e-7. Illegal drug market target community.

A person whose participation in the illegal drug market constitutes the following level offense shall be considered to have the following illegal drug market target community:

(1) Level 4: the county in which the defendant's place of participation is situated;

(2) Level 3: the target community described in Subsection (1) plus all counties with a border contiguous to that target community;

(3) Level 2: the target community described in Subsection (2) plus all counties with a border contiguous to that target community;

(4) Level 1: the state.   1997

58-37e-8. Joinder of parties.

(1) Two or more persons may join in one action under this chapter as plaintiffs if their respective actions have at least one place of illegal drug activity in common and if any portion of the period of illegal drug use overlaps with the period of illegal drug use for every other plaintiff.

(2) Two or more persons may be joined in one action under this chapter as defendants if those persons are liable to at least one plaintiff.

(3) A plaintiff need not be interested in obtaining and a defendant need not be interested in defending against all the relief demanded. Judgment may be given for one or more plaintiffs according to their respective rights to relief and against one or more defendants according to their respective liabilities.   1997

58-37e-9. Comparative responsibility.

(1) An action by an individual drug user is governed by the principles of comparative responsibility. Comparative responsibility attributed to the plaintiff does not bar recovery but diminishes the award of compensatory damages proportionally, according to the measure of responsibility attributed to the plaintiff.

(2) The burden of proving the comparative responsibility of the plaintiff is on the defendant, which shall be shown by clear and convincing evidence.

(3) Comparative responsibility may not be applied in an action brought by a third party who was not an individual drug user.   1997

58-37e-10. Contribution among and recovery from multiple defendants.

A person subject to liability under this chapter has a right of action for contribution against another person subject to liability under this chapter. Contribution may be enforced either in the original action or by a separate action brought for that purpose. A plaintiff may seek recovery in accordance with this chapter and existing law against a person whom a defendant has asserted a right of contribution.   1997

58-37e-11. Standard of proof — Effect of criminal drug conviction.

(1) Proof of participation in the illegal drug market in an action brought under this chapter shall be shown by clear and convincing evidence. Except as otherwise provided in this chapter, other elements of the cause of action shall be shown by a preponderance of the evidence.

(2) A person against whom recovery is sought who has a criminal conviction pursuant to state drug laws or the Comprehensive Drug Abuse Prevention and Control Act of 1970, Pub. L. 91-513, 84 Stat. 1236, codified at 21 U.S.C. Sec. 801 et seq., is estopped from denying participation in the illegal drug market. A conviction is also prima facie evidence of the person's participation in the illegal drug market during the two years preceding the date of an act giving rise to a conviction.

(3) The absence of a criminal drug conviction of a person against whom recovery is sought does not bar an action against that person.   1997

58-37e-12. Prejudgment attachment and execution on judgments.

(1) A plaintiff under this chapter, subject to Subsection (3), may request an ex parte prejudgment writ of attachment from the court pursuant to Utah Rules of Civil Procedure, Rule 64A against all assets of a defendant sufficient to satisfy a potential award. If attachment is instituted, a defendant is entitled to an immediate hearing. Attachment may be lifted if the defendant demonstrates that the assets will be available for a potential award or if the defendant posts a bond sufficient to cover a potential award.

(2) A person against whom a judgment has been rendered under this chapter is not eligible to exempt any property, of whatever kind, from process to levy or process to execute on the judgment, unless the property is exempt by operation of law.

(3) Any assets sought to satisfy a judgment under this chapter that are named in a forfeiture action or have been seized for forfeiture by any state or federal agency may not be used to satisfy a judgment unless and until the assets have been released following the conclusion of the forfeiture action or released by the agency that seized the assets.   1997

58-37e-13. Statute of limitations.

(1) Except as otherwise provided in this section, a claim under this chapter may not be brought more than two years after the cause of action accrues. A cause of action accrues under this chapter when a person who may recover has reason to know of the harm from illegal drug use that is the basis for the cause of action and has reason to know that the illegal drug use is the cause of the harm.

(2) (a) For a plaintiff, the statute of limitations under this section is tolled while the individual potential plaintiff is incapacitated by the use of an illegal drug to the extent that the individual cannot reasonably be expected to seek recovery under this chapter or as otherwise provided by law.

(b) For a defendant, the statute of limitations under this section is tolled until six months after the individual potential defendant is convicted of a criminal drug offense or as otherwise provided by law.

(3) The statute of limitations under this chapter for a claim based on participation in the illegal drug market that occurred prior to the effective date of this chapter does not begin to run until the effective date of this chapter.   1997

58-37e-14. Representation of governmental entities — Stay of action.

(1) A county attorney, district attorney, or city attorney may represent any political subdivision of the state, and the attorney general may represent the state in an action brought under this chapter.

(2) On motion by a governmental agency involved in a drug investigation or prosecution, an action brought under this chapter shall be stayed until the completion of the criminal investigation or prosecution that gave rise to the motion for a stay of the action.   1997

CHAPTER 63

SECURITY PERSONNEL LICENSING ACT

Part 3

Licensing

PART 3

LICENSING

58-63-301. Licensure required — License classifications.

(1) A license is required to engage in the practice of a contract security company, armed private security officer, or unarmed private security officer, except as specifically provided in Section 58-63-304, 58-63-310, or 58-1-307.

(2) The division shall issue to a person who qualifies under this chapter a license in the classifications:

(a) contract security company;

(b) armed private security officer; or

(c) unarmed private security officer.   2001

58-63-302. Qualifications for licensure.

(1) Each applicant for licensure as a contract security company shall:

(a) submit an application in a form prescribed by the division;

(b) pay a fee determined by the department under Section 63-38-3.2;

(c) have a qualifying agent who is a resident of the state and an officer, director, partner, proprietor, or manager of the applicant who:

(i) passes an examination component established by rule by the division in collaboration with the board; and

(ii) (A) demonstrates 6,000 hours of experience as a manager, supervisor, or administrator of a contract security company; or

(B) demonstrates 6,000 hours of supervisory experience acceptable to the division in collaboration with the board with a federal, United States military, state, county, or municipal law enforcement agency;

(d) if a corporation, provide:

(i) the names, addresses, dates of birth, and Social Security numbers of all corporate officers, directors, and those responsible management personnel employed within the state or having direct responsibility for managing operations of the applicant within the state; and

(ii) the names, addresses, dates of birth, and Social Security numbers, of all shareholders owning 5% or more of the outstanding shares of the corporation, except this may not be required if the stock is publicly listed and traded;

(e) if a limited liability company, provide:

(i) the names, addresses, dates of birth, and Social Security numbers of all company officers, and those responsible management personnel employed within the state or having direct responsibility for managing operations of the applicant within the state; and

(ii) the names, addresses, dates of birth, and Social Security numbers of all individuals owning 5% or more of the equity of the company;

(f) if a partnership, the names, addresses, dates of birth, and Social Security numbers of all general partners, and those responsible management personnel employed within the state or having direct responsibility for managing operations of the applicant within the state;

(g) if a proprietorship, the names, addresses, dates of birth, and Social Security numbers of the proprietor, and those responsible management personnel employed within the state or having direct responsibility for managing operations of the applicant within the state;

(h) be of good moral character in that officers, directors, shareholders described in Subsection (1)(d)(ii), partners, proprietors, and responsible management personnel have not been convicted of a felony, a misdemeanor involving moral turpitude, or any other crime that when considered with the duties and responsibilities of a contract security company is considered by the division and the board to indicate that the best interests of the public are not served by granting the applicant a license;

(i) document that none of the applicant's officers, directors, shareholders described in Subsection (1)(d)(ii), partners, proprietors, and responsible management personnel:

(i) have been declared by any court of competent jurisdiction incompetent by reason of mental defect or disease and not been restored; and

(ii) currently suffer from habitual drunkenness or from drug addiction or dependence;

(j) file and maintain with the division evidence of:

(i) comprehensive general liability insurance in form and in amounts to be established by rule by the division in collaboration with the board;

(ii) workers' compensation insurance that covers employees of the applicant in accordance with applicable Utah law;

(iii) registration with the Division of Corporations and Commercial Code; and

(iv) registration as required by applicable law with the:

(A) Unemployment Insurance Division in the Department of Workforce Services, for purposes of Title 35A, Chapter 4, Employment Security Act;

(B) State Tax Commission; and

(C) Internal Revenue Service; and

(k) meet with the division and board if requested by the division or board.

(2) Each applicant for licensure as an armed private security officer shall:

(a) submit an application in a form prescribed by the division;

(b) pay a fee determined by the department under Section 63-38-3.2;

(c) be of good moral character in that the applicant has not been convicted of a felony, a misdemeanor involving moral turpitude, or any other crime that when considered with the duties and responsibilities of an armed private security officer is considered by the division and the board to indicate that the best interests of the public are not served by granting the applicant a license;

(d) not have been declared by any court of competent jurisdiction incompetent by reason of mental defect or disease and not been restored;

(e) not be currently suffering from habitual drunkenness or from drug addiction or dependence;

(f) successfully complete basic education and training requirements established by rule by the division in collaboration with the board;

(g) successfully complete firearms training requirements established by rule by the division in collaboration with the board;

(h) pass the examination requirement established by rule by the division in collaboration with the board; and

(i) meet with the division and board if requested by the division or the board.

(3) Each applicant for licensure as an unarmed private security officer shall:

(a) submit an application in a form prescribed by the division;

(b) pay a fee determined by the department under Section 63-38-3.2;

(c) be of good moral character in that the applicant has not been convicted of a felony, a misdemeanor involving moral turpitude, or any other crime that when considered with the duties and responsibilities of an unarmed private security officer is considered by the division and the board to indicate that the best interests of the public are not served by granting the applicant a license;

(d) not have been declared by any court of competent jurisdiction incompetent by reason of mental defect or disease and not been restored;

(e) not be currently suffering from habitual drunkenness or from drug addiction or dependence;

(f) successfully complete basic education and training requirements established by rule by the division in collaboration with the board;

(g) pass the examination requirement established by rule by the division in collaboration with the board; and

(h) meet with the division and board if requested by the division or board.

(4) In accordance with Title 63, Chapter 46a, Utah Administrative Rulemaking Act, the division may make rules establishing when Federal Bureau of Investigation records shall be checked for applicants.

(5) To determine if an applicant meets the qualifications of Subsections (1)(h), (2)(c), and (3)(c), the division shall provide an appropriate number of copies of fingerprint cards to the Department of Public Safety with the division's request to:

(a) conduct a search of records of the Department of Public Safety for criminal history information relating to each applicant for licensure under this chapter and each applicant's officers, directors, shareholders described in Subsection (1)(d)(ii), partners, proprietors, and responsible management personnel; and

(b) forward to the Federal Bureau of Investigation a fingerprint card of each applicant requiring a check of records of the F.B.I. for criminal history information under this section.

(6) The Department of Public Safety shall send to the division:

(a) a written record of criminal history, or certification of no criminal history record, as contained in the records of the Department of Public Safety in a timely manner after receipt of a fingerprint card from the division and a request for review of Department of Public Safety records; and

(b) the results of the F.B.I. review concerning an applicant in a timely manner after receipt of information from the F.B.I.

(7) (a) The division shall charge each applicant a fee, in accordance with Section 63-38-3.2, equal to the cost of performing the records reviews under this section.

(b) The division shall pay the Department of Public Safety the costs of all records reviews, and the Department of Public Safety shall pay the F.B.I. the costs of records reviews under this chapter.

(8) Information obtained by the division from the reviews of criminal history records of the Department of Public Safety and the F.B.I. shall be used or disseminated by the division only for the purpose of determining if an applicant for licensure under this chapter is qualified for licensure. 2005

58-63-303. Term of license — Expiration — Renewal.

(1) The division shall issue each license under this chapter in accordance with a two-year renewal cycle established by rule. The division may by rule extend or shorten a renewal period by as much as one year to stagger the renewal cycles it administers.

(2) Each license automatically expires on the expiration date shown on the license unless the licensee renews it in accordance with Section 58-1-308. 1995

58-63-304. Exemptions from licensure.

(1) In addition to the exemptions from licensure in Section 58-1-307, the following individuals may engage in acts regulated under this chapter without being licensed under this chapter:

(a) a peace officer employed by or licensed as a contract security company; and

(b) a person employed by a contract security company for the sole purpose of operating or staffing security apparatus, including a magnetometer, magnetometer wand, x-ray viewing device, or other device approved by rule of the division.

(2) In accordance with Title 63, Chapter 46a, Utah Administrative Rulemaking Act, the division may make rules approving security apparatus under Subsection (1)(b). 2005

58-63-305. Status of licenses held on the effective date of this chapter.

An individual holding a valid Utah license as a contract security company, armed private security officer, or unarmed private security officer under Title 53, Chapter 5, Part 4, Security Personnel Licensing and Regulation Act, on July 1, 1995, is:

(1) on or after July 1, 1995, considered to hold a current license under this chapter in the comparable classification of contract security company, armed private security officer, or unarmed private security officer; and

(2) subject to this chapter. 2001

58-63-306. Replacement of qualifying agent.

If the qualifying agent of a contract security company ceases to perform the agent's duties on a regular basis, the licensee shall notify the division within 15 days by registered or certified mail, and shall replace the qualifying agent within 30 days after the time required for notification to the division. 1995

58-63-307. Use of firearms.

(1) An individual licensed as an armed private security officer may carry a firearm only while acting as an armed private security officer in accordance with this chapter and rules made under this chapter.

(2) An individual licensed as an armed private security officer is exempt from the provisions of Sections 76-10-505 and 53-5-704 while acting as an armed private security officer in accordance with this chapter and rules made under this chapter. 1995

58-63-308. Evidence of licensure.

An individual licensed as an armed private security officer or unarmed private security officer shall:

(1) carry a copy of the individual's license on the individual's person at all times while acting as a licensee; and

(2) display the license upon the request of a peace officer, a representative of the division, or a member of the public. 2001

58-63-309. Operating standards — Rulemaking.

The division in collaboration with the board shall establish by rule operating standards that shall apply to the conduct of licensees under this chapter, including rules relating to use of uniforms, badges, insignia, designations, and representations used by or associated with a licensees practice under this chapter. 1995

58-63-310. Interim permits.

(1) Upon receipt of a complete application for licensure in accordance with Section 58-63-302, an applicant for licensure as an armed private security officer or unarmed private security officer may be issued an interim permit.

(2) (a) Each interim permit shall expire 90 days after it is issued or on the date on which the applicant is issued a license, whichever is earlier.

(b) The division may reissue an interim permit if the delay in approving a license is beyond the control or influence of the interim permit holder.

(3) An interim permit holder may engage in the scope of practice defined for the license classification that the interim permit holder is seeking. 2001

TITLE 59

REVENUE AND TAXATION

CHAPTER 13

MOTOR AND SPECIAL FUEL TAX ACT

Part 3

Special Fuel

PART 3

SPECIAL FUEL

59-13-301. Tax basis — Rate — Exemptions — Revenue deposited with treasurer and credited to Transportation Fund — Reduction of tax in limited circumstances.

(1) (a) Except as provided in Subsections (2), (3), and (11) and Section 59-13-304, a tax is imposed at the same rate imposed under Subsection 59-13-201(1)(a) on the:

(i) removal of undyed diesel fuel from any refinery;

(ii) removal of undyed diesel fuel from any terminal;

(iii) entry into the state of any undyed diesel fuel for consumption, use, sale, or warehousing;

(iv) sale of undyed diesel fuel to any person who is not registered as a supplier under this part unless the tax has been collected under this section;

(v) any untaxed special fuel blended with undyed diesel fuel; or

(vi) use of untaxed special fuel, other than a clean special fuel.

(b) The tax imposed under this section shall only be imposed once upon any special fuel.

(2) (a) No special fuel tax is imposed or collected upon dyed diesel fuel which:

(i) is sold or used for any purpose other than to operate or propel a motor vehicle upon the public highways of the state, but this exemption applies only in those cases where the purchasers or the users of special fuel establish to the satisfaction of the commission that the special fuel was used for purposes other than to operate a motor vehicle upon the public highways of the state; or

(ii) is sold to this state or any of its political subdivisions.

(b) No special fuel tax is imposed on undyed diesel fuel which:

(i) is sold to the United States government or any of its instrumentalities or to this state or any of its political subdivisions;

(ii) is exported from this state if proof of actual exportation on forms prescribed by the commission is made within 180 days after exportation;

(iii) is used in a vehicle off-highway;

(iv) is used to operate a power take-off unit of a vehicle;

(v) is used for off-highway agricultural uses;

(vi) is used in a separately fueled engine on a vehicle that does not propel the vehicle upon the highways of the state; or

(vii) is used in machinery and equipment not registered and not required to be registered for highway use.

(3) No tax is imposed or collected on special fuel if it is:

(a) purchased for business use in machinery and equipment not registered and not required to be registered for highway use; and

(b) used pursuant to the conditions of a state implementation plan approved under Title 19, Chapter 2, Air Conservation Act.

(4) Upon request of a buyer meeting the requirements under Subsection (3), the Division of Air Quality shall issue an exemption certificate that may be shown to a seller.

(5) The special fuel tax shall be paid by the supplier.

(6) (a) The special fuel tax shall be paid by every user who is required by Sections 59-13-303 and 59-13-305 to obtain a special fuel user permit and file special fuel tax reports.

(b) The user shall receive a refundable credit for special fuel taxes paid on purchases which are delivered into vehicles and for which special fuel tax liability is reported.

(7) (a) Except as provided under Subsections (7)(b) and (c), all revenue received by the commission from taxes and license fees under this part shall be deposited daily with the state treasurer and credited to the Transportation Fund.

(b) An appropriation from the Transportation Fund shall be made to the commission to cover expenses incurred in the administration and enforcement of this part and the collection of the special fuel tax.

(c) Five dollars of each special fuel user trip permit fee paid under Section 59-13-303 may be used by the commission as a dedicated credit to cover the costs of electronic credentialing as provided in Section 41-1a-303.

(8) The commission may either collect no tax on special fuel exported from the state or, upon application, refund the tax paid.

(9) (a) The United States government or any of its instrumentalities, this state, or a political subdivision of this state that has purchased special fuel from a supplier or from a retail dealer of special fuel and has paid the tax on the special fuel as provided in this section is entitled to a refund of the tax and may file with the commission for a quarterly refund in a manner prescribed by the commission.

(b) In accordance with Title 63, Chapter 46a, Utah Administrative Rulemaking Act, the commission shall make rules governing the application and refund provided for in Subsection (9)(a).

(10) (a) The purchaser shall pay the tax on diesel fuel purchased for uses under Subsections (2)(b)(i), (iii), (iv), (v), (vi), and (vii) and apply for a refund for the tax paid as provided in Subsection (9) and this Subsection (10).

(b) In accordance with Title 63, Chapter 46a, Utah Administrative Rulemaking Act, the commission shall make rules governing the application and refund for off-highway and nonhighway uses provided under Subsections (2)(b)(iii), (iv), (vi), and (vii).

(c) A refund of tax paid under this part on diesel fuel used for nonhighway agricultural uses shall be made in accordance with the tax return procedures under Section 59-13-202.

(11) (a) Beginning on April 1, 2001, a tax imposed under this section on special fuel is reduced to the extent provided in Subsection (11)(b) if:

(i) the Navajo Nation imposes a tax on the special fuel;

(ii) the tax described in Subsection (11)(a)(i) is imposed without regard to whether the person required to pay the tax is an enrolled member of the Navajo Nation; and

(iii) the commission and the Navajo Nation execute and maintain an agreement as provided in this Subsection (11) for the administration of the reduction of tax.

(b) (i) If but for Subsection (11)(a) the special fuel is subject to a tax imposed by this section:

(A) the state shall be paid the difference described in Subsection (11)(b)(ii) if that difference is greater than $0; and

(B) a person may not require the state to provide a refund, a credit, or similar tax relief if the difference described in Subsection (11)(b)(ii) is less than or equal to $0.

(ii) The difference described in Subsection (11)(b)(i) is equal to the difference between:

(A) the amount of tax imposed on the special fuel by this section; less

(B) the tax imposed and collected by the Navajo Nation on the special fuel.

(c) For purposes of Subsections (11)(a) and (b), the tax paid to the Navajo Nation on the special fuel does not include any interest or penalties a taxpayer may be required to pay to the Navajo Nation.

(d) In accordance with Title 63, Chapter 46a, Utah Administrative Rulemaking Act, the commission shall make rules governing the procedures for administering the reduction of tax provided under this Subsection (11).

(e) The agreement required under Subsection (11)(a):

(i) may not:

(A) authorize the state to impose a tax in addition to a tax imposed under this chapter;

(B) provide a reduction of taxes greater than or different from the reduction described in this Subsection (11); or

(C) affect the power of the state to establish rates of taxation;

(ii) shall:

(A) be in writing;

(B) be signed by:

(I) the chair of the commission or the chair's designee; and

(II) a person designated by the Navajo Nation that may bind the Navajo Nation;

(C) be conditioned on obtaining any approval required by federal law;

(D) state the effective date of the agreement; and

(E) state any accommodation the Navajo Nation makes related to the construction and maintenance of state highways and other infrastructure within the Utah portion of the Navajo Nation; and

(iii) may:

(A) notwithstanding Section 59-1-403, authorize the commission to disclose to the Navajo Nation information that is:

(I) contained in a document filed with the commission; and

(II) related to the tax imposed under this section;

(B) provide for maintaining records by the commission or the Navajo Nation; or

(C) provide for inspections or audits of suppliers, distributors, carriers, or retailers located or doing business within the Utah portion of the Navajo Nation.

(f) (i) If, on or after April 1, 2001, the Navajo Nation changes the tax rate of a tax imposed on special fuel, any change in the amount of the reduction of taxes under this Subsection (11) as a result of the change in the tax rate is not effective until the first day of the calendar quarter after a 60-day period beginning on the date the commission receives notice:

(A) from the Navajo Nation; and

(B) meeting the requirements of Subsection (11)(f)(ii).

(ii) The notice described in Subsection (11)(f)(i) shall state:

(A) that the Navajo Nation has changed or will change the tax rate of a tax imposed on special fuel;

(B) the effective date of the rate change of the tax described in Subsection (11)(f)(ii)(A); and

(C) the new rate of the tax described in Subsection (11)(f)(ii)(A).

(g) If the agreement required by Subsection (11)(a) terminates, a reduction of tax is not permitted under this Subsection (11) beginning on the first day of the calender quarter after a 30-day period beginning on the day the agreement terminates.

(h) If there is a conflict between this Subsection (11) and the agreement required by Subsection (11)(a), this Subsection (11) governs. 2003

59-13-301.5. Refund of taxes impacting Ute tribe and Ute tribal members.

(1) In accordance with this section, the Ute tribe may receive a refund from the state of amounts paid in accordance with Section 59-13-301 if:

(a) the amounts paid by the Ute tribe when it purchases the special fuel includes the amount paid in taxes on the special fuel;

(b) the special fuel is purchased for use by:

(i) the Ute tribe; or

(ii) a Ute tribal member from a retail station that is:

(A) wholly owned by the Ute tribe; and

(B) located on Ute trust land; and

(c) the governor and the Ute tribe execute and maintain an agreement meeting the requirements of Subsection (3).

(2) In addition to the agreement required by Subsection (1), the commission shall enter into an agreement with the Ute tribe that:

(a) provides an allocation formula or procedure for determining:

(i) the amount of special fuel sold by the Ute tribe to a Ute tribal member; and

(ii) the amount of special fuel sold by the Ute tribe to a person who is not a Ute tribal member; and

(b) provides a process by which:

(i) the Ute tribe obtains a refund permitted by this section; and

(ii) reports and remits special fuel tax to the state for sales made to persons who are not Ute tribal members.

(3) The agreement required under Subsection (1):

(a) may not:

(i) authorize the state to impose a tax in addition to a tax imposed under this chapter;

(ii) provide a refund, credit, or similar tax relief that is greater or different than the refund permitted under this section; or

(iii) affect the power of the state to establish rates of taxation; and

(b) shall:

(i) provide that the state agrees to allow the refund described in this section;

(ii) be in writing;

(iii) be signed by:

(A) the governor; and

(B) the chair of the Business Committee of the Ute tribe;

(iv) be conditioned on obtaining any approval required by federal law; and

(v) state the effective date of the agreement.

(4) (a) The governor shall report to the commission by no later than February 1 of each year as to whether or not an agreement meeting the requirements of this Subsection (4) is in effect.

(b) If an agreement meeting the requirements of this Subsection (4) is terminated, the refund permitted under this section is not allowed beginning the January 1 following the date the agreement terminates.

(5) In accordance with Title 63, Chapter 46a, Utah Administrative Rulemaking Act, the commission may make rules regarding the procedures for seeking a refund agreed to under the agreement described in Subsection (2). 2001

59-13-302. Definitions — License requirements — Penalty — Application process and requirements — Fee not required — Bonds — Discontinuance of business — Liens upon property.

(1) As used in this section:

(a) "agent" means a person that:

(i) remits any amounts under this part for:

(A) an applicant; or

(B) a licensee; and

(ii) in accordance with an agreement between the person and the applicant or licensee described in Subsection (1)(a)(i), is required to collect, truthfully account for, and pay over an amount under this part for the:

(A) applicant; or

(B) licensee;

(b) "applicant" means a person that:

(i) is required by this section to obtain a license; and

(ii) submits an application:

(A) to the commission; and

(B) for a license under this section;

(c) "application" means an application for a license under this section;

(d) "fiduciary of the applicant" means a person that:

(i) is required to collect, truthfully account for, and pay over an amount under this part for an applicant;

(ii) is not an agent of the applicant described in Subsection (1)(d)(i); and

(iii) (A) is a corporate officer of the applicant described in Subsection (1)(d)(i);

(B) is a director of the applicant described in Subsection (1)(d)(i);

(C) is an employee of the applicant described in Subsection (1)(d)(i);

(D) is a partner of the applicant described in Subsection (1)(d)(i);

(E) is a trustee of the applicant described in Subsection (1)(d)(i); or

(F) has a relationship to the applicant described in Subsection (1)(d)(i) that is similar to a relationship described in Subsections (1)(d)(iii)(A) through (E) as determined by the commission by rule made in accordance with Title 63, Chapter 46a, Utah Administrative Rulemaking Act;

(e) "fiduciary of the licensee" means a person that:

(i) is required to collect, truthfully account for, and pay over an amount under this part for a licensee;

(ii) is not an agent of the licensee described in Subsection (1)(e)(i); and

(iii) (A) is a corporate officer of the licensee described in Subsection (1)(e)(i);

(B) is a director of the licensee described in Subsection (1)(e)(i);

(C) is an employee of the licensee described in Subsection (1)(e)(i);

(D) is a partner of the licensee described in Subsection (1)(e)(i);

(E) is a trustee of the licensee described in Subsection (1)(e)(i); or

(F) has a relationship to the licensee described in Subsection (1)(e)(i) that is similar to a relationship described in Subsections (1)(e)(iii)(A) through (E) as determined by the commission by rule made in accordance with Title 63, Chapter 46a, Utah Administrative Rulemaking Act;

(f) "license" means a license under this section; and

(g) "licensee" means a person that is licensed under this section by the commission.

(2) A person that is required to collect an amount under this part is guilty of a criminal violation as provided in Section 59-1-401 if before obtaining a license under this section that person engages in business within the state.

(3) The license described in Subsection (2):

(a) shall be granted and issued:

(i) by the commission in accordance with this section;

(ii) without a license fee; and

(iii) if:

(A) an applicant:

(I) states the applicant's name and address in the application; and

(II) provides other information in the application that the commission may require; and

(B) the person meets the requirements of this section to be granted a license as determined by the commission;

(b) may not be assigned to another person; and

(c) is valid:

(i) only for the person named on the license; and

(ii) until:

(A) the person described in Subsection (3)(c)(i):

(I) ceases to do business; or

(II) changes that person's business address; or

(B) the commission revokes the license.

(4) The commission shall review an application and determine whether the applicant meets the requirements of this section to be issued a license.

(5) (a) An applicant shall post a bond with the commission before the commission may issue the applicant a license.

(b) If the commission determines it is necessary to ensure compliance with this part, the commission may require a licensee to increase the amount of a bond posted with the commission.

(c) A bond under this Subsection (5) shall be:

(i) executed by:

(A) for an applicant, the applicant as principal, with a corporate surety; or

(B) for a licensee, the licensee as principal, with a corporate surety; and

(ii) payable to the commission conditioned upon the faithful performance of all of the requirements of this part including:

(A) the payment of all amounts under this part;

(B) the payment of any:

(I) penalty as provided in Section 59-1-401; or

(II) interest as provided in Section 59-1-402; or

(C) any other obligation of the:

(I) applicant under this part; or

(II) licensee under this part.

(d) Except as provided in Subsection (5)(f), the commission shall calculate the amount of a bond under this Subsection (5) on the basis of:

(i) commission estimates of:

(A) an applicant's liability for any amount under this part; or

(B) a licensee's liability for any amount under this part; and

(ii) the amount of a delinquency described in Subsection (5)(e) if:

(A) a license under this section was revoked for a delinquency under this part for:

(I) (Aa) an applicant; or

(Bb) a licensee;

(II) a fiduciary of the:

(Aa) applicant; or

(Bb) licensee; or

(III) a person for which the applicant, licensee, fiduciary of the applicant, or fiduciary of the licensee is required to collect, truthfully account for, and pay over an amount under this part; or

(B) there is a delinquency in paying an amount under this part for:

(I) (Aa) an applicant; or

(Bb) a licensee;

(II) a fiduciary of the:

(Aa) applicant; or

(Bb) licensee; or

(III) a person for which the applicant, licensee, fiduciary of the applicant, or fiduciary of the licensee is required to collect, truthfully account for, and pay over an amount under this part.

(e) Except as provided in Subsection (5)(f), for purposes of Subsection (5)(d)(ii):

(i) for an applicant, the amount of the delinquency is the sum of:

(A) the amount of any delinquency that served as a basis for revoking the license under this section of:

(I) the applicant;

(II) a fiduciary of the applicant; or

(III) a person for which the applicant or the fiduciary of the applicant is required to collect, truthfully account for, and pay over an amount under this part; or

(B) the amount that any of the following owe under this part:

(I) the applicant;

(II) a fiduciary of the applicant; and

(III) a person for which the applicant or the fiduciary of the applicant is required to collect, truthfully account for, and pay over an amount under this part; or

(ii) for a licensee, the amount of the delinquency is the sum of:

(A) the amount of any delinquency that served as a basis for revoking the license under this section of:

(I) the licensee;

(II) a fiduciary of the licensee; or

(III) a person for which the licensee or the fiduciary of the licensee is required to collect, truthfully account for, and pay over an amount under this part; or

(B) the amount that any of the following owe under this part:

(I) the licensee;

(II) a fiduciary of the licensee; and

(III) a person for which the licensee or the fiduciary of the licensee is required to collect, truthfully account for, and pay over an amount under this part.

(f) Notwithstanding Subsection (5)(d) or (e), a bond required by this Subsection (5) may not:

(i) be less than $50,000; or

(ii) exceed $500,000.

(6) (a) The commission shall revoke a license under this section if:

(i) a licensee violates any provision of this part; and

(ii) before the commission revokes the license the commission provides the licensee:

(A) reasonable notice; and

(B) a hearing.

(b) If the commission revokes a licensee's license in accordance with Subsection (6)(a), the commission may not issue another license to that licensee until that licensee complies with the requirements of this part, including:

(i) paying any:

(A) amounts due under this part;

(B) penalty as provided in Section 59-1-401; or

(C) interest as provided in Section 59-1-402; and

(ii) posting a bond in accordance with Subsection (5).

(7) (a) If any person ceases to be a supplier within the state by reason of the discontinuance, sale, or transfer of the person's business, the supplier shall notify the commission in writing at the time the discontinuance, sale, or transfer takes effect.

(b) The notice shall give the date of discontinuance and, in the event of a sale, the date of the sale and the name and address of the purchaser or transferee.

(c) Taxes on all special fuel delivery or removal made prior to the discontinuance, sale, or transfer, shall become due and payable on the date of discontinuance, sale, or transfer.

(d) The supplier shall make a report and pay all taxes, interest, and penalties and surrender to the commission the license certificate that was issued to the supplier by the commission.

(8) (a) The tax imposed by this part shall be a lien upon the property of any supplier liable for an amount of tax that is required to be collected, if the supplier sells the business, stock of goods, or quits business, and if the supplier fails to make a final return and payment within 15 days after the date of selling or quitting business.

(b) The successor or assigns, if any, shall be required to withhold a sufficient amount of the purchase money to cover the amount of the taxes that are required to be collected and interest or penalties due and paid under Sections 59-1-401 and 59-1-402 until the former owner produces a receipt from the commission showing that the taxes have been paid or a certificate stating that no amount of tax is due. If the purchaser of a business or stock of goods fails to withhold sufficient purchase money, the purchaser shall be personally liable for the payment of the amount that is due.　　　2005

59-13-303. Special fuel user permits — Application — Revocation of permits under certain circumstances.

(1) (a) Except as provided in Subsection (1)(b), each user shall, prior to the use of the fuel in a qualified motor vehicle, apply to the commission on forms prescribed by the commission for a special fuel user permit. When the application is approved by the commission, a single special fuel user permit shall be issued to the user.

(b) In place of the special fuel user permit issued under Subsection (1)(a), a user may purchase a special fuel user trip permit. A special fuel user trip permit is valid for 96 hours or until the qualified vehicle leaves the state, whichever occurs first.

(c) The fee for the special fuel user trip permit is $25.

(2) A special fuel user permit number shall be assigned to each licensed user and is nontransferable and valid until surrendered by the user for nonuse or until revoked by the commission.

(3) The special fuel user permit expires December 31 of each year. Special fuel user permits for the

calendar year shall be honored until February 28 of the following year. An application shall be filed with the commission each year for a new special fuel user permit for vehicles operated by a licensed user.

(4) (a) The special fuel user permit shall be kept in the passenger compartment of each vehicle, or as otherwise authorized by the commission.

(b) A user that does not comply with the requirements of this section may be required to purchase a special fuel user trip permit.

(5) The commission may revoke the special fuel user permit issued under this section from any person refusing or neglecting to comply with this part.

(6) Any user reporting Utah special fuel tax liability under Part 5, Interstate Agreements, is exempted from the permit requirements of this section.   2005

59-13-304. Exemptions from Special Fuel Tax — Clean Special Fuel Tax — Certificate required — Fees for certificates — Inspection of vehicles — Exemptions.

(1) (a) Except as provided in Subsection (4), a user of special fuel who owns a vehicle powered by a clean special fuel as defined under Section 59-13-102 shall pay a clean special fuel tax as provided under this section for use of clean special fuel.

(b) A user of special fuel who qualifies for the clean special fuel tax shall annually purchase from the commission a clean special fuel tax certificate for each vehicle owned or leased that is powered by a clean special fuel.

(c) Clean special fuel tax certificates are provided to encourage the use of clean fuels to reduce air pollution.

(2) (a) The fee for a clean special fuel tax certificate is:

(i) 70/.19 of the tax per gallon imposed under Subsection 59-13-201(1)(a), rounded up to the nearest dollar, for qualified motor vehicles as defined under Section 59-13-102; and

(ii) 36/.19 of the tax per gallon imposed under Subsection 59-13-201(1)(a), rounded up to the nearest dollar, for other vehicles.

(b) The commission may require each vehicle to be inspected for safe operation before issuing the certificate.

(c) Each vehicle shall be equipped with an approved and properly installed carburetion system if it is powered by a fuel that is gaseous at standard atmospheric conditions.

(3) (a) Beginning January 1, 2001 through December 31, 2010, there is imposed a surcharge of $35 on each clean special fuel tax certificate issued under this section.

(b) (i) Until Subsection (3)(b)(ii) applies, surcharges imposed under Subsection (3)(a) shall be deposited into the Centennial Highway Fund Restricted Account created under Section 72-2-118.

(ii) When the highway general obligation bonds have been paid off and the highway projects completed that are intended to be paid from revenues deposited in the Centennial Highway Fund Restricted Account as determined by the Executive Appropriations Committee under Subsection 72-2-118(6)(d), the surcharge imposed under Subsection (3)(a) shall be deposited into the Transportation Investment Fund of 2005 created by Section 72-2-124.

(4) A governmental entity identified in Subsection 59-13-301(9) that owns or leases a vehicle powered by a special fuel that qualifies as a clean special fuel is exempt from the clean special fuel tax imposed under this section.   2005 (1st S.S.)

59-13-305. User report required — Contents of report — Signature — Penalties — Exemptions from requirements — Change of exemption status — Duty to notify commission.

(1) Unless exempted by Subsection (5), each user shall file with the commission, on or before the last day of the month following the end of a reporting period, a report on forms prescribed by the commission showing:

(a) the amount of fuel purchased and the amount of fuel used during the preceding reporting period by that user in the state; and

(b) any other information the commission may require to carry out the purposes of this part.

(2) The report shall be signed by the user or a responsible representative. This signature need not be notarized, but when signed is considered to have been made under oath.

(3) A penalty is imposed under Section 59-1-401 for failure to file reports as provided in this section for each report not filed, regardless of the imposition of other penalties under this part.

(4) (a) Each user that has a registered special fuel-powered motor vehicle other than a qualified motor vehicle and has facilities for bulk storage of special fuels shall declare special fuel tax liability for any nonqualified motor vehicle on the user report required by Subsection (1).

(b) Credit shall be given on the report for any special fuel taxes paid on purchases for any nonqualified vehicle. Purchase records must be maintained to substantiate the amount of any credit claimed.

(5) (a) The following users are exempt from the filing requirements of Subsections (1) and (2) for the motor vehicles specified:

(i) a user who purchases a special fuel user trip permit for all of its operations for qualified vehicles for the reporting period, except a user having a special fuel user permit under Subsection 59-13-303 (1)(a);

(ii) a user that has a registered special fuel-powered motor vehicle other than a qualified motor vehicle and does not have facilities for bulk storage of special fuels;

(iii) a user of special fuel, for which the tax imposed by this chapter has already been paid; or

(iv) a user that has a motor vehicle powered by special fuel for which the tax is paid under an interstate fuel tax agreement under Section 59-13-502.

(b) (i) The exemption under Subsection (5)(a)(iii) applies only when the user retains records verifying that all special fuel purchases for the exempt vehicle were taxed as required under this part.

(ii) The commission may at the time of application or renewal of a special fuel user permit under Section 59-13-303 require that the user certify:

(A) that the user qualifies for an exemption under Subsection (5)(a)(iii); and

(B) whether the user has facilities for bulk storage of special fuel.   2005

59-13-306. Due date of special fuel tax.

The special fuel tax is due and payable at the offices of the commission on or before the last day of the month following each reporting period. If not paid at the offices of the commission or if the envelope enclosing the report or remittance does not bear a post office cancellation mark dated on or before the due date, the special fuel tax is delinquent.   1987

59-13-307. Supplier reports — Signature required — Penalties.

(1) Each supplier shall file with the commission, on or before the last day of each month, a report on forms prescribed by the commission showing the amount of fuel delivered or removed during the preceding calendar month and any other information the commission may require to carry out the purposes of this part.

(2) The report shall be signed by the supplier or a responsible representative. This signature need not be notarized, but when signed is considered to have been made under oath. The report shall be accompanied by a remittance payable to the commission for the amount of special fuel tax due.

(3) A penalty is imposed under Section 59-1-401 upon each licensee and bonded supplier who fails to file any report as prescribed regardless of the imposition of other penalties under this part.   2001

59-13-308. Delinquency — Penalties — Interest.

If any user becomes delinquent in tax payments under this part, all licenses or permits issued under this part are automatically revoked. In addition, the commission shall impose a penalty determined under Section 59-1-401. The amount of the delinquent tax and the penalty shall bear interest at the rate and in the manner prescribed in Section 59-1-402.   2005

59-13-309. Repealed.   1994

59-13-310. Special fuel from out of state — Reports required — Contents of reports.

(1) Every person who delivers special fuel from outside the state to any consignee within the state shall file with the commission on or before the last day of each month a report on forms prescribed by the commission showing:

(a) all deliveries of special fuel within the state during the preceding month; and

(b) the points of origin and original destination.

(2) Where any consignment of special fuel was diverted in transit and delivered within this state, the carrier making delivery of this consignment shall report to the commission:

(a) the place of the delivery of the consignment;

(b) to whom the consignment was delivered;

(c) the number of gallons of special fuel transported or delivered;

(d) the date of delivery and the name of the consignor and of the consignee; and

(e) any other information the commission may require.   1997

59-13-311. Tax is a lien against vehicle — Removal of lien.

The special fuel tax constitutes a lien upon, and has the effect of an execution duly levied against, any vehicle in which special fuel is used. The lien may not be removed until the special fuel tax is paid or the vehicle subject to the lien is sold in payment of the tax.
                    1987

59-13-312. User and supplier reports on special fuel — Commission examination of reports — Auditing requirements — Deposit of funds with treasurer as dedicated credits.

(1) Each user, supplier, and any other person importing, manufacturing, refining, dealing in, transporting, or storing fuel shall keep a record, in the form prescribed by the commission, of all deliveries, removals, purchases, receipts, sales, meter readings, inventories, and distribution of special fuel. The records shall include copies of all invoices or bills of all sales, and are subject to inspection by the commission or its authorized representative during regular business hours. All records shall be preserved for a period of three years.

(2) Any user claiming a refund for taxes paid to a supplier shall retain on file a receipt or invoice, or a microfilm or microfiche of the receipt or invoice, evidencing the purchase of special fuel and the payment of the tax. The commission may require the user to furnish summaries or copies of original documentation substantiating the amount of refund claimed.

(3) (a) The commission or its authorized representative may examine the books, papers, records, and equipment of any supplier, user, or person dealing in, transporting, or storing special fuel and may investigate the character of the disposition which any person makes of special fuel in order to determine whether all taxes due are being properly reported and paid.

(b) The fact that the books, papers, records, and equipment are not maintained in this state at the time of demand does not cause the commission to lose any right of examination under this part when and where the records become available.

(4) If the payer of this tax or the person dealing in special fuel does not maintain records in this state so that an audit of the records may be made by the commission or its representative, that person may be required to:

(a) forward the necessary records to the commission for examination; or

(b) pay the necessary expenses for an auditor of the commission to travel to the location of the records outside of this state to make an examination.

(5) Any funds collected under this section shall be deposited with the state treasurer and are dedicated credits for the commission.   1997

59-13-313. Commission to enforce laws — Estimates of tax — Penalties — Notice of determination — Information sharing with other states — Assessment procedures — Limitations.

(1) (a) The commission is charged with the enforcement of this part and may prescribe rules relating to administration and enforcement of this part.

(b) The commission may coordinate with state and federal agencies in the enforcement of this part.

(c) Enforcement procedures may include checking diesel fuel dye compliance of storage facilities and tanks of vehicles, in a manner consistent with state and federal law.

(2) (a) If the commission has reason to question the report filed or the amount of special fuel tax paid to the state by any user or supplier, it may compute and determine the amount to be paid based upon the best information available to it.

(b) Any added amount of special fuel tax determined to be due under this section shall have added to it a penalty as provided under Section 59-1-401, and shall bear interest at the rate and in the manner prescribed in Section 59-1-402.

(c) The commission shall give to the user or supplier written notice of its determination. The notice may be served personally or sent to the user or supplier at the user or supplier's last-known address as it appears in the records of the commission.

(3) The commission may, upon the duly received request of the officials to whom the enforcement of the special fuel laws of any other state are entrusted, forward to those officials any information which the commission may have in its possession relative to the delivery, removal, production, manufacture, refining, compounding, receipt, sale, use, transportation, or shipment of special fuel by any person.

(4) (a) Except as provided in Subsections (4)(c) through (f), the commission shall assess the amount of taxes imposed under this part, and any penalties and interest, within three years after a taxpayer files a return.

(b) Except as provided in Subsections (4)(c) through (f), if the commission does not make an assessment under Subsection (4)(a) within three years, the commission may not commence a proceeding for the collection of the taxes after the expiration of the three-year period.

(c) Notwithstanding Subsections (4)(a) and (b), the commission may make an assessment or commence a proceeding to collect a tax at any time if a deficiency is due to:

(i) fraud; or

(ii) failure to file a return.

(d) Notwithstanding Subsections (4)(a) and (b), beginning on July 1, 1998, the commission may extend the period to make an assessment or to commence a proceeding to collect the tax under this part if:

(i) the three-year period under this Subsection (4) has not expired; and

(ii) the commission and the taxpayer sign a written agreement:

(A) authorizing the extension; and

(B) providing for the length of the extension.

(e) If the commission delays an audit at the request of a taxpayer, the commission may make an assessment as provided in Subsection (4)(f) if:

(i) the taxpayer subsequently refuses to agree to an extension request by the commission; and

(ii) the three-year period under this Subsection (4) expires before the commission completes the audit.

(f) An assessment under Subsection (4)(e) shall be:

(i) for the time period for which the commission could not make an assessment because of the expiration of the three-year period; and

(ii) in an amount equal to the difference between:

(A) the commission's estimate of the amount of taxes the taxpayer would have been assessed for the time period described in Subsection (4)(f)(i); and

(B) the amount of taxes the taxpayer actually paid for the time period described in Subsection (4)(f)(i).   2000

59-13-314. Special fuel user permit required before registration of vehicle.

Before registering any motor vehicle which is operated by special fuels, the registered owner or lessee of the vehicle shall obtain:

(1) a valid special fuel user permit for the current year if required under Section 59-13-303; or

(2) a valid clean special fuel tax certificate for the current year if required under Section 59-13-304.   2003

59-13-315. Transfer of ownership of vehicle — Lien to be removed — Tax clearance by commission.

The transfer of registered ownership of any motor vehicle subject to a lien of the tax imposed by this part may be effected only after a certificate of clearance of the tax has been issued by the commission.   1987

59-13-316. Neglect or refusal to report — Estimate — Penalties — Notice to user or supplier.

(1) If any user or supplier neglects or refuses to make a report required by this part, the commission shall make an estimate based on the best information available to it, for the months in which the user or supplier failed to make a report, or for the amount of special fuel sold or used by the user or supplier subject to the special fuel tax.

(2) On the basis of the estimate, the commission shall compute and determine the amount required to be paid to the state, adding to this sum a penalty as provided under Section 59-1-401, and interest at the rate and in the manner prescribed in Section 59-1-402.

(3) The commission shall give to the user or supplier written notice of the estimate. The notice may be served personally or sent to the user or supplier at the user or supplier's last-known address as it appears in the records of the commission.   2000

59-13-317. Delinquency — Collection procedures.

(1) (a) In the event that any user or supplier is delinquent in the payment of any obligation imposed by this part, the commission may give notice of the amount of the delinquency by registered mail to all persons having in their possession or under their control, any credits or other personal property belonging to the user or supplier, or owing any debts to the user or supplier.

(b) At the time of receipt of the notice and thereafter, any person so notified may not transfer or make other disposition of the credits, personal property, or debts until the commission has consented to a transfer or disposition or until ten days have elapsed from and after the receipt of the notice.

(c) Any person so notified shall, within five days after the receipt of the notice, advise the commission of any and all credits, personal property, or debts in their possession, under their control, or owing by them.

(2) (a) If any user or supplier is delinquent in the payment of the obligations imposed by this chapter, the commission may at once bring an action to determine the amount of tax and collect all sums due the state from any user or supplier.

(b) In any suit brought to enforce the rights of the state, a certificate by the commission showing the delinquency is prima facie evidence of the levy of the special fuel tax, of the delinquency, and of compliance with this part in relation to the computation and levy of the special fuel tax.

(c) In this action a writ of attachment may be issued, and no bond or affidavit previous to the issuing of the attachment may be required.   1997

59-13-318. Errors in payments — Refunds.

(1) (a) If the commission, through error, collects or receives any special fuel tax, penalty, or interest imposed by this part, the amount of tax, penalty, or interest, upon written application, shall be refunded to the person paying it. The application shall state the specific grounds on which it is founded and whether the sums were paid voluntarily or under protest.

(b) Except as provided in Subsection (1)(c), a refund may not be made unless a claim has been filed within three years of the date of the overpayment.

(c) Notwithstanding Subsection (1)(b), beginning on July 1, 1998, the commission shall extend the period for a taxpayer to file a claim under Subsection (1)(b) if:

(i) the three-year period under Subsection (1)(b) has not expired; and

(ii) the commission and the taxpayer sign a written agreement:

(A) authorizing the extension; and

(B) providing for the length of the extension.

(d) A refund may not be made to successors or assigns in business of the person making the payment but shall be made to an estate or heir of the person if written application is made within the time limit, accompanied by proper authority from a probate court.

(e) Refunds to which taxpayers are entitled under this chapter shall be paid from the Transportation Fund.

(2) Any user who has paid taxes on purchases in the state which exceed the amount due based on the special fuel reported to be used in the state shall receive a refund of taxes overpaid in a timely manner.

(3) Interest shall be applied to refunds given under this section as prescribed in Section 59-1-402.   1998

59-13-319. Repealed.   1994

59-13-320. Penalties for violations of the special fuel tax provisions.

(1) The following offenses, unless otherwise provided, are class B misdemeanors:

(a) failing or refusing to pay the tax imposed by this part;

(b) engaging in business in this state as a supplier without being the holder of an uncancelled license to engage in this business;

(c) operating a motor vehicle, which requires special fuel, upon the highways of this state without a valid special fuel user permit;

(d) failing to make any of the reports required by this part;

(e) making any false statement in any application, report, or statement required by this part;

(f) refusing to permit the commission or any employee to examine records as provided by this part;

(g) failing to keep proper records of quantities of fuel received, produced, refined, manufactured, compounded, used, or delivered in this state as required by this part;

(h) making any false statement in connection with an application for the refund of any moneys or taxes provided in this part; or

(i) violating any of the provisions of this part for which no penalty is provided.

(2) Any person required to make, render, sign, or verify any report and who makes any false or fraudulent report with intent to defeat or evade the assessment required by law to be made, is subject to a criminal violation under Section 59-1-401.

(3) The remedies of the state are cumulative and no action taken by the commission or any of its officers to pursue any remedy may be construed to be an election on the part of the state to exclude any other allowed by law.   2003

59-13-320.5. Use of dyed diesel on highways prohibited — Penalty.

(1) A person may not operate a motor vehicle on a highway if a fuel supply tank of the motor vehicle contains dyed diesel fuel, unless:

(a) permitted under federal law;

(b) (i) the motor vehicle is used on the highway only to travel from one parcel of land owned or operated by the owner to another parcel of land owned or operated by the owner; and

(ii) the motor vehicle's travel on the highway is necessary for furtherance of agricultural purposes; or

(c) the motor vehicle is special mobile equipment, as defined in Section 41-1a-102, including off-road motorized construction or maintenance equipment, that is only incidentally operated or moved on a highway in connection with a construction project.

(2) A person who violates Subsection (1) shall pay a penalty assessed by the commission as follows:

(a) the greater of $500 or $5 per gallon of dyed diesel fuel within each fuel supply tank of the motor vehicle, based on the maximum storage capacity of each fuel supply tank; or

(b) for a second and subsequent offense, the greater of $1,000 or $10 per gallon of dyed diesel fuel within each fuel supply tank of the motor vehicle, based on the maximum storage capacity of each fuel supply tank.

(3) The penalty imposed under this section:

(a) is in addition to any other taxes, interest, or penalties imposed under this chapter; and

(b) shall be deposited in the Transportation Fund.

(4) Upon making a record of its actions, and upon reasonable cause shown, the commission may waive, reduce, or compromise the penalty imposed under this section.   2001

59-13-321. Wholesaler option for rack distributions tax payments — Notification — Security.

(1) As used in this section "wholesaler" means a person who receives a rack distribution of diesel fuel from a supplier for purposes of resale.

(2) (a) Upon agreement of wholesaler and supplier, the payment of the taxes to the supplier under this part may be made on or before one business day prior to the time that the supplier is required to remit those taxes to the commission.

(b) The wholesaler shall provide written notification to the supplier of the wholesaler's intent to exercise the payment option under Subsection (2)(a) at least 30 days prior to the payment.

(c) The wholesaler's payment of the taxes under Subsection (2)(a) shall be made by electronic funds transfer.

(3) Upon the wholesaler's exercise of the payment option provided in Subsection (2), the supplier may require security for the payment of the taxes if no security exists between the wholesaler and the supplier.

(4) At the option of the supplier, the wholesaler's exercise of the payment option provided under this section may be terminated if the wholesaler fails to:

(a) remit timely payment of the taxes as provided in Subsection (2); or

(b) provide security as provided in Subsection (3). ₁₉₉₇

59-13-322. Refunds of tax due to fire, flood, storm, accident, crime, or discharge in bankruptcy — Filing claims and affidavits — Commission approval — Rulemaking — Appeals — Penalties.

(1) (a) A retailer, wholesaler, or licensed supplier, who without fault, sustains a loss or destruction of 7,000 or more gallons of diesel fuel in a single incident due to fire, flood, storm, accident, or the commission of a crime and who has paid or is required to pay the tax on the special fuel as provided by this part, is entitled to a refund or credit of the tax subject to the conditions and limitations provided under this section.

(b) The claimant shall file a claim for a refund or credit with the commission within 90 days of the incident.

(c) Any part of a loss or destruction eligible for indemnification under an insurance policy for the taxes paid or required on the loss or destruction of special fuel is not eligible for a refund or credit under this section.

(d) Any claimant filing a claim for a refund or credit shall furnish any or all of the information outlined in this section upon request of the commission.

(e) The burden of proof of loss or destruction is on the claimant who shall provide evidence of loss or destruction to the satisfaction of the commission.

(f) (i) The claim shall include an affidavit containing the:

(A) name of claimant;

(B) claimant's address;

(C) date, time, and location of the incident;

(D) cause of the incident;

(E) name of the investigating agencies at the scene;

(F) number of gallons actually lost from sale; and

(G) information on any insurance coverages related to the incident.

(ii) The claimant shall support the claim by submitting the original invoices or copy of the original invoices.

(iii) This original claim and all information contained in it constitutes a permanent file with the commission in the name of the claimant.

(2) (a) A retailer, wholesaler, or licensed distributor who has paid the tax on special fuel as provided by this part is entitled to a refund for taxes paid on that portion of an account that:

(i) relates to 4,500 or more gallons of special fuel purchased in a single transaction for which no payment has been received; and

(ii) has been discharged in a bankruptcy proceeding.

(b) The claimant shall file a claim for refund with the commission within 90 days from the date of the discharge.

(c) Any claimant filing a claim for a refund shall furnish any or all of the information outlined in this section upon request of the commission.

(d) The burden of proof of discharge is on the claimant who shall provide evidence of discharge to the satisfaction of the commission.

(e) The claim shall include an affidavit containing the following:

(i) the name of the claimant;

(ii) the claimant's address;

(iii) the name of the debtor that received a discharge in bankruptcy; and

(iv) the portion of the account that is subject to an order granting a discharge.

(f) The claimant shall support the claim by submitting:

(i) the original invoices or a copy of the original invoices; and

(ii) a certified copy of the notice of discharge.

(g) This original claim and all information contained in it constitutes a permanent file with the commission in the name of the claimant.

(h) In accordance with Title 63, Chapter 46a, Utah Administrative Rulemaking Act, the commission shall promulgate rules for the allocation of the discharge under this Subsection (2) to maximize the claimant's refund amount.

(3) Upon commission approval of the claim for a refund, the commission shall pay the amount found due to the claimant. The total amount of claims for refunds shall be paid from the Transportation Fund.

(4) In accordance with Title 63, Chapter 46a, Utah Administrative Rulemaking Act, the commission may promulgate rules to enforce this part, and may refuse to accept unsubstantiated evidence for the claim. If the commission is not satisfied with the evidence submitted in connection with the claim, it may reject the claim or require additional evidence.

(5) Any person aggrieved by the decision of the commission with respect to a refund or credit may file a request for agency action, requesting a hearing before the commission.

(6) Any person who makes any false claim, report, or statement, either as claimant, agent, or creditor, with intent to defraud or secure a refund or credit to which the claimant is not entitled, is subject to the criminal penalties provided under Section 59-1-401, and the commission shall initiate the filing of a complaint for alleged violations of this part. In addition to these penalties, the person may not receive any refund or credit as a claimant or as a creditor of a claimant for refund or credit for a period of five years. ₂₀₀₃

CHAPTER 14

CIGARETTE AND TOBACCO TAX AND LICENSING

Part 2

Cigarettes

PART 2

CIGARETTES

59-14-207. Repealed.   ₂₀₀₂

CHAPTER 15

BEER TAX

Section
59-15-101.   Tax basis — Rate.

59-15-101.   Tax basis — Rate.

(1) (a) A tax is imposed at the rate specified in Subsection (1)(b) on all beer, as defined in Section 32A-1-105, that is imported or manufactured for sale, use, or distribution in this state.

(b) The tax described in Subsection (1)(a) shall be imposed at a rate of:

(i) $11 per 31-gallon barrel for beer imported or manufactured:

(A) before July 1, 2003; and

(B) for sale, use, or distribution in this state; and

(ii) $12.80 per 31-gallon barrel for beer imported or manufactured:

(A) on or after July 1, 2003; and

(B) for sale, use, or distribution in this state.

(c) The tax imposed under this Subsection (1):

(i) shall be imposed at a proportionate rate for:

(A) any quantity of beer other than a 31-gallon barrel; or

(B) the fractional parts of a 31-gallon barrel; and

(ii) may not be imposed more than once on the same beer.

(2) A tax may not be imposed on beer:

(a) sold to the United States and its agencies; or

(b) (i) manufactured or imported for sale, use, or distribution outside the state; and

(ii) exported from the state.   2003

CHAPTER 19

ILLEGAL DRUG STAMP TAX ACT

59-19-101.   Short title.

This chapter is known as the "Illegal Drug Stamp Tax Act."   1988

59-19-102.   Definitions.

As used in this chapter:

(1) "Controlled substance" means any drug or substance, whether real or counterfeit, as defined in Section 58-37-2, that is held, possessed, transported, transferred, sold, or offered to be sold in violation of Utah laws. It does not include marihuana.

(2) "Dealer" means a person who, in violation of Utah law, manufactures, produces, ships, transports, or imports into Utah or in any manner acquires or possesses more than 42 ½ grams of marihuana, or seven or more grams of any controlled substance, or ten or more dosage units of any controlled substance which is not sold by weight.

(3) "Marihuana" means any marihuana, whether real or counterfeit, as defined in Section 58-37-2, that is held, possessed, transported, transferred, sold, or offered to be sold in violation of Utah laws.   1988

59-19-103.   Tax imposed on marihuana and controlled substances.

(1) A tax is imposed on marihuana and controlled substances as defined under this chapter at the following rates:

(a) on each gram of marihuana, or each portion of a gram, $3.50;

(b) on each gram of controlled substance, or each portion of a gram, $200; and

(c) on each 50 dosage units of a controlled substance that is not sold by weight, or portion thereof, $2,000.

(2) For the purpose of calculating the tax under this chapter, a quantity of marihuana or other controlled substance is measured by the weight of the substance, whether pure or impure or dilute, or by dosage units when the substance is not sold by weight, in the dealer's possession. A quantity of a controlled substance is dilute if it consists of a detectable quantity of pure controlled substance and any excipients or fillers.   1988

59-19-104.   Stamps evidencing tax paid to be provided and sold by the commission.

(1) The commission shall adopt a uniform system of providing, affixing, and displaying official stamps, official labels, or other official indicia for marihuana and controlled substances on which a tax is imposed.

(2) A dealer may not possess any marihuana or controlled substance upon which a tax is imposed by this chapter, unless the tax has been paid on the marihuana or other controlled substance as evidenced by a stamp or other official indicia.

(3) Official stamps, labels, or other indicia to be affixed to all marihuana or controlled substances shall be purchased from the commission. The purchaser shall pay 100% of face value for each stamp, label, or other indicia at the time of the purchase.   1988

59-19-105.   Stamps to be affixed to marihuana and controlled substance — Anonymity provided when purchasing stamps — Collection and distribution of tax — Property in kind.

(1) When a dealer purchases, acquires, transports, or imports into this state marihuana or controlled substances, he shall permanently affix the official indicia on the marihuana or controlled substances evidencing the payment of the tax required under this chapter. A stamp or other official indicia may not be used more than once.

(2) Taxes imposed upon marihuana or controlled substances by this chapter are due and payable immediately upon acquisition or possession in this state by a dealer.

(3) Payments required by this chapter shall be made to the commission on forms provided by the commission.

(4) (a) A dealer is not required to give his name, address, Social Security number, or other identifying information on the form.

(b) The commission or its employees may not reveal any facts contained in any report, form, or return required by this chapter or any information obtained from a dealer.

(c) None of the information contained in a report, form, or return or otherwise obtained from a dealer in connection with this section may be used against the dealer in any criminal proceeding unless it is independently obtained, except in connection with a proceeding involving taxes due under this chapter from the dealer making the return. This subsection supersedes any provision to the contrary.

(d) A person who discloses information in violation of this subsection is guilty of a class A misdemeanor.

(5) This section does not prohibit the commission from publishing statistics that do not disclose the identity of a dealer or the actual contents of any reports, forms, or returns.

(6) (a) The commission shall collect all taxes imposed under this chapter. Amounts collected under this chapter, whether characterized as taxes, interest, or penalties, shall be deposited in the Drug Stamp Tax Fund as a dedicated credit and shall be applied and distributed under Section 63-38-9 of the Budgetary Procedures Act as follows:

(i) forty percent to the commission for administrative costs of recovery; and

(ii) sixty percent to the law enforcement agency conducting the controlled substance investigation, to be used and applied by the agency in the continued enforcement of controlled substance laws.

(b) If there is more than one participating law enforcement agency, the 60% under Subsection (6)(a)(ii) shall be divided equitably and distributed among the agencies by the administrative law judge conducting the hearing to determine taxpayer liability. The distribution shall be based upon the extent of agency participation as appears from evidence submitted by each agency relative to actual time and expense incurred in the investigation.

(c) If no law enforcement agency is involved in the collection of a specific amount under this chapter, the entire amount collected shall be applied under Subsection (6)(a)(i) to administrative costs of recovery.

(7) (a) If property in kind obtained from the taxpayer is of use or benefit to the commission in the enforcement of this chapter or is of use or benefit to the participating law enforcement agency in the continued enforcement of controlled substance laws, either the commission or the law enforcement agency may apply to the administrative law judge for the award of the property. If the administrative law judge finds the property is of use or benefit either to the commission or the law enforcement agency, the property shall be awarded accordingly.

(b) Before an award under this subsection is ordered, the property shall be appraised by a court-appointed appraiser and the appraised value shall be credited to the taxpayer. If the taxpayer objects to the results of the court-appointed appraisal, he may obtain his own appraisal at his own expense within ten days of the court-appointed appraisal. The decision of the administrative law judge as to value is controlling.

(c) The value of any property in kind awarded to the commission or to the participating law enforcement agency shall be counted as a portion of its percentage share under Subsection (6).

(8) Property of the taxpayer otherwise subject to forfeiture under Section 58-37-13 is not affected by this chapter if there is compliance with Section 58-37-13 regarding the forfeiture and the proceeds and property seized and forfeited are accordingly divided and distributed.   1989

59-19-106. Civil penalty — Criminal penalty — Statute of limitations — Burden of proof.

(1) Any dealer violating this chapter is subject to a penalty of 100% of the tax in addition to the tax imposed by Section 59-19-103. The penalty shall be collected as part of the tax.

(2) In addition to the tax penalty imposed, a dealer distributing or possessing marihuana or controlled substances without affixing the appropriate stamps, labels, or other indicia is guilty of a third degree felony.

(3) An information, indictment, or complaint may be filed upon any criminal offense under this chapter within six years after the commission of the offense. This subsection supersedes any provisions to the contrary.

(4) Any tax and penalties assessed by the commission are presumed to be valid and correct. The burden is on the taxpayer to show their incorrectness or invalidity.   1989

59-19-107. Commission to administer tax — No criminal immunity for dealers.

(1) The commission shall administer this chapter and may adopt rules necessary to enforce this chapter.

(2) Nothing in this chapter requires persons lawfully in possession of marihuana or a controlled substance to pay the tax required under this chapter.

(3) Nothing in this chapter provides immunity of any kind for a dealer from criminal prosecution under Utah law.   1988

TITLE 62A

UTAH HUMAN SERVICES CODE

Chapter

CHAPTER 4a

CHILD AND FAMILY SERVICES

Part 2

Child Welfare Services

PART 2

CHILD WELFARE SERVICES

62A-4a-201. Rights of parents — Children's rights — Interest and responsibility of state.

(1) (a) Under both the United States Constitution and the constitution of this state, a parent possesses a fundamental liberty interest in the care, custody, and management of the parent's children. A fundamentally fair process must be provided to parents if the state moves to challenge or interfere with parental rights. A governmental entity must support any actions or allegations made in opposition to the rights and desires of a parent regarding the parent's children by sufficient evidence to satisfy a parent's constitutional entitlement to heightened protection against government interference with the parent's fundamental rights and liberty interests.

(b) The fundamental liberty interest of a parent concerning the care, custody, and management of the parent's children is recognized, protected, and does not cease to exist simply because a parent may fail to be a model parent or because the parent's child is placed in the temporary custody of the state. At all times, a parent retains a vital interest in preventing the irretrievable destruction of family life. Prior to an adjudication of unfitness, government action in relation to parents and their children may not exceed the least restrictive means or alternatives available to accomplish a compelling state interest. Until the state proves parental unfitness, the child and the child's parents share a vital interest in preventing erroneous termination of their natural relationship and the state cannot presume that a child and the child's parents are adversaries.

(c) It is in the best interest and welfare of a child to be raised under the care and supervision of the child's natural parents. A child's need for a normal family life in a permanent home, and for positive, nurturing family relationships will usually best be met by the child's natural parents. Additionally, the integrity of the family unit, and the right of parents to conceive and raise their children have found protection in the due process clause of the Fourteenth Amendment to the United States Constitution. The right of a fit, competent parent to raise the parent's child without undue government interference is a fundamental liberty interest that has long been protected by the laws and Constitution of this state and of the United States.

(d) It is the public policy of this state that parents retain the fundamental right and duty to exercise primary control over the care, supervision, upbringing, and education of their children.

(e) Subsections (2) through (7) shall be interpreted and applied consistent with this Subsection (1).

(2) It is also the public policy of this state that children have the right to protection from abuse and neglect, and that the state retains a compelling interest in investigating, prosecuting, and punishing abuse and neglect, as defined in this chapter, and in Title 78, Chapter 3a, Juvenile Court Act of 1996. Therefore, the state, as parens patriae, has an interest in and responsibility to protect children whose parents abuse them or do not adequately provide for their welfare. There may be circumstances where a parent's conduct or condition is a substantial departure from the norm and the parent is unable or unwilling to render safe and proper parental care and protection. Under those circumstances, the state may take action for the welfare and protection of the parent's children.

(3) When the division intervenes on behalf of an abused, neglected, or dependent child, it shall take into account the child's need for protection from immediate harm. Throughout its involvement, the division shall utilize the least intrusive and least restrictive means available to protect a child, in an effort to ensure that children are brought up in stable, permanent families, rather than in temporary foster placements under the supervision of the state.

(4) When circumstances within the family pose a threat to the child's immediate safety or welfare, the division may obtain custody of the child for a planned period and place the child in a safe environment, in accordance with the requirements of Title 78, Chapter 3a, Part 3, Abuse, Neglect, and Dependency Proceedings.

(5) In determining and making "reasonable efforts" with regard to a child, pursuant to the provisions of Section 62A-4a-203, both the division's and the court's paramount concern shall be the child's health, safety, and welfare. The desires of a parent for the parent's child shall be given full and serious consideration by the division and the court.

(6) In cases where actual sexual abuse, abandonment, or serious physical abuse or neglect are established, the state has no duty to make "reasonable efforts" or to, in any other way, attempt to maintain a child in the child's home, provide reunification services, or to attempt to rehabilitate the offending parent or parents. This Subsection (6) does not exempt the division from providing court-ordered services.

(7) (a) It is the division's obligation, under federal law, to achieve permanency for children who are abused, neglected, or dependent. If the use or continuation of "reasonable efforts," as described in Subsections (5) and (6), is determined to be inconsistent with the permanency plan for a child, then measures shall be taken, in a timely manner, to place the child in accordance with the permanency plan, and to complete whatever steps are necessary to finalize the permanent placement of the child.

(b) If, because of his conduct or condition, a parent is determined to be unfit or incompetent based on the grounds for termination of parental rights described in Title 78, Chapter 3a, Part 4, Termination of Parental Rights Act, the welfare and best interest of the child is of paramount importance, and shall govern in determining whether that parent's rights should be terminated.   2005

62A-4a-202. Preventive services — Family preservation services.

(1) (a) Within appropriations from the Legislature and monies obtained under Subsection (5), the division shall provide preventive, in-home services and family preservation services for families whose children are at immediate risk of being removed from the home and for families in crisis, if:

    (i) the child's welfare is not immediately endangered; and

    (ii) the division determines that it is possible and appropriate.

(b) In determining whether preventive or family preservation services are reasonable and appropriate, in keeping with the provisions of Subsection 62A-4a-201(1) the child's health, safety, and welfare shall be the paramount concern. The division shall consider whether those services will be effective within a six-month period, and whether they are likely to prevent reabuse or continued neglect of the child.

(2) The division shall maintain a statewide inventory of early intervention, preventive, and family preservation services available through public and private agencies or individuals for use by caseworkers. The inventory shall include:

(a) the method of accessing each service;

(b) eligibility requirements for each service; and

(c) the geographic areas and the number of families that can be served by each service, and information regarding waiting lists for each service.

(3) As a part of its preventive services, the division shall provide family preservation services that are short-term, intensive, crisis intervention programs, and that address:

(a) the safety of children;

(b) the physical and emotional needs of parents and children, including evaluating specific needs of the family, including depression, addiction, and mental illness;

(c) the child's physical surroundings, including cleaning and repairing physical housing, and addressing needs for necessities such as food, heat, and electricity;

(d) personal cleanliness, nutrition, and provision of personal grooming supplies and clothing;

(e) budgeting, money management, and employment; and

(f) parenting skills, including nonviolent discipline, nurturing, and structure, and teaching responsibility, respect for others, cooperation, and moral values.

(4) (a) The division may use only specially trained caseworkers or private providers to provide the family preservation services described in Subsection (3).

(b) Family preservation caseworkers may only be assigned a minimum number of families, but the division shall require that they be available 24 hours for an intensive period of at least six weeks, and that they respond to an assigned family within 24 hours.

(c) The division shall allow family preservation caseworkers to be creative and flexible in responding to the needs of each individual family.

(5) To provide, expand, and improve the delivery of in-home services to prevent the removal of children from their homes and promote the preservation of families, the division shall make substantial effort to obtain funding, including:

(a) federal grants;

(b) federal waivers; and

(c) private monies.   2004

62A-4a-202.1. Entering home of a minor — Taking a minor into protective custody — Caseworker accompanied by peace officer — Preventive services — Shelter care or emergency kinship.

(1) A state officer, peace officer, or child welfare worker may not enter the home of a minor who is not under the jurisdiction of the court, remove a minor from the minor's home or school, or take a minor into protective custody unless:

(a) the state officer, peace officer, or child welfare worker has obtained:

    (i) the consent of the minor's parent or guardian; or

    (ii) a court order issued under Section 78-3a-106; or

(b) there exist exigent circumstances.

(2) A child welfare worker within the division may take action under Subsection (1) accompanied by a peace officer, or without a peace officer when a peace officer is not reasonably available.

(3) If possible, consistent with the minor's safety and welfare, before taking a minor into protective

custody, the worker shall also determine whether there are services reasonably available to the worker which, if provided to the minor's parent or to the minor, would eliminate the need to remove the minor from the custody of the minor's parent or guardian. If those services are reasonably available, they shall be utilized. In determining whether services are reasonably available, and in making reasonable efforts to provide those services, the minor's health, safety, and welfare shall be the worker's paramount concern.

(4) (a) A minor removed or taken into custody under this section may not be placed or kept in a secure detention facility pending court proceedings unless the minor is detainable based on guidelines promulgated by the Division of Juvenile Justice Services.

(b) A minor removed from the custody of the minor's parent or guardian but who does not require physical restriction shall be given temporary care in:

(i) a shelter facility; or

(ii) an emergency kinship placement in accordance with Section 62A-4a-209.   2004

62A-4a-202.2. Notice to parent upon removal of child — Written statement of procedural rights and preliminary proceedings.

(1) (a) Any peace officer or caseworker who takes a minor into protective custody pursuant to Section 62A-4a-202.1 shall immediately use reasonable efforts to locate and inform, through the most efficient means available, the parents, including a noncustodial parent, the guardian, or responsible relative:

(i) that the minor has been taken into protective custody;

(ii) the reasons for removal and placement in protective custody;

(iii) that a written statement is available that explains the parent's procedural rights and the preliminary stages of the investigation and shelter hearing; and

(iv) of a telephone number where the parent may access further information.

(b) For purposes of locating and informing the noncustodial parent as required in Subsection (1)(a), the division shall search for the noncustodial parent through the national parent locator database if the division is unable to locate the noncustodial parent through other reasonable efforts.

(2) The attorney general's office shall adopt, print, and distribute a form for the written statement described in Subsection (1)(a)(iii). The statement shall be made available to the division and for distribution in schools, health care facilities, local police and sheriff's offices, the division, and any other appropriate office within the Department of Human Services. The notice shall be in simple language and include at least the following information:

(a) the conditions under which a minor may be released, hearings that may be required, and the means by which the parent may access further specific information about a minor's case and conditions of protective and temporary custody; and

(b) the rights of a minor and of the parent or guardian to legal counsel and to appeal.

(3) If a good faith attempt was made by the peace officer or caseworker to notify the parent or guardian in accordance with the requirements of Subsection (1), failure to notify shall be considered to be due to circumstances beyond the control of the peace officer or caseworker and may not be construed to permit a new defense to any juvenile or judicial proceeding or to interfere with any rights, procedures, or investigations provided for by this chapter or Title 78, Chapter 3a, Juvenile Courts.   2000 (1st S.S.)

62A-4a-202.3. Investigation — Supported or unsupported reports — Child in protective custody.

(1) When a child is taken into protective custody in accordance with Section 62A-4a-202.1, 78-3a-106, or 78-3a-301, or when the division takes any other action which would require a shelter hearing under Subsection 78-3a-306(1), the division shall immediately initiate an investigation of the:

(a) circumstances of the minor; and

(b) grounds upon which the decision to place the minor into protective custody was made.

(2) The division's investigation shall conform to reasonable professional standards, and shall include:

(a) a search for and review of any records of past reports of abuse or neglect involving:

(i) the same child;

(ii) any sibling or other child residing in the same household as the child; and

(iii) the alleged perpetrator;

(b) with regard to a child who is five years of age or older, a personal interview with the child:

(i) outside of the presence of the alleged perpetrator; and

(ii) conducted in accordance with the requirements of Subsection (7);

(c) if a parent or guardian can be located, an interview with at least one of the child's parents or guardian;

(d) an interview with the person who reported the abuse, unless the report was made anonymously;

(e) where possible and appropriate, interviews with other third parties who have had direct contact with the child, including:

(i) school personnel; and

(ii) the child's health care provider;

(f) an unscheduled visit to the child's home, unless:

(i) the division has reasonable cause to believe that the reported abuse was committed by a person who:

(A) is not the child's parent; and

(B) does not:

(I) live in the child's home; or

(II) otherwise have access to the child in the child's home; or

(ii) an unscheduled visit is not necessary to obtain evidence for the investigation; and

(g) if appropriate and indicated in any case alleging physical injury, sexual abuse, or failure to meet the child's medical needs, a medical examination, obtained no later than 24 hours after the child is placed in protective custody.

(3) The division may rely on a written report of a prior interview rather than conducting an additional interview, if:

(a) law enforcement:

(i) previously conducted a timely and thorough investigation regarding the alleged abuse, neglect, or dependency; and

(ii) produced a written report;

(b) the investigation described in Subsection (3)(a)(i) included one or more of the interviews required by Subsection (2); and

(c) the division finds that an additional interview is not in the best interest of the child.

(4) (a) The division's determination of whether a report is supported or unsupported may be based on the child's statements alone.

(b) Inability to identify or locate the perpetrator may not be used by the division as a basis for:

(i) determining that a report is unsupported; or

(ii) closing the case.

(c) The division may not determine a case to be unsupported or identify a case as unsupported solely because the perpetrator was an out-of-home perpetrator.

(d) Decisions regarding whether a report is supported, unsupported, or without merit shall be based on the facts of the case at the time the report was made.

(5) The division should maintain protective custody of the child if it finds that one or more of the following conditions exist:

(a) the minor does not have a natural parent, guardian, or responsible relative who is able and willing to provide safe and appropriate care for the minor;

(b) (i) shelter of the minor is a matter of necessity for the protection of the minor; and

(ii) there are no reasonable means by which the minor can be protected in:

(A) the minor's home; or

(B) the home of a responsible relative;

(c) there is substantial evidence that the parent or guardian is likely to flee the jurisdiction of the court; or

(d) the minor has left a previously court ordered placement.

(6) (a) Within 24 hours after receipt of a child into protective custody, excluding weekends and holidays, the division shall:

(i) convene a child protection team to review the circumstances regarding removal of the child from the child's home or school; and

(ii) prepare the testimony and evidence that will be required of the division at the shelter hearing, in accordance with Section 78-3a-306.

(b) The child protection team described in Subsection (6)(a)(i) shall include:

(i) the caseworker assigned to the case;

(ii) the caseworker who made the decision to remove the child;

(iii) a representative of the school or school district where the child attends school;

(iv) the peace officer who removed the child from the home;

(v) a representative of the appropriate Children's Justice Center, if one is established within the county where the child resides;

(vi) if appropriate, and known to the division, a therapist or counselor who is familiar with the child's circumstances; and

(vii) any other individuals determined appropriate and necessary by the team coordinator and chair.

(c) At the 24-hour meeting, the division shall have available for review and consideration the complete child protective services and foster care history of the child and the child's parents and siblings.

(7) (a) After receipt of a child into protective custody and prior to the adjudication hearing, all investigative interviews with the child that are initiated by the division shall be:

(i) audio or video taped; and

(ii) except as provided in Subsection (7)(b), conducted with a support person of the child's choice present.

(b) Notwithstanding Subsection (7)(a)(ii), the support person who is present for an interview of a child may not be an alleged perpetrator.

(8) The division shall cooperate with law enforcement investigations regarding the alleged perpetrator.

(9) The division may not close an investigation solely on the grounds that the division investigator is unable to locate the child until all reasonable efforts have been made to locate the child and family members including:

(a) visiting the home at times other than normal work hours;

(b) contacting local schools;

(c) contacting local, county, and state law enforcement agencies; and

(d) checking public assistance records.   2005

62A-4a-202.4. Access to criminal background information.

(1) For purposes of background screening and investigation of child abuse under this chapter and Title 78, Chapter 3a, Part 3, Abuse, Neglect, and Dependency Proceedings, the division shall have direct access to criminal background information maintained pursuant to Title 53, Chapter 10, Part 2, Bureau of Criminal Identification.

(2) The division and the Office of the Guardian Ad Litem Director are also authorized to request the Department of Public Safety to conduct a complete Federal Bureau of Investigation criminal background check through the national criminal history system (NCIC).   1998

62A-4a-202.5. Law enforcement investigation of alleged abuse in foster care.

Investigations of any report or allegation of abuse or neglect of a child that allegedly occurs while the child is living in substitute care in the protective custody, temporary custody, or custody of the division shall be conducted by:

(1) a law enforcement officer, as defined in Section 53-13-103; or

(2) a child protective services investigator under Section 62A-4a-202.6.   2001

62A-4a-202.6. Child protective services investigators within attorney general's office — Authority.

(1) (a) Pursuant to Section 67-5-16 the attorney general may employ, with the consent of the division, child protective services investigators to investigate reports of abuse or neglect of a child that occur while the child is in the custody of the division.

(b) (i) Under the direction of the Board of Child and Family Services, the division shall, in accordance with Subsection 62A-4a-409(5), contract with an independent child protective service investigator to investigate reports of abuse or neglect of a child that occur while the child is in the custody of the division.

(ii) The executive director of the department shall designate an entity within the department, other than the division, to monitor the contract for the investigators described in Subsection (1)(b)(i).

(2) The investigators described in Subsection (1) may also investigate allegations of abuse or neglect of a child by a department employee or a licensed substitute care provider.

(3) The investigators described in Subsection (1), if not peace officers, shall have the same rights, duties, and authority of a child protective services investigator employed by the division to:

(a) make a thorough investigation upon receiving either an oral or written report of alleged abuse or neglect of a child, with the primary purpose of that investigation being the protection of the child;

(b) make an inquiry into the child's home environment, emotional, or mental health, the nature and extent of the child's injuries, and the child's physical safety;

(c) make a written report of their investigation, including determination regarding whether the alleged abuse or neglect was substantiated, unsubstantiated, or without merit, and forward a copy of that report to the division within the time mandates for investigations established by the division;

(d) immediately consult with school authorities to verify the child's status in accordance with Sections 53A-11-101 through 53A-11-103 when a report is based upon or includes an allegation of educational neglect;

(e) enter upon public or private premises, using appropriate legal processes, to investigate reports of alleged child abuse or neglect; and

(f) take a child into protective custody, and deliver the child to a law enforcement officer, or to the division. Control and jurisdiction over the child shall be determined by the provisions of Title 62A, Chapter 4a, Part 2, Child Welfare Services, Title 78, Chapter 3a, Juvenile Courts, and as otherwise provided by law.   2001

PART 4

CHILD ABUSE OR NEGLECT REPORTING REQUIREMENTS

62A-4a-401. Legislative purpose.

It is the purpose of this part to protect the best interests of children, offer protective services to prevent harm to children, stabilize the home environment, preserve family life whenever possible, and encourage cooperation among the states in dealing with the problem of child abuse.   1994

62A-4a-402. Definitions.

As used in this part:

(1) "A person responsible for a child's care" means the child's parent, guardian, or other person responsible for the child's care, whether in the same home as the child, a relative's home, a group, family, or center day care facility, a foster care home, or a residential institution.

(2) "Child" means a person under 18 years of age.

(3) "Child abuse or neglect" means causing harm or threatened harm to a child's health or welfare.

(4) "Harm or threatened harm" means damage or threatened damage to the physical or emotional health and welfare of a child through neglect or abuse, and includes but is not limited to:

(a) causing nonaccidental physical or mental injury;

(b) incest;

(c) sexual abuse;

(d) sexual exploitation;

(e) molestation; or

(f) repeated negligent treatment or maltreatment.

(5) "Incest" means having sexual intercourse with a person whom the perpetrator knows to be his or her ancestor, descendant, brother, sister, uncle, aunt, nephew, niece, or first cousin. The relationships referred to in this subsection include blood relationships of the whole or half blood without regard to legitimacy, and include relationships of parent and child by adoption, and relationships of stepparent and stepchild while the marriage creating the relationship of a stepparent and stepchild exists.

(6) "Molestation" means touching the anus or any part of the genitals of a child or otherwise taking indecent liberties with a child, or causing a child to take indecent liberties with the perpetrator or another with the intent to arouse or gratify the sexual desire of any person.

(7) "Sexual abuse" means acts or attempted acts of sexual intercourse, sodomy, or molestation directed towards a child.

(8) "Sexual exploitation of minors" means knowingly employing, using, persuading, inducing, enticing or coercing any minor to pose in the nude for the purpose of sexual arousal of any person or for profit, or to engage in any sexual or simulated sexual conduct for the purpose of photographing, filming, recording, or displaying in any way the sexual or simulated sexual conduct, and includes displaying, distributing, possessing for the purpose of distribution, or selling material depicting minors in the nude or engaging in sexual or simulated sexual conduct.

(9) "Subject" or "subject of the report" means any person reported under this part, including, but not limited to, a child, parent, guardian, or other person responsible for a child's care.   1998

62A-4a-403. Reporting requirements.

(1) Except as provided in Subsection (2), when any person including persons licensed under Title 58, Chapter 67, Utah Medical Practice Act, or Title 58, Chapter 31b, Nurse Practice Act, has reason to believe that a child has been subjected to incest, molestation, sexual exploitation, sexual abuse, physical abuse, or neglect, or who observes a child being subjected to conditions or circumstances which would reasonably result in sexual abuse, physical abuse, or neglect, he shall immediately notify the nearest peace officer, law enforcement agency, or office of the division. On receipt of this notice, the peace officer or law enforcement agency shall immediately notify the nearest office of the division. If an initial report of child abuse or neglect is made to the division, the division shall immediately notify the appropriate local law enforcement agency. The division shall, in addition to its own investigation, comply with and lend support to investigations by law enforcement undertaken pursuant to a report made under this section.

(2) The notification requirements of Subsection (1) do not apply to a clergyman or priest, without the consent of the person making the confession, with regard to any confession made to him in his professional character in the course of discipline enjoined by the church to which he belongs, if:

(a) the confession was made directly to the clergyman or priest by the perpetrator; and

(b) the clergyman or priest is, under canon law or church doctrine or practice, bound to maintain the confidentiality of that confession.

(3) (a) When a clergyman or priest receives information about abuse or neglect from any source other than confession of the perpetrator, he is required to give notification on the basis of that information even though he may have also received a report of abuse or neglect from the confession of the perpetrator.

(b) Exemption of notification requirements for a clergyman or priest does not exempt a clergyman or priest from any other efforts required by law to prevent further abuse or neglect by the perpetrator.   1999

62A-4a-404. Fetal alcohol syndrome and drug dependency — Reporting requirements.

When any person, including a licensee under the Medical Practice Act or the Nurse Practice Act, attends the birth of a child or cares for a child, and determines that the child, at the time of birth, has fetal alcohol syndrome or fetal drug dependency, he shall report that determination to the division as soon as possible.   1994

62A-4a-405. Death of child — Reporting requirements.

Any person who has reason to believe that a child has died as a result of child abuse or neglect shall report that fact to the local law enforcement agency, who shall report to the county attorney or district attorney as provided under Section 17-18-1 or 17-18-1.7 and to the appropriate medical examiner in accordance with Title 26, Chapter 4, Utah Medical Examiner Act. The medical examiner shall investigate and report his findings to the police, the appropriate county attorney or district attorney, the attorney general's office, the division, and if the institution making the report is a hospital, to that hospital.   1994

62A-4a-406. Photographs.

(1) Any physician, surgeon, medical examiner, peace officer, law enforcement official, or public health officer or official may take photographs of the areas of trauma visible on a child and, if medically indicated, perform radiological examinations.

(2) Photographs may be taken of the premises or of objects relevant to a reported circumstance of child abuse or neglect.

(3) Photographs or X-rays, and all other medical records pertinent to an investigation for child abuse or neglect shall be made available to the division, law enforcement officials, and the court.   1994

62A-4a-407. Protective custody.

(1) A physician examining or treating a child may take the child into protective custody not to exceed 72 hours, without the consent of the child's parent, guardian, or any other person responsible for the child's care or exercising temporary or permanent control over the child, when the physician has reason to believe that the child's life or safety will be in danger unless protective custody is exercised.

(2) The person in charge of a hospital or similar medical facility may retain protective custody of a child suspected of being abused or neglected, when he reasonably believes the facts warrant that retention. This action may be taken regardless of whether additional medical treatment is required, and regardless of whether the person responsible for the child's care requests the child's return.

(3) The division shall be immediately notified of protective custody exercised under this section. Protective custody under this section may not exceed 72 hours without an order of the district or juvenile court.   1995

62A-4a-408. Written reports.

Reports made pursuant to this part shall be followed by a written report within 48 hours, if requested by the division. The division shall immediately forward a copy of that report to the statewide central register, on forms supplied by the register.
                    1994

62A-4a-409. Investigation by division — Temporary protective custody — Preremoval interviews of children.

(1) The division shall make a thorough preremoval investigation upon receiving either an oral or written report of alleged abuse, neglect, fetal alcohol syndrome, or fetal drug dependency, when there is reasonable cause to suspect a situation of abuse, neglect, fetal alcohol syndrome, or fetal drug dependency. The primary purpose of that investigation shall be protection of the child.

(2) The preremoval investigation shall include the same investigative requirements described in Section 62A-4a-202.3.

(3) The division shall make a written report of its investigation. The written report shall include a determination regarding whether the alleged abuse or neglect was supported, unsupported, or without merit.

(4) (a) The division shall use an interdisciplinary approach whenever possible in dealing with reports made under this part.

(b) For this purpose, the division shall convene appropriate interdisciplinary "child protection teams" to assist it in its protective, diagnostic, assessment, treatment, and coordination services.

(c) A representative of the division shall serve as the team's coordinator and chair. Members of the team shall serve at the coordinator's invitation. Whenever possible, the team shall include representatives of:

(i) health, mental health, education, and law enforcement agencies;

(ii) the child;

(iii) parent and family support groups unless the parent is alleged to be the perpetrator; and

(iv) other appropriate agencies or individuals.

(5) In any case where the division supervises, governs, or directs the affairs of any individual, institution, or facility that has been alleged to be involved in acts or omissions of child abuse or neglect, the investigation of the reported child abuse or neglect shall be conducted by an agency other than the division.

(6) If a report of neglect is based upon or includes an allegation of educational neglect, the division shall immediately consult with school authorities to verify the child's status in accordance with Sections 53A-11-101 through 53A-11-103.

(7) When the division has completed its initial investigation under this part, it shall give notice of that completion to the person who made the initial report.

(8) Division workers or other child protection team members have authority to enter upon public or

private premises, using appropriate legal processes, to investigate reports of alleged child abuse or neglect, upon notice to parents of their rights under the Child Abuse Prevention and Treatment Act, 42 U.S.C. Sec. 5106, or any successor thereof.

(9) With regard to any interview of a child prior to removal of that child from the child's home:

(a) except as provided in Subsection (9)(b) or (c), the division shall notify a parent of the child prior to the interview;

(b) if a child's parent or stepparent, or a parent's paramour has been identified as the alleged perpetrator, the division need not notify a parent of the child prior to an initial interview with the child;

(c) if the perpetrator is unknown, or if the perpetrator's relationship to the child's family is unknown, the division may conduct a minimal interview, not to exceed 15 minutes, with the child prior to notification of the child's parent;

(d) in all cases described in Subsection (9)(b) or (c), a parent of the child shall be notified as soon as practicable after the child has been interviewed, but in no case later than 24 hours after the interview has taken place;

(e) a child's parents shall be notified of the time and place of all subsequent interviews with the child; and

(f) (i) the child shall be allowed to have a support person of the child's choice present; and

(ii) the person described in Subsection (9)(f)(i):

(A) may include:

(I) a school teacher;

(II) an administrator;

(III) a guidance counselor;

(IV) a child care provider; or

(V) clergy; and

(B) may not be a person who is alleged to be, or potentially may be, the perpetrator.

(10) In accordance with the procedures and requirements of Sections 62A-4a-202.1 through 62A-4a-202.3, a division worker or child protection team member may take a child into protective custody and deliver the child to a law enforcement officer, or place the child in an emergency shelter facility approved by the juvenile court, at the earliest opportunity subsequent to the child's removal from the child's original environment. Control and jurisdiction over the child is determined by the provisions of Title 78, Chapter 3a, Juvenile Court Act of 1996, and as otherwise provided by law.

(11) With regard to cases in which law enforcement has or is conducting an investigation of alleged abuse or neglect of a child:

(a) the division shall coordinate with law enforcement to ensure that there is an adequate safety plan to protect the child from further abuse or neglect; and

(b) the division is not required to duplicate an aspect of the investigation that, in the division's determination, has been satisfactorily completed by law enforcement.   2004

62A-4a-410.   Immunity from liability.

(1) Any person, official, or institution participating in good faith in making a report, taking photographs or X-rays, assisting an investigator from the division, serving as a member of a child protection team, or taking a child into protective custody pursuant to this part, is immune from any liability, civil or criminal, that otherwise might result by reason of those actions.

(2) This section does not provide immunity with respect to acts or omissions of a governmental employee except as provided in Title 63, Chapter 30d, Governmental Immunity Act of Utah.   2005

62A-4a-411.   Failure to report — Criminal penalty.

Any person, official, or institution required to report a case of suspected child abuse, child sexual abuse, neglect, fetal alcohol syndrome, or fetal drug dependency, who willfully fails to do so is guilty of a class B misdemeanor. Action for failure to report must be commenced within four years from the date of knowledge of the offense and the willful failure to report.
                                              1994

62A-4a-412.   Reports and information confidential.

(1) Except as otherwise provided in this chapter, reports made pursuant to this part, as well as any other information in the possession of the division obtained as the result of a report are private, protected, or controlled records under Title 63, Chapter 2, Government Records Access and Management Act, and may only be made available to:

(a) a police or law enforcement agency investigating a report of known or suspected child abuse or neglect;

(b) a physician who reasonably believes that a child may be the subject of abuse or neglect;

(c) an agency that has responsibility or authority to care for, treat, or supervise a child who is the subject of a report;

(d) a contract provider that has a written contract with the division to render services to a child who is the subject of a report;

(e) any subject of the report, the natural parents of the minor, and the guardian ad litem;

(f) a court, upon a finding that access to the records may be necessary for the determination of an issue before the court, provided that in a divorce, custody, or related proceeding between private parties, the record alone is:

(i) limited to objective or undisputed facts that were verified at the time of the investigation; and

(ii) devoid of conclusions drawn by the division or any of the division's workers on the ultimate issue of whether or not a person's acts or omissions constituted any level of abuse or neglect of another person;

(g) an office of the public prosecutor or its deputies in performing an official duty;

(h) a person authorized by a Children's Justice Center, for the purposes described in Section 67-5b-102;

(i) a person engaged in bona fide research, when approved by the director of the division, if the information does not include names and addresses;

(j) the State Office of Education, acting on behalf of itself or on behalf of a school district, for the purpose of evaluating whether an individual should be permitted to obtain or retain a license as an educator or serve as an employee or volunteer in a school, limited to information with substantiated findings involving an alleged sexual offense, an alleged felony or class A misdemeanor drug offense, or any alleged offense against the person under Title 76, Chapter 5, Offenses Against the Person, and with the understanding that the office must provide the subject of a report received under Subsection (1)(k) with an opportunity to respond to the report before making a decision concerning licensure or employment;

(k) any person identified in the report as a perpetrator or possible perpetrator of child abuse or neglect, after being advised of the screening prohibition in Subsection (2);

(l) a person filing a petition for a child protective order on behalf of a minor who is the subject of the report; and

(m) a licensed child-placing agency or person who is performing a preplacement adoptive evaluation in accordance with the requirements of Section 78-30-3.5.

(2) (a) A person, unless listed in Subsection (1), may not request another person to obtain or release a report or any other information in the possession of the division obtained as a result of the report that is available under Subsection (1)(k) to screen for potential perpetrators of child abuse or neglect.

(b) A person who requests information knowing that it is a violation of Subsection (2)(a) to do so is subject to the criminal penalty in Subsection (4).

(3) (a) Except as provided in Section 62A-4a-116.3 and Subsection (3)(b), the division and law enforcement officials shall ensure the anonymity of the person or persons making the initial report and any others involved in its subsequent investigation.

(b) Notwithstanding any other provision of law, excluding Section 78-3a-314, but including this chapter and Title 63, Chapter 2, Government Records Access and Management Act, when the division makes a report or other information in its possession available under Subsection (1)(e) to a subject of the report or a parent of a minor, the division shall remove from the report or other information only the names, addresses, and telephone numbers of individuals or specific information that could:

(i) identify the referent;

(ii) impede a criminal investigation; or

(iii) endanger a person's safety.

(4) Any person who wilfully permits, or aides and abets the release of data or information obtained as a result of this part, in the possession of the division or contained on any part of the Management Information System, in violation of this part or Sections 62A-4a-116 through 62A-4a-116.3, is guilty of a class C misdemeanor.

(5) The physician-patient privilege is not a ground for excluding evidence regarding a child's injuries or the cause of those injuries, in any proceeding resulting from a report made in good faith pursuant to this part.

(6) A child-placing agency or person who receives a report in connection with a preplacement adoptive evaluation pursuant to Section 78-30-3.5:

(a) may provide this report to the person who is the subject of the report; and

(b) may provide this report to a person who is performing a preplacement adoptive evaluation in accordance with the requirement of Section 78-30-3.5, or to a licensed child-placing agency or to an attorney seeking to facilitate an adoption.

2004

62A-4a-413.   Repealed.   2002

62A-4a-414.   Interviews of children — Recording required.

(1) (a) Interviews of children during an investigation in accordance with Section 62A-4a-409, and involving allegations of sexual abuse or serious physical abuse of a child, shall be conducted only under the following conditions:

(i) the interview shall be recorded visually and aurally on film, videotape, or by other electronic means;

(ii) both the interviewer and the child shall be simultaneously recorded and visible on the final product;

(iii) the time and date of the interview shall be continuously and clearly visible to any subsequent viewer of the recording; and

(iv) the recording equipment shall run continuously for the duration of the interview.

(b) This Subsection (1) does not apply to initial or minimal interviews conducted in accordance with Subsection 62A-4a-409(9)(b) or (c).

(2) Interviews conducted in accordance with Subsection (1) shall be carried out in an existing Children's Justice Center or in a soft interview room, when available.

(a) If the Children's Justice Center or a soft interview room is not available, the interviewer shall use the best setting available under the circumstances.

(b) If the equipment required under Subsection (1) is not available, the interview shall be audiotaped, provided that the interviewer shall clearly state at the beginning of the tape:

(i) the time, date, and place of the interview;

(ii) the full name and age of the child being interviewed; and

(iii) that the equipment required under Subsection (1) is not available and why.

(3) All other investigative interviews shall be audiotaped using electronic means. At the beginning of the tape, the worker shall state clearly the time, date, and place of the meeting, and the full name and age of the child in attendance.   2004

PART 5

RUNAWAYS

62A-4a-501.   Providing shelter to a runaway — Reporting requirements — Division to provide assistance — Penalty.

(1) Any person who knowingly and intentionally harbors a minor and who knows at the time of harboring the minor that the minor is away from the parent's or legal guardian's home, or other lawfully prescribed residence, without the permission of the parent or legal guardian, shall promptly notify the parent or legal guardian of the minor's location or report the location of the minor to the division. The report may be made by telephone or any other reasonable means.

(2) Unless the context clearly requires otherwise:

(a) "Promptly" means within eight hours after the person has knowledge that the minor is away from home without parental permission.

(b) "Shelter" means the person's home or any structure over which the person has any control.

(3) Upon receipt of a report that a minor is being harbored by a person the division shall notify the parent or legal guardian that a report has been made

and inform the parent or legal guardian of assistance available from the division.

(4) A parent or legal guardian who is aware that his minor is being harbored may notify the division or a law enforcement agency and request assistance in retrieving the minor from the place of shelter. The division or local law enforcement agency may assist the parent or legal guardian in retrieving the minor.

(5) Any person who knowingly and intentionally harbors a minor and who knows at the time of harboring the minor that the minor is away from the parent's or legal guardian's home, or other lawfully prescribed residence, without the permission of the parent or guardian and without making the notification required by this section is guilty of a class B misdemeanor.   1996

CHAPTER 7

JUVENILE JUSTICE SERVICES

Part 1

Division of Juvenile Justice Services — Functions and Duties

Part 4

Secure Facilities

PART 1

DIVISION OF JUVENILE JUSTICE SERVICES — FUNCTIONS AND DUTIES

62A-7-106.   Renumbered as § 62A-7-402.   2005

PART 4

Secure Facilities

62A-7-402.   Aiding or concealing youth offender — Trespass — Criminal penalties.

(1) A person who commits any of the following offenses is guilty of a class A misdemeanor:

(a) entering, or attempting to enter, a building or enclosure appropriated to the use of youth offenders, without permission;

(b) entering any premises belonging to a secure facility and committing or attempting to commit a trespass or damage on those premises; or

(c) willfully annoying or disturbing the peace and quiet of a secure facility or of a youth offender in a secure facility.

(2) A person is guilty of a third degree felony who:

(a) knowingly harbors or conceals a youth offender who has:

(i) escaped from a secure facility; or

(ii) absconded from:

(A) a facility or supervision; or

(B) supervision of the Division of Juvenile Justice Services; or

(b) willfully aided or assisted a youth offender who has been lawfully committed to a secure facility in escaping or attempting to escape from that facility.

(3) As used in this section:

(a) a youth offender absconds from a facility when he:

(i) leaves the facility without permission; or

(ii) fails to return at a prescribed time.

(b) A youth offender absconds from supervision when he:

(i) changes his residence from the residence that he reported to the division as his correct address to another residence, without notifying the Division of Juvenile Justice Services or obtaining permission; or

(ii) for the purpose of avoiding supervision:

(A) hides at a different location from his reported residence; or

(B) leaves his reported residence.   2005

CHAPTER 8

SUBSTANCE ABUSE [RENUMBERED]

CHAPTER 12

MENTAL HEALTH [RENUMBERED]

CHAPTER 15

SUBSTANCE ABUSE AND MENTAL HEALTH ACT

Part 1

Division and Board of Substance Abuse and Mental Health

Part 4

Alcohol Training and Education

Part 6

Utah State Hospital and Other Mental Health Facilities

Part 7

Commitment of Persons Under Age 18 to Division of Substance Abuse and Mental Health

PART 1

DIVISION AND BOARD OF SUBSTANCE ABUSE AND MENTAL HEALTH

62A-15-105. Authority and responsibilities of board.

The board is the policymaking body for the division and for programs funded with state and federal moneys under Sections 17-43-201, 17-43-301, 17-43-304, and 62A-15-110. The board shall:

(1) in establishing policy, seek input from local substance abuse authorities, local mental health authorities, consumers, providers, advocates, division staff, and other interested parties as determined by the board;

(2) establish, by rule, minimum standards for local substance abuse authorities and local mental health authorities;

(3) establish, by rule, procedures for developing its policies which ensure that local substance abuse authorities and local mental health authorities are given opportunity to comment and provide input on any new policy of the board or proposed changes in existing policy of the board;

(4) provide a mechanism for review of its existing policy, and for consideration of policy changes that are proposed by local substance abuse authorities or local mental health authorities;

(5) develop program policies, standards, rules, and fee schedules for the division; and

(6) in accordance with Title 63, Chapter 46a, Utah Administrative Rulemaking Act, make rules approving the form and content of substance abuse treatment, educational series, screening, and assessment that are described in Section 41-6a-501.   2005

PART 4

ALCOHOL TRAINING AND EDUCATION

62A-15-401. Alcohol training and education seminar.

(1) As used in this part:

(a) "instructor" means a person that directly provides the instruction during an alcohol training and education seminar for a seminar provider;

(b) "licensee" means a person who is:

(i) a new or renewing licensee under Title 32A, Alcoholic Beverage Control Act; and

(ii) engaged in the retail sale of alcoholic beverages for consumption on the premises of the licensee; and

(c) "seminar provider" means a person other than the division who provides an alcohol training and education seminar meeting the requirements of this section.

(2) (a) This section applies to a person who, as defined by the board by rule:

(i) manages operations at the premises of a licensee;

(ii) supervises the serving of alcoholic beverages to a customer for consumption on the premises of a licensee; or

(iii) serves alcoholic beverages to a customer for consumption on the premises of a licensee.

(b) A person described in Subsection (2)(a) shall:

(i) complete an alcohol training and education seminar within 30 days of:

(A) if the person is an employee, the day the person begins employment;

(B) if the person is an independent contractor, the day the person is first hired;

(C) if the person holds an ownership interest in the licensee, the day that person first engages in an activity that would result in that person being required to complete an alcohol training and education seminar; and

(ii) pay a fee:

(A) to the seminar provider; and

(B) that is equal to or greater than the amount established under Subsection (4)(h).

(c) Notwithstanding Subsection (2)(b)(i)(C), a person described in Subsection (2)(b)(i)(C) shall complete an alcohol training and education seminar by no later than July 31, 2001, if as of May 1, 2001 the person:

(i) holds an ownership interest in the licensee; and

(ii) has engaged in an activity that would result in that person being required to complete an alcohol training and education seminar.

(3) (a) A licensee may not permit a person who is not in compliance with Subsection (2) to:

(i) serve or supervise the serving of alcoholic beverages to a customer for consumption on the premises of the licensee; or

(ii) engage in any activity that would constitute managing operations at the premises of a licensee.

(b) A licensee that violates Subsection (3)(a) is subject to Section 32A-1-401.

(4) The division shall:

(a) (i) provide alcohol training and education seminars; or

(ii) certify one or more seminar providers;

(b) establish the curriculum for an alcohol training and education seminar that includes the following subjects:

(i) (A) alcohol as a drug; and

(B) alcohol's effect on the body and behavior;

(ii) recognizing the problem drinker;

(iii) an overview of state alcohol laws related to responsible beverage service, as determined in consultation with the Department of Alcoholic Beverage Control;

(iv) dealing with the problem customer, including ways to terminate service; and

(v) alternative means of transportation to get the customer safely home;

(c) recertify each seminar provider every three years;

(d) monitor compliance with the curriculum described in Subsection (4)(b);

(e) maintain for at least three years a record of every person who has completed an alcohol training and education seminar;

(f) provide the information described in Subsection (4)(e) on request to:

(i) the Department of Alcoholic Beverage Control; or

(ii) law enforcement;

(g) provide the Department of Alcoholic Beverage Control on request a list of any seminar provider certified by the division; and

(h) establish a fee amount for each person attending an alcohol training and education seminar that is sufficient to offset the division's cost of administering this section.

(5) The board shall by rule made in accordance with Title 63, Chapter 46a, Utah Administrative Rulemaking Act:

(a) define what constitutes under this section a person who:

(i) manages operations at the premises of a licensee;

(ii) supervises the serving of alcoholic beverages to a customer for consumption on the premises of a licensee; or

(iii) serves alcoholic beverages to a customer for consumption on the premises of a licensee;

(b) establish criteria for certifying and recertifying a seminar provider; and

(c) establish guidelines for the manner in which an instructor provides an alcohol education and training seminar.

(6) A seminar provider shall:

(a) obtain recertification by the division every three years;

(b) ensure that an instructor used by the seminar provider:

(i) follows the curriculum established under this section; and

(ii) conducts an alcohol training and education seminar in accordance with the guidelines established by rule;

(c) ensure that any information provided by the seminar provider or instructor of a seminar provider is consistent with:

(i) the curriculum established under this section; and

(ii) this section;

(d) provide the division with the names of all persons who complete an alcohol training and education seminar provided by the seminar provider;

(e) collect a fee for each person attending an alcohol training and education seminar in accordance with Subsection (2); and

(f) forward to the division the portion of the fee that is equal to the amount described in Subsection (4)(h).

(7) (a) If after a hearing conducted in accordance with Title 63, Chapter 46b, Administrative Procedures Act, the division finds that a seminar provider violates this section or that an instructor of the seminar provider violates this section, the division may:

(i) suspend the certification of the seminar provider for a period not to exceed 90 days;

(ii) revoke the certification of the seminar provider;

(iii) require the seminar provider to take corrective action regarding an instructor; or

(iv) prohibit the seminar provider from using an instructor until such time that the seminar provider establishes to the satisfaction of the division that the instructor is in compliance with Subsection (6)(b).

(b) The division may certify a seminar provider whose certification is revoked:

(i) no sooner than 90 days from the date the certification is revoked; and

(ii) if the seminar provider establishes to the satisfaction of the division that the seminar provider will comply with this section.

2002 (5th S.S.)

PART 6

UTAH STATE HOSPITAL AND OTHER MENTAL HEALTH FACILITIES

62A-15-620. Attempt to commit person contrary to requirements — Penalty.

Any person who attempts to place another person in the custody of a local mental health authority contrary to the provisions of this part is guilty of a class B misdemeanor, in addition to liability in an action for damages, or subject to other criminal charges.

2002 (5th S.S.)

62A-15-621. Trespass — Disturbance — Penalty.

Any person who, without permission, enters any of the buildings or enclosures appropriated to the use of patients, or makes any attempt to do so, or enters anywhere upon the premises belonging to or used by the division, a local mental health authority, or the state hospital and commits, or attempts to commit, any trespass or depredation thereon, or any person who, either from within or without the enclosures, willfully annoys or disturbs the peace or quiet of the premises or of any patient therein, is guilty of a class B misdemeanor. 2002 (5th S.S.)

62A-15-622. Abduction of patient — Penalty.

Any person who abducts a patient who is in the custody of a local mental health authority, or induces any patient to elope or escape from that custody, or attempts to do so, or aids or assists therein, is guilty of a class B misdemeanor, in addition to liability for damages, or subject to other criminal charges.

2002 (5th S.S.)

62A-15-623. Criminal's escape — Penalty.

Any person committed to the state hospital under the provisions of Title 77, Chapter 15, Inquiry into Sanity of Defendant, or Chapter 16, Mental Examination after Conviction, who escapes or leaves the state hospital without proper legal authority is guilty of a class A misdemeanor. 2002 (5th S.S.)

62A-15-628. Involuntary commitment — Procedures.

(1) An adult may not be involuntarily committed to the custody of a local mental health authority except under the following provisions:

(a) emergency procedures for temporary commitment upon medical or designated examiner certification, as provided in Subsection 62A-15-629(1);

(b) emergency procedures for temporary commitment without endorsement of medical or designated examiner certification, as provided in Subsection 62A-15-629(2); or

(c) commitment on court order, as provided in Section 62A-15-631.

(2) A person under 18 years of age may be committed to the physical custody of a local mental health authority only after a court commitment proceeding in accordance with the provisions of Part 7, Commitment of Persons Under Age 18 to Division of Substance Abuse and Mental Health. 2003

62A-15-629. Temporary commitment — Requirements and procedures.

(1) (a) An adult may be temporarily, involuntarily committed to a local mental health authority upon:

(i) written application by a responsible person who has reason to know, stating a belief that the individual is likely to cause serious injury to himself or others if not immediately restrained, and stating the personal knowledge of the individual's condition or circumstances which lead to that belief; and

    (ii) a certification by a licensed physician or designated examiner stating that the physician or designated examiner has examined the individual within a three-day period immediately preceding that certification, and that he is of the opinion that the individual is mentally ill and, because of his mental illness, is likely to injure himself or others if not immediately restrained.

  (b) Application and certification as described in Subsection (1)(a) authorizes any peace officer to take the individual into the custody of a local mental health authority and transport the individual to that authority's designated facility.

(2) If a duly authorized peace officer observes a person involved in conduct that gives the officer probable cause to believe that the person is mentally ill, as defined in Section 62A-15-602, and because of that apparent mental illness and conduct, there is a substantial likelihood of serious harm to that person or others, pending proceedings for examination and certification under this part, the officer may take that person into protective custody. The peace officer shall transport the person to be transported to the designated facility of the appropriate local mental health authority pursuant to this section, either on the basis of his own observation or on the basis of a mental health officer's observation that has been reported to him by that mental health officer. Immediately thereafter, the officer shall place the person in the custody of the local mental health authority and make application for commitment of that person to the local mental health authority. The application shall be on a prescribed form and shall include the following:

    (a) a statement by the officer that he believes, on the basis of personal observation or on the basis of a mental health officer's observation reported to him by the mental health officer, that the person is, as a result of a mental illness, a substantial and immediate danger to himself or others;

    (b) the specific nature of the danger;

    (c) a summary of the observations upon which the statement of danger is based; and

    (d) a statement of facts which called the person to the attention of the officer.

(3) A person committed under this section may be held for a maximum of 24 hours, excluding Saturdays, Sundays, and legal holidays. At the expiration of that time period, the person shall be released unless application for involuntary commitment has been commenced pursuant to Section 62A-15-631. If that application has been made, an order of detention may be entered under Subsection 62A-15-631(3). If no order of detention is issued, the patient shall be released unless he has made voluntary application for admission.

(4) Transportation of mentally ill persons pursuant to Subsections (1) and (2) shall be conducted by the appropriate municipal, or city or town, law enforcement authority or, under the appropriate law enforcement's authority, by ambulance to the extent that Subsection (5) applies. However, if the designated facility is outside of that authority's jurisdiction, the appropriate county sheriff shall transport the person or cause the person to be transported by ambulance to the extent that Subsection (5) applies.

(5) Notwithstanding Subsections (2) and (4), a peace officer shall cause a person to be transported by ambulance if the person meets any of the criteria in Section 26-8a-305. In addition, if the person requires physical medical attention, the peace officer shall direct that transportation be to an appropriate medical facility for treatment.   **2002 (5th S.S.)**

62A-15-643. Confidentiality of information and records — Exceptions — Penalty.

(1) All certificates, applications, records, and reports made for the purpose of this part, including those made on judicial proceedings for involuntary commitment, that directly or indirectly identify a patient or former patient or an individual whose commitment has been sought under this part, shall be kept confidential and may not be disclosed by any person except insofar as:

    (a) the individual identified or his legal guardian, if any, or, if a minor, his parent or legal guardian shall consent;

    (b) disclosure may be necessary to carry out the provisions of:

      (i) this part; or

      (ii) Section 53-10-208.1; or

    (c) a court may direct, upon its determination that disclosure is necessary for the conduct of proceedings before it, and that failure to make the disclosure would be contrary to the public interest.

(2) A person who knowingly or intentionally discloses any information not authorized by this section is guilty of a class B misdemeanor.   **2002 (5th S.S.)**

PART 7

COMMITMENT OF PERSONS UNDER AGE 18 TO DIVISION OF SUBSTANCE ABUSE AND MENTAL HEALTH

62A-15-707. Confidentiality of information and records — Exceptions — Penalty.

(1) Notwithstanding the provisions of Sections 63-2-101 through 63-2-909, Government Records Access Management Act, all certificates, applications, records, and reports made for the purpose of this part that directly or indirectly identify a patient or former patient or an individual whose commitment has been sought under this part, shall be kept confidential and may not be disclosed by any person except as follows:

    (a) the individual identified consents after reaching 18 years of age;

    (b) the child's parent or legal guardian consents;

    (c) disclosure is necessary to carry out any of the provisions of this part; or

    (d) a court may direct, upon its determination that disclosure is necessary for the conduct of proceedings before it, and that failure to make the disclosure would be contrary to the public interest.

(2) A person who violates any provision of this section is guilty of a class B misdemeanor.

    2002 (5th S.S.)

TITLE 63

STATE AFFAIRS IN GENERAL

Chapter

CHAPTER 2

GOVERNMENT RECORDS ACCESS AND MANAGEMENT

Part 3

Classification

PART 3

CLASSIFICATION

63-2-304. Protected records.

The following records are protected if properly classified by a governmental entity:

(1) trade secrets as defined in Section 13-24-2 if the person submitting the trade secret has provided the governmental entity with the information specified in Section 63-2-308;

(2) commercial information or nonindividual financial information obtained from a person if:

(a) disclosure of the information could reasonably be expected to result in unfair competitive injury to the person submitting the information or would impair the ability of the governmental entity to obtain necessary information in the future;

(b) the person submitting the information has a greater interest in prohibiting access than the public in obtaining access; and

(c) the person submitting the information has provided the governmental entity with the information specified in Section 63-2-308;

(3) commercial or financial information acquired or prepared by a governmental entity to the extent that disclosure would lead to financial speculations in currencies, securities, or commodities that will interfere with a planned transaction by the governmental entity or cause substantial financial injury to the governmental entity or state economy;

(4) records the disclosure of which could cause commercial injury to, or confer a competitive advantage upon a potential or actual competitor of, a commercial project entity as defined in Subsection 11-13-103(4);

(5) test questions and answers to be used in future license, certification, registration, employment, or academic examinations;

(6) records the disclosure of which would impair governmental procurement proceedings or give an unfair advantage to any person proposing to enter into a contract or agreement with a governmental entity, except that this Subsection (6) does not restrict the right of a person to see bids submitted to or by a governmental entity after bidding has closed;

(7) records that would identify real property or the appraisal or estimated value of real or personal property, including intellectual property, under consideration for public acquisition before any rights to the property are acquired unless:

(a) public interest in obtaining access to the information outweighs the governmental entity's need to acquire the property on the best terms possible;

(b) the information has already been disclosed to persons not employed by or under a duty of confidentiality to the entity;

(c) in the case of records that would identify property, potential sellers of the described property have already learned of the governmental entity's plans to acquire the property;

(d) in the case of records that would identify the appraisal or estimated value of property, the potential sellers have already learned of the governmental entity's estimated value of the property; or

(e) the property under consideration for public acquisition is a single family residence and the governmental entity seeking to acquire the property has initiated negotiations to acquire the property as required under Section 78-34-4.5;

(8) records prepared in contemplation of sale, exchange, lease, rental, or other compensated transaction of real or personal property including intellectual property, which, if disclosed prior to completion of the transaction, would reveal the appraisal or estimated value of the subject property, unless:

(a) the public interest in access outweighs the interests in restricting access, including the governmental entity's interest in maximizing the financial benefit of the transaction; or

(b) when prepared by or on behalf of a governmental entity, appraisals or estimates of the value of the subject property have already been disclosed to persons not employed by or under a duty of confidentiality to the entity;

(9) records created or maintained for civil, criminal, or administrative enforcement purposes or audit purposes, or for discipline, licensing, certification, or registration purposes, if release of the records:

(a) reasonably could be expected to interfere with investigations undertaken for enforcement, discipline, licensing, certification, or registration purposes;

(b) reasonably could be expected to interfere with audits, disciplinary, or enforcement proceedings;

(c) would create a danger of depriving a person of a right to a fair trial or impartial hearing;

(d) reasonably could be expected to disclose the identity of a source who is not generally known outside of government and, in the case of a record compiled in the course of an investigation, disclose information furnished by a source not generally known outside of government if disclosure would compromise the source; or

(e) reasonably could be expected to disclose investigative or audit techniques, procedures, policies, or orders not generally known outside of government if disclosure would interfere with enforcement or audit efforts;

(10) records the disclosure of which would jeopardize the life or safety of an individual;

(11) records the disclosure of which would jeopardize the security of governmental property, governmental programs, or governmental recordkeeping systems from damage, theft, or other appropriation or use contrary to law or public policy;

(12) records that, if disclosed, would jeopardize the security or safety of a correctional facility, or records relating to incarceration, treatment, probation, or parole, that would interfere with the control and supervision of an offender's incarceration, treatment, probation, or parole;

(13) records that, if disclosed, would reveal recommendations made to the Board of Pardons and Parole by an employee of or contractor for the Department of Corrections, the Board of Pardons and Parole, or the Department of Human Services that are based on the employee's or contractor's supervision, diagnosis, or treatment of any person within the board's jurisdiction;

(14) records and audit workpapers that identify audit, collection, and operational procedures and methods used by the State Tax Commission, if disclosure would interfere with audits or collections;

(15) records of a governmental audit agency relating to an ongoing or planned audit until the final audit is released;

(16) records prepared by or on behalf of a governmental entity solely in anticipation of litigation that are not available under the rules of discovery;

(17) records disclosing an attorney's work product, including the mental impressions or legal theories of an attorney or other representative of a governmental entity concerning litigation;

(18) records of communications between a governmental entity and an attorney representing, retained, or employed by the governmental entity if the communications would be privileged as provided in Section 78-24-8;

(19) personal files of a legislator, including personal correspondence to or from a member of the Legislature, provided that correspondence that gives notice of legislative action or policy may not be classified as protected under this section;

(20) (a) records in the custody or control of the Office of Legislative Research and General Counsel, that, if disclosed, would reveal a particular legislator's contemplated legislation or contemplated course of action before the legislator has elected to support the legislation or course of action, or made the legislation or course of action public; and

(b) notwithstanding Subsection (20)(a), the form to request legislation submitted to the Office of Legislative Research and General Counsel is a public document unless a legislator asks that the records requesting the legislation be maintained as protected records until such time as the legislator elects to make the legislation or course of action public;

(21) research requests from legislators to the Office of Legislative Research and General Counsel or the Office of the Legislative Fiscal Analyst

and research findings prepared in response to these requests;

(22) drafts, unless otherwise classified as public;

(23) records concerning a governmental entity's strategy about collective bargaining or pending litigation;

(24) records of investigations of loss occurrences and analyses of loss occurrences that may be covered by the Risk Management Fund, the Employers' Reinsurance Fund, the Uninsured Employers' Fund, or similar divisions in other governmental entities;

(25) records, other than personnel evaluations, that contain a personal recommendation concerning an individual if disclosure would constitute a clearly unwarranted invasion of personal privacy, or disclosure is not in the public interest;

(26) records that reveal the location of historic, prehistoric, paleontological, or biological resources that if known would jeopardize the security of those resources or of valuable historic, scientific, educational, or cultural information;

(27) records of independent state agencies if the disclosure of the records would conflict with the fiduciary obligations of the agency;

(28) records of an institution within the state system of higher education defined in Section 53B-1-102 regarding tenure evaluations, appointments, applications for admissions, retention decisions, and promotions, which could be properly discussed in a meeting closed in accordance with Title 52, Chapter 4, Open and Public Meetings, provided that records of the final decisions about tenure, appointments, retention, promotions, or those students admitted, may not be classified as protected under this section;

(29) records of the governor's office, including budget recommendations, legislative proposals, and policy statements, that if disclosed would reveal the governor's contemplated policies or contemplated courses of action before the governor has implemented or rejected those policies or courses of action or made them public;

(30) records of the Office of the Legislative Fiscal Analyst relating to budget analysis, revenue estimates, and fiscal notes of proposed legislation before issuance of the final recommendations in these areas;

(31) records provided by the United States or by a government entity outside the state that are given to the governmental entity with a requirement that they be managed as protected records if the providing entity certifies that the record would not be subject to public disclosure if retained by it;

(32) transcripts, minutes, or reports of the closed portion of a meeting of a public body except as provided in Section 52-4-7;

(33) records that would reveal the contents of settlement negotiations but not including final settlements or empirical data to the extent that they are not otherwise exempt from disclosure;

(34) memoranda prepared by staff and used in the decision-making process by an administrative law judge, a member of the Board of Pardons and Parole, or a member of any other body charged by law with performing a quasi-judicial function;

(35) records that would reveal negotiations regarding assistance or incentives offered by or requested from a governmental entity for the purpose of encouraging a person to expand or

locate a business in Utah, but only if disclosure would result in actual economic harm to the person or place the governmental entity at a competitive disadvantage, but this section may not be used to restrict access to a record evidencing a final contract;

(36) materials to which access must be limited for purposes of securing or maintaining the governmental entity's proprietary protection of intellectual property rights including patents, copyrights, and trade secrets;

(37) the name of a donor or a prospective donor to a governmental entity, including an institution within the state system of higher education defined in Section 53B-1-102, and other information concerning the donation that could reasonably be expected to reveal the identity of the donor, provided that:

(a) the donor requests anonymity in writing;

(b) any terms, conditions, restrictions, or privileges relating to the donation may not be classified protected by the governmental entity under this Subsection (37); and

(c) except for an institution within the state system of higher education defined in Section 53B-1-102, the governmental unit to which the donation is made is primarily engaged in educational, charitable, or artistic endeavors, and has no regulatory or legislative authority over the donor, a member of the donor's immediate family, or any entity owned or controlled by the donor or the donor's immediate family;

(38) accident reports, except as provided in Sections 41-6a-404, 41-12a-202, and 73-18-13;

(39) a notification of workers' compensation insurance coverage described in Section 34A-2-205;

(40) (a) the following records of an institution within the state system of higher education defined in Section 53B-1-102, which have been developed, discovered, disclosed to, or received by or on behalf of faculty, staff, employees, or students of the institution:

(i) unpublished lecture notes;

(ii) unpublished notes, data, and information:

(A) relating to research; and

(B) of:

(I) the institution within the state system of higher education defined in Section 53B-1-102; or

(II) a sponsor of sponsored research;

(iii) unpublished manuscripts;

(iv) creative works in process;

(v) scholarly correspondence; and

(vi) confidential information contained in research proposals;

(b) Subsection (40)(a) may not be construed to prohibit disclosure of public information required pursuant to Subsection 53B-16-302(2)(a) or (b); and

(c) Subsection (40)(a) may not be construed to affect the ownership of a record;

(41) (a) records in the custody or control of the Office of Legislative Auditor General that would reveal the name of a particular legislator who requests a legislative audit prior to the date that audit is completed and made public; and

(b) notwithstanding Subsection (41)(a), a request for a legislative audit submitted to the Office of the Legislative Auditor General is a public document unless the legislator asks that the records in the custody or control of the Office of Legislative Auditor General that would reveal the name of a particular legislator who requests a legislative audit be maintained as protected records until the audit is completed and made public;

(42) records that provide detail as to the location of an explosive, including a map or other document that indicates the location of:

(a) a production facility; or

(b) a magazine;

(43) information contained in the database described in Section 62A-3-311.1;

(44) information contained in the Management Information System and Licensing Information System described in Title 62A, Chapter 4a, Child and Family Services;

(45) information regarding National Guard operations or activities in support of the National Guard's federal mission;

(46) records provided by any pawnbroker or pawnshop to a law enforcement agency or to the central database in compliance with Title 13, Chapter 32a, Pawnshop Transaction Information Act;

(47) information regarding food security, risk, and vulnerability assessments performed by the Department of Agriculture and Food;

(48) except to the extent that the record is exempt from this chapter pursuant to Section 63-2-106, records related to an emergency plan or program prepared or maintained by the Division of Emergency Services and Homeland Security the disclosure of which would jeopardize:

(a) the safety of the general public; or

(b) the security of:

(i) governmental property;

(ii) governmental programs; or

(iii) the property of a private person who provides the Division of Emergency Services and Homeland Security information;

(49) records of the Department of Agriculture and Food relating to the National Animal Identification System or any other program that provides for the identification, tracing, or control of livestock diseases, including any program established under Title 4, Chapter 24, Utah Livestock Brand and Anti-theft Act or Title 4, Chapter 31, Utah Livestock Inspection and Quarantine; and

(50) as provided in Section 26-39-109:

(a) information or records held by the Department of Health related to a complaint regarding a child care program or residential child care which the department is unable to substantiate; and

(b) information or records related to a complaint received by the Department of Health from an anonymous complainant regarding a child care program or residential child care. **2005**

CHAPTER 11

PARKS AND RECREATION

Section
63-11-17.   Powers and duties of Board and Division of Parks and Recreation.

63-11-17. Powers and duties of Board and Division of Parks and Recreation.

(1) (a) The board may make rules:

(i) governing the use of the state park system;

(ii) to protect state parks and their natural and cultural resources from misuse or damage, including watersheds, plants, wildlife, and park amenities; and

(iii) to provide for public safety and preserve the peace within state parks.

(b) To accomplish the purposes stated in Subsection (1)(a), the board may enact rules that:

(i) close or partially close state parks; or

(ii) establish use or access restrictions within state parks.

(c) Rules made under Subsection (1) may not have the effect of preventing the transfer of livestock along a livestock highway established in accordance with Section 72-3-112.

(2) The Division of Wildlife Resources shall retain the power and jurisdiction conferred upon it by law within state parks and on property controlled by the Division of Parks and Recreation with reference to fish and game.

(3) The Division of Parks and Recreation shall permit multiple use of state parks and property controlled by it for purposes such as grazing, fishing and hunting, mining, and the development and utilization of water and other natural resources.

(4) (a) The division may acquire real and personal property in the name of the state by all legal and proper means, including purchase, gift, devise, eminent domain, lease, exchange, or otherwise, subject to the approval of the executive director and the governor.

(b) As used in this section, "real property" includes land under water, upland, and all other property commonly or legally defined as real property.

(c) In acquiring any real or personal property, the credit of the state may not be pledged without the consent of the legislature.

(5) (a) Before acquiring any real property, the division shall notify the county legislative body of the county where the property is situated of its intention to acquire the property.

(b) If the county legislative body requests a hearing within ten days of receipt of the notice, the board shall hold a public hearing in the county concerning the matter.

(6) Acceptance of gifts or devises of land or other property shall be at the discretion of the division, subject to the approval of the executive director of the Department of Natural Resources and the governor.

(7) Acquisition of property by eminent domain shall be in the manner authorized by Title 78, Chapter 34, Eminent Domain.

(8) (a) The Division of Parks and Recreation may make charges for special services and use of facilities, the income from which shall be available for park and recreation purposes.

(b) The division may conduct and operate those services necessary for the comfort and convenience of the public.

(c) The board shall adopt appropriate rules governing the collection of charges under this Subsection (8).

(9) (a) The division may lease or rent concessions of all lawful kinds and nature in state parks and property to persons, partnerships, and corporations for a valuable consideration upon the recommendation of the board.

(b) The division shall comply with Title 63, Chapter 56, Utah Procurement Code, in selecting concessionaires.

(10) The division shall proceed without delay to negotiate with the federal government concerning the Weber Basin and other recreation and reclamation projects.   2003

63-11-17.1. Division of Parks and Recreation — Creation — Powers and authority.

There is created the Division of Parks and Recreation, which shall be within the Department of Natural Resources under the administration and general supervision of the executive director of natural resources and under the policy direction of the Board of Parks and Recreation. The Division of Parks and Recreation shall be the parks and recreation authority for the state of Utah, shall assume all of the functions, powers, duties, rights and responsibilities of the Utah State Park and Recreation Commission except those which are delegated to the Board of Parks and Recreation by this act, and is vested with such other functions, powers, duties, rights and responsibilities as provided in this act and other law.   1969

63-11-17.2. Peace officer authority of park rangers.

(1) The Division of Parks and Recreation has the duty to protect state parks and park property from misuse or damage and to preserve the peace within state parks.

(2) Employees of the Division of Parks and Recreation who are POST certified peace officers and who are designated as park rangers by the division director, are law enforcement officers under Section 53-13-103, and have all the powers of law enforcement officers in the state, with the exception of the power to serve civil process.

(3) The Division of Parks and Recreation has the authority to deputize persons who are peace officers or special function officers to assist park rangers on a seasonal temporary basis.   1998

63-11-17.3. Violation of law or board regulations — Misdemeanor.

Any person who violates Section 63-11-17 or any of the rules of the board adopted pursuant to this chapter is guilty of a class B misdemeanor.   1997

CHAPTER 25a

CRIMINAL JUSTICE AND SUBSTANCE ABUSE

Part 4

Crime Victims' Reparations Act

PART 4

CRIME VICTIMS' REPARATIONS ACT

63-25a-401. Title.

This part is known as the "Crime Victims' Reparations Act" and may be abbreviated as the "CVRA."

1996

63-25a-402. Definitions.

As used in this chapter:

(1) "Accomplice" means a person who has engaged in criminal conduct as defined in Section 76-2-202.

(2) "Board" means the Crime Victims' Reparations Board created under Section 63-25a-404.

(3) "Bodily injury" means physical pain, illness, or any impairment of physical condition.

(4) "Claim" means:

(a) the victim's application or request for a reparations award; and

(b) the formal action taken by a victim to apply for reparations pursuant to Sections 63-25a-401 through 63-25a-428.

(5) "Claimant" means any of the following claiming reparations under this chapter:

(a) a victim;

(b) a dependent of a deceased victim;

(c) a representative other than a collateral source; or

(d) the person or representative who files a claim on behalf of a victim.

(6) "Child" means an unemancipated person who is under 18 years of age.

(7) "Collateral source" means the definition as provided in Section 63-25a-413.

(8) "Contested case" means a case which the claimant contests, claiming the award was either inadequate or denied, or which a county attorney, a district attorney, a law enforcement officer, or other individual related to the criminal investigation proffers reasonable evidence of the claimant's lack of cooperation in the prosecution of a case after an award has already been given.

(9) (a) "Criminally injurious conduct" other than acts of war declared or not declared means conduct that:

(i) is or would be subject to prosecution in this state under Section 76-1-201;

(ii) occurs or is attempted;

(iii) causes, or poses a substantial threat of causing, bodily injury or death;

(iv) is punishable by fine, imprisonment, or death if the person engaging in the conduct possessed the capacity to commit the conduct; and

(v) does not arise out of the ownership, maintenance, or use of a motor vehicle, aircraft, or water craft, unless the conduct is intended to cause bodily injury or death, or is conduct which is or would be punishable under Title 76, Chapter 5, Offenses Against the Person, or as any offense chargeable as driving under the influence of alcohol or drugs.

(b) "Criminally injurious conduct" includes an act of terrorism, as defined in 18 U.S.C. 2331 committed outside of the United States against a resident of this state. "Terrorism" does not include an "act of war" as defined in 18 U.S.C. 2331.

(10) "Dependent" means a natural person to whom the victim is wholly or partially legally responsible for care or support and includes a child of the victim born after his death.

(11) "Dependent's economic loss" means loss after the victim's death of contributions of things of economic value to his dependent, not including services the dependent would have received from the victim if he had not suffered the fatal injury, less expenses of the dependent avoided by reason of victim's death.

(12) "Dependent's replacement services loss" means loss reasonably and necessarily incurred by the dependent after the victim's death in obtaining services in lieu of those the decedent would have performed for his benefit if he had not suffered the fatal injury, less expenses of the dependent avoided by reason of the victim's death and not subtracted in calculating the dependent's economic loss.

(13) "Director" means the director of the Reparations Office.

(14) "Disposition" means the sentencing or determination of penalty or punishment to be imposed upon a person:

(a) convicted of a crime;

(b) found delinquent; or

(c) against whom a finding of sufficient facts for conviction or finding of delinquency is made.

(15) "Economic loss" means economic detriment consisting only of allowable expense, work loss, replacement services loss, and if injury causes death, dependent's economic loss and dependent's replacement service loss. Noneconomic detriment is not loss, but economic detriment is loss although caused by pain and suffering or physical impairment.

(16) "Elderly victim" means a person 60 years of age or older who is a victim.

(17) "Fraudulent claim" means a filed claim based on material misrepresentation of fact and intended to deceive the reparations staff for the purpose of obtaining reparation funds for which the claimant is not eligible as provided in Section 63-25a-410.

(18) "Fund" means the Crime Victim Reparation Fund created in Section 63-63a-4.

(19) "Law enforcement officer" means a law enforcement officer as defined in Section 53-13-103.

(20) "Medical examination" means a physical examination necessary to document criminally injurious conduct but does not include mental health evaluations for the prosecution and investigation of a crime.

(21) "Mental health counseling" means outpatient and inpatient counseling necessitated as a result of criminally injurious conduct. The definition of mental health counseling is subject to rules promulgated by the board pursuant to Title 63, Chapter 46a, Utah Administrative Rulemaking Act.

(22) "Misconduct" as provided in Subsection 63-25a-412(1)(b) means conduct by the victim which was attributable to the injury or death of the victim as provided by rules promulgated by the board pursuant to Title 63, Chapter 46a, Utah Administrative Rulemaking Act.

(23) "Noneconomic detriment" means pain, suffering, inconvenience, physical impairment, and other nonpecuniary damage, except as provided in this chapter.

(24) "Pecuniary loss" does not include loss attributable to pain and suffering except as otherwise provided in this chapter.

(25) "Offender" means a person who has violated the criminal code through criminally injurious conduct regardless of whether he is arrested, prosecuted, or convicted.

(26) "Offense" means a violation of the criminal code.

(27) "Perpetrator" means the person who actually participated in the criminally injurious conduct.

(28) "Personal property" has the same definition as provided in Section 68-3-12.

(29) "Reparations Office" means the office of the reparations staff for the purpose of carrying out this chapter.

(30) "Reparations officer" means a person employed by the Reparations Office to investigate claims of victims and award reparations under this chapter, and includes the director when he is acting as a reparations officer.

(31) "Reparations staff" means the director, the reparations officers, and any other staff employed to administer the Crime Victims' Reparations Act.

(32) "Replacement service loss" means expenses reasonably and necessarily incurred in obtaining ordinary and necessary services in lieu of those the injured person would have performed, not for income but the benefit of himself or his dependents if he had not been injured.

(33) "Representative" means the victim, immediate family member, legal guardian, attorney, conservator, executor, or an heir of a person but does not include service providers.

(34) "Restitution" means money or services an appropriate authority orders an offender to pay or render to a victim of the offender's conduct.

(35) "Secondary victim" means a person who is traumatically affected by the criminally injurious conduct subject to rules promulgated by the board pursuant to Title 63, Chapter 46a, Utah Administrative Rulemaking Act.

(36) "Service provider" means a person or agency who provides a service to crime victims for a monetary fee except attorneys as provided in Section 63-25a-424.

(37) (a) "Victim" means a person who suffers bodily or psychological injury or death as a direct result of criminally injurious conduct or of the production of pornography in violation of Sections 76-5a-1 through 76-5a-4 if the person is a minor.

(b) "Victim" does not include a person who participated in or observed the judicial proceedings against an offender unless otherwise provided by statute or rule.

(c) "Victim" includes a resident of this state who is injured or killed by an act of terrorism, as defined in 18 U.S.C. 2331, committed outside of the United States.

(38) "Work loss" means loss of income from work the injured victim would have performed if he had not been injured and expenses reasonably incurred by him in obtaining services in lieu of those he would have performed for income, reduced by any income from substitute work he was capable of performing but unreasonably failed to undertake.   2002

63-25a-403. Restitution — Reparations not to supplant restitution — Assignment of claim for restitution judgment to Reparations Office.

(1) A reparations award shall not supplant restitution as established under Title 77, Chapter 38a, Crime Victims Restitution Act, or as established by any other provisions.

(2) The court shall not consider a reparations award when determining the order of restitution nor when enforcing restitution.

(3) If, due to reparation payments to a victim, the Reparations Office is assigned under Section 63-25a-419 a claim for the victim's judgment for restitution or a portion of the restitution, the Reparations Office may file with the sentencing court a notice of the assignment. The notice of assignment shall be signed by the victim and a Reparations Officer and shall state the amount of the claim assigned.

(4) Upon conviction and sentencing of the defendant, the court shall enter a civil judgment for complete restitution as provided in Section 77-38a-401 and identify the Reparations Office as the assignee of the assigned portion of the judgment.

(5) If the notice of assignment is filed after sentencing, the court shall modify the civil judgment for restitution to identify the Reparations Office as the assignee of the assigned portion of the judgment.   2002

63-25a-404. Crime Victims' Reparations Board — Members.

(1) (a) A Crime Victims' Reparations Board is created, consisting of seven members appointed by the governor with the consent of the Senate.

(b) The membership of the board shall consist of:

(i) a member of the bar of this state;

(ii) a victim of criminally injurious conduct;

(iii) a licensed physician;

(iv) a representative of law enforcement;

(v) a mental health care provider; and

(vi) two other private citizens.

(c) The governor may appoint a chair of the board who shall serve for a period of time prescribed by the governor, not to exceed the length of the chair's term. The board may elect a vice chair to serve in the absence of the chair.

(d) The board may hear appeals from administrative decisions as provided in rules adopted pursuant to Section 63-25a-415.

(2) (a) Except as required by Subsection (2)(b), as terms of current board members expire, the governor shall appoint each new member or reappointed member to a four-year term.

(b) Notwithstanding the requirements of Subsection (2)(a), the governor shall, at the time of appointment or reappointment, adjust the length of terms to ensure that the terms of board members are staggered so that approximately half of the board is appointed every two years.

(c) A member may be reappointed to one successive term.

(3) (a) When a vacancy occurs in the membership for any reason, the replacement shall be appointed for the unexpired term.

(b) A member resigning from the board shall serve until his successor is appointed and qualified.

(4) (a) (i) Members who are not government employees shall receive no compensation or benefits for their services, but may receive per diem and expenses incurred in the performance of the member's official duties at the rates established by the Division of Finance under Sections 63A-3-106 and 63A-3-107.

(ii) Members may decline to receive per diem and expenses for their service.

(b) (i) State government officer and employee members who do not receive salary, per diem, or expenses from their agency for their service may receive per diem and expenses incurred in the performance of their official duties from the board at the rates established by the Division of Finance under Sections 63A-3-106 and 63A-3-107.

(ii) State government officer and employee members may decline to receive per diem and expenses for their service.

(5) The board shall meet at least once quarterly but may meet more frequently as necessary.   2002

63-25a-405. Board and office within Commission on Criminal and Juvenile Justice.

(1) The Crime Victims' Reparations Board and Reparations Office are placed within the Commission on Criminal and Juvenile Justice for the provision by the commission of administrative and support services to the Reparations Office.

(2) The board or the director may request assistance from the Commission on Criminal and Juvenile Justice, the Department of Public Safety, and other state agencies in conducting research or monitoring victims' programs.

(3) The fund shall appear as a separate line item in the Commission on Criminal and Juvenile Justice budget.   2002

63-25a-406. Functions of board.

(1) The board shall:

(a) adopt a description of the organization and prescribe the general operation of the board;

(b) prescribe policy for the Reparations Office;

(c) adopt rules to implement and administer Sections 63-25a-401 through 63-25a-428 pursuant to Title 63, Chapter 46a, Utah Administrative Rulemaking Act, which may include setting of ceilings on reparations, defining of terms not specifically stated in this chapter, and establishing of rules governing attorney fees;

(d) prescribe forms for applications for reparations;

(e) review all awards made by the reparations staff, although the board may not reverse or modify awards authorized by the reparations staff;

(f) render an annual report to the governor and the Legislature regarding the staff's and the board's activities;

(g) cooperate with the director and his staff in formulating standards for the uniform application of Section 63-25a-409, taking into consideration the rates and amounts of reparation payable for injuries and death under other laws of this state and the United States;

(h) advocate the adoption, repeal, or modification of laws or proposed legislation in the interest of victims of crime;

(i) allocate monies available in the Crime Victim Reparation Fund to victims of criminally injurious conduct for reparations claims; and

(j) allocate monies available to other victim services as provided by administrative rule once a sufficient reserve has been established for reparation claims.

(2) All rules, or other statements of policy, along with application forms specified by the board, are binding upon the director, the reparations officers, and other staff.   2002

63-25a-407. Director — Appointment and functions.

The executive director of the Commission on Criminal and Juvenile Justice, after consulting with the board, shall appoint a director to carry out the provisions of this chapter. The director shall be an experienced administrator with a background in at least one of the following fields: social work, psychology, criminal justice, law, or a related field. The director shall demonstrate an understanding of the needs of crime victims and of services to victims. The director shall devote his time and capacity to his duties. The director shall:

(1) hire staff, including reparations officers, as necessary;

(2) act when necessary as a reparations officer in deciding initial claims;

(3) possess the same investigation and decision-making authority as the reparations officers;

(4) hear appeals from the decisions of the reparations officers, unless he acted as a reparations officer on the initial claim;

(5) serve as a liaison between the reparations staff and the Reparations Office;

(6) serve as the public relations representative of the Reparations Office;

(7) provide for payment of all administrative salaries, fees, and expenses incurred by the staff of the board, to be paid out of appropriations from the fund;

(8) cooperate with the state treasurer and the state Division of Finance in causing the funds in the trust fund to be invested and its investments sold or exchanged and the proceeds and income collected;

(9) apply for, receive, allocate, disburse, and account for grants of funds made available by the United States, the state, foundations, corporations, and other businesses, agencies, or individuals;

(10) obtain and utilize the services of other governmental agencies upon request; and

(11) act in any other capacity or perform any other acts necessary for the Reparations Office or board to successfully fulfill its statutory objectives.   2002

63-25a-408. Reparations officers.

The reparations officers shall in addition to any assignments made by the director of the Reparations Office:

(1) hear and determine all matters relating to claims for reparations and reinvestigate or re-open claims without regard to statutes of limitation or periods of prescription;

(2) obtain from prosecuting attorneys, law enforcement officers, and other criminal justice agencies, investigations and data to enable the reparations officer to determine whether and to what extent a claimant qualifies for reparations;

(3) hold hearings, administer oaths or affirmations, examine any person under oath or affirmation, issue subpoenas requiring the attendance and giving of testimony of witnesses, require the production of any books, papers, documents, or other evidence which may contribute to the reparations officer's ability to determine particular reparation awards;

(4) determine who is a victim or dependent;

(5) award reparations or other benefits determined to be due under this chapter and the rules of the board;

(6) take notice of judicially recognized facts and general, technical, and scientific facts within their specialized knowledge;

(7) advise and assist the board in developing policies recognizing the rights, needs, and interests of crime victims;

(8) render periodic reports as requested by the board concerning:

(a) the officers' activities; and

(b) the manner in which the rights, needs, and interests of crime victims are being addressed by the state's criminal justice system;

(9) establish priorities for assisting elderly victims of crime or those victims facing extraordinary hardships;

(10) cooperate with the Commission on Criminal and Juvenile Justice to develop information regarding crime victims' problems and programs; and

(11) assist the director in publicizing the provisions of the Crime Victims' Reparations Act, including the procedures for obtaining reparation, and in encouraging law enforcement agencies, health providers, and other related officials to take reasonable care to ensure that victims are informed about the provisions of this chapter and the procedure for applying for reparation.   1996

63-25a-409. Grounds for eligibility.

In order to be eligible for a reparations award under this chapter:

(1) The claimant shall be:

(a) a victim of criminally injurious conduct;

(b) a dependent of a deceased victim of criminally injurious conduct; or

(c) a representative acting on behalf of one of the above.

(2) The victim shall be either a resident of Utah or the criminally injurious conduct shall have occurred in Utah.

(3) The application shall be made in writing in a form that conforms substantially to that prescribed by the board.

(4) The criminally injurious conduct shall be reported to a law enforcement officer, in his capacity as a law enforcement officer, or other federal or state investigative agencies.

(5) (a) The claimant or victim shall cooperate with the appropriate law enforcement agencies in their efforts to apprehend or convict the perpetrator of the alleged offense.

(b) An award to a victim may be made whether any person is arrested, prosecuted, or convicted of the criminally injurious conduct giving rise to the claim.

(6) The criminally injurious conduct shall have occurred after December 31, 1986.   2000

63-25a-410. Ineligible persons — Fraudulent claims — Penalties.

(1) The following individuals shall not be eligible to receive an award of reparations:

(a) persons who do not meet all of the provisions set forth in Section 63-25a-409;

(b) the offender;

(c) an accomplice of the offender;

(d) any person whose receipt of an award would unjustly benefit the offender, accomplice, or other person reasonably suspected of participating in the offense;

(e) the victim of a motor vehicle injury who was the owner or operator of the motor vehicle and was not at the time of the injury in compliance with the state motor vehicle insurance laws;

(f) any convicted offender serving a sentence of imprisonment for that conviction or residing in any other institution which provides for the maintenance of convicted persons; and

(g) residents of halfway houses or any other correctional facilities and all persons who are on probation or parole if the circumstances surrounding the offense of which they are victims constitute a violation of their parole or probation.

(2) A person who knowingly submits a fraudulent claim for reparations or who knowingly misrepresents material facts in making a claim, and who receives an award based on that claim, is guilty of an offense, based on the following award amounts:

(a) for value under $300, a class B misdemeanor;

(b) for value equal to or greater than $300, but less than $1,000, a class A misdemeanor;

(c) for value equal to or greater than $1,000, but less than $5,000, a third degree felony; and

(d) for value equal to or greater than $5,000, a second degree felony.

(3) A person who submits a claim described in Subsection (2) but receives no award based on that claim is guilty of a class B misdemeanor.

(4) The state attorney general may prosecute violations under this section or may make arrangements with county attorneys for the prosecution of violations under this section when the attorney general cannot conveniently prosecute.

(5) The state may also bring a civil action against a claimant who receives reparation payments that are later found to be unjustified and who does not return to the board the unjustified amount. 2000

63-25a-411. Compensable losses and amounts.

A reparations award under this chapter may be made if:

(1) the reparations officer finds the claim satisfies the requirements for the award under the provisions of this chapter and the rules of the board;

(2) monies are available in the fund;

(3) the person for whom the award of reparations is to be paid is otherwise eligible under this act;

(4) the claim is for an allowable expense incurred by the victim, as follows:

(a) reasonable and necessary charges incurred for products, services, and accommodations;

(b) inpatient and outpatient medical treatment and physical therapy, subject to rules promulgated by the board pursuant to Title 63, Chapter 46a, Utah Administrative Rulemaking Act;

(c) mental health counseling which:

(i) is set forth in a mental health treatment plan which has been approved prior to any payment by a reparations officer; and

(ii) qualifies within any further rules promulgated by the board pursuant to Title 63, Chapter 46a, Utah Administrative Rulemaking Act;

(d) actual loss of past earnings and anticipated loss of future earnings because of a death or disability resulting from the personal injury at a rate not to exceed 66-⅔% of the person's weekly gross salary or wages or the maximum amount allowed under the state workers' compensation statute;

(e) care of minor children enabling a victim or spouse of a victim, but not both of them, to continue gainful employment at a rate per child per week as determined under rules established by the board;

(f) funeral and burial expenses for death caused by the criminally injurious conduct, subject to rules promulgated by the board pursuant to Title 63, Chapter 46a, Utah Administrative Rulemaking Act;

(g) loss of support to the dependent or dependents not otherwise compensated for a pecuniary loss for personal injury, for as long as the dependence would have existed had the victim survived, at a rate not to exceed 66-⅔% of the person's weekly salary or wages or the maximum amount allowed under the state workers' compensation statute, whichever is less;

(h) personal property necessary and essential to the health or safety of the victim as defined by rules promulgated by the board pursuant to Title 63, Chapter 46a, Utah Administrative Rulemaking Act; and

(i) medical examinations as defined in Section 63-25a-402, subject to rules promulgated by the board pursuant to Title 63, Chapter 46a, Utah Administrative Rulemaking Act, which may allow for exemptions from Sec-

tions 63-25a-409, 63-25a-412, and 63-25a-413.

(5) If a Utah resident suffers injury or death as a result of criminally injurious conduct inflicted in a state, territory, or country that does not provide a reciprocal crime victims' compensation program, the Utah resident has the same rights under this chapter as if the injurious conduct occurred in this state.

(6) An award of reparations shall not exceed $25,000 in the aggregate unless the victim is entitled to proceeds in excess of that amount as provided in Subsection 77-38a-403(2). However, reparations for actual medical expenses incurred as a result of homicide, attempted homicide, aggravated assault, or DUI offenses, may be awarded up to $50,000 in the aggregate. 2002

63-25a-412. Reparations reduction.

(1) Reparations otherwise payable to a claimant may be reduced or denied as follows:

(a) the economic loss upon which the claim is based has been or could be recouped from other persons, including collateral sources, and the victim was not entitled to nor receiving monies prior to the criminally injurious conduct giving rise to the claim under this chapter;

(b) the reparations officer considers the claim unreasonable because of the misconduct of the claimant or of a victim through whom he claims; or

(c) the victim had not used a facility or health care provider that would be covered by a collateral source.

(2) When two or more dependents are entitled to an award as a result of a victim's death, the award shall be apportioned by the reparations officer among the dependents. 2000

63-25a-413. Collateral sources.

(1) Collateral source shall include any source of benefits or advantages for economic loss otherwise reparable under this chapter which the victim or claimant has received, or which is readily available to the victim from:

(a) the offender;

(b) the insurance of the offender;

(c) the United States government or any of its agencies, a state or any of its political subdivisions, or an instrumentality of two or more states, except in the case on nonobligatory state-funded programs;

(d) social security, Medicare, and Medicaid;

(e) state-required temporary nonoccupational income replacement insurance or disability income insurance;

(f) workers' compensation;

(g) wage continuation programs of any employer;

(h) proceeds of a contract of insurance payable to the victim for the loss he sustained because of the criminally injurious conduct;

(i) a contract providing prepaid hospital and other health care services or benefits for disability; or

(j) veteran's benefits, including veteran's hospitalization benefits.

(2) (a) An order of restitution shall not be considered readily available as a collateral source.

(b) Receipt of an award of reparations under this chapter shall be considered an assignment of the victim's rights to restitution from the offender.

(3) The victim shall not discharge a claim against a person or entity without the state's written permission and shall fully cooperate with the state in pursuing its right of reimbursement, including providing the state with any evidence in his possession.

(4) The state's right of reimbursement applies regardless of whether the victim has been fully compensated for his losses.

(5) Notwithstanding the collateral source provisions in Subsection (1) and Subsection 63-25a-412(1)(a), a victim of a sexual offense who requests testing of himself may be reimbursed for the costs of the HIV test only as provided in Subsection 76-5-503(4).   2001

63-25a-414.   Notification of claimant — Suspension of proceedings.

(1) The Reparations Office shall immediately notify the claimant in writing of any decision and shall forward to the Division of Finance a certified copy of the decision and a warrant request for the amount of the claim. The Division of Finance shall pay the claimant the amount submitted to the division, out of the fund. If monies in the fund are temporarily depleted, claimants entitled to receive awards shall be placed on a waiting list and shall receive their awards as funds are available in the order in which their claims were awarded.

(2) The reparations officer may suspend the proceedings pending disposition of a criminal prosecution that has been commenced or is imminent.   2002

63-25a-415.   Rules for contested claims — Exemption from Administrative Procedures Act.

(1) Rules for procedures for contested determinations by a reparations officer shall be adopted pursuant to Title 63, Chapter 46a, Utah Administrative Rulemaking Act.

(2) Crime Victims' Reparations is exempt from Title 63, Chapter 46b, Administrative Procedures Act. 2000

63-25a-416.   Waiver of privilege.

(1) A victim filing a claim under the provisions of this chapter shall be considered to have waived any privilege as to communications or records relevant to an issue of the physical, mental, or emotional conditions of the victim except for the attorney-client privilege. The waiver shall apply only to reparations officers, the director of reparations, the board, and legal counsel.

(2) The claimant may be required to supply any additional medical or psychological reports available relating to the injury or death for which compensation is claimed.

(3) The reparations officer hearing a claim or an appeal from a claim shall make available to the claimant a copy of the report. If the victim is deceased, the director or his appointee, on request, shall furnish the claimant a copy of the report unless dissemination of that copy is prohibited by law.   1996

63-25a-417.   Additional testing.

(1) If the mental, physical, or emotional condition of a victim is material to a claim, the reparations officer, director, or chair of the board who hears the claim or the appeal may order the claimant to submit to a mental or physical examination by a physician or psychologist and may recommend to the court to order an autopsy of a deceased victim.

(2) Any order for additional examination shall be for good cause shown and shall provide notice to the person to be examined and his representative.

(3) All reports from additional examinations shall set out findings, including results of all tests made, diagnoses, prognoses, other conclusions, and reports of earlier examinations of the same conditions.

(4) A copy of the report shall be made available to the victim or the representative of the victim unless dissemination of that copy is prohibited by law.   1996

63-25a-418.   Failure to comply.

If a person refuses to comply with an order under this chapter or asserts a privilege, except privileges arising from the attorney-client relationship, to withhold or suppress evidence relevant to a claim, the director or reparations officer may make any appropriate determination including denial of the claim.
          1996

63-25a-419.   Assignment of recovery — Reimbursement.

(1) By accepting an award of reparations, the victim automatically assigns to the state, subject to the provisions of Subsection (2), all claims against any third party to the lesser of:

(a) the amount paid by the state; or

(b) the amount recovered from the third party.

(2) The board, with the concurrence of the director, may reduce the state's right of reimbursement if it is determined that the reduction will benefit the fund.

(3) The state reserves the right to make a claim for reimbursement on behalf of the victim and the victim shall not impair the state's claim or the state's right of reimbursement.   2002

63-25a-420.   Special verdict — Allocation of damages.

In an action in a court of this state arising out of criminally injurious conduct, the judge, on timely motion, shall direct the jury to return a special verdict, indicating separately the awards to noneconomic detriment, punitive damages, and economic loss.
          1996

63-25a-421.   Award — Payment methods — Claims against the award.

(1) The reparations officer may provide for the payment of an award in a lump sum or in installments. The part of an award equal to the amount of economic loss accrued to the date of the award shall be paid in a lump sum. An award of allowable expense that would accrue after an initial award is made may not be paid in a lump sum. Except as provided in Subsection (2), the part of an award that may not be paid in a lump sum shall be paid in installments.

(2) At the request of the claimant, the reparations officer may convert future economic loss installment payments, other than allowable expense, to a lump sum payment, discounted to present value, but only upon a finding by the officer that the award in a lump sum will promote the interests of the claimant.

(3) An award for future economic loss payable in installments may be made only for a period for which the reparations officer can reasonably determine future economic loss. The reparations officer may reconsider and modify an award for future economic loss payable in installments, upon his finding that a material and substantial change of circumstances has occurred.

(4) An award is not subject to execution, attachment, or garnishment, except that an award for allowable expense is not exempt from a claim of a creditor to the extent that he provided products, services, or accommodations, the costs of which are included in the award.

(5) An assignment or agreement to assign a right to reparations for loss accruing in the future is unenforceable, except:

(a) an assignment of a right to reparations for work loss to secure payment of alimony, maintenance, or child support;

(b) an assignment of a right to reparations for allowable expense to the extent that the benefits are for the cost of products, services, or accommodations necessitated by the injury or death on which the claim is based and are provided or to be provided by the assignee; or

(c) an assignment to repay a loan obtained to pay for the obligations or expenses described in Subsection (5)(a) or (b). 1996

63-25a-422. Emergency award.

If the reparations officer determines that the claimant will suffer financial hardship unless an emergency award is made, and it appears likely that a final award will be made, an amount may be paid to the claimant, to be deducted from the final award or repaid by and recoverable from the claimant to the extent that it exceeds the final award. The board may limit emergency awards to any amount it considers necessary. 1996

63-25a-423. Review of award decision.

The reparations officer shall review at least annually every award being paid in installments. An order on review of an award does not require refund of amounts previously paid unless the award was obtained by fraud or a material mistake of fact. 1996

63-25a-424. Attorney fees.

(1) The claims procedures shall be sufficiently simple that the assistance of an attorney is unnecessary, and no attorney fees shall be paid for the assistance of an attorney or any other representative in filing the claim or providing information to the reparations officer.

(2) Attorney fees may be granted in the following circumstances and shall be paid out of the reparations award not to exceed 15% of the amount of the reparations award:

(a) when an award has been denied and, after a hearing, the decision to deny is overturned; or

(b) when minor dependents of a deceased victim require assistance in establishing a trust or determining a guardian.

(3) An attorney or any other person providing assistance in a reparations claim, who contracts for or receives sums not allowed under this chapter, is guilty of a class B misdemeanor. This provision shall not extend to attorneys who assist the victim in filing a civil action against the perpetrator. 1996

63-25a-425 to 63-25a-427. Repealed. 2000

63-25a-428. Purpose — Not entitlement program.

(1) Crime Victims' Reparations is a program with the purpose to assist victims of criminally injurious conduct. Reparation to a victim is limited to the monies available in the fund.

(2) This program is not an entitlement program. Awards may be limited or denied as determined appropriate by the board. Failure to grant an award does not create a cause of action against Crime Victims' Reparations, the state, or any of its subdivisions. There is no right to judicial review over the decision whether or not to grant an award.

(3) A cause of action based on a failure to give or receive the notice required by this chapter does not accrue to any person against the state, any of its agencies or local subdivisions, any of their law enforcement officers or other agents or employees, or any health care or medical provider or its agents or employees. The failure does not affect or alter any requirement for filing or payment of a claim. 2002

CHAPTER 30

GOVERNMENTAL IMMUNITY ACT [REPEALED]

63-30-1 to 63-30-38. Repealed. 1978, 1983, 2004

CHAPTER 30d

GOVERNMENTAL IMMUNITY ACT OF UTAH

Part 1

General Provisions

Part 2

Governmental Immunity — Statement, Scope, and Effect

Part 3

Waivers of Immunity

Part 4

Notice of Claim Against a Governmental Entity or a Government Employee

Part 5

Legal Actions Under This Chapter — Jurisdiction and Venue

Part 6

Legal Actions Under This Chapter — Procedures, Requirements, Damages, and Limitations on Judgments

PART 1

GENERAL PROVISIONS

63-30d-101. Title, scope, and intent.
(1) This chapter is known as the "Governmental Immunity Act of Utah."

(2) (a) The waivers and retentions of immunity found in this chapter apply to all functions of government, no matter how labeled.

(b) This single, comprehensive chapter governs all claims against governmental entities or against their employees or agents arising out of the performance of the employee's duties, within the scope of employment, or under color of authority. 2004

63-30d-102. Definitions.
As used in this chapter:
(1) "Claim" means any asserted demand for or cause of action for money or damages, whether arising under the common law, under state constitutional provisions, or under state statutes, against a governmental entity or against an employee in the employee's personal capacity.
(2) (a) "Employee" includes:
(i) a governmental entity's officers, employees, servants, trustees, or commissioners;
(ii) members of a governing body;
(iii) members of a government entity board;
(iv) members of a government entity commission;
(v) members of an advisory body, officers, and employees of a Children's Justice Center created in accordance with Section 67-5b-104;
(vi) student teachers holding a letter of authorization in accordance with Sections 53A-6-103 and 53A-6-104;
(vii) educational aides;
(viii) students engaged in providing services to members of the public in the course of an approved medical, nursing, or other professional health care clinical training program;
(ix) volunteers as defined by Subsection 67-20-2(3); and
(x) tutors.
(b) "Employee" includes all of the positions identified in Subsection (2)(a), whether or not the individual holding that position receives compensation.
(c) "Employee" does not include an independent contractor.
(3) "Governmental entity" means the state and its political subdivisions as both are defined in this section.
(4) (a) "Governmental function" means each activity, undertaking, or operation of a governmental entity.
(b) "Governmental function" includes each activity, undertaking, or operation performed by a department, agency, employee, agent, or officer of a governmental entity.
(c) "Governmental function" includes a governmental entity's failure to act.
(5) "Injury" means death, injury to a person, damage to or loss of property, or any other injury that a person may suffer to his person or estate, that would be actionable if inflicted by a private person or his agent.
(6) "Personal injury" means an injury of any kind other than property damage.
(7) "Political subdivision" means any county, city, town, school district, public transit district, redevelopment agency, special improvement or taxing district, special district, an entity created

by an interlocal agreement adopted under Title 11, Chapter 13, Interlocal Cooperation Act, or other governmental subdivision or public corporation.

(8) "Property damage" means injury to, or loss of, any right, title, estate, or interest in real or personal property.

(9) "State" means the state of Utah, and includes each office, department, division, agency, authority, commission, board, institution, hospital, college, university, Children's Justice Center, or other instrumentality of the state.

(10) "Willful misconduct" means the intentional doing of a wrongful act, or the wrongful failure to act, without just cause or excuse, where the actor is aware that his conduct will probably result in injury.   2004

PART 2

GOVERNMENTAL IMMUNITY — STATEMENT, SCOPE, AND EFFECT

63-30d-201. Immunity of governmental entities from suit.

(1) Except as may be otherwise provided in this chapter, each governmental entity and each employee of a governmental entity are immune from suit for any injury that results from the exercise of a governmental function.

(2) Notwithstanding the waiver of immunity provisions of Section 63-30d-301, a governmental entity, its officers, and its employees are immune from suit for any injury or damage resulting from the implementation of or the failure to implement measures to:

(a) control the causes of epidemic and communicable diseases and other conditions significantly affecting the public health or necessary to protect the public health as set out in Title 26A, Chapter 1, Local Health Departments;

(b) investigate and control suspected bioterrorism and disease as set out in Title 26, Chapter 23b, Detection of Public Health Emergencies Act; and

(c) respond to a national, state, or local emergency, a public health emergency as defined in Section 26-23b-102, or a declaration by the President of the United States or other federal official requesting public health related activities.   2004

63-30d-202. Act provisions not construed as admission or denial of liability — Effect of waiver of immunity — Exclusive remedy — Joinder of employee — Limitations on personal liability.

(1) (a) Nothing contained in this chapter, unless specifically provided, may be construed as an admission or denial of liability or responsibility by or for a governmental entity or its employees.

(b) If immunity from suit is waived by this chapter, consent to be sued is granted, and liability of the entity shall be determined as if the entity were a private person.

(c) No cause of action or basis of liability is created by any waiver of immunity in this chapter, nor may any provision of this chapter be construed as imposing strict liability or absolute liability.

(2) Nothing in this chapter may be construed as adversely affecting any immunity from suit that a governmental entity or employee may otherwise assert under state or federal law.

(3) (a) Except as provided in Subsection (3)(c), an action under this chapter against a governmental entity for an injury caused by an act or omission that occurs during the performance of an employee's duties, within the scope of employment, or under color of authority is a plaintiff's exclusive remedy.

(b) Judgment under this chapter against a governmental entity is a complete bar to any action by the claimant, based upon the same subject matter, against the employee whose act or omission gave rise to the claim.

(c) A plaintiff may not bring or pursue any civil action or proceeding based upon the same subject matter against the employee or the estate of the employee whose act or omission gave rise to the claim, unless:

(i) the employee acted or failed to act through fraud or willful misconduct;

(ii) the injury or damage resulted from the employee driving a vehicle, or being in actual physical control of a vehicle:

(A) with a blood alcohol content equal to or greater by weight than the established legal limit;

(B) while under the influence of alcohol or any drug to a degree that rendered the person incapable of safely driving the vehicle; or

(C) while under the combined influence of alcohol and any drug to a degree that rendered the person incapable of safely driving the vehicle;

(iii) injury or damage resulted from the employee being physically or mentally impaired so as to be unable to reasonably perform his or her job function because of:

(A) the use of alcohol;

(B) the nonprescribed use of a controlled substance as defined in Section 58-37-4; or

(C) the combined influence of alcohol and a nonprescribed controlled substance as defined by Section 58-37-4; or

(iv) in a judicial or administrative proceeding, the employee intentionally or knowingly gave, upon a lawful oath or in any form allowed by law as a substitute for an oath, false testimony material to the issue or matter of inquiry under this section.

(4) Except as permitted in Subsection (3)(c), no employee may be joined or held personally liable for acts or omissions occurring:

(a) during the performance of the employee's duties;

(b) within the scope of employment; or

(c) under color of authority.   2004

63-30d-203. Exemptions for certain takings actions.

An action that involves takings law, as defined in Section 63-34-13, is not subject to the requirements of Sections 63-30d-401, 63-30d-402, 63-30d-403, and 63-30d-601.   2004

PART 3

WAIVERS OF IMMUNITY

63-30d-301. Waivers of immunity — Exceptions.

(1) (a) Immunity from suit of each governmental entity is waived as to any contractual obligation.

(b) Actions arising out of contractual rights or obligations are not subject to the requirements of Sections 63-30d-401, 63-30d-402, 63-30d-403, or 63-30d-601.

(c) The Division of Water Resources is not liable for failure to deliver water from a reservoir or associated facility authorized by Title 73, Chapter 26, Bear River Development Act, if the failure to deliver the contractual amount of water is due to drought, other natural condition, or safety condition that causes a deficiency in the amount of available water.

(2) Immunity from suit of each governmental entity is waived:

(a) as to any action brought to recover, obtain possession of, or quiet title to real or personal property;

(b) as to any action brought to foreclose mortgages or other liens on real or personal property, to determine any adverse claim on real or personal property, or to obtain an adjudication about any mortgage or other lien that the governmental entity may have or claim on real or personal property;

(c) as to any action based on the negligent destruction, damage, or loss of goods, merchandise, or other property while it is in the possession of any governmental entity or employee, if the property was seized for the purpose of forfeiture under any provision of state law;

(d) subject to Subsection 63-30d-302(1), as to any action brought under the authority of Article I, Section 22, of the Utah Constitution, for the recovery of compensation from the governmental entity when the governmental entity has taken or damaged private property for public uses without just compensation;

(e) subject to Subsection 63-30d-302(2), as to any action brought to recover attorneys' fees under Sections 63-2-405 and 63-2-802;

(f) for actual damages under Title 67, Chapter 21, Utah Protection of Public Employees Act; or

(g) as to any action brought to obtain relief from a land use regulation that imposes a substantial burden on the free exercise of religion under Title 63, Chapter 90b, Utah Religious Land Use Act.

(3) (a) Except as provided in Subsection (3)(b), immunity from suit of each governmental entity is waived as to any injury caused by:

(i) a defective, unsafe, or dangerous condition of any highway, road, street, alley, crosswalk, sidewalk, culvert, tunnel, bridge, viaduct, or other structure located on them; or

(ii) any defective or dangerous condition of a public building, structure, dam, reservoir, or other public improvement.

(b) Immunity is not waived if the injury arises out of, in connection with, or results from:

(i) a latent dangerous or latent defective condition of any highway, road, street, alley, crosswalk, sidewalk, culvert, tunnel, bridge, viaduct, or other structure located on them; or

(ii) a latent dangerous or latent defective condition of any public building, structure, dam, reservoir, or other public improvement.

(4) Immunity from suit of each governmental entity is waived as to any injury proximately caused by a negligent act or omission of an employee committed within the scope of employment.

(5) Immunity is not waived under Subsections (3) and (4) if the injury arises out of, in connection with, or results from:

(a) the exercise or performance, or the failure to exercise or perform, a discretionary function, whether or not the discretion is abused;

(b) assault, battery, false imprisonment, false arrest, malicious prosecution, intentional trespass, abuse of process, libel, slander, deceit, interference with contract rights, infliction of mental anguish, or violation of civil rights;

(c) the issuance, denial, suspension, or revocation of, or by the failure or refusal to issue, deny, suspend, or revoke, any permit, license, certificate, approval, order, or similar authorization;

(d) a failure to make an inspection or by making an inadequate or negligent inspection;

(e) the institution or prosecution of any judicial or administrative proceeding, even if malicious or without probable cause;

(f) a misrepresentation by an employee whether or not it is negligent or intentional;

(g) riots, unlawful assemblies, public demonstrations, mob violence, and civil disturbances;

(h) the collection of and assessment of taxes;

(i) the activities of the Utah National Guard;

(j) the incarceration of any person in any state prison, county or city jail, or other place of legal confinement;

(k) any natural condition on publicly owned or controlled lands, any condition existing in connection with an abandoned mine or mining operation, or any activity authorized by the School and Institutional Trust Lands Administration or the Division of Forestry, Fire, and State Lands;

(l) research or implementation of cloud management or seeding for the clearing of fog;

(m) the management of flood waters, earthquakes, or natural disasters;

(n) the construction, repair, or operation of flood or storm systems;

(o) the operation of an emergency vehicle, while being driven in accordance with the requirements of Section 41-6a-208;

(p) the activities of:

(i) providing emergency medical assistance;

(ii) fighting fire;

(iii) regulating, mitigating, or handling hazardous materials or hazardous wastes;

(iv) emergency evacuations;

(v) transporting or removing injured persons to a place where emergency medical assistance can be rendered or where the person can be transported by a licensed ambulance service; or

(vi) intervening during dam emergencies;

(q) the exercise or performance, or the failure to exercise or perform, any function pursuant to Title 73, Chapter 10, Board of Water Resources — Division of Water Resources; or

(r) unauthorized access to government records, data, or electronic information systems by any person or entity.   2005

63-30d-302. Specific remedies — "Takings" actions — Government Records Access and Management Actions.

(1) In any action brought under the authority of Article I, Section 22, of the Utah Constitution for the recovery of compensation from the governmental entity when the governmental entity has taken or dam-

aged private property for public uses without just compensation, compensation and damages shall be assessed according to the requirements of Title 78, Chapter 34, Eminent Domain.

(2) (a) Notwithstanding Section 63-30d-401, a notice of claim for attorneys' fees under Subsection 63-30d-301(2)(e) may be filed contemporaneously with a petition for review under Section 63-2-404.

(b) The provisions of Subsection 63-30d-403(1), relating to the governmental entity's response to a claim, and the provisions of 63-30d-601, requiring an undertaking, do not apply to a notice of claim for attorneys' fees filed contemporaneously with a petition for review under Section 63-2-404.

(c) Any other claim under this chapter that is related to a claim for attorneys' fees under Subsection 63-30d-301(2)(e) may be brought contemporaneously with the claim for attorneys' fees or in a subsequent action. 2004

PART 4

NOTICE OF CLAIM AGAINST A GOVERNMENTAL ENTITY OR A GOVERNMENT EMPLOYEE

63-30d-401. Claim for injury — Notice — Contents — Service — Legal disability — Appointment of guardian ad litem.

(1) (a) Except as provided in Subsection (1)(b), a claim arises when the statute of limitations that would apply if the claim were against a private person begins to run.

(b) The statute of limitations does not begin to run until a claimant knew, or with the exercise of reasonable diligence should have known:

(i) that the claimant had a claim against the governmental entity or its employee; and

(ii) the identity of the governmental entity or the name of the employee.

(c) The burden to prove the exercise of reasonable diligence is upon the claimant.

(2) Any person having a claim against a governmental entity, or against its employee for an act or omission occurring during the performance of the employee's duties, within the scope of employment, or under color of authority shall file a written notice of claim with the entity before maintaining an action, regardless of whether or not the function giving rise to the claim is characterized as governmental.

(3) (a) The notice of claim shall set forth:

(i) a brief statement of the facts;

(ii) the nature of the claim asserted;

(iii) the damages incurred by the claimant so far as they are known; and

(iv) if the claim is being pursued against a governmental employee individually as provided in Subsection 63-30d-202(3)(c), the name of the employee.

(b) The notice of claim shall be:

(i) signed by the person making the claim or that person's agent, attorney, parent, or legal guardian; and

(ii) directed and delivered by hand or by mail according to the requirements of Section 68-3-8.5 to the office of:

(A) the city or town clerk, when the claim is against an incorporated city or town;

(B) the county clerk, when the claim is against a county;

(C) the superintendent or business administrator of the board, when the claim is against a school district or board of education;

(D) the presiding officer or secretary/clerk of the board, when the claim is against a special district;

(E) the attorney general, when the claim is against the State of Utah;

(F) a member of the governing board, the executive director, or executive secretary, when the claim is against any other public board, commission, or body; or

(G) the agent authorized by a governmental entity to receive the notice of claim by the governmental entity under Subsection (5)(e).

(4) (a) If an injury that may reasonably be expected to result in a claim against a governmental entity is sustained by a claimant who is under the age of majority or mentally incompetent, that governmental entity may file a request with the court for the appointment of a guardian ad litem for the potential claimant.

(b) If a guardian ad litem is appointed, the time for filing a claim under Section 63-30d-402 begins when the order appointing the guardian is issued.

(5) (a) Each governmental entity subject to suit under this chapter shall file a statement with the Division of Corporations and Commercial Code within the Department of Commerce containing:

(i) the name and address of the governmental entity;

(ii) the office or agent designated to receive a notice of claim; and

(iii) the address at which it is to be directed and delivered.

(b) Each governmental entity shall update its statement as necessary to ensure that the information is accurate.

(c) The Division of Corporations and Commercial Code shall develop a form for governmental entities to complete that provides the information required by Subsection (5)(a).

(d) (i) Newly incorporated municipalities shall file the statement required by Subsection (5)(a) at the time that the statement of incorporation and boundaries is filed with the lieutenant governor under Section 10-1-106.

(ii) Newly incorporated special districts shall file the statement required by Subsection (5)(a) at the time that the written notice of creation of the district is filed with the State Tax Commission and State Auditor under Sections 17A-1-102 and 17B-3-215.

(e) A governmental entity may, in its statement, identify an agent authorized by the entity to accept notices of claim on its behalf.

(6) The Division of Corporations and Commercial Code shall:

(a) maintain an index of the statements required by this section arranged both alphabetically by entity and by county of operation; and

(b) make the indices available to the public both electronically and via hard copy.

(7) A governmental entity may not challenge the validity of a notice of claim on the grounds that it was not directed and delivered to the proper office or agent if the error is caused by the governmental entity's failure to file or update the statement required by Subsection (5). 2004

63-30d-402. Time for filing notice of claim.

A claim against a governmental entity, or against an employee for an act or omission occurring during the performance of the employee's duties, within the scope of employment, or under color of authority, is barred unless notice of claim is filed with the person and according to the requirements of Section 63-30d-401 within one year after the claim arises regardless of whether or not the function giving rise to the claim is characterized as governmental.   2004

63-30d-403. Notice of claim — Approval or denial by governmental entity or insurance carrier within 60 days — Remedies for denial of claim.

(1) (a) Within 60 days of the filing of a notice of claim, the governmental entity or its insurance carrier shall inform the claimant in writing that the claim has either been approved or denied.

(b) A claim is considered to be denied if, at the end of the 60-day period, the governmental entity or its insurance carrier has failed to approve or deny the claim.

(2) (a) If the claim is denied, a claimant may institute an action in the district court against the governmental entity or an employee of the entity.

(b) The claimant shall begin the action within one year after denial of the claim or within one year after the denial period specified in this chapter has expired, regardless of whether or not the function giving rise to the claim is characterized as governmental.   2004

PART 5

LEGAL ACTIONS UNDER THIS CHAPTER — JURISDICTION AND VENUE

63-30d-501. Jurisdiction of district courts over actions.

(1) The district courts have exclusive, original jurisdiction over any action brought under this chapter.

(2) An action brought under this chapter may not be tried as a small claims action.   2004

63-30d-502. Venue of actions.

(1) Actions against the state may be brought in the county in which the claim arose or in Salt Lake County.

(2) (a) Actions against a county may be brought in the county in which the claim arose, or in the defendant county, or, upon leave granted by a district court judge of the defendant county, in any county contiguous to the defendant county.

(b) Leave may be granted ex parte.

(3) Actions against all other political subdivisions, including cities and towns, shall be brought in the county in which the political subdivision is located or in the county in which the claim arose.   2004

PART 6

LEGAL ACTIONS UNDER THIS CHAPTER — PROCEDURES, REQUIREMENTS, DAMAGES, AND LIMITATIONS ON JUDGMENTS

63-30d-601. Actions governed by Utah Rules of Civil Procedure — Undertaking required.

(1) An action brought under this chapter shall be governed by the Utah Rules of Civil Procedure to the extent that they are consistent with this chapter.

(2) At the time the action is filed, the plaintiff shall file an undertaking in a sum fixed by the court that is:

(a) not less than $300; and

(b) conditioned upon payment by the plaintiff of taxable costs incurred by the governmental entity in the action if the plaintiff fails to prosecute the action or fails to recover judgment.   2004

63-30d-602. Compromise and settlement of claims.

(1) A political subdivision, after conferring with its legal officer or other legal counsel if it does not have a legal officer, may compromise and settle any action as to the damages or other relief sought.

(2) The risk manager in the Department of Administrative Services may compromise and settle any action against the state for which the Risk Management Fund may be liable:

(a) on the risk manager's own authority, if the amount of the settlement is $25,000 or less;

(b) with the concurrence of the attorney general or the attorney general's representative and the executive director of the Department of Administrative Services if the amount of the settlement is $25,000.01 to $100,000; or

(c) by complying with the procedures and requirements of Title 63, Chapter 38b, State Settlement Agreements, if the amount of the settlement is more than $100,000.   2004

63-30d-603. Exemplary or punitive damages prohibited — Governmental entity exempt from execution, attachment, or garnishment.

(1) (a) A judgment may not be rendered against a governmental entity for exemplary or punitive damages.

(b) If a governmental entity would be required to pay the judgment under Section 63-30d-902 or 63-30d-903, the governmental entity shall pay any judgment or portion of any judgment entered against its employee in the employee's personal capacity even if the judgment is for or includes exemplary or punitive damages.

(2) Execution, attachment, or garnishment may not issue against a governmental entity.   2004

63-30d-604. Limitation of judgments against governmental entity or employee — Process for adjustment of limits.

(1) (a) Except as provided in Subsections (2) and (3), if a judgment for damages for personal injury against a governmental entity, or an employee whom a governmental entity has a duty to indemnify, exceeds $553,500 for one person in any one occurrence, or $1,107,000 for two or more persons in any one occurrence, the court shall reduce the judgment to that amount.

(b) A court may not award judgment of more than $553,500 for injury or death to one person regardless of whether or not the function giving rise to the injury is characterized as governmental.

(c) Except as provided in Subsection (2), if a judgment for property damage against a governmental entity, or an employee whom a governmental entity has a duty to indemnify, exceeds $221,400 in any one occurrence, the court shall reduce the judgment to that amount, regardless of whether or not the function giving rise to the damage is characterized as governmental.

(2) The damage limits established in this section do not apply to damages awarded as compensation when a governmental entity has taken or damaged private property for public use without just compensation.

(3) The limitations of judgments established in Subsection (1) shall be adjusted according to the methodology set forth in Subsection (4).

(4) (a) Each year, the risk manager shall:

(i) calculate the consumer price index as provided in Sections 1(f)(4) and 1(f)(5), Internal Revenue Code;

(ii) calculate the increase or decrease in the limitation of judgment amounts established in this section as a percentage equal to the percentage difference between the consumer price index for the preceding calendar year and the consumer price index for calendar year 2003; and

(iii) after making an increase or decrease under Subsection (4)(a)(ii), round up the limitation of judgment amounts established in Subsection (1) to the nearest $100.

(b) Each even-numbered year after 2004, the risk manager shall make rules, which become effective no later than July 1, that establish the new limitation of judgment amounts.

(c) Adjustments made by the risk manager to the limitation of judgment amounts established by this section have prospective effect only from the date the rules establishing the new limitation of judgment take effect and those adjusted limitations of judgment apply only to claims for injuries or losses that occur after the effective date of the rules that establish those new limitations of judgment.   2004

PART 7

PAYMENT PROCESS AND SOURCES FOR PAYING PROVED CLAIMS AGAINST GOVERNMENTAL ENTITIES

63-30d-701. Payment of claim or judgment against state — Presentment for payment.

(1) (a) Each claim, as defined by Subsection 63-30d-102(1), that is approved by the state or any final judgment obtained against the state shall be presented for payment to:

(i) the state risk manager; or

(ii) the office, agency, institution, or other instrumentality involved, if payment by that instrumentality is otherwise permitted by law.

(b) If payment of the claim is not authorized by law, the judgment or claim shall be presented to the board of examiners for action as provided in Section 63-6-10.

(c) If a judgment against the state is reduced by the operation of Section 63-30d-604, the claimant may submit the excess claim to the board of examiners.   2004

63-30d-702. Payment of claim or judgment against political subdivision — Procedure by governing body — Payment options.

(1) (a) Each claim approved by a political subdivision or any final judgment obtained against a political subdivision shall be submitted to the governing body of the political subdivision.

(b) The governing body shall pay the claim immediately from the general funds of the political subdivision unless:

(i) the funds are appropriated to some other use or restricted by law or contract for other purposes; or

(ii) the political subdivision opts to pay the claim or award in installments under Subsection (2).

(2) If the subdivision is unable to pay the claim or award during the current fiscal year, it may pay the claim or award in not more than ten ensuing annual installments of equal size or in whatever other installments that are agreeable to the claimant.   2004

63-30d-703. Reserve funds for payment of claims or purchase of insurance created by political subdivisions.

Any political subdivision may create and maintain a reserve fund or, may jointly with one or more other political subdivisions, make contributions to a joint reserve fund, for the purpose of:

(1) making payment of claims against the cooperating subdivisions when they become payable under this chapter; or

(2) for the purpose of purchasing liability insurance to protect the cooperating subdivisions from any or all risks created by this chapter.   2004

63-30d-704. Tax levy by political subdivisions for payment of claims, judgments, or insurance premiums.

(1) Notwithstanding any provision of law to the contrary, a political subdivision may levy an annual property tax sufficient to pay:

(a) any claim, settlement, or judgment;

(b) the costs to defend against any claim, settlement, or judgment; or

(c) for the establishment and maintenance of a reserve fund for the payment of claims, settlements, or judgments that may be reasonably anticipated.

(2) (a) The payments authorized to pay for punitive damages or to pay the premium for authorized insurance is money spent for a public purpose within the meaning of this section and Article XIII, Sec. 5, Utah Constitution, even though, as a result of the levy, the maximum levy as otherwise restricted by law is exceeded.

(b) No levy under this section may exceed .0001 per dollar of taxable value of taxable property.

(c) The revenues derived from this levy may not be used for any purpose other than those specified in this section.   2004

PART 8

SELF-INSURANCE AND PURCHASE OF LIABILITY INSURANCE BY GOVERMENTAL ENTITIES

63-30d-801. Insurance — Self-insurance or purchase of liability insurance by governmental entity authorized — Establishment of trust accounts for self-insurance.

(1) Any governmental entity within the state may self-insure, purchase commercial insurance, or self-insure and purchase excess commercial insurance in excess of the statutory limits of this chapter against:

(a) any risk created or recognized by this chapter; or

(b) any action for which a governmental entity or its employee may be held liable.

(2) (a) In addition to any other reasonable means of self-insurance, a governmental entity may self-insure with respect to specified classes of claims by establishing a trust account.

(b) In creating the trust account, the governmental entity shall ensure that:

(i) the trust account is managed by an independent private trustee; and

(ii) the independent private trustee has authority, with respect to claims covered by the trust, to:

(A) expend both principal and earnings of the trust account solely to pay the costs of investigation, discovery, and other pretrial and litigation expenses including attorneys' fees; and

(B) pay all sums for which the governmental entity may be adjudged liable or for which a compromise settlement may be agreed upon.

(c) Notwithstanding any law to the contrary, the trust agreement between the governmental entity and the trustee may authorize the trustee to:

(i) employ counsel to defend actions against the entity and its employees;

(ii) protect and safeguard the assets of the trust;

(iii) provide for claims investigation and adjustment services;

(iv) employ expert witnesses and consultants; and

(v) provide other services and functions that are necessary and proper to carry out the purposes of the trust.

(d) The monies and interest earned on the trust fund may be invested by following the procedures and requirements of Title 51, Chapter 7, State Money Management Act, and are subject to audit by the state auditor.   2004

63-30d-802. Insurance — Liability insurance — Government vehicles operated by employees outside scope of employment.

(1) A governmental entity that owns vehicles driven by an employee of the governmental entity with the express or implied consent of the entity, but which, at the time liability is incurred as a result of an automobile accident, is not being driven and used within the course and scope of the driver's employment is, subject to Subsection (2), considered to provide the driver with the insurance coverage required by Title 41, Chapter 12a, Financial Responsibility of Motor Vehicle Owners and Operators Act.

(2) The liability coverages considered provided are the minimum limits under Section 31A-22-304.   2004

63-30d-803. Liability insurance — Construction of policy not in compliance with act.

(1) If any insurance policy, rider, or endorsement issued after June 30, 2004 that was purchased to insure against any risk that may arise as a result of the application of this chapter contains any condition or provision not in compliance with the requirements of this chapter, that policy, rider, or endorsement is not invalid, but shall be construed and applied according to the conditions and provisions that would have applied had the policy, rider, or endorsement been in full compliance with this chapter, provided that the policy is otherwise valid.

(2) If any insurance policy, rider, or endorsement issued after June 30, 1966 and before July 1, 2004 that was purchased to insure against any risk that may arise as a result of the application of this chapter contains any condition or provision not in compliance with the requirements of the chapter, that policy, rider, or endorsement is not invalid, but shall be construed and applied according to the conditions and provisions that would have applied had the policy, rider, or endorsement been in full compliance with this chapter, provided that the policy is otherwise valid.   2004

63-30d-804. Liability insurance — Methods for purchase or renewal.

(1) Except as provided in Subsection (2), a contract or policy of insurance may be purchased or renewed under this chapter only upon public bid to be let to the lowest and best bidder.

(2) The purchase or renewal of insurance by the state shall be conducted in accordance with the provisions of Title 63, Chapter 56, Utah Procurement Code.   2004

63-30d-805. Liability insurance — Insurance for employees authorized — No right to indemnification or contribution from governmental agency.

(1) (a) A governmental entity may insure any or all of its employees against liability, in whole or in part, for injury or damage resulting from an act or omission occurring during the performance of an employee's duties, within the scope of employment, or under color of authority, regardless of whether or not that entity is immune from suit for that act or omission.

(b) Any expenditure for that insurance is for a public purpose.

(c) Under any contract or policy of insurance providing coverage on behalf of a governmental entity or employee for any liability defined by this section, regardless of the source of funding for the coverage, the insurer has no right to indemnification or contribution from the governmental entity or its employee for any loss or liability covered by the contract or policy.

(2) Any surety covering a governmental entity or its employee under any faithful performance surety bond has no right to indemnification or contribution from the governmental entity or its employee for any loss covered by that bond based on any act or omission for which the governmental entity would be obligated to defend or indemnify under the provisions of Section 63-30d-902.   2004

PART 9

COVERAGE AND REPRESENTATION OF STATE ENTITIES AND EMPLOYEES

63-30d-901. Expenses of attorney general, general counsel for state judiciary, and general counsel for the Legislature in representing the state, its branches, members, or employees.

(1) (a) The Office of the Attorney General has primary responsibility to provide legal representation to the judicial, executive, and legislative branches of state government in cases where coverage under the Risk Management Fund created by Section 63A-4-201 applies.

(b) When the attorney general has primary responsibility to provide legal representation to the judicial or legislative branches, the attorney general shall consult with the general counsel for the state judiciary and with the general counsel for the Legislature, to solicit their assistance in defending their respective branch, and in determining strategy and making decisions concerning the disposition of those claims.

(c) Notwithstanding Subsection (1)(b), the decision for settlement of monetary claims in those cases lies with the attorney general and the state risk manager.

(2) (a) If the Judicial Council, after consultation with the general counsel for the state judiciary, determines that the Office of the Attorney General cannot adequately defend the state judiciary, its members, or employees because of a conflict of interest, separation of powers concerns, or other political or legal differences, the Judicial Council may direct its general counsel to separately represent and defend it.

(b) If the general counsel for the state judiciary undertakes independent legal representation of the state judiciary, its members, or employees, the general counsel shall notify the state risk manager and the attorney general in writing before undertaking that representation.

(c) If the state judiciary elects to be represented by its own counsel under this section, the decision for settlement of claims against the state judiciary, its members, or employees, where Risk Management Fund coverage applies, lies with the general counsel for the state judiciary and the state risk manager.

(3) (a) If the Legislative Management Committee, after consultation with the general counsel for the Legislature, determines that the Office of the Attorney General cannot adequately defend the legislative branch, its members, or employees because of a conflict of interest, separation of powers concerns, or other political or legal differences, the Legislative Management Committee may direct its general counsel to separately represent and defend it.

(b) If the general counsel for the Legislature undertakes independent legal representation of the Legislature, its members, or employees, the general counsel shall notify the state risk manager and the attorney general in writing before undertaking that representation.

(c) If the legislative branch elects to be represented by its own counsel under this section, the decision for settlement of claims against the legislative branch, its members, or employees, where Risk Management Fund coverage applies, lies with the general counsel for the Legislature and the state risk manager.

(4) (a) Notwithstanding the provisions of Section 67-5-3 or any other provision of the Utah Code, the attorney general, the general counsel for the state judiciary, and the general counsel for the Legislature may bill the Department of Administrative Services for all costs and legal fees expended by their respective offices, including attorneys' and secretarial salaries, in representing the state or any indemnified employee against any claim for which the Risk Management Fund may be liable and in advising state agencies and employees regarding any of those claims.

(b) The risk manager shall draw funds from the Risk Management Fund for this purpose.

2004

63-30d-902. Defending government employee — Request — Cooperation — Payment of judgment.

(1) Except as provided in Subsections (2) and (3), a governmental entity shall defend any action brought against its employee arising from an act or omission occurring:

(a) during the performance of the employee's duties;

(b) within the scope of the employee's employment; or

(c) under color of authority.

(2) (a) Before a governmental entity may defend its employee against a claim, the employee shall make a written request to the governmental entity to defend him:

(i) within ten days after service of process upon him; or

(ii) within a longer period that would not prejudice the governmental entity in maintaining a defense on his behalf; or

(iii) within a period that would not conflict with notice requirements imposed on the entity in connection with insurance carried by the entity relating to the risk involved.

(b) If the employee fails to make a request, or fails to reasonably cooperate in the defense, including the making of an offer of judgment under Rule 68, Utah Rules of Civil Procedure, Offers of Judgment, the governmental entity need not defend or continue to defend the employee, nor pay any judgment, compromise, or settlement against the employee in respect to the claim.

(3) The governmental entity may decline to defend, or, subject to any court rule or order, decline to continue to defend, an action against an employee if it determines:

(a) that the act or omission in question did not occur:

(i) during the performance of the employee's duties;

(ii) within the scope of his employment; or

(iii) under color of authority; or

(b) that the injury or damage on which the claim was based resulted from conditions set forth in Subsection 63-30d-202(3)(c).

(4) (a) Within ten days of receiving a written request to defend an employee, the governmental entity shall inform the employee whether or not it shall provide a defense, and, if it refuses to provide a defense, the basis for its refusal.

(b) A refusal by the entity to provide a defense is not admissible for any purpose in the action in which the employee is a defendant.

(5) Except as provided in Subsection (6), if a governmental entity conducts the defense of an employee, the governmental entity shall pay any judgment based upon the claim.

(6) A governmental entity may conduct the defense of an employee under a reservation of rights under which the governmental entity reserves the right not to pay a judgment if any of the conditions set forth in Subsection (3) are established.

(7) (a) Nothing in this section or Section 63-30d-903 affects the obligation of a governmental entity to provide insurance coverage according to the requirements of Subsection 41-12a-301(3) and Section 63-30d-802.

(b) When a governmental entity declines to defend, or declines to continue to defend, an action against its employee under any of the conditions set forth in Subsection (3), it shall still provide coverage up to the amount specified in Section 31A-22-304.

2004

63-30d-903. Recovery of judgment paid and defense costs by government employee.

(1) Subject to Subsection (2), if an employee pays a judgment entered against him, or any portion of it,

that the governmental entity is required to pay under Section 63-30d-902, the employee may recover from the governmental entity the amount of the payment and the reasonable costs incurred in the employee's defense.

(2) (a) If a governmental entity does not conduct the defense of an employee against a claim, or conducts the defense under a reservation of rights as provided in Subsection 63-30d-902(6), the employee may recover from the governmental entity under Subsection (1) if the employee can prove that none of the conditions set forth in Subsection 63-30d-202(3)(c) applied.

(b) The employee has the burden of proof that none of the conditions set forth in Subsection 63-30d-202(3)(c) applied.   2004

63-30d-904. Indemnification of governmental entity by employee not required.

If a governmental entity pays all or part of a judgment, compromise, or settlement based on a claim against the governmental entity or an employee, the employee is not required to indemnify the governmental entity for the payment.   2004

CHAPTER 46b

ADMINISTRATIVE PROCEDURES ACT

63-46b-0.5.   Short title.

This act is known as the "Administrative Procedures Act."   1991

63-46b-1.   Scope and applicability of chapter.

(1) Except as set forth in Subsection (2), and except as otherwise provided by a statute superseding provisions of this chapter by explicit reference to this chapter, the provisions of this chapter apply to every agency of the state and govern:

(a) state agency action that determines the legal rights, duties, privileges, immunities, or other legal interests of an identifiable person, including agency action to grant, deny, revoke, suspend, modify, annul, withdraw, or amend an authority, right, or license; and

(b) judicial review of the action.

(2) This chapter does not govern:

(a) the procedure for making agency rules, or judicial review of the procedure or rules;

(b) the issuance of a notice of a deficiency in the payment of a tax, the decision to waive a penalty or interest on taxes, the imposition of and penalty or interest on taxes, or the issuance of a tax assessment, except that this chapter governs an agency action commenced by a taxpayer or by another person authorized by law to contest the validity or correctness of the action;

(c) state agency action relating to extradition, to the granting of a pardon or parole, a commutation or termination of a sentence, or to the rescission, termination, or revocation of parole or probation, to the discipline of, resolution of a grievance of, supervision of, confinement of, or the treatment of an inmate or resident of a correctional facility, the Utah State Hospital, the Utah State Developmental Center, or a person in the custody or jurisdiction of the Division of Substance Abuse and Mental Health, or a person on probation or parole, or judicial review of the action;

(d) state agency action to evaluate, discipline, employ, transfer, reassign, or promote a student or teacher in a school or educational institution, or judicial review of the action;

(e) an application for employment and internal personnel action within an agency concerning its own employees, or judicial review of the action;

(f) the issuance of a citation or assessment under Title 34A, Chapter 6, Utah Occupational Safety and Health Act, and Title 58, Chapter 3a, Architects Licensing Act, Chapter 11a, Cosmetologist/Barber, Esthetician, Electrologist, and Nail Technician Licensing Act, Chapter 17b, Pharmacy Practice Act, Chapter 22, Professional Engineers and Professional Land Surveyors Licensing Act, Chapter 53, Landscape Architects Licensing Act, Chapter 55, Utah Construction Trades Licensing Act, Chapter 63, Security Personnel Licensing Act, and Chapter 76, Professional Geologist Licensing Act, except that this chapter governs an agency action commenced by the employer, licensee, or other person authorized by law to contest the validity or correctness of the citation or assessment;

(g) state agency action relating to management of state funds, the management and disposal of school and institutional trust land assets, and contracts for the purchase or sale of products, real property, supplies, goods, or services by or for the state, or by or for an agency of the state, except as provided in those contracts, or judicial review of the action;

(h) state agency action under Title 7, Chapter 1, Article 3, Powers and Duties of Commissioner of Financial Institutions, Title 7, Chapter 2, Possession of Depository Institution by Commissioner, Title 7, Chapter 19, Acquisition of Failing Depository Institutions or Holding Companies, and Title 63, Chapter 30d, Governmental Immunity Act of Utah, or judicial review of the action;

(i) the initial determination of a person's eligibility for unemployment benefits, the initial determination of a person's eligibility for benefits under Title 34A, Chapter 2, Workers' Compensation Act, and Title 34A, Chapter 3, Utah Occupational Disease Act, or the initial determination of a person's unemployment tax liability;

(j) state agency action relating to the distribution or award of a monetary grant to or between governmental units, or for research, development, or the arts, or judicial review of the action;

(k) the issuance of a notice of violation or order under Title 26, Chapter 8a, Utah Emergency Medical Services System Act, Title 19, Chapter 2, Air Conservation Act, Title 19, Chapter 3, Radiation Control Act, Title 19, Chapter 4, Safe Drinking Water Act, Title 19, Chapter 5, Water Quality Act, Title 19, Chapter 6, Part 1, Solid and Hazardous Waste Act, Title 19, Chapter 6, Part 4, Underground Storage Tank Act, or Title 19, Chapter 6, Part 7, Used Oil Management Act, except that this chapter governs an agency action commenced by a person authorized by law to contest the validity or correctness of the notice or order;

(l) state agency action, to the extent required by federal statute or regulation, to be conducted according to federal procedures;

(m) the initial determination of a person's eligibility for government or public assistance benefits;

(n) state agency action relating to wildlife licenses, permits, tags, and certificates of registration;

(o) a license for use of state recreational facilities;

(p) state agency action under Title 63, Chapter 2, Government Records Access and Management Act, except as provided in Section 63-2-603;

(q) state agency action relating to the collection of water commissioner fees and delinquency penalties, or judicial review of the action;

(r) state agency action relating to the installation, maintenance, and repair of headgates, caps, values, or other water controlling works and weirs, flumes, meters, or other water measuring devices, or judicial review of the action;

(s) the issuance and enforcement of an initial order under Section 73-2-25;

(t) (i) a hearing conducted by the Division of Securities under Section 61-1-11.1; and

(ii) an action taken by the Division of Securities pursuant to a hearing conducted under Section 61-1-11.1, including a determination regarding the fairness of an issuance or exchange of securities described in Subsection 61-1-11.1(1); and

(u) state agency action relating to water well driller licenses, water well drilling permits, water well driller registration, or water well drilling

construction standards, or judicial review of the action.

(3) This chapter does not affect a legal remedy otherwise available to:

(a) compel an agency to take action; or

(b) challenge an agency's rule.

(4) This chapter does not preclude an agency, prior to the beginning of an adjudicative proceeding, or the presiding officer during an adjudicative proceeding from:

(a) requesting or ordering a conference with parties and interested persons to:

(i) encourage settlement;

(ii) clarify the issues;

(iii) simplify the evidence;

(iv) facilitate discovery; or

(v) expedite the proceeding; or

(b) granting a timely motion to dismiss or for summary judgment if the requirements of Rule 12(b) or Rule 56 of the Utah Rules of Civil Procedure are met by the moving party, except to the extent that the requirements of those rules are modified by this chapter.

(5) (a) A declaratory proceeding authorized by Section 63-46b-21 is not governed by this chapter, except as explicitly provided in that section.

(b) Judicial review of a declaratory proceeding authorized by Section 63-46b-21 is governed by this chapter.

(6) This chapter does not preclude an agency from enacting a rule affecting or governing an adjudicative proceeding or from following the rule, if the rule is enacted according to the procedures outlined in Title 63, Chapter 46a, Utah Administrative Rulemaking Act, and if the rule conforms to the requirements of this chapter.

(7) (a) If the attorney general issues a written determination that a provision of this chapter would result in the denial of funds or services to an agency of the state from the federal government, the applicability of the provision to that agency shall be suspended to the extent necessary to prevent the denial.

(b) The attorney general shall report the suspension to the Legislature at its next session.

(8) Nothing in this chapter may be interpreted to provide an independent basis for jurisdiction to review final agency action.

(9) Nothing in this chapter may be interpreted to restrict a presiding officer, for good cause shown, from lengthening or shortening a time period prescribed in this chapter, except the time period established for judicial review.   2005

63-46b-2. Definitions.

(1) As used in this chapter:

(a) "Adjudicative proceeding" means an agency action or proceeding described in Section 63-46b-1.

(b) "Agency" means a board, commission, department, division, officer, council, office, committee, bureau, or other administrative unit of this state, including the agency head, agency employees, or other persons acting on behalf of or under the authority of the agency head, but does not mean the Legislature, the courts, the governor, any political subdivision of the state, or any administrative unit of a political subdivision of the state.

(c) "Agency head" means an individual or body of individuals in whom the ultimate legal authority of the agency is vested by statute.

(d) "Declaratory proceeding" means a proceeding authorized and governed by Section 63-46b-21.

(e) "License" means a franchise, permit, certification, approval, registration, charter, or similar form of authorization required by statute.

(f) "Party" means the agency or other person commencing an adjudicative proceeding, all respondents, all persons permitted by the presiding officer to intervene in the proceeding, and all persons authorized by statute or agency rule to participate as parties in an adjudicative proceeding.

(g) "Person" means an individual, group of individuals, partnership, corporation, association, political subdivision or its units, governmental subdivision or its units, public or private organization or entity of any character, or another agency.

(h) (i) "Presiding officer" means an agency head, or an individual or body of individuals designated by the agency head, by the agency's rules, or by statute to conduct an adjudicative proceeding.

(ii) If fairness to the parties is not compromised, an agency may substitute one presiding officer for another during any proceeding.

(iii) A person who acts as a presiding officer at one phase of a proceeding need not continue as presiding officer through all phases of a proceeding.

(i) "Respondent" means a person against whom an adjudicative proceeding is initiated, whether by an agency or any other person.

(j) "Superior agency" means an agency required or authorized by law to review the orders of another agency.

(2) This section does not prohibit an agency from designating by rule the names or titles of the agency head or the presiding officers with responsibility for adjudicative proceedings before the agency.   1988

63-46b-2.1. Bases for certain recommendations and decisions limited.

(1) Except as provided in Subsection (2), no agency may recommend or rule on the custody, placement, including foster placement, or other disposition alternative for a minor, or the termination of parental rights, based on the fact that a parent or guardian of the minor lawfully does one or more of the following:

(a) legally possesses or uses a firearm or other weapon;

(b) espouses particular religious beliefs; or

(c) schools the minor or other minors outside the public education system or is otherwise sympathetic to schooling a minor outside the public education system.

(2) Subsection (1) does not prohibit a recommendation or ruling based on the compatibility of a minor with a particular custody, placement, or other disposition alternative as determined by the presence of any of the factors in Subsections (1)(a) through (1)(c).
2004

63-46b-3. Commencement of adjudicative proceedings.

(1) Except as otherwise permitted by Section 63-46b-20, all adjudicative proceedings shall be commenced by either:

(a) a notice of agency action, if proceedings are commenced by the agency; or

(b) a request for agency action, if proceedings are commenced by persons other than the agency.

(2) A notice of agency action shall be filed and served according to the following requirements:

(a) The notice of agency action shall be in writing, signed by a presiding officer, and shall include:

(i) the names and mailing addresses of all persons to whom notice is being given by the presiding officer, and the name, title, and mailing address of any attorney or employee who has been designated to appear for the agency;

(ii) the agency's file number or other reference number;

(iii) the name of the adjudicative proceeding;

(iv) the date that the notice of agency action was mailed;

(v) a statement of whether the adjudicative proceeding is to be conducted informally according to the provisions of rules adopted under Sections 63-46b-4 and 63-46b-5, or formally according to the provisions of Sections 63-46b-6 to 63-46b-11;

(vi) if the adjudicative proceeding is to be formal, a statement that each respondent must file a written response within 30 days of the mailing date of the notice of agency action;

(vii) if the adjudicative proceeding is to be formal, or if a hearing is required by statute or rule, a statement of the time and place of any scheduled hearing, a statement of the purpose for which the hearing is to be held, and a statement that a party who fails to attend or participate in the hearing may be held in default;

(viii) if the adjudicative proceeding is to be informal and a hearing is required by statute or rule, or if a hearing is permitted by rule and may be requested by a party within the time prescribed by rule, a statement that the parties may request a hearing within the time provided by the agency's rules;

(ix) a statement of the legal authority and jurisdiction under which the adjudicative proceeding is to be maintained;

(x) the name, title, mailing address, and telephone number of the presiding officer; and

(xi) a statement of the purpose of the adjudicative proceeding and, to the extent known by the presiding officer, the questions to be decided.

(b) When adjudicative proceedings are commenced by the agency, the agency shall:

(i) mail the notice of agency action to each party;

(ii) publish the notice of agency action, if required by statute; and

(iii) mail the notice of agency action to any other person who has a right to notice under statute or rule.

(3) (a) Where the law applicable to the agency permits persons other than the agency to initiate adjudicative proceedings, that person's request for agency action shall be in writing and signed by the person invoking the jurisdiction of the agency, or by that person's representative, and shall include:

(i) the names and addresses of all persons to whom a copy of the request for agency action is being sent;

(ii) the agency's file number or other reference number, if known;

(iii) the date that the request for agency action was mailed;

(iv) a statement of the legal authority and jurisdiction under which agency action is requested;

(v) a statement of the relief or action sought from the agency; and

(vi) a statement of the facts and reasons forming the basis for relief or agency action.

(b) The person requesting agency action shall file the request with the agency and shall mail a copy to each person known to have a direct interest in the requested agency action.

(c) An agency may, by rule, prescribe one or more forms eliciting the information required by Subsection (3)(a) to serve as the request for agency action when completed and filed by the person requesting agency action.

(d) The presiding officer shall promptly review a request for agency action and shall:

(i) notify the requesting party in writing that the request is granted and that the adjudicative proceeding is completed;

(ii) notify the requesting party in writing that the request is denied and, if the proceeding is a formal adjudicative proceeding, that the party may request a hearing before the agency to challenge the denial; or

(iii) notify the requesting party that further proceedings are required to determine the agency's response to the request.

(e) (i) Any notice required by Subsection (3)(d)(ii) shall contain the information required by Subsection 63-46b-5(1)(i) in addition to disclosure required by Subsection (3)(d)(ii).

(ii) The agency shall mail any notice required by Subsection (3)(d) to all parties, except that any notice required by Subsection (3)(d)(iii) may be published when publication is required by statute.

(iii) The notice required by Subsection (3)(d)(iii) shall:

(A) give the agency's file number or other reference number;

(B) give the name of the proceeding;

(C) designate whether the proceeding is one of a category to be conducted informally according to the provisions of rules enacted under Sections 63-46b-4 and 63-46b-5, with citation to the applicable rule authorizing that designation, or formally according to Sections 63-46b-6 to 63-46b-11;

(D) in the case of a formal adjudicative proceeding, and where respondent parties are known, state that a written response must be filed within 30 days of the date of the agency's notice if mailed, or within 30 days of the last publication date of the agency's notice, if published;

(E) if the adjudicative proceeding is to be formal, or if a hearing is to be held in an informal adjudicative proceeding, state the time and place of any scheduled hearing, the purpose for which the hearing is to be held, and that a party who fails to attend or participate in a scheduled and noticed hearing may be held in default;

(F) if the adjudicative proceeding is to be informal, and a hearing is required by statute or rule, or if a hearing is permitted by rule and may be requested by a party within the time prescribed by rule, state the parties' right to request a hearing and the time within which a hearing may be requested under the agency's rules; and

(G) give the name, title, mailing address, and telephone number of the presiding officer.

(4) When initial agency determinations or actions are not governed by this chapter, but agency and judicial review of those initial determinations or actions are subject to the provisions of this chapter, the request for agency action seeking review must be filed with the agency within the time prescribed by the agency's rules.

(5) For designated classes of adjudicative proceedings, an agency may, by rule, provide for a longer response time than allowed by this section, and may provide for a shorter response time if required or permitted by applicable federal law.

(6) Unless the agency provides otherwise by rule or order, applications for licenses filed under authority of Title 32A, Chapters 3, Packaging Agencies, 4, Public Liquor License, and 5, Private Club Liquor License are not considered to be a request for agency action under this chapter.

(7) If the purpose of the adjudicative proceeding is to award a license or other privilege as to which there are multiple competing applicants, the agency may, by rule or order, conduct a single adjudicative proceeding to determine the award of that license or privilege.

2001

63-46b-4. Designation of adjudicative proceedings as informal — Standards — Undesignated proceedings formal.

(1) The agency may, by rule, designate categories of adjudicative proceedings to be conducted informally according to the procedures set forth in rules enacted under the authority of this chapter if:

(a) the use of the informal procedures does not violate any procedural requirement imposed by a statute other than this chapter;

(b) in the view of the agency, the rights of the parties to the proceedings will be reasonably protected by the informal procedures;

(c) in the view of the agency, the agency's administrative efficiency will be enhanced by categorizations; and

(d) the cost of formal adjudicative proceedings outweighs the potential benefits to the public of a formal adjudicative proceeding.

(2) Subject to the provisions of Subsection (3), all agency adjudicative proceedings not specifically designated as informal proceedings by the agency's rules shall be conducted formally in accordance with the requirements of this chapter.

(3) Any time before a final order is issued in any adjudicative proceeding, the presiding officer may convert a formal adjudicative proceeding to an informal adjudicative proceeding, or an informal adjudicative proceeding to a formal adjudicative proceeding if:

(a) conversion of the proceeding is in the public interest; and

(b) conversion of the proceeding does not unfairly prejudice the rights of any party. 1987

63-46b-5. Procedures for informal adjudicative proceedings.

(1) If an agency enacts rules designating one or more categories of adjudicative proceedings as infor-

mal adjudicative proceedings, the agency shall, by rule, prescribe procedures for informal adjudicative proceedings that include the following:

(a) Unless the agency by rule provides for and requires a response, no answer or other pleading responsive to the allegations contained in the notice of agency action or the request for agency action need be filed.

(b) The agency shall hold a hearing if a hearing is required by statute or rule, or if a hearing is permitted by rule and is requested by a party within the time prescribed by rule.

(c) In any hearing, the parties named in the notice of agency action or in the request for agency action shall be permitted to testify, present evidence, and comment on the issues.

(d) Hearings will be held only after timely notice to all parties.

(e) Discovery is prohibited, but the agency may issue subpoenas or other orders to compel production of necessary evidence.

(f) All parties shall have access to information contained in the agency's files and to all materials and information gathered in any investigation, to the extent permitted by law.

(g) Intervention is prohibited, except that the agency may enact rules permitting intervention where a federal statute or rule requires that a state permit intervention.

(h) All hearings shall be open to all parties.

(i) Within a reasonable time after the close of an informal adjudicative proceeding, the presiding officer shall issue a signed order in writing that states the following:

(i) the decision;

(ii) the reasons for the decision;

(iii) a notice of any right of administrative or judicial review available to the parties; and

(iv) the time limits for filing an appeal or requesting a review.

(j) The presiding officer's order shall be based on the facts appearing in the agency's files and on the facts presented in evidence at any hearings.

(k) A copy of the presiding officer's order shall be promptly mailed to each of the parties.

(2) (a) The agency may record any hearing.

(b) Any party, at his own expense, may have a reporter approved by the agency prepare a transcript from the agency's record of the hearing.

(3) Nothing in this section restricts or precludes any investigative right or power given to an agency by another statute.   **1988**

63-46b-6. Procedures for formal adjudicative proceedings — Responsive pleadings.

(1) In all formal adjudicative proceedings, unless modified by rule according to Subsection 63-46b-3(5), the respondent, if any, shall file and serve a written response signed by the respondent or the respondent's representative within 30 days of the mailing date or last date of publication of the notice of agency action or the notice under Subsection 63-46b-3(3)(d), which shall include:

(a) the agency's file number or other reference number;

(b) the name of the adjudicative proceeding;

(c) a statement of the relief that the respondent seeks;

(d) a statement of the facts; and

(e) a statement summarizing the reasons that the relief requested should be granted.

(2) The respondent shall send a copy of the response filed under Subsection (1) to each party.

(3) The presiding officer, or the agency by rule, may permit or require pleadings in addition to the notice of agency action, the request for agency action, and the response. All documents permitted or required to be filed shall be filed with the agency and one copy shall be sent to each party.   2001

63-46b-7. Procedures for formal adjudicative proceedings — Discovery and subpoenas.

(1) In formal adjudicative proceedings, the agency may, by rule, prescribe means of discovery adequate to permit the parties to obtain all relevant information necessary to support their claims or defenses. If the agency does not enact rules under this section, the parties may conduct discovery according to the Utah Rules of Civil Procedure.

(2) Subpoenas and other orders to secure the attendance of witnesses or the production of evidence in formal adjudicative proceedings shall be issued by the presiding officer when requested by any party, or may be issued by the presiding officer on his own motion.

(3) Nothing in this section restricts or precludes any investigative right or power given to an agency by another statute.   1987

63-46b-8. Procedures for formal adjudicative proceedings — Hearing procedure.

(1) Except as provided in Subsections 63-46b-3(d)(i) and (ii), in all formal adjudicative proceedings, a hearing shall be conducted as follows:

(a) The presiding officer shall regulate the course of the hearing to obtain full disclosure of relevant facts and to afford all the parties reasonable opportunity to present their positions.

(b) On his own motion or upon objection by a party, the presiding officer:

(i) may exclude evidence that is irrelevant, immaterial, or unduly repetitious;

(ii) shall exclude evidence privileged in the courts of Utah;

(iii) may receive documentary evidence in the form of a copy or excerpt if the copy or excerpt contains all pertinent portions of the original document;

(iv) may take official notice of any facts that could be judicially noticed under the Utah Rules of Evidence, of the record of other proceedings before the agency, and of technical or scientific facts within the agency's specialized knowledge.

(c) The presiding officer may not exclude evidence solely because it is hearsay.

(d) The presiding officer shall afford to all parties the opportunity to present evidence, argue, respond, conduct cross-examination, and submit rebuttal evidence.

(e) The presiding officer may give persons not a party to the adjudicative proceeding the opportunity to present oral or written statements at the hearing.

(f) All testimony presented at the hearing, if offered as evidence to be considered in reaching a decision on the merits, shall be given under oath.

(g) The hearing shall be recorded at the agency's expense.

(h) Any party, at his own expense, may have a person approved by the agency prepare a transcript of the hearing, subject to any restrictions that the agency is permitted by statute to impose to protect confidential information disclosed at the hearing.

(i) All hearings shall be open to all parties.

(2) This section does not preclude the presiding officer from taking appropriate measures necessary to preserve the integrity of the hearing.   1988

63-46b-9. Procedures for formal adjudicative proceedings — Intervention.

(1) Any person not a party may file a signed, written petition to intervene in a formal adjudicative proceeding with the agency. The person who wishes to intervene shall mail a copy of the petition to each party. The petition shall include:

(a) the agency's file number or other reference number;

(b) the name of the proceeding;

(c) a statement of facts demonstrating that the petitioner's legal rights or interests are substantially affected by the formal adjudicative proceeding, or that the petitioner qualifies as an intervenor under any provision of law; and

(d) a statement of the relief that the petitioner seeks from the agency.

(2) The presiding officer shall grant a petition for intervention if the presiding officer determines that:

(a) the petitioner's legal interests may be substantially affected by the formal adjudicative proceeding; and

(b) the interests of justice and the orderly and prompt conduct of the adjudicative proceedings will not be materially impaired by allowing the intervention.

(3) (a) Any order granting or denying a petition to intervene shall be in writing and mailed to the petitioner and each party.

(b) An order permitting intervention may impose conditions on the intervenor's participation in the adjudicative proceeding that are necessary for a just, orderly, and prompt conduct of the adjudicative proceeding.

(c) The presiding officer may impose the conditions at any time after the intervention.   2001

63-46b-10. Procedures for formal adjudicative proceedings — Orders.

In formal adjudicative proceedings:

(1) Within a reasonable time after the hearing, or after the filing of any posthearing documents permitted by the presiding officer, or within the time required by any applicable statute or rule of the agency, the presiding officer shall sign and issue an order that includes:

(a) a statement of the presiding officer's findings of fact based exclusively on the evidence of record in the adjudicative proceedings or on facts officially noted;

(b) a statement of the presiding officer's conclusions of law;

(c) a statement of the reasons for the presiding officer's decision;

(d) a statement of any relief ordered by the agency;

(e) a notice of the right to apply for reconsideration;

(f) a notice of any right to administrative or judicial review of the order available to aggrieved parties; and

(g) the time limits applicable to any reconsideration or review.

(2) The presiding officer may use the presiding officer's experience, technical competence, and specialized knowledge to evaluate the evidence.

(3) A finding of fact that was contested may not be based solely on hearsay evidence unless that evidence is admissible under the Utah Rules of Evidence.

(4) This section does not preclude the presiding officer from issuing interim orders to:

(a) notify the parties of further hearings;

(b) notify the parties of provisional rulings on a portion of the issues presented; or

(c) otherwise provide for the fair and efficient conduct of the adjudicative proceeding.   2001

63-46b-11. Default.

(1) The presiding officer may enter an order of default against a party if:

(a) a party in an informal adjudicative proceeding fails to participate in the adjudicative proceeding;

(b) a party to a formal adjudicative proceeding fails to attend or participate in a properly scheduled hearing after receiving proper notice; or

(c) a respondent in a formal adjudicative proceeding fails to file a response under Section 63-46b-6.

(2) An order of default shall include a statement of the grounds for default and shall be mailed to all parties.

(3) (a) A defaulted party may seek to have the agency set aside the default order, and any order in the adjudicative proceeding issued subsequent to the default order, by following the procedures outlined in the Utah Rules of Civil Procedure.

(b) A motion to set aside a default and any subsequent order shall be made to the presiding officer.

(c) A defaulted party may seek agency review under Section 63-46b-12, or reconsideration under Section 63-46b-13, only on the decision of the presiding officer on the motion to set aside the default.

(4) (a) In an adjudicative proceeding begun by the agency, or in an adjudicative proceeding begun by a party that has other parties besides the party in default, the presiding officer shall, after issuing the order of default, conduct any further proceedings necessary to complete the adjudicative proceeding without the participation of the party in default and shall determine all issues in the adjudicative proceeding, including those affecting the defaulting party.

(b) In an adjudicative proceeding that has no parties other than the agency and the party in default, the presiding officer shall, after issuing the order of default, dismiss the proceeding.   1988

63-46b-12. Agency review — Procedure.

(1) (a) If a statute or the agency's rules permit parties to any adjudicative proceeding to seek review of an order by the agency or by a superior agency, the aggrieved party may file a written request for review within 30 days after the issuance of the order with the person or entity designated for that purpose by the statute or rule.

(b) The request shall:

(i) be signed by the party seeking review;

(ii) state the grounds for review and the relief requested;

(iii) state the date upon which it was mailed; and

(iv) be mailed to the presiding officer and to each party.

(2) (a) Within 15 days of the mailing date of the request for review, or within the time period provided by agency rule, whichever is longer, any party may file a response with the person designated by statute or rule to receive the response.

(b) The party who files a response under Subsection (2)(a) shall mail a copy of the response to each of the parties and to the presiding officer.

(3) If a statute or the agency's rules require review of an order by the agency or a superior agency, the agency or superior agency shall review the order within a reasonable time or within the time required by statute or the agency's rules.

(4) To assist in review, the agency or superior agency may by order or rule permit the parties to file briefs or other documents, or to conduct oral argument.

(5) Notice of hearings on review shall be mailed to all parties.

(6) (a) Within a reasonable time after the filing of any response, other filings, or oral argument, or within the time required by statute or applicable rules, the agency or superior agency shall issue a written order on review.

(b) The order on review shall be signed by the agency head or by a person designated by the agency for that purpose and shall be mailed to each party.

(c) The order on review shall contain:

(i) a designation of the statute or rule permitting or requiring review;

(ii) a statement of the issues reviewed;

(iii) findings of fact as to each of the issues reviewed;

(iv) conclusions of law as to each of the issues reviewed;

(v) the reasons for the disposition;

(vi) whether the decision of the presiding officer or agency is to be affirmed, reversed, or modified, and whether all or any portion of the adjudicative proceeding is to be remanded;

(vii) a notice of any right of further administrative reconsideration or judicial review available to aggrieved parties; and

(viii) the time limits applicable to any appeal or review.   2001

63-46b-13. Agency review — Reconsideration.

(1) (a) Within 20 days after the date that an order is issued for which review by the agency or by a superior agency under Section 63-46b-12 is unavailable, and if the order would otherwise constitute final agency action, any party may file a written request for reconsideration with the agency, stating the specific grounds upon which relief is requested.

(b) Unless otherwise provided by statute, the filing of the request is not a prerequisite for seeking judicial review of the order.

(2) The request for reconsideration shall be filed with the agency and one copy shall be mailed to each party by the person making the request.

(3) (a) The agency head, or a person designated for that purpose, shall issue a written order granting the request or denying the request.

(b) If the agency head or the person designated for that purpose does not issue an order within 20 days after the filing of the request, the request for reconsideration shall be considered to be denied.   2001

63-46b-14. Judicial review — Exhaustion of administrative remedies.

(1) A party aggrieved may obtain judicial review of final agency action, except in actions where judicial review is expressly prohibited by statute.

(2) A party may seek judicial review only after exhausting all administrative remedies available, except that:

(a) a party seeking judicial review need not exhaust administrative remedies if this chapter or any other statute states that exhaustion is not required;

(b) the court may relieve a party seeking judicial review of the requirement to exhaust any or all administrative remedies if:

(i) the administrative remedies are inadequate; or

(ii) exhaustion of remedies would result in irreparable harm disproportionate to the public benefit derived from requiring exhaustion.

(3) (a) A party shall file a petition for judicial review of final agency action within 30 days after the date that the order constituting the final agency action is issued or is considered to have been issued under Subsection 63-46b-13(3)(b).

(b) The petition shall name the agency and all other appropriate parties as respondents and shall meet the form requirements specified in this chapter.   1988

63-46b-15. Judicial review — Informal adjudicative proceedings.

(1) (a) The district courts have jurisdiction to review by trial de novo all final agency actions resulting from informal adjudicative proceedings, except that the juvenile courts have jurisdiction over all state agency actions relating to:

(i) the removal or placement of children in state custody;

(ii) the support of children under Subsection (1)(a)(i) as determined administratively under Section 78-3a-906; and

(iii) substantiated findings of abuse or neglect made by the Division of Child and Family Services, after an evidentiary hearing.

(b) Venue for judicial review of informal adjudicative proceedings shall be as provided in the statute governing the agency or, in the absence of such a venue provision, in the county where the petitioner resides or maintains the petitioner's principal place of business.

(2) (a) The petition for judicial review of informal adjudicative proceedings shall be a complaint governed by the Utah Rules of Civil Procedure and shall include:

(i) the name and mailing address of the party seeking judicial review;

(ii) the name and mailing address of the respondent agency;

(iii) the title and date of the final agency action to be reviewed, together with a copy, summary, or brief description of the agency action;

(iv) identification of the persons who were parties in the informal adjudicative proceedings that led to the agency action;

(v) a copy of the written agency order from the informal proceeding;

(vi) facts demonstrating that the party seeking judicial review is entitled to obtain judicial review;

(vii) a request for relief, specifying the type and extent of relief requested; and

(viii) a statement of the reasons why the petitioner is entitled to relief.

(b) All additional pleadings and proceedings in the district court are governed by the Utah Rules of Civil Procedure.

(3) (a) The district court, without a jury, shall determine all questions of fact and law and any constitutional issue presented in the pleadings.

(b) The Utah Rules of Evidence apply in judicial proceedings under this section.   2001

63-46b-16. Judicial review — Formal adjudicative proceedings.

(1) As provided by statute, the Supreme Court or the Court of Appeals has jurisdiction to review all final agency action resulting from formal adjudicative proceedings.

(2) (a) To seek judicial review of final agency action resulting from formal adjudicative proceedings, the petitioner shall file a petition for review of agency action with the appropriate appellate court in the form required by the appellate rules of the appropriate appellate court.

(b) The appellate rules of the appropriate appellate court shall govern all additional filings and proceedings in the appellate court.

(3) The contents, transmittal, and filing of the agency's record for judicial review of formal adjudicative proceedings are governed by the Utah Rules of Appellate Procedure, except that:

(a) all parties to the review proceedings may stipulate to shorten, summarize, or organize the record;

(b) the appellate court may tax the cost of preparing transcripts and copies for the record:

(i) against a party who unreasonably refuses to stipulate to shorten, summarize, or organize the record; or

(ii) according to any other provision of law.

(4) The appellate court shall grant relief only if, on the basis of the agency's record, it determines that a person seeking judicial review has been substantially prejudiced by any of the following:

(a) the agency action, or the statute or rule on which the agency action is based, is unconstitutional on its face or as applied;

(b) the agency has acted beyond the jurisdiction conferred by any statute;

(c) the agency has not decided all of the issues requiring resolution;

(d) the agency has erroneously interpreted or applied the law;

(e) the agency has engaged in an unlawful procedure or decision-making process, or has failed to follow prescribed procedure;

(f) the persons taking the agency action were illegally constituted as a decision-making body or were subject to disqualification;

(g) the agency action is based upon a determination of fact, made or implied by the agency, that is not supported by substantial evidence when viewed in light of the whole record before the court;

(h) the agency action is:

(i) an abuse of the discretion delegated to the agency by statute;

(ii) contrary to a rule of the agency;

(iii) contrary to the agency's prior practice, unless the agency justifies the inconsistency by giving facts and reasons that demonstrate a fair and rational basis for the inconsistency; or

(iv) otherwise arbitrary or capricious. 1988

63-46b-17. Judicial review — Type of relief.

(1) (a) In either the review of informal adjudicative proceedings by the district court or the review of formal adjudicative proceedings by an appellate court, the court may award damages or compensation only to the extent expressly authorized by statute.

(b) In granting relief, the court may:

(i) order agency action required by law;

(ii) order the agency to exercise its discretion as required by law;

(iii) set aside or modify agency action;

(iv) enjoin or stay the effective date of agency action; or

(v) remand the matter to the agency for further proceedings.

(2) Decisions on petitions for judicial review of final agency action are reviewable by a higher court, if authorized by statute.   1987

63-46b-18. Judicial review — Stay and other temporary remedies pending final disposition.

(1) Unless precluded by another statute, the agency may grant a stay of its order or other temporary remedy during the pendency of judicial review, according to the agency's rules.

(2) Parties shall petition the agency for a stay or other temporary remedies unless extraordinary circumstances require immediate judicial intervention.

(3) If the agency denies a stay or denies other temporary remedies requested by a party, the agency's order of denial shall be mailed to all parties and shall specify the reasons why the stay or other temporary remedy was not granted.

(4) If the agency has denied a stay or other temporary remedy to protect the public health, safety, or welfare against a substantial threat, the court may not grant a stay or other temporary remedy unless it finds that:

(a) the agency violated its own rules in denying the stay; or

(b) (i) the party seeking judicial review is likely to prevail on the merits when the court finally disposes of the matter;

(ii) the party seeking judicial review will suffer irreparable injury without immediate relief;

(iii) granting relief to the party seeking review will not substantially harm other parties to the proceedings; and

(iv) the threat to the public health, safety, or welfare relied upon by the agency is not sufficiently serious to justify the agency's action under the circumstances.   1987

63-46b-19. Civil enforcement.

(1) (a) In addition to other remedies provided by law, an agency may seek enforcement of an order by seeking civil enforcement in the district courts.

(b) The action seeking civil enforcement of an agency's order must name, as defendants, each alleged violator against whom the agency seeks to obtain civil enforcement.

(c) Venue for an action seeking civil enforcement of an agency's order shall be determined by the requirements of the Utah Rules of Civil Procedure.

(d) The action may request, and the court may grant, any of the following:

(i) declaratory relief;

(ii) temporary or permanent injunctive relief;

(iii) any other civil remedy provided by law; or

(iv) any combination of the foregoing.

(2) (a) Any person whose interests are directly impaired or threatened by the failure of an agency to enforce an agency's order may timely file a complaint seeking civil enforcement of that order, but the action may not be commenced:

(i) until at least 30 days after the plaintiff has given notice of his intent to seek civil enforcement of the alleged violation to the agency head, the attorney general, and to each alleged violator against whom the petitioner seeks civil enforcement;

(ii) if the agency has filed and is diligently prosecuting a complaint seeking civil enforcement of the same order against the same or a similarly situated defendant; or

(iii) if a petition for judicial review of the same order has been filed and is pending in court.

(b) The complaint seeking civil enforcement of an agency's order must name, as defendants, the agency whose order is sought to be enforced, the agency that is vested with the power to enforce the order, and each alleged violator against whom the plaintiff seeks civil enforcement.

(c) Except to the extent expressly authorized by statute, a complaint seeking civil enforcement of an agency's order may not request, and the court may not grant, any monetary payment apart from taxable costs.

(3) In a proceeding for civil enforcement of an agency's order, in addition to any other defenses allowed by law, a defendant may defend on the ground that:

(a) the order sought to be enforced was issued by an agency without jurisdiction to issue the order;

(b) the order does not apply to the defendant;

(c) the defendant has not violated the order; or

(d) the defendant violated the order but has subsequently complied.

(4) Decisions on complaints seeking civil enforcement of an agency's order are reviewable in the same manner as other civil cases.   1987

63-46b-20. Emergency adjudicative proceedings.

(1) An agency may issue an order on an emergency basis without complying with the requirements of this chapter if:

(a) the facts known by the agency or presented to the agency show that an immediate and significant danger to the public health, safety, or welfare exists; and

(b) the threat requires immediate action by the agency.

(2) In issuing its emergency order, the agency shall:

(a) limit its order to require only the action necessary to prevent or avoid the danger to the public health, safety, or welfare;

(b) issue promptly a written order, effective immediately, that includes a brief statement of findings of fact, conclusions of law, and reasons for the agency's utilization of emergency adjudicative proceedings; and

(c) give immediate notice to the persons who are required to comply with the order.

(3) If the emergency order issued under this section will result in the continued infringement or impairment of any legal right or interest of any party, the agency shall commence a formal adjudicative proceeding in accordance with the other provisions of this chapter.   1987

63-46b-21. Declaratory orders.

(1) Any person may file a request for agency action, requesting that the agency issue a declaratory order determining the applicability of a statute, rule, or order within the primary jurisdiction of the agency to specified circumstances.

(2) Each agency shall issue rules that:

(a) provide for the form, contents, and filing of petitions for declaratory orders;

(b) provide for the disposition of the petitions;

(c) define the classes of circumstances in which the agency will not issue a declaratory order;

(d) are consistent with the public interest and with the general policy of this chapter; and

(e) facilitate and encourage agency issuance of reliable advice.

(3) (a) An agency may not issue a declaratory order if:

(i) the request is one of a class of circumstances that the agency has by rule defined as being exempt from declaratory orders; or

(ii) the person requesting the declaratory order participated in an adjudicative proceeding concerning the same issue within 12 months of the date of the present request.

(b) An agency may issue a declaratory order that would substantially prejudice the rights of a person who would be a necessary party, only if that person consents in writing to the determination of the matter by a declaratory proceeding.

(4) Persons may intervene in declaratory proceedings if:

(a) they meet the requirements of Section 63-46b-9; and

(b) they file timely petitions for intervention according to agency rules.

(5) An agency may provide, by rule or order, that other provisions of Sections 63-46b-4 through 63-46b-13 apply to declaratory proceedings.

(6) (a) After receipt of a petition for a declaratory order, the agency may issue a written order:

(i) declaring the applicability of the statute, rule, or order in question to the specified circumstances;

(ii) setting the matter for adjudicative proceedings;

(iii) agreeing to issue a declaratory order within a specified time; or

(iv) declining to issue a declaratory order and stating the reasons for its action.

(b) A declaratory order shall contain:

(i) the names of all parties to the proceeding on which it is based;

(ii) the particular facts on which it is based; and

(iii) the reasons for its conclusion.

(c) A copy of all orders issued in response to a request for a declaratory proceeding shall be mailed promptly to the petitioner and any other parties.

(d) A declaratory order has the same status and binding effect as any other order issued in an adjudicative proceeding.

(7) Unless the petitioner and the agency agree in writing to an extension, if an agency has not issued a declaratory order within 60 days after receipt of the petition for a declaratory order, the petition is denied.
1988

63-46b-22. Transition procedures.

(1) The procedures for agency action, agency review, and judicial review contained in this chapter are applicable to all agency adjudicative proceedings commenced by or before an agency on or after January 1, 1988.

(2) Statutes and rules governing agency action, agency review, and judicial review that are in effect on December 31, 1987, govern all agency adjudicative proceedings commenced by or before an agency on or before December 31, 1987, even if those proceedings are still pending before an agency or a court on January 1, 1988.
1991

63-46b-23. Electronic records and conversion of written records by governmental agencies.

A governmental agency may make rules regarding electronic records and conversion of written records as prescribed by Title 46, Chapter 4, Part 5, Electronic Records in Government Agencies.
2001

CHAPTER 55

LEGISLATIVE OVERSIGHT AND SUNSET ACT

Part 2

Repeal Dates

PART 2

REPEAL DATES

63-55-269. Repeal dates, Title 69.

Section 69-2-5.6, Emergency services telephone charge to fund statewide unified E-911 emergency service, is repealed July 1, 2011.
2004

CHAPTER 55b

REPEAL DATES BY TITLE

63-55b-153. Repeal dates — Titles 53, 53A, and 53B.

(1) Subsection 53-3-205(9)(a)(i)(D) is repealed July 1, 2007.

(2) Subsection 53-3-804(2)(g) is repealed July 1, 2007.

(3) Section 53A-1-403.5 is repealed July 1, 2007.

(4) Subsection 53A-1a-511(7)(c) is repealed July 1, 2007.

(5) Section 53A-3-702 is repealed July 1, 2008.

(6) Section 53B-8-104.5 is repealed July 1, 2009.
2004

63-55b-177. Repeal dates, Title 77.

Section 77-2a-3.1 is repealed June 30, 2006. 2004

CHAPTER 63a

CRIME VICTIM REPARATION TRUST, PUBLIC SAFETY SUPPORT FUNDS, SUBSTANCE ABUSE PREVENTION ACCOUNT, AND SERVICES FOR VICTIMS OF DOMESTIC VIOLENCE ACCOUNT

63-63a-1. Surcharge — Application and exemptions.

(1) (a) A surcharge shall be paid on all criminal fines, penalties, and forfeitures imposed by the courts.

(b) The surcharge shall be:

(i) 85% upon conviction of a:

(A) felony;

(B) class A misdemeanor;

(C) violation of Title 41, Chapter 6a, Part 5, Driving Under the Influence and Reckless Driving; or

(D) class B misdemeanor not classified within Title 41, Motor Vehicles, including violation of comparable county or municipal ordinances; or

(ii) 35% upon conviction of any other offense, including violation of county or municipal ordinances not subject to the 85% surcharge.

(2) The surcharge may not be imposed:

(a) upon nonmoving traffic violations;

(b) upon court orders when the offender is ordered to perform compensatory service work in lieu of paying a fine; and

(c) upon penalties assessed by the juvenile court as part of the nonjudicial adjustment of a case under Section 78-3a-502.

(3) (a) The surcharge and the exceptions under Subsections (1) and (2) also apply to all fines, penalties, and forfeitures imposed on juveniles for conduct that would be criminal if committed by an adult.

(b) However, the surcharge does not include amounts assessed or collected separately by juvenile courts for the Juvenile Restitution Account, which is independent of this chapter and does not affect the imposition or collection of the surcharge.

(4) The surcharge under this section shall be imposed in addition to the fine charged for a civil or criminal offense, and no reduction may be made in the fine charged due to the surcharge imposition.

(5) Fees, assessments, and surcharges related to criminal or traffic offenses shall be authorized and managed by this chapter rather than attached to particular offenses.   2005

63-63a-2. Division of collected monies retained by state treasurer and local governmental collecting entity — Purpose of surcharge — Allocation of collections — Financial information.

(1) The amount of the surcharge imposed under this chapter by courts of record shall be collected before any fine and deposited with the state treasurer.

(2) The amount of the surcharge and the amount of criminal fines, penalties, and forfeitures imposed under this chapter by courts not of record shall be collected concurrently.

(a) As monies are collected on criminal fines, penalties, and forfeitures subject to the 85% surcharge, the monies shall be divided pro rata so that the local governmental collecting entity retains 54% of the collected monies and the state retains 46% of the collected monies.

(b) As monies are collected on criminal fines, penalties, and forfeitures subject to the 35% surcharge, the monies shall be divided pro rata so that the local governmental collecting entity retains 74% of the collected monies and the state retains 26% of the collected monies.

(c) The court shall deposit with the state treasurer the surcharge portion of all monies as they are collected.

(3) Courts of record, courts not of record, and administrative traffic proceedings shall collect financial information to determine:

(a) the total number of cases in which:

(i) a final judgment has been rendered;

(ii) surcharges and fines are paid by partial or installment payment; and

(iii) the judgment is fulfilled by an alternative method upon the court's order;

(b) the total dollar amounts of surcharges owed to the state and fines owed to the state and county or municipality, including:

(i) waived surcharges;

(ii) uncollected surcharges; and

(iii) collected surcharges.

(4) The courts of record, courts not of record, and administrative traffic proceedings shall report all collected financial information monthly to the Administrative Office of the Courts. The collected information shall be categorized by cases subject to the 85% and 35% surcharge.

(5) The purpose of the surcharge is to finance the trust funds and support accounts as provided in this chapter.

(6) (a) From the surcharge, the Division of Finance shall allocate in the manner and for the purposes described in Sections 63-63a-3 through 63-63a-9.

(b) The balance of the collected surcharge shall be deposited in the General Fund.

(c) Allocations shall be made on a fiscal year basis.

(7) The provisions of Sections 63-63a-1 and 63-63a-2 may not impact the distribution and allocation of fines and forfeitures imposed in accordance with Sections 23-14-13, 78-3-14.5, and 78-5-116.   2003

63-63a-3. EMS share of surcharge — Accounting.

(1) The Division of Finance shall allocate 14% of the collected surcharge established in Section 63-63a-1, but not to exceed the amount appropriated by the Legislature, to the Emergency Medical Services (EMS) Grants Program Account under Section 26-8a-207.

(2) The amount shall be recorded by the Department of Health as a dedicated credit.   1999

63-63a-4. Distribution of surcharge amounts.

(1) In this section:

(a) "Reparation fund" means the Crime Victim Reparation Fund.

(b) "Safety account" means the Public Safety Support Account.

(2) (a) There is created a restricted special revenue fund known as the "Crime Victim Reparation Fund" to be administered and distributed as provided in this chapter by the Reparations Office under Title 63, Chapter 25a, Part 4, Crime Victims' Reparations Act, in cooperation with the Division of Finance.

(b) Monies deposited in this fund are for victim reparations, criminal justice and substance abuse, other victim services, and, as appropriated, for administrative costs of the Commission on Criminal and Juvenile Justice under Title 63, Chapter 25a.

(3) (a) There is created a restricted account in the General Fund known as the "Public Safety Support Account" to be administered and distributed by the Department of Public Safety in cooperation with the Division of Finance as provided in this chapter.

(b) Monies deposited in this account shall be appropriated to:

(i) the Division of Peace Officer Standards and Training (POST) as described in Title 53, Chapter 6, Peace Officer Standards and Training Act; and

(ii) the Office of the Attorney General for the support of the Utah Prosecution Council established in Title 67, Chapter 5a, and the fulfillment of the council's duties.

(4) The Division of Finance shall allocate from the collected surcharge established in Section 63-63a-1:

(a) 35% to the reparation fund;

(b) 18.5% to the safety account for POST, but not to exceed the amount appropriated by the Legislature; and

(c) 3% to the safety account for support of the Utah Prosecution Council, but not to exceed the amount appropriated by the Legislature.

(5) (a) In addition to the funding provided by other sections of this chapter, a percentage of the income earned by inmates working for correctional industries in a federally certified private sector/prison industries enhancement program shall be deposited in the reparation fund.

(b) The percentage of income deducted from inmate pay under Subsection (5)(a) shall be determined by the executive director of the Department of Corrections in accordance with the requirements of the private sector/prison industries enhancement program.

(6) (a) In addition to other monies collected from the surcharge, judges are encouraged to, and may in their discretion, impose additional reparations to be paid into the reparation fund by convicted criminals.

(b) The additional discretionary reparations may not exceed the statutory maximum fine permitted by Title 76, Utah Criminal Code, for that offense. 2002 (5th S.S.)

63-63a-5. Substance Abuse Prevention Account established — Funding — Uses.

(1) There is created a restricted account within the General Fund known as the Substance Abuse Prevention Account.

(2) (a) The Division of Finance shall allocate to the Substance Abuse Prevention Account from the collected surcharge established in Section 63-63a-1:

(i) 2.5% for the juvenile court, but not to exceed the amount appropriated by the Legislature; and

(ii) 2.5% for the State Office of Education, but not to exceed the amount appropriated by the Legislature.

(b) The juvenile court shall use the allocation to pay for community service programs required by Subsection 78-3a-118(2)(m).

(c) The State Office of Education shall use the allocation in public school programs for:

(i) substance abuse prevention and education;

(ii) substance abuse prevention training for teachers and administrators; and

(iii) district and school programs to supplement, not supplant, existing local prevention efforts in cooperation with local substance abuse authorities. 1998

63-63a-6. Victims of Domestic Violence Services Account established — Funding — Uses.

(1) There is created a restricted account in the General Fund known as the Victims of Domestic Violence Services Account.

(2) (a) The Division of Finance shall allocate to the Victims of Domestic Violence Services Account from the collected surcharge established in Section 63-63a-1:

(i) 4% for the Division for Domestic Violence Services, but not to exceed the amount appropriated by the Legislature; and

(ii) .5% for the Office of the Attorney General, but not to exceed the amount appropriated by the Legislature.

(b) The attorney general shall use the allocation for training municipal and county attorneys in the prosecution of domestic violence offenses. 1993

63-63a-7. Intoxicated Driver Rehabilitation Account share of surcharge.

The Division of Finance shall allocate 7.5% of the collected surcharge established in Section 63-63a-1, but not to exceed the amount appropriated by the Legislature, to the Intoxicated Driver Rehabilitation Account established by Section 62A-15-503. 2002 (5th S.S.)

63-63a-8. Children's Legal Defense Account.

(1) There is created a restricted account within the General Fund known as the Children's Legal Defense Account.

(2) The purpose of the Children's Legal Defense Account is to provide for programs that protect and defend the rights, safety, and quality of life of children.

(3) The Legislature shall appropriate money from the account for the administrative and related costs of the following programs:

(a) implementing the Mandatory Educational Course on Children's Needs for Divorcing Parents relating to the effects of divorce on children as provided in Sections 30-3-4, 30-3-7, 30-3-10.3, 30-3-11.3, 30-3-15.3, and 30-3-18, and the Mediation Pilot Program — Child Custody or Parent-time as provided in Sections 30-3-15.3 and 30-3-18;

(b) implementing the use of guardians ad litem as provided in Sections 30-3-5.2, 78-3a-318, 78-3a-912, 78-11-6, and 78-7-9; the training of guardian ad litems and volunteers as provided in Section 78-3a-912; and termination of parental rights as provided in Sections 78-3a-118, 78-3a-119, 78-3a-903, and Title 78, Chapter 3a, Part 4, Termination of Parental Rights Act. This account may not be used to supplant funding for the guardian ad litem program in the juvenile court as provided in Section 78-3a-912; and

(c) implementing and administering the Expedited Parent-time Enforcement Pilot Program as provided in Section 30-3-38.

(4) The following withheld fees shall be allocated only to the Children's Legal Defense Account and used only for the purposes provided in Subsections (3)(a) through (c):

(a) the additional $10 fee withheld on every marriage license issued in the state of Utah as provided in Section 17-16-21; and

(b) a fee of $2 shall be withheld from the existing civil filing fee collected on any complaint, affidavit, or petition in a civil, probate, or adoption matter in every court of record.

(5) The Division of Finance shall allocate the monies described in Subsection (4) from the General Fund to the Children's Legal Defense Account.

(6) Any funds in excess of $200,000 remaining in the restricted account as of June 30 of any fiscal year shall lapse into the General Fund. 2001

63-63a-8.5. Guardian Ad Litem Services Account established — Funding — Uses.

There is created in the General Fund a restricted account known as the Guardian Ad Litem Services Account, for the purpose of funding the Office of the Guardian Ad Litem Director, in accordance with the provisions of Sections 78-3a-911 and 78-3a-912. The Division of Finance shall allocate 1.75% of the collected surcharge established in Section 63-63a-1 to the Guardian Ad Litem Services Account. That amount may not, however, exceed the amount appropriated by the Legislature. 1997

63-63a-9. Statewide Warrant Operations Account — Share of surcharge — Use.

(1) There is created a restricted account within the General Fund known as the Statewide Warrant Operations Account.

(2) The Division of Finance shall allocate 2.5% of the collected surcharge established under Section 63-63a-1, but not to exceed the amount appropriated by the Legislature, to this account.

(3) The Legislature may appropriate money from the restricted account to the Department of Public Safety to pay for statewide warrant system costs incurred under Section 53-10-208. 1998

CHAPTER 94

MCGRUFF SAFE HOUSE ACT

Section
63-94-101.   Title.
63-94-102.   Purpose.
63-94-103.   Designation — Administration.
63-94-104.   Program requirements.

63-94-101. Title.
This chapter is known as the "McGruff Safe House" Act.   1997

63-94-102. Purpose.
(1) The Legislature recognizes that children are often in dangerous situations that may be threatening or frightening to them and that there is a need for "safe homes" in our neighborhoods where a child may go for help.

(2) The Legislature also recognizes that along with the need for "safe homes" that children can recognize easily, there is needed a method by which these homes can be identified.

(3) The purpose of this chapter is to:
    (a) provide and designate a recognizable symbol for those "safe homes" that children can readily identify; and
    (b) establish a method by which local law enforcement agencies can identify and train volunteers who are willing to make their homes "safe homes".   1997

63-94-103. Designation — Administration.
(1) The National McGruff House Network Program is hereby designated as the officially recognized statewide "safe house" program for Utah.

(2) The program shall be administered through the Department of Public Safety by the Utah Council for Crime Prevention.   1997

63-94-104. Program requirements.
(1) The statewide program administrator shall:
    (a) provide support and training upon request to local law enforcement agencies interested in implementing the program in their area;
    (b) provide local programs with signs for display in approved "safe homes"; and
    (c) maintain a register of all "safe homes" that includes, at a minimum, the address of the home and the names of all persons living in the home.

(2) The local program shall:
    (a) recruit volunteer "safe homes" in neighborhoods with the help of local community groups;
    (b) provide training and education to volunteers regarding the program and its use;
    (c) provide for an application process for volunteers;
    (d) conduct criminal history background checks on volunteers and members of their households;
    (e) approve or disapprove applications for "safe homes";
    (f) provide education through community programs for parents and children on the program and the proper use of "safe homes";
    (g) provide approved "safe homes" with signs for display;
    (h) provide procedures by which a "safe home" may be removed from the register; and
    (i) provide for a method of renewal of the "safe home" designation in order to keep the registry current and provide for the periodic review of the "safe home", the volunteer, and all members of the household.   1997

CHAPTER 98

FIREARM LAWS

Section
63-98-101.   Title.
63-98-102.   Uniform firearm laws.

63-98-101. Title.
This chapter is known as "Firearm Laws."   2004

63-98-102. Uniform firearm laws.
(1) The individual right to keep and bear arms being a constitutionally protected right under Article I, Section 6 of the Utah Constitution, the Legislature finds the need to provide uniform civil and criminal firearm laws throughout the state.

(2) Except as specifically provided by state law, a local authority or state entity may not:
    (a) prohibit an individual from owning, possessing, purchasing, selling, transferring, transporting, or keeping a firearm at the individual's place of residence, property, business, or in any vehicle lawfully in the individual's possession or lawfully under the individual's control; or
    (b) require an individual to have a permit or license to purchase, own, possess, transport, or keep a firearm.

(3) In conjunction with Title 76, Chapter 10, Part 5, Weapons, this section is uniformly applicable throughout this state and in all its political subdivisions and municipalities.

(4) All authority to regulate firearms is reserved to the state except where the Legislature specifically delegates responsibility to local authorities or state entities.

(5) Unless specifically authorized by the Legislature by statute, a local authority or state entity may not enact, establish, or enforce any ordinance, regulation, rule, or policy pertaining to firearms that in any way inhibits or restricts the possession or use of firearms on either public or private property.

(6) As used in this section:
    (a) "firearm" has the same meaning as defined in Subsection 76-10-501(9); and
    (b) "local authority or state entity" includes public school districts, public schools, and state institutions of higher education.

(7) Nothing in this section restricts or expands private property rights.   2004

TITLE 69

TELEGRAPHIC AND TELEPHONIC TRANSACTIONS

Chapter
2.   Emergency Telephone Service Law.

CHAPTER 2

EMERGENCY TELEPHONE SERVICE LAW

Section
69-2-5.   Funding for 911 emergency telephone service.

69-2-5. Funding for 911 emergency telephone service.

(1) In providing funding of 911 emergency telephone service, any public agency establishing a 911 emergency telephone service may:

(a) seek assistance from the federal or state government, to the extent constitutionally permissible, in the form of loans, advances, grants, subsidies, and otherwise, directly or indirectly;

(b) seek funds appropriated by local governmental taxing authorities for the funding of public safety agencies; and

(c) seek gifts, donations, or grants from individuals, corporations, or other private entities.

(2) For purposes of providing funding of 911 emergency telephone service, special service districts may raise funds as provided in Section 17A-2-1322 and may borrow money and incur indebtedness as provided in Section 17A-2-1316.

(3) (a) Except as provided in Subsection (3)(b) and subject to the other provisions of this Subsection (3) a county, city, or town within which 911 emergency telephone service is provided may levy monthly an emergency services telephone charge on:

(i) each local exchange service switched access line within the boundaries of the county, city, or town; and

(ii) each revenue producing radio communications access line with a billing address within the boundaries of the county, city, or town.

(b) Notwithstanding Subsection (3)(a), an access line provided for public coin telephone service is exempt from emergency telephone charges.

(c) The amount of the charge levied under this section may not exceed:

(i) 65 cents per month for each local exchange service switched access line;

(ii) 65 cents per month for each radio communications access line; and

(iii) 4 cents of the amount of the charge levied under Subsections (3)(c)(i) and (ii), less the collection costs of the provider and Tax Commission permitted by Subsection (3)(h) and Subsection 53-10-604(2)(b), shall be deposited monthly in the statewide unified E-911 Emergency Service Fund created in Section 53-10-603, for the purposes outlined in that section.

(d) (i) For purposes of this Subsection (3)(d) the following terms shall be defined as provided in Section 59-12-102:

(A) "mobile telecommunications service";

(B) "primary place of use";

(C) "service address"; and

(D) "telephone service."

(ii) An access line described in Subsection (3)(a) is considered to be within the boundaries of a county, city, or town if the telephone services provided over the access line are located within the county, city, or town:

(A) for purposes of sales and use taxes under Title 59, Chapter 12, Sales and Use Tax Act; and

(B) determined in accordance with Section 59-12-207.4.

(iii) The rate imposed on an access line under this section shall be determined in accordance with Subsection (3)(d)(iv) if the location of an access line described in Subsection (3)(a) is determined under Subsection (3)(d)(ii) to be a county, city, or town other than county, city, or town in which is located:

(A) for telephone service other than mobile telecommunications service, the purchaser's service address; or

(B) for mobile telecommunications service, the purchaser's primary place of use.

(iv) The rate imposed on an access line under this section shall be the lower of:

(A) the rate imposed by the county, city, or town in which the access line is located under Subsection (3)(d)(ii); or

(B) the rate imposed by the county, city, or town in which it is located:

(I) for telephone service other than mobile telecommunications service, the purchaser's service address; or

(II) for mobile telecommunications service, the purchaser's primary place of use.

(e) (i) A county, city, or town shall notify the Public Service Commission of the intent to levy the charge under this Subsection (3) at least 30 days prior to the effective date of the charge being levied.

(ii) For purposes of this Subsection (3)(e):

(A) "Annexation" means an annexation to:

(I) a city or town under Title 10, Chapter 2, Part 4, Annexation; or

(II) a county under Title 17, Chapter 2, Annexation to County.

(B) "Annexing area" means an area that is annexed into a county, city, or town.

(iii) (A) Except as provided in Subsection (3)(e)(iii)(C) or (D), if on or after July 1, 2003, a county, city, or town enacts or repeals a charge or changes the amount of the charge under this section, the enactment, repeal, or change shall take effect:

(I) on the first day of a calendar quarter; and

(II) after a 90-day period beginning on the date the State Tax Commission receives notice meeting the requirements of Subsection (3)(e)(iii)(B) from the county, city, or town.

(B) The notice described in Subsection (3)(e)(iii)(A) shall state:

(I) that the county, city, or town will enact or repeal a charge or change the amount of the charge under this section;

(II) the statutory authority for the charge described in Subsection (3)(e)(iii)(B)(I);

(III) the effective date of the charge described in Subsection (3)(e)(iii)(B)(I); and

(IV) if the county, city, or town enacts the charge or changes the amount of the charge described in Subsection (3)(e)(iii)(B)(I), the amount of the charge.

(C) Notwithstanding Subsection (3)(e)(iii)(A), the enactment of a charge or a charge increase under this section shall take effect on the first day of the first billing period:

  (I) that begins after the effective date of the enactment of the charge or the charge increase; and

  (II) if the billing period for the charge begins before the effective date of the enactment of the charge or the charge increase imposed under this section.

(D) Notwithstanding Subsection (3)(e)(iii)(A), the repeal of a charge or a charge decrease under this section shall take effect on the first day of the last billing period:

  (I) that began before the effective date of the repeal of the charge or the charge decrease; and

  (II) if the billing period for the charge begins before the effective date of the repeal of the charge or the charge decrease imposed under this section.

(iv) (A) Except as provided in Subsection (3)(e)(iv)(C) or (D), if for an annexation that occurs on or after July 1, 2003, the annexation will result in the enactment, repeal, or a change in the amount of a charge imposed under this section for an annexing area, the enactment, repeal, or change shall take effect:

  (I) on the first day of a calendar quarter; and

  (II) after a 90-day period beginning on the date the State Tax Commission receives notice meeting the requirements of Subsection (3)(e)(iv)(B) from the county, city, or town that annexes the annexing area.

(B) The notice described in Subsection (3)(e)(iv)(A) shall state:

  (I) that the annexation described in Subsection (3)(e)(iv)(A) will result in an enactment, repeal, or a change in the charge being imposed under this section for the annexing area;

  (II) the statutory authority for the charge described in Subsection (3)(e)(iv)(B)(I);

  (III) the effective date of the charge described in Subsection (3)(e)(iv)(B)(I); and

  (IV) if the county, city, or town enacts the charge or changes the amount of the charge described in Subsection (3)(e)(iv)(B)(I), the amount of the charge.

(C) Notwithstanding Subsection (3)(e)(iv)(A), the enactment of a charge or a charge increase under this section shall take effect on the first day of the first billing period:

  (I) that begins after the effective date of the enactment of the charge or the charge increase; and

  (II) if the billing period for the charge begins before the effective date of the enactment of the charge or the charge increase imposed under this section.

(D) Notwithstanding Subsection (3)(e)(iv)(A), the repeal of a charge or a charge decrease under this section shall take effect on the first day of the last billing period:

  (I) that began before the effective date of the repeal of the charge or the charge decrease; and

  (II) if the billing period for the charge begins before the effective date of the repeal of the charge or the charge decrease imposed under this section.

(f) Subject to Subsection (3)(g), an emergency services telephone charge levied under this section shall:

  (i) be billed and collected by the person that provides the:

    (A) local exchange service switched access line services; or

    (B) radio communications access line services; and

  (ii) except for costs retained under Subsection (3)(h), remitted to the State Tax Commission.

(g) An emergency services telephone charge on a mobile telecommunications service may be levied, billed, and collected only to the extent permitted by the Mobile Telecommunications Sourcing Act, 4 U.S.C. Sec. 116 et seq.

(h) The person that bills and collects the charges levied under Subsection (3)(f) may:

  (i) bill the charge imposed by this section in combination with the charge levied under Section 69-2-5.6 as one line item charge; and

  (ii) retain an amount not to exceed 1.5% of the levy collected under this section as reimbursement for the cost of billing, collecting, and remitting the levy.

(i) The State Tax Commission shall:

  (i) collect, enforce, and administer the charge imposed under this Subsection (3) pursuant to the same procedures used in the administration, collection, and enforcement of the state sales and use taxes under:

    (A) Title 59, Chapter 1, General Taxation Policies; and

    (B) Title 59, Chapter 12, Part 1, Tax Collection, except for:

      (I) Section 59-12-104;

      (II) Section 59-12-104.1;

      (III) Section 59-12-104.2; and

      (IV) Sections 59-12-107.1 through 59-12-107.3.

  (ii) transmit monies collected under this Subsection (3):

    (A) monthly; and

    (B) by electronic funds transfer by the commission to the county, city, or town that imposes the charge; and

  (iii) charge the county, city, or town for the State Tax Commission's services under this Subsection (3) in an amount:

    (A) sufficient to reimburse the State Tax Commission for the cost to the State Tax Commission in rendering the services; and

    (B) that may not exceed an amount equal to 1.5% of the charges imposed under this Subsection (3).

(4) (a) Any money received by a public agency for the provision of 911 emergency telephone service

shall be deposited in a special emergency telephone service fund.

(b) (i) Except as provided in Subsection (5), the money in the emergency telephone service fund shall be expended by the public agency to pay the costs of establishing, installing, maintaining, and operating a 911 emergency telephone system or integrating a 911 system into an established public safety dispatch center, including contracting with the providers of local exchange service, radio communications service, and vendors of appropriate terminal equipment as necessary to implement the 911 emergency telephone service.

(ii) Revenues derived for the funding of 911 emergency telephone service may only be used for that portion of costs related to the operation of the 911 emergency telephone system when such a system is integrated with any public safety dispatch system.

(c) Any unexpended money in the emergency telephone service fund at the end of a fiscal year does not lapse, and must be carried forward to be used for the purposes described in this section.

(5) (a) Revenue received by a local entity from an increase in the levy imposed under Subsection (3) after the 2004 Annual General Session, or from grants from the Utah 911 Committee pursuant to Section 53-10-605:

(i) shall be deposited into the special emergency telephone service fund described in Subsection (4)(a); and

(ii) shall only be used for that portion of the costs related to the development and operation of wireless and land-based enhanced 911 emergency telephone service and the implementation of wireless E-911 Phase I and Phase II services as provided in Subsection (5)(b).

(b) The costs allowed under Subsection (5)(a)(ii) shall include the public service answering point's or local entity's costs for:

(i) acquisition, upgrade, modification, maintenance, and operation of public service answering point equipment capable of receiving E-911 information;

(ii) database development, operation, and maintenance; and

(iii) personnel costs associated with establishing, installing, maintaining, and operating wireless E-911 Phase I and Phase II services, including training emergency service personnel regarding receipt and use of E-911 wireless service information and educating consumers regarding the appropriate and responsible use of E-911 wireless service.

(6) A local entity that increases the levy it imposes under Subsection (3)(c) after the 2004 Annual General Session shall increase the levy to the maximum amount permitted by Subsection (3)(c).   2004

TITLE 72

TRANSPORTATION CODE

CHAPTER 1

DEPARTMENT OF TRANSPORTATION ADMINISTRATION

Part 1

General Provisions

Part 2

Department of Transportation

Part 3

Transportation Commission

PART 1

GENERAL PROVISIONS

72-1-101. Title.

(1) This title is known as the "Transportation Code."

(2) This chapter is known as the "Department of Transportation Administration Act."   **1998**

72-1-102. Definitions.

As used in this title:

(1) "Commission" means the Transportation Commission created under Section 72-1-301.

(2) "Construction" means the construction, reconstruction, replacement, and improvement of the highways, including the acquisition of rights-of-way and material sites.

(3) "Department" means the Department of Transportation created in Section 72-1-201.

(4) "Executive director" means the executive director of the department appointed under Section 72-1-202.

(5) "Farm tractor" has the meaning set forth in Section 41-1a-102.

(6) "Federal aid primary highway" means that portion of connected main highways located within this state officially designated by the department and approved by the United States Secretary of Transportation under Title 23, Highways, U.S.C.

(7) "Highway" means any public road, street, alley, lane, court, place, viaduct, tunnel, culvert, bridge, or structure laid out or erected for public use, or dedicated or abandoned to the public, or made public in an action for the partition of real property, including the entire area within the right-of-way.

(8) "Highway authority" means the department or the legislative, executive, or governing body of a county or municipality.

(9) "Implement of husbandry" has the meaning set forth in Section 41-1a-102.

(10) "Interstate system" means any highway officially designated by the department and included as part of the national interstate and defense highways, as provided in the Federal Aid Highway Act of 1956 and any supplemental acts or amendments.

(11) "Limited-access facility" means a highway especially designated for through traffic, and over, from, or to which neither owners nor occupants of abutting lands nor other persons have any right or easement, or have only a limited right or easement of access, light, air, or view.

(12) "Motor vehicle" has the same meaning set forth in Section 41-1a-102.

(13) "Municipality" has the same meaning set forth in Section 10-1-104.

(14) "National highway systems highways" means that portion of connected main highways located within this state officially designated by the department and approved by the United States Secretary of Transportation under Title 23, Highways, U.S.C.

(15) (a) "Port-of-entry" means a fixed or temporary facility constructed, operated, and maintained by the department where drivers, vehicles, and vehicle loads are checked or inspected for compliance with state and federal laws as specified in Section 72-9-501.

(b) "Port-of-entry" includes inspection and checking stations and weigh stations.

(16) "Port-of-entry agent" means a person employed at a port-of-entry to perform the duties specified in Section 72-9-501.

(17) "Right-of-way" means real property or an interest in real property, usually in a strip, acquired for or devoted to a highway.

(18) "Sealed" does not preclude acceptance of electronically sealed and submitted bids or proposals in addition to bids or proposals manually sealed and submitted.

(19) "Semitrailer" has the meaning set forth in Section 41-1a-102.

(20) "SR" means state route and has the same meaning as state highway as defined in this section.

(21) "State highway" means those highways designated as state highways in Title 72, Chapter 4, Designation of State Highways Act.

(22) "State highway purposes" has the meaning set forth in Section 72-5-102.

(23) "State transportation systems" means all streets, alleys, roads, highways, and thorough-fares of any kind, including connected structures, airports, spaceports, and all other modes and forms of conveyance used by the public.

(24) "Trailer" has the meaning set forth in Section 41-1a-102.

(25) "Truck tractor" has the meaning set forth in Section 41-1a-102.

(26) "UDOT" means the Utah Department of Transportation.

(27) "Vehicle" has the same meaning set forth in Section 41-1a-102.   2001

PART 2

DEPARTMENT OF TRANSPORTATION

72-1-201. Creation of Department of Transportation — Functions, powers, duties, rights, and responsibilities.

There is created the Department of Transportation which shall:

(1) have the general responsibility for planning, research, design, construction, maintenance, security, and safety of state transportation systems;

(2) provide administration for state transportation systems and programs;

(3) implement the transportation policies of the state;

(4) plan, develop, construct, and maintain state transportation systems that are safe, reliable, environmentally sensitive, and serve the needs of the traveling public, commerce, and industry;

(5) establish standards and procedures regarding the technical details of administration of the state transportation systems as established by statute and administrative rule;

(6) advise the governor and the Legislature about state transportation systems needs;

(7) coordinate with utility companies for the reasonable, efficient, and cost-effective installation, maintenance, operation, relocation, and upgrade of utilities within state highway rights-of-way; and

(8) in accordance with Title 63, Chapter 46a, Utah Administrative Rulemaking Act, make policy and rules for the administration of the department, state transportation systems, and programs.   1999

72-1-207. Department may sue and be sued — Legal adviser of department.

(1) The department may sue, and it may be sued only on written contracts made by it or under its authority.

(2) The department may sue in the name of the state.

(3) In all matters requiring legal advice in the performance of its duties and in the prosecution or defense of any action growing out of the performance of its duties, the attorney general is the legal adviser of the commission, and the department, and shall perform any and all legal services required by the commission and the department without other compensation than his salary.

(4) Upon request of the department, the attorney general shall aid in any investigation, hearing, or trial under the provisions of Chapter 9, Motor Carrier Safety Act, and institute and prosecute actions or proceedings for the enforcement of the provisions of the Constitution and statutes of this state or any rule or order of the department affecting motor carriers of persons and property.   1998

72-1-208. Cooperation with counties, cities, towns, the federal government, and all state departments.

(1) The department shall cooperate with the counties, cities, and towns in the construction, maintenance, and use of the highways and in all related matters, and may provide services to the counties, cities, and towns on terms mutually agreed upon.

(2) The department, with the approval of the governor, shall cooperate with the federal government in all federal-aid projects and with all state departments in all matters in connection with the use of the highways.   1998

72-1-208.5. Definition — Cooperation with metropolitan planning organizations — Cooperation in plans and programs required.

(1) As used in this section, "metropolitan planning organization" means an organization established under 23 U.S.C. Sec. 134.

(2) The department shall cooperate with a metropolitan planning organization in the metropolitan planning organization's responsibility to carry out a continuing, cooperative, and comprehensive process for transportation planning and project programming.

(3) If a metropolitan planning organization has a contiguous boundary with another metropolitan planning organization, the department shall cooperate with those organizations if the metropolitan planning organizations have:

(a) coordinated project priorities, transportation plans, and transportation improvement programs; and

(b) submitted joint priorities, plans, and programs to the department as comprehensive, integrated transportation plans.

(4) Subject to the provisions of 23 U.S.C. Sec. 134, if the governor and the affected local units of government jointly determine that metropolitan planning organizations have failed to meet the guidelines under Subsection (3), the governor and local units of government may redesignate or realign the metropolitan planning organizations.   2004

72-1-209. Department to cooperate in programs relating to scenic centers.

The department shall cooperate in planning and promoting road-building programs into the scenic centers of the state and in providing camping grounds and facilities in scenic centers for tourists with:

(1) the Governor's Office of Economic Development;

(2) other states;

(3) all national, state, and local planning and zoning agencies and boards;

(4) municipal and county officials; and

(5) other agencies.   2005

72-1-210. Department to be assisted by faculties and personnel of universities.

The engineering machinery and apparatus and the force of mechanics and instructors in the University of Utah and Utah State University are at the disposal of the department, and any faculty member of the institutions shall furnish any information or assistance desired upon request of the department.   1998

72-1-211. Department to develop strategic initiatives — Report — Rulemaking.

(1) The executive director shall develop strategic initiatives for the department.

(2) The strategic initiatives developed under Subsection (1) shall include consideration of the following factors:

(a) corridor preservation;

(b) development of new transportation capacity projects;

(c) long-term maintenance and operations of the transportation system;

(d) safety;

(e) incident management; and

(f) homeland security.

(3) (a) The executive director or the executive director's designee shall report the strategic initiatives of the department developed under Subsection (1) to the Transportation Commission.

(b) The report required under Subsection (3)(a) shall include the measure that will be used to determine whether the strategic initiatives have been achieved.

(4) After compliance with Subsection (3) and in accordance with Title 63, Chapter 46a, Utah Administrative Rulemaking Act, the department shall make rules establishing the strategic initiatives developed under this part.   2005

PART 3

TRANSPORTATION COMMISSION

72-1-301. Transportation Commission created — Members, appointment, terms — Qualifications — Pay and expenses — Chair — Quorum — Surety bond.

(1) (a) There is created the Transportation Commission which shall consist of seven members.

(b) The members of the commission shall be residents of Utah.

(c) No more than four of the commissioners shall be members of any one political party.

(d) (i) The commissioners shall be appointed by the governor, with the consent of the Senate, for a term of six years, beginning on April 1 of odd-numbered years, except as provided under Subsection (1)(d)(ii).

(ii) The first two additional commissioners serving on the seven member commission shall be appointed for terms of two years nine months and four years nine months, respectively, initially commencing on July 1, 1996, and subsequently commencing as specified under Subsection (1)(d)(i).

(e) The commissioners serve on a part-time basis.

(f) Each commissioner shall remain in office until a successor is appointed and qualified.

(2) The selection of the commissioners shall be as follows:

(a) one commissioner from Box Elder, Cache, or Rich county;

(b) one commissioner from Salt Lake or Tooele county;

(c) one commissioner from Carbon, Emery, Grand, or San Juan county;

(d) one commissioner from Beaver, Garfield, Iron, Kane, Millard, Piute, Sanpete, Sevier, Washington, or Wayne county;

(e) one commissioner from Weber, Davis, or Morgan county;

(f) one commissioner from Juab, Utah, Wasatch, Duchesne, Summit, Uintah, or Daggett county; and

(g) one commissioner selected from the state at large.

(3) (a) Members appointed before May 2, 1996, shall continue to receive the compensation, per diem, expenses, and benefits they were receiving as of January 1, 1996.

(b) Members appointed after May 2, 1996, shall receive no compensation or benefits for their services, but may receive per diem and expenses incurred in the performance of the member's official duties at the rates established by the Division of Finance under Sections 63A-3-106 and 63A-3-107.

(c) Members may decline to receive compensation, benefits, per diem, and expenses for their service.

(4) (a) One member of the commission shall be designated by the governor as chair.

(b) The commission shall select one member as vice chair to act in the chair's absence.

(5) Any four commissioners constitute a quorum.

(6) (a) Each member of the commission shall qualify by:

(i) taking the constitutional oath of office; and

(ii) giving a surety bond.

(b) The Division of Finance of the Department of Administrative Services shall determine the form and amount of the bond, and the state shall pay the bond premium.   2002

CHAPTER 3

HIGHWAY JURISDICTION AND CLASSIFICATION

Part 1

Highways in General

Part 2

State Park Access Highways

Part 3

Statewide Public Safety Interest Highways

PART 1

HIGHWAYS IN GENERAL

72-3-101.   Title.

This chapter is known as the "Highway Jurisdiction and Classification Act."   1998

72-3-102.   State highways — Class A state roads.

(1) State highways comprise highways, roads, and streets designated under Chapter 4, Designation of State Highways.

(2) State highways are class A state roads.

(3) The state has title to all rights-of-way for all state highways.

(4) The department has jurisdiction and control over all state highways.

(5) The department shall construct and maintain each state highway using funds made available for that purpose.   2000

72-3-103.   County roads — Class B roads — Construction and maintenance by counties.

(1) County roads comprise all public highways, roads, and streets within the state that:

(a) are situated outside of incorporated municipalities and not designated as state highways;

(b) have been designated as county roads; or

(c) are located on property under the control of a federal agency and constructed or maintained by the county under agreement with the appropriate federal agency.

(2) County roads are class B roads.

(3) The state and county have joint undivided interest in the title to all rights-of-way for all county roads.

(4) The county governing body exercises sole jurisdiction and control of county roads within the county.

(5) The county shall construct and maintain each county road using funds made available for that purpose.

(6) The county legislative body may expend funds allocated to each county from the Transportation Fund under rules made by the department.

(7) A county legislative body may use any portion of the class B road funds provided by this chapter for the construction and maintenance of class A state roads by cooperative agreement with the department.

(8) A county may enter into agreements with the appropriate federal agency for the use of federal

funds, county road funds, and donations to county road funds to construct, improve, or maintain county roads within or partly within national forests. 2000

72-3-104. City streets — Class C roads — Construction and maintenance.

(1) City streets comprise:

(a) highways, roads, and streets within the corporate limits of the municipalities that are not designated as class A state roads or as class B roads; and

(b) those highways, roads, and streets located within a national forest and constructed or maintained by the municipality under agreement with the appropriate federal agency.

(2) City streets are class C roads.

(3) Except for city streets within counties of the first and second class as defined in Section 17-50-501, the state and city have joint undivided interest in the title to all rights-of-way for all city streets.

(4) The municipal governing body exercises sole jurisdiction and control of the city streets within the municipality.

(5) The department shall cooperate with the municipal legislative body in the construction and maintenance of the class C roads within each municipality.

(6) The municipal legislative body shall expend or cause to be expended upon the class C roads the funds allocated to each municipality from the Transportation Fund under rules made by the department.

(7) Any town or city in the third, fourth, or fifth class may:

(a) contract with the county or the department for the construction and maintenance of class C roads within its corporate limits; or

(b) transfer, with the consent of the county, its:

(i) class C roads to the class B road system; and

(ii) funds allocated from the Transportation Fund to the municipality to the county legislative body for use upon the transferred class C roads.

(8) A municipal legislative body of any city of the third, fourth, or fifth class may use any portion of the class C road funds allocated to the municipality for the construction of sidewalks, curbs, and gutters on class A state roads within the municipal limits by cooperative agreement with the department. 2003

72-3-105. Class D roads — Maps to be prepared by county — Indication of roads.

(1) As used in this section, "class D road" means any road, way, or other land surface route that has been or is established by use or constructed and has been maintained to provide for usage by the public for vehicles with four or more wheels that is not a class A, class B, or class C road under this title.

(2) Each class D road is part of the highway and road system within the state with the same force and effect as if the class D road had been included within this system upon its being first established or constructed.

(3) The state and county have joint undivided interest in the title to all rights-of-way for class D roads.

(4) The county governing body exercises sole jurisdiction and control of class D roads within the county.

(5) Each county shall prepare maps showing to the best of its ability the class D roads within its boundaries which were in existence as of October 21, 1976. Preparation of these maps may be done by the county itself or through any multi-county planning district in which the county participates.

(6) Any class D road which is established or constructed after October 21, 1976, shall be reflected on maps prepared as provided in Subsection (5).

(7) The county shall provide a copy of any map under Subsection (5) or (6) upon completion to the department.

(8) The department shall scribe each road shown on its own county map series. The department is not responsible for the validity of any class D road and is not responsible for its being inventoried. The department shall also keep on file an historical map record of the roads as provided by the counties. 2000

72-3-106. Actions to determine priority of use of public roads.

(1) The county attorney under the direction of the county legislative body shall determine a priority of public use of all county roads.

(2) This action may be instigated by the written request of ten taxpayers of the county to the county legislative body.

(3) The county legislative body shall request the county attorney to instigate action within a reasonable length of time. 1998

72-3-107. County executive to keep plats of roads and highways.

(1) The county executive of each county shall determine all county roads existing in the county and prepare and keep current plats and specific descriptions of the county roads.

(2) The plats and specific descriptions shall be kept on file in the office of the county clerk or recorder. 1998

72-3-108. County roads — Vacation and narrowing.

(1) A county may, by ordinance, vacate, narrow, or change the name of a county road without petition or after petition by a property owner.

(2) A county may not vacate a county road unless notice of the hearing is:

(a) published in a newspaper of general circulation in the county once a week for four consecutive weeks prior to the hearing; or

(b) posted in three public places for four consecutive weeks prior to the hearing; and

(c) mailed to the department and all owners of property abutting the county road.

(3) The right-of-way and easements, if any, of a property owner and the franchise rights of any public utility may not be impaired by vacating or narrowing a county road.

(4) Except as provided in Section 72-5-305, if a county vacates a county road, the state's right-of-way interest in the county road is also vacated. 2000

72-3-109. Division of responsibility with respect to state highways in cities and towns.

(1) Except as provided in Subsection (3), the jurisdiction and responsibility of the department and the municipalities for state highways within municipalities is as follows:

(a) The department has jurisdiction over and is responsible for the construction and maintenance of:

(i) the portion of the state highway located between the back of the curb on either side of the state highway; or

(ii) if there is no curb, the traveled way, its contiguous shoulders, and appurtenances.

(b) The department may widen or improve state highways within municipalities.

(c) (i) A municipality has jurisdiction over all other portions of the right-of-way and is responsible for construction and maintenance of the right-of-way.

(ii) If a municipality grants permission for the installation of any pole, pipeline, conduit, sewer, ditch, culvert, billboard, advertising sign, or any other structure or object of any kind or character within the portion of the right-of-way under its jurisdiction:

(A) the permission shall contain the condition that any installation will be removed from the right-of-way at the request of the municipality; and

(B) the municipality shall cause any installation to be removed at the request of the department when the department finds the removal necessary:

(I) to eliminate a hazard to traffic safety;

(II) for the construction and maintenance of the state highway; or

(III) to meet the requirements of federal regulations.

(d) If it is necessary that a utility, as defined in Section 72-6-116, be relocated, reimbursement shall be made for the relocation as provided for in Section 72-6-116.

(e) (i) The department shall construct curbs, gutters, and sidewalks on the state highways if necessary for the proper control of traffic, driveway entrances, or drainage.

(ii) If a state highway is widened or altered and existing curbs, gutters, or sidewalks are removed, the department shall replace the curbs, gutters, or sidewalks.

(f) The department may furnish and install street lighting systems for state highways, but their operation and maintenance is the responsibility of the municipality.

(g) If new storm sewer facilities are necessary in the construction and maintenance of the state highways, the cost of the storm sewer facilities shall be borne by the state and the municipality in a proportion mutually agreed upon between the department and the municipality.

(2) (a) In accordance with Title 63, Chapter 46a, Utah Administrative Rulemaking Act, the department shall make rules governing the location and construction of approach roads and driveways entering the state highway. The rules shall:

(i) include criteria for the design, location, and spacing of approach roads and driveways based on the functional classification of the adjacent highway, including the urban or rural nature of the area;

(ii) be consistent with the "Manual on Uniform Traffic Control Devices" and the model access management policy or ordinance developed by the department under Subsection 72-2-117(9);

(iii) include procedures for:

(A) the application and review of a permit for approach roads and driveways including review of related site plans that have been recommended according to local ordinances; and

(B) approving, modifying, denying, or appealing the modification or denial of a permit for approach roads and driveways within 45 days of receipt of the application; and

(iv) require written justifications for modifying or denying a permit.

(b) The department may delegate the administration of the rules to the highway authorities of a municipality.

(c) In accordance with this section and Section 72-7-104, an approach road or driveway may not be constructed on a state highway without a permit issued under this section.

(3) The department has jurisdiction and control over the entire right-of-way of interstate highways within municipalities and is responsible for the construction, maintenance, and regulation of the interstate highways within municipalities.   2001

72-3-110. Proposal to bypass or provide alternate route through city or town — Notice and hearing required.

(1) Whenever the department proposes to construct a highway bypassing any city or town, or to provide an alternate route through or outside any city or town, the commission shall notify the governing officials of the city or town and hold a public hearing, on a date set, for the purpose of advising the citizens of the city or town of the reason or reasons for the highway proposed to be constructed.

(2) The hearing shall be held within the city or town to be bypassed, except that if the highway proposed will bypass or provide an alternate route through or outside of several cities or towns located within close proximity to each other, the commission may combine the hearings and hold them in one city or town centrally and conveniently located to the others at which time each city and town shall be given ample opportunity to be heard.

(3) Subsequent to the hearing, the commission shall notify in writing the officials of the city or town, or of each of the cities or towns if the hearings are combined, of the decision reached as a result of the hearing within ten days from the time the decision is reached.   1998

72-3-111. Roads and parking spaces in connection with state institutions and areas for recreational activities.

Subject to Section 72-1-303, the department is authorized to build and maintain roads:

(1) leading to roads and parking spaces on the grounds of state institutions to which roads have not been designated by the Legislature; and

(2) roads and parking spaces to serve areas in immediate proximity to a designated highway used for:

(a) salt flat races;

(b) ski meets; and

(c) activities which are promoted for the general welfare.   1998

72-3-112. Authority to designate, maintain, and build livestock highways.

(1) A highway authority may designate, survey, construct, protect, enter into agreements for, purchase rights-of-way for, and maintain livestock highways.

(2) If state highways with heavy traffic are regularly used for the movement of livestock, the department, county legislative bodies, and municipal legislative bodies shall construct and maintain livestock roads or trails for livestock travel.

(3) A livestock highway or trail is for the purpose of transferring livestock and may not be used for pastur-

ing purposes, except during regular transfer operations. The public may use livestock highways or trails but shall give preference to livestock when livestock is present.

(4) A person may not drive livestock upon the public highways when a livestock highway is available and can be used without undue inconvenience.

(5) A person who violates the provisions of Subsection (4) is guilty of a class B misdemeanor. The court shall impose a:

(a) fine of not more than $100;

(b) jail sentence of not more than 30 days; or

(c) fine and imprisonment. 1998

PART 2

STATE PARK ACCESS HIGHWAYS

72-3-201. Jurisdiction over highways leading to and within state parks.

(1) As used in this part, "state park access highways" means the highways specified under this part.

(2) The department, a county, or a municipality has jurisdiction over and responsibility for:

(a) primary access highways to state parks;

(b) highways to the main attraction within each state park; and

(c) highways through state parks providing access to land uses beyond state park boundaries.

(3) (a) The appropriate entities with jurisdiction over and responsibility for the highways referred to in Subsections (2)(a) and (b) are specified in Sections 72-3-202 through 72-3-206.

(b) Jurisdiction over and responsibility for highways under Subsection (2)(c) shall be determined by the commission as described in Sections 72-3-102, 72-3-103, and 72-3-104. 1998

72-3-202. State park access highways — Anasazi Indian Village State Park to Edge of the Cedars State Park.

State park access highways include:

(1) ANASAZI INDIAN VILLAGE STATE PARK. Access to the Anasazi Indian Village State Park is at the park entrance located in Garfield County at milepoint 87.8 on State Highway 12. No access road is defined.

(2) BEAR LAKE STATE PARK (Marina). Access to the Bear Lake Marina is at the pay gate located in Rich County at milepoint 413.2 on State Highway 89. No access road is defined.

(3) BEAR LAKE STATE PARK (East Shore). Access to the Bear Lake East Shore begins in Rich County at State Highway 30 and proceeds northerly on a county road (L326) a distance of 9.2 miles, to the camping area of the park and is under the jurisdiction of Rich County.

(4) BEAR LAKE STATE PARK (Rendezvous Beach). Access to the Bear Lake Rendezvous Beach is at the park entrance in Rich County at milepoint 124.5 on State Highway 30. No access road is defined.

(5) CAMP FLOYD/STAGECOACH INN STATE PARK. Access to the Camp Floyd/Stagecoach Inn State Park is at the parking area in Utah County at milepoint 20.6 on State Highway 73. No access road is defined.

(6) CORAL PINK SAND DUNES STATE PARK. Access to the Coral Pink Sand Dunes State Park begins in Kane County at State Highway 89 and proceeds southwesterly on a county road a distance of 12.0 miles to the visitor center of the park and is under the jurisdiction of Kane County.

(7) DEAD HORSE POINT STATE PARK. Access to Dead Horse Point State Park begins in Grand County at State Highway 191 and proceeds southwesterly on State Highway 313 a distance of 20.8 miles to the camping area at the park and is under the jurisdiction of UDOT.

(8) DEER CREEK STATE PARK. Access to Deer Creek State Park begins in Wasatch County at State Highway 189 and proceeds southwesterly on State Highway 314 a distance of 0.2 miles to the boat ramp at the park and is under the jurisdiction of UDOT.

(9) EAST CANYON STATE PARK. Access to East Canyon State Park begins in Morgan County at State Highway 66 and proceeds southeasterly on State Highway 306 a distance of 0.1 miles to the parking area at the park and is under the jurisdiction of UDOT.

(10) EDGE OF THE CEDARS STATE PARK. Access to Edge of the Cedars State Park begins in Blanding at U.S. Highway 191 and proceeds west on Center Street to 600 West then north on 600 West to the parking area and museum at 660 West 400 North. The access road is under jurisdiction of Blanding. 1998

72-3-203. State park access highways — Escalante State Park to Huntington State Park.

State park access highways include:

(1) ESCALANTE STATE PARK. Access to Escalante State Park begins in Garfield County at State Highway 12 and proceeds northwesterly on a county road a distance of 1 mile to the park's visitor center and is under the jurisdiction of Garfield County.

(2) FORT BUENAVENTURA STATE PARK. Access to Fort Buenaventura State Park is at the visitor center/contact station in Weber County at 2450 A Avenue in Ogden. No access road is defined.

(3) FREMONT INDIAN STATE PARK. Access to the Fremont Indian State Park begins in Sevier County at the Sevier Junction on Highway 89 and proceeds westerly on county road 2524 to interchange 17 on Interstate 70, a distance of 5.9 miles and is under the jurisdiction of Sevier County.

(4) GOBLIN VALLEY STATE PARK. Access to the Goblin Valley State Park begins in Emery County at State Highway 24 and proceeds southwesterly on a county road 11.7 miles to the overlook/parking area at the park and is under the jurisdiction of Emery County.

(5) GOOSENECKS STATE PARK. Access to Goosenecks State Park begins in San Juan County at State Highway 261 and proceeds southwesterly on State Highway 316 a distance of 3.6 miles to the parking area and overlook at the park and is under the jurisdiction of UDOT.

(6) ANTELOPE ISLAND STATE PARK. Access to Antelope Island State Park begins in Davis County at State Highway 127 and proceeds southwesterly on a county road a distance of 7.2 miles to the parking area and marina at the park and is under the jurisdiction of Davis County.

(7) GREAT SALT LAKE STATE PARK. Access to the Great Salt Lake State Park begins in Salt Lake County at Interstate Highway 80 and proceeds southwesterly on a county road a distance

of 1.5 miles to the parking area and marina at the park and is under the jurisdiction of Salt Lake County.

(8) GREEN RIVER STATE PARK. Access to Green River State Park is at the park entrance in Grand County at Green River Boulevard in Green River. No access road is defined.

(9) GUNLOCK STATE PARK. Access to the Gunlock State Park begins in Washington County at the junction of county road (L009) and a county road and proceeds northwesterly on a county road a distance of 0.1 miles to the parking area at the park and is under the jurisdiction of Washington County.

(10) HUNTINGTON STATE PARK. Access to the Huntington State Park begins in Emery County at State Highway 10 and proceeds northwesterly on a county road a distance of 0.3 miles to the park entrance and is under the jurisdiction of Emery County.   2002

72-3-204.   State park access highways — Hyrum State Park to Painted Rocks.

State park access highways include:

(1) HYRUM STATE PARK. Access to Hyrum State Park is at the pay gate in Cache County at 405 West 300 South in Hyrum and proceeds northerly on 400 West to State Highway 101. No access road is defined.

(2) IRON MISSION STATE PARK. Access to Iron Mission State Park is at the parking area and museum in Iron County at milepoint 3.3 on State Highway 130 at 585 North Main St. in Cedar City. No access road is defined.

(3) IRON MISSION STATE PARK (OLD IRON TOWN HISTORIC SITE). Access to Old Iron Town begins at the junction of a county road and State Highway 56, 19.0 miles west of Cedar City, and proceeds southwesterly 2.7 miles to the parking lot for Old Iron Town and is under the jurisdiction of Iron County.

(4) JORDAN RIVER STATE PARK. Access to Jordan River State Park is at the park entrance in Salt Lake County at milepoint 61.3 on State Highway 68 at 1084 North Redwood Road in Salt Lake City. No access road is defined.

(5) JORDANELLE STATE PARK (HAILSTONE MARINA). Access to the Jordanelle State Park Hailstone Marina begins in Wasatch County at State Highway 40 and proceeds southeasterly on State Highway 319 a distance of 1.4 miles to the marina parking area at the park and is under the jurisdiction of UDOT.

(6) JORDANELLE STATE PARK (ROCK CLIFF NATURE CENTER). Access to the Jordanelle State Park Rock Cliff Nature Center begins in Wasatch County at State Highway 32 and proceeds northwesterly on a county road a distance of 0.6 miles to the parking area at the park and is under the jurisdiction of the county.

(7) JORDANELLE STATE PARK (ROCK CREEK). Access to Jordanelle State Park Rock Creek begins in Wasatch County at State Highway 189 and proceeds southerly on a county road a distance of 0.1 miles to the parking area at the park and is under the jurisdiction of the county.

(8) KODACHROME BASIN STATE PARK. Access to the Kodachrome Basin State Park begins in Kane County at State Highway 12 and proceeds southeasterly on a county road 10.1 miles to the parking area at Kodachrome Lodge and is under the jurisdiction of Kane County.

(9) LOST CREEK STATE PARK. Access to the Lost Creek State Park begins in Morgan County at Interstate Highway 84 and proceeds northeasterly on a county road a distance of 12.8 miles to the parking/boat launch area at the park and is under the jurisdiction of Morgan County.

(10) MILLSITE STATE PARK. Access to the Millsite State Park begins in Emery County at State Highway 10 and proceeds northwesterly on a county road (L122) a distance of 4.6 miles to the parking area at the park and is under the jurisdiction of Emery County.

(11) MINERSVILLE STATE PARK. Access to the Minersville State Park begins in Beaver County at State Highway 21 and proceeds northwesterly on State Highway 310 a distance of 0.3 miles to the visitor center/contact station at the park and is under the jurisdiction of UDOT.

(12) NEWSPAPER ROCK STATE PARK. Access to the Newspaper Rock State Park begins in San Juan County at State Highway 191 and proceeds southwesterly on State Highway 211 a distance of 12.4 miles to the parking area at the park and is under the jurisdiction of UDOT.

(13) OTTER CREEK STATE PARK. Access to the Otter Creek State Park is at the pay gate/contact station in Piute County at milepoint 6.4 on State Highway 22. No access road is defined.

(14) PAINTED   ROCKS   (YUBA   EAST SHORE). Access to the Painted Rocks Yuba East Shore begins in Sanpete County at State Highway 28 and proceeds westerly on a county road a distance of 2.0 miles to the parking/boat launch area at the park and is under the jurisdiction of Sanpete County.   2002

72-3-205.   State park access highways — Palisade State Park to Starvation State Park.

State park access highways include:

(1) PALISADE STATE PARK. Access to the Palisade State Park begins in Sanpete County at State Highway 89 and proceeds northeasterly on a county road a distance of 2.2 miles to the golf club/contact station at the park and is under the jurisdiction of Sanpete County.

(2) PIONEER TRAILS STATE PARK. Access to Pioneer Trails State Park is at the park entrance in Salt Lake County at 2601 East Sunnyside Avenue in Salt Lake City. No access road is defined.

(3) PIUTE STATE PARK. Access to the Piute State Park begins in Piute County at State Highway 89 and proceeds southeasterly on a county road a distance of 1.0 miles to the parking area at the park and is under the jurisdiction of Piute County.

(4) QUAIL CREEK STATE PARK. Access to the Quail Creek State Park begins in Washington County at State Highway 9 and proceeds northerly on State Highway 318 a distance of 2.2 miles to the pay gate/contact station at the park and is under the jurisdiction of UDOT.

(5) RED FLEET STATE PARK. Access to the Red Fleet State Park begins in Uintah County at State Highway 191 and proceeds easterly on a county road a distance of 2.0 miles to the pay gate at the park and is under the jurisdiction of Uintah County.

(6) ROCKPORT STATE PARK. Access to the Rockport State Park begins in Summit County at State Highway 32 and proceeds northwesterly on

State Highway 302 a distance of 0.2 miles to the pay gate at the park and is under the jurisdiction of UDOT.

(7) SCOFIELD (Mountain View). Access to Scofield Mountain View is at the boat launch in Carbon County at milepoint 9.2 on State Highway 96. No access road is defined.

(8) SCOFIELD STATE PARK (Madsen Bay). Access to the Scofield State Park Madsen Bay is at the park entrance in Carbon County at milepoint 12.3 on State Highway 96. No access road is defined.

(9) SNOW CANYON STATE PARK. Access to the Snow Canyon State Park begins in Washington County at State Highway 18 near mile post 4 in St. George west on the Tuacahn Parkway to Federal Route 3200 then north on Federal Route 3200 to the south boundary of the Snow Canyon State Park.

(10) STARVATION STATE PARK. Access to the Starvation State Park begins in Duchesne County at State Highway 40 and proceeds northwesterly on State Highway 311 a distance of 2.2 miles to the boat ramp at the park and is under the jurisdiction of UDOT.   1998

**72-3-206. State park access highways —
Steinaker State Park to Yuba State
Park.**
State park access highways include:

(1) STEINAKER STATE PARK. Access to the Steinaker State Park begins in Uintah County at State Highway 191 and proceeds northwesterly on State Highway 301 a distance of 1.7 miles to the boat ramp at the park and is under the jurisdiction of UDOT.

(2) TERRITORIAL STATEHOUSE STATE PARK. Access to the Territorial Statehouse State Park is at the parking area in Millard County at milepoint 1.0 on State Highway 100. No access road is defined.

(3) UTAH FIELD HOUSE OF NATURAL HISTORY STATE PARK. Access to Utah Field House of Natural History State Park is at the parking area in Uintah County at milepoint 145.8 on State Highway 40 at 235 East Main in Vernal. No access road is defined.

(4) UTAH LAKE STATE PARK. Access to the Utah Lake State Park begins in Utah County at State Highway 114 and proceeds westerly on a county road a distance of 2.5 miles to the pay gate at the park and is under the jurisdiction of Utah County.

(5) VETERAN'S MEMORIAL CEMETERY. Access to the Veteran's Memorial Cemetery is at the cemetery entrance in Utah County at 17111 South Camp Williams Road in Bluffdale. No access road is defined.

(6) WASATCH MOUNTAIN STATE PARK. Access to the Wasatch Mountain State Park begins in Wasatch County on State Route 40 at the junction of Federal Route 3130, a county road, then westerly on Federal Route 3130 on River Road, Burgi Lane, and Cari Lane, county and city roads, to State Highway 224 then northwesterly on State Highway 224 to the campground entrance.

(7) WILLARD BAY STATE PARK (South). Access to the Willard Bay State Park South begins in Box Elder County at a county road and proceeds northwesterly on State Highway 312 a

distance of 0.2 miles to the marina parking at the park and is under the jurisdiction of UDOT.

(8) WILLARD BAY STATE PARK (North). Access to the Willard Bay State Park North begins in Box Elder County at Interstate Highway 15 and proceeds southwesterly on State Highway 315 a distance of 0.6 miles to the marina parking at the park and is under the jurisdiction of UDOT.

(9) YUBA STATE PARK. Access to the Yuba State Park begins in Juab County at Interstate Highway 15 and proceeds southerly on county road (L203) a distance of 4.1 miles to the pay gate at the park and is under the jurisdiction of Juab County.   1998

**72-3-207. State Park Access Highways Improvement Program — Distribution —
Rulemaking.**

(1) There is created the State Park Access Highways Improvement Program within the department.

(2) The program shall be funded from the following revenue sources:

(a) any voluntary contributions received for improvements to state park access highways; and

(b) appropriations made to the program by the Legislature.

(3) The department may use the program monies as matching grants to a county or municipality for the improvement of class B or class C roads specified as state park access highways under this part subject to:

(a) monies available in the program;

(b) prioritization of the program monies by the commission;

(c) a county or municipality providing at least 50% of the cost of each improvement project in matching funds; and

(d) rules made under Subsection (4).

(4) The department shall make rules in accordance with Title 63, Chapter 46a, Utah Administrative Rulemaking Act, necessary to administer the program and to establish the procedures for a county or municipality to apply for a grant of program monies.

(5) All appropriations made to the program by the Legislature are nonlapsing.   1998

PART 3

**STATEWIDE PUBLIC SAFETY INTEREST
HIGHWAYS**

**72-3-301. Statewide public safety interest highway defined — Designations — Control — Maintenance — Improvement
restrictions — Formula funding provisions.**

(1) As used in this part, "statewide public safety interest highway" means a designated state highway that serves a compelling statewide public safety interest.

(2) Statewide public safety interest highways include:

(a) SR-900. From near the east bound on and off ramps of the I-80 Delle Interchange on the I-80 south frontage road, traversing northwesterly, westerly, and northeasterly, including on portions of a county road and a Bureau of Land Management road for a distance of 9.24 miles. Then beginning again at the I-80 south frontage road traversing southwesterly and northwesterly on a county road for a distance of 4.33 miles. Then beginning again at the I-80 south frontage road traversing southwesterly, northerly, northwesterly, westerly, and northeasterly on a county road and a Bureau of Land Management road to near the east bound on and off ramps of I-80 Low/Lakeside Interchange for a distance of 2.61 miles. The entire length of SR-900 is a total distance of 16.18 miles.

(b) SR-901. From SR-196 traversing westerly and northwesterly on a county road to a junction with a Bureau of Land Management road described as part of SR-901, then northwesterly to a junction with a county road for a distance of 8.70 miles. Then beginning again at a junction with SR-901 traversing northwesterly on a Bureau of Land Management road to a junction with a county road for a distance of 6.52 miles. Then beginning again at a junction with SR-901 traversing southwesterly on a Bureau of Land Management road to a junction with a county road for a distance of 5.44 miles. Then beginning again from a junction with SR-901 traversing southwesterly on a county road to a junction with a county road a distance of 11.52 miles. Then beginning again at a junction with SR-196 traversing westerly on a Bureau of Land Management road to a junction with a county road for a distance of 11.30 miles. The entire length of SR-901 is a total distance of 43.48 miles.

(3) The department has jurisdiction and control over all statewide public safety interest highways.

(4) (a) A county shall maintain the portions of a statewide public safety interest highway that was a class B county road under the county's jurisdiction prior to the designation under this section.

(b) Notwithstanding the provisions of Section 17-50-305, a county may not abandon any portion of a statewide public safety interest highway.

(c) Except under written authorization of the executive director of the department, a statewide public safety interest highway shall remain the same class of highway that it was prior to the designation under this section with respect to grade, drainage, surface, and improvements and it may not be upgraded or improved to a higher class of highway.

(5) A class B county road that is designated a statewide public safety interest highway under this section is considered a class B county road for the purposes of the distribution formula and distributions of funds. The amount of funds received by any jurisdiction from the class B and C roads account under Section 72-2-107 may not be affected by the provisions of this section. 2001

CHAPTER 4

DESIGNATION OF STATE HIGHWAYS

Part 1

State Highways

Part 2

Special Designations

PART 1

STATE HIGHWAYS

72-4-101.   Title.

This chapter is known as the "Designation of State Highways Act."   1998

72-4-102.   Additions to or deletions from state highway system — Designation of highways as state highways between sessions.

(1) (a) The Legislature may add to or delete highways or sections of highways from the state highway system.

(b) The department shall annually submit to the Legislature a list of highways or sections of highways the commission recommends for addition to or deletion from the state highway system.

(c) All recommendations shall be based on the criteria for state highways under Section 72-4-102.5.

(2) Between general sessions of the Legislature, highways may be designated as state highways or deleted from the state highway system if:

(a) approved by the commission in accordance with the criteria for state highways under Section 72-4-102.5;

(b) a deletion is agreed upon by all highway authorities involved in the transfer; and

(c) the highways are included in the list of recommendations submitted to the Legislature in the next year for legislative approval or disapproval.

(3) All highway authorities involved in a highway transfer under this section shall consider available highway financing levels and operational abilities for the maintenance and construction of a transferred highway.

(4) (a) The list of recommendations under this section shall be submitted to the Transportation Interim Committee of the Legislature on or before November 1 of each year.

(b) The recommendations shall include:

(i) any fiscal and funding recommendations of each highway authority involved in the transfer of a highway or section of a highway; and

(ii) a cost estimate, fiscal analysis, and funding recommendation, or recommendation for further study from the Office of the Legislative Fiscal Analyst.   1999

72-4-102.5.   Definitions — Rulemaking — Criteria for state highways.

(1) As used in this section:

(a) "arterial highway" has the same meaning as provided under the Federal Highway Administration Functional Classification Guidelines;

(b) "collector highway," "collector road," or "collector street" has the same meaning as provided under the Federal Highway Administration Functional Classification Guidelines;

(c) "local street" or "local road" means a highway that is not an arterial highway or a collector highway and that is under the jurisdiction of a county or municipality;

(d) "major collector highway," "major collector road," or "major collector street" has the same meaning as provided under the Federal Highway Administration Functional Classification Guidelines;

(e) "minor collector road" or "minor collector street" has the same meaning as provided under the Federal Highway Administration Functional Classification Guidelines;

(f) "minor arterial highway" or "minor arterial street" has the same meaning as provided under the Federal Highway Administration Functional Classification Guidelines;

(g) "principal arterial highway" has the same meaning as provided under the Federal Highway Administration Functional Classification Guidelines;

(h) "rural area" has the same meaning as provided under the Federal Highway Administration Functional Classification Guidelines;

(i) "tourist area" means an area of the state frequented by tourists for the purpose of visiting national parks, national recreation areas, national monuments, or state parks; and

(j) "urban area" has the same meaning as provided under the Federal Highway Administration Functional Classification Guidelines.

(2) (a) Subject to the provisions of Title 72, Chapter 3, Highway Jurisdiction and Classification Act, and this chapter, a state highway shall meet the criteria provided under this section.

(b) The highway authorities of this state or their representatives shall cooperate to match the criteria provided under this section with the state highways designated under this title.

(c) The primary function of state highways is to provide for the safe and efficient movement of traffic, while providing access to property is a secondary function.

(d) The primary function of county and municipal highways is to provide access to property.

(e) For purposes of this section, if a highway is within ten miles of a location identified under this section, the location is considered to be served by that highway.

(3) A state highway shall:

(a) serve a statewide purpose by accommodating interstate movement of traffic or interregion movement of traffic within the state;

(b) primarily move higher traffic volumes over longer distances than highways under local jurisdiction;

(c) connect major population centers;

(d) be spaced so that:

(i) all developed areas in the state are within a reasonable distance of a state highway; and

(ii) duplicative state routes are avoided;

(e) provide state highway system continuity and efficiency of state highway system operation and maintenance activities;

(f) include all interstate routes, all expressways, and all highways on the National Highway System as designated by the Federal Highway Administration under 23 C.F.R. Section 470, Subpart A, as of January 1, 2005; and

(g) exclude parking lots, driving ranges, and campus roads.

(4) In addition to the provisions of Subsection (3), in rural areas a state highway shall:

(a) include all minor arterial highways;

(b) include a major collector highway that:

(i) serves a county seat;

(ii) serves a municipality with a population of 1,000 or more;

(iii) serves a major industrial, commercial, or recreation areas that generate traffic volumes equivalent to a population of 1,000 or more;

(iv) provides continuity for the state highway system by providing major connections between other state highways;

(v) provides service between two or more counties; or

(vi) serves a compelling statewide public safety interest; and

(c) exclude all minor collector streets and local roads.

(5) In addition to the provisions of Subsection (3), in urban areas a state highway shall:

(a) include all principal arterial highways;

(b) include a minor arterial highway that:

(i) provides continuity for the state highway system by providing major connections between other state highways;

(ii) is a route that is expected to be a principal arterial highway within ten years; or

(iii) is needed to provide access to state highways; and

(c) exclude all collector highways and local roads.

(6) In addition to the provisions of Subsections (3) and (4), in tourist areas, a state highway:

(a) shall include a highway that:

(i) serves a national park or a national recreational area; or

(ii) serves a national monument with visitation greater than 100,000 per year; or

(b) may include a highway that:

(i) serves a state park with visitation greater than 100,000 per year; or

(ii) serves a recreation site with visitation greater than 100,000 per year.

(7) (a) In accordance with Title 63, Chapter 46a, Utah Administrative Rulemaking Act, the department shall make rules:

(i) establishing and defining a functional classification of highways for the purpose of implementing this section;

(ii) defining and designating regionally significant arterial highways; and

(iii) establishing an access management policy consistent with the functional classification of roadways.

(b) The definitions under Subsection (7)(a) shall provide a separate functional classification system for urban and rural highways recognizing the unique differences in the character of services provided by urban and rural highways.

(c) The rules under Subsection (7)(a):

(i) shall conform as nearly as practical to the Federal Highway Administration Functional Classification Guidelines; and

(ii) may incorporate by reference, in whole or in part, the federal guidelines under Subsection (7)(c)(i).   2005

72-4-103. Deletion of highway from state highway system — Return to county or municipality or abandonment.

When a state highway or portion of a state highway is deleted from the state highway system by the Legislature or the commission, the department shall:

(1) return or relinquish the state highway or portion of the state highway to the county or municipality in which it is situated; or

(2) abandon the state highway or portion of the state highway if it no longer serves the purpose of a highway.   1998

72-4-104. Disposition of portion of highways realigned.

(1) The department may make changes in the alignment of state highways to provide for greater highway safety or more economical highway operation and maintenance.

(2) When a state highway is realigned, the former portion of it may be:

(a) returned or relinquished to the county or municipality in which it is situated to be maintained as a highway; or

(b) abandoned by the department if it no longer serves the purpose of a highway.   1998

72-4-105. Designation of state highways in municipalities.

If the route of a state highway extends into or through a municipality and the Legislature has not specifically designated the location of the highway within the municipality, the commission, in cooperation with the municipality, shall designate the streets of the municipality over which the state highway shall be routed. The designated streets shall be part of the state highway system without compensation to the municipality.   1998

72-4-106. State highways — SR-6, SR-8, SR-9, SR-10.

State highways include:

(1) SR-6. From the Utah-Nevada state line easterly through Delta and Tintic Junction to the northbound ramps of the North Santaquin Interchange of Route 15; then beginning again at the Moark Connection Interchange of Route 15 easterly through Spanish Fork Canyon and Price to Route 70 west of Green River.

(2) SR-8. From Route 18 in St. George on Sunset Boulevard to Dixie Downs Road.

(3) SR-9. From Route 15 at Harrisburg Junction easterly to Zion National Park south boundary through the Zion National Park east boundary to Route 89 at Mt. Carmel Junction.

(4) SR-10. From a junction with Route 70 east of Fremont Junction northeasterly to Route 55 in Price.   2000

72-4-107. State highways — SR-11 to SR-20.

State highways include:

(1) SR-11. From the Utah-Arizona state line south of Kanab northerly to Route 89 in Kanab.

(2) SR-12. From Route 89 at Bryce Canyon Junction easterly through Tropic Junction and Escalante then northerly through Boulder and Grover to Route 24 east of Torrey.

(3) SR-13. From Route 91 in Brigham City northerly through Bear River and Haws Corner to 20800 North, northwest of Plymouth, then

west to the southbound on- and off-ramps of Route 15 Plymouth Interchange.

(4) SR-14. From Route 130 in Cedar City southeasterly to Route 89 at Long Valley Junction.

(5) SR-15. From the Utah-Arizona state line near St. George to the Utah-Idaho state line south of Malad, Idaho, on interstate Route 15.

(6) SR-16. From the Utah-Wyoming state line northwesterly ten miles through Woodruff then northerly to Route 30 at Sage Creek Junction.

(7) SR-17. From Route 9 in LaVerkin northerly to Route 15 at Anderson Junction.

(8) SR-18. From Route 15 in south St. George northerly to Route 56 at Beryl Junction.

(9) SR-19. From Route 70 west of Green River easterly through Green River to Route 70 near Elgin.

(10) SR-20. From Route 15, 14 miles north of Paragonah easterly to Route 89 at Orton.   1998

72-4-108. State highways — SR-21 to SR-26, SR-28 to SR-30.

State highways include:

(1) SR-21. From the Utah-Nevada state line near Garrison southerly and easterly to Beaver to Route 160.

(2) SR-22. From Antimony Bridge northerly to Route 62.

(3) SR-23. From Route 91 south of Wellsville northerly through Wellsville, Mendon, Petersboro, Newton, and Cornish to the Utah-Idaho state line near Weston, Idaho.

(4) SR-24. From Route 50 near Salina southerly through Loa to Hanksville; then northeasterly to Route 70 at Buckmaster Interchange west of Green River.

(5) SR-25. From Fish Lake Junction on Route 24 northerly to near Bowery Haven Campground.

(6) SR-26. From Route 126 in Roy easterly to Route 89 in Ogden.

(7) SR-28. From Route 89 in Gunnison northerly through Levan to the southbound on- and off-ramps of Route 15 at the South Nephi Interchange.

(8) SR-29. From Joes Valley Reservoir easterly through Orangeville Junction to Route 10 north of Castle Dale.

(9) SR-30. From the Utah-Nevada state line northeasterly through Curlew Junction to Route 84 west of Snowville; then beginning again at a junction with Route 15 west of Riverside easterly through Collinston to Route 91 in Logan; then beginning again at a junction with Route 89 in Garden City southeasterly through Sage Creek Junction to the Utah-Wyoming state line.   1998

72-4-109. State highways — SR-31, SR-32, SR-34 to SR-40.

State highways include:

(1) SR-31. From Route 89 in Fairview southeasterly to Route 10 in Huntington.

(2) SR-32. From Route 40 north of Heber City, northeasterly to a junction with Route 35 at Francis; then north through Kamas to the Route 80 westbound off-ramp northeast of Wanship.

(3) SR-34. From Route 18 east on 100 North Street in St. George to the east side curb of River Road.

(4) SR-35. From Route 32 at Francis southeasterly through Tabiona to Route 87 north of Duchesne.

(5) SR-36. Two separate sections from Route 6 to Tintic Junction: the first, beginning near mile post 138 to Tintic Junction, and the second, beginning near mile post 136 to Tintic Junction, then northerly through Tooele and Mills Junction to Route 80 at the Tooele-Grantsville Interchange.

(6) SR-37. From Route 126 in Sunset west through Clinton to south of Hooper; then northerly through Hooper to west of West Haven; then east through West Haven to Route 108 near Roy.

(7) SR-38. From Route 13 in Brigham City northerly through Honeyville and Deweyville to Route 30 in Collinston.

(8) SR-39. From Route 134 easterly on Twelfth Street in Ogden and Ogden Canyon to Route 16 in Woodruff.

(9) SR-40. From Route 80 at Silver Creek Junction southerly through Heber City then easterly through Duchesne, Vernal, and Jensen to the Utah-Colorado state line.   1998

72-4-110. State highways — SR-41 to SR-46, SR-48, SR-50.

State highways include:

(1) SR-41. From Route 15 south of Nephi northerly through Nephi to Route 15 north of Nephi.

(2) SR-42. From the Utah-Idaho state line near Strevell, Idaho, easterly to Route 30 at Curlew Junction.

(3) SR-43. From the Utah-Wyoming state line about 6-½ miles west of Manila easterly through Manila to the Utah-Wyoming state line about three miles east of Manila.

(4) SR-44. From Route 191 at Greendale Junction northwesterly to Route 43 in Manila.

(5) SR-45. From the Evacuation Wash Area south of Bonanza northwesterly through Bonanza to Route 40 southeast of Vernal, near Naples.

(6) SR-46. From Route 191 at LaSal Junction easterly to the Utah-Colorado state line.

(7) SR-48. From the Kennecott gate in Copperton northeasterly to 7800 South then easterly on 7800 South to Route 68 in West Jordan; then beginning again at Route 68 easterly on 7000 South and 7200 South to Route 89.

(8) SR-50. From Route 6 in Delta southeasterly to Holden, then northerly to Route 15 and beginning again at Route 15 near Scipio; then easterly to Main Street in Scipio; then south on Main Street to Center Street in Scipio; then southeasterly to a junction with Route 89 in Salina.   2001

72-4-111. State highways — SR-51 to SR-60.

State highways include:

(1) SR-51. From Route 147 in Spanish Fork northeasterly to Route 89 in Springville.

(2) SR-52. From Route 114 easterly on 8th North in Orem to Route 189 at Olmstead.

(3) SR-53. From Route 15 easterly on Twenty-fourth Street in Ogden to Route 89.

(4) SR-54. From Mona easterly to the on and off ramps east of Route 15 at the Mona Interchange.

(5) SR-55. From Route 6 west of Price easterly on First North Street to 3rd East Street; then south on 3rd East Street to Main Street; then easterly and southerly to Route 6 near Price southeast corporate limits.

(6) SR-56. From the Utah-Nevada state line easterly to Route 130 in Cedar City.

(7) SR-57. From Route 10 northerly to the Wilberg Mine northwest of Orangeville.

(8) SR-58. From the Utah-Nevada state line easterly through Wendover to Route 80.

(9) SR-59. From the Utah-Arizona state line northwesterly to Route 9 in Hurricane.

(10) SR-60. From Route 26 at Riverdale Junction easterly to Route 89.　　　1998

72-4-112.　State highways — SR-61 to SR-66, SR-68, and SR-70.

State highways include:

(1) SR-61. From Route 23 in Cornish easterly to Route 91 at Webster Junction.

(2) SR-62. From Route 89 south of Junction easterly through Kingston to near Otter Creek Reservoir; then northerly to Route 24 at Plateau Junction.

(3) SR-63. From Bryce National Park north boundary northerly to Tropic Junction on Route 12.

(4) SR-64. From Route 15 south of Holden northerly to Route 50.

(5) SR-65. From Route 80 near Mt. Dell Reservoir northeasterly on the Brigham Young Memorial Highway to Henefer; then northeasterly to Route 84.

(6) SR-66. From Route 65 near East Canyon Reservoir northerly through Porterville to Route 84 in Morgan.

(7) SR-68. From Route 6 at Elberta northerly on Redwood Road and Fifth South Street in Bountiful; then southerly on 2nd West in Bountiful to Route 89 in Bountiful.

(8) SR-70. From Route 15 near Cove Fort to the Utah-Colorado state line west of Grand Junction, Colorado, on interstate Route 70.　　　2002

72-4-113.　State highways — SR-71 to SR-80.

State highways include:

(1) SR-71. From Route 154 in Riverton easterly to Seventh East Street in Draper; then northerly on Seventh East and Ninth East Streets to Route 186 at Seventh East Street and Fourth South Street in Salt Lake City.

(2) SR-72. From Route 24 in Loa northerly to a junction with Route 70 and Route 10 near Fremont Junction.

(3) SR-73. From Route 36 northeast of St. John Station southeasterly on Five Mile Pass; then northeasterly to Route 89 in Lehi.

(4) SR-74. From Route 89 in American Fork northerly to 200 feet south of the intersection with Canyon Crest Road in Alpine.

(5) SR-75. From Route 15 northwest of Springville easterly to Route 89 near Ironton.

(6) SR-76. From Route 70 easterly to old Fremont Junction on Route 72.

(7) SR-77. From Route 147 north of Benjamin north through Barney Corner; then easterly to Route 89 in Springville.

(8) SR-78. From Route 15 at the Mills Junction Interchange northerly to west of Levan; then east to Route 28 in Levan.

(9) SR-79. From Route 126 easterly on Thirty-first Street in Ogden to the lane separation, then on eastbound lane only to Route 89; then easterly on Thirtieth Street to Route 203; beginning again at Thirtieth Street and Route 89 then westerly on the westbound lane only to merge with eastbound lanes.

(10) SR-80. From the Utah-Nevada state line in Wendover to the Utah-Wyoming state line west of Evanston, Wyoming, on Interstate 80.　　　2004

72-4-114.　State highways — SR-81 to SR-84, SR-86 to SR-90.

State highways include:

(1) SR-81. From Route 30 north to Fielding.

(2) SR-82. From Route 102 north on 300 East Street in Tremonton to Garland; then east approximately 0.8 mile; then north to Route 13.

(3) SR-83. From Route 13 in Corinne westerly to Lampo Junction; then northerly to Route 84 at Howell Interchange.

(4) SR-84. From the Utah-Idaho state line near Snowville to a point on Route 15 at the Tremonton Interchange; then from another point on Route 15 near Roy to Route 80 near Echo, traversing the alignment of interstate Route 84.

(5) SR-86. From Route 65 at Henefer westerly to Route 84.

(6) SR-87. From Route 40 in Duchesne northerly; then easterly through Altamont; thence southeasterly through Upalco; then east to Route 40 southwest of Roosevelt.

(7) SR-88. From the south end of the Green River Bridge south of Ouray northerly to Route 40 east of Ft. Duchesne.

(8) SR-89. From the Utah-Arizona state line northwest of Page, Arizona, westerly to Kanab; then northerly to a junction with Route 70 near Sevier Junction; then beginning again at the junction with Route 70 south of Salina, northerly through Salina, Gunnison and Mt. Pleasant to a junction with Route 6 at Thistle Junction; beginning again at a junction with Route 6 at Moark Junction northerly through Springville, Provo, Orem, and American Fork to Route 15 north of Lehi; then beginning again at a junction with Route 71 in Draper northerly via Murray and Salt Lake City to a junction with Route 15 at Beck Interchange; then beginning again at a junction with Route 15 near Orchard Drive northerly through Bountiful to a junction with Route 15 at North Bountiful Interchange; then beginning again at a junction with Route 15 at Lagoon Junction northerly through Uintah Junction and Ogden to Route 91 near south city limits of Brigham City; then beginning again at a junction with Route 91 in Logan northeasterly to Garden City; then north to the Utah-Idaho state line.

(9) SR-90. From Route 13 in Brigham easterly on 2nd South Street to Route 91.　　　2005

72-4-115.　State highways — SR-91 to SR-100.

State highways include:

(1) SR-91. From Route 15 south of Brigham City; then easterly through Brigham Canyon and Logan to the Utah-Idaho state line near Franklin, Idaho.

(2) SR-92. From Route 15 near Point of the Mountain east through American Fork Canyon to Route 189 in Provo Canyon.

(3) SR-93. From the on- and off-ramps on the west side of Route 15, east along the south city limits of Woods Cross to Route 89.

(4) SR-94. From Route 70 northeasterly to Thompson.

(5) SR-95. From Route 24 east of Hanksville southerly crossing near the confluence of the Dirty Devil and Colorado Rivers to a point 4.3 miles south of Blanding on Route 191.

(6) SR-96. From Clear Creek northerly through Scofield to Route 6 near Colton.

(7) SR-97. From Route 108 east on 5600 South Street in Roy to the Hill Air Force Base Northwest gate.

(8) SR-98. From Route 37 at Hooper east to Route 108.

(9) SR-99. From Route 15 south of Fillmore northerly through Fillmore to Route 15.

(10) SR-100. From Route 99 in Fillmore westerly then northerly to Route 50 west of Holden.

2001

72-4-116. State highways — SR-101 to SR-110.
State highways include:

(1) SR-101. From Wellsville on Route 23 easterly through Hyrum to the Hardware Ranch with a stub connection to the visitors' center and parking area.

(2) SR-102. From Route 83 east of Lampo Junction northeasterly through Penrose to Thatcher; then easterly through Tremonton and Deweyville to Route 38.

(3) SR-103. From Route 126 in Clearfield easterly on 650 North Street in Clearfield to Hill Air Force Base main gate.

(4) SR-104. From Route 126 easterly on Wilson Lane, Twentieth Street, and Twenty-first Street in Ogden to Route 204.

(5) SR-105. From Route 15 east on Parrish Lane in Centerville to Route 106.

(6) SR-106. From Route 15 east on 400 North in Bountiful easterly to Second West in Bountiful; then northerly to Sheppard Lane in Farmington; then west on Sheppard Lane to Route 89 in Farmington.

(7) SR-107. From Route 110 west of West Point easterly through West Point to Route 126 in Clearfield.

(8) SR-108. From the I-15 north bound on- and off-ramps at the Hill Field South Gate Interchange in Layton west to Syracuse; then north into Weber County; then northeasterly to Route 126.

(9) SR-109. From Route 126 easterly through Layton to Route 89.

(10) SR-110. From Route 127 west of Syracuse north to Route 37 west of Clinton. 2002

72-4-117. State highways — SR-111 to SR-120.
State highways include:

(1) SR-111. From Route 48 east of Copperton northerly through Bacchus to Route 201 northeast of Magna.

(2) SR-112. From a point east of Grantsville on Route 138 southeasterly to Tooele on Route 36.

(3) SR-113. From Route 189 in Charleston northerly to Midway; then easterly to Route 40 in Heber City.

(4) SR-114. From Route 89 in Provo westerly on Center Street to Geneva Road; then northerly through Lakeview, Vineyard, and Geneva to Route 89 in Pleasant Grove.

(5) SR-115. From Route 6 in Payson northerly to Benjamin; then easterly to Route 156 in Spanish Fork.

(6) SR-116. From Route 132 in Moroni easterly to Route 89 in Mt. Pleasant.

(7) SR-117. From Wales easterly through Chester to Spring City; then northeasterly to Route 89.

(8) SR-118. From Route 70 easterly through Joseph and Monroe; then northerly to Route 120 in south Richfield. Beginning again with Route

120 at 300 North in Richfield, northeasterly to Route 24 near Sigurd.

(9) SR-119. From Route 118 in Richfield easterly to Route 24 at Kings Meadow Canyon.

(10) SR-120. From Route 70 easterly to Main Street in Richfield; then northerly on Main Street to Route 70 north of Richfield. 1998

72-4-118. State highways — SR-121 to SR-128, SR-130.
State highways include:

(1) SR-121. From Route 40 in Roosevelt northerly to Neola; then easterly through LaPoint and Maeser to Route 40 in Vernal.

(2) SR-122. From the Utah Railway right-of-way line near Hiawatha easterly to Route 10 near Carbon-Emery County line.

(3) SR-123. From Route 6 at Sunnyside Junction easterly to Sunnyside.

(4) SR-124. From Horse Canyon coal mine northerly through Columbia Junction to Route 123.

(5) SR-125. From Route 50 east of Delta easterly to Oak City; then northerly to Route 132 near Leamington.

(6) SR-126. From Route 15 south of Layton northerly to Route 89 at Hot Springs Junction.

(7) SR-127. From Route 110 easterly on Syracuse Road to a junction with Route 108 in Syracuse.

(8) SR-128. From Route 191 near Moab northeasterly along south bank of Colorado River to Dewey; then northerly to Route 70 approximately six miles west of Cisco.

(9) SR-130. From Route 15 northerly through Cedar City to Route 21 north of Minersville. 1998

72-4-119. State highways — SR-132 to SR-134, SR-136 to SR-140.
State highways include:

(1) SR-132. From Route 6 in Lynndyl northeasterly through Leamington to Nephi; then southeasterly through Fountain Green and Moroni to Route 89 at Pigeon Hollow Junction.

(2) SR-133. From Kanosh south city limits north through Meadow to Route 15 north of Meadow.

(3) SR-134. From Route 37 at Kanesville northerly to Plain City; then easterly to Route 235 in North Ogden.

(4) SR-136. From a junction with Route 50 and 125 east of Delta north to Route 6.

(5) SR-137. From Route 89 in Gunnison easterly to Mayfield; then northerly to Route 89.

(6) SR-138. From Route 80 at Stansbury Interchange southeasterly through Grantsville to Route 36 at Mills Junction.

(7) SR-139. From Route 6 northerly to Route 157 near Spring Glen.

(8) SR-140. From Route 68 at Bluffdale easterly coincident with the Bluffdale Road to the on and off access ramps on the east side of Route 15. 2005

72-4-120. State highways — SR-141 to SR-151.
State highways include:

(1) SR-141. From Route 6 in Genola to Route 147 west of Payson.

(2) SR-142. From Route 23 near Newton to Clarkston; then easterly through Trenton to Route 91 in Richmond.

(3) SR-143. From Route 15 west of Parowan easterly through Parowan, then southerly to the Panguitch Lake Road, then easterly and northerly coincident with the Panguitch Lake Road to Route 89 in Panguitch.

(4) SR-144. From Route 92 in American Fork Canyon northerly to Tibble Fork Reservoir.

(5) SR-145. From Route 15 east on Main Street in American Fork to Route 89.

(6) SR-146. From Route 89 at Pleasant Grove northerly to Route 92 near the mouth of American Fork Canyon.

(7) SR-147. From Route 141, McBeth Corner; then northerly four miles; then east approximately three miles to Benjamin; then north approximately one mile; then easterly crossing Route 89 one mile; then north to Mapleton; then west to Route 89.

(8) SR-148. From Route 14 north to Cedar Breaks National Monument south boundary.

(9) SR-149. From Route 40 at Jensen northerly to Dinosaur National Monument boundary.

(10) SR-150. From Route 32 in Kamas easterly to Mirror Lake and northerly to Utah-Wyoming state line.

(11) SR-151. From Route 154 east on 10400 South Street to 1300 West Street; then southeasterly to 10600 South Street; then east on 10600 South Street to Route 15.   2001

72-4-121. State highways — SR-152 to SR-160.
State highways include:

(1) SR-152. From Route 71 at 4800 South Street southeasterly on Van Winkle Expressway to the Route 215 Interchange near 6400 South Street.

(2) SR-153. From Route 160 in Beaver easterly by Puffer Lake to Route 89 in Junction City.

(3) SR-154. From Route 15 westerly near 13400 South on Bangerter Highway to near 3200 West; then northerly to the westbound off ramp of Route 80 near the Salt Lake International Airport.

(4) SR-155. From Route 10 in Huntington northeasterly to Cleveland; then northerly to Route 10 at Washboard Junction.

(5) SR-156. From Route 6 in Spanish Fork north on Main Street to I-15.

(6) SR-157. From Route 244 at Poplar and Main Streets in Helper southerly and northeasterly to Kenilworth.

(7) SR-158. From Eden Junction on Route 39 northerly to the parking lot of Powder Mountain Ski Resort.

(8) SR-159. From Route 21 near Garrison north to Route 6 near the Utah-Nevada state line.

(9) SR-160. From Route 15 south of Beaver northerly through Beaver to Route 15 north of Beaver.   1998

72-4-122. State highways — SR-161 to SR-165, SR-167, SR-168.
State highways include:

(1) SR-161. From Route 70 near Cove Fort northwesterly to Route 15.

(2) SR-162. From Route 191 at Bluff easterly to the Utah-Colorado state line.

(3) SR-163. From the Utah-Arizona state line southwest of Mexican Hat northeasterly to Route 191 near Bluff.

(4) SR-164. From Route 15 southwest of Spanish Fork easterly to Route 198 one-half mile south of Spanish Fork.

(5) SR-165. From Paradise northerly through Hyrum and Nibley to Route 91 in Logan.

(6) SR-167. From Route 84 near Mountain Green northerly on Trappers Loop Road to Route 39 south of Huntsville.

(7) SR-168. From the north entrance of Hill Air Force Base northerly to Route 60 in Riverdale.   2005

72-4-123. State highways — SR-171 to SR-174, SR-178, SR-180.
State highways include:

(1) SR-171. From Route 111 at Eighty-fourth West Street and Thirty-fifth South Street easterly on Thirty-fifth South Street and Thirty-third South Street to Route 215 at the east-side belt route.

(2) SR-172. From 6200 South north on 5600 West to Route 80.

(3) SR-173. From Route 111 southeast of Magna easterly through Kearns and Murray to Route 89 at 5300 South Street in Murray.

(4) SR-174. From Intermountain Power Plant maingate southeasterly to Route 6 south of Lynndyl.

(5) SR-178. From the southbound on and off ramps of Route 15 east on 800 South in Payson to Route 198.

(6) SR-180. From Route 15 southeast of American Fork northerly on Fifth East Street to Route 89 in American Fork.   2001

72-4-124. State highways — SR-181, SR-184, SR-186, SR-189, SR-190.
State highways include:

(1) SR-181. From Route 152 north on Thirteenth East Street to Route 186 in Salt Lake City.

(2) SR-184. From Route 89 at North Temple and State Streets in Salt Lake City northerly on State Street to the State Capitol; then westerly on Second North and northerly on Columbus Street and Victory Road to Route 89 at Beck Street.

(3) SR-186. From Route 89 east on North Temple Street in Salt Lake City to Third West Street; then south on Third West Street to Fourth South Street; then easterly on Fourth South, Tenth East, Fifth South Streets, and Foothill Boulevard to Route 80 near the mouth of Parley's Canyon.

(4) SR-189. From Route 15 south of Provo northerly on University Avenue and Provo Canyon to Route 40 south of Heber.

(5) SR-190. From Route 215 at Knudsen's Corner southeasterly to Route 210 at the mouth of Big Cottonwood Canyon; then easterly through Big Cottonwood Canyon to Brighton, including Brighton Loop; then easterly through Guardsman Pass to the Salt Lake-Wasatch County line.   1998

72-4-125. State highways — SR-191, SR-193, SR-195, SR-197 to SR-200.
State highways include:

(1) SR-191. From the Utah-Arizona state line south of Bluff northerly through Blanding, Monticello, and Moab to Route 70 at Crescent Junction; then beginning again from Route 6 north of Helper northerly through Indian Canyon to Route 40 at Duchesne; then beginning again from Route 40 at Vernal northerly through Greendale Junction and Dutch John to the Utah-Wyoming state line.

(2) SR-193. From Route 126 in Clearfield east through the south entrance to Hill Air Force Base to Route 89.

(3) SR-195. From Route 266 near Holladay north on Twenty-third East Street to Route 80.

(4) SR-196. From Route 199 near the control gate at Dugway Proving Grounds northerly via the Skull Valley Road to the west bound on and off ramps of Route 80 at the Rowley Junction Interchange.

(5) SR-197. From Route 73 northerly on Fifth West Street to Route 89 in Lehi.

(6) SR-198. From Route 15 northbound ramps of the North Santaquin Interchange northeasterly through Spring Lake, to 100 North in Payson; then easterly and northeasterly through Salem to 300 South in Spanish Fork; then easterly and southeasterly to Route 6 at Moark Junction.

(7) SR-199. From Dugway Proving Grounds main gate northeasterly through Clover to Route 36.

(8) SR-200. From Route 61 in Lewiston, approximately three miles west of Route 91, north to the Utah-Idaho state line.   1998

72-4-126.   State highways — SR-201 to SR-204, SR-208 to SR-211.

State highways include:

(1) SR-201. From Route 80 at Lake Point Junction east on Twenty-first South Street to Route 89 in Salt Lake City.

(2) SR-202. From Route 201 near Garfield northwesterly through the Garfield Cutoff to Route 80.

(3) SR-203. From Route 89 near Uintah northerly on Harrison Boulevard in Ogden to Route 39.

(4) SR-204. From Route 26 north on Wall Avenue in Ogden to Route 89.

(5) SR-208. From Route 40 east of Fruitland northerly to Route 35 near Tabiona.

(6) SR-209. From Route 68 easterly on Ninetieth South Street; then southeasterly to Ninety-fourth South Street; then easterly to Route 210 near the mouth of Little Cottonwood Canyon.

(7) SR-210. From Route 190 at the mouth of Big Cottonwood Canyon southeasterly on Wasatch Boulevard and through Little Cottonwood Canyon, to Alta, including the Alta Bypass.

(8) SR-211. From Dugout Ranch southeasterly; then northeasterly to Route 191 near Church Rock.   1998

72-4-127.   State highways — SR-212, SR-215, SR-218, SR-219.

State highways include:

(1) SR-212. From the northwest frontage road of Washington Interchange southeasterly; then northeasterly and easterly to 300 East Street in Washington.

(2) SR-215. From a junction with Route 80 near the mouth of Parley's Canyon southeast of Salt Lake City, southwesterly to near the south city limits of Murray, junctioning with Route 15, then northwesterly, northerly, and easterly to a junction with Route 15 north of Salt Lake City, on interstate Route 215.

(3) SR-218. From Route 23 east of Newton easterly to Route 91 in Smithfield.

(4) SR-219. From the 1984 west corporate limits of Enterprise east to Route 18.   1998

72-4-128.   State highways — SR-222, SR-224 to SR-228.

State highways include:

(1) SR-222. From Route 113 in Midway northerly to Pine Creek Campground.

(2) SR-224. From the Wasatch-Summit County line south of Park City through Ontario Canyon and Park City to Route 80 at Kimball Junction.

(3) SR-225. From Route 15 east on Burke Lane to Route 106 in Farmington.

(4) SR-226. From Snow Basin Ski Lodge lower parking lot in Weber County southeasterly to Route 167 the Trappers Loop Road.

(5) SR-227. From Route 15 near Glover Lane north on Walker Lane to State Street; then east to Route 106 in Farmington.

(6) SR-228. From the northbound off-ramp of Route 15 at the South Leeds Interchange; then northerly on Main Street in Leeds to the northbound on-ramp of Route 15; then westerly to the southbound off-ramp of Route 15; and from the southbound on-ramp of Route 15 easterly to Main Street in Leeds.   2005

72-4-129.   State highways — SR-232, SR-235, SR-237 to SR-240.

State highways include:

(1) SR-232. From Route 126 in Layton north to the south entrance to Hill Air Force Base.

(2) SR-235. From Route 89 in Ogden north to Route 134 in North Ogden.

(3) SR-237. From Seventh North Street and Eighth East Street in Logan northerly to Hyde Park; then west to Route 91 west of Hyde Park.

(4) SR-238. From Route 165 east to Millville; then northerly through Providence and River Heights to Route 91 in Logan.

(5) SR-239. From Route 91 in Logan east on 1400 North Street to Route 237.

(6) SR-240. From Route 15 east to Route 38 in Honeyville.   2005

72-4-130.   State highways — SR-241, SR-243, SR-244, SR-248.

State highways include:

(1) SR-241. From SR-114 east on 1600 North in Orem to the on- and off-ramps on the east side of interstate Route 15.

(2) SR-243. From Route 89 in Logan Canyon to Beaver Mountain Ski Resort.

(3) SR-244. From Route 6 in Helper easterly on Poplar Street to Main Street; then northerly on Main Street to Route 6.

(4) SR-248. From Route 224 at Park City Junction to Route 40 at the Park City Interchange; then southeasterly and easterly to Route 32 in Kamas.   1998

72-4-131.   State highways — SR-256 to SR-260.

State highways include:

(1) SR-256. From 89 north of Salina northerly through Redmond to Route 89 south of Axtell.

(2) SR-257. From Route 21 at Milford northeasterly through Black Rock and Deseret to Route 6 near Hinckley.

(3) SR-258. From Route 70 near Elsinore easterly to Route 118 east of Elsinore.

(4) SR-259. From Route 24 near Sigurd, north to I-70 at the Sigurd Interchange.

(5) SR-260. From Route 24 south of Aurora to Route 50 west of Salina.   1998

72-4-132.   State highways — SR-261, SR-262, SR-264 to SR-266, SR-268 to SR-270.

State highways include:

(1) SR-261. From Route 163 north of Mexican Hat to Route 95 east of Natural Bridges National Monument.

(2) SR-262. From Route 191 approximately eleven miles north of Bluff easterly and southerly to Route 162 near Montezuma Creek.

(3) SR-264. From Route 31 easterly through Flat Canyon and Eccles Canyon to Route 96 south of Scofield.

(4) SR-265. From Route 114 near Twelfth South Street in Orem southeasterly to Route 189 in Provo.

(5) SR-266. From Route 215 easterly on Forty-seventh South Street and Forty-fifth South Street to Route 215.

(6) SR-268. From Route 15 easterly on 600 North Street to Route 89 in Salt Lake City.

(7) SR-269. From Route 15 easterly on Fifth and Sixth South Streets to Route 89 in Salt Lake City, providing one-way couplets.

(8) SR-270. From Route 15 easterly and northerly on West Temple Street to Route 186 in Salt Lake City.   2005

72-4-133.   State highways — SR-271, SR-273 to SR-276, SR-279, SR-280.

State highways include:

(1) SR-271. From Route 274 in Parowan northeasterly to Route 15 north of Paragonah.

(2) SR-273. From Route 89 at North Farmington Interchange northerly to Kaysville; then west on Cherry Street to Route 15.

(3) SR-274. From Route 143 in Parowan north on Main Street to Route 15 north of Parowan.

(4) SR-275. From Route 95 northwesterly to the east boundary of Natural Bridges National Monument.

(5) SR-276. From Route 95 southerly to Glen Canyon National Recreation Area boundary near Bullfrog Basin then beginning again at the Glen Canyon National Recreation Area boundary east of Halls Crossing easterly to Route 95.

(6) SR-279. From the Potash Plant north along the Colorado River to Route 191 north of Moab.

(7) SR-280. From Route 80 near the south limits of Coalville easterly to Main Street in Coalville.   2002

72-4-134.   State highways — SR-282 and SR-284 to SR-290.

State highways include:

(1) SR-282. At University of Utah.

(a) From 500 South Street north on Campus Center Drive to South Campus Drive.

(b) From University Street and 400 South Street easterly and northeasterly on South Campus Drive to Wasatch Drive.

(c) From Foothill Boulevard Route 186 northerly on Wasatch Drive to South Medical Drive.

(d) From Wasatch Drive northerly on South Medical Drive and West Medical Drive to North Campus Drive; then south and southwest to University Street and 100 South Street.

(2) SR-284. At Weber State University in Ogden.

(a) From 4100 South Street northerly on the peripheral road to Edvalson Street; then northwesterly and westerly on 3700 South Street to Route 203, Harrison Boulevard.

(b) From Route 203 easterly on 4100 South Street to Taylor Avenue.

(c) Campus North Road from the north-south peripheral road easterly on Edvalson Street to Foothill Drive.

(d) From Route 203, Harrison Boulevard, easterly on 3850 South Street to north-south peripheral road.

(e) From Route 203, Harrison Boulevard, easterly on 4000 South Street to the north-south peripheral road.

(3) SR-285. The Institute for the Deaf. From Twentieth Street in Ogden northwesterly to Monroe Avenue.

(4) SR-286. From Route 235 to and including a peripheral road at the State Industrial School in Ogden.

(5) SR-287. From Route 140 northerly to the Utah State Prison Vehicle Direction Station.

(6) SR-288. From Route 89 at 1200 East in Logan, at Utah State University, on 1200 East and 1000 North to Route 237.

(7) SR-289. At College of Southern Utah. From Route 130 in Cedar City westerly on Center Street to 1150 West Street; then south to Second South Street; then east to Third West Street; then north to Center Street, providing a peripheral road around the College of Southern Utah.

(8) SR-290. At Snow College. From Route 89 in Ephraim easterly on First North Street to Fourth East Street; then south to Center Street; then west to Route 89, providing a peripheral road around Snow College.   2002

72-4-135.   State highways — SR-291 to SR-294, SR-296, SR-298, SR-299.

State highways include:

(1) SR-291. The Institute for the Blind. From Route 203, Harrison Boulevard, near Seventh Street in Ogden easterly and southerly to the hospital, including the loop on the southwest side of the hospital.

(2) SR-292. At Salt Lake Community College.

(a) From 2200 West Street easterly on 4520 South for 0.17 miles; beginning again at 0.47 miles easterly on 4520 South to Route 68.

(b) From Route 68 westerly on 4600 South for 0.80 miles; then northerly on 1900 West to 4520 South.

(c) From 4600 South northerly paralleling Route 68 to 4520 South.

(d) From 2200 West easterly on Bruin Boulevard to Route 68.

(3) SR-293. At State Capitol Building. All roads and parking areas within the capitol grounds.

(4) SR-294. At State Mental Hospital. From the main gate on Center Street in Provo easterly to the administration building.

(5) SR-296. At American Fork Training School. From 700 North in American Fork northerly.

(6) SR-298. Roads at the Browning Armory in South Ogden used for automotive drivers' ability tests including parking areas.

(7) SR-299. Those roads used for drivers' tests at 2780 West and 4700 South in Salt Lake County.   2004

72-4-136.   State highways — SR-301 to SR-304, SR-306, SR-309, SR-310.

State highways include:

(1) SR-301. From the boat ramp at Steinaker State Park northeasterly to Route 191 near the north end of Steinaker Reservoir.

(2) SR-302. From Route 32 near the south end of Rockport Reservoir northwesterly to a point near the north boundary of Rockport State Park.

(3) SR-303. From the Goblin Valley Overlook northerly to the Goblin Valley State Park north boundary.

(4) SR-304. From the parking lot at the beach area in Hyrum State Park northwesterly to a junction with Center Street and Fifth South Street in Hyrum City.

(5) SR-306. From the parking area north to Route 66 near the north end of East Canyon Lake State Park.

(6) SR-309. From a local road northerly to the parking area at Millsite Lake State Park.

(7) SR-310. From the parking area at Minersville Lake State Park east to Route 21.

2004

72-4-137. State highways — SR-311 to SR-320, SR-491.

State highways include:

(1) SR-311. From Route 40 northerly to the boat ramp at Starvation Lake State Park.

(2) SR-312. From the parking area at the south marina of Willard Bay State Park east to a local road.

(3) SR-313. From the camping area at Dead Horse Point northerly to Route 191 near Seven Mile Canyon.

(4) SR-314. From Route 189 northwesterly to the boat ramp at Deer Creek Lake State Recreation area.

(5) SR-315. From the parking area at the marina of Willard Bay North State Recreation Area northerly to 750 North in Willard, then east to Route 89.

(6) SR-316. From the Great Goosenecks of the San Juan State Park northeasterly to Route 261.

(7) SR-317. Roads and parking areas at the Calvin L. Rampton Complex.

(8) SR-318. From Route 9 northerly to Quail Creek State Park pay gate.

(9) SR-319. From the southbound on and off ramps of Route 40, Mayflower Interchange southeasterly to the Jordanelle State Park fee station.

(10) SR-320. Department of Public Safety Emergency Vehicle Operation Range at Camp Williams.

(11) SR-491. From Route 191 at Monticello east to the Utah-Colorado state line.   2004

PART 2

SPECIAL DESIGNATIONS

72-4-201. I-15 designated as Veterans' Memorial Highway.

(1) There is established the Veterans' Memorial Highway composed of the existing Interstate Highway 15 from the Utah-Idaho border to the Utah-Arizona border.

(2) The department shall designate Interstate 15 as the "Veterans' Memorial Highway" on all future state highway maps.   1998

72-4-201.5. Tenth Mountain Division Memorial Highway.

(1) There is established the Tenth Mountain Division Memorial Highway composed of the existing Route 224 from Kimball Junction southeasterly to the junction with Route 248 in Park City.

(2) The department shall designate this portion of Route 224 as the "Tenth Mountain Division Memorial Highway" on all future state highway maps.   2002

72-4-202. Legacy Loop Highway.

(1) There is established the Legacy Loop Highway comprising the existing highway from Route 15 south of St. George, northerly on Route 18 to Route 56 at Beryl Junction, then easterly on Route 56 to Route 130 in Cedar City, and then northeasterly on Route 130 and county routes 1788 and 1786 to Route 143 in Parowan.

(2) The Department of Transportation shall designate the portions of the highways identified in Subsection (1) as the Legacy Loop Highway on all future state highway maps.   1998

72-4-203. Utah National Parks Highway.

(1) There is established the Utah National Parks Highway comprising the existing highway from Route 89 at the Utah-Arizona border near Big Water westerly on Route 89 to Route 9 near Mount Carmel Junction then westerly on Route 9 to Route 17 near La Verkin then northerly on Route 17 to Interstate Highway 15 then northerly on Interstate Highway 15 frontage roads, the Veterans' Memorial Highway, to Route 14 near Cedar City then southeasterly on Route 14 to Route 148 near Cedar Breaks National Monument then northerly on Route 148 to Route 143 near the north end of Cedar Breaks National Monument then northeasterly on Route 143 to Route 89 near Panguitch then southerly on Route 89 to Route 12 near Red Canyon then northeasterly on Route 12, the Clem Church Memorial Highway, to Route 24 near Torrey then easterly on Route 24 to Route 95 near Hanksville then southeasterly on Route 95, the Bicentennial Highway, to Route 191 near Blanding then northerly on Route 191 to the junction with Interstate Highway 70 near Crescent Junction.

(2) In addition to other official designations, the Department of Transportation shall designate and highlight the portions of the highways identified in Subsection (1) as the Utah National Parks Highway on all future state highway maps.   1998

72-4-204. Dinosaur Diamond Prehistoric Highway.

(1) There is established the Dinosaur Diamond Prehistoric Highway comprising the existing highways beginning on Route 191 in Blanding north to the frontage road of Route 70 at Crescent Junction, then west on the frontage road of Route 70 to Green River, then northerly on Route 191 and Route 6 to Route 10 near Price, then:

(a) south on Route 10 to Castle Dale, then North on Route 10 to Route 155, then south on Route 155 to the Cleveland Lloyd Dinosaur Quarry via its access road; and

(b) northerly on Route 191 and Route 6 to Helper and the State of Utah Indian Canyon Scenic Byway, then northeasterly on Route 191 to Route 40 in Duchesne, then east on Route 40 and Route 191 to Vernal, and then east on Route 40 to Route 149, then northeasterly on Route 149 to the Dinosaur National Monument, then southwesterly on Route 149 to Route 40, then east on Route 40 to the Utah and Colorado state boundary line.

(2) In addition to other official designations, the Department of Transportation shall designate and highlight the portions of the highways identified in Subsection (1) as the Dinosaur Diamond Prehistoric Highway on all future state highway maps.   1998

72-4-205. Ram Boulevard.

(1) There is established Ram Boulevard comprising a section of Route 118 in Monroe from 1450 West along 100 South to Main Street.

(2) In addition to other official designations, the Department of Transportation shall designate the portions of the highway identified in Subsection (1) as Ram Boulevard.   2001

72-4-206. The Utah Fruitway.

(1) There is established the Utah Fruitway comprising a section of Route 89 beginning at the Box Elder and Weber County line north to the south city limit of Brigham City.

(2) In addition to other official designations, the Department of Transportation shall designate the portions of the highway identified in Subsection (1) as the Utah Fruitway on future state highway maps.
2002

72-4-207. The Purple Heart Trail.

(1) There is established the Purple Heart Trail comprising Route 80, which is also known as Interstate 80, the Dwight D. Eisenhower Highway, beginning at the Nevada-Utah state line in Wendover, east to the Wyoming-Utah state line west of Evanston, Wyoming.

(2) In addition to other official designations, the Department of Transportation shall designate the highway identified in Subsection (1) as the Purple Heart Trail on future state highway maps.   2002

72-4-208. James V. Hansen Highway.

(1) There is established the James V. Hansen Highway comprising a section of Route 89 beginning in Farmington at the Route 89 and Interstate Highway 15 interchange north to Route 203, Harrison Boulevard in South Ogden.

(2) In addition to other official designations, the Department of Transportation shall designate the portions of the highway identified in Subsection (1) as the James V. Hansen Highway on future state highway maps.   2003

72-4-209. Mormon Pioneer Heritage Area.

(1) There is established a state heritage area known as the Mormon Pioneer Heritage Area comprising a section of Route 89 beginning in Fairview to Kanab and including the Boulder Loop in Garfield and Wayne Counties.

(2) In addition to other official designations, the Department of Transportation shall designate the portions of the highway identified in Subsection (1) as the Mormon Pioneer Heritage Area on future state highway maps.   2004

PART 3

UTAH STATE SCENIC BYWAY PROGRAM

72-4-301. Definitions.

As used in this part, "committee" means the Utah State Scenic Byway Committee created in Section 72-4-302.   2004

72-4-302. Utah State Scenic Byway Committee — Creation — Membership — Meetings — Expenses.

(1) There is created the Utah State Scenic Byway Committee.

(2) The committee shall consist of the following members:

(a) a representative from each of the following entities appointed by each respective entity:

(i) the Governor's Office of Economic Development;

(ii) the Utah Department of Transportation;

(iii) the Utah Association of Governments;

(iv) the Division of State Parks and Recreation;

(v) the Federal Highway Administration;

(vi) the National Park Service;

(vii) the National Forest Service;

(viii) the Bureau of Land Management; and

(ix) the Utah Travel Regions Association;

(b) two local government tourism representatives selected by the state entities identified in Subsection (2)(a); and

(c) a representative from the private sector selected by the state entities identified in Subsection (2)(a).

(3) (a) The representative from the Governor's Office of Economic Development shall chair the committee.

(b) The members appointed under Subsections (2)(a)(v), (vi), (vii), and (viii) serve as nonvoting, ex officio members of the committee.

(4) The Governor's Office of Economic Development and the department shall provide staff support to the committee.

(5) (a) The chair may call a meeting of the committee only with the concurrence of the department.

(b) A majority of the voting members of the committee constitute a quorum.

(c) Action by a majority vote of a quorum of the committee constitutes action by the committee.

(6) (a) (i) Members who are not state government employees shall receive no compensation or benefits for their services, but may receive per diem and expenses incurred in the performance of the member's official duties at the rates established by the Division of Finance under Sections 63A-3-106 and 63A-3-107.

(ii) Members may decline to receive per diem and expenses for their service.

(b) (i) State government officer and employee members who do not receive salary, per diem, or expenses from their agency for their service may receive per diem and expenses incurred in the performance of their official duties at the rates established by the Division of Finance under Sections 63A-3-106 and 63A-3-107.

(ii) State government officer and employee members may decline to receive per diem and expenses for their service.

(c) (i) Local government members who do not receive salary, per diem, or expenses from the entity that they represent for their service may receive per diem and expenses incurred in the performance of their official duties at the rates established by the Division of Finance under Sections 63A-3-106 and 63A-3-107.

(ii) Local government members may decline to receive per diem and expenses for their service.   2005

72-4-303. Powers and duties of the Utah State Scenic Byway Committee — Rulemaking authority — Designation on state maps — Outdoor advertising.

(1) The committee shall have the responsibility to:

(a) administer a coordinated scenic byway program within the state that:

(i) preserves and protects the intrinsic qualities described in Subsection (1)(b) unique to scenic byways;

(ii) enhances recreation; and

(iii) promotes economic development through tourism and education;

(b) ensure that a highway nominated for a scenic byway designation possesses at least one of the following six intrinsic qualities:

(i) scenic quality;

(ii) natural quality;

(iii) historic quality;

(iv) cultural quality;

(v) archaeological quality; or

(vi) recreational quality;

(c) designate highways as state scenic byways from nominated highways within the state if the committee determines that the highway possesses the criteria for a state scenic byway; and

(d) remove the designation of a highway as a scenic byway if the committee determines that the highway no longer meets the criteria under which it was designated.

(2) In accordance with Title 63, Chapter 46a, Utah Administrative Rulemaking Act, the department shall make rules in consultation with the committee:

(a) for the administration of a scenic byway program;

(b) establishing the criteria that a highway shall possess to be designated as a scenic byway, including the criteria described in Subsection (1)(b);

(c) establishing the process for nominating a highway to be designated as a state scenic byway;

(d) specifying the process for hearings to be conducted in the area of proposed designation prior to the highway being designated as a scenic byway;

(e) identifying the highways within the state designated as scenic byways; and

(f) establishing the process and criteria for removing the designation of a highway as a scenic byway.

(3) The department shall designate scenic byway routes on future state highway maps.

(4) A highway within the state designated as a scenic byway is subject to federal outdoor advertising regulations in accordance with 23 U.S.C. Sec. 131.

2004

CHAPTER 5

RIGHTS-OF-WAY

Part 1

Public Highways

Part 2

Rights-of-Way Across State Lands

Part 3

Rights-of-Way Across Federal Lands Act

Part 4

Transportation Corridor Preservation

PART 1

PUBLIC HIGHWAYS

72-5-101. Title.

This chapter is known as the "Rights-of-way Act."

1998

72-5-102. Definitions.

As used in this part, "state transportation purposes" includes:

(1) highway and public transportation rights-of-way, including those necessary within cities and towns;

(2) the construction, reconstruction, relocation, improvement, maintenance, and mitigation from the effects of these activities on state highways and other transportation facilities under the control of the department;

(3) limited access facilities, including rights of access, air, light, and view and frontage and service roads to highways;

(4) adequate drainage in connection with any highway, cut, fill, or channel change and the maintenance of any highway, cut, fill, or channel change;

(5) weighing stations, shops, offices, storage buildings and yards, and road maintenance or construction sites;

(6) road material sites, sites for the manufacture of road materials, and access roads to the sites;

(7) the maintenance of an unobstructed view of any portion of a highway to promote the safety of the traveling public;

(8) the placement of traffic signals, directional signs, and other signs, fences, curbs, barriers, and obstructions for the convenience of the traveling public;

(9) the construction and maintenance of storm sewers, sidewalks, and highway illumination;

(10) the construction and maintenance of livestock highways;

(11) the construction and maintenance of roadside rest areas adjacent to or near any highway; and

(12) the mitigation of impacts from public transportation projects.   2001

72-5-103. Acquisition of rights-of-way and other real property — Title to property acquired.

(1) The department may acquire any real property or interests in real property necessary for temporary, present, or reasonable future state transportation purposes by gift, agreement, exchange, purchase, condemnation, or otherwise.

(2) (a) (i) Title to real property acquired by the department or the counties, cities, and towns by gift, agreement, exchange, purchase, condemnation, or otherwise for highway rights-of-way or other transportation purposes may be in fee simple or any lesser estate or interest.

(ii) Title to real property acquired by the department for a public transit project shall be transferred to the public transit district responsible for the project.

(iii) A public transit district shall cover all costs associated with any condemnation on its behalf.

(b) If the highway is a county road, city street under joint title as provided in Subsection 72-3-104(3), or right-of-way described in Title 72, Chapter 5, Part 3, Rights-of-way Across Federal Lands Act, title to all interests in real property less than fee simple held under this section is held jointly by the state and the county, city, or town holding the interest.

(3) A transfer of land bounded by a highway on a right-of-way for which the public has only an easement passes the title of the person whose estate is transferred to the middle of the highway.   2001

72-5-104. Public use constituting dedication — Scope.

(1) A highway is dedicated and abandoned to the use of the public when it has been continuously used as a public thoroughfare for a period of ten years.

(2) The dedication and abandonment creates a right-of-way held by the state in accordance with Sections 72-3-102, 72-3-104, 72-3-105, and 72-5-103.

(3) The scope of the right-of-way is that which is reasonable and necessary to ensure safe travel according to the facts and circumstances.   2000

72-5-105. Highways, streets, or roads once established continue until abandoned.

(1) All public highways, streets, or roads once established shall continue to be highways, streets, or roads until abandoned or vacated by order of the highway authorities having jurisdiction or by other competent authority.

(2) For purposes of assessment, upon the recordation of an order executed by the proper authority with the county recorder's office, title to the vacated or abandoned highway, street, or road shall vest to the adjoining record owners, with ½ of the width of the highway, street, or road assessed to each of the adjoining owners. Provided, however, that should a description of an owner of record extend into the vacated or abandoned highway, street, or road that portion of the vacated or abandoned highway, street, or road shall vest in the record owner, with the remainder of the highway, street, or road vested as otherwise provided in this Subsection (2).   2002

72-5-106. Expiration of franchise of toll bridge or road.

If the franchise of any toll bridge or road expires by limitation, forfeiture, or nonuser it is a free public highway, and no claim shall be valid against the public for right-of-way or for land or material comprising the bridge or road.   1998

72-5-107. United States patents — Patentee and county to assert claims to roads crossing land.

(1) (a) If any person acquires title from the United States to any land in this state over which any public highway extends that has not been duly platted, and that has not been continuously used as a public highway for a period of ten years, the person shall within three months after receipt of the person's patent assert the person's claim for damages in writing to the county executive of the county in which the land is situated.

(b) The county legislative body shall have an additional period of three months in which to begin proceedings to condemn the land according to law.

(2) (a) The highway shall continue open as a public highway during the periods described under Subsection (1).

(b) If no action is begun by the county executive within the period described under Subsection (1)(b), the highway shall be considered to be abandoned by the public.

(3) In case of a failure by the person so acquiring title to public lands to assert his claim for damage during the three months from the time the person received a patent to the lands, the person shall thereafter be barred from asserting or recovering any damages by reason of the public highway, and the public highway shall remain open.   1998

72-5-108. Width of rights-of-way for public highways.

The width of rights-of-way for public highways shall be set as the highway authorities of the state, counties, or municipalities may determine for the highways under their respective jurisdiction.   1998

72-5-109. Contributions of property by counties and municipalities.

Counties and municipalities may contribute real or personal property to the department for state transportation purposes.   2001

72-5-110. Acquisition of personal property.

The department may acquire by gift, agreement, exchange, purchase, or otherwise machinery, tools, equipment, materials, supplies, or other personal property necessary for the administration, construction, maintenance, and operation of the state highways, and may sell, exchange, or otherwise dispose of the machinery, tools, equipment, materials, supplies, and other personal property when no longer suitable or required for state transportation purposes.   2001

72-5-111. Disposal of real property.

(1) (a) If the department determines that any real property or interest in real property, acquired for a highway purpose, is no longer necessary for the purpose, the department may lease, sell, exchange, or otherwise dispose of the real property or interest in the real property.

     (b) (i) Real property may be sold at private or public sale.

         (ii) Except as provided in Subsection (1)(c) related to exchanges, proceeds of any sale shall be deposited with the state treasurer and credited to the Transportation Fund.

     (c) If approved by the commission, real property or an interest in real property may be exchanged by the department for other real property or interest in real property, including improvements, for highway purposes.

(2) (a) In the disposition of real property at any private sale, first consideration shall be given to the original grantor or the original grantor's heirs.

     (b) Notwithstanding the provisions of Section 78-34-20, if no portion of a parcel of real property acquired by the department is used for transportation purposes, then the original grantor or the grantor's heirs shall be given the opportunity to repurchase the parcel of real property at the department's original purchase price from the grantor.

     (c) In accordance with Section 72-5-404, this Subsection (2) does not apply to property rights acquired in proposed transportation corridors using funds from the Transportation Corridor Preservation Revolving Loan Fund created in Section 72-2-117.

(3) (a) Any sale, exchange, or disposal of real property or interest in real property made by the department under this section, is exempt from the mineral reservation provisions of Title 65A, Chapter 6, Mineral Leases.

     (b) Any deed made and delivered by the department under this section without specific reservations in the deed is a conveyance of all the state's right, title, and interest in the real property or interest in the real property.   2003

72-5-112. Acquisition of real property from county, city, or other political subdivision — Exchange.

The department may purchase or otherwise acquire from any county, city, or other political subdivision of the state real property or interests in real property which may be exchanged for or used in the purchase of other real property or interests in real property to be used in connection with the construction, maintenance, or operation of state highways.   1998

72-5-113. Acquisition of entire lot, block, or tract — Sale or exchange of remainder.

If a part of an entire lot, block, tract of land, or interest or improvement in real property is to be acquired by the department and the remainder is to be left in a shape or condition of little value to its owner or to give rise to claims or litigation concerning damages, the department may acquire the whole of the property and may sell the remainder or may exchange it for other property needed for highway purposes.   1998

72-5-114. Property acquired in advance of construction — Lease or rental.

(1) (a) The department may acquire real property or interests or improvements in real property in advance of the actual construction, reconstruction, or improvement of highways in order to save on acquisition costs or avoid the payment of excessive damages.

     (b) The real property or interests or improvements in real property may be leased or rented by the department in a manner, for a period of time, and for a sum determined by the department to be in the best interest of the state.

(2) (a) The department may employ private agencies to manage rental properties when it is more economical and in the best interests of the state.

     (b) All moneys received for leases and rentals, after deducting any portion to which the federal government may be entitled, shall be deposited with the state treasurer and credited to the Transportation Fund.   1998

72-5-115. Acquisition of property devoted to or held for other public use.

(1) If property devoted to or held for some other public use for which the power of eminent domain might be exercised is to be taken for state transportation purposes, the department may, with the consent of the person or agency in charge of the other public use, condemn real property to be exchanged with the person or agency for the real property to be taken for state transportation purposes.

(2) This section does not limit the department's authorization to acquire, other than by condemnation, property for exchange purposes.   2001

PART 2

RIGHTS-OF-WAY ACROSS STATE LANDS

72-5-201. Purpose statement.

(1) (a) The Legislature recognizes that highways provide tangible benefits to private and public lands of the state by providing access, allowing development, and facilitating production of income.

     (b) Many of those highways traverse state lands, including lands held by the state in trust for the school children and public institutions of the state.

     (c) Many of the existing highways have been previously established without an official grant of an easement or right of entry from this state, yet these highways often are the only access to private and public lands of the state.

(2) The Legislature intends to establish a means for ensuring continued access to the private and public lands of the state for the good of the people, while fulfilling its fiduciary responsibilities toward the schoolchildren by protecting their trust holdings against loss.   1998

72-5-202. Definitions.

As used in this part:

(1) "Responsible authority" means a private party, the state of Utah, or a political subdivision of the state claiming rights to a highway right-of-way, easement, or right of entry across state lands.

(2) "Sovereign lands" has the same meaning as provided in Section 65A-1-1.

(3) "State lands" means sovereign and trust lands, as well as all other lands held by or on behalf of the departments, divisions, or institutions of the state.

(4) "Trust lands" has the same meaning as "school and institutional trust lands" as defined in Section 53C-1-103.   1998

72-5-203. Public easement or right of entry — Grant — Application — Conditions.

(1) (a) (i) Subject to Section 53C-1-302 and Subsection 53C-1-204(1), a temporary public easement or right of entry is granted for each highway existing prior to January 1, 1992, that terminates at or within or traverses any state lands and that has been constructed and maintained or used by a responsible authority.

(ii) The temporary public easement or right of entry granted under Subsection (1)(a)(i) is 100 feet wide for each class A and B highway.

(b) Each easement shall remain in effect through June 30, 2004, or until a permanent easement or right of entry has been established under Subsection (2), whichever is greater.

(2) (a) The School and Institutional Trust Lands Administration and the Division of Forestry, Fire and State Lands shall make rules in accordance with Title 63, Chapter 46a, Utah Administrative Rulemaking Act, establishing an application process for a responsible authority to obtain a permanent easement or right of entry over any temporary public easement granted under Subsection (1), subject to the provisions of Subsections (2)(b), (c), and (d).

(b) A grant of a permanent easement or right of entry across sovereign lands shall be made upon a showing to the Division of Forestry, Fire and State Lands that continued use of the easement will provide a public benefit commensurate with the value of the permanent easement or right of entry.

(c) A grant of a permanent easement or right of entry across trust lands shall be made upon a showing to the School and Institutional Trust Lands Administration that the grant is consistent with the state's fiduciary responsibilities under Section 53C-1-302 and Subsection 53C-1-204(1).

(d) A grant of a permanent easement or right of entry across state lands other than sovereign and trust lands shall be made upon a showing to the managing unit of state government that the continued use will provide a public benefit commensurate with the value of the easement and will not unreasonably interfere with the purposes for which the land was obtained or is now held.

(3) The grant of the temporary public easement or right of entry under Subsection (1) is consistent with the trust responsibilities of the state and in the best interest of the state.

(4) A responsible authority that has been granted a permanent easement or right of entry over state lands may maintain the permanent easement or right of entry for the uses to which the permanent easement or right of entry was put prior to and including January 1, 1992, subject to the right of the managing unit of state government or private party to relocate the permanent easement or right of entry.

(5) The grant of a permanent easement or right of entry under this section is effective on the date the highway was originally constructed or established for public use.   2003

PART 3

RIGHTS-OF-WAY ACROSS FEDERAL LANDS ACT

72-5-301. Definitions.

As used in this part:

(1) "Acceptance," "acceptance of a right-of-way for the construction of a highway over public lands, not reserved for public uses," or "accepted" so as to vest the R.S. 2477 dominant estate in the right-of-way in the state and any applicable political subdivision of the state, means one or more of the following acts prior to October 21, 1976:

(a) by the state or any political subdivision of the state:

(i) construction or maintenance of a highway;

(ii) inclusion of the highway in a state, county, or municipal road system;

(iii) expenditure of any public funds on the highway;

(iv) execution of a memorandum of understanding or other agreement with any other public or private entity or an agency of the federal government that recognizes the right or obligation of the state or a political subdivision of the state to construct or maintain the highway or a portion of the highway; or

(v) (A) the acceptance at statehood of the school or institutional trust lands accessed or traversed by the right-of-way; or

(B) the selection and receipt by the state of a clear list, indemnity list, or other document conveying title to the state of school, institutional trust lands, or other state lands accessed or traversed by the highway;

(b) use by the public for a period in excess of ten years in accordance with Section 72-5-104; or

(c) any other act consistent with state or federal law indicating acceptance of a right-of-way.

(2) (a) "Construction" means any physical act of readying a highway for use by the public according to the available or intended mode of transportation, including, foot, horse, vehicle, pipeline, or other mode.

(b) "Construction" includes:

(i) removing vegetation;

(ii) moving obstructions, including rocks, boulders, and outcroppings;

(iii) filling low spots;

(iv) maintenance over several years;

(v) creation of an identifiable route by use over time; and

(vi) other similar activities.

(3) "Cut-off date" means the earlier of the date the underlying land was reserved for public use or October 21, 1976.

(4) (a) "Highway" means:

(i) any road, street, trail, or other access or way that is open to the public to come and go or transport water at will, without regard to how or by whom the way was constructed or maintained; and

(ii) appurtenant land and structures including road drainage ditches, back and front slopes, turnouts, rest areas, and other areas that facilitate use of the highway by the public.

(b) "Highway" includes:

(i) pedestrian trails, horse paths, livestock trails, wagon roads, jeep trails, logging roads, homestead roads, mine-to-market roads, alleys, tunnels, bridges, and all other ways and their attendant access for maintenance; and

(ii) irrigation canals, waterways, viaducts, ditches, pipelines, or other means of water transmission and their attendant access for maintenance.

(c) To be a "highway" a right-of-way need not have destinations or termini that are some kind of landmarks distinguishable from other points along the right-of-way, as long as the right-of-way accommodates travelers from one point along the right-of-way to another point as often as convenient or necessary.

(5) "Maintenance" means any physical act of upkeep of a highway or repair of wear or damage whether from natural or other causes, including the following:

(a) vertical and horizontal alignment alterations to meet applicable safety standards;

(b) widening an existing road or flattening of shoulders or side slopes to meet applicable safety standards;

(c) grooming and grading of the previously constructed road surface;

(d) establishing and maintaining the road crown with materials gathered along the road;

(e) filling ruts;

(f) spot filling with the same materials of the road, or improved materials;

(g) leveling or smoothing washboards;

(h) clearing the roadway of obstructing debris;

(i) cleaning culverts, including head basins and outlets;

(j) resurfacing with the same or improved materials;

(k) installing, maintaining, repairing and replacing rip rap;

(l) maintaining drainage;

(m) maintaining and repairing washes and gullies;

(n) installing, maintaining, repairing, and replacing culverts as necessary to protect the existing surface from erosion;

(o) repairing washouts;

(p) installing, maintaining, repairing and replacing marker posts;

(q) installing, maintaining, and repairing water crossings;

(r) installing, maintaining, and repairing and replacing cattle guards;

(s) installing, maintaining, and repairing and replacing road signs;

(t) installing, maintaining, and repairing and replacing road striping;

(u) repair, stabilization and improvement of cut and fill slopes;

(v) application of seal coats; or

(w) snow removal.

(6) "Public lands not reserved for public uses" means the surface of federal lands open to entry and location and includes the surface of lands that are subject to subsurface coal withdrawals or mining claims.

(7) "R.S. 2477 right-of-way" means a right-of-way for a highway constructed in this state on public lands not reserved for public uses in accordance with Revised Statute 2477, codified as 43 U.S.C. Section 932, and accepted by the state or a political subdivision of the state prior to October 21, 1976.   2003

**72-5-302. Rights-of-way across federal lands —
Title — Presumption — Scope.**

(1) This part applies to all R.S. 2477 rights-of-way.

(2) The state and its political subdivisions have title to the R.S. 2477 rights-of-ways in accordance with Sections 72-3-102, 72-3-103, 72-3-104, 72-3-105, and 72-5-103.

(3) (a) Acceptance of a right-of-way for the construction of a highway over public lands, not reserved for public uses, is presumed if the state or a political subdivision of the state makes a finding that the highway was constructed and the right-of-way was accepted prior to October 21, 1976.

(b) The existence of a highway in a condition suitable for public use establishes a presumption that the highway has continued in use in its present location since the land over which it is built was public land not reserved for public use.

(4) (a) Unless specifically determined prior to the cut-off date provided in Section 72-5-301 by the state or a political subdivision of the state with authority over the R.S. 2477 right-of-way, the scope of the R.S. 2477 right-of-way is that which is reasonable and necessary for all highway uses as of the cut-off date determined according to the facts and circumstances, including:

(i) highway drainage facilities;

(ii) shoulders adjacent to the right-of-way; and

(iii) maintenance activities defined in Section 72-5-301 that are reasonable and necessary.

(b) Unless specifically determined by the state or political subdivision of the state with the authority over the R.S. 2477 right-of-way, an R.S. 2477 right-of-way is presumed to be at least 66 feet wide if that is the usual width of highway rights-of-way in the area.

(c) The scope of the R.S. 2477 right-of-way includes the right to widen the highway as necessary to accommodate the increased travel associated with those uses, up to, where applicable, improving a highway to two lanes so travelers can safely pass each other.

(5) The safety standards established by the Department of Transportation in accordance with Section 72-6-102 apply to all determinations of safety on R.S. 2477 rights-of-way used for vehicular travel.   2003

72-5-303. Maintenance — Impact on adjacent land owners.

(1) (a) The state and its political subdivisions are not required to maintain highways within R.S. 2477 rights-of-way for vehicular travel unless the R.S. 2477 right-of-way encompasses a highway included on a highway system for vehicular travel.

(b) A decision to improve or not improve an R.S. 2477 right-of-way is a purely discretionary function.

(2) The holder of an R.S. 2477 right-of-way and the owner of the servient estate shall exercise their rights without unreasonably interfering with one another.

(3) The holder of the R.S. 2477 right-of-way shall design and conduct construction and maintenance activities so as to minimize impacts on adjacent federal public lands, consistent with applicable safety standards.   1998

72-5-304. Mapping and survey requirements.

(1) The Department of Transportation, counties, and cities are not required to possess centerline surveys for R.S. 2477 rights-of-ways.

(2) To be accepted, highways within R.S. 2477 rights-of-way do not need to be included in the plats, descriptions, and maps of county roads required by Sections 72-3-105 and 72-3-107 or on the State Geographic Information Database, created in Section 63F-1-507, required to be maintained by Subsection (3).

(3) (a) The Automated Geographic Reference Center, created in Section 63F-1-506, shall create and maintain a record of R.S. 2477 rights-of-way on the Geographic Information Database.

(b) The record of R.S. 2477 rights-of-way shall be based on information maintained by the Department of Transportation and cartographic, topographic, photographic, historical, and other data available to or maintained by the Automated Geographic Reference Center.

(c) Agencies and political subdivisions of the state may provide additional information regarding R.S. 2477 rights-of-way when information is available.   2005

72-5-305. Term of grant — Abandonment.

(1) In accordance with the terms of the R.S. 2477 right-of-way grant, once accepted, an R.S. 2477 right-of-way is established for a perpetual term.

(2) (a) Abandonment of any R.S. 2477 right-of-way shall only take place in accordance with the procedures in Part 1, Public Highways, of this chapter.

(b) If any R.S. 2477 right-of-way is abandoned by a political subdivision of the state, the right-of-way shall revert to the state.

(3) The passage of time or the frequency of use of an R.S. 2477 right-of-way is not evidence of waiver or abandonment of the R.S. 2477 right-of-way.

(4) An R.S. 2477 right-of-way continues even if the servient estate is transferred out of the public domain.   1998

72-5-306. Assumption of risk — Immunity — Public safety.

(1) An R.S. 2477 right-of-way not designated under Section 72-3-102, 72-3-103, or 72-3-104 as a Class A, B, or C road is traveled at the risk of the user.

(2) The state and its political subdivisions do not waive immunity under Title 63, Chapter 30d, Governmental Immunity Act of Utah, for injuries or damages occurring in or associated with any R.S. 2477 right-of-way.

(3) The state and its political subdivisions assume no liability for injury or damage resulting from a failure to maintain any:

(a) R.S. 2477 right-of-way for vehicular travel; or

(b) highway sign on an R.S. 2477 right-of-way.

(4) If the state or any political subdivision of the state chooses to maintain an R.S. 2477 right-of-way, the basic governmental objective involved in providing the improvements is the consistent promotion of public safety.

(5) (a) The state recognizes that there are limited funds available to upgrade all R.S. 2477 rights-of-way to applicable safety standards.

(b) A decision by the state or a political subdivision of the state to allocate funds for maintaining an R.S. 2477 right-of-way is the result of evaluation and assigning of priorities for the promotion of public safety.

(c) The state or a political subdivision of the state must use its judgment and expertise to evaluate which safety feature improvements should be made first. In making this policy determination the state or a political subdivision of the state may:

(i) perform on-site inspections and weigh all factors relating to safety, including the physical characteristics and configuration of the R.S. 2477 right-of-way and the volume and type of traffic on the R.S. 2477 right-of-way; and

(ii) consult with transportation experts who have expertise to make an evaluation of the relative dangerousness of R.S. 2477 rights-of-way within their jurisdiction.   2005

72-5-307. Agreement affecting R.S. 2477 right-of-way.

(1) Before a political subdivision of the state enters into an agreement with the federal government affecting the rights, status, or scope of an R.S. 2477 right-of-way, the political subdivision shall give written notice of its intent to enter the agreement, together with a copy of the proposed final agreement, to the governing body of every county of the state through which the right-of-way extends.

(2) After receiving notice of the proposed agreement, the governing body of a county shall, within 60 days, give written notice to the political subdivision that:

(a) the county does not object to the proposed agreement; or

(b) the county objects to the proposed agreement.

(3) If the governing body of a county through which an R.S. 2477 right-of-way extends objects to a proposed agreement in accordance with Subsection (2), the political subdivision proposing to enter into the agreement may only enter into the agreement if it obtains declaratory relief from the district court. The relief shall be granted if the political subdivision shows by a preponderance of evidence that the proposed agreement does not materially affect the objecting county's interests.

(4) If the governing body of a county through which an R.S. 2477 right-of-way extends fails to object within 60 days after receiving notice, in accordance with Subsection (2), the county is considered not to have an objection.

(5) If a political subdivision fails to provide notice of a proposed agreement to a county as required by Subsection (1), the political subdivision is considered without authority to enter into the agreement, and the agreement is void.

(6) In accordance with the joint title provisions in Subsection 72-5-302(2), an agreement between a political subdivision of the state and the federal government may not affect the interests of the state regarding an R.S. 2477 right-of-way, unless the state is also a party to the agreement.

(7) This section does not affect an agreement made solely for the purpose of:

(a) maintenance, as defined under Section 72-5-301; or

(b) preserving safe travel of an R.S. 2477 right-of-way.   2001

72-5-308. Provisions govern determinations — Determinations effective dates.

The provisions of this part pertaining to substantive standards for acceptance of the R.S. 2477 grant shall govern the R.S. 2477 assessments of the governor or the governor's designee and the decisions of the courts to the extent that the provisions are consistent with state law, including common law, applicable as of the cut-off date.   2003

72-5-309. Acceptance of rights-of-way — Notice of acknowledgment required.

(1) The governor or the governor's designee may assess whether the grant of the R.S. 2477 has been accepted with regard to any right-of-way so as to vest title of the right-of-way in the state and the applicable subdivision as provided for in Section 72-5-103.

(2) If the governor or governor's designee concludes that the grant has been accepted as to any right-of-way, the governor or a designee shall issue a notice of acknowledgment of the acceptance of the R.S. 2477 grant as to that right-of-way.

(3) A notice of acknowledgment of the R.S. 2477 grant shall include:

(a) a statement of reasons for the acknowledgment;

(b) a general description of the right-of-way or rights-of-way subject to the notice of acknowledgment, including the county in which it is located, and notice of where a full legal description may be viewed or obtained;

(c) a statement that the owner of the servient estate in the land over which the right-of-way subject to the notice runs may file an action in district court for a decision regarding the correctness or incorrectness of the acknowledgment; and

(d) a statement of the time limit provided in Section 72-5-310 for filing an appeal.

(4) (a) A notice of acknowledgment may be recorded in the office of the county recorder in the county where the right-of-way or rights-of-way exist.

(b) A notice of acknowledgment recorded in the county recorder's office is conclusive evidence of acceptance of the R.S. 2477 grant upon:

(i) expiration of the 60-day period for filing an action under Section 72-5-310 without the filing of an action; or

(ii) a final court decision that the notice of acknowledgment was not incorrect.   2003

72-5-310. Notice of acknowledgment — Court determination — Presumption of acceptance.

(1) The governor or his designee shall provide a copy of the notice of acknowledgement by certified mail and return receipt requested to the owner of the servient estate in land over which a notice of acknowledgment runs.

(2) (a) A person with a servient estate or dominant estate ownership claim to the right-of-way may petition for a decision of the district court as to the correctness of the acknowledgment of acceptance of the R.S. 2477 grant issued under Section 72-5-309.

(b) Venue for the court action shall be the district court for Salt Lake County.

(c) The petition shall be filed no later than 60 days after the date of the notice of acknowledgment.

(d) The state, through the governor or the governor's designee, shall be named as a respondent and served with a copy of the petition in accordance with the Utah Rules of Civil Procedure.

(e) No one other than a person with a servient estate or dominant estate claim to the right-of-way may challenge the correctness of a notice of acknowledgment.

(3) The petition for a court decision of the correctness of the notice of acknowledgment shall be a complaint governed by the Utah Rules of Civil Procedure and shall contain:

(a) the petitioner's name and mailing address;

(b) a copy of the notice of acknowledgment the petitioner asserts is incorrect;

(c) a request for relief specifying the type and extent of relief requested; and

(d) a statement of the reasons why the petitioner is entitled to relief.

(4) Except as provided under this Part 3, all pleadings and proceedings to determine the correctness of a notice of acknowledgment in the district court are governed by the Utah Rules of Civil Procedure.

(5) The court shall make its decision without deference to the notice of acknowledgment.

(6) (a) In accordance with Section 72-5-302, a rebuttable presumption that the R.S. 2477 grant has been accepted is created when:

(i) a highway existed on public lands not reserved for public uses as of the cut-off date under Section 72-5-301; and

(ii) the highway currently exists in a condition suitable for public use.

(b) The proponent of the R.S. 2477 status of the highway bears the burden of proving acceptance of the grant by a preponderance of the evidence for all decisions that are not subject to Subsection (6)(a).   2003

PART 4

TRANSPORTATION CORRIDOR PRESERVATION

72-5-401. Definitions.

As used in this part:

(1) "Corridor" means the path or proposed path of a transportation facility that exists or that may exist in the future. A corridor may include the land occupied or to be occupied by a transportation facility, and any other land that may be needed for expanding a transportation facility or for controlling access to it.

(2) "Corridor preservation" means planning or acquisition processes intended to:

(a) protect or enhance the capacity of existing corridors; and

(b) protect the availability of proposed corridors in advance of the need for and the actual commencement of the transportation facility construction.

(3) "Development" means:

(a) the subdividing of land;

(b) the construction of improvements, expansions, or additions; or

(c) any other action that will appreciably increase the value of and the future acquisition cost of land.

(4) "Official map" means a map, drawn by government authorities and recorded in county recording offices that:

(a) shows actual and proposed rights-of-way, centerline alignments, and setbacks for highways and other transportation facilities;

(b) provides a basis for restricting development in designated rights-of-way or between designated setbacks to allow the government authorities time to purchase or otherwise reserve the land; and

(c) for counties and municipalities may be adopted as an element of the general plan, pursuant to Title 17, Chapter 27a, Part 4, General Plan, or Title 10, Chapter 9a, Part 4, General Plan.

(5) "Taking" means an act or regulation, either by exercise of eminent domain or other police power, whereby government puts private property to public use or restrains use of private property for public purposes, and that requires compensation to be paid to private property owners.   2005

72-5-402. Public purpose.

(1) The Legislature finds and declares that the planning and preservation of transportation corridors is a public purpose, that the acquisition of public rights in private property for possible use as a transportation corridor years in advance is a public purpose, and that acquisition of public rights in private property for possible use as alternative transportation corridors is a public purpose, even if one or more of the transportation corridors is eventually not used for a public purpose, so long as reasonable evidence exists at the time of acquisition that the transportation facility will be developed within the time period established under this part.

(2) The Legislature finds and declares that the acquisition of private property rights for the preservation of transportation corridors should be done on a voluntary basis and not by the use of eminent domain powers.   2003

72-5-403. Transportation corridor preservation powers.

(1) The department, counties, and municipalities may:

(a) act in cooperation with one another and other government entities to promote planning for and enhance the preservation of transportation corridors and to more effectively use the monies available in the Transportation Corridor Preservation Revolving Loan Fund created in Section 72-2-117;

(b) undertake transportation corridor planning, review, and preservation processes; and

(c) acquire fee simple rights and other rights of less than fee simple, including easement and development rights, or the rights to limit development, including rights in alternative transportation corridors, and to make these acquisitions

up to a projected 30 years in advance of using those rights in actual transportation facility construction.

(2) In addition to the powers described under Subsection (1), counties and municipalities may:

(a) limit development for transportation corridor preservation by land use regulation and by official maps; and

(b) by ordinance prescribe procedures for approving limited development in transportation corridors until the time transportation facility construction begins.   2003

72-5-404. Disposition of excess property rights.

If the department has acquired property rights in land in proposed transportation corridors, and some or all of that land is eventually not used for the proposed transportation corridors, the department shall dispose of the property rights in accordance with the provisions of Section 78-34-20.   2003

72-5-405. Private owner rights.

(1) The department, counties, and municipalities shall observe all protections conferred on private property rights, including Title 63, Chapter 90, Private Property Protection Act, Title 63, Chapter 90a, Constitutional Taking Issues, and compensation for takings.

(2) Private property owners from whom less than fee simple rights are obtained for transportation corridors or transportation corridor preservation have the right to petition the department, a county, or a municipality to acquire the entire fee simple interest in the affected property.

(3) (a) A private property owner whose property's development is limited or restricted by a power granted under this part may petition the county or municipality that adopted the official map to acquire less than or the entire fee simple interest in the affected property, at the option of the property owner.

(b) If the county or municipality petitioned under Subsection (3)(a) does not acquire the interest in the property requested by the property owner, then the county or municipality may not exercise any of the powers granted under this part to limit or restrict the affected property's development.   2000

72-5-406. Rulemaking.

In accordance with Title 63, Chapter 46a, Utah Administrative Rulemaking Act, the department shall make rules providing for private property owner petition procedures described in Section 72-5-405.   2000

CHAPTER 6

CONSTRUCTION, MAINTENANCE, AND OPERATIONS

72-6-101. Title.

This chapter is known as the "Construction, Maintenance, and Operations Act." 1998

72-6-102. Uniform plans and specifications for construction and maintenance.

The department shall:

(1) prepare and adopt uniform standard plans and specifications for the construction and maintenance of state highways; and

(2) issue a manual containing plans and specifications for the information and guidance of officials having supervision of the construction and maintenance of state highways. 1998

72-6-103. Plans, specifications, and estimates for culverts, bridges, and road construction.

The department shall furnish plans, specifications, and estimates for culverts, bridges, road construction, and other related information desired by local highway authorities for use on county roads and city streets on terms mutually agreed upon. 1998

72-6-104. Highways to conform to grade and direction in municipalities.

Except for the highways part of the interstate system, a highway that extends through a municipality shall conform to the direction and grade of other streets in the municipality unless permission is obtained from the highway authorities of the municipality for a variance in the direction and grade. 1998

72-6-105. Contracts for construction and maintenance — Agreements with county or municipality.

The department may enter into written agreements on behalf of the state with any county or municipality for rights-of-way and the construction or maintenance of any part of a state highway:

(1) at the expense of the state;

(2) at the expense of any county or municipality; or

(3) at the joint expense of the state and any county and any municipality. 1998

72-6-106. Use of recycled asphalt.

(1) In making plans, specifications, and estimates, and in advertising for bids under this chapter, the department shall allow up to 25% but may allow up to 60% reclaimed asphalt pavement to be incorporated into hot asphaltic concrete used for road construction and maintenance.

(2) The department shall ensure that hot asphaltic concrete incorporating reclaimed asphalt pavement meets or exceeds the department quality standards for roads constructed or maintained with hot asphaltic concrete not containing reclaimed asphalt pavement.

(3) If the department rejects any hot asphaltic concrete containing reclaimed asphalt pavement, the department shall give a written statement to the provider indicating the specific reasons the hot asphaltic concrete was rejected.

(4) This section does not authorize the state to directly or indirectly subsidize the production of hot asphaltic concrete containing reclaimed asphalt pavement. 1998

72-6-107. Construction or improvement of highway — Contracts — Retainage.

(1) (a) The department shall make plans, specifications, and estimates prior to the construction or improvement of any state highway.

(b) Except as provided in Section 63-56-502 and except for construction or improvements performed with state prison labor, a construction or improvement project with an estimated cost exceeding the bid limit as defined in Section 72-6-109 for labor and materials shall be performed under contract awarded to the lowest responsible bidder.

(c) The advertisement for bids shall be published in a newspaper of general circulation in the county in which the work is to be performed, at least once a week for two consecutive weeks, with the last publication at least ten days before bids are opened.

(d) The department shall receive sealed bids and open the bids at the time and place designated in the advertisement. The department may then award the contract but may reject any and all bids.

(e) If the department's estimates are substantially lower than any responsible bid received, the department may perform any work by force account.

(2) If any payment on a contract with a private contractor for construction or improvement of a state highway is retained or withheld, the payment shall be retained or withheld and released as provided in Section 13-8-5.

(3) If the department performs a construction or improvement project by force account, the department shall:

(a) provide an accounting of the costs and expenditures of the improvement including material and labor;

(b) disclose the costs and expenditures to any person upon request and allow the person to make a copy and pay for the actual cost of the copy; and

(c) perform the work using the same specifications and standards that would apply to a private contractor.

(4) In accordance with Title 63, Chapter 46a, Utah Administrative Rulemaking Act, the department shall establish procedures for:

(a) hearing evidence that a region within the department violated this section; and

(b) administering sanctions against the region if the region is found in violation.   2005

72-6-108. Class B and C roads — Improvement projects — Contracts — Retainage.

(1) A county executive for class B roads and the municipal executive for class C roads shall cause plans, specifications, and estimates to be made prior to the construction of any improvement project, as defined in Section 72-6-109, on a class B or C road if the estimated cost for any one project exceeds the bid limit as defined in Section 72-6-109 for labor, equipment, and materials.

(2) (a) All projects in excess of the bid limit shall be performed under contract to be let to the lowest responsible bidder.

(b) If the estimated cost of the improvement project exceeds the bid limit for labor, equipment, and materials, the project may not be divided to permit the construction in parts, unless each part is done by contract.

(3) The advertisement on bids shall be published in a newspaper of general circulation in the county in which the work is to be performed at least once a week for three consecutive weeks. If there is no newspaper of general circulation, the notice shall be posted for at least 20 days in at least five public places in the county.

(4) The county or municipal executive or their designee shall receive sealed bids and open the bids at the time and place designated in the advertisement. The county or municipal executive or their designee may then award the contract but may reject any and all bids.

(5) The person, firm, or corporation that is awarded a contract under this section is subject to the provisions of Title 63, Chapter 56, Utah Procurement Code.

(6) If any payment on a contract with a private contractor for construction or improvement of a class B or C road is retained or withheld, the payment shall be retained or withheld and released as provided in Section 13-8-5.   1999

72-6-109. Class B and C roads — Construction and maintenance — Definitions — Estimates lower than bids — Accountability.

(1) As used in this section and Section 72-6-108:

(a) "Bid limit" means:

(i) for the year 2003, $125,000; and

(ii) for each year after 2003, the amount of the bid limit for the previous year, plus an amount calculated by multiplying the amount of the bid limit for the previous year by the lesser of 3% or the actual percent change in the Consumer Price Index during the previous calendar year.

(b) "Consumer Price Index" means the Consumer Price Index for All Urban Consumers as published by the Bureau of Labor Statistics of the United States Department of Labor.

(c) (i) "Construction" means the work that would apply to:

(A) any new roadbed either by addition to existing systems or relocation;

(B) resurfacing of existing roadways with more than two inches of bituminous pavement; or

(C) new structures or replacement of existing structures, except the replacement of drainage culverts.

(ii) "Construction" does not include maintenance, emergency repairs, or the installation of traffic control devices as described in Section 41-6a-301.

(d) "Improvement project" means construction and maintenance as defined in this section except for that maintenance excluded under Subsection (2).

(e) "Maintenance" means the keeping of a road facility in a safe and usable condition to which it was constructed or improved, and includes:

(i) the reworking of an existing surface by the application of up to and including two inches of bituminous pavement;

(ii) the installation or replacement of guardrails, seal coats, and culverts;

(iii) the grading or widening of an existing unpaved road or flattening of shoulders or side slopes to meet current width and safety standards; and

(iv) horizontal or vertical alignment changes necessary to bring an existing road in compliance with current safety standards.

(f) "Project" means the performance of a clearly identifiable group of associated road construction activities or the same type of maintenance process, where the construction or maintenance is performed on any one class B or C road, within a half-mile proximity and occurs within the same calendar year.

(2) The following types of maintenance work are not subject to the contract or bid limit requirements of this section:

(a) the repair of less than the entire surface by crack sealing or patching; and

(b) road repairs incidental to the installation, replacement, or repair of water mains, sewers, drainage pipes, culverts, or curbs and gutters.

(3) (a) (i) If the estimates of a qualified engineer referred to in Section 72-6-108 are substantially lower than any responsible bid received or in the event no bids are received, the county or municipality may perform the work by force account.

(ii) In no event shall "substantially lower" mean estimates that are less than 10% below the lowest responsible bid.

(b) If a county or municipality performs an improvement project by force account, it shall:

(i) provide an accounting of the costs and expenditures of the improvement including material, labor, and direct equipment costs to be calculated using the Cost Reference Guide for Construction Equipment by Dataquest Inc.;

(ii) disclose the costs and expenditures to any person upon request and allow the person to make a copy and pay for the actual cost of the copy; and

(iii) perform the work using the same specifications and standards that would apply to a private contractor.   2005

72-6-110. Supervision and standards of construction for class B and C roads.

(1) All construction plans, specifications, and estimates and all construction work under Section 72-6-108 shall be prepared and performed under the direct supervision of a registered professional engineer.

(2) The supervising engineer shall certify to the county legislative body or the municipal executive that all road construction projects conform to design and construction standards as currently adopted by the American Association of State Highway and Transportation officials.   1998

72-6-111. Construction and maintenance of appurtenances — Noise abatement measures.

(1) The department is authorized to construct and maintain appurtenances along the state highway system necessary for public safety, welfare, and information. Appurtenances include highway illumination, sidewalks, curbs, gutters, steps, driveways, retaining walls, fire hydrants, guard rails, noise abatement measures, storm sewers, and rest areas.

(2) A noise abatement measure may only be constructed by the department along a highway when:

(a) the department is constructing a new state highway or performing major reconstruction on an existing state highway;

(b) the Legislature provides an appropriation or the federal government provides funding for construction of retrofit noise abatement along an existing state highway; or

(c) the cost for the noise abatement measure is provided by citizens, adjacent property owners, developers, or local governments.

(3) In addition to the requirements under Subsection (2), the department may only construct noise abatement measures within the unincorporated area of a county or within a municipality that has an ordinance or general plan that requires:

(a) a study to be conducted to determine the noise levels along new development adjacent to an existing state highway or a dedicated right-of-way; and

(b) the construction of noise abatement measures at the expense of the developer if required to be constructed under standards established by a rule of the department.

(4) In accordance with Title 63, Chapter 46a, Utah Administrative Rulemaking Act, the department shall make rules establishing:

(a) when noise abatement measures are required to be constructed, including standards for decibel levels of traffic noise;

(b) the decibel level of traffic noise which identifies the projects to be programmed by the commission for the earliest construction of retrofit noise abatement measures funded under Subsection (2)(b) based on availability of funding; and

(c) a priority system for the construction of other retrofit noise abatement measures that meet or exceed the standards established under this section and are funded under Subsection (2)(b) which includes:

(i) the number of residential dwellings adversely affected by the traffic noise;

(ii) the cost effectiveness of mitigating the traffic noise; and

(iii) the length of time the decibel level of traffic noise has met or exceeded the standards established under this section.   1998

72-6-112. Traffic Noise Abatement Program — Uses.

(1) There is created the Traffic Noise Abatement Program.

(2) The program consists of monies generated from the following revenue sources:

(a) any voluntary contributions received for traffic noise abatement; and

(b) appropriations made to the program by the Legislature.

(3) The department shall use program monies as prioritized by the commission and as provided by law for the study, design, construction, and maintenance of noise abatement measures.

(4) All funding for the Traffic Noise Abatement Program shall be nonlapsing.   1998

72-6-113. Acquisition and improvement of land for preservation of scenic beauty — Authority of department.

(1) The department is authorized to acquire and improve strips of land necessary for the restoration, preservation, and enhancement of scenic beauty within and adjacent to a federal-aid highway of this state, including acquisition of publicly owned and controlled rest and recreation areas, sanitary, and other facilities within or adjacent to the highway right-of-way reasonably necessary to accommodate the traveling public.

(2) Acquisition may be by gift, purchase, or exchange but may not be by condemnation.

(3) The interest in any land authorized to be acquired and maintained under this section may be fee simple or any lesser interest, as determined by the department to be reasonably necessary to accomplish the purposes of this section.

(4) (a) Real property, or any interest in real property, acquired under this section is part of the adjacent or nearest highway and is under the jurisdiction of the department.

(b) The department may enter into an agreement with any state agency for maintenance of land acquired in accordance with this section.   1998

72-6-114. Restricting use of or closing highway — Penalty for failure to observe barricade, warning light, etc.

(1) A highway authority may close or restrict travel on a highway under their jurisdiction due to construction, maintenance work, or emergency.

(2) If a highway or portion of a highway is closed or restricted to travel, a highway authority shall cause suitable barriers and notices to be posted and maintained in accordance with Section 41-6a-301.

(3) A person who willfully fails to observe any barricade, warning light, sign, or flagman, used in accordance with this section, is guilty of a class B misdemeanor.   2005

72-6-115. Traffic Management Committee — Appointment — Duties.

(1) As used in this section, "committee" means the Traffic Management Committee created in this section.

(2) (a) There is created within the Department of Transportation the Traffic Management Commit-

tee comprising up to 13 members knowledgeable about traffic engineering, traffic flow, air quality, or intelligent transportation systems as follows:

(i) two members designated by the executive director of the department;

(ii) one member designated by the Utah Association of Counties;

(iii) one member designated by the Department of Environmental Quality;

(iv) one member designated by the Wasatch Front Regional Council;

(v) one member designated by the Mountainland Association of Governments;

(vi) one member designated by the Commissioner of Public Safety; and

(vii) one member designated by the Utah League of Cities and Towns;

(viii) one member designated by the general manager of a public transit district with more than 200,000 people residing within the public transit district boundaries;

(ix) up to four additional members designated by the committee for one-year terms; and

(x) a designating entity under Subsections (2)(a)(i) through (viii) may designate an alternative member to serve in the absence of its designated member.

(b) The committee shall:

(i) advise the department on matters related to the implementation and administration of this section;

(ii) make recommendations to law enforcement agencies related to traffic flow and incident management during heavy traffic periods;

(iii) make recommendations to the department, counties, and municipalities on increasing the safety and efficiency of highways using current traffic management systems, including traffic signal coordination, traffic monitoring, freeway ramp metering, variable message signing, and incident management; and

(iv) evaluate the cost effectiveness of implementing a specific traffic management system on a highway considering:

(A) existing traffic volume in the area;

(B) the necessity and potential of reducing vehicle emissions in the area;

(C) the feasibility of the traffic management system on the highway; and

(D) whether traffic congestion will be reduced by the system.

(c) The committee shall annually elect a chair and a vice chair from its members.

(d) When a vacancy occurs in the membership for any reason, the replacement shall be appointed.

(e) The committee shall meet as it determines necessary to accomplish its duties.

(f) Reasonable notice shall be given to each member of the committee prior to any meeting.

(g) A majority of the committee constitutes a quorum for the transaction of business.

(h) (i) (A) Members who are not government employees shall receive no compensation or benefits for their services, but may receive per diem and expenses incurred in the performance of the member's official duties at the rates established by the

Division of Finance under Sections 63A-3-106 and 63A-3-107.

(B) Members may decline to receive per diem and expenses for their service.

(ii) (A) State government officer and employee members who do not receive salary, per diem, or expenses from their agency for their service may receive per diem and expenses incurred in the performance of their official duties from the committee at the rates established by the Division of Finance under Sections 63A-3-106 and 63A-3-107.

(B) State government officer and employee members may decline to receive per diem and expenses for their service.

(iii) (A) Local government members who do not receive salary, per diem, or expenses from the entity that they represent for their service may receive per diem and expenses incurred in the performance of their official duties at the rates established by the Division of Finance under Sections 63A-3-106 and 63A-3-107.

(B) Local government members may decline to receive per diem and expenses for their service.

(3) (a) The Department of Transportation shall implement and administer traffic management systems to facilitate the efficient flow of motor vehicle traffic on state highways to improve regional mobility, and to reduce motor vehicle emissions where those improvements are cost effective, as determined by the committee in accordance with criteria under Subsection (2)(b).

(b) A traffic management system shall be designed to allow safe, efficient, and effective:

(i) integration of existing traffic management systems;

(ii) additions of highways and intersections under county and city administrative jurisdiction;

(iii) incorporation of other traffic management systems; and

(iv) adaptation to future traffic needs.

(4) (a) The cost of implementing and administering a traffic management system shall be shared pro rata by the department and the counties and municipalities using it.

(b) The department shall enter into an agreement or contract under Title 11, Chapter 13, Interlocal Cooperation Act, with a county or municipality to share costs incurred under this section.

(5) Additional highways and intersections under the administrative jurisdiction of a county or municipality may be added to a traffic management system upon application of the county or municipality after:

(a) a recommendation of the committee;

(b) approval by the department;

(c) determination of the appropriate cost share of the addition under Subsection (4)(a); and

(d) an agreement under Subsection (4)(b).

(6) The committee may establish technical advisory committees as needed to assist in accomplishing its duties under this section.   2001

72-6-116. Regulation of utilities — Relocation of utilities.

(1) As used in this section:

(a) "Cost of relocation" includes the entire amount paid by the utility company properly attributable to the relocation of the utility after deducting any increase in the value of the new utility and any salvage value derived from the old utility.

(b) "Utility" includes telecommunication, gas, electricity, cable television, water, sewer, data, and video transmission lines, drainage and irrigation systems, and other similar utilities located in, on, along, across, over, through, or under any state highway.

(c) "Utility company" means a privately, cooperatively, or publicly owned utility, including utilities owned by political subdivisions.

(2) (a) In accordance with Title 63, Chapter 46a, Utah Administrative Rulemaking Act, the department may make rules for the installation, construction, maintenance, repair, renewal, system upgrade, and relocation of all utilities.

(b) If the department determines under the rules established in this section that it is necessary that any utilities should be relocated, the utility company owning or operating the utilities shall relocate the utilities in accordance with this section and the order of the department.

(3) (a) The department shall pay 100% of the cost of relocation of a utility on a state highway if the:

(i) utility is owned or operated by a political subdivision of the state; or

(ii) utility company owns the easement or fee title to the right-of-way in which the utility is located.

(b) Except as provided in Subsection (3)(a) or (c), the department shall pay 50% of the cost of relocation of a utility on a state highway and the utility company shall pay the remainder of the cost of relocation.

(c) This Subsection (3) does not affect the provisions of Subsection 72-7-108(5).

(4) If a utility is relocated, the utility company owning or operating the utility, its successors or assigns, may maintain and operate the utility, with the necessary appurtenances, in the new location.

(5) In accordance with this section, the cost of relocating a utility in connection with any project on a highway is a cost of highway construction.

(6) (a) The department shall notify affected utility companies whenever the relocation of utilities is likely to be necessary because of a reconstruction project.

(b) The notification shall be made during the preliminary design of the project or as soon as practical in order to minimize the number, costs, and delays of utility relocations.

(c) A utility company notified under this Subsection (6) shall coordinate with the department and the department's contractor on the utility relocations, including the scheduling of the utility relocations. 2000

72-6-117. Limited-access facilities and service roads — Access — Right-of-way acquisition — Grade separation — Written permission required.

(1) A highway authority, acting alone or in cooperation with the federal government, another highway authority, or another state may plan, designate, establish, regulate, vacate, alter, improve, maintain, and provide a limited-access facility including a service road to the limited-access facility.

(2) A highway authority may regulate, restrict, or prohibit the use of a limited-access facility by pedestrians, animals, or by the various classes of vehicles or traffic.

(3) A highway authority may divide and separate any limited-access facility into separate roadways by the construction of raised curbing, central dividing sections, or other physical separations, or by designating separate roadways by signs, markers, stripes, and other appropriate devices.

(4) A person may not enter, exit, or cross a limited-access facility, except at designated points at which access is permitted by the highway authority.

(5) A highway authority may acquire, by gift, devise, purchase, or condemnation, private or public property and property rights for a limited-access facility and service road, including rights of access, air, view, and light. All property rights acquired under this section may be in fee simple or in any lesser estate or interest. A highway authority may acquire an entire lot, block, or tract of land, if needed, even though the entire lot, block, or tract is not immediately needed for the right-of-way of the limited-access facility or service road.

(6) A highway authority may designate and establish limited-access highways as new facilities or may designate and establish an existing highway as part of a limited-access facility.

(7) (a) A highway authority may provide for the elimination of at grade intersections of a limited-access facility and an existing highway by grade separation, service road, or by closing the intersecting highway.

(b) A highway authority may not connect or intersect a limited-access facility without the written consent and previous approval of the highway authority having jurisdiction over the limited-access facility.

(8) Highway authorities may enter into agreements with each other, or with the federal government, on the financing, planning, establishment, improvement, maintenance, use, regulation, or vacation of limited-access facilities or other public ways in their respective jurisdiction, to facilitate the purposes of this section. 1998

72-6-118. Definitions — Establishment and operation of tollways — Imposition and collection of tolls — Amount of tolls — Rulemaking.

(1) As used in this section:

(a) "High occupancy toll lane" means a high occupancy vehicle lane designated under Section 41-6a-702 that may be used by an operator of a vehicle carrying less than the number of persons specified for the high occupancy vehicle lane if the operator of the vehicle pays a toll or fee.

(b) "Toll" means any tax, fee, or charge assessed for the specific use of a tollway.

(c) "Toll lane" means a designated new highway or additional lane capacity that is constructed, operated, or maintained for which a toll is charged for its use.

(d) (i) "Tollway" means a highway, highway lane, bridge, path, tunnel, or right-of-way designed and used as a transportation route that is constructed, operated, or maintained through the use of toll revenues.

(ii) "Tollway" includes a high occupancy toll lane and a toll lane.

(2) Subject to the provisions of Subsection (3), the department may:

(a) establish and operate tollways and related facilities for the purpose of funding in whole or in part the acquisition of right-of-way and the design, construction, reconstruction, operation, enforcement, and maintenance of or impacts from a transportation route for use by the public;

(b) enter into contracts, agreements, licenses, franchises, or other arrangements to implement this section; and

(c) impose and collect tolls on any tollway established under this section.

(3) (a) Except as provided under Subsection (3)(d), the department or other entity may not establish or operate a tollway on an existing state highway, except as approved by the commission and the Legislature.

(b) Between sessions of the Legislature, a state tollway may be designated or deleted if:

(i) approved by the commission in accordance with the standards made under this section; and

(ii) the tollways are submitted to the Legislature in the next year for legislative approval or disapproval.

(c) In conjunction with a proposal submitted under Subsection (3)(b)(ii), the department shall provide a description of the tollway project, projected traffic, the anticipated amount of tolls to be charged, and projected toll revenue.

(d) If approved by the commission, the department may:

(i) establish high occupancy toll lanes on existing state highways; and

(ii) establish tollways on new state highways or additional capacity lanes.

(4) In accordance with Title 63, Chapter 46a, Utah Administrative Rulemaking Act, the commission shall set the amount of any toll imposed or collected on a tollway on a state highway.

(5) (a) In accordance with Title 63, Chapter 46a, Utah Administrative Rulemaking Act, the department shall make rules:

(i) necessary to establish and operate tollways on state highways; and

(ii) that establish standards and specifications for automatic tolling systems.

(b) The rules shall:

(i) include minimum criteria for having a tollway; and

(ii) conform to regional and national standards for automatic tolling.

(6) (a) The commission may provide funds for public or private tollway pilot projects or high occupancy toll lanes from General Fund monies appropriated by the Legislature to the commission for that purpose.

(b) The commission may determine priorities and funding levels for tollways designated under this section.

(7) All revenue generated from a tollway on a state highway shall be deposited into the Tollway Restricted Account created in Section 72-2-120 and used for acquisition of right-of-way and the design, construction, reconstruction, operation, maintenance, and enforcement of transportation facilities within the corridor served by the tollway.   2005

72-6-119. "511" traveler information services — Lead agency — Implementation — Cooperation — Rulemaking — Costs.

(1) As used in this section, "511" or "511 service" means three-digit telecommunications dialing to access intelligent transportation system — traveler information service provided in the state in accordance with the Federal Communications Commission and United States Department of Transportation.

(2) The department is the state's lead agency for implementing 511 service and is the state's point of contact for coordinating 511 service with telecommunications service providers.

(3) The department shall:

(a) implement and administer 511 service in the state;

(b) coordinate with the highway authorities and public transit districts to provide advanced multimodal traveler information through 511 service and other means; and

(c) in accordance with Title 63, Chapter 46a, Utah Administrative Rulemaking Act, make rules as necessary to implement this section.

(4) (a) In accordance with Title 11, Chapter 13, Interlocal Cooperation Act, the department shall enter into agreements or contracts with highway authorities and public transit districts to share the costs of implementing and administering 511 service in the state.

(b) The department shall enter into other agreements or contracts relating to the 511 service to offset the costs of implementing and administering 511 service in the state.   2001

CHAPTER 7

PROTECTION OF HIGHWAYS

Part 1

Protection of Rights-of-Way

Part 2

Junkyard Control Act

PART 1

PROTECTION OF RIGHTS-OF-WAY

72-7-101. Title.

This chapter is known as the "Protection of Highways Act." 1998

72-7-102. Excavations, structures, or objects prohibited within right-of-way except in accordance with law — Permit and fee requirements — Rulemaking — Penalty for violation.

(1) As used in this section, "management costs" means the reasonable, direct, and actual costs a highway authority incurs in exercising authority over the highways under its jurisdiction.

(2) Except as provided in Subsection (3) and Section 54-4-15, a person may not:

(a) dig or excavate, within the right-of-way of any state highway, county road, or city street; or

(b) place, construct, or maintain any approach road, driveway, pole, pipeline, conduit, sewer, ditch, culvert, billboard, advertising sign, or any other structure or object of any kind or character within the right-of-way.

(3) (a) A highway authority having jurisdiction over the right-of-way may allow excavating, installation of utilities and other facilities or access under rules made by the highway authority and

in compliance with federal, state, and local law as applicable.

    (b) (i) The rules may require a permit for any excavation or installation and may require a surety bond or other security.

    (ii) The application for a permit for excavation or installation on a state highway shall be accompanied by a fee established under Subsection (4)(f).

    (iii) The permit may be revoked and the surety bond or other security may be forfeited for cause.

(4) (a) Except as provided in Section 72-7-108 with respect to the department concerning the interstate highway system, a highway authority may require compensation from a utility service provider for access to the right-of-way of a highway only as provided in this section.

    (b) A highway authority may recover from a utility service provider, only those management costs caused by the utility service provider's activities in the right-of-way of a highway under the jurisdiction of the highway authority.

    (c) (i) A fee or other compensation under this Subsection (4) shall be imposed on a competitively neutral basis.

    (ii) If a highway authority's management costs cannot be attributed to only one entity, the management costs shall be allocated among all privately owned and government agencies using the highway right-of-way for utility service purposes, including the highway authority itself. The allocation shall reflect proportionately the management costs incurred by the highway authority as a result of the various utility uses of the highway.

    (d) A highway authority may not use the compensation authority granted under this Subsection (4) as a basis for generating revenue for the highway authority that is in addition to its management costs.

    (e) (i) A utility service provider that is assessed management costs or a franchise fee by a highway authority is entitled to recover those management costs.

    (ii) If the highway authority that assesses the management costs or franchise fees is a political subdivision of the state and the utility service provider serves customers within the boundaries of that highway authority, the management costs may be recovered from those customers.

    (f) In accordance with Title 63, Chapter 46a, Utah Administrative Rulemaking Act, the department shall adopt a schedule of fees to be assessed for management costs incurred in connection with issuing and administering a permit on a state highway under this section.

    (g) In addition to the requirements of this Subsection (4), a telecommunications tax or fee imposed by a municipality on a telecommunications provider, as defined in Section 10-1-402, is subject to Section 10-1-406.

(5) Permit fees collected by the department under this section shall be deposited with the state treasurer and credited to the Transportation Fund.

(6) Nothing in this section shall affect the authority of a municipality under:

    (a) Section 10-1-203;

    (b) Section 11-26-1;

    (c) Title 10, Chapter 1, Part 3, Municipal Energy Sales and Use Tax Act; or

    (d) Title 10, Chapter 1, Part 4, Municipal Telecommunications License Tax Act.

(7) A person who violates the provisions of Subsection (2) is guilty of a class B misdemeanor.   2003

72-7-103. Limitation on access authority.

A highway authority may not deny reasonable ingress and egress to property adjoining a public highway except where:

    (1) the highway authority acquires right of ingress and egress by gift, agreement, purchase, eminent domain, or otherwise; or

    (2) no right of ingress or egress exists between the right-of-way and the adjoining property.   1998

72-7-104. Installations constructed in violation of rules — Rights of highway authorities to remove or require removal.

(1) If any person, firm, or corporation installs, places, constructs, alters, repairs, or maintains any approach road, driveway, pole, pipeline, conduit, sewer, ditch, culvert, outdoor advertising sign, or any other structure or object of any kind or character within the right-of-way of any highway without complying with this title, the highway authority having jurisdiction over the right-of-way may:

    (a) remove the installation from the right-of-way or require the person, firm, or corporation to remove the installation; or

    (b) give written notice to the person, firm, or corporation to remove the installation from the right-of-way.

(2) Notice under Subsection (1)(b) may be served by:

    (a) personal service; or

    (b) (i) mailing the notice to the person, firm, or corporation by certified mail; and

    (ii) posting a copy on the installation for ten days.

(3) If the installation is not removed within ten days after the notice is complete, the highway authority may remove the installation at the expense of the person, firm, or corporation.

(4) A highway authority may recover:

    (a) the costs and expenses incurred in removing the installation, serving notice, and the costs of a lawsuit if any; and

    (b) $10 for each day the installation remained within the right-of-way after notice was complete.

(5) (a) If the person, firm, or corporation disputes or denies the existence, placement, construction, or maintenance of the installation, or refuses to remove or permit its removal, the highway authority may bring an action to abate the installation as a public nuisance.

    (b) If the highway authority is granted a judgment, the highway authority may recover the costs of having the public nuisance abated as provided in Subsection (4).

(6) The department, its agents, or employees, if acting in good faith, incur no liability for causing removal of an installation within a right-of-way of a highway as provided in this section.

(7) The actions of the department under this section are not subject to the provisions of Title 63, Chapter 46b, the Administrative Procedures Act.   1998

72-7-105. Obstructing traffic on sidewalks or highways prohibited.

(1) A person may not:

    (a) drive or place any vehicle, animal, or other thing upon or along any sidewalk except in crossing the sidewalk to or from abutting property; or

(b) permit the vehicle, animal, or other thing to remain on or across any sidewalk in a way that impedes or obstructs the ordinary use of the sidewalk.

(2) (a) Except under Subsection (2)(b), vehicles, building material, or other similar things may be placed temporarily on highways in a manner that will not impede, endanger, or obstruct ordinary traffic.

(b) A highway authority may prohibit or may require the removal of vehicles, building material, or other obstructions on any highway under their jurisdiction. 1998

72-7-106. Gates on class B and D roads.

(1) As used in this section, "county road" means:

(a) a class B road as defined in Section 72-3-103; and

(b) a class D road as defined in Section 72-3-105.

(2) The county executive of a county may authorize the erection or maintenance of a gate on a county road in order to avoid the necessity of building highway fences.

(3) The person for whose immediate benefit a gate is erected or maintained shall in all cases bear the expense.

(4) Nothing contained in Section 72-7-105 shall be construed to prohibit a person from placing an unlocked, nonrestrictive gate across a county road, or maintaining the same, with the authorization of the county executive of that county.

(5) (a) A gate is not allowed on a county road unless authorized by the county executive in accordance with the provisions of this section.

(b) If the expense of the erection and maintenance of the gate is not paid or if a lock or other device is placed upon the gate so as to make it restrictive, the county executive of that county shall notify the responsible party that county approval is terminated and the gate is considered to be an obstruction under Section 72-7-105.

(6) The placement or maintenance of a gate with the authorization of the county executive across a county road does not constitute or establish an abandonment under Section 72-5-105 or 72-5-305 by the county and does not establish an easement on behalf of the person establishing the gate.

(7) A person who commits any of the following acts is guilty of a class B misdemeanor and is liable for all damages suffered by a party as a result of the acts:

(a) leaves open a gate, erected or maintained under this section;

(b) unnecessarily drives over the ground adjoining the highway on which a gate is erected;

(c) places a lock or other restrictive device on a gate; or

(d) violates a rule or regulation of a county legislative body relating to the gates within the county. 2003

72-7-107. Public safety program signs — Permits.

(1) As used in this section, "public safety program sign" means a sign, placed on or adjacent to a highway, that is promoting a highway safety program or highway safety practice, or a crime or drug abuse prevention program that is being sponsored by the department, the Department of Public Safety, or a local law enforcement agency.

(2) In accordance with Title 63, Chapter 46a, Utah Administrative Rulemaking Act, the department shall make rules to allow public safety program signs on state highways by permit. The rules shall contain reasonable terms and conditions:

(a) that are no more restrictive than motorist service signing requirements of the Manual on Uniform Traffic Control Devices for Streets and Highways adopted under Section 41-6a-301; and

(b) for granting and maintaining a permit. 2005

72-7-108. Longitudinal telecommunication access in the interstate highway system — Definitions — Agreements — Compensation — Restrictions — Rulemaking.

(1) As used in this section:

(a) "Longitudinal access" means access to or use of any part of a right-of-way of a highway on the interstate system that extends generally parallel to the right-of-way for a total of 30 or more linear meters.

(b) "Statewide telecommunications purposes" means the further development of the statewide network that meets the telecommunications needs of state agencies and enhances the learning purposes of higher and public education.

(c) "Telecommunication facility" means any telecommunication cable, line, fiber, wire, conduit, innerduct, access manhole, handhole, tower, hut, pedestal, pole, box, transmitting equipment, receiving equipment, power equipment, or other equipment, system, and device used to transmit, receive, produce, or distribute via wireless, wireline, electronic, or optical signal for communication purposes.

(2) (a) Except as provided in Subsection (4), the department may allow a telecommunication facility provider longitudinal access to the right-of-way of a highway on the interstate system for the installation, operation, and maintenance of a telecommunication facility.

(b) The department shall enter into an agreement with a telecommunication facility provider and issue a permit before granting it any longitudinal access under this section.

(i) Except as specifically provided by the agreement, a property interest in a right-of-way may not be granted under the provisions of this section.

(ii) An agreement entered into by the department under this section shall:

(A) specify the terms and conditions for the renegotiation of the agreement;

(B) specify maintenance responsibilities for each telecommunication facility;

(C) be nonexclusive; and

(D) be limited to a maximum term of 30 years.

(3) (a) The department shall require compensation from a telecommunication facility provider under this section for longitudinal access to the right-of-way of a highway on the interstate system.

(b) The compensation charged shall be:

(i) fair and reasonable;

(ii) competitively neutral;

(iii) nondiscriminatory;

(iv) open to public inspection;

(v) established to promote access by multiple telecommunication facility providers;

(vi) established for zones of the state, with zones determined based upon factors that include population density, distance, numbers of telecommunication subscribers, and the impact upon private right-of-way users;

(vii) established to encourage the deployment of digital infrastructure within the state;

(viii) set after the department conducts a market analysis to determine the fair and reasonable values of the right-of-way based upon adjacent property values;

(ix) a lump sum payment or annual installment, at the option of the telecommunications facility provider; and

(x) set in accordance with Subsection (3)(f).

(c) (i) The compensation charged may be cash, in-kind compensation, or a combination of cash and in-kind compensation.

(ii) In-kind compensation requires the agreement of both the telecommunication facility provider and the department.

(iii) The department shall, in consultation with the Telecommunications Advisory Council created in Section 72-7-109, determine the present value of any in-kind compensation based upon the incremental cost to the telecommunication facility provider.

(iv) The value of in-kind compensation or a combination of cash and in-kind compensation shall be equal to or greater than the amount of cash compensation that would be charged if the compensation is cash only.

(d) (i) The department shall provide for the proportionate sharing of costs among the department and telecommunications providers for joint trenching or trench sharing based on the amount of conduit innerduct space that is authorized in the agreement for the trench.

(ii) If two or more telecommunications facility providers are required to share a single trench, each telecommunications facility provider in the trench shall share the cost and benefits of the trench in accordance with Subsection (3)(d)(i) on a fair, reasonable, competitively neutral, and nondiscriminatory basis.

(e) The market analysis under Subsection (3)(b)(viii) shall be conducted at least every five years and any adjustments warranted shall apply only to agreements entered after the date of the new market analysis.

(f) In accordance with Title 63, Chapter 46a, Utah Administrative Rulemaking Act, the department shall establish a schedule of rates of compensation for any longitudinal access granted under this section.

(4) The department may not grant any longitudinal access under this section that results in a significant compromise of the safe, efficient, and convenient use of the interstate system for the traveling public.

(5) The department may not pay any cost of relocation of a telecommunication facility granted longitudinal access to the right-of-way of a highway on the interstate system under this section.

(6) (a) Monetary compensation collected by the department in accordance with this section shall be deposited with the state treasurer and credited to the Transportation Fund.

(b) Any telecommunications capacity acquired as in-kind compensation shall be used:

(i) exclusively for statewide telecommunications purposes and may not be sold or leased in competition with telecommunication or Internet service providers; and

(ii) as determined by the department after consultation with the Telecommunications Advisory Council created in Section 72-7-109.

(7) In accordance with Title 63, Chapter 46a, Utah Administrative Rulemaking Act, the department shall make rules:

(a) governing the installation, operation, and maintenance of a telecommunication facility granted longitudinal access under this section;

(b) specifying the procedures for establishing an agreement for longitudinal access for a telecommunication facility provider;

(c) providing for the relocation or removal of a telecommunication facility for:

(i) needed changes to a highway on the interstate system;

(ii) expiration of an agreement; or

(iii) a breach of an agreement; and

(d) providing an opportunity for all interested providers to apply for access within open right-of-way segments.

(8) (a) Except for a right-of-way of a highway on the interstate system, nothing in this section shall be construed to allow a highway authority to require compensation from a telecommunication facility provider for longitudinal access to the right-of-way of a highway under the highway authority's jurisdiction.

(b) Nothing in this section shall affect the authority of a municipality under:

(i) Section 10-1-203;

(ii) Section 11-26-1;

(iii) Title 10, Chapter 1, Part 3, Municipal Energy Sales and Use Tax Act; or

(iv) Title 10, Chapter 1, Part 4, Municipal Telecommunications License Tax Act.

(9) Compensation paid to the department under Subsection (3) may not be used by any person as evidence of the market or other value of the access for any other purpose, including condemnation proceedings, other litigation, or the application of rates of taxation or the establishment of franchise fees relating to longitudinal access rights.   2003

72-7-109. Telecommunications Advisory Council — Membership — Duties.

(1) As used in this section:

(a) "Council" means the Telecommunications Advisory Council created in this section.

(b) "Statewide telecommunications purposes" has the same meaning provided in Section 72-7-108.

(2) (a) There is created within the department the Telecommunication Advisory Council consisting of six members who represent:

(i) the governor's chief advisor on telecommunications;

(ii) the Public Service Commission;

(iii) the department;

(iv) the Utah Education Network;

(v) the Division of Purchasing and General Services within the Department of Administrative Services; and

(vi) the Division of Public Utilities within the Department of Commerce.

(b) The members shall be appointed by the governor with the consent of the Senate.

(3) (a) The members shall annually elect a chair from its members.

(b) The council shall meet as it determines necessary to accomplish its duties.

(c) A majority of the council constitutes a quorum for the transaction of business.

(d) Members shall receive no compensation or benefits for their services.

(4) (a) The department shall provide staff support for the council.

(b) The council may request assistance from other technical advisors as it determines necessary to accomplish its duties.

(5) The council shall:

(a) provide information, suggestions, strategic plans, priorities, and recommendations to assist the department in administering telecommunications access to interstate highway rights-of-way for statewide telecommunications purposes;

(b) assist the department in valuing in-kind compensation in accordance with Subsection 72-7-108(3)(c);

(c) seek input from telecommunications providers and the public;

(d) coordinate and exchange information with other technology and telecommunications entities of the state and its political subdivisions; and

(e) provide other assistance as requested by the department.   2002

PART 2

JUNKYARD CONTROL ACT

72-7-201. Purpose.

The regulation of junkyards in areas adjacent to any state highway included in the national system of interstate and primary highways is a statewide public purpose and necessary to promote the public safety, health, welfare, convenience, and enjoyment of public travel, to protect the public investment in public highways, and to preserve and enhance the scenic beauty of lands bordering on the highways.   1998

72-7-202. Definitions.

As used in this part:

(1) "Automobile graveyard" means any establishment or place of business which is maintained, used, or operated for storing, keeping, buying, or selling wrecked, scrapped, ruined, or dismantled motor vehicles or motor vehicle parts.

(2) "Junk" means old or scrap copper, brass, rope, rags, batteries, plastic, paper, trash, rubber, waste, junked, dismantled, or wrecked automobiles or their parts, and iron, steel, and other old or scrap ferrous or nonferrous material.

(3) "Junkyard" means any place, establishment, or business maintained, used, or operated for storing, keeping, buying, or selling junk, or for the maintenance or operation of an automobile graveyard. Junkyard includes a salvage yard, war surplus yard, garbage dump, recycling facility, garbage processing facility, and sanitary land fill.   1998

72-7-203. License required.

(1) A person may not establish, operate, or maintain a junkyard, any portion of which is within 1,000 feet of the nearest edge of the right-of-way of any interstate or federal-aid primary highway, without obtaining a license from the department under this part.

(2) A municipality may adopt ordinances, not in conflict with this part, to regulate the creation or maintenance of junkyards of any type within 660 feet of the right-of-way of designated state and federal highways within the jurisdictional limits of the adopting municipality.

(3) In accordance with Title 63, Chapter 46a, Utah Administrative Rulemaking Act, the department may make rules, not in conflict with this part, to regulate the creation and maintenance of junkyards within 660 feet of the right-of-way of designated federal and state highways outside the jurisdictional limits of a municipality.   1998

72-7-204. Issuance of licenses — Fees — Duration — Renewal — Disposition of proceeds.

(1) The department has the sole authority to issue licenses for the establishment, maintenance, and operation of junkyards within the limits defined in Section 72-7-203, and shall charge a $10 license fee payable annually in advance.

(2) All licenses issued under this section expire on the first day of January following the date of issue. Licenses may be renewed from year to year upon payment of the requisite fee.

(3) Proceeds from the license fee shall be deposited with the state treasurer and credited to the Transportation Fund.   1999

72-7-205. Conditions for licensing of junkyard within 1,000 feet of highway.

(1) The department may not grant a license for the establishment, maintenance, or operation of a junkyard within 1,000 feet of the nearest edge of the right-of-way of any highway on the interstate or primary systems unless the junkyard is:

(a) screened by natural objects, plantings, fences, or other appropriate means so the junkyard is not visible from the main-traveled-way of the system; and

(b) (i) located within areas that are zoned for industrial use under county or municipal ordinances; or

(ii) located within unzoned industrial areas, determined by actual land uses as defined by rules made by the department in accordance with Title 63, Chapter 46a, Utah Administrative Rulemaking Act.

(2) A junkyard controlled by this part may not be expanded or have its use extended except by permission of the department under rules made by the department.   1998

72-7-206. Screening of existing junkyards.

(1) The department shall screen any junkyard lawfully in existence on May 9, 1967, which is located within 1,000 feet of the nearest edge of the right-of-way and visible from the main-traveled-way of any highway on the interstate or primary system.

(2) The screening shall be at locations on the right-of-way or in areas outside the right-of-way acquired for that purpose and may not be visible from the main-traveled-way of the interstate or federal-aid primary systems.

(3) The department may not install junkyard screening under this section unless:

(a) the necessary federal funds for participation have been appropriated by the federal government and are immediately available to the state; and

(b) the department has received approval to seek federal grants, loans, or participation in federal programs under Title 63, Chapter 38e, Federal Funds Procedures.   2004

72-7-207. Junkyards not adaptable to screening — Authority of department to acquire land — Compensation.

(1) If the department determines that the topography of the land adjoining the interstate and primary systems will not permit adequate screening of junkyards or that screening would not be economically feasible, the department may acquire by gift, purchase, exchange, or eminent domain the interests in lands necessary to secure the relocation, removal, or disposal of the junkyards.

(2) If the department determines that it is in the best interests of the state, it may acquire lands, or interests in lands, necessary to provide adequate screening of junkyards.

(3) The acquisitions provided for in this section may not be undertaken unless:

(a) the necessary federal funds for participation have been appropriated by the federal government and are immediately available to the state; and

(b) the department has received approval to seek federal grants, loans, or participation in federal programs under Title 63, Chapter 38e, Federal Funds Procedures.

(4) Damages resulting from any taking of property in eminent domain shall be ascertained in the manner provided by law.

(5) Just compensation shall be paid the owner for the relocation, removal, or disposal of a junkyard lawfully established under the laws of this state and which must be relocated, removed, or disposed of under this part. 2004

72-7-208. Junkyard operated in violation of provisions is public nuisance — Abatement — Correction notice.

(1) The establishment, operation, or maintenance of any junkyard contrary to the provisions of this part is a public nuisance, and the department, with the advice of the attorney general, may apply to the district court of the county in which the junkyard is located for an injunction to abate the nuisance.

(2) A correction notice of 30 days shall be given the owner prior to filing for an injunction to abate the nuisance.

(3) A notice is not required prior to filing a misdemeanor complaint under Section 72-7-211. 1998

72-7-209. Enforcement authority — Agreements with United States.

(1) In accordance with Title 63, Chapter 46a, Utah Administrative Rulemaking Act, the department may make rules:

(a) governing the materials that may be used for screening and the location, construction, and maintenance of screening for junkyards; and

(b) implementing and enforcing this part.

(2) The department may:

(a) enter into agreements with the secretary pursuant to Title 23, United States Code as amended, relating to the control of junkyards in areas adjacent to the interstate and primary systems; and

(b) take action in the name of the state to comply with the terms of the agreements. 1998

72-7-210. Present ordinances or regulations may be stricter.

Nothing in this part affects the provisions of any lawful ordinance or regulation which is more restrictive than the provisions of this part. 1998

72-7-211. Violations — Misdemeanor.

A person who violates any provision of this part or rules of the department made under this part is guilty of a class B misdemeanor. 1998

PART 3

HIGHWAY DAMAGE LIABILITY

72-7-301. Liability for damage to highway, highway equipment, or highway sign — Liability for damage to highway from illegal operation of oversize or overweight vehicles — Recovery.

(1) A person who by any means willfully or negligently injures or damages any highway, highway equipment, or highway sign is liable for the damage.

(2) A person who operates or moves any vehicle or object on any highway is liable for all damage that the highway sustains from:

(a) any illegal operation or movement of a vehicle or object; and

(b) any vehicle or object that exceeds the maximum size, weight, or load limitations specified by law, with or without authority of an oversize or overweight permit.

(3) (a) Except under Subsection (3)(b), if the operator is not the owner of the vehicle or object but is operating or moving the vehicle or object with the express or implied permission of the owner, the owner and operator are jointly and severally liable under Subsection (2) for any damage caused to a highway by the operation or movement of the vehicle or object.

(b) An operator who is not the owner of the vehicle or object and who under an express or implied condition of his employment or any privilege related to his employment is required to operate or move a vehicle or object in violation of Part 4, Vehicle Size, Weight, and Load Limitations, is not liable for any damage caused to a highway by the illegal operation or movement of the vehicle or object.

(4) The value of the property damaged may be recovered in a civil action brought by the highway authority having jurisdiction over the property damaged. 1998

72-7-302. Violations of rules as to use — Damage to signs, warnings, or barriers — Penalty.

(1) A person is guilty of a class B misdemeanor who:

(a) willfully violates any of the rules of the department or the commission on the use of state highways or traffic on them; or

(b) willfully and unlawfully removes, defaces, or interferes with any highway sign, signal, notice, warning, or barrier.

(2) A person who commits an offense under Subsection (1)(b) that results in any injury to persons or damage to property is guilty of a class A misdemeanor. 1998

72-7-303. Escaping water and other obstructions — Injuring or obstructing highway — Penalty for violations.

(1) A person may not willfully or carelessly:

(a) obstruct or damage any public highway by causing or permitting flow or seepage of water;

(b) permit water under the person's control to escape in any manner that results in damage to a public highway;

(c) place or leave, or cause to be placed or left, anything upon a public highway in a way that obstructs travel or that endangers property or persons passing on the highway.

(2) A person who violates this section is guilty of a class B misdemeanor. 1998

72-7-304. Injury to trees on highways — Penalty for violations.

(1) A person may not dig up, cut down, or otherwise willfully damage or destroy any shade, ornamental, or other tree, planted and standing on any public highway in conformity to law.

(2) A person who violates this section is guilty of a class B misdemeanor and is liable to the owner of the tree for treble the amount of damages sustained. 1998

72-7-305. Driving animals over highways — Liability for damages.

(1) Except for a livestock highway, a person who drives a herd of domestic animals over a public highway is liable for any damage done by the animals in destroying the banks or rolling rocks into or upon the highway.

(2) The damage may be recovered in a civil action brought by a highway authority having jurisdiction over the highway. 1998

72-7-306. Limited highways — Penalty for driving animals over.

(1) A highway authority may declare a public highway that is laid out through improved lands that are not protected by fences along the lines of the highway passing through it, to be limited highways. A notice to that effect shall be posted at each end of a limited highway.

(2) A person who willfully drives any band or herd of domestic animals over a limited highway except during the time that the abutting lands are thrown open to the public by the owners for grazing purposes, is guilty of a class B misdemeanor. 1998

PART 4

VEHICLE SIZE, WEIGHT, AND LOAD LIMITATIONS

72-7-401. Application of size, weight, and load limitations for vehicles — Exceptions.

(1) (a) Except as provided in Subsection (2), the maximum size, weight, and load limitations on vehicles under this part apply to all highways throughout the state.

(b) Local authorities may not alter the limitations except as expressly provided under Sections 41-6a-204 and 72-7-408.

(2) Except as specifically made applicable, the size, weight, and load limitations in this chapter do not apply to:

(a) fire-fighting apparatus;

(b) highway construction and maintenance equipment being operated at the site of maintenance or at a construction project as authorized by a highway authority;

(c) highway construction and maintenance equipment temporarily being operated between a material site and a highway maintenance site or a highway construction project if:

(i) the section of any highway being used is not located within a county of the first or second class;

(ii) authorized for a specific highway project by the highway authority having jurisdiction over each highway being used;

(iii) the distance between the material site and maintenance site or highway construction project does not exceed ten miles; and

(iv) the operator carries in the vehicle written verification of the authorization from the highway authority having jurisdiction over each highway being used;

(d) implements of husbandry incidentally moved on a highway while engaged in an agricultural operation or incidentally moved for repair or servicing, subject to the provisions of Section 72-7-407;

(e) vehicles transporting logs or poles from forest to sawmill:

(i) when required to move upon a highway other than the national system of interstate and defense highways;

(ii) if the gross vehicle weight does not exceed 80,000 pounds; and

(iii) the vehicle or combination of vehicles are in compliance with Subsections 72-7-404(1) and (2)(a); and

(f) tow trucks or towing vehicles under emergency conditions when:

(i) it becomes necessary to move a vehicle, combination of vehicles, special mobile equipment, or objects to the nearest safe area for parking or temporary storage;

(ii) no other alternative is available; and

(iii) the movement is for the safety of the traveling public.

(3) (a) Except when operating on the national system of interstate and defense highways, a motor vehicle carrying livestock as defined in Section 4-1-8, or a motor vehicle carrying raw grain if the grain is being transported by the farmer from his farm to market prior to bagging, weighing, or processing, may exceed by up to 2,000 pounds the tandem axle weight limitations specified under Section 72-7-404 without obtaining an overweight permit under Section 72-7-406.

(b) Subsection (3)(a) is an exception to Sections 72-7-404 and 72-7-406. 2005

72-7-402. Limitations as to vehicle width, height, length, and load extensions.

(1) (a) Except as provided by statute, all state or federally approved safety devices and any other lawful appurtenant devices, including refrigeration units, hitches, air line connections, and load securing devices related to the safe operation of a vehicle are excluded for purposes of measuring the width and length of a vehicle under the provisions of this part, if the devices are not designed or used for carrying cargo.

(b) Load-induced tire bulge is excluded for purposes of measuring the width of vehicles under the provisions of this part.

(c) Appurtenances attached to the sides or rear of a recreational vehicle that is not a commercial motor vehicle are excluded for purposes of measuring the width and length of the recreational vehicle if the additional width or length of the appurtenances does not exceed six inches.

(2) A vehicle unladen or with a load may not exceed a width of 8-½ feet.

(3) A vehicle unladen or with a load may not exceed a height of 14 feet.

(4) (a) (i) A single-unit vehicle, unladen or with a load, may not exceed a length of 45 feet including front and rear bumpers.

(ii) In this section, a truck tractor coupled to one or more semitrailers or trailers is not considered a single-unit vehicle.

(b) (i) Except as provided under Subsection (4)(b)(iii), a semitrailer, unladen or with a load, may not exceed a length of 48 feet excluding refrigeration units, hitches, air line connections, and safety appurtenances.

(ii) There is no overall length limitation on a truck tractor and semitrailer combination when the semitrailer length is 48 feet or less.

(iii) A semitrailer that exceeds a length of 48 feet but does not exceed a length of 53 feet may operate on a route designated by the department or within one mile of that route.

(c) (i) Two trailers coupled together, unladen or with a load, may not exceed an overall length of 61 feet, measured from the front of the first trailer to the rear of the second trailer.

(ii) There is no overall length limitation on a truck tractor and double trailer combination when the trailers coupled together measure 61 feet or less.

(d) All other combinations of vehicles, unladen or with a load, when coupled together, may not exceed a total length of 65 feet, except the length limitations do not apply to combinations of vehicles operated at night by a public utility when required for emergency repair of public service facilities or properties, or when operated under a permit under Section 72-7-406.

(5) (a) Subject to Subsection (4), a vehicle or combination of vehicles may not carry any load extending more than three feet beyond the front of the body of the vehicle or more than six feet beyond the rear of the bed or body of the vehicle.

(b) A passenger vehicle may not carry any load extending beyond the line of the fenders on the left side of the vehicle nor extending more than six inches beyond the line of the fenders on the right side of the vehicle.

(6) Any exception to this section must be authorized by a permit as provided under Section 72-7-406.

(7) In accordance with Title 63, Chapter 46a, Utah Administrative Rulemaking Act, the department shall make rules designating routes where a semitrailer that exceeds a length of 48 feet but that does not exceed a length of 53 feet may operate as provided under Subsection (4)(b)(iii).

(8) Any person who violates this section is guilty of a class B misdemeanor. 2002

72-7-403. Towing requirements and limitations on towing.

(1) (a) The draw-bar or other connection between any two vehicles, one of which is towing or drawing the other on a highway, may not exceed 15 feet in length from one vehicle to the other except in the case of a connection between any two vehicles transporting poles, pipe, machinery, or structural material that cannot be dismembered when transported upon a pole trailer as defined in Section 41-6a-102.

(b) When the connection between the two vehicles is a chain, rope, or cable, a red flag or other signal or cloth not less than 12 inches both in length and width shall be displayed on or near the midpoint of the connection.

(2) A person may not operate a combination of vehicles when any trailer, semitrailer, or other vehicle being towed:

(a) whips or swerves from side to side dangerously or unreasonably; or

(b) fails to follow substantially in the path of the towing vehicle.

(3) A person who violates this section is guilty of a class B misdemeanor. 2005

72-7-404. Maximum gross weight limitation for vehicles — Bridge formula for weight limitations — Minimum mandatory fines.

(1) (a) As used in this section:

(i) "Axle load" means the total load on all wheels whose centers may be included between two parallel transverse vertical planes 40 inches apart.

(ii) "Tandem axle" means two or more axles spaced not less than 40 inches nor more than 96 inches apart and having at least one common point of weight suspension.

(b) The tire load rating shall be marked on the tire sidewall. A tire, wheel, or axle may not carry a greater weight than the manufacturer's rating.

(2) (a) A vehicle may not be operated or moved on any highway in the state with:

(i) a gross weight in excess of 10,500 pounds on one wheel;

(ii) a single axle load in excess of 20,000 pounds; or

(iii) a tandem axle load in excess of 34,000 pounds.

(b) Subject to the limitations of Subsection (3), the gross vehicle weight of any vehicle or combination of vehicles may not exceed 80,000 pounds.

(3) (a) Subject to the limitations in Subsection (2), no group of two or more consecutive axles between the first and last axle of a vehicle or combination of vehicles and no vehicle or combination of vehicles may carry a gross weight in excess of the weight provided by the following bridge formula, except as provided in Subsection (3)(b):

$$W = 500 \{LN/(N-1) + 12N+36\}$$

(i) W = overall gross weight on any group of two or more consecutive axles to the nearest 500 pounds.

(ii) L = distance in feet between the extreme of any group of two or more consecutive axles. When the distance in feet includes a fraction of a foot of one inch or more the next larger number of feet shall be used.

(iii) N = number of axles in the group under consideration.

(b) Two consecutive sets of tandem axles may carry a gross weight of 34,000 pounds each if the overall distance between the first and last axles of the consecutive sets of tandem axles is 36 feet or more.

(4) Any exception to this section must be authorized by an overweight permit as provided in Section 72-7-406.

(5) (a) Any person who violates this section is guilty of a class B misdemeanor except that, notwithstanding Sections 76-3-301 and 76-3-302, the violator shall pay the largest minimum mandatory fine of either:

(i) $50 plus the sum of the overweight axle fines calculated under Subsection (5)(b); or

(ii) $50 plus the gross vehicle weight fine calculated under Subsection (5)(b).

(b) The fine for each axle and a gross vehicle weight violation shall be calculated according to the following schedule:

Number of Pounds Overweight	Axle Fine (Cents per Pound for Each Overweight Axle)	Gross Vehicle Weight Fine (Cents per Pound)
1 — 2,000	0	0
2,001 — 5,000	4	5
5,001 — 8,000	5	5
8,001 — 12,000	6	5
12,001 — 16,000	7	5
16,001 — 20,000	9	5
20,001 — 25,000	11	5
25,001 or more	13	5

1999

72-7-405. Measuring vehicles for size and weight compliance — Summary powers of peace officers — Penalty for violations.

(1) Any peace officer having reason to believe that the height, width, length, or weight of a vehicle and load is unlawful may require the operator to stop the vehicle and submit to a measurement or weighing of the vehicle and load.

(2) A peace officer may require that the vehicle be driven to the nearest scales or port-of-entry if the scales or port-of-entry is within three miles.

(3) (a) A peace officer, special function officer, or port-of-entry agent may measure or weigh a vehicle and vehicle load for compliance with this chapter.

(b) If, upon measuring or weighing a vehicle and load, it is determined that the height, width, length, or weight is unlawful, the measuring or weighing peace officer, special function officer, or port-of-entry agent may require the operator to park the vehicle in a suitable place. The vehicle shall remain parked until the vehicle or its load is adjusted or a portion of the load is removed to conform to legal limits. All materials unloaded shall be cared for by the owner or operator of the vehicle at his risk.

(4) An operator who fails or refuses to stop and submit the vehicle and load to a measurement or weighing, or who fails or refuses when directed by a peace officer, special function officer, or port-of-entry agent to comply with this section is guilty of a class B misdemeanor.

(5) Any driver or owner of a vehicle who violates Section 72-7-404 or 72-7-406 is guilty of a class B misdemeanor. 1998

72-7-406. Oversize permits and oversize and overweight permits for vehicles of excessive size or weight — Applications — Restrictions — Fees — Rulemaking provisions — Penalty.

(1) (a) The department may, upon receipt of an application and good cause shown, issue in writing an oversize permit or an oversize and overweight permit. The oversize permit or oversize and overweight permit may authorize the applicant to operate or move upon a highway:

(i) a vehicle or combination of vehicles, unladen or with a load weighing more than the maximum weight specified in Section 72-7-404 for any wheel, axle, group of axles, or total gross weight; or

(ii) a vehicle or combination of vehicles that exceeds the vehicle width, height, or length provisions under Section 72-7-402.

(b) Except as provided under Subsection (8), an oversize and overweight permit may not be issued under this section to allow the transportation of a load that is reasonably divisible.

(c) The maximum size or weight authorized by a permit under this section shall be within limits that do not impair the state's ability to qualify for federal-aid highway funds.

(d) The department may deny or issue a permit under this section to protect the safety of the traveling public and to protect highway foundation, surfaces, or structures from undue damage by one or more of the following:

(i) limiting the number of trips the vehicle may make;

(ii) establishing seasonal or other time limits within which the vehicle may operate or move on the highway indicated;

(iii) requiring security in addition to the permit to compensate for any potential damage by the vehicle to any highway; and

(iv) otherwise limiting the conditions of operation or movement of the vehicle.

(e) Prior to granting a permit under this section, the department shall approve the route of any vehicle or combination of vehicles.

(2) An application for a permit under this section shall state:

(a) the proposed maximum wheel loads, maximum axle loads, all axle spacings of each vehicle or combination of vehicles;

(b) the proposed maximum load size and maximum size of each vehicle or combination of vehicles;

(c) the specific roads requested to be used under authority of the permit; and

(d) if the permit is requested for a single trip or if other seasonal limits or time limits apply.

(3) Each oversize permit or oversize and overweight permit shall be carried in the vehicle or combination of vehicles to which it refers and shall be available for inspection by any peace officer, special function officer, port of entry agent, or other personnel authorized by the department.

(4) A permit under this section may not be issued or is not valid unless the vehicle or combination of vehicles is:

(a) properly registered for the weight authorized by the permit; or

(b) registered for a gross laden weight of 78,001 pounds or over, if the gross laden weight authorized by the permit exceeds 80,000 pounds.

(5) (a) (i) An oversize permit may be issued under this section for a vehicle or combination of vehicles that exceeds one or more of the maximum width, height, or length provisions under Section 72-7-402.

(ii) Except for an annual oversize permit for an implement of husbandry under Section 72-7-407, only a single trip oversize permit may be issued for a vehicle or combination of vehicles that is more than 14 feet six inches wide, 14 feet high, or 105 feet long.

(b) The fee is $25 for a single trip oversize permit under this Subsection (5). This permit is valid for not more than 96 continuous hours.

(c) The fee is $60 for a semiannual oversize permit under this Subsection (5). This permit is valid for not more than 180 continuous days.

(d) The fee is $75 for an annual oversize permit under this Subsection (5). This permit is valid for not more than 365 continuous days.

(6) (a) An oversize and overweight permit may be issued under this section for a vehicle or combination of vehicles carrying a nondivisible load that exceeds one or more of the maximum weight provisions of Section 72-7-404 by not more than 25%, except that the gross weight may not exceed 125,000 pounds.

(b) The fee is $50 for a single trip oversize and overweight permit under this Subsection (6). This permit is valid for not more than 96 continuous hours.

(c) A semiannual oversize and overweight permit under this Subsection (6) is valid for not more than 180 continuous days. The fee for this permit is:

(i) $150 for a vehicle or combination of vehicles with gross vehicle weight of more than 80,000 pounds, but not exceeding 84,000 pounds;

(ii) $260 for a vehicle or combination of vehicles with gross vehicle weight of more than 84,000 pounds, but not exceeding 112,000 pounds; and

(iii) $350 for a vehicle or combination of vehicles with gross vehicle weight of more than 112,000 pounds, but not exceeding 125,000 pounds.

(d) An annual oversize and overweight permit under this Subsection (6) is valid for not more than 365 continuous days. The fee for this permit is:

(i) $200 for a vehicle or combination of vehicles with gross vehicle weight of more than 80,000 pounds, but not exceeding 84,000 pounds;

(ii) $400 for a vehicle or combination of vehicles with gross vehicle weight of more than 84,000 pounds, but not exceeding 112,000 pounds; and

(iii) $450 for a vehicle or combination of vehicles with gross vehicle weight of more than 112,000 pounds, but not exceeding 125,000 pounds.

(7) (a) A single trip oversize and overweight permit may be issued under this section for a vehicle or combination of vehicles carrying a nondivisible load that exceeds one or more of the maximum weight provisions of Section 72-7-404 by more than 25% or that exceeds a gross weight of 125,000 pounds.

(b) (i) The fee for a single trip oversize and overweight permit under this Subsection (7), which is valid for not more than 96 continuous hours, is $.01 per mile for each 1,000 pounds above 80,000 pounds subject to the rounding described in Subsection (7)(c).

(ii) The minimum fee that may be charged under this Subsection (7) is $65.

(iii) The maximum fee that may be charged under this Subsection (7) is $450.

(c) (i) The miles used to calculate the fee under this Subsection (7) shall be rounded up to the nearest 50 mile increment.

(ii) The pounds used to calculate the fee under this Subsection (7) shall be rounded up to the nearest 25,000 pound increment.

(8) (a) An oversize and overweight permit may be issued under this section for a vehicle or combination of vehicles carrying a divisible load if:

(i) the bridge formula under Subsection 72-7-404(3) is not exceeded; and

(ii) the length of the vehicle or combination of vehicles is:

(A) more than the limitations specified under Subsections 72-7-402(4)(c) and (d) but not exceeding 81 feet in cargo carrying length and the application is for a single trip, semiannual trip, or annual trip permit; or

(B) more than 81 feet in cargo carrying length but not exceeding 95 feet in cargo carrying length and the application is for an annual trip permit.

(b) The fee is $50 for a single trip oversize and overweight permit under this Subsection (8). The permit is valid for not more than 96 continuous hours.

(c) The fee for a semiannual oversize and overweight permit under this Subsection (8), which permit is valid for not more than 180 continuous days is:

(i) $150 for a vehicle or combination of vehicles with gross vehicle weight of more than 80,000 pounds, but not exceeding 84,000 pounds;

(ii) $260 for a vehicle or combination of vehicles with gross vehicle weight of more than 84,000 pounds, but not exceeding 112,000 pounds; and

(iii) $350 for a vehicle or combination of vehicles with gross vehicle weight of more than 112,000 pounds, but not exceeding 129,000 pounds.

(d) The fee for an annual oversize and overweight permit under this Subsection (8), which permit is valid for not more than 365 continuous days is:

(i) $200 for a vehicle or combination of vehicles with gross vehicle weight of more than 80,000 pounds, but not exceeding 84,000 pounds;

(ii) $400 for a vehicle or combination of vehicles with gross vehicle weight of more than 84,000 pounds, but not exceeding 112,000 pounds; and

(iii) $450 for a vehicle or combination of vehicles with gross vehicle weight of more than 112,000 pounds, but not exceeding 129,000 pounds.

(9) Permits under Subsections (7) and (8) may be issued only upon authorization of the commission.

(10) Permit fees collected under this section shall be credited monthly to the Transportation Fund.

(11) The department shall prepare maps, drawings, and instructions as guidance when issuing permits under this section.

(12) In accordance with Title 63, Chapter 46a, Utah Administrative Rulemaking Act, the department shall make rules governing the issuance and revocation of all permits under this section and Section 72-7-407.

(13) Any person who violates any of the terms or conditions of a permit issued under this section:

(a) may have his permit revoked; and

(b) is guilty of a class B misdemeanor.   2001

72-7-407. Implements of husbandry — Escort vehicle requirements — Oversize permit — Rulemaking — Penalty.

(1) As used in this section, "escort vehicle" means a motor vehicle, as defined under Section 41-1a-102, that has its emergency warning lights operating, and that is being used to warn approaching motorists by either preceding or following a slow or oversized

vehicle, object, or implement of husbandry being moved on the highway.

(2) An implement of husbandry being moved on a highway shall be accompanied by:

(a) front and rear escort vehicles when the implement of husbandry is 16 feet in width or greater unless the implement of husbandry is moved by a farmer or rancher or his employees in connection with an agricultural operation; or

(b) one or more escort vehicles when the implement of husbandry is traveling on a highway where special hazards exist related to weather, pedestrians, other traffic, or highway conditions.

(3) In addition to the requirements of Subsection (2), a person may not move an implement of husbandry on a highway during hours of darkness without lights and reflectors as required under Section 41-6a-1608 or 41-6a-1609.

(4) (a) Except for an implement of husbandry moved by a farmer or rancher or the farmer's or rancher's employees in connection with an agricultural operation, a person may not move an implement of husbandry on the highway without:

(i) an oversize permit obtained under Section 72-7-406 if required;

(ii) trained escort vehicle drivers and approved escort vehicles when required under Subsection (2); and

(iii) compliance with the vehicle weight requirements of Section 72-7-404.

(b) (i) The department shall issue an annual oversize permit for the purpose of allowing the movement of implements of husbandry on the highways in accordance with this chapter.

(ii) The permit shall require the applicant to obtain verbal permission from the department for each trip involving the movement of an implement of husbandry 16 feet or greater in width.

(c) In accordance with Title 63, Chapter 46a, Utah Administrative Rulemaking Act, the department shall make rules specifying training for escort vehicle drivers and equipment requirements for escort vehicles as provided in Subsection (4)(a).

(5) Any person who violates this section is guilty of a class B misdemeanor.   2005

72-7-408. Highway authority — Restrictions on highway use — Erection and maintenance of signs designating restrictions — Penalty.

(1) (a) Subject to Subsection (1)(b), a highway authority may by rule or ordinance prescribe procedures and criteria which prohibit the operation of any vehicle or impose restrictions on the weight of a vehicle upon any highway under its jurisdiction.

(b) A highway authority may impose restrictions for a highway under Subsection (1)(a) if an engineering inspection concludes that, due to deterioration caused by climatic conditions, a highway will be seriously damaged or destroyed unless certain vehicles are prohibited or vehicle weights are restricted.

(2) The highway authority imposing restrictions under this section shall erect signs citing the provisions of the rule or ordinance at each end of that portion of any highway affected. The restriction is effective only when the signs are erected and maintained.

(3) Any person who violates any restriction imposed under the authority of this section is guilty of a class B misdemeanor.   2001

72-7-409. Loads on vehicles — Limitations — Confining, securing, and fastening load required — Penalty.

(1) As used in this section:

(a) "Agricultural product" means any raw product which is derived from agriculture, including silage, hay, straw, grain, manure, and other similar product.

(b) "Vehicle" has the same meaning set forth in Section 41-1a-102.

(2) A vehicle may not be operated or moved on any highway unless the vehicle is constructed or loaded to prevent its contents from dropping, sifting, leaking, or otherwise escaping.

(3) (a) In addition to the requirements under Subsection (2), a vehicle carrying dirt, sand, gravel, rock fragments, pebbles, crushed base, aggregate, any other similar material, or scrap metal shall have a covering over the entire load unless:

(i) the highest point of the load does not extend above the top of any exterior wall or sideboard of the cargo compartment of the vehicle; and

(ii) the outer edges of the load are at least six inches below the top inside edges of the exterior walls or sideboards of the cargo compartment of the vehicle.

(b) The following material is exempt from the provisions of Subsection (3)(a):

(i) hot mix asphalt;

(ii) construction debris or scrap metal if the debris or scrap metal is a size and in a form not susceptible to being blown out of the vehicle;

(iii) material being transported across a highway between two parcels of property that would be contiguous but for the highway that is being crossed; and

(iv) material listed under Subsection (3)(a) that is enclosed on all sides by containers, bags, or packaging.

(c) A chemical substance capable of coating or bonding a load so that the load is confined on a vehicle, may be considered a covering for purposes of Subsection (3)(a) so long as the chemical substance remains effective at confining the load.

(4) Subsections (2) and (3) do not apply to a vehicle or implement of husbandry carrying an agricultural product, if the agricultural product is:

(a) being transported in a manner which is not a hazard or a potential hazard to the safe operation of the vehicle or to other highway users; and

(b) loaded in a manner that only allows minimal spillage.

(5) (a) An authorized vehicle performing snow removal services on a highway is exempt from the requirements of this section if the vehicle's load is screened to a particle size established by a rule of the department.

(b) This section does not prohibit the necessary spreading of any substance connected with highway maintenance, construction, securing traction, or snow removal.

(6) A person may not operate a vehicle with a load on any highway unless the load and any load covering is fastened, secured, and confined to prevent the covering or load from becoming loose, detached, or in

any manner a hazard to the safe operation of the vehicle, or to other highway users.

(7) Before entering a highway, the operator of a vehicle carrying any material listed under Subsection (3), shall remove all loose material on any portion of the vehicle not designed to carry the material.

(8) Any person who violates this section is guilty of a class B misdemeanor.   1998

PART 5

UTAH OUTDOOR ADVERTISING ACT

72-7-501. Purpose of part — Utah-Federal Agreements ratified.

(1) The purpose of this part is to provide the statutory basis for the regulation of outdoor advertising consistent with zoning principles and standards and the public policy of this state in providing public safety, health, welfare, convenience and enjoyment of public travel, to protect the public investment in highways, to preserve the natural scenic beauty of lands bordering on highways, and to ensure that outdoor advertising shall be continued as a standardized medium of communication throughout the state so that it is preserved and can continue to provide general information in the specific interest of the traveling public safely and effectively.

(2) It is the purpose of this part to provide a statutory basis for the reasonable regulation of outdoor advertising consistent with the customary use, zoning principles and standards, the protection of private property rights, and the public policy relating to areas adjacent to the interstate, federal aid primary highway existing as of June 1, 1991, and the national highway systems highways.

(3) The agreement entered into between the governor of the state of Utah and the Secretary of Transportation of the United States dated January 18, 1968, regarding the size, lighting, and spacing of outdoor advertising which may be erected and maintained within areas adjacent to the interstate, federal aid primary highway existing as of June 1, 1991, and national highway systems highways which are zoned commercial or industrial or in other unzoned commercial or industrial areas as defined pursuant to the terms of the agreement is hereby ratified and approved, subject to subsequent amendments.   1998

72-7-502. Definitions.

As used in this part:

(1) "Commercial or industrial activities" means those activities generally recognized as commercial or industrial by zoning authorities in this state, except that none of the following are commercial or industrial activities:

(a) agricultural, forestry, grazing, farming, and related activities, including wayside fresh produce stands;

(b) transient or temporary activities;

(c) activities not visible from the main-traveled way;

(d) activities conducted in a building principally used as a residence; and

(e) railroad tracks and minor sidings.

(2) "Commercial or industrial zone" means only:

(a) those areas within the boundaries of cities or towns that are used or reserved for business, commerce, or trade, or zoned as a highway service zone, under enabling state legislation or comprehensive local zoning ordinances or regulations;

(b) those areas within the boundaries of urbanized counties that are used or reserved for business, commerce, or trade, or zoned as a highway service zone, under enabling state legislation or comprehensive local zoning ordinances or regulations;

(c) those areas outside the boundaries of urbanized counties and outside the boundaries of cities and towns that:

(i) are used or reserved for business, commerce, or trade, or zoned as a highway service zone, under comprehensive local zoning ordinances or regulations or enabling state legislation; and

(ii) are within 8420 feet of an interstate highway exit, off-ramp, or turnoff as measured from the nearest point of the beginning or ending of the pavement widening at the exit from or entrance to the main-traveled way; or

(d) those areas outside the boundaries of urbanized counties and outside the boundaries of cities and towns and not within 8420 feet of an interstate highway exit, off-ramp, or turnoff as measured from the nearest point of the beginning or ending of the pavement widening at the exit from or entrance to the main-traveled way that are reserved for business, commerce, or trade under enabling state legislation or comprehensive local zoning ordinances or regulations, and are actually used for commercial or industrial purposes.

(3) "Commercial or industrial zone" does not mean areas zoned for the sole purpose of allowing outdoor advertising.

(4) "Comprehensive local zoning ordinances or regulations" means a municipality's comprehensive plan required by Section 10-9a-401, the municipal zoning plan authorized by Section 10-9a-501, the county master plan authorized by Sections 17-27a-401 and 17-27a-501. Property that is rezoned by comprehensive local zoning ordinances or regulations is rebuttably presumed to have not been zoned for the sole purpose of allowing outdoor advertising.

(5) "Directional signs" means signs containing information about public places owned or operated by federal, state, or local governments or their agencies, publicly or privately owned natural phenomena, historic, cultural, scientific, educational, or religious sites, and areas of natural scenic beauty or naturally suited for outdoor recreation, that the department considers to be in the interest of the traveling public.

(6) (a) "Erect" means to construct, build, raise, assemble, place, affix, attach, create, paint, draw, or in any other way bring into being.

(b) "Erect" does not include any activities defined in Subsection (6)(a) if they are performed incident to the change of an advertising message or customary maintenance of a sign.

(7) "Highway service zone" means a highway service area where the primary use of the land is used or reserved for commercial and roadside services other than outdoor advertising to serve the traveling public.

(8) "Information center" means an area or site established and maintained at rest areas for the purpose of informing the public of:

(a) places of interest within the state; or

(b) any other information that the department considers desirable.

(9) "Interchange or intersection" means those areas and their approaches where traffic is channeled off or onto an interstate route, excluding the deceleration lanes, acceleration lanes, or feeder systems, from or to another federal, state, county, city, or other route.

(10) "Maintain" means to allow to exist, subject to the provisions of this chapter.

(11) "Maintenance" means to repair, refurbish, repaint, or otherwise keep an existing sign structure safe and in a state suitable for use, including signs destroyed by vandalism or an act of God.

(12) "Main-traveled way" means the through traffic lanes, including auxiliary lanes, acceleration lanes, deceleration lanes, and feeder systems, exclusive of frontage roads and ramps. For a divided highway, there is a separate main-traveled way for the traffic in each direction.

(13) "Official signs and notices" means signs and notices erected and maintained by public agencies within their territorial or zoning jurisdictions for the purpose of carrying out official duties or responsibilities in accordance with direction or authorization contained in federal, state, or local law.

(14) "Off-premise signs" means signs located in areas zoned industrial, commercial, or H-1 and in areas determined by the department to be unzoned industrial or commercial.

(15) "On-premise signs" means signs used to advertise the major activities conducted on the property where the sign is located.

(16) "Outdoor advertising" means any outdoor advertising structure or outdoor structure used in combination with an outdoor advertising sign or outdoor sign.

(17) "Outdoor advertising corridor" means a strip of land 350 feet wide, measured perpendicular from the edge of a controlled highway right-of-way.

(18) "Outdoor advertising structure" or "outdoor structure" means any sign structure, including any necessary devices, supports, appurtenances, and lighting that is part of or supports an outdoor sign.

(19) "Point of widening" means the point of the gore or the point where the intersecting lane begins to parallel the other lanes of traffic, but the point of widening may never be greater than 2,640 feet from the center line of the intersecting highway of the interchange or intersection at grade.

(20) "Public assembly facility" means a convention facility as defined under Section 59-12-602 and that:

(a) is wholly or partially funded by public moneys; and

(b) requires a person attending an event at the public assembly facility to purchase a ticket or that otherwise charges for the use of the public assembly facility as part of its regular operation.

(21) "Relocation" includes the removal of a sign from one situs together with the erection of a new sign upon another situs in a commercial or industrial zoned area as a substitute.

(22) "Relocation and replacement" means allowing all outdoor advertising signs or permits the right to maintain outdoor advertising along the interstate, federal aid primary highway existing as of June 1, 1991, and national highway system highways to be maintained in a commercial or industrial zoned area to accommodate the displacement, remodeling, or widening of the highway systems.

(23) "Remodel" means the upgrading, changing, alteration, refurbishment, modification, or complete substitution of a new outdoor advertising structure for one permitted pursuant to this part and that is located in a commercial or industrial area.

(24) "Rest area" means an area or site established and maintained within or adjacent to the right-of-way by or under public supervision or control for the convenience of the traveling public.

(25) "Scenic or natural area" means an area determined by the department to have aesthetic value.

(26) "Traveled way" means that portion of the roadway used for the movement of vehicles, exclusive of shoulders and auxiliary lanes.

(27) (a) "Unzoned commercial or industrial area" means:

(i) those areas not zoned by state law or local law, regulation, or ordinance that are occupied by one or more industrial or commercial activities other than outdoor advertising signs;

(ii) the lands along the highway for a distance of 600 feet immediately adjacent to those activities; and

(iii) lands covering the same dimensions that are directly opposite those activities on the other side of the highway, if the department determines that those lands on the opposite side of the highway do not have scenic or aesthetic value.

(b) In measuring the scope of the unzoned commercial or industrial area, all measurements shall be made from the outer edge of the regularly used buildings, parking lots, storage, or processing areas of the activities and shall be along or parallel to the edge of pavement of the highway.

(c) All signs located within an unzoned commercial or industrial area become nonconforming if the commercial or industrial activity used in defining the area ceases for a continuous period of 12 months.

(28) "Urbanized county" means a county with a population of at least 125,000 persons.　　2005

72-7-503. Advertising — Permit required — Penalty for violation.

(1) It is unlawful for any person to place any form of advertising upon any part of the public domain, or within 300 feet of a public highway, except within the corporate limits of a city or town, and except upon land in private ownership situated along the highway, without first receiving a permit from the department, if a state highway, or from the county executive, if a county road.

(2) Any person who violates this section is guilty of a class B misdemeanor.　　1998

72-7-504. Advertising prohibited near interstate or primary system — Exceptions — Logo advertising — Department rules.

(1) Outdoor advertising that is capable of being read or comprehended from any place on the main-

traveled way of an interstate or primary system may not be erected or maintained, except:

(a) directional and other official signs and notices authorized or required by law, including signs and notices pertaining to natural wonders and scenic and historic attractions, informational or directional signs regarding utility service, emergency telephone signs, buried or underground utility markers, and above ground utility closure signs;

(b) signs advertising the sale or lease of property upon which they are located;

(c) signs advertising activities conducted on the property where they are located, including signs on the premises of a public assembly facility as provided in Section 72-7-504.5;

(d) signs located in a commercial or industrial zone;

(e) signs located in unzoned industrial or commercial areas as determined from actual land uses; and

(f) logo advertising under Subsection (2).

(2) (a) The department may itself or by contract erect, administer, and maintain informational signs on the main-traveled way of an interstate or primary system for the display of logo advertising and information of interest to the traveling public if:

(i) the department complies with Title 63, Chapter 56, Utah Procurement Code, in the lease or other contract agreement with a private party for the sign or sign space; and

(ii) the private party for the lease of the sign or sign space pays an amount set by the department to be paid to the department or the party under contract with the department under this Subsection (2).

(b) The amount shall be sufficient to cover the costs of erecting, administering, and maintaining the signs or sign spaces.

(c) The department may consult the Governor's Office of Economic Development in carrying out this Subsection (2).

(3) (a) Revenue generated under Subsection (2) shall be:

(i) applied first to cover department costs under Subsection (2); and

(ii) deposited in the Transportation Fund.

(b) Revenue in excess of costs under Subsection (2)(a) shall be deposited in the General Fund as a dedicated credit for use by the Governor's Office of Economic Development no later than the following fiscal year.

(4) Outdoor advertising under Subsections (1)(a), (d), (e), and (f) shall conform to the rules made by the department under Sections 72-7-506 and 72-7-507.

2005

72-7-504.5. Public assembly facility signs — Restrictions.

Signs on the premises of a public assembly facility that do not bring rental income to the owner of the public assembly facility may advertise:

(1) the name of the facility, including identifiable venues or stores within the facility; and

(2) principal or accessory products or services offered on the property and activities conducted on the property as permitted by 23 C.F.R. Section 750.709, including:

(a) events being conducted in the facility or upon the premises, including the sponsor of the current event; and

(b) products or services sold at the facility and activities conducted on the property that produce significant income to the operation of the facility.   2003

72-7-505. Sign size — Sign spacing — Location in outdoor advertising corridor — Limit on implementation.

(1) (a) Except as provided in Subsection (2), a sign face within the state may not exceed the following limits:

(i) maximum area — 1,000 square feet;

(ii) maximum length — 60 feet; and

(iii) maximum height — 25 feet.

(b) No more than two facings visible and readable from the same direction on the main-traveled way may be erected on any one sign structure. Whenever two facings are so positioned, neither shall exceed the maximum allowed square footage.

(c) Two or more advertising messages on a sign face and double-faced, back-to-back, stacked, side-by-side, and V-type signs are permitted as a single sign or structure if both faces enjoy common ownership.

(d) A changeable message sign is permitted if the interval between message changes is not more frequent than at least eight seconds and the actual message rotation process is accomplished in three seconds or less.

(2) (a) An outdoor sign structure located inside the unincorporated area of a nonurbanized county may have the maximum height allowed by the county for outdoor advertising structures in the commercial or industrial zone in which the sign is located. If no maximum height is provided for the location, the maximum sign height may be 65 feet above the ground or 25 feet above the grade of the main traveled way, whichever is greater.

(b) An outdoor sign structure located inside an incorporated municipality or urbanized county may have the maximum height allowed by the municipality or urbanized county for outdoor advertising structures in the commercial or industrial zone in which the sign is located. If no maximum height is provided for the location, the maximum sign height may be 65 feet above the ground or 25 feet above the grade of the main traveled way, whichever is greater.

(3) Except as provided in Section 72-7-509:

(a) Any sign allowed to be erected by reason of the exceptions set forth in Subsection 72-7-504(1) or in H-1 zones may not be closer than 500 feet to an existing off-premise sign adjacent to an interstate highway or limited access primary highway, except that signs may be erected closer than 500 feet if the signs on the same side of the interstate highway or limited access primary highway are not simultaneously visible.

(b) Signs may not be located within 500 feet of any of the following which are adjacent to the highway, unless the signs are in an incorporated area:

(i) public parks;

(ii) public forests;

(iii) public playgrounds;

(iv) areas designated as scenic areas by the department or other state agency having and exercising this authority; or

(v) cemeteries.

(c) (i) (A) Except under Subsection (3)(c)(ii), signs may not be located on an interstate highway or limited access highway on the primary system within 500 feet of an interchange, or intersection at grade, or rest area measured along the interstate highway or freeway from the sign to the nearest point of the beginning or ending of pavement widening at the exit from or entrance to the main-traveled way.

(B) Interchange and intersection distance limitations shall be measured separately for each direction of travel. A measurement for each direction of travel may not control or affect any other direction of travel.

(ii) A sign may be placed closer than 500 feet from the nearest point of the beginning or ending of pavement widening at the exit from or entrance to the main-traveled way, if:

(A) the sign is replacing an existing outdoor advertising use or structure which is being removed or displaced to accommodate the widening, construction, or reconstruction of an interstate, federal aid primary highway existing as of June 1, 1991, or national highway system highway; and

(B) it is located in a commercial or industrial zoned area inside an urbanized county or an incorporated municipality.

(d) The location of signs situated on nonlimited access primary highways in commercial, industrial, or H-1 zoned areas between streets, roads, or highways entering the primary highway shall not exceed the following minimum spacing criteria:

(i) Where the distance between centerlines of intersecting streets, roads, or highways is less than 1,000 feet, a minimum spacing between structures of 150 feet may be permitted between the intersecting streets or highways.

(ii) Where the distance between centerlines of intersecting streets, roads, or highways is 1,000 feet or more, minimum spacing between sign structures shall be 300 feet.

(e) All outdoor advertising shall be erected and maintained within the outdoor advertising corridor.

(4) Subsection (3)(c)(ii) may not be implemented until:

(a) the Utah-Federal Agreement for carrying out national policy relative to control of outdoor advertising in areas adjacent to the national system of interstate and defense highways and the federal-aid primary system is modified to allow the sign placement specified in Subsection (3)(c)(ii); and

(b) the modified agreement under Subsection (4)(a) is signed on behalf of both the state and the United States Secretary of Transportation. 2002

72-7-506. Advertising — Regulatory power of department — Notice requirements.

(1) In accordance with Title 63, Chapter 46a, Utah Administrative Rulemaking Act, the department may make rules no more restrictive than this chapter to:

(a) control the erection and maintenance of outdoor advertising along the interstate and primary highway systems;

(b) provide for enforcement of this chapter;

(c) establish the form, content, and submittal of applications to erect outdoor advertising; and

(d) establish administrative procedures.

(2) In addition to all other statutory notice requirements:

(a) the department shall give reasonably timely written notice to all outdoor advertising permit holders of any changes or proposed changes in administrative rules made under authority of this part; and

(b) any county, municipality, or governmental entity shall, upon written request, give reasonably timely written notice to all outdoor advertising permit holders within its jurisdiction of any change or proposed change to the outdoor or off-premise advertising provisions of its zoning provisions, codes, or ordinances. 1998

72-7-507. Advertising — Permits — Application requirements — Duration — Fees.

(1) (a) Outdoor advertising may not be maintained without a current permit.

(b) Applications for permits shall be made to the department on forms furnished by it.

(c) A permit must be obtained prior to installing each outdoor sign.

(d) The application for a permit shall be accompanied by an initial fee established under Section 63-38-3.2.

(2) (a) Each permit issued by the department is valid for a period of up to five years and shall expire on June 30 of the fifth year of the permit, or upon the expiration or termination of the right to use the property, whichever is sooner.

(b) Upon renewal, each permit may be renewed for periods of up to five years upon the filing of a renewal application and payment of a renewal fee established under Section 63-38-3.2.

(3) Sign owners residing outside the state shall provide the department with a continuous performance bond in the amount of $2,500.

(4) Fees may not be prorated for fractions of the permit period. Advertising copy may be changed at any time without payment of an additional fee.

(5) (a) Each sign shall have its permit continuously affixed to the sign in a position visible from the nearest traveled portion of the highway.

(b) The permit shall be affixed to the sign structure within 30 days after delivery by the department to the permit holder, or within 30 days of the installation date of the sign structure.

(c) Construction of the sign structure shall begin within 180 days after delivery of the permit by the department to the permit holder and construction shall be completed within 365 days after delivery of the permit.

(6) The department may not accept any applications for a permit or issue any permit to erect or maintain outdoor advertising within 500 feet of a permitted sign location except to the permit holder or the permit holder's assigns until the permit has expired or has been terminated pursuant to the procedures under Section 72-7-508.

(7) Permits are transferrable if the ownership of the permitted sign is transferred.

(8) Conforming, permitted sign structures may be altered, changed, remodeled, and relocated subject to the provisions of Subsection (6). 1998

72-7-508. Unlawful outdoor advertising — Adjudicative proceedings — Judicial review — Costs of removal — Civil and criminal liability for damaging regulated signs — Immunity for Department of Transportation.

(1) Outdoor advertising is unlawful when:

(a) erected after May 9, 1967, contrary to the provisions of this chapter;

(b) a permit is not obtained as required by this part;

(c) a false or misleading statement has been made in the application for a permit that was material to obtaining the permit; or

(d) the sign for which a permit was issued is not in a reasonable state of repair, is unsafe, or is otherwise in violation of this part.

(2) The establishment, operation, repair, maintenance, or alteration of any sign contrary to this chapter is also a public nuisance.

(3) Except as provided in Subsection (4), in its enforcement of this section, the department shall comply with the procedures and requirements of Title 63, Chapter 46b, Administrative Procedures Act.

(4) (a) The district courts shall have jurisdiction to review by trial de novo all final orders of the department under this part resulting from formal and informal adjudicative proceedings.

(b) Venue for judicial review of final orders of the department shall be in the county in which the sign is located.

(5) If the department is granted a judgment, the department is entitled to have any nuisance abated and recover from the responsible person, firm, or corporation, jointly and severally:

(a) the costs and expenses incurred in removing the sign; and

(b) $10 for each day the sign was maintained following the expiration of ten days after notice of agency action was filed and served under Section 63-46b-3.

(6) (a) Any person, partnership, firm, or corporation who vandalizes, damages, defaces, destroys, or uses any sign controlled under this chapter without the owner's permission is liable to the owner of the sign for treble the amount of damage sustained and all costs of court, including a reasonable attorney's fee, and is guilty of a class C misdemeanor.

(b) This subsection does not apply to the department, its agents, or employees if acting to enforce this part.   1998

72-7-509. Existing outdoor advertising not in conformity with part — When removal required — When relocation allowed.

(1) Any outdoor advertising lawfully in existence along the interstate or the primary systems on May 9, 1967, and which is not then in conformity with its provisions is not required to be removed until five years after it becomes nonconforming or pursuant to the provisions of Section 72-7-510.

(2) Any existing outdoor advertising structure that does not comply with Section 72-7-505, but that is located in an industrial and commercial area, an unzoned industrial and commercial area, or an area where outdoor advertising would otherwise be permitted, may be remodeled and relocated on the same property in a commercial or industrial zoned area, or another area where outdoor advertising would otherwise be permitted under this part.   1998

72-7-510. Existing outdoor advertising not in conformity with part — Procedure — Eminent domain — Compensation — Relocation.

(1) As used in this section, "nonconforming sign" means a sign that has been erected in a zone or area other than commercial or industrial or where outdoor advertising is not permitted under this part.

(2) (a) The department may acquire by gift, purchase, agreement, exchange, or eminent domain, any existing outdoor advertising and all property rights pertaining to the outdoor advertising which were lawfully in existence on May 9, 1967, and which by reason of this part become nonconforming.

(b) If the department, or any town, city, county, governmental entity, public utility, or any agency or the United States Department of Transportation under this part, prevents the maintenance as defined in Section 72-7-502, or requires that maintenance of an existing sign be discontinued, the sign in question shall be considered acquired by the entity and just compensation will become immediately due and payable.

(c) Eminent domain shall be exercised in accordance with the provision of Title 78, Chapter 34, Eminent Domain.

(3) (a) Just compensation shall be paid for outdoor advertising and all property rights pertaining to the same, including the right of the landowner upon whose land a sign is located, acquired through the processes of eminent domain.

(b) For the purposes of this part, just compensation shall include the consideration of damages to remaining properties, contiguous and noncontiguous, of an outdoor advertising sign company's interest, which remaining properties, together with the properties actually condemned, constituted an economic unit.

(c) The department is empowered to remove signs found in violation of Section 72-7-508 without payment of any compensation.

(4) Except as specifically provided in this section or Section 72-7-513, this part may not be construed to permit a person to place or maintain any outdoor advertising adjacent to any interstate or primary highway system which is prohibited by law or by any town, city, or county ordinance. Any town, city, county, governmental entity, or public utility which requires the removal, relocation, alteration, change, or termination of outdoor advertising shall pay just compensation as defined in this part and in Title 78, Chapter 34, Eminent Domain.

(5) Except as provided in Section 72-7-508, no sign shall be required to be removed by the department nor sign maintenance as described in this section be discontinued unless at the time of removal or discontinuance there are sufficient funds, from whatever source, appropriated and immediately available to pay the just compensation required under this section and unless at that time the federal funds required to be contributed under 23 U.S.C., Sec. 131, if any, with respect to the outdoor advertising being removed, have been appropriated and are immediately available to this state.

(6) (a) If any outdoor advertising use, structure, or permit may not be continued because of the widening, construction, or reconstruction along an interstate, federal aid primary highway existing as of June 1, 1991, or national highway systems highway, the owner shall have the option

to relocate and remodel the use, structure, or permit to another location:

    (i) on the same property;

    (ii) on adjacent property;

    (iii) on the same highway within 5280 feet of the previous location, which may be extended 5280 feet outside the areas described in Subsection 72-7-505(3)(c)(i)(A), on either side of the same highway; or

    (iv) mutually agreed upon by the owner and the county or municipality in which the use, structure, or permit is located.

  (b) The relocation under Subsection (6)(a) shall be in a commercial or industrial zoned area or where outdoor advertising is permitted under this part.

  (c) The county or municipality in which the use or structure is located shall, if necessary, provide for the relocation and remodeling by ordinance for a special exception to its zoning ordinance.

  (d) The relocated and remodeled use or structure may be:

    (i) erected to a height and angle to make it clearly visible to traffic on the main-traveled way of the highway to which it is relocated or remodeled;

    (ii) the same size and at least the same height as the previous use or structure, but the relocated use or structure may not exceed the size and height permitted under this part;

    (iii) relocated to a comparable vehicular traffic count.

  (7) (a) The governmental entity, quasi-governmental entity, or public utility that causes the need for the outdoor advertising relocation or remodeling as provided in Subsection (6)(a) shall pay the costs related to the relocation, remodeling, or acquisition.

  (b) If a governmental entity prohibits the relocation and remodeling as provided in Subsection (6)(a), it shall pay just compensation as provided in Subsection (3).   1999

72-7-510.5. Height adjustments for outdoor advertising signs.

  (1) If the view and readability of an outdoor advertising sign including a nonconforming sign as defined in Section 72-7-510 is obstructed due to a noise abatement or safety measure, grade change, construction, aesthetic improvement made by an agency of this state, directional sign, or widening along an interstate, federal aid primary highway existing as of June 1, 1991, or national highway systems highway, the owner of the sign may:

  (a) adjust the height of the sign; or

  (b) relocate the sign to a point within 500 feet of its prior location, if the sign complies with the spacing requirements under Section 72-7-505 and is in a commercial or industrial zone.

  (2) A height adjusted sign under this section does not constitute a substantial change to the sign.

  (3) The county or municipality in which the outdoor advertising sign is located shall, if necessary, provide for the height adjustment or relocation by ordinance for a special exception to its zoning ordinance.

  (4) (a) The height adjusted sign may be erected to a height and angle to make it clearly visible to traffic on the main-traveled way of the highway and shall be the same size as the previous sign.

  (b) The provisions of Subsection (4)(a) are an exception to the height requirements under Section 72-7-505.   2002

72-7-511. Violation of part — Misdemeanor.

A person who violates any provision of this part is guilty of a class B misdemeanor.   1998

72-7-512. Appeals by attorney general.

The attorney general may take such appeals as are provided for in 23 U.S.C., Sec. 131.   1998

72-7-513. Relocation on state highways.

  (1) As used in this section, "state highway" means those highways designated as state highways in Title 72, Chapter 4, Designation of State Highways, on July 1, 1999, and any subsequently designated state highway.

  (2) If any outdoor advertising use or structure may not be continued because of the widening, construction, or reconstruction along a state highway, the owner shall have the option to relocate and remodel the use or structure to another location:

  (a) on the same property;

  (b) on adjacent property;

  (c) within 2640 feet of the previous location on either side of the same highway; or

  (d) mutually agreed upon by the owner and the county or municipality in which the use, structure, or permit is located.

  (3) The relocation under Subsection (2) shall be in a commercial or industrial zoned area or where outdoor advertising is permitted under this part.

  (4) The county or municipality in which the use or structure is located shall, if necessary, provide for the relocation and remodeling by ordinance for a special exception to its zoning ordinance.

  (5) The relocated and remodeled use or structure may be:

    (a) erected to a height and angle to make it clearly visible to traffic on the main-traveled way of the highway to which it is relocated or remodeled;

    (b) the same size and at least the same height as the previous use or structure, but the relocated use or structure may not exceed the size and height permitted under this part;

    (c) relocated to a comparable vehicular traffic count.

  (6) (a) The governmental entity, quasi-governmental entity, or public utility that causes the need for the outdoor advertising relocation or remodeling as provided in Subsection (2) shall pay the costs related to the relocation, remodeling, or acquisition.

    (b) If a governmental entity prohibits the relocation and remodeling as provided in Subsection (2)(a), (b), or (c), it shall pay just compensation as provided in Subsection 72-7-510(3).   1999

72-7-514. Landscape control program.

  (1) As used in this section, "landscape control" means trimming or removal of seedlings, saplings, trees and vegetation along the interstate, federal aid primary highway existing as of June 1, 1991, and national highway system right-of-way to provide clear visibility of outdoor advertising.

  (2) (a) The department shall establish a landscape control program as provided under this section.

    (b) Except as provided in this section, a person, including an outdoor advertising sign owner or business owner may not perform or cause landscape control to be performed.

  (3) (a) An outdoor advertising sign owner or business owner may submit a request for landscape control to the department.

(b) Within 60 days of the request under Subsection (3)(a), the department shall:

(i) conduct a field review of the request with a representative of the sign or business owner, the department, and the Federal Highway Administration to consider the following issues listed in their order of priority:

(A) safety;

(B) protection of highway features, including right-of-way and landscaping;

(C) aesthetics; and

(D) motorists' view of the sign or business; and

(ii) notify the sign or business owner what, if any, trimming, removal, restoration, banking, or other landscape control shall be allowed as decided by the department, after consultation with the Federal Highway Administration.

(c) If the sign or business owner elects to proceed, in accordance with the decision issued under this subsection, the department shall issue a permit that describes what landscape control may be allowed, assigns responsibility for costs, describes the safety measures to be observed, and attaches any explanatory plans or other information.

(4) The department shall establish an appeals process within the department for landscape control decisions made under Subsection (3).

(5) (a) A person who performs landscape control in violation of this section is guilty of a class C misdemeanor, and is liable to the owner for treble the amount of damages sustained to the landscape.

(b) Each permit issued under this section shall notify the permit holder of the penalties under Subsection (5)(a).   1998

72-7-515. Utah-Federal Agreement — Severability clause.

(1) As used in this section, "Utah-Federal Agreement" means the agreement relating to outdoor advertising that is described under Section 72-7-501, and it includes any modifications to the agreement that are signed on behalf of both the state and the United States Secretary of Transportation.

(2) The provisions of this part are subject to and shall be superseded by conflicting provisions of the Utah-Federal Agreement.

(3) If any provision of this part or its application to any person or circumstance is found to be unconstitutional, or in conflict with or superseded by the Utah-Federal Agreement, the remainder of this part and the application of the provision to other persons or circumstances shall not be affected by it.   1999

72-7-516. Relocating outdoor advertising structure to maintain required distance from high voltage overhead lines.

If an outdoor advertising structure needs to be moved so that the sign can be reposted or maintenance performed without having to comply with the distance or notification requirements of Section 54-8c-2, or in order to comply with distance or notification requirements imposed by the National Electrical Safety Code or any other similar applicable regulation promulgated by a federal agency, then:

(1) the owner shall have the right to relocate the same or similar type structure to the minimal number of feet necessary:

(a) on the same property; or

(b) if the same property is not available, on another property; and

(2) the county or municipality in which the outdoor advertising structure is located shall, if necessary, accommodate the move by a special exception to its zoning ordinance.   2002

CHAPTER 8

PEDESTRIAN SAFETY AND FACILITIES ACT

72-8-101. Title.

This chapter is known as the "Pedestrian Safety and Facilities Act."   1998

72-8-102. Definitions.

As used in this chapter:

(1) "Construction" means the function of constructing or reconstructing a sidewalk with or without curb and gutter and includes land acquisition and engineering or inspection as defined by the rules and regulations of the department.

(2) "Curb and gutter" means the area between the roadway and sidewalk designed for water runoff and providing a barrier for safety of pedestrian and vehicular traffic.

(3) "Participating municipality" means a city of the third, fourth, or fifth class or a town.

(4) "Pedestrian safety devices" means any device or method designed to foster the safety of pedestrian traffic including sidewalks, curbs, gutters, and pedestrian overpasses.   2003

72-8-103. Designated county and municipal sidewalks — Construction on easements granted by transportation department.

(1) All sidewalks, including curbs and gutters within the unincorporated areas of a county and within nonparticipating municipalities situated within the county, are designated county sidewalks. All sidewalks within participating municipalities are designated municipal sidewalks.

(2) Counties and participating municipalities may construct and maintain curbs, gutters, sidewalks, and pedestrian safety devices adjacent to the traveled portion of state highways upon easements that may be granted by the department. The department shall cooperate with counties and participating municipalities to accomplish pedestrian safety construction and maintenance.

(3) A county or municipality may construct and maintain pedestrian safety devices on state highways in compliance with rules made by the department.   1998

72-8-104. Funding priorities by county and municipality officials — Factors.

(1) A county or municipality may use a portion of their B and C road funds for pedestrian safety devices under this part.

(2) The county legislative body of the counties and the governing officials of participating municipalities may establish funding priorities relating to construction of curbs, gutters, sidewalks, or other pedestrian safety construction, with funds permitted to be expended by this part, based on factors including, but not limited to:

(a) existing useable rights-of-way;

(b) vehicle-pedestrian accident experience;

(c) average daily vehicle traffic;

(d) average daily pedestrian traffic;

(e) average daily school age pedestrian traffic; and

(f) speed of vehicle traffic.

(3) All construction performed under this part shall be barrier free to wheelchairs at crosswalks and intersections. 1998

72-8-105. Pedestrian safety to be considered in highway planning.

A highway authority shall consider pedestrian safety in all highway engineering and planning where pedestrian traffic may be a significant factor on all projects within the state or any of its political subdivisions. 1998

72-8-106. Rules and regulations — Cooperation with the county legislative body.

The department shall:

(1) make rules providing for uniform accounting of the funds permitted to be expended for curbs, gutters, sidewalks, and pedestrian safety devices, as provided in this part; and

(2) cooperate with the county executives and county legislative bodies and the governing officials of participating municipalities in order to implement this part and make rules required by this part. 1998

72-8-107. County or city granting exemption from construction — Not eligible to utilize funds under part.

(1) This part may not be construed to substitute or replace the construction of curbs, gutters, sidewalks, or pedestrian safety devices by any counties or participating municipalities. Funds expended under this part are in addition to funds normally used by counties and participating municipalities for pedestrian safety devices and may not be used in substitution for local funding.

(2) If any county or participating municipalities or any of their agencies grant an exemption or deferral agreement for the construction of sidewalks, curbs, gutters, or pedestrian safety devices which are otherwise normally required, the area for which the exemption or deferral agreement applies is not be eligible to utilize funds permitted to be expended by this part. 1998

72-8-108. Repealed. 2003

CHAPTER 9

MOTOR CARRIER SAFETY ACT

Part 1

General Provisions

Part 2

Motor Carrier Advisory Board

Part 3

Department Duties

Part 4

Motor Carrier Liability — Duties

Part 5

Ports-of-Entry

Part 6

Tow Truck Provisions

Part 7

Penalties, Fines, and Fees

PART 1

GENERAL PROVISIONS

72-9-101. Title.

This chapter is known as the "Motor Carrier Safety Act."   1998

72-9-102. Definitions.

As used in this chapter:

(1) (a) "Commercial vehicle" means a motor vehicle, vehicle, trailer, or semitrailer used or maintained for business, compensation, or profit to transport passengers or property on a highway if the commercial vehicle:

(i) has a manufacturer's gross vehicle weight rating or gross combination weight rating of 10,001 or more pounds;

(ii) is designed to transport more than 15 passengers, including the driver; or

(iii) is used in the transportation of hazardous materials and is required to be placarded in accordance with 49 C.F.R. Part 172, Subpart F.

(b) The following vehicles are not considered a commercial vehicle for purposes of this chapter:

(i) equipment owned and operated by the United States Department of Defense when driven by any active duty military personnel and members of the reserves and national guard on active duty including personnel on full-time national guard duty, personnel on part-time training, and national guard military technicians and civilians who are required to wear military uniforms and are subject to the code of military justice;

(ii) firefighting and emergency vehicles, operated by emergency personnel, not including commercial tow trucks; and

(iii) recreational vehicles that are driven solely as family or personal conveyances for noncommercial purposes.

(2) "Motor carrier" means a person engaged in or transacting the business of transporting passengers, freight, merchandise, or other property by a commercial vehicle on a highway within this state and includes a tow truck business.

(3) "Tow truck" means a motor vehicle constructed, designed, altered, or equipped primarily for the purpose of towing or removing damaged, disabled, abandoned, seized, or impounded vehicles from a highway or other place by means of a crane, hoist, tow bar, tow line, dolly, tilt bed, or other means.

(4) "Tow truck service" means the functions and any ancillary operations associated with recovering, removing, and towing a vehicle and its load from a highway or other place by means of a tow truck.

(5) "Transportation" means the actual movement of property or passengers by motor vehicle, including loading, unloading, and any ancillary service provided by the motor carrier in connection with movement by motor vehicle, which is performed by or on behalf of the motor carrier, its employees or agents, or under the authority of the motor carrier, its employees or agents, or under the apparent authority and with the knowledge of the motor carrier.   2003

72-9-103. Rulemaking — Adjudicative proceedings.

(1) In accordance with Title 63, Chapter 46a, Utah Administrative Rulemaking Act, the department shall make rules:

(a) adopting by reference in whole or in part the Federal Motor Carrier Safety Regulations including minimum security requirements for motor carriers;

(b) specifying the equipment required to be carried in each tow truck, including limits on loads that may be moved based on equipment capacity and load weight;

(c) specifying collection procedures, in conjunction with the administration and enforcement of the safety or security requirements, for the motor carrier fee under Section 72-9-706; and

(d) providing for the necessary administration and enforcement of this chapter.

(2) The department shall comply with Title 63, Chapter 46b, Administrative Procedures Act, in its adjudicative proceedings.   1998

72-9-104. Motor carriers to operate under chapter.

A motor carrier may not operate any commercial vehicle for the transportation of persons or property on any public highway in this state except in accordance with this chapter, and rules and orders of the department.   1998

72-9-105. Information lettered on vehicle — Exceptions.

(1) Except under Subsection (4), a motor carrier shall have lettered on both sides of any vehicle used for transportation of persons or property:

(a) the name of the motor carrier company; and

(b) the location of domicile by city and state.

(2) The lettering shall be free from obstruction and legible from a distance of at least 50 feet.

(3) (a) In addition to the lettering required under Subsection (1), the department may require an identification number assigned by the department to be displayed in accordance with this section.

(b) The number may be used to assist the department in conjunction with the U.S. Department of Transportation to develop a program to improve motor carrier safety enforcement.

(4) A commercial vehicle primarily used by a farmer for the production of agricultural products is exempt from the provisions of this section.   1998

72-9-106. Exemption for public utilities from regulations establishing hours of service.

(1) As used in this section, "emergency" means a condition which jeopardizes life or property or that endangers public health and safety.

(2) A person who is an employee of an electrical corporation, a gas corporation, or a telephone corporation, as these corporations are defined in Section

54-2-1, is exempt from any hours of service rules and regulations for drivers while operating a public utility vehicle within the state during the emergency restoration of public utility service. 1998

72-9-107. Medical exemptions for farm vehicle operators.

Except as provided in Section 53-3-206, an operator of a farm vehicle or combination of farm vehicles that are under 26,001 pounds gross vehicle weight rating and not operated as a commercial motor vehicle, in accordance with Subsection 53-3-102(5)(b)(ii), is exempt from additional requirements for physical qualifications, medical examinations, and medical certification. 2000

PART 2

MOTOR CARRIER ADVISORY BOARD

72-9-201. Motor Carrier Advisory Board created — Appointment — Terms — Meetings — Per diem and expenses — Duties.

(1) There is created within the department the Motor Carrier Advisory Board consisting of five members appointed by the governor.

(2) Each member of the board shall:

(a) represent experience and expertise in the areas of motor carrier transportation, commerce, agriculture, economics, shipping, or highway safety;

(b) be selected at large on a nonpartisan basis; and

(c) have been a legal resident of the state for at least one year immediately preceding the date of appointment.

(3) (a) Except as required by Subsection (3)(b), as terms of current board members expire, the governor shall appoint each new member or reappointed member to a four-year term.

(b) The governor shall, at the time of appointment or reappointment, adjust the length of terms to ensure that the terms of board members are staggered so that approximately half of the board is appointed every two years.

(c) A member shall serve from the date of appointment until a replacement is appointed.

(4) When a vacancy occurs in the membership for any reason, the replacement shall be appointed for the unexpired term beginning the day following the expiration of the preceding term.

(5) The board shall elect its own chair and vice chair at the first regular meeting of each calendar year.

(6) The board shall meet at least quarterly or as needed when called by the chair.

(7) Any three voting members constitute a quorum for the transaction of business that comes before the board.

(8) (a) Members shall receive no compensation or benefits for their services, but may receive per diem and expenses incurred in the performance of the member's official duties at the rates established by the Division of Finance under Sections 63A-3-106 and 63A-3-107.

(b) Members may decline to receive per diem and expenses for their service.

(9) The board shall advise the department and the commission on interpretation, adoption, and implementation of this chapter and other motor carrier related issues.

(10) The department shall provide staff support to the board. 1998

PART 3

DEPARTMENT DUTIES

72-9-301. Duties — Enforcement — Federal safety regulations — Audits — Rights of entry for audits.

(1) The department shall administer and in cooperation with the Department of Public Safety, Utah Highway Patrol Division, as specified under Section 53-8-105, shall enforce state and federal laws related to the operation of a motor carrier within the state, including:

(a) the operation of ports-of-entry under Section 72-9-501;

(b) vehicle size, weight, and load restrictions;

(c) security requirements;

(d) safety requirements; and

(e) the Federal Motor Carrier Safety Regulations as contained in Title 49, Code of Federal Regulations.

(2) The department shall conduct compliance audits and inspections as needed to enforce state and federal laws related to the operation of a motor carrier.

(3) (a) In accordance with Subsection (3)(b), the department's authorized employees or agents may enter, inspect, and examine any lands, buildings, and equipment of a motor carrier subject to this chapter, to inspect and copy any accounts, books, records, and documents in order to administer and enforce state and federal laws related to the operation of a motor carrier provided:

(i) the department's authorized employees or agents schedule an appointment with the motor carrier prior to entering, inspecting, or examining any facility or records of a motor carrier;

(ii) if the department's authorized employees or agents believe that a criminal violation is involved and that a scheduled appointment would compromise the detection of the alleged criminal violation, no appointment is necessary.

(b) A motor carrier shall submit its lands, buildings, and equipment for inspection and examination and shall submit its accounts, books, records, and documents for inspection and copying in accordance with this section. 1998

72-9-302. Interstate agreements.

(1) The department may enter into agreements with other states to allow the cooperative base state safety and insurance regulation of motor carriers transporting property or passengers in interstate commerce.

(2) An agreement may authorize another state to:

(a) accept the filing of a certificate and affidavit of insurance;

(b) issue a revocation, suspension, restriction, probation, and reinstatement order or notice; and

(c) collect and disburse any fee to and from another state that participates in the base state program.

(3) An agreement may allow the exchange of information for audit, reporting, and enforcement purposes. 1998

72-9-303. Cease and desist orders — Registration sanctions.

(1) The department may issue cease and desist orders to any person:

(a) who engages in or represents himself to be engaged in a motor carrier operation that is in violation of this chapter;

(b) to prevent the violation of any of the provisions of this title; and

(c) who otherwise violates this chapter or any rules adopted under this chapter.

(2) (a) The department shall notify the Motor Vehicle Division of the State Tax Commission upon having reasonable grounds to believe that a motor carrier is in violation of this chapter. Upon receiving notice by the department, the Motor Vehicle Division shall refuse registration or shall suspend or revoke a registration as provided in Sections 41-1a-109 and 41-1a-110.

(b) The department shall notify the Motor Vehicle Division immediately upon being satisfied that a motor carrier, reported as being in violation under Subsection (2)(a), is in compliance with this chapter. Upon receiving notice by the department, the Motor Vehicle Division shall remove any restriction made on a registration under this chapter. 1998

PART 4

MOTOR CARRIER LIABILITY — DUTIES

72-9-401. Liability of motor carriers for loss or damage to freight.

(1) (a) A motor carrier receiving property for transportation from one point in this state to another point in this state shall issue a receipt or bill of lading for the property, and shall be liable to the lawful holder of the property for any loss, damage, or injury to the property caused by the motor carrier, or by any motor carrier to which the property may be delivered or over whose line or lines the property may pass within this state when transported on a through bill of lading.

(b) A contract, receipt, rule, regulation, or other limitation of any character whatsoever may not exempt the motor carrier from this liability.

(2) A motor carrier that receives property for transportation or any motor carrier delivering the property to the consignee shall be liable to the lawful holder of the receipt or bill of lading, or to any party entitled to recover on the property whether the receipt or bill of lading has been issued or not, for the full actual loss, damage or injury to the property caused by the motor carrier, or by any motor carrier to which the property may have been delivered or over whose line or lines the property may have passed within this state when transported on a through bill of lading.

(3) (a) The provisions of Subsection (2) apply notwithstanding any limitation of liability or of the amount of recovery, or any representation or agreement as to the value of the property in any receipt or bill of lading or in any contract, rule, or regulation.

(b) Any limitation of liability is unlawful and void if the provisions respecting liability for full actual loss, damage, or injury notwithstanding any limitation of liability or of recovery, or any representation or agreement or release as to value to property, except livestock, received for transportation concerning which the motor carrier expressly authorizes or requires, by order of the commission, the establishment and maintenance of rates dependent upon the value declared in writing by the shipper or agreed to in writing as the released value of the property.

(c) The declaration or agreement shall have no other effect than to limit liability and recovery to an amount not exceeding the value so declared or agreed upon. 1998

72-9-402. Limitation of time for presenting claims and bringing suit.

(1) A motor carrier shall allow at least:

(a) 90 days for giving notice of claims for any loss, damage, or injury to property;

(b) four months for the filing of claims; and

(c) two years for the institution of suits.

(2) If the loss or injury complained of is due to delay or damage while being loaded or unloaded, or damage in transit caused by carelessness or negligence, a notice of claim or a filing of claim is not required as a condition precedent to recovery. 1998

72-9-403. Contribution between connecting motor carriers.

(1) The motor carrier paying for the loss or damage to property transported or received is entitled to recovery from the motor carrier responsible for the loss or damage, or on the motor carrier's line the loss, damage, or injury was sustained.

(2) The amount of the loss or damage is equal to the amount the motor carrier is required to pay to the persons entitled to the recovery. 1998

72-9-404. Bills of lading — Form.

Bills of lading issued by any motor carrier for the transportation of goods within this state shall conform to this chapter, rules made under this chapter, and Title 70A, Chapter 7, Part 3, Bills of Lading — Special Provisions, that are not in conflict with this chapter. 1998

PART 5

PORTS-OF-ENTRY

72-9-501. Construction, operation, and maintenance of ports-of-entry by the department — Function of ports-of-entry — Checking and citation powers of port-of-entry agents.

(1) (a) The department shall construct ports-of-entry for the purpose of checking motor carriers, drivers, vehicles, and vehicle loads for compliance with state and federal laws including laws relating to:

(i) driver qualifications;

(ii) Title 53, Chapter 3, Part 4, Uniform Commercial Driver License Act;

(iii) vehicle registration;

(iv) fuel tax payment;

(v) vehicle size, weight, and load;

(vi) security or insurance;

(vii) this chapter;

(viii) hazardous material as defined under 49 U.S.C. 5102;

(ix) livestock transportation; and

(x) safety.

(b) The ports-of-entry shall be located on state highways at sites determined by the department.

(2) (a) The ports-of-entry shall be operated and maintained by the department.

(b) A port-of-entry agent may check, inspect, or test drivers, vehicles, and vehicle loads for compliance with state and federal laws specified in Subsection (1).

(3) (a) A port-of-entry agent, in whose presence an offense described in this section is committed, may:

(i) issue and deliver a misdemeanor or infraction citation under Section 77-7-18;

(ii) request and administer chemical tests to determine blood alcohol concentration in compliance with Section 41-6a-515;

(iii) place a driver out-of-service in accordance with Section 53-3-417; and

(iv) serve a driver with notice of the Driver License Division of the Department of Public Safety's intention to disqualify the driver's privilege to drive a commercial motor vehicle in accordance with Section 53-3-418.

(b) This section does not grant actual arrest powers as defined in Section 77-7-1 to a port-of-entry agent who is not a peace officer or special function officer designated under Title 53, Chapter 13, Peace Officer Classifications.   2005

72-9-502. Motor vehicles to stop at ports-of-entry — Signs — Exceptions — Rulemaking — By-pass permits.

(1) Except under Subsection (3), a motor carrier operating a motor vehicle with a gross vehicle weight of 10,001 pounds or more or any motor vehicle carrying livestock as defined in Section 4-24-2, shall stop at a port-of-entry as required under this section.

(2) The department may erect and maintain signs directing motor vehicles to a port-of-entry as provided in this section.

(3) A motor vehicle required to stop at a port-of-entry under Subsection (1) is exempt from this section if:

(a) the total one-way trip distance for the motor vehicle would be increased by more than 5% or three miles, whichever is greater if diverted to a port-of-entry; or

(b) the motor vehicle is operating under a temporary port-of-entry by-pass permit issued under Subsection (4).

(4) (a) In accordance with Title 63, Chapter 46a, Utah Administrative Rulemaking Act, the department shall make rules for the issuance of a temporary port-of-entry by-pass permit exempting a motor vehicle from the provisions of Subsection (1) if the department determines that the permit is needed to accommodate highway transportation needs due to multiple daily or weekly trips in the proximity of a port-of-entry.

(b) The rules under Subsection (4)(a) shall provide that one permit may be issued to a motor carrier for multiple motor vehicles.   2005

72-9-503. Authority to enter agreement with other states for joint port-of-entry operation.

(1) The executive director of the department may negotiate and enter into bilateral agreements with a representative designated by a contiguous state for the construction, operation, maintenance, and staffing of a jointly occupied port-of-entry.

(2) The agreement may provide for the collection of highway user fees, registration fees, permit fees, fuel taxes, and any other fees and taxes by either state jointly occupying a port-of-entry.

(3) The agreement may provide for the enforcement of state and federal laws as provided in this chapter.   1998

PART 6

TOW TRUCK PROVISIONS

72-9-601. Tow truck motor carrier requirements — Authorized towing certificates.

(1) In addition to the requirements of this chapter, a tow truck motor carrier shall:

(a) ensure that all the motor carrier's tow truck drivers are properly:

(i) trained to operate tow truck equipment;

(ii) licensed, as required under Title 53, Chapter 3, Uniform Driver License Act; and

(iii) complying with the requirements under Sections 41-6a-1406 and 72-9-603; and

(b) obtain and display a current authorized towing certificate for the tow truck motor carrier, and each tow truck and driver, as required under Section 72-9-602.

(2) A tow truck motor carrier may only perform a towing service described in Section 41-6a-1406, 41-6a-1407, or 72-9-603, with a tow truck and driver that has a current authorized towing certificate under this part.   2005

72-9-602. Towing inspections, investigations, and certification — Equipment requirements — Consumer information.

(1) (a) The department shall inspect, investigate, and certify tow truck motor carriers, tow trucks, and tow truck drivers to ensure compliance with this chapter and compliance with Sections 41-6a-1406 and 41-6a-1407.

(b) The inspection, investigation, and certification shall be conducted prior to any tow truck operation and at least every two years thereafter.

(c) (i) The department shall issue an authorized towing certificate for each tow truck motor carrier, tow truck, and driver that complies with this part.

(ii) The certificate shall expire two years from the month of issuance.

(d) The department may charge a biennial fee established under Section 63-38-3.2 to cover the cost of the inspection, investigation, and certification required under this part.

(2) The department shall make consumer protection information available to the public that may use a tow truck motor carrier.   2005

72-9-603. Towing notice requirements — Cost responsibilities — Abandoned vehicle title restrictions — Rules for maximum rates and certification.

(1) Except for tow truck service that was ordered by a peace officer, or a person acting on behalf of a law enforcement agency, or a highway authority, as defined in Section 72-1-102, after performing a tow truck service that is being done without the vehicle, vessel, or outboard motor owner's knowledge, the tow truck operator or the tow truck motor carrier shall:

(a) immediately upon arriving at the place of storage or impound of the vehicle, vessel, or outboard motor, contact the law enforcement agency having jurisdiction over the area where the vehicle, vessel, or outboard motor was picked up and notify the agency of the:

(i) location of the vehicle, vessel, or outboard motor;

(ii) date, time, and location from which the vehicle, vessel, or outboard motor was removed;

(iii) reasons for the removal of the vehicle, vessel, or outboard motor;

(iv) person who requested the removal of the vehicle, vessel, or outboard motor; and

(v) vehicle, vessel, or outboard motor's description, including its identification number and license number or other identification number issued by a state agency; and

(b) within two business days of performing the tow truck service, send a certified letter to the last-known address of the registered owner and lien holder of the vehicle, vessel, or outboard motor obtained from the Motor Vehicle Division or if the person has actual knowledge of the owner's address to the current address, notifying him of the:

    (i) location of the vehicle, vessel, or outboard motor;

    (ii) date, time, location from which the vehicle, vessel, or outboard motor was removed;

    (iii) reasons for the removal of the vehicle, vessel, or outboard motor;

    (iv) person who requested the removal of the vehicle, vessel, or outboard motor;

    (v) a description, including its identification number and license number or other identification number issued by a state agency; and

    (vi) costs and procedures to retrieve the vehicle, vessel, or outboard motor.

(2) Until the tow truck operator or tow truck motor carrier reports the removal as required under Subsection (1)(a), a tow truck motor carrier or impound yard may not:

    (a) collect any fee associated with the removal; and

    (b) begin charging storage fees.

(3) The owner of a vehicle, vessel, or outboard motor lawfully removed is only responsible for paying:

    (a) the tow truck service and storage fees set in accordance with Subsection (7); and

    (b) the administrative impound fee set in Section 41-6a-1406, if applicable.

(4) The fees under Subsection (3) are a possessory lien on the vehicle, vessel, or outboard motor until paid.

(5) A person may not request a transfer of title to an abandoned vehicle until at least 30 days after notice has been sent under Subsection (1)(b).

(6) A tow truck motor carrier or impound yard shall clearly and conspicuously post and disclose all its current fees and rates for tow truck service and storage of a vehicle in accordance with rules established under Subsection (7).

(7) In accordance with Title 63, Chapter 46a, Utah Administrative Rulemaking Act, the Department of Transportation shall:

    (a) set maximum rates that:

        (i) tow truck motor carriers may charge for the tow truck service of a vehicle, vessel, or outboard motor that are transported in response to:

            (A) a peace officer dispatch call;

            (B) a motor vehicle division call; and

            (C) any other call where the owner of the vehicle, vessel, or outboard motor has not consented to the removal; and

        (ii) impound yards may charge for the storage of a vehicle, vessel, or outboard motor stored as a result of one of the conditions listed under Subsection (7)(a)(i);

    (b) establish authorized towing certification requirements, not in conflict with federal law, related to incident safety, clean-up, and hazardous material handling; and

    (c) specify the form and content of the posting and disclosure of fees and rates charged by a tow truck motor carrier or impound yard.   **2005**

72-9-604. Regulatory powers of local authorities — Tow trucks.

(1) A county or municipal legislative or governing body may not enact or enforce any ordinance, regulation, rule, or fee pertaining to a tow truck or tow truck motor carrier that conflicts with this part.

(2) A tow truck motor carrier that has a county or municipal business license for a place of business located within that county or municipality may not be required to obtain another business license in order to perform a tow truck service in another county or municipality if there is not a business location in the other county or municipality.

(3) A county or municipal legislative body may require an annual tow truck safety inspection in addition to the inspections required under Sections 53-8-205 and 72-9-602 if:

    (a) no fee is charged for the inspection; and

    (b) the inspection complies with federal motor carrier safety regulations.

(4) A tow truck shall be subject to only one annual safety inspection under Subsection (3). A county or municipality that requires the additional annual safety inspection shall accept the same inspection performed by another county or municipality.   **1998**

72-9-605. Exception from part.

This part does not apply to a person who is towing a vehicle owned by that person in a noncommercial operation.   **1998**

PART 7

PENALTIES, FINES, AND FEES

72-9-701. Penalty for unlawful conduct.

(1) Unless otherwise specified, any person who violates the provisions of this chapter or who aids or abets another person in a violation of this chapter is guilty of a class B misdemeanor. A second or subsequent conviction for a violation of this chapter or of aiding or abetting another person in a violation of this chapter is a class A misdemeanor.

(2) Unless otherwise specified, any person who fails to obey any lawful order or rule made under this chapter is guilty of a class B misdemeanor. A second or subsequent conviction for failing to obey any lawful order or rule made under this chapter is a class A misdemeanor.   **1998**

72-9-702. Existing rights of action unaffected — Penalties cumulative.

(1) This chapter may not be construed to have the effect of releasing or waiving any right of action by the state, the department or any person for any right, penalty, or forfeiture which may have arisen or occurred under any law of this state before May 10, 1983, or which arises or occurs after May 10, 1983.

(2) All penalties accruing under this chapter are cumulative, and a suit for the recovery of one penalty is not a bar to and shall not affect the recovery of any other penalty or forfeiture, and is not a bar to any criminal prosecution against any motor carrier, or any officer, director, agent, or employee of a motor carrier, or any other corporation or person, or a bar to the exercise by the department, through the court, of its power to punish for contempt.   **1998**

72-9-703. Civil penalties for violations — Compromise.

(1) In addition to any other penalties, a motor carrier that fails or neglects to comply with any provision of the Constitution of this state, statute, or any rule or order of the department is subject to a civil

penalty of not less than $500 nor more than $2,000 for each offense.

(2) Every violation of any provision of the constitution of this state, statute, or any rule or order of the department, is a separate and distinct offense. Each day's continuance of the violation is a separate and distinct offense.

(3) (a) The civil penalty may be compromised by the department and a determination of compromise is appealable by the person alleged to have committed the violation. In determining the amount of the penalty or the amount agreed upon in compromise, the department shall consider the:

(i) gravity of the violation; and

(ii) good faith of the person charged in attempting to achieve compliance after notification of the violation.

(b) The amount of the penalty when finally determined or the amount agreed upon in compromise may be deducted from any sums owing by the state to the person charged or may be recovered in a civil action in the courts of this state.

(4) In construing and enforcing the provisions of this chapter relating to penalties, the act, omission, or failure of any officer, agent, or employee of any motor carrier, acting within the scope of his official duties or employment, is deemed to be the act, omission, or failure of the motor carrier. 1998

72-9-704. Assignment of administrative law judge.

(1) The department shall assign an administrative law judge to hear contested matters.

(2) The administrative law judge's orders shall be reviewed by the department. 1998

72-9-705. Disposition of fees and civil fines.

All fees and civil fines received and collected under this chapter shall be transmitted daily to the state treasurer and deposited in the Transportation Fund. 1998

72-9-706. Motor carrier fee for certain vehicles — Collection.

(1) A motor carrier, not subject to the fee under Section 41-1a-1219, who operates a commercial vehicle on a highway within this state shall pay an annual motor carrier fee at the same rate provided under Section 41-1a-1219 for each motor vehicle or combination of motor vehicles operated in this state.

(2) The department shall collect the fee required under this section. 1998

CHAPTER 10

AERONAUTICS

Part 1

Uniform Aeronautical Regulatory Act

Part 2

Uniform Airports Act

PART 1

UNIFORM AERONAUTICAL REGULATORY ACT

72-10-101. Title.

This chapter is known as the "Aeronautics Act."

1998

72-10-102. Definitions.

As used in this chapter:

(1) "Acrobatics" means the intentional maneuvers of an aircraft not necessary to air navigation.

(2) "Aeronautics" means transportation by aircraft, air instruction, the operation, repair, or maintenance of aircraft, and the design, operation, repair, or maintenance of airports, or other air navigation facilities.

(3) "Aeronautics instructor" means any individual engaged in giving or offering to give instruction in aeronautics, flying, or ground subjects, either with or without:

(a) compensation or other reward;

(b) advertising the occupation;

(c) calling his facilities an air school, or any equivalent term; or

(d) employing or using other instructors.

(4) "Aircraft" means any contrivance now known or in the future invented, used, or designed for navigation of or flight in the air.

(5) "Air instruction" means the imparting of aeronautical information by any aviation instructor or in any air school or flying club.

(6) "Airport" means any area of land, water, or both, that:

(a) is used or is made available for landing and takeoff;

(b) provides facilities for the shelter, supply, and repair of aircraft, and handling of passengers and cargo; and

(c) meets the minimum requirements established by the division as to size and design, surface, marking, equipment, and operation.

(7) "Airport authority" means a political subdivision of the state, other than a county or municipality, that is authorized by statute to operate an airport.

(8) "Air school" means any person engaged in giving, offering to give, or advertising, representing, or holding himself out as giving, with or without compensation or other reward, instruc-

tion in aeronautics, flying, or ground subjects, or in more than one of these subjects.

(9) "Airworthiness" means conformity with requirements prescribed by the Federal Aviation Administration regarding the structure or functioning of aircraft, engine, parts, or accessories.

(10) "Antique aircraft" means a civil aircraft that is:

(a) 30 years old or older, calculated as to include the current year;

(b) primarily a collector's item and used solely for recreational or display purposes;

(c) not used for daily or regular transportation; and

(d) not used for commercial operations.

(11) "Civil aircraft" means any aircraft other than a public aircraft.

(12) "Commercial aircraft" means aircraft used for commercial purposes.

(13) "Commercial airport" means a landing area, landing strip, or airport that may be used for commercial operations.

(14) "Commercial flight operator" means a person who conducts commercial operations.

(15) "Commercial operations" means:

(a) any operations of an aircraft for compensation or hire or any services performed incidental to the operation of any aircraft for which a fee is charged or compensation is received, including the servicing, maintaining, and repairing of aircraft, the rental or charter of aircraft, the operation of flight or ground schools, the operation of aircraft for the application or distribution of chemicals or other substances, and the operation of aircraft for hunting and fishing; or

(b) the brokering or selling of any of these services; but

(c) does not include any operations of aircraft as common carriers certificated by the federal government or the services incidental to those operations.

(16) "Dealer" means any person who is actively engaged in the business of flying for demonstration purposes, or selling or exchanging aircraft, and who has an established place of business.

(17) "Division" means the Operations Division in the Department of Transportation, created in Section 72-1-204.

(18) "Experimental aircraft" means:

(a) any aircraft designated by the Federal Aviation Administration or the military as experimental and used solely for the purpose of experiments, or tests regarding the structure or functioning of aircraft, engines, or their accessories; and

(b) any aircraft designated by the Federal Aviation Administration as:

(i) being custom or amateur built; and

(ii) used for recreational, educational, or display purposes.

(19) "Flight" means any kind of locomotion by aircraft while in the air.

(20) "Flying club" means five or more persons who for neither profit nor reward own, lease, or use one or more aircraft for the purpose of instruction, pleasure, or both.

(21) "Glider" means an aircraft heavier than air, similar to an airplane, but without a power plant.

(22) "Mechanic" means a person who constructs, repairs, adjusts, inspects, or overhauls aircraft, engines, or accessories.

(23) "Parachute jumper" means any person who has passed the required test for jumping with a parachute from an aircraft, and has passed an examination showing that he possesses the required physical and mental qualifications for the jumping.

(24) "Parachute rigger" means any person who has passed the required test for packing, repairing, and maintaining parachutes.

(25) "Passenger aircraft" means aircraft used for transporting persons, in addition to the pilot or crew, with or without their necessary personal belongings.

(26) "Person" means any individual, corporation, limited liability company, or association of individuals.

(27) "Pilot" means any person who operates the controls of an aircraft while in-flight.

(28) "Primary glider" means any glider that has a gliding angle of less than ten to one.

(29) "Public aircraft" means an aircraft used exclusively in the service of any government or of any political subdivision, including the government of the United States, of the District of Columbia, and of any state, territory, or insular possession of the United States, but not including any government-owned aircraft engaged in carrying persons or goods for commercial purposes.

(30) "Reckless flying" means the operation or piloting of any aircraft recklessly, or in a manner as to endanger the property, life, or body of any person, due regard being given to the prevailing weather conditions, field conditions, and to the territory being flown over.

(31) "Registration number" means the number assigned by the Federal Aviation Administration to any aircraft, whether or not the number includes a letter or letters.

(32) "Secondary glider" means any glider that has a gliding angle between ten to one and 16 to one, inclusive.

(33) "Soaring glider" means any glider that has a gliding angle of more than 16 to one.   2003

72-10-103. Rulemaking requirement.

(1) In accordance with Title 63, Chapter 46a, Utah Administrative Rulemaking Act, the department shall make rules:

(a) governing the establishment, location, and use of air navigation facilities;

(b) regulating the use, licensing, and supervision of airports;

(c) establishing minimum standards with which all air navigation facilities, flying clubs, aircraft, gliders, pilots, and airports must comply; and

(d) safeguarding from accident and protecting the safety of persons operating or using aircraft and persons and property on the ground.

(2) The rules may:

(a) require that any device or accessory that forms part of any aircraft or its equipment be certified as complying with this chapter;

(b) limit the use of any device or accessory as necessary for safety; and

(c) develop and promote aeronautics within this state.

(3) (a) To avoid the danger of accident incident to confusion arising from conflicting rules governing aeronautics, the rules shall conform as nearly as possible with federal legislation, rules, regulations, and orders on aeronautics.

(b) The rules may not be inconsistent with paramount federal legislation, rules, regulations, and orders on the subject.

(4) The department may not require any pilot, aircraft, or mechanic who has procured a license under the Civil Aeronautics Authority of the United States to obtain a license from this state, other than required by this chapter.

(5) The department may not make rules that conflict with the regulations of:

(a) the Civil Aeronautics Authority; or

(b) other federal agencies authorized to regulate the particular activity.

(6) All schedules of charges, tolls, and fees established by the division shall be approved and adopted by the department.

(7) The department shall comply with the procedures and requirements of Title 63, Chapter 46b, Administrative Procedures Act, in its adjudicative proceedings.   1998

72-10-104. Investigations and hearings — Powers.

(1) The department may conduct investigations, inquiries, and hearings concerning matters covered by this chapter and accidents or injuries incident to the operation of aircraft occurring within this state.

(2) The department may:

(a) administer oaths and affirmations;

(b) certify to all official acts;

(c) issue subpoenas;

(d) compel the attendance and testimony of witnesses; and

(e) compel the production of papers, books, and documents.

(3) (a) If any person fails to comply with any subpoena or order issued by the department, the department may petition any district court in this state to order compliance.

(b) The district court may order the person to comply with the requirements of the subpoena or order of the department, or to give evidence upon the matter in question.

(c) Any failure to obey the order of the court may be punished by the court as contempt.   1998

72-10-105. Reports of investigations or hearings — Restrictions on use — Employees of division not required to testify.

(1) The reports of investigations or hearings, or any part of them, may not be admitted in evidence or used for any purpose in any suit, action, or proceeding growing out of any matter referred to in the investigations or hearings, or in any report of them, except in case of criminal or other proceedings instituted by or on behalf of the division under this title.

(2) An employee of the division may not be required to testify to any fact ascertained in or information gained by reason of his official capacity.

(3) The employees of the division may not be required to testify as expert witnesses in any suit, action, or proceeding involving any aircraft or any navigation facility.   1998

72-10-106. Enforcement of chapter — Fees for services by division.

(1) (a) The division and every county and municipal officer required to enforce state laws shall enforce and assist in the enforcement of this chapter.

(b) The division may enforce this chapter by injunction in the district courts of this state.

(c) Other departments and political subdivisions of this state may cooperate with the department and the division in the development of aeronautics within this state.

(2) (a) Unless otherwise provided by statute, the division may adopt a schedule of fees assessed for services provided by the division.

(b) Each fee shall be reasonable and fair, and shall reflect the cost of the service provided.

(c) Each fee established in this manner shall be submitted to and approved by the Legislature as part of the division's annual appropriations request.

(d) The division may not charge or collect any fee proposed in this manner without approval by the Legislature.   1998

72-10-107. Procedures — Adjudicative proceedings.

The division shall conduct adjudicative proceedings in accordance with Title 63, Chapter 46b, Administrative Procedures Act.   1998

72-10-108. Payment of expenses of administration.

The division shall pay the expenses of the administration of this part out of the special funds set up by the state treasurer for that purpose.   1998

72-10-109. Certificate of registration of aircraft required — Exceptions.

(1) (a) A person may not operate, pilot, or navigate, or cause or authorize to be operated, piloted, or navigated within this state any civil aircraft located in this state unless the aircraft has a current certificate of registration issued by this state through the county in which the aircraft is located.

(b) This restriction does not apply to aircraft licensed by a foreign country with which the United States has a reciprocal agreement covering the operations of the registered aircraft or to a non-passenger-carrying flight solely for inspection or test purposes authorized by the Federal Aviation Administration to be made without the certificate of registration.

(2) Aircraft assessed by the State Tax Commission are exempt from the state registration requirement under Subsection (1).   1998

72-10-110. Aircraft registration information requirements — Registration fee — Administration — Partial year registration.

(1) All applications for aircraft registration, including under Section 72-10-111, shall contain:

(a) a description of the aircraft, including:

(i) the manufacturer or builder;

(ii) the aircraft registration number, type, year of manufacture, or if an experimental aircraft, the year the aircraft was completed and certified for air worthiness by an inspector of the Federal Aviation Administration; and

(iii) gross weight;

(b) the name and address of the owner of the aircraft; and

(c) where the aircraft is located, or the address where the aircraft is usually used or based.

(2) (a) Except as provided in Section 72-10-111, at the time application is made for registration or renewal of registration of an aircraft under this

chapter, an annual registration fee shall be paid as follows:

(i) $25 for each balloon, glider, ultralight, helicopter, or propellor driven aircraft;

(ii) $5,000 for each jet aircraft with a maximum gross takeoff weight under 20,000 lbs.; and

(iii) $10,000 for each jet aircraft with a maximum gross takeoff weight of 20,000 lbs. or more.

(b) The registration fees assessed under this chapter shall be collected by the county and remitted to the Tax Commission to be distributed as provided in Subsection (2)(c).

(c) After deducting the costs of administering all aircraft registrations under this chapter, the Tax Commission shall deposit all remaining aircraft registration fees in the Transportation Fund's Restricted Revenue Account for aeronautical operations of the Department of Transportation to be used as provided in Subsection 59-13-402(2).

(d) Aircraft which are registered under this chapter for less than a full calendar year shall be charged a registration fee which is reduced in proportion to the fraction of the calendar year during which the aircraft is registered in this state.   1999

72-10-111. Registration of antique or experimental aircraft.

(1) In lieu of the annual registration fees under Section 72-10-110, the registration fee for antique aircraft and experimental aircraft is a single fee of $50.

(2) Registration under this section shall comply with the registration requirements of Section 72-10-110, but need not be renewed while an aircraft is operated as an antique aircraft or experimental aircraft under this chapter.

(3) An aircraft to be registered as an antique aircraft or experimental aircraft shall meet applicable airworthiness standards established by state and federal aviation regulatory agencies.   1998

72-10-112. Failure to register — Penalty.

Failure to register any aircraft required to be registered with the state in the county in which the aircraft is located subjects the owners of the aircraft to the same penalties provided for motor vehicles under Sections 41-1a-1101, 41-1a-1301, and 41-1a-1307.
                                                    1998

72-10-113. Pilot's certificate of competency required — Exceptions.

(1) A person may not pilot within this state any civil aircraft unless that person is the holder of a currently effective pilot's certificate of competency issued by the government of the United States.

(2) This restriction does not apply to any person operating any aircraft licensed by a foreign country with which the United States has a reciprocal agreement covering the operation of the licensed aircraft.
                                                    1998

72-10-114. Mechanic's certificate of competency.

(1) Mechanics will be rated as airframe or power-plant mechanics.

(2) A person may hold a plurality of certificate of competency, including both classes of mechanic's certificate of competency or a pilot's and mechanic's certificate of competency.

(3) The certificate shall be a currently effective certificate of competency issued by the government of the United States.

(4) This restriction does not apply to mechanics employed by the United States government.   1998

72-10-115. Certificate carried subject to inspection — Burden of proving validity of certificate in criminal proceedings.

(1) The certificate of license or permit required of a pilot or a student shall be kept in the personal possession of a licensee or permittee operating an aircraft within the state.

(2) The certificate of license required for an aircraft shall be carried in the aircraft at all times and shall be conspicuously posted in clear view of passengers.

(3) The certificate of pilot's license, student's permit, or aircraft license shall be presented for inspection upon the demand of any peace officer of this state, any authorized official or employee of the division, or any official, manager, or person in charge of any airport in this state upon which it shall land, or upon the reasonable request of any other person.

(4) In any criminal prosecution under this title, a defendant who relies upon a license or permit of any kind has the burden of proving that the defendant is properly licensed or is the possessor of a proper license or permit.

(5) The fact of nonissuance of a license or permit may be evidenced by a certificate signed by the official having power of issuance, or his deputy, under seal of office, stating that a diligent search in the office records has been made and that from the records it appears that no license or permit was issued.   1998

72-10-116. Airport license required — Issuance by division — Restrictions on use of lands or waters of another — Annual fee.

(1) (a) An airport open to public use may not be used or operated unless it is duly licensed by the division.

(b) Any person who owns or operates an airport open to public use shall file an application with the division for a license for the facility.

(2) (a) A license shall be granted whenever it is reasonably necessary for the accommodation and convenience of the public and may be granted in other cases in the discretion of the division.

(b) The division may not issue a license if the division finds that the facility is not constructed, equipped, and operated in accordance with the standards set by the department.

(3) (a) The landing or taking off of aircraft on or from the lands or waters of another without consent is unlawful, except in the case of a forced landing.

(b) For damages caused by a takeoff or landing, the owner, lessee of the aircraft, operator, or any of them is liable.

(4) (a) A student pilot may not land on any area without the knowledge of the operator, instructor, or school from which the student is flying.

(b) The use of private landing fields must not impose a hazard upon the person or property of others.

(5) A certificate of registration is not required of, and the rules made under this title do not apply to an airport owned or operated by the government of the United States.

(6) The division, with the approval of the commission, may charge a fee determined by the division pursuant to Section 63-38-3.2 for the issuance of an annual airport license.   1998

72-10-117. Aircraft landing permits — Eligible aircraft — Special licenses — Rules — Proof of insurance — Bonds.

(1) (a) The county executive of any county may issue permits authorizing aircraft to land on or take off from designated county roads.

(b) Permits may be issued to aircraft operated:

(i) as air ambulances;

(ii) as pesticide applicators; or

(iii) by or under contract with public utilities and used in connection with inspection, maintenance, installation, operation, construction, or repair of property owned or operated by the public utility.

(2) Permits may also be issued by the county executive to other aircraft under rules made by the division.

(3) (a) In accordance with Title 63, Chapter 46a, Utah Administrative Rulemaking Act, the division shall make rules for issuing a special license to:

(i) an aircraft permitted by a county executive to land on a county road; and

(ii) a pilot permitted to operate an aircraft licensed under this subsection from a county road.

(b) The rules made under this subsection shall include provisions for the safety of the flying and motoring public.

(4) In accordance with Title 63, Chapter 46a, Utah Administrative Rulemaking Act, the department shall make rules for the landing and taking off of aircraft to which permits have been issued, which may include annual reports of activities of the aircraft.

(5) Prior to obtaining a permit or license to any aircraft, the applicant shall file with the county executive and the division a certificate of insurance executed by an insurance company or association authorized to transact business in this state upon a form prescribed by the division that there is in full force and effect a policy of insurance covering the aircraft for liability against:

(a) personal injury or death for any one person in an amount of $50,000 or more;

(b) any one accident in an amount of $100,000 or more; and

(c) property damage in an amount of $50,000 or more.

(6) In addition to the insurance required under this section, either the county executive or the division may require the posting of a bond to indemnify the county or division against liability resulting from issuing the permit or license. 1998

72-10-118. Reason for division order to be stated — Closing airports — Notice — Right of inspection.

(1) If the division rejects an application for permission to operate or establish an airport, or issues any order under this chapter that requires or prohibits certain actions, its order shall:

(a) contain the reasons for the rejection or order; and

(b) state the requirements to be met before approval will be given or the order changed.

(2) The division may order the closing of any airport until its requirements have been fulfilled.

(3) (a) An airport not meeting the standards required by the division shall:

(i) be given notice of its noncompliance; and

(ii) have ten days from the receipt of that notice to respond to the division with a plan and schedule for compliance.

(b) If the airport fails to respond within the required time, the division may revoke the airport license and close the airport.

(4) The division and any state, county, or municipal officer charged with the duty of enforcing this chapter may inspect and examine at reasonable hours any premises, buildings, or other structures where regulated airports are operated. 1998

72-10-119. Judicial review.

(1) Any person against whom an order has been entered may obtain judicial review.

(2) Venue for judicial review of informal adjudicative proceedings is in the district court of the county in which the order was made or the county in which property affected by the order is located. 1998

72-10-120. Violations — Penalty.

A person who fails to comply with the requirements or violating any of the provisions of this part, or the rules or orders adopted by the department is guilty of a class B misdemeanor. 1998

72-10-121. Severability clause.

If any provision of this part or its application to any person or circumstances is held invalid, this invalidity may not affect other provisions or applications of the part which can be given effect without the invalid provision or application and to this end the provisions of this part are declared to be severable. 1998

72-10-122. Construction of chapter.

This chapter shall be so interpreted and construed as to effectuate its general purpose to make uniform the law of those states which enact it. 1998

72-10-123. Sovereignty in space above land and water in state.

Sovereignty in the space above the lands and waters of this state is declared to rest in the state, except where granted to and assumed by the United States pursuant to a constitutional grant from the people of this state. 1998

72-10-124. Report of death or serious injury to person or property.

If in the operation of civil aircraft death or serious injury to person or to property results, a report shall be made in accordance with federal aviation regulations. 1998

72-10-125. Report of injury to aircraft or property.

All accidents in the operation of civil aircraft which cause injury to aircraft or property shall be reported in accordance with federal aviation regulations. 1998

72-10-126. Marking buildings to aid navigation.

(1) The division may cooperate with the officials of all state institutions for the purpose of marking one building within their group as an aid to aerial navigation.

(2) The marking is subject to the approval of the division and shall comply with the requirements of the United States civil aeronautics authority for air marking. 1998

72-10-127. Tampering with aircraft forbidden.

It shall be unlawful for any person, without express or implied authority of the owner, to operate, climb upon, enter, manipulate the controls or accessories of, set in motion, remove parts or contents of, or other-

wise tamper with any civil aircraft within this state, or knowingly cause or permit the same to be done.
1998

72-10-128. Tampering with airport or equipment forbidden.

A person may not interfere or tamper with any airport, landing field, or airway, or the equipment thereof.
1998

72-10-129. Expenditures for Civil Air Patrol.

(1) The division may expend state aeronautics funds for the Utah wing of the Civil Air Patrol to be used to:

(a) purchase aviation facilities, training, supplies, and equipment;

(b) defray maintenance and rental costs of hangar facilities and aircraft;

(c) purchase maintenance supplies and equipment for the communications network of the Civil Air Patrol; and

(d) provide administrative costs approved by the division.

(2) The expenditures may not exceed in any fiscal year the amount appropriated to the Utah wing of the Civil Air Patrol by the Legislature.
1998

72-10-130. Approval of expenditures for Civil Air Patrol.

An expenditure of state funds for the civil air patrol may not be made unless a purchase order is first approved by the director of aeronautics under guidelines established by the department and unless the funds are specifically used as required in this chapter.
1998

72-10-131. Tax-exempt status of Civil Air Patrol equipment.

Equipment, aircraft and vehicles owned by the civil air patrol and used for the emergency service needs of the state of Utah are given tax-exempt status.
1998

PART 2

UNIFORM AIRPORTS ACT

72-10-201. Powers of division — Acceptance of property.

The division, a county, or municipal legislative body may accept contributions of money or real or personal property for the purpose of establishing, developing, operating, or maintaining airports under this part.
1998

72-10-202. Cooperation with counties, municipalities, and federal government — Expenditures by division.

(1) The division may:

(a) cooperate with counties and municipalities in developing and constructing airports;

(b) make agreements on behalf of the state with any county or municipality regarding the financial participation, construction, and operation of any airports;

(c) cooperate with the federal government in establishing airports; and

(d) accept from the United States of America, money to be matched with the funds of the state and funds appropriated by any county or municipality in developing and constructing airports under the Uniform Airports Act.

(2) The division may expend not to exceed 10% of its annual appropriation upon any one project under this chapter.
1998

72-10-203. Division and counties, municipalities, and airport authorities authorized to acquire and regulate airports.

(1) The division and municipalities, counties, and airport authorities may acquire, establish, construct, expand, own, lease, control, equip, improve, maintain, operate, regulate, and police airports for the use of aircraft and may use for these purposes any available property that is owned or controlled by the division or by a municipality, county, or airport authority.

(2) A county may not exercise the authority conferred in this section outside of its geographical limits except jointly with an adjoining county.
1998

72-10-204. Lands acquired by division and counties, municipalities, and airport authorities — Declaration of public purpose.

Any land acquired, owned, leased, controlled, or occupied by the division or by a county, municipality, or airport authority for the purposes enumerated in Section 72-10-203, is acquired, owned, leased, controlled, or occupied for public, governmental, and municipal purposes.
1998

72-10-205. Acquisition of property — Condemnation.

(1) Private property needed by the division or a county, municipality, or airport authority for an airport or landing field or for the expansion of an airport or landing field may be acquired by grant, purchase, lease, or other means if the division or the political subdivision is able to agree with the owners of the property on the terms of acquisition.

(2) If no agreement can be reached, the private property may be obtained by condemnation in the manner provided for the state or a political subdivision to acquire real property for public purposes.
1998

72-10-206. Payment by appropriation or sale of bonds.

The purchase price or award for real property acquired, in accordance with the provisions of this part, for an airport or landing field may be paid for by appropriation of money available for the property or wholly or partly from the proceeds of the sale of bonds of the county, municipality, or other political subdivision, as the legislative body of the political subdivision shall determine, subject to the adoption of a proposition at a regular or special election, if the adoption of a proposition is a prerequisite to the issuance of bonds of the political subdivision for public purposes generally.
1998

72-10-207. Powers of department and political subdivisions over airports — Security unit.

(1) The department, and counties, municipalities, or other political subdivisions of this state that have established or may establish airports or that acquire, lease, or set apart real property for those purposes, may:

(a) construct, equip, improve, maintain, and operate the airports or may vest the authority for their construction, equipment, improvement, maintenance, and operation in an officer of the department or in an officer, board, or body of the political subdivision;

(b) adopt rules, establish charges, fees, and tolls for the use of airports and landing fields, fix penalties for the violation of the rules, and establish liens to enforce payment of the charges, fees, and tolls, subject to approval by the commission;

(c) lease the airports to private parties for operation for a term not exceeding 50 years, as long as the public is not deprived of its rightful, equal, and uniform use of the facility;

(d) lease or assign space, area, improvements, equipment, buildings, and facilities on the airports to private parties for operation for a term not exceeding 50 years;

(e) lease or assign real property comprising all or any part of the airports to private parties for the construction and operation of hangars, shop buildings, or office buildings for a term not exceeding 50 years, if the projected construction cost of the hangar, shop building, or office building is $100,000 or more; and

(f) establish, maintain, operate, and staff a security unit for the purpose of enforcing state and local laws at any airport that is subject to federal airport security regulations.

(2) The department or political subdivision shall pay the construction, equipment, improvement, maintenance, and operations expenses of any airport established by them under Subsection (1).

(3) (a) If the department or political subdivision establishes a security unit under Subsection (1)(f), the department head or the governing body of the political subdivision shall appoint persons qualified as peace officers under Title 53, Chapter 13, Peace Officer Classifications to staff the security unit.

(b) A security unit appointed by the department or political subdivision is exempt from civil service regulations.   1998

72-10-208. Providing for levying of taxes.

The local public authorities having power to appropriate money within the counties, municipalities, or other public subdivisions of this state for the purpose of acquiring, establishing, developing, operating, maintaining, or controlling airports under the provisions of this part, are authorized to appropriate and cause to be raised by taxation or otherwise in such political subdivisions money sufficient to carry out therein the provisions of this part, also to use for such purpose or purposes money derived from the airports.   1998

72-10-209. Acquisition of air rights — Condemnation.

(1) To provide unobstructed air space for the landing and taking off of aircraft using airports acquired or maintained under this chapter, the division and a county, municipality, or airport authority may acquire the air rights over private property necessary to insure safe approaches to the landing areas of the airports.

(2) The air rights may be acquired by grant, purchase, lease, or condemnation in the same manner provided under Section 72-10-205 for the acquisition or expansion of airports.   1998

72-10-210. Easements for marks or lights — Condemnation.

(1) The division and a county, municipality, or airport authority may acquire the right or easement for a term of years or perpetually to place and maintain suitable marks for the daytime, and to place, operate, and maintain suitable lights for the nighttime marking of buildings or other structures or obstructions for the safe operation of aircraft using airports and landing fields acquired or maintained under this chapter.

(2) The rights or easements may be acquired by grant, purchase, lease, or condemnation in the same manner provided under Section 72-10-205 for the acquisition or expansion of airports.   1998

72-10-211. Police regulations.

The division and a county, municipality, or airport authority acquiring, establishing, developing, operating, maintaining, or controlling airports outside the geographical limits of the subdivisions, under this chapter may amend and enforce police regulations for the airports.   1998

72-10-212. General provisions of law applicable in condemnation proceedings, issuing bonds, and levying taxes.

It is the intent and purpose of this part that all provisions herein relating to the issuance of bonds and the levying of taxes for airport purposes and the condemnation for airports and airport facilities shall be construed in accordance with general provisions of the law of this state governing the right and procedure of municipalities to condemn property, issue bonds, and levy taxes.   1998

72-10-213. Severability clause.

If any provision of this part or its application is held invalid, this invalidity does not affect provisions or applications of the part which can be given effect without the invalid provision or application, and to this end the provisions of this part are declared to be severable.   1998

72-10-214. Construction of part.

This part shall be so interpreted and construed as to effectuate the general purpose of those states which enact it.   1998

PART 3

FEDERAL AIRPORT FUNDS ACT

72-10-301. Definitions.

As used in this part:

(1) "Airport" means any area of land or water which is used, or intended for use for the landing and taking-off of aircraft, and any appurtenant areas which are used, or intended for use, for aircraft buildings or other airport facilities or rights of way, together with all airport buildings and facilities located on them.

(2) "Air navigation facility" means any facility — other than one owned and operated by the United States — used in, available for use in, or designed for use in aid of air navigation, including any structures, mechanisms, lights, beacons, markers, communicating systems, or other instrumentalities, or devices used or useful as an aid, or constituting an advantage or convenience, to the safe taking-off, navigation, and landing of aircraft, or the safe and efficient operation or maintenance of an airport, and any combination of any or all of the facilities.

(3) "Airport hazard" means any structure, object of natural growth, or use of land which obstructs the air space required for the flight of aircraft in landing or taking-off at an airport or is otherwise hazardous to the landing or taking-off of aircraft.

(4) "Municipality" means any county, city, town, or political subdivision of this state.

(5) "Person" means any individual, firm, partnership, corporation, company, association, joint stock association, or body politic and includes any

trustee, receiver, assignee, or other similar representation thereof.

(6) "Public agency" means the United States government or any of its agencies, a state or its agencies, a municipality or other political subdivision, or a tax-supported organization. 1998

72-10-302. Purpose and policy of part.

It is declared that the purpose of this part is to further the public interest in aeronautical progress:

(1) by authorizing public agencies of this state to accept, channel, and disburse federal, state, and other funds for the planning, acquisition, construction, maintenance, operation, and regulation of airports and air navigation facilities;

(2) by granting to a state agency the powers and imposing upon it the duties that the state may obtain the full benefit of financial assistance made available by the federal government, as well as assistance from other sources;

(3) by providing authority that may be exercised by a public agency independently or jointly with other public agencies, and enabling two or more cities, towns, counties, and other political subdivisions jointly to establish, acquire, develop, and operate an airport or airports for their joint or common use. 1998

72-10-303. Submission of requests for aid — Approval by division — Receipt and disbursement of funds.

(1) The state, a county, municipality, or airport authority may not submit to any federal agency or department of the United States any requests for aid under any act of congress that provides funds for airports or commercial airport construction, development, expansion, or improvements, unless the project and the requests for aid have been first approved by the division.

(2) The state, a county, municipality, or airport authority may not directly accept, receive, receipt for, or disburse any funds granted by the United States under the act, but it shall designate the division as its agent and in its behalf to accept, receive, receipt for, and disburse the funds.

(3) The state, a county, municipality, or airport authority shall enter into an agreement with the division, prescribing the terms and conditions of the agency in accordance with federal laws, rules, and regulations and applicable laws of this state.

(4) Moneys paid by the United States government shall be retained by the state or paid to a county, municipality, or airport authority under terms and conditions imposed by the United States government in making the grant. 1998

72-10-304. Powers and duties of division.

(1) The division may make available its engineering and other technical services, with or without charge, to the state, a county, municipality, or airport authority or person desiring them in connection with the planning, acquisition, construction, improvement, maintenance, or operation of airports or air navigation facilities.

(2) (a) The division may render financial assistance by grant, loan, or both, to any county, municipality, or airport authority, in the planning, acquisition, construction, improvement, maintenance, or operation of an airport owned or controlled, or to be owned or controlled by the county, municipality, or airport authority, out of appropriations made by the Legislature for these purposes.

(b) Financial assistance may be furnished in connection with federal or other financial aid for the same purposes.

(3) (a) The division may use the facilities and services of other state agencies and of the counties and municipalities to the utmost extent possible.

(b) The state agencies, counties, and municipalities shall make available their facilities and services.

(4) All powers granted to any county, municipality, or airport authority by this chapter may be exercised jointly with any county, municipality, or airport authority, and jointly with any state agency or the United States if the laws of the other state or of the United States permit the joint exercise. 1998

72-10-305. Mutual assistance — Gifts, leases, and loans.

(1) If any public agency determines that the public interest and the interest of the public agency will be served by assisting any other public agency in exercising the powers and authority granted by this part, the public agency may furnish assistance by gift of real or personal property or money or lease or loan with or without charge or interest.

(2) In appropriating the property or money and providing for the assistance by taxation, the issuance of bonds, or other means, the public agency may exercise all of its powers as though used for its own direct purposes as provided in this part. 1998

72-10-306. Contractual powers of public agencies.

A public agency may enter into any contracts necessary to the execution of the powers granted it, and for the purposes provided by this part. 1998

72-10-307. Powers of governing bodies.

The governing body of any public agency having power to appropriate and raise money is authorized to appropriate, and to raise by taxation or otherwise, sufficient moneys to carry out the provisions and purposes of this part. 1998

72-10-308. Construction of part.

This part shall be so interpreted and construed as to make uniform so far as possible the laws and regulations of this state and other states and of the government of the United States having to do with the subject of public airports. 1998

72-10-309. Severability clause.

If any provision of this part or its application to any person or circumstance shall be held invalid, this invalidity does not affect the provisions or applications of this part which can be given effect without the invalid provision or application, and to this end the provisions of this part are declared to be severable.

1998

PART 4

AIRPORT ZONING ACT

72-10-401. Definitions.

As used in this part, unless the context otherwise requires:

(1) "Airport" means any area of land or water designed and set aside for the landing and taking-off of aircraft and utilized or to be utilized in the interest of the public for these purposes.

(2) "Airport hazard" means any structure or tree or use of land which obstructs the airspace required for the flight of aircraft in landing or

taking-off at an airport or is otherwise hazardous to the landing or taking-off of aircraft.

(3) "Airport hazard area" means any area of land or water upon which an airport hazard might be established if not prevented as provided in this part.

(4) "Political subdivision" means any municipality, city, town, or county.

(5) "Structure" means any object constructed or installed by man, including buildings, towers, smokestacks, and overhead transmission lines.

(6) "Tree" means any object of natural growth.
1998

72-10-402. Declaration with respect to airport hazards.

The Legislature finds that:

(1) an airport hazard endangers the lives and property of users of the airport and of occupants of land in its vicinity;

(2) an obstruction of the type that reduces the size of the area available for the landing, taking-off, and maneuvering of aircraft tends to destroy or impair the utility of the airport and the public investment in the airport;

(3) the creation or establishment of an airport hazard is a public nuisance and an injury to the community served by the airport in question;

(4) it is necessary in the interest of the public health, public safety, and general welfare that the creation or establishment of airport hazards be prevented;

(5) this should be accomplished, to the extent legally possible, by exercise of the police power, without compensation; and

(6) both the prevention of the creation or establishment of airport hazards and the elimination, removal, alteration, mitigation, or marking and lighting of existing airport hazards are public purposes for which political subdivisions may raise and expend public funds and acquire land or property interests in land.
1998

72-10-403. Airport zoning regulations — Joint airport zoning board — Powers of board — Membership.

(1) (a) In order to prevent the creation or establishment of airport hazards, every political subdivision having an airport hazard area within its territorial limits may adopt, administer, and enforce, under the police power and in the manner and upon the conditions prescribed in this part, airport zoning regulations for the airport hazard area.

(b) The regulations may divide the area into zones, and, within the zones, specify the land uses permitted and regulate and restrict the height to which structures and trees may be erected or allowed to grow.

(2) (a) If an airport is owned or controlled by a political subdivision and any airport hazard area appertaining to the airport is located outside the territorial limits of the political subdivision, the political subdivision owning or controlling the airport and the political subdivision within which the airport hazard area is located may, by ordinance or resolution duly adopted, create a joint airport zoning board.

(b) The board shall have the same power to adopt, administer, and enforce airport zoning regulations applicable to the airport hazard area in question as that vested by Subsection (1) in the political subdivision within which the area is located.

(c) Each joint board shall have as members two representatives appointed by each political subdivision participating in its creation and in addition a chair elected by a majority of the appointed members.
1998

72-10-404. Zoning ordinances — Governing law in event of conflict.

(1) In the event that a political subdivision has adopted or adopts a comprehensive zoning ordinance regulating the height of buildings, any airport zoning regulations applicable to the same area or a portion of the area may be incorporated in and made a part of comprehensive zoning regulations, and be administered and enforced in connection with the comprehensive zoning regulations.

(2) In the event of conflict between any airport zoning regulations adopted under this part and any other regulations applicable to the same area, whether the conflict be with respect to the height of structures or trees, the use of land, or any other matter, and whether the other regulations were adopted by the political subdivision which adopted the airport zoning regulations or by some other political subdivision, the more stringent limitation or requirement shall govern and prevail.
1998

72-10-405. Airport zoning regulations — Adoption and amendment — Airport zoning commission — Powers and duties.

(1) (a) An airport zoning regulation may not be adopted, amended, or changed under this part except by action of the legislative body of the political subdivision in question, or the joint board provided for in Subsection 72-10-403(2), after a public hearing at which parties in interest and citizens shall have an opportunity to be heard.

(b) At least 15 days' notice of the hearing shall be published in an official paper, or a paper of general circulation, in the political subdivision or subdivisions in which is located the airport hazard area to be zoned.

(2) (a) Prior to the initial zoning of any airport hazard area under this part, the political subdivision or joint airport zoning board which is to adopt the regulations shall appoint a commission, to be known as the airport zoning commission, to recommend the boundaries of the various zones to be established and the regulations to be adopted.

(b) The commission shall make a preliminary report and hold public hearings before submitting its final report, and the legislative body of the political subdivision or the joint airport zoning board may not hold its public hearings or take other action until it has received the final report of the commission.

(c) If a comprehensive zoning commission already exists, it may be appointed as the airport zoning commission.
1998

72-10-406. Airport zoning regulations — Validity, limitations, and restrictions.

(1) (a) All airport zoning regulations adopted under this part shall be reasonable and none shall impose any requirement or restriction which is not reasonably necessary to effectuate the purposes of this part.

(b) In determining what regulations it may adopt, each political subdivision and joint airport zoning board shall consider the character of the flying operations expected to be conducted at the airport, the nature of the terrain within the airport hazard area, the character of the neighborhood, and the uses to which the property to be zoned is put and adaptable.

(2) Any airport zoning regulations adopted under this part may not require the removal, lowering, or other change or alteration of any structure or tree not conforming to the regulations when adopted or amended, or otherwise interfere with the continuance of any nonconforming use, except as provided in Subsection 72-10-407(3).   1998

72-10-407. Permit for new or changed structures or uses — Nonconforming structures — Airport hazards — Application to board of adjustment for variance — Allowance of variance — Conditioning permit or variance.

(1) (a) Any airport zoning regulations adopted under this part may require that a permit be obtained before any new structure or use may be constructed or established and before any existing use or structure may be substantially changed or substantially altered or repaired.

(b) All regulations shall provide that before any nonconforming structure or tree may be replaced, substantially altered or repaired, rebuilt, allowed to grow higher, or replanted, a permit shall be secured from the administrative agency authorized to administer and enforce the regulations, authorizing the replacement, change, or repair.

(c) A permit may not be granted that allows the establishment or creation of an airport hazard or permit a nonconforming structure or tree or nonconforming use to be made or become higher or become a greater hazard to air navigation than it was when the applicable regulation was adopted or when the application for a permit is made.

(d) Except as provided in this Subsection (1), all applications for permits shall be granted.

(2) (a) Any person desiring to erect any structure, or increase the height of any structure, or permit the growth of any tree, or otherwise use the person's property in violation of airport zoning regulations adopted under this part, may apply to the board of adjustment for a variance from the zoning regulations in question.

(b) A variance shall be allowed where a literal application or enforcement of the regulations would result in practical difficulty or unnecessary hardship and the relief granted would not be contrary to the public interest but do substantial justice and be in accordance with the spirit of the regulations and this part.

(c) Any variance may be allowed subject to any reasonable conditions that the board of adjustment may deem necessary to effectuate the purposes of this part.

(3) In granting any permit or variance under this section, the administrative agency or board of adjustment may, if it considers the action advisable to effectuate the purposes of this part and reasonable in the circumstances, so condition a permit or variance as to require the owner of the structure or tree in question to permit the political subdivision, at its own expense, to install, operate, and maintain thereon markers and lights as may be necessary to indicate to flyers the presence of an airport hazard.   1998

72-10-408. Appeals to board of adjustment — Procedure — Stay of proceedings — Hearing and judgment.

(1) Any person aggrieved, or taxpayer affected, by any decision of any administrative agency made in its administration of airport zoning regulations adopted under this part, or any governing body of a political subdivision, or any joint airport zoning board, which is of the opinion that a decision of an administrative agency is an improper application of airport zoning regulations of concern to the governing body or board, may appeal to the board of adjustment authorized to hear and decide appeals from the decisions of the administrative agency.

(2) (a) All appeals taken under this section shall be taken within a reasonable time, as provided by the rules of the board, by filing with the agency from which the appeal is taken and with the board, a notice of appeal specifying the grounds of the appeal.

(b) The agency from which the appeal is taken shall transmit to the board all the papers constituting the record upon which the action appealed from was taken.

(3) (a) An appeal shall stay all proceedings in furtherance of the action appealed from, unless the agency from which the appeal is taken certifies to the board, after the notice of appeal has been filed with it, that by reason of the facts stated in the certificate a stay would, in its opinion, cause imminent peril to life or property.

(b) In these cases, proceedings shall not be stayed otherwise than by order of the board on notice to the agency from which the appeal is taken and on due cause shown.

(4) (a) The board shall fix a reasonable time for the hearing of appeals, give public notice and due notice to the parties in interest, and decide the appeal within a reasonable time.

(b) Upon the hearing any party may appear in person or by agent or by attorney.

(5) The board may, in conformity with the provisions of this part, reverse or affirm wholly or partly, or modify, the order, requirement, decision, or determination appealed from and may make an order, requirement, decision, or determination as ought to be made, and to that end shall have all the powers of the administrative agency from which the appeal is taken.   1998

72-10-409. Airport zoning regulations — Administration and enforcement.

(1) (a) All airport zoning regulations adopted under this part shall provide for the administration and enforcement of the regulations by an administrative agency which may be an agency created by the regulations or any official, board, or other existing agency of the political subdivision adopting the regulations or of one of the political subdivisions which participated in the creation of the joint airport zoning board adopting the regulations, if satisfactory to that political subdivision.

(b) The administrative agency may not be or include any member of the board of adjustment.

(2) The duties of any administrative agency designated pursuant to this part shall include that of hearing and deciding all permits under Subsection 72-10-407(1), but the agency may not have or exercise any of the powers delegated to the board of adjustment.   1998

72-10-410. Board of adjustment — Powers — Appointment and membership of board — Hearings and decisions by board — Meetings — Adoption of rules.

(1) All airport zoning regulations adopted under this part shall provide for a board of adjustment to have and exercise the following powers:

    (a) to hear and decide appeals from any order, requirement, decision, or determination made by the administrative agency in the enforcement of the airport zoning regulations, as provided in Section 72-10-408;

    (b) to hear and decide any special exceptions to the terms of the airport zoning regulations upon which the board may be required to pass under the regulations;

    (c) to hear and decide specific variances under Subsection 72-10-407(2).

(2) (a) If a zoning board of appeals or adjustment already exists, it may be appointed as the board of adjustment.

    (b) Otherwise, the board of adjustment shall consist of five members, each to be appointed for a term of three years, by the authority adopting the regulations and to be removable by the appointing authority for cause, upon written charges and after public hearing.

(3) The concurring vote of a majority of the members of the board of adjustment shall be sufficient to reverse any order, requirement, decision, or determination of the administrative agency, or to decide in favor of the applicant on any matter upon which it is required to pass under the airport zoning regulations, or to effect any variation in the regulations.

(4) (a) The board shall adopt rules in accordance with the provisions of the ordinance or resolution by which it was created.

    (b) Meetings of the board shall be held at the call of the chair and at other times as the board may determine.

    (c) The chair, or in the chair's absence, the acting chair, may administer oaths and compel the attendance of witnesses.

    (d) All hearings of the board shall be public.

    (e) The board shall keep minutes of its proceedings, showing the vote of each member upon each question, or, if absent or failing to vote, indicating the fact, and shall keep records of its examinations and other official actions, all of which shall immediately be filed in the office of the board and shall be a public record.   1998

72-10-411. Appeals to district courts — Procedure — Findings, judgment, and costs — Regulations invalid as to one structure or parcel of land.

(1) (a) Any person aggrieved, or taxpayer affected, by any decision of a board of adjustment, or any governing body of a political subdivision or any joint airport zoning board, which is of the opinion that a decision of a board of adjustment is illegal, may present to the district court a verified petition setting forth that the decision is illegal, in whole or in part, and specifying the grounds of the illegality.

    (b) The petition shall be presented to the court within 30 days after the decision is filed in the office of the board.

(2) (a) Upon presentation of the petition the court may allow a writ of certiorari directed to the board of adjustment to review the decision of the board.

    (b) The allowance of the writ may not stay proceedings upon the decision appealed from, but the court may, on application, on notice to the board and on due cause shown, grant a restraining order.

(3) (a) The board of adjustment may not be required to return the original papers acted upon by it, but it shall be sufficient to return certified or sworn copies of the papers or of any portions as may be called for by the writ.

    (b) The return shall concisely set forth any other facts as may be pertinent and material to show the grounds of the decision appealed from and shall be verified.

(4) (a) The court shall have exclusive jurisdiction to affirm, modify, or set aside the decision brought up for review, in whole or in part, and if necessary, to order further proceedings by the board of adjustment.

    (b) The findings of fact of the board shall be considered by the court unless an objection shall have been urged before the board, or, if it was not so urged, unless there were reasonable grounds for failure to do so.

(5) Costs may not be allowed against the board of adjustment unless it appears to the court that it acted with gross negligence, in bad faith, or with malice, in making the decision appealed from.

(6) In any case in which airport zoning regulations adopted under this part, although generally reasonable, are held by a court to interfere with the use or enjoyment of a particular structure or parcel of land to an extent, or to be so onerous in their application to a structure or parcel of land, as to constitute a taking or deprivation of that property in violation of the Constitution of this state or the Constitution of the United States, the holding shall not affect the application of the regulations to other structures and parcels of land.   1998

72-10-412. Violations of chapter or rulings — Misdemeanor — Remedies of political subdivisions.

(1) Each violation of this part or of any regulations, orders, or rulings promulgated or made pursuant to this part, shall constitute a misdemeanor.

(2) (a) A political subdivision or agency adopting zoning regulations under this part may institute in any court of competent jurisdiction, an action to prevent, restrain, correct, or abate any violation of this part, or of airport zoning regulations adopted under this part, or of any order or ruling made in connection with their administration or enforcement.

    (b) The court shall adjudge to the plaintiff the relief, by way of injunction or otherwise, as may be proper under all the facts and circumstances of the case, in order fully to effectuate the purposes of this part and of the regulations adopted and orders and rulings made pursuant to them.   1998

72-10-413. Purchase or condemnation of air rights or navigation easements.

A political subdivision within which the property or nonconforming use is located or the political subdivision owning the airport or served by it may acquire, by purchase, grant, or condemnation in the manner provided by the law under which political subdivisions are authorized to acquire real property for public purposes, an air right, navigation easement, or other estate or interest in the property or nonconforming structure or use in question if:

(1) it is desired to remove, lower, or otherwise terminate a nonconforming structure or use;

(2) the approach protection necessary cannot, because of constitutional limitations, be provided by airport zoning regulations under this part; or

(3) it appears advisable that the necessary approach protection be provided by acquisition of property rights rather than by airport zoning regulations.　　　1998

72-10-414. Exchange of private property near federal airports.

(1) If any governmental entity or agency adopts any measure which infringes upon the use of privately owned property, or which is designed to assure development compatible with the continued operation of a federal airport, the owner of that private property, if the owner has continuously owned the land from the date of the measure and whose land is wholly or partially within the area directly affected by the measure, may request an exchange of the affected land for state land outside the affected area.

(2) (a) Upon a request pursuant to Subsection (1), the Board of State Lands, without cost to the affected landowner, shall appraise the subject land taking into consideration the fair market value of any and all improvements, and may offer a land exchange at the earliest practicable time.

(b) The state may identify at least one, and may identify up to three parcels of state land of a substantially equal value to the land requested to be exchanged, and which can otherwise be exchanged in a manner which will not prejudice the interest of the state and which will not be inconsistent with proper management, control, protection, and use of state land.

(c) The state may provide for the use of qualified appraisers to expedite the process of the request.　　　1998

72-10-415. Severability clause.

If any provision of this part or its application to any person or circumstances is held invalid, this invalidity does not affect the provisions or applications of the part which can be given effect without the invalid provision or application, and to this end the provisions of this part are declared to be severable.　　　1998

PART 5

FLYING WHILE INTOXICATED

72-10-501. Flying under the influence of alcohol, drugs, or with specified or unsafe blood alcohol concentration — Calculations of blood or breath alcohol — Criminal punishment — Arrest without warrant.

(1) (a) A person may not operate or be in actual physical control of an aircraft within this state if the person:

(i) has sufficient alcohol in his body that a subsequent chemical test shows that the person has a blood or breath alcohol concentration of .04 grams or greater at the time of the test;

(ii) is under the influence of alcohol, any drug, or the combined influence of alcohol and any drug to a degree that renders the person incapable of safely operating an aircraft; or

(iii) has a blood or breath alcohol concentration of .04 grams or greater at the time of operation or actual physical control.

(b) The fact that a person charged with violating this section is or has been legally entitled to use alcohol or a drug is not a defense against any charge of violating this section.

(2) Calculations of blood or breath alcohol concentration under this section shall be made in accordance with Subsection 41-6a-502(1).

(3) (a) A person convicted of a violation of Subsection (1) is guilty of a:

(i) class B misdemeanor; or

(ii) class A misdemeanor if the person has also inflicted bodily injury upon another as a proximate result of having operated the aircraft in a negligent manner.

(b) In this section, the standard of negligence is that of simple negligence, the failure to exercise that degree of care that an ordinarily reasonable and prudent person exercises under like or similar circumstances.

(4) A peace officer may, without a warrant, arrest a person for a violation of this section when the officer has probable cause to believe:

(a) the violation has occurred, although not in the officer's presence; and

(b) the violation was committed by that person.　　　2005

72-10-502. Implied consent to chemical tests for alcohol or drugs — Number of tests — Refusal — Person incapable of refusal — Results of test available — Who may give test — Evidence.

(1) (a) A person operating an aircraft in this state consents to a chemical test or tests of the person's breath, blood, urine, or oral fluids:

(i) for the purpose of determining whether the person was operating or in actual physical control of an aircraft while having a blood or breath alcohol content statutorily prohibited under Section 72-10-501, or while under the influence of alcohol, any drug, or combination of alcohol and any drug under Section 72-10-501, if the test is or tests are administered at the direction of a peace officer having grounds to believe that person to have been operating or in actual physical control of an aircraft in violation of Section 72-10-501; or

(ii) if the person operating the aircraft is involved in an accident that results in death, serious injury, or substantial aircraft damage.

(b) (i) The peace officer determines which of the tests are administered and how many of them are administered.

(ii) The peace officer may order any or all tests of the person's breath, blood, urine, or oral fluids.

(iii) If an officer requests more than one test, refusal by a person to take one or more requested tests, even though the person does submit to any other requested test or tests, is a refusal under this section.

(c) (i) A person who has been requested under this section to submit to a chemical test or tests of the person's breath, blood, urine, or oral fluids may not select the test or tests to be administered.

(ii) The failure or inability of a peace officer to arrange for any specific chemical test is not a defense to taking a test requested by a peace officer, and it is not a defense in any criminal, civil, or administrative proceeding resulting from a person's refusal to submit to the requested test or tests.

(2) (a) If the person has been placed under arrest and has then been requested by a peace officer to submit to any one or more of the chemical tests provided in Subsection (1) and refuses to submit to any chemical test, the person shall be warned by the peace officer requesting the test that a refusal to submit to the test is admissible in civil or criminal proceedings as provided under Subsection (8).

(b) Following this warning, unless the person immediately requests that the chemical test offered by a peace officer be administered, a test may not be given.

(3) Any person who is dead, unconscious, or in any other condition rendering the person incapable of refusal to submit to any chemical test or tests is considered to not have withdrawn the consent provided for in Subsection (1), and the test or tests may be administered whether the person has been arrested or not.

(4) Upon the request of the person who was tested, the results of the test or tests shall be made available to that person.

(5) (a) Only a physician, registered nurse, practical nurse, or person authorized under Section 26-1-30 to draw blood under Section 41-6a-523, acting at the request of a peace officer, may withdraw blood to determine the alcohol or drug content. This limitation does not apply to the taking of a urine, breath, or oral fluid specimen.

(b) Any physician, registered nurse, practical nurse, or person authorized under Section 26-1-30 to draw blood under Section 41-6a-523 who, at the direction of a peace officer, draws a sample of blood from any person whom a peace officer has reason to believe is flying in violation of this chapter, or hospital or medical facility at which the sample is drawn, is immune from any civil or criminal liability arising from drawing the sample, if the test is administered according to standard medical practice.

(6) (a) The person to be tested may, at the person's own expense, have a physician of the person's own choice administer a chemical test in addition to the test or tests administered at the direction of a peace officer.

(b) The failure or inability to obtain the additional test does not affect admissibility of the results of the test or tests taken at the direction of a peace officer, or preclude or delay the test or tests to be taken at the direction of a peace officer.

(c) The additional test shall be subsequent to the test or tests administered at the direction of a peace officer.

(7) For the purpose of determining whether to submit to a chemical test or tests, the person to be tested does not have the right to consult an attorney or have an attorney, physician, or other person present as a condition for the taking of any test.

(8) If a person under arrest refuses to submit to a chemical test or tests or any additional test under this section, evidence of any refusal is admissible in any civil or criminal action or proceeding arising out of acts alleged to have been committed while the person was operating or in actual physical control of an aircraft while under the influence of alcohol, any drug, or combination of alcohol and any drug.

(9) The results of any test taken under this section or the refusal to be tested shall be reported to the Federal Aviation Administration by the peace officer requesting the test.   2005

72-10-503. Standards for chemical analysis of breath or oral fluids — Evidence.

(1) The Commissioner of the Department of Public Safety shall establish standards for the administration and interpretation of chemical analysis of a person's breath or oral fluids, including standards of training.

(2) In any action or proceeding in which it is material to prove that a person was operating or in actual physical control of an aircraft while under the influence of alcohol or any drug or operating with a blood or breath alcohol content statutorily prohibited, documents offered as memoranda or records of acts, conditions, or events to prove that the analysis was made and the instrument used was accurate, according to standards established in Subsection (1), are admissible if:

(a) the judge finds that they were made in the regular course of the investigation at or about the time of the act, condition, or event; and

(b) the source of information from which made and the method and circumstances of their preparation indicate their trustworthiness.

(3) If the judge finds that the standards established under Subsection (1) and the conditions of Subsection (2) have been met, there is a presumption that the test results are valid and further foundation for introduction of the evidence is unnecessary.   2004

72-10-504. Admissibility of chemical test results in actions for flying under the influence — Weight of evidence.

(1) (a) In any civil or criminal action or proceeding in which it is material to prove that a person was operating or in actual physical control of an aircraft while under the influence of alcohol, drugs, or with a blood or breath alcohol content statutorily prohibited, the results of a chemical test or tests as authorized in Section 72-10-502 are admissible as evidence.

(b) (i) In a criminal proceeding, noncompliance with Section 72-10-502 does not render the results of the chemical test inadmissible.

(ii) Evidence of a defendant's blood or breath alcohol content or drug content is admissible except when prohibited by Rules of Evidence or the constitution.

(2) This section does not prevent a court from receiving otherwise admissible evidence as to a defendant's blood or breath alcohol level or drug level at the time relevant to the alleged offense.   2002

CHAPTER 12

TRAVEL REDUCTION

Section
72-12-110.   Vehicles used and drivers excluded from definitions for regulatory purposes.

72-12-101. Title.
This chapter is known as the "Travel Reduction Act."   1998

72-12-102. Legislative findings and policy.
(1) The Legislature finds that:
(a) increasingly heavy commuting burdens on Utah's freeways and major transportation arteries are gradually aggravating driving conditions for all Utah motorists;
(b) single-occupant driving is the predominant mode of transportation used by commuters in Utah;
(c) single-occupant driving represents the most costly and most excessive use of dwindling petroleum reserves; and
(d) rapidly increasing energy costs represent an ever-growing burden on commuters' work-related expenses.
(2) The policy of this state is to support and encourage transportation modes and ride-sharing programs that reduce the number of vehicle miles traveled, thereby reducing gasoline consumption and protecting the environment.   1998

72-12-103. Definitions.
As used in this chapter:
(1) "Car-pool" means a mode of transportation in which:
(a) six or fewer persons, including the driver, ride together in a motor vehicle;
(b) that transportation is incidental to another purpose of the driver; and
(c) the vehicle manufacturer's design capacity of any one seat is not exceeded.
(2) "Van-pool" means a nonprofit mode of pre-arranged commuter transportation of a relatively fixed group of seven to 15 persons, including the driver, between home and work, or termini near home and work, in a vehicle the group occupancy of which does not exceed the vehicle manufacturer's design capacity and that:
(a) is owned or leased and operated by an individual:
(i) who owns only one van-pool vehicle;
(ii) whose provision of transportation is incidental to another purpose of the operator;
(iii) who does not transport people as a business; and
(iv) who accepts money from riders in the vehicle, if at all, only to recover some or all expenses directly related to the transportation, including fuel, maintenance, insurance, and depreciation;
(b) is owned or leased by a nonprofit employee organization and used to transport employees between home and work, or termini near home and work to provide incentives to employees to make the commute by a mode other than single occupant motor vehicle, the operating, administration, and reasonable depreciation costs of which are paid, if at all, by the persons using the vehicles; or
(c) is owned or leased by an employer, a public agency, or a public transit district, either alone or in cooperation with others to provide incentives to employees to make the commute by a mode other than single occupant motor vehicle, the driver and passengers of which are employees and fees charged, if at all, for which are nonprofit and only to recover operating, maintenance, administration, and reasonable depreciation costs.
(3) "Ride-sharing arrangement" means either a car-pool, van-pool, or both.   1998

72-12-104. Ride-sharing arrangements — Exemption from specified laws and rules.
The following laws and rules do not apply to ride-sharing arrangements:
(1) laws and rules containing insurance requirements that are specifically applicable to motor carriers or commercial vehicles;
(2) laws imposing a higher standard of care on drivers or owners of motor carriers or commercial vehicles than that imposed on drivers or owners of other motor vehicles;
(3) laws and rules with equipment requirements and special accident reporting requirements that are specifically applicable to motor carriers or commercial vehicles; and
(4) laws imposing a tax on fuel purchased in other states by motor carriers or road user taxes on commercial buses.   1998

72-12-105. Worker compensation inapplicable to injuries in ride-sharing.
Section 34A-2-401 providing compensation for workers injured during the course of their employment does not apply to persons injured while participating in a ride-sharing arrangement between their places of residence and places of employment.   1998

72-12-106. Employer's liability for ride-sharing injuries.
(1) An employer is not liable for injuries to passengers or other persons or both resulting from the operation or use of a motor vehicle not owned, leased, or contracted for by the employer in a ride-sharing arrangement.
(2) An employer is not liable for injuries to passengers or other persons or both on account of the employer having provided information or incentives or otherwise having encouraged employees to participate in ride-sharing arrangements.   1998

72-12-107. Benefits of ride-sharing driver not taxable income.
Money and other benefits, other than salary, received by a driver in a ride-sharing arrangement does not constitute income for the purpose of computing gross income under Title 59, Chapter 10, Individual Income Tax.   1998

72-12-108. Local taxation and licensing.
A county or municipality may not impose a tax on, or require a license for, a ride-sharing arrangement.   1998

72-12-109. Wage and hour regulations unaffected by ride-sharing.
The fact that an employee participates in any kind of ride-sharing arrangement does not affect the application of any laws requiring payment of a minimum wage or overtime pay or otherwise regulating the hours a person may work.   1999

72-12-110. Vehicles used and drivers excluded from definitions for regulatory purposes.
(1) A motor vehicle used in a ride-sharing arrangement is not a bus or commercial vehicle under:

(a) Title 41, Chapter 1a, Motor Vehicle Act, relating to registration; and

(b) Title 41, Chapter 6a, Traffic Code, relating to equipment requirements and rules of the road.

(2) The driver of a vehicle used in a ride-sharing arrangement is not a chauffeur and he is not transporting persons for compensation under the driver licensing provisions of Title 53, Chapter 3, Uniform Driver License Act. 2005

CHAPTER 13

UTAH SPACEPORT AUTHORITY ACT [REPEALED]

72-13-101 to 72-13-104. Repealed. 2003

TITLE 73

WATER AND IRRIGATION

CHAPTER 18

STATE BOATING ACT

73-18-1.   Statement of policy.

It is the policy of this state to regulate and promote safety for persons and property in and connected with the use, operation and equipment of vessels and to promote uniformity of laws and to adopt and pursue an educational program in relation thereto. 1971

73-18-2. Definitions.

As used in this chapter:

(1) "Board" means the Board of Parks and Recreation.

(2) "Boat livery" means an entity which holds any vessel for renting, leasing, or chartering.

(3) "Carrying passengers for hire" means to transport persons on vessels or to lead persons on vessels for consideration.

(4) "Consideration" means something of value given or done in exchange for something given or done by another.

(5) "Dealer" means any person who is licensed by the appropriate authority to engage in and who is engaged in the business of buying and selling vessels or of manufacturing them for sale.

(6) "Division" means the Division of Parks and Recreation.

(7) "Motorboat" means any vessel propelled by machinery, whether or not the machinery is the principal source of propulsion.

(8) "Operate" means to navigate, control, or otherwise use a vessel.

(9) "Operator" means the person who is in control of a vessel while it is in use.

(10) "Outfitting company" means any person who, for consideration:

(a) provides equipment to transport persons on rivers; and

(b) supervises guides who operate vessels to transport passengers or to lead persons on vessels.

(11) "Owner" means a person, other than a lien holder, holding a proprietary interest in or the title to a vessel. The term includes a person entitled to the use or possession of a vessel subject to an interest by another person, reserved or created by agreement and securing payment or performance of an obligation. The term does not include a lessee under a lease not intended as security.

(12) "Personal watercraft" means a motorboat that is:

(a) less than 16 feet in length;

(b) propelled by a water jet pump; and

(c) designed to be operated by a person sitting, standing, or kneeling on the vessel, rather than sitting or standing inside the vessel.

(13) "Sailboat" means any vessel having one or more sails and propelled by wind.

(14) "Vessel" means every type of watercraft, other than a seaplane on the water, used or capable of being used as a means of transportation on water.

(15) "Wakeless speed" means an operating speed at which the vessel does not create or make a wake or white water trailing the vessel. This speed is not in excess of five miles per hour.

(16) "Waters of this state" means any waters within the territorial limits of this state.　　1998

73-18-3. Enforcement of State Boating Act to be supervised by division.

The administration and enforcement of the State Boating Act shall be under the supervision and direction of the division.　　1986

73-18-3.5. Advisory council.

The board may appoint an advisory council representing various boating interests to seek recommendations on state boating policies.　　1987

73-18-4. Board may promulgate rules and set fees.

(1) The board may promulgate rules:

(a) creating a uniform waterway marking system which shall be obeyed by all vessel operators;

(b) regulating the placement of waterway markers and other permanent or anchored objects on the waters of this state;

(c) zoning certain waters of this state for the purpose of prohibiting the operation of vessels or motors for safety and health purposes only; and

(d) regulating vessel operators who carry passengers for hire and outfitting companies.

(2) (a) The board may set fees for licensing vessel operators who carry passengers for hire and registering outfitting companies in accordance with Section 63-38-3.2.

(b) The license and registration fees imposed pursuant to Subsection (2)(a) shall be deposited into the Boating Account created in Section 73-18-22.　　1998

73-18-5. Repealed.　　1969

73-18-6. Numbering of motorboats and sailboats required — Exception.

(1) Every motorboat and sailboat on the waters of this state shall be numbered. No person shall operate or give permission for the operation of any motorboat or sailboat on the waters of this state unless the motorboat or sailboat is numbered in accordance with:

(a) this chapter;

(b) applicable federal law; or

(c) a federally-approved numbering system of another state, if the owner is a resident of that state and his motorboat or sailboat has not been in this state in excess of 60 days for the calendar year.

(2) The number assigned to a motorboat or sailboat in accordance with this chapter, applicable federal law, or a federally-approved numbering system of another state shall be displayed on each side of the bow of the motorboat or sailboat, except this requirement does not apply to any vessel which has a valid marine document issued by the United States Coast Guard.　　1987

73-18-7. Registration requirements — Exemptions — Agents — Records — Period of registration and renewal — Expiration — Notice of transfer of interest or change of address — Duplicate registration card — Invalid registration — Powers of board.

(1) (a) Each motorboat and sailboat on the waters of this state shall be registered, unless it is exempt from registration as provided for in Section 73-18-9.

(b) A person may not place, or give permission for the placement of, a motorboat or sailboat on any waters of this state or operate or give permission for the operation of a motorboat or sailboat on the waters of this state, unless the motorboat or sailboat is registered in accordance with this chapter or is exempt from registration as provided for in Section 73-18-9.

(2) (a) The owner of each motorboat or sailboat required to be registered by this state shall file an application for registration with the division on forms approved by the division.

(b) (i) The application shall be signed by the owner of the motorboat or sailboat and accompanied by a fee set by the board.

(ii) This fee may not exceed $10 per year.

(c) The division, before issuing a registration card and registration decals, shall require from each applicant a certificate from the county assessor of the county in which the motorboat or sailboat has situs for taxation containing one of the following statements:

(i) the property tax on the motorboat or sailboat for the current year has been paid;

(ii) in the county assessor's opinion, the property tax is a lien on real property sufficient to secure the payment of the property tax; or

(iii) the motorboat or sailboat is exempt by law from payment of property tax for the current year.

(3) (a) Upon receipt of the application in the approved form, the division shall record the receipt and issue to the applicant registration decals and a registration card which state the number assigned to the motorboat or sailboat and the name and address of the owner.

(b) The registration card shall be available for inspection on the motorboat or sailboat for which it was issued, whenever that motorboat or sailboat is in operation.

(4) The assigned number shall:

(a) be painted or permanently attached to each side of the forward half of the motorboat or sailboat;

(b) consist of plain vertical block characters not less than three inches in height;

(c) contrast with the color of the background and be distinctly visible and legible;

(d) have spaces or hyphens equal to the width of a letter between the letter and numeral groupings; and

(e) read from left to right.

(5) Any vessel with a valid marine document issued by the United States Coast Guard is exempt from the number display requirements of Subsection (4).

(6) The nonresident owner of any motorboat or sailboat already covered by a valid number, which has been assigned to it pursuant to federal law or a federally-approved numbering system of his resident state, shall be exempt from registration while operating the motorboat or sailboat on the waters of this state unless he is operating in excess of the reciprocity period provided for in Subsection 73-18-9(1).

(7) (a) If the ownership of a motorboat or sailboat changes, a new application form with the fee shall be filed with the division and a new registration card and registration decals shall be issued in the same manner as provided for in Subsections (2) and (3).

(b) The current number assigned to the vessel shall be reassigned to the new owner to display on the motorboat or sailboat.

(8) If the United States Coast Guard has in force an overall system of identification numbering for motorboats or sailboats within the United States, the numbering system employed under this chapter by the board shall be in conformity with that system.

(9) The division may authorize any person to act as its agent for the registration of motorboats and sailboats. Any number assigned and any registration card and registration decals issued by an agent of the division in conformity with this chapter and rules of the board shall be valid.

(10) (a) All records of the division made or kept pursuant to this section shall be classified by the Motor Vehicle Division in the same manner as motor vehicle records are classified under Section 41-1a-116.

(b) Division records are available for inspection in the same manner as motor vehicle records pursuant to Section 41-1a-116.

(11) (a) Each registration, registration card, and decal issued under this chapter shall continue in effect for a period of 12 months beginning with the first day of the calendar month of registration. A registration may be renewed by the owner in the same manner provided for in the initial application. The current number assigned to the vessel shall be reassigned when the registration is renewed.

(b) Each registration, registration card, and registration decal expires the last day of the month in the year following the calendar month of registration.

(c) If the last day of the registration period falls on a day in which the appropriate state or county offices are not open for business, the registration of the motorboat or sailboat is extended to 12 midnight of the next business day.

(d) The division may receive applications for registration renewal and issue new registration cards at any time prior to the expiration of the registration, subject to the availability of renewal materials.

(e) The new registration shall retain the same expiration month as recorded on the original registration even if the registration has expired.

(f) The year of registration shall be changed to reflect the renewed registration period.

(g) If the registration renewal application is an application generated by the division through its automated system, the owner need not surrender the last registration card or duplicate.

(12) (a) The owner shall notify the division of the transfer of all or any part of his interest, other than creation of a security interest, in a motorboat or sailboat registered in this state under Subsections (2) and (3) or of the destruction or abandonment of the motorboat or sailboat.

(b) This notification must take place within 15 days of the transfer, destruction, or abandonment.

(c) The transfer, destruction, or abandonment of a motorboat or sailboat terminates its registration except if a transfer of a part interest which does not affect the owner's right to operate a motorboat or sailboat, the transfer shall not terminate the registration.

(13) (a) The registered owner shall notify the division within 15 days if his address changes from the address appearing on the registration card and shall, as a part of this notification, furnish the division with his new address.

(b) The board may provide in its rules for the surrender of the registration card bearing the former address and its replacement with a new registration card bearing the new address, or for the alteration of an outstanding registration card to show the new address of the holder.

(14) (a) If the registration card is lost or stolen, a fee of $4 may be collected by the division for the issuance of a duplicate.

(b) If the registration decals are lost or stolen, a fee of $3 may be collected by the division for the issuance of duplicate decals.

(15) A number other than the number assigned to a motorboat or sailboat or a number for a motorboat or sailboat granted reciprocity under this chapter may

not be painted, attached, or otherwise displayed on either side of the bow of a motorboat or sailboat.

(16) A motorboat or sailboat registration and number shall be invalid if obtained by knowingly falsifying an application for registration.

(17) The board may:

(a) designate the suffix to assigned numbers;

(b) adopt rules for the display of registration decals;

(c) adopt rules for the issuance and display of dealer numbers and registrations; and

(d) adopt rules for the issuance and display of temporary registrations.   2003

73-18-7.1. Fraudulent application for registration or certificate of title.

A person is guilty of a third degree felony if he:

(1) fraudulently uses a false or fictitious name in any application for a registration or certificate of title for a motorboat, sailboat, or outboard motor; or

(2) in making an application specified in Subsection (1), he:

(a) knowingly makes a false statement;

(b) knowingly conceals a material fact; or

(c) otherwise commits a fraud.   1990

73-18-7.2. Falsified registration or certificate of title.

It is a third degree felony for any person to:

(1) alter with fraudulent intent any motorboat or sailboat certificate of title, registration card, or registration decal or outboard motor certificate of title issued by the division or its authorized agent;

(2) forge or counterfeit any motorboat or sailboat certificate of title, registration card, or registration decal or outboard motor certificate of title purporting to have been issued by the division or its authorized agent;

(3) alter, falsify, or forge any assignment upon a motorboat, sailboat, or outboard motor certificate of title; or

(4) hold or use any motorboat or sailboat certificate of title, registration card, or registration decal or outboard motor certificate of title knowing it has been altered, forged, or falsified.   1990

73-18-7.3. Suspension or revocation of a registration or certificate of title.

The division or its authorized agent may suspend or revoke the registration or certificate of title of a motorboat, sailboat, or outboard motor if:

(1) the division or its authorized agent determines that the registration or certificate of title was fraudulently or erroneously issued;

(2) the division or its authorized agent determines that a registered motorboat or sailboat is mechanically unfit or unseaworthy for operation on the waters of this state;

(3) a registered motorboat or sailboat has been dismantled or wrecked so that it loses its character as a vessel;

(4) the division or its authorized agent determines that the required registration or titling fee has not been paid or is not paid upon reasonable notice and demand;

(5) a registration decal or number is knowingly displayed upon a motorboat or sailboat other than the one for which the decal or number was issued;

(6) the division or its authorized agent determines that the owner has committed any offense under this chapter or Title 41, Chapter 1a, Part 5,

involving the registration or certificate of title of a motorboat, sailboat, or outboard motor; or

(7) the division or authorized agent is so authorized under any other provision of law.   1992

73-18-7.4. Canceled, suspended, or revoked registration or certificate of title to be returned.

If the division or its authorized agent cancels, suspends, or revokes the registration or certificate of title of a motorboat, sailboat, or outboard motor, the owner shall immediately return the canceled, suspended, or revoked registration card, registration decal, or certificate of title to the division or authorized agent.   1990

73-18-8. Safety equipment required to be on board vessels.

(1) (a) Except as provided in Subsection (1)(c), each vessel shall have, for each person on board, one personal flotation device which is approved for the type of use by the commandant of the United States Coast Guard.

(b) Each personal flotation device shall be:

(i) in serviceable condition;

(ii) legally marked with the United States Coast Guard approval number; and

(iii) of an appropriate size for the person for whom it is intended.

(c) (i) Sailboards are exempt from the provisions of Subsection (1)(a).

(ii) The board may exempt certain types of vessels from the provisions of Subsection (1)(a) under certain conditions or upon certain waters.

(d) The board may require by rule for personal flotation devices to be worn:

(i) while a person is on board a certain type of vessel;

(ii) by a person under a certain age; or

(iii) on certain waters of the state.

(e) For vessels 16 feet or more in length, there shall also be on board, one Type IV throwable personal flotation device which is approved for this use by the commandant of the United States Coast Guard.

(2) Each vessel shall display navigation lights when the vessel is on the waters of this state between sunset and sunrise.

(3) If a vessel is not entirely open and it carries or uses any flammable or toxic fluid in any enclosure for any purpose, the vessel must be equipped with an efficient natural or mechanical ventilation system which is capable of removing resulting gases prior to and during the time the vessel is occupied by any person.

(4) Each vessel shall have fire extinguishing equipment on board.

(5) Any inboard gasoline engine shall be equipped with a carburetor backfire flame control device.

(6) The board may:

(a) require additional safety equipment by rule; and

(b) adopt rules conforming with the requirements of this section which govern specifications for and the use of safety equipment.

(7) A person may not operate or give permission for the operation of a vessel which is not equipped as required by this section or rules promulgated under this section.   1995

73-18-8.1. Capacity and certification label.

(1) Each vessel manufactured after November 1, 1972, which is less than 20 feet in length, except a

sailboat, canoe, kayak, inflatable vessel, or homemade motor boat must have a United States Coast Guard capacity and certification label permanently affixed to the vessel and clearly visible to the operator when boarding or operating the vessel. The capacity and certification information may be combined together and displayed on one label.

(2) No person shall operate, or give permission for the operation of, any vessel on the waters of this state if it is loaded or powered in excess of the maximum capacity information on the United States Coast Guard capacity label.

(3) No person shall alter, deface, or remove any United States Coast Guard capacity or certification information label affixed to a vessel.

(4) No person shall operate, or give permission for the operation of, a vessel on the waters of this state if the required United States Coast Guard capacity or certification information label has been altered, defaced, or removed.   1990

73-18-9. Exemptions from registration.

Registration under this chapter is not required for any of the following:

(1) a motorboat or sailboat already covered by a valid registration issued by its nonresident owner's resident state and it has not been within this state in excess of 14 days for the calendar year;

(2) a motorboat or sailboat from a country other than the United States temporarily using the waters of this state;

(3) a motorboat or sailboat whose owner is the United States, a state or subdivision thereof;

(4) a ship's lifeboat; or

(5) a motorboat or sailboat belonging to a class of vessels which is exempted from registration by the board after the board finds:

(a) that the registration of motorboats or sailboats of this class will not materially aid in their identification; and

(b) that the United States Coast Guard has a numbering system applicable to the class of motorboats or sailboats to which the motorboat or sailboat in question belongs, and the motorboat or sailboat would also be exempt from numbering if it were subject to federal law.   1987

73-18-10. Owner of boat livery — Duties.

(1) The owner of a boat livery shall keep a record of the following: the name and address of the person hiring any vessel; the identification number of the vessel; the vessel's departure date and time; and the vessel's expected time of return. The record shall be preserved for at least one year.

(2) Neither the owner of a boat livery nor his agent or employee may permit any vessel to depart from the premises of the boat livery unless the owner has equipped it as required under this chapter and unless he has advised the lessee or renter of the vessel of all rules promulgated under this chapter which the lessee or renter must obey.   1986

73-18-11. Regulation of muffling devices.

The board shall adopt rules for the regulating of muffling devices on all vessels.   1986

73-18-12. Operation in willful or wanton disregard for safety — Penalty.

(1) A person may not operate any nonmotorized vessel, or manipulate any water skis or any device

towed by a motorboat in a willful or wanton disregard for the safety of persons or property.

(2) A violation of Subsection (1) is a class B misdemeanor.   2002

73-18-12.1 to 73-18-12.8. Repealed.   2002

73-18-13. Duties of operator involved in accident — Notification and reporting procedures — Use of accident reports — Giving false information as misdemeanor.

(1) As used in this section, "agent" has the same meaning as provided in Section 41-6a-404.

(2) It is the duty of the operator of a vessel involved in an accident, if he can do so without seriously endangering his own vessel, crew, or passengers, to render aid to those affected by the accident as may be practicable. The operator shall also give his name, address, and identification of his vessel in writing to any person injured or to the owner of any property damaged in the accident.

(3) (a) The board shall adopt rules governing the notification and reporting procedure for vessels involved in accidents.

(b) The rules shall be consistent with federal requirements.

(4) (a) Except as provided in Subsection (4)(b), all accident reports:

(i) are protected and shall be for the confidential use of the division or other state, local, or federal agencies having use for the records for official governmental statistical, investigative, and accident prevention purposes; and

(ii) may be disclosed only in a statistical form that protects the privacy of any person involved in the accident.

(b) The division shall disclose a written accident report and its accompanying data to:

(i) a person involved in the accident, excluding a witness to the accident;

(ii) a person suffering loss or injury in the accident;

(iii) an agent, parent, or legal guardian of a person described in Subsections (4)(b)(i) and (ii);

(iv) a member of the press or broadcast news media;

(v) a state, local, or federal agency that uses the records for official governmental, investigative, or accident prevention purposes;

(vi) law enforcement personnel when acting in their official governmental capacity; and

(vii) a licensed private investigator.

(c) Information provided to a member of the press or broadcast news media under Subsection (4)(b)(iv) may only include:

(i) the name, age, sex, and city of residence of each person involved in the accident;

(ii) the make and model year of each vehicle involved in the accident;

(iii) whether or not each person involved in the accident was covered by a vehicle insurance policy;

(iv) the location of the accident; and

(v) a description of the accident that excludes personal identifying information not listed in Subsection (4)(c)(i).

(5) (a) Except as provided in Subsection (5)(b), an accident report may not be used as evidence in

any civil or criminal trial, arising out of an accident.

(b) Upon demand of any person who has, or claims to have, made the report, or upon demand of any court, the division shall furnish a certificate showing that a specified accident report has or has not been made to the division solely to prove a compliance or a failure to comply with the requirement that a report be made to the division. Accident reports may be used as evidence when necessary to prosecute charges filed in connection with a violation of Subsection (6).

(6) Any person who gives false information, knowingly or having reason to believe it is false, in an oral or written report as required in this chapter, is guilty of a class A misdemeanor.   2005

73-18-13.5. Personal watercraft accidents — Investigation and report of operator security — Agency action if no security — Surrender of registration materials.

(1) Upon request of a peace officer investigating an accident involving a personal watercraft, the operator of the personal watercraft shall provide evidence of the owner's or operator's security required under Section 73-18c-301.

(2) The peace officer shall record on a form approved by the division:

(a) the information provided by the operator;

(b) whether the operator provided insufficient or no information; and

(c) whether the peace officer finds reasonable cause to believe that any information given is not correct.

(3) The peace officer shall deposit all completed forms with the peace officer's agency, which shall forward the forms to the division no later than ten days after receipt.

(4) (a) The division shall revoke the registration of a personal watercraft involved in an accident unless the owner or operator can demonstrate to the division compliance with the owner's or operator's security requirement of Section 73-18c-301 at the time of the accident.

(b) Any registration revoked may not be renewed for a period of one year following the date of revocation.

(5) A person may appeal a revocation issued under Subsection (4) in accordance with procedures established by the board by rule that are consistent with Title 63, Chapter 46b, Administrative Procedures Act.

(6) (a) Any person whose registration is revoked under Subsection (4) shall return the registration card and decals for the personal watercraft to the division.

(b) If the person fails to return the registration materials as required, they shall be confiscated under Section 73-18-13.6.

(7) The board may make rules for the enforcement of this section.

(8) In this section, "evidence of owner's or operator's security" includes any one of the following:

(a) the operator's:

(i) insurance policy;

(ii) binder notice;

(iii) renewal notice; or

(iv) card issued by an insurance company as evidence of insurance;

(b) a copy of a surety bond, certified by the surety, which conforms to Section 73-18c-102;

(c) a certificate of the state treasurer issued under Section 73-18c-305; or

(d) a certificate of self-funded coverage issued under Section 73-18c-306.   1997

73-18-13.6. Grounds for confiscation of registration materials by state — Additional fee for reinstatement.

(1) (a) The division, any peace officer acting in an official capacity, or a person authorized under Subsection (2) may take possession of any registration card or decal issued by the state:

(i) upon revocation of it;

(ii) that is fictitious;

(iii) that has been unlawfully or erroneously issued; or

(iv) that is unlawfully or erroneously displayed.

(b) A receipt shall be issued that describes each confiscated item.

(2) The division may enter into contractual agreements with constables or other law enforcement agencies to facilitate confiscation of items listed in Subsection (1) if a person fails or refuses to surrender any of those documents to the division upon demand.

(3) The division shall assess against a person making an application to renew a registration, a fee, which shall be paid before the person's registration is renewed, to cover any costs of confiscating that person's registration materials.   1997

73-18-14. Transmittal of information to official or agency of United States.

In accordance with any request duly made by an authorized official or agency of the United States, any information compiled or otherwise available to the division under Section 73-18-13 shall be transmitted to the official or agency of the United States.   2000

73-18-15. Board to adopt rules concerning water skiing and aquaplane riding and use of other devices towed behind a vessel.

The board shall adopt rules for the regulation and safety of water skiing and aquaplane riding, and the use of other devices which are towed behind a vessel.   1986

73-18-15.1. Vessel navigation and steering rules.

(1) The operator of a vessel shall maintain a proper lookout by sight and hearing at all times to avoid the risk of collision.

(2) When the operators of two motorboats approach each other where there is risk of collision, each operator shall alter course to the right and pass on the left side of the other.

(3) When the operators of two motorboats are crossing paths and are at risk of a collision, the operator of the vessel which has the other vessel on its right side shall keep out of the way and yield right-of-way if necessary.

(4) The operator of any vessel overtaking any other vessel shall keep out of the way of the vessel being overtaken.

(5) The operator of a vessel underway shall keep out of the way of a:

(a) vessel not under command;

(b) vessel restricted in its ability to maneuver;

(c) vessel engaged in fishing; and

(d) sailing vessel.

(6) If the operator of one of two vessels is to keep out of the way, the other vessel operator shall maintain his course and speed unless it becomes apparent the other vessel is not taking the appropriate action.

(7) In narrow channels an operator of a vessel underway shall keep to the right of the middle of the channel.

(8) The operator of a vessel shall proceed at a safe speed at all times so that he can take proper and effective action to avoid collision and be stopped within a distance appropriate to the prevailing circumstances or conditions.

(9) (a) When the operators of two sailboats are approaching one another so as to involve risk of collision, one of the operators shall keep out of the way of the other as follows:

(i) when each has the wind on a different side, the operator of the vessel which has the wind on the left side shall keep out of the way of the other;

(ii) when both have the wind on the same side, the operator of the vessel which is to the windward shall keep out of the way of the vessel which is to leeward; and

(iii) if the operator of a vessel with the wind on the left side sees a vessel to windward and cannot determine with certainty whether the other vessel has the wind on the left or on the right side, the operator shall keep out of way of the other vessel.

(b) For purposes of this Subsection (9), the windward side shall be the side opposite that on which the mainsail is carried.

(10) The operator of any vessel may not exceed a wakeless speed when:

(a) within 150 feet of:

(i) another vessel;

(ii) a person in or floating on the water;

(iii) a water skier being towed by another boat;

(iv) a shore fisherman;

(v) a launching ramp;

(vi) a dock; or

(vii) a designated swimming area; or

(b) in an area designated as a wakeless speed area.

(11) The operator of a motorboat is responsible for any damage or injury caused by the wake produced by the operator's motorboat.

(12) (a) Except as provided in Subsection (12)(b), the operator of a motorboat that is less than 65 feet in length may not exceed a wakeless speed while any person is riding upon the bow decking, gunwales, transom, seatbacks, or motor cover.

(b) Subsection (12)(a) does not apply if the motorboat is:

(i) between 16 feet and 65 feet in length; and

(ii) the motorboat is equipped with adequate rails or other safeguards to prevent a person from falling overboard.

(13) If a person is riding upon the bow decking of a motorboat which does not have designed seating for passengers, the person shall straddle one of the upright supports of the bow rail and may not block the vision of the operator.

(14) The operator of a vessel may not tow a water skier or a person on another device:

(a) unless an onboard observer, who is at least eight years of age, is designated by the operator to watch the person being towed; or

(b) between sunset and sunrise.

(15) The operator of a vessel being operated between sunset and sunrise shall display lighted navigation lights approved by the division.

(16) A person who violates this section is guilty of a class C misdemeanor.   2002

73-18-15.2. Minimum age of operators — Boating safety course for youth to operate personal watercraft.

(1) (a) A person under 16 years of age may not operate a motorboat on the waters of this state unless the person is under the on-board and direct supervision of a person who is at least 18 years of age.

(b) A person under 16 years of age may operate a sailboat, if the person is under the direct supervision of a person who is at least 18 years of age.

(2) A person who is at least 12 years of age or older but under 16 years of age may operate a personal watercraft provided he:

(a) is under the direct supervision of a person who is at least 18 years of age;

(b) completes a boating safety course approved by the division; and

(c) has in his possession a boating safety certificate issued by the boating safety course provider.

(3) A person who is at least 16 years of age but under 18 years of age may operate a personal watercraft, if the person:

(a) completes a boating safety course approved by the division; and

(b) has in his possession a boating safety certificate issued by the boating safety course provider.

(4) A person required to attend a boating safety course under Subsection (3)(a) need not be accompanied by a parent or legal guardian while completing a boating safety course.

(5) A person may not give permission to another person to operate a vessel in violation of this section.

(6) As used in this section, "direct supervision" means oversight at a distance within which visual contact is maintained.

(7) (a) The division may collect a fee not to exceed $12 from each person who takes the division's boating safety course to help defray the cost of the boating safety course.

(b) Money collected from the fee collected under Subsection (7)(a) shall be deposited in the Boating Account.   2002

73-18-15.3. Personal watercraft — Prohibition on operation between sunset and sunrise.

A person may not operate a personal watercraft on the waters of this state between sunset and sunrise.   1998

73-18-15.5. Authorizing or permitting driving a vessel in violation of law.

(1) A person may not authorize or knowingly permit a vessel owned by him or that is under his control to be driven by a person in violation of this chapter or Title 41, Chapter 6a, Part 5, Driving Under the Influence and Reckless Driving.

(2) A person who violates Subsection (1) is guilty of a class C misdemeanor.   2005

73-18-16. Regattas, races, exhibitions — Rules.

The division may authorize the holding of regattas, motorboat or other boat races, marine parades, tournaments, or exhibitions on any waters of this state. The board may adopt rules concerning the safety of vessels and persons, either as observers or participants.   1987

73-18-17. Scope of application of chapter — Identical local ordinances authorized — Application for special local rules.

(1) This chapter, and other applicable laws of this state govern the operation, equipment, and numbering of vessels whenever any vessel is operated on the waters of this state, or when any activity regulated by this chapter takes place on the waters of this state. Nothing in this chapter prevents the adoption of any ordinance or local law relating to operation and equipment of vessels, the provisions of which are identical to the provisions of this chapter, amendments to this chapter, and rules promulgated under this chapter. Ordinances or local laws shall be operative only so long as and to the extent that they continue to be identical to provisions of this chapter, amendments to this chapter, and rules promulgated under this chapter.

(2) Any political subdivision of this state may, at any time, but only after public notice, formally apply to the board for special rules concerning the operation of vessels on any waters within its territorial limits. The political subdivision shall set forth in the application the reasons which make special rules necessary or appropriate. 1987

73-18-18. Liability of owner for injury or damage occasioned by negligent operation of vessel by minor.

The owner of a vessel shall be liable for any injury or damage occasioned by the negligent operation of such vessel, by a minor under the age of 18 years operating such vessel with the express or implied consent of the owner, whether under the laws of this state or by neglecting to observe such ordinary care and such operation as the rules of common law require. 1961

73-18-19. Publication of rules and regulations.

The rules promulgated under this chapter shall be published as required by Title 63, Chapter 46a, the Utah Administrative Rulemaking Act. 1987

73-18-20. Enforcement of chapter — Authority to stop and board vessels — Disregarding law enforcement signal to stop as misdemeanor — Procedure for arrest.

(1) Any law enforcement officer authorized under Title 53, Chapter 13, Peace Officer Classifications, may enforce the provisions of this chapter and the rules promulgated under this chapter.

(2) Any law enforcement officer authorized under Title 53, Chapter 13, Peace Officer Classifications, has the authority to stop and board any vessel subject to this chapter, whether the vessel is on water or land. If that officer determines the vessel is overloaded, unseaworthy, or the safety equipment required by this chapter or rules of the board is not on the vessel, that officer may prohibit the launching of the vessel or stop the vessel from operating.

(3) An operator who, having received a visual or audible signal from a law enforcement officer authorized under Title 53, Chapter 13, Peace Officer Classifications, to bring his vessel to a stop, operates his vessel in willful or wanton disregard of the signal so as to interfere with or endanger the operation of any vessel or endanger any person, or who attempts to flee or elude the officer whether by vessel or otherwise is guilty of a class A misdemeanor.

(4) Whenever any person is arrested for any violation of the provisions of this chapter or of the rules promulgated under this chapter, the procedure for arrest is the same as outlined in Sections 77-7-22 through 77-7-24. 2005

73-18-20.1. Seizure of a vessel.

(1) A peace officer, without a warrant, may seize and take possession of a vessel:

(a) that is placed or being operated on the waters of this state with improper registration;

(b) that the peace officer has reason to believe has been stolen;

(c) on which any hull identification number or serial number for an engine or outboard motor has been defaced, altered, or obliterated;

(d) that has been abandoned on public land, highways, or waters of this state; or

(e) if the registration or title fees for the vessel or outboard motor have not been paid.

(2) If necessary for the transportation of a seized vessel, the vessel's trailer may be seized to transport and store the vessel.

(3) Any peace officer seizing or taking possession of a vessel under this section shall comply with the provisions of Section 41-6a-1406. 2005

73-18-20.2. Defaced, altered, or obliterated identification or serial number — Release of vessel.

If the hull identification number or serial number for the engine or outboard motor of a vessel seized under Section 73-18-20.1 has been defaced, altered, or obliterated, the vessel may not be released until:

(1) the original manufacturer's hull identification number or engine or outboard motor serial number has been replaced; or

(2) a new number assigned by the division or its authorized agent has been provided and has been affixed to the vessel, engine, or outboard motor. 2001

73-18-20.3. Falsified hull identification, engine, or motor number.

(1) A person is guilty of a third degree felony if he:

(a) with fraudulent intent defaces, destroys, or alters a vessel hull identification number or serial number for an engine or outboard motor;

(b) places or stamps any vessel hull identification number upon a vessel or serial number upon an engine or outboard motor, except one assigned by the division or its authorized agent;

(c) knowingly buys, receives, disposes of, sells, offers for sale, or has in his possession any vessel, or engine or outboard motor removed from a vessel, from which the vessel hull identification number or engine or outboard motor serial number, has been removed, defaced, covered, altered, or destroyed for the purpose of concealing or misrepresenting the identity of the vessel, engine, or outboard motor;

(d) with intent to procure or pass title to a vessel or outboard motor, receives or transfers possession of a vessel or outboard motor which he knows or has reason to believe has been stolen or unlawfully taken; or

(e) has in his possession a vessel or outboard motor which he knows or has reason to believe has been stolen or unlawfully taken, unless the person is a peace officer engaged at the time in the performance of his duty.

(2) (a) This section does not prohibit the restoration by an owner of an original vessel hull identification number or manufacturer's serial number for an engine or outboard motor if the restoration is made by application to the division or its authorized agent.

(b) This section does not prohibit any manufacturer from placing, in the ordinary course of business, numbers or marks upon vessels, motors, outboard motors, or parts.   1990

73-18-20.4. Duty to report falsified vessel or motor number.

Any person owning or operating a marina, marine dealership, service station, public garage, paint shop, or a vessel repair shop shall immediately notify the local police authorities of any vessel or outboard motor that has any numbers that have apparently been altered, obliterated, or removed.   1990

73-18-20.5. Reporting of theft and recovery of vessels.

(1) (a) Any peace officer upon receiving reliable information that any vessel or outboard motor has been stolen shall immediately report the theft to the Criminal Investigations and Technical Services Division of the Department of Public Safety, established in Section 53-10-103.

(b) Any peace officer upon receiving information that any vessel or outboard motor which was previously reported as stolen has been recovered shall immediately report the recovery to his law enforcement agency and to the Criminal Investigations and Technical Services Division.

(2) The reporting and recovery procedures for vessels and outboard motors shall be the same as those specified in Section 41-1a-1401 for motor vehicles.   1998

73-18-20.6. Report by owners or lienholders of thefts and recoveries.

(1) The owner, or person having a lien or encumbrance upon a registered vessel or outboard motor which has been stolen or embezzled, may notify the law enforcement agency having jurisdiction where the theft or embezzlement occurred. If a vessel or outboard motor was embezzled, a report may be made only after having procured the issuance of a warrant for the arrest of the person charged with embezzlement.

(2) Any person who has given any notice under Subsection (1) shall notify the law enforcement agency where the theft or embezzlement was reported of a recovery of the vessel or outboard motor.   1990

73-18-20.7. Unlawful control over vessels — Penalties — Effect of prior consent — Accessory or accomplice.

(1) Any person who exercises unauthorized control over a vessel, not his own, without the consent of the owner or lawful custodian and with intent to temporarily deprive the owner or lawful custodian of possession of the vessel, is guilty of a class A misdemeanor.

(2) An offense under this section is a third degree felony if the actor does not return the vessel to the owner or lawful custodian within 24 hours after the exercise of unauthorized control.

(3) The consent of the owner or legal custodian of a vessel to its control by the actor is not in any case presumed or implied because of the owner's or legal custodian's consent on a previous occasion to the control of the vessel by the same or a different person.

(4) Any person who assists in, or is a party or accessory to or an accomplice in, an unauthorized taking or operating of a vessel is guilty of a class A misdemeanor.   1990

73-18-21. Violation of chapter as class B misdemeanor.

Unless otherwise specified, any person who violates any provision of this chapter or rule promulgated under this chapter is guilty of a class B misdemeanor.   1987

73-18-22. Boating Account created — Contents — Use of money.

(1) There is created within the General Fund a restricted account known as the Boating Account.

(2) Except as provided under Sections 73-18-24 and 73-18-25, all registration fees and related moneys collected by the division or any authorized agent, less the costs of collecting motorboat and sailboat registration fees by an authorized agent, shall be deposited into the Boating Account.

(3) The amount retained by an authorized agent may not exceed 20% of the fees charged in Section 73-18-7.

(4) Money in the Boating Account may be used for:

(a) the construction, improvement, operation, and maintenance of publicly owned boating facilities;

(b) boater education; and

(c) the payment of the costs and expenses of the division in administering and enforcing this chapter.   2003

73-18-23. Separability clause.

If any provision of this act, or the application of any provision to any person or circumstance, is held invalid, the rest of this act shall not be affected thereby.   1961

73-18-24. Search and rescue fee — Amount — Deposition.

(1) In addition to the fee imposed under Section 73-18-7, there is imposed a search and rescue fee of 50 cents on each motorboat or sailboat required to pay the fee imposed under Subsection 73-18-7(2) to be registered or renewed under Section 73-18-7.

(2) The fees imposed under this section shall be collected in the same manner and by the same agency designated to collect the fees imposed under this chapter.

(3) The fees collected under this section shall be deposited in the General Fund as dedicated credits for the Search and Rescue Financial Assistance Program created under Section 53-2-107.   1997

73-18-25. Fees to cover the costs of electronic payments.

(1) In accordance with Section 63-38a-105, the Division of Motor Vehicles may collect an electronic payment fee on all registrations and renewals of registration under Section 73-18-7.

(2) The division shall establish the fee according to the procedures and requirements of Section 63-38-3.2.   2003

CHAPTER 18a

BOATING — LITTER AND POLLUTION CONTROL

73-18a-1. Definitions.

As used in this chapter:

(1) "Board" means the Board of Parks and Recreation.

(2) "Division" means the Division of Parks and Recreation.

(3) "Human body waste" means excrement, feces, or other waste material discharged from the human body.

(4) "Litter" means any bottles, glass, crockery, cans, scrap metal, junk, paper, garbage, rubbish, or similar refuse discarded as no longer useful.

(5) "Marine toilet" means any toilet or other receptacle permanently installed on or within any vessel for the purpose of receiving human body waste. This term does not include portable toilets which may be removed from a vessel in order to empty its contents.

(6) "Operate" means to navigate, control, or otherwise use a vessel.

(7) "Operator" means the person who is in control of a vessel while it is in use.

(8) "Owner" means a person, other than a lien holder, holding a proprietary interest in or the title to a vessel. The term does not include a lessee under a lease not intended as security.

(9) "Vessel" means every type of watercraft, other than a seaplane on the water, used or capable of being used as a means of transportation on water.

(10) "Waters of this state" means all waters within the territorial limits of this state except those used exclusively for private purposes.   1986

73-18a-2. Littering and pollution of water or lands prohibited — Penalty.

(1) A person may not place, throw, deposit, discard, drop, or discharge and the operator of a vessel may not permit to be placed, thrown, deposited, discarded, dropped, or discharged into or upon the waters of this state, or lands adjacent to these waters any litter, human body waste, or other liquid or solid materials which may render the water or lands unsightly, nox-ious, or otherwise unwholesome or detrimental to the public health or welfare or the enjoyment of the water or lands for all legitimate uses, including recreational purposes.

(2) A person violating any provision of Subsection (1) is guilty of a class B misdemeanor and shall be fined not less than $100 for each violation.   1991

73-18a-3. Marine toilets — Use without pollution control device prohibited — Containers of body waste — Discharge into waters prohibited.

(1) No marine toilet on any vessel used or operated upon the waters of this state may be operated so as to discharge any inadequately treated human body waste into or upon waters of this state directly or indirectly.

(2) No person owning or operating a vessel with a marine toilet may use, or permit the use of, a toilet on the waters of this state, unless the toilet is equipped with facilities that will adequately treat, hold, incinerate, or otherwise handle human body waste in a manner that is capable of preventing water pollution.

(3) No container of human body waste may be placed, left, discharged, or caused to be placed, left, or discharged into or upon any waters of this state or lands adjacent to these waters by any person at any time.   1986

73-18a-4. Marine toilets — Pollution control devices required — Rules established by board.

(1) Every marine toilet on a vessel used or operated upon the waters of this state shall be equipped with an approved pollution control device in operative condition.

(2) The board shall make rules in accordance with Title 63, Chapter 46a, Utah Administrative Rulemaking Act, as provided in this chapter, establishing criteria or standards for definition and approval of acceptable pollution control devices for vessels.   1991

73-18a-5. Chemical treatment of marine toilet contents — Rules established by board and Department of Environmental Quality.

The board shall establish by rule, in accordance with Title 63, Chapter 46a, Utah Administrative Rulemaking Act, with approval by the Department of Environmental Quality, as provided in this chapter, standards relating to chemical treatment of marine toilet contents.   1991

73-18a-6, 73-18a-7. Repealed.   1987

73-18a-8. Public marinas — Duty to maintain waste disposal facilities.

The owner or whoever is lawfully vested with the possession, management, or control of a public marina or other public waterside facility used by a vessel for launching, docking, mooring, and related purposes shall be required to have, and properly maintain, waste receptacles or similar devices of proper design for the depositing of waste, litter, and human body waste, as required at locations where they can be conveniently used by a vessel's occupants. Waterside toilet facilities may be required if their absence contributes to or creates unsightliness or a hazard to the public health and welfare.   1986

73-18a-9. Public educational program.

The division may undertake and enlist the support and cooperation of all agencies, political subdivisions, and organizations to conduct a public educational program designed to inform the public of the undesirability of depositing trash, litter, and other objectionable materials in the waters of this state and the penalties provided by this chapter for such action. The division may use funds provided by the Legislature for this purpose. The division may utilize all means of communication in the conduct of this program.   1986

73-18a-10. Enforcement — Inspection of vessels, marinas, and other boating facilities.

Enforcement of this chapter or the rules promulgated under it shall be by law enforcement officers. Any vessel in this state is subject to inspection by the officers for the purpose of determining whether the vessel is equipped in compliance with this chapter. If the vessel is not so equipped, the division may suspend its registration until the proper installation is completed or the marine toilet is sealed in a manner which prohibits its use. The division may inspect marinas or other waterside public facilities used by vessels for launching, docking, or mooring purposes to determine whether they are adequately equipped for proper handling, storing, or disposal of waste, litter, or human body waste.   1987

73-18a-11. Regulation by political subdivisions prohibited — Exception.

Through the passage of this chapter, the state fully reserves to itself the exclusive right to establish requirements concerning the disposal of human body waste and litter from a vessel. To ensure statewide uniformity of the disposal of litter or human body waste from a vessel, regulation, other than the adoption for local enforcement of state rules, by any political subdivision of the state is prohibited.   1986

73-18a-12. Rules promulgated by board — Subject to approval by Department of Environmental Quality.

The board may promulgate rules under Title 63, Chapter 46a, Utah Administrative Rulemaking Act, which are necessary for the carrying out of duties, obligations, and powers conferred on the division by this chapter. These rules shall be subject to review and approval by the Department of Environmental Quality. This approval shall be recorded as part of the rules.   1991

73-18a-13. Publication of rules.

The rules promulgated under this chapter shall be published as required by the Utah Administrative Rulemaking Act.   1987

73-18a-14. Violation of chapter as class B misdemeanor.

Unless otherwise specified, any person who violates any provision of this chapter or rule promulgated under this chapter is guilty of a class B misdemeanor.   1987

73-18a-15. Arrest for violation — Procedure.

Whenever any person is arrested for any violation of the provisions of this chapter or rule promulgated under this chapter, the procedure for arrest is the same as specified in Sections 77-7-22 through 77-7-24.   2005

73-18a-16, 73-18a-17. Repealed.   1987

73-18a-18. Act supplemental to other laws.

This act shall not be construed as repealing any laws of the state relating to the pollution or littering of waters or lands thereof or any conservation laws, but shall be held and construed as auxiliary and supplemental thereto.   1967

CHAPTER 18b

WATER SAFETY

73-18b-1. Water safety rules and regulations — Adoption.

(1) The Board of Parks and Recreation may make rules necessary to promote safety in swimming, scuba diving, and related activities on any waters where public boating is permitted.

(2) The commission may consider recommendations of and cooperate with other state agencies and the owners or operators of those waters.   1997

73-18b-2. Filing and publishing regulations.

A copy of the regulations adopted pursuant to this act and any amendments thereto shall be filed in the office of the commission and with the Division of Archives and shall be published in a convenient form.   1984

73-18b-3. Violation of regulations — Misdemeanor.

Any person who violates any rules made by the Board of Parks and Recreation under authority of this chapter is guilty of a class B misdemeanor.   1997

73-18b-4. Enforcement of regulations.

(1) The Board of Parks and Recreation shall designate officers to enforce board rules made under the authority of this chapter.

(2) Those officers have the same authority in making arrests and responsibility in arrest procedures as they have in their other enforcement activities.   1997

CHAPTER 18c

FINANCIAL RESPONSIBILITY OF PERSONAL WATERCRAFT OWNERS AND OPERATORS ACT

Part 3

Owner's or Operator's Security Requirement

PART 3

OWNER'S OR OPERATOR'S SECURITY REQUIREMENT

73-18c-301.   Requirement of owner's or operator's security.

(1) Each resident owner of a personal watercraft shall maintain owner's or operator's security in effect at any time that the personal watercraft is operated on waters of the state.

(2) Each nonresident owner of a personal watercraft that has been physically present in this state for 90 or fewer days during the preceding 365 days shall maintain the type and amount of owner's or operator's security required in his or her place of residence at any time the personal watercraft is operated on waters of the state.

(3) Each nonresident owner of a personal watercraft that has been physically present in this state more than 90 days during the preceding 365 days shall thereafter maintain owner's or operator's security in effect at any time the personal watercraft is operated on waters of the state.

(4) The state and each of its political subdivisions and their respective departments, institutions, or agencies shall maintain owner's or operator's security in effect at any time their personal watercraft are operated on waters of the state.

(5) Any other state is considered a nonresident owner of its personal watercraft and is subject to Subsection (2) or (3).

(6) The United States, any political subdivision of it, or any of its agencies may maintain owner's or operator's security in effect for their personal watercraft.   1997

73-18c-302.   Operating personal watercraft without owner's or operator's security — Penalty.

(1) Any owner of a personal watercraft on which owner's or operator's security is required under Section 73-18c-301, who operates the personal watercraft or permits it to be operated on waters of the state without owner's security being in effect is guilty of a class B misdemeanor.

(2) Any other person who operates a personal watercraft upon waters of the state with the knowledge that the owner does not have owner's security in effect for the personal watercraft is also guilty of a class B misdemeanor, unless that person has in effect owner's or operator's security on a Utah-registered personal watercraft or its equivalent that covers the operation, by him or her, of the personal watercraft in question.   1997

73-18c-303.   Condition to obtaining registration.

The owner of a personal watercraft required to maintain owner's security under Section 73-18c-301 shall be required to swear or affirm, in writing, that he or she has owner's security in effect at the time of registering the personal watercraft.   1997

73-18c-304.   Evidence of owner's or operator's security to be carried when operating personal watercraft — Defense — Penalties.

(1) (a) (i) Except as provided in Subsection (1)(a)(ii), a person operating a personal watercraft shall:

     (A) have in the person's immediate possession evidence of owner's or operator's security for the personal watercraft the person is operating; and

     (B) display it upon demand of a peace officer.

(ii) A person operating a government-owned or government-leased personal watercraft is exempt from the requirements of Subsection (1)(a)(i).

(b) Evidence of owner's or operator's security includes any one of the following:

     (i) the operator's:

         (A) insurance policy;

         (B) binder notice;

         (C) renewal notice; or

         (D) card issued by an insurance company as evidence of insurance;

     (ii) a copy of a surety bond, certified by the surety, which conforms to Section 73-18c-102;

     (iii) a certificate of the state treasurer issued under Section 73-18c-305; or

     (iv) a certificate of self-funded coverage issued under Section 73-18c-306.

(2) It is an affirmative defense to a charge under this section that the person had owner's or operator's security in effect for the personal watercraft the person was operating at the time of the person's citation or arrest.

(3) (a) A letter from an insurance producer or company verifying that the person had the required liability insurance coverage on the date specified is considered proof of owner's or operator's security for purposes of Subsection (2).

(b) The court considering a citation issued under this section shall allow the letter under Subsection (3)(a) and a copy of the citation to be faxed or mailed to the clerk of the court to satisfy Subsection (2).

(4) A violation of this section is a class B misdemeanor.

(5) If a person is convicted of a violation of this section and if the person is the owner of a personal watercraft, the court shall:

     (a) require the person to surrender the person's registration materials to the court; and

     (b) forward the registration materials, together with a copy of the conviction, to the division.

(6) (a) Upon receiving notification from a court of a conviction for a violation of this section, the division shall revoke the person's personal watercraft registration.

(b) Any registration revoked may not be renewed for a period of one year following the date of revocation.   2003

73-18c-305.   State treasurer's certificate to satisfy owner's or operator's security requirement.

(1) A certificate of the state treasurer that conforms to this section satisfies the owner's or operator's security requirement of Section 73-18c-301.

(2) The certificate of the state treasurer shall certify that the person named in it has deposited in trust with the state treasurer cash in an amount equal to twice the single limit under Subsection 31A-22-1503(2) or securities with a fair market value of a similar amount, which securities are legal investments for insurers under Section 31A-18-105. The state treasurer may not accept a deposit and issue a certificate for it, unless the deposit is accompanied by evidence that there are no unsatisfied liens of any character on the assets deposited.

(3) The deposit shall be held by the state treasurer in trust to satisfy any execution on a judgment that would be paid under an insurance policy conforming to Sections 31A-22-1502 and 31A-22-1503 had the treasurer issued such a policy.

(4) Except as provided under Subsection (3), assets deposited with the treasurer under this chapter are exempt from attachment or execution.   1997

73-18c-306.   Certificate of self-funded coverage as proof of owner's or operator's security.

(1) The division may, upon the application of any person, issue a certificate of self-funded coverage when it is satisfied that the person has:

(a) more than 24 personal watercraft; and

(b) deposits, in a form approved by the division, securities in an amount of $200,000 plus $100 for each personal watercraft up to and including 1,000 personal watercraft and $50 for each personal watercraft over 1,000 personal watercraft.

(2) Persons holding a certificate of self-funded coverage under this chapter shall pay benefits to persons injured from the self-funded person's operation, maintenance, and use of personal watercraft as would an insurer issuing a policy to the self-funded person containing the coverages under Sections 31A-22-1502 and 31A-22-1503.

(3) In accordance with Title 63, Chapter 46b, Administrative Procedures Act, the division may, upon reasonable grounds, cancel the certificate. Failure to pay any judgment up to the limit under Subsection 31A-22-1503(2) within 30 days after the judgment is final is a reasonable ground to cancel the certificate.

(4) Any government entity with self-funded coverage for government-owned personal watercraft under Title 63, Chapter 30d, Governmental Immunity Act of Utah, meets the requirements of this section.   2005

73-18c-307.   Claims adjustment by persons with owner's or operator's security other than insurance.

(1) An owner or operator of a personal watercraft who maintains owner's or operator's security by a means other than an insurance policy under Section 73-18c-102, shall refer all bodily injury claims against the owner's or operator's security to an independent adjuster licensed under Title 31A, Chapter 26, Insurance Adjusters, or to an attorney.

(2) Unless otherwise provided by contract, any personal watercraft claim adjustment expense incurred by a person maintaining owner's or operator's security by a means other than an insurance policy under Section 73-18c-102, shall be paid by the person who maintains this type of owner's or operator's security.

(3) Owners and operators of personal watercraft maintaining owner's or operator's security by a means other than an insurance policy under Section 73-18c-102 are subject to the claim adjustment provisions of Title 31A, Chapter 26, Part 3, Claim Practices, in connection with claims against persons which arise out of the ownership, maintenance, or use of a personal watercraft.   2004

73-18c-308.   Providing false evidence of owner's or operator's security — Penalty.

(1) A person who provides evidence of owner's or operator's security to a peace officer under Section 73-18-13.5 or 73-18c-304 knowing or having reason to believe that the evidence of owner's or operator's security is false or that it is evidence of owner's or operator's security that is not in effect is guilty of a class B misdemeanor.

(2) A person is guilty of a class A misdemeanor if the person:

(a) forges or, without authority, signs any evidence of proof of owner's or operator's security; or

(b) falsely swears or affirms when obtaining a registration under Section 73-18c-303.   1997

TITLE 76

UTAH CRIMINAL CODE

Chapter
1.   General Provisions.
2.   Principles of Criminal Responsibility.
3.   Punishments.
4.   Inchoate Offenses.
5.   Offenses Against the Person.
5a. Sexual Exploitation of Children.
6.   Offenses Against Property.
6a. Pyramid Schemes.
7.   Offenses Against the Family.
8.   Offenses Against the Administration of Government.
9.   Offenses Against Public Order and Decency.
10. Offenses Against Public Health, Safety, Welfare, and Morals.

CHAPTER 1

GENERAL PROVISIONS

Part 1

Introductory Provisions

Part 2

Jurisdiction and Venue

Part 3

Limitations of Actions

PART 1

INTRODUCTORY PROVISIONS

76-1-101. Short title.

This title shall be known and may be cited as the "Utah Criminal Code." 1973

76-1-102. Effective date.

This code shall become effective on July 1, 1973. 1973

76-1-103. Application of code — Offense prior to effective date.

(1) The provisions of this code shall govern the construction of, the punishment for, and defenses against any offense defined in this code or, except where otherwise specifically provided or the context otherwise requires, any offense defined outside this code; provided such offense was committed after the effective date of this code.

(2) Any offense committed prior to the effective date of this code shall be governed by the law, statutory and non-statutory, existing at the time of commission thereof, except that a defense or limitation on punishment available under this code shall be available to any defendant tried or retried after the effective date. An offense under the laws of this state shall be deemed to have been committed prior to the effective date of this act if any of the elements of the offense occurred prior thereto. 1973

76-1-104. Purposes and principles of construction.

The provisions of this code shall be construed in accordance with these general purposes.

(1) Forbid and prevent the commission of offenses.

(2) Define adequately the conduct and mental state which constitute each offense and safeguard conduct that is without fault from condemnation as criminal.

(3) Prescribe penalties which are proportionate to the seriousness of offenses and which permit recognition or differences in rehabilitation possibilities among individual offenders.

(4) Prevent arbitrary or oppressive treatment of persons accused or convicted of offenses. 1973

76-1-105. Common law crimes abolished.

Common law crimes are abolished and no conduct is a crime unless made so by this code, other applicable statute or ordinance. 1974

76-1-106. Strict construction rule not applicable.

The rule that a penal statute is to be strictly construed shall not apply to this code, any of its provisions, or any offense defined by the laws of this state. All provisions of this code and offenses defined by the laws of this state shall be construed according to the fair import of their terms to promote justice and to effect the objects of the law and general purposes of Section 76-1-104. 1973

76-1-107. Procedure — Applicable provisions — Military codes, enforcement of court orders, and liability for civil damages not affected.

(1) Except as otherwise provided, the procedure governing the accusation, prosecution, conviction, and punishment of offenders and offenses is not regulated by this act but by the code of criminal procedure.

(2) This code does not affect any power conferred by law upon any court-martial or other military authority or officer to impose and inflict punishment upon offenders violating military codes or laws; nor does it affect any power of a court to punish for contempt or to employ any sanction authorized by law for the enforcement of an order or a civil judgment or decree.

(3) This act does not bar, suspend, or otherwise affect any right or liability to damages, penalty, forfeiture, impeachment, or other remedy authorized by law to be recovered or enforced in a civil action, administrative proceeding, or otherwise, regardless of whether the conduct involved in the proceeding constitutes an offense defined in this code. 1973

76-1-108. Separability clause.

If any provision of this act, or the application of any provision to any person or circumstance, is held invalid, the remainder of this act shall not be affected thereby. 1973

PART 2

JURISDICTION AND VENUE

76-1-201. Jurisdiction of offenses.

(1) A person is subject to prosecution in this state for an offense which he commits, while either within or outside the state, by his own conduct or that of another for which he is legally accountable, if:

(a) the offense is committed either wholly or partly within the state;

(b) the conduct outside the state constitutes an attempt to commit an offense within the state;

(c) the conduct outside the state constitutes a conspiracy to commit an offense within the state and an act in furtherance of the conspiracy occurs in the state; or

(d) the conduct within the state constitutes an attempt, solicitation, or conspiracy to commit in another jurisdiction an offense under the laws of both this state and the other jurisdiction.

(2) An offense is committed partly within this state if either the conduct which is any element of the offense, or the result which is an element, occurs within this state.

(3) In homicide offenses, the "result" is either the physical contact which causes death or the death itself.

(a) If the body of a homicide victim is found within the state, the death shall be presumed to have occurred within the state.

(b) If jurisdiction is based on this presumption, this state retains jurisdiction unless the defendant proves by clear and convincing evidence that:

(i) the result of the homicide did not occur in this state; and

(ii) the defendant did not engage in any conduct in this state which is any element of the offense.

(4) An offense which is based on an omission to perform a duty imposed by the law of this state is committed within the state regardless of the location of the offender at the time of the omission.

(5) (a) If no jurisdictional issue is raised, the pleadings are sufficient to establish jurisdiction.

(b) The defendant may challenge jurisdiction by filing a motion before trial stating which facts exist that deprive the state of jurisdiction.

(c) The burden is upon the state to initially establish jurisdiction over the offense by a preponderance of the evidence by showing under the provisions of Subsections (1) through (4) that the offense was committed either wholly or partly within the borders of the state.

(d) If after the prosecution has met its burden of proof under Subsection (5)(c) the defendant claims that the state is deprived of jurisdiction or may not exercise jurisdiction, the burden is upon the defendant to prove by a preponderance of the evidence:

(i) any facts claimed; and

(ii) why those facts deprive the state of jurisdiction.

(6) Facts that deprive the state of jurisdiction or prohibit the state from exercising jurisdiction include the fact that the:

(a) defendant is serving in a position that is entitled to diplomatic immunity from prosecution and that the defendant's country has not waived that diplomatic immunity;

(b) defendant is a member of the armed forces of another country and that the crime that he is alleged to have committed is one that due to an international agreement, such as a status of forces agreement between his country and the United States, cedes the exercise of jurisdiction over him for that offense to his country;

(c) defendant is an enrolled member of an Indian tribe, as defined in Section 9-9-101, and that the Indian tribe has a legal status with the United States or the state that vests jurisdiction in either tribal or federal courts for certain offenses committed within the exterior boundaries of a tribal reservation, and that the facts establish that the crime is one that vests jurisdiction in tribal or federal court; or

(d) offense occurred on land that is exclusively within federal jurisdiction.

(7) (a) The Legislature finds that identity fraud under Chapter 6, Part 11, Identity Fraud Act, involves the use of personal identifying information which is uniquely personal to the consumer or business victim of that identity fraud and which information is considered to be in lawful possession of the consumer or business victim wherever the consumer or business victim currently resides or is found.

(b) For purposes of Subsection (1)(a), an offense which is based on a violation of Chapter 6, Part 11, Identity Fraud Act, is committed partly within this state, regardless of the location of the offender at the time of the offense, if the victim of the identity fraud resides or is found in this state.

(8) The judge shall determine jurisdiction.   2004

76-1-202. Venue of actions.

(1) Criminal actions shall be tried in the county, district, or precinct where the offense is alleged to have been committed. In determining the proper place of trial, the following provisions shall apply:

(a) If the commission of an offense commenced outside the state is consummated within this state, the offender shall be tried in the county where the offense is consummated.

(b) When conduct constituting elements of an offense or results that constitute elements, whether the conduct or result constituting elements is in itself unlawful, shall occur in two or more counties, trial of the offense may be held in any of the counties concerned.

(c) If a person committing an offense upon the person of another is located in one county and his victim is located in another county at the time of the commission of the offense, trial may be held in either county.

(d) If a cause of death is inflicted in one county and death ensues in another county, the offender may be tried in either county.

(e) A person who commits an inchoate offense may be tried in any county in which any act that is an element of the offense, including the agreement in conspiracy, is committed.

(f) Where a person in one county solicits, aids, abets, agrees, or attempts to aid another in the planning or commission of an offense in another county, he may be tried for the offense in either county.

(g) When an offense is committed within this state and it cannot be readily determined in which county or district the offense occurred, the following provisions shall be applicable:

(i) When an offense is committed upon any railroad car, vehicle, watercraft, or aircraft passing within this state, the offender may be tried in any county through which such railroad car, vehicle, watercraft, or aircraft has passed.

(ii) When an offense is committed on any body of water bordering on or within this state, the offender may be tried in any county adjacent to such body of water. The words "body of water" shall include but not be limited to any stream, river, lake, or reservoir, whether natural or man-made.

(iii) A person who commits theft may be tried in any county in which he exerts control over the property affected.

(iv) If an offense is committed on or near the boundary of two or more counties, trial of the offense may be held in any of such counties.

(v) For any other offense, trial may be held in the county in which the defendant resides, or, if he has no fixed residence, in the county in which he is apprehended or to which he is extradited.

(h) A person who commits an offense based on Chapter 6, Part 11, Identity Fraud Act, may be tried in the county:

(i) where the victim's personal identifying information was obtained;

(ii) where the defendant used or attempted to use the personally identifying information;

(iii) where the victim of the identity fraud resides or is found; or

(iv) if multiple offenses of identity fraud occur in multiple jurisdictions, in any county where the victim's identity was used or obtained, or where the victim resides or is found.

(2) All objections of improper place of trial are waived by a defendant unless made before trial. 2004

PART 3

LIMITATIONS OF ACTIONS

76-1-301. Offenses for which prosecution may be commenced at any time.

A prosecution for a capital felony, aggravated murder, murder, manslaughter, child abuse homicide which is a second degree felony, aggravated kidnapping, or child kidnapping may be commenced at any time. 2002

76-1-301.5. Time limitations for prosecution of misusing public monies, falsification or alteration of government records, and bribery.

(1) A prosecution for misusing public monies, falsification or alteration of government records, or for a bribery offense shall be commenced within two years after facts constituting the offense have been reported to a prosecutor having responsibility and jurisdiction to prosecute the offense.

(2) This section does not shorten the limitation of actions under Section 76-1-302 or Subsection 76-1-303(3). 2002

76-1-302. Time limitations for prosecution of offenses — Provisions if DNA evidence would identify the defendant — Commencement of prosecution.

(1) Except as otherwise provided, a prosecution for:

(a) a felony or negligent homicide shall be commenced within four years after it is committed, except that prosecution for the offenses under Subsection (2) shall be commenced within eight years after the offense is committed, if within four years after its commission the offense is reported to a law enforcement agency;

(b) a misdemeanor other than negligent homicide shall be commenced within two years after it is committed; and

(c) any infraction shall be commenced within one year after it is committed.

(2) Offenses referred to in Subsection (1) are:

(a) rape under Section 76-5-402;

(b) object rape under Section 76-5-402.2;

(c) forcible sodomy under Subsection 76-5-403(2);

(d) forcible sexual abuse under Section 76-5-404; and

(e) aggravated sexual assault under Section 76-5-405.

(3) (a) Notwithstanding Subsection (1), prosecution for the offenses listed in Subsections 76-3-203.5(1)(c)(i)(A) through (AA) may be commenced at any time if the identity of the person who committed the crime is unknown but DNA evidence is collected that would identify the person at a later date.

(b) Subsection (3)(a) does not apply if the statute of limitations on a crime has run as of May 5, 2003, and no charges have been filed.

(4) If the statute of limitations would have run but for the provisions of Subsection (3) and identification of a perpetrator is made through DNA, a prosecution shall be commenced within one year of the discovery of the identity of the perpetrator.

(5) A prosecution is commenced upon the finding and filing of an indictment by a grand jury or upon the filing of a complaint or information. 2005

76-1-303. Time limitations for fraud or breach of fiduciary obligation and misconduct of public officer or employee.

(1) If the period prescribed in Section 76-1-302 has expired, a prosecution may be commenced for any offense a material element of which is either fraud or a breach of fiduciary obligation within one year after discovery of the offense by an aggrieved party or by a person who has a legal duty to represent an aggrieved party and who is himself not a party to the offense.

(2) Subsection (1) may not extend the period of limitation as provided in Section 76-1-302 by more than three years.

(3) If the period prescribed in Section 76-1-301.5 or 76-1-302 has expired, a prosecution may be commenced for:

(a) any offense based upon misconduct in office by a public officer or public employee:

(i) at any time during which the defendant holds a public office or during the period of his public employment; or

(ii) within two years after termination of defendant's public office or public employment.

(b) Except as provided in Section 76-1-301.5, Subsection (3) shall not extend the period of limitation otherwise applicable by more than three years. 1995

76-1-303.5. Sexual offense against a child.

If the period prescribed in Subsection 76-1-302(1) has expired, a prosecution may nevertheless be commenced for rape of a child, object rape of a child, sodomy upon a child, sexual abuse of a child, or aggravated sexual abuse of a child within four years after the report of the offense to a law enforcement agency.   1996

76-1-304. Defendant out of state — Plea held invalid — New prosecutions.

(1) The period of limitation does not run against any defendant during any period of time in which the defendant is out of the state following the commission of an offense.

(2) If the defendant has entered into a plea agreement with the prosecution and later successfully moves to invalidate his conviction, the period of limitation is suspended from the time of the entry of the plea pursuant to the plea agreement until the time at which the conviction is determined to be invalid, and that determination becomes final.

(3) For purposes of this section, "final" means:

    (a) all appeals have been exhausted;

    (b) no judicial review is pending; and

    (c) no application for judicial review is pending.

(4) When the period of limitation is suspended pursuant to Subsection (2), the suspension includes any charges to which the defendant pleaded guilty pursuant to a plea agreement, charges which were dismissed as a result of a plea agreement, as well as any known charges which were not barred at the time of entry of the plea.

(5) Notwithstanding any other limitation, a prosecution may be commenced for charges described in Subsection (4) within one year after a plea entered pursuant to a plea agreement has been determined to be invalid, and that determination becomes final.   1998

76-1-305. Lesser included offense for which period of limitations has run.

Whenever a defendant is charged with an offense for which the period of limitations has not run and the defendant should be found guilty of a lesser offense for which the period of limitations has run, the finding of the lesser and included offense against which the statute of limitations has run shall not be a bar to punishment for the lesser offense.   1973

76-1-306. Judge to determine.

When an issue concerning the statute of limitations is raised, the judge shall determine by a preponderance of the evidence whether the prosecution is barred by the limitations in this part.   1998

PART 4

MULTIPLE PROSECUTIONS AND DOUBLE JEOPARDY

76-1-401. "Single criminal episode" defined — Joinder of offenses and defendants.

In this part unless the context requires a different definition, "single criminal episode" means all conduct which is closely related in time and is incident to an attempt or an accomplishment of a single criminal objective.

Nothing in this part shall be construed to limit or modify the effect of Section 77-8a-1 in controlling the joinder of offenses and defendants in criminal proceedings.   1995

76-1-402. Separate offenses arising out of single criminal episode — Included offenses.

(1) A defendant may be prosecuted in a single criminal action for all separate offenses arising out of a single criminal episode; however, when the same act of a defendant under a single criminal episode shall establish offenses which may be punished in different ways under different provisions of this code, the act shall be punishable under only one such provision; an acquittal or conviction and sentence under any such provision bars a prosecution under any other such provision.

(2) Whenever conduct may establish separate offenses under a single criminal episode, unless the court otherwise orders to promote justice, a defendant shall not be subject to separate trials for multiple offenses when:

    (a) The offenses are within the jurisdiction of a single court; and

    (b) The offenses are known to the prosecuting attorney at the time the defendant is arraigned on the first information or indictment.

(3) A defendant may be convicted of an offense included in the offense charged but may not be convicted of both the offense charged and the included offense. An offense is so included when:

    (a) It is established by proof of the same or less than all the facts required to establish the commission of the offense charged; or

    (b) It constitutes an attempt, solicitation, conspiracy, or form of preparation to commit the offense charged or an offense otherwise included therein; or

    (c) It is specifically designated by a statute as a lesser included offense.

(4) The court shall not be obligated to charge the jury with respect to an included offense unless there is a rational basis for a verdict acquitting the defendant of the offense charged and convicting him of the included offense.

(5) If the district court on motion after verdict or judgment, or an appellate court on appeal or certiorari, shall determine that there is insufficient evidence to support a conviction for the offense charged but that there is sufficient evidence to support a conviction for an included offense and the trier of fact necessarily found every fact required for conviction of that included offense, the verdict or judgment of conviction may be set aside or reversed and a judgment of conviction entered for the included offense, without necessity of a new trial, if such relief is sought by the defendant.   1974

76-1-403. Former prosecution barring subsequent prosecution for offense out of same episode.

(1) If a defendant has been prosecuted for one or more offenses arising out of a single criminal episode, a subsequent prosecution for the same or a different offense arising out of the same criminal episode is barred if:

    (a) The subsequent prosecution is for an offense that was or should have been tried under Subsection 76-1-402(2) in the former prosecution; and

    (b) The former prosecution:

        (i) resulted in acquittal; or

        (ii) resulted in conviction; or

        (iii) was improperly terminated; or

        (iv) was terminated by a final order or judgment for the defendant that has not been reversed, set aside, or vacated and that necessarily required a determination inconsistent with a fact that must be established to secure conviction in the subsequent prosecution.

(2) There is an acquittal if the prosecution resulted in a finding of not guilty by the trier of facts or in a determination that there was insufficient evidence to warrant conviction. A finding of guilty of a lesser included offense is an acquittal of the greater offense even though the conviction for the lesser included offense is subsequently reversed, set aside, or vacated.

(3) There is a conviction if the prosecution resulted in a judgment of guilt that has not been reversed, set aside, or vacated; a verdict of guilty that has not been reversed, set aside, or vacated and that is capable of supporting a judgment; or a plea of guilty accepted by the court.

(4) There is an improper termination of prosecution if the termination takes place before the verdict, is for reasons not amounting to an acquittal, and takes place after a jury has been impanelled and sworn to try the defendant, or, if the jury trial is waived, after the first witness is sworn. However, termination of prosecution is not improper if:

(a) The defendant consents to the termination; or

(b) The defendant waives his right to object to the termination;

(c) The court finds and states for the record that the termination is necessary because:

(i) It is physically impossible to proceed with the trial in conformity with the law; or

(ii) There is a legal defect in the proceeding not attributable to the state that would make any judgment entered upon a verdict reversible as a matter of law; or

(iii) Prejudicial conduct in or out of the courtroom not attributable to the state makes it impossible to proceed with the trial without injustice to the defendant or the state; or

(iv) The jury is unable to agree upon a verdict; or

(v) False statements of a juror on voir dire prevent a fair trial. 1974

76-1-404. Concurrent jurisdiction — Prosecution in other jurisdiction barring prosecution in state.

If a defendant's conduct establishes the commission of one or more offenses within the concurrent jurisdiction of this state and of another jurisdiction, federal or state, the prosecution in the other jurisdiction is a bar to a subsequent prosecution in this state if (1) the former prosecution resulted in an acquittal, conviction, or termination of prosecution, as those terms are defined in Section 76-1-403, and (2) the subsequent prosecution is for the same offense or offenses. 1973

76-1-405. Subsequent prosecution not barred — Circumstances.

A subsequent prosecution for an offense shall not be barred under the following circumstances:

(1) The former prosecution was procured by the defendant without the knowledge of the prosecuting attorney bringing the subsequent prosecution and with intent to avoid the sentence that might otherwise be imposed; or

(2) The former prosecution resulted in a judgment of guilt held invalid in a subsequent proceeding on writ of habeas corpus, coram nobis, or similar collateral attack. 1973

PART 5

BURDEN OF PROOF

76-1-501. Presumption of innocence — "Element of the offense" defined.

(1) A defendant in a criminal proceeding is presumed to be innocent until each element of the offense charged against him is proved beyond a reasonable doubt. In absence of such proof, the defendant shall be acquitted.

(2) As used in this part the words "element of the offense" mean:

(a) The conduct, attendant circumstances, or results of conduct proscribed, prohibited, or forbidden in the definition of the offense;

(b) The culpable mental state required.

(3) The existence of jurisdiction and venue are not elements of the offense but shall be established by a preponderance of the evidence. 1973

76-1-502. Negating defense by allegation or proof — When not required.

Section 76-1-501 does not require negating a defense:

(1) By allegation in an information, indictment, or other charge; or

(2) By proof, unless:

(a) The defense is in issue in the case as a result of evidence presented at trial, either by the prosecution or the defense; or

(b) The defense is an affirmative defense, and the defendant has presented evidence of such affirmative defense. 1973

76-1-503. Presumption of fact.

An evidentiary presumption established by this code or other penal statute has the following consequences:

(1) When evidence of facts which support the presumption exist, the issue of the existence of the presumed fact must be submitted to the jury unless the court is satisfied that the evidence as a whole clearly negates the presumed fact;

(2) In submitting the issue of the existence of a presumed fact to the jury, the court shall charge that while the presumed fact must on all evidence be proved beyond a reasonable doubt, the law regards the facts giving rise to the presumption as evidence of the presumed fact. 1973

76-1-504. Affirmative defense presented by defendant.

Evidence of an affirmative defense as defined by this code or other statutes shall be presented by the defendant. 1973

PART 6

DEFINITIONS

76-1-601. Definitions.

Unless otherwise provided, the following terms apply to this title:

(1) "Act" means a voluntary bodily movement and includes speech.

(2) "Actor" means a person whose criminal responsibility is in issue in a criminal action.

(3) "Bodily injury" means physical pain, illness, or any impairment of physical condition.

(4) "Conduct" means an act or omission.

(5) "Dangerous weapon" means:

(a) any item capable of causing death or serious bodily injury; or

(b) a facsimile or representation of the item; and:

(i) the actor's use or apparent intended use of the item leads the victim to reasonably believe the item is likely to cause death or serious bodily injury; or

(ii) the actor represents to the victim verbally or in any other manner that he is in control of such an item.

(6) "Offense" means a violation of any penal statute of this state.

(7) "Omission" means a failure to act when there is a legal duty to act and the actor is capable of acting.

(8) "Person" means an individual, public or private corporation, government, partnership, or unincorporated association.

(9) "Possess" means to have physical possession of or to exercise dominion or control over tangible property.

(10) "Serious bodily injury" means bodily injury that creates or causes serious permanent disfigurement, protracted loss or impairment of the function of any bodily member or organ, or creates a substantial risk of death.

(11) "Substantial bodily injury" means bodily injury, not amounting to serious bodily injury, that creates or causes protracted physical pain, temporary disfigurement, or temporary loss or impairment of the function of any bodily member or organ.

(12) "Writing" or "written" includes any handwriting, typewriting, printing, electronic storage or transmission, or any other method of recording information or fixing information in a form capable of being preserved.   **1996**

CHAPTER 2

PRINCIPLES OF CRIMINAL RESPONSIBILITY

Part 1

Culpability Generally

Part 2

Criminal Responsibility for Conduct of Another

Part 3

Defenses to Criminal Responsibility

Part 4

Justification Excluding Criminal Responsibility

PART 1

CULPABILITY GENERALLY

76-2-101. Requirements of criminal conduct and criminal responsibility.

(1) (a) A person is not guilty of an offense unless the person's conduct is prohibited by law; and

(b) (i) the person acts intentionally, knowingly, recklessly, with criminal negligence, or with a mental state otherwise specified in the statute defining the offense, as the definition of the offense requires; or

(ii) the person's acts constitute an offense involving strict liability.

(2) These standards of criminal responsibility do not apply to the violations set forth in Title 41, Chapter 6a, Traffic Code, unless specifically provided by law.   **2005**

76-2-102. Culpable mental state required — Strict liability.

Every offense not involving strict liability shall require a culpable mental state, and when the definition of the offense does not specify a culpable mental state and the offense does not involve strict liability, intent, knowledge, or recklessness shall suffice to establish criminal responsibility. An offense shall involve strict liability if the statute defining the offense clearly indicates a legislative purpose to impose criminal responsibility for commission of the conduct prohibited by the statute without requiring proof of any culpable mental state.   **1983**

76-2-103. Definitions.

A person engages in conduct:

(1) Intentionally, or with intent or willfully with respect to the nature of his conduct or to a result of his conduct, when it is his conscious objective or desire to engage in the conduct or cause the result.

(2) Knowingly, or with knowledge, with respect to his conduct or to circumstances surrounding his conduct when he is aware of the nature of his conduct or the existing circumstances. A person acts knowingly, or with knowledge, with respect to a result of his conduct when he is aware that

his conduct is reasonably certain to cause the result.

(3) Recklessly, or maliciously, with respect to circumstances surrounding his conduct or the result of his conduct when he is aware of but consciously disregards a substantial and unjustifiable risk that the circumstances exist or the result will occur. The risk must be of such a nature and degree that its disregard constitutes a gross deviation from the standard of care that an ordinary person would exercise under all the circumstances as viewed from the actor's standpoint.

(4) With criminal negligence or is criminally negligent with respect to circumstances surrounding his conduct or the result of his conduct when he ought to be aware of a substantial and unjustifiable risk that the circumstances exist or the result will occur. The risk must be of such a nature and degree that the failure to perceive it constitutes a gross deviation from the standard of care that an ordinary person would exercise in all the circumstances as viewed from the actor's standpoint. 1974

76-2-104. Culpable mental state — Higher mental states included.

(1) If acting with criminal negligence is sufficient to establish the culpable mental state for an element of an offense, that element is also established if a person acts intentionally, knowingly, or recklessly.

(2) If acting recklessly is sufficient to establish the culpable mental state for an element of an offense, that element is also established if a person acts intentionally or knowingly.

(3) If acting knowingly is sufficient to establish the culpable mental state for an element of an offense, that element is also established if a person acts intentionally. 1998

76-2-105. Transferred intent.

Where intentionally causing a result is an element of an offense, that element is established even if a different person than the actor intended was killed, injured, or harmed, or different property than the actor intended was damaged or otherwise affected. 2004

PART 2

CRIMINAL RESPONSIBILITY FOR CONDUCT OF ANOTHER

76-2-201. Definitions.

As used in this part:

(1) "Agent" means any director, officer, employee, or other person authorized to act in behalf of a corporation or association.

(2) "High managerial agent" means:

(a) A partner in a partnership;

(b) An officer of a corporation or association;

(c) An agent of a corporation or association who has duties of such responsibility that his conduct reasonably may be assumed to represent the policy of the corporation or association.

(3) "Corporation" means all organizations required by the laws of this state or any other state to obtain a certificate of authority, a certificate of incorporation, or other form of registration to transact business as a corporation within this state or any other state and shall include domestic, foreign, profit and nonprofit corporations, but

shall not include a corporation sole, as such term is used in Title 16, Chapter 7, Utah Code Annotated 1953. Lack of an appropriate certificate of authority, incorporation, or other form of registration shall be no defense when such organization conducted its business in a manner as to appear to have lawful corporate existence. 1973

76-2-202. Criminal responsibility for direct commission of offense or for conduct of another.

Every person, acting with the mental state required for the commission of an offense who directly commits the offense, who solicits, requests, commands, encourages, or intentionally aids another person to engage in conduct which constitutes an offense shall be criminally liable as a party for such conduct. 1973

76-2-203. Defenses unavailable in prosecution based on conduct of another.

In any prosecution in which an actor's criminal responsibility is based on the conduct of another, it is no defense:

(1) That the actor belongs to a class of persons who by definition of the offense is legally incapable of committing the offense in an individual capacity, or

(2) That the person for whose conduct the actor is criminally responsible has been acquitted, has not been prosecuted or convicted, has been convicted of a different offense or of a different type or class of offense or is immune from prosecution. 1973

76-2-204. Criminal responsibility of corporation or association.

A corporation or association is guilty of an offense when:

(1) The conduct constituting the offense consists of an omission to discharge a specific duty of affirmative performance imposed on corporations or associations by law; or

(2) The conduct constituting the offense is authorized, solicited, requested, commanded, or undertaken, performed, or recklessly tolerated by the board of directors or by a high managerial agent acting within the scope of his employment and in behalf of the corporation or association. 1973

76-2-205. Criminal responsibility of person for conduct in name of corporation or association.

A person is criminally liable for conduct constituting an offense which he performs or causes to be performed in the name of or on behalf of a corporation or association to the same extent as if such conduct were performed in his own name or behalf. 1973

PART 3

DEFENSES TO CRIMINAL RESPONSIBILITY

76-2-301. Person under fourteen years old not criminally responsible.

A person is not criminally responsible for conduct performed before he reaches the age of fourteen years. This section shall in no way limit the jurisdiction of or proceedings before the juvenile courts of this state. 1973

76-2-302. Compulsion.

(1) A person is not guilty of an offense when he engaged in the proscribed conduct because he was coerced to do so by the use or threatened imminent

use of unlawful physical force upon him or a third person, which force or threatened force a person of reasonable firmness in his situation would not have resisted.

(2) The defense of compulsion provided by this section shall be unavailable to a person who intentionally, knowingly, or recklessly places himself in a situation in which it is probable that he will be subjected to duress.

(3) A married woman is not entitled, by reason of the presence of her husband, to any presumption of compulsion or to any defense of compulsion except as in Subsection (1) provided.   1973

76-2-303.   Entrapment.

(1) It is a defense that the actor was entrapped into committing the offense. Entrapment occurs when a peace officer or a person directed by or acting in cooperation with the officer induces the commission of an offense in order to obtain evidence of the commission for prosecution by methods creating a substantial risk that the offense would be committed by one not otherwise ready to commit it. Conduct merely affording a person an opportunity to commit an offense does not constitute entrapment.

(2) The defense of entrapment shall be unavailable when causing or threatening bodily injury is an element of the offense charged and the prosecution is based on conduct causing or threatening the injury to a person other than the person perpetrating the entrapment.

(3) The defense provided by this section is available even though the actor denies commission of the conduct charged to constitute the offense.

(4) Upon written motion of the defendant, the court shall hear evidence on the issue and shall determine as a matter of fact and law whether the defendant was entrapped to commit the offense. Defendant's motion shall be made at least ten days before trial except the court for good cause shown may permit a later filing.

(5) Should the court determine that the defendant was entrapped, it shall dismiss the case with prejudice, but if the court determines the defendant was not entrapped, such issue may be presented by the defendant to the jury at trial. Any order by the court dismissing a case based on entrapment shall be appealable by the state.

(6) In any hearing before a judge or jury where the defense of entrapment is an issue, past offenses of the defendant shall not be admitted except that in a trial where the defendant testifies he may be asked of his past convictions for felonies and any testimony given by the defendant at a hearing on entrapment may be used to impeach his testimony at trial.   1998

76-2-304.   Ignorance or mistake of fact or law.

(1) Unless otherwise provided, ignorance or mistake of fact which disproves the culpable mental state is a defense to any prosecution for that crime.

(2) Ignorance or mistake concerning the existence or meaning of a penal law is no defense to a crime unless:

(a) Due to his ignorance or mistake, the actor reasonably believed his conduct did not constitute an offense, and

(b) His ignorance or mistake resulted from the actor's reasonable reliance upon:

(i) An official statement of the law contained in a written order or grant of permission by an administrative agency charged by law with responsibility for interpreting the law in question; or

(ii) A written interpretation of the law contained in an opinion of a court of record or made by a public servant charged by law with responsibility for interpreting the law in question.

(3) Although an actor's ignorance or mistake of fact or law may constitute a defense to the offense charged, he may nevertheless be convicted of a lesser included offense of which he would be guilty if the fact or law were as he believed.   1974

76-2-304.5.   Mistake as to victim's age not a defense.

(1) It is not a defense to the crime of child kidnaping, a violation of Section 76-5-301.1; rape of a child, a violation of Section 76-5-402.1; object rape of a child, a violation of Section 76-5-402.3; sodomy upon a child, a violation of Section 76-5-403.1; or sexual abuse of a child, a violation of Section 76-5-404.1; or aggravated sexual abuse of a child, a violation of Subsection 76-5-404.1(4); or an attempt to commit any of those offenses, that the actor mistakenly believed the victim to be 14 years of age or older at the time of the alleged offense or was unaware of the victim's true age.

(2) It is not a defense to the crime of unlawful sexual activity with a minor, a violation of Section 76-5-401, sexual abuse of a minor, a violation of Section 76-5-401.1, or an attempt to commit either of these offenses, that the actor mistakenly believed the victim to be 16 years of age or older at the time of the alleged offense or was unaware of the victim's true age.   2003

76-2-305.   Mental illness — Use as a defense — Influence of alcohol or other substance voluntarily consumed — Definition.

(1) (a) It is a defense to a prosecution under any statute or ordinance that the defendant, as a result of mental illness, lacked the mental state required as an element of the offense charged.

(b) Mental illness is not otherwise a defense, but may be evidence in mitigation of the penalty in a capital felony under Section 76-3-207 and may be evidence of special mitigation reducing the level of a criminal homicide or attempted criminal homicide offense under Section 76-5-205.5.

(2) The defense defined in this section includes the defenses known as "insanity" and "diminished mental capacity."

(3) A person who asserts a defense of insanity or diminished mental capacity, and who is under the influence of voluntarily consumed, injected, or ingested alcohol, controlled substances, or volatile substances at the time of the alleged offense is not excused from criminal responsibility on the basis of mental illness if the alcohol or substance caused, triggered, or substantially contributed to the mental illness.

(4) (a) "Mental illness" means a mental disease or defect that substantially impairs a person's mental, emotional, or behavioral functioning. A mental defect may be a congenital condition, the result of injury, or a residual effect of a physical or mental disease and includes, but is not limited to, mental retardation.

(b) "Mental illness" does not mean an abnormality manifested primarily by repeated criminal conduct.

(5) "Mental retardation" means a significant subaverage general intellectual functioning, existing concurrently with deficits in adaptive behavior, and manifested prior to age 22.   2003

76-2-306. Voluntary intoxication.

Voluntary intoxication shall not be a defense to a criminal charge unless such intoxication negates the existence of the mental state which is an element of the offense; however, if recklessness or criminal negligence establishes an element of an offense and the actor is unaware of the risk because of voluntary intoxication, his unawareness is immaterial in a prosecution for that offense.   1973

76-2-307. Voluntary termination of efforts prior to offense.

It is an affirmative defense to a prosecution in which an actor's criminal responsibility arises from his own conduct or from being a party to an offense under Section 76-2-202 that prior to the commission of the offense, the actor voluntarily terminated his effort to promote or facilitate its commission and either:

(1) gave timely warning to the proper law enforcement authorities or the intended victim; or

(2) wholly deprives his prior efforts of effectiveness in the commission.   1995

76-2-308. Affirmative defenses.

Defenses enumerated in this part constitute affirmative defenses.   1973

PART 4

JUSTIFICATION EXCLUDING CRIMINAL RESPONSIBILITY

76-2-401. Justification as defense — When allowed.

(1) Conduct which is justified is a defense to prosecution for any offense based on the conduct. The defense of justification may be claimed:

(a) when the actor's conduct is in defense of persons or property under the circumstances described in Sections 76-2-402 through 76-2-406 of this part;

(b) when the actor's conduct is reasonable and in fulfillment of his duties as a governmental officer or employee;

(c) when the actor's conduct is reasonable discipline of minors by parents, guardians, teachers, or other persons in loco parentis, as limited by Subsection (2);

(d) when the actor's conduct is reasonable discipline of persons in custody under the laws of the state; or

(e) when the actor's conduct is justified for any other reason under the laws of this state.

(2) The defense of justification under Subsection (1)(c) is not available if the offense charged involves causing serious bodily injury, as defined in Section 76-1-601, serious physical injury, as defined in Section 76-5-109, or the death of the minor.   2000

76-2-402. Force in defense of person — Forcible felony defined.

(1) A person is justified in threatening or using force against another when and to the extent that he or she reasonably believes that force is necessary to defend himself or a third person against such other's imminent use of unlawful force. However, that person is justified in using force intended or likely to cause death or serious bodily injury only if he or she reasonably believes that force is necessary to prevent death or serious bodily injury to himself or a third person as a result of the other's imminent use of unlawful force, or to prevent the commission of a forcible felony.

(2) A person is not justified in using force under the circumstances specified in Subsection (1) if he or she:

(a) initially provokes the use of force against himself with the intent to use force as an excuse to inflict bodily harm upon the assailant;

(b) is attempting to commit, committing, or fleeing after the commission or attempted commission of a felony; or

(c) (i) was the aggressor or was engaged in a combat by agreement, unless he withdraws from the encounter and effectively communicates to the other person his intent to do so and, notwithstanding, the other person continues or threatens to continue the use of unlawful force; and

(ii) for purposes of Subsection (i) the following do not, by themselves, constitute "combat by agreement":

(A) voluntarily entering into or remaining in an ongoing relationship; or

(B) entering or remaining in a place where one has a legal right to be.

(3) A person does not have a duty to retreat from the force or threatened force described in Subsection (1) in a place where that person has lawfully entered or remained, except as provided in Subsection (2)(c).

(4) For purposes of this section, a forcible felony includes aggravated assault, mayhem, aggravated murder, murder, manslaughter, kidnapping, and aggravated kidnapping, rape, forcible sodomy, rape of a child, object rape, object rape of a child, sexual abuse of a child, aggravated sexual abuse of a child, and aggravated sexual assault as defined in Title 76, Chapter 5, and arson, robbery, and burglary as defined in Title 76, Chapter 6. Any other felony offense which involves the use of force or violence against a person so as to create a substantial danger of death or serious bodily injury also constitutes a forcible felony. Burglary of a vehicle, defined in Section 76-6-204, does not constitute a forcible felony except when the vehicle is occupied at the time unlawful entry is made or attempted.

(5) In determining imminence or reasonableness under Subsection (1), the trier of fact may consider, but is not limited to, any of the following factors:

(a) the nature of the danger;

(b) the immediacy of the danger;

(c) the probability that the unlawful force would result in death or serious bodily injury;

(d) the other's prior violent acts or violent propensities; and

(e) any patterns of abuse or violence in the parties' relationship.   1994

76-2-403. Force in arrest.

Any person is justified in using any force, except deadly force, which he reasonably believes to be necessary to effect an arrest or to defend himself or another from bodily harm while making an arrest.   1973

76-2-404. Peace officer's use of deadly force.

(1) A peace officer, or any person acting by his command in his aid and assistance, is justified in using deadly force when:

(a) the officer is acting in obedience to and in accordance with the judgment of a competent court in executing a penalty of death under Subsection 77-18-5.5(3) or (4);

(b) effecting an arrest or preventing an escape from custody following an arrest, where the officer reasonably believes that deadly force is necessary to prevent the arrest from being defeated by escape; and

(i) the officer has probable cause to believe that the suspect has committed a felony offense involving the infliction or threatened infliction of death or serious bodily injury; or

(ii) the officer has probable cause to believe the suspect poses a threat of death or serious bodily injury to the officer or to others if apprehension is delayed; or

(c) the officer reasonably believes that the use of deadly force is necessary to prevent death or serious bodily injury to the officer or another person.

(2) If feasible, a verbal warning should be given by the officer prior to any use of deadly force under Subsection (1)(b) or (1)(c). 2004

76-2-405. Force in defense of habitation.

(1) A person is justified in using force against another when and to the extent that he reasonably believes that the force is necessary to prevent or terminate the other's unlawful entry into or attack upon his habitation; however, he is justified in the use of force which is intended or likely to cause death or serious bodily injury only if:

(a) the entry is made or attempted in a violent and tumultuous manner, surreptitiously, or by stealth, and he reasonably believes that the entry is attempted or made for the purpose of assaulting or offering personal violence to any person, dwelling, or being in the habitation and he reasonably believes that the force is necessary to prevent the assault or offer of personal violence; or

(b) he reasonably believes that the entry is made or attempted for the purpose of committing a felony in the habitation and that the force is necessary to prevent the commission of the felony.

(2) The person using force or deadly force in defense of habitation is presumed for the purpose of both civil and criminal cases to have acted reasonably and had a reasonable fear of imminent peril of death or serious bodily injury if the entry or attempted entry is unlawful and is made or attempted by use of force, or in a violent and tumultuous manner, or surreptitiously or by stealth, or for the purpose of committing a felony. 1985

76-2-406. Force in defense of property.

A person is justified in using force, other than deadly force, against another when and to the extent that he reasonably believes that force is necessary to prevent or terminate criminal interference with real property or personal property:

(1) lawfully in his possession; or

(2) lawfully in the possession of a member of his immediate family; or

(3) belonging to a person whose property he has a legal duty to protect. 1973

76-2-407. Deadly force in defense of persons on real property.

(1) A person is justified in using force intended or likely to cause death or serious bodily injury against another in his defense of persons on real property other than his habitation if:

(a) he is in lawful possession of the real property;

(b) he reasonably believes that the force is necessary to prevent or terminate the other person's trespass onto the real property;

(c) the trespass is made or attempted by use of force or in a violent and tumultuous manner; and

(d) (i) the person reasonably believes that the trespass is attempted or made for the purpose of committing violence against any person on the real property and he reasonably believes that the force is necessary to prevent personal violence; or

(ii) the person reasonably believes that the trespass is made or attempted for the purpose of committing a forcible felony as defined in Section 76-2-402 that poses imminent peril of death or serious bodily injury to a person on the real property and that the force is necessary to prevent the commission of that forcible felony.

(2) The person using deadly force in defense of persons on real property under Subsection (1) is presumed for the purpose of both civil and criminal cases to have acted reasonably and had a reasonable fear of imminent peril of death or serious bodily injury if the trespass or attempted trespass is unlawful and is made or attempted by use of force, or in a violent and tumultuous manner, or for the purpose of committing a forcible felony. 2002

CHAPTER 3

PUNISHMENTS

Part 1

Classification of Offenses

PART 1

CLASSIFICATION OF OFFENSES

76-3-101. Sentencing in accordance with chapter.

(1) A person adjudged guilty of an offense under this code shall be sentenced in accordance with the provisions of this chapter.

(2) Penal laws enacted after the effective date of this code shall be classified for sentencing purposes in accordance with this chapter. 1973

76-3-102. Designation of offenses.

Offenses are designated as felonies, misdemeanors, or infractions. 1973

76-3-103. Felonies classified.

(1) Felonies are classified into four categories:

(a) Capital felonies;

(b) Felonies of the first degree;

(c) Felonies of the second degree;

(d) Felonies of the third degree.

(2) An offense designated as a felony either in this code or in another law, without specification as to punishment or category, is a felony of the third degree. 1973

76-3-104. Misdemeanors classified.

(1) Misdemeanors are classified into three categories:

(a) Class A misdemeanors;

(b) Class B misdemeanors;

(c) Class C misdemeanors.

(2) An offense designated a misdemeanor, either in this code or in another law, without specification as to punishment or category, is a class B misdemeanor. 1973

76-3-105. Infractions.

(1) Infractions are not classified.

(2) Any offense which is an infraction within this code is expressly designated and any offense defined outside this code which is not designated as a felony or misdemeanor and for which no penalty is specified is an infraction. 1973

PART 2

SENTENCING

76-3-201. Definitions — Sentences or combination of sentences allowed — Civil penalties — Hearing.

(1) As used in this section:

(a) "Conviction" includes a:

(i) judgment of guilt; and

(ii) plea of guilty.

(b) "Criminal activities" means any offense of which the defendant is convicted or any other criminal conduct for which the defendant admits responsibility to the sentencing court with or without an admission of committing the criminal conduct.

(c) "Pecuniary damages" means all special damages, but not general damages, which a person could recover against the defendant in a civil action arising out of the facts or events constituting the defendant's criminal activities and includes the money equivalent of property taken, destroyed, broken, or otherwise harmed, and losses including earnings and medical expenses.

(d) "Restitution" means full, partial, or nominal payment for pecuniary damages to a victim, and payment for expenses to a governmental entity for extradition or transportation and as further defined in Title 77, Chapter 38a, Crime Victims Restitution Act.

(e) (i) "Victim" means any person who the court determines has suffered pecuniary damages as a result of the defendant's criminal activities.

(ii) "Victim" does not include any coparticipant in the defendant's criminal activities.

(2) Within the limits prescribed by this chapter, a court may sentence a person convicted of an offense to any one of the following sentences or combination of them:

(a) to pay a fine;

(b) to removal or disqualification from public or private office;

(c) to probation unless otherwise specifically provided by law;

(d) to imprisonment;

(e) on or after April 27, 1992, to life in prison without parole; or

(f) to death.

(3) (a) This chapter does not deprive a court of authority conferred by law to:

(i) forfeit property;

(ii) dissolve a corporation;

(iii) suspend or cancel a license;

(iv) permit removal of a person from office;

(v) cite for contempt; or

(vi) impose any other civil penalty.

(b) A civil penalty may be included in a sentence.

(4) (a) When a person is convicted of criminal activity that has resulted in pecuniary damages, in addition to any other sentence it may impose, the court shall order that the defendant make restitution to the victims, or for conduct for which the defendant has agreed to make restitution as part of a plea agreement.

(b) In determining whether restitution is appropriate, the court shall follow the criteria and procedures as provided in Title 77, Chapter 38a, Crime Victims Restitution Act.

(5) (a) In addition to any other sentence the court may impose, the court shall order the defendant to pay restitution of governmental transportation expenses if the defendant was:

(i) transported pursuant to court order from one county to another within the state at governmental expense to resolve pending criminal charges;

(ii) charged with a felony or a class A, B, or C misdemeanor; and

(iii) convicted of a crime.

(b) The court may not order the defendant to pay restitution of governmental transportation expenses if any of the following apply:

(i) the defendant is charged with an infraction or on a subsequent failure to appear a warrant is issued for an infraction; or

(ii) the defendant was not transported pursuant to a court order.

(c) (i) Restitution of governmental transportation expenses under Subsection (5)(a)(i) shall be calculated according to the following schedule:

(A) $75 for up to 100 miles a defendant is transported;

(B) $125 for 100 up to 200 miles a defendant is transported; and

(C) $250 for 200 miles or more a defendant is transported.

(ii) The schedule of restitution under Subsection (5)(c)(i) applies to each defendant transported regardless of the number of defendants actually transported in a single trip.

(d) If a defendant has been extradited to this state under Title 77, Chapter 30, Extradition, to resolve pending criminal charges and is convicted of criminal activity in the county to which he has been returned, the court may, in addition to any other sentence it may impose, order that the defendant make restitution for costs expended by any governmental entity for the extradition.

(6) (a) In addition to any other sentence the court may impose, the court shall order the defendant to pay court-ordered restitution to the county for the cost of incarceration in the county correctional facility before and after sentencing if:

(i) the defendant is convicted of criminal activity that results in incarceration in the county correctional facility; and

(ii) (A) the defendant is not a state prisoner housed in a county correctional facility through a contract with the Department of Corrections; or

(B) the reimbursement does not duplicate the reimbursement provided under Section 64-13c-301 if the defendant is a state prisoner housed in a county correctional facility as a condition of probation under Subsection 77-18-1(8).

(b) (i) The costs of incarceration under Subsection (6)(a) are:

(A) the daily core inmate incarceration costs and medical and transportation costs established under Section 64-13c-302; and

(B) the costs of transportation services and medical care that exceed the negotiated reimbursement rate established under Subsection 64-13c-302(2).

(ii) The costs of incarceration under Subsection (6)(a) do not include expenses incurred by the county correctional facility in providing reasonable accommodation for an inmate qualifying as an individual with a disability as defined and covered by the federal Americans with Disabilities Act of 1990, 42 U.S.C. 12101 through 12213, including medical and mental health treatment for the inmate's disability.

(c) In determining the monetary sum and other conditions for the court-ordered restitution under this Subsection (6), the court shall consider the criteria provided under Subsections 77-38a-302(5)(c)(i) through (iv).

(d) If on appeal the defendant is found not guilty of the criminal activity under Subsection (6)(a)(i) and that finding is final as defined in Section 76-1-304, the county shall reimburse the defendant for restitution the defendant paid for costs of incarceration under Subsection (6)(a).

(7) (a) If a statute under which the defendant was convicted mandates that one of three stated minimum terms shall be imposed, the court shall order imposition of the term of middle severity unless there are circumstances in aggravation or mitigation of the crime.

(b) Prior to or at the time of sentencing, either party may submit a statement identifying circumstances in aggravation or mitigation or presenting additional facts. If the statement is in writing, it shall be filed with the court and served on the opposing party at least four days prior to the time set for sentencing.

(c) In determining whether there are circumstances that justify imposition of the highest or lowest term, the court may consider the record in the case, the probation officer's report, other reports, including reports received under Section 76-3-404, statements in aggravation or mitigation submitted by the prosecution or the defendant, and any further evidence introduced at the sentencing hearing.

(d) The court shall set forth on the record the facts supporting and reasons for imposing the upper or lower term.

(e) In determining a just sentence, the court shall consider sentencing guidelines regarding aggravating and mitigating circumstances promulgated by the Sentencing Commission.

(8) If during the commission of a crime described as child kidnapping, rape of a child, object rape of a child, sodomy upon a child, or sexual abuse of a child, the defendant causes substantial bodily injury to the child, and if the charge is set forth in the information or indictment and admitted by the defendant, or found true by a judge or jury at trial, the defendant shall be sentenced to the highest minimum term in state prison. This Subsection (8) takes precedence over any conflicting provision of law.   2003

76-3-201.1.   Collection of criminal judgment accounts receivable.

(1) As used in this section:

(a) "Criminal judgment accounts receivable" means any amount due the state arising from a criminal judgment for which payment has not been received by the state agency that is servicing the debt.

(b) "Accounts receivable" includes unpaid fees, overpayments, fines, forfeitures, surcharges, costs, interest, penalties, restitution to victims, third party claims, claims, reimbursement of a reward, and damages.

(2) (a) A criminal judgment account receivable ordered by the court as a result of prosecution for a criminal offense may be collected by any means authorized by law for the collection of a civil judgment.

(b) (i) The court may permit a defendant to pay a criminal judgment account receivable in installments.

(ii) In the district court, if the criminal judgment account receivable is paid in installments, the total amount due shall include all fines, surcharges, postjudgment interest, and fees.

(c) Upon default in the payment of a criminal judgment account receivable or upon default in the payment of any installment of that receivable, the criminal judgment account receivable may be collected as provided in this section or Subsection 77-18-1(9) or (10), and by any means authorized by law for the collection of a civil judgment.

(3) When a defendant defaults in the payment of a criminal judgment account receivable or any installment of that receivable, the court, on motion of the prosecution, victim, or upon its own motion may:

(a) order the defendant to appear and show cause why the default should not be treated as contempt of court; or

(b) issue a warrant of arrest.

(4) (a) Unless the defendant shows that the default was not attributable to an intentional refusal to obey the order of the court or to a failure to make a good faith effort to make the payment, the court may find that the default constitutes contempt.

(b) Upon a finding of contempt, the court may order the defendant committed until the criminal judgment account receivable, or a specified part of it, is paid.

(5) If it appears to the satisfaction of the court that the default is not contempt, the court may enter an order for any of the following or any combination of the following:

(a) require the defendant to pay the criminal judgment account receivable or a specified part of it by a date certain;

(b) restructure the payment schedule;

(c) restructure the installment amount;

(d) except as provided in Section 77-18-8, execute the original sentence of imprisonment;

(e) start the period of probation anew;

(f) except as limited by Subsection (6), convert the criminal judgment account receivable or any part of it to community service;

(g) except as limited by Subsection (6), reduce or revoke the unpaid amount of the criminal judgment account receivable; or

(h) in the district court, record the unpaid balance of the criminal judgment account receivable as a civil judgment and transfer the responsibility for collecting the judgment to the Office of State Debt Collection.

(6) In issuing an order under this section, the court may not modify the amount of the judgment of complete restitution.

(7) Whether or not a default constitutes contempt, the court may add to the amount owed the fees established under Subsection 63A-8-201(4)(g) and postjudgment interest.

(8) (a) (i) If a criminal judgment account receivable is past due in a case supervised by the Department of Corrections, the judge shall determine whether or not to record the unpaid balance of the account receivable as a civil judgment.

(ii) If the judge records the unpaid balance of the account receivable as a civil judgment, the judge shall transfer the responsibility for collecting the judgment to the Office of State Debt Collection.

(b) If a criminal judgment account receivable in a case not supervised by the Department of Corrections is past due, the district court may, without a motion or hearing, record the unpaid balance of the criminal judgment account receivable as a civil judgment and transfer the responsibility for collecting the account receivable to the Office of State Debt Collection.

(c) If a criminal judgment account receivable in a case not supervised by the Department of Corrections is more than 90 days past due, the district court shall, without a motion or hearing, record the unpaid balance of the criminal judgment account receivable as a civil judgment and transfer the responsibility for collecting the criminal judgment account receivable to the Office of State Debt Collection.

(9) (a) When a fine, forfeiture, surcharge, cost permitted by statute, fee, or an order of restitution is imposed on a corporation or unincorporated association, the person authorized to make disbursement from the assets of the corporation or association shall pay the obligation from those assets.

(b) Failure to pay the obligation may be held to be contempt under Subsection (3).

(10) The prosecuting attorney may collect restitution in behalf of a victim.   2003

76-3-201.2, 76-3-201.3.   Repealed.   1996, 2002

76-3-202. Paroled persons — Termination or discharge from sentence — Time served on parole — Discretion of Board of Pardons and Parole.

(1) Except as otherwise provided in this section, every person committed to the state prison to serve an indeterminate term and later released on parole shall, upon completion of three years on parole outside of confinement and without violation, be terminated from his sentence unless the person is earlier terminated by the Board of Pardons and Parole. Any person who violates the terms of his parole, while serving parole, shall at the discretion of the Board of Pardons and Parole be recommitted to prison to serve the portion of the balance of his term as determined by the Board of Pardons and Parole, but not to exceed the maximum term.

(2) Every person convicted of a second degree felony for violating Section 76-5-404 or 76-5-404.1, or attempting to violate any of those sections, upon completion of ten years parole outside of confinement and without violation, shall be terminated from his sentence unless the person is earlier terminated by the Board of Pardons and Parole. Any person who violates the terms of his parole, while serving parole, shall at the discretion of the Board of Pardons and Parole be recommitted to prison to serve the portion of the balance of his term as determined by the Board of Pardons and Parole, but not to exceed the maximum term.

(3) Every person convicted of a first degree felony for violating Section 76-5-301.1, Subsection 76-5-302(1)(b)(vi), Section 76-5-402, 76-5-402.1, 76-5-402.2, 76-5-402.3, 76-5-403, 76-5-403.1, 76-5-404.1, or 76-5-405, or attempting to violate any of those sections, shall complete a term of lifetime parole outside of confinement and without violation unless the person is earlier terminated by the Board of Pardons and Parole. Any person who violates the terms of his parole, while serving parole, shall at the discretion of the Board of Pardons and Parole be recommitted to prison to serve the portion of the balance of his term as determined by the Board of Pardons and Parole, but not to exceed the maximum term.

(4) In order for a parolee convicted on or after May 5, 1997, to be eligible for early termination from parole, the parolee must provide:

(a) evidence to the Board of Pardons and Parole that the parolee has completed high school classwork and has obtained a high school graduation diploma, a GED certificate, or a vocational certificate; or

(b) documentation of the inability to obtain one of the items listed in Subsection (4)(a) because of:

(i) a diagnosed learning disability; or

(ii) other justified cause.

(5) Any person paroled following a former parole revocation may not be discharged from his sentence until either:

(a) he has served three years or ten years as provided in Subsection (2) on parole outside of confinement and without violation, or in the case of a person convicted of a first degree felony violation of Section 76-5-301.1, Subsection 76-5-302(1)(b)(vi), Section 76-5-402, 76-5-402.1, 76-5-402.3, 76-5-403, 76-5-403.1, 76-5-404.1, or 76-5-405, or attempting to violate any of those sections, lifetime parole outside of confinement and without violation;

(b) his maximum sentence has expired; or

(c) the Board of Pardons and Parole so orders.

(6) (a) All time served on parole, outside of confinement and without violation constitutes service of the total sentence but does not preclude the requirement of serving a three-year, ten-year, or lifetime parole term, as the case may be, outside of confinement and without violation.

(b) Any time a person spends outside of confinement after commission of a parole violation does not constitute service of the total sentence unless the person is exonerated at a hearing to revoke the parole.

(c) Any time spent in confinement awaiting a hearing before the Board of Pardons and Parole or a decision by the board concerning revocation of parole constitutes service of the sentence. In the case of exoneration by the board, the time spent shall be included in computing the total parole term.

(7) When any parolee without authority from the Board of Pardons and Parole absents himself from the state or avoids or evades parole supervision, the period of absence, avoidance, or evasion tolls the parole period.

(8) While on parole, time spent in confinement outside the state may not be credited toward the service of any Utah sentence. Time in confinement outside the state for a conviction obtained in another jurisdiction shall toll the expiration of the Utah sentence.

(9) This section does not preclude the Board of Pardons and Parole from paroling or discharging an inmate at any time within the discretion of the Board of Pardons and Parole unless otherwise specifically provided by law.

(10) The parolee may petition the Board of Pardons and Parole for termination of lifetime parole as provided by this section in the case of a person convicted of a first degree felony violation Section 76-5-301.1, Subsection 76-5-302(1)(b)(vi), Section 76-5-402, 76-5-402.1, 76-5-402.2, 76-5-402.3, 76-5-403, 76-5-403.1, 76-5-404.1, or 76-5-405, or attempting to violate any of those sections.   2001

76-3-203. Felony conviction — Indeterminate term of imprisonment.

A person who has been convicted of a felony may be sentenced to imprisonment for an indeterminate term as follows:

(1) In the case of a felony of the first degree, unless the statute provides otherwise, for a term of not less than five years and which may be for life.

(2) In the case of a felony of the second degree, unless the statute provides otherwise, for a term of not less than one year nor more than 15 years.

(3) In the case of a felony of the third degree, unless the statute provides otherwise, for a term not to exceed five years.   2003

76-3-203.1. Offenses committed in concert with two or more persons — Notice — Enhanced penalties.

(1) (a) A person who commits any offense listed in Subsection (4) is subject to an enhanced penalty for the offense as provided in Subsection (3) if the trier of fact finds beyond a reasonable doubt that the person acted in concert with two or more persons.

(b) "In concert with two or more persons" as used in this section means the defendant was aided or encouraged by at least two other persons in committing the offense and was aware that he was so aided or encouraged, and each of the other persons:

(i) was physically present; or

(ii) participated as a party to any offense listed in Subsection (4).

(c) For purposes of Subsection (1)(b)(ii):

(i) other persons participating as parties need not have the intent to engage in the same offense or degree of offense as the defendant; and

(ii) a minor is a party if the minor's actions would cause him to be a party if he were an adult.

(2) The prosecuting attorney, or grand jury if an indictment is returned, shall cause to be subscribed upon the information or indictment notice that the defendant is subject to the enhanced penalties provided under this section.

(3) The enhanced penalty for a:

(a) class B misdemeanor is a class A misdemeanor;

(b) class A misdemeanor is a third degree felony;

(c) third degree felony is a second degree felony;

(d) second degree felony is a first degree felony; and

(e) first degree felony is an indeterminate prison term of not less than nine years and which may be for life.

(4) Offenses referred to in Subsection (1) are:

(a) any criminal violation of Title 58, Chapter 37, 37a, 37b, or 37c, regarding drug-related offenses;

(b) assault and related offenses under Title 76, Chapter 5, Part 1;

(c) any criminal homicide offense under Title 76, Chapter 5, Part 2;

(d) kidnapping and related offenses under Title 76, Chapter 5, Part 3;

(e) any felony sexual offense under Title 76, Chapter 5, Part 4;

(f) sexual exploitation of a minor as defined in Section 76-5a-3;

(g) any property destruction offense under Title 76, Chapter 6, Part 1;

(h) burglary, criminal trespass, and related offenses under Title 76, Chapter 6, Part 2;

(i) robbery and aggravated robbery under Title 76, Chapter 6, Part 3;

(j) theft and related offenses under Title 76, Chapter 6, Part 4;

(k) any fraud offense under Title 76, Chapter 6, Part 5, except Sections 76-6-504, 76-6-505, 76-6-507, 76-6-508, 76-6-509, 76-6-510, 76-6-511, 76-6-512, 76-6-513, 76-6-514, 76-6-516, 76-6-517, 76-6-518, and 76-6-520;

(l) any offense of obstructing government operations under Title 76, Chapter 8, Part 3, except Sections 76-8-302, 76-8-303, 76-8-304, 76-8-307, 76-8-308, and 76-8-312;

(m) tampering with a witness or other violation of Section 76-8-508;

(n) extortion or bribery to dismiss criminal proceeding as defined in Section 76-8-509;

(o) any explosives offense under Title 76, Chapter 10, Part 3;

(p) any weapons offense under Title 76, Chapter 10, Part 5;

(q) pornographic and harmful materials and performances offenses under Title 76, Chapter 10, Part 12;

(r) prostitution and related offenses under Title 76, Chapter 10, Part 13;

(s) any violation of Title 76, Chapter 10, Part 15, Bus Passenger Safety Act;

(t) any violation of Title 76, Chapter 10, Part 16, Pattern of Unlawful Activity Act;

(u) communications fraud as defined in Section 76-10-1801;

(v) any violation of Title 76, Chapter 10, Part 19, Money Laundering and Currency Transaction Reporting Act; and

(w) burglary of a research facility as defined in Section 76-10-2002.

(5) It is not a bar to imposing the enhanced penalties under this section that the persons with whom the actor is alleged to have acted in concert are not identified, apprehended, charged, or convicted, or that any of those persons are charged with or convicted of a different or lesser offense.   2005

76-3-203.2. Definitions — Use of dangerous weapon in offenses committed on or about school premises — Enhanced penalties.

(1) (a) As used in this section and Section 76-10-505.5, "on or about school premises" means any of the following:

(i) in a public or private elementary, secondary, or on the grounds of any of those schools;

(ii) in a public or private vocational school or postsecondary institution or on the grounds of any of those schools or institutions;

(iii) in those portions of any building, park, stadium, or other structure or grounds which are, at the time of the act, being used for an activity sponsored by or through a school or institution under Subsections (1)(a)(i) and (ii);

(iv) in or on the grounds of a preschool or child-care facility; and

(v) within 1,000 feet of any structure, facility, or grounds included in Subsections (1)(a)(i), (ii), (iii), and (iv).

(b) As used in this section:

(i) "Dangerous weapon" has the same definition as in Section 76-1-601.

(ii) "Educator" means any person who is employed by a public school district and who is required to hold a certificate issued by the State Board of Education in order to perform duties of employment.

(iii) "Within the course of employment" means that an educator is providing services or engaging in conduct required by the educator's employer to perform the duties of employment.

(2) Any person who, on or about school premises, commits any offense and uses or threatens to use a dangerous weapon, as defined in Section 76-1-601, in the commission of the offense is subject to an enhanced degree of offense as provided in Subsection (4).

(3) (a) Any person who commits an offense against an educator when the educator is acting within the course of employment is subject to an enhanced degree of offense as provided in Subsection (4).

(b) As used in Subsection (3)(a), "offense" means:

(i) an offense under Title 76, Chapter 5, Offenses Against The Person; and

(ii) an offense under Title 76, Chapter 6, Part 3, Robbery.

(4) If the trier of fact finds beyond a reasonable doubt that the defendant, while on or about school premises, commits any offense and in the commission of the offense uses or threatens to use a dangerous weapon, or that the defendant committed an offense against an educator when the educator was acting within the course of his employment, the enhanced penalty for a:

(a) class B misdemeanor is a class A misdemeanor;

(b) class A misdemeanor is a third degree felony;

(c) third degree felony is a second degree felony; or

(d) second degree felony is a first degree felony.

(5) The enhanced penalty for a first degree felony offense of a convicted person:

(a) is imprisonment for a term of not less than five years and which may be for life, and imposition or execution of the sentence may not be suspended unless the court finds that the interests of justice would be best served and states the specific circumstances justifying the disposition on the record; and

(b) is subject also to the dangerous weapon enhancement provided in Section 76-3-203.8 except for an offense committed under Subsection (3) that does not involve a firearm.

(6) The prosecuting attorney, or grand jury if an indictment is returned, shall provide notice upon the information or indictment that the defendant is subject to the enhanced degree of offense or penalty under Subsection (4) or (5).

(7) In cases where an offense is enhanced pursuant to Subsection (4)(a), (b), (c), or (d), or under Subsection (5)(a) for an offense committed under Subsection (2) that does not involve a firearm, the convicted person is not subject to the dangerous weapon enhancement in Section 76-3-203.8.   2003

76-3-203.3. Penalty for hate crimes — Civil rights violation.

As used in this section:

(1) "Primary offense" means those offenses provided in Subsection (5).

(2) A person who commits any primary offense with the intent to intimidate or terrorize another person or with reason to believe that his action would intimidate or terrorize that person is guilty of a third degree felony.

(3) "Intimidate or terrorize" means an act which causes the person to fear for his physical safety or damages the property of that person or another. The act must be accompanied with the intent to cause a person to fear to freely exercise or enjoy any right secured by the Constitution or laws of the state or by the Constitution or laws of the United States.

(4) (a) The prosecuting attorney, or grand jury if an indictment is returned, shall provide notice on the complaint in misdemeanor cases that the defendant is subject to a third degree felony provided under this section. The notice shall be in a clause separate from and in addition to the substantive offense charged.

(b) If the notice is not included initially, the court may subsequently allow the prosecutor to amend the charging document to include the notice if the court finds:

(i) that the amended charging documents, including any statement of probable cause, provide notice that the defendant is subject to a third degree felony provided under this section; and

(ii) that the defendant has not otherwise been substantially prejudiced by the amendment.

(5) Primary offenses referred to in Subsection (2) are the misdemeanor offenses for:

(a) assault and related offenses under Sections 76-5-102, 76-5-102.4, 76-5-106, 76-5-107, and 76-5-108;

(b) any misdemeanor property destruction offense under Sections 76-6-102, 76-6-104, and 76-8-714, and Subsection 76-6-106(2)(b);

(c) any criminal trespass offense under Sections 76-6-204 and 76-6-206;

(d) any misdemeanor theft offense under Section 76-6-412;

(e) any offense of obstructing government operations under Sections 76-8-301, 76-8-302, 76-8-304, 76-8-305, 76-8-306, 76-8-307, 76-8-308, and 76-8-313;

(f) any offense of interfering or intending to interfere with activities of colleges and universities under Title 76, Chapter 8, Part 7;

(g) any misdemeanor offense against public order and decency as defined in Title 76, Chapter 9, Part 1;

(h) any telephone abuse offense under Title 76, Chapter 9, Part 2;

(i) any cruelty to animals offense under Section 76-9-301; and

(j) any weapons offense under Section 76-10-506.   2004

76-3-203.5. Habitual violent offender — Definition — Procedure — Penalty.

(1) As used in this section:

(a) "Felony" means any violation of a criminal statute of the state, any other state, the United States, or any district, possession, or territory of the United States for which the maximum punishment the offender may be subjected to exceeds one year in prison.

(b) "Habitual violent offender" means a person convicted within the state of any violent felony and who on at least two previous occasions has been convicted of a violent felony and committed to either prison in Utah or an equivalent correctional institution of another state or of the United States either at initial sentencing or after revocation of probation.

(c) (i) "Violent felony" means any of the following offenses, or any attempt, solicitation, or conspiracy to commit any of these offenses punishable as a felony:

(A) aggravated arson, arson, knowingly causing a catastrophe, and criminal mischief, Title 76, Chapter 6, Part 1, Property Destruction;

(B) assault by prisoner, Section 76-5-102.5;

(C) disarming a police officer, Section 76-5-102.8;

(D) aggravated assault, Section 76-5-103;

(E) aggravated assault by prisoner, Section 76-5-103.5;

(F) mayhem, Section 76-5-105;

(G) stalking, Subsection 76-5-106.5(6);

(H) terroristic threat, Section 76-5-107;

(I) child abuse, Subsections 76-5-109(2)(a) and (b);

(J) commission of domestic violence in the presence of a child, Section 76-5-109.1;

(K) abuse or neglect of disabled child, Section 76-5-110;

(L) abuse, neglect, or exploitation of a vulnerable adult, Section 76-5-111;

(M) endangerment of child or elder adult, Section 76-5-112.5;

(N) criminal homicide offenses under Title 76, Chapter 5, Part 2, Criminal Homicide;

(O) kidnapping, child kidnapping, and aggravated kidnapping under Title 76, Chapter 5, Part 3, Kidnapping;

(P) rape, Section 76-5-402;

(Q) rape of a child, Section 76-5-402.1;

(R) object rape, Section 76-5-402.2;

(S) object rape of a child, Section 76-5-402.3;

(T) forcible sodomy, Section 76-5-403;

(U) sodomy on a child, Section 76-5-403.1;

(V) forcible sexual abuse, Section 76-5-404;

(W) aggravated sexual abuse of a child and sexual abuse of a child, Section 76-5-404.1;

(X) aggravated sexual assault, Section 76-5-405;

(Y) sexual exploitation of a minor, Section 76-5a-3;

(Z) aggravated burglary and burglary of a dwelling under Title 76, Chapter 6, Part 2, Burglary and Criminal Trespass;

(AA) aggravated robbery and robbery under Title 76, Chapter 6, Part 3, Robbery;

(BB) theft by extortion under Subsection 76-6-406(2)(a) or (b);

(CC) tampering with a witness under Subsection 76-8-508(1);

(DD) retaliation against a witness, victim, or informant under Section 76-8-508.3;

(EE) tampering with a juror under Subsection 76-8-508.5(2)(c);

(FF) extortion to dismiss a criminal proceeding under Section 76-8-509 if by any threat or by use of force theft by extortion has been committed pursuant to Subsections 76-6-406(2)(a), (b), and (i);

(GG) damage or destruction of school or institution of higher education property by explosives or flammable materials under Section 76-8-715;

(HH) possession, use, or removal of explosive, chemical, or incendiary devices under Subsections 76-10-306(3) through (6);

(II) unlawful delivery of explosive, chemical, or incendiary devices under Section 76-10-307;

(JJ) purchase or possession of a dangerous weapon or handgun by a restricted person under Section 76-10-503;

(KK) unlawful discharge of a firearm under Section 76-10-508;

(LL) aggravated exploitation of prostitution under Subsection 76-10-1306(1)(a);

(MM) bus hijacking under Section 76-10-1504; and

(NN) discharging firearms and hurling missiles under Section 76-10-1505; or

(ii) any felony violation of a criminal statute of any other state, the United States, or any district, possession, or territory of the United States which would constitute a violent felony as defined in this Subsection (1) if committed in this state.

(2) If a person is convicted in this state of a violent felony by plea or by verdict and the trier of fact determines beyond a reasonable doubt that the person is a habitual violent offender under this section, the penalty for a:

(a) third degree felony is as if the conviction were for a first degree felony;

(b) second degree felony is as if the conviction were for a first degree felony; or

(c) first degree felony remains the penalty for a first degree penalty except:

(i) the convicted person is not eligible for probation; and

(ii) the Board of Pardons and Parole shall consider that the convicted person is a habitual violent offender as an aggravating factor in determining the length of incarceration.

(3) (a) The prosecuting attorney, or grand jury if an indictment is returned, shall provide notice in the information or indictment that the defendant is subject to punishment as a habitual violent offender under this section. Notice shall include the case number, court, and date of conviction or commitment of any case relied upon by the prosecution.

(b) (i) The defendant shall serve notice in writing upon the prosecutor if the defendant intends to deny that:

(A) the defendant is the person who was convicted or committed;

(B) the defendant was represented by counsel or had waived counsel; or

(C) the defendant's plea was understandingly or voluntarily entered.

(ii) The notice of denial shall be served not later than five days prior to trial and shall state in detail the defendant's contention regarding the previous conviction and commitment.

(4) (a) If the defendant enters a denial under Subsection (3)(b) and if the case is tried to a jury, the jury may not be told until after it returns its verdict on the underlying felony charge, of the:

(i) defendant's previous convictions for violent felonies, except as otherwise provided in the Utah Rules of Evidence; or

(ii) allegation against the defendant of being a habitual violent offender.

(b) If the jury's verdict is guilty, the defendant shall be tried regarding the allegation of being an habitual violent offender by the same jury, if practicable, unless the defendant waives the jury, in which case the allegation shall be tried immediately to the court.

(c) (i) Prior to or at the time of sentencing the trier of fact shall determine if this section applies.

(ii) The trier of fact shall consider any evidence presented at trial and the prosecution and the defendant shall be afforded an opportunity to present any necessary additional evidence.

(iii) Prior to sentencing under this section, the trier of fact shall determine whether this section is applicable beyond a reasonable doubt.

(d) If any previous conviction and commitment is based upon a plea of guilty or no contest, there is a rebuttable presumption that the conviction and commitment were regular and lawful in all respects if the conviction and commitment occurred after January 1, 1970. If the conviction and commitment occurred prior to January 1, 1970, the burden is on the prosecution to establish by a preponderance of the evidence that the defendant was then represented by counsel or had lawfully waived his right to have counsel present, and that his plea was understandingly and voluntarily entered.

(e) If the trier of fact finds this section applicable, the court shall enter that specific finding on the record and shall indicate in the order of judgment and commitment that the defendant has been found by the trier of fact to be a habitual violent offender and is sentenced under this section.

(5) (a) The sentencing enhancement provisions of Sections 76-3-407 and 76-3-408 apply to a felony conviction defined in Title 76, Chapter 5, Part 4, Sexual Offenses, and supersede the provisions of this section.

(b) Notwithstanding Subsection (5)(a):

(i) the convictions under Sections 76-5-404 and 76-5a-3 are governed by the enhancement provisions of this section; and

(ii) the "violent felony" offense defined in Subsection (1)(c) shall include any felony sexual offense violation of Title 76, Chapter 5, Part 4, Sexual Offenses, to determine if the convicted person is a habitual violent offender.   2005

76-3-203.6. Enhanced penalty for certain offenses committed by prisoner.

(1) As used in this section, "serving a sentence" means a prisoner is sentenced and committed to the custody of the Department of Corrections, the sentence has not been terminated or voided, and the prisoner:

(a) has not been paroled; or

(b) is in custody after arrest for a parole violation.

(2) If the trier of fact finds beyond a reasonable doubt that a prisoner serving a sentence for a capital felony or a first degree felony commits any offense listed in Subsection (3), the court shall sentence the defendant to life in prison without parole. However, the court may sentence the defendant to an indeterminate prison term of not less than 20 years and which may be for life if the court finds that the interests of justice would best be served and states the specific circumstances justifying the disposition on the record.

(3) Offenses referred to in Subsection (2) are:

(a) aggravated assault, Subsection 76-5-103(2);

(b) mayhem, Section 76-5-105;

(c) attempted murder, Section 76-5-203;

(d) kidnapping, Section 76-5-301;

(e) child kidnapping, Section 76-5-301.1;

(f) aggravated kidnapping, Section 76-5-302;

(g) rape, Section 76-5-402;

(h) rape of a child, Section 76-5-402.1;

(i) object rape, Section 76-5-402.2;

(j) object rape of a child, Section 76-5-402.3;

(k) forcible sodomy, Section 76-5-403;

(l) sodomy on a child, Section 76-5-403.1;

(m) aggravated sexual abuse of a child, Section 76-5-404.1;

(n) aggravated sexual assault, Section 76-5-405;

(o) aggravated arson, Section 76-6-103;

(p) aggravated burglary, Section 76-6-203; and

(q) aggravated robbery, Section 76-6-302.   2001

76-3-203.7. Increase of sentence for violent felony if body armor used.

(1) As used in this section:

(a) "Body armor" means any material designed or intended to provide bullet penetration resistance or protection from bodily injury caused by a dangerous weapon.

(b) "Dangerous weapon" has the same definition as in Section 76-1-601.

(c) "Violent felony" has the same definition as in Section 76-3-203.5.

(2) A person convicted of a violent felony may be sentenced to imprisonment for an indeterminate term, as provided in Section 76-3-203, but if the trier of fact finds beyond a reasonable doubt that the defendant used, carried, or possessed a dangerous weapon and also used or wore body armor, with the intent to facilitate the commission of the violent felony, and the violent felony is:

(a) a first degree felony, the court shall sentence the person convicted for a term of not less than six years, and which may be for life;

(b) a second degree felony, the court shall sentence the person convicted for a term of not less than two years nor more than 15 years, and the court may sentence the person convicted for a term of not less than two years nor more than 20 years; and

(c) a third degree felony, the court shall sentence the person convicted for a term of not less than one year nor more than five years, and the court may sentence the person convicted for a term of not less than one year nor more than ten years.   2001

76-3-203.8. Increase of sentence if dangerous weapon used.

(1) As used in this section, "dangerous weapon" has the same definition as in Section 76-1-601.

(2) If the trier of fact finds beyond a reasonable doubt that a dangerous weapon was used in the commission or furtherance of a felony, the court:

(a) (i) shall increase by one year the minimum term of the sentence applicable by law; and

(ii) if the minimum term applicable by law is zero, shall set the minimum term as one year; and

(b) may increase by five years the maximum sentence applicable by law in the case of a felony of the second or third degree.

(3) A defendant who is a party to a felony offense shall be sentenced to the increases in punishment provided in Subsection (2) if the trier of fact finds beyond a reasonable doubt that:

(a) a dangerous weapon was used in the commission or furtherance of the felony; and

(b) the defendant knew that the dangerous weapon was present.

(4) If the trier of fact finds beyond a reasonable doubt that a person has been sentenced to a term of imprisonment for a felony in which a dangerous weapon was used in the commission of or furtherance of the felony and that person is subsequently convicted of another felony in which a dangerous weapon was used in the commission of or furtherance of the felony, the court shall, in addition to any other sentence imposed including those in Subsection (2), impose an indeterminate prison term to be not less than five nor more than ten years to run consecutively and not concurrently. 2004

76-3-204. Misdemeanor conviction — Term of imprisonment.

A person who has been convicted of a misdemeanor may be sentenced to imprisonment as follows:

(1) In the case of a class A misdemeanor, for a term not exceeding one year;

(2) In the case of a class B misdemeanor, for a term not exceeding six months;

(3) In the case of a class C misdemeanor, for a term not exceeding ninety days. 1973

76-3-205. Infraction conviction — Fine, forfeiture, and disqualification.

(1) A person convicted of an infraction may not be imprisoned but may be subject to a fine, forfeiture, and disqualification, or any combination.

(2) Whenever a person is convicted of an infraction and no punishment is specified, the person may be fined as for a class C misdemeanor. 1973

76-3-206. Capital felony — Penalties.

(1) A person who has pled guilty to or been convicted of a capital felony shall be sentenced in accordance with Section 76-3-207. That sentence shall be death, an indeterminate prison term of not less than 20 years and which may be for life, or, on or after April 27, 1992, life in prison without parole.

(2) (a) The judgment of conviction and sentence of death is subject to automatic review by the Utah State Supreme Court within 60 days after certification by the sentencing court of the entire record unless time is extended an additional period not to exceed 30 days by the Utah State Supreme Court for good cause shown.

(b) The review by the Utah State Supreme Court has priority over all other cases and shall be heard in accordance with rules promulgated by the Utah State Supreme Court. 2001

76-3-207. Capital felony — Sentencing proceeding.

(1) (a) When a defendant has pled guilty to or been found guilty of a capital felony, there shall be further proceedings before the court or jury on the issue of sentence.

(b) In the case of a plea of guilty to a capital felony, the sentencing proceedings shall be conducted before a jury or, upon request of the defendant and with the approval of the court and the consent of the prosecution, by the court which accepted the plea.

(c) (i) When a defendant has been found guilty of a capital felony, the proceedings shall be conducted before the court or jury which found the defendant guilty, provided the defendant may waive hearing before the jury with the approval of the court and the con-

sent of the prosecution, in which event the hearing shall be before the court.

(ii) If circumstances make it impossible or impractical to reconvene the same jury for the sentencing proceedings, the court may dismiss that jury and convene a new jury for the proceedings.

(d) If a retrial of the sentencing proceedings is necessary as a consequence of a remand from an appellate court, the sentencing authority shall be determined as provided in Subsection (6).

(2) (a) In capital sentencing proceedings, evidence may be presented on:

(i) the nature and circumstances of the crime;

(ii) the defendant's character, background, history, and mental and physical condition;

(iii) the victim and the impact of the crime on the victim's family and community without comparison to other persons or victims; and

(iv) any other facts in aggravation or mitigation of the penalty that the court considers relevant to the sentence.

(b) Any evidence the court considers to have probative force may be received regardless of its admissibility under the exclusionary rules of evidence. The state's attorney and the defendant shall be permitted to present argument for or against the sentence of death.

(3) Aggravating circumstances include those outlined in Section 76-5-202.

(4) Mitigating circumstances include:

(a) the defendant has no significant history of prior criminal activity;

(b) the homicide was committed while the defendant was under the influence of mental or emotional disturbance;

(c) the defendant acted under duress or under the domination of another person;

(d) at the time of the homicide, the capacity of the defendant to appreciate the wrongfulness of his conduct or to conform his conduct to the requirement of law was impaired as a result of a mental condition, intoxication, or influence of drugs, except that "mental condition" under this Subsection (4)(d) does not mean an abnormality manifested primarily by repeated criminal conduct;

(e) the youth of the defendant at the time of the crime;

(f) the defendant was an accomplice in the homicide committed by another person and the defendant's participation was relatively minor; and

(g) any other fact in mitigation of the penalty.

(5) (a) The court or jury, as the case may be, shall retire to consider the penalty. Except as provided in Subsection 76-3-207.5(2), in all proceedings before a jury, under this section, it shall be instructed as to the punishment to be imposed upon a unanimous decision for death and that the penalty of either an indeterminate prison term of not less than 20 years and which may be for life or life in prison without parole, shall be imposed if a unanimous decision for death is not found.

(b) The death penalty shall only be imposed if, after considering the totality of the aggravating and mitigating circumstances, the jury is persuaded beyond a reasonable doubt that total aggravation outweighs total mitigation, and is further persuaded, beyond a reasonable doubt, that the imposition of the death penalty is justified and appropriate in the circumstances. If the jury reports unanimous agreement to impose the sentence of death, the court shall discharge the jury and shall impose the sentence of death.

(c) If the jury is unable to reach a unanimous decision imposing the sentence of death or the state is not seeking the death penalty, the jury shall then determine whether the penalty of life in prison without parole shall be imposed, except as provided in Subsection 76-3-207.5(2). The penalty of life in prison without parole shall only be imposed if the jury determines that the sentence of life in prison without parole is appropriate. If the jury reports agreement by ten jurors or more to impose the sentence of life in prison without parole, the court shall discharge the jury and shall impose the sentence of life in prison without parole. If ten jurors or more do not agree upon a sentence of life in prison without parole, the court shall discharge the jury and impose an indeterminate prison term of not less than 20 years and which may be for life.

(d) If the defendant waives hearing before the jury as to sentencing, with the approval of the court and the consent of the prosecution, the court shall determine the appropriate penalty according to the standards of Subsections (5)(b) and (c).

(e) If the defendant is sentenced to more than one term of life in prison with or without the possibility of parole, or in addition to a sentence of life in prison with or without the possibility of parole the defendant is sentenced for other offenses which result in terms of imprisonment, the judge shall determine whether the terms of imprisonment shall be imposed as concurrent or consecutive sentences in accordance with Section 76-3-401.

(6) Upon any appeal by the defendant where the sentence is of death, the appellate court, if it finds prejudicial error in the sentencing proceeding only, may set aside the sentence of death and remand the case to the trial court for new sentencing proceedings to the extent necessary to correct the error or errors. An error in the sentencing proceedings may not result in the reversal of the conviction of a capital felony. In cases of remand for new sentencing proceedings, all exhibits and a transcript of all testimony and other evidence properly admitted in the prior trial and sentencing proceedings are admissible in the new sentencing proceedings, and if the sentencing proceeding was before a:

(a) jury, a new jury shall be impaneled for the new sentencing proceeding unless the defendant waives the hearing before the jury with the approval of the court and the consent of the prosecution, in which case the proceeding shall be held according to Subsection (6)(b) or (c), as applicable;

(b) judge, the original trial judge shall conduct the new sentencing proceeding; or

(c) judge, and the original trial judge is unable or unavailable to conduct a new sentencing proceeding, then another judge shall be designated to conduct the new sentencing proceeding, and the new proceeding will be before a jury unless the defendant waives the hearing before the jury with the approval of the court and the consent of the prosecution.

(7) In the event the death penalty is held to be unconstitutional by the Utah Supreme Court or the United States Supreme Court, the court having jurisdiction over a person previously sentenced to death for a capital felony shall cause the person to be brought before the court, and the court shall sentence the person to:

(a) an indeterminate prison term of not less than 20 years and which may be for life, if the death penalty is held unconstitutional prior to April 27, 1992; or

(b) life in prison without parole if the death penalty is held unconstitutional on or after April 27, 1992, and any person who is thereafter convicted of a capital felony shall be sentenced to an indeterminate prison term of not less than 20 years and which may be for life or life in prison without parole.

(8) (a) If the appellate court's final decision regarding any appeal of a sentence of death precludes the imposition of the death penalty due to mental retardation or subaverage general intellectual functioning under Section 77-15a-101, the court having jurisdiction over a defendant previously sentenced to death for a capital felony shall cause the defendant to be brought before the sentencing court, and the court shall sentence the defendant to life in prison without parole.

(b) If the appellate court precludes the imposition of the death penalty under Subsection (8)(a), but the appellate court finds that sentencing the defendant to life in prison without parole is likely to result in a manifest injustice, it may remand the case to the sentencing court for further sentencing proceedings to determine if the defendant should serve a sentence of life in prison without parole or an indeterminate prison term of not less than 20 years and which may be for life.   2003

76-3-207.5. Applicability — Effect on sentencing — Options of offenders.

(1) (a) The sentencing option of life without parole provided in Sections 76-3-201 and 76-3-207 applies only to those capital felonies for which the offender is sentenced on or after April 27, 1992.

(b) The sentencing option of life without parole provided in Sections 76-3-201 and 76-3-207 has no effect on sentences imposed in capital cases prior to April 27, 1992.

(2) An offender, who commits a capital felony prior to April 27, 1992, but is sentenced on or after April 27, 1992, shall be given the option, prior to a sentencing hearing pursuant to Section 76-3-207, to proceed either under the law which was in effect at the time the offense was committed or under the additional sentencing option of life in prison without parole provided in Sections 76-3-201 and 76-3-207.   2001

76-3-208. Imprisonment — Custodial authorities.

(1) Persons sentenced to imprisonment shall be committed to the following custodial authorities:

(a) felony commitments shall be to the Utah State Prison;

(b) (i) class A misdemeanor commitments shall be to the jail, or other facility designated by the town, city, or county where the defendant was convicted, unless the defendant consents to commitment to the Utah State Prison for an indeterminate term not to exceed one year;

(ii) if the defendant consents to commitment to the Utah State Prison for an indeterminate term not to exceed one year, the court may impose the sentence. The court may not order the imprisonment of a defendant to the Utah State Prison for a fixed term or other term that is inconsistent with this section and Section 77-18-4;

(c) all other misdemeanor commitments shall be to the jail or other facility designated by the town, city or county where the defendant was convicted.

(2) Custodial authorities may place a prisoner in a facility other than the one to which he was committed when:

(a) it does not have space to accommodate him; or

(b) the security of the institution or inmate requires it. 1995

PART 3

FINES AND SPECIAL SANCTIONS

76-3-301. Fines of persons.

(1) A person convicted of an offense may be sentenced to pay a fine, not exceeding:

(a) $10,000 for a felony conviction of the first degree or second degree;

(b) $5,000 for a felony conviction of the third degree;

(c) $2,500 for a class A misdemeanor conviction;

(d) $1,000 for a class B misdemeanor conviction;

(e) $750 for a class C misdemeanor conviction or infraction conviction; and

(f) any greater amounts specifically authorized by statute.

(2) This section does not apply to a corporation, association, partnership, government, or governmental instrumentality. 1995

76-3-301.5. Uniform fine schedule — Judicial Council.

(1) The Judicial Council shall establish a uniform recommended fine schedule for each offense under Subsection 76-3-301(1).

(a) The fine for each offense shall proportionally reflect the seriousness of the offense and other factors as determined in writing by the Judicial Council.

(b) The schedule shall be reviewed annually by the Judicial Council.

(c) The fines shall be collected under Section 77-18-1.

(2) The schedule shall incorporate:

(a) criteria for determining aggravating and mitigating circumstances; and

(b) guidelines for enhancement or reduction of the fine, based on aggravating or mitigating circumstances.

(3) Presentence investigation reports shall include documentation of aggravating and mitigating circumstances as determined under the criteria, and a recommended fine under the schedule.

(4) The Judicial Council shall also establish a separate uniform recommended fine schedule for the juvenile court and by rule provide for its implementation.

(5) This section does not prohibit the court from in its discretion imposing no fine, or a fine in any amount up to and including the maximum fine, for the offense. 1988

76-3-302. Fines of corporations, associations, partnerships, or government instrumentalities.

A corporation, association, partnership, or governmental instrumentality shall pay a fine for an offense defined in this code for which no special corporate fine is specified. The fine shall not exceed:

(1) $20,000 for a felony conviction;

(2) $10,000 for a class A misdemeanor conviction;

(3) $5,000 for a class B misdemeanor conviction; and

(4) $1,000 for a class C misdemeanor conviction or for an infraction conviction. 1995

76-3-303. Additional sanctions against corporation or association — Advertising of conviction — Disqualification of officer.

(1) When a corporation or association is convicted of an offense, the court may, in addition to or in lieu of imposing other authorized sanctions, require the corporation or association to give appropriate publicity of the conviction by notice to the class or classes of persons or section of the public interested in or affected by the conviction, by advertising in designated areas, or by designated media or otherwise.

(2) When an executive or high managerial officer of a corporation or association is convicted of an offense committed in furtherance of the affairs of the corporation or association, the court may include in the sentence an order disqualifying him from exercising similar functions in the same or other corporations or associations for a period of not exceeding five years if it finds the scope or willfulness of his illegal actions make it dangerous or inadvisable for such functions to be entrusted to him. 1973

PART 4

LIMITATIONS AND SPECIAL PROVISIONS ON SENTENCES

76-3-401. Concurrent or consecutive sentences — Limitations — Definition.

(1) A court shall determine, if a defendant has been adjudged guilty of more than one felony offense, whether to impose concurrent or consecutive sentences for the offenses. The court shall state on the record and shall indicate in the order of judgment and commitment:

(a) if the sentences imposed are to run concurrently or consecutively to each other; and

(b) if the sentences before the court are to run concurrently or consecutively with any other sentences the defendant is already serving.

(2) In determining whether state offenses are to run concurrently or consecutively, the court shall consider the gravity and circumstances of the offenses, the number of victims, and the history, character, and rehabilitative needs of the defendant.

(3) The court shall order that sentences for state offenses run consecutively if the later offense is committed while the defendant is imprisoned or on parole, unless the court finds and states on the record that consecutive sentencing would be inappropriate.

(4) If a written order of commitment does not clearly state whether the sentences are to run consecutively or concurrently, the Board of Pardons and Parole shall request clarification from the court. Upon receipt of the request, the court shall enter a clarified order of commitment stating whether the sentences are to run consecutively or concurrently.

(5) A court may impose consecutive sentences for offenses arising out of a single criminal episode as defined in Section 76-1-401.

(6) (a) If a court imposes consecutive sentences, the aggregate maximum of all sentences imposed

may not exceed 30 years imprisonment, except as provided under Subsection (6)(b).

(b) The limitation under Subsection (6)(a) does not apply if:

(i) an offense for which the defendant is sentenced authorizes the death penalty or a maximum sentence of life imprisonment; or

(ii) the defendant is convicted of an additional offense based on conduct which occurs after his initial sentence or sentences are imposed.

(7) The limitation in Subsection (6)(a) applies if a defendant:

(a) is sentenced at the same time for more than one offense;

(b) is sentenced at different times for one or more offenses, all of which were committed prior to imposition of the defendant's initial sentence; or

(c) has already been sentenced by a court of this state other than the present sentencing court or by a court of another state or federal jurisdiction, and the conduct giving rise to the present offense did not occur after his initial sentencing by any other court.

(8) When the limitation of Subsection (6)(a) applies, determining the effect of consecutive sentences and the manner in which they shall be served, the Board of Pardons and Parole shall treat the defendant as though he has been committed for a single term that consists of the aggregate of the validly imposed prison terms as follows:

(a) if the aggregate maximum term exceeds the 30-year limitation, the maximum sentence is considered to be 30 years; and

(b) when indeterminate sentences run consecutively, the minimum term, if any, constitutes the aggregate of the validly imposed minimum terms.

(9) When a sentence is imposed or sentences are imposed to run concurrently with the other or with a sentence presently being served, the term that provides the longer remaining imprisonment constitutes the time to be served.

(10) This section may not be construed to restrict the number or length of individual consecutive sentences that may be imposed or to affect the validity of any sentence so imposed, but only to limit the length of sentences actually served under the commitments.

(11) This section may not be construed to limit the authority of a court to impose consecutive sentences in misdemeanor cases.

(12) As used in this section, "imprisoned" means sentenced and committed to a secure correctional facility as defined in Section 64-13-1, the sentence has not been terminated or voided, and the person is not on parole, regardless of where the person is located.
                                                    2002

76-3-402. Conviction of lower degree of offense.

(1) If the court, having regard to the nature and circumstances of the offense of which the defendant was found guilty and to the history and character of the defendant, concludes it would be unduly harsh to record the conviction as being for that degree of offense established by statute and to sentence the defendant to an alternative normally applicable to that offense, the court may unless otherwise specifically provided by law enter a judgment of conviction for the next lower degree of offense and impose sentence accordingly.

(2) If a conviction is for a third degree felony the conviction is considered to be for a class A misdemeanor if:

(a) the judge designates the sentence to be for a class A misdemeanor and the sentence imposed is within the limits provided by law for a class A misdemeanor; or

(b) (i) the imposition of the sentence is stayed and the defendant is placed on probation, whether committed to jail as a condition of probation or not;

(ii) the defendant is subsequently discharged without violating his probation; and

(iii) the judge upon motion and notice to the prosecuting attorney, and a hearing if requested by either party or the court, finds it is in the interest of justice that the conviction be considered to be for a class A misdemeanor.

(3) An offense may be reduced only one degree under this section unless the prosecutor specifically agrees in writing or on the court record that the offense may be reduced two degrees. In no case may an offense be reduced under this section by more than two degrees.

(4) This section may not be construed to preclude any person from obtaining or being granted an expungement of his record as provided by law.   1991

76-3-403. Credit for good behavior against jail sentence for misdemeanors and certain felonies.

In any commitment for incarceration in a county jail or detention facility, other than the Utah State Prison, the custodial authority may in its discretion and upon good behavior of the inmate allow up to ten days credit against the sentence to be served for every 30 days served or up to two days credit for every ten days served when the period to be served is less than 30 days if:

(1) the incarceration is for a misdemeanor offense, and the sentencing judge has not entered an order to the contrary; or

(2) the incarceration is part of a probation agreement for a felony offense, and the sentencing district judge has not entered an order to the contrary.   1998

76-3-403.5. Work release from county jail or detention facility.

When an inmate is committed for incarceration in a county jail or in a detention facility, the custodial authority may in its discretion allow the inmate to work outside of the jail or facility as part of a jail or facility supervised work detail if the inmate's incarceration:

(1) is for a misdemeanor offense, and the sentencing judge has not entered an order to the contrary;

(2) is part of a probation agreement for a felony offense, and the sentencing district judge has not entered an order to the contrary; or

(3) is in a county facility pursuant to a contract with the Department of Corrections.   2000

76-3-404. Presentence investigation and diagnostic evaluation — Commitment of defendant — Sentencing procedure.

(1) (a) (i) In felony cases where the court is of the opinion imprisonment may be appropriate but desires more detailed information as a basis for determining the sentence to be imposed than has been provided by the presentence report, the court may in its discretion commit a convicted defendant to the custody of the Department of Corrections for

a diagnostic evaluation for a period not exceeding 90 days.

(ii) The Department of Corrections shall conduct a complete study and evaluation of the defendant during that time, inquiring into matters including:

(A) the defendant's previous delinquency or criminal experience;

(B) his social background;

(C) his capabilities;

(D) his mental, emotional, and physical health; and

(E) the rehabilitative resources or programs which may be available to suit his needs.

(b) (i) By the expiration of the commitment period, or by the expiration of additional commitment time the court may grant, not exceeding a further period of 90 days, the defendant shall be returned to the court for sentencing and the court, prosecutor, and the defendant or his attorney shall be provided with a written diagnostic evaluation report of results of the study, including any recommendations the Department of Corrections or the Utah State Hospital believes will be helpful to a proper resolution of the case.

(ii) Any diagnostic evaluation report ordered by the court is supplemental to and becomes a part of the presentence investigation report.

(iii) After receiving the diagnostic evaluation report and recommendations, the court shall proceed to sentence a defendant in accordance with the sentencing alternatives provided under Section 76-3-201.

(2) Any commitment for presentence investigation under this section does not constitute a commitment to prison. However, any person who is committed to prison following proceedings under this section shall be given credit against his sentence for the time spent in confinement for a presentence investigation report.
1991

76-3-405. Limitation on sentence where conviction or prior sentence set aside.

(1) Where a conviction or sentence has been set aside on direct review or on collateral attack, the court shall not impose a new sentence for the same offense or for a different offense based on the same conduct which is more severe than the prior sentence less the portion of the prior sentence previously satisfied.

(2) This section does not apply when:

(a) the increased sentence is based on facts which were not known to the court at the time of the original sentence, and the court affirmatively places on the record the facts which provide the basis for the increased sentence; or

(b) a defendant enters into a plea agreement with the prosecution and later successfully moves to invalidate his conviction, in which case the defendant and the prosecution stand in the same position as though the plea bargain, conviction, and sentence had never occurred.
1997

76-3-406. Crimes for which probation, suspension of sentence, lower category of offense, or hospitalization may not be granted.

Notwithstanding Sections 76-3-201 and 77-18-1 and Title 77, Chapter 16a, except as provided in Section 76-5-406.5, probation shall not be granted, the execution or imposition of sentence shall not be suspended, the court shall not enter a judgment for a lower category of offense, and hospitalization shall not be ordered, the effect of which would in any way shorten the prison sentence for any person who commits a capital felony or a first degree felony involving:

(1) Section 76-5-202, aggravated murder;

(2) Section 76-5-203, murder;

(3) Section 76-5-301.1, child kidnaping;

(4) Section 76-5-302, aggravated kidnaping;

(5) Section 76-5-402.1, rape of a child;

(6) Section 76-5-402.3, object rape of a child;

(7) Section 76-5-403.1, sodomy on a child;

(8) Subsections 76-5-404.1(4) and (5), aggravated sexual abuse of a child;

(9) Section 76-5-405, aggravated sexual assault; or

(10) any attempt to commit a felony listed in Subsections (5), (6), and (7).
2003

76-3-407. Repeat and habitual sex offenders — Additional prison term for prior felony convictions.

Notwithstanding any other provision of law, if the new offense is an attempt to commit or the commission of a felony of the first or second degree described in Title 76, Chapter 5, Part 4, the court shall impose in addition to and consecutive with any other prison term therefor, a three year term for each prior conviction for a felony sexual offense in Utah or any other state or federal jurisdiction which constitutes or would constitute a crime, assault with intent to commit a crime, or an attempt to commit a crime which, if committed in Utah, is punishable under Title 76, Chapter 5, Part 4, if the existence of the felony conviction has been charged and admitted or found true in the action for the new offense and if the prior felony conviction was entered before the commission of the new offense.
1984

76-3-408. Repeat and habitual sex offenders — Life imprisonment without parole on third conviction.

Notwithstanding any other provision of law, a person who has been convicted in two or more separate prosecutions of any sexual offense which, if committed in Utah or any other state or federal jurisdiction, would contain elements sufficient to constitute any of the offenses described in Sections 76-5-402, 76-5-402.1, 76-5-402.2, 76-5-402.3, 76-5-403, 76-5-403.1, 76-5-404, 76-5-404.1, and 76-5-405, shall, upon a conviction of any offense set forth in this section, be sentenced to a term of imprisonment for life without the possibility of parole if the existence of the prior felony convictions has been charged and admitted or found true in the action for the new offense and if the prior felony convictions were entered before the commission of the new offense. A prior felony conviction can be alleged for purposes of this section only if it was entered before the actual commission of the crime which constitutes the basis for the next felony conviction, subsequently entered against the accused, which is also alleged under this section.
1984

76-3-409. Child abuse or sex offense against child — Treatment of offender or victim — Payment of costs.

(1) Any person convicted in the district court of child abuse, or a sexual offense if the victim is under 18 years of age, may be ordered to participate in treatment or therapy under the supervision of the adult probation and parole section of the Department of Corrections, in cooperation with the division of children, youth, and families until the court is satis-

fied that such treatment or therapy has been successful or that no further benefit to the convicted offender would result if such treatment or therapy were continued. The court may also order treatment of the victim if it believes the same would be beneficial under the circumstances. Nothing in this section shall preclude the court from imposing any additional sentence as provided by law.

(2) The convicted offender shall be ordered to pay, to the extent that he or she is able, the costs of his or her treatment, together with treatment costs incurred by the victim and any administrative costs incurred by the appropriate state agency in the supervision of such treatment. If the convicted offender is unable to pay all or part of the costs of treatment, the court may order the appropriate state agency to pay such costs to the extent funding is provided by the Legislature for such purpose and shall order the convicted offender to perform public service work as compensation for the cost of treatment.   1985

PART 5

FORFEITURE

76-3-501. Vehicle subject to forfeiture — Seizure — Procedure.

(1) Any vehicle used in the commission of, attempt to commit, or flight after commission of any felony in which a firearm or other dangerous weapon as defined in Section 76-10-501, or explosive, chemical, or incendiary device or parts as defined in Section 76-10-306 is used, or any vehicle used in the commission of the illegal possession or sale of a firearm in or from the vehicle, is subject to forfeiture.

(2) Vehicles subject to forfeiture under this section may be seized by any peace officer of this state upon process issued by any court having jurisdiction over the vehicle. However, seizure without process may be made when:

(a) the seizure is incident to a lawful arrest, with or without an arrest warrant;

(b) the vehicle is seized incident to a lawful search with or without a search warrant or an inspection under an administrative inspection warrant;

(c) the vehicle subject to seizure has been the subject of a prior judgment in favor of the state in a criminal injunction or forfeiture proceeding; or

(d) the peace officer seizing the vehicle has probable cause to believe that the vehicle has been used or is intended to be used in violation of this section and the peace officer reasonably believes that the vehicle will be lost, damaged, or used in further violation of law if the officer delays seizure to obtain a warrant.

(3) Forfeiture proceedings under this section shall be instituted promptly in accordance with the procedures and substantive protections of Title 24, Chapter 1, Utah Uniform Forfeiture Procedures Act.

(4) Any vehicle taken or detained under this section is not repleviable but is in custody of the law enforcement agency making the seizure, subject only to the orders and decrees of the court or the official having jurisdiction. When a vehicle is seized under this chapter the appropriate person or agency may:

(a) remove the vehicle to a place designated by the court, official, or the warrant under which the vehicle was seized; or

(b) take custody of the vehicle and remove it to an appropriate location for disposition in accordance with law.   2002

CHAPTER 4

INCHOATE OFFENSES

Part 1

Attempt

Part 2

Criminal Conspiracy

Part 3

Exemptions and Restrictions

Part 4

Enticement of a Minor

PART 1

ATTEMPT

76-4-101. Attempt — Elements of offense.

(1) For purposes of this part, a person is guilty of an attempt to commit a crime if he:

(a) engages in conduct constituting a substantial step toward commission of the crime; and

(b) (i) intends to commit the crime; or

(ii) when causing a particular result is an element of the crime, he acts with an awareness that his conduct is reasonably certain to cause that result.

(2) For purposes of this part, conduct constitutes a substantial step if it strongly corroborates the actor's mental state as defined in Subsection (1)(b).

(3) A defense to the offense of attempt does not arise:

(a) because the offense attempted was actually committed; or

(b) due to factual or legal impossibility if the offense could have been committed if the attendant circumstances had been as the actor believed them to be.   2004

76-4-102. Attempt — Classification of offenses.

Criminal attempt to commit:

(1) a capital felony is a first degree felony;

(2) a first degree felony is a second degree felony, except that an attempt to commit any of the following offenses is a first degree felony punishable by imprisonment for an indeterminate term of not fewer than three years and which may be for life:

(a) murder, a violation of Subsection 76-5-203(2)(a), if the victim or another suffers serious bodily injury in the course of the actor's commission of the offense;

(b) child kidnapping, a violation of Section 76-5-301.1; or

(c) any of the felonies described in Title 76, Chapter 5, Part 4, Sexual Offenses, that are first degree felonies;

(3) a second degree felony is a third degree felony;

(4) a third degree felony is a class A misdemeanor;

(5) a class A misdemeanor is a class B misdemeanor;

(6) a class B misdemeanor is a class C misdemeanor; and

(7) a class C misdemeanor is punishable by a penalty not exceeding one half the penalty for a class C misdemeanor.   2002

PART 2

CRIMINAL CONSPIRACY

76-4-201. Conspiracy — Elements of offense.

For purposes of this part a person is guilty of conspiracy when he, intending that conduct constituting a crime be performed, agrees with one or more persons to engage in or cause the performance of the conduct and any one of them commits an overt act in pursuance of the conspiracy, except where the offense is a capital felony, a felony against the person, arson, burglary, or robbery, the overt act is not required for the commission of conspiracy.   2001

76-4-202. Conspiracy — Classification of offenses.

Conspiracy to commit:

(1) a capital felony is a first degree felony;

(2) a first degree felony is a second degree felony; except that conspiracy to commit child kidnaping, in violation of Section 76-5-301.1 or to commit any of those felonies described in Title 76, Chapter 5, Part 4, which are first degree felonies, is a first degree felony punishable by imprisonment for an indeterminate term of not less than three years and which may be for life;

(3) a second degree felony is a third degree felony;

(4) a third degree felony is a class A misdemeanor;

(5) a class A misdemeanor is a class B misdemeanor;

(6) a class B misdemeanor is a class C misdemeanor;

(7) A class C misdemeanor is punishable by a penalty not exceeding one half the penalty for a class C misdemeanor.   1996

76-4-203. Criminal solicitation — Elements.

(1) An actor commits criminal solicitation if with intent that a felony be committed, he solicits, requests, commands, offers to hire, or importunes another person to engage in specific conduct that under the circumstances as the actor believes them to be would be a felony or would cause the other person to be a party to the commission of a felony.

(2) An actor may be convicted under this section only if the solicitation is made under circumstances strongly corroborative of the actor's intent that the offense be committed.

(3) It is not a defense under this section that the person solicited by the actor:

(a) does not agree to act upon the solicitation;

(b) does not commit an overt act;

(c) does not engage in conduct constituting a substantial step toward the commission of any offense;

(d) is not criminally responsible for the felony solicited;

(e) was acquitted, was not prosecuted or convicted, or was convicted of a different offense or of a different type or degree of offense; or

(f) is immune from prosecution.

(4) It is not a defense under this section that the actor:

(a) belongs to a class of persons that by definition is legally incapable of committing the offense in an individual capacity; or

(b) fails to communicate with the person he solicits to commit an offense, if the intent of the actor's conduct was to effect the communication.

(5) Nothing in this section prevents an actor who otherwise solicits, requests, commands, encourages, or intentionally aids another person to engage in conduct which constitutes an offense from being prosecuted and convicted as a party to the offense under Section 76-2-202 if the person solicited actually commits the offense.   1993

76-4-204. Criminal solicitation — Penalties.

Criminal solicitation to commit:

(1) a capital felony is a first degree felony;

(2) a first degree felony is a second degree felony;

(3) a second degree felony is a third degree felony; and

(4) a third degree felony is a class A misdemeanor.   1990

PART 3

EXEMPTIONS AND RESTRICTIONS

76-4-301. Specific attempt or conspiracy offense prevails.

Whenever any offense specifically designates or defines an attempt or conspiracy and provides a penalty for the attempt or conspiracy other than provided in this chapter, the specific offense shall prevail over the provisions of this chapter.   1995

76-4-302. Conviction of inchoate and principal offense or attempt and conspiracy to commit offense prohibited.

No person shall be convicted of both an inchoate and principal offense or of both an attempt to commit an offense and a conspiracy to commit the same offense.   1974

PART 4

ENTICEMENT OF A MINOR

76-4-401. Enticing a minor over the Internet — Elements — Penalties.

(1) A person commits enticement of a minor over the Internet when the person knowingly uses a computer to solicit, seduce, lure, or entice, or attempts to use a computer to solicit, seduce, lure, or entice a minor or a person the defendant believes to be a minor to engage in any sexual activity which is a violation of state criminal law.

(2) It is not a defense to the crime of enticing a minor under Subsection (1), or an attempt to commit this offense, that a law enforcement officer or an undercover operative who is working with a law enforcement agency was involved in the detection or investigation of the offense.

(3) An enticement of a minor under Subsection (1) with the intent to commit:

(a) a first degree felony is a second degree felony;

(b) a second degree felony is a third degree felony;

(c) a third degree felony is a class A misdemeanor;

(d) a class A misdemeanor is a class B misdemeanor; and

(e) a class B misdemeanor is a class C misdemeanor.   2003

CHAPTER 5

OFFENSES AGAINST THE PERSON

Part 1

Assault and Related Offenses

Part 2

Criminal Homicide

Part 3

Kidnapping

Part 4

Sexual Offenses

Part 5

HIV Testing — Sexual Offenders and Victims

Section

— Costs paid by Crime Victim Reparations.

76-5-504. Victim notification and counseling.

PART 1

ASSAULT AND RELATED OFFENSES

76-5-101. "Prisoner" defined.

For purposes of this part "prisoner" means any person who is in custody of a peace officer pursuant to a lawful arrest or who is confined in a jail or other penal institution or a facility used for confinement of delinquent juveniles operated by the Division of Juvenile Justice Services regardless of whether the confinement is legal. 2003

76-5-102. Assault.

(1) Assault is:

(a) an attempt, with unlawful force or violence, to do bodily injury to another;

(b) a threat, accompanied by a show of immediate force or violence, to do bodily injury to another; or

(c) an act, committed with unlawful force or violence, that causes bodily injury to another or creates a substantial risk of bodily injury to another.

(2) Assault is a class B misdemeanor.

(3) Assault is a class A misdemeanor if:

(a) the person causes substantial bodily injury to another; or

(b) the victim is pregnant and the person has knowledge of the pregnancy.

(4) It is not a defense against assault, that the accused caused serious bodily injury to another. 2003

76-5-102.3. Assault against school employees.

(1) Any person who assaults an employee of a public or private school, with knowledge that the individual is an employee, and when the employee is acting within the scope of his authority as an employee, is guilty of a class A misdemeanor.

(2) As used in this section, "employee" includes a volunteer. 1992

76-5-102.4. Assault against peace officer — Penalty.

(1) Any person who assaults a peace officer, with knowledge that he is a peace officer, and when the peace officer is acting within the scope of his authority as a peace officer, is guilty of a class A misdemeanor.

(2) A person who violates this section shall serve, in jail or another correctional facility, a minimum of:

(a) 90 consecutive days for a second offense; and

(b) 180 consecutive days for each subsequent offense.

(3) The court may suspend the imposition or execution of the sentence required under Subsection (2) if the court finds that the interests of justice would be best served and makes specific findings concerning the disposition in writing or on the record. 1998

76-5-102.5. Assault by prisoner.

Any prisoner who commits assault, intending to cause bodily injury, is guilty of a felony of the third degree. 1974

76-5-102.6. Propelling substance or object at a correctional or peace officer — Penalties.

(1) Any prisoner who throws or otherwise propels any substance or object at a peace or correctional officer is guilty of a class A misdemeanor, except as provided under Subsection (2).

(2) A violation of Subsection (1) is a third degree felony if:

(a) the object or substance is:

(i) blood, urine, or fecal material; or

(ii) saliva, and the prisoner is infected with HIV, hepatitis B, or hepatitis C; and

(b) the object or substance comes into contact with any portion of the officer's face, including the eyes or mouth, or comes into contact with any open wound on the officer's body.

(3) If an offense committed under this section amounts to an offense subject to a greater penalty under another provision of state law than under this section, this section does not prohibit prosecution and sentencing for the more serious offense. 2005

76-5-102.7. Assault against health care provider and emergency medical service worker — Penalty.

(1) A person who assaults a health care provider or emergency medical service worker is guilty of a class A misdemeanor if:

(a) the person knew that the victim was a health care provider or emergency medical service worker; and

(b) the health care provider or emergency medical service worker was performing emergency or life saving duties within the scope of his authority at the time of the assault.

(2) As used in this section:

(a) "Emergency medical service worker" means a person certified under Section 26-8a-302.

(b) "Health care provider" has the meaning as provided in Section 78-14-3. 1999

76-5-102.8. Disarming a peace officer.

A person is guilty of a first degree felony who intentionally takes or removes, or attempts to take or remove, a firearm from the person or immediate presence of a person he knows is a peace officer:

(1) without the consent of the peace officer; and

(2) while the peace officer is acting within the scope of his authority as a peace officer. 1999

76-5-103. Aggravated assault.

(1) A person commits aggravated assault if he commits assault as defined in Section 76-5-102 and he:

(a) intentionally causes serious bodily injury to another; or

(b) under circumstances not amounting to a violation of Subsection (1)(a), uses a dangerous weapon as defined in Section 76-1-601 or other means or force likely to produce death or serious bodily injury.

(2) A violation of Subsection (1)(a) is a second degree felony.

(3) A violation of Subsection (1)(b) is a third degree felony. 1995

76-5-103.5. Aggravated assault by prisoner.

(1) Any prisoner, not serving a sentence for a capital felony or a felony of the first degree, who commits aggravated assault is guilty of:

(a) a felony of the second degree if no serious bodily injury was intentionally caused; or

(b) a felony of the first degree if serious bodily injury was intentionally caused.

(2) For the purpose of this section, "serving a sentence" means sentenced and committed to the custody of the Department of Corrections, the sentence has not been terminated or voided, and the prisoner is:

(a) not on parole; or

(b) in custody after arrest for a parole violation. 2001

76-5-104. Consensual altercation.

In any prosecution for criminal homicide under Part 2 of this chapter or assault, it is no defense to the prosecution that the defendant was a party to any duel, mutual combat, or other consensual altercation if during the course of the duel, combat, or altercation any dangerous weapon as defined in Section 76-1-601 was used or if the defendant was engaged in an ultimate fighting match as defined in Section 76-9-705. 1997

76-5-105. Mayhem.

(1) Every person who unlawfully and intentionally deprives a human being of a member of his body, or disables or renders it useless, or who cuts out or disables the tongue, puts out an eye, or slits the nose, ear, or lip, is guilty of mayhem.

(2) Mayhem is a felony of the second degree. 1973

76-5-106. Harassment.

(1) A person is guilty of harassment if, with intent to frighten or harass another, he communicates a written or recorded threat to commit any violent felony.

(2) Harassment is a class B misdemeanor. 1995

76-5-106.5. Definitions — Stalking — Injunction — Hearing.

(1) As used in this section:

(a) "Course of conduct" means repeatedly maintaining a visual or physical proximity to a person or repeatedly conveying verbal or written threats or threats implied by conduct or a combination thereof directed at or toward a person.

(b) "Immediate family" means a spouse, parent, child, sibling, or any other person who regularly resides in the household or who regularly resided in the household within the prior six months.

(c) "Repeatedly" means on two or more occasions.

(2) A person is guilty of stalking who:

(a) intentionally or knowingly engages in a course of conduct directed at a specific person that would cause a reasonable person:

(i) to fear bodily injury to himself or a member of his immediate family; or

(ii) to suffer emotional distress to himself or a member of his immediate family;

(b) has knowledge or should have knowledge that the specific person:

(i) will be placed in reasonable fear of bodily injury to himself or a member of his immediate family; or

(ii) will suffer emotional distress or a member of his immediate family will suffer emotional distress; and

(c) whose conduct:

(i) induces fear in the specific person of bodily injury to himself or a member of his immediate family; or

(ii) causes emotional distress in the specific person or a member of his immediate family.

(3) A person is also guilty of stalking who intentionally or knowingly violates a stalking injunction issued pursuant to Title 77, Chapter 3a, Stalking Injunctions, or intentionally or knowingly violates a permanent criminal stalking injunction issued pursuant to this section.

(4) Stalking is a class A misdemeanor:

(a) upon the offender's first violation of Subsection (2); or

(b) if the offender violated a stalking injunction issued pursuant to Title 77, Chapter 3a, Stalking Injunctions.

(5) Stalking is a third degree felony if the offender:

(a) has been previously convicted of an offense of stalking;

(b) has been convicted in another jurisdiction of an offense that is substantially similar to the offense of stalking;

(c) has been previously convicted of any felony offense in Utah or of any crime in another jurisdiction which if committed in Utah would be a felony, in which the victim of the stalking or a member of the victim's immediate family was also a victim of the previous felony offense; or

(d) violated a permanent criminal stalking injunction issued pursuant to Subsection (7).

(6) Stalking is a felony of the second degree if the offender:

(a) used a dangerous weapon as defined in Section 76-1-601 or used other means or force likely to produce death or serious bodily injury, in the commission of the crime of stalking;

(b) has been previously convicted two or more times of the offense of stalking;

(c) has been convicted two or more times in another jurisdiction or jurisdictions of offenses that are substantially similar to the offense of stalking;

(d) has been convicted two or more times, in any combination, of offenses under Subsection (5); or

(e) has been previously convicted two or more times of felony offenses in Utah or of crimes in another jurisdiction or jurisdictions which, if committed in Utah, would be felonies, in which the victim of the stalking was also a victim of the previous felony offenses.

(7) A conviction for stalking or a plea accepted by the court and held in abeyance for a period of time shall operate as an application for a permanent criminal stalking injunction limiting the contact of the defendant and the victim.

(a) A permanent criminal stalking injunction shall be issued without a hearing unless the defendant requests a hearing at the time of the verdict, finding, or plea of guilty, guilty and mentally ill, plea of no contest, or acceptance of plea in abeyance. The court shall give the defendant notice of his right to request a hearing.

(i) If the defendant requests a hearing, it shall be held at the time of the verdict, finding, or plea of guilty, guilty and mentally ill, plea of no contest, or acceptance of plea in abeyance unless the victim requests otherwise, or for good cause.

(ii) If the verdict, finding, or plea of guilty, guilty and mentally ill, plea of no contest, or acceptance of plea in abeyance was entered in a justice court, a certified copy of the judgment and conviction or a certified copy of the court's order holding the plea in abeyance must be filed by the victim in the district court as an application and request for hearing for a permanent criminal stalking injunction.

(b) A permanent criminal stalking injunction may grant the following relief:

(i) an order restraining the defendant from entering the residence, property, school, or place of employment of the victim and requiring the defendant to stay away from the victim and members of the victim's immediate family or household and to stay away from any specified place that is named in the order and is frequented regularly by the victim; and

(ii) an order restraining the defendant from making contact with the victim, including an order forbidding the defendant from personally or through an agent initiating any communication likely to cause annoyance or alarm, including personal, written, or telephone contact with the victim, the victim's employers, employees, fellow workers, or others with whom communication would be likely to cause annoyance or alarm to the victim.

(c) A permanent criminal stalking injunction may be dissolved upon application of the victim to the court which granted the order.

(d) Notice of permanent criminal stalking injunctions issued pursuant to this section shall be sent by the court to the statewide warrants network or similar system.

(e) A permanent criminal stalking injunction issued pursuant to this section shall be effective statewide.

(f) Violation of an injunction issued pursuant to this section shall constitute an offense of stalking. Violations may be enforced in a civil action initiated by the stalking victim, a criminal action initiated by a prosecuting attorney, or both.

(g) Nothing in this section shall preclude the filing of a criminal information for stalking based on the same act which is the basis for the violation of the stalking injunction issued pursuant to Title 77, Chapter 3a, Stalking Injunctions, or permanent criminal stalking injunction.   2001

76-5-107. Terroristic threat — Penalty.

(1) A person commits a terroristic threat if he threatens to commit any offense involving bodily injury, death, or substantial property damage, and:

(a) he threatens the use of a weapon of mass destruction, as defined in Section 76-10-401, or threatens by the use of a hoax weapon of mass destruction, as defined in Section 76-10-401; or

(b) he acts with intent to:

(i) intimidate or coerce a civilian population or to influence or affect the conduct of a government or a unit of government;

(ii) cause action of any nature by an official or volunteer agency organized to deal with emergencies;

(iii) place a person in fear of imminent serious bodily injury, substantial bodily injury, or death; or

(iv) prevent or interrupt the occupation of a building or a portion of the building, a place to which the public has access, or a facility or vehicle of public transportation operated by a common carrier.

(2) (a) A violation of Subsection (1)(a) or (1)(b)(i) is a second degree felony.

(b) A violation of Subsection (1)(b)(iv) is a third degree felony.

(c) Any other violation of this section is a class B misdemeanor.

(3) It is not a defense under this section that the person did not attempt to or was incapable of carrying out the threat.

(4) A threat under this section may be express or implied.

(5) A person who commits an offense under this section is subject to punishment for that offense, in addition to any other offense committed, including the carrying out of the threatened act.

(6) In addition to any other penalty authorized by law, a court shall order any person convicted of any violation of this section to reimburse any federal, state, or local unit of government, or any private business, organization, individual, or entity for all expenses and losses incurred in responding to the violation, unless the court states on the record the reasons why the reimbursement would be inappropriate.   2002

76-5-107.5. Prohibition of "hazing" — Definitions — Penalties.

(1) A person is guilty of hazing if that person intentionally, knowingly, or recklessly commits an act or causes another to commit an act that:

(a) (i) endangers the mental or physical health or safety of another; or

(ii) involves any brutality of a physical nature such as whipping, beating, branding, calisthenics, bruising, electric shocking, placing of a harmful substance on the body, or exposure to the elements; or

(iii) involves consumption of any food, liquor, drug, or other substance or any other physical activity that endangers the mental or physical health and safety of an individual; or

(iv) involves any activity that would subject the individual to extreme mental stress, such as sleep deprivation, extended isolation from social contact, or conduct that subjects another to extreme embarrassment, shame, or humiliation; or

(v) involves cruelty to any animal as provided in Section 76-9-301; and

(b) (i) is for the purpose of initiation, admission into, affiliation with, holding office in, or as a condition for continued membership in any organization; or

(ii) if the actor knew that the victim is a member of or candidate for membership with a school team or school organization to which the actor belongs or did belong within the preceding two years.

(2) It is not a defense to prosecution of hazing that a person under 21, against whom the hazing was directed, consented to or acquiesced in the hazing activity.

(3) An actor who hazes another is guilty of a:

(a) class C misdemeanor if the conduct violates Section 76-9-301;

(b) class B misdemeanor if there are no aggravating circumstances;

(c) class A misdemeanor if the act involves the operation or other use of a motor vehicle;

(d) third degree felony if the act involves the use of a dangerous weapon as defined in Section 76-1-601;

(e) third degree felony if the hazing results in serious bodily injury to a person; or

(f) second degree felony if hazing under Subsection (3)(e) involves the use of a dangerous weapon as defined in Section 76-1-601.

(4) A person who in good faith reports or participates in reporting of an alleged hazing is not subject to any civil or criminal liability regarding the reporting.

(5) (a) This section does not apply to military training or other official military activities.

(b) Military conduct is governed by Title 39, Chapter 6, Utah Code of Military Justice.

(6) (a) A prosecution under this section does not bar a prosecution of the actor for:

(i) any other offense for which the actor may be liable as a party for conduct committed by the person hazed; or

(ii) any offense, caused in the course of the hazing, that the actor commits against the person who is hazed.

(b) Under Subsection (6)(a)(i) a person may be separately punished, both for the hazing offense and the conduct committed by the person hazed.

(c) Under Subsection (6)(a)(ii) a person may not be punished both for hazing and for the other offense, but shall be punished for the offense carrying the greater maximum penalty.   1997

76-5-108. Protective orders restraining abuse of another — Violation.

(1) Any person who is the respondent or defendant subject to a protective order, child protective order, ex parte protective order, or ex parte child protective order issued under Title 30, Chapter 6, Cohabitant Abuse Act, or Title 78, Chapter 3a, Juvenile Court Act of 1996, Title 77, Chapter 36, Cohabitant Abuse Procedures Act, or a foreign protective order as described in Section 30-6-12, who intentionally or knowingly violates that order after having been properly served, is guilty of a class A misdemeanor, except as a greater penalty may be provided in Title 77, Chapter 36, Cohabitant Abuse Procedures Act.

(2) Violation of an order as described in Subsection (1) is a domestic violence offense under Section 77-36-1 and subject to increased penalties in accordance with Section 77-36-1.1.   2003

76-5-109. Child abuse.

(1) As used in this section:

(a) "Child" means a human being who is under 18 years of age.

(b) "Child abuse" means any offense described in Subsection (2) or (3), or in Section 76-5-109.1.

(c) "Physical injury" means an injury to or condition of a child which impairs the physical condition of the child, including:

(i) a bruise or other contusion of the skin;

(ii) a minor laceration or abrasion;

(iii) failure to thrive or malnutrition; or

(iv) any other condition which imperils the child's health or welfare and which is not a serious physical injury as defined in Subsection (1)(d).

(d) (i) "Serious physical injury" means any physical injury or set of injuries that:

(A) seriously impairs the child's health;

(B) involves physical torture;

(C) causes serious emotional harm to the child; or

(D) involves a substantial risk of death to the child.

(ii) "Serious physical injury" includes:

(A) fracture of any bone or bones;

(B) intracranial bleeding, swelling or contusion of the brain, whether caused by blows, shaking, or causing the child's head to impact with an object or surface;

(C) any burn, including burns inflicted by hot water, or those caused by placing a hot object upon the skin or body of the child;

(D) any injury caused by use of a dangerous weapon as defined in Subsection 76-1-601(5);

(E) any combination of two or more physical injuries inflicted by the same person, either at the same time or on different occasions;

(F) any damage to internal organs of the body;

(G) any conduct toward a child that results in severe emotional harm, severe developmental delay or retardation, or severe impairment of the child's ability to function;

(H) any injury that creates a permanent disfigurement or protracted loss or impairment of the function of a bodily member, limb, or organ;

(I) any conduct that causes a child to cease breathing, even if resuscitation is successful following the conduct; or

(J) any conduct that results in starvation or failure to thrive or malnutrition that jeopardizes the child's life.

(2) Any person who inflicts upon a child serious physical injury or, having the care or custody of such child, causes or permits another to inflict serious physical injury upon a child is guilty of an offense as follows:

(a) if done intentionally or knowingly, the offense is a felony of the second degree;

(b) if done recklessly, the offense is a felony of the third degree; or

(c) if done with criminal negligence, the offense is a class A misdemeanor.

(3) Any person who inflicts upon a child physical injury or, having the care or custody of such child, causes or permits another to inflict physical injury upon a child is guilty of an offense as follows:

(a) if done intentionally or knowingly, the offense is a class A misdemeanor;

(b) if done recklessly, the offense is a class B misdemeanor; or

(c) if done with criminal negligence, the offense is a class C misdemeanor.

(4) A parent or legal guardian who provides a child with treatment by spiritual means alone through prayer, in lieu of medical treatment, in accordance with the tenets and practices of an established church or religious denomination of which the parent or legal guardian is a member or adherent shall not, for that reason alone, be considered to have committed an offense under this section.

(5) A parent or guardian of a child does not violate this section by selecting a treatment option for the medical condition of the child, if the treatment option is one that a reasonable parent or guardian would believe to be in the best interest of the child.   2005

76-5-109.1. Commission of domestic violence in the presence of a child.

(1) As used in this section:

(a) "Cohabitant" has the same meaning as defined in Section 30-6-1.

(b) "Domestic violence" has the same meaning as in Section 77-36-1.

(c) "In the presence of a child" means:

(i) in the physical presence of a child; or

(ii) having knowledge that a child is present and may see or hear an act of domestic violence.

(2) A person is guilty of child abuse if the person:

(a) commits or attempts to commit criminal homicide, as defined in Section 76-5-201, against a cohabitant in the presence of a child; or

(b) intentionally causes serious bodily injury to a cohabitant or uses a dangerous weapon, as defined in Section 76-1-601, or other means or force likely to produce death or serious bodily injury against a cohabitant, in the presence of a child; or

(c) under circumstances not amounting to a violation of Subsection (2)(a) or (b), commits an act of domestic violence in the presence of a child.

(3) (a) A person who violates Subsection (2)(a) or (b) is guilty of a third degree felony.

(b) A person who violates Subsection (2)(c) is guilty of a class B misdemeanor.

(4) A charge under this section is separate and distinct from, and is in addition to, a charge of domestic violence where the victim is the cohabitant. Either or both charges may be filed by the prosecutor.

2002

76-5-110. Abuse or neglect of disabled child.

(1) As used in this section:

(a) "Abuse" means:

(i) inflicting physical injury, as that term is defined in Section 76-5-109;

(ii) having the care or custody of a disabled child, causing or permitting another to inflict physical injury, as that term is defined in Section 76-5-109; or

(iii) unreasonable confinement.

(b) "Caretaker" means:

(i) any parent, legal guardian, or other person having under that person's care and custody a disabled child; or

(ii) any person, corporation, or public institution that has assumed by contract or court order the responsibility to provide food, shelter, clothing, medical, and other necessities to a disabled child.

(c) "Disabled child" means any person under 18 years of age who is impaired because of mental illness, mental deficiency, physical illness or disability, or other cause, to the extent that the person is unable to care for the person's own personal safety or to provide necessities such as food, shelter, clothing, and medical care.

(d) "Neglect" means failure by a caretaker to provide care, nutrition, clothing, shelter, supervision, or medical care.

(2) Any caretaker who abuses or neglects a disabled child is guilty of a third degree felony.

(3) (a) A parent or legal guardian who provides a child with treatment by spiritual means alone through prayer, in lieu of medical treatment, in accordance with the tenets and practices of an established church or religious denomination of which the parent or legal guardian is a member or adherent shall not, for that reason alone, be considered to be in violation of this section.

(b) The exception under Subsection (3)(a) shall not preclude a court from ordering medical services from a physician licensed to engage in the practice of medicine to be provided to the child where there is substantial risk of harm to the child's health or welfare.

(c) A caretaker of a disabled child does not violate this section by selecting a treatment option for a disabled child's medical condition, if the treatment option is one that a reasonable caretaker would believe to be in the best interest of the disabled child.

2005

76-5-111. Abuse, neglect, or exploitation of a vulnerable adult — Penalties.

(1) As used in this section:

(a) "Abandonment" means a knowing or intentional action or inaction, including desertion, by a person or entity acting as a caretaker for a vulnerable adult that leaves the vulnerable adult without the means or ability to obtain necessary food, clothing, shelter, or medical or other health care.

(b) "Abuse" means:

(i) attempting to cause harm, intentionally or knowingly causing harm, or intentionally or knowingly placing another in fear of imminent harm;

(ii) causing physical injury by knowing or intentional acts or omissions;

(iii) unreasonable or inappropriate use of physical restraint, medication, or isolation that causes or is likely to cause harm to a vulnerable adult that is in conflict with a physician's orders or used as an unauthorized substitute for treatment, unless that conduct furthers the health and safety of the adult; or

(iv) deprivation of life-sustaining treatment, except:

(A) as provided in Title 75, Chapter 2, Part 11, Personal Choice and Living Will Act; or

(B) when informed consent, as defined in this section, has been obtained.

(c) "Business relationship" means a relationship between two or more individuals or entities where there exists an oral or written agreement for the exchange of goods or services.

(d) "Caretaker" means any person, entity, corporation, or public institution that assumes the responsibility to provide a vulnerable adult with care, food, shelter, clothing, supervision, medical or other health care, or other necessities. "Caretaker" includes a relative by blood or marriage, a household member, a person who is employed or who provides volunteer work, or a person who contracts or is under court order to provide care.

(e) "Deception" means:

(i) a misrepresentation or concealment:

(A) of a material fact relating to services rendered, disposition of property, or use of property intended to benefit a vulnerable adult;

(B) of the terms of a contract or agreement entered into with a vulnerable adult; or

(C) relating to the existing or pre-existing condition of any property involved in a contract or agreement entered into with a vulnerable adult; or

(ii) the use or employment of any misrepresentation, false pretense, or false promise in order to induce, encourage, or solicit a vulnerable adult to enter into a contract or agreement.

(f) "Elder adult" means a person 65 years of age or older.

(g) "Endeavor" means to attempt or try.

(h) "Exploitation" means the offense described in Subsection (4).

(i) "Harm" means pain, mental anguish, emotional distress, hurt, physical or psychological damage, physical injury, suffering, or distress inflicted knowingly or intentionally.

(j) "Informed consent" means:

(i) a written expression by the person or authorized by the person, stating that the person fully understands the potential risks and benefits of the withdrawal of food, water, medication, medical services, shelter, cooling, heating, or other services necessary to maintain minimum physical or mental health, and that the person desires that the services be withdrawn. A written expression is valid only if the person is of sound mind when the consent is given, and the consent is witnessed by at least two individuals who do not benefit from the withdrawal of services; or

(ii) consent to withdraw food, water, medication, medical services, shelter, cooling, heating, or other services necessary to maintain minimum physical or mental health, as permitted by court order.

(k) "Intimidation" means communication conveyed through verbal or nonverbal conduct which threatens deprivation of money, food, clothing, medicine, shelter, social interaction, supervision, health care, or companionship, or which threatens isolation or harm.

(l) (i) "Isolation" means knowingly or intentionally preventing a vulnerable adult from having contact with another person by:

(A) preventing the vulnerable adult from receiving visitors, mail, or telephone calls, contrary to the express wishes of the vulnerable adult, including communicating to a visitor that the vulnerable adult is not present or does not want to meet with or talk to the visitor, knowing that communication to be false;

(B) physically restraining the vulnerable adult in order to prevent the vulnerable adult from meeting with a visitor; or

(C) making false or misleading statements to the vulnerable adult in order to induce the vulnerable adult to refuse to receive communication from visitors or other family members.

(ii) The term "isolation" does not include an act intended to protect the physical or mental welfare of the vulnerable adult or an act performed pursuant to the treatment plan or instructions of a physician or other professional advisor of the vulnerable adult.

(m) "Lacks capacity to consent" means an impairment by reason of mental illness, developmental disability, organic brain disorder, physical illness or disability, chronic use of drugs, chronic intoxication, short-term memory loss, or other cause to the extent that a vulnerable adult lacks sufficient understanding of the nature or consequences of decisions concerning the adult's person or property.

(n) "Neglect" means:

(i) failure of a caretaker to provide nutrition, clothing, shelter, supervision, personal care, or dental or other health care, or failure to provide protection from health and safety hazards or maltreatment;

(ii) failure of a caretaker to provide care to a vulnerable adult in a timely manner and with the degree of care that a reasonable person in a like position would exercise;

(iii) a pattern of conduct by a caretaker, without the vulnerable adult's informed consent, resulting in deprivation of food, water, medication, health care, shelter, cooling, heating, or other services necessary to maintain the vulnerable adult's well being;

(iv) intentional failure by a caretaker to carry out a prescribed treatment plan that results or could result in physical injury or physical harm; or

(v) abandonment by a caretaker.

(o) "Physical injury" includes damage to any bodily tissue caused by nontherapeutic conduct, to the extent that the tissue must undergo a healing process in order to be restored to a sound and healthy condition, or damage to any bodily tissue to the extent that the tissue cannot be restored to a sound and healthy condition. "Physical injury" includes skin bruising, a dislocation, physical pain, illness, impairment of physical function, a pressure sore, bleeding, malnutrition, dehydration, a burn, a bone fracture, a subdural hematoma, soft tissue swelling, injury to any internal organ, or any other physical condition that imperils the health or welfare of the vulnerable adult and is not a serious physical injury as defined in this section.

(p) "Position of trust and confidence" means the position of a person who:

(i) is a parent, spouse, adult child, or other relative by blood or marriage of a vulnerable adult;

(ii) is a joint tenant or tenant in common with a vulnerable adult;

(iii) has a legal or fiduciary relationship with a vulnerable adult, including a court-appointed or voluntary guardian, trustee, attorney, or conservator; or

(iv) is a caretaker of a vulnerable adult.

(q) "Serious physical injury" means any physical injury or set of physical injuries that:

(i) seriously impairs a vulnerable adult's health;

(ii) was caused by use of a dangerous weapon as defined in Section 76-1-601;

(iii) involves physical torture or causes serious emotional harm to a vulnerable adult; or

(iv) creates a reasonable risk of death.

(r) "Sexual exploitation" means the production, distribution, possession, or possession with the intent to distribute material or a live performance depicting a nude or partially nude vulnerable adult who lacks the capacity to consent, for the purpose of sexual arousal of any person.

(s) "Undue influence" occurs when a person uses the person's role, relationship, or power to exploit, or knowingly assist or cause another to exploit, the trust, dependency, or fear of a vulnerable adult, or uses the person's role, relationship, or power to gain control deceptively over the decision making of the vulnerable adult.

(t) "Vulnerable adult" means an elder adult, or an adult 18 years of age or older who has a mental or physical impairment which substantially affects that person's ability to:

(i) provide personal protection;

(ii) provide necessities such as food, shelter, clothing, or medical or other health care;

(iii) obtain services necessary for health, safety, or welfare;

(iv) carry out the activities of daily living;

(v) manage the adult's own resources; or

(vi) comprehend the nature and consequences of remaining in a situation of abuse, neglect, or exploitation.

(2) Under any circumstances likely to produce death or serious physical injury, any person, including a caretaker, who causes a vulnerable adult to suffer serious physical injury or, having the care or custody of a vulnerable adult, causes or permits that adult's person or health to be injured, or causes or permits a vulnerable adult to be placed in a situation where the adult's person or health is endangered, is guilty of the offense of aggravated abuse of a vulnerable adult as follows:

(a) if done intentionally or knowingly, the offense is a second degree felony;

(b) if done recklessly, the offense is third degree felony; and

(c) if done with criminal negligence, the offense is a class A misdemeanor.

(3) Under circumstances other than those likely to produce death or serious physical injury any person, including a caretaker, who causes a vulnerable adult to suffer harm, abuse, or neglect; or, having the care or custody of a vulnerable adult, causes or permits that adult's person or health to be injured, abused, or neglected, or causes or permits a vulnerable adult to be placed in a situation where the adult's person or health is endangered, is guilty of the offense of abuse of a vulnerable adult as follows:

(a) if done intentionally or knowingly, the offense is a class A misdemeanor;

(b) if done recklessly, the offense is a class B misdemeanor; and

(c) if done with criminal negligence, the offense is a class C misdemeanor.

(4) (a) A person commits the offense of exploitation of a vulnerable adult when the person:

(i) is in a position of trust and confidence, or has a business relationship, with the vulnerable adult or has undue influence over the vulnerable adult and knowingly, by deception or intimidation, obtains or uses, or endeavors to obtain or use, the vulnerable adult's funds, credit, assets, or other property with the intent to temporarily or permanently deprive the vulnerable adult of the use, benefit, or possession of the adult's property, for the benefit of someone other than the vulnerable adult;

(ii) knows or should know that the vulnerable adult lacks the capacity to consent, and obtains or uses, or endeavors to obtain or use, or assists another in obtaining or using or endeavoring to obtain or use, the vulnerable adult's funds, assets, or property with the intent to temporarily or permanently deprive the vulnerable adult of the use, benefit, or possession of his property for the benefit of someone other than the vulnerable adult;

(iii) unjustly or improperly uses or manages the resources of a vulnerable adult for the profit or advantage of someone other than the vulnerable adult;

(iv) unjustly or improperly uses a vulnerable adult's power of attorney or guardianship for the profit or advantage of someone other than the vulnerable adult;

(v) involves a vulnerable adult who lacks the capacity to consent in the facilitation or furtherance of any criminal activity; or

(vi) commits sexual exploitation of a vulnerable adult.

(b) A person is guilty of the offense of exploitation of a vulnerable adult as follows:

(i) if done intentionally or knowingly and the aggregate value of the resources used or the profit made is or exceeds $5,000, the offense is a second degree felony;

(ii) if done intentionally or knowingly and the aggregate value of the resources used or the profit made is less than $5,000 or cannot be determined, the offense is a third degree felony;

(iii) if done recklessly, the offense is a class A misdemeanor; or

(iv) if done with criminal negligence, the offense is a class B misdemeanor.

(5) It does not constitute a defense to a prosecution for any violation of this section that the accused did not know the age of the victim.

(6) An adult is not considered abused, neglected, or a vulnerable adult for the reason that the adult has chosen to rely solely upon religious, nonmedical forms of healing in lieu of medical care.   2002

76-5-111.1. Reporting requirements — Investigation — Immunity — Violation — Penalty — Physician-patient privilege — Nonmedical healing.

(1) As provided in Section 62A-3-305, any person who has reason to believe that any vulnerable adult has been the subject of abuse, neglect, or exploitation shall immediately notify the nearest peace officer, law enforcement agency, or Adult Protective Services intake within the Department of Human Services, Division of Aging and Adult Services.

(2) Anyone who makes that report in good faith to a law enforcement agency, the Division of Aging and Adult Services, or Adult Protective Services of suspected abuse, neglect, or exploitation is immune from civil and criminal liability in connection with the report or other notification.

(3) (a) When the initial report is made to a peace officer or law enforcement agency, the officer or law enforcement agency shall immediately notify Adult Protective Services intake. Adult Protective Services and law enforcement shall coordinate, as appropriate, their investigations and provide protection to the vulnerable adult as necessary.

(b) Adult Protective Services will notify the Long-Term Care Ombudsman, as defined in Section 62A-3-202, when the initial report to Adult Protective Services involves a resident of a long-term care facility as defined in Section 62A-3-202. The Long-Term Care Ombudsman and Adult Protective Services shall coordinate, as appropriate, in conducting their investigations.

(c) When the initial report or subsequent investigation by Adult Protective Services indicates that a criminal offense may have occurred against a vulnerable adult, Adult Protective Services shall immediately notify the nearest local law enforcement agency. That law enforcement agency shall initiate an investigation in cooperation with Adult Protective Services.

(4) A person who is required to report suspected abuse, neglect, or exploitation of a vulnerable adult under Subsection (1), and who willfully fails to do so, is guilty of a class B misdemeanor.

(5) Under circumstances not amounting to a violation of Section 76-8-508, a person who threatens, intimidates, or attempts to intimidate a vulnerable adult who is the subject of a report, a witness, the person who made the report, or any other person cooperating with an investigation conducted pursuant to this chapter is guilty of a class B misdemeanor.

(6) The physician-patient privilege does not constitute grounds for excluding evidence regarding a vulnerable adult's injuries, or the cause of those injuries, in any judicial or administrative proceeding resulting from a report made in good faith pursuant to this part.

(7) An adult is not considered abused, neglected, or a vulnerable adult for the reason that the adult has chosen to rely solely upon religious, nonmedical forms of healing in lieu of medical care.   2004

76-5-112. Reckless endangerment — Penalty.

(1) A person commits reckless endangerment if, under circumstances not amounting to a felony offense, the person recklessly engages in conduct that creates a substantial risk of death or serious bodily injury to another person.

(2) Reckless endangerment is a class A misdemeanor.   1999

76-5-112.5. Endangerment of child or elder adult.

(1) For purposes of this section:

(a) "Chemical substance" means a substance intended to be used as a precursor in the manufacture of a controlled substance, or any other chemical intended to be used in the manufacture of a controlled substance. Intent under this subsection may be demonstrated by the substance's use, quantity, manner of storage, or proximity to other precursors, or to manufacturing equipment.

(b) "Child" means the same as that term is defined in Subsection 76-5-109(1)(a).

(c) "Controlled substance" means the same as that term is defined in Section 58-37-2.

(d) "Drug paraphernalia" means the same as that term is defined in Section 58-37a-3.

(e) "Elder adult" means the same as that term is defined in Section 76-5-111.

(2) Unless a greater penalty is otherwise provided by law, any person who knowingly or intentionally causes or permits a child or elder adult to be exposed to, to ingest or inhale, or to have contact with a controlled substance, chemical substance, or drug paraphernalia as defined in Subsection (1), is guilty of a felony of the third degree.

(3) Unless a greater penalty is otherwise provided by law, any person who violates Subsection (2), and a child or elder adult actually suffers bodily injury, substantial bodily injury, or serious bodily injury by exposure to, ingestion of, inhalation of, or contact with a controlled substance, chemical substance, or drug paraphernalia, is guilty of a felony of the second degree unless the exposure, ingestion, inhalation, or contact results in the death of the child or elder adult, in which case the person is guilty of a felony of the first degree.

(4) (a) It is an affirmative defense to a violation of this section that the controlled substance was provided by lawful prescription for the child or elder adult, and that it was administered to the

child or elder adult in accordance with the prescription instructions provided with the controlled substance.

(b) As used in this Subsection (4), "prescription" has the same definition as in Section 58-37-2.   2002

76-5-113. Surreptitious administration of certain substances — Definitions — Penalties — Defenses.

(1) As used in this section:

(a) "Administer" means the introduction of a substance into the body by injection, inhalation, ingestion, or by any other means.

(b) "Alcoholic beverage" has the same meaning as "alcoholic beverages" in Section 32A-1-105.

(c) "Bodily injury" has the same definition as in Section 76-1-601.

(d) "Controlled substance" has the same definition as in Section 58-37-2.

(e) "Deleterious substance" means a substance which, if administered, would likely cause bodily injury.

(f) "Poisonous" means a substance which, if administered, would likely cause serious bodily injury or death.

(g) "Prescription drug" has the same definition as in Section 58-17b-102.

(h) "Serious bodily injury" has the same definition as in Section 19-2-115.

(i) "Substance" means a controlled substance, poisonous substance, or deleterious substance as defined in this Subsection (1).

(2) In addition to any other offense the actor's conduct may constitute, it is a criminal offense for a person, surreptitiously or by means of fraud, deception, or misrepresentation, to cause another person to unknowingly consume or receive the administration of:

(a) any poisonous, deleterious, or controlled substance; or

(b) any alcoholic beverage.

(3) A violation of Subsection (2) is:

(a) a second degree felony if the substance is a poisonous substance, regardless of whether the substance is a controlled substance or a prescription drug;

(b) a third degree felony if the substance is not within the scope of Subsection (3)(a), and is a controlled substance or a prescription drug; and

(c) a class A misdemeanor if the substance is a deleterious substance or an alcoholic beverage.

(4) (a) It is an affirmative defense to a prosecution under Subsection (2) that the actor:

(i) provided the appropriate administration of a prescription drug; and

(ii) acted on the reasonable belief that his conduct was in the best interest of the well-being of the person to whom the prescription drug was administered.

(b) (i) The defendant shall file and serve on the prosecuting attorney a notice in writing of his intention to claim a defense under Subsection (4)(a) not fewer than 20 days before the trial.

(ii) The notice shall specifically identify the factual basis for the defense and the names and addresses of the witnesses the defendant proposes to examine to establish the defense.

(c) The prosecuting attorney shall file and serve the defendant with a notice containing the names and addresses of the witnesses the prosecutor proposes to examine in order to contradict or rebut the defendant's claim of an affirmative defense under Subsection (4)(a). This notice shall be filed or served not more than ten days after receipt of the defendant's notice under Subsection (4)(b), or at another time as the court may direct.

    (d) (i) Failure of a party to comply with the requirements of Subsection (4)(b) or (4)(c) entitles the opposing party to a continuance to allow for preparation.

       (ii) If the court finds that a party's failure to comply is the result of bad faith, it may impose appropriate sanctions.

(5) This section does not diminish the scope of authorized health care by a health care provider as defined in Section 26-23a-1.   2004

PART 2

CRIMINAL HOMICIDE

76-5-201. Criminal homicide — Elements — Designations of offenses.

(1) (a) A person commits criminal homicide if he intentionally, knowingly, recklessly, with criminal negligence, or acting with a mental state otherwise specified in the statute defining the offense, causes the death of another human being, including an unborn child at any stage of its development.

    (b) There shall be no cause of action for criminal homicide for the death of an unborn child caused by an abortion.

(2) Criminal homicide is aggravated murder, murder, manslaughter, child abuse homicide, homicide by assault, negligent homicide, or automobile homicide.
                       2002

76-5-202. Aggravated murder.

(1) Criminal homicide constitutes aggravated murder if the actor intentionally or knowingly causes the death of another under any of the following circumstances:

    (a) the homicide was committed by a person who is confined in a jail or other correctional institution;

    (b) the homicide was committed incident to one act, scheme, course of conduct, or criminal episode during which two or more persons were killed, or during which the actor attempted to kill one or more persons in addition to the victim who was killed;

    (c) the actor knowingly created a great risk of death to a person other than the victim and the actor;

    (d) the homicide was committed while the actor was engaged in the commission of, or an attempt to commit, or flight after committing or attempting to commit, aggravated robbery, robbery, rape, rape of a child, object rape, object rape of a child, forcible sodomy, sodomy upon a child, forcible sexual abuse, sexual abuse of a child, aggravated sexual abuse of a child, child abuse as defined in Subsection 76-5-109(2)(a), or aggravated sexual assault, aggravated arson, arson, aggravated burglary, burglary, aggravated kidnapping, kidnapping, or child kidnapping;

    (e) the homicide was committed incident to one act, scheme, course of conduct, or criminal episode during which the actor committed the crime of abuse or desecration of a dead human body as defined in Subsection 76-9-704(2)(e);

    (f) the homicide was committed for the purpose of avoiding or preventing an arrest of the defendant or another by a peace officer acting under color of legal authority or for the purpose of effecting the defendant's or another's escape from lawful custody;

    (g) the homicide was committed for pecuniary or other personal gain;

    (h) the defendant committed, or engaged or employed another person to commit the homicide pursuant to an agreement or contract for remuneration or the promise of remuneration for commission of the homicide;

    (i) the actor previously committed or was convicted of:

       (i) aggravated murder, Section 76-5-202;

       (ii) attempted aggravated murder, Section 76-5-202;

       (iii) murder, Section 76-5-203;

       (iv) attempted murder, Section 76-5-203; or

       (v) an offense committed in another jurisdiction which if committed in this state would be a violation of a crime listed in this Subsection (1)(i);

    (j) the actor was previously convicted of:

       (i) aggravated assault, Subsection 76-5-103(2);

       (ii) mayhem, Section 76-5-105;

       (iii) kidnapping, Section 76-5-301;

       (iv) child kidnapping, Section 76-5-301.1;

       (v) aggravated kidnapping, Section 76-5-302;

       (vi) rape, Section 76-5-402;

       (vii) rape of a child, Section 76-5-402.1;

       (viii) object rape, Section 76-5-402.2;

       (ix) object rape of a child, Section 76-5-402.3;

       (x) forcible sodomy, Section 76-5-403;

       (xi) sodomy on a child, Section 76-5-403.1;

       (xii) aggravated sexual abuse of a child, Section 76-5-404.1;

       (xiii) aggravated sexual assault, Section 76-5-405;

       (xiv) aggravated arson, Section 76-6-103;

       (xv) aggravated burglary, Section 76-6-203;

       (xvi) aggravated robbery, Section 76-6-302; or

       (xvii) an offense committed in another jurisdiction which if committed in this state would be a violation of a crime listed in this Subsection (1)(j);

    (k) the homicide was committed for the purpose of:

       (i) preventing a witness from testifying;

       (ii) preventing a person from providing evidence or participating in any legal proceedings or official investigation;

       (iii) retaliating against a person for testifying, providing evidence, or participating in any legal proceedings or official investigation; or

       (iv) disrupting or hindering any lawful governmental function or enforcement of laws;

    (l) the victim is or has been a local, state, or federal public official, or a candidate for public office, and the homicide is based on, is caused by, or is related to that official position, act, capacity, or candidacy;

(m) the victim is or has been a peace officer, law enforcement officer, executive officer, prosecuting officer, jailer, prison official, firefighter, judge or other court official, juror, probation officer, or parole officer, and the victim is either on duty or the homicide is based on, is caused by, or is related to that official position, and the actor knew, or reasonably should have known, that the victim holds or has held that official position;

(n) the homicide was committed:

(i) by means of a destructive device, bomb, explosive, incendiary device, or similar device which was planted, hidden, or concealed in any place, area, dwelling, building, or structure, or was mailed or delivered; or

(ii) by means of any weapon of mass destruction as defined in Section 76-10-401;

(o) the homicide was committed during the act of unlawfully assuming control of any aircraft, train, or other public conveyance by use of threats or force with intent to obtain any valuable consideration for the release of the public conveyance or any passenger, crew member, or any other person aboard, or to direct the route or movement of the public conveyance or otherwise exert control over the public conveyance;

(p) the homicide was committed by means of the administration of a poison or of any lethal substance or of any substance administered in a lethal amount, dosage, or quantity;

(q) the victim was a person held or otherwise detained as a shield, hostage, or for ransom;

(r) the homicide was committed in an especially heinous, atrocious, cruel, or exceptionally depraved manner, any of which must be demonstrated by physical torture, serious physical abuse, or serious bodily injury of the victim before death; or

(s) the actor dismembers, mutilates, or disfigures the victim's body, whether before or after death, in a manner demonstrating the actor's depravity of mind.

(2) Aggravated murder is a capital felony.

(3) (a) It is an affirmative defense to a charge of aggravated murder or attempted aggravated murder that the defendant caused the death of another or attempted to cause the death of another:

(i) under the influence of extreme emotional distress for which there is a reasonable explanation or excuse; or

(ii) under a reasonable belief that the circumstances provided a legal justification or excuse for his conduct although the conduct was not legally justifiable or excusable under the existing circumstances.

(b) Under Subsection (3)(a)(i), emotional distress does not include:

(i) a condition resulting from mental illness as defined in Section 76-2-305; or

(ii) distress that is substantially caused by the defendant's own conduct.

(c) The reasonableness of an explanation or excuse under Subsection (3)(a)(i) or the reasonable belief of the actor under Subsection (3)(a)(ii) shall be determined from the viewpoint of a reasonable person under the then existing circumstances.

(d) This affirmative defense reduces charges only as follows:

(i) aggravated murder to murder; and

(ii) attempted aggravated murder to attempted murder. 2005

76-5-203. Murder.

(1) As used in this section, "predicate offense" means:

(a) a violation of Section 58-37d-4 or 58-37d-5, Clandestine Drug Lab Act;

(b) child abuse, under Subsection 76-5-109(2)(a), when the victim is younger than 18 years of age;

(c) kidnapping under Section 76-5-301;

(d) child kidnapping under Section 76-5-301.1;

(e) aggravated kidnapping under Section 76-5-302;

(f) rape of a child under Section 76-5-402.1;

(g) object rape of a child under Section 76-5-402.3;

(h) sodomy upon a child under Section 76-5-403.1;

(i) forcible sexual abuse under Section 76-5-404;

(j) sexual abuse of a child or aggravated sexual abuse of a child under Section 76-5-404.1;

(k) rape under Section 76-5-402;

(l) object rape under Section 76-5-402.2;

(m) forcible sodomy under Section 76-5-403;

(n) aggravated sexual assault under Section 76-5-405;

(o) arson under Section 76-6-102;

(p) aggravated arson under Section 76-6-103;

(q) burglary under Section 76-6-202;

(r) aggravated burglary under Section 76-6-203;

(s) robbery under Section 76-6-301;

(t) aggravated robbery under Section 76-6-302; or

(u) escape or aggravated escape under Section 76-8-309.

(2) Criminal homicide constitutes murder if:

(a) the actor intentionally or knowingly causes the death of another;

(b) intending to cause serious bodily injury to another, the actor commits an act clearly dangerous to human life that causes the death of another;

(c) acting under circumstances evidencing a depraved indifference to human life, the actor engages in conduct which creates a grave risk of death to another and thereby causes the death of another;

(d) (i) the actor is engaged in the commission, attempted commission, or immediate flight from the commission or attempted commission of any predicate offense, or is a party to the predicate offense;

(ii) a person other than a party as defined in Section 76-2-202 is killed in the course of the commission, attempted commission, or immediate flight from the commission or attempted commission of any predicate offense; and

(iii) the actor acted with the intent required as an element of the predicate offense;

(e) the actor recklessly causes the death of a peace officer while in the commission or attempted commission of:

(i) an assault against a peace officer under Section 76-5-102.4; or

(ii) interference with a peace officer while making a lawful arrest under Section 76-8-

305 if the actor uses force against a peace officer;

(f) commits a homicide which would be aggravated murder, but the offense is reduced pursuant to Subsection 76-5-202(3); or

(g) the actor commits aggravated murder, but special mitigation is established under Section 76-5-205.5.

(3) Murder is a first degree felony.

(4) (a) It is an affirmative defense to a charge of murder or attempted murder that the defendant caused the death of another or attempted to cause the death of another:

(i) under the influence of extreme emotional distress for which there is a reasonable explanation or excuse; or

(ii) under a reasonable belief that the circumstances provided a legal justification or excuse for his conduct although the conduct was not legally justifiable or excusable under the existing circumstances.

(b) Under Subsection (4)(a)(i) emotional distress does not include:

(i) a condition resulting from mental illness as defined in Section 76-2-305; or

(ii) distress that is substantially caused by the defendant's own conduct.

(c) The reasonableness of an explanation or excuse under Subsection (4)(a)(i) or the reasonable belief of the actor under Subsection (4)(a)(ii) shall be determined from the viewpoint of a reasonable person under the then existing circumstances.

(d) This affirmative defense reduces charges only as follows:

(i) murder to manslaughter; and

(ii) attempted murder to attempted manslaughter.   2003

76-5-204. Death of other than intended victim no defense.

In any prosecution for criminal homicide, evidence that the actor caused the death of a person other than the intended victim shall not constitute a defense for any purpose to criminal homicide.   1973

76-5-205. Manslaughter.

(1) Criminal homicide constitutes manslaughter if the actor:

(a) recklessly causes the death of another;

(b) commits a homicide which would be murder, but the offense is reduced pursuant to Subsection 76-5-203(4); or

(c) commits murder, but special mitigation is established under Section 76-5-205.5.

(2) Manslaughter is a felony of the second degree.   2001 (1st S.S.)

76-5-205.5. Special mitigation reducing the level of criminal homicide offense — Burden of proof — Application to reduce offense.

(1) Special mitigation exists when:

(a) the actor causes the death of another under circumstances that are not legally justified, but the actor acts under a delusion attributable to a mental illness as defined in Section 76-2-305; and

(b) the nature of the delusion is such that, if the facts existed as the defendant believed them to be in his delusional state, those facts would provide a legal justification for his conduct.

(2) This section applies only if the defendant's actions, in light of his delusion, were reasonable from the objective viewpoint of a reasonable person.

(3) A defendant who was under the influence of voluntarily consumed, injected, or ingested alcohol, controlled substances, or volatile substances at the time of the alleged offense may not claim mitigation of the offense under this section on the basis of mental illness if the alcohol or substance caused, triggered, or substantially contributed to the mental illness.

(4) (a) If the trier of fact finds the elements of an offense as listed in Subsection (4)(b) are proven beyond a reasonable doubt, and also that the existence of special mitigation under this section is established by a preponderance of the evidence, it shall return a verdict on the reduced charge as provided in Subsection (4)(b).

(b) If under Subsection (4)(a) the offense is:

(i) aggravated murder, the defendant shall instead be found guilty of murder;

(ii) attempted aggravated murder, the defendant shall instead be found guilty of attempted murder;

(iii) murder, the defendant shall instead be found guilty of manslaughter; or

(iv) attempted murder, the defendant shall instead be found guilty of attempted manslaughter.

(5) (a) If a jury is the trier of fact, a unanimous vote of the jury is required to establish the existence of the special mitigation.

(b) If the jury does find special mitigation by a unanimous vote, it shall return a verdict on the reduced charge as provided in Subsection (4).

(c) If the jury finds by a unanimous vote that special mitigation has not been established, it shall convict the defendant of the greater offense for which the prosecution has established all the elements beyond a reasonable doubt.

(d) If the jury is unable to unanimously agree whether or not special mitigation has been established, the result is a hung jury.

(6) (a) If the issue of special mitigation is submitted to the trier of fact, it shall return a special verdict indicating whether the existence of special mitigation has been found.

(b) The trier of fact shall return the special verdict at the same time as the general verdict, to indicate the basis for its general verdict.

(7) Special mitigation under this section does not, in any case, reduce the level of an offense by more than one degree from that offense, the elements of which the evidence has established beyond a reasonable doubt.   1999

76-5-206. Negligent homicide.

(1) Criminal homicide constitutes negligent homicide if the actor, acting with criminal negligence, causes the death of another.

(2) Negligent homicide is a class A misdemeanor.   1973

76-5-207. Automobile homicide.

(1) As used in this section, "motor vehicle" means any self-propelled vehicle and includes any automobile, truck, van, motorcycle, train, engine, watercraft, or aircraft.

(2) (a) Criminal homicide is automobile homicide, a third degree felony, if the person operates a motor vehicle in a negligent manner causing the death of another and:

(i) has sufficient alcohol in his body that a subsequent chemical test shows that the person has a blood or breath alcohol concentration of .08 grams or greater at the time of the test;

(ii) is under the influence of alcohol, any drug, or the combined influence of alcohol and any drug to a degree that renders the person incapable of safely operating a vehicle; or

(iii) has a blood or breath alcohol concentration of .08 grams or greater at the time of operation.

(b) A conviction for a violation of this Subsection (2) is a second degree felony if it is subsequent to a conviction as defined in Subsection 41-6a-502(2).

(c) As used in this Subsection (2), "negligent" means simple negligence, the failure to exercise that degree of care that reasonable and prudent persons exercise under like or similar circumstances.

(3) (a) Criminal homicide is automobile homicide, a second degree felony, if the person operates a motor vehicle in a criminally negligent manner causing the death of another and:

(i) has sufficient alcohol in his body that a subsequent chemical test shows that the person has a blood or breath alcohol concentration of .08 grams or greater at the time of the test;

(ii) is under the influence of alcohol, any drug, or the combined influence of alcohol and any drug to a degree that renders the person incapable of safely operating a vehicle; or

(iii) has a blood or breath alcohol concentration of .08 grams or greater at the time of operation.

(b) As used in this Subsection (3), "criminally negligent" means criminal negligence as defined by Subsection 76-2-103(4).

(4) The standards for chemical breath analysis as provided by Section 41-6a-515 and the provisions for the admissibility of chemical test results as provided by Section 41-6a-516 apply to determination and proof of blood alcohol content under this section.

(5) Calculations of blood or breath alcohol concentration under this section shall be made in accordance with Subsection 41-6a-502(1).

(6) The fact that a person charged with violating this section is or has been legally entitled to use alcohol or a drug is not a defense.

(7) Evidence of a defendant's blood or breath alcohol content or drug content is admissible except when prohibited by Rules of Evidence or the constitution.

2005

76-5-208. Child abuse homicide.

(1) Criminal homicide constitutes child abuse homicide if the actor causes the death of a person under 18 years of age and the death results from child abuse, as defined in Subsection 76-5-109(1):

(a) if done recklessly as provided in Subsection 76-5-109(2)(b);

(b) if done with criminal negligence as provided in Subsection 76-5-109(2)(c); or

(c) if done with the mental culpability as provided in Subsection 76-5-109(3)(a), (b), or (c).

(2) Child abuse homicide as described in Subsection (1)(a) is a second degree felony.

(3) Child abuse homicide as described in Subsections (1)(b) and (c) is a third degree felony.   2000

76-5-209. Homicide by assault — Penalty.

(1) A person commits homicide by assault if, under circumstances not amounting to aggravated murder, murder, or manslaughter, a person causes the death of another while intentionally or knowingly attempting, with unlawful force or violence, to do bodily injury to another.

(2) Homicide by assault is a third degree felony.

1995

PART 3

KIDNAPPING

76-5-301. Kidnapping.

(1) An actor commits kidnapping if the actor intentionally or knowingly, without authority of law, and against the will of the victim:

(a) detains or restrains the victim for any substantial period of time;

(b) detains or restrains the victim in circumstances exposing the victim to risk of bodily injury;

(c) holds the victim in involuntary servitude;

(d) detains or restrains a minor without the consent of the minor's parent or legal guardian or the consent of a person acting in loco parentis, if the minor is 14 years of age or older but younger than 18 years of age; or

(e) moves the victim any substantial distance or across a state line.

(2) As used in this section, acting "against the will of the victim" includes acting without the consent of the legal guardian or custodian of a victim who is a mentally incompetent person.

(3) Kidnapping is a second degree felony.   2001

76-5-301.1. Child kidnapping.

(1) An actor commits child kidnapping if the actor intentionally or knowingly, without authority of law, and by any means and in any manner, seizes, confines, detains, or transports a child under the age of 14 without the consent of the victim's parent or guardian, or the consent of a person acting in loco parentis.

(2) Violation of Section 76-5-303 is not a violation of this section.

(3) Child kidnapping is a first degree felony punishable by imprisonment for an indeterminate term of not less than 6, 10, or 15 years and which may be for life. Imprisonment is mandatory in accordance with Section 76-3-406.   2001

76-5-302. Aggravated kidnapping.

(1) An actor commits aggravated kidnapping if the actor, in the course of committing unlawful detention or kidnapping:

(a) possesses, uses, or threatens to use a dangerous weapon as defined in Section 76-1-601; or

(b) acts with intent:

(i) to hold the victim for ransom or reward, or as a shield or hostage, or to compel a third person to engage in particular conduct or to forbear from engaging in particular conduct;

(ii) to facilitate the commission, attempted commission, or flight after commission or attempted commission of a felony;

(iii) to hinder or delay the discovery of or reporting of a felony;

(iv) to inflict bodily injury on or to terrorize the victim or another;

(v) to interfere with the performance of any governmental or political function; or

(vi) to commit a sexual offense as described in Title 76, Chapter 5, Part 4, Sexual Offenses.

(2) As used in this section, "in the course of committing unlawful detention or kidnapping" means in the course of committing, attempting to commit, or in

the immediate flight after the attempt or commission of a violation of:

    (a) Section 76-5-301, kidnapping; or

    (b) Section 76-5-304, unlawful detention.

(3) Aggravated kidnapping is a first degree felony punishable by imprisonment for an indeterminate term of not less than 6, 10, or 15 years and which may be for life. Imprisonment is mandatory in accordance with Section 76-3-406.   2001

76-5-303. Custodial interference.

(1) A person, whether a parent or other, is guilty of custodial interference if, without good cause, the actor takes, entices, conceals, or detains a child under the age of 16 from its parent, guardian, or other lawful custodian:

    (a) knowing the actor has no legal right to do so; and

    (b) with intent to hold the child for a period substantially longer than the parent-time or custody period previously awarded by a court of competent jurisdiction.

(2) A person, whether a parent or other, is guilty of custodial interference if, having actual physical custody of a child under the age of 16 pursuant to a judicial award of any court of competent jurisdiction which grants to another person parent-time, visitation, or custody rights, and without good cause the actor conceals or detains the child with intent to deprive the other person of lawful parent-time, visitation, or custody rights.

(3) Custodial interference is a class A misdemeanor unless the child is removed and taken from one state to another, in which case it is a felony of the third degree.   2001

76-5-304. Unlawful detention.

(1) An actor commits unlawful detention if the actor intentionally or knowingly, without authority of law, and against the will of the victim, detains or restrains the victim under circumstances not constituting a violation of:

    (a) kidnapping, Section 76-5-301;

    (b) child kidnapping, Section 76-5-301.1; or

    (c) aggravated kidnapping, Section 76-5-302.

(2) As used in this section, acting "against the will of the victim" includes acting without the consent of the legal guardian or custodian of a victim who is a mentally incompetent person.

(3) Unlawful detention is a class B misdemeanor.   2001

76-5-305. Defenses.

It is a defense under this part that:

    (1) the actor was acting under a reasonable belief that:

        (a) the conduct was necessary to protect any person from imminent bodily injury or death; or

        (b) the detention or restraint was authorized by law; or

    (2) the alleged victim is younger than 18 years of age or is mentally incompetent, and the actor was acting under a reasonable belief that the custodian, guardian, legal guardian, custodial parent, or person acting in loco parentis to the victim would, if present, have consented to the actor's conduct.   2001

76-5-306. Lesser included offenses.

In this part, the following offenses are lesser included offenses of Section 76-5-302, aggravated kidnapping:

    (1) Section 76-5-301, kidnapping; and

    (2) Section 76-5-304, unlawful detention.   2001

PART 4

SEXUAL OFFENSES

76-5-401. Unlawful sexual activity with a minor — Elements — Penalties — Evidence of age raised by defendant.

(1) For purposes of this section "minor" is a person who is 14 years of age or older, but younger than 16 years of age, at the time the sexual activity described in this section occurred.

(2) A person commits unlawful sexual activity with a minor if, under circumstances not amounting to rape, in violation of Section 76-5-402, object rape, in violation of Section 76-5-402.2, forcible sodomy, in violation of Section 76-5-403, or aggravated sexual assault, in violation of Section 76-5-405, the actor:

    (a) has sexual intercourse with the minor;

    (b) engages in any sexual act with the minor involving the genitals of one person and the mouth or anus of another person, regardless of the sex of either participant; or

    (c) causes the penetration, however slight, of the genital or anal opening of the minor by any foreign object, substance, instrument, or device, including a part of the human body, with the intent to cause substantial emotional or bodily pain to any person or with the intent to arouse or gratify the sexual desire of any person, regardless of the sex of any participant.

(3) A violation of Subsection (2) is a third degree felony unless the defendant establishes by a preponderance of the evidence the mitigating factor that the defendant is less than four years older than the minor at the time the sexual activity occurred, in which case it is a class B misdemeanor.   1998

76-5-401.1. Sexual abuse of a minor.

(1) For purposes of this section "minor" is a person who is 14 years of age or older, but younger than 16 years of age, at the time the sexual activity described in this section occurred.

(2) A person commits sexual abuse of a minor if the person is seven years or more older than the minor and, under circumstances not amounting to rape, in violation of Section 76-5-402, object rape, in violation of Section 76-5-402.2, forcible sodomy, in violation of Section 76-5-403, aggravated sexual assault, in violation of Section 76-5-405, unlawful sexual activity with a minor, in violation of Section 76-5-401, or an attempt to commit any of those offenses, the person touches the anus, buttocks, or any part of the genitals of the minor, or touches the breast of a female minor, or otherwise takes indecent liberties with the minor, or causes a minor to take indecent liberties with the actor or another person, with the intent to cause substantial emotional or bodily pain to any person or with the intent to arouse or gratify the sexual desire of any person regardless of the sex of any participant.

(3) A violation of this section is a class A misdemeanor.   1998

76-5-401.2. Unlawful sexual conduct with a 16 or 17 year old.

(1) For purposes of this section "minor" means a person who is 16 years of age or older, but younger than 18 years of age, at the time the sexual conduct described in this section occurred.

(2) A person commits unlawful sexual conduct with a minor if, under circumstances not amounting to rape, in violation of Section 76-5-402, object rape, in

violation of Section 76-5-402.2, forcible sodomy, in violation of Section 76-5-403, or aggravated sexual assault, in violation of Section 76-5-405, the actor who is ten or more years older than the minor at the time of the sexual conduct:

(a) has sexual intercourse with the minor;

(b) engages in any sexual act with the minor involving the genitals of one person and the mouth or anus of another person, regardless of the sex of either participant; or

(c) causes the penetration, however slight, of the genital or anal opening of the minor by any foreign object, substance, instrument, or device, including a part of the human body, with the intent to cause substantial emotional or bodily pain to any person or with the intent to arouse or gratify the sexual desire of any person, regardless of the sex of any participant.

(3) A violation of Subsection (2) is a third degree felony.   1998

76-5-402. Rape.

(1) A person commits rape when the actor has sexual intercourse with another person without the victim's consent.

(2) This section applies whether or not the actor is married to the victim.

(3) Rape is a felony of the first degree.   1991

76-5-402.1. Rape of a child.

(1) A person commits rape of a child when the person has sexual intercourse with a child who is under the age of 14.

(2) Rape of a child is a first degree felony punishable by imprisonment for an indeterminate term of not less than 6, 10, or 15 years and which may be for life. Imprisonment is mandatory in accordance with Section 76-3-406.   1996

76-5-402.2. Object rape.

A person who, without the victim's consent, causes the penetration, however slight, of the genital or anal opening of another person who is 14 years of age or older, by any foreign object, substance, instrument, or device, not including a part of the human body, with intent to cause substantial emotional or bodily pain to the victim or with the intent to arouse or gratify the sexual desire of any person, commits an offense which is punishable as a felony of the first degree.   1984

76-5-402.3. Object rape of a child — Penalty.

(1) A person commits object rape of a child when the person causes the penetration or touching, however slight, of the genital or anal opening of a child who is under the age of 14 by any foreign object, substance, instrument, or device, not including a part of the human body, with intent to cause substantial emotional or bodily pain to the child or with the intent to arouse or gratify the sexual desire of any person.

(2) (a) Object rape of a child is a first degree felony punishable by imprisonment for an indeterminate term of not less than 6, 10, or 15 years and which may be for life.

(b) Imprisonment is mandatory in accordance with Section 76-3-406.   2000

76-5-403. Sodomy — Forcible sodomy.

(1) A person commits sodomy when the actor engages in any sexual act with a person who is 14 years of age or older involving the genitals of one person and mouth or anus of another person, regardless of the sex of either participant.

(2) A person commits forcible sodomy when the actor commits sodomy upon another without the other's consent.

(3) Sodomy is a class B misdemeanor. Forcible sodomy is a felony of the first degree.   1983

76-5-403.1. Sodomy on a child.

(1) A person commits sodomy upon a child if the actor engages in any sexual act upon or with a child who is under the age of 14, involving the genitals or anus of the actor or the child and the mouth or anus of either person, regardless of the sex of either participant.

(2) Sodomy upon a child is a first degree felony punishable by imprisonment for an indeterminate term of not less than 6, 10, or 15 years and which may be for life. Imprisonment is mandatory in accordance with Section 76-3-406.   1996

76-5-404. Forcible sexual abuse.

(1) A person commits forcible sexual abuse if the victim is 14 years of age or older and, under circumstances not amounting to rape, object rape, sodomy, or attempted rape or sodomy, the actor touches the anus, buttocks, or any part of the genitals of another, or touches the breast of a female, or otherwise takes indecent liberties with another, or causes another to take indecent liberties with the actor or another, with intent to cause substantial emotional or bodily pain to any person or with the intent to arouse or gratify the sexual desire of any person, without the consent of the other, regardless of the sex of any participant.

(2) Forcible sexual abuse is a felony of the second degree.   1984

76-5-404.1. Sexual abuse of a child — Aggravated sexual abuse of a child.

(1) As used in this section, "child" means a person under the age of 14.

(2) A person commits sexual abuse of a child if, under circumstances not amounting to rape of a child, object rape of a child, sodomy upon a child, or an attempt to commit any of these offenses, the actor touches the anus, buttocks, or genitalia of any child, the breast of a female child, or otherwise takes indecent liberties with a child, or causes a child to take indecent liberties with the actor or another with intent to cause substantial emotional or bodily pain to any person or with the intent to arouse or gratify the sexual desire of any person regardless of the sex of any participant.

(3) Sexual abuse of a child is punishable as a second degree felony.

(4) A person commits aggravated sexual abuse of a child when in conjunction with the offense described in Subsection (2) any of the following circumstances have been charged and admitted or found true in the action for the offense:

(a) the offense was committed by the use of a dangerous weapon as defined in Section 76-1-601, or by force, duress, violence, intimidation, coercion, menace, or threat of harm, or was committed during the course of a kidnaping;

(b) the accused caused bodily injury or severe psychological injury to the victim during or as a result of the offense;

(c) the accused was a stranger to the victim or made friends with the victim for the purpose of committing the offense;

(d) the accused used, showed, or displayed pornography or caused the victim to be photographed in a lewd condition during the course of the offense;

(e) the accused, prior to sentencing for this offense, was previously convicted of any felony, or of a misdemeanor involving a sexual offense;

(f) the accused committed the same or similar sexual act upon two or more victims at the same time or during the same course of conduct;

(g) the accused committed, in Utah or elsewhere, more than five separate acts, which if committed in Utah would constitute an offense described in this chapter, and were committed at the same time, or during the same course of conduct, or before or after the instant offense;

(h) the offense was committed by a person who occupied a position of special trust in relation to the victim; "position of special trust" means that position occupied by a person in a position of authority, who, by reason of that position is able to exercise undue influence over the victim, and includes, but is not limited to, a youth leader or recreational leader who is an adult, adult athletic manager, adult coach, teacher, counselor, religious leader, doctor, employer, foster parent, baby-sitter, adult scout leader, natural parent, stepparent, adoptive parent, legal guardian, grandparent, aunt, uncle, or adult cohabitant of a parent;

(i) the accused encouraged, aided, allowed, or benefited from acts of prostitution or sexual acts by the victim with any other person, or sexual performance by the victim before any other person; or

(j) the accused caused the penetration, however slight, of the genital or anal opening of the child by any part or parts of the human body other than the genitals or mouth.

(5) Aggravated sexual abuse of a child is a first degree felony punishable by imprisonment for an indeterminate term of not less than five years and which may be for life. Imprisonment is mandatory in accordance with Section 76-3-406.　　　2003

76-5-405. Aggravated sexual assault — Penalty.

(1) A person commits aggravated sexual assault if in the course of a rape or attempted rape, object rape or attempted object rape, forcible sodomy or attempted forcible sodomy, or forcible sexual abuse or attempted forcible sexual abuse the actor:

(a) causes bodily injury to the victim;

(b) uses or threatens the victim with use of a dangerous weapon as defined in Section 76-1-601;

(c) compels, or attempts to compel, the victim to submit to rape, object rape, forcible sodomy, or forcible sexual abuse, by threat of kidnaping, death, or serious bodily injury to be inflicted imminently on any person; or

(d) is aided or abetted by one or more persons.

(2) Aggravated sexual assault is a first degree felony punishable by imprisonment for an indeterminate term of not less than 6, 10, or 15 years and which may be for life. Imprisonment is mandatory in accordance with Section 76-3-406.　　　1997

76-5-406. Sexual offenses against the victim without consent of victim — Circumstances.

An act of sexual intercourse, rape, attempted rape, rape of a child, attempted rape of a child, object rape, attempted object rape, object rape of a child, attempted object rape of a child, sodomy, attempted sodomy, forcible sodomy, attempted forcible sodomy, sodomy upon a child, attempted sodomy upon a child, forcible sexual abuse, attempted forcible sexual abuse, sexual abuse of a child, attempted sexual abuse of a child, aggravated sexual abuse of a child, attempted aggravated sexual abuse of a child, or simple sexual abuse is without consent of the victim under any of the following circumstances:

(1) the victim expresses lack of consent through words or conduct;

(2) the actor overcomes the victim through the actual application of physical force or violence;

(3) the actor is able to overcome the victim through concealment or by the element of surprise;

(4) (a) (i) the actor coerces the victim to submit by threatening to retaliate in the immediate future against the victim or any other person, and the victim perceives at the time that the actor has the ability to execute this threat; or

(ii) the actor coerces the victim to submit by threatening to retaliate in the future against the victim or any other person, and the victim believes at the time that the actor has the ability to execute this threat;

(b) as used in this Subsection (4) "to retaliate" includes but is not limited to threats of physical force, kidnaping, or extortion;

(5) the victim has not consented and the actor knows the victim is unconscious, unaware that the act is occurring, or physically unable to resist;

(6) the actor knows that as a result of mental disease or defect, the victim is at the time of the act incapable either of appraising the nature of the act or of resisting it;

(7) the actor knows that the victim submits or participates because the victim erroneously believes that the actor is the victim's spouse;

(8) the actor intentionally impaired the power of the victim to appraise or control his or her conduct by administering any substance without the victim's knowledge;

(9) the victim is younger than 14 years of age;

(10) the victim is younger than 18 years of age and at the time of the offense the actor was the victim's parent, stepparent, adoptive parent, or legal guardian or occupied a position of special trust in relation to the victim as defined in Subsection 76-5-404.1(4)(h);

(11) the victim is 14 years of age or older, but younger than 18 years of age, and the actor is more than three years older than the victim and entices or coerces the victim to submit or participate, under circumstances not amounting to the force or threat required under Subsection (2) or (4); or

(12) the actor is a health professional or religious counselor, as those terms are defined in this Subsection (12), the act is committed under the guise of providing professional diagnosis, counseling, or treatment, and at the time of the act the victim reasonably believed that the act was for medically or professionally appropriate diagnosis, counseling, or treatment to the extent that resistance by the victim could not reasonably be expected to have been manifested. For purposes of this Subsection (12):

(a) "health professional" means an individual who is licensed or who holds himself out to be licensed, or who otherwise provides professional physical or mental health services, diagnosis, treatment, or counseling including, but not limited to, a physician, osteopathic physician, nurse, dentist, physical therapist, chiropractor, mental health therapist, social service worker, clinical social worker, certified social worker, marriage and family therapist, professional counselor, psychiatrist, psychologist, psychiatric mental health nurse specialist, or substance abuse counselor; and

(b) "religious counselor" means a minister, priest, rabbi, bishop, or other recognized member of the clergy. **2003**

76-5-406.3. Applicability of sentencing provisions.

A person convicted of a violation of Section 76-5-301.1, child kidnaping; Section 76-5-302, aggravated kidnaping; Section 76-5-402.1, rape of a child; Section 76-5-402.3, object rape of a child; Section 76-5-403.1, sodomy on a child; Section 76-5-404.1, aggravated sexual abuse of a child; or Section 76-5-405, aggravated sexual assault shall be sentenced as follows:

(1) If the person is sentenced prior to April 29, 1996, he shall be sentenced in accordance with the statutory provisions in effect prior to that date.

(2) If the person commits the crime and is sentenced on or after April 29, 1996, he shall be punished in accordance with the statutory provisions in effect after April 29, 1996.

(3) If the person commits the crime prior to April 29, 1996, but is sentenced on or after April 29, 1996, he shall be given the option prior to sentencing to proceed either under the law which was in effect at the time the offense was committed or the law which was in effect at the time of sentencing. If the person refuses to select, the court shall sentence the person in accordance with the law in effect at the time of sentencing. The provisions of Subsections 77-27-9(2)(a) and (b) apply to the sentence of any person who selects under this section to be sentenced in accordance with the law in effect prior to April 29, 1996. **1996**

76-5-406.5. Circumstances required for probation or suspension of sentence for certain sex offenses against a child.

(1) In a case involving a conviction for a violation of Section 76-5-402.1, rape of a child; Section 76-5-402.3, object rape of a child; Section 76-5-403.1, sodomy on a child; or any attempt to commit a felony under those sections or a conviction for a violation of Subsections 76-5-404.1(4) and (5), aggravated sexual abuse of a child, the court may suspend execution of sentence and consider probation to a residential sexual abuse treatment center only if all of the following circumstances are found by the court to be present and the court in its discretion, considering the circumstances of the offense, including the nature, frequency, and duration of the conduct, and considering the best interests of the public and the child victim, finds probation to a residential sexual abuse treatment center to be proper:

(a) the defendant did not use a weapon, force, violence, substantial duress or menace, or threat of harm, in committing the offense or before or after committing the offense, in an attempt to frighten the child victim or keep the child victim from reporting the offense;

(b) the defendant did not cause bodily injury to the child victim during or as a result of the offense and did not cause the child victim severe psychological harm;

(c) the defendant, prior to the offense, had not been convicted of any public offense in Utah or elsewhere involving sexual misconduct in the commission of the offense;

(d) the defendant did not commit an offense described in this Part 4, Sexual Offenses, against more than one child victim or victim, at the same time, or during the same course of conduct, or previous to or subsequent to the instant offense;

(e) the defendant did not use, show, or display pornography or create sexually-related photographs or tape recordings in the course of the offense;

(f) the defendant did not act in concert with another offender during the offense or knowingly commit the offense in the presence of a person other than the victim or with lewd intent to reveal the offense to another;

(g) the defendant did not encourage, aid, allow, or benefit from any act of prostitution or sexual act by the child victim with any other person or sexual performance by the child victim before any other person;

(h) the defendant admits the offense of which he has been convicted and has been accepted for mental health treatment in a residential sexual abuse treatment center that has been approved by the Department of Corrections under Subsection (3);

(i) rehabilitation of the defendant through treatment is probable, based upon evidence provided by a treatment professional who has been approved by the Department of Corrections under Subsection (3) and who has accepted the defendant for treatment;

(j) prior to being sentenced, the defendant has undergone a complete psychological evaluation conducted by a professional approved by the Department of Corrections and:

(i) the professional's opinion is that the defendant is not an exclusive pedophile and does not present an immediate and present danger to the community if released on probation and placed in a residential sexual abuse treatment center; and

(ii) the court accepts the opinion of the professional;

(k) if the offense is committed by a parent, stepparent, adoptive parent, or legal guardian of the child victim, the defendant shall, in addition to establishing all other conditions of this section, establish it is in the child victim's best interest that the defendant not be imprisoned, by presenting evidence provided by a treatment professional who:

(i) is treating the child victim and understands he will be treating the family as a whole; or

(ii) has assessed the child victim for purposes of treatment as ordered by the court based on a showing of good cause; and

(l) if probation is imposed, the defendant, as a condition of probation, may not reside in a home where children younger than 18 years of age reside for at least one year beginning with the commencement of treatment, and may not again take up residency in a home where children younger than 18 years of age reside during the period of probation until allowed to do so by order of the court.

(2) A term of incarceration of at least 90 days is to be served prior to treatment and continue until the

time when bed space is available at a residential sexual abuse treatment center as provided under Subsection (3) and probation is to be imposed for up to a maximum of ten years.

(3) (a) The Department of Corrections shall develop qualification criteria for the approval of the sexual abuse treatment programs and professionals under this section. The criteria shall include the screening criteria employed by the department for sexual offenders.

(b) The sexual abuse treatment program shall be at least one year in duration, shall be residential, and shall specifically address the sexual conduct for which the defendant was convicted.

(4) Establishment by the defendant of all the criteria of this section does not mandate the granting under this section of probation or modification of the sentence that would otherwise be imposed by Section 76-3-406 regarding sexual offenses against children. The court has discretion to deny the request based upon its consideration of the circumstances of the offense, including:

(a) the nature, frequency, and duration of the conduct;

(b) the effects of the conduct on any child victim involved;

(c) the best interest of the public and any child victim; and

(d) the characteristics of the defendant, including any risk the defendant presents to the public and specifically to children.

(5) The defendant has the burden to establish by a preponderance of evidence eligibility under all of the criteria of this section.

(6) If the court finds a defendant granted probation under this section fails to cooperate or succeed in treatment or violates probation to any substantial degree, the sentence previously imposed for the offense shall be immediately executed.

(7) The court shall enter written findings of fact regarding the conditions established by the defendant that justify the granting of probation under this section.

(8) In cases involving conviction of any sexual offense against a child other than those offenses provided in Subsection (1), the court shall consider the circumstances described in Subsection (1) as advisory in determining whether or not execution of sentence should be suspended and probation granted. The defendant is not required to satisfy all of those circumstances for eligibility pursuant to this Subsection (8).   2004

76-5-407.   Applicability of part — "Penetration" or "touching" sufficient to constitute offense.

(1) The provisions of this part do not apply to consensual conduct between persons married to each other.

(2) In any prosecution for:

(a) the following offenses, any sexual penetration, however slight, is sufficient to constitute the relevant element of the offense:

(i) unlawful sexual activity with a minor, a violation of Section 76-5-401, involving sexual intercourse;

(ii) unlawful sexual conduct with a 16 or 17 year old, a violation of Subsection 76-5-401.2, involving sexual intercourse; or

(iii) rape, a violation of Section 76-5-402; or

(b) the following offenses, any touching, however slight, is sufficient to constitute the relevant element of the offense:

(i) unlawful sexual activity with a minor, a violation of Section 76-5-401, involving acts of sodomy;

(ii) unlawful sexual conduct with a 16 or 17 year old, a violation of Section 76-5-401.2, involving acts of sodomy;

(iii) sodomy, a violation of Subsection 76-5-403(1);

(iv) forcible sodomy, a violation of Subsection 76-5-403(2);

(v) rape of a child, a violation of Section 76-5-402.1; or

(vi) object rape of a child, a violation of Section 76-5-402.3.

(3) In any prosecution for the following offenses, any touching, even if accomplished through clothing, is sufficient to constitute the relevant element of the offense:

(a) sodomy on a child, a violation of Section 76-5-403.1; or

(b) sexual abuse of a child or aggravated sexual abuse of a child, a violation of Section 76-5-404.1.
                                                    2000

76-5-408.   Reserved.

76-5-409.   Corroboration of admission by child's statement.

(1) Notwithstanding any provision of law requiring corroboration of admissions or confessions, and notwithstanding any prohibition of hearsay evidence, a child's statement indicating in any manner the occurrence of the sexual offense involving the child is sufficient corroboration of the admission or the confession regardless of whether or not the child is available to testify regarding the offense.

(2) A child, for purposes of Subsection (1), is a person under the age of 14.   1983

76-5-410.   Child victim of sexual abuse as competent witness.

A child victim of sexual abuse under the age of ten is a competent witness and shall be allowed to testify without prior qualification in any judicial proceeding. The trier of fact shall determine the weight and credibility of the testimony.   1985

76-5-411.   Admissibility of out-of-court statement of child victim of sexual abuse.

(1) Notwithstanding any rule of evidence, a child victim's out-of-court statement regarding sexual abuse of that child is admissible as evidence although it does not qualify under an existing hearsay exception, if:

(a) the child is available to testify in court or under Rule 15.5(2) or (3), Utah Rules of Criminal Procedure;

(b) if the child is not available to testify in court or under Rule 15.5(2) or (3), Utah Rules of Criminal Procedure, there is other corroborative evidence of the abuse; or

(c) the statement qualifies for admission under Rule 15.5(1), Utah Rules of Criminal Procedure.

(2) Prior to admission of any statement into evidence under this section, the judge shall determine whether the interest of justice will best be served by admission of that statement. In making this determination the judge shall consider the age and maturity of the child, the nature and duration of the abuse, the

relationship of the child to the offender, and the reliability of the assertion and of the child.

(3) A statement admitted under this section shall be made available to the adverse party sufficiently in advance of the trial or proceeding, to provide him with an opportunity to prepare to meet it.

(4) For purposes of this section, a child is a person under the age of 14 years.   1989

76-5-412. Custodial sexual relations — Custodial sexual misconduct — Definitions — Penalties — Defenses.

(1) As used in this section:

  (a) "Actor" means:

    (i) a correctional officer, as defined in Section 53-13-104;

    (ii) a law enforcement officer, as defined in Section 53-13-103; or

    (iii) an employee of, or private provider or contractor for, the Department of Corrections or a county jail.

  (b) "Person in custody" means a person, either an adult 18 years of age or older, or a minor younger than 18 years of age, who is:

    (i) a prisoner, as defined in Section 76-5-101, and includes a prisoner who is in the custody of the Department of Corrections created under Section 64-13-2, but who is being housed at the Utah State Hospital established under Section 62A-15-601 or other medical facility;

    (ii) under correctional supervision, such as at a work release facility or as a parolee or probationer; or

    (iii) under lawful or unlawful arrest, either with or without a warrant.

  (c) "Private provider or contractor" means any person or entity that contracts with the Department of Corrections or with a county jail to provide services or functions that are part of the operation of the Department of Corrections or a county jail under state or local law.

(2) (a) An actor commits custodial sexual relations if the actor commits any of the acts under Subsection (3):

    (i) under circumstances not amounting to commission of, or an attempt to commit, an offense under Subsection (6); and

    (ii) (A) the actor knows that the individual is a person in custody; or

      (B) a reasonable person in the actor's position should have known under the circumstances that the individual was a person in custody.

  (b) A violation of Subsection (2)(a) is a third degree felony, but if the person in custody is younger than 18 years of age, a violation of Subsection (2)(a) is a second degree felony.

  (c) If the act committed under this Subsection (2) amounts to an offense subject to a greater penalty under another provision of state law than is provided under this Subsection (2), this Subsection (2) does not prohibit prosecution and sentencing for the more serious offense.

(3) Acts referred to in Subsection (2)(a) are:

  (a) having sexual intercourse with a person in custody;

  (b) engaging in any sexual act with a person in custody involving the genitals of one person and the mouth or anus of another person, regardless of the sex of either participant; or

  (c) causing the penetration, however slight, of the genital or anal opening of a person in custody by any foreign object, substance, instrument, or device, including a part of the human body, with the intent to cause substantial emotional or bodily pain to any person, regardless of the sex of any participant.

(4) (a) An actor commits custodial sexual misconduct if the actor commits any of the acts under Subsection (5):

    (i) under circumstances not amounting to commission of, or an attempt to commit, an offense under Subsection (6); and

    (ii) (A) the actor knows that the individual is a person in custody; or

      (B) a reasonable person in the actor's position should have known under the circumstances that the individual was a person in custody.

  (b) A violation of Subsection (4)(a) is a class A misdemeanor, but if the person in custody is younger than 18 years of age, a violation of Subsection (4)(a) is a third degree felony.

  (c) If the act committed under this Subsection (4) amounts to an offense subject to a greater penalty under another provision of state law than is provided under this Subsection (4), this Subsection (4) does not prohibit prosecution and sentencing for the more serious offense.

(5) Acts referred to in Subsection (4)(a) are the following acts when committed with the intent to cause substantial emotional or bodily pain to any person or with the intent to arouse or gratify the sexual desire of any person, regardless of the sex of any participant:

  (a) touching the anus, buttocks, or any part of the genitals of a person in custody;

  (b) touching the breast of a female person in custody;

  (c) otherwise taking indecent liberties with a person in custody; or

  (d) causing a person in custody to take indecent liberties with the actor or another person.

(6) The offenses referred to in Subsections (2)(a)(i) and (4)(a)(i) are:

  (a) Section 76-5-401, unlawful sexual activity with a minor;

  (b) Section 76-5-402, rape;

  (c) Section 76-5-402.1, rape of a child;

  (d) Section 76-5-402.2, object rape;

  (e) Section 76-5-402.3, object rape of a child;

  (f) Section 76-5-403, forcible sodomy;

  (g) Section 76-5-403.1, sodomy on a child;

  (h) Section 76-5-404, forcible sexual abuse;

  (i) Section 76-5-404.1, sexual abuse of a child or aggravated sexual abuse of a child; or

  (j) Section 76-5-405, aggravated sexual assault.

(7) (a) It is not a defense to the commission of the offense of custodial sexual relations under Subsection (2) or custodial sexual misconduct under Subsection (4), or an attempt to commit either of these offenses, if the person in custody is younger than 18 years of age, that the actor:

    (i) mistakenly believed the person in custody to be 18 years of age or older at the time of the alleged offense; or

    (ii) was unaware of the true age of the person in custody.

  (b) Consent of the person in custody is not a defense to any violation or attempted violation of Subsection (2) or (4).

(8) It is a defense that the commission by the actor of an act under Subsection (2) or (4) is the result of compulsion, as the defense is described in Subsection 76-2-302(1).   2002 (5th S.S.)

**76-5-413. Custodial sexual relations or miscon-
        duct with youth receiving state ser-
        vices — Definitions — Penalties — De-
        fenses.**

(1) As used in this section:

(a) "Actor" means:

(i) a person employed by the Department of Human Services, as created in Section 62A-1-102, or an employee of a private provider or contractor; or

(ii) a person employed by the juvenile court of the state, or an employee of a private provider or contractor.

(b) "Department" means the Department of Human Services created in Section 62A-1-102.

(c) "Juvenile court" means the juvenile court of the state created in Section 78-3a-102.

(d) "Private provider or contractor" means any person or entity that contracts with the:

(i) department to provide services or functions that are part of the operation of the department; or

(ii) juvenile court to provide services or functions that are part of the operation of the juvenile court.

(e) "Youth receiving state services" means a person:

(i) younger than 18 years of age, except as provided under Subsection (1)(e)(ii), who is:

(A) in the custody of the department under Subsection 78-3a-118(2)(c)(ii); or

(B) receiving services from any division of the department if any portion of the costs of these services is covered by public monies as defined in Section 76-8-401; or

(ii) younger than 21 years of age who is:

(A) in the custody of the Division of Juvenile Justice Services, or the Division of Child and Family Services; or

(B) under the jurisdiction of the juvenile court.

(2) (a) An actor commits custodial sexual relations with a youth receiving state services if the actor commits any of the acts under Subsection (3):

(i) under circumstances not amounting to commission of, or an attempt to commit, an offense under Subsection (6); and

(ii) (A) the actor knows that the individual is a youth receiving state services; or

(B) a reasonable person in the actor's position should have known under the circumstances that the individual was a youth receiving state services.

(b) A violation of Subsection (2)(a) is a third degree felony, but if the youth receiving state services is younger than 18 years of age, a violation of Subsection (2)(a) is a second degree felony.

(c) If the act committed under this Subsection (2) amounts to an offense subject to a greater penalty under another provision of state law than is provided under this Subsection (2), this Subsection (2) does not prohibit prosecution and sentencing for the more serious offense.

(3) Acts referred to in Subsection (2)(a) are:

(a) having sexual intercourse with a youth receiving state services;

(b) engaging in any sexual act with a youth receiving state services involving the genitals of one person and the mouth or anus of another person, regardless of the sex of either participant; or

(c) causing the penetration, however slight, of the genital or anal opening of a youth receiving state services by any foreign object, substance, instrument, or device, including a part of the human body, with the intent to cause substantial emotional or bodily pain to any person, regardless of the sex of any participant or with the intent to arouse or gratify the sexual desire of any person, regardless of the sex of any participant.

(4) (a) An actor commits custodial sexual misconduct with a youth receiving state services if the actor commits any of the acts under Subsection (5):

(i) under circumstances not amounting to commission of, or an attempt to commit, an offense under Subsection (6); and

(ii) (A) the actor knows that the individual is a youth receiving state services; or

(B) a reasonable person in the actor's position should have known under the circumstances that the individual was a youth receiving state services.

(b) A violation of Subsection (4)(a) is a class A misdemeanor, but if the youth receiving state services is younger than 18 years of age, a violation of Subsection (4)(a) is a third degree felony.

(c) If the act committed under this Subsection (4) amounts to an offense subject to a greater penalty under another provision of state law than is provided under this Subsection (4), this Subsection (4) does not prohibit prosecution and sentencing for the more serious offense.

(5) Acts referred to in Subsection (4)(a) are the following acts when committed with the intent to cause substantial emotional or bodily pain to any person or with the intent to arouse or gratify the sexual desire of any person, regardless of the sex of any participant:

(a) touching the anus, buttocks, or any part of the genitals of a youth receiving state services;

(b) touching the breast of a female youth receiving state services;

(c) otherwise taking indecent liberties with a youth receiving state services; or

(d) causing a youth receiving state services to take indecent liberties with the actor or another person.

(6) The offenses referred to in Subsections (2)(a)(i) and (4)(a)(i) are:

(a) Section 76-5-401, unlawful sexual activity with a minor;

(b) Section 76-5-402, rape;

(c) Section 76-5-402.1, rape of a child;

(d) Section 76-5-402.2, object rape;

(e) Section 76-5-402.3, object rape of a child;

(f) Section 76-5-403, forcible sodomy;

(g) Section 76-5-403.1, sodomy on a child;

(h) Section 76-5-404, forcible sexual abuse;

(i) Section 76-5-404.1, sexual abuse of a child or aggravated sexual abuse of a child; or

(j) Section 76-5-405, aggravated sexual assault.

(7) (a) It is not a defense to the commission of the offense of custodial sexual relations with a youth receiving state services under Subsection (2) or custodial sexual misconduct with a youth receiving state services under Subsection (4), or an

attempt to commit either of these offenses, if the youth receiving state services is younger than 18 years of age, that the actor:

    (i) mistakenly believed the youth receiving state services to be 18 years of age or older at the time of the alleged offense; or

    (ii) was unaware of the true age of the youth receiving state services.

  (b) Consent of the youth receiving state services is not a defense to any violation or attempted violation of Subsection (2) or (4).

(8) It is a defense that the commission by the actor of an act under Subsection (2) or (4) is the result of compulsion, as the defense is described in Subsection 76-2-302(1).   2003

PART 5

HIV TESTING — SEXUAL OFFENDERS AND VICTIMS

76-5-501. Definitions.

For purposes of this part:

  (1) "Convicted sexual offender" means a person or a juvenile as provided in Subsection 76-5-502(1).

  (2) "Department of Health" means the state Department of Health as defined in Section 26-1-2.

  (3) "HIV infection" means an indication of Human Immunodeficiency Virus (HIV) infection determined by current medical standards and detected by any of the following:

    (a) presence of antibodies to HIV, verified by a positive "confirmatory" test, such as Western blot or other method approved by the Utah State Health Laboratory. Western blot interpretation will be based on criteria currently recommended by the Association of State and Territorial Public Health Laboratory Directors;

    (b) presence of HIV antigen;

    (c) isolation of HIV; or

    (d) demonstration of HIV proviral DNA.

  (4) "HIV positive individual" means a person who is HIV positive as determined by the State Health Laboratory.

  (5) "Local department of health" means the department as defined in Subsection 26A-1-102(5).

  (6) "Positive" means an indication of the HIV infection as defined in Subsection (3).

  (7) "Sexual offense" means a violation of state law prohibiting a sexual offense under Title 76, Chapter 5, Part 4.

  (8) "Test" or "testing" means a test or tests for HIV infection conducted by and in accordance with standards recommended by the Department of Health.   1993

76-5-502. Mandatory testing — Liability for costs.

  (1) (a) A person who has entered a plea of guilty, a plea of no contest, a plea of guilty and mentally ill, a plea of not guilty by reason of insanity or been found guilty for violation of a sexual offense or an attempted sexual offense under Title 76, Chapter 5, Part 4, or a juvenile who is adjudicated to have violated or attempted to violate state law prohibiting a sexual offense under Title 76, Chapter 5, Part 4, shall be required to submit to a mandatory test upon the request of a victim or the parent or legal guardian of the minor victim or

victim of a sexual offense within six months of conviction to determine if the offender is an HIV positive individual.

  (b) The court shall order the convicted sexual offender to submit to the test upon sentencing or as a condition of probation. The order to the convicted sexual offender shall not include the identity and address of the victim requesting the test. The court shall forward the order to the Department of Health, including separate information about the victim's identity and address for notification and counseling purposes.

(2) If the mandatory test has not been conducted, and the convicted offender or adjudicated juvenile is already confined in a county jail, state prison, or a secure youth corrections facility, the person shall be tested while in confinement.

(3) The secure youth corrections facility or county jail shall cause the blood specimen of the offender as defined in Subsection (1) confined in that facility to be taken and shall forward the specimen to the Department of Health.

(4) The Department of Corrections shall cause the blood specimen of the offender defined in Subsection (1) confined in any state prison to be taken and shall forward the specimen to the Department of Health as provided in Section 64-13-36.

(5) The person tested shall be responsible for the costs of testing, unless the person is indigent. The costs will then be paid by the Department of Health from the General Fund.   1993

76-5-503. Voluntary testing — Victim to request — Costs paid by Crime Victim Reparations.

(1) A victim or minor victim of a sexual offense as provided under Title 76, Chapter 5, Part 4, may request a test for the HIV infection.

(2) (a) The local health department shall obtain the blood specimen from the victim and forward the specimen to the Department of Health.

  (b) The Department of Health shall analyze the specimen of the victim.

(3) The testing shall consist of a base-line test of the victim at the time immediately or as soon as possible after the alleged occurrence of the sexual offense. If the base-line test result is not positive, follow-up testing shall occur at three months and six months after the alleged occurrence of the sexual offense.

(4) The Crime Victim Reparations Fund shall pay for the costs of the victim testing if the victim provides a substantiated claim of the sexual offense, does not test HIV positive at the base-line testing phase, and complies with eligibility criteria established by the Crime Victim Reparations Act.   1993

76-5-504. Victim notification and counseling.

(1) The Department of Health shall provide the victim who requests testing of the convicted sexual offender's human immunodeficiency virus status counseling regarding HIV disease and referral for appropriate health care and support services. If the local health department where the victim resides and the Department of Health agree, the Department of Health shall forward a report of the convicted sexual offender's human immunodeficiency virus status to the local health department and the local health department shall provide the victim who requests the test with the test results, counseling regarding HIV disease, and referral for appropriate health care and support services.

(2) Notwithstanding the provisions of Section 26-6-27, the Department of Health and a local health department acting pursuant to an agreement made under Subsection (1) may disclose to the victim the results of the convicted sexual offender's human immunodeficiency virus status as provided in this section. **1997**

CHAPTER 5a

SEXUAL EXPLOITATION OF CHILDREN

Section

76-5a-1. Legislative determinations — Purpose of chapter.

The Legislature of Utah determines that the sexual exploitation of minors is excessively harmful to their physiological, emotional, social, and mental development; that minors cannot intelligently and knowingly consent to sexual exploitation; that regardless of whether it is classified as legally obscene, material that sexually exploits minors is not protected by the First Amendment of the United States Constitution or by the First or Fifteenth sections of Article I of the Utah Constitution and may be prohibited; and that prohibition of and punishment for the distribution, possession, possession with intent to distribute, and production of materials that sexually exploit minors is necessary and justified to eliminate the market for those materials and to reduce the harm to the minor inherent in the perpetuation of the record of his sexually exploitive activities. It is the purpose of this chapter to prohibit the production, possession, possession with intent to distribute, and distribution of materials which sexually exploit minors, regardless of whether the materials are classified as legally obscene. **1985**

76-5a-2. Definitions.

As used in this chapter:

(1) "Child pornography" means any visual depiction, including any live performance, photograph, film, video, picture, or computer or computer-generated image or picture, whether made or produced by electronic, mechanical, or other means, of sexually explicit conduct, where:

(a) the production of the visual depiction involves the use of a minor engaging in sexually explicit conduct;

(b) the visual depiction is of a minor engaging in sexually explicit conduct; or

(c) the visual depiction has been created, adapted, or modified to appear that an identifiable minor is engaging in sexually explicit conduct.

(2) "Distribute" means the selling, exhibiting, displaying, wholesaling, retailing, providing, giving, granting admission to, or otherwise transferring or presenting child pornography with or without consideration.

(3) "Identifiable minor":

(a) means a person:

(i) (A) who was a minor at the time the visual depiction was created, adapted, or modified; or

(B) whose image as a minor was used in creating, adapting, or modifying the visual depiction; and

(ii) who is recognizable as an actual person by the person's face, likeness, or other distinguishing characteristic, such as a birthmark, or other recognizable feature; and

(b) does not require proof of the actual identity of the identifiable minor.

(4) "Live performance" means any act, play, dance, pantomime, song, or other activity performed by live actors in person.

(5) "Minor" means a person younger than 18 years of age.

(6) "Nudity or partial nudity" means any state of dress or undress in which the human genitals, pubic region, buttocks, or the female breast, at a point below the top of the areola, is less than completely and opaquely covered.

(7) "Produce" means the photographing, filming, taping, directing, producing, creating, designing, or composing of child pornography or the securing or hiring of persons to engage in the production of child pornography.

(8) "Sexually explicit conduct" means actual or simulated:

(a) sexual intercourse, including genital-genital, oral-genital, anal-genital, or oral-anal, whether between persons of the same or opposite sex;

(b) masturbation;

(c) bestiality;

(d) sadistic or masochistic activities;

(e) lascivious exhibition of the genitals or pubic area of any person;

(f) the visual depiction of nudity or partial nudity for the purpose of causing sexual arousal of any person;

(g) the fondling or touching of the genitals, pubic region, buttocks, or female breast; or

(h) the explicit representation of the defecation or urination functions.

(9) "Simulated sexually explicit conduct" means a feigned or pretended act of sexually explicit conduct which duplicates, within the perception of an average person, the appearance of an actual act of sexually explicit conduct. **2001**

76-5a-3. Sexual exploitation of a minor — Offenses.

(1) A person is guilty of sexual exploitation of a minor:

(a) when the person knowingly produces, distributes, possesses, or possesses with intent to distribute, child pornography; or

(b) if the person is a minor's parent or legal guardian and knowingly consents to or permits that minor to be sexually exploited under Subsection (1)(a).

(2) Sexual exploitation of a minor is a felony of the second degree.

(3) It is a separate offense under this section:

(a) for each minor depicted, and if more than one minor is depicted in the child pornography in violation of this section, the depiction of each individual minor in the child pornography is a separate offense; and

(b) each time the same minor is depicted in different child pornography.

(4) It is an affirmative defense to a charge of violating this section that no person under 18 years of age was actually depicted in the visual depiction or used in producing or advertising the visual depiction.

2001

76-5a-4. Determination whether material violates chapter.

In determining whether material is in violation of this chapter, the material need not be considered as a whole, but may be examined by the trier of fact in part only. It is not an element of the offense of sexual exploitation of a minor that the material appeal to the prurient interest in sex of the average person nor that prohibited conduct need be portrayed in a patently offensive manner.

1985

CHAPTER 6

OFFENSES AGAINST PROPERTY

Part 1

Property Destruction

Part 2

Burglary and Criminal Trespass

Part 3

Robbery

Part 4

Theft

Part 5

Fraud

PART 1

PROPERTY DESTRUCTION

76-6-101. Definitions.

For purposes of this chapter:

(1) "Property" means any form of real property or tangible personal property which is capable of being damaged or destroyed and includes a habitable structure.

(2) "Habitable structure" means any building, vehicle, trailer, railway car, aircraft, or watercraft used for lodging or assembling persons or conducting business whether a person is actually present or not.

(3) "Property" is that of another, if anyone other than the actor has a possessory or proprietary interest in any portion thereof.

(4) "Value" means:

(a) The market value of the property, if totally destroyed, at the time and place of the offense, or where cost of replacement exceeds the market value; or

(b) Where the market value cannot be ascertained, the cost of repairing or replacing the property within a reasonable time following the offense.

(5) If the property damaged has a value that cannot be ascertained by the criteria set forth in Subsections (a) and (b) above, the property shall be deemed to have a value less than $300.   **1995**

76-6-102. Arson.

(1) A person is guilty of arson if under circumstances not amounting to aggravated arson, by means of fire or explosives, the person unlawfully and intentionally damages:

(a) any property with intention of defrauding an insurer; or

(b) the property of another.

(2) A violation of Subsection (1)(a) is a second degree felony.

(3) A violation of Subsection (1)(b) is:

(a) a second degree felony if:

(i) the damage caused is or exceeds $5,000 in value; or

(ii) as a proximate result of the fire or explosion, any person not a participant in the offense suffers serious bodily injury as defined in Section 76-1-601;

(b) a third degree felony if:

(i) the damage caused is or exceeds $1,000 but is less than $5,000 in value;

(ii) as a proximate result of the fire or explosion, any person not a participant in the offense suffers substantial bodily injury as defined in Section 76-1-601; or

(iii) the fire or explosion endangers human life;

(c) a class A misdemeanor if the damage caused is or exceeds $300 but is less than $1,000 in value; and

(d) a class B misdemeanor if the damage caused is less than $300.   2004

76-6-103. Aggravated arson.

(1) A person is guilty of aggravated arson if by means of fire or explosives he intentionally and unlawfully damages:

(a) a habitable structure; or

(b) any structure or vehicle when any person not a participant in the offense is in the structure or vehicle.

(2) Aggravated arson is a felony of the first degree.   1986

76-6-104. Reckless burning.

(1) A person is guilty of reckless burning if the person:

(a) recklessly starts a fire or causes an explosion which endangers human life;

(b) having started a fire, whether recklessly or not, and knowing that it is spreading and will endanger the life or property of another, either fails to take reasonable measures to put out or control the fire or fails to give a prompt fire alarm;

(c) builds or maintains a fire without taking reasonable steps to remove all flammable materials surrounding the site of the fire as necessary to prevent the fire's spread or escape; or

(d) damages the property of another by reckless use of fire or causing an explosion.

(2) (a) A violation of Subsection (1)(a) or (b) is a class A misdemeanor.

(b) A violation of Subsection (1)(c) is a class B misdemeanor.

(c) A violation of Subsection (1)(d) is:

(i) a class A misdemeanor if damage to property is or exceeds $1,000 in value;

(ii) a class B misdemeanor if the damage to property is or exceeds $300 but is less than $1,000 in value; and

(iii) a class C misdemeanor if the damage to property is or exceeds $150 but is less than $300 in value.

(d) Any other violation under Subsection (1)(d) is an infraction.   1998

76-6-104.5. Abandoned fire — Penalties.

(1) A person is guilty of abandoning a fire if, under circumstances not amounting to the offense of arson, aggravated arson, or causing a catastrophe under Title 76, Chapter 6, Part 1, Offenses Against Property, he leaves a fire:

(a) without first completely extinguishing it; and

(b) with the intent to not return to the fire.

(2) A person does not commit a violation of Subsection (1) or (2) if he leaves a fire to report an uncontrolled fire.

(3) A violation of Subsection (1):

(a) is a class C misdemeanor if the property damage is or exceeds $150 but is less than $300 in value;

(b) is a class B misdemeanor if property damage is or exceeds $300 but is less than $1,000 in value; and

(c) is a class A misdemeanor if property damage is or exceeds $1,000 in value.

(4) If a violation of Subsection (3) involves a wildland fire, the violator is also liable for suppression costs under Section 65A-3-4.   1998

76-6-105. Causing a catastrophe — Penalties.

(1) Any person is guilty of causing a catastrophe if the person causes widespread injury or damage to persons or property by:

(a) use of a weapon of mass destruction as defined in Section 76-10-401; or

(b) explosion, fire, flood, avalanche, collapse of a building, or other harmful or destructive force or substance that is not a weapon of mass destruction.

(2) Causing a catastrophe is:

(a) a first degree felony if the person causes the catastrophe knowingly and by the use of a weapon of mass destruction;

(b) a second degree felony if the person causes the catastrophe knowingly and by a means other than a weapon of mass destruction; and

(c) a class A misdemeanor if the person causes the catastrophe recklessly.

(3) In addition to any other penalty authorized by law, a court shall order any person convicted of any violation of this section to reimburse any federal, state, or local unit of government, or any private business, organization, individual, or entity for all expenses incurred in responding to the violation, unless the court states on the record the reasons why the reimbursement would be inappropriate.   2002

76-6-106. Criminal mischief.

(1) As used in this section, "critical infrastructure" includes:

(a) information and communication systems;

(b) financial and banking systems;

(c) transportation systems;

(d) any public utility service, including the power, energy, and water supply systems;

(e) sewage and water treatment systems;

(f) health care facilities as listed in Section 26-21-2, and emergency fire, medical, and law enforcement response systems;

(g) public health facilities and systems;

(h) food distribution systems; and

(i) other government operations and services.

(2) A person commits criminal mischief if the person:

(a) under circumstances not amounting to arson, damages or destroys property with the intention of defrauding an insurer;

(b) intentionally and unlawfully tampers with the property of another and as a result:

(i) recklessly endangers:

(A) human life; or

(B) human health or safety; or

(ii) recklessly causes or threatens a substantial interruption or impairment of any critical infrastructure;

(c) intentionally damages, defaces, or destroys the property of another; or

(d) recklessly or willfully shoots or propels a missile or other object at or against a motor vehicle, bus, airplane, boat, locomotive, train, railway car, or caboose, whether moving or standing.

(3) (a) (i) A violation of Subsection (2)(a) is a third degree felony.

(ii) A violation of Subsection (2)(b)(i)(A) is a class A misdemeanor.

(iii) A violation of Subsection (2)(b)(i)(B) is a class B misdemeanor.

(iv) A violation of Subsection (2)(b)(ii) is a second degree felony.

(b) Any other violation of this section is a:

(i) second degree felony if the actor's conduct causes or is intended to cause pecuniary loss equal to or in excess of $5,000 in value;

(ii) third degree felony if the actor's conduct causes or is intended to cause pecuniary loss equal to or in excess of $1,000 but is less than $5,000 in value;

(iii) class A misdemeanor if the actor's conduct causes or is intended to cause pecuniary loss equal to or in excess of $300 but is less than $1,000 in value; and

(iv) class B misdemeanor if the actor's conduct causes or is intended to cause pecuniary loss less than $300 in value.

(4) In determining the value of damages under this section, or for computer crimes under Section 76-6-703, the value of any item, computer, computer network, computer property, computer services, software, or data includes the measurable value of the loss of use of the items and the measurable cost to replace or restore the items.

(5) In addition to any other penalty authorized by law, a court shall order any person convicted of any violation of this section to reimburse any federal, state, or local unit of government, or any private business, organization, individual, or entity for all expenses incurred in responding to a violation of Subsection (2)(b)(ii), unless the court states on the record the reasons why the reimbursement would be inappropriate.   2002

76-6-107. Graffiti defined — Penalties — Removal costs — Reimbursement liability.

(1) "Graffiti" means any form of unauthorized printing, writing, spraying, scratching, affixing, or inscribing on the property of another regardless of the content or nature of the material used in the commission of the act.

(2) "Victim" means the person or entity whose property was defaced by the graffiti and bears the expense for its removal.

(3) Graffiti is a:

(a) second degree felony if the damage caused is in excess of $5,000;

(b) third degree felony if the damage caused is in excess of $1,000;

(c) class A misdemeanor if the damage caused is equal to or in excess of $300; and

(d) class B misdemeanor if the damage caused is less than $300.

(4) Damages under Subsection (3) include removal costs, repair costs, or replacement costs, whichever is less.

(5) The court, upon conviction or adjudication, shall order restitution to the victim in the amount of removal, repair, or replacement costs.

(6) An additional amount of $1,000 in restitution shall be added to removal costs if the graffiti is positioned on an overpass or an underpass, requires that traffic be interfered with in order to remove it, or the entity responsible for the area in which the clean-up is to take place must provide assistance in order for the removal to take place safely.

(7) A person who voluntarily and at his own expense, removes graffiti for which he is responsible may be credited for the removal costs against restitution ordered by a court.   1996

76-6-108. Damage to or interruption of a communication device — Penalty.

(1) As used in this section:

(a) "Communication device" means any device, including a telephone, cellular telephone, computer, or radio, which may be used in an attempt to summon police, fire, medical, or other emergency aid.

(b) "Emergency aid" means aid or assistance, including law enforcement, fire, or medical services, commonly summoned by persons concerned with imminent or actual:

(i) jeopardy to any person's health or safety; or

(ii) damage to any person's property.

(2) A person is guilty of damage to or interruption of a communication device if the actor attempts to prohibit or interrupt, or prohibits or interrupts, another person's use of a communication device when the other person is attempting to summon emergency aid or has communicated a desire to summon emergency aid, and in the process the actor:

(a) uses force, intimidation, or any other form of violence;

(b) destroys, disables, or damages a communication device; or

(c) commits any other act in an attempt to prohibit or interrupt the person's use of a communication device to summon emergency aid.

(3) Damage to or interruption of a communication device is a class B misdemeanor.   2000

76-6-109. Offenses committed against timber, mining, or agricultural industries — Enhanced penalties.

(1) A person who commits any criminal offense with the intent to halt, impede, obstruct, or interfere with the lawful management, cultivation, or harvesting of trees or timber, or the management or operations of agricultural or mining industries is subject to an enhanced penalty for the offense as provided below. However, this section does not apply to action protected by the National Labor Relations Act, 29 U.S.C. Section 151 et seq., or the Federal Railway Labor Act, 45 U.S.C. Section 151 et seq.

(2) The prosecuting attorney, or grand jury if an indictment is returned, shall cause to be subscribed upon the complaint in misdemeanor cases or the information or indictment in felony cases notice that the defendant is subject to the enhanced penalties provided under this section.

(3) If the trier of fact finds beyond a reasonable doubt that the defendant committed any criminal offense with the intent to halt, impede, obstruct, or interfere with the lawful management, cultivation, or

harvesting of trees or timber, or the management or operations of agricultural or mining industries, the penalties are enhanced as provided in this Subsection (3):

(a) a class C misdemeanor is a class B misdemeanor, with a mandatory fine of not less than $1,000, which is in addition to any term of imprisonment the court may impose;

(b) a class B misdemeanor is a Class A misdemeanor, with a fine of not less than $2,500, which is in addition to any term of imprisonment the court may impose;

(c) a class A misdemeanor is a third degree felony, with a fine of not less than $5,000, which is in addition to any term of imprisonment the court may impose;

(d) a third degree felony is a second degree felony, with a fine of not less than $7,500, which is in addition to any term of imprisonment the court may impose; and

(e) a second degree felony is subject to a fine of not less than $10,000, which is in addition to any term of imprisonment the court may impose.

2000

76-6-110. Offenses committed against animal enterprises — Definitions — Enhanced penalties.

(1) As used in this section:

(a) "Animal enterprise" means a commercial or academic enterprise that:

(i) uses animals for food or fiber production;

(ii) is an agricultural operation, including a facility for the production of crops or livestock, or livestock products;

(iii) operates a zoo, aquarium, circus, rodeo, or lawful competitive animal event; or

(iv) any fair or similar event intended to advance agricultural arts and sciences.

(b) "Livestock" means cattle, sheep, goats, swine, horses, mules, poultry, domesticated elk as defined in Section 4-39-102, or any other domestic animal or domestic furbearer raised or kept for profit.

(c) "Property" includes any buildings, vehicles, animals, data, or records.

(2) (a) A person who commits any criminal offense with the intent to halt, impede, obstruct, or interfere with the lawful operation of an animal enterprise or to damage, take, or cause the loss of any property owned by, used by, or in the possession of a lawful animal enterprise, is subject to an enhanced penalty under Subsection (3).

(b) Subsection (2)(a) does not apply to action protected by the National Labor Relations Act, 29 U.S.C. Section 151 et seq., or the Federal Railway Labor Act, 45 U.S.C. Section 151 et seq.

(c) The prosecuting attorney, or grand jury if an indictment is returned, shall cause to be subscribed upon the information or indictment notice that the defendant is subject to the enhanced penalties provided under this section.

(3) If the trier of fact finds beyond a reasonable doubt that the defendant committed any criminal offense with the intent to halt, impede, obstruct, or interfere with the lawful operation of an animal enterprise or to damage, take, or cause the loss of any property owned by, used by, or in the possession of a lawful animal enterprise, the penalties are enhanced as provided in this Subsection (3):

(a) a class C misdemeanor is a class B misdemeanor, with a mandatory fine of not less than $1,000, which is in addition to any term of imprisonment the court may impose;

(b) a class B misdemeanor is a class A misdemeanor, with a fine of not less than $2,500, which is in addition to any term of imprisonment the court may impose;

(c) a class A misdemeanor is a third degree felony, with a fine of not less than $5,000, which is in addition to any term of imprisonment the court may impose;

(d) a third degree felony is a second degree felony, with a fine of not less than $7,500, which is in addition to any term of imprisonment the court may impose; and

(e) a second degree felony is subject to a fine of not less than $10,000, which is in addition to any term of imprisonment the court may impose.

2001

PART 2

BURGLARY AND CRIMINAL TRESPASS

76-6-201. Definitions.

For the purposes of this part:

(1) "Building," in addition to its ordinary meaning, means any watercraft, aircraft, trailer, sleeping car, or other structure or vehicle adapted for overnight accommodation of persons or for carrying on business therein and includes:

(a) each separately secured or occupied portion of the structure or vehicle; and

(b) each structure appurtenant to or connected with the structure or vehicle.

(2) "Dwelling" means a building which is usually occupied by a person lodging therein at night, whether or not a person is actually present.

(3) A person "enters or remains unlawfully" in or upon premises when the premises or any portion thereof at the time of the entry or remaining are not open to the public and when the actor is not otherwise licensed or privileged to enter or remain on the premises or such portion thereof.

(4) "Enter" means:

(a) intrusion of any part of the body; or

(b) intrusion of any physical object under control of the actor.   1973

76-6-202. Burglary.

(1) An actor is guilty of burglary if he enters or remains unlawfully in a building or any portion of a building with intent to commit:

(a) a felony;

(b) theft;

(c) an assault on any person;

(d) lewdness, a violation of Subsection 76-9-702(1);

(e) sexual battery, a violation of Subsection 76-9-702(3);

(f) lewdness involving a child, in violation of Section 76-9-702.5; or

(g) voyeurism against a child under Subsection 76-9-702.7(2) or (5).

(2) Burglary is a felony of the third degree unless it was committed in a dwelling, in which event it is a felony of the second degree.

(3) A violation of this section is a separate offense from any of the offenses listed in Subsections (1)(a) through (g), and which may be committed by the actor while he is in the building.   2003

76-6-203. Aggravated burglary.

(1) A person is guilty of aggravated burglary if in attempting, committing, or fleeing from a burglary the actor or another participant in the crime:

(a) causes bodily injury to any person who is not a participant in the crime;

(b) uses or threatens the immediate use of a dangerous weapon against any person who is not a participant in the crime; or

(c) possesses or attempts to use any explosive or dangerous weapon.

(2) Aggravated burglary is a first degree felony.

(3) As used in this section, "dangerous weapon" has the same definition as under Section 76-1-601.   1989

76-6-204. Burglary of a vehicle — Charge of other offense.

(1) Any person who unlawfully enters any vehicle with intent to commit a felony or theft is guilty of a burglary of a vehicle.

(2) Burglary of a vehicle is a class A misdemeanor.

(3) A charge against any person for a violation of Subsection (1) shall not preclude a charge for a commission of any other offense.   1973

76-6-205. Manufacture or possession of instrument for burglary or theft.

Any person who manufactures or possesses any instrument, tool, device, article, or other thing adapted, designed, or commonly used in advancing or facilitating the commission of any offense under circumstances manifesting an intent to use or knowledge that some person intends to use the same in the commission of a burglary or theft is guilty of a class B misdemeanor.   1973

76-6-206. Criminal trespass.

(1) For purposes of this section, "enter" means intrusion of the entire body.

(2) A person is guilty of criminal trespass if, under circumstances not amounting to burglary as defined in Section 76-6-202, 76-6-203, or 76-6-204 or a violation of Section 76-10-2402 regarding commercial terrorism:

(a) he enters or remains unlawfully on property and:

(i) intends to cause annoyance or injury to any person or damage to any property, including the use of graffiti as defined in Section 76-6-107;

(ii) intends to commit any crime, other than theft or a felony; or

(iii) is reckless as to whether his presence will cause fear for the safety of another;

(b) knowing his entry or presence is unlawful, he enters or remains on property as to which notice against entering is given by:

(i) personal communication to the actor by the owner or someone with apparent authority to act for the owner;

(ii) fencing or other enclosure obviously designed to exclude intruders; or

(iii) posting of signs reasonably likely to come to the attention of intruders; or

(c) he enters a condominium unit in violation of Subsection 57-8-7(7).

(3) (a) A violation of Subsection (2)(a) is a class C misdemeanor unless it was committed in a dwelling, in which event it is a class B misdemeanor.

(b) A violation of Subsection (2)(b) is an infraction.

(4) It is a defense to prosecution under this section that the:

(a) property was open to the public when the actor entered or remained; and

(b) actor's conduct did not substantially interfere with the owner's use of the property.   2001

76-6-206.1. Criminal trespass of abandoned or inactive mines — Penalty.

(1) For purposes of this section:

(a) "Abandoned or inactive mine" means an underground mine which is no longer open for access or no longer under excavation and has been clearly marked as closed or protected from entry.

(b) "Enter" means intrusion of the entire body.

(2) A person is guilty of criminal trespass of an abandoned or inactive mine if, under circumstances not amounting to burglary as defined in Section 76-6-202, 76-6-203, or 76-6-204:

(a) the person intentionally enters and remains unlawfully in the underground workings of an abandoned or inactive mine; or

(b) intentionally and without authority removes, destroys, or tampers with any warning sign, covering, fencing, or other method of protection from entry placed on, around, or over any mine shaft, mine portal, or other abandoned or inactive mining excavation property.

(3) A violation of Subsection (2)(a) is a class B misdemeanor.

(4) A violation of Subsection (2)(b) is a class A misdemeanor.   1997

76-6-206.2. Criminal trespass on state park lands — Penalties.

(1) For purposes of this section:

(a) "Authorization" means specific written permission by, or contractual agreement with, the Division of Parks and Recreation.

(b) "Criminal trespass" means the elements of the crime of criminal trespass, as set forth in Section 76-6-206.

(c) "Division" means the Division of Parks and Recreation, as referred to in Section 63-11-3.1.

(d) "State park lands" means all lands administered by the division.

(2) A person is guilty of criminal trespass on state park lands and is liable for the civil damages prescribed in Subsection (5) if, under circumstances not amounting to a greater offense, and without authorization, the person:

(a) constructs improvements or structures on state park lands;

(b) uses or occupies state park lands for more than 30 days after the cancellation or expiration of authorization;

(c) knowingly or intentionally uses state park lands for commercial gain;

(d) intentionally or knowingly grazes livestock on state park lands, except as provided in Section 72-3-112; or

(e) remains, after being ordered to leave by someone with actual authority to act for the division, or by a law enforcement officer.

(3) A person is not guilty of criminal trespass if that person enters onto state park lands:

(a) without first paying the required fee; and

(b) for the sole purpose of pursuing recreational activity.

(4) A violation of Subsection (2) is a class B misdemeanor.

(5) In addition to restitution, as provided in Section 76-3-201, a person who commits any act described in

Subsection (2) may also be liable for civil damages in the amount of three times the value of:

(a) damages resulting from a violation of Subsection (2);

(b) the water, mineral, vegetation, improvement, or structure on state park lands that is removed, destroyed, used, or consumed without authorization;

(c) the historical, prehistorical, archaeological, or paleontological resource on state park lands that is removed, destroyed, used, or consumed without authorization; or

(d) the consideration which would have been charged by the division for unauthorized use of the land and resources during the period of trespass.

(6) Civil damages under Subsection (5) may be collected in a separate action by the division, and shall be deposited in the State Parks Fees Restricted Account as established in Section 63-11-66.   2004

PART 3

ROBBERY

76-6-301. Robbery.

(1) A person commits robbery if:

(a) the person unlawfully and intentionally takes or attempts to take personal property in the possession of another from his person, or immediate presence, against his will, by means of force or fear, and with a purpose or intent to deprive the person permanently or temporarily of the personal property; or

(b) the person intentionally or knowingly uses force or fear of immediate force against another in the course of committing a theft or wrongful appropriation.

(2) An act is considered to be "in the course of committing a theft or wrongful appropriation" if it occurs:

(a) in the course of an attempt to commit theft or wrongful appropriation;

(b) in the commission of theft or wrongful appropriation; or

(c) in the immediate flight after the attempt or commission.

(3) Robbery is a felony of the second degree.   2004

76-6-302. Aggravated robbery.

(1) A person commits aggravated robbery if in the course of committing robbery, he:

(a) uses or threatens to use a dangerous weapon as defined in Section 76-1-601;

(b) causes serious bodily injury upon another; or

(c) takes or attempts to take an operable motor vehicle.

(2) Aggravated robbery is a first degree felony.

(3) For the purposes of this part, an act shall be considered to be "in the course of committing a robbery" if it occurs in an attempt to commit, during the commission of, or in the immediate flight after the attempt or commission of a robbery.   2003

PART 4

THEFT

76-6-401. Definitions.

For the purposes of this part:

(1) "Property" means anything of value, including real estate, tangible and intangible personal property, captured or domestic animals and birds, written instruments or other writings representing or embodying rights concerning real or personal property, labor, services, or otherwise containing anything of value to the owner, commodities of a public utility nature such as telecommunications, gas, electricity, steam, or water, and trade secrets, meaning the whole or any portion of any scientific or technical information, design, process, procedure, formula or invention which the owner thereof intends to be available only to persons selected by him.

(2) "Obtain" means, in relation to property, to bring about a transfer of possession or of some other legally recognized interest in property, whether to the obtainer or another; in relation to labor or services, to secure performance thereof; and in relation to a trade secret, to make any facsimile, replica, photograph, or other reproduction.

(3) "Purpose to deprive" means to have the conscious object:

(a) To withhold property permanently or for so extended a period or to use under such circumstances that a substantial portion of its economic value, or of the use and benefit thereof, would be lost; or

(b) To restore the property only upon payment of a reward or other compensation; or

(c) To dispose of the property under circumstances that make it unlikely that the owner will recover it.

(4) "Obtain or exercise unauthorized control" means, but is not necessarily limited to, conduct heretofore defined or known as common-law larceny by trespassory taking, larceny by conversion, larceny by bailee, and embezzlement.

(5) "Deception" occurs when a person intentionally:

(a) Creates or confirms by words or conduct an impression of law or fact that is false and that the actor does not believe to be true and that is likely to affect the judgment of another in the transaction; or

(b) Fails to correct a false impression of law or fact that the actor previously created or confirmed by words or conduct that is likely to affect the judgment of another and that the actor does not now believe to be true; or

(c) Prevents another from acquiring information likely to affect his judgment in the transaction; or

(d) Sells or otherwise transfers or encumbers property without disclosing a lien, security interest, adverse claim, or other legal impediment to the enjoyment of the property, whether the lien, security interest, claim, or impediment is or is not valid or is or is not a matter of official record; or

(e) Promises performance that is likely to affect the judgment of another in the transaction, which performance the actor does not intend to perform or knows will not be performed; provided, however, that failure to perform the promise in issue without other evidence of intent or knowledge is not sufficient proof that the actor did not intend to perform or knew the promise would not be performed.   1973

76-6-402. Presumptions and defenses.

The following presumption shall be applicable to this part:

(1) Possession of property recently stolen, when no satisfactory explanation of such possession is made, shall be deemed prima facie evidence that the person in possession stole the property.

(2) It is no defense under this part that the actor has an interest in the property or service stolen if another person also has an interest that the actor is not entitled to infringe, provided an interest in property for purposes of this subsection shall not include a security interest for the repayment of a debt or obligation.

(3) It is a defense under this part that the actor:

(a) Acted under an honest claim of right to the property or service involved; or

(b) Acted in the honest belief that he had the right to obtain or exercise control over the property or service as he did; or

(c) Obtained or exercised control over the property or service honestly believing that the owner, if present, would have consented.
1974

76-6-403. Theft — Evidence to support accusation.

Conduct denominated theft in this part constitutes a single offense embracing the separate offenses such as those heretofore known as larceny, larceny by trick, larceny by bailees, embezzlement, false pretense, extortion, blackmail, receiving stolen property. An accusation of theft may be supported by evidence that it was committed in any manner specified in Sections 76-6-404 through 76-6-410, subject to the power of the court to ensure a fair trial by granting a continuance or other appropriate relief where the conduct of the defense would be prejudiced by lack of fair notice or by surprise.
1974

76-6-404. Theft — Elements.

A person commits theft if he obtains or exercises unauthorized control over the property of another with a purpose to deprive him thereof.
1973

76-6-404.5. Wrongful appropriation — Penalties.

(1) A person commits wrongful appropriation if he obtains or exercises unauthorized control over the property of another, without the consent of the owner or legal custodian and with intent to temporarily appropriate, possess, or use the property or to temporarily deprive the owner or legal custodian of possession of the property.

(2) The consent of the owner or legal custodian of the property to its control by the actor is not presumed or implied because of the owner's or legal custodian's consent on a previous occasion to the control of the property by any person.

(3) Wrongful appropriation is punishable one degree lower than theft, as provided in Section 76-6-412, so that a violation which would have been:

(a) a second degree felony under Section 76-6-412 if it had been theft is a third degree felony if it is wrongful appropriation;

(b) a third degree felony under Section 76-6-412 if it had been theft is a class A misdemeanor if it is wrongful appropriation;

(c) a class A misdemeanor under Section 76-6-412 if it had been theft is a class B misdemeanor if it is wrongful appropriation; and

(d) a class B misdemeanor under Section 76-6-412 if it had been theft is a class C misdemeanor if it is wrongful appropriation.

(4) Wrongful appropriation is a lesser included offense of the offense of theft under Section 76-6-404.
2001

76-6-405. Theft by deception.

(1) A person commits theft if he obtains or exercises control over property of another by deception and with a purpose to deprive him thereof.

(2) Theft by deception does not occur, however, when there is only falsity as to matters having no pecuniary significance, or puffing by statements unlikely to deceive ordinary persons in the group addressed. "Puffing" means an exaggerated commendation of wares or worth in communications addressed to the public or to a class or group.
1973

76-6-406. Theft by extortion.

(1) A person is guilty of theft if he obtains or exercises control over the property of another by extortion and with a purpose to deprive him thereof.

(2) As used in this section, extortion occurs when a person threatens to:

(a) Cause physical harm in the future to the person threatened or to any other person or to property at any time; or

(b) Subject the person threatened or any other person to physical confinement or restraint; or

(c) Engage in other conduct constituting a crime; or

(d) Accuse any person of a crime or expose him to hatred, contempt, or ridicule; or

(e) Reveal any information sought to be concealed by the person threatened; or

(f) Testify or provide information or withhold testimony or information with respect to another's legal claim or defense; or

(g) Take action as an official against anyone or anything, or withhold official action, or cause such action or withholding; or

(h) Bring about or continue a strike, boycott, or other similar collective action to obtain property which is not demanded or received for the benefit of the group which the actor purports to represent; or

(i) Do any other act which would not in itself substantially benefit him but which would harm substantially any other person with respect to that person's health, safety, business, calling, career, financial condition, reputation, or personal relationships.
1973

76-6-407. Theft of lost, mislaid, or mistakenly delivered property.

A person commits theft when:

(1) He obtains property of another which he knows to have been lost or mislaid, or to have been delivered under a mistake as to the identity of the recipient or as to the nature or amount of the property, without taking reasonable measures to return it to the owner; and

(2) He has the purpose to deprive the owner of the property when he obtains the property or at any time prior to taking the measures designated in paragraph (1).
1973

76-6-408. Receiving stolen property — Duties of pawnbrokers.

(1) A person commits theft if he receives, retains, or disposes of the property of another knowing that it has been stolen, or believing that it probably has been stolen, or who conceals, sells, withholds or aids in concealing, selling, or withholding the property from

the owner, knowing the property to be stolen, intending to deprive the owner of it.

(2) The knowledge or belief required for Subsection (1) is presumed in the case of an actor who:

    (a) is found in possession or control of other property stolen on a separate occasion;

    (b) has received other stolen property within the year preceding the receiving offense charged; or

    (c) is a pawnbroker or person who has or operates a business dealing in or collecting used or secondhand merchandise or personal property, or an agent, employee, or representative of a pawnbroker or person who buys, receives, or obtains property and fails to require the seller or person delivering the property to:

        (i) certify, in writing, that he has the legal rights to sell the property;

        (ii) provide a legible print, preferably the right thumb, at the bottom of the certificate next to his signature; and

        (iii) provide at least one positive form of identification.

(3) Every pawnbroker or person who has or operates a business dealing in or collecting used or secondhand merchandise or personal property, and every agent, employee, or representative of a pawnbroker or person who fails to comply with the requirements of Subsection (2)(c) is presumed to have bought, received, or obtained the property knowing it to have been stolen or unlawfully obtained. This presumption may be rebutted by proof.

(4) When, in a prosecution under this section, it appears from the evidence that the defendant was a pawnbroker or a person who has or operates a business dealing in or collecting used or secondhand merchandise or personal property, or was an agent, employee, or representative of a pawnbroker or person, that the defendant bought, received, concealed, or withheld the property without obtaining the information required in Subsection (2)(d), then the burden shall be upon the defendant to show that the property bought, received, or obtained was not stolen.

(5) Subsections (2)(c), (3), and (4) do not apply to scrap metal processors as defined in Section 76-10-901.

(6) As used in this section:

    (a) "Dealer" means a person in the business of buying or selling goods.

    (b) "Pawnbroker" means a person who:

        (i) loans money on deposit of personal property, or deals in the purchase, exchange, or possession of personal property on condition of selling the same property back again to the pledge or depositor;

        (ii) loans or advances money on personal property by taking chattel mortgage security on the property and takes or receives the personal property into his possession and who sells the unredeemed pledges; or

        (iii) receives personal property in exchange for money or in trade for other personal property.

    (c) "Receives" means acquiring possession, control, or title or lending on the security of the property.   2004

76-6-409. Theft of services.

(1) A person commits theft if he obtains services which he knows are available only for compensation by deception, threat, force, or any other means designed to avoid the due payment for them.

(2) A person commits theft if, having control over the disposition of services of another, to which he knows he is not entitled, he diverts the services to his own benefit or to the benefit of another who he knows is not entitled to them.

(3) In this section "services" includes, but is not limited to, labor, professional service, public utility and transportation services, restaurant, hotel, motel, tourist cabin, rooming house, and like accommodations, the supplying of equipment, tools, vehicles, or trailers for temporary use, telephone or telegraph service, steam, admission to entertainment, exhibitions, sporting events, or other events for which a charge is made.

(4) Under this section "services" includes gas, electricity, water, sewer, or cable television services, only if the services are obtained by threat, force, or a form of deception not described in Section 76-6-409.3.

(5) Under this section "services" includes telephone services only if the services are obtained by threat, force, or a form of deception not described in Sections 76-6-409.5 through 76-6-409.9.   1994

76-6-409.1. Devices for theft of services — Seizure and destruction — Civil actions for damages.

(1) A person may not knowingly:

    (a) make or possess any instrument, apparatus, equipment, or device for the use of, or for the purpose of, committing or attempting to commit theft under Section 76-6-409 or 76-6-409.3; or

    (b) sell, offer to sell, advertise, give, transport, or otherwise transfer to another any information, instrument, apparatus, equipment, or device, or any information, plan, or instruction for obtaining, making, or assembling the same, with intent that it be used, or caused to be used, to commit or attempt to commit theft under Section 76-6-409 or 76-6-409.3.

(2) (a) Any information, instrument, apparatus, equipment, or device, or information, plan, or instruction referred to in Subsection (1) may be seized pursuant to a court order, lawful search and seizure, lawful arrest, or other lawful process.

    (b) Upon the conviction of any person for a violation of any provision of this section, any information, instrument, apparatus, equipment, device, plan, or instruction shall be destroyed as contraband by the sheriff of the county in which the person was convicted.

(3) A person who violates any provision of Subsection (1) or (2) is guilty of a class A misdemeanor.

(4) Criminal prosecutions under this section do not affect any person's right of civil action for redress for damages suffered as a result of any violation of this section.   1987

76-6-409.3. Theft of utility or cable television services — Restitution — Civil action for damages.

(1) As used in this section:

    (a) "Cable television service" means any audio, video, or data service provided by a cable television company over its cable system facilities for payment, but does not include the use of a satellite dish or antenna.

    (b) "Owner" includes any part-owner, joint owner, tenant in common, joint tenant, or tenant by the entirety of the whole or a part of any building and the property on which it is located.

(c) "Person" means any individual, firm, partnership, corporation, company, association, or other legal entity.

(d) "Tenant or occupant" includes any person, including the owner, who occupies the whole or part of any building, whether alone or with others.

(e) "Utility" means any public utility, municipally-owned utility, or cooperative utility which provides electricity, gas, water, or sewer, or any combination of them, for sale to consumers.

(2) A person is guilty of theft of a utility or cable television service if the person commits any prohibited acts which make gas, electricity, water, sewer, or cable television available to a tenant or occupant, including himself, with intent to avoid due payment to the utility or cable television company. Any person aiding and abetting in these prohibited acts is a party to the offense under Section 76-2-202. Prohibited acts include:

(a) connecting any tube, pipe, wire, cable, or other instrument with any meter, device, or other instrument used for conducting gas, electricity, water, sewer, or cable television in a manner as permits the use of the gas, electricity, water, sewer, or cable television without its passing through a meter or other instrument recording the usage for billing;

(b) altering, injuring, or preventing the normal action of a meter, valve, stopcock, or other instrument used for measuring quantities of gas, electricity, water, or sewer service, or making or maintaining any modification or alteration to any device installed with the authorization of a cable television company for the purpose of intercepting or receiving any program or other service carried by the company which the person is not authorized by the company to receive;

(c) reconnecting gas, electricity, water, sewer, or cable television connections or otherwise restoring service when one or more of those utilities or cable service have been lawfully disconnected or turned off by the provider of the utility or cable service;

(d) intentionally breaking, defacing, or causing to be broken or defaced any seal, locking device, or other part of a metering device for recording usage of gas, electricity, water, or sewer service, or a security system for the recording device, or a cable television control device;

(e) removing a metering device designed to measure quantities of gas, electricity, water, or sewer service;

(f) transferring from one location to another a metering device for measuring quantities of public utility services of gas, electricity, water, or sewer service;

(g) changing the indicated consumption, jamming the measuring device, bypassing the meter or measuring device with a jumper so that it does not indicate use or registers use incorrectly, or otherwise obtaining quantities of gas, electricity, water, or sewer service from the utility without their passing through a metering device for measuring quantities of consumption for billing purposes;

(h) using a metering device belonging to the utility that has not been assigned to the location and installed by the utility;

(i) fabricating or using a device to pick or otherwise tamper with the locks used to deter utility service diversion, meter tampering, meter thefts, and unauthorized cable television service;

(j) assisting or instructing any person in obtaining or attempting to obtain any cable television service without payment of all lawful compensation to the company providing the service;

(k) making or maintaining a connection or connections, whether physical, electrical, mechanical, acoustical, or by other means, with any cables, wires, components, or other devices used for the distribution of cable television services without authority from the cable television company; or

(l) possessing without authority any device or printed circuit board designed in whole or in part to receive any cable television programming or services offered for sale over a cable television system with the intent that the device or printed circuit be used for the reception of the cable television company's services without payment. For purposes of this subsection, device or printed circuit board does not include the use of a satellite dish or antenna.

(3) The presence on property in the possession of a person of any device or alteration which permits the diversion or use of utility or cable service to avoid the registration of the use by or on a meter installed by the utility or to otherwise avoid the recording of use of the service for payment or otherwise avoid payment gives rise to an inference that the person in possession of the property installed the device or caused the alteration if:

(a) the presence of the device or alteration can be attributed only to a deliberate act in furtherance of an intent to avoid payment for utility or cable television service; and

(b) the person charged has received the direct benefit of the reduction of the cost of the utility or cable television service.

(4) A person who violates this section is guilty of the offense of theft of utility or cable television service.

(a) In the case of theft of utility services, if the value of the gas, electricity, water, or sewer service:

(i) is less than $300, the offense is a class B misdemeanor;

(ii) is or exceeds $300 but is not more than $1,000, the offense is a class A misdemeanor;

(iii) is or exceeds $1,000 but is not more than $5,000, the offense is a third degree felony; and

(iv) is or exceeds $5,000 or if the offender has previously been convicted of a violation of this section, the offense is a second degree felony.

(b) In the case of theft of cable television services, the penalties are prescribed in Section 76-6-412.

(5) A person who violates this section shall make restitution to the utility or cable television company for the value of the gas, electricity, water, sewer, or cable television service consumed in violation of this section plus all reasonable expenses and costs incurred on account of the violation of this section. Reasonable expenses and costs include expenses and costs for investigation, disconnection, reconnection, service calls, employee time, and equipment use.

(6) Criminal prosecution under this section does not affect the right of a utility or cable television company to bring a civil action for redress for damages suffered as a result of the commission of any of the acts prohibited by this section.

(7) This section does not abridge or alter any other right, action, or remedy otherwise available to a utility or cable television company.   1995

76-6-409.5. Definitions.

As used in this section and Sections 76-6-409.6 through 76-6-409.10:

(1) "Access device" means any telecommunication device including the telephone calling card number, electronic serial number, account number, mobile identification number, or personal identification number that can be used to obtain telephone service.

(2) "Clone cellular telephone" or "counterfeit cellular telephone" means a cellular telephone whose electronic serial number has been altered from the electronic serial number that was programmed in the telephone by the manufacturer by someone other than the manufacturer.

(3) "Cloning paraphernalia" means materials that, when possessed in combination, are capable of the creation of a cloned cellular telephone. These materials include scanners to intercept the electronic serial number and mobile identification number, cellular telephones, cables, EPROM chips, EPROM burners, software for programming the cloned telephone with a false electronic serial number and mobile identification number combination, a computer containing such software, and lists of electronic serial number and mobile identification number combinations.

(4) "Electronic serial number" means the unique number that:

   (a) was programmed into a cellular telephone by its manufacturer;

   (b) is transmitted by the cellular telephone; and

   (c) is used by cellular telephone providers to validate radio transmissions to the system as having been made by an authorized device.

(5) "EPROM" or "Erasable programmable read-only memory" means an integrated circuit memory that can be programmed from an external source and erased, for reprogramming, by exposure to ultraviolet light.

(6) "Intercept" means to electronically capture, record, reveal, or otherwise access, the signals emitted or received during the operation of a cellular telephone without the consent of the sender or receiver, by means of any instrument, device or equipment.

(7) "Manufacture of an unlawful telecommunication device" means to produce or assemble an unlawful telecommunication device, or to modify, alter, program, or reprogram a telecommunication device to be capable of acquiring or facilitating the acquisition of telecommunication service without the consent of the telecommunication service provider.

(8) "Mobile identification number" means the cellular telephone number assigned to the cellular telephone by the cellular telephone carrier.

(9) "Possess" means to have physical possession or otherwise to exercise control over tangible property.

(10) "Sell" means to offer to, agree to offer to, or to sell, exchange, give, or dispose of an unlawful telecommunications device to another.

(11) "Telecommunication device" means:

   (a) any type of instrument, device, machine, or equipment which is capable of transmitting or receiving telephonic, electronic, or radio communications; or

   (b) any part of an instrument, device, machine, or equipment, or other computer circuit, computer chip, electronic mechanism, or other component, which is capable of facilitating the transmission or reception of telephonic or electronic communications within the radio spectrum allocated to cellular radio telephony.

(12) "Telecommunication service" includes any service provided for a charge or compensation to facilitate the origination, transmission, emission, or reception of signs, signals, writings, images, and sounds or intelligence of any nature by telephone, including cellular telephones, wire, radio, television optical or other electromagnetic system.

(13) "Telecommunication service provider" means any person or entity providing telecommunication service including a cellular telephone or paging company or other person or entity which, for a fee, supplies the facility, cell site, mobile telephone switching office, or other equipment or telecommunication service.

(14) "Unlawful telecommunication device" means any telecommunication device that is capable of, or has been altered, modified, programmed, or reprogrammed, alone or in conjunction with another access device, so as to be capable of, acquiring or facilitating the acquisition of a telecommunication service without the consent of the telecommunication service provider. Unlawful devices include tumbler phones, counterfeit phones, tumbler microchips, counterfeit microchips, and other instruments capable of disguising their identity or location or of gaining access to a communications system operated by a telecommunication service provider.   1997

76-6-409.6. Use of telecommunication device to avoid lawful charge for service — Penalty.

(1) Any person who uses a telecommunication device with the intent to avoid the payment of any lawful charge for telecommunication service or with the knowledge that it was to avoid the payment of any lawful charge for telecommunication service is guilty of:

   (a) a class B misdemeanor, if the value of the telecommunication service is less than $300 or cannot be ascertained;

   (b) a class A misdemeanor, if the value of the telecommunication service charge is or exceeds $300 but is not more than $1,000;

   (c) a third degree felony, if the value of the telecommunication service is or exceeds $1,000 but is not more than $5,000;

   (d) a second degree felony, if:

      (i) the value of the telecommunication service is or exceeds $5,000; or

      (ii) the cloned cellular telephone was used to facilitate the commission of a felony.

(2) Any person who has been convicted previously of an offense under this section is guilty of a second degree felony upon a second conviction and any subsequent conviction.   1997

76-6-409.7. Possession of any unlawful telecommunication device — Penalty.

(1) Any person who knowingly possesses an unlawful telecommunication device is guilty of a class B misdemeanor.

(2) Any person who knowingly possesses five or more unlawful telecommunication devices in the same criminal episode is guilty of a third degree felony.

(3) Any person is guilty of a second degree felony who:

(a) knowingly and unlawfully possesses an instrument capable of intercepting electronic serial number and mobile identification number combinations under circumstances evidencing an intent to clone; or

(b) knowingly and unlawfully possesses cloning paraphernalia under circumstances evidencing an intent to clone.   1997

76-6-409.8. Sale of an unlawful telecommunication device — Penalty.

(1) Any person is guilty of a third degree felony who intentionally sells an unlawful telecommunication device or material, including hardware, data, computer software, or other information or equipment, knowing that the purchaser or a third person intends to use such material in the manufacture of an unlawful telecommunication device.

(2) If the offense under this section involves the intentional sale of five or more unlawful telecommunication devices within a six-month period, the person committing the offense is guilty of a second degree felony.   1997

76-6-409.9. Manufacture of an unlawful telecommunication device — Penalty.

(1) Any person who intentionally manufactures an unlawful telecommunication device is guilty of a third degree felony.

(2) If the offense under this section involves the intentional manufacture of five or more unlawful telecommunication devices within a six-month period, the person committing the offense is guilty of a second degree felony.   1997

76-6-409.10. Payment of restitution — Civil action — Other remedies retained.

(1) A person who violates Sections 76-6-409.5 through 76-6-409.9 shall make restitution to the telecommunication service provider for the value of the telecommunication service consumed in violation of this section plus all reasonable expenses and costs incurred on account of the violation of this section. Reasonable expenses and costs include expenses and costs for investigation, service calls, employee time, and equipment use.

(2) Criminal prosecution under this section does not affect the right of a telecommunication service provider to bring a civil action for redress for damages suffered as a result of the commission of any of the acts prohibited by this section.

(3) This section does not abridge or alter any other right, action, or remedy otherwise available to a telecommunication service provider.   1996

76-6-410. Theft by person having custody of property pursuant to repair or rental agreement.

A person is guilty of theft if:

(1) Having custody of property pursuant to an agreement between himself or another and the owner thereof whereby the actor or another is to perform for compensation a specific service for the owner involving the maintenance, repair, or use of such property, he intentionally uses or operates it, without the consent of the owner, for his own purposes in a manner constituting a gross deviation from the agreed purpose; or

(2) Having custody of any property pursuant to a rental or lease agreement where it is to be returned in a specified manner or at a specified time, intentionally fails to comply with the terms of the agreement concerning return so as to render such failure a gross deviation from the agreement.   1973

76-6-410.5. Theft of a rental vehicle.

(1) As used in this section:

(a) "Motor vehicle" means a self-propelled vehicle that is intended primarily for use and operation on the highways.

(b) "Rental agreement" means any written agreement stating the terms and conditions governing the use of a motor vehicle provided by a rental company.

(c) "Rental company" means any person or organization in the business of providing motor vehicles to the public.

(d) "Renter" means any person or organization obtaining the use of a motor vehicle from a rental company under the terms of a rental agreement.

(2) A renter is guilty of theft of a rental vehicle if, without notice to and permission of the rental company, the renter knowingly fails without good cause to return the vehicle within 72 hours after the time established for the return in the rental agreement.

(3) If the motor vehicle is not rented on a periodic tenancy basis, the rental company shall include the following information, legibly written, as part of the terms of the rental agreement:

(a) the date and time the motor vehicle is required to be returned; and

(b) the maximum penalties under state law if the motor vehicle is not returned within 72 hours from the date and time stated in compliance with Subsection (3)(a).   2001

76-6-411. Repealed.   1974

76-6-412. Theft — Classification of offenses — Action for treble damages.

(1) Theft of property and services as provided in this chapter shall be punishable:

(a) as a felony of the second degree if the:

(i) value of the property or services is or exceeds $5,000;

(ii) property stolen is a firearm or an operable motor vehicle;

(iii) actor is armed with a dangerous weapon, as defined in Section 76-1-601, at the time of the theft; or

(iv) property is stolen from the person of another;

(b) as a felony of the third degree if:

(i) the value of the property or services is or exceeds $1,000 but is less than $5,000;

(ii) the actor has been twice before convicted of theft, any robbery, or any burglary with intent to commit theft; or

(iii) in a case not amounting to a second-degree felony, the property taken is a stallion, mare, colt, gelding, cow, heifer, steer, ox, bull, calf, sheep, goat, mule, jack, jenny, swine, poultry, or a fur-bearing animal raised for commercial purposes;

(c) as a class A misdemeanor if the value of the property stolen is or exceeds $300 but is less than $1,000; or

(d) as a class B misdemeanor if the value of the property stolen is less than $300.

(2) Any person who violates Subsection 76-6-408(1) or Section 76-6-413, or commits theft of property described in Subsection 76-6-412(1)(b)(iii), is civilly liable for three times the amount of actual damages, if any sustained by the plaintiff, and for costs of suit and reasonable attorneys' fees.   1997

76-6-413. Release of fur-bearing animals — Penalty — Finding.

(1) In any case not amounting to a felony of the second degree, any person who intentionally and without permission of the owner releases any fur-bearing animal raised for commercial purposes is guilty of a felony of the third degree.

(2) The Legislature finds that the release of fur-bearing animals raised for commercial purposes subjects the animals to unnecessary suffering through deprivation of food and shelter and compromises their genetic integrity, thereby permanently depriving the owner of substantial value.   1997

PART 5

FRAUD

76-6-501. Forgery — "Writing" defined.

(1) A person is guilty of forgery if, with purpose to defraud anyone, or with knowledge that he is facilitating a fraud to be perpetrated by anyone, he:

(a) alters any writing of another without his authority or utters any such altered writing; or

(b) makes, completes, executes, authenticates, issues, transfers, publishes, or utters any writing so that the writing or the making, completion, execution, authentication, issuance, transference, publication or utterance purports to be the act of another, whether the person is existent or nonexistent, or purports to have been executed at a time or place or in a numbered sequence other than was in fact the case, or to be a copy of an original when no such original existed.

(2) As used in this section, "writing" includes printing, electronic storage or transmission, or any other method of recording valuable information including forms such as:

(a) checks, tokens, stamps, seals, credit cards, badges, trademarks, money, and any other symbols of value, right, privilege, or identification;

(b) a security, revenue stamp, or any other instrument or writing issued by a government or any agency; or

(c) a check, an issue of stocks, bonds, or any other instrument or writing representing an interest in or claim against property, or a pecuniary interest in or claim against any person or enterprise.

(3) Forgery is a felony of the third degree.   1996

76-6-502. Possession of forged writing or device for writing — Penalty.

Any person who, with intent to defraud, knowingly possesses any writing that is a forgery as defined in Section 76-6-501, or who with intent to defraud knowingly possesses any device for making any writing that is a forgery as defined in Section 76-6-501, is guilty of a third degree felony.   2001

76-6-503. Repealed.   2005

76-6-503.5. Wrongful liens and fraudulent handling of recordable writings — Penalties.

(1) "Lien" means:

(a) an instrument or document filed pursuant to Section 70A-9a-516;

(b) an instrument or document described in Subsection 38-9-1(6); and

(c) any instrument or document that creates or purports to create a lien or encumbrance on an owner's interest in real or personal property or a claim on another's assets.

(2) A person is guilty of the crime of wrongful lien if that person knowingly makes, utters, records, or files a lien:

(a) having no objectively reasonable basis to believe he has a present and lawful property interest in the property or a claim on the assets; or

(b) if the person files the lien in violation of a civil wrongful lien injunction pursuant to Title 38, Chapter 9a, Wrongful Lien Injunctions.

(3) A violation of this section is a third degree felony unless the person has been previously convicted of an offense under this section, in which case the violation is a second degree felony.

(4) (a) Any person who with intent to deceive or injure anyone falsifies, destroys, removes, records, or conceals any will, deed, mortgage, security instrument, lien, or other writing for which the law provides public recording is guilty of fraudulent handling of recordable writings.

(b) A violation of Subsection (4)(a) is a third degree felony unless the person has been previously convicted of an offense under this section, in which case the violation is a second degree felony.

(5) This section does not prohibit prosecution for any act in violation of Section 76-8-414 or for any offense greater than an offense under this section.
                  2005

76-6-504. Tampering with records — Penalty.

(1) Any person who, having no privilege to do so, knowingly falsifies, destroys, removes, or conceals any writing, other than the writings enumerated in Section 76-6-503.5 for which the law provides public recording or any record, public or private, with intent to deceive or injure any person or to conceal any wrongdoing is guilty of tampering with records.

(2) Tampering with records is a class B misdemeanor.   2005

76-6-505. Issuing a bad check or draft — Presumption.

(1) Any person who issues or passes a check or draft for the payment of money, for the purpose of obtaining from any person, firm, partnership, or corporation, any money, property, or other thing of value or paying for any services, wages, salary, labor, or rent, knowing it will not be paid by the drawee and payment is refused by the drawee, is guilty of issuing a bad check or draft.

For purposes of this subsection, a person who issues a check or draft for which payment is refused by the drawee is presumed to know the check or draft would not be paid if he had no account with the drawee at the time of issue.

(2) Any person who issues or passes a check or draft for the payment of money, for the purpose of obtaining from any person, firm, partnership, or corporation, any money, property, or other thing of value or paying for any services, wages, salary, labor, or rent, payment of which check or draft is legally refused by the drawee, is guilty of issuing a bad check or draft if he fails to make good and actual payment to the payee in the amount of the refused check or draft

within 14 days of his receiving actual notice of the check or draft's nonpayment.

(3) An offense of issuing a bad check or draft shall be punished as follows:

(a) If the check or draft or series of checks or drafts made or drawn in this state within a period not exceeding six months amounts to a sum that is less than $300, the offense is a class B misdemeanor.

(b) If the check or draft or checks or drafts made or drawn in this state within a period not exceeding six months amounts to a sum that is or exceeds $300 but is less than $1,000, the offense is a class A misdemeanor.

(c) If the check or draft or checks or drafts made or drawn in this state within a period not exceeding six months amounts to a sum that is or exceeds $1,000 but is less than $5,000, the offense is a felony of the third degree.

(d) If the check or draft or checks or drafts made or drawn in this state within a period not exceeding six months amounts to a sum that is or exceeds $5,000, the offense is a second degree felony.   1995

76-6-506.   Financial transaction card offenses — Definitions.

For purposes of this part:

(1) "Authorized credit card merchant" means a person as defined in Section 68-3-12 who is authorized by an issuer to furnish money, goods, services, or anything else of value upon presentation of a financial transaction card by a card holder and to present valid credit card sales drafts to the issuer for payment.

(2) "Automated banking device" means any machine which, when properly activated by a financial transaction card or a personal identification code, may be used for any of the purposes for which a financial transaction card may be used.

(3) "Card holder" means any person or organization named on the face of a financial transaction card to whom or for whose benefit a financial transaction card is issued by an issuer.

(4) "Credit card sales draft" means any sales slip, draft, or other written or electronic record of a sale of money, goods, services, or anything else of value made or purported to be made to or at the request of a card holder with a financial transaction card, financial transaction card credit number, or personal identification code, whether the record of the sale or purported sale is evidenced by a sales draft, voucher, or other similar document in writing or electronically recorded and transmitted.

(5) "Financial transaction card" means:

(a) any credit card, credit plate, bank services card, banking card, check guarantee card, debit card, telephone credit card, or any other card, issued by an issuer for the use of the card holder in obtaining money, goods, services, or anything else of value on credit, or in certifying or guaranteeing to a person or business the availability to the card holder of the funds on deposit that are equal to or greater than the amount necessary to honor a draft or check payable to the order of the person or business; or

(b) any instrument or device used in providing the card holder access to a demand or time deposit account for the purpose of making deposits of money or checks in the account, or withdrawing funds from the account in the form of money, money orders, travelers' checks or other form representing value, or transferring funds from any demand or time deposit account to any credit card account in full or partial satisfaction of any outstanding balance existing in the credit card account.

(6) "Issuer" means a business organization or financial institution or its agent that issues a financial transaction card.

(7) "Personal identification code" means any numerical or alphabetical code assigned to a card holder by the issuer to permit the authorized electronic use of his financial transaction card.
1991

76-6-506.1.   Financial transaction card offenses — Falsely making, coding, or signing card — Falsely signing evidence of card transaction.

Any person is guilty of a third degree felony who, with intent to defraud:

(1) counterfeits, falsely makes, embosses, or encodes magnetically or electronically any financial transaction card;

(2) knowingly possesses any financial transaction card produced or altered as described in Subsection (1);

(3) uses through carbon or other impressions or copies of credit card sales drafts or through any other means, the account number or personal identification code of a card holder in the creation of a fictitious or counterfeit credit card sales draft; or

(4) signs the name of another or a fictitious name to a financial transaction card, credit card sales draft, or any instrument for the payment of money which evidences a financial transaction card transaction.   1997

76-6-506.2.   Financial transaction card offenses — Unlawful use of card or automated banking device — False application for card.

It is unlawful for any person to:

(1) knowingly, with intent to defraud, obtain or attempt to obtain credit or purchase or attempt to purchase goods, property, or services, by the use of a false, fictitious, altered, counterfeit, revoked, expired, stolen, or fraudulently obtained financial transaction card, by any financial transaction card credit number, personal identification code, or by the use of a financial transaction card not authorized by the issuer or the card holder;

(2) use a financial transaction card, with intent to defraud, to knowingly and willfully exceed the actual balance of a demand or time deposit account;

(3) use a financial transaction card, with intent to defraud, to willfully exceed an authorized credit line by $500 or more, or by 50% of such line, whichever is greater;

(4) willfully, with intent to defraud, deposit into his or any other account by means of an automated banking device a false, fictitious, forged, altered, or counterfeit check, draft, money order, or any other similar document;

(5) make application for a financial transaction card to an issuer, while knowingly making or causing to be made a false statement or report relative to his name, occupation, financial condi-

tion, assets, or to willfully and substantially undervalue or understate any indebtedness for the purposes of influencing the issuer to issue the financial transaction card; or

(6) knowingly, with intent to defraud any authorized credit card merchant, card holder, or issuer, sell or attempt to sell credit card sales drafts to an authorized credit card merchant or any other person or organization, for any consideration whether at a discount or otherwise, or present or cause to be presented to the issuer or an authorized credit card merchant, for payment or collection, any such credit card sales draft, if:

(i) the draft is counterfeit or fictitious;

(ii) the purported sales evidenced by any such credit card sales draft did not take place;

(iii) the purported sale was not authorized by the card holder;

(iv) the items or services purported to be sold as evidenced by the credit card sales drafts are not delivered or rendered to the card holder or person intended to receive them; or

(v) when delivered or rendered, the goods or services are materially different or of materially lesser value or quality than represented by the seller or his agent to the purchaser, or have substantial discrepancies from goods or services impliedly represented by the purchase price when compared with the actual goods or services delivered or rendered. 1991

76-6-506.3. Financial transaction card offenses — Unlawful acquisition, possession, or transfer of card.

Any person is guilty of a third degree felony who:

(1) acquires a financial transaction card from another without the consent of the card holder or the issuer, or, with the knowledge that it has been acquired without consent, and with intent to use it in violation of Section 76-6-506.2;

(2) receives a financial transaction card with intent to use it in violation of Section 76-6-506.2;

(3) sells or transfers a financial transaction card to another person with the knowledge that it will be used in violation of Section 76-6-506.2;

(4) (a) acquires a financial transaction card that the person knows was lost, mislaid, or delivered under a mistake as to the identity or address of the card holder; and

(b) (i) retains possession with intent to use it in violation of Section 76-6-506.2; or

(ii) sells or transfers a financial transaction card to another person with the knowledge that it will be used in violation of Section 76-6-506.2; or

(5) possesses, sells, or transfers any information necessary for the use of a financial transaction card, including the credit number of the card, the expiration date of the card, or the personal identification code related to the card:

(a) (i) without the consent of the card holder or the issuer; or

(ii) with the knowledge that the information has been acquired without consent of the card holder or the issuer; and

(b) with intent to use the information in violation of Section 76-6-506.2. 2003

76-6-506.4. Financial transaction card offenses — Property obtained by unlawful conduct.

It is unlawful for any person to receive, retain, conceal, possess, or dispose of personal property, cash, or other form representing value, if he knows or has reason to believe the property, cash, or other form representing value has been obtained through unlawful conduct described in Section 76-6-506.1, 76-6-506.2, or 76-6-506.3. 1983

76-6-506.5. Financial transaction card offenses — Classification — Multiple violations.

(1) Any person found guilty of unlawful conduct described in Section 76-6-506.2, 76-6-506.4, or 76-6-506.6 shall be punished for:

(a) a class B misdemeanor when the value of the property, money, or thing obtained or sought to be obtained is less than $300;

(b) a class A misdemeanor when the value of the property, money, or thing obtained or sought to be obtained is or exceeds $300 but is less than $1,000;

(c) a third degree felony when the value of the property, money, or thing obtained or sought to be obtained is or exceeds $1,000 but is less than $5,000; and

(d) a second degree felony when the value of the property, money, or thing obtained or sought to be obtained is or exceeds $5,000.

(2) Multiple violations of Subsection 76-6-506.2(1), Sections 76-6-506.4, and 76-6-506.6 may be aggregated into a single offense, and the degree of the offense is determined by the total value of all property, money, or things obtained or sought to be obtained through the multiple violations.

(3) The court shall make appropriate findings in any prosecution under this section that the card holder did not commit the crime if:

(a) another person uses the financial transaction card without the card holder's consent; and

(b) that person commits a crime in addition to a financial transaction card offense with the card holder's financial transaction card. 2000

76-6-506.6. Financial transaction card offenses — Unauthorized factoring of credit card sales drafts.

It is unlawful for any person, knowingly, with intent to defraud, acting without the express authorization of the issuer, to employ, solicit, or otherwise cause an authorized credit card merchant, or for the authorized credit card merchant himself, to present any credit card sales draft to the issuer for payment pertaining to any sale or purported sale of goods or services which was not made by the authorized credit card merchant in the ordinary course of business. 1991

76-6-506.7. Obtaining encoded information on a financial transaction card with the intent to defraud the issuer, holder, or merchant.

(1) As used in this section:

(a) "Financial transaction card" or "card" means any credit card, credit plate, bank services card, banking card, check guarantee card, debit card, telephone credit card, or any other card, issued by an issuer for the use of the card holder in:

(i) obtaining money, goods, services, or anything else of value on credit; or

(ii) certifying or guaranteeing to a merchant the availability to the card holder of the funds on deposit that are equal to or greater than the amount necessary to honor a draft or check as the instrument for obtaining, purchasing, or receiving goods, services, money, or any other thing of value from the merchant.

(b) (i) "Merchant" means an owner or operator of any retail mercantile establishment or any agent, employee, lessee, consignee, officer, director, franchisee, or independent contractor of the owner or operator.

(ii) "Merchant" also means a person:

(A) who receives from a card holder, or a third person the merchant believes to be the card holder, a financial transaction card or information from a financial transaction card, or what the merchant believes to be a financial transaction card or information from a card; and

(B) who accepts the financial transaction card or information from a card under Subsection (1)(a)(ii)(A) as the instrument for obtaining, purchasing, or receiving goods, services, money, or any other thing of value from the merchant.

(c) "Reencoder" means an electronic device that places encoded information from the magnetic strip or stripe of a financial transaction card onto the magnetic strip or stripe of a different financial transaction card.

(d) "Scanning device" means a scanner, reader, or any other electronic device used to access, read, scan, obtain, memorize, or store, temporarily or permanently, information encoded on the magnetic strip or stripe of a financial transaction card.

(2) (a) A person is guilty of a third degree felony who uses:

(i) a scanning device to access, read, obtain, memorize, or store, temporarily or permanently, information encoded on the magnetic strip or stripe of a financial transaction card without the permission of the card holder and with intent to defraud the card holder, the issuer, or a merchant; or

(ii) a reencoder to place information encoded on the magnetic strip or stripe of a financial transaction card onto the magnetic strip or stripe of a different card without the permission of the authorized user of the card from which the information is being reencoded and with the intent to defraud the card holder, the issuer, or a merchant.

(b) Any person who has been convicted previously of an offense under Subsection (2)(a) is guilty of a second degree felony upon a second conviction and any subsequent conviction for the offense.   2003

76-6-507. Deceptive business practices — Definitions — Defense.

(1) A person is guilty of a class B misdemeanor if, in the course of business, he:

(a) uses or possesses for use a false weight or measure, or any other device for falsely determining or recording any quality or quantity;

(b) takes or attempts to take more than the represented quantity of any commodity or service when as buyer he furnishes the weight or measure; or

(c) sells, offers, or exposes for sale adulterated or mislabeled commodities.

(2) (a) "Adulterated" means varying from the standard of composition or quality prescribed, or pursuant to any statute providing criminal penalties for a variance, or set by established commercial usage.

(b) "Mislabeled" means varying from the standard of truth or disclosure in labeling prescribed by or pursuant to any statute providing criminal penalties for a variance, or set by established commercial usage[.]

(3) It is an affirmative defense to prosecution under this section that the defendant's conduct was not knowing or reckless.   1985

76-6-508. Bribery of or receiving bribe by person in the business of selection, appraisal, or criticism of goods or services.

(1) A person is guilty of a class A misdemeanor when, without the consent of the employer or principal, contrary to the interests of the employer or principal:

(a) he confers, offers, or agrees to confer upon the employee, agent, or fiduciary of an employer or principal any benefit with the purpose of influencing the conduct of the employee, agent, or fiduciary in relating to his employer's or principal's affairs; or

(b) he, as an employee, agent, or fiduciary of an employer or principal, solicits, accepts, or agrees to accept any benefit from another upon an agreement or understanding that such benefit will influence his conduct in relation to his employer's or principal's affairs; provided that this section does not apply to inducements made or accepted solely for the purpose of causing a change in employment by an employee, agent, or fiduciary.

(2) A person is guilty of violation of this section if he holds himself out to the public as being engaged in the business of making disinterested selection, appraisal, or criticism of goods or services and he solicits, accepts, or agrees to accept any benefit to influence his selection, appraisal, or criticism.   1991

76-6-509. Bribery of a labor official.

(1) Any person who offers, confers, or agrees to confer upon a labor official any benefit with intent to influence him in respect to any of his acts, decisions, or duties as a labor official is guilty of bribery of a labor official.

(2) Bribery of a labor official is a felony of the third degree.   1973

76-6-510. Bribe receiving by a labor official.

(1) Any labor official who solicits, accepts, or agrees to accept any benefit from another person upon an agreement or understanding that the benefit will influence him in any of his acts, decisions, or duties as a labor official is guilty of bribe receiving by a labor official.

(2) Bribe receiving by a labor official is a felony of the third degree.   1973

76-6-511. Defrauding creditors.

A person is guilty of a class A misdemeanor if:

(1) he destroys, removes, conceals, encumbers, transfers, or otherwise deals with property subject to a security interest with a purpose to hinder enforcement of that interest; or

(2) knowing that proceedings have been or are about to be instituted for the appointment of a

person entitled to administer property for the benefit of creditors, he:

(a) destroys, removes, conceals, encumbers, transfers, or otherwise deals with any property with a purpose to defeat or obstruct the claim of any creditor, or otherwise to obstruct the operation of any law relating to administration of property for the benefit of creditors; or

(b) presents to any creditor or to an assignee for the benefit of creditors, orally or in writing, any statement relating to the debtor's estate, knowing that a material part of such statement is false.   1991

76-6-512. Acceptance of deposit by insolvent financial institution.

A person is guilty of a felony of the third degree if:

(1) as an officer, manager, or other person participating in the direction of a financial institution, as defined in Section 7-1-103, he receives or permits receipt of a deposit or other investment knowing that the institution is or is about to become unable, from any cause, to pay its obligations in the ordinary course of business; and

(2) he knows that the person making the payment to the institution is unaware of such present or prospective inability.   1997

76-6-513. Definitions — Unlawful dealing of property by a fiduciary — Penalties.

(1) As used in this section:

(a) "Fiduciary" is as defined in Section 22-1-1.

(b) "Financial institution" means "depository institution" and "trust company" as defined in Section 7-1-103.

(c) "Governmental entity" is as defined in Section 63-30d-102.

(d) "Person" does not include a financial institution whose fiduciary functions are supervised by the Department of Financial Institutions or a federal regulatory agency.

(e) "Property" is as defined in Section 76-6-401.

(f) "Public monies" is as defined in Section 76-8-401.

(2) A person is guilty of unlawfully dealing with property by a fiduciary if he deals with property that has been entrusted to him as a fiduciary, or property of a governmental entity, public monies, or of a financial institution, in a manner which he knows is a violation of his duty and which involves substantial risk of loss or detriment to the owner or to a person for whose benefit the property was entrusted. A violation of this Subsection (2) is punishable under Section 76-6-412.

(3) (a) A person acting as a fiduciary is guilty of a violation of this subsection if, without permission of the owner of the property or some other person with authority to give permission, he pledges as collateral for a personal loan, or as collateral for the benefit of some party, other than the owner or the person for whose benefit the property was entrusted, the property that has been entrusted to the fiduciary.

(b) An offense under Subsection (3)(a) is punishable as:

(i) a felony of the second degree if the value of the property wrongfully pledged is or exceeds $5,000;

(ii) a felony of the third degree if the value of the property wrongfully pledged is or exceeds $1,000 but is less than $5,000;

(iii) a class A misdemeanor if the value of the property is or exceeds $300, but is less than $1,000 or the actor has been twice before convicted of theft, robbery, burglary with intent to commit theft, or unlawful dealing with property by a fiduciary; or

(iv) a class B misdemeanor if the value of the property is less than $300.   2004

76-6-514. Bribery or threat to influence contest.

A person is guilty of a felony of the third degree if:

(1) With a purpose to influence any participant or prospective participant not to give his best efforts in a publicly exhibited contest, he confers or offers or agrees to confer any benefit upon or threatens any injury to a participant or prospective participant; or

(2) With a purpose to influence an official in a publicly exhibited contest to perform his duties improperly, he confers or offers or agrees to confer any benefit upon or threatens any injury to such official; or

(3) With a purpose to influence the outcome of a publicly exhibited contest, he tampers with any person, animal, or thing contrary to the rules and usages purporting to govern the contest; or

(4) He knowingly solicits, accepts, or agrees to accept any benefit, the giving of which would be criminal under [Subsection] (1) or (2).   1973

76-6-515. Using or making slugs.

(1) A person is guilty of a class B misdemeanor if:

(a) With a purpose to defraud the supplier of property or a service offered or sold by means of a coin machine, he inserts, deposits, or uses a slug in that machine; or

(b) He makes, possesses, or disposes of a slug with the purpose of enabling a person to use it fraudulently in a coin machine.

(2) As used in this section:

(a) "Coin machine" means any mechanical or electronic device or receptacle designed to receive a coin or bill of a certain denomination, or a token made for the purpose, and, in return for the insertion or deposit thereof, automatically to offer, provide, assist in providing or permit the acquisition of property or a public or private service.

(b) "Slug" means any object which, by virtue of its size, shape, or other quality, is capable of being inserted, deposited, or otherwise used in a coin machine as an improper substitute for a genuine coin, bill, or token.   1973

76-6-516. Conveyance of real estate by married man without wife's consent.

Any married man who falsely represents himself as unmarried and under such representation knowingly conveys or mortgages real estate situate in this state, without the assent or concurrence of his wife when such consent or concurrence is necessary to relinquish her inchoate statutory interest therein, is guilty of a felony of the third degree.   1973

76-6-517. Making a false credit report.

(1) Any person who knowingly makes a materially false or misleading written statement to obtain property or credit for himself or another is guilty of making a false credit report.

(2) Making a false credit report is a class A misdemeanor.   1973

76-6-518. Criminal simulation.

(1) A person is guilty of criminal simulation if, with intent to defraud another:

(a) he makes or alters an object in whole or in part so that it appears to have value because of age, antiquity, rarity, source, or authorship that it does not have;

(b) he sells, passes, or otherwise utters an object so made or altered;

(c) he possesses an object so made or altered with intent to sell, pass, or otherwise utter it; or

(d) he authenticates or certifies an object so made or altered as genuine or as different from what it is.

(2) Criminal simulation is punishable as follows:

(a) If the value defrauded or intended to be defrauded is less than $300, the offense is a class B misdemeanor.

(b) If the value defrauded or intended to be defrauded is or exceeds $300 but is less than $1,000, the offense is a class A misdemeanor.

(c) If the value defrauded or intended to be defrauded is or exceeds $1,000 but is less than $5,000, the offense is a felony of the third degree.

(d) If the value defrauded or intended to be defrauded is or exceeds $5,000, the offense is a felony of the second degree.   1995

76-6-519. Repealed.   1983

76-6-520. Criminal usury.

(1) A person is guilty of criminal usury when he knowingly engages in or directly or indirectly provides financing for the business of making loans at a higher rate of interest or consideration therefor than is authorized by law.

(2) Criminal usury is a felony of the third degree.   1973

76-6-521. Fraudulent insurance act.

(1) A person commits a fraudulent insurance act if that person with intent to defraud:

(a) presents or causes to be presented any oral or written statement or representation knowing that the statement or representation contains false or fraudulent information concerning any fact material to an application for the issuance or renewal of an insurance policy, certificate, or contract;

(b) presents, or causes to be presented, any oral or written statement or representation:

(i) (A) as part of or in support of a claim for payment or other benefit pursuant to an insurance policy, certificate, or contract; or

(B) in connection with any civil claim asserted for recovery of damages for personal or bodily injuries or property damage; and

(ii) knowing that the statement or representation contains false or fraudulent information concerning any fact or thing material to the claim;

(c) knowingly accepts a benefit from proceeds derived from a fraudulent insurance act;

(d) intentionally, knowingly, or recklessly devises a scheme or artifice to obtain fees for professional services, or anything of value by means of false or fraudulent pretenses, representations, promises, or material omissions;

(e) knowingly employs, uses, or acts as a runner, as defined in Section 31A-31-102, for the purpose of committing a fraudulent insurance act;

(f) knowingly assists, abets, solicits, or conspires with another to commit a fraudulent insurance act; or

(g) knowingly supplies false or fraudulent material information in any document or statement required by the Department of Insurance.

(2) (a) A violation of Subsection (1)(a) is a class B misdemeanor.

(b) A violation of Subsections (1)(b) through (1)(g) is punishable as in the manner prescribed by Section 76-10-1801 for communication fraud for property of like value.

(3) A corporation or association is guilty of the offense of insurance fraud under the same conditions as those set forth in Section 76-2-204.

(4) The determination of the degree of any offense under Subsections (1)(b) through (1)(g) shall be measured by the total value of all property, money, or other things obtained or sought to be obtained by the fraudulent insurance act or acts described in Subsections (1)(b) through (1)(g).   2004

76-6-522. Definitions — Equity skimming of a vehicle — Penalties.

(1) As used in this section:

(a) "Broker" means any person who, for compensation of any kind, arranges for the sale, lease, sublease, or transfer of a vehicle.

(b) "Dealer" means any person engaged in the business of selling, leasing, or exchanging vehicles for compensation of any kind.

(c) "Lease" means any grant of use or possession of a vehicle for consideration, with or without an option to buy.

(d) "Security interest" means an interest in a vehicle that secures payment or performance of an obligation.

(e) "Transfer" means any delivery or conveyance of a vehicle to another from one person to another.

(f) "Vehicle" means every device in, upon, or by which any person or property is or may be transported or drawn upon a highway, or through the air or water, or over land and includes a manufactured home or mobile home as defined in Section 41-1a-102.

(2) A dealer or broker or any other person in collusion with a dealer or broker is guilty of equity skimming of a vehicle if he transfers or arranges the transfer of a vehicle for consideration or profit, when he knows or should have known the vehicle is subject to a lease or security interest, without first obtaining written authorization of the lessor or holder of the security interest.

(3) Equity skimming of a vehicle is a third degree felony.

(4) It is a defense to the crime of equity skimming of a vehicle if the accused proves by a preponderance of the evidence that the lease obligation or security interest has been satisfied within 30 days following the transfer of the vehicle.   1992

PART 6

RETAIL THEFT

76-6-601. Definitions.

As used in this chapter:

(1) "Merchandise" means any personal property displayed, held or offered for sale by a merchant.

(2) "Merchant" means an owner or operator of any retail mercantile establishment where merchandise is displayed, held or offered for sale and includes the merchant's employees, servants or agents.

(3) "Minor" means any unmarried person under 18 years of age.

(4) "Peace officer" has the same meaning as provided in Title 53, Chapter 13, Peace Officer Classifications.

(5) "Premises of a retail mercantile establishment" includes, but is not limited to, the retail mercantile establishment; any common use areas in shopping centers and all parking lots or areas set aside for the benefit of those patrons of the retail mercantile establishment.

(6) "Retail mercantile establishment" means any place where merchandise is displayed, held, or offered for sale to the public.

(7) "Retail value" means the merchant's stated or advertised price of the merchandise.

(8) "Shopping cart" means those push carts of the types which are commonly provided by grocery stores, drug stores, or other mercantile establishments or markets for the use of the public in transporting commodities in stores and markets from the store to a place outside the store.

(9) "Under-ring" means to cause the cash register or other sales recording device to reflect less than the retail value of the merchandise.   1998

76-6-602. Retail theft, acts constituting.

A person commits the offense of retail theft when he knowingly:

(1) Takes possession of, conceals, carries away, transfers or causes to be carried away or transferred, any merchandise displayed, held, stored or offered for sale in a retail mercantile establishment with the intention of retaining such merchandise or with the intention of depriving the merchant permanently of the possession, use or benefit of such merchandise without paying the retail value of such merchandise; or

(2) Alters, transfers, or removes any label, price tag, marking, indicia of value or any other markings which aid in determining value of any merchandise displayed, held, stored or offered for sale, in a retail mercantile establishment and attempts to purchase such merchandise personally or in consort with another at less than the retail value with the intention of depriving the merchant of the retail value of such merchandise; or

(3) Transfers any merchandise displayed, held, stored or offered for sale in a retail mercantile establishment from the container in or on which such merchandise is displayed to any other container with the intention of depriving the merchant of the retail value of such merchandise; or

(4) Under-rings with the intention of depriving the merchant of the retail value of the merchandise; or

(5) Removes a shopping cart from the premises of a retail mercantile establishment with the intent of depriving the merchant of the possession, use or benefit of such cart.   1979

76-6-603. Detention of suspected violator by merchant — Purposes.

Any merchant who has probable cause to believe that a person has committed retail theft may detain such person, on or off the premises of a retail mercantile establishment, in a reasonable manner and for a reasonable length of time for all or any of the following purposes:

(1) To make reasonable inquiry as to whether such person has in his possession unpurchased merchandise and to make reasonable investigation of the ownership of such merchandise;

(2) To request identification;

(3) To verify such identification;

(4) To make a reasonable request of such person to place or keep in full view any merchandise such individual may have removed, or which the merchant has reason to believe he may have removed, from its place of display or elsewhere, whether for examination, purchase or for any other reasonable purpose;

(5) To inform a peace officer of the detention of the person and surrender that person to the custody of a peace officer;

(6) In the case of a minor, to inform a peace officer, the parents, guardian or other private person interested in the welfare of that minor immediately, if possible, of this detention and to surrender custody of such minor to such person.

A merchant may make a detention as permitted herein off the premises of a retail mercantile establishment only if such detention is pursuant to an immediate pursuit of such person.   1979

76-6-604. Defense to action by person detained.

In any action for false arrest, false imprisonment, unlawful detention, defamation of character, assault, trespass, or invasion of civil rights brought by any person detained by the merchant, it shall be a defense to such action that the merchant detaining such person had probable cause to believe that the person had committed retail theft and that the merchant acted reasonably under all circumstances.   1979

76-6-605. Photographs of items allegedly taken or converted — Admissibility — Procedure.

(1) As used in this section "items" means:

(a) goods or merchandise as defined in Section 76-6-601; and

(b) library materials, as defined in Title 76, Chapter 6, Part 8.

(2) In any prosecution for a violation of Section 76-6-602 or Title 76, Chapter 6, Part 8, Library Theft, photographs of the items alleged to have been taken or converted are competent evidence of the items and are admissible in any proceeding, hearing, or trial as if the items themselves were introduced as evidence.

(3) The photographs shall bear a written description of the items alleged to have been taken or converted, the name of the owner, or the store, establishment, or library, as appropriate, where the alleged offense occurred, the name of the accused, the name of the arresting peace officer, the date of the photograph, and the name of the photographer.

(4) The writing shall be made under oath by the arresting peace officer, and the photographs identified by the signature of the photographer. Upon the filing of the photograph and writing with the authority or court holding the items as evidence, they shall be returned to their owner, or returned to the proprietor or manager of the store or establishment, or to an employee of the library, as is appropriate.   1989

76-6-606. Penalty.

An act of theft committed in violation of this part shall be punished in accordance with Subsection 76-6-412(1).   2000

76-6-607. Report of arrest to division.

Any arrest made for a violation of this part shall be reported by the appropriate jurisdiction to the Criminal Investigations and Technical Services Division of the Department of Public Safety, established in Section 53-10-103, which shall keep a record of the arrest together with the disposition of the arrest for purposes of inquiry by any law enforcement agency. 1998

76-6-608. Theft detection shielding devices prohibited — Penalties.

(1) A person may not knowingly:

(a) make or possess any container or device used for, intended for use for, or represented as having the purpose of shielding merchandise from any electronic or magnetic theft alarm sensor, with the intent to commit a theft of merchandise;

(b) sell, offer to sell, advertise, give, transport, or otherwise transfer to another any container or device intended for use for or represented as having the purpose of shielding merchandise from any electronic or magnetic theft alarm sensor;

(c) possess any tool or instrument designed to remove any theft detection device from any merchandise, with the intent to use the tool or instrument to remove any theft detection device from any merchandise without the permission of the merchant or the person owning or in possession of the merchandise; or

(d) intentionally remove a theft detection device from merchandise prior to purchase and without the permission of the merchant.

(2) (a) A violation of Subsection (1)(a), (b), or (c) is a class A misdemeanor.

(b) A violation of Subsection (1)(d) is a:

(i) class B misdemeanor if the value of the merchandise from which the theft detection device is removed is less than $300; or

(ii) class A misdemeanor if the value of the merchandise from which the theft detection device is removed is or exceeds $300.

(3) A violation of Subsection (1) is a separate offense from any offense listed in Title 76, Chapter 6, Part 4, Theft, or Part 6, Retail Theft.

(4) Criminal prosecutions under this section do not affect any person's right of civil action for redress for damages suffered as a result of any violation of this section. 2003

PART 7

COMPUTER CRIMES

76-6-701. Computer Crimes Act — Short title.

This part is known as the "Utah Computer Crimes Act." 1986

76-6-702. Definitions.

As used in this part:

(1) "Access" means to directly or indirectly use, attempt to use, instruct, communicate with, cause input to, cause output from, or otherwise make use of any resources of a computer, computer system, computer network, or any means of communication with any of them.

(2) "Authorization" means having the express or implied consent or permission of the owner, or of the person authorized by the owner to give consent or permission to access a computer, computer system, or computer network in a manner not exceeding the consent or permission.

(3) "Computer" means any electronic device or communication facility that stores, retrieves, processes, or transmits data.

(4) "Computer system" means a set of related, connected or unconnected, devices, software, or other related computer equipment.

(5) "Computer network" means:

(a) the interconnection of communication or telecommunication lines between:

(i) computers; or

(ii) computers and remote terminals; or

(b) the interconnection by wireless technology between:

(i) computers; or

(ii) computers and remote terminals.

(6) "Computer property" includes electronic impulses, electronically produced data, information, financial instruments, software, or programs, in either machine or human readable form, any other tangible or intangible item relating to a computer, computer system, computer network, and copies of any of them.

(7) "Confidential" means data, text, or computer property that is protected by a security system that clearly evidences that the owner or custodian intends that it not be available to others without the owner's or custodian's permission.

(8) "Information" does not include information obtained:

(a) through use of:

(i) an electronic product identification or tracking system; or

(ii) other technology used by a retailer to identify, track, or price goods; and

(b) by a retailer through the use of equipment designed to read the electronic product identification or tracking system data located within the retailer's location.

(9) "License or entitlement" includes:

(a) licenses, certificates, and permits granted by governments;

(b) degrees, diplomas, and grades awarded by educational institutions;

(c) military ranks, grades, decorations, and awards;

(d) membership and standing in organizations and religious institutions;

(e) certification as a peace officer;

(f) credit reports; and

(g) another record or datum upon which a person may be reasonably expected to rely in making decisions that will have a direct benefit or detriment to another.

(10) "Security system" means a computer, computer system, network, or computer property that has some form of access control technology implemented, such as encryption, password protection, other forced authentication, or access control designed to keep out unauthorized persons.

(11) "Services" include computer time, data manipulation, and storage functions.

(12) "Financial instrument" includes any check, draft, money order, certificate of deposit, letter of credit, bill of exchange, electronic fund transfer, automated clearing house transaction, credit card, or marketable security.

(13) "Software" or "program" means a series of instructions or statements in a form acceptable to a computer, relating to the operations of the computer, or permitting the functioning of a computer system in a manner designed to provide results including system control programs, application programs, or copies of any of them. 2005

76-6-703. Computer crimes and penalties.

(1) A person who without authorization gains or attempts to gain access to and alters, damages, destroys, discloses, or modifies any computer, computer network, computer property, computer system, computer program, computer data or software, and thereby causes damage to another, or obtains money, property, information, or a benefit for any person without legal right, is guilty of:

(a) a class B misdemeanor when:

(i) the damage caused or the value of the money, property, or benefit obtained or sought to be obtained is less than $300; or

(ii) the information obtained is not confidential;

(b) a class A misdemeanor when the damage caused or the value of the money, property, or benefit obtained or sought to be obtained is or exceeds $300 but is less than $1,000;

(c) a third degree felony when the damage caused or the value of the money, property, or benefit obtained or sought to be obtained is or exceeds $1,000 but is less than $5,000;

(d) a second degree felony when the damage caused or the value of the money, property, or benefit obtained or sought to be obtained is or exceeds $5,000; or

(e) a third degree felony when:

(i) the property or benefit obtained or sought to be obtained is a license or entitlement;

(ii) the damage is to the license or entitlement of another person; or

(iii) the information obtained is confidential; or

(iv) in gaining access the person breaches or breaks through a security system.

(2) (a) Except as provided in Subsection (2)(b), a person who intentionally or knowingly and without authorization gains or attempts to gain access to a computer, computer network, computer property, or computer system under circumstances not otherwise constituting an offense under this section is guilty of a class B misdemeanor.

(b) Notwithstanding Subsection (2)(a), a retailer that uses an electronic product identification or tracking system, or other technology to identify, track, or price goods is not guilty of a violation of Subsection (2)(a) if the equipment designed to read the electronic product identification or tracking system data and used by the retailer to identify, track, or price goods is located within the retailer's location.

(3) A person who uses or knowingly allows another person to use any computer, computer network, computer property, or computer system, program, or software to devise or execute any artifice or scheme to defraud or to obtain money, property, services, or other things of value by false pretenses, promises, or representations, is guilty of an offense based on the value of the money, property, services, or things of value, in the degree set forth in Subsection 76-10-1801(1).

(4) A person who intentionally or knowingly and without authorization, interferes with or interrupts computer services to another authorized to receive the services is guilty of a class A misdemeanor.

(5) It is an affirmative defense to Subsections (1) and (2) that a person obtained access or attempted to obtain access in response to, and for the purpose of protecting against or investigating, a prior attempted or successful breach of security of a computer, computer network, computer property, computer system whose security the person is authorized or entitled to protect, and the access attempted or obtained was no greater than reasonably necessary for that purpose.

2005

76-6-704. Attorney general, county attorney, or district attorney to prosecute — Conduct violating other statutes.

(1) The attorney general, district attorney, or the county attorney shall prosecute suspected criminal violations of this part.

(2) Prosecution under this part does not prevent any prosecutions under any other law. 1993

76-6-705. Reporting violations.

Every person, except those to whom a statutory or common law privilege applies, who has reason to believe that the provisions of Section 76-6-703 are being or have been violated shall report the suspected violation to the attorney general, or county attorney, or, if within a prosecution district, the district attorney of the county or prosecution district in which part or all of the violations occurred. 1993

PART 8

LIBRARY THEFT

76-6-801. Acts constituting library theft.

A person is guilty of the crime of library theft when he willfully, for the purpose of converting to personal use, and depriving the owner, conceals on his person or among his belongings library materials while on the premises of the library or willfully and without authority removes library materials from the library building with the intention of converting them to his own use. 1987

76-6-802. Presumption of intent.

A person who willfully conceals library materials on his person or among his belongings while on the premises of the library or in its immediate vicinity is prima facie presumed to have concealed library materials with the intention of converting them to his own use. If library materials are found concealed upon his person or among his belongings, or electronic security devices are activated by the person's presence, it is prima facie evidence of willful concealment. 1987

76-6-803. Mutilation or damaging of library material as library theft.

A person is guilty of the crime of library theft when he intentionally or recklessly writes upon, injures, defaces, tears, cuts, mutilates, destroys, or otherwise damages library materials. 1987

76-6-803.30. Failure to return library material as library theft — Notice — Failure to pay replacement value — Written notice.

(1) A person is guilty of library theft when, having possession or having been in possession of library materials, he:

(a) fails to return the materials within 30 days after receiving written notice demanding return of the materials; or

(b) if the materials are lost or destroyed, fails to pay the replacement value of the materials within 30 days after being notified.

(2) Written notice is considered received upon the sworn affidavit of the person delivering the notice with a statement as to the date, place, and manner of delivery, or upon proof that the notice was mailed

postage prepaid, via the United States Postal Service, to the current address listed for the person in the library records.   1987

76-6-803.60. Detention of theft suspect by library employee — Purposes.

(1) Any employee of the library who has probable cause to believe that a person has committed library theft may detain the person, on or off the premises of a library, in a reasonable manner and for a reasonable length of time for all or any of the following purposes:

(a) to make reasonable inquiry as to whether the person has in his possession concealed library materials;

(b) to request identification;

(c) to verify identification;

(d) to make a reasonable request of the person to place or keep in full view any library materials the individual may have removed, or which the employee has reason to believe he may have removed, from its place of display or elsewhere, whether for examination, or for any other reasonable purpose;

(e) to inform a peace officer of the detention of the person and surrender that person to the custody of a peace officer; or

(f) in the case of a minor, to inform a peace officer, the parents, guardian, or other private person interested in the welfare of the minor as soon as possible of this detention and to surrender custody of the minor to this person.

(2) An employee may make a detention under this section off the library premises only if the detention is pursuant to an immediate pursuit of the person.   1987

76-6-803.90. Liability — Defense — Probable cause — Reasonableness.

In any action for false arrest, false imprisonment, unlawful detention, defamation of character, assault, trespass, or invasion of civil rights brought by any person detained by an employee of the library, it is a defense to the action that the employee of the library detaining the person had probable cause to believe that the person had committed library theft and that the employee acted reasonably under all circumstances.   1987

76-6-804. "Book or other library materials" defined.

The terms "book or other library materials" as used in this act include any book, plate, picture, photograph, engraving, painting, drawing, map, newspaper, magazine, pamphlet, broadside, manuscript, document, letter, public record, microfilm, sound recording, audiovisual materials in any format, electronic data processing records, artifacts, or other documentary, written or printed materials regardless of physical form or characteristics, belonging to, on loan to, or otherwise in the custody of the following:

(1) any public library;

(2) any library of an educational or historical society;

(3) any museum; or

(4) any repository of public records.   1981

76-6-805. Penalty.

Any person violating the provisions of this act shall be subject to provisions of Section 76-6-412.   1981

PART 9

CULTURAL SITES PROTECTION

76-6-901. Definitions.

(1) "Antiquities" means:

(a) all material remains and their associations, recoverable through excavation or surface collection, that provide information pertaining to the historic or prehistoric peoples in the state; and

(b) vertebrate fossils and other exceptional fossils and fossil sites designated as state landmarks.

(2) "Persons" means an individual, corporation, partnership, trust, institution, association, or any other private entity or any officer, employee, agent, department, or instrumentality of the United States, of any Native American tribe, or of any state or political subdivision of any state.

(3) "State lands" means all lands owned by Utah, including all lands owned by political subdivisions, and school and institutional trust lands.   1990

76-6-902. Prohibitions.

(1) It is unlawful for any person to intentionally alter, remove, injure, or destroy antiquities without the landowner's consent.

(2) It is unlawful to intentionally reproduce, rework, or forge any antiquities or make any object, whether copies or not, or falsely label, describe, identify, or offer for sale or exchange any object with the intent to represent the object as original and genuine, nor may any person offer any object for sale or exchange that was collected or excavated in violation of this chapter.   1999

76-6-903. Penalties.

(1) A person is guilty of a class B misdemeanor if that person:

(a) violates this part; or

(b) counsels, procures, solicits, or employs any other person to violate this part.

(2) A person is guilty of a third degree felony if:

(a) that person commits a second or subsequent violation described in Subsection (1); or

(b) the amount calculated under Subsection (3) for a violation described in Subsection (1) exceeds $500.

(3) The amount described in Subsection (2)(b) is calculated by adding the:

(a) commercial or archaeological value of the antiquities involved in the violation; and

(b) cost of the restoration and repair of the antiquities involved in the violation.

(4) (a) All property used in conjunction with the criminal activity, together with all photographs and records, shall be forfeited to the state.

(b) All articles and material discovered, collected, excavated, or offered for sale or exchange shall be surrendered to the landowner.   1999

PART 10

MAIL BOX DAMAGE AND MAIL THEFT

76-6-1001. Definitions.

As used in this part:

(1) "Key" means any instrument used by the postal service and postal customer, and which is designed to operate the lock on a mail receptacle.

(2) "Mail" means any letter, card, parcel, or other material, along with its contents, that:

(a) has postage affixed by the postal customer or postal service;

(b) has been accepted for delivery by the postal service;

(c) the postal customer leaves for collection by the postal service; or

(d) the postal service delivers to the postal customer.

(3) "Mail receptacle" means a mail box, post office box, rural box, or any place intended or used by postal customers or the postal service for the collection or delivery of mail.

(4) "Postage" means a postal service stamp, permit imprint, meter strip, or other indication of either prepayment for postal service provided or authorization by the postal service for collection and delivery of mail.

(5) "Postal service" means the United States Postal Service and any motor carrier engaged in the business of collecting, transporting, and delivering mail.   1998

76-6-1002. Damage to mail receptacle — Penalties — Greater offenses.

(1) A person commits the crime of damage to a mail receptacle if the person knowingly damages the condition of a mail receptacle, including:

(a) taking, concealing, damaging, or destroying a key; or

(b) breaking open, tearing down, taking, damaging, or destroying a mail receptacle.

(2) (a) In determining the degree of an offense committed under Subsection (1), the penalty levels in Subsection 76-6-106(3)(b) apply.

(b) If the act committed amounts to an offense subject to a greater penalty, this subsection does not prohibit prosecution and sentencing for the more serious offense.   2002

76-6-1003. Mail theft — Penalties.

(1) A person commits the crime of mail theft if the person:

(a) knowingly, and with the intent to deprive another:

(i) takes, destroys, hides, or embezzles mail; or

(ii) obtains any mail by fraud or deception; or

(b) buys, receives, conceals, or possesses mail and knows or reasonably should have known that the mail was unlawfully taken or obtained.

(2) Mail theft is a:

(a) felony of the second degree if the value of the mail is or exceeds $5,000;

(b) felony of the third degree if the value of the mail is or exceeds $1,000, but is less than $5,000 in value; and

(c) class A misdemeanor if the value of the mail is less than $1,000 in value or the value cannot be ascertained.   2004

76-6-1004. Presumptions and defenses.

(1) The presumptions and defenses regarding the theft of property in Section 76-6-402 apply to this part, in addition to the provisions of this section.

(2) It is a defense to a charge of mail theft that:

(a) the defendant was unaware that the mail belonged to another person;

(b) the defendant reasonably believed he was entitled to the mail or had a right to acquire or dispose of the mail as he did; or

(c) the mail belonged to the defendant's spouse, unless the parties were either legally separated or living in separate residences at the time of the alleged mail theft.   1998

PART 11

IDENTITY FRAUD ACT

76-6-1101. Identity fraud.

This part is known as the "Identity Fraud Act."   2000

76-6-1102. Identity fraud crime.

(1) For purposes of this part, "personal identifying information" may include:

(a) name;

(b) address;

(c) telephone number;

(d) driver's license number;

(e) Social Security number;

(f) place of employment;

(g) employee identification numbers or other personal identification numbers;

(h) mother's maiden name;

(i) electronic identification numbers;

(j) digital signatures or a private key; or

(k) any other numbers or information that can be used to access a person's financial resources or medical information in the name of another person without the consent of that person except for numbers or information that can be prosecuted as financial transaction card offenses under Sections 76-6-506 through 76-6-506.4.

(2) A person is guilty of identity fraud when that person knowingly or intentionally:

(a) obtains personal identifying information of another person whether that person is alive or deceased; and

(b) uses, or attempts to use, that information with fraudulent intent, including to obtain, or attempt to obtain, credit, goods, services, any other thing of value, or medical information in the name of another person.

(3) Identity fraud is:

(a) a third degree felony if the value of the credit, goods, services, or any other thing of value is less than $5,000; or

(b) a second degree felony if the value of the credit, goods, services, or any other thing of value is or exceeds $5,000.

(4) Multiple violations may be aggregated into a single offense, and the degree of the offense is determined by the total value of all credit, goods, services, or any other thing of value used, or attempted to be used, through the multiple violations.   2005

76-6-1103. Investigation of violation.

In addition to investigations conducted by law enforcement agencies, the Office of the Attorney General also has responsibility for investigating violations of this part where identity fraud is the primary violation that is alleged to have been committed.   2004

76-6-1104. Court records.

In any case in which a person commits identify fraud and uses the personal identifying information obtained to commit a crime in addition to the identity fraud, the court shall make appropriate findings in any prosecution of such a crime that the person whose identity was falsely used to commit the crime did not commit the crime.   2000

76-6-1105. Unlawful possession of another's identification documents.

(1) For purposes of this section "identifying document" means:

(a) a government issued identifying document;

(b) a vehicle registration certificate; or

(c) any other document containing personal identifying information as defined in Subsections 76-6-1102(1)(d) through (k).

(2) (a) Notwithstanding the provisions of Subsection 76-6-1102(3), a person is guilty of a class A misdemeanor if he:

(i) obtains or possesses an identifying document with knowledge that he is not entitled to obtain or possess the identifying document; or

(ii) assists another person in obtaining or possessing an identifying document with knowledge that the person is not entitled to obtain or possess the identifying document.

(b) A person is guilty of a third degree felony if he:

(i) obtains or possesses multiple identifying documents with knowledge that he is not entitled to obtain or possess the multiple identifying documents; or

(ii) assists another person in obtaining or possessing multiple identifying documents with knowledge that the person is not entitled to obtain or possess the multiple identifying documents.

(c) For purposes of Subsection (2)(b), "multiple identifying documents" means identifying documents of two or more people.   2004

CHAPTER 6a

PYRAMID SCHEMES

76-6a-1.   Short title.

This act shall be known and may be cited as the "Pyramid Scheme Act."   1983

76-6a-2.   Definitions.

As used in this chapter:

(1) "Consideration" does not include payment for sales demonstration equipment and materials furnished at cost for use in making sales and not for resale, or time or effort spent in selling or recruiting activities.

(2) "Compensation" means money bonuses, commissions, overrides, prizes, or other real or personal property, tangible or intangible.

(3) "Person" includes a business trust, estate, trust, joint venture, or any other legal or commercial entity.

(4) "Pyramid scheme" means any sales device or plan under which a person gives consideration to another person in exchange for compensation or the right to receive compensation which is derived primarily from the introduction of other persons into the sales device or plan rather than from the sale of goods, services, or other property.   1983

76-6a-3.   Schemes prohibited — Violation as deceptive consumer sales practice — Prosecution of civil violations.

(1) A person may not organize, establish, promote, or administer any pyramid scheme.

(2) A criminal conviction under this chapter is prima facie evidence of a violation of Section 13-11-4, the Utah Consumer Sales Practices Act.

(3) Any violation of this chapter constitutes a violation of Section 13-11-4, the Utah Consumer Sales Practices Act.

(4) All civil violations of this chapter shall be investigated and prosecuted as prescribed by the Utah Consumer Sales Practices Act.   1983

76-6a-4.   Operation as felony — Investigation — Prosecution.

(1) Any person who knowingly organizes, establishes, promotes, or administers a pyramid scheme is guilty of a third degree felony.

(2) The appropriate county attorney or district attorney has primary responsibility for investigating and prosecuting criminal violations of this chapter.   1993

76-6a-5.   Plan provisions not constituting defenses.

It is not a defense to an action brought under this chapter if:

(1) The sales device or plan limits the number of persons who may be introduced into it;

(2) The sales device or plan includes additional conditions affecting eligibility for introduction into it or when compensation is received from it; or

(3) A person receives property or services in addition to the compensation or right to receive compensation in connection with a pyramid scheme.   1983

76-6a-6.   Rights of persons giving consideration in scheme.

(1) Any person giving consideration in connection with a pyramid scheme may, notwithstanding any agreement to the contrary, declare his giving of consideration and the related sale or contract for sale void, and may bring a court action to recover the consideration. In the action, the court shall, in addition to any judgment awarded to the plaintiff, require the defendant to pay to the plaintiff interest as provided in Section 15-1-4, reasonable attorneys' fees, and the costs of the action reduced by any compensation paid by the defendant to the plaintiff in connection with the pyramid scheme.

(2) The rights, remedies, and penalties provided in this chapter are independent of and supplemental to each other and to any other right, remedy or penalty available in law or equity. Nothing contained in this chapter shall be construed to diminish or abrogate any other right, remedy or penalty.   1983

CHAPTER 7

OFFENSES AGAINST THE FAMILY

Part 1

Marital Violations

Part 2

Nonsupport and Sale of Children

PART 1

MARITAL VIOLATIONS

76-7-101. Bigamy — Defense.

(1) A person is guilty of bigamy when, knowing he has a husband or wife or knowing the other person has a husband or wife, the person purports to marry another person or cohabits with another person.

(2) Bigamy is a felony of the third degree.

(3) It shall be a defense to bigamy that the accused reasonably believed he and the other person were legally eligible to remarry.　　1997

76-7-101.5. Child bigamy — Penalty.

(1) An actor 18 years of age or older is guilty of child bigamy when, knowing he or she has a wife or husband, or knowing that a person under 18 years of age has a wife or husband, the actor carries out the following with the person who is under 18 years of age:

(a) purports to marry the person who is under 18 years of age; or

(b) cohabits with the person who is under 18 years of age.

(2) A violation of Subsection (1) is a second degree felony.　　2003

76-7-102. Incest.

(1) A person is guilty of incest when, under circumstances not amounting to rape, rape of a child or aggravated sexual assault, he has sexual intercourse with a person whom he knows to be an ancestor, descendant, brother, sister, uncle, aunt, nephew, niece, or first cousin. The relationships referred to herein include blood relationships of the whole or half blood without regard to legitimacy, relationship of parent and child by adoption, and relationship of stepparent and stepchild while the marriage creating the relationship of a stepparent and stepchild exists.

(2) Incest is a felony of the third degree.　　1983

76-7-103. Adultery.

(1) A married person commits adultery when he voluntarily has sexual intercourse with a person other than his spouse.

(2) Adultery is a class B misdemeanor.　　1991

76-7-104. Fornication.

(1) Any unmarried person who shall voluntarily engage in sexual intercourse with another is guilty of fornication.

(2) Fornication is a class B misdemeanor.　　1973

PART 2

NONSUPPORT AND SALE OF CHILDREN

76-7-201. Criminal nonsupport.

(1) A person commits criminal nonsupport if, having a spouse, a child, or children under the age of 18 years, he knowingly fails to provide for the support of the spouse, child, or children when any one of them:

(a) is in needy circumstances; or

(b) would be in needy circumstances but for support received from a source other than the defendant or paid on the defendant's behalf.

(2) Except as provided in Subsection (3), criminal nonsupport is a class A misdemeanor.

(3) Criminal nonsupport is a felony of the third degree if the actor:

(a) has been convicted one or more times of nonsupport, whether in this state, any other state, or any court of the United States;

(b) committed the offense while residing outside of Utah; or

(c) commits the crime of nonsupport in each of 18 individual months within any 24-month period, or the total arrearage is in excess of $10,000.

(4) For purposes of this section "child" includes a child born out of wedlock whose paternity has been admitted by the actor or has been established in a civil suit.

(5) (a) In a prosecution for criminal nonsupport under this section, it is an affirmative defense that the accused is unable to provide support. Voluntary unemployment or underemployment by the defendant does not give rise to that defense.

(b) Not less than 20 days before trial the defendant shall file and serve on the prosecuting attorney a notice, in writing, of his intention to claim the affirmative defense of inability to provide support. The notice shall specifically identify the factual basis for the defense and the names and addresses of the witnesses who the defendant proposes to examine in order to establish the defense.

(c) Not more than ten days after receipt of the notice described in Subsection (5)(b), or at such other time as the court may direct, the prosecuting attorney shall file and serve the defendant with a notice containing the names and addresses of the witnesses who the state proposes to examine in order to contradict or rebut the defendant's claim.

(d) Failure to comply with the requirements of Subsection (5)(b) or (5)(c) entitles the opposing party to a continuance to allow for preparation. If the court finds that a party's failure to comply is the result of bad faith, it may impose appropriate sanctions. 1999

76-7-202. Orders for support in criminal nonsupport proceedings.

(1) In any proceeding under Section 76-7-201, the court may, instead of imposing the punishments otherwise prescribed, issue an order directing the defendant to periodically pay a sum to the Office of Recovery Services, or otherwise as the court may direct, to be used for the support of the dependents who are the subject of the proceeding under Section 76-7-201.

(2) The order to periodically pay a sum for the support of the dependents:

(a) may be issued with the consent of the defendant prior to trial, or after conviction, having regard to the circumstances, financial ability, and earning capacity of the defendant;

(b) shall be subject to change from time to time as circumstances may require;

(c) may not require payments for a period exceeding the term of probation provided for the offense with which the defendant is charged, or of which he is found guilty; and

(d) shall be conditioned upon the defendant either entering a recognizance in accordance with Subsection (3), or providing security in a sum as the court directs.

(3) The condition of recognizance shall require the defendant to:

(a) make personal appearance in court whenever ordered to do so within the period of probation; and

(b) comply with the terms of the order and any subsequent modifications of the order.

(4) If the court is satisfied by information and due proof under oath that at any time during the period of probation the defendant has violated the terms of the order, it may proceed with the trial of defendant under the original charge or sentence him under the original conviction or enforce the original sentence as the case may be. In the case of forfeiture of bail or bond in any proceeding under Section 76-7-201, the sum recovered may, in the discretion of the court, be paid in whole or in part to the Office of Recovery Services, or otherwise as the court may direct, to be used for the support of the dependents involved. 1995

76-7-203. Sale of child — Felony — Payment of adoption related expenses.

(1) For purposes of this section:

(a) "adoption related expenses" means expenses that:

(i) are reasonably related to the adoption of a child;

(ii) are incurred for a reasonable amount; and

(iii) may include expenses:

(A) of the mother or father of the child being adopted, including:

(I) legal expenses;

(II) maternity expenses;

(III) medical expenses;

(IV) hospital expenses;

(V) counseling expenses;

(VI) temporary living expenses during the pregnancy or confinement of the mother; or

(VII) expenses for travel between the mother's or father's home and the location where the child will be born or placed for adoption; or

(B) of a directly affected person for:

(I) travel between the directly affected person's home and the location where the child will be born or placed for adoption; or

(II) temporary living expenses during the pregnancy or confinement of the mother; and

(b) "directly affected person" means a person who is:

(i) a parent or guardian of a minor when the minor is the mother or father of the child being adopted;

(ii) a dependant of:

(A) the mother or father of the child being adopted; or

(B) the parent or guardian described in Subsection (1)(b)(i); or

(iii) the spouse of the mother or father of the child being adopted.

(2) Except as provided in Subsection (3), a person is guilty of a third degree felony if the person, while having custody, care, control, or possession of a child, sells, or disposes of, or attempts to sell or dispose of, the child for and in consideration of the payment of money or other thing of value.

(3) A person does not violate this section by paying adoption related expenses:

(a) as an act of charity; and

(b) if the payment is not made for the purpose of inducing the mother, parent, or legal guardian of a child to:

(i) place the child for adoption;

(ii) consent to an adoption; or

(iii) cooperate in the completion of an adoption.   2005

76-7-204. Repealed.   2005

PART 3

ABORTION

76-7-301. Definitions.

As used in this part:

(1) "Abortion" means the intentional termination or attempted termination of human pregnancy after implantation of a fertilized ovum, and includes any and all procedures undertaken to kill a live unborn child and includes all procedures undertaken to produce a miscarriage. "Abortion" does not include removal of a dead unborn child.

(2) "Medical emergency" means that condition which, on the basis of the physician's good faith clinical judgment, so threatens the life of a pregnant woman as to necessitate the immediate abortion of her pregnancy to avert her death, or for which a delay will create serious risk of substantial and irreversible impairment of major bodily function.

(3) (a) "Partial birth abortion" means an abortion in which the person performing the abortion:

(i) deliberately and intentionally vaginally delivers a living fetus until, in the case of a head first presentation, the entire fetal head is outside the body of the mother, or, in the case of breech presentation, any part of the fetal trunk past the navel is outside the body of the mother, for the purpose of performing an overt act that the person knows will kill the partially delivered living fetus; and

(ii) performs the overt act, other than completion of delivery, that kills the partially living fetus.

(b) "Partial birth abortion" does not include the dilation and evacuation procedure involving dismemberment prior to removal, the suction curettage procedure, or the suction aspiration procedure for abortion.

(4) "Physician" means a medical doctor licensed to practice medicine and surgery under Title 58, Chapter 67, Utah Medical Practice Act, a physician in the employment of the government of the United States who is similarly qualified, or an osteopathic physician licensed to practice osteopathic medicine under Title 58, Chapter 68, Utah Osteopathic Medical Practice Act.

(5) "Hospital" means a general hospital licensed by the Department of Health according to Title 26, Chapter 21, Health Care Facility Licensing and Inspection Act, and includes a clinic or other medical facility to the extent that such clinic or other medical facility provides equipment and personnel sufficient in quantity and quality to provide the same degree of safety to the pregnant woman and the unborn child as would be provided for the particular medical procedures undertaken by a general hospital licensed by the Department of Health. It shall be the responsibility of the Department of Health to determine if such clinic or other medical facility so qualifies and to so certify.   2004

76-7-301.1. Preamble — Findings and policies of Legislature.

(1) It is the finding and policy of the Legislature, reflecting and reasserting the provisions of Article I, Sections 1 and 7, Utah Constitution, which recognize that life founded on inherent and inalienable rights is entitled to protection of law and due process; and that unborn children have inherent and inalienable rights that are entitled to protection by the state of Utah pursuant to the provisions of the Utah Constitution.

(2) The state of Utah has a compelling interest in the protection of the lives of unborn children.

(3) It is the intent of the Legislature to protect and guarantee to unborn children their inherent and inalienable right to life as required by Article I, Sections 1 and 7, Utah Constitution.

(4) It is also the policy of the Legislature and of the state that, in connection with abortion, a woman's liberty interest, in limited circumstances, may outweigh the unborn child's right to protection. These limited circumstances arise when the abortion is necessary to save the pregnant woman's life or prevent grave damage to her medical health, and when pregnancy occurs as a result of rape or incest. It is further the finding and policy of the Legislature and of the state that a woman may terminate the pregnancy if the unborn child would be born with grave defects.
                                                1991 (1st S.S.)

76-7-302. Circumstances under which abortion authorized.

(1) An abortion may be performed in this state only by a physician licensed to practice medicine under Title 58, Chapter 67, Utah Medical Practice Act or an osteopathic physician licensed to practice medicine under Title 58, Chapter 68, Utah Osteopathic Medical Practice Act and, if performed 90 days or more after the commencement of the pregnancy as defined by competent medical practices, it shall be performed in a hospital.

(2) An abortion may be performed in this state only under the following circumstances:

(a) in the professional judgment of the pregnant woman's attending physician, the abortion is necessary to save the pregnant woman's life;

(b) the pregnancy is the result of rape or rape of a child, as defined by Sections 76-5-402 and 76-5-402.1, that was reported to a law enforcement agency prior to the abortion;

(c) the pregnancy is the result of incest, as defined by Subsection 76-5-406(10) or Section 76-7-102, and the incident was reported to a law enforcement agency prior to the abortion;

(d) in the professional judgment of the pregnant woman's attending physician, to prevent grave damage to the pregnant woman's medical health; or

(e) in the professional judgment of the pregnant woman's attending physician, to prevent the birth of a child that would be born with grave defects.

(3) After 20 weeks gestational age, measured from the date of conception, an abortion may be performed only for those purposes and circumstances described in Subsections (2)(a), (d), and (e).

(4) The name of a victim reported pursuant to Subsection (2)(b) or (c) is confidential and may not be revealed by law enforcement or any other party except upon approval of the victim. This subsection does not effect or supersede parental notification requirements otherwise provided by law.   2004

76-7-303. Concurrence of attending physician based on medical judgment.
No abortion may be performed in this state without the concurrence of the attending physician, based on his best medical judgment.   1974

76-7-304. Considerations by physician — Notice to minor's parents or guardian or married woman's husband.
To enable the physician to exercise his best medical judgment, he shall:
(1) Consider all factors relevant to the well-being of the woman upon whom the abortion is to be performed including, but not limited to,
(a) her physical, emotional and psychological health and safety,
(b) her age,
(c) her familial situation.
(2) Notify, if possible, the parents or guardian of the woman upon whom the abortion is to be performed, if she is a minor or the husband of the woman, if she is married.   1974

76-7-305. Informed consent requirements for abortion — 24-hour wait mandatory — Emergency exceptions.
(1) No abortion may be performed unless a voluntary and informed written consent, consistent with Section 8.08 of the American Medical Association's Code of Medical Ethics, Current Opinions, is first obtained by the attending physician from the woman upon whom the abortion is to be performed. Except in the case of a medical emergency, consent to an abortion is voluntary and informed only if:
(a) at least 24 hours prior to the abortion, the physician who is to perform the abortion, the referring physician, a registered nurse, nurse practitioner, advanced practice registered nurse, certified nurse midwife, or physician's assistant shall, in a face-to-face consultation, orally inform the woman of:
(i) the nature of the proposed abortion procedure or treatment, specifically how that procedure will affect the fetus, and the risks and alternatives to an abortion procedure or treatment that any person would consider material to the decision of whether or not to undergo an abortion. The alternatives required to be provided under this subsection shall include a description of adoption services, including private and agency adoption methods, and a statement that it is legal for adoptive parents to financially assist in pregnancy and birth expenses;
(ii) the probable gestational age and a description of the development of the unborn child at the time the abortion would be performed; and
(iii) the medical risks associated with carrying her child to term;
(b) at least 24 hours prior to the abortion the physician who is to perform the abortion, the referring physician, or, as specifically delegated by either of those physicians, a registered nurse, licensed practical nurse, certified nurse-midwife, advanced practice registered nurse, clinical labo-

ratory technologist, psychologist, marriage and family therapist, clinical social worker, or certified social worker has orally, in a face-to-face consultation, informed the pregnant woman that:
(i) the Department of Health, in accordance with Section 76-7-305.5, publishes printed material and an informational video that:
(A) provides medically accurate information regarding all abortion procedures that may be used;
(B) describes the gestational stages of an unborn child; and
(C) includes information regarding public and private services and agencies available to assist her through pregnancy, at childbirth, and while the child is dependent, including private and agency adoption alternatives; and
(ii) the printed material and a viewing of or a copy of the informational video shall be provided to her free of charge;
(iii) medical assistance benefits may be available for prenatal care, childbirth, and neonatal care, and that more detailed information on the availability of that assistance is contained in the printed materials and the informational video published by the Department of Health;
(iv) the father of the unborn child is legally required to assist in the support of her child, even in instances where he has offered to pay for the abortion, and that the Office of Recovery Services within the Department of Human Services will assist her in collecting child support. In the case of rape, this information may be omitted; and
(v) she has the right to view an ultrasound of the unborn child, at no expense to her, upon her request;
(c) the information required to be provided to the pregnant woman under Subsection (a) is also provided by the physician who is to perform the abortion, in a face-to-face consultation, prior to performance of the abortion, unless the attending or referring physician was the individual providing the information under Subsection (a);
(d) a copy of the printed materials published by the Department of Health has been provided to the pregnant woman;
(e) the informational video, published by the Department of Health, has been provided to the pregnant woman in accordance with Subsection (2); and
(f) the pregnant woman has certified in writing, prior to the abortion, that the information required to be provided under Subsections (a), (b), (c), (d), and (e) was provided, in accordance with the requirements of those subsections.
(2) When the informational video is provided to a pregnant woman, the person providing the information shall first request that the woman view the video at that time or at another specifically designated time and location. If the woman chooses not to do so, a copy of the video shall be provided to her.
(3) When a serious medical emergency compels the performance of an abortion, the physician shall inform the woman prior to the abortion, if possible, of the medical indications supporting his judgment that an abortion is necessary.
(4) Any physician who violates the provisions of this section is guilty of unprofessional conduct as

defined in Section 58-67-102 or 58-68-102, and his license for the practice of medicine and surgery shall be subject to suspension or revocation in accordance with Sections 58-67-401 and 58-67-402, Utah Medical Practice Act, or Sections 58-68-401 and 58-68-402, Utah Osteopathic Medical Practice Act.

(5) A physician is not guilty of violating this section for failure to furnish any of the information described in Subsection (1), if:

(a) he can demonstrate by a preponderance of the evidence that he reasonably believed that furnishing the information would have resulted in a severely adverse effect on the physical or mental health of the pregnant woman;

(b) in his professional judgment, the abortion was necessary to save the pregnant woman's life;

(c) the pregnancy was the result of rape or rape of a child, as defined in Sections 76-5-402 and 76-5-402.1;

(d) the pregnancy was the result of incest, as defined in Subsection 76-5-406(10) and Section 76-7-102;

(e) in his professional judgment the abortion was to prevent the birth of a child who would have been born with grave defects; or

(f) the pregnant woman was 14 years of age or younger.

(6) A physician who complies with the provisions of this section may not be held civilly liable to his patient for failure to obtain informed consent under Section 78-14-5.　　　　1997

76-7-305.5.　Requirements for printed materials and informational video — Annual report of Department of Health.

(1) In order to insure that a woman's consent to an abortion is truly an informed consent, the Department of Health shall publish printed materials and produce an informational video in accordance with the requirements of this section. The department and each local health department shall make those materials and a viewing of the video available at no cost to any person. The printed material and the informational video shall be comprehensible and contain all of the following:

(a) geographically indexed materials informing the woman of public and private services and agencies available to assist her, financially and otherwise, through pregnancy, at childbirth, and while the child is dependent, including services and supports available under Section 35A-3-308. Those materials shall contain a description of available adoption services, including a comprehensive list of the names, addresses, and telephone numbers of public and private agencies and private attorneys whose practice includes adoption, and explanations of possible available financial aid during the adoption process. The information regarding adoption services shall include the fact that private adoption is legal, and that the law permits adoptive parents to pay the costs of prenatal care, childbirth, and neonatal care. The printed information and video shall present adoption as a preferred and positive choice and alternative to abortion. The department may, at its option, include printed materials that describe the availability of a toll-free 24-hour telephone number that may be called in order to obtain, orally, the list and description of services, agencies, and adoption attorneys in the locality of the caller;

(b) truthful and nonmisleading descriptions of the probable anatomical and physiological characteristics of the unborn child at two-week gestational increments from fertilization to full term, accompanied by pictures or video segments representing the development of an unborn child at those gestational increments. The descriptions shall include information about brain and heart function and the presence of external members and internal organs during the applicable stages of development. Any pictures used shall contain the dimensions of the fetus and shall be realistic and appropriate for that woman's stage of pregnancy. The materials shall be designed to convey accurate scientific information about an unborn child at the various gestational ages, and to convey the state's preference for childbirth over abortion;

(c) truthful, nonmisleading descriptions of abortion procedures used in current medical practice at the various stages of growth of the unborn child, the medical risks commonly associated with each procedure, including those related to subsequent childbearing, the consequences of each procedure to the fetus at various stages of fetal development, the possible detrimental psychological effects of abortion, and the medical risks associated with carrying a child to term;

(d) any relevant information on the possibility of an unborn child's survival at the two-week gestational increments described in Subsection (1)(b);

(e) information on the availability of medical assistance benefits for prenatal care, childbirth, and neonatal care;

(f) a statement conveying that it is unlawful for any person to coerce a woman to undergo an abortion;

(g) a statement conveying that any physician who performs an abortion without obtaining the woman's informed consent or without according her a private medical consultation in accordance with the requirements of this section, may be liable to her for damages in a civil action at law;

(h) a statement conveying that the state of Utah prefers childbirth over abortion; and

(i) information regarding the legal responsibility of the father to assist in child support, even in instances where he has agreed to pay for an abortion, including a description of the services available through the Office of Recovery Services, within the Department of Human Services, to establish and collect that support.

(2) (a) The materials described in Subsection (1) shall be produced and printed in a way that conveys the state's preference for childbirth over abortion.

(b) The printed material described in Subsection (1) shall be printed in a typeface large enough to be clearly legible.

(3) Every facility in which abortions are performed shall immediately provide the printed informed consent materials and a viewing of or a copy of the informational video described in Subsection (1) to any patient or potential patient prior to the performance of an abortion, unless the patient's attending or referring physician certifies in writing that he reasonably believes that provision of the materials or video to that patient would result in a severely adverse effect on her physical or mental health.

(4) The Department of Health shall produce a standardized videotape that may be used statewide, con-

taining all of the information described in Subsection (1), in accordance with the requirements of that subsection and Subsection (2). In preparing the video, the department may summarize and make reference to the printed comprehensive list of geographically indexed names and services described in Subsection (1)(a). The videotape shall, in addition to the information described in Subsection (1), show an ultrasound of the heart beat of an unborn child at three weeks gestational age, at six to eight weeks gestational age, and each month thereafter, until 14 weeks gestational age. That information shall be presented in a truthful, nonmisleading manner designed to convey accurate scientific information, the state's preference for childbirth over abortion, and the positive aspects of adoption.

(5) The Department of Health and local health departments shall provide ultrasounds in accordance with the provisions of Subsection 76-7-305(1)(b), at no expense to the pregnant woman.

(6) The Department of Health shall compile and report the following information annually, preserving physician and patient anonymity:

(a) the total amount of informed consent material described in Subsection (1) that was distributed;

(b) the number of women who obtained abortions in this state without receiving those materials;

(c) the number of statements signed by attending physicians certifying to his opinion regarding adverse effects on the patient under Subsection (3); and

(d) any other information pertaining to protecting the informed consent of women seeking abortions.

(7) The Department of Health shall annually report to the Health and Human Services Interim Committee regarding the information described in Subsection (6), and provide a copy of the printed materials and the videotape produced in accordance with this section to that committee. 1998

76-7-306. Physician, hospital employee, or hospital not required to participate in abortion.

(1) A physician, or any other person who is a member of or associated with the staff of a hospital, or any employee of a hospital in which an abortion has been authorized, who states an objection to an abortion or the practice of abortion in general on moral or religious grounds shall not be required to participate in the medical procedures which will result in the abortion, and the refusal of any person to participate shall not form the basis of any claim for damages on account of the refusal or for any disciplinary or recriminatory action against such person, nor shall any moral or religious scruples or objections to abortions be the grounds for any discrimination in hiring in this state.

(2) Nothing in this part shall require any private and/or denominational hospital to admit any patient for the purpose of performing an abortion. 1995

76-7-307. Medical procedure required to save life of unborn child.

If an abortion is performed when the unborn child is sufficiently developed to have any reasonable possibility of survival outside its mother's womb, the medical procedure used must be that which, in the best medical judgment of the physician will give the unborn child the best chance of survival. No medical procedure designed to kill or injure that unborn child

may be used unless necessary, in the opinion of the woman's physician, to prevent grave damage to her medical health. 1991 (1st S.S.)

76-7-308. Medical skills required to preserve life of unborn child.

Consistent with the purpose of saving the life of the woman or preventing grave damage to the woman's medical health, the physician performing the abortion must use all of his medical skills to attempt to promote, preserve and maintain the life of any unborn child sufficiently developed to have any reasonable possibility of survival outside of the mother's womb.
1991 (1st S.S.)

76-7-309. Pathologist's report.

Any human tissue removed during an abortion shall be submitted to a pathologist who shall make a report, including, but not limited to whether there was a pregnancy, and if possible, whether the pregnancy was aborted by evacuating the uterus. 1974

76-7-310. Experimentation with unborn children prohibited — Testing for genetic defects.

Live unborn children may not be used for experimentation, but when advisable, in the best medical judgment of the physician, may be tested for genetic defects. 1974

76-7-310.5. Prohibition of specified abortion procedures — Viability defined.

(1) As used in this section, "saline abortion procedure" means performance of amniocentesis and injection of saline into the amniotic sac within the uterine cavity.

(2) (a) After viability has been determined in accordance with Subsection (2)(b), no person may knowingly perform a saline abortion procedure unless all other available abortion procedures would pose a risk to the life or the health of the pregnant woman.

(b) For purposes of this section determination of viability shall be made by the physician, based upon his own best clinical judgment. The physician shall determine whether, based on the particular facts of a woman's pregnancy that are known to him, and in light of medical technology and information reasonably available to him, there is a realistic possibility of maintaining and nourishing a life outside of the womb, with or without temporary, artificial life-sustaining support.

(3) Intentional, knowing, and willful violation of this section is a third degree felony. 2004

76-7-311. Selling and buying unborn children prohibited.

Selling, buying, offering to sell and offering to buy unborn children is prohibited. 1974

76-7-312. Intimidation or coercion to obtain abortion prohibited.

No person shall intimidate or coerce in any way any person to obtain an abortion. 1974

76-7-313. Physician's report to Department of Health.

In order for the state Department of Health to maintain necessary statistical information and ensure enforcement of the provisions of this part, any physician performing an abortion must obtain and record in writing: the age of the pregnant woman; her marital status and county of residence; the number of previous abortions performed on her; the hospital or other facility where performed; the weight in grams of the unborn child aborted, if it is possible to ascertain; the pathological description of the unborn child; the given menstrual age of the unborn child; the measurements, if possible to ascertain; and the medical procedure used. This information, and a copy of the pathologist's report, as required in Section 76-7-309, together with an affidavit that the required consent was obtained pursuant to Section 76-7-305 and a certificate by the physician that the unborn child was or was not capable of survival outside of the mother's womb, must be filed by the physician with the state Department of Health within 10 days after the abortion. All information supplied to the state Department of Health shall be confidential and privileged pursuant to Title 26, Chapter 25.   1981

76-7-314. Violations of abortion laws — Classifications.

(1) (a) Any person who intentionally performs an abortion other than as authorized by this part is guilty of a felony of the third degree.

    (b) (i) Notwithstanding any other provision of law, a woman who seeks to have or obtains an abortion for herself is not criminally liable.

      (ii) A woman upon whom a partial birth abortion is performed may not be prosecuted under Section 76-7-326 or 76-7-329 for a conspiracy to violate Section 76-7-326 or 76-7-329.

(2) A willful violation of Section 76-7-307, 76-7-308, 76-7-310, 76-7-310.5, 76-7-311, or 76-7-312 is a felony of the third degree.

(3) A violation of Section 76-7-326 or 76-7-329 is a felony of the third degree.

(4) A violation of any other provision of this part is a class A misdemeanor.   2004

76-7-315. Exceptions to certain requirements in serious medical emergencies.

When due to a serious medical emergency, time does not permit compliance with Section 76-7-302, 76-7-304, 76-7-305, 76-7-305.5, or 76-7-310.5 the provisions of those sections do not apply.   1996

76-7-316. Actions not precluded.

Nothing in this part shall preclude any person believing himself aggrieved by another under this part, from bringing any other action at common law or other statutory provision.   1995

76-7-317. Separability clause.

If any one or more provision, section, subsection, sentence, clause, phrase or word of this part or the application thereof to any person or circumstance is found to be unconstitutional, the same is hereby declared to be severable and the balance of this part shall remain effective notwithstanding such unconstitutionality. The legislature hereby declares that it would have passed this part, and each provision, section, subsection, sentence, clause, phrase or word thereof, irrespective of the fact that any one or more provision, section, subsection, sentence, clause, phrase, or word be declared unconstitutional.   1974

76-7-317.1. Creation of Abortion Litigation Trust Account.

(1) (a) There is created in the General Fund a restricted account known as the Abortion Litigation Trust Account. All money received by the state from private sources for litigation expenses connected with the defense of Senate Bill 23,

passed in the 1991 Annual General Session, shall be deposited in that account.

    (b) On behalf of the Abortion Litigation Trust Account, the Division of Finance may accept grants, gifts, bequests, or any money made available from any private sources to implement this section.

(2) Money shall be appropriated by the Legislature from the account to the Office of the Attorney General under Title 63, Chapter 38, Budgetary Procedures Act.

(3) The Abortion Litigation Trust Account may be used only for costs, expenses, and attorneys fees connected with the defense of the abortion law identified in Subsection (1).

(4) Any funds remaining in the abortion litigation trust account after final appellate procedures shall revert to the General Fund, to be first used to offset the monies expended by the state in connection with litigation regarding Senate Bill 23.   1991

76-7-317.2. Finding of unconstitutionality — Revival of old law.

If Section 76-7-302 as amended by Senate Bill 23, 1991 Annual General Session, is ever held to be unconstitutional by the United States Supreme Court, Section 76-7-302, as enacted by Chapter 33, Laws of Utah 1974, is reenacted and immediately effective.   1991

76-7-318 to 76-7-320. Repealed.   1974

76-7-321. Contraceptive and abortion services — Funds — Minor — Definitions.

As used in Sections 76-7-321 through 76-7-325:

(1) "Abortion services" means any material, program, plan, or undertaking which seeks to promote abortion, encourages individuals to obtain an abortion, or provides abortions.

(2) "Contraceptive services" means any material, program, plan, or undertaking that is used for instruction on the use of birth control devices and substances, encourages individuals to use birth control methods, or provides birth control devices.

(3) "Funds" means any money, supply, material, building, or project provided by this state or its political subdivisions.

(4) "Minor" means any person under the age of 18 who is not otherwise emancipated, married, or a member of the armed forces of the United States.   1995

76-7-322. Public funds for provision of contraceptive or abortion services restricted.

No funds of the state or its political subdivisions shall be used to provide contraceptive or abortion services to an unmarried minor without the prior written consent of the minor's parent or guardian.   1988

76-7-323. Public funds for support entities providing contraceptive or abortion services restricted.

No agency of the state or its political subdivisions shall approve any application for funds of the state or its political subdivisions to support, directly or indirectly, any organization or health care provider that provides contraceptive or abortion services to an unmarried minor without the prior written consent of the minor's parent or guardian. No institution shall be denied state or federal funds under relevant provisions of law on the ground that a person on its staff

provides contraceptive or abortion services in that person's private practice outside of such institution.
1988

76-7-324. Violation of restrictions on public funds for contraceptive or abortion services as misdemeanor.
Any agent of a state agency or political subdivision, acting alone or in concert with others, who violates Section 76-7-322, 76-7-323, or 76-7-331 is guilty of a class B misdemeanor.
2004

76-7-325. Notice to parent or guardian of minor requesting contraceptive — Definition of contraceptives — Penalty for violation.
(1) Any person before providing contraceptives to a minor shall notify, whenever possible, the minor's parents or guardian of the service requested to be provided to such minor. Contraceptives shall be defined as appliances (including but not limited to intrauterine devices), drugs, or medicinal preparations intended or having special utility for prevention of conception.
(2) Any person in violation of this section shall be guilty of a class C misdemeanor.
1983

76-7-326. Partial birth abortions prohibited.
Any physician who knowingly performs a partial birth abortion and thereby kills a human fetus shall be fined or imprisoned, or both, as provided under this part. This section does not apply to a partial birth abortion that is necessary to save the life of a mother whose life is endangered by a physical disorder, physical illness, or physical injury, including a life endangering physical condition caused by or arising from the pregnancy itself.
2004

76-7-327. Remedies for father or maternal grandparents.
(1) The father, if married to the mother at the time she receives a partial birth abortion, and if the mother has not attained the age of 18 years at the time of the abortion, the maternal grandparents of the fetus, may in a civil action obtain appropriate relief, unless the pregnancy resulted from the plaintiff's criminal conduct or the plaintiff consented to the abortion.
(2) Such relief shall include:
(a) money damages for all injuries, psychological and physical, occasioned by the violation of Section 76-7-326 or 76-7-329; and
(b) statutory damages equal to three times the cost of the partial birth abortion.
2004

76-7-328. Hearing to determine necessity of physician's conduct.
(1) A physician accused of an offense under Section 76-7-326 may seek a hearing before the Physicians Licensing Board created in Section 58-67-201, or the Osteopathic Physician and Surgeon's Licensing Board created in Section 58-68-201 on whether the physician's conduct was necessary to save the life of the mother whose life was endangered by a physical disorder, physical illness, or physical injury, including a life endangering physical condition caused by or arising from the pregnancy itself.
(2) The findings on that issue are admissible on that issue at the trial of the physician. Upon a motion from the physician, the court shall delay the beginning of the trial for not more than 30 days to permit such a hearing to take place.
2004

76-7-329. Person unauthorized to perform abortions — Penalties.
A person who is not legally authorized by the state to perform abortions, but who nevertheless directly performs a partial birth abortion, is subject to Sections 76-7-301, 76-7-314, 76-7-326, and 76-7-327.
2004

76-7-330. Contingent continuance of prior law.
(1) If the implementation of Section 76-7-326 enacted by this bill is stayed or otherwise ordered by a court of competent jurisdiction to not be implemented, beginning on the day on which the implementation of Section 76-7-326 is stayed or otherwise ordered not to be implemented the statutes listed in Subsection (2) shall:
(a) be given effect as if this bill did not amend those statutes; and
(b) remain in effect as if not amended by this bill until the day on which a court orders that Section 76-7-326 may be implemented.
(2) Subsection (1) applies to:
(a) Section 76-7-301;
(b) Section 76-7-310.5; and
(c) Section 76-7-314.
(3) Nothing in this section prevents the Legislature from amending, repealing, or taking any other action regarding the sections listed in Subsection (2) in this or a subsequent session.
2004

76-7-331. Public funding of abortion forbidden.
(1) As used in this section, "damage to a major bodily function" refers only to injury or impairment of a physical nature and may not be interpreted to mean mental, psychological, or emotional harm, illness, or distress.
(2) Public funds of the state, its institutions, or its political subdivisions may not be used to pay or otherwise reimburse, either directly or indirectly, any person, agency, or facility for the performance of any induced abortion services unless:
(a) in the professional judgment of the pregnant woman's attending physician, the abortion is necessary to save the pregnant woman's life;
(b) the pregnancy is the result of rape or incest reported to law enforcement agencies, unless the woman was unable to report the crime for physical reasons or fear of retaliation; or
(c) in the professional judgment of the pregnant woman's attending physician, the abortion is necessary to prevent permanent, irreparable, and grave damage to a major bodily function of the pregnant woman provided that a caesarian procedure or other medical procedure that could also save the life of the child is not a viable option.
(3) Any officer or employee of the state who knowingly authorizes the use of funds prohibited by this section shall be dismissed from that person's office or position and the person's employment shall be immediately terminated.
2004

CHAPTER 8

OFFENSES AGAINST THE ADMINISTRATION OF GOVERNMENT

Part 1

Corrupt Practices

PART 1

CORRUPT PRACTICES

76-8-101. Definitions.

For the purposes of this chapter:

(1) "Candidate for electoral office" means a person who has filed as a candidate for office under the laws of the state.

(2) "Party official" means any person holding any post in a political party whether by election, appointment, or otherwise.

(3) "Peace officer" means any employee of a police or law enforcement agency that is part of or administered by the state or any of its political subdivisions, and whose duties consist primarily of the prevention and detection of crime and the enforcement of criminal statutes or ordinances of this state or any of its political subdivisions.

(4) (a) "Pecuniary benefit" means any advantage in the form of money, property, commercial interest, or anything else, the primary significance of which is economic gain.

(b) "Pecuniary benefit" does not include economic advantage applicable to the public generally, such as tax reduction or increased prosperity generally.

(5) (a) "Public servant" means any officer or employee of the state or any political subdivision of the state, including judges, legislators, consultants, and persons otherwise performing a governmental function.

(b) A person is considered a public servant upon his election, appointment, or other designation as such, although he may not yet officially occupy that position.   1993

76-8-102. Campaign contributions not prohibited.

Nothing in this chapter shall be construed to prohibit the giving or receiving of campaign contributions made for the purpose of defraying the costs of a political campaign. No person shall be convicted of an offense solely on the evidence that a campaign contribution was made and that an appointment or nomination was subsequently made by the person to whose campaign or political party the contribution was made.   1973

76-8-103. Bribery or offering a bribe.

(1) A person is guilty of bribery or offering a bribe if that person promises, offers, or agrees to give or gives, directly or indirectly, any benefit to another with the purpose or intent to influence an action, decision, opinion, recommendation, judgment, vote, nomination, or exercise of discretion of a public servant, party official, or voter.

(2) It is not a defense to a prosecution under this statute that:

(a) the person sought to be influenced was not qualified to act in the desired way, whether because the person had not assumed office, lacked jurisdiction, or for any other reason;

(b) the person sought to be influenced did not act in the desired way; or

(c) the benefit is not conferred, solicited, or accepted until after:

(i) the action, decision, opinion, recommendation, judgment, vote, nomination, or exercise of discretion, has occurred; or

(ii) the public servant ceases to be a public servant.

(3) Bribery or offering a bribe is:

(a) a third degree felony when the value of the benefit asked for, solicited, accepted, or conferred is less than $1,000; and

(b) a second degree felony when the value of the benefit asked for, solicited, accepted, or conferred is $1,000 or more.   1998

76-8-104. Threats to influence official or political action.

(1) A person is guilty of a class A misdemeanor if he threatens any harm to a public servant, party official, or voter with a purpose of influencing his action, decision, opinion, recommendation, nomination, vote, or other exercise of discretion.

(2) As used in this section:

(a) "Harm" means any disadvantage or injury, pecuniary or otherwise, including disadvantage or injury to any other person or entity in whose welfare the public servant, party official, or voter is interested.

(b) "Public servant" does not include jurors.   1991

76-8-105. Receiving or soliciting bribe or bribery by public servant.

(1) A person is guilty of receiving or soliciting a bribe if that person asks for, solicits, accepts, or receives, directly or indirectly, any benefit with the understanding or agreement that the purpose or intent is to influence an action, decision, opinion, recommendation, judgment, vote, nomination, or exercise of discretion, of a public servant, party official, or voter.

(2) It is not a defense to a prosecution under this statute that:

(a) the person sought to be influenced was not qualified to act in the desired way, whether because the person had not assumed office, lacked jurisdiction, or for any other reason;

(b) the person sought to be influenced did not act in the desired way; or

(c) the benefit is not asked for, conferred, solicited, or accepted until after:

(i) the action, decision, opinion, recommendation, judgment, vote, nomination, or exercise of discretion, has occurred; or

(ii) the public servant ceases to be a public servant.

(3) Receiving or soliciting a bribe is:

(a) a third degree felony when the value of the benefit asked for, solicited, accepted, or conferred is $1,000 or less; and

(b) a second degree felony when the value of the benefit asked for, solicited, accepted, or conferred exceeds $1,000.   1998

76-8-106. Receiving bribe or bribery for endorsement of person as public servant.

A person is guilty of a class B misdemeanor if:

(1) He solicits, accepts, agrees to accept for himself, another person, or a political party, money or any other pecuniary benefit as compensation for his endorsement, nomination, appointment, approval, or disapproval of any person for a position as a public servant or for the advancement of any public servant; or

(2) He knowingly gives, offers, or promises any pecuniary benefit prohibited by paragraph (1).   1973

76-8-107. Alteration of proposed legislative bill or resolution.

Every person who fraudulently alters the draft of any bill or resolution which has been presented to either of the houses composing the Legislature to be passed or adopted, with intent to procure its being passed or adopted by either house, or certified by the presiding officer of either house in language different from that intended by such house, is guilty of a felony of the third degree.   1974

76-8-108. Alteration of enrolled legislative bill or resolution.

Every person who fraudulently alters the enrolled copy of any bill or resolution which has been passed or adopted by the Legislature with intent to procure it to be approved by the governor or certified by the Division of Archives, or printed or published by the printer of statutes in language different from that in which it was passed or adopted by the Legislature, is guilty of a felony of the third degree.   1985

76-8-109. Failure of member of Legislature to disclose interest in measure or bill.

(1) As used in this section:

(a) "Business in which the legislator is associated" means any business in which a legislator is a director, officer, owner, member, partner, employee, or is a holder of stocks or bonds in the company that have a fair market value of $10,000 or more. This does not include business associations by members of the legislator's immediate family.

(b) "Conflict of interest" means legislation or action by a legislator that the legislator reasonably believes may cause direct financial benefit or detriment to him, a member of the legislator's immediate family, or a business in which the legislator is associated, and that benefit or detriment is distinguishable from the effects of that action on the public or on the legislator's profession, occupation, or association generally.

(c) "Immediate family" means the legislator's spouse and children living in the legislator's immediate household.

(2) In addition to the Declaration of Conflict of Interest form provided for in Subsection (3), before or during any vote on legislation or any legislative matter in which a legislator has actual knowledge that he has a conflict of interest which is not stated on the conflict of interest form, that legislator shall orally declare to the committee or body before which the matter is pending that the legislator may have a conflict of interest and what that conflict is. This declaration of conflict of interest shall be noted in the minutes of any committee meeting or in the Senate or House Journal.

(3) (a) A legislator shall file a Declaration of Conflict of Interest form with the Secretary of the Senate if the legislator is a senator or with the Chief Clerk of the House of Representatives if the legislator is a representative to satisfy that legislator's disclosure of any conflict of interest as required by Subsection (2).

(b) This Declaration of Conflict of Interest form shall include the businesses in which the legislator is associated and the general legislative subject areas in which the legislator may have a conflict of interest.

(c) This Declaration of Conflict of Interest form is available to the public.

(d) This requirement of disclosure of any conflict of interest does not prohibit a legislator from voting on any legislation or legislative matter.

(4) Every member of the Legislature who has a conflict of interest in any measure or bill proposed or pending before the Legislature of which he is a member and does not disclose the fact to the house of which he is a member and votes thereon is guilty of a class B misdemeanor.   1995

76-8-110. Peace officer prohibited from acting as compensated collection agent for collection agencies or creditors.

(1) A peace officer may not have any interest in any collection agency or act as a compensated collection agent for any creditor or collection agency.

(2) A person that violates this section is guilty of a class C misdemeanor.   1992

PART 2

ABUSE OF OFFICE

76-8-201. Official misconduct — Unauthorized acts or failure of duty.

A public servant is guilty of a class B misdemeanor if, with an intent to benefit himself or another or to harm another, he knowingly commits an unauthorized act which purports to be an act of his office, or knowingly refrains from performing a duty imposed on him by law or clearly inherent in the nature of his office.   1973

76-8-202. Official misconduct — Unlawful acts based on "inside" information.

A public servant is guilty of a class A misdemeanor if, knowing that official action is contemplated or in reliance on information which he has acquired by virtue of his office or from another public servant, which information has not been made public, he:

(1) acquires or divests himself of a pecuniary interest in any property, transaction, or enterprise which may be affected by such action or information;

(2) speculates or wagers on the basis of such action or information; or

(3) knowingly aids another to do any of the foregoing.   1991

76-8-203. Unofficial misconduct.

(1) A person is guilty of unofficial misconduct if he exercises or attempts to exercise any of the functions of a public office when:

(a) he has not taken and filed the required oath of office;

(b) he has failed to execute and file the required bond;

(c) he has not been elected or appointed to office;

(d) he exercises any of the functions of his office after his term has expired and the successor has been elected or appointed and has qualified, or after his office has been legally removed; or

(e) he knowingly withholds or retains from his successor in office or other person entitled to the official seal or any records, papers, documents, or other writings appertaining or belonging to his office or mutilates or destroys or takes away the same.

(2) Unofficial misconduct is a class B misdemeanor.   1996

PART 3

OBSTRUCTING GOVERNMENTAL OPERATIONS

76-8-301. Interference with public servant.

(1) A person is guilty of interference with a public servant if he:

(a) uses force, violence, intimidation, or engages in any other unlawful act with a purpose to interfere with a public servant performing or purporting to perform an official function; or

(b) knowingly or intentionally interferes with the lawful service of process by a public servant.

(2) Interference with a public servant is a class B misdemeanor.

(3) For purposes of this section, "public servant" does not include jurors.   1998

76-8-302. Picketing or parading in or near court.

A person is guilty of a class B misdemeanor if he pickets or parades in or near a building which houses a court of this state with intent to obstruct access to that court or to affect the outcome of a case pending before that court.   1973

76-8-303. Prevention of Legislature or public servants from meeting or organizing.

A person is guilty of a felony of the third degree if he intentionally and by force or fraud:

(1) Prevents the Legislature, or either of the houses composing it, or any of the members thereof, from meeting or organizing; or

(2) Prevents any other public servant from meeting or organizing to perform a lawful governmental function.   1973

76-8-304. Disturbing Legislature or official meeting.

(1) A person is guilty of a class B misdemeanor if he intentionally:

(a) disturbs the Legislature, or either of the houses composing it, while in session;

(b) commits any disorderly conduct in the immediate view and presence of either house of the Legislature, tending to interrupt its proceedings or impair the respect of its authority; or

(c) disturbs an official meeting or commits any disorderly conduct in immediate view and presence of participants in an official meeting tending to interrupt its proceedings.

(2) "Official meeting," as used in this section, means any lawful meeting of public servants for the purposes of carrying on governmental functions. 1992

76-8-305. Interference with arresting officer.

A person is guilty of a class B misdemeanor if he has knowledge, or by the exercise of reasonable care should have knowledge, that a peace officer is seeking to effect a lawful arrest or detention of that person or another and interferes with the arrest or detention by:

(1) use of force or any weapon;

(2) the arrested person's refusal to perform any act required by lawful order:

(a) necessary to effect the arrest or detention; and

(b) made by a peace officer involved in the arrest or detention; or

(3) the arrested person's or another person's refusal to refrain from performing any act that would impede the arrest or detention.   1990

76-8-305.5. Failure to stop at the command of a law enforcement officer.

A person is guilty of a class A misdemeanor who flees from or otherwise attempts to elude a law enforcement officer:

(1) after the officer has issued a verbal or visual command to stop;

(2) for the purpose of avoiding arrest; and

(3) by any means other than a violation of Section 41-6a-210 regarding failure to stop a vehicle at the command of a law enforcement officer.   2005

76-8-306. Obstruction of justice — Elements — Penalties — Exceptions.

(1) An actor commits obstruction of justice if the actor, with intent to hinder, delay, or prevent the investigation, apprehension, prosecution, conviction, or punishment of any person regarding conduct that constitutes a criminal offense:

(a) provides any person with a weapon;

(b) prevents by force, intimidation, or deception, any person from performing any act that might aid in the discovery, apprehension, prosecution, conviction, or punishment of any person;

(c) alters, destroys, conceals, or removes any item or other thing;

(d) makes, presents, or uses any item or thing known by the actor to be false;

(e) harbors or conceals a person;

(f) provides a person with transportation, disguise, or other means of avoiding discovery or apprehension;

(g) warns any person of impending discovery or apprehension;

(h) conceals information that is not privileged and that concerns the offense, after a judge or magistrate has ordered the actor to provide the information; or

(i) provides false information regarding a suspect, a witness, the conduct constituting an offense, or any other material aspect of the investigation.

(2) (a) As used in this section, "conduct that constitutes a criminal offense" means conduct that would be punishable as a crime and is separate from a violation of this section, and includes:

(i) any violation of a criminal statute or ordinance of this state, its political subdivisions, any other state, or any district, possession, or territory of the United States; and

(ii) conduct committed by a juvenile which would be a crime if committed by an adult.

(b) A violation of a criminal statute that is committed in another state, or any district, possession, or territory of the United States, is a:

(i) capital felony if the penalty provided includes death or life imprisonment without parole;

(ii) a first degree felony if the penalty provided includes life imprisonment with parole or a maximum term of imprisonment exceeding 15 years;

(iii) a second degree felony if the penalty provided exceeds five years;

(iv) a third degree felony if the penalty provided includes imprisonment for any period exceeding one year; and

(v) a misdemeanor if the penalty provided includes imprisonment for any period of one year or less.

(3) The penalties for obstruction of justice are:

(a) a second degree felony if the conduct which constitutes an offense would be a capital felony or first degree felony;

(b) a third degree felony if:

(i) the conduct that constitutes an offense would be a second or third degree felony and the actor violates Subsection (1)(b), (c), (d), (e), or (f);

(ii) the conduct that constitutes an offense would be any offense other than a capital or first degree felony and the actor violates Subsection (1)(a); or

(iii) the obstruction of justice is presented or committed before a court of law; or

(c) a class A misdemeanor for any violation of this section that is not enumerated under Subsection (3)(a) or (b).

(4) It is not a defense that the actor was unaware of the level of penalty for the conduct constituting an offense.

(5) Subsection (1)(e) does not apply to harboring a youth offender, which is governed by Section 62A-7-402.

(6) Subsection (1)(b) does not apply to:

(a) tampering with a juror, which is governed by Section 76-8-508.5;

(b) influencing, impeding, or retaliating against a judge or member of the Board of Pardons and Parole, which is governed by Section 76-8-316;

(c) tampering with a witness or soliciting or receiving a bribe, which is governed by Section 76-8-508;

(d) retaliation against a witness, victim, or informant, which is governed by Section 76-8-508.3; or

(e) extortion or bribery to dismiss a criminal proceeding, which is governed by Section 76-8-509.

(7) Notwithstanding Subsection (1), (2), or (3), an actor commits a third degree felony if the actor harbors or conceals an offender who has escaped from official custody as defined in Section 76-8-309.　2005

76-8-307. Failure to aid peace officer.

A person is guilty of a class B misdemeanor if, upon command by a peace officer identifiable or identified by him as such, he unreasonably fails or refuses to aid the peace officer in effecting an arrest or in preventing the commission of any offense by another person.

1973

76-8-308. Acceptance of bribe or bribery to prevent criminal prosecution — Defense.

(1) A person is guilty of a class A misdemeanor if he:

(a) solicits, accepts, or agrees to accept any benefit as consideration for his refraining from initiating or aiding in a criminal prosecution; or

(b) confers, offers, or agrees to confer any benefit upon another as consideration for the person refraining from initiating or aiding in a criminal prosecution.

(2) It is an affirmative defense that the value of the benefit did not exceed an amount which the actor believed to be due as restitution or indemnification for the loss caused or to be caused by the offense.　1991

76-8-309. Escape and aggravated escape — Consecutive sentences — Definitions.

(1) (a) (i) A prisoner is guilty of escape if he leaves official custody without lawful authorization.

(ii) If a prisoner obtains authorization to leave official custody by means of deceit, fraud, or other artifice, the prisoner has not received lawful authorization.

(b) Escape under this Subsection (1) is a third degree felony except as provided under Subsection (1)(c).

(c) Escape under this Subsection (1) is a second degree felony if:

(i) the actor escapes from a state prison; or

(ii) (A) the actor is convicted as a party to the offense, as defined in Section 76-2-202; and

(B) the actor is an employee at or a volunteer of a law enforcement agency, the Department of Corrections, a county or district attorney's office, the office of the state attorney general, the Board of Pardons and Parole, or the courts, the Judicial Council, the Office of the Court Administrator, or similar administrative units in the judicial branch of government.

(2) (a) A prisoner is guilty of aggravated escape if in the commission of an escape he uses a dangerous weapon, as defined in Section 76-1-601, or causes serious bodily injury to another.

(b) Aggravated escape is a first degree felony.

(3) Any prison term imposed upon a prisoner for escape under this section shall run consecutively with any other sentence.

(4) For the purposes of this section:

(a) "Confinement" means the prisoner is:

(i) housed in a state prison or any other facility pursuant to a contract with the Utah Department of Corrections after being sentenced and committed and the sentence has not been terminated or voided or the prisoner is not on parole;

(ii) lawfully detained in a county jail prior to trial or sentencing or housed in a county jail after sentencing and commitment and the sentence has not been terminated or voided or the prisoner is not on parole; or

(iii) lawfully detained following arrest.

(b) "Escape" is considered to be a continuing activity commencing with the conception of the design to escape and continuing until the escaping prisoner is returned to official custody or the prisoner's attempt to escape is thwarted or abandoned.

(c) "Official custody" means arrest, whether with or without warrant, or confinement in a state prison, jail, institution for secure confinement of juvenile offenders, or any confinement pursuant to an order of the court or sentenced and committed and the sentence has not been terminated or voided or the prisoner is not on parole. A person is considered confined in the state prison if he:

(i) without authority fails to return to his place of confinement from work release or home visit by the time designated for return;

(ii) is in prehearing custody after arrest for parole violation;

(iii) is being housed in a county jail, after felony commitment, pursuant to a contract with the Department of Corrections; or

(iv) is being transported as a prisoner in the state prison by correctional officers.

(d) "Prisoner" means any person who is in official custody and includes persons under trusty status.

(e) "Volunteer" means any person who donates service without pay or other compensation except expenses actually and reasonably incurred as approved by the supervising agency.　2004

76-8-309.5 to 76-8-311. Repealed.　1990, 2004

76-8-311.1. Secure areas — Items prohibited — Penalty.

(1) In addition to the definitions in Section 76-10-501, as used in this section:

(a) "Correctional facility" has the same meaning as defined in Section 76-8-311.3.

(b) "Explosive" has the same meaning as defined for "explosive, chemical, or incendiary device" defined in Section 76-10-306.

(c) "Law enforcement facility" means a facility which is owned, leased, or operated by a law enforcement agency.

(d) "Mental health facility" has the same meaning as defined in Section 62A-15-602.

(e) (i) "Secure area" means any area into which certain persons are restricted from transporting any firearm, ammunition, dangerous weapon, or explosive.

(ii) A "secure area" may not include any area normally accessible to the public.

(2) (a) A person in charge of a correctional, law enforcement, or mental health facility may establish secure areas within the facility and may prohibit or control by rule any firearm, ammunition, dangerous weapon, or explosive.

(b) Subsections (2)(a), (3), (4), (5), and (6) apply to higher education secure area hearing rooms referred to in Subsections 53B-3-103(2)(a)(ii) and (b).

(3) At least one notice shall be prominently displayed at each entrance to an area in which a firearm, ammunition, dangerous weapon, or explosive is restricted.

(4) (a) Provisions shall be made to provide a secure weapons storage area so that persons entering the secure area may store their weapons prior to entering the secure area.

(b) The entity operating the facility shall be responsible for weapons while they are stored in the storage area.

(5) It is a defense to any prosecution under this section that the accused, in committing the act made criminal by this section, acted in conformity with the facility's rule or policy established pursuant to this section.

(6) (a) Any person who knowingly or intentionally transports into a secure area of a facility any firearm, ammunition, or dangerous weapon is guilty of a third degree felony.

(b) Any person violates Section 76-10-306 who knowingly or intentionally transports, possesses, distributes, or sells any explosive in a secure area of a facility.   2002 (5th S.S.)

76-8-311.3. Items prohibited in correctional and mental health facilities — Penalties.

(1) As used in this section:

(a) "Contraband" means any item not specifically prohibited for possession by offenders under this section or Title 58, Chapter 37, Utah Controlled Substances Act.

(b) "Controlled substance" means any substance defined as a controlled substance under Title 58, Chapter 37, Utah Controlled Substances Act.

(c) "Correctional facility" means:

(i) any facility operated by or contracting with the Department of Corrections to house offenders in either a secure or nonsecure setting;

(ii) any facility operated by a municipality or a county to house or detain criminal offenders;

(iii) any juvenile detention facility; and

(iv) any building or grounds appurtenant to the facility or lands granted to the state, municipality, or county for use as a correctional facility.

(d) "Medicine" means any prescription drug as defined in Title 58, Chapter 17b, Pharmacy Practice Act, but does not include any controlled substances as defined in Title 58, Chapter 37, Utah Controlled Substances Act.

(e) "Mental health facility" has the same meaning as defined in Section 62A-15-602.

(f) "Offender" means a person in custody at a correctional facility.

(g) "Secure area" has the same meaning as provided in Section 76-8-311.1.

(2) Notwithstanding Section 76-10-500, a correctional or mental health facility may provide by rule that no firearm, ammunition, dangerous weapon, implement of escape, explosive, controlled substance, spirituous or fermented liquor, medicine, or poison in any quantity may be:

(a) transported to or upon a correctional or mental health facility;

(b) sold or given away at any correctional or mental health facility;

(c) given to or used by any offender at a correctional or mental health facility; or

(d) knowingly or intentionally possessed at a correctional or mental health facility.

(3) It is a defense to any prosecution under this section if the accused in committing the act made criminal by this section:

(a) with respect to a correctional facility operated by the Department of Corrections, acted in conformity with departmental rule or policy;

(b) with respect to a correctional facility operated by a municipality, acted in conformity with the policy of the municipality;

(c) with respect to a correctional facility operated by a county, acted in conformity with the policy of the county; or

(d) with respect to a mental health facility, acted in conformity with the policy of the mental health facility.

(4) (a) Any person who transports to or upon a correctional facility, or into a secure area of a mental health facility, any firearm, ammunition, dangerous weapon, or implement of escape with intent to provide or sell it to any offender, is guilty of a second degree felony.

(b) Any person who provides or sells to any offender at a correctional facility, or any detainee at a secure area of a mental health facility, any firearm, ammunition, dangerous weapon, or implement of escape is guilty of a second degree felony.

(c) Any offender who possesses at a correctional facility, or any detainee who possesses at a secure area of a mental health facility, any firearm, ammunition, dangerous weapon, or implement of escape is guilty of a second degree felony.

(d) Any person who, without the permission of the authority operating the correctional facility or the secure area of a mental health facility, knowingly possesses at a correctional facility or a secure area of a mental health facility any firearm, ammunition, dangerous weapon, or implement of escape is guilty of a third degree felony.

(e) Any person violates Section 76-10-306 who knowingly or intentionally transports, possesses, distributes, or sells any explosive in a correctional facility or mental health facility.

(5) (a) A person is guilty of a third degree felony who, without the permission of the authority operating the correctional facility or secure area of a mental health facility, knowingly transports to or upon a correctional facility or into a secure area of a mental health facility any:

(i) spirituous or fermented liquor;

(ii) medicine, whether or not lawfully prescribed for the offender; or

(iii) poison in any quantity.

(b) A person is guilty of a third degree felony who knowingly violates correctional or mental health facility policy or rule by providing or selling to any offender at a correctional facility or detainee within a secure area of a mental health facility any:

(i) spirituous or fermented liquor;

(ii) medicine, whether or not lawfully prescribed for the offender; or

(iii) poison in any quantity.

(c) An inmate is guilty of a third degree felony who, in violation of correctional or mental health facility policy or rule, possesses at a correctional facility or in a secure area of a mental health facility any:

(i) spirituous or fermented liquor;

(ii) medicine, other than medicine provided by the facility's health care providers in compliance with facility policy; or

(iii) poison in any quantity.

(d) A person is guilty of a class A misdemeanor who, with the intent to directly or indirectly provide or sell any tobacco product to an offender, directly or indirectly:

(i) transports, delivers, or distributes any tobacco product to an offender or on the grounds of any correctional facility;

(ii) solicits, requests, commands, coerces, encourages, or intentionally aids another person to transport any tobacco product to an offender or on any correctional facility, if the person is acting with the mental state required for the commission of an offense; or

(iii) facilitates, arranges, or causes the transport of any tobacco product in violation of this section to an offender or on the grounds of any correctional facility.

(e) A person is guilty of a class A misdemeanor who, without the permission of the authority operating the correctional or mental health facility, fails to declare or knowingly possesses at a correctional facility or in a secure area of a mental health facility any:

(i) spirituous or fermented liquor;

(ii) medicine; or

(iii) poison in any quantity.

(f) A person is guilty of a class B misdemeanor who, without the permission of the authority operating the correctional facility, knowingly engages in any activity that would facilitate the possession of any contraband by an offender in a correctional facility. The provisions of Subsection (5)(d) regarding any tobacco product take precedence over this Subsection (5)(f).

(g) Exemptions may be granted for worship for Native American inmates pursuant to Section 64-13-40.

(6) The possession, distribution, or use of a controlled substance at a correctional facility or in a secure area of a mental health facility shall be prosecuted in accordance with Title 58, Chapter 37, Utah Controlled Substances Act.

(7) The department shall make rules under Title 63, Chapter 46a, Utah Administrative Rulemaking Act, to establish guidelines for providing written notice to visitors that providing any tobacco product to offenders is a class A misdemeanor. 2004

76-8-312. Bail-jumping.

(1) A person is guilty of an offense when having been released on bail or on his own recognizance by court order or by other lawful authority upon condition that he subsequently appear personally upon a charge of an offense, he fails without just cause to appear at the time and place which have been lawfully designated for his appearance.

(2) An offense under this section is a felony of the third degree when the offense charged is a felony, a class B misdemeanor when the offense charged is a misdemeanor, and an infraction when the offense charged is an infraction. 1974

76-8-313. Threatening elected officials — Assault.

A person commits assault on an elected official when he attempts or threatens, irrespective of a showing of immediate force or violence, to inflict bodily injury to the elected official with the intent to impede, intimidate, or interfere with the elected official in the performance of his official duties or with the intent to retaliate against the elected official because of the performance of his official duties. 1996

76-8-314. Threatening elected officials — "Elected official" defined.

As used in this section, "elected official" means:

(1) any elected official of the state, county, or city and includes the members of the official's immediate family;

(2) any temporary judge appointed to fill a vacant judicial position;

(3) any judge not yet retained by a retention election;

(4) any member of a school board; and

(5) any person appointed to fill a vacant position of an elected official as defined in Subsection (1). 1996

76-8-315. Threatening elected officials — Penalties for assault.

Assault on an elected official is a felony of the third degree if bodily injury is attempted or occurs, otherwise the assault is a class B misdemeanor. 1983

76-8-316. Influencing, impeding, or retaliating against a judge or member of the Board of Pardons and Parole.

(1) A person is guilty of a third degree felony if the person threatens to assault, kidnap, or murder a judge or a member of the Board of Pardons and Parole with the intent to impede, intimidate, or interfere with the judge or member of the board while engaged in the performance of the judge's or member's official duties or with the intent to retaliate against the judge or member on account of the performance of those official duties.

(2) A person is guilty of a second degree felony if the person commits an assault on a judge or a member of the Board of Pardons and Parole with the intent to impede, intimidate, or interfere with the judge or member of the board while engaged in the performance of the judge's or member's official duties, or with the intent to retaliate against the judge or member on account of the performance of those official duties.

(3) A person is guilty of a first degree felony if the person commits aggravated assault or attempted murder on a judge or a member of the Board of Pardons and Parole with the purpose to impede, intimidate, or interfere with the judge or member of the board while engaged in the performance of the judge's or member's official duties or with the purpose to retaliate against the judge or member on account of the performance of those official duties.

(4) As used in this section:

(a) "Immediate family" means parents, spouse, surviving spouse, children, and siblings of the officer.

(b) "Judge" means judges of all courts of record and courts not of record.

(c) "Judge or member" includes the members of the judge's or member's immediate family.

(d) "Member of the Board of Pardons and Parole" means appointed members of the board.

(5) A member of the Board of Pardons and Parole is an executive officer for purposes of Subsection 76-5-202(1)(k).   2001

PART 4

OFFENSES AGAINST PUBLIC PROPERTY

76-8-401. "Public monies," "public funds," and "public officer" defined.

As used in this title:

(1) "Public monies" and "public funds" mean monies, funds, and accounts, regardless of the source from which they are derived, that are owned, held, or administered by the state or any of its boards, commissions, institutions, departments, divisions, agencies, bureaus, laboratories, or other similar instrumentalities, or any county, city, school district, political subdivision, or other public body. "Public monies" also includes monies, funds, or accounts that have been transferred by any of those public entities to a private contract provider of programs or services. Those monies, funds, or accounts maintain the nature of public monies while in the possession of the private entity that has contracted with a public entity to provide programs or services.

(2) "Public officer" means:

(a) all elected officials of the state, a political subdivision of the state, a county, town, city, precinct, or district;

(b) a person appointed to or serving an unexpired term of an elected office;

(c) a judge of a court of record and not of record including justice court judges; and

(d) a member of the Board of Pardons and Parole.   1999

76-8-402. Misusing public monies.

(1) Every public officer of this state or a political subdivision, or of any county, city, town, precinct, or district of this state, and every other person charged, either by law or under contract, with the receipt, safekeeping, transfer, disbursement, or use of public monies commits an offense if the officer or other charged person:

(a) appropriates the money or any portion of it to his own use or benefit or to the use or benefit of another without authority of law;

(b) loans or transfers the money or any portion of it without authority of law;

(c) fails to keep the money in his possession until disbursed or paid out by authority of law;

(d) unlawfully deposits the money or any portion in any bank or with any other person;

(e) knowingly keeps any false account or makes any false entry or erasure in any account of or relating to the money;

(f) fraudulently alters, falsifies, conceals, destroys, or obliterates any such account;

(g) willfully refuses or omits to pay over, on demand, any public monies in his hands, upon the presentation of a draft, order, or warrant drawn upon such monies by competent authority;

(h) willfully omits to transfer the money when the transfer is required by law; or

(i) willfully omits or refuses to pay over, to any officer or person authorized by law to receive it, any money received by him under any duty imposed by law so to pay over the same.

(2) A violation of Subsection (1) is a felony of the third degree, except it is a felony of the second degree if:

(a) the value of the money exceeds $5,000;

(b) the amount of the false account exceeds $5,000;

(c) the amount falsely entered exceeds $5,000;

(d) the amount that is the difference between the original amount and the fraudulently altered amount exceeds $5,000; or

(e) the amount falsely erased, fraudulently concealed, destroyed, obliterated, or falsified in the account exceeds $5,000.

(3) In addition to the penalty described in Subsection (2), a public officer who violates Subsection (1) is subject to the penalties described in Section 76-8-404.   1999

76-8-403. Failure to keep and pay over public monies.

Every person who receives, safekeeps, transfers, or disburses public monies who neglects or fails to keep and pay over the money in the manner prescribed by law is guilty of a felony of the third degree.   1995

76-8-404. Making profit from or misusing public monies — Disqualification from office — Criminal penalty.

A public officer, regardless of whether or not the officer receives, safekeeps, transfers, disburses, or has a fiduciary relationship with public monies, who makes a profit from or out of public monies, or who uses public monies in a manner or for a purpose not authorized by law, is guilty of a felony as provided in Section 76-8-402 and shall, in addition to the punishment provided by law, be disqualified to hold public office.   1999

76-8-405. Failure to pay over fine, forfeiture or fee.

Every public officer who receives any fine, forfeiture, or fee and refuses or neglects to pay it over within the time prescribed by law is guilty of a class B misdemeanor.   1973

76-8-406. Obstructing collection of revenue.

Every person who willfully obstructs or hinders any public officer from collecting any revenue, taxes, or other sums of money in which the people of this state are interested, and which such officer is by law empowered to collect, is guilty of a class B misdemeanor.   1973

76-8-407. Refusing to give tax assessment information, or giving false information.

Every person who unlawfully refuses, upon demand, to give to any county assessor or deputy county

assessor a list of his property subject to taxation, or to swear to such list, or who gives a false name, or fraudulently refuses to give his true name when demanded by the assessor in the discharge of his official duties, is guilty of a class B misdemeanor.
1973

76-8-408. Giving false tax receipt or failing to give receipt.

Every person who uses or gives any receipt, except that prescribed by law, as evidence of the payment for any tax or license of any kind, or who receives payment for the tax or license without delivering the receipt prescribed by law, is guilty of a class B misdemeanor.
1973

76-8-409. Refusing to give tax assessor or tax or license collector list of, or denying access to, employees.

Every person who, when requested by the assessor or collector of taxes or license fees, refuses to give to the assessor or collector the name and residence of each person in his employ, or to give the assessor or collector access to the building or place of employment, is guilty of a class B misdemeanor.
1991

76-8-410. Doing business without license.

Every person who commences or carries on any business, trade, profession, or calling, for the transaction or carrying on of which a license is required by any law, or by any county, city, or town ordinance, without taking out the license required by law or ordinance is guilty of a class B misdemeanor.
1973

76-8-411. Trafficking in warrants.

No state, county, city, town, or district officer shall, either directly or indirectly, contract for or purchase any warrant or order issued by the state, county, city, town, or district of which he is an officer, at any discount whatever upon the sum due on the warrant or order, and, if any state, county, city, town, or district officer shall so contract for or purchase any such order or warrant on a discount, he is guilty of a class B misdemeanor.
1973

76-8-412. Stealing, destroying or mutilating public records by custodian.

Every officer having the custody of any record, map, or book, or of any paper or proceedings of any court, filed or deposited in any public office, or placed in his hands for any purpose, who is guilty of stealing, willfully destroying, mutilating, defacing, altering, falsifying, removing, or secreting the whole or any part thereof, or who permits any other person so to do, is guilty of a felony of the third degree.
1973

76-8-413. Stealing, destroying or mutilating public records by one not custodian.

Every person, not an officer such as is referred to in the preceding section, who is guilty of any of the acts specified in that section is guilty of a class A misdemeanor.
1973

76-8-414. Recording false or forged instruments.

Every person who knowingly procures or offers any false or forged instrument to be filed, registered, or recorded in any public office, which instrument, if genuine, might be filed or registered or recorded under any law of this state or of the United States, is guilty of a felony of the third degree.
1973

76-8-415. Damaging or removing monuments of official surveys.

Every person who willfully injures, defaces, or removes any signal, monument, building, or appurtenance thereto, placed, erected, or used by persons engaged in the United States or state survey is guilty of a class B misdemeanor.
1973

76-8-416. Taking toll or maintaining road, bridge, or ferry without authority — Refusal to pay lawful toll.

Any person who demands or receives compensation for the use of any bridge or ferry, or who sets up or keeps any road, bridge, or ferry, or constructed ford, for the purpose of receiving remuneration for its use without authority of law; and any person who refuses to pay on demand the compensation or fee authorized to be collected for use of a licensed toll road, bridge, ferry, or constructed ford after having used it is guilty of a class B misdemeanor.
1973

76-8-417. Tampering with official notice or proclamation.

Every person who intentionally defaces, obliterates, tears down, or destroys any copy or transcript or extract from or of any law of the United States or of this state, or any proclamation, advertisement, or notice, set up at any place in this state by authority of any law of the United States or of this state, or by order of any court or of any public officer, before the expiration of the time for which the same was to remain set up, is guilty of an infraction.
1973

76-8-418. Damaging jails.

A person who willfully and intentionally breaks down, pulls down, destroys, floods, or otherwise damages any public jail or other place of confinement, including a detention, shelter, or secure confinement facility for juveniles, is guilty of a felony of the third degree.
2005

76-8-419. Damaging highways or bridges.

(1) Every person who intentionally, knowingly, or recklessly digs up, removes, displaces, breaks, or otherwise damages or destroys any public highway, or any private way laid out by authority of law, or any bridge upon the highway or private way is guilty of a class A misdemeanor.

(2) If the violation of this section constitutes an offense subject to a greater penalty under another provision of Title 76, Utah Criminal Code, than is provided under this section, this section does not prohibit the prosecution and sentencing for the offense subject to a greater penalty.
2002

76-8-420. Removing or damaging road signs.

Every person who maliciously removes or injures any milepost or milestone or guidepost or any inscription on them, erected upon any highway, is guilty of a class B misdemeanor.
1973

PART 5

FALSIFICATION IN OFFICIAL MATTERS

76-8-501. Definitions.

For the purposes of this part:

(1) "Official proceeding" means any proceeding before a legislative, judicial, administrative, or other governmental body or official authorized by law to take evidence under oath or affirmation, including a notary or other person taking evidence in connection with any of these proceedings.

(2) "Material" means capable of affecting the course or outcome of the proceeding. A statement is not material if it is retracted in the course of the official proceeding in which it was made before it

became manifest that the falsification was or would be exposed and before it substantially affected the proceeding. 1997

76-8-502. False or inconsistent material statements.

A person is guilty of a felony of the second degree if in any official proceeding:

(1) He makes a false material statement under oath or affirmation or swears or affirms the truth of a material statement previously made and he does not believe the statement to be true; or

(2) He makes inconsistent material statements under oath or affirmation, both within the period of limitations, one of which is false and not believed by him to be true. 1997

76-8-503. False or inconsistent statements.

A person is guilty of a class B misdemeanor if:

(1) (a) he makes a false statement under oath or affirmation or swears or affirms the truth of the statement previously made and he does not believe the statement to be true if:

(i) the falsification occurs in an official proceeding, or is made with a purpose to mislead a public servant in performing his official functions; or

(ii) the statement is one which is authorized by law to be sworn or affirmed before a notary or other person authorized to administer oaths; or

(b) he makes inconsistent statements under oath or affirmation, both within the period of limitations, one of which is false and not believed by him to be true.

(2) A person is not guilty under this section if the falsification is retracted before it becomes manifest that the falsification was or would be exposed. 1997

76-8-504. Written false statement.

A person is guilty of a class B misdemeanor if:

(1) He makes a written false statement which he does not believe to be true on or pursuant to a form bearing a notification authorized by law to the effect that false statements made therein are punishable; or

(2) With intent to deceive a public servant in the performance of his official function, he:

(a) Makes any written false statement which he does not believe to be true; or

(b) Knowingly creates a false impression in a written application for any pecuniary or other benefit by omitting information necessary to prevent statements therein from being misleading; or

(c) Submits or invites reliance on any writing which he knows to be lacking in authenticity; or

(d) Submits or invites reliance on any sample, specimen, map, boundary mark, or other object which he knows to be false.

(3) No person shall be guilty under this section if he retracts the falsification before it becomes manifest that the falsification was or would be exposed. 1973

76-8-504.5. False statements — Preliminary hearing.

(1) A person is guilty of a class A misdemeanor if the person makes a false statement:

(a) which the person does not believe to be true;

(b) that the person has reason to believe will be used in a preliminary hearing; and

(c) after having been notified either verbally or in writing that:

(i) the statement may be used in a preliminary hearing before a magistrate or a judge; and

(ii) if the person makes a false statement after having received this notification, he is subject to a criminal penalty.

(2) Notification under Subsection (1) is sufficient if it is verbal or written and is in substantially the following form: "You are notified that statements you are about to make may be presented to a magistrate or a judge in lieu of your sworn testimony at a preliminary examination. Any false statement you make and that you do not believe to be true may subject you to criminal punishment as a class A misdemeanor." 1999

76-8-504.6. False or misleading information.

(1) A person is guilty of a class B misdemeanor if the person, not under oath or affirmation, intentionally or knowingly gives false or misleading material information to an officer of the court for the purpose of influencing a criminal proceeding.

(2) For the purposes of this section "officer of the court" means:

(a) prosecutor;

(b) judge;

(c) court clerk;

(d) interpreter;

(e) presentence investigator;

(f) probation officer;

(g) parole officer; and

(h) any other person reasonably believed to be gathering information for a criminal proceeding.

(3) This section does not apply under circumstances amounting to Section 76-8-306 or any other provision of this code carrying a greater penalty. 2004

76-8-505. False or inconsistent statements — Proof of falsity of statements — Irregularities no defense.

(1) On any prosecution for a violation of Subsection 76-8-502(1) or 76-8-503(1)(a), falsity of a statement may not be established solely through contradiction by the testimony of a single witness.

(2) In prosecutions for violation of Subsection 76-8-502(2) or 76-8-503(1)(b), it need not be alleged or proved which of the statements are false but only that one or the other is false and not believed by the defendant to be true.

(3) It is not a defense to a charge under this part that the oath or affirmation was administered or taken in an irregular manner. 1997

76-8-506. Providing false information to law enforcement officers, government agencies, or specified professionals.

A person is guilty of a class B misdemeanor if he:

(1) knowingly gives or causes to be given false information to any peace officer or any state or local government agency or personnel with a purpose of inducing the recipient of the information to believe that another has committed an offense;

(2) knowingly gives or causes to be given to any peace officer, any state or local government agency or personnel, or to any person licensed in this state to practice social work, psychology, or marriage and family therapy, information concerning the commission of an offense, knowing that the offense did not occur or knowing that he

has no information relating to the offense or danger; or

(3) knowingly gives or causes to be given false information to any state or local government agency or personnel with a purpose of inducing a change in the person's licensing or certification status or the licensing or certification status of another.   2005

76-8-507. False personal information to peace officer.

(1) A person commits a class C misdemeanor if, with intent of misleading a peace officer as to the person's identity, birth date, or place of residence, the person knowingly gives a false name, birth date, or address to a peace officer in the lawful discharge of the peace officer's official duties.

(2) A person commits a class A misdemeanor if, with the intent of leading a peace officer to believe that the person is another actual person, he gives the name, birth date, or address of another person to a peace officer acting in the lawful discharge of the peace officer's official duties.   2002

76-8-508. Tampering with witness — Receiving or soliciting a bribe.

(1) A person is guilty of the third degree felony of tampering with a witness if, believing that an official proceeding or investigation is pending or about to be instituted, or with the intent to prevent an official proceeding or investigation, he attempts to induce or otherwise cause another person to:

(a) testify or inform falsely;

(b) withhold any testimony, information, document, or item;

(c) elude legal process summoning him to provide evidence; or

(d) absent himself from any proceeding or investigation to which he has been summoned.

(2) A person is guilty of the third degree felony of soliciting or receiving a bribe as a witness if he solicits, accepts, or agrees to accept any benefit in consideration of his doing any of the acts specified under Subsection (1).

(3) The offense of tampering with a witness or soliciting or receiving a bribe under this section does not merge with any other substantive offense committed in the course of committing any offense under this section.   2004

76-8-508.3. Retaliation against a witness, victim, or informant.

(1) As used in this section:

(a) A person is "closely associated" with a witness, victim, or informant if the person is a member of the witness', victim's, or informant's family, has a close personal or business relationship with the witness or victim, or resides in the same household with the witness, victim, or informant.

(b) "Harm" means physical, emotional, or economic injury or damage to a person or to his property, reputation, or business interests.

(2) A person is guilty of the third degree felony of retaliation against a witness, victim, or informant if, believing that an official proceeding or investigation is pending, is about to be instituted, or has been concluded, he:

(a) (i) makes a threat of harm; or

(ii) causes harm; and

(b) directs the threat or action:

(i) against a witness or an informant regarding any official proceeding, a victim of

any crime, or any person closely associated with a witness, victim, or informant; and

(ii) as retaliation or retribution against the witness, victim, or informant.

(3) This section does not prohibit any person from seeking any legal redress to which the person is otherwise entitled.

(4) The offense of retaliation against a witness, victim, or informant under this section does not merge with any other substantive offense committed in the course of committing any offense under this section.   2004

76-8-508.5. Tampering with juror — Retaliation against juror — Penalty.

(1) As used in this section "juror" means a person:

(a) summoned for jury duty; or

(b) serving as or having served as a juror or alternate juror in any court or as a juror on any grand jury of the state.

(2) A person is guilty of tampering with a juror if he attempts to or actually influences a juror in the discharge of the juror's service by:

(a) communicating with the juror by any means, directly or indirectly, except for attorneys in lawful discharge of their duties in open court;

(b) offering, conferring, or agreeing to confer any benefit upon the juror; or

(c) communicating to the juror a threat that a reasonable person would believe to be a threat to injure:

(i) the juror's person or property; or

(ii) the person or property of any other person in whose welfare the juror is interested.

(3) A person is guilty of tampering with a juror if he commits any unlawful act in retaliation for anything done by the juror in the discharge of the juror's service:

(a) to the juror's person or property; or

(b) to the person or property of any other person in whose welfare the juror is interested.

(4) Tampering with a juror is a third degree felony.   1992

76-8-509. Extortion or bribery to dismiss criminal proceeding.

(1) A person is guilty of a felony of the second degree if by the use of force or by any threat which would constitute a means of committing the crime of theft by extortion under this code, if the threat were employed to obtain property, or by promise of any reward or pecuniary benefits, he attempts to induce an alleged victim of a crime to secure the dismissal of or to prevent the filing of a criminal complaint, indictment, or information.

(2) "Victim," as used in this section, includes a child or other person under the care or custody of a parent or guardian.   1973

76-8-510. Repealed.   2001

76-8-510.5. Tampering with evidence — Elements — Penalties.

(1) A person is guilty of tampering with evidence if, believing that an official proceeding or investigation is pending or about to be instituted, or with the intent to prevent an official proceeding or investigation, the person knowingly or intentionally:

(a) alters, destroys, conceals, or removes any thing or item with the purpose of impairing the veracity or availability of the thing or item in the proceeding or investigation; or

(b) makes, presents, or uses any thing or item which he knows to be false with the purpose of deceiving a public servant who is or may be engaged in the proceeding or investigation.

(2) Subsection (1) does not apply to any offense that amounts to a violation of Section 76-8-306.

(3) (a) Tampering with evidence is a third degree felony if the offense is committed in an official proceeding.

(b) Any violation of this section except under Subsection (3)(a) is a class A misdemeanor.   2005

76-8-511. Falsification or alteration of government record — Penalty.

A person is guilty of a class B misdemeanor if under circumstances not amounting to an offense subject to a greater penalty under Title 76, Chapter 6, Part 5, Fraud, the person:

(1) knowingly makes a false entry in or false alteration of anything belonging to, received, or kept by the government for information or record, or required by law to be kept for information of the government;

(2) presents or uses anything knowing it to be false and with a purpose that it be taken as a genuine part of information or records referred to in Subsection (1); or

(3) intentionally destroys, conceals, or otherwise impairs the verity or availability of the information or records, knowing that the destruction, concealment, or impairment is unlawful.   2003

76-8-512. Impersonation of officer.

A person is guilty of a class B misdemeanor who:

(1) impersonates a public servant or a peace officer with intent to deceive another or with intent to induce another to submit to his pretended official authority or to rely upon his pretended official act;

(2) falsely states he is a public servant or a peace officer with intent to deceive another or to induce another to submit to his pretended official authority or to rely upon his pretended official act; or

(3) displays or possesses without authority any badge, identification card, other form of identification, any restraint device, or the uniform of any state or local governmental entity, or a reasonable facsimile of any of these items, with the intent to deceive another or with the intent to induce another to submit to his pretended official authority or to rely upon his pretended official act.   1991

76-8-513. False judicial or official notice.

A person is guilty of a class B misdemeanor who, with a purpose to procure the compliance of another with a request made by the person, knowingly sends, mails, or delivers to the person a notice or other writing which has no judicial or other sanction but which in its format or appearance simulates a summons, complaint, court order, or process, or an insignia, seal, or printed form of a federal, state, or local government or an instrumentality thereof, or is otherwise calculated to induce a belief that it does have a judicial or other official sanction.   1973

76-8-514. False wearing or use of military or organization medal or insignia.

(1) It is an offense for any person to wear or use any military medal awarded by the United States, or the state of Utah, or of any society, order, or organization of ten years' standing in this state, unless the person is entitled to wear or use it, and it is unlawful for any person to use the name of the society, order, or organization, the titles of its officers, or its insignia, ritual, or ceremonies, unless the person is authorized thereunto by the society, order, or organization or by the state of Utah or the United States.

(2) A violation of this section is a class B misdemeanor.   1973

PART 6

ABUSE OF PROCESS

76-8-601. Wrongful commencement of action in justice court.

Any party to any suit or proceeding, and any attorney or agent for the party, who knowingly commences, prosecutes, or maintains any action, suit, or proceeding in any justice court other than as provided in Sections 78-5-103 and 78-5-104, is guilty of a class B misdemeanor.   1998

76-8-602. Assuming liability for conferring jurisdiction upon justice court judge.

Any person who binds himself, or voluntarily becomes liable jointly or jointly and severally with any other person, for the purpose of conferring jurisdiction of any cause upon any justice court judge in any precinct or city that would be without jurisdiction except for the liability of the joint obligor, and any person who induces a person to assume the liability for the purpose of conferring jurisdiction upon the justice court judge, is guilty of a class B misdemeanor.   1990

76-8-603. Wrongful attachment by justice court judge — Liability.

It is unlawful for any justice court judge to issue any writ of attachment, and for any party, agent, or attorney of the party, to advise, induce, or procure the issuance thereof, in any action, suit, or proceeding before the affidavit is filed, or where the affidavit filed does not conform substantially with the requirements of Rule 64C of the Utah Rules of Civil Procedure. Any person violating any of the provisions of this section is guilty of a class B misdemeanor and shall be liable to the person whose property, credits, money, or earnings are attached for double the value of the attached property, together with all costs paid by him, and all damages incurred in the attachment proceedings.   1990

PART 7

COLLEGES AND UNIVERSITIES

76-8-701. Definitions.

For the purposes of this part:

(1) "Chief administrative officer" means the president of a private or state institution of higher education or the officer designated by the president or by the governing board of the institution to administer the affairs of a campus or other facility owned by the institution or operated or controlled by the governing board of the institution.

(2) "School" or "institution of higher education" means any private institution of higher education or any state institution of higher education as defined in Section 53B-1-102.

(3) "State institution of higher education" includes the University of Utah, Utah State University, Southern Utah University, Weber State University, Snow College, Dixie State College of Utah, the College of Eastern Utah, Utah Valley

State College, Salt Lake Community College, and any other university or college which may be established and maintained by the state, and includes any branch or affiliated institution and any campus or facility owned, operated, or controlled by the governing board of the university or college.   2000

76-8-702. Purpose.

It is the purpose of this part to supplement and clarify the power vested in the governing board of each private or state institution of higher education and to regulate, conduct, and enforce law and order on property owned or controlled by it.   1973

76-8-703. Interfering or intending to interfere with activities — Failure to leave when ordered.

If any person on the campus of a private or state institution of higher education or on any other facility owned by the institution or operated or controlled by the governing board of the institution, commits any act which interferes with the peaceful conduct of the activities of the campus or facility, or has entered the campus or facility with the intent to commit any such act, the chief administrative officer or officer or employee designated by him to maintain order on the campus or facility may direct a person to leave the campus or facility, and if the person fails so to do, he is guilty of a class C misdemeanor.   1973

76-8-704. Violation of rule or regulation of institution — Failure to leave when ordered.

If a person enters upon the campus of a private or state institution of higher education or other facility owned or controlled by the governing board of the institution and violates any rule or regulation of the institution, the chief administrative officer or an officer or employee designated by him to maintain order on the campus or facility may inform the person of the regulation and its violation. If the person does not immediately cease and desist from violating the rule or regulation, the chief administrative officer, or officer or employee designated by him to maintain order on the campus or related facility, may direct the person to leave the campus or facility, and if the person fails so to do, he is guilty of a class C misdemeanor.   1973

76-8-705. Willful interference with lawful activities of students or faculty.

(1) If any person on the campus of a private or state institution of higher education or upon any other facility owned or controlled by the governing board of the institution, willfully denies to students, school officials, employees, or invitees:

(a) lawful freedom of movement,

(b) lawful use of the property or facilities, or

(c) lawful ingress or egress to the institution's physical facilities,

that person is guilty of a class C misdemeanor.

(2) If any person upon the campus of a private or state institution of higher education or upon any other facility owned or controlled by the governing board of the institution, willfully impedes the faculty or staff of the institution in the lawful performance of their duties, or willfully impedes a student of the institution in the lawful pursuit of his educational activities, that person is guilty of a class C misdemeanor.   1973

76-8-706. Injury or destruction of property.

Every person who maliciously injures or destroys any real or personal property belonging to or under the control of an institution of higher education or maliciously injures or destroys any personal property not his own which is lawfully present upon the campus or other facility of such institution shall be guilty of a class A misdemeanor.   1973

76-8-707. Assistance by local authorities.

(1) If, in the judgment of the chief administrative officer of any institution of higher education, or in the judgment of any officer or employee designated by him to maintain order on a campus or related facility, the law enforcement agency or security department of that institution lacks sufficient manpower to deal effectively with any condition of unrest existing or developing on a campus or related facility of the institution, he may call for assistance from the county sheriff of the county or any city law enforcement agency or from the Department of Public Safety.

(2) Upon receipt of the request, the county sheriff, city law enforcement agency, or Department of Public Safety must render all necessary assistance without expense to the institution of higher education.

(3) All personnel while rendering assistance shall serve under the general direction of the chief administrative officer of the institution or the officer or employee designated by him to maintain order on the campus or related facility.   1993

76-8-708. Enforcement of rules or regulations of institutions — Privilege of information acquired in proceedings.

(1) Nothing herein shall be deemed to prevent any state institution of higher education from proceeding to enforce against any invitee, student, faculty member, or other employee of an institution any rule or regulation of the institution in accordance with procedural regulations as may be established by the president and institutional council of the institution and as authorized by the state board of higher education.

(2) The chief administrative officer of any state institution of higher education, or any person designated by him to enforce any rule or regulation against any student, faculty member, or other employee of the institution cannot be examined as to information, written or oral, which has been acquired by him in the process of the enforcement proceedings or related activities, without the permission of the person against whom the rule or regulation was to be enforced.   1973

76-8-709. Enforcement of laws by local agencies not limited.

Nothing in this act shall limit the right or duty of any local law enforcement agency to enforce the law which it had prior to this enactment.   1973

76-8-710. Disruption of activities in or near school building — Failure to leave or re-entry.

Any person who comes into any school building or upon any school ground, or street, sidewalk, or public way adjacent to any school building or ground and whose presence or acts interfere with the peaceful conduct of the activities of any school or disrupt the school or its pupils or school activities, and who remains there, or who re-enters or comes upon the place within 72 hours, after being asked to leave by the chief administrative official of that school or his representative or agent is guilty of an offense and shall be punished as provided in Section 76-8-717.   1973

76-8-711. Withdrawal of consent to remain on campus or facility — Report and confirmation of action — Reinstatement — Hearing — Re-entry — Powers of suspension, dismissal or expulsion not affected.

(1) The chief administrative officer of a campus or other facility of an institution of higher education, or his agent or representative, whenever there is reasonable cause to believe that any student has willfully disrupted the orderly operation of the campus or facility, may notify any student that consent to remain on the campus or other facility under the control of the chief administrative officer has been withdrawn.

(2) (a) Whenever consent is withdrawn by any authorized officer or employee, other than the chief administrative officer, the officer or employee shall as soon as is reasonably possible submit a written report to the chief administrative officer. The report shall contain the following:

(i) The description of the person from whom consent was withdrawn, including, if available, the person's name and address.

(ii) A brief statement of the facts giving rise to the withdrawal of consent.

(b) If the chief administrative officer or, in his absence, his agent or representative upon reviewing the report finds there was reasonable cause to believe that the person willfully disrupted the orderly operation of the campus or facility, he may enter written confirmation upon the report of the action taken by the officer or employee. If the chief administrative officer or, in his absence, his agent or representative does not confirm the action of the officer or employee within 24 hours after the time consent was withdrawn, the action of the officer or employee shall be deemed void and of no force or effect, except that any arrest made during that period shall not, for this reason, be deemed not to have been made for probable cause.

(3) Consent shall be reinstated by the chief administrative officer whenever he has reason to believe that the presence of the student from whom consent was withdrawn will not constitute a substantial and material threat to the orderly operation of the campus or facility. In no case shall consent be withdrawn for longer than fourteen days from the date upon which consent was initially withdrawn. The student from whom consent has been withdrawn may submit a written request for a hearing on the withdrawal within the two-week period. The written request shall state the address to which notice of hearing is to be sent. The chief administrative officer shall grant a hearing not later than seven days from the date of receipt of a request and immediately mail a written notice of the time, place, and date of hearing.

(4) (a) Any student who has been notified by the chief administrative officer of a campus or other facility of an institution of higher education or by an officer or employee designated by the chief administrative officer to maintain order on the campus or facility, that consent to remain on the campus or facility has been withdrawn pursuant to Subsections (1) and (2), who has not had consent reinstated, and who willfully and knowingly enters or remains upon the campus or facility during the period for which consent has been withdrawn is guilty of an offense.

(b) This subsection shall not apply to any student who re-enters the campus or facility eight hours after notification of the withdrawal of consent for the sole purpose of applying to the chief administrative officer for reinstatement of consent or for the sole purpose of attending a hearing on withdrawal.

(5) This section shall not affect the power of the duly constituted authorities of an institution of higher education to suspend, dismiss, or expel any student or employee at the university or college.

(6) Any student convicted under this section shall be punished as provided in Section 76-8-717.   1973

76-8-712. Re-entry of campus or facility after denial of access as condition of suspension or dismissal — Presumption of knowledge.

(1) Every student or employee who, after a hearing, has been suspended or dismissed from an institution of higher education for disrupting the orderly operation of a campus or facility and as a condition of suspension or dismissal has been denied access to the campus or facility of the institution for the period of the suspension or for a period not to exceed one year in the case of dismissal, who has been served by registered or certified mail at the last address given by the person with a written notice of suspension or dismissal and condition; and who willfully and knowingly enters upon the campus or facility of the institution to which he has been denied access without the express written permission of the chief administrative officer is guilty of a misdemeanor and shall be punished as provided in Section 76-8-717.

(2) Knowledge shall be presumed if notice has been given as prescribed in this section. The presumption established by this section is a presumption affecting the burden of proof.   1973

76-8-713. Person not a student, officer or employee — Re-entry of campus or facility after direction to leave.

If a person who is not a student, officer, or employee of an institution of higher education and is not required by his employment to be on the campus or other facility owned, operated, or controlled by an institution of higher education, enters the campus or facility, and it reasonably appears to the chief administrative officer of the campus or facility or his agent or representative that the person is committing an act likely to interfere with the peaceful conduct of the activities of the campus or facility or has entered the campus or facility for the purpose of committing any such act, the chief administrative officer or his agent or representative may direct the person to leave the campus or facility, and if he fails to do so or willfully and knowingly re-enters upon the campus or facility within 72 hours after being directed to leave, he is guilty of an offense and shall be punished as provided in Section 76-8-717.   1973

76-8-714. Injury or destruction of property of school or person.

Every person who maliciously injures or destroys any real or personal property belonging to or under the control of a school or institution of higher education or maliciously injures or destroys any person's property which is lawfully present upon the campus or other facility is guilty of a class A misdemeanor.   1973

76-8-715. Damage or destruction of property by explosives or flammable materials.

Any person who willfully and maliciously damages or destroys any building, structure, machinery, equipment, or other real or personal property owned or leased to a school or institution of higher education by the use of explosives or highly flammable materials shall be guilty of a felony of the second degree.   1973

76-8-716. Request for assistance from state and local law enforcement authorities.

If, in the judgment of the chief administrative officer of any school or institution of higher education, his agent, or representative, the police or security department of that institution lacks sufficient manpower to deal effectively with any condition of unrest existing or developing on a campus or facility of the institution, he may request assistance from state and local law enforcement authorities. All state and local law enforcement officers while rendering assistance shall serve in co-operation with the chief administrative officer of the institution or his agent or representative and without expense to the institution.   1973

76-8-717. Violations — Classifications of offenses.

Any student or employee found guilty of a violation of those sections which specify this section as prescribing the punishment shall be punished as follows:

(1) Upon the first and second conviction, shall be punished as a class B misdemeanor.

(2) If the defendant has been convicted two or more times of a violation of any offense specified punishable under this section, he shall be punished for a class A misdemeanor.   1973

76-8-718. Enforcement rights of state or local law enforcement authority not limited.

Nothing in this act shall limit the right of any state or local law enforcement authority to enforce the laws of this state.   1973

PART 8

SABOTAGE PREVENTION

76-8-801. Definitions.

For the purpose of this part:

(1) "Highway" includes any private or public street, way, or other place used for travel to or from property.

(2) "Highway commissioners" means any individual, board, or other body having authority under then existing law to discontinue the use of the highway which it is desired to restrict or close to public use and travel.

(3) "Public utility" includes any pipeline, gas, electric, heat, water, oil, sewer, telephone, telegraph, radio, railway, railroad, airplane, transportation communication or other system by whomsoever owned or operated for public use.   1973

76-8-802. Destruction of property to interfere with preparation for defense or war.

Whoever intentionally destroys, impairs, injures, interferes, or tampers with real or personal property with reasonable grounds to believe that the act will hinder, delay, or interfere with the preparation of the United States or of any of the states for defense or for war, or with the prosecution of war by the United States, shall be guilty of a felony of the second degree.   1973

76-8-803. Causing or omitting to note defects in articles used in preparation for defense or war.

Whoever intentionally makes or causes to be made or omits to note on inspection any defect in any article

or thing with reasonable grounds to believe that the article or thing is intended to be used in connection with the preparation of the United States or any of the states for defense or for war, or for the prosecution of war by the United States, or that the article or thing is one of a number of similar articles or things, some of which are intended so to be used, shall be guilty of a felony of the third degree.   1973

76-8-804. Attempts to commit crimes of sabotage.

Whoever attempts to commit any of the crimes defined by this part shall be punishable for the attempt as prescribed in [Section] 76-4-102. In addition to the acts which constitute an attempt to commit crime under the law of this state, the solicitation or incitement of another to commit any of the crimes defined by this part not allowed by the commission of the crime, the collection or assemblage of any materials with the intent that they are to be used then or at a later time in the commission of the crime, or the entry, with or without permission, of a building, enclosure or other premises of another with the intent to commit any such crime therein or thereon shall constitute an attempt to commit the crime.   1973

76-8-805. Conspiracy to commit crimes of sabotage.

If two or more persons conspire to commit any crime defined by this part each of the persons is guilty of conspiracy and subject to the same punishment as if he had committed the crime which he conspired to commit, whether or not any act be done in furtherance of the conspiracy. It shall not constitute any defense or ground of suspension of judgment, sentence, or punishment on behalf of any person prosecuted under this section that any of his fellow conspirators has been acquitted, has not been arrested or convicted, or is amenable to justice or has been pardoned or otherwise discharged before or after conviction.   1973

76-8-806. Facts kept secret until complaint filed.

A person may not make public any evidence of fact or the name of the person accused of violating the provisions of Sections 76-8-802, 76-8-803, 76-8-804, and 76-8-805 prior to the filing of a formal complaint by the prosecuting attorney or committing magistrate charged with the performance of that duty.   1997

76-8-807. Posting of signs at war or defense facilities — Entering posted premises without permission.

(1) Any individual, partnership, association, corporation, municipal corporation, or state or any political subdivision thereof engaged in, or preparing to engage in, the manufacture, transportation or storage of any product to be used in the preparation of the United States or of any of the states for defense or for war or in the prosecution of war by the United States, or the manufacture, transportation, distribution or storage of gas, oil, coal, electricity or water, or any natural or artificial persons operating any public utility, whose property, except where it fronts on water or where there are entrances for railway cars, vehicles, persons, or things, is surrounded by a fence or wall, or a fence or wall and buildings, may post around his or its property at each gate, entrance, dock, or railway entrance and every one hundred feet of water front a sign reading "No Entry Without Permission." The sign shall also designate a point of entrance or place where application may be made for permission to enter, and

permission shall not be denied to any loyal citizen who has a valid right to enter.

(2) Any person willfully entering property enumerated in Subsection (1), without permission of the owner, shall be guilty of a class C misdemeanor.   1973

76-8-808. Detention and arrest without warrant of unauthorized persons on posted premises.

Any peace officer or any person employed as watchman, guard, or in a supervisory capacity on premises posted as provided in Section 76-8-807 may stop any person found on any premises to which entry without permission is forbidden by Section 76-8-807 and may detain him for the purpose of demanding, and may demand, of him, his name, address, and business in such place. If the peace officer or employee has reason to believe that the person has no right to be in the place, he shall release the person or he may arrest him without a warrant on the charge of violating the provisions of Section 76-8-807; and the employee shall release him or turn him over to the peace officer, or may arrest him without a warrant on the charge of violating the provisions of Section 76-8-807.   1973

76-8-809. Closing or restricting use of highways abutting defense or war facilities — Posting of notices.

Any individual, partnership, association, corporation, municipal corporation or state or any political subdivision thereof engaged in or preparing to engage in the manufacture, transportation or storage of any product to be used in the preparation of the United States or any of the states for defense or for war or in the prosecution of war by the United States, or in the manufacture, transportation, distribution or storage of gas, oil, coal, electricity or water, or any of said natural or artificial persons operating any public utility who has property so used which he or it believes will be endangered if public use and travel is not restricted or prohibited on one or more highways or parts thereof upon which the property abuts, may petition the highway commissioners of any city, town, or county to close one or more of the highways or parts thereof to public use and travel or to restrict by order the use and travel upon one or more of the highways or parts thereof.

Upon receipt of the petition, the highway commissioners shall set a day for hearing and give notice thereof by publication in a newspaper having general circulation in the city, town, or county in which the property is located, the publication shall be made at least seven days prior to the date set for hearing. If, after hearing, the highway commissioners determine that the public safety and the safety of the property of the petitioner so require, they shall by suitable order close to public use and travel or reasonably restrict the use of and travel upon one or more of the highways or parts thereof; provided the highway commissioners may issue written permits to travel over the highway so closed or restricted to responsible and reputable persons for a term, under conditions and in a form as the commissioners may prescribe. Appropriate notices in letters at least three inches high shall be posted conspicuously at each end of any highway so closed or restricted by an order. The highway commissioners may at any time revoke or modify any order so made.   1973

76-8-810. Violation of order relating to use of highways — Classification of offense.

Whoever violates any order made under the immediate preceding section shall be guilty of a class C misdemeanor.   1973

76-8-811. Bargaining rights of employees not impaired by sabotage prevention laws.

Nothing in this part shall be construed to impair, curtail, or destroy the rights of employees and their representatives to self organize, to form, join, or assist labor organizations, to bargain collectively through representatives of their own choosing, and to engage in concerted activities, for the purpose of collective bargaining or other mutual aid or protection as provided by state or federal laws.   1995

PART 9

SYNDICALISM AND SABOTAGE

76-8-901. "Criminal syndicalism" and "sabotage" defined.

For the purpose of this part:

(1) "Criminal syndicalism" is the doctrine which advocates crime, violence, force, arson, destruction of property, sabotage, or other unlawful acts or methods, as a means of accomplishing or effecting industrial or political ends, or as a means of effecting industrial or political revolution.

(2) "Sabotage" means the unlawful and intentional damage or injury to, or destruction of, real or personal property, in any form whatsoever, of any employer or owner by his employees, or by any employer, or by any person at the instance of any employer, or at the instance, request, or instigation of employees, or any other person.

1973

76-8-902. Advocating criminal syndicalism or sabotage.

Any person who by word of mouth or writing advocates, suggests, or teaches the duty, necessity, propriety, or expediency of crime, criminal syndicalism or sabotage, or who advocates, suggests or teaches the duty, necessity, propriety, or expediency or doing any act of violence, the destruction of or damage to any property, the bodily injury to any person, or the commission of any crime or unlawful act as a means of accomplishing or effecting any industrial or political ends, change or revolution, or who prints, publishes, edits, or issues, or knowingly circulates, sells, or distributes, or publicly displays, any books, pamphlets, paper, handbill, poster, document, or written or printed matter in any form whatsoever, containing, advocating, advising, suggesting, or teaching crime, criminal syndicalism, sabotage, the doing of any act of violence, the destruction of or damage to any property, the injury to any person, or the commission of any crime or unlawful act, as a means of accomplishing, effecting, or bringing about any industrial or political ends or change, or as a means of accomplishing, effecting, or bringing about any industrial or political revolution, or who openly or at all attempts to justify by word of mouth or writing the commission or the attempt to commit sabotage, any act of violence, the destruction of or damage to any property, the injury of any person, or the commission of any crime or unlawful act, with the intent to exemplify, spread, or teach or suggest criminal syndicalism, or organizes, or helps to organize, or becomes a member of, or voluntarily assembles with, any society or assemblage of persons formed to teach or advocate, or which teaches, advocates, or suggests the doctrine of criminal syndicalism or sabotage, or the necessity, propriety, or expediency of doing any act of violence or the commission of any crime or unlawful act as a means of accomplishing or effecting any industrial or political ends, change or revolution, is guilty of a felony of the third degree.

1973

76-8-903. Assembly for advocating criminal syndicalism or sabotage.

The assembly or consorting of two or more persons for the purpose of advocating, teaching, or suggesting the doctrine of criminal syndicalism, or to advocate, teach, suggest or encourage sabotage, or the duty, necessity, propriety or expediency of doing any act of violence, the destruction of or damage to any property, the bodily injury to any person, or the commission of any crime or unlawful act as a means of accomplishing or effecting any industrial or political ends, change or revolution, is hereby declared unlawful, and every person voluntarily participating therein, or by his presence aiding and instigating the same is guilty of a felony of the third degree.

1973

76-8-904. Permitting use of property for assembly advocating criminal syndicalism or sabotage.

The owner, lessee, agent, superintendent, or person in charge or occupation of any place, building, room, or structure, who knowingly permits therein any assembly or consorting of persons prohibited by the provisions of Section 76-8-903, or who after notification that the place or premises, or any part thereof, is so used, permits such use to be continued, is guilty of a class B misdemeanor.

1973

PART 10

HABITUAL CRIMINALS [REPEALED]

76-8-1001, 76-8-1002. Repealed.

1995

PART 11

TAXATION

76-8-1101. Criminal offenses and penalties relating to revenue and taxation — Rulemaking authority — Statute of limitations.

(1) (a) As provided in Section 59-1-401, criminal offenses and penalties are as provided in Subsections (1)(b) through (e).

(b) (i) Any person who is required by Title 59, Revenue and Taxation, or any laws the State Tax Commission administers or regulates to register with or obtain a license or permit from the State Tax Commission, who operates without having registered or secured a license or permit, or who operates when the registration, license, or permit is expired or not current, is guilty of a class B misdemeanor.

(ii) Notwithstanding Section 76-3-301, for purposes of Subsection (1)(b)(i), the penalty may not:

(A) be less than $500; or

(B) exceed $1,000.

(c) (i) Any person who, with intent to evade any tax or requirement of Title 59, Revenue and Taxation, or any lawful requirement of the State Tax Commission, fails to make, render, sign, or verify any return or to supply any information within the time required by law, or who makes, renders, signs, or verifies any false or fraudulent return or statement, or who supplies any false or fraudulent information, is guilty of a third degree felony.

(ii) Notwithstanding Section 76-3-301, for purposes of Subsection (1)(c)(i), the penalty may not:

(A) be less than $1,000; or

(B) exceed $5,000.

(d) (i) Any person who intentionally or willfully attempts to evade or defeat any tax or the payment of a tax is, in addition to other penalties provided by law, guilty of a second degree felony.

(ii) Notwithstanding Section 76-3-301, for purposes of Subsection (1)(d)(i), the penalty may not:

(A) be less than $1,500; or

(B) exceed $25,000.

(e) (i) A person is guilty of a second degree felony if that person commits an act:

(A) described in Subsection (1)(e)(ii) with respect to one or more of the following documents:

(I) a return;

(II) an affidavit;

(III) a claim; or

(IV) a document similar to Subsections (1)(e)(i)(A)(I) through (III); and

(B) subject to Subsection (1)(e)(iii), with knowledge that the document described in Subsection (1)(e)(i)(A):

(I) is false or fraudulent as to any material matter; and

(II) could be used in connection with any material matter administered by the State Tax Commission.

(ii) The following acts apply to Subsection (1)(e)(i):

(A) preparing any portion of a document described in Subsection (1)(e)(i)(A);

(B) presenting any portion of a document described in Subsection (1)(e)(i)(A);

(C) procuring any portion of a document described in Subsection (1)(e)(i)(A);

(D) advising in the preparation or presentation of any portion of a document described in Subsection (1)(e)(i)(A);

(E) aiding in the preparation or presentation of any portion of a document described in Subsection (1)(e)(i)(A);

(F) assisting in the preparation or presentation of any portion of a document described in Subsection (1)(e)(i)(A); or

(G) counseling in the preparation or presentation of any portion of a document described in Subsection (1)(e)(i)(A).

(iii) This Subsection (1)(e) applies:

(A) regardless of whether the person for which the document described in Subsection (1)(e)(i)(A) is prepared or presented:

(I) knew of the falsity of the document described in Subsection (1)(e)(i)(A); or

(II) consented to the falsity of the document described in Subsection (1)(e)(i)(A); and

(B) in addition to any other penalty provided by law.

(iv) Notwithstanding Section 76-3-301, for purposes of this Subsection (1)(e), the penalty may not:

(A) be less than $1,500; or

(B) exceed $25,000.

(v) In accordance with Title 63, Chapter 46a, Utah Administrative Rulemaking Act, the State Tax Commission may make rules prescribing the documents that are similar to Subsections (1)(e)(i)(A)(I) through (III).

(2) The statute of limitations for prosecution for a violation of this section is the later of six years:

(a) from the date the tax should have been remitted; or

(b) after the day on which the person commits the criminal offense.   2004

PART 12

PUBLIC ASSISTANCE FRAUD

76-8-1201. Definitions.

As used in this part:

(1) "Client" means a person who receives or has received public assistance.

(2) "Overpayment" means the same as that term is defined in Section 35A-3-602.

(3) "Provider" means the same as that term is defined in Section 62A-11-103.

(4) "Public assistance" means the same as that term is defined in Section 35A-1-102.   2003

76-8-1202. Application of part.

(1) This part does not apply to offenses by providers under the state's Medicaid program that are actionable under Title 26, Chapter 20, False Claims Act.

(2) (a) Section 35A-1-503 applies to criminal actions taken under this part.

(b) The repayment of funds or other benefits obtained in violation of the provisions of this chapter shall not constitute a defense or grounds for dismissal of a criminal action.   1997

76-8-1203. Disclosure required — Penalty.

(1) Each person who applies for public assistance shall disclose to the state agency administering the public assistance each fact that may materially affect the determination of his eligibility to receive public assistance, including his current:

(a) marital status;

(b) household composition;

(c) employment;

(d) income;

(e) receipt of monetary and in-kind gifts; and

(f) other resources.

(2) Any person applying for public assistance who intentionally, knowingly, or recklessly fails to disclose any material fact required to be disclosed under Subsection (1) is guilty of public assistance fraud as provided in Section 76-8-1206.

(3) Any client who intentionally, knowingly, or recklessly fails to disclose to the state agency administering the public assistance any change in a material fact required to be disclosed under Subsection (1), within ten days after the date of the change, is guilty of public assistance fraud as provided in Section 76-8-1206.   2000

76-8-1204. Disclosure by provider required — Penalty.

(1) (a) Any provider who solicits, requests, or receives, actually or constructively, any payment or contribution through a payment, assessment, gift, devise, bequest, or other means, directly or indirectly, from a client or client's family shall notify the state agency administering the public assistance the client is receiving of the amount of payment or contribution in writing within ten days after receiving that payment or contribution.

(b) If the payment or contribution is to be made under an agreement, written or oral, the provider shall notify the state agency administering the public assistance the client is receiving of the payment or contribution within ten days after entering into the agreement.

(2) Any person who intentionally, knowingly, or recklessly fails to notify the state agency administering the public assistance the client is receiving as required by this section is guilty of public assistance fraud as provided in Section 76-8-1206.   2000

76-8-1205. Public assistance fraud defined.

Each of the following persons, who intentionally, knowingly, or recklessly commits any of the following acts, is guilty of public assistance fraud:

(1) any person who uses, transfers, acquires, traffics in, falsifies, or possesses any food stamp, food stamp identification card, certificate of eligibility for medical services, Medicaid identification card, fund transfer instrument, payment instrument, or public assistance warrant in a manner not allowed by law;

(2) any person who fraudulently misappropriates any funds exchanged for food stamps, any food stamp, food stamp identification card, certificate of eligibility for medical services, Medicaid identification card, or other public assistance with which he has been entrusted or that has come into his possession in connection with his duties in administering any state or federally funded public assistance program;

(3) any person who receives an unauthorized payment as a result of acts described in this section;

(4) any provider who receives payment or any client who receives benefits after failing to comply with any applicable requirement in Sections 76-8-1203 and 76-8-1204;

(5) any provider who files a claim for payment under any state or federally funded public assistance program for goods or services not provided to or for a client of that program;

(6) any provider who files or falsifies a claim, report, or document required by state or federal law, rule, or provider agreement for goods or services not authorized under the state or federally funded public assistance program for which the goods or services were provided;

(7) any provider who fails to credit the state for payments received from other sources;

(8) any provider who bills a client or a client's family for goods or services not provided, or bills in an amount greater than allowed by law or rule;

(9) any client who, while receiving public assistance, acquires income or resources in excess of the amount he previously reported to the state agency administering the public assistance, and fails to notify the state agency to which the client previously reported within ten days after acquiring the excess income or resources;

(10) any person who fails to act as required under Section 76-8-1203 or 76-8-1204 with intent to obtain or help another obtain an "overpayment" as defined in Section 35A-3-602; and

(11) any person who obtains an overpayment by violation of Section 76-8-1203 or 76-8-1204.
                                                2003

76-8-1206. Penalties for public assistance fraud.

(1) The severity of the offense of public assistance fraud is classified in accordance with the value of

payments, assistance, or other benefits received, misappropriated, claimed, or applied for as follows:

(a) second degree felony if the value is or exceeds $5,000;

(b) third degree felony if the value is or exceeds $1,000 but is less than $5,000;

(c) class A misdemeanor if the value is or exceeds $300 but is less than $1,000; and

(d) class B misdemeanor if the value is less than $300.

(2) For purposes of Subsection (1), the value of an offense is calculated by aggregating the values of each instance of public assistance fraud committed by the defendant as part of the same facts and circumstances or a related series of facts and circumstances.

(3) Incidents of trafficking in food stamps that occur within a six-month period, committed by an individual or coconspirators, are deemed to be a related series of facts and circumstances regardless of whether the transactions are conducted with a variety of unrelated parties.   1995

76-8-1207. Legal actions — Evidence — Value of benefits — Repayment no defense to criminal action.

In any criminal action pursuant to this part:

(1) a paid state warrant made to the order of a party or a payment made through an electronic benefit card issued to a party constitutes prima facie evidence that the party received financial assistance from the state;

(2) all of the records in the custody of the department relating to the application for, verification of, issuance of, receipt of, and use of public assistance constitute records of regularly conducted activity within the meaning of the exceptions to the hearsay rule of evidence;

(3) the value of the benefits received shall be based on the ordinary or usual charge for similar benefits in the private sector; and

(4) the repayment of funds or other benefits obtained in violation of the provisions of this part constitutes no defense to, or ground for dismissal of, that action.   2000

PART 13

UNEMPLOYMENT INSURANCE FRAUD

76-8-1301. False statements regarding unemployment compensation — Penalties.

(1) (a) A person who makes a false statement or representation knowing it to be false or knowingly fails to disclose a material fact, to obtain or increase a benefit or other payment under Title 35A, Chapter 4, Employment Security Act, or under the Unemployment Compensation Law of any state or of the federal government for any person is guilty of unemployment insurance fraud.

(b) A violation of Subsection (1)(a) is:

(i) a class B misdemeanor when the value of the money obtained or sought to be obtained is less than $300;

(ii) a class A misdemeanor when the value of the money obtained or sought to be obtained is or exceeds $300 but is less than $1,000;

(iii) a third degree felony when the value of the money obtained or sought to be obtained is or exceeds $1,000 but is less than $5,000; or

(iv) a second degree felony when the value of the money obtained or sought to be obtained is or exceeds $5,000.

(c) The determination of the degree of an offense under Subsection (1)(b) shall be measured by the total value of all money obtained or sought to be obtained by the unlawful conduct.

(2) (a) An officer or agent of an employing unit as defined in Section 35A-4-202 or any other person who makes a false statement or representation knowing it to be false, or who knowingly fails to disclose a material fact, to prevent or reduce the payment of unemployment compensation benefits to an individual entitled to those benefits, or to avoid becoming or remaining a subject employer or to avoid or reduce any contribution or other payment required from an employing unit under Title 35A, Chapter 4, Employment Security Act, or under the Unemployment Compensation Law of any state or of the federal government, or who willfully fails or refuses to make a contribution or other payment or to furnish any report required in Title 35A, Chapter 4, Employment Security Act, or to produce or permit the inspection or copying of records as required under that chapter is guilty of unemployment insurance fraud.

(b) A violation of Subsection (2)(a) is:

(i) a class B misdemeanor when the value of the money obtained or sought to be obtained is less than $300;

(ii) a class A misdemeanor when the value of the money obtained or sought to be obtained is or exceeds $300 but is less than $1,000;

(iii) a third degree felony when the value of the money obtained or sought to be obtained is or exceeds $1,000 but is less than $5,000; or

(iv) a second degree felony when the value of the money obtained or sought to be obtained is or exceeds $5,000.

(3) (a) A person who willfully violates any provision of Title 35A, Chapter 4, Employment Security Act, or any order or rule made under that chapter, the violation of which is made unlawful or the observance of which is required under the terms of that chapter, and for which a penalty is neither prescribed in that chapter nor provided by any other applicable statute is guilty of a class A misdemeanor.

(b) Each day a violation of Subsection (3)(a) continues shall be a separate offense.

(4) A person is guilty of a class A misdemeanor if:

(a) as an employee of the Department of Workforce Services, in willful violation of Section 35A-4-312, the employee makes a disclosure of information obtained from an employing unit or individual in the administration of Title 35A, Chapter 4, Employment Security Act; or

(b) the person has obtained a list of applicants for work or of claimants or recipients of benefits under Title 35A, Chapter 4, Employment Security Act, and uses or permits the use of the list for any political purpose.   2003

PART 14

DISRUPTION OF SCHOOL ACTIVITIES

76-8-1401. Definitions.

As used in this part:

(1) "Chief administrator" means the principal of a school or the chief administrator of a school

that does not have a principal, and includes the administrator's designee or representative.

    (2) "School" means an elementary school or a secondary school that:

        (a) is a public or private school; and

        (b) provides instruction for one or more of the grades kindergarten through 12.   2004

76-8-1402. Disruption of activities in or near school building — Failure to leave — Reentry — Penalties.

    (1) In the absence of a local ordinance or other controlling law governing the conduct described in this Subsection (1), a person is guilty of an offense under Subsection (2) who, while on a street, sidewalk, or public way adjacent to any school building or ground:

        (a) by his or her presence or acts, materially disrupts the peaceful conduct of school activities; and

        (b) remains upon the place under Subsection (1)(a) after being asked to leave by the chief administrator of that school.

    (2) (a) A violation of Subsection (1) is subject to the penalties under Subsection (2)(b) unless the violation constitutes another offense subject to a greater penalty.

        (b) (i) The first and second violation of Subsection (1) are class B misdemeanors.

            (ii) A third and any subsequent violations of Subsection (1) are class A misdemeanors.   2004

CHAPTER 9

OFFENSES AGAINST PUBLIC ORDER AND DECENCY

Part 1

Breaches of the Peace and Related Offenses

Part 2

Telephone Abuse

Part 3

Cruelty to Animals

Part 4

Offenses Against Privacy

Part 5

Libel and Slander

Part 6

Offenses Against the Flag

Part 7

Miscellaneous Provisions

PART 1

BREACHES OF THE PEACE AND RELATED OFFENSES

76-9-101. Riot — Penalties.

(1) A person is guilty of riot if:

(a) simultaneously with two or more other persons he engages in tumultuous or violent conduct and thereby knowingly or recklessly creates a substantial risk of causing public alarm; or

(b) he assembles with two or more other persons with the purpose of engaging, soon thereafter, in tumultuous or violent conduct, knowing, that two or more other persons in the assembly have the same purpose; or

(c) he assembles with two or more other persons with the purpose of committing an offense against a person or property of another who he supposes to be guilty of a violation of law, believing that two or more other persons in the assembly have the same purpose.

(2) Any person who refuses to comply with a lawful order to withdraw given to him immediately prior to, during, or immediately following a violation of Subsection (1) is guilty of riot. It is no defense to a prosecution under this Subsection (2) that withdrawal must take place over private property; provided, however, that no persons so withdrawing shall incur criminal or civil liability by virtue of acts reasonably necessary to accomplish the withdrawal.

(3) Riot is a felony of the third degree if, in the course of and as a result of the conduct, any person suffers bodily injury, or substantial property damage, arson occurs or the defendant was armed with a dangerous weapon, as defined in Section 76-1-601; otherwise it is a class B misdemeanor. 1997

76-9-102. Disorderly conduct.

(1) A person is guilty of disorderly conduct if:

(a) he refuses to comply with the lawful order of the police to move from a public place, or knowingly creates a hazardous or physically offensive condition, by any act which serves no legitimate purpose; or

(b) intending to cause public inconvenience, annoyance, or alarm, or recklessly creating a risk thereof, he:

(i) engages in fighting or in violent, tumultuous, or threatening behavior;

(ii) makes unreasonable noises in a public place;

(iii) makes unreasonable noises in a private place which can be heard in a public place; or

(iv) obstructs vehicular or pedestrian traffic.

(2) "Public place," for the purpose of this section, means any place to which the public or a substantial group of the public has access and includes but is not limited to streets, highways, and the common areas of schools, hospitals, apartment houses, office buildings, transport facilities, and shops.

(3) Disorderly conduct is a class C misdemeanor if the offense continues after a request by a person to desist. Otherwise it is an infraction. 1999

76-9-103. Disrupting a meeting or procession.

(1) A person is guilty of disrupting a meeting or procession if, intending to prevent or disrupt a lawful meeting, procession, or gathering, he obstructs or interferes with the meeting, procession, or gathering by physical action, verbal utterance, or any other means.

(2) Disrupting a meeting or procession is a class B misdemeanor. 1973

76-9-104. Failure to disperse.

(1) A person is guilty of failure to disperse when he remains at the scene of a riot, disorderly conduct, or an unlawful assembly after having been ordered to disperse by a peace officer.

(2) This section shall not apply to a person who attempted to but was unable to leave the scene of the riot or unlawful assembly.

(3) Failure to disperse is a class C misdemeanor. 1973

76-9-105. Making a false alarm — Penalties.

(1) A person is guilty of making a false alarm if he initiates or circulates a report or warning of any fire, impending bombing, or other crime or catastrophe, knowing that the report or warning is false or baseless and is likely to cause evacuation of any building, place of assembly, or facility of public transport, to cause public inconvenience or alarm or action of any sort by any official or volunteer agency organized to deal with emergencies.

(2) (a) Making a false alarm relating to a weapon of mass destruction as defined in Section 76-10-401 is a second degree felony.

(b) Making a false alarm other than under Subsection (2)(a) is a class B misdemeanor.

(3) In addition to any other penalty authorized by law, a court shall order any person convicted of a felony violation of this section to reimburse any federal, state, or local unit of government, or any private business, organization, individual, or entity for all expenses and losses incurred in responding to the violation, unless the court states on the record the reasons why the reimbursement would be inappropriate. 2002

76-9-106. Disrupting the operation of a school.

(1) A person is guilty of disrupting the operation of a school if the person, after being asked to leave by a school official, remains on school property for the purpose of encouraging or creating an unreasonable and substantial disruption or risk of disruption of a class, activity, program, or other function of a public or private school.

(2) For purposes of this section, "school property" includes property being used by a public or private school for a school function.

(3) Disrupting the operation of a school is a class B misdemeanor. 1992

76-9-107. Unauthorized entry of school bus — Posting of warning on school buses.

(1) As used in this section:

(a) "Driver" means the driver of the school bus.

(b) "School bus" means every publicly or privately owned motor vehicle designed for transporting ten or more passengers and operated for the transportation of children to or from school or school activities.

(2) A person is guilty of a class B misdemeanor if the person:

(a) enters a school bus with the intent to commit a criminal offense;

(b) enters a school bus and disrupts or interferes with the driver; or

(c) enters a school bus and refuses to leave the bus after being ordered to leave by the driver and the person:

(i) is not a peace officer acting within the scope of his or her authority as a peace officer;

(ii) is not authorized by the school district to board the bus as a student or as an individual employed by the school district or volunteering as a participant in a school activity;

(iii) causes or attempts to cause a disruption or an annoyance to any passenger on the bus; or

(iv) is reckless as to whether the person's presence or behavior will cause fear on the part of any passenger on the bus.

(3) Each school district shall ensure that clearly legible signs be placed on each school bus, next to each entrance to the bus, warning that unauthorized entry of a school bus is a violation of state law.   2003

PART 2

TELEPHONE ABUSE

76-9-201. Electronic communication harassment — Definitions — Penalties.

(1) As used in this section:

(a) "Electronic communication" means any communication by electronic, electro-mechanical, or electro-optical communication device for the transmission and reception of audio, image, or text but does not include broadcast transmissions or similar communications that are not targeted at any specific individual.

(b) "Electronic communication device" includes telephone, facsimile, electronic mail, or pager.

(2) A person is guilty of electronic communication harassment and subject to prosecution in the jurisdiction where the communication originated or was received if with intent to annoy, alarm, intimidate, offend, abuse, threaten, harass, frighten, or disrupt the electronic communications of another, the person:

(a) (i) makes repeated contact by means of electronic communications, whether or not a conversation ensues; or

(ii) after the recipient has requested or informed the person not to contact the recipient, and the person repeatedly or continuously:

(A) contacts the electronic communication device of the recipient; or

(B) causes an electronic communication device of the recipient to ring or to receive other notification of attempted contact by means of electronic communication;

(b) makes contact by means of electronic communication and insults, taunts, or challenges the recipient of the communication or any person at the receiving location in a manner likely to provoke a violent or disorderly response;

(c) makes contact by means of electronic communication and threatens to inflict injury, physical harm, or damage to any person or the property of any person; or

(d) causes disruption, jamming, or overload of an electronic communication system through excessive message traffic or other means utilizing an electronic communication device.

(3) Electronic communication harassment is a class B misdemeanor.

(4) This section does not create any civil cause of action based on electronic communications made for legitimate business purposes.   2005

76-9-202. Emergency reporting — Interference — False report.

(1) As used in this section:

(a) "Emergency" means a situation in which property or human life is in jeopardy and the prompt summoning of aid is essential to the preservation of human life or property.

(b) "Party line" means a subscriber's line or telephone circuit consisting of two or more main telephone stations connected therewith, each station with a distinctive ring or telephone number.

(2) A person is guilty of emergency reporting abuse if he:

(a) intentionally refuses to yield or surrender the use of a party line or a public pay telephone to another person upon being informed that the telephone is needed to report a fire or summon police, medical, or other aid in case of emergency, unless the telephone is likewise being used for an emergency call;

(b) asks for or requests the use of a party line or a public pay telephone on the pretext that an emergency exists, knowing that no emergency exists; or

(c) reports an emergency or causes an emergency to be reported to any public, private, or volunteer entity whose purpose is to respond to fire, police, or medical emergencies, when the actor knows the reported emergency does not exist.

(3) (a) A violation of Subsection (2)(a) or (b) is a class C misdemeanor.

(b) A violation of Subsection (2)(c) is a class B misdemeanor, except as provided under Subsection (3)(c).

(c) A violation of Subsection (2)(c) is a second degree felony if the report is regarding a weapon of mass destruction, as defined in Section 76-10-401.

(4) In addition to any other penalty authorized by law, a court shall order any person convicted of a violation of this section to reimburse any federal, state, or local unit of government, or any private business, organization, individual, or entity for all expenses and losses incurred in responding to the violation, unless the court states on the record the reasons why the reimbursement would be inappropriate.   2002

PART 3

CRUELTY TO ANIMALS

76-9-301. Cruelty to animals.

(1) A person is guilty of cruelty to animals if the person intentionally, knowingly, recklessly, or with criminal negligence:

(a) fails to provide necessary food, care, or shelter for an animal in his custody;

(b) abandons an animal in the person's custody;

(c) transports or confines an animal in a cruel manner;

(d) injures an animal;

(e) causes any animal, not including a dog, to fight with another animal of like kind for amusement or gain; or

(f) causes any animal, including a dog, to fight with a different kind of animal or creature for amusement or gain.

(2) A violation of Subsection (1) is:

(a) a class B misdemeanor if committed intentionally or knowingly; and

(b) a class C misdemeanor if committed recklessly or with criminal negligence.

(3) A person is guilty of aggravated cruelty to an animal if the person:

(a) tortures an animal;

(b) administers poison or poisonous substances to an animal without having a legal privilege to do so;

(c) kills or causes to be killed an animal without having a legal privilege to do so.

(4) A violation of Subsection (3) is:

(a) a class A misdemeanor if committed intentionally or knowingly;

(b) a class B misdemeanor if committed recklessly; and

(c) a class C misdemeanor if committed with criminal negligence.

(5) It is a defense to prosecution under this section that the conduct of the actor towards the animal was:

(a) by a licensed veterinarian using accepted veterinary practice;

(b) directly related to bona fide experimentation for scientific research, provided that if the animal is to be destroyed, the manner employed will not be unnecessarily cruel unless directly necessary to the veterinary purpose or scientific research involved;

(c) permitted under Section 18-1-3;

(d) by a person who humanely destroys any animal found suffering past recovery for any useful purpose; or

(e) by a person who humanely destroys any apparently abandoned animal found on the person's property.

(6) For purposes of Subsection (5)(d), before destroying the suffering animal, the person who is not the owner of the animal shall obtain:

(a) the judgment of a veterinarian of the animal's nonrecoverable condition;

(b) the judgment of two other persons called by the person to view the unrecoverable condition of the animal in the person's presence;

(c) the consent from the owner of the animal to the destruction of the animal; or

(d) a reasonable conclusion that the animal's suffering is beyond recovery, through the person's own observation, if the person is in a location or circumstance where the person is unable to contact another person.

(7) This section does not affect or prohibit the training, instruction, and grooming of animals, so long as the methods used are in accordance with accepted husbandry practices.

(8) (a) This section does not affect or prohibit the use of an electronic locating or training collar by the owner of an animal for the purpose of lawful animal training, lawful hunting practices, or protecting against loss of that animal.

(b) County and municipal governments may not prohibit the use of an electronic locating or training collar.

(9) Upon conviction under this section, the court may in its discretion, in addition to other penalties:

(a) order the defendant to be evaluated to determine the need for psychiatric or psychological counseling, to receive counseling as the court determines to be appropriate, and to pay the costs of the evaluation and counseling;

(b) require the defendant to forfeit any rights the defendant has to the animal subjected to a violation of this section and to repay the reasonable costs incurred by any person or agency in caring for each animal subjected to violation of this section;

(c) order the defendant to no longer possess or retain custody of any animal, as specified by the court, during the period of the defendant's probation or parole or other period as designated by the court; and

(d) order the animal to be placed for the purpose of adoption or care in the custody of a county and municipal animal control agency, an animal welfare agency registered with the state, sold at public auction, or humanely destroyed.

(10) This section does not prohibit the use of animals in lawful training.

(11) As used in this section:

(a) "Abandons" means to intentionally deposit, leave, or drop off any live animal:

(i) without providing for the care of that animal; or

(ii) in a situation where conditions present an immediate, direct, and serious threat to the life, safety, or health of the animal.

(b) (i) "Animal" means a live, nonhuman vertebrate creature.

(ii) "Animal" does not include animals kept or owned for agricultural purposes and cared for in accordance with accepted husbandry practices, animals used for rodeo purposes, and does not include protected and unprotected wildlife as defined in Section 23-13-2.

(c) "Custody" means ownership, possession, or control over an animal.

(d) "Legal privilege" means an act authorized by state law, including Division of Wildlife Resources statutes and rules, and conducted in conformance with local ordinances.

(e) "Necessary food, care, and shelter" means appropriate and essential food and other needs of the animal, including veterinary care, and adequate protection against extreme weather conditions.   1996 (2nd S.S.)

76-9-301.1. Dog fighting — Training dogs for fighting — Dog fighting exhibitions.

(1) It is unlawful for any person to:

(a) own, possess, keep, or train a dog with the intent to engage it in an exhibition of fighting with another dog;

(b) cause a dog to fight with another dog or cause a dog to injure another dog for amusement or gain;

(c) tie, attach, or fasten any live animal to a machine or device propelled by any power, for the purpose of causing the animal to be pursued by a dog; or

(d) permit or allow any act which violates Subsection (a), (b), or (c) on any premises under his charge; or to control, aid, or abet any such act.

(2) Possession of any breaking stick, treadmill, wheel, hot walker, cat mill, cat walker, jenni, or other paraphernalia together with evidence that the paraphernalia is being used or is intended for use in the unlawful training of a dog to fight with another dog, together with the possession of any such dog, is prima facie evidence of violation of Subsections (1)(b) and (1)(c).

(3) A person who violates Subsection (1) is guilty of a third degree felony, and any fine imposed may not exceed $25,000.

(4) It is unlawful for a person to knowingly and intentionally be present as a spectator at any place, building, or tenement where preparations are being

made for an exhibition of dog fighting, or to knowingly and intentionally be present at a dog fighting exhibition or any other occurrence of fighting or injury described in this section. A person who violates this subsection is guilty of a class B misdemeanor.

(5) Nothing in this section prohibits any of the following:

(a) the use of dogs for management of livestock by the owner, his employees or agents, or any other person in the lawful custody of livestock;

(b) the use of dogs for hunting; or

(c) the training of dogs or the possession or use of equipment in the training of dogs for any purpose not prohibited by law.   1987

76-9-301.5. Spectator at organized animal fighting exhibitions.

It is unlawful for a person to knowingly be present as a spectator at any place, building, or tenement where preparations are being made for an exhibition of the fighting of animals, as prohibited by Subsection 76-9-301(1)(e) and (f), or to be present at such exhibition, regardless of whether any entrance fee has been charged. A person who violates this subsection is guilty of a class B misdemeanor.   1996 (2nd S.S.)

76-9-301.6. Dog fighting exhibition — Authority to arrest and take possession of dogs and property.

(1) A peace officer as defined in Title 53, Chapter 13, Peace Officer Classifications, may enter any place, building, or tenement where an exhibition of dog fighting is occurring, or where preparations are being made for such an exhibition and, without a warrant, arrest all persons present.

(2) (a) Notwithstanding the provisions of Section 76-9-305, any authorized officer who makes an arrest under Subsection (1) may lawfully take possession of all dogs, paraphernalia, implements, or other property or things used or employed, or to be employed, in an exhibition of dog fighting prohibited by Subsection 76-9-301(1)(f) or Section 76-9-301.1.

(b) The officer, at the time of the taking of property pursuant to Subsection (2)(a), shall state his name and provide other identifying information to the person in charge of the dogs or property taken.

(3) (a) After taking possession of dogs, paraphernalia, implements, or other property or things under Subsection (2), the officer shall file an affidavit with the judge or magistrate before whom a complaint has been made against any person arrested under this section.

(b) The affidavit shall include:

(i) the name of the person charged in the complaint;

(ii) a description of all property taken;

(iii) the time and place of the taking of the property;

(iv) the name of the person from whom the property was taken;

(v) the name of the person who claims to own the property, if known; and

(vi) a statement that the officer has reason to believe and believes that the property taken was used or employed, or was to be used or employed, in violation of Section 76-9-301 or 76-9-301.1, and the grounds for the belief.

(4) (a) The officer shall deliver the confiscated property to the judge or magistrate who shall, by order, place the property in the custody of the officer or any other person designated in the order, and that person shall keep the property until conviction or final discharge of the person against whom the complaint was made.

(b) The person designated in Subsection (4)(a) shall assume immediate custody of the property, and retain the property until further order of the court.

(c) Upon conviction of the person charged, all confiscated property shall be forfeited and destroyed or otherwise disposed of, as the court may order.

(d) If the person charged is acquitted or discharged without conviction, the court shall, on demand, order the property to be returned to its owner.   1998

76-9-301.7. Cruelty to animals — Enhanced penalties.

(1) "Conviction" means a conviction by plea or by verdict.

(2) A person who commits any violation of Section 76-9-301, Section 76-9-301.5, or Subsection 76-9-301.1(4) within the state and on at least one previous occasion has been convicted of violating Section 76-9-301, Section 76-9-301.5, or Subsection 76-9-301.1(4) shall be subject to an enhanced penalty as provided in Subsection (3).

(3) The enhanced degree of offense for offenses committed under this section are:

(a) if the offense is a class C misdemeanor, it is a class B misdemeanor; and

(b) if the offense is a class B misdemeanor, it is a class A misdemeanor.

(4) (a) The prosecuting attorney, or grand jury if an indictment is returned, shall provide written notice upon the information or indictment that the defendant is subject to an enhanced degree of offense or penalty under Subsection (3). The notice shall be served upon the defendant or his attorney not later than ten days prior to trial.

(b) If the notice is not included initially, the court may subsequently allow the prosecutor to amend the charging document to include the notice if the court finds:

(i) that the amended charging documents, including any statement of probable cause, provide notice that the defendant is subject to an enhanced penalty provided under this section; and

(ii) that the defendant has not otherwise been substantially prejudiced by the amendment.   1996 (2nd S.S.)

76-9-301.8. Bestiality — Definitions — Penalty.

(1) A person commits the crime of bestiality if the actor engages in any sexual activity with an animal with the intent of sexual gratification of the actor.

(2) For purposes of this section only:

(a) "Animal" means any live, nonhuman vertebrate creature, including fowl.

(b) "Sexual activity" means physical sexual contact:

(i) between the actor and the animal involving the genitals of the actor and the genitals of the animal;

(ii) the genitals of the actor or the animal and the mouth or anus of the actor or the animal; or

(iii) through the actor's use of an object in contact with the genitals or anus of the animal.

(3) A crime of bestiality is a class B misdemeanor.

1999

76-9-302, 76-9-303. Repealed. 1977, 1998

76-9-304. Allowing vicious animal to go at large.

Any owner of a vicious animal, knowing its propensities, who willfully allows it to go at large or who keeps it without ordinary care, and any animal, while at large, or while not kept with ordinary care, causes injury to another animal or to any human being who has taken reasonable precaution which the circumstances permitted, is guilty of a class B misdemeanor unless the animal causes the death of a human being, whereupon the owner is guilty of a felony of the third degree. 1977

76-9-305. Officer's authority to take possession of animals — Lien for care.

(1) Any law enforcement officer may take possession of any animals being treated cruelly and, after reasonable efforts to notify the owner, may provide shelter and care for them or upon permission from the owner may destroy them.

(2) Officers caring for animals pursuant to this section have a lien for the reasonable value of the care and/or destruction. Any court upon proof that the owner has been notified of the lien and amount due, at least five days prior, shall order the animal sold at public auction or destroyed.

(3) Any law enforcement officer may humanely destroy any animal found suffering past recovery for any useful purpose. Before destroying the animal the officer shall obtain the judgment to the effect of a veterinarian, or of two reputable citizens called by him to view the animal in his presence, or shall obtain consent to the destruction from the owner of the animal. 1977

76-9-306. Police service animals — Causing injury or interfering with handler — Penalties.

(1) As used in this section:
(a) "Handler" means a law enforcement officer who is specially trained, and uses a police service animal during the course of the performance of his law enforcement duties.
(b) "Police service animal" means any dog or horse used by a law enforcement agency, which is specially trained for law enforcement work, or any animal contracted to assist a law enforcement agency in the performance of law enforcement duties.

(2) It is a third degree felony for a person to intentionally:
(a) cause bodily injury or death to a police service animal;
(b) engage in conduct likely to cause bodily injury or death to a police service animal;
(c) lay out, place, or administer any poison, trap, substance, or object which is likely to produce bodily injury or death to a police service animal; or
(d) offer or agree with one or more persons to engage in or cause the performance of an act which constitutes a violation of this section.

(3) It is a class A misdemeanor for a person to intentionally or knowingly:
(a) taunt, torment, strike, or otherwise assault a police service animal;
(b) throw any object or substance at, or in the path of, a police service animal;

(c) interfere with or obstruct a police service animal, or attempt to, or interfere with the handler of the animal in a manner that inhibits, restricts, or deprives the handler of his control of the animal;
(d) release a police service animal from its area of control, such as a vehicle, kennel, or pen, or trespass in that area; or
(e) place any food, object, or substance into a police service animal's area of control without the permission of the handler.

(4) A police service animal is exempt from quarantine or other animal control ordinances if it bites any person while under proper police supervision or routine veterinary care. The law enforcement agency and the animal's handler shall make the animal available for examination at any reasonable time and shall notify the local health officer if the animal exhibits any abnormal behavior.

(5) In addition to any other penalty, a person convicted of a violation of this section is liable for restitution to the owning or employing law enforcement agency or individual owner of the police service animal for the replacement, training, and veterinary costs incurred as a result of the violation of this section. 2000

76-9-307. Injury to service animals — Penalties.

(1) As used in this section:
(a) "Assistance animal" means an animal that is trained or is in training to:
(i) lead or guide a person who is blind or has a visual disability;
(ii) assist a person who has a physical disability, including hearing impairment or deafness; or
(iii) assist a person who has a mental disability.
(b) "Person with a disability" means a person who is blind, visually impaired, deaf, hearing impaired, or otherwise has a physical or mental disability.

(2) It is a class A misdemeanor for a person to knowingly, intentionally, or recklessly cause substantial bodily injury or death to an assistance animal.

(3) It is a class A misdemeanor for a person who owns, keeps, harbors, or exercises control over an animal to knowingly, intentionally, or recklessly fail to exercise sufficient control over the animal to prevent it from causing:
(a) any substantial bodily injury or the death of an assistance animal; or
(b) the assistance animal's subsequent inability to function as an assistance animal as a result of the animal's attacking, chasing, or harassing the assistance animal.

(4) It is a class B misdemeanor for a person to chase or harass an assistance animal.

(5) It is a class B misdemeanor for a person who owns, keeps, harbors, or exercises control over an animal to knowingly, intentionally, or recklessly fail to exercise sufficient control over the animal to prevent it from chasing or harassing an assistance animal while it is carrying out its functions as an assistance animal, to the extent that the animal temporarily interferes with the assistance animal's ability to carry out its functions.

(6) (a) An assistance animal is exempt from quarantine or other animal control ordinances if it bites any person while it is subject to an offense under Subsection (2), (3), (4), or (5).

(b) The owner of the assistance animal or the person with a disability whom the assistance animal serves shall make the animal available for examination at any reasonable time and shall notify the local health officer if the animal exhibits any abnormal behavior.

(7) In addition to any other penalty, a person convicted of any violation of this section is liable for restitution to the owner of the assistance animal or the person with disabilities whom the assistance animal serves for the replacement, training, and veterinary costs incurred as a result of the violation of this section.

(8) If the act committed under this section amounts to an offense subject to a greater penalty under another provision of Title 76, Utah Criminal Code, than is provided under this section, this section does not prohibit prosecution and sentencing for the more serious offense.   2000

PART 4

OFFENSES AGAINST PRIVACY

76-9-401. Definitions.

For purposes of this part:

(1) "Private place" means a place where one may reasonably expect to be safe from casual or hostile intrusion or surveillance.

(2) "Eavesdrop" means to overhear, record, amplify, or transmit any part of a wire or oral communication of others without the consent of at least one party thereto by means of any electronic, mechanical, or other device.

(3) "Public" includes any professional or social group of which the victim of a defamation is a member.   1973

76-9-402. Privacy violation.

(1) A person is guilty of privacy violation if, except as authorized by law, he:

(a) Trespasses on property with intent to subject anyone to eavesdropping or other surveillance in a private place; or

(b) Installs in any private place, without the consent of the person or persons entitled to privacy there, any device for observing, photographing, recording, amplifying, or broadcasting sounds or events in the place or uses any such unauthorized installation; or

(c) Installs or uses outside of a private place any device for hearing, recording, amplifying, or broadcasting sounds originating in the place which would not ordinarily be audible or comprehensible outside, without the consent of the person or persons entitled to privacy there.

(2) Privacy violation is a class B misdemeanor.   1973

76-9-403. Communication abuse.

(1) A person commits communication abuse if, except as authorized by law, he:

(a) Intercepts, without the consent of the sender or receiver, a message by telephone, telegraph, letter, or other means of communicating privately; this paragraph does not extend to:

(i) Overhearing of messages through a regularly installed instrument on a telephone party line or on an extension; or

(ii) Interception by the telephone company or subscriber incident to enforcement of regulations limiting use of the facilities or to other normal operation and use; or

(b) Divulges without consent of the sender or receiver the existence or contents of any such message if the actor knows that the message was illegally intercepted or if he learned of the message in the course of employment with an agency engaged in transmitting it.

(2) Communication abuse is a class B misdemeanor.   1973

76-9-404. Criminal defamation.

(1) A person is guilty of criminal defamation if he knowingly communicates to any person orally or in writing any information which he knows to be false and knows will tend to expose any other living person to public hatred, contempt, or ridicule.

(2) Criminal defamation is a class B misdemeanor.   1973

76-9-405. Repealed.   1981

76-9-406. Injunctive relief against privacy offenses — Damages.

Any person, or the heirs of any deceased person, who has been injured by a violation of this part may bring an action against the person who committed the violation. If in the action the court finds the defendant is violating or has violated any of the provisions of this part, it shall enjoin the defendant from a continuance thereof. It shall not be necessary that actual damages to the plaintiffs be alleged or proved, but if damages are alleged and proved, the plaintiff in the action shall be entitled to recover from the defendant the actual damages, if any, sustained in addition to injunctive relief. A finding that the defendant is in violation of this part shall entitle the plaintiff to reasonable attorney's fees. Exemplary damages may be awarded where the violation is found to be malicious.   1973

76-9-407. Crime of abuse of personal identity — Penalty — Defense — Permitting civil action.

(1) The definitions in Section 45-3-2 apply to this section.

(2) Any person is guilty of a class B misdemeanor who knowingly or intentionally causes the publication of an advertisement in which the personal identity of an individual is used in a manner which expresses or implies that the individual approves, endorses, has endorsed, or will endorse the specific subject matter of the advertisement without the consent for such use by the individual.

(3) It is an affirmative defense that the person causing the publication of the advertisement reasonably believed that the person whose personal identity was to be used had consented to its use.

(4) Upon conviction of an offense under this section, unless waived by the victim, the court shall order that, within 30 days of the conviction, the person convicted shall issue a public apology or retraction to whomever received the advertisement. The apology or retraction shall be of similar size and placement as the original advertisement.

(5) Nothing in this section prohibits a civil action under Title 45, Chapter 3, Abuse of Personal Identity.   1999

PART 5

LIBEL AND SLANDER

76-9-501. "Libel" defined.

For the purpose of this part: "Libel" means a malicious defamation, expressed either by printing or by signs or pictures or the like, tending to defame or darken the memory of one who is dead, or to impeach the honesty, integrity, virtue, or reputation, or publish the natural defects of one who is alive and thereby expose him to public hatred, contempt, or ridicule.

1973

76-9-502. Libel — Elements — Classification of offense.

(1) A person is guilty of libel if he intentionally and with a malicious intent to injure another publishes or procures to be published any libel.

(2) Libel is a class B misdemeanor. 1991

76-9-503. Presumption of malice — Reading or seeing by another not necessary — Liability of newspaper or serial publication personnel.

(1) An injurious publication is presumed to have been malicious if no justifiable motive for making it is shown.

(2) To sustain a charge of publishing a libel, it is not essential that the words or things complained of should have been read or seen by another. It is adequate that the accused knowingly parted with the immediate custody of the libel under circumstances which exposed it to be read or seen by any other person than himself.

(3) Each author, editor, and proprietor of any newspaper or serial publication is chargeable with the publication of any words contained in any part of a book or number or a newspaper or serial. 1973

76-9-504. Fair reporting privilege of newspaper or broadcasting station personnel as to public official proceedings — Privilege as to defamatory matter not subject to censorship.

No reporter, editor, or proprietor of any newspaper, and no owner, licensee, or operator of a visual or sound radio broadcasting station, or network of stations, nor the agents or employees of a newspaper or broadcasting station, is liable to any prosecution for a fair and true report or broadcast of any judicial, legislative, or other public official proceedings, or of any statement, speech, argument, or debate in course of the same, except upon proof of malice in making the report, which shall not be implied from the mere fact of publication. In no event shall any owner, licensee, or operator of a visual or sound radio broadcasting station or network of stations, or the agents or employees thereof, be liable for prosecution for any defamatory matter or statement published or uttered in such radio or television broadcast where the publication cannot be censored by reason of the provisions of federal statute or the regulations of the federal communications commission. 1973

76-9-505. Libelous matter not privileged.

Libelous remarks or comments connected with matter privileged by the next preceding section receive no privilege by reason of their being so connected. 1973

76-9-506. Privilege as to communications between interested persons.

A communication made to a person interested in the communication by one who is also interested, or who stands in a relation to the former as to afford a reasonable ground for supposing his motive innocent, is not presumed to be malicious, and is a privileged communication. 1973

76-9-507. Slander — Imputing unchastity to female.

(1) A person is guilty of slander if he orally, falsely and knowingly, imputes to any female, married or unmarried, a lack of chastity.

(2) Slander is a class B misdemeanor. 1991

76-9-508. Slander — Imputation need not be proven false — Truth as defense.

In any prosecution under Section 76-9-507, it is not necessary for the state to show that the imputation was false, but the defendant may in justification show the truth of the imputation and inquiry into the general reputation for chastity of the female alleged to have been slandered may be made. 1995

76-9-509. Conveying false or libelous material to newspaper or broadcasting stations.

Any person who willfully states, conveys, delivers, or transmits, by any means whatsoever, to the manager, editor, publisher, reporter, or agent of any radio station, television station, newspaper, magazine, periodical, or serial for publication therein, any false or libelous statement concerning any person, and thereby secures actual publication of the same, is guilty of a class B misdemeanor. 1973

PART 6

OFFENSES AGAINST THE FLAG

76-9-601. Abuse of a flag.

(1) A person is guilty of abuse of a flag if he:

   (a) Intentionally places any unauthorized inscription or other thing upon any flag of the United States or of any state of the United States; or

   (b) Knowingly exhibits any such flag, knowing the inscription or other thing to be unauthorized; or

   (c) For purposes of advertising a product or service for sale or for distribution, affixes a representation of the flag of the United States or of a state of the United States to the product or on any display whereon the product or service is advertised; or

   (d) Knowingly casts contempt upon the flag of the United States or of any state of the United States by publicly mutilating, defacing, defiling, burning, or trampling upon it.

(2) Abuse of a flag is a class B misdemeanor. 1973

PART 7

MISCELLANEOUS PROVISIONS

76-9-701. Intoxication — Release of arrested person or placement in detoxification center.

(1) A person is guilty of intoxication if he is under the influence of alcohol, a controlled substance, or any substance having the property of releasing toxic vapors, to a degree that the person may endanger himself or another, in a public place or in a private place where he unreasonably disturbs other persons.

(2) A peace officer or a magistrate may release from custody an individual arrested under this section if he believes imprisonment is unnecessary for the protection of the individual or another; or a peace officer may take the arrested person to a detoxification center or other special facility as an alternative to incarceration or release from custody.

(3) When a person who is at least 13 years old, but younger than 18 years old, is found by the court to have violated this section, the provisions regarding suspension of the driver's license under Section 78-3a-506 apply to the violation.

(4) When the court has issued an order suspending a person's driving privileges for a violation of this

section, the person's driver license shall be suspended under Section 53-3-219.

(5) An offense under this section is a class C misdemeanor.   1997

76-9-702.   Lewdness — Sexual battery — Public urination.

(1) A person is guilty of lewdness if the person under circumstances not amounting to rape, object rape, forcible sodomy, forcible sexual abuse, aggravated sexual assault, or an attempt to commit any of these offenses, performs any of the following acts in a public place or under circumstances which the person should know will likely cause affront or alarm to, on, or in the presence of another who is 14 years of age or older:

(a) an act of sexual intercourse or sodomy;

(b) exposes his or her genitals, the female breast below the top of the areola, the buttocks, the anus, or the pubic area;

(c) masturbates; or

(d) any other act of lewdness.

(2) Lewdness is a class B misdemeanor.

(3) A person is guilty of sexual battery if the person under circumstances not amounting to rape, rape of a child, object rape, object rape of a child, forcible sodomy, sodomy upon a child, forcible sexual abuse, sexual abuse of a child, aggravated sexual abuse of a child, aggravated sexual assault, or an attempt to commit any of these offenses intentionally touches, whether or not through clothing, the anus, buttocks, or any part of the genitals of another person, or the breast of a female, and the actor's conduct is under circumstances the actor knows or should know will likely cause affront or alarm to the person touched.

(4) Sexual battery is a class A misdemeanor.

(5) A person is guilty of public urination if the person urinates or defecates:

(a) in a public place, other than a public rest room; and

(b) under circumstances which the person should know will likely cause affront or alarm to another.

(6) Public urination is a class C misdemeanor.

(7) A woman's breast feeding, including breast feeding in any location where the woman otherwise may rightfully be, does not under any circumstance constitute a lewd or grossly lewd act, irrespective of whether or not the breast is covered during or incidental to feeding.   2003

76-9-702.5.   Lewdness involving a child.

(1) A person is guilty of lewdness involving a child if the person under circumstances not amounting to rape of a child, object rape of a child, sodomy upon a child, sexual abuse of a child, aggravated sexual abuse of a child, or an attempt to commit any of those offenses, intentionally or knowingly does any of the following to, or in the presence of a child who is under 14 years of age:

(a) performs an act of sexual intercourse or sodomy;

(b) exposes his or her genitals, the female breast below the top of the areola, the buttocks, the anus, or the pubic area:

(i) in a public place; or

(ii) in a private place:

(A) under circumstances the person should know will likely cause affront or alarm; or

(B) with the intent to arouse or gratify the sexual desire of the actor or the child;

(c) masturbates;

(d) under circumstances not amounting to sexual exploitation of a child under Section 76-5a-3, causes a child under the age of 14 years to expose his or her genitals, anus, or breast, if female, to the actor, with the intent to arouse or gratify the sexual desire of the actor or the child; or

(e) performs any other act of lewdness.

(2) Lewdness involving a child is a class A misdemeanor.   2003

76-9-702.7.   Voyeurism offenses — Penalties.

(1) A person is guilty of voyeurism who intentionally uses a camcorder, motion picture camera, photographic camera of any type, or other equipment that is concealed or disguised to secretly or surreptitiously videotape, film, photograph, record, or view by electronic means an individual:

(a) for the purpose of viewing any portion of the individual's body regarding which the individual has a reasonable expectation of privacy, whether or not that portion of the body is covered with clothing;

(b) without the knowledge or consent of the individual; and

(c) under circumstances in which the individual has a reasonable expectation of privacy.

(2) A violation of Subsection (1) is a class A misdemeanor, except that a violation of Subsection (1) committed against a child under 14 years of age is a third degree felony.

(3) Distribution or sale of any images, including in print, electronic, magnetic, or digital format, obtained under Subsection (1) by transmission, display, or dissemination is a third degree felony, except that if the violation of this Subsection (3) includes images of a child under 14 years of age, the violation is a second degree felony.

(4) A person is guilty of voyeurism who, under circumstances not amounting to a violation of Subsection (1), views or attempts to view an individual, with or without the use of any instrumentality:

(a) with the intent of viewing any portion of the individual's body regarding which the individual has a reasonable expectation of privacy, whether or not that portion of the body is covered with clothing;

(b) without the knowledge or consent of the individual; and

(c) under circumstances in which the individual has a reasonable expectation of privacy.

(5) A violation of Subsection (4) is a class B misdemeanor, except that a violation of Subsection (4) committed against a child under 14 years of age is a class A misdemeanor.   2004

76-9-703.   Repealed.   1995

76-9-704.   Abuse or desecration of a dead human body — Penalties.

(1) For purposes of this section, "dead human body" includes any part of a human body in any stage of decomposition, including ancient human remains.

(2) A person is guilty of abuse or desecration of a dead human body if the person intentionally and unlawfully:

(a) fails to report the finding of a dead human body to a local law enforcement agency;

(b) disturbs, moves, removes, conceals, or destroys a dead human body or any part of it;

(c) disinters a buried or otherwise interred dead human body, without authority of a court order;

(d) dismembers a dead human body to any extent, or damages or detaches any part or portion of a dead human body; or

(e) (i) commits or attempts to commit upon any dead human body any act of sexual penetration, regardless of the sex of the actor and of the dead human body; and

(ii) as used in Subsection (2)(e)(i), "sexual penetration" means penetration, however slight, of the genital or anal opening by any object, substance, instrument, or device, including a part of the human body, or penetration involving the genitals of the actor and the mouth of the dead human body.

(3) A person does not violate this section if when that person directs or carries out procedures regarding a dead human body, that person complies with:

(a) Title 9, Chapter 8, Part 3, Antiquities;

(b) Title 26, Chapter 4, Utah Medical Examiner Act;

(c) Title 26, Chapter 28, Uniform Anatomical Gift Act;

(d) Title 53B, Chapter 17, Part 3, Use of Dead Bodies for Medical Purposes;

(e) Title 58, Chapter 9, Funeral Services Licensing Act; or

(f) Title 58, Chapter 67, Utah Medical Practice Act, which concerns licensing to practice medicine.

(4) (a) Failure to report the finding of a dead human body as required under Subsection (2)(a) is a class B misdemeanor.

(b) Abuse or desecration of a dead human body as described in Subsections (2)(b) through (e) is a third degree felony.   2005

76-9-705. Participation in an ultimate fighting match.

(1) For purposes of this section, "ultimate fighting match" means a live match in which:

(a) an admission fee is charged;

(b) match rules permit professional contestants to use a combination of boxing, kicking, wrestling, hitting, punching, or other combative, contact techniques; and

(c) match rules do not:

(i) incorporate a formalized system of combative techniques against which a contestant's performance is judged to determine the prevailing contestant;

(ii) divide a match into two or more equal and specified time periods for a match total of no more than 50 minutes; or

(iii) prohibit contestants from:

(A) using anything that is not part of the human body, except for boxing gloves, to intentionally inflict serious bodily injury upon an opponent through direct contact or the expulsion of a projectile;

(B) striking a person who demonstrates an inability to protect himself from the advances of an opponent;

(C) biting; or

(D) direct, intentional, and forceful strikes to the eyes, groin area, adam's apple area of the neck, and temple area of the head.

(2) Any person who publicizes, promotes, conducts, or engages in an ultimate fighting match is guilty of a class A misdemeanor.   1997

CHAPTER 10

OFFENSES AGAINST PUBLIC HEALTH, SAFETY, WELFARE, AND MORALS

Part 1

Cigarettes and Tobacco and Psychotoxic Chemical Solvents

PART 1

CIGARETTES AND TOBACCO AND PSYCHOTOXIC CHEMICAL SOLVENTS

76-10-101. Definitions.

As used in this part:

(1) "Place of business" means any and all places such as shops, stores, factories, public garages, offices, theaters, recreation and dance halls, poolrooms, cafes, cafeterias, cabarets, restaurants, hotels, lodging houses, streetcars, buses, interurban and railway passenger coaches and waiting rooms.

(2) "Smoking" means the possession of any lighted cigar, cigarette, pipe, or other lighted smoking equipment. 1998

76-10-102. Cigarettes and tobacco — Advertising restrictions — Warnings in smokeless tobacco advertisements.

(1) It is a class B misdemeanor for any person to display on any billboard, streetcar sign, streetcar, bus, placard, or on any other object or place of display, any advertisement of cigarettes, cigarette papers, cigars, chewing tobacco, or smoking tobacco or any disguise or substitute of either, except that a dealer in cigarettes, cigarette papers, tobacco or cigars, or their substitutes, may have a sign on the front of his place of business stating that he is a dealer in the articles; provided that nothing herein shall be construed to prohibit the advertising of cigarettes, cigarette papers, chewing tobacco or smoking tobacco, or any substitute of either, in any newspaper, magazine or periodical printed or circulating in this state.

(2) Any advertisement for smokeless tobacco placed in a newspaper, magazine, or periodical published in this state must bear a warning which states: "Use of smokeless tobacco may cause oral cancer and other mouth disorders and is addictive." This warning must be in a conspicuous location and in conspicuous and legible type, in contrast with the typography, layout, and color of all other printed material in the advertisement. For purposes of this subsection, "smokeless tobacco" means any finely cut, ground, powdered, or leaf tobacco that is intended to be placed in the oral cavity or nasal passage. In the event the United States Congress passes legislation which requires warnings in advertisements of smokeless tobacco, the specific language required to be placed in advertisements by that legislation shall take precedence over this subsection. 1986

76-10-103. Permitting minors to use tobacco in place of business.

It is a class C misdemeanor for the proprietor of any place of business to knowingly permit persons under age nineteen to frequent a place of business while they are using tobacco. 1973

76-10-104.   Providing cigars, cigarettes, or tobacco to minors — Penalties.

(1) Any person who knowingly, intentionally, recklessly, or with criminal negligence provides any cigar, cigarette, or tobacco in any form, to any person under 19 years of age, is guilty of a class C misdemeanor on the first offense, a class B misdemeanor on the second offense, and a class A misdemeanor on subsequent offenses.

(2) For purposes of this section "provides":

(a) includes selling, giving, furnishing, sending, or causing to be sent; and

(b) does not include the acts of the United States Postal Service or other common carrier when engaged in the business of transporting and delivering packages for others or the acts of a person, whether compensated or not, who transports or delivers a package for another person without any reason to know of the package's content.   **2000**

76-10-105.   Buying or possessing cigars, cigarettes, or tobacco by minors — Penalty — Compliance officer authority — Juvenile court jurisdiction.

(1) Any 18 year old person who buys or attempts to buy, accepts, or has in his possession any cigar, cigarette, or tobacco in any form is guilty of a class C misdemeanor and subject to:

(a) a minimum fine or penalty of $60; and

(b) participation in a court-approved tobacco education program, which may include a participation fee.

(2) Any person under the age of 18 who buys or attempts to buy, accepts, or has in his possession any cigar, cigarette, or tobacco in any form is subject to the jurisdiction of the Juvenile Court and:

(a) a minimum fine or penalty of $60; and

(b) participation in a court-approved tobacco education program, which may include a participation fee.

(3) A compliance officer appointed by a board of education under Section 53A-3-402 may issue citations for violations of this section committed on school property. Cited violations shall be reported to the appropriate juvenile court.   **2002**

76-10-105.1.   Requirement of direct, face-to-face sale of tobacco products.

(1) As used in this section:

(a) (i) "Cigarette" means any product which contains nicotine, is intended to be burned under ordinary conditions of use, and consists of:

(A) any roll of tobacco wrapped in paper or in any substance not containing tobacco; or

(B) any roll of tobacco wrapped in any substance containing tobacco which, because of its appearance, the type of tobacco used in the filler, or its packaging and labeling, is likely to be offered to, or purchased by, consumers as a cigarette described in Subsection (1)(a)(i).

(ii) "Cigarette" does not include a standard 60 carton case.

(b) "Cigarette tobacco" means any product that consists of loose tobacco that contains or delivers nicotine and is intended for use by consumers in a cigarette. Unless otherwise stated, the requirements pertaining to cigarettes shall also apply to cigarette tobacco.

(c) "Retailer" means any person who sells cigarettes or smokeless tobacco to individuals for personal consumption or who operates a facility where vending machines or self-service displays are permitted under this section.

(d) "Self-service display" means any display of cigarettes or smokeless tobacco products to which the public has access without the intervention of a retail employee.

(e) "Smokeless tobacco" means any product that consists of cut, ground, powdered, or leaf tobacco that contains nicotine and that is intended to be placed in the oral cavity. "Smokeless tobacco" does not include multi-container packs of smokeless tobacco.

(2) (a) Except as provided in Subsection (3), a retailer may sell cigarettes and smokeless tobacco only in a direct, face-to-face exchange between the retailer and the consumer. Examples of methods that are not permitted include vending machines and self-service displays.

(b) Subsection (2)(a) does not prohibit the use or display of locked cabinets containing cigarettes or smokeless tobacco if the locked cabinets are only accessible to the retailer or its employees.

(3) The following sales are permitted as exceptions to Subsection (2):

(a) mail-order sales, if the retailer requires the postal authority or other common carrier to:

(i) verify that the person who takes possession of the delivery and who signs for the delivery is 19 years of age or older;

(ii) obtain the signature of the person taking the delivery; and

(iii) include as part of the shipping documents a clear and conspicuous statement providing as follows: "This package contains tobacco products: Utah law prohibits possession of tobacco products by individuals under the age of 19"; and

(b) vending machines, including vending machines that sell packaged, single cigarettes, and self-service displays that are located in a separate and defined area within a facility where the retailer ensures that no person younger than 19 years of age is present, or permitted to enter, at any time, unless accompanied by a parent or legal guardian.

(4) Any ordinance, regulation, or rule adopted by the governing body of a political subdivision or state agency that affects the sale, placement, or display of cigarettes or smokeless tobacco that is not essentially identical to the provisions of this section and Section 76-10-102 is superceded.

(5) (a) A parent or legal guardian who accompanies a person younger than 19 years of age into an area described in Subsection (3) and permits the person younger than 19 years of age to purchase or otherwise take a cigar, cigarette, or tobacco in any form is guilty of providing tobacco as provided for in Section 76-10-104 and the penalties provided for in that section.

(b) Nothing in this section may be construed as permitting a person to provide tobacco to a minor in violation of Section 76-10-104.

(6) Violation of Subsection (2) or (3) is a:

(a) class C misdemeanor on the first offense;

(b) class B misdemeanor on the second offense; and

(c) class A misdemeanor on the third and all subsequent offenses.   **2004**

76-10-105.3. Prohibition of sale or gift of clove cigarettes.

It is unlawful for any person to knowingly sell, offer for sale, give or furnish any clove cigarette in this state. For purposes of this section "clove cigarette" means any cigarette which contains more than 10%, by weight, of raw eugenia caryophyllata or caryophyllus, commonly known as clove. Any person who violates this section is guilty of a class B misdemeanor. 1986

76-10-105.5, 76-10-106. Repealed. 1989

76-10-107. Abuse of psychotoxic chemical solvents.

(1) A person is guilty of abuse of psychotoxic chemical solvents if:

(a) for the purpose of causing a condition of intoxication, inebriation, excitement, stupefaction, or the dulling of his brain or nervous system, he intentionally:

(i) smells or inhales the fumes of any psychotoxic chemical solvent; or

(ii) possesses, purchases, or attempts to possess or purchase any psychotoxic chemical solvent; or

(b) the person offers, sells, or provides a psychotoxic chemical solvent to another person, knowing that other person or a third party intends to possess or use that psychotoxic chemical solvent in violation of Subsection (1)(a).

(2) This section does not apply to the prescribed use, distribution, or sale of those substances for medical or dental purposes.

(3) Abuse of psychotoxic chemical solvents is a class B misdemeanor.

(4) As used in this section, psychotoxic chemical solvent includes any glue, cement, or other substance containing one or more of the following chemical compounds: acetone and acetate, amyl nitrite or amyl nitrate or their isomers, benzene, butyl alcohol, butyl nitrite, butyl nitrate, or their isomers, ethyl alcohol, ethyl nitrite or ethyl nitrate, ethylene dichloride, isobutyl alcohol, methyl alcohol, methyl ethyl ketone, n-propyl alcohol, pentachlorophenol, petroleum ether, propyl nitrite or propyl nitrate or their isomers, toluene or xylene, or other chemical substance capable of causing a condition of intoxication, inebriation, excitement, stupefaction, or the dulling of the brain or nervous system as a result of the inhalation of the fumes or vapors of such chemical substance. Nothing in this section shall be construed to include any controlled substance regulated by the provisions of Title 58, Chapter 37, Utah Controlled Substances Act. 2002

76-10-107.5. Abuse of nitrous oxide — Penalty.

(1) As used in this section, "nitrous oxide" means:

(a) N_2O, a colorless gas or liquid that is also referred to as dinitrogen monoxide, nitrogen oxide, or laughing gas; and

(b) any substance containing nitrous oxide.

(2) A person is guilty of abuse of nitrous oxide who:

(a) possesses nitrous oxide with the intent to breathe, inhale, or ingest it for the purpose of:

(i) causing a condition of intoxication, elation, euphoria, dizziness, stupefaction, or dulling of the senses;

(ii) in any manner changing, distorting, or disturbing the audio, visual, or mental processes;

(b) knowingly and intentionally is under the influence of nitrous oxide; or

(c) offers, sells, or provides nitrous oxide to another person, knowing that other person or a third party intends to possess or use the nitrous oxide in violation of Subsection (2)(a) or (b).

(3) Subsection (2)(b) does not apply to any person who is under the influence of nitrous oxide pursuant to an administration for the purpose of medical, surgical, or dental care by a person holding a license under state law that authorizes the administration of nitrous oxide.

(4) Subsection (2)(c) does not apply to any person who administers nitrous oxide for the purpose of medical, surgical, or dental care and who holds a license under state law that authorizes the administration of nitrous oxide.

(5) A violation of this section is a class A misdemeanor. 2002

76-10-108 to 76-10-110. Repealed. 1994, 1996

76-10-111. Prohibition of gift or free distribution of smokeless tobacco — Exceptions.

(1) The Legislature finds that smokeless tobacco, or chewing tobacco, is harmful to the health of individuals who use those products because research indicates that they may cause mouth or oral cancers; that the use of smokeless tobacco among juveniles in this state is increasing rapidly; and that it is necessary to restrict the gift of these products in the interest of the health of the citizens of this state.

(2) Except as provided in Subsection (3), it is unlawful for a manufacturer, wholesaler, and retailer to give or distribute without charge any smokeless tobacco or chewing tobacco in this state. Any person who violates this section is guilty of a class C misdemeanor for the first offense, and is guilty of a class B misdemeanor for any subsequent offense.

(3) (a) Smokeless tobacco or chewing tobacco may be distributed to adults without charge at professional conventions where the general public is excluded.

(b) Subsection (2) does not apply to retailers, manufacturers, or distributors who give smokeless tobacco or chewing tobacco to persons of legal age upon their purchase of other tobacco products. 1990

76-10-112. Prohibition of distribution of cigarettes or other tobacco products — Exceptions.

(1) Except as provided in Subsection (2), it is unlawful for a manufacturer, wholesaler, or retailer to give or distribute cigarettes or other tobacco products in this state without charge. Any person who violates this subsection is guilty of a class C misdemeanor for the first offense and a class B misdemeanor for any subsequent offense.

(2) Cigarettes and other tobacco products may be distributed to adults without charge at professional conventions where the general public is excluded.

(3) The prohibition described in Subsection (1) does not apply to retailers, manufacturers, or distributors who give cigarettes or other tobacco products to persons of legal age upon their purchase of cigarettes or other tobacco products. 1989

PART 2

WATERS

76-10-201. Interference with water flow.

Every person who knowingly or intentionally interferes with or alters the flow of water in any stream, ditch, or lateral while under the control or management of any water commissioner is guilty of a crime punishable under Section 73-2-27.   2005

76-10-202. Taking water out of turn or excess amount — Damaging facilities.

(1) No person may, in violation of any right of any other person knowingly or intentionally:

(a) turn or use the water, or any part thereof, of any canal, ditch, pipeline, or reservoir, except at a time when the use of the water has been duly distributed to the person;

(b) use any greater quantity of the water than has been duly distributed to him;

(c) in any way change the flow of water when lawfully distributed for irrigation or other useful purposes, except when duly authorized to make the change; or

(d) break or injure any dam, canal, pipeline, watergate, ditch, or other means of diverting or conveying water for irrigation or other useful purposes.

(2) Subsection (1) applies to violations of any right to the use of water, including:

(a) a water right; or

(b) authorization of a person's use of water by:

(i) a water company, as defined in Subsection 73-3-3.5(1)(b); or

(ii) an entity having a valid water right under Utah law.

(3) Any person who violates this section is guilty of a crime punishable under Section 73-2-27.   2005

76-10-203. Obstruction of watergates.

Every person who rafts or floats logs, timber, or wood down any river or stream and allows the logs, timber, or wood to accumulate at or obstruct the watergates owned by any person or irrigation company taking or diverting the water of the river or stream for irrigation or manufacturing purposes is guilty of a crime punishable under Section 73-2-27.   2005

76-10-204. Damaging bridge, dam, canal or other water-related structure.

(1) A person is guilty of a third degree felony who intentionally, knowingly, or recklessly commits an offense under Subsection (2) that does not amount to a violation of Subsection 76-6-106(2)(b)(ii).

(2) Offenses referred to in Subsection (1) are when a person:

(a) cuts, breaks, damages, or destroys any bridge, dam, canal, flume, aqueduct, levee, embankment, reservoir, or other structure erected to create hydraulic power, to drain or reclaim any swamp and overflowed or marsh land, to conduct water for mining, manufacturing, reclamation, or agricultural purposes, or for the supply of the inhabitants of any city or town;

(b) makes or causes to be made any aperture in any dam, canal, flume, aqueduct, reservoir, embankment, levee, or structure with intent to injure or destroy it; or

(c) draws up, cuts, or injures any piles fixed in the ground and used for securing any lake or river bank or walls or any dock, quay, jetty, or lock.   2002

76-10-205. Repealed.   1986

PART 3

EXPLOSIVES

76-10-301. Repealed.   1999

76-10-302. Marking of containers of explosives before transportation or storage.

Every person who knowingly leaves with or delivers to another, or to any express or railway company or other common carrier, or to any warehouse or storehouse, any package containing nitroglycerin, dynamite, guncotton, gunpowder, or other highly explosive compound, or any benzine, gasoline, phosphorus, or other highly inflammable substance, or any vitriol, sulphuric, nitric, carbolic, muriatic, or other dangerous acid, chemical or compound, to be handled, stored, shipped, or transported, without plainly marking and indicating on such package the name and nature of the contents thereof, is guilty of a class B misdemeanor.   1973

76-10-303. Powder houses.

Every person who builds, constructs, or uses within 300 feet of any residence or traveled county road any powder house, magazine, or building in which powder, dynamite, or other explosive is kept in quantities exceeding 500 pounds is guilty of a class B misdemeanor; provided that this section shall not apply to any magazine maintained at any mine or stone quarry.   1973

76-10-304. Marking of containers of explosives held for sale or use.

It shall be a class A misdemeanor to sell or offer for sale or take or solicit orders of sale, or purchase or use, or have on hand or in store for the purpose of sale or use, any giant, hercules, atlas, venture or any other high explosive containing nitroglycerin, unless on each box or package and wrapper containing any such high explosive there shall be plainly stamped or printed the name and place of business of the person, partnership, or corporation by whom or by which it was manufactured, and the exact and true date of its manufacture, and the percentage of nitroglycerin or other high explosive contained therein.   1973

76-10-305. Different dates on containers of explosives prohibited — Reuse of containers prohibited.

It shall be unlawful for any person or persons, partnership, or corporation to have two or more different dates on any box or package containing giant, hercules, atlas, or venture, or any other high explosive containing nitroglycerin. It shall further be unlawful to use any box, package, or wrapper formerly used by any other person or persons, partnership, or corporation in the packing of such giant, hercules, atlas, venture, or other high explosive containing nitroglycerin, and the name and date on the box or package shall be the same as on the wrapper containing the giant, hercules, atlas, venture, or other explosive containing nitroglycerin.   1973

76-10-306. Explosive, chemical, or incendiary device and parts — Definitions — Persons exempted — Penalties.

(1) As used in this section:

(a) "Explosive, chemical, or incendiary device" means:

(i) dynamite and all other forms of high explosives, including water gel, slurry, military C-4 (plastic explosives), blasting agents to include nitro-carbon-nitrate, ammonium nitrate, fuel oil mixtures, cast primers and boosters, R.D.X., P.E.T.N., electric and non-electric blasting caps, exploding cords commonly called detonating cord, detcord, or primacord, picric acid explosives, T.N.T. and

T.N.T. mixtures, nitroglycerin and nitroglycerin mixtures, or any other chemical mixture intended to explode with fire or force;

(ii) any explosive bomb, grenade, missile, or similar device; and

(iii) any incendiary bomb, grenade, fire bomb, chemical bomb, or similar device, including any device, except kerosene lamps, if criminal intent has not been established, which consists of or includes a breakable container including a flammable liquid or compound and a wick composed of any material which, when ignited, is capable of igniting the flammable liquid or compound or any breakable container which consists of, or includes a chemical mixture that explodes with fire or force and can be carried, thrown, or placed.

(b) "Explosive, chemical, or incendiary device" does not include rifle, pistol, or shotgun ammunition, reloading components, or muzzleloading equipment.

(c) "Explosive, chemical, or incendiary parts" means any substances or materials or combinations which have been prepared or altered for use in the creation of an explosive, chemical, or incendiary device. These substances or materials include:

(i) timing device, clock, or watch which has been altered in such a manner as to be used as the arming device in an explosive;

(ii) pipe, end caps, or metal tubing which has been prepared for a pipe bomb; and

(iii) mechanical timers, mechanical triggers, chemical time delays, electronic time delays, or commercially made or improvised items which, when used singly or in combination, may be used in the construction of a timing delay mechanism, booby trap, or activating mechanism for any explosive, chemical, or incendiary device.

(d) "Explosive, chemical, or incendiary parts" does not include rifle, pistol, or shotgun ammunition, or any signaling device customarily used in operation of railroad equipment.

(2) The provisions in Subsections (3) and (6) do not apply to:

(a) any public safety officer while acting in his official capacity transporting or otherwise handling explosives, chemical, or incendiary devices;

(b) any member of the armed forces of the United States or Utah National Guard while acting in his official capacity;

(c) any person possessing a valid permit issued under the provisions of Uniform Fire Code, Article 77, or any employee of the permittee acting within the scope of his employment;

(d) any person possessing a valid license as an importer, wholesaler, or display operator under the provisions of Sections 11-3-3.5 and 53-7-223; and

(e) any person or entity possessing or controlling an explosive, chemical, or incendiary device as part of its lawful business operations.

(3) Any person is guilty of a second degree felony who, under circumstances not amounting to a violation of Title 76, Chapter 10, Part 4, Weapons of Mass Destruction, knowingly, intentionally, or recklessly possesses or controls an explosive, chemical, or incendiary device.

(4) Any person is guilty of a first degree felony who, under circumstances not amounting to a violation of Title 76, Chapter 10, Part 4, Weapons of Mass Destruction, knowingly or intentionally:

(a) uses or causes to be used an explosive, chemical, or incendiary device in the commission of or an attempt to commit a felony;

(b) injures another or attempts to injure another in his person or property through the use of an explosive, chemical, or incendiary device; or

(c) transports, possesses, distributes, or sells any explosive, chemical, or incendiary device in a secure area established pursuant to Section 76-8-311.1, 76-8-311.3, 76-10-529, or 78-7-6.

(5) Any person who, under circumstances not amounting to a violation of Title 76, Chapter 10, Part 4, Weapons of Mass Destruction, knowingly, intentionally, or recklessly removes or causes to be removed or carries away any explosive, chemical, or incendiary device from the premises where the explosive, chemical, or incendiary device is kept by the lawful user, vendor, transporter, or manufacturer without the consent or direction of the lawful possessor is guilty of a second degree felony.

(6) Any person who, under circumstances not amounting to a violation of Title 76, Chapter 10, Part 4, Weapons of Mass Destruction, knowingly, intentionally, or recklessly possesses any explosive, chemical, or incendiary parts is guilty of a felony of the third degree. 2002

76-10-307. Explosive, chemical, or incendiary device — Delivery to common carrier or mailing.

Any person is guilty of a felony of the second degree who delivers or causes to be delivered to any express or railway company or other common carrier, or to any person, any explosive, chemical, or incendiary device, knowing it to be the device, without informing the common carrier or person of its nature or sends it through the mail. 1999

76-10-308. Explosive, chemical, or incendiary device — Venue of prosecution for shipping.

Any person who knowingly, intentionally, or recklessly delivers any explosive, chemical, or incendiary device to any person for transmission without the consent or direction of the lawful possessor may be prosecuted in the county in which he delivers it or in the county to which it is transmitted. 1993

76-10-309. Repealed. 1993

PART 4

WEAPONS OF MASS DESTRUCTION

76-10-401. Definitions.

As used in this part:

(1) "Biological agent" means any microorganism, virus, infectious substance, or biological product that may be engineered as a result of biotechnology, or any naturally occurring or bioengineered component of any microorganism, virus, infectious substance, or biological product, that is capable of causing:

(a) death, disease, or other biological malfunction in a human, an animal, a plant, or another living organism;

(b) deterioration of food, water, equipment, supplies, or material of any kind; or

(c) deleterious alteration of the environment.

(2) "Delivery system" means:

(a) any apparatus, equipment, device, or means of delivery specifically designed to deliver or disseminate a biological agent, toxin, or vector; or

(b) any vector.

(3) "Hoax weapon of mass destruction" means any device or object that by its design, construction, content, or characteristics appears to be or to contain, or is represented to be, constitute, or contain, a weapon of mass destruction as defined in this section, but which is, in fact, an inoperative facsimile, imitation, counterfeit, or representation of a weapon of mass destruction which does not:

(a) meet the definition of a weapon of mass destruction; or

(b) actually contain or constitute a weapon, biological agent, toxin, vector, or delivery system prohibited by this section.

(4) "Toxin" means the toxic material of plants, animals, microorganisms, viruses, fungi, or infectious substances, or a recombinant molecule, whatever its origin or method of production, including:

(a) any poisonous substance or biological product that may be engineered as a result of biotechnology produced by a living organism; or

(b) any poisonous isomer or biological product, homolog, or derivative of the substance under Subsection (4)(a).

(5) "Vector" means a living organism, or molecule, including a recombinant molecule, or biological product that may be engineered as a result of biotechnology, capable of carrying a biological agent or toxin to a host.

(6) (a) "Weapon of mass destruction" means:

(i) any item or instrumentality that is designed or intended to cause widespread death or serious bodily injury to multiple victims;

(ii) any item or instrumentality that is designed or intended to cause death or serious bodily injury through the release, dissemination, or impact of toxic or poisonous chemicals, or their precursors;

(iii) any disease organism, including any biological agent, toxin, or vector which is used or intended to be used as a weapon;

(iv) any item or instrumentality that is designed to release radiation or radioactivity at a level dangerous to human life and that is used or intended to be used as a weapon; or

(v) any substance or material or combination which has been prepared or altered for use in the creation of a weapon described in Subsections (6)(a)(i) through (iv).

(b) "Weapon of mass destruction" does not include firearms or rifle, pistol, or shotgun ammunition, reloading components, or muzzleloading equipment.   2002

76-10-402. Manufacture, possession, sale, use, or attempted use of a weapon of mass destruction prohibited — Penalties.

A person who without lawful authority intentionally or knowingly manufactures, possesses, sells, delivers, displays, uses, attempts to use, solicits the use of, or conspires to use a weapon of mass destruction or a delivery system for a weapon of mass destruction, including any biological agent, toxin, vector, or delivery system as those terms are defined in this section, is guilty of a first degree felony.   2002

76-10-403. Manufacture, possession, sale, use, or attempted use of a hoax weapon of mass destruction prohibited — Penalty.

Any person who without lawful authority intentionally or knowingly manufactures, possesses, sells, delivers, displays, uses, attempts to use, solicits the use of, or conspires to use a hoax weapon of mass destruction with the intent to deceive or otherwise mislead another person into believing that the hoax weapon of mass destruction is a weapon of mass destruction is guilty of a second degree felony.   2002

76-10-404. Exemptions.

This part does not apply to any member or employee of the Armed Forces of the United States, allied armed forces personnel, a federal or state governmental agency, or a private entity, who is engaged in lawful activity within the scope of his or her employment, if the person is authorized or licensed to manufacture, possess, sell, deliver, display, or otherwise engage in activity relative to this section and if the person is in compliance with applicable federal and state law.

2002

76-10-405. Reimbursement of government response expenses.

In addition to any other penalty authorized by law, a court shall order any person convicted of any violation of this part to reimburse any federal, state, or local unit of government, or any private business, organization, individual, or entity for all expenses and losses incurred in responding to the violation, unless the court states on the record the reasons why the reimbursement would be inappropriate.   2002

PART 5

WEAPONS

76-10-500. Uniform law.

(1) The individual right to keep and bear arms being a constitutionally protected right, the Legislature finds the need to provide uniform laws throughout the state. Except as specifically provided by state law, a citizen of the United States or a lawfully admitted alien shall not be:

(a) prohibited from owning, possessing, purchasing, selling, transferring, transporting, or keeping any firearm at his place of residence, property, business, or in any vehicle lawfully in his possession or lawfully under his control; or

(b) required to have a permit or license to purchase, own, possess, transport, or keep a firearm.

(2) This part is uniformly applicable throughout this state and in all its political subdivisions and municipalities. All authority to regulate firearms shall be reserved to the state except where the Legislature specifically delegates responsibility to local authorities or state entities. Unless specifically authorized by the Legislature by statute, a local authority or state entity may not enact or enforce any ordinance, regulation, or rule pertaining to firearms.   1999

76-10-501. Definitions.

As used in this part:

(1) (a) "Antique firearm" means any firearm:

(i) (A) with a matchlock, flintlock, percussion cap, or similar type of ignition system; and

(B) that was manufactured in or before 1898; or

(ii) that is a replica of any firearm described in this Subsection (1)(a), if the replica:

(A) is not designed or redesigned for using rimfire or conventional centerfire fixed ammunition; or

(B) uses rimfire or centerfire fixed ammunition which is:

(I) no longer manufactured in the United States; and

(II) is not readily available in ordinary channels of commercial trade; or

(iii) (A) that is a muzzle loading rifle, shotgun, or pistol; and

(B) is designed to use black powder, or a black powder substitute, and cannot use fixed ammunition.

(b) "Antique firearm" does not include:

(i) any weapon that incorporates a firearm frame or receiver;

(ii) any firearm that is converted into a muzzle loading weapon; or

(iii) any muzzle loading weapon that can be readily converted to fire fixed ammunition by replacing the:

(A) barrel;

(B) bolt;

(C) breechblock; or

(D) any combination of Subsection (1)(b)(iii)(A), (B), or (C).

(2) (a) "Concealed dangerous weapon" means a dangerous weapon that is covered, hidden, or secreted in a manner that the public would not be aware of its presence and is readily accessible for immediate use.

(b) A dangerous weapon shall not be considered a concealed dangerous weapon if it is a firearm which is unloaded and is securely encased.

(3) "Criminal history background check" means a criminal background check conducted by a licensed firearms dealer on every purchaser of a handgun through the division or the local law enforcement agency where the firearms dealer conducts business.

(4) "Curio or relic firearm" means any firearm that:

(a) is of special interest to a collector because of a quality that is not associated with firearms intended for:

(i) sporting use;

(ii) use as an offensive weapon; or

(iii) use as a defensive weapon;

(b) (i) was manufactured at least 50 years prior to the current date; and

(ii) is not a replica of a firearm described in Subsection (4)(b)(i);

(c) is certified by the curator of a municipal, state, or federal museum that exhibits firearms to be a curio or relic of museum interest;

(d) derives a substantial part of its monetary value:

(i) from the fact that the firearm is:

(A) novel;

(B) rare; or

(C) bizarre; or

(ii) because of the firearm's association with an historical:

(A) figure;

(B) period; or

(C) event; and

(e) has been designated as a curio or relic firearm by the director of the United States Treasury Department Bureau of Alcohol, Tobacco, and Firearms under 27 C.F.R. Sec. 178.11.

(5) (a) "Dangerous weapon" means any item that in the manner of its use or intended use is capable of causing death or serious bodily injury. The following factors shall be used in determining whether a knife, or any other item, object, or thing not commonly known as a dangerous weapon is a dangerous weapon:

(i) the character of the instrument, object, or thing;

(ii) the character of the wound produced, if any;

(iii) the manner in which the instrument, object, or thing was used; and

(iv) the other lawful purposes for which the instrument, object, or thing may be used.

(b) "Dangerous weapon" does not include any explosive, chemical, or incendiary device as defined by Section 76-10-306.

(6) "Dealer" means every person who is licensed under crimes and criminal procedure, 18 U.S.C. 923 and engaged in the business of selling, leasing, or otherwise transferring a handgun, whether the person is a retail or wholesale dealer, pawnbroker, or otherwise.

(7) "Division" means the Criminal Investigations and Technical Services Division of the Department of Public Safety, created in Section 53-10-103.

(8) "Enter" means intrusion of the entire body.

(9) (a) "Firearm" means a pistol, revolver, shotgun, sawed-off shotgun, rifle or sawed-off rifle, or any device that could be used as a dangerous weapon from which is expelled a projectile by action of an explosive.

(b) As used in Sections 76-10-526 and 76-10-527, "firearm" does not include an antique firearm.

(10) "Firearms transaction record form" means a form created by the division to be completed by a person purchasing, selling, or transferring a handgun from a dealer in the state.

(11) "Fully automatic weapon" means any firearm which fires, is designed to fire, or can be readily restored to fire, automatically more than one shot without manual reloading by a single function of the trigger.

(12) (a) "Handgun" means a pistol, revolver, or other firearm of any description, loaded or unloaded, from which any shot, bullet, or other missile can be discharged, the length of which, not including any revolving, detachable, or magazine breech, does not exceed 12 inches.

(b) As used in Sections 76-10-520, 76-10-521, and 76-10-522, "handgun" and "pistol or revolver" do not include an antique firearm.

(13) "House of worship" means a church, temple, synagogue, mosque, or other building set apart primarily for the purpose of worship in which religious services are held and the main

body of which is kept for that use and not put to any other use inconsistent with its primary purpose.

(14) "Prohibited area" means any place where it is unlawful to discharge a firearm.

(15) "Readily accessible for immediate use" means that a firearm or other dangerous weapon is carried on the person or within such close proximity and in such a manner that it can be retrieved and used as readily as if carried on the person.

(16) "Residence" means an improvement to real property used or occupied as a primary or secondary residence.

(17) "Sawed-off shotgun" or "sawed-off rifle" means a shotgun having a barrel or barrels of fewer than 18 inches in length, or in the case of a rifle, having a barrel or barrels of fewer than 16 inches in length, or any dangerous weapon made from a rifle or shotgun by alteration, modification, or otherwise, if the weapon as modified has an overall length of fewer than 26 inches.

(18) "Securely encased" means not readily accessible for immediate use, such as held in a gun rack, or in a closed case or container, whether or not locked, or in a trunk or other storage area of a motor vehicle, not including a glove box or console box.

(19) "State entity" means each department, commission, board, council, agency, institution, officer, corporation, fund, division, office, committee, authority, laboratory, library, unit, bureau, panel, or other administrative unit of the state.

(20) "Violent felony" means the same as defined in Section 76-3-203.5.   2001

76-10-502. When weapon deemed loaded.

(1) For the purpose of this chapter, any pistol, revolver, shotgun, rifle, or other weapon described in this part shall be deemed to be loaded when there is an unexpended cartridge, shell, or projectile in the firing position.

(2) Pistols and revolvers shall also be deemed to be loaded when an unexpended cartridge, shell, or projectile is in a position whereby the manual operation of any mechanism once would cause the unexpended cartridge, shell, or projectile to be fired.

(3) A muzzle loading firearm shall be deemed to be loaded when it is capped or primed and has a powder charge and ball or shot in the barrel or cylinders.
                                                1990

76-10-503. Restrictions on possession, purchase, transfer, and ownership of dangerous weapons by certain persons.

(1) For purposes of this section:

(a) A Category I restricted person is a person who:

(i) has been convicted of any violent felony as defined in Section 76-3-203.5;

(ii) is on probation or parole for any felony;

(iii) is on parole from a secure facility as defined in Section 62A-7-101; or

(iv) within the last ten years has been adjudicated delinquent for an offense which if committed by an adult would have been a violent felony as defined in Section 76-3-203.5.

(b) A Category II restricted person is a person who:

(i) has been convicted of or is under indictment for any felony;

(ii) within the last seven years has been adjudicated delinquent for an offense which if committed by an adult would have been a felony;

(iii) is an unlawful user of a controlled substance as defined in Section 58-37-2;

(iv) is in possession of a dangerous weapon and is knowingly and intentionally in unlawful possession of a Schedule I or II controlled substance as defined in Section 58-37-2;

(v) has been found not guilty by reason of insanity for a felony offense;

(vi) has been found mentally incompetent to stand trial for a felony offense;

(vii) has been adjudicated as mentally defective as provided in the Brady Handgun Violence Prevention Act, Pub. L. No. 103-159, 107 Stat. 1536 (1993), or has been committed to a mental institution;

(viii) is an alien who is illegally or unlawfully in the United States;

(ix) has been dishonorably discharged from the armed forces; or

(x) has renounced his citizenship after having been a citizen of the United States.

(2) A Category I restricted person who intentionally or knowingly agrees, consents, offers, or arranges to purchase, transfer, possess, use, or have under his custody or control, or who intentionally or knowingly purchases, transfers, possesses, uses, or has under his custody or control:

(a) any firearm is guilty of a second degree felony; or

(b) any dangerous weapon other than a firearm is guilty of a third degree felony.

(3) A Category II restricted person who purchases, transfers, possesses, uses, or has under his custody or control:

(a) any firearm is guilty of a third degree felony; or

(b) any dangerous weapon other than a firearm is guilty of a class A misdemeanor.

(4) A person may be subject to the restrictions of both categories at the same time.

(5) If a higher penalty than is prescribed in this section is provided in another section for one who purchases, transfers, possesses, uses, or has under this custody or control any dangerous weapon, the penalties of that section control.

(6) It is an affirmative defense to a charge based on the definition in Subsection (1)(b)(iv) that the person was:

(a) in possession of a controlled substance pursuant to a lawful order of a practitioner for use of a member of the person's household or for administration to an animal owned by the person or a member of the person's household; or

(b) otherwise authorized by law to possess the substance.   2003

76-10-504. Carrying concealed dangerous weapon — Penalties.

(1) Except as provided in Section 76-10-503 and in Subsections (2) and (3):

(a) a person who carries a concealed dangerous weapon, as defined in Section 76-10-501, which is not a firearm on his person or one that is readily accessible for immediate use which is not securely encased, as defined in this part, in a place other than his residence, property, or business under his control is guilty of a class B misdemeanor; and

(b) a person without a valid concealed firearm permit who carries a concealed dangerous weapon which is a firearm and that contains no ammunition is guilty of a class B misdemeanor, but if the firearm contains ammunition the person is guilty of a class A misdemeanor.

(2) A person who carries concealed a sawed-off shotgun or a sawed-off rifle is guilty of a second degree felony.

(3) If the concealed firearm is used in the commission of a violent felony as defined in Section 76-3-203.5, and the person is a party to the offense, the person is guilty of a second degree felony.

(4) Nothing in Subsection (1) shall prohibit a person engaged in the lawful taking of protected or unprotected wildlife as defined in Title 23, Wildlife Resources Code, from carrying a concealed weapon or a concealed firearm with a barrel length of four inches or greater as long as the taking of wildlife does not occur:

(a) within the limits of a municipality in violation of that municipality's ordinances; or

(b) upon the highways of the state as defined in Section 41-6a-102. 2005

76-10-505. Carrying loaded firearm in vehicle, on street, or in prohibited area.

(1) Unless otherwise authorized by law, a person may not carry a loaded firearm:

(a) in or on a vehicle;

(b) on any public street; or

(c) in a posted prohibited area.

(2) A violation of this section is a class B misdemeanor. 1990

76-10-505.5. Possession of a dangerous weapon, firearm, or sawed-off shotgun on or about school premises — Penalties.

(1) A person may not possess any dangerous weapon, firearm, or sawed-off shotgun, as those terms are defined in Section 76-10-501, at a place that the person knows, or has reasonable cause to believe, is on or about school premises as defined in Subsection 76-3-203.2(1).

(2) (a) Possession of a dangerous weapon on or about school premises is a class B misdemeanor.

(b) Possession of a firearm or sawed-off shotgun on or about school premises is a class A misdemeanor.

(3) This section does not apply if:

(a) the person is authorized to possess a firearm as provided under Section 53-5-704, 53-5-705, 76-10-511, or 76-10-523, or as otherwise authorized by law;

(b) the possession is approved by the responsible school administrator;

(c) the item is present or to be used in connection with a lawful, approved activity and is in the possession or under the control of the person responsible for its possession or use; or

(d) the possession is:

(i) at the person's place of residence or on the person's property;

(ii) in any vehicle lawfully under the person's control, other than a vehicle owned by the school or used by the school to transport students; or

(iii) at the person's place of business which is not located in the areas described in Subsection 76-3-203.2(1)(a)(i), (ii), or (iv).

(4) This section does not prohibit prosecution of a more serious weapons offense that may occur on or about school premises. 2003

76-10-506. Threatening with or using dangerous weapon in fight or quarrel.

Every person, except those persons described in Section 76-10-503, who, not in necessary self defense in the presence of two or more persons, draws or exhibits any dangerous weapon in an angry and threatening manner or unlawfully uses the same in any fight or quarrel is guilty of a class A misdemeanor. 1992

76-10-507. Possession of deadly weapon with intent to assault.

Every person having upon his person any dangerous weapon with intent to unlawfully assault another is guilty of a class A misdemeanor. 1973

76-10-508. Discharge of firearm from a vehicle, near a highway, or in direction of any person, building, or vehicle — Penalties.

(1) (a) A person may not discharge any kind of dangerous weapon or firearm:

(i) from an automobile or other vehicle;

(ii) from, upon, or across any highway;

(iii) at any road signs placed upon any highways of the state;

(iv) at any communications equipment or property of public utilities including facilities, lines, poles, or devices of transmission or distribution;

(v) at railroad equipment or facilities including any sign or signal;

(vi) within Utah State Park buildings, designated camp or picnic sites, overlooks, golf courses, boat ramps, and developed beaches; or

(vii) without written permission to discharge the dangerous weapon from the owner or person in charge of the property within 600 feet of:

(A) a house, dwelling, or any other building; or

(B) any structure in which a domestic animal is kept or fed, including a barn, poultry yard, corral, feeding pen, or stockyard.

(b) It shall be a defense to any charge for violating this section that the person being accused had actual permission of the owner or person in charge of the property at the time in question.

(2) A violation of any provision of this section is a class B misdemeanor unless the actor discharges a firearm under any of the following circumstances not amounting to criminal homicide or attempted criminal homicide, in which case it is a third degree felony and the convicted person shall be sentenced to an enhanced minimum term of three years in prison:

(a) the actor discharges a firearm in the direction of any person or persons, knowing or having reason to believe that any person may be endangered;

(b) the actor, with intent to intimidate or harass another or with intent to damage a habitable structure as defined in Subsection 76-6-101(2), discharges a firearm in the direction of any building; or

(c) the actor, with intent to intimidate or harass another, discharges a firearm in the direction of any vehicle.

(3) The court shall:

(a) notify the Driver License Division of the conviction for purposes of any revocation, denial, suspension, or disqualification of a driver license under Section 53-3-220(1)(a)(xi); and

(b) specify in court at the time of sentencing the length of the revocation under Subsection 53-3-225(1)(c).

(4) This section does not apply to a person:

(a) who discharges any kind of firearm when that person is in lawful defense of self or others; or

(b) who is performing official duties as provided in Sections 23-20-1.5 and 76-10-523 and as otherwise provided by law.   2005

76-10-509. Possession of dangerous weapon by minor.

(1) A minor under 18 years of age may not possess a dangerous weapon unless he:

(a) has the permission of his parent or guardian to have the weapon; or

(b) is accompanied by a parent or guardian while he has the weapon in his possession.

(2) Any minor under 14 years of age in possession of a dangerous weapon shall be accompanied by a responsible adult.

(3) Any person who violates this section is guilty of:

(a) a class B misdemeanor upon the first offense; and

(b) a class A misdemeanor for each subsequent offense.   1993 (2nd S.S.)

76-10-509.4. Prohibition of possession of certain weapons by minors.

(1) A minor under 18 years of age may not possess a handgun.

(2) Except as provided by federal law, a minor under 18 years of age may not possess the following:

(a) a sawed-off rifle or sawed-off shotgun; or

(b) a fully automatic weapon.

(3) Any person who violates Subsection (1) is guilty of:

(a) a class B misdemeanor upon the first offense; and

(b) a class A misdemeanor for each subsequent offense.

(4) Any person who violates Subsection (2) is guilty of a third degree felony.   1995

76-10-509.5. Penalties for providing certain weapons to a minor.

(1) Any person who provides a handgun to a minor when the possession of the handgun by the minor is a violation of Section 76-10-509.4 is guilty of:

(a) a class B misdemeanor upon the first offense; and

(b) a class A misdemeanor for each subsequent offense.

(2) Any person who transfers in violation of applicable state or federal law a sawed-off rifle, sawed-off shotgun, or fully automatic weapon to a minor is guilty of a third degree felony.   1994

76-10-509.6. Parent or guardian providing firearm to violent minor.

(1) A parent or guardian may not intentionally or knowingly provide a firearm to, or permit the possession of a firearm by, any minor who has been convicted of a violent felony as defined in Section 76-3-203.5 or any minor who has been adjudicated in juvenile court for an offense which would constitute a violent felony if the minor were an adult.

(2) Any person who violates this section is guilty of:

(a) a class A misdemeanor upon the first offense; and

(b) a third degree felony for each subsequent offense.   2000

76-10-509.7. Parent or guardian knowing of minor's possession of dangerous weapon.

Any parent or guardian of a minor who knows that the minor is in possession of a dangerous weapon in violation of Section 76-10-509 or a firearm in violation of Section 76-10-509.4 and fails to make reasonable efforts to remove the firearm from the minor's possession is guilty of a class B misdemeanor.   1993 (2nd S.S.)

76-10-509.9. Sales of firearms to juveniles.

(1) A person may not sell any firearm to a minor under 18 years of age unless the minor is accompanied by a parent or guardian.

(2) Any person who violates this section is guilty of a third degree felony.   1993 (2nd S.S.)

76-10-510. Repealed.   1995

76-10-511. Possession of loaded firearm at residence authorized.

Except for persons described in Section 76-10-503, a person may have a loaded firearm at his place of residence, including any temporary residence or camp.   1993

76-10-512. Target concessions, shooting ranges, competitions, and hunting excepted from prohibitions.

The provisions of Section 76-10-509 and Subsection 76-10-509.4(1) regarding possession of handguns by minors shall not apply to any of the following:

(1) Patrons firing at lawfully operated target concessions at amusement parks, piers, and similar locations provided that the firearms to be used are firmly chained or affixed to the counters.

(2) Any person in attendance at a hunter's safety course or a firearms safety course.

(3) Any person engaging in practice or any other lawful use of a firearm at an established range or any other area where the discharge of a firearm is not prohibited by state or local law.

(4) Any person engaging in an organized competition involving the use of a firearm, or participating in or practicing for such competition.

(5) Any minor under 18 years of age who is on real property with the permission of the owner, licensee, or lessee of the property and who has the permission of a parent or legal guardian or the owner, licensee, or lessee to possess a firearm not otherwise in violation of law.

(6) Any resident or nonresident hunters with a valid hunting license or other persons who are lawfully engaged in hunting.

(7) Any person traveling to or from any activity described in Subsection (2), (3), (4), (5), or (6) with an unloaded firearm in his possession.   2000

76-10-513, 76-10-513.5. Renumbered as §§ 53-5-704 and 53-5-705.   1993

76-10-514. Repealed.   1986

76-10-515 to 76-10-518. Renumbered as §§ 53-5-706 to 53-5-709.   1993

76-10-519. Repealed.   1977

76-10-520. Number or mark assigned to pistol or revolver by Department of Public Safety.

The Department of Public Safety upon request may assign a distinguishing number or mark of identification to any pistol or revolver whenever it is without a manufacturer's number, or other mark of identification or whenever the manufacturer's number or other mark of identification or the distinguishing number or mark assigned by the Department of Public Safety has been destroyed or obliterated.   1993

76-10-521. Unlawful marking of pistol or revolver.

(1) Any person who places or stamps on any pistol or revolver any number except one assigned to it by the Department of Public Safety is guilty of a class A misdemeanor.

(2) This section does not prohibit restoration by the owner of the name of the maker, model, or of the original manufacturer's number or other mark of identification when the restoration is authorized by the Department of Public Safety, nor prevent any manufacturer from placing in the ordinary course of business the name of the make, model, manufacturer's number, or other mark of identification upon a new pistol or revolver.   1993

76-10-522. Alteration of number or mark on pistol or revolver.

Any person who changes, alters, removes, or obliterates the name of the maker, the model, manufacturer's number, or other mark of identification, including any distinguishing number or mark assigned by the Department of Public Safety, on any pistol or revolver, without first having secured written permission from the Department of Public Safety to make the change, alteration, or removal, is guilty of a class A misdemeanor.   1993

76-10-523. Persons exempt from weapons laws.

(1) This part and Title 53, Chapter 5, Part 7, Concealed Weapon Act, do not apply to any of the following:

(a) a United States marshal;

(b) a federal official required to carry a firearm;

(c) a peace officer of this or any other jurisdiction;

(d) a law enforcement official as defined and qualified under Section 53-5-711;

(e) a judge as defined and qualified under Section 53-5-711;

(f) a common carrier while engaged in the regular and ordinary transport of firearms as merchandise; or

(g) a nonresident traveling in or through the state, provided that any firearm is:

(i) unloaded; and

(ii) securely encased as defined in Section 76-10-501.

(2) The provisions of Subsections 76-10-504(1)(a), (1)(b), and Section 76-10-505 do not apply to any person to whom a permit to carry a concealed firearm has been issued:

(a) pursuant to Section 53-5-704; or

(b) by another state or county.   2003

76-10-523.5. Compliance with rules for secure facilities.

Any person, including a person licensed to carry a concealed firearm under Title 53, Chapter 5, Part 7, Concealed Weapons, shall comply with any rule established for secure facilities pursuant to Sections 53B-3-103, 76-8-311.1, 76-8-311.3, and 78-7-6 and shall be subject to any penalty provided in those sections.   2002

76-10-524. Purchase of firearms pursuant to federal law.

This part will allow purchases of firearms and ammunition pursuant to U.S.C. Title 18 Chapter 44 Sec. 922b(3).   2004

76-10-525. Disposition of weapons after use for court purposes.

All police departments and/or sheriff's departments which have in their possession a weapon after it has been used for court purposes shall determine the true owner of the weapon and return it to him; however, if unable to determine the true owner of the weapon, or if the true owner is the person committing the crime for which the weapon was used as evidence, the department shall confiscate it and it shall revert to that agency for their use and/or disposal as the head of the department determines.   1973

76-10-526. Criminal background check prior to purchase of a firearm — Fee — Exemption for concealed firearm permit holders.

(1) For purposes of this section, "valid permit to carry a concealed firearm" does not include a temporary permit issued pursuant to Section 53-5-705.

(2) To establish personal identification and residence in this state for purposes of this part, a dealer shall require an individual receiving a firearm to present one photo identification on a form issued by a governmental agency of the state.

(3) A criminal history background check is required for the sale of a firearm by a licensed firearm dealer in the state.

(4) (a) An individual, except a dealer, purchasing a firearm from a dealer shall consent in writing to a criminal background check, on a form provided by the division.

(b) The form shall contain the following information:

(i) the dealer identification number;

(ii) the name and address of the individual receiving the firearm;

(iii) the date of birth, height, weight, eye color, and hair color of the individual receiving the firearm; and

(iv) the Social Security number or any other identification number of the individual receiving the firearm.

(5) (a) The dealer shall send the form required by Subsection (4) to the division immediately upon its completion.

(b) No dealer shall sell or transfer any firearm to an individual until the dealer has provided the division with the information in Subsection (4) and has received approval from the division under Subsection (7).

(6) The dealer shall make a request for criminal history background information by telephone or other electronic means to the division and shall receive approval or denial of the inquiry by telephone or other electronic means.

(7) When the dealer calls for or requests a criminal history background check, the division shall:

(a) review the criminal history files, including juvenile court records, to determine if the individual is prohibited from purchasing, possessing, or transferring a firearm by state or federal law;

(b) inform the dealer that:

(i) the records indicate the individual is so prohibited; or

(ii) the individual is approved for purchasing, possessing, or transferring a firearm;

(c) provide the dealer with a unique transaction number for that inquiry; and

(d) provide a response to the requesting dealer during the call for a criminal background, or by return call, or other electronic means, without delay, except in case of electronic failure or other circumstances beyond the control of the division, the division shall advise the dealer of the reason for the delay and give the dealer an estimate of the length of the delay.

(8) (a) The division shall not maintain any records of the criminal history background check longer than 20 days from the date of the dealer's request if the division determines that the individual receiving the gun is not prohibited from purchasing, possessing, or transferring the firearm under state or federal law.

(b) However, the division shall maintain a log of requests containing the dealer's federal firearms number, the transaction number, and the transaction date for a period of 12 months.

(9) If the criminal history background check discloses information indicating that the individual attempting to purchase the firearm is prohibited from purchasing, possessing, or transferring a firearm, the division shall inform the law enforcement agency in the jurisdiction where the person resides.

(10) If an individual is denied the right to purchase a firearm under this section, the individual may review his criminal history information and may challenge or amend the information as provided in Section 53-10-108.

(11) The division shall make rules as provided in Title 63, Chapter 46a, Utah Administrative Rulemaking Act, to ensure the identity, confidentiality, and security of all records provided by the division pursuant to this part are in conformance with the requirements of the Brady Handgun Violence Prevention Act, Pub. L. No. 103-159, 107 Stat. 1536 (1993).

(12) (a) (i) All dealers shall collect a criminal history background check fee which is $7.50.

(ii) This fee remains in effect until changed by the division through the process under Section 63-38-3.2.

(b) (i) The dealer shall forward at one time all fees collected for criminal history background checks performed during the month to the division by the last day of the month following the sale of a firearm.

(ii) The division shall deposit the fees in the General Fund as dedicated credits to cover the cost of administering and conducting the criminal history background check program.

(13) An individual with a concealed firearm permit issued pursuant to Title 53, Chapter 5, Part 7, Concealed Weapon Act, shall be exempt from the background check and corresponding fee required in this section for the purchase of a firearm if:

(a) the individual presents his concealed firearm permit to the dealer prior to purchase of the firearm; and

(b) the dealer verifies with the division that the individual's concealed firearm permit is valid.

2004

76-10-527.   Penalties.

(1) This section shall apply only to a handgun until federal law requires the background check in Section 76-10-526 to extend to other firearms at which time this section shall also apply to those firearms.

(2) A dealer is guilty of a class A misdemeanor who willfully and intentionally:

(a) requests, obtains, or seeks to obtain criminal history background information under false pretenses; or

(b) disseminates criminal history background information.

(3) A person who purchases or transfers a firearm is guilty of a felony of the third degree who willfully and intentionally makes a false statement of the information required for a criminal background check in Section 76-10-526.

(4) A dealer is guilty of a felony of the third degree if the dealer willfully and intentionally sells or transfers a firearm in violation of this part.

(5) A person is guilty of a felony of the third degree who purchases a firearm with the intent to:

(a) resell or otherwise provide a firearm to any person who is ineligible to purchase or receive from a dealer a firearm; or

(b) transport a firearm out of this state to be resold to an ineligible person.   1998

76-10-528.   Carrying a dangerous weapon while under influence of alcohol or drugs unlawful.

(1) Any person who carries a dangerous weapon while under the influence of alcohol or a controlled substance as defined in Section 58-37-2 is guilty of a class B misdemeanor. Under the influence means the same level of influence or blood or breath alcohol concentration as provided in Subsections 41-6a-502(1)(a)(i) through (iii).

(2) It is not a defense to prosecution under this section that the person:

(a) is licensed in the pursuit of wildlife of any kind; or

(b) has a valid permit to carry a concealed firearm.   2005

76-10-529.   Possession of dangerous weapons, firearms, or explosives in airport secure areas prohibited — Penalty.

(1) As used in this section:

(a) "Airport authority" has the same meaning as defined in Section 72-10-102.

(b) "Dangerous weapon" is the same as defined in Section 76-10-501.

(c) "Explosive" is the same as defined for "explosive, chemical, or incendiary device" in Section 76-10-306.

(d) "Firearm" is the same as defined in Section 76-10-501.

(2) (a) Within a secure area of an airport established pursuant to this section, a person, including a person licensed to carry a concealed firearm under Title 53, Chapter 5, Part 7, Concealed Weapon Act, is guilty of:

(i) a class A misdemeanor if the person knowingly or intentionally possesses any dangerous weapon or firearm;

(ii) an infraction if the person recklessly or with criminal negligence possesses any dangerous weapon or firearm; or

(iii) a violation of Section 76-10-306 if the person transports, possesses, distributes, or sells any explosive, chemical, or incendiary device.

(b) Subsection (2)(a) does not apply to:

(i) persons exempted under Section 76-10-523; and

(ii) members of the state or federal military forces while engaged in the performance of their official duties.

(3) An airport authority, county, or municipality regulating the airport may:

(a) establish any secure area located beyond the main area where the public generally buys tickets, checks and retrieves luggage; and

(b) use reasonable means, including mechanical, electronic, x-ray, or any other device, to detect dangerous weapons, firearms, or explosives concealed in baggage or upon the person of any individual attempting to enter the secure area.

(4) At least one notice shall be prominently displayed at each entrance to a secure area in which a dangerous weapon, firearm, or explosive is restricted.

(5) Upon the discovery of any dangerous weapon, firearm, or explosive, the airport authority, county, or municipality, the employees, or other personnel administering the secure area may:

(a) require the individual to deliver the item to the air freight office or airline ticket counter;

(b) require the individual to exit the secure area; or

(c) obtain possession or retain custody of the item until it is transferred to law enforcement officers.   2004

76-10-530. Trespass with a firearm in a house of worship or private residence — Notice — Penalty.

(1) A person, including a person licensed to carry a concealed firearm pursuant to Title 53, Chapter 5, Part 7, Concealed Weapon Act, after notice has been given as provided in Subsection (2) that firearms are prohibited, may not knowingly and intentionally:

(a) transport a firearm into:

(i) a house of worship; or

(ii) a private residence; or

(b) while in possession of a firearm, enter or remain in:

(i) a house of worship; or

(ii) a private residence.

(2) Notice that firearms are prohibited may be given by:

(a) personal communication to the actor by:

(i) the church or organization operating the house of worship;

(ii) the owner, lessee, or person with lawful right of possession of the private residence; or

(iii) a person with authority to act for the person or entity in Subsections (2)(a)(i) and (ii);

(b) posting of signs reasonably likely to come to the attention of persons entering the house of worship or private residence;

(c) announcement, by a person with authority to act for the church or organization operating the house of worship, in a regular congregational meeting in the house of worship;

(d) publication in a bulletin, newsletter, worship program, or similar document generally circulated or available to the members of the congregation regularly meeting in the house of worship; or

(e) publication in a newspaper of general circulation in the county in which the house of worship is located or the church or organization operating the house of worship has its principal office in this state.

(3) A church or organization operating a house of worship and giving notice that firearms are prohibited may:

(a) revoke the notice, with or without supersedure, by giving further notice in any manner provided in Subsection (2); and

(b) provide or allow exceptions to the prohibition as the church or organization considers advisable.

(4) (a) (i) Within 30 days of giving or revoking any notice pursuant to Subsection (2)(c), (d), or (e), a church or organization operating a house of worship shall notify the division on a form and in a manner as the division shall prescribe.

(ii) The division shall post on its website a list of the churches and organizations operating houses of worship who have given notice under Subsection (4)(a)(i).

(b) Any notice given pursuant to Subsection (2)(c), (d), or (e) shall remain in effect until revoked or for a period of one year from the date the notice was originally given, whichever occurs first.

(5) Nothing in this section permits an owner who has granted the lawful right of possession to a renter or lessee to restrict the renter or lessee from lawfully possessing a firearm in the residence.

(6) A violation of this section is an infraction.   2003

76-10-531. Repealed.   2002

PART 6

CHARITY DRIVES

76-10-601. Definitions.

As used in this part:

(1) "Person" means any individual, organization, group, association, partnership, corporation, or any combination of them;

(2) "Professional fund raiser" means any person who for compensation or any other consideration plans, conducts, or manages in this state, the solicitation of contributions for or on behalf of any charitable organization or any other person, or who engages in the business of, or holds himself out to persons in this state as independently engaged in the business of soliciting contributions for such purpose, but shall not include a bona fide officer or employee of a charitable organization;

(3) "Professional solicitor" means any person who is employed or retained for compensation by a professional fund raiser to solicit contributions in this state for charitable purposes;

(4) "Charitable organization" means any organization that is benevolent, philanthropic, patriotic, or eleemosynary or one purporting to be such;

(5) "Contribution" means the promise or grant of any money or property of any kind or value.   1973

76-10-602. Use of person's name without consent for soliciting contributions prohibited — Exception.

No charitable organization, professional fund raiser, or professional solicitor, seeking to raise funds for charitable purposes, shall use the name of any other person for the purpose of soliciting contributions, in this state, without written consent of the person; provided that this section shall not apply to religious corporations or organizations, charities, agencies, and organizations operated, supervised, or controlled by or in connection with a religious corporation or organization.   1973

76-10-603. Use of name without consent on stationery or as one who contributed to organization prohibited.

It is a violation of this part to use, without written consent, the name of a person for the purpose of soliciting contributions if the person's name is listed on any stationery, advertisement, brochure, or correspondence of a charitable organization, or his name is listed or referred to as one who has contributed to, sponsored, or endorsed the charitable organization or its activities.   1995

76-10-604. Violations — Classification of offense.

Any person who violates the provisions of this part is guilty of a class B misdemeanor.   1995

PART 7

CORPORATION FRAUDS

76-10-701. Definitions.

As used in this part:

(1) "Bona fide stockholder of record" means a stockholder of record who has acquired stock in good faith and is acting for a proper purpose reasonably related to his interests as a stockholder.

(2) "Director" means any of the persons having by law the direction or management of the affairs of a corporation, by whatever name the persons are described in its charter or known by law.   1973

76-10-702. Fraudulent signing of stock subscriptions.

Every person who signs the name of a fictitious person to any subscription for, or agreement to take, stock in any corporation existing or proposed, and every person who signs to any subscription or agreement the name of any person, knowing that the person has no means or does not intend in good faith to comply with all the terms thereof, or under any understanding or agreement that the terms of the subscription or agreement are not to be complied with or enforced, is guilty of a class B misdemeanor.   1973

76-10-703. Fraudulent documents relating to organization or increase of capital stock.

Every officer, agent, or clerk of any corporation, or any person proposing to organize a corporation, or to increase the capital stock of any corporation, who knowingly exhibits any false, forged, or altered book, paper, voucher, security, or other instrument of evidence to any public officer or board authorized by law to examine the organization of the corporation, or to investigate its affairs, or to allow an increase of its capital, with intent to deceive the officer or board in respect thereto, shall be guilty of a felony of the third degree.   1973

76-10-704. Misrepresenting person as officer, agent, member or promoter.

Every person who, without being authorized so to do, subscribes the name of another to, or inserts the name of another in, any prospectus, circular, or other advertisement or announcement of any corporation or joint stock association, existing or intended to be formed, with intent to permit it to be published, and thereby to lead persons to believe that the person

whose name is so subscribed is an officer, agent, member, or promoter of such corporation or association, is guilty of a class B misdemeanor.   1973

76-10-705. Concurrence by director in dividend or division of capital in violation of law.

Every director of any stock corporation except savings and loan or building and loan associations who concurs in any vote or act of the directors of the corporation or any of them, by which it is intended either:

(1) to make any dividend except as permitted by Title 16, Chapter 10a, Utah Revised Business Corporation Act; or

(2) to divide, withdraw, or in any manner pay to the stockholders, or any of them, any part of the stated capital of the corporation except as permitted by Title 16, Chapter 10a, Utah Revised Business Corporation Act,

is guilty of a class B misdemeanor.   1992 (3rd S.S.)

76-10-706. Unlawful acts by director, officer or agent.

Every director, officer, or agent of any corporation or association who knowingly receives or possesses himself of any property of such corporation or association, otherwise than in payment of a just demand, and who, with intent to defraud, omits to make, or to cause or direct to be made, a full and true entry thereof in the books or accounts of the corporation or association; and every director, officer, agent, or member of any corporation or association who embezzles, abstracts, or willfully misapplies any of the money, funds, or credits of the corporation or association; or who, without authority from the directors, issues or puts in circulation any of the notes of the corporation or association; or who, without the authority, issues or puts forth any certificate of deposit, draws any order or bill of exchange, makes any acceptance, assigns any note, bond, draft, bill of exchange, mortgage, judgment, or decree; or who makes any false entry in any book, report, or statement of the corporation or association; or who issues any fraudulent, fictitious, or illegal stock in any such corporation or association, with intent in either case to injure or defraud the corporation or association, or any other company, body politic, or corporate, or any individual person, or to deceive any officer of the corporation or association, or any agent appointed to examine the affairs of any such corporation or association; and every person who, with like intent, aids or abets any officer, clerk, or agent in any violation of this section is guilty of a felony of the third degree.   1973

76-10-707. False reports.

Every director, officer, or agent of any corporation or joint stock association who knowingly makes or concurs in making or publishing any written report, exhibit, or statement of its affairs or pecuniary condition, containing any material statement which is false is guilty of a class B misdemeanor.   1973

76-10-708. Refusing inspection of books.

Every officer or agent of any corporation having or keeping an office within this state, who has in his custody or control the books of such corporation, and who refuses to give to a bona fide stockholder of record or member of the corporation, lawfully demanding during office hours, the right to inspect or take a copy of it or of any part thereof, is guilty of a class B misdemeanor.   1973

76-10-709. Presumption of director's knowledge of affairs.

Every director of a corporation or joint stock association is deemed to possess a knowledge of the affairs of his corporation as to enable him to determine whether any act, proceeding, or omission of its directors is a violation of this part. 1995

76-10-710. Presumption of director's concurrence in action if present at meeting — Written dissent required.

Every director of a corporation or joint stock association who is present at a meeting of the directors at which any act, proceeding, or omission of the directors in violation of this part occurs is deemed to have concurred therein, unless he at the time causes, or in writing requires, his dissent therefrom to be entered in the minutes of the directors or forwards his dissent by registered mail to the secretary of the corporation immediately after the adjournment of the meeting. 1973

76-10-711. Foreign corporations subject to laws.

It is no defense to a prosecution for a violation of any of the provisions of this part that the corporation was one created by the laws of another state, government, or country if it was one carrying on business or keeping an office therefor within this state. 1995

PART 8

NUISANCES

76-10-801. "Nuisance" defined — Violation — Classification of offense.

(1) A nuisance is any item, thing, manner, condition whatsoever that is dangerous to human life or health or renders soil, air, water, or food impure or unwholesome.

(2) Any person, whether as owner, agent, or occupant who creates, aids in creating, or contributes to a nuisance, or who supports, continues, or retains a nuisance, is guilty of a class B misdemeanor. 1973

76-10-802. Befouling waters.

A person is guilty of a class B misdemeanor if he:

(1) Constructs or maintains a corral, sheep pen, goat pen, stable, pigpen, chicken coop, or other offensive yard or outhouse where the waste or drainage therefrom shall flow directly into the waters of any stream, well, or spring of water used for domestic purposes; or

(2) Deposits, piles, unloads, or leaves any manure heap, offensive rubbish, or the carcass of any dead animal where the waste or drainage therefrom will flow directly into the waters of any stream, well, or spring of water used for domestic purposes; or

(3) Dips or washes sheep in any stream, or constructs, maintains, or uses any pool or dipping vat for dipping or washing sheep in such close proximity to any stream used by the inhabitants of any city or town for domestic purposes as to make the waters thereof impure or unwholesome; or

(4) Constructs or maintains any corral, yard, or vat to be used for the purpose of shearing or dipping sheep within twelve miles of any city or town, where the refuse or filth from the corral or yard would naturally find its way into any stream of water used by the inhabitants of any city or town for domestic purposes; or

(5) Establishes and maintains any corral, camp, or bedding place for the purpose of herding, holding, or keeping any cattle, horses, sheep, goats, or hogs within seven miles of any city or town, where the refuse or filth from the corral, camp, or bedding place will naturally find its way into any stream of water used by the inhabitants of any city or town for domestic purposes. 1973

76-10-803. "Public nuisance" defined — Agricultural operations.

(1) A public nuisance is a crime against the order and economy of the state and consists in unlawfully doing any act or omitting to perform any duty, which act or omission:

(a) annoys, injures, or endangers the comfort, repose, health, or safety of three or more persons;

(b) offends public decency;

(c) unlawfully interferes with, obstructs, or tends to obstruct, or renders dangerous for passage, any lake, stream, canal, or basin, or any public park, square, street, or highway;

(d) is a nuisance as defined in Section 78-38-9; or

(e) in any way renders three or more persons insecure in life or the use of property.

(2) An act which affects three or more persons in any of the ways specified in this section is still a nuisance regardless of the extent to which the annoyance or damage inflicted on individuals is unequal.

(3) (a) Agricultural operations that are consistent with sound agricultural practices are presumed to be reasonable and do not constitute a public nuisance under Subsection (1) unless the agricultural operation has a substantial adverse effect on the public health and safety.

(b) Agricultural operations undertaken in conformity with federal, state, and local laws and regulations, including zoning ordinances, are presumed to be operating within sound agricultural practices. 2002

76-10-804. Maintaining, committing or failing to remove public nuisance — Classification of offense.

Every person who maintains or commits any public nuisance, the punishment for which is not otherwise prescribed, or who willfully omits to perform any legal duty relating to the removal of a public nuisance, is guilty of a class B misdemeanor. 1973

76-10-805. Carcass or offal — Prohibitions relating to disposal — Classification of offense.

Every person who puts the carcass of any dead animal, or the offal from any slaughter pen, corral, or butcher shop into any river, creek, pond, street, alley, or public highway, or road in common use, or who attempts to destroy it by fire, within one-fourth of a mile of any city or town is guilty of a class B misdemeanor. 1973

76-10-806. Action for abatement of public nuisance.

The county attorney of the county where the public nuisance exists, upon direction of the county executive, or city attorney of the city where the public nuisance exists, upon direction of the board of city commissioners, or attorney general, upon direction of the governor, or any of the above attorneys without the necessity of direction, is empowered to institute an action in the name of the county, city, or state, as the case may be, to abate a public nuisance. The action shall be brought in the district court of the district where the public nuisance exists and shall be in the form prescribed by the Rules of Civil Procedure of the State of Utah for injunctions, but none of the above attorneys shall be required to execute a bond with respect to the action. If the action is instituted, however, to abate the distribution or exhibition of material alleged to offend public decency, the action shall be in the form prescribed by the Rules of Civil Procedure of Utah for injunctions, but no restraining order or injunction shall issue except upon notice to the person sought to be enjoined; and that person shall be entitled to a trial of the issues commencing within three days after filing of an answer to the complaint and a decision shall be rendered by the court within two days after the conclusion of the trial. As used in this part, "distribute," "exhibit," and "material" mean the same as provided in Section 76-10-1201.   1993

76-10-807. Reserved.

76-10-808. Relief granted for public nuisance.

If the existence of a public nuisance as defined by Subsection 76-10-803(1)(b) is admitted or established, either in a civil or criminal proceeding, a judgment shall be entered which shall:

(a) Permanently enjoin each defendant and any other person from further maintaining the nuisance at the place complained of and each defendant from maintaining such nuisance elsewhere;

(b) Direct the person enjoined to surrender to the sheriff of the county in which the action was brought any material in his possession which is subject to the injunction, and the sheriff shall seize and destroy this material; and

(c) Without proof of special injury direct that an accounting be had and all monies and other consideration paid as admission to view any motion picture film determined to constitute a public nuisance, or paid for any publication determined to constitute a public nuisance, in either case without deduction for expenses, be forfeited and paid into the general fund of the county where the nuisance was maintained.   1977

PART 9

TRADE AND COMMERCE

76-10-901. "Junk dealer" and "scrap metal processor" defined.

For the purpose of this part:

(1) "Junk dealer" means all persons, firms, or corporations engaged in the business of purchasing or selling secondhand, or castoff material of any kind, such as old iron, copper, brass, lead, zinc, tin, steel, aluminum, and other metals, metallic cables, wires, ropes, cordage, bottles, bagging, rags, rubber, paper, and other like materials.

(2) "Scrap metal processor" means any person who, from a fixed location, utilizes machinery and equipment for processing and manufacturing iron, steel, or nonferrous scrap into prepared grades, and whose principal product is scrap iron, scrap steel, or nonferrous metallic scrap, not including precious metals, for sale for remelting purposes.   1993

76-10-902. Fraudulent practices to affect market price.

Every person who willfully makes or publishes any false statement, spreads any false rumor, or employs any other false or fraudulent means or device, with intent to affect the market price of any kind of property, is guilty of a class B misdemeanor.   1973

76-10-903. Unfair discrimination in competitive practices.

Every person engaged in the production, manufacture, or distribution of any commodity in general use who intentionally for the purpose of destroying the competition of any regular, established dealer in such commodity, or to prevent the competition of any person who in good faith intends and attempts to become a dealer, discriminates between different sections, communities, or cities of this state by selling the commodity at a lower rate in one section, community, or city, or any portion thereof, than the person charges for the commodity in another section, community, or city, after equalizing the distance from the point of production, manufacture, or distribution and freight rates therefrom, is guilty of unfair discrimination.   1973

76-10-904. Corporation guilty of unfair discrimination — Action by attorney general.

If complaint is made to the attorney general that any corporation is guilty of unfair discrimination as defined by the preceding section, he shall investigate the complaint, and for that purpose, he may subpoena witnesses, administer oaths, take testimony, and require the production of books or other documents, and, if in his opinion sufficient grounds exist therefor, he may prosecute an action in the name of the state in the proper court to annul the charter or revoke the license of the corporation, as the case may be, and to permanently enjoin the corporation from doing business in this state, and, if in the action the court finds that the corporation is guilty of unfair discrimination as defined by the preceding section, the court shall annul the charter or revoke the license of the corporation and may permanently enjoin it from transacting business in this state.   1973

76-10-905. Penalty for violation.

Any person, firm, or corporation violating any of the provisions of this part shall be fined not less than $500 nor more than $4,000 for each offense.   1973

76-10-906. Unfair discrimination by buyer of milk, cream or butterfat — Classification of offense.

Any person doing business in this state and engaged in the business of buying milk, cream, or butterfat for the purpose of sale or storage, who, for the purpose of creating a monopoly or destroying the business of a competitor, discriminates between different sections, communities, localities, cities, or towns of this state by purchasing the commodity or commodities at a higher price or rate in one section, community, location, city, or town than is paid for the same commodity by the person in another section, community, locality, city, or town, after making due allowance for the difference, if any, in the grade or quality, and in the actual cost of transportation from the point of purchase to the point of manufacture, sale, or storage, is guilty of unfair discrimination, which is hereby prohibited and declared to be unlawful; and any person, firm, company, association, or corporation, or any officer, agent, receiver, or member of such firm, company, association, or corporation, found guilty of unfair discrimination as herein defined shall be guilty of a class B misdemeanor.   1991

76-10-907. Records of sales and purchases — Identification required.

(1) Every junk dealer and scrap metal processor shall keep a receipt book in which shall be recorded for each purchase and sale, in ink in the English language:

(a) a complete description of the property, including weight and metallic description if scrap metal;

(b) the full name and residence of the person or persons selling the junk or scrap metal;

(c) the vehicle type and license plate number, if applicable;

(d) the price per pound and the amount paid for each type of metal or junk purchased;

(e) the date and place of the purchase or sale; and

(f) the type and number of identification provided in Subsection (2)(a).

(2) In addition, the seller shall be required by the junk dealer or scrap metal processor to provide:

(a) at least one form of picture identification to consummate the transaction; and

(b) his signature on a certificate stating that he has the legal right to sell the scrap metal or junk.

(3) No entry in the receipt book may be erased, mutilated, or changed.

(4) The receipt book and entries shall at all times be open to inspection by the following officials in the area in which the junk dealer or scrap metal processor does business:

(a) the sheriff of the county or any of his deputies;

(b) any member of the police force in the city or town; and

(c) any constable or other state, municipal, or county official in the county in which the junk dealer or scrap metal processor does business.

(5) This section shall not apply to any sale or purchase if the value given is less than $20.   1993

76-10-908. Violation by junk dealer — Classification of offense — Local regulation not impaired.

Any junk dealer who is found guilty of a violation of any of the provisions of this part is guilty of a class B misdemeanor; provided that this part shall not be construed to in any way impair the power of counties, cities, or incorporated municipalities in this state to license, tax, and regulate any junk dealer.   1995

76-10-909. Junk dealer to obtain statement from sellers.

At the time of purchase by any junk dealer of any copper wire, pig, or pigs of metal or of any junk, as defined in this part, he shall obtain a signed and dated statement from the person or persons selling it as to when, where, and from whom the property was obtained and also the residence, address, and place of employment of the seller or sellers. The statement shall be retained for five years by the junk dealer and shall be subject to the provisions of section 76-10-907 relating to erasure, mutilation, or change and also to inspection.   1995

76-10-910. Falsification of seller's statement to junk dealer.

Any seller who, in making his statement as contemplated by this part in selling, offering, or trying to sell junk willfully makes a false statement or gives untrue information, shall be guilty of a class B misdemeanor.   1995

76-10-911. Antitrust Act — Short title.

This act shall be known, and may be cited, as the "Utah Antitrust Act."   1979

76-10-912. Legislative findings — Purpose of act.

The Legislature finds and determines that competition is fundamental to the free market system and that the unrestrained interaction of competitive forces will yield the best allocation of our economic resources, the lowest prices, the highest quality and the greatest material progress, while at the same time providing an environment conducive to the preservation of our democratic, political and social institutions.

The purpose of this act is, therefore, to encourage free and open competition in the interest of the general welfare and economy of this state by prohibiting monopolistic and unfair trade practices, combinations and conspiracies in restraint of trade or commerce and by providing adequate penalties for the enforcement of its provisions.   1979

76-10-913. Definitions.

As used in this act:

(1) "Attempt to monopolize" means action taken without a legitimate business purpose and with a specific intent of destroying competition or controlling prices to substantially lessen competition, or creating a monopoly, where there is a dangerous probability of creating a monopoly.

(2) "Commodity" includes any product of the soil, any article of merchandise or trade or commerce, and any other kind of real or personal property.

(3) "Manufacturer" means the producer or originator of any commodity or service.

(4) "Service" includes any activity that is performed in whole or in part for the purpose of financial gain including, but not limited to, personal service, professional service, rental, leasing or licensing for use.

(5) "Trade or commerce" includes all economic activity involving, or relating to, any commodity, service, or business activity, including the cost of exchange or transportation.   1979

76-10-914. Illegal anticompetitive activities.

(1) Every contract, combination in the form of trust or otherwise, or conspiracy in restraint of trade or commerce is declared to be illegal.

(2) It shall be unlawful for any person to monopolize, or attempt to monopolize, or combine or conspire with any other person or persons to monopolize, any part of trade or commerce.   1979

76-10-915. Exempt activities.

(1) No provision of this act shall be construed to prohibit:

(a) the activities of any public utility to the extent that those activities are subject to regulation by the public service commission, the state or federal department of transportation, the federal energy regulatory commission, the federal communications commission, the interstate commerce commission, or successor agencies;

(b) the activities of any insurer, insurance producer, independent insurance adjuster or rating organization including, but not limited to, making or participating in joint underwriting or reinsurance arrangements, to the extent that those activities are subject to regulation by the commissioner of insurance;

(c) the activities of securities dealers, issuers or agents, to the extent that those activities are subject to regulation under the laws of either this state or the United States;

(d) the activities of any state or national banking institution, to the extent that such activities are regulated or supervised by state government officers or agencies under the banking laws of this state or by federal government officers or agencies under the banking laws of the United States;

(e) the activities of any state or federal savings and loan association to the extent that those activities are regulated or supervised by state government officers or agencies under the banking laws of this state or federal government officers or agencies under the banking laws of the United States;

(f) the activities of a municipality to the extent authorized or directed by state law; or

(g) the activities of an emergency medical service provider licensed under Title 26, Chapter 8a, Utah Emergency Medical Service System Act, to the extent that those activities are regulated by state government officers or agencies under that act.

(2) The labor of a human being is not a commodity or article of commerce. Nothing contained in the antitrust laws shall be construed to forbid the existence and operation of labor, agricultural or horticultural organizations, instituted for the purpose of mutual help and not having capital stock or conducted for profit, or to forbid or restrain individual members of such organizations from lawfully carrying out the legitimate object thereof; nor shall such organizations or membership in them be held to be illegal combinations or conspiracies in restraint of trade under the antitrust laws.   2003

76-10-916. Attorney general's powers — Investigations — Institution of actions — Cooperation.

(1) The attorney general may investigate suspected violations of this act and institute appropriate actions regarding those suspected violations as provided in this act.

(2) Any violations of this act which come to the attention of any state government officer or agency shall be reported to the attorney general. All state government officers and agencies shall cooperate with, and assist in, any prosecution for violation of this act.

(3) The attorney general may proceed under any antitrust laws in the state or federal courts on behalf of this state, any of its political subdivisions or agencies, or as parens patriae on behalf of natural persons in this state.   1991

76-10-917. Civil antitrust investigations — Demand for production of documents and responses to written interrogatories — Oral examination — Judicial order for compliance — Confidentiality — Subpoenas precluded.

(1) When the attorney general has reasonable cause to believe that any person may be in possession, custody, or control of any information relevant to a civil antitrust investigation, he may, prior to the commencement of a civil action thereon, issue and cause to be served upon that person a written civil investigative demand requesting that person to:

(a) produce the documentary material for inspection, copying, or reproduction by the state where the documents are located or produced;

(b) give oral testimony under oath, concerning the subject of the investigation;

(c) respond to written interrogatories; or

(d) furnish any combination of these.

(2) (a) Each demand shall state:

(i) The nature of the activities under investigation, constituting the alleged antitrust violation, which may result in a violation of this act and the applicable provision of law;

(ii) that the recipient is entitled to counsel;

(iii) that the documents, materials, or testimony in response to the demand may be used in a civil or criminal proceeding;

(iv) that if the recipient does not comply with the demand the Office of the Attorney General may compel compliance by appearance, upon reasonable notice to the recipient, before the district court in the judicial district wherein the recipient resides or does business and only upon a showing before that district court that the requirements of Subsection (7) have been met;

(v) that the recipient has the right at any time before the return date of the demand, or within 30 days, whichever period is shorter, to seek a court order determining the validity of the demand; and

(vi) that at any time during the proceeding the person may assert any applicable privilege.

(b) If the demand is for production of documentary material, it shall also:

(i) describe the documentary material to be produced with sufficient definiteness and certainty as to permit the material to be fairly identified;

(ii) prescribe return dates that provide a reasonable period of time within which the material demanded may be assembled and made available for inspection and reproduction; and

(iii) identify the individual at the attorney general's office to whom the material shall be made available.

(c) If the demand is for the giving of oral testimony, it shall also:

(i) prescribe the date, time, and place at which oral testimony shall be commenced;

(ii) state that a member of the attorney general's office staff shall conduct the examination; and

(iii) state that the recording or the transcript of such examination shall be submitted to and maintained by the Office of the Attorney General.

(d) If the demand is for responses to written interrogatories, it shall also:

(i) state that each interrogatory shall be answered separately and fully in writing and under oath, unless the person objects to the interrogatory, in which event the reasons for objection shall be stated in lieu of an answer;

(ii) state that the answers are to be signed by the person making them, and the objections are to be signed by the attorney making them;

(iii) identify by name and address the individual at the Office of the Attorney General on whom answers and objections provided under this Subsection (2)(d) are to be served; and

(iv) prescribe the date on or before which these answers and objections are to be served on the identified individual.

(3) The civil investigative demand may be served upon any person who is subject to the jurisdiction of any Utah court and shall be served upon the person in the manner provided for service of a subpoena.

(4) (a) The documents submitted in response to a demand served under this section shall be accompanied by an affidavit, in the form the demand designates, by the person, if a natural person, to whom the demand is directed or, if not a natural person, by a person having knowledge of the facts and circumstances relating to the production.

(b) The affidavit shall state that all of the documentary material required by the demand and in the possession, custody, or control of the person to whom the demand is directed has in good faith been produced and made available to the Office of the Attorney General.

(c) The affidavit shall identify any demanded documents that are not produced and state the reason why each document was not produced.

(5) (a) The examination of any person pursuant to a demand for oral testimony served under this section shall be taken before an officer authorized to administer oaths or affirmations by the laws of the United States or of the place where the examination is held. The officer before whom the testimony is to be taken shall put the witness on oath or affirmation and shall personally, or by someone acting under his direction and in his presence, record the testimony of the witness. If the testimony is taken stenographically, it shall be transcribed and the officer before whom the testimony is taken shall promptly transmit the transcript of the testimony to the Office of the Attorney General.

(b) When taking oral testimony, all persons other than personnel from the attorney general's office, the witness, counsel for the witness, and the officer before whom the testimony is to be taken shall be excluded from the place where the examination is held.

(c) The oral testimony of any person taken pursuant to a demand served under this section shall be taken in the county where the person resides or transacts business or in any other place agreed upon by the attorney general and the person.

(d) When testimony is fully transcribed, the transcript shall be certified by the officer before whom the testimony was taken and submitted to the witness for examination and signing, in accordance with Rule 30(e) of the Utah Rules of Civil Procedure. A copy of the deposition shall be furnished free of charge to each witness upon his request.

(e) Any change in testimony recorded by nonstenographic means shall be made in the manner provided in Rule 30 of the Utah Rules of Civil Procedure for changing deposition testimony recorded by nonstenographic means.

(f) Any person compelled to appear under a demand for oral testimony under this section may be accompanied, represented, and advised by counsel. Counsel may advise the person, in confidence, either upon the request of the person or upon counsel's own initiative, with respect to any question asked of the person. The person or counsel may object on the record to any question, in whole or in part, and shall briefly state for the record the reason for the objection. An objection may properly be made, received, and entered upon the record when it is claimed that the person is entitled to refuse to answer the question on grounds of any constitutional or other legal right or privilege, including the privilege against self-incrimination. If the person refuses to answer any question, the attorney general may petition the district court for an order compelling the person to answer the question.

(g) If any person compelled to appear under a demand for oral testimony or other information pursuant to this section refuses to answer any questions or produce information on grounds of the privilege against self-incrimination, the testimony of that person may be compelled as in criminal cases.

(h) Any person appearing for oral examination pursuant to a demand served under this section is entitled to the same fees and mileage which are paid to witnesses in the district courts of the state of Utah. Witness fees and expenses shall be tendered and paid as in any civil action.

(6) The providing of any testimony, documents, or objects in response to a civil investigative demand issued pursuant to the provisions of this act shall be considered part of an official proceeding as defined in Section 76-8-501.

(7) (a) If a person fails to comply with the demand served upon him under this section, the attorney general may file in the district court of the county in which the person resides, is found, or does business, a petition for an order compelling compliance with the demand. Notice of hearing of the petition and a copy of the petition shall be served upon the person, who may appear in opposition to the petition. If the court finds that the demand is proper, that there is reasonable cause to believe there has been a violation of this act, and that the information sought or document or object demanded is relevant to the violation, it shall order the person to comply with the demand, subject to modifications the court may prescribe.

(b) (i) At any time before the return date specified in a demand or within 30 days after the demand has been served, whichever period is shorter, the person who has been served may file a petition for an order modifying or setting aside the demand. This petition shall be filed in the district court in the county of the person's residence, principal office, or place of business, or in the district court in Salt Lake County. The petition shall specify each ground upon which the petitioner relies in seeking the relief sought. The petition may be based upon any failure of the demand to comply with the provisions of this section or upon any constitutional or other legal right or privilege of the petitioner. The petitioner shall serve notice of hearing of the petition and a copy of the petition upon the attorney general. The attorney general may submit an answer to the petition within 30 days after receipt of the petition.

(ii) After hearing on the petition described in Subsection (7)(b)(i), and for good cause shown, the court may make any further order in the proceedings that justice requires to protect the person from unreasonable annoyance, embarrassment, oppression, burden, or expense. At any hearing pursuant to this section it is the attorney general's burden to establish that the demand is proper, that there is reasonable cause to believe that there has been a violation of this act, and that the information sought or document or object demanded is relevant to the violation.

(8) (a) Any procedure, testimony taken, or material produced under this section shall be kept confidential by the attorney general unless confidentiality is waived in writing by the person who has testified, or produced documents or objects.

(b) Notwithstanding any other provision of this section, the attorney general may disclose testimony or documents obtained under this section, without either the consent of the person from whom it was received or the person being investigated, to:

(i) any grand jury; and

(ii) officers and employees of federal or state law enforcement agencies, provided the person from whom the information, documents, or objects were obtained is notified 20 days prior to disclosure, and the federal or state law enforcement agency certifies that the information will be:

(A) maintained in confidence, as required by Subsection (8)(a); and

(B) used only for official law enforcement purposes.

(9) Use of a civil investigative demand under this action precludes the invocation by the attorney general of Section 77-22-2.   1999

76-10-918. Attorney general may bring action for injunctive relief, damages or civil penalty.

(1) The attorney general may bring an action for appropriate injunctive relief, and for damages or a civil penalty in the name of the state, any of its political subdivisions or agencies, or as parens patriae on behalf of natural persons in this state, for a violation of this act.

(2) Any individual who violates this act is subject to a civil penalty of not more than $100,000 for each violation. Any person, other than an individual, who violates this act is subject to a civil penalty of not more than $500,000 for each violation.   1991

76-10-919. Person may bring action for injunctive relief and damages — Treble damages — Recovery of actual damages or civil penalty by state or political subdivisions — Immunity of political subdivisions from damages, costs, or attorney's fees.

(1) (a) A person who is injured or is threatened with injury in his business or property by a violation of the Utah Antitrust Act may bring an action for injunctive relief and damages.

(b) Subject to the provisions of Subsections (3), (4), and (5), the court shall award three times the amount of damages sustained, plus the cost of suit and a reasonable attorney's fee, in addition to granting any appropriate temporary, preliminary, or permanent injunctive relief.

(2) (a) If the court determines that a judgment in the amount of three times the damages awarded plus attorney's fees and costs will directly cause the insolvency of the defendant, the court shall reduce the amount of judgment to the highest sum that would not cause the defendant's insolvency.

(b) The court may not reduce a judgment to an amount less than the amount of damages sus-

tained plus the costs of suit and a reasonable attorney's fee.

(3) The state or any of its political subdivisions may recover the actual damages it sustains, or the civil penalty provided by the Utah Antitrust Act, in addition to injunctive relief, costs of suit, and a reasonable attorney's fee.

(4) No damages, costs, or attorney's fee may be recovered under this section:

(a) from any political subdivision;

(b) from the official or employee of any political subdivision acting in an official capacity; or

(c) against any person based on any official action directed by a political subdivision or its official or employee acting in an official capacity.

(5) (a) Subsection (4) does not apply to cases filed before April 27, 1987, unless the defendant establishes and the court determines that in light of all the circumstances, including the posture of litigation and the availability of alternative relief, it would be inequitable not to apply Subsection (4) to a pending case.

(b) In determining the application of Subsection (4), existence of a jury verdict, court judgment, or any subsequent litigation is prima facie evidence that Subsection (4) is not applicable.   1987

76-10-920. Fine and imprisonment for violation — Certain vertical agreements excluded — Nolo contendere.

(1) (a) Any person who violates Section 76-10-914 by price fixing, bid rigging, agreeing among competitors to divide customers or territories, or by engaging in a group boycott with specific intent of eliminating competition shall be punished, notwithstanding Sections 76-3-301 and 76-3-302:

(i) if an individual, by a fine not to exceed $100,000 or by imprisonment for an indeterminate time not to exceed three years, or both; or

(ii) if by a person other than an individual, a fine not to exceed $500,000.

(b) Subsection (a) may not be construed to include vertical agreements between a manufacturer, its distributors, or their subdistributors dividing customers and territories solely involving the manufacturer's commodity or service where the manufacturer distributes its commodity or service both directly and through distributors or subdistributors in competition with itself.

(2) A defendant may plead nolo contendere to a charge brought under this title but only with the consent of the court. Such a plea shall be accepted by the court only after due consideration of the views of the parties and the interest of the public in the effective administration of justice.   1995

76-10-921. Conviction as prima facie evidence in action for injunctive relief or damages.

In any action brought by the state, a final judgment or decree determining that a person has criminally violated this act, other than a judgment entered pursuant to a nolo contendere plea or a decree entered prior to the taking of any testimony, shall be prima facie evidence against that person in any action brought pursuant to Section 76-10-919, as to all matters with respect to which the judgment or decree would be an estoppel between the parties thereto.   1979

76-10-922. Attorney General Litigation Fund.

(1) (a) There is created a special revenue fund known as the Attorney General Litigation Fund for the purpose of providing funds to pay for any costs and expenses incurred by the state attorney general in relation to actions under state or federal antitrust or criminal laws. These funds are in addition to other funds as may be appropriated by the Legislature to the attorney general for the administration and enforcement of the laws of this state.

(b) At the close of any fiscal year, any balance in the fund in excess of $2,000,000 shall be transferred to the General Fund.

(c) The attorney general may expend monies from the Attorney General Litigation Fund for the purposes in Subsection (1)(a).

(2) (a) All monies received by the state or its agencies by reason of any judgment, settlement, or compromise as the result of any action commenced, investigated, or prosecuted by the attorney general, after payment of any fines, restitution, payments, costs, or fees allocated by the court, shall be deposited in the Attorney General Litigation Fund, except as provided in Subsection (2)(b).

(b) (i) Any expenses advanced by the attorney general in any of the actions under Subsection (1)(a) shall be credited to the Attorney General Litigation Fund.

(ii) Any monies recovered by the attorney general on behalf of any private person or public body other than the state shall be paid to those persons or bodies from funds remaining after payment of expenses under Subsection (2)(b)(i).

(3) The Division of Finance shall transfer any monies remaining in the Antitrust Revolving Account on July 1, 2002, to the Attorney General Litigation Fund created in Subsection (1).   2002

76-10-923. Attorney general to advocate competition.

The attorney general shall have the authority and responsibility to advocate the policy of competition before all political subdivisions of this state and all public agencies whose actions may affect the interests of persons in this state.   1979

76-10-924. Venue of actions by state — Transfer.

Any action brought by the state pursuant to this act shall be brought in any county wherein the defendant resides or does business, or at the option of the defendant, such action shall be transferred, upon motion made within 30 days after commencement of the action, to Salt Lake County.   1979

76-10-925. Statute of limitations.

(1) Any action brought by the attorney general pursuant to this act is barred if it is not commenced within four years after the cause of action accrues.

(2) Any other action pursuant to this act is barred if it is not commenced within four years after the cause of action accrues, or within one year after the conclusion of an action brought by the state pursuant to this act based in whole or in part on any matter complained of in the subsequent action, whichever is the latter.   1979

76-10-926. Interpretation of act.

The Legislature intends that the courts, in construing this act, will be guided by interpretations given by the federal courts to comparable federal antitrust statutes and by other state courts to comparable state antitrust statutes.   1979

PART 10

TRADEMARKS, TRADE NAMES AND DEVICES

76-10-1001. Definitions.

For the purpose of this part:

(1) "Forged trademark," "forged trade name," "forged trade device," and "counterfeited trademark," "counterfeited trade name," "counterfeited trade device," or their equivalents, as used in this part, include every alteration or imitation of any trademark, trade name, or trade device so resembling the original as to be likely to deceive.

(2) "Trademark" or "trade name" or "trade device," as used in this part, includes every trademark registrable with the Division of Corporations and Commercial Code.   1984

76-10-1002. Forging or counterfeiting trademark, trade name or trade device.

Every person who willfully forges or counterfeits, or procures to be forged or counterfeited, any trademark, trade name, or trade device, usually affixed by any person, or by any association or union of workingmen, to his or its goods, which has been filed with the Division of Corporations and Commercial Code, with intent to pass off any goods to which the forged or counterfeited trademark, trade name, or trade device is affixed, or intended to be affixed, as the goods of the person or association or union of workingmen, is guilty of a class B misdemeanor.   1984

76-10-1003. Selling goods under counterfeited trademark, trade name or trade device.

Every person who sells or keeps for sale any goods upon or to which any counterfeited trademark, trade name, or trade device has been affixed, after it has been filed with the Division of Corporations and Commercial Code, intending to represent the goods as the genuine goods of another, knowing it to be counterfeited, is guilty of a class B misdemeanor.   1984

76-10-1004. Sales in containers bearing registered trademark of substituted articles.

Every person who has or uses any container or similar article bearing or having in any way connected with it the registered trademark of another for the purpose of disposing, with intent to deceive or defraud, of any article or substance other than that which the container or similar article originally contained or was connected with by the owner of such trademark is guilty of a class B misdemeanor.   1973

76-10-1005. Using, destroying, concealing or possessing articles with registered trademark or service mark to deprive owner of use or possession — Exception.

Every person who, without the consent of the owner of an article bearing the owner's validly registered trademark or service mark, uses, destroys, conceals, or possesses the article or who defaces or otherwise conceals the trademark or service mark upon the article with intent to deprive the owner of the use or possession of the article is guilty of a class B misdemeanor; provided, however, that nothing contained in this part shall be construed to apply to or restrict the transfer or use of wooden boxes or the re-use of burlap or cotton bags or sacks when those bags or sacks have been reversed inside out or the markings thereon have been concealed or obliterated to effectively demonstrate that the products contained therein do not purport to be the products of the owner of the registered trademark or service mark theretofore put upon those bags. 1995

76-10-1006. Selling or dealing with articles bearing registered trademark or service mark with intent to defraud.

Every person who, without the consent of the owner of an article bearing the owner's validly registered trademark or service mark, knowingly sells or traffics in the articles or who withholds the articles from the owner thereof with intent to defraud the owner thereof is guilty of a class B misdemeanor. 1973

76-10-1007. Use of registered trademark without consent.

Every person who adopts or in any way uses the registered trademark of another, without the consent of the owner thereof, is guilty of a class B misdemeanor. 1973

76-10-1008. Inspections by trade commission.

Subject to the provisions of Section 76-10-1009 of this part, the Utah State Trade Commission may, for purposes of enforcement of this part, inspect the premises of any business operating in this state during regular business hours. 1995

76-10-1009. Violation as unfair trade practice and unfair competition — Investigation and enforcement proceedings by trade commission.

Violation of a provision of this part is hereby declared to be an unfair trade practice and an unfair method of competition. The Utah State Trade Commission shall have jurisdiction over violations and may proceed against a violator as provided by the Trade Commission Act. The trade commission may institute an investigation upon receiving an informal complaint from a person who claims to have been injured by the violation of this part. Upon receiving a sworn complaint from a person claiming to be injured by a violation of this part, the trade commission must institute an investigation. If evidence of a violation is found by the commission or is produced by the complainant, the commission must take appropriate enforcement proceedings as provided in the Trade Commission Act. 1973

76-10-1010. Action by law enforcement agencies on complaints.

Nothing in this part providing for enforcement by the trade commission shall be construed to deprive law enforcement agencies from assuming jurisdiction and acting upon a proper complaint as provided by law. 1973

PART 11

GAMBLING

76-10-1101. Definitions.

For the purpose of this part:

(1) "Gambling" means risking anything of value for a return or risking anything of value upon the outcome of a contest, game, gaming scheme, or gaming device when the return or outcome is based upon an element of chance and is in accord with an agreement or understanding that someone will receive something of value in the event of a certain outcome, and gambling includes a lottery; gambling does not include:

(a) a lawful business transaction, or

(b) playing an amusement device that confers only an immediate and unrecorded right of replay not exchangeable for value.

(2) "Gambling bet" means money, checks, credit, or any other representation of value.

(3) "Gambling device or record" means anything specifically designed for use in gambling or used primarily for gambling.

(4) "Gambling proceeds" means anything of value used in gambling.

(5) "Lottery" means any scheme for the disposal or distribution of property by chance among persons who have paid or promised to pay any valuable consideration for the chance of obtaining property, or portion of it, or for any share or any interest in property, upon any agreement, understanding, or expectation that it is to be distributed or disposed of by lot or chance, whether called a lottery, raffle, or gift enterprise, or by whatever name it may be known.

(6) "Video gaming device" means any device that possesses all of the following characteristics:

(a) a video display and computer mechanism for playing a game;

(b) the length of play of any single game is not substantially affected by the skill, knowledge, or dexterity of the player;

(c) a meter, tracking, or recording mechanism that records or tracks any money, tokens, games, or credits accumulated or remaining;

(d) a play option that permits a player to spend or risk varying amounts of money, tokens, or credits during a single game, in which the spending or risking of a greater amount of money, tokens, or credits:

(i) does not significantly extend the length of play time of any single game; and

(ii) provides for a chance of greater return of credits, games, or money; and

(e) an operating mechanism that requires inserting money, tokens, or other valuable consideration in order to function. 1998

76-10-1102. Gambling.

(1) A person is guilty of gambling if he:

(a) participates in gambling;

(b) knowingly permits any gambling to be played, conducted, or dealt upon or in any real or personal property owned, rented, or under the control of the actor, whether in whole or in part; or

(c) knowingly allows the use of any video gaming device that is:

(i) in any business establishment or public place; and

(ii) accessible for use by any person within the establishment or public place.

(2) Gambling is a class B misdemeanor, provided, however, that any person who is twice convicted under this section shall be guilty of a class A misdemeanor. 1998

76-10-1103. Gambling fraud.

(1) A person is guilty of gambling fraud if he participates in gambling and wins or acquires to himself or another any gambling proceeds when he knows he has a lesser risk of losing or greater chance

of winning than one or more of the other participants, and the risk is not known to all participants.

(2) A person convicted of gambling fraud shall be punished as in the case of theft of property of like value. 1973

76-10-1104. Gambling promotion.

(1) A person is guilty of gambling promotion if he derives or intends to derive an economic benefit other than personal winnings from gambling and:

(a) he induces or aids another to engage in gambling; or

(b) he knowingly invests in, finances, owns, controls, supervises, manages, or participates in any gambling.

(2) Gambling promotion is a class B misdemeanor, provided, however, that any person who is twice convicted under this section shall be guilty of a felony of the third degree. 1991

76-10-1104.5. Advertisement or solicitation for participation in lotteries — Void in Utah.

(1) For purposes of this section:

(a) "Conspicuously printed" means printed in either larger or bolder type size than the adjacent and surrounding material so as to be clearly legible to any person viewing the print.

(b) "Lottery" means the same as defined in Section 76-10-1101.

(2) It is unlawful for any person to distribute or disseminate any advertisement or other written or printed material containing an advertisement or solicitation for participation in any lottery unless the advertisement or solicitation contains or includes the words "Void in Utah" conspicuously printed.

(3) (a) Any person who is convicted of violating Subsection (2) shall be fined the sum of $2,500.

(b) Any person who is twice or more convicted under this section shall be fined the sum of $10,000. 2001

76-10-1105. Possessing a gambling device or record.

(1) A person is guilty of possessing a gambling device or record if he knowingly possesses it with intent to use it in gambling.

(2) Possession of a gambling device or record is a class B misdemeanor, provided, however, that any person who is twice convicted under this section shall be guilty of a class A misdemeanor, and any person who is convicted three or more times under this section shall be guilty of a felony of the third degree. 1973

76-10-1106. Duty of prosecuting attorney or law enforcement officer to prosecute offenses.

All prosecuting attorneys, sheriffs, constables, and peace officers who have reasonable cause to believe any person has violated any provisions of this part shall diligently prosecute those persons. 1990

76-10-1107. Seizure and sale of devices or equipment used for gambling.

(1) Whenever any magistrate shall determine that any devices or equipment is used or kept for the purpose of being used for gambling, the magistrate may authorize the county commissioner of the county wherein the seizure occurred, in conjunction with the sheriff, or if the seizure occurred within the limits of an incorporated city or town, may authorize its governing body, in conjunction with its chief law enforcement officer, to seize the devices or equipment and

institute forfeiture proceedings in accordance with the procedures and substantive protections of Title 24, Chapter 1, Utah Uniform Forfeiture Procedures Act.

(2) The proceeds of any sale shall be paid to the Uniform School Fund, as provided in Section 53A-16-101. 2002

76-10-1108. Seizure and disposition of gambling debts or proceeds.

(1) Any gambling bets or gambling proceeds which are reasonably identifiable as having been used or obtained in violation of this part may be seized for forfeiture pursuant to the procedures and substantive protections of the Utah Uniform Forfeiture Procedures Act, Title 24, Chapter 1 of the Utah Code.

(2) All sums forfeited under this section shall be paid to the Uniform School Fund, Title 53A, Chapter 16, Section 101 of the Utah Code. 2000

76-10-1109. Confidence game — Punishment as for theft — Description in charge.

(1) Any person who obtains or attempts to obtain from any other person any money or property by any means, instrument or device commonly called a confidence game shall be punished as in the case of theft of property of like value.

(2) In every indictment, information, or complaint under this section, it shall be deemed and held a sufficient description of the offense to charge that the accused did, on _____ (insert the date) unlawfully and knowingly obtain or attempt to obtain (as the case may be) from _____, (insert the name of the person or persons defrauded or attempted to be defrauded) his money or property (as the case may be) by means and by use of a confidence game. 1973

PART 12

PORNOGRAPHIC AND HARMFUL MATERIALS AND PERFORMANCES

76-10-1201. Definitions.

For the purpose of this part:

(1) "Contemporary community standards" means those current standards in the vicinage where an offense alleged under this act has occurred, is occurring, or will occur.

(2) "Distribute" means to transfer possession of materials whether with or without consideration.

(3) "Exhibit" means to show.

(4) "Harmful to minors" means that quality of any description or representation, in whatsoever form, of nudity, sexual conduct, sexual excitement, or sadomasochistic abuse when it:

(a) taken as a whole, appeals to the prurient interest in sex of minors;

(b) is patently offensive to prevailing standards in the adult community as a whole with respect to what is suitable material for minors; and

(c) taken as a whole, does not have serious value for minors. Serious value includes only serious literary, artistic, political or scientific value for minors.

(5) "Knowingly" means an awareness, whether actual or constructive, of the character of material or of a performance. A person has constructive knowledge if a reasonable inspection or observation under the circumstances would have disclosed the nature of the subject matter and if a failure to inspect or observe is either for the purpose of avoiding the disclosure or is criminally negligent.

(6) "Material" means anything printed or written or any picture, drawing, photograph, motion picture, or pictorial representation, or any statue or other figure, or any recording or transcription, or any mechanical, chemical, or electrical reproduction, or anything which is or may be used as a means of communication. Material includes undeveloped photographs, molds, printing plates, and other latent representational objects.

(7) "Minor" means any person less than eighteen years of age.

(8) "Nudity" means the showing of the human male or female genitals, pubic area, or buttocks, with less than an opaque covering, or the showing of a female breast with less than an opaque covering, or any portion thereof below the top of the nipple, or the depiction of covered male genitals in a discernibly turgid state.

(9) "Performance" means any physical human bodily activity, whether engaged in alone or with other persons, including but not limited to singing, speaking, dancing, acting, simulating, or pantomiming.

(10) "Public place" includes a place to which admission is gained by payment of a membership or admission fee, however designated, notwithstanding its being designated a private club or by words of like import.

(11) "Sado-masochistic abuse" means flagellation or torture by or upon a person who is nude or clad in undergarments, a mask, or in a revealing or bizarre costume, or the condition of being fettered, bound, or otherwise physically restrained on the part of one so clothed.

(12) "Sexual conduct" means acts of masturbation, sexual intercourse, or any touching of a person's clothed or unclothed genitals, pubic area, buttocks, or, if the person is a female, breast, whether alone or between members of the same or opposite sex or between humans and animals in an act of apparent or actual sexual stimulation or gratification.

(13) "Sexual excitement" means a condition of human male or female genitals when in a state of sexual stimulation or arousal, or the sensual experiences of humans engaging in or witnessing sexual conduct or nudity.   2001

76-10-1202. Repealed.   1975

76-10-1203. Pornographic material or performance — Expert testimony not required.

(1) Any material or performance is pornographic if:
(a) The average person, applying contemporary community standards, finds that, taken as a whole, it appeals to prurient interest in sex;
(b) It is patently offensive in the description or depiction of nudity, sexual conduct, sexual excitement, sado-masochistic abuse, or excretion; and
(c) Taken as a whole it does not have serious literary, artistic, political or scientific value.

(2) In prosecutions under this part, where circumstances of production, presentation, sale, dissemination, distribution, exhibition, or publicity indicate that the matter is being commercially exploited by the defendant for the sake of its prurient appeal, this evidence is probative with respect to the nature of the matter and can justify the conclusion that, in the context in which it is used, the matter has no serious literary, artistic, political, or scientific value.

(3) Neither the prosecution nor the defense shall be required to introduce expert witness testimony as to whether the material or performance is or is not harmful to adults or minors or is or is not pornographic, or as to any element of the definition of pornographic, including contemporary community standards.   1977

76-10-1204. Distributing pornographic material.

(1) A person is guilty of distributing pornographic material when he knowingly:
(a) sends or brings any pornographic material into the state with intent to distribute or exhibit it to others;
(b) prepares, publishes, prints, or possesses any pornographic material with intent to distribute or exhibit it to others;
(c) distributes or offers to distribute, exhibits or offers to exhibit any pornographic material to others;
(d) writes, creates, or solicits the publication or advertising of pornographic material;
(e) promotes the distribution or exhibition of material he represents to be pornographic; or
(f) presents or directs a pornographic performance in any public place or any place exposed to public view or participates in that portion of the performance which makes it pornographic.

(2) Each distributing of pornographic material as defined in Subsection (1) is a separate offense.

(3) It is a separate offense under this section for:
(a) each day's exhibition of any pornographic motion picture film; and
(b) each day in which any pornographic publication is displayed or exhibited in a public place with intent to distribute or exhibit it to others.

(4) (a) An offense under this section is a third degree felony punishable by:
(i) a minimum mandatory fine of not less than $1,000 plus $10 for each article exhibited up to the maximum allowed by law; and
(ii) incarceration, without suspension of sentence in any way, for a term of not less than 30 days.
(b) This Subsection (4) supersedes Section 77-18-1.

(5) A service provider, as defined in Section 76-10-1230, complies with this section if it complies with Sections 76-10-1231 and 76-10-1232.   2005

76-10-1205. Inducing acceptance of pornographic material.

(1) A person is guilty of inducing acceptance of pornographic material when he knowingly:
(a) requires or demands as a condition to a sale, allocation, consignment, or delivery for resale of any newspaper, magazine, periodical, book, publication, or other merchandise that the purchaser or consignee receive any pornographic material or material reasonably believed by the purchaser or consignee to be pornographic; or
(b) denies, revokes, or threatens to deny or revoke a franchise, or to impose any penalty, financial or otherwise, because of the failure or refusal to accept pornographic material or material reasonably believed by the purchaser or consignee to be pornographic.

(2) (a) An offense under this section is a third degree felony punishable by:
(i) a minimum mandatory fine of not less than $1,000 plus $10 for each article exhibited up to the maximum allowed by law; and

(ii) incarceration, without suspension of sentence in any way, for a term of not less than 30 days.

(b) This Subsection (2) supersedes Section 77-18-1.

(3) A service provider, as defined in Section 76-10-1230, complies with this section if it complies with Sections 76-10-1231 and 76-10-1232.   2005

76-10-1206. Dealing in material harmful to a minor.

(1) A person is guilty of dealing in material harmful to minors when, knowing that a person is a minor, or having negligently or recklessly failed to determine the proper age of a minor, he:

(a) intentionally distributes or offers to distribute, exhibits or offers to exhibit to a minor any material harmful to minors;

(b) intentionally produces, presents, or directs any performance before a minor, that is harmful to minors; or

(c) intentionally participates in any performance before a minor, that is harmful to minors.

(2) (a) Each separate offense under this section is a third degree felony punishable by:

(i) a minimum mandatory fine of not less than $300 plus $10 for each article exhibited up to the maximum allowed by law; and

(ii) incarceration, without suspension of sentence, for a term of not less than 14 days.

(b) This section supersedes Section 77-18-1.

(3) (a) If a defendant has already been convicted once under this section, each separate further offense is a second degree felony punishable by:

(i) a minimum mandatory fine of not less than $5,000 plus $10 for each article exhibited up to the maximum allowed by law; and

(ii) incarceration, without suspension of sentence, for a term of not less than one year.

(b) This section supersedes Section 77-18-1.

(4) (a) A service provider, as defined in Section 76-10-1230, complies with this section if it complies with Sections 76-10-1231 and 76-10-1232.

(b) A content provider, as defined in Section 76-10-1230, complies with this section if it complies with Section 76-10-1233.   2005

76-10-1206.5. Repealed.   1983

76-10-1207. Use of real property by tenant or occupant — Voiding of lease — Allowance of such use by owner or lessor.

(1) If a tenant or occupant of real property uses this property for an activity for which he or his employee is convicted under any provision of this part, the conviction makes void the lease or other title under which he holds at the option of the fee owner or any intermediate lessor; and 10 days after the fee owner or any intermediate lessor gives notice in writing to the tenant or occupant that he is exercising the option, the right of possession to the property reverts in the person exercising the option. This option does not arise until all avenues of direct appeal from the conviction have been exhausted or abandoned by the tenant or occupant, or his employee.

(2) It shall be unlawful for a fee owner or intermediate lessor of real property to knowingly allow this property to be used for the purpose of distributing or exhibiting pornographic materials, or for pornographic performances, by a tenant or occupant if the tenant or occupant, or his employee, has been convicted under any provision of this part of an offense occurring on the same property and all avenues of direct appeal from the conviction have been exhausted or abandoned.

(a) "Allow" under this Subsection (2) means a failure to exercise the option arising under Subsection (1) within 10 days after the fee owner or lessor receives notice in writing from the county attorney of the county where the property is situated, or if situated in a city of the first or second class, from the city attorney of that city, that the property is being used for a purpose prohibited by this Subsection (2).

(b) A willful violation of this Subsection (2) is a class A misdemeanor and any fine assessed, if not paid within 30 days after judgment, shall become a lien upon the property.

(3) Any tenant or occupant who receives a notice in writing that the fee owner or intermediate lessor is exercising the option provided by Subsection (1) and who does not quit the premises within 10 days after the giving of that notice is guilty of a class A misdemeanor.   1977

76-10-1207.5. Exemption — Corrections treatment, programs.

This part does not apply to the Department of Corrections or any treatment program by or under contract with the department when the use of sexually explicit material that is pornographic is limited to the assessment or treatment of an offender as defined under Section 64-13-1.   1990

76-10-1208. Affirmative defenses.

(1) It is an affirmative defense to prosecution under this part that the distribution of pornographic material was restricted to institutions or persons having scientific, educational, governmental, or other similar justification for possessing pornographic material.

(2) It is not a defense to prosecution under this part that the actor was a motion picture projectionist, usher, ticket-taker, bookstore employee, or otherwise was required to violate any provision of this part incident to his employment.   1977

76-10-1209. Injunctive relief — Jurisdiction — Consent to be sued — Service of process.

(1) The district courts of this state shall have full power, authority, and jurisdiction, upon application by any county attorney or city attorney within their respective jurisdictions or the attorney general, to issue any and all proper restraining orders, preliminary and permanent injunctions, and any other writs and processes appropriate to carry out and enforce the provisions of this part. No restraining order or injunction, however, shall issue except upon notice to the person sought to be enjoined. That person shall be entitled to a trial of the issues commencing within three days after filing of an answer to the complaint and a decision shall be rendered by the court within two days after the conclusion of the trial. If a final order or judgment of injunction is entered against the person sought to be enjoined, this final order or judgment shall contain a provision directing the person to surrender to the sheriff of the county in which the action was brought any pornographic material in his possession which is subject to the injunction; and the sheriff shall be directed to seize and destroy this material.

(2) Any person not qualified to do business in the state who sends or brings any pornographic material into the state with the intent to distribute or exhibit it to others in this state thereby consents that he may be sued in any proceedings commenced under this sec-

tion and therefor appoints the director of the Division of Corporations and Commercial Code to be the agent upon whom may be served all legal process against that person. Service of process shall be made by serving a copy of same upon the director of the Division of Corporations and Commercial Code or by filing the copy in that office, together with payment of a fee determined by the division pursuant to Section 63-38-3.2. This service shall be sufficient service upon the defendant if:

    (a) notice of the service and a copy of the process are within ten days thereafter sent by mail by the prosecuting attorney to the defendant at the address of the defendant that appears on any material exhibited or distributed, and if no address appears, then the last known address of the defendant; and

    (b) the prosecuting attorney's affidavit of compliance with the provisions of this subsection are attached to the summons. The Division of Corporations and Commercial Code shall keep a record of all the process served upon it under this section, showing the day and hour of the service. Nothing in this subsection shall be construed to limit the operation of Rule 17(e) of the Utah Rules of Civil Procedure.

(3) This section shall not be construed in any way to limit the district courts in the exercise of their jurisdiction under any other provision of law.   1995

76-10-1210. Local regulation of pornographic materials or materials harmful to minors.

(1) It is not the intent of this part to prescribe or limit the regulation of pornographic materials or materials harmful to minors, and counties, cities, and other political subdivisions of the State of Utah are specifically given the right hereby to further regulate the materials. Specifically, without limitation, these political subdivisions may further regulate materials by ordinances relating to zoning, licensing, public nuisances, or relating to a specific type of business such as adult bookstores or drive-in movies.

(2) It is not the intent of this part to preclude the application of other laws of the State of Utah to pornographic materials or materials harmful to minors. Specifically, without limitation, this part is not in derogation of Sections 76-10-803 and 76-10-806.

(3) The commission of a crime under this part shall be deemed to offend public decency under Section 76-10-803. It is the intent of this part to give the broadest meaning permissible under the federal and state constitutions to the words "offends public decency" in Section 76-10-803.   1977

76-10-1211. Separability clause.

If any clause, sentence, paragraph, or part of this part or its application to any person or circumstance shall for any reason be adjudged by any court of competent jurisdiction to be invalid, the judgment shall not affect, impair, or invalidate the remainder of this part or its application to other persons or circumstances but shall be confined in its operation to the clause, sentence, paragraph, persons, or circumstances, or part thereof directly involved in the controversy in which the judgment shall have been rendered.   1995

76-10-1212. Search and seizure — Affidavit — Issuance of warrant — Hearing upon claim that material seized not pornographic or harmful to minors — Procedures cumulative.

(1) An affidavit for a search warrant shall be filed with the magistrate describing with specificity the material sought to be seized. Where practical, the material alleged to be pornographic or harmful to minors shall be attached to the affidavit for search warrant to afford the magistrate the opportunity to examine this material.

(2) Upon the filing of an affidavit for a search warrant, the magistrate shall determine, by examination of the material sought to be seized if attached, by examination of the affidavit describing the material, or by other manner or means that he finds necessary, whether probable cause exists to believe that the material is pornographic or harmful to minors and whether probable cause exists for the immediate issuance of a search warrant. Upon making this determination, he shall issue a search warrant ordering the seizure of the material described in the affidavit for a search warrant according to the provisions of the Utah Rules of Criminal Procedure.

(3) (a) If a search warrant is issued and material alleged to be pornographic or harmful to minors is seized under the provisions of this section, any person claiming to be in possession of this material or claiming ownership of it at the time of its seizure may file a notice in writing with the magistrate within ten days after the date of the seizure, alleging that the material is not pornographic or harmful to minors.

    (b) The magistrate shall set a hearing within seven days after the filing of this notice, or at another time to which the claimant might agree. At this hearing evidence may be presented as to whether there is probable cause to believe the material seized is pornographic or harmful to minors, and at the conclusion of the hearing magistrate shall make a further determination of whether probable cause exists to believe that the material is pornographic or harmful to minors.

    (c) A decision as to whether there is probable cause to believe the seized material is pornographic or harmful to minors shall be rendered by the court within two days after the conclusion of the hearing.

    (d) If at the hearing the magistrate finds that no probable cause exists to believe that the material is pornographic or harmful to minors, then the material shall be returned to the person or persons from whom it was seized.

    (e) If the material seized is a film, and the claimant demonstrates that no other copy of the film is available to him, the court shall allow the film to be copied at the claimant's expense pending the hearing.

(4) If a motion to suppress the evidence is granted on the grounds of an unlawful seizure, the property shall be restored unless it is subject to confiscation as contraband, in which case it may not be returned.

(5) (a) Procedures under this section for the seizure of allegedly pornographic material or material harmful to minors are cumulative of all other lawful means of obtaining evidence as provided by the laws of this state.

    (b) This section does not prevent the obtaining of allegedly pornographic material or material harmful to minors by purchase, subpoena duces tecum, or under injunction proceedings as authorized by this act or by any other provision of law of the state.   2000

76-10-1213. Corporate defendants — Summons — Subpoena duces tecum.

(1) (a) The attendance in court of a corporation for purposes of commencing or prosecuting a crimi-

nal action against it under this part may be accomplished by the issuance and service of a summons. A summons shall be issued by a magistrate if he finds probable cause that material in the possession of the corporation against which the summons is sought is pornographic or harmful to minors, which finding shall be upon affidavit describing with specificity the material alleged to be pornographic or harmful to minors or by another manner or means the magistrate finds necessary.

(b) Where practical, the material alleged to be pornographic or harmful to minors shall be attached to the affidavit so as to afford the magistrate the opportunity to examine this material.

(c) The summons must be served upon the corporation by delivery of it to an officer, director, managing or general agent, or cashier, or assistant cashier of the corporation.

(2) The production of material alleged to be pornographic or harmful to minors in any proceedings under this part against a corporation may be compelled by the issuance and service of a subpoena duces tecum. This section does not prohibit or limit the use of a subpoena duces tecum in proceedings against natural persons under this part.   2000

76-10-1214. Conspiracy an offense — Punishment.

(1) A conspiracy of two or more persons to commit any offense proscribed by this part is a third degree felony punishable for each separate offense by a minimum mandatory fine of not less than $1,000 and by imprisonment, without suspension of sentence in any way, for a term of not less than 60 days. This subsection supersedes Section 77-18-1.

(2) If a defendant has already been convicted once under this section, each separate further offense is a second degree felony punishable by a minimum mandatory fine of not less than $5,000 and by imprisonment, without suspension of sentence in any way, for a term of not less than one year. This subsection supersedes Section 77-18-1.   1990

76-10-1215. Prosecution by county, district, or city attorney — Fines payable to county or city.

Prosecution for violation of any section of this part, including a felony violation, shall be brought by the county attorney or, if within a prosecution district, the district attorney of the county where the violation occurs. If the violation occurs, however, in a city of the first or second class, prosecution may be brought by either the county, district, or city attorney, notwithstanding any provision of law limiting the powers of city attorneys. All fines imposed for the violation of this part shall be paid to the county or city of the prosecuting attorney, as the case may be.   1993

76-10-1216. Distribution of motion picture films — Definitions.

As used in this act:

(1) "Exhibit" means to show in a public place or in a place where the public is admitted, whether or not an admission fee is charged.

(2) "Distributor" means any person from which a film is acquired by sale, loan, or any other means, directly or indirectly, for the purpose of exhibiting it in this state or elsewhere but shall not include any person whose function with respect to any film is limited to the transportation or storage thereof.

(3) "Film" means what is usually known as a motion picture film and which is intended to be shown commercially for profit by devices of any kind whatsoever.

(4) "Person" includes a natural person, firm, association, partnership, or corporation.

(5) "Public place" includes any place to which admission is gained by payment of a membership or admission fee, however designated, notwithstanding it is designated as a private club or by words of like import.   1977

76-10-1217. Intent to prevent commercial distribution and exhibition of pornographic films — Local regulation and other laws not limited.

(1) It is the intent of this act to prevent the commercial distribution and exhibition of films in this state which are pornographic. There is substantial evidence that elements of organized crime have engaged to an increasing degree in the production and distribution of such films and, therefore, it is the further intent of this act to facilitate the criminal prosecution of distributors of pornographic films.

(2) It is not the intent of this act to limit the regulation of films by counties, cities, towns, and other political subdivisions within the state, and these subdivisions are specifically given the right by this act to further regulate films. Nor is it the intent of this act to limit or abridge the power to otherwise prosecute violations of any other provisions of law including, but not limited to, those provisions of Title 76, Chapter 10, Part 12.   1977

76-10-1218. Qualification for exhibition and distribution of films required.

No person shall distribute any film for exhibition in this state unless that person is first qualified to do so nor exhibit any film in this state which was not acquired for exhibition, directly or indirectly, from a distributor qualified to distribute films in this state.   1977

76-10-1219. Qualification for distribution of films — Corporations and others to file statements.

(1) A distributor which is a corporation shall be qualified to distribute films within this state if:

(a) it is a domestic corporation in good standing or a foreign corporation authorized to transact business in this state;

(b) it has filed with the Division of Corporations and Commercial Code a statement upon forms prescribed and furnished by that office, signed and verified on behalf of the corporation by an officer qualified and authorized to bind the corporation for such purpose, a statement indicating that it desires to be qualified to distribute films in this state and that it submits itself to the jurisdiction and laws of this state relating thereto and, further, indicating the following:

(i) the address of its principal office;

(ii) the name under which it wishes to distribute films in this state;

(iii) the names and addresses of all directors and officers;

(iv) the address of the registered office in this state; and

(v) the name of its registered agent in this state;

(c) it files a current statement on or before March 1 of each year thereafter indicating that information specified in Subsection (b) of this Subsection (1) in the manner provided therein.

(2) A distributor which is not a corporation shall be qualified to distribute films within this state if:

(a) it has and continuously maintains a registered office in this state;

(b) it has a registered agent whose business address is at that registered office and which is either an individual residing and domiciled in this state, a domestic corporation in good standing, or a foreign corporation authorized to transact business in this state;

(c) it has filed with the Division of Corporations and Commercial Code a statement, upon forms prescribed and furnished by that office, signed and verified, indicating that it desires to be qualified to distribute films in this state and that it submits itself to the jurisdiction and laws of this state relating thereto and, further, indicating the following:

(i) the address of its principal office;

(ii) the name under which it wishes to distribute films in this state;

(iii) the names and address of each partner or the sole proprietor, owning the distributorship;

(iv) the address of its registered office in this state; and

(v) the name of its registered agent in this state;

(d) it files a current statement on or before March 1 of each year thereafter indicating that information specified in Subsection (b) of this Subsection (2) in the manner provided therein.

(3) The Division of Corporations and Commercial Code shall keep a record of all processes, notices and demands served upon it pursuant to this section, together with the time of such service and its action relating thereto.

(4) This section shall not affect the right to serve any process, notice, or demand, required or permitted by law to be served upon a distributor, in any other manner provided by law.   1984

76-10-1220. Change of registered office or agent by film distributor — Resignation of registered agent.

(1) A distributor qualified to distribute films in this state may change its registered office or registered agent by filing with the Division of Corporations and Commercial Code a statement setting forth:

(a) the name of the distributor;

(b) the address of its present registered office;

(c) the name of its present registered agent; and

(d) the address of the new registered office or name of the new registered agent.

(2) The statement provided for in this section must be signed, verified, and filed in the same manner as specified in Section 76-10-1219.

(3) If the Division of Corporations and Commercial Code finds that the statement conforms to the provisions of this act, it shall file the statement in its office and the change in the registered office or agent shall thereupon take effect.

(4) Any registered agent may resign that position by filing a signed and verified notice of that resignation in duplicate with the Division of Corporations and Commercial Code which shall forthwith mail a copy thereof to the distributor at its principal office.

That resignation shall take effect 30 days after receipt thereof by the Division of Corporations and Commercial Code.   1984

76-10-1221. Service of process, notice or demand on registered agent of film distributor — Director of Division of Corporations and Commercial Code as agent for process.

(1) Any process, notice, or demand required or permitted by law to be served upon the distributor may be served upon the registered agent of that distributor.

(2) If the registered agent cannot with reasonable diligence be found at the registered office, the director of the Division of Corporations and Commercial Code shall constitute the agent of the distributor for the service of any process, notice, or demand required or permitted by law to be served upon the distributor. Service of any such process, notice, or demand upon the director of the Division of Corporations and Commercial Code shall be made in duplicate and the Division of Corporations and Commercial Code shall thereupon cause one of the copies thereof to be forwarded by registered mail to the distributor at its principal office indicated in that statement filed pursuant to Section 76-10-1219. Such service shall be deemed complete upon the tenth day following that service.   1984

76-10-1222. Distribution of pornographic film — Penalties for violations.

(1) Any person who knowingly or by criminal negligence distributes for exhibition within this state a film which is pornographic as that term is defined in the Utah criminal code shall be guilty of a class A misdemeanor and shall, for each separate offense, be fined not less than $1,000 and imprisoned, without suspension of sentence in any way, for a term of not less than 60 days.

(2) Any person convicted of a violation of this section who has been convicted before of a violation of this section, shall be guilty of a felony of the third degree and shall, for each separate offense, be fined not less than $5,000 and imprisoned, without suspension of sentence in any way, for a term of not less than six months.

(3) Each copy of a pornographic film distributed for exhibition within this state in violation of this section shall constitute a separate offense.   1977

76-10-1223. Distribution of film without being qualified — Exhibition of film not acquired from qualified distributor — Penalties for violations.

(1) Any person who knowingly distributes any film for exhibition within this state without being qualified to do so, or who knowingly exhibits a film in this state which has not been acquired from a distributor qualified to distribute films in this state is guilty of a class B misdemeanor and shall, for each separate offense, be fined not less than $299 and imprisoned, without suspension of sentence in any way, for a term of not less than 30 days.

(2) Any person convicted of a violation of this section, who has been convicted before of a violation of this section, shall be guilty of a class A misdemeanor and shall, for each separate offense, be fined not less than $1,000 and imprisoned, without suspension of sentence in any way, for a term of not less than 60 days.

(3) Each day's exhibition of such a film, and each copy of a film distributed for exhibition within this state, shall constitute a separate offense.   1977

76-10-1224. Defense to prosecution for distribution or exhibition of pornographic film — Status as projectionist or other employee no defense.

(1) It shall be an affirmative defense to any prosecution under Section 76-10-1222 or 76-10-1223 that the distribution is exempt from the restrictions of this act by the provisions of Section 76-10-1226.

(2) It shall not constitute a defense to any prosecution under Section 76-10-1222 or 76-10-1223 that the actor was a motion picture projectionist or was otherwise required by his employment to commit the violation complained of.   1977

76-10-1225. Prosecution of pornographic film violations by county attorney, district attorney, or city attorney.

The county attorney of the county where the violation occurred or within a prosecution district where the violation occurred, the district attorney shall file and prosecute any action for violations of this act unless the violation occurs in a city of the first or second class. If the violation occurs in such a city, the action may be commenced and prosecuted by either the city attorney or the county attorney. All fines imposed for any violation of this act shall be paid to the political subdivision employing the prosecuting attorney.   1993

76-10-1226. Exemptions from application of film distribution act.

This part does not apply to any film:

(1) distributed to or exhibited by any accredited university, college, school, library, or other educational institution, church, or museum, if there is scientific, religious, or educational justification for the exhibition of the film; or

(2) exhibited by the Department of Corrections or exhibited as part of any treatment program operated by or under contract with the department if the exhibition of the film is solely for the assessment or treatment of an offender as defined under Section 64-13-1.   1990

76-10-1227. Indecent public displays — Definitions.

For purposes of this part:

(1) "Description or depictions of illicit sex or sexual immorality" means:

(a) human genitals in a state of sexual stimulation or arousal;

(b) acts of human masturbation, sexual intercourse, or sodomy;

(c) fondling or other erotic touching of human genitals or pubic region; or

(d) fondling or other erotic touching of the human buttock or female breast.

(2) "Nude or partially denuded figures" means:

(a) less than completely and opaquely covered:

(i) human genitals;

(ii) pubic regions;

(iii) buttock; and

(iv) female breast below a point immediately above the top of the areola; and

(b) human male genitals in a discernibly turgid state, even if completely and opaquely covered.

(3) (a) This section does not apply to any material which, when taken as a whole, has serious value for persons younger than 18 years of age, except as provided under Subsection (3)(c).

(b) As used in Subsection (3)(a), "serious value" means having serious literary, artistic, political, or scientific value for persons younger than 18 years of age, taking into consideration the ages of all minors who could be exposed to the material.

(c) Descriptions or depictions of illicit sex or sexual immorality as defined in Subsection (1)(a), (b), or (c) have no serious value for persons younger than 18 years of age.   2002

76-10-1228. Indecent public displays — Prohibitions — Penalty.

(1) A person is guilty of a class A misdemeanor who willfully or knowingly:

(a) engages in the business of selling, lending, giving away, showing, advertising for sale, or distributing to any person under the age of 18 or has in his possession with intent to engage in that business or to otherwise offer for sale or commercial distribution to any individual under the age of 18 any material with descriptions or depictions of illicit sex, sexual immorality, or nude or partially denuded figures; or

(b) publicly displays at newsstands or any other establishment frequented by minors under the age of 18, or where the minors are or may be invited as a part of the general public, any motion picture, or any live, taped, or recorded performance, or any still picture or photograph, or any book, pocket book, pamphlet, or magazine the cover or content of which exploits, is devoted to, or is principally made up of indecent descriptions or depictions of illicit sex or sexual immorality, or that consists of pictures of nude or partially denuded figures posed or presented in a manner to provoke or arouse lust or passion or to exploit lust or perversion.

(2) A violation of this section is punishable by a minimum mandatory fine of not less than $500 and by incarceration, without suspension of sentence in any way, for a term of not less than 30 days. This section supersedes Section 77-18-1.   2002

76-10-1229. Distribution of pornographic material through cable television prohibited — Definitions — Prosecution of violation.

(1) No person, including a franchisee, shall knowingly distribute by wire or cable any pornographic or indecent material to its subscribers.

(2) For purposes of this section "material" means any visual display shown on a cable television system, whether or not accompanied by sound, or any sound recording played on a cable television system.

(3) For purposes of this section "pornographic material" is any material defined as pornographic in Sections 76-10-1201 and 76-10-1203.

(4) For purposes of this section "indecent material" means any material described in Section 76-10-1227.

(5) For purposes of this section "distribute" means to send, transmit, retransmit, or otherwise pass through a cable television system.

(6) Prosecution for violation of this section may be initiated at the instance of the attorney general or any county or city attorney of an interested political subdivision or at the instance of the governing body of any such political subdivision.

(7) Any person who violates this section is guilty of a class A misdemeanor.   1981

76-10-1229.5. Breast feeding is not violation of this part.

A woman's breast feeding, including breast feeding in any location where the woman otherwise may rightfully be, does not under any circumstance constitute a violation of this part, irrespective of whether or not the breast is covered during or incidental to feeding.   1995

76-10-1230. Definitions.

As used in Sections 76-10-1231, 76-10-1232, and 76-10-1233:

(1) "Access restricted" means that a content provider limits access to material harmful to minors by:

(a) properly rating content;

(b) providing an age verification mechanism designed to prevent a minor's access to material harmful to minors, including requiring use of a credit card, adult access code, or digital certificate verifying age; or

(c) any other reasonable measures feasible under available technology.

(2) "Adult content registry" means the adult content registry created by Section 67-5-19.

(3) "Consumer" means a natural person residing in this state who subscribes to a service provided by a service provider for personal or residential use.

(4) "Content provider" means a person that creates, collects, acquires, or organizes electronic data for electronic delivery to a consumer with the intent of making a profit.

(5) (a) "Hosting company" means a person that provides services or facilities for storing or distributing content over the Internet without editorial or creative alteration of the content.

(b) A hosting company may have policies concerning acceptable use without becoming a content provider under Subsection (4).

(6) (a) "Internet service provider" means a person engaged in the business of providing a computer and communications facility through which a consumer may obtain access to the Internet.

(b) "Internet service provider" does not include a common carrier if it provides only telecommunications service.

(7) "Properly rated" means content using a labeling system to label material harmful to minors provided by the content provider in a way that:

(a) accurately apprises a consumer of the presence of material harmful to minors; and

(b) allows the consumer the ability to control access to material harmful to minors based on the material's rating by use of reasonably priced commercially available software, including software in the public domain.

(8) (a) Except as provided in Subsection (8)(b), "service provider" means:

(i) an Internet service provider; or

(ii) a person who otherwise provides an Internet access service to a consumer.

(b) "Service provider" does not include a person who does not terminate a service in this state, but merely transmits data through:

(i) a wire;

(ii) a cable; or

(iii) an antenna.

(c) "Service provider," notwithstanding Subsection (8)(b), includes a person who meets the requirements of Subsection (8)(a) and leases or rents a wire or cable for the transmission of data.   2005

76-10-1231. Data service providers — Internet content harmful to minors [Effective January 1, 2006].

(1) (a) Upon request by a consumer, a service provider shall filter content to prevent the transmission of material harmful to minors to the consumer.

(b) A service provider complies with Subsection (1)(a) if it uses a generally accepted and commercially reasonable method of filtering.

(2) At the time of a consumer's subscription to a service provider's service, or at the time this section takes effect if the consumer subscribes to the service provider's service at the time this section takes effect, the service provider shall notify the consumer in a conspicuous manner that the consumer may request to have material harmful to minors blocked under Subsection (1).

(3) (a) A service provider may comply with Subsection (1) by:

(i) providing in-network filtering to prevent receipt of material harmful to minors; or

(ii) providing software for contemporaneous installation on the consumer's computer that blocks, in an easy-to-enable and commercially reasonable manner, receipt of material harmful to minors.

(b) (i) Except as provided in Subsection (3)(b)(ii), a service provider may not charge a consumer for blocking material or providing software under this section, except that a service provider may increase the cost to all subscribers to the service provider's services to recover the cost of complying with this section.

(ii) A service provider with fewer than 7,500 subscribers may charge a consumer for providing software under Subsection (3)(a)(ii) if the charge does not exceed the service provider's cost for the software.

(4) If the attorney general determines that a service provider violates Subsection (1) or (2), the attorney general shall:

(a) notify the service provider that the service provider is in violation of Subsection (1) or (2); and

(b) notify the service provider that the service provider has 30 days to comply with the provision being violated or be subject to Subsection (5).

(5) A service provider that violates Subsection (1) or (2) is:

(a) subject to a civil fine of $2,500 for each separate violation of Subsection (1) or (2), up to $10,000 per day; and

(b) guilty of a class A misdemeanor if:

(i) the service provider knowingly or intentionally fails to comply with Subsection (1); or

(ii) the service provider fails to provide the notice required by Subsection (2).

(6) A proceeding to impose a civil fine under Subsection (5)(a) may only be brought by the attorney general in a court of competent jurisdiction.

(7) (a) The Division of Consumer Protection within the Department of Commerce shall, in consultation with other entities as the Division of Consumer Protection considers appropriate, test the effectiveness of a service provider's system for blocking material harmful to minors under Subsection (1) at least annually.

(b) The results of testing by the Division of Consumer Protection under Subsection (7)(a) shall be made available to:

(i) the service provider that is the subject of the test; and

(ii) the public.

(c) The Division of Consumer Protection shall make rules in accordance with Title 63, Chapter 46a, Utah Administrative Rulemaking Act, to fulfil its duties under this section.   2005

76-10-1232. Data service providers — Adult content registry [Effective May 1, 2006].

(1) (a) Upon request by a consumer, a service provider may not transmit material from a content provider site listed on the adult content registry created by Section 67-5-19 to a consumer.

(b) A service provider complies with Subsection (1)(a) if it uses a generally accepted and commercially reasonable method of filtering.

(c) At the time of a consumer's subscription to a service provider's service, or at the time this section takes effect if the consumer subscribes to the service provider's service at the time this section takes effect, the service provider shall notify the consumer in a conspicuous manner that:

(i) the consumer may request to have material on the adult content registry blocked under Subsection (1)(a); and

(ii) the consumer's request to have material harmful to minors blocked under Subsection (1)(a) may also result in blocking material that is not harmful to minors.

(2) (a) A service provider may comply with Subsection (1) by:

(i) providing in-network filtering to prevent receipt of material harmful to minors;

(ii) providing software for contemporaneous installation on the consumer's computer that blocks, in an easy-to-enable and commercially reasonable manner, receipt of material harmful to minors; or

(iii) complying with any federal law in effect that requires the blocking of content from a registry of sites containing material harmful to minors.

(b) A service provider may block material from the adult content registry by domain name or Internet Protocol address.

(c) (i) A service provider may not charge a consumer for blocking material or providing software under this section, except that a service provider may increase the cost to all subscribers to the service provider's services to recover the cost of complying with this section.

(ii) A service provider with fewer than 7,500 subscribers may charge a consumer for providing software under Subsection (2)(a)(ii) if the charge does not exceed the service provider's cost for the software.

(d) A service provider shall coordinate the service provider's list of content providers on the adult content registry with the attorney general's list of content providers on the adult content registry at least weekly.

(3) If the attorney general determines that the service provider violates Subsection (1) or (2), the attorney general shall:

(a) notify the service provider that the service provider is in violation of Subsection (1) or (2); and

(b) notify the service provider that the service provider has 30 days to comply with the provision being violated or be subject to Subsection (4).

(4) A service provider that violates Subsection (1) or (2) is:

(a) subject to a civil fine of $2,500 for each separate violation of Subsection (1) or (2), up to $10,000 per day; and

(b) guilty of a class A misdemeanor if the service provider knowingly or intentionally fails to comply with Subsection (1) or (2).

(5) A proceeding to impose a civil fine under Subsection (4)(a) may only be brought by the attorney general in a court of competent jurisdiction.   2005

76-10-1233. Content providers — Material harmful to minors [Effective May 1, 2006].

(1) A content provider that is domiciled in Utah, or generates or hosts content in Utah, shall restrict access to material harmful to minors.

(2) The Division of Consumer Protection shall make rules in accordance with Title 63, Chapter 46a, Utah Administrative Rulemaking Act, to establish acceptable rating methods to be implemented by a content provider under Subsection (1).

(3) If the attorney general determines that a content provider violates Subsection (1), the attorney general shall:

(a) notify the content provider that the content provider is in violation of Subsection (1); and

(b) notify the content provider that the content provider has 30 days to comply with Subsection (1) or be subject to Subsection (4).

(4) If a content provider violates this section more than 30 days after receiving the notice provided in Subsection (3), the content provider is guilty of a third degree felony.   2005

PART 13

PROSTITUTION

76-10-1301. Definitions.

For the purposes of this part:

(1) "House of prostitution" means a place where prostitution or promotion of prostitution is regularly carried on by one or more persons under the control, management, or supervision of another.

(2) "Inmate" means a person who engages in prostitution in or through the agency of a house of prostitution.

(3) "Public place" means any place to which the public or any substantial group of the public has access.

(4) "Sexual activity" means acts of masturbation, sexual intercourse, or any sexual act involving the genitals of one person and the mouth or anus of another person, regardless of the sex of either participant.   1988

76-10-1302. Prostitution.

(1) A person is guilty of prostitution when:

(a) he engages in any sexual activity with another person for a fee;

(b) is an inmate of a house of prostitution; or

(c) loiters in or within view of any public place for the purpose of being hired to engage in sexual activity.

(2) Prostitution is a class B misdemeanor. However, any person who is convicted a second time, and on all subsequent convictions, under this section or under a local ordinance adopted in compliance with Section 76-10-1307 is guilty of a class A misdemeanor, except as provided in Section 76-10-1309.   1993

76-10-1303. Patronizing a prostitute.

(1) A person is guilty of patronizing a prostitute when:

(a) he pays or offers or agrees to pay another person a fee for the purpose of engaging in an act of sexual activity; or

(b) he enters or remains in a house of prostitution for the purpose of engaging in sexual activity.

(2) Patronizing a prostitute is a class B misdemeanor, except as provided in Section 76-10-1309.   1993

76-10-1304. Aiding prostitution.

(1) A person is guilty of aiding prostitution if he:

(a) solicits a person to patronize a prostitute;

(b) procures or attempts to procure a prostitute for a patron;

(c) leases or otherwise permits a place controlled by the actor, alone or in association with another, to be used for prostitution or the promotion of prostitution; or

(d) solicits, receives, or agrees to receive any benefit for doing any of the acts prohibited by this subsection.

(2) Aiding prostitution is a class B misdemeanor. However, a person who is convicted a second time, and on all subsequent convictions, under this section or under a local ordinance adopted in compliance with Section 76-10-1307 is guilty of a class A misdemeanor.   1991

76-10-1305. Exploiting prostitution.

(1) A person is guilty of exploiting prostitution if he:

(a) procures an inmate for a house of prostitution or place in a house of prostitution for one who would be an inmate;

(b) encourages, induces, or otherwise purposely causes another to become or remain a prostitute;

(c) transports a person into or within this state with a purpose to promote that person's engaging in prostitution or procuring or paying for transportation with that purpose;

(d) not being a child or legal dependent of a prostitute, shares the proceeds of prostitution with a prostitute pursuant to their understanding that he is to share therein; or

(e) owns, controls, manages, supervises, or otherwise keeps, alone or in association with another, a house of prostitution or a prostitution business.

(2) Exploiting prostitution is a felony of the third degree.   2000

76-10-1306. Aggravated exploitation of prostitution.

(1) A person is guilty of aggravated exploitation if:

(a) in committing an act of exploiting prostitution, as defined in Section 76-10-1305, he uses any force, threat, or fear against any person; or

(b) the person procured, transported, or persuaded or with whom he shares the proceeds of prostitution is under eighteen years of age or is the wife of the actor.

(2) Aggravated exploitation of prostitution is a felony of the second degree.   2001

76-10-1307. Local ordinance consistent with code provisions.

An ordinance adopted by a local authority governing prostitution or aiding prostitution shall be consistent with the provisions of this part which govern those matters.   1991

76-10-1308. Prosecution.

The following class A misdemeanors may be prosecuted by attorneys of cities and towns, as well as by prosecutors authorized elsewhere in this code to prosecute these alleged violations:

(1) class A misdemeanor violations of Section 76-10-1302; and

(2) class A misdemeanor violations of Section 76-10-1304.   1991

76-10-1309. Enhanced penalties — HIV positive offender.

A person who is an HIV positive individual and has actual knowledge of that fact and has received written personal notice of the positive test results from a law enforcement agency pursuant to Section 76-10-1312 and is convicted of:

(1) prostitution under Section 76-10-1302 shall be guilty of a felony of the third degree;

(2) patronizing a prostitute under Section 76-10-1303 shall be guilty of a felony of a third degree; or

(3) sexual solicitation under Section 76-10-1313 shall be guilty of a felony of the third degree.   1993

76-10-1310. Definitions.

(1) "HIV infection" means an indication of Human Immunodeficiency Virus (HIV) infection determined by current medical standards and detected by any of the following:

(a) presence of antibodies to HIV, verified by a positive confirmatory test, such as Western blot or other method approved by the Utah State Health Laboratory. Western blot interpretation will be based on criteria currently recommended by the Association of State and Territorial Public Health Laboratory Directors;

(b) presence of HIV antigen;

(c) isolation of HIV; or

(d) demonstration of HIV proviral DNA.

(2) "HIV positive individual" means a person who is HIV positive and has actual knowledge of his disease.

(3) "Local law enforcement agency" means the agency responsible for investigation of the violations of Sections 76-10-1302, 76-10-1303, and 76-10-1313, the filing of charges which may lead to conviction, and the conducting of tests for HIV infection.

(4) "Notice" means the HIV positive individual has been notified by the law enforcement agency as provided in Section 76-10-1312.

(5) "Positive" means an indication of the HIV infection as defined in Subsection (1).

(6) "Test" or "testing" means a test or tests for HIV infection in accordance with standards recommended by the Department of Health.   1993

76-10-1311. Mandatory testing — Retention of offender medical file — Civil liability.

(1) A person who has entered a plea of guilty, a plea of no contest, a plea of guilty and mentally ill, or been

found guilty for violation of Section 76-10-1302, 76-10-1303, or 76-10-1313 shall be required to submit to a mandatory test to determine if the offender is an HIV positive individual. The mandatory test shall be required and conducted prior to sentencing.

(2) If the mandatory test has not been conducted prior to sentencing, and the convicted offender is already confined in a county jail or state prison, such person shall be tested while in confinement.

(3) The local law enforcement agency shall cause the blood specimen of the offender as defined in Subsection (1) confined in county jail to be taken and tested.

(4) The Department of Corrections shall cause the blood specimen of the offender defined in Subsection (1) confined in any state prison to be taken and tested.

(5) The local law enforcement agency shall collect and retain in the offender's medical file the following data:

    (a) the HIV infection test results;

    (b) a copy of the written notice as provided in Section 76-10-1312;

    (c) photographic identification; and

    (d) fingerprint identification.

(6) The local law enforcement agency shall classify the medical file as a private record pursuant to Subsection 63-2-302(1)(b) or a controlled record pursuant to Section 63-2-303.

(7) The person tested shall be responsible for the costs of testing, unless the person is indigent. The costs will then be paid by the local law enforcement agency or the Department of Corrections from the General Fund.

(8) (a) The laboratory performing testing shall report test results to only designated officials in the Department of Corrections, the Department of Health, and the local law enforcement agency submitting the blood specimen.

    (b) Each department or agency shall designate those officials by written policy.

    (c) Designated officials may release information identifying an offender under Section 76-10-1302, 76-10-1303, or 76-10-1313 who has tested HIV positive as provided under Subsection 63-2-202(1) and for purposes of prosecution pursuant to Section 76-10-1309.

(9) (a) An employee of the local law enforcement agency, the Department of Corrections, or the Department of Health who discloses the HIV test results under this section is not civilly liable except when disclosure constitutes fraud or willful misconduct as provided in Section 63-30d-202.

    (b) An employee of the local law enforcement agency, the Department of Corrections, or the Department of Health who discloses the HIV test results under this section is not civilly or criminally liable, except when disclosure constitutes a knowing violation of Section 63-2-801.

(10) When the medical file is released as provided in Section 63-2-803, the local law enforcement agency, the Department of Corrections, or the Department of Health or its officers or employees are not liable for damages for release of the medical file. 2005

76-10-1312. Notice to offender of HIV positive test results.

(1) A person convicted under Section 76-10-1302, 76-10-1303, or 76-10-1313 who has tested positive for the HIV infection shall be notified of the test results in person at the sentencing hearing in the presence of the judge and counsel only.

(2) Whenever practicable, prior to notification in the district court, the offender shall be served personally with written notice by the local law enforcement agency at a meeting with a local law enforcement officer and a person from the state or county health department.

    (a) At that meeting, the offender shall be informed of the test results and counseled on HIV infection and its effects.

    (b) The local law enforcement agency shall arrange the time and place of notification and counseling.

(3) The notice shall contain the following information:

    (a) the date of the test;

    (b) the positive test results;

    (c) the name of the HIV positive individual; and

    (d) the following language:

"A person who has been convicted of prostitution under Section 76-10-1302, patronizing a prostitute under Section 76-10-1303, or sexual solicitation under Section 76-10-1313 after being tested and diagnosed as an HIV positive individual and receiving actual notice and personal written notice of the positive test results shall be guilty of a felony of the third degree pursuant to Section 76-10-1309."

(4) Upon conviction under Section 76-10-1309, and as a condition of probation, the offender shall receive treatment and counseling for HIV infection and drug abuse as provided in Title 62A, Chapter 15, Substance Abuse and Mental Health Act. 2002 (5th S.S.)

76-10-1313. Sexual solicitation — Penalty.

(1) A person is guilty of sexual solicitation when:

    (a) he offers or agrees to commit any sexual activity with another person for a fee; or

    (b) he pays or offers or agrees to pay another person to commit any sexual activity for a fee.

(2) Sexual solicitation is a class B misdemeanor. However, any person who is convicted a second time, and on all subsequent convictions, under this section or under a local ordinance adopted in compliance with Section 76-10-1307, is guilty of a class A misdemeanor, except as provided in Section 76-10-1309. 1993

76-10-1314. Examination of testing procedures and results in legal proceedings.

(1) Employees of the laboratory who conduct laboratory analysis of blood samples for presence of antibody to HIV provided pursuant to a request by a law enforcement agency or the Department of Corrections under Section 76-10-1311, may be examined in a legal proceeding of any kind or character as to:

    (a) the nature of the testing;

    (b) the validity of the testing;

    (c) the results of the test;

    (d) the HIV positivity or negativity of the person tested;

    (e) the evidentiary chain of custody; and

    (f) other factors relevant to the prosecution, subject to the court's ruling.

(2) This section applies only to the criminal investigation and prosecution under Section 76-10-1309 which permits enhanced penalties upon a subsequent conviction for:

    (a) prostitution, Section 76-10-1302;

    (b) patronizing a prostitute, Section 76-10-1303; or

    (c) sexual solicitation, Section 76-10-1313. 1993

PART 14

REPEALER [REPEALED]

76-10-1401.   Repealed.   1996

PART 15

BUS PASSENGER SAFETY ACT

76-10-1501.   Short title.

This act shall be known and may be cited as the "Bus Passenger Safety Act."   1979

76-10-1502.   Legislative findings.

The Legislature finds that the continued orderly operation of bus transportation is beneficial to the commerce of the state and to the convenience of its citizens; that it is essential to the comfort, safety and well-being of bus passengers that orderly conduct be maintained; that the promotion of bus transportation is beneficial to the economy of the state and conservation of energy; and that an increasing number of citizens avail themselves of this mode of transportation.   1979

76-10-1503.   Definitions.

As used in this act:

(1) "Bus" means any passenger bus or coach or other motor vehicle having a seating capacity of 15 or more passengers operated by a bus company for the purpose of carrying passengers or cargo for hire and includes a transit vehicle, as defined in Section 17A-2-1004, of a public transit district under Title 17A, Chapter 2, Part 10, Utah Public Transit District Act.

(2) "Bus company" or "company" means any person, group of persons or corporation providing for-hire transportation to passengers or cargo by bus upon the highways in the state, including passengers and cargo in interstate or intrastate travel. These terms also include local public bodies, public transit districts, municipalities, public corporations, boards and commissions established under the laws of the state providing transportation to passengers or cargo by bus upon the highways in the state, whether or not for hire.

(3) "Charter" means a group of persons, pursuant to a common purpose and under a single contract, and at a fixed charge in accordance with a bus company's tariff, which has acquired the exclusive use of a bus to travel together to a specified destination or destinations.

(4) "Passenger" means any person transported or served by a bus company, including persons accompanying or meeting another being transported, any person shipping or receiving cargo and any person purchasing a ticket or receiving a pass.

(5) "Terminal" means a bus station or depot or any other facility operated or leased by or operated on behalf of a bus company and includes a transit facility, as defined in Section 17A-2-1004, of a public transit district under Title 17A, Chapter 2, Part 10, Utah Public Transit District Act. This term includes a reasonable area immediately adjacent to any designated stop along the route traveled by any bus operated by a bus company and parking lots or areas adjacent to terminals.   1998

76-10-1504.   Bus hijacking — Assault with intent to commit hijacking — Use of a dangerous weapon or firearm — Penalties.

(1) A person is guilty of bus hijacking if he seizes or exercises control, by force or violence or threat of force or violence, of any bus within the state. Bus hijacking is a first degree felony.

(2) A person is guilty of assault with the intent to commit bus hijacking if he intimidates, threatens, or commits assault or battery toward any driver, attendant, guard, or any other person in control of a bus so as to interfere with the performance of duties by such person. Assault with the intent to commit bus hijacking is a second degree felony.

(3) Any person who, in the commission of assault with intent to commit bus hijacking, uses a dangerous weapon, as defined in Section 76-1-601, is guilty of a first degree felony.

(4) (a) Any person who boards a bus with a concealed dangerous weapon or firearm upon his person or effects is guilty of a second degree felony.

(b) The prohibition of Subsection (4)(a) does not apply to elected or appointed peace officers or commercial security personnel who are in possession of weapons or firearms used in the course and scope of their employment, or a person licensed to carry a concealed weapon; nor shall the prohibition apply to persons in possession of weapons or firearms with the consent of the owner of the bus or his agent, or the lessee or bailee of the bus.   1998

76-10-1505.   Discharging firearms and hurling missiles into buses and terminals — Exception.

(1) Any person who discharges a firearm or hurls a missile at or into any bus or terminal shall be guilty of a third degree felony.

(2) The prohibition of this section does not apply to elected or appointed peace officers or commercial security personnel who discharge firearms or hurl missiles in the course and scope of their employment.   1999

76-10-1506.   Threatening breach of peace — Disorderly conduct — Foul language — Refusing requests — Use of controlled substance, liquor, or tobacco — Ejection of passenger.

(1) A person is guilty of a class C misdemeanor, if the person:

(a) threatens a breach of the peace, is disorderly, or uses obscene, profane, or vulgar language on a bus;

(b) is in or upon any bus while unlawfully under the influence of a controlled substance as defined in Section 58-37-2;

(c) fails to obey a reasonable request or order of a bus driver, bus company representative, a nondrinking designee other than the driver as provided in Subsection 32A-12-213(3)(c)(ii), or other person in charge or control of a bus or terminal;

(d) ingests any controlled substance, unless prescribed by a physician or medical facility, in or upon any bus, or drinks intoxicating liquor in or upon any bus, except a chartered bus as defined and provided in Sections 32A-1-105 and 41-6a-526; or

(e) smokes tobacco or other products in or upon any bus, except a chartered bus.

(2) If any person violates Subsection (1), the driver of the bus or person in charge thereof may stop at the place where the offense is committed or at the next regular or convenient stopping place and remove such person, using only such force as may be necessary to accomplish the removal, and the driver or person in

charge may request the assistance of passengers to assist in the removal.

(3) The driver or person in charge may cause the person so removed to be detained and delivered to the proper authorities. 2005

76-10-1507. Exclusion of persons without bona fide business from terminal — Firearms and dangerous materials — Surveillance devices and seizure of offending materials — Detention of violators — Private security personnel.

(1) In order to provide for the safety, welfare and comfort of passengers, a bus company may refuse admission to terminals to any person not having bona fide business within the terminal. Any such refusal shall not be inconsistent or contrary to state or federal laws or regulations, or to any ordinance of the political subdivision in which the terminal is located. An authorized bus company representative may require any person in a terminal to identify himself and state his business. Failure to comply with such request or to state an acceptable business purpose shall be grounds for the representative to request that the person depart the terminal. Any person who refuses to comply with such a request shall be guilty of a class C misdemeanor.

(2) Any person who carries a concealed dangerous weapon, firearm, or any explosive, highly inflammable or hazardous materials or devices into a terminal or aboard a bus shall be guilty of a third degree felony. The bus company may employ reasonable means, including mechanical, electronic or x-ray devices to detect such items concealed in baggage or upon the person of any passenger. Upon the discovery of any such item, the company may obtain possession and retain custody thereof until it is transferred to a peace officer.

(3) An authorized bus company representative may detain within a terminal or bus any person violating the provisions of this act for a reasonable time until law enforcement authorities arrive. Such detention shall not constitute unlawful imprisonment and neither the bus company nor the representative shall be civilly or criminally liable upon grounds of unlawful imprisonment or assault, provided that only reasonable and necessary force is exercised against any person so detained.

(4) A bus company may employ or contract for private security personnel. Such personnel may detain within a terminal or bus any person violating the provisions of this act for a reasonable time until law enforcement authorities arrive, and may use reasonable and necessary force in subduing or detaining any person violating this act. 1998

76-10-1508. Theft of baggage or cargo.

Any person who removes any baggage, cargo or other item transported upon a bus or stored in a terminal without consent of the owner of the property or the bus company, or its duly authorized representative is guilty of theft and shall be punished pursuant to Section 76-6-412. 1979

76-10-1509. Obstructing operation of bus.

Any person who unlawfully obstructs or impedes by force or violence, or any means of intimidation, the regular operation of a bus is guilty of a class C misdemeanor. 1979

76-10-1510. Obstructing operation of bus — Conspiracy.

Two or more persons who willfully or maliciously combine or conspire to violate Section 76-10-1509 shall each be guilty of a class C misdemeanor. 1979

76-10-1511. Cumulative and supplemental nature of act.

The provisions of this act shall be cumulative and supplemental to the provisions of any other law of the state. 1979

PART 16

PATTERN OF UNLAWFUL ACTIVITY ACT

76-10-1601. Short title.

This act is the "Pattern of Unlawful Activity Act." 1987

76-10-1602. Definitions.

As used in this part:

(1) "Enterprise" means any individual, sole proprietorship, partnership, corporation, business trust, association, or other legal entity, and any union or group of individuals associated in fact although not a legal entity, and includes illicit as well as licit entities.

(2) "Pattern of unlawful activity" means engaging in conduct which constitutes the commission of at least three episodes of unlawful activity, which episodes are not isolated, but have the same or similar purposes, results, participants, victims, or methods of commission, or otherwise are interrelated by distinguishing characteristics. Taken together, the episodes shall demonstrate continuing unlawful conduct and be related either to each other or to the enterprise. At least one of the episodes comprising a pattern of unlawful activity shall have occurred after July 31, 1981. The most recent act constituting part of a pattern of unlawful activity as defined by this part shall have occurred within five years of the commission of the next preceding act alleged as part of the pattern.

(3) "Person" includes any individual or entity capable of holding a legal or beneficial interest in property, including state, county, and local governmental entities.

(4) "Unlawful activity" means to directly engage in conduct or to solicit, request, command, encourage, or intentionally aid another person to engage in conduct which would constitute any offense described by the following crimes or categories of crimes, or to attempt or conspire to engage in an act which would constitute any of those offenses, regardless of whether the act is in fact charged or indicted by any authority or is classified as a misdemeanor or a felony:

(a) any act prohibited by the criminal provisions of Title 13, Chapter 10, Unauthorized Recording Practices Act;

(b) any act prohibited by the criminal provisions of Title 19, Environmental Quality Code, Sections 19-1-101 through 19-7-109;

(c) taking, destroying, or possessing wildlife or parts of wildlife for the primary purpose of sale, trade, or other pecuniary gain, in violation of Title 23, Chapter 13, Wildlife Resources Code of Utah, or Section 23-20-4;

(d) false claims for medical benefits, kickbacks, and any other act prohibited by False Claims Act, Sections 26-20-1 through 26-20-12;

(e) any act prohibited by the criminal provisions of Title 32A, Chapter 12, Criminal Offenses;

(f) any act prohibited by the criminal provisions of Title 57, Chapter 11, Utah Uniform Land Sales Practices Act;

(g) any act prohibited by the criminal provisions of Title 58, Chapter 37, Utah Controlled Substances Act, or Title 58, Chapter 37b, Imitation Controlled Substances Act, Title 58, Chapter 37c, Utah Controlled Substance Precursor Act, or Title 58, Chapter 37d, Clandestine Drug Lab Act;

(h) any act prohibited by the criminal provisions of Title 61, Chapter 1, Utah Uniform Securities Act;

(i) any act prohibited by the criminal provisions of Title 63, Chapter 56, Utah Procurement Code;

(j) assault or aggravated assault, Sections 76-5-102 and 76-5-103;

(k) a terroristic threat, Section 76-5-107;

(l) criminal homicide, Sections 76-5-201, 76-5-202, and 76-5-203;

(m) kidnapping or aggravated kidnapping, Sections 76-5-301 and 76-5-302;

(n) sexual exploitation of a minor, Section 76-5a-3;

(o) arson or aggravated arson, Sections 76-6-102 and 76-6-103;

(p) causing a catastrophe, Section 76-6-105;

(q) burglary or aggravated burglary, Sections 76-6-202 and 76-6-203;

(r) burglary of a vehicle, Section 76-6-204;

(s) manufacture or possession of an instrument for burglary or theft, Section 76-6-205;

(t) robbery or aggravated robbery, Sections 76-6-301 and 76-6-302;

(u) theft, Section 76-6-404;

(v) theft by deception, Section 76-6-405;

(w) theft by extortion, Section 76-6-406;

(x) receiving stolen property, Section 76-6-408;

(y) theft of services, Section 76-6-409;

(z) forgery, Section 76-6-501;

(aa) fraudulent use of a credit card, Sections 76-6-506.1, 76-6-506.2, and 76-6-506.4;

(bb) deceptive business practices, Section 76-6-507;

(cc) bribery or receiving bribe by person in the business of selection, appraisal, or criticism of goods, Section 76-6-508;

(dd) bribery of a labor official, Section 76-6-509;

(ee) defrauding creditors, Section 76-6-511;

(ff) acceptance of deposit by insolvent financial institution, Section 76-6-512;

(gg) unlawful dealing with property by fiduciary, Section 76-6-513;

(hh) bribery or threat to influence contest, Section 76-6-514;

(ii) making a false credit report, Section 76-6-517;

(jj) criminal simulation, Section 76-6-518;

(kk) criminal usury, Section 76-6-520;

(ll) fraudulent insurance act, Section 76-6-521;

(mm) computer crimes, Section 76-6-703;

(nn) identity fraud, Section 76-6-1102;

(oo) sale of a child, Section 76-7-203;

(pp) bribery to influence official or political actions, Section 76-8-103;

(qq) threats to influence official or political action, Section 76-8-104;

(rr) receiving bribe or bribery by public servant, Section 76-8-105;

(ss) receiving bribe or bribery for endorsement of person as public servant, Section 76-8-106;

(tt) official misconduct, Sections 76-8-201 and 76-8-202;

(uu) obstruction of justice, Section 76-8-306;

(vv) acceptance of bribe or bribery to prevent criminal prosecution, Section 76-8-308;

(ww) false or inconsistent material statements, Section 76-8-502;

(xx) false or inconsistent statements, Section 76-8-503;

(yy) written false statements, Section 76-8-504;

(zz) tampering with a witness or soliciting or receiving a bribe, Section 76-8-508;

(aaa) retaliation against a witness, victim, or informant, Section 76-8-508.3;

(bbb) extortion or bribery to dismiss criminal proceeding, Section 76-8-509;

(ccc) public assistance fraud in violation of Section 76-8-1203, 76-8-1204, or 76-8-1205;

(ddd) unemployment insurance fraud, Section 76-8-1301;

(eee) intentionally or knowingly causing one animal to fight with another, Subsection 76-9-301(1)(f);

(fff) possession, use, or removal of explosives, chemical, or incendiary devices or parts, Section 76-10-306;

(ggg) delivery to common carrier, mailing, or placement on premises of an incendiary device, Section 76-10-307;

(hhh) possession of a deadly weapon with intent to assault, Section 76-10-507;

(iii) unlawful marking of pistol or revolver, Section 76-10-521;

(jjj) alteration of number or mark on pistol or revolver, Section 76-10-522;

(kkk) forging or counterfeiting trademarks, trade name, or trade device, Section 76-10-1002;

(lll) selling goods under counterfeited trademark, trade name, or trade devices, Section 76-10-1003;

(mmm) sales in containers bearing registered trademark of substituted articles, Section 76-10-1004;

(nnn) selling or dealing with article bearing registered trademark or service mark with intent to defraud, Section 76-10-1006;

(ooo) gambling, Section 76-10-1102;

(ppp) gambling fraud, Section 76-10-1103;

(qqq) gambling promotion, Section 76-10-1104;

(rrr) possessing a gambling device or record, Section 76-10-1105;

(sss) confidence game, Section 76-10-1109;

(ttt) distributing pornographic material, Section 76-10-1204;

(uuu) inducing acceptance of pornographic material, Section 76-10-1205;

(vvv) dealing in harmful material to a minor, Section 76-10-1206;

(www) distribution of pornographic films, Section 76-10-1222;

(xxx) indecent public displays, Section 76-10-1228;

(yyy) prostitution, Section 76-10-1302;

(zzz) aiding prostitution, Section 76-10-1304;

(aaaa) exploiting prostitution, Section 76-10-1305;

(bbbb) aggravated exploitation of prostitution, Section 76-10-1306;

(cccc) communications fraud, Section 76-10-1801;

(dddd) any act prohibited by the criminal provisions of Title 76, Chapter 10, Part 19, Money Laundering and Currency Transaction Reporting Act;

(eeee) any act prohibited by the criminal provisions of the laws governing taxation in this state; and

(ffff) any act illegal under the laws of the United States and enumerated in Title 18, Section 1961 (1)(B), (C), and (D) of the United States Code.   2004

76-10-1603. Unlawful acts.

(1) It is unlawful for any person who has received any proceeds derived, whether directly or indirectly, from a pattern of unlawful activity in which the person has participated as a principal, to use or invest, directly or indirectly, any part of that income, or the proceeds of the income, or the proceeds derived from the investment or use of those proceeds, in the acquisition of any interest in, or the establishment or operation of, any enterprise.

(2) It is unlawful for any person through a pattern of unlawful activity to acquire or maintain, directly or indirectly, any interest in or control of any enterprise.

(3) It is unlawful for any person employed by or associated with any enterprise to conduct or participate, whether directly or indirectly, in the conduct of that enterprise's affairs through a pattern of unlawful activity.

(4) It is unlawful for any person to conspire to violate any provision of Subsection (1), (2), or (3).   1987

76-10-1603.5. Violation a felony — Costs — Forfeiture — Fines — Divestiture — Restrictions — Dissolution or reorganization — Prior restraint.

(1) A person who violates any provision of Section 76-10-1603 is guilty of a second degree felony. In addition to penalties prescribed by law, the court may order the person found guilty of the felony to pay to the state, if the attorney general brought the action, or to the county, if the county attorney or district attorney brought the action, the costs of investigating and prosecuting the offense and the costs of securing the forfeitures provided for in this section. The person shall forfeit to the Uniform School Fund, as provided in Section 53A-16-101:

(a) any interest acquired or maintained in violation of any provision of Section 76-10-1603;

(b) any interest in, security of, claim against, or property or contractual right of any kind affording a source of influence over any enterprise which the person has established, operated, controlled, conducted, or participated in the conduct of in violation of Section 76-10-1603; and

(c) any property constituting or derived from the net proceeds which the person obtained, directly or indirectly, from the conduct constituting the pattern of unlawful activity or from any act or conduct constituting the pattern of unlawful activity proven as part of the violation of any provision of Section 76-10-1603.

(2) If a violation of Section 76-10-1603 is based on a pattern of unlawful activity consisting of acts or conduct in violation of Section 76-10-1204, 76-10-1205, 76-10-1206, or 76-10-1222, the property subject to forfeiture under this section is limited to property, the seizure or forfeiture of which would not constitute a prior restraint on the exercise of an affected party's rights under the First Amendment to the Constitution of the United States or Article I, Sec. 15 of the Utah Constitution, or would not otherwise unlawfully interfere with the exercise of those rights.

(3) In lieu of a fine otherwise authorized by law for a violation of Section 76-10-1603, a defendant who derives net proceeds from a conduct prohibited by Section 76-10-1603 may be fined not more than twice the amount of the net proceeds.

(4) Property subject to criminal forfeiture in accord with the procedures and substantive protections of Title 24, Chapter 1, Utah Uniform Forfeiture Procedures Act:

(a) includes:

(i) real property, including things growing on, affixed to, and found in land; and

(ii) tangible and intangible personal property including money, rights, privileges, interests, claims, and securities of any kind; but

(b) does not include property exchanged or to be exchanged for services rendered in connection with the defense of the charges or any related criminal case.

(5) Upon conviction for violating any provision of Section 76-10-1603, and in addition to any penalty prescribed by law and in addition to any forfeitures provided for in this section, the court may do any or all of the following:

(a) order the person to divest himself of any interest in or any control, direct or indirect, of any enterprise;

(b) impose reasonable restrictions on the future activities or investments of any person, including prohibiting the person from engaging in the same type of endeavor as the enterprise engaged in, to the extent the Utah Constitution and the Constitution of the United States permit; or

(c) order the dissolution or reorganization of any enterprise.

(6) If a violation of Section 76-10-1603 is based on a pattern of unlawful activity consisting of acts or conduct in violation of Section 76-10-1204, 76-10-1205, 76-10-1206, or 76-10-1222, the court may not enter any order that would amount to a prior restraint on the exercise of an affected party's rights under the First Amendment to the Constitution of the United States or Article I, Section 15, Utah Constitution.

(7) All rights, title, and interest in forfeitable property described in Subsections (1) and (2) vest in the state treasurer, on behalf of the Uniform School Fund, upon the commission of the act or conduct giving rise to the forfeiture under this section.

(8) For purposes of this section, the "net proceeds" of an offense means property acquired as a result of the violation minus the direct costs of acquiring the property.   2002

76-10-1604. Enforcement authority of peace officers.

Notwithstanding any law to the contrary, peace officers in the state of Utah shall have authority to enforce the criminal provisions of this act by initiating investigations, assisting grand juries, obtaining indictments, filing informations, and assisting in the prosecution of criminal cases through the attorney general or county attorneys' offices.   1981

76-10-1605. Remedies of person injured by a pattern of unlawful activity — Double damages — Costs, including attorney's fee — Arbitration — Agency — Burden of proof — Actions by attorney general, county attorney, or district attorney — Dismissal — Statute of limitations — Authorized orders of district court.

(1) A person injured in his person, business, or property by a person engaged in conduct forbidden by any provision of Section 76-10-1603 may sue in an appropriate district court and recover twice the damages he sustains, regardless of whether:

(a) the injury is separate or distinct from the injury suffered as a result of the acts or conduct constituting the pattern of unlawful conduct alleged as part of the cause of action; or

(b) the conduct has been adjudged criminal by any court of the state or of the United States.

(2) A party who prevails on a cause of action brought under this section recovers the cost of the suit, including a reasonable attorney's fee.

(3) All actions arising under this section which are grounded in fraud are subject to arbitration under Title 78, Chapter 31a.

(4) In all actions under this section, a principal is liable for actual damages for harm caused by an agent acting within the scope of either his employment or apparent authority. A principal is liable for double damages only if the pattern of unlawful activity alleged and proven as part of the cause of action was authorized, solicited, requested, commanded, undertaken, performed, or recklessly tolerated by the board of directors or a high managerial agent acting within the scope of his employment.

(5) In all actions arising under this section, the burden of proof is clear and convincing evidence.

(6) The attorney general, county attorney, or, if within a prosecution district, the district attorney may maintain actions under this section on behalf of the state, the county, or any person injured by a person engaged in conduct forbidden by any provision of Section 76-10-1603, to prevent, restrain, or remedy injury as defined in this section and may recover the damages and costs allowed by this section.

(7) In all actions under this section, the elements of each claim or cause of action shall be stated with particularity against each defendant.

(8) If an action, claim, or counterclaim brought or asserted by a private party under this section is dismissed prior to trial or disposed of on summary judgment, or if it is determined at trial that there is no liability, the prevailing party shall recover from the party who brought the action or asserted the claim or counterclaim the amount of its reasonable expenses incurred because of the defense against the action, claim, or counterclaim, including a reasonable attorney's fee.

(9) An action or proceeding brought under this section shall be commenced within three years after the conduct prohibited by Section 76-10-1603 terminates or the cause of action accrues, whichever is later. This provision supersedes any limitation to the contrary.

(10) (a) In any action brought under this section, the district court has jurisdiction to prevent, restrain, or remedy injury as defined by this section by issuing appropriate orders after making provisions for the rights of innocent persons.

(b) Before liability is determined in any action brought under this section, the district court may:

(i) issue restraining orders and injunctions;

(ii) require satisfactory performance bonds or any other bond it considers appropriate and necessary in connection with any property or any requirement imposed upon a party by the court; and

(iii) enter any other order the court considers necessary and proper.

(c) After a determination of liability, the district court may, in addition to granting the relief allowed in Subsection (1), do any one or all of the following:

(i) order any person to divest himself of any interest in or any control, direct or indirect, of any enterprise;

(ii) impose reasonable restrictions on the future activities or investments of any person, including prohibiting any person from engaging in the same type of endeavor as the enterprise engaged in, to the extent the Utah Constitution and the Constitution of the United States permit; or

(iii) order the dissolution or reorganization of any enterprise.

(d) However, if an action is brought to obtain any relief provided by this section, and if the conduct prohibited by Section 76-10-1603 has for its pattern of unlawful activity acts or conduct illegal under Section 76-10-1204, 76-10-1205, 76-10-1206, or 76-10-1222, the court may not enter any order that would amount to a prior restraint on the exercise of an affected party's rights under the First Amendment to the Constitution of the United States, or Article I, Sec. 15 of the Utah Constitution. The court shall, upon the request of any affected party, and upon the notice to all parties, prior to the issuance of any order provided for in this subsection, and at any later time, hold hearings as necessary to determine whether any materials at issue are obscene or pornographic and to determine if there is probable cause to believe that any act or conduct alleged violates Section 76-10-1204, 76-10-1205, 76-10-1206, or 76-10-1222. In making its findings the court shall be guided by the same considerations required of a court making similar findings in criminal cases brought under Section 76-10-1204, 76-10-1205, 76-10-1206, or 76-10-1222, including, but not limited to, the definitions in Sections 76-10-1201, 76-10-1203, and 76-10-1216, and the exemptions in Section 76-10-1226.   1993

76-10-1606. Repealed.   1987

76-10-1607. Evidentiary value of criminal judgment in civil proceeding.

A final judgment or decree rendered in favor of the state or a county in any criminal proceeding brought by this state or a county shall preclude the defendant from denying the essential allegations of the criminal offense in any subsequent civil proceeding.   1981

76-10-1608. Severability clause.

If any part or application of the Utah Pattern of Unlawful Activity Act is held invalid, the remainder of this part, or its application to other situations or persons, is not affected.   1987

76-10-1609. Prospective application.

The amendments to the Utah Pattern of Unlawful Activity Act are prospective in nature and apply only to civil causes of action accruing after the effective date of this act. However, crimes committed prior to the effective date of this act may comprise part of a pattern of unlawful activity if at least one of the criminal episodes comprising that pattern occurs after the effective date of this act and the pattern otherwise meets the definition of pattern of unlawful activity as defined in Section 76-10-1602.   1987

PART 17

CABLE TELEVISION PROGRAMMING DECENCY ACT [REPEALED]

76-10-1701 to 76-10-1708. Repealed.   1988

PART 18

COMMUNICATIONS FRAUD

76-10-1801. Communications fraud — Elements — Penalties.

(1) Any person who has devised any scheme or artifice to defraud another or to obtain from another money, property, or anything of value by means of false or fraudulent pretenses, representations, promises, or material omissions, and who communicates directly or indirectly with any person by any means for the purpose of executing or concealing the scheme or artifice is guilty of:

(a) a class B misdemeanor when the value of the property, money, or thing obtained or sought to be obtained is less than $300;

(b) a class A misdemeanor when the value of the property, money, or thing obtained or sought to be obtained is or exceeds $300 but is less than $1,000;

(c) a third degree felony when the value of the property, money, or thing obtained or sought to be obtained is or exceeds $1,000 but is less than $5,000;

(d) a second degree felony when the value of the property, money, or thing obtained or sought to be obtained is or exceeds $5,000; and

(e) a second degree felony when the object of the scheme or artifice to defraud is other than the obtaining of something of monetary value.

(2) The determination of the degree of any offense under Subsection (1) shall be measured by the total value of all property, money, or things obtained or sought to be obtained by the scheme or artifice described in Subsection (1) except as provided in Subsection (1)(e).

(3) Reliance on the part of any person is not a necessary element of the offense described in Subsection (1).

(4) An intent on the part of the perpetrator of any offense described in Subsection (1) to permanently deprive any person of property, money, or thing of value is not a necessary element of the offense.

(5) Each separate communication made for the purpose of executing or concealing a scheme or artifice described in Subsection (1) is a separate act and offense of communication fraud.

(6) (a) To communicate as described in Subsection (1) means to bestow, convey, make known, recount, impart; to give by way of information; to talk over; or to transmit information.

(b) Means of communication include but are not limited to use of the mail, telephone, telegraph, radio, television, newspaper, computer, and spoken and written communication.

(7) A person may not be convicted under this section unless the pretenses, representations, promises,

or material omissions made or omitted were made or omitted intentionally, knowingly, or with a reckless disregard for the truth.   1995

PART 19

MONEY LAUNDERING AND CURRENCY TRANSACTION REPORTING

76-10-1901. Short title.

This part is known as the Money Laundering and Currency Transaction Reporting Act.   1989

76-10-1902. Definitions.

As used in this part:

(1) "Bank" means each agent, agency, or office in this state of any person doing business in any one of the following capacities:

(a) a commercial bank or trust company organized under the laws of this state or of the United States;

(b) a private bank;

(c) a savings and loan association or a building and loan association organized under the laws of this state or of the United States;

(d) an insured institution as defined in Section 401 of the National Housing Act;

(e) a savings bank, industrial bank, or other thrift institution;

(f) a credit union organized under the laws of this state or of the United States; or

(g) any other organization chartered under Title 7, Financial Institutions, and subject to the supervisory authority set forth in that title.

(2) "Conducts" includes initiating, concluding, or participating in initiating or concluding a transaction.

(3) (a) "Currency" means the coin and paper money of the United States or of any other country that is designated as legal tender, that circulates, and is customarily used and accepted as a medium of exchange in the country of issuance.

(b) "Currency" includes United States silver certificates, United States notes, Federal Reserve notes, and foreign bank notes customarily used and accepted as a medium of exchange in a foreign country.

(4) "Financial institution" means any agent, agency, branch, or office within this state of any person doing business, whether or not on a regular basis or as an organized business concern, in one or more of the following capacities:

(a) a bank, except bank credit card systems;

(b) a broker or dealer in securities;

(c) a currency dealer or exchanger, including a person engaged in the business of check cashing;

(d) an issuer, seller, or redeemer of travelers checks or money orders, except as a selling agent exclusively who does not sell more than $150,000 of the instruments within any 30-day period;

(e) a licensed transmitter of funds or other person engaged in the business of transmitting funds;

(f) a telegraph company;

(g) a person subject to supervision by any state or federal supervisory authority; or

(h) the United States Postal Service regarding the sale of money orders.

(5) "Financial transaction" means a transaction:

(a) involving the movement of funds by wire or other means or involving one or more monetary instruments, which in any way or degree affects commerce; or

(b) involving the use of a financial institution that is engaged in, or its activities affect commerce in any way or degree.

(6) The phrase "knows that the property involved represents the proceeds of some form of unlawful activity" means that the person knows or it was represented to the person that the property involved represents proceeds from a form of activity, although the person does not necessarily know which form of activity, that constitutes a crime under state or federal law, regardless of whether or not the activity is specified in Subsection (12).

(7) "Monetary instruments" means coins or currency of the United States or of any other country, travelers checks, personal checks, bank checks, money orders, and investment securities or negotiable instruments in bearer form or in other form so that title passes upon delivery.

(8) "Person" means an individual, corporation, partnership, trust or estate, joint stock company, association, syndicate, joint venture, or other unincorporated organization or group, and all other entities cognizable as legal personalities.

(9) "Proceeds" means property acquired or derived directly or indirectly from, produced through, realized through, or caused by an act or omission and includes any property of any kind.

(10) "Property" means anything of value, and includes any interest in property, including any benefit, privilege, land, or right with respect to anything of value, whether real or personal, tangible or intangible.

(11) "Prosecuting agency" means the office of the attorney general or the office of the county attorney, including any attorney on the staff whether acting in a civil or criminal capacity.

(12) "Specified unlawful activity" means any unlawful activity defined as an unlawful activity in Section 76-10-1602, except an illegal act under Title 18, Section 1961(1)(B), (C), and (D), United States Code, and includes activity committed outside this state which, if committed within this state, would be unlawful activity.

(13) "Transaction" means a purchase, sale, loan, pledge, gift, transfer, delivery, or other disposition. With respect to a financial institution, "transaction" includes a deposit, withdrawal, transfer between accounts, exchange of currency, loan, extension of credit, purchase or sale of any stock, bond, certificate of deposit, or other monetary instrument, or any other payment, transfer, or delivery by, through, or to a financial institution, by whatever means effected.

(14) "Transaction in currency" means a transaction involving the physical transfer of currency from one person to another. A transaction that is a transfer of funds by means of bank check, bank draft, wire transfer, or other written order that does not include the physical transfer of currency is not a transaction in currency under this chapter.   2000

76-10-1903. Money laundering.

(1) A person commits the offense of money laundering who:

(a) transports, receives, or acquires the property which is in fact proceeds of the specified unlawful activity, knowing that the property involved represents the proceeds of some form of unlawful activity;

(b) makes proceeds of unlawful activity available to another by transaction or transportation, or other means, knowing that it is intended to be used for the purpose of continuing or furthering the commission of specified unlawful activity;

(c) conducts a transaction knowing the property involved in the transaction represents the proceeds of some form of unlawful activity with the intent:

(i) to promote the unlawful activity;

(ii) to conceal or disguise the nature, location, source, ownership, or control of the property; or

(iii) to avoid a transaction reporting requirement under this chapter; or

(d) knowingly accepts or receives property which is represented to be proceeds of unlawful activity.

(2) Under Subsection (1)(d), knowledge that the property represents the proceeds of unlawful activity may be established by proof that a law enforcement officer or person acting at the request of a law enforcement officer made such representations and the person's subsequent statements or actions indicate that the person believed those representations to be true.   1996

76-10-1904. Money laundering — Penalty.

(1) A person who violates Subsection 76-10-1903(1)(a), (b), or (c) is guilty of a second degree felony.

(2) A person who violates Subsection 76-10-1903(1)(d) is guilty of a third degree felony.   1996

76-10-1905. Repealed.   1993

76-10-1906. Reporting by financial institutions — Criminal and civil penalties — Enforcement.

(1) (a) All financial institutions in this state required to file reports under Title 31, Sections 5311 through 5313, United States Code Annotated, as prescribed by 31 Code of Federal Regulations Sections 103.21 and 103.22, shall file a duplicate copy of the required report with the Utah Division of Investigation.

(b) All persons engaged in a trade or business, except financial institutions referred to in Subsection (1)(a), who receive more than $10,000 in domestic or foreign currency in one transaction, or who receive this amount through two or more related transactions during any one business day, shall complete and file with the Utah Division of Investigation the information required by Title 26, Section 6050I, United States Code Annotated, concerning returns relating to currency received in trade or business.

(c) Any person who knowingly and intentionally fails to comply with the reporting requirements of this subsection is:

(i) on a first conviction, guilty of a class C misdemeanor; and

(ii) on a second or subsequent conviction, guilty of a class A misdemeanor.

(d) A person is guilty of a third degree felony who knowingly and intentionally violates any part of this subsection and the violation is committed either:

(i) in furtherance of the commission of any other violation of state law; or

(ii) as part of a pattern of illegal activity involving transactions exceeding $100,000 in any 12-month period.

(2) (a) The Utah Division of Investigation and the Office of the Attorney General shall enforce compliance with Subsection (1) and are custodians of and have access to all information and documents filed under Subsection (1).

(b) The information is confidential except any law enforcement agency, county attorney, or district attorney, when establishing a clear need for the information for investigative purposes, shall have access and shall maintain the information in a confidential manner except as otherwise provided by the Utah Rules of Criminal Procedure.
1998

76-10-1907. Separate offenses.

(1) Under this part each individual currency transaction exceeding $10,000 and made in violation of Subsection 76-10-1906(1) or each financial transaction in violation of Section 76-10-1903 or 76-10-1904 involving the movement of funds in excess of $10,000 is a separate punishable offense.

(2) Under this part each failure to file a report as required under Subsection 76-10-1906(1) is a separate punishable offense.   1989

76-10-1908. Forfeiture — Grounds — Procedure — Disposition of property seized.

(1) (a) Any of the following property shall be subject to civil or criminal forfeiture:

(i) any conveyance including vehicles, aircraft, watercraft, or other vessel used in violation of Section 76-10-1904; and

(ii) any property which is the net proceeds of a violation of Section 76-10-1903, 76-10-1904, or 76-10-1906.

(b) For purposes of this section, the "net proceeds" of an offense means property acquired as a result of the violation minus the direct costs of acquiring the property.

(2) Property subject to forfeiture under Subsection (1) may be seized by any peace officer of this state upon process issued by any court having jurisdiction over the property. However, seizure without process may be made when:

(a) the seizure is incident to an arrest or search under a search warrant, an inspection under an administrative inspection warrant, under a writ of attachment, or under a writ of garnishment;

(b) the property subject to seizure has been the subject of a prior judgment in favor of the state in a criminal injunction or forfeiture proceeding under this section; or

(c) the peace officer has probable cause to believe that the property has been used in violation of Section 76-10-1903, 76-10-1904, or 76-10-1906.

(3) Forfeiture proceedings under this section shall be commenced in accordance with the procedures and substantive protections of Title 24, Chapter 1, Utah Uniform Forfeiture Procedures Act.

(4) Property taken or detained under this section is not repleviable but is in custody of the law enforcement agency making the seizure, subject only to the orders and decrees of the court or the official having jurisdiction. When property is seized under this chapter, the appropriate person or agency may:

(a) place the property under seal;

(b) remove the property to a place designated by it or the warrant under which it was seized; or

(c) take custody of the property and remove it to an appropriate location for disposition in accordance with law.   2002

PART 20

SECURITY OF RESEARCH FACILITIES

76-10-2001. Definitions.

As used in this part:

(1) "Building," in addition to its commonly-accepted meaning, means any watercraft, aircraft, trailer, sleeping car, or other structure or vehicle adapted for overnight accommodations of persons or for carrying on business and includes:

(a) each separately secured or occupied portion of the building or vehicle; and

(b) each structure appurtenant or connected to the building or vehicle.

(2) "Enter" means:

(a) an intrusion of any part of the body; or

(b) the intrusion of any physical object, sound wave, light ray, electronic signal, or other means of intrusion under the control of the actor.

(3) "Research" means studious and serious inquiry, examination, investigation, or experimentation aimed at the discovery, examination, or accumulation of facts, data, devices, theories, technologies, or applications done for any public, governmental, proprietorial, or teaching purpose.

(4) "Research facility" means any building, or separately secured yard, pad, pond, laboratory, pasture, pen, or corral which is not open to the public, the major use of which is to conduct research, to house research subjects, to store supplies, equipment, samples, specimens, records, data, prototypes, or other property used in or generated from research.   1989

76-10-2002. Burglary of a research facility — Penalties.

(1) A person is guilty of burglary of a research facility if he enters or remains unlawfully in a research facility with the intent to:

(a) obtain unauthorized control over any property, sample, specimen, record, data, test result, or proprietary information in the facility;

(b) alter or eradicate any sample, specimen, record, data, test result, or proprietary information in the facility;

(c) damage, deface, or destroy any property in the facility;

(d) release from confinement or remove any animal or biological vector in the facility regardless of whether or not that animal or vector is dangerous;

(e) commit an assault on any person;

(f) commit any other felony; or

(g) interfere with the personnel or operations of a research facility through any conduct that does not constitute an assault.

(2) A person who violates Subsection (1)(g) is guilty of a class A misdemeanor. A person who violates any other provision in this section is guilty of a felony of the second degree.   1989

PART 21

MISUSE OF RECYCLING BINS

76-10-2101. Use of recycling bins — Prohibited items — Penalties.

(1) As used in this section:

(a) "Recycling" means the process of collecting materials diverted from the waste stream for reuse.

(b) "Recycling bin" means any receptacle made available to the public by a governmental entity or private business for the collection of any source-separated item for recycling purposes.

(2) It is an infraction to place any prohibited item or substance in a recycling bin if the bin is posted with the following information printed legibly in basic English:

(a) a descriptive list of the items that may be deposited in the recycling bin, entitled in boldface capital letters: "ITEMS YOU MAY DEPOSIT IN THIS RECYCLING BIN:";

(b) at the end of the list in Subsection (a), the following statement in boldface capital letters: "REMOVING FROM THIS BIN ANY ITEM THAT IS LISTED ABOVE AND THAT YOU DID NOT PLACE IN THE CONTAINER IS THE CRIMINAL OFFENSE OF THEFT, PUNISHABLE BY LAW.";

(c) the following statement in boldface capital letters: "DEPOSIT OF ANY OTHER ITEM IN THIS RECYCLING BIN IS AGAINST THE LAW.";

(d) the following statement in boldface capital letters, posted on the recycling collection container in close proximity to the notices required under Subsections (2)(a), (b), and (c): "PLACING ANY ITEM OR SUBSTANCE IN THIS RECYCLING BIN OTHER THAN THOSE ALLOWED IN THE LIST POSTED ON THIS BIN IS AN INFRACTION, PUNISHABLE BY A MAXIMUM FINE OF $750."; and

(e) the name and telephone number of the entity that owns the recycling bin or is responsible for its placement and maintenance.   1992

PART 22

PUBLIC HEALTH OFFENSES

76-10-2201.   Unlawful body piercing and tattooing of a minor.

(1) As used in this section:

(a) "Body piercing" means the creation of an opening in the body, excluding the ear, for the purpose of inserting jewelry or other decoration.

(b) "Consent of a minor's parent or legal guardian" means the presence of a parent or legal guardian during the performance of body piercing or tattooing upon the minor after the parent or legal guardian has provided reasonable proof of personal identity and familial relationship.

(c) "Minor" means a person younger than 18 years of age who:

(i) is not married; and

(ii) has not been declared emancipated by a court of law.

(d) "Personal identification number" means the number of an apparently valid driver's license or other picture identification card that expressly states that the person is 18 years of age or older.

(e) "Tattoo" means to fix an indelible mark or figure upon the body by inserting a pigment under the skin or by producing scars.

(2) A person is guilty of unlawful body piercing of a minor if he performs or offers to perform a body piercing:

(a) upon a minor;

(b) without receiving the consent of the minor's parent or legal guardian; and

(c) for remuneration or in the course of a business or profession.

(3) A person is guilty of unlawful tattooing of a minor if he performs or offers to perform a tattooing:

(a) upon a minor;

(b) without receiving the consent of the minor's parent or legal guardian;

(c) for remuneration or in the course of a business or profession.

(4) A person is not guilty of Subsection (2) or (3) if the person:

(a) had no actual knowledge of the minor's age; and

(b) reviewed, recorded, and has maintained a personal identification number for the minor prior to performing an unlawful body piercing or unlawful tattooing.

(5) (a) A person who violates Subsection (2) or (3) is guilty of a class C misdemeanor.

(b) The owner or operator of a business in which a violation of Subsection (2) or (3) occurs is subject to a civil penalty of $750 for each violation.   1998

PART 23

CONTRIBUTING TO THE DELINQUENCY OF A MINOR

76-10-2301.   Contributing to the delinquency of a minor — Definitions — Penalties.

(1) For purposes of this part:

(a) "Adult" means a person 18 years of age or older.

(b) "Minor" means a person younger than 18 years of age.

(2) Any adult who commits any act or engages in any conduct which he knows or should know would have the effect of causing or encouraging a minor to commit an act which would be a misdemeanor or infraction criminal violation of any federal or state statute or any county or municipal ordinance if committed by an adult is guilty of a class B misdemeanor.

(3) A violation of Subsection (2) does not require that the minor be found to be delinquent or to have committed a delinquent act.

(4) An offense committed under Subsection (2) is in addition to any completed or inchoate offense which the actor may have committed personally or as a party.   2000

PART 24

COMMERCIAL TERRORISM

76-10-2401.   Definitions.

As used in this part:

(1) "Building", in addition to its commonly accepted meaning, means any watercraft, aircraft, trailer, sleeping car, or other structure or vehicle adapted for overnight accommodations of persons or for carrying on business and includes:

(a) each separately secured or occupied portion of the building or vehicle; and

(b) each structure appurtenant or connected to the building or vehicle.

(2) "Business" means a retail business dealing in tangible personal property.

(3) "Enter" means:

(a) an intrusion of any part of the body; or

(b) the intrusion of any physical object under the control of the actor.   2002

76-10-2402. Commercial terrorism — Penalties.

(1) A person is guilty of a misdemeanor if he enters or remains unlawfully on the premises of or in a building of any business with the intent to interfere with the employees, customers, personnel, or operations of a business through any conduct that does not constitute an offense listed under Subsection (2). A violation of this Subsection (1) is a class A misdemeanor.

(2) A person is guilty of felony commercial terrorism if he enters or remains unlawfully on the premises or in a building of any business with the intent to interfere with the employees, customers, personnel, or operations of a business and also with the intent to:

    (a) obtain unauthorized control over any merchandise, property, records, data, or proprietary information of the business;

    (b) alter, eradicate, or remove any merchandise, records, data, or proprietary information of the business;

    (c) damage, deface, or destroy any property on the premises of the business;

    (d) commit an assault on any person; or

    (e) commit any other felony.

(3) A person who violates any provision in Subsection (2) is guilty of a felony of the second degree.

(4) This section does not apply to action protected by the National Labor Relations Act, 29 U.S.C. Section 151 et seq., or the Federal Railway Labor Act, 45 U.S.C. Section 151 et seq.

(5) This section does not apply to a person's exercise of the rights under the First Amendment to the Constitution of the United States or under Article I, Sec. 15 of the Utah Constitution.   2002

PART 25

UNLAWFUL USE OF A LASER POINTER

76-10-2501. Unlawful use of a laser pointer — Definitions — Penalties.

(1) As used in this section:

    (a) "Laser light" means light that is amplified by stimulated emission of radiation.

    (b) "Laser pointer" means any portable device that emits a visible beam of laser light that may be directed at a person.

    (c) "Law enforcement officer" means an officer under Section 53-13-103.

(2) A person is guilty of unlawful use of a laser pointer if the person directs a beam of laser light from a laser pointer at:

    (a) a moving motor vehicle or its occupants; or

    (b) one whom the person knows or has reason to know is a law enforcement officer.

(3) It is an affirmative defense to a charge under Subsection (2)(b) that:

    (a) the law enforcement officer was:

        (i) not in uniform;

        (ii) not traveling in a vehicle identified as a law enforcement vehicle; and

        (iii) not otherwise engaged in an activity that would give the person reason to know him to be a law enforcement officer; and

    (b) the law enforcement officer was not otherwise known by the person to be a law enforcement officer.

(4) Violation of Subsection (2)(a) is an infraction. Violation of Subsection (2)(b) is a class C misdemeanor.

(5) If the violation of this section constitutes an offense subject to a greater penalty under another provision of Title 76, Utah Criminal Code, than is provided under this section, this section does not prohibit the prosecution and sentencing for the offense subject to a greater penalty.   2001

PART 26

SHAFTS AND WELLS — SAFETY

76-10-2601. Fencing of shafts and wells.

(1) Any person who has sunk or sinks a shaft or well on the public domain for any purpose shall enclose it with a substantial curb or fence, which shall be at least 4 ½ feet high.

(2) Any person violating this section is guilty of a class B misdemeanor.   2002

TITLE 77

UTAH CODE OF CRIMINAL PROCEDURE

CHAPTER 2

PROSECUTION, SCREENING, AND DIVERSION

77-2-4.2. Compromise of traffic charges — Limitations.

(1) As used in this section:

    (a) "Compromise" means referral of a person charged with a traffic violation to traffic school or other school, class, or remedial or rehabilitative program.

    (b) "Traffic violation" means any charge, by citation or information, of a violation of:

        (i) Title 41, Chapter 6a, Traffic Code, amounting to:

            (A) a class B misdemeanor;

            (B) a class C misdemeanor; or

            (C) an infraction; or

        (ii) any local traffic ordinance.

(2) Any compromise of a traffic violation shall be done pursuant to a plea in abeyance agreement as provided in Title 77, Chapter 2a, Pleas in Abeyance, except:

    (a) when the criminal prosecution is dismissed pursuant to Section 77-2-4; or

(b) when there is a plea by the defendant to and entry of a judgment by a court for the offense originally charged or for an amended charge.

(3) In all cases which are compromised pursuant to the provisions of Subsection (2):

    (a) the court, taking into consideration the offense charged, shall collect a plea in abeyance fee which shall:

        (i) be subject to the same surcharge as if imposed on a criminal fine; and

        (ii) be allocated subject to the surcharge as if paid as a criminal fine under Section 78-3-14.5 and a surcharge under Title 63, Chapter 63a, Crime Victim Reparation Trust, Public Safety Support Funds, Substance Abuse Prevention Account, and Services for Victims of Domestic Violence Account; or

    (b) if no plea in abeyance fee is collected, a surcharge on the fee charged for the traffic school or other school, class, or rehabilitative program shall be collected, which surcharge shall:

        (i) be computed, assessed, collected, and remitted in the same manner as if the traffic school fee and surcharge had been imposed as a criminal fine and surcharge; and

        (ii) be subject to the financial requirements contained in Title 63, Chapter 63a, Crime Victim Reparation Trust, Public Safety Support Funds, Substance Abuse Prevention Account, and Services for Victims of Domestic Violence Account.   2005

CHAPTER 2a

PLEAS IN ABEYANCE

Section

77-2a-1.   Definitions.

For the purposes of this chapter:

    (1) "Plea in abeyance" means an order by a court, upon motion of the prosecution and the defendant, accepting a plea of guilty or of no contest from the defendant but not, at that time, entering judgment of conviction against him nor imposing sentence upon him on condition that he comply with specific conditions as set forth in a plea in abeyance agreement.

    (2) "Plea in abeyance agreement" means an agreement entered into between the prosecution and the defendant setting forth the specific terms and conditions upon which, following acceptance of the agreement by the court, a plea may be held in abeyance.   1993

77-2a-2.   Plea in abeyance agreement — Negotiation — Contents — Terms of agreement — Waiver of time for sentencing.

(1) At any time after acceptance of a plea of guilty or no contest but prior to entry of judgment of conviction and imposition of sentence, the court may, upon motion of both the prosecuting attorney and the defendant, hold the plea in abeyance and not enter judgment of conviction against the defendant nor impose sentence upon the defendant within the time periods contained in Rule 22(a), Utah Rules of Criminal Procedure.

(2) The defendant shall be represented by counsel during negotiations for a plea in abeyance and at the time of acknowledgment and affirmation of any plea in abeyance agreement unless the defendant shall have knowingly and intelligently waived his right to counsel.

(3) The defendant has the right to be represented by counsel at any court hearing relating to a plea in abeyance agreement.

(4) (a) Any plea in abeyance agreement entered into between the prosecution and the defendant and approved by the court shall include a full, detailed recitation of the requirements and conditions agreed to by the defendant and the reason for requesting the court to hold the plea in abeyance.

    (b) If the plea is to a felony or any combination of misdemeanors and felonies, the agreement shall be in writing and shall, prior to acceptance by the court, be executed by the prosecuting attorney, the defendant, and the defendant's counsel in the presence of the court.

(5) A plea shall not be held in abeyance for a period longer than 18 months if the plea was to any class of misdemeanor or longer than three years if the plea was to any degree of felony or to any combination of misdemeanors and felonies.

(6) A plea in abeyance agreement shall not be approved unless the defendant, before the court, and any written agreement, knowingly and intelligently waives time for sentencing as designated in Rule 22(a), Utah Rules of Criminal Procedure.   1993

77-2a-3.   Manner of entry of plea — Powers of court [Effective until July 1, 2006].

(1) (a) Acceptance of any plea in anticipation of a plea in abeyance agreement shall be done in full compliance with the provisions of Rule 11, Utah Rules of Criminal Procedure.

    (b) In cases charging offenses for which bail may be forfeited, a plea in abeyance agreement may be entered into without a personal appearance before a magistrate.

(2) A plea in abeyance agreement may provide that the court may, upon finding that the defendant has successfully completed the terms of the agreement:

    (a) reduce the degree of the offense and enter judgment of conviction and impose sentence for a lower degree of offense; or

    (b) allow withdrawal of defendant's plea and order the dismissal of the case.

(3) Upon finding that a defendant has successfully completed the terms of a plea in abeyance agreement, the court may reduce the degree of the offense or dismiss the case only as provided in the plea in abeyance agreement or as agreed to by all parties. Upon sentencing a defendant for any lesser offense pursuant to a plea in abeyance agreement, the court may not invoke Section 76-3-402 to further reduce the degree of the offense.

(4) The court may require the Department of Corrections to assist in the administration of the plea in abeyance agreement as if the defendant were on probation to the court under Section 77-18-1.

(5) The terms of a plea in abeyance agreement may include:

(a) an order that the defendant pay a nonrefundable plea in abeyance fee, with a surcharge based on the amount of the plea in abeyance fee, both of which shall be allocated in the same manner as if paid as a fine for a criminal conviction under Section 78-3-14.5 and a surcharge under Title 63, Chapter 63a, Crime Victim Reparation Trust, Public Safety Support Funds, Substance Abuse Prevention Account, and Services for Victims of Domestic Violence Account, and which may not exceed in amount the maximum fine and surcharge which could have been imposed upon conviction and sentencing for the same offense;

(b) an order that the defendant pay restitution to the victims of his actions as provided in Title 77, Chapter 38a, Crime Victims Restitution Act;

(c) an order that the defendant pay the costs of any remedial or rehabilitative program required by the terms of the agreement; and

(d) an order that the defendant comply with any other conditions which could have been imposed as conditions of probation upon conviction and sentencing for the same offense.

(6) A court may not hold a plea in abeyance without the consent of both the prosecuting attorney and the defendant. A decision by a prosecuting attorney not to agree to a plea in abeyance is not subject to judicial review.

(7) No plea may be held in abeyance in any case involving a sexual offense against a victim who is under the age of 14.   2004

Manner of entry of plea — Powers of court [Effective July 1, 2006].

(1) (a) Acceptance of any plea in anticipation of a plea in abeyance agreement shall be done in full compliance with the provisions of Rule 11, Utah Rules of Criminal Procedure.

(b) In cases charging offenses for which bail may be forfeited, a plea in abeyance agreement may be entered into without a personal appearance before a magistrate.

(2) A plea in abeyance agreement may provide that the court may, upon finding that the defendant has successfully completed the terms of the agreement:

(a) reduce the degree of the offense and enter judgment of conviction and impose sentence for a lower degree of offense; or

(b) allow withdrawal of defendant's plea and order the dismissal of the case.

(3) Upon finding that a defendant has successfully completed the terms of a plea in abeyance agreement, the court may reduce the degree of the offense or dismiss the case only as provided in the plea in abeyance agreement or as agreed to by all parties. Upon sentencing a defendant for any lesser offense pursuant to a plea in abeyance agreement, the court may not invoke Section 76-3-402 to further reduce the degree of the offense.

(4) The court may require the Department of Corrections to assist in the administration of the plea in abeyance agreement as if the defendant were on probation to the court under Section 77-18-1.

(5) The terms of a plea in abeyance agreement may include:

(a) an order that the defendant pay a nonrefundable plea in abeyance fee, with a surcharge based on the amount of the plea in abeyance fee, both of which shall be allocated in the same manner as if paid as a fine for a criminal conviction under Section 78-3-14.5 and a surcharge under Title 63, Chapter 63a, Crime Victim Reparation Trust, Public Safety Support Funds, Substance Abuse Prevention Account, and Services for Victims of Domestic Violence Account, and which may not exceed in amount the maximum fine and surcharge which could have been imposed upon conviction and sentencing for the same offense;

(b) an order that the defendant pay restitution to the victims of his actions as provided in Title 77, Chapter 38a, Crime Victims Restitution Act;

(c) an order that the defendant pay the costs of any remedial or rehabilitative program required by the terms of the agreement; and

(d) an order that the defendant comply with any other conditions which could have been imposed as conditions of probation upon conviction and sentencing for the same offense.

(6) A court may not hold a plea in abeyance without the consent of both the prosecuting attorney and the defendant. A decision by a prosecuting attorney not to agree to a plea in abeyance is final.

(7) No plea may be held in abeyance in any case involving:

(a) a sexual offense against a victim who is under the age of 14; or

(b) a driving under the influence violation under Section 41-6a-502.   2004

77-2a-3.1. Restrictions on pleas to driving under the influence violations.

(1) As used in this section, an "education or treatment incentive program" means a program that includes:

(a) a screening as defined in Section 41-6a-501 that is approved by the Board of Substance Abuse and Mental Health in accordance with Section 62A-15-105;

(b) an assessment as defined in Section 41-6a-501 that is approved by the Board of Substance Abuse and Mental Health in accordance with Section 62A-15-105, if found appropriate in a screening under Subsection (1)(a);

(c) (i) an educational series as defined in Section 41-6a-501 that is approved by the Board of Substance Abuse and Mental Health in accordance with Section 62A-15-105; or

(ii) a substance abuse treatment program as defined in Section 41-6a-501 that is approved by the Board of Substance Abuse and Mental Health in accordance with Section 62A-15-105, if found appropriate in an assessment under Subsection (1)(b);

(d) regular court reviews for compliance;

(e) random drug and alcohol testing; and

(f) if a substance abuse treatment program is found appropriate under Subsection (1)(c), at least monthly reports from the substance abuse treatment program to the court.

(2) (a) A plea may not be held in abeyance in any case involving a driving under the influence violation under Section 41-6a-502 that is punishable as a felony or class A misdemeanor.

(b) A plea to a driving under the influence violation under Section 41-6a-502 that is punishable as a class B misdemeanor may not be held in abeyance unless:

    (i) (A) the plea is entered pursuant to an education or treatment incentive program; and

        (B) the education or treatment incentive program is approved by the district attorney, county attorney, attorney general, or chief prosecutor of a municipality; or

    (ii) evidentiary issues or other circumstances justify resolution of the case with a plea in abeyance.

(3) A plea to a driving under the influence violation under Section 41-6a-502 may not be dismissed or entered as a conviction of a lesser offense pursuant to Subsection (2)(b)(i) if the defendant:

    (a) has been convicted of any other violation which is defined as a conviction under Subsection 41-6a-501(2);

    (b) has had a plea to any other violation of Section 41-6a-502 held in abeyance; or

    (c) in the current case:

        (i) operated a vehicle in a negligent manner proximately resulting in bodily injury to another or property damage to an extent requiring reporting to a law enforcement agency under Section 41-6a-401;

        (ii) had a blood or breath alcohol level of .16 or higher; or

        (iii) had a passenger under 18 years of age in the vehicle at the time of the offense.

(4) A decision by a prosecuting attorney not to establish an education or treatment incentive program is final.   **2005**

77-2a-4. Violation of plea in abeyance agreement — Hearing — Entry of judgment and imposition of sentence — Subsequent prosecutions.

(1) If, at any time during the term of the plea in abeyance agreement, information comes to the attention of the prosecuting attorney or the court that the defendant has violated any condition of the agreement, the court, at the request of the prosecuting attorney, made by appropriate motion and affidavit, or upon its own motion, may issue an order requiring the defendant to appear before the court at a designated time and place to show cause why the court should not find the terms of the agreement to have been violated and why the agreement should not be terminated. If, following an evidentiary hearing, the court finds that the defendant has failed to substantially comply with any term or condition of the plea in abeyance agreement, it may terminate the agreement and enter judgment of conviction and impose sentence against the defendant for the offense to which the original plea was entered. Upon entry of judgment of conviction and imposition of sentence, any amounts paid by the defendant as a plea in abeyance fee prior to termination of the agreement shall be credited against any fine imposed by the court.

(2) The termination of a plea in abeyance agreement and subsequent entry of judgment of conviction and imposition of sentence shall not bar any independent prosecution arising from any offense that constituted a violation of any term or condition of an agreement whereby the original plea was placed in abeyance.   **1993**

CHAPTER 3a

STALKING INJUNCTIONS

77-3a-101. Civil stalking injunction — Petition — Ex parte injunction.

(1) As used in this chapter, "stalking" means the crime of stalking as defined in Section 76-5-106.5. Stalking injunctions may not be obtained against law enforcement officers, governmental investigators, or licensed private investigators, acting in their official capacity.

(2) Any person who believes that he or she is the victim of stalking may file a verified written petition for a civil stalking injunction against the alleged stalker with the district court in the district in which the petitioner or respondent resides or in which any of the events occurred. A minor with his or her parent or guardian may file a petition on his or her own behalf, or a parent, guardian, or custodian may file a petition on the minor's behalf.

(3) The Administrative Office of the Courts shall develop and adopt uniform forms for petitions, ex parte civil stalking injunctions, civil stalking injunctions, service and any other necessary forms in accordance with the provisions of this chapter on or before July 1, 2001. The office shall provide the forms to the clerk of each district court.

    (a) All petitions, injunctions, ex parte injunctions, and any other necessary forms shall be issued in the form adopted by the Administrative Office of the Courts.

    (b) The offices of the court clerk shall provide the forms to persons seeking to proceed under this chapter.

(4) The petition for a civil stalking injunction shall include:

    (a) the name of the petitioner; however, the petitioner's address shall be disclosed to the court for purposes of service, but, on request of the petitioner, the address may not be listed on the petition, and shall be protected and maintained in a separate document or automated database, not subject to release, disclosure, or any form of public access except as ordered by the court for good cause shown;

    (b) the name and address, if known, of the respondent;

    (c) specific events and dates of the actions constituting the alleged stalking;

    (d) if there is a prior court order concerning the same conduct, the name of the court in which the order was rendered; and

    (e) corroborating evidence of stalking, which may be in the form of a police report, affidavit, record, statement, item, letter, or any other evidence which tends to prove the allegation of stalking.

(5) If the court determines that there is reason to believe that an offense of stalking has occurred, an ex parte civil stalking injunction may be issued by the court that includes any of the following:

    (a) respondent may be enjoined from committing stalking;

    (b) respondent may be restrained from coming near the residence, place of employment, or school of the other party or specifically designated locations or persons;

(c) respondent may be restrained from contacting, directly or indirectly, the other party, including personal, written or telephone contact with the other party, the other party's employers, employees, fellow workers or others with whom communication would be likely to cause annoyance or alarm to the other party; or

(d) any other relief necessary or convenient for the protection of the petitioner and other specifically designated persons under the circumstances.

(6) Within ten days of service of the ex parte civil stalking injunction, the respondent is entitled to request, in writing, an evidentiary hearing on the civil stalking injunction.

(a) A hearing requested by the respondent shall be held within ten days from the date the request is filed with the court unless the court finds compelling reasons to continue the hearing. The hearing shall then be held at the earliest possible time. The burden is on the petitioner to show by a preponderance of the evidence that stalking of the petitioner by the respondent has occurred.

(b) An ex parte civil stalking injunction issued under this section shall state on its face:

(i) that the respondent is entitled to a hearing, upon written request within ten days of the service of the order;

(ii) the name and address of the district court where the request may be filed;

(iii) that if the respondent fails to request a hearing within ten days of service, the ex parte civil stalking injunction is automatically modified to a civil stalking injunction without further notice to the respondent and that the civil stalking injunction expires three years after service of the ex parte civil stalking injunction; and

(iv) that if the respondent requests, in writing, a hearing after the ten-day period after service, the court shall set a hearing within a reasonable time from the date requested.

(7) At the hearing, the court may modify, revoke, or continue the injunction. The burden is on the petitioner to show by a preponderance of the evidence that stalking of the petitioner by the respondent has occurred.

(8) The ex parte civil stalking injunction and civil stalking injunction shall include the following statement: "Attention. This is an official court order. If you disobey this order, the court may find you in contempt. You may also be arrested and prosecuted for the crime of stalking and any other crime you may have committed in disobeying this order."

(9) The ex parte civil stalking injunction shall be served on the respondent within 90 days from the date it is signed. An ex parte civil stalking injunction is effective upon service. If no hearing is requested in writing by the respondent within ten days of service of the ex parte civil stalking injunction, the ex parte civil stalking injunction automatically becomes a civil stalking injunction without further notice to the respondent and expires three years from the date of service of the ex parte civil stalking injunction.

(10) If the respondent requests a hearing after the ten-day period after service, the court shall set a hearing within a reasonable time from the date requested. At the hearing, the burden is on the respon-

dent to show good cause why the civil stalking injunction should be dissolved or modified.

(11) Within 24 hours after the affidavit or acceptance of service has been returned, excluding weekends and holidays, the clerk of the court from which the ex parte civil stalking injunction was issued shall enter a copy of the ex parte civil stalking injunction and proof of service or acceptance of service in the statewide network for warrants or a similar system.

(a) The effectiveness of an ex parte civil stalking injunction or civil stalking injunction shall not depend upon its entry in the statewide system and, for enforcement purposes, a certified copy of an ex parte civil stalking injunction or civil stalking injunction is presumed to be a valid existing order of the court for a period of three years from the date of service of the ex parte civil stalking injunction on the respondent.

(b) Any changes or modifications of the ex parte civil stalking injunction are effective upon service on the respondent. The original ex parte civil stalking injunction continues in effect until service of the changed or modified civil stalking injunction on the respondent.

(12) Within 24 hours after the affidavit or acceptance of service has been returned, excluding weekends and holidays, the clerk of the court shall enter a copy of the changed or modified civil stalking injunction and proof of service or acceptance of service in the statewide network for warrants or a similar system.

(13) The ex parte civil stalking injunction or civil stalking injunction may be dissolved at any time upon application of the petitioner to the court which granted it.

(14) The court clerk shall provide, without charge, to the petitioner one certified copy of the injunction issued by the court and one certified copy of the proof of service of the injunction on the respondent. Charges may be imposed by the clerk's office for any additional copies, certified or not certified in accordance with Rule 4-202.08 of the Code of Judicial Administration.

(15) The remedies provided in this chapter for enforcement of the orders of the court are in addition to any other civil and criminal remedies available. The district court shall hear and decide all matters arising pursuant to this section.

(16) After a hearing with notice to the affected party, the court may enter an order requiring any party to pay the costs of the action, including reasonable attorney's fees.

(17) This chapter does not apply to protective orders or ex parte protective orders issued pursuant to Title 30, Chapter 6, Cohabitant Abuse Act, or to preliminary injunctions issued pursuant to an action for dissolution of marriage or legal separation.   2001

77-3a-102. Fees — Service of process.

(1) Ex parte civil stalking injunctions and civil stalking injunctions shall be served by a sheriff or constable.

(2) All service shall be in accordance with applicable law.

(3) Fees may not be imposed by a court clerk, constable, or law enforcement agency for:

(a) filing a petition under this chapter;

(b) obtaining an ex parte civil stalking injunction; or

(c) service of a civil stalking injunction, ex parte or otherwise.   2001

77-3a-103. Enforcement.

(1) A peace or law enforcement officer shall, without a warrant, arrest a person if the peace or law

enforcement officer has probable cause to believe that the person has violated an ex parte civil stalking injunction or civil stalking injunction issued pursuant to this chapter or has violated a permanent criminal stalking injunction issued pursuant to Section 76-5-106.5, whether or not the violation occurred in the presence of the officer.

(2) A violation of an ex parte civil stalking injunction or of a civil stalking injunction issued pursuant to this chapter constitutes the criminal offense of stalking as defined in Section 76-5-106.5 and is also a violation of the civil stalking injunction. Violations may be enforced by a civil action initiated by the petitioner, a criminal action initiated by a prosecuting attorney, or both.   2001

CHAPTER 7

ARREST, BY WHOM, AND HOW MADE

77-7-1. "Arrest" defined — Restraint allowed.

An arrest is an actual restraint of the person arrested or submission to custody. The person shall not be subjected to any more restraint than is necessary for his arrest and detention.   1980

77-7-2. Arrest by peace officers.

A peace officer may make an arrest under authority of a warrant or may, without warrant, arrest a person:

(1) for any public offense committed or attempted in the presence of any peace officer; "presence" includes all of the physical senses or any device that enhances the acuity, sensitivity, or range of any physical sense, or records the observations of any of the physical senses;

(2) when he has reasonable cause to believe a felony or a class A misdemeanor has been committed and has reasonable cause to believe that the person arrested has committed it;

(3) when he has reasonable cause to believe the person has committed a public offense, and there is reasonable cause for believing the person may:

(a) flee or conceal himself to avoid arrest;

(b) destroy or conceal evidence of the commission of the offense; or

(c) injure another person or damage property belonging to another person.   1999

77-7-3. By private persons.

A private person may arrest another:

(1) For a public offense committed or attempted in his presence; or

(2) When a felony has been committed and he has reasonable cause to believe the person arrested has committed it.   1980

77-7-4. Magistrate may orally order arrest.

A magistrate may orally require a peace officer to arrest anyone committing or attempting to commit a public offense in the presence of the magistrate, and, in the case of an emergency, when probable cause exists, a magistrate may orally authorize a peace officer to arrest a person for a public offense, and thereafter, as soon as practical, an information shall be filed against the person arrested.   1980

77-7-5. Issuance of warrant — Time and place arrests may be made — Contents of warrant — Responsibility for transporting prisoners — Court clerk to dispense restitution for transportation.

(1) A magistrate may issue a warrant for arrest upon finding probable cause to believe that the person to be arrested has committed a public offense. If the offense charged is:

(a) a felony, the arrest upon a warrant may be made at any time of the day or night; or

(b) a misdemeanor, the arrest upon a warrant can be made at night only if:

(i) the magistrate has endorsed authorization to do so on the warrant;

(ii) the person to be arrested is upon a public highway, in a public place, or in a place open to or accessible to the public; or

(iii) the person to be arrested is encountered by a peace officer in the regular course of that peace officer's investigation of a criminal offense unrelated to the misdemeanor warrant for arrest.

(2) For the purpose of Subsection (1):

(a) daytime hours are the hours of 6 a.m. to 10 p.m.; and

(b) nighttime hours are the hours after 10 p.m. and before 6 a.m.

(3) (a) If the magistrate determines that the accused must appear in court, the magistrate shall include in the arrest warrant the name of the law enforcement agency in the county or municipality with jurisdiction over the offense charged.

(b) (i) The law enforcement agency identified by the magistrate under Subsection (3)(a) is responsible for providing inter-county transportation of the defendant, if necessary, from the arresting law enforcement agency to the court site.

(ii) The law enforcement agency named on the warrant may contract with another law enforcement agency to have a defendant transported.

(c) (i) The law enforcement agency identified by the magistrate under Subsection (a) as responsible for transporting the defendant shall provide to the court clerk of the court in which the defendant is tried, an affidavit stating that the defendant was transported, indicating the law enforcement agency responsible for the transportation, and stating the number of miles the defendant was transported.

(ii) The court clerk shall account for restitution paid under Subsection 76-3-201(5) for governmental transportation expenses and dispense restitution monies collected by the court to the law enforcement agency responsible for the transportation of a convicted defendant. 2002

77-7-5.5. Repealed. 1991

77-7-6. Manner of making arrest.

(1) The person making the arrest shall inform the person being arrested of his intention, cause, and authority to arrest him. Such notice shall not be required when:

(a) there is reason to believe the notice will endanger the life or safety of the officer or another person or will likely enable the party being arrested to escape;

(b) the person being arrested is actually engaged in the commission of, or an attempt to commit, an offense; or

(c) the person being arrested is pursued immediately after the commission of an offense or an escape.

(2) (a) If a hearing-impaired person, as defined in Subsection 78-24a-1(2), is arrested for an alleged violation of a criminal law, including a local ordinance, the arresting officer shall assess the communicative abilities of the hearing-impaired person and conduct this notification, and any

further notifications of rights, warnings, interrogations, or taking of statements, in a manner that accurately and effectively communicates with the hearing-impaired person including qualified interpreters, lip reading, pen and paper, typewriters, computers with print-out capability, and telecommunications devices for the deaf.

(b) Compliance with this subsection is a factor to be considered by any court when evaluating whether statements of a hearing-impaired person were made knowingly, voluntarily, and intelligently. 1995

77-7-7. Force in making arrest.

If a person is being arrested and flees or forcibly resists after being informed of the intention to make the arrest, the person arresting may use reasonable force to effect the arrest. Deadly force may be used only as provided in Section 76-2-404. 1980

77-7-8. Forcible entry to make arrest — Conditions requiring a warrant.

(1) (a) Subject to Subsection (2), a peace officer when making an arrest may forcibly enter the building in which the person to be arrested is, or in which there are reasonable grounds for believing him to be.

(b) Before making the forcible entry, the officer shall demand admission and explain the purpose for which admission is desired.

(c) The officer need not give a demand and explanation before making a forcible entry under the exceptions in Section 77-7-6 or where there is reason to believe evidence will be secreted or destroyed.

(2) If the building to be entered under Subsection (1) appears to be a private residence or the officer knows the building is a private residence, and if there is no consent to enter or there are no exigent circumstances, the officer shall, before entering the building:

(a) obtain an arrest or search warrant if the building is the residence of the person to be arrested; or

(b) obtain a search warrant if the building is a residence, but not the residence of the person whose arrest is sought. 2003

77-7-9. Weapons may be taken from prisoner.

Any person making an arrest may seize from the person arrested all weapons which he may have on or about his person. 1980

77-7-10. Telegraph or telephone authorization of execution of arrest warrant.

Any magistrate may, by an endorsement on a warrant of arrest, authorize by telegraph, telephone or other reasonable means, its execution. A copy of the warrant or notice of its issuance and terms may be sent to one or more peace officers. The copy or notice communicated authorizes the officer to proceed in the same manner under it as if he had an original warrant. 1980

77-7-11. Possession of warrant by arresting officer not required.

Any peace officer who has knowledge of an outstanding warrant of arrest may arrest a person he reasonably believes to be the person described in the warrant, without the peace officer having physical possession of the warrant. 1980

77-7-12. Detaining persons suspected of shoplifting or library theft — Persons authorized.

(1) A peace officer, merchant, or merchant's employee, servant, or agent who has reasonable grounds

to believe that goods held or displayed for sale by the merchant have been taken by a person with intent to steal may, for the purpose of investigating the unlawful act and attempting to effect a recovery of the goods, detain the person in a reasonable manner for a reasonable length of time.

(2) A peace officer or employee of a library may detain a person for the purposes and under the limits of Subsection (1) if there are reasonable grounds to believe the person violated Title 76, Chapter 6, Part 8, Library Theft.   1987

77-7-13. Arrest without warrant by peace officer — Reasonable grounds, what constitutes — Exemption from civil or criminal liability.

(1) A peace officer may arrest, without warrant, any person the officer has reasonable ground to believe has committed a theft under Title 76, Chapter 6, Part 8, Library Theft, or of goods held or displayed for sale.

(2) A charge of theft made to a peace officer under Part 8, Library Theft, by an employee of a library, or by a merchant, merchant's employee, servant, or agent constitutes a reasonable ground for arrest, and the peace officer is relieved from any civil or criminal liability.   1998

77-7-14. Person causing detention or arrest of person suspected of shoplifting or library theft — Civil and criminal immunity.

(1) A peace officer, merchant, or merchant's employee, servant, or agent who causes the detention of a person as provided in Section 77-7-12, or who causes the arrest of a person for theft of goods held or displayed for sale, is not criminally or civilly liable where he has reasonable and probable cause to believe the person detained or arrested committed a theft of goods held or displayed for sale.

(2) A peace officer or employee of a library who causes a detention or arrest of a person under Title 76, Chapter 6, Part 8, Library Theft, is not criminally or civilly liable where he has reasonable and probable cause to believe that the person committed a theft of library materials.   1987

77-7-15. Authority of peace officer to stop and question suspect — Grounds.

A peace officer may stop any person in a public place when he has a reasonable suspicion to believe he has committed or is in the act of committing or is attempting to commit a public offense and may demand his name, address and an explanation of his actions.   1980

77-7-16. Authority of peace officer to frisk suspect for dangerous weapon — Grounds.

A peace officer who has stopped a person temporarily for questioning may frisk the person for a dangerous weapon if he reasonably believes he or any other person is in danger.   1980

77-7-17. Authority of peace officer to take possession of weapons.

A peace officer who finds a dangerous weapon pursuant to a frisk may take and keep it until the completion of the questioning, at which time he shall either return it if lawfully possessed, or arrest such person.   1980

77-7-18. Citation on misdemeanor or infraction charge.

A peace officer, in lieu of taking a person into custody, any public official of any county or municipality charged with the enforcement of the law, a port-of-entry agent as defined in Section 72-1-102, and a volunteer authorized to issue a citation under Section 41-6a-213 may issue and deliver a citation requiring any person subject to arrest or prosecution on a misdemeanor or infraction charge to appear at the court of the magistrate before whom the person should be taken pursuant to law if the person had been arrested.   2005

77-7-19. Appearance required by citation — Arrest for failure to appear — Transfer of cases — Motor vehicle violations — Disposition of fines and costs.

(1) Persons receiving misdemeanor citations shall appear before the magistrate designated in the citation on or before the time and date specified in the citation unless the uniform bail schedule adopted by the Judicial Council or Subsection 77-7-21(1) permits forfeiture of bail for the offense charged.

(2) A citation may not require a person to appear sooner than five days or later than 14 days following its issuance.

(3) A person who receives a citation and who fails to comply with Section 77-7-21 on or before the time and date and at the court specified is subject to arrest. The magistrate may issue a warrant of arrest.

(4) Except where otherwise provided by law, a citation or information issued for violations of Title 41, Motor Vehicles, shall state that the person receiving the citation or information shall appear before the magistrate who has jurisdiction over the offense charged.

(5) Any justice court judge may, upon the motion of either the defense attorney or prosecuting attorney, based on a lack of territorial jurisdiction or the disqualification of the judge, transfer cases to a justice court with territorial jurisdiction or the district court within the county.

(6) (a) Clerks and other administrative personnel serving the courts shall ensure that all citations for violation of Title 41, Motor Vehicles, are filed in a court with jurisdiction and venue and shall refuse to receive citations that should be filed in another court.

(b) Fines, fees, costs, and forfeitures imposed or collected for violations of Title 41, Motor Vehicles, which are filed contrary to this section shall be paid to the entitled municipality or county by the state, county, or municipal treasurer who has received the fines, fees, costs, or forfeitures from the court which collected them.

(c) The accounting and remitting of sums due shall be at the close of the fiscal year of the municipality or county which has received fines, fees, costs, or forfeitures as a result of any improperly filed citations.   2001

77-7-20. Service of citation on defendant — Filing in court — Contents of citations.

(1) If a citation is issued pursuant to Section 77-7-18, the peace officer or public official shall issue one copy to the person cited and shall within five days file a duplicate copy with the court specified in the citation.

(2) Each copy of the citation issued under authority of this chapter shall contain:

(a) the name of the court before which the person is to appear;

(b) the name of the person cited;

(c) a brief description of the offense charged;

(d) the date, time and place at which the offense is alleged to have occurred;

(e) the date on which the citation was issued;

(f) the name of the peace officer or public official who issued the citation, and the name of the arresting person if an arrest was made by a private party and the citation was issued in lieu of taking the arrested person before a magistrate;

(g) the time and date on or before and after which the person is to appear;

(h) the address of the court in which the person is to appear;

(i) a certification above the signature of the officer issuing the citation in substantially the following language: "I certify that a copy of this citation or information (Summons and Complaint) was duly served upon the defendant according to law on the above date and I know or believe and so allege that the above-named defendant did commit the offense herein set forth contrary to law. I further certify that the court to which the defendant has been directed to appear is the proper court pursuant to Section 77-7-21."; and

(j) a notice containing substantially the following language:

READ CAREFULLY

This citation is not an information and will not be used as an information without your consent. If an information is filed you will be provided a copy by the court. You MUST appear in court on or before the time set in this citation. IF YOU FAIL TO APPEAR AN INFORMATION WILL BE FILED AND THE COURT MAY ISSUE A WARRANT FOR YOUR ARREST.   1980

77-7-21. Proceeding on citation — Voluntary forfeiture of bail — Parent signature required — Information, when required.

(1) (a) A copy of the citation issued under Section 77-7-18 that is filed with the magistrate may be used in lieu of an information to which the person cited may plead guilty or no contest and be sentenced or on which bail may be forfeited.

(b) With the magistrate's approval, a person may voluntarily forfeit bail without appearance being required in any case of a class B misdemeanor or less.

(c) Voluntary forfeiture of bail shall be entered as a conviction and treated the same as if the accused pleaded guilty.

(d) If the person cited is under 18 years of age, and if any of the charges allege a violation of Title 41, the court shall promptly mail a copy of the citation or a notice of the citation to the address as shown on the citation, to the attention of the parent or guardian of the defendant.

(2) An information shall be filed and proceedings held in accordance with the Rules of Criminal Procedure and all other applicable provisions of this code if the person cited:

(a) willfully fails to appear before a magistrate pursuant to a citation issued under Section 77-7-18;

(b) pleads not guilty to the offense charged; or

(c) does not deposit bail on or before the date set for the person's appearance.

(3) (a) The information is an original pleading.

(b) If a person cited waives by written agreement the filing of the information, the prosecution may proceed on the citation.   1994

77-7-22. Failure to appear as misdemeanor.

Any person who willfully fails to appear before a court pursuant to a citation issued under the provisions of Section 77-7-18 is guilty of a class B misdemeanor, regardless of the disposition of the charge upon which he was originally cited.   1980

77-7-23. Delivery of prisoner arrested without warrant to magistrate — Transfer to court with jurisdiction — Violation as misdemeanor.

(1) (a) When an arrest is made without a warrant by a peace officer or private person, the person arrested shall be taken without unnecessary delay to the magistrate in the district court, the precinct of the county, or the municipality in which the offense occurred, except under Subsection (2). An information stating the charge against the person shall be made before the magistrate.

(b) If the justice court judge of the precinct or municipality or the district court judge is not available, the arrested person shall be taken before the magistrate within the same county who is nearest to the scene of the alleged offense or nearest to the jail under Subsection (2), who may act as committing magistrate for arraigning the accused, setting bail, or issuing warrants.

(2) If the arrested person under Subsection (1) must be transported from jail to a magistrate, the person may be taken before the magistrate nearest to the jail rather than the magistrate specified in Subsection (1) for arraignment, setting bail, or issuing warrants.

(3) The case shall then be transferred to the court having jurisdiction. This section does not confer jurisdiction upon a court unless otherwise provided by law.

(4) Any officer or person violating this section is guilty of a class B misdemeanor.   1997

77-7-24. Notice to appear in court — Contents — Promise to comply — Signing — Release from custody — Official misconduct.

(1) If a person who is arrested for a violation of Title 41, Chapter 6a, Traffic Code, that is punishable as a misdemeanor is immediately taken before a magistrate as provided under Section 77-7-23, the peace officer shall prepare, in triplicate or more copies, a written notice to appear in court containing:

(a) the name and address of the person;

(b) the number, if any, of the person's driver license;

(c) the license plate number of the person's vehicle;

(d) the offense charged; and

(e) the time and place the person shall appear in court.

(2) The time specified in the notice to appear must be at least five days after the arrest of the person unless the person demands an earlier hearing.

(3) The place specified in the notice to appear shall be made before a magistrate of competent jurisdiction in the county in which the alleged violation occurred.

(4) (a) In order to secure release as provided in this section, the arrested person shall promise to appear in court by signing at least one copy of the written notice prepared by the arresting officer.

(b) The arresting peace officer shall immediately:

(i) deliver a copy of the notice to the person promising to appear; and

(ii) release the person arrested from custody.

(5) A peace officer violating any of the provisions of this section shall be:

(a) guilty of misconduct in office; and

(b) subject to removal from office.   2005

77-7-25. Keeping of records — Making and forwarding of abstract upon conviction or forfeiture of bail — Form and contents — Official misconduct.

(1) A magistrate or judge of a court shall keep a full record of each case in which a person is charged with:

(a) a violation of this chapter; or

(b) any other law regulating the operation of a motor vehicle on the highway.

(2) (a) Within ten days after the conviction or forfeiture of bail of a person on a charge of violating a provision of this chapter or other law regulating the operation of a motor vehicle on the highway, the magistrate of the court or clerk of the court in which the conviction was made or bail was forfeited shall prepare and immediately forward to the department an abstract of the record of the court covering the case in which the person was convicted or forfeited bail.

(b) The abstract shall be certified by the person required to prepare the abstract to be true and correct.

(c) A report under this Subsection (2) is not required for a conviction involving the illegal parking or standing of a vehicle.

(3) The abstract must be made in a manner specified by the Driver License Division and shall include the:

(a) name and address of the party charged;

(b) number, if any, of the person's driver license;

(c) license plate number of the vehicle involved;

(d) nature of the offense;

(e) date of hearing;

(f) plea;

(g) judgment, or whether bail was forfeited; and

(h) amount of the fine or forfeiture.

(4) A court shall provide a copy of the report to the Driver License Division on the conviction of a person of manslaughter or other felony in which a vehicle was used.

(5) The failure, refusal, or neglect of a judicial officer to comply with the requirements of this section constitutes misconduct in office and is grounds for removal.

(6) The Driver License Division shall classify and disclose all abstracts received in accordance with Section 53-3-109.   2005

77-7-26. Improper disposition or cancellation of notice to appear or traffic citation — Official misconduct — Misdemeanor.

(1) (a) It is unlawful and official misconduct for any peace officer or other officer or public employee to dispose of:

(i) a notice to appear; or

(ii) traffic citation.

(b) The provisions of Subsection (1)(a) do not apply if the disposal is done with the consent of the magistrate before whom the arrested person was to appear.

(2) A person who cancels or solicits the cancellation of a notice to appear or a traffic citation, in any manner other than as provided by law, is guilty of a class B misdemeanor.   2005

CHAPTER 9

UNIFORM ACT ON FRESH PURSUIT

77-9-1. Authority of peace officer of another state.

A peace officer of another state or the District of Columbia who enters this state in fresh pursuit and continues in fresh pursuit of a person in order to arrest him on the ground that he is reasonably believed to have committed a felony in another state, has the same authority to arrest and hold a person in custody as a peace officer of this state. Fresh pursuit does not require instant action, but pursuit without unreasonable delay.   1980

77-9-2. Procedure after arrest.

An officer who has made an arrest pursuant to Section 77-9-1 shall without unnecessary delay take the person arrested before a magistrate of the county in which the arrest was made. The magistrate shall conduct a hearing to determine the lawfulness of the arrest. If he finds the arrest was lawful, the magistrate may commit the person arrested for a reasonable time or may admit the person to bail pending extradition proceedings.   1980

77-9-3. Authority of peace officer of this state beyond normal jurisdiction.

(1) Any peace officer authorized by any governmental entity of this state may exercise a peace officer's authority beyond the limits of such officer's normal jurisdiction as follows:

(a) when in fresh pursuit of an offender for the purpose of arresting and holding that person in custody or returning the suspect to the jurisdiction where the offense was committed;

(b) when a public offense is committed in such officer's presence;

(c) when participating in an investigation of criminal activity which originated in the officer's normal jurisdiction in cooperation with the local authority; or

(d) when called to assist peace officers of another jurisdiction.

(2) (a) Any peace officer, prior to taking any action authorized by Subsection (1), shall notify and receive approval of the local law enforcement authority, or if the prior contact is not reasonably possible, notify the local law enforcement authority as soon as reasonably possible.

(b) Unless specifically requested to aid a peace officer of another jurisdiction or otherwise as provided for by law, no legal responsibility for a peace officer's action outside his normal jurisdiction, except as provided in this section, shall attach to the local law enforcement authority.   1998

77-18-9. Definitions.

As used in this chapter:

(1) "Administrative finding" means a decision upon a question of fact reached by an administrative agency following an administrative hearing or other procedure satisfying the requirements of due process.

(2) "Certificate of eligibility" means a document issued by the division stating that the criminal record which is the subject of a petition for expungement is eligible for expungement.

(3) "Conviction" means judgment by a criminal court on a verdict or finding of guilty after trial, a plea of guilty, or a plea of nolo contendere.

(4) "Division" means the Criminal Investigations and Technical Services Division of the Department of Public Safety established in Section 53-10-103.

(5) "Expungement" means the sealing or destruction of a criminal record, including records of the investigation, arrest, detention, or conviction of the petitioner.

(6) "Jurisdiction" means an area of authority.

(7) "Petitioner" means a person seeking expungement under this chapter.

(8) Second degree forcible felony includes:
(a) aggravated assault, if the person intentionally causes serious bodily injury;
(b) aggravated assault by a prisoner;
(c) aggravated assault on school premises;
(d) intentional child abuse;
(e) criminally negligent automobile homicide;
(f) reckless child abuse homicide;
(g) mayhem;
(h) manslaughter;
(i) kidnaping;
(j) forcible sexual abuse;
(k) robbery;
(l) felony fleeing causing death or serious bodily injury; or
(m) delivery of an explosive to a common carrier.   1999

77-18-10. Petition — Expungement of records of arrest, investigation, and detention — Eligibility conditions — No filing fee.

(1) A person who has been arrested with or without a warrant may petition the court in which the proceeding occurred or, if there were no court proceedings, any court in the jurisdiction where the arrest occurred, for an order expunging any and all records of arrest, investigation, and detention which may have been made in the case, subject to the following conditions:
(a) at least 30 days have passed since the arrest for which expungement is sought;
(b) there have been no intervening arrests; and
(c) one of the following occurred:
(i) the person was released without the filing of formal charges;
(ii) proceedings against the person were dismissed;
(iii) the person was discharged without a conviction and no charges were refiled within 30 days;
(iv) the person was acquitted at trial; or
(v) the record of any proceedings against the person has been sealed.

(2) (a) A person seeking expungement under Subsection (1) may petition the court for expungement before the expiration of the 30 days required by Subsection (1)(a) if he believes extraordinary circumstances exist and the court orders the division to proceed with the eligibility process.

(b) A court may, with the receipt of a certificate of eligibility, order expungement if the court finds that the petitioner is eligible for relief under this subsection and in the interest of justice the order should be issued prior to the expiration of the 30-day period required by Subsection (1)(a).

(3) As provided in Subsection 78-7-35(1)(i), there is no fee for a petition filed under Subsection (2).

(4) The petitioner shall file a certificate of eligibility issued by the division to be reviewed by the prosecuting attorney and the court prior to issuing an order granting the expungement.

(5) If the court finds that the petitioner is eligible for relief under this section, it shall issue an order granting the expungement.

(6) No filing fees or other administrative charges shall be assessed against a successful petitioner under this section.

(7) A person who has received expungement of an arrest under this section may respond to any inquiry as though the arrest did not occur, unless otherwise provided by law.   2001

77-18-11. Petition — Expungement of conviction — Certificate of eligibility — Fee — Notice — Written evaluation — Objections — Hearing.

(1) A person convicted of a crime may petition the convicting court for an expungement of the record of conviction.

(2) (a) The court shall require receipt of a certificate of eligibility issued by the division under Section 77-18-12.

(b) The fee for each certificate of eligibility is $25. This fee remains in effect until changed by the division through the process under Section 63-38-3.2.

(c) Funds generated under Subsection (2)(b) shall be deposited in the General Fund as a dedicated credit by the department to cover the costs incurred in providing the information.

(3) The petition and certificate of eligibility shall be filed with the court and served upon the prosecuting attorney and the Department of Corrections.

(4) A victim shall receive notice of a petition for expungement if, prior to the entry of an expungement order, the victim or, in the case of a minor or a person who is incapacitated or deceased, the victim's next of kin or authorized representative, submits a written and signed request for notice to the office of the Department of Corrections in the judicial district in which the crime occurred or judgment was entered.

(5) The Department of Corrections shall serve notice of the expungement request by first-class mail to the victim at the most recent address of record on file with the department. The notice shall include a copy of the petition, certificate of eligibility, and statutes and rules applicable to the petition.

(6) The court in its discretion may request a written evaluation by Adult Parole and Probation of the Department of Corrections.

    (a) The evaluation shall include a recommendation concerning the petition for expungement.

    (b) If expungement is recommended, the evaluation shall include certification that the petitioner has completed all requirements of sentencing and probation or parole and state any rationale that would support or refute consideration for expungement.

    (c) The conclusions and recommendations contained in the evaluation shall be provided to the petitioner and the prosecuting attorney.

(7) If the prosecuting attorney or a victim submits a written objection to the court concerning the petition within 30 days after service of the notice, or if the petitioner objects to the conclusions and recommendations in the evaluation within 15 days after receipt of the conclusions and recommendations, the court shall set a date for a hearing and notify the prosecuting attorney for the jurisdiction, the petitioner, and the victim of the date set for the hearing.

(8) Any person who has relevant information about the petitioner may testify at the hearing.

(9) The prosecuting attorney may respond to the court with a recommendation or objection within 30 days.

(10) If an objection is not received under Subsection (7), the expungement may be granted without a hearing.

(11) A court may not expunge a conviction of:

    (a) a capital felony;

    (b) a first degree felony;

    (c) a second degree forcible felony;

    (d) any sexual act against a minor; or

    (e) an offense for which a certificate of eligibility may not be issued under Section 77-18-12.

2004

77-18-12. Grounds for denial of certificate of eligibility — Effect of prior convictions.

(1) The division shall issue a certificate of eligibility to a petitioner seeking to obtain expungement for a criminal record unless prior to issuing a certificate of eligibility the division finds, through records of a governmental agency, including national criminal data bases that:

    (a) the conviction for which expungement is sought is:

        (i) a capital felony;

        (ii) a first degree felony;

        (iii) a second degree forcible felony;

        (iv) automobile homicide;

        (v) a felony violation of Section 41-6a-502;

        (vi) a conviction involving a sexual act against a minor;

        (vii) any registerable sex offense as defined in Subsection 77-27-21.5(1)(d); or

        (viii) an attempt, solicitation, or conspiracy to commit any offense listed in Subsection 77-27-21.5(1)(d);

    (b) the petitioner's record includes two or more convictions for any type of offense which would be classified as a felony under Utah law, not arising out of a single criminal episode, regardless of the jurisdiction in which the convictions occurred;

    (c) the petitioner has previously obtained expungement in any jurisdiction of a crime which would be classified as a felony in Utah;

    (d) the petitioner has previously obtained expungement in any jurisdiction of two or more convictions which would be classified as misdemeanors in Utah unless the convictions would be classified as class B or class C misdemeanors in Utah and 15 years have passed since these misdemeanor convictions;

    (e) the petitioner was convicted in any jurisdiction, subsequent to the conviction for which expungement is sought and within the time periods as provided in Subsection (2), of a crime which would be classified in Utah as a felony, misdemeanor, or infraction;

    (f) the person has a combination of three or more convictions not arising out of a single criminal episode including any conviction for an offense which would be classified under Utah law as a class B or class A misdemeanor or as a felony, including any misdemeanor and felony convictions previously expunged, regardless of the jurisdiction in which the conviction or expungement occurred; or

    (g) a proceeding involving a crime is pending or being instituted in any jurisdiction against the petitioner.

(2) A conviction may not be included for purposes of Subsection (1)(e), and a conviction may not be considered for expungement until, after the petitioner's release from incarceration, parole, or probation, whichever occurs last and all fines ordered by the court have been satisfied, at least the following period of time has elapsed:

    (a) seven years in the case of a felony;

    (b) ten years in the case of:

        (i) a misdemeanor conviction or the equivalent of a misdemeanor conviction as defined in Subsection 41-6a-501(2); or

        (ii) a felony violation of Subsection 58-37-8(2)(g);

    (c) five years in the case of a class A misdemeanor;

    (d) three years in the case of any other misdemeanor or infraction under Title 76, Utah Criminal Code; or

    (e) 15 years in the case of multiple class B or class C misdemeanors.

(3) A petitioner who would not be eligible to receive a certificate of eligibility under Subsection (1)(d) or (f) may receive a certificate of eligibility for one additional expungement if at least 15 years have elapsed since the last of any of the following:

    (a) release from incarceration, parole, or probation relating to the most recent conviction; and

(b) any other conviction which would have prevented issuance of a certificate of eligibility under Subsection (1)(e).

(4) If, after reasonable research, a disposition for an arrest on the criminal history file is unobtainable, the division may issue a special certificate giving discretion of eligibility to the court.   2005

77-18-13. Hearing — Standard of proof — Exception.

(1) The court shall review the petition, certificate of eligibility, and any written evaluation and receive any testimony or writing submitted by a victim or prosecuting attorney.

(2) The court shall issue a certificate to the petitioner, stating the court's finding that the petition and certificate of eligibility are sufficient and the statutory requirements for expungement have been satisfied unless there is clear and convincing evidence to persuade the court that it would be contrary to the interest of the public to grant a requested expungement.

(3) Except as otherwise provided by law, a person receiving expungement of a conviction under this section may respond to any inquiry as though the conviction did not occur.   1996

77-18-14. Order to expunge — Distribution of order — Redaction — Receipt of order — Administrative proceedings — Division requirements.

(1) Except as otherwise provided in this chapter, upon approval of a petition for expungement, the court shall enter an order to expunge all records in the petitioner's case which are in the custody of that court or in the custody of any other court, agency, or official.

(2) The petitioner shall be responsible for service of the order of expungement to all affected state, county, and local entities, agencies, and officials including the court, arresting agency, booking agency, Department of Corrections, and the division.

(3) The division shall forward a copy of the expungement order to the Federal Bureau of Investigation.

(4) In order to avoid destruction or sealing of the records in whole or in part, any state, county, or local entity, agency, or official receiving an expungement order shall only expunge all references to the petitioner's name. The petitioner, based on good cause, may petition the court to expunge the records in whole or in part.

(5) No state, county, or local entity, agency, or official may, after receiving service of an expungement order, divulge information contained in the expunged portion of the record.

(6) (a) An order of expungement shall not restrict an agency's use or dissemination of records in its ordinary course of business until the agency has received service of a copy of the order.

(b) Any action taken by an agency after issuance of the order but prior to the agency's receipt of a copy of the order may not be invalidated by the order.

(7) An order of expungement may not:

(a) terminate or invalidate any pending administrative proceedings or actions of which the petitioner had notice according to the records of the administrative body prior to issuance of the expungement order;

(b) affect the enforcement of any order or findings issued by an administrative body pursuant to its lawful authority prior to issuance of the expungement order; or

(c) remove any evidence relating to the petitioner including records of arrest, which the administrative body has used or may use in these proceedings.

(8) The division shall provide the petitioner with a list of the agencies affected by this subsection with clear written directions regarding the requirements of this section.   1999

77-18-15. Retention of expunged records — Agencies.

(1) The division shall keep, index, and maintain all expunged records of arrests and convictions.

(2) Employees of the division may not divulge any information contained in its index to any person or agency without a court order, except to the following:

(a) the Board of Pardons and Parole;

(b) the Peace Officer Standards and Training;

(c) federal authorities, unless prohibited by federal law;

(d) the Division of Occupational and Professional Licensing; and

(e) the State Office of Education.

(3) The division may also use the information in its index for the purpose of establishing good character for issuance of a concealed firearm permit as provided in Section 53-5-704.

(4) A person whose records are released under Subsection (2) shall be given a reasonable opportunity by the recipient agency to challenge and explain any information in the records and to challenge the relevancy of that information before a final determination is made by the agency.

(5) A court may permit inspection or release of an expunged record only upon petition by the person who is the subject of the record and only to the persons named in the petition.

(6) (a) For judicial sentencing, a court may order any records sealed under this section to be opened and admitted into evidence.

(b) The records are confidential and are available for inspection only by the court, parties, counsel for the parties, and any other person who is authorized by the court to inspect them.

(c) At the end of the action or proceeding, the court shall order the records sealed again.

(7) Records released under this section are classified as protected under Section 63-2-304 and are accessible only as provided under Title 63, Chapter 2, Part 2, Access to Records.   1999

77-18-16. Penalty.

Any person who willfully violates any prohibition in this chapter is guilty of a class A misdemeanor.   1994

77-18-17. Retroactive application.

The provisions of Sections 77-18-9 through 77-18-17 apply retroactively to all arrests and convictions regardless of the date on which the arrests were made or convictions were entered.   1994

CHAPTER 23

SEARCH AND ADMINISTRATIVE WARRANTS

Part 1

Administrative Traffic Checkpoints

PART 1

ADMINISTRATIVE TRAFFIC CHECKPOINTS

77-23-101. Title of act.

Sections 77-23-101 through 77-23-105 may be cited as the "Administrative Traffic Checkpoint Act." 1992

77-23-102. Definitions.

As used in this part:

(1) "Administrative traffic checkpoint" means a roadblock procedure where enforcement officers stop all, or a designated sequence of, motor vehicles traveling on highways and roads and subject those vehicles to inspection or testing and the drivers or occupants to questioning or the production of documents.

(2) "Command level officer" includes all sheriffs, heads of law enforcement agencies, and all supervisory enforcement officers of sergeant rank or higher.

(3) "Emergency circumstances" means circumstances where enforcement officers reasonably believe road conditions, weather conditions, or persons present a significant hazard to persons or the property of other persons.

(4) "Enforcement officer" includes:

  (a) peace officers as defined in Title 53, Chapter 13, Peace Officer Classifications;

  (b) correctional officers as defined in Title 53, Chapter 13;

  (c) special function officers as defined and under the restrictions of Title 53, Chapter 13; and

  (d) federal officers as defined in Title 53, Chapter 13.

(5) "Magistrate" includes all judicial officers enumerated in Subsection 77-1-3(4).

(6) "Motor vehicle" includes all vehicles as defined in Title 41, Chapter 1a. 1998

77-23-103. Circumstances permitting an administrative traffic checkpoint.

A motor vehicle may be stopped and the occupants detained by an enforcement officer when the enforcement officer:

(1) is acting pursuant to a duly authorized search warrant or arrest warrant;

(2) has probable cause to arrest or search;

(3) has reasonable suspicion that criminal activity has occurred or is occurring;

(4) is acting under emergency circumstances; or

(5) is acting pursuant to duly authorized administrative traffic checkpoint authority granted by a magistrate in accordance with Section 77-23-104. 1992

77-23-104. Written plan — Approval of magistrate.

(1) An administrative traffic checkpoint may be established and operated upon written authority of a magistrate.

(2) A magistrate may issue written authority to establish and operate an administrative traffic checkpoint if:

  (a) a command level officer submits to the magistrate a written plan signed by the command level officer describing:

    (i) the location of the checkpoint including geographical and topographical information;

    (ii) the date, time, and duration of the checkpoint;

    (iii) the sequence of traffic to be stopped;

    (iv) the purpose of the checkpoint, including the inspection or inquiry to be conducted;

    (v) the minimum number of personnel to be employed in operating the checkpoint, including the rank of the officer or officers in charge at the scene;

    (vi) the configuration and location of signs, barriers, and other means of informing approaching motorists that they must stop and directing them to the place to stop;

    (vii) any advance notice to the public at large of the establishment of the checkpoint; and

    (viii) the instructions to be given to the enforcement officers operating the checkpoint;

  (b) the magistrate makes an independent judicial determination that the plan appropriately:

    (i) minimizes the length of time the motorist will be delayed;

    (ii) minimizes the intrusion of the inspection or inquiry;

    (iii) minimizes the fear and anxiety the motorist will experience;

    (iv) minimizes the degree of discretion to be exercised by the individual enforcement officers operating the checkpoint; and

    (v) maximizes the safety of the motorist and the enforcement officers; and

  (c) the administrative traffic checkpoint has the primary purpose of inspecting, verifying, or detecting:

    (i) drivers that may be under the influence of alcohol or drugs;

    (ii) license plates, registration certificates, insurance certificates, or driver licenses;

(iii) violations of Title 23, Wildlife Resources Code of Utah; or

(iv) other circumstances that are specifically distinguishable by the magistrate from a general interest in crime control.

(3) Upon determination by the magistrate that the plan meets the requirements of Subsection (2), the magistrate shall sign the authorization and issue it to the command level officer, retaining a copy for the court's file.

(4) A copy of the plan and signed authorization shall be issued to the checkpoint command level officer participating in the operation of the checkpoint.

(5) Any enforcement officer participating in the operation of the checkpoint shall conform his activities as nearly as practicable to the procedures outlined in the plan.

(6) The checkpoint command level officer shall be available to exhibit a copy of the plan and signed authorization to any motorist who has been stopped at the checkpoint upon request of the motorist.   2001

77-23-104.5. Signs — Prohibitions.

An enforcement officer may not display a sign that notifies motorists of an administrative traffic checkpoint unless the checkpoint is being operated under the authority of a magistrate as provided in Section 77-23-104.   2001

77-23-105. Failure to stop — Criminal liability.

Any person who intentionally and knowingly passes, without stopping as required, any administrative traffic checkpoint operated under the authority of a magistrate as provided in Section 77-23-104 is guilty of a class B misdemeanor.   1992

PART 2

SEARCH WARRANTS

77-23-201. Search warrants — Definitions.

As used in this part:

(1) "Daytime" means the hours beginning at 6 a.m. and ending at 10 p.m. local time.

(2) "Search warrant" is an order issued by a magistrate in the name of the state and directed to a peace officer, describing with particularity the thing, place, or person to be searched and the property or evidence to be seized by him and brought before the magistrate.   2001

77-23-202. Grounds for issuance.

Property or evidence may be seized pursuant to a search warrant if there is probable cause to believe it:

(1) was unlawfully acquired or is unlawfully possessed;

(2) has been used or is possessed for the purpose of being used to commit or conceal the commission of an offense; or

(3) is evidence of illegal conduct.   1994

77-23-203. Conditions precedent to issuance.

(1) A search warrant shall not issue except upon probable cause supported by oath or affirmation particularly describing the person or place to be searched and the person, property, or evidence to be seized.

(2) If the item sought to be seized is evidence of illegal conduct, and is in the possession of a person or entity for which there is insufficient probable cause shown to the magistrate to believe that such person or entity is a party to the alleged illegal conduct, no search warrant shall issue except upon a finding by the magistrate that the evidence sought to be seized cannot be obtained by subpoena, or that such evidence would be concealed, destroyed, damaged, or altered if sought by subpoena. If such a finding is made and a search warrant issued, the magistrate shall direct upon the warrant such conditions that reasonably afford protection of the following interests of the person or entity in possession of such evidence:

(a) protection against unreasonable interference with normal business;

(b) protection against the loss or disclosure of protected confidential sources of information; or

(c) protection against prior or direct restraints on constitutionally protected rights.   1994

77-23-204. Remotely communicated search warrants served in written form.

A remotely communicated search warrant issued under Rule 40 of the Rules of Criminal Procedure shall be served in a written form upon the person or place to be served.   2005

77-23-205. Time for service — Officer may request assistance.

(1) The magistrate shall insert a direction in the warrant that it be served in the daytime, unless the affidavits or oral testimony state a reasonable cause to believe a search is necessary in the night to seize the property prior to it being concealed, destroyed, damaged, altered, or for other good reason; in which case he may insert a direction that it be served any time of the day or night. An officer may request other persons to assist him in conducting the search.

(2) The search warrant shall be served within ten days from the date of issuance. Any search warrant not executed within this time shall be void and shall be returned to the court or magistrate as not executed.   1994

77-23-206. Receipt for property taken.

When the officer seizes property pursuant to a search warrant, he shall give a receipt to the person from whom it was seized or in whose possession it was found. If no person is present, the officer shall leave the receipt in the place where he found the property. Failure to give or leave a receipt shall not render the evidence seized inadmissible at trial.   1994

77-23-207. Return — Inventory of property taken.

The officer, after execution of the warrant, shall promptly make a verified return of the warrant to the magistrate and deliver a written inventory of anything seized, stating the place where it is being held.   1994

77-23-208. Safekeeping of property.

The officer seizing the property shall be responsible for its safekeeping and maintenance until the court otherwise orders.   1994

77-23-209. Return of recorded testimony and warrant to district court.

(1) The magistrate shall annex the search warrant, the return, and the inventory to the depositions, affidavits, or recorded testimony upon which the search warrant is based.

(2) If the magistrate does not have authority to proceed further with respect to the offense regarding which the warrant was issued, the magistrate shall forward the warrant and the depositions, affidavits, or recorded testimony to the appropriate court of the county having jurisdiction over the offense within 15 days after the return.   2005

77-23-210. Force used in executing warrant — When notice of authority is required as a prerequisite.

When a search warrant has been issued authorizing entry into any building, room, conveyance, compartment, or other enclosure, the officer executing the warrant may use such force as is reasonably necessary to enter:

(1) if, after notice of his authority and purpose, there is no response or he is not admitted with reasonable promptness; or

(2) without notice of his authority and purpose, if the magistrate issuing the warrant directs in the warrant that the officer need not give notice. The magistrate shall so direct only upon proof, under oath, that the object of the search may be quickly destroyed, disposed of, or secreted, or that physical harm may result to any person if notice were given. 1994

77-23-211. Violation of health, safety, building, or animal cruelty laws or ordinances — Warrants to obtain evidence.

In addition to other warrants provided by this chapter, magistrates, upon a showing of probable cause to believe a state, county, or city law or ordinance, has been violated in relation to health, safety, building, or animal cruelty, may issue a warrant for the purpose of obtaining evidence of a violation. Warrants may be obtained from a magistrate upon request of peace officers and state, county, and municipal health, fire, building, and animal control personnel only after approval by a prosecuting attorney. A search warrant issued under this section shall be directed to any peace officer within the county where the warrant is to be executed, who shall serve the same. Other concerned personnel may accompany the officer. 1994

77-23-212. Evidence seized pursuant to warrant not excluded unless unlawful search or seizure substantial — "Substantial" defined.

(1) Property or evidence seized pursuant to a search warrant may not be suppressed at a motion, trial, or other proceeding, unless the unlawful conduct of the peace officer is shown to be substantial.

(2) Any unlawful search or seizure shall be considered substantial and in bad faith if the warrant was obtained with malicious purpose and without probable cause or was executed maliciously and willfully beyond the authority of the warrant or with unnecessary severity. 1997

CHAPTER 27

PARDONS AND PAROLES

77-27-21.5. Sex offender registration — Information system — Law enforcement and courts to report — Registration — Penalty — Effect of expungement.

(1) As used in this section:

(a) "Department" means the Department of Corrections.

(b) "Employed" or "carries on a vocation" includes employment that is full time or part time for a period of time exceeding 14 days or for an aggregate period of time exceeding 30 days during any calendar year, whether financially compensated, volunteered, or for the purpose of government or educational benefit.

(c) "Notification" means a person's acquisition of information from the department about a sex offender, including his place of habitation, physical description, and other information as provided in Subsections (11) and (12).

(d) "Register" means to comply with the rules of the department made under this section.

(e) "Sex offender" means any person:

(i) convicted by this state of:

(A) a felony or class A misdemeanor violation of Section 76-4-401, enticing a minor over the Internet;

(B) Section 76-5-301.1, kidnapping of a child;

(C) a felony violation of Section 76-5-401, unlawful sexual activity with a minor;

(D) Section 76-5-401.1, sexual abuse of a minor;

(E) Section 76-5-401.2, unlawful sexual conduct with a 16 or 17 year old;

(F) Section 76-5-402, rape;

(G) Section 76-5-402.1, rape of a child;

(H) Section 76-5-402.2, object rape;

(I) Section 76-5-402.3, object rape of a child;

(J) a felony violation of Section 76-5-403, forcible sodomy;

(K) Section 76-5-403.1, sodomy on a child;

(L) Section 76-5-404, forcible sexual abuse;

(M) Section 76-5-404.1, sexual abuse of a child or aggravated sexual abuse of a child;

(N) Section 76-5-405, aggravated sexual assault;

(O) Section 76-5a-3, sexual exploitation of a minor;

(P) Section 76-7-102, incest;

(Q) Section 76-9-702.5, lewdness involving a child;

(R) Section 76-10-1306, aggravated exploitation of prostitution; or

(S) attempting, soliciting, or conspiring to commit any felony offense listed in Subsection (1)(e)(i);

(ii) convicted by any other state or the United States government of an offense which if committed in this state would be punishable as one or more of the offenses listed in Subsection (1)(e)(i) and who is:

(A) a Utah resident; or

(B) not a Utah resident, but who is in the state for a period exceeding 14 consecutive days, or for an aggregate period exceeding 30 days, during any calendar year; or

(iii) who is found not guilty by reason of insanity of one or more offenses listed in Subsection (1)(e)(i).

(2) The department, to assist in investigating sex-related crimes and in apprehending offenders, shall:

(a) develop and operate a system to collect, analyze, maintain, and disseminate information on sex offenders and sex offenses; and

(b) make information collected and developed under this section available to the public.

(3) Any law enforcement agency shall, in the manner prescribed by the department, inform the department of:

(a) the receipt of a report or complaint of an offense listed in Subsection (1)(e), within three working days; and

(b) the arrest of a person suspected of any of the offenses listed in Subsection (1)(e), within five working days.

(4) Upon convicting a person of any of the offenses listed in Subsection (1)(e), the convicting court shall within three working days forward a copy of the judgment and sentence to the department.

(5) A sex offender in the custody of the department shall be registered by agents of the department upon:

(a) being placed on probation;

(b) commitment to a secure correctional facility operated by or under contract to the department;

(c) release from confinement to parole status, termination or expiration of sentence, or escape;

(d) entrance to and release from any community-based residential program operated by or under contract to the department; or

(e) termination of probation or parole.

(6) A sex offender not in the custody of the department and who is confined in a correctional facility not operated by or under contract to the department shall be registered with the department by the sheriff of the county in which the offender is confined upon:

(a) commitment to the correctional facility; and

(b) release from confinement.

(7) A sex offender committed to a state mental hospital shall be registered with the department by the hospital upon admission and upon discharge.

(8) A sex offender convicted by any other state or by the United States government is required to register under Subsection (1)(e)(ii) and shall register with the department within ten days after entering the state.

(9) (a) Except as provided in Subsections (9)(b) and (c), a sex offender shall, for the duration of the sentence and for ten years after termination of sentence, register annually and again within ten days of every change of his place of habitation.

(b) (i) A sex offender convicted of any of the offenses listed in Subsection (9)(b)(ii) shall, for the offender's lifetime, register annually and again within ten days of every change of the offender's place of habitation. This registration requirement is not subject to exemptions and may not be terminated or altered during the offender's lifetime.

(ii) Offenses referred to in Subsection (9)(b)(i) are:

(A) any offense listed in Subsection (1)(e) if the offender has previously been convicted of an offense listed in Subsection (1)(e);

(B) Section 76-5-402.1, rape of a child;

(C) Section 76-5-402.3, object rape of a child;

(D) Section 76-5-403, forcible sodomy;

(E) Section 76-5-403.1, sodomy on a child; and

(F) Section 76-5-405, aggravated sexual assault.

(c) Notwithstanding Subsections (9)(a) and (b), a sex offender who is confined in a secure facility

or in a state mental hospital is not required to register annually.

(10) An agency in the state that registers a sex offender on probation, a sex offender who has been released from confinement to parole status or termination, or a sex offender whose sentence has expired shall inform the offender of the duty to comply with the continuing registration requirements of this section during the period of registration required in Subsection (9), including:

(a) notification to the state agencies in the states where the registrant presently resides and plans to reside when moving across state lines;

(b) verification of address at least every 60 days pursuant to a parole agreement for lifetime parolees; and

(c) notification to the out-of-state agency where the offender is living, whether or not the offender is a resident of that state.

(11) A sex offender shall provide the department with the following information:

(a) all names or aliases the sex offender is or has been known by;

(b) the sex offender's name and residential address;

(c) a physical description, including the sex offender's age, height, weight, eye and hair color;

(d) the type of vehicle or vehicles the sex offender drives;

(e) a current photograph of the sex offender; and

(f) each institution of higher education in Utah at which the sex offender is employed, carries on a vocation, or is a student, and any change of enrollment or employment status of the sex offender at any institution of higher education.

(12) The department shall:

(a) provide the following additional information when available:

(i) the crimes the sex offender was convicted of; and

(ii) a description of the sex offender's primary and secondary targets; and

(b) ensure that the registration information collected regarding a sex offender's enrollment or employment at an institution of higher education is:

(i) promptly made available to any law enforcement agency that has jurisdiction where the institution is located; and

(ii) entered into the appropriate state records or data system.

(13) (a) A sex offender who knowingly fails to register under this section is guilty of a class A misdemeanor and shall be sentenced to serve a term of incarceration for not fewer than 90 days and also at least one year of probation.

(b) Neither the court nor the Board of Pardons and Parole may release a person who violates this section from serving a term of at least 90 days and of completing probation of at least one year. This Subsection (13)(b) supersedes any other provision of the law contrary to this section.

(14) Notwithstanding Title 63, Chapter 2, Government Records Access and Management Act, information in Subsections (11) and (12) collected and released under this section is public information.

(15) (a) If a sex offender is to be temporarily sent outside a secure facility in which he is confined on any assignment, including, without limitation, firefighting or disaster control, the official who has custody of the offender shall, within a reason-

able time prior to removal from the secure facility, notify the local law enforcement agencies where the assignment is to be filled.

(b) This Subsection (15) does not apply to any person temporarily released under guard from the institution in which he is confined.

(16) Notwithstanding Sections 77-18-9 through 77-18-14 regarding expungement, a person convicted of any offense listed in Subsection (1)(e) is not relieved from the responsibility to register as required under this section.

(17) Notwithstanding Section 42-1-1, a sex offender:

(a) may not change his name:

(i) while under the jurisdiction of the department; and

(ii) until the registration requirements of this statute have expired; or

(b) may not change his name at any time, if registration is under Subsection (9)(b).

(18) The department may make rules necessary to implement this section, including:

(a) the method for dissemination of the information; and

(b) instructions to the public regarding the use of the information.

(19) Any information regarding the identity or location of a victim shall be redacted by the department from information provided under Subsections (11) and (12).

(20) Nothing in this section shall be construed to create or impose any duty on any person to request or obtain information regarding any sex offender from the department.

(21) If the department chooses to post registry information on the Internet, the website shall contain a disclaimer informing the public of the following:

(a) the information contained on the site is obtained from sex offenders and the department does not guarantee its accuracy;

(b) members of the public are not allowed to publicize the information or use it to harass or threaten sex offenders or members of their families; and

(c) harassment, stalking, or threats against sex offenders or their families are prohibited and doing so may violate Utah criminal laws.

(22) The department shall construct the website so that users, before accessing registry information, must indicate that they have read the disclaimer, understand it, and agree to comply with its terms.

(23) The department, its personnel, and any individual or entity acting at the request or upon the direction of the department are immune from civil liability for damages for good faith compliance with this section and will be presumed to have acted in good faith by reporting information.

(24) The department shall redact information that, if disclosed, could reasonably identify a victim.   2002

CHAPTER 28c

INTERSTATE COMPACT FOR ADULT OFFENDER SUPERVISION

Part 1

Purpose and Functions

Part 2

Authority of the Governor to Enter Into Compact

PART 1

PURPOSE AND FUNCTIONS

77-28c-101. Title.

This chapter is known as the "Interstate Compact for Adult Offender Supervision."   2001

77-28c-102. Preamble.

PREAMBLE

Whereas: The Interstate Compact for the supervision of Parolees and Probationers was established in 1937, it is the earliest corrections "compact" established among the states and has not been amended since its adoption over 62 years ago;

Whereas: This compact is the only vehicle for the controlled movement of adult parolees and probationers across state lines, and it currently has jurisdiction over more than a quarter of a million offenders;

Whereas: The complexities of the compact have become more difficult to administer, and many jurisdictions have expanded supervision expectations to include currently unregulated practices such as victim input, victim notification requirements, and sex offender registration;

Whereas: After hearings, national surveys, and a detailed study by a task force appointed by the National Institute of Corrections, the overwhelming recommendation has been to amend the document to bring about an effective management capacity that addresses public safety concerns and offender accountability;

Whereas: Upon the adoption of this Interstate Compact for Adult Offender Supervision, it is the intention of the legislature to repeal the previous Interstate Compact for the Supervision of Parolees and Probationers on the effective date of this Compact.   2001

77-28c-103. Compact.

ARTICLE I

PURPOSE

(a) The compacting states to this Interstate Compact recognize that each state is responsible for the supervision of adult offenders in the community who are authorized pursuant to the by-laws and rules of this compact to travel across state lines both to and from each compacting state in such a manner as to track the location of offenders, transfer supervision authority in an orderly and efficient manner, and when necessary, return offenders to the originating jurisdictions. The compacting states also recognize that Congress, by enacting the Crime Control Act, 4 U.S.C. Section 112 (1965), has authorized and encouraged compacts for cooperative efforts and mutual assistance in the prevention of crime.

(b) It is the purpose of this compact and the Interstate Commission created hereunder, through means of joint and cooperative action among the compacting states: To provide the framework for the promotion of public safety and protect the rights of victims through the control and regulation of the interstate movement of offenders in the community; to provide for the effective tracking, supervision, and rehabilitation of these offenders by the sending and receiving states; and to equitably distribute the costs, benefits, and obligations of the compact among the compacting states.

(c) In addition, this compact will: Create an Interstate Commission which will establish uniform procedures to manage the movement between states of adults placed under community supervision and released to the community under the jurisdiction of courts, paroling authorities, corrections, or other criminal justice agencies which will promulgate rules to achieve the purpose of this compact; ensure an opportunity for input and timely notice to victims and to jurisdictions where defined offenders are authorized to travel or to relocate across state lines; establish a system of uniform data collection, access to information on active cases by authorized criminal justice officials, and regular reporting of compact activities to heads of state councils, state executive, judicial, and legislative branches, and criminal justice administrators; monitor compliance with rules governing interstate movement of offenders and initiate interventions to address and correct noncompliance; and coordinate training and education regarding regulations of interstate movement of offenders for officials involved in such activity.

(d) The compacting states recognize that there is no "right" of any offender to live in another state and that duly accredited officers of a sending state may at all times enter a receiving state and there apprehend and retake any offender under supervision subject to the provisions of this compact and by-laws and rules promulgated hereunder. It is the policy of the compacting states that the activities conducted by the Interstate Commission created herein are the formation of public policies and are therefore public business.

ARTICLE II

DEFINITIONS

(a) As used in this compact, unless the context clearly requires a different construction:

(1) "Adult" means both individuals legally classified as adults and juveniles treated as adults by court order, statute, or operation of law.

(2) "By-laws" mean those by-laws established by the Interstate Commission for its governance, or for directing or controlling the Interstate Commission's actions or conduct.

(3) "Compact administrator" means the individual in each compacting state appointed pursuant to the terms of this compact responsible for the administration and management of the state's supervision and transfer of offenders subject to the terms of this compact, the rules adopted by the Interstate Commission and policies adopted by the state council under this compact.

(4) "Compacting state" means any state which has enacted the enabling legislation for this compact.

(5) "Commissioner" means the voting representative of each compacting state appointed pursuant to Article III of this compact.

(6) "Interstate Commission" means the Interstate Commission for Adult Offender Supervision established by this compact.

(7) "Member" means the commissioner of a compacting state or designee, who shall be a person officially connected with the commissioner.

(8) "Noncompacting state" means any state which has not enacted the enabling legislation for this compact.

(9) "Offender" means an adult placed under or subject to supervision as the result of the commission of a criminal offense and released to the community under the jurisdiction of courts, paroling authorities, corrections, or other criminal justice agencies.

(10) "Person" means any individual, corporation, business enterprise, or other legal entity, either public or private.

(11) "Rules" means acts of the Interstate Commission, duly promulgated pursuant to Article VIII of this compact, substantially affecting interested parties in addition to the Interstate Commission, which shall have the force and effect of law in the compacting states.

(12) "State" means a state of the United States, the District of Columbia, and any other territorial possessions of the United States.

(13) "State council" means the resident members of the State Council for Interstate Adult Offender Supervision created by each state under Article IV of this compact.

ARTICLE III

THE COMPACT COMMISSION

(a) The compacting states hereby create the "Interstate Commission for Adult Offender Supervision." The Interstate Commission shall be a body corporate and joint agency of the compacting states. The Interstate Commission shall have all the responsibilities, powers, and duties set forth herein; including the power to sue and be sued, and such additional powers as may be conferred upon it by subsequent action of the respective legislatures of the compacting states in accordance with the terms of this compact.

(b) The Interstate Commission shall consist of Commissioners selected and appointed by resident members of a State Council for Interstate Adult Offender Supervision for each state. In addition to the commissioners who are the voting representatives of each state, the Interstate Commission shall include individuals who are not commissioners but who are members of interested organizations. Such noncommissioner members must include a member of the national organizations of governors, legislators, state chief justices, attorneys general, and crime victims. All noncommissioner members of the Interstate Commission shall be ex-officio (nonvoting) members. The Interstate Commission may provide in its by-laws for such additional, ex-officio, nonvoting members as it deems necessary.

(c) Each compacting state represented at any meeting of the Interstate Commission is entitled to one vote. A majority of the compacting states shall constitute a quorum for the transaction of business, unless a larger quorum is required by the by-laws of the Interstate Commission.

(d) The Interstate Commission shall meet at least once each calendar year. The chairperson may call additional meetings and, upon the request of 27 or more compacting states, shall call additional meetings. Public notice shall be given of all meetings and meetings shall be open to the public.

(e) The Interstate Commission shall establish an executive committee which shall include commission officers, members, and others as shall be determined by the by-laws. The Executive Committee shall have the power to act on behalf of the Interstate Commission during periods when the Interstate Commission is not in session, with the exception of rulemaking and/or amendment to the Compact. The Executive Committee oversees the day-to-day activities managed by the Executive Director and Interstate Commission staff; administers enforcement and compliance with the provisions of the compact, its by-laws, and as directed by the Interstate Commission; and performs other duties as directed by the Commission or set forth in the by-laws.

ARTICLE IV

THE STATE COUNCIL

(a) Each member state shall create a State Council for Interstate Adult Offender Supervision which shall be responsible for the appointment of the commissioner who shall serve on the Interstate Commission from that state. Each state council shall appoint as its commissioner the Compact Administrator from that state to serve on the Interstate Commission in such capacity under or pursuant to applicable law of the member state. While each member state may determine the membership of its own state council, its membership must include at least one representative from the legislative, judicial, and executive branches of government, victims groups, and compact administrators.

(b) Each compacting state retains the right to determine the qualifications of the compact administrator, who shall be appointed by the state council or by the Governor in consultation with the legislature and the judiciary.

(c) In addition to appointment of its commissioner to the National Interstate Commission, each state council shall exercise oversight and advocacy concerning its participation in Interstate Commission activities and other duties as may be determined by each member state including, but not limited to, development of policy concerning operations and procedures of the compact within that state.

ARTICLE V

POWERS AND DUTIES OF THE INTERSTATE COMMISSION

(a) The Interstate Commission shall have the following powers:

(1) To adopt a seal and suitable by-laws governing the management and operation of the Interstate Commission.

(2) To promulgate rules which shall have the force and effect of statutory law and shall be binding in the compacting states to the extent and in the manner provided in this compact.

(3) To oversee, supervise, and coordinate the interstate movement of offenders subject to the terms of this compact and any by-laws adopted and rules promulgated by the compact commission.

(4) To enforce compliance with compact provisions, Interstate Commission rules, and by-laws, using all necessary and proper means including, but not limited to, the use of judicial process.

(5) To establish and maintain offices.

(6) To purchase and maintain insurance and bonds.

(7) To borrow, accept, or contract for services of personnel including, but not limited to, members and their staffs.

(8) To establish and appoint committees and hire staff which it deems necessary for the carrying out of its functions including, but not limited to, an executive committee as required by Article III which shall have the power to act on behalf of the Interstate Commission in carrying out its powers and duties hereunder.

(9) To elect or appoint such officers, attorneys, employees, agents, or consultants, and to fix their compensation, define their duties, and determine their qualifications; and to establish the Interstate Commission's personnel policies and programs relating to, among other things, conflicts of interest, rates of compensation, and qualifications of personnel.

(10) To accept any and all donations and grants of money, equipment, supplies, materials, and services, and to receive, utilize, and dispose of same.

(11) To lease, purchase, accept contributions or donations of, or otherwise to own, hold, improve, or use any property, real, personal, or mixed.

(12) To sell, convey, mortgage, pledge, lease, exchange, abandon, or otherwise dispose of any property, real, personal, or mixed.

(13) To establish a budget and make expenditures and levy dues as provided in Article X of this compact.

(14) To sue and be sued.

(15) To provide for dispute resolution among compacting states.

(16) To perform such functions as may be necessary or appropriate to achieve the purposes of this compact.

(17) To report annually to the legislatures, governors, judiciary, and state councils of the compacting states concerning the activities of the Interstate Commission during the preceding year. Such reports shall also include any recommendations that may have been adopted by the Interstate Commission.

(18) To coordinate education, training, and public awareness regarding the interstate movement of offenders for officials involved in such activity.

(19) To establish uniform standards for the reporting, collecting, and exchanging of data.

ARTICLE VI

ORGANIZATION AND OPERATION OF THE INTERSTATE COMMISSION

(a) By-laws. The Interstate Commission shall, by a majority of the members, within 12 months of the first Interstate Commission meeting, adopt by-laws to govern its conduct as may be necessary or appropriate to carry out the purposes of the compact including, but not limited to:

(1) Establishing the fiscal year of the Interstate Commission;

(2) Establishing an executive committee and such other committees as may be necessary, providing reasonable standards and procedures:

(i) For the establishment of committees, and

(ii) Governing any general or specific delegation of any authority or function of the Interstate Commission;

(3) Providing reasonable procedures for calling and conducting meetings of the Interstate Commission, and ensuring reasonable notice of each such meeting;

(4) Establishing the titles and responsibilities of the officers of the Interstate Commission;

(5) Providing reasonable standards and procedures for the establishment of the personnel policies and programs of the Interstate Commission. Notwithstanding any civil service or other similar laws of any compacting state, the by-laws shall exclusively govern the personnel policies and programs of the Interstate Commission; and

(6) Providing a mechanism for winding up the operations of the Interstate Commission and the equitable return of any surplus funds that may exist upon the termination of the compact after the payment and/or reserving of all of its debts and obligations;

(7) Providing transition rules for "start up" administration of the compact;

(8) Establishing standards and procedures for compliance and technical assistance in carrying out the compact.

(b) Officers and Staff.

(1) The Interstate Commission shall, by a majority of the members, elect from among its members a chairperson and a vice chairperson, each of whom shall have such authorities and duties as may be specified in the by-laws. The chairperson or, in his or her absence or disability, the vice chairperson, shall preside at all meetings of the Interstate Commission. The officers so elected shall serve without compensation or remuneration from the Interstate Commission; provided that subject to the availability of budgeted funds, the officers shall be reimbursed for any actual and necessary costs and expenses incurred by them in the performance of their duties and responsibilities as officers of the Interstate Commission.

(2) The Interstate Commission shall, through its executive committee, appoint or retain an executive director for such period, upon such terms and conditions and for such compensation as the Interstate Commission may deem appropriate. The executive director shall serve as secretary to the Interstate Commission, and hire and supervise such other staff as may be authorized by the Interstate Commission, but shall not be a member.

(c) Corporate Records of the Interstate Commission. The Interstate Commission shall maintain its corporate books and records in accordance with the by-laws.

(d) Qualified Immunity, Defense, and Indemnification.

(1) The members, officers, executive director, and employees of the Interstate Commission shall be immune from suit and liability, either personally or in their official capacity, for any claim for damage to or loss of property or personal injury or other civil liability caused or arising out of any actual or alleged act, error or omission that occurred within the scope of Interstate Commission employment, duties, or responsibilities; provided, that nothing in this paragraph shall be construed to protect any such person from suit and/or liability for any damage, loss, injury, or liability caused by the intentional or willful and wanton misconduct of any such person.

(2) The Interstate Commission shall defend the commissioner of a compacting state, or his or her representatives or employees, or the Interstate Commission's representatives or employees, in any civil action seeking to impose liability, arising out of any actual or alleged act, error or omission that occurred within the scope of Interstate Commission employment, duties, or responsibilities, or that the defendant had a reasonable basis for believing occurred within the scope of Interstate Commission employment, duties, or responsibilities; provided, that the actual or alleged act, error, or omission did not result from intentional wrongdoing on the part of such person.

(3) The Interstate Commission shall indemnify and hold the commissioner of a compacting state, the appointed designee, or employees, or the Interstate Commission's representatives or employees, harmless in the amount of any settlement or judgement obtained against such persons arising out of any actual or alleged act, error, or omission that occurred within the scope of Interstate Commission employment, duties, or responsibilities, or that such persons had a reasonable basis for believing occurred within the scope of Interstate Commission employment, duties, or responsibilities, provided, that the actual or alleged act, error, or omission did not result from gross negligence or intentional wrongdoing on the part of such person.

ARTICLE VII

ACTIVITIES OF THE INTERSTATE COMMISSION

(a) The Interstate Commission shall meet and take such actions as are consistent with the provisions of this compact.

(b) Except as otherwise provided in this compact and unless a greater percentage is required by the by-laws, in order to constitute an act of the Interstate Commission, such act shall have been taken at a meeting of the Interstate Commission and shall have received an affirmative vote of a majority of the members present.

(c) Each member of the Interstate Commission shall have the right and power to cast a vote to which that Compacting State is entitled and to participate in the business and affairs of the Interstate Commission. A member shall vote in person on behalf of the state and shall not delegate a vote to another member state. However, a state council shall appoint another authorized representative, in the absence of the commissioner from that state, to cast a vote on behalf of the member state at a specified meeting. The by-laws may provide for members' participation in meetings by telephone or other means of telecommunication or electronic communication. Any voting conducted by telephone, or other means of telecommunication or electronic communication, shall be subject to the same quorum requirements of meetings where members are present in person.

(d) The Interstate Commission shall meet at least once during each calendar year. The chairperson of the Interstate Commission may call additional meetings at any time and, upon the request of a majority of the members, shall call additional meetings.

(e) The Interstate Commission's by-laws shall establish conditions and procedures under which the Interstate Commission shall make its information and official records available to the public for inspection or copying. The Interstate Commission may exempt from disclosure any information or official records to the extent they would adversely affect personal privacy rights or proprietary interests. In promulgating such rules, the Interstate Commission may make available to law enforcement agencies records and information otherwise exempt from disclosure, and may enter into agreements with law enforcement agencies to receive or exchange information or records subject to nondisclosure and confidentiality provisions.

(f) Public notice shall be given of all meetings and all meetings shall be open to the public, except as set forth in the rules or as otherwise provided in the compact. The Interstate Commission shall promulgate rules consistent with the principles contained in the "Government in Sunshine Act," 5 U.S.C. Section 552(b), as may be amended. The Interstate Commission and any of its committees may close a meeting to the public where it determines by two-thirds vote that an open meeting would be likely to:

(1) Relate solely to the Interstate Commission's internal personnel practices and procedures;

(2) Disclose matters specifically exempted from disclosure by statute;

(3) Disclose trade secrets or commercial or financial information which is privileged or confidential;

(4) Involve accusing any person of a crime, or formally censuring any person;

(5) Disclose information of a personal nature where disclosure would constitute a clearly unwarranted invasion of personal privacy;

(6) Disclose investigatory records compiled for law enforcement purposes;

(7) Disclose information contained in or related to examination, operating, or condition reports prepared by, or on behalf of or for the use of, the Interstate Commission with respect to a regulated entity for the purpose of regulation or supervision of such entity;

(8) Disclose information, the premature disclosure of which would significantly endanger the life of a person or the stability of a regulated entity;

(9) Specifically relate to the Interstate Commission's issuance of a subpoena, or its participation in a civil action or proceeding.

(g) For every meeting closed pursuant to this provision, the Interstate Commission's chief legal officer shall publicly certify that, in his or her opinion, the meeting may be closed to the public, and shall reference each relevant provision authorizing closure of the meeting. The Interstate Commission shall keep minutes which shall fully and clearly describe all matters discussed in any meeting and shall provide a full and accurate summary of any actions taken, and the reasons therefor, including a description of each of the views expressed on any item and the record of any roll call vote (reflected in the vote of each member on the question). All documents considered in connection with any action shall be identified in such minutes.

(h) The Interstate Commission shall collect standardized data concerning the Interstate movement of offenders as directed through its by-laws and rules which shall specify the data to be collected, the means of collection, and data exchange and reporting requirements.

ARTICLE VIII

RULEMAKING FUNCTIONS OF THE INTERSTATE COMMISSION

(a) The Interstate Commission shall promulgate rules in order to effectively and efficiently achieve the purposes of the compact, including transition rules governing administration of the compact during the period in which it is being considered and enacted by the states.

(b) Rulemaking shall occur pursuant to the criteria set forth in this article and the by-laws and rules adopted pursuant thereto. Such rulemaking shall substantially conform to the principles of the federal Administrative Procedure Act, 5 U.S.C.S. Section 551 et seq., and the Federal Advisory Committee Act, 5 U.S.C.S. App. 2, Section 1 et seq., as may be amended (hereinafter "APA"). All rules and amendments shall become binding as of the date specified in each rule or amendment.

(c) If a majority of the legislatures of the compacting states rejects a rule, by enactment of a statute or resolution in the same manner used to adopt the compact, then such rule shall have no further force and effect in any compacting state.

(d) When promulgating a rule, the Interstate Commission shall:

(1) Publish the proposed rule, stating with particularity the text of the rule which is proposed and the reason for the proposed rule;

(2) Allow persons to submit written data, facts, opinions, and arguments, which information shall be publicly available;

(3) Provide an opportunity for an informal hearing; and

(4) Promulgate a final rule and its effective date, if appropriate, based on the rulemaking record. Not later than 60 days after a rule is promulgated, any interested person may file a petition in the United States District Court for the District of Columbia or in the Federal District Court where the Interstate Commission's principal office is located for judicial review of such rule. If the court finds that the Interstate Commission's action is not supported by substantial evidence, (as defined in the APA), in the rulemaking record, the court shall hold the rule unlawful and set it aside.

(e) Subjects to be addressed within 12 months after the first meeting must at a minimum include:

(i) notice to victims and opportunity to be heard;

(ii) offender registration and compliance;

(iii) violations/returns;

(iv) transfer procedures and forms;

(v) eligibility for transfer;

(vi) collection of restitution and fees from offenders;

(vii) data collection and reporting;

(viii) the level of supervision to be provided by the receiving state;

(ix) transition rules governing the operation of the compact and the Interstate Commission during all or part of the period between the effective date of the compact and the date on which the last eligible state adopts the compact; and

(x) mediation, arbitration, and dispute resolution.

(f) The existing rules governing the operation of the previous compact superceded by this act shall be null and void 12 months after the first meeting of the Interstate Commission created hereunder.

(g) Upon determination by the Interstate Commission that an emergency exists, it may promulgate an emergency rule which shall become effective immediately upon adoption, provided that the usual rulemaking procedures provided hereunder shall be retroactively applied to said rule as soon as reasonably possible, in no event later than 90 days after the effective date of the rule.

ARTICLE IX

OVERSIGHT, ENFORCEMENT, AND DISPUTE RESOLUTION BY THE INTERSTATE COMMISSION

(a) Oversight.

(1) The Interstate Commission shall oversee the Interstate movement of adult offenders in the compacting states and shall monitor such activities being administered in noncompacting states which may significantly affect compacting states.

(2) The courts and executive agencies in each compacting state shall enforce this compact and shall take all actions necessary and appropriate to effectuate the compact's purposes and intent. In any judicial or administrative proceeding in a compacting state pertaining to the subject matter of this compact which may affect the powers, responsibilities, or actions of the Interstate Commission, the Interstate Commission shall be entitled to receive all service of process in any such proceeding, and shall have standing to intervene in the proceeding for all purposes.

(b) Dispute Resolution.

(1) The compacting states shall report to the Interstate Commission on issues or activities of concern to them, and cooperate with and support the Interstate Commission in the discharge of its duties and responsibilities.

(2) The Interstate Commission shall attempt to resolve any disputes or other issues which are subject to the compact and which may arise among compacting states and noncompacting states.

(3) The Interstate Commission shall enact a by-law or promulgate a rule providing for both mediation and binding dispute resolution for disputes among the compacting states.

(c) Enforcement. The Interstate Commission, in the reasonable exercise of its discretion, shall enforce the provisions of this compact using any or all means set forth in Article XII (b) of this compact.

ARTICLE X

FINANCE

(a) The Interstate Commission shall pay or provide for the payment of the reasonable expenses of its establishment, organization, and ongoing activities.

(b) The Interstate Commission shall levy on and collect an annual assessment from each compacting state to cover the cost of the internal operations and activities of the Interstate Commission and its staff which must be in a total amount sufficient to cover the Interstate Commission's annual budget as approved each year. The aggregate annual assessment amount shall be allocated based upon a formula to be determined by the Interstate Commission, taking into consideration the population of the state and the volume of interstate movement of offenders in each compacting state and shall promulgate a rule binding upon all compacting states which governs said assessment.

(c) The Interstate Commission shall not incur any obligations of any kind prior to securing the funds adequate to meet the same; nor shall the Interstate Commission pledge the credit of any of the compacting states, except by and with the authority of the compacting state.

(d) The Interstate Commission shall keep accurate accounts of all receipts and disbursements. The receipts and disbursements of the Interstate Commission shall be subject to the audit and accounting procedures established under its by-laws. However, all receipts and disbursements of funds handled by the Interstate Commission shall be audited yearly by a certified or licensed public accountant and the report of the audit shall be included in and become part of the annual report of the Interstate Commission.

ARTICLE XI

COMPACTING STATES, EFFECTIVE DATE, AND AMENDMENT

(a) Any state, as defined in Article II of this compact, is eligible to become a compacting state.

(b) The compact shall become effective and binding upon legislative enactment of the compact into law by no less than 35 of the states. The initial effective date shall be the later of July 1, 2001, or upon enactment into law by the thirty-fifth jurisdiction. Thereafter it shall become effective and binding, as to any other compacting state, upon enactment of the compact into law by that state. The governors of nonmember states or their designees will be invited to participate in Interstate Commission activities on a nonvoting basis prior to adoption of the compact by all states and territories of the United States.

(c) Amendments to the compact may be proposed by the Interstate Commission for enactment by the compacting states. No amendment shall become effective and binding upon the Interstate Commission and the compacting states unless and until it is enacted into law by unanimous consent of the compacting states.

ARTICLE XII

WITHDRAWAL, DEFAULT, TERMINATION, AND JUDICIAL ENFORCEMENT

(a) Withdrawal.

(1) Once effective, the compact shall continue in force and remain binding upon each and every compacting state; provided, that a compacting state may withdraw from the compact ("withdrawing state") by enacting a statute specifically repealing the statute which enacted the compact into law.

(2) The effective date of withdrawal is the effective date of the repeal.

(3) The withdrawing state shall immediately notify the chairperson of the Interstate Commission in writing upon the introduction of legislation repealing this compact in the withdrawing state. The Interstate Commission shall notify the other compacting states of the withdrawing state's intent to withdraw within 60 days of its receipt thereof.

(4) The withdrawing state is responsible for all assessments, obligations, and liabilities incurred through the effective date of withdrawal, including any obligations, the performance of which extend beyond the effective date of withdrawal.

(5) Reinstatement following withdrawal of any compacting state shall occur upon the withdrawing state reenacting the compact or upon such later date as determined by the Interstate Commission.

(b) Default.

(1) If the Interstate Commission determines that any compacting state has at any time de-

faulted ("defaulting state") in the performance of any of its obligations or responsibilities under this compact, the by-laws, or any duly promulgated rules, the Interstate Commission may impose any or all of the following penalties:

(i) Fines, fees, and costs in such amounts as are deemed to be reasonable as fixed by the Interstate Commission;

(ii) Remedial training and technical assistance as directed by the Interstate Commission;

(iii) Suspension and termination of membership in the compact. Suspension shall be imposed only after all other reasonable means of securing compliance under the by-laws and rules have been exhausted. Immediate notice of suspension shall be given by the Interstate Commission to the governor, the chief justice or chief judicial officer of the state, the majority and minority leaders of the defaulting state's legislature, and the state council.

(2) The grounds for default include, but are not limited to, failure of a compacting state to perform such obligations or responsibilities imposed upon it by this compact, Interstate Commission by-laws, or duly promulgated rules. The Interstate Commission shall immediately notify the defaulting state in writing of the penalty imposed by the Interstate Commission on the defaulting state pending a cure of the default. The Interstate Commission shall stipulate the conditions and the time period within which the defaulting state must cure its default. If the defaulting state fails to cure the default within the time period specified by the Interstate Commission, in addition to any other penalties imposed herein, the defaulting state may be terminated from the compact upon an affirmative vote of a majority of the compacting states and all rights, privileges, and benefits conferred by this compact shall be terminated from the effective date of suspension. Within 60 days of the effective date of termination of a defaulting state, the Interstate Commission shall notify the governor, the chief justice or chief judicial officer, and the majority and minority leaders of the defaulting state's legislature and the state council of such termination.

(3) The defaulting state is responsible for all assessments, obligations, and liabilities incurred through the effective date of termination including any obligations, the performance of which extends beyond the effective date of termination.

(4) The Interstate Commission shall not bear any costs relating to the defaulting state unless otherwise mutually agreed upon between the Interstate Commission and the defaulting state. Reinstatement following termination of any compacting state requires both a reenactment of the compact by the defaulting state and the approval of the Interstate Commission pursuant to the rules.

(c) Judicial Enforcement. The Interstate Commission may, by majority vote of the members, initiate legal action in the United States District Court for the District of Columbia or, at the discretion of the Interstate Commission, in the federal district where the Interstate Commission has its offices, to enforce compliance with the provisions of the compact and its duly promulgated rules and by-laws, against any compacting state in default. In the event judicial enforcement is necessary the prevailing party shall be awarded all costs of such litigation including reasonable attorneys' fees.

(d) Dissolution of Compact.

(1) The compact dissolves effective upon the date of the withdrawal or default of the compacting state which reduces membership in the compact to one compacting state.

(2) Upon the dissolution of this compact, the compact becomes null and void and shall be of no further force or effect, and the business and affairs of the Interstate Commission shall be wound up and any surplus funds shall be distributed in accordance with the by-laws.

ARTICLE XIII

SEVERABILITY AND CONSTRUCTION

(a) The provisions of this compact shall be severable, and if any phrase, clause, sentence, or provision is deemed unenforceable, the remaining provisions of the compact shall be enforceable.

(b) The provisions of this compact shall be liberally constructed to effectuate its purposes.

ARTICLE XIV

BINDING EFFECT OF COMPACT AND OTHER LAWS

(a) Other Laws.

(1) Nothing herein prevents the enforcement of any other law of a compacting state that is not inconsistent with this compact.

(2) All compacting states' laws conflicting with this compact are superseded to the extent of the conflict.

(b) Binding Effect of the Compact.

(1) All lawful actions of the Interstate Commission, including all rules and by-laws promulgated by the Interstate Commission, are binding upon the compacting states.

(2) All agreements between the Interstate Commission and the compacting states are binding in accordance with their terms.

(3) Upon the request of a party to a conflict over meaning or interpretation of Interstate Commission actions, and upon a majority vote of the compacting states, the Interstate Commission may issue advisory opinions regarding such meaning or interpretation.

(4) In the event any provision of this compact exceeds the constitutional limits imposed on the legislature of any compacting state, the obligations, duties, powers, or jurisdiction sought to be conferred by such provision upon the Interstate Commission shall be ineffective and such obligations, duties, powers, or jurisdiction shall remain in the compacting state and shall be exercised by the agency thereof to which such obligations, duties, powers, or jurisdiction are delegated by law in effect at the time this compact becomes effective.   2001

77-28c-104. Definitions — Compact transfer application fee.

(1) As used in this section:

(a) "Department" means the Department of Corrections.

(b) "Offender" has the same meaning as provided in Section 77-28c-103, Article II(a)(9).

(2) (a) Offenders desiring a transfer of supervision to another state under the Interstate Compact for Adult Offender Supervision shall apply to the department for transfer.

(b) In accordance with Title 63, Chapter 46a, Utah Administrative Rulemaking Act, the department shall make rules governing the transfer of supervision of an offender.

(3) The department shall collect a fee of $50 from each offender applying for transfer of supervision to another state under the Interstate Compact for Adult Offender Supervision.　　　　2004

77-28c-105. Compact for Adult Offender Supervision Restricted Account.

(1) There is created within the General Fund, a restricted account known as the Interstate Compact for Adult Offender Supervision Restricted Account.

(2) Monies in the account shall consist of the compact application fee collected by the department for a transfer of supervision under the provisions of Subsection 77-28c-104(3).

(3) Upon appropriation by the Legislature, monies in the account shall be used:

(a) to cover costs incurred in the collection of the fee; and

(b) for the administration of the Interstate Compact for Adult Offender Supervision, including the payment of the annual assessment levied under Subsection 77-28c-103, Article X(b).　2004

PART 2

AUTHORITY OF THE GOVERNOR TO ENTER INTO COMPACT

77-28c-201. Authority of governor to join compact.

The governor of Utah is authorized and directed to execute a compact on behalf of this state with any other state or states joining the Interstate Compact for Adult Offender Supervision as provided in Section 77-28c-103.　　　　2001

CHAPTER 30

EXTRADITION

77-30-1. Definitions.

Where appearing in this act, the term "governor" includes any person performing the functions of governor by authority of the law of this state. The term "executive authority" includes the governor and any person performing the functions of governor in a state other than this state. The term "state," referring to a state other than this state, includes any other state or territory, organized or unorganized, of the United States of America.　　　　1980

77-30-2. Duty of governor to deliver person charged with crime upon demand by other state.

Subject to the provisions of this act, the provisions of the Constitution of the United States controlling, and any and all Acts of Congress enacted in pursuance thereof, it is the duty of the governor of this state to have arrested and delivered up to the executive authority of any other state of the United States any person charged in that state with treason, felony or other crime who has fled from justice and is found in this state.　　　　1980

77-30-3. Form of demand — What documents presented must show.

No demand for the extradition of a person charged with a crime in another state shall be recognized by the governor unless in writing alleging, except in cases arising under Section 77-30-6, that the accused was present in the demanding state at the time of the commission of the alleged crime, and that thereafter he fled from the state, and accompanied by a copy of an indictment found or by information supported by affidavit in the state having jurisdiction of the crime, or by a copy of an affidavit made before a magistrate there, together with a copy of any warrant which was issued thereupon or by a copy of a judgment of conviction or of a sentence composed in execution, together with a statement by the executive authority of the demanding state that the person claimed has escaped from confinement or has broken the terms of

his bail, probation or parole. The indictment, information or affidavit made before the magistrate must substantially charge the person demanded with having committed a crime under the law of that state and the copy of the indictment, information, affidavit, judgment of conviction or sentence must be authenticated by the executive authority making the demand.
1980

77-30-4. Governor may investigate demand.

When a demand shall be made upon the governor of this state by the executive authority of another state for the surrender of a person so charged with a crime, the governor may call upon the attorney general or any prosecuting officer in this state to investigate or assist in investigating the demand, and to report to him the situation and circumstances of the person so demanded, and whether he ought to be surrendered.
1980

77-30-5. Extradition for prosecution before conclusion of trial or term in other state — Return of person involuntarily leaving demanding state.

When it is desired to have returned to this state a person charged in this state with a crime, and such person is imprisoned or is held under criminal proceedings then pending against him in another state, the governor of this state may agree with the executive authority of such other state for the extradition of such person before the conclusion of such proceedings or his term of sentence in such other state, upon condition that such person be returned to such other state at the expense of this state as soon as the prosecution in this state is terminated.

The governor of this state may also surrender on demand of the executive authority of any other state any person in this state who is charged in the manner provided in Section 77-30-23 with having violated the laws of the state whose executive authority is making the demand, even though such person left the demanding state involuntarily.
1980

77-30-6. Extradition for crime committed in another state by person while in this state.

The governor of this state may also surrender, on demand of the executive authority of any other state, any person in this state charged in such other state, in the manner provided in Section 77-30-3, with committing an act in this state, or in a third state, intentionally resulting in a crime in the state whose executive authority is making the demand, and the provisions of this act not otherwise inconsistent shall apply to such cases even though the accused was not in that state at the time of the commission of the crime, and has not fled therefrom.
1980

77-30-7. Governor's warrant of arrest — Recitals.

If the governor decides that the demand should be complied with he shall sign a warrant of arrest, which shall be sealed with the state seal, directed to any peace officer or other person whom he may think fit to entrust with the execution thereof. The warrant must substantially recite the facts necessary to the validity of its issuance.
1980

77-30-8. Execution of warrant of arrest.

Such warrant shall authorize the peace officer or other person to whom directed to arrest the accused at any time and any place where he may be found within the state and to command the aid of all peace officers or other persons in the execution of the warrant, and

to deliver the accused, subject to the provisions of this act to the duly authorized agent of the demanding state.
1980

77-30-9. Authority of officers under warrant of arrest.

Every such peace officer or other person empowered to make the arrest shall have the same authority in arresting the accused, to command assistance therein, as peace officers have by law in the execution of any criminal process directed to them, with like penalties against those who refuse their assistance.
1980

77-30-10. Time to apply for habeas corpus allowed.

No person arrested upon such warrant shall be delivered over to the agent whom the executive authority demanding him shall have appointed to receive him unless he shall first be taken forthwith before a judge of a court of record in this state who shall inform him of the demand made for his surrender and of the crime with which he is charged and that he has the right to demand and procure legal counsel and if the prisoner or his counsel shall state that he or they desire to test the legality of his arrest, the judge of such court of record shall fix a reasonable time to be allowed him within which to apply for a writ of habeas corpus. When such writ is applied for, notice thereof and the time and place of hearing thereon shall be given to the prosecuting officer of the county in which the arrest is made and in which the accused is in custody, and to the said agent of the demanding state.
1980

77-30-11. Penalty for disobedience of habeas corpus.

Any officer who shall deliver to the agent for extradition of the demanding state a person in his custody under the governor's warrant, in willful disobedience to Section 77-30-10, shall be guilty of a misdemeanor and on conviction shall be fined not more than $1,000 or be imprisoned in the county jail not more than six months, or both.
1995

77-30-12. Officers entitled to use local jails.

The officer or persons executing the governor's warrant of arrest or the agent of the demanding state to whom the prisoner may have been delivered may, when necessary, confine the prisoner in the jail of any county or city through which he may pass and the keeper of such jail must receive and safely keep the prisoner until the officer or person having charge of him is ready to proceed on his route, such officer or person being chargeable with the expense of keeping.

The officer or agent of a demanding state to whom a prisoner may have been delivered following extradition proceedings in another state, or to whom a prisoner may have been delivered after waiving extradition in such other state, and who is passing through this state with such a prisoner for the purpose of immediately returning such prisoner to the demanding state may, when necessary, confine the prisoner in the jail of any county or city through which he may pass, and the keeper of such jail must receive and safely keep the prisoner until the officer or agent having charge of him is ready to proceed on his route, such officer or agent being chargeable with the expense of keeping; provided, such officer or agent shall produce and show to the keeper of such jail satisfactory written evidence of the fact that he is actually transporting such prisoner to the demanding state after a requisition by the executive authority of such demanding state. Such prisoner shall not be entitled to demand a new requisition while in this state.
1980

77-30-13. Fugitives from justice — Warrant of arrest.

Whenever any person within this state shall be charged on the oath of any credible person before any judge or magistrate of this state with the commission of any crime in any other state, and, except in cases arising under Section 77-30-6 that he has fled from justice, or with having been convicted of a crime in that state and having escaped from confinement, or having broken the terms of his bail, probation or parole, or whenever complaint shall have been made before any judge or magistrate in this state setting forth on the affidavit of any credible person in another state that a crime has been committed in such other state and that the accused has been charged in such state with the commission of the crime, and except in cases arising under Section 77-30-6, has fled from justice, or with having been convicted of a crime in that state and having escaped from confinement, or having broken the terms of his bail, probation or parole, and is believed to be in this state, the judge or magistrate shall issue a warrant directed to any peace officer commanding him to apprehend the person named therein, wherever he may be found in this state, and to bring him before the same or any judge, magistrate or court who or which may be available in or convenient of access to the place where the arrest may be made, to answer the charge or complaint and affidavit, and a certified copy of the sworn charge or complaint and affidavit upon which the warrant is issued shall be attached to the warrant.   1980

77-30-14. Arrest without warrant.

The arrest of a person may be lawfully made also by any peace officer or a private person without a warrant upon reasonable information that the accused stands charged in the courts of a state with a crime punishable by death or imprisonment for a term exceeding one year, but when so arrested the accused must be taken before a judge or magistrate with all practicable speed and complaint must be made against him under oath setting forth the ground for the arrest as in Section 77-30-13, and thereafter his answer shall be heard as if he had been arrested on a warrant.   1995

77-30-15. Commitment pending arrest under warrant of governor.

If from the examination before the judge or magistrate it appears that the person held is the person charged with having committed the crime alleged, and, except in cases arising under Section 77-30-6 that he has fled from justice, the judge or magistrate must, by a warrant reciting the accusation, commit him to the county jail for such a time not exceeding thirty days and specified in the warrant as will enable the arrest of the accused to be made under a warrant of the governor on a requisition of the executive authority of the state having jurisdiction of the offense, unless the accused gives bail as provided in the next section or until he shall be legally discharged.   1980

77-30-16. Amount of bail.

(1) Except as provided in Subsection (2), a judge or magistrate in this state may admit the person arrested to bail by bond with sufficient sureties and in an amount he considers proper, conditioned for his appearance before him at a time specified in the bond and for his surrender, to be arrested upon the warrant of the governor of this state.

(2) A person arrested under Section 77-30-13 shall be admitted to bail as a matter of right, except the court has discretion to deny bail as provided in Utah Constitution Article I, Section 8, and when a judge or magistrate in the demanding state has ordered that the person charged be held without bail or the person has waived extradition.

(3) There is a rebuttable presumption that the bail set by the court or magistrate in the demanding state is the proper amount of bail in this state.   1997

77-30-17. Procedure when no arrest made under warrant of governor.

If the accused is not arrested under warrant of the governor by the expiration of the time specified in the warrant or bond, a judge or magistrate may discharge him or may recommit him for a further period not to exceed sixty days, or a judge or magistrate may again take bail for his appearance and surrender, as provided in Section 77-30-16, but within a period not to exceed sixty days after the date of such new bond.   1980

77-30-18. Forfeiture of bail.

If the prisoner is admitted to bail and fails to appear and surrender himself according to the conditions of his bond the judge or magistrate by proper order shall declare the bond forfeited and order his immediate arrest without warrant if he be within this state. Recovery may be had on such bond in the name of the state as in the case of other bonds given by the accused in criminal proceedings within this state.   1980

77-30-19. Procedure if prosecution pending in this state.

If a criminal prosecution has been instituted against such person under the laws of this state and is still pending the governor, in his discretion, may either surrender him on demand of the executive authority of another state or hold him until he has been tried and discharged or convicted and punished in this state.   1980

77-30-20. Governor not to inquire into guilt or innocence.

The guilt or innocence of the accused as to the crime of which he is charged in another state may not be inquired into by the governor or in any proceeding after the demand for extradition accompanied by a charge of crime in legal form as above provided shall have been presented to the governor, except as it may be involved in identifying the person held as the person charged with the crime.   1980

77-30-21. Governor's warrant of arrest recalled or another issued.

The governor may recall his warrant of arrest or may issue another warrant whenever he deems proper.   1980

77-30-22. Fugitives from this state — Issuance of governor's warrant.

Whenever the governor of this state shall demand a person charged with a crime or with escaping from confinement or breaking the terms of his bail, probation, or parole in this state from the executive authority of any other state or from the chief justice or an associate justice of the superior court of the District of Columbia authorized to receive such demand under the laws of the United States, he shall issue a warrant under the seal of this state to some agent, commanding him to receive the person so charged if delivered to him and convey him to the proper officer of the county in this state in which the offense was committed.   1980

77-30-23. Fugitives from this state — Applications for requisition for return.

(1) When the return to this state of a person charged with a crime in this state is required, the prosecuting attorney shall present to the governor his written application for a requisition for the return of the person charged, in which application shall be stated the name of the person so charged, the crime charged against him, the approximate time, place, and circumstances of its commission, the state in which he is believed to be, including the location of the accused therein at the time the application is made, and certifying that in the opinion of the said prosecuting attorney the ends of justice require the arrest and return of the accused to this state for trial and that the proceeding is not instituted to enforce a private claim.

(2) When the return to this state is required of a person who has been convicted of a crime in this state and has escaped from confinement or broken the terms of his bail, probation, or parole, the prosecuting attorney of the county in which the offense was committed, the parole board, or the warden of the institution or sheriff of the county from which escape was made shall present to the governor a written application for a requisition for the return of such person, in which application shall be stated the name of the person, the crime of which he was convicted, the circumstances of his escape from confinement, or of the breach of the terms of his bail, probation, or parole, the state in which he is believed to be, including the location of the person therein at the time application is made.

(3) The application shall be verified by affidavit, shall be executed in duplicate, and shall be accompanied by two certified copies of the indictment returned, or information and affidavit filed, or of the complaint made to the judge or magistrate stating the offense with which the accused is charged, or of the judgment or conviction, or of the sentence.

The prosecuting officer, parole board, warden, or sheriff may also attach such further affidavits and other documents in duplicate as he shall deem proper to be submitted with such application. One copy of the application with the action of the governor indicated by endorsement thereon and one of the certified copies of the indictment, complaint, information, and affidavits or of the judgment of conviction or of the sentence shall be filed in the office of the governor to remain of record in that office. The other copies of all papers shall be forwarded with the governor's requisition.
                                                      1984

77-30-24. Payment of expenses — Extradition costs.

(1) When the punishment of the crime is the confinement of the defendant in prison, the expenses shall be paid out of the state treasury on the certificate of the governor and warrant of the auditor, and in all other cases they shall be paid out of the treasury of the county where the crime is alleged to have been committed. The expenses shall be the fees paid to the officers of the state on whose governor the requisition is made.

(2) Any person who is returned to the state under this chapter, and who is convicted of, or pleads guilty or no contest to, the criminal charge or to a lesser criminal charge may, under Sections 76-3-201, 77-27-5, and 77-27-6, be required to make restitution to the appropriate governmental entities for the costs of his extradition.   1987

77-30-25. Person brought into state on extradition exempt from civil process — Waiver of extradition proceedings — Non-waiver by this state.

(1) A person brought into this state by or after waiver of extradition based on a criminal charge shall not be subject to service of personal process in civil actions arising out of the same facts as the criminal proceedings to answer which he is being or has been returned until he has been convicted in the criminal proceedings, or, if acquitted, until he has had reasonable opportunity to return to the state from which he was extradited.

(2) Any person arrested in this state charged with having committed any crime in another state or alleged to have escaped from confinement or broken the terms of his bail, probation or parole may waive the issuance and service of the warrant provided for in Sections 77-30-7 and 77-30-8, and all other procedure incidental to extradition proceedings, by executing or subscribing in the presence of a judge of any court of record within this state a writing which states that he consents to return to the demanding state; provided, before such waiver shall be executed or subscribed by such person it shall be the duty of such judge to inform such person of his rights to the issuance and service of a warrant of extradition and to obtain a writ of habeas corpus as provided for in Section 77-30-10.

If and when such consent has been duly executed it shall forthwith be forwarded to the office of the governor of this state and filed therein. The judge shall direct the officer having such person in custody to deliver forthwith such person to the duly accredited agent or agents of the demanding state and shall deliver or cause to be delivered to such agent or agents a copy of such consent; provided, nothing in this section shall be deemed to limit the rights of the accused person to return voluntarily and without formality to the demanding state, or shall this waiver procedure be deemed to be an exclusive procedure or to limit the powers, rights, or duties of the officers of the demanding state or of this state.

(3) Nothing in this act shall be deemed to constitute a waiver by this state of its right, power or privilege to try such demanded person for a crime committed within this state, or of its right, power or privilege to regain custody of such person by extradition proceedings or otherwise for the purpose of trial, sentence or punishment for any crime committed within this state, or shall any proceedings had under this act which result in or fail to result in extradition be deemed a waiver by this state of any of its rights, privileges or jurisdiction in any way whatsoever.   1980

77-30-26. Prosecution not limited to crime specified in requisition.

After a person has been brought back to this state by or after waiver of extradition proceedings he may be tried in this state for other crimes which he may be charged with having committed here as well as that specified in the requisition for his extradition.   1980

77-30-27. Uniformity of interpretation.

The provisions of this act shall be so interpreted and construed as to effectuate its general purposes to make uniform the law of those states which enact it.
                                                      1980

77-30-28. Citation — Uniform Criminal Extradition Act.

This act may be cited as the Uniform Criminal Extradition Act.   1980

CHAPTER 36

COHABITANT ABUSE PROCEDURES ACT

77-36-1. Definitions.

As used in this chapter:

(1) "Cohabitant" has the same meaning as in Section 30-6-1.

(2) "Domestic violence" means any criminal offense involving violence or physical harm or threat of violence or physical harm, or any attempt, conspiracy, or solicitation to commit a criminal offense involving violence or physical harm, when committed by one cohabitant against another. "Domestic violence" also means commission or attempt to commit, any of the following offenses by one cohabitant against another:

(a) aggravated assault, as described in Section 76-5-103;

(b) assault, as described in Section 76-5-102;

(c) criminal homicide, as described in Section 76-5-201;

(d) harassment, as described in Section 76-5-106;

(e) telephone harassment, as described in Section 76-9-201;

(f) kidnaping, child kidnaping, or aggravated kidnaping, as described in Sections 76-5-301, 76-5-301.1, and 76-5-302;

(g) mayhem, as described in Section 76-5-105;

(h) sexual offenses, as described in Title 76, Chapter 5, Part 4, and Title 76, Chapter 5a;

(i) stalking, as described in Section 76-5-106.5;

(j) unlawful detention, as described in Section 76-5-304;

(k) violation of a protective order or ex parte protective order, as described in Section 76-5-108;

(l) any offense against property described in Title 76, Chapter 6, Part 1, 2, or 3;

(m) possession of a deadly weapon with intent to assault, as described in Section 76-10-507;

(n) discharge of a firearm from a vehicle, near a highway, or in the direction of any person, building, or vehicle, as described in Section 76-10-508;

(o) disorderly conduct, as defined in Section 76-9-102, if a conviction of disorderly conduct is the result of a plea agreement in which the defendant was originally charged with any of the domestic violence offenses otherwise described in this Subsection (2). Conviction of disorderly conduct as a domestic violence offense, in the manner described in this Subsection (2)(o), does not constitute a misdemeanor crime of domestic violence under 18 U.S.C. Section 921, and is exempt from the provisions of the federal Firearms Act, 18 U.S.C. Section 921 et seq.; or

(p) child abuse as described in Section 76-5-109.1.

(3) "Victim" means a cohabitant who has been subjected to domestic violence.   2002

77-36-1.1. Enhancement of offense and penalty for subsequent domestic violence offenses.

(1) For purposes of this section, "qualifying domestic violence offense" means:

(a) a domestic violence offense in Utah; or

(b) an offense in any other state, or in any district, possession, or territory of the United States, that would be a domestic violence offense under Utah law.

(2) A person who is convicted of a domestic violence offense is:

(a) guilty of a class B misdemeanor if:

(i) the domestic violence offense described in this Subsection (2) is designated by law as a class C misdemeanor; and

(ii) (A) the domestic violence offense described in this Subsection (2) is committed within five years after the person is convicted of a qualifying domestic violence offense; or

(B) the person is convicted of the domestic violence offense described in this Subsection (2) within five years after the person is convicted of a qualifying domestic violence offense;

(b) guilty of a class A misdemeanor if:

(i) the domestic violence offense described in this Subsection (2) is designated by law as a class B misdemeanor; and

(ii) (A) the domestic violence offense described in this Subsection (2) is committed within five years after the person is convicted of a qualifying domestic violence offense; or

(B) the person is convicted of the domestic violence offense described in this Subsection (2) within five years after the person is convicted of a qualifying domestic violence offense; or

(c) guilty of a felony of the third degree if:

(i) the domestic violence offense described in this Subsection (2) is designated by law as a class A misdemeanor; and

(ii) (A) the domestic violence offense described in this Subsection (2) is committed within five years after the person is convicted of a qualifying domestic violence offense; or

(B) the person is convicted of the domestic violence offense described in this Subsection (2) within five years after the person is convicted of a qualifying domestic violence offense.

(3) For purposes of this section, a plea of guilty or no contest to any qualifying domestic violence offense in Utah which plea is held in abeyance under Title 77, Chapter 2a, Pleas in Abeyance, is the equivalent of a conviction, even if the charge has been subsequently reduced or dismissed in accordance with the plea in abeyance agreement.   2005

77-36-2. Repealed.   1995

77-36-2.1. Duties of law enforcement officers — Notice to victims.

(1) A law enforcement officer who responds to an allegation of domestic violence shall use all reasonable means to protect the victim and prevent further violence, including:

(a) taking the action that, in the officer's discretion, is reasonably necessary to provide for the safety of the victim and any family or household member;

(b) confiscating the weapon or weapons involved in the alleged domestic violence;

(c) making arrangements for the victim and any child to obtain emergency housing or shelter;

(d) providing protection while the victim removes essential personal effects;

(e) arrange, facilitate, or provide for the victim and any child to obtain medical treatment; and

(f) arrange, facilitate, or provide the victim with immediate and adequate notice of the rights of victims and of the remedies and services available to victims of domestic violence, in accordance with Subsection (2).

(2) (a) A law enforcement officer shall give written notice to the victim in simple language, describing the rights and remedies available under this chapter, Title 30, Chapter 6, Cohabitant Abuse Act, and Title 78, Chapter 3h, Child Protective Orders.

(b) The written notice shall also include:

(i) a statement that the forms needed in order to obtain an order for protection are available from the court clerk's office in the judicial district where the victim resides or is temporarily domiciled;

(ii) a list of shelters, services, and resources available in the appropriate community, together with telephone numbers, to assist the victim in accessing any needed assistance; and

(iii) the information required to be provided to both parties in accordance with Subsection 77-36-2.5(7).   2003

77-36-2.2. Powers and duties of law enforcement officers to arrest.

(1) The primary duty of law enforcement officers responding to a domestic violence call is to protect the victim and enforce the law.

(2) (a) In addition to the arrest powers described in Section 77-7-2, when a peace officer responds to a domestic violence call and has probable cause to believe that an act of domestic violence has been committed, the peace officer shall arrest without a warrant or issue a citation to any person that he has probable cause to believe has committed an act of domestic violence.

(b) If the peace officer has probable cause to believe that there will be continued violence against the alleged victim, or if there is evidence that the perpetrator has either recently caused serious bodily injury or used a dangerous weapon in the domestic violence offense, the officer shall arrest and take the alleged perpetrator into custody, and may not utilize the option of issuing a citation under this section. For purposes of this section "serious bodily injury" and "dangerous weapon" mean the same as those terms are defined in Section 76-1-601.

(c) If a peace officer does not immediately exercise arrest powers or initiate criminal proceedings by citation or otherwise, he shall notify the victim of his or her right to initiate a criminal proceeding and of the importance of preserving evidence, in accordance with the requirements of Section 77-36-2.1.

(3) If a law enforcement officer receives complaints of domestic violence from two or more opposing persons, the officer shall evaluate each complaint separately to determine who the predominant aggressor was. If the officer determines that one person was the predominant physical aggressor, the officer need not arrest the other person alleged to have committed domestic violence. In determining who the predominant aggressor was, the officer shall consider:

(a) any prior complaints of domestic violence;

(b) the relative severity of injuries inflicted on each person;

(c) the likelihood of future injury to each of the parties; and

(d) whether one of the parties acted in self defense.

(4) A law enforcement officer may not threaten, suggest, or otherwise indicate the possible arrest of all parties in order to discourage any party's request for intervention by law enforcement.

(5) (a) A law enforcement officer who does not make an arrest after investigating a complaint of domestic violence, or who arrests two or more parties, shall submit a detailed, written report specifying the grounds for not arresting or for arresting both parties.

(b) A law enforcement officer who does not make an arrest shall notify the victim of his or her right to initiate a criminal proceeding and of the importance of preserving evidence.

(6) (a) A law enforcement officer responding to a complaint of domestic violence shall prepare an incident report that includes the officer's disposition of the case.

(b) That report shall be made available to the victim, upon request, at no cost.

(c) The law enforcement agency shall forward a copy of the incident report to the appropriate prosecuting attorney within five days after the complaint of domestic violence occurred.

(7) Each law enforcement agency shall, as soon as practicable, make a written record and maintain records of all incidents of domestic violence reported to it, and shall be identified by a law enforcement agency code for domestic violence.   1998

77-36-2.3. Law enforcement officer's training.

All training of law enforcement officers relating to domestic violence shall stress protection of the victim, enforcement of criminal laws in domestic situations, and the availability of community shelters, services, and resources. Law enforcement agencies and community organizations with expertise in domestic violence shall cooperate in all aspects of that training.   1995

77-36-2.4. Violation of protective orders — Mandatory arrest.

(1) A law enforcement officer shall, without a warrant, arrest an alleged perpetrator whenever there is probable cause to believe that the alleged perpetrator has violated any of the provisions of an ex parte protective order or protective order.

(2) (a) Intentional or knowing violation of any ex parte protective order or protective order is a class A misdemeanor, in accordance with Section 76-5-108, and is a domestic violence offense, pursuant to Section 77-36-1.

(b) Second or subsequent violations of ex parte protective orders or protective orders carry increased penalties, in accordance with Section 77-36-1.1.

(3) As used in this section, "ex parte protective order" or "protective order" includes any protective order or ex parte protective order issued under Title 30, Chapter 6, Cohabitant Abuse Act, or Title 77, Chapter 36, Cohabitant Abuse Procedures Act, any child protective order or ex parte child protective order issued under Title 78, Chapter 3h, Child Protective Orders, or a foreign protective order enforceable under Section 30-6-12.   2003

77-36-2.5. Conditions for release after arrest for domestic violence.

(1) Upon arrest for domestic violence, a person may not be released on bail, recognizance, or otherwise prior to the close of the next court day following the arrest, unless as a condition of that release he is ordered by the court or agrees in writing that until the expiration of that time he will:

(a) have no personal contact with the alleged victim;

(b) not threaten or harass the alleged victim; and

(c) not knowingly enter onto the premises of the alleged victim's residence or any premises temporarily occupied by the alleged victim.

(2) As a condition of release, the court may order the defendant to participate in an electronic monitoring program and pay the costs associated with the program.

(3) (a) Subsequent to an arrest for domestic violence, an alleged victim may waive in writing any or all of the requirements described in Subsection (1). Upon waiver, those requirements shall not apply to the alleged perpetrator.

(b) A court or magistrate may modify the requirements described in Subsections (1)(a) or (c), in writing or on the record, and only for good cause shown.

(4) (a) Whenever a person is released pursuant to Subsection (1), the releasing agency shall notify the arresting law enforcement agency of the release, conditions of release, and any available information concerning the location of the victim. The arresting law enforcement agency shall then make reasonable effort to notify the victim of that release.

(b) (i) When a person is released pursuant to Subsection (1) based on a written agreement, the releasing agency shall transmit that information to the statewide domestic violence network described in Section 30-6-8.

(ii) When a person is released pursuant to Subsection (1) based upon a court order, the court shall transmit that order to the statewide domestic violence network described in Section 30-6-8.

(c) This Subsection (4) does not create or increase liability of a law enforcement officer or agency, and the good faith immunity provided by Section 77-36-8 is applicable.

(5) (a) If a law enforcement officer has probable cause to believe that a person has violated a court order or agreement executed pursuant to Subsection (1) the officer shall, without a warrant, arrest the alleged violator.

(b) Any person who knowingly violates a court order or agreement executed pursuant to Subsection (1) shall be guilty as follows:

(i) if the original arrest was for a felony, an offense under this section is a third degree felony; or

(ii) if the original arrest was for a misdemeanor, an offense under this section is a class A misdemeanor.

(c) City attorneys may prosecute class A misdemeanor violations under this section.

(6) An individual who was originally arrested for a felony under this chapter and released pursuant to this section may subsequently be held without bail if there is substantial evidence to support a new felony charge against him.

(7) At the time an arrest for domestic violence is made, the arresting officer shall provide the alleged victim with written notice containing the following information:

(a) the requirements described in Subsection (1), and notice that those requirements shall be ordered by a court or must be agreed to by the alleged perpetrator prior to release;

(b) notification of the penalties for violation of the court order or any agreement executed under Subsection (1);

(c) the date and time, absent modification by a court or magistrate, that the requirements expire;

(d) the address of the appropriate court in the district or county in which the alleged victim resides;

(e) the availability and effect of any waiver of the requirements; and

(f) information regarding the availability of and procedures for obtaining civil and criminal protective orders with or without the assistance of an attorney.

(8) At the time an arrest for domestic violence is made, the arresting officer shall provide the alleged perpetrator with written notice containing the following information:

(a) the requirements described in Subsection (1) and notice that those requirements shall be ordered by a court or must be agreed to by the alleged perpetrator prior to release;

(b) notification of the penalties for violation of the court or any agreement executed under Subsection (1); and

(c) the date and time absent modification by a court or magistrate that the requirements expire.

(9) In addition to the provisions of Subsections (1) through (6), because of the unique and highly emotional nature of domestic violence crimes, the high recidivism rate of violent offenders, and the demonstrated increased risk of continued acts of violence subsequent to the release of an offender who has been arrested for domestic violence, it is the finding of the Legislature that domestic violence crimes, as defined in Section 77-36-1, are crimes for which bail may be denied if there is substantial evidence to support the charge, and if the court finds by clear and convincing evidence that the alleged perpetrator would constitute a substantial danger to an alleged victim of domestic violence if released on bail. If bail is denied under this Subsection (9), it shall be under the terms and conditions described in Subsections (1) through (6).   2004

77-36-2.6. Appearance of defendant required — Determinations by court.

(1) A defendant who has been arrested for an offense involving domestic violence shall appear in person before the court or a magistrate within one judicial day after the arrest.

(2) A defendant who has been charged by citation, indictment, or information with an offense involving domestic violence but has not been arrested, shall appear before the court in person for arraignment as soon as practicable, but no later than 14 days after the next day on which court is in session following the issuance of the citation or the filing of the indictment or information.

(3) At the time of an appearance under Subsection (1) or (2), the court shall determine the necessity of imposing a protective order or other condition of pretrial release including, but not limited to, participating in an electronic monitoring program, and shall state its findings and determination in writing.

(4) Appearances required by this section are mandatory and may not be waived.   2003

77-36-2.7. Dismissal — Diversion prohibited — Plea in abeyance — Release before trial.

(1) Because of the serious nature of domestic violence, the court, in domestic violence actions:

(a) may not dismiss any charge or delay disposition because of concurrent divorce or other civil proceedings;

(b) may not require proof that either party is seeking a dissolution of marriage before instigation of criminal proceedings;

(c) shall waive any requirement that the victim's location be disclosed other than to the defendant's attorney, upon a showing that there is any possibility of further violence, and order the defendant's attorney not to disclose the victim's location to his client;

(d) shall identify, on the docket sheets, the criminal actions arising from acts of domestic violence;

(e) may dismiss a charge on stipulation of the prosecutor and the victim; and

(f) may hold a plea in abeyance, in accordance with the provisions of Chapter 2a, making treatment or any other requirement for the defendant a condition of that status.

(2) When the court holds a plea in abeyance in accordance with Subsection (1)(f), the case against a perpetrator of domestic violence may be dismissed only if the perpetrator successfully completes all conditions imposed by the court. If the defendant fails to complete any condition imposed by the court under Subsection (1)(f), the court may accept the defendant's plea.

(3) (a) Because of the likelihood of repeated violence directed at those who have been victims of domestic violence in the past, when any defendant charged with a crime involving domestic violence is released from custody before trial, the court authorizing the release may issue an order:

(i) enjoining the defendant from threatening to commit or committing acts of domestic violence or abuse against the victim and any designated family or household member;

(ii) prohibiting the defendant from harassing, telephoning, contacting, or otherwise communicating with the victim, directly or indirectly;

(iii) removing and excluding the defendant from the victim's residence and the premises of the residence;

(iv) ordering the defendant to stay away from the residence, school, place of employment of the victim, and the premises of any of these, or any specified place frequented by the victim and any designated family member; and

(v) ordering any other relief that the court considers necessary to protect and provide for the safety of the victim and any designated family or household member.

(b) Violation of an order issued pursuant to this section is punishable as follows:

(i) if the original arrest or subsequent charge filed is a felony, an offense under this section is a third degree felony; and

(ii) if the original arrest or subsequent charge filed is a misdemeanor, an offense under this section is a class A misdemeanor.

(c) The court shall provide the victim with a certified copy of any order issued pursuant to this section if the victim can be located with reasonable effort.

(4) When a court dismisses criminal charges or a prosecutor moves to dismiss charges against a defendant accused of a domestic violence offense, the specific reasons for dismissal shall be recorded in the court file and made a part of the statewide domestic violence network described in Section 30-6-8.

(5) When the privilege of confidential communication between spouses, or the testimonial privilege of spouses is invoked in any criminal proceeding in which a spouse is the victim of an alleged domestic violence offense, the victim shall be considered to be an unavailable witness under the Utah Rules of Evidence.

(6) The court may not approve diversion for a perpetrator of domestic violence.   1999

77-36-3, 77-36-3.1. Renumbered as §§ 77-36-2.7 and 77-36-2.5.   1995

77-36-3.5. Repealed.   1991

77-36-4. Renumbered as § 77-36-2.6.   1995

77-36-5. Sentencing — Restricting contact with victim — Electronic monitoring — Counseling — Cost assessed against defendant.

(1) When a defendant is found guilty of a crime and a condition of the sentence restricts the defendant's

contact with the victim, an order may be issued or, if one has already been issued, it may be extended for the length of the defendant's probation. The order shall be in writing, and the prosecutor shall provide a certified copy of that order to the victim.

(2) In determining its sentence the court, in addition to penalties otherwise provided by law, may require the defendant to participate in an electronic monitoring program.

(3) The court may also require the defendant to pay all or part of the costs of counseling incurred by the victim, as well as the costs for defendant's own counseling.

(4) The court shall:

(a) assess against the defendant, as restitution, any costs for services or treatment provided to the abused spouse by the Division of Child and Family Services under Section 62A-4a-106; and

(b) order those costs to be paid directly to the division or its contracted provider.

(5) The court shall order the defendant to obtain and satisfactorily complete treatment or therapy in a domestic violence treatment program, as defined in Section 62A-2-101, that is licensed by the Department of Human Services, unless the court finds that there is no licensed program reasonably available or that the treatment or therapy is not necessary. 2003

77-36-5.1. Conditions of probation for person convicted of domestic violence offense.

(1) Before any perpetrator who has been convicted of a domestic violence offense may be placed on probation, the court shall consider the safety and protection of the victim and any member of the victim's family or household.

(2) The court may condition probation or a plea in abeyance on the perpetrator's compliance with one or more orders of the court which may include, but are not limited to, an order:

(a) enjoining the perpetrator from threatening to commit or committing acts of domestic violence against the victim or other family or household member;

(b) prohibiting the perpetrator from harassing, telephoning, contacting, or otherwise communicating with the victim, directly or indirectly;

(c) requiring the perpetrator to stay away from the victim's residence, school, place of employment, and the premises of any of these, or a specified place frequented regularly by the victim or any designated family or household member;

(d) prohibiting the perpetrator from possessing or consuming alcohol or controlled substances;

(e) prohibiting the perpetrator from purchasing, using, or possessing a firearm or other specified weapon;

(f) directing the perpetrator to surrender any weapons that he owns or possesses;

(g) directing the perpetrator to participate in and complete, to the satisfaction of the court, a program of intervention for perpetrators, treatment for alcohol or substance abuse, or psychiatric or psychological treatment;

(h) directing the perpetrator to pay restitution to the victim; and

(i) imposing any other condition necessary to protect the victim and any other designated family or household member or to rehabilitate the perpetrator.

(3) The perpetrator is responsible for the costs of any condition of probation, according to his ability to pay.

(4) (a) Adult Probation and Parole, or other provider, shall immediately report to the court and notify the victim of any assault by the perpetrator, the perpetrator's failure to comply with any condition imposed by the court, and any threat of harm made by the perpetrator.

(b) Notification of the victim under Subsection (4)(a) shall consist of a good faith reasonable effort to provide prompt notification, including mailing a copy of the notification to the last-known address of the victim. 1996

77-36-6. Enforcement of orders.

Each law enforcement agency in this state shall enforce all orders of the court issued pursuant to the requirements and procedures described in this chapter, and shall enforce all protective orders and ex parte protective orders issued pursuant to Title 30, Chapter 6. The requirements of this section apply statewide, regardless of the jurisdiction in which the order was issued or the location of the victim or the perpetrator. 1995

77-36-7. Prosecutor to notify victim of decision as to prosecution.

(1) The prosecutor who is responsible for making the decision of whether to prosecute a case shall advise the victim, if the victim has requested notification, of the status of the victim's case and shall notify the victim of a decision within five days after the decision has been made.

(2) Notification to the victim that charges will not be filed against an alleged perpetrator shall include a description of the procedures available to the victim in that jurisdiction for initiation of criminal and other protective proceedings. 1996

77-36-8. Peace officers' immunity from liability.

A peace officer may not be held liable in any civil action brought by a party to an incident of domestic violence for making or failing to make an arrest or for issuing or failing to issue a citation in accordance with this chapter, for enforcing in good faith an order of the court, or for acting or omitting to act in any other way in good faith under this chapter, in situations arising from an alleged incident of domestic violence. 1995

77-36-9. Separability clause.

If any provision of this chapter or its application to any person or circumstance is held invalid, the remainder of the chapter or the application of the provision to other persons or circumstances is not affected. 1983

77-36-10. Authority to prosecute class A misdemeanor violations.

Alleged class A misdemeanor violations of this chapter may be prosecuted by city attorneys. 1996

CHAPTER 37

VICTIMS' RIGHTS

77-37-1. Legislative intent.

(1) The Legislature recognizes the duty of victims and witnesses of crime to fully and voluntarily coop-

erate with law enforcement and prosecutorial agencies, the essential nature of citizen cooperation to state and local law enforcement efforts, and the general effectiveness and well-being of the criminal justice system of this state. In this chapter, the Legislature declares its intent to ensure that all victims and witnesses of crime are treated with dignity, respect, courtesy, and sensitivity, and that the rights extended in this chapter to victims and witnesses of crime are honored and protected by law in a manner no less vigorous than protections afforded criminal defendants.

(2) The Legislature finds it is necessary to provide child victims and child witnesses with additional consideration and different treatment than that usually afforded to adults. The treatment should ensure that children's participation in the criminal justice process be conducted in the most effective and least traumatic, intrusive, or intimidating manner.   1987

77-37-2. Definitions.

In this chapter:

(1) "Child" means a person who is younger than 18 years of age, unless otherwise specified in statute. The rights to information as extended in this chapter also apply to the parents, custodian, or legal guardians of children.

(2) "Family member" means spouse, child, sibling, parent, grandparent, or legal guardian.

(3) "Victim" means a person against whom a crime has allegedly been committed, or against whom an act has allegedly been committed by a juvenile or incompetent adult, which would have been a crime if committed by a competent adult.

(4) "Witness" means any person who has been subpoenaed or is expected to be summoned to testify for the prosecution or who by reason of having relevant information is subject to call or likely to be called as a witness for the prosecution, whether any action or proceeding has commenced.   1987

77-37-3. Bill of Rights.

(1) The bill of rights for victims and witnesses is:

(a) Victims and witnesses have a right to be informed as to the level of protection from intimidation and harm available to them, and from what sources, as they participate in criminal justice proceedings as designated by Section 76-8-508, regarding witness tampering, and Section 76-8-509, regarding threats against a victim. Law enforcement, prosecution, and corrections personnel have the duty to timely provide this information in a form that is useful to the victim.

(b) Victims and witnesses, including children and their guardians, have a right to be informed and assisted as to their role in the criminal justice process. All criminal justice agencies have the duty to provide this information and assistance.

(c) Victims and witnesses have a right to clear explanations regarding relevant legal proceedings; these explanations shall be appropriate to the age of child victims and witnesses. All criminal justice agencies have the duty to provide these explanations.

(d) Victims and witnesses should have a secure waiting area that does not require them to be in close proximity to defendants or the family and friends of defendants. Agencies controlling facilities shall, whenever possible, provide this area.

(e) Victims are entitled to restitution or reparations, including medical costs, as provided in Title 63, Chapter 25a, Criminal Justice and Substance Abuse, and Sections 62A-7-109, 77-38a-302, and 77-27-6. State and local government agencies that serve victims have the duty to have a functional knowledge of the procedures established by the Utah Crime Victims' Reparations Board and to inform victims of these procedures.

(f) Victims and witnesses have a right to have any personal property returned as provided in Sections 77-24-1 through 77-24-5. Criminal justice agencies shall expeditiously return the property when it is no longer needed for court law enforcement or prosecution purposes.

(g) Victims and witnesses have the right to reasonable employer intercession services, including pursuing employer cooperation in minimizing employees' loss of pay and other benefits resulting from their participation in the criminal justice process. Officers of the court shall provide these services and shall consider victims' and witnesses' schedules so that activities which conflict can be avoided. Where conflicts cannot be avoided, the victim may request that the responsible agency intercede with employers or other parties.

(h) Victims and witnesses, particularly children, should have a speedy disposition of the entire criminal justice process. All involved public agencies shall establish policies and procedures to encourage speedy disposition of criminal cases.

(i) Victims and witnesses have the right to timely notice of judicial proceedings they are to attend and timely notice of cancellation of any proceedings. Criminal justice agencies have the duty to provide these notifications. Defense counsel and others have the duty to provide timely notice to prosecution of any continuances or other changes that may be required.

(j) Victims of sexual offenses have a right to be informed of their right to request voluntary testing for themselves for HIV infection as provided in Section 76-5-503 and to request mandatory testing of the convicted sexual offender for HIV infection as provided in Section 76-5-502. The law enforcement office where the sexual offense is reported shall have the responsibility to inform victims of this right.

(2) Informational rights of the victim under this chapter are based upon the victim providing his current address and telephone number to the criminal justice agencies involved in the case.   2005

77-37-4. Additional rights — Children.

In addition to all rights afforded to victims and witnesses under this chapter, child victims and witnesses shall be afforded these rights:

(1) Children have the right to protection from physical and emotional abuse during their involvement with the criminal justice process.

(2) Children are not responsible for inappropriate behavior adults commit against them and have the right not to be questioned, in any manner, nor to have allegations made, implying this responsibility. Those who interview children have the responsibility to consider the interests of the child in this regard.

(3) Child victims and witnesses have the right to have interviews relating to a criminal prosecution kept to a minimum. All agencies shall coordinate interviews and ensure that they are conducted by persons sensitive to the needs of children.

(4) Child victims have the right to be informed of available community resources that might assist them and how to gain access to those resources. Law enforcement and prosecutors have the duty to ensure that child victims are informed of community resources, including counseling prior to the court proceeding, and have those services available throughout the criminal justice process. 1987

77-37-5. Remedies — Victims' Rights Committee.

Remedies available are:

(1) In each judicial district, the presiding district court judge shall appoint a person who shall establish and chair a victims' rights committee consisting of:

  (a) a county attorney or district attorney;

  (b) a sheriff;

  (c) a corrections field services administrator;

  (d) an appointed victim advocate;

  (e) a municipal attorney;

  (f) a municipal chief of police; and

  (g) other representatives as appropriate.

(2) The committee shall meet at least semiannually to review progress and problems related to this chapter, Title 77, Chapter 38, and Utah Constitution Article I, Section 28. Victims and other interested parties may submit matters of concern to the victims' rights committee. The committee may hold a hearing open to the public on any appropriate matter of concern and may publish its findings. These matters shall also be considered at the meetings of the victims' rights committee. The committee shall forward minutes of all meetings to the Commission on Criminal and Juvenile Justice and the Office of Crime Victims' Reparations for review and other appropriate action.

(3) The Office of Crime Victims' Reparations shall provide materials to local law enforcement to inform every victim of a sexual offense of the right to request testing of the convicted sexual offender and of the victim as provided in Section 76-5-502.

(4) If a person acting under color of state law willfully or wantonly fails to perform duties so that the rights in this chapter are not provided, an action for injunctive relief may be brought against the individual and the government entity that employs the individual. The failure to provide the rights in this chapter or Title 77, Chapter 38, does not constitute cause for a judgment against the state or any government entity, or any individual employed by the state or any government entity, for monetary damages, attorney's fees, or the costs of exercising any rights under this chapter.

(5) The person accused of and subject to prosecution for the crime or the act which would be a crime if committed by a competent adult, has no standing to make a claim concerning any violation of the provisions of this chapter. 1995

CHAPTER 38

RIGHTS OF CRIME VICTIMS ACT

77-38-1. Title.

This act shall be known and may be cited as the "Rights of Crime Victims Act." 1994

77-38-2. Definitions.

For the purposes of this chapter and the Utah Constitution:

(1) "Abuse" means treating the crime victim in a manner so as to injure, damage, or disparage.

(2) "Dignity" means treating the crime victim with worthiness, honor, and esteem.

(3) "Fairness" means treating the crime victim reasonably, even-handedly, and impartially.

(4) "Harassment" means treating the crime victim in a persistently annoying manner.

(5) "Important criminal justice hearings" or "important juvenile justice hearings" means the following proceedings in felony criminal cases or cases involving a minor's conduct which would be a felony if committed by an adult:

  (a) any preliminary hearing to determine probable cause;

  (b) any court arraignment where practical;

  (c) any court proceeding involving the disposition of charges against a defendant or minor or the delay of a previously scheduled trial date but not including any unanticipated proceeding to take an admission or a plea of guilty as charged to all charges previously filed or any plea taken at an initial appearance;

  (d) any court proceeding to determine whether to release a defendant or minor and, if so, under what conditions release may occur, excluding any such release determination made at an initial appearance;

  (e) any criminal or delinquency trial, excluding any actions at the trial that a court might take in camera, in chambers, or at a sidebar conference;

(f) any court proceeding to determine the disposition of a minor or sentence, fine, or restitution of a defendant or to modify any disposition of a minor or sentence, fine, or restitution of a defendant; and

(g) any public hearing concerning whether to grant a defendant or minor parole or other form of discretionary release from confinement.

(6) "Reliable information" means information worthy of confidence, including any information whose use at sentencing is permitted by the United States Constitution.

(7) "Representative of a victim" means a person who is designated by the victim or designated by the court and who represents the victim in the best interests of the victim.

(8) "Respect" means treating the crime victim with regard and value.

(9) (a) "Victim of a crime" means any natural person against whom the charged crime or conduct is alleged to have been perpetrated or attempted by the defendant or minor personally or as a party to the offense or conduct or, in the discretion of the court, against whom a related crime or act is alleged to have been perpetrated or attempted, unless the natural person is the accused or appears to be accountable or otherwise criminally responsible for or criminally involved in the crime or conduct or a crime or act arising from the same conduct, criminal episode, or plan as the crime is defined under the laws of this state.

(b) For purposes of the right to be present, "victim of a crime" does not mean any person who is in custody as a pretrial detainee, as a prisoner following conviction for an offense, or as a juvenile who has committed an act that would be an offense if committed by an adult, or who is in custody for mental or psychological treatment.

(c) For purposes of the right to be present and heard at a public hearing as provided in Subsection 77-38-2(5)(g) and the right to notice as provided in Subsection 77-38-3(7)(a), "victim of a crime" includes any victim originally named in the allegation of criminal conduct who is not a victim of the offense to which the defendant entered a negotiated plea of guilty.   1997

77-38-3. Notification to victims — Initial notice, election to receive subsequent notices — Form of notice — Protected victim information.

(1) Within seven days of the filing of felony criminal charges against a defendant, the prosecuting agency shall provide an initial notice to reasonably identifiable and locatable victims of the crime contained in the charges, except as otherwise provided in this chapter.

(2) The initial notice to the victim of a crime shall provide information about electing to receive notice of subsequent important criminal justice hearings listed in Subsections 77-38-2(5)(a) through (f) and rights under this chapter.

(3) The prosecuting agency shall provide notice to a victim of a crime for the important criminal justice hearings, provided in Subsections 77-38-2(5)(a) through (f) which the victim has requested.

(4) (a) The responsible prosecuting agency may provide initial and subsequent notices in any reasonable manner, including telephonically, electronically, orally, or by means of a letter or form prepared for this purpose.

(b) In the event of an unforeseen important criminal justice hearing, listed in Subsections 77-38-2(5)(a) through (f) for which a victim has requested notice, a good faith attempt to contact the victim by telephone shall be considered sufficient notice, provided that the prosecuting agency subsequently notifies the victim of the result of the proceeding.

(5) (a) The court shall take reasonable measures to ensure that its scheduling practices for the proceedings provided in Subsections 77-38-2(5)(a) through (f) permit an opportunity for victims of crimes to be notified.

(b) The court shall also consider whether any notification system that it might use to provide notice of judicial proceedings to defendants could be used to provide notice of those same proceedings to victims of crimes.

(6) A defendant or, if it is the moving party, Adult Probation and Parole, shall give notice to the responsible prosecuting agency of any motion for modification of any determination made at any of the important criminal justice hearings provided in Subsections 77-38-2(5)(a) through (f) in advance of any requested court hearing or action so that the prosecuting agency may comply with its notification obligation.

(7) (a) Notice to a victim of a crime shall be provided by the Board of Pardons and Parole for the important criminal justice hearing provided in Subsection 77-38-2(5)(g).

(b) The board may provide notice in any reasonable manner, including telephonically, electronically, orally, or by means of a letter or form prepared for this purpose.

(8) Prosecuting agencies and the Board of Pardons and Parole are required to give notice to a victim of a crime for the proceedings provided in Subsections 77-38-2(5)(a) through (f) only where the victim has responded to the initial notice, requested notice of subsequent proceedings, and provided a current address and telephone number if applicable.

(9) (a) Law enforcement and criminal justice agencies shall refer any requests for notice or information about crime victim rights from victims to the responsible prosecuting agency.

(b) In a case in which the Board of Pardons and Parole is involved, the responsible prosecuting agency shall forward any request for notice that it has received from a victim to the Board of Pardons and Parole.

(10) In all cases where the number of victims exceeds ten, the responsible prosecuting agency may send any notices required under this chapter in its discretion to a representative sample of the victims.

(11) (a) A victim's address, telephone number, and victim impact statement maintained by a peace officer, prosecuting agency, Youth Parole Authority, Division of Juvenile Justice Services, Department of Corrections, and Board of Pardons and Parole, for purposes of providing notice under this section, is classified as protected as provided in Subsection 63-2-304(10).

(b) The victim's address, telephone number, and victim impact statement is available only to the following persons or entities in the performance of their duties:

(i) a law enforcement agency, including the prosecuting agency;

(ii) a victims' right committee as provided in Section 77-37-5;

(iii) a governmentally sponsored victim or witness program;

(iv) the Department of Corrections;

(v) Office of Crime Victims' Reparations;

(vi) Commission on Criminal and Juvenile Justice; and

(vii) the Board of Pardons and Parole.

(12) The notice provisions as provided in this section do not apply to misdemeanors as provided in Section 77-38-5 and to important juvenile justice hearings as provided in Section 77-38-2.   2003

77-38-4. Right to be present and to be heard — Control of disruptive acts or irrelevant statements — Statements from persons in custody.

(1) The victim of a crime shall have the right to be present at the important criminal or juvenile justice hearings provided in Subsections 77-38-2(5)(a) through (f), the right to be heard at the important criminal or juvenile justice hearings provided in Subsections 77-38-2(5)(b), (c), (d), and (f), and, upon request to the judge hearing the matter, the right to be present and heard at the initial appearance of the person suspected of committing the conduct or criminal offense against the victim on issues relating to whether to release a defendant or minor and, if so, under what conditions release may occur.

(2) This chapter shall not confer any right to the victim of a crime to be heard:

(a) at any criminal trial, including the sentencing phase of a capital trial under Section 76-3-207 or at any preliminary hearing, unless called as a witness; and

(b) at any delinquency trial or at any preliminary hearing in a minor's case, unless called as a witness.

(3) The right of a victim or representative of a victim to be present at trial is subject to Rule 615 of the Utah Rules of Evidence.

(4) Nothing in this chapter shall deprive the court of the right to prevent or punish disruptive conduct nor give the victim of a crime the right to engage in disruptive conduct.

(5) The court shall have the right to limit any victim's statement to matters that are relevant to the proceeding.

(6) In all cases where the number of victims exceeds five, the court may limit the in-court oral statements it receives from victims in its discretion to a few representative statements.

(7) Except as otherwise provided in this section, a victim's right to be heard may be exercised at the victim's discretion in any appropriate fashion, including an oral, written, audiotaped, or videotaped statement or direct or indirect information that has been provided to be included in any presentence report.

(8) If the victim of a crime is a person who is in custody as a pretrial detainee, as a prisoner following conviction for an offense, or as a juvenile who has committed an act that would be an offense if committed by an adult, or who is in custody for mental or psychological treatment, the right to be heard under this chapter shall be exercised by submitting a written statement to the court.

(9) The court may exclude any oral statement from a victim on the grounds of the victim's incompetency as provided in Rule 601(a) of Utah Rules of Evidence.

(10) Except in juvenile court cases, the Constitution may not be construed as limiting the existing rights of the prosecution to introduce evidence in support of a capital sentence.   1995

77-38-5. Application to felonies and misdemeanors of the declaration of the rights of crime victims.

The provisions of this chapter shall apply to:

(1) any felony filed in the courts of the state;

(2) to any class A and class B misdemeanor filed in the courts of the state; and

(3) to cases in the juvenile court as provided in Section 78-3a-115.   1997

77-38-6. Victim's right to privacy.

(1) The victim of a crime has the right, at any court proceeding, including any juvenile court proceeding, not to testify regarding the victim's address, telephone number, place of employment, or other locating information unless the victim specifically consents or the court orders disclosure on finding that a compelling need exists to disclose the information. A court proceeding on whether to order disclosure shall be in camera.

(2) A defendant may not compel any witness to a crime, at any court proceeding, including any juvenile court proceeding, to testify regarding the witness's address, telephone number, place of employment, or other locating information unless the witness specifically consents or the court orders disclosure on finding that a compelling need for the information exists. A court proceeding on whether to order disclosure shall be in camera.   1995

77-38-7. Victim's right to a speedy trial.

(1) In determining a date for any criminal trial or other important criminal or juvenile justice hearing, the court shall consider the interests of the victim of a crime to a speedy resolution of the charges under the same standards that govern a defendant's or minor's right to a speedy trial.

(2) The victim of a crime has the right to a speedy disposition of the charges free from unwarranted delay caused by or at the behest of the defendant or minor and to prompt and final conclusion of the case after the disposition or conviction and sentence, including prompt and final conclusion of all collateral attacks on dispositions or criminal judgments.

(3) (a) In ruling on any motion by a defendant or minor to continue a previously established trial or other important criminal or juvenile justice hearing, the court shall inquire into the circumstances requiring the delay and consider the interests of the victim of a crime to a speedy disposition of the case.

(b) If a continuance is granted, the court shall enter in the record the specific reason for the continuance and the procedures that have been taken to avoid further delays.   1995

77-38-8. Age-appropriate language at judicial proceedings — Advisor.

(1) In any criminal proceeding or juvenile court proceeding regarding or involving a child, examination and cross-examination of a victim or witness 13 years of age or younger shall be conducted in age-appropriate language.

(2) (a) The court may appoint an advisor to assist a witness 13 years of age or younger in understanding questions asked by counsel.

(b) The advisor is not required to be an attorney.   1995

77-38-9. Representative of victim — Court designation — Representation in cases involving minors — Photographs in homicide cases.

(1) (a) A victim of a crime may designate, with the approval of the court, a representative who may exercise the same rights that the victim is entitled to exercise under this chapter.

(b) Except as otherwise provided in this section, the victim may revoke the designation at any time.

(c) In cases where the designation is in question, the court may require that the designation of the representative be made in writing by the victim.

(2) In cases in which the victim is deceased or incapacitated, upon request from the victim's spouse, parent, child, or close friend, the court shall designate a representative or representatives of the victim to exercise the rights of a victim under this chapter on behalf of the victim. The responsible prosecuting agency may request a designation to the court.

(3) (a) If the victim is a minor, the court in its discretion may allow the minor to exercise the rights of a victim under this chapter or may allow the victim's parent or other immediate family member to act as a representative of the victim.

(b) The court may also, in its discretion, designate a person who is not a member of the immediate family to represent the interests of the minor.

(4) The representative of a victim of a crime shall not be:

(a) the accused or a person who appears to be accountable or otherwise criminally responsible for or criminally involved in the crime or conduct, a related crime or conduct, or a crime or act arising from the same conduct, criminal episode, or plan as the crime or conduct is defined under the laws of this state;

(b) a person in the custody of or under detention of federal, state, or local authorities; or

(c) a person whom the court in its discretion considers to be otherwise inappropriate.

(5) Any notices that are to be provided to a victim pursuant to this chapter shall be sent to the victim or the victim's lawful representative.

(6) On behalf of the victim, the prosecutor may assert any right to which the victim is entitled under this chapter, unless the victim requests otherwise or exercises his own rights.

(7) In any homicide prosecution, the prosecution may introduce a photograph of the victim taken before the homicide to establish that the victim was a human being, the identity of the victim, and for other relevant purposes.   **1995**

77-38-10. Victim's discretion.

(1) (a) The victim may exercise any rights under this chapter at his discretion to be present and to be heard at a court proceeding, including a juvenile delinquency proceeding.

(b) The absence of the victim at the court proceeding does not preclude the court from conducting the proceeding.

(2) A victim shall not refuse to comply with an otherwise lawful subpoena under this chapter.

(3) A victim shall not prevent the prosecution from complying with requests for information within a prosecutor's possession and control under this chapter.   **1995**

77-38-11. Enforcement — Appellate review — No right to money damages.

(1) If a person acting under color of state law willfully or wantonly fails to perform duties so that the rights in this chapter are not provided, an action for injunctive relief, including prospective injunctive relief, may be brought against the individual and the governmental entity that employs the individual.

(2) (a) The victim of a crime or representative of a victim of a crime, including any Victims' Rights Committee as defined in Section 77-37-5 may:

(i) bring an action for declaratory relief or for a writ of mandamus defining or enforcing the rights of victims and the obligations of government entities under this chapter; and

(ii) petition to file an amicus brief in any court in any case affecting crime victims.

(b) Adverse rulings on these actions or on a motion or request brought by a victim of a crime or a representative of a victim of a crime may be appealed under the rules governing appellate actions, provided that no appeal shall constitute grounds for delaying any criminal or juvenile proceeding.

(c) An appellate court shall review all such properly presented issues, including issues that are capable of repetition but would otherwise evade review.

(3) The failure to provide the rights in this chapter or Title 77, Chapter 37, Victims Rights, shall not constitute cause for a judgment against the state or any government entity, or any individual employed by the state or any government entity, for monetary damages, attorneys' fees, or the costs of exercising any rights under this chapter.   **1996**

77-38-12. Construction of this chapter — No right to set aside conviction, adjudication, admission, or plea — Severability clause.

(1) All of the provisions contained in this chapter shall be construed to assist the victims of crime.

(2) This chapter may not be construed as creating a basis for dismissing any criminal charge or delinquency petition, vacating any adjudication or conviction, admission or plea of guilty or no contest, or for appellate, habeas corpus, except in juvenile cases, or other relief from a judgment in any criminal or delinquency case.

(3) This chapter may not be construed as creating any right of a victim to appointed counsel at state expense.

(4) All of the rights contained in this chapter shall be construed to conform to the Constitution of the United States.

(5) (a) In the event that any portion of this chapter is found to violate the Constitution of the United States, the remaining provisions of this chapter shall continue to operate in full force and effect.

(b) In the event that a particular application of any portion of this chapter is found to violate the Constitution of the United States, all other applications shall continue to operate in full force and effect.

(6) The enumeration of certain rights for crime victims in this chapter shall not be construed to deny or disparage other rights granted by the Utah Constitution or the Legislature or retained by victims of crimes.   **1995**

77-38-13. Declaration of legislative authority.

It is the view of the Legislature that the provisions of this chapter, and other provisions enacted simultaneously with it, are substantive provisions within inherent legislative authority. In the event that any of the provisions of this chapter, and other provisions enacted simultaneously with it, are interpreted to be procedural in nature, the Legislature also intends to invoke its powers to modify procedural rules under the Utah Constitution. 1994

77-38-14. Notice of expungement petition — Victim's right to object.

(1) The Department of Corrections or the Juvenile Probation Department shall prepare a document explaining the right of a victim or a victim's representative to object to a petition for expungement under Section 77-18-11 or 78-3a-905 and the procedures for obtaining notice of any such petition. The department or division shall also provide each trial court a copy of the document which has jurisdiction over delinquencies or criminal offenses subject to expungement.

(2) The prosecuting attorney in any case leading to a conviction or an adjudication subject to expungement shall provide a copy of the document to each person who would be entitled to notice of a petition for expungement under Sections 77-18-11 and 78-3a-905. 1996

CHAPTER 38a

CRIME VICTIMS RESTITUTION ACT

Part 1

General Provisions

Part 2

Restitution Determination

Part 3

Restitution Requirements

Part 4

Restitution Judgments

Part 5

Enforcement and Collection

Part 6

Preservation of Assets

PART 1

GENERAL PROVISIONS

77-38a-101. Title.

This chapter is known as the "Crime Victims Restitution Act." 2001

77-38a-102. Definitions.

As used in this chapter:

(1) "Conviction" includes a:
  (a) judgment of guilt;
  (b) a plea of guilty; or
  (c) a plea of no contest.

(2) "Criminal activities" means any offense of which the defendant is convicted or any other criminal conduct for which the defendant admits responsibility to the sentencing court with or without an admission of committing the criminal conduct.

(3) "Department" means the Department of Corrections.

(4) "Diversion" means suspending criminal proceedings prior to conviction on the condition that a defendant agree to participate in a rehabilitation program, make restitution to the victim, or fulfill some other condition.

(5) "Party" means the prosecutor, defendant, or department involved in a prosecution.

(6) "Pecuniary damages" means all demonstrable economic injury, whether or not yet incurred, which a person could recover in a civil action arising out of the facts or events constituting the defendant's criminal activities and includes the fair market value of property taken, destroyed, broken, or otherwise harmed, and losses including lost earnings and medical expenses, but excludes punitive or exemplary damages and pain and suffering.

(7) "Plea agreement" means an agreement entered between the prosecution and defendant setting forth the special terms and conditions and criminal charges upon which the defendant will enter a plea of guilty or no contest.

(8) "Plea in abeyance" means an order by a court, upon motion of the prosecution and the defendant, accepting a plea of guilty or of no contest from the defendant but not, at that time, entering judgment of conviction against him nor imposing sentence upon him on condition that he comply with specific conditions as set forth in a plea in abeyance agreement.

(9) "Plea in abeyance agreement" means an agreement entered into between the prosecution and the defendant setting forth the specific terms and conditions upon which, following acceptance of the agreement by the court, a plea may be held in abeyance.

(10) "Plea disposition" means an agreement entered into between the prosecution and defendant including diversion, plea agreement, plea in abeyance agreement, or any agreement by which the defendant may enter a plea in any other jurisdiction or where charges are dismissed without a plea.

(11) "Restitution" means full, partial, or nominal payment for pecuniary damages to a victim, including prejudgment interest, the accrual of interest from the time of sentencing, insured damages, reimbursement for payment of a reward, and payment for expenses to a governmental entity for extradition or transportation and as may be further defined by law.

(12) (a) "Reward" means a sum of money:

(i) offered to the public for information leading to the arrest and conviction of an offender; and

(ii) that has been paid to a person or persons who provide this information, except that the person receiving the payment may not be a codefendant, an accomplice, or a bounty hunter.

(b) "Reward" does not include any amount paid in excess of the sum offered to the public.

(13) "Screening" means the process used by a prosecuting attorney to terminate investigative action, proceed with prosecution, move to dismiss a prosecution that has been commenced, or cause a prosecution to be diverted.

(14) (a) "Victim" means any person whom the court determines has suffered pecuniary damages as a result of the defendant's criminal activities.

(b) "Victim" may not include a codefendant or accomplice.   2005

PART 2

RESTITUTION DETERMINATION

77-38a-201. Restitution determination — Law enforcement duties and responsibilities.

Any law enforcement agency conducting an investigation for criminal conduct which would constitute a felony or class A misdemeanor shall provide in the investigative reports whether a claim for restitution exists, the basis for the claim, and the estimated or actual amount of the claim.   2001

77-38a-202. Restitution determination — Prosecution duties and responsibilities.

(1) At the time of entry of a conviction or entry of any plea disposition of a felony or class A misdemeanor, the attorney general, county attorney, municipal attorney, or district attorney shall provide to the district court:

(a) the names of all victims, including third parties, asserting claims for restitution;

(b) the actual or estimated amount of restitution determined at that time; and

(c) whether or not the defendant has agreed to pay the restitution specified as part of the plea disposition.

(2) In computing actual or estimated restitution, the attorney general, county attorney, municipal attorney, or district attorney shall:

(a) use the criteria set forth in Section 77-38a-302 for establishing restitution amounts; and

(b) in cases involving multiple victims, incorporate into any conviction or plea disposition all claims for restitution arising out of the investigation for which the defendant is charged.

(3) If charges are not to be prosecuted as part of a plea disposition, restitution claims from victims of those crimes shall also be provided to the court.   2001

77-38a-203. Restitution determination — Department of Corrections — Presentence investigation.

(1) (a) The department shall prepare a presentence investigation report in accordance with Subsection 77-18-1(5). The prosecutor and law enforcement agency involved shall provide all available victim information to the department upon request. The victim impact statement shall:

(i) identify all victims of the offense;

(ii) itemize any economic loss suffered by the victim as a result of the offense;

(iii) include for each identifiable victim a specific statement of the recommended amount of complete restitution as defined in Section 77-38a-302, accompanied by a recommendation from the department regarding the payment by the defendant of court-ordered restitution with interest as defined in Section 77-38a-302;

(iv) identify any physical, mental, or emotional injuries suffered by the victim as a result of the offense, and the seriousness and permanence;

(v) describe any change in the victim's personal welfare or familial relationships as a result of the offense;

(vi) identify any request for mental health services initiated by the victim or the victim's family as a result of the offense; and

(vii) contain any other information related to the impact of the offense upon the victim or the victim's family that the court requires.

(b) The crime victim shall be responsible to provide to the department upon request all invoices, bills, receipts, and other evidence of injury, loss of earnings, and out-of-pocket loss. The crime victim shall also provide upon request:

(i) all documentation and evidence of compensation or reimbursement from insurance companies or agencies of the state of Utah, any other state, or federal government received as a direct result of the crime for injury, loss, earnings, or out-of-pocket loss; and

(ii) proof of identification, including date of birth, Social Security number, drivers license number, next of kin, and home and work address and telephone numbers.

(c) The inability, failure, or refusal of the crime victim to provide all or part of the requested information shall result in the court determining restitution based on the best information available.

(2) (a) The court shall order the defendant as part of the presentence investigation to submit to the department any information determined necessary to be disclosed for the purpose of ascertaining the restitution.

(b) The willful failure or refusal of the defendant to provide all or part of the requisite information shall constitute a waiver of any grounds to appeal or seek future amendment or alteration of the restitution order predicated on the undisclosed information.

(c) If the defendant objects to the imposition, amount, or distribution of the restitution recommended in the presentence investigation, the court shall set a hearing date to resolve the matter.

(d) If any party fails to challenge the accuracy of the presentence investigation report at the time of sentencing, that matter shall be considered to be waived.   2005

PART 3

RESTITUTION REQUIREMENTS

77-38a-301. Restitution — Convicted defendant may be required to pay.

In a criminal action, the court may require a convicted defendant to make restitution.   2001

77-38a-302. Restitution criteria.

(1) When a defendant is convicted of criminal activity that has resulted in pecuniary damages, in addition to any other sentence it may impose, the court shall order that the defendant make restitution to victims of crime as provided in this chapter, or for conduct for which the defendant has agreed to make restitution as part of a plea disposition. For purposes of restitution, a victim has the meaning as defined in Subsection 77-38a-102(14) and in determining whether restitution is appropriate, the court shall follow the criteria and procedures as provided in Subsections (2) through (5).

(2) In determining restitution, the court shall determine complete restitution and court-ordered restitution.

(a) "Complete restitution" means restitution necessary to compensate a victim for all losses caused by the defendant.

(b) "Court-ordered restitution" means the restitution the court having criminal jurisdiction orders the defendant to pay as a part of the criminal sentence at the time of sentencing or within one year after sentencing.

(c) Complete restitution and court-ordered restitution shall be determined as provided in Subsection (5).

(3) If the court determines that restitution is appropriate or inappropriate under this part, the court shall make the reasons for the decision part of the court record.

(4) If the defendant objects to the imposition, amount, or distribution of the restitution, the court shall allow the defendant a full hearing on the issue.

(5) (a) For the purpose of determining restitution for an offense, the offense shall include any criminal conduct admitted by the defendant to the sentencing court or to which the defendant agrees to pay restitution. A victim of an offense that involves as an element a scheme, a conspiracy, or a pattern of criminal activity, includes any person directly harmed by the defendant's criminal conduct in the course of the scheme, conspiracy, or pattern.

(b) In determining the monetary sum and other conditions for complete restitution, the court shall consider all relevant facts, including:

(i) the cost of the damage or loss if the offense resulted in damage to or loss or destruction of property of a victim of the offense;

(ii) the cost of necessary medical and related professional services and devices relating to physical or mental health care, including nonmedical care and treatment rendered in accordance with a method of healing recognized by the law of the place of treatment;

(iii) the cost of necessary physical and occupational therapy and rehabilitation;

(iv) the income lost by the victim as a result of the offense if the offense resulted in bodily injury to a victim;

(v) up to five days of the individual victim's determinable wages that are lost due to theft of or damage to tools or equipment items of a trade that were owned by the victim and were essential to the victim's current employment at the time of the offense; and

(vi) the cost of necessary funeral and related services if the offense resulted in the death of a victim.

(c) In determining the monetary sum and other conditions for court-ordered restitution, the court shall consider the factors listed in Subsections (5)(a) and (b) and:

(i) the financial resources of the defendant and the burden that payment of restitution will impose, with regard to the other obligations of the defendant;

(ii) the ability of the defendant to pay restitution on an installment basis or on other conditions to be fixed by the court;

(iii) the rehabilitative effect on the defendant of the payment of restitution and the method of payment; and

(iv) other circumstances which the court determines may make restitution inappropriate.

(d) (i) Except as provided in Subsection (5)(d)(ii), the court shall determine complete restitution and court-ordered restitution, and shall make all restitution orders at the time of sentencing if feasible, otherwise within one year after sentencing.

(ii) Any pecuniary damages that have not been determined by the court within one year after sentencing may be determined by the Board of Pardons and Parole.

(e) The Board of Pardons and Parole may, within one year after sentencing, refer an order of judgment and commitment back to the court for determination of restitution. 2005

PART 4

RESTITUTION JUDGMENTS

77-38a-401. Entry of judgment — Interest — Civil actions — Lien.

(1) Upon the court determining that a defendant owes restitution, the clerk of the court shall enter an order of complete restitution as defined in Section 77-38a-302 on the civil judgment docket and provide notice of the order to the parties.

(2) The order shall be considered a legal judgment, enforceable under the Utah Rules of Civil Procedure. In addition, the department may, on behalf of the person in whose favor the restitution order is entered, enforce the restitution order as judgment creditor under the Utah Rules of Civil Procedure.

(3) If the defendant fails to obey a court order for payment of restitution and the victim or department elects to pursue collection of the order by civil process, the victim shall be entitled to recover reasonable attorney's fees.

(4) A judgment ordering restitution when recorded in a registry of judgments docket shall have the same affect and is subject to the same rules as a judgment in a civil action. Interest shall accrue on the amount ordered from the time of sentencing, including prejudgment interest.

(5) The department shall make rules permitting the restitution payments to be credited to principal first and the remainder of payments credited to interest in accordance with Title 63, Chapter 46a, Utah Administrative Rulemaking Act. 2001

77-38a-402. Nondischargeability in bankruptcy.

Restitution imposed under this chapter and interest accruing in accordance with Subsection 77-38a-401(4) is considered a debt and may not be discharged in bankruptcy. 2001

77-38a-403. Civil action by victim for damages.

(1) Provisions in this part concerning restitution do not limit or impair the right of a person injured by a defendant's criminal activities to sue and recover damages from the defendant in a civil action. Evidence that the defendant has paid or been ordered to pay restitution under this part may not be introduced in any civil action arising out of the facts or events which were the basis for the restitution. However, the court shall credit any restitution paid by the defendant to a victim against any judgment in favor of the victim in the civil action.

(2) If conviction in a criminal trial necessarily decides the issue of a defendant's liability for pecuniary damages of a victim, that issue is conclusively determined as to the defendant if it is involved in a subsequent civil action.   2001

77-38a-404. Priority.

(1) If restitution to more than one person, agency, or entity is set at the same time, the department shall establish the following priorities of payment, except as provided in Subsection (3):

(a) the crime victim;

(b) the Office of Crime Victim Reparations;

(c) any other government agency which has provided reimbursement to the victim as a result of the offender's criminal conduct;

(d) the person, entity, or governmental agency that has offered and paid a reward under Section 76-3-201.1 or 78-3a-118;

(e) any insurance company which has provided reimbursement to the victim as a result of the offender's criminal conduct; and

(f) any county correctional facility to which the court has ordered the defendant to pay restitution under Subsection 76-3-201(6).

(2) Restitution ordered under Subsection (1)(f) is paid after criminal fines and surcharges are paid.

(3) If the offender is required under Section 53-10-404 to reimburse the department for the cost of obtaining the offender's DNA specimen, this reimbursement is the next priority after restitution to the crime victim under Subsection (1)(a).

(4) All money collected for court-ordered obligations from offenders by the department will be applied:

(a) first, to victim restitution, except the $30 per month required to be collected by the department under Section 64-13-21, if applicable; and

(b) second, if applicable, to the cost of obtaining a DNA specimen under Subsection (3).   2003

PART 5

ENFORCEMENT AND COLLECTION

77-38a-501. Default and sanctions.

(1) When a defendant defaults in the payment of a judgment for restitution or any installment ordered, the court, on motion of the prosecutor, parole or probation agent, victim, or on its own motion may impose sanctions against the defendant as provided in Section 76-3-201.1.

(2) The court may not impose a sanction against the defendant under Subsection (1) if:

(a) the defendant's sole default in the payment of a judgement for restitution is the failure to pay restitution ordered under Subsection 76-3-201(6) regarding costs of incarceration in a county correctional facility; and

(b) the sanction would extend the defendant's term of probation or parole.   2003

77-38a-502. Collection from inmate offenders.

In addition to the remedies provided in Section 77-38a-501, the department upon written request of the prosecutor, victim, or parole or probation agent, shall collect restitution from offender funds held by the department as provided in Section 64-13-23.   2001

PART 6

PRESERVATION OF ASSETS

77-38a-601. Preservation of assets.

(1) At the time a criminal information, indictment charging a violation, or a petition alleging delinquency is filed, or at any time during the prosecution of the case, a prosecutor may petition the court to enter a restraining order or injunction, require the execution of a satisfactory performance bond, or take any other action to preserve the availability of property which may be necessary to satisfy an anticipated restitution order if, in the prosecutor's best judgement, there is a substantial likelihood that a conviction will be obtained and restitution will be ordered.

(a) Upon receiving a petition from a prosecutor under this Subsection (1), and after notice and a hearing, the court may enter a restraining order or injunction, require the execution of a satisfactory performance bond, or take any action necessary to preserve the availability of property which may be necessary to satisfy an anticipated restitution order.

(b) An order entered under this Subsection (1) is effective for up to 90 days, unless extended by the court for good cause shown.

(2) Prior to the filing of a criminal information, indictment charging a violation, or a petition alleging delinquency, a prosecutor may petition the court to enter a restraining order or injunction, require the execution of a satisfactory performance bond, or take any other action to preserve the availability of property which may be necessary to satisfy an anticipated restitution order if, in the prosecutor's best judgement, there is a substantial likelihood that a conviction will be obtained and restitution will be ordered.

(a) Upon receiving a request from a prosecutor under this Subsection (2), the court may enter a restraining order or injunction, require the execution of a satisfactory performance bond, or take any action necessary to preserve the availability of property which may be necessary to satisfy an anticipated restitution order after notice to persons appearing to have an interest in the property and affording them an opportunity to be heard, if the court determines that:

(i) there is probable cause to believe that a crime has been committed and that the defendant committed it, and that failure to enter the order will result in the property being sold, distributed, exhibited, destroyed, or removed from the jurisdiction of the court, or otherwise be made unavailable for restitution; and

(ii) the need to preserve the availability of the property or prevent its sale, distribution, exhibition, destruction, or removal through the entry of the requested order outweighs the hardship on any party against whom the order is to be entered.

(b) An order entered under this Subsection (2) is effective for the period of time given in the order.

(3) (a) Upon receiving a request from a prosecutor under Subsection (2), and notwithstanding Sub-

section (2)(a)(i), a court may enter a temporary restraining order against an owner with respect to specific property without notice or opportunity for a hearing if:

    (i) the prosecutor demonstrates that there is a substantial likelihood that the property with respect to which the order is sought appears to be necessary to satisfy an anticipated restitution order under this chapter; and

    (ii) that provision of notice would jeopardize the availability of the property to satisfy any restitution order or judgment.

(b) The temporary order in this Subsection (3) expires not more than ten days after it is entered unless extended for good cause shown or the party against whom it is entered consents to an extension.

(4) A hearing concerning an order entered under this section shall be held as soon as possible, and prior to the expiration of the temporary order.   2004

CHAPTER 39

SALE OF TOBACCO AND ALCOHOL TO UNDER AGE PERSONS

Section
77-39-101.   Investigation of sales of alcohol and tobacco to under age persons.

77-39-101. Investigation of sales of alcohol and tobacco to under age persons.

(1) (a) A peace officer, as defined by Title 53, Chapter 13, Peace Officer Classifications, may investigate the possible violation of Section 32A-12-203 or Section 76-10-104 by requesting a person under the legal age to attempt to purchase alcohol as provided in Section 32A-12-203, or tobacco as provided in Section 76-10-104, to enter into and attempt to purchase or make a purchase of alcohol or tobacco products from a retail establishment.

(b) A peace officer who is present at the site of a proposed purchase shall direct, supervise, and monitor the person requested to make the purchase.

(c) Immediately following the purchase or attempted purchase or as soon as practical the supervising peace officer shall inform the cashier and the proprietor or manager of the retail establishment that the attempted purchaser was under the legal age to purchase alcohol or tobacco.

(d) If a citation or information is issued, it shall be issued within seven days of the purchase.

(2) (a) If a person under the age of 18 years old is requested to attempt a purchase, a written consent of that person's parent or guardian shall be obtained prior to that person participating in any attempted purchase.

(b) A person requested by the peace officer to attempt a purchase may be a trained volunteer or receive payment but may not be paid based on the number of successful purchases of alcohol or tobacco.

(3) The person requested by the peace officer to attempt a purchase and anyone accompanying the person attempting a purchase may not during the attempted purchase misrepresent the age of the person by false or misleading identification documentation in attempting the purchase.

(4) A person requested to purchase alcohol or tobacco pursuant to this section is immune from prosecution, suit, or civil liability for the purchase of, attempted purchase of, or possession of alcohol or tobacco if a peace officer directs, supervises, and monitors the person.

(5) (a) Except as provided in Subsection (5)(b), a purchase attempted under this section shall be conducted on a random basis, but not more often than four times within a 12-month period at any one retail establishment location.

(b) Nothing in this section shall prohibit an investigation under this section if:

    (i) there is reasonable suspicion to believe the retail establishment has sold alcohol or tobacco to a person under the age established by Section 32A-12-203 or 76-10-104; and

    (ii) the supervising peace officer makes a written record of the grounds for the reasonable suspicion.

(6) (a) The peace officer exercising direction, supervision, and monitoring of the attempted purchase shall make a report of the attempted purchase, whether or not a purchase was made.

(b) The report shall include:

    (i) the name of the supervising peace officer;

    (ii) the name of the person attempting the purchase;

    (iii) a photograph of the person attempting the purchase showing how that person appeared at the time of the attempted purchase;

    (iv) the name and description of the cashier or proprietor from whom the person attempted the purchase;

    (v) the name and address of the retail establishment; and

    (vi) the date and time of the attempted purchase.   1998

TITLE 78

JUDICIAL CODE

PART I

COURTS

PART III

PROCEDURE

PART IV

PARTICULAR PROCEEDINGS

Chapter
31b. Alternative Dispute Resolution.
32. Contempt.
38. Nuisance, Waste, and Other Damage.

PART VIII

DIVERSION PROGRAMS

57. Utah Youth Court Diversion Act.

PART IX

MISCELLANEOUS PROVISIONS

58. Citizen Participation in Government Act.
61. Profits From Crime Memorabilia.

PART I

COURTS

CHAPTER 1

ENUMERATION OF COURTS

78-1-1. Courts of justice enumerated — Courts of record enumerated.

(1) The following are the courts of justice of this state:

(a) the Supreme Court;

(b) the Court of Appeals;

(c) the district courts;

(d) the juvenile courts; and

(e) the justice courts.

(2) All courts are courts of record, except the justice courts, which are courts not of record.   1996

78-1-2. Merger of district court and circuit court.

(1) Effective July 1, 1996, the circuit court shall be merged into the district court. The district court shall have jurisdiction as provided by law for the district court and shall have jurisdiction over all matters filed in the court formerly denominated the circuit court.

(2) The district court shall continue the judicial offices, judges, staff, cases, authority, duties, and all other attributes of the court formerly denominated the circuit court.

(3) Judges of the court formerly denominated the circuit court shall:

(a) on July 1, 1996, be judges of the district court; and

(b) next stand for retention election at the first general election held more than three years after their appointment or at the general election held in the sixth year after their last retention election, as applicable.   1996

78-1-2.1. Trial courts of record — Divisions.

The trial courts of record shall be divided into eight geographical divisions:

(1) First District — Box Elder, Cache, and Rich Counties;

(2) Second District — Weber, Davis, and Morgan Counties;

(3) Third District — Salt Lake, Summit, and Tooele Counties;

(4) Fourth District — Utah, Wasatch, Juab, and Millard Counties;

(5) Fifth District — Beaver, Iron, and Washington Counties;

(6) Sixth District — Garfield, Kane, Piute, Sanpete, Sevier, and Wayne Counties;

(7) Seventh District — Carbon, Emery, Grand, and San Juan Counties; and

(8) Eighth District — Daggett, Duchesne, and Uintah Counties.   1988

78-1-2.2. Number of district judges.

The number of district court judges shall be:

(1) four district judges in the First District;

(2) 14 district judges in the Second District;

(3) 28 district judges in the Third District;

(4) 12 district judges in the Fourth District;

(5) five district judges in the Fifth District;

(6) two district judges in the Sixth District;

(7) three district judges in the Seventh District; and

(8) two district judges in the Eighth District.   2004

78-1-2.3. Number of juvenile judges and jurisdictions.

The number of juvenile court judges shall be:

(1) two juvenile judges in the First Juvenile District;

(2) six juvenile judges in the Second Juvenile District;

(3) nine juvenile judges in the Third Juvenile District;

(4) four juvenile judges in the Fourth Juvenile District;

(5) two juvenile judges in the Fifth Juvenile District;

(6) one juvenile judge in the Sixth Juvenile District;

(7) two juvenile judges in the Seventh Juvenile District; and

(8) one juvenile judge in the Eighth Juvenile District.   2005

CHAPTER 2

SUPREME COURT

78-2-2. Supreme Court jurisdiction.

(1) The Supreme Court has original jurisdiction to

answer questions of state law certified by a court of the United States.

(2) The Supreme Court has original jurisdiction to issue all extraordinary writs and authority to issue all writs and process necessary to carry into effect its orders, judgments, and decrees or in aid of its jurisdiction.

(3) The Supreme Court has appellate jurisdiction, including jurisdiction of interlocutory appeals, over:

(a) a judgment of the Court of Appeals;

(b) cases certified to the Supreme Court by the Court of Appeals prior to final judgment by the Court of Appeals;

(c) discipline of lawyers;

(d) final orders of the Judicial Conduct Commission;

(e) final orders and decrees in formal adjudicative proceedings originating with:

(i) the Public Service Commission;

(ii) the State Tax Commission;

(iii) the School and Institutional Trust Lands Board of Trustees;

(iv) the Board of Oil, Gas, and Mining;

(v) the state engineer; or

(vi) the executive director of the Department of Natural Resources reviewing actions of the Division of Forestry, Fire and State Lands;

(f) final orders and decrees of the district court review of informal adjudicative proceedings of agencies under Subsection (3)(e);

(g) a final judgment or decree of any court of record holding a statute of the United States or this state unconstitutional on its face under the Constitution of the United States or the Utah Constitution;

(h) interlocutory appeals from any court of record involving a charge of a first degree or capital felony;

(i) appeals from the district court involving a conviction or charge of a first degree felony or capital felony;

(j) orders, judgments, and decrees of any court of record over which the Court of Appeals does not have original appellate jurisdiction; and

(k) appeals from the district court of orders, judgments, or decrees ruling on legislative subpoenas.

(4) The Supreme Court may transfer to the Court of Appeals any of the matters over which the Supreme Court has original appellate jurisdiction, except:

(a) capital felony convictions or an appeal of an interlocutory order of a court of record involving a charge of a capital felony;

(b) election and voting contests;

(c) reapportionment of election districts;

(d) retention or removal of public officers;

(e) matters involving legislative subpoenas; and

(f) those matters described in Subsections (3)(a) through (d).

(5) The Supreme Court has sole discretion in granting or denying a petition for writ of certiorari for the review of a Court of Appeals adjudication, but the Supreme Court shall review those cases certified to it by the Court of Appeals under Subsection (3)(b).

(6) The Supreme Court shall comply with the requirements of Title 63, Chapter 46b, Administrative Procedures Act, in its review of agency adjudicative proceedings. **2001**

78-2-7.5. Service of sheriff to court.

The court may at any time require the attendance and services of any sheriff in the state. **1988**

CHAPTER 2a

COURT OF APPEALS

Section
78-2a-3. Court of Appeals jurisdiction.

78-2a-3. Court of Appeals jurisdiction.

(1) The Court of Appeals has jurisdiction to issue all extraordinary writs and to issue all writs and process necessary:

(a) to carry into effect its judgments, orders, and decrees; or

(b) in aid of its jurisdiction.

(2) The Court of Appeals has appellate jurisdiction, including jurisdiction of interlocutory appeals, over:

(a) the final orders and decrees resulting from formal adjudicative proceedings of state agencies or appeals from the district court review of informal adjudicative proceedings of the agencies, except the Public Service Commission, State Tax Commission, School and Institutional Trust Lands Board of Trustees, Division of Forestry, Fire and State Lands actions reviewed by the executive director of the Department of Natural Resources, Board of Oil, Gas, and Mining, and the state engineer;

(b) appeals from the district court review of:

(i) adjudicative proceedings of agencies of political subdivisions of the state or other local agencies; and

(ii) a challenge to agency action under Section 63-46a-12.1;

(c) appeals from the juvenile courts;

(d) interlocutory appeals from any court of record in criminal cases, except those involving a charge of a first degree or capital felony;

(e) appeals from a court of record in criminal cases, except those involving a conviction or charge of a first degree felony or capital felony;

(f) appeals from orders on petitions for extraordinary writs sought by persons who are incarcerated or serving any other criminal sentence, except petitions constituting a challenge to a conviction of or the sentence for a first degree or capital felony;

(g) appeals from the orders on petitions for extraordinary writs challenging the decisions of the Board of Pardons and Parole except in cases involving a first degree or capital felony;

(h) appeals from district court involving domestic relations cases, including, but not limited to, divorce, annulment, property division, child custody, support, parent-time, visitation, adoption, and paternity;

(i) appeals from the Utah Military Court; and

(j) cases transferred to the Court of Appeals from the Supreme Court.

(3) The Court of Appeals upon its own motion only and by the vote of four judges of the court may certify to the Supreme Court for original appellate review and determination any matter over which the Court of Appeals has original appellate jurisdiction.

(4) The Court of Appeals shall comply with the requirements of Title 63, Chapter 46b, Administrative Procedures Act, in its review of agency adjudicative proceedings. **2001**

CHAPTER 3

DISTRICT COURTS

Section
78-3-4.   Jurisdiction — Appeals.

78-3-4. Jurisdiction — Appeals.

(1) The district court has original jurisdiction in all matters civil and criminal, not excepted in the Utah Constitution and not prohibited by law.

(2) The district court judges may issue all extraordinary writs and other writs necessary to carry into effect their orders, judgments, and decrees.

(3) The district court has jurisdiction over matters of lawyer discipline consistent with the rules of the Supreme Court.

(4) The district court has jurisdiction over all matters properly filed in the circuit court prior to July 1, 1996.

(5) The district court has appellate jurisdiction to adjudicate trials de novo of the judgments of the justice court and of the small claims department of the district court.

(6) Appeals from the final orders, judgments, and decrees of the district court are under Sections 78-2-2 and 78-2a-3.

(7) The district court has jurisdiction to review:

(a) agency adjudicative proceedings as set forth in Title 63, Chapter 46b, Administrative Procedures Act, and shall comply with the requirements of that chapter, in its review of agency adjudicative proceedings; and

(b) municipal administrative proceedings in accordance with Section 10-3-703.7.

(8) Notwithstanding Subsection (1), the district court has subject matter jurisdiction in class B misdemeanors, class C misdemeanors, infractions, and violations of ordinances only if:

(a) there is no justice court with territorial jurisdiction;

(b) the matter was properly filed in the circuit court prior to July 1, 1996;

(c) the offense occurred within the boundaries of the municipality in which the district courthouse is located and that municipality has not formed a justice court; or

(d) they are included in an indictment or information covering a single criminal episode alleging the commission of a felony or a class A misdemeanor.

(9) The district court has jurisdiction of actions under Title 78, Chapter 3h, Child Protective Orders, if the juvenile court transfers the case to the district court.   2004

CHAPTER 3a

JUVENILE COURTS

Part 1

General Provisions

PART 1

GENERAL PROVISIONS

78-3a-101. Title.
This chapter is known as the "Juvenile Court Act of 1996." 1996

78-3a-102. Establishment of juvenile court — Organization and status of court — Purpose.
(1) There is established for the state a juvenile court.
(2) The juvenile court is a court of record. It shall have a seal, and its judges, clerks, and referees have the power to administer oaths and affirmations.
(3) The juvenile court is of equal status with the district courts of the state.
(4) The juvenile court is established as a forum for the resolution of all matters properly brought before it, consistent with applicable constitutional and statutory requirements of due process.
(5) The purpose of the court under this chapter is to:
(a) promote public safety and individual accountability by the imposition of appropriate sanctions on persons who have committed acts in violation of law;
(b) order appropriate measures to promote guidance and control, preferably in the minor's own home, as an aid in the prevention of future unlawful conduct and the development of responsible citizenship;
(c) where appropriate, order rehabilitation, reeducation, and treatment for persons who have committed acts bringing them within the court's jurisdiction;
(d) adjudicate matters that relate to minors who are beyond parental or adult control and to establish appropriate authority over these minors by means of placement and control orders;
(e) adjudicate matters that relate to abused, neglected, and dependent minors and to provide care and protection for these minors by placement, protection, and custody orders;
(f) remove a minor from parental custody only where the minor's safety or welfare, or the public safety, may not otherwise be adequately safeguarded; and
(g) consistent with the ends of justice, act in the best interests of the minor in all cases and preserve and strengthen family ties. 2005

78-3a-103. Definitions.
(1) As used in this chapter:
(a) "Abused child" includes a minor less than 18 years of age who:
(i) has suffered or been threatened with nonaccidental physical or mental harm, negligent treatment, or sexual exploitation; or
(ii) has been the victim of any sexual abuse.
(b) "Adjudication" means a finding by the court, incorporated in a decree, that the facts alleged in the petition have been proved.
(c) "Adult" means a person 18 years of age or over, except that persons 18 years or over under the continuing jurisdiction of the juvenile court

pursuant to Section 78-3a-121 shall be referred to as minors.

(d) "Board" means the Board of Juvenile Court Judges.

(e) "Child placement agency" means:

(i) a private agency licensed to receive minors for placement or adoption under this code; or

(ii) a private agency receiving minors for placement or adoption in another state, which agency is licensed or approved where such license or approval is required by law.

(f) "Commit" means to transfer legal custody.

(g) "Court" means the juvenile court.

(h) "Dependent child" includes a minor who is homeless or without proper care through no fault of the minor's parent, guardian, or custodian.

(i) "Deprivation of custody" means transfer of legal custody by the court from a parent or the parents or a previous legal custodian to another person, agency, or institution.

(j) "Detention" means home detention and secure detention as defined in Section 62A-7-101 for the temporary care of minors who require secure custody in physically restricting facilities:

(i) pending court disposition or transfer to another jurisdiction; or

(ii) while under the continuing jurisdiction of the court.

(k) "Division" means the Division of Child and Family Services.

(l) "Formal referral" means a written report from a peace officer or other person informing the court that a minor is or appears to be within the court's jurisdiction and that a petition may be filed.

(m) "Group rehabilitation therapy" means psychological and social counseling of one or more persons in the group, depending upon the recommendation of the therapist.

(n) "Guardianship of the person" includes the authority to consent to marriage, to enlistment in the armed forces, to major medical, surgical, or psychiatric treatment, and to legal custody, if legal custody is not vested in another person, agency, or institution.

(o) "Habitual truant" is a school-age minor who:

(i) has received:

(A) more than two truancy citations within one school year from the school in which the minor is or should be enrolled; and

(B) eight absences without a legitimate or valid excuse; or

(ii) in defiance of efforts on the part of school authorities as required under Section 53A-11-103, refuses to regularly attend school or any scheduled period of the school day.

(p) "Legal custody" means a relationship embodying the following rights and duties:

(i) the right to physical custody of the minor;

(ii) the right and duty to protect, train, and discipline the minor;

(iii) the duty to provide the minor with food, clothing, shelter, education, and ordinary medical care;

(iv) the right to determine where and with whom the minor shall live; and

(v) the right, in an emergency, to authorize surgery or other extraordinary care.

(q) (i) "Minor" means a person under the age of 18 years.

(ii) "Minor" includes the term "child" as used in other parts of this chapter.

(r) "Natural parent" means a minor's biological or adoptive parent, and includes the minor's non-custodial parent.

(s) (i) "Neglected child" means a minor:

(A) whose parent, guardian, or custodian has abandoned the minor, except as provided in Title 62A, Chapter 4a, Part 8, Safe Relinquishment of a Newborn Child;

(B) whose parent, guardian, or custodian has subjected the minor to mistreatment or abuse;

(C) who lacks proper parental care by reason of the fault or habits of the parent, guardian, or custodian;

(D) whose parent, guardian, or custodian fails or refuses to provide proper or necessary subsistence, education, or medical care, including surgery or psychiatric services when required, or any other care necessary for health, safety, morals, or well-being; or

(E) who is at risk of being a neglected or abused child as defined in this chapter because another minor in the same home is a neglected or abused child as defined in this chapter.

(ii) The aspect of neglect related to education, described in Subsection (1)(s)(i)(D), means that, after receiving notice that a minor has been frequently absent from school without good cause, or that the minor has failed to cooperate with school authorities in a reasonable manner, a parent or guardian fails to make a good faith effort to ensure that the minor receives an appropriate education.

(iii) A parent or guardian legitimately practicing religious beliefs and who, for that reason, does not provide specified medical treatment for a minor, is not guilty of neglect.

(iv) Notwithstanding Subsection (1)(s)(i), a health care decision made for a child by the child's parent or guardian does not constitute neglect unless the state or other party to the proceeding shows, by clear and convincing evidence, that the health care decision is not reasonable and informed.

(v) Nothing in Subsection (1)(s)(iv) may prohibit a parent or guardian from exercising the right to obtain a second health care opinion.

(t) "Nonjudicial adjustment" means closure of the case by the assigned probation officer without judicial determination upon the consent in writing of the minor, the parent, legal guardian or custodian, and the assigned probation officer.

(u) "Probation" means a legal status created by court order following an adjudication on the ground of a violation of law or under Section 78-3a-104, whereby the minor is permitted to remain in the minor's home under prescribed conditions and under supervision by the probation department or other agency designated by the court, subject to return to the court for violation of any of the conditions prescribed.

(v) "Protective supervision" means a legal status created by court order following an adjudication on the ground of abuse, neglect, or dependency, whereby the minor is permitted to remain in the minor's home, and supervision and assistance to correct the abuse, neglect, or dependency is provided by the probation department or other agency designated by the court.

(w) (i) "Residual parental rights and duties" means those rights and duties remaining with the parent after legal custody or guardianship, or both, have been vested in another person or agency, including:

(A) the responsibility for support;

(B) the right to consent to adoption;

(C) the right to determine the child's religious affiliation; and

(D) the right to reasonable parent-time unless restricted by the court.

(ii) If no guardian has been appointed, "residual parental rights and duties" also include the right to consent to:

(A) marriage;

(B) enlistment; and

(C) major medical, surgical, or psychiatric treatment.

(x) "Secure facility" means any facility operated by or under contract with the Division of Juvenile Justice Services, that provides 24-hour supervision and confinement for youth offenders committed to the division for custody and rehabilitation.

(y) "Shelter" means the temporary care of minors in physically unrestricted facilities pending court disposition or transfer to another jurisdiction.

(z) "State supervision" means a disposition that provides a more intensive level of intervention than standard probation but is less intensive or restrictive than a community placement with the Division of Juvenile Justice Services.

(aa) "Substantiated" has the same meaning as defined in Subsection 62A-4a-101(29).

(bb) "Supported" has the same meaning as defined in Subsection 62A-4a-101(31).

(cc) "Termination of parental rights" means the permanent elimination of all parental rights and duties, including residual parental rights and duties, by court order.

(dd) "Therapist" means a person employed by a state division or agency for the purpose of conducting psychological treatment and counseling of a minor in its custody, or any other person licensed or approved by the state for the purpose of conducting psychological treatment and counseling.

(ee) "Unsubstantiated" has the same meaning as defined in Subsection 62A-4a-101(34).

(ff) "Without merit" has the same meaning as defined in Subsection 62A-4a-101(36).

(2) As used in Part 3, Abuse, Neglect, and Dependency Proceedings, with regard to the Division of Child and Family Services:

(a) "Custody" means the custody of a minor in the Division of Child and Family Services as of the date of disposition.

(b) "Protective custody" means the shelter of a minor by the Division of Child and Family Services from the time the minor is removed from home until the earlier of:

(i) the shelter hearing; or

(ii) the minor's return home.

(c) "Temporary custody" means the custody of a minor in the Division of Child and Family Services from the date of the shelter hearing until disposition.   2005

78-3a-104. Jurisdiction of juvenile court — Original — Exclusive.

(1) Except as otherwise provided by law, the juvenile court has exclusive original jurisdiction in proceedings concerning:

(a) a minor who has violated any federal, state, or local law or municipal ordinance or a person younger than 21 years of age who has violated any law or ordinance before becoming 18 years of age, regardless of where the violation occurred, excluding traffic laws and boating and ordinances;

(b) a person 21 years of age or older who has failed or refused to comply with an order of the juvenile court to pay a fine or restitution, if the order was imposed prior to the person's 21st birthday; however, the continuing jurisdiction is limited to causing compliance with existing orders;

(c) a minor who is an abused child, neglected child, or dependent child, as those terms are defined in Section 78-3a-103;

(d) a protective order for a minor pursuant to the provisions of Title 78, Chapter 3h, Child Protective Orders, which the juvenile court may transfer to the district court if the juvenile court has entered an ex parte protective order and finds that:

(i) the petitioner and the respondent are the natural parent, adoptive parent, or step parent of the child who is the object of the petition;

(ii) the district court has a petition pending or an order related to custody or parent-time entered under Title 30, Chapter 3, Divorce, Title 30, Chapter 6, Cohabitant Abuse Act, or Title 78, Chapter 45a, Uniform Act on Paternity, in which the petitioner and the respondent are parties; and

(iii) the best interests of the child will be better served in the district court;

(e) appointment of a guardian of the person or other guardian of a minor who comes within the court's jurisdiction under other provisions of this section;

(f) the termination of the legal parent-child relationship in accordance with Part 4, Termination of Parental Rights Act, including termination of residual parental rights and duties;

(g) the treatment or commitment of a mentally retarded minor;

(h) a minor who is a habitual truant from school;

(i) the judicial consent to the marriage of a minor under age 16 upon a determination of voluntariness or where otherwise required by law, employment, or enlistment of a minor when consent is required by law;

(j) any parent or parents of a minor committed to a secure youth corrections facility, to order, at the discretion of the court and on the recommendation of a secure youth corrections facility, the parent or parents of a minor committed to a secure youth corrections facility for a custodial term, to undergo group rehabilitation therapy under the direction of a secure youth corrections facility therapist, who has supervision of that parent's or parents' minor, or any other therapist the court may direct, for a period directed by the court as recommended by a secure youth corrections facility;

(k) a minor under Title 55, Chapter 12, Interstate Compact on Juveniles;

(l) the treatment or commitment of a mentally ill child. The court may commit a child to the physical custody of a local mental health authority in accordance with the procedures and requirements of Title 62A, Chapter 15, Part 7, Commitment of Persons Under Age 18 to Division of Substance Abuse and Mental Health. The court may not commit a child directly to the Utah State Hospital;

(m) the commitment of a minor in accordance with Section 62A-15-301;

(n) de novo review of final agency actions resulting from an informal adjudicative proceeding as provided in Section 63-46b-15; and

(o) adoptions conducted in accordance with the procedures described in Title 78, Chapter 30, Adoption, when the juvenile court has previously entered an order terminating the rights of a parent and finds that adoption is in the best interest of the minor.

(2) In addition to the provisions of Subsection (1)(a) the juvenile court has exclusive jurisdiction over any traffic or boating offense committed by a minor under 16 years of age and concurrent jurisdiction over all other traffic or boating offenses committed by a minor 16 years of age or older, except that the court shall have exclusive jurisdiction over the following offenses committed by a minor under 18 years of age:

(a) Section 76-5-207, automobile homicide;

(b) Section 41-6a-502, operating a vehicle while under the influence of alcohol or drugs;

(c) Section 41-6a-528, reckless driving or Section 73-18-12, reckless operation;

(d) Section 41-1a-1314, unauthorized control over a motor vehicle, trailer, or semitrailer for an extended period of time; and

(e) Section 41-6a-206 or 73-18-20, fleeing a peace officer.

(3) The court also has jurisdiction over traffic and boating offenses that are part of a single criminal episode filed in a petition that contains an offense over which the court has jurisdiction.

(4) The juvenile court has jurisdiction over an ungovernable or runaway minor who is referred to it by the Division of Child and Family Services or by public or private agencies that contract with the division to provide services to that minor where, despite earnest and persistent efforts by the division or agency, the minor has demonstrated that he:

(a) is beyond the control of his parent, guardian, lawful custodian, or school authorities to the extent that his behavior or condition endangers his own welfare or the welfare of others; or

(b) has run away from home.

(5) This section does not restrict the right of access to the juvenile court by private agencies or other persons.

(6) The juvenile court has jurisdiction of all magistrate functions relative to cases arising under Section 78-3a-602.

(7) The juvenile court has jurisdiction to make a finding of substantiated, unsubstantiated, or without merit, in accordance with Section 78-3a-320.   2005

78-3a-105. Concurrent jurisdiction — District court and juvenile court.

(1) The district court or other court has concurrent jurisdiction with the juvenile court as follows:

(a) when a person who is 18 years of age or older and who is under the continuing jurisdiction of the juvenile court under Section 78-3a-118 violates any federal, state, or local law or municipal ordinance; and

(b) in establishing paternity and ordering testing for the purposes of establishing paternity, in accordance with Title 78, Chapter 45a, Uniform Act on Paternity, with regard to proceedings initiated under Part 3, Abuse, Neglect, and Dependency Proceedings, or Part 4, Termination of Parental Rights Act.

(2) The juvenile court has jurisdiction over petitions to modify a minor's birth certificate if the court otherwise has jurisdiction over the minor.

(3) This section does not deprive the district court of jurisdiction to appoint a guardian for a minor, or to determine the support, custody, and parent-time of a minor upon writ of habeas corpus or when the question of support, custody, and parent-time is incidental to the determination of a cause in the district court.

(4) (a) Where a support, custody, or parent-time award has been made by a district court in a divorce action or other proceeding, and the jurisdiction of the district court in the case is continuing, the juvenile court may acquire jurisdiction in a case involving the same minor if the minor is dependent, abused, neglected, or otherwise comes within the jurisdiction of the juvenile court under Section 78-3a-104.

(b) The juvenile court may, by order, change the custody, subject to Subsection 30-3-10(4), support, parent-time, and visitation rights previously ordered in the district court as necessary to implement the order of the juvenile court for the safety and welfare of the minor. The juvenile court order remains in effect so long as the jurisdiction of the juvenile court continues.

(c) When a copy of the findings and order of the juvenile court has been filed with the district court, the findings and order of the juvenile court are binding on the parties to the divorce action as though entered in the district court.

(5) The juvenile court has jurisdiction over questions of custody, support, and parent-time, of a minor who comes within the court's jurisdiction under this section or Section 78-3a-104.   2004

78-3a-106. Search warrants and subpoenas — Authority to issue.

(1) The court has authority to issue search warrants, subpoenas, or investigative subpoenas in criminal cases, delinquency, and abuse, neglect, and dependency proceedings for the same purposes, in the same manner and pursuant to the same procedures set forth in the code of criminal procedure for the issuance of search warrants, subpoenas, or investigative subpoenas in other trial courts in the state.

(2) (a) The court may issue a warrant authorizing a child protective services worker or peace officer to search for a child and take the child into protective custody if it appears to the court upon a verified petition, recorded sworn testimony or an affidavit sworn to by a peace officer or any other person, and upon the examination of other witnesses, if required by the judge, that there is probable cause to believe that:

(i) there is an immediate threat to the safety of a child; and

(ii) the applicant certifies to the court in writing or by recorded sworn testimony as to the efforts, if any, that have been made to give notice to the minor's parent or guardian and the reasons supporting the claim that notice and an opportunity to be heard should not be required.

(b) A warrant removing a child from his home or school, or having the effect of depriving a parent or guardian of the care, custody, and control of their minor child, may not be issued without notice to the minor's parents and opportunity to be heard unless the requirements of Subsections (2)(a)(i) and (ii) have been satisfied.

(c) Pursuant to Section 77-23-210, a peace officer making the search may enter a house or premises by force, if necessary, in order to remove the child.

(d) The person executing the warrant shall then take the child to the place of shelter designated by the court.

(3) The parent or guardian to be notified must be the minor's primary caregiver, or the person who has custody of the minor, when the order is sought.   2003

78-3a-107. Judges of juvenile court — Appointments — Terms.

(1) Judges of the juvenile court shall be appointed initially to serve until the first general election held more than three years after the effective date of the appointment. Thereafter, the term of office of a judge of a juvenile court is six years and commences on the first Monday in January next following the date of election.

(2) A judge whose term expires may serve, upon request of the Judicial Council, until a successor is appointed and qualified.   1996

78-3a-108. Sessions of juvenile court.

(1) In each county, regular juvenile court sessions shall be held at a place designated by the judge or judges of the juvenile court district, with the approval of the board.

(2) Court sessions shall be held in each county when the presiding judge of the juvenile court directs, except that a judge of the district may hold court in any county within the district at any time, if required by the urgency of the case.   1996

78-3a-109. Title of petition and other court documents — Form and contents of petition — Order for temporary custody — Physical or psychological examination of minor, parent, or guardian — Dismissal of petition.

(1) The petition and all subsequent court documents in the proceeding shall be entitled:

"State of Utah, in the interest of ...., a person under 18 years of age (or a person under 21 years of age)."

(2) The petition shall be verified and statements in the petition may be made upon information and belief.

(3) The petition shall be written in simple and brief language and include the facts which bring the minor within the jurisdiction of the court, as provided in Section 78-3a-104.

(4) The petition shall further state:

(a) the name, age, and residence of the minor;

(b) the names and residences of the minor's parents;

(c) the name and residence of the guardian, if there is one;

(d) the name and address of the nearest known relative, if no parent or guardian is known; and

(e) the name and residence of the person having physical custody of the minor. If any of the

facts required are not known by the petitioner, the petition shall so state.

(5) At any time after a petition is filed, the court may make an order providing for temporary custody of the minor.

(6) The court may order that a minor concerning whom a petition has been filed shall be examined by a physician, surgeon, psychiatrist, or psychologist and may place the minor in a hospital or other facility for examination. After notice and a hearing set for the specific purpose, the court may order a similar examination of a parent or guardian whose ability to care for a minor is at issue, if the court finds from the evidence presented at the hearing that the parent's or guardian's physical, mental, or emotional condition may be a factor in causing the neglect, dependency, or delinquency of the minor.

(7) Pursuant to Rule 506(d)(3), Utah Rules of Evidence, examinations conducted pursuant to Subsection (6) are not privileged communications, but are exempt from the general rule of privilege.

(8) The court may dismiss a petition at any stage of the proceedings.

(9) If the petition is filed under Section 78-3a-305 or 78-3a-405 or if the matter is referred to the court under Subsection 78-3a-105(5):

(a) the court may require the parties to participate in mediation in accordance with Title 78, Chapter 31b, Alternative Dispute Resolution; and

(b) the Division of Child and Family Services or a party to the petition may request and the court may order the parties to participate in a family unity conference under the authority of the Division of Child and Family Services in accordance with Subsection (10).

(10) (a) A family unity conference may be ordered by the court for any of the following purposes:

(i) discussing and reviewing the case history;

(ii) designing a service plan for the child and family, including concurrent planning;

(iii) discussing a visitation schedule and rules for visitation;

(iv) identifying possible kinship placements under the requirements of Subsection 78-3a-307(5), and designing services to support the kinship placement;

(v) conflict resolution between the family and Division of Child and Family Services staff;

(vi) discussing child custody issues; or

(vii) crisis clinical intervention to reduce trauma to the child and family.

(b) The family unity conference may be attended by individuals chosen by the family and the Division of Child and Family Services, and may include extended family members, friends, clergy, service providers, and others who may support the family in keeping the child safe.

(c) A family unity conference may not be held in the following circumstances:

(i) when there is a criminal charge pending in the case;

(ii) to resolve petition disputes; and

(iii) when a family unity conference may pose a threat to the safety of a child or other family member.

(d) With regard to a family unity conference ordered by a court under Subsection (9)(b):

(i) the requirements of Subsection 78-31b-7(3)(b) apply except all parties to the proceeding:

    (A) shall be given no less than five days notice of any recommendation made to the court from the family unity conference; and

    (B) shall be given an opportunity to be heard by the court; and

  (ii) the confidentiality requirements of Section 78-31b-8 apply, except that admissions by a party to the allegations on the petition are admissible at any proceeding.

2005

78-3a-110. Summons — Service and process — Issuance and contents — Notice to absent parent or guardian — Emergency medical or surgical treatment — Compulsory process for attendance of witnesses when authorized.

(1) After a petition is filed the court shall promptly issue a summons, unless the judge directs that a further investigation is needed. No summons is required as to any person who appears voluntarily or who files a written waiver of service with the clerk of the court at or prior to the hearing.

(2) The summons shall contain:

  (a) the name of the court;

  (b) the title of the proceedings; and

  (c) except for a published summons, a brief statement of the substance of the allegations in the petition.

(3) A published summons shall state:

  (a) that a proceeding concerning the minor is pending in the court; and

  (b) an adjudication will be made.

(4) The summons shall require the person or persons who have physical custody of the minor to appear personally and bring the minor before the court at a time and place stated. If the person or persons summoned are not the parent, parents, or guardian of the minor, the summons shall also be issued to the parent, parents, or guardian, as the case may be, notifying them of the pendency of the case and of the time and place set for the hearing.

(5) Summons may be issued requiring the appearance of any other person whose presence the court finds necessary.

(6) If it appears to the court that the welfare of the minor or of the public requires that the minor be taken into custody, the court may by endorsement upon the summons direct that the person serving the summons take the minor into custody at once.

(7) Upon the sworn testimony of one or more reputable physicians, the court may order emergency medical or surgical treatment that is immediately necessary for a minor concerning whom a petition has been filed pending the service of summons upon his parents, guardian, or custodian.

(8) A parent or guardian is entitled to the issuance of compulsory process for the attendance of witnesses on his own behalf or on behalf of the minor. A guardian ad litem or a probation officer is entitled to compulsory process for the attendance of witnesses on behalf of the minor.

(9) Service of summons and process and proof of service shall be made in the manner provided in the Utah Rules of Civil Procedure.

(10) Service of summons or process shall be made by the sheriff of the county where the service is to be made, or by his deputy; but upon request of the court service shall be made by any other peace officer, or by another suitable person selected by the court.

(11) Service of summons in the state shall be made personally, by delivering a copy to the person summoned; provided, however, that parents of a minor living together at their usual place of abode may both be served by personal delivery to either parent of copies of the summons, one copy for each parent.

(12) If the judge makes a written finding that he has reason to believe that personal service of the summons will be unsuccessful, or will not accomplish notification within a reasonable time after issuance of the summons, he may order service by registered mail, with a return receipt to be signed by the addressee only, to be addressed to the last-known address of the person to be served in the state. Service shall be complete upon return to the court of the signed receipt.

(13) If the parents, parent, or guardian required to be summoned under Subsection (4) cannot be found within the state, the fact of their minor's presence within the state shall confer jurisdiction on the court in proceedings in minor's cases under this chapter as to any absent parent or guardian, provided that due notice has been given in the following manner:

  (a) If the address of the parent or guardian is known, due notice is given by sending him a copy of the summons by registered mail with a return receipt to be signed by the addressee only, or by personal service outside the state, as provided in the Utah Rules of Civil Procedure. Service by registered mail shall be complete upon return to the court of the signed receipt.

  (b) If the address or whereabouts of the parent or guardian outside the state cannot after diligent inquiry be ascertained, due notice is given by publishing a summons in a newspaper having general circulation in the county in which the proceeding is pending. The summons shall be published once a week for four successive weeks. Service shall be complete on the day of the last publication.

  (c) Service of summons as provided in this subsection shall vest the court with jurisdiction over the parent or guardian served in the same manner and to the same extent as if the person served was served personally within the state.

(14) In the case of service in the state, service completed not less than 48 hours before the time set in the summons for the appearance of the person served, shall be sufficient to confer jurisdiction. In the case of service outside the state, service completed not less than five days before the time set in the summons for appearance of the person served, shall be sufficient to confer jurisdiction.

(15) Computation of periods of time under this chapter shall be made in accordance with the Utah Rules of Civil Procedure. 1997

78-3a-111. Venue — Transfer or certification to other districts — Dismissal without adjudication on merits.

(1) Proceedings in minor's cases shall be commenced in the court of the district in which the minor is living or is found, or in which an alleged violation of law or ordinance occurred.

(2) After the filing of a petition, the court may transfer the case to the district where the minor resides or to the district where the violation of law or ordinance is alleged to have occurred. The court may, in its discretion, after adjudication certify the case for disposition to the court of the district in which the minor resides.

(3) The transferring or certifying court shall transmit all documents and legal and social records, or certified copies to the receiving court, and the receiving court shall proceed with the case as if the petition had been originally filed or the adjudication had been originally made in that court.

(4) The dismissal of a petition in one district where the dismissal is without prejudice and where there has been no adjudication upon the merits shall not preclude refiling within the same district or another district where there is venue of the case.   1997

78-3a-112. Appearances — Parents to appear with minor — Failure to appear — Contempt — Warrant of arrest, when authorized — Parent's employer to grant time off — Appointment of guardian ad litem.

(1) Any person required to appear who, without reasonable cause, fails to appear may be proceeded against for contempt of court, and the court may cause a bench warrant to issue to produce the person in court.

(2) In all cases when a minor is required to appear in court, the parents, guardian, or other person with legal custody of the minor shall appear with the minor unless excused by the judge.

(a) An employee may request permission to leave the workplace for the purpose of attending court if the employee has been notified by the juvenile court that his minor is required to appear before the court.

(b) An employer must grant permission to leave the workplace with or without pay if the employee has requested permission at least seven days in advance or within 24 hours of the employee receiving notice of the hearing.

(3) If a parent or other person who signed a written promise to appear and bring the minor to court under Section 78-3a-113 or 78-3a-114, fails to appear and bring the minor to court on the date set in the promise, or, if the date was to be set, after notification by the court, a warrant may be issued for the apprehension of that person or the minor, or both.

(4) Willful failure to perform the promise is a misdemeanor if, at the time of the execution of the promise, the promisor is given a copy of the promise which clearly states that failure to appear and have the minor appear as promised is a misdemeanor. The juvenile court shall have jurisdiction to proceed against the promisor in adult proceedings pursuant to Part 8, Adult Offenses.

(5) The court shall endeavor, through use of the warrant of arrest if necessary, as provided in Subsection (6), or by other means, to ensure the presence at all hearings of one or both parents or of the guardian of the minor. If neither a parent nor guardian is present at the court proceedings, the court may appoint a guardian ad litem to protect the interest of the minor. A guardian ad litem may also be appointed whenever necessary for the welfare of the minor, whether or not a parent or guardian is present.

(6) A warrant may be issued for the parent, the guardian, the custodian, or the minor if:

(a) a summons is issued but cannot be served;

(b) it is made to appear to the court that the person to be served will not obey the summons;

(c) serving the summons will be ineffectual; or

(d) the welfare of the minor requires that he be brought immediately into the custody of the court.   1997

78-3a-113. Minor taken into custody by peace officer, private citizen, or probation officer — Grounds — Notice requirements — Release or detention — Grounds for peace officer to take adult into custody.

(1) A minor may be taken into custody by a peace officer without order of the court if:

(a) in the presence of the officer the minor has violated a state law, federal law, local law, or municipal ordinance;

(b) there are reasonable grounds to believe the minor has committed an act which if committed by an adult would be a felony;

(c) the minor is seriously endangered in his surroundings or if the minor seriously endangers others, and immediate removal appears to be necessary for his protection or the protection of others;

(d) there are reasonable grounds to believe the minor has run away or escaped from his parents, guardian, or custodian; or

(e) there is reason to believe the minor is subject to the state's compulsory education law and that the minor is absent from school without legitimate or valid excuse, subject to Section 53A-11-105.

(2) (a) A private citizen or a probation officer may take a minor into custody if under the circumstances he could make a citizen's arrest if the minor was an adult.

(b) A probation officer may also take a minor into custody under Subsection (1) or if the minor has violated the conditions of probation, if the minor is under the continuing jurisdiction of the juvenile court or in emergency situations in which a peace officer is not immediately available.

(3) (a) (i) If an officer or other person takes a minor into temporary custody, he shall without unnecessary delay notify the parents, guardian, or custodian.

(ii) The minor shall then be released to the care of his parent or other responsible adult, unless his immediate welfare or the protection of the community requires his detention.

(b) If the minor is taken into custody or detention for a violent felony, as defined in Section 76-3-203.5, or an offense in violation of Title 76, Chapter 10, Part 5, Weapons, the officer or other law enforcement agent taking the minor into custody shall, as soon as practicable or as established under Subsection 53A-11-1001(2), notify the school superintendent of the district in which the minor resides or attends school for the purposes of the minor's supervision and student safety.

(i) The notice shall disclose only:

(A) the name of the minor;

(B) the offense for which the minor was taken into custody or detention; and

(C) if available, the name of the victim, if the victim:

(I) resides in the same school district as the minor; or

(II) attends the same school as the minor.

(ii) The notice shall be classified as a protected record under Section 63-2-304.

(iii) All other records disclosures are governed by Title 63, Chapter 2, Government Records Access and Management Act and the

Federal Family Educational Rights and Privacy Act.

(c) Employees of a governmental agency are immune from any criminal liability for providing or failing to provide the information required by this section unless the person acts or fails to act due to malice, gross negligence, or deliberate indifference to the consequences.

(d) Before the minor is released, the parent or other person to whom the minor is released shall be required to sign a written promise on forms supplied by the court to bring the minor to the court at a time set or to be set by the court.

(4) (a) A minor may not be held in temporary custody by law enforcement any longer than is reasonably necessary to obtain his name, age, residence, and other necessary information and to contact his parents, guardian, or custodian.

(b) If the minor is not released under Subsection (3), he shall be taken to a place of detention or shelter without unnecessary delay.

(5) (a) The person who takes a minor to a detention or shelter facility shall promptly file with the detention or shelter facility a written report on a form provided by the division stating the details of the presently alleged offense, the facts which bring the minor within the jurisdiction of the juvenile court, and the reason the minor was not released by law enforcement.

(b) (i) The designated youth corrections facility staff person shall immediately review the form and determine, based on the guidelines for detention admissions established by the Division of Juvenile Justice Services under Section 62A-7-202, whether to admit the minor to secure detention, admit the minor to home detention, place the minor in a placement other than detention, or return the minor home upon written promise to bring the minor to the court at a time set, or without restriction.

(ii) If the designated youth corrections facility staff person determines to admit the minor to home detention, that staff person shall notify the juvenile court of that determination. The court shall order that notice be provided to the designated persons in the local law enforcement agency and the school or transferee school, if applicable, which the minor attends of the home detention. The designated persons may receive the information for purposes of the minor's supervision and student safety.

(iii) Any employee of the local law enforcement agency and the school which the minor attends who discloses the notification of home detention is not:

(A) civilly liable except when disclosure constitutes fraud or willful misconduct as provided in Section 63-30d-202; and

(B) civilly or criminally liable except when disclosure constitutes a knowing violation of Section 63-2-801.

(c) A minor may not be admitted to detention unless the minor is detainable based on the guidelines or the minor has been brought to detention pursuant to a judicial order or division warrant pursuant to Section 62A-7-504.

(d) If a minor taken to detention does not qualify for admission under the guidelines established by the division under Sections 62A-7-104

and 62A-7-205, detention staff shall arrange appropriate placement.

(e) If a minor is taken into custody and admitted to a secure detention or shelter facility, facility staff shall immediately notify the minor's parents, guardian, or custodian and shall promptly notify the court of the placement.

(f) If the minor is admitted to a secure detention or shelter facility outside the county of his residence and it is determined in the hearing held under Subsection 78-3a-114(3) that detention shall continue, the judge or commissioner shall direct the sheriff of the county of the minor's residence to transport the minor to a detention or shelter facility as provided in this section.

(6) A person may be taken into custody by a peace officer without a court order if the person is in apparent violation of a protective order or if there is reason to believe that a minor is being abused by the person and any of the situations outlined in Section 77-7-2 exist.   2005

78-3a-114. Placement of minor in detention or shelter facility — Grounds — Detention hearings — Period of detention — Notice — Confinement of minors for criminal proceedings — Bail laws inapplicable, exception.

(1) (a) A minor may not be placed or kept in a secure detention facility pending court proceedings unless it is unsafe for the public to leave the minor with his parents, guardian, or custodian and the minor is detainable based on guidelines promulgated by the Division of Juvenile Justice Services.

(b) A minor who must be taken from his home but who does not require physical restriction shall be given temporary care in a shelter facility and may not be placed in a detention facility.

(c) A minor may not be placed or kept in a shelter facility pending court proceedings unless it is unsafe for the minor to leave him with his parents, guardian, or custodian.

(2) After admission to a detention facility pursuant to the guidelines established by the Division of Juvenile Justice Services and immediate investigation by an authorized officer of the court, the judge or the officer shall order the release of the minor to his parents, guardian, or custodian if it is found he can be safely returned to their care, either upon written promise to bring the minor to the court at a time set or without restriction.

(a) If the minor's parent, guardian, or custodian fails to retrieve the minor from a facility within 24 hours after notification of release, the parent, guardian, or custodian is responsible for the cost of care for the time the minor remains in the facility.

(b) The facility shall determine the cost of care.

(c) Any money collected under this Subsection (2) shall be retained by the Division of Juvenile Justice Services to recover the cost of care for the time the minor remains in the facility.

(3) (a) When a minor is detained in a detention or shelter facility, the parents or guardian shall be informed by the person in charge of the facility that they have the right to a prompt hearing in court to determine whether the minor is to be further detained or released.

(b) Detention hearings shall be held by the judge or by a commissioner.

(c) The court may, at any time, order the release of the minor, whether a detention hearing is held or not.

(d) If the minor is released, and the minor remains in the facility, because the parents, guardian, or custodian fails to retrieve the minor, the parents, guardian, or custodian shall be responsible for the cost of care as provided in Subsections (2)(a), (b), and (c).

(4) (a) A minor may not be held in a detention facility longer than 48 hours prior to a detention hearing, excluding weekends and holidays, unless the court has entered an order for continued detention.

(b) A minor may not be held in a shelter facility longer than 48 hours prior to a shelter hearing, excluding weekends and holidays, unless a court order for extended shelter has been entered by the court after notice to all parties described in Section 78-3a-306.

(c) A hearing for detention or shelter may not be waived. Detention staff shall provide the court with all information received from the person who brought the minor to the detention facility.

(d) If the court finds at a detention hearing that it is not safe to release the minor, the judge or commissioner may order the minor to be held in the facility or be placed in another appropriate facility, subject to further order of the court.

(e) (i) After a detention hearing has been held, only the court may release a minor from detention. If a minor remains in a detention facility, periodic reviews shall be held pursuant to the Utah State Juvenile Court Rules of Practice and Procedure to ensure that continued detention is necessary.

(ii) After a detention hearing for a violent felony, as defined in Section 76-3-203.5, or an offense in violation of Title 76, Chapter 10, Part 5, Weapons, the court shall direct that notice of its decision, including any disposition, order, or no contact orders, be provided to designated persons in the appropriate local law enforcement agency and district superintendent or the school or transferee school, if applicable, which the minor attends. The designated persons may receive the information for purposes of the minor's supervision and student safety.

(iii) Any employee of the local law enforcement agency, school district, and the school which the minor attends who discloses the court's order of probation is not:

(A) civilly liable except when the disclosure constitutes fraud or willful misconduct as provided in Section 63-30d-202; and

(B) civilly or criminally liable except when disclosure constitutes a knowing violation of Section 63-2-801.

(5) A minor may not be held in a detention facility, following a dispositional order of the court for nonsecure substitute care as defined in Section 62A-4a-101, or for community-based placement under Section 62A-7-101 for longer than 72 hours, excluding weekends and holidays. The period of detention may be extended by the court for one period of seven calendar days if:

(a) the Division of Juvenile Justice Services or another agency responsible for placement files a written petition with the court requesting the extension and setting forth good cause; and

(b) the court enters a written finding that it is in the best interests of both the minor and the community to extend the period of detention.

(6) The agency requesting an extension shall promptly notify the detention facility that a written petition has been filed.

(7) The court shall promptly notify the detention facility regarding its initial disposition and any ruling on a petition for an extension, whether granted or denied.

(8) (a) A minor under 16 years of age may not be held in a jail, lockup, or other place for adult detention except as provided by Section 62A-7-201 or unless certified as an adult pursuant to Section 78-3a-603. The provisions of Section 62A-7-201 regarding confinement facilities apply to this Subsection (8).

(b) A minor 16 years of age or older whose conduct or condition endangers the safety or welfare of others in the detention facility for minors may, by court order that specifies the reasons, be detained in another place of confinement considered appropriate by the court, including a jail or other place of confinement for adults. However, a secure youth corrections facility is not an appropriate place of confinement for detention purposes under this section.

(9) A sheriff, warden, or other official in charge of a jail or other facility for the detention of adult offenders or persons charged with crime shall immediately notify the juvenile court when a minor who is or appears to be under 18 years of age is received at the facility and shall make arrangements for the transfer of the minor to a detention facility, unless otherwise ordered by the juvenile court.

(10) This section does not apply to a minor who is brought to the adult facility under charges pursuant to Section 78-3a-602 or by order of the juvenile court to be held for criminal proceedings in the district court under Section 78-3a-603.

(11) A minor held for criminal proceedings under Section 78-3a-602 or 78-3a-603 may be detained in a jail or other place of detention used for adults charged with crime.

(12) Provisions of law regarding bail are not applicable to minors detained or taken into custody under this chapter, except that bail may be allowed:

(a) if a minor who need not be detained lives outside this state; or

(b) when a minor who need not be detained comes within one of the classes in Subsection 78-3a-503(11).

(13) Section 76-8-418 is applicable to a minor who willfully and intentionally commits an act against a jail or other place of confinement, including a Division of Juvenile Justice Services detention, shelter, or secure confinement facility which would be a third degree felony if committed by an adult. 2004

78-3a-115. Hearings — Public excluded, exceptions — Victims admitted — Minor's cases heard separately from adult cases — Minor or parents or custodian heard separately — Continuance of hearing — Consolidation of proceedings involving more than one minor.

(1) Hearings in minor's cases shall be held before the court without a jury and may be conducted in an informal manner.

(a) In abuse, neglect, and dependency cases in all districts other than pilot districts selected by the Judicial Council under Subsection 78-3-

21(15)(a), the court shall exclude the general public from hearings held prior to July 1, 2004.

(b) In delinquency cases the court shall admit all persons who have a direct interest in the case and may admit persons requested by the parent or legal guardian to be present. The court shall exclude all other persons except as provided in Subsection (1)(c).

(c) In delinquency cases in which the minor charged is 14 years of age or older, the court shall admit any person unless the hearing is closed by the court upon findings on the record for good cause if:

(i) the minor has been charged with an offense which would be a felony if committed by an adult; or

(ii) the minor is charged with an offense that would be a class A or B misdemeanor if committed by an adult, and the minor has been previously charged with an offense which would be a misdemeanor or felony if committed by an adult.

(d) The victim of any act charged in a petition or information involving an offense committed by a minor which if committed by an adult would be a felony or a class A or class B misdemeanor shall, upon request, be afforded all rights afforded victims in Title 77, Chapter 36, Cohabitant Abuse Procedures Act, Title 77, Chapter 37, Victims' Rights, and Title 77, Chapter 38, Rights of Crime Victims Act. The notice provisions in Section 77-38-3 do not apply to important juvenile justice hearings as defined in Section 77-38-2.

(e) A victim, upon request to appropriate juvenile court personnel, shall have the right to inspect and duplicate juvenile court legal records that have not been expunged concerning:

(i) the scheduling of any court hearings on the petition;

(ii) any findings made by the court; and

(iii) any sentence or decree imposed by the court.

(2) Minor's cases shall be heard separately from adult cases. The minor or the minor's parents or custodian may be heard separately when considered necessary by the court. The hearing may be continued from time to time to a date specified by court order.

(3) When more than one minor is involved in a home situation which may be found to constitute neglect or dependency, or when more than one minor is alleged to be involved in the same law violation, the proceedings may be consolidated, except that separate hearings may be held with respect to disposition.

2004

78-3a-115.1. Access to abuse, neglect, and dependency hearings.

(1) This section applies:

(a) beginning November 1, 2003, to districts selected by the Judicial Council as pilot districts under Subsection 78-3-21(15)(a); and

(b) beginning July 1, 2004, to all other districts.

(2) (a) In abuse, neglect, and dependency cases the court shall admit any person to a hearing, including a hearing under Subsection 78-3a-320(3), unless the court makes a finding upon the record that the person's presence at the hearing would:

(i) be detrimental to the best interest of a child who is a party to the proceeding;

(ii) impair the fact-finding process; or

(iii) be otherwise contrary to the interests of justice.

(b) The court may exclude a person from a hearing under Subsection (2)(a) on its own motion or by motion of a party to the proceeding.   2004

78-3a-116. Hearings — Record — County attorney or district attorney responsibilities — Attorney general responsibilities — Disclosure — Admissibility of evidence.

(1) (a) A verbatim record of the proceedings shall be taken by an official court reporter or by means of a mechanical recording device in all cases that might result in deprivation of custody as defined in this chapter. In all other cases a verbatim record shall also be made unless dispensed with by the court.

(b) (i) Notwithstanding any other provision, including Title 63, Chapter 2, Government Records Access and Management Act, a record of a proceeding made under Subsection (1)(a) shall be released by the court to any person upon a finding on the record for good cause.

(ii) Following a petition for a record of a proceeding made under Subsection (1)(a), the court shall:

(A) provide notice to all subjects of the record that a request for release of the record has been made; and

(B) allow sufficient time for the subjects of the record to respond before making a finding on the petition.

(iii) A record of a proceeding may not be released under this Subsection (1)(b) if the court's jurisdiction over the subjects of the proceeding ended more than 12 months prior to the request.

(iv) For purposes of this Subsection (1)(b):

(A) "record of a proceeding" does not include documentary materials of any type submitted to the court as part of the proceeding, including items submitted under Subsection (4)(a); and

(B) "subjects of the record" includes the child's guardian ad litem, the child's legal guardian, the Division of Child and Family Services, and any other party to the proceeding.

(v) This Subsection (1)(b) applies:

(A) to records of proceedings made on or after November 1, 2003 in districts selected by the Judicial Council as pilot districts under Subsection 78-3-21(15)(a); and

(B) to records of proceedings made on or after July 1, 2004 in all other districts.

(2) (a) Except as provided in Subsection (2)(b), the county attorney or, if within a prosecution district, the district attorney shall represent the state in any proceeding in a minor's case.

(b) The attorney general shall enforce all provisions of Title 62A, Chapter 4a, Child and Family Services, and Title 78, Chapter 3a, Juvenile Courts, relating to:

(i) protection or custody of an abused, neglected, or dependent child; and

(ii) petitions for termination of parental rights.

(c) The attorney general shall represent the Division of Child and Family Services in actions involving minors who have not been adjudicated as abused or neglected, but who are otherwise committed to the custody of that division by the juvenile court, and who are classified in the division's management information system as having been placed in custody primarily on the basis of delinquent behavior or a status offense. Nothing in this Subsection (2)(c) may be construed to affect the responsibility of the county attorney or district attorney to represent the state in those matters, in accordance with the provisions of Subsection (2)(a).

(3) The board may adopt special rules of procedure to govern proceedings involving violations of traffic laws or ordinances, fish and game laws, and boating laws. However, proceedings involving offenses under Section 78-3a-506 are governed by that section regarding suspension of driving privileges.

(4) (a) For the purposes of determining proper disposition of the minor in dispositional hearings and establishing the fact of abuse, neglect, or dependency in adjudication hearings and in hearings upon petitions for termination of parental rights, written reports and other material relating to the minor's mental, physical, and social history and condition may be received in evidence and may be considered by the court along with other evidence. The court may require that the person who wrote the report or prepared the material appear as a witness if the person is reasonably available.

(b) For the purpose of determining proper disposition of a minor alleged to be or adjudicated as abused, neglected, or dependent, dispositional reports prepared by Foster Care Citizen Review Boards pursuant to Section 78-3g-103 may be received in evidence and may be considered by the court along with other evidence. The court may require any person who participated in preparing the dispositional report to appear as a witness, if the person is reasonably available.

(5) (a) In an abuse, neglect, or dependency proceeding occurring after the commencement of a shelter hearing under Section 78-3a-306 or the filing of a petition under Section 78-3a-305, each party to the proceeding shall provide in writing to the other parties or their counsel any information which the party:

(i) plans to report to the court at the proceeding; or

(ii) could reasonably expect would be requested of the party by the court at the proceeding.

(b) The disclosure required under Subsection (5)(a) shall be made:

(i) for dispositional hearings under Sections 78-3a-310 and 78-3a-311, no less than five days before the proceeding;

(ii) for proceedings under Title 78, Chapter 3a, Part 4, Termination of Parental Rights Act, in accordance with Utah Rules of Civil Procedure; and

(iii) for all other proceedings, no less than five days before the proceeding.

(c) If a party to a proceeding obtains information after the deadline in Subsection (5)(b), the information is exempt from the disclosure required under Subsection (5)(a) if the party certifies to the court that the information was obtained after the deadline.

(d) Subsection (5)(a) does not apply to:

(i) pretrial hearings; and

(ii) the frequent, periodic review hearings held in a dependency drug court case to assess and promote the parent's progress in substance abuse treatment.

(6) For the purpose of establishing the fact of abuse, neglect, or dependency, the court may, in its discretion, consider evidence of statements made by a minor under eight years of age to a person in a trust relationship. 2004

78-3a-117. Minor's cases considered civil proceedings — Adjudication of jurisdiction by juvenile court not conviction of crime, exceptions — Minor not to be charged with crime, exception — Traffic violation cases, abstracts to Department of Public Safety.

(1) Except as provided in Sections 78-3a-602 and 78-3a-603, proceedings in minor's cases shall be regarded as civil proceedings with the court exercising equitable powers.

(2) An adjudication by a juvenile court that a minor is within its jurisdiction under Section 78-3a-104 is not considered a conviction of a crime, except in cases involving traffic violations. An adjudication may not operate to impose any civil disabilities upon the minor nor to disqualify the minor for any civil service or military service or appointment.

(3) A minor may not be charged with a crime or convicted in any court except as provided in Sections 78-3a-602 and 78-3a-603, and in cases involving traffic violations. When a petition has been filed in the juvenile court, the minor may not later be subjected to criminal prosecution based on the same facts except as provided in Section 78-3a-602 or 78-3a-603.

(4) An adjudication by a juvenile court that a minor is within its jurisdiction under Section 78-3a-104 is considered a conviction for the purposes of determining the level of offense for which a juvenile may be charged and enhancing the level of an offense in the juvenile court. A prior adjudication may be used to enhance the level or degree of an offense committed by an adult only as otherwise specifically provided.

(5) Abstracts of court records for all adjudications of traffic violations shall be submitted to the Department of Public Safety as provided in Section 53-3-218.

(6) Information necessary to collect unpaid fines, fees, assessments, bail, or restitution may be forwarded to employers, financial institutions, law enforcement, constables, the Office of Recovery Services, or other agencies for purposes of enforcing the order as provided in Section 78-3a-118. 2000

78-3a-118. Adjudication of jurisdiction of juvenile court — Disposition of cases — Enumeration of possible court orders — Considerations of court — Obtaining DNA sample.

(1) (a) When a minor is found to come within the provisions of Section 78-3a-104, the court shall so adjudicate. The court shall make a finding of the facts upon which it bases its jurisdiction over the minor. However, in cases within the provisions of Subsection 78-3a-104(1), findings of fact are not necessary.

(b) If the court adjudicates a minor for a crime of violence or an offense in violation of Title 76, Chapter 10, Part 5, Weapons, it shall order that notice of the adjudication be provided to the school superintendent of the district in which the minor resides or attends school. Notice shall be made to the district superintendent within three days of the adjudication and shall include:

(i) the specific offenses for which the minor was adjudicated; and

(ii) if available, if the victim:

(A) resides in the same school district as the minor; or

(B) attends the same school as the minor.

(2) Upon adjudication the court may make the following dispositions by court order:

(a) (i) The court may place the minor on probation or under protective supervision in the minor's own home and upon conditions determined by the court, including compensatory service as provided in Section 78-11-20.7.

(ii) The court may place the minor in state supervision with the probation department of the court, under the legal custody of:

(A) his parent or guardian;

(B) the Division of Juvenile Justice Services; or

(C) the Division of Child and Family Services.

(iii) If the court orders probation or state supervision, the court shall direct that notice of its order be provided to designated persons in the local law enforcement agency and the school or transferee school, if applicable, which the minor attends. The designated persons may receive the information for purposes of the minor's supervision and student safety.

(iv) Any employee of the local law enforcement agency and the school which the minor attends who discloses the court's order of probation is not:

(A) civilly liable except when the disclosure constitutes fraud or willful misconduct as provided in Section 63-30d-202; and

(B) civilly or criminally liable except when the disclosure constitutes a knowing violation of Section 63-2-801.

(b) The court may place the minor in the legal custody of a relative or other suitable person, with or without probation or protective supervision, but the juvenile court may not assume the function of developing foster home services.

(c) (i) The court may:

(A) vest legal custody of the minor in the Division of Child and Family Services, Division of Juvenile Justice Services, or the Division of Substance Abuse and Mental Health; and

(B) order the Department of Human Services to provide dispositional recommendations and services.

(ii) For minors who may qualify for services from two or more divisions within the Department of Human Services, the court may vest legal custody with the department.

(iii) (A) Minors who are committed to the custody of the Division of Child and Family Services on grounds other than abuse or neglect are subject to the provisions of Title 78, Chapter 3a, Part 3A, Minors in Custody on Grounds Other Than Abuse or Neglect, and Title 62A, Chapter 4a, Part 2A, Minors in Custody on Grounds Other Than Abuse or Neglect.

(B) Prior to the court entering an order to place a minor in the custody of the Division of Child and Family Services on grounds other than abuse or neglect, the court shall provide the division with notice of the hearing no later than five days before the time specified for the hearing so the division may attend the hearing.

(C) Prior to committing a minor to the custody of the Division of Child and Family Services, the court shall make a finding as to what reasonable efforts have been attempted to prevent the minor's removal from his home.

(d) (i) The court may commit the minor to the Division of Juvenile Justice Services for secure confinement.

(ii) A minor under the jurisdiction of the court solely on the ground of abuse, neglect, or dependency under Subsection 78-3a-104(1)(c) may not be committed to the Division of Juvenile Justice Services.

(e) The court may commit the minor, subject to the court retaining continuing jurisdiction over him, to the temporary custody of the Division of Juvenile Justice Services for observation and evaluation for a period not to exceed 45 days, which period may be extended up to 15 days at the request of the director of the Division of Juvenile Justice Services.

(f) (i) The court may commit the minor to a place of detention or an alternative to detention for a period not to exceed 30 days subject to the court retaining continuing jurisdiction over the minor. This commitment may be stayed or suspended upon conditions ordered by the court.

(ii) This Subsection (2)(f) applies only to those minors adjudicated for:

(A) an act which if committed by an adult would be a criminal offense; or

(B) contempt of court under Section 78-3a-901.

(g) The court may vest legal custody of an abused, neglected, or dependent minor in the Division of Child and Family Services or any other appropriate person in accordance with the requirements and procedures of Title 78, Chapter 3a, Part 3, Abuse, Neglect, and Dependency Proceedings.

(h) The court may place the minor on a ranch or forestry camp, or similar facility for care and also for work, if possible, if the person, agency, or association operating the facility has been approved or has otherwise complied with all applicable state and local laws. A minor placed in a forestry camp or similar facility may be required to work on fire prevention, forestation and reforestation, recreational works, forest roads, and on other works on or off the grounds of the facility and may be paid wages, subject to the approval of and under conditions set by the court.

(i) (i) The court may order the minor to repair, replace, or otherwise make restitution for damage or loss caused by the minor's wrongful act, including costs of treatment as stated in Section 78-3a-318 and impose fines in limited amounts.

(ii) The court may also require the minor to reimburse an individual, entity, or governmental agency who offered and paid a reward to a person or persons for providing information resulting in a court adjudication that the minor is within the jurisdiction of the juvenile court due to the commission of a criminal offense.

(iii) If a minor has been returned to this state under the Interstate Compact on Juveniles, the court may order the minor to make restitution for costs expended by any governmental entity for the return.

(j) The court may issue orders necessary for the collection of restitution and fines ordered by the court, including garnishments, wage withholdings, and executions.

(k) (i) The court may through its probation department encourage the development of employment or work programs to enable minors to fulfill their obligations under Subsection (2)(i) and for other purposes considered desirable by the court.

(ii) Consistent with the order of the court, the probation officer may permit the minor found to be within the jurisdiction of the court to participate in a program of work restitution or compensatory service in lieu of paying part or all of the fine imposed by the court.

(l) (i) In violations of traffic laws within the court's jurisdiction, the court may, in addition to any other disposition authorized by this section:

(A) restrain the minor from driving for periods of time the court considers necessary; and

(B) take possession of the minor's driver license.

(ii) The court may enter any other disposition under Subsection (2)(l)(i); however, the suspension of driving privileges for an offense under Section 78-3a-506 are governed only by Section 78-3a-506.

(m) (i) When a minor is found within the jurisdiction of the juvenile court under Section 78-3a-104 because of violating Section 58-37-8, Title 58, Chapter 37a, Utah Drug Paraphernalia Act, or Title 58, Chapter 37b, Imitation Controlled Substances Act, the court shall, in addition to any fines or fees otherwise imposed, order that the minor perform a minimum of 20 hours, but no more than 100 hours, of compensatory service. Satisfactory completion of an approved substance abuse prevention or treatment program may be credited by the court as compensatory service hours.

(ii) When a minor is found within the jurisdiction of the juvenile court under Section 78-3a-104 because of a violation of Section 32A-12-209 or Subsection 76-9-701(1), the court may, upon the first adjudication, and shall, upon a second or subsequent adjudication, order that the minor perform a minimum of 20 hours, but no more than 100 hours of compensatory service, in addition to any fines or fees otherwise imposed. Satisfactory completion of an approved substance abuse prevention or treatment program may be credited by the court as compensatory service hours.

(n) The court may order that the minor be examined or treated by a physician, surgeon, psychiatrist, or psychologist or that he receive other special care. For these purposes the court may place the minor in a hospital or other suitable facility.

(o) (i) The court may appoint a guardian for the minor if it appears necessary in the interest of the minor, and may appoint as guardian a public or private institution or agency in which legal custody of the minor is vested.

(ii) In placing a minor under the guardianship or legal custody of an individual or of a private agency or institution, the court shall give primary consideration to the welfare of the minor. When practicable, the court may take into consideration the religious preferences of the minor and of the minor's parents.

(p) (i) In support of a decree under Section 78-3a-104, the court may order reasonable conditions to be complied with by the parents or guardian, the minor, the minor's custodian, or any other person who has been made a party to the proceedings. Conditions may include:

(A) parent-time by the parents or one parent;

(B) restrictions on the minor's associates;

(C) restrictions on the minor's occupation and other activities; and

(D) requirements to be observed by the parents or custodian.

(ii) A minor whose parents or guardians successfully complete a family or other counseling program may be credited by the court for detention, confinement, or probation time.

(q) The court may order the minor to be committed to the physical custody of a local mental health authority, in accordance with the procedures and requirements of Title 62A, Chapter 15, Part 7, Commitment of Persons Under Age 18 to Division of Substance Abuse and Mental Health.

(r) (i) The court may make an order committing a minor within its jurisdiction to the Utah State Developmental Center if the minor has mental retardation in accordance with the provisions of Title 62A, Chapter 5, Part 3, Admission to Mental Retardation Facility.

(ii) The court shall follow the procedure applicable in the district courts with respect to judicial commitments to the Utah State Developmental Center when ordering a commitment under Subsection (2)(r)(i).

(s) The court may terminate all parental rights upon a finding of compliance with the provisions of Title 78, Chapter 3a, Part 4, Termination of Parental Rights Act.

(t) The court may make any other reasonable orders for the best interest of the minor or as required for the protection of the public, except that a person younger than 18 years of age may not be committed to jail or prison.

(u) The court may combine the dispositions listed in this section if they are compatible.

(v) Before depriving any parent of custody, the court shall give due consideration to the rights of parents concerning their minor. The court may transfer custody of a minor to another person, agency, or institution in accordance with the requirements and procedures of Title 78, Chapter 3a, Part 3, Abuse, Neglect, and Dependency Proceedings.

(w) Except as provided in Subsection (2)(y)(i), an order under this section for probation or placement of a minor with an individual or an agency shall include a date certain for a review of the case by the court. A new date shall be set upon each review.

(x) In reviewing foster home placements, special attention shall be given to making adoptable minors available for adoption without delay.

(y) (i) The juvenile court may enter an order of permanent custody and guardianship with a relative or individual of a minor where the court has previously acquired jurisdiction as a result of an adjudication of abuse, neglect, or dependency. The juvenile court may enter an order for child support on behalf of the minor child against the natural or adoptive parents of the child.

(ii) Orders under Subsection (2)(y)(i):

(A) shall remain in effect until the minor reaches majority;

(B) are not subject to review under Section 78-3a-119; and

(C) may be modified by petition or motion as provided in Section 78-3a-903.

(iii) Orders permanently terminating the rights of a parent, guardian, or custodian and permanent orders of custody and guardianship do not expire with a termination of jurisdiction of the juvenile court.

(3) In addition to the dispositions described in Subsection (2), when a minor comes within the court's jurisdiction he may be given a choice by the court to serve in the National Guard in lieu of other sanctions, provided:

(a) the minor meets the current entrance qualifications for service in the National Guard as determined by a recruiter, whose determination is final;

(b) the minor is not under the jurisdiction of the court for any act that:

(i) would be a felony if committed by an adult;

(ii) is a violation of Title 58, Chapter 37, Utah Controlled Substances Act; or

(iii) was committed with a weapon; and

(c) the court retains jurisdiction over the minor under conditions set by the court and agreed upon by the recruiter or the unit commander to which the minor is eventually assigned.

(4) (a) A DNA specimen shall be obtained from a minor who is under the jurisdiction of the court as described in Subsection 53-10-403(3). The specimen shall be obtained by designated employees of the court or, if the minor is in the legal custody of the Division of Juvenile Justice Services, then by designated employees of the division under Subsection 53-10-404(5)(b).

(b) The responsible agency shall ensure that employees designated to collect the saliva DNA specimens receive appropriate training and that the specimens are obtained in accordance with accepted protocol.

(c) Reimbursements paid under Subsection 53-10-404(2)(a) shall be placed in the DNA Specimen Restricted Account created in Section 53-10-407.

(d) Payment of the reimbursement is second in priority to payments the minor is ordered to make for restitution under this section and treatment under Section 78-3a-318.   **2004**

78-3a-119. Period of operation of judgment, decree, or order — Rights and responsibilities of agency or individual granted legal custody.

(1) A judgment, order, or decree of the juvenile court does not operate after the minor becomes 21 years of age, except for:

(a) orders of commitment to the Utah State Developmental Center or to the custody of the Division of Substance Abuse and Mental Health;

(b) adoption orders under Subsection 78-3a-104(1)(o);

(c) orders permanently terminating the rights of a parent, guardian, or custodian, and permanent orders of custody and guardianships; and

(d) unless terminated by the court, orders to pay any fine or restitution.

(2) (a) Except as provided in Part 3, Abuse, Neglect, and Dependency Proceedings, an order vesting legal custody or guardianship of a minor in an individual, agency, or institution may be for an indeterminate period. A review hearing shall be held, however, upon the expiration of 12 months, and, with regard to petitions filed by the Division of Child and Family Services, no less than once every six months thereafter. The individual, agency, or institution involved shall file the petition for that review hearing. The court may terminate the order, or after notice and hearing, continue the order if it finds continuation of the order necessary to safeguard the welfare of the minor or the public interest. The findings of the court and its reasons shall be entered with the continuation order or with the order denying continuation.

(b) Subsection (2)(a) does not apply to minors who are in the custody of the Division of Child and Family Services, and who are placed in foster care, a secure youth corrections facility, the Division of Substance Abuse and Mental Health, the Utah State Developmental Center, or any agency licensed for child placements and adoptions, in cases where all parental rights of the natural parents have been terminated by the court under Part 4, Termination of Parental Rights Act, and custody of the minor has been granted to the agency for adoption or other permanent placement.

(3) (a) An agency granted legal custody may determine where and with whom the minor will live, provided that placement of the minor does not remove him from the state without court approval.

(b) An individual granted legal custody shall personally exercise the rights and responsibilities involved in legal custody, unless otherwise authorized by the court.   2002 (5th S.S.)

78-3a-120. Modification of order or decree — Requirements for changing or terminating custody, probation, or protective supervision.

(1) The court may modify or set aside any order or decree made by it, however a modification of an order placing a minor on probation may not be made upon an alleged violation of the terms of probation unless there has been a hearing in accordance with the procedures in Section 78-3a-903.

(2) Notice of the hearing shall be required in any case in which the effect of modifying or setting aside

an order or decree may be to make any change in the minor's legal custody.

(3) Notice of an order terminating probation or protective supervision shall be given to the parents, guardian, custodian, and, where appropriate, to the minor.   1997

78-3a-121. Continuing jurisdiction of juvenile court — Period of and termination of jurisdiction — Notice of discharge from custody of local mental health authority or Utah State Developmental Center — Transfer of continuing jurisdiction to other district.

(1) Jurisdiction of a minor obtained by the court through adjudication under Section 78-3a-118 continues for purposes of this chapter until he becomes 21 years of age, unless terminated earlier. However, the court retains jurisdiction beyond the age of 21 of a person who has refused or failed to pay any fine or victim restitution ordered by the court, but only for the purpose of causing compliance with existing orders.

(2) (a) The continuing jurisdiction of the court terminates:

(i) upon order of the court;

(ii) upon commitment to a secure youth corrections facility; or

(iii) upon commencement of proceedings in adult cases under Section 78-3a-801.

(b) The continuing jurisdiction of the court is not terminated by marriage.

(3) When a minor has been committed by the court to the physical custody of a local mental health authority or its designee or to the Utah State Developmental Center, the local mental health authority or its designee or the superintendent of the Utah State Developmental Center shall give the court written notice of its intention to discharge, release, or parole the minor not fewer than five days prior to the discharge, release, or parole.

(4) Jurisdiction over a minor on probation or under protective supervision, or of a minor who is otherwise under the continuing jurisdiction of the court, may be transferred by the court to the court of another district, if the receiving court consents, or upon direction of the chair of the Board of Juvenile Court Judges. The receiving court has the same powers with respect to the minor that it would have if the proceedings originated in that court.   2003

PART 5

DELINQUENCY AND CRIMINAL ACTIONS

78-3a-501. Criminal proceedings involving minors — Transfer to juvenile court — Exception.

(1) If, during the pendency of a criminal or quasi-criminal proceeding in another court, including a preliminary hearing, it is determined that the person charged is under 21 years of age and was less than 18 years of age at the time of committing the alleged offense, that court shall transfer the case to the juvenile court, together with all the papers, documents, and transcripts of any testimony except as provided in Sections 78-3a-602 and 78-3a-603.

(2) The court making the transfer shall order the person to be taken immediately to the juvenile court or to a place of detention designated by the juvenile court, or shall release him to the custody of his parent or guardian or other person legally responsible for him, to be brought before the juvenile court at a time designated by it. The juvenile court shall then proceed as provided in this chapter.   1996

78-3a-502. Petition — Preliminary inquiry — Nonjudicial adjustments — Formal referral — Citation — Failure to appear.

(1) Proceedings in minor's cases are commenced by petition.

(2) (a) A peace officer or any public official of the state, any county, city, or town charged with the enforcement of the laws of the state or local jurisdiction shall file a formal referral with the juvenile court within ten days of the minor's arrest. If the arrested minor is taken to a detention facility, the formal referral shall be filed with the juvenile court within 72 hours, excluding weekends and holidays. There shall be no requirement to file a formal referral with the juvenile court on an offense that would be a class B misdemeanor or less if committed by an adult.

(b) When the court is informed by a peace officer or other person that a minor is or appears to be within the court's jurisdiction, the probation department shall make a preliminary inquiry to determine whether the interests of the public or of the minor require that further action be taken.

(c) Based on the preliminary inquiry, the court may authorize the filing of or request that the county attorney or district attorney as provided under Sections 17-18-1 and 17-18-1.7 file a petition. In its discretion, the court may, through its probation department, enter into a written consent agreement with the minor and the minor's parent, guardian, or custodian for the nonjudicial adjustment of the case if the facts are admitted and establish prima facie jurisdiction. Efforts to effect a nonjudicial adjustment may not extend for a period of more than two months without leave of a judge of the court, who may extend the period for an additional two months. The probation department may not in connection with any nonjudicial adjustment compel any person to appear at any conference, produce any papers, or visit any place.

(d) The nonjudicial adjustment of a case may include conditions agreed upon as part of the nonjudicial closure:

(i) payment of a financial penalty of not more than $100 to the Juvenile Court;

(ii) payment of victim restitution;

(iii) satisfactory completion of compensatory service;

(iv) referral to an appropriate provider for counseling or treatment;

(v) attendance at substance abuse programs or counseling programs;

(vi) compliance with specified restrictions on activities and associations; and

(vii) other reasonable actions that are in the interest of the minor and the community.

(e) Proceedings involving offenses under Section 78-3a-506 are governed by that section regarding suspension of driving privileges.

(f) A violation of Section 76-10-105 that is subject to the jurisdiction of the Juvenile Court shall include a minimum fine or penalty of $60 and participation in a court-approved tobacco education program, which may include a participation fee.

(3) Except as provided in Section 78-3a-602, in the case of a minor 14 years of age or older, the county

attorney, district attorney, or attorney general may commence an action by filing a criminal information and a motion requesting the juvenile court to waive its jurisdiction and certify the minor to the district court.

(4) (a) In cases of violations of fish and game laws, boating laws, class B and class C misdemeanors, other infractions or misdemeanors as designated by general order of the Board of Juvenile Court Judges, and violations of Section 76-10-105 subject to the jurisdiction of the Juvenile Court, a petition is not required and the issuance of a citation as provided in Section 78-3a-503 is sufficient to invoke the jurisdiction of the court. A preliminary inquiry is not required unless requested by the court.

(b) Any failure to comply with the time deadline on a formal referral may not be the basis of dismissing the formal referral.   2002

78-3a-503. Citation procedure — Citation — Offenses — Time limits — Failure to appear.

(1) As used in this section, "citation" means an abbreviated referral and is sufficient to invoke the jurisdiction of the court in lieu of a petition.

(2) A citation shall be submitted to the court within five days of its issuance.

(3) Each copy of the citation shall contain:

(a) the name and address of the juvenile court before which the minor is to appear;

(b) the name of the minor cited;

(c) the statute or local ordinance that is alleged to have been violated;

(d) a brief description of the offense charged;

(e) the date, time, and location at which the offense is alleged to have occurred;

(f) the date the citation was issued;

(g) the name and badge or identification number of the peace officer or public official who issued the citation;

(h) the name of the arresting person if an arrest was made by a private party and the citation was issued in lieu of taking the arrested minor into custody as provided in Section 78-3a-113;

(i) the date and time when the minor is to appear, or a statement that the minor and parent or legal guardian are to appear when notified by the juvenile court; and

(j) the signature of the minor and the parent or legal guardian, if present, agreeing to appear at the juvenile court as designated on the citation.

(4) Each copy of the citation shall contain space for the following information to be entered if known:

(a) the minor's address;

(b) the minor's date of birth;

(c) the name and address of the minor's custodial parent or legal guardian, if different from the minor; and

(d) if there is a victim, the victim's name, address, and an estimate of loss, except that this information shall be removed from the documents the minor receives.

(5) A citation received by the court beyond the time designated in Subsection (2) shall include a written explanation for the delay.

(6) The following offenses may be sent to the juvenile court as a citation:

(a) violations of fish and game laws;

(b) violations of boating laws;

(c) violations of curfew laws;

(d) any class B misdemeanor or less traffic violations where the person is under the age of 16;

(e) any class B or class C misdemeanor or infraction;

(f) any other infraction or misdemeanor as designated by general order of the Board of Juvenile Court Judges; and

(g) violations of Section 76-10-105 subject to the jurisdiction of the Juvenile Court.

(7) A preliminary inquiry is not required unless requested by the court.

(8) The provisions of Subsection (5) may not apply to a runaway, ungovernable, or habitually truant minor.

(9) In the case of Section 76-10-105 violations committed on school property when a citation is issued under this section, the peace officer, public official, or compliance officer shall issue one copy to the minor cited, provide the parent or legal guardian with a copy, and file a duplicate with the juvenile court specified in the citation within five days.

(10) (a) A minor receiving a citation described in this section shall appear at the juvenile court designated in the citation on the time and date specified in the citation or when notified by the juvenile court.

(b) A citation may not require a minor to appear sooner than five days following its issuance.

(11) A minor who receives a citation and willfully fails to appear before the juvenile court pursuant to a citation is subject to arrest and may be found in contempt of court. The court may proceed against the minor as provided in Section 78-3a-901 regardless of the disposition of the offense upon which the minor was originally cited.

(12) When a citation is issued under this section, bail may be posted and forfeited under Subsection 78-3a-114(12) with the consent of the court and parent or legal guardian of the minor cited.   2003

78-3a-504. Minor held in detention — Credit for good behavior.

(1) The judge may order whether a minor held in detention under Subsection 78-3a-118(2)(f) or 78-3a-901(3) is eligible to receive credit for good behavior against the period of detention. The rate of credit is one day for every three days served. The Division of Juvenile Justice Services shall, in accordance with Title 63, Chapter 46a, Utah Administrative Rulemaking Act, establish rules describing good behavior for which credit may be earned.

(2) Any disposition including detention under Subsection 78-3a-118(2)(f) or 78-3a-901(3) shall be concurrent with any other order of detention.   2005

78-3a-505. Dispositional report required in minor's cases — Exceptions.

(1) The probation department or other agency designated by the court shall make a dispositional report in writing in all minor's cases in which a petition has been filed, except that the court may dispense with the study and report in cases involving violations of traffic laws or ordinances, violations of fish and game laws, boating laws, and other minor cases.

(2) When preparing a dispositional report and recommendation in a delinquency action, the probation department or other agency designated by the court shall consider the juvenile sentencing guidelines developed in accordance with Section 63-25a-304 and any aggravating or mitigating circumstances.

(3) Where the allegations of a petition filed under Subsection 78-3a-104(1) are denied, the investigation may not be made until the court has made an adjudication.   1997

78-3a-506. Suspension of license for certain offenses.

(1) This section applies to minors who are at least 13 years of age when found by the court to be within its jurisdiction by the commission of any offense under Section 58-37-8 or 32A-12-209, Title 58, Chapter 37a, Utah Drug Paraphernalia Act, Title 58, Chapter 37b, Imitation Controlled Substances, or Subsection 76-9-701(1).

(2) If the court hearing the case determines that the minor committed an offense under Section 58-37-8 or Title 58, Chapter 37a or 37b, the court shall prepare and send to the Driver License Division of the Department of Public Safety an order to suspend that minor's driving privileges.

(3) If the court hearing the case determines that the minor violated Section 32A-12-209 or Subsection 76-9-701(1), and the violation is the minor's:

(a) first violation, the court may suspend the minor's driving privileges; or

(b) second or subsequent violation, the court shall suspend the minor's driving privileges.

(4) When a court has issued an order suspending a minor's driving privileges for a violation of Section 32A-12-209 or 58-37-8, Title 58, Chapter 37a or 37b, or Subsection 76-9-701(1), the minor's license shall be suspended under Section 53-3-219.

(5) When the Department of Public Safety receives the arrest or conviction record of a person for a driving offense committed while his license is suspended under this section, the department shall extend the suspension for a like period of time. **1997**

78-3a-507 to 78-3a-521. Renumbered as §§ 78-3a-112 to 78-3a-121, 78-3a-913, 78-3a-914.

1997

PART 6

TRANSFER OF JURISDICTION

78-3a-601. Jurisdiction of district court.

(1) The district court shall have exclusive original jurisdiction over all persons 16 years of age or older charged by information or indictment with:

(a) an offense which would be murder or aggravated murder if committed by an adult; or

(b) an offense which would be a felony if committed by an adult if the minor has been previously committed to a secure facility as defined in Section 62A-7-101. This Subsection (1)(b) shall not apply if the offense is committed in a secure facility.

(2) When the district court has exclusive original jurisdiction over a minor under this section, it also has exclusive original jurisdiction over the minor regarding all offenses joined with the qualifying offense, and any other offenses, including misdemeanors, arising from the same criminal episode. The district court is not divested of jurisdiction by virtue of the fact that the minor is allowed to enter a plea to, or is found guilty of, a lesser or joined offense.

(3) (a) Any felony, misdemeanor, or infraction committed after the offense over which the district court takes jurisdiction under Subsection (1) or (2) shall be tried against the defendant as an adult in the district court or justice court having jurisdiction.

(b) If the qualifying charge under Subsection (1) results in an acquittal, a finding of not guilty, or a dismissal of the charge in the district court, the juvenile court under Section 78-3a-104 and the Division of Juvenile Justice Services regain jurisdiction and any authority previously exercised over the minor. **2003**

78-3a-602. Serious youth offender — Procedure.

(1) Any action filed by a county attorney, district attorney, or attorney general charging a minor 16 years of age or older with a felony shall be by criminal information and filed in the juvenile court if the information charges any of the following offenses:

(a) any felony violation of:

(i) Section 76-6-103, aggravated arson;

(ii) Subsection 76-5-103(1)(a), aggravated assault, involving intentionally causing serious bodily injury to another;

(iii) Section 76-5-302, aggravated kidnaping;

(iv) Section 76-6-203, aggravated burglary;

(v) Section 76-6-302, aggravated robbery;

(vi) Section 76-5-405, aggravated sexual assault;

(vii) Section 76-10-508, discharge of a firearm from a vehicle;

(viii) Section 76-5-202, attempted aggravated murder; or

(ix) Section 76-5-203, attempted murder; or

(b) an offense other than those listed in Subsection (1)(a) involving the use of a dangerous weapon which would be a felony if committed by an adult, and the minor has been previously adjudicated or convicted of an offense involving the use of a dangerous weapon which also would have been a felony if committed by an adult.

(2) All proceedings before the juvenile court related to charges filed under Subsection (1) shall be conducted in conformity with the rules established by the Utah Supreme Court.

(3) (a) If the information alleges the violation of a felony listed in Subsection (1), the state shall have the burden of going forward with its case and the burden of proof to establish probable cause to believe that one of the crimes listed in Subsection (1) has been committed and that the defendant committed it. If proceeding under Subsection (1)(b), the state shall have the additional burden of proving by a preponderance of the evidence that the defendant has previously been adjudicated or convicted of an offense involving the use of a dangerous weapon.

(b) If the juvenile court judge finds the state has met its burden under this Subsection (3), the court shall order that the defendant be bound over and held to answer in the district court in the same manner as an adult unless the juvenile court judge finds that all of the following conditions exist:

(i) the minor has not been previously adjudicated delinquent for an offense involving the use of a dangerous weapon which would be a felony if committed by an adult;

(ii) that if the offense was committed with one or more other persons, the minor appears to have a lesser degree of culpability than the codefendants; and

(iii) that the minor's role in the offense was not committed in a violent, aggressive, or premeditated manner.

(c) Once the state has met its burden under this Subsection (3) as to a showing of probable cause, the defendant shall have the burden of going forward and presenting evidence as to the existence of the above conditions.

(d) If the juvenile court judge finds by clear and convincing evidence that all the above conditions are satisfied, the court shall so state in its findings and order the minor held for trial as a minor and shall proceed upon the information as though it were a juvenile petition.

(4) If the juvenile court judge finds that an offense has been committed, but that the state has not met its burden of proving the other criteria needed to bind the defendant over under Subsection (1), the juvenile court judge shall order the defendant held for trial as a minor and shall proceed upon the information as though it were a juvenile petition.

(5) At the time of a bind over to district court a criminal warrant of arrest shall issue. The defendant shall have the same right to bail as any other criminal defendant and shall be advised of that right by the juvenile court judge. The juvenile court shall set initial bail in accordance with Title 77, Chapter 20, Bail.

(6) If an indictment is returned by a grand jury charging a violation under this section, the preliminary examination held by the juvenile court judge need not include a finding of probable cause that the crime alleged in the indictment was committed and that the defendant committed it, but the juvenile court shall proceed in accordance with this section regarding the additional considerations listed in Subsection (3)(b).

(7) When a defendant is charged with multiple criminal offenses in the same information or indictment and is bound over to answer in the district court for one or more charges under this section, other offenses arising from the same criminal episode and any subsequent misdemeanors or felonies charged against him shall be considered together with those charges, and where the court finds probable cause to believe that those crimes have been committed and that the defendant committed them, the defendant shall also be bound over to the district court to answer for those charges.

(8) A minor who is bound over to answer as an adult in the district court under this section or on whom an indictment has been returned by a grand jury, is not entitled to a preliminary examination in the district court.

(9) Allegations contained in the indictment or information that the defendant has previously been adjudicated or convicted of an offense involving the use of a dangerous weapon, or is 16 years of age or older, are not elements of the criminal offense and do not need to be proven at trial in the district court.

(10) If a minor enters a plea to, or is found guilty of, any of the charges filed or any other offense arising from the same criminal episode, the district court retains jurisdiction over the minor for all purposes, including sentencing.

(11) The juvenile court under Section 78-3a-104 and the Division of Juvenile Justice Services regain jurisdiction and any authority previously exercised over the juvenile when there is an acquittal, a finding of not guilty, or dismissal of all charges in the district court.   2003

78-3a-603. Certification hearings — Juvenile court to hold preliminary hearing — Factors considered by juvenile court for waiver of jurisdiction to district court.

(1) If a criminal information filed in accordance with Subsection 78-3a-502(3) alleges the commission of an act which would constitute a felony if committed by an adult, the juvenile court shall conduct a preliminary hearing.

(2) At the preliminary hearing the state shall have the burden of going forward with its case and the burden of establishing:

(a) probable cause to believe that a crime was committed and that the defendant committed it; and

(b) by a preponderance of the evidence, that it would be contrary to the best interests of the minor or of the public for the juvenile court to retain jurisdiction.

(3) In considering whether or not it would be contrary to the best interests of the minor or of the public for the juvenile court to retain jurisdiction, the juvenile court shall consider, and may base its decision on, the finding of one or more of the following factors:

(a) the seriousness of the offense and whether the protection of the community requires isolation of the minor beyond that afforded by juvenile facilities;

(b) whether the alleged offense was committed by the minor in concert with two or more persons under circumstances which would subject the minor to enhanced penalties under Section 76-3-203.1 were he an adult;

(c) whether the alleged offense was committed in an aggressive, violent, premeditated, or willful manner;

(d) whether the alleged offense was against persons or property, greater weight being given to offenses against persons, except as provided in Section 76-8-418;

(e) the maturity of the minor as determined by considerations of his home, environment, emotional attitude, and pattern of living;

(f) the record and previous history of the minor;

(g) the likelihood of rehabilitation of the minor by use of facilities available to the juvenile court;

(h) the desirability of trial and disposition of the entire offense in one court when the minor's associates in the alleged offense are adults who will be charged with a crime in the district court;

(i) whether the minor used a firearm in the commission of an offense; and

(j) whether the minor possessed a dangerous weapon on or about school premises as provided in Section 76-10-505.5.

(4) The amount of weight to be given to each of the factors listed in Subsection (3) is discretionary with the court.

(5) (a) Written reports and other materials relating to the minor's mental, physical, educational, and social history may be considered by the court.

(b) If requested by the minor, the minor's parent, guardian, or other interested party, the court shall require the person or agency preparing the report and other material to appear and be subject to both direct and cross-examination.

(6) At the conclusion of the state's case, the minor may testify under oath, call witnesses, cross-examine adverse witnesses, and present evidence on the factors required by Subsection (3).

(7) If the court finds the state has met its burden under Subsection (2), the court may enter an order:

(a) certifying that finding; and

(b) directing that the minor be held for criminal proceedings in the district court.

(8) If an indictment is returned by a grand jury, the preliminary examination held by the juvenile court

need not include a finding of probable cause, but the juvenile court shall proceed in accordance with this section regarding the additional consideration referred to in Subsection (2)(b).

(9) The provisions of Section 78-3a-116, Section 78-3a-913, and other provisions relating to proceedings in juvenile cases are applicable to the hearing held under this section to the extent they are pertinent.

(10) A minor who has been directed to be held for criminal proceedings in the district court is not entitled to a preliminary examination in the district court.

(11) A minor who has been certified for trial in the district court shall have the same right to bail as any other criminal defendant and shall be advised of that right by the juvenile court judge. The juvenile court shall set initial bail in accordance with Title 77, Chapter 20, Bail.

(12) When a minor has been certified to the district court under this section or when a criminal information or indictment is filed in a court of competent jurisdiction before a committing magistrate charging the minor with an offense described in Section 78-3a-602, the jurisdiction of the Division of Juvenile Justice Services and the jurisdiction of the juvenile court over the minor is terminated regarding that offense, any other offenses arising from the same criminal episode, and any subsequent misdemeanors or felonies charged against him, except as provided in Subsection (14).

(13) If a minor enters a plea to, or is found guilty of any of the charges filed or on any other offense arising out of the same criminal episode, the district court retains jurisdiction over the minor for all purposes, including sentencing.

(14) The juvenile court under Section 78-3a-104 and the Division of Juvenile Justice Services regain jurisdiction and any authority previously exercised over the minor when there is an acquittal, a finding of not guilty, or dismissal of all charges in the district court.   2003

78-3a-604. Appeals from serious youth offender and certification proceedings.

(1) A minor may, as a matter of right, appeal from:
(a) an order of the juvenile court binding the minor over to the district court as a serious youth offender pursuant to Section 78-3a-602; or
(b) an order of the juvenile court, after certification proceedings pursuant to Section 78-3a-603, directing that the minor be held for criminal proceedings in the district court.

(2) The prosecution may, as a matter of right, appeal from:
(a) an order of the juvenile court that a minor charged as a serious youth offender pursuant to Section 78-3a-602 be held for trial in the juvenile court; or
(b) a refusal by the juvenile court, after certification proceedings pursuant to Section 78-3a-603, to order that a minor be held for criminal proceedings in the district court.   2005

PART 8

ADULT OFFENSES

78-3a-801. Jurisdiction of adults for offenses against minors — Proof of delinquency not required for conviction.

(1) The court shall have jurisdiction, concurrent with the district court or justice court otherwise having subject matter jurisdiction, to try adults for the following offenses committed against minors:
(a) unlawful sale or supply of alcohol beverage or product to minors in violation of Section 32A-12-203;
(b) failure to report child abuse or neglect, as required by Title 62A, Chapter 4a, Part 4, Child Abuse or Neglect Reporting Requirements;
(c) harboring a minor in violation of Section 62A-4a-501;
(d) misdemeanor custodial interference in violation of Section 76-5-303;
(e) contributing to the delinquency of a minor in violation of Section 76-10-2301;
(f) failure to comply with compulsory education requirements in violation of Section 53A-11-101.

(2) It is not necessary for the minor to be found to be delinquent or to have committed a delinquent act for the court to exercise jurisdiction under Subsection (1).   1999

PART 9

MISCELLANEOUS PROVISIONS

78-3a-904. When photographs, fingerprints, or HIV infection tests may be taken — Distribution — Expungement.

(1) Photographs may be taken of a minor 14 years of age or older who:
(a) is taken into custody for the alleged commission of an offense under Sections 78-3a-104, 78-3a-601, and 78-3a-602 that would also be an offense if the minor were 18 years of age or older; or
(b) has been determined to be a serious habitual offender for tracking under Section 63-92-2 and is under the continuing jurisdiction of the Juvenile Court or the Division of Juvenile Justice Services.

(2) (a) Fingerprints may be taken of a minor 14 years of age or older who:
(i) is taken into custody for the alleged commission of an offense that would be a felony if the minor were 18 years of age or older;
(ii) has been determined to be a serious habitual offender for tracking under Section 63-92-2 and is under the continuing jurisdiction of the Juvenile Court or the Division of Juvenile Justice Services; or
(iii) is required to provide a DNA specimen under Section 53-10-403.
(b) Fingerprints shall be forwarded to the Bureau of Criminal Identification and may be stored by electronic medium.

(3) HIV testing may be conducted on a minor who is taken into custody after having been adjudicated to have violated state law prohibiting a sexual offense under Title 76, Chapter 5, Part 4, Sexual Offenses, upon the request of the victim or the parent or guardian of a minor victim.

(4) HIV tests, photographs, and fingerprints may not be taken of a minor younger than 14 years of age without the consent of the court.

(5) (a) Photographs may be distributed or disbursed to individuals or agencies other than state or local law enforcement agencies only when a minor 14 years of age or older is charged with an offense which would be a felony if committed by an adult.

(b) Fingerprints may be distributed or disbursed to individuals or agencies other than state or local law enforcement agencies.

(6) When a minor's juvenile record is expunged, all photographs and other records as ordered shall upon court order be destroyed by the law enforcement agency. Fingerprint records may not be destroyed.

2003

78-3a-905. Expungement of juvenile court record — Petition — Procedure.

(1) (a) A person who has been adjudicated under this chapter may petition the court for the expungement of his record in the juvenile court if:

(i) he has reached 18 years of age; and

(ii) one year has elapsed from the date of termination of the continuing jurisdiction of the juvenile court or, in case he was committed to a secure youth corrections facility, one year from the date of his unconditional release from the custody of the Division of Juvenile Justice Services.

(b) The court may waive the requirements in Subsection (1)(a), if the court finds, and states on the record, the reason why the waiver is appropriate.

(c) The petitioner shall include with his petition the original criminal history report obtained from the Bureau of Criminal Identification in accordance with the provisions of Subsection 53-10-108(8).

(d) The petitioner shall send a copy of the petition to the county attorney or, if within a prosecution district, the district attorney.

(e) (i) Upon the filing of a petition, the court shall set a date for a hearing and shall notify the county attorney or district attorney, and the agency with custody of the records of the pendency of the petition and of the date of the hearing. Notice shall be given at least 30 days prior to the hearing.

(ii) The court shall provide a victim with the opportunity to request notice of a petition for expungement. A victim shall receive notice of a petition for expungement at least 30 days prior to the hearing if, prior to the entry of an expungement order, the victim or, in the case of a minor or a person who is incapacitated or deceased, the victim's next of kin or authorized representative, submits a written and signed request for notice to the court in the judicial district in which the crime occurred or judgment was entered. The notice shall include a copy of the petition and statutes and rules applicable to the petition.

(2) (a) At the hearing, the county attorney or district attorney, a victim, and any other person who may have relevant information about the petitioner may testify.

(b) In deciding whether to grant a petition for expungement, the court shall consider whether the rehabilitation of the petitioner has been attained to the satisfaction of the court, taking into consideration the petitioner's response to programs and treatment, his behavior subsequent to adjudication, and the nature and seriousness of the conduct.

(c) The court may order sealed all petitioner's records under the control of the juvenile court and any of petitioner's records under the control of any other agency or official pertaining to the petitioner's adjudicated juvenile court cases if the court finds that:

(i) the petitioner has not, since the termination of the court's jurisdiction or his unconditional release from the Division of Juvenile Justice Services, been convicted of a:

(A) felony; or

(B) misdemeanor involving moral turpitude; and

(ii) no proceeding involving a felony or misdemeanor is pending or being instituted against him.

(3) The petitioner shall be responsible for service of the order of expungement to all affected state, county, and local entities, agencies, and officials. To avoid destruction or sealing of the records in whole or in part, the agency or entity receiving the expungement order shall only expunge all references to the petitioner's name in the records pertaining to the petitioner's adjudicated juvenile court cases.

(4) Upon the entry of the order, the proceedings in the petitioner's case shall be considered never to have occurred and the petitioner may properly reply accordingly upon any inquiry in the matter. Inspection of the records may thereafter only be permitted by the court upon petition by the person who is the subject of the records, and only to persons named in the petition.

(5) The court may not expunge a juvenile court record if the record contains an adjudication of:

(a) Section 76-5-202, aggravated murder; or

(b) Section 76-5-203, murder.

(6) (a) A person whose juvenile court record consists solely of nonjudicial adjustments as provided in Section 78-3a-502 may petition the court for expungement of his record if the person:

(i) has reached 18 years of age; and

(ii) has completed the conditions of the nonjudicial adjustments.

(b) The court shall, without a hearing, order sealed all petitioner's records under the control of the juvenile court and any of petitioner's records under the control of any other agency or official pertaining to the petitioner's nonjudicial adjustments.

2003

78-3a-913. Right to counsel — Appointment of counsel for indigent — Cost — Court hearing to determine compelling reason to appoint a noncontracting attorney — Rate of pay.

(1) (a) The parents, guardian, custodian, and the minor, if competent, shall be informed that they have the right to be represented by counsel at every stage of the proceedings. They have the right to employ counsel of their own choice and if any of them requests an attorney and is found by the court to be indigent, counsel shall be appointed by the court as provided in Subsection (3). The court may appoint counsel without a request if it considers representation by counsel necessary to protect the interest of the minor or of other parties.

(b) The cost of appointed counsel for an indigent minor or other indigent party, including the cost of counsel and expense of appeal, shall be paid by the county in which the trial court proceedings are held. Counties may levy and collect taxes for these purposes.

(c) The court shall take into account the income and financial ability to retain counsel of the parents or guardian of a minor in determining the indigency of the minor.

(2) If the state or county responsible to provide legal counsel for an indigent under Subsection (1)(b) has arranged by contract to provide services, the court if it has received notice or a copy of such contract shall appoint the contracting attorney as legal counsel to represent that indigent.

(3) In the absence of contrary contractual provisions regarding the selection and appointment of parental defense counsel, the court shall select and appoint the attorney or attorneys if:

(a) the contract for indigent legal services is with multiple attorneys; or

(b) the contract is with an additional attorney or attorneys in the event of a conflict of interest.

(4) If the court considers the appointment of a noncontracting attorney to provide legal services to an indigent despite the existence of an indigent legal services contract and the court has a copy or notice of such contract, before the court may make the appointment, it shall:

(a) set the matter for a hearing;

(b) give proper notice to the attorney general and the Office of Child Welfare Parental Defense created in Section 63A-11-103; and

(c) make findings that there is a compelling reason to appoint a noncontracting attorney before it may make such appointment.

(5) The indigent's mere preference for other counsel shall not be considered a compelling reason justifying the appointment of a noncontracting attorney.

(6) The court may order a minor, parent, guardian, or custodian for whom counsel is appointed and the parents or guardian of any minor for whom counsel is appointed to reimburse the county for the cost of appointed counsel.　　　　2004

78-3a-914. Exchange of information with agency or institution having legal custody — Transfer of minor to state prison or other adult facility prohibited.

(1) Whenever legal custody of a minor is vested in an institution or agency, the court shall transmit with the court order copies of the social study, any clinical reports, and other information pertinent to the care and treatment of the minor. The institution or agency shall give the court any information concerning the minor that the court may at any time require.

(2) The Division of Juvenile Justice Services or any other institution or agency to whom a minor is committed under Section 78-3a-118 may not transfer custody of the minor to the state prison or any other institution for the correction of adult offenders.　　2003

CHAPTER 3e

REPORTING SCHOOL-RELATED CONTROLLED SUBSTANCE ABUSE

78-3e-1. Definitions.

(1) The definitions in Sections 58-37-2, 58-37a-3, and 58-37b-2 apply to this chapter.

(2) As used in this chapter:

(a) "Prohibited act" means an act punishable under Section 53A-3-501, Section 58-37-8, Section 58-37a-5, or Title 58, Chapter 37b.

(b) "School" means a public or private elementary or secondary school.　　1988

78-3e-2. Reporting of prohibited acts affecting a school — Confidentiality.

A person who has reasonable cause to believe that an individual has committed a prohibited act shall immediately notify the nearest law enforcement agency, the principal, or an administrator of the affected school, or the superintendent or an administrator of the affected school district. If notice is given to a school official, the official may authorize an investigation into allegations involving school property, students, or school district employees. School officials may refer a complaint of an alleged prohibited act reported as occurring on school grounds or in connection with school-sponsored activities to an appropriate law enforcement agency. Referrals shall be made by school officials if the complaint alleges the prohibited act occurred elsewhere. The identity of persons making reports pursuant to this section shall be kept confidential.　　1986

78-3e-3. Immunity from civil or criminal liability.

Any person, official, or institution, other than a law enforcement officer or law enforcement agency, participating in good faith in making a report or conducting an investigation under the direction of school or law enforcement authorities under this chapter, is immune from any liability, civil or criminal, that otherwise might result by reason of that action.　　1986

78-3e-4. Admissibility of evidence in civil and criminal actions.

Evidence relating to violations of this chapter which is seized by school authorities acting alone and on their own authority and not in conjunction with or at the behest of law enforcement authorities is admissible in civil and criminal actions. A search under this section must be based on at least a reasonable belief that the search will turn up evidence of a violation of this chapter. The measures adopted for the search must be reasonably related to the objectives of the search and not excessively intrusive in light of the circumstances, including the age and sex of the person involved and the nature of the infraction.　　1986

78-3e-5. Board rules to ensure protection of individual rights.

The State Board of Education and local boards of education shall adopt rules to implement this chapter. The rules shall establish procedures to ensure protection of individual rights against excessive and unreasonable intrusion.　　1986

CHAPTER 3h

CHILD PROTECTIVE ORDERS

78-3h-101.   Definitions.

As used in this chapter:

(1) "Abuse" means physical abuse or sexual abuse.

(2) "Court" means the district court or juvenile court.

(3) All other terms have the same meaning as defined in Section 78-3a-103.   2004

78-3h-102.   Petition — Ex parte determination — Guardian ad litem — Referral to division.

(1) Any interested person may file a petition for a protective order on behalf of a child who is being abused or is in imminent danger of being abused. The petitioner shall first make a referral to the division.

(2) Upon the filing of a petition, the clerk of the court shall:

(a) review the records of the juvenile court, the district court, and the management information system of the division to find any petitions, orders, or investigations related to the child or the parties to the case;

(b) request the records of any law enforcement agency identified by the petitioner as having investigated abuse of the child; and

(c) identify and obtain any other background information that may be of assistance to the court.

(3) Upon the filing of a petition, the court shall immediately determine, based on the evidence and information presented, whether the minor is being abused or is in imminent danger of being abused. If so, the court shall enter an ex parte child protective order.

(4) The court may appoint an attorney guardian ad litem for the child who is the subject of the petition.
          2004

78-3h-103.   Hearing.

(1) The court shall schedule a hearing within 20 days after the ex parte determination.

(2) The petition, ex parte child protective order, and notice of hearing shall be served on the respondent, the minor's parent or guardian, and, if appointed, the guardian ad litem. The notice shall contain:

(a) the name and address of the person to whom it is directed;

(b) the date, time, and place of the hearing;

(c) the name of the minor on whose behalf a petition is being brought; and

(d) a statement that a person is entitled to have an attorney present at the hearing.

(3) The court shall provide an opportunity for any person having relevant knowledge to present evidence or information. The court may hear statements by counsel.

(4) An agent of the division served with a subpoena in compliance with the Utah Rules of Civil Procedure shall testify in accordance with the Utah Rules of Evidence.

(5) If the court determines, based on a preponderance of the evidence, that the minor is being abused or is in imminent danger of being abused, the court shall enter a child protective order. With the exception of the provisions of Section 78-3a-320, a child protective order does not constitute an adjudication of abuse, neglect, or dependency under Title 78, Chapter 3a, Part 3, Abuse Neglect and Dependency Proceedings.
          2004

78-3h-104.   Content of order.

(1) A child protective order or an ex parte child protective order may contain the following provisions the violation of which is a class A misdemeanor under Section 77-36-2.4:

(a) enjoin the respondent from threatening to commit or committing abuse of the minor;

(b) prohibit the respondent from harassing, telephoning, contacting, or otherwise communicating with the minor, directly or indirectly;

(c) prohibit the respondent from entering or remaining upon the residence, school, or place of employment of the minor and the premises of any of these or any specified place frequented by the minor;

(d) upon finding that the respondent's use or possession of a weapon may pose a serious threat of harm to the minor, prohibit the respondent from purchasing, using, or possessing a firearm or other specified weapon; and

(e) determine ownership and possession of personal property and direct the appropriate law enforcement officer to attend and supervise the petitioner's or respondent's removal of personal property.

(2) A child protective order or an ex parte child protective order may contain the following provisions the violation of which is contempt of court:

(a) determine temporary custody of a minor who is the subject of the petition;

(b) determine parent-time with a minor who is the subject of the petition, including denial of parent-time if necessary to protect the safety of the minor, and require supervision of parent-time by a third party;

(c) determine support in accordance with Title 78, Chapter 45, Uniform Civil Liability for Support Act; and

(d) order any further relief the court considers necessary to provide for the safety and welfare of the minor.

(3) A child protective order and an ex parte child protective order shall include:

(a) a statement that violation of a criminal provision is a class A misdemeanor and violation of a civil provision is contempt of court; and

(b) information the petitioner is able to provide to facilitate identification of the respondent, such as Social Security number, driver license number, date of birth, address, telephone number, and physical description.

(4) A child protective order shall include:

(a) a statement that:

(i) two years from entry of the order, the respondent may petition to dismiss the criminal portion of the order;

(ii) the petitioner should, within the 30 days prior to the end of the two-year period, advise the court of the petitioner's address for notice of any hearing; and

(iii) the address provided by the petitioner will not be made available to the respondent;

(b) the date when the civil portion of the order will expire or be reviewed; and

(c) the following statement: "Respondent was afforded notice and opportunity to be heard in the hearing that gave rise to this order. Pursuant to the Violence Against Women Act of 1994, P.L. 103-322, 108 Stat. 1796, 18 U.S.C.A. 2265, this order is valid in all the United States, the District of Columbia, tribal lands, and United States territories."   2004

78-3h-105. Service — Income withholding — Expiration.

(1) If the court enters an ex parte child protective order or a child protective order, the court shall:

(a) make reasonable efforts to ensure that the order is understood by the petitioner and the respondent, if present;

(b) as soon as possible transmit the order to the county sheriff for service; and

(c) by the end of the next business day after the order is entered transmit a copy of the order to any law enforcement agency designated by the petitioner and to the statewide domestic violence network described in Section 30-6-8.

(2) The county sheriff shall serve the order and transmit verification of service to the statewide domestic violence network described in Section 30-6-8 in an expeditious manner. Any law enforcement agency may serve the order and transmit verification of service to the statewide domestic violence network if the law enforcement agency has contact with the respondent or if service by that law enforcement agency is in the best interests of the child.

(3) When an order is served on a respondent in a jail, prison, or other holding facility, the law enforcement agency managing the facility shall notify the petitioner of the respondent's release. Notice to the petitioner consists of a prompt, good faith effort to provide notice, including mailing the notice to the petitioner's last-known address.

(4) Child support orders issued as part of a child protective order are subject to mandatory income withholding under Title 62A, Chapter 11, Part 4, Income Withholding in IV-D Cases, and Title 62A, Chapter 11, Part 5, Income Withholding in Non IV-D Cases.

(5) After notice and hearing a court may modify or vacate a child protective order without a showing of substantial and material change in circumstances, except that the criminal provisions of the child protective order may not be vacated within two years of issuance unless the petitioner:

(a) is personally served with notice of the hearing as provided in Rule 4, Utah Rules of Civil Procedure, and the petitioner personally appears before the court and gives specific consent to the vacation of the criminal provisions of the protective order; or

(b) submits a verified affidavit, stating agreement to the vacation of the criminal provisions of the protective order.

(6) The civil provisions of the child protective order expire 150 days after the date of the order unless a different date is set by the court. The court may not set a date more than 150 days after the date of the order without a finding of good cause. The court may review and extend the expiration date, but may not extend it to more than 150 days after the date of the order without a finding of good cause.   2004

78-3h-106. Statewide domestic violence network.

The Administrative Office of the Courts, in cooperation with the Department of Public Safety and the Criminal Investigations and Technical Services Division, shall post ex parte child protective orders, child protective orders, and any modifications to them on the statewide network established in Section 30-6-8.
2003

78-3h-107. Forms and assistance — No fees.

(1) The Administrative Office of the Courts shall adopt and make available uniform forms for petitions and orders conforming to this part. The forms shall notify the petitioner that:

(a) a knowing falsehood in any statement under oath may subject the petitioner to felony prosecution;

(b) the petitioner may provide a copy of the order to the principal of the minor's school; and

(c) the petitioner may enforce a court order through the court if the respondent violates or fails to comply with a provision of the order.

(2) If the petitioner is not represented, the clerk of the court shall provide, directly or through an agent:

(a) the forms adopted pursuant to Subsection (1);

(b) clerical assistance in completing the forms and filing the petition;

(c) information regarding means for service of process;

(d) a list of organizations with telephone numbers that may represent the petitioner; and

(e) information regarding the procedure for transporting a jailed or imprisoned respondent to hearings, including transportation order forms when necessary.

(3) No fee may be imposed by a court, constable, or law enforcement agency for:

(a) filing a petition under this chapter;

(b) obtaining copies necessary for service or delivery to law enforcement officials; or

(c) service of a petition, ex parte child protective order, or child protective order.   2003

CHAPTER 5

JUSTICE COURTS

78-5-101. Creation of justice court — Not of record.

Under Article VIII, Section 1, Utah Constitution, there is created a court not of record known as the justice court. The judges of this court are justice court judges.   1999

78-5-102. Offices of justice court judges.

(1) Justice court judges holding office in:

(a) county precincts are county justice court judges; and

(b) cities or towns are municipal justice court judges.

(2) With the concurrence of the governing bodies of both the county and municipality, a justice court judge may hold both the offices of county and municipal justice court judge.

(3) The county legislative body may establish a single precinct or divide the county into multiple precincts to create county justice courts for public convenience.

(4) (a) The governing body may assign as many justice court judges to a court as required for efficient judicial administration.

(b) If more than one judge is assigned to a court, any citations, informations, or complaints within that court shall be assigned to the judges at random.

(5) A municipality or county may contract with any other municipality or municipalities within the county under Title 11, Chapter 13, Interlocal Cooperation Act, to establish a justice court. A justice court established under Title 11, Chapter 13, shall meet the requirements for certification under Section 78-5-139. A justice court established under Title 11, Chapter 13, shall have territorial jurisdiction as if established separately.   1999

78-5-103. Territorial jurisdiction — Voting.

(1) The territorial jurisdiction of county justice courts extends to the limits of the precinct for which the justice court is created and includes all cities or towns within the precinct, except cities where a municipal justice court exists.

(2) The territorial jurisdiction of municipal justice courts extends to the corporate limits of the municipality in which the justice court is created.

(3) The territorial jurisdiction of county and municipal justice courts functioning as magistrates extends beyond the boundaries in Subsections (1) and (2):

(a) as set forth in Section 78-7-17.5; and

(b) to the extent necessary to carry out magisterial functions under Subsection 77-7-23(2) regarding jailed persons.

(4) For election of county justice court judges, all registered voters in the county justice court precinct may vote at the judge's retention election.   1999

78-5-104. Jurisdiction.

(1) Justice courts have jurisdiction over class B and C misdemeanors, violation of ordinances, and infractions committed within their territorial jurisdiction, except those offenses over which the juvenile court has exclusive jurisdiction.

(2) Justice courts have jurisdiction of small claims cases under Title 78, Chapter 6, Small Claims Courts, if the defendant resides in or the debt arose within the territorial jurisdiction of the justice court.   1997

78-5-105. Jurisdiction of justice court and juvenile court.

(1) Justice courts have jurisdiction over traffic misdemeanors and infractions committed by persons 16 or 17 years of age and that occur within the territorial jurisdiction of the court, except those offenses exclusive to the juvenile court under Section 78-3a-104.

(2) If the traffic offense involves the conviction of a person 16 years of age or older but younger than 18 years of age for an offense under Section 78-3a-506, the justice court judge shall notify the juvenile court of the conviction.

(3) The justice court has authority to take the juvenile's driver license and return it to the Driver License Division, Department of Public Safety, for suspension under Section 53-3-221.

(4) Justice court judges may transfer matters within the court's jurisdiction under this section to the juvenile court for postjudgment proceedings according to rules of the Judicial Council.   1997

78-5-106. Justice court judge authority.

Justice court judges:

(1) have the same authority regarding matters within their jurisdiction as judges of courts of record;

(2) may issue search warrants and warrants of arrest upon a finding of probable cause; and

(3) may conduct proceedings to determine:

(a) probable cause for any case within their jurisdiction; and

(b) an accused person's release on bail or his own recognizance.   1989

78-5-109. Laws, ordinances, and reference materials provided by counties, cities, and towns.

Each county, city, or town shall provide and keep current for each justice court in its jurisdiction a copy of the motor vehicle laws of Utah, appropriate copies of the Utah code, the justice court manual published by the state court administrator, state laws affecting local government, the county, city, or town ordinances, and other legal reference materials as determined to be necessary by the judge.   1989

78-5-111. Justice court staff to be provided.

(1) Each county, city, or town creating and maintaining a justice court shall provide:

(a) sufficient staff public prosecutors to attend the court and perform the duties of prosecution before the justice court;

(b) adequate funding for the costs of defense for persons charged with a public offense who are determined by the court to be indigent under Title 77, Chapter 32; and

(c) sufficient local peace officers to attend the justice court when required and provide security for the court.

(2) The county attorney or district attorney may appoint city prosecutors as deputies to prosecute state offenses in municipal justice courts.   1998

78-5-113. Process to any part of the state — Service.

(1) Process from a justice court may be issued to any place in the state.

(2) Subpoenas in any action or proceeding of a justice court may be issued to any place in the state.

(3) All warrants issued by a justice court for violation of any state law or local ordinance within a court's jurisdiction are directed to the sheriff, any constable of the county, or to the marshal or city police of the town or city.   1989

78-5-116.5. Security surcharge — Application — Deposit in restricted accounts.

(1) In addition to any fine, penalty, forfeiture, or other surcharge, a security surcharge of $32 shall be assessed on all convictions for offenses listed in the uniform bail schedule adopted by the Judicial Council and moving traffic violations.

(2) The security surcharge shall be collected and distributed pro rata with any fine collected. A fine that would otherwise have been charged may not be reduced due to the imposition of the security surcharge.

(3) The security surcharge shall be allocated as follows:

(a) the assessing court shall retain 20% of the amount collected for deposit into the general fund of the governmental entity; and

(b) 80% shall be remitted to the state treasurer to be distributed as follows:

(i) 62.5% to the treasurer of the county in which the justice court which remitted the amount is located;

(ii) 25% to the Court Security Account created in Section 63-63c-102; and

(iii) 12.5% to the Justice Court Technology, Security, and Training Account created in Section 78-5-116.7.

(4) The court shall remit money collected in accordance with Title 51, Chapter 7, State Money Management Act. 2004

78-5-116.7. Justice Court Technology, Security, and Training Account established — Funding — Uses.

There is created a restricted account in the General Fund known as the Justice Court Technology, Security, and Training Account.

(1) The state treasurer shall deposit in the account monies collected from the surcharge established in Subsection 78-5-116.5(3)(b)(iii).

(2) Monies shall be appropriated from the account to the Administrative Office of the Courts to only be used for technology, security, and training needs in justice courts throughout the state. 2004

78-5-120. Appeals from justice court — Trial or hearing de novo in district court.

(1) In a criminal case, a defendant is entitled to a trial de novo in the district court only if the defendant files a notice of appeal within 30 days of:

(a) sentencing after a bench or jury trial, or a plea of guilty in the justice court resulting in a finding or verdict of guilt; or

(b) a plea of guilty in the justice court that is held in abeyance.

(2) If an appeal under Subsection (1) is of a plea entered pursuant to negotiation with the prosecutor, and the defendant did not reserve the right to appeal as part of the plea negotiation, the negotiation is voided by the appeal.

(3) A defendant convicted and sentenced in justice court is entitled to a hearing de novo in the district court on the following matters, if he files a notice of appeal within 30 days of:

(a) an order revoking probation;

(b) an order entering a judgment of guilt pursuant to the person's failure to fulfil the terms of a plea in abeyance agreement;

(c) a sentence entered pursuant to Subsection (3)(b); or

(d) an order denying a motion to withdraw a plea.

(4) The prosecutor is entitled to a hearing de novo in the district court on:

(a) a final judgment of dismissal;

(b) an order arresting judgment;

(c) an order terminating the prosecution because of a finding of double jeopardy or denial of a speedy trial;

(d) a judgment holding invalid any part of a statute or ordinance;

(e) a pretrial order excluding evidence, when the prosecutor certifies that exclusion of that evidence prevents continued prosecution; or

(f) an order granting a motion to withdraw a plea of guilty or no contest.

(5) Upon entering a decision in a hearing de novo, the district court shall remand the case to the justice court unless:

(a) the decision results in immediate dismissal of the case;

(b) with agreement of the parties, the district court consents to retain jurisdiction; or

(c) the defendant enters a plea of guilty in the district court.

(6) The district court shall retain jurisdiction over the case on trial de novo.

(7) The decision of the district court is final and may not be appealed unless the district court rules on the constitutionality of a statute or ordinance.

2001 (1st S.S.)

78-5-125. All papers issued, except subpoenas, to be filled out without blanks.

Every paper made or issued by a justice court judge except a subpoena is valid only if issued without any blank space to be filled or completed by another person. 1989

CHAPTER 6

SMALL CLAIMS COURTS

Section
78-6-10. Appeals — Who may take and jurisdiction.

78-6-10. Appeals — Who may take and jurisdiction.

(1) Either party may appeal the judgment in a small claims action to the district court of the county by filing a notice of appeal in the original trial court within 30 days of entry of the judgment. If the judgment in a small claims action is entered by a judge or judge pro tempore of the district court, the notice of appeal shall be filed with the district court.

(2) The appeal is a trial de novo and shall be tried in accordance with the procedures of small claims actions, except a record of the trial shall be maintained. The trial de novo may not be heard by a judge pro tempore appointed under Section 78-6-1.5. The decision of the trial de novo may not be appealed unless the court rules on the constitutionality of a statute or ordinance. 2004

CHAPTER 7

GENERAL PROVISIONS APPLICABLE TO COURTS AND JUDGES

Section
78-7-17.5. Authority of magistrate.

78-7-17.5. Authority of magistrate.

(1) Except as otherwise provided by law, a magistrate as defined in Section 77-1-3 shall have the authority to:

(a) commit a person to incarceration prior to trial;

(b) set or deny bail under Section 77-20-1 and release upon the payment of bail and satisfaction of any other conditions of release;

(c) issue to any place in the state summonses and warrants of search and arrest and authorize administrative traffic checkpoints under Section 77-23-104;

(d) conduct an initial appearance in a felony;

(e) conduct arraignments;

(f) conduct a preliminary examination to determine probable cause;

(g) appoint attorneys and order recoupment of attorney fees;

(h) order the preparation of presentence investigations and reports;

(i) issue temporary orders as provided by rule of the Judicial Council; and

(j) perform any other act or function authorized by statute.

(2) A judge of the justice court may exercise the authority of a magistrate specified in Subsection (1) with the following limitations:

(a) a judge of the justice court may conduct an initial appearance, preliminary examination, or arraignment in a felony case as provided by rule of the Judicial Council;

(b) a judge of the justice court may not set bail in a capital felony nor deny bail in any case; and

(c) a judge of the justice court may authorize administrative traffic checkpoints under Section 77-23-104 and issue search warrants only within the judicial district.   2004

CHAPTER 13

PLACE OF TRIAL — VENUE

Section
78-13-9.   Grounds.

78-13-9. Grounds.

The court may, on motion, change the place of trial in the following cases:

(1) when the county designated in the complaint is not the proper county;

(2) when there is reason to believe that an impartial trial cannot be had in the county, city, or precinct designated in the complaint;

(3) when the convenience of witnesses and the ends of justice would be promoted by the change;

(4) when all the parties to an action, by stipulation or by consent in open court entered in the minutes, agree that the place of trial may be changed to another county.   2004

CHAPTER 18

PUNITIVE DAMAGES AWARDS

Section
78-18-1.   Basis for punitive damages awards — Section inapplicable to DUI cases — Division of award with state.

78-18-1. Basis for punitive damages awards — Section inapplicable to DUI cases — Division of award with state.

(1) (a) Except as otherwise provided by statute, punitive damages may be awarded only if compensatory or general damages are awarded and it is established by clear and convincing evidence that the acts or omissions of the tortfeasor are the result of willful and malicious or intentionally fraudulent conduct, or conduct that manifests a knowing and reckless indifference toward, and a disregard of, the rights of others.

(b) The limitations, standards of evidence, and standards of conduct of Subsection (1)(a) do not apply to any claim for punitive damages arising out of the tortfeasor's operation of a motor vehicle or motorboat while voluntarily intoxicated or under the influence of any drug or combination of alcohol and drugs as prohibited by Section 41-6a-502.

(c) The award of a penalty under Section 78-11-15 or 78-11-16 regarding shoplifting is not subject to the prior award of compensatory or general damages under Subsection (1)(a) whether or not restitution has been paid to the merchant prior to or as a part of a civil action under Section 78-11-15 or 78-11-16.

(2) Evidence of a party's wealth or financial condition shall be admissible only after a finding of liability for punitive damages has been made.

(3) (a) In any case where punitive damages are awarded, the judgment shall provide that 50% of the amount of the punitive damages in excess of $20,000 shall, after an allowable deduction for the payment of attorneys' fees and costs, be remitted by the judgment debtor to the state treasurer for deposit into the General Fund.

(b) For the purposes of this Subsection (3), an "allowable deduction for the payment of attorneys' fees and costs" shall equal the amount of actual and reasonable attorneys' fees and costs incurred by the judgment creditor minus the amount of any separate judgment awarding attorneys' fees and costs to the judgment creditor.

(c) The state shall have all rights due a judgment creditor until the judgment is satisfied, and stand on equal footing with the judgment creditor of the original case in securing a recovery.

(d) Unless all affected parties, including the state, expressly agree otherwise or the application is contrary to the terms of the judgment, any payment on the judgment by or on behalf of any judgment debtor, whether voluntary or by execution or otherwise, shall be applied in the following order:

(i) compensatory damages, and any applicable attorneys fees and costs;

(ii) the initial $20,000 punitive damages; and

(iii) the balance of the punitive damages.   2005

Part III

Procedure

CHAPTER 28

ONLINE COURT ASSISTANCE

Section
78-28-1.   Online court assistance program — Purpose of program — User's fee.
78-28-2.   Creation of policy board — Membership — Terms — Chair — Quorum — Expenses.

78-28-1. Online court assistance program — Purpose of program — User's fee.

(1) There is established an online court assistance program administered by the Administrative Office of the Courts to provide the public with information about civil procedures and to assist the public in preparing and filing civil pleadings and other papers in:

(a) uncontested divorces;

(b) enforcement of orders in the divorce decree;

(c) landlord and tenant actions; and

(d) other types of proceedings approved by the Online Court Assistance Program Policy Board.

(2) The purpose of the online court assistance program shall be to:

(a) minimize the costs of civil litigation;

(b) improve access to the courts; and

(c) provide for informed use of the courts and the law by pro se litigants.

(3) (a) An additional $20 shall be added to the filing fee established by Section 78-7-35 if a person files a complaint, petition, answer, or response prepared through the program. There shall be no fee for using the program or for papers filed subsequent to the initial pleading.

(b) There is created within the General Fund a restricted account known as the Online Court Assistance Account. The fee collected under this Subsection (3) shall be deposited in the restricted account and appropriated by the Legislature to the Administrative Office of the Courts to develop, operate, and maintain the program and to support the use of the program through education of the public.   2001

78-28-2. Creation of policy board — Membership — Terms — Chair — Quorum — Expenses.

(1) There is created a 13 member policy board to be known as the "Online Court Assistance Program Policy Board" which shall:

(a) identify the subject matter included in the Online Court Assistance Program;

(b) develop information and forms in conformity with the rules of procedure and evidence; and

(c) advise the Administrative Office of the Courts regarding the administration of the program.

(2) The voting membership shall consist of:

(a) two members of the House of Representatives to be designated by the speaker, with one member from each party;

(b) two members of the Senate designated by the president, with one member from each party;

(c) two attorneys actively practicing in domestic relations designated by the Family Law Section of the Utah State Bar;

(d) one attorney actively practicing in civil litigation designated by the Civil Litigation Section of the Utah State Bar;

(e) one court commissioner designated by the chief justice of the Utah Supreme Court;

(f) one district court judge designated by the chief justice of the Utah Supreme Court;

(g) one attorney from Utah Legal Services designated by its director;

(h) one attorney from Legal Aid designated by its director; and

(i) two persons from the Administrative Office of the Courts designated by the state court administrator.

(3) (a) The terms of the members shall be four years and staggered so that approximately half of the board expires every two years.

(b) The board shall meet as needed.

(4) The board shall select one of its members to serve as chair.

(5) A majority of the members of the board constitutes a quorum.

(6) (a) (i) Members who are not government employees shall receive no compensation or benefits for their services, but may receive per diem and expenses incurred in the performance of the member's official duties at the rates established by the Division of Finance under Sections 63A-3-106 and 63A-3-107.

(ii) Members may decline to receive per diem and expenses for their service.

(b) (i) State government officer and employee members who do not receive salary, per diem, or expenses from their agency for their service may receive per diem and expenses incurred in the performance of their official duties from the board at the rates established by the Division of Finance under Sections 63A-3-106 and 63A-3-107.

(ii) State government officer and employee members may decline to receive per diem and expenses for their service.

(c) Legislators on the committee shall receive compensation and expenses as provided by law and legislative rule.   2000

CHAPTER 29

DISEASE TESTING FOR AT-RISK PUBLIC SAFETY OFFICERS

78-29-101. Definitions.

For purposes of this chapter:

(1) "Blood or contaminated body fluids" includes blood, amniotic fluid, pericardial fluid, peritoneal fluid, pleural fluid, synovial fluid, cerebrospinal fluid, semen, and vaginal secretions, and any body fluid visibly contaminated with blood.

(2) "Disease" means Human Immunodeficiency Virus infection, acute or chronic Hepatitis B infection, Hepatitis C infection, and any other infectious disease specifically designated by the Labor Commission in consultation with the Department of Health for the purposes of this chapter.

(3) "Emergency medical services provider" means an individual certified under Section 26-8a-302, a public safety officer, local fire department personnel, or personnel employed by the Department of Corrections or by a county jail, who provide prehospital emergency medical care for an emergency medical services provider either as an employee or as a volunteer.

(4) "First aid volunteer" means a person who provides voluntary emergency assistance or first aid medical care to an injured person prior to the arrival of an emergency medical services provider or public safety officer.

(5) "Public safety officer" means a peace officer as defined in Title 53, Chapter 13, Peace Officer Classifications.

(6) "Significant exposure" and "significantly exposed" mean:

(a) exposure of the body of one person to the blood or body fluids of another person by:

(i) percutaneous injury, including a needle stick or cut with a sharp object or instrument; or

(ii) contact with an open wound, mucous membrane, or nonintact skin because of a cut, abrasion, dermatitis, or other damage; or

(b) exposure that occurs by any other method of transmission defined by the Department of Health as a significant exposure.

2005

78-29-102. Petition — Disease testing — Notice — Payment for testing.

(1) An emergency medical services provider, or first aid volunteer who is significantly exposed during the course of performing the emergency medical services provider's duties or during the course of performing emergency assistance or first aid may:

(a) request that the person to whom he was significantly exposed voluntarily submit to testing; or

(b) petition the district court for an order requiring that the person to whom he was significantly exposed submit to testing to determine the presence of a disease, as defined in Section 78-29-101, and that the results of that test be disclosed to the petitioner by the Department of Health.

(2) (a) The petitioner shall file a petition with the district court seeking an order to submit to testing and to disclose the results in accordance with the provisions of this section.

(b) The petition shall be sealed upon filing and made accessible only to the petitioner, the subject of the petition, and their attorneys, upon court order.

(3) (a) The petition described in Subsection (2) shall be accompanied by an affidavit in which the emergency medical services provider or first aid volunteer certifies that he has been significantly exposed to the individual who is the subject of the petition and describes that exposure.

(b) The petitioner shall submit to testing to determine the presence of a disease, when the petition is filed or within three days after the petition is filed.

(4) The petitioner shall cause the petition required under this section to be served on the person who the petitioner is requesting to be tested in a manner that will best preserve the confidentiality of that person.

(5) (a) The court shall set a time for a hearing on the matter within ten days after the petition is filed and shall give the petitioner and the individual who is the subject of the petition notice of the hearing at least 72 hours prior to the hearing.

(b) The individual who is the subject of the petition shall also be notified that he may have an attorney present at the hearing, and that his attorney may examine and cross-examine witnesses.

(c) The hearing shall be conducted in camera.

(6) The district court may enter an order requiring that an individual submit to testing for a disease if the court finds probable cause to believe:

(a) the petitioner was significantly exposed; and

(b) the exposure occurred during the course of the emergency medical services provider's duties, or the provision of emergency assistance or first aid by a first aid volunteer.

(7) The court may order that additional, follow-up testing be conducted, and that the individual submit to that testing, as it determines to be necessary and appropriate.

(8) The court is not required to order an individual to submit to a test under this section if it finds that there is a substantial reason, relating to the life or health of the individual, not to enter the order.

(9) (a) Upon order of the district court that a person submit to testing for a disease, that person shall report to the designated local health department to have his blood drawn within ten days from the issuance of the order, and thereafter as designated by the court, or be held in contempt of court.

(b) The court shall send the order to the Department of Health and to the local health department ordered to draw the blood.

(c) Notwithstanding the provisions of Section 26-6-27, the Department of Health and a local health department may disclose the test results pursuant to a court order as provided in this section.

(d) Under this section, anonymous testing as provided under Section 26-6-3.5 shall not satisfy the requirements of the court order.

(10) The local health department or the Department of Health shall inform the subject of the petition and the petitioner of the results of the test and advise both parties that the test results are confidential. That information shall be maintained as confidential by all parties to the action.

(11) The court, its personnel, the process server, the Department of Health, local health department, and petitioner shall maintain confidentiality of the name and any other identifying information regarding the individual tested and the results of the test as they relate to that individual, except as specifically authorized by this chapter.

(12) (a) Except as provided in Subsection (12)(b), the petitioner shall remit payment for the drawing of the blood specimen and the analysis of the specimen for the mandatory disease testing to the entity that draws the blood.

(b) If the petitioner is an emergency medical services provider, the agency which employs the emergency medical services provider shall remit payment for the drawing of the blood specimen and the analysis of the specimen for the mandatory disease testing to the entity that draws the blood.

(13) The entity that draws the blood shall cause the blood and the payment for the analysis of the specimen to be delivered to the Department of Health for analysis.

(14) If the individual is incarcerated, the incarcerating authority shall either draw the blood specimen or shall pay the expenses of having the individual's blood drawn.

2005

78-29-103. Confidentiality — Disclosure — Penalty.

Any person or entity entitled to receive confidential information under this chapter, other than the individual tested and identified in the information, who violates the provisions of this chapter by releasing or making public that confidential information, or by otherwise breaching the confidentiality requirements of this chapter, is guilty of a class B misdemeanor.

2005

78-29-104. Department authority — Rules.

The Labor Commission in consultation with the Department of Health has authority to establish rules necessary for the purposes of Subsections 78-29-101(2) and (6). 2005

78-29-105. Construction.

Nothing in this chapter may be construed as prohibiting:

(1) a person from voluntarily consenting to the request of a health care provider, as defined in Section 78-14-3, to submit to testing following a significant exposure; or

(2) a court from considering the petition of a health care provider for an order requiring that a person submit to testing to determine the presence of a disease if a significant exposure has occurred in connection with the health care provider's treatment of that person. 2005

Part IV

Particular Proceedings

CHAPTER 31b

ALTERNATIVE DISPUTE RESOLUTION

Section
78-31b-7. Minimum procedures for mediation.

78-31b-7. Minimum procedures for mediation.

(1) A judge or court commissioner may refer to mediation any case for which the Judicial Council and Supreme Court have established a program or procedures. A party may file with the court an objection to the referral which may be granted for good cause.

(2) (a) Unless all parties and the neutral or neutrals agree only parties, their representatives, and the neutral may attend the mediation sessions.

(b) If the mediation session is pursuant to a referral under Subsection 78-3a-109(9), the ADR provider or ADR organization shall notify all parties to the proceeding and any person designated by a party. The ADR provider may notify any person whose rights may be affected by the mediated agreement or who may be able to contribute to the agreement. A party may request notice be provided to a person who is not a party.

(3) (a) Except as provided in Subsection (3)(b), any settlement agreement between the parties as a result of mediation may be executed in writing, filed with the clerk of the court, and enforceable as a judgment of the court. If the parties stipulate to dismiss the action, any agreement to dismiss shall not be filed with the court.

(b) With regard to mediation affecting any petition filed under Section 78-3a-305 or 78-3a-405:

(i) all settlement agreements and stipulations of the parties shall be filed with the court;

(ii) all timelines, requirements, and procedures described in Title 78, Chapter 3a, Parts 3 and 4, and in Title 62A, Chapter 4a, shall be complied with; and

(iii) the parties to the mediation may not agree to a result that could not have been ordered by the court in accordance with the procedures and requirements of Title 78, Chapter 3a, Parts 3 and 4, and Title 62A, Chapter 4a. 2004

CHAPTER 32

CONTEMPT

Section
78-32-17. Noncompliance with child support order.

78-32-17. Noncompliance with child support order.

(1) When a court of competent jurisdiction, or the Office of Recovery Services pursuant to an action under Title 63, Chapter 46b, Administrative Procedures Act, makes an order requiring a parent to furnish support or necessary food, clothing, shelter, medical care, or other remedial care for his child, and the parent fails to do so, proof of noncompliance shall be prima facie evidence of contempt of court.

(2) Proof of noncompliance may be demonstrated by showing that:

(a) the order was made, and filed with the district court; and

(b) the parent knew of the order because:

(i) the order was mailed to the parent at his last-known address as shown on the court records;

(ii) the parent was present in court at the time the order was pronounced;

(iii) the parent entered into a written stipulation and the parent or counsel for the parent was sent a copy of the order;

(iv) counsel was present in court and entered into a stipulation which was accepted and the order based upon the stipulation was then sent to counsel for the parent; or

(v) the parent was properly served and failed to answer.

(3) Upon establishment of a prima facie case of contempt under Subsection (2), the obligor under the child support order has the burden of proving inability to comply with the child support order.

(4) A court may, in addition to other available sanctions, withhold, suspend, or restrict the use of driver's licenses, professional and occupational licenses, and recreational licenses and impose conditions for reinstatement upon a finding that:

(a) an obligor has:

(i) made no payment for 60 days on a current obligation of support as set forth in an administrative or court order and, thereafter, has failed to make a good faith effort under the circumstances to make payment on the support obligation in accordance with the order; or

(ii) made no payment for 60 days on an arrearage obligation of support as set forth in a payment schedule, written agreement with the Office of Recovery Services, or an administrative or judicial order and, thereafter, has failed to make a good faith effort under the circumstances to make payment on the arrearage obligation in accordance with the payment schedule, agreement, or order; and

(iii) not obtained a judicial order staying enforcement of the support or arrearage obligation for which the obligor would be otherwise delinquent;

(b) a custodial parent has:

(i) violated a parent-time order by denying contact for 60 days between a noncustodial parent and a child and, thereafter, has failed to make a good faith effort under the circumstances to comply with a parent-time order; and

 (ii) not obtained a judicial order staying enforcement of the parent-time order; or

 (c) an obligor or obligee, after receiving appropriate notice, has failed to comply with a subpoena or order relating to a paternity or child support proceeding.   2001

CHAPTER 38

NUISANCE, WASTE, AND OTHER DAMAGE

78-38-.5. Legislative intent.

(1) The Legislature finds:

 (a) the federal Environmental Protection Agency (EPA) has determined that environmental tobacco smoke is a Group A carcinogen, in the same category as other cancer-causing chemicals such as asbestos;

 (b) the EPA has determined that there is no acceptable level of exposure to Class A carcinogens; and

 (c) the EPA has determined that exposure to environmental tobacco smoke also causes an increase in respiratory diseases and disorders among exposed persons.

(2) The Legislature finds that environmental tobacco smoke generated in a rental or condominium unit may drift into other units, exposing the occupants of those units to tobacco smoke, and that standard construction practices are not effective in preventing this drift of tobacco smoke.

(3) The Legislature further finds that persons who desire to not be exposed to drifting environmental tobacco smoke should be able to determine in advance of entering into a rental, lease, or purchase agreement whether the subject unit may be exposed to environmental tobacco smoke.   1997

78-38-1. Nuisance defined — Right of action for — Judgment.

(1) A nuisance is anything which is injurious to health, indecent, offensive to the senses, or an obstruction to the free use of property, so as to interfere with the comfortable enjoyment of life or property. A nuisance may be the subject of an action.

(2) A nuisance may include the following:

 (a) drug houses and drug dealing as provided in Section 78-38-9;

 (b) gambling as provided in Title 76, Chapter 10, Part 11;

 (c) criminal activity committed in concert with two or more persons as provided in Section 76-3-203.1;

 (d) party houses which frequently create conditions defined in Subsection (1); and

 (e) prostitution as provided in Title 76, Chapter 10, Part 13.

(3) A nuisance under this section includes tobacco smoke that drifts into any residential unit a person rents, leases, or owns, from another residential or commercial unit and this smoke:

 (a) drifts in more than once in each of two or more consecutive seven-day periods; and

 (b) creates any of the conditions under Subsection (1).

(4) Subsection (3) does not apply to:

 (a) residential rental units available for temporary rental, such as for vacations, or available for only 30 or fewer days at a time; or

 (b) hotel or motel rooms.

(5) Subsection (3) does not apply to any unit that is part of a timeshare project, as defined in Section 57-19-2, or subject to a timeshare interest as defined in Section 57-19-2.

(6) An action may be brought by any person whose property is injuriously affected, or whose personal enjoyment is lessened by the nuisance.

(7) Upon judgment, the nuisance may be enjoined or abated, and damages may be recovered.

(8) There is no cause of action for a nuisance under Subsection (3) if the rental, lease, restrictive covenant, or purchase agreement for the unit states in writing that:

 (a) smoking is allowed in other units, either residential or commercial, and that tobacco smoke from those units may drift into the unit that is subject of the agreement; and

 (b) by his signature the renter, lessee, or buyer acknowledges he has been informed that tobacco smoke may drift into the unit he is renting, leasing, or purchasing, and he waives any right to a cause of action for a nuisance under Subsection (3).

(9) A cause of action for a nuisance under Subsection (3) may be brought against:

 (a) the individual generating the tobacco smoke;

(b) the renter or lessee who permits or fails to control the generation of tobacco smoke, in violation of the terms of his rental or lease agreement, on the premises he rents or leases; or

(c) the landlord, but only if:

(i) the terms of the renter's or lessee's contract provide the unit will not be subject to the nuisance of drifting tobacco smoke;

(ii) the complaining renter or lessee has provided to the landlord a statement in writing indicating that tobacco smoke is creating a nuisance in the renter's or lessee's unit; and

(iii) the landlord knowingly allows the continuation of a nuisance under Subsection (3) after receipt of written notice under Subsection (c)(ii), and in violation of the terms of the rental or lease agreement under Subsection (c)(i).   1997

78-38-2. Right of action for waste — Damages.

If a guardian, tenant for life or years, joint tenant or tenant in common, of real property commits waste thereon, any person aggrieved by the waste may bring an action against him therefor, in which action there may be a judgment for treble damages.   1953

78-38-3. Right of action for injuries to trees — Damage.

Any person who cuts down or carries off any wood or underwood, tree or timber, or girdles or otherwise injures any tree [or] timber on the land of another person, or on the street or highway in front of any person's house, town or city lot, or cultivated grounds, or on the commons or public grounds of any city or town, or on the street or highway in front thereof, without lawful authority, is liable to the owner of such land, or to such city or town, for treble the amount of damages which may be assessed therefor in a civil action.   1953

78-38-4. Limited damages in certain cases.

Nothing in Section 78-38-3 authorizes the recovery of more than the just value of the timber taken from uncultivated woodland for the repair of a public highway or bridge upon the land, or adjoining it.   1995

78-38-4.5. Proof of ownership required to harvest or transport forest products or native vegetation — Definitions — Requirements for proof of ownership.

(1) It is unlawful for any person, firm, company, partnership, corporation, or business to harvest or transport timber, forest products, or other native vegetation without proof of ownership. For purposes of this chapter:

(a) "Forest products" means any tree or portion thereof before it is manufactured into dimensional lumber, timbers, and ties, or mill peeled and made into power poles or house logs, including but not limited to coniferous and deciduous trees, Christmas trees, sawlogs, poles, posts, pulp logs, and fuelwood; and

(b) "Native vegetation" means all other forest, desert, or rangeland vegetation including but not limited to shrubs, flora, roots, bulbs, and seed.

(2) Proof of ownership requires possession of:

(a) a contract, permit, or other writing issued by the landowner or proper state or federal agency;

(b) a bill of sale, or other sales receipt;

(c) a bill of lading or product load receipt;

(d) a ticket issued by the seller authorizing harvesting or removal; or

(e) any other legal instrument.

(3) The document required in Subsection (2) shall be issued by the landowner or proper state or federal agency and shall provide the following information:

(a) date of execution;

(b) name and address of person authorized to harvest or transport the products, if different from the purchaser;

(c) a legal or other sufficient description of the property from which the products are harvested or removed;

(d) the estimated amount or volume, species, and other pertinent information regarding the products harvested or transported;

(e) the delivery or scaling point;

(f) the name and address of the purchaser of the products;

(g) the name and address of the landowner, agency, or vendor; and

(h) an expiration date.   1987

78-38-4.6. Enforcement.

Any law enforcement officer specified in Section 53-13-103, or ranger, or special agent of the United States Forest Service or the United States Bureau of Land Management may:

(1) stop any vehicle or means of conveyance, including common carriers, containing timber, forest products, or native vegetation upon any road or highway of this state for the purpose of making an inspection and investigation but may not unduly detain a driver of such vehicle or means of conveyance;

(2) inspect the timber, forest product, or native vegetation in any vehicle, or other means of conveyance, including common carrier, to determine whether the provisions of this chapter have been complied with;

(3) seize and hold any timber, forest product, or native vegetation harvested, removed, or transported in violation of this chapter; and

(4) sell or dispose of the timber, forest product, or native vegetation as provided by rule by the appropriate agency.   1998

78-38-4.7. Transportation of forest products or native vegetation into or through the state.

Timber, forest products, or native vegetation transported into or through the state must be accompanied by a shipping permit or proof of ownership.   1987

78-38-4.8. Exemptions.

The provisions of this chapter do not apply to the transportation of:

(1) wood chips, sawdust, and bark;

(2) products transported by the owner of the property or his agent from which the products were removed; or

(3) products for personal consumption incidental to camping and picnicking which is limited to the amount:

(a) needed for the duration of the picnic or campout; and

(b) used at the campsite.   1987

78-38-4.9. Violation as misdemeanor.

Violation of Sections 78-38-4.5 through 78-38-4.7 is a class B misdemeanor.   1992

78-38-5. Manufacturing facility in operation over three years — Limited application of nuisance provisions.

(1) Notwithstanding Sections 78-38-1 and 76-10-803, no manufacturing facility or the operation

thereof shall be or become a nuisance, private or public, by virtue of any changed conditions in and about the locality thereof after the same has been in operation for more than three years when such manufacturing facility or the operation thereof was not a nuisance at the time the operation thereof began; provided, the manufacturing facility does not increase the condition asserted to be a nuisance and that the provisions of this subsection shall not apply whenever a nuisance results from the negligent or improper operation of any such manufacturing facility.

(2) The provisions of Subsection (1) of this section shall not affect or defeat the right of any person to recover damages for any injuries or damage sustained on account of any pollution of, or change in the condition of, the waters of any stream or on account of any overflow of the lands of any person.

(3) Any and all ordinances now or hereafter adopted by any county or municipal corporation in which such manufacturing facility is located, which makes the operation thereof a nuisance or providing for an abatement thereof as a nuisance in the circumstances set forth in this section are null and void; provided, however, that the provisions of this subsection shall not apply whenever a nuisance results from the negligent or improper operation of any such manufacturing facility.   1981

78-38-6. "Manufacturing facility" defined.

As used in this act, "manufacturing facility" means any factory, plant, or other facility including its appurtenances, where the form of raw materials, processed materials, commodities, or other physical objects is converted or otherwise changed into other materials, commodities, or physical objects or where such materials, commodities, or physical objects are combined to form a new material, commodity, or physical object.   1981

78-38-7. Agricultural operations — Nuisance liability.

(1) Agricultural operations that are consistent with sound agricultural practices are presumed to be reasonable and do not constitute a nuisance unless the agricultural operation has a substantial adverse effect on the public health and safety.

(2) Agricultural operations undertaken in conformity with federal, state, and local laws and regulations, including zoning ordinances, are presumed to be operating within sound agricultural practices.   1995

78-38-8. "Agricultural operation" defined.

As used in this act, "agricultural operation" means any facility for the production for commercial purposes of crops, livestock, poultry, livestock products, or poultry products.   1981

78-38-9. Nuisance — Right of action to abate nuisances — Drug houses and drug dealing — Gambling — Group criminal activity — Prostitution — Weapons.

(1) Every building or place is a nuisance where:

(a) the unlawful sale, manufacture, service, storage, distribution, dispensing, or acquisition occurs of any controlled substance, precursor, or analog specified in Title 58, Chapter 37, Controlled Substances;

(b) gambling is permitted to be played, conducted, or dealt upon as prohibited in Title 76, Chapter 10, Part 11, Gambling, which creates the conditions of a nuisance as defined in Subsection 78-38-1(1);

(c) criminal activity is committed in concert with two or more persons as provided in Section 76-3-203.1;

(d) parties occur frequently which create the conditions of a nuisance as defined in Subsection 78-38-1(1);

(e) prostitution or promotion of prostitution is regularly carried on by one or more persons as provided in Title 76, Chapter 10, Part 13, Prostitution; and

(f) a violation of Title 76, Chapter 10, Part 5, Weapons, occurs on the premises.

(2) It is a defense to nuisance under Subsection (1)(a) if the defendant can prove that the defendant is lawfully entitled to possession of a controlled substance.

(3) Sections 78-38-10 through 78-38-16 govern only an abatement by eviction of the nuisance as defined in Subsection (1).   1999

78-38-10. Nuisance — Abatement by eviction.

(1) Whenever there is reason to believe that a nuisance under Sections 78-38-9 through 78-38-16 is kept, maintained, or exists in any county, the county attorney of the county, the city attorney of any incorporated city, any citizen or citizens of the state residing in the county, or any corporation, partnership or business doing business in the county, in his or their own names, may maintain an action in a court of competent jurisdiction to abate the nuisance and obtain an order for the automatic eviction of the tenant.

(2) The court may designate a spokesperson of any group of citizens who would otherwise have the right to maintain an action in their individual names against the defendant under this section.   1992

78-38-11. Abatement by eviction order — Grounds.

An order of abatement by eviction may issue only upon a showing by the applicant by a preponderance of the evidence that:

(1) the applicant will suffer irreparable harm unless the order of abatement by eviction issues;

(2) the threatened injury to the applicant outweighs whatever damage the proposed order of abatement by eviction may cause the party so ordered;

(3) the order of abatement by eviction, if issued, would not be adverse to the public interest; and

(4) there is a substantial likelihood that the applicant will prevail on the merits of the underlying claim, or the case presents serious issues on the merits which should be the subject of further litigation.   1992

78-38-12. Prior acts of threats of violence — Protection of witnesses.

At the time of application for abatement of the nuisance by eviction pursuant to Sections 78-38-10 and 78-38-11, if proof of the existence of the nuisance depends, in whole or in part, upon the affidavits of witnesses who are not peace officers, upon a showing of prior threats of violence or acts of violence by any defendant or other person, the court may issue orders to protect those witnesses, including, nondisclosure of the name, address, or any other information which may identify those witnesses.   1992

78-38-13. Landlord, owner, or designated agent — Necessary party — Automatic eviction.

(1) A landlord, owner, or designated agent is a necessary party defendant in a nuisance action under Sections 78-38-9 through 78-38-16 for entry of an order to abate the nuisance by eviction where the acts complained of are those of third parties upon the premises of the landlord, owner, or designated agent.

(2) In the presence of the applicant, the tenant and the landlord, owner, or designated agent at the court's hearing on the action to abate the nuisance by eviction, the court shall notify the necessary parties of its finding that:

(a) a nuisance exists as defined in Section 78-38-9; and

(b) as a result, the court is issuing an order to evict the tenant subject to compliance with the security requirement in Section 78-38-14.

(3) In all cases, including default judgments, the order of abatement by eviction may be issued and enforced immediately. 1992

78-38-14. Security requirement — Amount not a limitation — Jurisdiction over surety.

(1) The court shall condition issuance of the order of abatement by eviction on the giving of security by the applicant, in such sum and form as the court determines proper, unless it appears that none of the parties will incur or suffer costs, attorney fees, or damage as the result of any wrongful order of abatement by eviction, or unless there exists some other substantial reason for dispensing with the requirement of security. No such security shall be required of the United States, the State of Utah, or of an officer, agency, or subdivision of either; nor shall it be required when it is prohibited by law.

(2) The amount of security shall not establish or limit the amount of costs, including reasonable attorney fees incurred in connection with the order of abatement by eviction, or damages that may be awarded to a party who is found to have been wrongfully evicted.

(3) A surety upon a bond or undertaking under this section submits to the jurisdiction of the court and irrevocably appoints the clerk of the court as agent upon whom any papers affecting the surety's liability on the bond or undertaking may be served. The surety's liability may be enforced on motion without the necessity of an independent action. The motion and such notice of the motion as the court prescribes may be served on the clerk of the court who shall immediately mail copies to the persons giving the security if their addresses are known.

(4) The plaintiff, upon demand, shall be granted a hearing to be held prior to the expiration of three days from the date the defendant is served with notice of the plaintiff's giving of security as provided in Subsection 78-38-14(1). 1992

78-38-15. Evidence of nuisance.

In any action for abatement by eviction instituted pursuant to Sections 78-38-9 through 78-38-16, all evidence otherwise authorized by law, including evidence of reputation in a community, is admissible to prove the existence of a nuisance by a preponderance of the evidence. 1992

78-38-16. Award of costs and attorneys' fees.

(1) The court may award costs, including the costs of investigation and discovery, and reasonable attorneys' fees, which are not compensated for pursuant to some other provision of law, to the prevailing party in any case in which a governmental agency, private citizen or citizens, corporation, partnership, or business seeks to abate the nuisance by eviction in or upon any building or place where the nuisance occurs as provided in Section 78-38-9.

(2) The court may award costs, including the costs of investigation and discovery, and reasonable attorneys' fees against a defendant landlord, owner, or designated agent only when the court finds that the defendant landlord, owner, or designated agent had actual notice of the nuisance action and willfully failed to take reasonable action within a reasonable time to abate the nuisance. 1996

PART VIII

DIVERSION PROGRAMS

CHAPTER 57

UTAH YOUTH COURT DIVERSION ACT

78-57-101. Title.

This chapter is known as the "Utah Youth Court Diversion Act." 1999

78-57-102. Definitions.

(1) "Adult" means a person 18 years of age or older.

(2) "Gang activity" means any criminal activity that is conducted as part of an organized youth gang. It includes any criminal activity that is done in concert with other gang members, or done alone if it is to fulfill gang purposes. "Gang activity" does not include graffiti.

(3) "Minor offense" means any unlawful act that is a status offense or would be a class B or C misdemeanor, infraction, or violation of a municipal or county ordinance if the youth were an adult. "Minor offense" does not include:

(a) class A misdemeanors;

(b) felonies of any degree;

(c) any offenses that are committed as part of gang activity;

(d) any of the following offenses which would carry mandatory dispositions if referred to the juvenile court under Section 78-3a-506:

(i) a second violation of Section 32A-12-209, Unlawful Purchase, Possession or Consumption by Minors — Measurable Amounts in Body;

(ii) a violation of Section 41-6a-502, Driving Under the Influence;

(iii) a violation of Section 58-37-8, Controlled Substances Act;

(iv) a violation of Title 58, Chapter 37a, Utah Drug Paraphernalia Act;

(v) a violation of Title 58, Chapter 37b, Imitation Controlled Substances Act; or

(vi) a violation of Section 76-9-701, Intoxication; or

(e) any offense where a dangerous weapon, as defined in Subsection 76-1-601(5), is used in the commission of the offense.

(4) "Sponsoring entity" means any political subdivision of the state, including a school or school district, juvenile court, law enforcement agency, prosecutor's office, county, city, or town.

(5) "Status offense" means a violation of the law that would not be a violation but for the age of the offender.

(6) "Youth" means a person under the age of 18 years or who is 18 but still attending high school.

2005

78-57-103.　Youth Court — Authorization — Referral.

(1) Youth Court is a diversion program which provides an alternative disposition for cases involving juvenile offenders in which youth participants, under the supervision of an adult coordinator, may serve in various capacities within the courtroom, acting in the role of jurors, lawyers, bailiffs, clerks, and judges.

(a) Youth who appear before youth courts have been identified by law enforcement personnel, school officials, a prosecuting attorney, or the juvenile court as having committed acts which indicate a need for intervention to prevent further development toward juvenile delinquency, but which appear to be acts that can be appropriately addressed outside the juvenile court process.

(b) Youth Courts may only hear cases as provided for in this chapter.

(c) Youth Court is a diversion program and not a court established under the Utah Constitution, Article VIII.

(2) Any person may refer youth to a Youth Court for minor offenses. Once a referral is made, the case shall be screened by an adult coordinator to determine whether it qualifies as a Youth Court case.

(3) Youth Courts have authority over youth:

(a) referred for a minor offense or offenses, or who are granted permission for referral under this chapter;

(b) who, along with a parent, guardian, or legal custodian, voluntarily and in writing, request Youth Court involvement;

(c) who admit having committed the referred offense;

(d) who, along with a parent, guardian, or legal custodian, waive any privilege against self-incrimination and right to a speedy trial; and

(e) who, along with their parent, guardian, or legal custodian, agree to follow the Youth Court disposition of the case.

(4) Except with permission granted under Subsection (5), Youth Courts may not exercise authority over youth who are under the continuing jurisdiction of the juvenile court for law violations, including any youth who may have a matter pending which has not yet been adjudicated. Youth Courts may, however, exercise authority over youth who are under the continuing jurisdiction of the juvenile court as set forth in this Subsection (4) if the offense before the Youth Court is not a law violation, and the referring agency has notified the juvenile court of the referral.

(5) Youth Courts may exercise authority over youth described in Subsection (4), and over any other offense with the permission of the juvenile court and the prosecuting attorney in the county or district that would have jurisdiction if the matter were referred to juvenile court.

(6) Permission of the juvenile court may be granted by a probation officer of the court in the district that would have jurisdiction over the offense being referred to Youth Court.

(7) Youth Courts may decline to accept a youth for Youth Court disposition for any reason and may terminate a youth from Youth Court participation at any time.

(8) A youth or the youth's parent, guardian, or custodian may withdraw from the Youth Court process at any time. The Youth Court shall immediately notify the referring source of the withdrawal.

(9) The Youth Court may transfer a case back to the referring source for alternative handling at any time.

(10) Referral of a case of Youth Court may not prohibit the subsequent referral of the case to any court.

2002

78-57-104.　Parental involvement — Victims — Restitution.

(1) Every youth appearing before the Youth Court shall be accompanied by a parent, guardian, or legal custodian.

(2) Victims shall have the right to attend hearings and be heard.

(3) Any restitution due a victim of an offense shall be made in full prior to the time the case is completed by the Youth Court. Restitution shall be agreed upon between the youth and victim.

1999

78-57-105.　Dispositions.

(1) Youth Court dispositional options include:

(a) community service;

(b) participation in law-related educational classes, appropriate counseling, treatment, or other educational programs;

(c) providing periodic reports to the Youth Court;

(d) participating in mentoring programs;

(e) participation by the youth as a member of a Youth Court;

(f) letters of apology;

(g) essays; and

(h) any other disposition considered appropriate by the Youth Court and adult coordinator.

(2) Youth Courts may not impose a term of imprisonment or detention and may not impose fines.

(3) Youth Court dispositions shall be completed within 180 days from the date of referral.

(4) Youth Court dispositions shall be reduced to writing and signed by the youth and a parent, guardian, or legal custodian indicating their acceptance of the disposition terms.

(5) Youth Court shall notify the referring source if a participant fails to successfully complete the Youth Court disposition. The referring source may then take any action it considers appropriate.

1999

78-57-106.　Liability.

(1) A person or entity associated with the referral, evaluation, adjudication, disposition, or supervision of matters under this chapter may not be held civilly liable for any injury occurring to any person performing community service or any other activity associated with a certified Youth Court unless the person causing the injury acted in a willful or wanton manner.

(2) Persons participating in a certified Youth Court shall be considered to be volunteers for purposes of Workers' Compensation and other risk-related issues.

1999

78-57-107. Fees.

(1) Youth Courts may require that the youth pay a reasonable fee, not to exceed $30, to participate in Youth Court. This fee may be reduced or waived by the Youth Court in exigent circumstances. This fee shall be paid to and accounted for by the sponsoring entity.

(2) Fees for classes, counseling, treatment, or other educational programs that are the disposition of the Youth Court are the responsibility of the participant.

1999

78-57-108. Youth Court Board — Membership — Responsibilities.

(1) The Utah attorney general's office shall provide staff support and assistance to a Youth Court Board comprised of the following:

(a) the Utah attorney general or his designee;

(b) one member of the Utah Prosecution Council;

(c) one member from the Board of Juvenile Court Judges;

(d) the juvenile court administrator or his designee;

(e) one person from the Office of Juvenile Justice and Delinquency Prevention;

(f) the state superintendent of education or his designee;

(g) two representatives from Youth Courts based primarily in schools;

(h) two representatives from Youth Courts based primarily in communities;

(i) one member from the law enforcement community; and

(j) one member from the community at large.

(2) The members selected to fill the positions in Subsections (1)(a) through (f) shall jointly select the members to fill the positions in Subsections (1)(g) through (j).

(3) Members shall serve two-year staggered terms beginning July 1, 1999, except the initial terms of the members designated by Subsections (1)(a), (c), (e), and (i), and one of the members from Subsections (1)(g) and (h) shall serve one-year terms, but may be reappointed for a full two-year term upon the expiration of their initial term.

(4) The Youth Court Board shall meet at least quarterly to:

(a) set minimum standards for the establishment of Youth Courts, including an application process, membership and training requirements, and the qualifications for the adult coordinator;

(b) review certification applications; and

(c) provide for a process to recertify each Youth Court every three years.

(5) In accordance with Title 63, Chapter 46a, Utah Administrative Rulemaking Act, the Youth Court Board shall make rules to accomplish the requirements of Subsection (3).

(6) The Youth Court Board may deny certification or recertification, or withdraw the certification of any Youth Court for failure to comply with program requirements.

(7) (a) Members shall receive no compensation or benefits for their services, but may receive per diem and expenses incurred in the performance of the member's official duties at the rates established by the Division of Finance under Sections 63A-3-106 and 63A-3-107.

(b) Members may decline to receive per diem and expenses for their service.

(8) The Youth Court Board shall provide a list of certified Youth Courts to the Board of Juvenile Court Judges, all law enforcement agencies in the state, all school districts, and the Utah Prosecution Council by December 31 of each year.

1999

78-57-109. Establishing a Youth Court — Sponsoring entity responsibilities.

(1) Youth Courts may be established by a sponsoring entity or by a private nonprofit entity which contracts with a sponsoring entity.

(2) The sponsoring entity shall:

(a) oversee the formation of the Youth Court;

(b) provide assistance with the application for certification from the Youth Court Board; and

(c) provide assistance for the training of Youth Court members.

1999

78-57-110. School credit.

Local school boards may provide school credit for participation as a member of a Youth Court.

1999

PART IX

MISCELLANEOUS PROVISIONS

CHAPTER 58

CITIZEN PARTICIPATION IN GOVERNMENT ACT

78-58-101. Title.

This chapter is known as the "Citizen Participation in Government Act."

2001

78-58-102. Definitions.

As used in this chapter:

(1) "Action involving public participation in the process of government" means any lawsuit, cause of action, claim, cross-claim, counterclaim, or other judicial pleading or filing requesting relief to which this act applies.

(2) "Government" includes a branch, department, agency, instrumentality, official, employee, agent, or other person acting under color of law of the United States, a state, or subdivision of a state or other public authority.

(3) "Moving party" means any person on whose behalf the motion is filed.

(4) "Person" means the same as defined in Section 68-3-12.

(5) "Process of government" means the mechanisms and procedures by which the legislative and executive branches of government make decisions, and the activities leading up to the decisions, including the exercise by a citizen of the right to influence those decisions under the First Amendment to the U.S. Constitution.

(6) "Responding party" means any person against whom the motion described in Section 78-58-103 is filed.

(7) "State" means the same as defined in Section 68-3-12.   2001

78-58-103. Applicability.

(1) A defendant in an action who believes that the action is primarily based on, relates to, or is in response to an act of the defendant while participating in the process of government and is done primarily to harass the defendant, may file:

(a) an answer supported by an affidavit of the defendant detailing his belief that the action is designed to prevent, interfere with, or chill public participation in the process of government, and specifying in detail the conduct asserted to be the participation in the process of government believed to give rise to the complaint; and

(b) a motion for judgment on the pleadings in accordance with the Utah Rules of Civil Procedure Rule 12(c).

(2) Affidavits detailing activity not adequately detailed in the answer may be filed with the motion.

2001

78-58-104. Procedures.

(1) On the filing of a motion for judgment on the pleadings:

(a) all discovery shall be stayed pending resolution of the motion unless the court orders otherwise;

(b) the trial court shall hear and determine the motion as expeditiously as possible with the moving party providing by clear and convincing evidence that the primary reason for the filing of the complaint was to interfere with the first amendment right of the defendant; and

(c) the moving party shall have a right to seek interlocutory appeal from a trial court order denying the motion or from a trial court failure to rule on the motion in expedited fashion.

(2) The court shall grant the motion and dismiss the action upon a finding that the primary purpose of the action is to prevent, interfere with, or chill the moving party's proper participation in the process of government.

(3) Any government body to which the moving party's acts were directed or the attorney general may intervene to defend or otherwise support the moving party.   2001

78-58-105. Counter actions — Attorney's fees — Damages.

(1) A defendant in an action involving public participation in the process of government may maintain an action, claim, cross-claim, or counterclaim to recover:

(a) costs and reasonable attorney's fees, upon a demonstration that the action involving public participation in the process of government was commenced or continued without a substantial basis in fact and law and could not be supported by a substantial argument for the extension, modification, or reversal of existing law; and

(b) other compensatory damages upon an additional demonstration that the action involving public participation in the process of government was commenced or continued for the purpose of harassing, intimidating, punishing, or otherwise maliciously inhibiting the free exercise of rights granted under the First Amendment to the U.S. Constitution.

(2) Nothing in this section shall affect or preclude the right of any party to any recovery otherwise authorized by law.   2001

CHAPTER 61

PROFITS FROM CRIME MEMORABILIA

Section
78-61-101.   Definitions.
78-61-102.   Profit from sale of memorabilia — Deposit in Crime Victim Reparation Fund — Penalty.

78-61-101. Definitions.

As used in this chapter:

(1) "Conviction" means an adjudication by a federal or state court resulting from a trial or plea, including a plea of no contest, nolo contendere, a finding of not guilty due to insanity, or not guilty but mentally ill regardless of whether the sentence was imposed or suspended.

(2) "Fund" means the Crime Victim Reparation Fund created in Section 63-63a-4.

(3) "Memorabilia" means any tangible property of a person convicted of a first degree or capital felony, the value of which is enhanced by the notoriety gained from the conviction.

(4) "Profit" means any income or benefit over and above the fair market value of the property that is received upon the sale or transfer of memorabilia.   2004

78-61-102. Profit from sale of memorabilia — Deposit in Crime Victim Reparation Fund — Penalty.

(1) Any person who receives a profit from the sale or transfer of memorabilia shall remit to the fund:

(a) a complete, itemized accounting of the transaction, including:

(i) a description of each item sold;

(ii) the amount received for each item;

(iii) the estimated fair market value of each item; and

(iv) the name and address of the purchaser of each item; and

(b) a check or money order for the amount of the profit, which shall be the difference between the amount received for the item and the estimated fair market value of the item.

(2) Any person who willfully violates Subsection (1) may be assessed a civil penalty of up to $1,000 per item sold or transferred or three times the amount of the unremitted profit, whichever is greater.   2004

Index

A

ABANDONED ANIMALS.
Cruelty to animals, §§76-9-301 to 76-9-305.

ABANDONED VEHICLES.
Police officer removing.
Procedure if not reclaimed, §41-6a-1408.

ABANDONING A FIRE, §76-6-104.5.

ABANDONMENT.
Motor vehicles.
Removal and impoundment of vehicles generally, §41-6a-1406.

ABORTION.
Abortion litigation trust account.
Created, §76-7-317.1.
Actions.
Provisions not to preclude bringing civil action, §76-7-316.
Birth defects.
Prevention of birth of child born with grave defects.
Circumstances under which abortion authorized, §76-7-302.
Woman's liberty interest outweighing unborn child's right to protection, §76-7-301.1.
Circumstances under which abortion authorized, §76-7-302.
Abortion litigation trust fund.
Created, §76-7-317.1.
Finding of unconstitutionality.
Revival of old law, §76-7-317.2.
Coercion.
Intimidation or coercion of person to obtain abortion prohibited, §76-7-312.
Confidentiality.
Circumstances under which abortion authorized.
Pregnancy as result of rape or incest.
Name of victim confidential, §76-7-302.
Consent.
Informed consent, §§76-7-305, 76-7-305.5.
Constitutionality of abortion law.
Finding of unconstitutionality.
Revival of old law, §76-7-317.2.
Construction and interpretation.
Separability clause, §76-7-317.
Contraceptive and abortion services, §§76-7-321 to 76-7-325.
Entities providing services.
Restriction on public funds, §76-7-323.
Misdemeanor for violation of restrictions, §76-7-324.
Notice to parent or guardian of minor requesting contraceptive.
Misdemeanor for violation, §76-7-325.
Criminal homicide for death caused by abortion.
No cause of action, §76-5-201.
Defense of abortion law.
Abortion litigation trust account.
Created, §76-7-317.1.
Definitions, §76-7-301.
Contraceptive and abortion services, §76-7-321.

ABORTION —Cont'd
Definitions —Cont'd
Notice to parent or guardian of minor requesting contraceptive.
Definition of contraceptive, §76-7-325.
Dilation and extraction procedure.
Prohibition of specific procedures, §76-7-310.5.
Emergencies.
Exceptions to provisions in serious medical emergency, §76-7-315.
Experimentation with unborn children.
Prohibited, §76-7-310.
Violations of abortion laws.
When felony, §76-7-314.
Findings of the legislature, §76-7-301.1.
Funding of abortion.
Public funding prohibited, exception, §76-7-331.
Genetic defects.
Testing for genetic defects.
Permitted, §76-7-310.
Grave damage to pregnant woman's medical health.
Circumstances under which abortion authorized, §76-7-302.
Woman's liberty interest outweighing unborn child's right to protection, §76-7-301.1.
Guardians.
Notice to minor's parent or guardian, §76-7-304.
Request for contraceptive services, §76-7-325.
Homicide.
Criminal homicide caused by abortion.
No cause of action for, §76-5-201.
Hospitals.
Circumstances under which abortion authorized, §76-7-302.
Definition of hospital, §76-7-301.
Definition of medical emergency, §76-7-301.
Participation in abortion.
Employees not required to participate, §76-7-306.
Husband and wife.
Notice to married woman's husband, §76-7-304.
Incest.
Circumstances under which abortion authorized, §76-7-302.
Pregnancy occurring as result of.
Woman's liberty interest outweighing unborn child's right to protection, §76-7-301.1.
Intimidation.
Coercion or intimidation of person to obtain abortion prohibited, §76-7-312.
Minors.
Notice to minor's parent or guardian.
Request for contraceptive services, §76-7-325.
Notice.
Duties of physicians, §76-7-304.
Informed consent.
Information to be furnished to patient upon request, §76-7-305.5.
Parent or guardian of minor requesting contraceptive, §76-7-325.
Definition of contraceptive, §76-7-325.
Misdemeanor for violation, §76-7-325.

767

ADOPTION.
Court of appeals.
Appellate jurisdiction, §78-2a-3.
Juvenile courts.
Jurisdiction, §78-3a-105.
Concurrent jurisdiction in certain cases,
§78-3a-105.
Orders.
Period of operation, §78-3a-119.
Payment of adoption-related expenses.
Sale of children, §76-7-203.
Sale of children.
Payment of adoption-related expenses, §76-7-203.

ADULTERATION.
Alcoholic beverages.
Unlawful adulteration, §32A-12-219.
Fraud.
Deceptive business practices.
Criminal offense, §76-6-507.
Definition of adulterated, §76-6-507.

ADULTERY.
Conduct constituting, §76-7-103.

ADULT PROTECTIVE SERVICES.
Disabled adults, §§76-5-111, 76-5-111.1.

ADVERTISING.
Abuse of personal identity, §76-9-407.
Alcoholic beverages, §32A-12-401.
Convention centers.
Signs on premises, §72-7-504.5.
Lotteries, §76-10-1104.5.
Outdoor advertising, §§72-7-501 to 72-7-516.
See OUTDOOR ADVERTISING.
Sentencing.
Conviction of corporations or associations.
Advertising conviction, §76-3-303.
Unauthorized signs, signals, lights or
markings.
Prohibited, §41-6a-309.

AFFIRMATIVE DEFENSES.
Criminal culpability, §§76-2-301 to 76-2-308.

AFFRONT.
Lewdness, §§76-9-702, 76-9-702.5.

AFTERMARKET CRASH PARTS.
Motor vehicle insurance companies,
§§31A-22-316 to 31A-22-320.

AGE.
Operation of vehicle by persons under sixteen
and a half, §41-8-3.
Passenger restrictions, §41-8-3.
Operation of vehicle by persons under 16,
§41-8-1.
Operation of vehicle by persons under 17.
Prohibited during night hours, §41-8-2.

AGED PERSONS.
Endangerment, §76-5-112.5.
Identification cards.
Continuation in effect until death, §53-3-807.
Motor vehicle insurance.
Premium rate reduction for persons fifty-five
years of age or older, §31A-19a-211.
Neglect, §76-5-111.
Reporting requirements, §76-5-111.1.
Sexual offenses.
Abuse, neglect or exploitation of disabled or elder
adults.
Reporting requirements, §76-5-111.1.

AGGRAVATED ARSON, §76-6-103.

AGGRAVATED ASSAULT.
Generally, §76-5-103.
Prisoner committing aggravated assault,
§76-5-103.5.

AGGRAVATED BURGLARY, §76-6-203.

AGGRAVATED ESCAPE, §76-8-309.

AGGRAVATED KIDNAPPING, §76-5-302.
Sentencing, §76-5-406.3.

AGGRAVATED MURDER.
Sentencing leniency restrictions, §76-3-406.

AGGRAVATED ROBBERY, §76-6-302.

AGGRAVATED SEXUAL ASSAULT, §76-5-405.
Sentencing, §76-5-406.3.

AGGRAVATION OF SENTENCE, §76-3-201.
Capital punishment, §76-3-207.

AGRICULTURE.
Farm tractors.
Defined, §41-6a-102.
Nuisance liability, §78-38-7.

AIDING AND ABETTING.
Criminal responsibility, §76-2-202.
Prostitution.
Aiding prostitution generally, §76-10-1304.
Local ordinances to be consistent with code
provisions, §76-10-1307.
Wildlife.
Violation of title, §23-20-23.

AIDS.
Juvenile courts.
HIV testing of child violating laws prohibiting
sexual offenses, §78-3a-904.
Public safety officers.
At-risk officer testing, §§78-29-101 to 78-29-105.

AIRBAGS.
Failure to repair a damaged or deployed
motor vehicle airbag, §41-6a-1624.

AIRCRAFT.
General provisions, §§72-10-102 to 72-10-131.
Short title of act, §72-10-101.

AIRCRAFT ACCIDENTS.
Reporting requirements, §§72-10-124, 72-10-125.

AIR-DRIVEN PIPES.
Drug paraphernalia, §§58-37a-1 to 58-37a-6.

AIRPLANES.
General provisions, §§72-10-102 to 72-10-131.
Short title of act, §72-10-101.

AIR POLLUTION.
Clean fuel.
Special group license plates, §41-1a-418.
Fees, §41-1a-1211.
Vehicles permitted to use HOV lanes, §41-6a-702.
Motor vehicles.
Equipment.
Air pollution control devices, §41-6a-1626.
Inspections.
Emissions inspections, §41-6a-1642.
Low-speed vehicles, §41-6a-1508.

AIRPORTS.
Bond issues.
Acquisition of property.
Payment for, §72-10-206.
Contracts.
Federal airport funds.
Public agencies.
Contractual powers, §72-10-306.

ANTITRUST —Cont'd
Public utilities.
Exempt activities, §76-10-915.
Purpose of act, §76-10-912.
Securities.
Exempt activities, §76-10-915.
Sentencing.
Fine and/or imprisonment for violation,
§76-10-920.
Service of process.
Investigations.
Civil antitrust investigations.
Demand to produce documentary materials or
give oral testimony, §76-10-917.
Services.
Defined, §76-10-913.
Short title of act, §76-10-911.
State of Utah.
Recovery of actual damages or civil penalty by
state or political subdivisions, §76-10-919.
No recovery from political subdivisions,
§76-10-919.
Title of act.
Short title, §76-10-911.
Vertical agreements.
Certain vertical agreements excluded from
provisions of act, §76-10-920.

APPEALS.
Drunk driving.
Drivers' licenses.
Revocation, §41-6a-521.
Juvenile courts.
Transfer of jurisdiction to district court.
Serious youth offenders and certification
proceedings, §78-3a-604.
Small claims actions, §78-6-10.

APPEARANCES.
Citations.
Misdemeanor or infraction charges.
Failure to appear.
Arrest, §§77-7-19, 77-7-22.
Juvenile courts.
Citation procedure.
Failure to appear, §78-3a-503.
Contempt proceedings.
Failure to appear, §78-3a-112.
Spouse abuse procedures.
Mandatory, §77-36-2.6.

APPLICABILITY OF CRIMINAL CODE,
§76-1-103.

ARBITRATION.
Motor vehicle insurance.
Claims resolution by, §31A-22-303.
Third party claims, §31A-22-321.

ARCADES.
Controlled substances.
Possession violation, §58-37-8.

ARCHERY.
Hunter orange.
Requirement to wear, §23-20-31.

ARCHITECTS.
Child support or visitation violations by
licensees, §78-32-17.

ARENAS.
Controlled substances.
Prohibited acts committed in, §58-37-8.

ARMS.
See WEAPONS.

ARRAIGNMENT.
Magistrates.
Authority to conduct, §78-7-17.5.

ARREST.
Aircraft operated while intoxicated.
Warrantless arrest, §72-10-501.
Alcoholic beverages.
Criminal procedure.
Applicable provisions, §32A-13-102.
Appearance, §77-7-19.
Boating.
Litter and pollution control.
Violation of chapter or rules.
Procedure, §73-18a-15.
Violations of provisions, §73-18-20.
Bus passenger safety.
Detention of violators.
Authorized bus company representatives may
detain, §76-10-1507.
Citations.
Misdemeanor or infraction charges, §§77-7-18 to
77-7-22.
Citizen's arrest.
Doors and windows.
Breaking.
When proper, §77-7-8.
Felonies.
Reasonable cause, §77-7-3.
Force, §76-2-403.
Public offenses committed or attempted in
presence, §77-7-3.
Cohabitant abuse.
Prevention of abuse in absence of protective order,
§30-6-8.
Criminal identification.
Arrest based on warrant.
Peace officers to supply information, §53-10-207.
School employee for controlled substance or sex
offense, §53-10-211.
Deaf persons.
Procedure following, §77-7-6.
Defined, §77-7-1.
Delivery of prisoner.
Arrested without warrant, §77-7-23.
Doors.
Breaking.
When proper, §77-7-8.
Driving while intoxicated.
Warrantless arrest, §41-6a-508.
Evading arrest, §76-8-305.5.
Execution.
Warrants.
Telegraph or telephone authorization, §77-7-10.
Extradition.
See EXTRADITION.
Fleeing from or otherwise eluding a law
enforcement officer to avoid arrest,
§76-8-305.5.
Flying under the influence.
Warrantless arrest, §72-10-501.
Force in making, §§76-2-403, 77-7-7.
Forcible entry.
Peace officers, §77-7-8.
Fresh pursuit.
Procedure after, §77-9-2.
Frisking suspect for dangerous weapons,
§§77-7-15 to 77-7-17.
Goods held or displayed for sale, §77-7-13.
Hearing-impaired persons.
Procedure following, §77-7-6.
Highway patrol powers, §53-8-106.

C

CABLE TELEVISION.
Fraud.
Communications fraud generally, §76-10-1801.
Pornography.
Distribution of pornographic material through cable television, §76-10-1229.
Theft.
Cable television services, §76-6-409.3.

CAMOUFLAGE.
Hunter orange apparel, §23-20-31.

CAMPERS.
Defined, §41-1a-102.
Display of decal, §41-1a-227.
Registration, §41-1a-227.

CAMP FLOYD/STAGECOACH INN STATE PARK.
Jurisdiction over highways, §§72-3-201, 72-3-202.

CANALS.
Injuring canal.
Felony, §76-10-204.

CANES.
Motor vehicles.
White cane law, §41-6a-1007.

CANYONS.
Motor vehicles.
Driving in canyons and on mountain highways, §41-6a-1708.
Railroads.
Right of way in canyons, §56-1-9.

CAPITAL PUNISHMENT.
Mental health of defendant.
Sentencing proceedings for capital felonies, §76-3-207.
Pardons and paroles.
Life imprisonment without parole.
Applicability of sentencing option, §76-3-207.5.

CAPITOL.
Motor vehicles.
Traffic and parking rules.
Enforcement, §53-1-109.

CARAVANS.
Motor vehicles.
Following another vehicle.
Restrictions, §41-6a-711.

CARBURETOR PIPES.
Drug paraphernalia, §§58-37a-1 to 58-37a-6.

CARCASSES.
Nuisances.
Misdemeanor for improper disposal, §76-10-805.

CAR INSURANCE.
General provisions.
See MOTOR VEHICLE INSURANCE.

CARPOOLS.
Ridesharing.
General provisions, §§72-12-102 to 72-12-110.
See RIDESHARING.

CARRIERS.
Motor carriers.
General provisions.
See MOTOR CARRIERS.

CATALOGUE SALES.
City or town option sales and use tax.
Botanical, cultural, recreational and zoological organizations funding, §59-12-1402.

CATASTROPHE.
Causing a catastrophe, §76-6-105.

CERAMIC PIPES.
Drug paraphernalia, §§58-37a-1 to 58-37a-6.

CHAIN LETTERS.
Pyramid schemes.
Generally, §§76-6a-1 to 76-6a-6.

CHAMBER PIPES.
Drug paraphernalia, §§58-37a-1 to 58-37a-6.

CHARITIES.
Charitable organizations, §§76-10-601 to 76-10-603.
Violations of provisions of part, §76-10-604.

CHECKS.
Bad checks, §76-6-505.
Presumptions.
Issuing bad check or draft, §76-6-505.

CHEMICAL WEAPONS.
Detection of public health emergencies act, §§26-23b-101 to 26-23b-110.
Weapons of mass destruction generally, §§76-10-401 to 76-10-405.

CHILD ABUSE OR NEGLECT.
Alcoholic beverages.
Child born with fetal alcohol syndrome.
Duty to report, §62A-4a-404.
Child protective orders.
Violating, §76-5-108.
Child protective services investigator, §62A-4a-202.6.
Children's justice center.
Definitions, §78-3a-103.
Clergy.
Reporting requirements.
Exceptions, §62A-4a-403.
Cohabitant abuse.
Generally, §§30-6-1 to 30-6-15.
Conduct constituting child abuse, §76-5-109.
Disabled child, §76-5-110.
Controlled substances.
Child born with fetal drug dependency.
Duty to report, §62A-4a-404.
Death.
Due to abuse or neglect.
Duty to report, §62A-4a-405.
Definitions, §76-5-109.
Abused child, §78-3a-103.
Disabled child, §76-5-110.
Reporting, §62A-4a-402.
Disabled child, §76-5-110.
Domestic violence in presence of child, §76-5-109.1.
Elements of child abuse, §76-5-109.
Disabled child, §76-5-110.
Homicide, §76-5-208.
Death from child abuse, §76-5-201.
Immunities.
Legal action, §62A-4a-410.
Interdisciplinary child protection teams, §62A-4a-409.
Interview with child prior to removal from home, §62A-4a-409.
Investigations.
Children in custody of child and family services division.
Duty of peace officers to investigate, §53-13-110.
Interviews of children.
Allegations of sexual abuse or serious physical abuse, §62A-4a-414.

DEALERS —Cont'd
Junk dealers.
  See JUNK DEALERS.
Motor vehicle dealers.
  See MOTOR VEHICLE DEALERS.

DEATH.
Child abuse or neglect.
  Death of child due to abuse or neglect.
    Duty to report, §62A-4a-405.
Emergency medical services.
  Workers' compensation presumption for providers.
    Time limit for death benefits, §34A-2-903.
Homicide generally.
  See HOMICIDE.
Hospitals.
  Routine inquiry and required request.
    Search and notification, §26-28-6.
Sentencing.
  Capital punishment.
    See CAPITAL PUNISHMENT.

DEBIT CARDS.
Financial transaction cards generally.
  See FINANCIAL TRANSACTION CARDS.

DECEPTION, THEFT BY, §§76-6-401, 76-6-405.

DECEPTIVE BUSINESS PRACTICES,
  §76-6-507.

DEEDS.
Fraud.
  Recordation.
    Fraudulent handling of recordable writings,
      §76-6-503.5.

DEER CREEK STATE PARK.
Jurisdiction over highways, §§72-3-201,
  72-3-202.

DEFAMATION.
Criminal defamation, §76-9-404.
  Imputing unchastity to female, §§76-9-507,
    76-9-508.

DEFENSES.
Abuse of personal identity.
  Consent as affirmative defense, §76-9-407.
Affirmative defenses.
  Possessing controlled substance and weapon,
    §76-10-503.
Controlled substances.
  Possessing controlled substance and weapon,
    §76-10-503.
**Custodial sexual relations or misconduct with
  youth receiving state services,** §76-5-413.
Drunk driving.
  Legal entitlement to use alcohol or drug.
    Defense not available, §41-6a-504.
Kidnapping, §76-5-305.
Murder.
  Aggravated murder, §76-5-202.
**Operation of vehicle by person under sixteen
  and a half.**
  Passenger restrictions, §41-8-3.
Traffic signal preemption devices.
  Inoperative device.
    Affirmative defense, §41-6a-311.

DEFINED TERMS.
Abuse.
  Child protective orders, §78-3h-101.
Access restricted.
  Adult content on internet, §76-10-1230.
Accompanying data.
  Accident reports, §41-6a-404.

DEFINED TERMS —Cont'd
Account.
  Alcoholic beverages, §32A-1-115.
**Action involving public participation in the
  process of government.**
  Citizen participation in government, §78-58-102.
Activity regulated under this title.
  Wildlife, §23-13-2.
Actor.
  Custodial sexual relations or misconduct with
    youth receiving state services, §76-5-413.
Administration of criminal justice.
  Criminal investigations and technical services
    division, §53-10-102.
Adult.
  Youth courts, §78-57-102.
Adult content registry.
  Adult content on internet, §76-10-1230.
Agency.
  Uniform forfeiture procedures, §24-1-3.
Agent.
  Motor vehicle accident reports, §41-6a-404.
Agricultural operations.
  Limited application of nuisance provisions,
    §78-38-8.
Alcoholic beverage.
  Drinking alcoholic beverage and open containers
    in motor vehicles, §41-6a-526.
Alcohol-related offense.
  Alcoholic beverages, §32A-1-115.
Alcohol restricted driver, §41-6a-529.
All-terrain type I vehicle, §41-6a-102.
Annexation.
  Funding for 911 emergency telephone service,
    §69-2-5.
Annual conviction time period.
  Alcoholic beverages, §32A-1-115.
Aquaculture facility.
  Wildlife, §23-13-2.
Aquatic animal.
  Wildlife, §23-13-2.
Aquatic wildlife.
  Wildlife, §23-13-2.
Assessment.
  Driving under the influence and reckless driving,
    §41-6a-501.
Authorized emergency vehicle, §41-6a-102.
Bag limit.
  Wildlife, §23-13-2.
Banquet.
  Alcoholic beverages, §32A-1-105.
Bar.
  Alcoholic beverages, §32A-1-105.
Bicycle, §41-6a-102.
Big game.
  Wildlife, §23-13-2.
Biological agent.
  Weapons of mass destruction, §76-10-401.
Bioterrorism.
  Public health emergencies, §26-23b-102.
Blood or blood-contaminated body fluids.
  Disease testing for at-risk public safety officers,
    §78-29-101.
Booby trap.
  Controlled substances, §58-37d-3.
Bus, §41-6a-102.
Carcass.
  Wildlife, §23-13-2.
Card.
  Financial transaction card, §76-6-506.7.
Cash bar.
  Alcoholic beverages, §32A-1-105.

DERAILMENT.
Defined as technical hazard, §53-2-102.

DERRICKS.
Duties respecting derricks, power equipment, etc., §41-6a-1206.

DESTRUCTION OF PROPERTY, §§76-6-101 to 76-6-110.
Arson.
  Aggravated arson.
    Conduct constituting, §76-6-103.
  Conduct constituting, §76-6-102.
Burning.
  Reckless burning.
    Conduct constituting, §76-6-104.
Catastrophes.
  Causing a catastrophe.
    Conduct constituting, §76-6-105.
Definitions, §76-6-101.
Graffiti, §76-6-107.
Habitable structure.
  Defined, §76-6-101.
Mischief.
  Criminal mischief.
    Conduct constituting, §76-6-106.

DETECTION OF PUBLIC HEALTH EMERGENCIES ACT, §§26-23b-101 to 26-23b-110.

DETECTION OF PUBLIC HEALTH EMERGENCIES.
Definitions, §26-23b-102.
Enforcement, §26-23b-109.
Investigations, §26-23b-108.
Liability, §26-23b-107.
Reports, §26-23b-103.
  Authorization, §26-23b-104.
  Medical laboratories, §26-23b-106.
  Pharmacies, §26-23b-105.
Title, §26-23b-101.

DETECTIVES.
Private investigators, §§53-9-101 to 53-9-119.
  See PRIVATE INVESTIGATORS.

DETENTION.
Unlawful detention.
  Conduct constituting, §76-5-304.
  Elements of offense, §76-5-304.

DIACETYLMORPHINE.
Narcotic drugs, §§58-37-1 to 58-37-21.
  See CONTROLLED SUBSTANCES.

DINOSAUR DIAMOND PREHISTORIC HIGHWAY, §72-4-204.

DIPLOMATS.
Traffic violations by, §41-6a-1901.

DISABLED PERSONS.
Abuse, neglect or exploitation of disabled adults.
  Reporting requirements, §76-5-111.1.
Child abuse or neglect.
  Abuse or neglect of disabled child.
    Conduct constituting, §76-5-110.
Exploitation, §76-5-111.
  Reporting requirements, §76-5-111.1.
Identification cards.
  Extension of expiration, §53-3-807.
License plates.
  Disability special group license plates or windshield placards, §41-1a-420.
Medication neglect, §76-5-110.

DISABLED PERSONS —Cont'd
Minors.
  Child abuse or neglect.
    Abuse or neglect of disabled child, §76-5-110.
  Medication neglect, §76-5-110.
Motor vehicles.
  License plates.
    Disability special group license plates or windshield placards, §41-1a-420.
Neglect, §76-5-111.
  Reporting requirements, §76-5-111.1.
Public schools.
  Standards, §53A-1-402.
Sexual offenses.
  Abuse, neglect or exploitation of disabled or elder adults, §76-5-111.
  Reporting requirements, §76-5-111.1.
Wildlife.
  Licenses.
    Fishing licenses, §23-19-36.

DISAPPEARANCES.
Missing children.
  Public schools.
    Missing children identification, §§53A-11-501 to 53A-11-504.

DISARMING A PEACE OFFICER, §76-5-102.8.

DISCRIMINATION.
Alcoholic beverages.
  Dramshop liability.
    Employees refusing to sell alcoholic beverages. Sanctions or termination of employment by employers, §32A-14a-103.
Commerce.
  Competitive practices.
    Unfair discrimination in competitive practices.
      Corporation guilty, §76-10-904.
      Criminal offense, §76-10-903.
      Penalty, §76-10-905.
Dramshop liability.
  Employees refusing to sell alcoholic beverages. Sanctions or termination of employment by employers, §32A-14a-103.

DISEASES.
Detection of public health emergencies, §§26-23b-101 to 26-23b-110.
Public safety officers.
  Disease testing for at-risk public safety officers, §§78-29-101 to 78-29-105.
Rabies.
  See RABIES.

DISMEMBERMENT.
Personal injury protection, §31A-22-309.

DISORDERLY CONDUCT.
Bus passenger safety.
  Ejection of passenger, §76-10-1506.
Conduct constituting, §76-9-102.
Definitions.
  Public places, §76-9-102.
Elements of offense, §76-9-102.
Failure to disperse.
  Misdemeanor, §76-9-104.
Infractions.
  When infraction, §76-9-102.
Public places.
  Defined, §76-9-102.

DISPATCHERS.
Annual training requirement, §53-6-306.
Application for certification exam.
  Requirements, §53-6-302.

EDGE OF THE CEDARS STATE PARK.
Jurisdiction over highways, §§72-3-201, 72-3-202.

EDUCATION.
Boards of education.
General provisions.
See PUBLIC SCHOOLS.
Disruption of school activities, failure to leave, reentry, §§76-8-1401, 76-8-1402.
Youth courts.
School credit for participation, §78-57-110.

EFFECTIVE DATE OF CRIMINAL CODE, §76-1-102.
Offenses prior to effective date.
Application of code, §76-1-102.

EGGS.
Protected wildlife or eggs.
Taking unlawful except as authorized, §23-15-7.

ELECTIONS.
Appeals.
Supreme court.
Appellate jurisdiction, §78-2-2.
Corrupt practices.
Campaign contributions not prohibited, §76-8-102.
Party officials.
Defined, §76-8-101.
Juvenile court judges.
Retention election, §78-1-2.3.
Supreme court.
Appellate jurisdiction involving, §78-2-2.

ELECTRICAL COOPERATIVES.
Rates and charges.
Wholesale electrical cooperatives.
Exemption from rate regulation, §54-4-1.1.
Increase of rates.
Requirements, §54-4-1.1.

ELECTRIC ASSISTED BICYCLES.
Definition, §41-6a-102.
Protective headgear for operators, §41-6a-1505.

ELECTRICIANS.
Licenses.
Child support or visitation violations, §78-32-17.

ELECTRICITY.
High voltage overhead lines.
Outdoor advertising structures relocated from high voltage overhead lines, §72-7-516.
Theft of services, §§76-6-409, 76-6-409.3.
Devices for theft of services, §76-6-409.1.

ELECTRIC PIPES.
Drug paraphernalia, §§58-37a-1 to 58-37a-6.

ELECTRONIC COMMUNICATIONS.
Harassment.
Electronic communication harassment, §76-9-201.

EMAIL.
Harassment.
Electronic communication harassment, §76-9-201.

EMBEZZLEMENT.
Municipal corporations.
Public property offenses, §§76-8-402, 76-8-403.
Public money.
Limitation of actions, §76-1-301.5.
Theft generally.
See THEFT.

EMBRACERY, §76-8-508.5.

EMERGENCIES.
Alcoholic beverages.
Unlawful sale or supply during, §32A-12-207.

EMERGENCIES —Cont'd
Department of public safety.
Drivers' license compact.
Licensing authority, §53-3-605.
Detection of public health emergencies, §§26-23b-101 to 26-23b-110.
Disaster response and recovery.
Expenditures authorized, §53-2-106.
Division of comprehensive emergency management.
Creation, §53-2-103.
Director, §53-2-103.
Division of emergency services and homeland security.
Energy emergency plan, §53-2-110.
Loan program, §53-2-102.5.
Emergency management assistance compact, §§53-2-201, 53-2-202.
Authority of governor to enter into compact, §53-2-301.
Energy emergency plan.
Division of emergency services and homeland security, §53-2-110.
Telephones.
Emergency dispatchers, §§53-6-301 to 53-6-310.
See DISPATCHERS.

EMERGENCY MEDICAL SERVICES.
Death.
Workers' compensation presumption for providers.
Time limit for death benefits, §34A-2-903.
Licenses.
Child support or visitation violations, §78-32-17.
Presumptions.
Workers' compensation presumption for providers, §§34A-2-901 to 34A-2-905. See within this heading, "Workers' compensation presumption for providers."
Rules and regulations.
Workers' compensation presumption for providers, §34A-2-905.
Volunteers.
Workers' compensation presumption for providers.
Volunteer providers, §34A-2-904.
Workers' compensation presumption for providers.
Claims.
Time limits, §34A-2-902.
Death benefits.
Time limit, §34A-2-903.
Failure to be tested.
Effect, §34A-2-903.
Generally, §34A-2-901.
Rebuttable presumption, §34A-2-905.
Rules and regulations, §34A-2-905.
Time limits for claims, §34A-2-902.
Time limits for death benefits, §34A-2-903.
Volunteer emergency medical services providers, §34A-2-904.

EMERGENCY VEHICLES.
Authorized emergency vehicles.
Applicability and exemptions to and from chapter, §41-6a-212.
Defined, §41-6a-102.
Policy regarding vehicle pursuits, §41-6a-212.
Private vehicle as emergency vehicle.
Defined.
Rules, §41-6a-310.
Right of way, §41-6a-904.

EMINENT DOMAIN.
Governmental immunity.
Takings actions.
Exemptions, §63-30d-203.
Waiver of immunity, §63-30d-302.

EXPLOSIVES —Cont'd
Motor vehicles.
Definition of explosives, §41-6a-102.
Possession and mailing.
Generally, §§76-10-306 to 76-10-308.
Powder houses.
Misdemeanor for violations, §76-10-303.
Transportation.
Marking containers before transportation or storage.
Misdemeanor for violation, §76-10-302.
Universities and colleges.
Damage or destruction of property by explosives or flammable material, §76-8-715.
Wildlife.
Use by division employees and certain federal game agents, §23-13-7.

EXPUNGEMENT OF RECORDS.
Applicability of provisions.
Retroactive application, §77-18-17.
Certificate of eligibility, §77-18-11.
Defined, §77-18-9.
Denial.
Grounds, §77-18-12.
Issuance, §77-18-12.
Definitions, §77-18-9.
Hearings, §§77-18-11, 77-18-13.
Juvenile courts, §§78-3a-904, 78-3a-905.
Notice.
Petition for expungement of conviction record, §77-18-11.
Victims.
Right to notice of expungement petition, §77-38-14.
Orders, §77-18-14.
Petition, §§77-18-10, 77-18-11.
Prior convictions.
Effect on eligibility, §77-18-12.
Retention of expunged record, §77-18-15.
Retroactive application of provisions, §77-18-17.
Sentencing.
Opening of sealed records and admission into evidence, §77-18-15.
Sex offender registration.
Effect of expungement, §77-27-21.5.
Victims of crime.
Notice of expungement petition.
Rights of crime victims, §77-38-14.
Violations of provisions as misdemeanors, §77-18-16.

EXTORTION.
Theft by extortion.
Elements of offense, §76-6-406.
Use of extortion or bribery to dismiss criminal proceedings.
Felony, §76-8-509.

EXTRADITION.
Actions.
Civil actions.
Service of process.
Persons brought into state exempt from, §77-30-25.
Arrest.
Commitment.
Pending governor's warrant of arrest, §77-30-15.
Fugitives.
Warrants, §77-30-13.
Governor's warrant, §77-30-7.
Commitment pending, §77-30-15.
Execution, §77-30-8.

EXTRADITION —Cont'd
Arrest —Cont'd
Governor's warrant —Cont'd
Habeas corpus, §77-30-10.
Misdemeanor.
Disobedience of section, §77-30-11.
Penalty.
Disobedience of section, §77-30-11.
Issuance, §77-30-22.
No arrest made.
Procedure, §77-30-17.
Officers.
Authority of, §77-30-9.
Recall or another issued, §77-30-21.
Recitals, §77-30-7.
Habeas corpus.
Governor's warrant, §77-30-10.
Misdemeanor.
Disobedience of section, §77-30-11.
Warrants.
Fugitives from justice, §77-30-13.
Without, §77-30-14.
Without warrant, §77-30-14.
Bail, §77-30-16.
Capital cases, §77-30-16.
Forfeiture, §77-30-18.
Capital cases.
Bail.
Exception in, §77-30-16.
Citation of act, §77-30-28.
Cities.
Jails.
Officers entitled to use, §77-30-12.
Commitment.
Governor's warrant of arrest.
Pending arrest under, §77-30-15.
Construction and interpretation.
Uniformity of, §77-30-27.
Costs.
Payment of expenses, §77-30-24.
Counties.
Jails.
Officers entitled to use, §77-30-12.
Crime committed in another state by person while in this state, §77-30-6.
Definitions, §77-30-1.
Demand by other state, §§77-30-2 to 77-30-4.
Execution.
Governor's warrant of arrest, §77-30-8.
Executive authority.
Defined, §77-30-1.
Expenses.
Payment of, §77-30-24.
Forfeitures.
Bail, §77-30-18.
Forms.
Demand by other state, §77-30-3.
Governor.
Arrest.
Warrant, §77-30-7.
Commitment pending, §77-30-15.
Execution, §77-30-8.
Habeas corpus, §77-30-10.
Penalty for disobedience, §77-30-11.
Issuance, §77-30-22.
No arrest made.
Procedure, §77-30-17.
Officers.
Authority of, §77-30-9.
Recall or another issued, §77-30-21.
Recitals, §77-30-7.
Defined, §77-30-1.

FIRST-AID VOLUNTEERS —Cont'd
Transportation —Cont'd
Forest products or native vegetation —Cont'd
Seizure and disposal of products, §78-38-4.6.
Stopping vehicles, §78-38-4.6.
Violations, §78-38-4.9.

FIRST DEGREE MURDER, §76-5-202.

FISH.
Aquatic wildlife.
General provisions, §§23-15-2 to 23-15-9.
See WILDLIFE.

FLAGMAN.
Highway maintenance, §§41-6a-1203, 41-6a-1206,
72-6-114.

FLAGS.
Abuse of a flag, §76-9-601.
Motor vehicle equipment.
Load extending beyond rear of vehicles,
§41-6a-1606.

FLARES.
Motor vehicle equipment.
Trucks and buses to carry, §41-6a-1637.

FLOTATION DEVICES.
Boating requirement, §73-18-8.

FLYING UNDER THE INFLUENCE, §§72-10-501
to 72-10-504.
Arrest.
Warrantless arrest, §72-10-501.
Blood or breath alcohol concentration,
§72-10-501.
Chemical tests, §§72-10-502 to 72-10-504.
Criminal punishment, §72-10-501.

FOLLOWING ANOTHER VEHICLE.
Caravan or motorcade, §41-6a-711.
Funeral processions.
Exceptions for funeral processions, §41-6a-711.
Proximity and distance, §41-6a-711.

FORCE.
Justification.
Arrest, §76-2-403.
Deadly force.
Peace officers, §76-2-404.
Defense of habitation, §76-2-405.
Defense of person, §76-2-402.
Defense of property, §76-2-406.
Real property other than habitation, §76-2-407.

FORCIBLE SEXUAL ABUSE, §76-5-405.
Aggravated murder.
Homicide in connection with, §76-5-202.

FORCIBLE SODOMY, §76-5-403.

FOREIGN VEHICLES.
Defined, §41-1a-102.
Registration, §41-1a-224.
Compliance with federal law, §41-1a-225.
English translation, §41-1a-225.
Transfer of ownership.
Compliance with federal law required, §41-1a-711.
Disclosure requirements, §41-1a-712.

FORENSIC SERVICES, BUREAU OF,
§§53-10-401 to 53-10-406.
Blood analysis.
Convicted murderers, §53-10-403.
Medically certified professions to draw sample,
§53-10-405.
Requirement to obtain sample, §53-10-404.
Rulemaking authority, §53-10-406.

FORENSIC SERVICES, BUREAU OF —Cont'd
Blood analysis —Cont'd
Sex offenders, §53-10-403.
Transmittal of sample to department, §53-10-404.
When no sample required, §53-10-405.
Who may draw sample, §53-10-405.
Bureau chief.
Appointment, §53-10-401.
Bureau duties, §53-10-402.
Blood analysis, §53-10-406.
Chain of incoming evidence.
Protection of chain of custody, §53-10-402.
Creation, §53-10-401.
Crime scenes.
Analysis of physical evidence, §53-10-402.
DNA specimen restricted account, §53-10-407.
Expert testimony.
Scientific evidence, §53-10-402.
Expungement of record, §53-10-406.
Health care personnel.
Blood analysis.
Medically certified to draw sample, §53-10-405.
Infectious diseases.
Crime lab employee safety, §53-10-402.
Satellite laboratories.
Establishment, §53-10-402.

FORESTS AND FORESTRY.
Abandoning fire, §76-6-104.5.
Fire protection of forests and wildlands.
Abandoning fire, §76-6-104.5.
Transportation.
Forest products or native vegetation, §§78-38-4.5
to 78-38-4.9.
Transportation of forest products and native
vegetation violations, §78-38-4.9.

FORFEITURES, §41-6a-211.
Uniform forfeiture procedures, §§24-1-1 to
24-1-20.
See UNIFORM FORFEITURE PROCEDURES.

FORGERY.
Alcoholic beverages.
Prohibited act, §32A-12-310.
Commercial drivers' licenses, §41-3-703.
Conduct constituting, §76-6-501.
Cultural sites protection.
Prohibited acts, §76-6-902.
Drivers' licenses, §41-3-703.
Elements of offense, §76-6-501.
License plates, §41-3-703.
Military justice, §76-6-502.
When misdemeanor, §76-6-501.
Motor vehicles.
False evidences of title and registration,
§41-1a-1315.
Licenses, plates, permits or decals, §41-3-703.
Possession of forged writing or device for
writing.
Conduct constituting, §76-6-502.
Recordation.
Recording false or forged instruments.
Criminal offense, §76-8-414.
Records.
Recording false or forged instruments, §76-8-414.
Trademarks and service marks.
Misdemeanor, §76-10-1002.
Trade names.
Definition of forged trade names, §76-10-1001.
Misdemeanors, §76-10-1002.
Writing.
Defined, §76-6-501.

FORNICATION.
Conduct constituting, §76-7-104.

FORT BUENAVENTURA STATE PARK.
Jurisdiction over highways, §§72-3-201, 72-3-203.

FOSTER CARE.
Abuse of child in substitute care.
Investigation by law enforcement officer, §62A-4a-202.5.
Citizen review board.
Reports as evidence in juvenile court hearings, §78-3a-116.
Investigations.
Law enforcement investigation of alleged abuse, §62A-4a-202.5.

FOUR WHEELERS.
Motor vehicle chassis and equipment restrictions, §§41-6a-1629 to 41-6a-1632.

FRAUD.
Adulteration.
Deceptive business practices.
Criminal offense, §76-6-507.
Definition of adulterated, §76-6-507.
Aircraft.
Equity skimming of vehicles, §76-6-522.
Alcoholic beverages.
Forgery of writings with intent to defraud, §32A-12-310.
Appraisals.
Bribery of or receiving bribe by person in business of selection, appraisal or criticism of goods or services, §76-6-508.
Athletic contests.
Bribery or threat to influence contest.
Conduct constituting, §76-6-514.
Bail bond recovery licensure.
False representation as licensee, §53-11-121.
Grounds for disciplinary action, §53-11-119.
Boating.
Certificate of title.
Fraudulent application, §73-18-7.1.
Equity skimming of vehicles, §76-6-522.
Registration.
Fraudulent application, §73-18-7.1.
Bribery.
Contests.
Bribery or threat to influence contest, §76-6-514.
Brokers.
Equity skimming of vehicles, §76-6-522.
Cable television.
Communications fraud generally, §76-10-1801.
Checks.
Fraudulent checks.
Issuing bad checks or drafts, §76-6-505.
Coin operated machines.
Slugs.
Using or making slugs, §76-6-515.
Commerce.
Price.
Fraudulent practices to affect market price.
Misdemeanor, §76-10-902.
Communications fraud, §76-10-1801.
Computer crimes, §§76-6-701 to 76-6-705.
Communications fraud, §76-10-1801.
Contests.
Bribery or threat to influence contest.
Conduct constituting, §76-6-514.
Conveyances.
Real property conveyed by husband without wife's consent, §76-6-516.

FRAUD —Cont'd
Corporations, §§76-10-701 to 76-10-711.
Creditors.
Defrauding creditors.
Conduct constituting, §76-6-511.
Credit reporting.
Making false credit report.
Conduct constituting, §76-6-517.
Crime victims reparations.
Claims.
Actions.
Civil action, §63-25a-410.
Definition of "fraudulent claims," §63-25a-402.
Penalties, §63-25a-410.
Criminal simulation.
Generally, §76-6-518.
Data processing.
Communications fraud generally, §76-10-1801.
Computer crimes generally, §§76-6-701 to 76-6-705.
Dealers.
Equity skimming of vehicles, §76-6-522.
Deceptive business practices, §76-6-507.
Deeds.
Recordation.
Fraudulent handling of recordable writings, §76-6-503.5.
Defenses.
Communications fraud, §76-10-1801.
Deceptive business practices, §76-6-507.
Definitions.
Deceptive business practices, §76-6-507.
Vehicles.
Equity skimming of vehicles, §76-6-522.
Definitions.
Defenses.
Deceptive business practices, §76-6-507.
Financial transaction card offenses, §76-6-506.
Forgery.
Writing, §76-6-501.
Vehicles.
Equity skimming of vehicles, §76-6-522.
Drafts.
Issuing bad check or draft.
Criminal offense, §76-6-505.
Fiduciaries.
Unlawful dealing with property by fiduciary.
Conduct constituting, §76-6-513.
Elements of offense, §76-6-513.
Financial institutions, §§76-6-512, 76-6-513.
Financial transaction cards.
Acquisition, possession or transfer of card in unlawful manner.
Elements of offense, §76-6-506.3.
Application.
False application for card.
Elements of offense, §76-6-506.2.
Authorized credit card merchants.
Defined, §76-6-506.
Unauthorized factoring of credit card sales drafts, §76-6-506.6.
Automated banking devices.
Defined, §76-6-506.
Card holders.
Defined, §76-6-506.
Classification of offenses, §76-6-506.5.
Credit card sales drafts.
Defined, §76-6-506.
Unauthorized factoring, §76-6-506.6.
Definitions, §76-6-506.
Degree of offense.
Value of property, money or things obtained, §76-6-506.5.

FRAUD —Cont'd
Financial transaction cards —Cont'd
Evidence of card transaction.
Falsely signing.
Elements of offense, §76-6-506.1.
Falsely making, coding or signing card.
Elements of offense, §76-6-506.1.
Felonies.
When offenses felony, §76-6-506.5.
Issuers.
Defined, §76-6-506.
Misdemeanors.
When unlawful acts misdemeanor, §76-6-506.5.
Personal identification code.
Defined, §76-6-506.
Property obtained by unlawful conduct.
Elements of offense, §76-6-506.4.
Unauthorized factoring of credit card sales drafts, §76-6-506.6.
Use.
Unlawful use of card or automated banking device.
Elements of offense, §76-6-506.2.
Value of property, money or things obtained.
Determination of degree of offense, §76-6-506.5.
Gambling.
Conduct constituting, §76-10-1103.
Confidence games.
Punishment as for theft, §76-10-1109.
Elements of offense, §76-10-1103.
Sentencing, §76-10-1103.
Husband and wife.
Conveyance of real property by husband without wife's consent, §76-6-516.
Identity fraud, §§76-6-1101 to 76-6-1104.
Insurance, §76-6-521.
Arson, §76-6-102.
Unemployment insurance fraud, §76-8-1301.
Labels.
Deceptive business practices.
Mislabeling.
Criminal offense, §76-6-507.
Leases.
Equity skimming of vehicles, §76-6-522.
Mail fraud.
Communications fraud generally, §76-10-1801.
Mobile or manufactured homes.
Equity skimming of vehicles, §76-6-522.
Mortgages.
Recordation.
Fraudulent handling of recordable writings, §76-6-503.5.
Motor vehicles.
Equity skimming of vehicles, §76-6-522.
False evidences of title and registration, §41-1a-1315.
Identification numbers.
Fraudulent alteration, §41-1a-1318.
Negotiable instruments.
Issuing bad check or draft, §76-6-505.
Newspapers.
Communications fraud generally, §76-10-1801.
Private investigators.
Disciplinary action, §53-9-118.
Unprofessional conduct, §53-9-102.
Public assistance, §§76-8-1201 to 76-8-1207.
Public safety department.
Criminal investigations and technical services division.
False information, §53-10-111.
Radio.
Communications fraud generally, §76-10-1801.

FRAUD —Cont'd
Recordation.
Fraudulent handling of recordable writings.
Conduct constituting, §76-6-503.5.
Elements of offense, §76-6-503.5.
Felony of third degree, §76-6-503.5.
Records.
Tampering with records.
Conduct constituting, §76-6-504.
Security interest.
Equity skimming of vehicles, §76-6-522.
Simulation.
Criminal simulation.
Conduct constituting, §76-6-518.
Slugs.
Using or making.
Conduct constituting, §76-6-515.
Taxation.
Tax evasion.
Criminal offense, §76-8-1101.
Telecommunications.
Communications fraud generally, §76-10-1801.
Telegraphs.
Communications fraud generally, §76-10-1801.
Telephones.
Communications fraud generally, §76-10-1801.
Television.
Communications fraud generally, §76-10-1801.
Threats.
Contests.
Bribery or threat to influence contest, §76-6-514.
Trademarks and service marks.
Selling or dealing with articles bearing registered trademark or service mark with intent to defraud.
Misdemeanor, §76-10-1006.
Usury.
Conduct constituting, §76-6-520.
Uttering.
Simulation.
Criminal simulation generally, §76-6-518.
Vehicles.
Equity skimming of vehicles.
Conduct constituting, §76-6-522.
Defenses.
Satisfaction of lease obligation or security interest, §76-6-522.
Vending machines.
Slugs.
Using or making slugs, §76-6-515.
Weights and measures.
Deceptive business practices.
Criminal offense, §76-6-507.
Wildlife.
Licenses, permits, tags or certificates.
Fraud, deceit or misrepresentation in obtaining, §23-19-5.
Wills.
Recordation.
Fraudulent handling of recordable writings, §76-6-503.5.

FREEDOM OF INFORMATION.
Protected records, §63-2-304.

FREIGHT.
See MOTOR CARRIERS.

FREMONT INDIAN STATE PARK.
Jurisdiction over highways, §§72-3-201, 72-3-203.

FRESH PURSUIT.
Arrest.
Procedure, §77-9-2.
Authority, §§77-9-1 to 77-9-3.

MOPEDS —Cont'd
Rights of way.
  Pedestrians.
    Yielding to pedestrians on sidewalk,
      §41-6a-1106.
Sidewalks.
  Use of sidewalks.
    Where prohibited, §41-6a-1106.
Streets.
  Operation on public highways, §41-6a-1502.
Turns, §41-6a-1108.
  Signals, §41-6a-1109.

MORMON PIONEER HERITAGE AREA,
  §72-4-209.

MORPHINE.
  Narcotic drugs, §§58-37-1 to 58-37-21.
  See CONTROLLED SUBSTANCES.

MORTGAGES.
Recordation.
  Fraudulent handling of recordable writings,
    §76-6-503.5.

MOTION PICTURES.
Corporations.
  Distribution.
    Registered office or agent of distributor,
      §§76-10-1219 to 76-10-1221.
Distribution.
  Pornographic films.
    Defenses, §§76-10-1224, 76-10-1226.
      Status as projectionist or other employee no
        defense, §76-10-1224.
    Misdemeanors.
      When misdemeanor, §76-10-1222.
  Qualification for exhibition and distribution of
    films required, §76-10-1218.
  Corporations and others to file statements,
    §76-10-1219.
  Exhibition of film not acquired from qualified
    distributor.
    Misdemeanor, §76-10-1223.
  Misdemeanor for distribution without
    qualification, §76-10-1223.
  Registered office or agent of distributor.
    Change, §76-10-1220.
    Resignation of registered agent, §76-10-1220.
  Service of process, notice or demand.
    Agent for process.
      Appointment of director of division of
        corporations and commercial code as
        agent for process, §76-10-1221.
      Director of division of corporations and
        commercial code as agent for process,
        §76-10-1221.
      Registered agent of film distributor to receive,
        §76-10-1221.
Pornography.
  General provisions, §§76-10-1201 to 76-10-1229.
  See PORNOGRAPHY.
  Sexual exploitation of minors, §§76-5a-1 to
    76-5a-4.

MOTOR ASSISTED SCOOTERS.
Subject to bicycle regulations, §41-6a-1115.

MOTOR CARRIERS.
Accidents.
  Department of transportation.
    Powers as to, §54-4-16.
Actions.
  Enforcement of provisions.
    Existing rights of action unaffected, §72-9-702.
Advisory board, §72-9-201.

MOTOR CARRIERS —Cont'd
Alcoholic beverages.
  Criminal offenses.
    Division of shipments, §32A-12-502.
    Records, §32A-12-506.
    Removal from conveyances, §32A-12-502.
    Unlawful transportation, §32A-12-504.
Bills of lading.
  Conformance with provisions, §72-9-404.
Bus passenger safety.
  General provisions, §§76-10-1501 to 76-10-1511.
  See BUSES.
Cease and desist orders.
  Safety.
    Department of transportation, §72-9-303.
Commercial drivers' licenses.
  General provisions, §§53-3-401 to 53-3-420.
    See COMMERCIAL DRIVERS' LICENSES.
Commercial driver training schools.
  General provisions, §§53-3-501 to 53-3-510.
    See COMMERCIAL DRIVER TRAINING
      SCHOOLS.
Compromise and settlement.
  Civil penalties for violations, §72-9-703.
Damages.
  Freight.
    Loss or damage.
      Contribution between connecting carriers,
        §72-9-403.
      Liability, §72-9-401.
      Limitation of actions, §72-9-402.
Definitions.
  Safety, §72-9-102.
Department of transportation.
  Accidents.
    Powers as to, §54-4-16.
  Motor carrier advisory board, §72-9-201.
  Safety.
    Administrative law judge.
      Assignment by department, §72-9-704.
    Cease and desist orders, §72-9-303.
    Compliance audits and inspections, §72-9-301.
    Duties of department, §72-9-301.
    Interstate agreements, §72-9-302.
    Motor carrier advisory board, §72-9-201.
    Rules and regulations, §72-9-103.
    Sanctions for violations.
      Refusal, suspension or revocation of
        registration, §72-9-303.
Drivers' licenses.
  Commercial drivers' licenses, §§53-3-401 to
    53-3-420.
  See COMMERCIAL DRIVERS' LICENSES.
Electronic credentialing.
  Cooperation with department and federal
    agencies, §41-1a-303.
Farm vehicle operators.
  Medical exemptions for, §72-9-107.
Freight.
  Loss or damage.
    Contribution between connecting carriers,
      §72-9-403.
    Liability, §72-9-401.
    Limitation of actions, §72-9-402.
Information lettered on vehicle, §72-9-105.
Inspections.
  Safety.
    Compliance audits and inspections by
      department, §72-9-301.
    Tow truck requirements, §§72-9-601, 72-9-602.
Insurance.
  Liability insurance.
    Regulations specifying, §72-9-103.

MOTORCYCLES —Cont'd
Rider education —Cont'd
Instructors —Cont'd
Exemption, §53-3-909.
Licensing skills test exemption, §53-3-907.
Programs.
Administration, §53-3-903.
Exemption, §53-3-909.
Standards, §53-3-903.
Streets.
Operation on public highways, §41-6a-1502.

MOTOR-DRIVEN CYCLES.
Personal motorized mobility devices.
Definitions, §41-6a-102.
Restrictions on operation, §41-6a-1116.

MOTOR FUELS.
Bonds, surety.
Special fuels.
Supplier, §59-13-302.
Users, §59-13-303.
Clean fuels.
Taxation.
Exemptions from special fuel tax, §59-13-304.
Low-speed vehicles, §41-6a-1508.
Use of HOV lanes, §41-6a-702.
Dyed diesel fuel.
Use on highways, §59-13-320.5.
Purpose of act.
Aviation fuel.
Special fuels, §59-13-301.
Special fuels.
Commission.
Enforcement of provisions, §59-13-313.
Dyed diesel fuel.
Use on highways, §59-13-320.5.
Inspection of vehicles, §59-13-304.
Liens.
Tax a lien against vehicle, §59-13-311.
Payment of tax.
Delinquency, §59-13-308.
Permits, §59-13-303.
Special fuel vehicle permit, §59-13-314.
Refunds.
Fire, flood, storm or accident, §59-13-322.
Shipments from outside state.
Reports.
Contents, §59-13-310.
Required, §59-13-310.
Supplier.
Bonds, surety, §59-13-302.
Discontinuance of business, §59-13-302.
Licenses, §§59-13-302, 59-13-308.
Liens.
Tax to be lien upon property, §59-13-302.
Monthly reports, §59-13-302.
Neglect or refusal to report, §59-13-316.
Records, §59-13-312.
Reports, §59-13-307.
Taxation.
Delinquency, collection procedures, §59-13-317.
Due date of special fuel tax, §59-13-306.
Liens.
Property of user-dealer, §59-13-302.
Rack distribution tax payment option,
§59-13-321.
Ute Indian Tribe.
Exemption.
Refunds, §59-13-301.5.
Violations of provisions, §59-13-320.
User reports, §59-13-305.

MOTOR FUELS —Cont'd
Taxation.
Electronic credentialing of motor carriers.
Cooperation with department and federal
agencies, §41-1a-303.

MOTOR VEHICLE ACCIDENTS.
**Accident involving injury, death or property
damage.**
Violation of duties by operator, occupant or owner,
§41-6a-401.
Airbags.
Failure to repair a damaged or deployed airbag,
§41-6a-1624.
Assistance.
Rendering assistance, §41-6a-401.
Department of public safety.
Adjudicative proceedings, §41-6a-514.
Fences.
Broken fences.
Duties of police officer, §41-6a-408.
Financial responsibility.
General provisions, §§41-12a-101 to 41-12a-806.
See MOTOR VEHICLE FINANCIAL
RESPONSIBILITY.
Penalty for giving false information, §41-6a-403.
Post-accident security, §§41-12a-501 to
41-12a-513.
See MOTOR VEHICLE FINANCIAL
RESPONSIBILITY.
Report and investigation of driver security.
Duties of officer, §41-6a-403.
Hit-and-run.
Operators' licenses.
Mandatory revocation or suspension, §53-3-220.
Information to be given, §41-6a-401.
Livestock on highway.
Collision with livestock.
Action for damages, §§41-6a-407, 41-6a-408.
Notice to owner or brand inspector if livestock or
broken fence involved, §41-6a-408.
Name.
Giving name, §41-6a-401.
No fault insurance.
Limitations, exclusions and conditions to personal
injury protection, §31A-22-309.
Notice.
Duty to give notice of accident, §41-6a-401.
Police officers.
Financial responsibility of driver.
Report and investigation, §41-6a-403.
Livestock on highway.
Investigating officer's duties, §41-6a-408.
Reports.
Duty to forward or render, §41-6a-402.
Post-accident security, §§41-12a-501 to
41-12a-513.
See MOTOR VEHICLE FINANCIAL
RESPONSIBILITY.
Property damage.
Rendering assistance, §41-6a-401.
Reports.
Confidentiality, §41-6a-404.
Diplomats.
Traffic violations by, §41-6a-1901.
Disclosures allowed, §41-6a-404.
Duty to render.
Driver, witnesses and investigative officer,
§41-6a-402.
Evidence.
Use as evidence, §41-6a-404.
False information.
Penalty for giving false information, §41-6a-404.

MOTOR VEHICLE EQUIPMENT —Cont'd
Seat belts.
See SEAT BELTS.
Semitrailers.
Warning signal around disabled vehicle,
§41-6a-1638.
Sirens.
Emergency vehicles, §41-6a-1625.
Restrictions, §41-6a-1625.
Special mobile equipment.
Defined, §41-1a-102.
Exceptions, §41-6a-1601.
Spot lamps.
Restrictions, §41-6a-1610.
Streets and highways.
Construction and maintenance of vehicles.
Transportation department to adopt rules for
lighting, §41-6a-1617.
Substandard devices.
Injunction against sale, §41-6a-1622.
Appeal, §41-6a-1622.
Review, §41-6a-1622.
Sale prohibited, §41-6a-1622.
Television receivers.
Restrictions on receivers in vehicles, §41-6a-1641.
Theft alarm signals, §41-6a-1625.
Tires, §41-6a-1636.
Metal tires.
Permits.
Special permits to use metal tires,
§41-6a-1636.
Prohibited tires, §41-6a-1636.
Pneumatic tires.
Defined, §41-1a-102.
Prohibited tires, §41-6a-1636.
Regulatory powers of state transportation
department, §41-6a-1636.
Studded tires.
Winter use, §41-6a-1636.
Tread depth, §41-6a-1636.
Tracks.
Movable tracks on traction engines, tractors, etc.
Permits.
Special permits to use, §41-6a-1636.
Unapproved equipment.
Sale.
Prohibited, §41-6a-1619.
Unsafe or improperly equipped vehicles.
Misdemeanor, §41-6a-1601.
Violation of chapter.
Generally, §41-6a-203.
Warning lamps.
Requirements, §41-6a-1611.
Windows.
Nontransparent materials, §41-6a-1635.
Obstructions reducing visibility, §41-6a-1635.
Windshields.
Nontransparent materials, §41-6a-1635.
Obstructions reducing visibility, §41-6a-1635.
Wipers.
Requirements, §41-6a-1635.
Wipers.
Requirements, §41-6a-1635.
Wreckers.
Safety chains on towed vehicles required,
§41-6a-1634.

**MOTOR VEHICLE FINANCIAL
RESPONSIBILITY,** §§41-12a-101 to
41-12a-806.
Accidents.
Penalty for giving false information, §41-6a-403.

**MOTOR VEHICLE FINANCIAL
RESPONSIBILITY** —Cont'd
Accidents —Cont'd
Report and investigation of driver security.
Duties of officer, §41-6a-403.
Reports.
Access to, §41-12a-202.
Administration of chapter, §41-12a-201.
Construction and interpretation, §41-12a-104.
Definitions, §41-12a-103.
Department of public safety.
Accident reports.
Access to accident reports, §41-12a-202.
Administration of chapter, §41-12a-201.
Definition of department, §41-12a-103.
Post-accident security.
Cooperation with other states, §41-12a-507.
Insurance.
Payments by insurers as evidence to
department, §41-12a-504.
Proof of security.
Keeping proof current, §41-12a-411.
Power to require proof in other form,
§41-12a-409.
Drivers' licenses.
Definition of license or license certificate,
§41-12a-103.
Nonresident's operating privilege.
Defined, §41-12a-103.
Operating without license.
Misdemeanor, §41-12a-603.
Post-accident security.
Applicability of provisions to persons without
license or registration, §41-12a-506.
Conditions to licensing, §41-12a-503.
Revocation, §41-12a-604.
Security.
Filing false report to obtain.
Misdemeanor, §41-12a-602.
Enforcement.
Accident reports.
Filing false report, §41-12a-602.
Collusive transfers prohibited, §41-12a-601.
Operating vehicle without license or registration.
Misdemeanor, §41-12a-603.
Revocation of license and registration,
§41-12a-604.
Violations of chapter.
Misdemeanor, §41-12a-605.
Evidence of security, §41-12a-303.2.
Former safety responsibility act.
Superseded, §41-12a-102.
Inspections.
Security.
Condition to obtaining inspection, §41-12a-303.
Judgments.
Defined, §41-12a-103.
Installment payments, §41-12a-513.
Satisfaction.
Failure to satisfy, §41-12a-511.
When satisfied, §41-12a-512.
"Motor vehicle" defined, §41-12a-103.
Nonresidents.
Defined, §41-12a-103.
Post-accident security.
Service of process, §41-12a-505.
Proof of security.
Insurance certificate, §41-12a-403.
Security, §41-12a-301.
Operators.
Definition of operator, §41-12a-103.

NUISANCES —Cont'd
Highways.
Junkyard control.
Junkyards operated in violation of provisions, §72-7-208.
Injunctions.
Public nuisances, §76-10-808.
Judgments, §78-38-1.
Limited application of nuisance provisions.
Agricultural operations of over three years duration.
"Agricultural operations" defined, §78-38-8.
Manufacturing facility in operation over three years, §78-38-5.
"Manufacturing facility" defined, §78-38-6.
Motor vehicles.
Traffic-control devices.
Unauthorized signs, signals, lights or markings, §41-6a-309.
Offal.
Disposal.
Misdemeanor for violation of provisions, §76-10-805.
Party houses.
Abatement of nuisances.
Right of action, §78-38-9.
Public nuisances.
Abatement of public nuisance.
Action for abatement, §76-10-806.
Defined, §76-10-803.
Forfeiture of money, §76-10-808.
Injunctions, §76-10-808.
Maintaining, committing or failing to remove.
Misdemeanor, §76-10-804.
Relief granted for public nuisance, §76-10-808.
Smoking in leased, rented, etc., residential units, §78-38-.5.
Waters and watercourses.
Befouling waters.
Misdemeanor, §76-10-802.
Water supply and waterworks.
Befouling waters.
Misdemeanor, §76-10-802.
Weapons.
Right of action to abate nuisance, §78-38-9.

NURSE MIDWIVES.
Licenses.
Child support or visitation violations, §78-32-17.

NURSES.
Child abuse or neglect.
Reporting.
General provisions, §§62A-4a-401 to 62A-4a-412.
See CHILD ABUSE OR NEGLECT.
Requirement, §62A-4a-403.
Dispatchers.
Investigations or certification hearings, §53-6-308.
Falsification in official matters, §§76-8-501 to 76-8-514.
Forensic services, bureau of.
Blood analysis.
Medically certified to draw sample, §53-10-405.
Licenses.
Child support or visitation violations, §78-32-17.

O

OATHS.
Division of motor vehicles.
Authority to administer, §41-1a-112.

OATHS —Cont'd
Drivers' licenses.
Division officers and employees.
Authority to administer oaths, §53-3-108.
Peace officers.
Authority to administer oaths, §53-13-113.

OBJECT RAPE.
See RAPE.

OBSCENITY.
Pornography generally.
See PORNOGRAPHY.

OBSTRUCTING COLLECTION OF REVENUE, §76-8-406.

OBSTRUCTING GOVERNMENTAL OPERATIONS.
Bail-jumping.
Conduct constituting, §76-8-312.
Bribery.
Prevention of criminal prosecution.
Acceptance of bribe or bribery to prevent criminal prosecution, §76-8-308.
Escape, §76-8-309.
Influencing, impeding or retaliating.
Judge or member of board of pardons and parole, §76-8-316.
Interference with peace officer making lawful arrest, §76-8-305.
Interference with public servant generally, §76-8-301.
Legislature.
Disturbing legislature or official meeting, §76-8-304.
Prevention of legislature or public servants from meeting or organizing, §76-8-303.
Obstructing justice, §76-8-306.
Picketing or parading in or near court.
Misdemeanors, §76-8-302.
Prisons and prisoners.
Contraband.
Items prohibited in correctional facilities.
Prohibited acts, §76-8-311.3.
Public officers and employees.
Threatening elected officials, §§76-8-313, 76-8-315.
Definition of elected official, §76-8-314.
Taxation.
Obstructing collection of revenue, §76-8-406.

OBSTRUCTING JUSTICE.
Conduct constituting, §76-8-306.
Interception of communications.
Giving notice or attempting to give notice of possible interception to persons, §76-8-306.
Judge or member of board of pardons and parole.
Influencing, impeding or retaliating against, §76-8-316.

OCCUPATIONAL THERAPISTS.
Licenses.
Child support or visitation violations, §78-32-17.

ODOMETERS.
Certificates of title.
Mileage requirements, §41-1a-905.
Odometer statement as prerequisite to titling, §41-1a-508.
Recordation, §41-1a-904.
Violations, §41-1a-1319.
Defined, §41-1a-102.
Disclosure statement, §§41-1a-902 to 41-1a-904.
Inspection, §41-1a-904.
Mandatory, §41-1a-901.

OFF-HIGHWAY VEHICLES —Cont'd
Public lands.
Definition of public land, §41-22-2.
Facilities and programs.
  Agencies administering public lands to develop
    facilities and programs, §41-22-20.
Restrictions on use of public lands, §41-22-12.
Signs.
  Agencies authorized to erect regulatory signs on
    public land, §41-22-11.
Vehicles operated on public land.
  Authorized, §41-22-10.1.
Racing.
Permission required for race or organized event,
  §41-22-15.
Registration.
Application, §41-22-3.
  Falsification of documents, §41-22-4.
    Revocation or suspension of registration,
      §41-22-17.
Cards, §41-22-3.
  Duplicate cards, §41-22-7.
Electronic payments.
  Fee to cover costs, §41-22-36.
Exemptions from registration.
  Vehicles exempt from registration, §§41-1a-202,
    41-22-9.
Fees, §41-22-8.
  Deposit in off-highway vehicle account,
    §41-22-19.
  Electronic payments, costs of, §41-22-36.
  Matching fund requests, §41-22-19.
  Use, §41-22-19.
Off-highway husbandry vehicles, §41-22-5.5.
Register.
  Defined, §41-22-2.
Renewal, §41-22-3.5.
Revocation or suspension.
  Falsified application, §41-22-17.
Serial numbers.
  Alteration or removal of serial numbers
    unlawful, §41-22-4.
Staggered registration dates, §41-22-3.5.
Stickers.
  Display, §41-22-4.
    Rules of board, §41-22-5.1.
  Duplicate stickers, §41-22-7.
  Issuance, §41-22-3.
  Off-highway implements of husbandry,
    §41-22-5.5.
Taxation.
  Proof of property tax payment, §41-22-3.
Roadways.
Defined, §41-22-2.
Rules and regulations.
Publication, §41-22-21.
Safety.
Education and training program, §§41-22-31 to
  41-22-33.
Safety certificates.
Issuance, §41-22-31.
Operation requirements, §41-22-30.
Serial numbers.
Registration.
  Alteration or removal of serial numbers
    unlawful, §41-22-4.
Signs.
Agencies authorized to erect regulatory signs on
  public land, §41-22-11.
Privately-owned lands.
  Tampering with signs on.
    Prohibited, §41-22-12.5.

OFF-HIGHWAY VEHICLES —Cont'd
Snowmobiles.
Defined, §41-22-2.
Helmets.
  Protective headgear requirements, §41-22-10.8.
Operation, §41-22-10.4.
Trails.
  Restrictions on use, §41-22-12.1.
Sovereign immunity.
Vehicle safety education and training program.
  State immunity from suit, §41-22-31.
Special group license plates, §§41-1a-418,
  41-1a-1211.
State of Utah.
Safety education and training program.
  State immunity from suit, §41-22-31.
Streets.
Definition of street, §41-22-2.
Snowmobiles.
  Operation on streets or highways, §41-22-10.4.
Supervision.
Cooperation, §41-22-30.
Supervision of operator.
Local ordinances, §41-22-10.5.
Taxation.
Registration.
  Proof of property tax payment, §41-22-3.
Tires.
Low pressure tires.
  Defined, §41-22-2.
Traffic regulation.
Compliance.
  Required, §41-22-10.6.
Vandalism.
Prohibited uses of off-highway vehicles, §41-22-13.
Wildlife.
Prohibited uses of off-highway vehicles, §41-22-13.

OFFICE OF EXECUTIVE PROTECTION,
  §§53-1-112 to 53-1-115.

**OFFICIAL MISCONDUCT OF PUBLIC
  SERVANT,** §76-8-201.

OLYMPIC PUBLIC SAFETY COMMAND.
Sunset provision, §63-55b-153.

ONE-WAY TRAFFIC, §41-6a-709.

OPEN SEASON.
Defined, §23-13-2.

OPERATORS' LICENSES.
Motor vehicles.
Commercial drivers' licenses, §§53-3-401 to
  53-3-420.
  See COMMERCIAL DRIVERS' LICENSES.
General provisions, §§53-3-201 to 53-3-229.
  See DRIVERS' LICENSES.

OPIATES.
Definition, §58-37-2.

OPTOMETRISTS.
Licensure.
Child support or visitation violations, §78-32-17.
Suspension or revocation.
  Child support or visitation violations, §78-32-17.

ORAL SEX.
Sodomy generally, §§76-5-403, 76-5-403.1.

ORDERS.
Crime victims restitution.
Preservation of assets, §77-38a-601.
Juvenile courts.
See JUVENILE COURTS.

ORDERS —Cont'd
Railroads.
See RAILROADS.

ORDINANCES.
Driving while intoxicated and reckless driving.
Municipal attorneys authorized to prosecute for driving while license suspended or revoked for conviction of driving while intoxicated, §41-6a-519.
Uniform application of provisions.
Effect of local ordinances, §41-6a-207.

ORGAN DONATION.
Drivers' licenses.
License fee checkoff, §53-3-214.7.
Motor vehicle registration.
Registration checkoff, §41-1a-230.5.

ORGAN DONATION CONTRIBUTION FUND,
§26-18b-101.

OSTEOPATHS.
Licenses.
Child support or visitation violations, §78-32-17.

OTTER CREEK STATE PARK.
Jurisdiction over highways, §§72-3-201, 72-3-204.

OUTBOARD MOTORS.
Abandoned and inoperative motors.
Disposal, §41-1a-1009.
Acquisition or resale of motor.
Certificate of origin required, §41-1a-710.
Dealer transfer of ownership, §41-1a-709.
Defined, §41-1a-102.
Exempt from title requirements, §41-1a-505.
Prerequisites for titling, §41-1a-508.
Salvage motors.
Destruction or change, §41-1a-1012.
Stolen and recovered outboard motors.
Examination of registration records and indices, §41-1a-513.

OUTDOOR ADVERTISING.
Appeals.
Attorney general, §72-7-512.
Decisions of department, §72-7-508.
Attorney general.
Appeals by, §72-7-512.
Definitions, §72-7-502.
Department of transportation.
Appeals from decisions of department, §72-7-508.
Definition of "department," §72-7-502.
Rules and regulations, §72-7-506.
Violations of provisions, §72-7-508.
Eminent domain.
Existing outdoor advertising not in conformity with act, §72-7-510.
Existing outdoor advertising not in conformity with act.
Eminent domain, §72-7-510.
Height adjustments, §72-7-510.5.
Relocation, §§72-7-509, 72-7-510.
Removal, §§72-7-509, 72-7-510.
Height adjustments for nonconforming signs, §72-7-510.5.
Information centers.
Defined, §72-7-502.
Interstate system.
Defined, §72-7-502.
Prohibited near interstate system, §72-7-504.
Exceptions, §72-7-504.
Landscape control program, §72-7-514.

OUTDOOR ADVERTISING —Cont'd
Legislative declaration.
Purpose of act, §72-7-501.
Logo advertising, §72-7-504.
Permit violations, §72-7-503.
Violations of provisions, §72-7-511.
Nonconforming signs.
Height adjustments, §72-7-510.5.
Notice of rule changes, §72-7-506.
Outdoor advertising corridor.
Defined, §72-7-502.
Location in, §72-7-504.
Permits.
Generally, §72-7-507.
Required, §§72-7-503, 72-7-504, 72-7-507.
Primary system.
Defined, §72-7-502.
Prohibited near primary system, §72-7-504.
Purpose of act, §72-7-501.
Relocation.
Procedure, §72-7-510.
State highways, §72-7-513.
Structures from high voltage overhead lines, §72-7-516.
When allowable, §72-7-509.
Removal of unlawful advertising, §72-7-508.
Existing outdoor advertising not in conformity with act, §§72-7-509, 72-7-510.
Rest areas.
Defined, §72-7-502.
Rules and regulations.
Department of transportation, §72-7-506.
Scenic or natural areas.
Defined, §72-7-502.
Severability of act, §72-7-515.
Signs, §§72-7-502, 72-7-504, 72-7-505.
Utah-federal agreement.
Conflicts of law, §72-7-515.
Ratification, §72-7-501.
Violations of provisions.
Penalty, §72-7-511.
Permits, §72-7-503.

OVERTAKING.
Passing vehicles proceeding in same direction, §41-6a-704.
Passing on right.
When permissible, §41-6a-705.
Signs and markings on roadway, §41-6a-708.

OVERWORKING ANIMALS.
Cruelty to animals, §§76-9-301 to 76-9-305.

P

PAGERS.
Telecommunication device restrictions.
Generally, §§76-6-409.5 to 76-6-409.10.

PAINTED ROCKS, STATE PARK.
Jurisdiction over highways, §§72-3-201, 72-3-204.

PALISADES STATE PARK.
Jurisdiction over highways, §§72-3-201, 72-3-205.

PANDERING.
Aiding prostitution generally, §76-10-1304.
Local ordinances to be consistent with code provisions, §76-10-1307.

PARACHUTING.
Defined, §72-10-102.

PEACE OFFICERS —Cont'd
Training —Cont'd
Division of peace officer standards and training
　—Cont'd
　Gifts.
　　Acceptance and disposition, §53-6-108.
　Hearings.
　　Powers of division, §53-6-210.
　Investigations.
　　Powers of division, §53-6-210.
　Purpose, §53-6-103.
　Rules and regulations.
　　Promulgation by director, §53-6-105.
　Municipal corporations.
　　Higher minimum standards.
　　　Power to set, §53-6-207.
　Notice.
　　Revocation or suspension of certification,
　　　§53-6-211.
　Peace officer training and certification act.
　　Citation of part, §53-6-201.
　Reparation fund.
　　Appropriations from, §53-6-213.
　Requirements, §§53-6-202, 53-6-205.
　Rules and regulations.
　　Division of peace officer standards and training.
　　　Director.
　　　　Promulgation, §53-6-105.
　Temporary presence in state for training.
　　Certification.
　　　Considered to be certified, §53-13-107.
　Termination of employment.
　　Change of status form, §53-6-209.
　Waiver of training course requirement, §§53-6-204
　　to 53-6-206.
Training academy.
Basic course completion at.
　Required, §53-13-103.
Trees and timber.
Transportation of forest products or native
　vegetation.
　Enforcement of provisions, §78-38-4.6.
Universities and colleges.
Assistance by local authorities, §76-8-707.
　Request for assistance from state and local law
　　enforcement authorities, §76-8-716.
Enforcement of laws by local agencies.
　Not limited by part, §76-8-709.
Enforcement rights of state and local law
　enforcement authorities not limited by part,
　§76-8-718.
Police or security personnel considered,
　§53B-3-105.
Weapons.
Concealed weapons permit, §53-5-704.
　Qualifications for exemption, §53-5-711.
Disarming a peace officer, §76-5-102.8.
Frisking suspect for dangerous weapons.
　Authority, §§77-7-16, 77-7-17.
Special function officers.
　Carrying, §53-13-105.
Who may exercise authority, §53-13-102.

**PEARL HARBOR SURVIVOR LICENSE
　PLATES,** §41-1a-421.

PEARL HARBOR SURVIVORS.
Motor vehicles.
Special license plates, §41-1a-418.
　Fees, §41-1a-1211.
　Identification requirements, §41-1a-421.

PEDESTRIANS.
Alcoholic beverages.
Walking under the influence.
　Restrictions, §41-6a-1009.
Applicability of chapter, §41-6a-1001.
**Avoiding pedestrians in human-powered
　vehicles.**
Vehicles to exercise due care to avoid,
　§41-6a-1006.
Bicycles.
Yielding right of way to pedestrians, §41-6a-1106.
Blind pedestrians.
Drivers to yield right of way, §41-6a-1007.
Bridges.
Passing closed railroad or bridge gate or barrier
　prohibited, §41-6a-1005.
Crosswalks.
Unmarked crosswalk locations.
　Restrictions on pedestrians, §41-6a-1010.
Definitions, §41-6a-102.
Emergency vehicles.
Duties of driver and pedestrian, §41-6a-1004.
Motor vehicle insurance.
Policies.
　Definition of pedestrian, §31A-22-301.
Pedestrian vehicles, §41-6a-1011.
Railroads.
Passing closed railroad or bridge gate or barrier
　prohibited, §41-6a-1005.
Right of way.
Bicyclists to yield right of way to pedestrians,
　§41-6a-1106.
Blind persons.
　Drivers to yield right of way to blind persons,
　　§41-6a-1007.
Crosswalks.
　Unmarked crosswalk location.
　　Pedestrians to yield to vehicles, §41-6a-1010.
Determination, §41-6a-1002.
Emergency vehicles.
　Duty of driver and pedestrian, §41-6a-1004.
Roadways.
　Pedestrian upon roadway to yield to vehicles,
　　§41-6a-1009.
Sidewalks.
　Vehicle crossing sidewalk.
　　Driver to yield, §41-6a-1008.
Vehicle or pedestrian working upon highway,
　§41-6a-905.
Yielding right of way by pedestrian, §41-6a-1003.
Sidewalks.
Vehicle crossing sidewalk.
　Driver to yield, §41-6a-1008.
Signals.
Special pedestrian-control signals, §41-6a-306.
　Meaning, §41-6a-306.
　Rights and duties, §41-6a-306.
Vehicles to exercise due care to avoid pedestrians
　and human-powered vehicles.
　Audible signals to be given, §41-6a-1006.
Streets and highways, §41-6a-1009.
Traffic-control devices, §41-6a-1001.
Walking under the influence.
Restrictions, §41-6a-1009.

PEDESTRIAN VEHICLES, §41-6a-1011.

PEEPING TOMS.
Criminal offenses, §76-9-702.

PENAL INSTITUTIONS.
See PRISONS AND PRISONERS.

PROBATION —Cont'd
Sexual offenses.
Child victim of sex offense.
Circumstances required for probation or
suspension of sentence for sex offense
against child, §76-5-406.5.
Crimes for which probation restricted, §76-3-406.
Registration of sex offenders, §77-27-21.5.
Sodomy, §§76-3-406, 76-5-406.5.
Weapons.
Possession of dangerous weapons.
Person on probation for felony.
Persons not permitted to possess, §76-10-503.

PROCESS.
Service of process.
See SERVICE OF PROCESS.

PROCESSIONS.
Breach of the peace.
Disrupting meeting or procession, §76-9-103.
Disrupting meeting or procession.
Misdemeanors, §76-9-103.

PROCLAMATIONS.
Tampering with official proclamation,
§76-8-417.

**PRODUCTION OF DOCUMENTS AND
THINGS.**
Antitrust.
Investigations.
Civil antitrust investigations.
Demand to produce documentary materials,
§76-10-917.
Subpoena duces tecum.
Pornography.
Corporate defendants, §76-10-1213.

PROFANITY.
Bus passenger safety act, §76-10-1506.

PROFESSIONAL COUNSELORS.
Licenses.
Child support or visitation violations, §78-32-17.

PROSECUTING ATTORNEYS.
Gambling.
Failure to prosecute offense, §76-10-1106.

PROSTITUTION.
Aiding prostitution.
Conduct constituting, §76-10-1304.
Elements of offense, §76-10-1304.
Local ordinances to be consistent with code
provisions, §76-10-1307.
Misdemeanors, §76-10-1304.
Conduct constituting, §76-10-1302.
Definitions, §76-10-1301.
Elements of offense, §76-10-1302.
Exploiting prostitution, §§76-10-1305,
76-10-1306.
Felonies, §§76-10-1305, 76-10-1306.
Houses of prostitution.
Abatement of nuisance.
Right of action, §78-38-9.
Defined, §76-10-1301.
Inmates.
Defined, §76-10-1301.
Loitering, §76-10-1302.
Misdemeanors, §76-10-1302.
Aiding prostitution, §76-10-1304.
Patronizing a prostitute, §76-10-1303.
Prosecution, §76-10-1308.
Municipal corporations.
Corporation counsel.
Prosecution of misdemeanor, §76-10-1308.

PROSTITUTION —Cont'd
Ordinances.
Local ordinance to be consistent with code
provisions, §76-10-1307.
Pandering.
Aiding prostitution generally, §76-10-1304.
Local ordinances to be consistent with code
provisions, §76-10-1307.
Patronizing a prostitute, §76-10-1303.
Pimps, §§76-10-1305, 76-10-1306.
Prosecution of offenses, §76-10-1308.
Public places.
Defined, §76-10-1301.
Sexual activity.
Defined, §76-10-1301.

PROTECTIVE ORDERS.
Child protective order violations, §76-5-108.
Cohabitant abuse.
Generally, §§30-6-1 to 30-6-15.
See COHABITANT ABUSE.
Juvenile courts.
Abuse, neglect and dependency proceedings,
§§78-3h-101 to 78-3h-107.

PSYCHOLOGISTS.
Falsification in official matters.
False reports of offenses to.
Misdemeanor, §76-8-506.

PSYCHOTOXIC CHEMICAL SOLVENTS.
Abuse, §76-10-107.

PUBLIC AIRPORTS ACT.
General provisions, §§72-10-201 to 72-10-214.
See AIRPORTS.

PUBLIC ASSISTANCE FRAUD, §§76-8-1201 to
76-8-1207.
Application of provisions, §76-8-1202.
Defined terms, §§76-8-1201, 76-8-1205.
Disclosures, §§76-8-1203, 76-8-1204.
Evidence, §76-8-1207.
Penalties, §76-8-1206.
Repayments as defense to actions, §76-8-1207.
Value of benefits received, §§76-8-1206,
76-8-1207.

PUBLIC BUILDINGS.
Alcoholic beverages.
Unlawful consumption in public places,
§32A-12-220.

PUBLIC EMPLOYEES.
General provisions.
See PUBLIC OFFICERS AND EMPLOYEES.

PUBLIC HEALTH EMERGENCIES.
Detection of public health emergencies act,
§§26-23b-101 to 26-23b-110.
Weapons of mass destruction generally,
§§76-10-401 to 76-10-405.

PUBLIC LANDS.
Off-highway vehicles.
Definition of public land, §41-22-2.
Facilities and programs.
Agencies administering public lands to develop
facilities and programs, §41-22-20.
Restrictions on use of public lands, §41-22-12.
Signs.
Agencies authorized to erect regulatory signs on
public land, §41-22-11.
Vehicles operated on public land.
Authorized, §41-22-10.1.
Rights of way across federal lands act,
§§72-5-301 to 72-5-306.
Agreements affecting R.S. 2477 right-of-way,
§72-5-307.

RAPE —Cont'd
Object rape —Cont'd
Consent.
Circumstances showing absence of consent,
§76-5-406.
Dead bodies.
Abuse or desecration of dead body.
Committing or attempting to commit object
rape, §76-9-704.
Defenses.
Force in defense of person, §76-2-402.
Elements of offense, §76-5-402.2.
Felonies.
First degree felony, §76-5-402.2.
Homicide.
Murder.
Causing death of another while committing
object rape, §76-5-203.
Limitation of actions, §76-1-302.
Penetration.
Degree sufficient to constitute offense, §76-5-407.
Child victim, §76-5-407.
Probation.
Child rape.
Circumstances required for probation or
suspension of sentence for sex offense
against child, §76-5-406.5.
Crimes for which probation, suspension of
sentence, lower category of offenses or
hospitalization restricted, §76-3-406.
Self defense.
Force in defense of person.
Justified to prevent commission of forcible
felony, §76-2-402.
Sentencing.
Child rape, §§76-3-406, 76-5-406.5.
Statutory rape.
Child rape generally, §76-5-402.1.
Unlawful sexual activity with a minor.
Lesser offense than rape, §76-5-401.

**REAL ESTATE BROKERS AND SALES
       AGENTS.**
Licenses.
Child support or visitation violations, §78-32-17.

REAL PROPERTY.
Governmental immunity.
Waiver of immunity.
Actions involving property, §63-30d-301.
Owners of real property.
Right to regulate traffic, §41-6a-215.

RECKLESS BURNING, §76-6-104.

RECKLESS DRIVING.
Drivers' licenses.
Two charges of reckless driving committed within
period of twelve months.
Mandatory revocation or suspension of license,
§53-3-220.
Elements of offense, §41-6a-528.
Misdemeanors, §41-6a-528.
Ordinances.
Local ordinances to be consistent with code,
§41-6a-510.
Penalties, §41-6a-528.

RECKLESS ENDANGERMENT, §76-5-112.

RECKLESS FLYING.
Defined, §72-10-102.

RECKLESSLY OR MALICIOUSLY.
Defined for criminal culpability, §76-2-103.

RECORDATION.
Crimes and offenses.
Fraudulent handling of recordable writings.
Elements of offense, §76-6-503.5.
Felony of third degree, §76-6-503.5.
Deeds.
Fraudulent handling of recordable writings,
§76-6-503.5.
Forgery.
Recording false or forged instruments.
Criminal offense, §76-8-414.
Fraudulent handling of recordable writings.
Conduct constituting, §76-6-503.5.
Public property offenses.
Recording false or forged instruments, §76-8-414.

RECORDS.
Driving while intoxicated.
School speed zones.
Recordkeeping system, §41-6a-604.
Speed restrictions.
Reduced speed school zones, §41-6a-604.

RECREATIONAL THERAPISTS.
Licenses.
Child support or visitation violations, §78-32-17.

RECREATIONAL VEHICLES.
Defined, §41-1a-102.

RECREATION CENTERS.
Controlled substances.
Prohibited acts committed in, §58-37-8.

RECYCLING.
Misuse of recycling bins.
Generally, §76-10-2101.

RED FLEET STATE PARK.
Jurisdiction over highways, §§72-3-201,
72-3-205.

RED FOXES.
Spotlighting, §23-13-17.

REFUSE.
Litter generally.
See LITTER.

REGISTRATION.
Boating.
See BOATING.
Service marks.
See TRADEMARKS AND SERVICE MARKS.
Trademarks and service marks.
See TRADEMARKS AND SERVICE MARKS.

RENT.
Theft.
Theft by person having custody of property
pursuant to repair or rental agreement,
§76-6-410.

RENTAL MOTOR VEHICLES.
Collision damages.
Defense costs, coverage requirement, §31A-22-314.
Definitions, §31A-22-311.
Liability generally, §31A-22-312.
Mandatory coverage, §31A-22-314.
Provisions inapplicable to rental companies
disclosing charges, §31A-22-312.
Reports of insurance, §31A-22-315.
Security.
None required, §31A-22-312.
Waivers of coverage, §31A-22-312.
Mandatory insurance coverage, §31A-22-314.
Operators' licenses.
Requirements for renting of motor vehicles,
§53-3-203.

SPEED RESTRICTIONS —Cont'd
Streets and highways.
Speed contest or exhibition on highway.
Barricade or obstruction for speed contest or
exhibition.
Prohibited, §41-6a-606.
Prohibited, §41-6a-606.
Vintage vehicles.
Minimum speed inapplicable, §41-21-3.
Violation.
Pleading.
Contents, §41-6a-607.

SPEEDY TRIAL.
Victims.
Right of victim to speedy trial, §77-38-7.

SPIRITUAL HEALING.
Medication neglect.
Exemption from prohibition, §76-5-110.

SPORTS.
**Bribery or threat to influence athletic
contests, §76-6-514.**

SPORTS FACILITIES.
Alcoholic beverages.
Sports center, defined, §32A-1-105.
Controlled substances.
Prohibited acts committed in, §58-37-8.

SPOTLIGHTING WILDLIFE, §§23-13-2, 23-13-17.

SPOUSE ABUSE.
Cohabitant abuse generally.
See COHABITANT ABUSE.
Spouse abuse procedures, §§77-36-1 to 77-36-10.

STADIUMS.
Controlled substances.
Prohibited acts committed in, §58-37-8.

STALKING, §76-5-106.5.
Injunctions, §§77-3a-101 to 77-3a-103.

STAMPS.
Illegal drug stamp tax, §§59-19-101 to 59-19-107.
See ILLEGAL DRUG STAMP TAX.

STANDING.
Definition of standing, §41-6a-102.
Restrictions and exceptions, §41-6a-1401.

STARTING VEHICLES, §41-6a-803.

STARVATION STATE PARK.
**Jurisdiction over highways, §§72-3-201,
72-3-205.**

STATE BOARD OF EDUCATION.
Generally.
See PUBLIC SCHOOLS.

STATE DEVELOPMENTAL CENTER.
Juvenile courts.
Custody of state training school.
Notice of discharge from, §78-3a-121.
Orders of commitment to.
Period of operation, §78-3a-119.

STATE HIGHWAY PATROL.
General provisions, §§53-8-103 to 53-8-107.
See HIGHWAY PATROL.

STATE HIGHWAYS, §§72-4-101 to 72-4-137.
Appurtenances.
Construction and maintenance, §72-6-111.
Class A state roads, §72-3-102.
**Construction and maintenance, §§72-6-101 to
72-6-118.**
Defined, §72-3-102.

STATE HIGHWAYS —Cont'd
Deletions from state highway system,
§§72-4-102, 72-4-103.
**Designation of state highways, §§72-4-105 to
72-4-137.**
General provisions.
See HIGHWAYS.
Noise abatement measures, §72-6-111.
Traffic noise abatement program, §72-6-112.
Realignment of highways.
Disposition of portion of highways realigned,
§72-4-104.
Title of act, §72-4-101.

**STATE LABORATORY DRUG TESTING
ACCOUNT, §26-1-34.**

STATE LANDS.
Division of forestry, fire and state lands.
Appeals.
Supreme court.
Appellate jurisdiction over final orders and
decrees, §78-2-2.

**STATE OLYMPIC PUBLIC SAFETY
COMMAND.**
See OLYMPIC PUBLIC SAFETY COMMAND.

STATE TAX COMMISSION.
Administration of chapter, §41-1a-103.
Duties, §41-1a-104.
Prescribing forms, §41-1a-105.

STATUTE OF LIMITATIONS.
Alcoholic beverages.
Dramshop liability, §32A-14a-102.
Liability for injuries and damages resulting from
distribution, §32A-14a-102.
Antitrust, §76-10-925.
Barred prosecution.
Judge to determine, §76-1-306.
Child abuse or neglect.
Reporting.
Actions for failure to report, §62A-4a-411.
Dramshop liability, §32A-14a-102.
Embezzlement of public money, §76-1-301.5.
Felonies, §76-1-302.
Capital felonies, §76-1-301.
Fiduciaries.
Breach of fiduciary obligation, §76-1-303.
Fraud.
Criminal fraud, §76-1-303.
Homicide, §§76-1-301, 76-1-302.
Infractions, §76-1-302.
Insurance.
Motor vehicle insurance.
No fault provisions.
Limitations, exclusions and conditions to
personal injury protection, §31A-22-309.
Minors.
Sexual offenses against children, §76-1-303.5.
Motor carriers.
Freight.
Loss or damage.
Presenting claims and bringing suit,
§72-9-402.
Motor fuels tax.
Special fuels.
Assessment or commencing proceeding for
collection, §59-13-313.
Refund claimed by taxpayer, §59-13-318.
Public officers and employees.
Misconduct of public officer or employee,
§76-1-303.

TAMPERING.
Aircraft, §§72-10-127, 72-10-128.
Alcoholic beverages.
Records, §32A-12-303.
Bribery.
Witnesses.
Use of bribery to effect tampering, §76-8-508.
Evidence, §76-8-510.5.
Fences.
Privately-owned lands.
Tampering with fences on, §41-22-12.5.
Jury.
Tampering with jury, §76-8-508.5.
Motor vehicles.
Tampering with, §41-1a-1305.
Official notice or proclamation, §76-8-417.
Records, §76-6-504.

TAMPERING WITH EVIDENCE, §76-8-510.5.

TAXATION.
Motor vehicles.
Low-speed vehicles, §41-6a-1508.

TAXICABS.
Defined, §53-3-102.
Endorsements on drivers' licenses.
Application and fee, §53-3-205.
Required, §53-3-202.

TELECOMMUNICATIONS.
Device restrictions, §§76-6-409.5 to 76-6-409.10.
Fraud.
Communications fraud generally, §76-10-1801.
Interstate highway system.
Longitudinal telecommunication access in, §72-7-108.
Public safety department.
Bureau of communications, §§53-10-501, 53-10-502.
Criminal investigations and technical services division, §53-10-109.
Telecommunications advisory council, §72-7-109.
Towers and related facilities.
Interstate highways.
Access to right of way, §72-7-108.

TELECOMMUNICATIONS ADVISORY COUNCIL, §72-7-109.

TELEGRAPHS.
Arrest.
Warrants.
Execution of.
Authorization by, §77-7-10.
Communication abuse, §76-9-403.
Fraud.
Communications fraud generally, §76-10-1801.
Telecommunication device restrictions generally, §§76-6-409.5 to 76-6-409.10.
See TELECOMMUNICATIONS.
Theft of services, §76-6-409.
Devices for theft of services, §76-6-409.1.
Telecommunication devices.
Manufacture of unlawful telecommunication device, §76-6-409.9.
Possession of unlawful telecommunication device, §76-6-409.7.
Unlawful use, §76-6-409.6.

TELEPHONES.
Abuse.
Emergency telephone abuse.
Misdemeanor, §76-9-202.

TELEPHONES —Cont'd
Abuse —Cont'd
Telephone harassment.
Misdemeanor, §76-9-201.
Arrest.
Warrants.
Execution of.
Authorization by, §77-7-10.
Cohabitant abuse act.
Telephone harassment.
Making telephone call in violation of protective order, §76-9-201.
Communication abuse.
Criminal offense, §76-9-403.
Emergency telephone service.
Annexation.
Emergency services telephone charge in annexing area, §69-2-5.
Definitions.
Funding service, §69-2-5.
Dispatchers, §§53-6-301 to 53-6-310.
See DISPATCHERS.
Emergency services telephone charge.
Levy by county, city or town, §69-2-5.
Funding of service, §69-2-5.
Mobile telecommunications service.
Emergency services telephone charge levied on, §69-2-5.
Notice.
Charge.
Emergency telephone charge, §69-2-5.
Public agency establishing.
Funding, §69-2-5.
Rates and charges.
Emergency telephone charge, §69-2-5.
Special emergency telephone service fund, §69-2-5.
Special service districts.
Funding service, §69-2-5.
Statewide unified E-911 emergency services fund, §§53-10-603 to 53-10-605.
Telephone abuse.
Emergency telephone abuse, §76-9-202.
Utah 911 committee, §§53-10-601 to 53-10-606.
Fraud.
Communications fraud generally, §76-10-1801.
Harassment.
Telephone abuse.
Misdemeanor, §76-9-201.
911 service.
Statewide unified E-911 emergency services fund, §§53-10-603 to 53-10-605.
Utah 911 committee, §§53-10-601 to 53-10-606.
Notice.
Emergency telephone service.
Charge.
Emergency telephone charge, §69-2-5.
Telecommunication device restrictions generally, §§76-6-409.5 to 76-6-409.10.
Theft of services, §76-6-409.
Devices for theft of services, §76-6-409.1.
Telecommunication devices.
Manufacture of unlawful telecommunication device, §76-6-409.9.
Possession of unlawful telecommunication device, §76-6-409.7.
Unlawful use, §76-6-409.6.
Utah 911 committee, §§53-10-601 to 53-10-606.
Creation, §53-10-601.
Duties, §53-10-602.
Expenses, §53-10-604.
Members, §53-10-601.
Powers, §53-10-602.

Notes

Notes

Notes